The Sporting News

BASEBALL GUIDE

1996 EDITION

Editors/Baseball Guide

CRAIG CARTER
DAVE SLOAN

The Sporting News

PUBLISHING CO.

Efrem Zimbalist III, President and Chief Executive Officer, Times Mirror Magazines; **Nicholas H. Niles,** President and Chief Executive Officer; **Francis X. Farrell,** Senior Vice President, Publisher; **John D. Rawlings,** Senior Vice President, Editorial Director; **John Kastberg,** Vice President, General Manager; **Kathy Kinkeade,** Vice President, Production; **Mike Nahrstedt,** Managing Editor; **Mike Huguenin,** Assistant Managing Editor; **Joe Hoppel and Bill Marx,** Senior Editors; **Tom Dienhart and Dave Sloan,** Associate Editors; **Craig Carter,** Statistical Editor; **Kyle Veltrop,** Assistant Editor; **Fred Barnes,** Director of Graphics; **Angie Blackwell,** Art Director; **Albert Dickson,** Chief Photographer; **Paul Nisely,** Photo Editor; **Gary Brinker,** Director/Information Systems; **Bob Parajon,** Prepress Director; **Patrick Kolieboi,** Network Manager; **Terry Shea,** Database Analyst; **Marilyn Kasal,** Production Manager; **Mike Bruner,** Graphics Network Manager; **Michael Behrens,** Macintosh Production Artist.

A Times Mirror
Company

EXPLANATION OF STATISTICAL ABBREVIATIONS

A: assists. **AB:** at-bats. **Avg.:** batting average (hits divided by at-bats). **BB:** bases on balls. **Bk.:** balks. **CG:** complete games. **CS:** caught stealing. **E:** errors. **ER:** earned runs. **ERA:** earned-run average (earned runs times nine divided by innings pitched). **G:** games. **GB:** games behind. **GF:** games finished. **GDP:** grounding into double plays. **GS:** games started. **H:** hits. **HB:** hit batsmen. **HP:** hit by pitches. **HR:** home runs. **IBB:** intentional bases on balls. **IP:** innings pitched. **L:** losses. **OBP:** on-base percentage (hits plus bases on balls plus hit by pitches divided by at-bats plus bases on balls plus hit by pitches plus sacrifice flies). **Pct.:** winning percentage. **PO:** putouts. **Pos.:** position. **R:** runs. **RBI:** runs batted in. **SB:** stolen bases. **SF:** sacrifice flies (run-scoring flyouts). **SH:** sacrifice hits (bunts that advance one or more runners but result in the batter being retired at first base or reaching first on an error). **ShO:** shutouts. **Slg.:** slugging percentage (total bases divided by at-bats). **SO:** strikeouts. **Sv.:** saves. **TB:** total bases (hits plus doubles plus two times the number of triples plus three times the number of home runs). **TBF:** total batters faced. **TC:** total chances (putouts plus assists plus errors). **TPA:** total plate appearances (at-bats plus bases on balls plus sacrifice hits plus sacrifice flies plus hit by pitches plus times reaching base on catcher's interference). **W:** wins. **WP:** wild pitches. **2B:** doubles. **3B:** triples.

World Series, A.L. Championship Series, N.L. Championship Series, A.L. Division Series, N.L. Division Series, A.L. West playoff and All-Star Game highlights written by Joe Hoppel, Mike Huguenin, Bill Marx, Dave Sloan and Kyle Veltrop of THE SPORTING NEWS.

Major league statistics compiled by STATS, Inc., Lincolnwood, Ill.

Minor league statistics compiled by Howe Sportsdata International Inc., Boston.

ISBN: 0-89204-544-2 (perfect-bound)
       0-89204-547-7 (comb-bound)

10 9 8 7 6 5 4 3 2 1

CONTENTS

ON THE COVER: Los Angeles' Hideo Nomo led the National League with 236 strikeouts and finished second with a 2.54 ERA en route to winning N.L. Rookie of the Year honors in 1995 (Photo by Michael Ponzini)

Spine photo of Ken Griffey Jr. by Albert Dickson/The Sporting News.

1996 SEASON

Major League Baseball directories

Team by team

MAJOR LEAGUE BASEBALL

COMMISSIONER'S OFFICE

Address
350 Park Avenue
New York, NY 10022
Telephone
212-339-7800
FAX
212-355-0007
Director of governmental relations
Eugene Callahan
Executive director, market development
Katherine Francis

Director, special events
Carolyn Taylor
Exec. dir., security/facility management
Kevin Hallinan
Executive director, public relations
Richard Levin
Executive director, baseball operations
William Murray
General counsel
Thomas J. Ostertag

Director, minor league relations
Jimmie Lee Solomon
Chief financial officer
Jeffrey White
**Executive director, licensing operations
and president, MLBP**
Don Gibson

AMERICAN LEAGUE

Address
350 Park Avenue
New York, NY 10022
Telephone
212-339-7600
President
Gene A. Budig
Vice president
Gene Autry
Executive director of umpiring
Martin J. Springstead
Coordinator of umpire operations
Artesia Basta-Marino
V.p., administration and media affairs
Phyllis Merhige
Director of finance
Derek Irwin
Director, waivers and player records
John G. Ricco

Assistant media affairs director
Joe Fitzgerald
Administrator of umpires/travel
Tess Basta-Marino
Administrative assistant
Carolyn Coen
Umpires
Larry Barnett
Joseph Brinkman
Alan Clark
Drew Coble
Derryl Cousins
Terry Craft
Donald Denkinger
James Evans
Dale Ford
Richard Garcia
Ted Hendry
John Hirschbeck
Mark Johnson

Jim Joyce
Kenneth Kaiser
Greg Kosc
Tim McClelland
Larry McCoy
James McKean
Chuck Meriwether
Durwood Merrill
Dan Morrison
Steve Palermo*
David Phillips
Rick Reed
Michael Reilly
John (Rocky) Roe
Dale Scott
John Shulock
Tim Tschida
Vic Voltaggio
Tim Welke
Larry Young
*Inactive status.

NATIONAL LEAGUE

Address
350 Park Avenue
New York, NY 10022
Telephone
212-339-7700
President and treasurer
Leonard S. Coleman Jr.
Senior vice president and secretary
Katy Feeney
Executive director, public affairs
Ricky Clemons
Director of umpire supervision
Ed Vargo
**Assistant secretary and executive director,
player records**
Nancy Crofts
Executive secretary
Rita Aughavin

Administrative assistant, umpires
Cathy Davis
Public relations assistant
Glenn Wilburn
Umpires
Wally Bell
Greg Bonin
Jerry Crawford
Gary Darling
Bob Davidson
Gerry Davis
Dana DeMuth
Bruce Froemming
Brian Gorman
Eric Gregg
Tom Hallion
Angel Hernandez
Mark Hirschbeck
Bill Hohn
Jeff Kellogg

Jerry Layne
Randy Marsh
John McSherry
Ed Montague
Larry Poncino
Frank Pulli
Jim Quick
Ed Rapuano Jr.
Charlie Reliford
Steve Rippley
Paul Runge
Terry Tata
Larry Vanover
Harry Wendelstedt
Joe West
Charlie Williams
Mike Winters

OTHER ORGANIZATIONS

PLAYER RELATIONS COMMITTEE

Address
350 Park Avenue
New York, NY 10022
Telephone
212-339-7400
212-371-2242 (FAX)

Chief labor negotiator and general counsel
Randy L. Levine
General counsel
Charles P. O'Connor
Associate counsels
Louis Melendez
John Westhoff

Contract administrator
Barbara Ernst
Director, public relations
Richard Levin

NATIONAL BASEBALL HALL OF FAME AND MUSEUM

Address
P.O. Box 590
Cooperstown, NY 13326
Telephone
607-547-7200
607-547-2044 (FAX)
Chairman of Hall of Fame
Edward W. Stack
President
Donald C. Marr Jr.
Vice presidents
William J. Guilfoile
Frank Simio
Curator
William T. Spencer Jr.
Registrar
Peter P. Clark
Director of merchandising
Barbara Shinn
Controller
Frances L. Althiser
Librarian
James L. Gates
Director of public relations
Jeff Idelson

NATIONAL ASSOCIATION OF PROFESSIONAL BASEBALL LEAGUES

Address
P.O. Box A
St. Petersburg, FL 33731
Telephone
813-822-6937
813-821-5819 (FAX)
President
Mike Moore
Vice president/administration
Pat O'Conner
Chief operating officer
Rob Dlugozima
General counsel
Ben Hayes
Exec. dir./business and finance
Bob Miller
Exec. director/special events
Bob Sparks
Director/licensing
Misann Ellmaker
Director/marketing
Ron Myers
Director/media relations
Jim Ferguson

MAJOR LEAGUE SCOUTING BUREAU

Address
23712 Birtcher Dr., Suite A
Lake Forest, CA 92630
Telephone
714-458-7600
714-458-9454 (FAX)
Director
Donald F. Pries

BASEBALL WRITERS' ASSOCIATION OF AMERICA

President
Jerome Holtzman, Chicago Tribune
Vice president
Hal McCoy, Dayton Daily News
Secretary/treasurer
Jack O'Connell, Hartford Courant

HOWE SPORTSDATA INTERNATIONAL INC.

Address
Boston Fish Pier
West Building No. 2, Suite 306
Boston, MA 02210
Telephone
617-951-0070
617-951-1379 (stats request)
617-737-9960 (FAX)
President
Jay Virshbo
Historical consultant
William Weiss

MAJOR LEAGUE BASEBALL PLAYERS ASSOCIATION

Address
12 E. 49th St., 24th Floor
New York, NY 10017
Telephone
212-826-0808
212-752-3649 (FAX)
Executive director and general counsel
Donald M. Fehr
Special assistant
Tony Bernazard
Associate general counsel
Eugene D. Orza
Assistant general counsels
Doyle R. Pryor
Counsel
Arthur Schack
Director of licensing
Judy Heeter

ELIAS SPORTS BUREAU

Address
500 Fifth Ave.
New York, NY 10110
Telephone
212-869-1530
212-354-0980 (FAX)
General manager
Seymour Siwoff

MAJOR LEAGUE BASEBALL UMPIRE DEVELOPMENT

Address
P.O. Box A
St. Petersburg, FL 33731
Telephone
813-823-1286
813-823-7212 (FAX)
Executive director
Edwin W. Lawrence
Director of field supervision
Mike Fitzpatrick

MAJOR LEAGUE UMPIRES ASSOCIATION

Address
1735 Market St., Suite 3420
Philadelphia, PA 19103
Telephone
215-979-3220
215-979-3201 (FAX)
General counsel
Richard G. Phillips

MAJOR LEAGUE BASEBALL PLAYERS ALUMNI ASSOC.

Address
3637 4th St., North, Suite 480
St. Petersburg, FL 33704
Telephone
813-822-3399
813-822-6300 (FAX)
President
Brooks Robinson
Vice presidents
Bob Boone
Carl Erskine
Mike Hegan
Chuck Hinton
Al Kaline
Mike Schmidt
Rusty Staub
Billy Williams
Secretary/treasurer
Fred Valentine

BASEBALL ASSISTANCE TEAM INC.

Address
350 Park Avenue
New York, NY 10022
Telephone
212-339-7884
Chairman
Ralph Branca
President
Joe Garagiola
Vice presidents
Joe Black
Earl Wilson
Executive director
Frank Slocum
Secretary/treasurer
Tom Ostertag

ASSOCIATION OF PROFESSIONAL BASEBALL PLAYERS OF AMERICA

Address
12062 Valley View, Suite 211
Garden Grove, CA 92645
Telephone
714-892-9900
714-897-0233 (FAX)
President
John J. McHale
Secretary/treasurer
Chuck Stevens

BALTIMORE ORIOLES
AMERICAN LEAGUE EAST DIVISION

1996 ORIOLES SCHEDULE

Home games shaded.
* — All-Star Game at Veterans Stadium (Philadelphia)
N — Night game (any game starting after 5 p.m.)

MARCH
SUN	MON	TUE	WED	THU	FRI	SAT
31						

APRIL
SUN	MON	TUE	WED	THU	FRI	SAT
	1 KC	2	3 N KC	4 KC	5 N MIN	6 N MIN
7 MIN	8	9 N CLE	10 N CLE	11	12 N MIN	13 MIN
14 MIN	15	16 N BOS	17 N BOS	18 BOS	19 N TEX	20 N TEX
21 TEX	22 N CLE	23 N CLE	24 N KC	25 N KC	26 N TEX	27 TEX
28 TEX	29 N TEX	30 N NY				

MAY
SUN	MON	TUE	WED	THU	FRI	SAT
			1 N NY	2	3 N MIL	4 MIL
5 MIL	6	7 N CHI	8 N CHI	9 N CHI	10 N MIL	11 MIL
12 MIL	13 N OAK	14 N OAK	15 OAK	16	17 N SEA	18 N SEA
19 SEA	20 N CAL	21 N CAL	22 N CAL	23	24 N OAK	25 OAK
26 OAK	27	28 N SEA	29 N SEA	30	31 N CAL	

JUNE
SUN	MON	TUE	WED	THU	FRI	SAT
						1 N CAL
2 CAL	3	4 N DET	5 N DET	6 N DET	7 N CHI	8 CHI
9 CHI	10 N DET	11 N DET	12 DET	13 N KC	14 N KC	15 KC
16 N KC	17 N TEX	18 N TEX	19 N TEX	20	21 N KC	22 KC
23 KC	24 N TEX	25 N TEX	26 N TEX	27	28 N NY	29 NY
30 NY						

JULY
SUN	MON	TUE	WED	THU	FRI	SAT
	1	2 N TOR	3 N TOR	4 N BOS	5 N BOS	6 BOS
7 N BOS	8 *	9 ALL-STAR GAME	10	11 N NY	12 N NY	13 N NY
14 N NY	15 N TOR	16 N TOR	17 N TOR	18 N BOS	19 N BOS	20 BOS
21 BOS	22 N MIN	23 N MIN	24 N MIN	25 N CLE	26 N CLE	27 CLE
28 CLE	29	30 N MIN	31 N MIN			

AUGUST
SUN	MON	TUE	WED	THU	FRI	SAT
				1 MIN	2 N CLE	3 CLE
4 CLE	5 N CLE	6 N MIL	7 N MIL	8 MIL	9 N CHI	10 N CHI
11 CHI	12 N MIL	13 N MIL	14 MIL	15 N OAK	16 OAK	17 OAK
18 OAK	19	20 N SEA	21 N SEA	22 N SEA	23 N CAL	24 N CAL
25 CAL	26 N OAK	27 N OAK	28 OAK	29 N SEA	30 N SEA	31 SEA

SEPTEMBER
SUN	MON	TUE	WED	THU	FRI	SAT
1 N SEA	2 N CAL	3 N CAL	4 N CAL	5	6 N DET	7 N DET
8 DET	9 N DET	10 N CHI	11 N CHI	12 N CHI	13 N DET	14 DET
15 DET	16	17 N NY	18 N NY	19 N NY	20 N TOR	21 TOR
22 TOR	23	24 N BOS	25 N BOS	26 N TOR	27 N TOR	28 TOR
29 TOR						

1996 SEASON

CLUB DIRECTORY

Managing general partner
Peter Angelos

Vice chairman, business & finance
Joe Foss

General manager
Pat Gillick

Assistant general manager
Kevin Malone

Director of player development
Syd Thrift

Asst. director of player development
Don Buford

Scouting director
Gary Nickels

Special assistants to the g.m.
Gordon Goldsberry
Fred Uhlman Sr.

Assistant, scouting
Matt Slater

Assistant, player development/scouting
Mike Wong

Director of business affairs
Walter Gutowski

Director of finance
Robert Ames

Traveling secretary
Philip Itzoe

Director of public relations
John Maroon

Asst. director of public relations
Bill Stetka

Director of marketing and advertising
Scott Nickle

Assistant director of marketing
Michael Fiorelli

Director of stadium operations
Roy Sommerhof

Director of community relations
Julie Wagner

Asst. director of community relations
Stacey Beckwith

Coordinator of events
Spiro Alafassos

Publishing coordinator
Stephanie Parrillo

Director of computer services
James Kline

Director of ticket operations
Audrey Brown

Trainers
Richard Bancells
Jamie Reed

Strength and conditioning
Tim Bishop

Scouts
Rick Arnold
Carlos Bernhardt
Jesus Carmona
Lane Decker
Manny Estrada
Jim Gilbert
John Green
Jesus Halabi
Jim Howard
Deacon Jones
Leo Labossiere
Mike Ledna
Curt Motton
Lamar North
Fred Petersen
Harry Shelton
Ed Sprague
John Stokic
Mike Tullier
Earl Winn
Jerry Zimmerman

MINOR LEAGUE AFFILIATES

Class	Team	League	Manager
AAA	Rochester	International	Marv Foley
AA	Bowie	Eastern	Bob Miscik
A	High Desert	California	Tim Blackwell
A	Frederick	Carolina	Mike O'Berry
Rookie	Bluefield	Appalachian	To be announced
Rookie	Gulf Coast Orioles	Gulf Coast	Geno Petralli

BROADCAST INFORMATION

Radio: WBAL-AM (1090).
TV: WJZ (Channel 13), WNUV (Channel 54), WFTY (Channel 50, Washington, D.C.).
Cable TV: Home Team Sports.

SPRING TRAINING

Ballpark (city): Ft. Lauderdale Stadium (Ft. Lauderdale, Fla.).
Ticket information: To be announced.

SPRING TRAINING ROSTER

Manager—Davey Johnson.
Coaches—Pat Dobson, Rick Down, Andy Etchebarren, Elrod Hendricks (44), Sam Perlozzo, John Stearns.

No.	PITCHERS	B/T	Ht./Wt.	Born	1995 clubs
49	Benitez, Armando	R/R	6-4/180	11-3-72	Baltimore, Rochester
21	Erickson, Scott	R/R	6-4/222	2-2-68	Minnesota, Baltimore
60	Haynes, Jimmy	R/R	6-4/185	9-5-72	Rochester, Baltimore
37	Krivda, Rick	R/L	6-1/180	1-19-70	Rochester, Baltimore
52	Lee, Mark	L/L	6-3/200	7-20-64	Rochester, Baltimore
	Maduro, Calvin	R/R	6-0/175	9-5-74	Frederick, Bowie
	McDowell, Roger	R/R	6-1/197	12-21-60	Texas
	Mercker, Kent	L/L	6-2/195	2-1-68	Atlanta
75	Mills, Alan	B/R	6-1/192	10-18-66	Baltimore, Rochester, Gulf Coast Orioles
	Munoz, Oscar	R/R	6-3/210	9-25-69	Salt Lake, Minnesota
35	Mussina, Mike	R/R	6-2/185	12-8-68	Baltimore
	Myers, Randy	L/L	6-1/230	9-19-62	Chicago N.L.
47	Orosco, Jesse	R/L	6-2/205	4-21-57	Baltimore
	Percibal, Billy	R/R	6-1/156	2-2-74	High Desert, Bowie
53	Rhodes, Arthur	L/L	6-2/206	10-24-69	Rochester, Baltimore
	Sackinsky, Brian	R/R	6-4/220	6-22-71	Rochester
	Stephenson, Garrett	R/R	6-4/195	1-2-72	Bowie
	Wells, David	L/L	6-4/225	5-20-63	Detroit, Cincinnati

No.	CATCHERS	B/T	Ht./Wt.	Born	1995 clubs
59	Devarez, Cesar	R/R	5-10/175	9-22-69	Rochester, Baltimore
23	Hoiles, Chris	R/R	6-0/213	3-20-65	Baltimore
	Waszgis, B.J.	R/R	6-2/210	8-24-70	Bowie
24	Zaun, Greg	B/R	5-10/170	4-14-71	Rochester, Baltimore

No.	INFIELDERS	B/T	Ht./Wt.	Born	1995 clubs
6	Alexander, Manny	R/R	5-10/165	3-20-71	Baltimore
	Alomar, Roberto	B/R	6-0/185	2-5-68	Toronto
	Bautista, Juan	R/R	6-0/165	6-24-75	High Desert, Bowie
30	Huson, Jeff	L/R	6-3/180	8-15-64	Rochester, Baltimore
12	Manto, Jeff	R/R	6-3/210	8-23-64	Baltimore, Bowie, Frederick
	McClain, Scott	R/R	6-4/210	5-19-72	Bowie, Rochester
25	Palmeiro, Rafael	L/L	6-0/188	9-24-64	Baltimore
8	Ripken, Cal	R/R	6-4/220	8-24-60	Baltimore
	Surhoff, B.J.	L/R	6-1/200	8-4-64	Milwaukee
	Tyler, Brad	L/R	6-2/175	3-3-69	Rochester

No.	OUTFIELDERS	B/T	Ht./Wt.	Born	1995 clubs
9	Anderson, Brady	L/L	6-1/195	1-18-64	Baltimore
	Bartee, Kim	B/R	6-0/175	7-21-72	Gulf Coast Orioles, Bowie, Rochester
26	Bonilla, Bobby	B/R	6-3/240	2-23-63	New York N.L., Baltimore
	Devereaux, Mike	R/R	6-0/195	4-10-63	Chicago A.L., Atlanta
11	Hammonds, Jeffrey	R/R	6-0/195	3-5-71	Baltimore, Bowie
42	Obando, Sherman	R/R	6-4/215	1-23-70	Baltimore, Rochester
34	Smith, Mark	R/R	6-4/195	5-7-70	Rochester, Baltimore

BALLPARK INFORMATION

Ballpark (capacity, surface)
Oriole Park at Camden Yards (48,876, grass)

Address
333 W. Camden St.
Baltimore, MD 21201

Business phone
410-685-9800

Ticket information
410-481-SEAT

Ticket prices
$25 (club level seats)
$20 (lower box between bases)
$18 (lower box beyond bases)
$16 (If club level, terrace boxes)
$14 (upper box, lf box)
$12 (left field upper box)
$9 (upper & lower reserved)
$7 (lf upper reserved)
$5 (bleachers)
$3 (standing room)

Field dimensions (from home plate)
To left field at foul line, 333 feet
To center field, 400 feet
To right field at foul line, 318 feet

First game played
April 6, 1992 (Orioles 2, Indians 0)

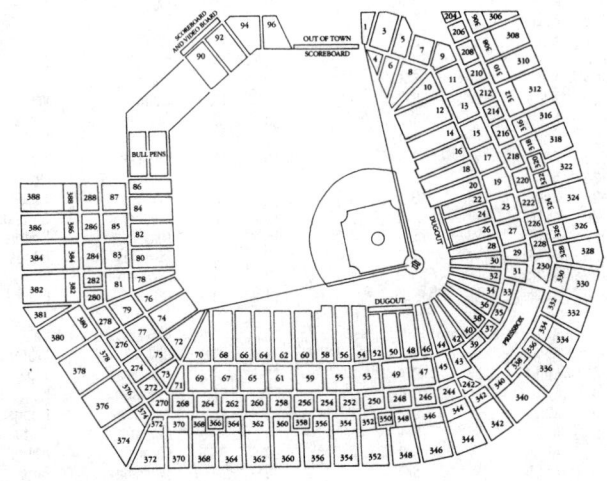

DAY BY DAY

1996 SEASON *Baltimore Orioles*

Date	Opp.	Res.	Score	(inn.*)	Hits	Opp. hits	Winning pitcher	Losing pitcher	Save	Record	Pos.	GB
4-26	At K.C.	L	1-5		2	8	Appier	Moyer		0-1	5th	1
4-27	At Min.	L	4-7		10	9	Stevens	Pennington	Aguilera	0-2	5th	2
4-28	At Min.	L	9-12		11	17	Guthrie	Benitez	Aguilera	0-3	5th	2½
4-29	At Min.	W	13-7		15	7	K. Brown	Hawkins		1-3	T4th	2½
4-30	At Min.	W	6-3		8	6	Rhodes	Erickson	Jones	2-3	T4th	1½
5-1	Mil.	L	0-7		2	12	Bones	Mussina		2-4	5th	2½
5-3	Mil.	L	4-7		5	9	Kiefer	Jones	Lloyd	2-5	5th	3
5-4	Mil.	W	5-2		8	5	Mills	Mercedes	Jones	3-5	T4th	3
5-5	Tor.	W	9-2		11	6	K. Brown	Leiter		4-5	4th	3
5-6	Tor.	L	3-7		12	12	Darwin	Rhodes		4-6	4th	3
5-7	Tor.	W	6-2		10	6	Mussina	Cone		5-6	4th	2
5-9	At Bos.	L	3-4		6	4	Belinda	Benitez		5-7	4th	3
5-10	At Bos.	L	2-6		7	8	Hanson	Fernandez		5-8	4th	4
5-12	Cle.	L	2-3		9	8	Martinez	K. Brown	Mesa	5-9	4th	4½
5-13	Cle.	W	6-1		8	3	Mussina	Clark		6-9	4th	4
5-14	Cle.	L	1-3		4	4	Hershiser	Rhodes	Mesa	6-10	5th	5
5-16	Det.	L	8-9		16	11	Boever	Jones	Henneman	6-11	5th	6
5-17	Det.	W	7-4		11	8	K. Brown	Lira	Benitez	7-11	5th	6
5-18	Det.	W	3-2		6	4	Mussina	Wells	Jones	8-11	4th	6
5-19	At N.Y.	W	7-5		10	5	Mills	Wetteland	Jones	9-11	4th	5
5-20	At N.Y.	L	2-7		4	7	Perez	Fernandez		9-12	4th	5
5-21	At N.Y.	L	0-5		4	12	Hitchcock	McDonald		9-13	5th	5
5-23	At Oak.	W	8-1		11	4	K. Brown	Harkey		10-13	T4th	5
5-24	At Oak.	L	3-5		9	10	Corsi	Mussina	Eckersley	10-14	T4th	5
5-25	At Oak.	L	6-9		7	9	Honeycutt	Benitez	Eckersley	10-15	5th	5
5-26	At Sea.	L	3-8		11	10	Johnson	McDonald		10-16	5th	6
5-27	At Sea.	W	11-4		16	7	Mills	Wells		11-16	5th	6
5-28	At Sea.	L	2-5		7	9	Bosio	K. Brown	Ayala	11-17	5th	6
5-29	At Cal.	L	5-6		10	7	Boskie	Mussina	Smith	11-18	5th	7
5-30	At Cal.	W	5-4	(10)	10	8	Orosco	Patterson	Jones	12-18	5th	7
5-31	At Cal.	W	5-3		10	8	McDonald	Sanderson	Jones	13-18	5th	7
6-2	Oak.	W	2-1		9	5	K. Brown	Honeycutt	Jones	14-18	T3rd	7
6-3	Oak.	W	9-5		8	8	Mussina	Harkey		15-18	2nd	7
6-4	Oak.	L	6-14		12	14	Stewart	Fernandez		15-19	T2nd	8
6-5	Sea.	L	0-2		3	5	Johnson	McDonald		15-20	T2nd	9
6-6	Sea.	W	12-6		15	8	Moyer	Fleming		16-20	2nd	8
6-7	Sea.	L	2-10		10	8	Bosio	K. Brown		16-21	2nd	9
6-8	Sea.	W	8-2		9	7	Mussina	Torres		17-21	2nd	8
6-9	Cal.	W	10-4		14	7	Klingenbeck	Springer		18-21	2nd	8
6-10	Cal.	W	6-2		9	7	McDonald	Bielecki		19-21	2nd	8
6-11	Cal.	L	4-5		10	10	Langston	Moyer	Smith	19-22	2nd	7
6-12	At Cle.	L	3-4		5	8	Nagy	K. Brown	Mesa	19-23	T2nd	7
6-13	At Cle.	L	0-11		8	14	Martinez	Mussina		19-24	T2nd	8
6-14	At Cle.	L	2-5		9	7	Ogea	Klingenbeck	Mesa	19-25	T2nd	8
6-16	At Det.	L	3-5		9	9	Lira	McDonald	Henneman	19-26	T3rd	8
6-17	At Det.	L	3-5		4	11	Wells	K. Brown	Boever	19-27	T4th	8
6-18	At Det.	L	8-10		12	14	Maxcy	Mussina	Henneman	19-28	5th	9
6-19	N.Y.	W	5-4		10	7	Klingenbeck	Perez	Jones	20-28	T4th	8
6-20	N.Y.	W	8-7		11	11	Oquist	Wickman	Jones	21-28	T3rd	7
6-21	N.Y.	L	1-2		5	6	Pettitte	Moyer	Wetteland	21-29	T3rd	8
6-22	Bos.	L	1-4		8	6	Clemens	K. Brown	Belinda	21-30	T4th	9
6-23	Bos.	W	7-5		10	12	Mussina	Smith	Lee	22-30	4th	8
6-24	Bos.	L	5-6		7	14	Cormier	Orosco	Belinda	22-31	4th	9
6-25	Bos.	W	10-1		15	8	Rhodes	Eshelman		23-31	4th	8
6-26	At Mil.	W	2-0		11	2	Moyer	Miranda	Jones	24-31	4th	8
6-27	At Mil.	W	11-3		15	6	DeSilva	Sparks		25-31	4th	8
6-28	At Mil.	W	4-2		7	5	Mussina	Bones	Jones	26-31	4th	7
6-29	At Tor.	L	1-5		7	8	Guzman	Fernandez		26-32	4th	8
6-30	At Tor.	L	5-6		11	8	Cox	Clark		26-33	4th	8
7-1	At Tor.	W	6-2		10	7	Moyer	Leiter		27-33	4th	7
7-2	At Tor.	W	9-7		8	5	Benitez	Crabtree	Jones	28-33	T3rd	7
7-3	Min.	W	9-4		11	9	Mussina	Tapani		29-33	T3rd	7
7-4	Min.	L	3-6		7	11	Erickson	Klingenbeck		29-34	4th	8
7-5	Min.	L	2-8		7	12	Trombley	Rhodes		29-35	4th	8
7-6	At Chi.	W	2-1		10	7	Moyer	Fortugno	Jones	30-35	T3rd	7
7-7	At Chi.	W	5-2		8	8	Clark	Abbott	Jones	31-35	3rd	6
7-8	At Chi.	W	5-2		8	9	Mussina	Bere		32-35	3rd	6
7-9	At Chi.	W	11-2		14	10	Erickson	Fernandez		33-35	3rd	6
7-13	K.C.	L	8-9		13	12	Meacham	Jones	Montgomery	33-36	3rd	6
7-14	K.C.	L	2-7		7	8	Gordon	McDonald		33-37	3rd	7

Date	Opp.	Res.	Score	(inn.*)	Hits	Opp. hits	Winning pitcher	Losing pitcher	Save	Record	Pos.	GB
7-15	K.C.	W	9-1		17	7	Erickson	Appier		34-37	3rd	6
7-16	K.C.	W	3-2		4	4	Moyer	Bunch	Jones	35-37	3rd	5
7-17	At Tex.	W	3-2	(13)	10	5	Lee	Cook	Jones	36-37	T2nd	4
7-18	At Tex.	W	4-2		5	5	Mussina	Pavlik	Jones	37-37	2nd	4
7-19	At Min.	L	3-5		5	8	Radke	McDonald	Stevens	37-38	2nd	5
7-20	At Min.	L	2-5		5	8	Rodriguez	Erickson	Stevens	37-39	2nd	6
7-21	At K.C.	W	10-6		11	12	Oquist	Bunch		38-39	2nd	6
7-22	At K.C.	L	3-5		10	8	Brewer	Rhodes	Montgomery	38-40	2nd	6
7-23	At K.C.	W	6-2		8	6	Mussina	Gordon		39-40	2nd	5
7-25	Tex.	W	4-3		7	7	Orosco	McDowell		40-40	T2nd	4¹/₂
7-26	Tex.	W	7-6		10	7	Moyer	Cook	Jones	41-40	2nd	4¹/₂
7-27	Tex.	L	1-2		7	7	Vosberg	Orosco	Russell	41-41	T2nd	4¹/₂
7-28	Chi.	W	4-3		5	9	Mussina	Alvarez	Jones	42-41	2nd	4¹/₂
7-29	Chi.	L	4-7		9	12	Bertotti	Oquist	Hernandez	42-42	T2nd	5¹/₂
7-30	Chi.	W	8-3		9	11	Erickson	Bere		43-42	T2nd	4¹/₂
7-31	Tor.	L	3-6		8	9	Hentgen	Moyer	Jordan	43-43	3rd	5
8-1	Tor.	L	10-12		10	13	Robinson	Jones	Castillo	43-44	3rd	6
8-2	Tor.	W	1-0		1	4	Mussina	Menhart		44-44	3rd	5
8-3	Tor.	L	2-8	(10)	4	8	Jordan	Clark		44-45	3rd	6
8-4	Mil.	L	4-12		8	16	Karl	Erickson		44-46	3rd	7
8-5	Mil.	W	6-5		12	8	Clark	Fetters		45-46	3rd	7
8-6	Mil.	L	2-3		3	6	Ignasiak	K. Brown	Fetters	45-47	3rd	8
8-7	At N.Y.	L	0-3		3	3	McDowell	Mussina		45-48	3rd	9
8-8	At N.Y.	L	4-11		8	11	Cone	Krivda		45-49	3rd	10
8-9	At N.Y.	W	7-2		10	6	Moyer	Kamieniecki		46-49	3rd	10
8-10	At Bos.	L	1-11		5	17	Cormier	Erickson		46-50	3rd	11
8-11	At Bos.	L	4-5	(12)	8	11	Aguilera	Clark		46-51	3rd	12
8-12	At Bos.	L	0-7		6	15	Clemens	Mussina		46-52	3rd	13
8-13	At Bos.	L	2-3		2	6	Wakefield	Krivda	Belinda	46-53	3rd	14
8-14	Cle.	L	6-9		11	13	Assenmacher	Benitez	Mesa	46-54	3rd	15
8-15	Cle.	W	8-3		11	7	Erickson	Nagy		47-54	3rd	14
8-16	Cle.	L	5-8		10	11	Hershiser	K. Brown	Mesa	47-55	3rd	15
8-17	K.C.	L	2-3	(10)	10	7	Olson	Orosco	Montgomery	47-56	3rd	16
8-18	At Oak.	W	8-4		7	9	Krivda	Prieto	Clark	48-56	3rd	15
8-19	At Oak.	W	12-6		14	8	Moyer	Wojciechowski		49-56	3rd	15
8-20	At Oak.	L	3-6		2	13	Johns	Erickson	Eckersley	49-57	3rd	16
8-21	At Sea.	L	0-6		7	10	Nelson	Benitez		49-58	3rd	17
8-22	At Sea.	W	2-1		6	8	Mussina	Belcher	Jones	50-58	3rd	17
8-23	At Sea.	W	7-1		13	9	Krivda	Wolcott	Benitez	51-58	3rd	17
8-24	At Cal.	L	4-6		9	11	Finley	Rhodes	Smith	51-59	3rd	18
8-25	At Cal.	W	11-2		12	6	Erickson	Langston		52-59	3rd	17
8-26	At Cal.	W	5-2		14	5	K. Brown	B. Anderson		53-59	3rd	16
8-27	At Cal.	W	4-0		15	4	Mussina	Harkey		54-59	3rd	16
8-29	Oak.	L	1-3		8	5	Reyes	Clark	Eckersley	54-60	3rd	16
8-30	Oak.	L	2-7		8	11	Johns	Moyer	Eckersley	54-61	3rd	17
8-31	Oak.	L	7-8		10	13	Reyes	Clark	Eckersley	54-62	3rd	17
9-1	Sea.	L	3-4		9	9	Belcher	Mussina	Charlton	54-63	3rd	18
9-2	Sea.	W	3-2		7	6	K. Brown	Bosio	Jones	55-63	3rd	18
9-3	Sea.	L	6-9		10	12	Carmona	Krivda	Charlton	55-64	3rd	19
9-4	Cal.	L	3-5		8	11	Abbott	Moyer	Smith	55-65	3rd	19¹/₂
9-5	Cal.	W	8-0		17	3	Erickson	B. Anderson		56-65	3rd	19¹/₂
9-6	Cal.	W	4-2		9	6	Mussina	Boskie	Orosco	57-65	3rd	19¹/₂
9-8	At Cle.	L	2-3		5	6	Hershiser	K. Brown	Mesa	57-66	3rd	19¹/₂
9-9	At Cle.	L	1-2		2	5	Ogea	Krivda	Mesa	57-67	3rd	19¹/₂
9-10	At Cle.	L	3-5		6	12	Tavarez	Orosco	Mesa	57-68	3rd	19¹/₂
9-11	Bos.	W	10-7		9	11	Lee	Gunderson	Jones	58-68	3rd	18¹/₂
9-12	Bos.	W	6-5		11	9	Hartley	Hudson	Orosco	59-68	3rd	17¹/₂
9-13	Bos.	L	0-2		2	7	Wakefield	Haynes	Aguilera	59-69	3rd	18¹/₂
9-14	N.Y.	L	4-5		7	10	Pettitte	Krivda	Wetteland	59-70	3rd	18¹/₂
9-15	N.Y.	W	8-1		5	8	Erickson	Hitchcock		60-70	3rd	18¹/₂
9-16	N.Y.	L	5-6	(6)	9	10	McDowell	Mussina	Wickman	60-71	3rd	18¹/₂
9-17	N.Y.	W	2-0		6	4	K. Brown	Kamieniecki	Orosco	61-71	3rd	18¹/₂
9-18	At Det.	W	6-2		9	5	Haynes	Lira		62-71	3rd	17¹/₂
9-19	At Det.	L	4-7		11	9	Myers	Krivda	Henry	62-72	3rd	18¹/₂
9-20	At Det.	W	6-3		10	8	Erickson	Sodowsky		63-72	3rd	18¹/₂
9-21	At Det.	W	13-1		16	3	Mussina	Doherty		64-72	3rd	18
9-22	At Mil.	W	10-3		14	9	K. Brown	Givens		65-72	3rd	17¹/₂
9-23	At Mil.	W	9-3		11	3	Haynes	Bones		66-72	3rd	17
9-24	At Mil.	L	1-5		5	7	Sparks	Krivda		66-73	3rd	17
9-26	At Tor.	W	5-0		10	5	Mussina	Hentgen		67-73	3rd	16¹/₂
9-27	At Tor.	W	7-0		12	3	Erickson	Menhart		68-73	3rd	15¹/₂
9-29	Det.	W	6-0		10	5	K. Brown	Lira		69-73	3rd	16
9-30	Det.	W	12-0		14	2	McDonald	Bergman		70-73	3rd	16
10-1	Det.	W	4-0		10	2	Mussina	Sodowsky		71-73	3rd	15

Monthly records: April (2-3), May (11-15), June (13-15), July (17-10), August (11-19), September (16-11), October (1-0).
*Innings, if other than nine.

HIGHLIGHTS

High point: The Orioles won 11 of their last 13 games and closed the season with five shutouts—well after they had ceased to be a contender in either the division race or the wild-card scramble.

Low point: Beginning with a 3-1 loss to Oakland on August 29, the Orioles dropped six of seven games leading up to the night Cal Ripken tied Lou Gehrig's consecutive-games record. That dropped them 10 games under .500 and removed any realistic hope of competing for a wild-card berth.

Turning point: There really wasn't one, since the Orioles opened the season with only six victories in their first 17 games, but they did make a midseason run that could have carried them into contention. They went 21-11 from June 25-July 30 to get to 43-42 but slipped eight games below .500 by August 14.

Most valuable player: First baseman Rafael Palmeiro. He batted .310 with 39 home runs and 104 RBIs and further vindicated the club's decision to sign him to a rich five-year contract.

Most valuable pitcher: Righthander Mike Mussina. He went 19-9 with a 3.29 ERA. He is 71-30 in his first 4½ big-league seasons.

Most improved player: Third baseman Jeff Manto. A minor league journeyman, Manto became a Camden Yards sensation in June by rapping home runs in four consecutive at-bats over three games. He finished with a .256 average and 17 homers in just 254 at-bats.

Most pleasant surprise: Rookie righthander Jimmy Haynes. Haynes went 2-1 with a 2.25 ERA in four appearances (three starts). He gave up just 11 hits in 24 innings and had 22 strikeouts.

Biggest disappointments: Catcher Chris Hoiles. He signed a five-year contract soon after the labor situation cleared up, then batted .250 with 19 homers and 58 RBIs. Third baseman Leo Gomez also returned with enhanced expectations after a strong 1994 performance, only to lose his job because of injuries and inconsistency at the plate.

Key injuries: Righthander Ben McDonald

struggled with shoulder tendinitis and managed just three victories in 13 starts. Jeffrey Hammonds, seemingly ready to establish himself in the outfield, was limited to 178 at-bats because of knee and shoulder problems.

Notable: Ripken broke Gehrig's consecutive-games record on September 6 in what almost everyone considered the high point of the major league season. . . . Harold Baines hit his 300th career homer on September 22. . . . The Orioles acquired outfielder Bobby Bonilla (from the Mets) and pitcher Scott Erickson (Twins) in July.

—PETER SCHMUCK

RECORDS

1995 regular-season record: 71-73 (3rd in A.L. East); 36-36 at home; 35-37 on road; 25-27 vs. East; 22-27 vs. Central; 24-19 vs West; 22-17 vs. lefthanded starters; 49-56 vs. righthanded starters; 62-64 on grass; 9-9 on turf; 20-20 in daytime; 51-53 at night; 16-21 in one-run games; 2-3 in extra-inning games; 0-0-0 in doubleheaders.

Team record past five years: 375-367 (.505, ranks 5th in league in that span).

TEAM LEADERS

Batting average: Rafael Palmeiro (.310).
At-bats: Brady Anderson, Rafael Palmeiro (554).
Runs: Brady Anderson (108).
Hits: Rafael Palmeiro (172).
Total bases: Rafael Palmeiro (323).
Doubles: Brady Anderson (33).
Triples: Brady Anderson (10).
Home runs: Rafael Palmeiro (39).
Runs batted in: Rafael Palmeiro (104).
Stolen bases: Brady Anderson (26).
Slugging percentage: Rafael Palmeiro (.583).
On-base percentage: Harold Baines (.403).
Wins: Mike Mussina (19).
Earned-run average: Mike Mussina (3.29).
Complete games: Scott Erickson, Mike Mussina (7).
Shutouts: Mike Mussina (4).
Saves: Doug Jones (22).
Innings pitched: Mike Mussina (221.2).
Strikeouts: Mike Mussina (158).

GAMES BY POSITION

Catcher: Chris Hoiles 107, Greg Zaun 39, Matt Nokes 16, Cesar Devarez 6.
First base: Rafael Palmeiro 142, Jeff Manto 4, Leo Gomez 3, Jack Voigt 1.
Second base: Manny Alexander 81, Bret Barberie 74, Jeff Huson 21.
Third base: Jeff Manto 69, Leo Gomez 44, Jeff Huson 33, Bobby Bonilla 24, Bret Barberie 3, Manny Alexander 2.
Shortstop: Cal Ripken 144, Manny Alexander 7, Jeff Huson 1.
Outfield: Brady Anderson 142, Curtis Goodwin 84, Kevin Bass 77, Jeffrey Hammonds 46, Bobby Bonilla 39, Mark Smith 32, Damon Buford 24, Jarvis Brown 17, Andy Van Slyke 17, Sherman Obando 7.
Designated hitter: Harold Baines 122, Kevin Bass 19, Jeff Manto 13, Sherman Obando 7, Chris Hoiles 6, Bret Barberie 5, Leo Gomez 5, Jeffrey Hammonds 5, Mark Smith 5, Curtis Goodwin 2, Jeff Huson 2, Matt Nokes 2, Manny Alexander 1, Jack Voigt 1.

TOP DRAFT CHOICES

1. **Alvie Shepherd,** RHP, University of Nebraska.
2. **Charles Alley,** C, Palm Beach (Fla.) Lakes H.S.
3. **Darrell Dent,** OF, Montclair Prep, Panorama City, Calif.
4. **Louis Fisher,** RHP, Fremont H.S., Oakland.
5. **Luke Hudson,** RHP, Fountain Valley (Calif.) H.S.
6. **John Bale,** LHP, University of Southern Mississippi.
7. **Kevin Miller,** 3B, Ballard H.S., Seattle.
8. **Scott Eibey,** LHP, University of Northern Iowa.
9. **Joel Stephens,** OF, Notre Dame H.S., Elmira, N.Y.
10. **David Dellucci,** OF, University of Mississippi.

BOSTON RED SOX
AMERICAN LEAGUE EAST DIVISION

1996 RED SOX SCHEDULE

▢ Home games shaded.
* – All-Star Game at Veterans Stadium (Philadelphia)
N – Night game (any game starting after 5 p.m.)

MARCH

SUN	MON	TUE	WED	THU	FRI	SAT
31						

APRIL

SUN	MON	TUE	WED	THU	FRI	SAT
	1 TEX	2	3 N TEX	4 N TEX	5 KC	6 KC
7 KC	8 MIN	9	10 MIN	11 N MIN	12 N CLE	13 CLE
14 CLE	15 CLE	16 N BAL	17 N BAL	18 BAL	19 N CLE	20 CLE
21 CLE	22 N MIN	23 MIN	24 N TEX	25 N TEX	26 N KC	27 KC
28 KC	29	30 N DET				

MAY

SUN	MON	TUE	WED	THU	FRI	SAT
			1 N DET	2	3 N TOR	4 TOR
5 TOR	6	7 N MIL	8 N MIL	9 MIL	10 N TOR	11 TOR
12 TOR	13	14 N CAL	15 N CAL	16	17 N OAK	18 OAK
19 OAK	20 N SEA	21 N SEA	22 N SEA	23 N SEA	24 N CAL	25 CAL
26 CAL	27 OAK	28 N OAK	29 N OAK	30 N SEA	31 N SEA	

JUNE

SUN	MON	TUE	WED	THU	FRI	SAT
						1 SEA
2 SEA	3	4 N CHI	5 N CHI	6 N CHI	7 N MIL	8 MIL
9 MIL	10 N CHI	11 N CHI	12 N CHI	13 N TEX	14 N TEX	15 TEX
16 TEX	17	18 N CLE	19 N CLE	20 N CLE	21 N TEX	22 N TEX
23 N TEX	24	25 N CLE	26 N CLE	27 N DET	28 N DET	29 N DET
30 DET						

JULY

SUN	MON	TUE	WED	THU	FRI	SAT
	1 N NY	2 N NY	3 NY	4 BAL	5 N BAL	6 BAL
7 N BAL	8 *	9 ALL-STAR GAME	10	11 N DET	12 N DET	13 DET
14 DET	15 N NY	16 N NY	17 N NY	18 N BAL	19 N BAL	20 BAL
21 BAL	22 N KC	23 N KC	24 N KC	25 N MIN	26 N MIN	27 N MIN
28 MIN	29	30 N KC	31 N KC			

AUGUST

SUN	MON	TUE	WED	THU	FRI	SAT
				1 N KC	2 N MIN	3 N MIN
4 MIN	5 N TOR	6 N TOR	7 N TOR	8	9 N MIL	10 N MIL
11 MIL	12 N TOR	13 N TOR	14 N TOR	15	16 N CAL	17 N CAL
18 N CAL	19 N CAL	20 N OAK	21 N OAK	22 N OAK	23 N SEA	24 SEA
25 SEA	26 N CAL	27 N CAL	28 N CAL	29	30 N OAK	31 N OAK

SEPTEMBER

SUN	MON	TUE	WED	THU	FRI	SAT
1 OAK	2 N SEA	3 N SEA	4 N SEA	5	6 N CHI	7 N CHI
8 CHI	9 N MIL	10 N MIL	11 N MIL	12	13 N CHI	14 CHI
15 CHI	16	17 N DET	18 N DET	19 DET	20 N NY	21 NY
22 N NY	23	24 N BAL	25 N BAL	26 N NY	27 N NY	28 NY
29 NY						

1996 SEASON
CLUB DIRECTORY

Chief executive officer
John L. Harrington
Exec. v.p., baseball operations
James (Lou) Gorman
Exec. v.p. and general manager
Daniel F. Duquette
Exec. v.p. for administration
John S. Buckley
V.p. and chief financial officer
Robert C. Furbush
V.p. broadcasting and special projects
James P. Healey
Vice president marketing
Lawrence C. Cancro
Vice president public relations
Richard L. Bresciani
Vice president stadium operations
Joseph F. McDermott
Assistant general managers
Michael D. Port
Elaine W. Steward
Director of scouting
W. Wayne Britton
Dir. of player dev. and administration
Edward P. Kenney
Director of field operations
Robert W. Schaefer
Asst. to player dev. and scouting
Erwin L. Bryant
Special asst. for player development
John M. Pesky
Traveling secretary
Stephen W. August
Director of Florida operations
William A. MacKay
Major league scout
Frank Malzone
Medical director
Arthur M. Pappas, M.D.
Trainer
James W. Rowe Jr.
Physical therapist
Richard M. Zawacki
Instructors
Theodore S. Williams
Carl M. Yastrzemski
Executive administrative assistant
Lorraine Leong
Equip. manager and clubhouse operations
J. Joseph Cochran

Controller
Stanley H. Tran
Director of facilities management
Thomas L. Queenan Jr.
Director of food services
Patricia T. Flanagan
Director of ticket operations
Joseph P. Helyar
Superintendent of grounds and maint.
Joseph Mooney
Manager of box office
Richard J. Beaton Jr.
Manager of communications
Jeffrey E. Goldenberg
Manager of community relations
Ronald E. Burton Jr.
Manager of corporate sales
Robert G. Capilli
Manager of functions
Daniel E. Lyons
Manager of property maintenance
John M. Caron
Manager of publications
Debra A. Matson
Manager of publicity
Kevin J. Shea
Manager of 600 Club
John F. McCormick
Coordinator of central purchasing
Eileen M. Murphy-Tagrin
Coordinator of computer operations
Scott A. LeLievre
Coordinator of credentials
Mary Jane Ryan
Coordinator of marketing services
Susan E. Salerno
Scouts
Ray Blanco, Charles (Buzz) Bowers, Wayne Britton, Martin Crespo, Ray Crone, Luis Delgado, Ray Fagnant, Eddie Haas, Frank Malzone, Steve McAllister, Howard McCullouch, Danny Monzon, Mike Rizzo, Phillip Rossi, Gary Rajsich, Alex Scott, Matt Sczesny, Jerry Stephenson, Fay Thompson, Luke Wrenn, Jeffrey Zona

MINOR LEAGUE AFFILIATES

Class	Team	League	Manager
AAA	Pawtucket	International	Buddy Bailey
AA	Trenton	Eastern	Ken Macha
A	Sarasota	Florida State	Tommy Barrett
A	Battle Creek	Midwest	DeMarlo Hale
A	Lowell	New York-Pennsylvania	Bob Geren
Rookie	Gulf Coast Red Sox	Gulf Coast	Felix Maldonado

BROADCAST INFORMATION
Radio: WEEI-AM (680).
TV: To be announced.
Cable TV: New England Sports Network.

SPRING TRAINING
Ballpark (city): City of Palms Park (Ft. Myers, Fla.).
Ticket information: 813-334-4700.

1996 SEASON *Boston Red Sox*

SPRING TRAINING ROSTER

Manager—Kevin Kennedy (44).
Coaches—Dave Carlucci (59), Tim Johnson (17), Al Nipper (47), Dave Oliver (16), Jim Rice (14), Frank White (20).

No.	PITCHERS	B/T	Ht./Wt.	Born	1995 clubs
57	Bark, Brian	L/L	5-9/170	8-26-68	Richmond, Pawtucket, Boston
43	Belinda, Stan	R/R	6-3/215	8-6-66	Sarasota, Boston
	Betti, Rich	R/L	5-11/170	9-16-73	Gulf Coast Red Sox, Utica, Michigan
21	Clemens, Roger	R/R	6-4/230	8-4-62	Sarasota, Pawtucket, Boston
	Crawford, Joe	L/L	6-3/225	5-2-70	Binghamton, Norfolk
52	Eshelman, Vaughn	L/L	6-3/215	5-22-69	Boston, Trenton
	Eversgerd, Bryan	R/L	6-1/190	2-11-69	Montreal, Ottawa
	Gordon, Tom	R/R	5-9/180	11-18-67	Kansas City
28	Gunderson, Eric	R/L	6-0/195	3-29-66	New York N.L., Boston
	Henry, Butch	L/L	6-1/205	10-7-68	Montreal
54	Hudson, Joe	R/R	6-1/180	9-29-70	Trenton, Boston
19	Maddux, Mike	L/R	6-2/185	8-27-61	Pittsburgh, Boston
	Moyer, Jamie	L/L	6-0/170	11-18-62	Baltimore
45	Murray, Matt	L/R	6-5/235	9-26-70	Greenville, Richmond, Atlanta, Boston
	Orellano, Rafael	L/L	6-2/160	4-28-73	Trenton
	Pennington, Brad	L/L	6-5/215	4-14-69	Baltimore, Cincinnati, Indianapolis
50	Ryan, Ken	R/R	6-3/230	10-24-68	Boston, Trenton, Pawtucket
36	Sele, Aaron	R/R	6-5/218	6-25-70	Boston, Trenton, Sarasota, Pawtucket
32	Stanton, Mike	L/L	6-1/190	6-2-67	Atlanta, Boston
55	Suppan, Jeff	R/R	6-2/203	1-2-75	Trenton, Boston, Pawtucket
49	Wakefield, Tim	R/R	6-2/205	8-2-66	Pawtucket, Boston

No.	CATCHERS	B/T	Ht./Wt.	Born	1995 clubs
37	Haselman, Bill	R/R	6-3/220	5-25-66	Boston
30	Hatteberg, Scott	L/R	6-1/192	12-14-69	Pawtucket, Boston
22	Stanley, Mike	R/R	6-0/190	6-25-63	New York A.L.

No.	INFIELDERS	B/T	Ht./Wt.	Born	1995 clubs
10	Alicea, Luis	B/R	5-9/176	7-29-65	Boston
	Cordero, Wil	R/R	6-2/195	10-3-71	Montreal
18	Jefferson, Reggie	L/L	6-4/215	9-25-68	Boston
11	Naehring, Tim	R/R	6-2/203	2-1-67	Boston
	Tatum, Jim	R/R	6-2/200	10-9-67	Colorado Springs, Colorado
13	Valentin, John	R/R	6-0/185	2-18-67	Boston
42	Vaughn, Mo	L/R	6-1/240	12-15-67	Boston

No.	OUTFIELDERS	B/T	Ht./Wt.	Born	1995 clubs
38	Canseco, Jose	R/R	6-4/240	7-2-64	Boston, Pawtucket
	Cookson, Brent	R/R	6-0/195	9-7-69	Phoenix, Omaha, Kansas City
39	Greenwell, Mike	L/R	6-0/200	7-18-63	Boston, Pawtucket
46	Hosey, Dwayne	B/R	5-10/175	3-11-67	Omaha, Boston
65	Malave, Jose	R/R	6-2/212	5-31-71	Pawtucket
58	Murray, Glenn	R/R	6-2/225	11-23-70	Pawtucket
	Nixon, Trot	L/L	6-2/196	4-11-74	Trenton, Sarasota
25	O'Leary, Troy	L/L	6-0/196	8-4-69	Boston
26	Tinsley, Lee	B/R	5-10/196	3-4-69	Boston, Trenton

BALLPARK INFORMATION

Ballpark (capacity, surface)
Fenway Park (33,871, grass)

Address
4 Yawkey Way
Boston, MA 02215

Business phone
617-267-9440

Ticket information
617-267-8661

Ticket prices
$23 (field box)
$18 (upper box, right field roof box)
$14 (grandstand)
$9 (bleachers, standing room)

Field dimensions (from home plate)
To left field at foul line, 315 feet
To center field, 420 feet
To right field at foul line, 302 feet

First game played
April 20, 1912
(Red Sox 7, New York Highlanders 6)

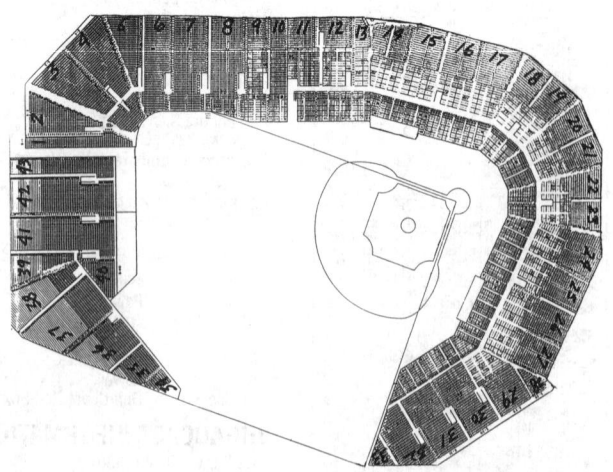

DAY BY DAY

Date	Opp.	Res.	Score	(inn.*)	Hits	Opp. hits	Winning pitcher	Losing pitcher	Save	Record	Pos.	GB
4-26	Min.	W	9-0		14	2	Sele	Erickson		1-0	T1st	...
4-28	Chi.	W	10-4		8	7	Cormier	Bere		2-0	T1st	...
4-29	Chi.	W	8-0		10	5	Hanson	Alvarez		3-0	T1st	...
4-30	Chi.	L	11-17		14	17	DeLeon	F. Rodriguez		3-1	T1st	...
5-1	At N.Y.	L	3-5		9	11	Howe	Lilliquist	Wetteland	3-2	2nd	1
5-2	At N.Y.	W	8-0		8	3	Eshelman	Hitchcock		4-2	T1st	...
5-3	At N.Y.	L	3-4	(13)	8	16	Wickman	Pierce		4-3	3rd	1
5-4	At N.Y.	L	3-5		6	10	Ausanio	Johnston	Wetteland	4-4	3rd	2
5-5	At Det.	W	10-7		17	6	Lilliquist	Lira	Ryan	5-4	T2nd	2
5-6	At Det.	W	5-3		6	7	Sele	Bergman	Belinda	6-4	T1st	1
5-7	At Det.	W	12-1		17	5	Eshelman	Groom		7-4	T1st	...
5-9	Bal.	W	4-3		4	6	Belinda	Benitez		8-4	1st	+1
5-10	Bal.	W	6-2		8	7	Hanson	Fernandez		9-4	1st	+1
5-12	N.Y.	L	2-12		4	11	Hitchcock	Sele		9-5	2nd	1/2
5-13	N.Y.	W	6-4		12	3	Eshelman	Wickman	Ryan	10-5	1st	+1/2
5-14	N.Y.	W	3-2		8	9	Pena	Howe		11-5	1st	+11/2
5-16	At Mil.	W	5-0		7	4	Hanson	Scanlan		12-5	1st	+21/2
5-17	At Mil.	W	8-2		8	8	Sele	Bones		13-5	1st	+3
5-18	Cle.	W	4-3		10	10	Belinda	Poole		14-5	1st	+31/2
5-19	Cle.	L	5-9		8	13	Tavarez	Ryan		14-6	1st	+31/2
5-20	Cle.	L	5-7		11	12	Plunk	Pena	Mesa	14-7	1st	+21/2
5-21	Cle.	L	10-12		18	17	Assenmacher	Pierce	Mesa	14-8	1st	+11/2
5-23	At Sea.	W	5-4	(10)	11	9	Belinda	Frey	Ryan	15-8	1st	+21/2
5-24	At Sea.	L	6-15		8	16	Carmona	Pierce	Nelson	15-9	1st	+21/2
5-25	At Sea.	L	3-4		6	7	Belcher	Smith	Ayala	15-10	1st	+21/2
5-26	At Cal.	W	8-3		8	8	Hanson	Williams		16-10	1st	+3
5-27	At Cal.	W	12-1		13	5	Wakefield	Bielecki		17-10	1st	+4
5-28	At Cal.	L	3-8		8	12	Finley	Vanegmond		17-11	1st	+31/2
5-29	At Oak.	W	9-6		10	9	Smith	Stewart		18-11	1st	+41/2
5-30	At Oak.	W	1-0		4	3	Wakefield	Darling	Ryan	19-11	1st	+5
5-31	At Oak.	W	6-5		14	10	Hanson	Stottlemyre	Ryan	20-11	1st	+6
6-2	Sea.	W	6-5	(10)	14	10	Belinda	Torres		21-11	1st	+61/2
6-3	Sea.	W	10-8		12	14	Cormier	Carmona	Ryan	22-11	1st	+7
6-4	Sea.	W	2-1	(10)	7	6	Wakefield	Ayala		23-11	1st	+8
6-5	Cal.	W	3-2		7	11	Hanson	Bielecki	Ryan	24-11	1st	+9
6-6	Cal.	L	3-12		10	17	Langston	Looney	James	24-12	1st	+8
6-7	Cal.	W	5-1		10	6	Clemens	Finley		25-12	1st	+9
6-8	Cal.	L	8-10		11	18	Butcher	Cormier	Smith	25-13	1st	+8
6-9	Oak.	W	4-1		8	3	Wakefield	Stewart		26-13	1st	+8
6-10	Oak.	L	5-8		13	13	Corsi	Maddux		26-14	1st	+7
6-11	Oak.	L	1-8		8	13	Stottlemyre	Smith		26-15	1st	+7
6-12	At Tor.	L	3-4	(12)	8	11	Timlin	Ryan		26-16	1st	+7
6-13	At Tor.	W	11-7		13	10	Maddux	Hentgen		27-16	1st	+8
6-14	At Tor.	L	3-5		9	8	Leiter	Wakefield	Castillo	27-17	1st	+8
6-16	Mil.	L	3-4		9	10	Miranda	Hanson	Fetters	27-18	1st	+61/2
6-17	Mil.	L	1-9		5	16	Sparks	Clemens		27-19	1st	+51/2
6-18	Mil.	W	4-2		9	10	Smith	Bones	Belinda	28-19	1st	+51/2
6-19	At Cle.	L	3-4	(10)	12	11	Plunk	Ryan		28-20	1st	+51/2
6-20	At Cle.	L	2-9		6	15	Ogea	Eshelman	Belinda	28-21	1st	+51/2
6-21	At Cle.	W	3-1		6	5	Hanson	Hershiser	Belinda	29-21	1st	+51/2
6-22	At Bal.	W	4-1		6	8	Clemens	K. Brown	Belinda	30-21	1st	+6
6-23	At Bal.	L	5-7		12	10	Mussina	Smith	Lee	30-22	1st	+5
6-24	At Bal.	W	6-5		14	7	Cormier	Orosco	Belinda	31-22	1st	+5
6-25	At Bal.	L	1-10		8	15	Rhodes	Eshelman		31-23	1st	+4
6-26	Tor.	W	4-3		5	9	Belinda	Castillo		32-23	1st	+5
6-27	Tor.	W	6-5	(11)	7	8	Lilliquist	Williams		33-23	1st	+6
6-28	Tor.	L	4-8		6	12	Cone	Smith		33-24	1st	+5
6-29	Det.	W	7-1		10	8	Wakefield	Moore		34-24	1st	+6
6-30	Det.	L	6-7		12	10	Boever	Ryan	Henneman	34-25	1st	+5
7-1	Det.	L	2-11		12	15	Lira	Hanson	Doherty	34-26	1st	+4
7-2	Det.	W	12-11		15	13	Belinda	Boever		35-26	1st	+5
7-3	At K.C.	W	12-5		11	9	Smith	Appier	Maddux	36-26	1st	+5
7-4	At K.C.	W	6-5		9	11	Wakefield	Gubicza	Belinda	37-26	1st	+5
7-5	At K.C.	L	2-3		7	8	Pichardo	F. Rodriguez		37-27	1st	+4
7-6	At Min.	L	4-6		9	11	Radke	Smith	Stevens	37-28	1st	+3
7-7	At Min.	W	5-4		9	10	Belinda	Guardado	Aguilera	38-28	1st	+3
7-8	At Min.	L	5-9		5	11	Guthrie	Belinda		38-29	1st	+3
7-9	At Min.	W	7-0		10	4	Wakefield	Rodriguez		39-29	1st	+3
7-13	Tex.	L	8-9		11	11	Vosberg	Clemens	Russell	39-30	1st	+3
7-14	Tex.	W	5-2		10	9	Wakefield	Pavlik	Aguilera	40-30	1st	+4
7-15	Tex.	L	2-7		6	14	Gross	Hanson		40-31	1st	+31/2

– 15 –

Date	Opp.	Res.	Score	(inn.*)	Hits	Opp. hits	Winning pitcher	Losing pitcher	Save	Record	Pos.	GB
7-16	Tex.	L	2-5		7	4	Rogers	Smith	Russell	40-32	1st	+4
7-17	K.C.	L	3-4		8	12	Gubicza	Suppan	Montgomery	40-33	1st	+4
7-18	K.C.	W	4-1		13	6	Clemens	Gordon	Aguilera	41-33	1st	+4
7-19	At Chi.	W	5-3		13	8	Wakefield	Sirotka	Aguilera	42-33	1st	+5
7-20	At Chi.	W	3-1		6	10	Hanson	McCaskill	Aguilera	43-33	1st	+6
7-21	Min.	W	13-5		17	11	Smith	Trombley	Hudson	44-33	1st	+6
7-22	Min.	L	7-8		12	13	Guthrie	Suppan	Stevens	44-34	1st	+6
7-23	Min.	L	3-8		11	9	Tapani	Clemens		44-35	1st	+5
7-24	Min.	W	4-1		7	9	Wakefield	Radke	Aguilera	45-35	1st	+5½
7-25	Chi.	L	3-8		5	10	Bere	Cormier	Hernandez	45-36	1st	+4½
7-26	Chi.	W	5-3		13	9	Smith	Fernandez	Aguilera	46-36	1st	+4½
7-27	Chi.	L	4-5		11	12	Karchner	Aguilera	Hernandez	46-37	1st	+4½
7-28	At Tex.	W	6-2		11	5	Maddux	Taylor		47-37	1st	+4½
7-29	At Tex.	W	7-1		11	6	Wakefield	Gross		48-37	1st	+5½
7-30	At Tex.	L	6-7		11	8	Whiteside	Hanson	Russell	48-38	1st	+4½
8-1	At Det.	W	13-3		15	9	Smith	Moore		49-38	1st	+4½
8-2	At Det.	L	0-5		4	5	Bergman	Clemens		49-39	1st	+4½
8-3	At Det.	W	10-2		10	7	Wakefield	Nitkowski		50-39	1st	+4½
8-4	At Tor.	W	7-1		7	6	Hanson	Rogers		51-39	1st	+4½
8-5	At Tor.	W	9-3		11	8	Cormier	Hentgen		52-39	1st	+4½
8-6	At Tor.	W	6-4		10	12	Eshelman	Hurtado	Aguilera	53-39	1st	+5½
8-7	At Tor.	W	5-4	(10)	6	10	Belinda	Crabtree		54-39	1st	+5½
8-8	Cle.	W	5-1		12	6	Wakefield	Clark		55-39	1st	+5½
8-9	Cle.	W	9-5		8	6	Hanson	Plunk		56-39	1st	+6½
8-10	Bal.	W	11-1		17	5	Cormier	Erickson		57-39	1st	+8
8-11	Bal.	W	5-4	(12)	11	8	Aguilera	Clark		58-39	1st	+9
8-12	Bal.	W	7-0		15	6	Clemens	Mussina		59-39	1st	+9
8-13	Bal.	W	3-2		6	2	Wakefield	Krivda	Belinda	60-39	1st	+9
8-14	N.Y.	W	9-3		13	8	Hanson	Kamieniecki		61-39	1st	+10
8-15	N.Y.	L	2-9		10	14	Hitchcock	Cormier		61-40	1st	+9
8-16	N.Y.	W	7-4		11	9	Gunderson	Wickman	Belinda	62-40	1st	+10
8-17	At Cal.	W	4-3		11	8	Gunderson	Habyan	Belinda	63-40	1st	+10½
8-18	At Sea.	L	3-9		11	10	Wolcott	Wakefield		63-41	1st	+9½
8-19	At Sea.	W	4-3		6	4	Hanson	Benes	Aguilera	64-41	1st	+10½
8-20	At Sea.	W	7-6		10	12	Cormier	Bosio	Aguilera	65-41	1st	+11½
8-21	At Cal.	W	6-4		7	8	Eshelman	B. Anderson	Belinda	66-41	1st	+12½
8-22	At Cal.	W	6-4		9	7	Clemens	Harkey	Aguilera	67-41	1st	+13½
8-23	At Cal.	W	6-5	(10)	11	9	Stanton	Smith	Aguilera	68-41	1st	+14½
8-24	At Oak.	W	13-6		14	14	Hanson	Ontiveros		69-41	1st	+15½
8-25	At Oak.	L	1-6		3	13	Johns	Cormier		69-42	1st	+15½
8-26	At Oak.	L	4-11		10	16	Stottlemyre	Smith		69-43	1st	+15½
8-27	At Oak.	W	4-1		8	7	Clemens	Van Poppel	Aguilera	70-43	1st	+15½
8-29	Sea.	L	4-6		7	10	Benes	Wakefield	Charlton	70-44	1st	+15
8-30	Sea.	W	7-6		13	11	Maddux	Nelson	Aguilera	71-44	1st	+15
8-31	Sea.	L	2-11		9	19	Wolcott	Cormier	Guetterman	71-45	1st	+14
9-1	Cal.	W	11-3		18	11	Clemens	Boskie		72-45	1st	+14
9-2	Cal.	W	5-4		10	11	Smith	Langston	Aguilera	73-45	1st	+14
9-3	Cal.	W	8-1		11	4	Wakefield	Finley		74-45	1st	+15
9-5	Oak.	W	7-4	(14)	13	12	Aguilera	Reyes		75-45	1st	+15½
9-6	Oak.	W	8-2		13	7	Clemens	Johns		76-45	1st	+15½
9-8	At N.Y.	L	4-8		7	5	Cone	Wakefield	Howe	76-46	1st	+14½
9-9	At N.Y.	L	1-9		7	11	Pettitte	Smith		76-47	1st	+13½
9-10	At N.Y.	L	3-9		7	10	Hitchcock	Hanson		76-48	1st	+12½
9-11	At Bal.	L	7-10		11	9	Lee	Gunderson	Jones	76-49	1st	+11½
9-12	At Bal.	L	5-6		9	11	Hartley	Hudson	Orosco	76-50	1st	+10½
9-13	At Bal.	W	2-0		7	2	Wakefield	Haynes	Aguilera	77-50	1st	+11½
9-14	At Cle.	L	3-5		4	10	Hershiser	Eshelman	Mesa	77-51	1st	+10½
9-15	At Cle.	W	6-3		11	8	Hanson	Embree		78-51	1st	+11½
9-16	At Cle.	L	5-6		7	11	Clark	Clemens	Mesa	78-52	1st	+10½
9-17	At Cle.	W	9-6		12	9	Suppan	Shuey	Aguilera	79-52	1st	+11½
9-18	Mil.	L	1-6		7	12	Bones	Wakefield		79-53	1st	+10½
9-19	Mil.	W	5-3		9	5	Eshelman	Sparks	Aguilera	80-53	1st	+10½
9-20	Mil.	W	3-2		9	4	Cormier	Karl	Aguilera	81-53	1st	+10½
9-23†	Tor.	W	5-0		9	7	Clemens	Leiter		82-53		
9-23‡	Tor.	L	6-8		8	11	Ware	Wakefield	Castillo	82-54	1st	+9
9-24	Tor.	L	1-2		4	6	Guzman	Aguilera	Timlin	82-55	1st	+9
9-25	Det.	L	4-7		8	10	Gohr	Murray	Doherty	82-56	1st	+8½
9-26	Det.	W	5-1		11	6	Smith	Nitkowski		83-56	1st	+8½
9-27	Det.	L	5-7		16	14	Lima	Wakefield	Blomdahl	83-57	1st	+7½
9-28	At Mil.	W	11-6		14	10	Clemens	Scanlan		84-57	1st	+8
9-29	At Mil.	W	11-9		16	15	Hanson	Bones	Aguilera	85-57	1st	+8
9-30	At Mil.	W	9-1		16	9	Maddux	Sparks		86-57	1st	+8
10-1	At Mil.	L	1-8		6	9	Karl	Wakefield		86-58	1st	+7

Monthly records: April (3-1), May (17-10), June (14-14), July (14-13), August (23-7), September (15-12), October (0-1).
*Innings, if other than nine. †First game of doubleheader. ‡Second game of doubleheader.

HIGHLIGHTS

High point: A 12-game winning streak that began August 3 in Detroit and catapulted the Red Sox from a 4½-game lead in the A.L. East to a 10-game bulge on August 14.

Low point: Being swept by Cleveland in the best-of-five division playoffs, which extended the Red Sox's postseason losing streak to a major league-record 13 games.

Turning point: The July 6 trade that brought closer Rick Aguilera from Minnesota for rookie righthander Frank Rodriguez. The bullpen was a shambles at that stage of the season. Aguilera's presence not only gave the Red Sox a first-rate closer but also allowed other relievers to settle into defined roles.

Most valuable player: First baseman Mo Vaughn, who was the league's MVP as well. With Jose Canseco injured most of the first half of the season, Vaughn carried the team. Not even a woeful postseason (0-for-14) could detract from Vaughn's eye-popping regular season (.300 average, 39 homers, 126 RBIs).

Most valuable pitcher: Tim Wakefield. Knuckleballer Wakefield fluttered his way to a 14-1 record and a league-leading 1.65 ERA before stumbling in the late going (seven losses in his last nine decisions). With Roger Clemens and Aaron Sele out with injuries, Wakefield became the staff ace.

Most improved player: Wakefield. In 1994, he was 5-15 with a 5.84 ERA in Class AAA ball. After being released by the Pirates in the spring of 1995, Wakefield signed with the Red Sox organization and, after a stint at Pawtucket, was summoned by Boston in late May.

Most pleasant surprise: Wakefield. He wound up 16-8 with a 2.95 ERA.

Biggest disappointment: Righthander Ken Ryan and outfielder Mark Whiten. Ryan was projected as the closer of the future. By mid-June, though, he had lost the stopper job—and his confidence. He no longer figures in the team's plans. Whiten was supposed to be the everyday rightfielder but was a bust. After hitting .185 in 32

games, he was traded to Philadelphia.

Key injuries: Sele made only six starts because of shoulder tendinitis. Clemens, hampered by shoulder problems, didn't start a game until June 2.

Notable: Shortstop John Valentin set career highs in homers (27), RBIs (102), runs (108), hits (155), total bases (277), walks (81) and steals (20). . . . Outfielder Troy O'Leary, claimed off waivers from Milwaukee, played his first full season in the majors and hit .308. . . . Aguilera converted 20 of 21 save chances during the regular season but blew a big one in the first game of the playoffs.

—JOE GIULIOTTI

RECORDS

1995 regular-season record: 86-58 (1st in A.L. East); 42-30 at home; 44-28 on road; 30-22 vs. East; 27-20 vs. Central; 29-16 vs. West; 20-17 vs. lefthanded starters; 66-41 vs. righthanded starters; 76-51 on grass; 10-7 on turf; 26-18 in daytime; 60-40 at night; 25-15 in one-run games; 8-3 in extra-inning games; 0-0-0 in doubleheaders.

Team record past five years: 377-368 (.506, ranks 4th in league in that span).

TEAM LEADERS

Batting average: Tim Naehring (.307).
At-bats: Mo Vaughn (550).
Runs: John Valentin (108).
Hits: Mo Vaughn (165).
Total bases: Mo Vaughn (316).
Doubles: John Valentin (37).
Triples: Troy O'Leary (6)
Home runs: Mo Vaughn (39).
Runs batted in: Mo Vaughn (126).
Stolen bases: John Valentin (20).
Slugging percentage: Mo Vaughn (.575).
On-base percentage: Tim Naehring (.415).
Wins: Tim Wakefield (16).
Earned-run average: Tim Wakefield (2.95).
Complete games: Tim Wakefield (6).
Shutouts: Erik Hanson, Tim Wakefield (1).
Saves: Rick Aguilera (20).
Innings pitched: Tim Wakefield (195.1).
Strikeouts: Erik Hanson (139).

GAMES BY POSITION

Catcher: Mike Macfarlane 111, Bill Haselman 48, Rich Rowland 11, Scott Hatteberg 2.
First base: Mo Vaughn 138, Chris Donnels 8, Reggie Jefferson 7, Bill Haselman 1.
Second base: Luis Alicea 132, Terry Shumpert 8, Carlos Rodriguez 7, Juan Bell 5, Chris Donnels 3, Steve Rodriguez 1.
Third base: Tim Naehring 124, Chris Donnels 27, Terry Shumpert 5, Juan Bell 1, Bill Haselman 1, Carlos Rodriguez 1.
Shortstop: John Valentin 135, Juan Bell 6, Carlos Rodriguez 6, Steve Rodriguez 4, Terry Shumpert 3.
Outfield: Mike Greenwell 118, Troy O'Leary 105, Lee Tinsley 97, Willie McGee 64, Mark Whiten 31, Matt Stairs 23, Dwayne Hosey 21, Wes Chamberlain 12, Tuffy Rhodes 9, Chris James 8, Ron Mahay 5, Dave Hollins 2, Reggie Jefferson 2, Jose Canseco 1.
Designated hitter: Jose Canseco 101, Reggie Jefferson 32, Bill Haselman 11, Wes Chamberlain 5, Chris James 5, Dave Hollins 3, Mike Macfarlane 3, Troy O'Leary 3, Rich Rowland 3, Mike Greenwell 2, Matt Stairs 2, Mo Vaughn 2, Dwayne Hosey 1, Tim Naehring 1, Steve Rodriguez 1, Terry Shumpert 1, Mark Whiten 1.

TOP DRAFT CHOICES

1a. **Andy Yount,** RHP, Kingwood (Tex.) H.S.
1b. **Corey Jenkins,** OF, Dreher H.S., Columbia, S.C.
2. **Jose Olmeda,** SS, Fajardo, Puerto Rico.
3. **Jay Yennaco,** RHP, Pinkerton Academy, Windham, N.H.
4. **Mike Spinelli,** LHP, Revere (Mass.) H.S.
5. **Steve Lomasney,** C, Peabody (Mass.) H.S.
6. **Matt Kinney,** RHP, Bangor (Maine) H.S.
7. **Cole Liniak,** SS, San Dieguito H.S., Encinitas, Calif.
8. **Luis Cardona,** C, San Sebastian, Puerto Rico.
9. **Paxton Crawford,** RHP, Carlsbad (N.M.) H.S.
10. **Kevie Austin,** RHP, Emmanuel (Ga.) College.

CALIFORNIA ANGELS
AMERICAN LEAGUE WEST DIVISION

1996 ANGELS SCHEDULE

Home games shaded.
* — All-Star Game at Veterans Stadium (Philadelphia)
N — Night game (any game starting after 5 p.m.)

MARCH

SUN	MON	TUE	WED	THU	FRI	SAT
31						

APRIL

SUN	MON	TUE	WED	THU	FRI	SAT
	1	2 N MIL	3 N MIL	4	5 N CHI	6 N CHI
7 CHI	8	9 N TOR	10 N TOR	11 N TOR	12 N DET	13 DET
14 DET	15 N SEA	16 N SEA	17 N TOR	18 N TOR	19 N DET	20 N DET
21 N DET	22 N DET	23	24 N MIL	25 MIL	26 N CHI	27 N CHI
28 CHI	29 N CHI	30 N OAK				

MAY

SUN	MON	TUE	WED	THU	FRI	SAT
			1 N OAK	2 OAK	3 N MIN	4 N MIN
5 MIN	6 N KC	7 N KC	8 N KC	9 N KC	10 N CLE	11 N CLE
12 N CLE	13	14 N BOS	15 N BOS	16	17 N NY	18 NY
19 NY	20 N BAL	21 N BAL	22 N BAL	23	24 N BOS	25 N BOS
26 BOS	27 N NY	28 N NY	29 N NY	30	31 N BAL	

JUNE

SUN	MON	TUE	WED	THU	FRI	SAT
						1 N BAL
2 BAL	3 N MIN	4 N MIN	5 N MIN	6	7 N CLE	8 CLE
9 CLE	10 N KC	11 N KC	12 KC	13 N TOR	14 N TOR	15 N TOR
16 TOR	17 N CHI	18 N CHI	19 CHI	20 N MIL	21 N MIL	22 N MIL
23 MIL	24 N CHI	25 N CHI	26	27 N OAK	28 N OAK	29 OAK
30 N OAK						

JULY

SUN	MON	TUE	WED	THU	FRI	SAT
	1 N TEX	2 N TEX	3 N TEX	4 OAK	5 N OAK	6 OAK
7 OAK	8 * 9 ALL-STAR GAME	10	11 N SEA	12 N SEA	13 SEA	
14 SEA	15 N TEX	16 N TEX	17 N TEX	18 N SEA	19 N SEA	20 N SEA
21 SEA	22 N DET	23 N DET	24	25 N MIL	26 N MIL	27 N MIL
28 MIL	29	30 N DET	31 N DET			

AUGUST

SUN	MON	TUE	WED	THU	FRI	SAT
				1 DET	2 N TOR	3 TOR
4 TOR	5	6 N MIN	7 N MIN	8 N MIN	9 N KC	10 N KC
11 KC	12 N CLE	13 N CLE	14	15 N CLE	16 N BOS	17 BOS
18 N BOS	19 N NY	20 N NY	21 N NY	22	23 N BAL	24 N BAL
25 BAL	26 N BOS	27 N BOS	28 N BOS	29 N NY	30 N NY	31 N NY

SEPTEMBER

SUN	MON	TUE	WED	THU	FRI	SAT
1 NY	2 N BAL	3 N BAL	4 N BAL	5	6 N MIN	7 N MIN
8 MIN	9 N CLE	10 N CLE	11 N CLE	12 N KC	13 N KC	14 KC
15 KC	16 N OAK	17 N OAK	18 N OAK	19	20 N TEX	21 N TEX
22 TEX	23 N SEA	24 N SEA	25 SEA	26 N TEX	27 N TEX	28 N TEX
29 TEX						

1996 SEASON

CLUB DIRECTORY

Chairman of the board
Gene Autry

Board of directors
Gene Autry
Jackie Autry
Richard M. Brown
Stanley B. Schneider
John P. Singleton
Peter V. Ueberroth

President and chief executive officer
Richard M. Brown

Executive vice president
Jackie Autry

Vice president and general manager
W.J. Bavasi

Vice president and chief financial officer
Ronald C. Shirley

Vice president, civic affairs
Tom Seeberg

Vice president, operations
Kevin Uhlich

Vice president, marketing
Joe Schrier

Asst. v.p., media relations & broadcasting
John Sevano

Asst. v.p., scouting & player personnel
Bob Fontaine Jr.

Asst. vice president, sales
Lynn Biggs

Assistant general manager
Tim Mead

Special assistants to the g.m.
Preston Gomez
Bob Harrison

Exec. secretary to general manager
Cathy Carey

Legal counsel/contract negotiator
Mark Rosenthal

Director, player development
Ken Forsch

Asst. dir., scouting/player development
Jeff Parker

Traveling secretary
Frank Sims

Equipment manager
Ken Higdon

Video coordinator
Diego Lopez

Director, baseball information
Larry Babcock

Asst. director, baseball information
Kraig Kojian

Assistant, media relations
Carolyn LaPierre

Club photographers
V.J. Lovero
John Cordes

Manager, publications
Doug Ward

Director, community relations
Marie Moreno

Medical director
Dr. Lewis Yocum

Trainers
Ned Bergert
Rick Smith

Sports psychologist
Ken Ravizza

Director, international operations
Ta Honda

Scouts
Don Archer, Ted Brzenk, John Burden, Tom Burns, Mike Cadahia, Pete Coachman, Marco Davalillo, Pompeyo Davalillo, Tom Davis, Red Gaskill, Steve Gruwell, Ta Honda, Rick Ingalls, Hal Keller, Tim Kelly, Kris Kline, Tom Kotchman, Tony LaCava, Ron Marigny, Jim McLaughlin, Darrell Miller, Jon Neiderer, Tom Osowski, Eusebio Perez, Dick Probola, Bob Protexter, Paul Robinson, Rick Schlenker, Jerry Streeter, Rip Tutor, Jack Uhey, Dick Wilson

Major league scouts
Joe Coleman, Dave Garcia, Jay Hankins, Bob Harrison, Nick Kamzic, Matt Keough, Joe McDonald, Tom Romenesko, Moose Stubing, Dale Sutherland

MINOR LEAGUE AFFILIATES

Class	Team	League	Manager
AAA	Vancouver	Pacific Coast	Don Long
AA	Midland	Texas	Mario Mendoza
A	Lake Elsinore	California	Mitch Seoane
A	Cedar Rapids	Midwest	Tom Lawless
A	Boise	Northwest	Tom Kotchman
Rookie	Mesa Angels	Arizona	Bruce Hines

BROADCAST INFORMATION
Radio: KMPC-AM (710).
TV: KCAL-TV (Channel 9).
Cable TV: Prime Sports.

SPRING TRAINING
Ballpark (city): Diablo Stadium (Tempe, Ariz.).
Ticket information: 602-678-2222 (Ticketron); 619-323-4143 (Angels Stadium).

SPRING TRAINING ROSTER

Manager—Marcel Lachemann (53).
Coaches—Rick Burleson (39), Rod Carew (29), Chuck Hernandez (55), Bobby Knoop (2), Bill Lachemann (38), Joe Maddon (70).

No.	PITCHERS	B/T	Ht./Wt.	Born	1995 clubs
	Abbott, Jim	L/L	6-3/210	9-19-67	Chicago A.L., California
56	Anderson, Brian	B/L	6-1/190	4-26-72	California, Lake Elsinore
48	Edenfield, Ken	R/R	6-1/165	3-18-67	California, Vancouver
58	Edsell, Geoff	R/R	6-3/190	12-12-71	Lake Elsinore, Midland
	Finley, Chuck	L/L	6-6/214	11-26-62	California
60	Hancock, Ryan	R/R	6-2/215	11-11-71	Midland
34	Harvey, Bryan	R/R	6-2/212	6-2-63	Florida
41	Holdridge, David	R/R	6-3/185	2-5-69	Vancouver, Lake Elsinore, Midland
42	Holzemer, Mark	L/L	6-0/165	8-20-69	Vancouver, California
46	James, Mike	R/R	6-4/216	8-15-67	California, Lake Elsinore
37	Janicki, Pete	R/R	6-4/190	1-26-71	Lake Elsinore, Vancouver
12	Langston, Mark	R/L	6-2/184	8-20-60	California
45	Leftwich, Phil	R/R	6-5/205	5-19-69	Arizona Angels, Vancouver
40	Percival, Troy	R/R	6-3/200	8-9-69	California
51	Schmidt, Jeff	R/R	6-5/190	2-21-71	Midland
47	Smith, Lee	R/R	6-6/269	12-4-57	California
64	VanRyn, Ben	L/L	6-5/185	8-9-71	Chattanooga, Vancouver, Midland
59	Williams, Shad	R/R	6-0/185	3-10-71	Vancouver

No.	CATCHERS	B/T	Ht./Wt.	Born	1995 clubs
14	Fabregas, Jorge	L/R	6-3/205	3-13-70	California, Vancouver
8	Greene, Todd	R/R	5-9/195	5-8-71	Midland, Vancouver
20	Turner, Chris	R/R	6-1/190	3-23-69	Vancouver, California

No.	INFIELDERS	B/T	Ht./Wt.	Born	1995 clubs
17	Arias, George	R/R	5-11/190	3-12-72	Midland
5	Correia, Rod	R/R	5-11/185	9-13-67	Vancouver, California
33	DiSarcina, Gary	R/R	6-1/178	11-19-67	California
1	Easley, Damion	R/R	5-11/185	11-11-69	California
28	Harkrider, Timothy	B/R	6-0/180	9-5-71	Midland
10	Hudler, Rex	R/R	6-0/195	9-2-60	California
38	Jordan, Ricky	R/R	6-3/205	5-26-65	Vancouver
24	Perez, Eduardo	R/R	6-4/215	9-11-69	Vancouver, California
6	Snow, J.T.	B/L	6-2/202	2-26-68	California
18	Velarde, Randy	R/R	6-0/192	11-24-62	New York A.L.

No.	OUTFIELDERS	B/T	Ht./Wt.	Born	1995 clubs
16	Anderson, Garret	L/L	6-3/190	6-30-72	California, Vancouver
44	Davis, Chili	B/R	6-3/217	1-17-60	California
25	Edmonds, Jim	L/L	6-1/190	6-27-70	California
3	Palmeiro, Orlando	L/R	5-11/155	1-19-69	Vancouver, California
13	Riley, Marquis	R/R	5-11/170	12-27-70	Vancouver
15	Salmon, Tim	R/R	6-3/220	8-24-68	California

BALLPARK INFORMATION

Ballpark (capacity, surface)
Anaheim Stadium (64,593, grass)

Address
2000 Gene Autry Way
Anaheim, CA 92806

Business phones
714-937-7200
213-625-1123

Ticket information
714-634-2000

Ticket prices
$14.50 (field & club level, MVP)
$12 (field & club level, box)
$11 (terrace level, MVP)
$9 (terrace level, box)
$8 (view level, lower box)
$7 (view level, upper box)
$5 (pavillion, reserved)

Field dimensions (from home plate)
To left field at foul line, 333 feet
To center field, 404 feet
To right field at foul line, 333 feet

First game played
April 19, 1966 (White Sox 3, Angels 1)

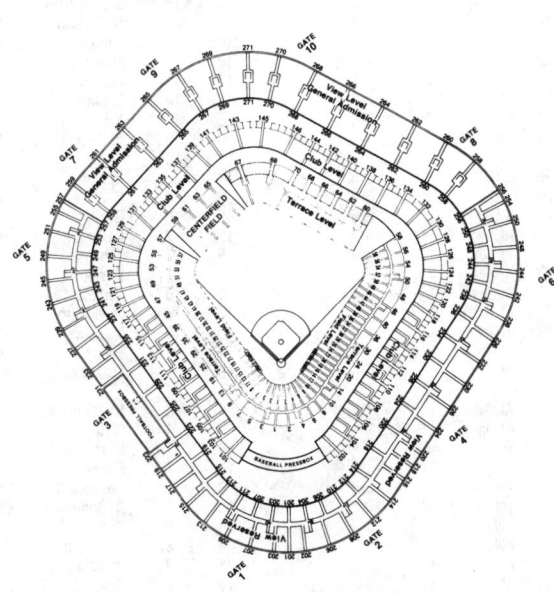

DAY BY DAY

Date	Opp.	Res.	Score	(inn.*)	Hits	Opp. hits	Winning pitcher	Losing pitcher	Save	Record	Pos.	GB
4-26	Det.	L	4-5		8	9	Moore	Finley	Groom	0-1	T2nd	1/2
4-28	At Tor.	W	7-6	(10)	10	12	Butcher	Castillo	Smith	1-1	2nd	1
4-29	At Tor.	L	0-3		5	10	Leiter	Sanderson	Hall	1-2	3rd	2
4-30	At Tor.	W	5-3		7	8	Butcher	Menhart	Smith	2-2	2nd	1
5-1	At Tor.	W	2-0		6	5	Boskie	Cone	Smith	3-2	2nd	1
5-2	Oak.	L	0-2		3	5	Stewart	Finley	Eckersley	3-3	2nd	2
5-3	Oak.	W	8-7	(10)	13	9	Butcher	Reyes		4-3	2nd	2
5-4	Oak.	L	6-9		10	9	Stottlemyre	Williams	Eckersley	4-4	2nd	2 1/2
5-5	Sea.	W	10-0		8	8	Patterson	Fleming		5-4	2nd	1 1/2
5-6	Sea.	W	7-5		11	8	Williams	Wells	Smith	6-4	2nd	1/2
5-7	Sea.	L	2-3		7	7	Johnson	Finley	Ayala	6-5	2nd	1 1/2
5-9	Tex.	W	3-2		8	7	Langston	Helling	Smith	7-5	2nd	1/2
5-10	Tex.	W	11-2		16	7	Sanderson	Tewksbury		8-5	1st	+1/2
5-11	Tex.	L	2-6		7	9	Rogers	Springer	Russell	8-6	1st	+1/2
5-12	At K.C.	W	3-2		9	4	Butcher	Brewer	Smith	9-6	1st	+1/2
5-13	At K.C.	L	2-4		3	7	Appier	Patterson		9-7	1st	1/2
5-14	At K.C.	W	8-1		9	5	Langston	Browning		10-7	1st	+1/2
5-15	At Min.	L	6-9		11	14	Erickson	Sanderson	Aguilera	10-8	T1st	...
5-16	At Min.	W	9-6		14	8	Bielecki	Guardado	Smith	11-8	1st	+1
5-17	At Min.	L	3-7		9	10	Tapani	Finley		11-9	T1st	...
5-18	At Min.	W	15-9		16	14	Boskie	Mahomes		12-9	1st	+1
5-19	At Chi.	W	6-5		11	10	Percival	McCaskill	Smith	13-9	1st	+2
5-20	At Chi.	W	7-5	(10)	9	11	Patterson	Dibble	Smith	14-9	1st	+2
5-21	At Chi.	W	8-6		11	11	Bielecki	Bere	Smith	15-9	1st	+2
5-23	N.Y.	W	10-0		12	2	Finley	M. Rivera		16-9	1st	+3
5-24	N.Y.	W	3-1		4	7	Patterson	McDowell	Smith	17-9	1st	+3
5-25	N.Y.	W	15-2		12	6	Langston	Perez		18-9	1st	+3
5-26	Bos.	L	3-8		8	8	Hanson	Williams		18-10	1st	+2
5-27	Bos.	L	1-12		5	13	Wakefield	Bielecki		18-11	1st	+1
5-28	Bos.	W	8-3		12	8	Finley	Vanegmond		19-11	1st	+2
5-29	Bal.	W	6-5		7	10	Boskie	Mussina	Smith	20-11	1st	+2 1/2
5-30	Bal.	L	4-5	(10)	8	10	Orosco	Patterson	Jones	20-12	1st	+1 1/2
5-31	Bal.	L	3-5		8	10	McDonald	Sanderson	Jones	20-13	1st	+1/2
6-2	At N.Y.	W	3-2		7	5	Finley	Pettitte	Smith	21-13	1st	+1 1/2
6-3	At N.Y.	W	4-2		5	8	Boskie	McDowell	Smith	22-13	1st	+2 1/2
6-4	At N.Y.	L	3-11		13	13	Perez	Langston		22-14	1st	+1 1/2
6-5	At Bos.	L	2-3		11	7	Hanson	Bielecki	Ryan	22-15	1st	+1 1/2
6-6	At Bos.	W	12-3		17	10	Langston	Looney	James	23-15	1st	+1 1/2
6-7	At Bos.	L	1-5		6	10	Clemens	Finley		23-16	1st	+1/2
6-8	At Bos.	W	10-8		18	11	Butcher	Cormier	Smith	24-16	1st	+1/2
6-9	At Bal.	L	4-10		7	14	Klingenbeck	Springer		24-17	2nd	1/2
6-10	At Bal.	L	2-6		7	9	McDonald	Bielecki		24-18	2nd	1
6-11	At Bal.	W	5-4		10	10	Langston	Moyer	Smith	25-18	2nd	1
6-12	Min.	W	9-1		10	5	Finley	Guardado		26-18	2nd	1
6-13	Min.	W	7-2		13	8	Boskie	Tapani		27-18	T1st	...
6-14	Min.	L	5-8		13	14	Erickson	Butcher	Aguilera	27-19	T1st	...
6-15	Chi.	W	5-1		8	6	Bielecki	Keyser	Smith	28-19	1st	+1/2
6-17	Chi.	W	4-3	(11)	10	9	Patterson	Fortugno		29-19	1st	+1
6-18	Chi.	W	8-4		12	10	Finley	Bere		30-19	1st	+2
6-19	K.C.	W	5-8		11	8	Appier	Boskie		30-20	1st	+1
6-20	K.C.	W	3-2		9	4	B. Anderson	Gubicza	Smith	31-20	1st	+1
6-21	K.C.	L	3-6		5	8	Gordon	Bielecki	Montgomery	31-21	1st	+1
6-23	At Sea.	W	14-4		13	7	Langston	Belcher		32-21	1st	+1
6-24	At Sea.	L	2-3		5	7	Johnson	Finley		32-22	T1st	...
6-25	At Sea.	W	7-5		12	12	Boskie	Bosio	Smith	33-22	1st	+1
6-26	At Sea.	L	3-7		8	10	Torres	B. Anderson		33-23	1st	+1
6-27	At Tex.	L	6-10		10	15	Tewksbury	Bielecki	Cook	33-24	1st	...
6-28	At Tex.	L	8-9		10	11	McDowell	Smith		33-25	2nd	1
6-29	At Tex.	W	20-4		21	7	Finley	Pavlik	Springer	34-25	T1st	...
6-30	At Oak.	L	5-8		9	8	Eckersley	Smith		34-26	2nd	1
7-1	At Oak.	L	1-5		5	6	Stottlemyre	B. Anderson	Eckersley	34-27	2nd	1
7-2	At Oak.	W	7-1		9	4	Bielecki	Harkey		35-27	T1st	...
7-3	Tor.	W	4-2		8	7	Langston	Cone	Smith	36-27	1st	+1
7-4	Tor.	W	14-0		15	3	Finley	Guzman		37-27	1st	+1
7-5	Tor.	L	5-6		9	12	Hentgen	Boskie	Castillo	37-28	1st	+1
7-6	Tor.	W	10-1		14	4	B. Anderson	Leiter		38-28	1st	+1
7-7	Mil.	L	3-9		4	10	Sparks	Bielecki		38-29	T1st	...
7-8	Mil.	W	1-0		3	3	Langston	Bones		39-29	1st	+1
7-9	Mil.	L	7-9		11	8	Ignasiak	Finley	Fetters	39-30	T1st	...
7-13	At Det.	W	8-5	(10)	10	10	Percival	Boever	Smith	40-30	T1st	...
7-14	At Det.	W	7-3		9	9	Patterson	Lira	Percival	41-30	1st	+1

Date	Opp.	Res.	Score	(inn.*)	Hits	Opp. hits	Winning pitcher	Losing pitcher	Save	Record	Pos.	GB
7-16†	At Det.	W	6-4		10	7	Finley	Boever	Smith	42-30		
7-16‡	At Det.	W	13-6		19	9	James	Moore		43-30	1st	+1
7-17	At Cle.	W	8-3		15	5	B. Anderson	Ogea		44-30	1st	+2
7-18	At Cle.	L	5-7		8	12	Assenmacher	Smith		44-31	1st	+2
7-19	At Tor.	W	10-2		15	7	Springer	Guzman		45-31	1st	+3
7-20	At Tor.	W	10-3		17	6	Butcher	Hentgen		46-31	1st	+4
7-21	Det.	L	3-4		8	10	Wells	Habyan	Henneman	46-32	1st	+4
7-22	Det.	W	13-3		17	6	B. Anderson	Bergman		47-32	1st	+5
7-23	Det.	W	13-2		14	9	Langston	Lima		48-32	1st	+6
7-24	Cle.	L	7-9	(10)	12	13	Assenmacher	Smith	Mesa	48-33	1st	+6
7-25	Cle.	W	6-5		9	10	Finley	Hershiser	Smith	49-33	1st	+7
7-26	Cle.	W	6-3		7	8	Harkey	Martinez	Smith	50-33	1st	+8
7-27	At Mil.	W	9-3		12	7	B. Anderson	Wegman		51-33	1st	+8
7-28	At Mil.	W	13-6		17	12	Langston	Roberson		52-33	1st	+9
7-29	At Mil.	W	4-0		12	6	Abbott	Bones		53-33	1st	+10
7-30	At Mil.	W	8-3		13	10	Finley	Karl		54-33	1st	+10
8-1	Sea.	W	7-2		10	7	B. Anderson	Johnson		55-33	1st	+11
8-2	Sea.	W	5-4		9	11	Harkey	Belcher	Smith	56-33	1st	+11
8-3	Sea.	L	7-10		12	15	Benes	Abbott	Charlton	56-34	1st	+11
8-4	Tex.	L	4-6		7	7	Rogers	Finley	Vosberg	56-35	1st	+10
8-5	Tex.	W	5-3		12	8	Langston	Darwin	Smith	57-35	1st	+11
8-6	Tex.	L	2-5		8	10	Pavlik	B. Anderson	Vosberg	57-36	1st	+10
8-7	Tex.	W	9-2		13	6	Harkey	Taylor		58-36	1st	+11
8-8	At K.C.	W	4-0		11	7	Abbott	Gordon	Percival	59-36	1st	+11
8-9	At K.C.	W	9-1		17	5	Finley	Bunch		60-36	1st	+11
8-10	At K.C.	L	0-5		7	9	Jacome	Langston		60-37	1st	+10
8-11	At Min.	W	8-5		9	9	James	Guardado	Smith	61-37	1st	+10½
8-12	At Min.	L	4-6		7	12	Parra	Harkey	Stevens	61-38	1st	+10
8-13	At Min.	W	2-1		5	7	Abbott	Radke	Smith	62-38	1st	+10
8-14	At Chi.	W	11-10	(10)	15	15	James	McCaskill	Smith	63-38	1st	+10½
8-15	At Chi.	W	7-3		12	9	Langston	Bolton	Percival	64-38	1st	+10½
8-16	At Chi.	L	2-9		5	14	Fernandez	B. Anderson		64-39	1st	+10½
8-17	Bos.	L	3-4		8	11	Gunderson	Habyan	Belinda	64-40	1st	+9½
8-18	N.Y.	L	3-7		11	12	McDowell	Abbott	Wetteland	64-41	1st	+9½
8-19	N.Y.	W	5-3		9	7	Finley	Cone	Smith	65-41	1st	+9½
8-20	N.Y.	W	10-5		12	10	Langston	Hitchcock		66-41	1st	+9½
8-21	Bos.	L	4-6		8	7	Eshelman	B. Anderson	Belinda	66-42	1st	+8½
8-22	Bos.	L	4-6		7	9	Clemens	Harkey	Aguilera	66-43	1st	+8½
8-23	Bos.	L	5-6	(10)	9	11	Stanton	Smith	Aguilera	66-44	1st	+7½
8-24	Bal.	W	6-4		11	9	Finley	Rhodes	Smith	67-44	1st	+8½
8-25	Bal.	L	2-11		6	12	Erickson	Langston		67-45	1st	+8½
8-26	Bal.	L	2-5		5	14	K. Brown	B. Anderson		67-46	1st	+7½
8-27	Bal.	L	0-4		4	15	Mussina	Harkey		67-47	1st	+7½
8-29	At N.Y.	L	4-12		5	13	Cone	Finley		67-48	1st	+8
8-30	At N.Y.	L	1-4		5	12	Pettitte	Abbott		67-49	1st	+8
8-31	At N.Y.	L	6-11		14	15	Hitchcock	B. Anderson		67-50	1st	+7½
9-1	At Bos.	L	3-11		11	18	Clemens	Boskie		67-51	1st	+6½
9-2	At Bos.	L	4-5		11	10	Smith	Langston	Aguilera	67-52	1st	+6½
9-3	At Bos.	L	1-8		4	11	Wakefield	Finley		67-53	1st	+5½
9-4	At Bal.	W	5-3		11	8	Abbott	Moyer	Smith	68-53	1st	+6½
9-5	At Bal.	L	0-8		3	17	Erickson	B. Anderson		68-54	1st	+5½
9-6	At Bal.	L	2-4		6	9	Mussina	Boskie	Orosco	68-55	1st	+5½
9-8	Min.	W	9-3		12	5	Langston	Parra		69-55	1st	+6
9-9	Min.	W	6-5		11	11	Monteleone	Mahomes	Smith	70-55	1st	+6
9-10	Min.	L	8-9	(10)	9	11	Stevens	Holzemer	Mahomes	70-56	1st	+5
9-11	Chi.	W	4-1		11	5	Boskie	Sirotka		71-56	1st	+6
9-12	Chi.	W	3-1		6	7	Langston	Alvarez	Smith	72-56	1st	+6
9-13	Chi.	L	1-6		4	13	Andujar	Percival		72-57	1st	+5
9-15	K.C.	L	0-5		3	10	Appier	Abbott		72-58	1st	+4
9-16	K.C.	L	6-7		12	10	Gordon	Boskie	Montgomery	72-59	1st	+3
9-17	K.C.	L	8-10		13	11	Pichardo	Langston	Montgomery	72-60	1st	+3
9-18	At Oak.	L	0-4		2	6	Johns	Finley		72-61	1st	+2
9-19	At Oak.	L	2-3	(10)	8	7	Reyes	Percival		72-62	1st	+1
9-20	At Oak.	L	6-9		16	13	Stottlemyre	Boskie	Eckersley	72-63	T1st	...
9-22	At Tex.	L	3-8		7	10	Rogers	Langston		72-64	2nd	1
9-23	At Tex.	L	1-5		4	10	Pavlik	Finley		72-65	2nd	2
9-24	At Tex.	W	5-0		11	3	Abbott	Witt		73-65	2nd	2
9-26	At Sea.	L	2-10		9	10	Benes	Boskie		73-66	2nd	3
9-27	At Sea.	W	2-0		5	3	Finley	Belcher	Smith	74-66	2nd	2
9-28	Oak.	W	4-1		5	7	Percival	Johns	Smith	75-66	2nd	2
9-29	Oak.	W	9-6		15	12	Habyan	Ontiveros	Smith	76-66	2nd	2
9-30	Oak.	W	9-3		12	9	Harkey	Wasdin		77-66	2nd	1
10-1	Oak.	W	8-2		14	4	Finley	Stottlemyre		78-66	T1st	...
10-2	At Sea.	L	1-9		3	12	Johnson	Langston		78-67	2nd	1

Monthly records: April (2-2), May (18-11), June (14-13), July (20-7), August (13-17), September (10-16), October (1-1).
*Innings, if other than nine. †First game of doubleheader. ‡Second game of doubleheader.

HIGHLIGHTS

High point: As late as August 9, the Angels headed the A.L. West by 11 games, the biggest lead in franchise history.

Low point: From August 25-September 26, California experienced two nine-game losing streaks and won only six games. The slide, which came as Seattle was getting hot, dropped the Angels three games behind the Mariners.

Turning point: Trying to break up a double play against Seattle on August 3, shortstop Gary DiSarcina slid into second base and tore a ligament in his left thumb. During his absence, the Angels went 16-25 en route to a deadlock with Seattle after 144 regular-season games.

Most valuable player: Outfielder Tim Salmon. He hit .330 (the third-best figure in the A.L.), with 34 homers and 105 RBIs. He played in all but two games.

Most valuable pitcher: Reliever Lee Smith. The veteran saved 37 games, the second-highest season total in club history.

Most improved player: Outfielder Jim Edmonds. Not even the Angels expected Edmonds to provide the power he demonstrated in '95. He hadn't hit more than 14 home runs in any pro season before bashing 33 and driving in a team-high 107 runs to go with a .290 average.

Most pleasant surprise: DiSarcina. A career .242 hitter entering the season, DiSarcina put together a breakthrough year. He batted .307, became an All-Star, established himself among the league's defensive elite and emerged as a clubhouse leader.

Biggest disappointment: Reliever Mitch Williams. He came to camp as a potential closer or setup man, hoping to resurrect his career. Instead, he retired after being released on June 18. He left with a 1-2 record and a 6.75 ERA.

Key injuries: Designated hitter Chili Davis missed 26 games because of two hamstring injuries, and DiSarcina was sidelined for 41.

Notable: The Walt Disney Co. bought controlling interest in the club from Gene Autry and will be calling all the shots in 1996. . . . Outfielder Garret Anderson was named The Sporting News' A.L. Rookie Player of the

Year. He hit .321 with 16 homers. . . . Davis was fined $5,000 for reaching into the stands to confront a fan in Milwaukee. . . . Five Angels hit 20 or more homers, with third baseman/outfielder Tony Phillips (27), first baseman J.T. Snow (24) and Davis (20) joining Salmon and Edmonds. . . . The Angels were the Orioles' opponents on September 6 when Cal Ripken played his record-breaking 2,131st consecutive game. . . . Mark Langston tied Chuck Finley for the team lead with 15 victories but came up a loser in the most crucial game—the A.L. West playoff against Seattle and Randy Johnson.

—DAVE CUNNINGHAM

RECORDS

1995 regular-season record: 78-67 (2nd in A.L. West); 39-33 at home; 39-34 on road; 28-29 vs. East; 31-18 vs. Central; 19-20 vs. West; 23-18 vs. lefthanded starters; 55-49 vs. righthanded starters; 66-59 on grass; 12-8 on turf; 23-17 in daytime; 55-50 at night; 16-14 in one-run games; 6-5 in extra-inning games; 1-0-0 in doubleheaders.

Team record past five years: 349-397 (.468, ranks 14th in league in that span).

TEAM LEADERS

Batting average: Tim Salmon (.330).
At-bats: Jim Edmonds (558).
Runs: Jim Edmonds (120).
Hits: Tim Salmon (177).
Total bases: Tim Salmon (319).
Doubles: Tim Salmon (34).
Triples: Gary DiSarcina (6).
Home runs: Tim Salmon (34).
Runs batted in: Jim Edmonds (107).
Stolen bases: Tony Phillips (13).
Slugging percentage: Tim Salmon (.594).
On-base percentage: Tim Salmon (.429).
Wins: Chuck Finley, Mark Langston (15).
Earned-run average: Chuck Finley (4.21).
Complete games: Chuck Finley, Mark Langston (2).
Shutouts: Jim Abbott, Chuck Finley, Mark Langston (1).
Saves: Lee Smith (37).
Innings pitched: Chuck Finley (203.0).
Strikeouts: Chuck Finley (195).

GAMES BY POSITION

Catcher: Jorge Fabregas 73, Greg Myers 61, Andy Allanson 35, Mark Dalesandro 8, Chris Turner 4.
First base: J.T. Snow 143, Carlos Martinez 4, Rex Hudler 2, Mike Aldrete 1.
Second base: Damion Easley 88, Rex Hudler 52, Spike Owen 16, Jose Lind 15, Rene Gonzales 2, Rod Correia 1.
Third base: Tony Phillips 88, Spike Owen 29, Eduardo Perez 23, Rene Gonzales 18, Carlos Martinez 16, Rod Correia 2.
Shortstop: Gary DiSarcina 98, Damion Easley 25, Spike Owen 25, Dick Schofield 12, Rod Correia 7, Rene Gonzales 1.
Outfield: Tim Salmon 142, Jim Edmonds 139, Garret Anderson 100, Tony Phillips 48, Rex Hudler 22, Orlando Palmeiro 7, Dave Gallagher 6, Mike Aldrete 2, Mark Dalesandro 1.
Designated hitter: Chili Davis 119, Greg Myers 16, Rex Hudler 3, Mike Aldrete 2, Carlos Martinez 2, Tony Phillips 2, Garret Anderson 1, Rod Correia 1, Mark Dalesandro 1, Kevin Flora 1, Dave Gallagher 1, Orlando Palmeiro 1, Eduardo Perez 1, Tim Salmon 1.

TOP DRAFT CHOICES

1. **Darin Erstad,** OF, University of Nebraska.
2. **Jarrod Washburn,** LHP, University of Wisconsin-Oshkosh.
3. **Jeremy Blevins,** RHP, Sullivan East H.S., Bristol, Tenn.
4. **Brian Cooper,** RHP, University of Southern California.
5. **Justin Baughman,** SS, Lewis & Clark (Ore.) College.
6. **Ryan Kane,** 3B, Presbyterian (S.C.) College.
7. **Chris Pine,** RHP, Tualatin (Ore.) H.S.
8. **Brian Scutero,** RHP, University of Central Florida.
9. **Jason Stockstill,** LHP, Katella H.S., Anaheim, Calif.
10. **Brandon McGuire,** RHP-SS, Coahoma (Tex.) H.S.

CHICAGO WHITE SOX
AMERICAN LEAGUE CENTRAL DIVISION

1996 WHITE SOX SCHEDULE

Home games shaded.
* — All-Star Game at Veterans Stadium (Philadelphia)
N — Night game (any game starting after 5 p.m.)

MARCH

SUN	MON	TUE	WED	THU	FRI	SAT
31 N SEA						

APRIL

SUN	MON	TUE	WED	THU	FRI	SAT
	1 N SEA	2 SEA	3	4 N CAL	5 N CAL	6
7 CAL	8	9 TEX	10	11 TEX	12 OAK	13 OAK
14 OAK	15 N KC	16 N KC	17 N KC	18	19 N OAK	20 OAK
21 OAK	22 N TEX	23 TEX	24 N SEA	25 N SEA	26 N CAL	27 N CAL
28 CAL	29 N CAL	30 N CLE				

MAY

SUN	MON	TUE	WED	THU	FRI	SAT
			1 N CLE	2 N NY	3 N NY	4 NY
5 NY	6	7 N BAL	8 N BAL	9 N BAL	10 N NY	11 N NY
12 NY	13 N MIL	14 N MIL	15 N MIL	16 MIL	17 N DET	18 DET
19 N DET	20	21 N TOR	22 TOR	23	24 N MIL	25 N MIL
26 MIL	27 N TOR	28 N TOR	29 N TOR	30 N DET	31 N DET	

JUNE

SUN	MON	TUE	WED	THU	FRI	SAT
						1 N DET
2 DET	3	4 N BOS	5 N BOS	6 N BOS	7 N BAL	8 BAL
9 BAL	10 N BOS	11 N BOS	12 BOS	13	14 N SEA	15 N SEA
16 SEA	17 N CAL	18 N CAL	19 CAL	20 N SEA	21 N SEA	22 SEA
23 SEA	24 N CAL	25 N CAL	26	27 N CLE	28 N CLE	29 N CLE
30 N CLE						

JULY

SUN	MON	TUE	WED	THU	FRI	SAT
	1 N MIN	2 N MIN	3 N MIN	4 CLE	5 N CLE	6 CLE
7 CLE	8 *	9 ALL-STAR GAME	10	11 N KC	12 N KC	13 KC
14 KC	15 N MIN	16 N MIN	17 N MIN	18 N KC	19 N KC	20 KC
21 KC	22 N OAK	23 OAK	24 OAK	25 N TEX	26 N TEX	27 TEX
28 TEX	29	30 N OAK	31 OAK			

AUGUST

SUN	MON	TUE	WED	THU	FRI	SAT
				1 OAK	2 N TEX	3 N TEX
4 N TEX	5 N TEX	6 N NY	7 N NY	8	9 N BAL	10 N BAL
11 BAL	12 N NY	13 N NY	14 NY	15	16 N MIL	17 N MIL
18 MIL	19 N DET	20 N DET	21 DET	22 N TOR	23 N TOR	24 TOR
25 TOR	26 N MIL	27 N MIL	28 MIL	29	30 N TOR	31 TOR

SEPTEMBER

SUN	MON	TUE	WED	THU	FRI	SAT
1 TOR	2 N DET	3 N DET	4 N DET	5	6 N BOS	7 N BOS
8 BOS	9	10 N BAL	11 N BAL	12 N BAL	13 N BOS	14 BOS
15 BOS	16 N CLE	17 N CLE	18 N CLE	19 N MIN	20 N MIN	21 MIN
22 MIN	23 N KC	24 N KC	25	26 N MIN	27 N MIN	28 MIN
29 MIN						

1996 SEASON

CLUB DIRECTORY

Chairman
Jerry Reinsdorf
Vice chairman
Eddie Einhorn
Executive vice president
Howard Pizer
Senior v.p., major league operations
Ron Schueler
Senior v.p., marketing and broadcasting
Rob Gallas
Senior vice president, baseball
Jack Gould
Vice president, finance
Tim Buzard
Vice president, stadium operations
Terry Savarise
V.p., free agent and major league scouting
Larry Monroe
Director of baseball operations
Dan Evans
Special assistants to Ron Schueler
Ed Brinkman
Bart Johnson
Dave Yoakum
Director of scouting
Duane Shaffer
Director of player development
Steve Noworyta
Director of minor league instruction
Jim Snyder
Traveling secretary
Glen Rosenbaum
Assistant to the director of scouting
Grace Guerrero Zwit
Director of marketing and broadcasting
Mike Bucek
Director of public relations
Doug Abel
Dir. of sponsorship sales and promotions
Bob Grim
Director of community relations
Christine Makowski
Director of ticket sales
Jim Munro

Director of ticket operations
Bob Devoy
Dir. of management information services
Don Brown
Director of human resources
Moira Foy
Controller
Bill Waters
Assistant director of public relations
Scott Reifert
Trainers
Herm Schneider
Mark Anderson
Director of conditioning
Steve Odgers
Team physicians
Dr. James Boscardin
Dr. Hugo Cuadros
Dr. Bernard Feldman
Dr. David Orth
Dr. Scott Price
Dr. Lowell Scott Weil
Scouting national cross-checker
George Bradley
Scouting supervisors
Mark Bernstein
Doug Laumann
Ed Pebley
Full-time scouts
Juan Ramon Bernhardt, Joseph Butler, Scott Cerny, Hernan Cortes, Alex Cosmidis, Ed Crosby, Larry Grefer, Warren Hughes, Miguel Ibarra, John Kazanas, Reginald Lewis, William Meyer, Jose Ortega, David Owen, Gary Pellant, Paul Provas, Michael Sgobba, Ken Stauffer, John Tumminia, Mark Weidemaier
Part-time scouts
Jose Bernhardt, John Doldeorian, Joe Ingalls, Jack Jolly, George Kachigian, Joe Karp, Dario Lodigiani, Donald Metzger, Al Otto, Michael Paris, Joe Thurman, Frank Trucchio

MINOR LEAGUE AFFILIATES

Class	Team	League	Manager
AAA	Nashville	American Assoc.	Rick Renick
AA	Birmingham	Southern	To be announced
A	Hickory	South Atlantic	Chris Cron
A	South Bend	Midwest	To be announced
A	Prince William	Carolina	To be announced
Rookie	Bristol	Appalachian	Nick Capra
Rookie	Gulf Coast White Sox	Gulf Coast	Mike Gellinger

BROADCAST INFORMATION

Radio: WMVP-AM (1000).
TV: WGN-TV (Channel 9).
Cable TV: SportsChannel.

SPRING TRAINING

Ballpark (city): Ed Smith Stadium (Sarasota, Fla.).
Ticket information: 813-287-8844.

1996 SEASON — Chicago White Sox

SPRING TRAINING ROSTER

Manager—Terry Bevington (18).
Coaches—Bill Buckner, Roly de Armas (56), Ron Jackson (52), Doug Mansolino (17), Joe Nossek (21), Mike Pazik (25), Mark Salas (55).

No.	PITCHERS	B/T	Ht./Wt.	Born	1995 clubs
40	Alvarez, Wilson	L/L	6-1/235	3-24-70	Chicago A.L.
49	Andujar, Luis	R/R	6-2/175	11-22-72	Birmingham, Chicago A.L.
37	Baldwin, James	R/R	6-3/210	7-15-71	Chicago A.L., Nashville
46	Bere, Jason	R/R	6-3/185	5-26-71	Chicago A.L., Nashville
52	Bertotti, Mike	L/L	6-1/185	1-18-70	Birmingham, Nashville, Chicago A.L.
	Darwin, Jeff	R/R	6-3/180	7-6-69	Tacoma
44	Ellis, Robert	R/R	6-5/220	12-15-70	Nashville
32	Fernandez, Alex	R/R	6-1/215	8-13-69	Chicago A.L.
39	Hernandez, Roberto	R/R	6-4/235	11-11-64	Chicago A.L.
60	Karchner, Matt	R/R	6-4/210	6-28-67	Nashville, Chicago A.L.
26	Keyser, Brian	R/R	6-1/180	10-31-66	Nashville, Chicago A.L.
34	Lorraine, Andrew	L/L	6-3/195	8-11-72	Vancouver, Nashville, Chicago A.L.
15	McCaskill, Kirk	R/R	6-1/205	4-9-61	Chicago A.L.
36	Ruffcorn, Scott	R/R	6-4/210	12-29-69	Nashville, Birmingham, Gulf Coast White Sox, Chicago A.L.
43	Schrenk, Steve	R/R	6-3/185	11-20-68	Gulf Coast White Sox
41	Simas, Bill	L/R	6-3/220	11-28-71	Vancouver, Nashville, Chicago A.L.
38	Sirotka, Mike	L/L	6-1/200	5-13-71	Birmingham, Chicago A.L., Nashville
50	Thomas, Larry	R/L	6-1/195	10-25-69	Birmingham, Chicago A.L.
	Woods, Brian	R/R	6-6/212	6-7-71	Prince William

No.	CATCHERS	B/T	Ht./Wt.	Born	1995 clubs
20	Karkovice, Ron	R/R	6-1/219	8-8-63	Chicago A.L.
	Kreuter, Chad	B/R	6-2/200	8-26-64	Seattle, Tacoma
	Vinas, Julio	R/R	6-1/205	2-14-73	Birmingham
	Vollmer, Scott	R/R	6-1/185	2-9-71	Birmingham

No.	INFIELDERS	B/T	Ht./Wt.	Born	1995 clubs
33	Brady, Doug	B/R	5-11/165	11-23-69	Nashville, Chicago A.L.
5	Durham, Ray	B/R	5-8/170	11-30-71	Chicago A.L.
13	Guillen, Ozzie	L/R	5-11/164	1-20-64	Chicago A.L.
7	Martin, Norberto	R/R	5-10/164	12-10-66	Chicago A.L.
	Norton, Greg	B/R	6-1/190	7-6-72	Birmingham
	Saenz, Olmedo	R/R	6-0/185	10-8-70	Nashville
27	Snopek, Chris	R/R	6-1/185	9-20-70	Nashville, Chicago A.L.
35	Thomas, Frank	R/R	6-5/257	5-27-68	Chicago A.L.
23	Ventura, Robin	L/R	6-1/198	7-14-67	Chicago A.L.

No.	OUTFIELDERS	B/T	Ht./Wt.	Born	1995 clubs
3	Baines, Harold	L/L	6-2/195	3-15-59	Baltimore
24	Cameron, Mike	R/R	6-2/190	1-8-73	Chicago A.L., Birmingham
	Hurst, Jimmy	R/R	6-6/225	3-1-72	Birmingham
	Lewis, Darren	R/R	6-0/189	8-28-67	San Francisco, Cincinnati
14	Martinez, Dave	L/L	5-10/175	9-26-64	Chicago A.L.
28	Mouton, Lyle	R/R	6-4/240	5-13-69	Nashville, Chicago A.L.

BALLPARK INFORMATION

Ballpark (capacity, surface)
Comiskey Park (44,321, grass)

Address
333 W. 35th St.
Chicago, IL 60616

Business phone
312-924-1000

Ticket information
312-924-1000

Ticket prices
$20 (club level)
$20 (lower deck box)
$15 (lower deck reserved)
$13 (upper deck box)
$12 (bleacher reserved)
$8 (upper deck reserved)

Field dimensions (from home plate)
To left field at foul line, 347 feet
To center field, 400 feet
To right field at foul line, 347 feet

First game played
April 18, 1991 (Tigers 16, White Sox 0)

DAY BY DAY

Date	Opp.	Res.	Score	(inn.*)	Hits	Opp. hits	Winning pitcher	Losing pitcher	Save	Record	Pos.	GB
4-26	At Mil.	L	3-12		7	12	Miranda	Fernandez		0-1	T4th	1
4-27	Mil.	L	4-9		9	11	Eldred	Abbott		0-2	5th	2
4-28	At Bos.	L	4-10		7	8	Cormier	Bere		0-3	5th	3
4-29	At Bos.	L	0-8		5	10	Hanson	Alvarez		0-4	5th	3
4-30	At Bos.	W	17-11		17	14	DeLeon	F. Rodriguez		1-4	5th	3
5-2	At Tor.	L	8-9		12	12	Timlin	Marquez		1-5	5th	4
5-3	At Tor.	L	7-8	(10)	13	9	Menhart	Hernandez		1-6	5th	5
5-5	K.C.	L	1-3	(12)	6	13	Meacham	McCaskill	Montgomery	1-7	5th	4 1/2
5-6	K.C.	W	7-4		12	5	Alvarez	Gubicza	Hernandez	2-7	5th	4 1/2
5-7	K.C.	L	5-7		13	12	Gordon	Baldwin	Montgomery	2-8	5th	5 1/2
5-8	Min.	W	4-2		6	12	Fernandez	Mahomes	Hernandez	3-8	5th	5
5-9	Min.	W	6-1		9	2	Abbott	Hawkins		4-8	4th	4
5-10	Min.	W	8-7		8	9	McCaskill	Guthrie	Hernandez	5-8	4th	4
5-12	At Sea.	L	4-6		9	12	Johnson	Alvarez	Risley	5-9	4th	5
5-13	At Sea.	L	5-6		9	8	Davis	Fernandez	Ayala	5-10	4th	5
5-14	At Sea.	W	10-2		13	7	Abbott	Converse		6-10	4th	5
5-16	Oak.	L	1-7	(6)	3	9	Ontiveros	Bere		6-11	4th	6
5-17	Oak.	W	6-4		11	8	DeLeon	Acre	Hernandez	7-11	4th	5 1/2
5-18	Oak.	W	4-2		10	6	Fernandez	Stewart	Hernandez	8-11	4th	4 1/2
5-19	Cal.	L	5-6		10	11	Percival	McCaskill	Smith	8-12	4th	5 1/2
5-20	Cal.	L	5-7	(10)	11	9	Patterson	Dibble	Smith	8-13	4th	6 1/2
5-21	Cal.	L	6-8		11	11	Bielecki	Bere	Smith	8-14	4th	7 1/2
5-24†	Tex.	W	10-8		10	12	Radinsky	Burrows	Hernandez	9-14		
5-24‡	Tex.	L	6-13		15	12	Oliver	Fernandez		9-15	4th	7
5-26	At Det.	L	7-8		12	11	Maxcy	Hernandez		9-16	4th	8
5-27	At Det.	W	1-0		6	3	Bere	Lira	Hernandez	10-16	4th	7
5-28	At Det.	W	14-12		14	17	Radinsky	Groom	Hernandez	11-16	4th	7
5-29	At Cle.	L	6-7		10	12	Tavarez	DeLeon	Mesa	11-17	4th	8
5-30	At Cle.	L	1-2		7	5	Assenmacher	Fernandez	Mesa	11-18	4th	9
5-31	At Cle.	L	3-6		7	8	Hershiser	Abbott	Mesa	11-19	4th	10
6-1	At Cle.	L	4-7		9	12	Black	Bere	Plunk	11-20	4th	11
6-2	Det.	W	5-4	(15)	14	16	Hernandez	Henneman		12-20	4th	10
6-3	Det.	W	10-6		17	9	McCaskill	Boever		13-20	4th	10
6-4	Det.	L	5-8		7	10	Maxcy	Hernandez	Henneman	13-21	4th	11
6-5	Tor.	W	3-2		8	7	Abbott	Guzman	Hernandez	14-21	4th	11
6-6	Tor.	W	6-4		9	9	Bere	Hentgen	Hernandez	15-21	4th	11
6-7	Tor.	L	3-4		10	11	Leiter	Keyser	Timlin	15-22	4th	12
6-9	At Tex.	L	1-6		6	10	Oliver	Alvarez		15-23	4th	13 1/2
6-11	At Tex.	L	2-3		8	8	McDowell	DeLeon		15-24	4th	14
6-12	At Oak.	L	0-1		7	5	Ontiveros	Bere	Eckersley	15-25	4th	15
6-13	At Oak.	W	7-6	(10)	10	15	Hernandez	Leiper		16-25	4th	15
6-14	At Oak.	L	5-8		9	7	Honeycutt	DeLeon	Eckersley	16-26	4th	16
6-15	At Cal.	L	1-5		6	8	Bielecki	Keyser	Smith	16-27	4th	16 1/2
6-17	At Cal.	L	3-4	(11)	9	10	Patterson	Fortugno		16-28	4th	17
6-18	At Cal.	L	4-8		10	12	Finley	Bere		16-29	4th	17
6-19	Sea.	W	8-6		15	10	McCaskill	Fleming	Hernandez	17-29	4th	17
6-20	Sea.	L	5-9		8	9	Johnson	Alvarez		17-30	4th	18
6-21	Sea.	W	5-4	(10)	11	8	McCaskill	Risley		18-30	4th	17
6-22	Sea.	L	2-3		4	10	Torres	Abbott	Ayala	18-31	4th	17 1/2
6-23	Cle.	W	12-5		20	8	Bere	Nagy		19-31	4th	16 1/2
6-24	Cle.	W	8-3		11	5	Fernandez	Black		20-31	4th	15 1/2
6-25	Cle.	W	3-2		4	7	DeLeon	Assenmacher	Radinsky	21-31	4th	14 1/2
6-26	At Min.	W	6-5		11	12	Keyser	Radke	Hernandez	22-31	4th	14 1/2
6-27	At Min.	W	8-6		12	13	Abbott	Harris		23-31	4th	14 1/2
6-28	At Min.	W	4-3		8	7	Bere	Tapani	Dibble	24-31	4th	14 1/2
6-29	At Mil.	W	17-13		22	14	Fernandez	Givens		25-31	3rd	14 1/2
6-30	At K.C.	L	0-1		4	11	Gubicza	Alvarez	Pichardo	25-32	4th	15 1/2
7-1	At K.C.	W	11-5		14	11	Keyser	Gordon		26-32	3rd	14 1/2
7-2	At K.C.	W	6-5	(10)	12	12	Fortugno	Pichardo		27-32	3rd	14 1/2
7-3	N.Y.	L	4-8		6	11	McDowell	Radinsky		27-33	4th	15 1/2
7-4	N.Y.	L	1-4		4	8	M. Rivera	Fernandez		27-34	4th	15 1/2
7-5	N.Y.	W	11-5		14	7	Alvarez	Boehringer	McCaskill	28-34	4th	15 1/2
7-6	Bal.	L	1-2		7	10	Moyer	Fortugno	Jones	28-35	4th	16 1/2
7-7	Bal.	L	2-5		8	8	Clark	Abbott	Jones	28-36	4th	16 1/2
7-8	Bal.	L	2-5		9	8	Mussina	Bere		28-37	4th	17 1/2
7-9	Bal.	L	2-11		10	14	Erickson	Fernandez		28-38	4th	17 1/2
7-12	Mil.	W	8-2		11	8	Alvarez	Sparks		29-38	4th	17
7-13	At Mil.	L	7-8	(10)	8	11	Reyes	Hernandez		29-39	4th	17 1/2
7-14	At Mil.	L	7-8		12	7	Bones	Bere	Fetters	29-40	4th	19
7-15	At Mil.	L	5-9		11	16	Wegman	Fortugno		29-41	4th	20
7-16	At Mil.	L	1-6		3	10	Givens	Keyser		29-42	4th	21

Date	Opp.	Res.	Score	(inn.*)	Hits	Opp. hits	Winning pitcher	Losing pitcher	Save	Record	Pos.	GB
7-17	At N.Y.	T	1-1	(7)	9	2	......	......		29-42	4th	20½
7-18†	At N.Y.	W	9-4		18	13	Abbott	Boehringer		30-42		
7-18‡	At N.Y.	W	11-4		19	11	Righetti	McDowell		31-42	4th	20
7-19	Bos.	L	3-5		8	13	Wakefield	Sirotka	Aguilera	31-43	4th	21
7-20	Bos.	L	1-3		10	6	Hanson	McCaskill	Aguilera	31-44	4th	22
7-21	Mil.	L	2-5		7	7	Wegman	Keyser	Fetters	31-45	4th	23
7-22	Mil.	W	4-2		7	5	Alvarez	Sparks	Hernandez	32-45	4th	23
7-23	Mil.	W	11-6		12	12	Abbott	Roberson		33-45	4th	23
7-25	At Bos.	W	8-3		10	5	Bere	Cormier	Hernandez	34-45	4th	22½
7-26	At Bos.	L	3-5		9	13	Smith	Fernandez	Aguilera	34-46	4th	22½
7-27	At Bos.	W	5-4		12	11	Karchner	Aguilera	Hernandez	35-46	4th	21½
7-28	At Bal.	L	3-4		9	5	Mussina	Alvarez	Jones	35-47	4th	22½
7-29	At Bal.	W	7-4		12	9	Bertotti	Oquist	Hernandez	36-47	4th	21½
7-30	At Bal.	L	3-8		11	9	Erickson	Bere		36-48	4th	22½
7-31	K.C.	W	6-4		12	9	Fernandez	Jacome	Hernandez	37-48	4th	22
8-1	K.C.	W	4-3		9	8	Righetti	Gubicza	Hernandez	38-48	4th	21
8-2	K.C.	W	5-2		7	9	Keyser	Pichardo	Hernandez	39-48	4th	21
8-3	K.C.	L	0-9		7	10	Bunch	Bertotti		39-49	4th	22
8-4	At Cle.	L	3-13		12	16	Nagy	Bere		39-50	4th	23
8-5	At Cle.	L	7-11		11	21	Hershiser	Fernandez		39-51	4th	24
8-6	At Cle.	W	5-1		8	7	Righetti	Martinez		40-51	4th	23
8-7	At Sea.	L	4-6		6	7	Belcher	Alvarez	Charlton	40-52	4th	23½
8-8	At Sea.	L	9-10		16	14	Ayala	Hernandez		40-53	4th	23½
8-9	At Sea.	L	8-11		12	11	Bosio	Keyser	Ayala	40-54	4th	23½
8-11	Oak.	W	13-5		16	9	Fernandez	Stottlemyre		41-54	4th	24½
8-12	Oak.	L	2-8		6	16	Van Poppel	Righetti		41-55	4th	24½
8-13	Oak.	W	8-7		14	14	DeLeon	Reyes	Hernandez	42-55	4th	23½
8-14	Cal.	L	10-11	(10)	15	15	James	McCaskill	Smith	42-56	4th	24½
8-15	Cal.	L	3-7		9	12	Langston	Bolton	Percival	42-57	4th	24½
8-16	Cal.	W	9-2		14	5	Fernandez	B. Anderson		43-57	4th	24½
8-17	Tex.	L	1-2	(10)	4	6	McDowell	Karchner		43-58	4th	24½
8-18	Tex.	W	3-1		9	7	Alvarez	Witt	Hernandez	44-58	4th	24½
8-19	Tex.	L	6-9		7	13	Gross	Bolton		44-59	4th	25½
8-20	Tex.	L	4-6		8	11	Rogers	Bere	McDowell	44-60	4th	26½
8-21	At Det.	W	7-3		10	8	Fernandez	Moore	McCaskill	45-60	4th	26½
8-22	At Det.	W	15-7		22	13	DeLeon	Lima		46-60	4th	25½
8-23	At Det.	L	5-7		8	8	Lira	Hernandez		46-61	4th	26½
8-25	At Tor.	W	8-7		9	12	Bere	Hentgen	Hernandez	47-61	4th	26½
8-26	At Tor.	L	2-3		9	10	Rogers	Hernandez		47-62	4th	27½
8-27	At Tor.	L	1-2		3	9	Leiter	Righetti	Castillo	47-63	4th	28½
8-28	Mil.	W	6-5		11	10	Alvarez	McAndrew	Hernandez	48-63	4th	28½
8-29	Det.	L	5-7		11	14	Bergman	Keyser	Lira	48-64	4th	29½
8-30	Det.	W	10-7		16	10	Karchner	Maxcy	Hernandez	49-64	4th	29½
8-31	Det.	W	9-0		10	5	Fernandez	Moore		50-64	4th	29½
9-1	Tor.	W	5-3		8	7	Keyser	Leiter	Hernandez	51-64	4th	29½
9-2	Tor.	W	10-4		13	10	Alvarez	Ware		52-64	4th	28½
9-3	Tor.	W	6-5		11	13	Simas	Guzman	Hernandez	53-64	4th	28½
9-4	At Tex.	W	14-3		18	4	Bere	Gross		54-64	4th	27½
9-5	At Tex.	W	2-1	(11)	11	6	Karchner	Vosberg		55-64	4th	27½
9-6	At Tex.	W	7-5		13	9	Keyser	Tewksbury	Hernandez	56-64	4th	27½
9-7	At Tex.	L	0-2		3	5	Pavlik	Alvarez		56-65	4th	28½
9-8	At Oak.	W	7-3		11	5	Andujar	Van Poppel	Hernandez	57-65	4th	28½
9-9	At Oak.	L	2-8		5	13	Ontiveros	Bere		57-66	4th	29½
9-10	At Oak.	W	5-3		8	11	Fernandez	Stottlemyre	Hernandez	58-66	4th	29½
9-11	At Cal.	L	1-4		5	11	Boskie	Sirotka		58-67	4th	29½
9-12	At Cal.	L	1-3		7	6	Langston	Alvarez	Smith	58-68	4th	29½
9-13	At Cal.	W	6-1		13	4	Andujar	Percival		59-68	4th	29½
9-15	Sea.	L	2-3		8	8	Benes	Bere	Charlton	59-69	4th	30
9-16	Sea.	L	3-5		5	11	Belcher	Karchner	Charlton	59-70	4th	31
9-17	Sea.	W	2-1		5	8	McCaskill	Wolcott	Hernandez	60-70	4th	30
9-18	Cle.	L	1-11		6	13	Hill	Alvarez		60-71	4th	31
9-19	Cle.	L	2-8		7	13	Nagy	Andujar		60-72	4th	32
9-20	Cle.	W	4-3		10	10	Bere	Roa	Hernandez	61-72	4th	31
9-21	Mil.	W	5-1		10	5	Fernandez	Scanlan		62-72	4th	30½
9-22	At Min.	W	5-4	(10)	12	8	McCaskill	Mahomes	Hernandez	63-72	3rd	30½
9-23	At Min.	W	14-4		20	7	Alvarez	Parra		64-72	3rd	30½
9-24	At Min.	L	3-4		5	10	Hawkins	Simas		64-73	3rd	30½
9-25	At Min.	L	1-6		4	7	Robertson	Bere		64-74	T3rd	31
9-26	At K.C.	W	7-0		8	6	Fernandez	Gordon		65-74	3rd	30
9-27	At K.C.	W	6-0		9	3	Sirotka	Jacome		66-74	3rd	30
9-28	At K.C.	L	0-4		4	5	Gubicza	Alvarez		66-75	3rd	31
9-29	Min.	W	4-3		8	6	Karchner	Guardado		67-75	3rd	31
9-30	Min.	L	6-7		9	10	O. Munoz	Bere	Stevens	67-76	3rd	32
10-1	Min.	W	2-1	(11)	7	5	Hernandez	Stevens		68-76	3rd	32

Monthly records: April (1-4), May (10-15), June (14-13), July (12-16), August (13-16), September (17-12), October (1-0).
*Innings, if other than nine. †First game of doubleheader. ‡Second game of doubleheader.

HIGHLIGHTS

High point: The White Sox won 18 of their last 30 games, which was good enough to get interim Manager Terry Bevington rehired for two years.

Low point: On June 2, with the team's hope of winning the Central Division title already slipping away, Manager Gene Lamont was fired. The Sox were 11-20 at the time, having just been swept by Cleveland in a four-game series.

Turning point: The beginning of the season set the trend. Chicago started 1-7 and allowed 70 runs in those eight games while making 23 errors. The White Sox never recovered.

Most valuable player: First baseman Frank Thomas. He became the first player in baseball history to bat .300 with at least 20 homers, 100 RBIs, 100 runs and 100 walks in five consecutive seasons.

Most valuable pitcher: Righthander Alex Fernandez. He proved he could handle the No. 1 starting role. Fernandez didn't lose in his last 11 games, going 7-0 with a 1.35 ERA. For the season, he was 12-8 with a 3.80 ERA.

Most improved player: Second baseman Ray Durham. The White Sox had such confidence he would succeed that they didn't re-sign Joey Cora. After a slow start, the multi-talented Durham finished with a .257 average and seven homers, 51 RBIs and 18 steals.

Most pleasant surprise: Outfielder Lyle Mouton. Mouton, obtained from the Yankees in the Jack McDowell deal, became the everyday right fielder for the last six weeks and hit .302 with five homers and 27 RBIs in just 179 at-bats.

Biggest disappointments: Pitcher Jason Bere and designated hitters Chris Sabo and John Kruk. Bere lost 15 games and had a 7.19 ERA one season after he had the best winning percentage in the league. Neither Sabo nor Kruk could pick up the slack left by Julio Franco and both players went by the wayside.

Key injuries: The White Sox had no major injuries. But Scott Ruffcorn, considered a future member of the rotation, missed much of the Class AAA season with non-surgical shoulder problems that could set back his career.

Notable: Outfielder Lance Johnson finished with 186 hits, the first White Sox player to lead the league in that category since Minnie Minoso in 1960. . . . The Sox had their first losing record since 1989. . . . After winning the league ERA title the previous two seasons, the Chicago pitching staff was 10th in '95.

—**DAVE VAN DYCK**

RECORDS

1995 regular-season record: 68-76 (3rd in A.L. Central); 38-34 at home; 30-42 on road; 21-22 vs. East; 29-23 vs. Central; 18-31 vs. West; 15-25 vs. lefthanded starters; 53-51 vs. righthanded starters; 61-65 on grass; 7-11 on turf; 20-19 in daytime; 48-57 at night; 22-25 in one-run games; 7-7 in extra-inning games; 1-0-1 in doubleheaders.
Team record past five years: 402-341 (.541, ranks 1st in league in that span).

TEAM LEADERS

Batting average: Frank Thomas (.308).
At-bats: Lance Johnson (607).
Runs: Frank Thomas (102).
Hits: Lance Johnson (186).
Total bases: Frank Thomas (299).
Doubles: Ray Durham, Frank Thomas (27).
Triples: Lance Johnson (12).
Home runs: Frank Thomas (40).
Runs batted in: Frank Thomas (111).
Stolen bases: Lance Johnson (40).
Slugging percentage: Frank Thomas (.606).
On-base percentage: Frank Thomas (.454).
Wins: Alex Fernandez (12).
Earned-run average: Alex Fernandez (3.80).
Complete games: Alex Fernandez (5).
Shutouts: Alex Fernandez (2).
Saves: Roberto Hernandez (32).
Innings pitched: Alex Fernandez (203.2).
Strikeouts: Alex Fernandez (159).

GAMES BY POSITION

Catcher: Ron Karkovice 113, Mike LaValliere 46, Barry Lyons 16, Chris Tremie 9.
First base: Frank Thomas 90, Dave Martinez 47, Robin Ventura 18, Barry Lyons 4, John Kruk 1, Chris Sabo 1.
Second base: Ray Durham 122, Norberto Martin 17, Craig Grebeck 8, Doug Brady 6.
Third base: Robin Ventura 121, Craig Grebeck 18, Chris Snopek 17, Norberto Martin 9, Chris Sabo 1.
Shortstop: Ozzie Guillen 120, Craig Grebeck 31, Norberto Martin 7, Chris Snopek 6.
Outfield: Lance Johnson 140, Tim Raines 107, Mike Devereaux 90, Dave Martinez 59, Lyle Mouton 53, Mike Cameron 28, Warren Newson 24, Norberto Martin 12.
Designated hitter: Frank Thomas 53, John Kruk 42, Tim Raines 22, Chris Sabo 15, Norberto Martin 10, Barry Lyons 7, Warren Newson 7, Dave Martinez 4, Doug Brady 2, Lyle Mouton 2, Ray Durham 1, Ozzie Guillen 1, Lance Johnson 1, Chris Tremie 1, Robin Ventura 1.

TOP DRAFT CHOICES

1. **Jeff Liefer,** 3B, Long Beach State University.
2. **Brian Simmons,** OF, University of Michigan.
3. **J.J. Putz,** RHP, Trenton (Mich.) H.S.
4. **Ryan Topham,** OF, University of Notre Dame.
5. **Tighe Brown,** RHP, St. Xavier H.S., Louisville, Ky.
6. **John Hunt,** LHP, Ohio University.
7. **Jason Lakman,** RHP, Woodinville (Wash.) H.S.
8. **Adam Virchis,** RHP, San Diego State University.
9. **Jason Secoda,** RHP, Cal State Los Angeles.
10. **Chuck Klee,** SS, Cardinal Gibbons H.S., Fort Lauderdale, Fla.

CLEVELAND INDIANS
AMERICAN LEAGUE CENTRAL DIVISION

1996 INDIANS SCHEDULE

☐ Home games shaded.
* — All-Star Game at Veterans Stadium (Philadelphia)
N — Night game (any game starting after 5 p.m.)

MARCH

SUN	MON	TUE	WED	THU	FRI	SAT
31						

APRIL

SUN	MON	TUE	WED	THU	FRI	SAT
	1 NY	2 N NY	3 N NY	4 N TOR	5 N TOR	6 TOR
7 TOR	8 N BAL	9 N BAL	10	11 N BOS	12 N BOS	13 BOS
14 BOS	15 N MIN	16 N MIN	17	18 N BOS	19 N BOS	20 BOS
21 BOS	22 N BAL	23 N BAL	24 N NY	25 N NY	26 N TOR	27 TOR
28 TOR	29 N CHI	30				

MAY

SUN	MON	TUE	WED	THU	FRI	SAT
			1 N CHI	2 N SEA	3 N SEA	4 N SEA
5 SEA	6 N OAK	7 OAK	8 N OAK	9	10 N CAL	11 N CAL
12 N CAL	13	14 N DET	15 N DET	16 N DET	17 N TEX	18 TEX
19 TEX	20	21 N MIL	22 N MIL	23 N MIL	24 N DET	25 DET
26 DET	27 N TEX	28 N TEX	29 N TEX	30 N MIL	31 N MIL	

JUNE

SUN	MON	TUE	WED	THU	FRI	SAT
						1 MIL
2 MIL	3	4 N SEA	5 N SEA	6 N SEA	7 N CAL	8 CAL
9 CAL	10 N OAK	11 N OAK	12 N OAK	13 N NY	14 N NY	15 NY
16 NY	17	18 N BOS	19 N BOS	20 N NY	21 N NY	22 NY
23 NY	24	25 N BOS	26 N BOS	27 N CHI	28 N CHI	29 N CHI
30 N CHI						

JULY

SUN	MON	TUE	WED	THU	FRI	SAT
	1 N KC	2 N KC	3 N KC	4 CHI	5 N CHI	6 CHI
	8 *	9 ALL-STAR GAME	10	11 N MIN	12 N MIN	13 N MIN
14	15 N KC	16 N KC	17 N KC	18 N MIN	19 N MIN	20 MIN
21	22 N TOR	23 N TOR	24 N TOR	25 N BAL	26 N BAL	27 BAL
28 BAL	29	30 N TOR	31 N TOR			

AUGUST

SUN	MON	TUE	WED	THU	FRI	SAT
				1 N TOR	2 N BAL	3 BAL
4 BAL	5 N BAL	6 N SEA	7 N SEA	8	9 SEA	10 OAK
11 OAK	12 N CAL	13 N CAL	14 N CAL	15	16 N DET	17 DET
18 DET	19 N TEX	20 N TEX	21 N TEX	22	23 N MIL	24 MIL
25 MIL	26 N DET	27 N DET	28 DET	29	30 N TEX	31 N TEX

SEPTEMBER

SUN	MON	TUE	WED	THU	FRI	SAT
1 TEX	2 MIL	3 N MIL	4 N MIL	5	6 N SEA	7 SEA
8 SEA	9 N CAL	10 N CAL	11 N CAL	12 N OAK	13 OAK	14 OAK
15 OAK	16 N CHI	17 N CHI	18 N KC	19 N KC	20 N KC	21 KC
22 KC	23 N MIN	24 N MIN	25 N MIN	26	27 N KC	28 KC
29 KC						

1996 SEASON

CLUB DIRECTORY

Board of directors
Richard E. Jacobs
Martin J. Cleary
Gary L. Bryenton

Chairman of the board and CEO
Richard E. Jacobs

Executive vice president, general manager
John Hart

Executive vice president, business
Dennis Lehman

V.p., marketing and communications
Jeff Overton

Vice president
Martin J. Cleary

Vice president, public relations
Bob DiBiasio

Vice president, finance
Ken Stefanov

Dir. of baseball operations/asst. g.m.
Dan O'Dowd

Director, scouting
Jay Robertson

Director, team travel
Mike Seghi

Director, minor league operations
Mark Shapiro

Administrator, player personnel
Wendy Hoppel

Administrator, scouting
Brad Grant

Director, media relations
Bart Swain

Assistant director, media relations
Susie Gharrity

Director, community relations
Allen Davis

Manager, community relations
Melissa Zapanta

Manager, promotions
Chris Previte

Director, broadcasting
Mike Lehr

Manager, advertising/publications
Kim Carpinello

Controller
Ron McQuate

Director, ticket services
Connie Minadeo

Director, ticket sales
Vic Gregovits

Coordinator, season/group sales
Diane Stack

Director, ballpark operations
Jim Folk

Director, merchandising/licensing
Jayne Churchmack

Home clubhouse manager
Stan Hunter

Equipment manager
Jeff Sipos

Visiting clubhouse manager
Cy Buynak

Medical director
William T. Wilder, M.D.

Head trainer
Jim Warfield

Assistant trainer
Paul Spicuzza

Strength and conditioning coach
Fernando Montes

Team physicians
Ronald Golovan M.D.
Godofredo Domingo, M.D.
K.V. Gopal, M.D.
Zenos Vangelos, M.D.

Major league/spec. assignment scouts
Dan Carnevale, Tom Giordano, Ted Simmons, Bill Werle

Full-time scouts
Luis Aponte, Steve Avila, Brad Cameron, Tom Couston, Rene Gayo, Mark Germann, Winston Llenas, Guy Mader, Bob Mayer, Kasey McKeon, Jim Richardson, Max Semler, Jim Stevenson, Gene Thompson, Gary Tuck, Craig Wallenbrock, Mark Weidemaier

MINOR LEAGUE AFFILIATES

Class	Team	League	Manager
AAA	Buffalo	American Association	Brian Graham
AA	Canton-Akron	Eastern	Jeff Datz
A	Kinston	Carolina	Jack Mull
A	Columbus	South Atlantic	Joel Skinner
A	Watertown	New York-Pennsylvania	Ted Kubiak
Rookie	Burlington	Appalachian	Harry Spilman

BROADCAST INFORMATION

Radio: WKNR-AM (1220).
TV: WUAB-TV (Channel 43).
Cable TV: SportsChannel.

SPRING TRAINING

Ballpark (city): Chain O'Lakes (Winter Haven, Fla.).
Ticket information: 813-293-3900.

SPRING TRAINING ROSTER

Manager—Mike Hargrove (21).
Coaches—Toby Harrah, Luis Isaacs (6), Charlie Manuel (42), Dave Nelson (1), Jeff Newman (29), Mark Wiley (28), Dan Williams (43).

No.	PITCHERS	B/T	Ht./Wt.	Born	1995 clubs
45	Assenmacher, Paul	L/L	6-3/210	12-10-60	Cleveland
54	Clark, Mark	R/R	6-5/225	5-12-68	Cleveland, Buffalo
	De La Rosa, Maximo	R/R	5-11/170	7-12-71	Kinston, Canton/Akron
56	Embree, Alan	L/L	6-2/190	1-23-70	Buffalo, Cleveland
	Harris, Pep	R/R	6-2/185	9-23-72	Canton/Akron, Buffalo
55	Hershiser, Orel	R/R	6-3/195	9-16-58	Cleveland
	Kirkreit, Daron	R/R	6-6/225	8-7-72	Kinston, Canton/Akron
	Kline, Steve	B/L	6-2/200	8-22-72	Canton/Akron
51	Lewis, James	R/R	6-4/190	1-31-70	Buffalo
59	Lopez, Albie	R/R	6-2/205	8-18-71	Buffalo, Cleveland
32	Martinez, Dennis	R/R	6-1/180	5-14-55	Cleveland
	McDowell, Jack	R/R	6-5/188	1-16-66	New York A.L.
49	Mesa, Jose	R/R	6-3/225	5-22-66	Cleveland
41	Nagy, Charles	L/R	6-3/200	5-5-67	Cleveland
37	Ogea, Chad	L/R	6-2/200	11-9-70	Buffalo, Cleveland
38	Plunk, Eric	R/R	6-6/220	9-3-63	Cleveland
52	Poole, Jim	L/L	6-2/203	4-28-66	Buffalo, Cleveland
47	Roa, Joe	R/R	6-1/195	10-11-71	Buffalo, Cleveland
	Sexton, Jeff	R/R	6-2/190	10-4-71	Columbus, Kinston
53	Shuey, Paul	R/R	6-3/215	9-16-70	Cleveland, Buffalo
50	Tavarez, Julian	R/R	6-2/165	5-22-73	Cleveland
	Whitten, Casey	L/L	6-0/175	5-23-72	Canton/Akron

No.	CATCHERS	B/T	Ht./Wt.	Born	1995 clubs
15	Alomar, Sandy	R/R	6-5/215	6-18-66	Canton/Akron, Cleveland
60	Diaz, Einar	R/R	5-10/165	12-28-72	Kinston
12	Levis, Jesse	L/R	5-9/180	4-14-68	Buffalo, Cleveland
17	Pena, Tony	R/R	6-0/185	6-4-57	Cleveland

No.	INFIELDERS	B/T	Ht./Wt.	Born	1995 clubs
9	Baerga, Carlos	B/R	5-11/200	11-4-68	Cleveland
	Franco, Julio	R/R	6-1/190	8-23-61	Chiba Lotte
	Jackson, Damian	R/R	5-10/160	8-16-73	Canton/Akron
33	Murray, Eddie	B/R	6-2/220	2-24-56	Cleveland
36	Perry, Herbert	R/R	6-2/215	9-15-69	Buffalo, Cleveland
25	Thome, Jim	L/R	6-4/220	8-27-70	Cleveland
13	Vizquel, Omar	B/R	5-9/165	4-24-67	Cleveland
	Wilson, Enrique	B/R	5-11/160	7-27-75	Kinston

No.	OUTFIELDERS	B/T	Ht./Wt.	Born	1995 clubs
8	Belle, Albert	R/R	6-2/210	8-25-66	Cleveland
23	Burnitz, Jeromy	L/R	6-0/190	4-15-69	Buffalo, Cleveland
58	Giles, Brian	L/L	5-11/195	1-21-71	Buffalo, Cleveland
35	Kirby, Wayne	L/R	5-10/190	1-22-64	Cleveland
7	Lofton, Kenny	L/L	6-0/180	5-31-67	Cleveland
24	Ramirez, Manny	R/R	6-0/190	5-30-72	Cleveland

BALLPARK INFORMATION

Ballpark (capacity, surface)
Jacobs Field (42,865, grass)

Address
2401 Ontario St.
Cleveland, OH 44115

Business phone
216-420-4200

Ticket information
216-241-8888

Ticket prices
$21 (field box)
$17 (lower box & view box)
$14 (lower reserved, upper box & mezzanine seating)
$10 (upper reserved)
$6 (reserved g.a.)
$8 (bleachers)
$6 (Standing room only)

Field dimensions (from home plate)
To left field at foul line, 325 feet
To center field, 405 feet
To right field at foul line, 325 feet

First game played
April 4, 1994
(Indians 4, Mariners 3, 11 innings)

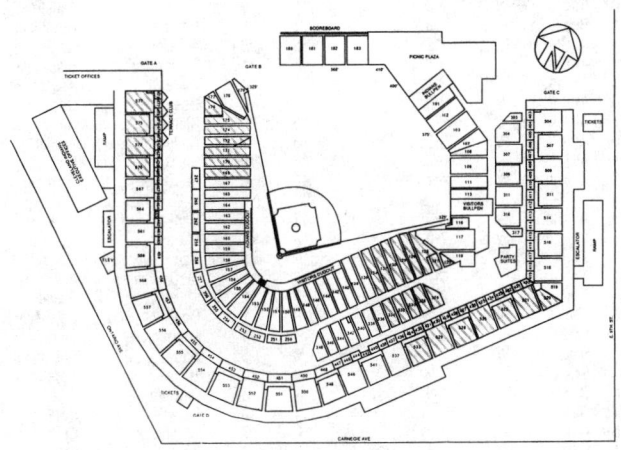

DAY BY DAY

Date	Opp.	Res.	Score	(inn.*)	Hits	Opp. hits	Winning pitcher	Losing pitcher	Save	Record	Pos.	GB
4-27	At Tex.	W	11-6		13	8	Martinez	Gross		1-0	T2nd	½
4-28	At Tex.	L	9-10		11	11	Whiteside	Poole	Russell	1-1	T3rd	1½
4-29	At Tex.	L	5-6		10	8	Burrows	Shuey		1-2	T3rd	1½
4-30	At Tex.	W	7-6	(12)	12	13	Mesa	Whiteside		2-2	T2nd	1½
5-2	At Det.	W	11-1		15	8	Martinez	Bergman		3-2	T2nd	1½
5-3	At Det.	W	14-7		18	10	Clark	Doherty		4-2	2nd	1½
5-4	At Det.	L	3-4		7	6	Wells	Hershiser	Henneman	4-3	T2nd	1½
5-5	Min.	W	5-1		9	5	Nagy	Erickson	Mesa	5-3	T2nd	½
5-6	Min.	L	2-5		8	10	Radke	Black	Aguilera	5-4	T2nd	1½
5-7	Min.	W	10-9	(17)	26	18	Poole	Guthrie		6-4	T2nd	1½
5-8	K.C.	W	6-2		11	10	Clark	Appier	Grimsley	7-4	2nd	1
5-9	K.C.	W	10-0		8	4	Hershiser	Linton		8-4	T1st	...
5-10	K.C.	W	3-2	(10)	11	4	Plunk	Meacham		9-4	T1st	...
5-12	At Bal.	W	3-2		8	9	Martinez	K. Brown	Mesa	10-4	1st	+½
5-13	At Bal.	L	1-6		3	8	Mussina	Clark		10-5	1st	+½
5-14	At Bal.	W	3-1		4	4	Hershiser	Rhodes	Mesa	11-5	1st	+1½
5-16	At N.Y.	W	10-5		15	8	Nagy	Key		12-5	1st	+2½
5-18	At Bos.	L	3-4		10	10	Belinda	Poole		12-6	1st	+3
5-19	At Bos.	W	9-5		13	8	Tavarez	Ryan		13-6	1st	+3
5-20	At Bos.	W	7-5		12	11	Plunk	Pena	Mesa	14-6	1st	+4
5-21	At Bos.	W	12-10		17	18	Assenmacher	Pierce	Mesa	15-6	1st	+5
5-22	Mil.	L	5-7		6	16	Bones	Nagy	Fetters	15-7	1st	+4
5-23	Mil.	W	5-3		13	7	Martinez	Sparks	Mesa	16-7	1st	+5
5-24	Mil.	L	5-7		9	13	Rightnowar	Clark	Fetters	16-8	1st	+4
5-26	At Tor.	W	7-4		11	7	Hershiser	Hentgen	Mesa	17-8	1st	+5
5-27	At Tor.	L	0-3		6	6	Leiter	Plunk	Hall	17-9	1st	+4½
5-28	At Tor.	W	5-4		5	10	Nagy	Darwin		18-9	1st	+4½
5-29	Chi.	W	7-6		12	10	Tavarez	DeLeon	Mesa	19-9	1st	+4½
5-30	Chi.	W	2-1		5	7	Assenmacher	Fernandez	Mesa	20-9	1st	+4½
5-31	Chi.	W	6-3		8	7	Hershiser	Abbott	Mesa	21-9	1st	+5½
6-1	Chi.	W	7-4		12	9	Black	Bere	Plunk	22-9	1st	+6
6-2	Tor.	L	0-5		3	9	Leiter	Nagy	Timlin	22-10	1st	+5
6-3	Tor.	W	3-0		7	9	Martinez	Darwin		23-10	1st	+5
6-4	Tor.	W	9-8		17	8	Tavarez	Hall		24-10	1st	+5
6-5	Det.	W	8-0		10	6	Hershiser	Bergman		25-10	1st	+5
6-6	Det.	W	4-3		9	4	Tavarez	Boever	Mesa	26-10	1st	+6
6-7	Det.	W	3-2	(10)	8	6	Plunk	Maxcy		27-10	1st	+7
6-8	At Mil.	W	8-7		12	14	Tavarez	Lloyd	Mesa	28-10	1st	+8
6-9	At Mil.	W	7-4		13	8	Ogea	Roberson	Mesa	29-10	1st	+8½
6-10	At Mil.	L	1-6		3	9	Miranda	Hershiser	Reyes	29-11	1st	+7½
6-11	At Mil.	W	11-5		19	10	Black	Scanlan		30-11	1st	+7½
6-12	Bal.	W	4-3		8	5	Nagy	K. Brown	Mesa	31-11	1st	+7½
6-13	Bal.	W	11-0		14	8	Martinez	Mussina		32-11	1st	+7½
6-14	Bal.	W	5-2		7	9	Ogea	Klingenbeck	Mesa	33-11	1st	+7½
6-16	N.Y.	L	2-4		6	6	Wickman	Poole	Wetteland	33-12	1st	+6
6-17	N.Y.	W	7-4		12	9	Black	Pettitte	Mesa	34-12	1st	+7
6-18	N.Y.	L	5-9		11	12	McDowell	Nagy	Wetteland	34-13	1st	+7
6-19	Bos.	W	4-3	(10)	11	12	Plunk	Ryan		35-13	1st	+7
6-20	Bos.	W	9-2		15	6	Ogea	Eshelman		36-13	1st	+8
6-21	Bos.	L	1-3		5	6	Hanson	Hershiser	Belinda	36-14	1st	+7
6-23	At Chi.	L	5-12		8	20	Bere	Nagy		36-15	1st	+6
6-24	At Chi.	L	3-8		5	11	Fernandez	Black		36-16	1st	+6
6-25	At Chi.	L	2-3		7	4	DeLeon	Assenmacher	Radinsky	36-17	1st	+5½
6-26	At K.C.	W	2-0		8	7	Ogea	Gordon	Mesa	37-17	1st	+6½
6-27	At K.C.	W	7-1		15	5	Clark	Haney		38-17	1st	+7½
6-28	At K.C.	W	5-2		8	7	Nagy	Appier	Mesa	39-17	1st	+8½
6-29	At Min.	W	10-5		16	10	Black	Erickson		40-17	1st	+9
6-30	At Min.	W	4-1		10	6	Martinez	Trombley	Mesa	41-17	1st	+9
7-1	At Min.	L	5-6		12	6	Radke	Ogea	Aguilera	41-18	1st	+9
7-2	At Min.	W	7-0		14	7	Clark	Harris		42-18	1st	+10
7-3	Tex.	W	9-1		11	5	Nagy	Rogers		43-18	1st	+11
7-4	Tex.	L	6-7		8	12	McDowell	Assenmacher	Whiteside	43-19	1st	+11
7-5	Tex.	W	2-0		7	2	Martinez	Gross	Mesa	44-19	1st	+11
7-6	Sea.	W	8-1		9	3	Ogea	Belcher		45-19	1st	+12
7-7	Sea.	L	3-5		8	11	Johnson	Clark		45-20	1st	+12
7-8	Sea.	W	7-3		9	5	Nagy	Bosio		46-20	1st	+12
7-9	Sea.	L	3-9		9	10	Torres	Hershiser		46-21	1st	+12
7-14†	Oak.	W	1-0		4	5	Embree	Prieto	Mesa	47-21		
7-14‡	Oak.	W	7-6		11	10	Nagy	Darling	Mesa	48-21	1st	+12½
7-15	Oak.	W	7-2		8	7	Hershiser	Ontiveros	Plunk	49-21	1st	+13½
7-16	Oak.	W	5-4	(12)	13	9	Embree	Eckersley		50-21	1st	+14½

Date	Opp.	Res.	Score	(inn.*)	Hits	Opp. hits	Winning pitcher	Losing pitcher	Save	Record	Pos.	GB
7-17	Cal.	L	3-8		5	15	B. Anderson	Ogea		50-22	1st	+13½
7-18	Cal.	W	7-5		12	8	Assenmacher	Smith		51-22	1st	+13½
7-19	At Tex.	W	14-5		19	12	Nagy	Gross		52-22	1st	+13½
7-20	At Tex.	W	6-3		11	10	Hershiser	Brandenburg	Mesa	53-22	1st	+14½
7-21	At Oak.	W	6-1		7	6	Martinez	Stottlemyre		54-22	1st	+14½
7-22	At Oak.	W	6-4		8	7	Tavarez	Eckersley	Mesa	55-22	1st	+15½
7-23	At Oak.	W	2-0		5	6	Clark	Prieto	Mesa	56-22	1st	+16½
7-24	At Cal.	W	9-7	(10)	13	12	Assenmacher	Smith	Mesa	57-22	1st	+16½
7-25	At Cal.	L	5-6		10	9	Finley	Hershiser	Smith	57-23	1st	+16½
7-26	At Cal.	L	3-6		8	7	Harkey	Martinez	Smith	57-24	1st	+15½
7-27	At Sea.	L	5-11		6	14	Belcher	Ogea		57-25	1st	+15½
7-28	At Sea.	W	6-5		12	12	Plunk	Frey	Mesa	58-25	1st	+16½
7-29	At Sea.	L	3-5		9	7	Bosio	Embree	Ayala	58-26	1st	+16½
7-30	At Sea.	W	5-2		7	5	Hershiser	Torres	Mesa	59-26	1st	+17
8-1	Min.	L	5-6		10	12	Mahomes	Tavarez	Stevens	59-27	1st	+17½
8-2	Min.	W	12-6		15	13	Clark	Harris		60-27	1st	+17½
8-3	Min.	W	6-4		10	9	Hill	Radke	Mesa	61-27	1st	+18½
8-4	Chi.	W	13-3		16	12	Nagy	Bere		62-27	1st	+18½
8-5	Chi.	W	11-7		21	11	Hershiser	Fernandez		63-27	1st	+19½
8-6	Chi.	L	1-5		7	8	Righetti	Martinez		63-28	1st	+18½
8-8	At Bos.	L	1-5		6	12	Wakefield	Clark		63-29	1st	+17½
8-9	At Bos.	L	5-9		6	8	Hanson	Plunk		63-30	1st	+16½
8-10†	At N.Y.	W	10-9		13	16	Poole	Wetteland	Mesa	64-30		
8-10‡	At N.Y.	W	5-2		9	8	Ogea	Hitchcock	Mesa	65-30	1st	+18
8-11	At N.Y.	W	5-4	(11)	15	13	Tavarez	Wetteland	Mesa	66-30	1st	+18
8-12	At N.Y.	L	2-3		7	6	McDowell	Martinez		66-31	1st	+18
8-13	At N.Y.	L	1-4		6	10	Cone	Clark		66-32	1st	+17
8-14	At Bal.	W	9-6		13	11	Assenmacher	Benitez	Mesa	67-32	1st	+17
8-15	At Bal.	L	3-8		7	11	Erickson	Nagy		67-33	1st	+17
8-16	At Bal.	W	8-5		11	10	Hershiser	K. Brown	Mesa	68-33	1st	+17
8-17	Mil.	L	3-7		9	11	McAndrew	Martinez	Fetters	68-34	1st	+16
8-18	Mil.	W	7-5		11	10	Clark	Bones	Mesa	69-34	1st	+17
8-19	Mil.	W	4-3		6	8	Plunk	Wegman		70-34	1st	+18
8-20	Mil.	W	8-5		12	10	Tavarez	Sparks	Mesa	71-34	1st	+19
8-21	At Tor.	W	7-3		8	10	Hershiser	Hurtado	Embree	72-34	1st	+19½
8-22	At Tor.	L	4-5		7	9	Castillo	Tavarez		72-35	1st	+18½
8-23	At Tor.	W	6-5		7	9	Poole	Carrara	Mesa	73-35	1st	+19
8-25	Det.	W	6-5	(11)	10	9	Tavarez	Lira		74-35	1st	+18½
8-26	Det.	W	6-2		8	11	Nagy	Moore		75-35	1st	+18½
8-27	Det.	W	9-2		11	5	Hershiser	Lima		76-35	1st	+18½
8-28	Tor.	W	9-1		13	10	Ogea	Carrara		77-35	1st	+19½
8-29	Tor.	W	4-1		7	3	Clark	Guzman		78-35	1st	+20½
8-30	Tor.	W	4-3	(14)	12	18	Assenmacher	Castillo		79-35	1st	+21½
8-31	Tor.	W	6-4	(10)	12	10	Mesa	Rogers		80-35	1st	+21½
9-1	At Det.	W	14-4		21	9	Nagy	Lima		81-35	1st	+21½
9-2	At Det.	L	2-3		5	7	Lira	Hershiser	Doherty	81-36	1st	+21½
9-3	At Det.	W	9-8	(10)	14	11	Mesa	Boever		82-36	1st	+21½
9-4	At Det.	L	2-3		3	4	Sodowsky	Clark	Henry	82-37	1st	+21
9-5	At Mil.	W	7-3		15	8	Martinez	Sparks		83-37	1st	+21
9-6	At Mil.	W	12-2		13	7	Hill	Givens		84-37	1st	+22
9-7	Sea.	W	4-1		8	7	Nagy	Bosio	Mesa	85-37	1st	+22½
9-8	Bal.	W	3-2		6	5	Hershiser	K. Brown	Mesa	86-37	1st	+23½
9-9	Bal.	W	2-1		5	2	Ogea	Krivda	Mesa	87-37	1st	+24½
9-10	Bal.	W	5-3		12	6	Tavarez	Orosco	Mesa	88-37	1st	+25½
9-11	N.Y.	L	0-4		4	7	McDowell	Martinez		88-38	1st	+25
9-12	N.Y.	L	2-9		8	13	Kamieniecki	Hill		88-39	1st	+24
9-13	N.Y.	W	5-0		10	3	Nagy	Cone		89-39	1st	+25
9-14	Bos.	W	5-3		10	4	Hershiser	Eshelman	Mesa	90-39	1st	+25
9-15	Bos.	L	3-6		8	11	Hanson	Embree		90-40	1st	+24
9-16	Bos.	W	6-5		11	7	Clark	Clemens	Mesa	91-40	1st	+24
9-17	Bos.	L	6-9		9	12	Suppan	Shuey	Aguilera	91-41	1st	+23
9-18	At Chi.	W	11-1		13	6	Hill	Alvarez		92-41	1st	+23½
9-19	At Chi.	W	8-2		13	7	Nagy	Andujar		93-41	1st	+24½
9-20	At Chi.	L	3-4		10	10	Bere	Roa	Hernandez	93-42	1st	+24½
9-22	At K.C.	W	5-3		8	8	Hershiser	Olson	Mesa	94-42	1st	+26
9-23	At K.C.	W	7-3		13	7	Martinez	Gubicza		95-42	1st	+27
9-24	At K.C.	L	2-4		5	10	Appier	Clark		95-43	1st	+26
9-26	At Min.	L	4-13		9	17	Trombley	Nagy		95-44	1st	+26
9-27	At Min.	W	9-6		15	9	Hill	Radke	Mesa	96-44	1st	+27
9-28	At Min.	W	12-4		17	7	Martinez	Rodriguez		97-44	1st	+27
9-29	K.C.	W	9-2		12	5	Hershiser	Appier		98-44	1st	+28
9-30	K.C.	W	3-2	(10)	10	5	Embree	Montgomery		99-44	1st	+29
10-1	K.C.	W	17-7		19	13	Nagy	Gordon		100-44	1st	+30

Monthly records: April (2-2), May (19-7), June (20-8), July (18-9), August (21-9), September (19-9), October (1-0).
*Innings, if other than nine. †First game of doubleheader. ‡Second game of doubleheader.

1996 SEASON *Cleveland Indians*

HIGHLIGHTS

High point: On September 8, Orel Hershiser beat the Orioles, 3-2, to enable the Indians to clinch the A.L. Central title, Cleveland's first championship of any kind in 41 years.

Low point: It's not much of a descent, but Cleveland's 4-3 loss to the Tigers on May 4 dropped the Indians' record to 4-3—the last time the club was a mere one game over .500. More troublesome that day, reliever Paul Shuey joined catcher Sandy Alomar on the disabled list.

Turning point: During a 35-game stretch in April and early May, the Indians went 28-7 and turned the Central Division race into a runaway.

Most valuable player: Outfielder Albert Belle. He hit 31 homers in the last two months of the season and finished with a club-record 50. Belle tied for the league lead in RBIs (126) with Boston's Mo Vaughn and became the first major leaguer to reach 50 homers and 50 doubles in a season.

Most valuable pitcher: Reliever Jose Mesa. The biggest difference between the Indians of 1994 and 1995 was Mesa. Cleveland didn't have a legitimate closer in '94; in '95, Mesa led the league with 46 saves (in 48 opportunities).

Most improved player: Third baseman Jim Thome. He made strides defensively and also raised his batting average 46 points, to .314, and added 25 home runs and 73 RBIs. He walked 97 times and compiled an on-base percentage of .438.

Most pleasant surprise: Righthander Julian Tavarez. By the time the season was half over, rookie Tavarez—a starter in the minors—had become co-setup man with Eric Plunk and ultimately posted a 10-2 record with a 2.44 ERA.

Biggest disappointment: Outfielder Wayne Kirby. The club's fourth outfielder, Kirby hit .293 with 11 steals in 78 games in '94. In '95, he never got on track, posting a .207 average.

Key injuries: Alomar was lost for two months after undergoing arthroscopic knee surgery late in April, and designated hitter Eddie Murray missed a month because of broken ribs.

Notable: The Indians won the A.L. Central by 30 games over Kansas City, the largest championship margin in major league history. . . . Murray got the 3,000th hit of his career June 30 against Minnesota. His RBI total of 82 gave him 19 consecutive seasons with 75 or more, tying him with Henry Aaron for the major league record. . . . Mesa had more saves than any other major league *team.* . . . Including postseason play, Cleveland won 29 games in its last at-bat. . . . Starters Hershiser, Charles Nagy, Dennis Martinez, Chad Ogea and Ken Hill combined for a 56-21 record.

—SHELDON OCKER

RECORDS

1995 regular-season record: 100-44 (1st in A.L. Central); 54-18 at home; 46-26 on road; 43-20 vs. East; 37-14 vs. Central; 20-10 vs. West; 27-14 vs. lefthanded starters; 73-30 vs. righthanded starters; 89-38 on grass; 11-6 on turf; 30-13 in daytime; 70-31 at night; 28-14 in one-run games; 13-0 in extra-inning games; 2-0-0 in double-headers.

Team record past five years: 375-368 (.505, ranks 6th in league in that span).

TEAM LEADERS

Batting average: Eddie Murray (.323).
At-bats: Carlos Baerga (557).
Runs: Albert Belle (121).
Hits: Carlos Baerga (175).
Total bases: Albert Belle (377).
Doubles: Albert Belle (52).
Triples: Kenny Lofton (13).
Home runs: Albert Belle (50).
Runs batted in: Albert Belle (126).
Stolen bases: Kenny Lofton (54).
Slugging percentage: Albert Belle (.690).
On-base percentage: Jim Thome (.438).
Wins: Charles Nagy, Orel Hershiser (16).
Earned-run average: Dennis Martinez (3.08).
Complete games: Dennis Martinez (3).
Shutouts: Dennis Martinez (2).
Saves: Jose Mesa (46).
Innings pitched: Dennis Martinez (187.0).
Strikeouts: Charles Nagy (139).

GAMES BY POSITION

Catcher: Tony Pena 91, Sandy Alomar 61, Scooter Tucker 17, Jesse Levis 12.
First base: Paul Sorrento 91, Herbert Perry 45, Eddie Murray 18, Alvaro Espinoza 2.
Second base: Carlos Baerga 134, Alvaro Espinoza 22, Billy Ripken 7.
Third base: Jim Thome 134, Alvaro Espinoza 22, David Bell 2, Herbert Perry 1, Billy Ripken 1.
Shortstop: Omar Vizquel 136, Alvaro Espinoza 19.
Outfield: Albert Belle 142, Manny Ramirez 131, Kenny Lofton 114, Wayne Kirby 68, Ruben Amaro 22, Jeromy Burnitz 6, Brian Giles 3.
Designated hitter: Eddie Murray 95, Dave Winfield 39, Paul Sorrento 11, Wayne Kirby 7, Herbert Perry 5, Manny Ramirez 5, Ruben Amaro 3, Jeromy Burnitz 2, Kenny Lofton 2, Carlos Baerga 1, Albert Belle 1, Alvaro Espinoza 1, Brian Giles 1, Jim Thome 1.

TOP DRAFT CHOICES

1. **David Miller,** 1B, Clemson University.
2. **Sean Casey,** 1B, University of Richmond.
3. **Chad Whitaker,** OF, St. Thomas Aquinas H.S., Fort Lauderdale, Fla.
4. **Scott Harrison,** RHP, Swett H.S., Pinole, Calif.
5. **Scott Schultz,** RHP, Louisiana State University.
6. **Jake Messner,** OF, Rio Americano H.S., Sacramento, Calif.
7. **Scott Morgan,** OF, Gonzaga University.
8. **Tim Jorgensen,** SS, University of Wisconsin-Oshkosh.
9. **Mike Edwards,** SS, Mechanicsburg (Pa.) Area H.S.
10. **Jason Bennett,** RHP, Shippensburg (Pa.) University.

DETROIT TIGERS
AMERICAN LEAGUE EAST DIVISION

1996 TIGERS SCHEDULE

☐ Home games shaded.
* — All-Star Game at Veterans Stadium (Philadelphia)
N — Night game (any game starting after 5 p.m.)

MARCH

SUN	MON	TUE	WED	THU	FRI	SAT
31						

APRIL

SUN	MON	TUE	WED	THU	FRI	SAT
	1 MIN	2 N MIN	3 MIN	4 OAK	5 N OAK	6 OAK
7 OAK	8	9 SEA	10 SEA	11 N CAL	12 CAL	13 CAL
14 CAL	15 N TOR	16 TOR	17 N SEA	18 N SEA	19 N CAL	20 N CAL
21 N CAL	22 N CAL	23	24 MIN	25 N MIN	26 N OAK	27 OAK
28 OAK	29	30 N BOS				

MAY

SUN	MON	TUE	WED	THU	FRI	SAT
			1 N BOS	2 N TEX	3 N TEX	4 TEX
5 TEX	6 N NY	7 N NY	8 N NY	9 N NY	10 N TEX	11 N TEX
12 TEX	13	14 N CLE	15 N CLE	16 N CLE	17 N CHI	18 CHI
19 N CHI	20	21 N KC	22 KC	23	24 N CLE	25 CLE
26 CLE	27 N KC	28	29 N KC	30 N CHI	31 N CHI	

JUNE

SUN	MON	TUE	WED	THU	FRI	SAT
						1 N CHI
2 CHI	3	4 N BAL	5 N BAL	6 N BAL	7 N NY	8 NY
9 NY	10 N BAL	11 N BAL	12 BAL	13	14 N MIN	15 N MIN
16 MIN	17 N OAK	18 N OAK	19 OAK	20 N MIN	21 N MIN	22 MIN
23 MIN	24 N OAK	25 OAK	26	27 N BOS	28 N BOS	29 N BOS
30 BOS						

JULY

SUN	MON	TUE	WED	THU	FRI	SAT
	1 N MIL	2 N MIL	3 N MIL	4 N TOR	5 N TOR	6 TOR
7 TOR	8	9 *ALL-STAR GAME	10	11 N BOS	12 N BOS	13 BOS
14 BOS	15 N MIL	16 MIL	17 N TOR	18 N TOR	19 N TOR	20 TOR
21 TOR	22 N CAL	23 N CAL	24	25 N SEA	26 N SEA	27 N SEA
28 SEA	29	30 N CAL	31 N CAL			

AUGUST

SUN	MON	TUE	WED	THU	FRI	SAT
				1 CAL	2 N SEA	3 N SEA
4 SEA	5	6 N TEX	7 N TEX	8 N TEX	9 N NY	10 NY
11 NY	12 N TEX	13 N TEX	14 N TEX	15	16 N CLE	17 CLE
18 CLE	19 N CHI	20 N CHI	21 CHI	22 N KC	23 N KC	24 KC
25 KC	26 N CLE	27 N CLE	28 CLE	29 N KC	30 N KC	31 KC

SEPTEMBER

SUN	MON	TUE	WED	THU	FRI	SAT
1 KC	2 N CHI	3 N CHI	4 N CHI	5	6 N BAL	7 BAL
8 BAL	9 N BAL	10 N NY	11 N NY	12 NY	13 N BAL	14 BAL
15 BAL	16	17 N BOS	18 N BOS	19 BOS	20 N MIL	21 N MIL
22 MIL	23 N TOR	24 N TOR	25 TOR	26	27 N MIL	28 N MIL
29 MIL						

1996 SEASON

CLUB DIRECTORY

Owners
Michael Ilitch
Marian Ilitch

Board of directors
Michael Ilitch, Chairman
Marian Ilitch
Charles P. Jones
Jay Bielfield
Denise Ilitch Lites
Ronald Ilitch
Michael Ilitch Jr.
Lisa Ilitch Murray
Atanas Ilitch
Christopher Ilitch
Carole Ilitch

Owner, chairman
Michael Ilitch

Owner, secretary treasurer
Marian Ilitch

President, chief executive officer
John McHale Jr.

Vice presidents
Atanas Ilitch
Christopher Ilitch

Vice president, business operations
Dave Glazier

Vice president, baseball operations/g.m.
Randy Smith

Assistant general manager
Steve Lubratich

Special assistant to the g.m.
Randy Johnson

Chief financial officer
Gerald Pasternak

League affairs
John Ziegler

Urban development
Emmett Moten

Senior director, assistant general manager
Gary Vitto

Director minor league operations
Dave Miller

Director field operations
John Lipon

Assistant director equipment
Jim Schmakel

Asst. manager equipment and clubhouse
John Nelson

Traveling secretary
Bill Brown

Team physicians
Clarence S. Livingood, M.D.
David J. Collon, M.D.
Terry Lock, M.D.
Louis Saco, M.D. (Florida)

Head trainer
Russ Miller

Strength and conditioning coach
Brad Andress

Scouting
Gary Blaylock
Gwen Keating

Minor league staff
Audrey Zielinski

Senior director public relations
Daniel Ewald

Director of marketing
Michael Dietz

Director of stadium operations
John Pettit

Controller
Scott Fisher

Director of community relations
Jim Price

Director ticket operations
Ken Marchetti

Director ticket sales
Gino D'Ambrosio

Marketing coordinator
James Brylewski

Season/group sales coordinator
Jodi Schroeder

Director of scouting
Jeff Scott

Scouts
Ruben Amaro, Arnie Beyeler, Wayne Blackburn, Gary Blaylock, Nathan Durst, Andy Hancock, Jack Hays, Harvey Koepf, Lou Laslo, Joe Lewis, Dennis Lieberthal, Juan Lopez, Jeff Malinoff, Stan Meek, John Mirabelli, Mark Monahan, Glenn Murdock, Ramon Pena, Dee Phillips, Dave Roberts, Joe Robinson, Don Rowland, Bill Schudlich, Steve Souchock, Clyde Weir, Dick Wiencek, Rob Wilfong

MINOR LEAGUE AFFILIATES

Class	Team	League	Manager
AAA	Toledo	International	Tom Runnells
AA	Jacksonville	Southern	Bill Plummer
A	Lakeland	Florida State	Dave Anderson
A	Fayetteville	South Atlantic	Dwight Lowry
A	Jamestown	New York-Pennsylvania	Bruce Fields
Rookie	Gulf Coast Tigers	Gulf Coast	Kevin Bradshaw

BROADCAST INFORMATION

Radio: WJR-AM (760).
TV: WKBD-TV (Channel 50).
Cable TV: Pro Am Sports Systems.

SPRING TRAINING

Ballpark (city): Marchant Stadium (Lakeland, Fla.).
Ticket information: 813-499-8229.

SPRING TRAINING ROSTER

Manager—Buddy Bell (25).
Coaches—Glenn Ezell (10), Terry Francona (55), Larry Herndon (31), Fred Kendall (18), Jon Matlack (54), Ron Oester (16).

No.	PITCHERS	B/T	Ht./Wt.	Born	1995 clubs
43	Bergman, Sean	R/R	6-4/205	4-11-70	Detroit, Toledo
26	Blomdahl, Ben	R/R	6-2/185	12-30-70	Detroit, Toledo
37	Boever, Joe	R/R	6-1/200	10-4-60	Detroit
33	Christopher, Mike	R/R	6-5/205	11-3-63	Toledo, Detroit
44	Doherty, John	R/R	6-4/210	6-11-67	Detroit
34	Gohr, Greg	R/R	6-3/205	10-29-67	Toledo, Detroit
48	Greene, Rick	R/R	6-5/200	1-2-71	Jacksonville
57	Keagle, Greg	R/R	6-1/185	6-20-71	Memphis, Rancho Cucamonga, Las Vegas
32	Lima, Jose	R/R	6-2/170	9-30-72	Lakeland, Toledo, Detroit
40	Lira, Felipe	R/R	6-0/170	4-26-72	Detroit
15	Maxcy, Brian	R/R	6-1/170	5-4-71	Toledo, Detroit
21	McCurry, Jeff	R/R	6-7/210	1-21-70	Calgary, Pittsburgh
36	Miller, Trever	R/L	6-3/175	5-29-73	Jacksonville
20	Moehler, Brian	R/R	6-3/195	12-3-71	Jacksonville
27	Myers, Mike	L/L	6-3/195	6-26-69	Charlotte, Florida, Toledo, Detroit
49	Nitkowski, C.J.	L/L	6-3/190	3-3-73	Chattanooga, Indianapolis, Cincinnati, Detroit
28	Olivares, Omar	R/R	6-1/193	7-6-67	Colorado Springs, Colorado, Philadelphia, Scranton/Wilkes-Barre
39	Ratliff, Jon	R/R	6-5/200	12-22-71	Orlando
30	Santos, Henry	L/L	6-1/175	1-17-73	Lakeland, Toledo
38	Smith, Cam	R/R	6-3/195	9-20-73	Fayetteville
46	Sodowsky, Clint	L/R	6-3/180	7-13-72	Jacksonville, Toledo, Detroit
14	Thompson, Justin	L/L	6-3/175	3-8-73	Lakeland, Jacksonville

No.	CATCHERS	B/T	Ht./Wt.	Born	1995 clubs
12	Flaherty, John	R/R	6-1/202	10-21-67	Detroit
	Parent, Mark	R/R	6-5/240	9-16-61	Pittsburgh, Chicago N.L.

No.	INFIELDERS	B/T	Ht./Wt.	Born	1995 clubs
17	Clark, Tony	B/R	6-8/250	6-15-72	Toledo, Detroit
45	Fielder, Cecil	R/R	6-3/250	9-21-63	Detroit
24	Fryman, Travis	R/R	6-1/194	3-25-69	Detroit
35	Gomez, Chris	R/R	6-1/183	6-16-71	Detroit
51	Hyers, Tim	L/L	6-1/195	10-3-71	San Diego, Las Vegas
22	Lewis, Mark	R/R	6-1/190	11-30-69	Cincinnati
42	Nevin, Phil	R/R	6-2/180	1-19-71	Tucson, Houston, Toledo, Detroit
8	Penn, Shannon	B/R	5-10/163	9-11-69	Detroit, Toledo
19	Schmidt, Tom	R/R	6-3/200	2-12-73	New Haven
23	Williams, Eddie	R/R	6-0/210	11-1-64	San Diego

No.	OUTFIELDERS	B/T	Ht./Wt.	Born	1995 clubs
29	Bautista, Danny	R/R	5-11/170	5-24-72	Detroit, Toledo
9	Curtis, Chad	R/R	5-10/175	11-6-68	Detroit
52	Franklin, Micah	B/R	6-0/200	4-25-72	Calgary
4	Higginson, Bobby	L/R	5-11/180	8-18-70	Detroit
7	Plantier, Phil	L/R	5-11/195	1-27-69	Houston, Tucson, San Diego
13	Steverson, Todd	R/R	6-2/194	11-15-71	Detroit, Toledo

BALLPARK INFORMATION

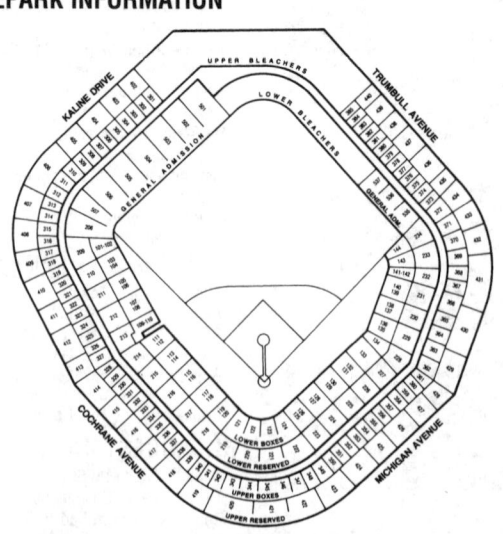

Ballpark (capacity, surface)
Tiger Stadium (52,416, grass)

Address
Tiger Stadium
Detroit, MI 48216

Business phone
313-962-4000

Ticket information
313-963-2050

Ticket prices
$15 (box seats)
$12 (reserved seats)
$8 (grandstand reserved seats)
$2.50 (bleacher seats)
$1 (bleachers—youths 14 and under)

Field dimensions (from home plate)
To left field at foul line, 340 feet
To center field, 440 feet
To right field at foul line, 325 feet

First game played
April 20, 1912
(Tigers 6, Cleveland Naps 5, 11 innings)

DAY BY DAY

Date	Opp.	Res.	Score	(inn.*)	Hits	Opp. hits	Winning pitcher	Losing pitcher	Save	Record	Pos.	GB
4-26	At Cal.	W	5-4		9	8	Moore	Finley	Groom	1-0	T1st	...
4-27	At Sea.	L	0-3		3	7	Johnson	Bergman	Ayala	1-1	4th	1
4-28	At Sea.	L	2-9		11	14	Bosio	Doherty		1-2	4th	1½
4-29	At Sea.	L	1-11		7	14	Fleming	Wells	Converse	1-3	T4th	2½
4-30	At Sea.	W	10-1		12	6	Moore	Wells		2-3	T4th	1½
5-2	Cle.	L	1-11		8	15	Martinez	Bergman		2-4	T4th	2
5-3	Cle.	L	7-14		10	18	Clark	Doherty		2-5	T4th	3
5-4	Cle.	W	4-3		6	7	Wells	Hershiser	Henneman	3-5	T4th	3
5-5	Bos.	L	7-10		6	17	Lilliquist	Lira	Ryan	3-6	5th	4
5-6	Bos.	L	3-5		7	6	Sele	Bergman	Belinda	3-7	5th	4
5-7	Bos.	L	1-12		5	17	Eshelman	Groom		3-8	5th	4
5-9	At Mil.	W	4-2	(10)	12	7	Doherty	Lloyd		4-8	5th	4
5-10	At Mil.	L	2-13		9	15	Scanlan	Moore		4-9	5th	5
5-11	At Mil.	W	8-0		12	8	Bergman	Wegman		5-9	5th	4½
5-12	At Tex.	W	6-1		8	5	Groom	Gross		6-9	4th	4
5-13	At Tex.	L	3-5		7	9	Pavlik	Wells	Russell	6-10	4th	4½
5-14	At Tex.	W	8-3		14	5	Moore	Helling		7-10	4th	4½
5-16	At Bal.	W	9-8		11	16	Boever	Jones	Henneman	8-10	4th	4½
5-17	At Bal.	L	4-7		8	11	K. Brown	Lira	Benitez	8-11	4th	5½
5-18	At Bal.	L	2-3		4	6	Mussina	Wells	Jones	8-12	5th	6½
5-19	Tor.	L	2-4		4	10	Cone	Moore		8-13	5th	6½
5-20	Tor.	W	10-6		9	11	Doherty	Hentgen		9-13	5th	5½
5-21	Tor.	W	2-1		4	5	Boever	Cox	Henneman	10-13	T3rd	4½
5-22	Sea.	W	10-8		9	12	Boever	Carmona	Henneman	11-13	3rd	4
5-23	Min.	W	6-4	(7)	8	8	Wells	Guardado		12-13	3rd	4
5-24	Min.	W	14-3		18	5	Moore	Radke		13-13	3rd	3
5-25	Min.	L	3-4		7	11	Guthrie	Boever	Aguilera	13-14	3rd	3
5-26	Chi.	W	8-7		11	12	Maxcy	Hernandez		14-14	2nd	3
5-27	Chi.	L	0-1		3	6	Bere	Lira	Hernandez	14-15	2nd	4
5-28	Chi.	L	12-14		17	14	Radinsky	Groom	Hernandez	14-16	3rd	4
5-29	At Tor.	L	4-5		9	12	Cone	Moore	Timlin	14-17	3rd	5
5-30	At Tor.	W	8-6		8	10	Lira	Cox	Henneman	15-17	2nd	5
5-31	At Tor.	L	3-5		7	13	Hentgen	Doherty		15-18	2nd	6
6-2	At Chi.	L	4-5	(15)	16	14	Hernandez	Henneman		15-19	T3rd	7
6-3	At Chi.	L	6-10		9	17	McCaskill	Boever		15-20	4th	8
6-4	At Chi.	W	8-5		10	7	Maxcy	Hernandez	Henneman	16-20	T2nd	8
6-5	At Cle.	L	0-8		6	10	Hershiser	Bergman		16-21	T2nd	9
6-6	At Cle.	L	3-4		4	9	Tavarez	Boever	Mesa	16-22	3rd	9
6-7	At Cle.	L	2-3	(10)	6	8	Plunk	Maxcy		16-23	5th	10
6-8	At Min.	L	2-9		7	14	Tapani	Moore		16-24	5th	10
6-9	At Min.	W	6-5		8	9	Doherty	Guthrie	Henneman	17-24	4th	10
6-10	At Min.	W	7-5		12	16	Bergman	Trombley	Henneman	18-24	3rd	9
6-11	At Min.	W	8-2		12	7	Lira	Radke	Boever	19-24	3rd	8
6-12	N.Y.	W	6-1		14	4	Wells	Pettitte		20-24	T2nd	7
6-13	N.Y.	L	4-10		6	11	McDowell	Moore		20-25	T2nd	8
6-14	N.Y.	L	3-12		4	15	Perez	Ahearne		20-26	T2nd	8
6-15	N.Y.	W	9-2		10	7	Bergman	Boehringer		21-26	2nd	7½
6-16	Bal.	W	5-3		9	9	Lira	McDonald	Henneman	22-26	2nd	6½
6-17	Bal.	W	5-3		11	4	Wells	K. Brown	Boever	23-26	2nd	5½
6-18	Bal.	W	10-8		14	12	Maxcy	Mussina	Henneman	24-26	2nd	5½
6-19	Tex.	L	4-6		8	10	Gross	Ahearne	Russell	24-27	2nd	5½
6-20	Tex.	L	6-8		9	8	Oliver	Bergman	Russell	24-28	2nd	5½
6-21	Tex.	W	1-0		9	6	Lira	Tewksbury	Henneman	25-28	2nd	5½
6-23	Mil.	W	5-2		8	11	Wells	Bones	Henneman	26-28	2nd	5
6-24	Mil.	W	7-2		9	8	Moore	Givens	Boever	27-28	2nd	5
6-25	Mil.	W	6-3		7	9	Maxcy	Rightnowar	Henneman	28-28	2nd	4
6-26	At N.Y.	L	3-7		8	13	Pettitte	Lira		28-29	2nd	5
6-27	At N.Y.	L	1-7		7	10	MacDonald	Bohanon	Ausanio	28-30	2nd	6
6-28	At N.Y.	W	8-4		14	9	Wells	McDowell		29-30	2nd	5
6-29	At Bos.	L	1-7		8	10	Wakefield	Moore		29-31	2nd	6
6-30	At Bos.	W	7-6		10	12	Boever	Ryan	Henneman	30-31	2nd	5
7-1	At Bos.	W	11-2		15	12	Lira	Hanson	Doherty	31-31	2nd	4
7-2	At Bos.	L	11-12		13	15	Belinda	Boever		31-32	2nd	5
7-3	Sea.	W	4-2		6	7	Wells	Bosio	Henneman	32-32	2nd	5
7-4	Sea.	W	9-8		11	14	Christopher	Ayala		33-32	2nd	5
7-5	Sea.	W	8-6		10	14	Christopher	Carmona	Henneman	34-32	2nd	4
7-6	K.C.	W	12-5		18	12	Doherty	Haney	Wickander	35-32	2nd	3
7-7	K.C.	W	3-1		3	7	Wells	Appier		36-32	2nd	3
7-8	K.C.	L	1-4		3	10	Gubicza	Moore	Montgomery	36-33	2nd	3
7-9	K.C.	W	4-2		6	5	Lira	Gordon	Henneman	37-33	2nd	3
7-13	Cal.	L	5-8	(10)	10	10	Percival	Boever	Smith	37-34	2nd	3

Date	Opp.	Res.	Score	(inn.*)	Hits	Opp. hits	Winning pitcher	Losing pitcher	Save	Record	Pos.	GB
7-14	Cal.	L	3-7		9	9	Patterson	Lira	Percival	37-35	2nd	4
7-16†	Cal.	L	4-6		7	10	Finley	Boever	Smith	37-36		
7-16‡	Cal.	L	6-13		9	19	James	Moore		37-37	2nd	4
7-17	At Sea.	L	6-10	(10)	8	14	Ayala	Groom		37-38	T2nd	4
7-18	At Sea.	L	6-10		9	15	Belcher	Lima		37-39	3rd	5
7-19	At Oak.	L	1-2		5	9	Prieto	Doherty	Honeycutt	37-40	3rd	6
7-20	At Oak.	L	3-6		6	12	Darling	Moore	Eckersley	37-41	3rd	7
7-21	At Cal.	W	4-3		10	8	Wells	Habyan	Henneman	38-41	3rd	7
7-22	At Cal.	L	3-13		6	17	B. Anderson	Bergman		38-42	4th	7
7-23	At Cal.	L	2-13		9	14	Langston	Lima		38-43	4th	7
7-25	Oak.	W	6-3		9	11	Lira	Darling		39-43	4th	6½
7-26	Oak.	W	10-4		11	8	Wells	Reyes		40-43	4th	6½
7-27	Oak.	L	3-11		13	16	Stottlemyre	Moore		40-44	4th	6½
7-28	At K.C.	L	3-4		7	9	Montgomery	Doherty		40-45	4th	7½
7-29	At K.C.	L	4-5	(16)	6	22	Pichardo	Doherty		40-46	4th	8½
7-30	At K.C.	L	2-3		10	9	Anderson	Lira	Montgomery	40-47	4th	8½
8-1	Bos.	L	3-13		9	15	Smith	Moore		40-48	4th	9½
8-2	Bos.	W	5-0		5	4	Bergman	Clemens		41-48	4th	8½
8-3	Bos.	L	2-10		7	10	Wakefield	Nitkowski		41-49	4th	9½
8-4	N.Y.	L	1-4		3	11	Kamieniecki	Lima	Wetteland	41-50	4th	10½
8-5	N.Y.	L	1-7		5	11	Hitchcock	Lira		41-51	4th	11½
8-6	N.Y.	W	6-5	(12)	13	8	Boever	Eiland		42-51	4th	11½
8-8	At Tex.	L	1-4		8	12	Gross	Bergman	Whiteside	42-52	4th	13
8-9	At Tex.	L	5-13		9	17	Rogers	Doherty		42-53	4th	14
8-10	At Tex.	L	2-7		5	8	Darwin	Lira		42-54	4th	15
8-11	At Mil.	L	4-5		9	8	Givens	Moore	Fetters	42-55	T4th	16
8-12	At Mil.	W	8-2		11	6	Lima	McAndrew	Doherty	43-55	4th	16
8-13	At Mil.	L	3-8		11	11	Bones	Bergman		43-56	4th	17
8-14	At Mil.	L	2-3		10	7	Karl	Maxcy	Fetters	43-57	4th	18
8-15	Tor.	W	11-5		14	14	Bohanon	Hentgen		44-57	4th	17
8-16	Tor.	L	4-7		10	10	Hurtado	Maxcy	Castillo	44-58	4th	18
8-17	Tor.	L	0-3		5	6	Leiter	Lima	Castillo	44-59	5th	19
8-18	Min.	W	3-1		7	9	Bergman	Parra	Doherty	45-59	4th	18
8-19	Min.	L	5-9		7	16	Radke	Nitkowski	Mahomes	45-60	5th	19
8-20	Min.	L	7-8	(10)	11	14	Mahomes	Doherty		45-61	5th	20
8-21	Chi.	L	3-7		8	10	Fernandez	Moore	McCaskill	45-62	5th	21
8-22	Chi.	L	7-15		13	22	DeLeon	Lima		45-63	5th	22
8-23	Chi.	W	7-5		8	8	Lira	Hernandez		46-63	5th	22
8-25	At Cle.	L	5-6	(11)	9	10	Tavarez	Lira		46-64	5th	22½
8-26	At Cle.	L	2-6		11	8	Nagy	Moore		46-65	5th	22½
8-27	At Cle.	L	2-9		5	11	Hershiser	Lima		46-66	5th	23½
8-29	At Chi.	W	7-5		14	11	Bergman	Keyser	Lira	47-66	5th	22½
8-30	At Chi.	L	7-10		10	16	Karchner	Maxcy	Hernandez	47-67	5th	23½
8-31	At Chi.	L	0-9		5	10	Fernandez	Moore		47-68	5th	23½
9-1	Cle.	L	4-14		9	21	Nagy	Lima		47-69	5th	24½
9-2	Cle.	W	3-2		7	5	Lira	Hershiser	Doherty	48-69	5th	24½
9-3	Cle.	L	8-9	(10)	11	14	Mesa	Boever		48-70	5th	25½
9-4	Cle.	W	3-2		4	3	Sodowsky	Clark	Henry	49-70	5th	25
9-5	At Min.	W	6-4		10	6	Nitkowski	O. Munoz	Christopher	50-70	4th	25
9-6	At Min.	L	1-9		4	8	Rodriguez	Maxcy		50-71	5th	26
9-8	At Tor.	L	5-9		7	7	Ware	Lira		50-72	5th	26
9-9	At Tor.	W	5-2		8	7	Bergman	Guzman	Henry	51-72	5th	25
9-10	At Tor.	W	5-2	(11)	7	9	Doherty	Timlin	Henry	52-72	4th	24
9-11	At Tor.	W	3-2	(10)	8	10	Christopher	Rogers	Bohanon	53-72	4th	23
9-12	Mil.	W	5-1		8	4	Lima	Givens	Doherty	54-72	4th	22
9-13	Mil.	W	5-3		7	9	Henry	Fetters		55-72	4th	22
9-14	Mil.	L	3-6		6	8	Sparks	Bergman	Fetters	55-73	4th	22
9-15	Tex.	W	3-2		4	6	Sodowsky	Gross	Henry	56-73	4th	22
9-16	Tex.	L	3-7		7	17	Rogers	Nitkowski		56-74	4th	22
9-17	Tex.	L	0-5		3	7	Pavlik	Lima		56-75	4th	23
9-18	Bal.	L	2-6		5	9	Haynes	Lira		56-76	4th	23
9-19	Bal.	W	7-4		9	11	Myers	Krivda	Henry	57-76	4th	23
9-20	Bal.	L	3-6		8	10	Erickson	Sodowsky		57-77	4th	24
9-21	Bal.	L	1-13		3	16	Mussina	Doherty		57-78	4th	24½
9-23†	At N.Y.	L	2-5		4	6	Cone	Lima	Wetteland	57-79		
9-23‡	At N.Y.	L	1-3		5	8	Kamieniecki	Lira	Wetteland	57-80		25½
9-24	At N.Y.	W	8-3		12	9	Christopher	Pettitte		58-80	4th	24½
9-25	At Bos.	W	7-4		10	8	Gohr	Murray	Doherty	59-80	4th	23½
9-26	At Bos.	L	1-5		6	11	Smith	Nitkowski		59-81	4th	24½
9-27	At Bos.	W	7-5		14	16	Lima	Wakefield	Blomdahl	60-81	4th	23½
9-29	At Bal.	L	0-6		5	10	K. Brown	Lira		60-82	4th	25
9-30	At Bal.	L	0-12		2	14	McDonald	Bergman		60-83	4th	26
10-1	At Bal.	L	0-4		2	10	Mussina	Sodowsky		60-84	4th	26

Monthly records: April (2-3), May (13-15), June (15-13), July (10-16), August (7-21), September (13-15), October (0-1).
*Innings, if other than nine. †First game of doubleheader. ‡Second game of doubleheader.

HIGHLIGHTS

High point: On the day before the All-Star break, the Tigers won for the sixth time in seven games by defeating Kansas City, 4-2, with Kirk Gibson bowling over catcher Pat Borders on a key eighth-inning play. The Detroit crowd roared as Gibson pumped his fists on the way to the dugout, and the surprising Tigers ended the day at 37-33, just three games behind the A.L. East-leading Red Sox.

Low points: In the early going, the Tigers were 16-24—10 games behind the Red Sox and in last place—after a loss in Minnesota on June 8; in the season finale, they skidded to a season-low 24 games below .500.

Turning point: The Tigers were a different team after the All-Star Game, starting with a four-game sweep at the hands of the Angels in Detroit. That snowballed into an eight-game slide, and the team went 23-51 after the break.

Most valuable player: Outfielder Chad Curtis. Curtis, acquired from California for Tony Phillips, played every game and blended power, speed and defense. He scored 96 runs and stole 27 bases, and his 21 homers and 67 RBIs were career highs.

Most valuable pitcher: Lefthander David Wells. He was 10-3 in 18 games with a 3.04 ERA before being traded to Cincinnati. Mike Christopher was the most dependable reliever, going 4-0 in 36 games with a 3.82 ERA.

Most improved player: Catcher John Flaherty. He shed the label of career backup with a surprising 11 homers and good defense.

Most pleasant surprise: Christopher. A journeyman reliever and replacement player in the spring, Christopher was the team's only consistent reliever after closer Mike Henneman was traded in August.

Biggest disappointment: Reliever Joe Boever. A bullpen savior the previous year, Boever was pounded time and again (128 hits in 98⅔ innings and a 6.39 ERA).

Key injuries: Righthanders Greg Gohr and Jose Lima, two of the club's best prospects, spent much of the season rebuilding arm strength after offseason surgery. Both showed improvement in the final month.

Notable: Alan Trammell and Lou Whitaker finished the season by appearing in their 1,918th game together; the American League record for teammates had been set by the Royals' George Brett and Frank White (1,914). . . . . Sparky Anderson (2,194) passed Bucky Harris and moved into third place on the all-time managerial victory list before he and the team parted company at season's end. . . . On August 11, one day after Henneman was dealt to Houston and 11 days after Wells was traded to the Reds in rebuilding moves, Gibson retired.

—REID CREAGER

RECORDS

1995 regular-season record: 60-84 (4th in A.L. East); 35-37 at home; 25-47 on road; 22-30 vs. East; 25-32 vs. Central; 13-22 vs. West; 15-21 vs. lefthanded starters; 45-63 vs. righthanded starters; 51-74 on grass; 9-10 on turf; 21-30 in daytime; 39-54 at night; 15-17 in one-run games; 4-9 in extra-inning games; 0-2-0 in doubleheaders.
Team record past five years: 357-388 (.479, ranks 13th in league in that span).

TEAM LEADERS

Batting average: Travis Fryman (.275).
At-bats: Chad Curtis (586).
Runs: Chad Curtis (96).
Hits: Chad Curtis (157).
Total bases: Chad Curtis (255).
Doubles: Chad Curtis (29).
Triples: Travis Fryman, Bob Higginson (5).
Home runs: Cecil Fielder (31).
Runs batted in: Cecil Fielder (82).
Stolen bases: Chad Curtis (27).
Slugging percentage: Cecil Fielder (.472).
On-base percentage: Chad Curtis (.349).
Wins: David Wells (10).
Earned-run average: Felipe Lira (4.31).
Complete games: David Wells (3).
Shutouts: Sean Bergman (1).
Saves: Mike Henneman (18).
Innings pitched: Felipe Lira (146.1).
Strikeouts: Felipe Lira (89).

GAMES BY POSITION

Catcher: John Flaherty 112, Ron Tingley 53.
First base: Cecil Fielder 77, Juan Samuel 37, Tony Clark 27, Franklin Stubbs 20, Derrick White 16, Scott Fletcher 1, Ron Tingley 1.
Second base: Scott Fletcher 63, Lou Whitaker 63, Chris Gomez 31, Steve Rodriguez 12, Juan Samuel 6, Shannon Penn 3.
Third base: Travis Fryman 144.
Shortstop: Chris Gomez 97, Alan Trammell 60, Scott Fletcher 3, Steve Rodriguez 1.
Outfield: Chad Curtis 144, Bob Higginson 123, Danny Bautista 86, Milt Cuyler 36, Phil Nevin 27, Todd Steverson 27, Franklin Stubbs 20, Juan Samuel 9, Derrick White 9, Rudy Pemberton 8, Joe Hall 5, Kirk Gibson 1.
Designated hitter: Kirk Gibson 63, Cecil Fielder 58, Juan Samuel 16, Lou Whitaker 8, Derrick White 8, Alan Trammell 6, Rudy Pemberton 3, Franklin Stubbs 3, Milt Cuyler 2, Bob Higginson 2, Phil Nevin 2, Chris Gomez 1, Joe Hall 1, Todd Steverson 1.

TOP DRAFT CHOICES

1. **Mike Drumright,** RHP, Wichita State University.
2. **Brian Powell,** RHP, University of Georgia.
3. **Chuck Crowder,** LHP, Crestwood H.S., Mantua, Ohio.
4. **Clay Bruner,** RHP, Weatherford (Okla.) H.S.
5. **Rosario Ortiz,** RHP, Arizona Western J.C.
6. **Jeremiah Lignitz,** C, Davison (Mich.) H.S.
7. **Chris Manser,** RHP-OF, Hillsborough H.S., Tampa, Fla.
8. **Scott Weaver,** OF, University of Michigan.
9. **Ron Marietta,** LHP, Bishop Ford H.S., Brooklyn.
10. **John Foran,** RHP, University of Central Florida.

KANSAS CITY ROYALS
AMERICAN LEAGUE CENTRAL DIVISION

1996 ROYALS SCHEDULE

Home games shaded.
* — All-Star Game at Veterans Stadium (Philadelphia)
N — Night game (any game starting after 5 p.m.)

MARCH

SUN	MON	TUE	WED	THU	FRI	SAT
31						

APRIL

SUN	MON	TUE	WED	THU	FRI	SAT
	1 BAL	2	3 N BAL	4 BAL	5 BOS	6 BOS
7 BOS	8	9 NY	10	11 NY	12 N MIL	13 MIL
14 MIL	15 N CHI	16 N CHI	17 N CHI	18 N MIL	19 N MIL	20 MIL
21 MIL	22 N NY	23 N NY	24 N BAL	25 N BAL	26 N BOS	27 BOS
28 BOS	29 N MIN	30 N MIN				

MAY

SUN	MON	TUE	WED	THU	FRI	SAT
		1 N MIN	2	3 N OAK	4 N OAK	
5 OAK	6 N CAL	7 N CAL	8 N CAL	9 N CAL	10 N SEA	11 N SEA
12 SEA	13 N TEX	14 N TEX	15 N TEX	16	17 N TOR	18 N TOR
19 TOR	20 N TOR	21 N DET	22 DET	23 N TEX	24 N TEX	25 N TEX
26 TEX	27 N DET	28	29 N DET	30	31 N TOR	

JUNE

SUN	MON	TUE	WED	THU	FRI	SAT
						1 TOR
2 TOR	3 N OAK	4 OAK	5 N OAK	6	7 N SEA	8 N SEA
9 SEA	10 N CAL	11 N CAL	12 CAL	13 N BAL	14 N BAL	15 BAL
16 N BAL	17 N MIL	18 N MIL	19 MIL	20 N BAL	21 N BAL	22 BAL
23 BAL	24	25 N MIL	26 N MIL	27 N MIL	28 N MIN	29 N MIN
30 MIN						

JULY

SUN	MON	TUE	WED	THU	FRI	SAT
	1 N CLE	2 N CLE	3 N CLE	4 N MIN	5 N MIN	6 N MIN
7 N MIN	8 *	9 ALL-STAR GAME	10	11 N CHI	12 N CHI	13 N CHI
14 CHI	15 N CLE	16 N CLE	17 N CLE	18 N CHI	19 N CHI	20 N CHI
21 CHI	22 N BOS	23 N BOS	24 N BOS	25 N NY	26 N NY	27 NY
28 NY	29	30 N BOS	31 N BOS			

AUGUST

SUN	MON	TUE	WED	THU	FRI	SAT
				1 N BOS	2 N NY	3 N NY
4 NY	5 N NY	6 N OAK	7 N OAK	8 OAK	9 N CAL	10 N CAL
11 CAL	12 N SEA	13 N SEA	14 N SEA	15	16 N TEX	17 N TEX
18 N TEX	19 N TOR	20 N TOR	21 N TOR	22 N DET	23 N DET	24 N DET
25 DET	26	27 N TEX	28 N TEX	29 N DET	30 N DET	31 DET

SEPTEMBER

SUN	MON	TUE	WED	THU	FRI	SAT
1 DET	2 TOR	3 N TOR	4 N TOR	5	6 N OAK	7 N OAK
8 OAK	9	10 N SEA	11 N SEA	12 N CAL	13 N CAL	14 CAL
15 CAL	16 N MIN	17 N MIN	18 N MIN	19 N CLE	20 N CLE	21 CLE
22 CLE	23	24 N CHI	25 N CHI	26	27 N CLE	28 N CLE
29 CLE						

1996 SEASON
CLUB DIRECTORY

Board of directors
David D. Glass
Mike Herman
Paul H. Henson
Larry Kauffman
Janice C. Kreamer
Louis Smith
Joseph T. McGuff

Chairman of the board & CEO
David D. Glass

President
Mike Herman

Exec. v.p. and general manager
Spencer (Herk) Robinson

V.p., finance/corporate secretary
Dale Rohr

Vice president, baseball operations
George Brett

V.p., govt. and consumer affairs
Merle Wood

V.p., administration and development
Dennis Cryder

V.p., marketing and communications
Mike Levy

Dir., communications and com. relations
Dennis Cryder

Director, administration
John Johnson

Director, human resources
Lauris P. Hawthorne

Director of scouting
Art Stewart

Assistant general manager
Jay Hinrichs

Director of minor league operations
Bob Hegman

Director of marketing and sales
Mike Behymer

Director of stadium operations
Tom Folk

Director of season ticket sales
Joe Grigoli

Dir. of information service/operations
Loretta Kratzberg

Controller
Patrick Fleischmann

Director of team travel
Dave Witty

Director, player personnel
Larry Doughty

Assistant director, player personnel
Dan Glass

Special assistant to the g.m.
Brian Murphy

Director of information services
Joe Pettelkow

Director of ticket operations
John Walker

Manager of media relations
Steve Fink

Manager of community relations
Barry Holmes

Stadium engineer
Duane Robinson

Equipment manager
Mike Burkhalter

Team physician
Dr. Steve Joyce

Trainer
Nick Swartz

Assistant trainer
Steve Morrow

Scouts
Frank Baez, Allard Baird, Bob Bishop, Carl Blando, Bob Carter, Balos Davis, Steve Flores, Guy Hansen, Dave Herrera, Ray Jackson, Gary Johnson, Tony Levato, Tom McDevitt, Jeff McKay, Chuck McMichael, Brian Murphy, Cliff Pastornicky, Herb Raybourn, Wil Rutenschroer, Luis Silverio, Jerry Stephens, Jerry Terrell, Terry Wetzel, Dick Wiencek, Stan Williams, Dennis Woody

MINOR LEAGUE AFFILIATES

Class	Team	League	Manager
AAA	Omaha	American Assoc.	Mike Jirschle
AA	Wichita	Texas	Ron Johnson
A	Lansing	Midwest	Brian Poldberg
A	Wilmington	Carolina	John Mizerock
A	Spokane	Northwest	Bob Herold
Rookie	Gulf Coast Royals	Gulf Coast	Al Pedrique

BROADCAST INFORMATION
Radio: WIBW-AM (580).
TV: KSMO-TV (Channel 62).
Cable TV: None.

SPRING TRAINING
Ballpark (city): Baseball City Stadium (Baseball City, Fla.).
Ticket information: 941-424-2500.

SPRING TRAINING ROSTER

Manager—Bob Boone (8).
Coaches—Tim Foli (56), Guy Hansen (55), Bruce Kison (54), Greg Luzinski (19), Mitchell Page (39), Jamie Quirk (9).

No.	PITCHERS	B/T	Ht./Wt.	Born	1995 clubs
17	Appier, Kevin	R/R	6-2/195	12-6-67	Kansas City
61	Bevil, Brian	R/R	6-3/190	9-5-71	Wichita, Omaha
62	Bovee, Mike	R/R	5-10/200	8-21-73	Wichita
50	Bunch, Melvin	R/R	6-1/170	11-4-71	Kansas City, Omaha
38	Converse, Jim	R/R	5-9/185	8-17-71	Seattle, Tacoma, Omaha, Kansas City
53	Evans, Bart	R/R	6-1/190	12-30-70	Wichita, Wilmington
27	Granger, Jeff	R/L	6-4/200	12-16-71	Wichita
23	Gubicza, Mark	R/R	6-5/230	8-14-62	Kansas City
33	Haney, Chris	L/L	6-3/195	11-16-68	Kansas City
37	Huisman, Rick	R/R	6-3/210	5-17-69	Tucson, Omaha, Kansas City
45	Jacome, Jason	L/L	6-0/180	11-24-70	New York N.L., Norfolk, Kansas City
57	Magnante, Mike	L/L	6-1/195	6-17-65	Omaha, Kansas City
28	Meacham, Rusty	R/R	6-3/180	1-27-68	Kansas City
21	Montgomery, Jeff	R/R	5-11/180	1-7-62	Kansas City
35	Pichardo, Hipolito	R/R	6-1/185	8-22-69	Kansas City
34	Pittsley, James	R/R	6-7/215	4-3-74	Omaha, Kansas City
63	Ralston, Kris	R/R	6-2/200	8-8-71	Wichita
52	Torres, Dilson	R/R	6-3/200	5-31-70	Kansas City, Omaha

No.	CATCHERS	B/T	Ht./Wt.	Born	1995 clubs
26	Fasano, Sal	R/R	6-2/220	8-10-71	Wilmington, Wichita
15	Macfarlane, Mike	R/R	6-1/210	4-12-64	Boston
	Mercedes, Henry	R/R	6-1/210	7-23-69	Omaha, Kansas City
29	Sweeney, Mike	R/R	6-1/195	7-22-73	Wilmington, Kansas City

No.	INFIELDERS	B/T	Ht./Wt.	Born	1995 clubs
3	Hamelin, Bob	L/L	6-0/235	11-29-67	Kansas City, Omaha
6	Howard, David	B/R	6-0/175	2-26-67	Kansas City
4	Lockhart, Keith	L/R	5-10/170	11-10-64	Omaha, Kansas City
67	Lopez, Mendy	R/R	6-2/165	10-15-74	Wilmington
66	Nunez, Sergio	R/R	5-11/155	1-3-75	Wilmington
30	Offerman, Jose	B/R	6-0/190	11-8-68	Los Angeles
16	Randa, Joe	R/R	5-11/190	12-18-69	Omaha, Kansas City
	Roberts, Bip	B/R	5-7/165	10-27-63	San Diego, Rancho Cucamonga, Las Vegas
14	Stynes, Chris	R/R	5-9/175	1-19-73	Omaha, Kansas City
44	Vitiello, Joe	R/R	6-3/230	4-11-70	Kansas City, Omaha

No.	OUTFIELDERS	B/T	Ht./Wt.	Born	1995 clubs
43	Burton, Darren	B/R	6-1/185	9-16-72	Omaha, Wichita, Orlando
18	Damon, Johnny	L/L	6-0/175	11-5-73	Wichita, Kansas City
42	Goodwin, Tom	L/R	6-1/175	7-27-68	Kansas City
58	Myers, Rod	L/L	6-0/190	1-14-73	Wichita
25	Norman, Les	R/R	6-1/185	2-25-69	Omaha, Kansas City
22	Nunnally, Jon	L/R	5-10/190	11-9-71	Kansas City
31	Tucker, Michael	L/R	6-2/185	6-25-71	Kansas City, Omaha

BALLPARK INFORMATION

Ballpark (capacity, surface)
Kauffman Stadium (40,625, grass)

Address
P.O. Box 419969
Kansas City, MO 64141-6969

Business phone
816-921-2200

Ticket information
816-921-8000

Ticket prices
$14 (club box)
$13 (field box)
$11 (plaza reserved)
$10 (view upper box)
$9 (view upper reserved)
$4.50 (Royal nights)
$5 (general admission)

Field dimensions (from home plate)
To left field at foul line, 330 feet
To center field, 400 feet
To right field at foul line, 330 feet

First game played
April 10, 1973 (Royals 12, Rangers 1)

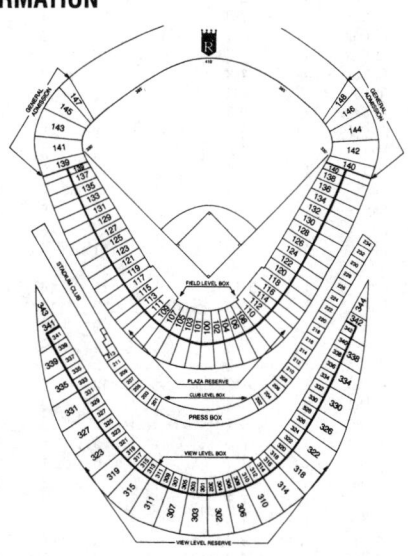

DAY BY DAY

Date	Opp.	Res.	Score	(inn.*)	Hits	Opp. hits	Winning pitcher	Losing pitcher	Save	Record	Pos.	GB
4-26	Bal.	W	5-1		8	2	Appier	Moyer		1-0	T1st	...
4-28	N.Y.	L	1-4		8	10	McDowell	Gubicza	Wetteland	1-1	T3rd	1½
4-29	N.Y.	L	3-10		8	11	Perez	Gordon		1-2	T3rd	1½
4-30	N.Y.	W	9-3		12	4	Appier	Kamieniecki		2-2	T2nd	1½
5-2	At Min.	W	4-3		7	8	Gubicza	Tapani	Montgomery	3-2	T2nd	1½
5-3	At Min.	L	9-10		13	15	Stevens	Meacham	Aguilera	3-3	3rd	2½
5-4	At Min.	W	6-0		8	7	Appier	Hawkins		4-3	T2nd	1½
5-5	At Chi.	W	3-1	(12)	13	6	Meacham	McCaskill	Montgomery	5-3	T2nd	½
56	At Chi.	L	4-7		5	12	Alvarez	Gubicza	Hernandez	5-4	T2nd	1½
5-7	At Chi.	W	7-5		12	13	Gordon	Baldwin	Montgomery	6-4	T2nd	1½
5-8	At Cle.	L	2-6		10	11	Clark	Appier	Grimsley	6-5	3rd	2
5-9	At Cle.	L	0-10		4	8	Hershiser	Linton		6-6	3rd	2
5-10	At Cle.	L	2-3	(10)	4	11	Plunk	Meacham		6-7	3rd	3
5-12	Cal.	L	2-3		4	9	Butcher	Brewer	Smith	6-8	3rd	4
5-13	Cal.	W	4-2		7	3	Appier	Patterson		7-8	3rd	3
5-14	Cal.	L	1-8		5	9	Langston	Browning		7-9	3rd	4
5-16	Sea.	W	4-2	(5)	7	4	Haney	Fleming		8-9	3rd	4
5-17	Sea.	L	0-4		4	9	Wells	Gubicza		8-10	3rd	4½
5-18	Sea.	W	3-2	(14)	16	7	Brewer	Converse		9-10	3rd	3½
5-19	Oak.	L	3-10		10	15	Darling	Browning		9-11	3rd	4½
5-20	Oak.	L	1-11		3	10	Stottlemyre	Haney		9-12	3rd	5½
5-21	Oak.	L	2-7		7	13	Ontiveros	Gubicza		9-13	3rd	6½
5-22	At Tor.	W	7-0		12	2	Appier	Darwin		10-13	3rd	5½
5-23	At Tor.	L	6-10		6	16	Timlin	Pichardo	Hall	10-14	3rd	6½
5-24	At Tor.	W	8-5		12	7	Gordon	Cone		11-14	3rd	5½
5-25	At Mil.	W	3-1		6	4	Haney	Roberson	Montgomery	12-14	3rd	5
5-26	At Mil.	W	8-3		11	12	Appier	Scanlan		13-14	2nd	5
5-28	At Mil.	W	7-4		13	10	Gubicza	Bones	Montgomery	14-14	2nd	4½
5-29	Tex.	W	12-0		18	6	Gordon	Gross		15-14	2nd	4½
5-30	Tex.	W	7-6		12	8	Pichardo	Vosberg		16-14	2nd	4½
5-31	Tex.	L	2-4		6	7	Tewksbury	Appier		16-15	2nd	5½
6-2	Mil.	W	3-2		10	6	Gubicza	Bones	Montgomery	17-15	2nd	5
6-3	Mil.	W	2-1		5	5	Gordon	Lloyd		18-15	2nd	5
6-4	Mil.	W	4-3		7	7	Pichardo	Lloyd	Montgomery	19-15	2nd	5
6-5	At Tex.	W	4-1		9	4	Appier	Tewksbury	Montgomery	20-15	T1st	5
6-6	At Tex.	L	1-2		7	9	Rogers	Gubicza		20-16	2nd	6
6-7	At Tex.	L	4-10		10	13	Burrows	Gordon		20-17	2nd	7
6-8	At Tex.	L	9-10	(10)	15	14	Vosberg	Brewer		20-18	2nd	8
6-10	Tor.	W	8-2		17	4	Appier	Darwin		21-18	2nd	7½
6-11	Tor.	W	3-2	(10)	8	9	Pichardo	Hall		22-18	2nd	7½
6-12	At Sea.	W	10-9		12	13	Meacham	Villone	Montgomery	23-18	2nd	7½
6-13	At Sea.	W	3-1		9	6	Haney	Torres	Montgomery	24-18	2nd	7½
6-14	At Sea.	W	2-1		7	9	Appier	Belcher	Montgomery	25-18	2nd	7½
6-15	At Oak.	W	7-0		11	1	Gubicza	Darling		26-18	2nd	7
6-16	At Oak.	W	3-1	(13)	6	8	Pichardo	Corsi	Montgomery	27-18	2nd	6
6-17	At Oak.	L	5-7		6	6	Harkey	Rasmussen	Eckersley	27-19	2nd	7
6-18	At Oak.	L	1-3		6	7	Honeycutt	Montgomery	Eckersley	27-20	2nd	7
6-19	At Cal.	W	8-5		8	11	Appier	Boskie		28-20	2nd	7
6-20	At Cal.	L	2-3		4	9	B. Anderson	Gubicza	Smith	28-21	2nd	8
6-21	At Cal.	W	6-3		8	5	Gordon	Bielecki	Montgomery	29-21	2nd	7
6-23	Min.	W	4-0		6	4	Appier	Tapani		30-21	2nd	6
6-24	Min.	L	5-6		11	9	Guthrie	Pichardo	Aguilera	30-22	2nd	6
6-26	Cle.	L	0-2		7	8	Ogea	Gordon	Mesa	30-23	2nd	6½
6-27	Cle.	L	1-7		5	15	Clark	Haney		30-24	2nd	7½
6-28	Cle.	L	2-5		7	8	Nagy	Appier	Mesa	30-25	2nd	8½
6-30	Chi.	W	1-0		11	4	Gubicza	Alvarez	Pichardo	31-25	2nd	9
7-1	Chi.	L	5-11		11	14	Keyser	Gordon		31-26	2nd	9
7-2	Chi.	L	5-6	(10)	12	12	Fortugno	Pichardo		31-27	2nd	10
7-3	Bos.	L	5-12		9	11	Smith	Appier	Maddux	31-28	2nd	11
7-4	Bos.	L	5-6		11	9	Wakefield	Gubicza	Belinda	31-29	2nd	11
7-5	Bos.	W	3-2		8	7	Pichardo	F. Rodriguez		32-29	2nd	11
7-6	At Det.	L	5-12		12	18	Doherty	Haney	Wickander	32-30	2nd	12
7-7	At Det.	L	1-3		7	3	Wells	Appier		32-31	2nd	12
7-8	At Det.	W	4-1		10	3	Gubicza	Moore	Montgomery	33-31	2nd	12
7-9	At Det.	L	2-4		5	6	Lira	Gordon	Henneman	33-32	2nd	12
7-12	At N.Y.	L	1-9		6	11	Pettitte	Haney		33-33	2nd	12½
7-13	At Bal.	W	9-8		12	13	Meacham	Jones	Montgomery	34-33	2nd	12
7-14	At Bal.	W	7-2		8	7	Gordon	McDonald		35-33	2nd	12½
7-15	At Bal.	L	1-9		7	17	Erickson	Appier		35-34	2nd	13½
7-16	At Bal.	L	2-3		4	4	Moyer	Bunch	Jones	35-35	T2nd	14½
7-17	At Bos.	W	4-3		12	8	Gubicza	Suppan	Montgomery	36-35	T2nd	13½

Date	Opp.	Res.	Score	(inn.*)	Hits	Opp. hits	Winning pitcher	Losing pitcher	Save	Record	Pos.	GB
7-18	At Bos.	L	1-4		6	13	Clemens	Gordon	Aguilera	36-36	3rd	14½
7-19	At N.Y.	L	2-5		5	8	Hitchcock	Torres	Wetteland	36-37	3rd	15½
7-20	At N.Y.	L	4-8		8	11	Howe	Brewer		36-38	3rd	16½
7-21	Bal.	L	6-10		12	11	Oquist	Bunch		36-39	3rd	17½
7-22	Bal.	W	5-3		8	10	Brewer	Rhodes	Montgomery	37-39	3rd	17½
7-23	Bal.	L	2-6		6	8	Mussina	Gordon		37-40	3rd	18½
7-25	N.Y.	L	1-8		8	13	Kamieniecki	Appier		37-41	3rd	19
7-26	N.Y.	W	6-5		11	10	Pichardo	Wickman		38-41	3rd	18
7-27	N.Y.	L	0-1		5	7	Pettitte	Gubicza	Wetteland	38-42	3rd	18
7-28	Det.	W	4-3		9	7	Montgomery	Doherty		39-42	3rd	18
7-29	Det.	W	5-4	(16)	22	6	Pichardo	Doherty		40-42	3rd	17
7-30	Det.	W	3-2		9	10	Anderson	Lira	Montgomery	41-42	2nd	17
7-31	At Chi.	L	4-6		9	12	Fernandez	Jacome	Hernandez	41-43	T2nd	17½
8-1	At Chi.	L	3-4		8	9	Righetti	Gubicza	Hernandez	41-44	T2nd	17½
8-2	At Chi.	L	2-5		9	7	Keyser	Pichardo	Hernandez	41-45	3rd	18½
8-3	At Chi.	W	9-0		10	7	Bunch	Bertotti		42-45	T2nd	18½
8-4	At Min.	W	12-4		13	8	Meacham	Mahomes	Montgomery	43-45	T2nd	18½
8-5	At Min.	L	8-13		11	16	Trombley	Jacome		43-46	3rd	19½
8-6	At Min.	W	11-1		15	4	Gubicza	Klingenbeck		44-46	3rd	18½
8-8	Cal.	L	0-4		7	11	Abbott	Gordon	Percival	44-47	3rd	18½
8-9	Cal.	L	1-9		5	17	Finley	Bunch		44-48	3rd	18½
8-10	Cal.	W	5-0		9	7	Jacome	Langston		45-48	3rd	19
8-11	Sea.	L	1-2		5	9	Johnson	Gubicza	Ayala	45-49	3rd	20
8-12	Sea.	W	7-2		12	3	Appier	Belcher	Meacham	46-49	3rd	19
8-13	Sea.	W	6-3		12	8	Gordon	Krueger	Montgomery	47-49	3rd	18
8-14	Oak.	L	5-13		7	14	Wojciechowski	Brewer		47-50	3rd	19
8-15	Oak.	W	7-4	(7)	9	6	Jacome	Darling	Olson	48-50	3rd	18
8-16	Oak.	L	4-8		9	12	Stottlemyre	Magnante	Mohler	48-51	3rd	19
8-17	At Bal.	W	3-2	(10)	7	10	Olson	Orosco	Montgomery	49-51	3rd	18
8-18	At Tor.	W	10-3		11	8	Gordon	Carrara		50-51	3rd	18
8-19	At Tor.	L	4-5	(13)	6	12	Rogers	Montgomery		50-52	3rd	19
8-20	At Tor.	L	3-4		7	10	Timlin	Olson		50-53	3rd	20
8-21†	At Mil.	L	1-3		6	9	Givens	Gubicza	Miranda	50-54		
8-21‡	At Mil.	W	18-9		19	13	Appier	Scanlan		51-54	3rd	20½
8-22	At Mil.	L	1-8		7	10	McAndrew	Gordon		51-55	3rd	20½
8-24	Tex.	W	5-3		8	7	Jacome	Gross	Montgomery	52-55	3rd	20½
8-25	Tex.	W	9-4		12	11	Gubicza	Rogers	Olson	53-55	3rd	20½
8-26	Tex.	L	3-10		7	16	Tewksbury	Appier	Cook	53-56	3rd	21½
8-27	Tex.	W	5-2		7	7	Gordon	Pavlik	Montgomery	54-56	3rd	21½
8-28	At N.Y.	W	4-3		9	9	Torres	McDowell	Montgomery	55-56	3rd	21½
8-29	Mil.	W	7-1		10	7	Jacome	Bones		56-56	3rd	21½
8-30	Mil.	W	2-1		5	4	Gubicza	Karl	Montgomery	57-56	T2nd	21½
8-31	Mil.	W	7-6		12	8	Montgomery	Fetters		58-56	2nd	21½
9-1	At Tex.	W	5-2		12	8	Gordon	Tewksbury	Olson	59-56	2nd	21½
9-2	At Tex.	L	1-4		7	5	Pavlik	Fleming	Russell	59-57	2nd	21½
9-3	At Tex.	W	8-5		15	10	Olson	Vosberg	Montgomery	60-57	2nd	21½
9-4†	Tor.	L	1-6		10	17	Hentgen	Gubicza	Timlin	60-58		
9-4‡	Tor.	W	9-7		13	12	Magnante	Castillo	Montgomery	61-58	2nd	21
9-5	Tor.	W	9-8	(10)	10	11	Olson	Robinson		62-58	2nd	21
9-6	Tor.	L	2-6		9	11	Leiter	Gordon		62-59	2nd	22
9-8	At Sea.	L	1-4		5	11	Johnson	Jacome	Charlton	62-60	2nd	23½
9-9	At Sea.	L	2-6		3	13	Benes	Gubicza		62-61	2nd	24½
9-10	At Sea.	L	4-5		10	7	Ayala	Olson	Charlton	62-62	2nd	25½
9-12	At Oak.	W	3-1		7	6	Gordon	Van Poppel	Montgomery	63-62	2nd	24
9-13	At Oak.	L	5-6		10	11	Johns	Jacome	Eckersley	63-63	2nd	25
9-14	At Oak.	W	5-4		6	10	Converse	Eckersley	Montgomery	64-63	2nd	25
9-15	At Cal.	W	5-0		10	3	Appier	Abbott		65-63	2nd	24
9-16	At Cal.	W	7-6		10	12	Gordon	Boskie	Montgomery	66-63	2nd	24
9-17	At Cal.	W	10-8		11	13	Pichardo	Langston	Montgomery	67-63	2nd	23
9-18†	Min.	W	16-7		20	13	Gubicza	Parra	Meacham	68-63		
9-18‡	Min.	L	4-10		12	16	Hawkins	Torres	Mahomes	68-64	2nd	23½
9-19	Min.	L	3-7		4	12	Robertson	Appier		68-65	2nd	24½
9-20	Min.	L	4-5	(12)	11	13	Stevens	Meacham		68-66	2nd	24½
9-21	Min.	L	2-5		8	8	Radke	Jacome		68-67	2nd	25
9-22	Cle.	L	3-5		8	8	Hershiser	Olson	Mesa	68-68	2nd	26
9-23	Cle.	L	3-7		7	13	Martinez	Gubicza		68-69	2nd	27
9-24	Cle.	W	4-2		10	5	Appier	Clark		69-69	2nd	26
9-26	Chi.	L	0-7		6	6	Fernandez	Gordon		69-70	2nd	26
9-27	Chi.	L	0-6		3	9	Sirotka	Jacome		69-71	2nd	27
9-28	Chi.	W	4-0		6	4	Gubicza	Alvarez		70-71	2nd	27
9-29	At Cle.	L	2-9		5	12	Hershiser	Appier		70-72	2nd	28
9-30	At Cle.	L	2-3	(10)	5	10	Embree	Montgomery		70-73	2nd	29
10-1	At Cle.	L	7-17		13	19	Nagy	Gordon		70-74	2nd	30

Monthly records: April (2-2), May (14-13), June (15-10), July (10-18), August (17-13), September (12-17), October (0-1).

*Innings, if other than nine. †First game of doubleheader. ‡Second game of doubleheader.

HIGHLIGHTS

High point: With no hope of catching Cleveland in the A.L. Central, the Royals got into the thick of the wild-card chase. Winning eight of 10 games, they took the wild-card lead on August 31 and held it for 10 days before fading.

Low point: Still in the wild-card hunt after their second West Coast trip, the Royals came home in mid-September and lost six consecutive games—four to lowly Minnesota and two to mighty Cleveland—and were out of it.

Turning point: After going nine games over .500 (30-21) on June 23, when they trailed the Indians by six games, the Royals went on a 7-20 spin and by July 25 were 19 games behind. They finished 30 out, the biggest deficit for a second-place team in major league history.

Most valuable player: Third baseman Gary Gaetti. Though he turned 37, Gaetti had 35 homers and 96 RBIs. He had six homers and 13 RBIs in one five-game span.

Most valuable pitcher: Righthander Kevin Appier. Off to an 11-2 start with a 2.03 ERA, Appier slumped and had shoulder problems but still finished 15-10 with a 3.89 ERA. Opponents hit just .221 against him.

Most improved player: Center fielder Tom Goodwin. Unable to make it with the Dodgers, Goodwin hit a surprising .288 and stole 50 bases.

Most pleasant surprise: Right fielder Jon Nunnally. Obtained from Cleveland in the Rule 5 draft, Nunnally jumped from Class A and became the Royals' right fielder. He had 14 homers and 42 RBIs.

Biggest disappointment: Designated hitter Bob Hamelin. The 1994 A.L. Rookie of the Year was shipped to the minors. He had seven homers, 25 RBIs and a .168 average.

Key injuries: Appier's sore shoulder sidelined him 2½ weeks. Lefthander Chris Haney, after a hot start, had back surgery and missed most of the season. Rookie righthander Jim Pittsley suffered an elbow injury just after joining the rotation and

underwent surgery. First baseman Wally Joyner missed the last two weeks with an ankle injury.

Notable: Second baseman Chico Lind, after leaving the club without permission June 1, was suspended and eventually released. . . . The Royals used a club-record 51 players, including 19 rookies. . . . Joyner's 83 RBIs were the most in his four years with the club. . . . Mark Gubicza pitched a one-hitter June 15 at Oakland. . . . The Royals, who were 14-27 against lefthanded starters, were last in the A.L. in runs scored (629) and homers (119).

—DICK KAEGEL

RECORDS

1995 regular-season record: 70-74 (2nd in A.L. Central); 35-37 at home; 35-37 on road; 21-22 vs. East; 22-28 vs. Central; 27-24 vs. West; 14-27 vs. lefthanded starters; 56-47 vs. righthanded starters; 60-66 on grass; 10-8 on turf; 21-18 in daytime; 49-56 at night; 24-19 in one-run games; 7-6 in extra-inning games; 0-0-3 in doubleheaders.

Team record past five years: 372-373 (.499, ranks 8th in league in that span).

TEAM LEADERS

Batting average: Wally Joyner (.310).
At-bats: Gary Gaetti (514).
Runs: Gary Gaetti (76).
Hits: Wally Joyner (144).
Total bases: Gary Gaetti (266).
Doubles: Wally Joyner (28).
Triples: Jon Nunnally (6).
Home runs: Gary Gaetti (35).
Runs batted in: Gary Gaetti (96).
Stolen bases: Tom Goodwin (50).
Slugging percentage: Gary Gaetti (.518).
On-base percentage: Wally Joyner (.394).
Wins: Kevin Appier (15).
Earned-run average: Mark Gubicza (3.75).
Complete games: Kevin Appier (4).
Shutouts: Mark Gubicza (2).
Saves: Jeff Montgomery (31).
Innings pitched: Mark Gubicza (213.1).
Strikeouts: Kevin Appier (185).

GAMES BY POSITION

Catcher: Brent Mayne 103, Pat Borders 45, Henry Mercedes 22, Mike Sweeney 4.
First base: Wally Joyner 126, Gary Gaetti 11, Bob Hamelin 8, Joe Vitiello 8, Edgar Caceres 6, Jeff Grotewold 1, David Howard 1, Russ McGinnis 1, Juan Samuel 1.
Second base: Keith Lockhart 61, David Howard 41, Edgar Caceres 36, Jose Lind 29, Chris Stynes 17, Joe Randa 9, Jose Mota 2.
Third base: Gary Gaetti 123, Joe Randa 22, Keith Lockhart 17, Edgar Caceres 3, Russ McGinnis 1.
Shortstop: Greg Gagne 118, David Howard 33, Edgar Caceres 8.
Outfield: Tom Goodwin 130, Jon Nunnally 107, Vince Coleman 69, Johnny Damon 47, Phil Hiatt 47, Michael Tucker 36, David Howard 30, Les Norman 17, Brent Cookson 12, Felix Jose 7, Chris James 5, Juan Samuel 5, Keith Miller 4, Russ McGinnis 1.
Designated hitter: Bob Hamelin 56, Joe Vitiello 38, Michael Tucker 22, Chris James 14, Keith Lockhart 14, Jeff Grotewold 11, Juan Samuel 7, Gary Gaetti 6, Les Norman 5, Vince Coleman 4, Keith Miller 4, Jon Nunnally 4, Pat Borders 3, Edgar Caceres 3, Brent Cookson 2, Greg Gagne 2, Tom Goodwin 2, Phil Hiatt 2, Wally Joyner 2, Joe Randa 2, David Howard 1, Chris Stynes 1.

TOP DRAFT CHOICES

1. **Juan LeBron,** OF, Arroyo, Puerto Rico.
2. **Carlos Beltran,** OF, Manati, Puerto Rico.
3. **Doug Blosser,** 1B, Sarasota (Fla.) H.S.
4. **Vic Radcliff,** SS, North Augusta (S.C.) H.S.
5. **Steve Medrano,** SS, Bishop Amat H.S., La Puente, Calif.
6. **Melvin Dasher,** OF, Palatka (Fla.) H.S.
7. **James Sanders,** RHP, Lee (Tex.) J.C.
8. **Jeff Martin,** RHP, Bishop Gorman H.S., Las Vegas, Nev.
9. **Mike Robbins,** LHP, Stanford University.
10. **David Moore,** RHP, Northeast H.S., Oakland Park, Fla.

MILWAUKEE BREWERS
AMERICAN LEAGUE CENTRAL DIVISION

1996 BREWERS SCHEDULE

Home games shaded.
* — All-Star Game at Veterans Stadium (Philadelphia)
N — Night game (any game starting after 5 p.m.)

MARCH
SUN	MON	TUE	WED	THU	FRI	SAT
31						

APRIL
SUN	MON	TUE	WED	THU	FRI	SAT
	1 N CAL	2 N CAL	3	4 N SEA	5 N SEA	6
7 SEA	8 OAK	9 N	10	11 OAK	12 N KC	13 KC
14 KC	15 N NY	16 N NY	17 N	18 N KC	19 N KC	20 KC
21 KC	22 N OAK	23 OAK	24 N CAL	25 CAL	26 N SEA	27 SEA
28 SEA	29 SEA	30 N TOR				

MAY
SUN	MON	TUE	WED	THU	FRI	SAT
			1 N TOR	2 TOR	3 N BAL	4 BAL
5 BAL	6 N BOS	7 N BOS	8 BOS	9 N BAL	10 N BAL	11 BAL
12 BAL	13 N CHI	14 N CHI	15 N CHI	16 CHI	17 N MIN	18 N MIN
19 MIN	20 N MIN	21 N CLE	22 N CLE	23 N CLE	24 N CHI	25 N CHI
26 CHI	27 N MIN	28 MIN	29 N CLE	30 N CLE	31	

JUNE
SUN	MON	TUE	WED	THU	FRI	SAT
						1 CLE
2 CLE	3 N TEX	4 N TEX	5 N TEX	6	7 N BOS	8 N BOS
9 BOS	10 N TEX	11 N TEX	12 N TEX	13 N OAK	14 N OAK	15 OAK
16 OAK	17 N KC	18 N KC	19 KC	20 N CAL	21 N CAL	22 CAL
23 CAL	24 N KC	25 N KC	26 N KC	27 N TOR	28 TOR	29
30 TOR						

JULY
SUN	MON	TUE	WED	THU	FRI	SAT
	1 N DET	2 N DET	3 N DET	4 NY	5 N NY	6 N NY
7 NY	8 *	9 ALL-STAR GAME	10	11 N TOR	12 N TOR	13 N TOR
14 TOR	15 N DET	16 N DET	17 N DET	18 N NY	19 N NY	20 NY
21 NY	22 N SEA	23 N SEA	24 N CAL	25 N CAL	26 N CAL	27
28 CAL	29 N SEA	30 N SEA	31			

AUGUST
SUN	MON	TUE	WED	THU	FRI	SAT
				1 SEA	2 N OAK	3 OAK
4 N OAK	5 OAK	6 N BAL	7 N BAL	8 BAL	9 N BOS	10 N BOS
11 BOS	12 N BAL	13 N BAL	14 BAL	15	16 N CHI	17 N CHI
18 CHI	19 N MIN	20 N MIN	21 MIN	22	23 N CLE	24 CLE
25 CLE	26 N CHI	27 N CHI	28 CHI	29 N MIN	30 N MIN	31 N MIN

SEPTEMBER
SUN	MON	TUE	WED	THU	FRI	SAT
1 MIN	2 CLE	3 N CLE	4 N CLE	5	6 N TEX	7 TEX
8 TEX	9 N BOS	10 N BOS	11 N TEX	12 N TEX	13 N TEX	14 TEX
15 TEX	16 N TOR	17 N TOR	18	19	20 N DET	21 N DET
22 DET	23	24 N NY	25 N NY	26	27 N DET	28 N DET
29 DET						

1996 SEASON

CLUB DIRECTORY

President, chief executive officer
Allan H. (Bud) Selig
Senior vice president, baseball operations
Sal Bando
Vice president & general counsel
Wendy Selig-Prieb
Vice president, broadcast operations
Bill Haig
Vice president, broadcast sales
Mitch Nye
Director, finance
Paul Baniel
V.p., new ballpark development
Michael Bucek
Vice president, stadium operations
Gabe Paul Jr.
Director of Brewers Gold Club
Geoff Campion
Scouting director
Ken Califano
Senior consultant, baseball operations
Dee Fondy
Special assistants, baseball operations
Larry Haney
Chuck Tanner
Assistant general counsel
Eugene (Pepi) Randolph
Director of baseball administration
Brian Small
Vice president of corporate affairs
Laurel Prieb
Director of community relations
Michael Downs
Director of stadium administration
Terry Ann Peterson
Director of grounds
Gary Vandenberg
Director of media relations
Jon Greenberg
Director of player development
Fred Stanley
Dir. of admin. & human resources
Tom Gausden
Director of publications
Mario Ziino

Director of ticket operations
John Barnes
Vice president of ticket sales
Bob Voight
Traveling secretary
Steve Ethier
Trainers
John Adam
Al Price
Strength and conditioning coach
John Rewolinski
Team physicians
Dr. Dennis Sullivan
Dr. Drew Palin
Western crosschecker
Lou Snipp
Eastern crosschecker
Ed Durkin
Midwest supervisor
Fred Beene
Northeast supervisor
Ron Rizzi
West Coast supervisor
Kevin Christman
Southeast supervisor
Russ Bove
International scouting supervisor
Epy Guerrero
Special assignment scouts
Paul Tretiak
Walter Youse
Scouts
Jeff Brookens, Domingo Carrasquel, Rich Chiles, Ramon Conde, Felix Delgado, Bob Derksen, Walter Doggan, Dick Fanning, Bill Foley, Dick Foster, Danny Garcia, Mike Gibbons, Manolo Hernandez, Ken Houp, Elvio Jiminez, Harvey Kuenn Jr., John Logan, Demie Mainieri, Alex Morales, Mike Powers, Doug Reynolds, Corey Rodriguez, Bob Sloan, Jonathan Story, Tom Tanous, John Viney, Red Whitsett, Ric Wilson, David Young

MINOR LEAGUE AFFILIATES

Class	Team	League	Manager
AAA	New Orleans	American Assoc.	Tim Ireland
AA	El Paso	Texas	Dave Machemer
A	Stockton	California	Greg Mahberg
A	Beloit	Midwest	Luis Salazar
Rookie	Helena	Pioneer	Alex Morales
Rookie	Ogden	Pioneer	Bernie Moncallo

BROADCAST INFORMATION
Radio: WTMJ-AM (620).
TV: WVTV-TV (Channel 24).
Cable TV: None.

SPRING TRAINING
Ballpark (city): Compadre Stadium (Chandler, Ariz.).
Ticket information: 602-895-1200.

SPRING TRAINING ROSTER

Manager—Phil Garner (3).
Coaches—Chris Bando (12), Bill Castro (35), Jim Gantner (17), Lamar Johnson (28), Don Rowe (45).

No.	PITCHERS	T/B	Ht./Wt.	Born	1995 clubs
25	Bones, Ricky	R/R	6-0/193	4-7-69	Milwaukee
48	Boze, Marshall	R/R	6-1/214	5-23-71	New Orleans
40	Browne, Byron	R/R	6-7/200	8-8-70	El Paso
21	Eldred, Cal	R/R	6-4/235	11-24-67	Milwaukee
36	Fetters, Mike	R/R	6-4/224	12-19-64	Milwaukee
13	Givens, Brian	R/L	6-6/220	11-6-65	New Orleans, Milwaukee
42	Karl, Scott	L/L	6-2/195	8-9-71	New Orleans, Milwaukee
43	Kiefer, Mark	R/R	6-4/184	11-13-68	Milwaukee, New Orleans
37	Lloyd, Graeme	L/L	6-7/234	4-9-67	Milwaukee
31	McAndrew, Jamie	R/R	6-2/190	9-2-67	New Orleans, Milwaukee
38	Miranda, Angel	L/L	6-1/195	11-9-69	Milwaukee
39	Narcisse, Tyrone	R/R	6-5/205	2-4-72	Jackson
51	Roberson, Sid	L/L	5-9/170	9-7-71	New Orleans, Milwaukee
50	Sparks, Steve	R/R	6-0/187	7-2-65	Milwaukee
52	Wickander, Kevin	L/L	6-3/205	1-4-65	Toledo, Detroit, Milwaukee

No.	CATCHERS	T/B	Ht./Wt.	Born	1995 clubs
59	Hughes, Bobby	R/R	6-4/237	3-10-71	Stockton, El Paso
22	Matheny, Mike	R/R	6-3/205	9-22-70	New Orleans, Milwaukee

No.	INFIELDERS	T/B	Ht./Wt.	Born	1995 clubs
26	Cirillo, Jeff	R/R	6-2/188	9-23-69	Milwaukee
32	Jaha, John	R/R	6-1/222	5-27-66	Milwaukee, Beloit, New Orleans
16	Listach, Pat	B/R	5-9/180	9-12-67	Milwaukee
8	Loretta, Mark	R/R	6-0/175	8-14-71	New Orleans, Milwaukee
53	Martinez, Gabby	B/R	6-2/170	1-7-74	Stockton, El Paso
14	Nilsson, Dave	L/R	6-3/231	12-14-69	Beloit, El Paso, New Orleans, Milwaukee
20	Seitzer, Kevin	R/R	5-11/193	3-26-62	Milwaukee
7	Unroe, Tim	R/R	6-3/200	10-7-70	New Orleans, Milwaukee
2	Valentin, Jose	L/R	5-10/166	10-12-69	Milwaukee
1	Vina, Fernando	L/R	5-9/170	4-16-69	Milwaukee
13	Weger, Wes	R/R	6-0/176	10-3-70	El Paso, New Orleans

No.	OUTFIELDERS	T/B	Ht./Wt.	Born	1995 clubs
54	Banks, Brian	B/R	6-3/200	9-28-70	El Paso
29	Carr, Chuck	B/R	5-10/165	8-10-68	Florida, Charlotte
55	Dunn, Todd	R/R	6-5/220	7-29-70	Stockton
61	Felder, Ken	R/R	6-3/220	2-9-71	El Paso
15	Hulse, David	L/L	5-11/170	2-25-68	Milwaukee
30	Mieske, Matt	R/R	6-0/192	2-13-68	Milwaukee
60	Perez, Danny	R/R	5-10/188	2-26-71	New Orleans, El Paso
18	Singleton, Duane	L/R	6-1/177	8-6-72	New Orleans, Milwaukee
23	Vaughn, Greg	R/R	6-0/202	7-3-65	Milwaukee
27	Ward, Turner	B/R	6-2/198	4-11-65	Milwaukee, Beloit, New Orleans

BALLPARK INFORMATION

Ballpark (capacity, surface)
County Stadium (53,192, grass)

Address
County Stadium
P.O. Box 3099 Milwaukee, WI
53201-3099

Business phone
414-933-4114

Ticket information
414-933-9000

Ticket prices
$18 (diamond box)
$15 (mezzanine, lower box)
$12 (upper box, lower grandstand)
$8 (upper grandstand)
$7 (general admission)
$4 (bleachers)

Field dimensions (from home plate)
To left field at foul line, 315 feet
To center field, 402 feet
To right field at foul line, 315 feet

First game played
April 7, 1970 (Angels 12, Brewers 0)

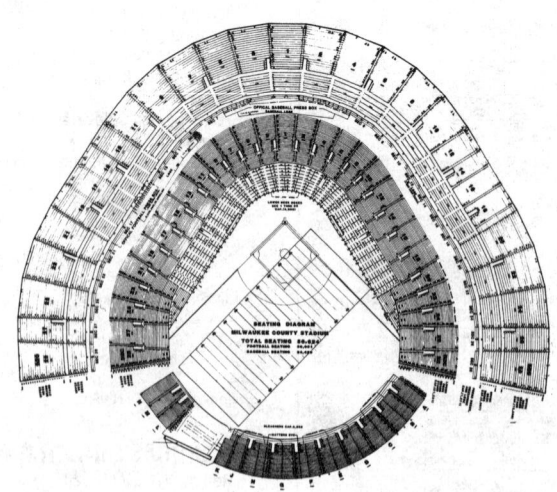

DAY BY DAY

Date	Opp.	Res.	Score	(inn.*)	Hits	Opp. hits	Winning pitcher	Losing pitcher	Save	Record	Pos.	GB
4-26	Chi.	W	12-3		12	7	Miranda	Fernandez		1-0	T1st	...
4-27	At Chi.	W	9-4		11	9	Eldred	Abbott		2-0	1st	+1/2
4-28	Oak.	W	8-7	(10)	8	9	Kiefer	Eckersley		3-0	1st	+1
4-29	Oak.	L	2-8		4	12	Ontiveros	Wegman	Honeycutt	3-1	1st	+1
4-30	Oak.	W	4-3		8	6	Kiefer	Wengert	Lloyd	4-1	1st	+11/2
5-1	At Bal.	W	7-0		12	2	Bones	Mussina		5-1	1st	+2
5-3	At Bal.	W	7-4		9	5	Kiefer	Jones	Lloyd	6-1	1st	+11/2
5-4	At Bal.	L	2-5		5	8	Mills	Mercedes	Jones	6-2	1st	+11/2
5-5	At N.Y.	L	4-6		9	9	Bankhead	Wegman	Wetteland	6-3	1st	+1/2
5-6	At N.Y.	W	5-2		10	8	Bones	Key	Lloyd	7-3	1st	+11/2
5-7	At N.Y.	W	9-1		14	7	Ignasiak	Hitchcock		8-3	1st	+11/2
5-9	Det.	L	2-4	(10)	7	12	Doherty	Lloyd		8-4	T1st	...
5-10	Det.	W	13-2		15	9	Scanlan	Moore		9-4	T1st	...
5-11	Det.	L	0-8		8	12	Bergman	Wegman		9-5	2nd	1/2
5-12	Tor.	W	14-5		18	12	Ignasiak	Darwin		10-5	2nd	1/2
5-13	Tor.	L	0-10		3	11	Cone	Miranda		10-6	2nd	1/2
5-14	Tor.	L	3-8		9	14	Hentgen	Eldred		10-7	2nd	11/2
5-16	Bos.	L	0-5		4	7	Hanson	Scanlan		10-8	2nd	21/2
5-17	Bos.	L	2-8		8	8	Sele	Bones		10-9	2nd	3
5-18	At Tex.	L	2-6		6	13	Pavlik	Lloyd		10-10	2nd	3
5-19	At Tex.	W	1-0		5	5	Sparks	Oliver	Fetters	11-10	2nd	3
5-20	At Tex.	L	6-7	(11)	17	13	Vosberg	Kiefer		11-11	2nd	4
5-21	At Tex.	L	0-6		5	8	Rogers	Scanlan		11-12	2nd	5
5-22	At Cle.	W	7-5		16	6	Bones	Nagy	Fetters	12-12	2nd	4
5-23	At Cle.	L	3-5		7	13	Martinez	Sparks	Mesa	12-13	2nd	5
5-24	At Cle.	L	7-5		13	9	Rightnowar	Clark	Fetters	13-13	2nd	4
5-25	K.C.	L	1-3		4	6	Haney	Roberson	Montgomery	13-14	2nd	41/2
5-26	K.C.	L	3-8		12	11	Appier	Scanlan		13-15	3rd	51/2
5-28	K.C.	L	4-7		10	13	Gubicza	Bones	Montgomery	13-16	3rd	6
5-29	Min.	L	5-7		7	11	Erickson	Miranda	Aguilera	13-17	3rd	7
5-30	Min.	W	5-3		11	9	Roberson	Tapani	Lloyd	14-17	3rd	7
5-31	Min.	W	8-1		13	8	Scanlan	Guardado		15-17	3rd	7
6-2	At K.C.	L	2-3		6	10	Gubicza	Bones	Montgomery	15-18	3rd	71/2
6-3	At K.C.	L	1-2		5	5	Gordon	Lloyd		15-19	3rd	81/2
6-4	At K.C.	L	3-4		7	7	Pichardo	Lloyd	Montgomery	15-20	3rd	91/2
6-6	At Min.	W	13-5		14	9	Scanlan	Radke		16-20	3rd	10
6-7	At Min.	W	6-3		8	11	Miranda	Erickson	Rightnowar	17-20	3rd	10
6-8	Cle.	L	7-8		14	12	Tavarez	Lloyd	Mesa	17-21	3rd	11
6-9	Cle.	L	4-7		8	13	Ogea	Roberson	Mesa	17-22	3rd	12
6-10	Cle.	W	6-1		9	3	Miranda	Hershiser	Reyes	18-22	3rd	11
6-11	Cle.	L	5-11		10	19	Black	Scanlan		18-23	3rd	12
6-12	Tex.	L	2-4		7	8	Pavlik	Sparks	Russell	18-24	3rd	13
6-13	Tex.	W	14-2		16	4	Bones	Gross		19-24	3rd	13
6-14	Tex.	W	4-2		8	6	Roberson	Oliver	Fetters	20-24	3rd	13
6-16	At Bos.	W	4-3		10	9	Miranda	Hanson	Fetters	21-24	3rd	12
6-17	At Bos.	W	9-1		16	5	Sparks	Clemens		22-24	3rd	12
6-18	At Bos.	L	2-4		10	9	Smith	Bones	Belinda	22-25	3rd	12
6-20	At Tor.	W	5-3		13	9	Roberson	Hentgen	Fetters	23-25	3rd	121/2
6-21	At Tor.	W	10-9		10	14	Wegman	Timlin	Fetters	24-25	3rd	111/2
6-22	At Tor.	W	9-0		13	4	Sparks	Darwin		25-25	3rd	11
6-23	At Det.	L	2-5		11	8	Wells	Bones	Henneman	25-26	3rd	11
6-24	At Det.	L	2-7		8	9	Moore	Givens	Boever	25-27	3rd	11
6-25	At Det.	L	3-6		9	7	Maxcy	Rightnowar	Henneman	25-28	3rd	11
6-26	Bal.	L	0-2		2	11	Moyer	Miranda	Jones	25-29	3rd	12
6-27	Bal.	L	3-11		6	15	DeSilva	Sparks		25-30	3rd	13
6-28	Bal.	L	2-4		5	7	Mussina	Bones	Jones	25-31	3rd	14
6-29	Chi.	L	13-17		14	22	Fernandez	Givens		25-32	4th	15
6-30	N.Y.	W	12-6		15	14	Roberson	Perez		26-32	3rd	15
7-1	N.Y.	L	1-3	(12)	8	10	Howe	Reyes	Wetteland	26-33	4th	15
7-2	N.Y.	W	7-6		11	10	Sparks	Pettitte	Fetters	27-33	4th	15
7-3	At Oak.	W	7-3	(10)	8	10	Rightnowar	Van Poppel		28-33	3rd	15
7-4	At Oak.	L	3-5		6	6	Honeycutt	Ignasiak	Eckersley	28-34	3rd	15
7-5	At Oak.	W	8-2		12	5	Roberson	Ontiveros	Wegman	29-34	3rd	15
7-6	At Oak.	W	5-2		7	7	Karl	Stottlemyre	Fetters	30-34	3rd	15
7-7	At Cal.	W	9-3		10	4	Sparks	Bielecki		31-34	3rd	14
7-8	At Cal.	L	0-1		3	3	Langston	Bones		31-35	3rd	15
7-9	At Cal.	W	9-7		8	11	Ignasiak	Finley	Fetters	32-35	3rd	14
7-12	At Chi.	L	2-8		8	11	Alvarez	Sparks		32-36	3rd	141/2
7-13	Chi.	W	8-7	(10)	11	8	Reyes	Hernandez		33-36	3rd	14
7-14	Chi.	W	8-7		7	12	Bones	Bere	Fetters	34-36	3rd	141/2
7-15	Chi.	W	9-5		16	11	Wegman	Fortugno		35-36	3rd	141/2

Date	Opp.	Res.	Score	(inn.*)	Hits	Opp. hits	Winning pitcher	Losing pitcher	Save	Record	Pos.	GB
7-16	Chi.	W	6-1		10	3	Givens	Keyser		36-36	T2nd	14½
7-17	Oak.	W	13-4		15	11	Sparks	Stewart		37-36	T2nd	13½
7-18	Oak.	W	4-0		12	3	Roberson	Wojciechowski		38-36	2nd	13½
7-19	Sea.	W	7-6	(12)	13	15	Wegman	Ayala		39-36	2nd	13½
7-20	Sea.	L	2-4	(13)	11	8	Krueger	McAndrew		39-37	2nd	14½
7-21	At Chi.	W	5-2		7	7	Wegman	Keyser	Fetters	40-37	2nd	14½
7-22	At Chi.	L	2-4		5	7	Alvarez	Sparks	Hernandez	40-38	2nd	15½
7-23	At Chi.	L	6-11		12	12	Abbott	Roberson		40-39	2nd	16½
7-24	At Sea.	W	6-4		9	13	Bones	Bosio	Fetters	41-39	2nd	16½
7-25	At Sea.	L	6-8		7	12	Johnson	Karl	Ayala	41-40	2nd	16½
7-26	At Sea.	W	4-3		8	6	Givens	Torres	Fetters	42-40	2nd	15½
7-27	Cal.	L	3-9		7	12	B. Anderson	Wegman		42-41	2nd	15½
7-28	Cal.	L	6-13		12	17	Langston	Roberson		42-42	2nd	16½
7-29	Cal.	L	0-4		6	12	Abbott	Bones		42-43	2nd	16½
7-30	Cal.	L	3-8		10	13	Finley	Karl		42-44	3rd	17½
8-1	At N.Y.	L	5-7		7	12	M. Rivera	Miranda	Wetteland	42-45	T2nd	17½
8-2	At N.Y.	W	5-2		11	7	Sparks	McDowell	Fetters	43-45	2nd	17½
8-3	At N.Y.	L	4-5		6	7	Cone	Miranda	Wetteland	43-46	T2nd	18½
8-4	At Bal.	W	12-4		16	8	Karl	Erickson		44-46	T2nd	18½
8-5	At Bal.	L	5-6		8	12	Clark	Fetters		44-47	T2nd	19½
8-6	At Bal.	W	3-2		6	3	Ignasiak	K. Brown	Fetters	45-47	2nd	18½
8-8	Tor.	W	6-5	(11)	12	13	Wegman	Rogers		46-47	2nd	17½
8-9	Tor.	W	12-7		11	12	Karl	Guzman		47-47	2nd	16½
8-10	Tor.	L	4-8		11	17	Hentgen	Sparks	Castillo	47-48	2nd	18
8-11	Det.	W	5-4		8	9	Givens	Moore	Fetters	48-48	2nd	18
8-12	Det.	L	2-8		6	11	Lima	McAndrew	Doherty	48-49	2nd	18
8-13	Det.	W	8-3		11	11	Bones	Bergman		49-49	2nd	17
8-14	Det.	W	3-2		7	10	Karl	Maxcy	Fetters	50-49	2nd	17
8-15	At Tex.	L	2-3		6	10	Whiteside	Dibble		50-50	2nd	17
8-16	At Tex.	W	15-6		17	6	Givens	Darwin		51-50	2nd	17
8-17	At Cle.	W	7-3		11	9	McAndrew	Martinez	Fetters	52-50	2nd	16
8-18	At Cle.	L	5-7		10	11	Clark	Bones	Mesa	52-51	2nd	17
8-19	At Cle.	L	3-4		8	6	Plunk	Wegman		52-52	2nd	18
8-20	At Cle.	L	5-8		10	12	Tavarez	Sparks	Mesa	52-53	2nd	19
8-21†	K.C.	W	3-1		9	6	Givens	Gubicza	Miranda	53-53		
8-21‡	K.C.	L	9-18		13	19	Appier	Scanlan		53-54	2nd	19½
8-22	K.C.	W	8-1		10	7	McAndrew	Gordon		54-54	2nd	18½
8-24	Min.	W	5-3		8	9	Bones	Radke	Fetters	55-54	2nd	18½
8-25	Min.	W	6-3		10	7	Karl	Trombley	Wegman	56-54	2nd	18½
8-26	Min.	W	7-6	(10)	10	11	Slusarski	Stevens		57-54	2nd	18½
8-27	Min.	W	14-7		18	12	Scanlan	Rodriguez		58-54	2nd	18½
8-28	At Chi.	L	5-6		10	11	Alvarez	McAndrew	Hernandez	58-55	2nd	19½
8-29	At K.C.	L	1-7		7	10	Jacome	Bones		58-56	2nd	20½
8-30	At K.C.	L	1-2		4	5	Gubicza	Karl	Montgomery	58-57	T2nd	21½
8-31	At K.C.	L	6-7		8	12	Montgomery	Fetters		58-58	3rd	22½
9-1	At Min.	L	5-9		8	12	Rodriguez	Wegman	Guardado	58-59	3rd	23½
9-2	At Min.	L	5-6		8	11	Guardado	Slusarski		58-60	3rd	23½
9-3	At Min.	W	7-6		7	13	Dibble	Mahomes	Fetters	59-60	3rd	23½
9-4	At Min.	L	6-9		8	16	Trombley	Karl	Guardado	59-61	3rd	23½
9-5	Cle.	L	3-7		8	15	Martinez	Sparks		59-62	3rd	24½
9-6	Cle.	L	2-12		7	13	Hill	Givens		59-63	3rd	25½
9-8	Tex.	W	10-1		13	7	Bones	Witt		60-63	3rd	26
9-9	Tex.	L	4-10		11	12	Gross	Sparks		60-64	3rd	27
9-10	Tex.	L	2-5		6	15	Rogers	Karl	Russell	60-65	3rd	28
9-12	At Det.	L	1-5		4	8	Lima	Givens	Doherty	60-66	3rd	27½
9-13	At Det.	L	3-5		9	7	Henry	Fetters		60-67	3rd	28½
9-14	At Det.	W	6-3		8	6	Sparks	Bergman	Fetters	61-67	3rd	28½
9-15	At Tor.	W	5-1	(15)	12	6	Kiefer	Robinson		62-67	3rd	27½
9-16	At Tor.	L	4-5	(11)	7	11	Carrara	Wegman		62-68	3rd	28½
9-17	At Tor.	L	0-5		6	10	Leiter	Givens		62-69	3rd	28½
9-18	At Bos.	W	6-1		12	7	Bones	Wakefield		63-69	3rd	28½
9-19	At Bos.	L	3-5		5	9	Eshelman	Sparks	Aguilera	63-70	3rd	29½
9-20	At Bos.	L	2-3		4	9	Cormier	Karl	Aguilera	63-71	3rd	29½
9-21	At Chi.	L	1-5		5	10	Fernandez	Scanlan		63-72	3rd	30
9-22	Bal.	L	3-10		9	14	K. Brown	Givens		63-73	4th	31
9-23	Bal.	L	3-9		3	11	Haynes	Bones		63-74	4th	32
9-24	Bal.	W	5-1		7	5	Sparks	Krivda		64-74	4th	31
9-26	N.Y.	L	4-5		9	8	Hitchcock	Karl	Wetteland	64-75	4th	31
9-27	N.Y.	L	3-6		8	8	Cone	Givens		64-76	4th	32
9-28	Bos.	L	6-11		10	14	Clemens	Scanlan		64-77	4th	33
9-29	Bos.	L	9-11		15	16	Hanson	Bones	Aguilera	64-78	4th	34
9-30	Bos.	L	1-9		9	16	Maddux	Sparks		64-79	4th	35
10-1	Bos.	W	8-1		9	6	Karl	Wakefield		65-79	4th	35

Monthly records: April (4-1), May (11-16), June (11-15), July (16-12), August (16-14), September (6-21), October (1-0).
*Innings, if other than nine. †First game of doubleheader. ‡Second game of doubleheader.

HIGHLIGHTS

High point: The Brewers won six of seven games during a late-August homestand against Kansas City and Minnesota to improve to 58-54 and were in the thick of the A.L. wild-card race.

Low point: A 10-3 loss to visiting Baltimore on September 22—Milwaukee's 19th loss in 24 games—eliminated the Brewers from wild-card contention and guaranteed their third consecutive losing season.

Turning point: Immediately after their successful homestand ended August 27, the Brewers embarked on a telling eight-game trip through Chicago, Kansas City and Minnesota and lost seven games—four by one run.

Most valuable player: Outfielder B.J. Surhoff. He carried the club through most of July and August and established career highs with 13 homers and a .320 average. Surhoff's ability to play the outfield, third base, first base and catcher made him a defensive asset.

Most valuable pitcher: Reliever Mike Fetters. Bothered by a sore shoulder early in the season, Fetters finished with 22 saves in 27 opportunities and was a steadying influence on an inexperienced bullpen.

Most improved player: Catcher Mike Matheny. Forced into the starting lineup when Joe Oliver was sidelined by a broken wrist, Matheny hit .247 and proved he can be an everyday player.

Most pleasant surprise: A quartet of rookie starters, headed by knuckleballer Steve Sparks (a nine-game winner), kept the Brewers in postseason contention for much of the season. Sparks played a huge role early in the year when he pitched out of the bullpen between starts.

Biggest disappointment: Designated hitter Greg Vaughn. He suffered through a season-long slump and wound up at .224.

Key injuries: Righthander Cal Eldred, expected to be the staff ace, made just four starts before being sidelined with a torn ligament in his elbow. He underwent Tommy John reconstructive surgery in June. The losses of setup men Al Reyes (elbow injury), Jose Mercedes (shoulder) and Graeme Lloyd (finger) also were costly. Shortstop Jose Valentin, usually one of the club's most durable players, was relegated to pinch-running duty in the last five weeks because of a broken finger.

Notable: Manager Phil Garner was suspended for four games in August for an on-field wrestling match with Chicago skipper Terry Bevington. . . . Milwaukee hit just 128 homers but tied a major league record with 10 grand slams. . . . Ricky Bones, the only member of Milwaukee's season-opening rotation to retain his role all year, won a staff-high 10 games. Nothing unusual there. In the previous three seasons, Bones won nine, 11 and 10 games. . . . The Brewers led the majors with 186 double plays.

—DREW OLSON

RECORDS

1995 regular-season record: 65-79 (4th in A.L. Central); 33-39 at home; 32-40 on road; 26-34 vs. East; 22-29 vs. Central; 17-16 vs. West; 13-29 vs. lefthanded starters; 52-50 vs. righthanded starters; 56-73 on grass; 9-6 on turf; 20-27 in daytime; 45-52 at night; 16-17 in one-run games; 7-5 in extra-inning games; 0-0-1 in doubleheaders.

Team record past five years: 362-383 (.486, ranks 11th in league in that span).

TEAM LEADERS

Batting average: B.J. Surhoff (.320).
At-bats: Kevin Seitzer (492).
Runs: B.J. Surhoff (72).
Hits: Kevin Seitzer (153).
Total bases: Kevin Seitzer (207).
Doubles: Kevin Seitzer (33).
Triples: Fernando Vina (7).
Home runs: John Jaha (20).
Runs batted in: B.J. Surhoff (73).
Stolen bases: Jose Valentin (16).
Slugging percentage: B.J. Surhoff (.492).
On-base percentage: Kevin Seitzer (.395).
Wins: Ricky Bones (10)
Earned-run average: Ricky Bones, Steve Sparks (4.63).
Complete games: Ricky Bones, Steve Sparks (3).
Shutouts: None.
Saves: Mike Fetters (22).
Innings pitched: Steve Sparks (202.0)
Strikeouts: Steve Sparks (96).

GAMES BY POSITION

Catcher: Joe Oliver 91, Mike Matheny 80, B.J. Surhoff 18, Dave Nilsson 2.
First base: John Jaha 81, B.J. Surhoff 55, Kevin Seitzer 36, Dave Nilsson 7, Jeff Cirillo 3, Joe Oliver 2, Tim Unroe 2.
Second base: Fernando Vina 99, Pat Listach 59, Jeff Cirillo 25, Mark Loretta 4.
Third base: Jeff Cirillo 108, Kevin Seitzer 88, Pat Listach 2, Fernando Vina 2, Jose Valentin 1.
Shortstop: Jose Valentin 104, Pat Listach 36, Mark Loretta 13, Fernando Vina 6, Jeff Cirillo 2.
Outfield: David Hulse 115, Darryl Hamilton 109, Matt Mieske 108, B.J. Surhoff 60, Dave Nilsson 58, Turner Ward 40, Derrick May 32, Pat Listach 11, Duane Singleton 11.
Designated hitter: Greg Vaughn 104, Dave Nilsson 14, Kevin Seitzer 14, John Jaha 6, Joe Oliver 6, B.J. Surhoff 3, Jose Valentin 3, Darryl Hamilton 2, Matt Mieske 2, Mark Loretta 1, Turner Ward 1.

TOP DRAFT CHOICES

1. **Geoff Jenkins,** OF, University of Southern California.
2. **Mike Pasqualicchio,** LHP, Lamar University.
3. **Greg Schaub,** RHP, Solanco H.S., Oxford, Pa.
4. **Jeff Alfano,** C, Mt. Whitney H.S., Visalia, Calif.
5. **Jared Camp,** RHP, Indian River (Fla.) J.C.
6. **Toby Kominek,** OF, Central Michigan University.
7. **Sam Singleton,** SS, DuPont H.S., Rand, W.Va.
8. **Ryan Ritter,** 2B-OF, Georgia Tech.
9. **Mike Kinkade,** C-OF, Washington State University.
10. **Jason Dawsey,** LHP, Clemson University.

1996 SEASON *Milwaukee Brewers*

MINNESOTA TWINS
AMERICAN LEAGUE CENTRAL DIVISION

1996 TWINS SCHEDULE

Home games shaded.
* — All-Star Game at Veterans Stadium (Philadelphia)
N — Night game (any game starting after 5 p.m.)

MARCH
SUN	MON	TUE	WED	THU	FRI	SAT
31						

APRIL
SUN	MON	TUE	WED	THU	FRI	SAT
	1 DET	2 N DET	3 DET	4	5 N BAL	6 N BAL
7 BAL	8 BOS	9	10 N BOS	11 BOS N BAL	12 N BAL	13 BAL
14 BAL	15	16 N CLE	17 N CLE	18	19 N NY	20 N NY
21 NY	22 N BOS	23 BOS	24 DET	25 DET N	26 N NY	27 NY
28 NY	29 N KC	30 N KC				

MAY
SUN	MON	TUE	WED	THU	FRI	SAT
			1 N KC	2	3 N CAL	4 N CAL
5 CAL	6 N SEA	7 N SEA	8 SEA	9	10 N OAK	11 OAK
12 OAK	13	14 N TOR	15 N TOR	16 TOR	17 N MIL	18 N MIL
19 MIL	20 N TEX	21 N TEX	22 TEX	23 N TOR	24 N TOR	25 TOR
26 TOR	27	28 N MIL	29 MIL	30 N TEX	31 N TEX	

JUNE
SUN	MON	TUE	WED	THU	FRI	SAT
						1 N TEX
2 TEX	3 N CAL	4 N CAL	5 N CAL	6	7 N OAK	8 N OAK
9 N OAK	10 N SEA	11 N SEA	12 N SEA	13	14 N DET	15 N DET
16 DET	17 N NY	18 N NY	19 NY	20 N DET	21 N DET	22 DET
23 DET	24 N NY	25 N NY	26 NY	27	28 N KC	29 N KC
30 KC						

JULY
SUN	MON	TUE	WED	THU	FRI	SAT
	1 N CHI	2 N CHI	3 N CHI	4 N KC	5 N KC	6 KC
7 KC	8 *	9 * ALL-STAR GAME	10	11 N CLE	12 N CLE	13 CLE
14 CLE	15 N CHI	16 N CHI	17 CHI	18 N CLE	19 N CLE	20 CLE
21 CLE	22 N BAL	23 N BAL	24 N BAL	25 N BOS	26 N BOS	27 BOS
28 BOS	29	30 N BAL	31 N BAL			

AUGUST
SUN	MON	TUE	WED	THU	FRI	SAT
				1 BAL	2 N BOS	3 N BOS
4 BOS	5	6 N CAL	7 N CAL	8 N CAL	9 N SEA	10 N SEA
11 SEA	12 N OAK	13 N OAK	14 OAK	15	16 N TOR	17 N TOR
18 TOR	19 N MIL	20 N MIL	21 MIL	22 N TEX	23 N TEX	24 N TEX
25 TEX	26 N TOR	27 N TOR	28 N TOR	29 N MIL	30 N MIL	31 N MIL

SEPTEMBER
SUN	MON	TUE	WED	THU	FRI	SAT
1 MIL	2 N TEX	3 N TEX	4 N TEX	5	6 N CAL	7 N CAL
8 CAL	9 N OAK	10 N OAK	11 N OAK	12 N OAK	13 N SEA	14 SEA
15 SEA	16 N KC	17 N KC	18 N KC	19 N CHI	20 N CHI	21 CHI
22 CHI	23 N CLE	24 N CLE	25 N CLE	26	27 N CHI	28 N CHI
29 CHI						

1996 SEASON

CLUB DIRECTORY

Owner
Carl R. Pohlad

President
Jerry Bell

Chairman of executive committee
Howard Fox

Directors
Donald E. Benson
Paul R. Christen
James O. Pohlad
Robert C. Pohlad
William M. Pohlad
Robert E. Woolley

Vice president, general manager
Terry Ryan

Vice president, asst. general manager
Bill Smith

Vice president, sales
Bill Mahre

Chief financial officer
Kevin Mather

Vice president, operations
Matt Hoy

Director of minor leagues
Jim Rantz

Director of scouting
Mike Radcliff

Director of baseball operations
Rob Antony

Traveling secretary
Remzi Kiratli

Manager, media relations
Sean Harlin

Club physicians
Dr. Leonard J. Michienzi
Dr. John Steubs

Scouts
Ellsworth Brown
Ray Coley
Gene DeBoer
Cal Ermer
Marty Esposito
Vern Followell
Earl Frishman
Scott Groot
Bill Harford
Deron Johnson
John Leavitt
Joel Lepel
Bill Lohr
Bill Milos
Kevin Murphy
Tim O'Neil
Mark Quimuyog
Clair Rierson
Eddie Robinson
Edwin Rodriguez
Mike Ruth
Ricky Taylor
Brad Weitzel
John Wilson

International scouts
Enrique Brito
Howard Norsetter
Johnny Sierra

MINOR LEAGUE AFFILIATES

Class	Team	League	Manager
AAA	Salt Lake	Pacific Coast	Phil Roof
AA	Hardware City	Eastern	Al Newman
A	Fort Myers	Florida State	John Russell
A	Fort Wayne	Midwest	Dan Rohn
Rookie	Elizabethton	Appalachian	Jose Maizon
Rookie	Gulf Coast Twins	Gulf Coast	Mike Boulanger

BROADCAST INFORMATION
Radio: WCCO-AM (830).
TV: WCCO-TV (Channel 4).
Cable TV: Midwest Sports Channel.

SPRING TRAINING
Ballpark (city): Lee County Sports Complex (Fort Myers, Fla.).
Ticket information: 800-33-TWINS.

SPRING TRAINING ROSTER

Manager—Tom Kelly (10).
Coaches—Terry Crowley (46), Ron Gardenhire (35), Rick Stelmaszek (43), Dick Such (42), Scott Ullger (45).

No.	PITCHERS	B/T	Ht./Wt.	Born	1995 clubs
38	Aguilera, Rick	R/R	6-5/203	12-31-61	Minnesota, Boston
53	Barcelo, Marc	R/R	6-3/215	1-10-72	Salt Lake
49	Gandarillas, Gus	R/R	6-0/183	7-19-71	Salt Lake, New Britain
18	Guardado, Eddie	R/L	6-0/193	10-2-70	Minnesota
31	Hansell, Greg	R/R	6-5/215	3-12-71	Los Angeles, Albuquerque, Salt Lake
32	Hawkins, LaTroy	R/R	6-5/193	12-21-72	Minnesota, Salt Lake
39	Jacobsen, Joe	R/R	6-3/225	12-26-71	Vero Beach, San Bernardino
52	Klingenbeck, Scott	R/R	6-2/205	2-3-71	Rochester, Baltimore, Minnesota
20	Mahomes, Pat	R/R	6-4/212	8-9-70	Minnesota
19	Naulty, Dan	R/R	6-6/211	1-6-70	Salt Lake
56	Parra, Jose	R/R	5-11/165	11-28-72	Albuquerque, Los Angeles, Minnesota
59	Radke, Brad	R/R	6-2/186	10-27-72	Minnesota
30	Ritchie, Todd	R/R	6-3/190	11-7-71	New Britain
54	Roberts, Brett	R/R	6-7/230	3-24-70	New Britain
47	Robertson, Rich	L/L	6-4/175	9-15-68	Salt Lake, Minnesota
33	Rodriguez, Frank	R/R	6-0/195	12-11-72	Boston, Pawtucket, Minnesota
22	Serafini, Dan	B/L	6-1/180	1-25-74	New Britain, Salt Lake
41	Stevens, Dave	R/R	6-3/205	3-4-70	Minnesota
48	Trinidad, Hector	R/R	6-2/190	9-8-73	New Britain
51	Watkins, Scott	L/L	6-3/180	5-15-70	Salt Lake, Minnesota

No.	CATCHERS	B/T	Ht./Wt.	Born	1995 clubs
27	Durant, Mike	R/R	6-2/200	9-14-69	Salt Lake
24	Myers, Greg	L/R	6-2/215	4-14-66	California
9	Walbeck, Matt	B/R	5-11/188	10-2-69	Minnesota

No.	INFIELDERS	B/T	Ht./Wt.	Born	1995 clubs
8	Coomer, Ron	R/R	5-11/195	11-18-66	Albuquerque, Minnesota
7	Hocking, Denny	B/R	5-10/174	4-2-70	Salt Lake, Minnesota
15	Hollins, Dave	B/R	6-1/210	5-25-66	Philadelphia, Boston
11	Knoblauch, Chuck	R/R	5-9/181	7-7-68	Minnesota
2	Meares, Pat	R/R	6-0/188	9-6-68	Minnesota
4	Molitor, Paul	R/R	6-0/190	8-22-56	Toronto
17	Reboulet, Jeff	R/R	6-0/171	4-30-64	Minnesota
23	Roper, Chad	R/R	6-1/210	3-29-74	New Britain
37	Stahoviak, Scott	L/R	6-5/222	3-6-70	Salt Lake, Minnesota

No.	OUTFIELDERS	B/T	Ht./Wt.	Born	1995 clubs
25	Becker, Rich	B/L	5-10/199	2-1-72	Salt Lake, Minnesota
40	Cordova, Marty	R/R	6-0/193	7-10-69	Minnesota
44	Johnson, J.J.	R/R	6-0/195	8-31-73	Sarasota, Trenton
26	Latham, Chris	B/R	6-0/195	5-26-73	Vero Beach, San Antonio, Albuquerque
50	Lawton, Matt	L/R	5-10/196	11-3-71	New Britain, Minnesota
55	Ogden, Jamie	L/L	6-5/233	1-19-72	New Britain
34	Puckett, Kirby	R/R	5-9/233	3-14-61	Minnesota

BALLPARK INFORMATION

Ballpark (capacity, surface)
Hubert H. Humphrey Metrodome (56,783, artificial)

Address
501 Chicago Ave. South
Minneapolis, MN 55415

Business phone
612-375-1366

Ticket information
612-375-7444

Ticket prices
$17 (VIP level)
$15 (lower deck club level)
$12 (lower deck reserved)
$11 (upper deck club level)
$10 (upper deck reserved)
$7 (g.a., lower left field)
$4 (g.a., upper deck)

Field dimensions (from home plate)
To left field at foul line, 343 feet
To center field, 408 feet
To right field at foul line, 327 feet

First game played
April 6, 1982 (Mariners 11, Twins 7)

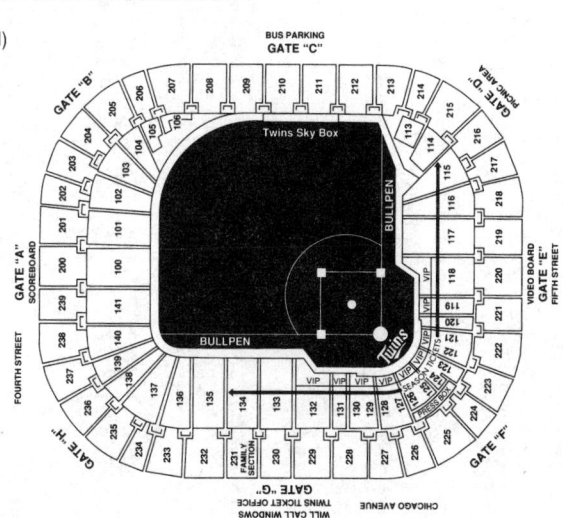

DAY BY DAY

Date	Opp.	Res.	Score	(inn.*)	Hits	Opp. hits	Winning pitcher	Losing pitcher	Save	Record	Pos.	GB
4-26	At Bos.	L	0-9		2	14	Sele	Erickson		0-1	T4th	1
4-27	Bal.	W	7-4		9	10	Stevens	Pennington	Aguilera	1-1	4th	1
4-28	Bal.	W	12-9		17	11	Guthrie	Benitez	Aguilera	2-1	2nd	1
4-29	Bal.	L	7-13		7	15	K. Brown	Hawkins		2-2	2nd	1
4-30	Bal.	L	3-6		6	8	Rhodes	Erickson	Jones	2-3	4th	2
5-2	K.C.	L	3-4		8	7	Gubicza	Tapani	Montgomery	2-4	4th	3
5-3	K.C.	W	10-9		15	13	Stevens	Meacham	Aguilera	3-4	4th	3
5-4	K.C.	L	0-6		7	8	Appier	Hawkins		3-5	4th	3
5-5	At Cle.	L	1-5		5	9	Nagy	Erickson	Mesa	3-6	4th	3
5-6	At Cle.	W	5-2		10	8	Radke	Black	Aguilera	4-6	4th	3
5-7	At Cle.	L	9-10	(17)	18	26	Poole	Guthrie		4-7	4th	4
5-8	At Chi.	L	2-4		12	6	Fernandez	Mahomes	Hernandez	4-8	4th	4½
5-9	At Chi.	L	1-6		2	9	Abbott	Hawkins		4-9	5th	4½
5-10	At Chi.	L	7-8		9	8	McCaskill	Guthrie	Hernandez	4-10	5th	5½
5-12	Oak.	W	9-5		13	10	Tapani	Stewart		5-10	5th	5½
5-13	Oak.	L	5-13		13	16	Acre	Mahomes	Corsi	5-11	5th	5½
5-14	Oak.	L	3-12		9	12	Stottlemyre	Radke		5-12	5th	6½
5-15	Cal.	W	9-6		14	11	Erickson	Sanderson	Aguilera	6-12	5th	6
5-16	Cal.	L	6-9		8	14	Bielecki	Guardado	Smith	6-13	5th	7
5-17	Cal.	W	7-3		10	9	Tapani	Finley		7-13	5th	6½
5-18	Cal.	L	9-15		14	16	Boskie	Mahomes		7-14	5th	6½
5-19	Sea.	W	8-6		12	11	Radke	Davis	Aguilera	8-14	5th	6½
5-20	Sea.	L	6-10		10	15	Belcher	Erickson		8-15	5th	7½
5-21	Sea.	L	2-5		6	8	Johnson	Tapani	Ayala	8-16	5th	8½
5-23	At Det.	L	4-6	(7)	8	8	Wells	Guardado		8-17	5th	9
5-24	At Det.	L	3-14		5	18	Moore	Radke		8-18	5th	9
5-25	At Det.	W	4-3		11	7	Guthrie	Boever	Aguilera	9-18	5th	8½
5-26	Tex.	L	5-6		13	12	Tewksbury	Tapani	Russell	9-19	5th	9½
5-27	Tex.	L	1-3		10	10	Rogers	Guardado	Russell	9-20	5th	9½
5-28	Tex.	L	2-4		6	10	Pavlik	Radke	McDowell	9-21	5th	10½
5-29	At Mil.	W	7-5		11	7	Erickson	Miranda	Aguilera	10-21	5th	10½
5-30	At Mil.	L	3-5		9	11	Roberson	Tapani	Lloyd	10-22	5th	11½
5-31	At Mil.	L	1-8		8	13	Scanlan	Guardado		10-23	5th	12½
6-1	At Tex.	L	3-6		8	11	Rogers	Radke	Russell	10-24	5th	13½
6-2	At Tex.	L	5-6		9	10	McDowell	Aguilera		10-25	5th	13½
6-3	At Tex.	W	4-0		12	6	Tapani	Gross		11-25	5th	13½
6-4	At Tex.	L	2-7		5	11	Oliver	Guardado		11-26	5th	14½
6-6	Mil.	L	5-13		9	14	Scanlan	Radke		11-27	5th	16
6-7	Mil.	L	3-6		11	8	Miranda	Erickson	Rightnowar	11-28	5th	17
6-8	Det.	W	9-2		14	7	Tapani	Moore		12-28	5th	17
6-9	Det.	L	5-6		9	8	Doherty	Guthrie	Henneman	12-29	5th	18
6-10	Det.	L	5-7		16	12	Bergman	Trombley	Henneman	12-30	5th	18
6-11	Det.	L	2-8		7	12	Lira	Radke	Boever	12-31	5th	19
6-12	At Cal.	L	1-9		5	10	Finley	Guardado		12-32	5th	20
6-13	At Cal.	L	2-7		8	13	Boskie	Tapani		12-33	5th	21
6-14	At Cal.	W	8-5		14	13	Erickson	Butcher	Aguilera	13-33	5th	21
6-16	At Sea.	W	10-1		13	5	Radke	Johnson		14-33	5th	20
6-17	At Sea.	L	4-6		7	6	Bosio	Trombley	Ayala	14-34	5th	21
6-18	At Sea.	L	1-2		5	8	Risley	Tapani		14-35	5th	21
6-19	At Oak.	W	8-5	(10)	10	11	Aguilera	Corsi		15-35	5th	21
6-20	At Oak.	L	2-5		11	10	Ontiveros	Mahomes	Eckersley	15-36	5th	22
6-21	At Oak.	W	3-2		9	6	Stevens	Corsi	Aguilera	16-36	5th	21
6-23	At K.C.	L	0-4		4	6	Appier	Tapani		16-37	5th	21
6-24	At K.C.	W	6-5		9	11	Guthrie	Pichardo	Aguilera	17-37	5th	20
6-26	Chi.	L	5-6		12	11	Keyser	Radke	Hernandez	17-38	5th	20½
6-27	Chi.	L	6-8		13	12	Abbott	Harris		17-39	5th	21½
6-28	Chi.	L	3-4		7	8	Bere	Tapani	Dibble	17-40	5th	22½
6-29	Cle.	L	5-10		10	16	Black	Erickson		17-41	4th	23½
6-30	Cle.	L	1-4		6	10	Martinez	Trombley	Mesa	17-42	5th	24½
7-1	Cle.	W	6-5		6	12	Radke	Ogea	Aguilera	18-42	5th	23½
7-2	Cle.	L	0-7		7	14	Clark	Harris		18-43	5th	24½
7-3	At Bal.	L	4-9		9	11	Mussina	Tapani		18-44	5th	25½
7-4	At Bal.	W	6-3		11	7	Erickson	Klingenbeck		19-44	5th	24½
7-5	At Bal.	W	8-2		12	7	Trombley	Rhodes		20-44	5th	24½
7-6	Bos.	W	6-4		11	9	Radke	Smith	Stevens	21-44	5th	24½
7-7	Bos.	L	4-5		10	9	Belinda	Guardado	Aguilera	21-45	5th	24½
7-8	Bos.	W	9-5		11	5	Guthrie	Belinda		22-45	5th	24½
7-9	Bos.	L	0-7		4	10	Wakefield	Rodriguez		22-46	5th	24½
7-13	At N.Y.	L	2-7		5	14	McDowell	Tapani		22-47	5th	25
7-14	At N.Y.	W	11-4		17	10	Radke	Hitchcock		23-47	5th	25½
7-15	At N.Y.	W	8-5		16	9	Guardado	Kamieniecki		24-47	5th	25½

Date	Opp.	Res.	Score	(inn.*)	Hits	Opp. hits	Winning pitcher	Losing pitcher	Save	Record	Pos.	GB
7-16	At N.Y.	L	1-5		7	10	M. Rivera	Trombley		24-48	5th	26$\frac{1}{2}$
7-17	Tor.	L	3-6		12	10	Leiter	Harris	Castillo	24-49	5th	26$\frac{1}{2}$
7-18	Tor.	L	0-7		4	14	Cone	Tapani		24-50	5th	27$\frac{1}{2}$
7-19	Bal.	W	5-3		8	5	Radke	McDonald	Stevens	25-50	5th	27$\frac{1}{2}$
7-20	Bal.	W	5-2		8	5	Rodriguez	Erickson	Stevens	26-50	5th	27$\frac{1}{2}$
7-21	At Bos.	L	5-13		11	17	Smith	Trombley	Hudson	26-51	5th	28$\frac{1}{2}$
7-22	At Bos.	W	8-7		13	12	Guthrie	Suppan	Stevens	27-51	5th	28$\frac{1}{2}$
7-23	At Bos.	W	8-3		9	11	Tapani	Clemens		28-51	5th	28$\frac{1}{2}$
7-24	At Bos.	L	1-4		9	7	Wakefield	Radke	Aguilera	28-52	5th	29$\frac{1}{2}$
7-25	At Tor.	W	7-3		14	5	Rodriguez	Guzman		29-52	5th	28$\frac{1}{2}$
7-26	At Tor.	L	2-6		8	9	Hentgen	Trombley		29-53	5th	28$\frac{1}{2}$
7-27	At Tor.	L	2-9		7	12	Hurtado	Harris		29-54	5th	28$\frac{1}{2}$
7-28	N.Y.	W	5-3		6	8	Tapani	McDowell		30-54	5th	28$\frac{1}{2}$
7-29	N.Y.	L	2-4		6	8	Cone	Radke	Wetteland	30-55	5th	28$\frac{1}{2}$
7-30	N.Y.	L	4-7		11	7	Kamieniecki	Rodriguez	Wetteland	30-56	5th	29$\frac{1}{2}$
8-1	At Cle.	W	6-5		12	10	Mahomes	Tavarez	Stevens	31-56	5th	28$\frac{1}{2}$
8-2	At Cle.	L	6-12		13	15	Clark	Harris		31-57	5th	29$\frac{1}{2}$
8-3	At Cle.	L	4-6		9	10	Hill	Radke	Mesa	31-58	5th	30$\frac{1}{2}$
8-4	K.C.	L	4-12		8	13	Meacham	Mahomes	Montgomery	31-59	5th	31$\frac{1}{2}$
8-5	K.C.	W	13-8		16	11	Trombley	Jacome		32-59	5th	31$\frac{1}{2}$
8-6	K.C.	L	1-11		4	15	Gubicza	Klingenbeck		32-60	5th	31$\frac{1}{2}$
8-7	Oak.	W	9-6		8	9	Mahomes	Reyes	Stevens	33-60	5th	31
8-8	Oak.	W	5-3		11	4	Radke	Prieto	Stevens	34-60	5th	30
8-9	Oak.	L	3-6	(10)	7	9	Mohler	Stevens	Eckersley	34-61	5th	30
8-11	Cal.	L	5-8		9	9	James	Guardado	Smith	34-62	5th	32
8-12	Cal.	W	6-4		12	7	Parra	Harkey	Stevens	35-62	5th	31
8-13	Cal.	L	1-2		7	5	Abbott	Radke	Smith	35-63	5th	31
8-14	Sea.	L	2-6		7	7	Benes	Trombley	Nelson	35-64	5th	32
8-15	Sea.	W	7-6		13	12	O. Munoz	Ayala		36-64	5th	31
8-16	Sea.	L	4-6		9	10	Risley	Stevens	Ayala	36-65	5th	32
8-18	At Det.	L	1-3		9	7	Bergman	Parra	Doherty	36-66	5th	32$\frac{1}{2}$
8-19	At Det.	W	9-5		16	7	Radke	Nitkowski	Mahomes	37-66	5th	32$\frac{1}{2}$
8-20	At Det.	W	8-7	(10)	14	11	Mahomes	Doherty		38-66	5th	32$\frac{1}{2}$
8-21	At Tex.	L	5-12		11	12	Darwin	Klingenbeck		38-67	5th	33$\frac{1}{2}$
8-22	At Tex.	W	9-4		10	10	Rodriguez	Pavlik		39-67	5th	32$\frac{1}{2}$
8-23	At Tex.	L	1-9		9	12	Witt	Parra		39-68	5th	33$\frac{1}{2}$
8-24	At Mil.	L	3-5		9	8	Bones	Radke	Fetters	39-69	5th	34
8-25	At Mil.	L	3-6		7	10	Karl	Trombley	Wegman	39-70	5th	35
8-26	At Mil.	L	6-7	(10)	11	10	Slusarski	Stevens		39-71	5th	36
8-27	At Mil.	L	7-14		12	18	Scanlan	Rodriguez		39-72	5th	37
8-28	Tex.	W	4-3	(10)	13	9	Guardado	McDowell		40-72	5th	37
8-29	Tex.	W	2-0		6	3	Radke	Gross		41-72	5th	37
8-30	Tex.	W	6-2		12	6	Guardado	Rogers		42-72	5th	37
9-1	Mil.	W	9-5		12	8	Rodriguez	Wegman	Guardado	43-72	5th	37$\frac{1}{2}$
9-2	Mil.	W	6-5		11	8	Guardado	Slusarski		44-72	5th	36$\frac{1}{2}$
9-3	Mil.	L	6-7		13	7	Dibble	Mahomes	Fetters	44-73	5th	37$\frac{1}{2}$
9-4	Mil.	W	9-6		16	8	Trombley	Karl	Guardado	45-73	5th	36$\frac{1}{2}$
9-5	Det.	L	4-6		6	10	Nitkowski	O. Munoz	Christopher	45-74	5th	37$\frac{1}{2}$
9-6	Det.	W	9-1		8	4	Rodriguez	Maxcy		46-74	5th	37$\frac{1}{2}$
9-8	At Cal.	L	3-9		5	12	Langston	Parra		46-75	5th	39
9-9	At Cal.	L	5-6		11	11	Monteleone	Mahomes	Smith	46-76	5th	40
9-10	At Cal.	W	9-8	(10)	11	9	Stevens	Holzemer	Mahomes	47-76	5th	40
9-11	At Sea.	W	12-10		17	11	Mahomes	Nelson	Stevens	48-76	5th	39
9-12	At Sea.	L	3-14		14	13	Bosio	Rodriguez	Carmona	48-77	5th	39
9-13	At Sea.	L	4-7		6	8	Nelson	Mahomes	Charlton	48-78	5th	40
9-15	At Oak.	L	5-6		11	13	Stottlemyre	Mahomes		48-79	5th	40$\frac{1}{2}$
9-16	At Oak.	L	1-6		5	7	Wasdin	Radke		48-80	5th	41$\frac{1}{2}$
9-17	At Oak.	L	1-4		6	9	Van Poppel	Rodriguez		48-81	5th	41$\frac{1}{2}$
9-18†	At K.C.	L	7-16		13	20	Gubicza	Parra	Meacham	48-82		
9-18‡	At K.C.	W	10-4		16	12	Hawkins	Torres	Mahomes	49-82	5th	42
9-19	At K.C.	W	7-3		12	4	Robertson	Appier		50-82	5th	42
9-20	At K.C.	W	5-4	(12)	13	11	Stevens	Meacham		51-82	5th	41
9-21	At K.C.	W	5-2		10	8	Radke	Jacome		52-82	5th	40$\frac{1}{2}$
9-22	Chi.	L	4-5	(10)	8	12	McCaskill	Mahomes	Hernandez	52-83	5th	41$\frac{1}{2}$
9-23	Chi.	L	4-14		7	20	Alvarez	Parra		52-84	5th	42$\frac{1}{2}$
9-24	Chi.	W	4-3		10	5	Hawkins	Simas		53-84	5th	41$\frac{1}{2}$
9-25	Chi.	W	6-1		7	4	Robertson	Bere		54-84	5th	41
9-26	Cle.	W	13-4		17	9	Trombley	Nagy		55-84	5th	40
9-27	Cle.	L	6-9		9	15	Hill	Radke	Mesa	55-85	5th	41
9-28	Cle.	L	4-12		7	17	Martinez	Rodriguez		55-86	5th	42
9-29	At Chi.	L	3-4		6	8	Karchner	Guardado		55-87	5th	43
9-30	At Chi.	W	7-6		10	9	O. Munoz	Bere	Stevens	56-87	5th	43
10-1	At Chi.	L	1-2	(11)	5	7	Hernandez	Stevens		56-88	5th	44

Monthly records: April (2-3), May (8-20), June (7-19), July (13-14), August (12-16), September (14-15), October (0-1).
*Innings, if other than nine. †First game of doubleheader. ‡Second game of doubleheader.

1996 SEASON *Minnesota Twins*

HIGHLIGHTS

High point: In a resurgence that came about when they got their young players in place, the Twins swept a three-game series against Texas in late August, took three of four against Milwaukee over Labor Day weekend and won four of five against Kansas City in mid-September to severely damage all three clubs' wild-card hopes.

Low point: Pick a date, any date. The Twins were 20 games out of first place by June 12, 25 back by July 13, 30 behind by August 3 and 40 back by September 9.

Turning point: The seventh inning of a game against Boston on July 6. Rick Aguilera was summoned from the bullpen to the dugout and told he had been traded to the Red Sox. It was the first move in the Twins' massive restructuring and indicated the club was looking past 1995. Starter Scott Erickson was dealt to Baltimore the next day.

Most valuable player: Second baseman Chuck Knoblauch. He was second in the league in hitting at .333 and contributed 11 homers and 46 stolen bases. All three figures were career highs.

Most valuable pitcher: Righthander Brad Radke. He made the jump from Class AA to the majors and became the Twins' most consistent pitcher, going 11-14. His ERA was 5.32 ERA, however.

Most improved player: Shortstop Pat Meares. One year after nearly losing his job to Denny Hocking, Meares developed into a solid all-around player. He was reliable defensively, hit a solid .269 and had a career-high 12 homers.

Most pleasant surprise: Outfielder Marty Cordova. He won the starting job in left field in spring training and never let up, winning A.L. Rookie of the Year honors after hitting .277 with 24 homers and 84 RBIs.

Biggest disappointment: Kevin Tapani, who went 6-11 with a 4.92 ERA and allowed 21 homers in 20 starts before being traded to Los Angeles on July 31. Erickson stumbled, too, and Pat Mahomes began the year in the starting rotation but was banished to the bullpen for good by the All-Star break.

Key injuries: Center fielder Alex Cole suffered a broken right leg, a dislocated ankle and torn ankle ligaments while trying to make a sliding catch in Milwaukee on May 30 and wasn't reactivated until September 19. Outfielder Jerald Clark strained a knee ligament in a game at Seattle in June; a month later, he reinjured the knee in his first game back and was lost for the season.

Notable: The Twins set club records for total players (46) and rookies (19) used in one season. . . . Minnesota got two victories all season from a left-handed starter—both by Rich Robertson in September.

—SCOTT MILLER

RECORDS

1995 regular-season record: 56-88 (5th in A.L. Central); 29-43 at home; 27-45 on road; 19-23 vs. East; 18-34 vs. Central; 19-31 vs. West; 19-26 vs. lefthanded starters; 37-62 vs. righthanded starters; 24-39 on grass; 32-49 on turf; 12-27 in daytime; 44-61 at night; 15-18 in one-run games; 5-5 in extra-inning games; 0-0-1 in doubleheaders.

Team record past five years: 365-378 (.491, ranks 10th in league in that span).

TEAM LEADERS

Batting average: Chuck Knoblauch (.333).
At-bats: Chuck Knoblauch, Kirby Puckett (538).
Runs: Chuck Knoblauch (107).
Hits: Chuck Knoblauch (179).
Total bases: Kirby Puckett (277).
Doubles: Kirby Puckett (39).
Triples: Chuck Knoblauch (8).
Home runs: Marty Cordova (24).
Runs batted in: Kirby Puckett (99).
Stolen bases: Chuck Knoblauch (46).
Slugging percentage: Kirby Puckett (.515).
On-base percentage: Chuck Knoblauch (.424).
Wins: Brad Radke (11).
Earned-run average: Brad Radke (5.32).
Complete games: Kevin Tapani (3).
Shutouts: Brad Radke, Kevin Tapani (1).
Saves: Rick Aguilera (12).
Innings pitched: Brad Radke (181.0).
Strikeouts: Kevin Tapani (88).

GAMES BY POSITION

Catcher: Matt Walbeck 113, Matt Merullo 46, Jeff Reboulet 1.
First base: Scott Stahoviak 69, Dan Masteller 48, Ron Coomer 22, David McCarty 18, Kevin Maas 8, Steve Dunn 3, Chip Hale 3, Pedro Munoz 3, Matt Merullo 2.
Second base: Chuck Knoblauch 136, Jeff Reboulet 15, Chip Hale 7, Brian Raabe 4, Kirby Puckett 1.
Third base: Scott Leius 112, Jeff Reboulet 22, Scott Stahoviak 22, Ron Coomer 13, Chip Hale 5, Brian Raabe 2, Kirby Puckett 1.
Shortstop: Pat Meares 114, Jeff Reboulet 39, Scott Leius 7, Denny Hocking 6, Chuck Knoblauch 2, Kirby Puckett 1.
Outfield: Marty Cordova 137, Kirby Puckett 109, Rich Becker 105, Pedro Munoz 25, Jerald Clark 23, Alex Cole 23, Dan Masteller 22, Matt Lawton 19, David McCarty 5, Pat Meares 3, Ron Coomer 1.
Designated hitter: Pedro Munoz 77, Kirby Puckett 28, Chip Hale 27, Matt Merullo 13, Kevin Maas 12, Dan Masteller 8, Ron Coomer 4, Bernardo Brito 3, Jerald Clark 3, Riccardo Ingram 3, Scott Leius 3, Alex Cole 2, Matt Lawton 1, Scott Stahoviak 1.

TOP DRAFT CHOICES

1. **Mark Redman,** LHP, University of Oklahoma.
2. **Jason Bell,** RHP, Oklahoma State University.
3. **A.J. Hinch,** C, Stanford University.
4. **Jay Hood,** SS, Germantown (Tenn.) H.S.
5. **Doug Mientkiewicz,** 1B, Florida State University.
6. **Shane Gunderson,** C-1B, University of Minnesota.
7. **Mike Moriarty,** SS, Seton Hall University.
8. **Will Rushing,** LHP, Georgia Southern University.
9. **Joe McHenry,** OF, Oakland H.S., Murfreesboro, Tenn.
10. **Kyle Kane,** OF, Linfield H.S., Temecula Valley, Calif.

NEW YORK YANKEES
AMERICAN LEAGUE EAST DIVISION

1996 YANKEES SCHEDULE

Home games shaded.
* — All-Star Game at Veterans Stadium (Philadelphia)
N — Night game (any game starting after 5 p.m.)

MARCH

SUN	MON	TUE	WED	THU	FRI	SAT
31						

APRIL

SUN	MON	TUE	WED	THU	FRI	SAT
	1 CLE	2	N 3 CLE	4 CLE	N 5 TEX	6 N TEX
7 N TEX	8	9 KC	10	11 KC	N 12 TEX	13 N TEX
14 TEX	15	N 16 MIL	17 MIL	18	N 19 MIN	20 N MIN
21 MIN	N 22 KC	N 23 KC	N 24 CLE	25 N CLE	N 26 MIN	27 MIN
28 MIN	29	N 30 BAL				

MAY

SUN	MON	TUE	WED	THU	FRI	SAT
			N 1 BAL	2 N CHI	3 N CHI	4 CHI
5 CHI	N 6 DET	N 7 DET	N 8 DET	N 9 DET	N 10 CHI	11 N CHI
12 CHI	13	N 14 SEA	15 N SEA	16	N 17 CAL	18 CAL
19 CAL	20	N 21 OAK	22 OAK	23 N OAK	N 24 SEA	25 N SEA
26 N SEA	27 N CAL	28 N CAL	29 N CAL	30	N 31 OAK	

JUNE

SUN	MON	TUE	WED	THU	FRI	SAT
						1 OAK
2 OAK	3	N 4 TOR	N 5 TOR	N 6 TOR	N 7 DET	8 DET
9 DET	N 10 TOR	N 11 TOR	N 12 TOR	N 13 CLE	N 14 CLE	15 CLE
16 CLE	N 17 MIN	N 18 MIN	19 MIN	20	N 21 CLE	22 CLE
23 CLE	24 N MIN	N 25 MIN	26 MIN	N 27 BAL	N 28 BAL	29 BAL
30 BAL						

JULY

SUN	MON	TUE	WED	THU	FRI	SAT
	N 1 BOS	N 2 BOS	3 BOS	N 4 MIL	N 5 MIL	6 MIL
7 MIL	8 *	9 ALL-STAR GAME	10	N 11 BAL	N 12 BAL	13 N BAL
14 BAL	N 15 BOS	N 16 BOS	N 17 BOS	18 N MIL	N 19 MIL	20 MIL
21 MIL	N 22 TEX	N 23 TEX	24 TEX	25 N KC	N 26 KC	27 KC
28 KC	29	N 30 TEX	N 31 TEX			

AUGUST

SUN	MON	TUE	WED	THU	FRI	SAT
				N 1 TEX	N 2 KC	3 KC
4 KC	N 5 KC	N 6 CHI	N 7 CHI	8	N 9 DET	10 DET
11 DET	N 12 CHI	13 CHI	14	15	N 16 SEA	17 SEA
18 SEA	N 19 SEA	N 20 CAL	21 CAL	N 22 CAL	N 23 OAK	24 N OAK
25 OAK	26 N SEA	27 N SEA	28 N SEA	29 N CAL	N 30 CAL	31 N CAL

SEPTEMBER

SUN	MON	TUE	WED	THU	FRI	SAT
1 CAL	2 OAK	N 3 OAK	N 4 OAK	5	N 6 TOR	7 N TOR
8 TOR	9	N 10 DET	N 11 DET	12 DET	N 13 TOR	14 TOR
15 TOR	N 16 TOR	N 17 BAL	N 18 BAL	N 19 BAL	N 20 BOS	21 BOS
22 N BOS	23	N 24 MIL	N 25 MIL	N 26 MIL	N 27 BOS	28 BOS
29 BOS						

1996 SEASON
CLUB DIRECTORY

Principal owner
George M. Steinbrenner

General partner
Joseph A. Molloy

Executive vice president, general counsel
David W. Sussman

Senior vice president
Arthur Richman

Vice president and general manager
Robert Watson

V.p., finance, chief financial officer
Barry Pincus

Vice president
Ed Weaver

Director of office admin. and services
Harvey C. Winston

Vice president, ticket operations
Frank Swaine

V.p., player development and scouting
Bill Livesey

Asst. g.m., baseball operations
Brian Cashman

Major League administrator
Tom May

Assistant, baseball operations
Gene Kechane

Dir. of player development and scouting
Mitch Lukevics

Director of scouting
Lin Garrett

Traveling secretary
David Szen

Director of stadium operations
Sonny Hight

Director of customer services
Joel S. White

Director of video operations
John J. Franzone

Executive director of ticket operations
Jeff Kline

Ticket director
Ken Skrypek

Director of media relations and publicity
To be announced

Asst. dir. of media relations and publicity
John Thursby

Director of marketing
Debbie Tymon

Director of special events
Bob Pelegrino

Dir. of public and com. relations, N.Y.
Brian Smith

Director of publications
Greg Mazzola

Minor league instructors
Darrell Evans
Chuck Estrada
Mick Kelleher
Roy White

Team physician
Dr. Stuart Hershon

Head trainer
Gene J. Monahan

Assistant trainer
Steve Donohue

Cross-checkers
John Cox, Cotton Nye, Donnie Rowland

Area supervisor scouts
Joe Arnold, Mark Batchko, Rudolfo Camejo, Stephen Chandler, Larry D'Amato, Lee Elder, Joel Grampietro, Tim Kelly, Mel Nelson, Greg Orr, Scott Pleis, Cesar Presbott, Joe Robison, Reggie Waller, Leon Wurth, Gary York

Foreign scouts
Mike Baker, Gordon Blakely, Dick Groch, Philip Elhage, J. Robert Grove, Ron Harvey, Karl Heron, Ruddy Jabalera, Mike LaBossiere, Francisco Lugo, Victor Mata, Manuel Medina, Jorge Oquendo, Raul Ortega, Carlos Paz, Jim Patterson, Jose Quintero, Arquimedes Rojas, Marc Picard, Bruce Ross, Bill Saunders, Dennis Springenatic, Dale Tilleman, Modesto Ulloa

MINOR LEAGUE AFFILIATES

Class	Team	League	Manager
AAA	Columbus	International	Stump Merrill
AA	Norwich	Eastern	Jim Essian
A	Tampa	Florida State	Trey Hillman
A	Greensboro	South Atlantic	Ricky Patterson
A	Oneonta	New York-Pennsylvania	Rob Thompson
Rookie	Gulf Coast Yankees	Gulf Coast	Ken Dominguez

BROADCAST INFORMATION
Radio: WABC-AM (770).
TV: WPIX (Channel 11).
Cable TV: Madison Square Garden Network.

SPRING TRAINING
Ballpark (city): Fort Lauderdale Stadium (Fort Lauderdale, Fla.).
Ticket information: 305-776-1921.

1996 SEASON New York Yankees

SPRING TRAINING ROSTER

Manager—Joe Torre.
Coaches—Jose Cardenal, Chris Chambliss, Tony Cloninger (40), Willie Randolph (30), Mel Stottlemyre, Don Zimmer.

No.	PITCHERS	B/T	Ht./Wt.	Born	1995 clubs
31	Boehringer, Brian	B/R	6-2/190	1-8-70	New York A.L., Columbus
	Cone, David	L/R	6-1/190	1-2-63	Toronto, New York A.L.
67	Croghan, Andy	R/R	6-5/220	10-26-69	Columbus
	Cumberland, Chris	R/L	6-1/190	1-15-73	Gulf Coast Yankees, Tampa
52	Hutton, Mark	R/R	6-6/240	2-6-70	Columbus
28	Kamieniecki, Scott	R/R	6-0/195	4-19-64	New York A.L., Tampa, Columbus
22	Key, Jimmy	R/L	6-1/185	4-22-61	New York A.L.
	Mecir, Jim	B/R	6-1/195	5-16-70	Tacoma, Seattle
	Mendoza, Ramiro	R/R	6-2/154	6-15-72	Norwich, Columbus
43	Nelson, Jeff	R/R	6-8/235	11-17-66	Seattle
60	Ojala, Kirt	L/L	6-2/210	12-24-68	Columbus
33	Perez, Melido	R/R	6-4/210	2-15-66	New York A.L., Norwich
46	Pettitte, Andy	L/L	6-5/235	6-15-72	Columbus, New York A.L.
58	Rivera, Mariano	R/R	6-4/168	11-29-69	Columbus, New York A.L.
	Rogers, Kenny	L/L	6-1/205	11-10-64	Texas
47	Taylor, Brien	L/L	6-3/220	12-26-71	Gulf Coast Yankees
	Wallace, Kent	L/R	6-3/195	8-22-70	Norwich, Columbus
35	Wetteland, John	R/R	6-2/215	8-21-66	New York A.L.
27	Wickman, Bob	R/R	6-1/212	2-6-69	New York A.L.

No.	CATCHERS	B/T	Ht./Wt.	Born	1995 clubs
	Figga, Mike	R/R	6-0/200	7-31-70	Norwich, Columbus
	Girardi, Joe	R/R	5-11/195	10-14-64	Colorado
13	Leyritz, Jim	R/R	6-0/195	12-27-63	New York A.L.
62	Posada, Jorge	B/R	6-2/205	8-17-71	Columbus, New York A.L.
	Ronan, Marc	L/R	6-2/190	9-19-69	Louisville

No.	INFIELDERS	B/T	Ht./Wt.	Born	1995 clubs
12	Boggs, Wade	L/R	6-2/197	6-15-58	New York A.L.
	Duncan, Mariano	R/R	6-0/185	3-13-63	Philadelphia, Cincinnati
50	Eenhoorn, Robert	R/R	6-3/185	2-9-68	Columbus, New York A.L.
2	Fernandez, Tony	B/R	6-2/175	6-30-62	New York A.L.
56	Fox, Andy	L/R	6-4/205	1-12-71	Norwich, Columbus
2	Jeter, Derek	R/R	6-3/185	6-26-74	Columbus, New York A.L.
14	Kelly, Pat	R/R	6-0/182	10-14-67	New York A.L., Gulf Coast Yankees, Tampa
24	Martinez, Tino	L/R	6-2/210	12-7-67	Seattle
66	Seefried, Tate	L/R	6-4/205	4-22-72	Columbus, Norwich

No.	OUTFIELDERS	B/T	Ht./Wt.	Born	1995 clubs
54	Luke, Matt	L/L	6-5/220	2-26-71	Norwich, Columbus
21	O'Neill, Paul	L/L	6-4/215	2-25-63	New York A.L.
30	Raines, Tim	B/R	5-8/186	9-16-59	Chicago A.L.
	Rivera, Ruben	R/R	6-3/200	11-14-73	Norwich, Columbus, New York A.L.
25	Sierra, Ruben	B/R	6-1/200	10-6-65	Oakland, New York A.L.
51	Williams, Bernie	B/R	6-2/205	9-13-68	New York A.L.
29	Williams, Gerald	R/R	6-2/190	8-10-66	New York A.L.

BALLPARK INFORMATION

Ballpark (capacity, surface)
Yankee Stadium (57,545, grass)

Address
Yankee Stadium
E. 161 St. and River Ave.
Bronx, NY 10451

Business phone
718-293-4300

Ticket information
718-293-6000

Ticket prices
$19 (lower and loge box seats)
$16.50 (tier box seats)
$16 (lower reserves)
$11.50 (tier reserves)
$2 (senior citizens)
$6 (bleachers)

Field dimensions (from home plate)
To left field at foul line, 312 feet
To center field, 410 feet
To right field at foul line, 310 feet

First game played
April 18, 1923 (Yankees 4, Red Sox 1)

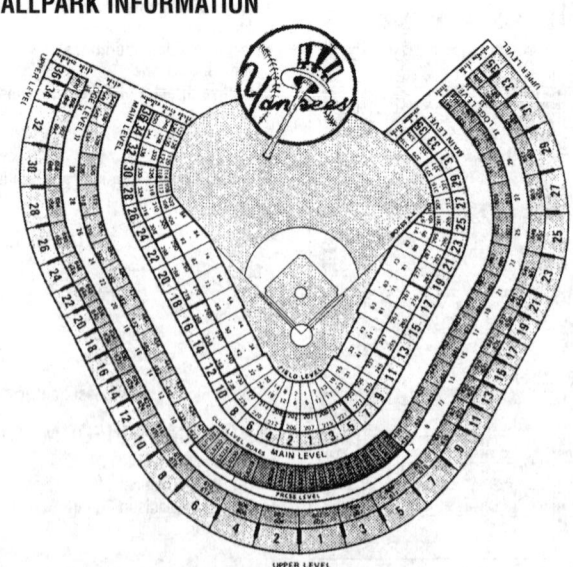

DAY BY DAY

Date	Opp.	Res.	Score	(inn.*)	Hits	Opp. hits	Winning pitcher	Losing pitcher	Save	Record	Pos.	GB
4-26	Tex.	W	8-6		14	10	Key	Rogers	Wetteland	1-0	T1st	...
4-28	At K.C.	W	4-1		10	8	McDowell	Gubicza	Wetteland	2-0	T1st	...
4-29	At K.C.	W	10-3		11	8	Perez	Gordon		3-0	T1st	...
4-30	At K.C.	L	3-9		4	12	Appier	Kamieniecki		3-1	T1st	...
5-1	Bos.	W	5-3		11	9	Howe	Lilliquist	Wetteland	4-1	1st	+1
5-2	Bos.	L	0-8		3	8	Eshelman	Hitchcock		4-2	T1st	...
5-3	Bos.	W	4-3	(13)	16	8	Wickman	Pierce		5-2	1st	+1/2
5-4	Bos.	W	5-3		10	6	Ausanio	Johnston	Wetteland	6-2	1st	+1
5-5	Mil.	W	6-4		9	9	Bankhead	Wegman	Wetteland	7-2	1st	+2
5-6	Mil.	L	2-5		8	10	Bones	Key	Lloyd	7-3	1st	+1
5-7	Mil.	L	1-9		7	14	Ignasiak	Hitchcock		7-4	T1st	...
5-9	At Tor.	L	6-9		12	14	Hentgen	McDowell		7-5	T2nd	1
5-10	At Tor.	W	6-4	(11)	14	12	Wetteland	Williams		8-5	2nd	1
5-11	At Tor.	W	12-11		15	14	Ausanio	Ward	Howe	9-5	2nd	1/2
5-12	At Bos.	W	12-2		11	4	Hitchcock	Sele		10-5	1st	+1/2
5-13	At Bos.	L	4-6		3	12	Eshelman	Wickman	Ryan	10-6	2nd	1/2
5-14	At Bos.	L	2-3		9	8	Pena	Howe		10-7	2nd	11/2
5-16	Cle.	L	5-10		8	15	Nagy	Key		10-8	2nd	21/2
5-19	Bal.	L	5-7		5	10	Mills	Wetteland	Jones	10-9	2nd	31/2
5-20	Bal.	W	7-2		7	4	Perez	Fernandez		11-9	2nd	21/2
5-21	Bal.	W	5-0		12	4	Hitchcock	McDonald		12-9	2nd	11/2
5-23	At Cal.	L	0-10		2	12	Finley	M. Rivera		12-10	2nd	21/2
5-24	At Cal.	L	1-3		7	4	Patterson	McDowell	Smith	12-11	2nd	21/2
5-25	At Cal.	L	2-15		6	12	Langston	Perez		12-12	2nd	21/2
5-26	At Oak.	L	3-4		4	3	Leiper	Hitchcock	Corsi	12-13	3rd	31/2
5-27	At Oak.	L	0-3		1	9	Ontiveros	Pettitte		12-14	3rd	41/2
5-28	At Oak.	W	4-1		10	8	M. Rivera	Harkey	Wetteland	13-14	2nd	31/2
5-29	At Sea.	L	7-8	(12)	11	18	Ayala	Bankhead		13-15	2nd	41/2
5-30	At Sea.	L	3-7		13	8	Nelson	Perez		13-16	3rd	51/2
5-31	At Sea.	L	9-11		13	13	Wells	MacDonald	Ayala	13-17	T3rd	61/2
6-2	Cal.	L	2-3		5	7	Finley	Pettitte	Smith	13-18	5th	71/2
6-3	Cal.	L	2-4		8	5	Boskie	McDowell	Smith	13-19	5th	81/2
6-4	Cal.	W	11-3		13	13	Perez	Langston		14-19	T4th	81/2
6-5	Oak.	L	5-11		10	13	Darling	Hitchcock		14-20	T4th	91/2
6-6	Oak.	L	6-8		14	9	Stottlemyre	M. Rivera	Eckersley	14-21	T4th	91/2
6-7	Oak.	W	6-1		14	5	Pettitte	Ontiveros		15-21	T3rd	91/2
6-8	Oak.	L	3-8		9	13	Harkey	McDowell		15-22	4th	91/2
6-9	Sea.	L	1-11		7	14	Belcher	Perez		15-23	4th	101/2
6-10	Sea.	L	2-3		6	7	Nelson	Howe	Ayala	15-24	5th	101/2
6-11	Sea.	W	10-7		13	12	Howe	Frey	Wetteland	16-24	T4th	91/2
6-12	At Det.	L	1-6		4	14	Wells	Pettitte		16-25	5th	91/2
6-13	At Det.	W	10-4		11	6	McDowell	Moore		17-25	T4th	91/2
6-14	At Det.	W	12-3		15	4	Perez	Ahearne		18-25	T4th	81/2
6-15	At Det.	L	2-9		7	10	Bergman	Boehringer		18-26	5th	9
6-16	At Cle.	W	4-2		6	6	Wickman	Poole	Wetteland	19-26	T3rd	8
6-17	At Cle.	L	4-7		9	12	Black	Pettitte	Mesa	19-27	T4th	8
6-18	At Cle.	W	9-5		12	11	McDowell	Nagy	Wetteland	20-27	4th	8
6-19	At Bal.	L	4-5		7	10	Klingenbeck	Perez	Jones	20-28	T4th	8
6-20	At Bal.	L	7-8		11	11	Oquist	Wickman	Jones	20-29	5th	8
6-21	At Bal.	W	2-1		6	5	Pettitte	Moyer	Wetteland	21-29	T3rd	8
6-23	Tor.	W	6-2		11	7	McDowell	Cone		22-29	3rd	71/2
6-24	Tor.	W	10-2		11	5	Perez	Guzman		23-29	3rd	71/2
6-25	Tor.	W	8-2		13	6	Hitchcock	Hentgen		24-29	3rd	61/2
6-26	Det.	W	7-3		13	8	Pettitte	Lira		25-29	3rd	61/2
6-27	Det.	W	7-1		10	7	MacDonald	Bohanon	Ausanio	26-29	3rd	61/2
6-28	Det.	L	4-8		9	14	Wells	McDowell		26-30	3rd	61/2
6-30	At Mil.	L	6-12		14	15	Roberson	Perez		26-31	3rd	7
7-1	At Mil.	W	3-1	(12)	10	8	Howe	Reyes	Wetteland	27-31	3rd	6
7-2	At Mil.	L	6-7		10	11	Sparks	Pettitte	Fetters	27-32	T3rd	7
7-3	At Chi.	W	8-4		11	6	McDowell	Radinsky		28-32	T3rd	7
7-4	At Chi.	W	4-1		8	4	M. Rivera	Fernandez		29-32	3rd	7
7-5	At Chi.	L	5-11		7	14	Alvarez	Boehringer	McCaskill	29-33	3rd	7
7-6	At Tex.	L	2-5		8	7	Pavlik	Hitchcock	Vosberg	29-34	3rd	7
7-7	At Tex.	L	0-10		6	15	Tewksbury	Pettitte		29-35	4th	8
7-8	At Tex.	W	7-3		11	6	J. McDowell	R. McDowell	Wetteland	30-35	4th	7
7-9	At Tex.	L	4-5	(12)	10	10	Vosberg	Howe		30-36	4th	8
7-12	K.C.	W	9-1		11	6	Pettitte	Haney		31-36	4th	71/2
7-13	Min.	W	7-2		14	5	McDowell	Tapani		32-36	4th	61/2
7-14	Min.	L	4-11		10	17	Radke	Hitchcock		32-37	4th	71/2
7-15	Min.	L	5-8		9	16	Guardado	Kamieniecki		32-38	4th	71/2
7-16	Min.	W	5-1		10	7	M. Rivera	Trombley		33-38	4th	61/2

Date	Opp.	Res.	Score	(inn.*)	Hits	Opp. hits	Winning pitcher	Losing pitcher	Save	Record	Pos.	GB
7-17	Chi.	T	1-1	(7)	2	9	......	......		33-38	4th	6
7-18†	Chi.	L	4-9		13	18	Abbott	Boehringer		33-39		
7-18‡	Chi.	L	4-11		11	19	Righetti	McDowell		33-40	4th	7¹/₂
7-19	K.C.	W	5-2		8	5	Hitchcock	Torres	Wetteland	34-40	4th	7¹/₂
7-20	K.C.	W	8-4		11	8	Howe	Brewer		35-40	4th	7¹/₂
7-21	Tex.	W	8-3		8	9	Eiland	Rogers	Wetteland	36-40	4th	7¹/₂
7-22	Tex.	W	7-4		9	7	Pettitte	Tewksbury	Wetteland	37-40	3rd	6¹/₂
7-23	Tex.	W	11-4		18	11	McDowell	Burrows		38-40	3rd	5¹/₂
7-24	Tex.	W	5-4		15	8	Howe	Whiteside		39-40	T2nd	5¹/₂
7-25	At K.C.	W	8-1		13	8	Kamieniecki	Appier		40-40	T2nd	4¹/₂
7-26	At K.C.	L	5-6		10	11	Pichardo	Wickman		40-41	3rd	5¹/₂
7-27	At K.C.	W	1-0		7	5	Pettitte	Gubicza	Wetteland	41-41	T2nd	4¹/₂
7-28	At Min.	L	3-5		8	6	Tapani	McDowell		41-42	3rd	5¹/₂
7-29	At Min.	W	4-2		8	6	Cone	Radke	Wetteland	42-42	T2nd	5¹/₂
7-30	At Min.	W	7-4		7	11	Kamieniecki	Rodriguez	Wetteland	43-42	T2nd	4¹/₂
8-1	Mil.	W	7-5		12	7	M. Rivera	Miranda	Wetteland	44-42	2nd	4¹/₂
8-2	Mil.	L	2-5		7	11	Sparks	McDowell	Fetters	44-43	2nd	4¹/₂
8-3	Mil.	W	5-4		7	6	Cone	Miranda	Wetteland	45-43	2nd	4¹/₂
8-4	At Det.	W	4-1		11	3	Kamieniecki	Lima	Wetteland	46-43	2nd	4¹/₂
8-5	At Det.	W	7-1		11	5	Hitchcock	Lira		47-43	2nd	4¹/₂
8-6	At Det.	L	5-6	(12)	8	13	Boever	Eiland		47-44	2nd	5¹/₂
8-7	Bal.	W	3-0		3	3	McDowell	Mussina		48-44	2nd	5¹/₂
8-8	Bal.	W	11-4		11	8	Cone	Krivda		49-44	2nd	5¹/₂
8-9	Bal.	L	2-7		6	10	Moyer	Kamieniecki		49-45	2nd	6¹/₂
8-10†	Cle.	L	9-10		16	13	Poole	Wetteland	Mesa	49-46		
8-10‡	Cle.	L	2-5		8	9	Ogea	Hitchcock	Mesa	49-47	2nd	8
8-11	Cle.	L	4-5	(11)	13	15	Tavarez	Wetteland	Mesa	49-48	2nd	9
8-12	Cle.	W	3-2		6	7	McDowell	Martinez		50-48	2nd	9
8-13	Cle.	W	4-1		10	6	Cone	Clark		51-48	2nd	9
8-14	At Bos.	L	3-9		8	13	Hanson	Kamieniecki		51-49	2nd	10
8-15	At Bos.	W	9-2		14	10	Hitchcock	Cormier		52-49	2nd	9
8-16	At Bos.	L	4-7		9	11	Gunderson	Wickman	Belinda	52-50	2nd	10
8-18	At Cal.	W	7-3		12	11	McDowell	Abbott	Wetteland	53-50	2nd	9¹/₂
8-19	At Cal.	L	3-5		7	9	Finley	Cone	Smith	53-51	2nd	10¹/₂
8-20	At Cal.	L	5-10		10	12	Langston	Hitchcock		53-52	2nd	11¹/₂
8-21	At Oak.	L	4-13		10	16	Stottlemyre	Pettitte		53-53	2nd	12¹/₂
8-22	At Oak.	L	2-6		5	10	Van Poppel	Kamieniecki		53-54	2nd	13¹/₂
8-23	At Oak.	L	1-2		8	5	Wojciechowski	McDowell	Eckersley	53-55	2nd	14¹/₂
8-24	At Sea.	L	7-9		9	9	Nelson	Wetteland		53-56	2nd	15¹/₂
8-25	At Sea.	L	4-7		11	7	Bosio	Pettitte		53-57	2nd	15¹/₂
8-26	At Sea.	L	0-7		3	12	Johnson	Hitchcock		53-58	2nd	15¹/₂
8-27	At Sea.	W	5-2		15	5	Kamieniecki	Belcher	Wetteland	54-58	2nd	15¹/₂
8-28	K.C.	L	3-4		9	9	Torres	McDowell	Montgomery	54-59	T2nd	16
8-29	Cal.	W	12-4		13	5	Cone	Finley		55-59	2nd	15
8-30	Cal.	W	4-1		12	5	Pettitte	Abbott		56-59	2nd	15
8-31	Cal.	W	11-6		15	14	Hitchcock	B. Anderson		57-59	2nd	14
9-1	Oak.	W	8-7		8	7	M. Rivera	Mohler	Wetteland	58-59	2nd	14
9-2	Oak.	W	5-0		9	2	McDowell	Wojciechowski		59-59	2nd	14
9-3	Oak.	L	9-10	(10)	18	15	Eckersley	Wetteland		59-60	2nd	15
9-4	Sea.	W	13-3		19	9	Pettitte	Torres		60-60	2nd	14¹/₂
9-5	Sea.	L	5-6		12	8	Wolcott	M. Rivera	Charlton	60-61	2nd	15¹/₂
9-6	Sea.	W	4-3		7	6	McDowell	Belcher		61-61	2nd	15¹/₂
9-8	Bos.	W	8-4		5	7	Cone	Wakefield	Howe	62-61	2nd	14¹/₂
9-9	Bos.	W	9-1		11	7	Pettitte	Smith		63-61	2nd	13¹/₂
9-10	Bos.	W	9-3		10	7	Hitchcock	Hanson		64-61	2nd	12¹/₂
9-11	At Cle.	W	4-0		7	4	McDowell	Martinez		65-61	2nd	11¹/₂
9-12	At Cle.	W	9-2		13	8	Kamieniecki	Hill		66-61	2nd	10¹/₂
9-13	At Cle.	L	0-5		3	10	Nagy	Cone		66-62	2nd	11¹/₂
9-14	At Bal.	W	5-4		10	7	Pettitte	Krivda	Wetteland	67-62	2nd	10¹/₂
9-15	At Bal.	L	1-8		8	5	Erickson	Hitchcock		67-63	2nd	11¹/₂
9-16	At Bal.	W	6-5	(6)	10	9	McDowell	Mussina	Wickman	68-63	2nd	10¹/₂
9-17	At Bal.	L	0-2		4	6	K. Brown	Kamieniecki	Orosco	68-64	2nd	11¹/₂
9-18	Tor.	W	9-2		12	9	Cone	Cox		69-64	2nd	10¹/₂
9-19	Tor.	W	5-3		3	5	Pettitte	Guzman	Wetteland	70-64	2nd	10¹/₂
9-20	Tor.	W	2-1		5	6	Hitchcock	Hentgen		71-64	2nd	10¹/₂
9-21	Tor.	W	6-4		11	9	Howe	Menhart	Wetteland	72-64	2nd	10
9-23†	Det.	W	5-2		6	4	Cone	Lima	Wetteland	73-64		
9-23‡	Det.	W	3-1		8	5	Kamieniecki	Lira	Wetteland	74-64	2nd	9
9-24	Det.	L	3-8		9	12	Christopher	Pettitte		74-65	2nd	9
9-26	At Mil.	W	5-4		8	9	Hitchcock	Karl	Wetteland	75-65	2nd	8¹/₂
9-27	At Mil.	W	6-3		8	8	Cone	Givens		76-65	2nd	7¹/₂
9-29	At Tor.	W	4-3		7	4	Pettitte	Castillo	Wetteland	77-65	2nd	8
9-30	At Tor.	W	6-1		7	4	Kamieniecki	Leiter		78-65	2nd	8
10-1	At Tor.	W	6-1		11	7	Hitchcock	Hentgen		79-65	2nd	7

Monthly records: April (3-1), May (10-16), June (13-14), July (17-11), August (14-17), September (21-6), October (1-0).
*Innings, if other than nine. †First game of doubleheader. ‡Second game of doubleheader.

HIGHLIGHTS

High point: The Yankees clinched a wild-card playoff spot in the season finale at Toronto on October 1. Longtime Yankees Randy Velarde and Don Mattingly slugged home runs in the 6-1 triumph.

Low point: On August 26, the Yankees dropped their eighth consecutive game as Seattle's Randy Johnson tossed a three-hit shutout. The losing streak was part of a 3-10 road swing that marked the first time since 1967 that the Yanks had absorbed that many defeats on one trip.

Turning point: The Yankees got it together in September, going 21-6 and reeling off a six-game winning streak against eventual division champions Seattle, Boston and Cleveland.

Most valuable player: Outfielder Bernie Williams. After the All-Star break, when the Yankees rallied, Williams hit .350 in 79 games and contributed 57 runs, 18 doubles, four triples and nine homers.

Most valuable pitcher: Righthander David Cone. Acquired July 28 from the Blue Jays for three minor leaguers, he went 9-2 for the Yankees. He won his last three starts as New York barely qualified for the playoffs.

Most improved player: Williams. He emerged as the star the Yankees were counting on. Overall, he batted .307 with 18 homers and 82 RBIs.

Most pleasant surprise: Lefthander Andy Pettitte. The rookie went 9-3 in the second half of the season, showing tremendous poise for a 23-year-old. He finished 12-9 with a 4.17 ERA.

Biggest disappointments: Second baseman Pat Kelly and shortstop Tony Fernandez. Kelly never seemed to fully recover from wrist surgery and wound up batting .237. Fernandez hit .245 after signing a two-year, $3 million deal.

Key injuries: Jimmy Key, who was 17-4 in 1994, reinjured his shoulder in May and needed surgery on July 5 to repair a partially torn rotator cuff. He pitched in five games. Melido Perez, 5-5 with a 5.58 ERA, suffered from shoulder inflammation and pitched only one inning after the All-Star break. Kelly tore a ligament in his left wrist and missed two months. Pitcher Scott Kamieniecki was hampered by an elbow strain that cost him most of the first half.

Notable: Mattingly made his first postseason appearance after 1,785 regular-season games. . . . It was the Yankees' first postseason action since 1981. . . . Third baseman Wade Boggs surpassed .300 (.324) for the 13th time in 14 seasons. . . . Paul O'Neill, coming off a monster '94 season, delivered once again. He hit .300, with 22 homers and 96 RBIs. . . . Jack McDowell won 15 games but saw his ERA climb for the third consecutive season, to 3.93.

—JON HEYMAN

RECORDS

1995 regular-season record: 79-65 (2nd in A.L. East); 46-26 at home; 33-39 on road; 35-17 vs. West; 25-20 vs. Central; 19-28 vs. West; 25-28 vs. lefthanded starters; 54-37 vs. righthanded starters; 71-57 on grass; 8-8 on turf; 26-25 in daytime; 53-40 at night; 14-17 in one-run games; 3-5 in extra-inning games; 1-2-0 in doubleheaders.

Team record past five years: 384-359 (.517, ranks 3rd in league in that span).

TEAM LEADERS

Batting average: Wade Boggs (.324).
At-bats: Bernie Williams (563).
Runs: Bernie Williams (93).
Hits: Bernie Williams (173).
Total bases: Bernie Williams (274).
Doubles: Don Mattingly (32).
Triples: Bernie Williams (9).
Home runs: Paul O'Neill (22).
Runs batted in: Paul O'Neill (96).
Stolen bases: Luis Polonia (10).
Slugging percentage: Paul O'Neill (.526).
On-base percentage: Wade Boggs (.412).
Wins: Jack McDowell (15).
Earned-run average: Jack McDowell (3.93).
Complete games: Jack McDowell (8).
Shutouts: Jack McDowell (2).
Saves: John Wetteland (31).
Innings pitched: Jack McDowell (217.2).
Strikeouts: Jack McDowell (157).

GAMES BY POSITION

Catcher: Mike Stanley 107, Jim Leyritz 46, Jorge Posada 1.
First base: Don Mattingly 125, Jim Leyritz 18, Wade Boggs 9, Dion James 6, Dave Silvestri 4, Russ Davis 2.
Second base: Pat Kelly 87, Randy Velarde 62, Dave Silvestri 7, Tony Fernandez 4, Robert Eenhoorn 3, Kevin Elster 1.
Third base: Wade Boggs 117, Russ Davis 34, Randy Velarde 19.
Shortstop: Tony Fernandez 103, Randy Velarde 28, Derek Jeter 15, Kevin Elster 10, Robert Eenhoorn 2, Dave Silvestri 1.
Outfield: Bernie Williams 144, Paul O'Neill 121, Gerald Williams 92, Luis Polonia 64, Dion James 29, Randy Velarde 20, Danny Tartabull 18, Darryl Strawberry 11, Ruben Sierra 10, Ruben Rivera 4.
Designated hitter: Ruben Sierra 46, Danny Tartabull 39, Dion James 27, Jim Leyritz 15, Darryl Strawberry 15, Mike Stanley 10, Russ Davis 4, Paul O'Neill 4, Dave Silvestri 4, Pat Kelly 1, Don Mattingly 1, Gerald Williams 1.

TOP DRAFT CHOICES

1. **Shea Morenz,** OF, University of Texas.
2a. **Richard Brown,** OF, Nova H.S., Fort Lauderdale, Fla.
2b. **Brian Buchanan,** LHP, Oviedo (Fla.) H.S.
3. **Luke Wilcox,** OF, Western Michigan University.
4. **Eric Boardman,** RHP, Cerritos (Calif.) J.C.
5. **Jason Wright,** RHP, Martinsville (Ind.) H.S.
6. **Brad Williams,** LHP, Sabino H.S., Tucson, Ariz.
7. **Bob St. Pierre,** RHP, University of Richmond.
8. **Scott Brand,** RHP, McLennan (Tex.) J.C.
9. **Mike Judd,** RHP, Grossmont (Calif.) J.C.
10. **Jeff Saffer,** OF, Pima (Ariz.) C.C.

OAKLAND ATHLETICS
AMERICAN LEAGUE WEST DIVISION

1996 ATHLETICS SCHEDULE

Home games shaded.
* — All-Star Game at Veterans Stadium (Philadelphia)
N — Night game (any game starting after 5 p.m.)

MARCH

SUN	MON	TUE	WED	THU	FRI	SAT
31						

APRIL

SUN	MON	TUE	WED	THU	FRI	SAT
	1 N TOR	2	3 N TOR	4 DET	5 N DET	6 DET
7 DET	8	9 MIL	10	11 MIL	12 N CHI	13 CHI
14 CHI	15 N TEX	16 N TEX	17 N TEX	18	19 N CHI	20 CHI
21 CHI	22 N MIL	23 MIL	24 N TOR	25 N TOR	26 N DET	27 DET
28 DET	29	30 N CAL				

MAY

SUN	MON	TUE	WED	THU	FRI	SAT
		1 N CAL	2 CAL	3 N KC	4 N KC
5 KC	6 N CLE	7 CLE	8 N CLE	9	10 N MIN	11 MIN
12 MIN	13 N BAL	14 N BAL	15 BAL	16	17 N BOS	18 BOS
19 BOS	20 N BOS	21 N NY	22 N NY	23 NY	24 N BAL	25 BAL
26 BAL	27 BOS	28 N BOS	29 N BOS	30	31 N NY	

JUNE

SUN	MON	TUE	WED	THU	FRI	SAT
						1 NY
2 NY	3 KC	4 N KC	5 KC	6	7 N MIN	8 MIN
9 N MIN	10 N CLE	11 N CLE	12 N CLE	13 N MIL	14 N MIL	15 MIL
16 MIL	17 N DET	18 N DET	19 DET	20 N TOR	21 N TOR	22 TOR
23 TOR	24 N DET	25 DET	26	27 N CAL	28 N CAL	29 CAL
30 N CAL						

JULY

SUN	MON	TUE	WED	THU	FRI	SAT
	1 N SEA	2 N SEA	3 SEA	4 CAL	5 N CAL	6 CAL
7 CAL	8 *	9 ALL-STAR GAME	10	11 N TEX	12 N TEX	13 N TEX
14 TEX	15 N SEA	16 N SEA	17 SEA	18 N SEA	19 N TEX	20 N TEX
21 N TEX	22 N CHI	23 CHI	24 N CHI	25 CHI	26 N TOR	27 TOR
28 TOR	29	30 N CHI	31 CHI			

AUGUST

SUN	MON	TUE	WED	THU	FRI	SAT
				1 CHI	2 N MIL	3 MIL
4 N MIL	5	6 N KC	7 N KC	8 KC	9 N CLE	10 CLE
11 CLE	12 N MIN	13 N MIN	14 MIN	15 N BAL	16 BAL	17 BAL
18 BAL	19	20 N BOS	21 N BOS	22 N BOS	23 N NY	24 NY
25 NY	26 N BAL	27 N BAL	28 BAL	29	30 N BOS	31 N BOS

SEPTEMBER

SUN	MON	TUE	WED	THU	FRI	SAT
1 BOS	2 NY	3 N NY	4 N NY	5	6 N KC	7 KC
8 KC	9 N MIN	10 N MIN	11 N MIN	12 N MIN	13 N CLE	14 CLE
15 CLE	16	17 N CAL	18 N CAL	19	20 N SEA	21 N SEA
22 SEA	23 N TEX	24 TEX	25	26 N SEA	27 N SEA	28 SEA
29 SEA						

1996 SEASON *Oakland Athletics*

1996 SEASON

CLUB DIRECTORY

Co-owner/president
Stephen C. Schott

Co-owner,/president of strategic planning
Ken Hoffman

Executive vice president, administration
Ed Alvarez

President and general manager
Sandy Alderson

Vice president, business operations
Alan Ledford

Vice president, finance
Goy Fuller

Special assistants to the g.m.
Bill Rigney
Dave Stewart

Assistant general manager
Billy Beane

Director of player development
Keith Lieppman

Baseball operations assistant
Dave Seifert

Director of scouting
Grady Fuson

Assistant director of scouting
Eric Kubota

Director of baseball administration
Pam Pitts

Director of team travel
Mickey Morabito

Baseball information manager
Mike Selleck

Administrative asst., baseball operations
Betty Shinoda

Director of broadcasting
Ken Pries

Director of community relations
Christina Centeno

Director of public relations
Jim Bloom

Director of stadium operations
David Rinetti

Director of corporate sales
Doug Nelson

Director of purchasing & merchandising
David Alioto

Media relations manager
Teddy Santiago

Director of events and promotions
Susan Bress

Dir. of tickets, skybox sales and operations
Paul Solby

Admin. assistant, executive office
Erin Buckert

Director of information resources
David Lozow

Personnel manager
Susan Larsen

Team physician
Dr. Allan Pont

Team orthopedist
Dr. Jerrald Goldman

Trainers
Barry Weinberg
Larry Davis

Equipment manager
Steve Vucinich

Visiting clubhouse manager
Mike Thalblum

Scouts
Tony Arias, Dick Bogard, Steve Bowden, Tom Clark, Ed Crosby, Ron Elam, Ruben Escalera, Grady Fuson, Ubaldo Heredia, Tim Holt, Ron Hopkins, Eric Kubota, John Kuehl, Miguel Machado, Rick Magnante, Gary McGraw, Billy Merkel, Marty Miller, Steve Nichols, Chris Pittaro, John Poloni, J.P. Ricciardi, Joe Robinson, Will Schock, Mike Soper, Rich Sparks, Ron Vaughn, Santiago Villalona

MINOR LEAGUE AFFILIATES

Class	Team	League	Manager
AAA	Edmonton	Pacific Coast	Gary Jones
AA	Huntsville	Southern	Dick Scott
A	Modesto	California	Jim Colborn
A	West Michigan	Midwest	Mike Quade
A	Southern Oregon	Northwest	Tony DeFrancesco
Rookie	Scotttsdale A's	Arizona	Juan Navarrete

BROADCAST INFORMATION

Radio: KFRC-AM (610); KNTA-AM (1430, Spanish language).
TV: KRON-TV (Channel 4).
Cable TV: SportsChannel.

SPRING TRAINING

Ballpark (city): Phoenix Stadium (Phoenix, Ariz.).
Ticket information: 602-392-0074.

SPRING TRAINING ROSTER

Manager—Art Howe (18).
Coaches—Bob Cluck (5), Duffy Dyer (11), Brad Fischer (35), Denny Walling (15), Ron Washington (38).

No.	PITCHERS	B/T	Ht./Wt.	Born	1995 clubs
55	Acre, Mark	R/R	6-8/240	9-16-68	Oakland
49	Adams, Willie	R/R	6-7/215	10-8-72	Huntsville, Edmonton
41	Corsi, Jim	R/R	6-1/220	9-9-61	Edmonton, Oakland
43	Eckersley, Dennis	R/R	6-2/195	10-3-54	Oakland
52	Fermin, Ramon	R/R	6-3/180	11-25-72	Huntsville, Oakland
57	Hollins, Stacy	R/R	6-3/180	7-31-72	Huntsville, Edmonton
51	Johns, Doug	R/L	6-2/185	12-19-67	Edmonton, Oakland
20	Karsay, Steve	R/R	6-3/205	3-24-72	Oakland
32	Mohler, Mike	R/L	6-2/195	7-26-68	Edmonton, Oakland
48	Prieto, Ariel	R/R	6-3/225	10-22-69	Oakland
17	Reyes, Carlos	B/R	6-1/190	4-4-69	Oakland
59	Van Poppel, Todd	R/R	6-5/210	12-9-71	Oakland
31	Wasdin, John	R/R	6-2/190	8-5-72	Edmonton, Oakland
56	Wengert, Don	R/R	6-2/205	11-6-69	Oakland, Edmonton
26	Williams, Todd	R/R	6-3/185	2-13-71	Los Angeles, Albuquerque
	Witasick, Jay	R/R	6-4/205	8-28-72	St. Petersburg, Arkansas
39	Wojciechowski, Steve	L/L	6-2/185	7-29-70	Edmonton, Oakland

No.	CATCHERS	B/T	Ht./Wt.	Born	1995 clubs
36	Steinbach, Terry	R/R	6-1/195	3-2-62	Oakland
19	Williams, George	B/R	5-10/190	4-22-69	Edmonton, Oakland

No.	INFIELDERS	B/T	Ht./Wt.	Born	1995 clubs
37	Batista, Tony	R/R	6-0/165	12-9-73	Huntsville
14	Bordick, Mike	R/R	5-11/175	7-21-65	Oakland, Modesto
7	Brosius, Scott	R/R	6-1/185	8-15-66	Oakland
47	Cox, Steve	L/L	6-4/200	10-31-74	Modesto
13	Cruz, Fausto	R/R	5-10/165	5-1-72	Edmonton, Oakland
8	Gates, Brent	B/R	6-1/180	3-14-70	Oakland
16	Giambi, Jason	L/R	6-2/200	1-8-71	Edmonton, Oakland
40	McDonald, Jason	B/R	5-8/175	3-20-72	Modesto
25	McGwire, Mark	R/R	6-5/250	10-1-63	Oakland
21	Paquette, Craig	R/R	6-0/190	3-28-69	Oakland
3	Spiezio, Scott	B/R	6-2/195	9-21-72	Huntsville

No.	OUTFIELDERS	B/T	Ht./Wt.	Born	1995 clubs
	Battle, Allen	R/R	6-0/170	11-29-68	St. Louis, Louisville
29	Berroa, Geronimo	R/R	6-0/195	3-18-65	Oakland
44	Herrera, Jose	L/L	6-0/165	8-30-72	Huntsville, Oakland
33	Lesher, Brian	R/L	6-5/205	3-5-71	Huntsville
23	Lydy, Scott	R/R	6-5/195	10-26-68	Edmonton
45	Tartabull, Danny	R/R	6-1/204	10-30-62	New York A.L., Oakland
9	Young, Ernie	R/R	6-1/190	7-8-69	Edmonton, Oakland

BALLPARK INFORMATION

Ballpark (capacity, surface)
Oakland-Alameda County Coliseum (45,000, grass)

Address
Oakland Athletics
7677 Oakport St., Second Floor
Oakland, CA 94621

Business phone
510-638-4900

Ticket information
510-568-6000

Ticket prices
$14 (field level)
$13 (plaza level)
$7 (upper reserved)
$4.50 (bleachers)

Field dimensions (from home plate)
To left field at foul line, 330 feet
To center field, 400 feet
To right field at foul line, 330 feet

First game played
April 17, 1968 (Orioles 4, Athletics 1)

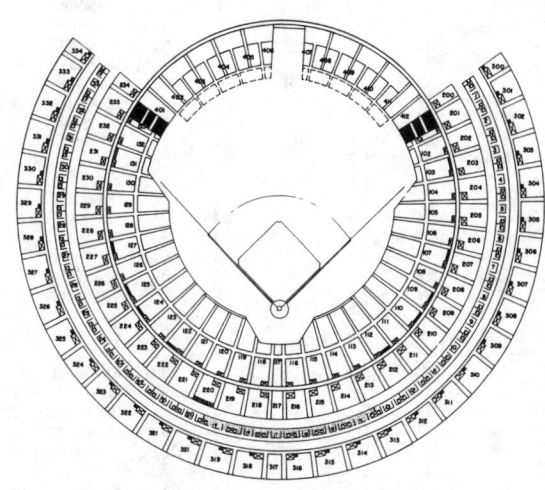

DAY BY DAY

1996 SEASON *Oakland Athletics*

Date	Opp.	Res.	Score	(inn.*)	Hits	Opp. hits	Winning pitcher	Losing pitcher	Save	Record	Pos.	GB
4-26	At Tor.	L	1-13		6	11	Cone	Stewart		0-1	T2nd	1/2
4-27	At Tor.	L	1-7		4	8	Hentgen	Darling		0-2	T3rd	1 1/2
4-28	At Mil.	L	7-8	(10)	9	8	Kiefer	Eckersley		0-3	4th	2 1/2
4-29	At Mil.	W	8-2		12	4	Ontiveros	Wegman	Honeycutt	1-3	4th	2 1/2
4-30	At Mil.	L	3-4		6	8	Kiefer	Wengert	Lloyd	1-4	4th	2 1/2
5-2	At Cal.	W	2-0		5	3	Stewart	Finley	Eckersley	2-4	3rd	3
5-3	At Cal.	L	7-8	(10)	9	13	Butcher	Reyes		2-5	3rd	4
5-4	At Cal.	W	9-6		9	10	Stottlemyre	Williams	Eckersley	3-5	3rd	3 1/2
5-5	Tex.	L	4-9		7	15	Tewksbury	Ontiveros		3-6	T3rd	3 1/2
5-6	Tex.	L	2-4		7	9	Rogers	Harkey	Russell	3-7	4th	3 1/2
5-7	Tex.	W	8-6		8	15	Stewart	Gross	Eckersley	4-7	T3rd	3 1/2
5-8	Tex.	L	4-7	(10)	9	12	Russell	Eckersley		4-8	4th	4
5-9	Sea.	W	7-5		12	11	Wengert	Converse		5-8	T3rd	3
5-10	Sea.	W	7-4		10	6	Ontiveros	Fleming	Eckersley	6-8	3rd	2 1/2
5-11	Sea.	W	3-1		6	6	Harkey	Villone	Eckersley	7-8	3rd	1 1/2
5-12	At Min.	L	5-9		10	13	Tapani	Stewart		7-9	3rd	2 1/2
5-13	At Min.	W	13-5		16	13	Acre	Mahomes	Corsi	8-9	3rd	2
5-14	At Min.	W	12-3		12	9	Stottlemyre	Radke		9-9	3rd	1 1/2
5-16	At Chi.	W	7-1	(6)	9	3	Ontiveros	Bere		10-9	T2nd	1
5-17	At Chi.	L	4-6		8	11	DeLeon	Acre	Hernandez	10-10	3rd	1
5-18	At Chi.	L	2-4		6	10	Fernandez	Stewart	Hernandez	10-11	4th	2
5-19	At K.C.	W	10-3		15	10	Darling	Browning		11-11	T2nd	2
5-20	At K.C.	W	11-1		10	3	Stottlemyre	Haney		12-11	T2nd	2
5-21	At K.C.	W	7-2		13	7	Ontiveros	Gubicza		13-11	T2nd	2
5-23	Bal.	L	1-8		4	11	K. Brown	Harkey		13-12	T2nd	3
5-24	Bal.	W	5-3		10	9	Corsi	Mussina	Eckersley	14-12	2nd	3
5-25	Bal.	W	9-6		9	7	Honeycutt	Benitez	Eckersley	15-12	2nd	3
5-26	N.Y.	W	4-3		3	4	Leiper	Hitchcock	Corsi	16-12	2nd	2
5-27	N.Y.	W	3-0		9	1	Ontiveros	Pettitte		17-12	2nd	1
5-28	N.Y.	L	1-4		8	10	M. Rivera	Harkey	Wetteland	17-13	T2nd	2
5-29	Bos.	L	6-9		9	10	Smith	Stewart		17-14	T3rd	3
5-30	Bos.	L	0-1		3	4	Wakefield	Darling	Ryan	17-15	T3rd	3
5-31	Bos.	L	5-6		10	14	Hanson	Stottlemyre	Ryan	17-16	4th	3
6-2	At Bal.	L	1-2		5	9	K. Brown	Honeycutt	Jones	17-17	4th	4
6-3	At Bal.	L	5-9		8	8	Mussina	Harkey		17-18	4th	5
6-4	At Bal.	W	14-6		14	12	Stewart	Fernandez		18-18	4th	4
6-5	At N.Y.	W	11-5		13	10	Darling	Hitchcock		19-18	4th	3
6-6	At N.Y.	W	8-6		9	14	Stottlemyre	M. Rivera	Eckersley	20-18	4th	3
6-7	At N.Y.	L	1-6		5	14	Pettitte	Ontiveros		20-19	4th	3
6-8	At N.Y.	W	8-3		13	9	Harkey	McDowell		21-19	4th	3
6-9	At Bos.	L	1-4		3	8	Wakefield	Stewart		21-20	4th	3 1/2
6-10	At Bos.	W	8-5		13	13	Corsi	Maddux		22-20	4th	3
6-11	At Bos.	W	8-1		13	8	Stottlemyre	Smith		23-20	4th	3
6-12	Chi.	W	1-0		5	7	Ontiveros	Bere	Eckersley	24-20	3rd	3
6-13	Chi.	L	6-7	(10)	15	10	Hernandez	Leiper		24-21	3rd	3
6-14	Chi.	W	8-5		7	9	Honeycutt	DeLeon	Eckersley	25-21	3rd	2
6-15	K.C.	L	0-7		1	11	Gubicza	Darling		25-22	3rd	3
6-16	K.C.	L	1-3	(13)	8	6	Pichardo	Corsi	Montgomery	25-23	3rd	3 1/2
6-17	K.C.	W	7-5		6	6	Harkey	Rasmussen	Eckersley	26-23	3rd	3 1/2
6-18	K.C.	W	3-1		7	6	Honeycutt	Montgomery	Eckersley	27-23	3rd	3 1/2
6-19	Min.	L	5-8	(10)	11	10	Aguilera	Corsi		27-24	3rd	3 1/2
6-20	Min.	W	5-2		10	11	Ontiveros	Mahomes	Eckersley	28-24	3rd	3 1/2
6-21	Min.	L	2-3		6	9	Stevens	Corsi	Aguilera	28-25	3rd	3 1/2
6-23	At Tex.	L	4-7		9	7	Rogers	Stewart	Russell	28-26	3rd	4 1/2
6-24	At Tex.	L	5-6		14	10	Whiteside	Van Poppel	Russell	28-27	4th	4 1/2
6-25	At Tex.	W	6-2		8	9	Ontiveros	Gross	Eckersley	29-27	3rd	4 1/2
6-26	At Tex.	W	4-3		8	8	Stottlemyre	Vosberg	Eckersley	30-27	3rd	3 1/2
6-27	At Sea.	W	6-4		11	8	Harkey	Belcher	Eckersley	31-27	3rd	2 1/2
6-28	At Sea.	W	7-5		12	9	Van Poppel	Nelson		32-27	3rd	2 1/2
6-29	At Sea.	L	2-5		6	7	Bosio	Acre	Ayala	32-28	3rd	2 1/2
6-30	Cal.	W	8-5		8	9	Eckersley	Smith		33-28	3rd	2 1/2
7-1	Cal.	W	5-1		6	5	Stottlemyre	B. Anderson	Eckersley	34-28	3rd	1 1/2
7-2	Cal.	L	1-7		4	9	Bielecki	Harkey		34-29	3rd	1 1/2
7-3	Mil.	L	3-7	(10)	10	8	Rightnowar	Van Poppel		34-30	3rd	2 1/2
7-4	Mil.	W	5-3		6	6	Honeycutt	Ignasiak	Eckersley	35-30	3rd	2 1/2
7-5	Mil.	L	2-8		5	12	Roberson	Ontiveros	Wegman	35-31	3rd	2 1/2
7-6	Mil.	L	2-5		7	7	Karl	Stottlemyre	Fetters	35-32	3rd	3 1/2
7-7	Tor.	L	2-4		8	11	Williams	Prieto	Castillo	35-33	3rd	3 1/2
7-8†	Tor.	L	6-9		12	12	Cone	Harkey		35-34		
7-8‡	Tor.	W	6-3		9	11	Eckersley	Guzman		36-34	3rd	4
7-9	Tor.	L	3-7		8	8	Hentgen	Darling		36-35	3rd	4

Date	Opp.	Res.	Score	(inn.*)	Hits	Opp. hits	Winning pitcher	Losing pitcher	Save	Record	Pos.	GB
7-12	Tor.	W	7-4		7	8	Stottlemyre	Leiter	Eckersley	37-35	3rd	3¹/₂
7-14†	At Cle.	L	0-1		5	4	Embree	Prieto	Mesa	37-36		
7-14‡	At Cle.	L	6-7		10	11	Nagy	Darling	Mesa	37-37	3rd	5¹/₂
7-15	At Cle.	L	2-7		7	8	Hershiser	Ontiveros	Plunk	37-38	3rd	6
7-16	At Cle.	L	4-5	(12)	9	13	Embree	Eckersley		37-39	3rd	7¹/₂
7-17	At Mil.	L	4-13		11	15	Sparks	Stewart		37-40	4th	8¹/₂
7-18	At Mil.	L	0-4		3	12	Roberson	Wojciechowski		37-41	4th	8¹/₂
7-19	Det.	W	2-1		9	5	Prieto	Doherty	Honeycutt	38-41	4th	8¹/₂
7-20	Det.	W	6-3		12	6	Darling	Moore	Eckersley	39-41	4th	8¹/₂
7-21	Cle.	L	1-6		6	7	Martinez	Stottlemyre		39-42	4th	8¹/₂
7-22	Cle.	L	4-6		7	8	Tavarez	Eckersley	Mesa	39-43	4th	9¹/₂
7-23	Cle.	L	0-2		6	5	Clark	Prieto	Mesa	39-44	4th	10¹/₂
7-25	At Det.	L	3-6		11	9	Lira	Darling		39-45	4th	11
7-26	At Det.	L	4-10		8	11	Wells	Reyes		39-46	4th	12
7-27	At Det.	W	11-3		16	13	Stottlemyre	Moore		40-46	4th	12
7-28	At Tor.	L	0-3		4	7	Leiter	Van Poppel	Castillo	40-47	4th	13
7-29	At Tor.	L	11-18		13	16	Carrara	Prieto		40-48	4th	14
7-30	At Tor.	W	11-3		15	10	Darling	Guzman		41-48	4th	14
8-1	Tex.	W	4-3	(11)	11	12	Reyes	Whiteside		42-48	4th	14
8-2	Tex.	L	4-5		12	7	Taylor	Van Poppel	McDowell	42-49	4th	15
8-3	Tex.	W	5-3		4	6	Prieto	Gross	Eckersley	43-49	4th	14
8-4	Sea.	W	9-8		12	12	Eckersley	Ayala		44-49	4th	13
8-5	Sea.	L	9-15		9	11	Wells	Briscoe		44-50	4th	14
8-6	Sea.	L	8-15		17	16	Krueger	Stottlemyre		44-51	4th	14
8-7	At Min.	L	6-9		9	8	Mahomes	Reyes	Stevens	44-52	4th	15
8-8	At Min.	L	3-5		4	11	Radke	Prieto	Stevens	44-53	4th	16
8-9	At Min.	W	6-3	(10)	9	7	Mohler	Stevens	Eckersley	45-53	4th	16
8-11	At Chi.	L	5-13		9	16	Fernandez	Stottlemyre		45-54	4th	16¹/₂
8-12	At Chi.	W	8-2		16	6	Van Poppel	Righetti		46-54	4th	15¹/₂
8-13	At Chi.	L	7-8		14	14	DeLeon	Reyes	Hernandez	46-55	4th	16¹/₂
8-14	At K.C.	W	13-5		14	7	Wojciechowski	Brewer		47-55	4th	16¹/₂
8-15	At K.C.	L	4-7	(7)	6	9	Jacome	Darling	Olson	47-56	4th	17¹/₂
8-16	At K.C.	W	8-4		12	9	Stottlemyre	Magnante	Mohler	48-56	4th	16¹/₂
8-17	Sea.	W	3-2		8	7	Honeycutt	Charlton		49-56	4th	15¹/₂
8-18	Bal.	L	4-8		9	7	Krivda	Prieto	Clark	49-57	4th	15¹/₂
8-19	Bal.	L	6-12		8	14	Moyer	Wojciechowski		49-58	4th	16¹/₂
8-20	Bal.	W	6-3		13	2	Johns	Erickson	Eckersley	50-58	4th	16¹/₂
8-21	N.Y.	W	13-4		16	10	Stottlemyre	Pettitte		51-58	4th	15¹/₂
8-22	N.Y.	W	6-2		10	5	Van Poppel	Kamieniecki		52-58	4th	14¹/₂
8-23	N.Y.	W	2-1		5	8	Wojciechowski	McDowell	Eckersley	53-58	4th	13¹/₂
8-24	Bos.	L	6-13		14	14	Hanson	Ontiveros		53-59	4th	14¹/₂
8-25	Bos.	W	6-1		13	3	Johns	Cormier		54-59	4th	13¹/₂
8-26	Bos.	W	11-4		16	10	Stottlemyre	Smith		55-59	4th	12¹/₂
8-27	Bos.	L	1-4		7	8	Clemens	Van Poppel	Aguilera	55-60	4th	12¹/₂
8-29	At Bal.	W	3-1		5	8	Reyes	Clark	Eckersley	56-60	4th	11¹/₂
8-30	At Bal.	W	7-2		11	8	Johns	Moyer	Eckersley	57-60	4th	10¹/₂
8-31	At Bal.	W	8-7		13	10	Reyes	Clark	Eckersley	58-60	4th	9¹/₂
9-1	At N.Y.	L	7-8		7	8	M. Rivera	Mohler	Wetteland	58-61	4th	9¹/₂
9-2	At N.Y.	L	0-5		2	9	McDowell	Wojciechowski		58-62	4th	9¹/₂
9-3	At N.Y.	W	10-9	(10)	15	18	Eckersley	Wetteland		59-62	4th	8¹/₂
9-5	At Bos.	L	4-7	(14)	12	13	Aguilera	Reyes		59-63	4th	9
9-6	At Bos.	L	2-8		7	13	Clemens	Johns		59-64	4th	9
9-8	Chi.	L	3-7		5	11	Andujar	Van Poppel	Hernandez	59-65	4th	10
9-9	Chi.	W	8-2		13	5	Ontiveros	Bere		60-65	4th	10
9-10	Chi.	L	3-5		11	8	Fernandez	Stottlemyre	Hernandez	60-66	4th	10
9-12	K.C.	L	1-3		6	7	Gordon	Van Poppel	Montgomery	60-67	4th	11¹/₂
9-13	K.C.	W	6-5		11	10	Johns	Jacome	Eckersley	61-67	4th	10¹/₂
9-14	K.C.	L	4-5		10	6	Converse	Eckersley	Montgomery	61-68	4th	11
9-15	Min.	W	6-5		13	11	Stottlemyre	Mahomes		62-68	4th	10
9-16	Min.	W	6-1		7	5	Wasdin	Radke		63-68	4th	9
9-17	Min.	W	4-1		9	6	Van Poppel	Rodriguez		64-68	4th	8
9-18	Cal.	W	4-0		6	2	Johns	Finley		65-68	4th	7
9-19	Cal.	W	3-2	(10)	7	8	Reyes	Percival		66-68	4th	6
9-20	Cal.	W	9-6		13	16	Stottlemyre	Boskie	Eckersley	67-68	4th	5
9-22	At Sea.	L	7-10		11	11	Nelson	Corsi	Charlton	67-69	4th	6
9-23	At Sea.	L	0-7		4	9	Johnson	Johns		67-70	4th	7
9-24	At Sea.	L	8-9		11	10	Charlton	Eckersley		67-71	4th	8
9-26	At Tex.	L	6-7		8	11	McDowell	Reyes	Russell	67-72	4th	9
9-27	At Tex.	L	2-11		7	12	Rogers	Van Poppel		67-73	4th	9
9-28	At Cal.	L	1-4		7	5	Percival	Johns	Smith	67-74	4th	10
9-29	At Cal.	L	6-9		12	15	Habyan	Ontiveros	Smith	67-75	4th	11
9-30	At Cal.	L	3-9		9	12	Harkey	Wasdin		67-76	4th	11
10-1	At Cal.	L	2-8		4	14	Finley	Stottlemyre		67-77	4th	11

Monthly records: April (1-4), May (16-12), June (16-12), July (8-20), August (17-12), September (9-16), October (0-1).
*Innings, if other than nine. †First game of doubleheader. ‡Second game of doubleheader.

1996 SEASON Oakland Athletics

HIGHLIGHTS

High point: From June 25 to July 1, the A's won six of seven games and moved 1¹/₂ games out of first place. The A's won only seven more games in July and didn't threaten again.

Low point: The A's were outscored 74-35 in their final nine games. They were 0-9 in those games and really didn't show up for any of them.

Turning point: A fastball that sailed from David Cone's right hand and didn't stop until it smacked Mark McGwire's head on July 8. After the incident, McGwire missed 18 of the next 21 games as the A's stumbled from four games behind first-place California to 15 games out.

Most valuable player: For the third consecutive season, McGwire wasn't durable; in '95, though, he at least played in more games than he missed. Even though he missed 40 games, McGwire hit 39 homers. He homered every 8.1 at-bats.

Most valuable pitcher: Righthander Todd Stottlemyre. Stottlemyre finished 14-7, but he had four leads blown by the bullpen and lost two 1-0 leads in the ninth inning. So even on one of the worst clubs in the majors, Stottlemyre could have won 20.

Most improved player: Righthander Jim Corsi. He had gone through two elbow surgeries in two years with Florida and decided to return to Oakland, where he had had his best success. Corsi gave up only 11 earned runs in 45 innings and became almost unhittable as the A's top setup man.

Most pleasant surprise: Lefthander Rick Honeycutt. Honeycutt, 41, was placed on the scrap heap after posting a 7.20 ERA with Texas in '94. He rebounded and at one time had 24¹/₃ consecutive scoreless innings.

Biggest disappointment: Outfielder Ruben Sierra. Sierra's ticket out of town started being written once he said he would like to throw fastballs at G.M. Sandy Alderson's head; he was shipped to the Yankees after Manager Tony La Russa called him a "village idiot."

Key injury: When McGwire was hit in the head by Cone and then suffered back spasms, the A's were a ship without a rudder. McGwire provided the A's with their only legitimate offensive threat.

Notable: La Russa left for St. Louis three weeks after the end of the season, ending 9¹/₂ seasons in Oakland. . . . McGwire passed Reggie Jackson to become the Oakland A's all-time leader in home runs (277).

—**PEDRO GOMEZ**

RECORDS

1995 regular-season record: 67-77 (4th in A.L. West); 38-34 at home; 29-43 on road; 26-26 vs. East; 22-31 vs. Central; 19-20 vs. West; 27-22 vs. lefthanded starters; 40-55 vs. righthanded starters; 61-66 on grass; 6-11 on turf; 30-28 in daytime; 37-49 at night; 13-18 in one-run games; 4-9 in extra-inning games; 0-1-1 in doubleheaders.

Team record past five years: 366-378 (.492, ranks 9th in league in that span).

TEAM LEADERS

Batting average: Rickey Henderson (.300).
At-bats: Geronimo Berroa (546).
Runs: Geronimo Berroa (87).
Hits: Geronimo Berroa (152).
Total bases: Geronimo Berroa (246).
Doubles: Rickey Henderson (31).
Triples: Brent Gates (4).
Home runs: Mark McGwire (39).
Runs batted in: Mark McGwire (90).
Stolen bases: Stan Javier (36).
Slugging percentage: Geronimo Berroa (.451).
On-base percentage: Rickey Henderson (.407).
Wins: Todd Stottlemyre (14).
Earned-run average: Todd Stottlemyre (4.55).
Complete games: Steve Ontiveros, Todd Stottlemyre (2).
Shutouts: Doug Johns, Steve Ontiveros (1).
Saves: Dennis Eckersley (29).
Innings pitched: Todd Stottlemyre (209.2).
Strikeouts: Todd Stottlemyre (205).

GAMES BY POSITION

Catcher: Terry Steinbach 111, Eric Helfand 36, George Williams 13, Brian Harper 2.
First base: Mark McGwire 91, Mike Aldrete 35, Jason Giambi 26, Scott Brosius 18, Craig Paquette 3, Terry Steinbach 2, Brent Gates 1.
Second base: Brent Gates 132, Mike Gallego 18, Scott Brosius 3.
Third base: Craig Paquette 75, Scott Brosius 60, Jason Giambi 30, Mike Gallego 12, Stan Javier 1.
Shortstop: Mike Bordick 126, Mike Gallego 14, Fausto Cruz 8, Craig Paquette 8, Scott Brosius 3.
Outfield: Stan Javier 124, Rickey Henderson 90, Geronimo Berroa 71, Ruben Sierra 62, Scott Brosius 49, Andy Tomberlin 42, Jose Herrera 25, Ernie Young 24, Craig Paquette 20, Mike Aldrete 16, Danny Tartabull 1.
Designated hitter: Geronimo Berroa 72, Danny Tartabull 22, Rickey Henderson 19, Mark McGwire 10, George Williams 10, Ruben Sierra 7, Jose Herrera 5, Brent Gates 3, Scott Brosius 2, Jason Giambi 2, Mike Bordick 1, Andy Tomberlin 1.

TOP DRAFT CHOICES

1. **Ariel Prieto,** RHP, Palm Springs/ Western League.
2. **Mark Bellhorn,** SS, Auburn University.
3. **Billy Brown,** OF, St. Thomas Aquinas H.S., Fort Lauderdale, Fla.
4. **Wayne Nix,** RHP, Monroe H.S., North Hills, Calif.
5. **Danny Ardoin,** C, McNeese State University.
6. **Jamey Price,** RHP, University of Mississippi.
7. **Tim Jones,** OF, Buena Park (Calif.) H.S.
8. **Tom Bennett,** RHP, Ohlone (Calif.) H.S.
9. **Tom Knickerbocker,** OF, Kirkwood (Iowa) J.C.
10. **Ryan Christensen,** OF, Pepperdine University.

SEATTLE MARINERS
AMERICAN LEAGUE WEST DIVISION

1996 MARINERS SCHEDULE

☐ Home games shaded.
* — All-Star Game at Veterans Stadium (Philadelphia)
N — Night game (any game starting after 5 p.m.)

MARCH

SUN	MON	TUE	WED	THU	FRI	SAT
31 N CHI						

APRIL

SUN	MON	TUE	WED	THU	FRI	SAT
	1 N CHI	2 CHI	3	4	5 N MIL	6 N MIL
7 MIL	8	9 DET	10 DET	11 DET	12 N TOR	13 TOR
14 TOR	15 N DET	16 N DET	17 N DET	18 N DET	19 N TOR	20 N TOR
21 TOR	22 N TOR	23	24 N CHI	25 N CHI	26 N MIL	27 MIL
28 MIL	29 MIL	30 N TEX				

MAY

SUN	MON	TUE	WED	THU	FRI	SAT
			1 N TEX	2 N CLE	3 N CLE	4 N CLE
5 CLE	6 N MIN	7 N MIN	8 MIN	9	10 N KC	11 KC
12 KC	13 N NY	14 N NY	15	16	17 N BAL	18 BAL
19 BAL	20 N BOS	21 N BOS	22 N BOS	23	24 N NY	25 N NY
26 NY	27 N BAL	28 N BAL	29	30 N BOS	31 N BOS	

JUNE

SUN	MON	TUE	WED	THU	FRI	SAT
						1 BOS
2 BOS	3	4 N CLE	5 N CLE	6 N CLE	7 N KC	8 N KC
9 KC	10 N MIN	11 N MIN	12 MIN	13	14 N CHI	15 N CHI
16 CHI	17	18 N TOR	19 N TOR	20 N TOR	21 N CHI	22 N CHI
23 CHI	24	25 N TOR	26 N TOR	27 TOR	28 N TEX	29 TEX
30 TEX						

JULY

SUN	MON	TUE	WED	THU	FRI	SAT
	1 N OAK	2 N OAK	3 OAK	4 N TEX	5 N TEX	6 N TEX
7 N TEX	8 *	9 ALL-STAR GAME	10	11 N CAL	12 N CAL	13 CAL
14 CAL	15 N OAK	16 OAK	17 N OAK	18 N CAL	19 N CAL	20 N CAL
21 CAL	22 N MIL	23 N MIL	24 N MIL	25 N DET	26 N DET	27 N DET
28 DET	29 N MIL	30 N MIL	31			

AUGUST

SUN	MON	TUE	WED	THU	FRI	SAT
				1 MIL	2 N DET	3 N DET
4 DET	5	6 N CLE	7 N CLE	8 CLE	9 N MIN	10 N MIN
11 MIN	12 N KC	13 N KC	14 KC	15	16 N NY	17 NY
18 NY	19 N BAL	20 N BAL	21 BAL	22	23 N BOS	24 BOS
25 BOS	26 N NY	27 N NY	28 N NY	29 N BAL	30 N BAL	31 BAL

SEPTEMBER

SUN	MON	TUE	WED	THU	FRI	SAT
1 N BAL	2 N BOS	3 N BOS	4 N BOS	5	6 N CLE	7 CLE
8 CLE	9	10 N KC	11 N KC	12 N KC	13 N MIN	14 MIN
15 MIN	16 N TEX	17 N TEX	18 N TEX	19	20 N OAK	21 OAK
22 OAK	23 N CAL	24 N CAL	25 CAL	26 N OAK	27 N OAK	28 OAK
29 OAK						

1996 SEASON
CLUB DIRECTORY

Chief executive officer
John Ellis

President and chief operating officer
Chuck Armstrong

Vice president, baseball operations
Woody Woodward

Vice president, communications
Randy Adamack

Vice president, finance and administration
Brian Beggs

Vice president, business development
Paul Isaki

Vice president, marketing and sales
Bob Gobrecht

V.p., scouting and player development
Roger Jongewaard

Controller
Denise Podosek

Sr. director of baseball administration
Lee Pelekoudas

Assistant to v.p., baseball operations
George Zuraw

Minor league director
Larry Beinfest

Coordinator of minor league instruction
George Zuraw

Director, team travel
Craig Detwiler

Director, community relations
Joe Chard

Director, corporate sponsorships
Beth Wojick

Director, marketing
Todd Vecchio

Director, public relations
Dave Aust

Director, stadium operations
Tony Pereira

Operations manager
Connie Zentner

Assistant director, public relations
Tim Hevly

Exec. asst. to chairman and president
Janet O'Brien

Payroll manager
Shirley Shreve

Trainer
Rick Griffin

Home clubhouse and equipment manager
Henry Genzale

Club physicians
Dr. Larry Pedegana
Dr. Mitchel Storey

Club dentist
Dr. Richard Leshgold

Head groundskeeper
Wilbur Loo

Public address announcer
Tom Hutyler

Major league and special assignment scouts
Bill Kearns
Ken Compton

National supervisor and assignment scout
Benny Looper

National cross-checker
Carroll Sembera

Scouting supervisors
Ken Madeja
Frank Mattox
Steve Pope

Area scouts
Dave Alexander, Maximo Alvarez, Fernando Arguelles, Brian Ballentine, Earl Battey, Jeff Brissom, Mark Brown, Darrin Chamberlain, Rodney Davis, Jesus de la Rosa, Ramon de los Santos, Curtis Dishman, Ron Hafner ,Larry Harper, Stan Lewis, John McMichen, Tom McNamara, Mauro Mazzotti, Billy Merkel, Julio Molina, Omer Munoz, Myron Pines, Don Poplin, Phil Pote, Jeff Shull, Alex Smith, Chris Smith, Jim Stewart, Roberto Valdez, Curtis Wallace, Ken Wandzel, Craig Weissmann, Bill Young, Fate Young

MINOR LEAGUE AFFILIATES

Class	Team	League	Manager
AAA	Tacoma	Pacific Coast League	Dave Myers
AA	Port City	Southern	Orlando Gomez
A	Lancaster	California	Dave Brundage
A	Wisconsin	Midwest	Mike Goff
A	Everett	Northwest	To be announced
Rookie	Peoria Mariners	Arizona	Tom LaVasseur

BROADCAST INFORMATION

Radio: KIRO-AM (710).
TV: KIRO-TV (Channel 7).
Cable TV: Prime Sports Northwest.

SPRING TRAINING

Ballpark: Peoria Stadium (Peoria, Ariz.).
Ticket information: 602-784-4444.

SPRING TRAINING ROSTER

Manager—Lou Piniella (14).
Coaches—Bobby Cuellar (5), Lee Elia (4), John McLaren (7), Sam Mejias (49), Steve Smith, Matt Sinatro (15).

No.	PITCHERS	B/T	Ht./Wt.	Born	1995 clubs
13	Ayala, Bobby	R/R	6-3/210	7-8-69	Seattle
26	Bosio, Chris	R/R	6-3/235	4-3-63	Seattle
22	Carmona, Rafael	L/R	6-2/185	10-2-72	Port City, Seattle, Tacoma
37	Charlton, Norm	B/L	6-3/205	1-6-63	Philadelphia, Seattle
	Crow, Dean	L/R	6-4/215	8-21-72	Riverside
47	Davis, Tim	L/L	5-11/165	7-14-70	Seattle, Tacoma
36	Davison, Scott	R/R	6-0/190	10-16-70	Tacoma, Port City, Seattle
39	Harikkala, Tim	R/R	6-2/185	7-15-71	Seattle, Tacoma
37	Hibbard, Greg	L/L	6-0/190	9-13-64	Seattle
	Hitchcock, Sterling	L/L	6-1/192	4-29-71	New York A.L.
	Hurtado, Edwin	R/R	6-3/215	2-1-70	Knoxville, Toronto
51	Johnson, Randy	R/L	6-10/230	9-10-63	Seattle
41	Lowe, Derek	R/R	6-6/170	6-1-73	Port City, Arizona Mariners
	Menhart, Paul	R/R	6-2/190	3-25-69	Toronto, Syracuse
96	Suzuki, Makoto	R/R	6-3/195	5-31-75	Riverside, Arizona Mariners
38	Torres, Salomon	R/R	5-11/165	3-11-72	San Francisco, Phoenix, Tacoma, Seattle
	Urso, Sal	R/L	5-11/190	1-19-72	Port City
33	Wolcott, Bob	R/R	6-0/190	9-8-73	Port City, Tacoma, Seattle

No.	CATCHERS	B/T	Ht./Wt.	Born	1995 clubs
	Ibanez, Raul	L/R	6-2/200	6-2-72	Riverside
31	Widger, Chris	R/R	6-3/195	5-21-71	Tacoma, Seattle
6	Wilson, Dan	R/R	6-3/202	3-25-69	Seattle

No.	INFIELDERS	B/T	Ht./Wt.	Born	1995 clubs
28	Cora, Joey	B/R	5-8/162	5-14-65	Seattle
	Davis, Russ	R/R	6-0/195	9-13-69	New York A.L.
10	Fermin, Felix	R/R	5-11/185	10-9-63	Seattle, Tacoma
29	Guevara, Giomar	B/R	5-8/150	10-23-72	Riverside
11	Martinez, Edgar	R/R	5-11/200	1-2-63	Seattle
	Otanez, Willis	R/R	5-11/150	4-19-73	Vero Beach, San Antonio
20	Pirkl, Greg	R/R	6-5/240	8-7-70	Seattle, Tacoma
26	Pozo, Arquimedez	R/R	5-10/160	8-24-73	Tacoma, Seattle
12	Relaford, Desi	B/R	5-8/155	9-16-73	Port City, Tacoma
3	Rodriguez, Alex	R/R	6-3/195	7-27-75	Tacoma, Seattle
	Sheets, Andy	R/R	6-2/180	11-19-71	Tacoma
9	Sojo, Luis	R/R	5-11/175	1-3-66	Seattle, Tacoma
	Sorrento, Paul	L/R	6-2/220	11-17-65	Cleveland
12	Strange, Doug	B/R	6-1/185	4-13-64	Seattle

No.	OUTFIELDERS	B/T	Ht./Wt.	Born	1995 clubs
8	Amaral, Rich	R/R	6-0/175	4-1-62	Seattle
40	Bragg, Darren	L/R	5-9/180	9-7-69	Seattle, Tacoma
19	Buhner, Jay	R/R	6-3/215	8-13-64	Seattle
27	Diaz, Alex	B/R	5-11/180	10-5-68	Seattle, Tacoma
24	Griffey, Ken	L/L	6-3/205	11-21-69	Seattle, Tacoma

BALLPARK INFORMATION

Ballpark (capacity, surface)
The Kingdome (59,158, artificial)

Address
P.O. Box 4100
83 King St.
Seattle, WA 98104

Business phone
206-628-3555

Ticket information
206-628-3555

Ticket prices
$20 (box)
$18 (field)
$15 (club)
$10 (view)
$8 (view, children 14 and under)
$7 (outfield reserved)
$7 (family)
$5 (family, children 14 and under)
$5 (of reserved, children 14 and under)
$5 ("no frills")

Field dimensions (from home plate)
To left field at foul line, 331 feet
To center field, 405 feet
To right field at foul line, 312 feet

First game played
April 6, 1977 (Angels 7, Mariners 0)

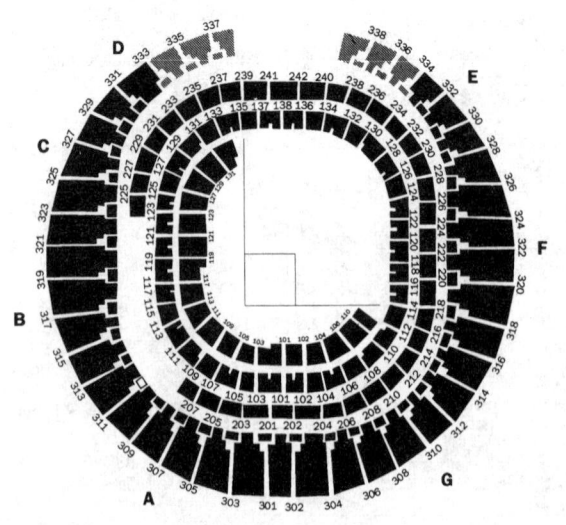

DAY BY DAY

Date	Opp.	Res.	Score	(inn.*)	Hits	Opp. hits	Winning pitcher	Losing pitcher	Save	Record	Pos.	GB
4-27	Det.	W	3-0		7	3	Johnson	Bergman	Ayala	1-0	1st	+1
4-28	Det.	W	9-2		14	11	Bosio	Doherty		2-0	1st	+1
4-29	Det.	W	11-1		14	7	Fleming	Wells	Converse	3-0	1st	+1½
4-30	Det.	L	1-10		6	12	Moore	Wells		3-1	1st	+1
5-1	At Tex.	W	4-1		8	5	Davis	Rogers	Ayala	4-1	1st	+1
5-2	At Tex.	W	15-3		15	8	Nelson	Heredia		5-1	1st	+2
5-3	At Tex.	W	5-1		12	6	Bosio	Pavlik		6-1	1st	+2
5-5	At Cal.	L	0-10		8	8	Patterson	Fleming		6-2	1st	+1½
5-6	At Cal.	L	5-7		8	11	Williams	Wells	Smith	6-3	1st	+½
5-7	At Cal.	W	3-2		7	7	Johnson	Finley	Ayala	7-3	1st	+1½
5-9	At Oak.	L	5-7		11	12	Wengert	Converse		7-4	1st	+½
5-10	At Oak.	L	4-7		6	10	Ontiveros	Fleming	Eckersley	7-5	2nd	½
5-11	At Oak.	L	1-3		6	6	Harkey	Villone	Eckersley	7-6	2nd	½
5-12	Chi.	W	6-4		12	9	Johnson	Alvarez	Risley	8-6	2nd	½
5-13	Chi.	W	6-5		8	9	Davis	Fernandez	Ayala	9-6	1st	+½
5-14	Chi.	L	2-10		7	13	Abbott	Converse		9-7	2nd	½
5-16	At K.C.	L	2-4	(5)	4	7	Haney	Fleming		9-8	T2nd	1
5-17	At K.C.	W	4-0		9	4	Wells	Gubicza		10-8	T1st	...
5-18	At K.C.	L	2-3	(14)	7	16	Brewer	Converse		10-9	2nd	1
5-19	At Min.	L	6-8		11	12	Radke	Davis	Aguilera	10-10	T2nd	2
5-20	At Min.	W	10-6		15	10	Belcher	Erickson		11-10	T2nd	2
5-21	At Min.	W	5-2		8	6	Johnson	Tapani	Ayala	12-10	T2nd	2
5-22	At Det.	L	8-10		12	9	Boever	Carmona	Henneman	12-11	T3rd	2½
5-23	Bos.	L	4-5	(10)	9	11	Belinda	Frey	Ryan	12-12	4th	3½
5-24	Bos.	W	15-6		16	8	Carmona	Pierce	Nelson	13-12	T3rd	3½
5-25	Bos.	W	4-3		7	6	Belcher	Smith	Ayala	14-12	3rd	3½
5-26	Bal.	W	8-3		10	11	Johnson	McDonald		15-12	3rd	2½
5-27	Bal.	L	4-11		7	16	Mills	Wells		15-13	4th	2½
5-28	Bal.	W	5-2		9	7	Bosio	K. Brown	Ayala	16-13	4th	2½
5-29	N.Y.	W	8-7	(12)	18	11	Ayala	Bankhead		17-13	2nd	2½
5-30	N.Y.	W	7-3		8	13	Nelson	Perez		18-13	2nd	1½
5-31	N.Y.	W	11-9		13	13	Wells	MacDonald	Ayala	19-13	2nd	½
6-2	At Bos.	L	5-6	(10)	10	14	Belinda	Torres		19-14	T2nd	1½
6-3	At Bos.	L	8-10		14	12	Cormier	Carmona	Ryan	19-15	T2nd	2½
6-4	At Bos.	L	1-2	(10)	6	7	Wakefield	Ayala		19-16	3rd	2½
6-5	At Bal.	W	2-0		5	3	Johnson	McDonald		20-16	T2nd	1½
6-6	At Bal.	L	6-12		8	15	Moyer	Fleming		20-17	3rd	2½
6-7	At Bal.	W	10-2		8	10	Bosio	K. Brown		21-17	3rd	1½
6-8	At Bal.	L	2-8		7	9	Mussina	Torres		21-18	3rd	2½
6-9	At N.Y.	W	11-1		14	7	Belcher	Perez		22-18	3rd	2
6-10	At N.Y.	W	3-2		7	6	Nelson	Howe	Ayala	23-18	3rd	1½
6-11	At N.Y.	L	7-10		12	13	Howe	Frey	Wetteland	23-19	3rd	2½
6-12	K.C.	L	9-10		13	12	Meacham	Villone	Montgomery	23-20	4th	3½
6-13	K.C.	L	1-3		6	9	Haney	Torres	Montgomery	23-21	4th	3½
6-14	K.C.	L	1-2		9	7	Appier	Belcher	Montgomery	23-22	4th	3½
6-16	Min.	L	1-10		5	13	Radke	Johnson		23-23	4th	4½
6-17	Min.	W	6-4		6	7	Bosio	Trombley	Ayala	24-23	4th	4½
6-18	Min.	W	2-1		8	5	Risley	Tapani		25-23	4th	4½
6-19	At Chi.	L	6-8		10	15	McCaskill	Fleming	Hernandez	25-24	4th	4½
6-20	At Chi.	W	9-5		9	8	Johnson	Alvarez		26-24	4th	4½
6-21	At Chi.	L	4-5	(10)	8	11	McCaskill	Risley		26-25	4th	4½
6-22	At Chi.	W	3-2		10	4	Torres	Abbott	Ayala	27-25	4th	4
6-23	Cal.	L	4-14		7	13	Langston	Belcher		27-26	4th	5
6-24	Cal.	W	3-2		7	5	Johnson	Finley		28-26	3rd	4
6-25	Cal.	L	5-7		12	12	Boskie	Bosio	Smith	28-27	4th	4
6-26	Cal.	W	7-3		10	8	Torres	B. Anderson		29-27	4th	4
6-27	Oak.	L	4-6		8	11	Harkey	Belcher	Eckersley	29-28	4th	4
6-28	Oak.	L	5-7		9	12	Van Poppel	Nelson		29-29	4th	5
6-29	Oak.	W	5-2		7	6	Bosio	Acre	Ayala	30-29	4th	4
6-30	Tex.	L	2-10		6	13	Gross	Torres		30-30	4th	5
7-1	Tex.	W	2-0		8	6	Belcher	Pavlik	Ayala	31-30	4th	4
7-2	Tex.	W	4-3		13	9	Ayala	Whiteside		32-30	4th	3
7-3	At Det.	L	2-4		7	6	Wells	Bosio	Henneman	32-31	4th	4
7-4	At Det.	L	8-9		14	11	Christopher	Ayala		32-32	4th	5
7-5	At Det.	L	6-8		14	10	Christopher	Carmona	Henneman	32-33	4th	5
7-6	At Cle.	L	1-8		3	9	Ogea	Belcher		32-34	4th	6
7-7	At Cle.	W	5-3		11	8	Johnson	Clark		33-34	4th	5
7-8	At Cle.	L	3-7		5	9	Nagy	Bosio		33-35	4th	6
7-9	At Cle.	W	9-3		10	9	Torres	Hershiser		34-35	4th	5
7-13	Tor.	L	1-4		6	5	Cone	Belcher	Castillo	34-36	4th	6
7-14	Tor.	L	1-5		3	14	Guzman	Bosio		34-37	4th	7

Date	Opp.	Res.	Score	(inn.*)	Hits	Opp. hits	Winning pitcher	Losing pitcher	Save	Record	Pos.	GB
7-15	Tor.	W	3-0		8	3	Johnson	Hentgen		35-37	4th	6¹/₂
7-16	Tor.	L	3-9		7	11	Hurtado	Carmona		35-38	4th	8
7-17	Det.	W	10-6	(10)	14	8	Ayala	Groom		36-38	3rd	8
7-18	Det.	W	10-6		15	9	Belcher	Lima		37-38	3rd	7
7-19	At Mil.	L	6-7	(12)	15	13	Wegman	Ayala		37-39	3rd	8
7-20	At Mil.	W	4-2	(13)	8	11	Krueger	Mcandrew		38-39	3rd	8
7-21	At Tor.	L	3-4		8	7	Hurtado	Torres	Castillo	38-40	3rd	8
7-22	At Tor.	W	7-2		13	5	Belcher	Leiter		39-40	3rd	8
7-23	At Tor.	W	6-4		12	11	Wells	Cone	Ayala	40-40	3rd	8
7-24	Mil.	L	4-6		13	9	Bones	Bosio	Fetters	40-41	3rd	8
7-25	Mil.	W	8-6		12	7	Johnson	Karl	Ayala	41-41	3rd	8
7-26	Mil.	L	3-4		6	8	Givens	Torres	Fetters	41-42	3rd	9
7-27	Cle.	W	11-5		14	6	Belcher	Ogea		42-42	3rd	9
7-28	Cle.	L	5-6		12	12	Plunk	Frey	Mesa	42-43	3rd	10
7-29	Cle.	W	5-3		7	9	Bosio	Embree	Ayala	43-43	T2nd	10
7-30	Cle.	L	2-5		5	7	Hershiser	Torres	Mesa	43-44	3rd	11
8-1	At Cal.	L	2-7		7	10	B. Anderson	Johnson		43-45	3rd	12
8-2	At Cal.	L	4-5		11	9	Harkey	Belcher	Smith	43-46	3rd	13
8-3	At Cal.	L	10-7		15	12	Benes	Abbott	Charlton	44-46	3rd	12
8-4	At Oak.	L	8-9		12	12	Eckersley	Ayala		44-47	3rd	12
8-5	At Oak.	W	15-9		11	9	Wells	Briscoe		45-47	3rd	12
8-6	At Oak.	W	15-8		16	17	Krueger	Stottlemyre		46-47	3rd	11
8-7	Chi.	W	6-4		7	6	Belcher	Alvarez	Charlton	47-47	T2nd	11
8-8	Chi.	W	10-9		14	16	Ayala	Hernandez		48-47	T2nd	11
8-9	Chi.	W	11-8		11	12	Bosio	Keyser	Ayala	49-47	T2nd	11
8-11	At K.C.	W	2-1		9	5	Johnson	Gubicza	Ayala	50-47	2nd	10¹/₂
8-12	At K.C.	L	2-7		3	12	Appier	Belcher	Meacham	50-48	3rd	10¹/₂
8-13	At K.C.	L	3-6		8	12	Gordon	Krueger	Montgomery	50-49	3rd	11¹/₂
8-14	At Min.	W	6-2		7	7	Benes	Trombley	Nelson	51-49	3rd	11¹/₂
8-15	At Min.	L	6-7		12	13	O. Munoz	Ayala		51-50	3rd	12¹/₂
8-16	At Min.	W	6-4		10	9	Risley	Stevens	Ayala	52-50	3rd	11¹/₂
8-17	At Oak.	L	2-3		7	8	Honeycutt	Charlton		52-51	3rd	11¹/₂
8-18	Bos.	W	9-3		10	11	Wolcott	Wakefield		53-51	3rd	10¹/₂
8-19	Bos.	L	3-4		4	6	Hanson	Benes	Aguilera	53-52	3rd	11¹/₂
8-20	Bos.	L	6-7		12	10	Cormier	Bosio	Aguilera	53-53	3rd	12¹/₂
8-21	Bal.	W	6-0		10	7	Nelson	Benitez		54-53	3rd	11¹/₂
8-22	Bal.	L	1-2		8	6	Mussina	Belcher	Jones	54-54	3rd	11¹/₂
8-23	Bal.	L	1-7		9	13	Krivda	Wolcott	Benitez	54-55	3rd	11¹/₂
8-24	N.Y.	W	9-7		9	9	Nelson	Wetteland		55-55	3rd	11¹/₂
8-25	N.Y.	W	7-4		7	11	Bosio	Pettitte		56-55	3rd	10¹/₂
8-26	N.Y.	W	7-0		12	3	Johnson	Hitchcock		57-55	3rd	9¹/₂
8-27	N.Y.	L	2-5		5	15	Kamieniecki	Belcher	Wetteland	57-56	3rd	9¹/₂
8-29	At Bos.	W	6-4		10	7	Benes	Wakefield	Charlton	58-56	3rd	8¹/₂
8-30	At Bos.	L	6-7		11	13	Maddux	Nelson	Aguilera	58-57	3rd	8¹/₂
8-31	At Bos.	W	11-2		19	9	Wolcott	Cormier	Guetterman	59-57	T2nd	7¹/₂
9-1	At Bal.	W	4-3		9	9	Belcher	Mussina	Charlton	60-57	2nd	6¹/₂
9-2	At Bal.	L	2-3		6	7	K. Brown	Bosio	Jones	60-58	T2nd	6¹/₂
9-3	At Bal.	W	9-6		12	10	Carmona	Krivda	Charlton	61-58	2nd	5¹/₂
9-4	At N.Y.	L	3-13		9	19	Pettitte	Torres		61-59	2nd	6¹/₂
9-5	At N.Y.	W	6-5		8	12	Wolcott	M. Rivera	Charlton	62-59	2nd	5¹/₂
9-6	At N.Y.	L	3-4		6	7	McDowell	Belcher		62-60	2nd	5¹/₂
9-7	At Cle.	L	1-4		7	8	Nagy	Bosio	Mesa	62-61	2nd	6
9-8	K.C.	W	4-1		11	5	Johnson	Jacome	Charlton	63-61	2nd	6
9-9	K.C.	W	6-2		13	3	Benes	Gubicza		64-61	2nd	6
9-10	K.C.	W	5-4		7	10	Ayala	Olson	Charlton	65-61	2nd	5
9-11	Min.	L	10-12		11	17	Mahomes	Nelson	Stevens	65-62	2nd	6
9-12	Min.	W	14-3		13	14	Bosio	Rodriguez	Carmona	66-62	2nd	6
9-13	Min.	W	7-4		8	6	Nelson	Mahomes	Charlton	67-62	2nd	5
9-15	At Chi.	W	3-2		8	8	Benes	Bere	Charlton	68-62	2nd	4
9-16	At Chi.	W	5-3		11	5	Belcher	Karchner	Charlton	69-62	2nd	3
9-17	At Chi.	L	1-2		8	5	McCaskill	Wolcott	Hernandez	69-63	2nd	3
9-18	Tex.	W	8-1		11	3	Johnson	Witt		70-63	2nd	2
9-19	Tex.	W	5-4	(11)	12	10	Charlton	McDowell		71-63	2nd	1
9-20	Tex.	W	11-3		20	8	Benes	Tewksbury		72-63	T1st	...
9-22	Oak.	W	10-7		11	11	Nelson	Corsi	Charlton	73-63	1st	+1
9-23	Oak.	W	7-0		9	4	Johnson	Johns		74-63	1st	+2
9-24	Oak.	W	9-8		10	11	Charlton	Eckersley		75-63	1st	+2
9-26	Cal.	W	10-2		10	9	Benes	Boskie		76-63	1st	+3
9-27	Cal.	L	0-2		3	5	Finley	Belcher	Smith	76-64	1st	+2
9-28	At Tex.	W	6-2		5	9	Johnson	Pavlik	Charlton	77-64	1st	+2
9-29	At Tex.	W	4-3		8	14	Ayala	Vosberg	Charlton	78-64	1st	+2
9-30	At Tex.	L	2-9		9	13	Gross	Benes		78-65	1st	+1
10-1	At Tex.	L	3-9		8	13	Rogers	Belcher	Whiteside	78-66	T1st	...
10-2	Cal.	W	9-1		12	3	Johnson	Langston		79-66	1st	+1

Monthly records: April (3-1), May (16-12), June (11-17), July (13-14), August (16-13), September (19-8), October (1-1).
*Innings, if other than nine. †First game of doubleheader. ‡Second game of doubleheader.

HIGHLIGHTS

High point: Eighteen years of frustration ended October 2 when Randy Johnson pitched the Mariners to a 9-1 victory over the Angels in a one-game playoff for the A.L. West title. The Mariners trailed the Angels by 12½ games on August 20.

Low point: Ken Griffey made a bone-shattering catch to rob Baltimore's Kevin Bass of an extra-base hit on May 26 at the Kingdome. The collision with the fence broke two bones in Griffey's left wrist, forcing him to miss 73 games.

Turning point: On August 24, nine days after Griffey returned to action, he hit a two-run homer off Yankees closer John Wetteland for a 9-7 Seattle victory. The Mariners went 24-11 the remainder of the regular season.

Most valuable player: Designated hitter Edgar Martinez. Martinez's longest hitless streak was 0-for-8, and he never went more than two games without a hit en route to his second A.L. batting title (.356 average).

Most valuable pitcher: Lefthander Randy Johnson. Johnson finished 18-2, and the Mariners won 27 of his 30 starts. Johnson's 294 strikeouts and 65 walks represented one of the best ratios this century.

Most improved player: Catcher Dan Wilson. A .216 hitter in his first season with the Mariners in '94, he hit a solid .278 with nine homers and 51 RBIs.

Most pleasant surprise: Reliever Norm Charlton. Charlton, unwanted in Philadelphia, returned to Seattle and virtually saved the season. When closer Bobby Ayala struggled, Charlton came on, going 14-for-15 in save opportunities.

Biggest disappointments: Lefthander Dave Fleming. Fleming, a 17-game winner as a rookie three years ago, pitched himself out of the rotation, out of the bullpen and ultimately out of the organization. Darren Bragg began the season as the Mariners' starting left fielder and leadoff batter. The team expected him to solve a 10-year problem in left field, but he didn't, batting .234 with three homers and 12 RBIs before returning to the minors.

Key injuries: Griffey missed 73 games with his broken left wrist. Right fielder Jay Buhner spent 15 days on the D.L. with a hamstring injury.

Notable: The Mariners' rise to the A.L. West championship was the first step in building a baseball tradition in Seattle. "Everything has to start somewhere," Manager Lou Piniella said, "and this organization has started its own tradition. This is not a one-year thing. We need to get better and better."

—JIM STREET

RECORDS

1995 regular-season record: 67-76 (4th in N.L. East). 37-34 at home; 30-42 on road; 22-30 vs. East; 27-29 vs. Central; 18-17 vs. West; 21-28 vs. lefthanded starters; 46-48 vs. righthanded starters; 52-54 on grass; 15-22 on turf; 15-15 in daytime; 52-61 at night; 18-17 in one-run games; 6-9 in extra-inning games; 0-1-1 in doubleheaders.

Team record past five years: 182-238 in three years (.433, ranks 14th in league in that span).

TEAM LEADERS

Batting average: Edgar Martinez (.356).
At-bats: Tino Martinez (519).
Runs: Edgar Martinez (121).
Hits: Edgar Martinez (182).
Total bases: Edgar Martinez (321).
Doubles: Edgar Martinez (52).
Triples: Tino Martinez, Dan Wilson (3).
Home runs: Jay Buhner (40).
Runs batted in: Jay Buhner (121).
Stolen bases: Vince Coleman (32).
Slugging percentage: Edgar Martinez (.628).
On-base percentage: Edgar Martinez (.479).
Wins: Randy Johnson (18).
Earned-run average: Randy Johnson (2.48).
Complete games: Randy Johnson (6).
Shutouts: Randy Johnson (3).
Saves: Bobby Ayala (19).
Innings pitched: Randy Johnson (214.1).
Strikeouts: Randy Johnson (294).

GAMES BY POSITION

Catcher: Dan Wilson 119, Chad Kreuter 23, Chris Widger 19.
First base: Tino Martinez 139, Mike Blowers 7, Greg Pirkl 6, Edgar Martinez 3.
Second base: Joey Cora 112, Felix Fermin 29, Luis Sojo 19, Doug Strange 5, Arquimedez Pozo 1.
Third base: Mike Blowers 126, Doug Strange 41, Edgar Martinez 4.
Shortstop: Luis Sojo 80, Felix Fermin 46, Alex Rodriguez 46, Joey Cora 1.
Outfield: Jay Buhner 120, Alex Diaz 88, Rich Amaral 73, Ken Griffey Jr. 70, Darren Bragg 47, Vince Coleman 38, Marc Newfield 24, Warren Newson 23, Gary Thurman 9, Luis Sojo 6, Mike Blowers 5, Doug Strange 4, Chris Widger 3.
Designated hitter: Edgar Martinez 138, Jay Buhner 4, Ken Griffey Jr. 2, Rich Amaral 1, Darren Bragg 1, Tino Martinez 1, Greg Pirkl 1, Alex Rodriguez 1, Doug Strange 1, Chris Widger 1.

TOP DRAFT CHOICES

1. **Jose Cruz Jr.,** OF, Rice University.
2. **Shane Monahan,** OF, Clemson University.
3. **Greg Wooten,** RHP, Portland State University.
4. **Duan Johnson,** SS, St. Paul's (N.C.) H.S.
5. **Gary Kinnie,** RHP, Chippewa Valley H.S., Clifton Township, Mich.
6. **Karl Thompson,** C, University of Santa Clara.
7. **Branden Nogowski,** LHP, Hood River (Ore.) Valley H.S.
8. **Seth Brizek,** SS, Clemson University.
9. **Marty Weymouth,** RHP, Brother Rice H.S., Bloomfield Hills, Mich.
10. **Ernest Tolbert,** OF, Lincoln H.S., San Diego.

TEXAS RANGERS
AMERICAN LEAGUE WEST DIVISION

1996 RANGERS SCHEDULE

Home games shaded.
* — All-Star Game at Veterans Stadium (Philadelphia)
N — Night game (any game starting after 5 p.m.)

MARCH

SUN	MON	TUE	WED	THU	FRI	SAT
31						

APRIL

SUN	MON	TUE	WED	THU	FRI	SAT
	1 DOS	2	3 N BOS	4 N BOS	5 N NY	6 N NY
7 N NY	8	9 CHI	10	11 CHI	12 N NY	13 NY
14 NY	15 N OAK	16 N OAK	17	18	19 N BAL	20 N BAL
21 BAL	22 N CHI	23 CHI	24	25 N BOS	26 N BOS	27 BAL
28 BAL	29 N BAL	30 N SEA				

MAY

SUN	MON	TUE	WED	THU	FRI	SAT
			1 N SEA	2 N DET	3 N DET	4 DET
5 DET	6	7 N TOR	8 N TOR	9 N TOR	10 N DET	11 N DET
12 DET	13 N KC	14 N KC	15 N KC	16	17 N CLE	18 CLE
19 CLE	20	21 N MIN	22 MIN	23 N KC	24 N KC	25 N KC
26 KC	27 N CLE	28 N CLE	29 N CLE	30	31 N MIN	

JUNE

SUN	MON	TUE	WED	THU	FRI	SAT
						1 N MIN
2 MIN	3 N MIL	4 N MIL	5 MIL	6	7 N TOR	8 N TOR
9 TOR	10 N MIL	11 N MIL	12 MIL	13 N BOS	14 N BOS	15 N BOS
16 BOS	17 N BAL	18 N BAL	19 BAL	20	21 N BOS	22 N BOS
23 N DOS	24 N BAL	25 N BAL	26 N BAL	27	28 N SEA	29 SEA
30 SEA						

JULY

SUN	MON	TUE	WED	THU	FRI	SAT
	1 N CAL	2 N CAL	3 N CAL	4 N SEA	5 N SEA	6 N SEA
7 N SEA	8 *	9 ALL-STAR GAME	10	11 N OAK	12 N OAK	13 N OAK
14 OAK	15 N CAL	16 N CAL	17 N CAL	18 N OAK	19 N OAK	20 N OAK
21 N OAK	22 N NY	23 N NY	24 N NY	25 N CHI	26 N CHI	27 CHI
28 CHI	29 N RY	30 N NY	31 N NY			

AUGUST

SUN	MON	TUE	WED	THU	FRI	SAT
				1 N NY	2 N CHI	3 N CHI
4 N CHI	5 N CHI	6 N DET	7 N DET	8 N DET	9 N TOR	10 TOR
11 TOR	12 N DET	13 N DET	14 N DET	15	16 N KC	17 KC
18 N KC	19 N CLE	20 N CLE	21 N CLE	22 N MIN	23 N MIN	24 N MIN
25 MIN	26	27 N KC	28 N KC	29	30 N CLE	31 N CLE

SEPTEMBER

SUN	MON	TUE	WED	THU	FRI	SAT
1 CLE	2 N MIN	3 N MIN	4 N MIN	5	6 N MIL	7 MIL
8 MIL	9 N TOR	10 N TOR	11 N TOR	12 N MIL	13 N MIL	14 N MIL
15 MIL	16 N SEA	17 N SEA	18 N SEA	19	20 N CAL	21 N CAL
22 CAL	23 N OAK	24 OAK	25	26 N CAL	27 N CAL	28 N CAL
29 CAL						

(side margin) **1996 SEASON** *Texas Rangers*

1996 SEASON
CLUB DIRECTORY

General partners
Edward W. (Rusty) Rose
J. Thomas Schieffer
President
J. Thomas Schieffer
Vice president, general manager
R. Douglas Melvin
V.p., business operations/treasurer
John F. McMichael
Vice president, marketing
David Dziedzic
Vice president, administration/secretary
Charles F. Wangner
Vice president, public relations
John C. Blake
Vice president, community development
Norman B. Lyons
Vice president, legal affairs
William D. Miller
V.p. and chief information officer
Steve McNeill
General counsel
Gerald W. Haddock
Director of grounds
Jim Anglea
Special asst. to the general manager
Sandy Johnson
Dir., professional and int'l scouting
Omar Minaya
Director of amateur scouting
Len Strelitz
Director, player development
Reid Nichols
Traveling secretary
Dan Schimek
Dir. of major league administration
Judy Johns
Admin. asst., baseball operations
Bob Garvey
Asst. to the general manager
Lee MacPhail IV
Dir. of minor league administration
Monty Clegg
Director of medical services
Dr. Mike Mycoskie

Visiting clubhouse manager
Joe Macko
Equipment and home clubhouse manager
Zack Minasian
Video coordinator
Brian Harbert
Controller
Chip Sawicki
Director, corporate marketing
Dave Fendrick
Director, in-park entertainment
Chuck Morgan
Director, merchandising
Nancy McCusker
Director, ticket operations
John Schriever
Director, sales
Ross Scott
Director, player relations
Taunee Taylor
Dir., Spanish broadcasting and Latin American liason
Luis R. Mayoral
Director, publications
Eric Kolb
Assistant director, public relations
John Ralph
Assistant director, player relations
Sheila Bolduc
Assistant, special projects
Bobby Bragan
Admin. asst., public relations
Michelle Baugh
Scouting supervisors
Bill Earnhart, Bryan Lambe, Omar Minaya, Len Strelitz, Rudy Terrasas
Scouts
Hector Acevedo, Manuel Batista, Joe Branzell, Mike Cadahia, Mike Daughtry, Marc Delpiano, Kip Fagg, Jim Fairey, Mark Giegler, Mike Grouse, Todd Guggiana, Tim Hallgren, Larry Izzo, Cornelio Pena, Alan Regier, Pat Rigby, Randy Jeff, Mike Toomey. Danilo Troncoso, Bob Zuk

MINOR LEAGUE AFFILIATES

Class	Team	League	Manager
AAA	Oklahoma City	American Association	Greg Biagini
AA	Tulsa	Texas	Bobby Jones
A	Charlotte	Florida State	Butch Wynegar
A	Charleston (SC)	South Atlantic	To be announced
A	Hudson Valley	New York-Penn.	Bump Wills
Rookie	Gulf Coast Rangers	Gulf Coast	Jim Byrd

BROADCAST INFORMATION

Radio: KRLD-AM (1080); KXEB-AM (910, Spanish language).
TV: KXAS-TV (Channel 5); KXTX-TV (Channel 39).
Cable TV: Prime Sports.

SPRING TRAINING

Ballpark (city): Charlotte County Stadium (Port Charlotte, Fla.).
Ticket information: 813-625-9500, 813-624-2211.

SPRING TRAINING ROSTER

Manager—Johnny Oates (26).
Coaches—Dick Bosman (17), Bucky Dent (20), Larry Hardy (25), Rudy Jaramillo (8), Ed Napoleon (12), Jerry Narron (5).

No.	PITCHERS	B/T	Ht./Wt.	Born	1995 clubs
48	Alberro, Jose	R/R	6-2/190	6-29-69	Texas, Oklahoma City
51	Brandenburg, Mark	R/R	6-0/180	7-14-70	Oklahoma City, Texas
42	Cook, Dennis	L/L	6-3/190	10-4-62	Cleveland, Texas
43	Curtis, Chris	R/R	6-2/185	5-8-71	Oklahoma City
47	Davis, Jeff	R/R	6-0/170	8-20-72	Charlotte, Tulsa
46	Gross, Kevin	R/R	6-5/227	6-8-61	Texas
32	Helling, Rick	R/R	6-3/215	12-15-70	Texas, Oklahoma City
39	Henneman, Mike	R/R	6-4/205	12-11-61	Detroit, Houston
44	Hill, Ken	R/R	6-2/205	12-14-65	St. Louis, Cleveland
41	Howard, Chris	R/L	6-0/185	11-18-65	Sarasota, Pawtucket, Texas
49	Lacy, Kerry	R/R	6-2/195	8-7-72	Tulsa, Oklahoma City
53	Mimbs, Mark	L/L	6-2/180	2-13-69	Albuquerque
54	Nichting, Chris	R/R	6-1/205	5-13-66	Oklahoma City, Texas
28	Oliver, Darren	R/L	6-2/200	10-6-70	Texas
56	Patterson, Danny	R/R	6-0/175	2-17-71	Tulsa, Oklahoma City
59	Pavlik, Roger	R/R	6-2/220	10-4-67	Texas
45	Rumer, Tim	L/L	6-3/205	8-8-69	Columbus
60	Santana, Julio	R/R	6-0/175	1-20-74	Oklahoma City, Charlotte, Tulsa
35	Smith, Danny	L/L	6-5/195	4-20-69	Texas
52	Vosberg, Ed	L/L	6-1/190	9-28-61	Oklahoma City, Texas
27	Whiteside, Matt	R/R	6-0/205	8-8-67	Texas
32	Witt, Bobby	R/R	6-2/205	5-11-64	Florida, Texas

No.	CATCHERS	B/T	Ht./Wt.	Born	1995 clubs
7	Rodriguez, Ivan	R/R	5-9/205	11-30-71	Texas
10	Valle, Dave	R/R	6-2/220	10-30-60	Texas

No.	INFIELDERS	B/T	Ht./Wt.	Born	1995 clubs
22	Clark, Will	L/L	6-1/196	3-13-64	Texas
23	Gil, Benji	R/R	6-2/182	10-6-72	Texas
3	McLemore, Mark	B/R	5-11/207	10-4-64	Texas
9	Ortiz, Luis	R/R	6-0/195	5-25-70	Oklahoma City, Texas
16	Palmer, Dean	R/R	6-2/195	12-27-68	Texas
24	Worthington, Craig	R/R	6-0/200	4-17-65	Indianapolis, Cincinnati, Texas

No.	OUTFIELDERS	B/T	Ht./Wt.	Born	1995 clubs
	Faneyte, Rikkert	R/R	6-1/170	5-31-69	Phoenix, San Francisco
14	Frazier, Lou	B/R	6-2/175	1-26-65	Montreal, Ottawa, Texas
19	Gonzalez, Juan	R/R	6-3/215	10-16-69	Texas
4	Hamilton, Darryl	L/R	6-1/180	12-3-64	Milwaukee
18	Lowery, Terrell	R/R	6-3/180	10-25-70	Gulf Coast Rangers, Charlotte
21	Newson, Warren	L/L	5-7/202	7-3-64	Chicago A.L., Seattle
15	Tettleton, Mickey	B/R	6-2/212	9-16-60	Texas

BALLPARK INFORMATION

Ballpark (capacity, surface)
The Ballpark in Arlington (49,178, grass)

Address
1000 Ballpark Way
Arlington, TX 76011

Business phone
817-273-5222

Ticket information
817-273-5100

Ticket prices
$20 (club box)
$15 (terrace club box)
$16 (field box)
$14 (terrace box)
$10 (upper box)
$9 (upper reserved)
$8 (left field reserved)
$8 (upper & lower porch)
$6 (grandstand reserved, adults)
$3 (grandstand reserved, children
13 and under)
$4 (outfield bleachers, adults)
$2 (outfield bleachers, children 13 and under)

Field dimensions (from home plate)
To left field at foul line, 332 feet
To center field, 400 feet
To right field at foul line, 325 feet

First game played
April 11, 1994 (Brewers 4, Rangers 3)

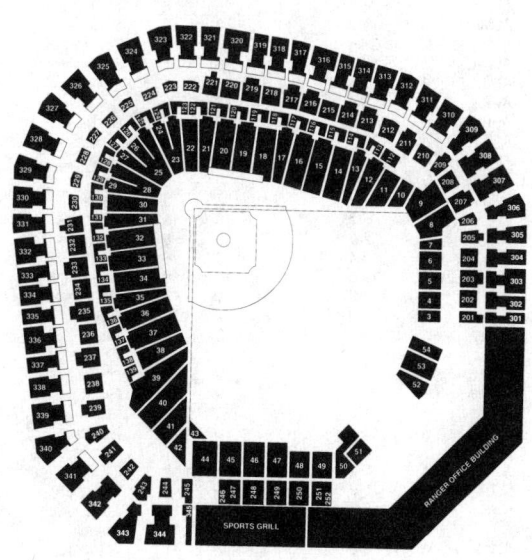

DAY BY DAY

1996 SEASON *Texas Rangers*

Date	Opp.	Res.	Score	(inn.*)	Hits	Opp. hits	Winning pitcher	Losing pitcher	Save	Record	Pos.	GB
4-26	At N.Y.	L	6-8		10	14	Key	Rogers	Wetteland	0-1	T2nd	1/2
4-27	Cle.	L	6-11		8	13	Martinez	Gross		0-2	T3rd	1 1/2
4-28	Cle.	W	10-9		11	11	Whiteside	Poole	Russell	1-2	3rd	1 1/2
4-29	Cle.	W	6-5		8	10	Burrows	Shuey		2-2	2nd	1 1/2
4-30	Cle.	L	6-7	(12)	13	12	Mesa	Whiteside		2-3	3rd	1 1/2
5-1	Sea.	L	1-4		5	8	Davis	Rogers	Ayala	2-4	3rd	2 1/2
5-2	Sea.	L	3-15		8	15	Nelson	Heredia		2-5	4th	3 1/2
5-3	Sea.	L	1-5		6	12	Bosio	Pavlik		2-6	4th	4 1/2
5-5	At Oak.	W	9-4		15	7	Tewksbury	Ontiveros		3-6	T3rd	3 1/2
5-6	At Oak.	W	4-2		9	7	Rogers	Harkey	Russell	4-6	3rd	2 1/2
5-7	At Oak.	L	6-8		15	8	Stewart	Gross	Eckersley	4-7	T3rd	3 1/2
5-8	At Oak.	W	7-4	(10)	12	9	Russell	Eckersley		5-7	3rd	3
5-9	At Cal.	L	2-3		7	8	Langston	Helling	Smith	5-8	T3rd	3
5-10	At Cal.	L	2-11		7	16	Sanderson	Tewksbury		5-9	4th	3 1/2
5-11	At Cal.	W	6-2		9	7	Rogers	Springer	Russell	6-9	4th	2 1/2
5-12	Det.	L	1-6		5	8	Groom	Gross		6-10	4th	3 1/2
5-13	Det.	W	5-3		9	7	Pavlik	Wells	Russell	7-10	4th	3
5-14	Det.	L	3-8		5	14	Moore	Helling		7-11	4th	3 1/2
5-15	Tor.	W	12-4		14	12	Tewksbury	Guzman		8-11	4th	2 1/2
5-16	Tor.	W	6-1		12	4	Rogers	Leiter	Burrows	9-11	4th	2 1/2
5-17	Tor.	W	12-7		16	11	Gross	Darwin	Vosberg	10-11	4th	1 1/2
5-18	Mil.	W	6-2		13	6	Pavlik	Lloyd		11-11	3rd	1 1/2
5-19	Mil.	L	0-1		5	5	Sparks	Oliver	Fetters	11-12	4th	2 1/2
5-20	Mil.	W	7-6	(11)	13	17	Vosberg	Kiefer		12-12	4th	2 1/2
5-21	Mil.	W	6-0		8	5	Rogers	Scanlan		13-12	4th	2 1/2
5-24†	At Chi.	L	8-10		12	10	Radinsky	Burrows	Hernandez	13-13		
5-24‡	At Chi.	W	13-6		12	15	Oliver	Fernandez		14-13	T3rd	3 1/2
5-26	At Min.	W	6-5		12	13	Tewksbury	Tapani	Russell	15-13	4th	3
5-27	At Min.	W	3-1		10	10	Rogers	Guardado	Russell	16-13	3rd	2
5-28	At Min.	W	4-2		10	6	Pavlik	Radke	McDowell	17-13	T2nd	2
5-29	At K.C.	L	0-12		6	18	Gordon	Gross		17-14	T3rd	3
5-30	At K.C.	L	6-7		8	12	Pichardo	Vosberg		17-15	T3rd	3
5-31	At K.C.	W	4-2		7	6	Tewksbury	Appier		18-15	3rd	2
6-1	Min.	W	6-3		11	8	Rogers	Radke	Russell	19-15	3rd	1 1/2
6-2	Min.	W	6-5		10	9	McDowell	Aguilera		20-15	T2nd	1 1/2
6-3	Min.	L	0-4		6	12	Tapani	Gross		20-16	T2nd	2 1/2
6-4	Min.	W	7-2		11	5	Oliver	Guardado		21-16	2nd	1 1/2
6-5	K.C.	L	1-4		4	9	Appier	Tewksbury	Montgomery	21-17	T2nd	1 1/2
6-6	K.C.	W	2-1		9	7	Rogers	Gubicza		22-17	2nd	1 1/2
6-7	K.C.	W	10-4		13	10	Burrows	Gordon		23-17	2nd	1/2
6-8	K.C.	W	10-9	(10)	14	15	Vosberg	Brewer		24-17	2nd	1/2
6-9	Chi.	W	6-1		10	6	Oliver	Alvarez		25-17	1st	+1/2
6-11	Chi.	W	3-2		8	8	McDowell	DeLeon		26-17	1st	+1
6-12	At Mil.	W	4-2		8	7	Pavlik	Sparks	Russell	27-17	1st	+1
6-13	At Mil.	L	2-14		4	16	Bones	Gross		27-18	T1st	...
6-14	At Mil.	L	2-4		6	8	Roberson	Oliver	Fetters	27-19	T1st	...
6-16	At Tor.	W	7-3		11	11	Tewksbury	Darwin		28-19	T1st	...
6-17	At Tor.	L	3-4		3	9	Cone	Rogers		28-20	2nd	1
6-18	At Tor.	L	2-7		10	6	Guzman	Pavlik		28-21	2nd	2
6-19	At Det.	W	6-4		10	8	Gross	Ahearne	Russell	29-21	2nd	1
6-20	At Det.	W	8-6		8	9	Oliver	Bergman	Russell	30-21	2nd	1
6-21	At Det.	L	0-1		6	7	Lira	Tewksbury	Henneman	30-22	2nd	1
6-23	Oak.	W	7-4		7	9	Rogers	Stewart	Russell	31-22	2nd	1
6-24	Oak.	W	6-5		10	14	Whiteside	Van Poppel	Russell	32-22	T1st	...
6-25	Oak.	L	2-6		9	8	Ontiveros	Gross	Eckersley	32-23	2nd	1
6-26	Oak.	L	3-4		6	6	Stottlemyre	Vosberg	Eckersley	32-24	2nd	1
6-27	Cal.	W	10-6		15	10	Tewksbury	Bielecki	Cook	33-24	T1st	...
6-28	Cal.	W	9-8		11	10	McDowell	Smith		34-24	1st	+1
6-29	Cal.	L	4-20		7	21	Finley	Pavlik	Springer	34-25	T1st	...
6-30	At Sea.	W	10-2		13	6	Gross	Torres		35-25	1st	+1
7-1	At Sea.	L	0-2		6	8	Belcher	Pavlik	Ayala	35-26	1st	+1
7-2	At Sea.	L	3-4		9	13	Ayala	Whiteside		35-27	T1st	...
7-3	At Cle.	L	1-9		5	11	Nagy	Rogers		35-28	2nd	1
7-4	At Cle.	W	7-6		12	8	McDowell	Assenmacher	Whiteside	36-28	2nd	1
7-5	At Cle.	L	0-2		2	7	Martinez	Gross	Mesa	36-29	2nd	1
7-6	N.Y.	W	4-2		7	8	Pavlik	Hitchcock	Vosberg	37-29	2nd	1
7-7	N.Y.	W	10-0		15	6	Tewksbury	Pettitte		38-29	T1st	...
7-8	N.Y.	L	3-7		6	11	J. McDowell	R. McDowell	Wetteland	38-30	2nd	1
7-9	N.Y.	W	5-4	(12)	10	10	Vosberg	Howe		39-30	T1st	...
7-13	At Bos.	W	9-8		11	11	Vosberg	Clemens	Russell	40-30	T1st	...
7-14	At Bos.	L	2-5		9	10	Wakefield	Pavlik	Aguilera	40-31	2nd	1

Date	Opp.	Res.	Score	(inn.*)	Hits	Opp. hits	Winning pitcher	Losing pitcher	Save	Record	Pos.	GB
7-15	At Bos.	W	7-2		14	6	Gross	Hanson		41-31	2nd	$^{1}/_{2}$
7-16	At Bos.	W	5-2		4	7	Rogers	Smith	Russell	42-31	2nd	1
7-17	Bal.	L	2-3	(13)	5	10	Lee	Cook	Jones	42-32	2nd	2
7-18	Bal.	L	2-4		5	5	Mussina	Pavlik	Jones	42-33	2nd	2
7-19	Cle.	L	5-14		12	19	Nagy	Gross		42-34	2nd	3
7-20	Cle.	L	3-6		10	11	Hershiser	Brandenburg	Mesa	42-35	2nd	4
7-21	At N.Y.	L	3-8		9	8	Eiland	Rogers	Wetteland	42-36	2nd	4
7-22	At N.Y.	L	4-7		7	9	Pettitte	Tewksbury	Wetteland	42-37	2nd	5
7-23	At N.Y.	L	4-11		11	18	McDowell	Burrows		42-38	2nd	6
7-24	At N.Y.	L	4-5		8	15	Howe	Whiteside		42-39	2nd	6
7-25	At Bal.	L	3-4		7	7	Orosco	McDowell		42-40	2nd	7
7-26	At Bal.	L	6-7		7	10	Moyer	Cook	Jones	42-41	2nd	8
7-27	At Bal.	W	2-1		7	7	Vosberg	Orosco	Russell	43-41	2nd	8
7-28	Bos.	L	2-6		5	11	Maddux	Taylor		43-42	2nd	9
7-29	Bos.	L	1-7		6	11	Wakefield	Gross		43-43	T2nd	10
7-30	Bos.	W	7-6		8	11	Whiteside	Hanson	Russell	44-43	2nd	10
8-1	At Oak.	L	3-4	(11)	12	11	Reyes	Whiteside		44-44	2nd	11
8-2	At Oak.	W	5-4		7	12	Taylor	Van Poppel	McDowell	45-44	2nd	11
8-3	At Oak.	L	3-5		6	4	Prieto	Gross	Eckersley	45-45	2nd	11
8-4	At Cal.	W	6-4		7	7	Rogers	Finley	Vosberg	46-45	2nd	10
8-5	At Cal.	L	3-5		8	12	Langston	Darwin	Smith	46-46	2nd	11
8-6	At Cal.	W	5-2		10	8	Pavlik	B. Anderson	Vosberg	47-46	2nd	10
8-7	At Cal.	L	2-9		6	13	Harkey	Taylor		47-47	T2nd	11
8-8	Det.	W	4-1		12	8	Gross	Bergman	Whiteside	48-47	T2nd	11
8-9	Det.	W	13-5		17	9	Rogers	Doherty		49-47	T2nd	11
8-10	Det.	W	7-2		8	5	Darwin	Lira		50-47	2nd	10
8-11	Tor.	L	5-14		6	17	Hurtado	Pavlik		50-48	3rd	11
8-12	Tor.	W	6-3		9	9	Witt	Leiter	McDowell	51-48	2nd	10
8-13	Tor.	W	6-1		10	6	Gross	Carrara		52-48	2nd	10
8-15	Mil.	W	3-2		10	6	Whiteside	Dibble		53-48	2nd	$10^{1}/_{2}$
8-16	Mil.	L	6-15		6	17	Givens	Darwin		53-49	2nd	$10^{1}/_{2}$
8-17	At Chi.	W	2-1	(10)	6	4	McDowell	Karchner		54-49	2nd	$9^{1}/_{2}$
8-18	At Chi.	L	1-3		7	9	Alvarez	Witt	Hernandez	54-50	2nd	$9^{1}/_{2}$
8-19	At Chi.	W	9-6		13	7	Gross	Bolton		55-50	2nd	$9^{1}/_{2}$
8-20	At Chi.	W	6-4		11	8	Rogers	Bere	McDowell	56-50	2nd	$9^{1}/_{2}$
8-21	Min.	W	12-5		12	11	Darwin	Klingenbeck		57-50	2nd	$8^{1}/_{2}$
8-22	Min.	L	4-9		10	10	Rodriguez	Pavlik		57-51	2nd	$8^{1}/_{2}$
8-23	Min.	W	9-1		12	9	Witt	Parra		58-51	2nd	$7^{1}/_{2}$
8-24	At K.C.	L	3-5		7	8	Jacome	Gross	Montgomery	58-52	2nd	$8^{1}/_{2}$
8-25	At K.C.	L	4-9		11	12	Gubicza	Rogers	Olson	58-53	2nd	$8^{1}/_{2}$
8-26	At K.C.	W	10-3		16	7	Tewksbury	Appier	Cook	59-53	2nd	$7^{1}/_{2}$
8-27	At K.C.	L	2-5		7	7	Gordon	Pavlik	Montgomery	59-54	2nd	$7^{1}/_{2}$
8-28	At Min.	L	3-4	(10)	9	13	Guardado	McDowell		59-55	2nd	8
8-29	At Min.	L	0-2		3	6	Radke	Gross		59-56	2nd	8
8-30	At Min.	L	2-6		6	12	Guardado	Rogers		59-57	2nd	8
9-1	K.C.	L	2-5		8	12	Gordon	Tewksbury	Olson	59-58	3rd	$7^{1}/_{2}$
9-2	K.C.	W	4-1		5	7	Pavlik	Fleming	Russell	60-58	T2nd	$6^{1}/_{2}$
9-3	K.C.	L	5-8		10	15	Olson	Vosberg	Montgomery	60-59	3rd	$6^{1}/_{2}$
9-4	Chi.	L	3-14		4	18	Bere	Gross		60-60	3rd	$7^{1}/_{2}$
9-5	Chi.	L	1-2	(11)	6	11	Karchner	Vosberg		60-61	3rd	$7^{1}/_{2}$
9-6	Chi.	L	5-7		9	13	Keyser	Tewksbury	Hernandez	60-62	3rd	$7^{1}/_{2}$
9-7	Chi.	W	2-0		5	3	Pavlik	Alvarez		61-62	3rd	7
9-8	At Mil.	L	1-10		7	13	Bones	Witt		61-63	3rd	8
9-9	At Mil.	W	10-4		12	11	Gross	Sparks		62-63	3rd	8
9-10	At Mil.	W	5-2		15	6	Rogers	Karl	Russell	63-63	3rd	7
9-12	At Tor.	W	6-5		10	11	McDowell	Leiter	Russell	64-63	3rd	$7^{1}/_{2}$
9-13	At Tor.	W	3-2	(11)	12	7	Whiteside	Timlin		65-63	3rd	$6^{1}/_{2}$
9-14	At Tor.	W	6-1		14	7	Witt	Guzman		66-63	3rd	6
9-15	At Det.	L	2-3		6	4	Sodowsky	Gross	Henry	66-64	3rd	6
9-16	At Det.	W	7-3		17	7	Rogers	Nitkowski		67-64	3rd	5
9-17	At Det.	W	5-0		7	3	Pavlik	Lima		68-64	3rd	4
9-18	At Sea.	L	1-8		3	11	Johnson	Witt		68-65	3rd	4
9-19	At Sea.	L	4-5	(11)	10	12	Charlton	McDowell		68-66	3rd	4
9-20	At Sea.	L	3-11		8	20	Benes	Tewksbury		68-67	3rd	4
9-22	Cal.	W	8-3		10	7	Rogers	Langston		69-67	3rd	4
9-23	Cal.	W	5-1		10	4	Pavlik	Finley		70-67	3rd	4
9-24	Cal.	L	0-5		3	11	Abbott	Witt		70-68	3rd	5
9-26	Oak.	W	7-6		11	8	McDowell	Reyes	Russell	71-68	3rd	5
9-27	Oak.	W	11-2		12	7	Rogers	Van Poppel		72-68	3rd	4
9-28	Sea.	L	2-6		9	5	Johnson	Pavlik	Charlton	72-69	3rd	5
9-29	Sea.	L	3-4		14	8	Ayala	Vosberg	Charlton	72-70	3rd	6
9-30	Sea.	W	9-2		13	9	Gross	Benes		73-70	3rd	5
10-1	Sea.	W	9-3		13	8	Rogers	Belcher	Whiteside	74-70	3rd	4

Monthly records: April (2-3), May (16-12), June (17-10), July (9-18), August (15-14), September (14-13), October (1-0).

*Innings, if other than nine. †First game of doubleheader. ‡Second game of doubleheader.

HIGHLIGHTS

High point: The Rangers went 17-10 in June and won three of four from the Red Sox in Fenway Park immediately after the All-Star break. The combination of the solid effort in June and the success in Boston left Texas one game out of first place with a 42-31 record, the team's highest over-.500 mark of the season.

Low point: After leaving Fenway, the Rangers suffered a 10-game losing streak that effectively removed them from title contention. The skid dropped the Rangers eight games out of first.

Turning point: The Rangers won seven of the first nine games of a 12-game September road swing to move one game behind Kenny race and four behind fading California in the division race. But the Rangers finished the trip by getting swept in Seattle.

Most valuable player: Outfielder Otis Nixon. Nixon had an impact at the top of the lineup, hitting .295 with 87 runs and 50 steals, and he played well in center field.

Most valuable pitcher: Lefthander Kenny Rogers. He went 17-7 with a 3.38 ERA and set a club record by throwing 39 consecutive scoreless innings.

Most improved player: Righthander Roger Pavlik. He recovered from a season of shoulder problems by going 10-10 with a club-high 149 strikeouts. He was 4-1 with a 1.90 ERA in his last six starts.

Most pleasant surprise: Rookie shortstop Benji Gil. He helped improve the defense dramatically.

Biggest disappointment: Righthander Kevin Gross. He signed a two-year contract and went 9-15 with a 5.54 ERA.

Key injuries: Third baseman Dean Palmer, off to the best start of his career, was lost for 3½ months with a torn biceps tendon. Outfielder Juan Gonzalez played in just 90 games because of back and shoulder injuries. Pitcher Bob Tewksbury missed 10 starts with a stress fracture in his rib cage and a pulled hamstring muscle. Closer Jeff Russell twice went on the disabled list with a herniated disk in his lower back. Pitcher Darren Oliver won a spot in the rotation

but, after seven starts, suffered a partially torn rotator cuff and missed the final three months.

Notable: The Rangers missed the playoffs for the 24th consecutive season (their entire existence in Texas) and are the only A.L. team never to have reached postseason play.

—T.R. SULLIVAN

RECORDS

1995 regular-season record: 74-70 (3rd in A.L. West); 41-31 at home; 33-39 on road; 25-20 vs. East; 31-29 vs. Central; 18-21 vs. West; 25-22 vs. lefthanded starters; 49-48 vs. righthanded starters; 66-60 on grass; 8-10 on turf; 14-17 in daytime; 60-53 at night; 21-18 in one-run games; 6-6 in extra-inning games; 0-0-1 in doubleheaders.

Team record past five years: 374-370 (.503, ranks 7th in league in that span).

TEAM LEADERS

Batting average: Ivan Rodriguez (.303).
At-bats: Otis Nixon (589).
Runs: Otis Nixon (87).
Hits: Otis Nixon (174).
Total bases: Mickey Tettleton (219).
Doubles: Ivan Rodriguez (32).
Triples: Mark McLemore (5).
Home runs: Mickey Tettleton (32).
Runs batted in: Will Clark (92).
Stolen bases: Otis Nixon (50).
Slugging percentage: Mickey Tettleton (.510).
On-base percentage: Mickey Tettleton (.396).
Wins: Kenny Rogers (17).
Earned-run average: Kenny Rogers (3.38).
Complete games: Kevin Gross, Bob Tewksbury (4).
Shutouts: Roger Pavlik, Kenny Rogers, Bob Tewksbury (1).
Saves: Jeff Russell (20).
Innings pitched: Kenny Rogers (208.0).
Strikeouts: Roger Pavlik (149).

GAMES BY POSITION

Catcher: Ivan Rodriguez 127, Dave Valle 29, Mickey Tettleton 3, John Marzano 2.
First base: Will Clark 122, Mike Pagliarulo 11, Mickey Tettleton 9, Dave Valle 7, Jack Voigt 5, Rusty Greer 3, Shawn Hare 1.
Second base: Jeff Frye 83, Mark McLemore 66, Esteban Beltre 15.
Third base: Mike Pagliarulo 68, Dean Palmer 36, Luis Ortiz 35, Craig Worthington 26, Steve Buechele 9, Esteban Beltre 1.
Shortstop: Benji Gil 130, Esteban Beltre 36.
Outfield: Otis Nixon 138, Rusty Greer 125, Mark McLemore 73, Mickey Tettleton 63, Lou Frazier 47, Jack Voigt 25, Candy Maldonado 11, Shawn Hare 9, Eric Fox 8, Juan Gonzalez 5, Billy Hatcher 5.
Designated hitter: Juan Gonzalez 83, Mickey Tettleton 58, Luis Ortiz 3, Lou Frazier 2, Shawn Hare 2, Will Clark 1, Eric Fox 1, Billy Hatcher 1, Sam Horn 1, Mark McLemore 1, Ivan Rodriguez 1, Jack Voigt 1.

TOP DRAFT CHOICES

1. **Jonathan Johnson,** RHP, Florida State University.
2. **Phill Lowery,** LHP, Casa Grande H.S., Petaluma, Calif.
3. **Ryan Dempster,** RHP, Elphinstone H.S., Gibsons, B.C.
4. **Ryan Glynn,** RHP, Virginia Military Institute.
5. **Shawn Gallagher,** 1B, New Hanover H.S., Wilmington, N.C.
6. **Dan Kolb,** RHP, Sterling, Ill.
7. **George Carrion,** RHP-SS, DeWitt Clinton H.S., Bronx, N.Y.
8. **Craig Monroe,** SS, Texarkana (Tex.) H.S.
9. **Juan Rivera,** C, Rio Grande, Puerto Rico.
10. **Julio Mercado,** OF, Brook Pointe H.S., Stafford, Va.

TORONTO BLUE JAYS
AMERICAN LEAGUE EAST DIVISION

1996 BLUE JAYS SCHEDULE

Home games shaded.
* — All-Star Game at Veterans Stadium (Philadelphia)
N — Night game (any game starting after 5 p.m.)

MARCH

SUN	MON	TUE	WED	THU	FRI	SAT
31						

APRIL

SUN	MON	TUE	WED	THU	FRI	SAT
	1 N OAK	2	3 N OAK	4	5 N CLE	6 CLE
7 CLE	8	9 N CAL	10 N CAL	11 N CAL	12 N SEA	13 SEA
14 SEA	15 N DET	16 DET	17 N CAL	18 N CAL	19 N SEA	20 N SEA
21 SEA	22 N SEA	23	24 N OAK	25 N OAK	26 N CLE	27 CLE
28 CLE	29	30 N MIL				

MAY

SUN	MON	TUE	WED	THU	FRI	SAT
			1 N MIL	2 MIL	3 N BOS	4 BOS
5 BOS	6	7 N TEX	8 N TEX	9 N TEX	10 N BOS	11 BOS
12 BOS	13	14 N MIN	15 N MIN	16 MIN	17 N KC	18 N KC
19 KC	20 N KC	21 N CHI	22 CHI	23 N MIN	24 N MIN	25 MIN
26 MIN	27 N CHI	28 N CHI	29 N CHI	30	31 N KC	

JUNE

SUN	MON	TUE	WED	THU	FRI	SAT
						1 KC
2 KC	3	4 N NY	5 N NY	6 N NY	7 N TEX	8 N TEX
9 TEX	10 N NY	11 N NY	12 N NY	13 N CAL	14 N CAL	15 N CAL
16 CAL	17	18 N SEA	19 N SEA	20 N OAK	21 N OAK	22 OAK
23 OAK	24	25 N SEA	26 N SEA	27 SEA	28 N MIL	29 MIL
30 MIL						

JULY

SUN	MON	TUE	WED	THU	FRI	SAT
	1 BAL	2 N BAL	3 N BAL	4 N DET	5 N DET	6 DET
7 DET	8	9 * ALL-STAR GAME	10	11 N MIL	12 N MIL	13 N MIL
14 MIL	15 N BAL	16 N BAL	17 N BAL	18 N DET	19 N DET	20 DET
21 DET	22 N CLE	23 N CLE	24 N CLE	25 N OAK	26 N OAK	27 OAK
28 OAK	29	30 N CLE	31 N CLE			

AUGUST

SUN	MON	TUE	WED	THU	FRI	SAT
				1 N CLE	2 N CAL	3 CAL
4 CAL	5 N BOS	6 N BOS	7 N BOS	8	9 N TEX	10 TEX
11 TEX	12 N BOS	13 N BOS	14 N BOS	15	16 N MIN	17 N MIN
18 MIN	19 N KC	20 N KC	21 N KC	22 N CHI	23 N CHI	24 N CHI
25 CHI	26 N MIN	27 N MIN	28 N MIN	29	30 N CHI	31 CHI

SEPTEMBER

SUN	MON	TUE	WED	THU	FRI	SAT
1 CHI	2 KC	3 N KC	4 N KC	5	6 N NY	7 N NY
8 NY	9 N TEX	10 N TEX	11 N TEX	12	13 N NY	14 N NY
15 NY	16 N NY	17 N MIL	18 MIL	19	20 N BAL	21 N BAL
22 BAL	23 N DET	24 N DET	25 DET	26 N BAL	27 N BAL	28 BAL
29 BAL						

1996 SEASON

CLUB DIRECTORY

President and chief executive officer
Paul Beeston

Vice president, business
Bob Nicholson

Vice president, development
Christine Legein

Vice president, general manager
Gord Ash

Vice presidents, baseball
Bob Mattick
Al LaMacchia

Special asst. to v.p., baseball, g.m.
Al Widmar

Assistant general managers
Bob Engle
Tim McCleary

Director, public relations
Howard Starkman

Director, stadium and ticket operations
George Holm

Director, marketing
Paul Markle

Director, finance
Susie Quigley

Director, scouting
Tim Wilken

Director, international scouting
Wayne Morgan

Director, player development
Karl Kuehl

Director, Canadian scouting
Bill Byckowski

Director, minor league business
Ken Carson

Administrator, player personnel
Bob Nelson

Asst. dir., tickets and box office manager
Randy Low

Assistant director, operations
Len Frejlich

Manager, group sales
Maureen Haffey

Manager, team travel
John Brioux

Manager, promotions and advertising
Rick Amos

Manager, accounting
Cathy McNamara

Manager, employee compensation
Perry Nicoletta

Manager, information systems
Hans Frauenlob

Manager, ticket vault
Paul Goodyear

Manager, game operations
Mario Coutinho

Supervisor, office service
Mick Bazinet

Trainers
Tommy Craig
Brent Andrews

Strength and conditioning coordinator
Geoffrey Horne

Team physician
Dr. Ron Taylor

Special assignment scouts
Moose Johnson
Gordon Lakey

Director, international scouting
Wayne Morgan

Advance scout
Don Welke

Scouts
Tony Arias, Ed Blankmeyer, David Blume, Chris Bourjos, Chris Buckley, Bus Campbell, John Cole, Ellis Dungan, Joe Ford, Tim Hewes, Tom Hinkle, Jim Hughes, Duane Larson, Ted Lekas, Ben McLure, Bill Moore, Andy Pienovi, Alvin Rittman, Jorge Rivera, Mike Russell, Joe Siers, Mark Snipp, Jerry Sobeck, Ron Tostenson, Steve Williams

MINOR LEAGUE AFFILIATES

Class	Team	League	Manager
AAA	Syracuse	International	Richie Hebner
AA	Knoxville	Southern	Omar Malave
A	Dunedin	Florida State	Dennis Holmberg
A	Hagerstown	South Atlantic	J.J. Cannon
A	St. Catharines	New York-Penn.	Rocket Wheeler
Rookie	Medicine Hat	Pioneer	To be announced

BROADCAST INFORMATION

Radio: THE-FAN (590).
TV: Baton Broadcasting, CBC-TV (Channel 6).
Cable TV: The Sports Network.

SPRING TRAINING

Ballpark (city): Dunedin Stadium at Grant Field (Dunedin, Fla.).
Ticket information: 813-733-0429.

SPRING TRAINING ROSTER

Manager—Cito Gaston (43).
Coaches—Alfredo Griffin (4), Nick Leyva (16), Mel Queen (34), Gene Tenace (18), Willie Upshaw (28).

No.	PITCHERS	B/T	Ht./Wt.	Born	1995 clubs
38	Carrara, Giovanni	R/R	6-2/230	3-4-68	Syracuse, Toronto
49	Castillo, Tony	L/L	5-10/190	3-1-63	Toronto
37	Crabtree, Tim	R/R	6-4/205	10-13-69	Syracuse, Toronto
39	Gordon, Mike	L/R	6-3/210	11-30-72	Tampa, Dunedin
66	Guzman, Juan	R/R	5-11/195	10-28-66	Toronto, Syracuse
	Hanson, Erik	R/R	6-6/215	5-18-65	Boston
41	Hentgen, Pat	R/R	6-2/200	11-13-68	Toronto
36	Janzen, Marty	R/R	6-3/197	5-31-73	Tampa, Norwich, Knoxville
51	Paige, Carey	R/R	6-3/175	3-2-74	Durham, Greenville
48	Quantrill, Paul	L/R	6-1/185	11-3-68	Philadelphia
55	Risley, Bill	R/R	6-2/215	5-29-67	Tacoma, Seattle
44	Robinson, Ken	R/R	5-9/170	11-3-69	Syracuse, Toronto
47	Rogers, Jimmy	R/R	6-2/205	1-3-67	Syracuse, Toronto
42	Sievert, Mark	L/R	6-4/195	2-16-73	Hagerstown
45	Silva, Jose	R/R	6-5/210	12-19-73	Knoxville
24	Spoljaric, Paul	R/L	6-3/212	9-24-70	Syracuse
40	Timlin, Mike	R/R	6-4/210	3-10-66	Toronto, Syracuse
52	Ware, Jeff	R/R	6-3/195	11-11-70	Syracuse, Toronto
54	Williams, Woody	R/R	6-0/190	8-19-66	Toronto, Syracuse

No.	CATCHERS	B/T	Ht./Wt.	Born	1995 clubs
27	Knorr, Randy	R/R	6-2/220	11-12-68	Toronto, Syracuse
35	Martinez, Sandy	L/R	6-2/200	10-3-72	Knoxville, Toronto
46	Mosquera, Julio	R/R	6-0/185	1-29-72	Hagerstown
22	O'Brien, Charlie	R/R	6-2/205	5-1-61	Atlanta

No.	INFIELDERS	B/T	Ht./Wt.	Born	1995 clubs
5	Boston, D.J.	L/L	6-7/230	9-6-71	Knoxville
14	Brito, Tilson	R/R	6-0/170	5-28-72	Syracuse
3	Cairo, Miguel	R/R	6-0/160	5-4-74	San Antonio
20	Cedeno, Domingo	B/R	6-1/170	11-4-68	Toronto
21	Crespo, Felipe	B/R	5-11/210	3-5-73	Syracuse
6	Delgado, Carlos	L/R	6-3/225	6-25-72	Toronto, Syracuse
25	Evans, Tom	R/R	6-1/208	7-9-74	Dunedin
8	Gonzalez, Alex	R/R	6-0/185	4-8-73	Toronto
9	Olerud, John	L/L	6-5/218	8-5-68	Toronto
1	Perez, Tomas	B/R	5-11/175	12-29-73	Toronto
33	Sprague, Ed	R/R	6-2/205	7-25-67	Toronto

No.	OUTFIELDERS	B/T	Ht./Wt.	Born	1995 clubs
29	Carter, Joe	R/R	6-3/225	3-7-60	Toronto
15	Green, Shawn	L/L	6-4/190	11-10-72	Toronto
2	Nixon, Otis	B/R	6-2/180	1-9-59	Texas
17	Perez, Robert	R/R	6-3/215	6-4-69	Syracuse, Toronto
30	Ramirez, Angel	R/R	6-0/170	1-24-73	Dunedin
23	Roberts, Lonell	B/R	6-0/180	6-7-71	Knoxville
7	Stewart, Shannon	R/R	6-1/195	2-25-74	Knoxville, Toronto

BALLPARK INFORMATION

Ballpark (capacity, surface)
SkyDome (50,516, artificial)

Address
One Blue Jays Way
Suite 3200
Toronto, Ontario M5V 1J1

Business phone
416-341-1000

Ticket information
416-341-1111

Ticket prices
$23 (esplanade IF, club level OF)
$18 (skydeck IF, esplanade OF)
$13 (skydeck)
$6 (skydeck outfield)

Field dimensions (from home plate)
To left field at foul line, 330 feet
To center field, 400 feet
To right field at foul line, 330 feet

First game played
June 5, 1989 (Brewers 5, Blue Jays 3)

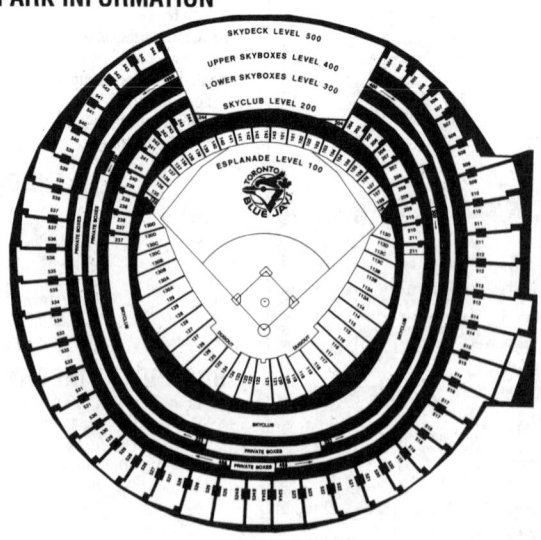

DAY BY DAY

Date	Opp.	Res.	Score	(inn.*)	Hits	Opp. hits	Winning pitcher	Losing pitcher	Save	Record	Pos.	GB
4-26	Oak.	W	13-1		11	6	Cone	Stewart		1-0	T1st	...
4-27	Oak.	W	7-1		8	4	Hentgen	Darling		2-0	1st	+1/2
4-28	Cal.	L	6-7	(10)	12	10	Butcher	Castillo	Smith	2-1	3rd	1/2
4-29	Cal.	W	3-0		10	5	Leiter	Sanderson	Hall	3-1	3rd	1/2
4-30	Cal.	L	3-5		8	7	Butcher	Menhart	Smith	3-2	3rd	1/2
5-1	Cal.	L	0-2		5	6	Boskie	Cone	Smith	3-3	3rd	11/2
5-2	Chi.	W	9-8		12	12	Timlin	Marquez		4-3	3rd	1/2
5-3	Chi.	W	8-7	(10)	9	13	Menhart	Hernandez		5-3	2nd	1/2
5-5	At Bal.	L	2-9		6	11	K. Brown	Leiter		5-4	T2nd	2
5-6	At Bal.	W	7-3		12	12	Darwin	Rhodes		6-4	T2nd	1
5-7	At Bal.	L	2-6		6	10	Mussina	Cone		6-5	3rd	1
5-9	N.Y.	W	9-6		14	12	Hentgen	McDowell		7-5	T2nd	1
5-10	N.Y.	L	4-6	(11)	12	14	Wetteland	Williams		7-6	3rd	2
5-11	N.Y.	L	11-12		14	15	Ausanio	Ward	Howe	7-7	3rd	21/2
5-12	At Mil.	L	5-14		12	18	Ignasiak	Darwin		7-8	3rd	3
5-13	At Mil.	W	10-0		11	3	Cone	Miranda		8-8	3rd	21/2
5-14	At Mil.	W	8-3		14	9	Hentgen	Eldred		9-8	3rd	21/2
5-15	At Tex.	L	4-12		12	14	Tewksbury	Guzman		9-9	3rd	3
5-16	At Tex.	L	1-6		4	12	Rogers	Leiter	Burrows	9-10	3rd	4
5-17	At Tex.	L	7-12		11	16	Gross	Darwin	Vosberg	9-11	3rd	5
5-19	At Det.	W	4-2		10	4	Cone	Moore		10-11	3rd	41/2
5-20	At Det.	L	6-10		11	9	Doherty	Hentgen		10-12	3rd	41/2
5-21	At Det.	L	1-2		5	4	Boever	Cox	Henneman	10-13	T3rd	41/2
5-22	K.C.	L	0-7		2	12	Appier	Darwin		10-14	T4th	5
5-23	K.C.	W	10-6		16	6	Timlin	Pichardo	Hall	11-14	T4th	5
5-24	K.C.	L	5-8		7	12	Gordon	Cone		11-15	T4th	5
5-26	Cle.	L	4-7		7	11	Hershiser	Hentgen	Mesa	11-16	4th	51/2
5-27	Cle.	W	3-0		6	6	Leiter	Plunk	Hall	12-16	4th	51/2
5-28	Cle.	L	4-5		10	5	Nagy	Darwin	Mesa	12-17	4th	51/2
5-29	Det.	W	5-4		12	9	Cone	Moore	Timlin	13-17	4th	51/2
5-30	Det.	L	6-8		10	8	Lira	Cox	Henneman	13-18	4th	61/2
5-31	Det.	W	5-3		13	7	Hentgen	Doherty		14-18	T3rd	61/2
6-2	At Cle.	W	5-0		9	3	Leiter	Nagy	Timlin	15-18	2nd	61/2
6-3	At Cle.	L	0-3		9	7	Martinez	Darwin		15-19	3rd	71/2
6-4	At Cle.	L	8-9		8	17	Tavarez	Hall		15-20	T4th	81/2
6-5	At Chi.	L	2-3		7	8	Abbott	Guzman	Hernandez	15-21	T4th	91/2
6-6	At Chi.	L	4-6		9	9	Bere	Hentgen	Hernandez	15-22	T4th	91/2
6-7	At Chi.	W	4-3		11	10	Leiter	Keyser	Timlin	16-22	T3rd	91/2
6-10	At K.C.	L	2-8		4	17	Appier	Darwin		16-23	4th	91/2
6-11	At K.C.	L	2-3	(10)	9	8	Pichardo	Hall		16-24	T4th	91/2
6-12	Bos.	W	4-3	(12)	11	8	Timlin	Ryan		17-24	4th	81/2
6-13	Bos.	L	7-11		10	13	Maddux	Hentgen		17-25	T4th	91/2
6-14	Bos.	W	5-3		8	9	Leiter	Wakefield	Castillo	18-25	T4th	81/2
6-16	Tex.	L	3-7		11	11	Tewksbury	Darwin		18-26	5th	81/2
6-17	Tex.	W	4-3		9	3	Cone	Rogers		19-26	3rd	71/2
6-18	Tex.	W	7-2		6	10	Guzman	Pavlik		20-26	3rd	71/2
6-20	Mil.	L	3-5		9	13	Roberson	Hentgen	Fetters	20-27	T3rd	7
6-21	Mil.	L	9-10		14	10	Wegman	Timlin	Fetters	20-28	T3rd	8
6-22	Mil.	L	0-9		4	13	Sparks	Darwin		20-29	T4th	9
6-23	At N.Y.	L	2-6		7	11	McDowell	Cone		20-30	5th	9
6-24	At N.Y.	L	2-10		5	11	Perez	Guzman		20-31	5th	10
6-25	At N.Y.	L	2-8		6	13	Hitchcock	Hentgen		20-32	5th	10
6-26	At Bos.	L	3-4		9	5	Belinda	Castillo		20-33	5th	11
6-27	At Bos.	L	5-6	(11)	8	7	Lilliquist	Williams		20-34	5th	12
6-28	At Bos.	W	8-4		12	6	Cone	Smith		21-34	5th	11
6-29	Bal.	W	5-1		8	7	Guzman	Fernandez		22-34	5th	11
6-30	Bal.	W	6-5		8	11	Cox	Clark		23-34	5th	10
7-1	Bal.	L	2-6		7	10	Moyer	Leiter		23-35	5th	10
7-2	Bal.	L	7-9		5	8	Benitez	Crabtree	Jones	23-36	5th	11
7-3	At Cal.	L	2-4		7	8	Langston	Cone	Smith	23-37	5th	12
7-4	At Cal.	L	0-14		3	15	Finley	Guzman		23-38	5th	13
7-5	At Cal.	W	6-5		12	9	Hentgen	Boskie	Castillo	24-38	5th	12
7-6	At Cal.	L	1-10		4	14	B. Anderson	Leiter		24-39	5th	12
7-7	At Oak.	W	4-2		11	8	Williams	Prieto	Castillo	25-39	5th	12
7-8†	At Oak.	W	9-6		12	12	Cone	Harkey		26-39		
7-8‡	At Oak.	L	3-6		11	9	Eckersley	Guzman		26-40	5th	111/2
7-9	At Oak.	W	7-3		8	8	Hentgen	Darling		27-40	5th	111/2
7-12	At Oak.	L	4-7		8	7	Stottlemyre	Leiter	Eckersley	27-41	5th	12
7-13	At Sea.	W	4-1		5	6	Cone	Belcher	Castillo	28-41	5th	11
7-14	At Sea.	W	5-1		14	3	Guzman	Bosio		29-41	5th	11
7-15	At Sea.	L	0-3		3	8	Johnson	Hentgen		29-42	5th	11

Date	Opp.	Res.	Score	(inn.*)	Hits	Opp. hits	Winning pitcher	Losing pitcher	Save	Record	Pos.	GB
7-16	At Sea.	W	9-3		11	7	Hurtado	Carmona		30-42	5th	10
7-17	At Min.	W	6-3		10	12	Leiter	Harris	Castillo	31-42	5th	9
7-18	At Min.	W	7-0		14	4	Cone	Tapani		32-42	5th	9
7-19	Cal.	L	2-10		7	15	Springer	Guzman		32-43	5th	10
7-20	Cal.	L	3-10		6	17	Butcher	Hentgen		32-44	5th	11
7-21	Sea.	W	4-3		7	8	Hurtado	Torres	Castillo	33-44	5th	11
7-22	Sea.	L	2-7		5	13	Belcher	Leiter		33-45	5th	11
7-23	Sea.	L	4-6		11	12	Wells	Cone	Ayala	33-46	5th	11
7-25	Min.	L	3-7		5	14	Rodriguez	Guzman		33-47	5th	11½
7-26	Min.	W	6-2		9	8	Hentgen	Trombley		34-47	5th	11½
7-27	Min.	W	9-2		12	7	Hurtado	Harris		35-47	5th	10½
7-28	Oak.	W	3-0		7	4	Leiter	Van Poppel	Castillo	36-47	5th	10½
7-29	Oak.	W	18-11		16	13	Carrara	Prieto		37-47	5th	10½
7-30	Oak.	L	3-11		10	15	Darling	Guzman		37-48	5th	10½
7-31	At Bal.	W	6-3		9	8	Hentgen	Moyer	Jordan	38-48	5th	10
8-1	At Bal.	W	12-10		13	10	Robinson	Jones	Castillo	39-48	5th	10
8-2	At Bal.	L	0-1		4	1	Mussina	Menhart		39-49	5th	10
8-3	At Bal.	W	8-2	(10)	8	4	Jordan	Clark		40-49	5th	10
8-4	Bos.	L	1-7		6	7	Hanson	Rogers		40-50	5th	11
8-5	Bos.	L	3-9		8	11	Cormier	Hentgen		40-51	5th	12
8-6	Bos.	L	4-6		12	10	Eshelman	Hurtado	Aguilera	40-52	5th	13
8-7	Bos.	L	4-5	(10)	10	6	Belinda	Crabtree		40-53	5th	14
8-8	At Mil.	L	5-6	(11)	13	12	Wegman	Rogers		40-54	5th	15
8-9	At Mil.	L	7-12		12	11	Karl	Guzman		40-55	5th	16
8-10	At Mil.	W	8-4		17	11	Hentgen	Sparks	Castillo	41-55	5th	16
8-11	At Tex.	W	14-5		17	6	Hurtado	Pavlik		42-55	T4th	16
8-12	At Tex.	L	3-6		9	9	Witt	Leiter	McDowell	42-56	5th	17
8-13	At Tex.	L	1-6		6	10	Gross	Carrara		42-57	5th	18
8-15	At Det.	L	5-11		14	14	Bohanon	Hentgen		42-58	5th	18½
8-16	At Det.	W	7-4		10	10	Hurtado	Maxcy	Castillo	43-58	5th	18½
8-17	At Det.	W	3-0		6	5	Leiter	Lima	Castillo	44-58	4th	18½
8-18	K.C.	L	3-10		8	11	Gordon	Carrara		44-59	5th	18½
8-19	K.C.	W	5-4	(13)	12	6	Rogers	Montgomery		45-59	4th	18½
8-20	K.C.	W	4-3		10	7	Timlin	Olson		46-59	4th	18½
8-21	Cle.	L	3-7		10	8	Hershiser	Hurtado	Embree	46-60	4th	19½
8-22	Cle.	W	5-4		9	7	Castillo	Tavarez		47-60	4th	19½
8-23	Cle.	L	5-6		9	7	Poole	Carrara	Mesa	47-61	4th	20½
8-25	Chi.	L	7-8		12	9	Bere	Hentgen	Hernandez	47-62	4th	21
8-26	Chi.	W	3-2		10	9	Rogers	Hernandez		48-62	4th	20
8-27	Chi.	W	2-1		9	3	Leiter	Righetti	Castillo	49-62	4th	20
8-28	At Cle.	L	1-9		10	13	Ogea	Carrara		49-63	4th	20½
8-29	At Cle.	L	1-4		3	7	Clark	Guzman		49-64	4th	20½
8-30	At Cle.	L	3-4	(14)	18	12	Assenmacher	Castillo		49-65	4th	21½
8-31	At Cle.	L	4-6	(10)	10	12	Mesa	Rogers		49-66	4th	21½
9-1	At Chi.	L	3-5		7	8	Keyser	Leiter	Hernandez	49-67	4th	22½
9-2	At Chi.	L	4-10		10	13	Alvarez	Ware		49-68	4th	23½
9-3	At Chi.	L	5-6		13	11	Simas	Guzman	Hernandez	49-69	4th	24½
9-4†	At K.C.	W	6-1		17	10	Hentgen	Gubicza	Timlin	50-69		
9-4‡	At K.C.	L	7-9		12	13	Magnante	Castillo	Montgomery	50-70	4th	24½
9-5	At K.C.	L	8-9	(10)	11	10	Olson	Robinson		50-71	5th	25½
9-6	At K.C.	W	6-2		11	9	Leiter	Gordon		51-71	4th	25½
9-8	Det.	W	9-5		7	7	Ware	Lira		52-71	4th	24½
9-9	Det.	L	2-5		7	8	Bergman	Guzman	Henry	52-72	4th	24½
9-10	Det.	L	2-5	(11)	9	7	Doherty	Timlin	Henry	52-73	5th	24½
9-11	Det.	L	2-3	(10)	10	8	Christopher	Rogers	Bohanon	52-74	4th	24½
9-12	Tex.	L	5-6		11	10	McDowell	Leiter	Russell	52-75	4th	24½
9-13	Tex.	L	2-3	(11)	7	12	Whiteside	Timlin		52-76	5th	25½
9-14	Tex.	L	1-6		7	14	Witt	Guzman		52-77	5th	25½
9-15	Mil.	L	1-5	(15)	6	12	Kiefer	Robinson		52-78	5th	26½
9-16	Mil.	W	5-4	(11)	11	7	Carrara	Wegman		53-78	5th	25½
9-17	Mil.	W	5-0		10	6	Leiter	Givens		54-78	5th	25½
9-18	At N.Y.	L	2-9		9	12	Cone	Cox		54-79	5th	25½
9-19	At N.Y.	L	3-5		5	3	Pettitte	Guzman	Wetteland	54-80	5th	26½
9-20	At N.Y.	L	1-2		6	5	Hitchcock	Hentgen	Wetteland	54-81	5th	27½
9-21	At N.Y.	L	4-6		9	11	Howe	Menhart	Wetteland	54-82	5th	28
9-23†	At Bos.	L	0-5		7	9	Clemens	Leiter		54-83		
9-23‡	At Bos.	W	8-6		11	8	Ware	Wakefield	Castillo	55-83	5th	28
9-24	At Bos.	W	2-1		6	4	Guzman	Aguilera	Timlin	56-83	5th	27
9-26	Bal.	L	0-5		5	10	Mussina	Hentgen		56-84	5th	27½
9-27	Bal.	L	0-7		3	12	Erickson	Menhart		56-85	5th	27½
9-29	N.Y.	L	3-4		4	7	Pettitte	Castillo	Wetteland	56-86	5th	29
9-30	N.Y.	L	1-6		4	7	Kamieniecki	Leiter		56-87	5th	30
10-1	N.Y.	L	1-6		7	11	Hitchcock	Hentgen		56-88	5th	30

Monthly records: April (3-2), May (11-16), June (9-16), July (15-14), August (11-18), September (7-21), October (0-1).
*Innings, if other than nine. †First game of doubleheader. ‡Second game of doubleheader.

HIGHLIGHTS

High point: In their worst season since 1981, the Jays' longest winning streak was four games. The high-water mark was the first 10 games when they went 6-4 to provide some early encouragement before falling apart.

Low point: Even though they were long out of it, the Jays sunk to new lows in the final month. Their 7-22 mark was their worst September-October since 1978.

Turning point: Milwaukee shortstop Jose Valentin hit a ninth-inning grand slam off Mike Timlin at SkyDome to hand Toronto a 10-9 loss June 21, the second game of a season-high eight-game losing streak.

Most valuable player: Second baseman Roberto Alomar. He played spectacular defense, hit .300 and drove in 66 runs, batting in four spots in the order.

Most valuable pitcher: Lefthander Al Leiter. Leiter finished 11-11 but was among the top 15 in the league in strikeouts and ERA most of the season. Opponents hit .238 off him, 30 points below the club average.

Most improved player: Third baseman Ed Sprague. Sprague's job was threatened in spring training by minor leaguer Howard Battle, but he responded by reaching career highs in homers (18), RBIs (74), walks and hit-by-pitches and played solid defense.

Most pleasant surprise: Right fielder Shawn Green. The rookie had trouble adjusting defensively but became a bona fide major league hitter with a .288 average and 15 homers in 379 at-bats.

Biggest disappointments: Juan Guzman was 4-14 with a 6.32 ERA and had no control. Pat Hentgen, after winning 32 games in the previous two seasons, finished 10-14 with a 5.11 ERA. Danny Darwin, whom the Jays signed without scouting, was 1-8 before he was released.

Key injuries: With the exception of Tony Castillo, the entire back end of Toronto's bullpen was on the D.L. at least once. Timlin had elbow surgery, Danny Cox had back and neck problems, Darren Hall had elbow problems and Duane Ward has pitched only 2⅔ innings in two seasons because of rotator cuff problems. Designated hitter Paul Molitor nursed shoulder problems all season, and outfielder Devon White missed the final month with a broken foot.

Notable: Toronto used 15 rookies, one short of the franchise record. . . . Alomar established A.L. records for second basemen with 104 consecutive error-free games and 484 consecutive chances without an error.

—STEVE MILTON

RECORDS

1995 regular-season record: 56-88 (5th in A.L. East); 29-43 at home; 27-45 on road; 18-34 vs. East; 22-31 vs. Central; 16-23 vs. West; 15-29 vs. lefthanded starters; 41-59 vs. righthanded starters; 22-44 on grass; 34-44 on turf; 23-27 in daytime, 33-61 at night; 16-23 in one-run games; 5-13 in extra-inning games; 0-0-2 in doubleheaders. **Team record past five years:** 393-352 (.528, ranks 2nd in league in that span).

TEAM LEADERS

Batting average: Roberto Alomar (.300).
At-bats: Joe Carter (558).
Runs: Ed Sprague (77).
Hits: Roberto Alomar (155).
Total bases: Joe Carter (239).
Doubles: John Olerud (32).
Triples: Roberto Alomar (7).
Home runs: Joe Carter (25).
Runs batted in: Joe Carter (76).
Stolen bases: Roberto Alomar (30).
Slugging percentage: Roberto Alomar (.449).
On-base percentage: John Olerud (.398).
Wins: Al Leiter (11).
Earned-run average: Al Leiter (3.64).
Complete games: Juan Guzman (3).
Shutouts: David Cone (2).
Saves: Tony Castillo (13).
Innings pitched: Pat Hentgen (200.2).
Strikeouts: Al Leiter (153).

GAMES BY POSITION

Catcher: Lance Parrish 67, Angel Martinez 61, Randy Knorr 45.
First base: John Olerud 133, Joe Carter 7, Ed Sprague 7, Carlos Delgado 4.
Second base: Roberto Alomar 128, Domingo Cedeno 20, Tomas Perez 7.
Third base: Ed Sprague 139, Alex Gonzalez 9, Howard Battle 6, Domingo Cedeno 1, Tomas Perez 1.
Shortstop: Alex Gonzalez 97, Tomas Perez 31, Domingo Cedeno 30.
Outfield: Joe Carter 128, Shawn Green 109, Devon White 99, Candy Maldonado 58, Mike Huff 55, Carlos Delgado 17, Robert Perez 15, Shannon Stewart 12.
Designated hitter: Paul Molitor 129, Carlos Delgado 7, Joe Carter 5, Alex Gonzalez 3, Ed Sprague 2, Howard Battle 1, Candy Maldonado 1, Lance Parrish 1.

TOP DRAFT CHOICES

1. **Roy Halladay,** RHP, West H.S., Arvada, Colo.
2. **Craig Wilson,** C, Marina H.S., Huntington Beach, Calif.
3. **Jeff Maloney,** SS, Ridge H.S., Basking Ridge, N.J.
4. **Mike Whitlock,** 1B, San Lorenzo (Calif.) H.S.
5. **Jay Veniard,** LHP, University of Central Florida.
6. **Blaine Fortin,** C, Lundar (Manitoba) H.S.
7. **Jeremi Rudolph,** OF, Apopka (Fla.) H.S.
8. **Dave Marciniak,** SS, Woodbridge (N.J.) H.S.
9. **Kyle Burchart,** RHP, Bixby (Okla.) H.S.
10. **Ryan Freel,** 2B, Tallahassee (Fla.) C.C.

ATLANTA BRAVES
NATIONAL LEAGUE EAST DIVISION

1996 BRAVES SCHEDULE

☐ Home games shaded.
* — All-Star Game at Veterans Stadium (Philadelphia)
N — Night game (any game starting after 5 p.m.)

MARCH

SUN	MON	TUE	WED	THU	FRI	SAT
31						

APRIL

SUN	MON	TUE	WED	THU	FRI	SAT
	1 SF	2	3 N SF	4 N	5 N STL	6 N STL
7 STL	8 LA	9 N LA	10 N LA	11 SD N	12 SD N	13 SD
14 SD	15	16 N FLA	17 N FLA	18 N FLA	19 N SD	20 N SD
21 SD N	22 LA	23 N LA	24 N SF	25 SF	26 N STL	27 STL
28 N STL	29	30 N HOU				

MAY

SUN	MON	TUE	WED	THU	FRI	SAT
		1 N HOU	2	3 N PHI	4 N PHI	
5 PHI	6 N COL	7 N COL	8 N COL	9	10 N PHI	11 N PHI
12 PHI	13 N PIT	14 N PIT	15 N PIT	16	17 N CIN	18 N CIN
19 CIN	20 N CHI	21 N CHI	22 CHI	23	24 N PIT	25 N PIT
26 PIT	27 CHI	28 N CHI	29 CHI	30	31 N CIN	

JUNE

SUN	MON	TUE	WED	THU	FRI	SAT
						1 CIN
2 N CIN	3 N NY	4 N NY	5 N NY	6	7 N COL	8 COL
9 COL	10 N NY	11 N NY	12 N NY	13 N LA	14 N LA	15 LA
16 LA	17 N SD	18 N SD	19 SD	20	21 N SF	22 N SF
23 SF	24 N STL	25 N STL	26 N STL	27 N STL	28 N FLA	29 N FLA
30 FLA						

JULY

SUN	MON	TUE	WED	THU	FRI	SAT
	1 MON	2 N MON	3 N MON	4 N HOU	5 N HOU	6 N HOU
7 HOU	8 *	9 N	10	11 N FLA	12 N FLA	13 N FLA
14 FLA	15 N MON	16 MON	17	18 N HOU	19 N HOU	20 N HOU
21 HOU	22 N STL	23 N STL	24 N STL	25 N SF	26 N SF	27 SF
28 SF	29	30 N SD	31 N SD			

AUGUST

SUN	MON	TUE	WED	THU	FRI	SAT
				1 SD N	2 N LA	3 N LA
4 LA	5	6 N PHI	7 N PHI	8 N PHI	9 N COL	10 COL
11 N COL	12 N PHI	13 N PHI	14 PHI	15 PHI	16 N PIT	17 N PIT
18 PIT	19	20 N CIN	21 N CIN	22 N CIN	23 N CHI	24 CHI
25 CHI	26	27 N PIT	28 N PIT	29 PIT	30 N CHI	31 CHI

SEPTEMBER

SUN	MON	TUE	WED	THU	FRI	SAT
1 CHI	2 N CIN	3 N CIN	4 N CIN	5	6 N NY	7 N NY
8 NY	9	10 N COL	11 N COL	12 COL	13 N NY	14 NY
15 NY	16 N NY	17 N HOU	18 HOU	19	20 N MON	21 N MON
22 MON	23 N MON	24 N FLA	25 N FLA	26 N FLA	27 N MON	28 N MON
29 MON						

1996 SEASON
CLUB DIRECTORY

Owner
R.E. Turner III
Chairman of the board of directors
William C. Bartholomay
President
Stanley H. Kasten
Exec. v.p. and general manager
John Schuerholz
Sr. v.p. and asst. to the president
Henry L. Aaron
Senior v.p., administration
Bob Wolfe
V.p., dir. of marketing and broadcasting
Wayne Long
Vice president
Lee Douglas
Assistant general manager
Dean Taylor
Asst. dir. of scouting and player dev.
Deric Ladnier
Special assistants/player personnel
Willie Stargell
Jose Martinez
Dir. of team travel and equipment manager
Bill Acree
Sr. dir. of promotions and civic affairs
Miles McRea
Controller
Chip Moore
Director of ticket sales
Paul Adams
Dir. of stadium operations and security
Larry Bowman
Director of Braves Foundation
Danny Goodwin
Field director
Ed Mangan
Director of ticket operations
Ed Newman
Director of minor league operations
Rod Gilbreath
Dir. of scouting and player development
Paul Snyder
Dir. of advertising
Amy Richter
Dir. of community rel. and fan dev.
Dexter Santos
Director of public relations
Jim Schultz

Media relations managers
Glen Serra
Phil Civins
Thurmond Brooks
Director of multicultural marketing
Peter Serrano
Director of sports human services
Lisa Stricklin
Trainer
Dave Pursley
Assistant trainer
Jeff Porter
Club physician
Dr. David T. Watson
Associate physicians
Dr. John Cantwell
Dr. Robert Crow
Dr. Norman Elliott
Club orthopedists
Dr. Joe Chandler
Dr. Marvin Royster
Special assistant to general manager
Bill Lajoie
Major league scouts
Scott Nethery, Fred Shaffer, Bill Wight, Don Williams, John Van Ornum
National supervisor
Roy Clark, Bob Wadsworth
Regional supervisors
Butch Baccala, Harold Cronin, John Flannery
International supervisor
Bill Clark
Area supervisors
Matt Anderson, Stu Cann, Phil Dale, Tom Ealy, Rob English, Rene Francisco, John Hagemann, Brian Kohlscheen, Scott Littlefield, Jim Martz, Dayton Moore, Marco Paddy, Julian Perez, Rolando Petit, John Ramey, Alan Regier, Malcolm Seibert, John Stewart, Reyes Vizcaino
Scouts
Ray Belanger, Steve Bishop, Jim Buchert, Joe Caputo, Bob Dunning, Edgar Fernandez, Pedro Flores, Felix Francisco, Bill Froberg, Ruben Garcia, Ralph Garr, Gil Garrido, James Guinn, Henry Herrera, Luis Herrera, Bob Irwin, Bob Isabelle, Al Kubski, Jose Leon, Vicente Melian, Giorgio Moretti, Dario Paulino, Ernie Pedersen, Jack Powell, Charlie Smith, Carlos Torres, Bob Turzilli, Giovanni Viceisza

MINOR LEAGUE AFFILIATES

Class	Team	League	Manager
AAA	Richmond	International	Bill Dancy
AA	Greenville	Southern	Jeff Cox
A	Durham	Carolina	Randy Ingle
A	Macon	South Atlantic	Paul Runge
A	Eugene	Northwest	Jim Saul
Rookie	Danville	Appalachian	Brian Snitker
Rookie	Gulf Coast Braves	Gulf Coast	Robert Lucas

BROADCAST INFORMATION
Radio: WSB-AM (750).
TV: TBS-TV (Channel 17).
Cable TV: SportSouth.

SPRING TRAINING
Ballpark (city): Municipal Stadium (West Palm Beach, Fla.).
Ticket information: 407-683-6100.

SPRING TRAINING ROSTER

Manager—Bobby Cox (6).
Coaches—Jim Beauchamp (37), Pat Corrales (39), Clarence Jones (28), Leo Mazzone (54), Jimy Williams (22).

No.	PITCHERS	B/T	Ht./Wt.	Born	1995 clubs
33	Avery, Steve	L/L	6-4/205	4-14-70	Atlanta
51	Borbon, Pedro	L/L	6-1/205	11-15-67	Atlanta
50	Borowski, Joe	R/R	6-2/225	5-4-71	Rochester, Bowie, Baltimore
56	Brock, Chris	R/R	6-0/175	2-5-70	Richmond
52	Clontz, Brad	R/R	6-1/180	4-25-71	Atlanta
64	Daniels, Lee	R/R	6-4/190	3-31-71	Durham
	Fox, Chad	R/R	6-3/183	9-3-70	Chattanooga
47	Glavine, Tom	L/L	6-1/185	3-25-66	Atlanta
65	Jacobs, Ryan	R/L	6-2/175	2-3-74	Durham
31	Maddux, Greg	R/R	6-0/175	4-14-66	Atlanta
68	Malloy, Marty	R/L	5-10/160	7-6-72	Greenville
34	May, Darrell	L/L	6-2/170	6-13-72	Greenville, Richmond, Atlanta
38	McMichael, Greg	R/R	6-3/215	12-1-66	Atlanta
59	Potts, Michael	L/L	5-9/170	9-5-70	Richmond
46	Schmidt, Jason	R/R	6-5/185	1-29-73	Atlanta, Richmond
62	Schutz, Carl	L/L	5-11/200	8-22-71	Greenville
29	Smoltz, John	R/R	6-3/185	5-15-67	Atlanta
49	Thobe, Tom	L/L	6-6/195	9-3-69	Richmond, Atlanta
36	Wade, Terrell	L/L	6-3/205	1-25-73	Richmond, Atlanta
43	Wohlers, Mark	R/R	6-4/207	1-23-70	Atlanta
48	Woodall, Brad	B/L	6-0/175	6-25-69	Atlanta, Richmond

No.	CATCHERS	B/T	Ht./Wt.	Born	1995 clubs
63	Ayrault, Joe	R/R	6-3/190	10-8-71	Greenville
61	Houston, Tyler	L/R	6-2/210	1-17-71	Richmond
8	Lopez, Javier	R/R	6-3/185	11-5-70	Atlanta
12	Perez, Eduardo	R/R	6-1/175	5-4-68	Richmond, Atlanta

No.	INFIELDERS	B/T	Ht./Wt.	Born	1995 clubs
2	Belliard, Rafael	R/R	5-6/160	10-24-61	Atlanta
4	Blauser, Jeff	R/R	6-0/180	11-8-65	Atlanta
30	Giovanola, Ed	L/R	5-10/170	3-4-69	Richmond, Atlanta
64	Graffanino, Tony	R/R	6-1/175	6-6-72	Richmond
10	Jones, Chipper	B/R	6-3/195	4-24-72	Atlanta
20	Lemke, Mark	B/R	5-9/167	8-13-65	Atlanta
27	McGriff, Fred	L/L	6-3/215	10-31-63	Atlanta
16	Mordecai, Mike	R/R	5-11/175	12-13-67	Atlanta
61	Smith, Bobby	R/R	6-3/190	5-10-74	Greenville

No.	OUTFIELDERS	B/T	Ht./Wt.	Born	1995 clubs
67	Dye, Jermaine	R/R	6-0/195	1-28-74	Greenville
9	Grissom, Marquis	R/R	5-11/190	4-17-67	Atlanta
66	Hollins, Damon	R/L	5-11/180	6-12-74	Greenville
23	Justice, David	L/L	6-3/200	4-14-66	Atlanta
18	Klesko, Ryan	L/L	6-3/220	6-12-71	Atlanta, Greenville
63	Monds, Wonderful	R/R	6-3/190	1-11-73	Gulf Coast Braves, Durham
	Smith, Dwight	L/R	5-11/195	11-8-63	Atlanta
	Walton, Jerome	R/R	6-1/185	7-8-65	Cincinnati

BALLPARK INFORMATION

Ballpark (capacity, surface)
Atlanta-Fulton County Stadium (52,769, grass)

Address
P.O. Box 4064
Atlanta, GA 30302

Business phone
404-522-7630

Ticket information
404-522-7630

Ticket prices
$25 (dugout level)
$20 (club level)
$17 (field level)
$15 (family level)
$12 (lower pavilion)
$10 (upper level)
$5 (upper pavilion)
$1 (g.a., children under 12)

Field dimensions (from home plate)
To left field at foul line, 330 feet
To center field, 402 feet
To right field at foul line, 330 feet

First game played
April 12, 1966 (Pirates 3, Braves 2)

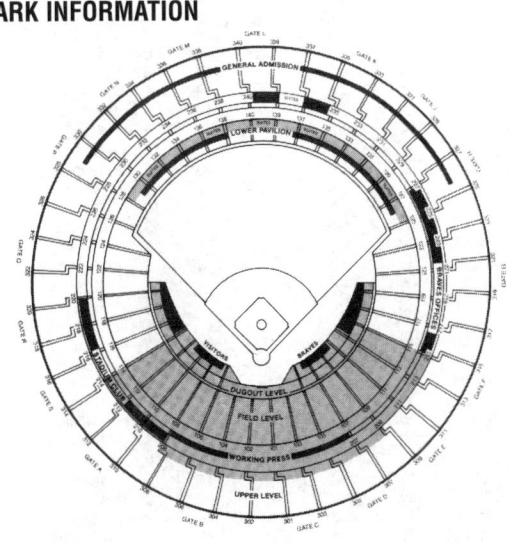

DAY BY DAY

1996 SEASON *Atlanta Braves*

Date	Opp.	Res.	Score	(inn.*)	Hits	Opp. hits	Winning pitcher	Losing pitcher	Save	Record	Pos.	GB
4-26	S.F.	W	12-5		17	6	Maddux	Mulholland		1-0	T1st	...
4-27	S.F.	W	6-4		6	6	Stanton	Burba	Clontz	2-0	T1st	...
4-28	At L.A.	L	1-9		4	9	Daal	Avery		2-1	T1st	...
4-29	At L.A.	W	4-3		6	7	McMichael	Murphy		3-1	1st	+1
4-30	At L.A.	W	6-3		9	8	Smoltz	Martinez	Clontz	4-1	1st	+1
5-2	At Fla.	W	7-1		7	3	Maddux	Gardner		5-1	1st	+1
5-3	At Fla.	W	6-4		8	12	Glavine	Witt	Clontz	6-1	1st	+1
5-4	At Fla.	W	6-3		11	8	Woodall	Nen	McMichael	7-1	1st	+2
5-5	Phi.	L	4-9		9	12	Green	Mercker	Borland	7-2	1st	+1 1/2
5-6	Phi.	L	1-3		4	8	Mimbs	Smoltz	Slocumb	7-3	1st	+1/2
5-7	Phi.	L	4-5		8	10	Schilling	Bedrosian	Slocumb	7-4	2nd	1/2
5-8	Phi.	L	2-3		8	6	Abbott	Glavine	Slocumb	7-5	T2nd	1 1/2
5-9	At N.Y.	W	3-2		5	8	McMichael	Manzanillo	Clontz	8-5	2nd	1 1/2
5-10	At N.Y.	L	2-5		7	7	Henry	Wohlers	Franco	8-6	2nd	2 1/2
5-11	At N.Y.	L	3-5		8	13	B. Jones	Smoltz	Franco	8-7	T2nd	2 1/2
5-12	Cin.	L	4-5	(11)	6	12	Brantley	Bedrosian		8-8	3rd	3 1/2
5-13	Cin.	W	9-6		10	10	Glavine	Smith	Borbon	9-8	3rd	3 1/2
5-14	Cin.	L	3-5	(10)	7	8	Carrasco	Clontz		9-9	3rd	4 1/2
5-15	Col.	W	4-0		7	5	Mercker	Olivares		10-9	3rd	3 1/2
5-16	Col.	W	15-3		20	6	Smoltz	Acevedo		11-9	3rd	3 1/2
5-17	Col.	L	5-6		8	8	Holmes	Maddux	Ruffin	11-10	3rd	4 1/2
5-18	Col.	W	3-2		8	11	McMichael	Munoz	Borbon	12-10	3rd	4
5-19	Fla.	W	4-0		6	5	Avery	Veres		13-10	2nd	3
5-20	Fla.	W	8-7		9	12	Wohlers	Nen		14-10	2nd	3
5-21	Fla.	W	5-1		8	2	Smoltz	Burkett		15-10	2nd	3
5-23	At St.L.	W	7-1		8	5	Maddux	Jackson		16-10	2nd	3
5-24	At St.L.	W	9-5		13	6	Glavine	Frascatore		17-10	2nd	3
5-25	At St.L.	L	1-4		6	8	Hill	Avery	Henke	17-11	2nd	3
5-26	At Hou.	W	8-3		12	7	Mercker	Swindell		18-11	2nd	3
5-27	At Hou.	L	2-3	(10)	6	10	Hudek	Stanton		18-12	2nd	4
5-28	At Hou.	W	3-1		5	1	Maddux	Kile		19-12	2nd	3
5-29	At Chi.	W	2-1		10	5	Glavine	Castillo		20-12	2nd	3
5-31	At Chi.	L	1-4		6	11	Morgan	Avery	Myers	20-13	2nd	3 1/2
6-1	L.A.	L	3-6		7	10	Valdes	Mercker		20-14	2nd	4 1/2
6-2	Hou.	L	2-7		5	8	Drabek	Smoltz		20-15	3rd	4 1/2
6-3	Hou.	L	1-2	(10)	4	7	Jones	Wohlers	Hudek	20-16	3rd	4 1/2
6-4	Hou.	L	2-6		10	13	Reynolds	Glavine		20-17	3rd	4 1/2
6-5	Chi.	W	7-5		8	13	Bedrosian	Hickerson	Wohlers	21-17	3rd	3 1/2
6-6	Chi.	W	17-3		20	5	Mercker	Trachsel		22-17	2nd	2 1/2
6-7	Chi.	W	4-3		10	6	Smoltz	Perez	Wohlers	23-17	2nd	2 1/2
6-9	St.L.	W	3-2	(10)	8	6	McMichael	Arocha		24-17	2nd	2 1/2
6-10	St.L.	L	3-7		7	12	DeLucia	Glavine		24-18	2nd	3 1/2
6-11	St.L.	L	4-8		13	14	Habyan	Avery	Henke	24-19	3rd	4 1/2
6-13	At Mon.	L	2-11		7	13	Perez	Mercker		24-20	3rd	4 1/2
6-14	At Mon.	W	7-3		11	9	Smoltz	Fassero		25-20	3rd	3 1/2
6-15	At Mon.	W	2-0		8	7	Maddux	Martinez		26-20	2nd	3 1/2
6-16	At Col.	W	2-0		8	6	Glavine	Swift		27-20	2nd	2 1/2
6-17	At Col.	W	7-1		12	6	Avery	Acevedo		28-20	2nd	2 1/2
6-18	At Col.	W	9-4		13	6	Mercker	Freeman		29-20	2nd	2 1/2
6-19	At Cin.	W	10-0		10	5	Smoltz	Schourek		30-20	2nd	2 1/2
6-20	At Cin.	W	10-2		18	9	Maddux	Nitkowski		31-20	2nd	2 1/2
6-21	At Cin.	L	1-3		3	4	Smiley	Glavine	Brantley	31-21	2nd	3 1/2
6-22	At Cin.	L	8-9		10	12	Hernandez	Borbon	Brantley	31-22	2nd	4 1/2
6-23	N.Y.	L	3-9		6	11	Saberhagen	Mercker		31-23	2nd	4 1/2
6-24	N.Y.	W	5-4		9	10	Smoltz	Mlicki	Wohlers	32-23	2nd	4 1/2
6-25	N.Y.	W	4-2		10	13	Maddux	Harnisch	Wohlers	33-23	2nd	4 1/2
6-26	Mon.	W	4-3		6	9	Glavine	Aquino	Wohlers	34-23	2nd	4
6-27	Mon.	L	0-3		4	5	Henry	Avery	Rojas	34-24	2nd	4
6-28	Mon.	W	4-3		4	6	Clontz	Rojas		35-24	2nd	3
6-30	At Phi.	L	1-3		5	5	Green	Smoltz	Slocumb	35-25	2nd	3 1/2
7-1	At Phi.	W	3-1		5	5	Maddux	West		36-25	2nd	2 1/2
7-2	At Phi.	W	5-3		7	8	Glavine	Mimbs	Wohlers	37-25	2nd	1 1/2
7-3	At Phi.	W	10-4		15	9	Avery	Schilling		38-25	2nd	1/2
7-4	L.A.	W	3-2		7	5	Clontz	Valdes	Wohlers	39-25	1st	+1/2
7-5	L.A.	W	4-1		6	9	Wohlers	Astacio		40-25	1st	+1 1/2
7-6	L.A.	W	1-0		5	5	McMichael	Seanez		41-25	1st	+1 1/2
7-7	S.F.	W	8-4		11	10	Glavine	Greer		42-25	1st	+2 1/2
7-8	S.F.	W	9-4		14	6	Avery	Portugal		43-25	1st	+3 1/2
7-9	S.F.	W	3-2		6	8	Wohlers	Beck		44-25	1st	+4 1/2
7-12	At Pit.	L	1-2		6	7	Parris	Smoltz	Miceli	44-26	1st	+4 1/2
7-13	At S.D.	W	4-1		8	5	Maddux	Hamilton		45-26	1st	+4 1/2

1996 SEASON *Atlanta Braves*

Date	Opp.	Res.	Score	(inn.*)	Hits	Opp. hits	Winning pitcher	Losing pitcher	Save	Record	Pos.	GB
7-14	At S.D.	W	6-2		9	8	Glavine	Benes		46-26	1st	+5$\frac{1}{2}$
7-15	At S.D.	W	7-6		6	6	Clontz	Florie	Wohlers	47-26	1st	+6$\frac{1}{2}$
7-16	At S.D.	L	1-3		3	12	Dishman	Mercker	Hoffman	47-27	1st	+6$\frac{1}{2}$
7-18	Pit.	L	4-5	(10)	11	8	Dyer	Wohlers	Miceli	47-28	1st	+6
7-19	Pit.	W	3-2		4	6	Maddux	Loaiza	Wohlers	48-28	1st	+7
7-20	Pit.	W	4-3		7	9	Clontz	Plesac		49-28	1st	+8
7-21	S.D.	L	6-9		11	13	Bochtler	McMichael	Hoffman	49-29	1st	+7
7-22	S.D.	W	3-2		9	7	Wohlers	Blair		50-29	1st	+8
7-23	S.D.	W	2-1		6	9	Smoltz	Hamilton	Wohlers	51-29	1st	+8
7-24	At Pit.	W	3-2		10	9	Clontz	Plesac	Wohlers	52-29	1st	+9
7-25	At Pit.	W	3-1	(10)	7	9	Clontz	Gott	Stanton	53-29	1st	+9
7-26	At L.A.	L	0-1		6	4	Valdes	Avery	Worrell	53-30	1st	+7$\frac{1}{2}$
7-27	At L.A.	L	4-9		9	14	Cummings	Mercker		53-31	1st	+6$\frac{1}{2}$
7-28	At S.F.	W	6-2		6	4	Clontz	Beck		54-31	1st	+7$\frac{1}{2}$
7-29	At S.F.	W	5-1		8	4	Maddux	Mulholland		55-31	1st	+8$\frac{1}{2}$
7-30	At S.F.	L	2-3		6	6	Brewington	Glavine	Beck	55-32	1st	+8$\frac{1}{2}$
8-1	Phi.	L	3-4		4	8	Fernandez	Avery	Slocumb	55-33	1st	+7$\frac{1}{2}$
8-2	Phi.	W	7-5		8	11	Mercker	Munoz	Wohlers	56-33	1st	+8$\frac{1}{2}$
8-3	Phi.	W	5-4		10	10	Borbon	Slocumb		57-33	1st	+9$\frac{1}{2}$
8-4	At Mon.	W	4-3		5	8	Maddux	Martinez	Wohlers	58-33	1st	+10$\frac{1}{2}$
8-5	At Mon.	W	9-6		17	11	Glavine	Henry	Wohlers	59-33	1st	+11
8-6	At Mon.	L	2-6		7	6	Perez	Avery		59-34	1st	+11$\frac{1}{2}$
8-7	At Mon.	W	5-1		11	8	Mercker	Fassero		60-34	1st	+12
8-8	Cin.	W	5-4		8	6	Smoltz	McElroy	Wohlers	61-34	1st	+13
8-9	Cin.	L	3-9		7	14	Burba	Maddux	Brantley	61-35	1st	+13
8-10	Cin.	W	2-1		6	6	Wohlers	Carrasco		62-35	1st	+14
8-11	Col.	W	5-3		5	6	Avery	Reynoso	Wohlers	63-35	1st	+14
8-12	Col.	L	4-16		8	18	Leskanic	Mercker		63-36	1st	+14
8-13	Col.	W	3-2		8	6	Wohlers	Holmes		64-36	1st	+15
8-14	Fla.	W	4-3		7	8	McMichael	Perez		65-36	1st	+15
8-15	Fla.	W	4-1		9	4	Glavine	Banks	Wohlers	66-36	1st	+15
8-16	Fla.	L	5-8		11	8	Rapp	Avery	Nen	66-37	1st	+15
8-18	At St.L.	L	3-4		8	10	Watson	Mercker	Henke	66-38	1st	+14
8-19	At St.L.	L	4-5		9	9	Urbani	Murray	Henke	66-39	1st	+13$\frac{1}{2}$
8-20	At St.L.	W	1-0		7	2	Maddux	Morgan		67-39	1st	+13$\frac{1}{2}$
8-21	At Hou.	W	5-4		9	11	Glavine	McMurtry	Wohlers	68-39	1st	+13$\frac{1}{2}$
8-22	At Hou.	W	6-4		8	8	Avery	Brocail	Wohlers	69-39	1st	+14$\frac{1}{2}$
8-23	At Hou.	W	6-2		10	4	Mercker	Hampton		70-39	1st	+14$\frac{1}{2}$
8-25	At Chi.	W	7-3		10	8	Smoltz	Castillo		71-39	1st	+14
8-26	At Chi.	W	7-2		11	7	Maddux	Trachsel		72-39	1st	+14
8-27	At Chi.	W	3-1		8	6	Glavine	Bullinger	Wohlers	73-39	1st	+15
8-28	At Chi.	L	5-7		7	13	Navarro	Avery	Myers	73-40	1st	+14$\frac{1}{2}$
8-29	Hou.	L	9-11	(13)	14	19	Swindell	Murray		73-41	1st	+14$\frac{1}{2}$
8-30	Hou.	L	0-2		7	6	Reynolds	Smoltz	Jones	73-42	1st	+14$\frac{1}{2}$
8-31	Hou.	W	5-2		7	6	Maddux	Drabek		74-42	1st	+14$\frac{1}{2}$
9-1	Chi.	L	5-7		6	11	Bullinger	Glavine	Myers	74-43	1st	+14$\frac{1}{2}$
9-2	Chi.	L	4-6		8	10	Navarro	Avery	Myers	74-44	1st	+14$\frac{1}{2}$
9-3	Chi.	W	2-0		6	6	Schmidt	Foster	Wohlers	75-44	1st	+14$\frac{1}{2}$
9-4	St.L.	W	6-5		12	9	Wohlers	Parrett		76-44	1st	+15$\frac{1}{2}$
9-5	St.L.	W	1-0		6	7	Maddux	Urbani		77-44	1st	+16$\frac{1}{2}$
9-6	St.L.	W	6-1		8	7	Glavine	Petkovsek		78-44	1st	+16$\frac{1}{2}$
9-7	At Fla.	L	1-5		4	7	Rapp	Avery		78-45	1st	+16
9-8	At Fla.	W	6-5		13	9	McMichael	Perez	Wohlers	79-45	1st	+17
9-9	At Fla.	W	9-5		13	13	Clontz	Nen	Wohlers	80-45	1st	+17
9-10	At Fla.	L	4-5	(11)	8	11	Mathews	Borbon		80-46	1st	+17
9-11	At Col.	L	4-5	(12)	15	13	Hickerson	Woodall		80-47	1st	+16$\frac{1}{2}$
9-12	At Col.	L	2-12		9	17	Painter	Avery	Ritz	80-48	1st	+15$\frac{1}{2}$
9-13	At Col.	W	9-7		11	13	Schmidt	Bailey		81-48	1st	+16$\frac{1}{2}$
9-15	At Cin.	W	3-1		7	7	Smoltz	McElroy	McMichael	82-48	1st	+17
9-16	At Cin.	W	6-1		10	8	Maddux	Portugal		83-48	1st	+18
9-17	At Cin.	W	4-1		9	6	Glavine	Smiley	Wohlers	84-48	1st	+19
9-18	N.Y.	W	7-1		9	4	Avery	B. Jones		85-48	1st	+19
9-19	N.Y.	L	3-10		11	13	Mlicki	Schmidt		85-49	1st	+19
9-20	N.Y.	L	4-8		9	11	Isringhausen	Smoltz	Franco	85-50	1st	+19
9-21	N.Y.	W	3-0		6	5	Maddux	Telgheder	Wohlers	86-50	1st	+19
9-22	Mon.	W	5-1		7	7	Glavine	Perez		87-50	1st	+20
9-23	Mon.	L	2-5		6	9	Martinez	McMichael	Rojas	87-51	1st	+19
9-24	Mon.	W	5-4	(10)	7	10	Borbon	Leiper		88-51	1st	+20
9-26	At Phi.	W	5-1		6	3	Smoltz	Quantrill		89-51	1st	+21
9-27	At Phi.	W	6-0		10	5	Maddux	Mimbs		90-51	1st	+22
9-29	At N.Y.	L	3-6		8	10	B. Jones	Glavine	Franco	90-52	1st	+22
9-30	At N.Y.	L	4-8		11	11	Minor	Schmidt	Franco	90-53	1st	+21
10-1	At N.Y.	L	0-1	(11)	5	5	Walker	Wade		90-54	1st	+21

Monthly records: April (4-1), May (16-12), June (15-12), July (20-7), August (19-10), September (16-11), October (0-1).
*Innings, if other than nine.

HIGHLIGHTS

High point: The Braves had their best July in Atlanta history by winning 20 of 27 games, matching the most wins the team had posted in any month since they moved from Milwaukee in 1966.

Low point: The Braves lost four in a row at home to begin June. The losses dropped the Braves five games behind the first-place Phillies.

Turning point: Starting July 1, the Braves won nine consecutive games to move from three games behind to four games in front at the All-Star break.

Most valuable player: First baseman Fred McGriff. Although he failed to hit 30 homers for the first time in eight seasons, McGriff's 27 homers and 93 RBIs led the team.

Most valuable pitcher: Righthander Greg Maddux. He set a record by winning his fourth consecutive Cy Young Award after posting a 19-2 record and 1.63 ERA. He became the first pitcher since Walter Johnson in 1918-19 to have an ERA of less than 1.80 in consecutive seasons.

Most improved player: Catcher Javier Lopez. His offensive numbers improved dramatically following a disappointing rookie season. He led the club with a .315 average, and had 14 home runs and 51 RBIs in 100 games.

Most pleasant surprises: Third baseman Chipper Jones and closer Mark Wohlers. Jones returned from knee surgery and had an impressive rookie year, hitting .265 with 23 homers and 86 RBIs, while playing a position he never had played. Wohlers emerged as one of the league's dominant closers, setting an Atlanta record with 21 consecutive saves, and finished with 25 saves and a 2.09 ERA.

Biggest disappointment: Shortstop Jeff Blauser. He hit a career-low .211 and drove in 31 runs in 431 at-bats. Hampered by injuries, he missed 29 games, yet still led the club with 107 strikeouts.

Key injuries: There were no major injuries, though a series of nagging aches and pains sidelined several players. Outfielder Ryan Klesko missed two weeks with a sprained thumb, and outfielder David Justice was gone for two weeks after tearing ligaments in his shoulder. Blauser missed 29 games with an assortment of injuries, including a bruised knee.

Notable: Maddux set a major league record by winning 18 consecutive road games and became the first Braves pitcher since Phil Niekro in 1980 to post four consecutive complete games.

—BILL ZACK

RECORDS

1995 regular-season records: 90-54 (1st in N.L. East); 44-28 at home; 46-26 on road; 31-21 vs. East; 33-22 vs. Central; 26-11 vs. West; 23-13 vs. lefthanded starters; 67-41 vs. righthanded starters; 65-44 on grass; 25-10 on turf; 25-14 in daytime; 65-40 at night; 31-17 in one-run games; 3-9 in extra-inning games; 0-0-0 in doubleheaders.

Team record past five years: 454-290 (.610, ranks 1st in league in that span).

TEAM LEADERS

Batting average: Fred McGriff (.280).
At-bats: Marquis Grissom (551).
Runs: Chipper Jones (87).
Hits: Fred McGriff (148).
Total bases: Fred McGriff (258).
Doubles: Fred McGriff (27).
Triples: Mark Lemke (5).
Home runs: Fred McGriff (27).
Runs batted in: Fred McGriff (93).
Stolen bases: Marquis Grissom (29).
Slugging percentage: Fred McGriff (.489).
On-base percentage: Dave Justice (.365).
Wins: Greg Maddux (19).
Earned-run average: Greg Maddux (1.63).
Complete games: Greg Maddux (10).
Shutouts: Greg Maddux (3).
Saves: Mark Wohlers (25).
Innings pitched: Greg Maddux (209.2)
Strikeouts: John Smoltz (193).

GAMES BY POSITION

Catcher: Javier Lopez 93, Charlie O'Brien 64, Eduardo Perez 5.
First base: Fred McGriff 144, Mike Mordecai 9, Ryan Klesko 4, Jose Oliva 1, Eduardo Perez 1.
Second base: Mark Lemke 115, Rafael Belliard 32, Mike Mordecai 21, Ed Giovanola 7.
Third base: Chipper Jones 123, Jose Oliva 25, Mike Mordecai 6, Ed Giovanola 3, Mike Sharperson 1.
Shortstop: Jeff Blauser 115, Rafael Belliard 40, Mike Mordecai 6, Ed Giovanola 1.
Outfield: Marquis Grissom 136, David Justice 120, Ryan Klesko 102, Mike Kelly 83, Mike Devereaux 27, Dwight Smith 25, Chipper Jones 20, Luis Polonia 15, Brian Kowitz 8, Mike Mordecai 1.

TOP DRAFT CHOICES

1. **Chad Hutchinson,** RHP, Torrey Pines H.S., San Diego.
2. **Jim Scharrer,** 1B, Cathedral Prep, Erie, Pa.
3. **Robbie Bell,** RHP, Marlboro (N.Y.) Central H.S.
4. **Jimmy Osting,** LHP, Trinity H.S., Louisville, Ky.
5. **Kevin McGlinchy,** RHP, Malden (Mass.) H.S.
6. **Matt Middleton,** SS, Graham H.S., Conover, Ohio.
7. **Gerald Vecchioni,** SS, Patapsco H.S., Baltimore.
8. **Chad Mead,** LHP-1B, Woodward (Okla.) H.S.
9. **Ben Wyatt,** LHP, Fair H.S., Little Rock, Ark.
10. **Ryan Schurman,** RHP, Tualatin (Ore.) H.S.

CHICAGO CUBS
NATIONAL LEAGUE CENTRAL DIVISION

1996 CUBS SCHEDULE

Home games shaded.
* — All-Star Game at Veterans Stadium (Philadelphia)
N — Night game (any game starting after 5 p.m.)

MARCH

SUN	MON	TUE	WED	THU	FRI	SAT
31						

APRIL

SUN	MON	TUE	WED	THU	FRI	SAT
	1 SD	2	3 SD	4 LA	5 LA	6 LA
7 LA	8 COL	9	10 COL	11	12 SF	13 SF
14 SF N	15 N COL	16 COL N	17 CIN	18 SF N	19 SF N	20 SF
21 SF N	22 N COL	23 COL N	24 N SD	25 SD N	26 N LA	27 N LA
28 LA N	29 N LA	30 N STL				

MAY

SUN	MON	TUE	WED	THU	FRI	SAT
			1 STL	2	3 NY	4 NY
5 NY	6 N MON	7 N MON	8 N MON	9 N	10 NY N	11 NY
12 NY	13 N HOU	14 HOU	15 N HOU	16 N HOU	17 FLA N	18 FLA
19 FLA N	20 ATL N	21 N ATL	22 ATL	23 N	24 HOU N	25 HOU
26 HOU	27 ATL N	28 N ATL	29 ATL	30 N	31 N FLA	

JUNE

SUN	MON	TUE	WED	THU	FRI	SAT
					N FLA	1 FLA
2 FLA N	3 PHI	4 PHI	5 PHI	6	7 MON N	8 MON
9 MON N	10 N PHI	11 N PHI	12 PHI N	13 SD	14 N SD	15 SD
16 SD N	17 LA	18 LA	19 LA	20 N	21 N SD	22 SD
23 SD	24 N LA	25 N LA	26	27	28 N CIN	29 CIN
30 CIN						

JULY

SUN	MON	TUE	WED	THU	FRI	SAT
	1 N PIT	2 N PIT	3 N PIT	4 CIN	5 CIN N	6 CIN
7 CIN	8 * ALL-STAR GAME	9	10	11 N STL	12 STL N	13 STL
14 STL N	15 N PIT	16 PIT N	17 PIT	18 N STL	19 N STL	20 STL
21 STL	22 SF	23 SF N	24 N SF	25 N COL	26 N COL	27 N COL
28 COL	29	30 N SF	31 SF			

AUGUST

SUN	MON	TUE	WED	THU	FRI	SAT
				1 COL	2 N COL	3 COL
4 COL	5 N NY	6	7 N NY	8	9 N MON	10 N MON
11 MON	12 N NY	13 N NY	14 N NY	15	16 N HOU	17 HOU
18 HOU N	19 N FLA	20 FLA N	21 FLA	22	23 N ATL	24 ATL
25 ATL	26	27 N HOU	28 N HOU	29 HOU	30 N ATL	31 ATL

SEPTEMBER

SUN	MON	TUE	WED	THU	FRI	SAT
1 ATL	2 FLA N	3 N FLA	4 N FLA	5 PHI N	6 N PHI	7 PHI
8 PHI	9 N MON	10 N MON	11 MON	12	13 N PHI	14 PHI
15 PHI	16	17 N STL	18 N STL	19 N STL	20 N PIT	21 PIT
22 PIT	23 N PIT	24 N CIN	25 N CIN	26 CIN	27 N PIT	28 PIT
29 PIT	30					

1996 SEASON

CLUB DIRECTORY

Board of directors
Jim Dowdle
Andrew B. MacPhail
Andrew McKenna

President and chief executive officer
Andrew B. MacPhail

General manager
Ed Lynch

Director, baseball administration
Scott Nelson

Dir., Arizona op./spec. assignment scout
Larry Himes

Special assistants to the g.m.
Al Goldis
John Young

Special player consultant
Hugh Alexander

Major league advance scout
Keith Champion

Traveling secretary
Jimmy Bank

Director, minor leagues
David Wilder

Field coordinator
Tom Gamboa

Hitting coordinator
Gary Matthews

Pitching coordinator
Rick Kranitz

Roving outfield instructor
Jimmy Piersall

Strength coordinator
Bruce Hammel

Director, scouting
Jim Hendry

Regional scouting supervisor (central)
John Stockstill

Regional scouting supervisor (northeast)
Billy Blitzer

Regional scouting supervisor (southeast)
Tony DeMacio

Regional scouting supervisor (west)
Larry Maxie

Director, media relations
Sharon Pannozzo

Media information coordinator
Chuck Wasserstrom

Media relations assistant
Wanda Taylor

Team physicians
John Marquardt, M.D.
Michael Schafer, M.D.

Head trainer
John Fierro

Assistant trainer
Brian McCann

Equipment manager
Yosh Kawano

Visiting clubhouse manager
Tom Hellmann

Exec. vice president, business operations
Mark McGuire

Dir., minor league business operations
Connie Kowal

V.p., marketing and broadcasting
John McDonough

Manager, broadcasting/special events
Phil Bedella

Mgr., Cubs Care/community relations
Rebecca Polihronis

Director, publications/special projects
Ernie Roth

Manager, publications
Ed McGregor

Photographer
Stephen Green

Director, stadium operations
Tom Cooper

Assistant director, stadium operations
Paul Rathje

Director, ticket operations
Frank Maloney

Full-time scouts
Tom Bourque, Mike Bricker, Bill Capps, Frank DeMoss, Jim Crawford, Preston Douglas, Oneri Fleita, Steve Fuller, Al Geddes, John Gracio, Gene Handley, Joe Housey, Spider Jorgensen, Buzzy Keller, Brad Kelley, Jose Lugo, Scott May, Brian Milner, Alberto Rondon, Marc Russo, Billy Swoope, Fermin Ubri

MINOR LEAGUE AFFILIATES

Class	Team	League	Manager
AAA	Iowa	American Association	Ron Clark
AA	Orlando	Southern	Bruce Kimm
A	Daytona	Florida State	Dave Trembley
A	Rockford	Midwest	Steve Roadcap
A	Williamsport	New York-Pennsylvania	Ruben Amaro
Rookie	Gulf Coast Cubs	Gulf Coast	Sandy Alomar

BROADCAST INFORMATION

Radio: WGN-AM (720).
TV: WGN-TV (Channel 9).
Cable TV: CLTV.

SPRING TRAINING

Ballpark (city): HoHoKam Park (Mesa, Ariz.).
Ticket information: 800-638-4253.

1996 SEASON *Chicago Cubs*

SPRING TRAINING ROSTER

Manager—Jim Riggleman (5).
Coaches—Dave Bialas (43), Ferguson Jenkins (31), Tony Muser (40), Mako Oliveras (3), Dan Radison (42), Billy Williams (26).

No.	PITCHERS	B/T	Ht./Wt.	Born	1995 clubs
51	Adams, Terry	R/R	6-3/205	3-6-73	Orlando, Iowa, Chicago N.L.
52	Bullinger, Jim	R/R	6-2/190	8-21-65	Chicago N.L., Orlando
55	Casian, Larry	R/L	6-0/175	10-28-65	Iowa, Chicago N.L.
49	Castillo, Frank	R/R	6-1/200	4-1-69	Chicago N.L.
49	Dibble, Rob	L/R	6-4/230	1-24-64	Birmingham, Chicago A.L., New Orleans, Milwaukee
32	Foster, Kevin	R/R	6-1/170	1-13-69	Chicago N.L.
29	Guzman, Jose	R/R	6-3/200	4-9-63	Gulf Coast Cubs
59	Myers, Rod	R/R	6-1/200	6-26-69	Omaha
38	Navarro, Jaime	R/R	6-4/230	3-27-68	Chicago N.L.
	Patterson, Bob	R/L	6-2/192	5-16-59	California
47	Perez, Mike	R/R	6-0/200	10-19-64	Chicago N.L.
41	Rivera, Roberto	L/L	6-0/200	1-1-69	Orlando, Chicago N.L.
36	Swartzbaugh, Dave	R/R	6-2/210	2-11-68	Iowa, Orlando, Chicago N.L.
44	Telemaco, Amaury	R/R	6-3/210	1-19-74	Orlando
46	Trachsel, Steve	R/R	6-4/205	10-31-70	Chicago N.L.
58	Walker, Wade	R/R	6-1/190	9-18-71	Daytona
13	Wendell, Turk	L/R	6-2/195	5-19-67	Daytona, Orlando, Chicago N.L.

No.	CATCHERS	B/T	Ht./Wt.	Born	1995 clubs
6	Hubbard, Mike	R/R	6-1/195	2-16-71	Iowa, Chicago N.L.
9	Servais, Scott	R/R	6-2/205	6-4-67	Houston, Chicago N.L.

No.	INFIELDERS	B/T	Ht./Wt.	Born	1995 clubs
37	Brown, Brant	L/R	6-3/205	6-22-71	Orlando
15	Franco, Matt	L/R	6-2/210	8-19-69	Iowa, Chicago N.L.
17	Grace, Mark	L/L	6-2/190	6-28-64	Chicago N.L.
24	Haney, Todd	R/R	5-9/165	7-30-65	Iowa, Chicago N.L.
18	Hernandez, Jose	R/R	6-1/180	7-14-69	Chicago N.L.
	Magadan, Dave	L/R	6-3/205	9-30-62	Houston
50	Maxwell, Jason	R/R	6-1/175	3-21-72	Daytona
54	Morris, Bobby	L/R	6-0/190	11-22-72	Daytona
57	Orie, Kevin	R/R	6-4/210	9-1-72	Daytona
11	Sanchez, Rey	R/R	5-9/175	10-5-67	Chicago N.L.
23	Sandberg, Ryne	R/R	6-2/180	9-18-59	Chicago N.L.

No.	OUTFIELDERS	B/T	Ht./Wt.	Born	1995 clubs
10	Bullett, Scott	L/L	6-2/220	12-25-68	Chicago N.L.
1	Glanville, Doug	R/R	6-2/170	8-25-70	Iowa
25	Gonzalez, Luis	L/R	6-2/185	9-3-67	Houston, Chicago N.L.
53	Hightower, Vee	B/R	6-5/215	4-25-72	Rockford
39	Jennings, Robin	L/L	6-2/205	4-11-72	Orlando
19	Kieschnick, Brooks	L/R	6-4/225	6-6-72	Iowa
56	McRae, Brian	B/R	6-0/190	8-27-67	Chicago N.L.
21	Sosa, Sammy	R/R	6-0/190	11-12-68	Chicago N.L.
30	Timmons, Ozzie	R/R	6-2/220	9-18-70	Chicago N.L.
45	Valdes, Pedro	L/L	6-1/180	6-29-73	Orlando

BALLPARK INFORMATION

Ballpark (capacity, surface)
Wrigley Field (38,765, grass)

Address
1060 W. Addison St.
Chicago, IL 60613-4397

Business phone
312-404-2827

Ticket information
312-404-2827

Ticket prices
$19 (club box)
$19 (field box)
$15 (terrace box)
$15 (upper deck box)
$15 (family section)
$12 (terrace reserved)
$9 (adult upper deck reserved)
$6 (under 14 upper deck reserved)
$10 (bleachers)
All weekday afternoon games in April, May and September are less.

Field dimensions (from home plate)
To left field at foul line, 355 feet
To center field, 400 feet
To right field at foul line, 353 feet

First game played
April 20, 1916 (Cubs 7, Reds 6)

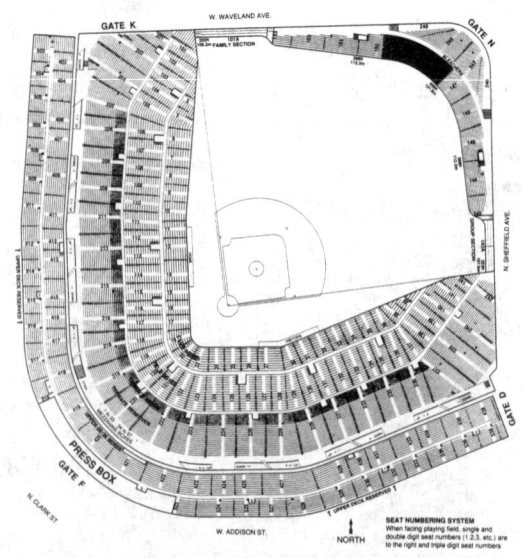

DAY BY DAY

Date	Opp.	Res.	Score	(inn.*)	Hits	Opp. hits	Winning pitcher	Losing pitcher	Save	Record	Pos.	GB
4-26	At Cin.	W	7-1		10	7	Bullinger	Rijo	Perez	1-0	T1st	...
4-27	At Cin.	W	6-5	(11)	11	12	Edens	McElroy	Myers	2-0	1st	+1
4-28	Mon.	W	4-3		10	7	Foster	Henry	Myers	3-0	1st	+2
4-29	Mon.	W	5-4		7	8	Navarro	Rueter	Myers	4-0	1st	+3
4-30	Mon.	L	2-4		8	10	Heredia	Castillo	Rojas	4-1	1st	+2
5-2	Hou.	L	2-5		7	9	Dougherty	Walker	Jones	4-2	1st	+1
5-3	Hou.	L	2-11		6	14	Kile	Trachsel		4-3	T1st	...
5-5	At Pit.	W	8-4		10	12	Foster	Lieber		5-3	2nd	1/2
5-6	At Pit.	W	13-5		14	10	Navarro	Wagner		6-3	1st	+1/2
5-7	At Pit.	L	3-4		7	7	Maddux	Banks	Miceli	6-4	1st	+1/2
5-8	At St.L.	W	7-4		8	8	Bullinger	Watson	Myers	7-4	1st	+1/2
5-9	At St.L.	W	3-0		5	7	Trachsel	Osborne	Myers	8-4	1st	+1/2
5-10	At St.L.	L	1-11		5	12	Hill	Foster		8-5	T1st	...
5-12	S.D.	W	8-4		11	10	Navarro	Benes		9-5	1st	+1/2
5-13	S.D.	W	5-0		8	3	Castillo	Ashby		10-5	1st	+11/2
5-14	S.D.	L	7-9		13	7	Hermanson	Perez	Hoffman	10-6	1st	+11/2
5-15	At S.F.	W	6-1		13	3	Trachsel	Leiter		11-6	1st	+2
5-16	At S.F.	W	2-0		6	3	Navarro	Mulholland	Myers	12-6	1st	+3
5-17	At S.F.	L	1-2		4	2	Portugal	Foster	Beck	12-7	1st	+2
5-19	At L.A.	W	7-3		11	7	Castillo	Candiotti	Myers	13-7	1st	+21/2
5-20	At L.A.	W	7-1		10	6	Bullinger	Martinez		14-7	1st	+21/2
5-21	At L.A.	W	2-1	(13)	9	5	Walker	F. Rodriguez	Myers	15-7	1st	+21/2
5-22	At Col.	L	8-9		9	18	Munoz	Myers		15-8	1st	+21/2
5-23	At Col.	W	7-6		14	9	Foster	Freeman	Myers	16-8	1st	+3
5-24	At Col.	W	5-3		8	6	Castillo	Bailey	Myers	17-8	1st	+3
5-25	Cin.	L	2-6		9	6	Smiley	Morgan	Hernandez	17-9	1st	+2
5-26	Fla.	L	3-5		10	8	Rapp	Perez	Nen	17-10	1st	+1
5-27	Fla.	W	3-1		5	5	Wendell	Burkett	Myers	18-10	1st	+1
5-28	Fla.	W	13-8		18	11	Foster	Weathers		19-10	1st	+1
5-29	Atl.	L	1-2		5	10	Glavine	Castillo		19-11	1st	+1/2
5-31	Atl.	W	4-1		11	6	Morgan	Avery	Myers	20-11	T1st	...
6-1	At Phi.	L	3-5		8	7	Charlton	Trachsel	Slocumb	20-12	T1st	...
6-2	At Fla.	W	5-1		9	4	Navarro	Burkett	Perez	21-12	1st	+1
6-3	At Fla.	L	4-5		9	10	Veres	Hickerson		21-13	T1st	...
6-4	At Fla.	W	5-3		10	7	Castillo	Hammond	Myers	22-13	T1st	...
6-5	At Atl.	L	5-7		13	8	Bedrosian	Hickerson	Wohlers	22-14	2nd	1
6-6	At Atl.	L	3-17		5	20	Mercker	Trachsel		22-15	2nd	2
6-7	At Atl.	L	3-4		6	10	Smoltz	Perez	Wohlers	22-16	2nd	2
6-8	Col.	L	3-5		6	10	Ritz	Foster	Reed	22-17	2nd	3
6-9	Col.	L	1-2	(10)	6	8	Holmes	Perez	Munoz	22-18	2nd	4
6-10	Col.	W	3-0		3	5	Morgan	Acevedo	Myers	23-18	2nd	4
6-11	Col.	L	1-5		6	9	Thompson	Trachsel	Leskanic	23-19	2nd	5
6-13	S.F.	L	4-8		6	13	Portugal	Navarro		23-20	2nd	51/2
6-14	S.F.	L	3-4	(13)	12	11	Mintz	Young	Beck	23-21	2nd	51/2
6-15	S.F.	W	3-1		8	4	Castillo	Leiter	Myers	24-21	2nd	5
6-16	L.A.	W	2-0		5	6	Hickerson	Seanez		25-21	2nd	4
6-17	L.A.	L	5-12		9	18	Martinez	Young		25-22	2nd	5
6-18	L.A.	L	0-6		5	9	Valdes	Navarro		25-23	2nd	6
6-19	At S.D.	L	3-5		4	8	Berumen	Foster	Hoffman	25-24	2nd	6
6-20	At S.D.	W	7-2		12	10	Castillo	Sanders		26-24	2nd	5
6-21	At S.D.	L	0-1		6	5	Benes	Trachsel		26-25	3rd	6
6-22	At Hou.	W	13-2		18	6	Bullinger	Drabek	Young	27-25	2nd	6
6-23	At Hou.	L	2-3	(12)	5	10	Jones	Walker		27-26	3rd	6
6-24	At Hou.	W	5-2		9	6	Foster	Kile	Myers	28-26	2nd	6
6-25	At Hou.	L	6-19		12	19	Reynolds	Castillo		28-27	3rd	6
6-26	Pit.	L	6-8		12	16	Parris	Trachsel	Miceli	28-28	3rd	61/2
6-27	Pit.	L	5-6		9	8	Neagle	Bullinger	Plesac	28-29	3rd	71/2
6-28	Pit.	W	10-3		14	8	Hickerson	Dyer		29-29	3rd	71/2
6-29	St.L.	L	4-6		10	9	Hill	Foster		29-30	3rd	81/2
6-30	St.L.	L	1-3		9	8	Urbani	Castillo	Henke	29-31	3rd	81/2
7-1	St.L.	W	8-7		10	10	Perez	Habyan	Myers	30-31	3rd	81/2
7-2	St.L.	W	7-6		8	13	Bullinger	Jackson	Myers	31-31	3rd	81/2
7-3	At N.Y.	W	4-2		7	6	Navarro	Pulsipher	Myers	32-31	3rd	71/2
7-4	At N.Y.	W	3-0		7	8	Foster	Saberhagen	Myers	33-31	3rd	71/2
7-5	At N.Y.	L	4-5		8	8	Franco	Hickerson		33-32	3rd	81/2
7-6	At N.Y.	W	8-4		14	8	Trachsel	Harnisch	Walker	34-32	3rd	71/2
7-7	At Phi.	W	8-2		12	8	Bullinger	Mimbs	Hickerson	35-32	3rd	71/2
7-8	At Phi.	W	3-1		7	2	Navarro	Schilling	Myers	36-32	3rd	61/2
7-9	At Phi.	W	7-6	(13)	12	14	Wendell	Williams		37-32	3rd	61/2
7-12	At Mon.	L	2-3		5	9	Urbina	Castillo	Rojas	37-33	3rd	7
7-13	Cin.	L	5-11		10	10	Rijo	Trachsel	Brantley	37-34	3rd	8

Date	Opp.	Res.	Score	(inn.*)	Hits	Opp. hits	Winning pitcher	Losing pitcher	Save	Record	Pos.	GB
7-14	Cin.	L	4-5		9	11	Jackson	Perez	Brantley	37-35	3rd	9
7-15	Cin.	L	3-4		9	12	Schourek	Navarro	Brantley	37-36	3rd	10
7-16	Cin.	W	7-5		12	6	Foster	Pugh	Myers	38-36	3rd	9
7-17	N.Y.	L	2-7		3	11	DiPoto	Walker		38-37	3rd	9
7-18	N.Y.	L	3-12		7	17	B. Jones	Trachsel		38-38	3rd	10
7-19	At Mon.	L	3-4		12	10	Martinez	Bullinger	Shaw	38-39	3rd	11
7-20	At Mon.	L	0-4		7	7	Henry	Navarro		38-40	3rd	11¹/₂
7-21	At Cin.	L	1-10		4	14	Schourek	Foster		38-41	3rd	12¹/₂
7-22	At Cin.	L	3-4		6	9	Jackson	Young	Brantley	38-42	3rd	13¹/₂
7-23	At Cin.	L	5-7	(10)	12	12	Hernandez	Myers		38-43	3rd	14¹/₂
7-24	N.Y.	W	5-3		6	9	Bullinger	Pulsipher	Myers	39-43	3rd	13¹/₂
7-25	Mon.	W	6-5		4	13	Navarro	Martinez	Young	40-43	3rd	12¹/₂
7-26	Mon.	L	2-4		12	11	Henry	Foster	Rojas	40-44	3rd	12¹/₂
7-28	Phi.	W	4-0		6	11	Castillo	Munoz	Myers	41-44	3rd	13
7-29	Phi.	W	8-7		10	16	Young	Slocumb		42-44	3rd	12
7-30	Phi.	W	8-0		11	3	Bullinger	Deshaies		43-44	3rd	11
8-1	At Pit.	W	7-5		11	8	Navarro	Ericks	Myers	44-44	3rd	11
8-2	At Pit.	L	3-4	(10)	10	8	Miceli	Young		44-45	3rd	12
8-3	At Pit.	W	7-2		9	8	Casian	Gott		45-45	3rd	12
8-4	At St.L.	W	5-3		8	5	Trachsel	Morgan	Myers	46-45	3rd	12
8-5	At St.L.	W	1-0		4	5	Bullinger	DeLucia	Myers	47-45	3rd	11¹/₂
8-6	At St.L.	L	3-4	(13)	12	13	Parrett	Nabholz		47-46	3rd	13
8-8	S.D.	L	1-3		11	8	Hamilton	Foster	Hoffman	47-47	3rd	13
8-10†	S.D.	L	2-3		6	6	Blair	Castillo	Hoffman	47-48		
8-10‡	S.D.	W	12-5		13	7	Trachsel	B. Williams		48-48	3rd	13
8-11	At S.F.	W	6-2		10	7	Bullinger	Leiter		49-48	3rd	12
8-12	At S.F.	W	4-0		8	8	Navarro	Bautista		50-48	3rd	11
8-13	At S.F.	L	3-6		9	10	S. Valdez	Foster	Beck	50-49	3rd	11
8-14	At L.A.	W	5-4	(11)	13	15	Myers	Guthrie	Adams	51-49	3rd	11
8-15	At L.A.	L	5-7		11	8	Nomo	Trachsel	Worrell	51-50	3rd	12
8-16	At L.A.	L	1-6		7	8	Valdes	Bullinger		51-51	3rd	12
8-17	At Col.	L	5-12		9	14	Bailey	Navarro		51-52	3rd	13
8-18	At Col.	W	26-7		27	10	Young	Saberhagen		52-52	3rd	13
8-19	At Col.	W	6-5		7	10	Castillo	Ritz	Myers	53-52	3rd	13
8-20	At Col.	L	2-4		5	5	Leskanic	Wendell		53-53	3rd	14
8-22	Fla.	L	6-8		10	11	Rapp	Bullinger	Nen	53-54	3rd	13¹/₂
8-23	Fla.	W	10-2		10	7	Navarro	Weathers		54-54	3rd	13¹/₂
8-24	Fla.	W	6-2		11	5	Foster	Hammond	Myers	55-54	3rd	12¹/₂
8-25	Atl.	L	3-7		8	10	Smoltz	Castillo		55-55	3rd	13¹/₂
8-26	Atl.	L	2-7		7	11	Maddux	Trachsel		55-56	3rd	14¹/₂
8-27	Atl.	L	1-3		6	8	Glavine	Bullinger	Wohlers	55-57	3rd	15¹/₂
8-28	Atl.	W	7-5		13	7	Navarro	Avery	Myers	56-57	3rd	15¹/₂
8-29	At Fla.	W	10-6		13	11	Foster	Hammond		57-57	3rd	15¹/₂
8-30	At Fla.	L	1-4		5	7	Burkett	Castillo		57-58	3rd	15¹/₂
8-31	At Fla.	W	12-3		13	9	Trachsel	Banks		58-58	3rd	14¹/₂
9-1	At Atl.	W	7-5		11	6	Bullinger	Glavine	Myers	59-58	3rd	14¹/₂
9-2	At Atl.	W	6-4		10	8	Navarro	Avery	Myers	60-58	3rd	13¹/₂
9-3	At Atl.	L	0-2		6	6	Schmidt	Foster	Wohlers	60-59	3rd	13¹/₂
9-4	Col.	W	2-0		4	5	Castillo	Rekar		61-59	T2nd	13¹/₂
9-6	Col.	L	4-10		12	14	Reynoso	Bullinger		61-60	3rd	14
9-8	S.F.	L	3-7		10	12	S. Valdez	Navarro	Beck	61-61	3rd	14
9-9	S.F.	L	3-8		8	14	Mulholland	Castillo		61-62	3rd	14
9-10	S.F.	L	7-8		10	12	VanLandingham	Trachsel	Beck	61-63	3rd	14
9-11	L.A.	W	12-1		17	6	Foster	Valdes		62-63	3rd	14
9-12	L.A.	L	1-7		6	11	Nomo	Bullinger		62-64	3rd	14
9-13	L.A.	W	7-6	(13)	15	14	Adams	Guthrie		63-64	3rd	14
9-15	At S.D.	W	6-2		12	6	Castillo	Bochtler	Myers	64-64	3rd	13¹/₂
9-16	At S.D.	L	4-12		9	17	Ashby	Trachsel		64-65	3rd	13¹/₂
9-17	At S.D.	L	3-11		8	13	Valenzuela	Foster		64-66	3rd	13¹/₂
9-18	At Hou.	L	1-3		7	7	Wall	Bullinger	Jones	64-67	3rd	14¹/₂
9-19	At Hou.	W	7-6		9	15	Navarro	Hampton	Myers	65-67	3rd	13¹/₂
9-20	At Hou.	L	0-4		7	9	Reynolds	Castillo		65-68	3rd	14¹/₂
9-21	Pit.	L	3-4		9	10	Neagle	Trachsel	Miceli	65-69	3rd	15
9-22	Pit.	W	6-3		7	2	Foster	Ericks	Myers	66-69	3rd	15
9-23	Pit.	W	8-5		11	9	Bullinger	Dyer	Myers	67-69	3rd	14
9-24	Pit.	W	3-2	(10)	9	7	Wendell	Miceli		68-69	3rd	14
9-25	St.L.	W	7-0		11	1	Castillo	Benes		69-69	3rd	13
9-26	St.L.	W	3-2		7	5	Trachsel	Parrett	Myers	70-69	3rd	12¹/₂
9-27	St.L.	W	5-3		8	10	Foster	Watson	Myers	71-69	3rd	11
9-28	Hou.	W	12-11	(11)	19	17	Young	Jones		72-69	3rd	11
9-29	Hou.	W	4-3	(10)	8	10	Perez	Brocail		73-69	3rd	11
9-30	Hou.	L	8-9		8	14	Swindell	Perez	Henneman	73-70	3rd	11
10-1	Hou.	L	7-8		13	16	Veres	Adams	Jones	73-71	3rd	12

Monthly records: April (4-1), May (16-10), June (9-20), July (14-13), August (15-14), September (15-12), October (0-1).
*Innings, if other than nine. †First game of doubleheader. ‡Second game of doubleheader.

HIGHLIGHTS

High point: The Cubs used an 8-1 run before the All-Star break to go five games over .500 and creep 6¹/₂ games behind N.L. Central-leading Cincinnati.

Low point: A 1-11 free fall after the All-Star break broke the euphoria. The Cubs spent the rest of the season flirting with .500, finishing two games over.

Turning point: Losing catcher Scott Servais to a twisted knee on a hard slide by Philadelphia's Darren Daulton on July 9. The Cubs proceeded to falter and were out of the race by the time Servais returned.

Most valuable player: Center fielder Brian McRae. Sammy Sosa and Mark Grace had superior years statistically, but McRae stabilized a sore-spot position. He batted .288 in an unfamiliar leadoff role, scored 92 runs and stole 27 steals.

Most valuable pitcher: Righthander Jaime Navarro. A free-agent pickup, Navarro rebounded from two poor seasons in Milwaukee and led a young rotation with 14 victories.

Most improved player: Righthander Frank Castillo. Coming back from his two-victory, injury-marred season of 1994, Castillo led the staff with a 3.21 ERA and had a late-season one-hitter against the Cardinals. He won 11 games.

Most pleasant surprise: Servais. The Cubs knew they had obtained a heady handler of pitchers when they acquired Servais from Houston in late June. What they didn't anticipate was his power. Servais drilled 12 homers for the Cubs in 175 at-bats.

Biggest disappointment: Righthander Steve Trachsel. He plummeted from a solid rookie season (9-7 record, 3.21 ERA) to a 7-13 mark and a 5.15 ERA. He allowed 25 home runs and a staff-high 76 walks.

Key injuries: Four players ended their seasons with hand/wrist injuries, including infielders Todd Zeile and Rey Sanchez. They couldn't contribute to the wild-card chase in the closing weeks.

Notable: The club finished below .500 at home for the second consecutive season, going 34-38. Conversely, the Cubs posted a plus-.500 road record—they were 39-33—for the third consecutive season. . . . Sosa had his second 30-30 season to go with 119 RBIs. . . . Grace's 51 doubles equaled the N.L. high over the past 42 seasons. . . . Grace's .326 average placed him in the top 10 in N.L. hitting for the sixth time in his eight big-league seasons. . . . Randy Myers won the league's Fireman of the Year award for the second time in three years.

—JOE GODDARD

RECORDS

1995 regular-season record: 73-71 (3rd in N.L. Central); 34-38 at home; 39-33; on road; 25-21 vs. East; 25-24 vs. Central; 23-26 vs. West; 24-20 vs. lefthanded starters; 49-51 vs. righthanded starters; 57-56 on grass; 16-15 on turf; 37-38 in daytime; 36-33 at night; 19-24 in one-run games; 8-6 in extra-ining games; 0-0-1 in doubleheaders. Longest winning streak: 8 (September 22-September 29); Longest losing streak: 7 (July 17-July 23).

Team record past five years: 361-380 (.487, ranks 10th in league in that span).

TEAM LEADERS

Batting average: Mark Grace (.326).
At-bats: Brian McRae (580).
Runs: Mark Grace (97).
Hits: Mark Grace (180).
Total bases: Mark Grace (285).
Doubles: Mark Grace (51).
Triples: Scott Bullett (7).
Home runs: Sammy Sosa (36).
Runs batted in: Sammy Sosa (119).
Stolen bases: Sammy Sosa (34).
Slugging percentage: Mark Grace (.516).
On-base percentage: Mark Grace (.395).
Wins: Jamie Navarro (14).
Earned-run average: Frank Castillo (3.21).
Complete games: Frank Castillo, Steve Trachsel (2).
Shutouts: Frank Castillo (2).
Saves: Randy Myers (38).
Innings pitched: Jamie Navarro (200.1).
Strikeouts: Kevin Foster (146).

GAMES BY POSITION

Catcher: Scott Servais 52, Rick Wilkins 49, Todd Pratt 25, Joe Kmak 18, Mark Parent 10, Mike Hubbard 9.
First base: Mark Grace 143, Howard Johnson 3, Rick Wilkins 2, Matt Franco 1, Todd Zeile 1.
Second base: Rey Sanchez 111, Jose Hernandez 29, Todd Haney 17, Howard Johnson 8, Matt Franco 3.
Third base: Todd Zeile 75, Howard Johnson 34, Steve Buechele 32, Jose Hernandez 20, Todd Haney 4, Matt Franco 1, Joe Kmak 1.
Shortstop: Shawon Dunston 125, Jose Hernandez 43, Rey Sanchez 4, Howard Johnson 1.
Outfield: Sammy Sosa 143, Brian McRae 137, Luis Gonzalez 76, Scott Bullett 64, Ozzie Timmons 55, Howard Johnson 13, Tuffy Rhodes 11, Kevin Roberson 11, Todd Zeile 2.

TOP DRAFT CHOICES

1. **Kerry Wood,** RHP, Grand Prairie (Tex.) H.S.
2. **Brian McNichol,** LHP, James Madison University.
3. **Jeff Yoder,** RHP, Pottsville Area (Pa.) H.S.
4. **Adam Everett,** SS, Harrison H.S., Marietta, Ga.
5. **Ismael Villegas,** RHP, Guaynabo, Puerto Rico.
6. **Tony Ellison,** OF, North Carolina State University.
7. **Dorian Speed,** OF, Florida International University.
8. **Denny Bair,** RHP, Northeast Louisiana University.
9. **Robert Ricketts,** RHP, Polk (Fla.) C.C.
10. **Richard Pressley,** 1B, Dr. Phillips H.S., Orlando, Fla.

CINCINNATI REDS
NATIONAL LEAGUE CENTRAL DIVISION

1996 REDS SCHEDULE

☐ Home games shaded.
* — All-Star Game at Veterans Stadium (Philadelphia)
N — Night game (any game starting after 5 p.m.)

MARCH
SUN	MON	TUE	WED	THU	FRI	SAT
31						

APRIL
SUN	MON	TUE	WED	THU	FRI	SAT
	1 MON	2 N MON	3 MON	4 N PHI	5 N PHI	6
7 PHI	8 N NY	9 N NY	10 N NY	11 N HOU	12 N HOU	13 HOU
14 HOU	15 N CHI	16 CHI	17 CHI	18	19 N HOU	20 N HOU
21 HOU	22 N NY	23 N NY	24 N MON	25 MON	26 N PHI	27 PHI
28 PHI	29	30 N PIT				

MAY
SUN	MON	TUE	WED	THU	FRI	SAT
			1 N PIT	2	3 N SF	4 SF
5 N SF	6	7 N LA	8 N LA	9	10 N SD	11 N SD
12 SD	13	14 N COL	15 N COL	16	17 N ATL	18 N ATL
19 ATL	20 N FLA	21 N FLA	22 FLA	23 N COL	24 N COL	25 N COL
26 COL	27 FLA	28 N FLA	29 N FLA	30	31 N ATL	

JUNE
SUN	MON	TUE	WED	THU	FRI	SAT
						1 ATL
2 N ATL	3 N SF	4 N SF	5 N SF	6 N SF	7 N LA	8 N LA
9 LA	10 N SD	11 N SD	12 N SD	13	14 N MON	15 N MON
16 MON	17 N HOU	18 N HOU	19 N HOU	20 N NY	21 N NY	22 N NY
23 N NY	24 N PHI	25 N PHI	26 N PHI	27	28 N CHI	29 CHI
30 CHI						

JULY
SUN	MON	TUE	WED	THU	FRI	SAT
	1 N STL	2 N STL	3 STL	4 CHI	5 N CHI	6 N CHI
7 CHI	8	* 9 ALL-STAR GAME	10	11 N PIT	12 N PIT	13 N PIT
14 PIT	15 N STL	16 N STL	17 STL	18 N PIT	19 N PIT	20 N PIT
21 PIT	22 N PHI	23 N PHI	24 PHI	25	26 N NY	27 NY
28 NY	29 N HOU	30 N HOU	31 HOU			

AUGUST
SUN	MON	TUE	WED	THU	FRI	SAT
				1 N MON	2 N MON	3 N MON
4 MON	5 N SF	6 SF	7 SF	8	9 N LA	10 LA
11 LA	12 N LA	13 N SD	14 N SD	15 SD	16 N COL	17 N COL
18 COL	19 N COL	20 N ATL	21 N ATL	22 N ATL	23 N FLA	24 FLA
25 FLA	26 N COL	27 N COL	28 COL	29	30 N FLA	31 N FLA

SEPTEMBER
SUN	MON	TUE	WED	THU	FRI	SAT
1 FLA	2 N ATL	3 N ATL	4 N ATL	5	6 N SF	7 SF
8 SF	9 N LA	10 N LA	11 N LA	12	13 N SD	14 SD
15 SD	16	17 N PIT	18 N PIT	19 N PIT	20 N STL	21 STL
22 STL	23 N STL	24 N CHI	25 N CHI	26 CHI	27 N STL	28 STL
29 STL						

1996 SEASON

CLUB DIRECTORY

General partner
Marge Schott

President and chief executive officer
Marge Schott

General manager
Jim Bowden

Director, player development
Sheldon Bender

Director, scouting
Julian Mock

Assistant/baseball operations
Brad Kullman

Special assistant to the general manager
Gene Bennett

Senior advisor/baseball operations
Larry Barton Jr.

Major league scouts
Jack McKeon
John Stearns

Controller
John Allen

Director, stadium operations
Jody Pettyjohn

Director, ticket department
John O'Brien

Director, season ticket sales
Pat McCaffrey

Director, group sales
Barb McManus

Director, marketing
Chip Baker

Director, publicity
Mike Ringering

Traveling secretary
Joel Pieper

Assistant ticket director
Ken Ayer

Administrative assistant, business
Ginny Kamp

Administrative assistant, scouting
Wilma Mann

Admin. assistant, player development
Lois Schneider

Scouting secretary
Lois Hudson

Trainers
Greg Lynn
Doug Spreen

Field superintendent
Gary Wahoff

Equipment manager
Bernie Stowe

Scouts
Johnny Almaraz
Jeff Barton
Ray Bellino
Fred Blair
George Brill
Robby Corsaro
Bobby Filotei
Jim Grief
Don Gust
Fred Hayes
Don Hill
Les Houser
David Jennings
Fred Leone
Anthony Lowe
John Luedtke
Mike Mangan
Jose Moreno
Denny Nagle
Miguel Nava
Jerry Raddatz
Tom Severtson
Douglas Stewart
Bob Szymkowski
Lee Toole
Marion (Bo) Trumbo
Mike Wallace
John Walsh
Tom Wilson
Jeff Zimmerman
Murray Zuk

MINOR LEAGUE AFFILIATES

Class	Team	League	Manager
AAA	Indianapolis	American Association	Dave Miley
AA	Chattanooga	Southern	Mark Berry
A	Winston-Salem	Carolina	Phillip Wellman
A	Charleston (WV)	South Atlantic	Tommy Thompson
Rookie	Princeton	Appalachian	Mark Wagner
Rookie	Billings	Pioneer	Matt Martin

BROADCAST INFORMATION
Radio: WLW-AM (700).
TV: WSTR-TV (Channel 64).
Cable TV: SportsChannel Cincinnati.

SPRING TRAINING
Ballpark (city): Plant City Stadium (Plant City, Fla.).
Ticket information: 813-752-7337.

SPRING TRAINING ROSTER

Manager—Ray Knight (25).
Coaches—Marc Bombard, Donald Gullett (35), Jim Lett, Hal McRae (4), Joel Youngblood (2).

No.	PITCHERS	B/T	Ht./Wt.	Born	1995 clubs
45	Brantley, Jeff	R/R	5-10/180	9-5-63	Cincinnati
34	Burba, Dave	R/R	6-4/240	7-7-66	San Francisco, Cincinnati
58	Carrasco, Hector	R/R	6-2/180	10-22-69	Cincinnati
37	Hernandez, Xavier	L/R	6-2/195	8-16-65	Cincinnati
32	Jarvis, Kevin	L/R	6-2/200	8-1-69	Indianapolis, Cincinnati
31	McElroy, Chuck	L/L	6-0/195	10-1-67	Cincinnati
48	Moore, Marcus	B/R	6-5/195	11-2-70	Indianapolis, Chattanooga
21	Portugal, Mark	R/R	6-0/190	10-30-62	San Francisco, Cincinnati
40	Pugh, Tim	R/R	6-6/225	1-26-67	Indianapolis, Cincinnati
27	Rijo, Jose	R/R	6-3/215	5-13-65	Cincinnati
44	Roper, John	R/R	6-0/175	11-21-71	Cincinnati, Chattanooga, Indianapolis, Phoenix, San Francisco
26	Ruffin, Johnny	R/R	6-3/170	7-29-71	Cincinnati, Indianapolis
42	Salkeld, Roger	R/R	6-5/215	3-6-71	Tacoma, Indianapolis
46	Schourek, Pete	L/L	6-5/205	5-10-69	Cincinnati
57	Smiley, John	L/L	6-4/210	3-17-65	Cincinnati
47	Sullivan, Scott	R/R	6-4/210	3-13-71	Indianapolis, Cincinnati
38	White, Gabe	L/L	6-2/200	11-20-71	Ottawa, Montreal

No.	CATCHERS	B/T	Ht./Wt.	Born	1995 clubs
6	Berryhill, Damon	B/R	6-0/205	12-3-63	Cincinnati
10	Taubensee, Eddie	L/R	6-4/205	10-31-68	Cincinnati

No.	INFIELDERS	B/T	Ht./Wt.	Born	1995 clubs
39	Belk, Tim	R/R	6-3/200	4-6-70	Indianapolis
29	Boone, Bret	R/R	5-10/180	4-6-69	Cincinnati
20	Branson, Jeff	L/R	6-0/180	1-26-67	Cincinnati
12	Greene, Willie	L/R	5-11/185	9-23-71	Cincinnati, Indianapolis
28	Harris, Lenny	L/R	5-10/210	10-28-64	Cincinnati
30	Hunter, Brian R.	R/L	6-0/195	3-4-68	Cincinnati, Indianapolis
11	Larkin, Barry	R/R	6-0/195	4-28-64	Cincinnati
23	Morris, Hal	L/L	6-4/210	4-9-65	Cincinnati, Indianapolis
51	Owens, Eric	R/R	6-1/185	2-3-71	Indianapolis, Cincinnati
53	Reese, Pokey	R/R	5-11/180	6-10-73	Indianapolis

No.	OUTFIELDERS	B/T	Ht./Wt.	Born	1995 clubs
9	Anthony, Eric	L/L	6-2/195	11-8-67	Cincinnati, Indianapolis
33	Gibralter, Steve	R/R	6-0/190	10-9-72	Indianapolis, Cincinnati
7	Goodwin, Curtis	L/L	5-11/180	9-30-72	Rochester, Baltimore
22	Howard, Thomas	B/R	6-2/205	12-11-64	Cincinnati
	Kelly, Mike	R/R	6-4/195	6-2-70	Richmond, Atlanta
36	King, Andre	R/R	6-1/180	11-26-73	Durham, Prince William
67	Ladell, Cleveland	R/R	5-11/170	9-19-70	Chattanooga
50	Mottola, Chad	R/R	6-3/220	10-15-71	Chattanooga, Indianapolis
16	Sanders, Reggie	R/R	6-1/185	12-1-67	Cincinnati
68	Watkins, Pat	R/R	6-2/185	9-2-72	Winston-Salem, Chattanooga
15	Wilson, Nigel	L/L	6-1/185	1-12-70	Indianapolis, Cincinnati

BALLPARK INFORMATION

Ballpark (capacity, surface)
Riverfront Stadium (52,952, artificial)

Address
100 Riverfront Stadium
Cincinnati, OH 45202

Business phone
513-421-4510

Ticket information
513-421-7337

Ticket prices
$11.50 (blue level box seats)
$10 (green level box seats)
$10 (yellow level box seats)
$9 (red level box seats)
$8 (green level reserved seats)
$6.50 (red level reserved seats)
$3.50 (``top six'' reserved seats)

Field dimensions (from home plate)
To left field at foul line, 330 feet
To center field, 404 feet
To right field at foul line, 330 feet

First game played
June 30, 1970 (Braves 8, Reds 2)

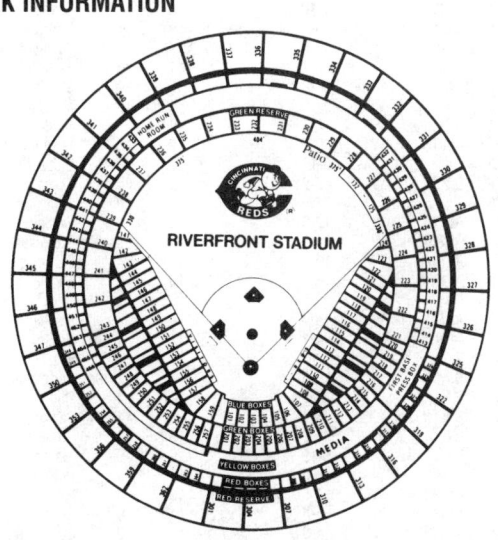

DAY BY DAY

Date	Opp.	Res.	Score	(inn.*)	Hits	Opp. hits	Winning pitcher	Losing pitcher	Save	Record	Pos.	GB
4-26	Chi.	L	1-7		7	10	Bullinger	Rijo	Perez	0-1	T4th	1
4-27	Chi.	L	5-6	(11)	12	11	Edens	McElroy	Myers	0-2	T4th	2
4-28	At S.D.	L	7-8		11	12	Berumen	Carrasco		0-3	T4th	3
4-29	At S.D.	L	5-9		8	10	Sanders	Schourek		0-4	5th	4
4-30	At S.D.	L	6-7		10	12	Hoffman	Carrasco		0-5	5th	4
5-2	Phi.	L	0-6		5	13	Schilling	Rijo		0-6	5th	4
5-3	Phi.	W	7-2		8	5	Hernandez	Charlton	Brantley	1-6	5th	3
5-4	Phi.	L	4-6		7	8	Harris	Carrasco	Slocumb	1-7	5th	4
5-5	N.Y.	L	0-3		5	7	B. Jones	Schourek	Franco	1-8	5th	5
5-6	N.Y.	W	13-11		15	14	Hernandez	Henry		2-8	5th	4½
5-7	N.Y.	W	8-4		11	11	Rijo	Jacome		3-8	5th	3½
5-9	At Fla.	W	9-1		13	8	Smiley	Rapp	Hernandez	4-8	4th	4
5-10	At Fla.	W	3-0		8	2	Jarvis	Burkett		5-8	4th	3
5-11	At Fla.	W	3-1	(15)	8	9	Pugh	Dunbar		6-8	4th	3
5-12	At Atl.	W	5-4	(11)	12	6	Brantley	Bedrosian		7-8	3rd	2½
5-13	At Atl.	L	6-9		10	10	Glavine	Smith	Borbon	7-9	4th	3½
5-14	At Atl.	W	5-3	(10)	8	7	Carrasco	Clontz		8-9	4th	2½
5-16	At Mon.	L	3-7		7	14	Perez	Jarvis	Rojas	8-10	T3rd	4
5-17	At Mon.	W	6-2		10	9	Rijo	Fassero	Carrasco	9-10	3rd	3
5-19	Col.	W	2-0		7	6	Schourek	Ritz	Brantley	10-10	3rd	3
5-20	Col.	W	10-9	(10)	14	13	Smith	Bailey		11-10	3rd	3
5-21	Col.	L	2-5		6	8	Acevedo	Jarvis	Holmes	11-11	3rd	4
5-22	Hou.	W	3-2	(10)	8	9	Brantley	Veres		12-11	3rd	3
5-23	Hou.	W	10-5		8	13	Hernandez	Kile	Carrasco	13-11	2nd	3
5-24	Hou.	W	4-2		9	5	Schourek	Reynolds	Brantley	14-11	2nd	3
5-25	At Chi.	W	6-2		6	9	Smiley	Morgan	Hernandez	15-11	2nd	2
5-26	At St.L.	W	4-3		11	12	Jarvis	Arocha	Carrasco	16-11	2nd	1
5-27	At St.L.	W	5-2		10	9	Rijo	Palacios		17-11	2nd	1
5-28	At St.L.	W	9-2		14	7	Pugh	Jackson		18-11	2nd	1
5-30	At Pit.	W	4-2		13	5	Schourek	Lieber	Brantley	19-11	T1st	...
5-31	At Pit.	W	11-1		17	7	Smiley	Wagner		20-11	T1st	...
6-1	At Pit.	L	3-5		7	9	Neagle	Rijo	Miceli	20-12	T1st	...
6-2	St.L.	L	7-10		8	16	Parrett	Smith	Henke	20-13	2nd	1
6-3	St.L.	W	8-4		12	12	Pugh	DeLucia		21-13	T1st	...
6-4	St.L.	W	4-0		5	2	Schourek	Hill		22-13	1st	...
6-5	Pit.	W	3-2		9	9	Smiley	Neagle	Brantley	23-13	1st	+1
6-6	Pit.	W	2-1	(10)	4	6	McElroy	Miceli		24-13	1st	+2
6-7	Pit.	L	3-7		7	10	Lieber	Jarvis	Plesac	24-14	1st	+2
6-8	At Hou.	W	6-3		9	8	Pugh	Kile	Brantley	25-14	1st	+3
6-9	At Hou.	W	5-2		9	7	Hernandez	Reynolds	Brantley	26-14	1st	+4
6-10	At Hou.	W	3-2		7	11	Smiley	Swindell	Carrasco	27-14	1st	+4
6-11	At Hou.	W	3-2	(10)	11	10	Brantley	Jones		28-14	1st	+5
6-12	At Col.	W	11-6		15	10	Jarvis	Freeman		29-14	1st	+5½
6-13	At Col.	L	4-6		8	12	Ritz	Pugh	Leskanic	29-15	1st	+5½
6-14	At Col.	L	4-10		8	14	Grahe	Schourek		29-16	1st	+5½
6-16	Mon.	L	3-6		9	14	Henry	Smiley		29-17	1st	+4
6-17	Mon.	W	5-4		9	7	Carrasco	Aquino	Brantley	30-17	1st	+5
6-18	Mon.	W	10-7		11	13	Jackson	G. White	Brantley	31-17	1st	+6
6-19	Atl.	L	0-10		5	10	Smoltz	Schourek		31-18	1st	+6
6-20	Atl.	L	2-10		9	18	Maddux	Nitkowski		31-19	1st	+5
6-21	Atl.	W	3-1		4	3	Smiley	Glavine	Brantley	32-19	1st	+5½
6-22	Atl.	W	9-8		12	10	Hernandez	Borbon	Brantley	33-19	1st	+6
6-23	Fla.	L	4-16		7	17	Burkett	Jarvis		33-20	1st	+5½
6-24	Fla.	W	5-2		9	5	Schourek	Hammond	Carrasco	34-20	1st	+6
6-25	Fla.	L	1-5		3	10	Weathers	Rijo	Mathews	34-21	1st	+5½
6-27	At Phi.	W	12-3		13	9	Smiley	Mimbs	Hernandez	35-21	1st	+5
6-28	At Phi.	W	1-0		4	3	Nitkowski	Schilling	Brantley	36-21	1st	+5
6-29	At Phi.	W	10-4		14	6	Schourek	Quantrill		37-21	1st	+5½
6-30	At N.Y.	L	6-7		10	11	Minor	McElroy	Franco	37-22	1st	+5½
7-1	At N.Y.	W	5-4		9	9	Pugh	Harnisch	Brantley	38-22	1st	+5½
7-2	At N.Y.	W	4-1		11	8	Smiley	B. Jones	Brantley	39-22	1st	+5½
7-3	S.F.	L	7-8		10	11	Burba	Hernandez	Beck	39-23	1st	+5½
7-4	S.F.	W	10-6		13	12	Schourek	Mulholland		40-23	1st	+5½
7-5	S.F.	W	9-0		10	4	Rijo	Leiter		41-23	1st	+6½
7-6	S.F.	L	5-7		9	14	Barton	Brantley	Beck	41-24	1st	+5½
7-7	L.A.	W	4-2		6	9	Smiley	Banks	Jackson	42-24	1st	+5½
7-8	L.A.	L	2-12		6	15	Martinez	Nitkowski		42-25	1st	+4
7-9	L.A.	W	8-0		15	6	Schourek	Valdes		43-25	1st	+5
7-13	At Chi.	W	11-5		10	10	Rijo	Trachsel	Brantley	44-25	1st	+6
7-14	At Chi.	W	5-4		11	9	Jackson	Perez	Brantley	45-25	1st	+6
7-15	At Chi.	W	4-3		12	9	Schourek	Navarro	Brantley	46-25	1st	+6

Date	Opp.	Res.	Score	(inn.*)	Hits	Opp. hits	Winning pitcher	Losing pitcher	Save	Record	Pos.	GB
7-16	At Chi.	L	5-7		6	12	Foster	Pugh	Myers	46-26	1st	+6
7-17	At S.D.	L	6-8		9	8	Blair	Nitkowski	Hoffman	46-27	1st	+5
7-18	At S.D.	W	5-1		7	6	McElroy	Hamilton		47-27	1st	+5
7-19	At S.D.	W	7-4		11	8	Jackson	Hoffman	Brantley	48-27	1st	+6
7-21	Chi.	W	10-1		14	4	Schourek	Foster		49-27	1st	+6¹/₂
7-22	Chi.	W	4-3		9	6	Jackson	Young	Brantley	50-27	1st	+6¹/₂
7-23	Chi.	W	7-5	(10)	12	12	Hernandez	Myers		51-27	1st	+6¹/₂
7-24	S.D.	L	8-10		11	14	Benes	Portugal	Hoffman	51-28	1st	+6¹/₂
7-25	S.D.	L	2-4		7	8	B. Williams	Pugh	Hoffman	51-29	1st	+5¹/₂
7-26	At S.F.	L	1-4		2	7	Leiter	Schourek		51-30	1st	+4¹/₂
7-27	At S.F.	W	14-6		14	12	Burba	Aquino		52-30	1st	+4¹/₂
7-28	At L.A.	W	3-2		6	3	Smiley	Candiotti	Brantley	53-30	1st	+5¹/₂
7-29	At L.A.	L	2-4		10	8	Martinez	Portugal	Worrell	53-31	1st	+4¹/₂
7-30	At L.A.	L	4-5		7	9	Nomo	Pugh		53-32	1st	+3¹/₂
8-1	N.Y.	W	4-3		6	6	Schourek	Harnisch	Brantley	54-32	1st	+4
8-2	N.Y.	W	6-2		11	10	Wells	B. Jones		55-32	1st	+4
8-3	N.Y.	W	3-2		6	6	McElroy	Cornelius	Brantley	56-32	1st	+5
8-4	Phi.	W	1-0		6	5	Smiley	Juden	Brantley	57-32	1st	+4¹/₂
8-6†	Phi.	W	6-1		7	3	Schourek	Greene		58-32		
8-6‡	Phi.	W	2-1	(10)	9	7	Jackson	Slocumb		59-32	1st	+6¹/₂
8-8	At Atl.	L	4-5		6	8	Smoltz	McElroy	Wohlers	59-33	1st	+6¹/₂
8-9	At Atl.	W	9-3		14	7	Burba	Maddux	Brantley	60-33	1st	+7¹/₂
8-10	At Atl.	L	1-2		6	6	Wohlers	Carrasco		60-34	1st	+7¹/₂
8-11	At Fla.	L	2-6		6	9	Rapp	Portugal		60-35	1st	+7¹/₂
8-12	At Fla.	L	3-7		9	12	Weathers	Schourek		60-36	1st	+6¹/₂
8-13	At Fla.	L	4-6		8	12	Gardner	Wells	Nen	60-37	1st	+5¹/₂
8-14	Col.	W	4-0		7	8	Burba	Ritz		61-37	1st	+6
8-15	Col.	W	11-3		15	9	Portugal	Rekar		62-37	1st	+7
8-16	Col.	L	4-6		10	7	Reynoso	Smiley	Painter	62-38	1st	+6
8-17	L.A.	W	6-2		10	7	Schourek	Tapani		63-38	1st	+7
8-18	Hou.	W	8-3		12	10	Wells	Hampton		64-38	1st	+8
8-19	Hou.	W	8-0		12	2	Burba	Reynolds		65-38	1st	+9
8-20	Hou.	W	11-4		17	13	Portugal	Swindell		66-38	1st	+10
8-21	At St.L.	L	6-8		12	9	Mathews	Jackson		66-39	1st	+10
8-22	At St.L.	L	3-7		8	10	Barber	Schourek		66-40	1st	+10
8-23	At St.L.	W	3-1		7	6	Wells	Watson		67-40	1st	+11
8-24	At St.L.	L	5-6		9	8	DeLucia	Carrasco	Henke	67-41	1st	+10¹/₂
8-25	At Pit.	W	19-3		19	7	Portugal	Parris		68-41	1st	+11¹/₂
8-26	At Pit.	W	7-6		19	14	Hernandez	Wagner	Brantley	69-41	1st	+12¹/₂
8-27	At Pit.	W	10-1		16	5	Schourek	Loaiza		70-41	1st	+13¹/₂
8-28	St.L.	W	5-2		9	6	Wells	Watson		71-41	1st	+14¹/₂
8-29	St.L.	W	4-1		9	6	Burba	Osborne		72-41	1st	+14¹/₂
8-30	St.L.	L	3-4		8	7	Morgan	Portugal	Henke	72-42	1st	+13¹/₂
8-31	Pit.	L	4-6	(10)	8	13	Plesac	Brantley	Miceli	72-43	1st	+13¹/₂
9-1	Pit.	W	7-1		8	5	Schourek	Loaiza		73-43	1st	+13¹/₂
9-2	Pit.	L	8-11		11	18	White	Wells		73-44	1st	+12¹/₂
9-3	Pit.	L	3-7		8	11	Wagner	Burba	Miceli	73-45	1st	+12¹/₂
9-4	At Hou.	W	6-1		10	6	Portugal	Reynolds		74-45	1st	+13¹/₂
9-5	At Hou.	L	1-10		5	12	Drabek	Viola		74-46	1st	+12¹/₂
9-6	At Hou.	W	7-3		12	4	Smiley	Wall		75-46	1st	+13¹/₂
9-8	At Col.	L	5-10		9	9	Leskanic	Carrasco		75-47	1st	+12¹/₂
9-9	At Col.	L	2-6		10	11	Swift	Wells	Ritz	75-48	1st	+12¹/₂
9-10	At Col.	L	4-5		13	8	Reed	Carrasco	Leskanic	75-49	1st	+11¹/₂
9-11	Fla.	W	2-1	(11)	7	9	Jackson	Garces		76-49	1st	+12
9-12	Fla.	L	4-5		7	11	Rapp	Smiley	Nen	76-50	1st	+11
9-13	Fla.	W	6-0		11	2	Schourek	Hammond		77-50	1st	+12
9-14	S.D.	W	8-1		8	4	Wells	Blair		78-50	1st	+13
9-15	Atl.	L	1-3		7	7	Smoltz	McElroy	McMichael	78-51	1st	+12
9-16	Atl.	L	1-6		8	10	Maddux	Portugal		78-52	1st	+11
9-17	Atl.	L	1-4		6	9	Glavine	Smiley	Wohlers	78-53	1st	+10
9-18	Mon.	W	7-4		14	9	Schourek	Alvarez		79-53	1st	+10
9-19	Mon.	L	1-4		7	10	Rueter	Wells	Rojas	79-54	1st	+10
9-20	Mon.	W	5-2		9	6	Portugal	Fassero	Jackson	80-54	1st	+10
9-22	At Phi.	W	3-2		6	7	Burba	Borland	Brantley	81-54	1st	+11
9-23	At Phi.	L	2-3	(13)	7	7	Ricci	Hernandez		81-55	1st	+10
9-24	At Phi.	W	6-4		8	8	Wells	D. Springer	Brantley	82-55	1st	+10
9-25	At N.Y.	L	1-2	(6)	6	5	Isringhausen	Pugh		82-56	1st	+9
9-27†	At N.Y.	L	4-5		8	13	Person	Smiley	Franco	82-57		
9-27‡	At N.Y.	L	2-9		5	9	Cornelius	Burba	Henry	82-58	1st	+8
9-28	At Mon.	W	9-7		8	10	Schourek	Martinez	Brantley	83-58	1st	+9
9-29	At Mon.	W	14-9		13	15	Portugal	Alvarez		84-58	1st	+10
9-30	At Mon.	L	1-6		5	7	Rueter	Wells		84-59	1st	+9
10-1	At Mon.	W	5-1		6	4	Pugh	Fassero		85-59	1st	+9

Monthly records: April (0-5), May (20-6), June (17-11), July (16-10), August (19-11), September (12-16), October (1-0).
*Innings, if other than nine. †First game of doubleheader. ‡Second game of doubleheader.

1996 SEASON *Cincinnati Reds*

HIGHLIGHTS

High point: The Reds went to Atlanta in early August riding a six-game winning streak. They dropped the first game but hammered eventual Cy Young Award winner Greg Maddux, 9-3, the next day. Maddux entered the game 12-1 and didn't lose again the rest of the regular season.

Low point: It's hard to believe anything could beat the team's 1-8 start. But losing 17 of 27 games from August 30 through September 27 was more disheartening, even though the team clinched the division during that stretch, because it left the Reds feeling vulnerable entering the playoffs.

Turning point: After losing eight of their first nine games, the Reds trailed the Mets, 11-4, in the eighth inning, but scored six runs in the eighth and three in the ninth to win, 13-11.

Most valuable player: Shortstop Barry Larkin. He not only was the team's MVP, but also the league's. Off the field, Larkin was the team's leader, calling meetings that helped shake the team from its slumps. On the field, he played his usual brilliant shortstop—and hit .319 with 15 homers, 66 RBIs and 51 steals.

Most valuable pitcher: Lefthander Pete Schourek. He finished 18-7 with a 3.22 ERA.

Most improved player: Schourek. Here's a guy who was waived by the Mets in April 1994. He was claimed by the Reds, then worked his way into the starting rotation by the end of the 1994 season.

Most pleasant surprise: Righthander Dave Burba. The late-season pickup from the Giants was expected to bolster the bullpen and maybe start, but he ended up solidifying the rotation, going 6-2 with a 3.27 ERA with the Reds in 15 games (4-1, 2.41 ERA in his nine starts). Then he adeptly filled the middle-relief gap between the starters and setup man Mike Jackson in the postseason.

Biggest disappointment: Third baseman Willie Greene. He was supposed to be a phenom, but he lasted 19 at-bats as a starter before the Reds had seen enough and farmed him out.

Key injury: The biggest injury was to starting pitcher Jose Rijo, who was limited to 14 games because of elbow problems that eventually required Tommy John surgery.

Notable: The Reds reached the NLCS for the first time since winning the World Series in 1990. . . . Ron Gant had four game-winning, extra-inning homers, tying Willie Mays' single-season record. . . . The Reds led the majors in steals (190).

—MIKE BASS

RECORDS

1995 regular-season record: 85-59 (1st N.L. Central); 44-28 at home; 41-31 on road; 35-26 vs. East; 35-14 vs. Central; 23-26 vs. West; 23-12 vs. lefthanded starters; 62-47 vs. righthanded starters; 17-23 on grass; 68-36 on turf; 23-16 in daytime; 62-43 at night; 23-15 in one-run games; 10-3 in extra-inning games; 1-1-0 in double-headers.

Team record past five years: 388-356 (.522, ranks 3rd in league in that span).

TEAM LEADERS

Batting average: Barry larkin (.319).
At-bats: Barry Larkin (496).
Runs: Barry Larkin (98).
Hits: Barry Larkin (158).
Total bases: Reggie Sanders (280).
Doubles: Reggie Sanders (36).
Triples: Barry Larkin, Reggie Sanders (6).
Home runs: Ron Gant (29).
Runs batted in: Reggie Sanders (99).
Stolen bases: Barry Larkin (51).
Slugging percentage: Reggie Sanders (.579).
On-base percentage: Reggie Sanders (.397).
Wins: Pete Schourek (18).
Earned-run average: Pete Schourek (3.22).
Complete games: David Wells (3).
Shutouts: Dave Burba (1).
Saves: Jeff Brantley (28).
Innings pitched: Mark Portugal (181.2).
Strikeouts: Pete Schourek (160).

GAMES BY POSITION

Catcher: Benito Santiago 75, Eddie Taubensee 65, Damon Berryhill 29.
First base: Hal Morris 99, Lenny Harris 23, Brian R. Hunter 23, Eric Anthony 17, Benito Santiago 8, Mariano Duncan 6, Craig Worthington 4, Eddie Taubensee 3, Jerome Walton 3, Damon Berryhill 1, Jeff Branson 1.
Second base: Bret Boone 138, Mariano Duncan 7, Jeff Branson 6, Mark Lewis 2, Lenny Harris 1.
Third base: Jeff Branson 98, Mark Lewis 72, Lenny Harris 24, Willie Greene 7, Eric Owens 2, Craig Worthington 2.
Shortstop: Barry Larkin 130, Jeff Branson 32, Mariano Duncan 6, Mark Lewis 2.
Outfield: Reggie Sanders 130, Ron Gant 117, Jerome Walton 89, Thomas Howard 82, Darren Lewis 57, Deion Sanders 33, Eric Anthony 24, Lenny Harris 8, Brian R. Hunter 4, Mariano Duncan 3, Steve Gibralter 2, Nigel Wilson 2.

TOP DRAFT CHOICES

1. None.
2. **Brett Tomko,** RHP, Florida Southern College.
3. **Andre Montgomery,** SS, Pleasure Ridge Park H.S., Louisville, Ky.
4. **Mark Corey,** RHP, Edinboro (Pa.) University.
5. **Mike LaRue,** C, Dallas Baptist University.
6. **Andy Burress,** C, Telfair County H.S., McRae, Ga.
7. **Herb Goodman,** OF, North Greenville (S.C.) J.C.
8. **Ray King,** LHP, Lambuth (Tenn.) University.
9. **Bobby Walters,** OF, Salisaw (Okla.) H.S.
10. **Ben Bailey,** RHP, Glen Oaks (Mich.) C.C.

COLORADO ROCKIES
NATIONAL LEAGUE WEST DIVISION

1996 ROCKIES SCHEDULE

☐ Home games shaded.
* — All-Star Game at Veterans Stadium (Philadelphia)
N — Night game (any game starting after 5 p.m.)

MARCH

SUN	MON	TUE	WED	THU	FRI	SAT
31						

APRIL

SUN	MON	TUE	WED	THU	FRI	SAT
	1	2 PHI	3 N PHI	4 N PHI	5 MON	6 MON
7 MON	8 CHI	9	10 CHI	11 N NY	12 N NY	13 NY
14 N NY	15 N SD	16 SD	17 SD	18	19 N NY	20 NY
21 NY	22 N CHI	23 CHI	24 N PHI	25 PHI	26 N MON	27 MON
28 MON	29	30 N LA				

MAY

SUN	MON	TUE	WED	THU	FRI	SAT
			1 N LA	2	3 N FLA	4 FLA
5 FLA	6 N ATL	7 N ATL	8 N ATL	9 N FLA	10 N FLA	11 FLA
12 FLA	13	14 N CIN	15 N CIN	16	17 N STL	18 STL
19 STL	20 N PIT	21 N PIT	22 PIT	23 N CIN	24 N CIN	25 CIN
26 CIN	27 N STL	28 N STL	29 N STL	30	31 N PIT	

JUNE

SUN	MON	TUE	WED	THU	FRI	SAT
						1 N PIT
2 PIT	3	4 N HOU	5 N HOU	6 N HOU	7 N ATL	8 ATL
9 ATL	10 N HOU	11 N HOU	12 HOU	13 N PHI	14 N PHI	15 PHI
16 PHI	17 N MON	18 N MON	19 MON	20	21 N PHI	22 PHI
23 PHI	24 N NY	25 N NY	26 NY	27 N LA	28 N LA	29 N LA
30 LA						

JULY

SUN	MON	TUE	WED	THU	FRI	SAT
	1 SF	2 N SF	3 N SF	4 N LA	5 N LA	6 LA
7 LA	8 *	9 ALL-STAR GAME	10	11 N SD	12 N SD	13 N SD
14 N SD	15 N SF	16 SF	17 SF	18	19 N SD	20 N SD
21 N SD	22	23 N NY	24 NY	25 N CHI	26 N CHI	27 N CHI
28 CHI	29 N MON	30 N MON	31 MON			

AUGUST

SUN	MON	TUE	WED	THU	FRI	SAT
				1 CHI	2 CHI	3 CHI
4 CHI	5 N FLA	6 N FLA	7 FLA	8	9 N ATL	10 ATL
11 ATL	12 N FLA	13 N FLA	14 N FLA	15 N CIN	16 N CIN	17 CIN
18 CIN	19 N CIN	20 N STL	21 N STL	22 STL	23 N PIT	24 PIT
25 PIT	26 N CIN	27 N CIN	28 CIN	29	30 N STL	31 N STL

SEPTEMBER

SUN	MON	TUE	WED	THU	FRI	SAT
1 STL	2 PIT	3	4 N PIT	5	6 N HOU	7 HOU
8 HOU	9 N HOU	10 N ATL	11 N ATL	12 ATL	13 N HOU	14 HOU
15 HOU	16 N LA	17 N LA	18	19 N SF	20 N SF	21 SF
22 SF	23 N SD	24 N SD	25 SD	26	27 N SF	28 SF
28 SF						

1996 SEASON

CLUB DIRECTORY

Chairman, president and CEO
Jerry McMorris

Exec. vice president/general manager
Bob Gebhard

Sr. v.p./secretary and corporate counsel
Clark Weaver

Senior vice president/chief financial officer
Hal Roth

Vice president/sales and marketing
Greg Feasel

Vice president/finance
Michael Kent

Vice president/player personnel
Dick Balderson

Assistant general manager
Tony Siegle

Vice president/ticket operations
Sue Ann McClaren

Sr. vice president/business operations
Keli McGregor

Director, scouting
Pat Daugherty

Director, team travel
Peter Durso

Director, public relations
Mike Swanson

Director, stadium services
Kevin Kahn

Director, ticket operations
Chuck Javernick

Director, publications
Jimmy Oldham

Dir., charitable and community affairs
Roger Kinney

Dir., management information systems
Mary Burns

Assistant director, player personnel
Paul Egins

Assistant director, scouting
Jay Darnell

Mgr. of promotions and special events
Alan Bossart

Director of broadcasting
Eric Brummond

Head groundskeeper
Mark Razum

Coordinator of instruction
Rick Mathews

National cross-checkers
Dave Holliday
Jeff Schugel

Regional cross-checkers
Bruce Andrew
Bill Gayton
Robyn Lynch

Major league scouts
Jack Bloomfield, Jim Fanning, Bill Harford, Larry High, Bill Wood

Scouts
Ty Coslow, Dar Cox, Mike Ericson, Abe Flores, Mike Garlatti, Bert Holt, Greg Hopkins, Bill Hughes, Damon Iannelli, Pat Jones, Bill Mackenzie, Frank Mattox, Danny Montgomery, Lance Nichols, Steve Payne, Art Pontarelli, Ed Santa, Nick Venuto, Tom Wheeler

International scouts
Phil Allen, Cristobal A. Giron, Julian Gonzalez, Angel Hermoso, Jim Hovorka, Brian McRobie, Atanacio Mendez, Jorge Posada, Reed Spencer, Ron Steele

MINOR LEAGUE AFFILIATES

Class	Team	League	Manager
AAA	Colorado Springs	Pacific Coast	Brad Mills
AA	New Haven	Eastern	Bill Hayes
A	Salem	Carolina	Bill McGuire
A	Asheville	South Atlantic	P.J. Carey
A	Portland	Northwest	Ron Gideon
Rookie	Mesa Rockies	Arizona	Jim Eppard

BROADCAST INFORMATION

Radio: KOA-AM (850).
TV: KWGN-TV (Channel 2).
Cable TV: None.

SPRING TRAINING

Ballpark (city): Hi Corbett Field (Tucson, Ariz.).
Ticket information: 602-327-9467.

1996 SEASON Colorado Rockies

SPRING TRAINING ROSTER

Manager—Don Baylor (25).
Coaches—Frank Funk (45), Gene Glynn (2), Ken Griffey Sr. (24), Jackie Moore (47), Paul Zuvella (46).

No.	PITCHERS	B/T	Ht./Wt.	Born	1995 clubs
50	Alston, Garvin	R/R	6-1/185	12-8-71	New Haven
51	Arteaga, Ivan	L/R	6-2/227	7-20-72	New Haven
38	Bailey, Roger	R/R	6-1/180	10-3-70	Colorado, Colorado Springs
45	Burke, John	B/R	6-4/215	2-9-70	Colorado Springs
41	DeJean, Mike	R/R	6-2/205	9-28-70	Norwich
36	Farmer, Mike	B/L	6-1/193	7-3-68	New Haven
44	Freeman, Marvin	R/R	6-7/222	4-10-63	Colorado
40	Holmes, Darren	R/R	6-0/202	4-25-66	Colorado
57	Jones, Bobby	R/L	6-0/175	4-11-72	New Haven, Colorado Springs
16	Leskanic, Curtis	R/R	6-0/180	4-2-68	Colorado
43	Munoz, Mike	L/L	6-2/192	7-12-65	Colorado
17	Nied, David	R/R	6-2/185	12-22-68	Portland, New Haven, Colorado Springs, Colorado
28	Painter, Lance	L/L	6-1/197	7-21-67	Colorado, Colorado Springs
39	Reed, Steve	R/R	6-2/212	3-11-66	Colorado
56	Rekar, Bryan	R/R	6-3/210	6-3-72	New Haven, Colorado Springs, Colorado
42	Reynoso, Armando	R/R	6-0/204	5-1-66	Colorado Springs, Colorado
30	Ritz, Kevin	R/R	6-4/222	6-8-65	Colorado
18	Ruffin, Bruce	B/L	6-2/215	10-4-63	Colorado, New Haven
31	Saberhagen, Bret	R/R	6-1/200	4-11-64	New York N.L., Colorado
20	Swift, Bill	R/R	6-0/197	10-27-61	Colorado
32	Thompson, Mark	R/R	6-2/205	4-7-71	Colorado, Colorado Springs
48	Thomson, John	R/R	6-3/175	10-1-73	New Haven
53	Viano, Jake	R/R	5-10/177	9-4-73	New Haven

No.	CATCHERS	B/T	Ht./Wt.	Born	1995 clubs
27	Brito, Jorge	R/R	6-1/190	6-22-66	Colorado, Colorado Springs
34	Owens, Jayhawk	R/R	6-1/213	2-10-69	Colorado Springs, Colorado
12	Reed, Jeff	L/R	6-2/190	11-12-62	San Francisco

No.	INFIELDERS	B/T	Ht./Wt.	Born	1995 clubs
6	Bates, Jason	B/R	5-11/181	1-5-71	Colorado
9	Castilla, Vinny	R/R	6-1/200	7-4-67	Colorado
4	Counsell, Craig	L/R	6-0/170	8-21-70	Colorado Springs, Colorado
14	Galarraga, Andres	R/R	6-3/235	6-18-61	Colorado
35	Vander Wal, John	L/L	6-2/198	4-29-66	Colorado
22	Weiss, Walt	B/R	6-0/178	11-28-63	Colorado
21	Young, Eric	R/R	5-9/170	5-18-67	Colorado

No.	OUTFIELDERS	B/T	Ht./Wt.	Born	1995 clubs
10	Bichette, Dante	R/R	6-3/235	11-18-63	Colorado
26	Burks, Ellis	R/R	6-2/198	9-11-64	Colorado Springs, Colorado
1	Hubbard, Trenidad	R/R	5-8/183	5-11-66	Colorado Springs, Colorado
52	Jones, Terry	B/R	5-10/165	2-15-71	New Haven
3	McCracken, Quinton	B/R	5-7/173	3-16-70	New Haven, Colorado Springs, Colorado
29	Pulliam, Harvey	R/R	6-0/218	10-20-67	Colorado Springs, Colorado
33	Walker, Larry	L/R	6-3/225	12-1-66	Colorado

BALLPARK INFORMATION

Ballpark (capacity, surface)
Coors Field (50,200, grass)

Address
2001 Blake St.
Denver, CO 80205-2000

Business phone
303-292-0200

Ticket information
303-762-5437

Ticket prices
$26 (club level)
$20 (infield box)
$16 (outfield box)
$12 (lower reserved)
$10 (upper reserved, RF box)
$8 (RF mezzanine)
$6 (lower RF reserved)
$5 (upper RF reserved, pavilion)
$4 (CF bleachers)
$1 (rockpile)

Field dimensions (from home plate)
To left field at foul line, 347 feet
To center field, 415 feet
To right field at foul line, 350

First game played
April 26, 1995 (Rockies 11, Mets 9, 14 innings)

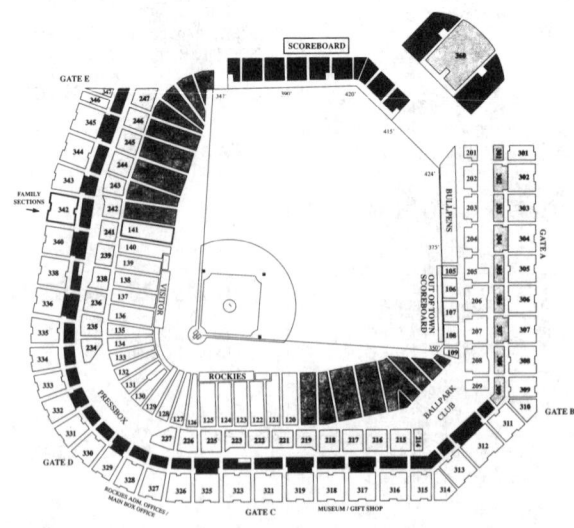

DAY BY DAY

Date	Opp.	Res.	Score	(inn.*)	Hits	Opp. hits	Winning pitcher	Losing pitcher	Save	Record	Pos.	GB
4-26	N.Y.	W	11-9	(14)	15	18	Thompson	Remlinger		1-0	2nd	$^1/_2$
4-27	N.Y.	W	8-7		13	10	Reed	Lomon		2-0	T1st	...
4-28	At Hou.	W	2-1		3	7	Leskanic	Kile	Ruffin	3-0	T1st	...
4-29	At Hou.	W	2-1		3	4	Olivares	Hampton	Ruffin	4-0	1st	+1
4-30	At Hou.	L	1-3		4	5	Brocail	Leskanic	Hudek	4-1	T1st	...
5-1	S.D.	W	8-3		11	7	Holmes	Mauser		5-1	1st	+1
5-2	S.D.	W	6-5	(11)	14	11	Bailey	B. Williams		6-1	1st	+2
5-3	S.D.	W	12-7		14	12	Bailey	Hamilton	Ruffin	7-1	1st	+3
5-5	L.A.	L	4-6		9	12	Martinez	Olivares	Seanez	7-2	1st	+1$^1/_2$
5-6	L.A.	L	11-17		17	21	T. Williams	Acevedo		7-3	1st	+$^1/_2$
5-7	L.A.	L	10-12		12	13	Daal	Reed	Valdes	7-4	T2nd	$^1/_2$
5-9	S.F.	W	10-6		13	10	Ritz	Wilson		8-4	1st	+$^1/_2$
5-10	S.F.	W	8-5		13	12	Holmes	Bautista		9-4	1st	+1$^1/_2$
5-11	S.F.	W	10-4		11	7	Acevedo	Mulholland	Reed	10-4	1st	+2
5-12	At Fla.	W	10-6		13	9	Swift	Gardner	Ruffin	11-4	1st	+2
5-13	At Fla.	L	2-8		6	11	Witt	Freeman		11-5	1st	+2
5-14	At Fla.	W	6-3		11	9	Ritz	Rapp	Ruffin	12-5	1st	+2$^1/_2$
5-15	At Atl.	L	0-4		5	7	Mercker	Olivares		12-6	1st	+2
5-16	At Atl.	L	3-15		6	20	Smoltz	Acevedo		12-7	1st	+2
5-17	At Atl.	W	6-5		8	8	Holmes	Maddux	Ruffin	13-7	1st	+2$^1/_2$
5-18	At Atl.	L	2-3		11	8	McMichael	Munoz	Borbon	13-8	1st	+2$^1/_2$
5-19	At Cin.	L	0-2		6	7	Schourek	Ritz	Brantley	13-9	1st	+1$^1/_2$
5-20	At Cin.	L	9-10	(10)	13	14	Smith	Bailey		13-10	1st	+$^1/_2$
5-21	At Cin.	W	5-2		8	6	Acevedo	Jarvis	Holmes	14-10	1st	+1$^1/_2$
5-22	Chi.	W	9-8		18	9	Munoz	Myers		15-10	1st	+2
5-23	Chi.	L	6-7		9	14	Foster	Freeman	Myers	15-11	1st	+2
5-24	Chi.	L	3-5		6	8	Castillo	Bailey	Myers	15-12	1st	+2
5-26	At Pit.	L	2-4		5	7	Wagner	Acevedo	Miceli	15-13	1st	+$^1/_2$
5-27	At Pit.	L	4-9		11	10	Neagle	Swift		15-14	1st	+$^1/_2$
5-28	At Pit.	W	6-3		11	9	Freeman	White	Ruffin	16-14	1st	+$^1/_2$
5-29	At St.L.	L	5-6	(11)	13	11	Habyan	Bailey		16-15	2nd	$^1/_2$
5-30	At St.L.	L	5-8		11	14	Hill	Grahe	Henke	16-16	2nd	1$^1/_2$
5-31	At St.L.	W	5-3		9	9	Acevedo	Petkovsek	Holmes	17-16	2nd	$^1/_2$
6-2	Pit.	W	7-4		10	13	Holmes	Mccurry		18-16	2nd	$^1/_2$
6-3	Pit.	W	7-6		13	10	Ritz	Lieber	Holmes	19-16	2nd	$^1/_2$
6-4	Pit.	W	4-1		6	8	Grahe	Wagner	Leskanic	20-16	2nd	$^1/_2$
6-5	St.L.	L	5-9		11	13	Petkovsek	Acevedo		20-17	2nd	$^1/_2$
6-6	St.L.	W	5-4		11	9	Leskanic	Parrett		21-17	2nd	$^1/_2$
6-7	St.L.	W	7-3		9	10	Freeman	Jackson		22-17	2nd	$^1/_2$
6-8	At Chi.	W	5-3		10	6	Ritz	Foster	Reed	23-17	1st	+$^1/_2$
6-9	At Chi.	W	2-1	(10)	8	6	Holmes	Perez	Munoz	24-17	1st	+1$^1/_2$
6-10	At Chi.	L	0-3		5	3	Morgan	Acevedo	Myers	24-18	1st	+1$^1/_2$
6-11	At Chi.	W	5-1		9	6	Thompson	Trachsel	Leskanic	25-18	1st	+2$^1/_2$
6-12	Cin.	L	6-11		10	15	Jarvis	Freeman		25-19	1st	+2
6-13	Cin.	W	6-4		12	8	Ritz	Pugh	Leskanic	26-19	1st	+2
6-14	Cin.	W	10-4		14	8	Grahe	Schourek		27-19	1st	+2
6-16	Atl.	L	0-2		6	8	Glavine	Swift		27-20	1st	+2$^1/_2$
6-17	Atl.	L	1-7		6	12	Avery	Acevedo		27-21	1st	+1$^1/_2$
6-18	Atl.	L	4-9		6	13	Mercker	Freeman		27-22	1st	+$^1/_2$
6-19	Fla.	L	2-7		12	10	Hammond	Ritz		27-23	1st	+$^1/_2$
6-20	Fla.	L	2-7		7	11	Mathews	Grahe		27-24	1st	+$^1/_2$
6-21	Fla.	W	6-3		11	7	Swift	Rapp	Reed	28-24	1st	+$^1/_2$
6-22	At S.D.	W	3-2		9	6	Reynoso	Dishman	Ruffin	29-24	1st	+1$^1/_2$
6-23	At S.D.	L	2-3		8	5	Ashby	Freeman	Hoffman	29-25	1st	+1
6-24	At S.D.	L	0-2		4	6	Hamilton	Ritz		29-26	T1st	...
6-25	At S.D.	W	11-3		14	7	Grahe	Sanders		30-26	T1st	...
6-27	At S.F.	W	5-1		9	3	Swift	Bautista		31-26	1st	+$^1/_2$
6-28	At S.F.	L	1-2	(11)	10	6	Barton	Munoz		31-27	1st	+$^1/_2$
6-29	At L.A.	L	0-3		6	10	Nomo	Freeman		31-28	2nd	$^1/_2$
6-30	At L.A.	W	2-1		5	5	Ritz	Candiotti	Munoz	32-28	1st	+$^1/_2$
7-1	At L.A.	L	4-5		7	10	Worrell	Bailey		32-29	2nd	$^1/_2$
7-2	At L.A.	W	10-1		8	6	Swift	Martinez		33-29	1st	+$^1/_2$
7-3	Hou.	W	15-10		21	13	Bailey	Dougherty	Holmes	34-29	1st	+1
7-4	Hou.	L	8-16		14	17	Hampton	Olivares		34-30	1st	+1
7-5	Hou.	W	4-2		6	4	Ritz	Kile	Holmes	35-30	1st	+2
7-6	Mon.	W	9-6		14	13	Grahe	Fassero	Holmes	36-30	1st	+3
7-7	Mon.	W	12-7		16	9	Acevedo	Heredia		37-30	1st	+4
7-8	Mon.	W	8-3		13	5	Reynoso	Henry	Leskanic	38-30	1st	+4
7-9	Mon.	W	4-1		6	7	Freeman	Martinez		39-30	1st	+5
7-13	At N.Y.	L	2-4		4	9	B. Jones	Ritz	Franco	39-31	1st	+5
7-14	At N.Y.	L	4-13		9	20	Pulsipher	Reynoso		39-32	1st	+4

1996 SEASON *Colorado Rockies*

Date	Opp.	Res.	Score	(inn.*)	Hits	Opp. hits	Winning pitcher	Losing pitcher	Save	Record	Pos.	GB
7-15	At N.Y.	W	5-4		12	13	Swift	Saberhagen	Holmes	40-32	1st	+4
7-16	At N.Y.	L	1-2	(10)	9	7	Franco	Thompson		40-33	1st	+4
7-17	Phi.	W	8-5		11	9	Munoz	Bottalico	Holmes	41-33	1st	+5
7-18	Phi.	L	5-7		9	14	Schilling	Ritz	Slocumb	41-34	1st	+5
7-19	Phi.	W	5-3		9	8	Rekar	Green	Holmes	42-34	1st	+5
7-20	Phi.	W	7-3		11	7	Swift	Quantrill		43-34	1st	+5
7-21	N.Y.	L	1-12		9	18	Harnisch	Reynoso		43-35	1st	+4
7-22	N.Y.	W	5-4		9	10	Leskanic	Henry	Holmes	44-35	1st	+5
7-23	N.Y.	W	8-5		9	11	Ritz	B. Jones	Holmes	45-35	1st	+5
7-24	At Phi.	W	11-3		10	8	Rekar	Green		46-35	1st	+5
7-25	At Phi.	L	6-7	(10)	11	12	Slocumb	Munoz		46-36	1st	+5
7-26	At Hou.	L	3-4		10	8	Kile	Reynoso	Jones	46-37	1st	+4
7-27	At Hou.	L	4-5	(12)	11	16	Jones	Munoz		46-38	1st	+3
7-28	At Mon.	W	8-3		11	9	Ritz	Urbina		47-38	1st	+4
7-29	At Mon.	W	5-3		13	5	Rekar	Fassero	Holmes	48-38	1st	+4
7-30	At Mon.	L	4-11		7	10	Martinez	Freeman		48-39	1st	+3
7-31	At Mon.	W	3-2		10	7	Reynoso	Henry	Holmes	49-39	1st	+3 1/2
8-1	L.A.	L	6-9		11	12	Valdes	Thompson	Worrell	49-40	1st	+2 1/2
8-2	L.A.	L	7-10		11	13	Tapani	Ritz		49-41	1st	+1 1/2
8-3	L.A.	W	9-4		10	14	Saberhagen	Martinez		50-41	1st	+2 1/2
8-4	S.D.	W	14-12		12	20	Reed	Berumen	Holmes	51-41	1st	+3 1/2
8-5	S.D.	W	7-3		15	9	Reynoso	Ashby		52-41	1st	+3 1/2
8-6	S.D.	L	8-16		12	19	Dishman	Thompson		52-42	1st	+3 1/2
8-8	At Fla.	L	4-5	(13)	10	12	Groom	Bailey		52-43	1st	+2
8-9	At Fla.	L	1-2		7	6	Burkett	Ritz	Nen	52-44	1st	+1
8-10	At Fla.	L	2-3		6	5	Pena	Reed		52-45	1st	+1
8-11	At Atl.	L	3-5		6	5	Avery	Reynoso	Wohlers	52-46	T1st	...
8-12	At Atl.	W	16-4		18	8	Leskanic	Mercker		53-46	T1st	...
8-13	At Atl.	L	2-3		6	8	Wohlers	Holmes		53-47	2nd	1
8-14	At Cin.	L	0-4		8	7	Burba	Ritz		53-48	2nd	1
8-15	At Cin.	L	3-11		9	15	Portugal	Rekar		53-49	2nd	2
8-16	At Cin.	W	6-4		7	10	Reynoso	Smiley	Painter	54-49	2nd	2
8-17	Chi.	W	12-5		14	9	Bailey	Navarro		55-49	2nd	1
8-18	Chi.	L	7-26		10	27	Young	Saberhagen		55-50	2nd	1
8-19	Chi.	L	5-6		10	7	Castillo	Ritz	Myers	55-51	2nd	1
8-20	Chi.	W	4-2		5	5	Leskanic	Wendell		56-51	T1st	...
8-22	Pit.	L	1-10		10	16	Loaiza	Reynoso		56-52	2nd	1 1/2
8-23	Pit.	W	9-5		17	10	Bailey	Neagle		57-52	2nd	1 1/2
8-24	Pit.	W	8-6		10	13	Painter	Wagner	Leskanic	58-52	2nd	1/2
8-25	St.L.	L	3-8		7	14	Morgan	Rekar	Mathews	58-53	2nd	1/2
8-26	St.L.	L	4-5		5	6	Fossas	Ruffin	Henke	58-54	2nd	1/2
8-27	St.L.	L	5-10		10	18	Barber	Reynoso		58-55	2nd	1 1/2
8-28	At Pit.	W	6-3		11	9	Bailey	Powell	Leskanic	59-55	2nd	1
8-29	At Pit.	L	0-4		1	7	Wagner	Ritz		59-56	2nd	1
8-30	At Pit.	W	6-0		8	7	Rekar	Ericks		60-56	T1st	...
9-1	At St.L.	L	4-5		6	8	DeLucia	Leskanic	Henke	60-57	2nd	1/2
9-2	At St.L.	W	6-1		4	5	Bailey	Watson		61-57	1st	+1/2
9-3	At St.L.	W	5-4	(11)	11	9	Holmes	Parrett	Ruffin	62-57	1st	+1/2
9-4	At Chi.	L	0-2		5	4	Castillo	Rekar		62-58	2nd	1/2
9-6	At Chi.	W	10-4		14	12	Reynoso	Bullinger		63-58	T1st	...
9-8	Cin.	W	10-5		9	9	Leskanic	Carrasco		64-58	T1st	...
9-9	Cin.	W	6-2		11	10	Swift	Wells	Ritz	65-58	T1st	...
9-10	Cin.	W	5-4		8	13	Reed	Carrasco	Leskanic	66-58	T1st	...
9-11	Atl.	W	5-4	(12)	13	15	Hickerson	Woodall		67-58	1st	+1
9-12	Atl.	W	12-2		17	9	Painter	Avery	Ritz	68-58	1st	+1
9-13	Atl.	L	7-9		13	11	Schmidt	Bailey		68-59	1st	+1
9-15	Fla.	W	6-3		13	10	Reed	Burkett	Leskanic	69-59	1st	+1
9-16	Fla.	W	8-7		12	9	Reed	Mathews	Ruffin	70-59	1st	+2
9-17	Fla.	L	0-17		1	21	Rapp	Rekar		70-60	1st	+1
9-18	At S.D.	W	5-1		11	4	Ritz	Hamilton	Ruffin	71-60	1st	+1 1/2
9-19	At S.D.	L	4-15		9	18	Blair	Reynoso		71-61	1st	+1 1/2
9-20	At S.D.	W	10-2		16	5	Swift	Dishman		72-61	1st	+1 1/2
9-21	At S.F.	L	3-5		9	10	S. Valdez	Grahe	Beck	72-62	1st	+1 1/2
9-22	At S.F.	W	6-1		10	2	Ritz	Estes		73-62	1st	+1 1/2
9-23	At S.F.	L	0-2		2	8	Brewington	Rekar	Beck	73-63	1st	+1/2
9-24	At S.F.	W	3-1		5	4	Reynoso	Leiter	Leskanic	74-63	1st	+1/2
9-25	At L.A.	L	3-4		8	7	Martinez	Swift	Worrell	74-64	2nd	1/2
9-26	At L.A.	W	7-3		9	9	Saberhagen	Candiotti		75-64	2nd	+1/2
9-27	At L.A.	L	4-7		10	12	Tapani	Ritz	Worrell	75-65	2nd	1/2
9-28	S.F.	L	4-12		12	18	Brewington	Rekar		75-66	2nd	1
9-29	S.F.	L	7-10		12	15	Service	Leskanic	Beck	75-67	2nd	1
9-30	S.F.	W	9-3		13	14	Swift	Mulholland		76-67	2nd	1
10-1	S.F.	W	10-9		15	13	Painter	Leiter	Leskanic	77-67	2nd	1

Monthly records: April (4-1), May (13-15), June (15-12), July (17-11), August (11-17), September (16-11), October (1-0).
*Innings, if other than nine.

HIGHLIGHTS

High point: In winning 12 of 17, the Rockies went 11 games above .500 on July 24 with a five-game lead. That night, rookie Bryan Rekar pitched the team's only complete game of the season, against Philadelphia.

Low point: Beginning with being swept in a three-game series at Florida, the Rockies stumbled through a 2-7 road trip that dropped them a season-high two games out of first in mid-August.

Turning point: Opening Day. With the Mets in town to christen Coors Field, the Rockies rallied to tie the score in the ninth and 13th innings and won, 11-9, in the 14th on Dante Bichette's three-run homer, the Rockies' first at Coors Field. The victory set the tone: The club would go 44-28 at home and set a record for homers at home with 134.

Most valuable player: Bichette. He hit .340 and led the N.L. with 40 homers and 128 RBIs.

Most valuable pitcher: Righthander Kevin Ritz. Two years removed from elbow surgery, Ritz was the only constant in the rotation, leading the team in victories (11), innings (173¹/₃) and starts (28).

Most improved player: Vinny Castilla. Castilla, a backup shortstop/second baseman the two previous years, was being counted on to platoon at third. He won the job outright and was the starting third baseman in the All-Star Game. Castilla hit .309 with 32 home runs and 90 RBIs.

Most pleasant surprise: Righthander Curtis Leskanic. Leskanic led the majors with 76 appearances, allowing 83 hits and striking out 107 in 98 innings. He was 10-for-16 in save opportunities, and stranded 38 of 46 inherited runners.

Biggest disappointments: Other than Ritz, the rotation was mediocre. The 12 starters the Rockies used averaged 5²/₃ innings per start. A starter lasted eight innings only 10 times.

Key injuries: Pitchers Bill Swift and Marvin Freeman missed time, and David Nied missed the season. Reliever Bruce Ruffin

was sidelined twice, facing only nine batters between May 28 and August 22.

Notable: The Rockies became the second team in history to have four players with 30 homers—Bichette (40), Castilla (32), Andres Galarraga (31) and Larry Walker (36). . . . John Vander Wal set a major league single-season record with 28 pinch-hits. . . . The Rockies earned the N.L. wild-card spot, making the postseason in their third year of existence, the fastest of any expansion team in history.

—**TRACY RINGOLSBY**

RECORDS

1995 regular-season record: 77-67 (2nd in West); 44-28 at home; 33-39 on road; 25-23 vs. East; 31-26 vs. Central; 21-18 vs. West; 28-17 vs. lefthanded starters; 49-50 vs. righthanded starters; 63-52 on grass; 14-15 on turf; 32-18 in daytime; 45-49 at night; 19-19 in one-run games; 5-7 in extra-inning games; 0-0-0 in doubleheaders.

Team record past five years: 197-226 in three years (.466, ranks 11th in league in that span).

TEAM LEADERS

Batting average: Dante Bichette (.340).
At-bats: Dante Bichette (579).
Runs: Dante Bichette (102).
Hits: Dante Bichette (197).
Total bases: Dante Bichette (359).
Doubles: Dante Bichette (38).
Triples: Eric Young (9).
Home runs: Dante Bichette (40).
Runs batted in: Dante Bichette (128).
Stolen bases: Eric Young (35).
Slugging percentage: Dante Bichette (.620).
On-base percentage: Walt Weiss (.403).
Wins: Kevin Ritz (11).
Earned-run average: Kevin Ritz (4.21).
Complete games: Bryan Rekar (1).
Shutouts: None.
Saves: Darren Holmes (14).
Innings pitched: Kevin Ritz (173.1).
Strikeouts: Kevin Ritz (120).

GAMES BY POSITION

Catcher: Joe Girardi 122, Jorge Brito 18, Jayhawk Owens 16, Matt Nokes 3, Jim Tatum 1.
First base: Andres Galarraga 142, John Vander Wal 10, Mike Kingery 5.
Second base: Jason Bates 82, Eric Young 77, Roberto Mejia 16.
Third base: Vinny Castilla 137, Jason Bates 15, Pedro Castellano 3.
Shortstop: Walt Weiss 136, Jason Bates 20, Vinny Castilla 5, Craig Counsell 3.
Outfield: Dante Bichette 136, Larry Walker 129, Mike Kingery 108, Ellis Burks 80, Eric Young 19, Trent Hubbard 16, John Vander Wal 10, Jim Tatum 2, Quinton McCracken 1, Harvey Pulliam 1.

TOP DRAFT CHOICES

1. **Todd Helton,** 1B-LHP, University of Tennessee.
2. **Ben Petrick,** C, Glencoe H.S., Hillsboro, Ore.
3. **Chris Macca,** RHP, St. Leo (Fla.) College.
4. **John Clark,** SS, Clemens H.S., Schertz, Tex.
5. **Mike Vavrek,** RHP, Lewis (Ill.) University.
6. **Chandler Martin,** RHP, University of Portland.
7. **Cristy Rosa,** RHP, Guanica, Puerto Rico.
8. **Tal Light,** 3B, Oklahoma State University.
9. **Jamie Emiliano,** RHP, Florida International University.
10. **Gary Gordon,** OF, Willingboro (N.J.) H.S.

FLORIDA MARLINS
NATIONAL LEAGUE EAST DIVISION

1996 MARLINS SCHEDULE

Home games shaded.
* — All-Star Game at Veterans Stadium (Philadelphia)
N — Night game (any game starting after 5 p.m.)

MARCH

SUN	MON	TUE	WED	THU	FRI	SAT
31						

APRIL

SUN	MON	TUE	WED	THU	FRI	SAT
	1 N PIT	2 N PIT	3	4 PIT	5 N SF	6 N SF
7 SF	8 N SD	9 N SD	10 N SD	11 N LA	12 N LA	13 N LA
14 LA	15	16 N ATL	17 N ATL	18 N ATL	19 N LA	20 N LA
21 N LA	22 N SD	23 N SD	24 N PIT	25 PIT	26 N SF	27 SF
28 SF	29	30 N PHI				

MAY

SUN	MON	TUE	WED	THU	FRI	SAT
			1 N PHI	2 N PHI	3 N COL	4 COL
5 COL	6 N NY	7 N NY	8 N NY	9 N COL	10 N COL	11 N COL
12 COL	13 N STL	14 N STL	15 N STL	16	17 N CHI	18 N CHI
19 CHI	20 N CIN	21 N CIN	22 N CIN	23	24 N STL	25 N STL
26 STL	27 N CIN	28 N CIN	29 N CIN	30	31 N CHI	

JUNE

SUN	MON	TUE	WED	THU	FRI	SAT
						1 N CHI
2 CHI	3	4 N MON	5 N MON	6	7 N NY	8 N NY
9 NY	10 N MON	11 N MON	12 N MON	13 N PIT	14 N PIT	15 N PIT
16 PIT	17 SF	18 SF	19 N SF	20	21 N PIT	22 N PIT
23 PIT	24 N SF	25 N SF	26 SF	27	28 N ATL	29 N ATL
30 ATL						

JULY

SUN	MON	TUE	WED	THU	FRI	SAT
	1 N HOU	2 N HOU	3 N HOU	4 PHI	5 N PHI	6 N PHI
7 PHI	8 *	9 ALL-STAR GAME	10	11 N ATL	12 N ATL	13 N ATL
14 ATL	15 N HOU	16 N HOU	17 N HOU	18 N PHI	19 N PHI	20 N PHI
21 PHI	22	23 N LA	24 N LA	25 N LA	26 N SD	27 N SD
28 SD	29 N SD	30 N LA	31 N LA			

AUGUST

SUN	MON	TUE	WED	THU	FRI	SAT
				1 N LA	2 N SD	3 N SD
4 SD	5 N COL	6 N COL	7 COL	8 N NY	9 N NY	10 N NY
11 NY	12	13 N COL	14 N COL	15 N COL	16 N STL	17 STL
18 STL	19 N CHI	20 CHI	21 CHI	22	23 N CIN	24 N CIN
25 CIN	26	27 N STL	28 N STL	29 N STL	30 N CIN	31 N CIN

SEPTEMBER

SUN	MON	TUE	WED	THU	FRI	SAT
1 CIN	2 CHI	3 N CHI	4 N CHI	5 N MON	6 N MON	7 N MON
8 MON	9 N NY	10 N NY	11 N NY	12 N MON	13 N MON	14 N MON
15 MON	16	17 N PHI	18 N PHI	19	20 N HOU	21 N HOU
22 HOU	23	24 N ATL	25 N ATL	26 N ATL	27 N HOU	28 N HOU
29 HOU						

1996 SEASON

CLUB DIRECTORY

Chairman
H. Wayne Huizenga
President
Donald A. Smiley
Exec. vice president and general manager
David Dombrowski
Vice president of broadcasting
Dean Jordan
Vice president of finance & administration
Jonathan Mariner
Vice president of sales and marketing
Bob Kramm
Special counsel
James J. Blosser
Special consultant
Richard C. Rochon
V.p. and assistant general manager
Frank Wren
Vice president of player personnel
Gary Hughes
Vice president of player development
John Boles
Senior adviser, player personnel
Whitey Lockman
Dir. of Latin American operations
Al Avila
Director of minor league administration
Dan Lunetta
Director of scouting
Orrin Freeman
Assistant, baseball operations
DeJon Watson
Director of team travel
Bill Beck
Director of international relations
Tony Perez
Director of season & group sales
Frank Gernert
Director of marketing communications
Mark Geddis
Director of community relations
Jose Sotolongo
Director of promotions and sponsorships
Ben Creed

Director of media relations
Chuck Pool
Assistant directors of media relations
Ron Colangelo
Adolfo Salgueiro
Director of Brevard County operations
Ken Lehner
Equipment manager
Mike Wallace
Team physician
Dr. Dan Kanell
Head trainer
Larry Starr
Major league scouts
Ken Kravec, Scott Reid
International crosschecker
Tim Schmidt
National crosschecker
Jax Robertson
Regional crosscheckers
Dick Egan, Murray Cook, Greg Zunino
Scouts
Kelvin Bowles, Ty Brown, Joe Campise,
John Castleberry, Jon Deeble, Brad
Del Barba, Louis Eljaua, David Finlely,
Lou Fitzgerald, William George, Jim
Hendry, Stan Saleski, Stan Zielinski,
Ed Bockman, Richard Bordi, David
Chadd, Matthew King, Robert Laurie,
Steve McFarland, Charlie Silvera, Keith
Snider, Grady Mack, Steve Minor,
Cucho Rodriguez, Tim Schmidt, Bill
Singer, Keith Snider, Wally Walker,
DeJon Watson, Jeff Wren
Director Dominican Republic operations
Jesus Alou
Dominican Republic scouts
Angel Santana, Julian Camilo, Carlos
de la Cruz, Pablo Lantigua
Puerto Rico scouts
Cucho Rodriguez, Pedro Cintron
Venezuela scout
Levy Ochoa
Colombia scout
Hobert Cabrera
Panama scout
Plinio Castillo

MINOR LEAGUE AFFILIATES

Class	Team	League	Manager
AAA	Charlotte	International	Sal Rende
AA	Portland	Eastern	Carlos Tosca
A	Brevard County	Florida State	Fredi Gonzalez
A	Kane County	Midwest	Lynn Jones
A	Utica	New York-Pennsylvania	Steve McFarland
Rookie	Gulf Coast Marlins	Gulf Coast	Juan Bustabad

BROADCAST INFORMATION
Radio: WQAM-AM (560); WCMQ-AM
(1210, Spanish language).
TV: WBFS-TV (Channel 33).
Cable TV: The Sunshine Network.

SPRING TRAINING
Ballpark (city): Space Coast Stadium
(Melbourne, Fla.).
Ticket information: 407-633-9200.

SPRING TRAINING ROSTER

Manager—Rene Lachemann (15).
Coaches—Rusty Kuntz (22), Jose Morales (34), Cookie Rojas (1), Larry Rothschild (47), Rick Williams (38).

No.	PITCHERS	B/T	Ht./Wt.	Born	1995 clubs
58	Adamson, Joel	L/L	6-4/185	7-2-71	Charlotte
57	Alfonseca, Antonio	R/R	6-4/180	4-16-72	Portland
43	Batista, Miguel	R/R	6-0/180	2-19-71	Charlotte
46	Bowen, Ryan	R/R	6-0/185	2-10-68	Brevard County, Charlotte, Florida
33	Burkett, John	R/R	6-2/211	11-28-64	Florida
54	Darensbourg, Vic	L/L	5-10/165	11-13-70	DID NOT PLAY
28	Gardner, Mark	R/R	6-1/205	3-1-62	Florida
11	Hammond, Chris	L/L	6-1/195	1-21-66	Brevard County, Charlotte, Florida
24	Heredia, Wilson	R/R	6-0/175	3-30-72	Texas, Oklahoma City, Tulsa, Portland
	Hernandez, Livan	R/R	6-2/220	2-20-75	Cuban national team
50	Hurst, Bill	R/R	6-7/215	4-28-70	Brevard County
55	Juelsgaard, Jarod	R/R	6-3/195	6-27-68	Portland
36	Larkin, Andy	R/R	6-4/175	6-27-74	Portland
25	Leiter, Al	L/L	6-3/215	10-23-65	Toronto
18	Mantei, Matt	R/R	6-1/181	7-7-73	Portland, Charlotte, Florida
51	Mathews, Terry	L/R	6-2/225	10-5-64	Florida, Charlotte
53	Miller, Kurt	R/R	6-5/205	8-24-72	Charlotte
31	Nen, Robb	R/R	6-4/200	11-28-69	Florida
58	Perez, Yorkis	L/L	6-0/180	9-30-67	Florida
59	Powell, Jay	R/R	6-4/225	1-19-72	Portland, Florida
48	Rapp, Pat	R/R	6-3/215	7-13-67	Charlotte, Florida
41	Seelbach, Chris	R/R	6-4/180	12-18-72	Richmond, Greenville
37	Small, Aaron	R/R	6-5/208	11-23-71	Syracuse, Charlotte, Florida
44	Valdes, Marc	R/R	6-0/187	12-20-71	Charlotte, Florida
52	Veres, Randy	R/R	6-3/210	11-25-65	Charlotte, Florida
42	Ward, Bryan	L/L	6-2/210	1-28-72	Brevard County, Portland
35	Weathers, Dave	R/R	6-3/220	9-25-69	Florida, , Charlotte
30	Whisenant, Matt	B/L	6-3/215	6-8-71	Portland, Portland

No.	CATCHERS	B/T	Ht./Wt.	Born	1995 clubs
23	Johnson, Charles	R/R	6-2/215	7-20-71	Florida, Portland
13	Natal, Bob	R/R	5-11/190	11-13-65	Florida, Charlotte

No.	INFIELDERS	B/T	Ht./Wt.	Born	1995 clubs
7	Abbott, Kurt	R/R	6-0/185	6-2-69	Charlotte, Florida
26	Arias, Alex	R/R	6-3/185	11-20-67	Florida
4	Colbrunn, Greg	R/R	6-0/200	7-26-69	Florida
9	Pendleton, Terry	B/R	5-9/195	7-16-60	Florida
16	Renteria, Edgar	R/R	6-1/172	8-7-75	Portland
3	Veras, Quilvio	B/R	5-9/166	4-3-71	Florida

No.	OUTFIELDERS	B/T	Ht./Wt.	Born	1995 clubs
19	Conine, Jeff	R/R	6-1/220	6-27-66	Florida
27	McMillon, Bill	L/L	5-11/172	11-17-71	Portland
6	Orsulak, Joe	L/L	6-1/205	5-31-62	New York N.L.
10	Sheffield, Gary	R/R	5-11/190	11-18-68	Florida
20	Tavarez, Jesus	B/B	6-0/170	3-26-71	Charlotte, Florida
2	White, Devon	B/R	6-2/190	12-29-62	Toronto

BALLPARK INFORMATION

Ballpark (capacity, surface)
Joe Robbie Stadium (40,585, grass)

Address
2267 N.W. 199th St.
Miami, Fla. 33056

Business phone
305-626-7400

Ticket information
305-626-7400

Ticket prices
$20 (club level section B)
$13 (club level section C)
$13 (terrace box)
$11 (mezzanine box)
$8 (outfield reserved, adult)
$7 (mezzanine reserved)
$3.50 (outfield res., 12 and under)
$4 (general admission, adult)
$1.50 (g.a., 12 and under)

Field dimensions (from home plate)
To left field at foul line, 335 feet
To center field, 410 feet
To right field at foul line, 345

First game played
April 5, 1993 (Marlins 6, Dodgers 3)

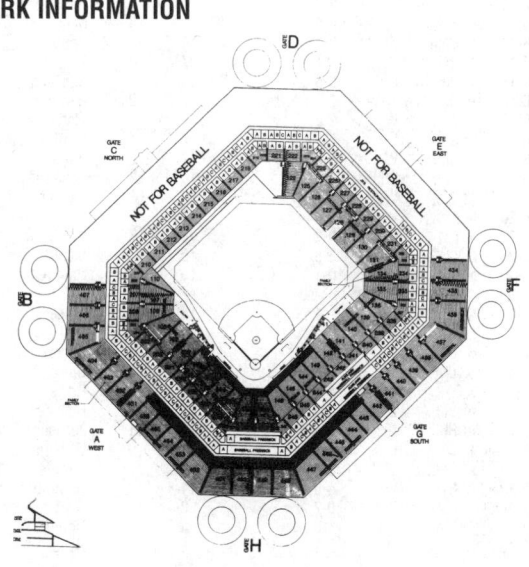

DAY BY DAY

1996 SEASON *Florida Marlins*

Date	Opp.	Res.	Score	(inn.*)	Hits	Opp. hits	Winning pitcher	Losing pitcher	Save	Record	Pos.	GB
4-25	L.A.	L	7-8		9	13	Martinez	Burkett	Seanez	0-1	5th	1/2
4-26	L.A.	L	2-4		7	9	Candiotti	Gardner	Seanez	0-2	5th	1 1/2
4-28	At S.F.	L	0-4		2	6	Leiter	Witt		0-3	5th	2
4-29	At S.F.	L	0-1		3	7	Wilson	Rapp	Beck	0-4	5th	3
4-30	At S.F.	W	10-3		11	6	Burkett	Torres		1-4	5th	3
5-2	Atl.	L	1-7		3	7	Maddux	Gardner		1-5	5th	4
5-3	Atl.	L	4-6		12	8	Glavine	Witt	Clontz	1-6	5th	5
5-4	Atl.	L	3-6		8	11	Woodall	Nen	McMichael	1-7	5th	6
5-5	At Mon.	W	11-6		11	10	Burkett	Heredia	Mathews	2-7	5th	5
5-6	At Mon.	W	10-3		12	10	Weathers	Rueter		3-7	5th	4
5-7	At Mon.	L	3-9		9	12	Fassero	Gardner		3-8	5th	4 1/2
5-8	At Mon.	L	5-7		4	10	Rojas	Perez		3-9	5th	5 1/2
5-9	Cin.	L	1-9		8	13	Smiley	Rapp	Hernandez	3-10	5th	6 1/2
5-10	Cin.	L	0-3		2	8	Jarvis	Burkett		3-11	5th	7 1/2
5-11	Cin.	L	1-3	(15)	9	8	Pugh	Dunbar		3-12	5th	7 1/2
5-12	Col.	L	6-10		9	13	Swift	Gardner	Ruffin	3-13	5th	8 1/2
5-13	Col.	W	8-2		11	6	Witt	Freeman		4-13	5th	8 1/2
5-14	Col.	L	3-6		9	11	Ritz	Rapp	Ruffin	4-14	5th	9 1/2
5-15	Phi.	W	9-1		10	6	Burkett	Green		5-14	5th	8 1/2
5-16	Phi.	L	7-9	(10)	10	13	Slocumb	Nen		5-15	5th	9 1/2
5-17	Phi.	L	1-3	(13)	8	4	Bottalico	Lewis	Slocumb	5-16	5th	10 1/2
5-19	At Atl.	L	0-4		5	6	Avery	Veres		5-17	5th	10 1/2
5-20	At Atl.	L	7-8		12	9	Wohlers	Nen		5-18	5th	11 1/2
5-21	At Atl.	L	1-5		2	8	Smoltz	Burkett		5-19	5th	12 1/2
5-22	At Mon.	L	2-5		3	9	Perez	Weathers	Rojas	5-20	5th	13
5-23	At Pit.	W	6-1		10	3	Hammond	Loaiza		6-20	5th	13
5-25	At Pit.	L	1-3		6	9	Plesac	Witt	Miceli	6-21	5th	13 1/2
5-26	At Chi.	W	5-3		8	10	Rapp	Perez	Nen	7-21	5th	13 1/2
5-27	At Chi.	L	1-3		5	5	Wendell	Burkett	Myers	7-22	5th	14 1/2
5-28	At Chi.	L	8-13		11	18	Foster	Weathers		7-23	5th	14 1/2
5-29	Hou.	W	9-7		19	8	Veres	Reynolds	Nen	8-23	5th	14 1/2
5-31	Hou.	L	4-7		8	10	Dougherty	Witt	Hudek	8-24	5th	15
6-2	Chi.	L	1-5		4	9	Navarro	Burkett	Perez	8-25	5th	15 1/2
6-3	Chi.	W	5-4		10	9	Veres	Hickerson		9-25	5th	14 1/2
6-4	Chi.	L	3-5		7	10	Castillo	Hammond	Myers	9-26	5th	14 1/2
6-5	At Hou.	L	5-6		10	8	Veres	Nen		9-27	5th	14 1/2
6-6	At Hou.	W	7-6	(11)	11	16	Gardner	Hudek	Nen	10-27	5th	13 1/2
6-7	At Hou.	W	8-3		12	8	Burkett	Drabek	Veres	11-27	5th	13 1/2
6-8	Pit.	W	7-3		10	11	Mathews	Wagner		12-27	5th	13
6-9	Pit.	W	5-4		12	8	Hammond	Neagle	Perez	13-27	5th	13
6-10	Pit.	L	2-6		6	10	Loaiza	Witt		13-28	5th	14
6-11	Pit.	L	3-4		7	7	Miceli	Nen		13-29	5th	15
6-13	At N.Y.	L	3-7		8	13	Saberhagen	Burkett		13-30	5th	15
6-14	At N.Y.	W	4-0		7	7	Hammond	Mlicki		14-30	5th	14
6-15	At N.Y.	L	4-5	(10)	10	13	Minor	Veres		14-31	5th	15
6-16	At Phi.	W	2-1		6	6	Rapp	West	Nen	15-31	5th	14
6-17	At Phi.	L	4-11		7	10	Mimbs	Weathers		15-32	5th	15
6-18	At Phi.	L	3-5		8	9	Schilling	Perez	Slocumb	15-33	5th	16
6-19	At Col.	W	7-2		10	12	Hammond	Ritz		16-33	5th	16
6-20	At Col.	W	7-2		11	7	Mathews	Grahe		17-33	5th	16
6-21	At Col.	L	3-6		7	11	Swift	Rapp	Reed	17-34	5th	17
6-23	At Cin.	W	16-4		17	7	Burkett	Jarvis		18-34	5th	16 1/2
6-24	At Cin.	L	2-5		5	9	Schourek	Hammond	Carrasco	18-35	5th	17 1/2
6-25	At Cin.	W	5-1		10	3	Weathers	Rijo	Mathews	19-35	T4th	17 1/2
6-26	N.Y.	W	9-4		14	7	Rapp	B. Jones		20-35	4th	17
6-27	N.Y.	L	0-2		3	7	Pulsipher	Murphy	Franco	20-36	T4th	17
6-28	N.Y.	L	3-8		10	11	Saberhagen	Burkett		20-37	5th	17
6-30	Mon.	W	10-1		19	6	Hammond	Perez		21-37	5th	16 1/2
7-1	Mon.	L	8-11		14	15	Fassero	Rapp	Rojas	21-38	5th	16 1/2
7-2	Mon.	L	6-7		17	13	Harris	Mathews	Rojas	21-39	5th	16 1/2
7-3	S.D.	W	5-2		10	7	Burkett	Dishman		22-39	T4th	15 1/2
7-4	S.D.	W	6-4		9	9	Gardner	Ashby		23-39	4th	15
7-5	S.D.	L	4-7	(10)	7	13	Florie	Perez	Hoffman	23-40	T4th	16
7-6	At St.L.	L	2-3	(12)	7	8	Habyan	Mantei		23-41	T4th	17
7-7	At St.L.	L	0-4		4	11	Jackson	Witt		23-42	5th	18
7-8	At St.L.	L	2-3		11	9	Watson	Burkett	Henke	23-43	5th	19
7-9	At St.L.	W	6-0		9	7	Gardner	Hill		24-43	T4th	19
7-13	At L.A.	W	4-0		11	3	Hammond	Candiotti		25-43	T4th	18 1/2
7-14	At L.A.	L	0-7		0	10	Martinez	Burkett		25-44	5th	19 1/2
7-15	At L.A.	L	1-3		3	5	Nomo	Witt		25-45	5th	20 1/2
7-16	At L.A.	W	5-2		8	6	Rapp	Valdes	Nen	26-45	5th	19 1/2

Date	Opp.	Res.	Score	(inn.*)	Hits	Opp. hits	Winning pitcher	Losing pitcher	Save	Record	Pos.	GB
7-17	At S.F.	W	10-8		12	10	Mathews	Beck	Nen	27-45	5th	19
7-18	At S.F.	W	12-10	(14)	15	16	Murphy	Bautista		28-45	5th	18
7-19	At S.F.	W	3-1		8	5	Burkett	Portugal		29-45	5th	18
7-20	L.A.	L	2-4	(10)	6	8	Astacio	Mathews	Worrell	29-46	5th	19
7-21	L.A.	L	3-5		7	9	Valdes	Rapp	Worrell	29-47	5th	19
7-22	L.A.	W	11-10		13	16	Veres	Astacio	Nen	30-47	5th	19
7-23	L.A.	L	2-4		8	6	Candiotti	Hammond	Worrell	30-48	5th	20
7-24	S.F.	L	3-8		8	14	Brewington	Burkett		30-49	5th	21
7-25	S.F.	W	9-3		15	7	Witt	Mulholland		31-49	T4th	21
7-27†	S.D.	L	2-8		10	13	Blair	Weathers		31-50	5th	20¹/₂
7-27‡	S.D.	W	8-5		11	6	Gardner	Dishman	Mathews	32-50	5th	20
7-28	St.L.	W	6-0		9	4	Hammond	Petkovsek		33-50	4th	20
7-29	St.L.	W	2-0		5	7	Burkett	Watson	Nen	34-50	4th	20
7-30	St.L.	W	3-1		7	6	Perez	Arocha	Nen	35-50	4th	19
8-1	At Mon.	W	5-2		12	8	Rapp	Perez	Nen	36-50	4th	18
8-2	At Mon.	W	7-6	(10)	11	14	Pena	Shaw	Nen	37-50	4th	18
8-4	At N.Y.	W	7-2		12	10	Burkett	Isringhausen		38-50	4th	18¹/₂
8-5	At N.Y.	W	6-3		8	9	Veres	Pulsipher	Nen	39-50	4th	18¹/₂
8-6	At N.Y.	L	3-7		5	8	B. Jones	Rapp		39-51	4th	18¹/₂
8-7	At N.Y.	L	2-5		7	10	Mlicki	Mathews	Franco	39-52	4th	19¹/₂
8-8	Col.	W	5-4	(13)	12	10	Groom	Bailey		40-52	4th	19¹/₂
8-9	Col.	W	2-1		6	7	Burkett	Ritz	Nen	41-52	4th	18¹/₂
8-10	Col.	W	3-2		5	6	Pena	Reed		42-52	4th	18¹/₂
8-11	Cin.	W	6-2		9	6	Rapp	Portugal		43-52	4th	18¹/₂
8-12	Cin.	W	7-3		12	9	Weathers	Schourek		44-52	4th	17¹/₂
8-13	Cin.	W	6-4		12	8	Gardner	Wells	Nen	45-52	4th	17¹/₂
8-14	At Atl.	L	3-4		8	7	McMichael	Perez		45-53	4th	18¹/₂
8-15	At Atl.	L	1-4		4	9	Glavine	Banks	Wohlers	45-54	4th	19¹/₂
8-16	At Atl.	W	8-5		8	11	Rapp	Avery	Nen	46-54	4th	18¹/₂
8-18†	At Pit.	L	7-13		15	16	Wagner	Groom		46-55		
8-18‡	At Pit.	L	6-7	(13)	13	14	Miceli	Groom		46-56	4th	19
8-19	At Pit.	L	5-10		8	13	Mccurry	Veres		46-57	4th	19
8-20	At Pit.	L	2-3		10	11	Parris	Burkett	Miceli	46-58	4th	20
8-21	At Pit.	L	3-5		10	7	Dyer	Gardner	Wagner	46-59	4th	21
8-22	At Chi.	W	8-6		11	10	Rapp	Bullinger	Nen	47-59	4th	21
8-23	At Chi.	L	2-10		7	10	Navarro	Weathers		47-60	4th	22
8-24	At Chi.	L	2-6		5	11	Foster	Hammond	Myers	47-61	4th	22¹/₂
8-25	Hou.	W	5-4		8	9	Burkett	Reynolds	Nen	48-61	4th	22¹/₂
8-26	Hou.	W	6-2		10	9	Banks	Swindell		49-61	4th	22¹/₂
8-27	Hou.	W	10-2		12	7	Rapp	Drabek		50-61	4th	22¹/₂
8-28	Hou.	W	6-4		12	7	Weathers	Brocail	Nen	51-61	4th	21¹/₂
8-29	Chi.	L	6-10		11	13	Foster	Hammond		51-62	4th	21¹/₂
8-30	Chi.	W	4-1		7	5	Burkett	Castillo		52-62	4th	20¹/₂
8-31	Chi.	L	3-12		9	13	Trachsel	Banks		52-63	4th	21¹/₂
9-1	At Hou.	L	3-7		9	13	Dougherty	Garces		52-64	4th	21¹/₂
9-2	At Hou.	L	8-10		8	13	Dougherty	Perez	Henneman	52-65	4th	21¹/₂
9-3	At Hou.	W	8-7	(11)	12	11	Small	Dougherty	Gardner	53-65	4th	21¹/₂
9-4	Pit.	W	7-3		10	13	Burkett	Parris		54-65	4th	21¹/₂
9-6	Pit.	W	2-1		7	7	Banks	Neagle	Nen	55-65	4th	22
9-7	Atl.	W	5-1		7	4	Rapp	Avery		56-65	4th	21
9-8	Atl.	L	5-6		9	13	McMichael	Perez	Wohlers	56-66	4th	22
9-9	Atl.	L	5-9		13	13	Clontz	Nen	Wohlers	56-67	4th	23
9-10	Atl.	W	5-4	(11)	11	8	Mathews	Borbon		57-67	4th	22
9-11	At Cin.	L	1-2	(11)	9	7	Jackson	Garces		57-68	4th	22
9-12	At Cin.	W	5-4		11	7	Rapp	Smiley	Nen	58-68	4th	21
9-13	At Cin.	L	0-6		2	11	Schourek	Hammond		58-69	4th	22
9-15	At Col.	L	3-6		10	13	Reed	Burkett	Leskanic	58-70	5th	23
9-16	At Col.	L	7-8		9	12	Reed	Mathews	Ruffin	58-71	5th	24
9-17	At Col.	W	17-0		21	1	Rapp	Rekar		59-71	5th	24
9-18	At Phi.	L	10-13		10	12	Bottalico	Veres	Slocumb	59-72	5th	25
9-19	At Phi.	W	5-4		7	10	Perez	Borland	Nen	60-72	5th	24
9-20	At Phi.	W	2-1		5	4	Burkett	Quantrill		61-72	5th	23
9-21	At Phi.	L	1-3		5	7	Mimbs	Banks	Frey	61-73	5th	24
9-22	N.Y.	W	3-0	(8)	5	4	Rapp	Cornelius		62-73	T4th	24
9-23	N.Y.	W	4-3		9	10	Hammond	B. Jones	Nen	63-73	T3rd	23
9-24	N.Y.	W	4-3		10	8	Bowen	Mlicki	Nen	64-73	3rd	23
9-25	Mon.	L	0-9		3	14	Rueter	Burkett	Heredia	64-74	T3rd	23¹/₂
9-26	Mon.	L	4-5		11	11	Fraser	Nen	Rojas	64-75	T4th	24¹/₂
9-27	Mon.	W	9-3		12	5	Rapp	G. White		65-75	T4th	24¹/₂
9-29	Phi.	W	5-2		7	3	Hammond	D. Springer		66-75	4th	23¹/₂
9-30	Phi.	L	2-3		10	7	Williams	Burkett	Slocumb	66-76	4th	23¹/₂
10-1	Phi.	W	8-2		16	8	Bowen	Quantrill		67-76	4th	22¹/₂

Monthly records: April (1-4), May (7-20), June (13-13), July (14-13), August (17-13), September (14-13), October (1-0).
*Innings, if other than nine. †First game of doubleheader. ‡Second game of doubleheader.

1996 SEASON *Florida Marlins*

HIGHLIGHTS

High point: The Marlins won a club-record eight consecutive games, beginning with a July 27 victory over the Padres in the second game of a doubleheader. That started a team-record 14-game home winning streak.

Low point: Robb Nen gave up a two-out, three-run homer in the ninth to Craig Biggio in a 6-5 loss at Houston on June 5. It dropped Florida to 9-27—the worst start in the majors and the worst in franchise history.

Turning point: Two games into the second half, the Marlins were no-hit by the Dodgers' Ramon Martinez. But after that loss, the Marlins closed the season 42-32 and finished 1½ games out of second in the N.L. East.

Most valuable player: Outfielder Jeff Conine. Conine, the MVP of the All-Star Game, hit .302 and had a club-record 25 homers and 105 RBIs.

Most valuable pitchers: Righthanders John Burkett (14-14) and Pat Rapp (14-7). Both were among league leaders in wins. Burkett led the team in innings, and Rapp was 11-2 with a 2.30 ERA in his last 15 starts.

Most improved player: Catcher Charles Johnson. On June 23, the rookie was hitting .143. From then on, he hit .337 and finished at .251. Of Johnson's last 57 hits, 24 were for extra bases.

Most pleasant surprise: First baseman Greg Colbrunn. Colbrunn hadn't played more than 70 major league games in a season because of injury. But in '95, he played in a team-high 138 games and was fourth among N.L. first basemen with 23 homers and 89 RBIs (both career highs).

Biggest disappointment: When closer Bryan Harvey blew out his right elbow in his first appearance of the season, it set the tone for a bullpen that finished 17-30 with a 4.45 ERA and 16 blown saves.

Key injuries: Harvey's was the most devastating, but setup man Jeremy Hernandez never fully recovered from '94 surgery to remove a herniated disk in his neck. Nine relievers spent time on the D.L. Outfielder Gary Sheffield tore ligaments in his left thumb and played in only 63 games.

Notable: Florida's .469 winning percentage was the third-highest in history among third-year expansion teams. . . . Second baseman Quilvio Veras finished among N.L. leaders in walks and steals and had the seventh-highest on-base percentage (.384) for a rookie since 1971.

—SCOTT TOLLEY

RECORDS

1995 regular-season record: 67-76 (4th in N.L. East); 37-34 at home; 30-42 on road; 22-30 vs. East; 27-29 vs. Central; 18-17 vs. West; 21-28 vs. lefthanded starters; 46-48 vs. righthanded starters; 52-54 on grass; 15-22 on turf; 15-15 in daytime; 52-61 at night; 18-17 in one-run games; 6-9 in extra-inning games; 0-1-1 in doubleheaders.

Team record past five years: 182-238 in three years (.433 ranks 14th in league in that span).

TEAM LEADERS

Batting average: Jeff Conine (.302).
At-bats: Terry Pendleton (513).
Runs: Quilvio Veras (86).
Hits: Terry Pendleton (149).
Total bases: Jeff Conine (251).
Doubles: Terry Pendleton (32).
Triples: Kurt Abbott, Quilvio Veras (7).
Home runs: Jeff Conine (25).
Runs batted in: Jeff Conine (105).
Stolen bases: Quilvio Veras (56).
Slugging percentage: Jeff Conine (.520).
On-base percentage: Quilvio Veras (.384).
Wins: John Burkett (14).
Earned-run average: Pat Rapp (3.44).
Complete games: John Burkett (4).
Shutouts: Chris Hammond, Pat Rapp (2).
Saves: Robb Nen (23).
Innings pitched: John Burkett (188.1).
Strikeouts: John Burkett, Chris Hammond (126).

GAMES BY POSITION

Catcher: Charles Johnson 97, Steve Decker 46, Bob Natal 13.
First base: Greg Colbrunn 134, Jeff Conine 14, Russ Morman 3, Steve Decker 2, Tommy Gregg 2.
Second base: Quilvio Veras 122, Jerry Browne 27, Mario Diaz 9, Alex Arias 6, Eddie Zosky 1.
Third base: Terry Pendleton 129, Alex Arias 21, Jerry Browne 7, Mario Diaz 3.
Shortstop: Kurt Abbott 115, Alex Arias 36, Mario Diaz 5, Eddie Zosky 4.
Outfield: Jeff Conine 118, Chuck Carr 103, Gary Sheffield 61, Jesus Tavarez 61, Andre Dawson 59, Tommy Gregg 38, Jerry Browne 29, Russ Morman 18, Darrell Whitmore 16, Quilvio Veras 2.

TOP DRAFT CHOICES

1. **Jaime Jones,** OF, Rancho Bernardo H.S., San Diego.
2. **Nate Rolison,** 1B, Petal (Miss.) H.S.
3. **Randy Winn,** OF, University of Santa Clara.
4. **Mike Marriott,** RHP, Spring (Tex.) H.S.
5. **Rene Rascon,** OF, Sonoma State (Calif.) University.
6. **Michael Tejera,** LHP, Southwest H.S., Miami.
7. **Hansel Izquierdo,** RHP, Southwest H.S., Miami.
8. **Mark Watson,** LHP, Clemson University.
9. **Tony Enard,** RHP, Fresno State University.
10. **Bob Pailthorpe,** RHP, University of Santa Clara.

1996 SEASON Florida Marlins

HOUSTON ASTROS
NATIONAL LEAGUE CENTRAL DIVISION

1996 ASTROS SCHEDULE

☐ Home games shaded.
* — All-Star Game at Veterans Stadium (Philadelphia)
N — Night game (any game starting after 5 p.m.)

MARCH

SUN	MON	TUE	WED	THU	FRI	SAT
31						

APRIL

SUN	MON	TUE	WED	THU	FRI	SAT
	1 LA	2 N LA	3 LA	4	5 N SD	6 N SB
7 SD	8 N SF	9 N SF	10 SF	11 N CIN	12 N CIN	13 CIN
14 CIN	15	16 N NY	17 NY	18	19 N CIN	20 N CIN
21 CIN	22 N SF	23 SF	24 N LA	25 N LA	26 N SD	27 N SD
28 SD	29 N SD	30 N ATL				

MAY

SUN	MON	TUE	WED	THU	FRI	SAT
			1 N ATL	2	3 N MON	4 N MON
5 MON	6 N PHI	7 N PHI	8 N PHI	9 N MON	10 N MON	11 N MON
12 MON	13 N CHI	14 CHI	15 CHI	16 CHI	17 N PIT	18 N PIT
19 PIT	20 N STL	21 N STL	22 STL	23	24 N CHI	25 N CHI
26 CHI	27 PIT	28 N PIT	29 N PIT	30	31 N STL	

JUNE

SUN	MON	TUE	WED	THU	FRI	SAT
						1 N STL
2 STL	3	4 N COL	5 N COL	6 N COL	7 N PHI	8 PHI
9 PHI	10 N COL	11 N COL	12 COL	13 N SF	14 N SF	15 SF
16 SF	17 N CIN	18 N CIN	19 CIN	20 N LA	21 N LA	22 LA
23 LA	24	25 N SD	26 N SD	27	28 N NY	29 N NY
30 NY						

JULY

SUN	MON	TUE	WED	THU	FRI	SAT
	1 N FLA	2 N FLA	3 N FLA	4 N ATL	5 N ATL	6 N ATL
7 ATL	8	9 ALL-STAR GAME *	10	11 N NY	12 N NY	13 N NY
14 NY	15 N FLA	16 N FLA	17 N FLA	18 N ATL	19 N ATL	20 N ATL
21 ATL	22 N SD	23 N SD	24 SD	25	26 N LA	27 N LA
28 LA	29 N CIN	30 N CIN	31 CIN			

AUGUST

SUN	MON	TUE	WED	THU	FRI	SAT
				1	2 N SF	3 N SF
4 SF	5	6 N MON	7 N MON	8 MON	9 N PHI	10 PHI
11 PHI	12 N MON	13 N MON	14 N MON	15	16 N CHI	17 CHI
18 CHI	19 N PIT	20 N PIT	21 N PIT	22 N PIT	23 N STL	24 STL
25 STL	26 N STL	27 N CHI	28 N CHI	29	30 N PIT	31 PIT

SEPTEMBER

SUN	MON	TUE	WED	THU	FRI	SAT
1 PIT	2 N STL	3 N STL	4 N STL	5	6 N COL	7 N COL
8 COL	9 N COL	10 N PHI	11 N PHI	12 PHI	13 N COL	14 COL
15 COL	16	17 N ATL	18 ATL	19	20 N FLA	21 N FLA
22 FLA	23	24 N NY	25 N NY	26 NY	27 N FLA	28 FLA
29 FLA						

1996 SEASON

CLUB DIRECTORY

Chairman and CEO
Drayton McLane Jr.

President
Tal Smith

Sr. vice president, business operations
Bob McClaren

General manager
Gerry Hunsicker

Director of baseball administration
Barry Waters

Special assistant to the general manager
Fred Nelson

Director of scouting & player development
Dan O'Brien

Asst. to director of player development
Trey Wilkinson

Dir. of major and minor league player rel.
Tim Purpura

Asst. dir. of scouting & dir. of int'l dev.
David Rawnsley

Director of media relations
Rob Matwick

Assistant director of media relations
Tyler Barnes

Director of marketing
Pam Gardner

Director of broadcasting & promotions
Jamie Hildreth

Director of community development
Gene Pemberton

Director of advertising
Amy Kress

Director of ticket sales & services
Rich Fromstein

Controller
Robert McBurnett

Scouts
Ricardo Aponte
Bob Blair
Stan Boroski
Ralph Bratton
George Brophy
Ruben Cabrera
Raphael Cariel
Gerry Craft
Jug Deford
Chuck Edmondson
Orlando Estevez
James Farrar
Brian Granger
Dick Hager
Dan Huston
Marc Johnson
Brian Keegan
Bill Kelso
Bob King
David Lakey
Julio Linares
Mike Maggart
Walt Matthews
Domingo Mercedes
Tom Mooney
Dan O'Brien Jr.
Joe Pittman
Jim Pransky
David Rawnsley
Andres Reiner
Anibal Reluz
Adriano Rodriguez
Deron Rombach
Nelson Rood
Rich Schroeder
Mark Servais
Bob Skinner
Tad Slowik
Lynwood Stallings
Kevin Stein
Frankie Thon
Pablo Torrealba
Paul Weaver
Grant Weir
Gene Wellman
Greg Whitworth

MINOR LEAGUE AFFILIATES

Class	Team	League	Manager
AAA	Tucson	Pacific Coast	Rick Sweet
AA	Jackson	Southern	Tim Tolman
A	Kissimmee	Florida State	To be announced
A	Quad City	Midwest	To be announced
A	Auburn	New York-Pennsylvania	To be announced
Rookie	Gulf Coast Astros	Gulf Coast	To be announced

BROADCAST INFORMATION
Radio: KPRC-AM (940); KXYZ-AM
(1320, Spanish language).
TV: KTXH-TV (Channel 20).
Cable TV: Home Sports Entertainment.

SPRING TRAINING
Ballpark (city): Osceola County
Stadium (Kissimmee, Fla.).
Ticket information: 407-933-2520.

1996 SEASON Houston Astros

SPRING TRAINING ROSTER

Manager—Terry Collins (2).
Coaches—Matt Galante (48), Steve Henderson (55), Julio Linares (1), Brent Strom (42), Rick Sweet (18).

No.	PITCHERS	B/T	Ht./Wt.	Born	1995 clubs
46	Brocail, Doug	L/R	6-5/235	5-16-67	Houston, Tucson
38	Creek, Ryan	R/R	6-1/180	9-24-72	Jackson
49	Dougherty, Jim	R/R	6-0/210	3-8-68	Houston, Tucson
15	Drabek, Doug	R/R	6-1/185	7-25-62	Houston
44	Gallaher, Kevin	R/R	6-3/190	8-1-68	Kissimmee, Tucson, Jackson
43	Grzanich, Mike	R/R	6-1/180	8-24-72	Jackson
10	Hampton, Mike	R/L	5-10/180	9-9-72	Houston
58	Hartgraves, Dean	R/L	6-0/185	8-12-66	Tucson, Houston
53	Henriquez, Oscar	R/R	6-6/220	1-28-74	Kissimmee
45	Holt, Chris	R/R	6-4/205	9-18-71	Jackson, Tucson
35	Hudek, John	B/R	6-1/200	8-8-66	Houston
59	Jones, Todd	L/R	6-3/200	4-24-68	Houston
57	Kile, Darryl	R/R	6-5/185	12-2-68	Houston, Tucson
54	Loiselle, Rich	R/R	6-5/225	1-12-72	Memphis, Las Vegas, Tucson
50	Mlicki, Doug	R/R	6-3/175	4-12-71	Jackson, Tucson
51	Morman, Alvin	L/L	6-3/210	1-6-69	Tucson
37	Reynolds, Shane	R/R	6-3/210	3-26-68	Houston
36	Small, Mark	R/R	6-3/205	11-12-67	Tucson
41	Swindell, Greg	R/L	6-3/225	1-2-65	Houston
31	Tabaka, Jeff	R/L	6-2/195	1-17-64	Las Vegas, San Diego, Houston
13	Wagner, Billy	L/L	5-11/180	6-25-71	Jackson, Tucson, Houston
66	Wall, Donne	R/R	6-1/180	7-11-67	Tucson, Houston

No.	CATCHERS	B/T	Ht./Wt.	Born	1995 clubs
20	Eusebio, Tony	R/R	6-2/180	4-27-67	Houston
3	Wilkins, Rick	L/R	6-2/215	6-4-67	Chicago N.L., Houston, Jackson, Tucson

No.	INFIELDERS	B/T	Ht./Wt.	Born	1995 clubs
5	Bagwell, Jeff	R/R	6-0/195	5-27-68	Houston, Jackson
17	Berry, Sean	R/R	5-11/200	3-22-66	Montreal
7	Biggio, Craig	R/R	5-11/180	12-14-65	Houston
12	Gutierrez, Ricky	R/R	6-1/175	5-23-70	Houston, Tucson
21	Hajek, Dave	R/R	5-10/165	10-14-67	Tucson, Houston
29	Holbert, Ray	R/R	6-0/175	9-25-70	San Diego, Las Vegas
24	Miller, Orlando	R/R	6-1/180	1-13-69	Houston

No.	OUTFIELDERS	B/T	Ht./Wt.	Born	1995 clubs
63	Abreu, Bob	L/R	6-0/160	3-11-74	Tucson
14	Bell, Derek	R/R	6-2/215	12-11-68	Houston
60	Hidalgo, Richard	R/R	6-3/190	7-2-75	Jackson
19	Hunter, Brian L.	R/R	6-4/180	3-5-71	Tucson, Houston, Jackson
16	May, Derrick	L/R	6-4/225	7-14-68	Milwaukee, Houston
6	Mouton, James	R/R	5-9/175	12-29-68	Houston, Tucson
23	Simms, Mike	R/R	6-4/185	1-12-67	Houston, Tucson

BALLPARK INFORMATION

Ballpark (capacity, surface)
The Astrodome (54,313, artificial)

Address
P.O. Box 288
Houston, TX 77001-0288

Business phone
713-799-9500

Ticket information
713-799-9555

Ticket prices
$19 (star deck)
$16 (field level)
$14 (mezzanine)
$11 (loge level)
$10 (skybox)
$7 (upper box)
$5 (upper reserved)
$5 (skybox club)
$4 (adult pavilion)
$1 (youth pavilion)

Field dimensions (from home plate)
To left field at foul line, 325 feet
To center field, 400 feet
To right field at foul line, 325 feet

First game played
April 12, 1965 (Phillies 2, Astros 0)

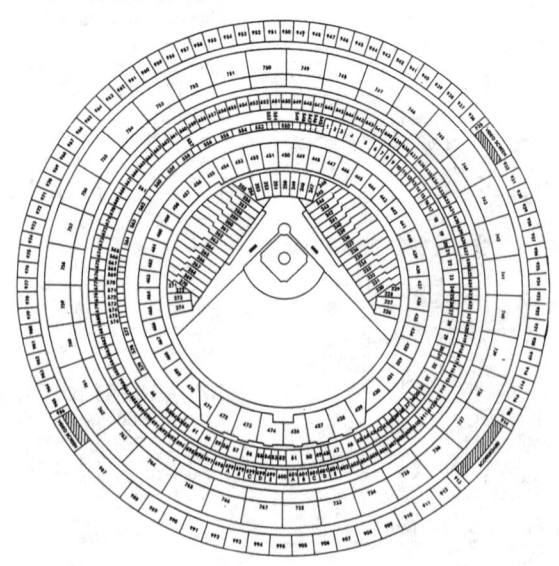

DAY BY DAY

Date	Opp.	Res.	Score	(inn.*)	Hits	Opp. hits	Winning pitcher	Losing pitcher	Save	Record	Pos.	GB
4-26	At S.D.	W	10-2		12	8	Drabek	Benes		1-0	T1st	...
4-27	At S.D.	L	1-13		5	21	Ashby	Reynolds		1-1	T2nd	1
4-28	Col.	L	1-2		7	3	Leskanic	Kile	Ruffin	1-2	T2nd	2
4-29	Col.	L	1-2		4	3	Olivares	Hampton	Ruffin	1-3	T2nd	3
4-30	Col.	W	3-1		5	4	Brocail	Leskanic	Hudek	2-3	T2nd	2
5-2	At Chi.	W	5-2		9	7	Dougherty	Walker	Jones	3-3	2nd	1
5-3	At Chi.	W	11-2		14	6	Kile	Trachsel		4-3	T1st	...
5-4	At St.L.	W	6-4		10	10	Jones	DeLucia	Hudek	5-3	1st	+1/2
5-5	At St.L.	W	9-4		11	8	Hampton	Urbani		6-3	1st	+1/2
5-6	At St.L.	L	5-7		7	11	Palacios	Swindell	Henke	6-4	2nd	1/2
5-7	At St.L.	L	5-6		14	7	Parrett	Drabek	Henke	6-5	2nd	1/2
5-8	At Pit.	W	6-3		8	7	Jones	Gott	Hudek	7-5	2nd	1/2
5-9	At Pit.	W	13-6		16	9	Reynolds	Lieber		8-5	2nd	1/2
5-11	At Pit.	W	12-4		17	9	Swindell	Wagner		9-5	1st	+1/2
5-12	Phi.	L	2-5		8	12	Schilling	Drabek	Slocumb	9-6	2nd	1/2
5-13	Phi.	L	5-7		7	9	Bottalico	Kile	Slocumb	9-7	2nd	11/2
5-14	Phi.	L	2-5		5	11	Quantrill	Hampton	Slocumb	9-8	2nd	11/2
5-16	N.Y.	L	0-1		3	6	B. Jones	Reynolds	Henry	9-9	2nd	3
5-17	N.Y.	W	7-2		14	8	Swindell	Jacome		10-9	2nd	2
5-18	N.Y.	L	1-8		6	10	Mlicki	Drabek		10-10	2nd	21/2
5-19	Mon.	W	10-2		9	5	Veres	Martinez		11-10	2nd	21/2
5-20	Mon.	W	2-1	(10)	9	4	Hudek	Shaw		12-10	2nd	21/2
5-21	Mon.	W	5-2		8	5	Swindell	Heredia	Hudek	13-10	2nd	21/2
5-22	At Cin.	L	2-3	(10)	9	8	Brantley	Veres		13-11	2nd	21/2
5-23	At Cin.	L	5-10		13	8	Hernandez	Kile	Carrasco	13-12	3rd	31/2
5-24	At Cin.	L	2-4		5	9	Schourek	Reynolds	Brantley	13-13	3rd	41/2
5-26	Atl.	L	3-8		7	12	Mercker	Swindell		13-14	3rd	4
5-27	Atl.	W	3-2	(10)	10	6	Hudek	Stanton		14-14	3rd	4
5-28	Atl.	L	1-3		1	5	Maddux	Kile		14-15	3rd	5
5-29	At Fla.	L	7-9		8	19	Veres	Reynolds	Nen	14-16	3rd	5
5-31	At Fla.	W	7-4		10	8	Dougherty	Witt	Hudek	15-16	3rd	5
6-2	At Atl.	W	7-2		8	5	Drabek	Smoltz		16-16	3rd	41/2
6-3	At Atl.	W	2-1	(10)	7	4	Jones	Wohlers	Hudek	17-16	3rd	31/2
6-4	At Atl.	W	6-2		13	10	Reynolds	Glavine		18-16	3rd	31/2
6-5	Fla.	W	6-5		8	10	Veres	Nen		19-16	3rd	31/2
6-6	Fla.	L	6-7	(11)	16	11	Gardner	Hudek	Nen	19-17	3rd	41/2
6-7	Fla.	L	3-8		8	12	Burkett	Drabek	Veres	19-18	3rd	41/2
6-8	Cin.	L	3-6		8	9	Pugh	Kile	Brantley	19-19	3rd	51/2
6-9	Cin.	L	2-5		7	9	Hernandez	Reynolds	Brantley	19-20	3rd	61/2
6-10	Cin.	L	2-3		11	7	Smiley	Swindell	Carrasco	19-21	3rd	71/2
6-11	Cin.	L	2-3	(10)	10	11	Brantley	Jones		19-22	3rd	81/2
6-13	At Phi.	W	6-5		6	10	Veres	Schilling	Hudek	20-22	3rd	8
6-14	At Phi.	W	9-5		12	7	Kile	Charlton	Jones	21-22	3rd	7
6-15	At Phi.	L	2-4		8	10	Bottalico	Hudek		21-23	3rd	71/2
6-16	At N.Y.	W	7-5	(16)	17	13	Dougherty	Gunderson	Brocail	22-23	3rd	61/2
6-17	At N.Y.	W	7-3		10	10	Drabek	Pulsipher		23-23	3rd	61/2
6-18	At N.Y.	L	4-10		9	13	Saberhagen	Hampton		23-24	3rd	71/2
6-19	At Mon.	W	6-3		8	10	Kile	Fassero	Jones	24-24	3rd	61/2
6-20	At Mon.	W	7-4		14	11	Reynolds	Martinez		25-24	3rd	51/2
6-21	At Mon.	W	5-3		10	9	Swindell	Henry	Jones	26-24	2nd	51/2
6-22	Chi.	L	2-13		6	18	Bullinger	Drabek	Young	26-25	3rd	51/2
6-23	Chi.	W	3-2	(12)	10	5	Jones	Walker		27-25	2nd	51/2
6-24	Chi.	L	2-5		6	9	Foster	Kile	Myers	27-26	3rd	61/2
6-25	Chi.	W	19-6		19	12	Reynolds	Castillo		28-26	2nd	51/2
6-26	St.L.	W	11-0		14	6	Swindell	Petkovsek		29-26	2nd	5
6-27	St.L.	W	6-2		9	8	Drabek	Jackson		30-26	2nd	5
6-28	St.L.	W	9-0		11	5	Hampton	Morgan		31-26	2nd	5
6-30	Pit.	L	9-12		15	17	Loaiza	Kile		31-27	2nd	51/2
7-1	Pit.	W	11-0		11	6	Reynolds	Parris		32-27	2nd	51/2
7-2	Pit.	W	5-3		12	9	Swindell	Neagle	Jones	33-27	2nd	51/2
7-3	At Col.	L	10-15		13	21	Bailey	Dougherty	Holmes	33-28	2nd	51/2
7-4	At Col.	W	16-8		17	14	Hampton	Olivares		34-28	2nd	51/2
7-5	At Col.	L	2-4		4	6	Ritz	Kile	Holmes	34-29	2nd	51/2
7-6	S.D.	W	5-4	(12)	10	6	Jones	B. Williams		35-29	2nd	51/2
7-7	S.D.	W	5-4		11	15	Dougherty	Kroon		36-29	2nd	51/2
7-8†	S.D.	W	3-2	(17)	10	10	Brocail	B. Williams		37-29		
7-8‡	S.D.	W	4-1		8	8	Hampton	Valenzuela	Jones	38-29	2nd	4
7-9	S.D.	L	2-9		6	8	Ashby	Kile		38-30	2nd	5
7-13	At S.F.	L	5-6	(12)	10	7	Hook	Dougherty		38-31	2nd	6
7-14	At S.F.	W	13-8		15	12	Dougherty	Portugal	Veres	39-31	2nd	6
7-15	At S.F.	W	15-9		18	12	Dougherty	Greer		40-31	2nd	6

Date	Opp.	Res.	Score	(inn.*)	Hits	Opp. hits	Winning pitcher	Losing pitcher	Save	Record	Pos.	GB
7-16	At S.F.	L	6-7	(14)	11	11	Hook	Brocail		40-32	2nd	6
7-17	At L.A.	W	3-1		6	6	Hampton	Banks	Jones	41-32	2nd	5
7-18	At L.A.	W	13-4		16	9	Reynolds	Candiotti		42-32	2nd	5
7-19	At L.A.	L	5-6		10	9	Astacio	Dougherty	Worrell	42-33	2nd	6
7-20	S.F.	W	11-4		15	9	Drabek	Mulholland		43-33	2nd	5¹/₂
7-21	S.F.	L	3-6		9	9	Leiter	Kile	Beck	43-34	2nd	6¹/₂
7-22	S.F.	W	7-6		12	11	Hampton	Wilson	Jones	44-34	2nd	6¹/₂
7-23	S.F.	W	3-2	(10)	9	7	Brocail	Service		45-34	2nd	6¹/₂
7-24	L.A.	L	5-6		8	14	Martinez	Swindell		45-35	2nd	6¹/₂
7-25	L.A.	W	4-0		7	3	Drabek	Nomo		46-35	2nd	5¹/₂
7-26	Col.	W	4-3		8	10	Kile	Reynoso	Jones	47-35	2nd	4¹/₂
7-27	Col.	W	5-4	(12)	16	11	Jones	Munoz		48-35	2nd	4¹/₂
7-28	At S.D.	L	2-3		11	7	Hamilton	Reynolds	Hoffman	48-36	2nd	5¹/₂
7-29	At S.D.	W	6-1		12	8	Swindell	Benes		49-36	2nd	4¹/₂
7-30	At S.D.	W	7-1		8	13	Drabek	B. Williams		50-36	2nd	3¹/₂
7-31	At S.D.	L	1-5		5	9	Ashby	Kile		50-37	2nd	4
8-1	At St.L.	W	8-6		14	10	Hampton	Jackson		51-37	2nd	4
8-2	At St.L.	W	4-2		7	7	Reynolds	Osborne	Jones	52-37	2nd	4
8-3	At St.L.	L	1-2		9	8	Watson	Swindell	Henke	52-38	2nd	5
8-4†	At Pit.	W	6-5		14	6	Veres	Christiansen	Jones	53-38		
8-4‡	At Pit.	W	5-4		13	10	Brocail	Parris	Jones	54-38	2nd	4¹/₂
8-5	At Pit.	L	1-3		6	7	Ericks	Kile	Miceli	54-39	2nd	5
8-6	At Pit.	L	3-6		7	8	Loaiza	Hampton	Miceli	54-40	2nd	6¹/₂
8-8	Mon.	L	0-6		6	11	Heredia	Reynolds		54-41	2nd	6¹/₂
8-9	Mon.	L	5-6		12	16	Martinez	Swindell	Fraser	54-42	2nd	7¹/₂
8-10	Mon.	L	2-6		7	13	Henry	Drabek	Leiper	54-43	2nd	7¹/₂
8-11	N.Y.	L	5-7		11	10	Henry	Jones	Franco	54-44	2nd	7¹/₂
8-12	N.Y.	W	3-1		8	6	Hampton	Mlicki	Henneman	55-44	2nd	6¹/₂
8-13	N.Y.	W	5-3		7	6	Reynolds	Cornelius	Henneman	56-44	2nd	5¹/₂
8-15	Phi.	L	2-3		6	6	Juden	Swindell	Slocumb	56-45	2nd	7
8-16	Phi.	W	5-4		9	10	Hartgraves	Slocumb		57-45	2nd	6
8-17	Phi.	L	2-3		8	10	Fletcher	Jones	Borland	57-46	2nd	7
8-18	At Cin.	L	3-8		10	12	Wells	Hampton		57-47	2nd	8
8-19	At Cin.	L	0-8		2	12	Burba	Reynolds		57-48	2nd	9
8-20	At Cin.	L	4-11		13	17	Portugal	Swindell		57-49	2nd	10
8-21	Atl.	L	4-5		11	9	Glavine	McMurtry	Wohlers	57-50	2nd	10
8-22	Atl.	L	4-6		8	8	Avery	Brocail	Wohlers	57-51	2nd	10
8-23	Atl.	L	2-6		4	10	Mercker	Hampton		57-52	2nd	11
8-25	At Fla.	L	4-5		9	8	Burkett	Reynolds	Nen	57-53	2nd	11¹/₂
8-26	At Fla.	L	2-6		9	10	Banks	Swindell		57-54	2nd	12¹/₂
8-27	At Fla.	L	2-10		7	12	Rapp	Drabek		57-55	2nd	13¹/₂
8-28	At Fla.	L	4-6		7	12	Weathers	Brocail	Nen	57-56	2nd	14¹/₂
8-29	At Atl.	W	11-9	(13)	19	14	Swindell	Murray		58-56	2nd	14¹/₂
8-30	At Atl.	W	2-0		6	7	Reynolds	Smoltz	Jones	59-56	2nd	13¹/₂
8-31	At Atl.	L	2-5		6	7	Maddux	Drabek		59-57	2nd	13¹/₂
9-1	Fla.	W	7-3		13	9	Dougherty	Garces		60-57	2nd	13¹/₂
9-2	Fla.	W	10-8		13	8	Dougherty	Perez	Henneman	61-57	2nd	12¹/₂
9-3	Fla.	L	7-8	(11)	11	12	Small	Dougherty	Gardner	61-58	2nd	12¹/₂
9-4	Cin.	L	1-6		6	10	Portugal	Reynolds		61-59	T2nd	13¹/₂
9-5	Cin.	W	10-1		12	5	Drabek	Viola		62-59	2nd	12¹/₂
9-6	Cin.	L	3-7		4	12	Smiley	Wall		62-60	2nd	13¹/₂
9-8	At Phi.	W	12-3		12	9	Hampton	Green		63-60	2nd	12¹/₂
9-9	At Phi.	L	4-6	(11)	14	15	Slocumb	Henneman		63-61	2nd	12¹/₂
9-10	At Phi.	W	5-4		9	9	Drabek	Juden	Henneman	64-61	2nd	11¹/₂
9-12	At N.Y.	W	8-6		12	11	Wall	Cornelius	Henneman	65-61	2nd	11
9-13	At N.Y.	L	5-10		10	14	B. Jones	Hampton		65-62	2nd	12
9-14	At N.Y.	L	2-4		6	9	Mlicki	Reynolds	Franco	65-63	2nd	13
9-15	At Mon.	W	7-3		10	10	Tabaka	Harris		66-63	2nd	12
9-16	At Mon.	W	7-4		11	9	Brocail	Perez		67-63	2nd	11
9-17	At Mon.	W	5-3		11	7	Drabek	Martinez	Henneman	68-63	2nd	10
9-18	Chi.	W	3-1		7	7	Wall	Bullinger	Jones	69-63	2nd	10
9-19	Chi.	L	6-7		15	9	Navarro	Hampton	Myers	69-64	2nd	10
9-20	Chi.	W	4-0		9	6	Reynolds	Castillo		70-64	2nd	10
9-22	St.L.	L	0-3		4	7	Watson	Drabek	Henke	70-65	2nd	11
9-23	St.L.	W	7-3		8	10	Wall	Petkovsek		71-65	2nd	10
9-24	St.L.	W	1-0	(10)	6	7	Hartgraves	DeLucia		72-65	2nd	10
9-25	Pit.	W	10-5		13	8	Brocail	White		73-65	2nd	9
9-26	Pit.	W	2-0		9	9	Swindell	Neagle	Henneman	74-65	2nd	8¹/₂
9-27	Pit.	L	3-6	(11)	7	15	Miceli	Jones	McCurry	74-66	2nd	8
9-28	At Chi.	L	11-12	(11)	17	19	Young	Jones		74-67	2nd	9
9-29	At Chi.	L	3-4	(10)	10	8	Perez	Brocail		74-68	2nd	10
9-30	At Chi.	W	9-8		14	8	Swindell	Perez	Henneman	75-68	2nd	9
10-1	At Chi.	W	8-7		16	13	Veres	Adams	Jones	76-68	2nd	9

Monthly records: April (2-3), May (13-13), June (16-11), July (19-10), August (9-20), September (16-11), October (1-0).
*Innings, if other than nine. †First game of doubleheader. ‡Second game of doubleheader.

HIGHLIGHTS

High point: The club scored 181 runs in July, the most by an N.L. team in one month since Cincinnati scored 182 in June 1977. Houston set a franchise record with a 19-10 record. Despite that, the Astros gained only 1½ games on first-place Cincinnati during the month.

Low point: After first baseman Jeff Bagwell suffered a broken hand July 30, the Astros went 9-20 in August, falling from four games out at the start of the month to 13½ back by the end of August. The club lost a team-record 11 in a row in August.

Turning point: The Astros went to Riverfront Stadium for a critical three-game series August 18-20 trailing Cincinnati by seven games. They were swept. The Reds won the season series, 12-1, outscoring the Astros, 75-39.

Most valuable player: Second baseman Craig Biggio. He led the majors with 123 runs and won a Gold Glove. He also had 22 homers and 33 steals.

Most valuable pitcher: Righthander Shane Reynolds. An excellent strikeout-walk ratio (175 strikeouts/37 walks) and a 3.47 ERA in 30 starts belied his 10-11 record.

Most improved player: Catcher Tony Eusebio. He went from being viewed as a backup to a full-time player on the basis of a .299 average, 58 RBIs and a strong throwing arm.

Most pleasant surprise: Lefthander Mike Hampton. The Astros weren't sure Hampton, 22, was ready for a spot in the rotation. Hampton responded with a 9-8 record and 3.35 ERA, lowest among the starters.

Biggest disappointment: Righthander Darryl Kile. Another out-of-control season landed Kile in the minors two years after he was an All-Star. He walked 73 in 127 innings and was 4-12 with a 4.96 ERA before being sent down.

Key injuries: The big blow was Bagwell's broken hand. The Astros went 9-21 without him. By the time he returned September 1, the Astros were out of the N.L. Central race

and had lost their lead for the wild-card berth.

Notable: No pitcher won more than 10 games, the first time the team leader had that few wins since 1962, the first year of the franchise. . . . The Astros were 36-36 at home, only the fifth time they didn't have a winning record since the Astrodome opened in 1965. . . . The Astros set a team record with 747 runs despite playing only 144 games.

—NEIL HOHLFELD

RECORDS

1995 regular-season record: 76-68 (2nd in N.L. Central); 36-36 at home; 40-32 on road; 30-30 vs. East; 27-25 vs. Central; 19-13 vs. West; 24-17 vs. lefthanded starters; 52-51 vs. righthanded starters; 21-19 on grass; 55-49 on turf; 20-20 in daytime; 56-48 at night; 20-23 in one-run games; 11-10 in extra-inning games; 2-0-0 in doubleheaders.

Team record past five years: 373-372 (.501, ranks 6th in league in that span).

TEAM LEADERS

Batting average: Derek Bell (.334).
At-bats: Craig Biggio (533).
Runs: Craig Biggio (123).
Hits: Craig Biggio (167).
Total bases: Craig Biggio (267).
Doubles: Jeff Bagwell (29).
Triples: Brian L. Hunter (5).
Home runs: Craig Biggio (22).
Runs batted in: Jeff Bagwell (87).
Stolen bases: Craig Biggio (33).
Slugging percentage: Derek Bell (.442).
On-base percentage: Jeff Bagwell (.399).
Wins: Doug Drabek, Shane Reynolds, Greg Swindell (10).
Earned-run average: Mike Hampton (3.35).
Complete games: Shane Reynolds (3).
Shutouts: Shane Reynolds (2).
Saves: Todd Jones (15).
Innings pitched: Shane Reynolds (189.1).
Strikeouts: Shane Reynolds (175).

GAMES BY POSITION

Catcher: Tony Eusebio 103, Scott Servais 28, Rick Wilkins 13, Pat Borders 11, Jerry Goff 11, Scooter Tucker 3.
First base: Jeff Bagwell 114, Mike Simms 25, Dave Magadan 11, Mike Brumley 1, Derrick May 1, Craig Shipley 1.
Second base: Craig Biggio 141, Andy Stankiewicz 6, Craig Shipley 5, Chris Donnels 1.
Third base: Dave Magadan 100, Craig Shipley 65, Phil Nevin 16, Chris Donnels 9, Andy Stankiewicz 3, Ricky Gutierrez 2, Mike Brumley 1.
Shortstop: Orlando Miller 89, Ricky Gutierrez 44, Andy Stankiewicz 14, Craig Shipley 11, Mike Brumley 3.
Outfield: Derek Bell 110, James Mouton 94, Brian L. Hunter 74, John Cangelosi 59, Luis Gonzalez 55, Derrick May 55, Milt Thompson 34, Phil Plantier 20, Mike Simms 12, Mike Brumley 3.

TOP DRAFT CHOICES

1. **Tony McKnight,** RHP, Arkansas H.S., Texarkana, Ark.
2. **Eric Ireland,** RHP, Millikan H.S., Long Beach, Calif.
3. **Chad Alexander,** OF, Texas A&M University.
4. **Brian Sikorski,** RHP, Western Michigan University.
5. **Mike Rose,** C, Jesuit H.S., Sacramento, Calif.
6. **Scott Chapman,** C, Alexander H.S., Albany, Ohio.
7. **Jason McCarter,** RHP, Monterey Peninsula (Calif.) J.C.
8. **Eric Smith,** RHP, Butler County (Kan.) C.C.
9. **Jason Adams,** SS, Wichita State University.
10. **Jeremy DeShazer,** OF, Lake Washington H.S., Kirkland, Wash.

LOS ANGELES DODGERS
NATIONAL LEAGUE WEST DIVISION

1996 DODGERS SCHEDULE

Home games shaded.
* — All-Star Game at Veterans Stadium (Philadelphia)
N — Night game (any game starting after 5 p.m.)

MARCH

SUN	MON	TUE	WED	THU	FRI	SAT
31						

APRIL

SUN	MON	TUE	WED	THU	FRI	SAT
	1 HOU	2 N HOU	3 HOU	4 CHI	5 CHI	6 CHI
7 CHI	8 ATL	9 N ATL	10 N ATL	11 N FLA	12 N FLA	13 N FLA
14 FLA	15	16 N SF	17 SF	18	19 N FLA	20 N FLA
21 N FLA	22 N ATL	23 ATL	24 N HOU	25 N HOU	26 N CHI	27 N CHI
28 CHI	29 N CHI	30 N COL				

MAY

SUN	MON	TUE	WED	THU	FRI	SAT
			N COL	2	3 N PIT	4 N PIT
5 PIT	6	7 N CIN	8 N CIN	9 N STL	10 N STL	11 N STL
12 STL	13 N MON	14 N MON	15 N MON	16 N PHI	17 N PHI	18 N PHI
19 PHI	20 N NY	21 N NY	22 N NY	23	24 N MON	25 N MON
26 MON	27	28 N PHI	29 N PHI	30 N PHI	31 N NY	

JUNE

SUN	MON	TUE	WED	THU	FRI	SAT
						1 NY
2 NY	3	4 N PIT	5 N PIT	6 N PIT	7 N CIN	8 N CIN
9 CIN	10 N STL	11 N STL	12	13 N ATL	14 N ATL	15 ATL
16 ATL	17 N CHI	18 N CHI	19 N CHI	20 N HOU	21 N HOU	22 N HOU
23 HOU	24	25 N CHI	26 N CHI	27 N COL	28 N COL	29 N COL
30 COL						

JULY

SUN	MON	TUE	WED	THU	FRI	SAT
	1 N SD	2 N SD	3 N SD	4 N COL	5 N COL	6 COL
7 COL	8	*9 ALL-STAR GAME	10	11 N SF	12 N SF	13 N SF
14 N SF	15 N SD	16 N SD	17 N SD	18 N SF	19 N SF	20 SF
21 SF	22	23 N FLA	24 N FLA	25 N FLA	26 N HOU	27 N HOU
28 HOU	29	30 N FLA	31 N FLA			

AUGUST

SUN	MON	TUE	WED	THU	FRI	SAT
				1 N FLA	2 N ATL	3 ATL
4 ATL	5	6 N PIT	7 N PIT	8	9 N CIN	10 CIN
11 CIN	12 N CIN	13 N STL	14 N STL	15 N STL	16 N MON	17 N MON
18 N MON	19	20 N PHI	21 N PHI	22 N PHI	23 N NY	24 NY
25 NY	26	27 N MON	28 N MON	29 N MON	30 N PHI	31 N PHI

SEPTEMBER

SUN	MON	TUE	WED	THU	FRI	SAT
1 N PHI	2	3 N NY	4 N NY	5 N NY	6 N SF	7 N SF
8 PIT	9 N CIN	10 N CIN	11 N CIN	12 N STL	13 N STL	14 STL
15 STL	16 N COL	17 N COL	18 COL	19 N SD	20 N SD	21 SD
22 SD	23	24 N SF	25 N SF	26 N SF	27 N SD	28 N SD
29 SD						

1996 SEASON

CLUB DIRECTORY

Board of directors
Peter O'Malley
Harry M. Bardt
Roland Seidler
Mrs. Roland (Terry) Seidler

President
Peter O'Malley

Executive vice president
Fred Claire

Vice president, communications
Tom Hawkins

Vice president, finance
Bob Graziano

Vice president, marketing
Barry Stockhamer

Director, stadium operations
Doug Duennes

Vice president, treasurer
Roland Seidler

Vice president, Campo Las Palmas
Ralph Avila

Assistant secretary and general counsel
Santiago Fernandez

Director, accounting and finance
Bill Foltz

Director, advertising and special events
Paul Kalil

Director, broadcasting and publications
Brent Shyer

Director, community relations
Don Newcombe

Director, community affairs
Monique Brandon

Director, human resources and admin.
Irene Tanji

Dir., management information services
Mike Mularky

Vice president, minor league operations
Charlie Blaney

Director, scouting
Terry Reynolds

Director, publicity
Jay Lucas

Assistant director, publicity
Derrick Hall

Traveling secretary
Bill DeLury

Director, ticket operations
Debra Duncan

Director, ticket marketing
Allan Erselius

Club physicians
Dr. Frank W. Jobe
Dr. Michael F. Mellman

Scouts
Eleodoro Arias, Eddie Bane, Bill Barkley, Rick Birmingham, Gib Bodet, Flores Bolivar, Mike Brito, Joe Campbell, Jim Chapman, Bob Darwin, Eddie Fajardo Rodriguez, Joe Ferrone, Rafael Gonzalez, Carl Greene, Michael Hankins, Dick, Hanlon, Dennis Haren, Hank Jones, Lon Joyce, John Keenan, Gary LaRocque, Don LeJohn, Carl Lowenstine, Teodoro Mata, Ed Mathes, Dale McReynolds, Tommy Mixon, Alberto Osorio, Deni Pacini, Camilo Pasqual, Pablo Peguero, Claude Pelletier, Bill Pleis, Silvano Quesada, Ross Sapp, Mark Sheehy, Jim Stoeckel, Tom Thomas, Glen Van Proyen

Special assignment scouts
Mel Didier, Gary Sutherland

MINOR LEAGUE AFFILIATES

Class	Team	League	Manager
AAA	Albuquerque	Pacific Coast	Phil Regan
AA	San Antonio	Texas	John Shelby
A	San Bernardino	California	Del Crandall
A	Vero Beach	Florida State	Jon Debus
A	Yakima	Northwest	Joe Vavra
A	Savannah	South Atlantic	John Shoemaker
Rookie	Great Falls	Pioneer	Mickey Hatcher

BROADCAST INFORMATION

Radio: KABC-AM (790); KWKW-AM (1330, Spanish language).
TV: KTLA-TV (Channel 5).

SPRING TRAINING

Ballpark (city): Holman Stadium (Vero Beach, Fla.).
Ticket information: 407-569-4900.

SPRING TRAINING ROSTER

Manager—Tommy Lasorda (2).
Coaches—Joe Amalfitano (8), Mark Cresse (58), Bill Russell (18), Reggie Smith (9), David Wallace (17).

No.	PITCHERS	B/T	Ht./Wt.	Born	1995 clubs
56	Astacio, Pedro	R/R	6-2/195	11-28-69	Los Angeles
	Brewer, Billy	L/L	6-1/175	4-15-68	Kansas City, Springfield, Omaha
49	Candiotti, Tom	R/R	6-2/215	8-31-57	Los Angeles
64	Correa, Ramser	R/R	6-5/200	11-13-70	DID NOT PLAY
41	Cummings, John	L/L	6-3/200	5-10-69	Seattle, Tacoma, San Antonio, Los Angeles
37	Dreifort, Darren	R/R	6-2/205	5-18-72	Los Angeles
63	Duran, Roberto	L/L	6-0/167	3-6-73	Vero Beach
51	Eischen, Joey	L/L	6-1/190	5-25-70	Ottawa, Los Angeles, Albuquerque
35	Gorecki, Rick	R/R	6-3/167	8-27-73	Vero Beach
52	Guthrie, Mark	R/L	6-4/207	9-22-65	Minnesota, Los Angeles
52	Hall, Darren	R/R	6-3/205	7-14-64	Toronto
47	Martinez, Jesus	L/L	6-2/145	3-13-74	San Antonio, Albuquerque
48	Martinez, Ramon J.	B/R	6-4/186	3-22-68	Los Angeles
16	Nomo, Hideo	R/R	6-2/210	8-31-68	Bakersfield, Los Angeles
13	Osuna, Antonio	R/R	5-11/160	4-12-73	Los Angeles, San Bernardino, Albuquerque
61	Park, Chan Ho	R/R	6-2/195	6-30-73	Albuquerque, Los Angeles
50	Rodriguez, Felix	R/R	6-1/180	12-5-72	Albuquerque, Los Angeles
59	Valdes, Ismael	R/R	6-3/207	8-21-73	Los Angeles
68	Watts, Brandon	L/L	6-3/195	9-13-72	Vero Beach
65	Weaver, Eric	R/R	6-5/230	8-4-73	San Antonio
38	Worrell, Todd	R/R	6-5/222	9-28-59	Los Angeles

No.	CATCHERS	B/T	Ht./Wt.	Born	1995 clubs
26	Hernandez, Carlos	R/R	5-11/215	5-24-67	Los Angeles
10	Huckaby, Kenneth	R/R	6-1/205	1-27-71	Albuquerque
31	Piazza, Mike	R/R	6-3/215	9-4-68	Los Angeles

No.	INFIELDERS	B/T	Ht./Wt.	Born	1995 clubs
20	Blowers, Mike	R/R	6-2/210	4-24-65	Seattle
25	Busch, Mike	R/R	6-5/220	7-7-68	Albuquerque, Los Angeles
60	Castro, Juan	R/R	5-10/163	6-20-72	Albuquerque, Los Angeles
14	DeShields, Delino	L/R	6-1/175	1-15-69	Los Angeles
3	Fonville, Chad	B/R	5-6/155	3-5-71	Montreal, Los Angeles
21	Gagne, Greg	R/R	5-11/180	11-12-61	Kansas City
62	Guerrero, Wilton	R/R	5-11/145	10-24-74	San Antonio, Albuquerque
5	Hansen, Dave	L/R	6-0/195	11-24-68	Los Angeles
33	Ingram, Garey	R/R	5-11/185	7-25-70	Los Angeles, Albuquerque
23	Karros, Eric	R/R	6-4/222	11-4-67	Los Angeles

No.	OUTFIELDERS	B/T	Ht./Wt.	Born	1995 clubs
7	Ashley, Billy	R/R	6-7/235	7-11-70	Los Angeles
22	Butler, Brett	L/L	5-10/161	6-15-57	New York N.L., Los Angeles
27	Cedeno, Roger	B/R	6-1/165	8-16-74	Albuquerque, Los Angeles
12	Garcia, Karim	L/L	6-0/172	10-29-75	Albuquerque, Los Angeles
28	Hollandsworth, Todd	L/L	6-2/193	4-20-73	Los Angeles, San Bernardino, Albuquerque
43	Mondesi, Raul	R/R	5-11/212	3-12-71	Los Angeles

BALLPARK INFORMATION

Ballpark (capacity, surface)
Dodger Stadium (56,000, grass)

Address
1000 Elysian Park Ave.
Los Angeles, CA 90012

Business phone
213-224-1500

Ticket information
213-224-1400

Ticket prices
$14, $12 & $11 (box seats)
$8 & $9 (reserved seats)
$6 (top deck and pavilion)
$3 (g.a., youth 12 and under)

Field dimensions (from home plate)
To left field at foul line, 330 feet
To center field, 395 feet
To right field at foul line, 330 feet

First game played
April 10, 1962 (Reds 6, Dodgers 3)

General Admission
(Left and Right Field Pavilion)
Reserved Level
Club Level
Loge Box
Field Box

DAY BY DAY

Date	Opp.	Res.	Score	(inn.*)	Hits	Opp. hits	Winning pitcher	Losing pitcher	Save	Record	Pos.	GB
4-25	At Fla.	W	8-7		13	9	Martinez	Burkett	Seanez	1-0	1st	+$^1/_2$
4-26	At Fla.	W	4-2		9	7	Candiotti	Gardner	Seanez	2-0	1st	+$^1/_2$
4-28	Atl.	W	9-1		9	4	Daal	Avery		3-0	T1st	...
4-29	Atl.	L	3-4		7	6	McMichael	Murphy		3-1	T2nd	1
4-30	Atl.	L	3-6		8	9	Smoltz	Martinez	Clontz	3-2	3rd	1
5-1	At S.F.	L	0-7		7	9	Mulholland	Candiotti		3-3	T3rd	2
5-2	At S.F.	L	3-4	(15)	12	9	Hook	Hansell		3-4	4th	3
5-3	At S.F.	W	7-6		13	14	Osuna	Beck	Worrell	4-4	T2nd	3
5-5	At Col.	W	6-4		12	9	Martinez	Olivares	Seanez	5-4	3rd	2
5-6	At Col.	W	17-11		21	17	T. Williams	Acevedo		6-4	3rd	1
5-7	At Col.	W	12-10		13	12	Daal	Reed	Valdes	7-4	T2nd	$^1/_2$
5-8	At S.D.	L	2-5		8	8	Hermanson	Osuna	Hoffman	7-5	3rd	1
5-9	At S.D.	L	2-9		7	13	Sanders	Candiotti		7-6	3rd	1$^1/_2$
5-10	At S.D.	W	3-1		5	8	Martinez	Valenzuela	Worrell	8-6	T2nd	1$^1/_2$
5-12	St.L.	W	8-4		10	5	T. Williams	Jackson		9-6	2nd	2
5-13	St.L.	L	2-3		10	6	Frascatore	Astacio	Henke	9-7	2nd	2
5-14	St.L.	L	5-6	(11)	10	8	Arocha	Osuna	Henke	9-8	3rd	3
5-15	Pit.	W	4-0		8	1	Martinez	Wagner		10-8	2nd	2
5-16	Pit.	L	0-2		9	6	Neagle	Valdes	Miceli	10-9	2nd	2
5-17	Pit.	L	2-3		8	6	Plesac	T. Williams	Miceli	10-10	3rd	3
5-18	Pit.	L	6-7		13	13	Christiansen	T. Williams	Gott	10-11	T3rd	3
5-19	Chi.	L	3-7		7	11	Castillo	Candiotti	Myers	10-12	T3rd	3
5-20	Chi.	L	1-7		6	10	Bullinger	Martinez		10-13	3rd	3
5-21	Chi.	L	1-2	(13)	5	9	Walker	F. Rodriguez	Myers	10-14	4th	4
5-23	At N.Y.	W	6-4		10	9	Daal	Henry	Worrell	11-14	T3rd	3$^1/_2$
5-24	At N.Y.	W	5-0		10	6	Astacio	Birkbeck		12-14	3rd	2$^1/_2$
5-25	At N.Y.	W	3-0		11	5	Candiotti	Harnisch		13-14	3rd	2
5-26	At Mon.	L	4-9		11	9	Heredia	Martinez	Scott	13-15	3rd	2
5-27	At Mon.	L	1-2		10	5	Perez	Valdes	Rojas	13-16	3rd	2
5-28	At Mon.	L	1-5		7	6	Fassero	Nomo	Scott	13-17	T3rd	3
5-29	At Phi.	L	6-8		8	14	Quantrill	Astacio	Slocumb	13-18	4th	3$^1/_2$
5-30	At Phi.	L	0-5		7	8	Green	Candiotti		13-19	4th	4$^1/_2$
5-31	At Phi.	W	4-1	(10)	8	3	Martinez	Bottalico	Worrell	14-19	T3rd	3$^1/_2$
6-1	At Atl.	W	6-3		10	7	Valdes	Mercker		15-19	3rd	3
6-2	N.Y.	W	2-1		7	2	Nomo	Saberhagen	Worrell	16-19	3rd	3
6-3	N.Y.	L	3-5		7	9	Mlicki	Astacio	Franco	16-20	3rd	4
6-4	N.Y.	W	5-3		6	9	F. Rodriguez	DiPoto	Worrell	17-20	3rd	4
6-5	Mon.	W	3-1		8	5	Martinez	Heredia	Worrell	18-20	3rd	3
6-6	Mon.	W	5-1		12	7	Valdes	Perez		19-20	3rd	3
6-7	Mon.	W	7-1		12	6	Nomo	Fassero		20-20	3rd	3
6-9	Phi.	L	0-4		6	8	Quantrill	Astacio		20-21	3rd	4
6-10	Phi.	L	0-3		5	9	Green	Candiotti		20-22	3rd	4
6-11	Phi.	L	1-2		7	11	Mimbs	Martinez	Slocumb	20-23	4th	5
6-13	At Pit.	W	5-3		14	7	Valdes	Lieber	Worrell	21-23	3rd	4$^1/_2$
6-14	At Pit.	W	8-5		13	8	Nomo	Wagner	Worrell	22-23	3rd	4$^1/_2$
6-15	At Pit.	L	7-11		13	13	Neagle	Astacio		22-24	3rd	5
6-16	At Chi.	L	0-2		6	5	Hickerson	Seanez		22-25	4th	5
6-17	At Chi.	W	12-5		18	9	Martinez	Young		23-25	4th	4
6-18	At Chi.	W	6-0		9	5	Valdes	Navarro		24-25	4th	3
6-19	At St.L.	W	5-2		9	3	Nomo	Hill	Worrell	25-25	4th	2
6-20	At St.L.	L	0-7		8	11	Petkovsek	Astacio		25-26	4th	2
6-21	At St.L.	W	10-1		9	5	Candiotti	Palacios		26-26	4th	2
6-22	S.F.	W	7-6		9	14	Seanez	Burba	Worrell	27-26	3rd	2
6-23	S.F.	W	7-2		13	5	Valdes	Portugal		28-26	2nd	1
6-24	S.F.	W	7-0		12	2	Nomo	Leiter		29-26	T1st	...
6-25	S.F.	W	3-2		8	9	Candiotti	VanLandingham	Worrell	30-26	T1st	...
6-26	S.D.	W	8-5		7	11	Worrell	B. Williams		31-26	1st	+$^1/_2$
6-27	S.D.	L	3-14		3	18	Dishman	Martinez		31-27	2nd	$^1/_2$
6-28	S.D.	L	2-8		4	11	Ashby	Valdes		31-28	2nd	$^1/_2$
6-29	Col.	W	3-0		10	6	Nomo	Freeman		32-28	1st	+$^1/_2$
6-30	Col.	L	1-2		5	5	Ritz	Candiotti	Munoz	32-29	2nd	$^1/_2$
7-1	Col.	W	5-4		10	7	Worrell	Bailey		33-29	1st	+$^1/_2$
7-2	Col.	L	1-10		6	8	Swift	Martinez		33-30	2nd	$^1/_2$
7-4	At Atl.	L	2-3		5	7	Clontz	Valdes	Wohlers	33-31	2nd	1
7-5	At Atl.	L	1-4		9	6	Wohlers	Astacio		33-32	2nd	2
7-6	At Atl.	L	0-1		5	6	McMichael	Seanez		33-33	T2nd	3
7-7	At Cin.	L	2-4		9	6	Smiley	Banks	Jackson	33-34	T2nd	4
7-8	At Cin.	W	12-2		15	6	Martinez	Nitkowski		34-34	2nd	4
7-9	At Cin.	L	0-8		6	15	Schourek	Valdes		34-35	2nd	5
7-13	Fla.	L	0-4		3	11	Hammond	Candiotti		34-36	T2nd	5
7-14	Fla.	W	7-0		10	0	Martinez	Burkett		35-36	2nd	4

Date	Opp.	Res.	Score	(inn.*)	Hits	Opp. hits	Winning pitcher	Losing pitcher	Save	Record	Pos.	GB
7-15	Fla.	W	3-1		5	3	Nomo	Witt		36-36	2nd	4
7-16	Fla.	L	2-5		6	8	Rapp	Valdes	Nen	36-37	2nd	4
7-17	Hou.	L	1-3		6	6	Hampton	Banks	Jones	36-38	2nd	5
7-18	Hou.	L	4-13		9	16	Reynolds	Candiotti		36-39	2nd	5
7-19	Hou.	W	6-5		9	10	Astacio	Dougherty	Worrell	37-39	2nd	5
7-20	At Fla.	W	4-2	(10)	8	6	Astacio	Mathews	Worrell	38-39	2nd	5
7-21	At Fla.	W	5-3		9	7	Valdes	Rapp	Worrell	39-39	2nd	4
7-22	At Fla.	L	10-11		16	13	Veres	Astacio	Nen	39-40	2nd	5
7-23	At Fla.	W	4-2		6	8	Candiotti	Hammond	Worrell	40-40	2nd	5
7-24	At Hou.	W	6-5		14	8	Martinez	Swindell		41-40	2nd	5
7-25	At Hou.	L	0-4		3	7	Drabek	Nomo		41-41	2nd	5
7-26	Atl.	W	1-0		4	6	Valdes	Avery	Worrell	42-41	2nd	4
7-27	Atl.	W	9-4		14	9	Cummings	Mercker		43-41	2nd	3
7-28	Cin.	L	2-3		3	6	Smiley	Candiotti	Brantley	43-42	2nd	4
7-29	Cin.	W	4-2		8	10	Martinez	Portugal	Worrell	44-42	2nd	4
7-30	Cin.	W	5-4		9	7	Nomo	Pugh		45-42	2nd	3
8-1	At Col.	W	9-6		12	11	Valdes	Thompson	Worrell	46-42	2nd	2 1/2
8-2	At Col.	W	10-7		13	11	Tapani	Ritz		47-42	2nd	1 1/2
8-3	At Col.	L	4-9		14	10	Saberhagen	Martinez		47-43	2nd	2 1/2
8-4	At S.F.	L	1-15		7	16	VanLandingham	Candiotti		47-44	2nd	3 1/2
8-5	At S.F.	W	3-0		7	1	Nomo	Brewington		48-44	2nd	3 1/2
8-6	At S.F.	L	1-3		5	7	Leiter	Valdes		48-45	2nd	3 1/2
8-7	At S.F.	W	3-1	(12)	6	6	Osuna	Bautista	Worrell	49-45	2nd	3
8-8	St.L.	W	4-3		9	6	Astacio	Parrett	Worrell	50-45	2nd	2
8-9	St.L.	W	4-2		8	10	Candiotti	Morgan	Worrell	51-45	2nd	1
8-10	St.L.	L	1-2		6	6	Petkovsek	Nomo	Henke	51-46	2nd	1
8-11	Pit.	W	3-2		7	6	Valdes	Ericks	Worrell	52-46	T1st	...
8-12	Pit.	W	11-10	(11)	17	22	Astacio	Mccurry		53-46	T1st	...
8-13	Pit.	W	4-1		9	4	Martinez	Neagle	Worrell	54-46	1st	+1
8-14	Chi.	L	4-5	(11)	15	13	Myers	Guthrie	Adams	54-47	1st	+1
8-15	Chi.	W	7-5		8	11	Nomo	Trachsel	Worrell	55-47	1st	+2
8-16	Chi.	W	6-1		8	7	Valdes	Bullinger		56-47	1st	+2
8-17	At Cin.	L	2-6		7	10	Schourek	Tapani		56-48	1st	+1
8-18	At N.Y.	L	2-3		8	6	Henry	Cummings		56-49	1st	+1
8-19	At N.Y.	L	1-2		6	3	Mlicki	Candiotti	Franco	56-50	1st	+1
8-20	At N.Y.	L	3-5		9	7	Isringhausen	Nomo	Franco	56-51	T1st	...
8-21	At Mon.	W	7-2		11	6	Valdes	Alvarez		57-51	1st	+1/2
8-22	At Mon.	W	7-4	(11)	14	9	Worrell	Fraser		58-51	1st	+1 1/2
8-23	At Mon.	W	5-0		10	5	Martinez	Fassero		59-51	1st	+1 1/2
8-24	At Phi.	L	6-7	(11)	13	13	Slocumb	Seanez		59-52	1st	+1/2
8-25	At Phi.	L	4-17		7	17	Juden	Nomo		59-53	1st	+1/2
8-26	At Phi.	L	4-9		7	10	Fernandez	Valdes		59-54	1st	+1/2
8-27	At Phi.	W	9-1		11	6	Tapani	Greene		60-54	1st	+1 1/2
8-29	N.Y.	L	3-4		6	7	DiPoto	Worrell	Franco	60-55	1st	+1
8-30	N.Y.	L	1-8		11	11	Mlicki	Candiotti	Henry	60-56	T1st	...
8-31	N.Y.	W	6-5		13	7	Worrell	DiPoto		61-56	1st	+1/2
9-1	Mon.	L	5-6		11	8	Harris	Valdes	Rojas	61-57	1st	+1/2
9-2	Mon.	L	8-9		14	14	Rueter	Tapani	Rojas	61-58	2nd	1/2
9-3	Mon.	W	6-3		9	4	Martinez	Fassero	Worrell	62-58	2nd	1/2
9-4	Phi.	W	5-1		4	6	Candiotti	Juden		63-58	1st	+1/2
9-5	Phi.	W	2-1		8	4	Cummings	Borland		64-58	1st	+1
9-6	Phi.	L	0-1		3	3	Grace	Valdes	Slocumb	64-59	T1st	...
9-8	At Pit.	W	8-2		13	6	Martinez	Loaiza		65-59	T1st	...
9-9	At Pit.	W	11-2		12	7	Tapani	Wagner		66-59	T1st	...
9-10	At Pit.	W	5-4		11	9	Cummings	Dyer	Worrell	67-59	T1st	...
9-11	At Chi.	L	1-12		6	17	Foster	Valdes		67-60	2nd	1
9-12	At Chi.	W	7-1		11	6	Nomo	Bullinger		68-60	2nd	1
9-13	At Chi.	L	6-7	(13)	14	15	Adams	Guthrie		68-61	2nd	1
9-15	At St.L.	W	7-6		12	13	Astacio	Henke	Worrell	69-61	2nd	1
9-16	At St.L.	L	4-5		9	11	Henke	Osuna		69-62	2nd	2
9-17	At St.L.	W	8-0		11	2	Valdes	Watson		70-62	2nd	1
9-19	S.F.	L	2-7		6	8	Leiter	Nomo	Barton	70-63	2nd	1 1/2
9-20	S.F.	W	4-2		5	7	Martinez	Mulholland	Worrell	71-63	2nd	1 1/2
9-21	S.D.	L	1-5		9	11	Ashby	Candiotti	Hoffman	71-64	2nd	1 1/2
9-22	S.D.	W	6-5		7	16	Astacio	Florie	Worrell	72-64	2nd	1 1/2
9-23	S.D.	W	4-2		7	7	Valdes	Bochtler		73-64	2nd	1/2
9-24	S.D.	W	6-2		10	7	Nomo	Blair		74-64	2nd	1/2
9-25	Col.	W	4-3		7	8	Martinez	Swift	Worrell	75-64	1st	+1/2
9-26	Col.	L	3-7		9	9	Saberhagen	Candiotti		75-65	2nd	1/2
9-27	Col.	W	7-4		12	10	Tapani	Ritz	Worrell	76-65	1st	+1/2
9-29	At S.D.	L	5-6		8	10	Worrell	Osuna	Hoffman	76-66	1st	+1
9-30	At S.D.	W	7-2		12	7	Nomo	Bochtler		77-66	1st	+1
10-1	At S.D.	W	4-1		10	4	Daal	B. Williams	Bruske	78-66	1st	+1

Monthly records: April (3-2), May (11-17), June (18-10), July (13-13), August (16-14), September (16-10), October (1-0).
*Innings, if other than nine.

HIGHLIGHTS

High point: Raul Mondesi slugged a two-run homer to snap a 1-1 tie in the Dodgers' 7-2 division-clinching victory over San Diego on the next-to-last day of the season. The Dodgers won 17 of their final 25 games to wrest the N.L. West lead from Colorado.

Low point: A 10-1 loss to Colorado on July 2 started a five-game losing streak; the Dodgers went on to lose 10 of 13 games and fall five games behind the Rockies. They didn't see first place again until August 11.

Turning point: Five games back after a 4-0 loss in Houston on July 25, the Dodgers got six-hit pitching the next night from Ismael Valdes and Todd Worrell and defeated Atlanta, 1-0, in Los Angeles. That started the Dodgers on a 15-6 run that propelled them back into first place for the first time in six weeks.

Most valuable player: First baseman Eric Karros. Karros had 18 game-winning hits, eight of them homers, and posted career highs in average (.298), homers (32) and RBIs (105). Catcher Mike Piazza hit .346 with 32 homers and 93 RBIs.

Most valuable pitcher: Righthander Ramon Martinez. Martinez finished 17-7 with a 3.66 ERA. On July 14, he tossed a no-hitter against Florida.

Most improved player: Karros. In his fourth full season, he improved every facet of his game, especially his defense.

Most pleasant surprises: Chad Fonville, a diminutive all-purpose player who was claimed on waivers from Montreal on May 31, unseated three starters at various times in the season: Delino DeShields at second base, Roberto Kelly in left field and Jose Offerman at shortstop. Entering 1995, Fonville hadn't played above Class A. Rookie righthander Hideo Nomo won seven of his first eight decisions, pitched three shutouts and led the N.L. in strikeouts.

Biggest disappointments: Outfielder Billy Ashley and Offerman. Ashley, coming off back-to-back blockbuster seasons in Class AAA (a combined 63 homers and 205 RBIs), won the starting job in left field during spring training but spent the second half of the year on the bench. Offerman made the All-Star team but lost his job to Fonville in the final month. He made a staggering 35 errors.

Key injuries: Piazza was lost for 22 games in May and early June after tearing a ligament in his thumb; the Dodgers lost 14 of those games. Third baseman Tim Wallach missed 47 games because of a sore back and a torn knee ligament.

Notable: Worrell established a franchise record with 32 saves. . . . Manager Tommy Lasorda gained his 1,500th career victory June 7.

—GORDON VERRELL

RECORDS

1995 regular-season record: 78-66 (1st in West); 39-33 at home; 39-33 on road; 28-28 vs. East; 26-23 vs. Central; 24-15 vs. West; 22-18 vs. lefthanded starters; 56-48 vs. righthanded starters; 62-51 on grass; 16-15 on turf; 17-15 in daytime; 61-51 at night; 19-26 in one-run games; 5-6 in extra-inning games; 0-0-0 in doubleheaders.

Team record past five years: 373-371 (.501, 5th in league in that span).

TEAM LEADERS

Batting average: Mike Piazza (.346).
At-bats: Raul Mondesi (536).
Runs: Raul Mondesi (91).
Hits: Eric Karros (164).
Total bases: Eric Karros (295).
Doubles: Eric Karros (29).
Triples: Raul Mondesi, Jose Offerman (6).
Home runs: Eric Karros, Mike Piazza (32).
Runs batted in: Eric Karros (105).
Stolen bases: Delano DeShields (39).
Slugging percentage: Mike Piazza (.606).
On-base percentage: Mike Piazza (.400).
Wins: Ramon Martinez (17).
Earned-run average: Hideo Nomo (2.54).
Complete games: Ismael Valdes (6).
Shutouts: Hideo Nomo (3).
Saves: Todd Worrell (32).
Innings pitched: Ramon Martinez (206.1).
Strikeouts: Hideo Nomo (236).

GAMES BY POSITION

Catcher: Mike Piazza 112, Carlos Hernandez 41, Tom Prince 17, Noe Munoz 2.
First base: Eric Karros 143, Mike Busch 2, Chris Gwynn 2, Henry Rodriguez 1, Tim Wallach 1.
Second base: Delino DeShields 113, Chad Fonville 36, Garey Ingram 7, Jeff Treadway 1.
Third base: Tim Wallach 96, Dave Hansen 58, Garey Ingram 12, Mike Busch 10, Juan Castro 7, Rick Parker 2, Eddie Pye 2, Jeff Treadway 2, Dick Schofield 1.
Shortstop: Jose Offerman 115, Chad Fonville 38, Juan Castro 4, Dick Schofield 3, Rick Parker 2.
Outfield: Raul Mondesi 138, Roberto Kelly 110, Billy Ashley 69, Brett Butler 38, Todd Hollandsworth 37, Roger Cedeno 36, Mitch Webster 25, Rick Parker 21, Henry Rodriguez 20, Chris Gwynn 17, Reggie Williams 14, Chad Fonville 11, Karim Garcia 5, Garey Ingram 4.

TOP DRAFT CHOICES

1. **David Yocum,** LHP, Florida State University.
2. **Darrin Babineaux,** RHP, University of Southwestern Louisiana.
3. **Onan Masaoka,** LHP, Waiakea H.S., Hilo, Hawaii.
4. **Judd Granzow,** OF, Faith Baptist H.S., Granada Hills, Calif.
5. **Sef Soto,** RHP, Palomar (Calif.) J.C.
6. **Kevin Gibbs,** OF, Old Dominion University.
7. **Trent Cuevas,** SS, El Dorado H.S., Placentia, Calif.
8. **Jon Tucker,** 1B, Chatsworth (Calif.) H.S.
9. **Eric Brown,** SS, East St. John H.S., LaPlace, La.
10. **Mike Carpentier,** SS, Cal State Sacramento.

MONTREAL EXPOS
NATIONAL LEAGUE EAST DIVISION

1996 EXPOS SCHEDULE

☐ Home games shaded.
* — All-Star Game at Veterans Stadium (Philadelphia)
N — Night game (any game starting after 5 p.m.)

MARCH
SUN	MON	TUE	WED	THU	FRI	SAT
31						

APRIL
SUN	MON	TUE	WED	THU	FRI	SAT
	1 CIN	2 N CIN	3 CIN	4 COL	5 COL	6 COL
7 CIN	8 N STL	9	10 STL	11 N PIT	12 N PIT	13 PIT
14 PIT	15 N PHI	16 N PHI	17 N PHI	18 N PHI	19 N PIT	20 PIT
21 PIT	22 N STL	23 N STL	24 N CIN	25 CIN	26 N COL	27 COL
28 COL	29 N NY	30 N NY				

MAY
SUN	MON	TUE	WED	THU	FRI	SAT
			1 N NY	2	3 N HOU	4 N HOU
5 HOU	6 N CHI	7 N CHI	8 N CHI	9 N HOU	10 N HOU	11 N HOU
12 HOU	13 N LA	14 N LA	15 N LA	16	17 N SD	18 N SD
19 SD	20 N SF	21 N SF	22 N SF	23	24 N LA	25 N LA
26 LA	27 N SD	28 N SD	29 N SD	30	31 N SF	

JUNE
SUN	MON	TUE	WED	THU	FRI	SAT
						1 N SF
2 SF	3	4 N FLA	5 N FLA	6	7 N CHI	8 N CHI
9 CHI	10 N FLA	11 N FLA	12 N FLA	13	14 N CIN	15 N CIN
16 CIN	17 N COL	18 N COL	19 N COL	20 N STL	21 N STL	22 N STL
23 STL	24 N PIT	25 N PIT	26 N PIT	27	28 N PHI	29 N PHI
30 PHI						

JULY
SUN	MON	TUE	WED	THU	FRI	SAT
	1 ATL	2 N ATL	3 N ATL	4 N NY	5 N NY	6 NY
7 NY	8 *	9 ALL-STAR GAME	10	11 N PHI	12 N PHI	13 N PHI
14 PHI	15 N ATL	16 N ATL	17	18 N NY	19 N NY	20 N NY
21 NY	22	23 N PIT	24 N PIT	25 N STL	26 N STL	27 N STL
28 STL	29 N COL	30 N COL	31 COL			

AUGUST
SUN	MON	TUE	WED	THU	FRI	SAT
				1 N CIN	2 N CIN	3 N CIN
4 CIN	5 N HOU	6 N HOU	7 HOU	8 N CHI	9 N CHI	10 CHI
11 CHI	12 N HOU	13 N HOU	14	15	16 N LA	17 N LA
18 N LA	19 N SD	20 N SD	21 N SD	22 N SF	23 N SF	24 SF
25 SF	26	27 N LA	28 N LA	29 N SD	30 N SD	31 N SD

SEPTEMBER
SUN	MON	TUE	WED	THU	FRI	SAT
1 SD	2 N SF	3 N SF	4 N SF	5 N FLA	6 N FLA	7 FLA
8 FLA	9 N CHI	10 N CHI	11 CHI	12 N FLA	13 N FLA	14 FLA
15 FLA	16	17 N NY	18 N NY	19 N ATL	20 N ATL	21 N ATL
22 ATL	23 N ATL	24 N PHI	25 N PHI	26 N PHI	27 N ATL	28 ATL
29 ATL						

1996 SEASON

CLUB DIRECTORY

President and general partner
Claude R. Brochu

Chairman of the partnership committee
Jacques Menard

Vice chairmen of the partnership comm.
Claude Blanchet
Jocelyn Proteau
Louis A. Tanguay

Vice president, baseball operations
Bill Stoneman

Vice president and general manager
Jim Beattie

Vice president, finance
Laurier M. Carpentier

Director, financial planning & admin.
Michel Bussiere

Director, accounting services
Constance Jodoin

Director, international operations
Fred Ferreira

Director, scouting
Ed Creech

Assistant director, scouting
Gregg Leonard

Director, player development
Bill Geivett

Asst. dir., player development, scouting
Neal Huntington

V.p., marketing and communications
Richard Morency

Vice president, stadium operations
Claude Delorme

Director, promotions
Luigi Carolo

Director, ticket office
Chantal Dalpe

Director, media services
Monique Giroux

Director, media relations
P.J. Loyello

Director, advertising
Johanne Heroux

Director, operations
Pierre Touzin

Director, merchandising and licensing
Susan LeBlanc

Director, group sales
Anne Dion

Director, season ticket sales
Gilles Beauregard

Public relations representative
Ron Piche

Club physician
Dr. Mike Thomassin

Club orthopedist
Dr. Larry Coughlin

Scouts
Carlos Acosta, Julio Acosta, Alex Agostino, Mark Baca, Mike Berger, Dennis Cardoza, Doug Carpenter, Michael Carter, Enrique Constante, Arturo DeFreitas, Luis Dorante, Phil Favia, Jim Fleming, Victor Franco, Dan Freed, Esthelio Gil, Scott Goldby, Freddy Gonzalez, Ton Hofstede, John Hughes, Bob Johnson, Jeff Kahn, Randy Kierce, Leo Lacle, Jimmy Lester, Dave Littlefield, Juan Loyola, Dave Malpass, Dario Marchisio, Willie Marrugo, Roy McMillan, Tomas Morales, Carlos Moreno, Bob Oldis, Rene Picota, Hank Sargent, Mark Shipley, Scott Stanley, Marv Thompson, Pedro Valarezo

MINOR LEAGUE AFFILIATES

Class	Team	League	Manager
AAA	Ottawa	International	Pete Mackanin
AA	Harrisburg	Eastern	Pat Kelly
A	West Palm Beach	Florida State	Rick Sofield
A	Delmarva	South Atlantic	Doug Sisson
A	Vermont	New York-Pennsylvania	To be announced
Rookie	Gulf Coast Expos	Gulf Coast	Jim Gabella

BROADCAST INFORMATION

Radio: CIQC-AM (600); CKAC-AM (73, French language).
TV: CBFT (2, French language).
Cable TV: The Sports Network; RDS (French language).

SPRING TRAINING

Ballpark (city): Municipal Stadium (West Palm Beach, Fla.).
Ticket information: 407-684-6801.

1996 SEASON Montreal Expos

– 113 –

SPRING TRAINING ROSTER

Manager—Felipe Alou (17).
Coaches—Tommy Harper (21), Joe Kerrigan (32), Jerry Manuel (6), Luis Pujols (55), Jim Tracy (23).

No.	PITCHERS	B/T	Ht./Wt.	Born	1995 clubs
48	Alvarez, Tavo	R/R	6-3/235	11-25-71	Harrisburg, Ottawa, Montreal
66	Aucoin, Derek	R/R	6-7/235	3-27-70	DID NOT PLAY
	Cormier, Rheal	L/L	5-10/187	4-23-67	Boston
	Daal, Omar	L/L	6-3/185	3-1-72	Albuquerque, Los Angeles
53	Falteisek, Steve	R/R	6-2/200	1-28-72	Harrisburg, Ottawa
13	Fassero, Jeff	L/L	6-1/195	1-5-63	Montreal
61	Gentile, Scott	R/R	5-10/205	12-21-70	Harrisburg
20	Henderson, Rod	R/R	6-4/193	3-11-71	Harrisburg
45	Martinez, Pedro J.	R/R	5-11/170	7-25-71	Montreal
59	Pacheco, Alex	R/R	6-3/200	7-19-73	Harrisburg, Ottawa
62	Paniagua, Jose	R/R	6-2/185	8-20-73	Harrisburg
33	Perez, Carlos	L/L	6-3/195	1-14-71	Montreal
51	Rojas, Mel	R/R	5-11/195	12-10-66	Montreal
42	Rueter, Kirk	L/L	6-3/195	12-1-70	Montreal, Ottawa
63	Schmidt, Curt	R/R	6-5/200	3-16-70	Montreal, Ottawa
54	Scott, Tim	R/R	6-2/205	11-16-66	Montreal
64	Stull, Everett	R/R	6-3/200	8-24-71	Harrisburg
41	Urbina, Ugueth	R/R	6-2/185	2-15-74	West Palm Beach, Ottawa, Montreal
	Veres, Dave	R/R	6-2/195	10-19-66	Houston
57	Weber, Neil	L/L	6-5/215	12-6-72	Harrisburg
	Witte, Trey	R/R	6-1/190	1-15-70	Port City
58	Yan, Esteban	R/R	6-4/230	6-22-74	Memphis, Rancho Cucamonga

No.	CATCHERS	B/T	Ht./Wt.	Born	1995 clubs
24	Fletcher, Darrin	L/R	6-1/200	10-3-66	Montreal
19	Laker, Tim	R/R	6-3/200	11-27-69	Montreal
2	Spehr, Tim	R/R	6-2/200	7-2-66	Montreal

No.	INFIELDERS	B/T	Ht./Wt.	Born	1995 clubs
56	Alcantara, Israel	R/R	6-2/180	5-6-73	Harrisburg, West Palm Beach
11	Andrews, Shane	R/R	6-1/215	8-28-71	Montreal
30	Floyd, Cliff	L/R	6-4/235	12-5-72	Montreal
4	Grudzielanek, Mark	R/R	6-1/185	6-30-70	Montreal, Ottawa
3	Lansing, Mike	R/R	6-0/185	4-3-68	Montreal
	McGuire, Ryan	L/L	6-1/195	11-23-71	Trenton
	Santangelo, F.P.	B/R	5-10/170	10-24-67	Ottawa, Montreal
25	Segui, David	B/L	6-1/202	7-19-66	New York N.L., Montreal
9	Silvestri, Dave	R/R	6-0/196	9-29-67	New York A.L., Montreal
4	Stankiewicz, Andy	R/R	5-9/165	8-10-64	Houston, Tucson

No.	OUTFIELDERS	B/T	Ht./Wt.	Born	1995 clubs
18	Alou, Moises	R/R	6-3/195	7-3-66	Montreal
15	Benitez, Yamil	R/R	6-2/195	5-10-72	Ottawa, Montreal
20	McDavid, Ray	L/R	6-2/200	7-20-71	Las Vegas, Arizona Padres, San Diego
40	Rodriguez, Henry	L/L	6-1/205	11-8-67	Los Angeles, Montreal, Ottawa
50	Stovall, DaRond	B/L	6-1/185	1-3-73	West Palm Beach
44	Tarasco, Tony	L/R	6-1/205	12-9-70	Montreal
22	White, Rondell	R/R	6-1/205	2-23-72	Montreal

BALLPARK INFORMATION

Ballpark (capacity, surface)
Olympic Stadium (46,500, artificial)

Address
4549 Pierre-de-Coubertin Ave.
Montreal, QC H1V 3N7

Business phone
514-253-3434

Ticket information
800-GO-EXPOS

Ticket prices
$28 (VIP box seats)
$19 (box seats)
$11 (terrace)
$7 (general admission)

Field dimensions (from home plate)
To left field at foul line, 325 feet
To center field, 404 feet
To right field at foul line, 325 feet

First game played
April 15, 1977 (Phillies 7, Expos 2)

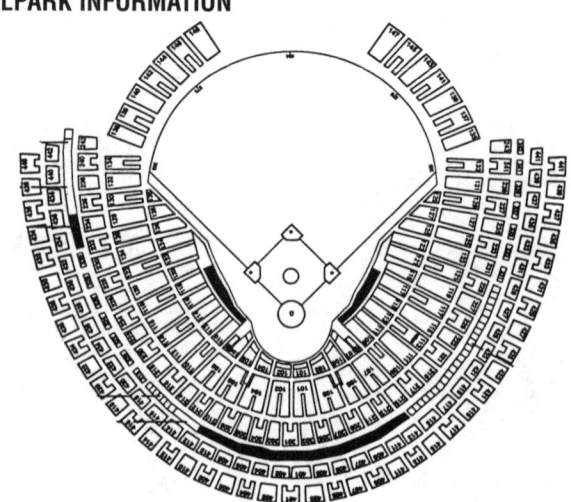

DAY BY DAY

Date	Opp.	Res.	Score	(inn.*)	Hits	Opp. hits	Winning pitcher	Losing pitcher	Save	Record	Pos.	GB
4-26	At Pit.	W	6-2		9	6	Fassero	Lieber		1-0	T1st	...
4-27	At Pit.	W	2-1		6	5	Martinez	Wagner	Rojas	2-0	T1st	...
4-28	At Chi.	L	3-4		7	10	Foster	Henry	Myers	2-1	T1st	...
4-29	At Chi.	L	4-5		8	7	Navarro	Rueter	Myers	2-2	T2nd	1
4-30	At Chi.	W	4-2		10	8	Heredia	Castillo	Rojas	3-2	2nd	1
5-2	N.Y.	W	9-6		14	10	Fassero	Jacome	Rojas	4-2	2nd	1
5-3	N.Y.	W	3-1		8	4	Martinez	Saberhagen	Rojas	5-2	2nd	1
5-4	N.Y.	L	1-5	(10)	7	4	Franco	Shaw		5-3	2nd	2
5-5	Fla.	L	6-11		10	11	Burkett	Heredia	Mathews	5-4	3rd	2
5-6	Fla.	L	3-10		10	12	Weathers	Rueter		5-5	3rd	2
5-7	Fla.	W	9-3		12	9	Fassero	Gardner		6-5	3rd	1½
5-8	Fla.	W	7-5		10	4	Rojas	Perez		7-5	T2nd	1½
5-9	At Phi.	L	3-8		9	15	Quantrill	Henry		7-6	3rd	2½
5-10	At Phi.	L	1-10		4	14	Green	Heredia		7-7	3rd	3½
5-11	At Phi.	W	13-1		16	6	Perez	Mimbs		8-7	T2nd	2½
5-12	At N.Y.	W	9-6		10	13	Fassero	Jacome		9-7	2nd	2½
5-13	At N.Y.	W	6-1		8	7	Martinez	Manzanillo	Aquino	10-7	2nd	2½
5-14	At N.Y.	W	3-2	(13)	9	8	Urbina	DiPoto	Rojas	11-7	2nd	2½
5-15	At N.Y.	L	3-5		5	10	Manzanillo	Shaw	Franco	11-8	2nd	2½
5-16	Cin.	W	7-3		14	7	Perez	Jarvis	Rojas	12-8	2nd	2½
5-17	Cin.	L	2-6		9	10	Rijo	Fassero	Carrasco	12-9	2nd	3½
5-19	At Hou.	L	2-10		5	9	Veres	Martinez		12-10	3rd	3½
5-20	At Hou.	L	1-2	(10)	4	9	Hudek	Shaw		12-11	3rd	4½
5-21	At Hou.	L	2-5		5	8	Swindell	Heredia	Hudek	12-12	3rd	5½
5-22	Fla.	W	5-2		9	3	Perez	Weathers	Rojas	13-12	3rd	5
5-23	S.D.	W	6-4		11	8	Fassero	Ashby	Rojas	14-12	3rd	5
5-24	S.D.	W	3-2		7	11	Shaw	Berumen	Aquino	15-12	3rd	5
5-25	S.D.	L	3-4		4	12	Sanders	Henry	Hoffman	15-13	3rd	5
5-26	L.A.	W	9-4		9	11	Heredia	Martinez	Scott	16-13	3rd	5
5-27	L.A.	W	2-1		5	10	Perez	Valdes	Rojas	17-13	3rd	5
5-28	L.A.	W	5-1		6	7	Fassero	Nomo	Scott	18-13	3rd	4
5-29	S.F.	L	6-11		9	8	Burba	Rojas		18-14	3rd	5
5-30	S.F.	L	3-4	(11)	10	7	Bautista	Shaw	Beck	18-15	3rd	6
5-31	S.F.	W	5-4		9	10	Heredia	Mulholland	Rojas	19-15	3rd	5
6-1	St.L.	W	6-2		11	7	Perez	Watson	Shaw	20-15	3rd	5
6-2	At S.D.	W	7-1		10	3	Fassero	Berumen		21-15	2nd	4
6-3	At S.D.	W	1-0	(10)	5	1	Martinez	B. Williams	Rojas	22-15	2nd	3
6-4	At S.D.	L	4-8		8	13	Sanders	Henry		22-16	2nd	3
6-5	At L.A.	L	1-3		5	8	Martinez	Heredia	Worrell	22-17	2nd	3
6-6	At L.A.	L	1-5		7	12	Valdes	Perez		22-18	3rd	3
6-7	At L.A.	L	1-7		6	12	Nomo	Fassero		22-19	3rd	4
6-9	At S.F.	W	9-3		14	12	Martinez	Leiter	Shaw	23-19	3rd	4
6-10	At S.F.	W	11-5		13	7	Henry	Bautista		24-19	3rd	4
6-11	At S.F.	W	10-8	(13)	20	16	G. White	Mintz		25-19	2nd	4
6-13	Atl.	W	11-2		13	7	Perez	Mercker		26-19	2nd	3
6-14	Atl.	L	3-7		9	11	Smoltz	Fassero		26-20	2nd	3
6-15	Atl.	L	0-2		7	8	Maddux	Martinez		26-21	3rd	4
6-16	At Cin.	W	6-3		14	9	Henry	Smiley		27-21	3rd	3
6-17	At Cin.	L	4-5		7	9	Carrasco	Aquino	Brantley	27-22	3rd	4
6-18	At Cin.	L	7-10		13	11	Jackson	G. White	Brantley	27-23	3rd	5
6-19	Hou.	L	3-6		10	8	Kile	Fassero	Jones	27-24	3rd	6
6-20	Hou.	L	4-7		11	14	Reynolds	Martinez		27-25	3rd	7
6-21	Hou.	L	3-5		9	10	Swindell	Henry	Jones	27-26	3rd	8
6-23	Pit.	L	0-2		2	6	Neagle	Martinez		27-27	3rd	8½
6-24	Pit.	W	5-0		7	6	Perez	Ericks		28-27	3rd	8½
6-25	Pit.	L	0-1		6	7	Loaiza	Fassero	Miceli	28-28	3rd	9½
6-26	At Atl.	L	3-4		9	6	Glavine	Aquino	Wohlers	28-29	3rd	10
6-27	At Atl.	W	3-0		5	4	Henry	Avery	Rojas	29-29	3rd	9
6-28	At Atl.	L	3-4		6	4	Clontz	Rojas		29-30	3rd	9
6-30	At Fla.	L	1-10		6	19	Hammond	Perez		29-31	3rd	9½
7-1	At Fla.	W	11-8		15	14	Fassero	Rapp	Rojas	30-31	3rd	8½
7-2	At Fla.	W	7-6		13	17	Harris	Mathews	Rojas	31-31	3rd	7½
7-3	At St.L.	L	0-6		1	6	Morgan	Henry		31-32	3rd	7½
7-4	At St.L.	W	5-0		10	4	Martinez	Hill		32-32	3rd	7
7-5	At St.L.	L	3-4	(10)	9	10	DeLucia	Rojas		32-33	3rd	8
7-6	At Col.	L	6-9		13	14	Grahe	Fassero	Holmes	32-34	3rd	9
7-7	At Col.	L	7-12		9	16	Acevedo	Heredia		32-35	3rd	10
7-8	At Col.	L	3-8		5	13	Reynoso	Henry	Leskanic	32-36	3rd	11
7-9	At Col.	L	1-4		7	6	Freeman	Martinez		32-37	3rd	12
7-12	Chi.	W	3-2		9	5	Urbina	Castillo	Rojas	33-37	3rd	11
7-13	Phi.	L	3-4		7	11	Schilling	Fassero	Slocumb	33-38	3rd	12

Date	Opp.	Res.	Score	(inn.*)	Hits	Opp. hits	Winning pitcher	Losing pitcher	Save	Record	Pos.	GB
7-14	Phi.	W	8-2		11	6	Martinez	Green		34-38	3rd	12
7-15	Phi.	W	5-3		12	12	Henry	Quantrill	Rojas	35-38	3rd	12
7-16	Phi.	W	5-1		9	7	Perez	Fernandez	Rojas	36-38	3rd	11
7-17	St.L.	L	5-8		9	10	DeLucia	Shaw	Henke	36-39	3rd	11¹/₂
7-18	St.L.	W	5-2		10	7	Fassero	Urbani	Rojas	37-39	3rd	10¹/₂
7-19	Chi.	W	4-3		10	12	Martinez	Bullinger	Shaw	38-39	3rd	10¹/₂
7-20	Chi.	W	4-0		7	7	Henry	Navarro		39-39	3rd	10¹/₂
7-21	At Pit.	L	6-7	(12)	10	9	Gott	Harris		39-40	3rd	10¹/₂
7-22	At Pit.	L	1-7		6	10	Parris	Urbina		39-41	3rd	11¹/₂
7-23	At Pit.	W	8-2		9	6	Fassero	Ericks		40-41	3rd	11¹/₂
7-25	At Chi.	L	5-6		13	4	Navarro	Martinez	Young	40-42	3rd	13
7-26	At Chi.	W	4-2		11	12	Henry	Foster	Rojas	41-42	3rd	12
7-27	St.L.	W	2-1		4	4	Perez	Jackson	Rojas	42-42	3rd	11
7-28	Col.	L	3-8		9	11	Ritz	Urbina		42-43	3rd	12
7-29	Col.	L	3-5		5	13	Rekar	Fassero	Holmes	42-44	3rd	13
7-30	Col.	W	11-4		10	7	Martinez	Freeman		43-44	3rd	12
7-31	Col.	L	2-3		7	10	Reynoso	Henry	Holmes	43-45	3rd	12¹/₂
8-1	Fla.	L	2-5		8	12	Rapp	Perez	Nen	43-46	3rd	12¹/₂
8-2	Fla.	L	6-7	(10)	14	11	Pena	Shaw	Nen	43-47	3rd	13¹/₂
8-4	Atl.	L	3-4		8	5	Maddux	Martinez	Wohlers	43-48	3rd	15
8-5	Atl.	L	6-9		11	17	Glavine	Henry	Wohlers	43-49	3rd	16
8-6	Atl.	W	6-2		6	7	Perez	Avery		44-49	3rd	15
8-7	Atl.	L	1-5		8	11	Mercker	Fassero		44-50	3rd	16
8-8	At Hou.	W	6-0		11	6	Heredia	Reynolds		45-50	3rd	16
8-9	At Hou.	W	6-5		16	12	Martinez	Swindell	Fraser	46-50	3rd	15
8-10	At Hou.	W	6-2		13	7	Henry	Drabek	Leiper	47-50	3rd	15
8-11	At Phi.	L	5-6		8	9	Fernandez	Perez	Slocumb	47-51	3rd	16
8-12	At Phi.	W	4-3		10	8	Fassero	Greene	Leiper	48-51	3rd	15
8-13	At Phi.	W	3-2		11	9	Scott	Bottalico	Rojas	49-51	T2nd	15
8-14	At Phi.	W	5-1		9	8	Martinez	Quantrill		50-51	2nd	15
8-15	At N.Y.	W	3-1		7	3	Scott	Isringhausen	Rojas	51-51	2nd	15
8-16	At N.Y.	L	0-1		6	3	Pulsipher	Perez	Franco	51-52	2nd	15
8-18	S.D.	W	7-3		11	6	Fassero	Dishman	Fraser	52-52	2nd	14
8-19	S.D.	L	5-9		11	17	Hamilton	Heredia		52-53	3rd	14
8-20	S.D.	L	0-3		5	7	Blair	Martinez	Hoffman	52-54	3rd	15
8-21	L.A.	L	2-7		6	11	Valdes	Alvarez		52-55	3rd	16
8-22	L.A.	L	4-7	(11)	9	14	Worrell	Fraser		52-56	3rd	17
8-23	L.A.	L	0-5		5	10	Martinez	Fassero		52-57	3rd	18
8-24	S.F.	L	3-5		7	8	Service	Leiper	Beck	52-58	3rd	18¹/₂
8-25	S.F.	W	12-1		15	3	Martinez	VanLandingham		53-58	3rd	18¹/₂
8-26	S.F.	L	1-2		4	10	Brewington	Alvarez	Beck	53-59	3rd	19¹/₂
8-27	S.F.	W	1-0		4	1	Rueter	Leiter		54-59	3rd	19¹/₂
8-29	At S.D.	W	2-1		7	9	Fassero	Hamilton	Rojas	55-59	3rd	18
8-30	At S.D.	L	2-3		8	13	Hoffman	Harris		55-60	3rd	18
8-31	At S.D.	W	5-4	(10)	10	8	Fraser	Villone	Rojas	56-60	3rd	18
9-1	At L.A.	W	6-5		8	11	Harris	Valdes	Rojas	57-60	3rd	17
9-2	At L.A.	W	9-8		14	14	Rueter	Tapani	Rojas	58-60	3rd	16
9-3	At L.A.	L	3-6		4	9	Martinez	Fassero	Worrell	58-61	3rd	17
9-4	At S.F.	L	1-2		7	4	Barton	Rojas		58-62	3rd	18
9-5	At S.F.	L	6-9		7	12	Bautista	DeLeon	Beck	58-63	3rd	19
9-6	At S.F.	W	8-2		12	2	Alvarez	Leiter		59-63	3rd	19
9-8	N.Y.	L	0-5		3	8	B. Jones	Rueter		59-64	3rd	19¹/₂
9-9	N.Y.	L	5-6		11	12	Byrd	Fassero	Franco	59-65	3rd	20¹/₂
9-10	N.Y.	L	2-6		9	11	Isringhausen	Perez		59-66	3rd	20¹/₂
9-11	N.Y.	W	5-0		13	4	Martinez	Pulsipher		60-66	3rd	19¹/₂
9-12	Phi.	L	2-8		9	13	Williams	Alvarez	Borland	60-67	3rd	19¹/₂
9-13	Phi.	W	5-4		9	11	Heredia	D. Springer	Rojas	61-67	3rd	19¹/₂
9-15	Hou.	L	3-7		10	10	Tabaka	Harris		61-68	3rd	20¹/₂
9-16	Hou.	L	4-7		9	11	Brocail	Perez		61-69	3rd	21¹/₂
9-17	Hou.	L	3-5		7	11	Drabek	Martinez	Henneman	61-70	T3rd	22¹/₂
9-18	At Cin.	L	4-7		9	14	Schourek	Alvarez		61-71	T3rd	23¹/₂
9-19	At Cin.	W	4-1		10	7	Rueter	Wells	Rojas	62-71	T3rd	22¹/₂
9-20	At Cin.	L	2-5		6	9	Portugal	Fassero	Jackson	62-72	4th	22¹/₂
9-22	At Atl.	L	1-5		7	7	Glavine	Perez		62-73	T4th	24
9-23	At Atl.	W	5-2		9	6	Martinez	McMichael	Rojas	63-73	T3rd	23
9-24	At Atl.	L	4-5	(10)	10	7	Borbon	Leiper		63-74	4th	24
9-25	At Fla.	W	9-0		14	3	Rueter	Burkett	Heredia	64-74	T3rd	23¹/₂
9-26	At Fla.	W	5-4		11	11	Fraser	Nen	Rojas	65-74	T3rd	23¹/₂
9-27	At Fla.	L	3-9		5	12	Rapp	G. White		65-75	T4th	24¹/₂
9-28	Cin.	L	7-9		10	8	Schourek	Martinez	Brantley	65-76	5th	25
9-29	Cin.	L	9-14		15	13	Portugal	Alvarez		65-77	5th	25
9-30	Cin.	W	6-1		7	5	Rueter	Wells		66-77	5th	24
10-1	Cin.	L	1-5		4	6	Pugh	Fassero		66-78	5th	24

Monthly records: April (3-2), May (16-13), June (10-16), July (14-14), August (13-15), September (10-17), October (0-1).
*Innings, if other than nine.

HIGHLIGHTS

High point: The Expos climbed into the N.L. wild-card race by winning eight of 10 from August 8-18, including a 7-2 record on a nine-game road trip.

Low point: A 7-6, 10-inning home loss to the Marlins on August 2 came on the same day catcher Tim Spehr learned he had testicular cancer. It also was just a few days after Moises Alou's father-in-law and brother-in-law were murdered in a robbery at the store they ran in Brooklyn.

Turning point: On August 16, Alou ran off the field at Shea Stadium with what the team called an "aggravation of a biceps tendon tear" that turned out to be one of two small shoulder tears. Alou never contributed on a regular basis after that and eventually underwent surgery. That robbed an already thin team of its one true offensive force.

Most valuable player: First baseman David Segui. Segui, who came over in a trade with the Mets for minor league righthander Reid Cornelius, solidified the defense and hit .309 with 12 homers and 68 RBIs.

Most valuable pitcher: Righthander Greg Harris. Harris (2-3, 2.61 ERA) was the team's most consistent reliever.

Most improved player: Center fielder Rondell White. He continued a career path similar to that of former Expo Marquis Grissom. White hit .295 with 13 homers, 57 RBIs and 25 steals.

Most pleasant surprise: Segui. His emergence as an everyday player will allow Cliff Floyd to move to the outfield. It didn't take long for Segui's strong personality to begin exerting itself in the clubhouse, either.

Biggest disappointment: Shortstop Wil Cordero. Cordero, an All-Star in 1994, had so much trouble throwing the ball that he eventually was moved to left field. He went 109 plate appearances between RBIs at one point.

Key injuries: Floyd shattered his left wrist in a collision with Mets catcher Todd Hundley on May 15 and saw only limited duty late in the year. Henry Rodriguez, acquired from the Dodgers as a replacement for Floyd, showed up limping and soon after went on the D.L. with a fractured right tibia. Lefthander Butch Henry is out until after the 1996 All-Star break, and Alou underwent surgery to close small tears in both shoulders.

Notable: On September, Harris became the first pitcher since Elton (Ice Box) Chamberlain in 1888 to pitch ambidextrously. . . . The Expos had eight players with 10 or more home runs for the first time in team history. . . . The Expos were 2-66 when trailing after eight innings.

—JEFF BLAIR

RECORDS

1995 regular-season record: 66-78 (4th in N.L. East); 31-41 at home; 35-37 on road; 26-26 vs. East; 20-27 vs. Central; 20-25 vs. West; 18-19 vs. lefthanded starters; 48-59 vs. righthanded starters; 22-23 on grass; 44-55 on turf; 21-20 in daytime; 45-58 at night; 20-23 in one-run games; 4-8 in extra-inning games; 0-0-0 in doubleheaders.
Team record past five years: 392-351 (.528, ranks 2nd in league in that span).

TEAM LEADERS

Batting average: Rondell White (.295).
At-bats: Wil Cordero (514).
Runs: Rondell White (87).
Hits: Wil Cordero (147).
Total bases: Wil Cordero (216).
Doubles: Wil Cordero (35).
Triples: David Segui, Tony Tarasco, Rondell White (4).
Home runs: Moises Alou, Sean Berry, Tony Tarasco (14).
Runs batted in: Mike Lansing (62).
Stolen bases: Mike Lansing (27).
Slugging percentage: Rondell White (.464).
On-base percentage: David Segui (.367).
Wins: Pedro Martinez (14).
Earned-run average: Pedro Martinez (3.47).
Complete games: Pedro Martinez (2).
Shutouts: Pedro Martinez (2).
Saves: Mel Rojas (30).
Innings pitched: Pedro Martinez (194.2).
Strikeouts: Pedro Martinez (174).

GAMES BY POSITION

Catcher: Darrin Fletcher 98, Tim Laker 61, Tim Spehr 38, Joe Siddall 7.
First base: David Segui 97, Shane Andrews 29, Cliff Floyd 18, Henry Rodriguez 10, Tom Foley 4, Dave Silvestri 4, Sean Berry 3.
Second base: Mike Lansing 127, Mark Grudzielanek 13, Jeff Treadway 11, F.P. Santangelo 5, Tom Foley 3, Dave Silvestri 3, Chad Fonville 2, Lou Frazier 1.
Third base: Sean Berry 83, Shane Andrews 51, Mark Grudzielanek 31, Dave Silvestri 8, Jeff Treadway 1.
Shortstop: Wil Cordero 105, Mark Grudzielanek 34, Dave Silvestri 9, Mike Lansing 2.
Outfield: Rondell White 119, Tony Tarasco 116, Moises Alou 92, Wil Cordero 26, Lou Frazier 25, F.P. Santangelo 25, Roberto Kelly 24, Curtis Pride 24, Yamil Benitez 14, Henry Rodriguez 8, Cliff Floyd 4, Dave Silvestri 3, David Segui 2.

TOP DRAFT CHOICES

1. **Michael Barrett,** SS, Pace Academy, Atlanta.
2. **Henry Mateo,** SS, Santurce, Puerto Rico.
3. **Kenny James,** OF, Sebring (Fla.) H.S.
4. **J.D. Smart,** RHP, University of Texas.
5. **Brian Schneider,** C, Northampton H.S., Cherryville, Pa.
6. **Ronney Daniels,** OF-LHP, Lake Wales (Fla.) H.S.
7. **Peter Fortune,** LHP, Rockland (N.Y.) C.C.
8. **Trey Martin,** RHP, Arcadia H.S., Phoenix.
9. **Bienvenido Sanchez,** RHP, Arecibo, Puerto Rico.
10. **Jeff Austin,** RHP, Kingwood (Tex.) H.S.

NEW YORK METS
NATIONAL LEAGUE EAST DIVISION

1996 METS SCHEDULE

Home games shaded.
* — All-Star Game at Veterans Stadium (Philadelphia)
N — Night game (any game starting after 5 p.m.)

MARCH

SUN	MON	TUE	WED	THU	FRI	SAT
						31

APRIL

SUN	MON	TUE	WED	THU	FRI	SAT
	1 STL	2	3 STL	4 STL	5 N PIT	6 PIT
7 PIT	8 N CIN	9 N CIN	10 N CIN	11 N COL	12 N COL	13 COL
14 N COL	15	16 N CIN	17 HOU	18 HOU	19 N COL	20 COL
21 COL	22 N CIN	23 N CIN	24 N STL	25 STL	26 N PIT	27 N PIT
28 PIT	29 N MON	30 N MON				

MAY

SUN	MON	TUE	WED	THU	FRI	SAT
		1 N MON	2	3 CHI	4 CHI
5 CHI	6 N FLA	7 N FLA	8 N FLA	9	10 N CHI	11 CHI
12 CHI	13 N SD	14 N SD	15 N SD	16 N SD	17 N SF	18 SF
19 SF	20 N LA	21 N LA	22 N LA	23	24 N SD	25 SD
26 SD	27	28 N SF	29 N SF	30 N SF	31 N LA	

JUNE

SUN	MON	TUE	WED	THU	FRI	SAT
						1 LA
2 LA	3 N ATL	4 N ATL	5 N ATL	6	7 N FLA	8 N FLA
9 FLA	10 N ATL	11 N ATL	12 N ATL	13 N STL	14 N STL	15 N STL
16 STL	17 PIT	18 N PIT	19 N PIT	20 N CIN	21 N CIN	22 N CIN
23 N CIN	24 N COL	25 N COL	26 COL	27	28 N HOU	29 N HOU
30 HOU						

JULY

SUN	MON	TUE	WED	THU	FRI	SAT
	1 N PHI	2 N PHI	3 N PHI	4 N MON	5 N MON	6 MON
7 MON	8 * ALL-STAR GAME	9	10	11 N HOU	12 N HOU	13 HOU
14 HOU	15 N PHI	16 N PHI	17 PHI	18 N MON	19 N MON	20 N MON
21 MON	22	23 N COL	24 COL	25	26 N CIN	27 CIN
28 CIN	29 N PIT	30 N PIT	31 N PIT			

AUGUST

SUN	MON	TUE	WED	THU	FRI	SAT
				1 N STL	2 N STL	3 STL
4 STL	5 N CHI	6 CHI	7 CHI	8 N FLA	9 N FLA	10 FLA
11 FLA	12 N CHI	13 N CHI	14 N CHI	15	16 N SD	17 N SD
18 SD	19 N SF	20 N SF	21 SF	22	23 N LA	24 LA
25 LA	26	27 N SD	28 N SD	29 N SD	30 N SF	31 N SF

SEPTEMBER

SUN	MON	TUE	WED	THU	FRI	SAT
1 SF	2 N LA	3 N LA	4 N LA	5	6 N ATL	7 N ATL
8 ATL	9 N FLA	10 N FLA	11 FLA	12	13 N ATL	14 ATL
15 ATL	16 N ATL	17 N MON	18 N MON	19 N PHI	20 N PHI	21 PHI
22 PHI	23	24 N HOU	25 N HOU	26 HOU	27 N PHI	28 PHI
29 PHI	30					

1996 SEASON

CLUB DIRECTORY

Chairman of the board
Nelson Doubleday
President and chief executive officer
Fred Wilpon
Directors
Nelson Doubleday
Fred Wilpon
Saul B. Katz
Joe McIlvaine
Marvin B. Tepper
Special advisor to the board of directors
Richard Cummins
Executive v.p., baseball operations
Joe McIlvaine
Assistant general manager
Steve Phillips
Director of scouting
John Barr
Director of minor league operations
Jack Zduriencik
Asst. dir. minor league & scouting
Jim Duquette
Baseball administrator
Maureen Cooke
Admin. asst., minor leagues
Thomas Hutchison
Senior v.p. and treasurer
Harold W. O'Shaughnessy
V.p. bus. aff., gen. counsel & secretary
David Howard
Vice president, marketing
Mark Bingham
Vice president, stadium operations
Bob Mandt
Vice president, ticket sales and services
Bill Ianniciello
Senior v.p. and consultant
J. Frank Cashen
Vice president, broadcasting
Mike Ryan
Dir., admin. and data processing
Russ Richardson

Director, community outreach
Jill Knee
Community outreach representative
Mookie Wilson
Director of promotions
James Plummer
Director of media relations
Jay Horwitz
Director, ticket operations
Dan DeMato
Manager, customer relations
Joann Galardy
Club physicians
Dr. David Altchek
Dr. David Dines
Club psychologist/E.A.P.
Dr. Allan Lans
Team trainers
Fred Hina
Sam McCrary
Scouts
Paul Baretta
Larry Chase
Carmen Fusco
Dick Gernert
Rob Guzik
Darrell Johnson
Roland Johnson
Buddy Kerr
Dave Lottsfeldt
Joe Mason
Marlin McPhail
Jim Miller
Bob Minor
Harry Minor
Joe Nigro
Carlos Pascual
Jim Reeves
Paul Ricciarini
Junior Roman
Bob Rossi
Eddy Toledo
Terry Tripp
Jim Woodward

MINOR LEAGUE AFFILIATES

Class	Team	League	Manager
AAA	Norfolk	International	Bobby Valentine
AA	Binghamton	Eastern	John Tamargo
A	St. Lucie	Florida State	John Gibbons
A	Capital City	South Atlantic	Howie Freiling
A	Pittsfield	New York-Pennsylvania	To be announced
Rookie	Kingsport	Appalachian	John Stephenson
Rookie	Gulf Coast Mets	Gulf Coast	Rafael Landestoy

BROADCAST INFORMATION

Radio: WFAN-AM (660).
TV: WWOR-TV (Channel 9).
Cable TV: SportsChannel.

SPRING TRAINING

Ballpark (city): St. Lucie County
Stadium (Port St. Lucie, Fla.).
Ticket information: 407-871-2115.

SPRING TRAINING ROSTER

Manager—Dallas Green (46).
Coaches—Mike Cubbage (4), Frank Howard (55), Thomas McCraw (3), Greg Pavlick (52), Steve Swisher (5), Bobby Wine (6).

No.	PITCHERS	B/T	Ht./Wt.	Born	1995 clubs
	Acevedo, Juan	R/R	6-2/195	5-5-70	Colorado, Colorado Springs, Norfolk
43	Byrd, Paul	R/R	6-1/185	12-3-70	Norfolk, New York N.L.
32	Carter, John	R/R	6-1/195	2-16-72	Canton/Akron
47	Cornelius, Reid	R/R	6-0/200	6-2-70	Montreal, Ottawa, Norfolk, New York N.L.
45	DiPoto, Jerry	R/R	6-2/200	5-24-68	New York N.L.
62	Edmondson, Brian	R/R	6-2/185	1-29-73	Binghamton
31	Franco, John	L/L	5-10/185	9-17-60	New York N.L.
27	Harnisch, Pete	R/R	6-0/207	9-23-66	New York N.L.
35	Henry, Doug	R/R	6-4/205	12-10-63	New York N.L.
44	Isringhausen, Jason	R/R	6-3/195	9-7-72	Binghamton, Norfolk, New York N.L.
28	Jones, Bobby	R/R	6-4/225	2-10-70	New York N.L.
61	Ludwick, Eric	R/R	6-5/210	12-14-71	Binghamton, Norfolk
48	Martinez, Pedro A.	R/L	6-2/185	11-29-68	Houston, Tucson
34	Minor, Blas	R/R	6-3/203	3-20-66	New York N.L.
38	Mlicki, Dave	R/R	6-4/190	6-8-68	New York N.L.
40	Nabholz, Chris	L/L	6-5/217	1-5-67	Iowa, Chicago N.L.
29	Person, Robert	R/R	5-11/180	10-6-69	Binghamton, Norfolk, New York N.L.
21	Pulsipher, Bill	L/L	6-3/200	10-9-73	Norfolk, New York N.L.
65	Ramirez, Hector	R/R	6-3/218	12-15-71	Binghamton
64	Rogers, Bryan	R/R	5-11/170	10-30-67	DID NOT PLAY
49	Walker, Pete	R/R	6-2/195	4-8-69	Norfolk, New York N.L.
63	Wallace, Derek	R/R	6-3/185	9-1-71	Wichita, Binghamton

No.	CATCHERS	B/T	Ht./Wt.	Born	1995 clubs
30	Castillo, Alberto	R/R	6-0/184	2-10-70	Norfolk, New York N.L.
66	Greene, Charlie	R/R	6-1/177	1-23-71	Binghamton, Norfolk
9	Hundley, Todd	B/R	5-11/185	5-27-69	New York N.L.
33	Stinnett, Kelly	R/R	5-11/195	2-14-70	New York N.L.

No.	INFIELDERS	B/T	Ht./Wt.	Born	1995 clubs
13	Alfonzo, Ed	R/R	5-11/187	8-11-73	New York N.L.
23	Bogar, Tim	R/R	6-2/198	10-28-66	New York N.L.
26	Brogna, Rico	L/L	6-2/200	4-18-70	New York N.L.
42	Huskey, Butch	R/R	6-3/244	11-10-71	Norfolk, New York N.L.
12	Kent, Jeff	R/R	6-1/185	3-7-68	New York N.L.
11	Ledesma, Aaron	R/R	6-2/200	6-3-71	Norfolk, New York N.L.
15	Vizcaino, Jose	B/R	6-1/180	3-26-68	New York N.L.

No.	OUTFIELDERS	B/T	Ht./Wt.	Born	1995 clubs
2	Buford, Damon	R/R	5-10/170	6-12-70	Baltimore, Rochester, New York N.L.
3	Everett, Carl	B/R	6-0/190	6-3-71	New York N.L., Norfolk
1	Johnson, Lance	L/L	5-11/160	7-6-63	Chicago A.L.
8	Jones, Chris	R/R	6-2/205	12-16-65	Norfolk, New York N.L.
22	Ochoa, Alex	R/R	6-0/185	3-29-72	Rochester, Norfolk, New York N.L.
20	Thompson, Ryan	R/R	6-3/215	11-4-67	Norfolk, New York N.L., Binghamton

BALLPARK INFORMATION

Ballpark (capacity, surface)
Shea Stadium (55,601, grass)

Address
Roosevelt Ave. and 126th St.
Flushing, NY 11368

Business phone
718-507-6387

Ticket information
718-507-8499

Ticket prices
$15 (box)
$12 (upper level box)
$12 (loge and mezzanine reserved)
$6.50 (back rows, loge & mezzanine reserved)
$6.50 (upper level reserved)
$1 (senior citizens)

Field dimensions (from home plate)
To left field at foul line, 338 feet
To center field, 410 feet
To right field at foul line, 338 feet

First game played
April 17, 1964 (Pirates 4, Mets 3)

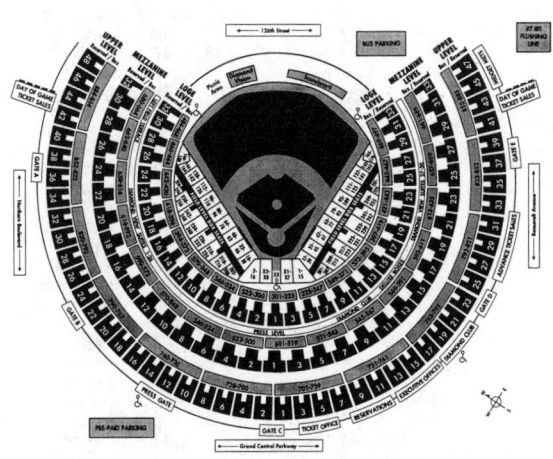

DAY BY DAY

Date	Opp.	Res.	Score	(inn.*)	Hits	Opp. hits	Winning pitcher	Losing pitcher	Save	Record	Pos.	GB
4-26	At Col.	L	9-11	(14)	18	15	Thompson	Remlinger		0-1	T3rd	1
4-27	At Col.	L	7-8		10	13	Reed	Lomon		0-2	T4th	2
4-28	St.L.	W	10-8		11	14	Minor	Arocha	Franco	1-2	4th	1
4-29	St.L.	W	5-4	(11)	10	8	Mlicki	Palacios		2-2	T2nd	1
4-30	St.L.	L	0-3		4	11	Urbani	B. Jones	Henke	2-3	4th	2
5-2	At Mon.	L	6-9		10	14	Fassero	Jacome	Rojas	2-4	4th	3
5-3	At Mon.	L	1-3		4	8	Martinez	Saberhagen	Rojas	2-5	4th	4
5-4	At Mon.	W	5-1	(10)	4	7	Franco	Shaw		3-5	4th	4
5-5	At Cin.	W	3-0		7	5	B. Jones	Schourek	Franco	4-5	4th	3
5-6	At Cin.	L	11-13		14	15	Hernandez	Henry		4-6	4th	3
5-7	At Cin.	L	4-8		11	11	Rijo	Jacome		4-7	4th	3½
5-9	Atl.	L	2-3		8	5	McMichael	Manzanillo	Clontz	4-8	4th	5
5-10	Atl.	W	5-2		7	7	Henry	Wohlers	Franco	5-8	4th	5
5-11	Atl.	W	5-3		13	8	B. Jones	Smoltz	Franco	6-8	4th	4
5-12	Mon.	L	6-9		13	10	Fassero	Jacome		6-9	4th	5
5-13	Mon.	L	1-6		7	8	Martinez	Manzanillo	Aquino	6-10	4th	6
5-14	Mon.	L	2-3	(13)	8	9	Urbina	DiPoto	Rojas	6-11	4th	7
5-15	Mon.	W	5-3		10	5	Manzanillo	Shaw	Franco	7-11	4th	6
5-16	At Hou.	W	1-0		6	3	B. Jones	Reynolds	Henry	8-11	4th	6
5-17	At Hou.	L	2-7		8	14	Swindell	Jacome		8-12	4th	7
5-18	At Hou.	W	8-1		10	6	Mlicki	Drabek		9-12	4th	6½
5-19	At Phi.	W	5-1		9	8	Gunderson	Quantrill		10-12	4th	5½
5-20	At Phi.	L	8-10		14	14	Green	Harnisch	Slocumb	10-13	4th	6½
5-21	At Phi.	L	3-5		8	10	Mimbs	B. Jones	Slocumb	10-14	4th	7½
5-23	L.A.	L	4-6		9	10	Daal	Henry	Worrell	10-15	4th	8½
5-24	L.A.	L	0-5		6	10	Astacio	Birkbeck		10-16	4th	9½
5-25	L.A.	L	0-3		5	11	Candiotti	Harnisch		10-17	4th	9½
5-26	S.F.	L	4-6		13	11	Dewey	Henry	Beck	10-18	4th	10½
5-27	S.F.	W	6-3		10	7	Saberhagen	Bautista		11-18	4th	10½
5-28	S.F.	L	1-5		7	10	Portugal	Mlicki		11-19	4th	10½
5-29	S.D.	L	2-3	(13)	8	14	Blair	Minor	Hoffman	11-20	4th	11½
5-30	S.D.	W	8-0		7	4	Harnisch	Sanders		12-20	4th	11½
5-31	S.D.	W	7-5	(10)	12	11	Franco	Hoffman		13-20	4th	10½
6-2	At L.A.	L	1-2		2	7	Nomo	Saberhagen	Worrell	13-21	4th	11
6-3	At L.A.	W	5-3		9	7	Mlicki	Astacio	Franco	14-21	4th	10
6-4	At L.A.	L	3-5		9	6	F. Rodriguez	DiPoto	Worrell	14-22	4th	10
6-5	At S.F.	W	7-2		11	11	B. Jones	Mulholland		15-22	4th	9
6-6	At S.F.	L	1-2		6	8	Hook	Franco		15-23	4th	9
6-7	At S.F.	L	8-9		12	12	Burba	Minor	Beck	15-24	4th	10
6-8	At S.F.	W	9-6		14	10	Mlicki	Wilson	Henry	16-24	4th	9½
6-9	At S.D.	L	4-8		6	11	Hamilton	Harnisch	Hoffman	16-25	4th	10½
6-10	At S.D.	L	2-4		4	6	Sanders	B. Jones		16-26	4th	11½
6-11	At S.D.	L	3-6		7	7	B. Williams	DiPoto		16-27	4th	12½
6-13	Fla.	W	7-3		13	8	Saberhagen	Burkett		17-27	4th	11½
6-14	Fla.	L	0-4		7	7	Hammond	Mlicki		17-28	4th	11½
6-15	Fla.	W	5-4	(10)	13	10	Minor	Veres		18-28	4th	11½
6-16	Hou.	L	5-7	(16)	13	17	Dougherty	Gunderson	Brocail	18-29	4th	11½
6-17	Hou.	L	3-7		10	10	Drabek	Pulsipher		18-30	4th	12½
6-18	Hou.	W	10-4		13	9	Saberhagen	Hampton		19-30	4th	12½
6-19	Phi.	L	3-6		7	10	Quantrill	Mlicki	Slocumb	19-31	4th	13½
6-20	Phi.	L	2-8		8	12	Green	Harnisch		19-32	4th	14½
6-21	Phi.	L	2-6		7	10	West	B. Jones	Bottalico	19-33	4th	15½
6-22	Phi.	L	2-8		10	19	Mimbs	Pulsipher		19-34	4th	16½
6-23	At Atl.	L	9-3		11	6	Saberhagen	Mercker		20-34	4th	15½
6-24	At Atl.	L	4-5		10	9	Smoltz	Mlicki	Wohlers	20-35	4th	16½
6-25	At Atl.	L	2-4		13	10	Maddux	Harnisch	Wohlers	20-36	T4th	17½
6-26	At Fla.	L	4-9		7	14	Rapp	B. Jones		20-37	5th	18
6-27	At Fla.	W	2-0		7	3	Pulsipher	Murphy	Franco	21-37	T4th	17
6-28	At Fla.	W	8-3		11	10	Saberhagen	Burkett		22-37	4th	16
6-30	Cin.	W	7-6		11	10	Minor	McElroy	Franco	23-37	4th	15½
7-1	Cin.	L	4-5		9	9	Pugh	Harnisch	Brantley	23-38	4th	15½
7-2	Cin.	L	1-4		8	11	Smiley	B. Jones	Brantley	23-39	4th	15½
7-3	Chi.	L	2-4		6	7	Navarro	Pulsipher	Myers	23-40	T4th	15½
7-4	Chi.	L	0-3		8	7	Foster	Saberhagen	Myers	23-41	5th	16
7-5	Chi.	W	5-4		8	8	Franco	Hickerson		24-41	T4th	16
7-6	Chi.	L	4-8		8	14	Trachsel	Harnisch	Walker	24-42	T4th	17
7-7	At Pit.	W	9-8		18	12	DiPoto	Miceli	Franco	25-42	4th	17
7-8	At Pit.	L	2-3		5	8	Ericks	Pulsipher		25-43	4th	18
7-9	At Pit.	L	3-6		5	10	Loaiza	Saberhagen		25-44	T4th	19
7-13	Col.	W	4-2		9	4	B. Jones	Ritz	Franco	26-44	T4th	18½
7-14	Col.	W	13-4		20	9	Pulsipher	Reynoso		27-44	4th	18½

Date	Opp.	Res.	Score	(inn.*)	Hits	Opp. hits	Winning pitcher	Losing pitcher	Save	Record	Pos.	GB
7-15	Col.	L	4-5		13	12	Swift	Saberhagen	Holmes	27-45	4th	19$^{1}/_{2}$
7-16	Col.	W	2-1	(10)	7	9	Franco	Thompson		28-45	4th	18$^{1}/_{2}$
7-17	At Chi.	W	7-2		11	3	DiPoto	Walker		29-45	4th	18
7-18	At Chi.	W	12-3		17	7	B. Jones	Trachsel		30-45	4th	17
7-19	At St.L.	W	5-4	(10)	13	8	DiPoto	DeLucia	Franco	31-45	4th	17
7-20	At St.L.	L	6-8		12	8	Watson	Mlicki	Henke	31-46	4th	18
7-21	At Col.	W	12-1		18	9	Harnisch	Reynoso		32-46	4th	17
7-22	At Col.	L	4-5		10	9	Leskanic	Henry	Holmes	32-47	4th	18
7-23	At Col.	L	5-8		11	9	Ritz	B. Jones	Holmes	32-48	4th	19
7-24	At Chi.	L	3-5		9	6	Bullinger	Pulsipher	Myers	32-49	4th	20
7-25	At St.L.	L	7-8	(11)	14	10	Petkovsek	DiPoto		32-50	T4th	21
7-26	At St.L.	L	2-3	(11)	9	8	Fossas	Henry		32-51	5th	21
7-28	Pit.	L	9-10		13	16	Gott	Franco		32-52	5th	21$^{1}/_{2}$
7-29	Pit.	W	2-1		10	5	Franco	Powell		33-52	5th	21$^{1}/_{2}$
7-30	Pit.	W	2-1		6	6	Isringhausen	Wagner	Franco	34-52	5th	20$^{1}/_{2}$
7-31	Pit.	W	4-1		9	9	Pulsipher	Parris		35-52	5th	20
8-1	At Cin.	L	3-4		6	6	Schourek	Harnisch	Brantley	35-53	5th	20
8-2	At Cin.	L	2-6		10	11	Wells	B. Jones		35-54	5th	21
8-3	At Cin.	L	2-3		6	6	McElroy	Cornelius	Brantley	35-55	5th	22
8-4	Fla.	L	2-7		10	12	Burkett	Isringhausen		35-56	5th	23
8-5	Fla.	L	3-6		9	8	Veres	Pulsipher	Nen	35-57	5th	24
8-6	Fla.	W	7-3		8	5	B. Jones	Rapp		36-57	5th	23
8-7	Fla.	W	5-2		10	7	Mlicki	Mathews	Franco	37-57	5th	23
8-8	At Phi.	W	12-10		17	15	Cornelius	Green	Franco	38-57	5th	23
8-9	At Phi.	W	4-0		10	6	Isringhausen	Quantrill		39-57	5th	22
8-10	At Phi.	W	5-1	(11)	10	4	Florence	Slocumb		40-57	5th	22
8-11	At Hou.	W	7-5		10	11	Henry	Jones	Franco	41-57	5th	22
8-12	At Hou.	L	1-3		6	8	Hampton	Mlicki	Henneman	41-58	5th	22
8-13	At Hou.	L	3-5		6	7	Reynolds	Cornelius	Henneman	41-59	5th	23
8-15	Mon.	L	1-3		3	7	Scott	Isringhausen	Rojas	41-60	5th	24$^{1}/_{2}$
8-16	Mon.	W	1-0		3	6	Pulsipher	Perez	Franco	42-60	5th	23$^{1}/_{2}$
8-18	L.A.	W	3-2		6	8	Henry	Cummings		43-60	5th	22$^{1}/_{2}$
8-19	L.A.	W	2-1		3	6	Mlicki	Candiotti	Franco	44-60	5th	21$^{1}/_{2}$
8-20	L.A.	W	5-3		7	9	Isringhausen	Nomo	Franco	45-60	5th	21$^{1}/_{2}$
8-21	S.F.	W	5-4	(11)	10	7	Byrd	Beck		46-60	5th	21$^{1}/_{2}$
8-22	S.F.	L	1-5		4	10	Leiter	Cornelius		46-61	5th	22$^{1}/_{2}$
8-23	S.F.	L	2-3		4	9	Mulholland	Telgheder		46-62	5th	23$^{1}/_{2}$
8-24	S.D.	W	5-4		8	9	Florence	Hoffman		47-62	5th	23
8-25	S.D.	W	10-5		14	7	Isringhausen	Blair	Minor	48-62	5th	23
8-26	S.D.	W	7-6		12	11	Pulsipher	Ashby	Franco	49-62	5th	23
8-27	S.D.	L	1-4		6	7	Valenzuela	Cornelius	Villone	49-63	5th	24
8-29	At L.A.	W	4-3		7	6	DiPoto	Worrell	Franco	50-63	5th	22$^{1}/_{2}$
8-30	At L.A.	W	8-1		11	11	Mlicki	Candiotti	Henry	51-63	5th	21$^{1}/_{2}$
8-31	At L.A.	L	5-6		7	13	Worrell	DiPoto		51-64	5th	22$^{1}/_{2}$
9-1	At S.F.	L	5-6		10	9	Barton	Franco		51-65	5th	22$^{1}/_{2}$
9-2	At S.F.	L	3-5		4	8	S. Valdez	Cornelius		51-66	5th	22$^{1}/_{2}$
9-3	At S.F.	W	11-6		16	11	Florence	C. Valdez	DiPoto	52-66	5th	22$^{1}/_{2}$
9-4	At S.D.	L	1-2	(10)	7	9	Hoffman	Henry		52-67	5th	23$^{1}/_{2}$
9-5	At S.D.	W	4-0		5	7	Isringhausen	Ashby	Franco	53-67	5th	23$^{1}/_{2}$
9-6	At S.D.	L	5-6		11	11	Bochtler	DiPoto		53-68	5th	24$^{1}/_{2}$
9-8	At Mon.	W	5-0		8	3	B. Jones	Rueter		54-68	5th	24
9-9	At Mon.	W	6-5		12	11	Byrd	Fassero	Franco	55-68	5th	24
9-10	At Mon.	W	6-2		11	9	Isringhausen	Perez		56-68	5th	23
9-11	At Mon.	L	0-5		4	13	Martinez	Pulsipher		56-69	5th	23
9-12	Hou.	L	6-8		11	12	Wall	Cornelius	Henneman	56-70	5th	23
9-13	Hou.	W	10-5		14	10	B. Jones	Hampton		57-70	5th	23
9-14	Hou.	W	4-2		9	6	Mlicki	Reynolds	Franco	58-70	5th	22$^{1}/_{2}$
9-15	Phi.	W	4-1		9	15	Isringhausen	Mimbs	Franco	59-70	4th	22$^{1}/_{2}$
9-16	Phi.	W	10-8		11	11	Telgheder	Greene	Franco	60-70	4th	22$^{1}/_{2}$
9-17	Phi.	W	8-2		12	9	Cornelius	Williams	DiPoto	61-70	T3rd	22$^{1}/_{2}$
9-18	At Atl.	L	1-7		4	9	Avery	B. Jones		61-71	T3rd	23$^{1}/_{2}$
9-19	At Atl.	W	10-3		13	11	Mlicki	Schmidt		62-71	T3rd	22$^{1}/_{2}$
9-20	At Atl.	W	8-4		11	9	Isringhausen	Smoltz	Franco	63-71	3rd	21$^{1}/_{2}$
9-21	At Atl.	L	0-3		5	6	Maddux	Telgheder	Wohlers	63-72	3rd	22$^{1}/_{2}$
9-22	At Fla.	L	0-3	(8)	4	5	Rapp	Cornelius		63-73	3rd	23$^{1}/_{2}$
9-23	At Fla.	L	3-4		10	9	Hammond	B. Jones	Nen	63-74	5th	23$^{1}/_{2}$
9-24	At Fla.	L	3-4		8	10	Bowen	Mlicki	Nen	63-75	5th	24$^{1}/_{2}$
9-25	Cin.	W	2-1	(6)	5	6	Isringhausen	Pugh		64-75	5th	24
9-27†	Cin.	W	5-4		13	8	Person	Smiley	Franco	65-75	T4th	24$^{1}/_{2}$
9-27‡	Cin.	W	9-2		9	5	Cornelius	Burba	Henry	66-75	3rd	24
9-29	Atl.	W	6-3		10	8	B. Jones	Glavine	Franco	67-75	3rd	23
9-30	Atl.	W	8-4		11	11	Minor	Schmidt	Franco	68-75	3rd	22
10-1	Atl.	W	1-0	(11)	5	5	Walker	Wade		69-75	T2nd	21

Monthly records: April (2-3), May (11-17), June (10-17), July (12-15), August (16-12), September (17-11), October (1-0).
*Innings, if other than nine. †First game of doubleheader. ‡Second game of doubleheader.

HIGHLIGHTS

High point: The Mets swept a three-game series from the Braves to complete their season. The sweep, by itself, was relatively insignificant. But it allowed the Mets to finish in a tie for second with the Phillies—albeit 21 games out.

Low point: Back-to-back losses in Pittsburgh in the two games preceding the All-Star break dropped the Mets into last place, 19 games below .500. The Mets were beaten in those two games by John Ericks (his only complete game in 18 major league starts) and Esteban Loaiza (his only complete game in 31 starts).

Turning point: Five consecutive losses followed the July 31 trade of Bret Saberhagen and dropped the Mets 23 1/2 games out of first. Beginning the next afternoon, the Mets won 34 of 52 (.654) and filled themselves with hope and anticipation.

Most valuable player: First baseman Rico Brogna. Had injury not struck catcher Todd Hundley, he might have been the MVP. But Brogna was there throughout with his excellent defense and lefthanded power (22 homers and 76 RBIs).

Most valuable pitcher: Reliever John Franco. Franco was there all year. Jason Isringhausen's impact didn't begin until after the All-Star break. Franco had 22 saves and three victories in his last 32 appearances.

Most improved player: Hundley. He was in the midst of a signature season when he injured his left wrist. Still, he finished with 15 homers, 51 RBIs and a .280 average in 275 at-bats. And his catching, throwing and pitch-calling improved.

Most pleasant surprise: Outfielder Carl Everett. Hitting .320 with 19 runs and 22 RBIs in his last 26 games made Everett, in the club's eyes, the only outfielder who secured some degree of job security for the '96 season.

Biggest disappointment: Outfielder Ryan Thompson. He finished with 267 at-bats and had seven homers and 31 RBIs; he also showed he still doesn't know what to expect from a pitcher in given situations.

Key injuries: Pete Harnisch was lost to significant shoulder surgery after 18 starts (2-8, 3.68). Hundley was assigned to the disabled list from July 23 to September 1

because of a sprained left wrist. And a herniated disk interrupted the fine work of rookie third baseman Edgardo Alfonzo.

Notable: The Mets' record (44-31) after the All-Star break was the second-best in the league. . . . Isringhausen won seven consecutive starts and pitched seven scoreless innings in the eighth (a no-decision). . . . The Mets batted .267, one point lower than the franchise best (1987). . . . The pitching staff, particularly the bullpen, reversed itself after a dreadful start and finished with the third-lowest ERA (3.88) in the league.

—MARTY NOBLE

RECORDS

1995 regular-season record: 69-75 (4th in N.L. East); 40-32 at home; 29-43 on road; 27-25 vs. East; 21-24 vs. Central; 21-26 vs. West; 21-24 vs. lefthanded starters; 48-51 vs. righthanded starters; 52-54 on grass; 14-18 on turf; 17-23 in daytime; 52-52 at night; 21-24 in one-run games; 9-7 in extra-inning games; 1-0-0 in doubleheaders. Longest winning streak: 6, twice (August 6-August 11; September 25-October 1); Longest losing streak: 6, twice (May 20-May 26; July 22-July 28).

Team record past five years: 332-410 (.447, ranks 13th in league in that span).

TEAM LEADERS

Batting average: Rico Brogna (.289).
At-bats: Jose Vizcaino (509).
Runs: Rico Brogna (72).
Hits: Jose Vizcaino (146).
Total bases: Rico Brogna (240).
Doubles: Rico Brogna (27).
Triples: Ed Alfonzo, Jose Vizcaino (5).
Home runs: Rico Brogna (22).
Runs batted in: Rico Brogna (76).
Stolen bases: Jose Vizcaino (8).
Slugging percentage: Rico Brogna (.485).
On-base percentage: Rico Brogna (.342).
Wins: Bobby Jones (10).
Earned-run average: Bobby Jones (4.19).
Complete games: Bobby Jones, Bret Saberhagen (3).
Shutouts: Bobby Jones (1).
Saves: John Franco (29).
Innings pitched: Bobby Jones (195.2).
Strikeouts: Bobby Jones (127).

GAMES BY POSITION

Catcher: Todd Hundley 89, Kelly Stinnett 67, Alberto Castillo 12.
First base: Rico Brogna 131, Tim Bogar 10, Bobby Bonilla 10, David Segui 7, Chris Jones 5, Aaron Ledesma 2, Joe Orsulak 1.
Second base: Jeff Kent 122, Ed Alfonzo 29, Tim Bogar 7, Bill Spiers 6, Jose Vizcaino 1.
Third base: Ed Alfonzo 58, Bobby Bonilla 46, Butch Huskey 27, Tim Bogar 25, Bill Spiers 11, Aaron Ledesma 10.
Shortstop: Jose Vizcaino 134, Tim Bogar 27, Ed Alfonzo 6, Aaron Ledesma 1.
Outfield: Brett Butler 90, Joe Orsulak 86, Carl Everett 77, Ryan Thompson 74, Chris Jones 52, Damon Buford 39, Bobby Bonilla 31, Ricky Otero 23, David Segui 18, Alex Ochoa 10, Jeff Barry 2, Tim Bogar 1, Butch Huskey 1.

TOP DRAFT CHOICES

1. **Ryan Jaroncyk,** SS, Orange Glen H.S., Escondido, Calif.
2. **Brett Herbison,** RHP-SS, Central H.S., Burlington, Ill.
3. **Ryan Bowers,** C, Pineview H.S., St. George, Utah.
4. **Corey Erickson,** SS, Lanphier H.S., Springfield, Ill.
5. **Jeff Parsons,** SS, University of Arkansas.
6. **Todd Cutchins,** LHP, Tallahassee (Fla.) C.C.
7. **Ryan Minor,** 1B-RHP, University of Oklahoma.
8. **Allan Burnett,** RHP, Central Arkansas Christian H.S., North Little Rock, Ark.
9. **Tydus Meadows,** OF, Evans (Ga.) H.S.
10. **Dan Murray,** RHP, San Diego State University.

PHILADELPHIA PHILLIES
NATIONAL LEAGUE EAST DIVISION

1996 PHILLIES SCHEDULE

Home games shaded.

* — All-Star Game at Veterans Stadium (Philadelphia)
N — Night game (any game starting after 5 p.m.)

MARCH

SUN	MON	TUE	WED	THU	FRI	SAT
31						

APRIL

SUN	MON	TUE	WED	THU	FRI	SAT
	1 COL	2	3 N COL	4 N COL	5 N CIN	6 N CIN
7 CIN	8 N PIT	9	10 PIT	11 N STL	12 N STL	13 STL
14 STL	15 N MON	16 N MON	17 N MON	18 N STL	19 N STL	20 STL
21 STL	22 N PIT	23 PIT	24 N COL	25 COL	26 N CIN	27 CIN
28 CIN	29	30 N FLA				

MAY

SUN	MON	TUE	WED	THU	FRI	SAT
		1 N FLA	2 N FLA	3 N ATL	4 N ATL
5 ATL	6 N HOU	7 N HOU	8 N HOU	9	10 N ATL	11 N ATL
12 ATL	13 N SF	14 N SF	15 SF	16 N LA	17 N LA	18 LA
19 LA	20	21 N SD	22 N SD	23 N SD	24 N SF	25 SF
26 SF	27	28 N LA	29 N LA	30 N LA	31 N SD	

JUNE

SUN	MON	TUE	WED	THU	FRI	SAT
						1 N SD
2 SD	3 N CHI	4	5 CHI	6 CHI	7 N HOU	8 HOU
9 HOU	10 N CHI	11 N CHI	12 CHI	13 N COL	14 N COL	15 COL
16 COL	17 N STL	18 STL	19	20 N COL	21 N COL	22 COL
23 COL	24 N CIN	25 N CIN	26 N CIN	27	28 N MON	29 N MON
30 MON						

JULY

SUN	MON	TUE	WED	THU	FRI	SAT
	1 N NY	2 N NY	3 N NY	4 N FLA	5 N FLA	6 N FLA
7 FLA	8 N NY	9 *	10 N MON	11 N MON	12 N MON
14 MON	15 N NY	16 N NY	17 N NY	18 N FLA	19 N FLA	20 FLA
21 FLA	22 N CIN	23 N CIN	24 CIN	25 N PIT	26 N PIT	27 PIT
28 N PIT	29	30 N STL	31 N STL			

AUGUST

SUN	MON	TUE	WED	THU	FRI	SAT
				1 N STL	2 N PIT	3 PIT
4 PIT	5 N PIT	6 N ATL	7 N ATL	8 N ATL	9 N HOU	10 HOU
11 HOU	12 N ATL	13 N ATL	14 N ATL	15 N ATL	16 N SF	17 SF
18 SF	19 N LA	20 N LA	21 N LA	22 N LA	23 N SD	24 SD
25 SD	26 SF	27 SF	28 N SF	29	30 N LA	31 LA

SEPTEMBER

SUN	MON	TUE	WED	THU	FRI	SAT
1 N LA	2 N SD	3 N SD	4 N SD	5 N CHI	6 N CHI	7 CHI
8 CHI	9	10 N HOU	11 N HOU	12 HOU	13 N CHI	14 CHI
15 N CHI	16	17 N FLA	18 N FLA	19 N FLA	20 N NY	21 NY
22 NY	23	24 N MON	25 N MON	26 N MON	27 N NY	28 NY
29 30 NY						

1996 SEASON Philadelphia Phillies

1996 SEASON

CLUB DIRECTORY

President/CEO/general partner
Bill Giles

Partners
Claire S. Betz
Estate of John Drew Betz
Tri-Play Associates (Alexander K. Buck, J. Mahlon Buck Jr., William C. Buck)
Double Play, Inc. (Herbert H. Middleton Jr.)
Fitz Eugene Dixon Jr.
Mrs. Rochelle Levy

Executive vice president and CEO
David Montgomery

Executive secretary
Nancy Nolan

Secretary and general counsel
William Y. Webb

Director, planning/development
Tom Hudson

Director, business development
Joseph W. Giles

Sr. vice president, general manager
Lee Thomas

Player personnel administrator
Ed Wade

Director, player development
Del Unser

Director, scouting
Mike Arbuckle

Assistant to the president
Paul Owens

Traveling secretary
Eddie Ferenz

Senior vice president, finance and planning
Jerry Clothier

Vice president, public relations
Larry Shenk

Broadcaster/director speakers' bureau
Chris Wheeler

Director, community relations
Regina Castellani

Administrator, public relations
Karen Nocella

Manager, media relations
Gene Dias

Manager, publicity
Leigh Tobin

Vice president, marketing
Dennis Mannion

Manager, advertising and broadcasting
Jo-Ann Levy-Lamoreaux

V.p., ticket sales and operations
Richard Deats

Director, ticket department
Dan Goroff

Director, stadium operations
Mike DiMuzio

Club physician
Dr. Phillip Marone

Club trainers
Jeff Cooper
Mark Anderson

National supervisor
Mark Wolever

Regional supervisor, scouts
Dick Lawlor

Spec. assignment, major league scouts
Ray Shore
Jimmy Stewart

Advance scout, major leagues
Hank King

Special assignment scouts
Bing Devine
Larry Rojas

Regular supervisor, scouts
Sonny Bowers
Dean Jongewood

Minor league and scouting
Maryann Skedzielewski

Regular scouts
Sal Agostinelli, Emil Belich, Tom Ferguson, Jim Fregosi Jr., Jose Gomez, Eli Grba, Bill Harper, Ken Hultzapple, John Kennedy, Jerry Lafferty, George Lauzerique, Jose Leiva, Terry Logan, Fred Mazuca, Lloyd Merritt, Willie Montanez, Arthur Parrack, Bob Poole, David Sirak, Mitch Sokel, Roy Tanner, Scott Trcka

MINOR LEAGUE AFFILIATES

Class	Team	League	Manager
AAA	Scranton/Wilkes-Barre	International	Butch Hobson
AA	Reading	Eastern	Bill Robinson
A	Clearwater	Florida State	Al LeBoeuf
A	Piedmont	South Atlantic	Roy Majtyka
A	Batavia	New York-Pennsylvania	Floyd Rayford
Rookie	Martinsville	Appalachian	Ramon Henderson

BROADCAST INFORMATION

Radio: WGMP-AM (1210).
TV: WPHL-TV (Channel 17).
Cable TV: To be announced.

SPRING TRAINING

Ballpark (city): Jack Russell Stadium (Clearwater, Fla.).
Ticket information: 215-463-1000, 813-442-8496.

SPRING TRAINING ROSTER

Manager—Jim Fregosi (11).
Coaches—Larry Bowa (2), Dave Cash (30), Denis Menke (14), Johnny Podres (46), John Vukovich (18).

No.	PITCHERS	B/T	Ht./Wt.	Born	1995 clubs
29	Banks, Willie	R/R	6-1/195	2-27-69	Chicago N.L., Los Angeles, Florida
61	Blazier, Ron	R/R	6-5/205	7-30-71	Reading
42	Borland, Toby	R/R	6-6/193	5-29-69	Philadelphia, Scranton/Wilkes-Barre
52	Bottalico, Ricky	L/R	6-1/208	8-26-69	Philadelphia
54	Crawford, Carlos	R/R	6-1/190	10-4-71	Buffalo, Canton/Akron
50	Fernandez, Sid	L/L	6-1/230	10-12-62	Baltimore, Bowie, Philadelphia
55	Gomes, Wayne	R/R	6-2/205	1-15-73	Reading
44	Grace, Mike	R/R	6-4/220	6-20-70	Reading, Scranton/Wilkes-Barre, Philadelphia
28	Green, Tyler	R/R	6-5/211	2-18-70	Philadelphia
49	Greene, Tommy	R/R	6-5/225	4-6-67	Clearwater, Philadelphia, Scranton/Wilkes-Barre
48	Jordan, Ricardo	L/L	6-0/180	6-27-70	Syracuse, Toronto
53	Karp, Ryan	L/L	6-4/214	4-5-70	Reading, Philadelphia, Scranton/Wilkes-Barre
45	Mimbs, Michael	L/L	6-2/190	2-13-69	Philadelphia
57	Mitchell, Larry	R/R	6-1/219	10-16-71	Reading
35	Munoz, Bobby	R/R	6-7/259	3-3-68	Reading, Scranton/Wilkes-Barre, Philadelphia
38	Schilling, Curt	R/R	6-4/226	11-14-66	Philadelphia
51	Slocumb, Heathcliff	R/R	6-3/220	6-7-66	Philadelphia
33	Springer, Russ	R/R	6-4/205	11-7-68	Vancouver, California, Philadelphia
63	Wallace, B.J.	R/L	6-3/195	5-18-71	Montreal
40	West, David	L/L	6-6/247	9-1-64	Philadelphia, Scranton/Wilkes-Barre, Reading
41	Williams, Mike	R/R	6-2/195	7-29-68	Philadelphia, Scranton/Wilkes-Barre

No.	CATCHERS	B/T	Ht./Wt.	Born	1995 clubs
10	Daulton, Darren	L/R	6-2/207	1-3-62	Philadelphia
24	Lieberthal, Mike	R/R	6-0/178	1-18-72	Philadelphia, Scranton/Wilkes-Barre
27	Webster, Lenny	R/R	5-9/202	2-10-65	Philadelphia

No.	INFIELDERS	B/T	Ht./Wt.	Born	1995 clubs
60	Battle, Howard	R/R	6-0/197	3-25-72	Syracuse, Toronto
5	Benjamin, Mike	R/R	6-0/169	11-22-65	San Francisco
58	Doster, Dave	R/R	5-10/185	10-8-70	Reading
25	Jefferies, Gregg	B/R	5-10/184	8-1-67	Philadelphia
23	Jordan, Kevin	R/R	6-1/193	10-9-69	Scranton/Wilkes-Barre, Philadelphia
12	Morandini, Mickey	L/R	5-11/176	4-22-66	Philadelphia
6	Schall, Gene	R/R	6-3/206	6-5-70	Scranton/Wilkes-Barre, Philadelphia
31	Sefcik, Kevin	R/R	5-10/175	2-10-71	Scranton/Wilkes-Barre, Reading, Philadelphia
19	Stocker, Kevin	B/R	6-1/175	2-13-70	Philadelphia
	Zeile, Todd	R/R	6-1/200	9-9-65	Louisville, St. Louis, Chicago N.L.

No.	OUTFIELDERS	B/T	Ht./Wt.	Born	1995 clubs
4	Dykstra, Lenny	L/L	5-10/188	2-10-63	Philadelphia
8	Eisenreich, Jim	L/L	5-11/195	4-18-59	Philadelphia
56	Holifield, Rick	L/L	6-2/180	3-25-70	Scranton/Wilkes-Barre, Reading
16	Longmire, Tony	L/R	6-1/218	8-12-68	Philadelphia
21	Marsh, Tom	R/R	6-2/196	12-27-65	Scranton/Wilkes-Barre, Philadelphia
22	Whiten, Mark	B/R	6-3/235	11-25-66	Boston, Pawtucket, Philadelphia

BALLPARK INFORMATION

Ballpark (capacity, surface)
Veterans Stadium (62,382, artificial)

Address
P.O. Box 7575
Philadelphia, PA 19101

Business phone
215-463-6000

Ticket information
215-463-1000

Ticket prices
$16 (field box)
$14 (sections 258-274)
$14 (terrace box)
$14 (loge box)
$10 (reserved, 600 level)
$5 (reserved, 700 level)

Field dimensions (from home plate)
To left field at foul line, 330 feet
To center field, 408 feet
To right field at foul line, 330 feet

First game played
April 10, 1971 (Phillies 4, Expos 1)

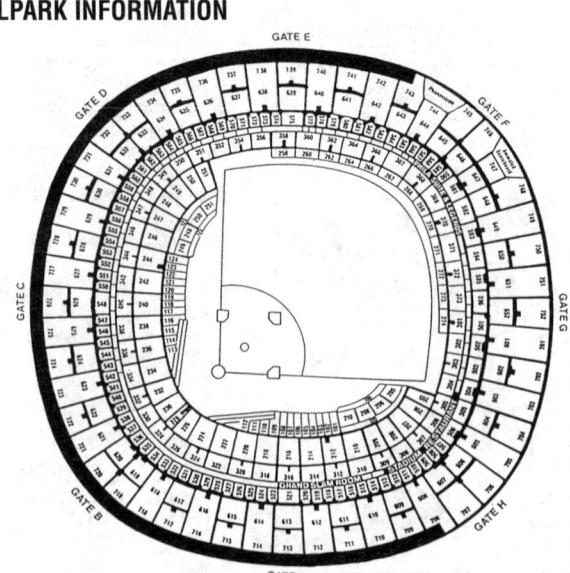

DAY BY DAY

Date	Opp.	Res.	Score	(inn.*)	Hits	Opp. hits	Winning pitcher	Losing pitcher	Save	Record	Pos.	GB
4-26	At St.L.	L	6-7		9	11	Arocha	Charlton		0-1	T3rd	1
4-27	At St.L.	W	6-2		8	10	West	Jackson		1-1	3rd	1
4-28	Pit.	W	5-2		7	8	Quantrill	Neagle	Slocumb	2-1	T1st	...
4-29	Pit.	L	2-3		7	8	Loaiza	Green	Gott	2-2	T2nd	1
5-2	At Cin.	W	6-0		13	5	Schilling	Rijo		3-2	3rd	1¹/₂
5-3	At Cin.	L	2-7		5	8	Hernandez	Charlton	Brantley	3-3	3rd	2¹/₂
5-4	At Cin.	W	6-4		8	7	Harris	Carrasco	Slocumb	4-3	3rd	2¹/₂
5-5	At Atl.	W	9-4		12	9	Green	Mercker	Borland	5-3	2nd	1¹/₂
5-6	At Atl.	W	3-1		8	4	Mimbs	Smoltz	Slocumb	6-3	2nd	¹/₂
5-7	At Atl.	W	5-4		10	8	Schilling	Bedrosian	Slocumb	7-3	1st	+¹/₂
5-8	At Atl.	W	3-2		6	8	Abbott	Glavine	Slocumb	8-3	1st	+1¹/₂
5-9	Mon.	W	8-3		15	9	Quantrill	Henry		9-3	1st	+1¹/₂
5-10	Mon.	W	10-1		14	4	Green	Heredia		10-3	1st	+2¹/₂
5-11	Mon.	L	1-13		6	16	Perez	Mimbs		10-4	1st	+2¹/₂
5-12	At Hou.	W	5-2		12	8	Schilling	Drabek	Slocumb	11-4	1st	+2¹/₂
5-13	At Hou.	W	7-5		9	7	Bottalico	Kile	Slocumb	12-4	1st	+2¹/₂
5-14	At Hou.	W	5-2		11	5	Quantrill	Hampton	Slocumb	13-4	1st	+2¹/₂
5-15	At Fla.	L	1-9		6	10	Burkett	Green		13-5	1st	+2¹/₂
5-16	At Fla.	W	9-7	(10)	13	10	Slocumb	Nen		14-5	1st	+2¹/₂
5-17	At Fla.	W	3-1	(13)	4	8	Bottalico	Lewis	Slocumb	15-5	1st	+3¹/₂
5-19	N.Y.	L	1-5		8	9	Gunderson	Quantrill		15-6	1st	+3
5-20	N.Y.	W	10-8		14	14	Green	Harnisch	Slocumb	16-6	1st	+3
5-21	N.Y.	W	5-3		10	8	Mimbs	B. Jones	Slocumb	17-6	1st	+3
5-23	S.F.	W	6-5		11	5	Harris	Beck		18-6	1st	+3
5-24	S.F.	W	2-1		7	7	Charlton	Wilson	Slocumb	19-6	1st	+3
5-25	S.F.	L	1-3	(6)	4	4	Leiter	Green		19-7	1st	+3
5-26	S.D.	W	2-0		5	2	Mimbs	Benes		20-7	1st	+3
5-27	S.D.	W	5-4	(10)	11	11	Abbott	Hermanson		21-7	1st	+4
5-28	S.D.	L	5-13	(10)	12	14	Hoffman	Harris		21-8	1st	+3
5-29	L.A.	W	8-6		14	8	Quantrill	Astacio	Slocumb	22-8	1st	+3
5-30	L.A.	W	5-0		8	7	Green	Candiotti		23-8	1st	+3¹/₂
5-31	L.A.	L	1-4	(10)	3	8	Martinez	Bottalico	Worrell	23-9	1st	+3¹/₂
6-1	Chi.	W	5-3		7	8	Charlton	Trachsel	Slocumb	24-9	1st	+4¹/₂
6-2	At S.F.	L	2-4		9	7	Beck	Harris		24-10	1st	+4
6-3	At S.F.	L	1-3		8	9	Wilson	Quantrill	Beck	24-11	1st	+3
6-4	At S.F.	L	0-4		4	8	Leiter	Green		24-12	1st	+3
6-5	At S.D.	L	4-5	(10)	7	13	Hoffman	Charlton		24-13	1st	+3
6-6	At S.D.	L	0-1		6	7	Valenzuela	Williams	Hoffman	24-14	1st	+2¹/₂
6-7	At S.D.	W	7-1		14	2	Schilling	Ashby		25-14	1st	+2¹/₂
6-9	At L.A.	W	4-0		8	6	Quantrill	Astacio		26-14	1st	+2¹/₂
6-10	At L.A.	W	3-0		9	5	Green	Candiotti		27-14	1st	+3¹/₂
6-11	At L.A.	W	2-1		11	7	Mimbs	Martinez	Slocumb	28-14	1st	+4
6-13	Hou.	L	5-6		10	6	Veres	Schilling	Hudek	28-15	1st	+3
6-14	Hou.	L	5-9		7	12	Kile	Charlton	Jones	28-16	1st	+3
6-15	Hou.	W	4-2		10	8	Bottalico	Hudek		29-16	1st	+3¹/₂
6-16	Fla.	L	1-2		6	6	Rapp	West	Nen	29-17	1st	+2¹/₂
6-17	Fla.	W	11-4		10	7	Mimbs	Weathers		30-17	1st	+2¹/₂
6-18	Fla.	W	5-3		9	8	Schilling	Perez	Slocumb	31-17	1st	+2¹/₂
6-19	At N.Y.	W	6-3		10	7	Quantrill	Mlicki	Slocumb	32-17	1st	+2¹/₂
6-20	At N.Y.	W	8-2		12	8	Green	Harnisch		33-17	1st	+2¹/₂
6-21	At N.Y.	W	6-2		10	7	West	B. Jones	Bottalico	34-17	1st	+3¹/₂
6-22	At N.Y.	W	8-2		19	10	Mimbs	Pulsipher		35-17	1st	+4¹/₂
6-23	At St.L.	L	1-7		9	10	Morgan	Schilling		35-18	1st	+4¹/₂
6-24	At St.L.	W	10-9		17	11	Quantrill	Hill	Slocumb	36-18	1st	+4¹/₂
6-25	At St.L.	W	5-3		10	6	Green	Urbani	Slocumb	37-18	1st	+4¹/₂
6-27	Cin.	L	3-12		9	13	Smiley	Mimbs	Hernandez	37-19	1st	+4
6-28	Cin.	L	0-1		3	4	Nitkowski	Schilling	Brantley	37-20	1st	+3
6-29	Cin.	L	4-10		6	14	Schourek	Quantrill		37-21	1st	+2¹/₂
6-30	Atl.	W	3-1		5	5	Green	Smoltz	Slocumb	38-21	1st	+3¹/₂
7-1	Atl.	L	1-3		5	5	Maddux	West		38-22	1st	+2¹/₂
7-2	Atl.	L	3-5		8	7	Glavine	Mimbs	Wohlers	38-23	1st	+1¹/₂
7-3	Atl.	L	4-10		9	15	Avery	Schilling		38-24	1st	+¹/₂
7-4	At Pit.	L	0-7		5	15	Ericks	Quantrill		38-25	2nd	¹/₂
7-5	At Pit.	L	4-7		6	8	Plesac	Charlton		38-26	2nd	1¹/₂
7-6	At Pit.	W	10-5		13	7	West	Parris		39-26	2nd	1¹/₂
7-7	Chi.	L	2-8		8	12	Bullinger	Mimbs	Hickerson	39-27	2nd	2¹/₂
7-8	Chi.	L	1-3		2	7	Navarro	Schilling	Myers	39-28	2nd	3¹/₂
7-9	Chi.	L	6-7	(13)	14	12	Wendell	Williams		39-29	2nd	4¹/₂
7-12	St.L.	L	3-4		9	5	Jackson	Mimbs	Henke	39-30	2nd	4¹/₂
7-13	At Mon.	W	4-3		11	7	Schilling	Fassero	Slocumb	40-30	2nd	4¹/₂
7-14	At Mon.	L	2-8		6	11	Martinez	Green		40-31	2nd	5¹/₂

Date	Opp.	Res.	Score	(inn.*)	Hits	Opp. hits	Winning pitcher	Losing pitcher	Save	Record	Pos.	GB
7-15	At Mon.	L	3-5		12	12	Henry	Quantrill	Rojas	40-32	2nd	6¹/₂
7-16	At Mon.	L	1-5		7	9	Perez	Fernandez	Rojas	40-33	2nd	6¹/₂
7-17	At Col.	L	5-8		9	11	Munoz	Bottalico	Holmes	40-34	2nd	7
7-18	At Col.	W	7-5		14	9	Schilling	Ritz	Slocumb	41-34	2nd	6
7-19	At Col.	L	3-5		8	9	Rekar	Green	Holmes	41-35	2nd	7
7-20	At Col.	L	3-7		7	11	Swift	Quantrill		41-36	2nd	8
7-21	St.L.	W	7-0		10	4	Fernandez	Osborne	Borland	42-36	2nd	7
7-22	St.L.	L	3-5	(11)	9	11	DeLucia	Olivares	Henke	42-37	2nd	8
7-23	St.L.	W	10-6		11	8	Quantrill	Hill	Borland	43-37	2nd	8
7-24	Col.	L	3-11		8	10	Rekar	Green		43-38	2nd	9
7-25	Col.	W	7-6	(10)	12	11	Slocumb	Munoz		44-38	2nd	9
7-26†	Pit.	W	2-1	(11)	6	2	Borland	Plesac		45-38		
7-26‡	Pit.	W	6-4		10	13	Quantrill	Dyer	Slocumb	46-38	2nd	7¹/₂
7-27	Pit.	W	6-4		15	7	Mimbs	Ericks	Slocumb	47-38	2nd	6¹/₂
7-28	At Chi.	L	0-4		11	6	Castillo	Munoz	Myers	47-39	2nd	7¹/₂
7-29	At Chi.	L	7-8		16	10	Young	Slocumb		47-40	2nd	8¹/₂
7-30	At Chi.	L	0-8		3	11	Bullinger	Deshaies		47-41	2nd	8¹/₂
8-1	At Atl.	W	4-3		8	4	Fernandez	Avery	Slocumb	48-41	2nd	7¹/₂
8-2	At Atl.	L	5-7		11	8	Mercker	Munoz	Wohlers	48-42	2nd	8¹/₂
8-3	At Atl.	L	4-5		10	10	Borbon	Slocumb		48-43	2nd	9¹/₂
8-4	At Cin.	L	0-1		5	6	Smiley	Juden	Brantley	48-44	2nd	10¹/₂
8-6†	At Cin.	L	1-6		3	7	Schourek	Greene		48-45		
8-6‡	At Cin.	L	1-2	(10)	7	9	Jackson	Slocumb		48-46	2nd	11¹/₂
8-8	N.Y.	L	10-12		15	17	Cornelius	Green	Franco	48-47	2nd	13
8-9	N.Y.	L	0-4		6	10	Isringhausen	Quantrill		48-48	2nd	13
8-10	N.Y.	L	1-5	(11)	4	10	Florence	Slocumb		48-49	2nd	14
8-11	Mon.	W	6-5		9	8	Fernandez	Perez	Slocumb	49-49	2nd	14
8-12	Mon.	L	3-4		8	10	Fassero	Greene	Leiper	49-50	2nd	14
8-13	Mon.	L	2-3		9	11	Scott	Bottalico	Rojas	49-51	T2nd	15
8-14	Mon.	L	1-5		8	9	Martinez	Quantrill		49-52	3rd	16
8-15	At Hou.	W	3-2		6	6	Juden	Swindell	Slocumb	50-52	3rd	16
8-16	At Hou.	L	4-5		10	9	Hartgraves	Slocumb		50-53	3rd	16
8-17	At Hou.	W	3-2		10	8	Fletcher	Jones	Borland	51-53	3rd	15¹/₂
8-18	S.F.	W	16-8		18	12	Mimbs	Hook		52-53	3rd	14¹/₂
8-19	S.F.	W	6-4		12	8	Bottalico	S. Valdez	Slocumb	53-53	2nd	13¹/₂
8-20	S.F.	W	8-7	(10)	15	15	Slocumb	Bautista		54-53	2nd	13¹/₂
8-21	S.D.	W	3-1		5	7	Fernandez	Ashby	Borland	55-53	2nd	13¹/₂
8-22	S.D.	L	3-5		10	11	Valenzuela	Greene	Hoffman	55-54	2nd	14¹/₂
8-23	S.D.	W	12-8		11	13	Williams	Dishman	Mimbs	56-54	2nd	14¹/₂
8-24	L.A.	W	7-6	(11)	13	13	Slocumb	Seanez		57-54	2nd	14
8-25	L.A.	W	17-4		17	7	Juden	Nomo		58-54	2nd	14
8-26	L.A.	W	9-4		10	7	Fernandez	Valdes		59-54	2nd	14
8-27	L.A.	L	1-9		6	11	Tapani	Greene		59-55	2nd	15
8-29	At S.F.	L	4-6		10	10	Mulholland	Quantrill	Beck	59-56	2nd	14¹/₂
8-30	At S.F.	L	1-4		5	6	VanLandingham	Juden	Beck	59-57	2nd	14¹/₂
8-31	At S.F.	W	6-0		8	5	Fernandez	Brewington		60-57	2nd	14¹/₂
9-1	At S.D.	L	3-6		10	11	Valenzuela	Grace	Hoffman	60-58	2nd	14¹/₂
9-2	At S.D.	L	5-6	(11)	10	10	Hoffman	Slocumb		60-59	2nd	14¹/₂
9-3	At S.D.	W	3-2		8	9	Quantrill	Hamilton	Slocumb	61-59	2nd	14¹/₂
9-4	At L.A.	L	1-5		6	4	Candiotti	Juden		61-60	2nd	15¹/₂
9-5	At L.A.	L	1-2		4	8	Cummings	Borland		61-61	2nd	16¹/₂
9-6	At L.A.	W	1-0		3	3	Grace	Valdes	Slocumb	62-61	2nd	16¹/₂
9-8	Hou.	L	3-12		9	12	Hampton	Green		62-62	2nd	17
9-9	Hou.	W	6-4	(11)	15	14	Slocumb	Henneman		63-62	2nd	17
9-10	Hou.	L	4-5		9	9	Drabek	Juden	Henneman	63-63	2nd	17
9-12	At Mon.	W	8-2		13	9	Williams	Alvarez	Borland	64-63	2nd	15¹/₂
9-13	At Mon.	L	4-5		11	9	Heredia	D. Springer	Rojas	64-64	2nd	16¹/₂
9-14	At Pit.	W	7-2		14	8	Quantrill	Wagner		65-64	2nd	16
9-15	At N.Y.	L	1-4		15	9	Isringhausen	Mimbs	Franco	65-65	2nd	17
9-16	At N.Y.	L	8-10		11	11	Telgheder	Greene	Franco	65-66	2nd	18
9-17	At N.Y.	L	2-8		9	12	Cornelius	Williams	DiPoto	65-67	2nd	19
9-18	Fla.	W	13-10		12	10	Bottalico	Veres	Slocumb	66-67	2nd	19
9-19	Fla.	L	4-5		10	7	Perez	Borland	Nen	66-68	2nd	19
9-20	Fla.	L	1-2		4	5	Burkett	Quantrill		66-69	2nd	19
9-21	Fla.	W	3-1		7	5	Mimbs	Banks	Frey	67-69	2nd	19
9-22	Cin.	L	2-3		7	6	Burba	Borland	Brantley	67-70	2nd	20
9-23	Cin.	W	3-2	(13)	7	7	Ricci	Hernandez		68-70	2nd	19
9-24	Cin.	L	4-6		8	8	Wells	D. Springer	Brantley	68-71	2nd	20
9-26	Atl.	L	1-5		3	6	Smoltz	Quantrill		68-72	2nd	21
9-27	Atl.	L	0-6		5	10	Maddux	Mimbs		68-73	2nd	22
9-29	At Fla.	L	2-5		3	7	Hammond	D. Springer		68-74	2nd	22
9-30	At Fla.	W	3-2		7	10	Williams	Burkett	Slocumb	69-74	2nd	21
10-1	At Fla.	L	2-8		8	16	Bowen	Quantrill		69-75	T2nd	21

Monthly records: April (2-2), May (21-7), June (15-12), July (9-20), August (13-16), September (9-17), October (0-1).
*Innings, if other than nine. †First game of doubleheader. ‡Second game of doubleheader.

HIGHLIGHTS

High points: By winning 37 of their first 55 games, the Phillies had a five-game lead in the N.L. East on June 25. After a brutal seven-week stretch that dropped them into third place, the Phillies then won 10 of 12 from August 15-26 to take a half-game lead in the N.L. wild-card race.

Low point: A 12-3 loss to Cincinnati on June 27 led to a stretch in which the Phillies went 12-34. Their five-game lead over Atlanta turned into a 15$\frac{1}{2}$-game deficit.

Turning point: In the span of three pitches by Heathcliff Slocumb on July 29 at Wrigley Field, the Phillies went from one out from a two-run victory to an 8-7 defeat, thanks to Shawon Dunston's three-run, ninth-inning homer.

Most valuable player: Third baseman Charlie Hayes. Signed almost as an after-thought, Hayes hit .276 with a club-leading 85 RBIs and tied for the team lead in homers with 11.

Most valuable pitcher: Slocumb. In his first chance as a closer, Slocumb converted 32 of 38 save chances and posted a 2.89 ERA.

Most improved player: Second baseman Mickey Morandini. He hit .283, including a team-high .346 with runners in scoring position, and was named to the All-Star team.

Most pleasant surprise: Reliever Ricky Bottalico. In 62 games, the rookie was 5-3 with a 2.46 ERA. He pitched 87$\frac{2}{3}$ innings, struck out 87 and allowed 50 hits. Opposing batters hit .167 off him.

Biggest disappointments: Tyler Green was 8-4 with a 2.81 ERA and was named to the N.L. All-Star team; he fell apart in the second half and finished 8-9 with a 5.31 ERA. First baseman Gregg Jefferies hit .306 but drove in only 56 runs. Shortstop Kevin Stocker, a career .298 hitter, batted .218.

Key injuries: Outfielder Lenny Dykstra played in 62 games because of back and knee injuries. Pitcher Curt Schilling's season consisted of 17 starts and ended with shoulder surgery. Pitchers Tommy Greene and Bobby Munoz experienced arm trouble

in spring training and never contributed. Munoz had ligament transplant surgery on his right elbow. Catcher Darren Daulton played 98 games but was hobbled by nagging injuries all year long until tearing the anterior cruciate ligament in his right knee August 25, which led to surgery.

Notable: The Phillies used a club-record 50 players; 26 were pitchers. . . . Twenty-four players made their Phillies debut and nine made their major league debuts.

—GEORGE A. KING III

RECORDS

1995 regular-season record: 69-75 (2nd in N.L. East); 35-37 at home; 34-38 on road; 24-28 vs. East; 22-27 vs. Central; 23-20 vs. West; 20-27 vs. lefthanded starters; 49-48 vs. righthanded starters; 20-25 on grass; 49-50 on turf; 16-25 in daytime; 53-50 at night; 20-23 in one-run games; 9-8 in extra-inning games; 1-1 in doubleheaders. **Team record past five years:** 368-377 (.494, ranks 9th in league in that span).

TEAM LEADERS

Batting average: Gregg Jefferies (.306).
At-bats: Charlie Hayes (529).
Runs: Gregg Jefferies (69).
Hits: Gregg Jefferies (147).
Total bases: Charlie Hayes, Gregg Jefferies (215).
Doubles: Mickey Morandini (34).
Triples: Mickey Morandini (7).
Home runs: Charlie Hayes, Gregg Jefferies, Mark Whiten (11).
Runs batted in: Charlie Hayes (85).
Stolen bases: Jim Eisenreich, Lenny Dykstra (10).
Slugging percentage: Gregg Jefferies (.448).
On-base percentage: Gregg Jefferies (.349).
Wins: Paul Quantrill (11).
Earned-run average: Paul Quantrill (4.67).
Complete games: Tyler Green (4).
Shutouts: Tyler Green (2).
Saves: Heathcliff Slocumb (32).
Innings pitched: Paul Quantrill (179.1).
Strikeouts: Curt Schilling (114).

GAMES BY POSITION

Catcher: Darren Daulton 95, Lenny Webster 43, Mike Lieberthal 14.
First base: Dave Hollins 61, Gregg Jefferies 59, Gene Schall 14, Mariano Duncan 12, Kevin Elster 4, Randy Ready 3.
Second base: Mickey Morandini 122, Mariano Duncan 24, Kevin Jordan 9, Randy Ready 1.
Third base: Charlie Hayes 141, Kevin Elster 2, Kevin Sefcik 2, Mariano Duncan 1, Kevin Jordan 1.
Shortstop: Kevin Stocker 125, Kevin Elster 19, Mariano Duncan 14.
Outfield: Jim Eisenreich 111, Lenny Dykstra 61, Andy Van Slyke 56, Dave Gallagher 55, Gregg Jefferies 55, Mark Whiten 55, Tom Marsh 29, Gary Varsho 25, Tony Longmire 23, Kevin Flora 20, Gene Schall 4.

TOP DRAFT CHOICES

1a. **Reggie Taylor,** OF, Newberry (S.C.) H.S.
1b. **Dave Coggin,** RHP, Upland (Calif.) H.S.
2. **Marlon Anderson,** 2B, University of South Alabama.
3. **Randy Knoll,** RHP-3B, Corona (Calif.) H.S.
4. **Steve Carver,** 3B, Stanford University.
5. **Pee Wee Lopez,** C, Westminster Christian H.S., Miami.
6. **Caleb Martinez,** LHP, Florida Bible Christian H.S., Miami.
7. **Chris Bauer,** RHP-SS, Wichita State University.
8. **Ricky Williams,** SS, Patrick Henry H.S., San Diego.
9. **Kirk Pierce,** C, Long Beach State University.
10. **Brian Mensink,** RHP, University of Minnesota.

PITTSBURGH PIRATES
NATIONAL LEAGUE CENTRAL DIVISION

1996 PIRATES SCHEDULE

Home games shaded.
* — All-Star Game at Veterans Stadium (Philadelphia)
N — Night game (any game starting after 5 p.m.)

MARCH

SUN	MON	TUE	WED	THU	FRI	SAT
31						

APRIL

SUN	MON	TUE	WED	THU	FRI	SAT
	1 N FLA	2 N FLA	3	4 FLA	5 N NY	6 N NY
7 NY	8 N PHI	9	10 PHI	11 N MON	12 N MON	13 N MON
14 MON	15 N STL	16 N STL	17 N STL	18 STL	19 N MON	20 MON
21 MON	22 N PHI	23 PHI	24 N FLA	25 FLA	26 N NY	27 N NY
28 NY	29	30 N CIN				

MAY

SUN	MON	TUE	WED	THU	FRI	SAT
			1 N CIN	2	3 N LA	4 N LA
5 LA	6 N LA	7 N SD	8 N SD	9 N SD	10 N SF	11 N SF
12 SF	13 N ATL	14 N ATL	15 N ATL	16	17 N HOU	18 N HOU
19 HOU	20 N COL	21 N COL	22 COL	23	24 N ATL	25 N ATL
26 ATL	27 HOU	28 N HOU	29 N HOU	30	31 N COL	

JUNE

SUN	MON	TUE	WED	THU	FRI	SAT
						1 N COL
2 COL	3 N LA	4 N LA	5 N LA	6 N LA	7 N SD	8 N SD
9 SD	10 N SF	11 N SF	12	13 N FLA	14 N FLA	15 N FLA
16 FLA	17 N NY	18 N NY	19 N NY	20	21 N FLA	22 N FLA
23 FLA	24 N MON	25 N MON	26 N MON	27	28 N STL	29 STL
30 STL						

JULY

SUN	MON	TUE	WED	THU	FRI	SAT
	1 N CHI	2 N CHI	3 N CHI	4 STL	5 N STL	6 N STL
7 STL	8	9 *	10	11 N CIN	12 N CIN	13 N CIN
14 CIN	15 N CHI	16 CHI	17 N CHI	18 N CIN	19 N CIN	20 N CIN
21 CIN	22	23 N MON	24 N MON	25 N PHI	26 N PHI	27 N PHI
28 N PHI	29 N NY	30 N NY	31 N NY			

AUGUST

SUN	MON	TUE	WED	THU	FRI	SAT
				1 NY	2 N PHI	3 PHI
4 PHI	5 N PHI	6 N LA	7 N LA	8 N SD	9 N SD	10 N SD
11 SD	12	13 N SF	14 N SF	15 N SF	16 N ATL	17 N ATL
18 ATL	19 N HOU	20 N HOU	21 N HOU	22 N HOU	23 N COL	24 N COL
25 COL	26	27 N ATL	28 N ATL	29 ATL	30 N HOU	31 HOU

SEPTEMBER

SUN	MON	TUE	WED	THU	FRI	SAT
1 HOU	2 N COL	3	4 N COL	5	6 N LA	7 N LA
8 LA	9 N SD	10 N SD	11 N SD	12 N SF	13 N SF	14 SF
15 SF	16	17 N CIN	18 N CIN	19 N CIN	20 N CHI	21 N CHI
22 CHI	23 N CHI	24 N STL	25 N STL	26	27 CHI	28 CHI
29 CHI	30					

(left margin) 1996 SEASON — Pittsburgh Pirates

1996 SEASON

CLUB DIRECTORY

Board of directors
Joe L. Brown
Frank V. Cahouet
Richard M. Cyert
Douglas D. Danforth
Robert M. Hernandez
Eugene Litman
John H. McConnell
Tom Murphy
Thomas H. O'Brien
Paul H. O'Neill
Fredric G. Reynolds
Vincent A. Sarni
Mark Sauer
Harvey M. Walken

Chairman of the exec. comm. of the board
Vincent Sarni

President and chief executive officer
Mark Sauer

Sr. v.p. and general manager
Cam Bonifay

Asst. g.m./dir. of player personnel
Pete Vuckovich

Special assistants to the g.m.
Leland Maddox
Chet Montgomery
Ken Parker
Lenny Yochim

V.p., finance and administration
Jim Plake

V.p., broadcasting and advertising sales
Mark Driscoll

Vice president, marketing and operations
Steven N. Greenberg

Treasurer
Ken Curcio

Manager of accounting
Patti Mistick

Traveling secretary
Greg Johnson

Director of ticket operations
Gary Remlinger

Sales mgr., broadcasting and promotions
Mark Ferraco

Dir. of major league baseball admin.
John Sirignano

Director of Bradenton baseball operations
Jeff Podobnik

Dir. of com. rel. and special events
Kathy Guy

Dir. of community services and sales
Al Gordon

Director of corporate relations
Nellie Briles

Director of information systems
Dale Dressler

Director of marketing communications
Mike Gordon

Director of media relations
Jim Trdinich

Director of merchandising
Joe Billetdeaux

Director of operations
Dennis DaPra

Director of scouting
Paul Tinnell

Club physician
Dr. Joseph Coroso

Team orthopedist
Dr. Jack Failla

Trainers
Kent Biggerstaff, Dave Tumbas

Equipment manager
Roger Wilson

Scouting coordinators
Ron King, Fred Wright

Special assignment scouts
Bill Bryk, Angel Figueroa
Boyd Odom

Latin America coordinators
Pablo Cruz, Jose Luna

Scouting supervisors
Tom Barnard, Grant Brittain, Dana Brown, Bill Bryk, Steve Demeter, Steve Fleming, Dave Klipstein, Scott Lovekamp, Ed Roebuck, Roy Smith, George Swain, Douglas Takaragawa, Mike Williams

MINOR LEAGUE AFFILIATES

Class	Team	League	Manager
AAA	Calgary	Pacific Coast	Trent Jewett
AA	Carolina	Southern	Marc Hill
A	Lynchburg	Carolina	Jeff Banister
A	Augusta	South Atlantic	Jay Loviglio
A	Erie	New York-Pennsylvania	Jeff Richardson
Rookie	Gulf Coast Pirates	Gulf Coast	Woody Huyke

BROADCAST INFORMATION
Radio: KDKA-AM (1020).
TV: To be announced.
Cable TV: To be announced.

SPRING TRAINING
Ballpark (city): McKechnie Field (Bradenton, Fla.).
Ticket information: 941-748-4610.

SPRING TRAINING ROSTER

Manager—Jim Leyland (10).
Coaches—Rich Donnelly (45), Gene Lamont, Milt May (39), Ray Miller (31), Tommy Sandt (37), Donald Williams (54).

No.	PITCHERS	B/T	Ht./Wt.	Born	1995 clubs
41	Christiansen, Jason	R/L	6-5/234	9-21-69	Pittsburgh
26	Cooke, Steve	R/L	6-6/236	1-14-70	Augusta, Carolina
62	Dyer, Mike	R/R	6-3/200	9-8-66	Pittsburgh
57	Ericks, John	R/R	6-7/251	9-16-67	Calgary, Pittsburgh
42	Hancock, Lee	L/L	6-4/220	6-27-67	Calgary, Pittsburgh
47	Lieber, Jon	L/R	6-3/220	4-2-70	Pittsburgh, Calgary
34	Loaiza, Esteban	R/R	6-4/190	12-31-71	Pittsburgh
32	Miceli, Dan	R/R	6-0/216	9-9-70	Pittsburgh
55	Morel, Ramon	R/R	6-2/193	8-15-74	Lynchburg, Carolina, Pittsburgh
15	Neagle, Denny	L/L	6-2/225	9-13-68	Pittsburgh
60	Parris, Steve	R/R	6-0/190	12-17-67	Carolina, Pittsburgh
	Peters, Chris	L/L	6-1/162	1-28-72	Lynchburg, Carolina
35	Pisciotta, Marc	R/R	6-5/227	8-7-70	Carolina
19	Plesac, Dan	L/L	6-5/217	2-4-62	Pittsburgh
28	Rogers, Kevin	L/L	6-1/198	8-20-68	San Jose, Phoenix
	Ruebel, Matt	L/L	6-2/180	10-16-69	Carolina
	Ryan, Matt	R/R	6-5/185	3-30-72	Carolina, Calgary
43	Wagner, Paul	R/R	6-1/209	11-14-67	Pittsburgh

No.	CATCHERS	B/T	Ht./Wt.	Born	1995 clubs
2	Encarnacion, Angelo	R/R	5-8/177	4-18-73	Calgary, Pittsburgh
	Kendall, Jason	R/R	6-0/181	6-26-74	Carolina

No.	INFIELDERS	B/T	Ht./Wt.	Born	1995 clubs
48	Aude, Rich	R/R	6-5/215	7-13-71	Pittsburgh, Calgary
3	Bell, Jay	R/R	6-0/182	12-11-65	Pittsburgh
13	Garcia, Carlos	R/R	6-1/205	10-15-67	Pittsburgh
22	Garcia, Freddy	R/R	6-2/205	8-1-72	Pittsburgh
36	Johnson, Mark	L/L	6-4/230	10-17-67	Pittsburgh, Calgary
7	King, Jeff	R/R	6-1/184	12-26-64	Pittsburgh
16	Liriano, Nelson	B/R	5-10/181	6-3-64	Pittsburgh
12	Wehner, John	R/R	6-3/206	6-29-67	Calgary, Pittsburgh
51	Womack, Tony	L/R	5-9/155	9-25-69	Calgary, Carolina
29	Young, Kevin	R/R	6-2/231	6-16-69	Calgary, Pittsburgh

No.	OUTFIELDERS	B/T	Ht./Wt.	Born	1995 clubs
	Allensworth, Jermaine	R/R	6-0/178	1-11-72	Carolina, Calgary
	Beamon, Trey	L/R	6-3/195	2-11-74	Calgary
5	Brumfield, Jacob	R/R	6-0/186	5-27-65	Pittsburgh, Carolina
35	Clark, Dave	L/R	6-2/213	9-3-62	Pittsburgh
	Claudio, Patricio	B/R	6-0/160	4-12-72	Bakersfield, Kinston
30	Cummings, Midre	L/R	6-0/203	10-14-71	Pittsburgh, Calgary
	Kingery, Mike	L/L	6-0/185	3-29-61	Colorado
28	Martin, Al	L/L	6-2/210	11-24-67	Pittsburgh
6	Merced, Orlando	L/R	5-11/183	11-2-66	Pittsburgh
	Peterson, Charles	R/R	6-3/203	5-8-74	Lynchburg, Carolina

BALLPARK INFORMATION

Ballpark (capacity, surface)
Three Rivers Stadium (47,972, artificial)

Address
600 Stadium Circle
Pittsburgh, PA 15212

Business phone
412-323-5000

Ticket information
800-289-2827

Ticket prices
$15 (club boxes)
$10 (terrace boxes)
$10 (family boxes)
$8 (reserved seats)
$5 (general admission)
$1 (g.a., children 14 and under)

Field dimensions (from home plate)
To left field at foul line, 335 feet
To center field, 400 feet
To right field at foul line, 335 feet

First game played
July 16, 1970 (Reds 3, Pirates 2)

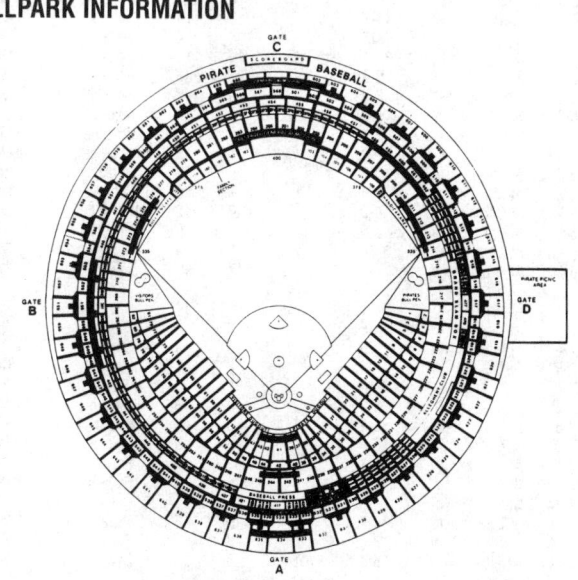

DAY BY DAY

Date	Opp.	Res.	Score	(inn.*)	Hits	Opp. hits	Winning pitcher	Losing pitcher	Save	Record	Pos.	GB
4-26	Mon.	L	2-6		6	9	Fassero	Lieber		0-1	T4th	1
4-27	Mon.	L	1-2		5	6	Martinez	Wagner	Rojas	0-2	T4th	2
4-28	At Phi.	L	2-5		8	7	Quantrill	Neagle	Slocumb	0-3	T4th	3
4-29	At Phi.	W	3-2		8	7	Loaiza	Green	Gott	1-3	T2nd	3
5-1	At St.L.	L	0-4		5	10	Hill	Wagner		1-4	4th	3
5-2	At St.L.	W	7-6		7	11	Dyer	Jackson	Gott	2-4	4th	2
5-3	At St.L.	L	6-8		14	14	Watson	Loaiza	Henke	2-5	4th	2
5-5	Chi.	L	4-8		12	10	Foster	Lieber		2-6	4th	3½
5-6	Chi.	L	5-13		10	14	Navarro	Wagner		2-7	4th	4
5-7	Chi.	W	4-3		7	7	Maddux	Banks	Miceli	3-7	4th	3
5-8	Hou.	L	3-6		7	8	Jones	Gott	Hudek	3-8	T4th	4
5-9	Hou.	L	6-13		9	16	Reynolds	Lieber		3-9	5th	5
5-11	Hou.	L	4-12		9	17	Swindell	Wagner		3-10	5th	5½
5-12	At S.F.	W	9-4		13	7	Neagle	Portugal		4-10	5th	5
5-13	At S.F.	L	4-6		9	11	Rosselli	Wilson	Beck	4-11	5th	6
5-14	At S.F.	L	1-2	(10)	5	8	Beck	Miceli		4-12	5th	6
5-15	At L.A.	L	0-4		1	8	Martinez	Wagner		4-13	5th	7
5-16	At L.A.	W	2-0		6	9	Neagle	Valdes	Miceli	5-13	5th	7
5-17	At L.A.	W	3-2		6	8	Plesac	T. Williams	Miceli	6-13	5th	6
5-18	At L.A.	W	7-6		13	13	Christiansen	T. Williams	Gott	7-13	5th	5½
5-19	At S.D.	W	8-6		10	12	Lieber	Hamilton	Miceli	8-13	5th	5½
5-20	At S.D.	L	6-9		13	9	Valenzuela	Gott		8-14	5th	6½
5-21	At S.D.	W	6-1		11	5	Neagle	Benes		9-14	5th	6½
5-23	Fla.	L	1-6		3	10	Hammond	Loaiza		9-15	5th	7
5-25	Fla.	W	3-1		9	6	Plesac	Witt	Miceli	10-15	5th	6½
5-26	Col.	W	4-2		7	5	Wagner	Acevedo	Miceli	11-15	4th	5½
5-27	Col.	W	9-4		10	11	Neagle	Swift		12-15	4th	5½
5-28	Col.	L	3-6		9	11	Freeman	White	Ruffin	12-16	4th	6½
5-30	Cin.	L	2-4		5	13	Schourek	Lieber	Brantley	12-17	T4th	6½
5-31	Cin.	L	1-11		7	17	Smiley	Wagner		12-18	T4th	7½
6-1	Cin.	W	5-3		9	7	Neagle	Rijo	Miceli	13-18	4th	6½
6-2	At Col.	L	4-7		13	10	Holmes	McCurry		13-19	T4th	7½
6-3	At Col.	L	6-7		10	13	Ritz	Lieber	Holmes	13-20	T4th	7½
6-4	At Col.	L	1-4		8	6	Grahe	Wagner	Leskanic	13-21	T4th	8½
6-5	At Cin.	L	2-3		9	9	Smiley	Neagle	Brantley	13-22	5th	9½
6-6	At Cin.	L	1-2	(10)	6	4	McElroy	Miceli		13-23	5th	10½
6-7	At Cin.	W	7-3		10	7	Lieber	Jarvis	Plesac	14-23	T4th	9½
6-8	At Fla.	L	3-7		11	10	Mathews	Wagner		14-24	5th	10½
6-9	At Fla.	L	4-5		8	12	Hammond	Neagle	Perez	14-25	5th	11½
6-10	At Fla.	W	6-2		10	6	Loaiza	Witt		15-25	5th	11½
6-11	At Fla.	W	4-3		7	7	Miceli	Nen		16-25	5th	11½
6-13	L.A.	L	3-5		7	14	Valdes	Lieber	Worrell	16-26	5th	12
6-14	L.A.	L	5-8		8	13	Nomo	Wagner	Worrell	16-27	5th	12
6-15	L.A.	W	11-7		13	13	Neagle	Astacio		17-27	5th	11½
6-16	S.D.	L	4-12		4	12	Benes	Loaiza		17-28	5th	11½
6-17	S.D.	L	8-11		10	18	Florie	Lieber	Hoffman	17-29	5th	12½
6-18	S.D.	L	0-2		4	6	Ashby	Wagner		17-30	5th	13½
6-19	S.F.	W	8-2		9	8	Neagle	Mintz		18-30	5th	12½
6-20	S.F.	W	5-3		10	10	Loaiza	Leiter	Miceli	19-30	5th	11½
6-21	S.F.	L	5-6		12	11	Burba	McCurry	Beck	19-31	5th	12½
6-23	At Mon.	W	2-0		6	2	Neagle	Martinez		20-31	5th	12
6-24	At Mon.	L	0-5		6	7	Perez	Ericks		20-32	5th	13
6-25	At Mon.	W	1-0		7	6	Loaiza	Fassero	Miceli	21-32	5th	12
6-26	At Chi.	W	8-6		16	12	Parris	Trachsel	Miceli	22-32	4th	11½
6-27	At Chi.	W	6-5		8	9	Neagle	Bullinger	Plesac	23-32	4th	11½
6-28	At Chi.	L	3-10		8	14	Hickerson	Dyer		23-33	4th	12½
6-30	At Hou.	W	12-9		17	15	Loaiza	Kile		24-33	4th	12
7-1	At Hou.	L	0-11		6	11	Reynolds	Parris		24-34	4th	13
7-2	At Hou.	L	3-5		9	12	Swindell	Neagle	Jones	24-35	4th	14
7-4	Phi.	W	7-0		15	5	Ericks	Quantrill		25-35	4th	13½
7-5	Phi.	W	7-4		8	6	Plesac	Charlton		26-35	4th	13½
7-6	Phi.	L	5-10		7	13	West	Parris		26-36	4th	13½
7-7	N.Y.	L	8-9		12	18	DiPoto	Miceli	Franco	26-37	5th	14½
7-8	N.Y.	W	3-2		8	5	Ericks	Pulsipher		27-37	5th	13½
7-9	N.Y.	W	6-3		10	5	Loaiza	Saberhagen		28-37	4th	13½
7-12	Atl.	W	2-1		7	6	Parris	Smoltz	Miceli	29-37	4th	13
7-13	St.L.	W	7-6		12	5	Dyer	Parrett	Miceli	30-37	4th	13
7-14	St.L.	L	4-6		10	11	Hill	Loaiza	Henke	30-38	4th	14
7-15	St.L.	W	9-2		10	6	Neagle	Watson		31-38	4th	14
7-16	St.L.	W	3-0		7	7	Parris	Osborne	Miceli	32-38	4th	13
7-18	At Atl.	W	5-4	(10)	8	11	Dyer	Wohlers	Miceli	33-38	4th	12½

Date	Opp.	Res.	Score	(inn.*)	Hits	Opp. hits	Winning pitcher	Losing pitcher	Save	Record	Pos.	GB
7-19	At Atl.	L	2-3		6	4	Maddux	Loaiza	Wohlers	33-39	4th	13½
7-20	At Atl.	L	3-4		9	7	Clontz	Plesac		33-40	4th	14
7-21	Mon.	W	7-6	(12)	9	10	Gott	Harris		34-40	4th	14
7-22	Mon.	W	7-1		10	6	Parris	Urbina		35-40	4th	14
7-23	Mon.	L	2-8		6	9	Fassero	Ericks		35-41	4th	15
7-24	Atl.	L	2-3		9	10	Clontz	Plesac	Wohlers	35-42	4th	15
7-25	Atl.	L	1-3	(10)	9	7	Clontz	Gott	Stanton	35-43	4th	15
7-26†	At Phi.	L	1-2	(11)	2	6	Borland	Plesac		35-44		
7-26‡	At Phi.	L	4-6		13	10	Quantrill	Dyer	Slocumb	35-45	T4th	15½
7-27	At Phi.	L	4-6		7	15	Mimbs	Ericks	Slocumb	35-46	T4th	16½
7-28	At N.Y.	W	10-9		16	13	Gott	Franco		36-46	4th	16½
7-29	At N.Y.	L	1-2		5	10	Franco	Powell		36-47	4th	16½
7-30	At N.Y.	L	1-2		6	6	Isringhausen	Wagner	Franco	36-48	4th	16½
7-31	At N.Y.	L	1-4		9	9	Pulsipher	Parris		36-49	4th	17
8-1	Chi.	L	5-7		8	11	Navarro	Ericks	Myers	36-50	4th	18
8-2	Chi.	W	4-3	(10)	8	10	Miceli	Young		37-50	4th	18
8-3	Chi.	L	2-7		8	9	Casian	Gott		37-51	4th	19
8-4†	Hou.	L	5-6		6	14	Veres	Christiansen	Jones	37-52		
8-4‡	Hou.	L	4-5		10	13	Brocail	Parris	Jones	37-53	T4th	20½
8-5	Hou.	W	3-1		7	6	Ericks	Kile	Miceli	38-53	4th	20
8-6	Hou.	W	6-3		8	7	Loaiza	Hampton	Miceli	39-53	4th	20½
8-8	At S.F.	W	9-5		11	8	Neagle	S. Valdez		40-53	4th	19½
8-9	At S.F.	L	3-4		8	8	VanLandingham	Christiansen	Beck	40-54	4th	20½
8-10	At S.F.	L	7-8		12	10	Beck	McCurry		40-55	4th	20½
8-11	At L.A.	L	2-3		6	7	Valdes	Ericks	Worrell	40-56	4th	20½
8-12	At L.A.	L	10-11	(11)	22	17	Astacio	McCurry		40-57	4th	20½
8-13	At L.A.	L	1-4		4	9	Martinez	Neagle	Worrell	40-58	4th	20½
8-14	At S.D.	L	5-6		6	9	Bochtler	Christiansen	Hoffman	40-59	4th	21½
8-15	At S.D.	W	6-0		7	7	Parris	Blair		41-59	4th	21½
8-16	At S.D.	L	0-2		5	7	Ashby	Ericks	Hoffman	41-60	4th	21½
8-18†	Fla.	W	13-7		16	15	Wagner	Groom		42-60		
8-18‡	Fla.	W	7-6	(13)	14	13	Miceli	Groom		43-60	4th	21½
8-19	Fla.	W	10-5		13	8	McCurry	Veres		44-60	4th	21½
8-20	Fla.	W	3-2		11	10	Parris	Burkett	Miceli	45-60	4th	21½
8-21	Fla.	W	5-3		7	10	Dyer	Gardner	Wagner	46-60	4th	20½
8-22	At Col.	W	10-1		16	10	Loaiza	Reynoso		47-60	4th	19½
8-23	At Col.	L	5-9		10	17	Bailey	Neagle		47-61	4th	20½
8-24	At Col.	L	6-8		13	10	Painter	Wagner	Leskanic	47-62	4th	20½
8-25	Cin.	L	3-19		7	19	Portugal	Parris		47-63	4th	21½
8-26	Cin.	L	6-7		14	19	Hernandez	Wagner	Brantley	47-64	4th	22½
8-27	Cin.	L	1-10		5	16	Schourek	Loaiza		47-65	5th	23½
8-28	Col.	L	3-6		9	11	Bailey	Powell	Leskanic	47-66	5th	24½
8-29	Col.	W	4-0		7	1	Wagner	Ritz		48-66	4th	24½
8-30	Col.	L	0-6		7	8	Rekar	Ericks		48-67	5th	24½
8-31	At Cin.	W	6-4	(10)	13	8	Plesac	Brantley	Miceli	49-67	T4th	23½
9-1	At Cin.	L	1-7		5	8	Schourek	Loaiza		49-68	5th	24½
9-2	At Cin.	W	11-8		18	11	White	Wells		50-68	T4th	23½
9-3	At Cin.	W	7-3		11	8	Wagner	Burba	Miceli	51-68	4th	22½
9-4	At Fla.	L	3-7		13	10	Burkett	Parris		51-69	4th	23½
9-6	At Fla.	L	1-2		7	7	Banks	Neagle	Nen	51-70	4th	24
9-8	L.A.	L	2-8		6	13	Martinez	Loaiza		51-71	T4th	24
9-9	L.A.	L	2-11		7	12	Tapani	Wagner		51-72	5th	24
9-10	L.A.	L	4-5		9	11	Cummings	Dyer	Worrell	51-73	5th	24
9-11	S.D.	W	7-5		8	13	Lieber	Ashby	Miceli	52-73	5th	24
9-12	S.D.	L	1-5		7	9	Valenzuela	Ericks		52-74	5th	24
9-13	S.D.	L	7-8		10	10	Villone	Plesac	Bochtler	52-75	5th	25
9-14	Phi.	L	2-7		8	14	Quantrill	Wagner		52-76	5th	26
9-15	S.F.	L	2-4	(10)	4	9	Service	Dyer	Beck	52-77	5th	26
9-16	S.F.	W	10-2		9	10	Neagle	Estes		53-77	5th	25
9-17	S.F.	W	5-4		8	13	Lieber	Brewington	Plesac	54-77	5th	24
9-18	St.L.	L	2-4		6	10	Osborne	Loaiza	Mathews	54-78	5th	25
9-19	St.L.	W	12-1		14	7	Wagner	Benes		55-78	5th	24
9-20	St.L.	L	3-9		10	12	Morgan	White		55-79	5th	25
9-21	At Chi.	W	4-3		10	9	Neagle	Trachsel	Miceli	56-79	5th	24½
9-22	At Chi.	L	3-6		2	7	Foster	Ericks	Myers	56-80	5th	25½
9-23	At Chi.	L	5-8		9	11	Bullinger	Dyer	Myers	56-81	5th	25½
9-24	At Chi.	L	2-3	(10)	7	9	Wendell	Miceli		56-82	5th	26½
9-25	At Hou.	L	5-10		8	13	Brocail	White		56-83	5th	26½
9-26	At Hou.	L	0-2		9	9	Swindell	Neagle	Henneman	56-84	5th	27
9-27	At Hou.	W	6-3	(11)	15	7	Miceli	Jones	McCurry	57-84	5th	25½
9-29	At St.L.	L	2-3		7	4	Osborne	Morel	Henke	57-85	5th	27
9-30	At St.L.	L	1-5		7	11	Benes	Wagner	Henke	57-86	5th	27
10-1	At St.L.	W	10-4		14	10	White	Barber		58-86	5th	27

Monthly records: April (1-3), May (11-15), June (12-15), July (12-16), August (13-18), September (8-19), October (1-0).
*Innings, if other than nine. †First game of doubleheader. ‡Second game of doubleheader.

HIGHLIGHTS

High point: The Pirates were 11-5 from July 4-22. That allowed them to get to 35-40, their best record in the season's second half.

Low point: A 3-10 start set the tone for a lost season.

Turning point: After the 11-5 streak in early July teased a run at respectability, the Pirates went 2-13 and lost any chance to stay near .500.

Most valuable player: A team as bad as the 1995 Pirates doesn't have a true MVP. Right fielder/first baseman Orlando Merced was the steadiest everyday player, setting career highs in doubles (29), homers (15) and RBIs (83) while hitting .300 for the second time in his career.

Most valuable pitcher: Lefthander Denny Neagle. He emerged from the pack of young starters and became an All-Star and the only consistently reliable member of the rotation. Neagle tied for the league lead in starts (31) and innings (209²/₃) and earned a trip to the All-Star Game.

Most improved player: Neagle. After compiling a 16-22 record in his first three seasons, he went 13-8.

Most pleasant surprise: Neagle again. The Pirates expected him to improve, but he probably took a bigger step than they anticipated. Another player who did better than expected was utility infielder Nelson Liriano, who batted .286 in 107 games.

Biggest disappointments: Starters Paul Wagner and Jon Lieber. Wagner has the arm to win 20 games, but his inability to harness that talent led to a 5-16 record. The Pirates thought they had something special in Lieber and penciled him in the original rotation. He wound up spending much of the season in the minors.

Key injuries: Lefthander Steve Cooke missed the season with a shoulder injury. Catcher Don Slaught was limited to 35 games because of a right hamstring strain. Outfielder Dave Clark missed nearly two months after breaking his left collarbone in a collision with teammate Jacob Brumfield. Righthander Jim Gott, counted on to stabi-

lize an inexperienced bullpen, wound up spending three separate stretches on the disabled list before he had shoulder surgery and was released.

Notable: The Pirates' 1-7 home start was the worst in club history. . . . The Pirates used 16 rookies, including four who never had played at Class AAA. . . . Jeff King homered twice in the second inning at San Francisco on August 8. He was the first Pirate to hit two homers in one inning since Jake Stenzel did it in 1894.

—JOHN MEHNO

RECORDS

1995 regular-season record: 58-86 (5th in N.L. Central); 31-41 at home; 27-45 on road; 20-23 vs. East; 20-32 vs. Central; 18-31 vs. West; 13-28 vs. lefthanded starters; 45-58 vs. righthanded starters; 16-29 on grass; 42-57 on turf; 14-26 in daytime; 44-60 at night; 19-27 in one-run games; 6-7 in extra- inning games; 1-2-0 in doubleheaders.

Team record past five years: 380-364 (.511, ranks 4th in league in that span).

TEAM LEADERS

Batting average: Orlando Merced (.300).
At-bats: Orlando Merced (487).
Runs: Orlando Merced (75).
Hits: Jay Bell (139).
Total bases: Orlando Merced (228).
Doubles: Orlando Merced (29).
Triples: Jay Bell, Orlando Merced (4).
Home runs: Jeff King (18).
Runs batted in: Jeff King (87).
Stolen bases: Jacob Brumfield (22).
Slugging percentage: Orlando Merced (.468).
On-base percentage: Orlando Merced (.365).
Wins: Denny Neagle (13).
Earned-run average: Denny Neagle (3.43).
Complete games: Denny Neagle (5).
Shutouts: Denny Neagle, Paul Wagner (1).
Saves: Dan Miceli (21).
Innings pitched: Denny Neagle (209.2).
Strikeouts: Denny Neagle (150).

GAMES BY POSITION

Catcher: Mark Parent 67, Angelo Encarnacion 55, Don Slaught 33, Mackey Sasser 11, John Wehner 1.
First base: Mark Johnson 70, Jeff King 35, Orlando Merced 35, Rich Aude 32, Kevin Young 6.
Second base: Carlos Garcia 92, Nelson Liriano 67, Jeff King 8.
Third base: Jeff King 84, Kevin Young 48, John Wehner 19, Freddy Garcia 8, Nelson Liriano 5, Jay Bell 3.
Shortstop: Jay Bell 136, Carlos Garcia 15, Jeff King 2, Nelson Liriano 1, John Wehner 1.
Outfield: Al Martin 121, Orlando Merced 107, Jacob Brumfield 104, Dave Clark 61, Steve Pegues 53, Midre Cummings 41, John Wehner 23, Freddy Garcia 10.

TOP DRAFT CHOICES

1. **Chad Hermansen,** SS, Green Valley H.S., Henderson, Nev.
2. **Garrett Long,** 1B, Bellaire H.S., Houston.
3. **Bronson Arroyo,** RHP, Brooksville-Hernando H.S., Brooksville, Fla.
4. **Alex Hernandez,** OF, Levittown, Puerto Rico.
5. **Dawan Elliott,** OF, Long Branch (N.J.) H.S.
6. **O.J. Cook,** RHP, Liberty H.S., Bethlehem, Pa.
7. **Josh Loggins,** C, Harrison H.S., West Lafayette, Ind.
8. **Brad Weber,** OF, DeKalb H.S., Auburn, Ind.
9. **Fred May,** OF, Kennedy H.S., Seattle.
10. **Daniel Delgado,** SS, Killian H.S., Miami.

ST. LOUIS CARDINALS
NATIONAL LEAGUE CENTRAL DIVISION

1996 CARDINALS SCHEDULE

MARCH

SUN	MON	TUE	WED	THU	FRI	SAT
31						

APRIL

SUN	MON	TUE	WED	THU	FRI	SAT
1 NY	2	3 NY	4 NY	5 N ATL	6 N ATL	
7 ATL	8 N MON	9	10 MON	11 N PHI	12 N PHI	13 PHI
14 PHI	15 N PIT	16 N PIT	17 N PIT	18 PIT	19 N PHI	20 N PHI
21 PHI	22 N MON	23 N MON	24 N NY	25 N NY	26 N ATL	27 ATL
28 N ATL	29 N CHI	30				

MAY

SUN	MON	TUE	WED	THU	FRI	SAT
		1 CHI	2 N SD	3 N SD	4	
5 SD	6 N SF	7 N SF	8 SF	9 N LA	10 N LA	11 LA
12 LA	13 N FLA	14 N FLA	15 N FLA	16	17 N COL	18 N COL
19 COL	20 N HOU	21 N HOU	22 N HOU	23	24 N FLA	25 N FLA
26 FLA	27 COL	28 N COL	29 N COL	30	31 N HOU	

JUNE

SUN	MON	TUE	WED	THU	FRI	SAT
						1 N HOU
2 HOU	3 N SD	4 N SD	5 N SD	6	7 N SF	8 SF
9 SF	10 N LA	11 N LA	12	13 N NY	14 N NY	15 N NY
16 NY	17	18 N PHI	19 N PHI	20 N MON	21 N MON	22 N MON
23 MON	24 N ATL	25 N ATL	26 N ATL	27 N PIT	28 PIT	29 PIT
30 PIT						

JULY

SUN	MON	TUE	WED	THU	FRI	SAT
	1 N CIN	2 N CIN	3 CIN	4 PIT	5 N PIT	6 N PIT
7 PIT	8 * ALL-STAR GAME	9	10	11 N CHI	12 N CHI	13 CHI
14 CHI	15 N CIN	16 N CIN	17	18 N CHI	19 N CHI	20 CHI
21 CHI	22 N ATL	23 N ATL	24 N ATL	25	26 N MON	27 N MON
28 MON	29	30 N PHI	31 N PHI			

AUGUST

SUN	MON	TUE	WED	THU	FRI	SAT
				1 N PHI	2 N NY	3 N NY
4 NY	5 N SD	6 N SD	7 N SD	8 N SF	9 N SF	10 SF
11 SF	12	13 N LA	14 N LA	15 N LA	16 N FLA	17 FLA
18 FLA	19	20 N COL	21 N COL	22 COL	23 N HOU	24 N HOU
25 HOU	26 N HOU	27 N FLA	28 N FLA	29 N FLA	30 N COL	31 N COL

SEPTEMBER

SUN	MON	TUE	WED	THU	FRI	SAT
1 COL	2 HOU	3 N HOU	4 N HOU	5	6 N SD	7 N SD
8 SD	9 N SF	10 SF	11 N LA	12 N LA	13 N LA	14 LA
15 LA	16 N CHI	17 N CHI	18 N CHI	19 N CIN	20 N CIN	21 CIN
22 CIN	23 N CIN	24 N PIT	25 N PIT	26	27 N CIN	28 CIN
29 CIN	30					

CLUB DIRECTORY

Chairman of the board
August A. Busch III

Vice chairman
Fred L. Kuhlmann

President
Mark Lamping

Vice president, business operations
Mark Gorris

Controller
Brad Wood

Vice president, general manager
Walt Jocketty

Admin. asst. to the president and CEO
Elaine Milo

Admin. asst. to the v.p., general manager
Judy Carpenter Barada

Admin. asst., business operations
Renee Garrett

Vice president, community relations
Marty Hendin

Admin. asst. to the v.p., com. relations
Mary Ellen Edmiston

Director of promotions
Thane Van Breusegen

Director of player development
Mike Jorgensen

Director of scouting
Marty Maier

Dir., major league player personnel
Jerry Walker

Assistants to player dev. and scouting
Scott Smulczenski
John Vuch

Public relations director
Brian Bartow

Dir. of broadcasting and market dev.
Dan Farrell

Promotions supervisor
Mike Ball

Director of group sales
Joe Strohm

Director, target marketing
Ted Savage

Director, ticket systems
Josephine Arnold

Director, human resources
Marian Rhodes

Director, ticket services
Kevin Wade

Manager, office services
Patti McCormick

Traveling secretary
C.J. Cherre

Club physician
Dr. Stan London

Scouting supervisors
Jorge Aranzamendi, Jim Bayens, Jim Belz, Randy Benson, Tim Conroy, Roberto Díaz, John DiPuglia, Charles Fick, Manuel Guerra, Mike Harris, Marty Keough, Tom McCormack, Joe Morlan, Scott Nichols, Jay North, Joe Rigoli, Mike Roberts, Hal Smith, Roger Smith

Special assignment scouts
Fred McAlister, Mike Squires

Part-time scouts
Sergio Beltre, Vern Benson, James Brown, David Clarkson, Manuel Espinosa, Cecil Espy, Jim Johnston, Charles Menzhuber, Joe Popek, Lionel Quijada, Ken Sharpe, Kenneth Thomas

MINOR LEAGUE AFFILIATES

Class	Team	League	Manager
AAA	Louisville	American Association	Joe Pettini
AA	Arkansas	Texas	Rick Mahler
A	St. Petersburg	Florida State	Chris Maloney
A	Peoria	Midwest	Roy Silver
A	New Jersey	New York-Pennsylvania	Scott Melvin
Rookie	Johnson City	Appalachian	Steve Turco

BROADCAST INFORMATION

Radio: KMOX-AM (1120).
TV: KPLR-TV (Channel 11).
Cable TV: Prime Network.

SPRING TRAINING

Ballpark (city): Al Lang Stadium (St. Petersburg, Fla.).
Ticket information: 813-896-4641.

1996 SEASON   St. Louis Cardinals

SPRING TRAINING ROSTER

Manager—Tony La Russa (10).
Coaches—Mark Dejohn (9), Dave Duncan (2), George Hendrick (25), Dave McKay (4), Tommie Reynolds (5).

No.	PITCHERS	B/T	Ht./Wt.	Born	1995 clubs
	Aybar, Manuel	R/R	6-1/165	10-5-74	Savannah, St. Petersburg
59	Bailey, Cory	R/R	6-1/208	1-24-71	Louisville, St. Louis
52	Barber, Brian	R/R	6-1/175	3-4-73	Louisville, St. Louis
41	Benes, Alan	R/R	6-5/215	1-21-72	Louisville, St. Louis
40	Benes, Andy	R/R	6-6/245	8-20-67	San Diego, Seattle
62	Busby, Mike	R/R	6-4/210	12-27-72	Arkansas, Louisville
48	Fossas, Tony	L/L	6-0/200	9-23-57	St. Louis
60	Frascatore, John	R/R	6-1/200	2-4-70	Louisville, St. Louis
38	Honeycutt, Rick	L/L	6-1/191	6-29-54	Oakland, New York A.L.
29	Jackson, Danny	R/L	6-0/220	1-5-62	St. Louis, Louisville
51	Mathews, T.J.	R/R	6-2/200	1-19-70	Louisville, St. Louis
57	Montgomery, Steve	R/R	6-4/210	12-25-70	Arkansas
36	Morgan, Mike	R/R	6-2/220	10-8-59	Orlando, Chicago N.L.
31	Osborne, Donovan	L/L	6-2/195	6-21-69	St. Louis, Arkansas, Louisville
49	Parrett, Jeff	R/R	6-3/195	8-26-61	St. Louis
46	Petkovsek, Mark	R/R	6-0/185	11-18-65	Louisville, St. Louis
	Stottlemyre, Todd	L/R	6-3/200	5-20-65	Oakland
24	Urbani, Tom	L/L	6-1/190	1-21-68	Louisville, St. Louis

No.	CATCHERS	B/T	Ht./Wt.	Born	1995 clubs
71	Marrero, Elieser	R/R	6-1/180	11-17-73	St. Petersburg
19	Pagnozzi, Tom	R/R	6-1/190	7-30-62	St. Louis, Louisville
4	Sheaffer, Danny	R/R	6-0/190	8-2-61	St. Louis

No.	INFIELDERS	B/T	Ht./Wt.	Born	1995 clubs
27	Bell, David	R/R	5-10/170	9-14-72	Buffalo, Cleveland, Louisville, St. Louis
12	Clayton, Royce	R/R	6-0/183	1-2-70	San Francisco
7	Cromer, Tripp	R/R	6-2/165	11-21-67	St. Louis
8	Gaetti, Gary	R/R	6-0/200	8-19-58	Kansas City
	Gallego, Mike	R/R	5-8/175	10-31-65	Oakland, Edmonton
53	Gulan, Mike	R/R	6-1/192	12-18-70	Arkansas, Louisville
68	Holbert, Aaron	R/R	6-0/160	1-9-73	Louisville
64	Johns, Keith	R/R	6-1/175	7-19-71	Arkansas, Louisville
42	Oliva, Jose	R/R	6-3/215	3-3-71	Atlanta, St. Louis
1	Smith, Ozzie	B/R	5-10/180	12-26-54	St. Louis
63	Young, Dmitri	B/R	6-2/210	10-11-73	Arkansas, Louisville

No.	OUTFIELDERS	B/T	Ht./Wt.	Born	1995 clubs
55	Bradshaw, Terry	L/R	6-0/180	2-3-69	Louisville, St. Louis
5	Gant, Ron	R/R	6-0/200	3-2-65	Cincinnati
23	Gilkey, Bernard	R/R	6-0/190	9-24-66	St. Louis, Louisville
3	Jordan, Brian	R/R	6-1/205	3-29-67	St. Louis
16	Lankford, Ray	L/L	5-11/198	6-5-67	St. Louis
47	Mabry, John	L/R	6-4/195	10-17-70	St. Louis, Louisville
70	Mejia, Miguel	R/R	6-1/155	3-25-75	Bluefield, High Desert
30	Sweeney, Mark	L/L	6-1/195	10-26-69	Vancouver, Louisville, St. Louis

BALLPARK INFORMATION

Ballpark (capacity, surface)
Busch Stadium (57,769, grass)

Address
250 Stadium Plaza
St. Louis, MO 63102

Business phone
314-421-3060

Ticket information
314-421-2400

Ticket prices
$25 (dugout level boxes)
$16 (baseline boxes)
$14 (field boxes, loge boxes)
$12 (loge and terrace boxes)
$10.50 (loge reserved)
$9.50 (terrace reserved)
$6 (terrace reserved-children)
$5.50 (general admission)
$5 (bleachers)
$2 (general admission-children)

Field dimensions (from home plate)
To left field at foul line, 330 feet
To center field, 402 feet
To right field at foul line, 330 feet

First game played
May 12, 1966 (Cardinals 4, Braves 3)

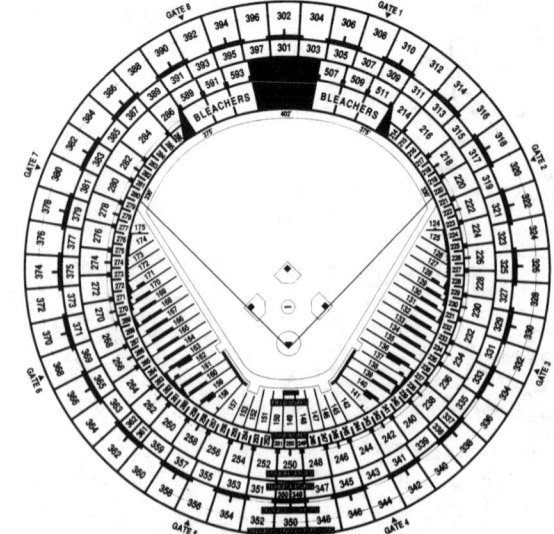

DAY BY DAY

Date	Opp.	Res.	Score	(inn.*)	Hits	Opp. hits	Winning pitcher	Losing pitcher	Save	Record	Pos.	GB
4-26	Phi.	W	7-6		11	9	Arocha	Charlton		1-0	T1st	...
4-27	Phi.	L	2-6		10	8	West	Jackson		1-1	T2nd	1
4-28	At N.Y.	L	8-10		14	11	Minor	Arocha	Franco	1-2	T2nd	2
4-29	At N.Y.	L	4-5	(11)	8	10	Mlicki	Palacios		1-3	T2nd	3
4-30	At N.Y.	W	3-0		11	4	Urbani	B. Jones	Henke	2-3	T2nd	2
5-1	Pit.	W	4-0		10	5	Hill	Wagner		3-3	2nd	1¹/₂
5-2	Pit.	L	6-7		11	7	Dyer	Jackson	Gott	3-4	3rd	1¹/₂
5-3	Pit.	W	8-6		14	14	Watson	Loaiza	Henke	4-4	3rd	¹/₂
5-4	Hou.	L	4-6		10	10	Jones	DeLucia	Hudek	4-5	3rd	1¹/₂
5-5	Hou.	L	4-9		8	11	Hampton	Urbani		4-6	3rd	2¹/₂
5-6	Hou.	W	7-5		11	7	Palacios	Swindell	Henke	5-6	3rd	2
5-7	Hou.	W	6-5		7	14	Parrett	Drabek	Henke	6-6	3rd	1
5-8	Chi.	L	4-7		8	8	Bullinger	Watson	Myers	6-7	3rd	2
5-9	Chi.	L	0-3		7	5	Trachsel	Osborne	Myers	6-8	3rd	3
5-10	Chi.	W	11-1		12	5	Hill	Foster		7-8	3rd	2
5-12	At L.A.	L	4-8		5	10	Jackson			7-9	4th	3
5-13	At L.A.	W	3-2		6	10	Frascatore	Astacio	Henke	8-9	3rd	3
5-14	At L.A.	W	6-5	(11)	8	10	Arocha	Osuna	Henke	9-9	3rd	2
5-15	At S.D.	L	5-7		9	12	Hermanson	DeLucia	Berumen	9-10	T3rd	3
5-16	At S.D.	L	0-1		6	7	Hoffman	Parrett		9-11	T3rd	4
5-17	At S.D.	L	1-2		8	7	Ashby	Jackson	Hoffman	9-12	4th	4
5-18	At S.F.	W	4-2	(10)	7	8	Arocha	Frey	Henke	10-12	4th	3¹/₂
5-19	At S.F.	L	5-6		9	9	Beck	Habyan		10-13	4th	4¹/₂
5-20	At S.F.	L	7-10		9	8	Beck	Arocha		10-14	4th	5¹/₂
5-21	At S.F.	W	9-7		12	17	DeLucia	Mulholland	Henke	11-14	4th	5¹/₂
5-23	Atl.	L	1-7		5	8	Maddux	Jackson		11-15	4th	6
5-24	Atl.	L	5-9		6	13	Glavine	Frascatore		11-16	4th	7
5-25	Atl.	W	4-1		8	6	Hill	Avery	Henke	12-16	4th	6
5-26	Cin.	L	3-4		12	11	Jarvis	Arocha	Carrasco	12-17	5th	6
5-27	Cin.	L	2-5		9	10	Rijo	Palacios		12-18	5th	7
5-28	Cin.	L	2-9		7	14	Pugh	Jackson		12-19	5th	8
5-29	Col.	W	6-5	(11)	11	13	Habyan	Bailey		13-19	5th	7
5-30	Col.	W	8-5		14	11	Hill	Grahe	Henke	14-19	T4th	6¹/₂
5-31	Col.	L	3-5		9	9	Acevedo	Petkovsek	Holmes	14-20	T4th	7¹/₂
6-1	At Mon.	L	2-6		7	11	Perez	Watson	Shaw	14-21	5th	7¹/₂
6-2	At Cin.	W	10-7		16	8	Parrett	Smith	Henke	15-21	T4th	7¹/₂
6-3	At Cin.	L	4-8		12	12	Pugh	DeLucia		15-22	T4th	7¹/₂
6-4	At Cin.	L	0-4		2	5	Schourek	Hill		15-23	4th	8¹/₂
6-5	At Col.	W	9-5		13	11	Petkovsek	Acevedo		16-23	4th	8¹/₂
6-6	At Col.	L	4-5		9	11	Leskanic	Parrett		16-24	4th	9¹/₂
6-7	At Col.	L	3-7		10	9	Freeman	Jackson		16-25	4th	9¹/₂
6-9	At Atl.	L	2-3	(10)	6	8	McMichael	Arocha		16-26	4th	11
6-10	At Atl.	W	7-3		12	7	DeLucia	Glavine		17-26	4th	11
6-11	At Atl.	W	8-4		14	13	Habyan	Avery	Henke	18-26	4th	11
6-13	S.D.	W	3-2		8	4	Fossas	B. Williams	Henke	19-26	4th	10¹/₂
6-14	S.D.	L	0-3		2	8	Hamilton	Hill		19-27	4th	10¹/₂
6-15	S.D.	W	2-1		5	5	Petkovsek	Sanders	Henke	20-27	4th	10
6-16	S.F.	W	6-5		8	10	Palacios	VanLandingham	Henke	21-27	4th	9
6-17	S.F.	L	1-4		4	10	Bautista	Urbani	Beck	21-28	4th	10
6-18	S.F.	L	1-6		5	11	Portugal	Morgan		21-29	4th	11
6-19	L.A.	L	2-5		3	9	Nomo	Hill	Worrell	21-30	4th	11
6-20	L.A.	W	7-0		11	8	Petkovsek	Astacio		22-30	4th	10
6-21	L.A.	L	1-10		5	9	Candiotti	Palacios		22-31	4th	11
6-23	Phi.	W	7-1		10	9	Morgan	Schilling		23-31	4th	10¹/₂
6-24	Phi.	L	9-10		11	17	Quantrill	Hill	Slocumb	23-32	4th	11¹/₂
6-25	Phi.	L	3-5		6	10	Green	Urbani	Slocumb	23-33	4th	11¹/₂
6-26	At Hou.	L	0-11		6	14	Swindell	Petkovsek		23-34	5th	12
6-27	At Hou.	L	2-6		8	9	Drabek	Jackson		23-35	5th	13
6-28	At Hou.	L	0-9		5	11	Hampton	Morgan		23-36	5th	14
6-29	At Chi.	W	6-4		9	10	Hill	Foster		24-36	5th	14
6-30	At Chi.	W	3-1		8	9	Urbani	Castillo	Henke	25-36	5th	13
7-1	At Chi.	L	7-8		10	10	Perez	Habyan	Myers	25-37	5th	14
7-2	At Chi.	L	6-7		13	8	Bullinger	Jackson	Myers	25-38	5th	15
7-3	Mon.	W	6-0		10	1	Morgan	Henry		26-38	5th	14
7-4	Mon.	L	0-5		4	10	Martinez	Hill		26-39	5th	15
7-5	Mon.	W	4-3	(10)	10	9	DeLucia	Rojas		27-39	5th	15
7-6	Fla.	W	3-2	(12)	8	7	Habyan	Mantei		28-39	5th	14
7-7	Fla.	W	4-0		11	4	Jackson	Witt		29-39	4th	14
7-8	Fla.	W	3-2		9	11	Watson	Burkett	Henke	30-39	4th	13
7-9	Fla.	L	0-6		7	9	Gardner	Hill		30-40	5th	14
7-12	At Phi.	W	4-3		5	9	Jackson	Mimbs	Henke	31-40	5th	13¹/₂

Date	Opp.	Res.	Score	(inn.*)	Hits	Opp. hits	Winning pitcher	Losing pitcher	Save	Record	Pos.	GB
7-13	At Pit.	L	6-7		5	12	Dyer	Parrett	Miceli	31-41	5th	14¹/₂
7-14	At Pit.	W	6-4		11	10	Hill	Loaiza	Henke	32-41	5th	14¹/₂
7-15	At Pit.	L	2-9		6	10	Neagle	Watson		32-42	5th	15¹/₂
7-16	At Pit.	L	0-3		7	7	Parris	Osborne	Miceli	32-43	5th	15¹/₂
7-17	At Mon.	W	8-5		10	9	DeLucia	Shaw	Henke	33-43	5th	14¹/₂
7-18	At Mon.	L	2-5		7	10	Fassero	Urbani	Rojas	33-44	5th	15¹/₂
7-19	N.Y.	L	4-5	(10)	8	13	DiPoto	DeLucia	Franco	33-45	5th	16¹/₂
7-20	N.Y.	W	8-6		8	12	Watson	Mlicki	Henke	34-45	5th	16
7-21	At Phi.	L	0-7		4	10	Fernandez	Osborne	Borland	34-46	5th	17
7-22	At Phi.	W	5-3	(11)	11	9	DeLucia	Olivares	Henke	35-46	5th	17
7-23	At Phi.	L	6-10		8	11	Quantrill	Hill	Borland	35-47	5th	18
7-25	N.Y.	W	8-7	(11)	10	14	Petkovsek	DiPoto		36-47	5th	16¹/₂
7-26	N.Y.	W	3-2	(11)	8	9	Fossas	Henry		37-47	T4th	15¹/₂
7-27	At Mon.	L	1-2		4	4	Perez	Jackson	Rojas	37-48	T4th	16¹/₂
7-28	At Fla.	L	0-6		4	9	Hammond	Petkovsek		37-49	5th	17¹/₂
7-29	At Fla.	L	0-2		7	5	Burkett	Watson	Nen	37-50	5th	17¹/₂
7-30	At Fla.	L	1-3		6	7	Perez	Arocha	Nen	37-51	5th	17¹/₂
8-1	Hou.	L	6-8		10	14	Hampton	Jackson		37-52	5th	18¹/₂
8-2	Hou.	L	2-4		7	7	Reynolds	Osborne	Jones	37-53	5th	19¹/₂
8-3	Hou.	W	2-1		8	9	Watson	Swindell	Henke	38-53	5th	19¹/₂
8-4	Chi.	L	3-5		5	8	Trachsel	Morgan	Myers	38-54	T4th	20¹/₂
8-5	Chi.	L	0-1		5	4	Bullinger	DeLucia	Myers	38-55	5th	21
8-6	Chi.	W	4-3	(13)	13	12	Parrett	Nabholz		39-55	5th	21¹/₂
8-8	At L.A.	L	3-4		6	9	Astacio	Parrett	Worrell	39-56	5th	21¹/₂
8-9	At L.A.	L	2-4		10	8	Candiotti	Morgan	Worrell	39-57	5th	22¹/₂
8-10	At L.A.	W	2-1		6	6	Petkovsek	Nomo	Henke	40-57	5th	21¹/₂
8-11†	At S.D.	L	0-3		5	7	Ashby	Jackson		40-58		
8-11‡	At S.D.	L	2-5		7	13	Bochtler	DeLucia	Hoffman	40-59	5th	22
8-12	At S.D.	L	5-6		8	9	Dishman	Mathews	Florie	40-60	5th	22
8-14	At S.F.	L	1-4		5	8	VanLandingham	Osborne	Beck	40-61	5th	22¹/₂
8-15	At S.F.	L	2-4		5	12	Brewington	Morgan	Beck	40-62	5th	23¹/₂
8-16	At S.F.	L	1-2		3	4	Leiter	Petkovsek		40-63	5th	23¹/₂
8-18	Atl.	W	4-3		10	8	Watson	Mercker	Henke	41-63	5th	24
8-19	Atl.	W	5-4		9	9	Urbani	Murray	Henke	42-63	5th	24
8-20	Atl.	L	0-1		2	7	Maddux	Morgan		42-64	5th	25
8-21	Cin.	W	8-6		9	12	Mathews	Jackson		43-64	5th	24
8-22	Cin.	W	7-3		10	8	Barber	Schourek		44-64	5th	23
8-23	Cin.	L	1-3		6	7	Wells	Watson		44-65	5th	24
8-24	Cin.	W	6-5		8	9	DeLucia	Carrasco	Henke	45-65	5th	23
8-25	At Col.	W	8-3		14	7	Morgan	Rekar	Mathews	46-65	5th	23
8-26	At Col.	W	5-4		6	5	Fossas	Ruffin	Henke	47-65	5th	23
8-27	At Col.	W	10-5		18	10	Barber	Reynoso		48-65	4th	23
8-28	At Cin.	L	2-5		6	9	Wells	Watson		48-66	4th	24
8-29	At Cin.	L	1-4		6	9	Burba	Osborne		48-67	5th	25
8-30	At Cin.	W	4-3		7	8	Morgan	Portugal	Henke	49-67	4th	24
9-1	Col.	W	5-4		8	6	DeLucia	Leskanic	Henke	50-67	4th	23¹/₂
9-2	Col.	L	1-6		5	4	Bailey	Watson		50-68	T4th	23¹/₂
9-3	Col.	L	4-5	(11)	9	11	Holmes	Parrett	Ruffin	50-69	5th	23¹/₂
9-4	At Atl.	L	5-6		9	12	Wohlers	Parrett		50-70	5th	24¹/₂
9-5	At Atl.	L	0-1		7	6	Maddux	Urbani		50-71	5th	24¹/₂
9-6	At Atl.	L	1-6		7	8	Glavine	Petkovsek		50-72	5th	25¹/₂
9-7	S.D.	W	5-2		8	7	Watson	Dishman	Henke	51-72	5th	25
9-8	S.D.	W	5-2		10	4	Osborne	Hamilton	Henke	52-72	T4th	24
9-9	S.D.	W	7-5		8	14	Parrett	Bochtler	Henke	53-72	4th	23
9-11	S.F.	W	13-4		13	8	Petkovsek	Brewington		54-72	4th	22¹/₂
9-12	S.F.	W	10-4		15	10	DeLucia	Leiter		55-72	4th	21¹/₂
9-13	S.F.	W	8-4		11	10	Osborne	S. Valdez		56-72	4th	21¹/₂
9-15	L.A.	L	6-7		13	12	Astacio	Henke	Worrell	56-73	4th	22
9-16	L.A.	W	5-4		11	9	Henke	Osuna		57-73	4th	21
9-17	L.A.	L	0-8		2	11	Valdes	Watson		57-74	4th	21
9-18	At Pit.	W	4-2		10	6	Osborne	Loaiza	Mathews	58-74	4th	21
9-19	At Pit.	L	1-12		7	14	Wagner	Benes		58-75	4th	21
9-20	At Pit.	W	9-3		12	10	Morgan	White		59-75	4th	21
9-22	At Hou.	W	3-0		7	4	Watson	Drabek	Henke	60-75	4th	21
9-23	At Hou.	L	3-7		10	8	Wall	Petkovsek		60-76	4th	21
9-24	At Hou.	L	0-1	(10)	7	6	Hartgraves	DeLucia		60-77	4th	22
9-25	At Chi.	L	0-7		1	11	Castillo	Benes		60-78	4th	22
9-26	At Chi.	L	2-3		5	7	Trachsel	Parrett	Myers	60-79	4th	22¹/₂
9-27	At Chi.	L	3-5		10	8	Foster	Watson	Myers	60-80	4th	22
9-29	Pit.	W	3-2		4	7	Osborne	Morel	Henke	61-80	4th	22¹/₂
9-30	Pit.	W	5-1		11	7	Benes	Wagner	Henke	62-80	4th	21¹/₂
10-1	Pit.	L	4-10		10	14	White	Barber		62-81	4th	22¹/₂

Monthly records: April (2-3), May (12-17), June (11-16), July (12-15), August (12-16), September (13-13), October (0-1).
*Innings, if other than nine. †First game of doubleheader. ‡Second game of doubleheader.

HIGHLIGHTS

High point: On August 27, the Cardinals completed their first sweep of a three-game series in 1995 by winning at Colorado, 10-5. That sweep represented three of only 23 road victories for the Cards, who had the worst away record in the majors.

Low point: An August West Coast trip in which the Cardinals went 1-8 (and scored only 18 runs) left them 23 games below .500. The lone victory came by forfeit in Los Angeles.

Turning point: After trading Todd Zeile and firing manager Joe Torre on June 16, the Cardinals dropped six of their last nine games on a homestand and never were close to contention again. They had won four of their last five before Torre's dismissal.

Most valuable player: Outfielder Ray Lankford. Lankford had his best power year with 25 homers and also led the club in RBIs (82) and tied for the team lead in steals (24).

Most valuable pitcher: Reliever Tom Henke. Henke, at 37, was thought to be on the downward slope but saved 36 games in 38 opportunities. Without him, the Cards would have finished in the American Association.

Most improved player: Outfielder Brian Jordan. In his first season as a regular, Jordan had 22 homers and 81 RBIs and made just one error. He had 490 at-bats; previously, his high had been 223.

Most pleasant surprise: First baseman John Mabry. He started the season in the minors. By the majors' belated opening day, Mabry was the Cardinals' first baseman. He wound up hitting .307 and also saw outfield duty.

Biggest disappointment: The list is lengthy. Danny Jackson, signed as the No. 1 starter, was plagued by illness and injury and finished 2-12. Third baseman Scott Cooper, acquired from Boston (where he was a two-time All-Star), batted .230 and drove in only 16 runs at home. Shortstop Ozzie Smith and catcher Tom Pagnozzi were injured and hit just .199 and .215, respectively. And Ken Hill was only 6-7 with a 5.06 ERA before being traded to Cleveland.

Key injuries: Smith went out in mid-May with shoulder problems and didn't return for three months. Pagnozzi missed two months with a broken bone below his left knee, then suffered a wrist fracture. Geronimo Pena had a wasted season at second base, turning up on the disabled list three times.

Notable: Lankford slammed 10 homers in September and connected in four consecutive games. . . . The Cardinals' road mark of 23-48 was their worst in 76 years. . . . Rookie Mark Sweeney had seven consecutive pinch hits, one short of the big-league record. . . . It was the Cards' last season on artificial turf; Busch Stadium will have grass in '96.

—RICK HUMMEL

RECORDS

1995 regular-season record: 62-81 (4th in Central); 39-33 at home; 23-48 on road; 19-23 vs. East; 20-32 vs. Central; 23-26 vs. West; 13-23 vs. lefthanded starters; 49-58 vs. righthanded starters; 14-30 on grass; 48-51 on turf; 17-27 in daytime; 45-54 at night; 25-25 in one-run games; 9-5 in extra-inning games; 0-1-0 in doubleheaders.
Team record past five years: 369-374 (.497, ranks 8th in league in that span).

TEAM LEADERS

Batting average: Bernard Gilkey (.298).
At-bats: Brian Jordan (490).
Runs: Brian Jordan (83).
Hits: Brian Jordan (145).
Total bases: Ray Lankford (248).
Doubles: Ray Lankford (35).
Triples: Bernard Gilkey, Brian Jordan (4).
Home runs: Ray Lankford (25).
Runs batted in: Ray Lankford (82).
Stolen bases: Brian Jordan, Ray Lankford (24).
Slugging percentage: Bernard Gilkey (.490).
On-base percentage: Ray Lankford (.360).
Wins: Rich DeLucia (8).
Earned-run average: No qualifiers.
Complete games: Danny Jackson (2).
Shutouts: Danny Jackson, Mark Petkovsek (1).
Saves: Tom Henke (36).
Innings pitched: Mike Morgan (131.1).
Strikeouts: Donovan Osborne (82).

GAMES BY POSITION

Catcher: Danny Sheaffer 67, Tom Pagnozzi 61, Scott Hemond 38.
First base: John Mabry 73, Todd Zeile 34, Mark Sweeney 19, Darnell Coles 18, Gerald Perry 11, Danny Sheaffer 3, Ray Giannelli 2, Jose Oliva 2, Chris Sabo 2.
Second base: Jose Oquendo 62, David Bell 37, Geronimo Pena 25, Ramon Caraballo 24, Tripp Cromer 11, Scott Hemond 6, Tim Hulett 2, Manny Lee 1.
Third base: Scott Cooper 110, Darnell Coles 22, Jose Oliva 18, David Bell 3, Jose Oquendo 2, Chris Sabo 1, Danny Sheaffer 1.
Shortstop: Tripp Cromer 95, Ozzie Smith 41, Jose Oquendo 24, Tim Hulett 1.
Outfield: Ray Lankford 129, Brian Jordan 126, Bernard Gilkey 118, John Mabry 39, Allen Battle 32, Terry Bradshaw 10, Ray Giannelli 2, Darnell Coles 1, Jose Oquendo 1, Mark Sweeney 1.

TOP DRAFT CHOICES

1a. **Matt Morris**, RHP, Seton Hall University.
1b. **Chris Haas**, 3B, St. Mary's H.S., Paducah, Ky.
2. **Jason Woolf**, SS, American H.S., Hialeah, Fla.
3. **Billy Deck**, 1B, Potomac H.S., Dumphries, Va.
4. **Brian Barfield**, RHP, DeKalb (Ga.) J.C.
5. **Cody McKay**, 3B, Arizona State University.
6. **Joe Freitas**, OF, Fresno State University.
7. **Matt King**, RHP, Galveston (Tex.) J.C.
8. **Jon Ward**, RHP, Cal State Fullerton.
9. **Ryan McHugh**, OF, Florida Southern College.
10. **Matt DeWitt**, RHP-3B, Valley H.S., Las Vegas, Nev.

1996 SEASON *St. Louis Cardinals*

SAN DIEGO PADRES
NATIONAL LEAGUE WEST DIVISION

1996 PADRES SCHEDULE

Home games shaded.
* — All-Star Game at Veterans Stadium (Philadelphia)
N — Night game (any game starting after 5 p.m.)

MARCH

SUN	MON	TUE	WED	THU	FRI	SAT
31						

APRIL

SUN	MON	TUE	WED	THU	FRI	SAT
	1 CHI	2	3 CHI	4	5 N HOU	6 N HOU
7 HOU	8 FLA	9 N FLA	10 N FLA	11 ATL	12 N ATL	13 N ATL
14 ATL	15 N COL	16 N COL	17 COL	18	19 N ATL	20 N ATL
21 ATL	22 N FLA	23 FLA	24 N CHI	25 CHI	26 N HOU	27 N HOU
28 HOU	29 HOU	30 N SF				

MAY

SUN	MON	TUE	WED	THU	FRI	SAT
			1 N SF	2	3 N STL	4 N STL
5 STL	6	7 N PIT	8 N PIT	9 N PIT	10 N CIN	11 N CIN
12 CIN	13 N NY	14 N NY	15 N NY	16 NY	17 N MON	18 N MON
19 MON	20	21 N PHI	22 N PHI	23 PHI	24 N NY	25 NY
26 NY	27 N MON	28 N MON	29 N MON	30	31 N PHI	

JUNE

SUN	MON	TUE	WED	THU	FRI	SAT
						1 N PHI
2 PHI	3 N STL	4 N STL	5 N STL	6	7 N PIT	8 N PIT
9 PIT	10 N CIN	11 N CIN	12 N CIN	13 N CHI	14 CHI	15 CHI
16 CHI	17 N ATL	18 N ATL	19 ATL	20 CHI	21 N CHI	22 N CHI
23 CHI	24	25 N HOU	26 N HOU	27 N SF	28 N SF	29 SF
30 SF						

JULY

SUN	MON	TUE	WED	THU	FRI	SAT
	1 N LA	2 N LA	3 N LA	4 SF	5 N SF	6 N SF
7 SF	8 *	9	10	11 N COL	12 N COL	13 N COL
14 COL	15 N LA	16 N LA	17 N LA	18 N COL	19 N COL	20 N COL
21 N COL	22 N HOU	23 N HOU	24 N HOU	25	26 N FLA	27 N FLA
28 FLA	29 FLA	30 N ATL	31 N ATL			

AUGUST

SUN	MON	TUE	WED	THU	FRI	SAT
				1 ATL	2 N FLA	3 N FLA
4 FLA	5 N STL	6 N STL	7 N STL	8 N PIT	9 N PIT	10 N PIT
11 PIT	12	13 N CIN	14 N CIN	15 N NY	16 N NY	17 N NY
18 NY	19 N MON	20 N MON	21 N MON	22	23 N PHI	24 N PHI
25 PHI	26	27 N NY	28 N NY	29 NY	30 N MON	31 N MON

SEPTEMBER

SUN	MON	TUE	WED	THU	FRI	SAT
1 MON	2 N PHI	3 N PHI	4 N PHI	5	6 N STL	7 N STL
8 STL	9 N PIT	10 N PIT	11 N PIT	12	13 N CIN	14 CIN
15 CIN	16 N SF	17 N SF	18 N SF	19 N LA	20 N LA	21 LA
22 LA	23 N COL	24 N COL	25 N LA	26 N LA	27 N LA	28 LA
29 LA						

1996 SEASON

CLUB DIRECTORY

Chairman
John Moores

President & chief executive officer
Larry Lucchino

Executive vice president
Bill Adams

V.p./baseball operations and g.m.
Kevin Towers

Vice president/marketing
Don Johnson

Vice president/public affairs
Charles Steinberg

Vice president/special projects
Andy Strasberg

Vice president/finance
Bob Wells

Assistant general manager
Fred Uhlman Jr.

Director/community relations
Michele Anderson

Director/merchandising
Michael Babida

Director/corporate development
Michael Dee

Controller
Steve Fitch

Director/administrative services
Lucy Freeman

Director/ticket operations & services
Dave Gilmore

Director/stadium operations
Mark Guglielmo

Director/Hispanic marketing
Enrique Morones

Director/Padres Foundation
Jennifer Moores

Director/player development
Russ Nixon

Director/minor league administration
Priscilla Oppenheimer

Club counsel
Alan Ostfield

Dir./media relations and team travel
Roger Riley

Director/sales
Louis Ruvane

Director/scouting
Brad Sloan

Trainer
Larry Duensing

Assistant trainer
Todd Hutcheson

Strength and conditioning coach
Dean Armitage

Club physicians
Cliff Colwell
Jan Fronek
Paul Hirshman
Blaine Phillips

Major league scouts
Ken Bracey
Ray Crone Sr.

Advance scout
Jeff Gardner

Supervisor
Bob Cummings

Area scouts
Chas Bolton, Howard Bowens, Eddie Dixon, Jimmy Dreyer, Denny Galehouse, Ronquito Garcia, Al Hargesheimer, Gary Kendall, Don Lyle, Rodney McCray, Tim McWilliam, Juan Melo, Rene Mons, Pat Murtaugh, Gary Roenicke, Bruce Seid, Greg Smith, Van Smith, Mark Wasinger, Jeff Wetherby

Part-time scouts
Pedro Avila, Bob Buob, Julio Coronado, Robert Gutierrez, Joe Ray Halsey, Timothy Harkness, Bill Killian, Darryl Milne, Chuck Pierce

MINOR LEAGUE AFFILIATES

Class	Team	League	Manager
AAA	Las Vegas	Pacific Coast	Jerry Royster
AA	Memphis	Southern	Ed Romero
A	Rancho Cucamonga	California	Mike Basso
A	Clinton	Midwest	Mike Ramsey
Rookie	Idaho Falls	Pioneer	Don Werner
Rookie	Peoria Padres	Arizona	Larry See

BROADCAST INFORMATION
Radio: KFMB-AM (760).
TV: KFMB-TV (Channel 8).
Cable TV: Prime Ticket Network.

SPRING TRAINING
Ballpark (city): Peoria Stadium (Peoria, Ariz.).
Ticket information: 602-878-4337.

SPRING TRAINING ROSTER

Manager—Bruce Bochy (15).
Coaches—Tim Flannery (4), Grady Little, Davey Lopes (42), Rob Picciolo (5), Merv Rettenmund (16), Dan Warthen.

No.	PITCHERS	B/T	Ht./Wt.	Born	1995 clubs
43	Ashby, Andy	R/R	6-5/190	7-11-67	San Diego
35	Beckett, Robbie	R/L	6-5/240	7-16-72	Memphis
55	Berumen, Andres	R/R	6-2/205	4-5-71	San Diego, Las Vegas, Rancho Cucamonga
45	Bochtler, Doug	R/R	6-3/200	7-5-70	Las Vegas, San Diego
33	Dishman, Glenn	R/L	6-1/195	11-5-70	Las Vegas, San Diego
39	Florie, Bryce	R/R	5-11/190	5-21-70	San Diego
50	Hamilton, Joey	R/R	6-4/230	9-9-70	San Diego
	Harriger, Denny	R/R	5-11/185	7-21-69	Las Vegas
48	Hermanson, Dustin	R/R	6-2/195	12-21-72	Las Vegas, San Diego
51	Hoffman, Trevor	R/R	6-0/205	10-13-67	San Diego
	Kaufman, Brad	R/R	6-2/210	4-26-72	Memphis
54	Kroon, Marc	R/R	6-2/195	4-2-73	Memphis, San Diego
	Long, Joey	R/L	6-2/220	7-15-70	Las Vegas, Memphis
27	Sanders, Scott	R/R	6-4/220	3-25-69	San Diego, Las Vegas
	Tewksbury, Bob	R/R	6-4/205	11-30-60	Texas, Charlotte
34	Valenzuela, Fernando	L/L	5-11/202	11-1-60	San Diego
49	Villone, Ron	L/L	6-3/235	1-16-70	Seattle, Tacoma, San Diego
36	Worrell, Tim	R/R	6-4/220	7-5-67	Rancho Cucamonga, Las Vegas, San Diego

No.	CATCHERS	B/T	Ht./Wt.	Born	1995 clubs
11	Ausmus, Brad	R/R	5-11/190	4-14-69	San Diego
53	Casanova, Raul	B/R	5-11/200	8-23-72	Memphis
25	Johnson, Brian	R/R	6-2/200	1-8-68	San Diego
59	Mulligan, Sean	R/R	6-2/210	4-25-70	Las Vegas

No.	INFIELDERS	B/T	Ht./Wt.	Born	1995 clubs
7	Bush, Homer	R/R	5-10/175	11-12-72	Memphis
21	Caminiti, Ken	B/R	6-0/200	4-21-63	San Diego
4	Cedeno, Andujar	R/R	6-1/170	8-21-69	San Diego
29	Cianfrocco, Archi	R/R	6-5/215	10-6-66	Las Vegas, San Diego
12	Joyner, Wally	L/L	6-2/200	6-16-62	Kansas City
9	Livingstone, Scott	L/R	6-0/190	7-15-65	San Diego
1	Lopez, Luis	B/R	5-11/175	9-4-70	San Diego
24	Petagine, Roberto	L/L	6-1/170	6-7-71	San Diego, Las Vegas
3	Reed, Jody	R/R	5-9/165	7-26-62	San Diego
	Velandia, Jorge	R/R	5-9/160	1-12-75	Memphis, Las Vegas

No.	OUTFIELDERS	B/T	Ht./Wt.	Born	1995 clubs
12	Finley, Steve	L/L	6-2/180	3-12-65	San Diego
19	Gwynn, Tony	L/L	5-11/215	5-9-60	San Diego
24	Henderson, Rickey	R/L	5-10/190	12-25-58	Oakland
58	Johnson, Earl	B/R	5-10/165	10-3-71	Memphis, Rancho Cucamonga
14	Newfield, Marc	R/R	6-4/205	10-19-72	Tacoma, Seattle, Las Vegas, San Diego
3	Nieves, Melvin	B/R	6-2/210	12-28-71	San Diego

BALLPARK INFORMATION

Ballpark (capacity, surface)
San Diego/Jack Murphy Stadium (46,510, grass)

Address
P.O. Box 2000
San Diego, CA 92112-2000

Business phone
619-283-4494

Ticket information
619-283-4494

Ticket prices
$14 (sky boxes, field level, IF)
$13 (field level/OF, plaza level/IF)
$12 (plaza level/OF)
$11 (loge level)
$10 (press level)
$7 (left field grandstand)
$5 (high fives, bleachers)

Field dimensions (from home plate)
To left field at foul line, 327 feet
To center field, 405 feet
To right field at foul line, 327 feet

First game played
April 8, 1969 (Padres 2, Astros 1)

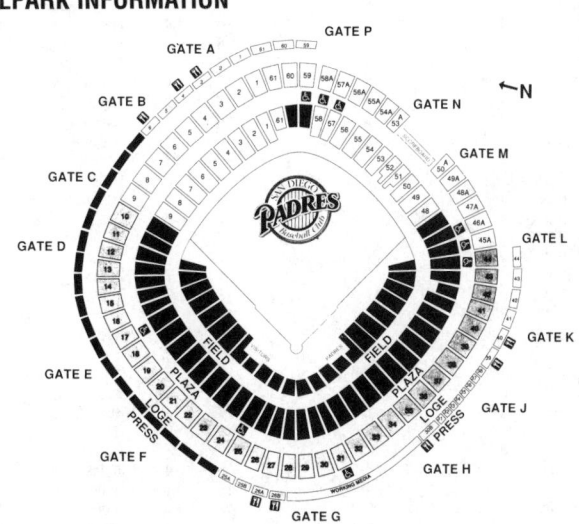

DAY BY DAY

San Diego Padres — 1996 SEASON

Date	Opp.	Res.	Score	(inn.*)	Hits	Opp. hits	Winning pitcher	Losing pitcher	Save	Record	Pos.	GB
4-26	Hou.	L	2-10		8	12	Drabek	Benes		0-1	T3rd	1 1/2
4-27	Hou.	W	13-1		21	5	Ashby	Reynolds		1-1	3rd	1
4-28	Cin.	W	8-7		12	11	Berumen	Carrasco		2-1	3rd	1
4-29	Cin.	W	9-5		10	8	Sanders	Schourek		3-1	T2nd	1
4-30	Cin.	W	7-6		12	10	Hoffman	Carrasco		4-1	T1st	...
5-1	At Col.	L	3-8		7	11	Holmes	Mauser		4-2	2nd	1
5-2	At Col.	L	5-6	(11)	11	14	Bailey	B. Williams		4-3	T2nd	2
5-3	At Col.	L	7-12		12	14	Bailey	Hamilton	Ruffin	4-4	T2nd	3
5-4	S.F.	L	4-5		10	7	Wilson	B. Williams	Beck	4-5	4th	3 1/2
5-5	S.F.	L	2-9		8	9	Rosselli	Valenzuela		4-6	4th	3 1/2
5-6	S.F.	L	6-13		16	18	Mulholland	Benes		4-7	4th	3 1/2
5-7	S.F.	L	4-11		8	12	Portugal	Ashby	Beck	4-8	4th	4
5-8	L.A.	W	5-2		8	8	Hermanson	Osuna	Hoffman	5-8	4th	3 1/2
5-9	L.A.	W	9-2		13	7	Sanders	Candiotti		6-8	4th	3
5-10	L.A.	L	1-3		8	5	Martinez	Valenzuela	Worrell	6-9	4th	4
5-12	At Chi.	L	4-8		10	11	Navarro	Benes		6-10	4th	5 1/2
5-13	At Chi.	L	0-5		3	8	Castillo	Ashby		6-11	4th	5 1/2
5-14	At Chi.	W	9-7		7	13	Hermanson	Perez	Hoffman	7-11	4th	5 1/2
5-15	St.L.	W	7-5		12	9	Hermanson	DeLucia	Berumen	8-11	4th	4 1/2
5-16	St.L.	W	1-0		7	6	Hoffman	Parrett		9-11	4th	3 1/2
5-17	St.L.	W	2-1		7	8	Ashby	Jackson	Hoffman	10-11	4th	3 1/2
5-19	Pit.	L	6-8		12	10	Lieber	Hamilton	Miceli	10-12	T3rd	3
5-20	Pit.	W	9-6		9	13	Valenzuela	Gott		11-12	3rd	2
5-21	Pit.	L	1-6		5	11	Neagle	Benes		11-13	3rd	3
5-23	At Mon.	L	4-6		8	11	Fassero	Ashby	Rojas	11-14	T3rd	3 1/2
5-24	At Mon.	L	2-3		11	7	Shaw	Berumen	Aquino	11-15	4th	3 1/2
5-25	At Mon.	W	4-3		12	4	Sanders	Henry	Hoffman	12-15	4th	3
5-26	At Phi.	L	0-2		2	5	Mimbs	Benes		12-16	4th	3
5-27	At Phi.	L	4-5	(10)	11	11	Abbott	Hermanson		12-17	4th	3
5-28	At Phi.	W	13-5	(10)	14	12	Hoffman	Harris		13-17	T3rd	3
5-29	At N.Y.	W	3-2	(13)	14	8	Blair	Minor	Hoffman	14-17	3rd	2 1/2
5-30	At N.Y.	L	0-8		4	7	Harnisch	Sanders		14-18	3rd	3 1/2
5-31	At N.Y.	L	5-7	(10)	11	12	Franco	Hoffman		14-19	T3rd	3 1/2
6-2	Mon.	L	1-7		3	10	Fassero	Berumen		14-20	4th	4 1/2
6-3	Mon.	L	0-1	(10)	1	5	Martinez	B. Williams	Rojas	14-21	4th	5 1/2
6-4	Mon.	W	8-4		13	8	Sanders	Henry		15-21	4th	5 1/2
6-5	Phi.	W	5-4	(10)	13	7	Hoffman	Charlton		16-21	4th	4 1/2
6-6	Phi.	W	1-0		7	6	Valenzuela	Williams	Hoffman	17-21	4th	4 1/2
6-7	Phi.	L	1-7		2	14	Schilling	Ashby		17-22	4th	5 1/2
6-9	N.Y.	W	8-4		11	6	Hamilton	Harnisch	Hoffman	18-22	4th	5 1/2
6-10	N.Y.	W	4-2		6	4	Sanders	B. Jones		19-22	4th	4 1/2
6-11	N.Y.	W	6-3		7	7	B. Williams	DiPoto		20-22	3rd	4 1/2
6-13	At St.L.	L	2-3		4	8	Fossas	B. Williams	Henke	20-23	4th	5
6-14	At St.L.	W	3-0		8	2	Hamilton	Hill		21-23	4th	5
6-15	At St.L.	L	1-2		5	5	Petkovsek	Sanders	Henke	21-24	4th	5 1/2
6-16	At Pit.	W	12-4		12	4	Benes	Loaiza		22-24	3rd	4 1/2
6-17	At Pit.	W	11-8		18	10	Florie	Lieber	Hoffman	23-24	3rd	3 1/2
6-18	At Pit.	W	2-0		6	4	Ashby	Wagner		24-24	3rd	2 1/2
6-19	Chi.	W	5-3		8	4	Berumen	Foster	Hoffman	25-24	3rd	1 1/2
6-20	Chi.	L	2-7		10	12	Castillo	Sanders		25-25	3rd	1 1/2
6-21	Chi.	W	1-0		5	6	Benes	Trachsel		26-25	3rd	1 1/2
6-22	Col.	L	2-3		6	9	Reynoso	Dishman	Ruffin	26-26	4th	2 1/2
6-23	Col.	W	3-2		5	8	Ashby	Freeman	Hoffman	27-26	T3rd	1 1/2
6-24	Col.	W	2-0		6	4	Hamilton	Ritz		28-26	3rd	1/2
6-25	Col.	L	3-11		7	14	Grahe	Sanders		28-27	3rd	1 1/2
6-26	At L.A.	L	5-8		11	7	Worrell	B. Williams		28-28	3rd	2 1/2
6-27	At L.A.	W	14-3		18	3	Dishman	Martinez		29-28	3rd	2
6-28	At L.A.	W	8-2		11	4	Ashby	Valdes		30-28	3rd	1
6-30	At S.F.	L	6-7		12	10	Hook	Hoffman		30-29	3rd	1 1/2
7-1	At S.F.	L	1-4		8	5	VanLandingham	Sanders	Beck	30-30	4th	2
7-2	At S.F.	W	15-3		14	5	Benes	Rosselli		31-30	3rd	1 1/2
7-3	At Fla.	L	2-5		7	10	Burkett	Dishman		31-31	4th	2 1/2
7-4	At Fla.	L	4-6		9	9	Gardner	Ashby		31-32	4th	2 1/2
7-5	At Fla.	W	7-4	(10)	13	7	Florie	Perez	Hoffman	32-32	3rd	2 1/2
7-6	At Hou.	L	4-5	(12)	6	10	Jones	B. Williams		32-33	4th	3 1/2
7-7	At Hou.	L	4-5		15	11	Dougherty	Kroon		32-34	4th	4 1/2
7-8†	At Hou.	L	2-3	(17)	10	10	Brocail	B. Williams		32-35		
7-8‡	At Hou.	L	1-4		8	8	Hampton	Valenzuela	Jones	32-36	4th	6
7-9	At Hou.	W	9-2		8	6	Ashby	Kile		33-36	T3rd	6
7-13	Atl.	L	1-4		5	8	Maddux	Hamilton		33-37	4th	6
7-14	Atl.	L	2-6		8	9	Glavine	Benes		33-38	4th	6

Date	Opp.	Res.	Score	(inn.*)	Hits	Opp. hits	Winning pitcher	Losing pitcher	Save	Record	Pos.	GB
7-15	Atl.	L	6-7		6	6	Clontz	Florie	Wohlers	33-39	4th	7
7-16	Atl.	W	3-1		12	3	Dishman	Mercker	Hoffman	34-39	4th	6
7-17	Cin.	W	8-6		8	9	Blair	Nitkowski	Hoffman	35-39	T3rd	6
7-18	Cin.	L	1-5		6	7	McElroy	Hamilton		35-40	T3rd	6
7-19	Cin.	L	4-7		8	11	Jackson	Hoffman	Brantley	35-41	T3rd	7
7-21	At Atl.	W	9-6		13	11	Bochtler	McMichael	Hoffman	36-41	3rd	6½
7-22	At Atl.	L	2-3		7	9	Wohlers	Blair		36-42	3rd	7½
7-23	At Atl.	L	1-2		9	6	Smoltz	Hamilton	Wohlers	36-43	3rd	8½
7-24	At Cin.	W	10-8		14	11	Benes	Portugal	Hoffman	37-43	3rd	8½
7-25	At Cin.	W	4-2		8	7	B. Williams	Pugh	Hoffman	38-43	3rd	7½
7-27†	At Fla.	W	8-2		13	10	Blair	Weathers		39-43		
7-27‡	At Fla.	L	5-8		6	11	Gardner	Dishman	Mathews	39-44	3rd	6½
7-28	Hou.	W	3-2		7	11	Hamilton	Reynolds	Hoffman	40-44	3rd	6½
7-29	Hou.	L	1-6		8	12	Swindell	Benes		40-45	3rd	7½
7-30	Hou.	L	1-7		13	8	Drabek	B. Williams		40-46	3rd	7½
7-31	Hou.	W	5-1		9	5	Ashby	Kile		41-46	3rd	7½
8-1	S.F.	L	3-4		6	8	Leiter	Dishman	Beck	41-47	3rd	7½
8-2	S.F.	W	11-3		16	9	Villone	Barton		42-47	3rd	6½
8-3	S.F.	W	3-0		10	4	Blair	S. Valdez	Hoffman	43-47	3rd	6½
8-4	At Col.	L	12-14		20	12	Reed	Berumen	Holmes	43-48	3rd	7½
8-5	At Col.	L	3-7		9	15	Reynoso	Ashby		43-49	3rd	8½
8-6	At Col.	W	16-8		19	12	Dishman	Thompson		44-49	3rd	7½
8-8	At Col.	W	3-1		8	11	Hamilton	Foster	Hoffman	45-49	3rd	6½
8-10†	At Chi.	W	3-2		6	6	Blair	Castillo	Hoffman	46-49		
8-10‡	At Chi.	L	5-12		7	13	Trachsel	B. Williams		46-50	3rd	5½
8-11†	St.L.	W	3-0		7	5	Ashby	Jackson		47-50		
8-11‡	St.L.	W	5-2		13	7	Bochtler	DeLucia	Hoffman	48-50	3rd	4
8-12	St.L.	W	6-5		9	8	Dishman	Mathews	Florie	49-50	3rd	4
8-14	Pit.	W	6-5		9	6	Bochtler	Christiansen	Hoffman	50-50	3rd	3½
8-15	Pit.	L	0-6		7	7	Parris	Blair		50-51	3rd	4½
8-16	Pit.	W	2-0		7	5	Ashby	Ericks	Hoffman	51-51	3rd	4½
8-18	At Mon.	L	3-7		6	11	Fassero	Dishman	Fraser	51-52	3rd	4
8-19	At Mon.	W	9-5		17	11	Hamilton	Heredia		52-52	3rd	3
8-20	At Mon.	W	3-0		7	5	Blair	Martinez	Hoffman	53-52	3rd	2
8-21	At Phi.	L	1-3		7	5	Fernandez	Ashby	Borland	53-53	3rd	3
8-22	At Phi.	W	5-3		11	10	Valenzuela	Greene	Hoffman	54-53	3rd	3
8-23	At Phi.	L	8-12		13	11	Williams	Dishman	Mimbs	54-54	3rd	4
8-24	At N.Y.	L	4-5		9	8	Florence	Hoffman		54-55	3rd	4
8-25	At N.Y.	L	5-10		7	14	Isringhausen	Blair	Minor	54-56	3rd	4
8-26	At N.Y.	L	6-7		11	12	Pulsipher	Ashby	Franco	54-57	3rd	4
8-27	At N.Y.	W	4-1		7	6	Valenzuela	Cornelius	Villone	55-57	3rd	4
8-29	Mon.	L	1-2		9	7	Fassero	Hamilton	Rojas	55-58	3rd	4
8-30	Mon.	W	3-2		13	8	Hoffman	Harris		56-58	3rd	3
8-31	Mon.	L	4-5	(10)	8	10	Fraser	Villone	Rojas	56-59	3rd	4
9-1	Phi.	W	6-3		11	10	Valenzuela	Grace	Hoffman	57-59	3rd	3
9-2	Phi.	W	6-5	(11)	10	10	Hoffman	Slocumb		58-59	3rd	2½
9-3	Phi.	L	2-3		9	8	Quantrill	Hamilton	Slocumb	58-60	3rd	3½
9-4	N.Y.	W	2-1	(10)	9	7	Hoffman	Henry		59-60	3rd	3
9-5	N.Y.	L	0-4		7	5	Isringhausen	Ashby	Franco	59-61	3rd	4
9-6	N.Y.	W	6-5		11	11	Bochtler	DiPoto		60-61	3rd	3
9-7	At St.L.	L	2-5		7	8	Watson	Dishman	Henke	60-62	3rd	3½
9-8	At St.L.	L	2-5		4	10	Osborne	Hamilton	Henke	60-63	3rd	4½
9-9	At St.L.	L	5-7		14	8	Parrett	Bochtler	Henke	60-64	T3rd	5½
9-11	At Pit.	L	5-7		13	8	Lieber	Ashby	Miceli	60-65	4th	7
9-12	At Pit.	W	5-1		9	7	Valenzuela	Ericks		61-65	3rd	7
9-13	At Pit.	W	8-7		10	10	Villone	Plesac	Bochtler	62-65	3rd	6
9-14	At Cin.	L	1-8		4	8	Wells	Blair		62-66	3rd	6½
9-15	Chi.	L	2-6		6	12	Castillo	Bochtler	Myers	62-67	T3rd	7½
9-16	Chi.	W	12-4		17	9	Ashby	Trachsel		63-67	3rd	7½
9-17	Chi.	W	11-3		13	8	Valenzuela	Foster		64-67	3rd	6½
9-18	Col.	L	1-5		4	11	Ritz	Hamilton	Ruffin	64-68	3rd	7½
9-19	Col.	W	15-4		18	9	Blair	Reynoso		65-68	3rd	6½
9-20	Col.	L	2-10		5	16	Swift	Dishman		65-69	3rd	7½
9-21	At L.A.	W	5-1		11	9	Ashby	Candiotti	Hoffman	66-69	3rd	6½
9-22	At L.A.	L	5-6		16	7	Astacio	Florie	Worrell	66-70	3rd	7½
9-23	At L.A.	L	2-4		7	7	Valdes	Bochtler		66-71	3rd	7½
9-24	At L.A.	L	2-6		7	10	Nomo	Blair		66-72	3rd	8½
9-25	At S.F.	W	7-4		12	10	B. Williams	Mulholland	Hoffman	67-72	3rd	8
9-26	At S.F.	W	6-3		10	10	Ashby	S. Valdez	Hoffman	68-72	3rd	7½
9-27	At S.F.	W	4-2		6	5	Valenzuela	Estes	Hoffman	69-72	3rd	7
9-29	L.A.	W	6-5		10	8	Worrell	Osuna	Hoffman	70-72	3rd	6
9-30	L.A.	L	2-7		7	12	Nomo	Bochtler		70-73	3rd	7
10-1	L.A.	L	1-4		4	10	Daal	B. Williams	Bruske	70-74	3rd	8

Monthly records: April (4-1), May (10-18), June (16-10), July (11-17), August (15-13), September (14-14), October (0-1).
*Innings, if other than nine. †First game of doubleheader. ‡Second game of doubleheader.

1996 SEASON San Diego Padres

HIGHLIGHTS

High point: The Padres won two in a row at Montreal to move two games out of first in the N.L. West on August 20. At that point, the club had won nine of its last 13.

Low point: The Padres lost all three games in St. Louis (September 7-9) to start a 2-5 trip that dropped them out of the race.

Turning point: Having won two in a row at Los Angeles to move 1 1/2 games out of first place, the Padres took a 6-4 lead into the ninth inning of their next game in San Francisco on June 30. But Barry Bonds' three-run homer defeated the Padres, who then plummeted.

Most valuable player: Center fielder Steve Finley. In addition to his superb defense, Finley more than offset the loss of leadoff hitter Bip Roberts from June 27 to August 22 to keep the Padres in contention.

Most valuable pitcher: Righthander Andy Ashby. He led the Padres in victories (12), shutouts (two) and ERA (2.94) and assumed the No. 1 starter's spot after Andy Benes was traded to Seattle on July 31.

Most improved player: Third baseman Ken Caminiti. Yes, he made a career-high 27 errors, but for the first time, he showed he could handle cleanup duty. He set career marks in batting average (.302), home runs (26), RBIs (94) and steals (12).

Most pleasant surprise: Lefthander Fernando Valenzuela. He had his first winning season (8-3) since 1986, and during a 24-game span in August and September, he was the only Padres starter to get a victory.

Biggest disappointments: Shortstop Andujar Cedeno and first baseman Eddie Williams. Cedeno's defense was lax at times; he also struck out 92 times and batted .210. Slowed by injuries, Williams struggled in the field, failed to anchor the cleanup spot and was benched down the stretch.

Key injuries: Roberts missed 71 games because of leg and back injuries. Pitcher Scott Sanders did not start after July 19 because of an elbow injury. Outfielder Tony Gwynn played the final 10 weeks despite a broken right big toe.

Notables: The Padres set club records for grand slams (nine), pinch-hit homers (10) and strikeouts (1,047). . . . Caminiti became the first major leaguer to hit homers from both sides of the plate three times in one season. . . . Gwynn won his sixth N.L. batting title with a .368 average, his 13th consecutive season over .300. . . . Director of scouting Kevin Towers became G.M., replacing Randy Smith, who resigned September 26.

—TOM KRASOVIC

RECORDS

1995 regular-season record: 70-74 (3rd in West); 40-32 at home; 30-42 on road; 22-27 vs. East; 32-24 vs. Central; 16-23 vs. West; 17-23 vs. lefthanded starters; 53-51 vs. righthanded starters; 56-56 on grass; 14-18 on turf; 24-24 in daytime; 46-50 at night; 20-22 in one-run games; 6-7 in extra-inning games; 1-1-2 in doubleheaders.

Team record past five years: 344-403 (.461, ranks 12th in league in that span).

TEAM LEADERS

Batting average: Tony Gwynn (.368).
At-bats: Tony Gwynn (535).
Runs: Steve Finley (104).
Hits: Tony Gwynn (197).
Total bases: Ken Caminiti (270).
Doubles: Ken Caminiti, Tony Gwynn (33).
Triples: Steve Finley (8).
Home runs: Ken Caminiti (26).
Runs batted in: Ken Caminiti (94).
Stolen bases: Steve Finley (36).
Slugging percentage: Ken Caminiti (.513).
On-base percentage: Tony Gwynn (.404).
Wins: Andy Ashby (12).
Earned-run average: Andy Ashby (2.94).
Complete games: Andy Ashby, Joey Hamilton (2).
Shutouts: Andy Ashby, Joey Hamilton (2).
Saves: Trevor Hoffman (31).
Innings pitched: Joey Hamilton (204.1).
Strikeouts: Andy Ashby (150).

GAMES BY POSITION

Catcher: Brad Ausmus 100, Brian Johnson 55.

First base: Eddie Williams 81, Roberto Petagine 51, Scott Livingstone 43, Archi Cianfrocco 30, Phil Clark 2, Brian Johnson 2, Melvin Nieves 2, Brad Ausmus 1, Tim Hyers 1.

Second base: Jody Reed 130, Bip Roberts 25, Ray Holbert 7, Scott Livingstone 4, Archi Cianfrocco 3.

Third base: Ken Caminiti 143, Scott Livingstone 13, Archi Cianfrocco 3, Andujar Cedeno 1.

Shortstop: Andujar Cedeno 116, Ray Holbert 30, Archi Cianfrocco 15, Bip Roberts 7, Jody Reed 5.

Outfield: Steve Finley 138, Tony Gwynn 133, Melvin Nieves 79, Bip Roberts 50, Phil Plantier 39, Phil Clark 34, Marc Newfield 19, Archi Cianfrocco 7, Ray McDavid 7, Billy Bean 4, Roberto Petagine 2, Ray Holbert 1.

TOP DRAFT CHOICES

1. **Ben Davis,** C, Malvern (Pa.) Prep.
2. **Gabe Alvarez,** SS, University of Southern California.
3. **Ryan Van de Weg,** RHP, Western Michigan University.
4. **Brandon Kolb,** RHP, Texas Tech.
5. **Kenny Henderson,** RHP, University of Miami.
6. **Kevin Walker,** LHP, Grand Prairie (Tex.) H.S.
7. **Jason Tolman,** 2B, Texas Tech.
8. **Sean Watkins,** 1B, Bradley University.
9. **Mike Martin,** C, Florida State University.
10. **James Sak,** RHP, Illinois Benedictine College.

SAN FRANCISCO GIANTS
NATIONAL LEAGUE WEST DIVISION

1996 SEASON San Francisco Giants

SPRING TRAINING ROSTER

Manager— Dusty Baker (12).
Coaches—Bobby Bonds (16), Robert E. Brenly (15), Wendall K. Kim (20), Robert P. Lillis (5), Dick Pole (48).

No.	PITCHERS	B/T	Ht./Wt.	Born	1995 clubs
	Barton, Shawn	R/L	6-3/195	5-14-63	Phoenix, San Francisco
38	Bautista, Jose	R/R	6-2/205	7-25-64	San Francisco
47	Beck, Rod	R/R	6-1/236	8-3-68	San Francisco
	Bourgeois, Steve	R/R	6-1/220	8-4-72	Shreveport, Phoenix
67	Brewington, Jamie	R/R	6-4/180	9-28-71	Shreveport, San Francisco
51	Creek, Doug	L/L	5-10/205	3-1-69	Louisville, Arkansas, St. Louis
46	DeLucia, Rich	R/R	6-0/185	10-7-64	St. Louis
40	Dewey, Mark	R/R	6-0/216	1-3-65	San Francisco
	Estes, Shawn	B/L	6-2/185	2-18-73	Wisconsin Rapids, Burlington, San Jose, Shreveport, San Francisco
	Fernandez, Osvaldo	R/R	6-1/190	11-4-68	Cuban national team
	Juden, Jeff	R/R	6-8/265	1-19-71	Scranton/Wilkes-Barre, Philadelphia
13	Leiter, Mark	R/R	6-3/210	4-13-63	San Francisco
	Pickett, Ricky	L/L	6-1/200	1-19-70	Chattanooga, Shreveport
53	Rosselli, Joe	R/L	6-1/170	5-28-72	San Francisco, Phoenix
34	Service, Scott	R/R	6-6/226	2-26-67	Indianapolis, San Francisco
	Valdez, Carlos	R/R	5-11/175	12-26-71	Shreveport, Phoenix, San Francisco
26	Valdez, Sergio	R/R	6-1/190	9-7-65	Phoenix, San Francisco
50	VanLandingham, William	R/R	6-2/210	7-16-70	San Jose, San Francisco
39	Watson, Allen	L/L	6-3/190	11-18-70	St. Louis, Louisville, Arkansas

No.	CATCHERS	B/T	Ht./Wt.	Born	1995 clubs
54	Jensen, Marcus	B/R	6-4/195	12-14-72	Shreveport
49	Lampkin, Tom	L/R	5-11/185	3-4-64	San Francisco
8	Manwaring, Kirt	R/R	5-11/203	7-15-65	San Francisco

No.	INFIELDERS	B/T	Ht./Wt.	Born	1995 clubs
26	Aurilia, Rich	R/R	6-1/170	9-2-71	Shreveport, Phoenix, San Francisco
18	Batiste, Kim	R/R	6-0/200	3-15-68	Scranton/Wilkes-Barre, Bowie, Rochester
	Canizaro, Jay	R/R	5-9/170	7-4-73	Shreveport
	Dunston, Shawon	R/R	6-1/180	3-21-63	Chicago N.L.
	King, Brett	R/R	6-1/190	7-20-72	San Jose
22	McCarty, David	R/L	6-5/213	11-23-69	Minnesota, Indianapolis, Phoenix, San Francisco
	Mueller, Bill	B/R	5-11/175	3-17-71	Shreveport, Phoenix
13	Phillips, J.R.	L/L	6-1/185	4-29-70	San Francisco
23	Scarsone, Steve	R/R	6-2/195	4-11-66	San Francisco
6	Thompson, Robby	R/R	5-11/173	5-10-62	San Francisco
9	Williams, Matt	R/R	6-2/216	11-28-65	San Francisco, San Jose

No.	OUTFIELDERS	B/T	Ht./Wt.	Born	1995 clubs
7	Benard, Marvin	L/L	5-9/180	1-20-70	Phoenix, San Francisco
25	Bonds, Barry	L/L	6-1/185	7-24-64	San Francisco
45	Carreon, Mark	R/L	6-0/195	7-9-63	San Francisco
4	Hill, Glenallen	R/R	6-2/220	3-22-65	San Francisco
28	Javier, Stan	B/R	6-0/185	1-9-64	Oakland
2	Leonard, Mark	L/R	6-0/212	8-14-64	Phoenix, San Francisco
	Singleton, Chris	L/L	6-2/195	8-15-72	San Jose
	Williams, Keith	R/R	6-0/190	4-21-72	Shreveport, Phoenix, Everett

BALLPARK INFORMATION

Ballpark (capacity, surface)
Candlestick Park (63,000, grass)

Address
Candlestick Park
San Francisco, CA 94124

Business phone
415-468-3700

Ticket information
415-467-8000

Ticket prices
$15 (lower box)
$12 (upper box)
$12 (lower reserved)
$7 (upper reserved)
$6 (pavilion)
$5 (bleachers)

Field dimensions (from home plate)
To left field at foul line, 335 feet
To center field, 400 feet
To right field at foul line, 328 feet

First game played
April 12, 1960 (Giants 3, Cardinals 1)

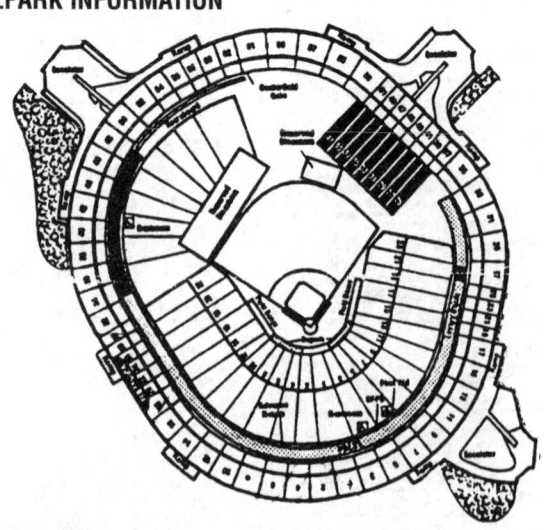

DAY BY DAY

Date	Opp.	Res.	Score	(inn.*)	Hits	Opp. hits	Winning pitcher	Losing pitcher	Save	Record	Pos.	GB
4-26	At Atl.	L	5-12		6	17	Maddux	Mulholland		0-1	T3rd	$1^1/2$
4-27	At Atl.	L	4-6		6	6	Stanton	Burba	Clontz	0-2	4th	2
4-28	Fla.	W	4-0		6	2	Leiter	Witt		1-2	4th	2
4-29	Fla.	W	1-0		7	3	Wilson	Rapp	Beck	2-2	4th	2
4-30	Fla.	L	3-10		6	11	Burkett	Torres		2-3	4th	2
5-1	L.A.	W	7-0		9	7	Mulholland	Candiotti		3-3	T3rd	2
5-2	L.A.	W	4-3	(15)	9	12	Hook	Hansell		4-3	T2nd	2
5-3	L.A.	L	6-7		14	13	Osuna	Beck	Worrell	4-4	T2nd	3
5-4	At S.D.	W	5-4		7	10	Wilson	B. Williams	Beck	5-4	2nd	$2^1/2$
5-5	At S.D.	W	9-2		9	8	Rosselli	Valenzuela		6-4	2nd	$1^1/2$
5-6	At S.D.	W	13-6		18	16	Mulholland	Benes		7-4	2nd	$^1/2$
5-7	At S.D.	W	11-4		12	8	Portugal	Ashby	Beck	8-4	1st	$+^1/2$
5-9	At Col.	L	6-10		10	13	Ritz	Wilson		8-5	2nd	$^1/2$
5-10	At Col.	L	5-8		12	13	Holmes	Bautista		8-6	T2nd	$1^1/2$
5-11	At Col.	L	4-10		7	11	Acevedo	Mulholland	Reed	8-7	3rd	$2^1/2$
5-12	Pit.	L	4-9		7	13	Neagle	Portugal		8-8	3rd	$3^1/2$
5-13	Pit.	W	6-4		11	9	Rosselli	Wilson	Beck	9-8	2nd	$2^1/2$
5-14	Pit.	W	2-1	(10)	8	5	Beck	Miceli		10-8	2nd	$2^1/2$
5-15	Chi.	L	1-6		3	13	Trachsel	Leiter		10-9	3rd	$2^1/2$
5-16	Chi.	L	0-2		3	6	Navarro	Mulholland	Myers	10-10	3rd	$2^1/2$
5-17	Chi.	W	2-1		2	4	Portugal	Foster	Beck	11-10	2nd	$2^1/2$
5-18	St.L.	L	2-4	(10)	8	7	Arocha	Frey	Henke	11-11	2nd	$2^1/2$
5-19	St.L.	W	6-5		9	9	Beck	Habyan		12-11	2nd	$1^1/2$
5-20	St.L.	W	10-7		8	9	Beck	Arocha		13-11	2nd	$^1/2$
5-21	St.L.	L	7-9		17	12	DeLucia	Mulholland	Henke	13-12	2nd	$1^1/2$
5-23	At Phi.	L	5-6		5	11	Harris	Beck		13-13	2nd	2
5-24	At Phi.	L	1-2		7	7	Charlton	Wilson	Slocumb	13-14	2nd	2
5-25	At Phi.	W	3-1	(6)	4	4	Leiter	Green		14-14	2nd	$1^1/2$
5-26	At N.Y.	W	6-4		11	13	Dewey	Henry	Beck	15-14	2nd	$^1/2$
5-27	At N.Y.	L	3-6		7	10	Saberhagen	Bautista		15-15	2nd	$1^1/2$
5-28	At N.Y.	W	5-1		10	7	Portugal	Mlicki		16-15	2nd	$^1/2$
5-29	At Mon.	W	11-6		8	9	Burba	Rojas		17-15	1st	$+^1/2$
5-30	At Mon.	W	4-3	(11)	7	10	Bautista	Shaw	Beck	18-15	1st	$+1^1/2$
5-31	At Mon.	L	4-5		10	9	Heredia	Mulholland	Rojas	18-16	1st	$+^1/2$
6-2	Phi.	W	4-2		7	9	Beck	Harris		19-16	1st	$+^1/2$
6-3	Phi.	W	3-1		9	8	Wilson	Quantrill	Beck	20-16	1st	$+^1/2$
6-4	Phi.	W	4-0		8	4	Leiter	Green		21-16	1st	$+^1/2$
6-5	N.Y.	L	2-7		11	11	B. Jones	Mulholland		21-17	1st	$+^1/2$
6-6	N.Y.	W	2-1		8	6	Hook	Franco		22-17	1st	$+^1/2$
6-7	N.Y.	W	9-8		12	12	Burba	Minor	Beck	23-17	1st	$+^1/2$
6-8	N.Y.	L	6-9		10	14	Mlicki	Wilson	Henry	23-18	2nd	$^1/2$
6-9	Mon.	L	3-9		12	14	Martinez	Leiter	Shaw	23-19	2nd	$1^1/2$
6-10	Mon.	L	5-11		7	13	Henry	Bautista		23-20	2nd	$1^1/2$
6-11	Mon.	L	8-10	(13)	16	20	G. White	Mintz		23-21	2nd	$2^1/2$
6-13	At Chi.	W	8-4		13	6	Portugal	Navarro		24-21	2nd	2
6-14	At Chi.	W	4-3	(13)	11	12	Mintz	Young	Beck	25-21	2nd	2
6-15	At Chi.	L	1-3		4	8	Castillo	Leiter	Myers	25-22	2nd	$2^1/2$
6-16	At St.L.	L	5-6		10	8	Palacios	VanLandingham	Henke	25-23	2nd	$2^1/2$
6-17	At St.L.	W	4-1		10	4	Bautista	Urbani	Beck	26-23	2nd	$1^1/2$
6-18	At St.L.	W	6-1		11	5	Portugal	Morgan		27-23	2nd	$^1/2$
6-19	At Pit.	L	2-8		8	9	Neagle	Mintz		27-24	2nd	$^1/2$
6-20	At Pit.	L	3-5		10	10	Loaiza	Leiter	Miceli	27-25	2nd	$^1/2$
6-21	At Pit.	W	6-5		11	12	Burba	Mccurry	Beck	28-25	2nd	$^1/2$
6-22	At L.A.	L	6-7		14	9	Seanez	Burba	Worrell	28-26	2nd	$1^1/2$
6-23	At L.A.	L	2-7		5	13	Valdes	Portugal		28-27	T3rd	$1^1/2$
6-24	At L.A.	L	0-7		2	12	Nomo	Leiter		28-28	4th	$1^1/2$
6-25	At L.A.	L	2-3		9	8	Candiotti	VanLandingham	Worrell	28-29	4th	$2^1/2$
6-27	Col.	L	1-5		3	9	Swift	Bautista		28-30	4th	$3^1/2$
6-28	Col.	W	2-1	(11)	6	10	Barton	Munoz		29-30	4th	$2^1/2$
6-30	S.D.	W	7-6		10	12	Hook	Hoffman		30-30	4th	2
7-1	S.D.	W	4-1		5	8	VanLandingham	Sanders	Beck	31-30	3rd	$1^1/2$
7-2	S.D.	L	3-15		5	14	Benes	Rosselli		31-31	4th	2
7-3	At Cin.	W	8-7		11	10	Burba	Hernandez	Beck	32-31	3rd	2
7-4	At Cin.	L	6-10		12	13	Schourek	Mulholland		32-32	3rd	2
7-5	At Cin.	L	0-9		4	10	Rijo	Leiter		32-33	4th	3
7-6	At Cin.	W	7-5		14	9	Barton	Brantley	Beck	33-33	T2nd	3
7-7	At Atl.	L	4-8		10	11	Glavine	Greer		33-34	T2nd	4
7-8	At Atl.	L	4-9		6	14	Avery	Portugal		33-35	3rd	5
7-9	At Atl.	L	2-3		8	6	Wohlers	Beck		33-36	T3rd	6
7-13	Hou.	W	6-5	(12)	7	10	Hook	Dougherty		34-36	T2nd	5
7-14	Hou.	L	8-13		12	15	Dougherty	Portugal	Veres	34-37	3rd	5

Date	Opp.	Res.	Score	(inn.*)	Hits	Opp. hits	Winning pitcher	Losing pitcher	Save	Record	Pos.	GB
7-15	Hou.	L	9-15		12	18	Dougherty	Greer		34-38	3rd	6
7-16	Hou.	W	7-6	(14)	11	11	Hook	Brocail		35-38	3rd	5
7-17	Fla.	L	8-10		10	12	Mathews	Beck	Nen	35-39	T3rd	6
7-18	Fla.	L	10-12	(14)	16	15	Murphy	Bautista		35-40	T3rd	6
7-19	Fla.	L	1-3		5	8	Burkett	Portugal		35-41	T3rd	7
7-20	At Hou.	L	4-11		9	15	Drabek	Mulholland		35-42	4th	8
7-21	At Hou.	W	6-3		9	9	Leiter	Kile	Beck	36-42	4th	7
7-22	At Hou.	L	6-7		11	12	Hampton	Wilson	Jones	36-43	4th	8
7-23	At Hou.	L	2-3	(10)	7	9	Brocail	Service		36-44	4th	9
7-24	At Fla.	W	8-3		14	8	Brewington	Burkett		37-44	4th	9
7-25	At Fla.	L	3-9		7	15	Witt	Mulholland		37-45	4th	9
7-26	Cin.	W	4-1		7	2	Leiter	Schourek		38-45	4th	8
7-27	Cin.	L	6-14		12	14	Burba	Aquino		38-46	4th	8
7-28	Atl.	L	2-6		4	6	Clontz	Beck		38-47	4th	8
7-29	Atl.	L	1-5		4	8	Maddux	Mulholland		38-48	4th	10
7-30	Atl.	W	3-2		6	6	Brewington	Glavine	Beck	39-48	4th	9
8-1	At S.D.	W	4-3		8	6	Leiter	Dishman	Beck	40-48	4th	8 1/2
8-2	At S.D.	L	3-11		9	16	Villone	Barton		40-49	4th	8 1/2
8-3	At S.D.	L	0-3		4	10	Blair	S. Valdez	Hoffman	40-50	4th	9 1/2
8-4	L.A.	W	15-1		16	7	VanLandingham	Candiotti		41-50	4th	9 1/2
8-5	L.A.	L	0-3		1	7	Nomo	Brewington		41-51	4th	10 1/2
8-6	L.A.	W	3-1		7	5	Leiter	Valdes		42-51	4th	9 1/2
8-7	L.A.	L	1-3	(12)	6	6	Osuna	Bautista	Worrell	42-52	4th	10
8-8	Pit.	L	5-9		8	11	Neagle	S. Valdez		42-53	4th	10
8-9	Pit.	W	4-3		8	8	VanLandingham	Christiansen	Beck	43-53	4th	9
8-10	Pit.	W	8-7		10	12	Beck	Mccurry		44-53	4th	8
8-11	Chi.	L	2-6		7	10	Bullinger	Leiter		44-54	4th	8
8-12	Chi.	L	0-4		8	8	Navarro	Bautista		44-55	4th	9
8-13	Chi.	W	6-3		10	9	S. Valdez	Foster	Beck	45-55	4th	9
8-14	St.L.	W	4-1		8	5	VanLandingham	Osborne	Beck	46-55	4th	8
8-15	St.L.	W	4-2		12	5	Brewington	Morgan	Beck	47-55	4th	8
8-16	St.L.	W	2-1		4	3	Leiter	Petkovsek		48-55	4th	8
8-18	At Phi.	L	8-16		12	18	Mimbs	Hook		48-56	4th	7 1/2
8-19	At Phi.	L	4-6		8	12	Bottalico	S. Valdez	Slocumb	48-57	4th	7 1/2
8-20	At Phi.	L	7-8	(10)	15	15	Slocumb	Bautista	Slocumb	48-58	4th	7 1/2
8-21	At N.Y.	L	4-5	(11)	7	10	Byrd	Beck		48-59	4th	8 1/2
8-22	At N.Y.	W	5-1		10	4	Leiter	Cornelius		49-59	4th	8 1/2
8-23	At N.Y.	W	3-2		9	4	Mulholland	Telgheder		50-59	4th	8 1/2
8-24	At Mon.	W	5-3		8	7	Service	Leiper	Beck	51-59	4th	7 1/2
8-25	At Mon.	L	1-12		3	15	Martinez	VanLandingham		51-60	4th	7 1/2
8-26	At Mon.	W	2-1		10	4	Brewington	Alvarez	Beck	52-60	4th	6 1/2
8-27	At Mon.	L	0-1		1	4	Rueter	Leiter		52-61	4th	7 1/2
8-29	Phi.	W	6-4		10	10	Mulholland	Quantrill	Beck	53-61	4th	6 1/2
8-30	Phi.	W	4-1		6	5	VanLandingham	Juden	Beck	54-61	4th	5 1/2
8-31	Phi.	L	0-6		5	8	Fernandez	Brewington		54-62	4th	6 1/2
9-1	N.Y.	W	6-5		9	10	Barton	Franco		55-62	4th	5 1/2
9-2	N.Y.	W	5-3		8	4	S. Valdez	Cornelius		56-62	4th	5
9-3	N.Y.	L	6-11		11	16	Florence	C. Valdez	DiPoto	56-63	4th	6
9-4	Mon.	W	2-1		4	7	Barton	Rojas		57-63	4th	5 1/2
9-5	Mon.	W	9-6		12	7	Bautista	DeLeon	Beck	58-63	4th	5 1/2
9-6	Mon.	L	2-8		2	12	Alvarez	Leiter		58-64	4th	5 1/2
9-8	At Chi.	W	7-3		12	10	S. Valdez	Navarro	Beck	59-64	4th	5 1/2
9-9	At Chi.	W	8-3		14	8	Mulholland	Castillo		60-64	T3rd	5 1/2
9-10	At Chi.	W	8-7		12	10	VanLandingham	Trachsel	Beck	61-64	3rd	5 1/2
9-11	At St.L.	L	4-13		8	13	Petkovsek	Brewington		61-65	3rd	6 1/2
9-12	At St.L.	L	4-10		10	15	DeLucia	Leiter		61-66	4th	7 1/2
9-13	At St.L.	L	4-8		10	11	Osborne	S. Valdez		61-67	4th	7 1/2
9-15	At Pit.	W	4-2	(10)	9	4	Service	Dyer	Beck	62-67	T3rd	7 1/2
9-16	At Pit.	L	2-10		10	9	Neagle	Estes		62-68	4th	8 1/2
9-17	At Pit.	L	4-5		13	8	Lieber	Brewington	Plesac	62-69	4th	8 1/2
9-19	At L.A.	W	7-2		8	6	Leiter	Nomo	Barton	63-69	4th	8
9-20	At L.A.	L	2-4		7	5	Martinez	Mulholland	Worrell	63-70	4th	9
9-21	Col.	W	5-3		10	9	S. Valdez	Grahe	Beck	64-70	4th	8
9-22	Col.	L	1-6		2	10	Ritz	Estes		64-71	4th	9
9-23	Col.	W	2-0		8	2	Brewington	Rekar	Beck	65-71	4th	8
9-24	Col.	L	1-3		4	5	Reynoso	Leiter	Leskanic	65-72	4th	9
9-25	S.D.	L	4-7		10	12	B. Williams	Mulholland	Hoffman	65-73	4th	9 1/2
9-26	S.D.	L	3-6		10	10	Ashby	S. Valdez	Hoffman	65-74	4th	10
9-27	S.D.	L	2-4		5	6	Valenzuela	Estes	Hoffman	65-75	4th	10 1/2
9-28	At Col.	W	12-4		18	12	Brewington	Rekar		66-75	4th	10
9-29	At Col.	W	10-7		15	12	Service	Leskanic	Beck	67-75	4th	9
9-30	At Col.	L	3-9		14	13	Swift	Mulholland		67-76	4th	10
10-1	At Col.	L	9-10		13	15	Painter	Leiter	Leskanic	67-77	4th	11

Monthly records: April (2-3), May (16-13), June (12-14), July (9-18), August (15-14), September (13-14), October (0-1).
*Innings, if other than nine.

HIGHLIGHTS

High point: On May 30, Barry Bonds and Matt Williams hit back-to-back homers in the ninth inning to tie the score against Montreal. Bonds then won the game in the 11th with an RBI double. The victory gave the Giants a 1$\frac{1}{2}$-game lead in the N.L. West, their biggest of the season.

Low point: The Giants dropped their final three games before the All-Star break—and 19 of their last 29—to drop six games out of first place.

Turning point: When Matt Williams fractured his right foot June 3, it devastated the Giants. At the time of his injury, they had a half-game lead in the N.L. West. During his 10-week absence, the Giants went 28-40 to fall to last place, 7$\frac{1}{2}$ games out of first.

Most valuable player: Outfielder Barry Bonds. Even without Williams to protect him for much of the season, Bonds hit .291 with 33 homers, 104 RBIs, 109 runs, 120 walks and 31 stolen bases.

Most valuable pitcher: Righthander Mark Leiter. He was the only Giants pitcher to remain in the rotation all season, and wound up leading the team in almost every category. He finished second in the league (behind Greg Maddux) in complete games with seven.

Most improved player: First baseman Mark Carreon. In his first chance to play every day, Carreon hit .301 with 17 homers after taking over at first. An outfielder throughout his career, Carreon was rocky defensively at the outset but quickly became adept around the bag.

Most pleasant surprise: Righthander Jamie Brewington. Brewington, 24, made the jump from Class AA after the All-Star break to clinch a spot in the starting rotation. Brewington was 6-4 in 13 starts.

Biggest disappointment: Second baseman Robby Thompson. For the second consecutive year, Thompson basically contributed nothing. Bothered by a series of injuries, including one to his left rotator cuff that required surgery, Thompson batted .223 with eight homers and 23 RBIs.

Key injuries: Williams' fractured foot, which knocked him out from June 4-August 18, was the biggest. Top setup man Mark Portugal missed nearly three months with a stress fracture in his rib cage.

Notable: The Giants made a blockbuster trade with the Reds on July 21, sending pitchers Mark Portugal and Dave Burba and outfielder Darren Lewis to Cincinnati for outfielder Deion Sanders, first baseman David McCarty and pitchers Scott Service, John Roper and Ricky Pickett. . . . The Giants finished last for the first time since 1985.

—LARRY STONE

RECORDS

1995 regular-season record: 67-77 (4th in West); 37-35 at home; 30-42 on road; 24-30 vs. East; 32-24 vs. Central; 16-23 vs. West; 17-23 vs. lefthanded starters; 53-51 vs. righthanded starters; 56-56 on grass; 14-18 on turf; 24-24 in daytime; 46-50 at night; 20-22 in one-run games; 6-7 in extra-inning games; 1-1-2 in doubleheaders.

Team record past five years: 344-403 (.461, ranks 12th in league in that span).

TEAM LEADERS

Batting average: Barry Bonds (.294).
At-bats: Royce Clayton (509).
Runs: Barry Bonds (109).
Hits: Barry Bonds (149).
Total bases: Barry Bonds (292).
Doubles: Barry Bonds (30).
Triples: Barry Bonds (7).
Home runs: Barry Bonds (33).
Runs batted in: Barry Bonds (104).
Stolen bases: Barry Bonds (31).
Slugging percentage: Barry Bonds (.577).
On-base percentage: Barry Bonds (.431).
Wins: Mark Leiter (10).
Earned-run average: Mark Leiter (3.82).
Complete games: Mark Leiter (7).
Shutouts: Mark Leiter (1).
Saves: Rod Beck (33).
Innings pitched: Mark Leiter (195.2).
Strikeouts: Mark Leiter (129).

GAMES BY POSITION

Catcher: Kirt Manwaring 118, Jeff Reed 42, Tom Lampkin 17.
First base: Mark Carreon 81, J.R. Phillips 79, Steve Scarsone 11, Todd Benzinger 5, David McCarty 2.
Second base: Robby Thompson 91, John Patterson 53, Steve Scarsone 13, Mike Benjamin 8.
Third base: Matt Williams 74, Steve Scarsone 50, Mike Benjamin 43.
Shortstop: Royce Clayton 136, Mike Benjamin 16, Rich Aurilia 6.
Outfield: Barry Bonds 143, Glenallen Hill 125, Darren Lewis 73, Deion Sanders 52, Rikkert Faneyte 34, Mark Carreon 22, Marvin Benard 7, Tom Lampkin 6, Mark Leonard 6, David McCarty 4, J.R. Phillips 1.

TOP DRAFT CHOICES

1. **Joe Fontenot,** RHP, Acadiana H.S., Lafayette, La.
2. **Jason Brester,** LHP, Burlington-Edison H.S., Burlington, Wash.
3. **Darin Blood,** RHP, Gonzaga University.
4. **Russ Ortiz,** RHP, University of Oklahoma.
5. **Jim Woodrow,** RHP, Flagler College (Fla.).
6. **Joe Nathan,** SS, SUNY Stonybrook.
7. **Alex Morales,** OF, University of Central Florida.
8. **Ben Tucker,** RHP, University of Southern California.
9. **Manny Bermudez,** RHP, Antioch (Calif.) H.S.
10. **Jeff Hutzler,** RHP, University of Texas-San Antonio.

1996 SEASON *San Francisco Giants*

1995 REVIEW

By STEVE GIETSCHIER
TSN Archivist

Major league baseball returned to the playing field in 1995 after a 234-day work stoppage, but the full enthusiasm and affection of its fans lagged far behind. Attendance dropped 20 percent from 1994, despite discounted ticket prices, as many people once deeply attached to the game simply professed indifference. Hearts were touched by the death of Mickey Mantle, one of baseball's greatest heroes, and by Cal Ripken's triumphant quest to eclipse Lou Gehrig's record for consecutive games played. But even these events and an exciting postseason, capped by the Atlanta Braves' victory in the World Series, served to rekindle only some of the dormant passion that once invigorated the sport. As the year drew to a close, skeptical observers were still waiting for a labor-management agreement to remove the cloud that had been hovering over the game and its future for more than two years.

As 1995 opened, the Major League Baseball Players Association was in the fifth month of a strike begun the previous August 12, and the owners were attempting to administer the game under rules they had imposed unilaterally in December 1994, pursuant to their declaration that the collective bargaining process was at an impasse. At issue, in general, was the protracted argument over baseball's economic health and, specifically, whether the players association should be willing to accept significant changes in a new Basic Agreement, including a salary cap or payroll tax, restrictions on free agency and an end to salary arbitration.

For several exasperating weeks early in the year, the two sides talked sporadically but did not come close to reaching an agreement. Outside intervention, including the continuing efforts of federal mediator W.J. (Bill) Usery and the direct intervention of President Bill Clinton, were equally unsuccessful. The owners opened spring training with the announced intention of playing the season with replacement players. Finally, on March 26, the National Labor Relations Board, acting on unfair labor practices complaints lodged by the players association, voted to authorize its general counsel to seek a preliminary injunction against the owners' imposition of new work rules. Three days later, the union voted to end its strike if the injunction were granted.

On March 31, U.S. District Court Judge Sonia Sotomayor issued the injunction. The strike came to an end, and on April 2, Acting Commissioner Bud Selig invited the union's membership back to work and announced that opening day would be delayed to allow time for a truncated spring training.

An abbreviated season, 144 regular-season games instead of the usual 162, began on April 25 and was

PRELIMINARY INJUNCTION TEXT

Partial text of the preliminary injunction issued March 31 by U.S. District Judge Sonia Sotomayor:

For the reasons discussed in the transcript of hearing before the court this day, the court issues an injunction directing and ordering respondents, the Major League Baseball Player Relations Committee Inc. and its 28 constituent member clubs of major league baseball, 1) to restore the terms and conditions of employment provided under the expired Basic Agreement which was effective Jan. 1, 1990, including its free agency-reserve systems with salary arbitration for eligible reserve players, Article XX (f) and all other of their constituent parts; 2) immediately to rescind by written notice to all club members any actions taken including the Feb. 6 letter from Charles P. O'Connor to Donald M. Fehr RE Exclusive Representation Status of PRC and the Feb. 6, 1995, memorandum with its attached questions and answers sent by Charles P. O'Connor to all major league clubs subject: Individual Club-Player Contract Negotiations, that are inconsistent with or conflict with the terms and conditions of employment, including all provisions of the free agency-reserve systems provided under the expired Basic Agreement; and 3) to bargain in good faith without unilateral changes to the Basic Agreement with the Major League Baseball Players Association (the "union") in compliance with secs. 8 (a) (1) and (5) of the National Labor Relations Act.

This injunction is to remain in effect until either (1) the players and owners enter into a new collective bargaining agreement that replaces the expired Basic Agreement, or (2) the final disposition of the matters pending before the National Labor Relations Board on the complaint and notice of hearing of the general counsel of the board in case No. 2-CA-28177, or (3) dissolution of the injunction demonstrating that an impasse in good faith bargaining has occurred despite a reasonable passage of time negotiating in good faith the full mandatory bargaining terms of the expired Basic Agreement.

SO ORDERED
New York, N.Y., March 31, 1995
Sonia Sotomayor
U.S. District Judge

played against this backdrop. At the end of the year, though, an agreement was still nowhere in sight.

(For details, see CHRONOLOGY OF KEY EVENTS IN BASEBALL'S 1995 LABOR NEGOTIATIONS.)

NEW CONTRACT FOR UMPIRES

Complicating baseball's labor situation even further was a dispute between the two leagues and their umpires, resolution of which was not reached until the season was a week old. The umpires, seeking a 60 percent raise in salary and other benefits increases, had been locked out when their contract expired December 31, 1994. Negotiations proceeded slowly and seemed to take a back seat to the turmoil of the players strike. When spring training games began, replacement umpires were officiating replacement players.

In mid-April, the two sides narrowed their differences and for a while discussed a no-strike, no-lockout deal that would have allowed regular umpires to return to work without a contract. Pressure to settle came from major league players and managers and from the decision of the Ontario Labor Relations Board prohibiting the use of replacements in that Canadian province. An agreement was concluded at a marathon bargaining session April 30.

The new five-year contract called for the umpires' base salary scale to increase from $60,000-$175,000 to $75,000-$225,000; a $20,000 postseason bonus for all umpires; increased bonuses to crew chiefs and to those selected to umpire the All-Star Game; increased pay for each round of the playoffs, and other benefits. The umpires returned to work May 3.

BRAVES WIN WORLD SERIES

The season that did transpire came to a close October 28 when Atlanta lefthander Tom Glavine defeated the Cleveland Indians, 1-0, in Game 6 of the World Series. Glavine, who yielded one hit over eight innings, and reliever Mark Wohlers, who pitched a perfect ninth, combined to fashion the fifth one-hitter in World Series history and the first since Jim Lonborg of the Boston Red Sox nearly no-hit the St. Louis Cardinals in 1967.

Glavine, who also won Game 2, 4-3, and was named Series MVP, was an ironic hero. Not only had his pitching achievements for the Braves (including three straight 20-win seasons and 16 victories in 1995) been overshadowed by the accomplishments of teammate Greg Maddux, who won his fourth straight Cy Young Award, but he also was frequently booed early in the year by fans who disagreed with his comments articulating the players' position in the labor dispute.

The Braves thus captured the third World Series crown in their franchise's long history, the first since 1957 and the first since they moved to Atlanta in 1966. In a sense, their triumph avenged a defeat that the Boston Braves had suffered in 1948 at the hands of the Indians and the losses Atlanta absorbed in 1991 to the Minnesota Twins and 1992 to the Toronto Blue Jays.

NEW ROUND OF PLAYOFFS

The 1995 season marked the debut of the Division Series, a first round of playoffs incorporating baseball's first use of the "wild card" concept. Qualifiers for the Division Series in each league included the winners of the East, Central and West divisions (a realignment introduced in 1994) and a wild card, the team with the best record among the trio of second-place clubs.

Baseball officials had argued that introducing a wild-card format into a sport that had long resisted such a change would boost fan interest by creating a fourth pennant race among wild-card contenders. But this proved not to be the case. Fans seemed confused about how the new system would operate, and attendance fell below expectations at crucial, late-season games bearing on the wild-card races. In addition, once the Division Series were set as best-of-five competitions with home-field advantage (the first two games on the road and the remainder at home) predetermined and

not based on performance, all the pennant races lost a certain luster.

In the National League, the Braves won the East Division and beat the wild-card Colorado Rockies, three games to one, in one series. The Cincinnati Reds, Central Division champs, won the other by sweeping the West Division winners, the Los Angeles Dodgers.

In the American League, the Indians, winners of the Central Division, swept the Red Sox, winners of the East Division, and the Seattle Mariners, West Division champs, defeated the wild-card New York Yankees, three games to two.

BRAVES OVERTAKE PHILLIES

By finishing first in the N.L. East, Atlanta became the first N.L. team to win four consecutive division titles (not including the interrupted 1994 season). The Philadelphia Phillies, N.L. pennant winners in 1993, held first place and a 3½-game lead over the Braves on June 30, but Atlanta won 20 of 27 games in July while the Phillies tumbled. By the end of the month, the Braves had built an 8½-game advantage and were never headed. They clinched the division flag September 13 and finished the season a franchise-record 21 games ahead of Philadelphia.

Atlanta's offense featured a balanced attack that did not lead the league in any category. The Braves were second in home runs, ninth in runs scored, 13th in hits and 13th in team batting average. Ryan Klesko led the team in hitting with a .310 average. Fred McGriff failed to reach the 30-home run mark for the first time since 1987, but he and three others (David Justice, Klesko and Chipper Jones) hit 23 or more, and McGriff drove in 93 runs.

The Braves' pitching was simply outstanding, finishing first in complete games, ERA, fewest hits allowed, fewest home runs allowed and strikeouts. Maddux dominated the league again, winning 19 games against only two losses, and was named The Sporting News' N.L. Pitcher of the Year for the fourth consecutive year. With a 1.63 ERA, he became the first major league pitcher since Walter Johnson in 1918-19 to post an ERA of less than 1.80 in back-to-back seasons. He won 10 straight games and had 10 complete games, including four in a row. John Smoltz added 12 wins, and Wohlers chalked up 25 saves.

REDS WIN N.L. CENTRAL

Cincinnati started the season 0-6 but came back to clinch the first official N.L. Central pennant September 21. The Reds won the division by nine games over the Houston Astros despite the lame-duck status of Manager Davey Johnson and a serious elbow injury to pitcher Jose Rijo. Cincinnati was led by shortstop Barry Larkin, whose .319 average with 15 homers, 66 RBIs and 51 stolen bases won him the N.L. MVP award, and pitcher Pete Schourek (18-7, 3.22), a former New York Mets castoff.

DODGERS BEST ROCKIES

The Dodgers won 17 of their final 25 games to eke out a one-game margin in the N.L. West over Colorado, clinching the title on the season's next-to-last day. Los Angeles, five games behind Colorado on July 25, won 11 of 16 to tie for first place August 11. The Dodgers were propelled by Mike Piazza (.346, 32 homers, 93 RBIs), Eric Karros (.298, 32, 105), Ramon Martinez (17-7, 3.66 ERA) and rookie pitcher Hideo Nomo, the first Japanese player to perform in the major leagues since Masanori Murakami pitched for the San Francisco Giants in 1964-65. Nomo created quite a sensation starting with his May 2 debut. He won seven of his first eight decisions, struck out 16 Pittsburgh Pirates on June 14 and pitched a one-hitter against the Giants on August 5. He started the All-Star Game and led the league in strikeouts.

The Rockies, in just their third season, waged a nip-and-tuck battle for the N.L. West flag and the wild-card spot simultaneously. Colorado never fell below second place and led the division for 109 days. The Rockies gave up first place for good September 27 but held off Houston for the wild card, clinching a playoff spot by winning their last two games.

The Rockies' strength was their offense. Dante Bichette led the league with 40 home runs and 128 RBIs while finishing third in the batting race. Colorado led the league in hitting, runs scored, hits, total bases, home runs and slugging percentage. Bichette joined Larry Walker (36), Vinny Castilla (32) and Andres Galarraga (31) to form the first quartet of teammates to hit 30 or more home runs apiece since the 1977 Los Angeles Dodgers (Steve Garvey, Reggie Smith, Dusty Baker and Ron Cey).

CLEVELAND ENDS PENNANT DROUGHT

The Indians won their first title of any kind in 41 years by 30 games, the largest pennant-winning margin in modern major league history. Cleveland went 31-9 from May 7-June 20 to turn the race into a rout and clinched the pennant September 8. The Indians led the league in hitting, runs, hits, total bases, home runs, RBIs and slugging percentage. Albert Belle, named Major League Player of the Year by The Sporting News, became the first player ever to reach the 50 mark in homers and doubles in the same season. He batted .317, drove in 126 runs and hit a major league-record 31 homers the last two months of the season. Manny Ramirez drove in 107 runs and hit 31 homers. Paul Sorrento and Jim Thome added 25 home runs each. Eddie Murray's 82 RBIs gave him 75 or more for 19 straight seasons, tying a major league mark.

Cleveland got strong and consistent starting pitching from Charles Nagy (16-6), Orel Hershiser (16-6) and Dennis Martinez (12-5). Julian Tavarez chalked up 10 wins as a setup man, and Jose Mesa led the majors with 46 saves, including a single-season record of 37 in succession.

RED SOX WIN A.L. EAST

The Red Sox took over first place for good May 13 and went on to win their first A.L. East title since 1990. Boston won 12 straight games in early August and 20 of 22 to open a 15½-game lead that proved decisive. The Red Sox clinched the division flag September 20. Mo

Vaughn hit .300 with 39 homers and 126 RBIs and won the A.L. MVP award. John Valentin added 27 homers and 102 RBIs. Knuckleballer Tim Wakefield, released by the Pirates in spring training, won 16 games. Rick Aguilera, acquired from the Twins in July, stabilized the bullpen and earned 20 saves.

A.L. WEST GOES TO PLAYOFF

The pennant race in the A.L. West was not decided until the day after the regular season ended when Seattle defeated the California Angels, 9-1, in the third one-game playoff in A.L. history. The Angels held first place by 10½ games on August 15 but proceeded to lose 28 of their next 37 to fall to second. The Mariners closed with a rush (24-9 from August 24 through September 29) but lost their last two regular-season games to allow California to catch them.

With Ken Griffey out of the lineup almost three months with a broken wrist, Seattle relied on the strong left arm of Randy Johnson to win its first division title ever. Johnson won 18 games, including the playoff, and led the league in ERA and strikeouts. He won the A.L. Cy Young Award and was named A.L. Pitcher of the Year by The Sporting News. Edgar Martinez hit .356 to win the batting title and drove in 113 runs.

California's playoff loss enabled the Yankees (21-6 in September) to snatch the A.L. wild-card berth. David Cone, acquired July 28 from Toronto, went 9-2 for New York and won his last three starts, key games all. Bernie Williams, who hit .350 after the All-Star break, finished at .307 with 18 homers and 82 RBIs.

ATLANTA SWEEPS REDS

The Braves made quick work of Cincinnati in the N.L. Championship Series, holding the Reds to only five runs in four games. Opening on the road, Atlanta won twice in extra innings, 2-1 and 6-2, behind Glavine and Smoltz. In Game 1, Schourek led, 1-0, only to have the Braves tie the score in the ninth on a pair of singles and a forceout. Atlanta won the game in the 11th when Mike Devereaux singled home McGriff. Game 2 was tied when Atlanta scored four runs in the 10th inning on a wild pitch and a three-run homer by catcher Javier Lopez.

Maddux won Game 3, 5-2, with home-run help from Charlie O'Brien and Jones. Lefthander Steve Avery gave up only two hits in six innings to win Game 4, 6-0. The Reds were just 3-for-29 with men in scoring position during the series and 6-for-52 with runners on base. Reggie Sanders, who hit .306 during the regular season, struck out 10 times in 16 NLCS at-bats.

A.L. TITLE SERIES GOES SIX GAMES

The Indians and Mariners split the first two games in the A.L. Championship Series. Short of starting pitching after the five-game Division Series against New York, Seattle Manager Lou Piniella gave the ball in Game 1 to 22-year-old rookie Bob Wolcott, who gave up eight hits and two runs in seven innings to earn a 3-2 victory. Cleveland rebounded in Game 2, winning 5-2 behind Hershiser's pitching and two RBIs each from

Ramirez and Carlos Baerga.

Game 3 at Jacobs Field saw Johnson and Nagy duel for eight innings and give up only two runs each. The Mariners won, 5-2, on Jay Buhner's two-out, three-run homer in the 11th inning off Eric Plunk. Cleveland came back, though, to win the next two games. Ken Hill shut out Seattle, 7-0, in Game 4, and Hershiser won Game 5, 3-2, with Thome hitting a game-winning home run in the sixth inning off Chris Bosio. Back in Seattle for Game 6, Martinez closed out the series for the Indians, 4-0, as Johnson's arm finally ran out of gas. Cleveland tallied one run in the fifth after an error and three in the eighth. Two runs scored on a passed ball before Baerga homered to straightaway center field.

BRAVES TOP TRIBE

Maddux opened the World Series with a pitching gem of his own, a two-hitter that the Braves won, 3-2, on a squeeze bunt by shortstop Rafael Belliard in the seventh inning. Atlanta won the second game, too, 4-3,

thanks to Lopez's two-run home run in the sixth.

After the Series moved to Jacobs Field, Cleveland rebounded to take Game 3, 7-6, in 11 innings. In the eighth inning, the Braves took a 6-5 lead on a pinch-single by Devereaux, but the Indians came right back to tie the score when catcher Sandy Alomar doubled home Ramirez. Designated hitter Murray drove home the winning run with a single.

Atlanta's Avery yielded only three hits as the Braves won Game 4, 5-2, but Hershiser bested Maddux to win Game 5, 5-4. Game 6 was scoreless until Justice, who had been critical of his team's fans for their lack of support, led off the bottom of the sixth inning with a line-drive home run off reliever Jim Poole. The Indians, who hit a meager .179 for the Series, had gotten their only hit, a bloop single to center by catcher Tony Pena, in the top of the sixth.

Each member of the winning Braves voted a full share received $206,635. Cleveland's full shares came to $121,945.

CHRONOLOGY OF KEY EVENTS IN BASEBALL'S 1995 LABOR NEGOTIATIONS

January 4—Sen. Daniel Moynihan (D-N.Y.) and Rep. Michael Bilirakis (R-Fla.) announce plans to introduce bills to remove baseball's exemption from federal antitrust laws.

January 10—Union's executive board passes a resolution banning agents from representing replacement players.

January 13—Executive council issues guidelines giving teams permission to hire replacement players.

January 26—President Bill Clinton orders the two sides to resume collective bargaining and to make significant progress toward a settlement by February 6.

January 27—Mediator W.J. Usery announces talks will resume February 1.

February 1—Owners submit a proposal to tax team payrolls between $35 million and $42 million at 75 percent and payrolls over $42 million at 100 percent, eliminate salary arbitration and grant restricted free agency to players with four to six years of major league service.

February 3—Owners, after being told that the NLRB was prepared to issue an unfair labor practices complaint alleging that the salary cap was implemented illegally, agree to rescind the system, effective February 6.

February 4—Players offer a counterproposal with salary-tax rates of 5 percent on payrolls between 50 and 130 percent of the average team payroll, 15 percent on payrolls between 130 and 160 percent and 25 percent on payrolls above 160 percent, plus an end to salary arbitration if all players with four years' service are made unrestricted free agents.

February 5—Usery announces that the sides cannot agree and that he will announce his plan for a settlement February 6.

February 6—The Player Relations Committee revokes salary arbitration and individual teams' authority to sign contracts.

February 7—After a one-day extension of the President's deadline, the sides fail to reach agreement at a White House bargaining session. Usery's report informally suggests a 50 percent salary tax on payrolls over $40 million and free agency after four years. The union rejects this plan, and the owners refuse the President's offer of binding arbitration.

February 16—Spring training opens with replacement players.

February 27—Negotiations resume in Scottsdale, Ariz.

March 4—Talks break off after the union proposes a 25 percent tax on payrolls above 133 percent of the average and the owners propose a 50 percent tax on all payrolls above the average.

March 9—Usery characterizes the dispute as "embarrassing and ridiculous" and urges the owners to make their "best" offer soon.

March 14—The NLRB announces that it will issue an unfair labor practices complaint against the owners.

March 17—NLRB General Counsel Fred Feinstein asks for permission to seek an injunction that would restore salary arbitration and free agency.

March 26—By a 3-2 vote, the NLRB authorizes its general counsel to seek a preliminary injunction against the owners to restore the pre-strike work rules.

March 27—The NLRB files in U.S. District Court in New York for a preliminary injunction. The owners propose keeping the current system of salary arbitration and free agency and instituting a 50 percent tax on payrolls above 108 percent of the average.

March 29—The union votes to end the strike if the NLRB request for an injunction is granted.

March 30—Owners vote 26-2 to begin the season with replacement players. The union makes a new proposal calling for a 25 percent tax on payrolls above 123 percent of the average.

March 31—Judge Sonia Sotomayor issues a preliminary injunction against the owners, ordering them to restore salary arbitration, free agency and the anti-collusion provisions of the expired Basic Agreement. The union ends its strike.

April 2—Owners decide not to lock players out. Selig announces an agreement to have players report to spring training and prepare for delayed opening day, later set for April 25.

April 4—The 2nd U.S. Circuit Court of Appeals denies a request by owners to stay the injunction.

April 5—Players and owners agree on a 144-game schedule.

May 11—The Court of Appeals reserves a decision on the appeal by the owners to have the injunction overturned.

June 21—Low-level talks resume with no progress reported.

August 3—The Senate Judiciary Committee votes 9-8 to repeal parts of baseball's antitrust exemption.

September 18—Randy Levine, former New York City commissioner of labor, is appointed the owners' chief negotiator.

September 29—The Court of Appeals rejects the owners' appeal of the injunction, ruling that their attempt to eliminate free agency, salary arbitration and the anti-collusion provisions was illegal.

November 15—Owners make a new proposal to the union at the first full-scale bargaining session since the injunction was issued. Details were kept confidential, but *The New York Times* later reported that the proposal called for a 25 percent tax on payrolls above $44 million in order to push player salaries down to 50 percent of revenues.

MANTLE SUCCUMBS TO CANCER

Baseball fans around the world held their collective breath when they learned that Mickey Mantle, Hall of Fame center fielder for the Yankees from 1951-68, had been hospitalized May 28 in Dallas with progressive liver failure. Doctors soon announced that Mantle's condition—linked to liver cancer, a long-dormant hepatitis C infection and damage from 40 years of alcohol abuse—would require a transplant. The operation was performed successfully June 8, the 26th anniversary of the day the Yankees retired Mantle's uniform number 7.

Amid ethical questions about the speed of the transplant, Mantle was released from the hospital June 29. Truly contrite for the life he had led, Mantle told his admirers he was a reverse role model. "Don't be like me," he said. A month later, his condition worsened, and he was readmitted to the hospital. On August 1, doctors found cancer in his right lung, and the killer cells soon spread to other vital organs. Mantle died August 13 at age 63.

IRON MAN CAL

A few weeks after Mantle's death, the season reached its emotional peak as Cal Ripken of the Baltimore Orioles approached Gehrig's record of 2,130 consecutive games, a mark once deemed insurmountable. Ripken's streak, begun May 30, 1982, had reached 2,009 games when the strike suspended play in 1994.

As the prospect loomed that the 1995 season would begin with replacement players and the streak would be jeopardized, Ripken stood firm with the union, refusing to consider a suggestion that he continue to play while the strike droned on. The players association, for its part, insisted that games using replacement players would never count in the official standings. Orioles Owner Peter Angelos added his own complication, refusing to field a team of replacements even for spring training games.

Ripken broke the record in style. He played in each of the Orioles' 144 games and departed only eight games early, missing a total of 18 innings. He hit .262 for the year with 17 home runs and 88 RBIs. In the record-tying and record-setting games on September 5 and 6, he batted a combined 5-for-9 with a homer in each game. In December, Ripken, whose streak stood at 2,153 games at season's end, was named Sportsman of the Year by The Sporting News.

HOME RUN BARRAGE

Despite the shortened season, major league hitters produced the second-highest home run total in history (4,081), surpassed only by the 4,458 homers hit in 1987. The Indians and Rockies led an offensive barrage in which every club except the Phillies hit more than 100 home runs and 21 players hit 30 or more. Both Albert Belle and Oakland's Mark McGwire tied a major league record by hitting five homers in two consecutive games. Baltimore's Jeff Manto tied another record by hitting home runs in four straight at-bats spread over three games. Andres Galarraga tied still another mark by hitting home runs in three consecutive innings. Ken

Caminiti of the San Diego Padres hit home runs from both sides of the plate three times, including two games in succession. Seattle's Mike Blowers hit three grand slams in the same month (August). Robin Ventura of the Chicago White Sox hit two in the same game (September 4).

Despite the short season, five players had 180 or more hits, including San Diego's Tony Gwynn (197), who shared the N.L. lead with Bichette. Gwynn hit .368 and won his sixth batting title. Eddie Murray garnered the 3,000th hit of his career June 30 when he singled in the sixth inning off the Twins' Mike Trombley. Galarraga got six hits in six at-bats July 3 against Houston. Rondell White of the Montreal Expos hit for the cycle (6-for-7 with two singles and two doubles) in a 13-inning game against the Giants on June 11. The Rockies' John Vander Wal set a major league record with 28 pinch hits.

ONE COMPLETE GAME NO-HITTER

The Dodgers' Ramon Martinez pitched the only complete-game, nine-inning no-hitter of the season July 14 when he beat the Florida Marlins, 7-0. Martinez was perfect through 7⅔ innings before walking Tommy Gregg on a 3-2 count.

Ramon's brother, Pedro, became the second pitcher ever to take a perfect game into extra innings. He pitched nine innings of perfect ball for the Expos against the Padres on June 3. Montreal scored the game's only run in the top of the 10th, and then Martinez gave up a double to Bip Roberts to open the bottom of the inning. Mel Rojas relieved Martinez and completed the shutout.

The Orioles' Mike Mussina led the A.L. with 19 wins, and Randy Myers of the Chicago Cubs led the N.L. with 38 saves. The Angels' Lee Smith extended his major league mark for career saves to 471 and broke his own major league record by recording saves in 19 consecutive appearances.

AMBIDEXTROUS HURLER

Expos pitcher Greg Harris donated his unusual six-finger glove to the National Baseball Hall of Fame after using it to become the first major leaguer in more than a century to pitch with both hands in the same game. Harris, normally a righthander, pitched the ninth inning against the Reds on September 28 with Montreal losing by six runs. He faced four batters, throwing righthanded to the first and fourth and left-handed to the middle two, the first of whom he walked.

DODGERS FORFEIT GAME

The Dodgers forfeited an August 10 home game to the Cardinals after fans showered the field with promotional baseballs on three occasions. The game was delayed for the first time in the bottom of the seventh when balls were thrown onto the field spontaneously. In the bottom of the ninth, fans again littered the field after home umpire Jim Quick ejected Dodger players Eric Karros and Raul Mondesi and Manager Tom Lasorda for arguing called strikes. After the field was cleared and a public-address announcement warned that offending fans could be arrested, more balls were thrown, including one that narrowly missed Cardinal outfielder Brian Jordan. At that point, Quick declared the forfeit, later upheld over the Dodgers' protest by N.L. President Leonard Coleman.

The forfeit was the first in the major leagues since July 12, 1979, when the White Sox staged Disco Demolition Night at Comiskey Park, and the first in the N.L. since July 18, 1954, when Philadelphia received a forfeit victory against the Cardinals.

SPEEDING UP THE GAME

Early in the season, owners asked former umpire Steve Palermo to make recommendations that would shorten the length of games. Effective July 28, three rule changes were implemented: First, except for nationally televised games, the interval between the third out in one half-inning and the start of the next half-inning was cut from 2:25 to 2:05; second, batters were ordered to remain within three feet of the side of the batter's box when stepping out; and, third, managers and coaches making pitching changes were ordered to signal their changes as they left the dugout.

ATTENDANCE DROPS

Major league attendance for the abbreviated season totaled 50,469,236. A.L. clubs outdrew N.L. clubs slightly, 25,358,988 to 25,110,248. The Rockies (3,390,037) and the Orioles (3,098,475) were the only teams to top the 3 million mark. Six other clubs surpassed 2 million. Only the Pirates (905,517) failed to exceed 1 million.

Average attendance for the season was 25,257, down from 31,612 in 1994.

EIGHT MANAGERIAL CHANGES

The White Sox became the first team to fire its manager in 1995, dismissing Gene Lamont on June 2 and replacing him with Terry Bevington, the team's third-base coach. Chicago, expected to contend in the A.L. Central, got off to an 11-20 start under Lamont, who was in his fourth season as manager. The White Sox did better for Bevington (57-56), but they still finished 32 games behind the Indians.

The Cardinals fired Joe Torre (20-27) on June 16 and gave the manager's job to their director of player development, Mike Jorgensen (41-55). On October 23, he was replaced by Tony La Russa, who took advantage of an opportunity to leave the Athletics with two years remaining on his contract. The A's hired Art Howe, former Astros manager, on November 16.

Four other teams changed managers after the season. The most unusual case occurred in Cincinnati, where Reds Owner Marge Schott—the year before—had announced her preference that coach Ray Knight be named manager. The Reds retained Davey Johnson for 1995 but offered him no more than a one-year contract extension. Johnson accepted and then guided his team to a division title and the NLCS. That success, however, did not change Schott's mind. On October 30, the Reds appointed Knight.

The same day, the Orioles hired Johnson to succeed Phil Regan, who had been fired after Baltimore finished third in the A.L. East with a 71-73 record. The

Detroit Tigers named Buddy Bell, a coach with Cleveland, as their new manager November 9. He replaced Sparky Anderson, who resigned October 2 as the third-winningest manager ever behind Connie Mack and John McGraw. Anderson managed the Reds for nine seasons and the Tigers for 17, compiling a record of 2,194-1,834 and three World Series titles.

On October 26, Buck Showalter declined the Yankees' offer to continue as their manager. They hired Torre on November 2, and Showalter agreed on November 15 to become the first manager of the expansion Arizona Diamondbacks, who begin play in 1998.

NEW GENERAL MANAGERS

Several teams changed general managers after the season. Kevin Malone resigned as Montreal G.M. on October 2. Bill Stoneman replaced him on an interim basis until Jim Beattie, a former major league pitcher, was hired October 27. Randy Smith resigned as G.M. of the Padres to accept the same position in Detroit, where he replaced Joe Klein. Kevin Towers, San Diego's scouting director since 1993, took Smith's old job.

Rather than accept a pay cut, Gene Michael resigned from the Yankees on October 18. He was replaced by Astros G.M. Bob Watson on October 23. Gerry Hunsicker, assistant G.M. of the Mets, succeeded Watson. Roland Hemond resigned as G.M. of the Orioles on October 20 and was replaced by Pat Gillick, former G.M. of the Blue Jays, on November 27.

OWNERSHIP CHANGES

On May 18, The Walt Disney Co. announced it would buy a 25 percent interest in the Angels from Gene Autry and his wife, Jackie. Disney agreed to become the managing general partner with an option to buy the remainder of the club later. Financial terms were not disclosed.

In May, the Internal Revenue Service approved a proposal by which title to the Kansas City Royals passed from the estate of the late Ewing Kauffman to the Greater Kansas City Community Foundation and Affiliated Trust. The foundation will operate the team for six years or until a new owner can be found who will keep the Royals in Kansas City.

Developers Steven Schott and Kenneth Hofmann purchased the Athletics from the Walter J. Haas family for a reported $85 million with the proviso that the team be kept in Oakland.

After months of negotiations between the Pirates and cable television entrepreneur John J. Rigas, an agreement for Rigas to purchase the team could not be concluded. The Pirates' future in Pittsburgh seemed very much in doubt until a new potential ownership group emerged. This group, headed by California newspaper executive Kevin McClatchy, agreed in November to buy the team for an estimated $85 million. In December, McClatchy filed papers confirming that he had met major league baseball's equity-to-debt guidelines. McClatchy's lease to use Three Rivers Stadium allows him to relocate the franchise should financing for a new baseball-only stadium not be secured by November 1, 1998.

Anheuser-Busch announced October 25 that it would sell the Cardinals, an A-B property since 1953. On December 22, a group headed by Frederick Hanser, William DeWitt Jr. and Andrew Baur reached a conditional agreement to buy the team, Busch Stadium and related properties for $150 million.

EXPANSION

Baseball's expansion committee, chaired by John Harrington, chief executive officer of the Red Sox, recommended on January 20 that two new teams be added, to begin play in 1997 or 1998, at a fee of $125-150 million each. On March 9, owners approved franchises for Phoenix and Tampa Bay at $130 million each. The Arizona Diamondbacks, owned by Jerry Colangelo, and the Tampa Bay Devil Rays, owned by a group headed by Vincent Naimoli, will begin play in 1998, albeit in which league was not decided. Both franchises hired general managers, Tampa Bay selecting assistant Braves G.M. Chuck LaMar on July 19 and Arizona picking Joe Garagiola Jr.

NEW TELEVISION PACT

On June 22, ABC and NBC notified baseball that they would pull out of The Baseball Network, a two-year-old partnership, at the end of the season. Economics aside, critics had assailed several features of The Baseball Network, including the end of the traditional Saturday afternoon "game of the week"; a package of night games that brought most fans nothing more than network broadcasts of games they might ordinarily see on local TV, and regionalized, simultaneous coverage of the Division Series and the League Championship Series.

Baseball hired Barry Frank to negotiate a new TV contract in July, and over the next few months he solicited the interest of all the networks in a new arrangement. On November 6, Frank concluded an agreement worth $1.7 billion over five years with NBC, Fox, ESPN and Liberty Media-Fox Cable. Under this contract, NBC will televise the All-Star Game in 1996, 1998 and 2000 and the World Series in 1997 and 1999. Fox will televise the All-Star Game in 1997 and 1999 and the World Series in 1996, 1998 and 2000. These two networks will each televise one League Championship Series per year and will divide telecasts of the Division Series three ways, bringing ESPN and perhaps ESPN2 into the mix to ensure national coverage of every postseason game.

Fox also agreed to resurrect the Saturday "game of the week," to be preceded by a one-hour show with 30 minutes of programming aimed at children. ESPN will televise a doubleheader on Wednesday nights and a single game on Sunday nights, and Liberty Media-Fox Cable will televise two games each week, choosing from Monday, Tuesday, Thursday and Friday nights, starting in 1997.

ARBITRATION DELAYED

Salary arbitration hearings, normally a preseason activity, did not begin until May 12. As an experiment, three cases were heard by three-person panels instead of the traditional single arbitrator. Sixty-one players filed for arbitration, but only eight cases advanced to the hearing and decision stage. Two players (Darren Lewis and Ben McDonald) won their cases, and six (Andy Benes, Jeff Fassero, Alex Fernandez, Leo Gomez, Carlos Hernandez and Mel Rojas) lost theirs.

SALARIES DECLINE

Figures announced by the players association November 28 showed the first substantial decrease in player salaries in 30 years. The average salary, calculated by the union at $1,110,766, was down 5 percent from the 1994 average, $1,168,263, due in part to a large increase in the number of rookies and an increase in the number of players on the disabled list. Total player compensation rose to about $924 million.

Eighteen teams paid an average salary of over $1 million, with the Yankees becoming the first team ever to surpass the $2 million mark. Montreal had the lowest average, $411,142, according to the association.

FREE-AGENT SIGNINGS

A total of 138 players filed for free agency during the period ending November 12. Devon White became the first major player to switch teams when he severed his ties with Toronto and agreed to a three-year, $10 million contract with the Marlins. Other prominent free agents who changed teams included Jack McDowell to Cleveland (two years, $10.15 million); Randy Myers to Baltimore (two years, $6.3 million); Mike Stanley to Boston (one year, $2.3 million); Lance Johnson to the Mets (two years, $5 million); Julio Franco to Cleveland (two years, $5 million); Rick Aguilera to Minnesota (three years, $9 million); Ron Gant to St. Louis (five years, $25 million); Andy Benes to St. Louis (two years, $8.1 million) and Roberto Alomar to Baltimore (three years, $18 million).

THEY'RE BACK

Two athletes who helped make uniform number 23 famous in Chicago reversed fields in 1995. After playing one year in the minor leagues, Michael Jordan gave up baseball March 18 to return to the Chicago Bulls. Ryne Sandberg, who had retired abruptly on June 13, 1994, in the second year of a four-year, $17 million contract, announced October 31 that he would return to baseball. Sandberg, 36, has won nine Gold Glove Awards at second base and hit 245 home runs in his career. The N.L.'s MVP in 1984, Sandberg signed a one-year contract for an estimated $2 million.

CONCLUSION

When Sparky Anderson resigned his position with the Tigers, he expressed a desire to manage again but declined to pursue another job actively. "If there is nobody that calls, I will not call anyone or apply," he said. "The game is all I care about."

As 1995 ended, baseball's future seemed as uncertain as Anderson's. Troubles aside, here's how the game on the field ended up:

AMERICAN LEAGUE

EAST DIVISION

Team	Bos.	N.Y.	Bal.	Det.	Tor.	Cle.	K.C.	Chi.	Mil.	Min.	Sea.	Cal.	Tex.	Oak.	W	L	Pct.	GB
Boston	...	5	9	8	8	6	3	5	8	5	7	11	3	8	86	58	.597	.....
New York	8	...	7	8	12	6	7	2	6	4	4	5	6	4	79	65	.549	7
Baltimore	4	6	...	8	7	2	4	6	7	3	6	9	4	5	71	73	.493	15
Detroit	5	5	5	...	7	3	3	4	8	7	5	2	4	2	60	84	.417	26
Toronto	5	1	6	6	...	3	5	5	5	4	4	2	3	7	56	88	.389	30

CENTRAL DIVISION

Team	Cle.	K.C.	Chi.	Mil.	Min.	Bos.	N.Y.	Bal.	Det.	Tor.	Sea.	Cal.	Tex.	Oak.	W	L	Pct.	GB
Cleveland	...	11	8	9	9	7	6	10	10	10	5	2	6	7	100	44	.694	.....
Kansas City	1	...	5	10	6	2	3	5	4	7	7	7	8	5	70	74	.486	30
Chicago	5	8	...	6	10	3	3	1	8	6	4	2	5	7	68	76	.472	32
Milwaukee	4	2	7	...	9	4	5	5	5	7	3	2	5	7	65	79	.451	35
Minnesota	4	7	3	4	...	4	3	6	5	1	4	5	5	5	56	88	.389	44

WEST DIVISION

Team	Sea.	Cal.	Tex.	Oak.	Bos.	N.Y.	Bal.	Det.	Tor.	Cle.	K.C.	Chi.	Mil.	Min.	W	L	Pct.	GB
Seattle	...	6	10	6	5	9	7	5	3	4	5	9	2	8	79	66	.545	.....
California	7	...	6	6	3	7	4	6	8	3	5	10	5	8	78	67	.538	1
Texas	3	7	...	8	4	3	1	8	9	3	6	7	7	8	74	70	.514	4 1/2
Oakland	7	7	5	...	4	9	7	3	3	0	8	5	2	7	67	77	.465	11 1/2

Tie game—Chicago at New York, July 17 (6 1/2 innings).
NOTE: Read across for wins, down for losses.
Clinching dates: Boston (East)—September 20; Cleveland (Central)—September 8; Seattle (West)—October 2; New York (wild card)—October 1.

NATIONAL LEAGUE

EAST DIVISION

Team	Atl.	N.Y.	Phi.	Fla.	Mon.	Cin.	Hou.	Chi.	St.L.	Pit.	L.A.	Col.	S.D.	S.F.	W	L	Pct.	GB
Atlanta	...	5	7	10	9	8	6	8	7	4	5	9	5	7	90	54	.625	.....
New York	8	...	7	6	6	5	6	3	3	4	6	4	6	5	69	75	.479	21
Philadelphia	6	6	...	7	5	3	7	1	5	6	9	2	6	6	69	75	.479	21
Florida	3	7	6	...	6	6	8	4	4	5	3	7	3	5	67	76	.469	22 1/2
Montreal	4	7	8	7	...	4	3	5	4	4	5	1	7	7	66	78	.458	24

CENTRAL DIVISION

Team	Cin.	Hou.	Chi.	St.L.	Pit.	Atl.	N.Y.	Phi.	Fla.	Mon.	L.A.	Col.	S.D.	S.F.	W	L	Pct.	GB
Cincinnati	...	12	7	8	8	5	7	9	6	8	4	5	3	3	85	59	.590	.....
Houston	1	...	8	9	9	6	6	5	4	9	3	4	7	5	76	68	.528	9
Chicago	3	5	...	9	8	4	6	4	8	3	7	6	5	5	73	71	.507	12
St. Louis	5	4	4	...	7	5	4	4	3	3	5	7	5	6	62	81	.434	22 1/2
Pittsburgh	5	4	5	6	...	2	3	3	8	4	4	4	4	6	58	86	.403	27

WEST DIVISION

Team	L.A.	Col.	S.D.	S.F.	Atl.	N.Y.	Phi.	Fla.	Mon.	Cin.	Hou.	Chi.	St.L.	Pit.	W	L	Pct.	GB
Los Angeles	...	9	7	8	4	6	4	7	7	3	2	5	7	9	78	66	.542	.....
Colorado	4	...	9	8	4	5	4	5	7	7	4	7	5	8	77	67	.535	1
San Diego	6	4	...	6	2	7	6	2	5	6	4	7	7	8	70	74	.486	8
San Francisco	5	5	7	...	1	8	6	3	6	3	3	7	7	6	67	77	.465	11

Forfeited game—St. Louis at Los Angeles, August 10 (game forfeited to St. Louis).
NOTE: Read across for wins, down for losses.
Clinching dates: Atlanta (East)—September 13; Cincinnati (Central)—September 21; Los Angeles (West)—September 30; Colorado (wild card)—October 1.

1995 REVIEW *Year in review*

A.L. WEST DIVISION PLAYOFF

HIGHLIGHTS

SEATTLE 9, CALIFORNIA 1

Why the Mariners won: Randy Johnson was menacing. He was perfect through 5⅔ innings and finished with a three-hitter and 12 strikeouts. He walked one and lost his shutout in the ninth on a homer by Tony Phillips. Rex Hudler's single broke up Johnson's perfect game. Johnson had the Kingdome's 52,356 fans screaming and on their feet and kept the momentum on his team's side long enough for the Mariners to break open the game with four runs in the seventh.

Why the Angels lost: Was it that the Angels fell apart in the seventh inning? Or that the psychological damage of allowing the Mariners to make up 13 games in the standings since August 2 still too heavy a burden to overcome? Mark Langston kept pace with Johnson, and the Angels trailed 1-0 going into the seventh. The Mariners loaded the bases with two out, and if Langston had retired Luis Sojo, the complexion of the game might have changed.

The turning points:

1. The coin flip that put the game in Seattle. Scoff if you want, but the Kingdome was rocking. The home-field advantage made a difference. Johnson had the Kingdome electric beyond anything Seattle had seen before.

2. The fateful seventh inning. Mike Blowers led off with a single to left. Then bad things began happening to the Angels. Tino Martinez sacrificed, and Langston fielded the ball. But Hudler, the second baseman, was late breaking for first to cover for J.T. Snow, who was playing in for the bunt. Langston had to delay the throw, and Martinez was safe. Dan Wilson bunted, and the runners advanced. Langston hit Joey Cora to load the bases. Vince Coleman followed with a liner to Tim Salmon in right. Blowers didn't score, and Coleman reacted angrily when he turned at first and realized Blowers had held. Then came the play that ended the Angels' season. Sojo hit a broken-bat double down the line just past Snow. The ball rolled into the bullpen as Blowers and Martinez scored. The relay came to Langston as Cora approached the plate. Langston seemed to double-clutch, and he threw the ball past catcher Andy Allanson. Sojo never stopped running, and he beat Allanson's throw to Langston at the plate.

Notable: This was baseball's first one-game playoff since 1980 (Houston over Los Angeles). . . . The Angels led the West by 11 games on August 9 before their big collapse. The Angels needed to win their last five to force the playoff. . . . The Mariners made the postseason for the

first time in their 19-year history. . . . Langston, then with the Mariners, was traded to Montreal for Johnson on May 25, 1989.

Quotable: Seattle outfielder Ken Griffey on Johnson: "When he stepped on the field today, there was something about him. It was like, 'Give me the one run and I'll take care of the rest.' " . . . Phillips, who played on two World Series teams in Oakland, on why he wanted all the younger Angels to remain in the dugout at the end of the game: "I wanted all the kids to stay and see what it's like to see someone else celebrate. It hurts. It hurts real bad. But maybe the next time this team, whoever is playing here, will remember and make sure they get to celebrate against someone else."

BOX SCORE

MONDAY, OCTOBER 2, AT SEATTLE

California	AB	R	H	RBI	PO	A
Phillips, 3b	4	1	1	1	2	5
DiSarcina, ss	3	0	0	0	1	1
Owen, ph	1	0	0	0	0	0
Edmonds, cf	3	0	0	0	1	0
Perez, ph	1	0	0	0	0	0
Salmon, rf	4	0	0	0	2	0
Davis, dh	2	0	0	0	0	0
Snow, 1b	3	0	0	0	7	0
Anderson, lf	2	0	0	0	0	0
Gallagher, ph-lf	1	0	0	0	1	1
Allanson, c	2	0	0	0	3	1
Gonzales, ph	1	0	1	0	0	0
Fabregas, c	0	0	0	0	1	0
Hudler, 2b	3	0	1	0	6	3
Langston, p	0	0	0	0	0	2
Patterson, p	0	0	0	0	0	0
James, p	0	0	0	0	0	0
Holzemer, p	0	0	0	0	0	0
Habyan, p	0	0	0	0	0	0
Totals	30	1	3	1	24	13

Seattle	AB	R	H	RBI	PO	A
Coleman, lf	5	0	2	1	0	0
Sojo, ss	3	1	2	3	0	1
Griffey, cf	3	0	0	0	4	0
E. Martinez, dh	3	1	2	0	0	0
Buhner, rf	4	1	1	0	1	0
Blowers, 3b	3	2	2	0	0	5
T. Martinez, 1b	2	2	1	1	8	0
Wilson, c	3	1	1	2	12	1
Cora, 2b	2	1	1	1	2	1
Johnson, p	0	0	0	0	0	1
Totals	28	9	12	8	27	9

California	0	0 0		0	0 0		0	0	1—1
Seattle	0	0 0		0	0 0		4	4	x—5

California	IP	H	R	ER	BB	SO
Langston (L)	6⅔	8	5	4	3	2
Patterson	⅓	0	0	0	0	1
James	*0	2	3	3	1	0
Holzemer	†0	1	1	1	0	0
Habyan	1	1	0	0	0	1

Seattle	IP	H	R	ER	BB	SO
Johnson (W)	9	3	1	1	1	12

*Pitched to three batters in eighth. †Pitched to one batter in eighth.

E—Langston. DP—California 4. LOB—California 3, Seattle 4. 2B—Gonzales, Sojo, Wilson. HR—Phillips. CS—Coleman. SH—Sojo, T. Martinez, Wilson. SF—Cora. HBP—By Langston (Cora). T—2:50. A—52,356. U—Shulock, plate; Evans, first; Young, second; Kosc, third; Johnson, left field; Kaiser, right field. Official scorer—Harland Beery.

A.L. DIVISION SERIES
CLEVELAND VS. BOSTON

HIGHLIGHTS
CLEVELAND 5, BOSTON 4

Why the Indians won: Having led the majors in 1995 with 207 home runs, they hauled out the heavy artillery from widely divergent sources—and did so at crunch time. After the Red Sox snapped a 3-3 tie in the top of the 11th on a solo homer by Tim Naehring, Albert Belle forged another deadlock with a solo shot in the bottom of the inning. Then, in the 13th, reserve catcher Tony Pena, who had hit only 12 homers in the past four seasons, delivered a two-out, game-deciding smash off Zane Smith.

Why the Red Sox lost: Blame it on their usual postseason funk. Entering this playoff, Boston had dropped 10 consecutive postseason games (and hadn't won a World Series since 1918). Or blame it on big boppers Mo Vaughn and Jose Canseco, who went a combined 0-for-12 at the plate, left 10 men on base and struck out four times. In the regular season, Vaughn and Canseco totaled 207 RBIs.

The turning points:

1. When Cleveland, trailing 2-0, finally demonstrated that longtime Red Sox ace Roger Clemens wasn't the invincible force of yesteryear, breaking through against the righthander for three sixth-inning runs. Belle's two-run double was the key blow.

2. When Boston had to go deep into its bullpen as the game wore on. By the time the fateful 13th inning rolled around, the Red Sox were relying on Smith, who had been rocked for a 5.61 ERA in the '95 season and had surrendered 144 hits in 110 2/3 innings. Smith wasn't up to the task.

Notable: The 5-hour, 1-minute game at Jacobs Field was the longest postseason contest in major league history. With two rain delays added to the night's proceedings, the game ended at 2:10 a.m., Eastern time. The record lasted all of 24 hours, though, as the Yankees and Mariners played a 5-hour, 13-minute game the next night. . . . The triumph was Cleveland's first in postseason play since the Indians won the decisive Game 6 of the 1948 World Series. The Indians were swept in the 1954 Series. . . . Boston, which scored first on John Valentin's two-run home run in the third, got a game-tying homer from Luis Alicea in the eighth. . . . After Belle's blast in the 11th, the Red Sox asked the umpires to confiscate—and check—his bat. Boston was suspicious about illegal substances therein, since one of Belle's bats was found to have been corked in 1994. . . . Fourteen pitchers were used in the game, with each club forced to call upon a starting pitcher—Smith for Boston, Ken Hill for Cleveland—for bullpen duty in the final two innings.

Quotable: "I don't need to use corked bats," Belle said. "I have muscles. It's a slap in the face, really." . . . More from Belle, after nothing illegal was discovered when his bat—as directed by A.L. representative Bobby Brown—was sawed in half: "He (Brown) knows what he can do with those two pieces." . . . Indians Manager Mike Hargrove called the marathon contest "the most intense, well-played game I've been associated with."

BOX SCORE

TUESDAY, OCTOBER 3, AT CLEVELAND

Boston	AB	R	H	RBI	PO	A
Hosey, rf	5	1	0	0	3	0
Valentin, ss	4	1	2	2	2	2
Vaughn, 1b	6	0	0	0	10	0
Canseco, dh	6	0	0	0	0	0
Greenwell, lf	6	0	3	0	4	0
Naehring, 3b	5	1	2	1	3	2
Tinsley, cf	5	0	0	0	1	0
Macfarlane, c	3	0	0	0	7	0
Stairs, ph	1	0	0	0	0	0
Haselman, c	2	0	0	0	6	0
Alicea, 2b	5	1	4	1	2	6
Clemens, p	0	0	0	0	0	0
Cormier, p	0	0	0	0	0	0
Belinda, p	0	0	0	0	0	0
Stanton, p	0	0	0	0	0	1
Aguilera, p	0	0	0	0	0	0
Maddux, p	0	0	0	0	0	1
Smith, p	0	0	0	0	0	0
Totals	48	4	11	4	38	12

Cleveland	AB	R	H	RBI	PO	A
Lofton, cf	5	0	1	0	6	0
Vizquel, ss	3	1	0	0	1	3
Baerga, 2b	5	1	2	0	3	0
Belle, lf	5	2	2	3	0	0
Murray, dh	6	0	1	1	0	0
Thome, 3b	6	0	1	0	2	3
Ramirez, rf	6	0	0	0	3	0
Sorrento, 1b	5	0	1	0	13	1
Perry, ph	1	0	0	0	0	0
Alomar, c	4	0	1	0	7	1
Kirby, pr	0	0	0	0	0	0
Pena, c	2	1	1	1	4	0
Martinez, p	0	0	0	0	0	1
Tavarez, p	0	0	0	0	0	0
Assenmacher, p	0	0	0	0	0	0
Plunk, p	0	0	0	0	0	1
Mesa, p	0	0	0	0	0	0
Poole, p	0	0	0	0	0	1
Hill, p	0	0	0	0	0	2
Totals	48	5	10	5	39	13

Boston	0 0 2	0 0 0	0 1 0	0 1 0	0—4
Cleveland	0 0 0	0 0 3	0 0 0	0 1 0	1—5

Two out when winning run scored.

Boston	IP	H	R	ER	BB	SO		Cleveland	IP	H	R	ER	BB	SO
Clemens	7	5	3	3	1	5		Martinez	6	5	2	2	0	2
Cormier	1/3	0	0	0	1	1		Tavarez	1 1/3	2	1	1	0	2
Belinda	1/3	0	0	0	0	0		Assenmacher	1/3	0	0	0	0	1
Stanton	2 1/3	1	0	0	0	4		Plunk	1 1/3	1	0	0	1	1
Aguilera	2/3	3	1	1	0	1		Mesa	1	0	0	0	2	0
Maddux	2/3	0	0	0	1	0		Poole	1 2/3	2	1	1	1	2
Smith (L)	1 1/3	1	1	1	0	0		Hill (W)	1 1/3	1	0	0	0	2

E—Alicea, Lofton, Sorrento, Macfarlane. DP—Cleveland 1. LOB—Boston 10, Cleveland 11. 2B—Alicea, Belle. HR—Pena, Belle, Naehring, Alicea, Valentin. SH—Vizquel, Naehring. SB—Vizquel, Alicea. CS—Valentin. HBP—By Maddux (Lofton), by Cormier (Baerga). T—5:01. A—44,218. U—Welke, plate; Hirschbeck, first; Brinkman, second; Roe, third; Denkinger, left field; Morrison, right field.

GAME 2

HIGHLIGHTS

CLEVELAND 4, BOSTON 0

Why the Indians won: They sent savvy postseason veteran Orel Hershiser to the mound. While it had been seven years since Hershiser won Championship Series and World Series MVP honors for the Dodgers in the same season, the righthander didn't disappoint. He lowered his career postseason ERA to 1.52 and improved his won-lost record to 5-0, shutting out the Red Sox on three hits over 7 1/3 innings.

Why the Red Sox lost: Their offense misfired again. While Mo Vaughn and Jose Canseco drew more heat with a combined 0-for-8, three-strikeout performance, they had plenty of accessories to the crime this time. In fact, the top six hitters in Boston's batting order went 0-for-24.

The turning points:

1. Boston's inability to get to Hershiser when it had opportunities. By the fourth pitch of the game, the Indians had committed two errors and Hershiser had thrown a wild pitch—but the Red Sox came up empty in the first inning. Third baseman Jim Thome's swipe tag of Dwayne Hosey, who was trying to advance to third on a ground ball, was pivotal. In the second inning, Boston loaded the bases with two out—but Hershiser again wriggled out of trouble.

2. Red Sox starter Erik Hanson kept the Indians' vaunted bashers at bay through four innings but couldn't handle one of Cleveland's lighter hitters in a critical situation in the fifth. With runners on first and third and one out in a scoreless game, Hanson faced Omar Vizquel, who was neither a double-digit home run hitter in '95 (the Indians had seven) nor a 70-or-more RBI producer (Cleveland had six). But glove wizard Vizquel unloaded a double to right-center, scoring Paul Sorrento and Kenny Lofton (both of whom had walked).

Notable: Cleveland's Jose Mesa, the majors' saves leader with 46 in 1995, pitched a 1-2-3 ninth to nail down the victory. Julian Tavarez and Paul Assenmacher also worked in relief for the Indians, each going one-third of an inning. . . . Eddie Murray, seeing his first postseason action since playing for Baltimore in the 1983 World

Series, accounted for the rest of the game's scoring with a two-run homer off Hanson in the eighth inning. It was the sixth postseason home run of Murray's career.

Quotable: Hershiser, who had career-threatening shoulder surgery in 1990 and was two games under .500 for the Dodgers from 1991-94, was almost nonplused by his performance. "I'm pretty much in awe that this is happening to me," said Hershiser, a 16-6 pitcher for Cleveland after signing with the Indians in April. "To continue to have success at this stage in my career after going through the surgery—the only thing I ask myself is to give my best. My movement and my velocity are back to where they were pre-surgery.". . . "If we go down in this situation because of my play, it'll be something I'll have to live with all winter," Vaughn said. "I haven't done my job."

BOX SCORE

WEDNESDAY, OCTOBER 4, AT CLEVELAND

Boston	AB	R	H	RBI	PO	A
Hosey, cf	4	0	0	0	2	0
Valentin, ss	4	0	0	0	3	1
Vaughn, 1b	4	0	0	0	9	1
Canseco, dh	4	0	0	0	0	0
Greenwell, lf	4	0	0	0	2	0
Naehring, 3b	4	0	0	0	1	0
McGee, rf	3	0	1	0	0	0
Macfarlane, c	3	0	2	0	5	0
Alicea, 2b	1	0	0	0	1	4
Hanson, p	0	0	0	0	1	3
Totals	31	0	3	0	24	9

Cleveland	AB	R	H	RBI	PO	A
Lofton, cf	3	1	0	0	1	0
Vizquel, ss	4	0	1	2	3	2
Baerga, 2b	4	0	0	0	1	3
Belle, lf	2	1	1	0	5	0
Murray, dh	4	1	2	2	0	0
Thome, 3b	4	0	0	0	2	2
Ramirez, rf	4	0	0	0	0	0
Kirby, rf	0	0	0	0	0	0
Sorrento, 1b	1	1	0	0	7	2
Alomar, c	2	0	0	0	8	0
Hershiser, p	0	0	0	0	0	0
Tavarez, p	0	0	0	0	0	0
Assenmacher, p	0	0	0	0	0	0
Mesa, p	0	0	0	0	0	0
Totals	28	4	4	4	27	9

Boston	0	0	0	0	0	0	0	0	0—0
Cleveland	0	0	0	0	2	0	0	2	x—4

Boston	IP	H	R	ER	BB	SO
Hanson (L)	8	4	4	4	4	5

Cleveland	IP	H	R	ER	BB	SO
Hershiser (W)	7⅓	3	0	0	2	7
Tavarez	⅓	0	0	0	0	0
Cleveland	IP	H	R	ER	BB	SO
Assenmacher	⅓	0	0	0	0	1
Mesa	1	0	0	0	0	0

E—Valentin, Sorrento, Belle. LOB—Boston 6, Cleveland 6. 2B—Vizquel. 3B—Murray. HR—Murray. SH—Alomar. SB—Hosey. HBP—By Hanson (Sorrento). WP—Hershiser. PB—Macfarlane. T—2:33. A—44,264. U—Hirschbeck, plate; Brinkman, first; Roe, second; Denkinger, third; Morrison, left field; Welke, right field.

GAME 3

HIGHLIGHTS
CLEVELAND 8, BOSTON 2

Why the Indians won: With a roster made up heavily of players without postseason experience, the Cleveland club showed remarkable poise and confidence as it ventured into the hostile territory known as Fenway Park. In fact, the Indians checked out of their Boston hotel before the game. And the Indians quickly showed they meant business, seizing a 2-0 lead in the second inning on a homer by Jim Thome (Eddie Murray was aboard with a walk) and scoring another run in third when Thome coaxed a bases-loaded walk.

Why the Red Sox lost: Not exactly brimming with confidence in view of their woeful postseason record (12 consecutive defeats stretching to Game 6 of the 1986 World Series), the Sox may have entered this do-or-die game with something less than total faith in starting pitcher Tim Wakefield. Knuckleballer Wakefield has been instrumental in Boston's sprint to the A.L. East title, forging a 14-1 record and 1.65 ERA by mid-August. But he lost seven of his last nine decisions and his ERA jumped to 2.95. Showing *that* late-season form, Wakefield yielded five hits, five walks and seven runs in 5⅓ innings.

The turning points:
1. Omar Vizquel's two-run single in the sixth off Boston reliever Rheal Cormier. The hit boosted Cleveland's lead to 7-1 and put the game out of reach for a Boston team that, out of character, was suddenly inept offensively.
2. With Red Sox runners on second and third base with one out in third and Cleveland ahead 3-0, Boston had Mo Vaughn and Jose Canseco coming up (and a chance to get back into the game). But Vaughn and Canseco remained in their 0-for-the-series stupor, Vaughn striking out and Canseco lining out to left fielder Albert Belle.

Notable: Boston muffed another big opportunity in the fourth inning. With two Red Sox runners on base and Cleveland leading 3-1, Indians first baseman Paul Sorrento made a diving stop of Dwayne Hosey's sharply hit grounder down the line and threw to pitcher Charles Nagy for the third out. It seemed to be Boston's last gasp. . . . Vaughn wound up hitless in 14 series at-bats and fanned seven times; Canseco was 0-for-13. . . . Known for their robust hitting, the Indians got

exemplary pitching in this series. Their staff fashioned a 1.74 ERA against the Red Sox and held Boston hitters to a collective .184 average. Cleveland actually led the A.L. in team batting *and* pitching in 1995.

Quotable: "Their (the Indians') pitching is the key," Boston Manager Kevin Kennedy said after Nagy and two relievers shut down his team on seven hits. "I think that's where it starts. The lineup I respect a lot, (but) I'm a big believer in pitching." . . . Cleveland Manager Mike Hargrove commiserated (well, sort of) with Vaughn, the darling of Red Sox fans, after the slugger's miserable showing in the series. "I can't say that I'm sorry that he didn't get a hit," Hargrove said, "but people like Mo Vaughn deserve better."

BOX SCORE
FRIDAY, OCTOBER 6, AT BOSTON

Cleveland	AB	R	H	RBI	PO	A
Lofton, cf	5	0	1	0	2	0
Vizquel, ss	5	1	1	2	0	6
Baerga, 2b	5	1	2	1	4	2
Belle, lf	4	0	0	0	2	0
Murray, dh	3	2	2	0	0	0
Thome, 3b	3	1	1	3	2	1
Espinoza, 3b	1	0	0	0	0	0
Ramirez, rf	2	1	0	0	0	0
Kirby, rf	1	0	1	0	0	0
Sorrento, 1b	4	1	2	1	7	2
Alomar, c	5	1	1	1	7	0
Pena, c	0	0	0	0	1	0
Nagy, p	0	0	0	0	2	1
Tavarez, p	0	0	0	0	0	0
Assenmacher, p	0	0	0	0	0	0
Totals	38	8	11	8	27	12

Boston	AB	R	H	RBI	PO	A
Hosey, cf	3	0	0	0	2	0
McGee, ph-cf	1	0	0	1	0	0
Valentin, ss	4	0	1	0	0	2
Vaughn, 1b	4	0	0	0	8	1
Canseco, rf	3	0	0	0	4	0
Greenwell, lf	5	0	0	0	2	0
Jefferson, dh	4	1	1	0	0	0
Naehring, 3b	4	1	2	0	1	3
Alicea, 2b	4	0	2	0	3	1
Macfarlane, c	3	0	1	1	6	0
Totals	35	2	7	2	27	8

Cleveland	0	2	1	0	0	5	0	0	0—8
Boston	0	0	0	1	0	0	0	1	0—2

Cleveland	IP	H	R	ER	BB	SO
Nagy (W)	7	4	1	1	5	6
Tavarez	1	3	1	1	0	1
Assenmacher	1	0	0	0	0	1

Boston	IP	H	R	ER	BB	SO
Wakefield (L)	5⅓	5	7	7	5	4
Cormier	⅓	2	1	1	0	1
Maddux	2⅓	2	0	0	0	1
Hudson	1	2	0	0	1	0

E—Lofton, Baerga, Macfarlane. LOB—Cleveland 10, Boston 12. 2B—Baerga, Alomar, Valentin. HR—Thome. SF—Macfarlane. HBP—By Wakefield (Ramirez). WP—Hudson. PB—Macfarlane. T—3:18. A—34,211. U—McKean, plate; McCoy, first; Garcia, second; Joyce, third; Reilly, left field; Scott, right field.

CLEVELAND INDIANS' BATTING AND FIELDING AVERAGES

Player, position	G	AB	R	H	TB	2B	3B	HR	RBI	BB	IBB	SO	Avg.	PO	A	E	Avg.
Kirby, pr-rf	2	1	0	1	1	0	0	0	0	0	0	0	1.000	0	0	0	.000
Pena, c	2	2	1	1	4	0	0	1	1	0	0	0	.500	5	0	0	1.000
Murray, dh	3	13	3	5	10	0	1	1	3	2	0	1	.385	0	0	0	.000
Sorrento, 1b	3	10	2	3	3	0	0	0	1	2	0	3	.300	27	5	2	.941
Baerga, 2b	3	14	2	4	5	1	0	0	1	0	0	1	.286	8	5	1	.929
Belle, lf	3	11	3	3	7	1	0	1	3	4	2	3	.273	7	0	1	.875
Alomar, c	3	11	1	2	3	1	0	0	1	0	0	1	.182	22	1	0	1.000
Vizquel, ss	3	12	2	2	3	1	0	0	4	2	0	2	.167	4	11	0	1.000
Lofton, cf	3	13	1	2	2	0	0	0	0	1	0	3	.154	9	0	2	.818
Thome, 3b	3	13	1	2	5	0	0	1	3	1	0	6	.154	6	6	0	1.000
Assenmacher, p	3	0	0	0	0	0	0	0	0	0	0	0	.000	0	0	0	.000
Hershiser, p	1	0	0	0	0	0	0	0	0	0	0	0	.000	0	0	0	.000
Hill, p	1	0	0	0	0	0	0	0	0	0	0	0	.000	0	2	0	1.000
Martinez, p	1	0	0	0	0	0	0	0	0	0	0	0	.000	0	1	0	1.000
Mesa, p	2	0	0	0	0	0	0	0	0	0	0	0	.000	0	0	0	.000
Nagy, p	1	0	0	0	0	0	0	0	0	0	0	0	.000	2	1	0	1.000
Plunk, p	1	0	0	0	0	0	0	0	0	0	0	0	.000	0	1	0	1.000
Poole, p	1	0	0	0	0	0	0	0	0	0	0	0	.000	0	1	0	1.000
Tavarez, p	3	0	0	0	0	0	0	0	0	0	0	0	.000	0	0	0	.000
Espinoza, 3b	1	1	0	0	0	0	0	0	0	0	0	0	.000	0	0	0	.000
Perry, ph	1	1	0	0	0	0	0	0	0	0	0	0	.000	0	0	0	.000
Ramirez, rf	3	12	1	0	0	0	0	0	0	1	0	2	.000	3	0	0	1.000
Totals	3	114	17	25	43	4	1	4	17	13	2	22	.219	93	34	6	.955

BOSTON RED SOX'S BATTING AND FIELDING AVERAGES

Player, position	G	AB	R	H	TB	2B	3B	HR	RBI	BB	IBB	SO	Avg.	PO	A	E	Avg.
Alicea, 2b	3	10	1	6	10	1	0	1	1	2	0	2	.600	6	11	1	.944
Macfarlane, c	3	9	0	3	3	0	0	0	1	0	0	3	.333	18	0	2	.900
Naehring, 3b	3	13	2	4	7	0	0	1	1	0	0	1	.308	5	5	0	1.000
Valentin, ss	3	12	1	3	7	1	0	1	2	3	1	1	.250	5	5	1	.909
Jefferson, dh	1	4	1	1	1	0	0	0	0	0	0	1	.250	0	0	0	.000
McGee, rf-cf-ph	2	4	0	1	1	0	0	0	1	0	0	2	.250	0	0	0	.000
Greenwell, lf	3	15	0	3	3	0	0	0	0	0	0	1	.200	8	0	0	1.000
Aguilera, p	1	0	0	0	0	0	0	0	0	0	0	0	.000	0	0	0	.000
Belinda, p	1	0	0	0	0	0	0	0	0	0	0	0	.000	0	0	0	.000
Clemens, p	1	0	0	0	0	0	0	0	0	0	0	0	.000	0	0	0	.000
Cormier, p	2	0	0	0	0	0	0	0	0	0	0	0	.000	0	0	0	.000
Hanson, p	1	0	0	0	0	0	0	0	0	0	0	0	.000	1	3	0	1.000
Hudson, p	1	0	0	0	0	0	0	0	0	0	0	0	.000	0	0	0	.000
Maddux, p	2	0	0	0	0	0	0	0	0	0	0	0	.000	1	2	0	1.000
Smith, p	1	0	0	0	0	0	0	0	0	0	0	0	.000	0	0	0	.000
Stanton, p	1	0	0	0	0	0	0	0	0	0	0	0	.000	0	1	0	1.000
Wakefield, p	1	0	0	0	0	0	0	0	0	0	0	0	.000	0	0	0	.000
Stairs, ph	1	1	0	0	0	0	0	0	0	0	0	1	.000	0	0	0	.000
Haselman, c	1	2	0	0	0	0	0	0	0	0	0	0	.000	6	0	0	1.000
Tinsley, cf	1	0	0	0	0	0	0	0	0	1	1	2	.000	1	0	0	1.000
Hosey, rf-cf	3	12	1	0	0	0	0	0	0	2	0	3	.000	7	0	0	1.000
Canseco, dh-rf	3	13	0	0	0	0	0	0	0	2	0	2	.000	4	0	0	1.000
Vaughn, 1b	3	14	0	0	0	0	0	0	0	1	0	7	.000	27	2	0	1.000
Totals	3	114	6	21	32	2	0	3	6	11	2	26	.184	89	29	4	.967

CLEVELAND INDIANS' PITCHING RECORDS

Pitcher	G	GS	CG	IP	H	R	ER	HR	BB	IBB	SO	HB	WP	W	L	Pct.	ERA
Hershiser	1	1	0	7 1/3	3	0	0	0	2	0	7	0	1	1	0	1.000	0.00
Mesa	2	0	0	2	0	0	0	0	2	0	0	0	0	0	0	.000	0.00
Assenmacher	3	0	0	1 2/3	0	0	0	0	0	0	3	0	0	0	0	.000	0.00
Hill	1	0	0	1 1/3	1	0	0	0	0	0	2	0	0	1	0	1.000	0.00
Plunk	1	0	0	1 1/3	1	0	0	0	1	1	1	0	0	0	0	.000	0.00
Nagy	1	1	0	7	4	1	1	0	5	0	6	0	0	1	0	1.000	1.29
Martinez	1	1	0	6	5	2	2	1	0	0	2	0	0	0	0	.000	3.00
Poole	1	0	0	1 2/3	2	1	1	1	1	1	2	0	0	0	0	.000	5.40
Tavarez	3	0	0	2 2/3	5	2	2	1	0	0	3	0	0	0	0	.000	6.75
Totals	3	3	0	31	21	6	6	3	11	2	26	0	0	3	0	1.000	1.74

1995 REVIEW A.L. Division Series

Pitcher	G	GS	CG	IP	H	R	ER	HR	BB	IBB	SO	HB	WP	W	L	Pct.	ERA
Maddux	2	0	0	3	2	0	0	0	1	1	1	1	0	0	0	.000	0.00
Stanton	1	0	0	2 1/3	1	0	0	0	0	0	4	0	0	0	0	.000	0.00
Hudson	1	0	0	1	2	0	0	1	0	0	0	0	1	0	0	.000	0.00
Belinda	1	0	0	0 1/3	0	0	0	0	0	0	0	0	0	0	0	.000	0.00
Clemens	1	1	0	7	5	3	3	0	1	0	5	0	0	0	0	.000	3.86
Hanson	1	1	0	8	4	4	4	1	4	1	5	1	0	0	1	.000	4.50
Smith	1	0	0	1 1/3	1	1	1	1	0	0	0	0	0	0	1	.000	6.75
Wakefield	1	1	0	5 1/3	5	7	7	1	5	0	4	1	0	0	1	.000	11.81
Aguilera	1	0	0	0 2/3	3	1	1	1	0	0	1	0	0	0	0	.000	13.50
Cormier	2	0	0	0 2/3	2	1	1	0	1	0	2	1	0	0	0	.000	13.50
Totals	3	3	1	29 2/3	25	17	17	4	13	2	22	4	0	0	3	.000	5.16

SCORE BY INNINGS

Cleveland	0	2	1		0	2	8		0	2	0		0	1	0	1—17
Boston	0	0	2		1	0	0		0	2	0		0	1	0	0— 6

MISCELLANEOUS STATISTICS

Sacrifice hits—Alomar, Naehring, Vizquel.
Sacrifice flies—Macfarlane.
Stolen bases—Alicea, Hosey, Vizquel.
Caught stealing—Valentin.
Double plays—Thome and Baerga.
Left on bases—Cleveland 11, 6, 10—27; Boston 10, 6, 12—28.
Hit by pitcher—By Maddux (Lofton), by Hanson (Sorrento), by Cormier (Baerga), by Wakefield (Ramirez).
Passed balls—Macfarlane 2.
Balks—None.
Time of games—First game, 5:01; second game, 2:33; third game, 3:18.
Attendance—First game, 44,218; second game, 44,264; third game, 34,211.
Umpires—Welke, Hirschbeck, Brinkman, Roe, Denkinger, McKean, McCoy, Garcia and Joyce.
Official scorers—Hank Kozloski, Charlie Scoggins.

SEATTLE VS. NEW YORK

GAME 1

HIGHLIGHTS

NEW YORK 9, SEATTLE 6

Why the Yankees won: A hobbled Wade Boggs missed the final three regular-season games because of a hamstring injury, but he was in top form for the opener. In the third inning, Boggs drove in the first two runs of the game with a homer off Chris Bosio. Then, with two Mariners on in the fourth, Boggs ended the threat when he went parallel to the ground to snare Dan Wilson's line drive. Boggs' night also included a single in the seventh and a double in the eighth.

Why the Mariners lost: Seattle pitchers were roughed up for 13 hits. The bullpen trio of Jeff Nelson, Bobby Ayala and Bob Wells was particularly ineffective, as it surrendered five runs on seven hits in just 1 2/3 innings. Ayala gave up three runs and four hits in the seventh and recorded only one out.

The turning points:

1. Ken Griffey belted his second homer of the game to tie it at 4 in the top of the seventh. But New York responded by putting the game away in the bottom of the inning. Five of the first six Yankees hitters reached base, with the only out coming on a sacrifice fly. Bernie Williams' go-ahead double and Ruben Sierra's two-run homer highlighted the uprising.

2. New York starter David Cone was in trouble in the sixth. He had just walked in the tying run and faced Luis Sojo with the bases loaded. But Cone escaped by getting Sojo to fly out to right fielder Paul O'Neill. In the inning, Seattle got two hits and two walks—but just one run.

Notable: Seattle made its first playoff appearance in its 19-year history. It was the first postseason appearance for the Yankees since 1981. . . . The Yankees' first two hitters, Boggs and Williams, were 6-for-10. Vince Coleman and Joey Cora, Seattle's No. 1 and No. 2 hitters, went 0-for-8. . . . The crowd of 57,178 was the largest at Yankee Stadium since it was remodeled for the 1976 season. . . . Cone picked up the win but labored throughout, as he walked six and needed 135 pitches to get through eight innings.

Quotable: "It was everything I had supposed it would be," said Don Mattingly, who was making his first postseason appearance after 14 years with the Yankees. "It was wild. It was a great place to be tonight." . . . New York Manager Buck Showalter on the atmosphere at Yankee Stadium: "I've talked with Willie (Randolph) and Reggie (Jackson) about what it's like to play a playoff game here, and tonight I really got a feel for it. There was such an electricity in the air."

BOX SCORE

TUESDAY, OCTOBER 3, AT NEW YORK

Seattle	AB	R	H	RBI	PO	A
Coleman, lf	4	1	0	0	3	0
Cora, 2b	4	1	0	0	0	4
Griffey, cf	5	3	3	3	3	0
E. Martinez, dh	4	1	3	1	0	0
T. Martinez, 1b	3	0	1	1	9	1
Buhner, rf	5	0	1	0	4	0
Blowers, 3b	4	0	0	0	0	1
Wilson, c	3	0	0	1	3	0
Sojo, ss	4	0	1	0	1	1
Bosio, p	0	0	0	0	1	0
Nelson, p	0	0	0	0	0	0
Ayala, p	0	0	0	0	0	0
Risley, p	0	0	0	0	0	0
Wells, p	0	0	0	0	0	0
Totals	36	6	9	6	24	7

New York	AB	R	H	RBI	PO	A
Boggs, 3b	5	2	2	2	1	1
Kelly, pr-2b	0	1	0	0	0	0
B. Williams, cf	5	2	3	2	2	0
O'Neill, rf	3	0	1	1	5	0
Sierra, dh	5	1	1	2	0	0
Mattingly, 1b	4	1	2	1	6	1
James, lf	3	0	1	0	3	0
G. Williams, pr-lf	1	0	0	0	2	0
Stanley, c	4	0	1	1	6	0
Fernandez, ss	3	0	0	0	0	2
Velarde, 2b-3b	3	2	1	0	1	1
Cone, p	0	0	0	0	1	0
Wetteland, p	0	0	0	0	0	0
Totals	36	9	13	9	27	5

Seattle	0	0	0	1	0	1	2	0	2—6
New York	0	0	2	0	0	2	4	1	x—9

Seattle	IP	H	R	ER	BB	SO
Bosio	5 2/3	6	4	4	1	1
Nelson (L)	*1/3	1	1	0	0	
Ayala	1/3	4	3	3	0	0
Risley	2/3	0	0	0	0	1
Wells	1	2	1	1	1	0

New York	IP	H	R	ER	BB	SO
Cone (W)	8	6	4	4	6	5
Wetteland	1	3	2	2	1	1

*Pitched to one batter in seventh.

LOB—Seattle 10, New York 7. 2B—Boggs, Mattingly, B. Williams. HR—Sierra, Griffey 2, Boggs. SF—O'Neill. HBP—By Nelson (Velarde). T—3:39. A—57,178.
U—Reilly, plate; Scott, first; McKean, second; McCoy, third; Garcia, left field; Joyce, right field.

GAME 2

HIGHLIGHTS

NEW YORK 7, SEATTLE 5 (15 INNINGS)

Why the Yankees won: Jim Leyritz vowed to get even against Seattle after he was hit in the face by a Randy Johnson pitch in May. In the 13th inning of Game 2, though, Leyritz couldn't deliver with the winning run at second base. So when the 15th inning came around, Leyritz decided it was time to make good on his promise. With one on and one out, Leyritz sent a Tim Belcher delivery over the right-field wall to give the Yankees a 2-0 lead in the series.

Why the Mariners lost: The Mariners took four leads, including one in the 12th inning, but didn't put away the Yankees. Seattle outhit New York 16-11, but couldn't get the Yankees out when it meant the most. Norm Charlton and Belcher each blew save opportunities for the Mariners.

The turning points:

1. Tino Martinez stroked an RBI single to give the Mariners a 2-1 lead in the sixth, but the Yankees responded with the long ball. Ruben Sierra and Don Mattingly opened the bottom of the inning with homers to right-center to give New York the lead. The back-to-back shots knocked starter Andy Benes from the game.

2. Ken Griffey homered for the third time in the series to give Seattle a 5-4 lead in the 12th. But walks to Wade Boggs and Bernie Williams set up Sierra, whose double off Belcher drove in the tying run. On that play, Seattle executed a perfect relay to throw out Williams—the winning run—at the plate.

Notable: Lou Piniella pulled his Mariners off the field after the Yankee Stadium crowd threw debris on the field in the sixth. . . . The heart of each lineup beat strongly as Seattle's 3-4-5 hitters—Griffey, Edgar Martinez and Jay Buhner—combined for eight hits and a homer. The New York trio of Paul O'Neill, Sierra and Mattingly homered three times and had seven hits. . . . Yankees rookie Mariano Rivera held the Mariners to two hits over the last 3 1/3 innings for the win. . . . At 5 hours, 13 minutes, it was the longest postseason game in major league history.

Quotable: "I got a look at his face as he rounded the bases and it looked like he had no idea what was going on," said Pat Kelly, who walked and scored on Leyritz's home run. . . . "When I saw the ball clear the fence, you can't describe how elated and exhausted I was," Leyritz said. "I could have floated around the bases." . . . Griffey: "This team is not out of it. Just because we're down 2-0 doesn't mean we won't sweep the next three at home."

BOX SCORE

WEDNESDAY, OCTOBER 4, AT NEW YORK

Seattle	AB	R	H	RBI	PO	A
Coleman, lf	5	2	2	1	1	0
Widger, c	2	0	0	0	7	0
Sojo, ss	7	0	1	1	3	8
Griffey, cf	6	1	2	2	6	1
E. Martinez, dh	6	1	3	0	0	0
Buhner, rf	6	0	3	0	2	0
Blowers, 3b	3	0	0	0	1	1
Strange, ph-3b	3	0	0	0	0	0
T. Martinez, 1b	7	0	2	1	11	2
Wilson, c	3	0	0	0	5	0
Diaz, ph-lf	3	0	1	0	1	1
Cora, 2b	4	1	2	0	4	1
Fermin, 2b	1	0	0	0	2	2
Benes, p	0	0	0	0	0	0
Risley, p	0	0	0	0	0	0
Charlton, p	0	0	0	0	0	0
Nelson, p	0	0	0	0	0	0
Belcher, p	0	0	0	0	0	1
Totals	56	5	16	5	43	17

New York	AB	R	H	RBI	PO	A
Boggs, 3b	4	1	0	0	2	4
Posada, pr	0	1	0	0	0	0
Davis, 3b	1	0	1	0	0	0
B. Williams, cf	6	0	1	1	4	0
O'Neill, rf	6	1	2	1	3	0
Sierra, dh	7	1	2	2	0	0
Mattingly, 1b	6	1	3	1	13	1
James, lf	3	0	0	0	0	0
G. Williams, lf	1	0	0	0	2	1
Strawberry, ph	1	0	0	0	0	0
Kelly, 2b	0	0	0	0	0	1
Leyritz, c	6	1	1	2	13	0
Fernandez, ss	5	0	1	0	1	5
Velarde, 2b-lf	5	0	0	0	6	5
Pettitte, p	0	0	0	0	0	3
Wickman, p	0	0	0	0	1	0
Wetteland, p	0	0	0	0	1	0
Rivera, p	0	0	0	0	0	0
Totals	51	7	11	7	45	21

Seattle .... 0 0 1 0 0 1 2 0 0 0 0 1 0 0 0—5
New York .... 0 0 0 0 1 2 1 0 0 0 0 1 0 0 2—7
One out when winning run scored.

Seattle	IP	H	R	ER	BB	SO
Benes	*5	6	3	3	3	3
Risley	1	0	0	0	0	0
Charlton	4	1	1	1	0	5
Nelson	1⅓	0	1	1	1	3
Belcher (L)	3	4	2	2	4	0

New York	IP	H	R	ER	BB	SO
Pettitte	7	9	4	4	3	0
Wickman	1⅓	2	0	0	0	2
Wetteland	3⅓	3	1	1	0	4
M. Rivera (W)	3⅓	2	0	0	0	5

*Pitched to two batters in sixth.

E—Cora, Sojo. DP—Seattle 2, New York 1. LOB—Seattle 11, New York 11. 2B—Sierra, Buhner, Cora, E. Martinez, B. Williams. HR—Leyritz, Griffey, O'Neill, Mattingly, Sierra, Coleman. SH—Kelly, Cora. SF—Griffey. CS—T. Martinez, Buhner. HBP—By Risley (Leyritz). T—5:13. A—57,126. U—Scott, plate; McKean, first; McCoy, second; Garcia, third; Joyce, left field; Reilly, right field.

GAME 3

HIGHLIGHTS

SEATTLE 7, NEW YORK 4

Why the Mariners won: For the second time in five days, ace Randy Johnson won for the Mariners when they faced a season-ending game. In the one-game playoff for the A.L. West title, Johnson pitched a three-hitter against California to propel Seattle into the divisional playoffs. Then with New York holding a 2-0 series lead, Johnson allowed just four hits and two runs while striking out 10.

Why the Yankees lost: While Johnson worked on three days' rest, Yankee starter Jack McDowell was trying to work off more than two weeks of rust. Sidelined by a back injury since September 21, McDowell allowed five runs and four walks in 5⅓ innings. The bullpen couldn't pick up McDowell, as it also was ineffective.

The turning points:

1. Tino Martinez proved to be the offensive spark for the Mariners. After Bernie Williams touched Johnson for a solo homer in the fourth, Martinez belted a McDowell pitch to center for a two-run shot in the fifth to give Seattle the lead for good.

2. Trailing 2-1 in the sixth, the Yankees reached Johnson for two hits and two walks but couldn't score. With one out and Randy Velarde on first, Williams singled to right. Velarde took too wide of a turn at second, though, and right fielder Jay Buhner threw him out. The next two Yankees reached base, but Johnson struck out Don Mattingly on three pitches to end the threat.

3. In the bottom of the sixth, McDowell was relieved after loading the bases. New York Manager Buck Showalter called on Steve Howe, who had a 7.70 ERA in September, to pitch to Martinez. Howe's only pitch of the night went for an RBI single. Seattle added three more runs in the inning to take a 6-1 lead.

Notable: The crowd of 57,944 was the largest for a Mariners game at the Kingdome. The only time the Kingdome drew more for baseball was the 1979 All-Star Game.... Williams, who raised his series average to .500 (7-for-14) with three hits, became the first player in postseason history to hit a home run from both sides of the plate in the same game.... Williams and Mike Stanley, who hit back-to-back homers off Bill Risley in the eighth, combined for five of New York's six hits. ... Seattle sent nine men to the plate in the sixth inning.

Quotable: "I was physically and mentally drained after my last start," said Johnson, who threw 116 pitches. "I was pitching on adrenaline, knowing the importance of tonight's game." ... Showalter on Johnson's seven-inning performance: "He wasn't carrying the same stuff he usually has, but when you're facing Randy Johnson, runs are at a premium." ... Martinez on Seattle's survival of the must-win situation: "We like to think now that the Yankees have their work cut out to win one game here."

BOX SCORE

FRIDAY, OCTOBER 6, AT SEATTLE

New York	AB	R	H	RBI	PO	A
Velarde, lf	3	0	0	0	1	0
B. Williams, cf	3	2	3	2	3	0
Stanley, c	4	1	2	1	7	0
Sierra, dh	3	0	0	0	0	0
Mattingly, 1b	4	0	0	0	7	0
G. Williams, rf	2	1	0	0	2	0
O'Neill, ph-rf	1	0	0	0	0	0
Davis, 3b	4	0	0	0	0	1
Fernandez, ss	4	0	1	0	2	3
Kelly, 2b	3	0	0	1	2	3
McDowell, p	0	0	0	0	0	0
Howe, p	0	0	0	0	0	0
Wickman, p	0	0	0	0	0	0
Hitchcock, p	0	0	0	0	0	1
Rivera, p	0	0	0	0	0	0
Totals	31	4	6	4	24	8

Seattle	AB	R	H	RBI	PO	A
Coleman, lf	4	2	2	0	3	0
Cora, 2b	2	1	0	0	1	3
Griffey, cf	3	0	0	0	1	0
E. Martinez, dh	1	2	0	0	0	0
T. Martinez, 1b	4	2	3	3	7	0
Buhner, rf	4	0	1	1	2	1
Blowers, 3b	2	0	1	1	0	1
Sojo, ss	3	0	0	1	1	2
Wilson, c	4	0	0	0	12	0
Johnson, p	0	0	0	0	0	0
Risley, p	0	0	0	0	0	0
Charlton, p	0	0	0	0	0	0
Totals	27	7	7	6	27	7

New York	0	0	0	1	0	0	1	2	0—4	
Seattle	0	0	0	0	2	4	1	0	x—7	

New York	IP	H	R	ER	BB	SO
McDowell (L)	5 1/3	3	5	5	4	4
Howe	*0	1	1	1	0	0
Wickman	2/3	2	0	0	0	1
Hitchcock	2/3	1	1	0	2	0
M. Rivera	1 1/3	0	0	0	0	2

Seattle	IP	H	R	ER	BB	SO
Johnson (W)	7	4	2	2	4	10
Risley	2/3	2	2	2	0	0
Charlton (S)	1 1/3	0	0	0	0	2

*Pitched to one batter in sixth.

E—Velarde, Stanley. DP—New York 2. LOB—New York 5, Seattle 5. 3B—Coleman. HR—Stanley, T. Martinez, B. Williams 2. SH—Cora. SF—Kelly, Sojo. SB—Griffey, Coleman, Cora, B. Williams. HBP—By McDowell (Blowers). WP—McDowell. T—3:04. A—57,944. U—Brinkman, plate; Roe, first; Evans, second; Morrison, third; Welke, left field; Hirschbeck, right field.

HIGHLIGHTS

SEATTLE 11, NEW YORK 8

Why the Mariners won: To put it simply: Edgar Martinez. Martinez drove in seven runs—the most ever in a postseason game. And his RBIs were dramatic. With Seattle trailing 5-0, Martinez helped make it a 5-4 game with a three-run homer in the third. And with it tied at 6 in the eighth, the A.L. batting champ showed his mettle by blasting a grand slam to center field off John Wetteland.

Why the Yankees lost: The Yankees handed starter Scott Kamieniecki three runs in the first and tacked on two more in the third, but he couldn't hold the lead. Kamieniecki needed 101 pitches to get through five innings. He was roughed up for five runs on nine hits and four walks.

The turning points:

1. After Chris Bosio was knocked out in the third by a two-run homer by Paul O'Neill, Seattle Manager Lou Piniella had to have a bleak outlook. After all, his bullpen entered Game 4 with a collective 0-2 record and 7.24 ERA. But Jeff Nelson held New York scoreless over the next four innings.

2. Don Mattingly was sensational at the plate with four hits, including two doubles and two RBIs. But two miscues in the field by the former Gold Glover cost New York. A wild throw by Mattingly allowed the Mariners to tie it at 5 in the fifth. Then, in the decisive eighth, Mattingly fielded a Joey Cora bunt and tried to beat Cora to the bag instead of flipping the ball to Wetteland. Cora eluded Mattingly's tag. The next hitter, Ken Griffey, was hit by a pitch and that brought up Martinez.

3. The Yankees weren't done after Martinez's blast. After Mike Stanley's RBI single made it 11-7, New York had the bases loaded and one out. Piniella brought in Bill Risley, who got Wade Boggs to hit into an RBI groundout. Bernie Williams then flew out to Griffey on the warning track to end the game.

Notable: The previous high for RBIs in a postseason game was shared by Bobby Richardson (1960 World Series) and Will Clark (1989 N.L. playoffs). . . . Despite allowing two hits, a walk and a wild pitch in two-thirds of an inning, Norm Charlton picked up the win. . . . After Martinez's grand slam, Jay Buhner hit a home run that glanced off Williams' glove in center field.

Quotable: "When I was a kid, I dreamed of being a hero in a game like this," Martinez said. . . . Piniella on Williams' drive that Griffey caught to end the game: "I held my breath on that last ball hit." . . . "I just made bad decisions on throwing the ball," Mattingly said of his fielding problems. "I'm disappointed with both decisions I made."

BOX SCORE

SATURDAY, OCTOBER 7, AT SEATTLE

New York	AB	R	H	RBI	PO	A
Boggs, 3b	5	1	2	1	1	3
Kelly, pr	0	0	0	0	0	0
B. Williams, cf	5	2	2	0	2	0
O'Neill, rf	3	2	2	2	2	0
Sierra, dh	4	0	1	1	0	0
Mattingly, 1b	5	1	4	2	7	0
James, lf	4	0	0	0	2	0
G. Williams, lf	0	0	0	0	1	0
Strawberry, ph	1	0	0	0	0	0
Stanley, c	4	1	1	1	5	0
Fernandez, ss	5	0	1	0	1	3
Velarde, ss	2	1	1	0	3	4
Kamieniecke, p	0	0	0	0	0	0
Hitchcock, p	0	0	0	0	0	0
Wickman, p	0	0	0	0	0	0
Wetteland, p	0	0	0	0	0	0
Howe, p	0	0	0	0	0	0
Totals	38	8	14	7	24	10

Seattle	AB	R	H	RBI	PO	A
Coleman, lf	4	1	0	0	1	0
Cora, 2b	4	2	2	0	2	4
Griffey, cf	4	3	2	1	3	0
E. Martinez, dh	4	2	3	7	0	0
T. Martinez, 1b	5	1	1	0	8	0
Buhner, rf	4	2	3	1	2	0
Blowers, 3b	4	0	1	0	1	1
Sojo, ss	4	0	3	1	3	3
Fermin, ss	0	0	0	0	1	0
Wilson, c	4	0	1	0	6	1
Bosio, p	0	0	0	0	0	0
Nelson, p	0	0	0	0	0	1
Belcher, p	0	0	0	0	0	0

1995 REVIEW A.L. Division Series

Seattle	AB	R	H	RBI	PO	A
Charlton, p	0	0	0	0	0	0
Ayala, p	0	0	0	0	0	0
Risley, p	0	0	0	0	0	0
Totals	37	11	16	10	27	11

New York ...... 3 0 2 0 0 0 0 1 2— 8
Seattle .... 0 0 4 0 1 1 0 5 x—11

New York	IP	H	R	ER	BB	SO
Kamieniecki	5	9	5	4	4	4
Hitchcock	1	1	1	1	0	1
Wickman	1	1	0	0	0	0

New York	IP	H	R	ER	BB	SO
Wetteland (L)	‡0	2	4	4	1	0
Howe	1	3	1	1	0	0

Seattle	IP	H	R	ER	BB	SO
Bosio	*2	4	5	5	3	1
Nelson	†4	6	0	0	2	4
Belcher	$1\frac{1}{3}$	0	1	1	1	0
Charlton (W)	§$\frac{2}{3}$	2	1	1	1	1
Ayala	$\frac{1}{3}$	2	1	1	1	0
Risley (S)	$\frac{2}{3}$	0	0	0	0	0

*Pitched to two batters in third. †Pitched to one batter in seventh. ‡Pitched to four batters in eighth. §Pitched to one batter in ninth.

E—Mattingly. DP—New York 1, Seattle 2. LOB—New York 12, Seattle 10. 2B—Sierra, Mattingly 2, Boggs. HR—Buhner, Griffey, E. Martinez 2, O'Neill. SH—Blowers. SF—Sojo, Sierra. CS—Velarde. HBP—By Wetteland (Griffey). WP—Charlton. T—4:08. A—57,180. U—Roe, plate; Evans, first; Morrison, second; Welke, third; Hirschbeck, left field; Brinkman, right field.

GAME 5

HIGHLIGHTS

SEATTLE 6, NEW YORK 5 (11 INNINGS)

Why the Mariners won: For the fourth time in seven days, the Mariners won when a loss would have ended their season. Seattle rallied to tie the score in the fourth and eighth innings. Then after Seattle fell behind 5-4 in the 11th, Game 4 hero Edgar Martinez doubled into the left-field corner with two on and no outs. Joey Cora scored from third and Ken Griffey raced from first and slid home well ahead of the throw to win the series for Seattle.

Why the Yankees lost: New York was hamstrung by a lack of confidence in its bullpen, which was hit hard all series. Starter David Cone threw 147 pitches before wilting in the eighth when he walked Doug Strange with the bases loaded to tie it at 4. In the ninth, Buck Showalter was forced to call on Game 3 starter Jack McDowell, who was making his first relief appearance in the majors. McDowell escaped jams in the ninth and 10th innings but gave up the tying and winning runs in the 11th.

The turning points:

1. With his team down 4-2 in the eighth, Griffey sparked the Mariners by hitting a solo homer to right off Cone. The home run was Griffey's fifth of the series, the most ever in a division or championship series.

2. After throwing 116 pitches just 48 hours earlier, Randy Johnson came on in relief in the ninth with two on and no out. He struck out Wade Boggs and got Bernie Williams and Paul O'Neill to pop out. Johnson then struck out the side in the 10th. In three innings, he gave up just one run on one hit and struck out six.

3. The Mariners had two on in the ninth when McDowell was brought in to pitch to Martinez. McDowell struck him out with a split-fingered fastball that was low and away. In the 11th, McDowell threw him the same pitch, but this one was up and in and Martinez pulled it into the corner.

Notable: For the series, Martinez hit .571 (12-for-21) with 10 RBIs. . . . Cora, who had seven homers in 2,028 career at-bats, hit one out to give Seattle a 1-0 lead in the third. . . . Seattle outhit New York 15-6 in Game 5. . . . Williams topped the Yankees with a .429 average for the series; Don Mattingly hit .417 in his first trip to the post-season.

Quotable: "I thought last night was the greatest game I ever played," Martinez said. "But tonight is the best game I ever played." . . . "It's the greatest feeling in the world when you're on the other side, but it made me sick to my stomach," O'Neill said. . . . Cone on his eighth-inning walk to Strange: "I rolled the dice with a 3-2 forkball and didn't make the pitch. I'm going to need some time to get over this one. This isn't going to be easy."

BOX SCORE

SUNDAY, OCTOBER 8, AT SEATTLE

New York	AB	R	H	RBI	PO	A
Boggs, 3b	5	0	0	0	0	0
Leyritz, ph-c	1	0	0	0	0	0
B. Williams, cf	2	2	0	0	2	0
O'Neill, rf	5	2	1	2	3	0
Sierra, dh	4	0	0	0	0	0
Mattingly, 1b	5	0	1	2	3	2
James, lf	2	0	0	0	1	0
G. Williams, pr-lf	1	0	0	0	0	0
Stanley, c	4	0	1	0	12	0
Kelly, pr-2b	0	1	0	0	0	0
Fernandez, ss	4	0	2	0	5	2
Velarde, 2b-3b	4	0	1	1	4	1
Cone, p	0	0	0	0	0	0
Rivera, p	0	0	0	0	0	0
McDowell, p	0	0	0	0	0	0
Totals	37	5	6	5	30	5

Seattle	AB	R	H	RBI	PO	A
Coleman, lf	6	0	1	0	6	0
Cora, 2b	5	2	2	1	3	0
Griffey, cf	5	2	2	1	2	0
E. Martinez, dh	6	0	3	2	0	0
T. Martinez, 1b	3	1	2	0	4	1
Rodriguez, pr-ss	1	1	0	0	0	0
Buhner, rf	5	0	3	1	1	0
Sojo, ss	2	0	0	0	1	1
Newson, ph	1	0	0	0	0	0
Fermin, ss	0	0	0	0	0	1
Diaz, ph	0	0	0	0	0	0
Widger, c	1	0	0	0	7	0
Wilson, c	3	0	1	0	8	0
Strange, ph-3b	1	0	0	1	0	0
Blowers, 3b-1b	5	0	1	0	0	2
Benes, p	0	0	0	0	1	0
Charlton, p	0	0	0	0	0	0
Johnson, p	0	0	0	0	0	0
Totals	44	6	15	6	33	5

New York									
New York	0 0 0	2 0 2	0 0 0	0	1—5
Seattle	0 0 1	1 0 0	0 2 0	0	2—6

None out when winning run scored.

New York	IP	H	R	ER	BB	SO
Cone	7²/₃	9	4	4	3	9
M. Rivera	²/₃	1	0	0	1	1
McDowell (L)	†1²/₃	5	2	2	0	2

Seattle	IP	H	R	ER	BB	SO
Benes	6²/₃	4	4	4	6	5
Charlton	*1¹/₃	1	0	0	2	1
Johnson (W)	3	1	1	1	2	6

*Pitched to two batters in ninth. †Pitched to three batters in 11th.

DP—Seattle 1. LOB—New York 10, Seattle 13. 2B—E. Martinez 2, Mattingly, Fernandez 2, T. Martinez. HR—Griffey, O'Neill, Cora. SH—Fernandez, Cora. WP—Cone 2. T—4:19. A—57,411. U—Evans, plate; Morrison, first; Welke, second; Hirschbeck, third; Brinkman, left field; Roe, right field.

STATISTICS

SEATTLE MARINERS' BATTING AND FIELDING AVERAGES

Player, position	G	AB	R	H	TB	2B	3B	HR	RBI	BB	IBB	SO	Avg.	PO	A	E	Avg.
E. Martinez, dh	5	21	6	12	21	3	0	2	10	6	2	2	.571	0	0	0	.000
Buhner, rf	5	24	2	11	15	1	0	1	3	2	0	4	.458	11	1	0	1.000
T. Martinez, 1b	5	22	4	9	13	1	0	1	5	3	0	4	.409	39	5	0	1.000
Griffey, cf	5	23	9	9	24	0	0	5	7	2	1	4	.391	15	1	0	1.000
Diaz, lf-ph	1	3	0	1	1	0	0	0	0	1	0	1	.333	1	1	0	1.000
Cora, 2b	5	19	7	6	10	1	0	1	1	3	0	0	.316	10	12	1	.957
Sojo, ss	5	20	0	5	5	0	0	0	3	0	0	3	.250	9	15	1	.960
Coleman, lf	5	23	6	5	10	0	1	1	1	2	0	4	.217	14	0	0	1.000
Blowers, 3b-1b	5	18	0	3	3	0	0	0	1	3	0	7	.167	2	6	0	1.000
Wilson, c	5	17	0	2	2	0	0	0	1	2	0	6	.118	34	1	0	1.000
Ayala, p	2	0	0	0	0	0	0	0	0	0	0	0	.000	0	0	0	.000
Belcher, p	2	0	0	0	0	0	0	0	0	0	0	0	.000	0	1	0	1.000
Benes, p	2	0	0	0	0	0	0	0	0	0	0	0	.000	1	0	0	1.000
Bosio, p	2	0	0	0	0	0	0	0	0	0	0	0	.000	1	0	0	1.000
Charlton, p	4	0	0	0	0	0	0	0	0	0	0	0	.000	0	0	0	.000
Johnson, p	2	0	0	0	0	0	0	0	0	0	0	0	.000	0	0	0	.000
Nelson, p	3	0	0	0	0	0	0	0	0	0	0	0	.000	0	1	0	1.000
Risley, p	4	0	0	0	0	0	0	0	0	0	0	0	.000	0	0	0	.000
Wells, p	1	0	0	0	0	0	0	0	0	0	0	0	.000	0	0	0	.000
Fermin, 2b-ss	3	1	0	0	0	0	0	0	0	0	0	1	.000	3	3	0	1.000
Newson, ph	1	1	0	0	0	0	0	0	0	0	0	1	.000	0	0	0	.000
Rodriguez, ss-pr	1	1	1	0	0	0	0	0	0	0	0	0	.000	0	0	0	.000
Widger, c	2	3	0	0	0	0	0	0	0	0	0	3	.000	14	0	0	1.000
Strange, 3b-ph	2	4	0	0	0	0	0	0	1	1	0	1	.000	0	0	0	.000
Totals	5	200	35	63	104	6	1	11	33	25	3	41	.315	154	47	2	.990

NEW YORK YANKEES' BATTING AND FIELDING AVERAGES

Player, position	G	AB	R	H	TB	2B	3B	HR	RBI	BB	IBB	SO	Avg.	PO	A	E	Avg.
B. Williams, cf	5	21	8	9	17	2	0	2	5	7	1	3	.429	13	0	0	1.000
Mattingly, 1b	5	24	3	10	17	4	0	1	6	1	0	5	.417	36	4	1	.976
O'Neill, rf-ph	5	18	5	6	15	0	0	3	6	5	0	5	.333	13	0	0	1.000
Stanley, c	4	16	2	5	8	0	0	1	3	2	0	1	.313	30	0	1	.968
Boggs, 3b	4	19	4	5	10	2	0	1	3	3	0	5	.263	4	8	0	1.000
Fernandez, ss	5	21	0	5	7	2	0	0	0	2	1	2	.238	9	15	0	1.000
Davis, 3b	2	5	0	1	1	0	0	0	0	0	0	2	.200	0	1	0	1.000
Velarde, 2b-3b-lf	5	17	3	3	3	0	0	0	1	6	0	4	.176	15	11	1	.963
Sierra, dh	5	23	2	4	12	2	0	2	5	2	0	7	.174	0	0	0	.000
Leyritz, c-ph	2	7	1	1	4	0	0	1	2	0	0	1	.143	13	0	0	1.000
James, lf	4	12	0	1	1	0	0	0	0	1	1	1	.083	6	0	0	1.000
Cone, p	2	0	0	0	0	0	0	0	0	0	0	0	.000	1	0	0	1.000
Hitchcock, p	2	0	0	0	0	0	0	0	0	0	0	0	.000	0	1	0	1.000
Howe, p	2	0	0	0	0	0	0	0	0	0	0	0	.000	0	0	0	.000
Kamieniecki, p	1	0	0	0	0	0	0	0	0	0	0	0	.000	0	0	0	.000
McDowell, p	2	0	0	0	0	0	0	0	0	0	0	0	.000	0	0	0	.000
Pettitte, p	1	0	0	0	0	0	0	0	0	0	0	0	.000	0	3	0	1.000
Posada, pr	1	0	1	0	0	0	0	0	0	0	0	0	.000	0	0	0	.000
Rivera, p	3	0	0	0	0	0	0	0	0	0	0	0	.000	0	0	0	.000
Wetteland, p	3	0	0	0	0	0	0	0	0	0	0	0	.000	1	0	0	1.000
Wickman, p	3	0	0	0	0	0	0	0	0	0	0	0	.000	0	1	0	1.000
Strawberry, ph	2	2	0	0	0	0	0	0	0	0	0	1	.000	0	0	0	.000
Kelly, 2b-pr	4	3	3	0	0	0	0	0	1	1	0	0	.000	2	4	0	1.000
G. Williams, lf-pr-rf	5	5	1	0	0	0	0	0	0	2	0	3	.000	7	1	0	1.000
Totals	5	193	33	50	95	12	0	11	32	32	3	43	.259	150	49	3	.985

SEATTLE MARINERS' PITCHING RECORDS

Pitcher	G	GS	CG	IP	H	R	ER	HR	BB	IBB	SO	HB	WP	W	L	Pct.	ERA
Charlton	4	0	0	7 1/3	4	2	2	1	3	0	9	0	1	1	0	1.000	2.45
Johnson	2	1	0	10	5	3	3	1	6	1	16	0	0	2	0	1.000	2.70
Nelson	3	0	0	5 2/3	7	2	2	0	3	0	7	1	0	0	1	.000	3.18
Benes	2	2	0	11 2/3	10	7	7	3	9	1	8	0	0	0	0	.000	5.40
Risley	4	0	0	3	2	2	2	2	0	0	1	1	0	0	0	.000	6.00
Belcher	2	0	0	4 1/3	4	3	3	1	5	1	0	0	0	0	1	.000	6.23
Wells	1	0	0	1	2	1	1	0	1	0	0	0	0	0	0	.000	9.00
Bosio	2	2	0	7 2/3	10	9	9	2	4	0	2	0	0	0	0	.000	10.57
Ayala	2	0	0	0 2/3	6	4	4	1	1	0	0	0	0	0	0	.000	54.00
Totals	5	5	0	51 1/3	50	33	33	11	32	3	43	2	0	3	2	.600	5.79

NEW YORK YANKEES' PITCHING RECORDS

Pitcher	G	GS	CG	IP	H	R	ER	HR	BB	IBB	SO	HB	WP	W	L	Pct.	ERA
Rivera	3	0	0	5 1/3	3	0	0	0	1	1	8	0	0	1	0	1.000	0.00
Wickman	3	0	0	3	5	0	0	0	0	0	3	0	0	0	0	.000	0.00
Cone	2	2	0	15 2/3	15	8	8	4	9	0	14	0	2	1	0	1.000	4.60
Pettitte	1	1	0	7	9	4	4	1	3	0	0	0	0	0	0	.000	5.14
Hitchcock	2	0	0	1 2/3	2	2	1	1	2	1	1	0	0	0	0	.000	5.40
Kamieniecki	1	1	0	5	9	5	4	1	4	0	4	0	0	0	0	.000	7.20
McDowell	2	1	0	7	8	7	7	1	4	1	6	1	1	0	2	.000	9.00
Wetteland	3	0	0	4 1/3	8	7	7	2	2	0	5	1	0	0	1	.000	14.54
Howe	2	0	0	1	4	2	2	1	0	0	0	0	0	0	0	.000	18.00
Totals	5	5	0	50	63	35	33	11	25	3	41	2	0	2	3	.400	5.94

SCORE BY INNINGS

Seattle	0	0	6	2	3	7	5	7	2	0	2	1	0	0	0—35
New York	3	0	4	3	1	6	6	4	2	0	1	1	0	0	2—33

MISCELLANEOUS STATISTICS

Sacrifice hits—Cora 3, Blowers, Fernandez, Kelly.
Sacrifice flies—Sojo 2, Griffey, Kelly, O'Neill, Sierra.
Stolen bases—Coleman, Cora, Griffey, B. Williams.
Caught stealing—Buhner, T. Martinez, Velarde.
Double plays—Boggs, Velarde and Mattingly; Cora, Sojo and T. Martinez; Fermin
and T. Martinez; Fernandez, Kelly and Mattingly; Kelly, Fernandez and Mattingly; Sojo and T. Martinez; T. Martinez, Sojo and T. Martinez.
Left on bases—Seattle 10, 11, 5, 10, 13—49; New York 7, 11, 5, 12, 10—45.
Hit by pitcher—By McDowell (Blowers), by Wetteland (Griffey), by Nelson (Velarde), by Risley (Leyritz).
Passed balls—None.
Balks—None.
Time of games—First game, 3:39; second game, 5:13; third game, 3:04; fourth game, 4:08; fifth game, 4:19.
Attendance—First game, 57,178; second game, 57,126; third game, 57,944; fourth game, 57,180; fifth game, 57,411.
Umpires—Reilly, Scott, McKean, McCoy, Garcia, Brinkman, Roe, Evans, Morrison, Welke and Hirschbeck.
Official scorers—Harland Beery, Red Foley.

1995 REVIEW A.L. Division Series

N.L. DIVISION SERIES
CINCINNATI VS. LOS ANGELES

GAME 1

HIGHLIGHTS
CINCINNATI 7, LOS ANGELES 2

Why the Reds won: Starting pitcher Pete Schourek was terrific, limiting the Dodgers to five hits in seven innings and allowing just two runs. Schourek, a former Mets castoff who won 18 games for Cincinnati during the regular season, was appearing in his first postseason game.

Why the Dodgers lost: They fell behind early and couldn't catch up. The Reds scored four times in the first inning and were ahead, 7-0, by the fifth inning. The early outburst took pressure off Schourek and took the partisan Dodgers crowd out of the game.

The turning points:

1. With one out in the top of the first, Barry Larkin and Ron Gant singled for Cincinnati. Reggie Sanders fouled out, but Hal Morris sliced a 1-2 pitch from Ramon Martinez to left-center field for a double, driving in two runs. Benito Santiago then hit a 2-1 pitch from Martinez over the left-field wall for a two-run homer, giving the Reds a 4-0 lead.

2. In the eighth inning, after a tiring Schourek had been lifted, the Dodgers put two men on with none out against reliever Mike Jackson. But Jackson worked his way out of the jam without allowing a run, and Jeff Brantley pitched a scoreless ninth.

Notable: Both starting pitchers were appearing in their first postseason games. . . . Martinez had won his last six starts against Cincinnati and was 9-1 since the All-Star break. . . . The announced crowd of 44,199 at Dodger Stadium was about 10,000 short of capacity. . . . Eight of the Reds' nine starting players hit safely against Martinez. The one who didn't—Schourek—hit a line drive that right fielder Raul Mondesi had to flag down on the warning track. . . . Before this game, the Reds had lost 18 of their last 31 games and the Dodgers had won 17 of 25. Cincinnati had lost in its previous 10 games on natural grass.

Quotable: Schourek on his first postseason start: "I had some butterflies, but I calmed myself down before the game. I kind of surprised myself by not being that nervous. The four-run first inning helped." . . . Morris, who entered the game batting .341 (15-for-44) lifetime against Martinez: "I can't really attribute it to anything. I'm a contact hitter, and tonight I just found some

gaps." . . . Reds outfielder Thomas Howard: "We came here trying to win both games. We weren't going to be happy with a split here." . . . Larkin on the Reds' early four-run lead: "It's tough to come back from that. We want the home-field advantage, and the only way to have the home-field advantage is to go home with at least one win. Hopefully, now we can get two wins and really have home-field advantage."

BOX SCORE

TUESDAY, OCTOBER 3, AT LOS ANGELES

Cincinnati	AB	R	H	RBI	PO	A
Howard, cf	3	0	1	0	1	0
Walton, ph-cf-lf	2	0	0	0	2	0
Larkin, ss	4	1	2	0	2	3
Gant, lf	5	1	1	0	2	0
D. Lewis, cf	0	0	0	0	1	0
Sanders, rf	5	1	1	0	2	0
Morris, 1b	4	2	3	2	6	1
Santiago, c	3	1	1	3	6	0
Boone, 2b	4	1	1	0	5	3
Branson, 3b	3	0	2	2	0	4
Schourek, p	2	0	0	0	0	1
Duncan, ph	1	0	0	0	0	0
Jackson, p	0	0	0	0	0	0
Brantley, p	0	0	0	0	0	0
Totals	36	7	12	7	27	12

Los Angeles	AB	R	H	RBI	PO	A
Butler, cf	5	0	1	1	0	0
Fonville, ss	4	0	1	0	0	2
Piazza, c	4	1	2	1	12	0
Karros, 1b	4	0	1	0	5	0
Wallach, 3b	3	0	0	0	0	1
Mondesi, rf	4	0	0	0	5	0
DeShields, 2b	3	1	2	0	3	3
Kelly, lf	4	0	1	0	2	0
Martinez, p	1	0	0	0	0	1
Cummings, p	0	0	0	0	0	0
Ashley, ph	0	0	0	0	0	0
Astacio, p	0	0	0	0	0	1
Webster, ph	1	0	0	0	0	0
Guthrie, p	0	0	0	0	0	0
Osuna, p	0	0	0	0	0	0
Hansen, ph	1	0	0	0	0	0
Totals	34	2	8	2	27	8

Cincinnati	4	0	0	0	3	0	0	0	0—7
Los Angeles	0	0	0	0	1	1	0	0	0—2

Cincinnati	IP	H	R	ER	BB	SO
Schourek (W)	7	5	2	2	3	5
Jackson	1	2	0	0	0	0
Brantley	1	1	0	0	0	0

Los Angeles	IP	H	R	ER	BB	SO
Martinez (L)	4 1/3	10	7	7	2	3
Cummings	2/3	1	0	0	0	1
Astacio	2	0	0	0	0	4
Guthrie	1	0	0	0	1	1
Osuna	1	1	0	0	1	1

DP—Cincinnati 1, Los Angeles 1. LOB—Cincinnati 8, Los Angeles 8. 2B—Branson, Boone, Sanders, Howard, Morris. HR—Piazza, Santiago. SH—Schourek. SF—Santiago. SB—Larkin 2. T—3:15. A—44,199. U—Montague, plate; Davidson, first; Gregg, second; Pulli, third; Froemming, left field; Darling, right field.

HIGHLIGHTS

CINCINNATI 5, LOS ANGELES 4

Why the Reds won: They were opportunistic, to say the least. Although they were outhit 14-6, the Reds took advantage of numerous Dodgers miscues to score all their runs. Cincinnati scored what proved to be the decisive runs in the ninth after loading the bases via three walks.

Why the Dodgers lost: Their defense, dreadful during the regular season, was downright horrible in this game. A throwing error by shortstop Chad Fonville set up Cincinnati's first two runs in the fourth inning, and a wide throw by catcher Mike Piazza on a pitchout led to the Reds' go-ahead run in the eighth.

The turning points:

1. With Los Angeles up 1-0 in the fourth and left-hander Ismael Valdes having retired the first 11 batters he faced, a wild throw by Fonville enabled Ron Gant to reach second with two out. The next batter, Reggie Sanders, homered to center field to give the Reds a 2-1 lead.

2. With the score tied at 2 in the sixth, the Dodgers loaded the bases on three singles with two outs. But the next batter was Valdes, who flied out to center. The Dodgers loaded the bases again in the seventh, but Cincinnati catcher Benito Santiago thwarted a possible big inning by cleanly fielding a one-hop throw from third baseman Jeff Branson to force out Brett Butler at home. Delino DeShields then hit a foul pop to end the inning.

Notable: Eric Karros (two homers and a double) drove in all four L.A. runs. . . . The announced crowd of 46,051 at Dodger Stadium was about 10,000 short of capacity. . . . The Dodgers stranded 11 runners, including eight in the fifth, sixth and seventh innings combined. . . . Los Angeles right fielder Raul Mondesi was ejected by plate umpire Bob Davidson for remarks he made to Davidson after DeShields fouled out with the bases loaded to end the seventh. . . . The Dodgers committed more errors (130) and had the lowest fielding percentage of any major league team (.976) during the 1995 season. . . . Valdes outpitched Reds starter John Smiley, but the L.A. bullpen was a disaster. Losing pitcher Antonio Osuna yielded a run-scoring single to Barry Larkin that broke a 2-2 tie in the eighth inning, and Kevin Tapani, normally a starting pitcher, gave up two earned runs in one-third of an inning.

Quotable: Cincinnati Manager Davey Johnson: "By all rights, we shouldn't have won this game. But we weren't going to be denied. Larkin got the key hit, and he's done that a lot." . . . L.A. Manager Tom Lasorda: "We've just got to come back now, pull an upset and win three straight games." . . . Larkin: "In these pressure games, we played well enough to win. But by no means is this series over."

BOX SCORE

WEDNESDAY, OCTOBER 4, AT LOS ANGELES

Cincinnati	AB	R	H	RBI	PO	A
Howard, cf	4	0	0	0	4	0
D. Lewis, cf	1	0	0	0	1	0
Larkin, ss	4	0	1	1	1	3
Gant, lf	4	1	0	0	4	0
Jackson, p	0	0	0	0	1	0
Brantley, p	0	0	0	0	0	0
Sanders, rf	3	2	1	2	2	0
Morris, 1b	3	1	0	0	8	0
Santiago, c	3	0	1	0	3	0
Boone, 2b	3	0	0	0	2	0
Burba, p	0	0	0	0	0	0
Walton, lf	0	0	0	0	0	0
Branson, 3b	3	0	0	0	1	3
M. Lewis, ph-3b	1	0	0	1	0	0
Smiley, p	2	0	0	0	0	1
Duncan, 2b	2	1	2	1	0	1
Totals	**33**	**5**	**6**	**5**	**27**	**8**

Los Angeles	AB	R	H	RBI	PO	A
Butler, cf	5	1	3	0	4	0
Fonville, ss	4	1	4	0	1	3
Piazza, c	5	0	0	0	7	0
Karros, 1b	4	2	3	4	6	0
Wallach, 3b	5	0	1	0	1	0
DeShields, 2b	5	0	0	0	4	3
Mondesi, rf	3	0	1	0	1	0
Hollandsworth, rf	1	0	0	0	0	0
Kelly, lf	4	0	1	0	3	0
Valdes, p	3	0	0	0	0	0
Osuna, p	0	0	0	0	0	0
Hansen, ph	1	0	1	0	0	0
Offerman, pr	0	0	0	0	0	0
Tapani, p	0	0	0	0	0	0
Guthrie, p	0	0	0	0	0	1
Astacio, p	0	0	0	0	0	0
Totals	**40**	**4**	**14**	**4**	**27**	**7**

Cincinnati	0	0	0	2	0	0	0	1	2—5
Los Angeles	1	0	0	1	0	0	0	0	2—4

Cincinnati	IP	H	R	ER	BB	SO
Smiley	6	9	2	2	0	1
Burba (W)	1	2	0	0	1	0
Jackson	1	1	0	0	0	0
Brantley (S)	1	2	2	2	0	1

Los Angeles	IP	H	R	ER	BB	SO
Valdes	7	3	2	0	1	6
Osuna (L)	1	2	1	1	0	0
Tapani	1/3	0	2	2	3	1
Guthrie	1/3	0	0	0	0	0
Astacio	1/3	1	0	0	0	0

E—Osuna, Fonville. DP—Los Angeles 1. LOB—Cincinnati 5, Los Angeles 11. 2B—Karros. HR—Karros 2, Sanders. SH—Fonville. SB—Morris, Sanders 2, Duncan. T—3:21. A—46,051. U—Davidson, plate; Gregg, first; Pulli, second; Froemming, third; Darling, left field; Montague, right field.

HIGHLIGHTS

CINCINNATI 10, LOS ANGELES 1

Why the Reds won: Their offense was overpowering. The Reds—who finished second in the league in slugging percentage (.440) and were shut out an N.L.-low three times in the regular season—battered six L.A. pitchers for 11 hits, including home runs by Ron Gant, Bret Boone and Mark Lewis.

Why the Dodgers lost: Hideo Nomo pitched like a rookie making his first postseason start. After going 13-6 with a 2.54 ERA during the regular season en route to winning N.L. Rookie of the Year honors, Nomo looked very ordinary against Cincinnati in the division series. He threw 91 pitches in five innings and allowed five earned runs. The Gant and Boone homers (in the third and fourth innings, respectively) clearly unsettled him.

The turning points:

1. With the game still scoreless in the third, the Dodgers appeared set to take the lead when Mike Piazza doubled with Chad Fonville on base. But Fonville stepped over the plate as he tried to avoid being tagged by catcher Benito Santiago. After sprawling in the dirt, Fonville got up and tried to dodge Santiago, who tagged him out.

2. Leading 3-1 in the sixth, the Reds blew the game open when Lewis, pinch-hitting for third baseman Jeff Branson, belted a grand slam off Mark Guthrie. Cincinnati scored three more times in the seventh to close out the scoring.

Notable: With the victory, the Reds advanced to the National League Championship Series for the eighth time, second only to Pittsburgh (nine) in N.L. history. . . . Cincinnati, which swept Oakland in the 1990 World Series, won its eighth consecutive postseason game. . . . The Dodgers were swept for only the second time in 27 postseason series. In 1966, Baltimore swept Los Angeles in the World Series. Ironically, Reds Manager Davey Johnson was the Orioles' second baseman in that series. . . . Lewis' blast was the first grand slam hit by a pinch-hitter in playoff history. Overall, it was the 17th pinch homer. . . . Reds right fielder Reggie Sanders, who hit .306 during the regular season, struck out five times in Game 3 and hit just .154 (2-for-13) in the series.

Quotable: Tom Lasorda, ending his 19th season as the Dodgers' manager: "I've been in a lot of playoffs, and this was the most devastating." . . . Johnson: "This is a remarkable team. We can beat you in a lot of ways." . . . Gant: "Once this team gets on a roll, it is capable of beating anyone."

BOX SCORE

FRIDAY, OCTOBER 6, AT CINCINNATI

Los Angeles	AB	R	H	RBI	PO	A
Butler, cf	5	0	0	0	3	0
Fonville, ss	4	0	1	0	0	2
Gwynn, ph	1	0	0	0	0	0
Piazza, c	5	0	1	0	12	0
Karros, 1b	4	1	2	0	3	0
Wallach, 3b	4	0	0	0	0	1
DeShields, 2b	4	0	1	0	1	1
Mondesi, rf	2	0	1	1	2	0
Hollandsworth, ph-rf	1	0	0	0	0	0
Kelly, lf	3	0	2	0	3	0
Nomo, p	2	0	0	0	0	0
Tapani, p	0	0	0	0	0	0
Guthrie, p	0	0	0	0	0	0
Astacio, p	0	0	0	0	0	0
Webster, ph	1	0	0	0	0	0
Cummings, p	0	0	0	0	0	0
Osuna, p	0	0	0	0	0	0
Hansen, ph	1	0	1	0	0	0
Totals	**37**	**1**	**9**	**1**	**24**	**4**

Cincinnati	AB	R	H	RBI	PO	A
Howard, cf	3	0	0	0	0	0
D. Lewis, ph-cf	2	0	0	0	1	0
Larkin, ss	5	1	2	0	0	2
Gant, lf	4	1	2	2	2	1
Walton, lf	1	0	0	0	1	0
Sanders, rf	5	0	0	0	3	0
Morris, 1b	3	2	1	0	8	1
Santiago, c	3	1	1	0	11	0
Boone, 2b	3	3	2	1	0	2
Branson, 3b	1	0	0	0	0	1
M. Lewis, ph-3b	1	2	1	4	0	0
Wells, p	3	0	1	0	1	1
Jackson, p	1	0	1	3	0	1
Brantley, p	0	0	0	0	0	0
Totals	**35**	**10**	**11**	**10**	**27**	**9**

Los Angeles	0	0 0	1	0 0	0	0 0—	1
Cincinnati	0	0 2	1	0 4	3	0 x—	10

Los Angeles	IP	H	R	ER	BB	SO
Nomo (L)	*5	7	5	5	2	6
Tapani	†0	0	1	1	1	0
Guthrie	‡0	2	1	1	0	0
Astacio	1	0	0	0	0	1
Cummings	²/₃	2	3	3	2	2
Osuna	1¹/₃	0	0	0	0	2

Cincinnati	IP	H	R	ER	BB	SO
Wells (W)	6¹/₃	6	1	0	1	8
Jackson	1²/₃	1	0	0	0	1
Brantley	1	2	0	0	0	1

*Pitched to two batters in sixth. †Pitched to one batter in sixth. ‡Pitched to two batters in sixth.

E—Kelly, M. Lewis, Sanders. LOB—Los Angeles 11, Cincinnati 6. 2B—Jackson, Piazza. HR—M. Lewis, Boone, Gant. SB—Boone, Larkin 2. HBP—By Wells (Mondesi). WP—Nomo. T—3:27. A—53,276. U—West, plate; Tata, first; Wendelstedt, second; Reliford, third; McSherry, left field; Layne, right field.

1995 REVIEW N.L. Division Series

CINCINNATI REDS' BATTING AND FIELDING AVERAGES

Player, position	G	AB	R	H	TB	2B	3B	HR	RBI	BB	IBB	SO	Avg.	PO	A	E	Avg.
Jackson, p	3	1	0	1	2	1	0	0	3	0	0	0	1.000	1	1	0	1.000
Duncan, ph-2b	1	3	1	2	2	0	0	0	1	0	0	0	.667	0	1	0	1.000
Morris, 1b	3	10	5	5	6	1	0	0	2	3	2	1	.500	22	2	0	1.000
M. Lewis, 3b-ph	2	2	2	1	4	0	0	1	5	1	1	0	.500	0	0	1	.000
Larkin, ss	3	13	2	5	5	0	0	0	1	1	0	2	.385	3	8	0	1.000
Santiago, c	3	9	2	3	6	0	0	1	3	3	0	3	.333	20	0	0	1.000
Wells, p	1	3	0	1	1	0	0	0	0	0	0	1	.333	1	1	0	1.000
Boone, 2b	3	10	4	3	7	0	0	1	1	1	0	3	.300	7	5	0	1.000
Branson, 3b	3	7	0	2	3	1	0	0	2	2	1	0	.286	1	8	0	1.000
Gant, lf	3	13	3	3	6	0	0	1	2	0	0	3	.231	8	1	0	1.000
Sanders, rf	3	13	3	2	6	1	0	1	2	1	0	9	.154	7	0	1	.875
Howard, cf	3	10	0	1	2	1	0	0	0	0	0	2	.100	5	0	0	1.000
Brantley, p	3	0	0	0	0	0	0	0	0	0	0	0	.000	0	0	0	.000
Burba, p	1	0	0	0	0	0	0	0	0	0	0	0	.000	0	0	0	.000
Schourek, p	1	2	0	0	0	0	0	0	0	0	0	1	.000	0	2	0	1.000
Smiley, p	1	2	0	0	0	0	0	0	0	0	0	1	.000	0	1	0	1.000
D. Lewis, cf-ph	3	3	0	0	0	0	0	0	0	0	0	1	.000	3	0	0	1.000
Walton, lf-cf-ph	3	3	0	0	0	0	0	0	0	1	0	1	.000	3	0	0	1.000
Totals	3	104	22	29	50	6	0	5	22	13	4	28	.279	81	30	2	.982

LOS ANGELES DODGERS' BATTING AND FIELDING AVERAGES

Player, position	G	AB	R	H	TB	2B	3B	HR	RBI	BB	IBB	SO	Avg.	PO	A	E	Avg.
Hansen, ph	3	3	0	2	2	0	0	0	0	0	0	0	.667	0	0	0	.000
Fonville, ss	3	12	1	6	6	0	0	0	0	0	0	1	.500	1	7	1	.889
Karros, 1b	3	12	3	6	13	1	0	2	4	1	0	0	.500	14	0	0	1.000
Kelly, lf	3	11	0	4	4	0	0	0	0	1	0	0	.364	8	0	1	.889
Butler, cf	3	15	1	4	4	0	0	0	1	0	0	3	.267	7	0	0	1.000
DeShields, 2b	3	12	1	3	3	0	0	0	0	1	0	3	.250	8	7	0	1.000
Mondesi, rf	3	9	0	2	2	0	0	0	1	0	0	2	.222	8	0	0	1.000
Piazza, c	3	14	1	3	7	1	0	1	1	0	0	2	.214	31	0	0	1.000
Wallach, 3b	3	12	0	1	1	0	0	0	0	1	0	3	.083	1	2	0	1.000
Ashley, ph	1	0	0	0	0	0	0	0	0	1	0	0	.000	0	0	0	.000
Astacio, p	3	0	0	0	0	0	0	0	0	0	0	0	.000	0	2	0	1.000
Cummings, p	2	0	0	0	0	0	0	0	0	0	0	0	.000	0	0	0	.000
Guthrie, p	3	0	0	0	0	0	0	0	0	0	0	0	.000	0	0	0	.000
Offerman, pr	1	0	0	0	0	0	0	0	0	0	0	0	.000	0	0	0	.000
Osuna, p	3	0	0	0	0	0	0	0	0	0	0	0	.000	0	0	1	.000
Tapani, p	2	0	0	0	0	0	0	0	0	0	0	0	.000	0	0	0	.000
Gwynn, ph	1	1	0	0	0	0	0	0	0	0	0	1	.000	0	0	0	.000
Martinez, p	1	1	0	0	0	0	0	0	0	0	0	0	.000	0	1	0	1.000
Hollandsworth, rf-ph	2	2	0	0	0	0	0	0	0	0	0	0	.000	0	0	0	.000
Nomo, p	1	2	0	0	0	0	0	0	0	0	0	2	.000	0	0	0	.000
Webster, ph	2	2	0	0	0	0	0	0	0	0	0	0	.000	0	0	0	.000
Valdes, p	1	3	0	0	0	0	0	0	0	0	0	0	.000	0	0	0	.000
Totals	3	111	7	31	42	2	0	3	7	5	0	17	.279	78	19	3	.970

CINCINNATI REDS' PITCHING RECORDS

Pitcher	G	GS	CG	IP	H	R	ER	HR	BB	IBB	SO	HB	WP	W	L	Pct.	ERA
Wells	1	1	0	6 1/3	6	1	0	0	1	0	8	1	0	1	0	1.000	0.00
Jackson	3	0	0	3 2/3	4	0	0	0	0	0	1	0	0	0	0	.000	0.00
Burba	1	0	0	1	2	0	0	0	1	0	0	0	0	1	0	1.000	0.00
Schourek	1	1	0	7	5	2	2	1	3	0	5	0	0	1	0	1.000	2.57
Smiley	1	1	0	6	9	2	2	1	0	0	1	0	0	0	0	.000	3.00
Brantley	3	0	0	3	5	2	2	1	0	0	2	0	0	0	0	.000	6.00
Totals	3	3	0	27	31	7	6	3	5	0	17	1	0	3	0	1.000	2.00

LOS ANGELES DODGERS' PITCHING RECORDS

Pitcher	G	GS	CG	IP	H	R	ER	HR	BB	IBB	SO	HB	WP	W	L	Pct.	ERA
Valdes	1	1	0	7	3	2	0	1	1	0	6	0	0	0	0	.000	0.00
Astacio	3	0	0	3 1/3	1	0	0	0	0	0	5	0	0	0	0	.000	0.00
Osuna	3	0	0	3 1/3	3	1	1	0	1	1	3	0	0	0	1	.000	2.70
Guthrie	3	0	0	1 1/3	2	1	1	1	1	0	1	0	0	0	0	.000	6.75
Nomo	1	1	0	5	7	5	5	2	2	1	6	0	1	0	1	.000	9.00
Martinez	1	1	0	4 1/3	10	7	7	1	2	0	3	0	0	0	1	.000	14.54

1995 REVIEW N.L. Division Series

Pitcher	G	GS	CG	IP	H	R	ER	HR	BB	IBB	SO	HB	WP	W	L	Pct.	ERA
Cummings	2	0	0	1 1/3	3	3	3	0	2	1	3	0	0	0	0	.000	20.25
Tapani	2	0	0	0 1/3	0	3	3	0	4	1	1	0	0	0	0	.000	81.00
Totals	3	3	0	26	29	22	20	5	13	4	28	0	0	0	3	.000	6.92

SCORE BY INNINGS

Cincinnati	4	0	2		3	3	4	3	1	2—22
Los Angeles	1	0	0		2	1	1	0	0	2— 7

MISCELLANEOUS STATISTICS

Sacrifice hits—Fonville, Schourek.
Sacrifice flies—Santiago.
Stolen bases—Larkin 4, Sanders 2, Boone, Duncan, Morris.
Caught stealing—None.
Double plays—Fonville, DeShields and Karros 2; Schourek, Larkin and Morris.
Left on bases—Cincinnati 8, 5, 6—19; Los Angeles 8, 11, 11—30.
Hit by pitcher—By Wells (Mondesi).
Passed balls—None.
Balks—None.
Time of games—First game, 3:15; second game, 3:21; third game, 3:27.
Attendance—First game, 44,199; second game, 46,051; third game, 53,276.
Umpires—Montague, Davidson, Gregg, Pulli, Froemming, West, Tata, Wendelstedt and Reliford.
Official scorers—Terry Bales, Glenn Sample.

ATLANTA VS. COLORADO

GAME 1

HIGHLIGHTS

ATLANTA 5, COLORADO 4

Why the Braves won: Rookie third baseman Chipper Jones, in his first postseason appearance, hit two solo home runs and made a defensive play in the eighth inning that saved the Braves. Jones' second homer, with two outs in the ninth, was the winner.

Why the Rockies lost: The hitting-crazy Rockies loaded the bases in the seventh, eighth and ninth innings—but scored only one run. A clutch hit in any of the three innings, and the Braves are losers. Instead, a double play ends the seventh, and the bases are left full in the eighth and ninth.

The turning points:

1. In the seventh inning, Rockies Manager Don Baylor made two costly moves. Because he uses his bullpen so much, Baylor brought 12 pitchers into the series and only five extra position players. With the score tied at 3 and Baylor sensing the opportunity to close out the Braves, he used two players off his bench at once. Vinny Castilla, whose two-run homer gave the Rockies their 3-1 lead, had doubled, and Greg Maddux hit the next batter, Walt Weiss. The pitcher was due to hit, so Baylor sent in Jason Bates to sacrifice. But that wasn't all Baylor did. He also sent in Trent Hubbard to run for Castilla as insurance against a force at third. Bates got the bunt down, and Braves Manager Bobby Cox countered by walking Eric Young to load the bases. With Joe Girardi due up, Baylor decided to use his ace pinch-hitter, John Vander Wal. Vander Wal, who set a major league record with 28 pinch-hits during the season, bounced into the Rockies' fourth double play. That not only was the end to the rally, but also three bench players.

2. With one out in the ninth and the Braves leading 5-4, the Rockies had the bases loaded and Andres Galarraga facing Mark Wohlers. Any kind of contact on a 100-mph Wohlers fastball should at least tie the score. But there is more on the line than Galarraga against Wohlers. On deck is Game 2 starting pitcher Lance Painter—not Vander Wal. The Rockies had run out of players. The game has come down to Galarraga, who had 31 homers and 106 RBIs during the season despite a league-leading 146 strikeouts, against Wohlers. Galarraga struck out, and so did Painter.

Notable: Maddux's performance was typical—for postseason play. He entered the game with a 1-2 record and an 8.10 ERA in two previous playoff appearances. . . . Marquis Grissom, Ryan Klesko and Jones were playing in their first postseason game. They combined to go 7-for-14 with a double, three home runs and three RBIs.

Quotable: Cox on Baylor's running out of players: "It happens. I've run out of players." . . . Baylor on using Vander Wal in the seventh inning: "I usually don't hit for Girardi, but I have the best pinch-hitter in the game in that spot. When you have the best pinch-hitter in the league, you go for it. I know Bobby Cox isn't going to take Greg Maddux out. But Maddux did what he always does—he got a ground ball." . . . Baylor on Painter's matchup with Wohlers: "That was not the ballgame. We had the bases loaded prior to that. We ran out of players. That is what beat us—not Lance Painter."

BOX SCORE

TUESDAY, OCTOBER 3, AT COLORADO

Atlanta	AB	R	H	RBI	PO	A
Grissom, cf	5	1	2	1	2	0
Lemke, 2b	5	0	1	0	3	8
Jones, 3b	5	2	2	2	0	2
McGriff, 1b	5	0	1	0	14	1
Justice, rf	2	1	1	0	1	0
Klesko, lf	4	1	3	0	0	0
McMichael, p	0	0	0	0	0	0
Pena, p	0	0	0	0	0	0
Wohlers, p	0	0	0	0	0	0
O'Brien, c	2	0	0	0	0	0
Polonia, ph	1	0	0	1	0	0
Lopez, c	1	0	1	0	4	1
Blauser, ss	2	0	0	0	2	5
Smith, ph	1	0	1	1	0	0
Belliard, ss	0	0	0	0	0	0
Maddux, p	3	0	0	0	1	4
Devereaux, ph-lf	1	0	0	0	0	0
Totals	37	5	12	5	27	21

Colorado	AB	R	H	RBI	PO	A
Young, 2b	4	0	2	0	2	2
Girardi, c	3	0	1	0	5	0
Vander Wal, ph	1	0	0	0	0	0
Munoz, p	0	0	0	0	0	0
Holmes, p	0	0	0	0	0	0
Kingery, cf	1	0	1	0	0	0
Bichette, lf	4	1	2	0	3	0
Walker, rf	3	1	1	0	0	0
Galarraga, 1b	5	1	2	0	11	1
Burks, cf	3	0	2	2	1	0

Colorado	AB	R	H	RBI	PO	A
Leskanic, p	0	0	0	0	0	0
Painter, ph	1	0	0	0	0	0
Castilla, 3b	3	1	2	2	1	5
Hubbard, pr	0	0	0	0	0	0
Owens, c	1	0	0	0	2	1
Weiss, ss	2	0	0	0	2	2
Ritz, p	2	0	0	0	0	1
Reed, p	0	0	0	0	0	1
Ruffin, p	0	0	0	0	0	0
Bates, ph-3b	1	0	0	0	0	1
Totals	34	4	13	4	27	14

Atlanta	0	0	1		0	0	2		0	1	1—5
Colorado	0	0	0		3	0	0		0	1	0—4

Atlanta	IP	H	R	ER	BB	SO
Maddux	7	9	3	3	2	0
McMichael	1/3	1	1	1	1	0
Pena (W)	2/3	1	0	0	1	1
Wohlers (S)	1	2	0	0	1	2

Colorado	IP	H	R	ER	BB	SO
Ritz	5 1/3	7	3	2	2	4
Reed	1	1	0	0	1	1
Ruffin	2/3	0	0	0	0	0
Munoz	2/3	1	1	1	0	1
Holmes	1/3	2	0	0	0	0
Leskanic (L)	1	1	1	1	0	1

E—Justice, Girardi, Burks, Castilla, Ritz. DP—Atlanta 4, Colorado 2. LOB—Atlanta 8, Colorado 11. 2B—Burks, Castilla, Grissom, Young. HR—Jones 2, Castilla, Grissom. SH—Bates. SF—Burks. SB—Polonia. HBP—By Maddux (Weiss). T—3:19. A—50,040. U—McSherry, plate; Layne, first; West, second; Tata, third; Wendelstedt, left field; Reliford, right field.

GAME 2

HIGHLIGHTS

ATLANTA 7, COLORADO 4

Why the Braves won: Experience and confidence. The Braves rallied for 25 victories in the regular season in their last at-bat and did the same in Game 1. So why panic? Down 4-3 in the top of the ninth, the Braves took care of business, scoring runs on RBI singles by Fred McGriff and pinch-hitter Mike Mordecai and getting two more on a throwing error by second baseman Eric Young.

Why the Rockies lost: The team again broke down in the ninth inning. It was more than the bullpen failing, too. The Braves scored three runs with two outs, but the devastating blow was Young's throwing error that let in two runs. If the Rockies could have escaped down only 5-4, the outcome could have been different.

The turning points:

1. Manager Bobby Cox gave Mordecai a green light on a 3-0 pitch from Darren Holmes with two outs and McGriff on second and Mike Devereaux on first. Mordecai was expecting the take sign, "but Bobby knows I can hit the fastball, and he's going to give me a chance to swing the bat in that situation." Mordecai also was expecting a different pitch: "I thought he might throw me a curve because he has a great one. But I got the green light and got a fastball, and I hit it hard."

2. After Mordecai singled, the next batter was weak-hitting Rafael Belliard—which is probably why Cox wanted Mordecai hitting away. Belliard bounced to Young, who botched a routine throw to first and allowed two runs to score. Mark Wohlers came into the game protecting a three-run lead rather than a one-run lead.

Notable: Marquis Grissom, who hit 12 home runs in 551 regular-season at-bats, hits two solo homers, giving him three in two games. It is the first two-homer game of his career. . . . Of the Braves' 25 last at-bat regular-season victories, two were won by Mordecai. One came against Holmes. . . . Lance Painter's start was only his second of the season for the Rockies. . . . Tom Glavine wasn't around to get the victory, making this his first postseason game in which he didn't figure in the decision. His postseason record is 3-6. . . . Alejandro Pena, who first appeared in postseason play in 1981 as a rookie with the Dodgers, picked up the victory. He also won Game 1. . . . The Rockies, 0-for-2 in save situations in the playoffs, blew 15 during the regular season.

Quotable: Grissom on the Braves' cardiac nature: "We've got a lot of experience to help come back in late innings. We never give up. We clutch up. Everyone wants to be a hero." . . . Cox on Mordecai, a utility player not known much outside of Atlanta: "All of our players know who 'Mordy' is. He works hard, he knows who he's going to face. He clutched it in." . . . Baylor: "We let another one get away. The disheartening thing is we should be 2-0 going to Atlanta."

BOX SCORE

WEDNESDAY, OCTOBER 4, AT COLORADO

Atlanta	AB	R	H	RBI	PO	A
Grissom, cf	6	2	2	2	3	0
Lemke, 2b	4	1	1	0	1	3
Jones, 3b	5	1	3	0	0	1
McGriff, 1b	4	1	1	1	11	1
Justice, rf	4	0	1	0	0	0
Lopez, c	4	0	1	1	6	1
Klesko, lf	3	0	0	0	2	0
Devereaux, ph-lf	2	1	1	0	1	0
Blauser, ss	2	0	0	0	2	5
Polonia, ph	1	0	0	0	0	0
Avery, p	0	0	0	0	0	0
Pena, p	0	0	0	0	0	0
Mordecai, ph	1	1	1	1	0	0
Wohlers, p	0	0	0	0	0	0
Glavine, p	3	0	1	0	1	1
Smith, ph	1	0	1	0	0	0
Belliard, ss	1	0	0	0	0	0
Totals	41	7	13	5	27	12

Colorado	AB	R	H	RBI	PO	A
Young, 2b	5	0	1	0	2	1
Burks, cf	3	1	0	0	3	0
Kingery, cf	2	0	0	0	1	0
Bichette, lf	4	2	3	0	2	0
Walker, rf	4	1	1	3	0	0
Galarraga, 1b	4	0	1	1	8	0
Castilla, 3b	3	0	0	0	0	6
Girardi, c	4	0	0	0	10	1
Weiss, ss	3	0	1	0	1	2

Colorado	AB	R	H	RBI	PO	A
Painter, p	1	0	0	0	0	0
Hubbard, ph	1	0	0	0	0	0
Reed, p	0	0	0	0	0	0
Ruffin, p	0	0	0	0	0	0
Bates, ph	1	0	1	0	0	0
Leskanic, p	0	0	0	0	0	0
Munoz, p	0	0	0	0	0	0
Holmes, p	0	0	0	0	0	0
Vander Wal, ph	1	0	0	0	0	0
Totals	36	4	8	4	27	10

Atlanta	1	0	1		1	0	0		0	0	4—7
Colorado	0	0	0		0	0	3		0	1	0—4

Atlanta	IP	H	R	ER	BB	SO
Glavine	7	5	3	2	1	3
Avery	2/3	1	1	1	0	1
Pena (W)	1/3	1	0	0	0	0
Wohlers (S)	1	1	0	0	0	2

Colorado	IP	H	R	ER	BB	SO
Painter	5	5	3	3	2	4
Reed	1 1/3	1	0	0	0	1
Ruffin	2/3	2	0	0	1	1
Leskanic	*1	2	1	1	0	2
Munoz (L)	1/3	1	1	1	0	0
Holmes	2/3	2	2	0	0	2

*Pitched to one batter in ninth.

E—Blauser, Young 2. LOB—Atlanta 12, Colorado 7. 2B—Jones, Galarraga, Smith, Bichette 2. HR—Walker, Grissom 2. SF—Lopez. HBP—By Pena (Castilla), by Reed (Blauser). T—3:08. A—50,063. U—Layne, plate; West, first; Tata, second; Wendelstedt, third; Reliford, left field; McSherry, right field.

GAME 3

HIGHLIGHTS

COLORADO 7, ATLANTA 5

Why the Rockies won: Despite allowing the Braves to rally in the ninth inning for the third game in a row, the Rockies didn't fold, coming back to score two in the 10th off Mark Wohlers. "When they tied it in the ninth, we never got down, not for a second," said Vinny Castilla, who homered and had three RBIs, including one in the 10th. "No one said, 'Here we go again.' Everyone said, 'We're going to win this game.'" With two outs in the 10th, Dante Bichette doubled and Larry Walker was walked intentionally. Andres Galarraga, who had struck out three times in a row, singled home Bichette, and Castilla followed with another run-scoring single.

Why the Braves lost: How many times can you ask a team to rally in the ninth or 10th? With everyone thinking sweep, starter John Smoltz failed to deliver. He didn't make it out of the sixth inning, giving up two homers and five runs. Through three games, the Braves' vaunted starters gave up 10 runs in 19⅔ innings (4.57 ERA). "It's just a shame," Smoltz said. "I was really trying to do my part to make sure that Greg (Maddux) doesn't pitch again until the Cincinnati series."

The turning points:

1. Smoltz wasn't consistent, and he hung two pitches that the Rockies jumped on for home runs. "It was a game where I dominated the first three innings, a game I should have gone the distance, but I made two mistakes," Smoltz said. Eric Young's two-run homer on a 1-2 pitch gave the Rockies a 3-0 lead in the third. Castilla's two-run homer with two outs in the fifth chased Smoltz.

2. The Braves couldn't make it three wins in a row with a rally in the ninth inning. With one out, Ryan Klesko singled. Darren Holmes came in for Bruce Ruffin and gave up a single to Javier Lopez. Mike Mordecai, who had the go-ahead ninth-inning single in Game 2, couldn't get Klesko home, flying to shallow left. Pinch-hitter Luis Polonia followed with a single to tie the score, but Marquis Grissom grounded out to end the inning.

Notable: Mark Thompson's save was his first in the major leagues. Thompson was 2-3 with a 6.53 ERA in the regular season. . . . Smoltz came into the game with a 5-1 record and 1.94 ERA in 10 postseason games. . . . The victory was only the Rockies' seventh in 39 games against the Braves. . . . Bichette was 0-for-14 lifetime against Smoltz when Bichette singled in the third, and Young's homer in the third was only his second hit off Smoltz in 13 at-bats.

Quotable: Wohlers on his performance: "I stunk. That's the way it goes. I had gotten them a couple of times; tonight they got me." . . . Bichette to the Braves' fans: "The only thing we really accomplished was to tell the people who brought those brooms they can take them home and maybe they can sweep off their porches."

BOX SCORE

FRIDAY, OCTOBER 6, AT ATLANTA

Colorado	AB	R	H	RBI	PO	A
Young, 2b	3	2	1	2	1	4
Reed, p	0	0	0	0	0	0
Munoz, p	0	0	0	0	0	0
Leskanic, p	0	0	0	0	0	0
Ruffin, p	0	0	0	0	0	0
Holmes, p	0	0	0	0	0	0
Vander Wal, ph	1	0	0	0	0	0
Thompson, p	0	0	0	0	1	0
Kingery, cf	4	0	0	0	1	0
Bichette, lf	5	2	3	0	2	0
Walker, rf	3	1	1	0	1	0
Galarraga, 1b	5	0	1	1	14	1
Castilla, 3b	5	1	2	3	1	2
Girardi, c	5	0	0	0	6	2
Weiss, ss	3	1	1	0	2	6
Swift, p	3	0	0	0	0	0
Bates, 2b	1	0	0	0	1	2
Totals	38	7	9	6	30	17

Atlanta	AB	R	H	RBI	PO	A
Grissom, cf	5	0	2	0	2	0
Lemke, 2b	5	0	0	0	1	2
Jones, 3b	5	0	1	0	3	0
McGriff, 1b	4	1	1	0	6	0
Justice, rf	3	1	0	0	3	0
Klesko, lf	4	3	3	1	0	0
Lopez, c	4	0	2	2	12	1
Blauser, ss	2	0	0	0	1	1
Belliard, ss	0	0	0	0	0	0
Smith, ph	0	0	0	0	0	0
Mordecai, ph-ss	2	0	1	1	1	0
Smoltz, p	2	0	0	0	1	1
Clontz, p	0	0	0	0	0	1
Devereaux, ph	1	0	0	0	0	0
Borbon, p	0	0	0	0	0	0
McMichael, p	0	0	0	0	0	0
Polonia, ph	1	0	1	1	0	0
Wohlers, p	0	0	0	0	0	0
Mercker, p	0	0	0	0	0	0
Totals	38	5	11	5	30	6

Colorado	1 0 2	0 0 2	0 0 0	2—7
Atlanta	0 0 0	3 0 0	1 0 1	0—5

Colorado	IP	H	R	ER	BB	SO
Swift	*6	7	4	4	2	3
Reed	1/3	0	0	0	0	1
Munoz	†0	1	0	0	0	0
Leskanic	1	0	0	0	0	1
Ruffin	1	1	1	1	0	1
Holmes (W)	2/3	2	0	0	0	0
Thompson (S)	1	0	0	0	0	0

Atlanta	IP	H	R	ER	BB	SO
Smoltz	5 2/3	5	5	5	1	6
Clontz	1 1/3	0	0	0	0	2
Borbon	1	1	0	0	0	3
McMichael	1	0	0	0	1	1
Wohlers (L)	2/3	3	2	2	1	0
Mercker	1/3	0	0	0	0	0

*Pitched to one batter in seventh. †Pitched to one batter in seventh.

DP—Colorado 3. LOB—Colorado 6, Atlanta 5. 2B—Bichette, Mordecai, Klesko. HR—Castilla, Young. SH—Kingery. SB—Walker, Weiss, Grissom. CS—Grissom, Lopez. HBP—By Smoltz (Walker). WP—Smoltz. T—3:16. A—51,300. U—Gregg, plate; Pulli, first; Froemming, second; Darling, third; Montague, left field; Davidson, right field.

GAME 4

HIGHLIGHTS

ATLANTA 10, COLORADO 4

Why the Braves won: Fred McGriff emerged from a 3-for-14 slump, hitting two homers and driving in five runs. Marquis Grissom went 5-for-5 and finished the series with a .524 average. For a change, the Braves struck early. McGriff's two-run homer highlighted a four-run third inning that erased a 3-0 deficit. The Braves then added six runs over the next three innings to put the game out of reach.

Why the Rockies lost: The pitching just wasn't there. Bret Saberhagen was shelled in his only appearance in the series. Saberhagen, bothered by a sore right shoulder, gave up six runs and seven hits in four innings. Dante Bichette staked Saberhagen to a 3-0 lead with his three-run homer off Greg Maddux in the third inning, but Saberhagen gave up four in the bottom of the inning and the rout was on. Kevin Ritz, the starter in Game 1, came on in relief but gave up four runs in 1²/₃ innings.

The turning points:

1. Bouncing back from the 3-0 deficit immediately was the difference. When the Braves hit, they win. It's that simple. For all the talk about their pitching, it is their hitting that determines their fate. In the regular season, the Braves hit .250. Only St. Louis and Detroit at .247 were worse. In Game 4, McGriff came up big—and did so early. When McGriff is hot, it seems to affect the rest of the team.

2. Did we say the Rockies' pitching was a problem? For the second time in the series, the Rockies pounced on Maddux, this time getting 10 hits and four runs, including two home runs. Bichette's three-run homer should have been a momentum-builder. Instead, the lead was gone minutes later. Roughing up Maddux twice and not winning either game were lost opportunities the Rockies could not overcome. For the series, the Rockies' bullpen allowed 25 hits in 15²/₃ innings, blew three saves and posted a 5.17 ERA. The staff's overall ERA was 5.75, and the Braves hit .331 in the series.

Notable: The victory enabled the Braves to become the first team to play in four consecutive N.L. Championship Series. Oakland (1971-75) holds the major league record for consecutive championship series appearances. . . . In six postseason starts, Maddux is 2-2 with a 6.62 ERA, quite a contrast from his 55-18 regular-season record in three seasons with the Braves.

Quotable: McGriff on his big game: "I hadn't helped much. I wanted to contribute." . . . Saberhagen: "If I am out there healthy, I think we probably win that game. To have me come in and let them down is tough to swallow." . . . Bichette: "If a couple of breaks go our way, then it turns around. I guess history is filled with a couple of breaks the other way."

BOX SCORE
SATURDAY, OCTOBER 7, AT ATLANTA

Colorado	AB	R	H	RBI	PO	A
Young, 2b	4	1	3	0	3	6
Kingery, cf	3	1	1	0	3	0
Bichette, lf	4	1	2	3	2	0
Walker, rf	4	0	0	0	2	0
Galarraga, 1b	4	0	1	0	8	0
Castilla, 3b	4	1	3	1	1	0
Girardi, c	4	0	1	0	4	0
Weiss, ss	4	0	0	0	1	2
Saberhagen, p	1	0	0	0	0	1
Hubbard, ph	1	0	0	0	0	0
Ritz, p	0	0	0	0	0	0
Munoz, p	0	0	0	0	0	0
Bates, ph	1	0	0	0	0	0
Reynoso, p	0	0	0	0	0	0
Ruffin, p	0	0	0	0	0	0
Vander Wal, ph	1	0	0	0	0	0
Totals	35	4	11	4	24	9

Atlanta	AB	R	H	RBI	PO	A
Grissom, cf	5	2	5	1	2	0
Lemke, 2b	5	2	2	1	3	3
Jones, 3b	3	1	1	2	0	1
McGriff, 1b	5	2	3	5	8	0
Justice, rf	4	0	1	0	2	0
Klesko, lf	4	1	1	0	1	0
Devereaux, lf	1	0	0	0	1	0
O'Brien, c	3	0	1	0	8	1
Belliard, ss	4	1	0	0	2	5
Maddux, p	3	1	1	0	0	1
Smith, ph	1	0	0	0	0	0
Pena, p	0	0	0	0	0	0
Totals	38	10	15	9	27	11

Colorado	0	0 3	0 0 1	0 0 0	—	4
Atlanta	0	0 4	2 1 3	0 0 x	—	10

Colorado	IP	H	R	ER	BB	SO
Saberhagen (L)	4	7	6	5	1	3
Ritz	1 2/3	5	4	4	1	1
Munoz	1/3	1	0	0	1	0
Reynoso	1	2	0	0	0	0
Ruffin	1	0	0	0	1	0

Atlanta	IP	H	R	ER	BB	SO
Maddux (W)	7	10	4	4	0	7
Pena	2	1	0	0	0	1

E—Young. DP—Colorado 1, Atlanta 1. LOB—Colorado 5, Atlanta 8. 2B—Lemke, Grissom, Jones. HR—Castilla, McGriff 2, Bichette. SH—Kingery. SB—Grissom, Young. T—2:38. A—50,027. U—Pulli, plate; Froemming, first; Darling, second; Montague, third; Davidson, left field; Gregg, right field.

STATISTICS

ATLANTA BRAVES' BATTING AND FIELDING AVERAGES

Player, position	G	AB	R	H	TB	2B	3B	HR	RBI	BB	IBB	SO	Avg.	PO	A	E	Avg.
Mordecai, ph-ss	1	3	1	2	3	1	0	0	2	0	0	0	.667	1	0	0	1.000
Smith, ph	3	3	0	2	3	1	0	0	1	0	0	0	.667	0	0	0	.000
Grissom, cf	4	21	5	11	22	2	0	3	4	0	0	3	.524	9	0	0	1.000
Klesko, lf	4	15	5	7	8	1	0	0	1	0	0	3	.467	3	0	0	1.000
Lopez, c	3	9	0	4	4	0	0	0	3	0	0	3	.444	22	3	0	1.000
Jones, 3b	4	18	4	7	15	2	0	2	4	2	1	2	.389	3	4	0	1.000
McGriff, 1b	4	18	4	6	12	0	0	2	6	2	0	3	.333	39	2	0	1.000
Glavine, p	1	3	0	1	1	0	0	0	0	0	0	1	.333	1	1	0	1.000
Polonia, ph	3	3	0	1	1	0	0	0	2	0	0	1	.333	0	0	0	.000
Justice, rf	4	13	2	3	3	0	0	0	5	0	0	2	.231	6	0	1	.857
Lemke, 2b	4	19	3	4	5	1	0	0	1	1	0	3	.211	8	16	0	1.000
Devereaux, lf-ph	3	5	1	1	1	0	0	0	0	0	0	0	.200	2	0	0	1.000
O'Brien, c	2	5	0	1	1	0	0	0	0	1	0	1	.200	8	1	0	1.000
Maddux, p	2	6	1	1	1	0	0	0	0	0	0	1	.167	1	4	0	1.000
Avery, p	1	0	0	0	0	0	0	0	0	0	0	0	.000	0	0	0	.000
Borbon, p	1	0	0	0	0	0	0	0	0	0	0	0	.000	0	0	0	.000
Clontz, p	1	0	0	0	0	0	0	0	0	0	0	0	.000	0	1	0	1.000
McMichael, p	2	0	0	0	0	0	0	0	0	0	0	0	.000	0	0	0	.000
Mercker, p	1	0	0	0	0	0	0	0	0	0	0	0	.000	0	0	0	.000
Pena, p	3	0	0	0	0	0	0	0	0	0	0	0	.000	0	0	0	.000
Wohlers, p	3	0	0	0	0	0	0	0	0	0	0	0	.000	0	0	0	.000
Smoltz, p	1	2	0	0	0	0	0	0	0	0	0	0	.000	1	1	0	1.000
Belliard, ss	4	5	1	0	0	0	0	0	0	0	0	1	.000	2	5	0	1.000
Blauser, ss	3	6	0	0	0	0	0	0	0	1	1	3	.000	5	11	1	.941
Totals	4	154	27	51	80	8	0	7	24	12	2	27	.331	111	49	2	.988

COLORADO ROCKIES' BATTING AND FIELDING AVERAGES

Player, position	G	AB	R	H	TB	2B	3B	HR	RBI	BB	IBB	SO	Avg.	PO	A	E	Avg.
Bichette, lf	4	17	6	10	16	3	0	1	3	1	0	3	.588	9	0	0	1.000
Castilla, 3b	4	15	3	7	17	1	0	3	6	0	0	1	.467	3	13	1	.941
Young, 2b	4	16	3	7	11	1	0	1	2	2	1	2	.438	8	13	3	.875
Burks, cf	2	6	1	2	3	1	0	0	2	0	0	1	.333	4	0	1	.800
Galarraga, 1b	4	18	1	5	6	1	0	0	2	0	0	6	.278	41	2	0	1.000
Bates, 3b-ph-2b	2	4	0	1	1	0	0	0	0	0	0	0	.250	1	3	0	1.000
Walker, rf	4	14	3	3	6	0	0	1	3	3	1	4	.214	3	0	0	1.000
Kingery, cf	4	10	1	2	2	0	0	0	0	0	0	1	.200	5	0	0	1.000
Weiss, ss	4	12	1	2	2	0	0	0	0	3	1	3	.167	6	12	0	1.000
Girardi, c	4	16	0	2	2	0	0	0	0	0	0	2	.125	25	3	1	.966
Holmes, p	3	0	0	0	0	0	0	0	0	0	0	0	.000	0	0	0	.000
Leskanic, p	3	0	0	0	0	0	0	0	0	0	0	0	.000	0	0	0	.000

Player, position	G	AB	R	H	TB	2B	3B	HR	RBI	BB	IBB	SO	Avg.	PO	A	E	Avg.
								BATTING								FIELDING	
Munoz, p	4	0	0	0	0	0	0	0	0	0	0	0	.000	0	0	0	.000
Reed, p	3	0	0	0	0	0	0	0	0	0	0	0	.000	0	1	0	1.000
Reynoso, p	1	0	0	0	0	0	0	0	0	0	0	0	.000	0	0	0	.000
Ruffin, p	4	0	0	0	0	0	0	0	0	0	0	0	.000	0	0	0	.000
Thompson, p	1	0	0	0	0	0	0	0	0	0	0	0	.000	1	0	0	1.000
Owens, c	1	1	0	0	0	0	0	0	0	0	0	1	.000	2	1	0	1.000
Saberhagen, p	1	1	0	0	0	0	0	0	0	0	0	0	.000	0	1	0	1.000
Hubbard, pr-ph	2	2	0	0	0	0	0	0	0	0	0	0	.000	0	0	0	.000
Painter, ph-p	1	2	0	0	0	0	0	0	0	0	0	1	.000	0	0	0	.000
Ritz, p	2	2	0	0	0	0	0	0	0	0	0	0	.000	0	1	1	.500
Swift, p	1	3	0	0	0	0	0	0	0	0	0	2	.000	0	0	0	.000
Vander Wal, ph	4	4	0	0	0	0	0	0	0	0	0	2	.000	0	0	0	.000
Totals	4	143	19	41	66	7	0	6	18	9	3	29	.287	108	50	7	.958

ATLANTA BRAVES' PITCHING RECORDS

Pitcher	G	GS	CG	IP	H	R	ER	HR	BB	IBB	SO	HB	WP	W	L	Pct.	ERA
Pena	3	0	0	3	3	0	0	0	1	1	2	1	0	2	0	1.000	0.00
Clontz	1	0	0	1⅓	0	0	0	0	0	0	2	0	0	0	0	.000	0.00
Borbon	1	0	0	1	1	0	0	0	0	0	3	0	0	0	0	.000	0.00
Mercker	1	0	0	0⅓	0	0	0	0	0	0	0	0	0	0	0	.000	0.00
Glavine	1	1	0	7	5	3	2	1	1	0	3	0	0	0	0		2.57
Maddux	2	2	0	14	19	7	7	3	2	1	7	1	0	1	0	1.000	4.50
Wohlers	3	0	0	2⅔	6	2	2	0	2	1	4	0	0	0	1	.000	6.75
McMichael	2	0	0	1⅓	1	1	1	0	2	0	1	0	0	0	0	.000	6.75
Smoltz	1	1	0	5⅔	5	5	5	2	1	0	6	1	1	0	0	.000	7.94
Avery	1	0	0	0⅔	1	1	1	0	0	0	1	0	0	0	0	.000	13.50
Totals	4	4	0	37	41	19	18	6	9	3	29	3	0	3	1	.750	4.38

COLORADO ROCKIES' PITCHING RECORDS

Pitcher	G	GS	CG	IP	H	R	ER	HR	BB	IBB	SO	HB	WP	W	L	Pct.	ERA
Reed	3	0	0	2⅔	2	0	0	0	1	1	3	1	0	0	0	.000	0.00
Holmes	3	0	0	1⅔	6	2	0	0	0	0	2	0	0	1	0	1.000	0.00
Reynoso	1	0	0	1	2	0	0	0	0	0	0	0	0	0	0	.000	0.00
Thompson	1	0	0	1	0	0	0	0	0	0	0	0	0	0	0	.000	0.00
Ruffin	4	0	0	3⅓	3	1	1	0	2	0	2	0	0	0	0	.000	2.70
Painter	1	1	0	5	5	3	3	2	2	0	4	0	0	0	0	.000	5.40
Swift	1	1	0	6	7	4	4	0	2	0	3	0	0	0	0	.000	6.00
Leskanic	3	0	0	3	3	2	2	1	0	0	4	0	0	0	1	.000	6.00
Ritz	2	1	0	7	12	7	6	3	3	1	5	0	0	0	0	.000	7.71
Saberhagen	1	1	0	4	7	6	5	1	1	0	3	0	0	0	1	.000	11.25
Munoz	4	0	0	1⅓	4	2	2	0	1	0	1	0	0	0	1	.000	13.50
Totals	4	4	0	36	51	27	23	7	12	2	27	1	0	1	3	.250	5.75

SCORE BY INNINGS

Atlanta	1	0	6	6	1	5	1	1	6	0—27
Colorado	0	0	5	3	0	6	0	2	0	2—19

MISCELLANEOUS STATISTICS

Sacrifice hits—Kingery 2, Bates.
Sacrifice flies—Burks, Lopez.
Stolen bases—Grissom 2, Polonia, Walker, Weiss, Young.
Caught stealing—Grissom, Lopez.
Double plays—Lemke, Blauser and McGriff 2; Belliard and McGriff; Blauser, Lemke and McGriff; Castilla, Young and Galarraga; Galarraga and Weiss; Maddux, Lopez and McGriff; Weiss and Galarraga; Young, Weiss and Galarraga.
Left on bases—Atlanta 8, 12, 5, 8—33; Colorado 11, 7, 6, 5—29.
Hit by pitcher—By Pena (Castilla), by Maddux (Weiss), by Smoltz (Walker), by Reed (Blauser).
Passed balls—None.
Balks—None.
Time of games—First game, 3:19; second game, 3:08; third game, 3:16; fourth game, 2:38.
Attendance—First game, 50,040; second game, 50,063; third game, 51,300; fourth game, 50,027.
Umpires—McSherry, Layne, West, Tata, Wendelstedt, Gregg, Pulli, Froemming, Darling and Montague.
Official scorers—Mark Frederickson, Frank Haraway.

A.L. CHAMPIONSHIP SERIES

GAME 1

HIGHLIGHTS

SEATTLE 3, CLEVELAND 2

Why the Mariners won: Rookie Bob Wolcott, making just his eighth major league appearance, went a career-high seven innings, allowing eight hits and five walks but just two earned runs. Wolcott had found out the day before the game that he had been added to the Mariners' roster. He spent most of the season in the minors, making six starts for the Mariners in August and September. Wolcott stranded three runners in the first, two more in the second and and got a bases-loaded double play to end the third.

Why the Indians lost: The Indians stranded 12 runners, one shy of the ALCS record set by Baltimore in 1971 and the Chicago White Sox in 1993. The Indians had three days' rest after finishing their sweep of the Red Sox, which may have been too much time off, said second baseman Carlos Baerga: "Maybe that's one of the things, that we didn't play for three days."

The turning points:

1. The Indians loaded the bases with no outs in the first as Wolcott threw balls on 12 of his first 13 pitches to Kenny Lofton, Omar Vizquel and Carlos Baerga. But Wolcott then struck out Albert Belle, retired Eddie Murray on a foul pop and got Jim Thome on a sharp grounder to second baseman Joey Cora.

2. After Belle tied it at 2 in the top of the seventh with a 441-foot solo homer, the Mariners retook the lead in the bottom of the seventh. Jay Buhner doubled, Mike Blowers reached on a throwing error by Thome at third and Luis Sojo's double scored Buhner and knocked Indians starter Dennis Martinez out of the game.

Notable: Wolcott began the season at Class AA Port City (Southern League). . . . Cleveland hit .294 with runners in scoring position during the regular season but went 2-for-11 in Game 1. . . . In five plate appearances, Lofton had two singles, a triple and two walks. But he failed to score. . . . Wolcott's performance was reminiscent of Game 1 of the 1980 World Series between Philadelphia and Kansas City. Because the Phillies' regular starting pitchers were tired after the NLCS against Houston, rookie Bob Walk got the start. The Phillies won, 7-6, as Walk went seven innings. The Phils won the Series, 4-2.

Quotable: "We let Wolcott get out of the first inning. That kind of set the tone," Indians Manager Mike Hargrove said. "We sure knew we missed a golden opportunity." . . . Wolcott on his performance: "I have to admit, I had my doubts in the first inning. But it all worked out." . . . "We were shocked that we didn't score in the first inning," Indians catcher Sandy Alomar Jr. said. "Unfortunately, we went after a lot of bad pitches." . . . Sojo on Wolcott: "Bob was unbelievable. When he got out of the first inning, everybody on our bench thought we had a chance to win the game."

BOX SCORE

TUESDAY, OCTOBER 10, AT SEATTLE

Cleveland	AB	R	H	RBI	PO	A
Lofton, cf	3	0	3	0	1	0
Vizquel, ss	4	0	0	0	1	7
Baerga, 2b	4	1	1	0	3	3
Belle, lf	4	1	1	1	1	0
Murray, dh	5	0	0	0	0	0
Thome, 3b	4	0	2	1	1	0
Ramirez, rf	4	0	1	0	0	0
Sorrento, 1b	4	0	1	0	10	0
Alomar, c	4	0	1	0	5	1
Amaro, pr	0	0	0	0	0	0
Pena, c	0	0	0	0	1	0
D. Martinez, p	0	0	0	0	1	0
Tavarez, p	0	0	0	0	0	1
Assenmacher, p	0	0	0	0	0	0
Plunk, p	0	0	0	0	0	0
Totals	36	2	10	2	24	12

Seattle	AB	R	H	RBI	PO	A
Coleman, lf	4	0	0	0	4	0
Cora, 2b	4	0	2	0	2	3
Griffey, cf	3	0	2	0	1	0
E. Martinez, dh	3	0	0	0	0	0
T. Martinez, 1b	3	0	0	0	6	1
Buhner, rf	3	2	1	0	3	0
Blowers, 3b	4	1	1	2	3	0
Sojo, ss	3	0	1	1	1	2
Wilson, c	3	0	0	0	6	0
Wolcott, p	0	0	0	0	1	1
Nelson, p	0	0	0	0	0	0
Charlton, p	0	0	0	0	0	0
Totals	30	3	7	3	27	7

Cleveland	0	0	1		0	0	0		1	0	0—2
Seattle	0	2	0		0	0	0		1	0	x—3

Cleveland	IP	H	R	ER	BB	SO
Martinez (L)	6⅓	6	3	3	2	4
Tavarez	1	1	0	0	1	1
Assenmacher	*0	0	0	0	1	0
Plunk	⅔	0	0	0	0	1

Seattle	IP	H	R	ER	BB	SO
Wolcott (W)	7	8	2	2	5	2
Nelson	⅔	1	0	0	0	1
Charlton (S)	1⅓	1	0	0	0	2

*Pitched to one batter in eighth.

E—Thome. DP—Cleveland 1, Seattle 1. LOB—Cleveland 12, Seattle 7. 2B—Griffey, Sojo, Buhner, Cora, Sorrento. 3B—Lofton. HR—Belle, Blowers. CS—Griffey. T—3:07. A—57,065. U—Phillips, plate; Cousins, first; Reed, second; Ford, third; McClelland, left field; Coble, right field.

HIGHLIGHTS

CLEVELAND 5, SEATTLE 2

Why the Indians won: Orel Hershiser continued his postseason mastery, allowing four hits and one earned run in eight innings; he struck out seven and his lone walk was intentional. While Hershiser was doing his part, the Indians' hitters also came through. Manny Ramirez homered twice and went 4-for-4, and Carlos Baerga broke a scoreless tie in the fifth with a two-out, two-run single with the bases loaded.

Why the Mariners lost: The Mariners couldn't get anything going off Hershiser. Seattle's No. 3-6 hitters—Ken Griffey, Edgar Martinez, Tino Martinez and Jay Buhner—went a combined 3-for-15. Mariners starter Tim Belcher tired noticeably in the sixth. He lasted 5²/₃ innings but threw 101 pitches; Hershiser threw 108 in eight innings.

The turning points:

1. With one on and no outs in the fifth, the Indians' Paul Sorrento grounded to Mariners first baseman Tino Martinez. Martinez's throw to shortstop Luis Sojo got the lead runner but was a little low and Sojo lost the handle trying to throw back to first to complete the double play. After a flyout, the Indians got a single and a walk to load the bases for Baerga, who got the type of clutch hit Cleveland couldn't come up with in Game 1.

2. The Indians added two runs in the sixth to put the game away. Ramirez homered and Sorrento followed with a single. Sandy Alomar then tripled Sorrento home.

Notable: Hershiser improved to 6-0 with a 1.47 ERA in 10 playoff and World Series games. . . . Seattle's Ken Griffey became the first A.L. player to homer six times in the postseason. Lenny Dykstra did it for Philadelphia in 1993 and Bob Robertson did it for Pittsburgh in 1971. . . . The crowd of 58,144 was the largest in Mariners history. . . . It was just the Mariners' fourth loss in their past 24 games at home.

Quotable: "The whole key in playoff baseball is to stay with your patterns, stay with your pitches," Hershiser said. "Don't let the crowd take your adrenaline away from you." . . . "The prospect of going down 0-2 and facing (Game 3 starter) Randy Johnson is not one that causes your appetite to stay with you very long," Indians Manager Mike Hargrove said. "As far as we were concerned, we had to win this game. I can't emphasize that enough. If this was a test of our character, we passed." . . . Hargrove on Hershiser: "Of all the people I've been around in baseball, and I've been around this game 20-25 years, he may be able to focus and concentrate more consistently than anyone I've been around." . . . Mariners Manager Lou Piniella: "Hershiser has been in a lot of these games. He's got the confidence to pitch well, and he did." . . . Mariners third baseman Mike Blowers was impressed with Hershiser: "It is one thing to throw strikes. It's another thing to be hitting his spots. He was hitting his spots."

BOX SCORE

WEDNESDAY, OCTOBER 11, AT SEATTLE

Cleveland	AB	R	H	RBI	PO	A
Lofton, cf	4	1	1	0	3	0
Vizquel, ss	3	0	0	0	0	4
Baerga, 2b	5	0	2	2	1	5
Belle, lf	3	0	1	0	0	0
Murray, dh	5	0	2	0	0	0
Thome, 3b	4	0	0	0	0	2
Espinoza, 3b	1	0	0	0	0	0
Ramirez, rf	4	2	4	2	3	0
Kirby, rf	0	0	0	0	0	0
Sorrento, 1b	4	2	1	0	14	0
Alomar, c	4	0	1	1	6	0
Hershiser, p	0	0	0	0	0	1
Mesa, p	0	0	0	0	0	1
Totals	37	5	12	5	27	13

Seattle	AB	R	H	RBI	PO	A
Coleman, lf	4	0	1	0	4	0
Cora, 2b	3	0	0	0	1	1
Griffey, cf	4	1	2	1	3	0
E. Martinez, dh	3	0	0	0	0	0
T. Martinez, 1b	4	0	0	0	6	3
Buhner, rf	4	1	1	1	3	0
Blowers, 3b	4	0	1	0	1	0
Sojo, ss	3	0	0	0	4	3
Diaz, ph	1	0	1	0	0	0
Wilson, c	3	0	0	0	4	0
Strange, ph	1	0	0	0	0	0
Belcher, p	0	0	0	0	1	0
Ayala, p	0	0	0	0	0	1
Risley, p	0	0	0	0	0	0
Totals	34	2	6	2	27	8

Cleveland	0	0	0	0	2	2	0	1	0—5
Seattle	0	0	0	0	0	1	0	0	1—2

Cleveland	IP	H	R	ER	BB	SO
Hershiser (W)	8	4	1	1	1	7
Mesa	1	2	1	1	0	0

Seattle	IP	H	R	ER	BB	SO
Belcher (L)	5²/₃	9	4	4	2	1
Ayala	2²/₃	2	1	1	3	2
Risley	²/₃	1	0	0	0	0

E—Sojo. DP—Seattle 2. LOB—Cleveland 10, Seattle 7. 3B—Alomar. HR—Buhner, Griffey, Ramirez 2. SB—Vizquel, Coleman. HBP—By Hershiser (Cora). WP—Hershiser. T—3:14. A—58,144. U—Cousins, plate; Reed, first; Ford, second; McClelland, third; Coble, left field; Phillips, right field.

HIGHLIGHTS

SEATTLE 5, CLEVELAND 2

Why the Mariners won: Jay Buhner homered in the top of the 11th inning to give Seattle the victory. Buhner had committed an error that allowed Cleveland to tie it at 2 in the eighth. Randy Johnson made his first start of the series for the Mariners and was superb. Johnson gave up two runs and four hits in eight innings, walking two and striking out six. Norm Charlton followed with three hitless innings of relief and gained the victory. The Indians put runners at first and second against Charlton in the ninth, but he got out of it with a strikeout and a ground-out and wasn't threatened again.

Why the Indians lost: The Indians couldn't touch Johnson or Charlton. Their defense also wasn't sterling. In the third, the Mariners' Ken Griffey singled with two outs, stole second, continued to third when Sandy Alomar's throw skipped into center, and scored when Alvaro Espinoza botched Edgar Martinez's grounder to third.

The turning points:

1. Buhner opened the door for Cleveland in the eighth by turning Espinoza's one-out fly ball into a two-base error. Buhner backpedaled to the warning track, then simply missed the ball, letting Espinoza scamper to second. Kenny Lofton then drove in pinch-runner Wayne Kirby with a single to left.

2. In the 11th, Julian Tavarez allowed a leadoff single to Joey Cora. Cora stole second with two outs. Eric Plunk walked Tino Martinez intentionally, and Buhner homered to right-center.

Notable: It was Cleveland's first loss in 15 extra-inning games this season. . . . Buhner also homered in the second. He became the ninth player this season to hit two homers in a postseason game. Before this year, only 15 players had multiple-homer games in playoff history. . . . Lofton had two hits off Johnson, just the 12th and 13th by lefthanders off Johnson this season.

Quotable: "Isn't this game funny? You can go from goat to hero so quick," Buhner said. "To do it in one game is really lucky. I came out smelling like a rose tonight." . . . "I was very aware that I was pitching against Randy," Indians starter Charles Nagy said. "To beat him, you almost have to throw a shutout. They have us backed into a corner." . . . Buhner on the error: "I got a good jump on the ball, but I went into my backpedal too soon. That was just a stupid, stupid mistake. The last major screw-up like that was in high school, when I let one hit me between the eyes. It knocked me out, so I didn't have to feel stupid walking off the field." . . . Mariners Manager Lou Piniella on Buhner's heroics in the 11th: "That's the way it should be. He gets up again and comes through. It doesn't always work out that way, you know?"

BOX SCORE

FRIDAY, OCTOBER 13, AT CLEVELAND

Seattle	AB	R	H	RBI	PO	A
Coleman, lf	5	0	0	0	0	0
Widger, c	0	0	0	0	1	0
Cora, 2b	4	1	1	0	4	1
Fermin, 2b	0	0	0	0	0	0
Griffey, cf	5	1	2	0	2	0
E. Martinez, dh	5	0	0	0	0	0
T. Martinez, 1b	4	1	1	0	11	1
Buhner, rf	5	2	2	4	4	0
Blowers, 3b	3	0	1	0	0	5
Diaz, ph-lf	2	0	0	0	0	0
Sojo, ss	4	0	2	0	1	4
Wilson, c	3	0	0	0	8	2
Strange, ph-3b	1	0	0	0	1	1
Johnson, p	0	0	0	0	1	1
Charlton, p	0	0	0	0	0	0
Totals	**41**	**5**	**9**	**4**	**33**	**15**

Cleveland	AB	R	H	RBI	PO	A
Lofton, cf	5	1	2	1	2	0
Vizquel, ss	4	0	0	1	2	3
Baerga, 2b	5	0	1	0	2	6
Belle, lf	4	0	0	0	0	0
Murray, dh	4	0	0	0	0	0
Amaro, pr-dh	1	0	0	0	0	0
Ramirez, rf	3	0	0	0	3	0
Perry, 1b	3	0	0	0	16	0
Alomar, c	3	0	0	0	7	2
Espinoza, 3b	3	0	1	0	0	1
Kirby, pr	0	1	0	0	0	0
Thome, 3b	1	0	0	0	0	0
Nagy, p	0	0	0	0	0	1
Mesa, p	0	0	0	0	1	1
Tavarez, p	0	0	0	0	0	0
Assenmacher, p	0	0	0	0	0	0
Plunk, p	0	0	0	0	0	0
Totals	**36**	**2**	**4**	**2**	**33**	**14**

Seattle	0	1	1	0 0 0	0 0 0	0	3—5
Cleveland	0	0	0	1 0 0	0 1 0	0	0—2

Seattle	IP	H	R	ER	BB	SO
Johnson	8	4	2	1	2	6
Charlton (W)	3	0	0	0	1	2

Cleveland	IP	H	R	ER	BB	SO
Nagy	8	5	2	1	0	6
Mesa	1	1	0	0	0	0
Tavarez (L)	*1	2	1	1	0	0
Assenmacher	1/3	0	0	0	0	0
Plunk	2/3	1	2	2	1	1

*Pitched to one batter in 11th.

E—Buhner, Espinoza, Alomar. DP—Cleveland 1. LOB—Seattle 5, Cleveland 6. 3B—Lofton. HR—Buhner 2. SF—Vizquel. SB—Cora, Lofton, Griffey. CS—Perry, E. Martinez. HBP—By Charlton (Belle), by Nagy (Cora). T—3:18. A—43,643. U—Reed, plate; Ford, first; McClelland, second; Coble, third; Phillips, left field; Cousins, right field.

HIGHLIGHTS

CLEVELAND 7, SEATTLE 0

Why the Indians won: Playing without Albert Belle, who led baseball in homers and RBIs, Cleveland scored three runs in the first inning and cruised from there. Belle twisted the ankle during Game 3, when he tried to get away from a pitch by Norm Charlton that hit him on the foot. Cleveland's Ken Hill, making his first postseason start, took advantage of the big early lead and pitched seven scoreless innings, allowing five hits. He and three relievers combined for the first shutout in the ALCS since Kansas City blanked Toronto in the 1985 playoffs.

Why the Mariners lost: Starter Andy Benes was roughed up early by the Indians. Benes, who threw 70 pitches, gave up six hits (including two homers), two walks and six earned runs in $2\frac{1}{3}$ innings.

The turning point: Kenny Lofton led off the bottom of the first with a single, stole second and continued to third when catcher Dan Wilson's throw bounced into center field. No. 2 hitter Omar Vizquel walked, and Carlos Baerga grounded out to score Lofton. Four pitches later, Eddie Murray hit a 435-foot shot into the seats in center, his seventh career homer in the postseason.

Notable: Seattle's Edgar Martinez, the A.L. batting champion at .356 this season, ended his 0-for-11 skid with an infield single in the second inning. His longest hitless streak during the regular season was 0-for-8. . . . The Indians' fuzzy purple mascot, Slider, was hurt when he fell off the eight-foot fence in right field in the fifth inning. Slider tore the anterior cruciate and medial collateral ligaments in his right knee. . . . The Mariners' only good news of the night came when Washington state lawmakers approved financing to build them a $320 million ballpark.

Quotable: Mariners Manager Lou Piniella on Benes' rough outing: "We didn't notice anything mechanically wrong. He got a few pitches up, and they hit 'em." . . . "Obviously you don't want to lose the guy who led the league in home runs (50) and RBIs (126)," Indians Manager Mike Hargrove said. "Anytime you lose someone with the ability Albert has, you need people to step up." . . . Pinella's summation of the game: "The story was Hill's pitching a good ballgame and our guy giving up six runs in three innings."

BOX SCORE

SATURDAY, OCTOBER 14, AT CLEVELAND

Seattle	AB	R	H	RBI	PO	A
Coleman, lf	3	0	0	0	1	0
Cora, 2b	4	0	0	0	0	3
Griffey, cf	3	0	0	0	1	0
E. Martinez, dh	4	0	1	0	0	0
T. Martinez, 1b	4	0	1	0	10	0
Buhner, rf	3	0	3	0	1	0
Blowers, 3b	4	0	0	0	1	2
Sojo, ss	3	0	1	0	2	4
Amaral, ph	1	0	0	0	0	0
Wilson, c	2	0	0	0	3	0
Widger, c	1	0	0	0	5	0
Strange, ph	0	0	0	0	0	0
Rodriguez, ph	1	0	0	0	0	0
Benes, p	0	0	0	0	0	0
Wells, p	0	0	0	0	0	1
Ayala, p	0	0	0	0	0	0
Nelson, p	0	0	0	0	0	2
Risley, p	0	0	0	0	0	0
Totals	**33**	**0**	**6**	**0**	**24**	**12**

Cleveland	AB	R	H	RBI	PO	A
Lofton, cf	3	1	1	1	3	0
Vizquel, ss	4	1	1	1	1	1
Baerga, 2b	4	1	2	1	1	1
Murray, dh	3	1	1	2	0	0
Thome, 3b	3	1	1	2	0	2
Ramirez, rf	3	0	1	0	1	0
Sorrento, 1b	3	0	0	0	6	1
Pena, c	3	1	1	0	11	0
Kirby, lf	4	1	1	0	3	0
Hill, p	0	0	0	0	1	1
Poole, p	0	0	0	0	0	0
Ogea, p	0	0	0	0	0	0
Embree, p	0	0	0	0	0	0
Totals	**30**	**7**	**9**	**7**	**27**	**6**

Seattle	0	0	0	0	0	0	0	0	0—0
Cleveland	3	1	2	0	0	1	0	0	x—7

Seattle	IP	H	R	ER	BB	SO
Benes (L)	$2\frac{1}{3}$	6	6	6	2	3
Wells	3	2	1	1	2	2
Ayala	1	1	0	0	0	1
Nelson	$1\frac{1}{3}$	0	0	0	2	0
Risley	$\frac{1}{3}$	0	0	0	1	0

Cleveland	IP	H	R	ER	BB	SO
Hill (W)	7	5	0	0	3	6
Poole	1	0	0	0	0	2
Ogea	$\frac{2}{3}$	0	0	0	0	2
Embree	$\frac{1}{3}$	0	0	0	0	1

E—Wilson. DP—Seattle 2. LOB—Seattle 9, Cleveland 7. 2B—Vizquel, Buhner. HR—Thome, Murray. SF—Lofton. SB—Kirby, Griffey, Coleman, Lofton. WP—Ogea. T—3:30. A—43,686. U—Ford, plate; McClelland, first; Coble, second; Phillips, third; Cousins, left field; Reed, right field.

HIGHLIGHTS

CLEVELAND 3, SEATTLE 2

Why the Indians won: Orel Hershiser allowed five hits and two runs—one earned—in six innings, striking out eight. He improved his career record in the playoffs and World Series to 7-0 with a 1.47 ERA. Four pitchers followed Hershiser, and none allowed a hit.

Why the Mariners lost: The Mariners failed in the clutch. They had two on and one out in the seventh and failed to score. Them, in the eighth, they had runners on first and second with one out, but Luis Sojo hit a liner that Indians short-stop Omar Vizquel grabbed and turned into a double play. Seattle finished with five hits; the top six in the order were a combined 3-for-22.

The turning points:

1. With one out in the sixth, Eddie Murray doubled off Chris Bosio. Three pitches later, Jim Thome homered into the mezzanine in right field to put the Indians ahead, 3-2, and end Bosio's night.

2. The Indians' Paul Assenmacher stranded the potential tying run at third base by striking out Ken Griffey and Jay Buhner back-to-back to end the seventh inning. Assenmacher got Griffey to chase a high fastball on a 1-and-2 count, then struck out Buhner on a 2-and-2 curveball.

Notable: Hershiser broke a tie with former Yankees pitcher Lefty Gomez for most postseason wins without a loss, and he matched former Cardinal Bob Gibson's record of seven consecutive postseason victories. . . . The Indians squandered a chance to blow it open in the seventh, leaving the bases loaded when Bill Risley struck out Thome and got Manny Ramirez to fly to right. Cleveland dropped to 1-for-13 with the bases loaded in the postseason. . . . Jose Mesa closed it out for Cleveland, his first postseason save after converting 46 of 48 opportunities during the regular season. . . . Winds gusting up to 30 mph played havoc with just about every ball in the air. . . . Five umpires, instead of the usual six, worked the game. Dave Phillips, who was to have worked the right-field line, had the flu.

Quotable: Hershiser on his performance: "The way I look at it is I'm just a human being trying to do my best and it's turning out OK. But I am grateful. I've been fortunate to have been given this ability and I almost lost it. I worked real hard to get it back, so this is very gratifying." . . . "I came in in a tough situation, back to the wall," Assenmacher said. "I didn't have whole lot to lose. I just went after them and tried to make some good pitches, and it worked." . . . Mariners Manager Lou Piniella: "We've played well all year under pressure situations. We would have liked to have won tonight, but I feel confident we're going to play well (in Game 6)."

BOX SCORE

SUNDAY, OCTOBER 15, AT CLEVELAND

Seattle	AB	R	H	RBI	PO	A
Cora, 2b	4	2	1	0	4	3
E. Martinez, dh	5	0	0	0	0	0
Griffey, cf	3	0	1	1	3	0
Buhner, rf	4	0	0	0	2	0
T. Martinez, 1b	4	0	1	0	5	0
Strange, 3b	2	0	0	0	1	2
Coleman, ph	0	0	0	0	0	0
Blowers, 3b	0	0	0	0	0	0
Diaz, lf	3	0	2	0	1	0
Sojo, ss	4	0	0	0	1	1
Wilson, c	3	0	0	0	7	0
Amaral, ph	1	0	0	0	0	0
Bosio, p	0	0	0	0	0	2
Nelson, p	0	0	0	0	0	1
Risley, p	0	0	0	0	0	0
Totals	33	2	5	1	24	9

Cleveland	AB	R	H	RBI	PO	A
Lofton, cf	5	0	2	0	4	0
Vizquel, ss	4	1	1	0	3	2
Baerga, 2b	3	0	1	0	2	1
Belle, lf	3	0	0	0	1	0
Kirby, lf	0	0	0	0	0	0
Murray, dh	3	1	3	1	0	0
Thome, 3b	3	1	1	2	0	1
Espinoza, 3b	0	0	0	0	0	0
Ramirez, rf	4	0	0	0	2	0
Sorrento, 1b	2	0	0	0	4	0
Perry, 1b	1	0	0	0	1	0
Alomar, c	4	0	2	0	10	0
Pena, c	0	0	0	0	0	0
Hershiser, p	0	0	0	0	0	3
Tavarez, p	0	0	0	0	0	0
Assenmacher, p	0	0	0	0	0	0
Plunk, p	0	0	0	0	0	0
Mesa, p	0	0	0	0	0	0
Totals	32	3	10	3	27	7

Seattle	0	0 1		0 1 0		0 0	0—2
Cleveland	1	0 0		0 0 2		0 0	x—3

Seattle	IP	H	R	ER	BB	SO
Bosio (L)	5 1/3	7	3	2	2	3
Nelson	1	2	0	0	3	2
Risley	1 2/3	1	0	0	0	2

Cleveland	IP	H	R	ER	BB	SO
Hershiser (W)	6	5	2	1	2	8
Tavarez	1/3	0	0	0	0	0
Assenmacher	1	0	0	0	0	2
Plunk	2/3	0	0	0	2	0
Mesa (S)	1	0	0	0	0	0

E—Griffey, Sorrento, Belle 2, T. Martinez. DP—Seattle 2, Cleveland 1. LOB—Seattle 9, Cleveland 11. 2B—Murray, Griffey, Alomar, Diaz. HR—Thome. SH—Kirby, Strange. SB—Coleman, Lofton 2, Cora, Vizquel 2. T—3:37. A—43,607. U—McClelland, plate; Coble, first; Cousins, second; Reed, third; Ford, left field.

GAME 6

HIGHLIGHTS

CLEVELAND 4, SEATTLE 0

Why the Indians won: They finally got to Mariners starter Randy Johnson. The Mariners had won four games this season when a loss would have meant the end of the season, and Johnson had won three of them. But the Indians took advantage of an error in the fifth to score a run, then broke it open with three runs in the eighth to qualify for the World Series for the first time since 1954. Dennis Martinez, 40, earned the first postseason victory of his career by holding the Mariners to four hits in seven innings.

Why the Mariners lost: The Mariners' potent offense failed them. The shutout was Cleveland's second in three games; Seattle was shut out only twice during the regular season. A slump by AL batting champion Edgar Martinez—who went 2-

for-23 in the series—and tough pitching against Ken Griffey shut down the Mariners.

The turning points:

1. Dennis Martinez, who struck out three and walked one, escaped his biggest jam in the sixth when he fanned Tino Martinez with runners on second and third to end the inning with a 1-0 lead. Twice he was helped by barehanded plays by shortstop Omar Vizquel.

2. In the eighth, Tony Pena led off with a double against the tiring Johnson. Kenny Lofton followed with a bunt single. Lofton stole second, then streaked home behind pinch-runner Ruben Amaro when a pitch glanced off catcher Dan Wilson's glove. One out later, Carlos Baerga capped the three-run inning with a homer off Johnson.

Notable: Martinez became the oldest pitcher to win a league championship series game. . . . The Indians complained that the Kingdome mound was too high. The grounds crew measured the mound, which was a half-inch too high. It was then lowered.

Quotable: Johnson on the Indians: "You don't win 100 games (in the regular season) just because of a great offense. They have some pretty good pitching over there, too." . . . Mariners Manager Lou Piniella was impressed by Dennis Martinez: "Martinez was a surgeon out there. Cleveland pitched so well this series and played so well all year." . . . Indians Manager Mike Hargrove on going to the World Series: "I guess maybe it was a situation where I had to pinch myself to make sure this was the Cleveland Indians and Mike Hargrove in this position. I found out that it really was." . . . Piniella reflecting on his team's season: "I told them that they had nothing to be ashamed of, they had a heck of a baseball season. This was a first step. Hopefully, next year we will take this further." . . . "It's so great to be able to accomplish something we haven't done for a long time," Dennis Martinez said. "Especially for the Cleveland people. They've waited a long time for this."

BOX SCORE

TUESDAY, OCTOBER 17, AT SEATTLE

Cleveland	AB	R	H	RBI	PO	A
Lofton, cf	4	1	2	1	3	0
Vizquel, ss	4	0	0	0	1	4
Baerga, 2b	4	1	3	1	3	6
Belle, lf	4	0	2	0	2	0
Murray, dh	4	0	0	0	0	0
Ramirez, rf	3	0	0	0	0	0
Kirby, rf	1	0	0	0	0	0
Perry, 1b	4	0	0	0	13	0
Espinoza, 3b	4	1	0	0	0	2
Pena, c	3	0	1	0	3	1
Amaro, pr	0	1	0	0	0	0
Alomar, c	0	0	0	0	2	0
D. Martinez, p	0	0	0	0	0	1
Tavarez, p	0	0	0	0	0	0
Mesa, p	0	0	0	0	0	0
Totals	35	4	8	2	27	14
Seattle	**AB**	**R**	**H**	**RBI**	**PO**	**A**
Coleman, lf	4	0	1	0	3	0
Widger, c	0	0	0	0	1	0
Cora, 2b	4	0	0	0	4	2
Griffey, cf	3	0	0	0	3	0
E. Martinez, dh	3	0	1	0	0	0
T. Martinez, 1b	3	0	0	0	7	0
Buhner, rf	4	0	0	0	2	0
Blowers, 3b	3	0	1	0	0	2
Sojo, ss	3	0	1	0	0	3
Fermin, ss	0	0	0	0	0	0
Wilson, c	2	0	0	0	7	1
Diaz, ph-lf	1	0	0	0	0	0
Johnson, p	0	0	0	0	0	0
Charlton, p	0	0	0	0	0	0
Totals	30	0	4	0	27	8

Cleveland	0	0	0	0	1	0	0	3	0—4
Seattle	0	0	0	0	0	0	0	0	0—0

Cleveland	IP	H	R	ER	BB	SO
Martinez (W)	7	4	0	0	1	3
Tavarez	1	0	0	0	0	1
Mesa	1	0	0	0	1	1
Seattle	**IP**	**H**	**R**	**ER**	**BB**	**SO**
Johnson (L)	7⅓	8	4	3	0	7
Charlton	1⅔	0	0	0	0	1

E—Cora. DP—Cleveland 1. LOB—Cleveland 4, Seattle 6. 2B—Pena, Belle, Sojo. HR—Baerga. SB—Lofton, E. Martinez, Coleman. HBP—By D. Martinez (E. Martinez). PB—Wilson. T—2:54. A—58,489. U—Coble, plate; Kaiser, first; Cousins, second; Reed, third; Ford, left field; McClelland, right field.

STATISTICS

CLEVELAND INDIANS' BATTING AND FIELDING AVERAGES

					BATTING								FIELDING			
Player, position	G	AB	R	H	TB	2B	3B	HR	RBI	BB	IBB	SO	Avg.	PO	A	E	Avg.
Lofton, cf	6	24	4	11	15	0	2	0	3	4	0	6	.458	15	0	0	1.000
Baerga, 2b	6	25	3	10	13	0	0	1	4	2	0	3	.400	12	22	0	1.000
Pena, c	4	6	1	2	3	1	0	0	1	0	0	0	.333	15	1	0	1.000
Ramirez, rf	6	21	2	6	12	0	0	2	2	2	0	5	.286	9	0	0	1.000
Alomar, c	5	15	0	4	7	1	1	0	1	1	0	1	.267	30	3	1	.971
Thome, 3b	5	15	2	4	10	0	0	2	5	2	0	3	.267	1	5	1	.857
Murray, dh	6	24	2	6	10	1	0	1	3	2	1	3	.250	0	0	0	.000
Belle, lf	5	18	1	4	8	1	0	1	1	3	0	5	.222	4	0	2	.667
Kirby, rf-pr-lf	4	5	2	1	1	0	0	0	0	0	0	0	.200	3	0	0	1.000
Sorrento, 1b	4	13	2	2	3	1	0	0	0	2	0	3	.154	34	1	2	.946
Espinoza, 3b	4	8	1	1	1	0	0	0	0	0	0	3	.125	0	3	1	.750
Vizquel, ss	6	23	2	2	3	1	0	0	2	5	0	2	.087	9	21	0	1.000
Assenmacher, p	3	0	0	0	0	0	0	0	0	0	0	0	.000	0	0	0	.000
Embree, p	1	0	0	0	0	0	0	0	0	0	0	0	.000	0	0	0	.000
Hershiser, p	2	0	0	0	0	0	0	0	0	0	0	0	.000	0	4	0	1.000

Player, position	G	AB	R	H	TB	2B	3B	HR	RBI	BB	IBB	SO	Avg.	PO	A	E	Avg.
Hill, p	1	0	0	0	0	0	0	0	0	0	0	0	.000	1	1	0	1.000
Martinez, p	2	0	0	0	0	0	0	0	0	0	0	0	.000	1	1	0	1.000
Mesa, p	4	0	0	0	0	0	0	0	0	0	0	0	.000	1	2	0	1.000
Nagy, p	1	0	0	0	0	0	0	0	0	0	0	0	.000	0	1	0	1.000
Ogea, p	1	0	0	0	0	0	0	0	0	0	0	0	.000	0	0	0	.000
Plunk, p	3	0	0	0	0	0	0	0	0	0	0	0	.000	0	0	0	.000
Poole, p	1	0	0	0	0	0	0	0	0	0	0	0	.000	0	0	0	.000
Tavarez, p	4	0	0	0	0	0	0	0	0	0	0	0	.000	0	1	0	1.000
Amaro, pr-dh	1	1	1	0	0	0	0	0	0	0	0	0	.000	0	0	0	.000
Perry, 1b	3	8	0	0	0	0	0	0	0	0	1	0	3	.000	30	0	0	1.000
Totals	6	206	23	53	86	6	3	7	21	25	1	37	.257	165	66	7	.971

SEATTLE MARINERS' BATTING AND FIELDING AVERAGES

Player, position	G	AB	R	H	TB	2B	3B	HR	RBI	BB	IBB	SO	Avg.	PO	A	E	Avg.
Diaz, ph-lf	3	7	0	3	4	1	0	0	0	1	0	1	.429	1	0	0	1.000
Griffey, cf	6	21	2	7	12	2	0	1	2	4	0	4	.333	13	0	1	.929
Buhner, rf	6	23	5	7	18	2	0	3	5	2	0	8	.304	15	0	1	.938
Sojo, ss	6	20	0	5	7	2	0	0	1	0	0	2	.250	9	18	1	.964
Blowers, 3b	6	18	1	4	7	0	0	1	2	0	0	4	.222	5	9	0	1.000
Cora, 2b	6	23	3	4	5	1	0	0	0	1	0	0	.174	15	12	1	.964
T. Martinez, 1b	6	22	1	3	3	0	0	0	0	3	1	7	.136	45	5	1	.980
Coleman, lf-ph	5	20	0	2	2	0	0	0	2	0	0	6	.100	12	0	0	1.000
E. Martinez, dh	6	23	0	2	2	0	0	0	0	2	2	5	.087	0	0	0	.000
Ayala, p	2	0	0	0	0	0	0	0	0	0	0	0	.000	0	1	0	1.000
Belcher, p	1	0	0	0	0	0	0	0	0	0	0	0	.000	1	0	0	1.000
Benes, p	1	0	0	0	0	0	0	0	0	0	0	0	.000	0	0	0	.000
Bosio, p	1	0	0	0	0	0	0	0	0	0	0	0	.000	0	2	0	1.000
Charlton, p	3	0	0	0	0	0	0	0	0	0	0	0	.000	0	0	0	.000
Fermin, 2b-ss	2	0	0	0	0	0	0	0	0	0	0	0	.000	0	0	0	.000
Johnson, p	2	0	0	0	0	0	0	0	0	0	0	0	.000	1	1	0	1.000
Nelson, p	3	0	0	0	0	0	0	0	0	0	0	0	.000	0	3	0	1.000
Risley, p	3	0	0	0	0	0	0	0	0	0	0	0	.000	0	0	0	.000
Wells, p	1	0	0	0	0	0	0	0	0	0	0	0	.000	0	1	0	1.000
Wolcott, p	1	0	0	0	0	0	0	0	0	0	0	0	.000	1	1	0	1.000
Rodriguez, ph	1	1	0	0	0	0	0	0	0	0	0	1	.000	0	0	0	.000
Widger, c	3	1	0	0	0	0	0	0	0	0	0	1	.000	7	0	0	1.000
Amaral, ph	2	2	0	0	0	0	0	0	0	0	0	1	.000	0	0	0	.000
Strange, ph-3b	2	4	0	0	0	0	0	0	0	0	0	2	.000	2	3	0	1.000
Wilson, c	6	16	0	0	0	0	0	0	0	0	0	4	.000	35	3	1	.974
Totals	6	201	12	37	60	8	0	5	10	15	3	46	.184	162	59	6	.974

CLEVELAND INDIANS' PITCHING RECORDS

Pitcher	G	GS	CG	IP	H	R	ER	HR	BB	IBB	SO	HB	WP	W	L	Pct.	ERA
Hill	1	1	0	7	5	0	0	0	3	0	6	0	0	1	0	1.000	0.00
Assenmacher	3	0	0	1 1/3	0	0	0	0	1	0	2	0	0	0	0	.000	0.00
Poole	1	0	0	1	0	0	0	0	0	0	2	0	0	0	0	.000	0.00
Ogea	1	0	0	0 2/3	1	0	0	0	0	0	2	0	1	0	0	.000	0.00
Embree	1	0	0	0 1/3	0	0	0	0	0	0	1	0	0	0	0	.000	0.00
Nagy	1	1	0	8	5	2	1	1	0	0	6	1	0	0	0	.000	1.13
Hershiser	2	2	0	14	9	3	2	1	3	0	15	1	1	2	0	1.000	1.29
Martinez	2	2	0	13 1/3	10	3	3	1	3	0	7	1	0	1	1	.500	2.03
Mesa	4	0	0	4	3	1	1	1	1	0	1	0	0	0	0	.000	2.25
Tavarez	4	0	0	3 1/3	3	1	1	0	1	1	2	0	0	0	1	.000	2.70
Plunk	3	0	0	2	1	2	2	1	3	1	2	0	0	0	0	.000	9.00
Totals	6	6	0	55	37	12	10	5	15	3	46	3	0	4	2	.667	1.64

SEATTLE MARINERS' PITCHING RECORDS

Pitcher	G	GS	CG	IP	H	R	ER	HR	BB	IBB	SO	HB	WP	W	L	Pct.	ERA
Charlton	3	0	0	6	1	0	0	0	1	0	5	1	0	1	0	1.000	0.00
Nelson	3	0	0	3	3	0	0	0	5	1	3	0	0	0	0	.000	0.00
Risley	3	0	0	2 2/3	2	0	0	0	1	0	2	0	0	0	0	.000	0.00
Johnson	2	2	0	15 1/3	12	6	4	4	2	0	13	0	0	0	1	.000	2.35
Ayala	2	0	0	3 2/3	3	1	1	1	3	0	3	0	0	0	0	.000	2.45
Wolcott	1	1	0	7	8	2	2	1	5	0	2	0	0	1	0	1.000	2.57
Wells	1	0	0	3	2	1	1	0	2	0	2	0	0	0	0	.000	3.00
Bosio	1	1	0	5 1/3	7	3	2	1	2	0	3	0	0	0	1	.000	3.38
Belcher	1	1	0	5 2/3	9	4	4	1	2	0	1	0	0	0	1	.000	6.35
Benes	1	1	0	2 1/3	6	6	6	2	2	1	3	0	0	0	1	.000	23.14
Totals	6	6	0	54	53	23	20	7	25	1	37	1	0	2	4	.333	3.33

SCORE BY INNINGS

Cleveland	4	1	3	1	3	5	1	5	0	0	0—23
Seattle	0	3	2	0	1	1	1	0	1	0	3—12

MISCELLANEOUS STATISTICS

Sacrifice hits—Kirby, Strange.

Sacrifice flies—Lofton, Vizquel.

Stolen bases—Lofton 5, Coleman 4, Vizquel 3, Cora 2, Griffey 2, Kirby, E. Martinez.

Caught stealing—Griffey, E. Martinez, Perry.

Double plays—Nelson, Sojo and T. Martinez 2; Ayala, Cora, Sojo and T. Martinez; Cora and Sojo; Mesa and Perry; Sojo and T. Martinez; Sojo, Cora and T. Martinez; T. Martinez, Sojo and T. Martinez; Vizquel (unassisted); Vizquel, Baerga and Perry; Vizquel, Baerga and Sorrento.

Left on bases—Cleveland 12, 10, 6, 7, 11, 4—50; Seattle 7, 7, 5, 9, 9, 6—43.

Hit by pitcher—By Hershiser (Cora), by Martinez (E. Martinez), by Charlton (Belle), by Nagy (Cora).

Passed balls—Wilson.

Balks—None.

Time of games—First game, 3:07; second game, 3:14; third game, 3:18; fourth game, 3:30; fifth game, 3:37; sixth game, 2:54.

Attendance—First game, 57,065; second game, 58,144; third game, 43,643; fourth game, 43,686; fifth game, 43,607; sixth game, 58,489.

Umpires—Phillips, Cousins, Reed, Ford, McClelland, Coble and Kaiser.

Official scorers—Harland Beery, Hank Kozloski.△45

N.L. CHAMPIONSHIP SERIES

GAME 1

HIGHLIGHTS
ATLANTA 2, CINCINNATI 1

Why the Braves won: The Braves rallied in the ninth inning for the fourth time in five postseason games. Pete Schourek was working on a four-hit shutout entering the ninth. But Chipper Jones and Fred McGriff singled to open the inning, and when David Justice followed with a fielder's choice force at second, the score was tied. The inning could have been bigger. The Braves went on to load the bases with two outs but pinch-hitter Dwight Smith flied to center. In the 11th, McGriff led off with a walk and scored on Mike Devereaux's two-out single.

Why the Reds lost: The Reds grounded into a playoff-record five double plays. Tom Glavine was the recipient of the first four. Fittingly, the game ended on one, when Greg McMichael induced Reggie Sanders into bouncing to Rafael Belliard at short. All five double plays ended innings.

The turning points:

1. The Reds' failure to avoid double plays is probably the overriding factor in the game. Which double play hurt the most? The last one? The one in the fourth with the bases loaded? "I think we hit into about three double plays that killed us," Reds Manager Davey Johnson said.

2. In the ninth, McGriff singled to right on a routine ground ball out of the reach of first baseman Hal Morris. Morris had been holding Jones on at first. If Morris' isn't holding Jones on, he makes the play.

3. The Reds got a leadoff double in the 11th from pinch-hitter Thomas Howard off Brad Clontz. Barry Larkin grounded out, moving Thomas to third. Steve Avery came in to pitch and walked Mariano Duncan. Braves Manager Bobby Cox then brought in McMichael, who had been a disaster in the 1993 championship series against the Phillies. Sanders, with only two hits in 16 postseason at-bats, grounded into double play No. 5.

Notable: Ironically, the Braves were last in the National League in turning double plays during the season, and only Seattle turned fewer in the majors. . . . In four at-bats, former Brave Ron Gant had two infield hits, one of which drove in the Reds' run. . . . Glavine is 13-1 lifetime at Riverfront Stadium. . . . Riverfront Stadium capacity is 52,952; 36,762 saw the game. There were 3,620 no-shows. . . . Braves shortstop Jeff Blauser suffered a series-ending deep bruise on his right thigh when Morris took him out at second base on a double play. Blauser already had a

sore right ankle.

Quotable: Glavine: "One thing that helps us is that we've been in some pretty gut-wrenching situations. Over the last four years, we don't do anything easy. The fact that we've been through this so many times certainly has to help settle your nerves when you get in that situation." . . . Devereaux: "This is like a second life for me. When I was with the White Sox, I knew we had no chance to get to the postseason. Before I got (here), I'd see on TV all the time how this team came back in the late innings. But until you're here in person, you really don't get a feel for how good this club is."

BOX SCORE

TUESDAY, OCTOBER 10, AT CINCINNATI

Atlanta	AB	R	H	RBI	PO	A
Grissom, cf	5	0	1	0	1	0
Lemke, 2b	5	0	0	0	2	6
Jones, 3b	5	1	2	0	0	3
McGriff, 1b	4	1	1	0	14	0
Justice, rf	4	0	1	1	1	0
Polonia, pr-lf	0	0	0	0	0	0
Lopez, c	5	0	1	0	10	0
Klesko, lf	2	0	0	0	0	0
Devereaux, rf	1	0	1	1	0	0
Blauser, ss	4	0	0	0	4	6
Clontz, p	0	0	0	0	0	0
Avery, p	0	0	0	0	0	0
McMichael, p	0	0	0	0	0	0
Glavine, p	1	0	0	0	0	1
Mordecai, ph	1	0	0	0	0	0
Pena, p	0	0	0	0	0	0
Smith, ph	1	0	0	0	0	0
Wohlers, p	0	0	0	0	0	0
Belliard, ss	0	0	0	0	1	1
Totals	38	2	7	2	33	17

Cincinnati	AB	R	H	RBI	PO	A
Walton, cf-lf	4	0	0	0	6	0
Howard, ph	1	0	1	0	0	0
Larkin, ss	5	1	2	0	1	1
Gant, lf	4	0	2	1	1	0
D. Lewis, cf	0	0	0	0	1	0
Harris, p	0	0	0	0	0	0
Duncan, ph	0	0	0	0	0	0
Sanders, rf	4	0	0	0	1	0
Santiago, c	3	0	1	0	9	1
Morris, 1b	3	0	1	0	5	1
Boone, 2b	4	0	0	0	5	4
M. Lewis, 3b	3	0	1	0	2	1
Branson, ph-3b	1	0	0	0	0	1
Schourek, p	3	0	0	0	1	1
Brantley, p	0	0	0	0	1	0
Anthony, ph	1	0	0	0	0	0
Jackson, p	0	0	0	0	0	1
Totals	36	1	8	1	33	11

Atlanta	0	0	0	0	0	0	0	0	1	0	1—2
Cincinnati	0	0	0	1	0	0	0	0	0	0	0—1

Atlanta	IP	H	R	ER	BB	SO
Glavine	7	7	1	1	2	5
Pena	1	0	0	0	0	1
Wohlers (W)	2	0	0	0	0	4
Clontz	1/3	1	0	0	0	0
Avery	*0	0	0	0	1	0
McMichael (S)	1/3	0	0	0	0	0

Cincinnati	IP	H	R	ER	BB	SO
Schourek	8⅓	6	1	1	2	8
Brantley	1⅔	0	0	0	2	1
Jackson (L)	1	1	1	1	1	0

*Pitched to one batter in 11th.

DP—Atlanta 5, Cincinnati 1. LOB—Atlanta 9, Cincinnati 6. 2B—Howard, Morris, Larkin. 3B—Larkin. SH—Polonia. CS—Klesko. HBP—By Glatine (Morris). WP—Schourek. T—3:18. A—40,382. U—Runge, plate; Quick, first; DeMuth, second; Davis, third; Marsh, left field; Crawford, right field.

GAME 2

HIGHLIGHTS

ATLANTA 6, CINCINNATI 2

Why the Braves won: Mark Portugal, in his first relief appearance of the season, gave up four runs in the 10th inning. Mark Lemke, hitless in the series, led off the 10th with a single and advanced to second on Chipper Jones' ground-out. Fred McGriff, who already had doubled a playoff-record three times in the game, was walked intentionally. Dave Justice lined a single to right, but Lemke couldn't score because he wasn't sure if Reggie Sanders would catch the ball. Portugal got ahead of Ryan Klesko, fooling him on two changeups. But Portugal went to the curveball on 0-2 and threw a wild pitch. He retired Klesko, but Javier Lopez followed with a three-run homer off the left-field foul pole.

Why the Reds lost: Lack of clutch hitting killed the Reds. They couldn't get runners home from third with none out in the eighth, or from second with one out in the ninth. In addition, Reds starter John Smiley pitched only five innings, and Manager Davey Johnson used his top three relievers—Dave Burba, Mike Jackson and Jeff Brantley—in innings six through nine, opening the door for Portugal in the 10th.

The turning points:

1. For the second consecutive game, Johnson decided to start Thomas Howard in center instead of the team's best defensive center fielder, Darren Lewis. In the second, McGriff hit a drive to deep left-center that glanced off the back of Howard's glove for a double. One out later, McGriff scored on Mike Devereaux's double. Howard would misplay another drive by McGriff that would go for a double, too.

2. With the score tied at 2, Barry Larkin led off the bottom of the eighth with a double off Alejandro Pena and stole third. But the heart of the Reds' order failed to produce. Ron Gant popped to second, Reggie Sanders struck out for the 10th time in his last 14 postseason at-bats and, after an intentional walk to Hal Morris, Benito Santiago struck out.

3. In the ninth inning, the Reds' Bret Boone was on third with two out. With Mariano Duncan at the plate, reliever Greg McMichael threw a 1-2 changeup in the dirt. Lopez made an exceptional play to avoid a wild pitch. "Ninth inning, winning run at third, I've got to be ready to block that ball," Lopez said. "I anticipated that it would be in the dirt."

Notable: The Braves became the first team to win the first two games on the road in a best-of-seven playoff series. . . . Jeff Branson stole home in the fifth inning on the back end of a double steal. It was the first steal of home in NLCS history. The only steal of home in the ALCS was by Oakland's Reggie Jackson in 1972.

Quotable: Lopez on his home run: "The happiest moment of my life." . . . Sanders on his strike-out binge: "I'm pressing. I'm trying to relax, but so far, it's not happening." . . . Portugal on his horrible 10th inning: "I feel like hell right now, but there's nothing you can do about it." On the home run pitch to Lopez, a sinking fastball: "Obviously, it wasn't a very good pitch." And on the wild pitch: "(Santiago) called the pitch I wanted to throw. I just threw a lousy pitch. And it ended up costing us the ballgame."

BOX SCORE

WEDNESDAY, OCTOBER 11, AT CINCINNATI

Atlanta	AB	R	H	RBI	PO	A
Grissom, cf	4	1	1	0	4	0
Lemke, 2b	4	1	1	0	5	3
Jones, 3b	5	0	1	1	1	4
McGriff, 1b	4	2	3	0	10	1
Justice, rf	4	1	1	0	2	0
Devereaux, lf	4	0	1	1	0	0
Klesko, ph-lf	1	0	0	0	0	0
Lopez, c	5	1	1	3	7	2
Belliard, ss	3	0	1	0	1	2
Polonia, ph	1	0	0	0	0	0
Mordecai, ss	1	0	0	0	0	0
Smoltz, p	3	0	1	0	0	1
Pena, p	0	0	0	0	0	0
Smith, p	1	0	0	0	0	0
McMichael, p	0	0	0	0	0	0
Wohlers, p	0	0	0	0	0	0
Totals	40	6	11	5	30	13

Cincinnati	AB	R	H	RBI	PO	A
Howard, cf	3	0	1	0	0	0
Jackson, p	0	0	0	0	0	0
Brantley, p	0	0	0	0	1	0
Duncan, ph	1	0	0	0	0	0
Portugal, p	0	0	0	0	0	0
Larkin, ss	5	0	3	0	3	7
Gant, lf	5	0	0	0	4	0
Sanders, rf	5	0	1	0	3	0
Morris, 1b	4	0	0	0	13	2
Santiago, c	4	0	1	0	2	0
Boone, 2b	3	1	2	0	2	4
Branson, 3b	3	1	0	0	0	0
Smiley, p	1	0	0	0	1	1
Harris, ph	1	0	1	1	0	0
Burba, p	0	0	0	0	0	0
Anthony, ph	0	0	0	0	0	0
D. Lewis, pr-cf	1	0	0	0	1	0
Totals	36	2	9	1	30	14

Atlanta	1	0	0	1	0	0	0	0	0	4	6
Cincinnati	0	0	0	0	2	0	0	0	0	0	2

Atlanta	IP	H	R	ER	BB	SO		Cincinnati	IP	H	R	ER	BB	SO
Smoltz	7	7	2	2	2	2		Smiley	5	5	2	2	0	1
Pena	1	1	0	0	1	2		Burba	2	2	0	0	3	0
McMichael (W)	1	0	0	0	1	0		Jackson	1	1	0	0	0	1
Wohlers	1	1	0	0	0	2		Brantley	1	0	0	0	0	0
								Portugal (L)	1	3	4	4	1	0

E—Smoltz, Sanders. DP—Cincinnati 1. LOB—Atlanta 8, Cincinnati 9. 2B—Larkin, Devereaux, McGriff 3. HR—Lopez. SH—Branson. SB—Morris, Larkin, Smoltz, Harris, Branson. CS—Sanders, Howard. WP—Portugal, Burba. Balks—Jackson. T—3:26. A—44,624. U—Quick, plate; DeMuth, first; Davis, second; Marsh, third; Crawford, left field; Runge, right field.

GAME 3

HIGHLIGHTS

ATLANTA 5, CINCINNATI 2

Why the Braves won: Greg Maddux finally pitched a good game in the postseason—and when that happened, what more would the Braves need? Maddux gave up one run and seven hits over eight innings, and his personal catcher, Charlie O'Brien, supplied all the offense he would need with a three-run homer in the sixth inning to break a scoreless tie.

Why the Reds lost: Reggie Sanders struck out three more times, including once with the bases loaded in the third inning. The Reds didn't score until it didn't matter, getting single runs in the eighth and ninth innings.

The turning points:

1. Just ask Reds Manager Davey Johnson. "Any time you strike out with the bases loaded, it can be classified as a turning point." In the Reds' third, pitcher David Wells (a .143 hitter) singled with one out, and Thomas Howard walked. Barry Larkin fouled out, but Maddux hit Ron Gant to load the bases. Sanders, with a chance to continue Maddux's postseason woes, fouled off four pitches before striking out on a high fastball. "It's not only Reggie," Larkin said. "I was up there with a man on first and second, and I popped out. We have to focus on the entire team, not just Reggie."

2. The Reds wasted another opportunity in the fourth. With two outs, center fielder Marquis Grissom tried to make a shoestring catch on Bret Boone's single. Grissom came up empty and the ball bounced to the wall. Dave Justice backed up Grissom and relayed the ball to second baseman Mark Lemke, whose strong throw home stopped Boone from scoring. Boone had some trouble rounding first and was flying around third when coach Ray Knight signaled for him to stop. "Bret has a tendency to watch the ball," Johnson said. "He was watching it instead of making his turn at first base. That's probably why he didn't score." Jeff Branson bounced to Maddux on the next pitch to end the inning.

Notable: When Maddux struck out Sanders in the sixth, it was Sanders' fifth consecutive strikeout, tying a NLCS record set by the Reds' Cesar Geronimo in 1973. In his next at-bat, Sanders reached on an infield hit. . . . Braves outfielder Dwight Smith sang the national anthem. Smith has sung the anthem before games but never in the playoffs.

Quotable: O'Brien on his first postseason homer: "I've been playing a long time. This is what you dream about when you're growing up and playing Johnny Bench in the back yard. Being a catcher, growing up in Oklahoma, I tried to be like him. I wore his number for a long time. I tried to catch like him. I tried to hit like him, too, but that didn't last long." In 10 major league seasons, O'Brien has 33 home runs, 356 fewer than Bench hit in his 17-year career. . . . Braves rookie Chipper Jones went 3-for-4 and hit a two-run homer. He is hitting .429 in the series. "Not one second of this postseason hasn't been fun," he said. "The only thing that's been a little bit of a surprise to me is how relaxed I've been. I think it's a big compliment when people come up to you and say, 'For a rookie, you're playing like a 10-year veteran.' "

BOX SCORE

FRIDAY, OCTOBER 13, AT ATLANTA

Cincinnati	AB	R	H	RBI	PO	A
Howard, cf	3	0	0	1	2	0
Larkin, ss	5	0	1	0	3	2
Gant, lf	3	1	1	0	2	0
Sanders, rf	4	0	1	0	3	0
Morris, 1b	4	0	1	1	5	0
Santiago, c	3	0	0	0	6	0
Boone, 2b	4	0	1	0	2	1
Branson, 3b	4	1	1	0	1	2
Wells, p	2	0	1	0	0	0
Harris, ph	1	0	1	0	0	0
Hernandez, p	0	0	0	0	0	0
Carrasco, p	0	0	0	0	0	0
Taubensee, ph	1	0	0	0	0	0
Totals	34	2	8	2	24	5

Atlanta	AB	R	H	RBI	PO	A
Grissom, cf	5	0	1	0	2	0
Lemke, 2b	4	1	1	0	2	3
Jones, 3b	4	1	3	2	1	5
McGriff, 1b	4	1	2	0	10	3
Justice, rf	3	0	1	0	1	0
Devereaux, lf	3	1	1	0	2	0
O'Brien, c	4	1	2	3	3	1
Belliard, ss	4	0	1	0	4	1
Maddux, p	3	0	0	0	1	1
Klesko, ph	1	0	0	0	0	0
Wohlers, p	0	0	0	0	1	0
Totals	35	5	12	5	27	14

Cincinnati	0	0	0	0	0	0	0	1	1—2
Atlanta	0	0	0	0	0	3	2	0	x—5

Cincinnati	IP	H	R	ER	BB	SO
Wells (L)	6	8	3	3	2	3
Hernandez	2/3	3	2	2	0	0
Carrasco	1 1/3	1	0	0	0	3

Atlanta	IP	H	R	ER	BB	SO
Maddux (W)	8	7	1	1	2	4
Wohlers	1	1	1	1	0	0

E—Grissom. DP—Cincinnati 1. LOB—Cincinnati 9, Atlanta 8. 2B—Branson, McGriff. HR—Jones, O'Brien. SF—Howard. SB—Jones. CS—Larkin. HBP—By Maddux (Gant). WP—Maddux. T—2:42. A—51,424. U—DeMuth, plate; Davis, first; Marsh, second; Crawford, third; Runge, left field; Quick, right field.

GAME 4

HIGHLIGHTS

ATLANTA 6, CINCINNATI 0

Why the Braves won: Steve Avery, making his first start of the postseason, limited the Reds to two hits over six innings, one an infield hit. His performance demoralized the Reds, who scored an NLCS-low five runs for a four-game series. The Braves scored five runs in the sixth inning to blow open a 1-0 game. The key hit was series MVP Mike Devereaux's three-run home run, the Braves' third three-run homer in three games.

Why the Reds lost: Besides the Reds not hitting, the bullpen failed again. Pete Schourek took the Reds through six innings, giving up one run. But ailing Mike Jackson (sore arm) could get only one out in the seventh while giving up three hits and walking three. All five runs were charged to Jackson. The Reds' bullpen gave up 12 runs in 11⅔ innings in the NLCS. By contrast, the Braves' bullpen allowed one meaningless run and struck out 14 in 11 innings.

The turning points:

1. Is it fair to keep dumping on Reggie Sanders? Probably not, but it's hard not to. Sanders, the cleanup hitter, had a horrible series. He struck out 10 times, including the final out of the series. He also was at the plate in the fourth inning with runners on first and second and one out. But he grounded to shortstop (breaking his bat), starting one of the three double plays the Reds would hit into in the game. Sanders had 19 strikeouts in the two playoff series and hit .138 (4-for-29).

2. Braves right fielder David Justice was hit on the right knee by a batted ball while warming up before the game. Justice had taken his turn in the batting cage and was running the bases when a one-hop grounder by Javier Lopez struck him on the already-sore knee. Justice had to be replaced in the lineup by Mike Devereaux. Fate worked its magic. Devereaux's three-run homer clinched the game and the MVP Award.

Notable: Atlanta's starters—Tom Glavine, John Smoltz, Greg Maddux and Avery—allowed four runs and 23 hits in 28 innings. . . . The Reds were outscored 19-5. The previous low for a four-game series was 10 by the Pirates in 1974. . . . How bad was it for the Reds? They produced more strikeouts than hits (31 to 28) and grounded into eight double plays. The Reds hit .103 with runners in scoring position and did not hit a home run. . . . Sanders' poor series took some of the focus off of teammate Ron Gant, who hit .188 (3-for-16). In his three previous NLCS series with the Braves, Gant hit .259, .182 and .185. . . . The game was the last

for Davey Johnson as manager of the Reds. It was no secret that he would be replaced at the end of the season by third base coach Ray Knight.

Quotable: Devereaux on his home run: "I was looking for a first-pitch fastball. He gave it to me." . . . Jackson: "Those guys hit everything I threw at them." . . . Avery, Atlanta's MVP in the 1991 playoffs, was dropped from the postseason rotation after going 7-13 with a 4.67 ERA. "I just wanted to feel part of the success that our pitchers have had," he said. "I also wanted to prove to myself that everything was fine. Obviously I wasn't happy with my season, but it's over. I was the same person. I just didn't win as many games."

BOX SCORE

SATURDAY, OCTOBER 14, AT ATLANTA

Cincinnati	AB	R	H	RBI	PO	A
Walton, cf	3	0	0	0	0	0
Howard, ph-cf	1	0	0	0	0	0
Larkin, ss	3	0	1	0	3	5
Gant, lf	4	0	0	0	2	0
Sanders, rf	3	0	0	0	0	0
Duncan, 1b	2	0	0	0	9	0
Morris, ph-1b	1	0	0	0	4	0
Santiago, c	3	0	1	0	6	0
Jackson, p	0	0	0	0	0	0
Burba, p	0	0	0	0	0	0
Boone, 2b	3	0	0	0	0	4
M. Lewis, 3b	1	0	0	0	0	2
Branson, ph-3b	1	0	0	0	0	0
Schourek, p	2	0	0	0	0	2
Taubensee, c	1	0	1	0	0	0
Totals	28	0	3	0	24	13

Atlanta	AB	R	H	RBI	PO	A
Grissom, cf	5	1	2	0	1	0
Lemke, 2b	5	0	1	1	4	4
Jones, 3b	2	1	1	0	2	1
McGriff, 1b	4	1	1	0	8	0
Devereaux, rf	5	1	1	3	0	0
Lopez, c	4	1	3	0	11	0
Klesko, lf	3	0	0	0	1	0
Belliard, ss	4	1	1	0	0	3
Avery, p	2	0	1	0	0	2
O'Brien, ph	1	0	0	0	0	0
McMichael, p	0	0	0	0	0	0
Polonia, ph	1	0	1	1	0	0
Pena, p	0	0	0	0	0	0
Wohlers, p	0	0	0	0	0	0
Totals	36	6	12	5	27	10

Cincinnati	0	0	0		0	0	0		0	0	0—0
Atlanta	0	0	1		0	0	0		5	0	x—6

Cincinnati	IP	H	R	ER	BB	SO
Schourek (L)	6	8	1	1	1	5
Jackson	⅓	3	5	5	3	0
Burba	1⅔	1	0	0	1	0

Atlanta	IP	H	R	ER	BB	SO
Avery (W)	6	2	0	0	3	6
McMichael	1	0	0	0	0	2
Pena	1	1	0	0	0	1
Wohlers	1	0	0	0	0	2

E—Belliard, Larkin. DP—Cincinnati 1, Atlanta 3. LOB—Cincinnati 4, Atlanta 11. 2B—Lopez. 3B—Grissom. HR—Devereaux. PB—Taubensee. T—2:54. A—52,067. U—Davis, plate; Marsh, first; Crawford, second; Runge, third; Quick, left field; DeMuth, right field.

ATLANTA BRAVES' BATTING AND FIELDING AVERAGES

Player, position	G	AB	R	H	TB	2B	3B	HR	RBI	BB	IBB	SO	Avg.	PO	A	E	Avg.
Avery, p	2	2	0	1	1	0	0	0	0	0	0	0	.500	0	2	0	1.000
Polonia, lf-pr-ph	1	2	0	1	1	0	0	0	1	0	0	0	.500	0	0	0	.000
Jones, 3b	4	16	3	7	10	0	0	1	3	3	0	1	.438	4	13	0	1.000
McGriff, 1b	4	16	5	7	11	4	0	0	0	3	2	0	.438	42	4	0	1.000
O'Brien, c-ph	1	5	1	2	5	0	0	1	3	0	0	1	.400	3	1	0	1.000
Lopez, c	3	14	2	5	9	1	0	1	3	0	0	1	.357	28	2	0	1.000
Smoltz, p	1	3	0	1	1	0	0	0	0	0	0	1	.333	0	1	1	.500
Devereaux, rf-lf	4	13	2	4	8	1	0	1	5	1	0	2	.308	2	0	0	1.000
Belliard, ss	4	11	1	3	3	0	0	0	0	0	0	3	.273	6	7	1	.929
Justice, rf	3	11	1	3	3	0	0	0	1	2	1	1	.273	4	0	0	1.000
Grissom, cf	4	19	2	5	7	0	1	0	0	1	0	4	.263	8	0	1	.889
Lemke, 2b	4	18	2	3	3	0	0	0	1	1	0	0	.167	13	16	0	1.000
Clontz, p	1	0	0	0	0	0	0	0	0	0	0	0	.000	0	0	0	.000
McMichael, p	3	0	0	0	0	0	0	0	0	0	0	0	.000	0	0	0	.000
Pena, p	3	0	0	0	0	0	0	0	0	0	0	0	.000	0	0	0	.000
Wohlers, p	4	0	0	0	0	0	0	0	0	0	0	0	.000	1	0	0	1.000
Glavine, p	1	1	0	0	0	0	0	0	0	1	0	0	.000	0	1	0	1.000
Mordecai, ph-ss	1	2	0	0	0	0	0	0	0	0	0	1	.000	0	0	0	.000
Smith, ph	2	2	0	0	0	0	0	0	0	0	0	0	.000	0	0	0	.000
Maddux, p	1	3	0	0	0	0	0	0	0	0	0	1	.000	1	1	0	1.000
Blauser, ss	1	4	0	0	0	0	0	0	0	1	0	2	.000	4	6	0	1.000
Klesko, lf-ph	3	7	0	0	0	0	0	0	0	3	2	4	.000	1	0	0	1.000
Totals	4	149	19	42	62	6	1	4	17	16	5	22	.282	117	54	3	.983

CINCINNATI REDS' BATTING AND FIELDING AVERAGES

Player, position	G	AB	R	H	TB	2B	3B	HR	RBI	BB	IBB	SO	Avg.	PO	A	E	Avg.
Harris, ph	2	2	0	2	2	0	0	0	1	0	0	0	1.000	0	0	0	.000
Taubensee, ph-c	1	2	0	1	1	0	0	0	0	0	0	0	.500	0	0	0	.000
Wells, p	1	2	0	1	1	0	0	0	0	0	0	0	.500	0	0	0	.000
Larkin, ss	4	18	1	7	11	2	1	0	0	1	0	1	.389	10	15	1	.962
Howard, ph-cf	3	8	0	2	3	1	0	0	1	2	0	1	.250	2	0	0	1.000
M. Lewis, 3b	2	4	0	1	1	0	0	0	0	1	0	1	.250	2	3	0	1.000
Santiago, c	4	13	0	3	3	0	0	0	0	2	0	3	.231	23	1	0	1.000
Boone, 2b	4	14	1	3	3	0	0	0	1	0	0	2	.214	9	13	0	1.000
Gant, lf	4	16	1	3	3	0	0	0	1	0	0	3	.188	9	0	0	1.000
Morris, 1b-ph	4	12	0	2	3	1	0	0	1	1	1	1	.167	27	3	0	1.000
Sanders, rf	4	16	0	2	2	0	0	0	0	2	1	10	.125	7	0	1	.875
Branson, 3b-ph	4	9	2	1	2	1	0	0	0	0	0	2	.111	1	3	0	1.000
Brantley, p	2	0	0	0	0	0	0	0	0	0	0	0	.000	2	0	0	1.000
Burba, p	2	0	0	0	0	0	0	0	0	0	0	0	.000	0	0	0	.000
Carrasco, p	1	0	0	0	0	0	0	0	0	0	0	0	.000	0	0	0	.000
Hernandez, p	1	0	0	0	0	0	0	0	0	0	0	0	.000	0	0	0	.000
Jackson, p	3	0	0	0	0	0	0	0	0	0	0	0	.000	0	1	0	1.000
Portugal, p	1	0	0	0	0	0	0	0	0	0	0	0	.000	0	0	0	.000
Anthony, ph	1	1	0	0	0	0	0	0	0	1	0	1	.000	0	0	0	.000
D. Lewis, cf-pr	2	1	0	0	0	0	0	0	0	0	0	0	.000	2	0	0	1.000
Smiley, p	1	1	0	0	0	0	0	0	0	0	0	0	.000	1	1	0	1.000
Duncan, ph-1b	1	3	0	0	0	0	0	0	1	0	0	1	.000	9	0	0	1.000
Schourek, p	2	5	0	0	0	0	0	0	0	0	0	4	.000	1	3	0	1.000
Walton, lf-cf	2	7	0	0	0	0	0	0	0	0	0	2	.000	6	0	0	1.000
Totals	4	134	5	28	35	5	1	0	4	12	2	31	.209	111	43	2	.987

ATLANTA BRAVES' PITCHING RECORDS

Pitcher	G	GS	CG	IP	H	R	ER	HR	BB	IBB	SO	HB	WP	W	L	Pct.	ERA
Avery	2	1	0	6	2	0	0	0	4	0	6	0	0	1	0	1.000	0.00
Pena	3	0	0	3	2	0	0	1	1	4	0	0	0	0	.000	0.00
McMichael	3	0	0	2 2/3	0	0	0	0	1	0	2	0	0	1	0	1.000	0.00
Clontz	1	0	0	0 1/3	1	0	0	0	0	0	0	0	0	0	0	.000	0.00
Maddux	1	1	0	8	7	1	1	0	2	0	4	1	1	1	0	1.000	1.13
Glavine	1	1	0	7	7	1	1	0	2	1	5	1	0	0	0	.000	1.29
Wohlers	4	0	0	5	2	1	1	0	0	0	8	0	0	1	0	1.000	1.80
Smoltz	1	1	0	7	7	2	2	0	2	0	2	0	0	0	0	.000	2.57
Totals	4	4	0	39	28	5	5	0	12	2	31	2	0	4	0	1.000	1.15

CINCINNATI REDS' PITCHING RECORDS

Pitcher	G	GS	CG	IP	H	R	ER	HR	BB	IBB	SO	HB	WP	W	L	Pct.	ERA
Burba	2	0	0	3 2/3	3	0	0	0	4	1	0	0	1	0	0	.000	0.00
Brantley	2	0	0	2 2/3	0	0	0	0	2	1	1	0	0	0	0	.000	0.00
Carrasco	1	0	0	1 1/3	1	0	0	0	0	0	3	0	0	0	0	.000	0.00
Schourek	2	2	0	14 1/3	14	2	2	0	3	0	13	0	1	0	1	.000	1.26
Smiley	1	1	0	5	5	2	2	0	0	0	1	0	0	0	0	.000	3.60
Wells	1	1	0	6	8	3	3	1	2	0	3	0	0	0	1	.000	4.50
Jackson	3	0	0	2 1/3	5	6	6	1	4	2	1	0	0	0	1	.000	23.14
Hernandez	1	0	0	0 2/3	3	2	2	1	0	0	0	0	0	0	0	.000	27.00
Portugal	1	0	0	1	3	4	4	1	1	1	0	0	1	0	1	.000	36.00
Totals	4	4	0	37	42	19	19	4	16	5	22	0	0	0	4	.000	4.62

SCORE BY INNINGS

Atlanta	1	0	1	1	0	3	7	0	1	4	1—19
Cincinnati	0	0	0	1	2	0	0	1	1	0	0— 5

MISCELLANEOUS STATISTICS

Sacrifice hits—Branson, Polonia.
Sacrifice flies—Howard.
Stolen bases—Branson, Harris, Jones, Larkin, Morris, Smoltz.
Caught stealing—Howard, Klesko, Larkin, Sanders.
Double plays—Belliard, Lemke and McGriff 2; Jones, Lemke and McGriff 2; Belliard and McGriff; Blauser and McGriff; Branson, Boone and Morris; Glavine, Blauser and McGriff; Larkin, Boone and Morris; Lemke, Blauser and McGriff; Schourek, Larkin and Duncan.
Left on bases—Atlanta 9, 8, 8, 11—36; Cincinnati 6, 9, 9, 4—28.
Hit by pitcher—By Maddux (Gant), by Glavine (Morris).
Passed balls—Taubensee.
Balks—Jackson.
Time of games—First game, 3:18; second game, 3:26; third game, 2:42; fourth game, 2:54.
Attendance—First game, 40,382; second game, 44,624; third game, 51,424; fourth game, 52,067.
Umpires—Runge, Quick, DeMuth, Davis, Marsh and Crawford.
Official scorers—Scott McGregor, Glenn Sample.

1995 REVIEW N.L. Championship Series

HIGHLIGHTS

ATLANTA 3, CLEVELAND 2

Why the Braves won: They sent the game's master pitcher, Greg Maddux, to the mound, and Maddux came through with a masterful effort. The performance was, in fact, *better* than that. Coming off a sensational season (19-2, 1.63 ERA) and en route to his fourth consecutive Cy Young Award, Maddux yielded only two singles to an Indians team loaded with offensive terrors, walked none, permitted four balls to be hit out of the infield, gave up no earned runs and made a grand total of 95 pitches. It wasn't perfection, but it will do until something better comes along.

Why the Indians lost: Kenny Lofton and his flying feet stirred up things offensively for Cleveland, but Lofton's teammates were overmatched against Maddux. Lofton reached on a first-inning error by Braves shortstop Rafael Belliard, stole second and third base, then scored on a groundout as the Indians quickly broke through against Maddux without benefit of a hit. With his team down 3-1 in the ninth inning, Lofton singled and, breaking with the pitch, sped around to third base on Omar Vizquel's soft grounder to the right side. When Atlanta first baseman Fred McGriff threw into left field while trying to make a play on Lofton at third, the Indians' center fielder dashed home. Try as he might, though, Lofton couldn't do it alone.

The turning points:

1. With runners on first and third and one out in Atlanta's seventh and the Braves having just broken a 1-1 tie on pinch-hitter Luis Polonia's forceout grounder, the Indians were caught flat-footed defensively by the light-hitting Belliard's squeeze bunt that increased the Braves' lead to 3-1. A one-run deficit against Maddux seemed a steep enough mountain for Cleveland to climb; a two-run deficit appeared virtually unscalable.

2. Indians starter Orel Hershiser, the postseason wonder and noted bulldog competitor, caught everyone by surprise by taking himself out of a 1-1 game after walking Atlanta's first two hitters in the seventh. Not that Hershiser could have extricated himself from the developing mess—the Braves went on to score two runs in that inning without managing a hit—but his willingness to leave the mound might have been an emotional blow for a young Cleveland team shy of postseason experience and leadership.

Notable: Lofton became the first American League player to steal two bases in one inning of a World Series game since Babe Ruth, of all people,

accomplished the feat in 1921. . . . Maddux's two-hitter marked the first time the Indians had been held to fewer than three hits in any game in 1995.

Quotable: Cleveland catcher Sandy Alomar said that while Maddux didn't have great velocity, "he's got great location. He throws strikes. He changes speeds. Location. Up. Down. Left. Right. He's got everything." McGriff on Maddux's *modus operandi:* "It was just bam-bam." . . . "When I looked around in the seventh inning and the score was tied, and I knew my (first-inning) error was responsible, I felt lousy," Belliard said. "I know I have to do the little things (laying down a crucial squeeze bunt, for example) to help us win."

BOX SCORE

SATURDAY, OCTOBER 21, AT ATLANTA

Cleveland	AB	R	H	RBI	PO	A
Lofton, cf	4	2	1	0	0	0
Vizquel, ss	4	0	0	0	2	5
Baerga, 2b	4	0	0	1	1	3
Belle, lf	3	0	0	0	0	0
Murray, 1b	3	0	0	0	9	0
Tavarez, p	0	0	0	0	0	2
Embree, p	0	0	0	0	0	0
Thome, 3b	3	0	1	0	0	1
Ramirez, rf	3	0	0	0	0	0
Alomar, c	3	0	0	0	9	0
Hershiser, p	2	0	0	0	0	2
Assenmacher, p	0	0	0	0	0	0
Sorrento, 1b	1	0	0	0	3	0
Totals	30	2	2	1	24	13

Atlanta	AB	R	H	RBI	PO	A
Grissom, cf	4	0	1	0	1	0
Lemke, 2b	3	0	1	0	0	8
Jones, 3b	4	0	0	0	1	2
McGriff, 1b	3	2	1	1	19	1
Justice, rf	1	1	0	0	1	0
Klesko, lf	2	0	0	0	0	0
‡Devereaux, ph-lf	0	0	0	0	0	0
O'Brien, c	2	0	0	0	4	1
§Polonia, ph	1	0	0	1	0	0
Lopez, c	0	0	0	0	0	0
Belliard, ss	2	0	0	1	0	3
Maddux, p	3	0	0	0	1	3
Totals	25	3	3	3	27	18

Cleveland	1 0 0	0 0 0	0 0 1—2
Atlanta	0 1 0	0 0 0	2 0 x—3

Cleveland	IP	H	R	ER	BB	SO
Hershiser (L)	*6	3	3	3	3	7
Assenmacher	†0	0	0	0	1	0
Tavarez	1⅓	0	0	0	1	0
Embree	⅔	0	0	0	0	2

Atlanta	IP	H	R	ER	BB	SO
Maddux (W)	9	2	2	0	0	4

*Pitched to two batters in seventh. †Pitched to one batter in seventh.

Bases on balls—Off Hershiser 3 (Justice 2, McGriff), off Assenmacher 1 (Devereaux), off Tavarez 1 (Lemke).

Strikeouts—By Hershiser 7 (Klesko 2, Grissom, Lemke, O'Brien, Maddux, Jones), by Embree 2 (Jones, McGriff), by Maddux 4 (Ramirez 2, Vizquel, Baerga).

‡Walked for Klesko in seventh. §Hit into force play for O'Brien in seventh. E—McGriff, Belliard. DP—Cleveland 1. LOB—Cleveland 1, Atlanta 4. HR—McGriff. SH—Belliard. SB—Lofton 2. T—2:37. A—51,876. U—Wendelstedt (N.L.), plate; McKean (A.L.), first; Froemming (N.L.), second; Hirschbeck (A.L.), third; Pulli (N.L.), left field; Brinkman (A.L.), right field.

PLAY BY PLAY

FIRST INNING

Cleveland—Lofton safe on shortstop's error. Vizquel struck out as Lofton stole second. Lofton stole third. Baerga grounded to short, Lofton scored. Belle grounded to short.

Atlanta—Grissom singled to right. Lemke grounded to second, Grissom went to second. Jones lined into a double play, shortstop to second baseman.

SECOND INNING

Cleveland—Murray grounded to the catcher. Thome grounded to first. Ramirez struck out.

Atlanta—McGriff homered to center. Justice grounded to short. Klesko struck out. O'Brien grounded to short.

THIRD INNING

Cleveland—Alomar grounded to second. Hershiser grounded to short. Lofton grounded to second.

Atlanta—Belliard grounded to the pitcher. Maddux grounded to third. Grissom struck out.

FOURTH INNING

Cleveland—Vizquel lined to center. Baerga grounded to the pitcher. Belle flied to right.

Atlanta—Lemke struck out. Jones grounded to second. McGriff grounded to the pitcher.

FIFTH INNING

Cleveland—Murray grounded to second. Thome singled to left. Ramirez struck out. Alomar grounded to second.

Atlanta—Justice walked. Klesko struck out. O'Brien struck out. Belliard grounded to second.

SIXTH INNING

Cleveland—Hershiser grounded to third. Lofton grounded to the pitcher. Vizquel grounded to second.

Atlanta—Maddux struck out. Grissom grounded to short. Lemke singled to center. Jones struck out.

SEVENTH INNING

Cleveland—Baerga struck out. Belle grounded to third. Murray grounded to the first baseman, who tossed to the pitcher covering first.

Atlanta—McGriff walked. Justice walked, McGriff went to second. Assenmacher now pitching. Devereaux, batting for Klesko, walked, advancing McGriff to third and Justice to second. Tavarez now pitching and Sorrento at first base. Polonia, batting for O'Brien, forced Devereaux at second, shortstop unassisted. McGriff scored and Justice went to third on the play. Belliard sacrificed to the pitcher. Justice scored and Polonia went to second on the play. Maddux grounded to the pitcher.

EIGHTH INNING

Cleveland—Devereaux now in left and Lopez catching. Thome grounded to second. Ramirez grounded to the pitcher. Alomar popped to first.

Atlanta—Grissom grounded to short. Lemke walked. Embree now pitching. Jones and McGriff struck out.

NINTH INNING

Cleveland—Sorrento grounded to second. Lofton singled to left. Vizquel grounded to second, Lofton went to third. Lofton then scored on the first baseman's throwing error. Baerga fouled to third.

GAME 2

HIGHLIGHTS

ATLANTA 4, CLEVELAND 3

Why the Braves won: The adage that good pitching stops good hitting— perhaps it should read *great* pitching stops *great* hitting—held up again. With Tom Glavine and three relievers limiting the Indians to six hits and two earned runs, Cleveland's monster lineup now had totals of eight hits (seven of them singles) and two earned runs in the first two games of the Series. Glavine wasn't as dominant as Greg Maddux in Game 1, but allowing three hits in six innings will win you a lot of games—including big games.

Why the Indians lost: Cleveland needed stand-out pitching to have a chance against the Braves' top-of-the-line staff—but veteran Dennis Martinez didn't supply it. Martinez, who last pitched in a World Series in 1979 (for Baltimore), was cuffed for eight hits and four runs in 5⅔ innings.

The turning points:

1. Javy Lopez's offense. The Atlanta catcher belted a two-run homer in the sixth off Martinez, breaking a 2-2 tie and positioning the Braves to seize a 2-0 lead in the Series.

2. Lopez's defense. After Cleveland cut the lead to 4-3 in the seventh, the Indians' Manny Ramirez became the potential tying run in the eighth after blooping a one-out single to center field. Lopez proceeded to pick off Ramirez.

Notable: Between Lopez's offensive and defensive heroics, Braves reliever Alejandro Pena came through in a sticky situation in the Indians' seventh. With one Cleveland run already in as a result of left fielder Mike Devereaux's two-base error and the Indians now trailing by one run, Pena entered the game with runners on third and first and two out—and induced slugger Albert Belle to foul out to Lopez. . . . The Indians had one last glimmer of hope in the ninth when, with two out, Omar Vizquel singled off Braves closer Mark Wohlers, then stole second base. But Wohlers got Carlos Baerga to pop out. . . . Cleveland's battery of Martinez, 40, and Tony Pena, 38, was the oldest in Series history.

Quotable: "They're just better pitchers than we've seen in a while, as a whole," Cleveland Manager Mike Hargrove said of Atlanta's rotation mainstays. "I'm not saying they're better than the pitchers in the American League. It's just that Greg Maddux and Tom Glavine are as good as we've seen in a long while." . . . Questioned about staying with Martinez when Lopez strode to the plate in the sixth, Hargrove said, "I didn't say Dennis stunk. I said he was struggling. There's a marked difference between the two. Dennis Martinez struggling is a lot better than a lot of people at the top of their game." . . . Glavine said he didn't have his best stuff, but his only real mistake was a second-inning gopher ball he served to Eddie Murray with a man aboard. "I certainly don't want to be the guy to characterize it as gutsy," Glavine said of his outing, "but, yeah, it probably was."

BOX SCORE

SUNDAY, OCTOBER 22, AT ATLANTA

Cleveland	AB	R	H	RBI	PO	A
Lofton, cf	5	1	1	0	1	0
Vizquel, ss	4	0	1	0	2	4
Baerga, 2b	4	0	0	0	2	5
Belle, lf	3	1	1	0	2	0
Murray, 1b	3	1	1	2	9	0
Ramirez, rf	4	0	2	0	4	0
Thome, 3b	3	0	0	0	1	1
T. Pena, c	3	0	0	0	3	0
‡Sorrento, ph	1	0	0	0	0	0
Alomar, c	0	0	0	0	0	0
Martinez, p	2	0	0	0	0	3
Embree, p	0	0	0	0	0	0
†Kirby, ph	1	0	0	0	0	0
Poole, p	0	0	0	0	0	0
Tavarez, p	0	0	0	0	0	0
§Amaro, ph	1	0	0	0	0	0
Totals	34	3	6	2	24	13

Atlanta	AB	R	H	RBI	PO	A
Grissom, cf	3	1	1	0	4	0
Lemke, 2b	3	1	1	0	1	2
Jones, 3b	3	0	2	1	2	3
McGriff, 1b	4	0	0	0	9	0
Justice, rf	3	1	2	1	3	0
Wohlers, p	0	0	0	0	0	0
Klesko, lf	3	0	0	0	1	0
Devereaux, lf-rf	1	0	0	0	0	0
Lopez, c	3	1	1	2	6	1
Belliard, ss	4	0	0	0	1	2
Glavine, p	1	0	0	0	0	0
*Smith, ph	1	0	1	0	0	0
McMichael, p	0	0	0	0	0	0
A. Pena, p	0	0	0	0	0	0
Polonia, lf	0	0	0	0	0	0
Totals	29	4	8	4	27	8

Cleveland	0	2	0	0	0	0	1	0	0—3
Atlanta	0	0	2	0	0	2	0	0	x—4

Cleveland	IP	H	R	ER	BB	SO
Martinez (L)	5²/₃	8	4	4	3	3
Embree	¹/₃	0	0	0	0	0
Poole	1	0	0	0	0	0
Tavarez	1	0	0	0	0	0

Atlanta	IP	H	R	ER	BB	SO
Glavine (W)	6	3	2	2	3	3
McMichael	²/₃	1	1	0	1	1
A. Pena	1	1	0	0	1	0
Wohlers (S)	1¹/₃	1	0	0	0	1

Bases on balls—Off Martinez 3 (Lemke, Justice, Glavine), off Glavine 3 (Murray, Vizquel, Belle), off McMichael 1 (Baerga), off A. Pena 1 (Thome).

Strikeouts—By Martinez 3 (Glavine, Klesko, Belliard), by Glavine 3 (Belle, Thome, Ramirez), by McMichael 1 (Kirby), by Wohlers 1 (Amaro).

*Singled for Glavine in sixth. †Struck out for Embree in seventh. ‡Flied out for T. Pena in eighth. §Struck out for Tavarez in ninth. E—Devereaux, Belle, Jones, Martinez. DP—Cleveland 2. LOB—Cleveland 9, Atlanta 7. 2B—Jones. HR—Lopez, Murray. SF—Jones. SB—Vizquel, Lofton 2. HBP—By Martinez (Grissom), by Tavarez (Lopez). WP—McMichael, Glavine. T—3:17. A—51,877. U—McKean (A.L.), plate; Froemming (N.L.), first; Hirschbeck (A.L.), second; Pulli (N.L.), third, Brinkman (A.L.), left field; Wendelstedt (N.L.), right field.

PLAY BY PLAY

FIRST INNING

Cleveland—Lofton grounded to short. Vizquel grounded to third. Baerga grounded to short.

Atlanta—Grissom flied to right. Lemke walked. Jones doubled to right, Lemke went to third. McGriff grounded to the pitcher. Justice walked. Klesko popped to third.

SECOND INNING

Cleveland—Belle singled to right. Murray homered to left, scoring Belle. Ramirez grounded to third. Thome grounded to second. Pena flied to center.

Atlanta—Lopez grounded to third. Belliard fouled to right. Glavine struck out.

THIRD INNING

Cleveland—Martinez lined to first. Lofton lined to second. Vizquel fouled to third.

Atlanta—Grissom was hit by a pitch. Lemke singled to center, Grissom went to second. Grissom went to third on the pitcher's error on a pickoff attempt. Jones hit a sacrifice fly to left, scoring Grissom. McGriff grounded to the pitcher, Lemke went to second. Justice singled to right, scoring Lemke. Klesko struck out.

FOURTH INNING

Cleveland—Baerga flied to left. Belle struck out. Murray walked. Ramirez singled to left, Murray went to second. Thome struck out.

Atlanta—Lopez flied to left. Belliard grounded to the pitcher. Glavine walked. Grissom forced Glavine at second, shortstop to second baseman.

FIFTH INNING

Cleveland—Pena lined to right. Martinez flied to right. Lofton reached on the third baseman's fielding error. Lofton stole second. Vizquel walked. Lofton went to third on a wild pitch. Baerga lined to right.

Atlanta—Lemke grounded to second. Jones singled to left. McGriff grounded into a double play, second baseman to shortstop to first baseman.

SIXTH INNING

Cleveland—Belle walked. Murray flied to center. Ramirez struck out. Thome forced Belle at second, shortstop unassisted.

Atlanta—Justice singled to left and went to second on the left fielder's error. Klesko grounded to second, Justice went to third. Lopez homered to center, scoring Lopez. Belliard struck out fouling off a bunt. Smith, batting for Glavine, singled to center. Grissom singled to right, Smith went to third. Embree now pitching. Lemke flied to center.

SEVENTH INNING

Cleveland—McMichael now pitching and Devereaux in left. Pena grounded to second. Kirby, batting for Embree, struck out. Lofton singled to right. Lofton stole second. Vizquel safe at second on the left fielder's fielding error, Lofton scored. Baerga walked. Vizquel went to third on a wild pitch. Pena now pitching. Belle fouled to the catcher.

Atlanta—Poole now pitching. Jones grounded to short. McGriff popped to short. Justice flied to right.

EIGHTH INNING

Cleveland—Murray flied to center. Ramirez singled to center. Ramirez was picked off first, catcher to first baseman. Thome walked.
Sorrento now batting for Pena. Wohlers now pitching, Devereaux in right and Polonia in left. Sorrento flied to center.

Atlanta—Tavarez now pitching and Alomar catching. Devereaux flied to right. Lopez was hit by a pitch. Belliard grounded into a double play, shortstop to second baseman to first baseman.

NINTH INNING

Cleveland—Amaro, batting for Tavarez, struck out. Lofton grounded to third. Vizquel singled to center. Vizquel stole second. Baerga popped to third.

HIGHLIGHTS

CLEVELAND 7, ATLANTA 6 (11 INNINGS)

Why the Indians won: With the pressure escalating—no team has come from a three games-to-zero deficit to win a World Series—Cleveland had a coolheaded old pro at the plate when it mattered most. With the game tied at 6 in the bottom of the 11th and runners on second and first, Eddie Murray strolled to the batter's box to face Braves reliever Alejandro Pena. Murray, a major leaguer since 1977 and a player who cracked the 3,000-hit barrier during the 1995 season, was having a miserable night against Atlanta starter John Smoltz and his successors. Hitless in five at-bats with three strikeouts, Murray didn't get down on himself; instead, the veteran designated hitter ripped a single to center field that scored pinch-runner Alvaro Espinoza, giving the Indians their first victory in a Series game in 47 years.

Why the Braves lost: Their beefed-up bullpen, hailed as the missing piece of Atlanta's championship puzzle (a mediocre relief corps took considerable heat for the Braves' Series failures in 1991 and 1992), faltered this time after the Braves had rallied for a 6-5 lead with three runs in the eighth. Mark Wohlers, who emerged as Atlanta's closer in '95, entered the game in the Indians' eighth and inherited a two-on, one-out predicament created by usually reliable setup man Greg McMichael. He promptly gave up a game-tying double to Sandy Alomar. And, three innings later, Pena yielded a leadoff double to Carlos Baerga (replaced by runner Espinoza), walked Albert Belle intentionally, then allowed Murray's game-deciding hit.

The turning points:

1. Just inserted into a 6-6 game (Cleveland once led 4-1), Indians first baseman Herbert Perry prevented Atlanta from inching ahead in the ninth when, with runners on second and first and two outs, he made a dazzling short-hop pickup of Chipper Jones' grounder down the line and outraced Jones to the bag.

2. While Atlanta's bullpen pitched well throughout most of the season, there's no question that driving a member of the Braves' elite rotation from the game would be a major breakthrough for Cleveland—and the Indians achieved just that when they routed Smoltz after the righthander was shelled for six hits and four runs in 2⅓ innings.

Notable: Kenny Lofton, whose basestealing and baserunning made the Braves jumpy in Games 1 and 2, was at his stir-it-up best. He went 3-for-3, reached base in all six of his trips to the plate (two singles, a double, two intentional walks and one walk) and stole his fifth base of the Series. . . . Cleveland relief ace Jose Mesa, who averaged almost exactly one inning of work per appearance

in the regular season, went three innings in this "must" contest and picked up the victory.

Quotable: "Jose worked his butt off out there," catcher Alomar said of his batterymate's overtime effort. . . . Indians Manager Mike Hargrove on Perry's ninth-inning fielding gem: "That was the play of the game. Herb is a good athlete, he has great hands, and exhibited all those traits on one play."

BOX SCORE

TUESDAY, OCTOBER 24, AT CLEVELAND

Atlanta	AB	R	H	RBI	PO	A
Grissom, cf	6	1	2	0	1	0
Polonia, lf	4	1	1	1	1	0
Jones, 3b	3	2	1	0	0	3
McGriff, 1b	5	1	3	2	14	0
Justice, rf	5	0	0	1	1	0
Klesko, dh	3	1	2	1	0	0
§Devereaux, ph-dh	2	0	1	1	0	0
Lopez, c	5	0	0	0	10	1
Lemke, 2b	5	0	2	0	3	7
Belliard, ss	2	0	0	0	0	0
‡Smith, ph	1	0	0	0	0	0
Mordecai, ss	1	0	0	0	0	3
Smoltz, p	0	0	0	0	0	0
Clontz, p	0	0	0	0	0	0
Mercker, p	0	0	0	0	0	0
McMichael, p	0	0	0	0	0	0
Wohlers, p	0	0	0	0	0	0
A. Pena, p	0	0	0	0	0	0
Totals	**42**	**6**	**12**	**6**	**30**	**14**

Cleveland	AB	R	H	RBI	PO	A
Lofton, cf	3	3	3	0	4	0
Vizquel, ss	6	2	2	1	3	6
Baerga, 2b	6	0	3	3	3	6
▲Espinoza, pr	0	1	0	0	0	0
Belle, lf	4	0	1	1	1	0
Murray, dh	6	0	1	1	0	0
Thome, 3b	4	0	0	0	1	1
Ramirez, rf	2	1	0	0	2	0
Sorrento, 1b	4	0	1	0	8	1
∞Kirby, pr	0	0	0	0	0	0
Perry, 1b	1	0	0	0	3	1
Alomar, c	5	0	1	1	7	0
Nagy, p	0	0	0	0	1	1
Assenmacher, p	0	0	0	0	0	0
Tavarez, p	0	0	0	0	0	0
Mesa, p	0	0	0	0	0	0
Totals	**41**	**7**	**12**	**7**	**33**	**16**

Atlanta	1 0 0	0 0 1	1 3 0	0 0—6
Cleveland	2 0 2	0 0 0	1 1 0	0 1—7

None out when winning run scored.

Atlanta	IP	H	R	ER	BB	SO
Smoltz	2⅓	6	4	4	2	4
Clontz	2⅓	1	0	0	0	1
Mercker	2	1	1	1	2	2
McMichael	⅔	1	1	1	1	1
Wohlers	2⅔	1	0	0	3	2
A. Pena (L)	†0	2	1	1	1	0

Cleveland	IP	H	R	ER	BB	SO
Nagy	*7	8	5	5	1	4
Assenmacher	⅓	0	1	1	1	0
Tavarez	⅔	1	0	0	0	0
Mesa (W)	3	3	0	0	1	3

*Pitched to two batters in eighth. †Pitched to three batters in 11th.
Bases on balls—Off Smoltz 2 (Ramirez, Thome), off Mercker 2 (Lofton, Belle), off McMichael 1 (Ramirez), off Wohlers 3 (Lofton 2, Ramirez), off A. Pena 1 (Belle), off Nagy 1 (Jones), off Assenmacher 1 (Jones), off Mesa 1 (Polonia).
Strikeouts—By Smoltz 4 (Thome, Sorrento, Alomar, Murray), by Clontz 1 (Sorrento), by Mercker 2 (Murray, Sorrento), by McMichael 1 (Murray), by Wohlers 2 (Vizquel, Perry), by Nagy 4 (Belliard, Grissom, McGriff, Polonia), by

1995 REVIEW *World Series*

Mesa 3 (Grissom, Devereaux, Mordecai).

‡Grounded out for Belliard in seventh. §Singled for Klesko in eighth. ∞Ran for Sorrento in eighth. ▲Ran for Baerga in 11th. E—Baerga, Belliard, Sorrento. DP—Atlanta 1, Cleveland 2. LOB—Atlanta 7, Cleveland 13. 2B—Baerga, Alomar, Grissom, Lofton, Jones. 3B—Vizquel. HR—Klesko, McGriff. SH—Mordecai. SB—Ramirez, McGriff, Polonia, Lofton. CS—Grissom, Lofton. T—4:09. A—43,584. U—Froemming (N.L.), plate; Hirschbeck (A.L.), first; Pulli (N.L.), second; Brinkman (A.L.), third; Wendelstedt (N.L.), left field; McKean (A.L.), right field.

PLAY BY PLAY

FIRST INNING

Atlanta—Grissom lined to center. Polonia grounded to second. Jones doubled to left. McGriff singled to right, scoring Jones. Justice popped to short.

Cleveland—Lofton singled to center. Vizquel tripled to right, scoring Lofton. Baerga grounded to first, scoring Vizquel. Belle grounded to third. Murray grounded to second.

SECOND INNING

Atlanta—Klesko grounded to short. Lopez flied to right. Lemke grounded to second.

Cleveland—Thome struck out. Ramirez walked. Sorrento and Alomar struck out.

THIRD INNING

Atlanta—Belliard and Grissom struck out. Polonia flied to left.

Cleveland—Lofton doubled to center. Vizquel singled to third, Lofton went to third. Baerga singled to left, scoring Lofton with Vizquel advancing to second. Belle singled to center, scoring Vizquel with Baerga advancing to second. Murray struck out. Thome walked, Baerga went to third and Belle to second. Clontz now pitching. Ramirez grounded into a double play, second baseman to first baseman.

FOURTH INNING

Atlanta—Jones walked. McGriff struck out. Justice forced Jones at second, third baseman to second baseman. Klesko singled to center, Justice went to second. Lopez forced Klesko at second, shortstop to second baseman.

Cleveland—Sorrento struck out . Alomar grounded to second. Lofton singled to center. Lofton was caught stealing, catcher to second baseman.

FIFTH INNING

Atlanta—Lemke grounded to second. Belliard grounded to short. Grissom singled to second and went to second on the first baseman's throwing error. Grissom was caught stealing, pitcher to the third baseman.

Cleveland—Vizquel flied to right. Baerga grounded to third. Belle reached on the shortstop's fielding error. Mercker now pitching. Murray struck out.

SIXTH INNING

Atlanta—Polonia struck out. Jones popped to center. McGriff homered to right. Justice grounded to short.

Cleveland—Thome flied to center. Ramirez grounded to third. Sorrento struck out.

SEVENTH INNING

Atlanta—Klesko homered to left-center. Lopez fouled to first. Lemke flied to center. Smith, batting for Belliard, grounded to the first baseman who tossed to the pitcher covering first.

Cleveland—Mordecai now at short. Alomar grounded to short. Lofton walked. Vizquel grounded to second, Lofton went to second. Lofton stole third. Baerga singled to short, scoring Lofton. Belle walked, Baerga went to second. McMichael now pitching. Murray struck out.

EIGHTH INNING

Atlanta—Grissom doubled to right. Polonia singled to right, scoring Grissom. Assenmacher now pitching. Polonia stole second. Jones walked. McGriff flied to center, Polonia went to third and Jones to second. Justice reached on the second baseman's fielding error, Polonia scored and Jones went to third. Tavarez now pitching. Devereaux, batting for Klesko, singled to left-center, scoring Jones as Justice went to second. Lopez grounded into a double play, second baseman to shortstop to first baseman.

Cleveland—Thome popped to second. Ramirez walked. Sorrento singled to right, Ramirez went to third. Kirby ran for Sorrento. Wohlers now pitching. Alomar doubled to right, scoring Ramirez as Kirby went to third. Lofton was intentionally walked. Vizquel struck out. Baerga grounded to second.

NINTH INNING

Atlanta—Mesa now pitching and Perry at first. Lemke singled to right. Mordecai sacrificed Lemke to second, first baseman to the second baseman covering first. Grissom struck out. Polonia walked. Jones grounded to first.

Cleveland—Belle grounded to short. Murray flied to left. Thome grounded to short.

10TH INNING

Atlanta—McGriff singled to left-center. Justice lined to right. Devereaux struck out. McGriff stole second. Lopez grounded to second.

Cleveland—Ramirez walked. Perry struck out. Ramirez stole second. Alomar grounded to second, Ramirez went to third. Lofton was intentionally walked. Vizquel grounded to second.

11TH INNING

Atlanta—Lemke singled to left-center. Mordecai struck out. Grissom grounded into a double play, second baseman to shortstop to first baseman.

Cleveland—Pena now pitching. Baerga doubled to center. Espinoza ran for Baerga. Belle was intentionally walked. Murray singled to center, scoring Espinoza scored as Belle went to second.

GAME 4

HIGHLIGHTS

ATLANTA 5, CLEVELAND 2

Why the Braves won: Even the No. 4 starter in Atlanta's rotation was too much for Cleveland. While Braves Manager Bobby Cox could have come back with premier pitcher Greg Maddux on three days' rest, he opted for Steve Avery. Lefthander Avery, who had compiled a 55-28 record from 1991-94 only to regress to a 7-13 mark in 1995, shut out the Indians on two hits over the first five innings and had a 4-1 cushion when Greg McMichael relieved him in the bottom of the seventh.

Why the Indians lost: As the tired-but-true baseball saying goes, Ken Hill pitched just well enough to lose. The righthander matched Avery zero for zero until the sixth, when Braves designated hitter Ryan Klesko homered to right with the bases empty. After Albert Belle answered with a solo homer off Avery in the Indians' half of the inning, Hill was nicked for two more runs in Atlanta's three-run seventh.

The turning points:

1. Cleveland lefthander Paul Assenmacher's inability to retire lefthanded-hitting David Justice with runners on second and third and two outs in the seventh. Atlanta had taken a 2-1 lead earlier in the inning on Luis Polonia's run-scoring double off Hill and sorely needed an insurance run or two. Assenmacher, taking over after Polonia's

hit, issued an intentional walk to Chipper Jones and, after both runners advanced on a passed ball, struck out lefthanded-hitting Fred McGriff. But Justice hit a 1-2 pitch up the middle for a single, scoring two runs and boosting Atlanta's edge to 4-1.

2. Atlanta lefthander Pedro Borbon's ability to put a quick end to the proceedings in the ninth. Summoned from the bullpen by Cox after closer Mark Wohlers gave up a home run (Manny Ramirez) and a double (Paul Sorrento) to the only two batters he faced, Borbon protected the Braves' 5-2 lead by striking out Jim Thome and Sandy Alomar and retiring Kenny Lofton on a drive to right.

Notable: In 90 previous World Series, only six teams wound up as champions after finding themselves in a three games-to-one hole—the Red Sox in 1903, the Pirates in 1925 and 1979, the Yankees in 1958, the Tigers in 1968 and the Royals in 1985. . . . Borbon's father, Pedro Sr., pitched in the 1972, 1975 and 1976 Series for the Reds. . . . Atlanta's Marquis Grissom, whose walk preceded Polonia's clutch double in the seventh, contributed three singles as well. . . . Cleveland's Lofton, who reached bases six times in Game 3, didn't reach base at all in a 0-for-5 performance in Game 4.

Quotable: "We've come back from tough situations, but this is the worst we've been in all year," Indians shortstop Omar Vizquel said of the Indians' 3-1 deficit and the fact his team would face Braves ace Greg Maddux in Game 5. "They've pretty much shut down the whole lineup. It's hard to get on first base, and after that it's hard to go beyond there." . . . Avery on Cox's decision to start him and give Maddux another day's rest: "I wanted to make it a good move for Bobby, because I knew he would get a lot of second-guessing." More from Avery: "I'm honored to be a part of this rotation. I think, somewhere down the road, it's going to be considered one of the best ever."

BOX SCORE

WEDNESDAY, OCTOBER 25, AT CLEVELAND

Atlanta	AB	R	H	RBI	PO	A
Grissom, cf	4	1	3	0	1	0
Polonia, lf	4	1	2	1	2	0
Devereaux, lf	0	0	0	0	0	0
Jones, 3b	4	1	0	0	0	4
McGriff, 1b	3	1	1	0	11	0
Justice, rf	5	0	1	2	4	0
Klesko, dh	3	1	1	1	0	0
‡Mordecai, ph-dh	1	0	0	0	0	0
Lopez, c	5	0	2	1	5	1
Lemke, 2b	5	0	1	0	4	3
Belliard, ss	3	0	0	0	0	4
Avery, p	0	0	0	0	0	0
McMichael, p	0	0	0	0	0	1
Wohlers, p	0	0	0	0	0	0
Borbon, p	0	0	0	0	0	0
Totals	37	5	11	5	27	13

Cleveland	AB	R	H	RBI	PO	A
Lofton, cf	5	0	0	0	6	0
Vizquel, ss	3	0	0	0	1	2
Baerga, 2b	4	0	1	0	3	1
Belle, lf	3	1	1	1	3	0
Murray, dh	2	0	0	0	0	0
Ramirez, rf	3	1	1	1	1	0
Perry, 1b	3	0	0	0	6	1
§Sorrento, ph	1	0	1	0	0	0
Espinoza, 3b	2	0	1	0	1	1
†Thome, ph-3b	2	0	1	0	1	0
Alomar, c	4	0	0	0	4	0
Hill, p	0	0	0	0	1	2
Assenmacher, p	0	0	0	0	0	0
Tavarez, p	0	0	0	0	0	0
Embree, p	0	0	0	0	0	0
Totals	32	2	6	2	27	7

Atlanta	0	0	0	0	0	1	3	0	1—5
Cleveland	0	0	0	0	0	1	0	0	1—2

Atlanta	IP	H	R	ER	BB	SO
Avery (W)	6	3	1	1	5	3
McMichael	2	1	0	0	0	0
Wohlers	*0	2	1	1	0	0
Borbon (S)	1	0	0	0	0	2

Cleveland	IP	H	R	ER	BB	SO
Hill (L)	6 1/3	6	3	3	4	1
Assenmacher	2/3	1	1	0	1	2
Tavarez	2/3	2	0	0	1	1
Embree	1 1/3	2	1	1	0	0

*Pitched to two batters in ninth.
Bases on balls—Off Avery 5 (Murray 2, Belle, Vizquel, Ramirez), off Hill 4 (McGriff 2, Klesko, Grissom), off Assenmacher 1 (Jones), off Tavarez 1 (Devereaux).
Strikeouts—By Avery 3 (Lofton, Belle, Perry), by Borbon 2 (Thome, Alomar), by Hill 1 (Belliard), by Assenmacher 2 (McGriff, Klesko), by Tavarez 1 (Lopez).
†Doubled for Espinoza in seventh. ‡Flied out for Klesko in ninth. §Doubled for Perry in ninth. E—Lemke. DP—Atlanta 1. LOB—Atlanta 12, Cleveland 8. 2B—Sorrento, McGriff, Thome, Polonia, Lopez 2. HR—Ramirez, Belle, Klesko. SH—Belliard. SB—Grissom 2. CS—Espinoza. Balk—Avery. PB—Alomar. T—3:14. A—43,578. U—Hirschbeck (A.L.), plate; Pulli (N.L.), first; Brinkman (A.L.), second; Wendelstedt (N.L.), third; McKean (A.L.), left field; Froemming (N.L.), right field.

PLAY BY PLAY

FIRST INNING

Atlanta—Grissom singled to center. Grissom stole second. Polonia popped to short. Jones flied to center, Grissom went to third. McGriff walked.
Justice forced McGriff at second, shortstop to the second baseman.
Cleveland—Lofton lined to right. Vizquel lined to second. Baerga singled to center. Belle walked, Baerga went to second. Murray forced Belle at second, third baseman to the second baseman.

SECOND INNING

Atlanta—Klesko walked. Lopez forced Klesko at second, third baseman to the second baseman. Lemke flied to left. Belliard grounded to the pitcher.
Cleveland—Ramirez grounded to short. Perry lined to left Polonia. Espinoza singled to right. Alomar forced Espinoza at second, shortstop to the second baseman.

THIRD INNING

Atlanta—Grissom singled to center. Polonia grounded to short, Grissom went to second. Jones grounded to the first baseman, who tossed to the pitcher covering first as Grissom went to third. McGriff walked. Justice grounded to first.
Cleveland—Lofton struck out. Vizquel grounded to third. Baerga lined to right.

FOURTH INNING

Atlanta—Klesko fouled to third. Lopez doubled to right. Lemke grounded to second, Lopez went to third. Belliard lined to second.
Cleveland—Belle struck out. Murray walked. Ramirez flied to center. Perry flied to left.

FIFTH INNING

Atlanta—Grissom flied to center. Polonia singled to center. Jones grounded to pitcher, Polonia went to second. McGriff flied to center.

Cleveland—Espinoza reached on the second baseman's fielding error. Espinoza was caught stealing, catcher to the second baseman to the first baseman. Alomar flied to right. Lofton grounded to short.

SIXTH INNING

Atlanta—Justice flied to center. Klesko homered to right. Lopez flied to center. Lemke flied to center.

Cleveland—Vizquel walked. Baerga grounded into a double play, third baseman to second baseman to first baseman. Belle homered to right. Murray walked. Murray went to second on a balk. Ramirez was intentionally walked. Perry struck out.

SEVENTH INNING

Atlanta—Belliard struck out. Grissom walked. Polonia doubled to right-center, scoring Grissom. Assenmacher now pitching. Jones was intentionally walked. Polonia went to third and Jones to second on a passed ball. McGriff struck out. Justice singled to center, scoring Polonia and Jones. Klesko struck out.

Cleveland—McMichael now pitching and Devereaux in left. Thome, batting for Espinoza, doubled to left. Alomar grounded to

second, Thome went to third. Lofton grounded to first. Vizquel grounded to third.

EIGHTH INNING

Atlanta—Tavarez now pitching and Thome at third. Lopez struck out. Lemke singled to left. Belliard sacrificed Lemke to second, first baseman unassisted. Grissom singled to third, Lemke went to third. Grissom stole second. Devereaux walked. Embree now pitching. Jones flied to right.

Cleveland—Baerga grounded to first. Belle grounded to the pitcher. Murray grounded to short.

NINTH INNING

Atlanta—McGriff doubled to left. Justice fouled to third. Mordecai, batting for Klesko, lined to left. Lopez doubled to left, scoring McGriff. Lemke flied to left.

Cleveland—Wohlers now pitching. Ramirez homered home run to left-center. Sorrento, batting for Perry, doubled to left. Borbon now pitching. Thome and Alomar struck out. Lofton lined to right.

GAME 5

HIGHLIGHTS

CLEVELAND 5, ATLANTA 4

Why the Indians won: Fully aware of the task at hand ("I've faced more pleasing prospects," Manager Mike Hargrove said) as they went against the best pitcher in baseball, Greg Maddux, the Indians never flinched. Instead, they took the offensive. Omar Vizquel, Cleveland's second batter of the game, drew a walk and, one out later, cleanup hitter Albert Belle cleaned up with a home run into the bullpen in right field. Before even an inning had been played, Maddux—coming off that splendid two-hitter in Game 1—had been exposed as a mere mortal.

Why the Braves lost: Cleveland righthander Orel Hershiser exhibited his old postseason magic. With his team on the brink of being ousted, he once again stepped to the fore and allowed only five hits and one earned run in eight innings.

The turning points:

1. With the game tied at 2 and Cleveland runners on first and third in the sixth inning, Maddux got careless with a two-out, 1-and-2 pitch to Jim Thome and the Indians' third baseman stroked it to center for an RBI single. Manny Ramirez followed with another run-scoring single.

2. With the potential tying run at the plate for Atlanta in the eighth and Cleveland ahead 4-2, Hershiser made a backhanded stab of Marquis Grissom's wicked liner and doubled Mike Mordecai off first base.

Notable: Atlanta's last nine defeats in World Series play—dating to 1991—were by one run. . . . Eddie Murray took none too kindly to an up-

and-in delivery from Maddux two pitches after Belle's first-inning homer. After starting toward the mound, Murray was intercepted by plate umpire Frank Pulli. After both benches emptied, order quickly was restored . . . . Thome belted a solo homer in the eighth, giving Cleveland a 5-2 lead. The blow, which at the time seemed to be mere icing on the cake, turned into a game-decider when Atlanta's Ryan Klesko slammed a two-run homer off Indians stopper Jose Mesa in the ninth. It was Klesko's third homer in three games.

Quotable: "Our guys really concentrated on getting him (Maddux)," Indians batting instructor Charlie Manuel said. "We felt like we wanted to get some swings on him. I thought a lot of it came from the second look (at Maddux in this World Series). Our players talked a lot about it and stayed focused. They were really determined." . . . Sandy Alomar concurred with Manuel. "He (threw) the same stuff as in Game 1," the Indians' catcher said, "but we made good adjustments." Such as? "We tried to cover the plate a little bit better than the last time," Alomar explained. "Everyone had been standing so far away from the plate that Maddux was hitting the outside corner. Tonight, we crowded the plate and forced him to pitch inside." . . . Hershiser called his crucial eighth-inning grab of Grissom's smash a matter of "self-defense. I was trying to protect myself." . . . Cleveland's Kenny Lofton said Maddux's high-and-tight pitch to Murray—while perhaps serving as a message of sorts from the pitcher—may have backfired. "It charged guys up because Maddux has great control," Lofton said. "He can pinpoint his pitches. For it to come that far up and in, we thought it was on purpose."

BOX SCORE

THURSDAY, OCTOBER 26, AT CLEVELAND

Atlanta	AB	R	H	RBI	PO	A
Grissom, cf	4	0	1	1	1	0
Polonia, lf	4	1	1	1	0	0
Jones, 3b	4	0	1	0	2	0
McGriff, 1b	4	1	1	0	10	0
Justice, rf	4	0	0	0	5	0
Klesko, dh	4	2	2	2	0	0
Lemke, 2b	4	0	0	0	0	4
O'Brien, c	1	0	0	0	3	1
†Lopez, ph-c	1	0	0	0	2	0
Belliard, ss	1	0	0	0	0	1
*Smith, ph	0	0	0	0	0	0
Mordecai, ss	1	0	1	0	0	3
Maddux, p	0	0	0	0	1	1
Clontz, p	0	0	0	0	0	0
Totals	32	4	7	4	24	10

Cleveland	AB	R	H	RBI	PO	A
Lofton, cf	4	0	0	0	0	0
Vizquel, ss	3	1	1	0	1	4
Baerga, 2b	4	1	1	0	2	4
Belle, lf	3	2	1	2	1	0
Murray, dh	3	0	0	0	0	0
Thome, 3b	4	1	2	2	0	0
Ramirez, rf	3	0	1	1	1	0
Perry, 1b	1	0	0	0	4	0
Sorrento, 1b	3	0	0	0	8	1
Kirby, rf	0	0	0	0	1	0
Alomar, c	3	0	2	0	8	0
Hershiser, p	0	0	0	0	1	5
Mesa, p	0	0	0	0	0	0
Totals	31	5	8	5	27	14

Atlanta	0	0	0		1	1	0		0	0	2—4
Cleveland	2	0	0		0	0	2		0	1	x—5

Atlanta	IP	H	R	ER	BB	SO
Maddux (L)	7	7	4	4	3	4
Clontz	1	1	1	1	0	1

Cleveland	IP	H	R	ER	BB	SO
Hershiser (W)	8	5	2	1	1	6
Mesa (S)	1	2	2	2	0	1

Bases on balls—Off Maddux 3 (Vizquel, Murray, Belle), off Hershiser 1 (Smith).

Strikeouts—By Maddux 4 (Ramirez, Sorrento, Belle, Vizquel), by Clontz 1 (Belle), by Hershiser 6 (McGriff 2, Justice, Belliard, Jones, Polonia), by Mesa 1 (Lemke).

*Was walked intentionally for Belliard in fifth. †Grounded out for O'Brien in seventh. E—Hershiser. DP—Cleveland 2. LOB—Atlanta 3, Cleveland 5. 2B—McGriff, Baerga, Alomar, Jones, Belle. HR—Klesko, Thome, Polonia, Belle. SH—O'Brien. T—2:33. A—43,595. U—Pulli (N.L.), plate; Brinkman (A.L.), first; Wendelstedt (N.L.), second; McKean (A.L.), third; Froemming (N.L.), left field; Hirschbeck (A.L.), right field.

PLAY BY PLAY

FIRST INNING

Atlanta—Grissom and Polonia grounded to the pitcher. Jones doubled to left. McGriff struck out .

Cleveland—Lofton popped to right. Vizquel walked. Baerga grounded to second, Vizquel went to second. Belle homered to right, scoring Vizquel. Murray walked. Murray was picked off first, catcher to the first baseman.

SECOND INNING

Atlanta—Justice struck out. Klesko grounded to second. Lemke popped to short.

Cleveland—Thome grounded to the pitcher. Ramirez and Sorrento struck out.

THIRD INNING

Atlanta—O'Brien grounded to short. Belliard struck out. Grissom flied to right.

Cleveland—Alomar grounded to short. Lofton flied to right. Vizquel singled to center. Baerga grounded to second.

FOURTH INNING

Atlanta—Polonia homered to right. Jones grounded to short. McGriff struck out. Justice grounded to the pitcher.

Cleveland—Belle struck out. Murray lined to the pitcher. Thome popped to third.

FIFTH INNING

Atlanta—Klesko singled to right. Lemke reached on a fielder's choice and a throwing error by the pitcher, Klesko went to second. O'Brien sacrificed Klesko to third and Lemke to second, first baseman to second baseman covering first. Smith, batting for Belliard, was intentionally walked. Grissom singled to the pitcher, scoring Klesko as Lemke went to third and Smith to second. Polonia grounded into a double play, shortstop to second baseman to first baseman.

Cleveland—Mordecai now at short. Ramirez grounded to short. Sorrento flied to right. Alomar doubled to left-center. Lofton flied to right.

SIXTH INNING

Atlanta—Jones struck out. McGriff grounded to the pitcher. Justice flied to left.

Cleveland—Vizquel grounded to short. Baerga doubled to left. Belle was intentionally walked. Murray flied to right, Baerga went to third. Thome singled past second, scoring Baerga and advancing Belle to third. Ramirez single past second, scoring Belle and advancing Thome to second. Sorrento popped to third.

SEVENTH INNING

Atlanta—Perry now at first and Kirby in right. Klesko grounded to short. Lemke grounded to second. Lopez, batting for O'Brien, grounded to the catcher.

Cleveland—Lopez now catching. Alomar singled to right. Lofton lined out to center. Vizquel struck out. Baerga grounded to second.

EIGHTH INNING

Atlanta—Mordecai singled to left. Grissom lined into a double play, pitcher to first baseman. Polonia struck out.

Cleveland—Clontz now pitching. Belle struck out. Murray grounded to second. Thome homered to center. Perry grounded to short.

NINTH INNING

Atlanta—Mesa now pitching.Jones flied to right. McGriff doubled to right. Justice grounded to second, McGriff went to third. Klesko homered to right, scoring McGriff. Lemke struck out.

HIGHLIGHTS

ATLANTA 1, CLEVELAND 0

Why the Braves won: They simply may have been too good *not* to win. Having lost in the 1991 and 1992 World Series and in the 1993 N.L. Championship Series, the 1990s Braves seemed in danger of being labeled "the best team never to win a World Series." But, at last, their early-'90s nucleus—blended with some key acquisitions and some highly skilled young talent—couldn't be denied.

Why the Indians lost: They seemed to be about where the Braves were in '92—a key player or two (in Cleveland's case, maybe two pitchers) short of having a championship team. In Game 6, Cleveland entrusted Dennis Martinez, 40, with the job of keeping the Indians alive. In Game 5, the task had been up to Orel Hershiser, 37. While

Hershiser won, Martinez lasted only 4⅔ innings—he gave up four hits and five walks and was often in trouble—despite being locked in a 0-0 tie.

The turning points:

1. When Tom Glavine, a member of the Braves since their sorry days of the late 1980s but overshadowed by Greg Maddux since 1993, took the mound as Atlanta's starter. Having experienced the emotional depths as a Braves pitcher (he was 7-17 for a 1988 Atlanta team that finished 54-106), he was determined to soar to the heights. He did just that, allowing one hit (Tony Pena's soft single to lead off the sixth) in eight innings.

2. When David Justice put his money where his mouth was in the sixth inning. Having ripped Atlanta fans the day before as being front-runners and nonchalant, Justice got the fans out of their seats when he rocketed a Jim Poole pitch into the right-field stands for what proved to be the only run of the game.

Notable: Kenny Lofton, whose hitting and basestealing contributed mightily to Cleveland's offense in the first three games, went 0-for-13 in the last three. Lofton did steal second in the sixth inning—Glavine had caught him off first but the Cleveland speedster made it safely to second—but Omar Vizquel fouled out to end the inning. . . . The Braves' triumph gave Atlanta its first championship in any major league sport. It was the third World Series crown overall for the Braves, who won the fall classic as a Boston team in 1914 and as a Milwaukee club in 1957.

Quotable: "I'm not saying that Greg Maddux isn't the best pitcher in baseball," Glavine said, "but I feel I can hold my own against any team." Incurring the wrath of many fans for his high-profile role in baseball's labor negotiations, Glavine said that "if in the end people like me now that haven't liked me all year, that's great. That's their choice, but I'm out there pitching because I'm proud of what I do. I'm proud of what this organization has done. I know how much they wanted to win, how much I wanted to win." . . . As for giving way to Mark Wohlers to start the ninth, Glavine said: "It was really hard to fight my emotions and keep my ego in check. You really want to be out there at the end, jumping around with everybody." . . . "I just wanted our fans to prove me wrong," said Justice, alluding to his tirade against the Atlanta faithful. "They were the biggest factor tonight. They were awesome."

BOX SCORE

SATURDAY, OCTOBER 28, AT ATLANTA

Cleveland	AB	R	H	RBI	PO	A
Lofton, cf	4	0	0	0	1	0
Vizquel, ss	3	0	0	0	3	1
‡Sorrento, ph	1	0	0	0	0	0
Baerga, 2b	4	0	0	0	4	5
Belle, lf	1	0	0	0	3	0
Murray, 1b	2	0	0	0	9	0
Ramirez, rf	3	0	0	0	0	0
Embree, p	0	0	0	0	0	1
Tavarez, p	0	0	0	0	0	0
Assenmacher, p	0	0	0	0	0	0
Thome, 3b	3	0	0	0	0	2
T. Pena, c	3	0	1	0	4	1
Martinez, p	1	0	0	0	0	0
Poole, p	1	0	0	0	0	0
Hill, p	0	0	0	0	0	0
Amaro, rf	1	0	0	0	0	0
Totals	27	0	1	0	24	10

Atlanta	AB	R	H	RBI	PO	A
Grissom, cf	4	0	1	0	5	0
Lemke, 2b	2	0	1	0	2	0
Jones, 3b	3	0	2	0	1	0
McGriff, 1b	4	0	0	0	5	1
Justice, rf	2	1	2	1	2	0
Klesko, lf	1	0	0	0	0	0
Devereaux, lf	1	0	0	0	0	0
Lopez, c	3	0	0	0	9	1
Belliard, ss	4	0	0	0	2	1
Glavine, p	3	0	0	0	1	3
†Polonia, ph	1	0	0	0	0	0
Wohlers, p	0	0	0	0	0	0
Totals	28	1	6	1	27	6

Cleveland	0	0	0	0	0	0	0	0	0—0
Atlanta	0	0	0	0	0	1	0	0	x—1

Cleveland	IP	H	R	ER	BB	SO
Martinez	4⅔	4	0	0	5	2
Poole (L)	1⅓	1	1	1	0	1
Hill	*0	1	0	0	0	0
Embree	1	0	0	0	2	0
Tavarez	⅔	0	0	0	0	0
Assenmacher	⅓	0	0	0	0	1

Atlanta	IP	H	R	ER	BB	SO
Glavine (W)	8	1	0	0	3	8
Wohlers (S)	1	0	0	0	0	0

*Pitched to one batter in seventh.

Bases on balls—Off Martinez 5 (Klesko 2, Justice, Lopez, Lemke), off Embree 2 (Jones, Justice), off Glavine 3 (Belle 2, Murray).

Strikeouts—By Martinez 2 (McGriff, Glavine), by Poole 1 (McGriff), by Assenmacher 1 (Polonia), by Glavine 8 (Vizquel 2, Thome 2, Murray, Ramirez, Martinez, Belle).

†Struck out for Glavine in eighth. ‡Flied out for Vizquel in ninth. E—Thome. DP—Cleveland 1. LOB—Cleveland 3, Atlanta 11. 2B—Justice. HR—Justice. SH—Lemke. SB—Grissom, Lofton. CS—Belle, Lemke. T—3:02. A—51,875. U—Brinkman (A.L.), plate; Wendelstedt (N.L.), first; McKean (A.L.), second; Froemming (N.L.), third; Hirschbeck (A.L.), left field; Pulli (N.L.), right field.

PLAY BY PLAY

FIRST INNING

Cleveland—Lofton flied to right. Vizquel struck out. Baerga grounded to the pitcher.

Atlanta—Grissom lined to first. Lemke singled to left. Lemke was caught stealing, catcher to shortstop. Jones singled to left. McGriff struck out.

SECOND INNING

Cleveland—Belle walked. Belle was caught stealing, catcher to second baseman. Murray and Ramirez struck out.

Atlanta—Justice and Klesko walked. Lopez popped to short. Belliard grounded into a double play, shortstop to second baseman to first baseman.

THIRD INNING

Cleveland—Thome struck out. Pena grounded to the pitcher. Martinez struck out.

Atlanta—Glavine grounded to third. Grissom fouled to first. Lemke grounded to second.

FOURTH INNING

Cleveland—Lofton grounded to first. Vizquel struck out. Baerga flied to center.

Atlanta—Jones and McGriff grounded to second. Justice doubled to center. Klesko was intentionally walked. Lopez walked, Justice went to third and Klesko to second. Belliard flied to center.

FIFTH INNING

Cleveland—Belle walked. Murray fouled to the catcher. Ramirez forced Belle at second, shortstop to second baseman. Thome struck out.

Atlanta—Glavine struck out. Grissom popped to second. Lemke walked. Jones singled to second, Lemke went to second. Poole now pitching. McGriff struck out.

SIXTH INNING

Cleveland—Pena singled to center. Poole fouled to first. Lofton forced Pena at second, pitcher to shortstop. Lofton stole second. Vizquel fouled to first.

Atlanta—Justice homered to right. Klesko grounded to second. Lopez grounded to third. Belliard safe on an error by the third baseman. Glavine lined to short.

SEVENTH INNING

Cleveland—Devereaux now in left field. Baerga lined to third. Belle struck out. Murray walked. Ramirez flied to center.

Atlanta—Hill now pitching. Grissom singled to left. Embree now pitching and Amaro in right. Lemke sacrificed Grissom to second, pitcher to the second baseman covering first. Jones was intentionally walked. McGriff flied to left. Grissom stole third. Justice walked, Jones went to second. Devereaux popped to second.

EIGHTH INNING

Cleveland—Thome flied to center. Pena flied to right. Amaro grounded to the first baseman, who tossed to the pitcher covering first.

Atlanta—Tavarez now pitching. Lopez flied to left. Belliard lined to left. Polonia now batting for Glavine. Assenmacher now pitching. Polonia struck out.

NINTH INNING

Cleveland—Wohlers now pitching. Lofton fouled to short. Sorrento, batting for Vizquel, flied to center. Baerga flied to center.

STATISTICS

ATLANTA BRAVES' BATTING AND FIELDING AVERAGES

Player, position	G	AB	R	H	TB	2B	3B	HR	RBI	BB	IBB	SO	Avg.	PO	A	E	Avg.
Smith, ph	2	2	0	1	1	0	0	0	0	1	1	0	.500	0	0	0	.000
Grissom, cf	6	25	3	9	10	1	0	0	1	1	0	3	.360	13	0	0	1.000
Mordecai, ss-dh	3	3	0	1	1	0	0	0	0	0	0	1	.333	0	6	0	1.000
Klesko, lf-dh	6	16	4	5	14	0	0	3	4	3	1	4	.313	1	0	0	1.000
Jones, 3b	6	21	3	6	9	3	0	0	1	4	2	3	.286	6	12	1	.947
Polonia, ph-lf	4	14	3	4	8	1	0	1	4	1	0	3	.286	3	0	0	1.000
Lemke, 2b	6	22	1	6	6	0	0	0	0	3	0	2	.273	10	24	1	.971
McGriff, 1b	6	23	5	6	14	2	0	2	3	3	0	7	.261	68	2	1	.986
Justice, rf	6	20	3	5	9	1	0	1	5	5	0	1	.250	16	0	0	1.000
Devereaux, lf-ph-rf-dh	5	4	0	1	1	0	0	0	1	2	0	1	.250	0	0	1	.000
Lopez, c-ph	6	17	1	3	8	2	0	1	3	1	0	1	.176	32	4	0	1.000
Avery, p	1	0	0	0	0	0	0	0	0	0	0	0	.000	0	0	0	.000
Borbon, p	1	0	0	0	0	0	0	0	0	0	0	0	.000	0	0	0	.000
Clontz, p	2	0	0	0	0	0	0	0	0	0	0	0	.000	0	0	0	.000
McMichael, p	3	0	0	0	0	0	0	0	0	0	0	0	.000	0	1	0	1.000
Mercker, p	1	0	0	0	0	0	0	0	0	0	0	0	.000	0	0	0	.000
Pena, p	2	0	0	0	0	0	0	0	0	0	0	0	.000	0	0	0	.000
Smoltz, p	1	0	0	0	0	0	0	0	0	0	0	0	.000	0	0	0	.000
Wohlers, p	4	0	0	0	0	0	0	0	0	0	0	0	.000	0	0	0	.000
Maddux, p	2	3	0	0	0	0	0	0	0	0	0	1	.000	2	4	0	1.000
O'Brien, c	2	3	0	0	0	0	0	0	0	0	0	1	.000	7	2	0	1.000
Glavine, p	2	4	0	0	0	0	0	0	0	1	0	2	.000	1	3	0	1.000
Belliard, ss	6	16	0	0	0	0	0	0	1	0	0	4	.000	3	11	2	.875
Totals	6	193	23	47	81	10	0	8	23	25	4	34	.244	162	69	6	.975

CLEVELAND INDIANS' BATTING AND FIELDING AVERAGES

Player, position	G	AB	R	H	TB	2B	3B	HR	RBI	BB	IBB	SO	Avg.	PO	A	E	Avg.
Espinoza, pr-3b	1	2	1	1	1	0	0	0	0	0	0	0	.500	1	1	0	1.000
Belle, lf	6	17	4	4	10	0	0	2	4	7	2	5	.235	10	0	1	.909
Ramirez, rf	6	18	2	4	7	0	0	1	2	4	1	5	.222	8	0	0	1.000
Thome, 3b-ph	6	19	1	4	8	1	0	1	2	2	0	5	.211	3	5	1	.889
Lofton, cf	6	25	6	5	6	1	0	0	0	3	2	1	.200	12	0	0	1.000
Alomar, c	5	15	0	3	5	2	0	0	1	0	0	2	.200	28	0	0	1.000
Baerga, 2b	6	26	1	5	7	2	0	0	4	1	0	1	.192	15	24	1	.975
Sorrento, 1b-ph	3	11	0	2	3	1	0	0	0	0	0	4	.182	19	2	1	.955
Vizquel, ss	6	23	3	4	6	0	0	1	1	3	0	5	.174	12	22	0	1.000
Pena, c	2	6	0	1	1	0	0	0	0	0	0	0	.167	7	1	0	1.000
Murray, 1b-dh	6	19	1	2	5	0	0	1	3	5	0	4	.105	27	0	0	1.000
Assenmacher, p	4	0	0	0	0	0	0	0	0	0	0	0	.000	0	0	0	.000
Embree, p	4	0	0	0	0	0	0	0	0	0	0	0	.000	0	1	0	1.000
Hill, p	2	0	0	0	0	0	0	0	0	0	0	0	.000	1	2	0	1.000
Mesa, p	2	0	0	0	0	0	0	0	0	0	0	0	.000	0	0	0	.000
Nagy, p	1	0	0	0	0	0	0	0	0	0	0	0	.000	1	1	0	1.000

Player, position	G	AB	R	H	TB	2B	3B	HR	RBI	BB	IBB	SO	Avg.	PO	A	E	Avg.
							BATTING								FIELDING		
Tavarez, p	5	0	0	0	0	0	0	0	0	0	0	0	.000	0	2	0	1.000
Kirby, ph-pr-rf	1	1	0	0	0	0	0	0	0	0	0	1	.000	1	0	0	1.000
Poole, p	2	1	0	0	0	0	0	0	0	0	0	0	.000	0	0	0	.000
Amaro, ph-rf	1	2	0	0	0	0	0	0	0	0	0	1	.000	0	0	0	.000
Hershiser, p	2	2	0	0	0	0	0	0	0	0	0	0	.000	1	7	1	.889
Martinez, p	2	3	0	0	0	0	0	0	0	0	0	1	.000	0	3	1	.750
Perry, 1b	3	5	0	0	0	0	0	0	0	0	0	2	.000	13	2	0	1.000
Totals	6	195	19	35	59	7	1	5	17	25	5	37	.179	159	73	6	.975

ATLANTA BRAVES' PITCHING RECORDS

Pitcher	G	GS	CG	IP	H	R	ER	HR	BB	IBB	SO	HB	WP	W	L	Pct.	ERA
Borbon	1	0	0	1	0	0	0	0	0	0	2	0	0	0	0	.000	0.00
Glavine	2	2	0	14	4	2	2	1	6	0	11	0	1	2	0	1.000	1.29
Avery	1	1	0	6	3	1	1	1	5	1	3	0	0	1	0	1.000	1.50
Wohlers	4	0	0	5	4	1	1	1	3	2	3	0	0	0	0	.000	1.80
Maddux	2	2	1	16	9	6	4	1	3	1	8	0	0	1	1	.500	2.25
Clontz	2	0	0	3 1/3	2	1	1	0	0	0	2	0	0	0	0	.000	2.70
McMichael	3	0	0	3 1/3	3	2	1	0	2	0	2	1	0	0	0	.000	2.70
Mercker	1	0	0	2	1	1	1	0	2	0	2	0	0	0	0	.000	4.50
Pena	2	0	0	1	3	1	1	0	2	1	0	0	0	0	1	.000	9.00
Smoltz	1	1	0	2 1/3	6	4	4	0	2	0	4	0	0	0	0	.000	15.43
Totals	6	6	1	54	35	19	16	5	25	5	37	0	0	4	2	.667	2.67

CLEVELAND INDIANS' PITCHING RECORDS

Pitcher	G	GS	CG	IP	H	R	ER	HR	BB	IBB	SO	HB	WP	W	L	Pct.	ERA
Tavarez	5	0	0	4 1/3	3	0	0	0	2	0	1	1	0	0	0	.000	0.00
Hershiser	2	2	0	14	8	5	4	2	4	1	13	0	0	1	1	.500	2.57
Embree	4	0	0	3 1/3	2	1	1	0	2	1	2	0	0	0	0	.000	2.70
Martinez	2	2	0	10 1/3	12	4	4	1	8	1	5	1	0	0	1	.000	3.48
Poole	2	0	0	2 1/3	1	1	1	1	0	0	1	0	0	0	1	.000	3.86
Hill	2	1	0	6 1/3	7	3	3	1	4	0	1	0	0	0	1	.000	4.26
Mesa	2	0	0	4	5	2	2	1	1	0	4	0	0	1	0	1.000	4.50
Nagy	1	1	0	7	8	5	5	2	1	0	4	0	0	0	0	.000	6.43
Assenmacher	4	0	0	1 1/3	1	2	1	0	3	1	3	0	0	0	0	.000	6.75
Totals	6	6	0	53	47	23	21	8	25	4	34	2	0	2	4	.333	3.57

SCORE BY INNINGS

Atlanta	1	1	2	1	1	5	6	3	3	0	0—23
Cleveland	5	2	2	0	0	3	2	2	2	0	1—19

MISCELLANEOUS STATISTICS

Sacrifice hits—Belliard 2, Lemke, Mordecai, O'Brien.
Sacrifice flies—Jones.
Stolen bases—Lofton 6, Grissom 3, McGriff, Polonia, Ramirez, Vizquel.
Caught stealing—Belle, Espinoza, Grissom, Lemke, Lofton.
Double plays—Vizquel, Baerga and Murray 2; Baerga, Vizquel and Murray; Baerga,
Vizquel and Perry; Baerga, Vizquel and Sorrento; Hershiser and Perry; Jones,
Lemke and McGriff; Lemke and McGriff; Vizquel and Baerga; Vizquel, Baerga and
Sorrento.
Left on bases—Atlanta 4, 7, 7, 12, 3, 11—44; Cleveland 1, 9, 13, 8, 5, 3—39.
Hit by pitcher—By Martinez (Grissom), by Tavarez (Lopez).
Passed balls—Alomar.
Balks—Avery.
Time of games—First game, 2:37; second game, 3:17; third game, 4:09; fourth game, 3:14; fifth game, 2:33; sixth game, 3:02.
Attendance—First game, 51,876; second game, 51,877; third game, 43,584; fourth game, 43,578; fifth game, 43,595; sixth game, 51,875.
Umpires—Wendelstedt, McKean, Froemming, Hirshbeck, Pulli, Hirschbeck, Brinkman and Polli.
Official scorers—Mark Frederickson, Hank Kozloski, Paul Meyer.

ALL-STAR GAME

HIGHLIGHTS

NATIONAL LEAGUE 3, AMERICAN LEAGUE 2

Why the National League won: The senior circuit managed only three hits but made each count. Craig Biggio, Mike Piazza and Jeff Conine homered for the N.L., marking the first time in All-Star Game history that all of a team's hits were home runs. Before Biggio's two-out blast in the sixth inning, three A.L. pitchers had held the N.L. hitless. That feat by Randy Johnson, Kevin Appier and Dennis Martinez was the longest no-hitter ever to open an All-Star Game.

Why the American League lost: The A.L. batted eight times with runners in scoring position—and went hitless each time. The junior circuit's two runs came on a fourth-inning homer by Frank Thomas following a single by Carlos Baerga.

The turning points:

1. Denny Neagle's escape from a dangerous situation in the sixth. Baerga led off with a double and pinch-runner Roberto Alomar stole third. Neagle then retired Edgar Martinez on a shallow fly ball, Mo Vaughn on strikes and Albert Belle on a grounder. "When Neagle got out of that inning, it gave us some momentum," Piazza said. Then in the seventh, Heathcliff Slocumb inherited a two-on, one-out situation from Carlos Perez and struck out Ivan Rodriguez and Jim Edmonds to earn the win.

2. N.L. Manager Felipe Alou's determination to use all of his position players. Alou, who did not bat in two of the three All-Star Games to which he had been named as a player, knew that Conine had been the only N.L. position player not to appear in the 1994 All-Star Game. "I'm not going to let that happen again," Alou said to himself and sent Conine in as a pinch-hitter leading off the eighth with the game tied, 2-2. The Florida outfielder promptly launched a Steve Ontiveros delivery into the left-field seats.

Notable: The Yankees' Buck Showalter and Montreal's Alou were named All-Star managers because their teams finished the strike-shortened 1994 season with the best records in their respective leagues. . . . N.L. starting pitcher Hideo Nomo was the first Japanese player selected as an All-Star. He struck out three and allowed one hit in two scoreless innings. . . . Conine was named the game's MVP as the N.L. won for the second consecutive year after losing six in a row.

Quotable: Showalter: "We were able to keep their hits down, but not the damage." . . . The 6-foot-10 Johnson on the Arlington heat (96

degrees at game time): "I felt like I shrunk a couple of inches." . . . Piazza: "I wasn't swinging the bat well coming in. It's amazing what a little adrenaline will do for you." . . . Tony Gwynn: "There's plenty of pleasure in beating the American League. They beat us like a drum for years."

BOX SCORE

National League	AB	R	H	RBI	PO	A
Dykstra, cf (Phillies)	2	0	0	0	1	0
Sosa, cf (Cubs)	1	0	0	0	2	0
Gwynn, rf (Padres)	2	0	0	0	1	0
Sanders, rf (Reds)	1	0	0	0	0	0
Mondesi, rf (Dodgers)	1	0	0	0	2	0
Bonds, lf (Giants)	3	0	0	0	0	0
Bichette, lf (Rockies)	1	0	0	0	2	0
Piazza, c (Dodgers)	3	1	1	1	6	1
Daulton, c (Phillies)	0	0	0	0	3	0
McGriff, 1b (Braves)	3	0	0	0	5	0
Grace, 1b (Cubs)	0	0	0	0	1	0
Gant, dh (Reds)	2	0	0	0	0	0
▲Conine, ph (Marlins)	1	1	1	1	0	0
Larkin, ss (Reds)	3	0	0	0	2	3
Offerman, ss (Dodgers)	0	0	0	0	0	0
Castilla, 3b (Rockies)	2	0	0	0	0	0
Bonilla, 3b (Mets)	1	0	0	0	0	0
Biggio, 2b (Astros)	2	1	1	1	2	1
Morandini, 2b (Phillies)	1	0	0	0	0	1
Nomo, p (Dodgers)	0	0	0	0	0	0
Smiley, p (Reds)	0	0	0	0	0	1
Green, p (Phillies)	0	0	0	0	0	1
Neagle, p (Pirates)	0	0	0	0	0	0
Perez, p (Expos)	0	0	0	0	0	0
Slocumb, p (Phillies)	0	0	0	0	0	0
Henke, p (Cardinals)	0	0	0	0	0	0
Myers, p (Cubs)	0	0	0	0	0	0
Totals	29	3	3	3	27	8

American League	AB	R	H	RBI	PO	A
Lofton, cf (Indians)	3	0	0	0	0	0
∞Edmonds, ph-cf (Angels)	1	0	0	0	0	0
Baerga, 2b (Indians)	3	1	3	0	1	2
*Alomar, pr-2b (Blue Jays)	1	0	0	0	0	0
E. Martinez, dh (Mariners)	3	0	0	0	0	0
◆T. Martinez, ph (Mariners)	1	0	1	0	0	0
Thomas, 1b (White Sox)	2	1	1	2	5	1
Vaughn, 1b (Red Sox)	2	0	0	0	4	0
Belle, lf (Indians)	3	0	0	0	1	0
O'Neill, lf (Yankees)	1	0	0	0	0	0
Ripken, ss (Orioles)	3	0	2	0	2	1
†DiSarcina, pr-ss (Angels)	1	0	0	0	0	0
Boggs, 3b (Yankees)	2	0	1	0	0	1
‡Seitzer, ph-3b (Brewers)	2	0	0	0	0	0
Puckett, rf (Twins)	2	0	0	0	2	0
§Ramirez, ph-rf (Indians)	0	0	0	0	2	0
Rodriguez, c (Rangers)	3	0	0	0	6	1
Stanley, c (Yankees)	1	0	0	0	3	0
Johnson, p (Mariners)	0	0	0	0	1	0
Appier, p (Royals)	0	0	0	0	0	1
D. Martinez, p (Indians)	0	0	0	0	0	1
Rogers, p (Rangers)	0	0	0	0	0	0
Ontiveros, p (Athletics)	0	0	0	0	0	1
Wells, p (Tigers)	0	0	0	0	0	0
Mesa, p (Indians)	0	0	0	0	0	0
Totals	34	2	8	2	27	9

National League	0	0	0	0	0	1	1	1	0	—3
American League	0	0	0	2	0	0	0	0	0	—2

National League	IP	H	R	ER	BB	SO
Nomo (Dodgers)	2	1	0	0	0	3
Smiley (Reds)	2	2	2	2	0	0
Green (Phillies)	1	2	0	0	0	1

National League	IP	H	R	ER	BB	SO
Neagle (Pirates)	1	1	0	0	0	1
Perez (Expos)	1/3	1	0	0	1	0
Slocumb (Phillies)	1	1	0	0	0	2
Henke (Cardinals)	2/3	0	0	0	0	1
Myers (Cubs)	1	0	0	0	1	0

American League	IP	H	R	ER	BB	SO
Johnson (Mariners)	2	0	0	0	1	3
Appier (Royals)	2	0	0	0	0	1
D. Martinez (Indians)	2	1	1	1	0	0
Rogers (Rangers)	1	1	1	1	0	2
Ontiveros (Athletics)	2/3	1	1	1	0	1
Wells (Tigers)	1/3	0	0	0	0	1
Mesa (Indians)	1	0	0	0	0	1

Winning pitcher—Slocumb. Losing pitcher—Ontiveros.
Save—Myers.

*Ran for Baerga in sixth. †Ran for Ripken in seventh. ‡Flied out for Boggs in seventh. §Walked for Puckett in seventh. ∞Struck out for Lofton in seventh. ▲Homered for Gant in eighth. ◆Singled for E. Martinez in eighth. E—None. LOB—N.L. 0, A.L. 7. 2B—Baerga. HR—Thomas, Biggio, Piazza, Conine. SB—Alomar. CS—Dykstra, Baerga. BB—Off Perez 1 (Ramirez), off Myers 1 (Ramirez), off Johnson 1 (Dykstra). SO—By Nomo 3 (Lofton, E. Martinez, Belle), by Green 1 (Puckett), by Neagle 1 (Vaughn), by Slocumb 2 (Rodriguez, Edmonds), by Henke 1 (Vaughn), by Johnson 3 (Bonds, McGriff, Gant), by Appier 1 (Castilla), by Rogers 2 (Sanders, McGriff), by Ontiveros 1 (Bonilla), by Wells 1 (Morandini), by Mesa 1 (Bichette). T—2:40. A—50,920. U—Merrill (A.L.), plate; Williams (N.L.), first; Clark (A.L.), second; Winters (N.L.), third; Hendry (A.L.), left field; Rapuano (N.L.), right field. Official scorers—Burt Hawkins, Paul Meyer, Jim Reeves.

Players listed on rosters but not used: A.L.—Finley, Hanson, L. Smith; N.L.—Worrell.

PLAY BY PLAY

FIRST INNING

N.L.—Dykstra walked. Gwynn flied to left. Dykstra caught stealing, catcher to shortstop. Bonds struck out.

A.L.—Lofton struck out. Baerga singled to right. Baerga caught stealing, catcher to second baseman. E. Martinez struck out.

SECOND INNING

N.L.—Piazza grounded to the first baseman, who tossed to the pitcher covering first. McGriff and Gant struck out.

A.L.—Thomas fouled to the catcher. Belle struck out. Ripken lined to right.

THIRD INNING

N.L.—Appier now pitching. Larkin grounded to second. Castilla struck out. Biggio grounded to short.

A.L.—Smiley now pitching. Boggs flied to center. Puckett grounded to the pitcher. Rodriguez grounded to short.

FOURTH INNING

N.L.—Dykstra grounded to second. Gwynn grounded to first. Bonds grounded to the pitcher.

A.L.—Lofton grounded to second. Baerga singled to left. E. Martinez popped to short. Thomas homered to left, scoring Baerga. Belle popped to short.

FIFTH INNING

N.L.—D. Martinez now pitching, Vaughn to first. Piazza lined to short. McGriff flied to right. Gant fouled to first.

A.L.—Green now pitching, Sanders to right. Ripken singled to center. Boggs singled to right, Ripken went to second. Puckett struck out. Rodriguez forced Boggs at second on a fielder's choice, shortstop to second baseman, as Ripken went to third. Lofton grounded to the pitcher.

SIXTH INNING

N.L.—Larkin lined to second. Castilla grounded to third. Biggio homered to left. Dykstra grounded to the pitcher.

A.L.—Neagle now pitching, Bonilla at third, Sosa in center. Baerga doubled to right. Alomar ran for Baerga. Alomar stole third. E. Martinez flied to center. Vaughn struck out. Belle grounded to short.

SEVENTH INNING

N.L.—Rogers now pitching, Alomar at second, O'Neill in left. Sanders struck out. Bonds flied to right. Piazza homered to right. McGriff struck out.

A.L.—Perez now pitching, Daulton catching, Grace at first, Morandini at second, Bichette in left, Mondesi in right. Ripken singled to left. DiSarcina ran for Ripken. Seitzer, pinch-hitting for Boggs, flied to right. Ramirez, pinch-hitting for Puckett, walked, and DiSarcina went to second. Slocumb now pitching. Rodriguez struck out. Edmonds, pinch-hitting for Lofton, struck out.

EIGHTH INNING

N.L.—Ontiveros now pitching, Stanley catching, DiSarcina at short, Seitzer at third, Ramirez in right, Edmonds in center. Conine, pinch-hitting for Gant, homered to left. Larkin grounded to the pitcher. Bonilla struck out. Wells now pitching. Morandini struck out.

A.L.—Offerman now at short. Alomar flied to left. T. Martinez, pinch-hitting for E. Martinez, singled to right. Henke now pitching. Vaughn struck out. O'Neill flied to center.

NINTH INNING

N.L.—Mesa now pitching. Sosa and Mondesi flied to right. Bichette struck out.

A.L.—Myers now pitching. DiSarcina flied to left. Seitzer grounded to second. Ramirez walked. Stanley lined to right.

NOTABLE PERFORMANCES

BOX SCORES OF NO-HIT GAMES

PEDRO MARTINEZ
JUNE 3

Montreal 1, San Diego 0 (N)

MONTREAL	AB	R	H	RBI	SAN DIEGO	AB	R	H	RBI
Frazier, cf	4	0	1	0	Roberts, lf	4	0	1	0
Treadway, 2b	5	0	1	1	Finley, cf	4	0	0	0
Cordero, ss	5	0	0	0	Gwynn, rf	4	0	0	0
Alou, lf	4	0	2	0	Caminiti, 3b	4	0	0	0
Fletcher, c	3	0	0	0	Petagine, 1b	3	0	0	0
Tarasco, rf	3	0	0	0	Ausmus, c	3	0	0	0
Grudzielanek, 3b	4	0	0	0	Reed, 2b	3	0	0	0
Andrews, 1b	3	1	1	0	Holbert, ss	2	0	0	0
Martinez, p	3	0	0	0	Livingstone, ph	1	0	0	0
Rojas, p	0	0	0	0	Cedeno, ss	0	0	0	0
					Hamilton, p	2	0	0	0
					E. Williams, ph	1	0	0	0
					B. Williams, p	0	0	0	0
TOTALS	34	1	5	1	**TOTALS**	31	0	1	0

Montreal	0 0 0	0 0 0	0 0 0	1—1
Los Angeles	0 0 0	0 0 0	0 0 0	0—0

E—Petagine, Holbert. DP—San Diego 2. LOB—Montreal 8, San Diego 1. 2B—Roberts (7). S—Martinez.

MONTREAL	IP	H	R	ER	BB	SO
Martinez (W, 4-1)	9	1	0	0	0	9
Rojas (S, 11)	1	0	0	0	0	0

LOS ANGELES	IP	H	R	ER	BB	SO
Hamilton	9	3	0	0	2	2
B. Williams (L, 0-3)	1	2	1	1	1	1

HBP—By Hamilton (Tarasco). WP—Rojas. T—2:22. A—9,707. Umpires—HP, Dantley. 1B, Williams. 2B, Bonin. 3B, Rieker.

NOTE: Pedro Martinez pitched nine perfect innings, but allowed a hit in the 10th. Mel Rojas relieved and finished the game.

RAMON MARTINEZ
JULY 14

Los Angeles 7, Florida 0 (N)

FLORIDA	AB	R	H	RBI	LOS ANGELES	AB	R	H	RBI
Veras, 2b	4	0	0	0	DeShields, 2b	2	2	0	0
Carr, cf	3	0	0	0	Offerman, ss	4	0	2	4
Conine, lf	3	0	0	0	Piazza, c	4	0	1	1
Pendleton, 3b	3	0	0	0	Karros, 1b	4	0	0	0
Colbrunn, 1b	3	0	0	0	Kelly, lf	4	1	2	0
Gregg, rf	2	0	0	0	Mondesi, rf	4	2	1	0
Nen, p	0	0	0	0	Wallach, 3b	4	0	1	0
Abbott, ss	3	0	0	0	Hollandsworth, cf	4	2	3	2
Johnson, c	3	0	0	0	Martinez, p	2	0	0	0
Burkett, p	1	0	0	0					
Diaz, ph	1	0	0	0					
Weathers, p	0	0	0	0					
Murphy, p	0	0	0	0					
Mathews, p	0	0	0	0					
Mantei, p	0	0	0	0					
Browne, rf	1	0	0	0					
TOTALS	27	0	0	0	**TOTALS**	32	7	10	7

Florida	0 0 0	0 0 0	0 0 0	0—0
Los Angeles	0 0 2	1 0 4	0 0 x—7

LOB—Florida 1, Los Angeles 5. 2B—Hollandsworth (1). 3B—Offerman (5). S—Martinez 2. SB—Mondesi.

FLORIDA	IP	H	R	ER	BB	SO
Burkett (L, 6-9)	5	6	3	3	1	5
Weathers	1/3	2	2	2	0	1
Murphy	1/3	1	2	2	1	0
Mathews	1/3	1	0	0	0	1
Mantei	1	0	0	0	0	2
Nen	1	0	0	0	0	1

LOS ANGELES	IP	H	R	ER	BB	SO
Martinez (W, 9-6)	9	0	0	0	1	8

T—2:21. A—30,988. Umpires—HP, Gregg. 1B, Davis. 2B, Tata. 3B, Winters.

LOW-HIT GAMES

AMERICAN LEAGUE
ONE-HIT GAMES

Date	Pitcher(s), Team, Opponent, Result—Player with hit
5-27	Steve Ontiveros, Oakland vs. New York, W 3-0—Luis Polonia (single in sixth)
6-15	Mark Gubicza, Kansas City at Oakland, W 7-0—Mark McGwire (single in fourth)
8-2	Paul Menhart, Toronto at Baltimore, L 0-1—Harold Baines (home run in second)

TWO-HIT GAMES

Date	Pitcher(s), Team, Opponent, Result—Player(s) with hit(s)
4-26	Aaron Sele (5 innings), Frank Rodriguez (1 inning), Alejandro Pena (1 inning), Jeff Pierce (1 inning) and Ken Ryan (1 inning), Boston vs. Minnesota, W 9-0—Kevin Maas (single in fifth), Scott Leius (single in eighth)
4-26	Kevin Appier (6²/₃ innings), Rusty Meacham (²/₃ inning), Billy Brewer (²/₃ inning) and Jeff Montgomery (1 inning), Kansas City vs. Baltimore, W 5-1—Leo Gomez (single in eighth), Sherman Obando (single in eighth)
5-1	Ricky Bones (7¹/₃ innings) and Graeme Lloyd (1²/₃ innings), Milwaukee at Baltimore, W 7-0—Chris Hoiles (single in fifth), Brady Anderson (single in eighth)
5-9	Jim Abbott (7 innings), Jose DeLeon (1 inning) and Kirk McCaskill (1 inning), Chicago vs. Minnesota, W 6-1—Chuck Knoblauch (single in fourth), Pedro Munoz (home run in seventh)
5-22	Kevin Appier (7 innings) and Hipolito Pichardo (2 innings), Kansas City at Toronto, W 7-0—Paul Molitor (single in fourth), Ed Sprague (single in fifth)
5-23	Chuck Finley, California vs. New York, W 10-0—Russ Davis (triple in sixth), Randy Velarde (single in ninth)
6-26	Jamie Moyer (7¹/₃ innings), Terry Clark (²/₃ inning) and Doug Jones (1 inning), Baltimore at Milwaukee, W 2-0—Jeff Cirillo (single in sixth), Darryl Hamilton (single in sixth)
7-5	Dennis Martinez (6 innings), Jim Poole (2 innings) and Jose Mesa (1 inning), Cleveland vs. Texas, W 2-0—Rusty Greer (single in first), Otis Nixon (single in ninth)
7-17	Wilson Alvarez, Chicago at New York, T 1-1—Mike Stanley (home run in fourth), Don Mattingly (double in seventh)
8-13	Tim Wakefield (8¹/₃ innings) and Stan Belinda (²/₃ inning), Boston vs. Baltimore, W 3-2—Rafael Palmeiro (home run in seventh), Brady Anderson (triple in ninth)
8-20	Doug Johns (5²/₃ innings), Jim Corsi (1 inning), Rick Honeycutt (1¹/₃ innings) and Dennis Eckersley (1 inning), Oakland vs. Baltimore, W 6-3—Jeff Manto (single in second), Brady Anderson (double in sixth)
9-2	Jack McDowell (8 innings) and Bob Wickman (1 inning), New York vs. Oakland, W 5-0—Stan Javier (single in fourth), Mike Bordick (single in eighth)

1995 REVIEW *Notable performances*

Date	Pitcher(s), Team, Opponent, Result—Player(s) with hit(s)

9-9 Chad Ogea (7 innings), Alan Embree (1 inning) and Jose Mesa (1 inning), Cleveland vs. Baltimore, W 2-1—Brady Anderson (double in first), Rafael Palmeiro (single in third)

9-13 Tim Wakefield (8⅓ innings) and Rick Aguilera (⅔ inning), Boston at Baltimore, W 2-0—Bret Barberie (single in third), Bobby Bonilla (single in seventh)

9-18 Doug Johns, Oakland vs. California, W 4-0—Jim Edmonds (single in first), Tim Salmon (single in seventh)

9-30 Ben McDonald (6 innings), Jimmy Haynes (2 innings) and Jesse Orosco (1 inning), Baltimore vs. Detroit, W 12-0—Chris Gomez (single in sixth), Tony Clark (single in ninth)

10-1 Mike Mussina, Baltimore vs. Detroit, W 4-0—Alan Trammell (single in first), Danny Bautista (double in sixth)

NATIONAL LEAGUE
ONE-HIT GAMES

Date	Pitcher(s), Team, Opponent, Result—Player with hit

5-15 Ramon Martinez (7 innings), Rudy Seanez (1 inning) and Todd Worrell (1 inning), Los Angeles vs. Pittsburgh, W 4-0—Jeff King (single in seventh)

5-28 Greg Maddux, Atlanta at Houston, W 3-1—Jeff Bagwell (home run in eighth)

6-3 Pedro Martinez (9 innings) and Mel Rojas (1 inning), Montreal at San Diego, W 1-0—Bip Roberts (double in 10th)

7-3 Mike Morgan (8⅓ innings) and Jeff Parrett (⅔ inning), St. Louis vs. Montreal, W 6-0—Wil Cordero (single in ninth)

8-5 Hideo Nomo, Los Angeles at San Francisco, W 3-0—Royce Clayton (single in seventh)

8-27 Kirk Rueter, Montreal vs. San Francisco, W 1-0—Kirt Manwaring (single in third)

8-29 Paul Wagner, Pittsburgh vs. Colorado, W 4-0—Andres Galarraga (single in ninth)

9-17 Pat Rapp, Florida at Colorado, W 17-0—Dante Bichette (single in fourth)

9-25 Frank Castillo, Chicago vs. St. Louis, W 7-0—Bernard Gilkey (triple in ninth)

TWO-HIT GAMES

Date	Pitcher(s), Team, Opponent, Result—Player(s) with hit(s)

4-28 Mark Leiter (6 innings), Mark Dewey (1 inning), Jose Bautista (1 inning) and Rod Beck (1 inning), San Francisco vs. Florida, W 4-0—Chuck Carr (single in third), Bobby Witt (single in third)

5-10 Kevin Jarvis, Cincinnati at Florida, W 3-0—Greg Colbrunn (double in second), Gary Sheffield (single in ninth)

5-17 Kevin Foster (7 innings) and Mike Perez (1 inning), Chicago at San Francisco, L 1-2—J.R. Phillips (single in sixth), Barry Bonds (home run in seventh)

5-21 John Smoltz (8 innings) and Mark Wohlers (1 inning), Atlanta vs. Florida, W 5-1—Quilvio Veras (double in sixth), Jerry Browne (single in sixth)

5-26 Michael Mimbs, Philadelphia vs. San Diego, W 2-0—Ken Caminiti (double in second), Andujar Cedeno (double in eighth)

6-2 Hideo Nomo (8 innings) and Todd Worrell (1 inning), Los Angeles vs. New York, W 2-1—Bobby Bonilla (home run in second and single in sixth)

6-4 Pete Schourek (7⅔ innings) and Jeff Brantley (1⅓ innings), Cincinnati vs. St. Louis, W 4-0—Darnell Coles (double in second), Tripp Cromer (single in ninth)

6-7 Curt Schilling, Philadelphia at San Diego, W 7-1—Eddie Williams (double in second), Ken Caminiti (home run in seventh)

6-14 Joey Hamilton, San Diego at St. Louis, W 3-0—Jose Oquendo (single in sixth), Brian Jordan (single in seventh)

6-23 Denny Neagle, Pittsburgh at Montreal, W 2-0—David Segui (double in third and single in sixth)

6-24 Hideo Nomo, Los Angeles vs. San Francisco, W 7-0—Darren Lewis (single in first and single in ninth)

7-8 Jaime Navarro (8⅓ innings) and Randy Myers (⅔ inning), Chicago at Philadelphia, W 3-1—Kevin Stocker (single in second), Charlie Hayes (double in eighth)

7-26 Sid Fernandez (7 innings), Ricky Bottalico (3 innings) and Toby Borland (1 inning), Philadelphia vs. Pittsburgh, W 2-1—Mark Parent (home run in fifth), John Wehner (single in 11th)

7-26 Mark Leiter, San Francisco vs. Cincinnati, W 4-1—Bret Boone (single in sixth), Ron Gant (home run in eighth)

8-19 Dave Burba, Cincinnati vs. Houston, W 8-0—Derrick May (double in seventh), Brian L. Hunter (single in ninth)

8-20 Greg Maddux, Atlanta at St. Louis, W 1-0—Brian Jordan (single in fifth), Danny Sheaffer (double in sixth)

9-6 Tavo Alvarez (7 innings), Dave Leiper (1 inning) and Tim Scott (1 inning), Montreal at San Francisco, W 8-2—Deion Sanders (triple in first), Kirt Manwaring (single in fifth)

9-13 Pete Schourek (7 innings) and Mike Jackson (2 innings), Cincinnati vs. Florida, W 6-0—Charles Johnson (single in sixth), Kurt Abbott (triple in eighth)

9-17 Ismael Valdes, Los Angeles at St. Louis, W 8-0—Scott Hemond (single in third), Bernard Gilkey (single in sixth)

9-22 Kevin Foster (8 innings) and Randy Myers (1 inning), Chicago vs. Pittsburgh, W 6-3—Midre Cummings (single in fourth), Jay Bell (single in fourth)

9-22 Kevin Ritz (6 innings), Roger Bailey (1 inning) and Curt Leskanic (2 innings), Colorado at San Francisco, W 6-1—Matt Williams (double in second), Glenallen Hill (home run in fifth)

9-23 Jamie Brewington (6 innings), Scott Service (1⅔ innings), Shawn Barton (⅓ inning) and Rod Beck (1 inning), San Francisco vs. Colorado, W 2-0—Joe Girardi (double in second), Bryan Rekar (single in fourth)

15-STRIKEOUT GAMES

Date	Pitcher, Team, Opponent	IP	H	R	ER	BB	SO	Result
5-23	Chuck Finley, California vs. New York	9	2	0	0	2	15	W 10-0
6-14	Hideo Nomo, Los Angeles at Pittsburgh	8	6	3	2	2	16	W 8-5
6-16	Todd Stottlemyre, Oakland vs. Kansas City	10	5	1	1	1	15	L 1-3
6-24	Randy Johnson, Seattle vs. California	9	5	2	2	3	15	W 3-2
7-15	Randy Johnson, Seattle vs. Toronto	9	3	0	0	2	16	W 3-0
9-23	Randy Johnson, Seattle vs. Oakland	7⅓	4	0	0	3	15	W 7-0

10-STRIKEOUT GAMES

AMERICAN LEAGUE

Team	No.	Pitchers
Seattle	16	Randy Johnson 16.
Oakland	8	Todd Stottlemyre 7, Dave Stewart 1.
Baltimore	6	Mike Mussina 2, Arthur Rhodes 2, Kevin Brown 1, Jimmy Haynes 1.
Chicago	5	Alex Fernandez 4, Jason Bere 1.
New York	5	David Cone 3, Jack McDowell 1, Mariano Rivera 1.
Kansas City	4	Kevin Appier 4.
Toronto	4	David Cone 2, Al Leiter 1, Juan Guzman 1.
California	3	Chuck Finley 2, Jim Abbott 1.
Texas	3	Bobby Witt 1, Roger Pavlik 1, Darren Oliver 1.
Boston	2	Roger Clemens 1, Erik Hanson 1.
Cleveland	2	Orel Hershiser 1, Charles Nagy 1.
Detroit	1	David Wells 1.
Milwaukee	1	Steve Sparks 1.
Minnesota	1	Mark Guthrie 1.

NATIONAL LEAGUE

Team	No.	Pitchers
Los Angeles	16	Hideo Nomo 11, Ramon Martinez 2, Ismael Valdes 2, Tom Candiotti 1.
Atlanta	9	John Smoltz 4, Greg Maddux 2, Steve Avery 2, Kent Mercker 1.
San Diego	7	Scott Sanders 3, Andy Benes 2, Andy Ashby 2.
Houston	6	Shane Reynolds 3, Doug Drabek 2, Darryl Kile 1.
Philadelphia	6	Curt Schilling 3, Sid Fernandez 2, Mike Williams 1.
Chicago	4	Frank Castillo 3, Kevin Foster 1.
Cincinnati	3	John Smiley 2, Pete Schourek 1.
San Francisco	3	Mark Leiter 2, William VanLandingham 1.
Florida	3	Bobby Witt 1, John Burkett 1, Chris Hammond 1.
Montreal	2	Jeff Fassero 1, Pedro Martinez 1.
New York	2	Bret Saberhagen 1, Dave Mlicki 1.
Pittsburgh	2	Denny Neagle 1, Paul Wagner 1.
St. Louis	2	Mark Petkovsek 1, Alan Benes 1.
Colorado	1	Bill Swift 1.

1-0 GAMES

AMERICAN LEAGUE

Date	Winner	Loser	Inn.*	Site
5-19	†Steve Sparks, Milwaukee	†Darren Oliver, Texas	4	Texas
5-27	†Jason Bere, Chicago	†Felipe Lira, Detroit	5	Detroit
5-30	†Tim Wakefield, Boston	Ron Darling, Oakland	5	Oakland
6-12	†Steve Ontiveros, Oakland	Jason Bere, Chicago	3	Oakland
6-21	†Felipe Lira, Detroit	Bob Tewksbury, Texas	1	Detroit
6-30	†Mark Gubicza, Kansas City	†Wilson Alvarez, Chicago	2	Kansas City
7-8	Mark Langston, California	Ricky Bones, Milwaukee	2	California
7-14‡	†Alan Embree, Cleveland	Ariel Prieto, Oakland	6	Cleveland
7-27	†Andy Pettitte, New York	†Mark Gubicza, Kansas City	4	Kansas City
8-2	Mike Mussina, Baltimore	Paul Menhart, Toronto	2	Baltimore

PLAYERS HITTING HOME RUNS IN 1-0 GAMES: 5-27—Ron Karkovice, Chicago; 6-21—Lou Whitaker, Detroit; 8-2—Harold Baines, Baltimore.
*Inning in which run scored. †Did not pitch complete game. ‡First game of doubleheader.

NATIONAL LEAGUE

Date	Winner	Loser	Inn.*	Site
4-29	†Trevor Wilson, San Francisco	†Pat Rapp, Florida	6	San Francisco
5-16	†Bobby Jones, New York	†Shane Reynolds, Houston	3	Houston
5-16	†Trevor Hoffman, San Diego	†Jeff Parrett, St. Louis	9	San Diego
6-3	†Pedro Martinez, Montreal	†Brian Williams, San Diego	10	San Diego
6-6	†Fernando Valenzuela, San Diego	†Mike Williams, Philadelphia	2	San Diego
6-21	Andy Benes, San Diego	Steve Trachsel, Chicago	6	San Diego
6-25	†Esteban Loaiza, Pittsburgh	†Jeff Fassero, Montreal	1	Montreal
6-28	†C.J. Nitkowski, Cincinnati	†Curt Schilling, Philadelphia	4	Philadelphia
7-6	†Greg McMichael, Atlanta	†Rudy Seanez, Los Angeles	9	Atlanta
7-26	†Ismael Valdes, Los Angeles	†Steve Avery, Atlanta	4	Los Angeles
8-4	†John Smiley, Cincinnati	†Jeff Juden, Philadelphia	1	Cincinnati
8-5	†Jim Bullinger, Chicago	†Rich DeLucia, St. Louis	8	St. Louis
8-16	†Bill Pulsipher, New York	†Carlos Perez, Montreal	4	New York
8-20	Greg Maddux, Atlanta	†Mike Morgan, St. Louis	3	St. Louis
8-27	Kirk Rueter, Montreal	Mark Leiter, San Francisco	5	Montreal
9-5	Greg Maddux, Atlanta	†Tom Urbani, St. Louis	2	Atlanta
9-6	†Mike Grace, Philadelphia	†Ismael Valdes, Los Angeles	8	Los Angeles
9-24	†Dean Hartgraves, Houston	†Rich DeLucia, St. Louis	10	Houston
10-1	†Pete Walker, New York	†Terrell Wade, Atlanta	11	New York

PLAYERS HITTING HOME RUNS IN 1-0 GAMES: 8-5—Scott Servais, Chicago; 9-5—Fred McGriff, Atlanta.
*Inning in which run scored. †Did not pitch complete game.

FOUR OR MORE HITS IN ONE GAME

AMERICAN LEAGUE

Team	No.	Hitters
Chicago	19	Lance Johnson 7, Robin Ventura 5, Ray Durham 2, Tim Raines 1, Dave Martinez 1, Mike Devereaux 1, Frank Thomas 1, Lyle Mouton 1.

Team	No.	Hitters
Cleveland	19	Albert Belle 4, Eddie Murray 3, Carlos Baerga 3, Kenny Lofton 3, Tony Pena 1, Alvaro Espinoza 1, Sandy Alomar 1, Paul Sorrento 1, Manny Ramirez 1, Herbert Perry 1.
California	18	Jim Edmonds 4, J.T. Snow 3, Tony Phillips 2, Rex Hudler 2, Gary DiSarcina 2, Tim Salmon 2, Chili Davis 1, Andy Allanson 1, Garret Anderson 1.
Boston	15	Tim Naehring 3, John Valentin 3, Mike Greenwell 2, Mo Vaughn 2, Lee Tinsley 2, Willie McGee 1, Jose Canseco 1, Dwayne Hosey 1.
Detroit	13	Travis Fryman 5, Chad Curtis 2, Chris Gomez 2, Lou Whitaker 1, Kirk Gibson 1, Franklin Stubbs 1, John Flaherty 1.
Milwaukee	13	Kevin Seitzer 3, B.J. Surhoff 3, John Jaha 2, Darryl Hamilton 1, Joe Oliver 1, David Hulse 1, Jose Valentin 1, Fernando Vina 1.
Minnesota	11	Chuck Knoblauch 3, Kirby Puckett 1, Matt Merullo 1, Pedro Munoz 1, Jeff Reboulet 1, Scott Stahoviak 1, Rich Becker 1, Marty Cordova 1, Dan Masteller 1.
Toronto	10	Paul Molitor 4, Joe Carter 2, Roberto Alomar 2, Ed Sprague 1, Alex Gonzalez 1.
Seattle	8	Vince Coleman 2, Gary Thurman 1, Jay Buhner 1, Doug Strange 1, Mike Blowers 1, Luis Sojo 1, Tino Martinez 1.
New York	7	Tony Fernandez 1, Dion James 1, Paul O'Neill 1, Mike Stanley 1, Luis Polonia 1, Randy Velarde 1, Jim Leyritz 1.
Oakland	7	Terry Steinbach 2, Geronimo Berroa 2, Stan Javier 1, Scott Brosius 1, Jason Giambi 1.
Baltimore	6	Harold Baines 2, Cal Ripken 2, Rafael Palmeiro 1, Jeff Manto 1.
Kansas City	6	Wally Joyner 2, Gary Gaetti 1, Greg Gagne 1, Vince Coleman 1, Keith Lockhart 1.
Texas	6	Otis Nixon 2, Mickey Tettleton 1, Will Clark 1, Juan Gonzalez 1, Rusty Greer 1.

NATIONAL LEAGUE

Team	No.	Hitters
San Diego	19	Steve Finley 4, Ken Caminiti 3, Jody Reed 3, Brad Ausmus 3, Tony Gwynn 1, Bip Roberts 1, Phil Plantier 1, Andujar Cedeno 1, Scott Livingstone 1, Archi Cianfrocco 1.
San Francisco	18	Matt Williams 4, Mark Carreon 4, Barry Bonds 3, Mike Benjamin 3, Jeff Reed 1, Deion Sanders 1, Steve Scarsone 1, Rich Aurilia 1.
Colorado	17	Dante Bichette 4, Joe Girardi 3, Vinny Castilla 3, Walt Weiss 2, Larry Walker 2, Andres Galarraga 1, Eric Young 1, Jayhawk Owens 1.
Houston	16	Derek Bell 5, Craig Biggio 2, Jeff Bagwell 2, Brian L. Hunter 2, John Cangelosi 1, Dave Magadan 1, Derrick May 1, Luis Gonzalez 1, Tony Eusebio 1.
Philadelphia	14	Jim Eisenreich 4, Mickey Morandini 3, Darren Daulton 2, Gregg Jefferies 2, Mariano Duncan 1, Tom Marsh 1, Tony Longmire 1.
Atlanta	11	Chipper Jones 4, Fred McGriff 2, Marquis Grissom 2, Mark Lemke 1, Dave Justice 1, Ryan Klesko 1.
Cincinnati	11	Hal Morris 2, Mark Lewis 2, Reggie Sanders 2, Barry Larkin 1, Benito Santiago 1, Ron Gant 1, Eric Anthony 1, Thomas Howard 1.
New York	11	Brett Butler 4, Jose Vizcaino 2, Jeff Kent 2, Joe Orsulak 1, Todd Hundley 1, Edgardo Alfonzo 1.
Montreal	10	Moises Alou 2, Sean Berry 2, Rondell White 2, Jeff Treadway 1, Darrin Fletcher 1, Wil Cordero 1, Tony Tarasco 1.
Los Angeles	9	Mike Piazza 3, Roberto Kelly 1, Delino DeShields 1, Eric Karros 1, Henry Rodriguez 1, Raul Mondesi 1, Chad Fonville 1.
Chicago	8	Mark Grace 2, Sammy Sosa 2, Shawon Dunston 1, Brian McRae 1, Scott Servais 1, Rey Sanchez 1.
Pittsburgh	8	Jay Bell 2, Orlando Merced 2, Dave Clark 1, Jeff King 1, John Wehner 1, Al Martin 1.
St. Louis	8	Ray Lankford 2, John Mabry 2, Jose Oquendo 1, Tom Pagnozzi 1, Bernard Gilkey 1, David Bell 1.
Florida	7	Jeff Conine 2, Terry Pendleton 1, Gary Sheffield 1, Alex Arias 1, Greg Colbrunn 1, Charles Johnson 1.

FIVE- AND SIX-HIT GAMES

Date	Player, Team, Opponent	AB	R	H	2B	3B	HR	RBI	Result
5-10	Chili Davis, California vs. Texas	5	2	5	1	0	1	5	W 11-2
5-21	Steve Scarsone, San Francisco vs. St. Louis	5	3	5	1	0	1	1	L 7-9
5-23	Derek Bell, Houston at Cincinnati	5	2	5	2	0	0	2	L 5-10
5-29	Terry Pendleton, Florida vs. Houston	5	2	5	1	1	0	1	W 9-7
6-2	John Valentin, Boston vs. Seattle	5	4	5	1	0	3	3	W 6-5
6-11	Rondell White, Montreal at San Francisco	7	5	6	2	1	1	3	W 10-8
6-14	Tony Phillips, California vs. Minnesota	5	2	5	2	0	0	1	L 5-8
6-14	Mike Benjamin, San Francisco at Chicago	7	0	6	1	0	0	2	W 4-3
6-24	Mickey Morandini, Philadelphia at St. Louis	6	2	5	2	0	0	3	W 10-9
6-29	Robin Ventura, Chicago at Milwaukee	6	4	5	0	0	1	3	W 17-13
7-3	Andres Galarraga, Colorado vs. Houston	6	4	6	1	0	2	5	W 15-10
7-5	Tino Martinez, Seattle at Detroit	5	2	5	1	0	2	5	L 6-8
7-16	Carlos Baerga, Cleveland vs. Oakland	6	1	5	1	0	0	0	W 5-4
7-25	Randy Velarde, New York at Kansas City	5	3	5	0	0	1	1	W 8-1
7-29	Vince Coleman, Kansas City vs. Detroit	8	0	5	0	0	0	1	W 5-4
8-5	Marquis Grissom, Atlanta at Montreal	5	1	5	0	0	2	2	W 9-6
9-4*	Paul Molitor, Toronto at Kansas City	5	1	5	1	0	1	3	W 6-1
9-17	Gary Sheffield, Florida at Colorado	5	4	5	1	0	1	4	W 17-0
9-23	Lance Johnson, Chicago at Minnesota	6	4	6	0	3	0	4	W 14-4
9-23	Robin Ventura, Chicago at Minnesota	6	1	5	3	0	0	1	W 14-4
9-23	Jose Vizcaino, New York at Florida	5	0	5	1	0	0	0	L 3-4

*First game of doubleheader.

HITTING STREAKS OF 15 OR MORE GAMES

AMERICAN LEAGUE

G	Player, Team	Span of streak
23	Jim Edmonds, California	June 4-June 29
20	Bobby Bonilla, Baltimore	Sept. 10-Oct. 1
19	Roberto Alomar, Toronto	Aug. 5-Aug. 25
18	Mark McGwire, Oakland	May 3-May 21
	Chad Curtis, Detroit	June 14-July 2
17	Vince Coleman, Kansas City	May 21-June 13
	Geronimo Berroa, Oakland	July 27-Aug. 14
	Brent Gates, Oakland	Aug. 9-Aug. 27
	Jose Canseco, Boston	Aug. 27-Sept. 15
16	Ed Sprague, Toronto	May 6-May 23
	Chili Davis, California	July 26-Aug. 11
	Jose Canseco, Boston	Aug. 10-Aug. 25
15	Lee Tinsley, Boston	June 10-June 25
	Ivan Rodriguez, Texas	June 18-July 4
	Chuck Knoblauch, Minnesota	July 19-Aug. 3
	Albert Belle, Cleveland	Aug. 8-Aug. 21
	Craig Paquette, Oakland	Aug. 17-Sept. 1
	Tim Salmon, California	Aug. 26-Sept. 11

NATIONAL LEAGUE

G	Player, Team	Span of streak
23	Dante Bichette, Colorado	May 22-June 18
21	Carlos Garcia, Pittsburgh	June 5-June 27
20	Bobby Bonilla, Baltimore	Sept. 10-Oct. 1
19	Eric Young, Colorado	July 18-Aug. 10
	Dante Bichette, Colorado	July 19-Aug. 8
18	David Segui, Montreal	July 20-Aug. 8
17	Eric Karros, Los Angeles	May 16-June 2
	Greg Colbrunn, Florida	Aug. 20-Sept. 6
16	Mike Piazza, Los Angeles	July 29-Aug. 16
	Ray Lankford, St. Louis	Aug. 29-Sept. 16
15	Mark Grace, Chicago	May 19-June 3
	Raul Mondesi, Los Angeles	June 13-June 27
	Tony Gwynn, San Diego	July 1-July 17
	Carlos Garcia, Pittsburgh	Sept. 2-Sept. 21

MULTI-HOMER GAMES

AMERICAN LEAGUE

Team	No.	Hitters
Cleveland	20	Albert Belle 8, Paul Sorrento 3, Eddie Murray 2, Sandy Alomar 2, Manny Ramirez 2, Carlos Baerga 1, Kenny Lofton 1, Herbert Perry 1.
Seattle	13	Jay Buhner 5, Mike Blowers 3, Tino Martinez 3, Edgar Martinez 2.
Oakland	11	Mark McGwire 5, Scott Brosius 2, Craig Paquette 2, Ruben Sierra 1, Geronimo Berroa 1.
Baltimore	10	Rafael Palmeiro 4, Jeff Manto 2, Harold Baines 1, Cal Ripken 1, Brady Anderson 1, Chris Hoiles 1.
Toronto	10	Joe Carter 4, Alex Gonzalez 2, Lance Parrish 1, Roberto Alomar 1, John Olerud 1, Ed Sprague 1.
Boston	9	Mo Vaughn 4, John Valentin 2, Mike Greenwell 1, Luis Alicea 1, Troy O'Leary 1.
Chicago	9	Robin Ventura 4, Frank Thomas 3, Ron Karkovice 1, Mike Devereaux 1.
Detroit	9	Cecil Fielder 3, John Flaherty 2, Kirk Gibson 1, Travis Fryman 1, Chad Curtis 1, Bob Higginson 1.
California	8	Tim Salmon 3, Jim Edmonds 3, Tony Phillips 1, Andy Allanson 1.
Texas	8	Mickey Tettleton 4, Dean Palmer 2, Juan Gonzalez 1, Ivan Rodriguez 1.
Kansas City	5	Gary Gaetti 3, Joe Vitiello 1, Jon Nunnally 1.
Milwaukee	4	B.J. Surhoff 2, Jose Valentin 1, Jeff Cirillo 1.
New York	3	Paul O'Neill 2, Mike Stanley 1.
Minnesota	2	Kirby Puckett 1, Pedro Munoz 1.

NATIONAL LEAGUE

Team	No.	Hitters
Colorado	17	Vinny Castilla 6, Andres Galarraga 3, Larry Walker 3, Ellis Burks 2, Dante Bichette 2, Jayhawk Owens 1.
Los Angeles	13	Mike Piazza 6, Raul Mondesi 3, Eric Karros 2, Billy Ashley 1, Todd Hollandsworth 1.
Cincinnati	12	Ron Gant 4, Barry Larkin 2, Benito Santiago 2, Reggie Sanders 2, Bret Boone 2.
San Francisco	10	Barry Bonds 3, Matt Williams 3, Robby Thompson 1, Kirt Manwaring 1, Mark Carreon 1, J.R. Phillips 1.
Chicago	8	Sammy Sosa 5, Howard Johnson 1, Scott Servais 1, Jose Hernandez 1.
Pittsburgh	7	Jeff King 2, Mark Johnson 2, Jay Bell 1, Orlando Merced 1, Steve Pegues 1.
San Diego	6	Ken Caminiti 4, Phil Plantier 1, Andujar Cedeno 1.
Florida	6	Jeff Conine 2, Greg Colbrunn 2, Andre Dawson 1, Gary Sheffield 1.
Atlanta	5	Fred McGriff 2, Ryan Klesko 2, Dave Justice 1.
New York	5	Bobby Bonilla 2, Rico Brogna 1, Damon Buford 1, Carl Everett 1.
Houston	3	Craig Biggio 2, Orlando Miller 1.
Philadelphia	3	Darren Daulton 1, Mark Whiten 1, Tom Marsh 1.
St. Louis	3	Brian Jordan 2, Todd Zeile 1.
Montreal	2	Sean Berry 1, Wil Cordero 1.

THREE-HOMER GAMES

Date	Player, Team, Opponent	AB	R	H	2B	3B	HR	RBI	Result
6-2	John Valentin, Boston vs. Seattle	5	4	5	1	0	3	3	W 6-5
6-11	Mark McGwire, Oakland at Boston	4	3	3	0	0	3	3	W 8-1
6-25	Andres Galarraga, Colorado at San Diego	3	3	3	0	0	3	7	W 11-3
8-10*	Mike Stanley, New York vs. Cleveland	4	3	3	0	0	3	7	L 9-10
8-15	Reggie Sanders, Cincinnati vs. Colorado	5	3	3	0	0	3	4	W 11-3
8-31	Paul O'Neill, New York vs. California	5	4	4	0	0	3	8	W 11-6
9-19	Albert Belle, Cleveland at Chicago	4	3	3	0	0	3	3	W 8-2

*First game of doubleheader.

AMERICAN LEAGUE

Date	Batter, Team	Pitcher, Team	Inn.*	Site
4-26	John Jaha, Milwaukee	Alex Fernandez, Chicago	1	Milwaukee
4-27	Ed Sprague, Toronto	Ron Darling, Oakland	4	Toronto
4-28	Joe Oliver, Milwaukee	Todd Stottlemyre, Oakland	2	Milwaukee
4-30	Ron Karkovice, Chicago	Alejandro Pena, Boston	8	Boston
5-2	John Valentin, Boston	Sterling Hitchcock, New York	3	New York
5-2	Mo Vaughn, Boston	Brian Boehringer, New York	4	New York
5-5	Travis Fryman, Detroit	Frank Rodriguez, Boston	1	Detroit
5-7	Kevin Seitzer, Milwaukee	Jeff Patterson, New York	8	New York
5-9	Paul Sorrento, Cleveland	Doug Linton, Kansas City	1	Cleveland
5-14	Terry Steinbach, Oakland	Mark Guthrie, Minnesota	9	Minnesota
5-18	Rusty Greer, Texas	Mark Kiefer, Milwaukee	8	Texas
5-22	Cecil Fielder, Detroit	Bob Wells, Seattle	1	Detroit
5-25	J.T. Snow, California	Melido Perez, New York	2	California
5-25	Terry Steinbach, Oakland	Armando Benitez, Baltimore	8	Oakland
5-26	Reggie Jefferson, Boston	Mike Butcher, California	6	California
5-29	Tim Salmon, California	Mike Mussina, Baltimore	3	California
5-29	Gary Gaetti, Kansas City	Terry Burrows, Texas	8	Kansas City
6-3	Cal Ripken, Baltimore	Mike Harkey, Oakland	5	Baltimore
6-3	Dave Martinez, Chicago	Joe Boever, Detroit	9	Chicago
6-4	Craig Paquette, Oakland	Alan Mills, Baltimore	6	Baltimore
6-6	Geronimo Berroa, Oakland	Mariano Rivera, New York	3	New York
6-7	Edgar Martinez, Seattle	Armando Benitez, Baltimore	8	Baltimore
6-13	Mike Stanley, New York	Mike Moore, Detroit	4	Detroit
6-16	Kirby Puckett, Minnesota	Randy Johnson, Seattle	6	Seattle
6-20	Gerald Williams, New York	Mike Oquist, Baltimore	5	Baltimore
6-21	Jose Valentin, Milwaukee	Mike Timlin, Toronto	9	Toronto
6-25	Alan Trammell, Detroit	Ron Rightnowar, Milwaukee	8	Detroit
6-30	Mark McGwire, Oakland	Lee Smith, California	9	Oakland
7-5	John Kruk, Chicago	Brian Boehringer, New York	1	Chicago
7-9	Matt Mieske, Milwaukee	Chuck Finley, California	1	California
7-9	Tino Martinez, Seattle	Bud Black, Cleveland	7	Cleveland
7-16	John Olerud, Toronto	Rafael Carmona, Seattle	4	Seattle
7-17	Tino Martinez, Seattle	Buddy Groom, Detroit	10	Seattle
7-18	Albert Belle, Cleveland	Lee Smith, California	9	Cleveland
7-21	Mo Vaughn, Boston	Scott Klingenbeck, Minnesota	5	Boston
7-21	Bret Barberie, Baltimore	Mel Bunch, Kansas City	4	Kansas City
7-21	Ed Sprague, Toronto	Salomon Torres, Seattle	3	Toronto
7-26	Chili Davis, California	Dennis Martinez, Cleveland	3	California
7-29	Bill Haselman, Boston	Kevin Gross, Texas	6	Texas
8-1	Harold Baines, Baltimore	Edwin Hurtado, Toronto	1	Baltimore
8-2	Paul Sorrento, Cleveland	Eddie Guardado, Minnesota	5	Cleveland
8-3	Mike Blowers, Seattle	Mike Butcher, California	7	California
8-3	Mo Vaughn, Boston	Joe Boever, Detroit	9	Detroit
8-4	Dave Nilsson, Milwaukee	Arthur Rhodes, Baltimore	4	Baltimore
8-4	Manny Ramirez, Cleveland	Jason Bere, Chicago	3	Cleveland
8-5	Matt Merullo, Minnesota	Billy Brewer, Kansas City	7	Minnesota
8-5	Mike Bordick, Oakland	Salomon Torres, Seattle	5	Oakland
8-8	Jay Buhner, Seattle	Mike Bertotti, Chicago	4	Seattle
8-10	Benji Gil, Texas	Joe Boever, Detroit	8	Texas
8-10†	Mike Stanley, New York	Charles Nagy, Cleveland	6	New York
8-11	Darryl Hamilton, Milwaukee	Mike Moore, Detroit	4	Milwaukee
8-11	Ruben Sierra, New York	Orel Hershiser, Cleveland	6	New York
8-14	George Williams, Oakland	Billy Brewer, Kansas City	6	Kansas City
8-14	Mike Blowers, Seattle	Pat Mahomes, Minnesota	7	Minnesota
8-16	John Jaha, Milwaukee	Danny Darwin, Texas	3	Texas
8-18	Mike Blowers, Seattle	Tim Wakefield, Boston	1	Seattle
8-18	Wally Joyner, Kansas City	Giovanni Carrara, Toronto	6	Toronto
8-19	Harold Baines, Baltimore	John Briscoe, Oakland	7	Oakland
8-21	Juan Gonzalez, Texas	Oscar Munoz, Minnesota	1	Texas
8-24	Jay Buhner, Seattle	David Cone, New York	1	Seattle
8-25	Ray Durham, Chicago	Pat Hentgen, Toronto	6	Toronto
8-25	Devon White, Toronto	Kirk McCaskill, Chicago	8	Toronto
8-26	Mike Macfarlane, Boston	Todd Stottlemyre, Oakland	4	Oakland
9-1	Albert Belle, Cleveland	Mike Myers, Detroit	8	Detroit
9-3	Ron Tingley, Detroit	Jose Mesa, Cleveland	9	Detroit
9-3	Matt Mieske, Milwaukee	Scott Watkins, Minnesota	7	Minnesota
9-4	John Jaha, Milwaukee	Mike Trombley, Minnesota	1	Minnesota
9-4	Robin Ventura, Chicago	Dennis Cook, Texas	4	Texas
9-4	Robin Ventura, Chicago	Danny Darwin, Texas	5	Texas

Date	Batter, Team	Pitcher, Team	Inn.*	Site
9-9	Mickey Tettleton, Texas	Joe Slusarski, Milwaukee	4	Milwaukee
9-15	Bobby Bonilla, Baltimore	Mariano Rivera, New York	6	Baltimore
9-22	Vince Coleman, Seattle	Todd Van Poppel, Oakland	4	Seattle
9-25	Travis Fryman, Detroit	Matt Murray, Boston	3	Boston
9-28	Ken Griffey, Seattle	Roger Pavlik, Texas	8	Texas
9-30	Brady Anderson, Baltimore	Sean Bergman, Detroit	2	Baltimore

*Inning in which grand slam was hit. †First game of doubleheader.

NATIONAL LEAGUE

Date	Batter, Team	Pitcher, Team	Inn.*	Site
4-26	Todd Hundley, New York	Bill Swift, Colorado	6	Colorado
5-4	Todd Hundley, New York	Bryan Eversgerd, Montreal	10	Montreal
5-5	Quilvio Veras, Florida	Curt Schmidt, Montreal	4	Montreal
5-7	Mike Piazza, Los Angeles	Bill Swift, Colorado	3	Colorado
5-9	Dante Bichette, Colorado	Trevor Wilson, San Francisco	1	Colorado
5-14	Brian Johnson, San Diego	Randy Myers, Chicago	8	Chicago
5-16	Gary Sheffield, Florida	Heathcliff Slocumb, Philadelphia	9	Florida
5-19	Dwight Smith, Atlanta	Richie Lewis, Florida	9	Atlanta
5-19	Tony Eusebio, Houston	Reid Cornelius, Montreal	7	Houston
5-20	Bip Roberts, San Diego	Danny Miceli, Pittsburgh	9	San Diego
5-23	Mike Lansing, Montreal	Andy Ashby, San Diego	1	Montreal
5-28	Rondell White, Montreal	Felix Rodriguez, Los Angeles	7	Montreal
5-29	Chris Hammond, Florida	Shane Reynolds, Houston	2	Florida
6-2	Sean Berry, Montreal	Willie Blair, San Diego	9	San Diego
6-6	Ryan Klesko, Atlanta	Willie Banks, Chicago	4	Atlanta
6-21	Delino DeShields, Los Angeles	Vince Palacios, St. Louis	2	St. Louis
6-27	Denny Neagle, Pittsburgh	Jim Bullinger, Chicago	6	Chicago
6-27	Ken Caminiti, San Diego	Greg Hansell, Los Angeles	6	Los Angeles
6-28	Brian McRae, Chicago	Mike Dyer, Pittsburgh	4	Chicago
6-28	Tony Eusebio, Houston	Jeff Parrett, St. Louis	8	Houston
7-2	Andres Galarraga, Colorado	Ramon Martinez, Los Angeles	3	Los Angeles
7-9	Eddie Williams, San Diego	Doug Brocail, Houston	7	Houston
7-9	Tommy Gregg, Florida	Ken Hill, St. Louis	7	St. Louis
7-14	Glenallen Hill, San Francisco	Greg Swindell, Houston	3	San Francisco
7-17	Ray Holbert, San Diego	C.J. Nitkowski, Chicago	5	San Diego
7-17	Kurt Abbott, Florida	Rod Beck, San Francisco	8	San Francisco
7-18	Greg Colbrunn, Florida	Chris Hook, San Francisco	14	San Francisco
7-21	Archi Cianfrocco, San Diego	Steve Bedrosian, Atlanta	8	Atlanta
8-2	Melvin Nieves, San Diego	Terry Mulholland, San Francisco	8	San Diego
8-10	Jeff King, Pittsburgh	Jamie Brewington, San Francisco	7	San Francisco
8-15	Raul Mondesi, Los Angeles	Steve Trachsel, Chicago	4	Los Angeles
8-16	Andre Dawson, Florida	Steve Avery, Atlanta	1	Atlanta
8-18†	Nelson Liriano, Pittsburgh	Yorkis Perez, Florida	8	Pittsburgh
8-20	Ron Gant, Cincinnati	Todd Jones, Houston	5	Cincinnati
8-22	Tony Gwynn, San Diego	Tommy Greene, Philadelphia	5	Philadelphia
8-23	Jim Eisenreich, Philadelphia	Dustin Hermanson, San Diego	5	Philadelphia
8-25	Carl Everett, New York	Willie Blair, San Diego	5	New York
8-25	Jeff Juden, Philadelphia	John Cummings, Los Angeles	4	Philadelphia
8-26	Melvin Nieves, San Diego	Doug Henry, New York	9	New York
8-26	Danny Sheaffer, St. Louis	Bruce Ruffin, Colorado	9	Colorado
8-27	Mike Piazza, Los Angeles	Tommy Greene, Philadelphia	6	Philadelphia
8-31	Jose Hernandez, Chicago	Buddy Groom, Florida	5	Florida
9-5	Derrick May, Houston	Kevin Jarvis, Cincinnati	7	Houston
9-5	David Segui, Montreal	Jose Bautista, San Francisco	4	San Francisco
9-8	Andres Galarraga, Colorado	Chuck McElroy, Cincinnati	7	Colorado
9-9	Matt Williams, San Francisco	Frank Castillo, Chicago	1	Chicago
9-17	Rico Brogna, New York	Mike Williams, Philadelphia	3	New York
9-28	Shane Andrews, Montreal	Chuck McElroy, Cincinnati	9	Montreal

*Inning in which grand slam was hit. †First game of doubleheader.

TRANSACTIONS

JANUARY 5
Dodgers organization signed C Tom Prince.

JANUARY 6
White Sox claimed P Tim Fortugno on waivers from Reds.

A's organization signed IF Paul Faries, IF Tim Jones, IF Jim Bowie, OF Andy Tomberlin, OF Scott Bryant, C Mike Maksudian, and P Roger Smithberg.

JANUARY 11
Cubs traded P Greg Hillman to Reds for IF Keith Kessinger.

JANUARY 16
Expos organization signed P Denis Boucher.

JANUARY 31
A's sold contract of 1B Troy Neel to Orix Blue Wave of the Japanese Pacific League.

FEBRUARY 1
Braves organization signed C Francisco Cabrera.

FEBRUARY 6
Giants released OF Darryl Strawberry.

FEBRUARY 7
Angels organization signed C Andy Allanson.

FEBRUARY 9
Dodgers organization signed OF Casey Candaele.

FEBRUARY 13
Dodgers organization signed P Hideo Nomo.

Phillies organization signed P Jeff Innis.

MARCH 3
Angels organization signed P Shawn Boskie.

MARCH 8
Angels organization signed P Mike Schooler.

Twins organization signed OF Jerald Clark.

Cardinals organization signed IF/OF Darnell Coles.

Giants organization signed P Randy Tomlin.

MARCH 14
Indians organization signed P Jim Poole.

MARCH 15
Indians organization signed P Gregg Olson.

MARCH 22
Indians organization signed IF Billy Ripken.

Rangers organization signed 3B Mike Pagliarulo.

MARCH 27
Dodgers organization signed OF Keith Mitchell.

Expos organization signed P Greg A. Harris.

MARCH 29
Padres organization signed IF/OF Cory Snyder.

MARCH 30
A's re-signed P Dennis Eckersley.

APRIL 4
Marlins signed P Mark Gardner.

Phillies organization signed C Lenny Webster.

APRIL 5
Orioles re-signed C Chris Hoiles.

White Sox signed P Jose DeLeon.

Indians signed DH Dave Winfield to a one-year contract.

Indians organization signed P Jack Armstrong and P Les Lancaster.

Brewers signed P Bob Scanlan.

A's organization signed P Greg Cadaret.

Royals traded OF Brian McRae to Cubs for P Derek Wallace and P Geno Morones.

Cubs organization signed C Todd Pratt and P Tom Edens.

Reds signed OF Eric Anthony.

Expos traded P John Wetteland to Yankees for OF Fernando Seguignol, a player to be named and cash.

Expos traded P Ken Hill to Cardinals for P Bryan Eversgerd, P Kirk Bullinger and OF Darond Stovall.

Mets signed P John Franco and P Pete Walker.

Padres signed P Fernando Valenzuela.

Giants signed P Mark Dewey.

APRIL 6
Tigers signed C Jeff Tackett.

Royals traded P David Cone to Blue Jays for P David Sinnes, IF Chris Stynes and IF Tony Medrano.

Brewers signed OF Turner Ward.

Twins signed OF Alex Cole and OF Pedro Munoz.

Twins organization signed P Carl Willis, P Vince Horsman, P Brad Radke and P Todd Ritchie.

Mariners signed 2B Joey Cora.

Expos traded OF Marquis Grissom to Braves for OF Roberto Kelly, OF Tony Tarasco and P Esteban Yan.

Cubs organization signed P Chris Nabholz.

Reds signed P Pete Schourek, C Ed Taubensee and 1B Brian Hunter.

Rockies signed OF Dante Bichette, P Mike Munoz, P Kevin Logsdon and IF John VanderWal.

Dodgers organization signed OF Chris Gwynn and OF Mitch Webster.

Expos signed P Jeff Shaw.

Mets signed P Pete Harnisch.

Phillies signed 3B Charlie Hayes.

Giants signed P Dave Burba and P Jose Bautista.

APRIL 7
White Sox signed P Kirk McCaskill.

Indians organization signed P Bud Black.

Tigers signed P Joe Boever, DH Kirk Gibson.

Tigers organization signe IF Juan Samuel.

Royals signed C Pat Borders and C Brent Mayne.

Brewers organization signed C B.J. Surhoff.

A's signed IF Mike Bordick and P Dave Leiper.

A's organization signed P Bob Welch.

Mariners signed P Dave Fleming, C Chad Kreuter and 1B Tino Martinez.

Rangers signed P Kenny Rogers.

Braves signed 2B Mark Lemke, 3B Jose Oliva and P Brad Woodall.

Cubs signed 1B Mark Grace.

Marlins signed 3B Terry Pendleton and IF Jerry Browne.

Astros signed OF Luis Gonzalez.

Dodgers signed 3B Dave Hansen, OF Roger Cedeno and P Rick Gorecki.

Mets signed 1B/OF David Segui.

Phillies signed P David West and 2B Mickey Morandini.

Pirates signed P Jim Gott and P Denny Neagle.

Cardinals signed P Vicente Palacios, 1B Gerald Perry and C Scott Hemond.

Padres signed IF Scott Livingston and P Bill Krueger.

Giants signed P Trevor Wilson.

Giants organization signed 1B Todd Benzinger.

APRIL 9

Orioles signed P Kevin Brown, P Joe Borowski, P Russell Brock, P Jimmy Haynes, P Doug Jones, P Scott Klingenbeck, P Rick Krivda, P Jesse Orosco, P Billy Percibal, P Brian Sackinsky, 1B Paul Carey, OF Alex Ochoa, OF Jim Wawruck and C Gregg Zaun.

Red Sox signed C Mike Macfarlane, 1B Reggie Jefferson, and P Stan Belinda.

Red Sox organization signed P Mike Hartley.

Red Sox traded 3B Scott Cooper, P Cory Bailey, and a player to be named to Cardinals for P Rheal Cormier and OF Mark Whiten.

Angels signed P Bob Patterson and IF Rene Gonzales.

White Sox signed P Jim Abbott and OF Mike Devereaux.

Indians signed P Orel Hershiser.

Tigers re-signed SS Alan Trammell.

Royals signed P Tom Browning and OF Chris James.

Royals organization signed P Jose DeJesus.

Yankees signed OF Dion James.

A's signed P Dave Stewart.

A's organization signed P Rick Honeycutt.

Mariners signed IF Rich Amaral, IF Greg Pirkl and P Bob Wells.

Rangers signed P Bob Tewksbury.

Cubs signed P Jaime Navarro.

Reds signed P Mike Jackson.

Rockies signed OF Larry Walker, P Bill Swift and P Omar Olivares.

Marlins signed P John Burkett, P Bobby Witt and OF Andre Dawson.

Mets signed P Robert Persto, P Hector Ramirez and 1B Omar Garcia.

Phillies organization signed OF Dave Gallagher and P Jose Melendez.

Cardinals re-signed OF Bernard Gilkey.

Giants signed P Mark Leiter, P Terry Mulholland and OF Glenallen Hill.

APRIL 10

White Sox signed 3B Chris Sabo.

Indians signed P Paul Assenmacher.

Rangers signed P Jose Alberro, P Ritchie Moody, P Roger McDowell, P Francisco Saneaux and SS Guillermo Mercedes.

Blue Jays signed P Danny Darwin, P Jose Silva, P Paul Spoljaric and OF Lonell Roberts.

Cubs organization signed P Mike Perez.

Rockies traded P Marcus Moore to Reds for IF Chris Sexton.

Dodgers organization signed P Rob Murphy

Mets organization signed OF Ricky Otero.

Phillies signed P Tyler Green, P Andy Carter and OF Rob Butler.

Pirates organization signed P Mike Maddux.

Padres organization signed P Ted Higuera.

Padres signed P Jeff Tabaka, P Tim Worrell, IF Roberto Petagine and C Brian Johnson.

APRIL 11

Red Sox signed P Erik Hanson.

Angels organization signed P Mike Bielecki and P Scott Sanderson.

Brewers organization signed OF Derrick May.

Twins organization signed P Greg W. Harris.

Yankees organization signed P Randy Velarde.

A's signed P Todd Stottlemyre.

Rangers signed P Jeff Russell.

Mets signed OF Brett Butler, IF Tito Navarro and IF Edgardo Alfonzo.

APRIL 12

Red Sox organization signed P Alejandro Pena.

Angels signed IF Luis Raven.

Yankees organization signed P Joe Hesketh.

A's organization signed IF Mike Gallego.

Rangers signed DH Mickey Tettleton.

Blue Jays signed P Mike Timlin, P Edwin Hurtado, IF Felipe Crespo and IF Tomas Perez.

Braves signed OF Dwight Smith.

Cubs claimed P Steve Dixon on waivers from the Indians.

Mets sent P Juan Castillo to Astros to complete the trade for P Pete Harnisch (November 28, 1994).

APRIL 13

Orioles signed P Alan Mills.

Tigers traded OF Tony Phillips to Angels for OF Chad Curtis.

Royals signed SS David Howard.

Brewers signed P Mike Fetters.

Cubs organization signed IF/OF Howard Johnson.

Cubs released P Jesse Hollins.

Dodgers organization signed SS Dick Schofield.

Phillies organization signed IF Mariano Duncan.

APRIL 14

Red Sox organization signed P Derek Lilliquist.

Red Sox claimed OF Troy O'Leary on waivers from Brewers.

Rangers traded OF David Hulse to Brewers for P Scott Taylor.

APRIL 16

Orioles organization signed OF Kevin Bass.

Angels organization signed 1B Ricky Jordan.

Blue Jays organization signed P Paul Gibson.

Cardinals organization signed IF Manuel Lee and IF Luis Rivera.

APRIL 17

Rangers returned P Francisco Saneaux, whom they had selected in Rule 5 Draft, to Baltimore organization.

Reds signed C Benito Santiago.

Expos organization signed P Luis Aquino.

Phillies signed OF Gary Varsho.

APRIL 19

Red Sox signed P Zane Smith.

Reds announced retirement of P Jack Morris.

APRIL 19

Royals organization signed OF Felix Jose.

Rangers signed P Darren Oliver and OF Rusty Greer.

Padres signed 2B Jody Reed.

APRIL 20

A's organization signed C Brian Harper.

Expos announced retirement of P Jeff Reardon.

Pirates released P Tim Wakefield.

APRIL 21

Orioles signed OF Andy Van Slyke.

Red Sox signed IF Tim Naehring.

Rangers signed 2B Jeff Frye and P Roger Pavlik.

Blue Jays organization signed P Frank Viola.

Dodgers released P Al Osuna.

Pirates sent OF Stanton Cameron to Rangers to complete an earlier trade for IF Erik Johnson.

APRIL 23

Red Sox returned OF Benji Simonton, whom they had selected in Rule 5 Draft, to Giants organization.

White Sox released OF Joe Hall.

Tigers organization signed IF Scott Fletcher.

Royals traded P Enrique Burgos to Giants for a player to be named.

Twins released C Derek Parks.

Yankees sent OF Lyle Mouton to White Sox to complete a December 14, 1994 trade for P Jack McDowell.

Cubs released P Ted Power.

Reds claimed OF Nigel Wilson on waivers from Marlins.

Expos organization signed IF Tom Foley.

Mets released OF Jim Lindeman and OF Tito Navarro.

Pirates released P Todd Frohwirth.

Giants signed 1B Todd Benzinger.

APRIL 24

Indians released P Willie Smith.

Yankees announced retirement of P Joe Hesketh.

A's released P Bob Welch and P Greg Cadaret.

APRIL 26

Royals organization signed OF Vince Coleman.

Blue Jays traded P Aaron Small to Marlins for a player to be named.

Astros traded P Jimmy Lewis and Of Buck McNabb to Indians for OF Tony Mitchell and C Mitch Melusky.

APRIL 30

Padres returned P Nate Cromwell, whom they had selected in Rule 5 Draft, to Astros organization.

MAY 1

Astros sent P Sean Fesh to Padres to complete a 12-player deal (December 28, 1994).

MAY 3

Yankees organization signed C Bob Melvin.

Rangers organization signed IF Luis Rivera.

Reds organization signed P Tim Belcher.

MAY 4

Twins released P Carl Willis.

A's announced retirement of C Brian Harper.

MAY 8

Royals signed P Rusty Meacham.

MAY 9

Indians organization signed IF Casey Candaele and OF Lloyd McClendon.

MAY 10

Red Sox organization signed P Brian Barnes.

MAY 11

Mets traded P Mike Remlinger to Reds for OF Cobi Cradle.

MAY 14

Royals released OF Felix Jose, IF Keith Miller and IF Russ McGinnis.

Cubs organization signed P Joe Magrane.

MAY 15

Indians claimed C Brook Fordyce on waivers from Mets.

Twins released P Kevin Campbell.

Mariners traded P Roger Salkeld to Reds for P Tim Belcher.

Dodgers released SS Dick Schofield and P Rob Murphy.

Pirates released P Mike Maddux and C Mackey Sasser.

Giants released 1B Todd Benzinger.

MAY 16

Orioles traded OF Jack Voigt to Rangers for P John Dettmer.

Cardinals released IF Tim Hulett.

MAY 18

Rangers traded C Roger Luce to Astros for P Domingo Jean.

MAY 19

Red Sox organization signed OF Cory Snyder.

MAY 21

Giants traded P Salomon Torres to Mariners for P Shawn Estes and IF Wilson Delgado.

Mariners acquired P Steve Frey from Giants for future considerations.

MAY 23

Expos traded OF Roberto Kelly and P Joey Eischen to Dodgers for OF Henry Rodriguez and IF Jeff Treadway.

MAY 24

Orioles signed IF Kim Batiste.

MAY 25

Yankees organization signed 1B Todd Benzinger.

Marlins returned P Matt Dunbar to Yankees for $25,000.

Dodgers claimed P John Cummings on waivers from Mariners.

MAY 26

Red Sox claimed OF Tuffy Rhodes on waivers from Cubs.

MAY 30

Red Sox signed P Mike Maddux.

MAY 31

Dodgers claimed IF Chad Fonville on waivers from Expos.

JUNE 2

Cubs released OF Felix Jose from Iowa of the American Association.

JUNE 4

White Sox released 3B Chris Sabo.

JUNE 5

Yankees claimed P Josias Manzanillo on waivers from Mets.

JUNE 6

Red Sox organization signed OF Willie McGee.

Red Sox released P Keith Shepherd.

Mets returned OF Kevin Northrup to Expos.

JUNE 8

Mets traded 1B/OF David Segui to Expos for P Reid Cornelius.

Cardinals organization signed 3B/OF Chris Sabo.

JUNE 9

Dodgers traded SS Rafael Bournigal to Expos for P John Foster.

JUNE 11

Astros traded IF Chris Donnels to Red Sox for a player to be named.

JUNE 13

Mets sold the contract of P Mike Birkbeck to Yokohama of the Japanese Baseball League.

JUNE 16

Orioles traded P Brad Pennington to Reds for OF Danny Clyburn and P Tony Nieto.

Cubs traded P Mike Morgan, IF/OF Paul Torres and C Francisco Morales to Cardinals for IF Todd Zeile and cash.

JUNE 18

Angels released P Mitch Williams.

Phillies traded P Gene Harris to Orioles for OF Andy Van Slyke.

JUNE 19

Orioles released C Matt Nokes.

Yankees signed OF/DH Darryl Strawberry.

Cubs traded P Willie Banks to Dodgers for P Dax Winslett.

JUNE 21

Brewers traded OF Derrick May to Astros for a player to be named; Astros sent IF Tommy Nevers to Brewers to complete deal (July 21).

JUNE 22

Rangers traded SS Guillermo Mercedes to Indians for P Dennis Cook.

JUNE 23

Angels organization signed P Carl Willis.

Expos organization signed P Joe Magrane.

JUNE 28

Cubs traded C Rick Wilkins to Astros for OF Luis Gonzalez and C Scott Servais.

JUNE 29

Braves claimed C Scooter Tucker on waivers from Indians.

Rockies organization signed C Matt Nokes.

JULY 6

Twins traded P Rick Aguilera to Red Sox for P Frankie Rodriguez and a player to be named; Red Sox sent OF J.J. Johnson to Twins to complete deal (October 11).

Cubs released 3B Steve Buechele.

JULY 7

Royals released P Dennis Rasmussen.

Twins traded P Scott Erickson to Orioles for P Scott Klingenbeck and a player to be named; Orioles sent OF Kimera Bartee to Twins to complete deal (September 19).

Royals traded P Bob Milacki to Mariners for P Dave Fleming.

Mariners claimed OF Kevin Roberson on waivers from the Cubs.

JULY 9

Orioles released P Sid Fernandez.

Phillies released P Norm Charlton.

Cardinals traded P John Habyan to Angels for OF Mark Sweeney.

JULY 11

Phillies claimed P Omar Olivares on waivers from the Rockies.

JULY 12

Rangers organization signed 3B Steve Buechele.

JULY 13

Royals released 2B Chico Lind.

Phillies signed P Sid Fernandez.

JULY 14

Indians released P Bud Black.

Mariners signed P Norm Charlton.

JULY 16

Red Sox released P Derek Lilliquist.

White Sox released P Rob Dibble.

JULY 17

Blue Jays released P Danny Darwin.

JULY 18

White Sox traded OF Warren Newson to Mariners for a player to be named; Mariners sent P Jeff Darwin to White Sox to complete deal (October 9).

JULY 19

Angels claimed P Mike Harkey on waivers from A's.

Astros traded OF Phil Plantier to Padres for P Jeff Tabaka and P Rich Loiselle.

JULY 21

Angels released IF Carlos Martinez.

Reds traded OF Deion Sanders, P John Roper, P Ricky Pickett, P Scott Service and IF Dave McCarty to Giants for P Mark Portugal, P Dave Burba and OF Darren Lewis.

Mets traded P Jason Jacome and P Allen McDill to Royals for P Eugenio Morones and P Derek Wallace; Royals sent P John Carter to Mets to complete deal (November 17).

JULY 23

A's announced retirement of P Dave Stewart.

Marlins released P Rob Murphy.

JULY 24

Red Sox traded OF Mark Whiten to Phillies for 3B Dave Hollins.

Angels organization signed 2B Jose Lind.

Indians sent P Gregg Olson outright to Buffalo of the American Association. Buffalo then traded Olson to Omaha of the American Association for cash.

JULY 27

White Sox traded P Jim Abbott and P Tim Fortugno to Angels for OF McKay Christensen, P Andrew Lorrain, P Bill Simas and P John Snyder.

Cardinals traded P Ken Hill to Indians for 3B David Bell, P Rick Heiserman and C Pepe McNeal.

JULY 28

Brewers organization signed P Rob Dibble.

Yankees traded OF Danny Tartabull to A's for OF Ruben Sierra and P Jason Beverlin.

Blue Jays traded P David Cone to Yankees for P Marty Janzen, P Jason Jarvis and P Mike Gordon.

Mets traded 3B/OF Bobby Bonilla and a player to be named to Orioles for OF Alex Ochoa and OF Damon Buford; Mets sent P Jimmy Williams to Orioles to complete deal (August 16).

JULY 30

White Sox announced retirement of DH John Kruk.

Rangers released 3B Steve Buechele.

Dodgers organization signed P Derek Lilliquist.

Expos traded OF Lou Frazier to Rangers for a player to be named.

JULY 31

Braves traded P Mike Stanton to Red Sox for a player to be named; Red Sox traded OF Marc Lewis and P Mike Jacobs to Braves for P Matt Murray to complete deal (August 31).

Rangers organization signed P Danny Darwin.

Tigers traded P David Wells to Reds for P C.J. Nitkowski and P Dave Tuttle; Reds sent IF Mark Lewis to Tigers to complete deal (November 16).

Cubs traded P Bryan Hickerson to Rockies for future considerations.

Mets traded P Bret Saberhagen to Rockies for P Juan Acevedo and P Arnold Gooch; Mets sent P David Swanson to Rockies to complete deal (August 4).

Padres traded P Andy Benes to Mariners for P Ron Villone and OF Marc Newfield; Padres sent P Greg Keagle to Mariners to complete deal (September 17).

Twins sent P Kevin Tapani and P Mark Guthrie to Dodgers for 3B Ron Coomer, P Greg Hansell, P Jose Parra and a player to be named; Dodgers sent OF Chris Latham to Twins to complete deal (October 30).

AUGUST 4

Angels organization signed SS Dick Schofield.

Mariners claimed P Eric Gunderson on waivers from Mets.

AUGUST 7

Tigers traded P Buddy Groom to Marlins for a player to be named.

AUGUST 8

Mariners released P Steve Frey.

Reds claimed IF Mariano Duncan on waivers from Phillies.

Marlins traded P Bobby Witt to Rangers for two players to be named; Rangers sent P Wilson Heredia (August 11) and OF Scott Podsednik (October 2) to Marlins to complete deal.

AUGUST 9

Phillies traded OF Dave Gallagher to Angels for OF Kevin Flora and a player to be named; Angels sent P Russ Springer to Phillies to complete deal (August 15).

AUGUST 10

Red Sox claimed P Eric Gunderson on waivers from Mariners.

Marlins claimed P Willie Banks on waivers from Dodgers.

Tigers traded P Mike Henneman to Astros for a player to be named; Astros sent IF/OF Phil Nevin to Astros to complete deal (August 15).

AUGUST 11

Tigers announced retirement of OF/DH Kirk Gibson.

Royals traded C Pat Borders to Astros for a player to named later later; Astros sent P Rick Huisman to Royals to complete deal (August 17).

Yankees traded OF Luis Polonia to Braves for OF Troy Hughes.

Braves announced retirement of P Steve Bedrosian.

AUGUST 14

Royals traded OF Chris James to Red Sox for OF Wes Chamberlain.

AUGUST 15

Royals traded OF Vince Coleman to Mariners for a player to be named; Mariners sent P Jim Converse to Royals to complete deal (August 18).

AUGUST 16

Rangers traded 1B/OF Stephen Larkin and an undisclosed amount of cash to Reds for 3B Craig Worthington.

AUGUST 18

Mets traded OF Brett Butler to Dodgers for OF Dwight Maness and OF Scott Hunter.

AUGUST 21

White Sox released P Atlee Hammaker.

AUGUST 25

Orioles released P James Hurst.

White Sox traded OF Mike Devereaux to Braves for OF Andre King.

Braves traded 3B Jose Oliva to Cardinals for OF Anton French.

AUGUST 28

White Sox traded P Jose DeLeon to Expos for P Jeff Shaw.

AUGUST 29

Tigers traded P Kevin Wickander to Brewers for a player to be named; Brewers sent OF Derek Hacopian to Tigers to complete deal (September 12).

AUGUST 30

Angels released Chico Lind.

AUGUST 31

Red Sox traded P Chris Howard to Rangers for OF Jack Voigt.

Red Sox claimed OF Dwayne Hosey on waivers from Royals.

Blue Jays traded OF Candy Maldonado to Rangers for a player to be named; Rangers sent an undisclosed amount of cash to Blue Jays to complete deal (November 21).

Marlins traded P Alejandro Pena to Braves for a player to be named; Braves sent P Chris Seelbach to Marlins to complete deal (September 15).

Pirates traded C Mark Parent to Cubs for a player to be named or cash considerations.

Reds claimed P Domingo Jean on waivers from Rangers.

SEPTEMBER 1

Tigers released P Mike Gardiner.

SEPTEMBER 4

Tigers released P Mike Moore.

SEPTEMBER 8

Tigers traded IF Juan Samuel to Royals for a player to be named; Royals sent OF Phil Hiatt to Tigers to complete deal (September 14).

Tigers claimed IF Steve Rodriguez on waivers from Red Sox.

SEPTEMBER 15

Expos announced retirement of IF Jeff Treadway.

SEPTEMBER 25

A's traded P Rick Honeycutt to Yankees for cash.

OCTOBER 4

Phillies claimed P Willie Banks on waivers from Marlins.

OCTOBER 6

Red Sox claimed OF Brent Cookson on waivers from Royals.

Giants traded IF Mike Benjamin to Phillies for P Jeff Juden and C/1B Tommy Eason.

Pirates released P Jim Gott.

OCTOBER 10

Astros traded P Pedro Martinez to Padres for IF Ray Holbert.

OCTOBER 11

Brewers released P Jeff Bronkey.

OCTOBER 12

Red Sox claimed P John Thobe on waivers from Expos.

Expos released P Hector Fajardo.

OCTOBER 13

Red Sox claimed P Butch Henry from Expos.

Angels released C Andy Allanson.

OCTOBER 16

Tigers released P Brian Bohanto, P Dwayne Henry, C Ron Tingley and OF Derrick White.

Yankees signed P Dwight Gooden.

OCTOBER 31

Cubs signed 2B Ryne Sandberg.

NOVEMBER 9

Dodgers re-signed OF Brett Butler.

NOVEMBER 14

White Sox re-signed OF Dave Martinez.

NOVEMBER 16

Mariners released C Chris Howard and OF Warren Newson.

Dodgers re-signed P Ramon Martinez.

Phillies claimed P Carlos Crawford on waivers from Indians.

NOVEMBER 17

Indians released Of Ruben Amaro.

Royals claimed P John Carter on waivers from Indians.

Phillies claimed P Carlos Crawford on waivers from Indians.

NOVEMBER 20

Orioles claimed P Oscar Munoz on waivers from Twins.

Tigers claimed OF Micah Franklin and P Jeff McCurry on waivers from Pirates.

Rockies traded C Joe Girardi to Yankees for P Mike DeJean and a player to be named.

Rockies re-signed SS Walt Weiss.

Mets signed P Chris Nabholz, P Joe Ausanio, P Steve Dixto, P Rick Reed, IF Luis Rivera and OF Kevin Roberson.

NOVEMBER 21

Marlins signed OF Devon White.

Cardinals released P Vicente Palacios and P Rich Rodriguez.

NOVEMBER 22

Angels signed IF Randy Velarde.

NOVEMBER 27

Royals claimed OF Darren Burton on waivers from Cubs.

Phillies re-signed P Sid Fernandez.

NOVEMBER 30

White Sox released C Barry Lyons.

Tigers released OF Milt Cuyler.

Dodgers signed SS Greg Gagne.

DECEMBER 1

Reds released OF Darren Lewis.

Giants traded OF Rikkert Faneyte to Rangers for a player to be named.

DECEMBER 2-3

Braves re-signed 1B Fred McGriff.

DECEMBER 4

Marlins traded P Tyrone Narcisse and OF Chuck Carr to Brewers for P Juan Gonzalez.

Reds acquired OF Andre King from Cardinals for IF Luis Ordaz, and traded P Mike Remlinger to Royals. The Reds then sent OF Miguel Mejia to Cardinals to complete deal.

DECEMBER 5

Angels organization signed IF Tim Wallach and IF Jack Howell.

Twins signed DH Paul Molitor.

Yankees re-signed 3B Wade Boggs.

Marlins signed OF Joe Orsulak.

DECEMBER 6

Rangers claimed Of Darren Lewis on waivers from Reds.
Rangers signed OF Warren Newson.
Blue Jays traded 3B Howard Battle and P Rickey Jordan to Phillies for P Paul Quantrill.

DECEMBER 7

Red Sox re-signed OF Jose Canseco.
Tigers signed OF Phil Plantier.
Mariners traded 1B Tino Martinez, P Jeff Nelsto and P Jim Mecir to Yankees for P Sterling Hitchcock and 3B Russ Davis.
Yankees signed 1B Tino Martinez.
Blue Jays signed OF Otis Nixon.
Cardinals re-signed P Mike Morgan.

DECEMBER 8

Brewers signed OF Chuck Carr.
Giants signed OF Stan Javier.

DECEMBER 11

White Sox signed OF Harold Baines.
White Sox organization signed C Chad Kreuter.
Twins signed P Rick Aguilera.
Yankees signed 2B Mariano Duncan.
Rangers signed C Mickey Tettleton.
Marlins organization signed P Alejandro Pena.
Giants re-signed OF Glenallen Hill.

DECEMBER 13

Tigers signed C Mark Parent.
Cubs organization signed P Rob Dibble.
Phillies organization signed OF Pete Incaviglia.

DECEMBER 14

Orioles signed P Randy Myers.
Red Sox signed C Mike Stanley.
Angels organization signed C Ron Tingley.
Indians signed P Jack McDowell.
Brewers signed P Kevin Wickander.
Rangers signed OF Darryl Hamilton.
Marlins signed P Al Leiter.
Astros re-signed 2B Craig Biggio.
Dodgers signed P Mark Guthrie and 3B Dave Hansen.
Mets signed OF Lance Johnson.
Phillies traded OF Phil Geisler to Mets for OF Ricky Otero.
Pirates signed OF Mike Kingery.
Giants traded SS Royce Clayton and a player to be named to Cardinals for P Allen Watson, P Rich DeLucia and P Doug Creek.

DECEMBER 15

Royals re-signed P Jeff Montgomery.
Blue Jays signed C Charlie O'Brien.
Expos traded P Rick Clelland to Dodgers for P Omar Daal.
Expos traded P Gabe White to Reds for 2B Jhonny Carvajal.
Mets signed OF Chris Jones.
Cardinals signed OF Willie McGee.
Mets traded OF Jeff Barry to Padres for P Pedro A. Martinez.

DECEMBER 17

Royals signed C Mike Macfarlane.
Braves traded P Kent Mercker to Orioles for P Joe Borowski and P Rachaad Stewart.
Dodgers traded SS Jose Offerman to Royals for P Billy Brewer.

DECEMBER 18

Orioles signed P Roger McDowell.
Red Sox signed P Butch Henry.
Brewers released P Bob Scanlan.
Mariners traded P Bill Risley and 2B Miguel Cairo to Blue Jays for P Edwin Hurtado and P Paul Menhart.

Rockies signed C Jeff Reed.
Cardinals signed 3B Gary Gaetti.
Padres signed P Bob Tewksbury.

DECEMBER 19

Orioles traded 1B Paul Carey to Red Sox for a player to be named.
Royals traded C Brent Mayne to Mets for OF Al Shirley.
Mariners signed IF Rich Amaral and IF Doug Strange.
Cubs re-signed 1B Mark Grace.
Giants re-signed P Rod Beck.
Red Sox signed 1B Reggie Jefferson and C/IF Bill Haselman.
Red Sox organization signed IF Juan Bell.
Indians organization signed C Eric Helfand.
Mets signed P Doug Henry.

DECEMBER 20

Orioles signed OF B.J. Surhoff.
Angels signed P Bryan Harvey.
Brewers signed OF David Hulse.
Astros traded P Dave Veres and C Raul Chavez to Expos for 3B Sean Berry.
Expos organization signed IF Andy Stankiewicz.
Mets organization signed OF Gary Thurman.

DECEMBER 21

Orioles signed 2B Roberto Alomar.
Orioles released 2B Bret Barberie, 3B Leo Gomez, P Terry Clark and P Ben McDonald.
Red Sox signed P Tom Gordon.
Red Sox organization signed OF Milt Cuyler.
Red Sox released P Tim Vanegmond and 3B Dave Hollins.
Angels released P Shawn Boskie, P Mike Harkey and P Rich Monteleone.
White Sox released SS Craig Grebeck, and P Scott Radinsky and P Jeff Shaw.
Indians released 1B Paul Sorrento.
Tigers released SS Alan Trammell.
Royals signed SS Jose Offerman.
Royals released P Dave Fleming.
Royals traded 1B Wally Joyner and P Aaron Dorlarque to Padres for IF Bip Roberts and P Bryan Wolff.
Brewers organization signed C Matt Nokes.
Twins released P Michael Misuraca, OF Pedro Munoz and 1B Tom Quinlan.
Yankees re-signed P David Cone and IF Pat Kelly.
Rangers released SS Esteban Beltre and 2B Jeff Frye.
Cubs released P Anthony Young and 3B Todd Zeile.
Reds released OF Jerome Walton.
Rockies released IF Roberto Mejia.
Marlins released P John Johnstone.
Astros released SS Craig Shipley.
Dodgers released P Kevin Tapani.
Expos released P Gil Heredia and P Dave Leiper.
Expos claimed OF Ray McDavid on waivers from Padres.
Phillies released P Dennis Springer.
Pirates released P Rick White.
Yankees traded P Rick Honeycutt to Cardinals for cash.
Cardinals released 3B Scott Cooper, 2B Geronimo Pena and C Scott Hemond.
Padres released P Willie Blair, P Brian Williams and 3B Eddie Williams.
Padres signed SS Andujar Cedeno.
Giants released OF Deion Sanders.

DECEMBER 22

Red Sox signed P Jamie Moyer.
Rangers signed P Ken Hill and P Mike Henneman.
Blue Jays signed P Erik Hanson.

DECEMBER 22

Marlins signed P Kevin Brown.
Marlins organization signed IF Craig Grebeck.
Phillies signed 3B Todd Zeile.

DECEMBER 23

Orioles organization signed IF Billy Ripken.
Twins signed 3B Dave Hollins.
Cardinals signed OF Ron Gant and P Andy Benes.

DECEMBER 26

Red Sox organization signed P Chuck Ricci.
Cubs signed 3B Dave Magadan.
Reds traded P David Wells to Orioles for OF Curtis Goodwin and OF Trovin Valdez.

DECEMBER 28

White Sox traded OF Tim Raines to Yankees for future considerations.
Cubs signed P Doug Jones.
Astros organization signed P John Johnstone, IF/OF Mike Brumley and C Jerry Goff.
Pirates signed 3B Charlie Hayes.

DECEMBER 29

Padres signed OF Rickey Henderson.

DECEMBER 30

Yankees signed P Kenny Rogers.

AWARD WINNERS

THE SPORTING NEWS

AMERICAN LEAGUE

Pitcher of the Year: Randy Johnson, Seattle
Rookie Player of the Year: Garret Anderson, California, OF
Rookie Pitcher of the Year: Julian Tavarez, Cleveland
Fireman of the Year: Jose Mesa, Cleveland
Comeback Player of the Year: Tim Wakefield, Boston, P
Manager of the Year: Mike Hargrove, Cleveland

MAJOR LEAGUE

Player of the Year: Albert Belle, Cleveland
Executive of the Year: John Hart, Cleveland

NATIONAL LEAGUE

Pitcher of the Year: Greg Maddux, Atlanta
Rookie Player of the Year: Chipper Jones, Atlanta, 3B
Rookie Pitcher of the Year: Hideo Nomo, Los Angeles
Fireman of the Year: Randy Myers, Chicago
Comeback Player of the Year: Ron Gant, Cincinnati, OF
Manager of the Year: Don Baylor, Colorado

MINOR LEAGUE

Player of the Year: Karim Garcia, OF, Albuquerque, Pacific Coast
Manager of the Year: Pete Mackanin, Ottawa, International
Executives of the Year: Jack and Mary Cain, Portland, Northwest

BASEBALL WRITERS' ASSOCIATION OF AMERICA

AMERICAN LEAGUE

MOST VALUABLE PLAYER

Player, Team	1	2	3	4	5	6	7	8	9	10	Pts.
Mo Vaughn, Boston	12	12	4	-	-	-	-	-	-	-	308
Albert Belle, Cleveland	11	10	7	-	-	-	-	-	-	-	300
Edgar Martinez, Seattle	4	5	12	5	2	-	-	-	-	-	244
Jose Mesa, Cleveland	1	-	1	6	6	4	1	1	1	1	130
Jay Buhner, Seattle	-	-	1	3	5	8	2	3	2	-	120
Randy Johnson, Seattle	-	1	2	3	5	5	2	-	1	-	111
Tim Salmon, California	-	-	-	6	3	4	2	6	1	2	110
Frank Thomas, Chicago	-	-	1	4	1	2	2	5	3	2	86
John Valentin, Boston	-	-	-	1	2	1	4	2	5	1	57
Gary Gaetti, Kansas City	-	-	-	-	2	1	4	2	1	4	45
Rafael Palmeiro, Baltimore	-	-	-	-	1	1	2	2	3	3	34
Manny Ramirez, Cleveland	-	-	-	-	1	-	4	1	2	1	30
Tim Wakefield, Boston	-	-	-	-	-	-	3	-	3	2	20
Jim Edmonds, California	-	-	-	-	-	1	-	2	2	3	18
Paul O'Neill, New York	-	-	-	-	-	-	1	1	1	-	2	14
Mark McGwire, Oakland	-	-	-	-	-	-	1	-	1	1	7
Chuck Knoblauch, Minnesota	-	-	-	-	-	-	-	1	-	2	5
Wade Boggs, New York	-	-	-	-	-	-	-	-	2	1	5
Gary DiSarcina, California	-	-	-	-	-	-	-	1	-	-	3
Cal Ripken, Baltimore	-	-	-	-	-	-	-	-	-	3	3
Kirby Puckett, Minnesota	-	-	-	-	-	-	-	-	1	-	2

Fourteen points awarded for a first-place vote, nine for second and down to one for 10th.

MANAGER OF THE YEAR

Manager, Team	1	2	3	Pts.
Lou Piniella, Seattle	9	12	5	86
Kevin Kennedy, Boston	11	5	4	74
Mike Hargrove, Cleveland	8	8	7	71
Buck Showalter, New York	-	1	5	8
Marcel Lachemann, California	-	1	2	5
Phil Garner, Milwaukee	-	1	1	4
Bob Boone, Kansas City	-	-	3	3
Johnny Oates, Texas	-	-	1	1

Five points awarded for a first-place vote, three for second and one for third.

CY YOUNG AWARD

Pitcher, Team	1	2	3	Pts.
Randy Johnson, Seattle	26	2	-	136
Jose Mesa, Cleveland	2	13	5	54
Tim Wakefield, Boston	-	6	11	29
David Cone, Tor.-N.Y.	-	5	3	18
Mike Mussina, Baltimore	-	2	8	14
Charles Nagy, Cleveland	-	-	1	1

Five points awarded for a first-place vote, three for second and one for third.

ROOKIE OF THE YEAR

Player, Team	1	2	3	Pts.
Marty Cordova, Minnesota	13	13	1	105
Garret Anderson, California	13	10	4	99
Andy Pettitte, New York	1	1	8	16
Troy Percival, California	1	2	2	13
Shawn Green, Toronto	-	2	2	8
Ray Durham, Chicago	-	-	3	3
Julian Tavarez, Cleveland	-	-	3	3
Jon Nunnally, Kansas City	-	-	2	2
Tom Goodwin, Kansas City	-	-	1	1
Brad Radke, Minnesota	-	-	1	1
Steve Sparks, Milwaukee	-	-	1	1

Five points awarded for a first-place vote, three for second and one for third.

NATIONAL LEAGUE
MOST VALUABLE PLAYER

Player, Team	1	2	3	4	5	6	7	8	9	10	Pts.
Barry Larkin, Cincinnati	11	5	7	2	1	1	-	-	-	1	281
Dante Bichette, Colorado	6	6	6	6	3	1	-	-	-	-	251
Greg Maddux, Atlanta	7	8	5	3	-	2	1	1	-	1	249
Mike Piazza, Los Angeles	3	7	6	4	3	-	2	1	2	-	214
Eric Karros, Los Angeles	-	2	3	3	7	3	1	1	4	-	135
Reggie Sanders, Cincinnati	-	-	-	3	7	3	5	6	1	2	120
Larry Walker, Colorado	-	-	1	1	-	8	3	6	1	1	88
Sammy Sosa, Chicago	-	-	-	2	1	6	2	2	7	3	81
Tony Gwynn, San Diego	-	-	-	2	4	1	2	3	3	6	72
Craig Biggio, Houston	-	-	-	2	1	1	5	2	2	3	58
Ron Gant, Cincinnati	1	-	-	-	-	1	1	2	-	2	31
Barry Bonds, San Francisco	-	-	-	-	-	-	3	1	2	2	21
Mark Grace, Chicago	-	-	-	-	1	-	-	1	1	3	14
Derek Bell, Houston	-	-	-	-	-	1	1	1	-	-	12
Jeff Bagwell, Houston	-	-	-	-	-	-	1	-	-	1	5
Charlie Hayes, Philadelphia	-	-	-	-	-	-	1	-	-	-	4
Andres Galarraga, Colorado	-	-	-	-	-	-	-	-	2	-	4
Chipper Jones, Atlanta	-	-	-	-	-	-	-	1	-	-	3
Vinny Castilla, Colorado	-	-	-	-	-	-	-	-	1	1	3
Fred McGriff, Atlanta	-	-	-	-	-	-	-	-	1	-	2
Pete Schourek, Cincinnati	-	-	-	-	-	-	-	-	1	-	2
Jeff Conine, Florida	-	-	-	-	-	-	-	-	-	1	1
Tom Henke, St. Louis	-	-	-	-	-	-	-	-	-	1	1

Fourteen points awarded for a first-place vote, nine for second and down to one for 10th.

MANAGER OF THE YEAR

Manager, Team	1	2	3	Pts.
Don Baylor, Colorado	19	9	-	122
Davey Johnson, Cincinnati	8	15	4	89
Bobby Cox, Atlanta	1	1	12	20
Terry Collins, Houston	-	2	5	11
Jim Riggleman, Chicago	-	1	3	6
Dallas Green, New York	-	-	3	3
Bruce Bochy, San Diego	-	-	1	1

Five points awarded for a first-place vote, three for second and one for third.

CY YOUNG AWARD

Pitcher, Team	1	2	3	Pts.
Greg Maddux, Atlanta	28	-	-	140
Pete Schourek, Cincinnati	-	16	7	55
Tom Glavine, Atlanta	-	6	12	30
Hideo Nomo, Los Angeles	-	5	4	19
Ramon Martinez, Los Angeles	-	1	5	8

Five points awarded for a first-place vote, three for second and one for third.

ROOKIE OF THE YEAR

Player, Team	1	2	3	Pts.
Hideo Nomo, Los Angeles	18	9	1	118
Chipper Jones, Atlanta	10	18	-	104
Quilvio Veras, Florida	-	1	11	14
Jason Isringhausen, New York	-	-	4	4
John Mabry, St. Louis	-	-	4	4
Carlos Perez, Montreal	-	-	4	4
Chad Fonville, Mon.-L.A.	-	-	1	1
Brian Hunter, Houston	-	-	1	1
Charles Johnson, Florida	-	-	1	1
Ismael Valdez, Los Angeles	-	-	1	1

Five points awarded for a first-place vote, three for second and one for third.

MISCELLANEOUS

ATTENDANCE

AMERICAN LEAGUE

	Home	Road
Baltimore	3,098,475	1,751,096
Boston	2,164,410	1,939,725
California	1,748,680	1,871,684
Chicago	1,609,773	1,749,175
Cleveland	2,842,745	2,009,149
Detroit	1,180,979	1,879,779
Kansas City	1,233,530	1,711,245
Milwaukee	1,087,560	1,790,661
Minnesota	1,057,667	1,634,586
New York	1,705,263	2,072,283
Oakland	1,174,310	1,753,085
Seattle	1,643,203	1,777,159
Texas	1,985,910	1,648,820
Toronto	2,826,483	1,770,541
Totals	**25,358,988**	**25,358,988**

NATIONAL LEAGUE

	Home	Road
Atlanta	2,561,831	2,024,693
Chicago	1,918,265	1,951,435
Cincinnati	1,837,649	1,781,065
Colorado	3,390,037	1,794,948
Florida	1,700,466	1,718,138
Houston	1,363,801	1,650,552
Los Angeles	2,766,251	1,917,341
Montreal	1,309,618	1,740,321
New York	1,273,183	1,827,201
Philadelphia	2,043,598	1,660,641
Pittsburgh	905,517	1,742,370
St. Louis	1,756,727	1,747,948
San Diego	1,041,805	1,725,753
San Francisco	1,241,500	1,827,842
Totals	**25,110,248**	**25,110,248**

DEBUTS

Player	Pos.	Team	Birth date	Birthplace	Debut
Acevedo, Juan	P	Colorado	5-5-70	Juarez, Mexico	4-30
Adams, Terry Wayne	P	Chicago N.L.	3-6-73	Mobile, Ala.	8-10
Ahearne, Patrick Howard	P	Detroit	12-10-69	San Francisco	6-14
Alberro, Jose E.	P	Texas	6-29-69	San Juan, Puerto Rico	4-27
Alfonzo, Edgardo Antonio	PH	New York N.L.	8-11-73	St. Teresa, Venezuela	4-26
Alvarez, Cesar Octavio	P	Montreal	11-25-71	Obregon, Mexico	8-21
Andrews, Darrell Shane	3B	Montreal	8-28-71	Dallas	4-26
Andujar, Luis	P	Chicago A.L.	11-22-72	Bani, Dominican Republic	9-8
Aurilia, Richard	SS	San Francisco	9-2-71	Brooklyn, N.Y.	9-6
Bailey, Charles Roger	P	Colorado	10-3-70	Chattahoochee, Fla.	4-27
Baker, Scott	P	Oakland	5-18-70	San Jose, Calif.	7-17
Baldwin, James	P	Chicago A.L.	7-15-71	Southern Pines, N.C.	4-30
Barber, Brian Scott	P	St. Louis	3-4-73	Hamilton, Ohio	8-12
Bark, Brian Stuart	P	Boston	8-26-68	Baltimore	7-6
Barry, Jeffrey Finas	OF	New York N.L.	9-22-68	Medford, Ore.	6-9
Bates, Jason Charles	2B	Colorado	1-5-71	Downey, Calif.	4-26
Battle, Allen Zelmo	PH	St. Louis	11-29-68	Grantham, N.C.	4-26
Battle, Howard Dion	PR	Toronto	3-25-72	Biloxi, Miss.	9-5
Bell, David Michael	PH	Cleveland	9-14-72	Cincinnati	5-3
Benard, Marvin Larry	PH	San Francisco	1-20-70	Bluefields, Nicaragua	9-5
Benes, Alan	P	St. Louis	1-21-72	Evansville, Ind.	9-19
Benitez, Yamil Antonio	OF	Montreal	5-10-72	San Juan, Puerto Rico	9-15
Bennett, Erik Hans	P	California	9-13-68	Yreka, Calif.	5-15
Bennett, Gary David	PH	Philadelphia	4-17-72	Waukegan, Ill.	9-24
Bertotti, Michael David	P	Chicago A.L.	1-18-70	Jersey City, N.J.	7-29
Berumen, Andres	P	San Diego	4-5-71	Tijuana, Mexico	4-27
Blomdahl, Benjamin Earl	P	Detroit	12-30-70	Long Beach, Calif.	4-28
Bochtler, Douglas Eugene	P	San Diego	7-5-70	West Palm Beach, Fla.	5-5
Boehringer, Brian Edward	P	New York A.L.	1-8-70	St. Louis	4-30
Borowski, Joseph Thomas	P	Baltimore	5-4-71	Bayonne, N.J.	7-9
Bradshaw, Terry Leon	PH	St. Louis	2-3-69	Franklin, Va.	5-4
Brady, Douglas Stephen	PR	Chicago A.L.	11-23-69	Jacksonville, Ill.	9-5
Brandenburg, Mark Clay	P	Texas	7-14-70	Houston	7-20
Brewington, Jamie Chancellor	P	San Francisco	9-28-71	Greenville, N.C.	7-24
Brito, Jorge Manuel	C	Colorado	6-22-66	Moncion, Dominican Republic	4-30
Bruske, James Scott	P	Los Angeles	10-7-64	East St. Louis, Ill.	8-25
Bunch, Melvin Lynn Jr.	P	Kansas City	11-4-71	Texarkana, Texas	5-6
Busch, Michael Anthony	PH	Los Angeles	7-7-68	Davenport, Iowa	8-30
Byrd, Paul Gregory	P	New York N.L.	12-3-70	Louisville, Ky.	7-28
Caceres, Edgar F.	1B	Kansas City	6-6-64	Lara, Venezuela	6-8
Cameron, Mike	OF	Chicago A.L.	1-8-73	La Grange, Ga.	8-27
Carmona, Rafael	P	Seattle	10-2-72	Rio Piedras, Puerto Rico	5-18
Carrara, Giovanni	P	Toronto	3-4-68	Anzuategui, Venezuela	7-29
Castillo, Alberto Terrero	C	New York N.L.	2-10-70	San Juan de la Maguana, D.R.	5-28
Castro, Juan	3B	Los Angeles	6-20-72	Los Mochis, Mexico	9-2
Cedeno, Roger Leandro	OF	Los Angeles	8-16-74	Valencia, Venezuela	6-20
Christiansen, Jason Samuel	P	Pittsburgh	9-21-69	Omaha, Neb.	4-26

Player	Pos.	Team	Birth date	Birthplace	Debut
Clark, Anthony Christopher	1B	Detroit	6-15-72	Newton, Kan.	9-3
Clontz, John Bradley	P	Atlanta	4-25-71	Stuart, Va.	4-26
Cookson, Brent Adam	DH	Kansas City	9-7-69	Van Nuys, Calif.	8-12
Coomer, Ronald Bryan	PH	Minnesota	11-18-66	Crest Hill, Ill.	8-1
Cordova, Martin Keevin	OF	Minnesota	7-10-69	Las Vegas	4-26
Cornelius, Jonathan Reid	P	Montreal	6-2-70	Thomasville, Ala.	4-29
Counsell, Craig John	SS	Colorado	8-21-70	South Bend, Ind.	9-17
Courtright, John Charles	P	Cincinnati	5-30-70	Marion, Ohio	5-6
Crabtree, Timothy Lyle	P	Toronto	10-13-69	Jackson, Mich.	6-23
Creek, Paul Douglas	P	St. Louis	3-1-69	Winchester, Va.	9-17
Damon, Johnny David	OF	Kansas City	11-5-73	Fort Riley, Kan.	8-12
Davison, Scott Ray	P	Seattle	10-16-70	Inglewood, Calif.	9-4
Dedrick, James Michael	P	Baltimore	4-4-68	Los Angeles	8-12
Devarez, Cesar Salvatore	PH	Baltimore	9-22-69	San Francisco de Macoris, D.R.	6-3
Dishman, Glenelg Edward	P	San Diego	11-5-70	Baltimore	6-22
Dougherty, James E.	P	Houston	3-8-68	Brentwood, N.Y.	4-27
Dunbar, Matthew Marshall	P	Florida	10-15-68	Tallahassee, Fla.	4-25
Durham, Ray	2B	Chicago A.L.	11-30-71	Charlotte, N.C.	4-26
Eddy, Christopher Mark	P	Oakland	11-27-69	Dallas	4-26
Edenfield, Kenneth Edward	P	California	3-18-67	Jesup, Ga.	5-11
Encarnacion, Angelo Benjamin	PH	Pittsburgh	4-18-73	Santo Domingo, Dominican Republic	5-2
Ericks, John Edward III	P	Pittsburgh	9-16-67	Oak Lawn, Ill.	6-24
Eshelman, Vaughn Michael	P	Boston	5-22-69	Philadelphia	5-2
Estes, Aaron Shawn	P	San Francisco	2-18-73	San Bernardino, Calif.	9-16
Fermin, Ramon Antonio Ventura	P	Oakland	11-25-72	San Francisco de Macoris, D.R.	8-6
Florence, Donald Emery	P	New York N.L.	3-16-67	Manchester, N.H.	8-8
Fonville, Chad Everette	PR	Montreal	3-5-71	Jacksonville, N.C.	4-28
Fordyce, Brook Alexander	PR	New York N.L.	5-7-70	New London, Conn.	4-26
Franco, Matthew Neil	PH	Chicago N.L.	8-19-69	Santa Monica, Calif.	9-6
Garcia, Freddy Adrian	PH	Pittsburgh	8-1-72	La Romana, Dominican Republic	5-2
Garcia, Gustavo (Karim)	OF	Los Angeles	10-29-75	Ciudad Obregon, Mexico	9-2
Giambi, Jason Gilbert	DH	Oakland	1-8-71	West Covina, Calif.	5-8
Giannelli, Raymond John	PH	St. Louis	2-5-66	Brooklyn, N.Y.	9-16
Gibralter, Stephan Benson	PH	Cincinnati	10-9-72	Dallas	6-1
Giles, Brian S.	OF	Cleveland	1-20-71	El Cajon, Calif.	9-16
Giovanola, Edward Thomas	2B	Atlanta	3-4-69	Los Gatos, Calif.	9-10
Givens, Brian Alan	P	Milwaukee	11-6-65	Lompac, Calif.	6-24
Goodwin, Curtin LaMar	OF	Baltimore	9-30-72	Oakland, Calif.	6-2
Grace, Michael James	P	Philadelphia	6-20-70	Joliet, Ill.	9-1
Grott, Matthew Allen	P	Cincinnati	12-5-67	La Porte, Ind.	5-4
Grudzielanek, Mark James	PH	Montreal	6-30-70	Milwaukee	4-28
Hajek, David Vincent	PH	Houston	10-14-67	Roseville, Calif.	9-15
Hancock, Leland David	P	Pittsburgh	6-27-67	Van Nuys, Calif.	9-3
Hansell, Gregory Michael	P	Los Angeles	3-12-71	Bellflower, Calif.	4-28
Harikkala, Timothy Allan	P	Seattle	7-15-71	West Palm Beach, Fla.	5-27
Hartgraves, Dean Charles	P	Houston	8-12-66	Bakersfield, Calif.	5-3
Hatteberg, Scott Allen	PH	Boston	12-14-69	Salem, Ore.	9-8
Hawkins, LaTroy	P	Minnesota	12-21-72	Gary, Ind.	4-29
Haynes, Jimmy Wayne	P	Baltimore	9-5-72	LaGrange, Ga.	9-13
Heredia, Wilson	P	Texas	3-30-72	La Romana, Dominican Republic	4-27
Hermanson, Dustin	P	San Diego	12-21-72	Springfield, Ohio	5-8
Herrera, Jose Ramon Catalino	OF	Oakland	8-30-72	Santo Domingo, Dominican Republic	8-12
Higginson, Robert Leigh	PH	Detroit	8-18-70	Philadelphia	4-26
Hollandsworth, Todd Mathew	OF	Los Angeles	4-20-73	Dayton, Ohio	4-25
Hook, Christopher Wayne	P	San Francisco	8-4-68	San Diego	4-30
Hosey, Dwayne Samuel	PR	Boston	3-11-67	Sharon, Pa.	9-1
Hubbard, Michael Wayne	PH	Chicago N.L.	2-16-71	Lynchburg, Va.	7-13
Hudson, Joseph Paul	P	Boston	9-29-70	Philadelphia	6-10
Huisman, Richard Allen	P	Kansas City	5-17-69	Oak Park, Ill.	9-4
Hurtado, Edwin Amilgar	P	Toronto	2-1-70	Barquisimeto, Venezuela	5-22
Isringhausen, Jason Derek	P	New York N.L.	9-7-72	Brighton, Ill.	7-17
James, Michael Elmo	P	California	8-15-67	Fort Walton Beach, Fla.	4-29
Jeter, Derek	SS	New York A.L.	6-26-74	Pequannock, N.J.	5-29
Johns, Douglas Alan	P	Oakland	12-19-67	South Bend, Ind.	7-8
Johnson, Mark Patrick	PH	Pittsburgh	10-17-67	Worcester, Mass.	4-26
Jordan, Kevin Wayne	PH	Philadelphia	10-9-69	San Francisco	8-8
Jordan, Ricardo	P	Toronto	6-27-70	Delray Beach, Fla.	6-23
Karchner, Matthew Dean	P	Chicago A.L.	6-28-67	Berwick, Pa.	7-18
Karl, Randall Scott	P	Milwaukee	8-9-71	Fontana, Calif.	5-4
Karp, Ryan Jason	P	Philadelphia	4-5-70	Los Angeles	6-23
Keyser, Brian	P	Chicago A.L.	10-31-66	Castro Valley, Calif.	6-2
Konuszewski, Dennis John	P	Pittsburgh	2-4-71	Bridgeport, Mich.	8-4
Kowitz, Brian Mark	PH	Atlanta	8-7-69	Baltimore	6-4

Player	Pos.	Team	Birth date	Birthplace	Debut
Krivda, Rick Michael	P	Baltimore	1-19-70	McKeesport, Pa.	7-7
Kroon, Marc Jason	P	San Diego	4-2-73	Bronx, N.Y.	7-7
Lawton, Matthew III	PH	Minnesota	11-3-71	Gulfport, Miss.	9-5
Ledesma, Aaron David	PH	New York N.L.	6-3-71	Union City, Calif.	7-2
Lira, Antonio Felipe	P	Detroit	4-26-72	Miranda, Venezuela	4-27
Loaiza, Esteban Antonio	P	Pittsburgh	12-31-71	Tijuana, Mexico	4-29
Lomon, Kevin Dale	P	New York N.L.	11-20-71	Fort Smith, Ark.	4-27
Loretta, Mark David	PH	Milwaukee	8-14-71	Santa Monica, Calif.	9-4
Mahay, Ronald Matthew	OF	Boston	6-28-71	Crestwood, Ill.	5-21
Mantei, Matthew Bruce	P	Florida	7-7-73	Tampa, Fla.	6-18
Marquez, Isidro Espinoza	P	Chicago A.L.	5-15-65	Navojoa, Sonora, Mexico	4-26
Martinez, Angel Sandy	C	Toronto	10-3-72	Villa Mella, Dominican Republic	6-24
Masteller, Dan Patrick	1B	Minnesota	3-17-68	Toledo, Ohio	6-23
Mathews, Timothy Jay	P	St. Louis	1-9-70	Belleville, Ill.	7-28
Maxcy, David Brian	P	Detroit	5-4-71	Amory, Miss.	5-26
May, Darrell Kevin	P	Atlanta	6-13-72	San Bernardino, Calif.	9-10
McAndrew, James Brian	P	Milwaukee	9-2-67	Williamsport, Pa.	7-17
McCracken, Quinton Antoine	PH	Colorado	3-16-70	Wilmington, N.C.	9-17
McCurry, Jeffrey Dee	P	Pittsburgh	1-21-70	Tokyo	5-6
Mecir, James Jason	P	Seattle	5-16-70	Queens, N.Y.	9-4
Menhart, Paul Gerard	P	Toronto	3-25-69	St. Louis	4-27
Mimbs, Michael Randall	P	Philadelphia	2-13-69	Macon, Ga.	5-6
Mintz, Stephen Wayne	P	San Francisco	11-28-68	Wilmington, N.C.	5-18
Morel, Ramon Rafael	P	Pittsburgh	8-15-74	Villa Gonzalez, Dominican Republic	7-6
Mouton, Lyle Joseph	OF	Chicago A.L.	5-13-69	Lafayette, La.	6-7
Munoz, Juan Oscar	P	Minnesota	9-4-69	Hialeah, Fla.	8-6
Munoz, Noe	C	Los Angeles	12-3-70	Ecatepec, Mexico	4-30
Murray, Matthew Michael	P	Atlanta	9-26-70	Boston	8-12
Myers, Michael Stanley	P	Florida	6-26-69	Cook County, Ill.	4-25
Nevin, Phillip Joseph	3B	Houston	1-19-71	Fullerton, Calif.	6-11
Nichting, Christopher Thomas	P	Texas	5-13-66	Cincinnati	5-15
Nitkowski, Christopher John	P	Cincinnati	3-3-73	Suffren, N.Y.	6-3
Nomo, Hideo	P	Los Angeles	8-31-68	Kobe, Japan	5-2
Norman, Leslie Eugene	PH	Kansas City	2-25-69	Warren, Mich.	5-29
Nunnally, Jonathan Keith	PR	Kansas City	11-9-71	Pelham, N.C.	4-26
Ochoa, Alex	PH	New York N.L.	3-29-72	Miami Lakes, Fla.	9-18
Osuna, Antonio Pedro	P	Los Angeles	4-12-73	Sinaloa, Mexico	4-25
Otero, Ricardo	OF	New York N.L.	4-15-72	Vega Baja, Puerto Rico	4-26
Owens, Eric Blake	3B	Cincinnati	2-3-71	Danville, Va.	6-6
Palmeiro, Orlando	PH	California	1-19-69	Hoboken, N.J.	7-1
Parra, Jose Miguel	P	Los Angeles	11-28-72	Jacagua Santiago, D.R.	5-7
Parris, Steven Michael	P	Pittsburgh	12-17-67	Joliet, Ill.	6-21
Patterson, Jeffrey Simmons	P	New York A.L.	10-1-68	Anaheim, Calif.	4-30
Pemberton, Rudy Hector	OF	Detroit	12-17-69	San Pedro de Macoris, D.R.	9-10
Penn, Shannon Dion	2B	Detroit	9-11-69	Cincinnati	4-28
Percival, Troy Eugene	P	California	8-9-69	Fontana, Calif.	4-26
Perez, Carlos Gross	P	Montreal	4-14-71	Nigua, Dominican Republic	4-27
Perez, Eduardo	PH	Atlanta	5-4-68	Cuidad Ojeda, Venezuela	9-10
Perez, Tomas Orlando	PR	Toronto	12-29-73	Barquisimeto, Venezuela	5-3
Person, Robert Alan	P	New York N.L.	10-6-69	Lowell, Mass.	9-18
Pettitte, Andrew Eugene	P	New York A.L.	6-15-72	Baton Rouge, La.	4-29
Pierce, Jeffrey Charles	P	Boston	6-7-69	Poughkeepsie, N.Y.	4-26
Pittsley, James Michael	P	Kansas City	4-3-74	DuBois, Pa.	5-23
Posada, Jorge Rafael	C	New York A.L.	8-17-71	Santurce, Puerto Rico	9-4
Powell, James Willard	P	Florida	1-9-72	Meridan, Miss.	9-10
Pozo, Arquimedez	PH	Seattle	8-24-73	Santo Domingo, Dominican Republic	9-12
Prieto, Ariel	P	Oakland	10-22-69	Havana, Cuba	7-2
Pulsipher, William Thomas	P	New York N.L.	10-9-73	Fort Benning, Ga.	6-17
Raabe, Brian Charles	2B	Minnesota	11-5-67	New Ulm, Minn.	9-17
Radke, Brad William	P	Minnesota	10-27-72	Eau Claire, Wis.	4-29
Randa, Joseph Gregory	2B	Kansas City	12-18-69	Milwaukee	4-30
Rekar, Bryan	P	Colorado	6-3-72	Oaklawn, Ill.	7-19
Reyes, Rafael Alberto	P	Milwaukee	4-10-71	San Cristobal, Dominican Republic	4-27
Ricci, Charles Mark	P	Philadelphia	11-20-68	Abington, Pa.	9-8
Rightnowar, Ronald Gene	P	Milwaukee	9-5-64	Toledo, Ohio	5-20
Rivera, Mariano	P	New York A.L.	11-29-69	Panama City, Panama	5-23
Rivera, Roberto	P	Chicago N.L.	1-1-69	Bayamon, Puerto Rico	9-3
Rivera, Ruben Moreno	PR	New York A.L.	11-14-73	La Chorrera, Panama	9-3
Roa, Joe Rodger	P	Cleveland	10-11-71	Southfield, Mich.	9-20
Roberson, Sidney Dean	P	Milwaukee	9-7-71	Jacksonville, Fla.	5-20
Robinson, Kenneth	P	Toronto	11-3-69	Barberton, Ohio	7-20
Rodriguez, Felix Antonio	P	Los Angeles	12-5-72	Monte Cristi, Dominican Republic	5-13
Rodriguez, Francisco	P	Boston	12-11-71	Brooklyn, N.Y.	4-26

Player	Pos.	Team	Birth date	Birthplace	Debut
Rodriguez, Steven James	PH	Boston	11-29-70	Las Vegas	4-30
Rogers, James Randall	P	Toronto	1-3-67	Tulsa, Okla.	7-30
Rosselli, Joseph D.	P	San Francisco	5-28-72	Burbank, Calif.	4-30
Santangelo, Frank	OF	Montreal	10-24-67	Livonia, Mich.	8-2
Schall, Eugene David	1B	Philadelphia	6-5-70	Abington, Pa.	6-16
Schmidt, Curtis Allen	P	Montreal	3-16-70	Miles City, Mont.	4-28
Schmidt, Jason David	P	Atlanta	1-29-73	Kelso, Wash.	4-28
Sefcik, Kevin John	3B	Philadelphia	2-10-71	Oak Lawn, Ill.	9-8
Simas, William Anthony	P	Chicago A.L.	11-28-71	Hanford, Calif.	8-15
Sirotka, Mike	P	Chicago A.L.	5-13-71	Chicago	7-19
Snopek, Christopher C.	3B	Chicago A.L.	9-20-70	Cynthiana, Ky.	7-31
Sodowsky, Clint Rea	P	Detroit	7-13-72	Ponca City, Okla.	9-4
Sparks, Steven William	P	Milwaukee	7-2-65	Tulsa, Okla.	4-28
Springer, Dennis L.	P	Philadelphia	2-12-65	Fresno, Calif.	9-13
Steverson, Todd Anthony	PR	Detroit	11-15-71	Los Angeles	4-28
Stewart, Shannon Harold	OF	Toronto	2-25-74	Cincinnati	9-2
Sturtze, Tanyon James	P	Chicago N.L.	10-12-70	Worcester, Mass.	5-3
Stynes, Christopher Desmond	PH	Kansas City	1-19-73	Queens, N.Y.	5-19
Sullivan, William Scott	P	Cincinnati	3-13-71	Tuscaloosa, Ala.	5-6
Suppan, Jeffrey Scot	P	Boston	1-2-75	Oklahoma City, Okla.	7-17
Swartzbaugh, David Theodore	P	Chicago N.L.	2-11-68	Middletown, Ohio	9-3
Sweeney, Mark	1B	St. Louis	10-26-69	Framingham, Maine	8-4
Sweeney, Michael John	C	Kansas City	7-22-73	Orange, Calif.	9-4
Taylor, Scott Michael	P	Texas	10-3-66	Topeka, Kan.	7-28
Thobe, John Joseph	P	Montreal	11-19-70	Covington, Ky.	9-18
Thobe, Thomas Neal	P	Atlanta	9-3-69	Covington, Ky.	9-12
Thomas, Larry Wayne Jr.	P	Chicago A.L.	10-25-69	Miami	8-11
Thomas, Michael Steven	P	Milwaukee	9-2-69	Sacramento, Calif.	7-12
Timmons, Osborne Llewellyn	PH	Chicago N.L.	9-18-70	Tampa, Fla.	4-26
Torres, Dilson Dario	P	Kansas City	5-31-70	Sur Edo Aragua, Venezuela	4-29
Tremie, Christopher J.	C	Chicago A.L.	10-17-69	Houston	7-1
Tucker, Michael Anthony	OF	Kansas City	6-25-71	South Boston, Va.	4-26
Unroe, Timothy Brian	1B	Milwaukee	10-7-70	Round Lake Beach, Ill.	5-30
Urbina, Ugueth Urtain	P	Montreal	2-15-74	Caracas, Venezuela	5-9
Valdes, Marc	P	Florida	12-20-71	Dayton, Ohio	8-28
Valdez, Carlos Luis	P	San Francisco	12-26-71	Nizao Bani, Dominican Republic	7-18
Veras, Quilvio Alberto	2B	Florida	4-3-71	Santo Domingo, Dominican Republic	4-25
Villone, Ronald Thomas	P	Seattle	1-16-70	Englewood, N.J.	4-28
Vitiello, Joseph David	PH	Kansas City	4-11-70	Cambridge, Mass.	4-29
Wade, Hawatha Terrell	P	Atlanta	1-25-73	Rembert, S.C.	9-12
Wagner, William Edward	P	Houston	6-25-71	Tannersville, Va.	9-13
Walker, Peter Brian	P	New York N.L.	4-8-69	Beverly, Mass.	6-7
Wall, Donne Lee	P	Houston	7-11-67	Potosi, Mo.	9-2
Ware, Jeffrey Allan	P	Toronto	11-11-70	Norfolk, Va.	9-2
Wasdin, John Truman	P	Oakland	8-5-72	Fort Belvoir, Va.	8-24
Watkins, Scott Allen	P	Minnesota	5-15-70	Tulsa, Okla.	8-1
Wengert, Donald Paul	P	Oakland	11-6-69	Sioux City, Iowa	4-30
White, Derrick Ramon	1B	Detroit	10-12-69	San Rafael, Calif.	7-22
Whiteside, David Sean	P	Detroit	4-19-71	Lakeland, Fla.	4-29
Widger, Christopher Jon	C	Seattle	5-21-71	Wilmington, Del.	6-23
Williams, George Erik	DH	Oakland	4-22-69	LaCrosse, Wis.	7-14
Williams, Todd Michael	P	Los Angeles	2-13-71	Syracuse, N.Y.	4-29
Wilson, Gary Morris	P	Pittsburgh	1-1-70	Arcata, Calif.	4-28
Wojciechowski, Steven Joseph	P	Oakland	7-29-70	Blue Island, Ill.	7-18
Wolcott, Robert William	P	Seattle	9-8-73	Huntington Beach, Calif.	8-18
Zaun, Gregory Owen	PR	Baltimore	4-14-71	Glendale, Calif.	6-24

SALARY ARBITRATION RESULTS

WINNERS

Player, Team	Salary awarded	Team's offer
Ben McDonald, Baltimore	$4,500,000	$3,200,000
Darren Lewis, San Francisco	$1,850,000	$1,025,000

LOSERS

Player, Team	Salary awarded	Player's request
Andy Benes, San Diego	$3,400,000	$4,400,000
Alex Fernandez, Chi. White Sox	$3,250,000	$3,900,000
Jeff Fassero, Montreal	$1,500,000	$2,450,000
Mel Rojas, Montreal	$1,300,000	$2,100,000
Leo Gomez, Baltimore	$1,850,000	$925,000
Carlos Hernandez, Los Angeles	$300,000	$525,000

AMERICAN LEAGUE

Baltimore: Harold Baines, Kevin Bass, Kevin Brown, Mark Eichhorn, Doug Jones, Jamie Moyer.

Boston: Rick Aguilera, Jose Canseco, Erik Hanson, Mike Macfarlane, Mike Maddux, Willie McGee, Zane Smith.

California: Jim Abbott, Mike Aldrete, Mike Bielecki, Chuck Finley, Dave Gallagher, Rene Gonzales, John Habyan, Greg Myers, Spike Owen, Bob Patterson, Tony Phillips, Scott Sanderson, Dick Schofield.

Chicago: Lance Johnson, Dave Martinez, Dave Righetti.

Cleveland: Alvaro Espinoza, John Farrell, Ken Hill, Eddie Murray, Tony Pena, Bill Ripken, Dave Winfield.

Detroit: Scott Fletcher, Franklin Stubbs, Lou Whitaker.

Kansas City: Tom Browning, Gary Gaetti, Greg Gagne, Tom Gordon, Mark Gubicza, Jeff Montgomery, Gregg Olson, Juan Samuel.

Milwaukee: Rob Dibble, Darryl Hamilton, Joe Oliver, Kevin Seitzer, B.J. Surhoff, Bill Wegman.

New York: Wade Boggs, David Cone, Rick Honeycutt, Steve Howe, Dion James, Don Mattingly, Jack McDowell, Mike Stanley, Randy Velarde.

Oakland: Mike Gallego, Brian Harper, Rickey Henderson, Stan Javier, Steve Ontiveros.

Seattle: Tim Belcher, Andy Benes, Vince Coleman, Lee Guetterman.

Texas: Danny Darwin, Candy Maldonado, Roger McDowell, Otis Nixon, Mike Pagliarulo, Kenny Rogers, Jeff Russell, Mickey Tettleton, Bob Tewksbury, Bobby Witt.

Toronto: Roberto Alomar, Danny Cox, Al Leiter, Paul Molitor, Lance Parrish, Duane Ward, Devon White.

NATIONAL LEAGUE

Atlanta: Mike Devereaux, Fred McGriff, Charlie O'Brien, Alejandro Pena, Luis Polonia, Dwight Smith.

Chicago: Shawon Dunston, Mark Grace, Howard Johnson, Randy Myers, Jaime Navarro, Mark Parent.

Cincinnati: Mariano Duncan, Ron Gant, Mike Jackson, Hal Morris, Benito Santiago, Frank Viola.

Colorado: Mike Kingery, Walt Weiss.

Florida: Jerry Browne, Andre Dawson, Bryan Harvey.

Houston: Craig Biggio, Pat Borders, John Cangelosi, Mike Henneman, Dave Magadan, Milt Thompson.

Los Angeles: Tom Candiotti, Roberto Kelly, Ramon Martinez, Tim Wallach.

New York: Joe Orsulak, Bill Spiers.

Philadelphia: Jim Eisenreich, Sid Fernandez, Charlie Hayes, Andy Van Slyke.

Pittsburgh: Don Slaught.

St. Louis: Tom Henke, Mike Morgan, Jeff Parrett, Jose Oquendo.

San Diego: Jody Reed, Fernando Valenzuela.

San Francisco: Terry Mulholland, Jeff Reed, Trevor Wilson.

(Listed in order of selection)

Player	Pos.	Drafted by	Drafted from (major league organization)
Joseph Jacobsen	P	Minnesota	Albuquerque, Pacific Coast League (Dodgers)
Patricio Claudio	OF	Pittsburgh	Buffalo, American Association (Indians)
Carey Paige	P	Toronto	Richmond, International League (Braves)
Andre King	OF	St. Louis	Nashville, American Association (White Sox)
Greg Keagle	P	Detroit	Tacoma, Pacific Coast League (Mariners)
Trey Witte	P	Montreal	Tacoma, Pacific Coast League (Mariners)
Tyron Narcisse	P	Milwaukee	Tucson, Pacific Coast League (Astros)
Kim Batiste	3B	San Francisco	Rochester, International League (Orioles)
Billy Wallace	P	Philadelphia	Ottawa, International League (Expos)
Miguel Mejia	OF	Kansas City	Rochester, International League (Orioles)
Kimera Bartee	OF	Baltimore	Salt Lake, Pacific Coast League (Twins)
Mark Mimbs	P	Texas	Albuquerque, Pacific Coast League (Dodgers)
Rodney Myers	P	Chicago N.L.	Omaha, American Association (Royals)
Marc Ronan	C	New York A.L.	New Orleans, American Association (Brewers)
Joe Crawford	P	Boston	Norfolk, International League (Mets)
Jon Ratliff	P	Detroit	Iowa, American Association (Cubs)
Tim Rumer	P	Texas	Columbus, International League (Yankees)

1995 REVIEW Miscellaneous

NECROLOGY

Bob Allison, 60, at Rio Verde, Ariz., on April 9. Allison, the 1959 American League Rookie of the Year when he hit 30 home runs and drove in 85 runs for the Senators, played 13 big-league seasons (all for the Senators/Twins franchise) and walloped 256 homers. He had 100-plus RBIs in 1961 and 1962, clubbed a career-high 35 homers in 1963 and had a 23-homer, 78-RBI season for the 1965 A.L. champion Twins.

Stan Andrews, 78, at Bradenton, Fla., on June 10. Andrews, a catcher, played a total of 70 games over four seasons (1939-40, 1944-45) for the Braves, Dodgers and Phillies.

Al Barlick, 80, at Springfield, Ill., on December 27. Barlick, known for his booming ball-and-strike calls, was an N.L. umpire from 1940-43, 1946-55 and 1958-71. He was inducted into baseball's Hall of Fame in 1989.

Dick Bartell, 87, at Alameda, Calif., on August 4. Bartell, the National League's starting shortstop in the first All-Star Game (1933), batted .284 and collected 2,165 hits in an 18-season career in the majors. He played for the Pirates, Phillies, Giants, Cubs and Tigers.

Russ Bauers, 80, at Maywood, Ill., on January 21. Righthander Bauers won 13 games for the Pirates in each of his first two full seasons in the majors (1937, 1938). Basically a reliever thereafter, Bauers finished with a 31-30 record in eight big-league seasons.

Ollie Bejma, 87, at South Bend., Ind., on January 3. Infielder Bejma spent three seasons (1934-36) with the Browns before finishing his major league career with the White Sox (1939). In his four years in the majors, Bejma batted .245 in 316 games.

Gus Bell, 66, at Cincinnati on May 7. Bell topped the 100-RBI mark four times for the power-hitting Reds of the 1950s and batted .292 or higher six times in one seven-year stretch. The right fielder for the Mets when that club made its N.L. debut in 1962, Bell was the initial part of a three-generation major league family. Son Buddy played 18 seasons in the big leagues and grandson David broke into the majors in 1995 with the Indians and Cardinals.

Norm Brown, 76, at Bennettsville, S.C., on May 31. Brown, who didn't give up an earned run over seven innings in his only major league start, pitched for the Athletics in 1943 and 1946 and was 0-1 in five appearances.

Billy Bruton, 69, at Marshalltown, Del., on December 5. Outfielder Bruton led the N.L. in stolen bases in his first three big-league seasons (1953-55) and was a key player for the Braves' powerful teams of the late 1950s. He was the top hitter in the 1958 World Series, batting .412. Bruton, who hit .273 over 12 big-league seasons, belted a game-winning home run for the Braves in their first game in Milwaukee—April 14, 1953—after the club's relocation from Boston.

Elmer Burkart, 78, at Baltimore on February 6. Burkart pitched for the Phillies from 1936-39, appearing in 16 games and going 1-1.

Glenn Burke, 42, at San Leandro, Calif., on May 30. Outfielder Burke spent four seasons in the majors (1976-79), dividing his time between the Dodgers (124 games) and the A's (101 games). He played in 83 games for the 1977 N.L. champion Dodgers and batted .254 in 169 at-bats. Burke started two games in the '77 N.L. playoffs and one game in that season's World Series.

Bruce Campbell, 85, on June 17. Outfielder Campbell, a .360 hitter for Detroit in the 1940 World Series, batted .290 over 13 big-league seasons. Besides the Tigers, Campbell played for the White Sox, Browns, Indians and Senators.

Jim Campbell, 71, at Lakeland, Fla., on October 31. A member of the Tigers' organization for 43 years in a career that ended in 1992, Campbell took over as the club's general manager in 1962 and later served as the franchise's chief executive officer. He oversaw the assembly of two World Series championship teams, the Tigers of 1968 and 1984.

John Campbell, 87, at Daytona Beach, Fla., on April 24. Campbell's big-league career consisted of a one-inning relief stint for the 1933 Senators.

Harry Craft, 80, at Conroe, Texas, on August 3. Craft, a Reds outfielder for six seasons (1937-42) and a World Series participant in 1939 and 1940, was Houston's manager when the N.L. expansion club made its debut in 1962. He also managed the Kansas City A's and was a member of the Cubs' "College of Coaches" managerial setup in 1961. Craft was Mickey Mantle's manager in Mantle's first two seasons of professional ball, 1949 (Independence, Kan.) and 1950 (Joplin, Mo.).

Tony Cuccinello, 87, at Tampa on September 21. Playing his 15th and last big-league season in 1945, White Sox infielder Cuccinello lost the A.L. batting title on the last day of that season when the Yankees' George Stirnweiss surged past him, .309 to .308. Cuccinello played most of his career in the N.L. and was a .280 hitter in 1,704 big-league games.

Jim Davis, 71, at San Mateo, Calif., on December 6. Lefthander Davis, who turned 30 in his first major league season, 1954, posted an 11-7 record for the Cubs that year. Used mostly as a reliever in a four-season major league career with the Cubs, Cardinals and Giants, Davis earned a place in the record books on May 27, 1956, when he struck out four batters in one inning (with one of the third strikes getting away from the Cubs' catcher).

Ray (Peaches) Davis, 89, at Duncan, Okla., on April 28. Davis was an 11-game winner for a 1937 Reds team that won only 56 games. He was 27-33 in four seasons in the majors.

Leon Day, 78, at Baltimore on March 13. Day, who died one week after he was elected to the Hall of Fame, was a Negro leagues star in the 1930s and 1940s as a pitcher, outfielder and second baseman.

Don Elston, 65, at Evanston, Ill., on January 2. Cubs reliever Elston led the N.L. in appearances with 69 in 1958 and 65 in 1959. The righthander pitched in 60, 58 and 57 games in the next three seasons and wound up a nine-year career in the majors in 1964 with a 49-54 record overall.

Rick Ferrell, 89, at Bloomfield Hills, Mich., on July 27. Hall of Famer Ferrell, whose 18-season major league career ended in 1947, caught in 1,806 A.L. games, which stood as a league record for 41 years. The A.L.'s catcher in the first All-Star Game (1933), he batted .281 in 1,884 big-league games. In the mid-1930s, Rick and brother Wes Ferrell formed a potent battery for the Red Sox.

Marc Filley, 82, at Yarmouth, Maine, on January 20. Filley pitched in one major league game—for the Senators in 1934.

Daniel Galbreath, 67, at Galloway, Ohio, on September 3. Galbreath, whose family was a longtime owner of the Pirates and prominent in horse-racing circles, served as president of the N.L. club from 1970-85.

Ed Gill, 99, at Brockton, Mass., on October 10. He pitched in 16 big-league games—all in 1919 (putting that time frame into perspective, Babe Ruth was still with the Red Sox). Gill posted a 1-1 record with the Senators.

Sal Gliatto, 93, at Tyler, Texas, on November 1. His major league career consisted of eight relief appearances for the 1930 Indians.

Harry Gumbert, 85, at Wimberley, Texas, on January 4. Gumbert, an 18-game winner for the 1939 Giants, won 143 games in 15 big-league seasons and pitched in three World Series (two with the Giants, one with the Cardinals).

Walter A. Haas Jr., 79, at San Francisco on September 20. He owned the A's from 1980-95 after purchasing the club from Charlie Finley.

Mickey Haefner, 82, at New Athens, Ill., on January 3. Lefthander Haefner won a career-high 16 games for the Senators in 1945, a season in which he was one of four knuckleballers in Washington's rotation. In eight seasons in the majors, Haefner went 78-91.

Johnny Hall, 71, at Midwest City, Okla., on January 17. Hall made three relief appearances for the 1948 Dodgers.

Burt Hawkins, 81, at Arlington, Texas, on November 27. Hawkins was media relations director for the Senators/Rangers franchise from its inception in 1961 through 1984.

Thelma Griffith Haynes, 82, at Orlando on October 15. A member of the Griffith family that owned the Senators/Twins franchise from 1920-84, she served in many capacities in the organization—including co-owner.

Herb Hippauf, 55, at Santa Clara, Calif., on July 17. Hippauf was 0-1 in three relief stints for the 1966 Braves. At the time of his death, he was a Rockies scout.

Herm Holshouser, 88, at Concord, N.C., on July 26. Holshouser made one start and 24 relief appearances for the 1930 Browns.

Roy Hughes, 84, at Asheville, N.C., on March 5. Hughes, whose best big-league season was 1936 when he hit .295 as the Indians' regular second baseman, was a member of the Cubs' last World Series team in 1945. He started at shortstop in six of that Series' seven games.

Nippy Jones, 70, at Sacramento on October 3. First baseman Jones, a .267 hitter over eight big-league seasons, appeared in the 1946 and 1957 World Series for the champion Cardinals and Braves. In the '57 Series, he figured prominently in Milwaukee's 10th-inning rally that won Game 4 by proving—via a smudge of shoe polish on the ball—that he had been hit by a pitch after umpire Augie Donatelli had first ruled otherwise.

Oscar Judd, 87, at Ingersoll, Ont., on December 27. Lefthander Judd compiled a 40-51 record in eight big-league seasons. The Canadian's best year was 1943, when he went 11-6 with a 2.90 ERA for the Red Sox and made the A.L. roster for the All-Star Game. At age 40, he tossed a seven-inning no-hitter in the International League.

Bill Kennedy, 76, at Alexandria, Va., on August 20. Lefthander Kennedy lost three of his four decisions while pitching for the Senators in 1942 and 1946-47.

Jack Kramer, 77, at Metairie, La., on May 18. Kramer won 17 games for the 1944 A.L. champion Browns and compiled an 18-5 record for a 1948 Red Sox team that lost a pennant-deciding playoff game to the Indians. Kramer, who didn't allow an earned run in 11 innings of work in the '44 World Series and led the A.L. in winning percentage (.783) in '48, won 95 games over 12 big-league seasons.

Eddie Lake, 79, at Castro Valley, Calif., on June 7. The No. 1 shortstop for the Red Sox in 1945 and for the Tigers the next two seasons, Lake played 835 games over 11 major league seasons.

Charlie Letchas, 79, at Tampa on March 14. Versatile infielder Letchas played 116 of his 136 major league games for the 1944 Phillies, batting .237 in 396 at-bats.

Eddie Logan, 83, at San Francisco on May 12. Logan served as equipment manager for the Giants for 40 years, the first 18 when the team was based in New York and the last 22 in San Francisco after the club's relocation.

Ron Luciano, 57, at Endicott, N.Y., on January 18. An A.L. umpire from 1968 through 1980, the flamboyant Luciano delighted fans and infuriated players and managers with his animated style of calling plays. Anecdotes about his career turned Luciano into an author and made him a popular guest on talk shows.

Mickey Mantle, 63, at Dallas on August 13. His rare mix of extraordinary power and blazing speed, combined with a small-town innocence that marked his arrival in the big leagues, made Mantle one of the most endearing players of his time. Nineteen years old and less than two years out of the Oklahoma high school ranks, he joined the Yankees in 1951 (Joe DiMaggio's last year with the team) and, except for a month's demotion to Class AAA ball, was with the club through 1968. Mantle, a Hall of Famer who slugged 536 home runs in 18 seasons with the Yankees, was a three-time A.L. MVP (1956-57, 1962), a Triple Crown winner ('56) and a member of pennant-winning Yankee teams in 12 of his first 14 seasons in the majors. He hit a record 18 homers in World Series play while helping the Yankees to seven Series championships. Switch-hitter Mantle, who flashed 3.1 speed to first base before incurring knee problems, clubbed a 565-foot homer at Washington's Griffith Stadium in 1953 and twice just missed becoming the first player to hit a fair ball out of Yankee Stadium. He is one of only five players in major league history to have two 50-homer seasons.

Von McDaniel, 56, at Hollis, Okla., on August 20. Going directly from high school ball to the majors in 1957, the Cardinals' McDaniel, 18, made two relief appearances before shutting out the Dodgers, 2-0, on two hits in his first major league start. In his seventh start, he tossed a one-hitter against the Pirates. After posting a 7-5 record and a 3.22 ERA in '57, McDaniel, brother of longtime reliever Lindy McDaniel, incurred arm problems and pitched in only two more big-league games.

George Metkovich, 73, at Costa Mesa, Calif., on May 17. Outfielder/first baseman Metkovich, who made two pinch-hit appearances for the Red Sox in the 1946 World Series, played for six big-league teams in 10 major league seasons. He batted .293 for the 1951 Pirates and .277 for the 1944 Red Sox.

Wally Millies, 88, at Oak Lawn, Ill., on February 28. Catcher Millies, who hit .312 in 74 games for the 1936 Senators, batted .243 overall in 246 big-league games.

Ray Moore, 68, at Clinton, Md., on March 3. Moore won 33 games for the Orioles from 1955-57 and was a member of the 1959 A.L. champion White Sox, for whom he went 3-6. He pitched one inning of relief in the '59 World Series.

Terry Moore, 82, at Collinsville, Ill., on March 29. Outstanding defensively, center fielder Moore joined the Cardinals the year after the club's Gas House Gang won the 1934 World Series and wound up playing on two Series champions himself. Moore spent all 11 of his major league seasons with the Cards—including the Series-winning years of 1942 and 1946—and hit .280 in 1,298 games.

Lindsey Nelson, 76, at Atlanta on June 10. Voted into the broadcasters' wing of baseball's Hall of Fame in 1988, Nelson was a member of the Mets' original broadcasting team in 1962 and spent 17 years as an announcer for the New York club. Besides other baseball assignments, Nelson was a veteran football broadcaster who was noted for his longtime Cotton Bowl coverage.

Chet Nichols, 64, at Lincoln, R.I., on March 27. As a rookie with the Braves, then based in Boston, Nichols captured the N.L. ERA title in 1951 with a figure of 2.88. He compiled an 11-8 record in '51 and tossed three shutouts. Nichols, son of a major leaguer, put together a 34-36 mark in nine big-league seasons.

Al Niemiec, 84, at Kirkland, Wash., on October 29. Infielder Niemiec played in nine games for the 1934 Red Sox and in 69 games for the 1936 Athletics.

Manuel Onis, 86, at Tampa on January 4. Catcher Onis, who played in just one big-league game, singled in his lone at-bat for the Dodgers in 1935.

Al Papai, 76, at Springfield, Ill., on September 7. Knuckleballer Papai made 70 of his 88 big-league appearances in relief despite being a standout starting pitcher in the minors (four 20-victory seasons in Class AA). Pitching for the Cardinals, Browns, Red Sox and White Sox, he was 9-14 over four years (1948-50, 1955).

Hal Peck, 77, at Milwaukee on April 13. Peck, who saw extensive outfield duty for the 1945 Athletics and the 1947 Indians, appeared in 45 games for Cleveland's 1948 World Series champions and was used primarily as a pinch-hitter. Peck reached the majors despite losing two toes in a 1942 shooting accident.

Kent Peterson, 69, at Highland, Utah, on April 27. Peterson, who broke into the majors at age 18, was 13-38 for the Reds and Phillies over eight big-league seasons (1944, 1947-53).

Vada Pinson, 59, at Oakland on October 21. Outfielder Pinson, who batted .343 for the pennant-winning Reds in 1961, collected 2,757 hits in an 18-year major league career. He had four 200-hit seasons, rapped 256 homers and stole more than 20 bases in a season nine times. Pinson twice led the N.L. in hits, doubles and triples.

Gus Polidor, 33, at Caracas, Venezuela, on April 28 when he was shot to death while two men tried to steal his car and abduct his child. Infielder Polidor saw part-time duty for the Angels, Brewers and Marlins in a big-league career that began in 1985 and ended in 1993.

Ray Prim, 88, at Monte Rio, Calif., on April 29. Prim was a 13-game winner for the Cubs' last N.L. pennant-winning team, the 1945 club. Prim, 38 years old at the time, fashioned a 2.40 ERA in '45. He went 22-21 in six big-league seasons.

Paul Pryor, 68, at St. Petersburg, Fla., on December 15. Pryor umpired in the N.L. from 1961-81.

Nap Reyes, 75, at Miami on September 15. Third baseman/first baseman Reyes played 278 of his 279 major league games in wartime duty (1943-45) with the Giants. He hit .289 in 116 games in

1944 and .288 in 122 games in '45. After jumping to the Mexican League in 1946, Reyes appeared in one more big-league box score—in 1950.

Lee Rogers, 82, at Little Rock, Ark., on November 23. In his lone major league season, 1938, Rogers pitched in 14 games for the Red Sox and 12 for the Dodgers. He compiled a 1-3 record overall.

Saul Rogovin, 72, at New York on January 23. The A.L.'s ERA leader in 1951 with a mark of 2.78, Rogovin pitched eight seasons in the majors and wound up with a 48-48 record. A year after winning the ERA title while pitching for the Tigers and White Sox, Rogovin won a career-high 14 games for the Chicago club.

Frank Secory, 82, at Port Huron, Mich., on April 7. A little-used outfielder for the Tigers (1940), Reds (1942) and (Cubs (1944-46), Secory enjoyed his best moments as a major league player when he went 2-for-5 as a pinch-hitter in the 1945 World Series. He later turned to umpiring, working in the N.L. from 1952-70.

David Shotkoski, 30, at West Palm Beach, Fla., on March 24. Contending for a job as a Braves replacement player in spring training, pitcher Shotkoski was fatally shot in an apparent robbery attempt.

William Suero, 29, in an automobile accident at Santo Domingo, Dominican Republic, on November 30. Infielder Suero appeared in 33 games for the Brewers in 1992-93.

Dick Tettelbach, 65, at East Harwich, Mass., on January 26. Outfielder Tettelbach played two games for the 1955 Yankees and a total of 27 games for the 1956-57 Senators.

Keith (Kite) Thomas, at Rocky Mount, N.C., on January 7. Outfielder Thomas' two-season career in the majors was highlighted by his six-homer output in 116 at-bats for the 1952 Athletics.

Jim Tyack, 83, at Bakersfield, Calif., on January 3. Outfielder Tyack, one of the few Montana-born players in major league history, batted .258 in 54 games for the 1943 Athletics.

Jimmy Uchrinsko, 94, at Mount Pleasant, Pa., on March 17. Uchrinsko made three relief appearances for the 1926 Senators.

Al Unser, 82, at Decatur, Ill., on July 7. Unser was a wartime catcher for the Tigers (1942-44) and Reds (1945) and a longtime minor league manager. He was the father of Del Unser, a major league outfielder for 15 seasons.

Cecil Upshaw, 52, at Lawrenceville, Ga., on February 7. Upshaw was Atlanta's bullpen stopper in 1969, the first year of divisional play in the majors, and helped the Braves to the N.L. West title by racking up 27 saves. He made 348 appearances (all in relief) in nine major league seasons and posted a 34-36 record.

Zoilo Versalles, 55, at Bloomington, Minn., on June 9. Shortstop Versalles was the A.L.'s MVP in 1965 when, playing for the A.L. champion Twins, he hit 19 homers, stole 27 bases and had league-high totals of 45 doubles, 12 triples and 126 runs scored. He wound up playing 12 seasons in the majors, nine of them for the Senators/Twins franchise, and batted .242 in 1,400 games.

Woody Williams, 82, at Appomattox, Va., on February 24. Used sparingly by the Reds in 1943, infielder Williams collected only 26 hits—but 10 of them came in succession, tying the N.L. record for consecutive hits. Furthermore, he had only 69 at-bats overall, resulting in a .377 batting average. Williams was Cincinnati's No. 1 second baseman the next two years, batting .240 and .237.

Jack Wilson, 83, at Edmonds, Wash., on April 19. Wilson was a double-digit winner for the Red Sox from 1937 through 1940, posting a career-high 16 victories in '37.

1995 A.L. STATISTICS

Batting

Designated hitting

Pinch-hitting

Pitching

Fielding

Miscellaneous

BATTING

TEAM

Team	Avg.	G	TPA	AB	R	H	TB	2B	3B	HR	RBI	SH	SF	HP	BB	IBB	SO	SB	CS	GDP	LOB	ShO	Slg.	OBP
Cleveland	.291	144	5686	5028	840	1461	2407	279	23	207	803	31	48	35	542	40	766	132	53	128	1012	3	.479	.361
Chicago	.280	145	5770	5060	755	1417	2181	252	37	146	712	46	56	32	576	54	767	110	39	106	1149	6	.431	.354
Boston	.280	144	5716	4997	791	1399	2272	286	31	175	754	45	49	45	560	38	923	99	44	129	1077	1	.455	.357
Minnesota	.279	144	5588	5005	703	1398	2096	270	34	120	662	18	36	58	471	32	916	105	57	152	1021	6	.419	.346
California	.277	145	5690	5019	801	1390	2250	252	25	186	761	33	38	36	564	40	889	58	39	115	1052	7	.448	.352
New York	.276	145	5699	4947	749	1365	2079	280	34	122	709	20	68	39	625	36	851	50	30	139	1119	7	.420	.357
Seattle	.276	145	5671	4996	796	1377	2239	276	20	182	767	52	34	39	549	53	871	110	41	109	1027	2	.448	.350
Milwaukee	.266	144	5631	5000	740	1329	2046	249	42	128	700	41	42	46	502	20	800	105	40	105	1049	8	.409	.336
Texas	.265	144	5566	4913	691	1304	2013	247	24	138	651	49	45	43	526	28	877	90	47	112	1023	8	.410	.338
Oakland	.264	144	5617	4916	730	1296	2067	228	18	169	694	32	58	45	565	25	911	112	46	108	1037	8	.420	.341
Baltimore	.262	144	5531	4837	704	1267	2069	229	27	173	668	40	41	39	574	36	803	92	45	119	1016	8	.428	.342
Kansas City	.260	144	5528	4903	629	1275	1942	240	35	119	578	66	39	43	475	33	849	120	53	105	1005	7	.396	.328
Toronto	.260	144	5650	5036	642	1309	2058	275	27	140	613	33	45	44	492	27	906	75	16	119	1064	10	.409	.328
Detroit	.247	144	5535	4865	654	1204	1967	228	29	159	619	35	43	41	551	30	987	73	36	121	1013	9	.404	.327
Totals	.270	1010	78878	69522	10225	18791	29686	3591	406	2164	9691	541	642	595	7572	492	12116	1331	586	1667	14620	90	.427	.344

INDIVIDUAL

TOP QUALIFIERS FOR BATTING CHAMPIONSHIP

Minimum 446 plate appearances. *Lefthanded batter. †Switch-hitter.

Player, Team	Avg.	G	TPA	AB	R	H	TB	2B	3B	HR	RBI	SH	SF	HP	BB	IBB	SO	SB	CS	GDP	Slg.	OBP
Martinez, Edgar, Seattle	.356	145	639	511	121	182	321	52	0	29	113	0	4	8	116	19	87	4	3	11	.628	.479
Knoblauch, Chuck, Minnesota	.333	136	629	538	107	179	262	34	8	11	63	0	3	10	78	3	95	46	18	15	.487	.424
Salmon, Tim, California	.330	143	638	537	111	177	319	34	3	34	105	0	4	6	91	2	111	5	5	9	.594	.429
Boggs, Wade, New York*	.324	126	541	460	76	149	194	22	4	5	63	0	7	0	74	5	50	1	1	13	.422	.412
Murray, Eddie, Cleveland†	.323	113	480	436	68	141	225	21	0	21	82	0	5	0	39	5	65	5	1	11	.516	.375
Surhoff, B.J., Milwaukee*	.320	117	462	415	72	133	204	26	3	13	73	2	4	4	37	4	43	7	3	6	.492	.378
Davis, Chili, California†	.318	119	522	424	81	135	218	23	0	20	86	0	9	0	89	12	79	3	3	12	.514	.429
Belle, Albert, Cleveland	.317	143	631	546	121	173	377	52	1	50	126	0	4	6	73	5	80	5	2	24	.690	.401
Baerga, Carlos, Cleveland†	.314	135	600	557	87	175	252	28	2	15	90	0	5	3	35	6	31	11	2	15	.452	.355
Thome, Jim, Cleveland*	.314	137	557	452	92	142	252	29	3	25	73	0	3	5	97	3	113	4	3	8	.558	.438
Puckett, Kirby, Minnesota	.314	137	602	538	83	169	277	39	0	23	99	0	5	3	56	18	89	3	2	15	.515	.379
Seitzer, Kevin, Milwaukee	.311	132	570	492	56	153	207	33	3	5	69	5	3	6	64	2	57	2	0	12	.421	.395
Palmeiro, Rafael, Baltimore*	.310	143	624	554	89	172	323	30	2	39	104	0	5	3	62	5	65	3	1	11	.583	.380
Lofton, Kenny, Cleveland*	.310	118	529	481	93	149	218	22	13	7	53	4	3	1	40	6	49	54	15	6	.453	.362
Joyner, Wally, Kansas City*	.310	131	550	465	69	144	208	28	0	12	83	5	9	2	69	10	65	3	2	7	.447	.394

DEPARTMENTAL LEADERS: G—E. Martinez, Sea., F. Thomas, Chi., 145; AB—Johnson, Chi., 607; R—Belle, Cle., E. Martinez, Sea., 121; H—Johnson, Chi., 186; TB—Belle, Cle., 377; 1B—Nixon, Tex., 151; 2B—Belle, Cle., E. Martinez, Sea., 52; 3B—Lofton, Cle., 13; HR—Belle, Cle., 50; RBI—Belle, Cle., Vaughn, Bos., 126; SH—Goodwin, K.C., 14; SF—F. Thomas, Chi., 12; HP—Sprague, Tor., 15; BB—F. Thomas, Chi., 136; IBB—F. Thomas, Chi., 29; SO—Vaughn, Bos., 150; SB—Lofton, Cle., 54; CS—Nixon, Tex., 21; GIDP—Belle, Cle., 24; Slg. Pct.—Belle, Cle., .690; OB. Pct.—E. Martinez, Sea., .479.

ALL PLAYERS

*Lefthanded batter. †Switch-hitter.

Player, Team	Avg.	G	TPA	AB	R	H	TB	2B	3B	HR	RBI	SH	SF	HP	BB	IBB	SO	SB	CS	GDP	Slg.	OBP
Aldrete, Mike, Oak.-Cal.*	.268	78	172	149	19	40	60	8	0	4	24	0	3	1	19	1	31	0	0	4	.403	.349
Alexander, Manny, Baltimore..	.236	94	268	242	35	57	77	9	1	3	23	4	0	2	20	0	30	11	4	2	.318	.299
Alicea, Luis, Boston†	.270	132	511	419	64	113	157	20	3	6	44	13	9	7	63	0	61	13	10	10	.375	.367
Allanson, Andy, California	.171	35	91	82	5	14	26	3	0	3	10	1	0	1	7	0	12	0	1	0	.317	.244
Alomar, Sandy, Cleveland	.300	66	218	203	32	61	97	6	0	10	35	4	1	3	7	0	26	3	1	8	.478	.332
Alomar, Roberto, Toronto†	.300	130	577	517	71	155	232	24	7	13	66	6	7	0	47	3	45	30	3	16	.449	.354
Amaral, Rich, Seattle	.282	90	261	238	45	67	91	14	2	2	19	1	0	1	21	0	33	21	2	3	.382	.342
Amaro, Ruben, Cleveland†	.200	28	68	60	5	12	18	3	0	1	7	2	0	2	4	0	6	1	3	1	.300	.273
Anderson, Brady, Baltimore*	.262	143	657	554	108	145	246	33	10	16	64	4	2	10	87	4	111	26	7	3	.444	.371
Anderson, Garret, California*	.321	106	400	374	50	120	189	19	1	16	69	2	4	1	19	4	65	6	2	8	.505	.352
Baerga, Carlos, Cleveland†	.314	135	600	557	87	175	252	28	2	15	90	0	5	3	35	6	31	11	2	15	.452	.355
Baines, Harold, Baltimore*	.299	127	459	385	60	115	208	19	1	24	63	0	4	0	70	13	45	0	2	17	.540	.403
Barberie, Bret, Baltimore†	.241	90	288	237	32	57	77	14	0	2	25	6	3	6	36	0	50	3	3	6	.325	.351
Bass, Kevin, Baltimore†	.244	111	327	295	32	72	99	12	0	5	32	4	2	2	24	0	47	8	8	15	.336	.303
Battle, Howard, Toronto	.200	9	19	15	3	3	3	0	0	0	0	0	0	0	4	0	8	1	0	0	.200	.368
Bautista, Danny, Detroit	.203	89	289	271	28	55	85	9	0	7	27	6	0	0	12	0	68	4	1	6	.314	.237
Becker, Rich, Minnesota*	.237	106	438	392	45	93	116	15	1	2	33	6	2	4	34	0	95	8	9	9	.296	.303
Bell, David, Cleveland	.000	2	2	2	0	0	0	0	0	0	0	0	0	0	0	0	0	0	0	0	.000	.000
Bell, Juan, Boston†	.154	17	29	26	7	4	9	2	0	1	2	0	1	0	2	0	10	0	0	0	.346	.207
Belle, Albert, Cleveland	.317	143	631	546	121	173	377	52	1	50	126	0	4	6	73	5	80	5	2	24	.690	.401
Beltre, Esteban, Texas	.217	54	99	92	7	20	28	8	0	0	7	3	0	0	4	0	15	0	0	1	.304	.250
Berroa, Geronimo, Oakland	.278	141	616	546	87	152	246	22	3	22	88	0	6	1	63	2	98	7	4	12	.451	.351
Blowers, Mike, Seattle	.257	134	498	439	59	113	208	24	1	23	96	3	3	0	53	0	128	2	1	18	.474	.335
Boggs, Wade, New York*	.324	126	541	460	76	149	194	22	4	5	63	0	7	0	74	5	50	1	1	13	.422	.412
Bonilla, Bobby, Baltimore†	.333	61	263	237	47	79	129	12	4	10	46	0	2	1	23	0	31	0	2	11	.544	.392
Borders, Pat, Kansas City	.231	52	150	143	14	33	55	8	1	4	13	0	0	0	7	1	22	0	0	1	.385	.267
Bordick, Mike, Oakland	.264	126	478	428	46	113	150	13	0	8	44	7	3	5	35	2	48	11	3	8	.350	.325
Brady, Doug, Chicago†	.190	12	23	21	4	4	5	1	0	0	3	0	0	0	2	0	4	0	1	1	.238	.261
Bragg, Darren, Seattle*	.234	52	170	145	20	34	50	5	1	3	12	1	2	4	18	1	37	9	0	4	.345	.331

Player, Team	Avg.	G	TPA	AB	R	H	TB	2B	3B	HR	RBI	SH	SF	HP	BB	IBB	SO	SB	CS	GDP	Slg.	OBP
Brito, Bernardo, Minnesota	.200	5	6	5	1	1	4	0	0	1	1	0	0	1	0	0	3	0	0	1	.800	.333
Brosius, Scott, Oakland	.262	123	443	389	69	102	176	19	2	17	46	1	4	8	41	0	67	4	2	5	.452	.342
Brown, Jarvis, Baltimore	.148	18	37	27	2	4	5	1	0	0	1	3	0	0	7	0	9	1	1	0	.185	.324
Buechele, Steve, Texas	.125	9	28	24	0	3	3	0	0	0	0	0	0	0	4	1	3	0	0	0	.125	.250
Buford, Damon, Baltimore	.063	24	42	32	6	2	2	0	0	0	2	3	1	0	6	0	7	3	1	0	.063	.205
Buhner, Jay, Seattle	.262	126	539	470	86	123	266	23	0	40	121	2	6	1	60	7	120	0	1	15	.566	.343
Burnitz, Jeromy, Cleveland*	.571	9	7	7	4	4	5	1	0	0	0	0	0	0	0	0	0	0	0	0	.714	.571
Caceres, Edgar, Kansas City†	.239	55	130	117	13	28	41	6	2	1	17	3	1	1	8	0	15	2	2	3	.350	.291
Cameron, Mike, Chicago	.184	28	44	38	4	7	12	2	0	1	2	3	0	0	3	0	15	0	0	0	.316	.244
Canseco, Jose, Boston	.306	102	450	396	64	121	220	25	1	24	81	0	5	7	42	4	93	4	0	9	.556	.378
Carter, Joe, Toronto	.253	139	603	558	70	141	239	23	0	25	76	0	5	3	37	5	87	12	1	11	.428	.300
Cedeno, Domingo, Toronto†	.236	51	174	161	18	38	58	6	1	4	14	1	0	2	10	0	35	0	1	3	.360	.289
Chamberlain, Wes, Boston	.119	19	45	42	4	5	9	1	0	1	1	0	0	0	3	0	11	1	0	2	.214	.178
Cirillo, Jeff, Milwaukee	.277	125	384	328	57	91	145	19	4	9	39	1	4	4	47	0	42	7	2	8	.442	.371
Clark, Jerald, Minnesota	.339	36	113	109	17	37	60	8	3	3	15	0	1	1	2	0	11	3	0	5	.550	.354
Clark, Tony, Detroit†	.238	27	109	101	10	24	40	5	1	3	11	0	0	0	8	0	30	0	0	2	.396	.294
Clark, Will, Texas*	.302	123	537	454	85	137	218	27	3	16	92	0	11	4	68	6	50	0	1	7	.480	.389
Cole, Alex, Minnesota*	.342	28	90	79	10	27	37	3	2	1	14	2	0	1	8	0	15	1	3	0	.468	.409
Coleman, Vince, K.C.-Sea.†	.288	115	500	455	66	131	181	23	6	5	29	5	1	2	37	2	80	42	16	8	.398	.343
Cookson, Brent, Kansas City	.143	22	38	35	2	5	6	1	0	0	5	1	0	0	2	0	7	1	0	0	.171	.189
Coomer, Ron, Minnesota	.257	37	111	101	15	26	46	3	1	5	19	0	0	1	9	0	11	0	1	9	.455	.324
Cora, Joey, Seattle†	.297	120	487	427	64	127	159	19	2	3	39	13	4	6	37	0	31	18	7	8	.372	.359
Cordova, Marty, Minnesota	.277	137	579	512	81	142	249	27	4	24	84	0	5	10	52	1	111	20	7	10	.486	.352
Correia, Rod, California	.238	14	22	21	3	5	8	1	1	0	3	1	0	0	0	0	5	0	0	1	.381	.238
Cruz, Fausto, Oakland	.217	8	30	23	0	5	5	0	0	0	5	2	2	0	3	0	5	1	1	1	.217	.286
Curtis, Chad, Detroit	.268	144	670	586	96	157	255	29	3	21	67	0	7	7	70	3	93	27	15	12	.435	.349
Cuyler, Milt, Detroit†	.205	41	98	88	15	18	27	1	4	0	5	2	0	0	8	0	16	2	1	0	.307	.271
Dalesandro, Mark, California	.100	11	10	10	1	1	2	1	0	0	0	0	0	0	0	0	2	0	0	0	.200	.100
Damon, Johnny, Kansas City*	.282	47	206	188	32	53	83	11	5	3	23	2	3	1	12	0	22	7	0	2	.441	.324
Davis, Chili, California†	.318	119	522	424	81	135	218	23	0	20	86	0	9	0	89	12	79	3	3	12	.514	.429
Davis, Russ, New York	.276	40	109	98	14	27	42	5	2	2	12	0	0	1	10	0	26	0	0	0	.429	.349
Delgado, Carlos, Toronto*	.165	37	99	91	7	15	27	3	0	3	11	0	2	0	6	0	26	0	0	1	.297	.212
Devarez, Cesar, Baltimore	.000	6	5	4	0	0	0	0	0	0	0	1	0	0	0	0	0	0	0	0	.000	.000
Devereaux, Mike, Chicago	.306	92	361	333	48	102	155	21	1	10	55	0	3	0	25	3	51	6	6	10	.465	.352
Diaz, Alex, Seattle†	.248	103	292	270	44	67	90	14	0	3	27	5	2	2	13	2	27	18	8	3	.333	.286
DiSarcina, Gary, California	.307	99	394	362	61	111	166	28	6	5	41	7	3	2	20	0	25	7	4	10	.459	.344
Donnels, Chris, Boston*	.253	40	101	91	13	23	35	2	2	2	11	0	1	0	9	0	18	0	0	1	.385	.317
Dunn, Steve, Minnesota*	.000	5	7	6	0	0	0	0	0	0	0	0	0	0	1	0	3	0	0	0	.000	.143
Durham, Ray, Chicago†	.257	125	517	471	68	121	181	27	6	7	51	5	4	6	31	2	83	18	5	8	.384	.309
Easley, Damion, California	.216	114	405	357	35	77	107	14	2	4	35	6	4	6	32	1	47	5	2	11	.300	.288
Edmonds, Jim, California*	.290	141	620	558	120	162	299	30	4	33	107	1	5	5	51	4	130	1	4	10	.536	.352
Eenhoorn, Robert, New York	.143	5	15	14	1	2	3	1	0	0	2	0	0	0	1	0	3	0	0	1	.214	.200
Elster, Kevin, New York	.118	10	18	17	1	2	3	1	0	0	0	0	0	0	1	0	5	0	0	0	.176	.167
Espinoza, Alvaro, Cleveland	.252	66	150	143	15	36	46	4	0	2	17	2	2	1	2	0	16	0	2	3	.322	.264
Fabregas, Jorge, California*	.247	73	248	227	24	56	69	10	0	1	22	3	1	0	17	0	28	0	2	9	.304	.298
Fermin, Felix, Seattle	.195	73	219	200	21	39	45	6	0	0	15	8	1	4	6	0	6	2	0	7	.225	.232
Fernandez, Tony, New York†	.245	108	438	384	57	94	133	20	2	5	45	3	5	4	42	4	40	6	6	14	.346	.322
Fielder, Cecil, Detroit	.243	136	578	494	70	120	233	18	1	31	82	0	4	5	75	8	116	0	1	17	.472	.346
Flaherty, John, Detroit	.243	112	385	354	39	86	143	22	1	11	40	8	2	3	18	0	47	0	0	8	.404	.284
Fletcher, Scott, Detroit	.231	67	209	182	19	42	57	10	1	1	17	4	1	3	19	0	27	1	0	2	.313	.312
Flora, Kevin, California	.000	2	1	1	1	0	0	0	0	0	0	0	0	0	0	0	1	0	0	0	.000	.000
Fox, Eric, Texas†	.000	10	19	15	2	0	0	0	0	0	0	1	0	0	3	0	4	0	0	0	.000	.167
Frazier, Lou, Texas†	.212	49	111	99	19	21	23	2	0	0	8	3	0	2	7	0	20	9	1	2	.232	.278
Frye, Jeff, Texas	.278	90	354	313	38	87	118	15	2	4	29	8	4	5	24	0	45	3	3	7	.377	.335
Fryman, Travis, Detroit	.275	144	640	567	79	156	232	21	5	15	81	0	7	3	63	4	100	4	2	18	.409	.347
Gaetti, Gary, Kansas City	.261	137	578	514	76	134	266	27	0	35	96	3	6	8	47	6	91	3	3	7	.518	.329
Gagne, Greg, Kansas City	.256	120	482	430	58	110	161	25	4	6	49	7	5	2	38	2	60	3	5	11	.374	.316
Gallagher, Dave, California	.188	11	18	16	1	3	4	1	0	0	0	0	0	0	2	0	1	0	0	0	.250	.278
Gallego, Mike, Oakland	.233	43	132	120	11	28	28	0	0	0	8	2	0	1	9	0	24	0	1	3	.233	.292
Gates, Brent, Oakland†	.254	136	585	524	60	133	180	24	4	5	56	4	11	0	46	2	84	3	3	15	.344	.308
Giambi, Jason, Oakland*	.256	54	210	176	27	45	70	7	0	6	25	1	2	3	28	0	31	2	1	4	.398	.364
Gibson, Kirk, Detroit*	.260	70	265	227	37	59	102	12	2	9	35	0	2	3	33	3	61	9	2	6	.449	.358
Gil, Benji, Texas	.219	130	454	415	36	91	144	20	3	9	46	10	2	1	26	0	147	2	4	5	.347	.266
Giles, Brian S., Cleveland*	.556	6	9	9	6	5	8	0	0	1	3	0	0	0	0	0	1	0	0	0	.889	.556
Gomez, Chris, Detroit	.223	123	482	431	49	96	153	20	2	11	50	3	4	3	41	0	96	4	1	13	.355	.292
Gomez, Leo, Baltimore	.236	53	149	127	16	30	47	5	0	4	12	0	2	2	18	1	23	0	1	0	.370	.336
Gonzales, Rene, California	.333	30	18	18	1	6	10	1	0	1	3	0	0	0	0	0	4	0	0	1	.556	.333
Gonzalez, Alex, Toronto	.243	111	425	367	51	89	146	19	4	10	42	9	4	1	44	1	114	4	4	7	.398	.322
Gonzalez, Juan, Texas	.295	90	374	352	57	104	209	20	2	27	82	0	5	0	17	3	66	0	0	15	.594	.324
Goodwin, Curtis, Baltimore*	.263	87	316	289	40	76	96	11	3	1	24	7	3	2	15	0	53	22	4	5	.332	.301
Goodwin, Tom, Kansas City*	.288	133	537	480	72	138	172	16	3	4	28	14	0	5	38	0	72	50	18	7	.358	.346
Grebeck, Craig, Chicago	.260	53	182	154	19	40	55	12	0	1	18	4	0	3	21	0	23	0	0	4	.357	.360
Green, Shawn, Toronto*	.288	121	405	379	52	109	193	31	4	15	54	0	3	3	20	3	68	1	2	4	.509	.326
Greenwell, Mike, Boston*	.297	120	525	481	67	143	221	25	4	15	76	0	4	2	38	4	35	9	5	18	.459	.349
Greer, Rusty, Texas*	.271	131	478	417	58	113	177	21	2	13	61	2	3	1	55	1	66	3	1	9	.424	.355
Griffey, Ken, Seattle*	.258	72	314	260	52	67	125	7	0	17	42	0	2	0	52	6	53	4	2	4	.481	.379
Grotewold, Jeff, Kansas City*	.278	15	46	36	4	10	14	1	0	1	6	0	0	0	9	0	7	0	0	2	.389	.422
Guillen, Ozzie, Chicago*	.248	122	433	415	50	103	132	20	3	1	41	4	1	0	13	1	25	6	7	11	.318	.270
Hale, Chip, Minnesota*	.262	69	114	103	10	27	37	4	0	2	18	0	0	0	11	1	20	0	0	6	.359	.333
Hall, Joe, Detroit	.133	7	17	15	2	2	2	0	0	0	0	0	0	0	2	0	3	0	0	1	.133	.235
Hamelin, Bob, Kansas City*	.168	72	242	208	20	35	65	7	1	7	25	0	1	6	26	1	56	0	1	6	.313	.278
Hamilton, Darryl, Milwaukee*	.271	112	459	398	54	108	155	20	6	5	44	8	3	3	47	3	35	11	1	9	.389	.350
Hammonds, Jeffrey, Baltimore	.242	57	191	178	18	43	66	9	1	4	23	1	2	1	9	0	30	4	2	3	.371	.279

Player, Team	Avg.	G	TPA	AB	R	H	TB	2B	3B	HR	RBI	SH	SF	HP	BB	IBB	SO	SB	CS	GDP	Slg.	OBP
Hare, Shawn, Texas*	.250	18	28	24	2	6	7	1	0	0	2	0	0	0	4	0	6	0	0	1	.292	.357
Harper, Brian, Oakland	.000	2	7	7	0	0	0	0	0	0	0	0	0	0	0	0	1	0	0	0	.000	.000
Haselman, Bill, Boston	.243	64	174	152	22	37	60	6	1	5	23	0	3	2	17	0	30	0	2	4	.395	.322
Hatcher, Billy, Texas	.083	6	13	12	2	1	2	1	0	0	0	0	0	0	1	0	1	0	0	0	.167	.154
Hatteberg, Scott, Boston*	.500	2	2	2	1	1	1	0	0	0	0	0	0	0	0	0	0	0	0	1	.500	.500
Helfand, Eric, Oakland*	.163	38	101	86	9	14	18	2	1	0	7	3	0	1	11	0	25	0	0	2	.209	.265
Henderson, Rickey, Oakland ..	.300	112	487	407	67	122	182	31	1	9	54	1	3	4	72	2	66	32	10	8	.447	.407
Herrera, Jose, Oakland*	.243	33	77	70	9	17	22	1	2	0	2	0	1	0	6	0	11	1	3	1	.314	.299
Hiatt, Phil, Kansas City	.204	52	124	113	11	23	41	6	0	4	12	2	0	0	9	0	37	1	0	3	.363	.262
Higginson, Bob, Detroit*	.224	131	486	410	61	92	161	17	5	14	43	2	7	5	62	3	107	6	4	5	.393	.329
Hocking, Denny, Minnesota†	.200	9	28	25	4	5	9	0	2	0	3	1	0	0	2	1	2	1	0	1	.360	.259
Hoiles, Chris, Baltimore	.250	114	426	352	53	88	162	15	1	19	58	0	3	4	67	3	80	1	0	11	.460	.373
Hollins, Dave, Boston†	.154	5	17	13	2	2	2	0	0	0	1	0	0	0	4	0	7	0	0	0	.154	.353
Horn, Sam, Texas*	.111	11	10	9	0	1	1	0	0	0	0	0	0	0	1	0	6	0	0	0	.111	.200
Hosey, Dwayne, Boston†	.338	24	77	68	20	23	42	8	1	3	7	1	0	0	8	0	16	6	0	0	.618	.408
Howard, David, Kansas City†	.243	95	287	255	23	62	83	13	4	0	19	6	1	1	24	1	41	6	1	7	.325	.310
Hudler, Rex, California	.265	84	241	223	30	59	93	16	0	6	27	2	1	5	10	1	48	13	0	2	.417	.310
Huff, Michael, Toronto	.232	61	168	138	14	32	46	9	1	1	9	5	2	1	22	0	21	1	1	4	.333	.337
Hulse, David, Milwaukee*	.251	119	364	339	46	85	117	11	6	3	47	2	5	0	18	2	60	15	3	3	.345	.285
Huson, Jeff, Baltimore*	.248	66	180	161	24	40	51	4	2	1	19	2	1	1	15	1	20	5	4	4	.317	.315
Ingram, Riccardo, Minnesota.	.125	4	10	8	0	1	1	0	0	0	1	0	0	0	2	0	1	0	0	1	.125	.300
Jaha, John, Milwaukee	.313	88	357	316	59	99	183	20	2	20	65	0	1	4	36	0	66	2	1	8	.579	.389
James, Chris, K.C.-Bos.	.268	42	94	82	8	22	32	4	0	2	8	2	2	1	7	0	14	1	0	2	.390	.326
James, Dion, New York*	.287	85	231	209	22	60	74	6	1	2	26	0	2	0	20	2	16	4	1	5	.354	.346
Javier, Stan, Oakland†	.278	130	504	442	81	123	171	20	2	8	56	5	4	4	49	3	63	36	5	8	.387	.353
Jefferson, Reggie, Boston*	.289	46	132	121	21	35	58	8	0	5	26	0	2	0	9	1	24	0	0	3	.479	.333
Jeter, Derek, New York	.250	15	51	48	5	12	18	4	1	0	7	0	0	0	3	0	11	0	0	0	.375	.294
Johnson, Lance, Chicago*	.306	142	645	607	98	186	258	18	12	10	57	2	3	1	32	2	31	40	6	7	.425	.341
Jose, Felix, Kansas City†	.133	9	32	30	2	4	5	1	0	0	1	0	0	0	2	0	9	0	0	1	.167	.188
Joyner, Wally, California*	.310	131	550	465	69	144	208	28	0	12	83	5	9	2	69	10	65	3	2	10	.447	.394
Karkovice, Ron, Chicago	.217	113	382	323	44	70	125	14	1	13	51	9	6	5	39	0	84	2	3	5	.387	.306
Kelly, Pat, New York	.237	89	310	270	32	64	90	12	1	4	29	10	2	5	23	0	65	8	3	5	.333	.307
Kirby, Wayne, Cleveland*	.207	101	205	188	29	39	56	10	2	1	14	1	2	1	13	0	32	10	3	4	.298	.260
Knoblauch, Chuck, Minnesota	.333	136	629	538	107	179	262	34	8	11	63	0	3	10	78	1	95	46	18	15	.487	.424
Knorr, Randy, Toronto	.212	45	144	132	18	28	45	8	0	3	16	1	0	0	11	0	28	0	0	5	.341	.273
Kreuter, Chad, Seattle†	.227	26	83	75	12	17	25	5	0	1	8	1	0	2	5	0	22	0	0	3	.333	.293
Kruk, John, Chicago*	.308	45	188	159	13	49	62	7	0	2	23	0	3	0	26	0	33	0	1	5	.390	.399
LaValliere, Mike, Chicago*	.245	46	109	98	7	24	33	6	0	1	19	0	2	0	9	0	15	0	0	3	.337	.303
Lawton, Matt, Minnesota*	.317	21	70	60	11	19	28	4	1	1	12	0	0	3	7	0	11	1	1	1	.467	.414
Leius, Scott, Minnesota	.247	117	427	372	51	92	130	16	5	4	45	0	4	2	49	3	54	2	1	14	.349	.335
Levis, Jesse, Cleveland*	.333	12	22	18	1	6	8	2	0	0	3	1	2	0	1	0	0	0	0	1	.444	.333
Leyritz, Jim, New York	.269	77	310	264	37	71	104	12	0	7	37	0	1	8	37	2	73	1	1	4	.394	.374
Lind, Jose, K.C.-Cal.	.236	44	147	140	9	33	38	5	0	0	7	1	0	0	6	0	12	0	1	5	.271	.267
Listach, Pat, Milwaukee†	.219	101	369	334	35	73	85	8	2	0	25	7	1	2	25	0	61	13	3	6	.254	.276
Lockhart, Keith, Kansas City*	.321	94	300	274	41	88	131	19	3	6	33	1	7	4	14	2	21	8	1	2	.478	.359
Lofton, Kenny, Cleveland*†	.310	118	529	481	93	149	218	22	13	7	53	4	3	1	40	6	49	54	15	6	.453	.362
Loretta, Mark, Milwaukee.	.260	19	56	50	13	13	19	3	0	1	3	1	0	1	4	0	7	1	1	1	.380	.327
Lyons, Barry, Chicago	.266	27	70	64	8	17	34	2	0	5	16	1	1	0	4	0	14	0	0	0	.531	.304
Maas, Kevin, Minnesota*	.193	22	64	57	5	11	18	4	0	1	5	0	0	0	7	2	11	0	0	4	.316	.281
Macfarlane, Mike, Boston	.225	115	420	364	45	82	147	18	1	15	51	0	4	14	38	0	78	2	1	9	.404	.319
Mahay, Ron, Boston*	.200	5	22	20	3	4	9	2	0	1	3	0	0	1	0	0	6	0	0	0	.450	.273
Maldonado, Candy, Tor.-Tex.	.263	74	227	190	28	50	93	16	0	9	30	0	3	2	32	0	50	1	2	6	.489	.370
Manto, Jeff, Baltimore	.256	89	280	254	31	65	125	9	0	17	38	0	0	2	24	0	69	0	3	6	.492	.325
Martin, Norberto, Chicago	.269	72	169	160	17	43	64	7	4	2	17	2	3	1	3	0	25	5	0	5	.400	.281
Martinez, Carlos, California	.180	26	68	61	7	11	15	1	0	1	9	0	0	1	6	2	7	0	0	2	.246	.265
Martinez, Dave, Chicago*	.307	119	349	303	49	93	132	16	4	5	37	9	4	1	32	2	41	8	2	6	.436	.371
Martinez, Edgar, Seattle	.356	145	639	511	121	182	321	52	0	29	113	0	4	8	116	19	87	4	3	11	.628	.479
Martinez, Angel, Toronto*	.241	62	200	191	12	46	64	12	0	2	25	0	1	1	7	0	45	0	0	1	.335	.270
Martinez, Tino, Seattle*	.293	141	593	519	92	152	286	35	3	31	111	2	6	4	62	15	91	0	0	10	.551	.369
Marzano, John, Texas	.333	2	6	6	1	2	2	0	0	0	0	0	0	0	0	0	0	0	0	0	.333	.333
Masteller, Dan, Minnesota*	.237	71	219	198	21	47	68	12	0	3	21	1	1	1	18	0	19	1	2	7	.343	.303
Matheny, Mike, Milwaukee	.247	80	181	166	13	41	52	9	1	0	21	1	0	2	12	0	28	2	1	3	.313	.306
Mattingly, Don, New York*	.288	128	507	458	59	132	189	32	2	7	49	0	8	1	40	7	35	0	2	17	.413	.341
May, Derrick, Milwaukee*	.248	32	119	113	15	28	36	3	1	1	9	0	0	1	5	0	18	0	1	1	.319	.286
Mayne, Brent, Kansas City*	.251	110	347	307	23	77	100	18	1	1	27	11	1	3	25	1	41	0	1	16	.326	.313
McCarty, Dave, Minnesota	.218	25	61	55	10	12	17	3	1	0	4	0	1	1	4	0	18	0	1	1	.309	.279
McGee, Willie, Boston†	.285	67	217	200	32	57	80	11	3	2	15	5	3	0	9	0	41	5	2	5	.400	.311
McGinnis, Russ, Kansas City .	.000	3	6	5	1	0	0	0	0	0	0	0	0	0	1	0	1	0	0	0	.000	.167
McGwire, Mark, Oakland	.274	104	422	317	75	87	217	13	0	39	90	0	6	11	88	5	77	1	1	9	.685	.441
McLemore, Mark, Texas†	.261	129	542	467	73	122	167	20	5	5	41	10	3	3	59	6	71	21	11	10	.358	.346
Meares, Pat, Minnesota	.269	116	425	390	57	105	168	19	4	12	49	4	5	11	15	0	68	10	4	17	.431	.311
Mercedes, Henry, Kansas City	.256	23	55	43	7	11	13	2	0	0	9	1	2	1	8	0	13	0	0	0	.302	.370
Merullo, Matt, Minnesota*	.282	76	216	195	19	55	74	14	1	1	27	1	3	3	14	0	27	0	1	5	.379	.335
Mieske, Matt, Milwaukee	.251	117	303	267	42	67	118	13	1	12	48	0	5	4	27	0	45	2	4	8	.442	.323
Miller, Keith, Kansas City	.333	9	17	15	2	5	8	0	0	1	3	0	0	0	2	0	4	0	0	1	.533	.412
Molitor, Paul, Toronto	.270	130	598	525	63	142	222	31	2	15	60	3	4	5	61	1	57	12	0	10	.423	.350
Mota, Jose, Kansas City†	.000	2	2	2	0	0	0	0	0	0	0	0	0	0	0	0	0	0	0	0	.000	.000
Mouton, Lyle, Chicago	.302	58	201	179	23	54	85	16	0	5	27	0	1	2	19	0	46	1	0	7	.475	.373
Munoz, Pedro, Minnesota	.301	104	400	376	45	113	184	17	0	18	58	0	3	2	19	0	86	0	3	14	.489	.338
Murray, Eddie, Cleveland†.	.323	113	480	436	68	141	225	21	0	21	82	0	5	0	39	5	65	5	1	12	.516	.375
Myers, Greg, California*	.260	85	294	273	35	71	114	12	2	9	38	1	2	1	17	3	49	0	1	4	.418	.304
Naehring, Tim, Boston .	.307	126	520	433	61	133	194	27	2	10	57	4	4	4	77	5	66	0	2	16	.448	.415
Nevin, Phil, Detroit	.219	29	110	96	9	21	32	3	1	2	12	0	0	3	11	0	27	0	0	3	.333	.318

Player, Team	Avg.	G	TPA	AB	R	H	TB	2B	3B	HR	RBI	SH	SF	HP	BB	IBB	SO	SB	CS	GDP	Slg.	OBP
Newfield, Marc, Seattle	.188	24	89	85	7	16	28	3	0	3	14	0	0	1	3	1	16	0	0	2	.329	.225
Newson, Warren, Chi.-Sea.* ..	.261	84	197	157	34	41	62	2	2	5	15	0	0	1	39	0	45	2	1	3	.395	.411
Nilsson, Dave, Milwaukee*	.278	81	294	263	41	73	123	12	1	12	53	0	5	2	24	4	41	2	0	9	.468	.337
Nixon, Otis, Texas†	.295	139	656	589	87	174	199	21	2	0	45	6	3	0	58	1	85	50	21	6	.338	.357
Nokes, Matt, Baltimore*	.122	26	54	49	4	6	13	1	0	2	6	0	1	0	4	0	11	0	0	2	.265	.185
Norman, Les, Kansas City......	.225	24	47	40	6	9	11	0	1	0	4	1	0	0	6	0	6	0	1	0	.275	.326
Nunnally, Jon, Kansas City*...	.244	119	360	303	51	74	143	15	6	14	42	4	0	2	51	5	86	6	4	4	.472	.357
Obando, Sherman, Baltimore.	.263	16	41	38	0	10	11	1	0	0	3	0	1	0	2	0	12	1	0	0	.289	.293
O'Leary, Troy, Boston*	.308	112	434	399	60	123	196	31	6	10	49	3	2	1	29	4	64	5	3	8	.491	.355
Olerud, John, Toronto*	.291	135	581	492	72	143	199	32	0	8	54	0	1	4	84	10	54	0	0	17	.404	.398
Oliver, Joe, Milwaukee	.273	97	369	337	43	92	148	20	0	12	51	2	0	3	27	1	66	2	4	11	.439	.332
O'Neill, Paul, New York*	.300	127	543	460	82	138	242	30	4	22	96	0	11	1	71	8	76	1	2	25	.526	.387
Ortiz, Luis, Texas....................	.231	41	115	108	10	25	37	5	2	1	18	0	1	0	6	0	18	0	1	7	.343	.270
Owen, Spike, California†	.229	82	237	218	17	50	68	9	3	1	28	1	0	0	18	1	22	3	2	7	.312	.288
Pagliarulo, Mike, Texas*	.232	86	262	241	27	56	84	16	0	4	27	2	3	1	15	2	49	0	0	10	.349	.277
Palmeiro, Orlando, California*	.350	15	21	20	3	7	7	0	0	0	1	0	0	0	1	0	1	0	0	0	.350	.381
Palmeiro, Rafael, Baltimore*..	.310	143	624	554	89	172	323	30	2	39	104	0	5	3	62	5	65	3	1	12	.583	.380
Palmer, Dean, Texas..............	.336	36	145	119	30	40	73	6	0	9	24	0	1	4	21	1	21	1	1	2	.613	.448
Paquette, Craig, Oakland........	.226	105	304	283	42	64	118	13	1	13	49	3	5	1	12	0	88	5	2	5	.417	.256
Parrish, Lance, Toronto..........	.202	70	202	178	15	36	57	9	0	4	22	6	2	1	15	0	52	0	0	4	.320	.265
Pemberton, Rudy, Detroit	.300	12	32	30	3	9	14	3	1	0	3	0	0	1	1	0	5	0	0	3	.467	.344
Pena, Tony, Cleveland	.262	91	279	263	25	69	99	15	0	5	28	1	0	1	14	1	44	1	0	9	.376	.302
Penn, Shannon, Detroit†	.333	3	10	9	0	3	3	0	0	0	0	0	0	0	1	0	2	0	0	2	.333	.400
Perez, Eduardo, California......	.169	29	86	71	9	12	21	4	1	1	7	0	1	2	12	0	9	0	2	3	.296	.302
Perez, Robert, Toronto...........	.188	17	48	48	2	9	14	2	0	1	3	0	0	0	0	0	5	0	0	1	.292	.188
Perez, Tomas, Toronto†	.245	41	106	98	12	24	32	3	1	1	8	0	1	0	7	0	18	0	1	6	.327	.292
Perry, Herbert, Cleveland	.315	52	184	162	23	51	75	13	1	3	23	3	2	4	13	0	28	1	3	5	.463	.376
Phillips, Tony, California†.......	.261	139	643	525	119	137	241	21	1	27	61	1	1	3	113	6	135	13	10	5	.459	.394
Pichardo, Hipolito, Kansas City	.000	44	2	2	0	0	0	0	0	0	0	0	0	0	0	0	0	0	0	0	.000	.000
Pirkl, Greg, Seattle	.235	10	18	17	2	4	4	0	0	0	0	0	0	0	1	0	7	0	0	0	.235	.278
Polonia, Luis, New York*	.261	67	269	238	37	62	83	9	3	2	15	2	4	0	25	1	29	10	4	3	.349	.326
Pozo, Arquimedez, Seattle	.000	1	1	1	0	0	0	0	0	0	0	0	0	0	0	0	0	0	0	0	.000	.000
Puckett, Kirby, Minnesota	.314	137	602	538	83	169	277	39	0	23	99	0	5	3	56	18	89	3	2	15	.515	.379
Raabe, Brian, Minnesota.........	.214	6	15	14	4	3	3	0	0	0	1	0	0	0	1	0	0	0	0	0	.214	.267
Raines, Tim, Chicago†	.285	133	581	502	81	143	212	25	4	12	67	3	3	3	70	3	52	13	2	8	.422	.374
Ramirez, Manny, Cleveland....	.308	137	571	484	85	149	270	26	1	31	107	2	5	5	75	6	112	6	6	13	.558	.402
Randa, Joe, Kansas City	.171	34	76	70	6	12	17	2	0	1	5	0	0	0	6	0	17	0	1	2	.243	.237
Reboulet, Jeff, Minnesota	.292	87	246	216	39	63	86	11	0	4	23	2	0	1	27	0	34	1	2	3	.398	.373
Rhodes, Karl, Boston*	.080	10	28	25	2	2	3	1	0	0	1	0	0	0	3	0	4	0	0	1	.120	.179
Ripken, Billy, Cleveland..........	.412	8	17	17	4	7	13	0	0	2	3	0	0	0	0	0	3	0	0	0	.765	.412
Ripken, Cal, Baltimore............	.262	144	613	550	71	144	232	33	2	17	88	1	8	2	52	6	59	0	1	15	.422	.324
Rivera, Ruben, New York	.000	5	1	1	0	0	0	0	0	0	0	0	0	0	0	0	1	0	0	0	.000	.000
Rodriguez, Alex, Seattle	.232	48	149	142	15	33	58	6	2	5	19	1	0	0	6	0	42	4	2	0	.408	.264
Rodriguez, Carlos, Boston† ...	.333	13	36	30	5	10	12	2	0	0	5	3	0	1	2	0	2	0	0	0	.400	.394
Rodriguez, Ivan, Texas...........	.303	130	517	492	56	149	221	32	2	12	67	0	5	4	16	2	48	0	2	11	.449	.327
Rodriguez, Steve, Bos.-Det. ...	.179	18	46	39	5	7	8	1	0	0	0	1	0	0	6	0	10	2	2	1	.205	.289
Rowland, Rich, Boston	.172	14	29	29	1	5	6	1	0	0	1	0	0	0	0	0	11	0	0	0	.207	.172
Sabo, Chris, Chicago..............	.254	20	80	71	10	18	26	5	0	1	8	2	2	2	3	1	12	2	0	0	.366	.295
Salmon, Tim, California..........	.330	143	638	537	111	177	319	34	3	34	105	0	4	6	91	2	111	5	5	9	.594	.429
Samuel, Juan, Det.-K.C.	.263	91	237	205	31	54	102	10	1	12	39	1	0	2	29	1	49	6	4	3	.498	.360
Schofield, Dick, California	.250	12	26	20	1	5	5	0	0	0	2	2	0	0	4	0	2	0	0	1	.250	.375
Seitzer, Kevin, Milwaukee.......	.311	132	570	492	56	153	207	33	3	5	69	5	3	6	64	2	57	2	0	13	.421	.395
Shumpert, Terry, Boston	.234	21	51	47	6	11	14	3	0	0	3	0	0	0	4	0	13	3	1	0	.298	.294
Sierra, Ruben, Oak.-N.Y.†	.263	126	533	479	73	126	215	32	0	19	86	0	8	0	46	4	76	5	4	8	.449	.323
Silvestri, Dave, New York........	.095	17	27	21	4	2	5	0	0	1	4	0	1	1	4	0	9	0	0	1	.238	.259
Singleton, Duane, Milwaukee*	.065	13	32	31	0	2	2	0	0	0	0	0	0	0	1	0	10	1	0	0	.065	.094
Smith, Mark, Baltimore	.231	37	120	104	11	24	38	5	0	3	15	2	1	1	12	2	22	3	0	4	.365	.314
Snopek, Chris, Chicago..........	.324	22	77	68	12	22	29	4	0	1	7	0	0	0	9	0	12	1	0	2	.426	.403
Snow, J.T., California†	.289	143	606	544	80	157	253	22	1	24	102	5	2	3	52	4	91	2	1	16	.465	.353
Sojo, Luis, Seattle..................	.289	102	370	339	50	98	141	18	2	7	39	6	1	1	23	0	19	4	2	9	.416	.335
Sorrento, Paul, Cleveland*.....	.235	104	378	323	50	76	165	14	0	25	79	0	4	0	51	6	71	1	1	10	.511	.336
Sprague, Ed, Toronto	.244	144	602	521	77	127	212	27	2	18	74	1	7	15	58	3	96	0	0	19	.407	.333
Stahoviak, Scott, Minnesota*	.266	94	296	263	28	70	98	19	0	3	23	0	2	1	30	1	61	5	1	3	.373	.341
Stairs, Matt, Boston*	.261	39	95	88	8	23	35	7	1	1	17	1	1	1	4	0	14	0	1	4	.398	.298
Stanley, Mike, New York	.268	118	470	399	63	107	192	29	1	18	83	0	9	5	57	1	106	1	1	14	.481	.360
Steinbach, Terry, Oakland	.278	114	440	406	43	113	186	26	1	15	65	1	4	3	25	4	74	1	3	15	.458	.322
Steverson, Todd, Detroit	.262	30	50	42	11	11	17	0	0	2	6	0	2	0	6	0	10	2	0	0	.405	.340
Stewart, Shannon, Toronto	.211	12	44	38	2	8	8	0	0	0	1	0	0	1	5	0	5	2	0	0	.211	.318
Stottlemyre, Todd, Oakland*..	.000	31	1	1	0	0	0	0	0	0	0	0	0	0	0	0	1	0	0	0	.000	.000
Strange, Doug, Seattle†	.271	74	169	155	19	42	61	9	2	2	21	1	0	2	10	0	25	0	3	3	.394	.323
Strawberry, Darryl, New York*	.276	32	99	87	15	24	39	4	1	3	13	0	0	2	10	1	22	0	0	0	.448	.364
Stubbs, Franklin, Detroit*	.250	62	137	116	13	29	46	11	0	2	19	0	1	1	19	1	27	0	1	3	.397	.358
Stynes, Chris, Kansas City	.171	22	39	35	7	6	7	1	0	0	2	0	0	0	4	0	3	0	0	3	.200	.256
Surhoff, B.J., Milwaukee*	.320	117	462	415	72	133	204	26	3	13	73	2	4	4	37	4	43	7	3	7	.492	.378
Sweeney, Mike, Kansas City...	.250	4	4	4	1	1	1	0	0	0	0	0	0	0	0	0	0	0	0	0	.250	.250
Tartabull, Danny, N.Y.-Oak......	.236	83	328	280	34	66	106	16	0	8	35	0	4	1	43	1	82	0	2	9	.379	.335
Tettleton, Mickey, Texas†	.238	134	547	429	76	102	219	19	1	32	78	1	3	7	107	5	110	0	0	8	.510	.396
Tewksbury, Bob, Texas...........	.000	22	1	1	0	0	0	0	0	0	0	0	0	0	0	0	1	0	0	0	.000	.000
Thomas, Frank, Chicago	.308	145	647	493	102	152	299	27	0	40	111	0	12	6	136	29	74	3	2	14	.606	.454
Thome, Jim, Cleveland*.........	.314	137	557	452	92	142	252	29	3	25	73	0	3	5	97	3	113	4	3	8	.558	.438
Thurman, Gary, Seattle	.320	13	27	25	3	8	10	2	0	0	3	0	1	0	1	0	3	5	2	0	.400	.333
Tingley, Ron, Detroit	.226	54	145	124	14	28	50	8	1	4	18	5	1	0	15	0	38	0	1	1	.403	.307
Tinsley, Lee, Boston†	.284	100	391	341	61	97	137	17	1	7	41	9	1	1	39	1	74	18	8	8	.402	.359

Player, Team	Avg.	G	TPA	AB	R	H	TB	2B	3B	HR	RBI	SH	SF	HP	BB	IBB	SO	SB	CS	GDP	Slg.	OBP
Tomberlin, Andy, Oakland*	.212	46	92	85	15	18	30	0	0	4	10	2	0	0	5	0	22	4	1	2	.353	.256
Trammell, Alan, Detroit	.269	74	255	223	28	60	78	12	0	2	23	3	2	0	27	4	19	3	1	8	.350	.345
Tremie, Chris, Chicago	.167	10	26	24	0	4	4	0	0	0	0	1	0	0	1	0	2	0	0	0	.167	.200
Tucker, Michael, Kansas City* ...	.260	62	198	177	23	46	68	10	0	4	17	2	0	1	18	2	51	2	3	3	.384	.332
Tucker, Scooter, Cleveland	.000	17	27	20	2	0	0	0	0	0	0	1	0	1	5	0	4	0	0	0	.000	.231
Turner, Chris, California	.100	5	10	10	0	1	1	0	0	0	1	0	0	0	0	0	3	0	0	0	.100	.100
Unroe, Tim, Milwaukee	.250	2	4	4	0	1	1	0	0	0	0	0	0	0	0	0	0	0	0	0	.250	.250
Valentin, John, Boston	.298	135	621	520	108	155	277	37	2	27	102	4	6	10	81	2	67	20	5	7	.533	.399
Valentin, Jose, Milwaukee†	.219	112	386	338	62	74	136	23	3	11	49	7	4	0	37	0	83	16	8	0	.402	.293
Valle, Dave, Texas	.240	36	83	75	7	18	21	3	0	0	5	1	0	1	6	0	18	1	0	2	.280	.305
Van Slyke, Andy, Baltimore* ..	.159	17	68	63	6	10	20	1	0	3	8	0	0	0	5	1	15	0	0	1	.317	.221
Vaughn, Greg, Milwaukee	.224	108	451	392	67	88	160	19	1	17	59	0	4	0	55	3	89	10	4	10	.408	.317
Vaughn, Mo, Boston*	.300	140	636	550	98	165	316	28	3	39	126	0	4	14	68	17	150	11	4	17	.575	.388
Velarde, Randy, New York......	.278	111	432	367	60	102	144	19	1	7	46	3	3	4	55	0	64	5	1	9	.392	.375
Ventura, Robin, Chicago*	.295	135	577	492	79	145	245	22	0	26	93	1	8	1	75	11	98	4	3	8	.498	.384
Vina, Fernando, Milwaukee* ...	.257	113	325	288	46	74	104	7	7	3	29	4	2	9	22	0	28	6	3	6	.361	.327
Vitiello, Joe, Kansas City	.254	53	142	130	13	33	58	4	0	7	21	0	4	8	0	0	25	0	0	4	.446	.317
Vizquel, Omar, Cleveland†	.266	136	622	542	87	144	190	28	0	6	56	10	10	1	59	0	59	29	11	4	.351	.333
Voigt, Jack, Bal.-Tex.	.175	36	74	63	9	11	20	3	0	2	8	0	1	0	10	0	14	0	0	2	.317	.284
Walbeck, Matt, Minnesota†	.257	115	422	393	40	101	124	18	1	1	44	1	2	1	25	2	71	3	1	11	.316	.302
Ward, Turner, Milwaukee†	.264	44	146	129	19	34	51	3	1	4	16	1	1	1	14	1	21	6	1	2	.395	.338
Whitaker, Lou, Detroit*	.293	84	285	249	36	73	129	14	0	14	44	0	3	2	31	4	41	4	0	6	.518	.372
White, Derrick, Detroit	.188	39	48	48	3	9	11	2	0	0	2	0	0	0	0	0	7	1	0	1	.229	.188
White, Devon, Toronto†	.283	101	465	427	61	121	184	23	5	10	53	1	3	5	29	1	97	11	2	5	.431	.334
Whiten, Mark, Boston†	.185	32	117	108	13	20	26	3	0	1	10	0	1	0	8	0	23	1	0	5	.241	.239
Widger, Chris, Seattle.............	.200	23	49	45	2	9	12	0	0	1	2	0	1	0	3	0	11	0	0	0	.267	.245
Williams, Bernie, New York†	.307	144	648	563	93	173	274	29	9	18	82	2	3	5	75	1	98	8	6	12	.487	.392
Williams, George, Oakland† ...	.291	29	94	79	13	23	39	5	1	3	14	0	2	2	11	2	21	0	0	1	.494	.383
Williams, Gerald, New York....	.247	100	208	182	33	45	85	18	2	6	28	0	3	1	22	1	34	4	2	4	.467	.327
Wilson, Dan, Seattle..............	.278	119	440	399	40	111	166	22	3	9	51	5	1	2	33	1	63	2	1	12	.416	.336
Winfield, Dave, Cleveland.......	.191	46	130	115	11	22	33	5	0	2	4	0	0	1	14	2	26	1	0	5	.287	.285
Worthington, Craig, Texas......	.221	26	77	68	4	15	25	4	0	2	6	2	0	0	7	0	8	0	0	6	.368	.293
Young, Ernie, Oakland	.200	26	58	50	9	10	19	3	0	2	5	0	0	0	8	0	12	0	0	1	.380	.310
Zaun, Greg, Baltimore†	.260	40	122	104	18	27	41	5	0	3	14	2	0	0	16	0	14	1	1	2	.394	.358

AWARDED FIRST BASE ON OBSTRUCTION OR CATCHER'S INTERFERENCE—Belle, Cleveland 2 (Martinez, Merullo); Grotewold, Kansas City (Pena); Hamelin, Kansas City (Kreuter); Steinbach, Oakland (Merullo); Strange, Seattle (Mayne).

PLAYERS WITH TWO OR MORE TEAMS

Player, Team	Avg.	G	TPA	AB	R	H	TB	2B	3B	HR	RBI	SH	SF	HP	BB	IBB	SO	SB	CS	GDP	Slg.	OBP
Aldrete, Mike, Oakland*	.272	60	147	125	18	34	54	8	0	4	21	0	2	1	19	1	23	0	0	3	.432	.367
Aldrete, Mike, California*	.250	18	25	24	1	6	6	0	0	0	3	0	1	0	0	0	8	0	0	1	.250	.240
Coleman, Vince, Kansas City† ...	.287	75	324	293	39	84	117	13	4	4	20	2	1	1	27	1	48	26	9	7	.399	.348
Coleman, Vince, Seattle†	.290	40	176	162	27	47	64	10	2	1	9	3	0	1	10	1	32	16	7	1	.395	.335
James, Chris, Kansas City.......	.310	26	67	58	6	18	27	3	0	2	7	0	2	1	6	0	10	1	0	1	.466	.373
James, Chris, Boston	.167	16	27	24	2	4	5	1	0	0	1	2	0	0	1	0	4	0	0	1	.208	.200
Lind, Jose, Kansas City	.268	29	101	97	4	26	29	3	0	0	6	1	0	0	3	0	8	0	1	2	.299	.290
Lind, Jose, California	.163	15	46	43	5	7	9	2	0	0	1	0	0	0	3	0	4	0	0	3	.209	.217
Maldonado, Candy, Toronto ...	.269	61	190	160	22	43	77	13	0	7	25	0	3	2	25	0	45	1	1	5	.481	.368
Maldonado, Candy, Texas.......	.233	13	37	30	6	7	16	3	0	2	5	0	0	0	7	0	5	0	1	1	.533	.378
Newson, Warren, Chicago* ...	.235	51	109	85	19	20	33	0	2	3	9	0	0	1	23	0	27	1	1	2	.388	.404
Newson, Warren, Seattle*	.292	33	88	72	15	21	29	2	0	2	6	0	0	0	16	0	18	1	0	1	.403	.420
Rodriguez, Steve, Boston.......	.125	6	9	8	1	1	1	0	0	0	0	0	0	0	1	0	1	0	0	0	.125	.222
Rodriguez, Steve, Detroit.......	.194	12	37	31	4	6	7	1	0	0	0	1	0	0	5	0	9	1	2	1	.226	.306
Samuel, Juan, Detroit	.281	76	198	171	28	48	90	10	1	10	34	1	0	2	24	0	38	5	4	3	.526	.376
Samuel, Juan, Kansas City......	.176	15	39	34	3	6	12	0	0	2	5	0	0	0	5	1	11	1	0	0	.353	.282
Sierra, Ruben, Oakland†	.265	70	291	264	40	70	123	17	0	12	42	0	3	0	24	2	42	4	4	2	.466	.323
Sierra, Ruben, New York†	.260	56	242	215	33	56	92	15	0	7	44	0	5	0	22	2	34	1	0	5	.428	.322
Tartabull, Danny, New York	.224	59	230	192	25	43	73	12	0	6	28	0	4	1	33	1	54	0	0	6	.380	.335
Tartabull, Danny, Oakland.......	.261	24	98	88	9	23	33	4	0	2	7	0	0	0	10	0	28	0	2	3	.375	.337
Voigt, Jack, Baltimore	1.000	3	1	1	1	1	1	0	0	0	0	0	0	0	0	0	0	0	0	0	1.000	1.000
Voigt, Jack, Texas	.161	33	73	62	8	10	19	3	0	2	8	0	1	0	10	0	14	0	0	2	.306	.274

DESIGNATED HITTING

TEAM

Team	Avg.	G	TPA	AB	R	H	TB	2B	3B	HR	RBI	SH	SF	HP	BB	IBB	SO	SB	CS	GDP	Slg.	OBP
Seattle	.355	145	647	519	122	184	325	54	0	29	113	0	3	8	117	20	89	4	4	12	.626	.478
California	.302	145	645	530	100	160	252	26	0	22	99	0	10	2	103	13	97	5	4	13	.475	.411
Cleveland	.297	144	624	556	83	165	254	26	0	21	91	0	4	2	62	5	95	7	2	16	.457	.367
Minnesota	.292	144	626	571	75	167	252	28	0	19	81	0	2	7	46	6	125	2	3	24	.441	.351
Boston	.291	144	645	571	83	166	285	33	1	28	113	0	10	9	55	4	126	4	0	13	.499	.357
Baltimore	.287	144	600	508	73	146	252	26	1	26	80	0	7	1	84	13	79	4	5	19	.496	.385
Chicago	.281	145	656	538	68	151	230	25	0	18	84	5	13	5	95	11	94	4	1	12	.428	.386
Texas	.270	144	630	552	94	149	293	25	1	39	109	1	8	4	65	5	117	0	0	20	.531	.347
Toronto	.262	144	668	584	68	153	240	35	2	16	69	4	8	7	65	1	75	15	0	11	.411	.339
New York	.262	145	636	558	87	146	227	31	1	16	95	0	9	3	66	3	119	3	1	11	.407	.338
Detroit	.258	144	623	534	75	138	229	25	3	20	71	1	1	5	82	7	138	9	4	11	.429	.362
Oakland	.256	144	645	566	83	145	233	24	2	20	77	0	6	1	72	3	128	7	5	8	.412	.338
Milwaukee	.234	144	641	563	89	132	236	25	2	25	84	1	4	1	72	5	121	11	5	13	.419	.320
Kansas City	.213	144	612	534	65	114	194	14	0	22	69	2	2	8	64	3	137	3	4	11	.363	.306
Totals	.275	2020	8898	7684	1165	2116	3502	397	13	321	1235	14	87	63	1048	99	1540	78	38	194	.456	.363

INDIVIDUAL

TOP DESIGNATED HITTERS

Minimum 90 at-bats. *Lefthanded batter. †Switch-hitter.

Player, Team	Avg.	G	TPA	AB	R	H	TB	2B	3B	HR	RBI	SH	SF	HP	BB	IBB	SO	SB	CS	GDP	Slg.	OBP
Martinez, Edgar, Seattle	.360	138	610	491	115	177	314	50	0	29	110	0	3	8	108	17	84	4	3	11	.640	.480
Murray, Eddie, Cleveland†	.344	95	403	363	61	125	195	19	0	17	75	0	4	0	36	4	50	5	1	9	.537	.400
Puckett, Kirby, Minnesota	.336	28	119	107	15	36	47	8	0	1	17	0	0	1	11	4	25	1	0	2	.439	.403
James, Dion, New York*	.327	27	107	101	12	33	40	4	0	1	13	0	1	0	5	0	7	3	1	2	.396	.355
Davis, Chili, California†	.318	119	522	424	81	135	218	23	0	20	86	0	9	0	89	12	79	3	3	12	.514	.429
Kruk, John, Chicago*	.318	42	182	154	13	49	62	7	0	2	23	0	3	0	25	0	31	0	1	4	.403	.407
Canseco, Jose, Boston	.306	101	445	392	62	120	218	24	1	24	81	0	5	7	41	4	91	4	0	9	.556	.378
Munoz, Pedro, Minnesota	.303	77	310	290	39	88	141	11	0	14	46	0	2	3	15	0	68	0	2	10	.486	.342
Gonzalez, Juan, Texas	.300	83	355	333	57	100	203	20	1	27	78	0	5	0	17	3	62	0	0	13	.610	.330
Baines, Harold, Baltimore*	.297	122	454	381	60	113	206	19	1	24	63	0	4	0	69	13	44	0	2	16	.541	.401
Jefferson, Reggie, Boston*	.295	32	105	95	17	28	47	7	0	4	22	0	2	0	8	0	18	0	0	3	.495	.343
Berroa, Geronimo, Oakland	.277	72	325	289	51	80	129	11	1	12	48	0	4	0	32	2	44	2	3	3	.446	.345
Molitor, Paul, Toronto	.270	129	597	525	63	142	222	31	2	15	60	3	4	5	60	1	57	12	0	10	.423	.348
Thomas, Frank, Chicago	.266	53	227	173	27	46	80	7	0	9	35	0	7	2	45	9	27	1	0	7	.462	.410
Gibson, Kirk, Detroit*	.253	63	258	221	35	56	96	12	2	8	28	0	1	3	33	3	60	8	2	5	.434	.357

ALL DESIGNATED HITTERS

*Lefthanded batter. †Switch-hitter.

Player, Team	Avg.	G	TPA	AB	R	H	TB	2B	3B	HR	RBI	SH	SF	HP	BB	IBB	SO	SB	CS	GDP	Slg.	OBP
Aldrete, Mike, California*	.143	2	7	7	0	1	1	0	0	0	0	0	0	0	0	0	2	0	0	0	.143	.143
Amaral, Rich, Seattle	.000	1	1	1	0	0	0	0	0	0	0	0	0	0	0	0	0	0	0	0	.000	.000
Amaro, Ruben, Cleveland†	.200	3	5	5	0	1	1	0	0	0	0	0	0	0	0	0	1	0	0	0	.200	.200
Anderson, Garret, California*	.000	1	4	4	0	0	0	0	0	0	0	0	0	0	0	0	1	0	0	0	.000	.000
Baerga, Carlos, Cleveland†	.000	1	4	4	0	0	0	0	0	0	0	0	0	0	0	0	0	0	0	0	.000	.000
Baines, Harold, Baltimore*	.297	122	454	381	60	113	206	19	1	24	63	0	4	0	69	13	44	0	2	16	.541	.401
Barberie, Bret, Baltimore†	.263	5	20	19	3	5	6	1	0	0	1	0	0	0	1	0	2	1	0	0	.316	.300
Bass, Kevin, Baltimore†	.385	19	45	39	5	15	21	3	0	1	10	0	0	1	5	0	9	2	3	2	.538	.467
Battle, Howard, Toronto	.000	1	3	3	0	0	0	0	0	0	0	0	0	0	0	0	3	0	0	0	.000	.000
Belle, Albert, Cleveland	.250	1	4	4	0	1	1	0	0	0	0	0	0	0	0	0	1	0	0	0	.250	.250
Berroa, Geronimo, Oakland	.277	72	325	289	51	80	129	11	1	12	48	0	4	0	32	2	44	2	3	3	.446	.345
Borders, Pat, Kansas City	.167	3	12	12	0	2	2	0	0	0	0	0	0	0	0	0	0	0	0	0	.167	.167
Bordick, Mike, Oakland	.500	1	2	2	0	1	2	1	0	0	1	0	0	0	0	0	0	0	0	0	1.000	.500
Brady, Doug, Chicago†	.000	2	1	1	0	0	0	0	0	0	0	0	0	0	0	0	1	0	0	0	.000	.000
Brito, Bernardo, Minnesota	.250	3	5	4	1	1	4	0	0	1	1	0	0	1	0	0	2	0	0	1	1.000	.400
Brosius, Scott, Oakland	.500	2	2	2	1	1	1	0	0	0	0	0	0	0	0	0	0	0	0	0	.500	.500
Buhner, Jay, Seattle	.267	4	18	15	3	4	7	3	0	0	3	0	0	0	3	1	2	0	0	0	.467	.389
Caceres, Edgar, Kansas City†	.667	3	4	3	2	2	5	0	0	1	3	1	0	0	0	0	0	0	0	0	1.667	.667
Canseco, Jose, Boston	.306	101	445	392	62	120	218	24	1	24	81	0	5	7	41	4	91	4	0	9	.556	.378
Carter, Joe, Toronto	.118	5	21	17	1	2	3	1	0	0	2	0	2	1	1	0	1	2	0	0	.176	.190
Chamberlain, Wes, Boston	.125	5	8	8	0	1	1	0	0	0	0	0	0	0	0	0	1	0	0	0	.125	.125
Clark, Jerald, Minnesota	1.000	3	4	4	2	4	8	1	0	1	4	0	0	0	0	0	0	0	0	0	2.000	1.000
Clark, Will, Texas*	.200	1	5	5	1	1	1	0	0	0	0	0	0	0	0	0	1	0	0	0	.200	.200
Cole, Alex, Minnesota*	.000	2	4	3	0	0	0	0	0	0	0	0	0	0	1	0	0	0	0	0	.000	.000
Coleman, Vince, Kansas City†	.500	4	14	12	4	6	6	0	0	0	0	0	0	0	2	0	3	3	2	0	.500	.571
Cookson, Brent, Kansas City	.333	2	4	3	0	1	2	1	0	0	2	0	0	0	1	0	1	0	0	0	.667	.500
Coomer, Ron, Minnesota	.333	4	9	6	2	2	5	0	0	1	2	0	0	0	3	0	1	0	0	1	.833	.556
Cuyler, Milt, Detroit†	.000	2	1	1	0	0	0	0	0	0	0	0	0	0	0	0	1	0	0	0	.000	.000
Dalesandro, Mark, California	.000	1	1	1	0	0	0	0	0	0	0	0	0	0	0	0	0	0	0	0	.000	.000
Davis, Chili, California†	.318	119	522	424	81	135	218	23	0	20	86	0	9	0	89	12	79	3	3	12	.514	.429
Davis, Russ, New York	.375	4	9	8	3	3	5	2	0	0	0	0	0	1	0	0	3	0	0	0	.625	.444
Delgado, Carlos, Toronto*	.150	7	22	20	1	3	4	1	0	0	2	0	1	0	1	0	10	0	0	0	.200	.182
Fielder, Cecil, Detroit	.251	58	249	215	30	54	92	6	1	10	31	0	0	1	33	4	62	0	0	6	.428	.353

Player, Team	Avg.	G	TPA	AB	R	H	TB	2B	3B	HR	RBI	SH	SF	HP	BB	IBB	SO	SB	CS	GDP	Slg.	OBP
Flora, Kevin, California	.000	1	1	1	0	0	0	0	0	0	0	0	0	0	0	0	1	0	0	0	.000	.000
Frazier, Lou, Texas†	.200	2	5	5	1	1	1	0	0	0	0	0	0	0	0	0	1	0	0	0	.200	.200
Gaetti, Gary, Kansas City	.118	6	19	17	2	2	8	0	0	2	3	0	0	0	2	0	1	0	0	0	.471	.211
Gagne, Greg, Kansas City	.000	2	3	2	0	0	0	0	0	0	0	0	0	0	1	0	1	0	0	0	.000	.333
Gallagher, Dave, California	.000	1	1	0	0	0	0	0	0	0	0	0	0	0	1	0	0	0	0	0	.000	1.000
Gates, Brent, Oakland†	.286	3	15	14	1	4	5	1	0	0	1	0	0	0	1	0	4	0	0	0	.357	.333
Giambi, Jason, Oakland*	.143	2	9	7	0	1	1	0	0	0	0	0	0	0	2	0	1	0	0	0	.143	.333
Gibson, Kirk, Detroit*	.253	63	258	221	35	56	96	12	2	8	28	0	1	3	33	3	60	8	2	5	.434	.357
Giles, Brian S., Cleveland*	.667	1	3	3	1	2	2	0	0	0	1	0	0	0	0	0	1	0	0	0	.667	.667
Gomez, Chris, Detroit	.000	1	1	1	0	0	0	0	0	0	0	0	0	0	0	0	0	0	0	0	.000	.000
Gomez, Leo, Baltimore	.167	5	6	6	1	1	1	0	0	0	0	0	0	0	0	0	2	0	0	0	.167	.167
Gonzalez, Alex, Toronto	.375	3	10	8	2	3	6	0	0	1	1	1	0	0	1	0	2	1	0	0	.750	.444
Gonzalez, Juan, Texas	.300	83	355	333	57	100	203	20	1	27	78	0	5	0	17	3	62	0	0	13	.610	.330
Goodwin, Tom, Kansas City*	.000	2	1	1	0	0	0	0	0	0	0	0	0	0	0	0	0	0	0	0	.000	.000
Greenwell, Mike, Boston*	.250	2	9	8	0	2	3	1	0	0	2	0	1	0	0	0	0	0	0	0	.375	.222
Griffey, Ken, Seattle*	.333	2	11	6	3	2	2	0	0	0	0	0	0	0	5	2	2	0	1	0	.333	.636
Grotewold, Jeff, Kansas City*	.281	11	41	32	2	9	12	0	0	1	4	0	0	0	8	0	7	0	0	0	.375	.425
Guillen, Ozzie, Chicago*	.000	1	1	1	0	0	0	0	0	0	0	0	0	0	0	0	0	0	0	0	.000	.000
Hale, Chip, Minnesota*	.262	27	65	61	6	16	22	3	0	1	4	0	0	0	4	1	11	0	0	4	.361	.308
Hall, Joe, Detroit	.000	1	1	0	0	0	0	0	0	0	0	0	0	0	1	0	0	0	0	0	.000	1.000
Hamelin, Bob, Kansas City*	.159	56	206	176	19	28	54	5	0	7	22	0	0	6	23	1	46	0	1	5	.307	.278
Hamilton, Darryl, Milwaukee*	.400	2	6	5	2	2	5	0	0	1	1	0	0	0	1	1	0	1	0	0	1.000	.500
Hammonds, Jeffrey, Baltimore	.200	5	7	5	0	1	2	1	0	0	1	0	1	0	1	0	1	0	0	0	.400	.286
Hare, Shawn, Texas*	.000	2	1	1	0	0	0	0	0	0	0	0	0	0	0	0	1	0	0	0	.000	.000
Haselman, Bill, Boston	.263	11	24	19	2	5	5	0	0	0	4	0	2	1	2	0	3	0	0	1	.263	.333
Hatcher, Billy, Texas	.000	1	1	1	0	0	0	0	0	0	0	0	0	0	0	0	0	0	0	0	.000	.000
Henderson, Rickey, Oakland	.224	19	81	67	8	15	23	2	0	2	10	0	1	0	13	0	16	5	0	1	.343	.346
Herrera, Jose, Oakland*	.667	5	3	3	1	2	5	1	1	0	0	0	0	0	0	0	0	0	0	0	1.667	.667
Hiatt, Phil, Kansas City	.250	2	4	4	1	1	1	0	0	0	1	0	0	0	0	0	2	0	0	0	.250	.250
Higginson, Bob, Detroit*	.400	2	6	5	1	2	3	1	0	0	0	0	0	0	1	0	2	0	0	0	.600	.500
Hoiles, Chris, Baltimore	.083	6	14	12	0	1	1	0	0	0	1	0	1	0	1	0	5	0	0	0	.083	.143
Hollins, Dave, Boston†	.222	3	10	9	0	2	2	0	0	0	1	0	0	0	1	0	4	0	0	0	.222	.300
Horn, Sam, Texas*	.000	1	1	1	0	0	0	0	0	0	0	0	0	0	0	0	1	0	0	0	.000	.000
Howard, David, Kansas City†	.000	1	1	0	0	0	0	0	0	0	0	0	0	0	1	0	0	0	0	0	.000	1.000
Hudler, Rex, California	.250	3	15	12	3	3	6	0	0	1	1	1	0	1	2	0	1	2	0	1	.500	.400
Huson, Jeff, Baltimore*	1.000	2	1	1	0	1	1	0	0	0	1	0	0	0	0	0	0	0	0	0	1.000	1.000
Ingram, Riccardo, Minnesota	.125	3	9	8	0	1	1	0	0	0	1	0	0	0	1	0	1	0	0	1	.125	.222
Jaha, John, Milwaukee	.160	6	29	25	2	4	9	2	0	1	2	0	0	1	3	0	8	0	0	1	.360	.276
James, Chris, K.C.-Bos.	.245	19	54	49	5	12	17	2	0	1	6	0	1	1	3	0	9	0	0	1	.347	.296
James, Dion, New York*	.327	27	107	101	12	33	40	4	0	1	13	0	1	0	5	0	7	3	1	2	.396	.355
Jefferson, Reggie, Boston*	.295	32	105	95	17	28	47	7	0	4	22	0	2	0	8	0	18	0	0	3	.495	.343
Joyner, Wally, Kansas City*	.200	2	5	5	0	1	1	0	0	0	0	0	0	0	0	0	0	0	0	0	.200	.200
Kelly, Pat, New York	.000	1	2	2	0	0	0	0	0	0	0	0	0	0	0	0	0	0	0	0	.000	.000
Kirby, Wayne, Cleveland*	.000	7	5	4	1	0	0	0	0	0	0	0	0	0	1	0	1	1	0	1	.000	.200
Kruk, John, Chicago*	.318	42	182	154	13	49	62	7	0	2	23	0	3	0	25	0	31	0	1	4	.403	.407
Lawton, Matt, Minnesota*	.000	1	2	2	1	0	0	0	0	0	0	0	0	0	0	0	1	0	0	0	.000	.000
Leius, Scott, Minnesota	.429	3	7	7	2	3	4	1	0	0	0	0	0	0	0	0	3	1	0	0	.571	.429
Leyritz, Jim, New York	.205	15	45	39	7	8	13	2	0	1	3	0	0	0	6	0	12	0	0	0	.333	.311
Lockhart, Keith, Kansas City*	.200	14	36	30	5	6	7	1	0	0	4	0	1	0	5	1	5	0	0	0	.233	.306
Lofton, Kenny, Cleveland*	.286	2	10	7	1	2	2	0	0	0	0	0	0	0	3	0	2	0	0	0	.286	.500
Loretta, Mark, Milwaukee	1.000	1	1	1	0	1	1	0	0	0	0	0	0	0	0	0	0	0	0	0	1.000	1.000
Lyons, Barry, Chicago	.222	7	21	18	1	4	7	0	0	1	3	1	1	0	1	0	2	0	0	0	.389	.250
Maas, Kevin, Minnesota*	.152	12	38	33	2	5	7	2	0	0	2	0	0	0	5	1	8	0	0	4	.212	.263
Macfarlane, Mike, Boston	.000	3	7	6	0	0	0	0	0	0	0	0	0	0	1	0	3	0	0	0	.000	.143
Maldonado, Candy, Toronto	1.000	1	3	1	0	1	2	1	0	0	1	0	0	1	1	0	0	0	0	0	2.000	1.000
Manto, Jeff, Baltimore	.167	13	29	24	4	4	8	1	0	1	1	0	0	0	5	0	10	0	0	0	.333	.310
Martin, Norberto, Chicago	.250	10	22	20	1	5	5	0	0	0	2	0	1	0	1	0	4	0	0	0	.250	.273
Martinez, Carlos, California	.167	2	6	6	0	1	1	0	0	0	0	0	0	0	0	0	2	0	0	0	.167	.167
Martinez, Dave, Chicago*	.500	4	4	2	1	1	1	0	0	0	0	0	0	0	2	1	0	0	0	0	.500	.750
Martinez, Edgar, Seattle	.360	138	610	491	115	177	314	50	0	29	110	0	3	8	108	17	84	4	3	11	.640	.480
Martinez, Tino, Seattle*	.000	1	4	3	0	0	0	0	0	0	0	0	0	0	1	0	0	0	0	1	.000	.250
Mastellar, Dan, Minnesota*	.154	8	16	13	1	2	2	0	0	0	0	0	0	0	3	0	0	0	0	0	.154	.313
Mattingly, Don, New York*	.500	1	2	2	0	1	1	0	0	0	0	0	0	0	0	0	0	0	0	0	.500	.500
McGwire, Mark, Oakland	.182	10	42	33	4	6	13	1	0	2	5	0	1	0	8	0	16	0	0	1	.394	.333
McLemore, Mark, Texas†	.000	1	4	4	0	0	0	0	0	0	0	0	0	0	0	0	1	0	0	1	.000	.000
Merullo, Matt, Minnesota*	.281	13	37	32	4	9	11	2	0	0	4	0	0	2	3	0	4	0	1	1	.344	.378
Mieske, Matt, Milwaukee	.000	2	4	4	0	0	0	0	0	0	0	0	0	0	0	0	1	0	0	1	.000	.000
Miller, Keith, Kansas City	.125	4	9	8	1	1	1	0	0	0	0	0	0	0	0	0	3	0	0	0	.125	.222
Molitor, Paul, Toronto	.270	129	597	525	63	142	222	31	2	15	60	3	4	5	60	1	57	12	0	10	.423	.348
Mouton, Lyle, Chicago	.250	2	4	4	0	1	1	0	0	0	1	0	0	0	0	0	2	0	0	0	.250	.250
Munoz, Pedro, Minnesota	.303	77	310	290	39	88	141	11	0	14	46	0	2	3	15	0	68	0	2	10	.486	.342
Murray, Eddie, Cleveland†	.344	95	403	363	61	125	195	19	0	17	75	0	4	0	36	4	50	5	1	9	.537	.400
Myers, Greg, California*	.266	16	74	64	13	17	22	2	0	1	10	0	1	1	8	1	9	0	1	0	.344	.351
Naehring, Tim, Boston	.000	1	4	3	0	0	0	0	0	0	0	0	0	0	1	0	0	0	0	0	.000	.250
Nevin, Phil, Detroit	.000	2	7	6	0	0	0	0	0	0	0	0	0	0	1	0	2	0	0	0	.000	.143
Newson, Warren, Chicago*	.235	7	21	17	3	4	10	0	0	2	3	0	0	0	4	0	6	0	0	0	.588	.381
Nilsson, Dave, Milwaukee*	.245	14	53	49	7	12	23	2	0	3	9	0	0	0	4	1	13	0	0	0	.469	.302
Nokes, Matt, Baltimore*	.000	2	2	1	0	0	0	0	0	0	0	0	0	0	1	0	0	0	0	0	.000	.500
Norman, Les, Kansas City	.000	5	2	2	0	0	0	0	0	0	0	0	0	0	0	0	1	0	0	0	.000	.000
Nunnally, Jon, Kansas City*	.000	4	2	2	0	0	0	0	0	0	0	0	0	0	0	0	2	0	0	0	.000	.000
Obando, Sherman, Baltimore	.263	7	20	19	0	5	6	1	0	0	2	0	1	0	0	0	6	1	0	0	.316	.250
O'Leary, Troy, Boston*	.444	3	9	9	0	4	4	0	0	0	1	0	0	0	0	0	0	0	0	0	.444	.444
Oliver, Joe, Milwaukee	.211	6	23	19	2	4	4	0	0	0	2	0	0	0	4	0	2	0	1	1	.211	.348

Player, Team	Avg.	G	TPA	AB	R	H	TB	2B	3B	HR	RBI	SH	SF	HP	BB	IBB	SO	SB	CS	GDP	Slg.	OBP
O'Neill, Paul, New York*	.111	4	12	9	0	1	1	0	0	0	2	0	1	0	2	0	3	0	0	2	.111	.250
Ortiz, Luis, Texas	.000	3	3	2	0	0	0	0	0	0	0	0	0	0	1	0	0	0	0	1	.000	.333
Parrish, Lance, Toronto	.000	1	4	3	0	0	0	0	0	0	0	0	0	0	1	0	1	0	0	0	.000	.250
Pemberton, Rudy, Detroit	.500	3	4	2	0	1	1	0	0	0	0	0	0	1	1	0	0	0	0	0	.500	.750
Perez, Eduardo, California	.000	1	1	1	0	0	0	0	0	0	0	0	0	0	0	0	0	0	0	0	.000	.000
Perry, Herbert, Cleveland	.333	5	16	15	2	5	6	1	0	0	5	0	0	0	1	0	2	0	0	0	.400	.375
Phillips, Tony, California†	.429	2	9	7	2	3	4	1	0	0	2	0	0	0	2	0	2	0	0	0	.571	.556
Pirkl, Greg, Seattle	.000	1	1	1	0	0	0	0	0	0	0	0	0	0	0	0	1	0	0	0	.000	.000
Puckett, Kirby, Minnesota	.336	28	119	107	15	36	47	8	0	1	17	0	0	1	11	4	25	1	0	2	.439	.403
Raines, Tim, Chicago†	.325	22	99	83	13	27	46	7	0	4	12	2	0	1	13	0	7	1	0	1	.554	.423
Ramirez, Manny, Cleveland	.188	5	19	16	4	3	10	1	0	2	4	0	0	1	2	0	5	0	1	0	.625	.316
Randa, Joe, Kansas City	.000	2	2	2	0	0	0	0	0	0	0	0	0	0	0	0	1	0	0	0	.000	.000
Rodriguez, Ivan, Texas	.333	1	4	3	1	1	1	0	0	0	0	0	0	0	1	0	1	0	0	0	.333	.500
Rodriguez, Steve, Boston	.000	1	1	1	0	0	0	0	0	0	0	0	0	0	0	0	0	0	0	0	.000	.000
Rowland, Rich, Boston	.000	3	3	3	0	0	0	0	0	0	0	0	0	0	0	0	2	0	0	0	.000	.000
Sabo, Chris, Chicago	.230	15	69	61	9	14	18	4	0	0	5	2	1	2	3	1	11	2	0	0	.295	.284
Salmon, Tim, California	.000	1	4	3	1	0	0	0	0	0	0	0	0	0	1	0	0	0	0	0	.000	.250
Samuel, Juan, Det.-K.C.	.231	23	46	39	6	9	20	2	0	3	11	1	0	0	6	1	12	0	2	0	.513	.333
Seitzer, Kevin, Milwaukee	.286	14	61	56	6	16	26	2	1	2	7	1	0	0	4	0	8	0	0	0	.464	.333
Sierra, Ruben, Oak.-N.Y.†	.252	53	232	206	33	52	89	13	0	8	46	0	4	0	22	3	33	0	0	5	.432	.319
Silvestri, Dave, New York	.250	4	7	4	3	1	4	0	0	1	3	0	0	1	2	0	1	0	0	1	1.000	.571
Smith, Mark, Baltimore	.000	3	2	1	0	0	0	0	0	0	0	0	0	0	1	0	0	0	0	1	.000	.500
Sorrento, Paul, Cleveland*	.174	11	27	23	1	4	4	0	0	0	2	0	0	0	4	0	6	0	0	1	.174	.296
Sprague, Ed, Toronto	.286	2	8	7	1	2	3	1	0	0	3	0	1	0	0	0	1	0	0	1	.429	.250
Stahoviak, Scott, Minnesota*	.000	1	1	1	0	0	0	0	0	0	0	0	0	0	0	0	1	0	0	0	.000	.000
Stairs, Matt, Boston*	.000	2	2	2	0	0	0	0	0	0	0	0	0	0	0	0	0	0	0	0	.000	.000
Stanley, Mike, New York	.216	10	42	37	3	8	9	1	0	0	2	0	0	0	5	0	12	0	0	0	.243	.310
Steverson, Todd, Detroit	1.000	1	1	1	0	1	1	0	0	0	0	0	0	0	0	0	0	0	0	0	1.000	1.000
Strange, Doug, Seattle†	1.000	1	1	1	1	1	2	1	0	0	0	0	0	0	0	0	0	0	0	0	2.000	1.000
Strawberry, Darryl, New York*	.265	15	53	49	10	13	24	0	1	3	10	0	1	0	3	0	11	0	0	0	.490	.321
Stubbs, Franklin, Detroit*	.222	3	11	9	1	2	2	0	0	0	0	0	0	0	2	0	1	0	0	0	.222	.364
Surhoff, B.J., Milwaukee*	.357	3	15	14	3	5	8	0	0	1	4	0	0	0	1	0	1	0	0	0	.571	.400
Tartabull, Danny, N.Y.-Oak.	.251	61	252	215	29	54	87	15	0	6	27	0	3	1	33	1	69	0	2	4	.405	.349
Tettleton, Mickey, Texas†	.234	58	251	197	34	46	87	5	0	12	30	1	3	4	46	2	49	0	0	5	.442	.384
Thomas, Frank, Chicago	.266	53	227	173	27	46	80	7	0	9	35	0	7	2	45	9	27	1	0	7	.462	.410
Thome, Jim, Cleveland*	.000	1	4	1	1	0	0	0	0	0	0	0	0	0	3	0	0	0	0	0	.000	.750
Tomberlin, Andy, Oakland*	.000	1	1	1	0	0	0	0	0	0	0	0	0	0	0	0	0	0	0	0	.000	.000
Trammell, Alan, Detroit	.316	6	21	19	1	6	8	2	0	0	3	0	0	0	2	0	2	0	0	0	.421	.381
Tremie, Chris, Chicago	.000	1	1	1	0	0	0	0	0	0	0	0	0	0	0	0	1	0	0	0	.000	.000
Tucker, Michael, Kansas City*	.279	22	72	61	10	17	29	3	0	3	7	1	0	0	10	0	27	0	1	1	.475	.380
Vaughn, Greg, Milwaukee	.224	104	448	389	66	87	159	19	1	17	59	0	4	0	55	3	88	10	4	10	.409	.317
Vaughn, Mo, Boston*	.429	2	9	7	2	3	4	1	0	0	1	0	0	1	1	0	1	0	0	0	.571	.556
Ventura, Robin, Chicago*	.000	1	4	3	0	0	0	0	0	0	0	0	0	0	1	0	2	0	0	0	.000	.250
Vitiello, Joe, Kansas City	.236	38	113	106	10	25	42	2	0	5	13	0	0	1	6	0	22	0	0	4	.396	.283
Ward, Turner, Milwaukee†	1.000	1	1	1	1	1	1	0	0	0	0	0	0	0	0	0	0	0	0	0	1.000	1.000
Whitaker, Lou, Detroit*	.360	8	28	25	4	9	14	2	0	1	2	0	0	0	3	0	2	1	0	0	.560	.429
White, Derrick, Detroit	.000	8	4	4	0	0	0	0	0	0	0	0	0	0	0	0	1	0	0	0	.000	.000
Whiten, Mark, Boston†	.000	1	2	2	0	0	0	0	0	0	0	0	0	0	0	0	2	0	0	0	.000	.000
Widger, Chris, Seattle	.000	1	1	1	0	0	0	0	0	0	0	0	0	0	0	0	0	0	0	0	.000	.000
Williams, George, Oakland†	.206	10	38	34	4	7	8	1	0	0	1	0	0	1	3	0	14	0	0	1	.235	.289
Winfield, Dave, Cleveland	.198	39	124	111	11	22	33	5	0	2	4	0	0	1	12	1	26	1	0	5	.297	.282

DESIGNATED HITTERS WITH TWO OR MORE TEAMS

Player, Team	Avg.	G	TPA	AB	R	H	TB	2B	3B	HR	RBI	SH	SF	HP	BB	IBB	SO	SB	CS	GDP	Slg.	OBP
James, Chris, Kansas City	.262	14	47	42	5	11	16	2	0	1	5	0	1	1	3	0	8	0	0	1	.381	.319
James, Chris, Boston	.143	5	7	7	0	1	1	0	0	0	1	0	0	0	0	0	1	0	0	0	.143	.143
Samuel, Juan, Detroit	.280	16	31	25	3	7	12	2	0	1	7	1	0	0	5	0	6	0	2	0	.480	.400
Samuel, Juan, Kansas City	.143	7	15	14	3	2	8	0	0	2	4	0	0	0	1	1	6	0	0	0	.571	.200
Sierra, Ruben, Oakland†	.207	7	32	29	4	6	14	2	0	2	4	0	0	0	3	1	5	0	0	0	.483	.281
Sierra, Ruben, New York†	.260	46	200	177	29	46	75	11	0	6	42	0	4	0	19	2	28	0	0	5	.424	.325
Tartabull, Danny, New York	.246	39	157	130	20	32	55	11	0	4	20	0	3	1	23	1	41	0	0	2	.423	.357
Tartabull, Danny, Oakland	.259	22	95	85	9	22	32	4	0	2	7	0	0	0	10	0	28	0	2	2	.376	.337

The following designated hitters, each of whom appeared in at least one game, had no plate appearances, runs scored or stolen-base attempts: Valentin, Jose, Milwaukee (3); Burnitz, Jeromy, Cleveland (2); Goodwin, Curtis, Baltimore (2); Alexander, Manny, Baltimore; Alomar, Roberto, Toronto; Bragg, Darren, Seattle; Correia, Rod, California; Durham, Ray, Chicago; Espinoza, Alvaro, Cleveland; Fox, Eric, Texas; Hosey, Dwayne, Boston; Johnson, Lance, Chicago; Palmeiro, Orlando, California; Rodriguez, Alex, Seattle; Shumpert, Terry, Boston; Stynes, Chris, Kansas City; Voigt, Jack, Baltimore; Voigt, Jack, Texas; Williams, Gerald, New York.

PINCH-HITTING

TEAM

Team	Avg.	G	TPA	AB	R	H	TB	2B	3B	HR	RBI	SH	SF	HP	BB	IBB	SO	SB	CS	GDP	Slg.	OBP
Baltimore	.308	91	152	130	15	40	55	9	0	2	14	1	1	0	20	2	30	0	1	4	.423	.397
Chicago	.307	84	132	114	12	35	49	8	0	2	21	0	2	2	14	4	27	2	0	0	.430	.386
Oakland	.284	73	111	88	18	25	47	3	2	5	17	2	3	3	15	1	23	1	0	2	.534	.394
Seattle	.281	71	134	121	15	34	42	2	0	2	23	0	0	0	13	1	32	3	1	3	.347	.351
Boston	.277	83	109	101	11	28	38	4	0	2	21	0	4	0	4	1	22	2	0	2	.376	.294
Minnesota	.270	95	184	159	19	43	62	7	0	4	33	2	1	3	19	0	34	0	0	14	.390	.357
New York	.269	75	122	93	15	25	37	4	1	2	26	0	4	0	25	3	19	1	0	3	.398	.410
California	.252	77	136	127	6	32	41	6	0	1	22	0	1	1	7	2	22	1	0	4	.323	.294
Detroit	.252	88	148	127	13	32	47	7	1	2	30	2	4	3	12	1	31	2	2	1	.370	.322
Texas	.244	61	106	90	11	22	30	2	0	2	19	1	1	2	12	0	29	0	0	2	.333	.343
Kansas City	.218	96	211	179	18	39	65	6	1	6	28	2	2	1	27	2	49	1	0	7	.363	.321
Milwaukee	.205	57	82	73	9	15	22	1	0	2	13	0	1	1	7	1	14	1	0	1	.301	.280
Toronto	.192	56	84	73	6	14	20	3	0	1	8	1	1	3	6	0	23	1	0	4	.274	.277
Cleveland	.163	66	100	86	8	14	18	1	0	1	9	0	2	0	12	1	24	2	0	4	.209	.260
Totals	.255	1073	1811	1561	176	398	573	63	5	34	284	11	27	19	193	19	379	17	4	51	.367	.339

TOP PINCH-HITTERS

Minimum 18 at-bats. *Lefthanded batter. †Switch-hitter.

Player, Team	Avg.	G	TPA	AB	R	H	TB	2B	3B	HR	RBI	SH	SF	HP	BB	IBB	SO	SB	CS	GDP	Slg.	OBP
Owen, Spike, California†	.395	40	40	38	2	15	18	3	0	0	14	0	0	0	2	1	1	1	0	3	.474	.425
Aldrete, Mike, Oak.-Cal.*	.355	40	40	31	6	11	18	1	0	2	8	0	3	0	6	1	7	0	0	1	.581	.425
Martin, Norberto, Chicago	.333	21	18	18	1	6	9	3	0	0	1	0	0	0	6	1	0	0	0		.500	.333
Strange, Doug, Seattle†	.313	35	34	32	5	10	15	2	0	1	7	0	0	0	2	0	8	0	0	2	.469	.353
Diaz, Alex, Seattle†	.300	23	23	20	4	6	9	0	0	1	6	0	0	3	1	2	2	0	0		.450	.391
Hale, Chip, Minnesota*	.298	51	50	47	3	14	18	1	0	1	15	0	0	0	3	0	7	0	0	5	.383	.340
Bass, Kevin, Baltimore†	.290	34	33	31	1	9	10	1	0	0	7	0	0	0	2	0	4	0	1	2	.323	.333
Lockhart, Keith, Kansas City*	.286	25	24	21	1	6	6	0	0	0	1	1	0	0	2	0	2	0	0	0	.286	.348
James, Dion, New York*	.280	31	30	25	2	7	7	0	0	0	2	0	0	0	5	2	3	1	0	1	.280	.400
Samuel, Juan, Det.-K.C.	.241	35	34	29	3	7	9	2	0	0	3	0	0	0	5	1	9	0	2	0	.310	.353
Whitaker, Lou, Detroit*	.238	23	22	21	1	5	9	1	0	1	7	0	1	0	0	0	6	0	0	0	.429	.227
Newson, Warren, Chi.-Sea.*	.231	36	33	26	4	6	6	0	0	0	3	0	0	1	6	0	9	0	0	0	.231	.394
Nunnally, Jon, Kansas City*	.211	20	20	19	1	4	8	1	0	1	4	0	0	1	1	1	8	0	0	1	.421	.250
Stubbs, Franklin, Detroit*	.200	31	30	25	2	5	7	2	0	0	7	0	1	1	3	1	6	0	0	1	.280	.300
Kirby, Wayne, Cleveland*	.185	30	30	27	3	5	5	0	0	0	5	0	0	0	3	0	7	2	0	1	.185	.267

ALL PINCH-HITTERS

*Lefthanded batter. †Switch-hitter.

Player, Team	Avg.	G	TPA	AB	R	H	TB	2B	3B	HR	RBI	SH	SF	HP	BB	IBB	SO	SB	CS	GDP	Slg.	OBP
Aldrete, Mike, Oak.-Cal.*	.355	40	40	31	6	11	18	1	0	2	8	0	3	0	6	1	7	0	0	1	.581	.425
Alexander, Manny, Baltimore	.143	7	7	7	0	1	1	0	0	0	0	0	0	0	0	0	0	0	0	0	.143	.143
Allanson, Andy, California	.000	1	1	1	0	0	0	0	0	0	0	0	0	0	0	0	0	0	0	0	.000	.000
Alomar, Sandy, Cleveland	.100	10	10	10	0	1	1	0	0	0	0	0	0	0	0	0	2	0	0	1	.100	.100
Alomar, Roberto, Toronto†	.000	3	2	2	0	0	0	0	0	0	0	0	0	0	0	0	0	0	0	0	.000	.000
Amaral, Rich, Seattle	.200	12	11	10	2	2	2	0	0	0	2	0	0	0	1	0	1	1	0	0	.200	.273
Amaro, Ruben, Cleveland†	.222	9	9	9	1	2	2	0	0	0	0	0	0	0	0	0	2	0	0	0	.222	.222
Anderson, Garret, California*	.167	8	7	6	0	1	1	0	0	0	1	0	0	1	0	0	1	0	0	0	.167	.286
Baerga, Carlos, Cleveland†	.000	1	1	0	0	0	0	0	0	0	0	1	0	1	0	0	0	0	0	0	.000	.000
Baines, Harold, Baltimore*	.556	14	14	9	4	5	6	1	0	0	0	0	0	0	5	2	2	0	0	0	.667	.714
Barberie, Bret, Baltimore†	.333	17	17	15	3	5	6	1	0	0	0	0	0	0	2	0	5	0	0	1	.400	.412
Bass, Kevin, Baltimore†	.290	34	33	31	1	9	10	1	0	0	7	0	0	0	2	0	4	0	1	2	.323	.333
Battle, Howard, Toronto	.000	1	1	1	0	0	0	0	0	0	0	0	0	0	0	0	1	0	0	0	.000	.000
Bautista, Danny, Detroit	.500	8	8	6	1	3	3	0	0	0	2	1	0	0	1	0	2	0	0	0	.500	.571
Becker, Rich, Minnesota*	1.000	1	1	1	0	1	1	0	0	0	0	0	0	0	0	0	0	0	0	0	1.000	1.000
Bell, David, Cleveland	.000	2	2	2	0	0	0	0	0	0	0	0	0	0	0	0	0	0	0	0	.000	.000
Bell, Juan, Boston†	.000	1	1	1	0	0	0	0	0	0	0	0	0	0	0	0	0	0	0	0	.000	.000
Beltre, Esteban, Texas	1.000	2	2	2	0	2	3	1	0	0	3	0	0	0	0	0	0	0	0	0	1.500	1.000
Berroa, Geronimo, Oakland	.000	3	3	2	1	0	0	0	0	0	0	0	0	0	1	0	1	0	0	1	.000	.333
Blowers, Mike, Seattle	.200	10	10	10	1	2	2	0	0	0	1	0	0	0	0	0	3	0	0	1	.200	.200
Boggs, Wade, New York*	.364	14	14	11	2	4	7	0	0	1	7	0	0	0	3	1	1	0	0	0	.636	.500
Borders, Pat, Kansas City	.250	8	8	8	1	2	4	2	0	0	0	0	0	0	0	0	3	0	0	1	.500	.250
Bordick, Mike, Oakland	.000	1	1	1	0	0	0	0	0	0	0	0	0	0	0	0	0	0	0	0	.000	.000
Brady, Doug, Chicago†	.333	3	3	3	0	1	1	0	0	0	0	0	0	0	0	0	1	0	0	0	.333	.333
Bragg, Darren, Seattle*	.333	6	6	6	0	2	2	0	0	0	0	0	0	0	0	0	1	0	0	1	.333	.333
Brito, Bernardo, Minnesota	.000	4	2	2	0	0	0	0	0	0	0	0	0	0	0	0	1	0	0	0	.000	.000
Brosius, Scott, Oakland	.000	5	5	4	0	0	0	0	0	0	0	0	0	0	1	0	1	0	0	1	.000	.200
Brown, Jarvis, Baltimore	.000	2	2	1	0	0	0	0	0	0	0	0	0	0	1	0	0	0	0	0	.000	.200
Buechele, Steve, Texas	.000	2	2	2	0	0	0	0	0	0	0	0	0	0	0	0	0	0	0	0	.000	.000
Buhner, Jay, Seattle	.000	2	2	1	0	0	0	0	0	0	0	0	0	0	2	0	0	0	0	0	.000	1.000
Caceres, Edgar, Kansas City†	.375	10	10	8	0	3	3	0	0	0	0	0	0	0	1	0	1	0	0	1	.375	.444
Cedeno, Domingo, Toronto†	.000	2	2	1	0	0	0	0	0	0	0	0	0	1	0	0	0	0	0	0	.000	.500
Chamberlain, Wes, Boston	.333	6	6	6	1	2	5	0	0	1	1	0	0	0	0	0	1	0	0	0	.833	.333
Cirillo, Jeff, Milwaukee	.000	5	5	4	0	0	0	0	0	0	0	0	0	0	1	0	0	0	0	0	.000	.200
Clark, Jerald, Minnesota	1.000	4	4	4	2	4	8	1	0	1	3	0	0	0	0	0	0	0	0	0	2.000	1.000
Cole, Alex, Minnesota*	.333	10	10	9	1	3	4	1	0	0	2	0	0	0	1	0	2	0	0	0	.444	.400

Player, Team	Avg.	G	TPA	AB	R	H	TB	2B	3B	HR	RBI	SH	SF	HP	BB	IBB	SO	SB	CS	GDP	Slg.	OBP
Coleman, Vince, K.C.-Sea.†	.500	2	2	2	1	1	1	0	0	0	0	0	0	0	0	0	0	1	0	0	.500	.500
Cookson, Brent, Kansas City	.091	13	12	11	0	1	1	0	0	0	2	0	0	1	0	0	3	0	0	0	.091	.167
Coomer, Ron, Minnesota	.000	6	6	5	0	0	0	0	0	0	0	0	0	1	0	0	1	0	0	2	.000	.167
Cora, Joey, Seattle†	.222	13	12	9	1	2	2	0	0	0	1	0	0	0	3	0	2	0	1	0	.222	.417
Correia, Rod, California	.000	1	1	1	0	0	0	0	0	0	0	0	0	0	0	0	0	0	0	0	.000	.000
Cuyler, Milt, Detroit†	.000	3	3	2	1	0	0	0	0	0	0	0	0	0	1	0	0	0	0	0	.000	.333
Dalesandro, Mark, California	.000	5	5	5	0	0	0	0	0	0	0	0	0	0	0	0	2	0	0	0	.000	.000
Damon, Johnny, Kansas City*	.000	2	2	1	0	0	0	0	0	0	1	0	1	0	0	0	0	0	0	0	.000	.000
Davis, Russ, New York	.667	5	4	3	0	2	3	1	0	0	1	0	0	0	1	0	1	0	0	0	1.000	.750
Delgado, Carlos, Toronto*	.077	15	15	13	1	1	4	0	0	1	2	0	1	0	1	0	3	0	0	1	.308	.133
Devarez, Cesar, Baltimore	.000	1	1	1	0	0	0	0	0	0	0	0	0	0	0	0	0	0	0	0	.000	.000
Devereaux, Mike, Chicago	.333	8	8	6	0	2	2	0	0	0	2	0	0	0	2	1	1	0	0	0	.333	.500
Diaz, Alex, Seattle†	.300	23	23	20	4	6	9	0	0	1	6	0	0	0	3	1	2	2	0	0	.450	.391
Donnels, Chris, Boston*	.250	5	5	4	0	1	1	0	0	0	2	0	1	0	0	0	1	0	0	0	.250	.200
Dunn, Steve, Minnesota*	.000	4	4	3	0	0	0	0	0	0	0	0	0	0	1	0	2	0	0	0	.000	.250
Durham, Ray, Chicago†	.250	5	5	4	1	1	2	1	0	0	0	0	0	1	0	0	1	1	0	0	.500	.400
Easley, Damion, California	.000	1	1	0	0	0	0	0	0	0	0	0	0	0	1	0	0	0	0	0	.000	1.000
Edmonds, Jim, California*	.000	3	3	3	0	0	0	0	0	0	0	0	0	0	0	0	1	0	0	0	.000	.000
Eenhoorn, Robert, New York	.000	1	1	1	0	0	0	0	0	0	0	0	0	0	0	0	0	0	0	0	.000	.000
Espinoza, Alvaro, Cleveland	.000	2	2	2	0	0	0	0	0	0	0	0	0	0	0	0	0	0	0	0	.000	.000
Fabregas, Jorge, California*	.333	3	3	3	0	1	2	1	0	0	0	0	0	0	0	0	0	0	0	0	.667	.333
Fernandez, Tony, New York†	.000	2	2	0	0	0	0	0	0	0	1	0	1	0	1	0	0	0	0	0	.000	.500
Fielder, Cecil, Detroit	.000	1	1	1	0	0	0	0	0	0	0	0	0	0	0	0	0	0	0	0	.000	.000
Flaherty, John, Detroit	.000	2	2	2	0	0	0	0	0	0	0	0	0	0	0	0	1	0	0	0	.000	.000
Fletcher, Scott, Detroit	.000	1	1	1	0	0	0	0	0	0	0	0	0	0	0	0	0	0	0	0	.000	.000
Flora, Kevin, California	.000	1	1	1	0	0	0	0	0	0	0	0	0	0	0	0	1	0	0	0	.000	.000
Fox, Eric, Texas†	.000	1	1	0	0	0	0	0	0	0	0	0	0	0	1	0	0	0	0	0	.000	1.000
Frazier, Lou, Texas†	.000	1	1	0	0	0	0	0	0	0	0	0	0	0	1	0	0	0	0	0	.000	1.000
Frye, Jeff, Texas	.000	7	7	6	0	0	0	0	0	0	0	1	0	0	0	0	1	0	0	0	.000	.000
Gaetti, Gary, Kansas City	.200	5	5	5	1	1	4	0	0	1	1	0	0	0	0	0	2	0	0	0	.800	.200
Gagne, Greg, Kansas City	.500	7	7	6	2	3	5	2	0	0	3	0	0	0	1	0	1	0	0	0	.833	.571
Gallagher, Dave, California	.250	5	5	4	1	1	1	0	0	0	0	0	0	0	0	0	0	0	0	0	.250	.400
Gallego, Mike, Oakland	1.000	3	2	1	1	1	1	0	0	0	0	0	0	0	1	0	0	0	0	0	1.000	1.000
Gates, Brent, Oakland†	.000	1	1	1	0	0	0	0	0	0	0	0	0	0	0	0	0	0	0	0	.000	.000
Giambi, Jason, Oakland*	.000	4	4	3	0	0	0	0	0	0	0	0	0	0	1	0	2	0	0	0	.000	.250
Gibson, Kirk, Detroit*	.500	7	7	6	2	3	6	0	0	1	7	0	1	0	0	0	1	1	0	0	1.000	.429
Giles, Brian, Cleveland*	1.000	2	2	2	2	2	5	0	0	1	3	0	0	0	0	0	0	0	0	0	2.500	1.000
Gomez, Chris, Detroit	.333	3	3	3	0	1	1	0	0	0	0	0	0	0	0	0	0	0	0	0	.333	.333
Gomez, Leo, Baltimore	.333	10	9	9	2	3	5	2	0	0	0	0	0	0	0	0	3	0	0	0	.556	.333
Gonzales, Rene, California	.400	5	5	5	0	2	3	1	0	0	1	0	0	0	0	0	0	0	0	0	.600	.400
Gonzalez, Alex, Toronto	.000	3	3	3	1	0	0	0	0	0	0	0	0	0	0	0	1	0	0	0	.000	.000
Gonzalez, Juan, Texas	.000	3	3	3	0	0	0	0	0	0	0	0	0	0	0	0	0	0	0	0	.000	.000
Goodwin, Curtis, Baltimore*	.500	2	2	2	0	1	1	0	0	0	0	0	0	0	0	0	1	0	0	0	.500	.500
Grebeck, Craig, Chicago	1.000	2	2	2	0	2	3	1	0	0	1	0	0	0	0	0	0	0	0	0	1.500	1.000
Green, Shawn, Toronto*	.200	16	16	15	0	3	4	1	0	0	1	0	0	1	0	0	8	1	0	0	.267	.250
Greer, Rusty, Texas*	.400	19	20	15	6	6	12	0	0	2	8	0	1	0	4	0	4	0	0	1	.800	.500
Grotewold, Jeff, Kansas City*	.000	3	3	2	1	0	0	0	0	0	0	0	0	0	1	0	0	0	0	1	.000	.333
Guillen, Ozzie, Chicago*	.375	8	8	8	1	3	3	0	0	0	3	0	0	0	0	0	0	0	0	0	.375	.375
Hale, Chip, Minnesota*	.298	51	50	47	3	14	18	1	0	1	15	0	0	0	3	0	7	0	0	5	.383	.340
Hall, Joe, Detroit	.000	2	2	1	0	0	0	0	0	0	0	0	0	0	1	0	0	0	0	0	.000	.500
Hamelin, Bob, Kansas City*	.333	14	13	9	1	3	7	1	0	1	3	0	0	0	4	0	3	0	0	0	.778	.538
Hamilton, Darryl, Milwaukee*	.125	9	9	8	2	1	1	0	0	0	0	0	0	0	1	1	3	1	0	0	.125	.222
Hammonds, Jeffrey, Baltimore	.167	8	8	6	0	1	2	1	0	0	1	0	1	0	1	0	1	0	0	0	.333	.250
Hare, Shawn, Texas*	.333	8	8	6	0	2	2	0	0	0	0	0	0	0	2	0	4	0	0	0	.333	.500
Haselman, Bill, Boston	.111	10	10	9	0	1	1	0	0	0	0	0	0	0	1	0	2	0	0	0	.111	.200
Hatcher, Billy, Texas	.000	1	1	1	0	0	0	0	0	0	0	0	0	0	0	0	0	0	0	0	.000	.000
Hatteberg, Scott, Boston*	1.000	1	1	1	1	1	1	0	0	0	0	0	0	0	0	0	0	0	0	0	1.000	1.000
Helfand, Eric, Oakland*	.000	5	5	5	0	0	0	0	0	0	0	0	0	0	0	0	1	0	0	0	.000	.000
Henderson, Rickey, Oakland	.400	5	5	5	2	2	5	0	0	1	3	0	0	0	0	0	1	0	0	0	1.000	.400
Herrera, Jose, Oakland*	.286	9	7	7	1	2	5	1	1	0	0	0	0	0	0	0	0	0	0	0	.714	.286
Hiatt, Phil, Kansas City	.250	20	19	16	2	4	7	0	0	1	3	0	0	0	3	0	6	0	0	0	.438	.368
Higginson, Bob, Detroit*	.214	17	16	14	2	3	5	0	1	0	0	0	0	1	1	0	6	1	0	0	.357	.313
Hocking, Denny, Minnesota†	.000	2	1	1	0	0	0	0	0	0	0	0	0	0	0	0	0	0	0	0	.000	.000
Hoiles, Chris, Baltimore	.250	9	9	8	2	2	5	0	0	1	1	0	0	0	1	0	3	0	0	0	.625	.333
Hollins, Dave, Boston†	1.000	1	1	1	0	1	1	0	0	0	0	0	0	0	0	0	0	0	0	0	1.000	1.000
Horn, Sam, Texas*	.111	11	10	9	0	1	1	0	0	0	0	0	0	0	1	0	6	0	0	0	.111	.200
Hosey, Dwayne, Boston†	.000	2	2	2	0	0	0	0	0	0	0	0	0	0	0	0	2	0	0	0	.000	.000
Howard, David, Kansas City†	.250	5	5	4	1	1	1	0	0	0	0	0	0	0	1	0	1	0	0	0	.250	.400
Hudler, Rex, California	.143	15	14	14	0	2	3	1	0	0	0	0	0	0	0	0	3	1	0	0	.214	.143
Huff, Michael, Toronto	.286	16	16	14	1	4	4	0	0	0	0	0	1	0	1	0	4	0	0	0	.286	.333
Hulse, David, Milwaukee*	.286	7	7	7	1	2	2	0	0	0	1	0	0	0	0	0	3	0	0	0	.286	.286
Huson, Jeff, Baltimore*	.286	9	9	7	1	2	2	0	0	0	1	0	0	0	2	0	0	0	0	0	.286	.444
Ingram, Riccardo, Minnesota	.000	2	2	1	0	0	0	0	0	0	0	0	0	0	1	0	1	0	0	0	.000	.000
Jaha, John, Milwaukee	1.000	1	1	1	0	1	1	0	0	0	0	0	0	0	0	0	0	0	0	0	1.000	1.000
James, Chris, K.C.-Bos.	.222	14	12	9	0	2	2	0	0	0	1	0	1	0	2	0	2	0	0	1	.222	.333
James, Dion, New York*	.280	31	30	25	2	7	7	0	0	0	2	0	0	0	5	2	3	1	0	1	.280	.400
Javier, Stan, Oakland†	.273	14	14	11	1	3	3	0	0	0	3	2	0	0	1	0	1	0	0	0	.273	.333
Jefferson, Reggie, Boston*	.375	12	11	8	1	3	3	0	0	0	2	0	2	0	1	1	2	0	0	0	.375	.364
Johnson, Lance, Chicago*	.400	5	5	5	0	2	2	0	0	0	1	0	0	0	0	0	1	0	0	1	.400	.400
Jose, Felix, Kansas City†	.000	2	2	2	0	0	0	0	0	0	0	0	0	0	0	0	0	0	0	0	.000	.000
Joyner, Wally, Kansas City*	.143	7	7	7	1	1	4	0	0	1	4	0	0	0	0	0	3	0	0	0	.571	.143
Karkovice, Ron, Chicago	.250	4	4	4	0	1	1	0	0	0	1	0	0	0	0	0	0	0	0	0	.250	.250
Kelly, Pat, New York	.000	2	2	2	0	0	0	0	0	0	0	0	0	0	0	0	2	0	0	0	.000	.000

Player, Team	Avg.	G	TPA	AB	R	H	TB	2B	3B	HR	RBI	SH	SF	HP	BB	IBB	SO	SB	CS	GDP	Slg.	OBP
Kirby, Wayne, Cleveland*	.185	30	30	27	3	5	5	0	0	0	5	0	0	0	3	0	7	2	0	1	.185	.267
Knorr, Randy, Toronto	.500	2	2	2	0	1	2	1	0	0	3	0	0	0	0	0	0	0	0	0	1.000	.500
Kreuter, Chad, Seattle†	.800	5	5	5	1	4	4	0	0	0	1	0	0	0	0	0	1	0	0	0	.800	.800
Kruk, John, Chicago*	.000	2	2	2	0	0	0	0	0	0	0	0	0	0	0	0	2	0	0	0	.000	.000
LaValliere, Mike, Chicago*	.000	1	1	1	0	0	0	0	0	0	0	0	0	0	0	0	1	0	0	0	.000	.000
Lawton, Matt, Minnesota*	.000	3	4	4	1	0	0	0	0	0	0	0	0	0	0	0	2	0	0	0	.000	.000
Leius, Scott, Minnesota	.375	8	9	8	1	3	3	0	0	0	3	0	0	0	1	0	3	0	0	1	.375	.444
Levis, Jesse, Cleveland*	.000	1	1	1	0	0	0	0	0	0	0	0	0	0	0	0	0	0	0	0	.000	.000
Leyritz, Jim, New York	.000	5	5	3	1	0	0	0	0	0	0	0	0	0	2	0	1	0	0	0	.000	.400
Lind, Jose, Kansas City	.000	1	1	1	0	0	0	0	0	0	0	0	0	0	0	0	0	0	0	0	.000	.000
Listach, Pat, Milwaukee†	.333	3	3	3	0	1	1	0	0	0	0	0	0	0	0	0	0	0	0	0	.333	.333
Lockhart, Keith, Kansas City*	.286	25	24	21	1	6	6	0	0	0	1	1	0	0	2	0	2	0	0	0	.286	.348
Lofton, Kenny, Cleveland*	.000	1	1	1	0	0	0	0	0	0	0	0	0	0	0	0	0	0	0	0	.000	.000
Loretta, Mark, Milwaukee	.500	4	4	4	1	2	3	1	0	0	0	0	0	0	0	0	1	0	0	0	.750	.500
Lyons, Barry, Chicago	.000	6	6	5	0	0	0	0	0	0	0	0	0	0	1	0	2	0	0	0	.000	.167
Maas, Kevin, Minnesota*	.000	7	7	6	0	0	0	0	0	0	0	0	0	0	1	0	1	0	0	1	.000	.143
Macfarlane, Mike, Boston	.000	4	3	3	0	0	0	0	0	0	0	0	0	0	0	0	1	0	0	0	.000	.000
Maldonado, Candy, Tor.-Tex.	.091	13	13	11	1	1	2	1	0	0	0	0	0	0	2	0	5	0	0	2	.182	.231
Manto, Jeff, Baltimore	.417	14	14	12	1	5	9	1	0	1	3	0	0	0	2	0	5	0	0	0	.750	.500
Martin, Norberto, Chicago	.333	21	18	18	1	6	9	3	0	0	1	0	0	0	0	0	6	1	0	0	.500	.333
Martinez, Carlos, California	.250	6	5	4	0	1	1	0	0	0	1	0	0	0	1	0	0	0	0	0	.250	.400
Martinez, Dave, Chicago*	.375	20	19	16	3	6	8	2	0	0	1	0	0	0	3	1	3	0	0	0	.500	.474
Martinez, Angel, Toronto*	.000	3	3	3	0	0	0	0	0	0	0	0	0	0	0	0	2	0	0	0	.000	.000
Martinez, Tino, Seattle*	.333	3	3	3	0	1	1	0	0	0	1	0	0	0	0	0	1	0	0	0	.333	.333
Masteller, Dan, Minnesota*	.308	16	16	13	2	4	8	1	0	1	4	0	0	0	3	0	2	0	0	2	.615	.438
Matheny, Mike, Milwaukee	.000	1	1	1	0	0	0	0	0	0	0	0	0	0	0	0	0	0	0	0	.000	.000
Mattingly, Don, New York*	.333	7	7	6	3	2	3	1	0	0	1	0	0	0	1	0	1	0	0	0	.500	.429
Mayne, Brent, Kansas City*	.000	9	8	7	0	0	0	0	0	0	0	0	0	0	1	0	0	0	0	1	.000	.125
McCarty, Dave, Minnesota	.667	5	5	3	1	2	2	0	0	0	0	0	0	0	2	0	0	0	0	0	.667	.800
McGee, Willie, Boston†	.286	16	16	14	2	4	4	0	0	0	1	0	1	0	1	0	1	2	0	1	.286	.313
McGinnis, Russ, Kansas City	.000	2	2	2	0	0	0	0	0	0	0	0	0	0	0	0	1	0	0	0	.000	.000
McGwire, Mark, Oakland	.000	4	4	1	0	0	0	0	0	0	0	0	0	2	1	0	0	0	0	0	.000	.750
McLemore, Mark, Texas†	.333	3	3	3	1	1	1	0	0	0	2	0	0	0	0	0	1	0	0	0	.333	.333
Meares, Pat, Minnesota	.333	3	3	3	2	1	1	0	0	0	1	0	0	0	0	0	0	0	0	0	.333	.333
Mercedes, Henry, Kansas City	.000	1	1	1	0	0	0	0	0	0	0	0	0	0	0	0	1	0	0	0	.000	.000
Merullo, Matt, Minnesota*	.158	22	21	19	2	3	4	1	0	0	1	0	0	1	1	0	4	0	0	0	.211	.238
Mieske, Matt, Milwaukee	.182	14	14	11	3	2	8	0	0	2	7	0	1	1	1	0	1	0	0	0	.727	.286
Miller, Keith, Kansas City	.200	7	7	5	0	1	1	0	0	0	0	0	0	0	2	0	2	0	0	1	.200	.429
Molitor, Paul, Toronto	.000	1	1	1	0	0	0	0	0	0	0	0	0	0	0	0	1	0	0	0	.000	.000
Mouton, Lyle, Chicago	.600	6	6	5	2	3	6	0	0	1	3	0	0	0	1	0	1	0	0	0	1.200	.667
Munoz, Pedro, Minnesota	.400	6	6	5	2	2	6	1	0	1	1	0	0	0	1	0	1	0	0	0	1.200	.500
Murray, Eddie, Cleveland†	1.000	1	1	1	0	1	2	1	0	0	0	0	0	0	0	0	0	0	0	0	2.000	1.000
Myers, Greg, California*	.000	13	13	12	0	0	0	0	0	0	0	0	0	0	1	1	5	0	0	0	.000	.077
Naehring, Tim, Boston	.500	2	2	2	0	1	1	0	0	0	1	0	0	0	0	0	1	0	0	0	.500	.500
Newson, Warren, Chi.-Sea.*	.231	36	33	26	4	6	6	0	0	0	1	0	0	1	6	0	9	0	0	0	.231	.394
Nilsson, Dave, Milwaukee*	.143	14	14	14	0	2	2	0	0	0	3	0	0	0	0	0	2	0	0	1	.143	.143
Nixon, Otis, Texas†	.000	1	1	0	1	0	0	0	0	0	0	0	0	0	1	0	0	0	0	0	.000	1.000
Nokes, Matt, Baltimore*	.125	11	10	8	0	1	1	0	0	0	0	0	0	0	2	0	3	0	0	0	.125	.300
Norman, Les, Kansas City	.200	6	5	5	1	1	3	0	1	0	2	0	0	0	0	0	1	0	0	0	.600	.200
Nunnally, Jon, Kansas City*	.211	20	20	19	1	4	8	1	0	1	4	0	0	0	1	1	8	0	0	1	.421	.250
Obando, Sherman, Baltimore	.333	6	6	6	0	2	2	0	0	0	1	0	0	0	0	0	1	0	0	0	.333	.333
O'Leary, Troy, Boston*	.417	12	12	12	1	5	9	1	0	1	3	0	0	0	0	0	3	0	0	0	.750	.417
Olerud, John, Toronto*	.333	3	3	3	0	1	1	0	0	0	1	0	0	0	0	0	0	0	0	0	.333	.333
Oliver, Joe, Milwaukee	.000	2	2	1	0	0	0	0	0	0	0	0	0	0	1	0	1	0	0	0	.000	.500
O'Neill, Paul, New York*	.400	8	8	5	0	2	4	0	1	0	3	0	0	0	3	0	1	0	0	0	.800	.625
Ortiz, Luis, Texas	.100	11	11	10	0	1	1	0	0	0	1	0	0	0	1	0	4	0	0	1	.100	.182
Owen, Spike, California†	.395	40	40	38	2	15	18	3	0	0	14	0	0	0	2	1	1	1	0	3	.474	.425
Pagliarulo, Mike, Texas*	.313	18	17	16	3	5	6	1	0	0	1	0	0	0	1	0	5	0	0	0	.375	.353
Palmeiro, Orlando, California*	.333	9	9	9	1	3	3	0	0	0	0	0	0	0	1	0	0	0	0	0	.333	.333
Palmeiro, Rafael, Baltimore*	.000	1	1	1	0	0	0	0	0	0	0	0	0	0	0	0	0	0	0	0	.000	.000
Palmer, Dean, Texas	.000	1	1	1	0	0	0	0	0	0	0	0	0	0	0	0	0	0	0	0	.000	.000
Paquette, Craig, Oakland	.375	9	9	8	1	3	4	1	0	0	3	0	0	0	1	0	3	0	0	1	.500	.444
Parrish, Lance, Toronto	.000	4	3	1	1	0	0	0	0	0	0	0	0	0	1	0	1	0	0	0	.000	.667
Pemberton, Rudy, Detroit	.000	3	3	1	0	0	0	0	0	0	0	0	0	0	1	0	0	0	0	0	.000	.667
Perez, Eduardo, California	.250	6	4	4	1	1	4	0	0	1	2	0	0	0	0	0	1	0	0	0	1.000	.250
Perez, Robert, Toronto	.500	4	4	4	0	2	2	0	0	0	1	0	0	0	0	0	1	0	0	0	.500	.500
Perez, Tomas, Toronto†	.500	2	2	2	1	1	1	0	0	0	0	0	0	0	0	0	0	0	0	0	.500	.500
Perry, Herbert, Cleveland	.000	3	3	3	0	0	0	0	0	0	0	0	0	0	0	0	1	0	0	0	.000	.000
Phillips, Tony, California†	.000	3	3	2	0	0	0	0	0	0	0	0	0	0	1	0	1	0	0	0	.000	.333
Pirkl, Greg, Seattle	.000	5	5	5	0	0	0	0	0	0	0	0	0	0	0	0	4	0	0	0	.000	.000
Polonia, Luis, New York*	.167	7	7	6	2	1	1	0	0	0	0	0	0	0	1	0	0	0	0	0	.167	.286
Pozo, Arquimedez, Seattle	.000	1	1	1	0	0	0	0	0	0	0	0	0	0	0	0	0	0	0	0	.000	.000
Puckett, Kirby, Minnesota	.000	1	1	1	0	0	0	0	0	0	0	0	0	0	0	0	0	0	0	0	.000	.000
Raabe, Brian, Minnesota	1.000	1	1	1	0	1	1	0	0	0	0	0	0	0	0	0	0	0	0	0	1.000	1.000
Raines, Tim, Chicago†	.111	9	9	9	0	1	1	0	0	0	0	0	0	0	0	0	1	0	0	0	.111	.111
Ramirez, Manny, Cleveland	.000	3	3	3	0	0	0	0	0	0	0	0	0	0	0	0	0	0	0	0	.000	.000
Randa, Joe, Kansas City	.000	6	6	5	1	0	0	0	0	0	0	0	0	0	1	0	3	0	0	0	.000	.167
Reboulet, Jeff, Minnesota	.300	15	15	10	2	3	3	0	0	0	1	2	0	0	3	0	4	0	0	0	.300	.462
Rhodes, Karl, Boston*	.000	2	2	2	0	0	0	0	0	0	0	0	0	0	0	0	0	0	0	0	.000	.000
Rodriguez, Carlos, Boston†	1.000	2	2	1	2	2	2	0	0	0	2	0	0	0	0	0	0	0	0	0	1.000	1.000
Rodriguez, Ivan, Texas	.667	7	7	6	0	4	4	0	0	0	3	0	0	1	0	0	1	0	0	0	.667	.714
Rodriguez, Steve, Boston	.000	3	3	3	0	0	0	0	0	0	0	0	0	0	0	0	0	0	0	0	.000	.000
Rowland, Rich, Boston	.250	4	4	4	0	1	1	0	0	0	1	0	0	0	0	0	2	0	0	0	.250	.250

Player, Team	Avg.	G	TPA	AB	R	H	TB	2B	3B	HR	RBI	SH	SF	HP	BB	IBB	SO	SB	CS	GDP	Slg.	OBP
Sabo, Chris, Chicago	.500	4	4	2	1	1	4	0	0	1	3	0	1	0	1	1	0	0	0	0	2.000	.500
Samuel, Juan, Det.-K.C.	.241	35	34	29	3	7	9	2	0	0	3	0	0	0	5	1	9	0	2	0	.310	.353
Seitzer, Kevin, Milwaukee	.500	2	2	2	0	1	1	0	0	0	1	0	0	0	0	0	0	0	0	0	.500	.500
Shumpert, Terry, Boston	.000	2	2	2	0	0	0	0	0	0	0	0	0	0	0	0	1	0	0	0	.000	.000
Sierra, Ruben, Oak.-N.Y.†	.400	5	5	5	0	2	2	0	0	0	2	0	0	0	0	0	2	0	0	0	.400	.400
Silvestri, Dave, New York	.500	2	2	2	1	1	4	0	0	1	3	0	0	0	0	0	0	0	0	0	2.000	.500
Smith, Mark, Baltimore	.250	7	7	4	1	1	2	1	0	0	0	0	0	0	3	0	1	0	0	1	.500	.571
Snopek, Chris, Chicago	1.000	1	1	1	0	1	1	0	0	0	1	0	0	0	0	0	0	0	0	0	1.000	1.000
Sojo, Luis, Seattle	.333	4	4	3	0	1	1	0	0	0	1	0	0	0	1	0	2	0	0	0	.333	.500
Sorrento, Paul, Cleveland*	.111	13	13	9	1	1	1	0	0	0	1	0	1	0	3	0	5	0	0	1	.111	.308
Stahoviak, Scott, Minnesota*	.200	15	12	10	0	2	3	1	0	0	1	0	1	0	1	0	3	0	0	0	.300	.333
Stairs, Matt, Boston*	.250	16	16	16	2	4	7	3	0	0	7	0	0	0	0	0	2	0	0	0	.438	.250
Stanley, Mike, New York	.000	4	4	2	0	0	0	0	0	0	2	0	2	0	0	0	1	0	0	0	.000	.000
Steinbach, Terry, Oakland	.333	4	4	3	1	1	1	0	0	0	1	0	1	0	0	0	0	1	0	0	.333	.250
Steverson, Todd, Detroit	.333	3	3	3	0	1	1	0	0	0	0	0	0	0	0	0	0	0	0	0	.333	.333
Strange, Doug, Seattle†	.313	35	34	32	5	10	15	2	0	1	7	0	0	0	2	0	8	0	0	2	.469	.353
Strawberry, Darryl, New York*	.200	8	8	5	0	1	2	1	0	0	1	0	0	0	3	0	2	0	0	0	.400	.500
Stubbs, Franklin, Detroit*	.200	31	30	25	2	5	7	2	0	0	7	0	1	1	3	1	6	0	0	1	.280	.300
Stynes, Chris, Kansas City	.333	4	3	3	0	1	1	0	0	0	0	0	0	0	0	0	1	0	0	0	.333	.333
Surhoff, B.J., Milwaukee*	.000	5	5	3	0	0	0	0	0	0	0	0	0	0	2	0	0	0	0	0	.000	.400
Sweeney, Mike, Kansas City	.333	3	3	3	1	1	1	0	0	0	0	0	0	0	0	0	0	0	0	0	.333	.333
Tartabull, Danny, N.Y.-Oak.	.500	9	9	6	2	3	3	0	0	0	1	0	0	0	3	0	2	0	0	0	.500	.667
Tettleton, Mickey, Texas†	.000	3	3	2	0	0	0	0	0	0	1	0	0	1	0	0	1	0	0	0	.000	.333
Tewksbury, Bob, Texas	.000	1	1	1	0	0	0	0	0	0	0	0	0	0	0	0	1	0	0	0	.000	.000
Thomas, Frank, Chicago	.000	3	3	3	0	0	0	0	0	0	0	0	0	0	0	0	0	0	0	0	.000	.000
Thome, Jim, Cleveland*	.000	8	8	5	0	0	0	0	0	0	0	0	0	0	3	0	4	0	0	0	.000	.375
Thurman, Gary, Seattle	.000	1	1	1	0	0	0	0	0	0	0	0	0	0	0	0	1	0	0	0	.000	.000
Tingley, Ron, Detroit	.000	1	1	0	0	0	0	0	0	0	1	0	1	0	0	0	0	0	0	0	.000	.000
Tinsley, Lee, Boston†	.500	5	5	4	2	2	2	0	0	0	1	0	0	0	1	0	1	0	0	0	.500	.600
Tomberlin, Andy, Oakland*	.333	6	6	6	2	2	8	0	0	2	2	0	0	0	0	0	2	0	0	0	1.333	.333
Trammell, Alan, Detroit	.364	13	13	11	2	4	6	2	0	0	2	1	0	0	1	0	0	0	0	0	.545	.417
Tremie, Chris, Chicago	.000	1	1	1	0	0	0	0	0	0	0	0	0	0	0	0	1	0	0	0	.000	.000
Tucker, Michael, Kansas City*	.000	9	8	6	1	0	0	0	0	0	0	0	0	0	2	0	2	0	0	0	.000	.250
Turner, Chris, California	.000	1	1	1	0	0	0	0	0	0	0	0	0	0	0	0	0	0	0	0	.000	.000
Valle, Dave, Texas	.000	2	2	2	0	0	0	0	0	0	0	0	0	0	0	0	1	0	0	0	.000	.000
Vaughn, Greg, Milwaukee	.250	5	4	4	0	1	1	0	0	0	0	0	0	0	0	0	1	0	0	0	.250	.250
Velarde, Randy, New York	.000	3	3	2	1	0	0	0	0	0	0	0	0	0	1	0	0	0	0	0	.000	.333
Ventura, Robin, Chicago*	.500	6	6	4	0	2	3	1	0	0	2	0	1	0	1	1	1	0	0	0	.750	.500
Vina, Fernando, Milwaukee*	.167	7	7	6	0	1	1	0	0	0	1	0	0	0	1	0	1	0	0	0	.167	.286
Vitiello, Joe, Kansas City	.182	15	14	11	1	2	5	0	0	1	2	0	0	1	2	0	3	0	0	0	.455	.357
Vizquel, Omar, Cleveland†	.000	1	1	1	0	0	0	0	0	0	0	0	0	0	0	0	0	0	0	0	.000	.000
Voigt, Jack, Bal.-Tex.	.333	4	3	3	0	1	1	0	0	0	0	0	0	0	0	0	0	0	0	0	.333	.333
Walbeck, Matt, Minnesota†	.000	4	4	3	0	0	0	0	0	0	1	0	1	0	0	0	0	0	0	2	.000	.000
Ward, Turner, Milwaukee†	.250	4	4	4	2	1	1	0	0	0	0	0	0	0	0	0	1	0	0	0	.250	.250
Whitaker, Lou, Detroit*	.238	23	22	21	1	5	9	1	0	1	7	0	1	0	0	0	6	0	0	0	.429	.227
White, Derrick, Detroit	.167	6	6	6	0	1	1	0	0	0	1	0	0	0	0	0	1	0	0	0	.167	.167
White, Devon, Toronto†	.000	1	1	1	0	0	0	0	0	0	0	0	0	0	0	0	0	0	0	1	.000	.000
Whiten, Mark, Boston†	.000	1	1	1	0	0	0	0	0	0	0	0	0	0	0	0	1	0	0	0	.000	.000
Widger, Chris, Seattle	.000	3	3	3	0	0	0	0	0	0	0	0	0	0	0	0	1	0	0	0	.000	.000
Williams, George, Oakland†	.429	9	9	7	2	3	5	0	1	0	0	0	0	1	1	0	2	0	0	0	.714	.556
Williams, Gerald, New York	.154	15	15	13	1	2	3	1	0	0	2	0	0	0	1	0	2	0	0	1	.231	.200
Wilson, Dan, Seattle	1.000	1	1	1	0	1	1	0	0	0	2	0	0	0	0	0	0	0	0	0	1.000	1.000
Winfield, Dave, Cleveland	.200	14	13	10	1	2	2	0	0	0	0	0	0	0	3	1	2	0	0	1	.200	.385
Young, Ernie, Oakland	.000	3	3	2	1	0	0	0	0	0	0	0	0	0	1	0	1	0	0	0	.000	.333
Zaun, Greg, Baltimore†	.500	2	2	2	0	1	2	1	0	0	0	0	0	0	0	0	0	0	0	0	1.000	.500

PINCH-HITTERS WITH TWO OR MORE TEAMS

Player, Team	Avg.	G	TPA	AB	R	H	TB	2B	3B	HR	RBI	SH	SF	HP	BB	IBB	SO	SB	CS	GDP	Slg.	OBP
Aldrete, Mike, Oakland*	.353	25	25	17	5	6	13	1	0	2	5	0	2	0	6	1	3	0	0	0	.765	.480
Aldrete, Mike, California*	.357	15	15	14	1	5	5	0	0	0	3	0	1	0	0	0	4	0	0	1	.357	.333
Coleman, Vince, Kansas City†	1.000	1	1	1	0	1	1	0	0	0	0	0	0	0	0	0	0	1	0	0	1.000	1.000
Coleman, Vince, Seattle†	.000	1	1	1	0	0	0	0	0	0	0	0	0	0	0	0	0	0	0	0	.000	.000
James, Chris, Kansas City	.400	9	8	5	0	2	2	0	0	0	1	0	1	0	2	0	2	0	0	0	.400	.500
James, Chris, Boston	.000	5	4	4	0	0	0	0	0	0	0	0	0	0	0	0	0	0	0	1	.000	.000
Maldonado, Candy, Toronto	.125	10	10	8	1	1	2	1	0	0	0	0	0	0	2	0	3	0	0	2	.250	.300
Maldonado, Candy, Texas	.000	3	3	3	0	0	0	0	0	0	0	0	0	0	0	0	2	0	0	0	.000	.000
Newson, Warren, Chicago*	.200	23	21	15	4	3	3	0	0	0	2	0	0	1	5	0	4	0	0	0	.200	.429
Newson, Warren, Seattle*	.273	13	12	11	0	3	3	0	0	0	1	0	0	0	1	0	5	0	0	0	.273	.333
Samuel, Juan, Detroit	.250	27	27	24	2	6	8	2	0	0	3	0	0	0	3	0	8	0	2	0	.333	.333
Samuel, Juan, Kansas City	.200	8	7	5	1	1	1	0	0	0	0	0	0	0	2	1	1	0	0	0	.200	.429
Sierra, Ruben, Oakland†	.333	3	3	3	0	1	1	0	0	0	0	0	0	0	0	0	1	0	0	0	.333	.333
Sierra, Ruben, New York†	.500	2	2	2	0	1	1	0	0	0	2	0	0	0	0	0	1	0	0	0	.500	.500
Tartabull, Danny, New York	.400	8	8	5	2	2	2	0	0	0	1	0	0	0	3	0	2	0	0	0	.400	.625
Tartabull, Danny, Oakland	1.000	1	1	1	0	1	1	0	0	0	0	0	0	0	0	0	0	0	0	0	1.000	1.000
Voigt, Jack, Baltimore	1.000	1	1	1	0	1	1	0	0	0	0	0	0	0	0	0	0	0	0	0	1.000	1.000
Voigt, Jack, Texas	.000	3	2	2	0	0	0	0	0	0	0	0	0	0	0	0	0	0	0	0	.000	.000

1995 A.L. STATISTICS Pinch-hitting

PITCHING

TEAM

Team	W	L	Pct.	ERA	G	ShO	GF	Sv.	IP	H	TBF	R	ER	HR	SH	SF	HB	BB	IBB	SO	WP	Bk.
Cleveland	100	44	.694	3.83	144	10	10	50	1301.0	1261	5512	607	554	135	32	44	45	445	16	926	48	5
Baltimore	71	73	.493	4.31	144	19	10	29	1267.0	1165	5382	640	607	149	33	34	37	523	40	930	30	9
Boston	86	58	.597	4.39	144	7	9	39	1292.2	1338	5600	698	631	127	32	47	46	476	28	888	57	1
Kansas City	70	74	.486	4.49	144	11	10	37	1288.0	1323	5561	691	642	142	39	42	38	503	38	763	45	5
Seattle	79	66	.545	4.50	145	9	8	39	1289.1	1343	5743	708	644	149	39	52	47	591	37	1068	50	7
California	78	67	.538	4.52	145	8	9	42	1284.1	1310	5571	697	645	163	48	45	43	486	23	901	42	10
New York	79	65	.549	4.56	145	18	5	35	1284.2	1286	5575	688	651	159	35	37	32	535	21	908	50	5
Texas	74	70	.514	4.66	144	14	4	34	1285.0	1385	5626	720	665	152	41	48	36	514	38	838	60	6
Milwaukee	65	79	.451	4.82	144	7	4	31	1286.0	1391	5707	747	689	146	34	62	47	603	39	699	45	7
Chicago	68	76	.472	4.85	145	12	4	36	1284.2	1374	5734	758	693	164	37	50	39	617	47	892	45	8
Toronto	56	88	.389	4.88	144	16	8	22	1292.2	1336	5773	777	701	145	36	37	51	654	42	894	73	4
Oakland	67	77	.465	4.93	144	8	4	34	1273.0	1320	5606	761	698	153	52	44	53	566	26	890	56	4
Detroit	60	84	.417	5.49	144	5	3	38	1275.0	1509	5774	844	778	170	42	50	45	536	79	729	67	7
Minnesota	56	88	.389	5.76	144	7	2	27	1272.2	1450	5714	889	815	210	41	50	36	533	18	790	52	4
Totals	1009	1009	.500	4.71	1010	151	90	493	17976.0	18791	78878	10225	9413	2164	541	642	595	7572	492	12116	720	82

NOTE—Totals for earned runs for several clubs do not agree with the composite total for all pitchers of each respective club due to instances in which provision 10.18(i) of the Scoring Rules were applied. The following differences are to be noted: Boston pitchers add to 634; Seattle pitchers add to 647; California pitchers add to 646; Texas pitchers add to 666; Oakland pitchers add to 703; Detroit pitchers add to 779; Minnesota pitchers add to 816.

INDIVIDUAL

TOP QUALIFIERS FOR EARNED-RUN AVERAGE TITLE

Minimum 144 innings. *Throws lefthanded.

Pitcher, Team	W	L	Pct.	ERA	G	GS	CG	ShO	GF	Sv.	IP	H	TBF	R	ER	HR	SH	SF	HB	BB	IBB	SO	WP	Bk.
Johnson, Randy, Seattle*	18	2	.900	2.48	30	30	6	3	0	0	214.1	159	866	65	59	12	2	1	6	65	1	294	5	2
Wakefield, Tim, Boston	16	8	.667	2.95	27	27	6	1	0	0	195.1	163	804	76	64	22	3	7	9	68	0	119	11	0
Martinez, Dennis, Cleveland	12	5	.706	3.08	28	28	3	2	0	0	187.0	174	771	71	64	17	4	4	12	46	2	99	3	0
Mussina, Mike, Baltimore	19	9	.679	3.29	32	32	7	4	0	0	221.2	187	882	86	81	24	2	1	50	4	158	2	0
Rogers, Kenny, Texas*	17	7	.708	3.38	31	31	3	1	0	0	208.0	192	877	87	78	26	3	5	2	76	1	140	8	1
Cone, David, Tor.-N.Y.	18	8	.692	3.57	30	30	6	2	0	0	229.1	195	954	95	91	24	2	3	6	88	2	191	11	1
Brown, Kevin, Baltimore	10	9	.526	3.60	26	26	3	1	0	0	172.1	155	706	73	69	10	5	2	9	48	1	117	3	0
Leiter, Al, Toronto*	11	11	.500	3.64	28	28	2	1	0	0	183.0	162	805	80	74	15	6	4	6	108	1	153	14	0
Abbott, Jim, Chi.-Cal.*	11	8	.579	3.70	30	30	4	1	0	0	197.0	209	842	93	81	14	8	4	2	64	1	86	1	0
Gubicza, Mark, Kansas City	12	14	.462	3.75	33	33	3	2	0	0	213.1	222	898	97	89	21	9	6	6	62	2	81	4	1
Fernandez, Alex, Chicago	12	8	.600	3.80	30	30	5	2	0	0	203.2	200	858	98	86	19	4	6	0	65	7	159	3	0
Hershiser, Orel, Cleveland	16	6	.727	3.87	26	26	1	1	0	0	167.1	151	683	76	72	21	3	4	5	51	1	111	3	0
Appier, Kevin, Kansas City	15	10	.600	3.89	31	31	4	1	0	0	201.1	163	832	90	87	14	3	3	8	80	1	185	5	0
McDowell, Jack, New York	15	10	.600	3.93	30	30	8	2	0	0	217.2	211	927	106	95	25	8	6	5	78	1	157	9	1
Pettitte, Andy, New York*	12	9	.571	4.17	31	26	3	0	1	0	175.0	183	745	86	81	15	4	5	1	63	3	114	8	1

DEPARTMENTAL LEADERS: W—Mussina, Bal., 19; L—Bere, Chi., Gross, Tex., Moore, Det., 15; G—Orosco, Bal., 65; GS—Gubicza, K.C., 33; CG—McDowell, N.Y., 8; ShO—Mussina, Bal., 4; GF—Hernandez, Chi., Mesa, Cle., 57; Sv.—Mesa, Cle., 46; IP—Cone, Tor.-N.Y., 229.1; H—Hentgen, Tor., 236; TBF—Cone, Tor.-N.Y., 954; R—Hentgen, Tor., 129; ER—Hentgen, Tor., 114; HR—Radke, Min., 32; SH—Langston, Cal., 11; SF—Sparks, Mil., 12; HB—Clemens, Bos., 14; BB—Leiter, Tor., 108; IBB—Boever, Det., 12; SO—Johnson, Sea., 294; WP—Leiter, Tor., 14; Bk.—B. Anderson, Cal., Fortugno, Chi., 3.

ALL PITCHERS

*Throws lefthanded.

Pitcher, Team	W	L	Pct.	ERA	G	GS	CG	ShO	GF	Sv.	IP	H	TBF	R	ER	HR	SH	SF	HB	BB	IBB	SO	WP	Bk.
Abbott, Jim, Chi.-Cal.*	11	8	.579	3.70	30	30	4	1	0	0	197.0	209	842	93	81	14	8	4	2	64	1	86	1	0
Acre, Mark, Oakland	1	2	.333	5.71	43	0	0	0	10	0	52.0	52	236	35	33	7	1	2	2	28	2	47	2	1
Aguilera, Rick, Min.-Bos.	3	3	.500	2.60	52	0	0	0	51	32	55.1	46	223	16	16	6	1	4	1	13	1	52	0	0
Ahearne, Pat, Detroit	0	2	.000	11.70	4	3	0	0	0	0	10.0	20	55	13	13	2	0	0	0	5	1	4	1	0
Alberro, Jose, Texas	0	0	.000	7.40	12	0	0	0	7	0	20.2	26	101	18	17	2	0	1	1	12	1	10	2	0
Alvarez, Wilson, Chicago*	8	11	.421	4.32	29	29	3	0	0	0	175.0	171	769	96	84	21	6	5	2	93	4	118	1	2
Anderson, Brian, California*	6	8	.429	5.87	18	17	1	0	0	0	99.2	110	433	66	65	24	5	5	3	30	2	45	1	3
Anderson, Scott, Kansas City	1	0	1.000	5.33	6	4	0	0	0	0	25.1	29	109	15	15	3	0	0	1	8	0	6	0	0
Andujar, Luis, Chicago	2	1	.667	3.26	5	5	0	0	0	0	30.1	26	128	12	11	4	0	0	1	14	2	9	0	0
Appier, Kevin, Kansas City	15	10	.600	3.89	31	31	4	1	0	0	201.1	163	832	90	87	14	3	3	8	80	1	185	5	0
Assenmacher, Paul, Clev.*	6	2	.750	2.82	47	0	0	0	12	0	38.1	32	160	13	12	3	1	2	3	12	3	40	1	0
Ausanio, Joe, New York	2	0	1.000	5.73	28	0	0	0	10	1	37.2	42	173	24	24	9	1	2	0	23	0	36	3	0
Ayala, Bobby, Seattle	6	5	.545	4.44	63	0	0	0	50	19	71.0	73	320	42	35	9	2	3	6	30	4	77	3	0
Baker, Scott, Oakland*	0	0	.000	9.82	1	0	0	0	0	0	3.2	5	22	4	4	0	0	1	1	5	0	3	0	0
Baldwin, James, Chicago	0	1	.000	12.89	6	4	0	0	0	0	14.2	32	81	22	21	6	0	0	0	9	1	10	1	0
Bankhead, Scott, New York	1	1	.500	6.00	20	1	0	0	8	0	39.0	44	175	26	26	9	0	1	0	16	0	20	1	0
Bark, Brian, Boston*	0	0	.000	0.00	1	0	0	0	0	0	2.1	2	8	0	0	0	0	0	1	0	0	1	0	0
Belcher, Tim, Seattle	10	12	.455	4.52	28	28	1	0	0	0	179.1	188	802	101	90	19	4	5	5	88	5	96	6	0
Belinda, Stan, Boston	8	1	.889	3.10	63	0	0	0	30	10	69.2	51	285	25	24	5	0	4	4	28	3	57	2	0
Benes, Andy, Seattle	7	2	.778	5.86	12	12	0	0	0	0	63.0	72	291	42	41	8	1	4	2	33	2	45	2	0
Benitez, Armando, Baltimore	1	5	.167	5.66	44	0	0	0	18	2	47.2	37	221	33	30	8	2	3	5	37	2	56	3	1
Bennett, Erik, California	0	0	.000	0.00	1	0	0	0	1	0	0.1	1	0	0	0	0	0	0	0	0	0	0	0	0
Bere, Jason, Chicago	8	15	.348	7.19	27	27	1	0	0	0	137.2	151	668	120	110	21	4	7	6	106	6	110	8	0
Bergman, Sean, Detroit	7	10	.412	5.12	28	28	1	1	0	0	135.1	169	630	95	77	19	5	3	4	67	8	86	13	0
Bertotti, Mike, Chicago*	1	1	.500	12.56	4	4	0	0	0	0	14.1	23	80	20	20	6	0	3	3	11	0	15	2	1

Pitcher, Team	W	L	Pct.	ERA	G	GS	CG	ShO	GF	Sv.	IP	H	TBF	R	ER	HR	SH	SF	HB	BB	IBB	SO	WP	Bk.
Bielecki, Mike, California	4	6	.400	5.97	22	11	0	0	2	0	75.1	80	334	56	50	15	2	5	3	31	1	45	3	0
Black, Bud, Cleveland*	4	2	.667	6.85	11	10	0	0	0	0	47.1	63	219	42	36	8	1	3	0	16	2	34	1	1
Blomdahl, Ben, Detroit	0	0	.000	7.77	14	0	0	0	5	1	24.1	36	115	21	21	5	1	0	0	13	0	15	2	0
Boehringer, Brian, New York	0	3	.000	13.75	7	3	0	0	0	0	17.2	24	99	27	27	5	0	1	1	22	1	10	3	0
Boever, Joe, Detroit	5	7	.417	6.39	60	0	0	0	27	3	98.2	128	463	74	70	17	7	8	3	44	12	71	1	1
Bohanon, Brian, Detroit*	1	1	.500	5.54	52	10	0	0	7	1	105.2	121	474	68	65	10	0	5	4	41	5	63	3	0
Bolton, Rodney, Chicago	0	2	.000	8.18	8	3	0	0	2	0	22.0	33	109	23	20	4	0	1	0	14	1	10	1	0
Bones, Ricky, Milwaukee	10	12	.455	4.63	32	31	3	0	0	0	200.1	218	877	108	103	26	3	11	4	83	2	77	5	2
Borowski, Joe, Baltimore	0	0	.000	1.23	6	0	0	0	3	0	7.1	5	30	1	1	0	0	0	0	4	0	3	0	0
Bosio, Chris, Seattle	10	8	.556	4.92	31	31	0	0	0	0	170.0	211	766	98	93	18	5	11	5	69	3	85	10	0
Boskie, Shawn, California	7	7	.500	5.64	20	20	1	0	0	0	111.2	127	494	73	70	16	4	6	7	25	0	51	4	0
Brandenburg, Mark, Texas	0	1	.000	5.93	11	0	0	0	5	0	27.1	36	123	18	18	5	0	1	1	7	1	21	0	1
Brewer, Billy, Kansas City*	2	4	.333	5.56	48	0	0	0	13	0	45.1	54	209	28	28	9	1	0	2	20	1	31	5	1
Briscoe, John, Oakland	0	1	.000	8.35	16	0	0	0	7	0	18.1	25	99	17	17	4	2	2	2	21	1	19	1	0
Bronkey, Jeff, Milwaukee	0	0	.000	3.65	8	0	0	0	4	0	12.1	15	56	6	5	0	2	0	0	6	0	5	1	0
Brown, Kevin, Baltimore	10	9	.526	3.60	26	26	3	1	0	0	172.1	155	706	73	69	10	5	2	9	48	1	117	3	0
Browning, Tom, Kansas City*	0	2	.000	8.10	2	2	0	0	0	0	10.0	13	49	9	9	2	1	0	0	5	0	3	0	0
Bunch, Mel, Kansas City	1	3	.250	5.63	13	5	0	0	3	0	40.0	42	175	25	25	11	0	0	0	14	1	19	6	0
Burrows, Terry, Texas*	2	2	.500	6.45	28	3	0	0	6	1	44.2	60	207	37	32	11	0	2	0	19	0	22	4	0
Butcher, Mike, California	6	1	.857	4.73	40	0	0	0	13	0	51.1	49	227	28	27	7	1	3	1	31	2	29	3	0
Campbell, Kevin, Minnesota	0	0	.000	4.66	6	0	0	0	1	0	9.2	8	39	5	5	0	0	0	0	5	0	5	1	0
Carmona, Rafael, Seattle	2	4	.333	5.66	15	3	0	0	6	1	47.2	55	230	31	30	9	1	5	2	34	1	28	3	1
Carrara, Giovanni, Toronto	2	4	.333	7.21	12	7	1	0	2	0	48.2	64	229	46	39	10	1	2	1	25	1	27	1	0
Castillo, Tony, Toronto*	1	5	.167	3.22	55	0	0	0	31	13	72.2	64	298	27	26	7	3	5	3	24	1	38	0	0
Charlton, Norm, Seattle*	2	1	.667	1.51	30	0	0	0	22	14	47.2	23	182	12	8	2	3	1	1	16	0	58	5	1
Christopher, Mike, Detroit	4	0	1.000	3.82	36	0	0	0	11	1	61.1	71	262	28	26	8	1	2	1	24	2	34	5	0
Clark, Mark, Cleveland	9	7	.563	5.27	22	21	2	0	0	0	124.2	143	552	77	73	13	3	6	4	42	0	68	8	0
Clark, Terry, Baltimore	2	5	.286	3.46	38	0	0	0	12	1	39.0	40	166	15	15	3	4	1	1	15	5	18	1	0
Clemens, Roger, Boston	10	5	.667	4.18	23	23	0	0	0	0	140.0	141	623	70	65	15	2	3	14	60	0	132	9	0
Cone, David, Tor.-N.Y.	18	8	.692	3.57	30	30	6	2	0	0	229.1	195	954	95	91	24	2	3	6	88	2	191	11	1
Converse, Jim, Sea.-K.C.	1	3	.250	6.56	15	1	0	0	4	1	23.1	28	109	17	17	2	2	0	0	16	2	14	2	0
Cook, Dennis, Cle.-Tex.*	0	2	.000	4.53	46	1	0	0	10	2	57.2	63	255	32	29	9	4	5	2	26	3	53	1	0
Cormier, Rheal, Boston*	7	5	.583	4.07	48	12	0	0	3	0	115.0	131	488	60	52	12	6	2	3	31	2	69	4	0
Cornett, Brad, Toronto	0	0	.000	9.00	5	0	0	0	2	0	5.0	9	25	6	5	1	0	0	1	3	0	4	1	0
Corsi, Jim, Oakland	2	4	.333	2.20	38	0	0	0	7	0	45.0	31	187	14	11	2	5	1	2	26	1	26	0	0
Cox, Danny, Toronto	1	3	.250	7.40	24	0	0	0	7	0	45.0	57	218	40	37	4	1	3	1	33	4	38	7	0
Crabtree, Tim, Toronto	0	2	.000	3.09	31	0	0	0	19	0	32.0	30	141	16	11	1	0	1	2	13	0	21	2	0
Cummings, John, Seattle*	0	0	.000	11.81	4	0	0	0	1	0	5.1	8	30	8	7	0	1	2	0	7	2	4	4	1
Darling, Ron, Oakland	4	7	.364	6.23	21	21	1	0	0	0	104.0	124	484	79	72	16	7	8	4	46	2	69	5	0
Darwin, Danny, Tor.-Tex.	3	10	.231	7.45	20	15	1	0	0	0	99.0	131	448	87	82	25	3	5	4	31	3	58	2	0
Davis, Tim, Seattle*	2	1	.667	6.38	5	5	0	0	0	0	24.0	30	117	21	17	2	0	1	0	18	2	19	0	0
Davison, Scott, Seattle	0	0	.000	6.23	3	0	0	0	3	0	4.1	7	21	3	3	1	0	0	0	1	0	3	0	0
Dedrick, Jim, Baltimore	0	0	.000	2.35	6	0	0	0	1	0	7.2	8	35	2	2	1	0	2	1	6	0	3	0	0
DeLeon, Jose, Chicago	5	3	.625	5.19	38	0	0	0	4	0	67.2	60	293	41	39	10	2	5	6	28	2	53	2	1
DeSilva, John, Baltimore	1	0	1.000	7.27	2	2	0	0	0	0	8.2	8	41	7	7	3	1	1	1	7	0	1	0	0
Dettmer, John, Texas	0	0	.000	27.00	1	0	0	0	0	0	0.1	2	4	1	1	0	0	0	0	0	0	0	0	0
Dibble, Rob, Chi.-Mil.	1	2	.333	7.18	31	0	0	0	8	1	26.1	16	143	21	21	2	3	6	3	46	2	26	8	0
Doherty, John, Detroit	5	9	.357	5.10	48	2	0	0	18	6	113.0	130	499	66	64	10	3	2	6	37	10	46	0	0
Eckersley, Dennis, Oakland	4	6	.400	4.83	52	0	0	0	48	29	50.1	53	212	29	27	5	1	2	1	11	0	40	0	0
Eddy, Chris, Oakland*	0	0	.000	7.36	6	0	0	0	0	0	3.2	7	22	3	3	0	2	0	2	2	0	2	1	0
Edenfield, Ken, California	0	0	.000	4.26	7	0	0	0	3	0	12.2	15	56	7	6	1	0	1	0	5	0	6	3	0
Eiland, Dave, New York	1	1	.500	6.30	4	1	0	0	1	0	10.0	16	51	10	7	1	0	1	0	3	1	6	1	0
Eldred, Cal, Milwaukee	1	1	.500	3.42	4	4	0	0	0	0	23.2	24	104	10	9	4	1	0	1	10	0	18	1	1
Embree, Alan, Cleveland*	3	2	.600	5.11	23	0	0	0	8	1	24.2	23	111	16	14	2	2	2	0	16	0	23	1	0
Erickson, Scott, Min.-Bal.	13	10	.565	4.81	32	31	7	2	1	0	196.1	213	836	108	105	18	3	3	5	67	0	106	3	2
Eshelman, Vaughn, Boston*	6	3	.667	4.85	23	14	0	0	4	0	81.2	86	356	47	44	3	0	3	1	36	0	41	4	0
Fajardo, Hector, Texas	0	0	.000	7.80	5	0	0	0	0	0	15.0	19	67	13	13	2	0	0	1	5	0	9	0	0
Farrell, John, Cleveland	0	0	.000	3.86	1	0	0	0	0	0	4.2	7	21	4	2	0	1	0	0	1	0	0	0	0
Fermin, Ramon, Oakland	0	0	.000	13.50	1	0	0	0	0	0	1.1	4	9	2	2	0	0	0	0	1	0	1	0	0
Fernandez, Alex, Chicago	12	8	.600	3.80	30	30	5	2	0	0	203.2	200	858	98	86	19	4	6	0	65	7	159	3	0
Fernandez, Sid, Baltimore*	0	4	.000	7.39	8	7	0	0	1	0	28.0	36	137	26	23	9	1	1	0	17	2	31	0	0
Fetters, Mike, Milwaukee	0	3	.000	3.38	40	0	0	0	34	22	34.2	40	163	16	13	3	2	1	0	20	4	33	5	0
Finley, Chuck, California*	15	12	.556	4.21	32	32	2	1	0	0	203.0	192	880	106	95	20	4	5	7	93	1	195	13	1
Fleming, Dave, Sea.-K.C.*	1	6	.143	5.96	25	12	1	0	3	0	80.0	84	374	61	53	19	3	4	2	53	4	40	5	0
Fortugno, Tim, Chicago*	1	3	.250	5.59	37	0	0	0	11	0	38.2	30	163	24	24	7	1	2	0	19	2	24	5	3
Frey, Steve, Seattle*	0	3	.000	4.76	13	0	0	0	3	0	11.1	16	56	7	6	0	3	1	1	6	1	7	0	0
Gardiner, Mike, Detroit	0	0	.000	14.59	9	0	0	0	1	0	12.1	27	66	20	20	5	3	2	0	2	1	7	1	0
Givens, Brian, Milwaukee*	5	7	.417	4.95	19	19	0	0	0	0	107.1	116	481	71	59	11	1	1	3	54	0	73	3	2
Gohr, Greg, Detroit	1	0	1.000	0.87	10	0	0	0	1	0	10.1	9	41	1	1	0	1	0	0	3	0	12	1	0
Gordon, Tom, Kansas City	12	12	.500	4.43	31	31	2	0	0	0	189.0	204	843	110	93	12	7	11	4	89	4	119	9	0
Grimsley, Jason, Cleveland	0	0	.000	6.09	15	2	0	0	2	1	34.0	37	165	24	23	4	1	2	2	32	1	25	7	0
Groom, Buddy, Detroit*	1	3	.250	7.52	23	4	0	0	6	1	40.2	55	203	35	34	6	2	2	2	26	4	23	0	0
Gross, Kevin, Texas	9	15	.375	5.54	31	30	4	0	0	0	183.2	200	825	124	113	27	5	7	8	89	8	106	5	0
Guardado, Eddie, Minnesota*	4	9	.308	5.12	51	5	0	0	10	2	91.1	99	410	54	52	13	6	5	0	45	2	71	5	1
Gubicza, Mark, Kansas City	12	14	.462	3.75	33	33	3	2	0	0	213.1	222	898	97	89	21	9	6	6	62	2	81	4	1
Guetterman, Lee, Seattle*	0	0	.000	6.88	23	0	0	0	3	1	17.0	21	85	13	13	1	1	0	3	10	0	11	0	0
Gunderson, Eric, Boston*	2	1	.667	5.11	19	0	0	0	1	0	12.1	13	58	7	7	0	2	1	2	9	1	9	0	0
Guthrie, Mark, Minnesota	5	3	.625	4.46	36	0	0	0	7	0	42.1	47	181	22	21	5	2	0	1	16	3	48	3	1
Guzman, Juan, Toronto	4	14	.222	6.32	24	24	3	0	0	0	135.1	151	619	101	95	13	3	2	3	73	6	94	8	0
Habyan, John, California*	1	2	.333	4.13	28	0	0	0	7	0	32.2	36	146	16	15	2	2	2	1	12	0	25	2	0
Hall, Darren, Toronto	0	2	.000	4.41	17	0	0	0	11	3	16.1	21	77	9	8	2	0	0	0	9	0	11	0	0
Hammaker, Atlee, Chicago*	0	0	.000	12.79	13	0	0	0	2	0	6.1	11	38	9	9	2	1	0	1	8	1	3	0	0
Haney, Chris, Kansas City*	3	4	.429	3.65	16	13	1	0	0	0	81.1	78	338	35	33	7	1	4	2	33	0	31	2	0

Pitcher, Team	W	L	Pct.	ERA	G	GS	CG	ShO	GF	Sv.	IP	H	TBF	R	ER	HR	SH	SF	HB	BB	IBB	SO	WP	Bk.
Hanson, Erik, Boston	15	5	.750	4.24	29	29	1	1	0	0	186.2	187	800	94	88	17	6	8	1	59	0	139	5	0
Harikkala, Tim, Seattle	0	0	.000	16.20	1	0	0	0	1	0	3.1	7	18	6	6	1	0	0	0	1	0	1	0	0
Harkey, Mike, Oak.-Cal.	8	9	.471	5.44	26	20	1	0	1	0	127.1	155	573	78	77	24	4	4	4	47	2	56	2	0
Harris, Gene, Baltimore	0	0	.000	4.50	3	0	0	0	0	0	4.0	4	17	2	2	0	1	0	0	1	0	4	2	0
Harris, Greg W., Minnesota	0	5	.000	8.82	7	6	0	0	0	0	32.2	50	160	35	32	5	1	2	0	16	0	21	3	0
Hartley, Mike, Bos.-Bal.	1	0	1.000	5.14	8	0	0	0	2	0	14.0	13	58	8	8	1	2	2	2	3	0	6	0	0
Hawkins, LaTroy, Minnesota	2	3	.400	8.67	6	6	1	0	0	0	27.0	39	131	29	26	3	0	3	1	12	0	9	1	1
Haynes, Jimmy, Baltimore	2	1	.667	2.25	4	3	0	0	0	0	24.0	11	94	6	6	2	1	0	0	12	1	22	0	0
Helling, Rick, Texas	0	2	.000	6.57	3	3	0	0	0	0	12.1	17	62	11	9	2	0	2	2	8	0	5	0	0
Henneman, Mike, Detroit	0	1	.000	1.53	29	0	0	0	26	18	29.1	24	118	5	5	0	1	0	0	9	1	24	2	0
Henry, Dwayne, Detroit	1	0	1.000	6.23	10	0	0	0	6	5	8.2	11	47	6	6	0	1	0	0	10	2	9	1	0
Hentgen, Pat, Toronto	10	14	.417	5.11	30	30	2	0	0	0	200.2	236	913	129	114	24	2	1	5	90	6	135	7	2
Heredia, Wilson, Texas	0	1	.000	3.75	6	0	0	0	0	0	12.0	9	58	5	5	2	2	1	0	15	2	6	0	0
Hernandez, Roberto, Chicago	3	7	.300	3.92	60	0	0	0	57	32	59.2	63	272	30	26	9	4	0	3	28	4	84	1	0
Hershiser, Orel, Cleveland	16	6	.727	3.87	26	26	1	1	0	0	167.1	151	683	76	72	21	3	4	5	51	1	111	3	0
Hill, Ken, Cleveland	4	1	.800	3.98	12	11	1	0	0	0	74.2	77	324	36	33	5	3	1	1	32	0	48	3	0
Hitchcock, Sterling, N.Y.*	11	10	.524	4.70	27	27	4	1	0	0	168.1	155	719	91	88	22	5	9	5	68	1	121	5	2
Holzemer, Mark, California*	0	1	.000	5.40	12	0	0	0	5	0	8.1	11	45	6	5	1	1	0	1	7	1	5	0	0
Honeycutt, Rick, Oak.-N.Y.*	5	1	.833	2.96	52	0	0	0	6	2	45.2	39	180	16	15	6	3	1	1	10	0	21	0	0
Horsman, Vince, Minnesota*	0	0	.000	7.00	6	0	0	0	3	0	9.0	12	43	8	7	2	2	1	0	4	1	4	0	0
Howard, Chris, Texas*	0	0	.000	0.00	4	0	0	0	1	0	4.0	3	15	0	0	0	0	1	0	1	0	2	1	0
Howe, Steve, New York*	6	3	.667	4.96	56	0	0	0	20	2	49.0	66	230	29	27	7	3	2	4	17	3	28	1	0
Hudson, Joe, Boston	0	1	.000	4.11	39	0	0	0	11	1	46.0	53	205	21	21	2	3	1	2	23	1	29	6	0
Huisman, Rick, Kansas City	0	0	.000	7.45	7	0	0	0	2	0	9.2	14	44	8	8	2	1	0	0	1	0	12	0	0
Hurtado, Edwin, Toronto	5	2	.714	5.45	14	10	1	0	0	0	77.2	81	345	50	47	11	2	3	5	40	3	33	11	0
Ignasiak, Mike, Milwaukee	4	1	.800	5.90	25	0	0	0	2	0	39.2	51	186	27	26	5	1	3	2	23	3	26	1	0
Jacome, Jason, Kansas City*	4	6	.400	5.36	15	14	1	0	0	0	84.0	101	364	52	50	15	2	3	1	21	2	39	0	1
James, Mike, California	3	0	1.000	3.88	46	0	0	0	11	1	55.2	49	237	27	24	6	2	0	3	26	2	36	1	0
Johns, Doug, Oakland*	5	3	.625	4.61	11	9	1	1	1	0	54.2	44	229	32	28	5	2	1	5	26	1	25	5	1
Johnson, Randy, Seattle*	18	2	.900	2.48	30	30	6	3	0	0	214.1	159	866	65	59	12	2	1	6	65	1	294	5	2
Johnston, Joel, Boston	0	1	.000	11.25	4	0	0	0	0	0	4.0	2	18	5	5	1	0	0	1	3	0	4	0	0
Jones, Doug, Baltimore	0	4	.000	5.01	52	0	0	0	47	22	46.2	55	211	30	26	6	1	0	2	16	2	42	0	0
Jordan, Ricardo, Toronto*	1	0	1.000	6.60	15	0	0	0	3	1	15.0	18	76	11	11	3	0	2	2	13	1	10	1	0
Kamieniecki, Scott, N.Y.	7	6	.538	4.01	17	16	1	0	1	0	89.2	83	391	43	40	8	1	0	3	49	1	43	4	0
Karchner, Matt, Chicago	4	2	.667	1.69	31	0	0	0	10	0	32.0	33	137	8	6	2	0	4	1	12	2	24	1	0
Karl, Scott, Milwaukee*	6	7	.462	4.14	25	18	1	0	3	0	124.0	141	548	65	57	10	3	3	3	50	6	59	0	0
Key, Jimmy, New York*	1	2	.333	5.64	5	5	0	0	0	0	30.1	40	134	20	19	3	3	1	0	6	1	14	1	0
Keyser, Brian, Chicago	5	6	.455	4.97	23	10	0	0	0	0	92.1	114	404	53	51	10	0	2	2	27	1	48	1	1
Kiefer, Mark, Milwaukee	4	1	.800	3.44	24	0	0	0	7	0	49.2	37	209	20	19	6	0	0	0	27	2	41	4	0
King, Kevin, Seattle*	0	0	.000	12.27	2	0	0	0	0	0	3.2	7	20	5	5	0	0	1	1	1	0	3	1	0
Klingenbeck, Scott, Bal.-Min.	2	4	.333	7.12	24	9	0	0	4	0	79.2	101	373	65	63	22	3	1	4	42	0	42	7	0
Krivda, Rick, Baltimore*	2	7	.222	4.54	13	13	1	0	0	0	75.1	76	319	40	38	9	0	4	4	25	1	53	2	2
Krueger, Bill, Seattle*	2	1	.667	5.85	6	5	0	0	1	0	20.0	37	96	17	13	4	1	0	0	4	1	10	1	0
Langston, Mark, California*	15	7	.682	4.63	31	31	2	1	0	0	200.1	212	859	109	103	21	11	3	3	64	1	142	5	1
Lee, Mark, Baltimore*	2	0	1.000	4.86	39	0	0	0	7	1	33.1	31	148	18	18	5	1	2	1	18	3	27	0	0
Leiper, Dave, Oakland*	1	1	.500	3.57	24	0	0	0	3	0	22.2	23	103	10	9	3	0	0	1	13	1	10	0	0
Leiter, Al, Toronto*	11	11	.500	3.64	28	28	2	1	0	0	183.0	162	805	80	74	15	6	4	6	108	1	153	14	0
Lilliquist, Derek, Boston*	2	1	.667	6.26	28	0	0	0	6	0	23.0	27	103	17	16	7	2	3	0	9	2	9	1	0
Lima, Jose, Detroit	3	9	.250	6.11	15	15	0	0	0	0	73.2	85	320	52	50	10	2	1	4	18	4	37	5	0
Linton, Doug, Kansas City	0	1	.000	7.25	7	2	0	0	0	0	22.1	22	98	21	18	4	0	0	2	10	1	13	0	0
Lira, Felipe, Detroit	9	13	.409	4.31	37	22	0	0	7	1	146.1	151	635	74	70	17	4	9	8	56	7	89	5	1
Lloyd, Graeme, Milwaukee*	0	5	.000	4.50	33	0	0	0	14	4	32.0	28	127	16	16	4	1	4	0	8	2	13	3	0
Looney, Brian, Boston*	0	1	.000	17.36	3	1	0	0	0	0	4.2	12	29	9	9	1	1	2	0	4	1	2	0	0
Lopez, Albie, Cleveland	0	0	.000	3.13	6	2	0	0	0	0	23.0	17	92	8	8	4	0	1	1	7	1	22	2	0
Lorraine, Andrew, Chicago*	0	0	.000	3.38	5	0	0	0	2	0	8.0	3	30	3	3	0	0	0	1	2	0	5	0	0
MacDonald, Bob, New York*	1	1	.500	4.86	33	0	0	0	5	0	46.1	50	202	25	25	7	2	0	1	22	0	41	1	0
Maddux, Mike, Boston	4	1	.800	3.61	36	4	0	0	6	1	89.2	86	367	40	36	5	1	1	2	15	3	65	5	0
Magnante, Mike, K.C.*	1	1	.500	4.23	28	0	0	0	7	0	44.2	45	190	23	21	6	2	2	2	16	1	28	2	0
Mahomes, Pat, Minnesota	4	10	.286	6.37	47	7	0	0	16	3	94.2	100	423	74	67	22	3	2	2	47	1	67	6	0
Manzanillo, Josias, New York	0	0	.000	2.08	11	0	0	0	4	0	17.1	19	81	4	4	1	2	0	2	9	2	11	1	0
Marquez, Isidro, Chicago	0	1	.000	6.75	7	0	0	0	2	0	6.2	9	31	5	5	3	1	0	0	2	0	8	0	0
Martinez, Dave, Chicago*	0	0	.000	0.00	1	0	0	0	1	0	1.0	0	5	0	0	0	0	0	0	2	0	0	0	0
Martinez, Dennis, Cleveland	12	5	.706	3.08	28	28	3	2	0	0	187.0	174	771	71	64	17	4	4	12	46	2	99	3	0
Maxcy, Brian, Detroit	4	5	.444	6.88	41	0	0	0	14	0	52.1	61	247	48	40	6	3	3	2	31	7	20	6	2
McAndrew, Jamie, Milw.	2	3	.400	4.71	10	4	0	0	2	0	36.1	37	153	21	19	2	1	0	1	12	2	19	0	0
McCaskill, Kirk, Chicago	6	4	.600	4.89	55	1	0	0	17	2	81.0	97	365	50	44	10	3	3	5	33	4	50	10	0
McDonald, Ben, Baltimore	3	6	.333	4.16	14	13	1	0	1	0	80.0	67	342	40	37	10	0	2	3	38	3	62	4	2
McDowell, Jack, New York	15	10	.600	3.93	30	30	8	2	0	0	217.2	211	927	106	95	25	8	6	5	78	1	157	9	1
McDowell, Roger, Texas	7	4	.636	4.02	64	0	0	0	26	4	85.0	86	362	39	38	5	6	5	6	34	7	49	1	1
Meacham, Rusty, K.C.	4	3	.571	4.98	49	0	0	0	26	2	59.2	72	262	36	33	6	1	4	1	19	5	30	0	0
Mecir, Jim, Seattle	0	0	.000	0.00	2	0	0	0	1	0	4.2	5	21	1	0	0	0	0	0	2	0	3	0	0
Menhart, Paul, Toronto	1	4	.200	4.92	21	9	1	0	6	0	78.2	72	350	49	43	9	3	4	6	47	4	50	6	0
Mercedes, Jose, Milwaukee	0	1	.000	9.82	5	0	0	0	0	0	7.1	12	42	9	8	1	0	2	0	8	0	6	1	0
Mesa, Jose, Cleveland	3	0	1.000	1.13	62	0	0	0	57	46	64.0	49	250	9	8	3	4	2	0	17	2	58	5	0
Mills, Alan, Baltimore	3	0	1.000	7.43	21	0	0	0	1	0	23.0	30	118	20	19	4	0	1	2	18	4	16	1	0
Miranda, Angel, Milwaukee*	4	5	.444	5.23	30	10	0	0	5	1	74.0	83	339	47	43	8	1	4	0	49	2	45	5	1
Mohler, Mike, Oakland*	1	1	.500	3.04	28	0	0	0	6	1	23.2	16	100	8	8	0	1	0	0	18	1	15	1	0
Monteleone, Rich, California	1	0	1.000	2.00	9	0	0	0	2	0	9.0	8	36	2	2	1	1	2	0	3	0	5	0	0
Montgomery, Jeff, K.C.	2	3	.400	3.43	54	0	0	0	46	31	65.2	60	275	27	25	7	5	5	2	25	4	49	1	1
Moore, Mike, Detroit	5	15	.250	7.53	25	25	1	0	0	0	132.2	179	632	118	111	24	4	4	2	68	3	64	8	0
Moyer, Jamie, Baltimore*	8	6	.571	5.21	27	18	0	0	3	0	115.2	117	483	70	67	18	5	3	3	30	0	65	0	0
Munoz, Oscar, Minnesota	2	1	.667	5.60	10	3	0	0	4	0	35.1	40	164	28	22	6	0	1	1	17	0	25	0	0
Murray, Matt, Boston	0	1	.000	18.90	2	1	0	0	0	0	3.1	11	24	10	7	1	0	0	0	3	0	1	0	0

Pitcher, Team	W	L	Pct.	ERA	G	GS	CG	ShO	GF	Sv.	IP	H	TBF	R	ER	HR	SH	SF	HB	BB	IBB	SO	WP	Bk.
Mussina, Mike, Baltimore	19	9	.679	3.29	32	32	7	4	0	0	221.2	187	882	86	81	24	2	2	1	50	4	158	2	0
Myers, Mike, Detroit*	1	0	1.000	9.95	11	0	0	0	3	0	6.1	10	33	7	7	1	0	1	2	4	0	4	0	0
Nagy, Charles, Cleveland	16	6	.727	4.55	29	29	2	1	0	0	178.0	194	771	95	90	20	2	5	6	61	0	139	2	0
Nelson, Jeff, Seattle	7	3	.700	2.17	62	0	0	0	24	2	78.2	58	318	21	19	4	5	3	6	27	5	96	1	0
Nichting, Chris, Texas	0	0	.000	7.03	13	0	0	0	3	0	24.1	36	122	19	19	1	1	2	1	13	1	6	3	0
Nitkowski, C.J., Detroit*	1	4	.200	7.09	11	11	0	0	0	0	39.1	53	184	32	31	7	0	3	3	20	2	13	1	0
Ogea, Chad, Cleveland	8	3	.727	3.05	20	14	1	0	3	0	106.1	95	442	38	36	11	0	5	1	29	0	57	3	1
Oliver, Darren, Texas*	4	2	.667	4.22	17	7	0	0	2	0	49.0	47	222	25	23	3	5	1	1	32	1	39	4	0
Olson, Gregg, Cle.-K.C.	3	3	.500	4.09	23	0	0	0	12	3	33.0	28	141	15	15	4	1	2	0	19	2	21	1	0
Ontiveros, Steve, Oakland	9	6	.600	4.37	22	22	2	1	0	0	129.2	144	558	75	63	12	2	6	4	38	0	77	5	0
Oquist, Mike, Baltimore	2	1	.667	4.17	27	0	0	0	2	0	54.0	51	255	27	25	6	1	4	2	41	3	27	2	0
Orosco, Jesse, Baltimore*	2	4	.333	3.26	65	0	0	0	23	3	49.2	28	200	19	18	4	2	4	1	27	7	58	2	1
Parra, Jose, Minnesota	1	5	.167	7.59	12	12	0	0	0	0	61.2	83	292	59	52	11	0	3	2	22	0	29	3	0
Patterson, Bob, California*	5	2	.714	3.04	62	0	0	0	20	0	53.1	48	212	18	18	6	2	1	1	13	3	41	0	1
Patterson, Jeff, New York	0	0	.000	2.70	3	0	0	0	3	0	3.1	3	16	1	1	1	0	0	0	3	0	3	0	0
Pavlas, Dave, New York	0	0	.000	3.18	4	0	0	0	1	0	5.2	8	24	2	2	0	0	0	0	0	0	3	0	0
Pavlik, Roger, Texas	10	10	.500	4.37	31	31	2	1	0	0	191.2	174	819	96	93	19	4	5	4	90	5	149	10	1
Pena, Alejandro, Boston	1	1	.500	7.40	17	0	0	0	5	0	24.1	33	117	23	20	5	0	0	0	12	2	25	0	0
Pennington, Brad, Baltimore*	0	1	.000	8.10	8	0	0	0	2	0	6.2	3	33	7	6	1	0	0	0	11	1	10	1	0
Percival, Troy, California	3	2	.600	1.95	62	0	0	0	16	3	74.0	37	284	19	16	6	4	1	1	26	2	94	2	2
Perez, Melido, New York	5	5	.500	5.58	13	12	1	0	1	0	69.1	70	304	46	43	10	1	3	1	31	2	44	4	0
Pettitte, Andy, New York*	12	9	.571	4.17	31	26	3	0	1	0	175.0	183	745	86	81	15	4	5	1	63	3	114	8	1
Phoenix, Steve, Oakland	0	0	.000	32.40	1	0	0	0	0	0	1.2	3	11	6	6	1	1	0	0	3	0	3	0	0
Pichardo, Hipolito, K.C.	8	4	.667	4.36	44	0	0	0	16	1	64.0	66	287	34	31	4	3	1	4	30	7	43	4	1
Pierce, Jeff, Boston	0	3	.000	6.60	12	0	0	0	2	0	15.0	16	72	12	11	0	1	1	0	14	4	12	0	0
Pittsley, Jim, Kansas City	0	0	.000	13.50	1	1	0	0	0	0	3.1	7	17	5	5	3	0	0	0	1	0	0	0	0
Plunk, Eric, Cleveland	6	2	.750	2.67	56	0	0	0	22	2	64.0	48	263	19	19	5	2	2	4	27	2	71	3	0
Poole, Jim, Cleveland*	3	3	.500	3.75	42	0	0	0	9	0	50.1	40	206	22	21	7	1	2	2	17	0	41	2	1
Prieto, Ariel, Oakland	2	6	.250	4.97	14	9	1	0	1	0	58.0	57	258	35	32	4	3	2	5	32	1	37	4	1
Radinsky, Scott, Chicago*	2	1	.667	5.45	46	0	0	0	10	1	38.0	46	171	23	23	7	1	4	0	17	4	14	0	0
Radke, Brad, Minnesota	11	14	.440	5.32	29	28	2	1	0	0	181.0	195	772	112	107	32	2	9	4	47	0	75	4	0
Rasmussen, Dennis, K.C.*	0	1	.000	9.00	5	1	0	0	1	0	10.0	13	51	10	10	3	0	0	0	8	2	6	2	0
Reyes, Al, Milwaukee	1	1	.500	2.43	27	0	0	0	13	1	33.1	19	138	9	9	3	1	2	3	18	2	29	0	0
Reyes, Carlos, Oakland	4	6	.400	5.09	40	1	0	0	19	0	69.0	71	306	43	39	10	4	0	5	28	4	48	5	0
Rhodes, Arthur, Baltimore*	2	5	.286	6.21	19	9	0	0	3	0	75.1	68	336	53	52	13	4	0	0	48	1	77	3	1
Righetti, Dave, Chicago*	3	2	.600	4.20	10	9	0	0	1	0	49.1	65	221	24	23	6	1	2	0	18	0	29	0	0
Rightnowar, Ron, Milwaukee	2	1	.667	5.40	34	0	0	0	13	1	36.2	35	160	23	22	3	5	3	5	18	3	22	1	0
Risley, Bill, Seattle	2	1	.667	3.13	45	0	0	0	5	1	60.1	55	249	21	21	7	2	3	1	18	1	65	2	0
Rivera, Mariano, New York	5	3	.625	5.51	19	10	0	0	2	0	67.0	71	301	43	41	11	0	2	2	30	0	51	0	1
Roa, Joe, Cleveland	0	1	.000	6.00	1	1	0	0	0	0	6.0	9	28	4	4	1	1	0	0	2	0	0	0	0
Roberson, Sid, Milwaukee*	6	4	.600	5.76	26	13	0	0	8	0	84.1	102	379	55	54	16	0	2	8	37	3	40	3	0
Robertson, Rich, Minnesota*	2	0	1.000	3.83	25	4	1	0	8	0	51.2	48	228	28	22	4	5	2	0	31	4	38	0	1
Robinson, Ken, Toronto	1	2	.333	3.69	21	0	0	0	9	0	39.0	25	167	21	16	7	1	2	2	22	1	31	1	0
Rodriguez, Frank, Bos.-Min.	5	8	.385	6.13	25	18	0	0	1	0	105.2	114	478	83	72	11	1	4	5	57	1	59	9	0
Rogers, Jimmy, Toronto	2	4	.333	5.70	19	0	0	0	9	0	23.2	21	110	15	15	4	3	1	0	18	4	13	0	0
Rogers, Kenny, Texas*	17	7	.708	3.38	31	31	3	1	0	0	208.0	192	877	87	78	26	3	5	2	76	1	140	8	1
Ruffcorn, Scott, Chicago	0	0	.000	7.88	4	0	0	0	0	0	8.0	10	46	7	7	0	1	0	2	13	0	5	0	0
Russell, Jeff, Texas	1	0	1.000	3.03	37	0	0	0	32	20	32.2	36	139	12	11	3	0	0	0	9	1	21	1	0
Ryan, Ken, Boston	0	4	.000	4.96	28	0	0	0	20	7	32.2	34	153	20	18	4	1	0	1	24	6	34	1	0
Sanderson, Scott, California	1	3	.250	4.12	7	7	0	0	0	0	39.1	48	170	23	18	6	1	2	2	4	1	23	0	1
Sanford, Mo, Minnesota	0	0	.000	5.30	11	0	0	0	6	0	18.2	16	89	11	11	7	0	0	2	16	0	17	1	0
Scanlan, Bob, Milwaukee	4	7	.364	6.59	17	14	0	0	1	0	83.1	101	389	66	61	9	0	6	7	44	3	29	3	0
Schullstrom, Erik, Minnesota	0	0	.000	6.89	37	0	0	0	16	0	47.0	66	225	36	36	8	2	1	1	22	1	21	5	0
Sele, Aaron, Boston	3	1	.750	3.06	6	6	0	0	0	0	32.1	32	146	14	11	3	1	1	3	14	0	21	3	0
Shaw, Jeff, Chicago	0	0	.000	6.52	9	0	0	0	1	0	9.2	12	41	7	7	2	1	0	1	1	0	6	0	0
Shepherd, Keith, Boston	0	0	.000	36.00	2	0	0	0	0	0	1.0	4	9	4	4	0	0	0	0	2	0	0	0	0
Shuey, Paul, Cleveland	0	2	.000	4.26	7	0	0	0	3	0	6.1	5	28	4	3	0	2	0	0	5	0	5	1	0
Simas, Bill, Chicago	1	1	.500	2.57	14	0	0	0	4	0	14.0	15	66	5	4	1	0	0	1	10	2	16	1	0
Sirotka, Mike, Chicago*	1	2	.333	4.19	6	6	0	0	0	0	34.1	39	152	16	16	2	1	3	0	17	0	19	2	0
Slusarski, Joe, Milwaukee	1	1	.500	5.40	12	0	0	0	6	0	15.0	21	73	11	9	3	1	1	2	6	1	6	0	0
Smith, Lee, California	0	5	.000	3.47	52	0	0	0	51	37	49.1	42	209	19	19	3	3	3	1	25	4	43	1	0
Smith, Zane, Boston*	8	8	.500	5.61	24	21	0	0	0	0	110.2	144	484	78	69	7	0	5	1	23	1	47	0	1
Sodowsky, Clint, Detroit	2	2	.500	5.01	6	6	0	0	0	0	23.1	24	112	15	13	4	1	0	0	18	0	14	1	1
Sparks, Steve, Milwaukee	9	11	.450	4.63	33	27	3	0	2	0	202.0	210	875	111	104	17	5	12	5	86	1	96	5	1
Springer, Russ, California	1	2	.333	6.10	19	6	0	0	3	1	51.2	60	238	37	35	11	1	0	5	25	1	38	1	0
Stanton, Mike, Boston*	1	0	1.000	3.00	22	0	0	0	12	0	21.0	17	84	9	7	3	0	0	0	8	0	10	1	0
Stevens, Dave, Minnesota	5	4	.556	5.07	56	0	0	0	34	10	65.2	74	302	40	37	14	4	5	1	32	1	47	2	0
Stewart, Dave, Oakland	3	7	.300	6.89	16	16	0	0	0	0	81.0	101	381	65	62	11	6	3	2	39	1	58	8	1
Stottlemyre, Todd, Oakland	14	7	.667	4.55	31	31	2	0	0	0	209.2	228	920	117	106	26	4	4	6	80	7	205	11	0
Suppan, Jeff, Boston	1	2	.333	5.96	8	3	0	0	1	0	22.2	29	100	15	15	4	1	1	0	5	1	19	0	0
Tapani, Kevin, Minnesota	6	11	.353	4.92	20	20	3	1	0	0	133.2	155	579	79	73	21	3	3	4	34	2	88	3	0
Tavarez, Julian, Cleveland	10	2	.833	2.44	57	0	0	0	15	0	85.0	76	350	36	23	7	0	2	3	21	0	68	3	2
Taylor, Scott M., Texas	1	2	.333	9.39	3	3	0	0	0	0	15.1	25	71	16	16	6	0	0	0	5	0	10	0	0
Tewksbury, Bob, Texas	8	7	.533	4.58	21	21	4	1	0	0	129.2	169	561	75	66	8	6	3	3	20	4	53	4	0
Thomas, Larry, Chicago*	0	0	.000	1.32	17	0	0	0	5	0	13.2	8	54	2	2	1	0	0	0	6	1	12	1	0
Thomas, Mike, Milwaukee*	0	0	.000	0.00	1	0	0	0	0	0	1.1	2	7	0	0	0	0	0	0	1	0	0	0	0
Timlin, Mike, Toronto	4	3	.571	2.14	31	0	0	0	19	5	42.0	38	179	13	10	1	3	0	2	17	5	36	3	1
Torres, Dilson, Kansas City	1	2	.333	6.09	24	2	0	0	7	0	44.1	56	198	30	30	6	0	0	1	17	2	28	1	0
Torres, Salomon, Seattle	3	8	.273	6.00	16	13	1	0	2	0	72.0	87	344	53	48	12	1	0	2	42	3	45	1	2
Trombley, Mike, Minnesota	4	8	.333	5.62	20	18	0	0	0	0	97.2	107	442	68	61	18	3	2	3	42	1	68	4	0
Vanegmond, Tim, Boston	0	1	.000	9.45	4	1	0	0	1	0	6.2	9	35	7	7	2	0	0	0	6	0	5	1	0
Van Poppel, Todd, Oakland	4	8	.333	4.88	36	14	1	0	10	0	138.1	125	582	77	75	16	3	6	4	56	1	122	4	0
Villone, Ron, Seattle*	0	2	.000	7.91	19	0	0	0	7	0	19.1	20	101	19	17	6	3	0	1	23	0	26	1	0

Pitcher, Team	W	L	Pct.	ERA	G	GS	CG	ShO	GF	Sv.	IP	H	TBF	R	ER	HR	SH	SF	HB	BB	IBB	SO	WP	Bk.
Vosberg, Ed, Texas*	5	5	.500	3.00	44	0	0	0	20	4	36.0	32	154	15	12	3	2	3	0	16	1	36	3	2
Wakefield, Tim, Boston	16	8	.667	2.95	27	27	6	1	0	0	195.1	163	804	76	64	22	3	7	9	68	0	119	11	0
Ward, Duane, Toronto	0	1	.000	27.00	4	0	0	0	0	0	2.2	11	25	10	8	0	0	0	1	5	0	3	2	0
Ware, Jeff, Toronto	2	1	.667	5.47	5	5	0	0	0	0	26.1	28	124	18	16	2	1	0	1	21	0	18	2	0
Wasdin, John, Oakland	1	1	.500	4.67	5	2	0	0	3	0	17.1	14	69	9	9	4	0	0	1	3	0	6	0	0
Watkins, Scott, Minnesota*	0	0	.000	5.40	27	0	0	0	7	0	21.2	22	94	14	13	2	1	3	0	11	1	11	0	0
Wegman, Bill, Milwaukee	5	7	.417	5.35	37	4	0	0	17	2	70.2	89	314	45	42	14	3	2	3	21	2	50	1	0
Wells, Bob, Seattle	4	3	.571	5.75	30	4	0	0	3	0	76.2	88	358	51	49	11	1	5	3	39	3	38	1	0
Wells, David, Detroit*	10	3	.769	3.04	18	18	3	0	0	0	130.1	120	539	54	44	17	3	2	2	37	5	83	6	1
Wengert, Don, Oakland	1	1	.500	3.34	19	0	0	0	10	0	29.2	30	129	14	11	3	1	1	1	12	2	16	1	0
Wetteland, John, New York*	1	5	.167	2.93	60	0	0	0	56	31	61.1	40	233	22	20	6	1	2	0	14	2	66	1	0
Whiteside, Matt, Texas	5	4	.556	4.08	40	0	0	0	18	3	53.0	48	223	24	24	5	2	3	1	19	2	46	4	0
Whiteside, Sean, Detroit*	0	0	.000	14.73	2	0	0	0	0	0	3.2	7	22	6	6	1	0	2	0	4	1	2	1	0
Wickander, Kevin, Det.-Mil.*	0	0	.000	1.93	29	0	0	0	9	1	23.1	19	99	6	5	1	1	2	1	12	5	11	1	1
Wickman, Bob, New York	2	4	.333	4.05	63	1	0	0	14	1	80.0	77	347	38	36	6	4	1	5	33	3	51	2	0
Williams, Mitch, California*	1	2	.333	6.75	20	0	0	0	3	0	10.2	13	65	10	8	1	0	1	2	21	0	9	2	1
Williams, Woody, Toronto	1	2	.333	3.69	23	3	0	0	10	0	53.2	44	232	23	22	6	2	0	2	28	1	41	0	0
Willis, Carl, Minnesota	0	0	.000	94.50	3	0	0	0	0	0	0.2	5	12	7	7	0	1	0	0	5	0	0	0	0
Witt, Bobby, Texas	3	4	.429	4.55	10	10	1	0	0	0	61.1	81	276	35	31	4	2	1	21	1	46	5	0
Wojciechowski, Steve, Oak.*	2	3	.400	5.18	14	7	0	0	3	0	48.2	51	219	28	28	7	1	2	1	28	1	13	0	0
Wolcott, Bob, Seattle	3	2	.600	4.42	7	6	0	0	0	0	36.2	43	164	18	18	6	0	3	2	14	0	19	0	0

COMBINATION SHUTOUTS: **Baltimore (3)**—Moyer-Clark-Jones, K. Brown-Orosco, McDonald-Hayes-Orosco. **Boston (7)**—Sele-F. Rodriguez-Pena-Pierce-Ryan, Hanson-Hartley-Lilliquist-Pierce-Ryan, Eshelman-Johnston-Ryan, Wakefield-Belinda-Cormier-Ryan, Wakefield-Aguilera, Clemens-Hudson, Clemens-Gunderson-Cormier-Belinda-Stanton-Hudson. **California (6)**—Boskie-Smith, B. Anderson-Patterson-Percival-Butcher-Williams, Abbott-Habyan-Patterson-Percival, Finley-James-Patterson, Abbott-Percival, Finley-Percival-Smith. **Chicago (2)**—Bere-Hernandez, Sirotka-Simas. **Cleveland (6)**—Martinez-Poole-Mesa, Hershiser-Assenmacher, Lopez-Embree-Tavarez-Mesa, Clark-Plunk-Mesa, Ogea-Poole-Tavarez-Mesa, Clark-Tavarez-Olson. **Detroit (2)**—Lira-Henneman, Bergman-Lira. **Kansas City (7)**—Gubicza-Brewer-Pichardo, Appier-Torres, Appier-Pichardo, Gordon-Torres-Pichardo, Appier-Brewer-Meacham, Bunch-Brewer-Montgomery, Jacome-Pichardo-Montgomery. **Milwaukee (4)**—Bones-Lloyd, Sparks-Lloyd-Fetters, Roberson-Rightnowar-Reyes, Sparks-Ignasiak-Lloyd. **New York (2)**—Pettitte-Wickman-Wetteland, McDowell-Wickman. **Oakland (2)**—Stewart-Honeycutt-Corsi-Leiper-Eckersley, Ontiveros-Corsi-Leiper-Eckersley. **Seattle (5)**—Johnson-Wells-Guetterman-Risley-Ayala, Johnson-Risley-Ayala, Belcher-Ayala, Johnson-Nelson, Johnson-Ayala. **Texas (1)**—Pavlik-McDowell. **Toronto (5)**—Leiter-Castillo 2, Leiter-Cornett-Hall, Leiter-Castillo-Hall, Leiter-Timlin.

PITCHERS WITH TWO OR MORE TEAMS

Pitcher, Team	W	L	Pct.	ERA	G	GS	CG	ShO	GF	Sv.	IP	H	TBF	R	ER	HR	SH	SF	HB	BB	IBB	SO	WP	Bk.
Abbott, Jim, Chicago*	6	4	.600	3.36	17	17	3	0	0	0	112.1	116	474	50	42	10	5	1	1	35	1	45	0	0
Abbott, Jim, California*	5	4	.556	4.15	13	13	1	1	0	0	84.2	93	368	43	39	4	3	3	1	29	0	41	1	0
Aguilera, Rick, Minnesota	1	1	.500	2.52	22	0	0	0	21	12	25.0	20	99	7	7	2	0	2	1	6	1	29	0	0
Aguilera, Rick, Boston	2	2	.500	2.67	30	0	0	0	30	20	30.1	26	124	9	9	4	1	2	0	7	0	23	0	0
Cone, David, Toronto	9	6	.600	3.38	17	17	5	2	0	0	130.1	113	537	53	49	12	2	2	5	41	2	102	6	1
Cone, David, New York	9	2	.818	3.82	13	13	1	0	0	0	99.0	82	417	42	42	12	0	1	1	47	0	89	5	0
Converse, Jim, Seattle	0	3	.000	7.36	6	1	0	0	3	1	11.0	16	55	9	9	2	1	0	0	8	0	9	0	0
Converse, Jim, Kansas City	1	0	1.000	5.84	9	0	0	0	1	0	12.1	12	54	8	8	0	1	0	0	8	2	5	2	0
Cook, Dennis, Cleveland*	0	0	.000	6.39	11	0	0	0	1	0	12.2	16	62	9	9	3	1	0	1	10	2	13	0	0
Cook, Dennis, Texas*	0	2	.000	4.00	35	1	0	0	9	2	45.0	47	193	23	20	6	3	5	1	16	1	40	1	0
Darwin, Danny, Toronto	1	8	.111	7.62	13	11	1	0	0	0	65.0	91	303	60	55	13	3	5	3	24	2	36	1	0
Darwin, Danny, Texas	2	2	.500	7.15	7	4	0	0	0	0	34.0	40	145	27	27	12	0	1	7	1	22	1	0
Dibble, Rob, Chicago	0	1	.000	6.28	16	0	0	0	4	1	14.1	7	78	10	10	1	1	2	3	27	2	16	5	0
Dibble, Rob, Milwaukee	1	1	.500	8.25	15	0	0	0	4	0	12.0	9	65	11	11	1	2	4	0	19	0	10	3	0
Erickson, Scott, Minnesota	4	6	.400	5.95	15	15	0	0	0	0	87.2	102	390	61	58	11	2	1	4	32	0	45	1	0
Erickson, Scott, Baltimore	9	4	.692	3.89	17	16	7	2	1	0	108.2	111	446	47	47	7	1	2	1	35	0	61	2	2
Fleming, Dave, Seattle*	1	5	.167	7.50	16	7	1	0	2	0	48.0	57	233	44	40	15	2	3	0	34	3	26	4	0
Fleming, Dave, Kansas City*	0	1	.000	3.66	9	5	0	0	1	0	32.0	27	141	17	13	4	1	2	19	1	14	1	0
Harkey, Mike, Oakland	4	6	.400	6.27	14	12	0	0	1	0	66.0	75	296	46	46	12	3	2	3	31	0	28	2	0
Harkey, Mike, California	4	3	.571	4.55	12	8	1	0	0	0	61.1	80	277	32	31	12	1	2	1	16	2	28	0	0
Hartley, Mike, Boston	0	0	.000	9.00	5	0	0	0	2	0	7.0	8	33	7	7	1	1	2	2	0	2	0	0
Hartley, Mike, Baltimore	1	0	1.000	7.00	3	0	0	0	2	0	7.0	5	25	1	1	0	1	0	0	1	0	4	0	0
Honeycutt, Rick, Oakland*	5	1	.833	2.42	49	0	0	0	6	2	44.2	37	174	13	12	5	3	1	9	0	21	0	0
Honeycutt, Rick, New York*	0	0	.000	27.00	3	0	0	0	1	0	1.0	2	6	3	3	1	0	0	1	0	0	1	0
Klingenbeck, Scott, Baltimore	2	2	.500	4.88	6	5	0	0	1	0	31.1	32	137	17	17	6	0	0	18	0	15	2	0
Klingenbeck, Scott, Minn.	0	2	.000	8.57	18	4	0	0	4	0	48.1	69	236	48	46	16	3	1	4	20	4	27	5	0
Olson, Gregg, Cleveland	0	0	.000	13.50	3	0	0	0	2	0	2.2	5	14	4	4	1	0	0	2	0	0	0	0
Olson, Gregg, Kansas City	3	3	.500	3.26	20	0	0	0	10	3	30.1	23	127	11	11	3	1	2	0	17	2	21	1	0
Rodriguez, Frank, Boston	0	2	.000	10.57	9	2	0	0	1	0	15.1	21	75	19	18	3	0	0	10	1	14	4	0
Rodriguez, Frank, Minn.	5	6	.455	5.38	16	16	0	0	0	0	90.1	93	403	64	54	8	1	4	5	47	0	45	5	0
Wickander, Kevin, Detroit*	0	0	.000	2.60	21	0	0	0	7	1	17.1	18	77	6	5	1	0	1	1	9	4	9	1	1
Wickander, Kevin, Milwaukee*	0	0	.000	0.00	8	0	0	0	2	0	6.0	1	23	0	0	0	1	1	0	3	1	2	0	0

FIELDING

TEAM

Team	Pct.	G	PO	A	E	TC	DP	PB	Team	Pct.	G	PO	A	E	TC	DP	PB
Baltimore	.986	144	3801	1441	72	5314	136	8	Milwaukee	.981	144	3858	1669	105	5632	179	34
New York	.986	145	3854	1411	74	5339	113	20	Oakland	.981	144	3819	1483	102	5404	145	4
Kansas City	.984	144	3864	1659	90	5613	160	11	Detroit	.981	144	3825	1592	106	5523	138	3
Texas	.982	144	3855	1586	98	5539	147	10	Seattle	.980	145	3868	1353	104	5325	101	13
California	.982	145	3853	1416	95	5364	117	13	Chicago	.980	145	3854	1411	108	5373	125	12
Cleveland	.982	144	3903	1595	101	5599	136	11	Boston	.978	144	3878	1579	120	5577	145	29
Toronto	.982	144	3878	1398	97	5373	128	31	Totals	.982	1010	53927	21078	1372	76377	1901	210
Minnesota	.981	144	3817	1485	100	5402	131	11									

TRIPLE PLAY: Seattle.

INDIVIDUAL

FIRST BASEMEN

NOTE: All caps denotes fielding-percentage leader based on 72 games for catchers, 96 for all other non-pitchers and 144 innings for pitchers. *Throws lefthanded.

Player, Team	Pct.	G	PO	A	E	TC	DP
Aldrete, Mike, Oak.-Cal.*	.989	36	176	10	2	188	16
Blowers, Mike, Seattle	.974	7	32	5	1	38	7
Boggs, Wade, New York	1.000	9	45	5	0	50	4
Brosius, Scott, Oakland	.984	18	110	17	2	129	26
Caceres, Edgar, Kansas City	1.000	6	11	0	0	11	2
Carter, Joe, Toronto	1.000	7	47	3	0	50	2
Cirillo, Jeff, Milwaukee	1.000	3	16	1	0	17	1
Clark, Jerald, Minnesota	1.000	11	33	3	0	36	4
Clark, Tony, Detroit	.985	27	252	18	4	274	25
Clark, Will, Texas*	.994	122	1076	88	7	1171	125
Coomer, Ron, Minnesota	.993	22	131	13	1	145	13
Davis, Russ, New York	1.000	2	1	0	0	1	0
Delgado, Carlos, Toronto	1.000	4	20	1	0	21	3
Donnels, Chris, Boston	1.000	8	36	6	0	42	8
Dunn, Steve, Minnesota*	1.000	3	5	0	0	5	2
Espinoza, Alvaro, Cleveland	1.000	2	9	0	0	9	1
Fielder, Cecil, Detroit	.993	77	631	73	5	709	66
Fletcher, Scott, Detroit	1.000	1	2	0	0	2	0
Gaetti, Gary, Kansas City	.990	11	92	10	1	103	10
Gates, Brent, Oakland	1.000	1	8	4	0	12	1
Giambi, Jason, Oakland	.994	26	167	10	1	178	20
Gomez, Leo, Baltimore	1.000	3	5	0	0	5	0
Greer, Rusty, Texas*	.935	3	29	0	2	31	4
Grotewold, Jeff, Kansas City	.750	1	3	0	1	4	1
Hale, Chip, Minnesota	1.000	3	13	0	0	13	0
Hamelin, Bob, Kansas City*	1.000	8	66	9	0	75	11
Hare, Shawn, Texas*	1.000	1	1	0	0	1	0
Haselman, Bill, Boston	1.000	1	2	0	0	2	0
Howard, David, Kansas City	1.000	1	3	0	0	3	1
Hudler, Rex, California	1.000	2	8	0	0	8	1
Jaha, John, Milwaukee	.997	81	649	60	2	711	86
James, Dion, New York*	1.000	6	31	4	0	35	1
Jefferson, Reggie, Boston*	1.000	7	26	4	0	30	4
JOYNER, WALLY, Kansas City*	.998	126	1111	118	3	1232	121
Kruk, John, Chicago*	.909	1	10	0	1	11	1
Leyritz, Jim, New York	.993	18	131	6	1	138	11
Lyons, Barry, Chicago	.974	4	33	4	1	38	4
Maas, Kevin, Minnesota*	.936	8	43	1	3	47	4
Manto, Jeff, Baltimore	1.000	4	28	2	0	30	5
Martinez, Carlos, California	1.000	4	20	0	0	20	2
Martinez, Dave, Chicago*	.997	47	311	23	1	335	38
Martinez, Edgar, Seattle	.968	3	29	1	1	31	0
Martinez, Tino, Seattle	.993	139	1048	101	8	1157	88
Masteller, Dan, Minnesota*	.994	48	333	21	2	356	35
Mattingly, Don, New York*	.994	125	946	81	7	1084	90
McCarty, Dave, Minnesota*	.993	18	128	10	1	139	13
McGinnis, Russ, Kansas City	1.000	1	8	0	0	8	0
McGwire, Mark, Oakland	.986	91	775	64	12	851	65
Merullo, Matt, Minnesota	1.000	2	5	2	0	7	0
Munoz, Pedro, Minnesota	.727	3	7	1	3	11	1
Murray, Eddie, Cleveland	.984	18	160	22	3	185	12
Nilsson, Dave, Milwaukee	1.000	7	16	2	0	18	1
Olerud, John, Toronto*	.997	133	1099	89	4	1192	103
Oliver, Joe, Milwaukee	1.000	2	6	0	0	6	1
Pagliarulo, Mike, Texas	.987	11	69	8	1	78	5
Palmeiro, Rafael, Baltimore*	.997	142	1181	119	4	1304	120
Paquette, Craig, Oakland	1.000	3	10	1	0	11	1
Perry, Herbert, Cleveland	1.000	45	388	30	0	418	30
Pirkl, Greg, Seattle	1.000	6	32	3	0	35	1
Reboulet, Jeff, Minnesota	1.000	17	80	13	0	93	7
Sabo, Chris, Chicago	.909	1	10	0	1	11	1
Samuel, Juan, Det.-K.C.	.984	38	279	23	5	307	26
Seitzer, Kevin, Milwaukee	.990	36	288	21	3	312	38
Silvestri, Dave, New York	1.000	4	26	2	0	28	2
Snow, J.T., California*	.997	143	1161	57	4	1222	105
Sorrento, Paul, Cleveland	.992	91	816	58	7	881	88
Sprague, Ed, Toronto	.971	7	34	0	1	35	3
Stahoviak, Scott, Minnesota	.998	69	494	61	1	556	48
Steinbach, Terry, Oakland	.833	2	5	0	1	6	3
Stubbs, Franklin, Detroit*	.972	20	134	5	4	143	13
Surhoff, B.J., Milwaukee	.992	55	348	29	3	380	45
Tettleton, Mickey, Texas	1.000	9	80	6	0	86	7
Thomas, Frank, Chicago	.991	90	738	34	7	779	67
Tingley, Ron, Detroit	1.000	1	1	0	0	1	0
Unroe, Tim, Milwaukee	1.000	2	11	0	0	11	3
Valle, Dave, Texas	1.000	7	20	1	0	21	2
Vaughn, Mo, Boston	.992	138	1262	95	11	1368	128
Ventura, Robin, Chicago	.981	18	95	10	2	107	12
Vitiello, Joe, Kansas City	.982	8	51	3	1	55	3
Voigt, Jack, Bal.-Tex.	.957	6	20	2	1	23	3
White, Derrick, Detroit	.981	16	47	5	1	53	4

FIRST BASEMEN WITH TWO OR MORE TEAMS

Player, Team	Pct.	G	PO	A	E	TC	DP
Aldrete, Mike, Oakland*	.989	35	175	10	2	187	16
Aldrete, Mike, California*	1.000	1	1	0	0	1	0
Samuel, Juan, Detroit	.983	37	271	23	5	299	26
Samuel, Juan, Kansas City	1.000	1	8	0	0	8	0
Voigt, Jack, Baltimore	1.000	1	1	1	0	2	0
Voigt, Jack, Texas	.952	5	19	1	1	21	3

SECOND BASEMEN

Player, Team	Pct.	G	PO	A	E	TC	DP
Alexander, Manny, Baltimore	.971	81	136	165	9	310	48
Alicea, Luis, Boston	.977	132	254	429	16	699	103
ALOMAR, ROBERTO, Toronto	.994	128	272	367	4	643	84
Baerga, Carlos, Cleveland	.973	134	231	444	19	694	99
Barberie, Bret, Baltimore	.977	74	114	186	7	307	45
Bell, Juan, Boston	1.000	5	9	11	0	20	4
Beltre, Esteban, Texas	.953	15	13	28	2	43	6
Brady, Doug, Chicago	1.000	6	14	21	0	35	4
Brosius, Scott, Oakland	1.000	3	3	4	0	7	1
Caceres, Edgar, Kansas City	.992	36	49	71	1	121	10
Cedeno, Domingo, Toronto	1.000	20	30	42	0	72	8
Cirillo, Jeff, Milwaukee	.984	25	52	75	2	129	16
Cora, Joey, Seattle	.955	112	205	262	22	489	53
Correia, Rod, California	1.000	3	0	3	0	3	0
Donnels, Chris, Boston	1.000	3	1	1	0	2	1
Durham, Ray, Chicago	.973	122	245	299	15	559	67
Easley, Damion, California	.981	88	145	209	7	361	41
Eenhoorn, Robert, New York	1.000	3	10	6	0	16	2
Elster, Kevin, New York	.000	1	0	0	0	0	0
Espinoza, Alvaro, Cleveland	.966	22	18	39	2	59	7
Fermin, Felix, Seattle	.991	29	32	75	1	108	12
Fernandez, Tony, New York	1.000	4	7	9	0	16	2
Fletcher, Scott, Detroit	1.000	63	109	161	0	270	49
Frye, Jeff, Texas	.975	83	173	248	11	432	55
Gallego, Mike, Oakland	.960	18	25	47	3	75	9
Gates, Brent, Oakland	.982	132	233	424	12	669	81
Gomez, Chris, Detroit	.979	31	55	82	3	140	20
Gonzales, Rene, California	1.000	6	4	6	0	10	0
Grebeck, Craig, Chicago	.988	8	11	14	0	25	2
Hale, Chip, Minnesota	1.000	7	2	5	0	7	1

1995 A.L. STATISTICS Fielding

Player, Team	Pct.	G	PO	A	E	TC	DP
Howard, David, Kansas City	.994	41	68	99	1	168	21
Hudler, Rex, California	.986	52	93	115	3	211	32
Huson, Jeff, Baltimore	1.000	21	38	45	0	83	14
Kelly, Pat, New York	.983	87	161	256	7	424	54
Knoblauch, Chuck, Minnesota	.985	136	253	400	10	663	88
Lind, Jose, K.C.-Cal.	.995	44	80	115	1	196	27
Listach, Pat, Milwaukee	1.000	59	104	169	0	273	44
Lockhart, Keith, Kansas City	.974	61	106	160	7	273	43
Loretta, Mark, Milwaukee	1.000	4	5	9	0	14	2
Martin, Norberto, Chicago	.950	17	35	41	4	80	12
McLemore, Mark, Texas	.993	66	108	184	2	294	42
Mota, Jose, Kansas City	1.000	2	1	3	0	4	0
Owen, Spike, California	1.000	16	27	21	0	48	7
Penn, Shannon, Detroit	.864	3	10	9	3	22	4
Perez, Tomas, Toronto	1.000	7	10	12	0	22	3
Pozo, Arquimedez, Seattle	1.000	1	0	1	0	1	0
Puckett, Kirby, Minnesota	1.000	1	0	1	0	1	0
Raabe, Brian, Minnesota	1.000	4	5	8	0	13	3
Randa, Joe, Kansas City	.957	9	7	15	1	23	3
Rebeoulet, Jeff, Minnesota	.979	15	17	29	1	47	5
Ripken, Billy, Cleveland	1.000	7	7	6	0	13	1
Rodriguez, Carlos, Boston	.960	7	9	15	1	25	3
Rodriguez, Steve, Bos.-Det.	.983	13	22	36	1	59	6
Samuel, Juan, Kansas City	.955	6	9	12	1	22	3
Shumpert, Terry, Boston	1.000	8	12	15	0	27	4
Silvestri, Dave, New York	1.000	7	2	11	0	13	1
Sojo, Luis, Seattle	.957	19	23	44	3	70	5
Strange, Doug, Seattle	1.000	5	3	5	0	8	1
Stynes, Chris, Kansas City	.982	17	21	35	1	57	14
Velarde, Randy, New York	.976	62	102	140	6	248	25
Vina, Fernando, Milwaukee	.983	99	183	225	7	415	71
Whitaker, Lou, Detroit	.985	63	107	163	4	274	32

TRIPLE PLAY: Cora, Sea.

SECOND BASEMEN WITH TWO OR MORE TEAMS

Player, Team	Pct.	G	PO	A	E	TC	DP
Lind, Jose, Kansas City	.992	29	56	75	1	132	17
Lind, Jose, California	1.000	15	24	40	0	64	10
Rodriguez, Steve, Boston	1.000	1	1	2	0	3	0
Rodriguez, Steve, Detroit	.982	12	21	34	1	56	6

THIRD BASEMEN

Player, Team	Pct.	G	PO	A	E	TC	DP
Alexander, Manny, Baltimore	.500	2	1	0	1	2	0
Barberie, Bret, Baltimore	1.000	3	0	1	0	1	0
Battle, Howard, Toronto	1.000	6	1	6	0	7	0
Bell, David, Cleveland	1.000	2	0	2	0	2	0
Bell, Juan, Boston	1.000	1	0	1	0	1	0
Beltre, Esteban, Texas	.000	1	0	0	0	0	0
Blowers, Mike, Seattle	.947	126	80	168	14	262	9
BOGGS, WADE, New York	.981	117	69	193	5	267	11
Bonilla, Bobby, Baltimore	.952	24	14	46	3	63	5
Brosius, Scott, Oakland	.918	60	27	96	11	134	8
Buechele, Steve, Texas	1.000	9	7	11	0	18	2
Caceres, Edgar, Kansas City	.000	3	2	3	0	5	2
Cedeno, Domingo, Toronto	.000	1	0	0	0	0	0
Cirillo, Jeff, Milwaukee	.938	108	45	153	13	211	22
Coomer, Ron, Minnesota	.962	13	6	19	1	26	1
Correia, Rod, California	.750	2	0	6	2	8	1
Davis, Russ, New York	.968	34	15	45	2	62	1
Donnels, Chris, Boston	.927	27	17	34	4	55	2
Espinoza, Alvaro, Cleveland	.974	22	10	27	1	38	1
Fryman, Travis, Detroit	.969	144	107	337	14	458	38
Gaetti, Gary, Kansas City	.954	123	90	218	15	323	21
Gallego, Mike, Oakland	.882	12	5	10	2	17	1
Giambi, Jason, Oakland	.960	30	27	45	3	75	4
Gomez, Leo, Baltimore	.978	44	23	68	2	93	3
Gonzales, Rene, California	1.000	18	2	6	0	8	0
Gonzalez, Alex, Toronto	.895	9	6	11	2	19	1
Grebeck, Craig, Chicago	.970	18	14	18	1	33	3
Hale, Chip, Minnesota	1.000	5	1	1	0	2	1
Haselman, Bill, Boston	.000	1	0	0	0	0	0
Huson, Jeff, Baltimore	1.000	33	21	44	0	65	5
Javier, Stan, Oakland	.000	1	0	0	0	0	0
Leius, Scott, Minnesota	.945	112	60	182	14	256	27
Listach, Pat, Milwaukee	1.000	2	1	0	0	1	0
Lockhart, Keith, Kansas City	.958	17	5	18	1	24	1
Manto, Jeff, Baltimore	.959	69	40	101	6	147	11
Martin, Norberto, Chicago	.818	9	2	7	2	11	2
Martinez, Carlos, California	.968	16	5	25	1	31	7
Martinez, Edgar, Seattle	.800	4	1	3	1	5	0
McGinnis, Russ, Kansas City	1.000	1	1	0	0	1	0
Naehring, Tim, Boston	.954	124	85	244	16	345	23

Player, Team	Pct.	G	PO	A	E	TC	DP
Ortiz, Luis, Texas	.867	35	9	43	8	60	2
Owen, Spike, California	.945	29	16	36	3	55	3
Pagliarulo, Mike, Texas	.963	68	42	113	6	161	12
Palmer, Dean, Texas	.948	36	19	72	5	96	9
Paquette, Craig, Oakland	.935	75	38	78	8	124	11
Perez, Eduardo, California	.883	23	16	37	7	60	3
Perez, Tomas, Toronto	.000	1	0	0	0	0	0
Perry, Herbert, Cleveland	1.000	1	3	0	0	3	0
Phillips, Tony, California	.924	88	53	178	19	250	17
Puckett, Kirby, Minnesota	.000	1	0	0	0	0	0
Raabe, Brian, Minnesota	.000	2	0	0	0	0	0
Randa, Joe, Kansas City	.949	22	8	29	2	39	1
Rebeoulet, Jeff, Minnesota	.960	22	14	34	2	50	2
Ripken, Billy, Cleveland	.000	1	0	0	0	0	0
Rodriguez, Carlos, Boston	1.000	1	0	1	0	1	0
Sabo, Chris, Chicago	1.000	1	0	1	0	1	0
Seitzer, Kevin, Milwaukee	.968	88	52	160	7	219	18
Shumpert, Terry, Boston	1.000	5	2	7	0	9	0
Snopek, Chris, Chicago	1.000	17	11	13	0	24	0
Sprague, Ed, Toronto	.958	139	133	234	16	383	20
Stahoviak, Scott, Minnesota	.907	22	9	30	4	43	3
Strange, Doug, Seattle	.948	41	28	64	5	97	2
Thome, Jim, Cleveland	.948	134	75	214	16	305	22
Valentin, Jose, Milwaukee	1.000	1	0	2	0	2	1
Velarde, Randy, New York	1.000	19	6	30	0	36	2
Ventura, Robin, Chicago	.948	121	106	206	17	329	15
Vina, Fernando, Milwaukee	.000	2	0	0	0	0	0
Worthington, Craig, Texas	.980	26	13	36	1	50	3

SHORTSTOPS

Player, Team	Pct.	G	PO	A	E	TC	DP
Alexander, Manny, Baltimore	1.000	7	2	5	0	7	1
Bell, Juan, Boston	.857	6	6	12	3	21	1
Beltre, Esteban, Texas	.969	36	40	53	3	96	13
Bordick, Mike, Oakland	.983	126	245	338	10	593	93
Brosius, Scott, Oakland	1.000	3	2	2	0	4	1
Caceres, Edgar, Kansas City	1.000	8	10	18	0	28	6
Cedeno, Domingo, Toronto	.980	30	55	90	3	148	18
Cirillo, Jeff, Milwaukee	1.000	2	0	1	0	1	0
Cora, Joey, Seattle	.000	1	0	0	1	1	0
Correia, Rod, California	.850	7	6	11	3	20	4
Cruz, Fausto, Oakland	.971	8	9	24	1	34	2
DiSarcina, Gary, California	.986	98	146	275	6	427	49
Easley, Damion, California	.973	25	41	67	3	111	18
Eenhoorn, Robert, New York	.750	2	1	2	1	4	0
Elster, Kevin, New York	1.000	10	10	14	0	24	2
Espinoza, Alvaro, Cleveland	.960	19	13	35	2	50	8
Fermin, Felix, Seattle	.971	46	75	94	5	174	31
Fernandez, Tony, New York	.976	103	141	274	10	425	63
Fletcher, Scott, Detroit	1.000	3	0	1	0	1	0
Gagne, Greg, Kansas City	.969	118	174	389	18	581	88
Gallego, Mike, Oakland	1.000	14	16	32	0	48	6
Gil, Benji, Texas	.974	130	226	408	17	651	95
Gomez, Chris, Detroit	.973	97	155	279	12	446	61
Gonzales, Rene, California	.000	1	0	0	0	0	0
Gonzalez, Alex, Toronto	.957	97	158	216	17	391	46
Grebeck, Craig, Chicago	.961	31	51	95	6	152	20
Guillen, Ozzie, Chicago	.976	120	167	318	12	497	58
Hocking, Denny, Minnesota	.971	6	13	20	1	34	5
Howard, David, Kansas City	.986	33	47	93	2	142	25
Huson, Jeff, Baltimore	.500	1	0	1	1	2	0
Jeter, Derek, New York	.962	15	17	34	2	53	7
Knoblauch, Chuck, Minn.	1.000	2	1	0	0	1	0
Leius, Scott, Minnesota	1.000	7	0	5	0	5	0
Listach, Pat, Milwaukee	.963	36	54	103	6	163	31
Loretta, Mark, Milwaukee	.979	13	13	33	1	47	5
Martin, Norberto, Chicago	.962	7	8	17	1	26	2
Meares, Pat, Minnesota	.965	114	186	317	18	521	69
Owen, Spike, California	.952	25	22	38	3	63	7
Paquette, Craig, Oakland	1.000	8	5	12	0	17	6
Perez, Tomas, Toronto	.954	31	38	65	5	108	14
Puckett, Kirby, Minnesota	.000	1	0	0	0	0	0
Rebeoulet, Jeff, Minnesota	.993	39	53	84	1	138	22
RIPKEN, CAL, Baltimore	.989	144	206	409	7	622	100
Rodriguez, Alex, Seattle	.953	46	56	106	8	170	14
Rodriguez, Carlos, Boston	1.000	6	7	11	0	18	3
Rodriguez, Steve, Bos.-Det.	.667	5	0	2	1	3	0
Schofield, Dick, California	1.000	12	8	23	0	31	2
Shumpert, Terry, Boston	.909	3	7	13	2	22	3
Silvestri, Dave, New York	.000	1	0	0	0	0	0
Snopek, Chris, Chicago	.941	6	14	18	2	34	5
Sojo, Luis, Seattle	.983	80	110	176	5	291	35

Player, Team	Pct.	G	PO	A	E	TC	DP
Trammell, Alan, Detroit	.980	60	86	158	5	249	34
Valentin, John, Boston	.973	135	227	414	18	659	95
Valentin, Jose, Milwaukee	.971	104	164	333	15	512	85
Velarde, Randy, New York	.976	28	37	87	3	127	21
Vina, Fernando, Milwaukee	.969	6	11	20	1	32	4
Vizquel, Omar, Cleveland	.986	136	210	405	9	624	84

TRIPLE PLAY: Sojo, Sea.

SHORTSTOPS WITH TWO OR MORE TEAMS

Player, Team	Pct.	G	PO	A	E	TC	DP
Rodriguez, Steve, Boston	.667	4	0	2	1	3	0
Rodriguez, Steve, Detroit	.000	1	0	0	0	0	0

OUTFIELDERS

Player, Team	Pct.	G	PO	A	E	TC	DP
Aldrete, Mike, Oak.-Cal.*	.958	18	23	0	1	24	0
Amaral, Rich, Seattle	.992	73	121	6	1	128	0
Amaro, Ruben, Cleveland	.000	22	35	0	0	35	0
Anderson, Brady, Baltimore*	.989	142	268	1	3	272	0
Anderson, Garret, California*	.978	100	213	7	5	225	0
Bass, Kevin, Baltimore	.984	77	123	3	2	128	1
Bautista, Danny, Detroit	.988	86	164	3	2	169	0
Becker, Rich, Minnesota*	.986	105	275	12	4	291	5
Belle, Albert, Cleveland	.981	142	304	7	6	317	1
Berroa, Geronimo, Oakland	.971	71	129	5	4	138	2
Blowers, Mike, Seattle	.800	5	4	0	1	5	0
Bonilla, Bobby, Baltimore	.971	39	66	2	2	70	0
Bragg, Darren, Seattle	.989	47	83	7	1	91	2
Brosius, Scott, Oakland	.971	49	66	2	2	70	0
Brown, Jarvis, Baltimore	1.000	17	16	0	0	16	0
Buford, Damon, Baltimore	1.000	24	40	0	0	40	0
Buhner, Jay, Seattle	.989	120	180	5	2	187	0
Burnitz, Jeromy, Cleveland	1.000	6	10	0	0	10	0
Cameron, Mike, Chicago	1.000	28	33	1	0	34	0
Canseco, Jose, Boston	1.000	1	1	0	0	1	0
Carter, Joe, Toronto	.975	128	269	9	7	285	1
Chamberlain, Wes, Boston	.955	12	20	1	1	22	0
Clark, Jerald, Minnesota	1.000	23	47	1	0	48	0
Cole, Alex, Minnesota*	.938	23	44	1	3	48	0
Coleman, Vince, K.C.-Sea.	.980	107	191	9	4	204	2
Cookson, Brent, Kansas City	1.000	12	14	0	0	14	0
Coomer, Ron, Minnesota	1.000	1	1	0	0	1	0
Cordova, Marty, Minnesota	.986	137	346	12	5	363	3
Curtis, Chad, Detroit	.992	144	362	5	3	370	1
Cuyler, Milt, Detroit	.929	36	50	2	4	56	0
Dalesandro, Mark, California	1.000	1	1	0	0	1	0
Damon, Johnny, Kansas City*	.991	47	110	0	1	111	0
Delgado, Carlos, Toronto	1.000	17	34	1	0	35	0
Devereaux, Mike, Chicago	.985	90	187	4	3	194	1
Diaz, Alex, Seattle	.987	88	145	4	2	151	2
Edmonds, Jim, California*	.998	139	401	8	1	410	2
Fox, Eric, Texas*	1.000	8	13	0	0	13	0
Frazier, Lou, Texas	.973	47	69	2	2	73	0
Gallagher, Dave, California	1.000	6	9	1	0	10	1
Gibson, Kirk, Detroit*	.000	1	0	0	0	0	0
Giles, Brian, Cleveland*	1.000	3	2	1	0	3	0
Gonzalez, Juan, Texas	1.000	5	6	1	0	7	0
Goodwin, Curtis, Baltimore*	.990	84	202	1	2	205	1
Goodwin, Tom, Kansas City	.990	130	292	6	3	301	2
Green, Shawn, Toronto*	.973	109	207	9	6	222	3
Greenwell, Mike, Boston	.972	118	201	11	6	218	1
Greer, Rusty, Texas*	.982	125	211	9	4	224	0
Griffey, Ken, Seattle*	.990	70	190	5	2	197	1
Hall, Joe, Detroit	1.000	5	11	1	0	12	0
Hamilton, Darryl, Milwaukee	.989	109	262	4	3	269	1
Hammonds, Jeffrey, Baltimore	.989	46	88	1	1	90	0
Hare, Shawn, Texas*	1.000	9	9	1	0	10	0
Hatcher, Billy, Texas	1.000	9	9	1	0	10	0
Henderson, Rickey, Oakland*	.988	90	162	5	2	169	1
Herrera, Jose, Oakland*	.956	25	41	2	2	45	1
Hiatt, Phil, Kansas City	.957	47	63	4	3	70	1
Higginson, Bob, Detroit	.985	123	247	13	4	264	3
Hollins, Dave, Boston	1.000	2	3	0	0	3	0
Hosey, Dwayne, Boston	1.000	21	46	1	0	47	0
Howard, David, Kansas City	.945	30	49	3	3	55	0
Hudler, Rex, California	.955	22	21	0	1	22	0
Huff, Michael, Toronto	.980	55	95	3	2	100	0
Hulse, David, Milwaukee*	.984	115	180	2	3	185	1
James, Chris, K.C.-Bos.	1.000	13	23	0	0	23	0
James, Dion, New York*	.968	29	30	0	1	31	0
JAVIER, STAN, Oakland	1.000	124	332	3	0	335	1
Jefferson, Reggie, Boston*	1.000	2	2	0	0	2	0
Johnson, Lance, Chicago*	.991	140	338	8	3	349	2
Jose, Felix, Kansas City	1.000	7	15	2	0	17	0
Kirby, Wayne, Cleveland	.990	68	94	2	1	97	1
Lawton, Matt, Minnesota	.972	19	34	1	1	36	0
Listach, Pat, Milwaukee	1.000	11	10	1	0	11	0
Lofton, Kenny, Cleveland*	.970	114	248	11	8	267	3
Mahay, Ron, Boston*	1.000	5	9	0	0	9	0
Maldonado, Candy, Tor.-Tex.	.990	69	98	3	1	102	0
Martin, Norberto, Chicago	1.000	12	7	2	0	9	0
Martinez, Dave, Chicago*	.976	59	81	2	2	85	1
Masteller, Dan, Minnesota*	1.000	22	32	0	0	32	0
May, Derrick, Milwaukee	.971	32	65	1	2	68	1
McCarty, Dave, Minnesota*	1.000	5	2	0	0	2	0
McGee, Willie, Boston	.973	64	101	7	3	111	1
McGinnis, Russ, Kansas City	.000	1	0	0	0	0	0
McLemore, Mark, Texas	.986	73	140	0	2	142	0
Meares, Pat, Minnesota	1.000	3	1	0	0	1	0
Mieske, Matt, Milwaukee	.979	108	177	7	4	188	2
Miller, Keith, Kansas City	1.000	4	5	1	0	6	0
Mouton, Lyle, Chicago	.990	53	93	5	1	99	1
Munoz, Pedro, Minnesota	.926	25	22	3	2	27	0
Nevin, Phil, Detroit	.963	27	50	2	2	54	0
Newfield, Marc, Seattle	1.000	24	44	0	0	44	0
Newson, Warren, Chi.-Sea.*	.975	47	77	2	2	81	0
Nilsson, Dave, Milwaukee	.981	58	99	5	2	106	0
Nixon, Otis, Texas	.989	138	357	4	4	365	1
Norman, Les, Kansas City	.958	17	22	1	1	24	0
Nunnally, Jon, Kansas City	.971	107	197	5	6	208	1
Obando, Sherman, Baltimore	.923	7	12	0	1	13	0
O'Leary, Troy, Boston*	.976	105	196	6	5	207	1
O'Neill, Paul, New York*	.987	121	220	3	3	226	0
Palmeiro, Orlando, California*	1.000	7	7	0	0	7	0
Paquette, Craig, Oakland	1.000	20	19	1	0	20	0
Pemberton, Rudy, Detroit	1.000	8	15	0	0	15	0
Perez, Robert, Toronto	1.000	15	30	0	0	30	0
Phillips, Tony, California	.991	48	113	1	1	115	0
Polonia, Luis, New York*	1.000	64	132	5	0	137	1
Puckett, Kirby, Minnesota	.981	109	194	9	4	207	1
Raines, Tim, Chicago	.980	107	193	7	4	204	1
Ramirez, Manny, Cleveland	.978	131	220	3	5	228	2
Rhodes, Kark, Boston*	.947	9	18	0	1	19	0
Rivera, Ruben, New York	1.000	4	2	0	0	2	0
Salmon, Tim, California	.988	142	320	7	4	331	0
Samuel, Juan, Det.-K.C.	.800	14	12	0	3	15	0
Sierra, Ruben, Oak.-N.Y.	.956	72	107	2	5	114	0
Singleton, Duane, Milwaukee	1.000	11	22	1	0	23	0
Smith, Mark, Baltimore	1.000	32	60	2	0	62	0
Sojo, Luis, Seattle	.900	6	8	1	1	10	0
Stairs, Matt, Boston	.913	23	19	2	2	23	0
Steverson, Todd, Detroit	1.000	27	22	1	0	23	0
Stewart, Shannon, Toronto	.955	12	20	1	1	22	0
Strange, Doug, Seattle	1.000	4	8	0	0	8	0
Strawberry, Darryl, New York*	.909	11	18	2	2	22	1
Stubbs, Franklin, Detroit*	.955	20	21	0	1	22	0
Surhoff, B.J., Milwaukee	.993	60	125	9	1	135	1
Tartabull, Danny, N.Y.-Oak.	1.000	19	28	1	0	29	1
Tettleton, Mickey, Texas	.972	63	100	3	3	106	1
Thurman, Gary, Seattle	1.000	9	15	0	0	15	0
Tinsley, Lee, Boston	.979	97	228	4	5	237	1
Tomberlin, Andy, Oakland*	.979	42	45	1	1	47	0
Tucker, Michael, Kansas City	.986	36	67	3	1	71	0
Van Slyke, Andy, Baltimore	.978	17	42	2	1	45	1
Velarde, Randy, New York	.960	20	23	1	1	25	0
Voigt, Jack, Texas	1.000	25	36	1	0	37	0
Ward, Turner, Milwaukee	.989	40	81	5	1	87	1
Wegman, Bill, Milwaukee	.000	1	0	0	0	0	0
White, Derrick, Detroit	.889	9	8	0	1	9	0
White, Devon, Toronto	.989	99	261	7	3	271	0
Whiten, Mark, Boston	1.000	31	52	4	0	56	1
Widger, Chris, Seattle	1.000	3	3	0	0	3	0
Williams, Bernie, New York	.982	144	432	1	8	441	0
Williams, Gerald, New York	.993	92	138	6	1	145	2
Young, Ernie, Oakland	.946	24	35	0	2	37	0

OUTFIELDERS WITH TWO OR MORE TEAMS

Player, Team	Pct.	G	PO	A	E	TC	DP
Aldrete, Mike, Oakland*	.941	16	16	0	1	17	0
Aldrete, Mike, California*	1.000	7	7	0	0	7	0
Coleman, Vince, Kansas City	.975	69	109	7	3	119	2
Coleman, Vince, Seattle	.988	38	82	2	1	85	0
James, Chris, Kansas City	1.000	5	9	0	0	9	0
James, Chris, Boston	1.000	8	14	0	0	14	0
Maldonado, Candy, Toronto	.988	58	78	2	1	81	0
Maldonado, Candy, Texas	1.000	11	20	1	0	21	0

Player, Team	Pct.	G	PO	A	E	TC	DP
Newson, Warren, Chicago*	.978	24	44	1	1	46	0
Newson, Warren, Seattle*	.971	23	33	1	1	35	0
Samuel, Juan, Detroit	.750	9	9	0	3	12	0
Samuel, Juan, Kansas City	1.000	5	3	0	0	3	0
Sierra, Ruben, Oakland	.957	62	89	1	4	94	0
Sierra, Ruben, New York	.950	10	18	1	1	20	0
Tartabull, Danny, New York	1.000	18	27	1	0	28	1
Tartabull, Danny, Oakland	1.000	1	1	0	0	1	0

CATCHERS

Player, Team	Pct.	G	PO	A	E	TC	DP	PB
Allanson, Andy, California	.994	35	164	15	1	180	1	3
Alomar, Sandy, Cleveland	.995	61	364	22	2	388	3	4
Borders, Pat, Kansas City	1.000	45	182	18	0	200	3	5
Dalesandro, Mark, California	1.000	8	10	0	0	10	0	0
Devarez, Cesar, Baltimore	1.000	6	14	0	0	14	0	0
Fabregas, Jorge, California	.986	73	391	36	6	433	4	8
Flaherty, John, Detroit	.982	112	569	33	11	613	5	0
Harper, Brian, Oakland	1.000	2	6	0	0	6	0	0
Haselman, Bill, Boston	.989	48	257	16	3	276	0	3
Hatteberg, Scott, Boston	1.000	2	4	0	0	4	0	0
Helfand, Eric, Oakland	.994	36	167	13	1	181	4	0
HOILES, CHRIS, Baltimore	.996	107	659	33	3	695	6	4
Karkovice, Ron, Chicago	.991	113	629	42	6	677	2	7
Knorr, Randy, Toronto	.971	45	243	22	8	273	2	8
Kreuter, Chad, Seattle	.976	23	151	12	4	167	3	3
LaValliere, Mike, Chicago	.996	46	202	20	1	223	1	1
Levis, Jesse, Cleveland	1.000	12	33	5	0	38	1	0
Leyritz, Jim, New York	.993	46	286	18	2	306	2	5
Lyons, Barry, Chicago	.987	16	64	10	1	75	2	4
Macfarlane, Mike, Boston	.993	111	618	49	5	672	8	26
Martinez, Sandy, Toronto	.986	61	329	28	5	362	6	14
Marzano, John, Texas	1.000	2	7	1	0	8	0	0
Matheny, Mike, Milwaukee	.986	80	261	18	4	283	2	10
Mayne, Brent, Kansas City	.995	103	540	40	3	583	11	4
Mercedes, Henry, K.C.	.986	22	62	8	1	71	1	2
Merullo, Matt, Minnesota	.987	46	210	11	3	224	2	3
Myers, Greg, California	.989	61	341	21	4	366	4	1
Nilsson, Dave, Milwaukee	1.000	2	2	0	0	2	0	0
Nokes, Matt, Baltimore	.989	16	83	5	1	89	0	1
Oliver, Joe, Milwaukee	.982	91	408	40	8	456	4	16
Parrish, Lance, Toronto	1.000	67	346	41	0	387	7	9
Pena, Tony, Cleveland	.987	91	508	36	7	551	6	6
Posada, Jorge, New York	1.000	1	1	0	0	1	0	0
Reboulet, Jeff, Minnesota	.000	1	0	0	0	0	0	0
Rodriguez, Ivan, Texas	.990	127	707	67	8	782	8	8
Rowland, Rich, Boston	.977	11	39	3	1	43	2	0
Stanley, Mike, New York	.993	107	651	35	5	691	10	15
Steinbach, Terry, Oakland	.993	111	681	57	5	743	8	3
Surhoff, B.J., Milwaukee	.984	18	57	6	1	64	0	8
Sweeney, Mike, Kansas City	.875	4	7	0	1	8	0	0
Tettleton, Mickey, Texas	1.000	3	5	1	0	6	0	0
Tingley, Ron, Detroit	.991	53	198	19	2	219	2	3
Tremie, Chris, Chicago	.976	9	39	2	1	42	0	0
Tucker, Scooter, Cleveland	.982	17	53	3	1	57	0	1
Turner, Chris, California	1.000	4	17	2	0	19	0	1
Valle, Dave, Texas	.993	29	137	12	1	150	0	2
Walbeck, Matt, Minnesota	.991	113	604	35	6	645	3	8
Widger, Chris, Seattle	1.000	19	61	1	0	62	0	2
Williams, George, Oakland	.956	13	58	7	3	68	0	1
Wilson, Dan, Seattle	.995	119	895	52	5	952	5	8
Zaun, Greg, Baltimore	.987	39	216	13	3	232	4	3

PITCHERS

Player, Team	Pct.	G	PO	A	E	TC	DP
Abbott, Jim, Chi.-Cal.*	1.000	30	8	32	0	40	0
Acre, Mark, Oakland	1.000	43	3	3	0	6	0
Aguilera, Rick, Min.-Bos.	1.000	52	2	8	0	10	0
Ahearne, Pat, Detroit	1.000	4	3	1	0	4	0
Alberro, Jose, Texas	1.000	12	2	4	0	6	0
Alvarez, Wilson, Chicago*	1.000	29	7	31	0	38	1
Anderson, Brian, California*	.909	18	4	16	2	22	0
Anderson, Scott, Kansas City	1.000	6	2	3	0	5	0
Andujar, Luis, Chicago	1.000	5	1	1	0	2	0
Appier, Kevin, Kansas City	1.000	31	16	20	0	36	3
Assenmacher, Paul, Cleveland*	1.000	47	0	5	0	5	1
Ausanio, Joe, New York	1.000	28	4	2	0	6	0
Ayala, Bobby, Seattle	.923	63	6	6	1	13	0
Baker, Scott, Oakland*	.000	1	0	0	0	0	0
Baldwin, James, Chicago	.750	6	0	3	1	4	0
Bankhead, Scott, New York	1.000	20	2	2	0	4	0
Bark, Brian, Boston*	.000	3	0	0	0	0	0
Belcher, Tim, Seattle	.974	28	22	16	1	39	5

Player, Team	Pct.	G	PO	A	E	TC	DP
Belinda, Stan, Boston	1.000	63	3	5	0	8	0
Benes, Andy, Seattle	1.000	12	2	7	0	9	0
Benitez, Armando, Baltimore	.500	44	1	0	1	2	1
Bennett, Erik, California	.000	1	0	0	0	0	0
Bere, Jason, Chicago	1.000	27	10	19	0	29	1
Bergman, Sean, Detroit	.889	28	9	15	3	27	0
Bertotti, Mike, Chicago*	.000	4	0	0	0	0	0
Bielecki, Mike, California	.875	22	6	8	2	16	0
Black, Bud, Cleveland*	1.000	11	0	8	0	8	0
Blomdahl, Ben, Detroit	1.000	14	1	6	0	7	0
Boehringer, Brian, New York	1.000	7	1	0	0	1	0
Boever, Joe, Detroit	.933	60	4	10	1	15	0
Bohanon, Brian, Detroit*	1.000	52	7	13	0	20	0
Bolton, Rodney, Chicago	1.000	8	2	3	0	5	0
Bones, Ricky, Milwaukee	1.000	32	19	32	0	51	8
Borowski, Joe, Baltimore	1.000	6	1	2	0	3	0
Bosio, Chris, Seattle	.972	31	12	23	1	36	3
Boskie, Shawn, California	1.000	20	4	19	0	23	1
Brandenburg, Mark, Texas	1.000	11	1	2	0	3	0
Brewer, Billy, Kansas City*	1.000	48	3	4	0	7	1
Briscoe, John, Oakland	1.000	16	2	2	0	4	1
Bronkey, Jeff, Milwaukee	1.000	8	3	0	0	3	0
Brown, Kevin, Baltimore	.976	26	40	42	2	84	2
Browning, Tom, Kansas City*	1.000	2	0	2	0	2	0
Bunch, Mel, Kansas City	.833	13	2	3	1	6	0
Burrows, Terry, Texas*	1.000	28	3	4	0	7	0
Butcher, Mike, California	1.000	40	4	3	0	7	1
Campbell, Kevin, Minnesota	1.000	6	2	0	0	2	0
Carmona, Rafael, Seattle	.933	15	9	5	1	15	1
Carrara, Giovanni, Toronto	1.000	12	1	3	0	4	0
Castillo, Tony, Toronto*	1.000	55	3	10	0	13	0
Charlton, Norm, Seattle*	1.000	30	2	6	0	8	0
Christopher, Mike, Detroit	1.000	36	4	8	0	12	0
Clark, Mark, Cleveland	1.000	22	8	16	0	24	3
Clark, Terry, Baltimore	.750	38	1	2	1	4	0
Clemens, Roger, Boston	.970	23	13	19	1	33	1
Cone, David, Tor.-N.Y.	.929	30	12	27	3	42	2
Converse, Jim, Sea.-K.C.	1.000	15	1	4	0	5	0
Cook, Dennis, Cle.-Tex.*	1.000	46	0	6	0	6	0
Cormier, Rheal, Boston*	.933	48	7	21	2	30	2
Cornett, Brad, Toronto	1.000	5	0	2	0	2	0
Corsi, Jim, Oakland	1.000	38	3	12	0	15	1
Cox, Danny, Toronto	.800	24	2	6	2	10	1
Crabtree, Tim, Toronto	1.000	31	2	8	0	10	1
Cummings, John, Seattle*	1.000	4	2	1	0	3	1
Darling, Ron, Oakland	1.000	21	10	20	0	30	2
Darwin, Danny, Tor.-Tex.	.833	20	3	7	2	12	1
Davis, Tim, Seattle*	1.000	5	1	8	0	9	0
Davison, Scott, Seattle	1.000	3	0	1	0	1	0
Dedrick, Jim, Baltimore	1.000	6	1	2	0	3	0
DeLeon, Jose, Chicago	.800	38	0	4	1	5	0
DeSilva, John, Baltimore	1.000	2	0	2	0	2	1
Dettmer, John, Texas	.000	1	0	0	0	0	0
Dibble, Rob, Chi.-Mil.	1.000	31	0	2	0	2	0
Doherty, John, Detroit	1.000	48	12	17	0	29	1
Eckersley, Dennis, Oakland	.889	52	3	5	1	9	2
Eddy, Chris, Oakland*	1.000	6	0	1	0	1	0
Edenfield, Ken, California	1.000	7	0	2	0	2	0
Eiland, Dave, New York	1.000	4	3	1	0	4	0
Eldred, Cal, Milwaukee	.800	4	2	2	1	5	0
Embree, Alan, Cleveland*	1.000	23	0	3	0	3	0
Erickson, Scott, Min.-Bal.	.986	32	27	41	1	69	2
Eshelman, Vaughn, Boston*	.933	23	6	8	1	15	1
Fajardo, Hector, Texas	1.000	5	0	3	0	3	1
Farrell, John, Cleveland	.500	1	1	0	1	2	1
Fermin, Ramon, Oakland	.000	1	0	0	0	0	0
Fernandez, Alex, Chicago	.927	30	11	27	3	41	5
Fernandez, Sid, Baltimore*	1.000	8	0	1	0	1	0
Fetters, Mike, Milwaukee	.750	40	2	1	1	4	0
Finley, Chuck, California*	.846	32	4	18	4	26	3
Fleming, Dave, Sea.-K.C.*	1.000	25	5	13	0	18	1
Fortugno, Tim, Chicago*	.800	37	1	7	2	10	0
Frey, Steve, Seattle*	1.000	13	1	4	0	5	0
Gardiner, Mike, Detroit	1.000	9	2	1	0	3	0
Givens, Brian, Milwaukee*	.875	19	3	11	2	16	1
Gohr, Greg, Detroit	1.000	10	0	1	0	1	0
Gordon, Tom, Kansas City	.962	31	25	26	2	53	3
Grimsley, Jason, Cleveland	1.000	15	0	8	0	8	1
Groom, Buddy, Detroit*	.833	23	2	3	1	6	0
Gross, Kevin, Texas	.946	31	15	20	2	37	5
Guardado, Eddie, Minnesota*	.917	51	4	7	1	12	0
GUBICZA, MARK, Kansas City	1.000	33	28	36	0	64	2
Guetterman, Lee, Seattle*	1.000	23	2	5	0	7	1

Player, Team	Pct.	G	PO	A	E	TC	DP
Gunderson, Eric, Boston*	1.000	19	0	3	0	3	0
Guthrie, Mark, Minnesota*	.500	36	0	2	2	4	0
Guzman, Juan, Toronto	.905	24	7	12	2	21	0
Habyan, John, California	.000	28	0	0	0	0	0
Hall, Darren, Toronto	1.000	17	2	1	0	3	0
Hammaker, Atlee, Chicago*	1.000	13	0	2	0	2	0
Haney, Chris, Kansas City*	1.000	16	1	15	0	16	0
Hanson, Erik, Boston	.949	29	17	20	2	39	1
Harikkala, Tim, Seattle	.000	1	0	0	0	0	0
Harkey, Mike, Oak.-Cal.	1.000	26	7	17	0	24	2
Harris, Gene, Baltimore	1.000	3	0	1	0	1	0
Harris, Greg W., Minnesota	1.000	7	7	3	0	10	0
Hartley, Mike, Bos.-Bal.	1.000	8	0	3	0	3	0
Hawkins, LaTroy, Minnesota	1.000	6	3	3	0	6	1
Haynes, Jimmy, Baltimore	1.000	4	0	3	0	3	0
Helling, Rick, Texas	1.000	3	0	1	0	1	0
Henneman, Mike, Detroit	1.000	29	2	1	0	3	0
Henry, Dwayne, Detroit	1.000	10	1	0	0	1	0
Hentgen, Pat, Toronto	.938	30	12	18	2	32	2
Heredia, Wilson, Texas	1.000	6	0	1	0	1	0
Hernandez, Roberto, Chicago	.875	60	2	5	1	8	0
Hershiser, Orel, Cleveland	.959	26	16	31	2	49	1
Hill, Ken, Cleveland	1.000	12	10	15	0	25	1
Hitchcock, Sterling, New York*	1.000	27	4	12	0	16	1
Holzemer, Mark, California*	1.000	12	1	3	0	4	0
Honeycutt, Rick, Oak.-N.Y.*	.889	52	3	5	1	9	0
Horsman, Vince, Minnesota*	1.000	6	1	3	0	4	0
Howard, Chris, Texas*	.000	4	0	0	0	0	0
Howe, Steve, New York*	1.000	56	3	11	0	14	1
Hudson, Joe, Boston	1.000	39	1	6	0	7	1
Huisman, Rick, Kansas City	1.000	7	0	1	0	1	0
Hurtado, Edwin, Toronto	1.000	14	5	8	0	13	3
Ignasiak, Mike, Milwaukee	1.000	25	3	2	0	5	1
Jacome, Jason, Kansas City*	.963	15	6	20	1	27	2
James, Mike, California	1.000	46	2	8	0	10	0
Johns, Doug, Oakland*	.944	11	6	11	1	18	0
Johnson, Randy, Seattle*	.969	30	7	24	1	32	0
Johnston, Joel, Boston	.000	4	0	0	0	0	0
Jones, Doug, Baltimore	.909	52	4	6	1	11	2
Jordan, Ricardo, Toronto*	1.000	15	1	2	0	3	0
Kamieniecki, Scott, New York	1.000	17	3	10	0	13	2
Karchner, Matt, Chicago	1.000	31	6	3	0	9	2
Karl, Scott, Milwaukee*	.897	25	5	21	3	29	3
Key, Jimmy, New York*	1.000	5	4	3	0	7	2
Keyser, Brian, Chicago	.963	23	9	17	1	27	1
Kiefer, Mark, Milwaukee	1.000	24	0	3	0	3	1
King, Kevin, Seattle*	.000	2	0	0	1	1	0
Klingenbeck, Scott, Bal.-Min.	.947	24	8	10	1	19	0
Krivda, Rick, Baltimore*	.875	13	0	7	1	8	0
Krueger, Bill, Seattle*	1.000	6	0	1	0	1	1
Langston, Mark, California*	.938	31	2	43	3	48	2
Lee, Mark, Baltimore*	.750	39	2	1	1	4	0
Leiper, Dave, Oakland*	1.000	24	1	2	0	3	0
Leiter, Al, Toronto*	1.000	28	7	15	0	22	2
Lilliquist, Derek, Boston*	1.000	28	2	2	0	4	0
Lima, Jose, Detroit	1.000	15	5	2	0	7	0
Linton, Doug, Kansas City	1.000	7	0	5	0	5	0
Lira, Felipe, Detroit	1.000	37	13	15	0	28	1
Lloyd, Graeme, Milwaukee*	1.000	33	2	7	0	9	0
Looney, Brian, Boston*	1.000	3	0	1	0	1	0
Lopez, Albie, Cleveland	1.000	6	1	2	0	3	0
Lorraine, Andrew, Chicago*	1.000	5	1	0	0	1	0
MacDonald, Bob, New York*	1.000	33	2	4	0	6	0
Maddux, Mike, Boston	.952	36	9	11	1	21	1
Magnante, Mike, Kansas City*	.895	28	8	9	2	19	3
Mahomes, Pat, Minnesota	1.000	47	10	9	0	19	3
Manzanillo, Josias, New York	1.000	11	1	3	0	4	1
Marquez, Isidro, Chicago	1.000	7	1	0	0	1	0
Martinez, Dave, Chicago*	.000	1	0	0	0	0	0
Martinez, Dennis, Cleveland	.938	28	15	46	4	65	3
Maxcy, Brian, Detroit	.909	41	6	14	2	22	1
McAndrew, Jamie, Milwaukee	.857	10	3	3	1	7	0
McCaskill, Kirk, Chicago	.900	55	5	13	2	20	0
McDonald, Ben, Baltimore	.947	14	5	13	1	19	0
McDowell, Jack, New York	.978	30	17	27	1	45	1
McDowell, Roger, Texas	.966	64	8	20	1	29	3
Meacham, Rusty, Kansas City	.933	49	5	9	1	15	3
Mecir, Jim, Seattle	.000	2	0	0	0	0	0
Menhart, Paul, Toronto	.929	21	2	11	1	14	1
Mercedes, Jose, Milwaukee	.000	5	0	0	0	0	0
Mesa, Jose, Cleveland	.941	62	6	10	1	17	0
Mills, Alan, Baltimore	1.000	21	0	1	0	1	0
Miranda, Angel, Milwaukee*	1.000	30	5	9	0	14	1
Mohler, Mike, Oakland*	1.000	28	2	2	0	4	0
Monteleone, Rich, California	1.000	9	0	1	0	1	0
Montgomery, Jeff, Kansas City	.944	54	13	4	1	18	1
Moore, Mike, Detroit	.971	25	14	20	1	35	3
Moyer, Jamie, Baltimore*	1.000	27	6	21	0	27	4
Munoz, Oscar, Minnesota	1.000	10	1	3	0	4	0
Murray, Matt, Boston	1.000	2	0	1	0	1	1
Mussina, Mike, Baltimore	.950	32	12	26	2	40	3
Myers, Mike, Detroit*	1.000	11	1	1	0	2	0
Nagy, Charles, Cleveland	.981	29	19	34	1	54	5
Nelson, Jeff, Seattle	.917	62	1	10	1	12	1
Nichting, Chris, Texas	1.000	13	5	7	0	12	0
Nitkowski, C.J., Detroit*	.889	11	2	6	1	9	0
Ogea, Chad, Cleveland	1.000	20	3	14	0	17	1
Oliver, Darren, Texas*	1.000	17	4	8	0	12	1
Olson, Gregg, Cle.-K.C.	1.000	23	1	5	0	6	0
Ontiveros, Steve, Oakland	1.000	22	17	26	0	43	4
Oquist, Mike, Baltimore	1.000	27	1	8	0	9	0
Orosco, Jesse, Baltimore*	1.000	65	3	8	0	11	1
Parra, Jose, Minnesota	.857	12	4	8	2	14	1
Patterson, Bob, California*	1.000	62	0	4	0	4	0
Patterson, Jeff, New York	.000	3	0	0	0	0	0
Pavlas, Dave, New York	.000	4	0	0	0	0	0
Pavlik, Roger, Texas	.981	31	20	32	1	53	4
Pena, Alejandro, Boston	1.000	17	1	1	0	2	0
Pennington, Brad, Baltimore*	.000	8	0	0	0	0	0
Percival, Troy, California	1.000	62	2	4	0	6	0
Perez, Melido, New York	.889	13	4	4	1	9	0
Pettitte, Andy, New York*	.970	31	5	27	1	33	0
Phoenix, Steve, Oakland	.000	1	0	0	0	0	0
Pichardo, Hipolito, K.C.	1.000	44	2	12	0	14	1
Pierce, Jeff, Boston	1.000	12	0	2	0	2	0
Pittsley, Jim, Kansas City	.000	1	0	0	0	0	0
Plunk, Eric, Cleveland	1.000	56	2	7	0	9	1
Poole, Jim, Cleveland*	.917	42	2	9	1	12	0
Prieto, Ariel, Oakland	.889	14	0	8	1	9	0
Radinsky, Scott, Chicago*	1.000	46	3	5	0	8	1
Radke, Brad, Minnesota	1.000	29	17	20	0	37	1
Rasmussen, Dennis, K.C.*	.000	5	0	0	0	0	0
Reyes, Al, Milwaukee	1.000	27	0	6	0	6	0
Reyes, Carlos, Oakland	1.000	40	3	13	0	16	0
Rhodes, Arthur, Baltimore*	.833	19	3	7	2	12	0
Righetti, Dave, Chicago*	.833	10	0	5	1	6	1
Rightnowar, Ron, Milwaukee	1.000	34	0	9	0	9	1
Risley, Bill, Seattle	1.000	45	2	3	0	5	0
Rivera, Mariano, New York	1.000	19	2	14	0	16	1
Roa, Joe, Cleveland	1.000	1	2	2	0	4	0
Roberson, Sid, Milwaukee*	.700	26	2	5	3	10	0
Robertson, Rich, Minnesota*	.875	25	3	4	1	8	0
Robinson, Ken, Toronto	1.000	21	2	1	0	3	0
Rodriguez, Frank, Bos.-Min.	1.000	25	12	23	0	35	3
Rogers, Jimmy, Toronto	1.000	19	0	2	0	2	0
Rogers, Kenny, Texas*	.958	31	11	35	2	48	3
Ruffcorn, Scott, Chicago	1.000	4	1	2	0	3	0
Russell, Jeff, Texas	1.000	37	2	2	0	4	0
Ryan, Ken, Boston	.667	28	1	1	1	3	1
Sanderson, Scott, California	1.000	7	3	4	0	7	1
Sanford, Mo, Minnesota	.000	11	0	0	0	0	0
Scanlan, Bob, Milwaukee	.909	17	6	14	2	22	1
Schullstrom, Erik, Minnesota	1.000	37	1	6	0	7	0
Sele, Aaron, Boston	.700	6	2	5	3	10	0
Shaw, Jeff, Chicago	1.000	9	1	2	0	3	1
Shepherd, Keith, Boston	1.000	2	0	1	0	1	0
Shuey, Paul, Cleveland	1.000	7	0	2	0	2	0
Simas, Bill, Chicago	.000	14	0	0	0	0	0
Sirotka, Mike, Chicago*	1.000	6	1	5	0	6	0
Slusarski, Joe, Milwaukee	1.000	12	2	1	0	3	0
Smith, Lee, California	1.000	52	1	4	0	5	0
Smith, Zane, Boston*	.958	24	5	18	1	24	1
Sodowsky, Clint, Detroit	1.000	6	2	1	0	3	0
Sparks, Steve, Milwaukee	.971	33	25	43	2	70	5
Springer, Russ, California	1.000	19	0	6	0	6	1
Stanton, Mike, Boston*	.667	22	1	3	2	6	0
Stevens, Dave, Minnesota	.941	56	9	7	1	17	1
Stewart, Dave, Oakland	1.000	16	5	11	0	16	0
Stottlemyre, Todd, Oakland	.944	31	16	18	2	36	1
Suppan, Jeff, Boston	1.000	8	2	2	0	4	0
Tapani, Kevin, Minnesota	1.000	20	16	11	0	27	1
Tavarez, Julian, Cleveland	.900	57	7	11	2	20	1
Taylor, Scott, Texas	1.000	3	1	3	0	4	2
Tewksbury, Bob, Texas	.973	21	12	24	1	37	3

Player, Team	Pct.	G	PO	A	E	TC	DP
Thomas, Larry, Chicago*	1.000	17	2	0	0	2	0
Thomas, Mike, Milwaukee*	.000	1	0	0	0	0	0
Timlin, Mike, Toronto	1.000	31	1	9	0	10	1
Torres, Dilson, Kansas City	1.000	24	6	12	0	18	1
Torres, Salomon, Seattle	1.000	16	7	15	0	22	1
Trombley, Mike, Minnesota	.950	20	9	10	1	20	2
Vanegmond, Tim, Boston	1.000	4	1	1	0	2	0
Van Poppel, Todd, Oakland	.938	36	4	11	1	16	0
Villone, Ron, Seattle*	.667	19	0	2	1	3	0
Vosberg, Ed, Texas*	.500	44	0	1	1	2	0
Wakefield, Tim, Boston	.943	27	15	18	2	35	4
Ward, Duane, Toronto	.000	4	0	0	1	1	0
Ware, Jeff, Toronto	1.000	5	2	4	0	6	1
Wasdin, John, Oakland	1.000	5	1	0	0	1	0
Watkins, Scott, Minnesota	1.000	27	1	4	0	5	0
Wegman, Bill, Milwaukee	.933	37	9	5	1	15	0
Wells, Bob, Seattle	1.000	30	7	8	0	15	0
Wells, David, Detroit*	.931	18	11	16	2	29	1
Wengert, Don, Oakland	1.000	19	3	1	0	4	0
Wetteland, John, New York	.833	60	2	3	1	6	1
Whiteside, Matt, Texas	1.000	40	0	5	0	5	0
Whiteside, Sean, Detroit*	.000	2	0	0	0	0	0
Wickander, Kevin, Det.-Mil.*	1.000	29	1	4	0	5	0
Wickman, Bob, New York	.944	63	4	13	1	18	1
Williams, Mitch, California*	1.000	20	1	1	0	2	0
Williams, Woody, Toronto	1.000	23	6	6	0	12	0
Willis, Carl, Minnesota	.000	3	0	0	0	0	0
Witt, Bobby, Texas	1.000	10	1	6	0	7	0
Wojciechowski, Steve, Oak.*	1.000	14	1	8	0	9	0
Wolcott, Bob, Seattle	1.000	7	4	1	0	5	0

TRIPLE PLAY: Nelson, Sea.

PITCHERS WITH TWO OR MORE TEAMS

Player, Team	Pct.	G	PO	A	E	TC	DP
Abbott, Jim, Chicago*	1.000	17	5	16	0	21	0
Abbott, Jim, California*	1.000	13	3	16	0	19	0
Aguilera, Rick, Minnesota	1.000	22	2	2	0	4	0
Aguilera, Rick, Boston	1.000	30	0	6	0	6	0
Cone, David, Toronto	.920	17	5	18	2	25	2
Cone, David, New York	.941	13	7	9	1	17	0
Converse, Jim, Seattle	1.000	6	0	1	0	1	0
Converse, Jim, Kansas City	1.000	9	1	3	0	4	0
Cook, Dennis, Cleveland*	1.000	11	0	2	0	2	0
Cook, Dennis, Texas*	1.000	35	0	4	0	4	0
Darwin, Danny, Toronto	.778	13	3	4	2	9	0
Darwin, Danny, Texas	1.000	7	0	3	0	3	1
Dibble, Rob, Chicago	1.000	16	0	2	0	2	0
Dibble, Rob, Milwaukee	.000	15	0	0	0	0	0
Erickson, Scott, Minnesota	1.000	15	8	19	0	27	0
Erickson, Scott, Baltimore	.976	17	19	22	1	42	2
Fleming, Dave, Seattle*	1.000	16	4	6	0	10	0
Fleming, Dave, Kansas City*	1.000	9	1	7	0	8	1
Harkey, Mike, Oakland	1.000	14	4	12	0	16	2
Harkey, Mike, California	1.000	12	3	5	0	8	0
Hartley, Mike, Boston	1.000	5	0	1	0	1	0
Hartley, Mike, Baltimore	1.000	3	0	2	0	2	0
Honeycutt, Rick, Oakland*	.889	49	3	5	1	9	0
Honeycutt, Rick, New York*	.000	3	0	0	0	0	0
Klingenbeck, Scott, Baltimore	1.000	6	3	8	0	11	0
Klingenbeck, Scott, Minnesota	.875	18	5	2	1	8	0
Olson, Gregg, Cleveland	.000	3	0	0	0	0	0
Olson, Gregg, Kansas City	1.000	20	1	5	0	6	0
Rodriguez, Frank, Boston	1.000	9	1	4	0	5	0
Rodriguez, Frank, Minnesota	1.000	16	11	19	0	30	3
Wickander, Kevin, Detroit*	1.000	21	1	4	0	5	0
Wickander, Kevin, Milwaukee*	.000	8	0	0	0	0	0

MISCELLANEOUS

SHUTOUT GAMES

Read across for wins, down for losses.

Team	Bos.	Sea.	Cle.	K.C.	Cal.	Bal.	Tor.	N.Y.	Chi.	Mil.	Oak.	Tex.	Det.	Min.	W	L	Pct.
Boston	..	0	0	0	0	2	1	1	1	1	1	0	0	2	9	1	.900
Seattle	0	..	0	1	0	2	1	1	0	0	1	1	1	0	8	2	.800
Cleveland	0	0	..	2	0	1	1	1	0	0	2	1	1	1	10	3	.769
Kansas City	0	0	0	..	2	0	1	0	3	0	1	1	0	2	10	7	.588
California	0	2	0	1	..	0	2	1	0	2	0	1	0	0	9	7	.563
Baltimore	0	0	0	0	2	..	3	1	0	1	0	0	3	0	10	8	.556
Toronto	0	0	2	0	1	0	..	0	0	2	1	0	1	1	8	10	.444
New York	0	0	1	1	0	2	0	..	0	0	1	0	0	0	5	7	.417
Chicago	0	0	0	2	0	0	0	0	..	0	0	0	2	0	4	6	.400
Milwaukee	0	0	0	0	0	1	1	0	0	..	0	1	1	0	4	8	.333
Oakland	0	0	0	0	2	0	0	1	1	0	..	0	0	0	4	8	.333
Texas	0	0	0	0	0	0	0	1	1	1	0	..	1	0	4	8	.333
Detroit	1	0	0	0	0	0	0	0	0	0	1	0	1	..	0	3	9	.250
Minnesota	0	0	0	0	0	0	0	0	0	0	0	0	2	0	..	2	6	.250
Lost	1	2	3	7	7	8	10	7	6	8	8	8	9	6	90	90	.500

HOME RECORD

Read across for home wins, down for road losses.

Team	Cle.	N.Y.	Sea.	Bos.	Tex.	Cal.	Chi.	Oak.	Bal.	Det.	K.C.	Mil.	Min.	Tor.	W	L	Pct.
Cleveland	..	2	3	4	2	1	6	4	6	6	6	4	4	6	54	18	.750
New York	2	..	3	6	5	4	0	3	4	4	3	3	2	7	46	26	.639
Seattle	2	6	..	3	5	4	5	4	3	5	3	1	4	1	46	27	.630
Boston	3	4	4	..	1	5	3	3	6	3	1	3	3	3	42	30	.583
Texas	2	3	2	1	..	4	3	4	0	4	4	4	5	5	41	31	.569
California	2	5	4	1	4	..	5	5	2	2	1	1	4	3	39	33	.542
Chicago	4	1	3	0	2	1	..	4	0	4	4	5	5	5	38	34	.528
Oakland	0	5	5	2	3	5	3	..	3	2	3	1	4	2	38	34	.528
Baltimore	2	4	3	4	2	4	2	2	..	5	2	2	1	3	36	36	.500
Detroit	3	3	4	1	2	0	2	2	4	..	3	5	3	3	35	37	.486
Kansas City	1	2	4	1	5	2	2	1	2	3	..	6	2	4	35	37	.486
Milwaukee	1	2	1	1	3	0	5	4	1	4	2	..	6	3	33	39	.458
Minnesota	2	1	2	2	3	3	2	3	4	2	2	3	..	0	29	43	.403
Toronto	2	1	1	2	2	1	4	4	2	3	3	2	2	..	29	43	.403
Lost on road	26	39	39	28	39	34	42	43	37	47	37	40	45	45	541	468	.536

ROAD RECORD

Read across for road wins, down for home losses.

Team	Cle.	Bos.	Cal.	Bal.	K.C.	N.Y.	Sea.	Tex.	Mil.	Chi.	Oak.	Min.	Tor.	Det.	W	L	Pct.
Cleveland	..	3	1	4	5	4	2	4	5	2	3	5	4	4	46	26	.639
Boston	3	..	6	3	2	1	3	2	5	2	5	2	5	5	44	28	.611
California	1	2	..	2	4	2	3	2	4	5	1	4	5	4	39	34	.534
Baltimore	0	0	5	..	2	2	3	2	5	4	3	2	4	3	35	37	.486
Kansas City	0	1	5	3	..	1	3	3	4	3	4	4	3	1	35	37	.486
New York	4	3	2	1	3	..	1	1	3	2	1	2	5	4	33	39	.458
Seattle	2	2	2	4	2	3	..	5	1	4	2	4	2	0	33	39	.458
Texas	1	3	3	1	2	0	1	..	3	4	4	3	4	4	33	39	.458
Milwaukee	3	3	2	4	0	3	2	2	..	2	3	3	4	1	32	40	.444
Chicago	1	3	1	1	4	2	1	3	1	..	3	5	1	4	30	42	.417
Oakland	0	2	2	4	5	4	2	2	1	2	..	3	1	1	29	43	.403
Minnesota	2	2	2	2	5	2	2	2	1	1	2	..	1	3	27	45	.375
Toronto	1	3	1	4	2	0	3	1	3	1	3	2	..	1	27	45	.375
Detroit	0	4	2	1	0	2	1	2	3	2	0	4	4	..	25	47	.347
Lost at home	18	30	33	36	37	26	27	31	39	34	34	43	43	37	468	541	.464

PITCHING AGAINST EACH CLUB

BALTIMORE—71-73

Pitcher	Bos. W-L	Cal. W-L	Chi. W-L	Cle. W-L	Det. W-L	K.C. W-L	Mil. W-L	Min. W-L	N.Y. W-L	Oak. W-L	Sea. W-L	Tex. W-L	Tor. W-L	Totals W-L
Benitez	0-1	0-0	0-0	0-1	0-0	0-0	0-0	0-1	0-0	0-1	0-1	0-0	1-0	1-5
K. Brown	0-1	1-0	0-0	0-4	2-1	0-0	1-1	1-0	1-0	2-0	1-2	0-0	1-0	10-9
Clark	0-1	0-0	1-0	0-0	0-0	0-0	1-0	0-0	0-0	0-2	0-0	0-0	0-2	2-5
DeSilva	0-0	0-0	0-0	0-0	0-0	0-0	1-0	0-0	0-0	0-0	0-0	0-0	0-0	1-0
Erickson	0-1	2-0	2-0	1-0	1-0	1-0	0-1	0-1	1-0	0-1	0-0	0-0	1-0	9-4
Fernandez	0-1	0-0	0-0	0-0	0-0	0-0	0-0	0-0	0-1	0-1	0-1	0-0	0-1	0-4
Hartley	1-0	0-0	0-0	0-0	0-0	0-0	0-0	0-0	0-0	0-0	0-0	0-0	0-0	1-0
Haynes	0-1	0-0	0-0	0-0	1-0	0-0	0-0	0-0	0-0	0-0	0-0	0-0	0-0	2-1
Jones	0-0	0-0	0-0	0-0	0-1	0-1	0-1	0-0	0-0	0-0	0-0	0-0	0-1	0-4
Klingenbeck	0-0	1-0	0-0	0-1	0-0	0-0	0-0	0-1	1-0	0-0	0-0	0-0	0-0	2-2

Pitcher	Bos. W-L	Cal. W-L	Chi. W-L	Cle. W-L	Det. W-L	K.C. W-L	Mil. W-L	Min. W-L	N.Y. W-L	Oak. W-L	Sea. W-L	Tex. W-L	Tor. W-L	Totals W-L
Krivda	0-1	0-0	0-0	0-1	0-1	0-0	0-1	0-0	0-2	1-0	1-1	0-0	0-0	2-7
Lee	1-0	0-0	0-0	0-0	0-0	0-0	0-0	0-0	0-0	0-0	0-0	1-0	0-0	2-0
McDonald	0-0	2-0	0-0	0-0	1-1	0-1	0-0	0-1	0-1	0-0	0-2	0-0	0-0	3-6
Mills	0-0	0-0	0-0	0-0	0-0	0-0	1-0	0-0	1-0	0-0	1-0	0-0	0-0	3-0
Moyer	0-0	0-2	1-0	0-0	0-0	1-1	1-0	0-0	1-1	1-1	1-0	1-0	1-1	8-6
Mussina	1-1	2-1	2-0	1-1	3-1	1-0	1-1	1-0	0-2	1-1	2-1	1-0	3-0	19-9
Oquist	0-0	0-0	0-1	0-0	0-0	1-0	0-0	0-0	1-0	0-0	0-0	0-0	0-0	2-1
Orosco	0-1	1-0	0-0	0-1	0-0	0-1	0-0	0-0	0-0	0-0	0-0	1-1	0-0	2-4
Pennington	0-0	0-0	0-0	0-0	0-0	0-0	0-0	0-1	0-0	0-0	0-0	0-0	0-0	0-1
Rhodes	1-0	0-1	0-0	0-1	0-0	0-1	0-0	1-1	0-0	0-0	0-0	0-0	0-1	2-5
Totals	4-9	9-4	6-1	2-10	8-5	4-5	7-5	3-6	6-7	5-7	6-7	4-1	7-6	71-73

NO-DECISIONS: Borowski, Dedrick, Harris.

BOSTON—86-58

Pitcher	Bal. W-L	Cal. W-L	Chi. W-L	Cle. W-L	Det. W-L	K.C. W-L	Mil. W-L	Min. W-L	N.Y. W-L	Oak. W-L	Sea. W-L	Tex. W-L	Tor. W-L	Totals W-L
Aguilera	1-0	0-0	0-1	0-0	0-0	0-0	0-0	0-0	0-0	1-0	0-0	0-0	0-1	2-2
Belinda	1-0	0-0	0-0	1-0	1-0	0-0	0-0	1-1	0-0	0-0	2-0	0-0	2-0	8-1
Clemens	2-0	3-0	0-0	0-1	0-1	1-0	1-1	0-1	0-0	2-0	0-0	0-1	1-0	10-5
Cormier	2-0	0-1	1-1	0-0	0-0	0-0	1-0	0-0	0-1	0-1	2-1	0-0	1-0	7-5
Eshelman	0-1	1-0	0-0	0-2	1-0	0-0	1-0	0-0	2-0	0-0	0-0	0-0	1-0	6-3
Gunderson	0-1	1-0	0-0	0-0	0-0	0-0	0-0	0-0	1-0	0-0	0-0	0-0	0-0	2-1
Hanson	1-0	2-0	2-0	3-0	0-1	0-0	2-1	0-0	1-1	2-0	1-0	0-2	1-0	15-5
Hudson	0-1	0-0	0-0	0-0	0-0	0-0	0-0	0-0	0-0	0-0	0-0	0-0	0-0	0-1
Johnston	0-0	0-0	0-0	0-0	0-0	0-0	0-0	0-0	0-1	0-0	0-0	0-0	0-0	0-1
Lilliquist	0-0	0-0	0-0	0-0	1-0	0-0	0-0	0-0	0-1	0-0	0-0	0-0	1-0	2-1
Looney	0-0	0-1	0-0	0-0	0-0	0-0	0-0	0-0	0-0	0-0	0-0	0-0	0-0	0-1
Maddux	0-0	0-0	0-0	0-0	0-0	0-0	1-0	0-0	0-0	0-1	1-0	1-0	1-0	4-1
Murray	0-0	0-0	0-0	0-0	0-1	0-0	0-0	0-0	0-0	0-0	0-0	0-0	0-0	0-1
Pena	0-0	0-0	0-0	0-1	0-0	0-0	0-0	0-0	1-0	0-0	0-0	0-0	0-0	1-1
Pierce	0-0	0-0	0-0	0-1	0-0	0-0	0-0	0-0	0-1	0-0	0-1	0-0	0-0	0-3
F. Rodriguez	0-0	0-0	0-1	0-0	0-0	0-1	0-0	0-0	0-0	0-0	0-0	0-0	0-0	0-2
Ryan	0-0	0-0	0-0	0-2	0-0	0-0	0-0	0-0	0-0	0-0	0-0	0-0	0-1	0-4
Sele	0-0	0-0	0-0	0-0	1-0	0-0	1-0	1-0	0-1	0-0	0-0	0-0	0-0	3-1
Smith	0-1	1-0	1-0	0-0	2-0	1-0	1-0	1-1	0-1	1-2	0-1	0-1	0-1	8-8
Stanton	0-0	1-0	0-0	0-0	0-0	0-0	0-0	0-0	0-0	0-0	0-0	0-0	0-0	1-0
Suppan	0-0	0-0	0-0	1-0	0-0	0-0	0-1	0-0	0-1	0-0	0-0	0-0	0-0	1-2
Vanegmond	0-0	0-1	0-0	0-0	0-0	0-0	0-0	0-0	0-0	0-0	0-0	0-0	0-0	0-1
Wakefield	2-0	0-0	1-0	1-0	2-1	1-0	0-2	2-0	0-1	2-0	1-2	2-0	0-2	16-8
Totals	9-4	11-3	5-3	6-7	8-5	3-2	8-4	5-4	5-8	8-4	7-5	3-4	8-5	86-58

NO-DECISIONS: Bark, Hartley, Shepherd.

CALIFORNIA—78-67

Pitcher	Bal. W-L	Bos. W-L	Chi. W-L	Cle. W-L	Det. W-L	K.C. W-L	Mil. W-L	Min. W-L	N.Y. W-L	Oak. W-L	Sea. W-L	Tex. W-L	Tor. W-L	Totals W-L
Abbott	1-0	0-0	0-0	0-0	0-0	1-1	1-0	1-0	0-2	0-0	0-1	1-0	0-0	5-4
B. Anderson	0-2	0-1	0-1	1-0	1-0	1-0	1-0	0-0	0-1	0-1	1-1	0-1	1-0	6-8
Bielecki	0-1	0-2	2-0	0-0	0-0	0-1	0-1	1-0	0-0	1-0	0-0	0-1	0-0	4-6
Boskie	1-1	0-1	1-0	0-0	0-0	0-2	0-0	2-0	1-0	0-1	1-1	0-0	1-1	7-7
Butcher	0-0	1-0	0-0	0-0	0-0	1-0	0-0	0-1	0-0	1-0	0-0	0-0	3-0	6-1
Finley	1-0	1-2	1-0	1-0	1-1	0-0	1-1	1-1	3-1	1-2	1-2	1-2	1-0	15-12
Habyan	0-0	0-1	0-0	0-0	0-1	0-0	0-0	0-0	0-0	1-0	0-0	0-0	0-0	1-2
Harkey	0-1	0-1	0-0	1-0	0-0	0-0	0-0	0-1	0-0	1-0	1-0	1-0	0-0	4-3
Holzemer	0-0	0-0	0-0	0-0	0-0	0-0	0-0	0-1	0-0	0-0	0-0	0-0	0-0	0-1
James	0-0	0-0	1-0	0-0	1-0	0-0	0-0	1-0	0-0	0-0	0-0	0-0	0-0	3-0
Langston	1-1	1-1	2-0	0-0	1-0	1-2	2-0	1-0	2-1	0-0	1-1	2-1	1-0	15-7
Monteleone	0-0	0-0	0-0	0-0	0-0	0-0	0-0	1-0	0-0	0-0	0-0	0-0	0-0	1-0
Patterson	0-1	0-0	2-0	0-0	1-0	0-1	0-0	0-0	1-0	0-0	1-0	0-0	0-0	5-2
Percival	0-0	0-0	1-1	0-0	1-0	0-0	0-0	0-0	0-0	1-1	0-0	0-0	0-0	3-2
Sanderson	0-1	0-0	0-0	0-0	0-0	0-0	0-1	0-0	0-0	0-0	0-0	1-0	0-1	1-3
Smith	0-0	0-1	0-0	0-2	0-0	0-0	0-0	0-0	0-0	0-0	0-1	0-0	0-1	0-5
Springer	0-1	0-0	0-0	0-0	0-0	0-0	0-0	0-0	0-0	0-0	0-0	0-0	1-0	1-2
Williams	0-0	0-1	0-0	0-0	0-0	0-0	0-0	0-0	0-0	0-1	1-0	0-0	0-0	1-2
Totals	4-9	3-11	10-2	3-2	6-2	5-7	5-2	8-5	7-5	6-7	7-6	6-7	8-2	78-67

NO-DECISIONS: Bennett, Edenfield.

CHICAGO—68-76

Pitcher	Bal. W-L	Bos. W-L	Cal. W-L	Cle. W-L	Det. W-L	K.C. W-L	Mil. W-L	Min. W-L	N.Y. W-L	Oak. W-L	Sea. W-L	Tex. W-L	Tor. W-L	Totals W-L
Abbott	0-1	0-0	0-0	0-1	0-0	0-0	1-1	2-0	0-0	0-0	1-1	0-0	1-0	6-4
Alvarez	0-1	0-1	0-1	0-1	0-0	1-2	3-0	1-0	1-0	0-0	0-3	1-2	1-0	8-11
Andujar	0-0	0-0	1-0	0-1	0-0	0-0	0-0	0-0	0-0	1-0	0-0	0-0	0-0	2-1
Baldwin	0-0	0-0	0-0	0-0	0-0	0-1	0-0	0-0	0-0	0-0	0-0	0-0	0-0	0-1
Bere	0-2	1-1	0-2	2-2	1-0	0-0	0-1	1-2	0-0	0-3	0-1	1-1	2-0	8-15
Bertotti	1-0	0-0	0-0	0-0	0-1	0-0	0-0	0-0	0-0	0-0	0-0	0-0	0-0	1-1
Bolton	0-0	0-0	0-1	0-0	0-0	0-0	0-0	0-0	0-0	0-0	0-0	0-1	0-0	0-2
DeLeon	0-0	1-0	0-0	1-1	1-0	0-0	0-0	0-0	0-0	2-1	0-0	0-1	0-0	5-3
Dibble	0-0	0-0	0-1	0-0	0-0	0-0	0-0	0-0	0-0	0-0	0-0	0-0	0-0	0-1
Fernandez	0-1	0-1	1-0	1-2	2-0	2-0	2-1	1-0	0-1	3-0	0-1	0-1	0-0	12-8
Fortugno	0-1	0-0	0-1	0-0	0-0	1-0	0-1	0-0	0-0	0-0	0-0	0-0	0-0	1-3

Pitcher	Bal. W-L	Bos. W-L	Cal. W-L	Cle. W-L	Det. W-L	K.C. W-L	Mil. W-L	Min. W-L	N.Y. W-L	Oak. W-L	Sea. W-L	Tex. W-L	Tor. W-L	Totals W-L
Hernandez	0-0	0-0	0-0	0-0	1-3	0-0	0-1	1-0	0-0	1-0	0-1	0-0	0-2	3-7
Karchner	0-0	1-0	0-0	0-0	1-0	0-0	0-0	1-0	0-0	0-0	0-1	1-1	0-0	4-2
Keyser	0-0	0-0	0-1	0-0	0-1	2-0	0-2	1-0	0-0	0-0	0-1	1-0	1-1	5-6
Marquez	0-0	0-0	0-0	0-0	0-0	0-0	0-0	0-0	0-0	0-0	0-0	0-0	0-1	0-1
McCaskill	0-0	0-1	0-2	0-0	1-0	0-1	0-0	2-0	0-0	3-0	0-0	0-0	0-0	6-4
Radinsky	0-0	0-0	0-0	0-0	1-0	0-0	0-0	0-0	0-1	0-0	0-0	1-0	0-0	2-1
Righetti	0-0	0-0	0-0	1-0	0-0	1-0	0-0	0-0	1-0	0-1	0-0	0-0	0-1	3-2
Simas	0-0	0-0	0-0	0-0	0-0	0-0	0-0	0-1	0-0	0-0	0-0	0-0	1-0	1-1
Sirotka	0-0	0-0	0-0	0-0	1-0	1-0	0-0	0-0	0-0	0-0	0-0	0-0	0-0	1-2
Totals	1-6	3-5	2-10	5-8	8-4	8-5	6-7	10-3	3-2	7-5	4-9	5-7	6-5	68-76

NO-DECISIONS: Hammaker, Lorraine, Martinez, Ruffcorn, Shaw, L. Thomas.

CLEVELAND—100-44

Pitcher	Bal. W-L	Bos. W-L	Cal. W-L	Chi. W-L	Det. W-L	K.C. W-L	Mil. W-L	Min. W-L	N.Y. W-L	Oak. W-L	Sea. W-L	Tex. W-L	Tor. W-L	Totals W-L
Assenmacher	1-0	1-0	2-0	1-1	0-0	0-0	0-0	0-0	0-0	0-0	0-0	0-1	1-0	6-2
Black	0-0	0-0	0-0	1-1	0-0	0-0	1-0	1-1	1-0	0-0	0-0	0-0	0-0	4-2
Clark	0-1	1-1	0-0	0-0	1-1	2-1	1-1	2-0	0-1	1-0	0-1	0-0	1-0	9-7
Embree	0-0	0-1	0-0	0-0	0-0	1-0	0-0	0-0	0-0	2-0	0-1	0-0	0-0	3-2
Hershiser	3-0	1-1	0-1	2-0	2-2	3-0	0-1	0-0	0-0	1-0	1-1	1-0	2-0	16-6
Hill	0-0	0-0	0-0	1-0	0-0	0-0	1-0	2-0	0-1	0-0	0-0	0-0	0-0	4-1
Martinez	2-0	0-0	0-1	0-1	1-0	1-0	2-1	2-0	0-2	0-0	0-0	2-0	1-0	12-5
Mesa	0-0	0-0	0-0	0-0	1-0	0-0	0-0	0-0	0-0	0-0	1-0	1-0	0-0	3-0
Nagy	1-1	0-0	0-0	2-1	2-0	2-0	0-1	1-1	2-1	1-0	2-0	2-0	1-1	16-6
Ogea	2-0	1-0	0-1	0-0	0-0	1-0	1-0	0-1	1-0	0-0	1-1	0-0	1-0	8-3
Plunk	0-0	2-1	0-0	0-0	1-0	1-0	1-0	0-0	0-0	0-0	1-0	0-0	0-1	6-2
Poole	0-0	0-1	0-0	0-0	0-0	0-0	0-0	1-0	1-1	0-0	0-0	0-1	0-0	3-3
Roa	0-0	0-0	0-0	0-1	0-0	0-0	0-0	0-0	0-0	0-0	0-0	0-0	0-0	0-1
Shuey	0-0	0-1	0-0	0-0	0-0	0-0	0-0	0-0	0-0	0-0	0-0	0-1	0-0	0-2
Tavarez	1-0	0-0	0-0	1-0	2-0	0-0	2-0	0-1	1-0	1-0	0-0	0-0	1-1	10-2
Totals	10-2	7-6	2-3	8-5	10-3	11-1	9-4	9-4	6-6	7-0	5-4	6-3	10-3	100-44

NO-DECISIONS: Cook, Farrell, Grimsley, Lopez, Olson.

DETROIT—60-84

Pitcher	Bal. W-L	Bos. W-L	Cal. W-L	Chi. W-L	Cle. W-L	K.C. W-L	Mil. W-L	Min. W-L	N.Y. W-L	Oak. W-L	Sea. W-L	Tex. W-L	Tor. W-L	Totals W-L
Ahearne	0-0	0-0	0-0	0-0	0-0	0-0	0-0	0-0	0-1	0-0	0-0	0-1	0-0	0-2
Bergman	0-1	1-1	0-1	1-0	0-2	0-0	1-2	2-0	1-0	0-0	0-1	0-2	1-0	7-10
Boever	1-0	1-1	0-2	0-1	0-2	0-0	0-0	0-1	1-0	0-0	1-0	0-0	1-0	5-7
Bohanon	0-0	0-0	0-0	0-0	0-0	0-0	0-0	0-0	0-1	0-0	0-0	0-0	1-0	1-1
Christopher	0-0	0-0	0-0	0-0	0-0	0-0	0-0	0-0	1-0	0-0	2-0	0-0	1-0	4-0
Doherty	0-1	0-0	0-0	0-0	0-1	1-2	1-0	1-1	0-0	0-1	0-1	0-1	2-1	5-9
Gohr	0-0	1-0	0-0	0-0	0-0	0-0	0-0	0-0	0-0	0-0	0-0	0-0	0-0	1-0
Groom	0-0	0-1	0-0	0-0	0-1	0-0	0-0	0-0	0-0	0-0	0-1	1-0	0-0	1-3
Henneman	0-0	0-0	0-0	0-0	0-0	0-0	0-0	0-0	0-0	0-0	0-0	0-0	0-0	0-1
Henry	0-0	0-0	0-0	0-0	0-0	0-0	1-0	0-0	0-0	0-0	0-0	0-0	0-0	0-1
Lima	0-0	1-0	0-1	0-1	0-2	0-0	2-0	0-0	0-2	0-0	0-1	0-1	0-1	3-9
Lira	1-3	1-1	0-1	1-1	1-1	1-1	0-0	1-0	0-3	1-0	0-0	1-1	1-1	9-13
Maxcy	1-0	0-0	0-0	2-1	0-1	0-0	1-1	0-1	0-0	0-0	0-0	0-0	0-1	4-5
Moore	0-0	0-2	1-1	0-0	0-0	0-1	1-2	1-1	0-1	0-2	1-0	1-0	0-2	5-15
Myers	1-0	0-0	0-0	0-0	0-0	0-0	0-0	0-0	0-0	0-0	0-0	0-0	0-0	1-0
Nitkowski	0-0	0-2	0-0	0-0	0-0	0-0	0-0	1-1	0-0	0-0	0-0	0-1	0-0	1-4
Sodowsky	0-2	0-0	0-0	0-0	1-0	0-0	0-0	0-0	0-0	0-0	0-0	1-0	0-0	2-2
Wells	1-1	0-0	1-0	0-0	1-0	1-0	1-0	1-0	2-0	1-0	1-1	0-1	0-0	10-3
Totals	5-8	5-8	2-6	4-8	3-10	3-4	8-5	7-5	5-8	2-3	5-5	4-8	7-6	60-84

NO-DECISIONS: Blomdahl, Gardiner, Whiteside, Wickander.

KANSAS CITY—70-74

Pitcher	Bal. W-L	Bos. W-L	Cal. W-L	Chi. W-L	Cle. W-L	Det. W-L	Mil. W-L	Min. W-L	N.Y. W-L	Oak. W-L	Sea. W-L	Tex. W-L	Tor. W-L	Totals W-L
Anderson	0-0	0-0	0-0	0-0	0-0	1-0	0-0	0-0	0-0	0-0	0-0	0-0	0-0	1-0
Appier	1-1	0-1	3-0	0-0	1-3	0-1	2-0	2-1	1-1	0-0	2-0	1-2	2-0	15-10
Brewer	1-0	0-0	0-1	0-0	0-0	0-0	0-0	0-0	0-1	0-1	1-0	0-1	0-0	2-4
Browning	0-0	0-0	0-1	0-0	0-0	0-0	0-0	0-0	0-0	0-0	0-0	0-0	0-0	0-2
Bunch	0-2	0-0	0-1	1-0	0-0	0-0	0-0	0-0	0-0	0-0	0-0	0-0	0-0	1-3
Converse	0-0	0-0	0-0	0-0	0-0	0-0	0-0	0-0	0-0	1-0	0-0	0-0	0-0	1-0
Fleming	0-0	0-0	0-0	0-0	0-0	0-0	0-0	0-0	0-0	0-0	0-0	0-1	0-0	0-1
Gordon	1-1	0-1	2-1	1-2	0-2	0-1	1-1	0-0	0-1	1-0	1-0	3-1	2-1	12-12
Gubicza	0-0	1-1	0-1	2-2	0-1	1-0	3-1	3-0	0-2	1-1	0-3	1-1	0-1	12-14
Haney	0-0	0-0	0-0	0-0	0-1	0-1	1-0	0-0	0-1	0-1	2-0	0-0	0-0	3-4
Jacome	0-0	0-0	1-0	0-0	0-0	0-0	1-0	0-2	0-0	1-1	0-1	1-0	0-0	4-6
Linton	0-0	0-0	0-0	0-0	0-0	0-0	0-0	0-0	0-0	0-0	0-0	0-0	0-1	0-1
Magnante	0-0	0-0	0-0	0-0	0-0	0-0	0-0	0-0	0-0	0-0	0-0	0-0	1-0	1-0
Meacham	1-0	0-0	0-0	0-0	0-0	0-0	0-0	1-2	0-0	0-0	1-0	0-0	0-1	4-3
Montgomery	0-0	0-0	0-0	0-0	0-1	1-0	1-0	0-0	0-0	0-1	0-0	0-0	0-1	2-3
Olson	1-0	0-0	0-0	0-0	0-1	0-0	0-0	0-0	0-0	0-0	0-1	1-0	1-1	3-3
Pichardo	0-0	1-0	1-0	0-2	0-0	1-0	1-0	0-1	1-0	0-0	1-0	1-1	1-0	8-4
Rasmussen	0-0	0-0	0-0	0-0	0-0	0-0	0-0	0-0	0-0	0-1	0-0	0-0	0-0	0-1
Torres	0-0	0-0	0-0	0-0	0-0	0-0	0-1	1-1	0-0	0-0	0-0	0-0	0-0	1-2
Totals	5-4	2-3	7-5	5-8	1-11	4-3	10-2	6-7	3-7	5-8	7-5	8-6	7-5	70-74

NO-DECISIONS: Huisman, Pittsley.

MILWAUKEE—65-79

Pitcher	Bal. W-L	Bos. W-L	Cal. W-L	Chi. W-L	Cle. W-L	Det. W-L	K.C. W-L	Min. W-L	N.Y. W-L	Oak. W-L	Sea. W-L	Tex. W-L	Tor. W-L	Totals W-L
Bones	1-2	1-3	0-2	1-0	1-1	1-1	0-3	1-0	1-0	0-0	1-0	2-0	0-0	10-12
Dibble	0-0	0-0	0-0	0-0	0-0	0-0	0-0	1-0	0-0	0-0	0-0	0-0	0-1	1-1
Eldred	0-0	0-0	0-0	1-0	0-0	0-0	0-0	0-0	0-0	0-0	0-0	0-0	0-1	1-1
Fetters	0-1	0-0	0-0	0-0	0-0	0-1	0-1	0-0	0-0	0-0	0-0	0-0	0-0	0-3
Givens	0-1	0-0	0-0	1-1	0-1	1-2	1-0	0-0	0-1	0-0	1-0	1-0	0-1	5-7
Ignasiak	1-0	0-0	1-0	0-0	0-0	0-0	0-0	0-0	1-0	0-1	0-0	0-0	1-0	4-1
Karl	1-0	1-1	0-1	0-0	0-0	1-0	0-1	1-1	0-1	1-0	0-1	0-1	1-0	6-7
Kiefer	1-0	0-0	0-0	0-0	0-0	0-0	0-0	0-0	0-0	2-0	0-0	0-1	1-0	4-1
Lloyd	0-0	0-0	0-0	0-0	0-1	0-1	0-2	0-0	0-0	0-0	0-0	0-1	0-0	0-5
Mcandrew	0-0	0-0	0-0	0-1	1-0	0-1	1-0	0-0	0-0	0-0	0-1	0-0	0-0	2-3
Mercedes	0-1	0-0	0-0	0-0	0-0	0-0	0-0	0-0	0-0	0-0	0-0	0-0	0-0	0-1
Miranda	0-1	1-0	0-0	1-0	1-0	0-0	0-0	1-1	0-2	0-0	0-0	0-0	0-1	4-5
Reyes	0-0	0-0	0-0	1-0	0-0	0-0	0-0	0-0	0-1	0-0	0-0	0-0	0-0	1-1
Rightnowar	0-0	0-0	0-0	0-0	1-0	0-1	0-0	0-0	0-0	1-0	0-0	0-0	0-0	2-1
Roberson	0-0	0-0	0-1	0-1	0-1	0-0	0-1	1-0	1-0	2-0	0-0	1-0	1-0	6-4
Scanlan	0-0	0-2	0-0	0-1	0-1	1-0	0-2	3-0	0-0	0-0	0-0	0-1	0-0	4-7
Slusarski	0-0	0-0	0-0	0-0	0-0	0-0	0-0	1-1	0-0	0-0	0-0	0-0	0-0	1-1
Sparks	1-1	1-2	1-0	0-2	0-3	1-0	0-0	0-0	2-0	1-0	0-0	1-2	1-1	9-11
Wegman	0-0	0-0	0-0	2-0	0-1	0-1	0-0	0-0	0-0	0-1	1-0	0-0	2-1	5-7
Totals	5-7	4-8	2-5	7-6	4-9	5-8	2-10	9-4	5-6	7-2	3-2	5-7	7-5	65-79

NO-DECISIONS: Bronkey, Thomas, Wickander.

MINNESOTA—56-88

Pitcher	Bal. W-L	Bos. W-L	Cal. W-L	Chi. W-L	Cle. W-L	Det. W-L	K.C. W-L	Mil. W-L	N.Y. W-L	Oak. W-L	Sea. W-L	Tex. W-L	Tor. W-L	Totals W-L
Aguilera	0-0	0-0	0-0	0-0	0-0	0-0	0-0	0-0	0-0	1-0	0-0	0-1	0-0	1-1
Erickson	1-1	0-1	2-0	0-0	0-2	0-0	0-0	1-1	0-0	0-0	0-1	0-0	0-0	4-6
Guardado	0-0	0-1	0-3	0-1	0-0	0-1	0-0	1-1	1-0	0-0	0-0	2-2	0-0	4-9
Guthrie	1-0	2-0	0-0	0-1	0-1	1-1	1-0	0-0	0-0	0-0	0-0	0-0	0-0	5-3
Harris	0-0	0-0	0-0	0-1	0-2	0-0	0-0	0-0	0-0	0-0	0-0	0-0	0-2	0-5
Hawkins	0-1	0-0	0-0	1-1	0-0	0-0	1-1	0-0	0-0	0-0	0-0	0-0	0-0	2-3
Klingenbeck	0-0	0-0	0-0	0-0	0-0	0-0	0-1	0-0	0-0	0-0	0-0	0-1	0-0	0-2
Mahomes	0-0	0-0	0-2	0-2	1-0	1-0	0-1	0-1	0-1	0-0	1-3	1-1	0-0	4-10
O. Munoz	0-0	0-0	0-0	1-0	0-0	0-0	0-1	0-0	0-0	0-0	1-0	0-0	0-0	2-1
Parra	0-0	0-0	1-1	0-0	1-0	0-0	0-1	0-1	0-0	0-0	0-0	0-1	0-0	1-5
Radke	1-0	1-1	0-1	0-1	2-2	1-2	1-0	0-2	1-1	1-2	2-0	1-2	0-0	11-14
Robertson	0-0	0-0	0-0	1-0	0-0	0-0	1-0	0-0	0-0	0-0	0-0	0-0	0-0	2-0
Rodriguez	1-0	0-1	0-0	0-0	0-1	1-0	0-0	1-1	0-1	0-0	0-1	1-0	1-0	5-6
Stevens	1-0	0-0	1-0	0-1	0-0	0-0	2-0	0-1	0-0	1-1	0-1	0-0	0-0	5-4
Tapani	0-1	1-0	1-1	0-1	0-0	1-0	0-2	0-1	1-1	1-0	0-2	1-1	0-1	6-11
Trombley	1-0	0-1	0-0	0-0	1-1	0-1	1-0	1-1	0-1	0-0	0-2	0-0	0-1	4-8
Totals	6-3	4-5	5-8	3-10	4-9	5-7	7-6	4-9	3-4	5-7	4-8	5-8	1-4	56-88

NO-DECISIONS: Campbell, Horsman, Sanford, Schullstrom, Watkins, Willis.

NEW YORK—79-65

Pitcher	Bal. W-L	Bos. W-L	Cal. W-L	Chi. W-L	Cle. W-L	Det. W-L	K.C. W-L	Mil. W-L	Min. W-L	Oak. W-L	Sea. W-L	Tex. W-L	Tor. W-L	Totals W-L
Ausanio	0-0	1-0	0-0	0-0	0-0	0-0	0-0	0-0	0-0	0-0	0-0	0-0	1-0	2-0
Bankhead	0-0	0-0	0-0	0-0	0-0	0-0	1-0	0-0	0-0	0-0	0-1	0-0	0-0	1-1
Boehringer	0-0	0-0	0-0	0-2	0-0	0-1	0-0	0-0	0-0	0-0	0-0	0-0	0-0	0-3
Cone	1-0	1-0	1-1	0-0	1-1	1-0	0-0	2-0	1-0	0-0	0-0	0-0	1-0	9-2
Eiland	0-0	0-0	0-0	0-0	0-0	0-1	0-0	0-0	0-0	0-0	0-0	1-0	0-0	1-1
Hitchcock	1-1	3-1	1-1	0-0	0-1	1-0	1-0	1-1	0-1	0-2	0-1	0-1	3-0	11-10
Howe	0-0	1-1	0-0	0-0	0-0	0-0	1-0	1-0	0-0	0-0	1-1	1-1	1-0	6-3
Kamieniecki	0-2	0-1	0-0	0-0	1-0	2-0	1-1	0-0	1-1	0-1	1-0	0-0	1-0	7-6
Key	0-0	0-0	0-0	0-0	0-1	0-0	0-0	0-1	0-0	0-0	1-0	0-0	0-0	1-2
MacDonald	0-0	0-0	0-0	0-0	0-0	1-0	0-0	0-0	0-0	0-0	0-1	0-0	0-0	1-1
McDowell	2-0	0-0	1-2	1-1	3-0	1-1	1-1	0-1	1-1	1-2	1-0	2-0	1-1	15-10
Perez	1-1	0-0	1-1	0-0	0-0	1-0	1-0	0-1	0-0	0-0	0-2	0-0	1-0	5-5
Pettitte	2-0	1-0	1-1	0-0	0-1	1-2	2-0	0-1	0-0	1-2	1-1	1-1	2-0	12-9
M. Rivera	0-0	0-0	0-1	1-0	0-0	0-0	0-0	1-0	1-0	2-1	0-1	0-0	0-0	5-3
Wetteland	0-1	0-0	0-0	0-0	0-2	0-0	0-0	0-0	0-0	0-1	0-0	0-0	1-0	1-5
Wickman	0-1	1-2	0-0	0-0	1-0	0-0	0-1	0-0	0-0	0-0	0-0	0-0	0-0	2-4
Totals	7-6	8-5	5-7	2-3	6-6	8-5	7-3	6-5	4-3	4-9	4-9	6-3	12-1	79-65

NO-DECISIONS: Honeycutt, Manzanillo, Patterson, Pavlas.

OAKLAND—67-77

Pitcher	Bal. W-L	Bos. W-L	Cal. W-L	Chi. W-L	Cle. W-L	Det. W-L	K.C. W-L	Mil. W-L	Min. W-L	N.Y. W-L	Sea. W-L	Tex. W-L	Tor. W-L	Totals W-L
Acre	0-0	0-0	0-0	0-1	0-0	0-0	0-0	0-0	1-0	0-0	0-1	0-0	0-0	1-2
Briscoe	0-0	0-0	0-0	0-0	0-0	0-0	0-0	0-0	0-0	0-0	0-1	0-0	0-0	0-1
Corsi	1-0	1-0	0-0	0-0	0-0	0-0	0-1	0-0	0-2	0-0	0-1	0-0	0-0	2-4
Darling	0-0	0-1	0-0	0-0	0-1	1-1	1-2	0-0	0-0	1-0	0-0	0-0	1-2	4-7
Eckersley	0-0	0-0	1-0	0-0	0-2	0-0	0-1	0-1	0-0	1-0	1-1	0-1	1-0	4-6
Harkey	0-2	0-0	0-1	0-0	0-0	0-0	1-0	0-0	0-0	1-1	2-0	0-1	0-1	4-6
Honeycutt	1-1	0-0	0-0	1-0	0-0	0-0	1-0	1-0	0-0	0-0	1-0	0-0	0-0	5-1
Johns	2-0	1-1	1-1	0-0	0-0	0-0	0-0	1-0	0-0	0-0	0-1	0-0	0-0	5-3
Leiper	0-0	0-0	0-0	0-1	0-0	0-0	0-0	0-0	0-0	1-0	0-0	0-0	0-0	1-1
Mohler	0-0	0-0	0-0	0-0	0-0	0-0	0-0	0-0	1-0	0-1	0-0	0-0	0-0	1-1
Ontiveros	0-0	0-1	0-1	3-0	0-1	0-0	1-0	1-1	1-0	1-1	1-0	1-1	0-0	9-6

Pitcher	Bal. W-L	Bos. W-L	Cal. W-L	Chi. W-L	Cle. W-L	Det. W-L	K.C. W-L	Mil. W-L	Min. W-L	N.Y. W-L	Sea. W-L	Tex. W-L	Tor. W-L	Totals W-L
Prieto	0-1	0-0	0-0	0-0	0-2	1-0	0-0	0-0	0-1	0-0	0-0	1-0	0-2	2-6
Reyes	2-0	0-1	1-1	0-1	0-0	0-1	0-0	0-0	0-1	0-0	0-0	1-1	0-0	4-6
Stewart	1-0	0-2	1-0	0-1	0-0	0-0	0-0	0-1	0-1	0-0	0-0	1-1	0-1	3-7
Stottlemyre	0-0	2-1	3-1	0-2	0-1	1-0	2-0	0-1	2-0	2-0	0-1	1-0	1-0	14-7
Van Poppel	0-0	0-1	0-0	1-1	0-0	0-0	0-1	0-1	1-0	1-0	1-0	0-3	0-1	4-8
Wasdin	0-0	0-0	0-1	0-0	0-0	0-0	0-0	0-0	1-0	0-0	0-0	0-0	0-0	1-1
Wengert	0-0	0-0	0-0	0-0	0-0	0-0	0-0	0-1	0-0	0-0	1-0	0-0	0-0	1-1
Wojciechowski	0-1	0-0	0-0	0-0	0-0	0-0	1-0	0-1	0-0	1-1	0-0	0-0	0-0	2-3
Totals	7-5	4-8	7-6	5-7	0-7	3-2	8-5	2-7	7-5	9-4	7-6	5-8	3-7	67-77

NO-DECISIONS: Baker, Eddy, Fermin, Phoenix.

SEATTLE—79-66

Pitcher	Bal. W-L	Bos. W-L	Cal. W-L	Chi. W-L	Cle. W-L	Det. W-L	K.C. W-L	Mil. W-L	Min. W-L	N.Y. W-L	Oak. W-L	Tex. W-L	Tor. W-L	Totals W-L
Ayala	0-0	0-1	0-0	1-0	0-0	1-1	1-0	0-1	0-1	1-0	0-1	2-0	0-0	6-5
Belcher	1-1	1-0	0-3	2-0	1-1	1-0	0-2	0-0	1-0	1-2	0-1	1-1	1-1	10-12
Benes	0-0	1-1	2-0	1-0	0-0	0-0	1-0	0-0	1-0	0-0	0-0	1-1	0-0	7-2
Bosio	2-1	0-1	0-1	1-0	1-2	1-1	0-0	0-1	2-0	1-0	1-0	1-0	0-1	10-8
Carmona	1-0	1-1	0-0	0-0	0-0	0-2	0-0	0-0	0-0	0-0	0-0	0-0	0-1	2-4
Charlton	0-0	0-0	0-0	0-0	0-0	0-0	0-0	0-0	0-0	0-0	1-1	1-0	0-0	2-1
Converse	0-0	0-0	0-0	0-1	0-0	0-0	0-1	0-0	0-0	0-0	0-1	0-0	0-0	0-3
Davis	0-0	0-0	0-0	1-0	0-0	0-0	0-0	0-0	0-1	0-0	0-0	1-0	0-0	2-1
Fleming	0-1	0-0	0-1	0-1	0-0	1-0	0-1	0-0	0-0	0-1	0-0	0-0	0-0	1-5
Frey	0-0	0-1	0-0	0-0	0-1	0-0	0-0	0-0	0-0	0-1	0-0	0-0	0-0	0-3
Johnson	2-0	0-0	3-1	2-0	1-0	1-0	2-0	1-0	1-1	1-0	1-0	2-0	1-0	18-2
Krueger	0-0	0-0	0-0	0-0	0-0	0-0	1-0	0-0	0-0	1-0	0-0	0-0	0-0	2-1
Nelson	1-0	0-1	0-0	0-0	0-0	0-0	0-0	0-0	1-1	3-0	1-1	1-0	0-0	7-3
Risley	0-0	0-0	0-0	0-1	0-0	0-0	0-0	0-0	2-0	0-0	0-0	0-0	0-0	2-1
Torres	0-1	0-1	1-0	1-0	1-1	0-0	0-1	0-1	0-0	0-1	0-0	0-1	0-1	3-8
Villone	0-0	0-0	0-0	0-0	0-0	0-0	0-1	0-0	0-0	0-0	0-1	0-0	0-0	0-2
Wells	0-1	0-0	0-1	0-0	0-0	0-1	1-0	0-0	0-0	1-0	1-0	0-0	1-0	4-3
Wolcott	0-1	2-0	0-0	0-1	0-0	0-0	0-0	0-0	0-0	1-0	0-0	0-0	0-0	3-2
Totals	7-6	5-7	6-7	9-4	4-5	5-5	5-7	2-3	8-4	9-4	6-7	10-3	3-4	79-66

NO-DECISIONS: Cummings, Davison, Guetterman, Harikkala, King, Mecir.

TEXAS—74-70

Pitcher	Bal. W-L	Bos. W-L	Cal. W-L	Chi. W-L	Cle. W-L	Det. W-L	K.C. W-L	Mil. W-L	Min. W-L	N.Y. W-L	Oak. W-L	Sea. W-L	Tor. W-L	Totals W-L
Brandenburg	0-0	0-0	0-0	0-0	0-1	0-0	0-0	0-0	0-0	0-0	0-0	0-0	0-0	0-1
Burrows	0-0	0-0	0-0	0-1	1-0	0-0	1-0	0-0	0-0	0-1	0-0	0-0	0-0	2-2
Cook	0-2	0-0	0-0	0-0	0-0	0-0	0-0	0-0	0-0	0-0	0-0	0-0	0-0	0-2
Darwin	0-0	0-0	0-1	0-0	0-0	1-0	0-0	0-1	1-0	0-0	0-0	0-0	0-0	2-2
Gross	0-0	1-1	0-0	1-1	0-3	2-2	0-2	1-1	0-2	0-0	0-3	2-0	2-0	9-15
Helling	0-0	0-0	0-1	0-0	0-0	0-1	0-0	0-0	0-0	0-0	0-0	0-0	0-0	0-2
Heredia	0-0	0-0	0-0	0-0	0-0	0-0	0-0	0-0	0-0	0-0	0-0	0-1	0-0	0-1
McDowell	0-1	0-0	1-0	2-0	1-0	0-0	0-0	0-0	1-1	0-1	1-0	0-1	1-0	7-4
Oliver	0-0	0-0	0-0	2-0	0-0	1-0	0-0	0-2	1-0	0-0	0-0	0-0	0-0	4-2
Pavlik	0-1	0-1	2-1	1-0	0-0	2-0	1-1	2-0	1-1	1-0	0-0	0-3	0-2	10-10
Rogers	0-0	1-0	3-0	1-0	0-1	2-0	1-1	2-0	2-1	0-2	3-0	1-1	1-1	17-7
Russell	0-0	0-0	0-0	0-0	0-0	0-0	0-0	0-0	0-0	1-0	0-0	0-0	0-0	1-0
Taylor	0-0	0-1	0-1	0-0	0-0	0-0	0-0	0-0	0-0	1-0	0-0	0-0	0-0	1-2
Tewksbury	0-0	0-0	1-1	0-1	0-0	0-1	2-2	0-0	1-0	1-1	1-0	0-1	2-0	8-7
Vosberg	1-0	1-0	0-0	0-1	0-0	0-0	1-2	1-0	0-0	1-0	0-1	0-1	0-0	5-5
Whiteside	0-0	1-0	0-0	0-0	1-1	0-0	0-0	1-0	0-0	0-1	1-1	0-1	1-0	5-4
Witt	0-0	0-0	0-1	0-1	0-0	0-0	0-0	0-1	1-0	0-0	0-0	0-1	2-0	3-4
Totals	1-4	4-3	7-6	7-5	3-6	8-4	6-8	7-5	8-5	3-6	8-5	3-10	9-3	74-70

NO-DECISIONS: Alberro, Dettmer, Fajardo, Howard, Nichting.

TORONTO—56-88

Pitcher	Bal. W-L	Bos. W-L	Cal. W-L	Chi. W-L	Cle. W-L	Det. W-L	K.C. W-L	Mil. W-L	Min. W-L	N.Y. W-L	Oak. W-L	Sea. W-L	Tex. W-L	Totals W-L
Carrara	0-0	0-0	0-0	0-0	0-2	0-0	0-1	1-0	0-0	0-0	1-0	0-0	0-1	2-4
Castillo	0-0	0-1	0-1	0-0	1-1	0-0	0-1	0-0	0-0	0-1	0-0	0-0	0-0	1-5
Cone	0-1	1-0	0-2	0-0	0-0	2-0	0-1	1-0	1-0	0-1	2-0	1-1	1-0	9-6
Cox	1-0	0-0	0-0	0-0	0-0	0-2	0-0	0-0	0-0	0-1	0-0	0-0	0-0	1-3
Crabtree	0-1	0-1	0-0	0-0	0-0	0-0	0-0	0-0	0-0	0-0	0-0	0-0	0-0	0-2
Darwin	1-0	0-0	0-0	0-0	0-2	0-0	0-2	0-2	0-0	0-0	0-0	0-0	0-2	1-8
Guzman	1-0	1-0	0-2	0-2	0-1	0-1	0-0	0-1	0-1	0-2	0-2	1-0	1-2	4-14
Hall	0-0	0-0	0-0	0-0	0-1	0-0	0-1	0-0	0-0	0-0	0-0	0-0	0-0	0-2
Hentgen	1-1	0-2	1-1	0-2	0-1	1-2	1-0	2-1	1-0	1-3	2-0	0-1	0-0	10-14
Hurtado	0-0	0-1	0-0	0-0	0-1	1-0	0-0	0-0	1-0	0-0	0-0	2-0	1-0	5-2
Jordan	1-0	0-0	0-0	0-0	0-0	0-0	0-0	0-0	0-0	0-0	0-0	0-0	0-0	1-0
Leiter	0-2	1-1	1-1	2-1	2-0	1-0	1-0	1-0	1-0	0-1	1-1	0-1	0-3	11-11
Menhart	0-2	0-0	0-1	1-0	0-0	0-0	0-0	0-0	0-0	0-0	0-0	0-0	0-1	1-4
Robinson	1-0	0-0	0-0	0-0	0-0	0-0	0-1	0-1	0-0	0-0	0-0	0-0	0-0	1-2
Rogers	0-0	0-0	0-0	1-0	0-1	0-1	1-0	0-1	0-0	0-0	0-0	0-0	0-0	2-4
Timlin	0-0	1-0	0-0	1-0	0-0	0-1	2-0	0-1	0-0	0-0	0-0	0-0	0-1	4-3
Ward	0-0	0-0	0-0	0-0	0-0	0-0	0-0	0-0	0-0	0-1	0-0	0-0	0-0	0-1
Ware	0-0	1-0	0-0	0-1	0-0	1-0	0-0	0-0	0-0	0-0	0-0	0-0	0-0	2-1
Williams	0-0	0-1	0-0	0-0	0-0	0-0	0-0	0-0	0-0	0-1	1-0	0-0	0-0	1-2
Totals	6-7	5-8	2-8	5-6	3-10	6-7	5-7	5-7	4-1	1-12	7-3	4-3	3-9	56-88

NO-DECISIONS: Cornett.

1995 A.L. STATISTICS Miscellaneous

HOME RUNS BY PARKS

	At Bal.	At Bos.	At Cal.	At Chi.	At Cle.	At Det.	At K.C.	At Mil.	At Min.	At N.Y.	At Oak.	At Sea.	At Tex.	At Tor.	Totals 1995	Totals 1994
Baltimore	90	5	11	3	2	8	5	9	10	5	10	5	3	7	173	139
Boston	11	70	12	4	6	12	4	9	9	8	10	3	9	8	175	120
California	8	5	90	11	4	10	10	4	15	4	6	8	6	5	186	120
Chicago	4	6	6	59	7	15	7	5	8	3	7	7	8	4	146	121
Cleveland	6	11	5	10	99	13	6	7	16	4	3	5	10	12	207	167
Detroit	4	6	3	6	4	92	2	6	8	6	1	9	4	8	159	161
Kansas City	5	2	11	5	3	1	49	6	13	3	5	4	5	7	119	100
Milwaukee	9	2	4	2	6	6	1	56	11	10	7	3	3	8	128	99
Minnesota	2	2	9	4	8	6	3	6	59	4	2	7	5	3	120	103
New York	8	2	2	4	4	8	6	3	1	69	2	4	2	7	122	139
Oakland	10	8	6	8	4	2	8	2	11	11	80	8	7	4	169	113
Seattle	9	6	9	7	6	3	2	2	10	11	8	101	4	4	182	153
Texas	3	6	6	6	1	6	4	5	1	5	6	6	81	2	138	124
Toronto	5	2	4	3	5	3	8	8	3	6	9	4	7	73	140	115
1995 total	174	133	178	132	159	185	117	127	179	145	155	174	154	152	2164	....
1994 total	145	135	167	105	131	161	89	111	136	125	105	107	130	127	....	1774

AT BALTIMORE (174):

Baltimore (90)—Palmeiro 21, Manto 12, Ripken 10, Anderson 10, Hoiles 9, Baines 7, Bonilla 7, Gomez 3, Bass 2, Alexander 2, Hammonds 2, Van Slyke 1, Nokes 1, Barberie 1, Smith 1, Zaun 1. **Boston (11)**—Vaughn 4, Greenwell 3, Canseco 2, Tinsley 1, Hosey 1. **California (8)**—Salmon 3, Davis 2, Phillips 1, Hudler 1, Edmonds 1. **Chicago (4)**—Devereaux 2, Johnson 1, F. Thomas 1. **Cleveland (6)**—Thome 2, Ramirez 2, Espinoza 1, Murray 1. **Detroit (4)**—Fielder 2, Curtis 1, Higginson 1. **Kansas City (5)**—Gaetti 2, Hamelin 2, Nunnally 1. **Milwaukee (9)**—Jaha 3, Seitzer 1, Oliver 1, Vaughn 1, Nilsson 1, Mieske 1, Cirillo 1. **Minnesota (2)**—P. Munoz 1, Cordova 1. **New York (8)**—B. Williams 3, Tartabull 1, O'Neill 1, Stanley 1, Velarde 1, G. Williams 1. **Oakland (10)**—Bordick 3, Steinbach 2, Paquette 2, Sierra 1, McGwire 1, Brosius 1. **Seattle (9)**—E. Martinez 3, Cora 1, Buhner 1, Strange 1, Amaral 1, Wilson 1, Newfield 1. **Texas (3)**—Tettleton 2, Rodriguez 1. **Toronto (5)**—Maldonado 1, Carter 1, Sprague 1, Knorr 1, Cedeno 1.

AT BOSTON (133):

Baltimore (5)—Baines 1, Ripken 1, Palmeiro 1, Hoiles 1, Manto 1. **Boston (70)**—Vaughn 15, Valentin 11, Canseco 10, Macfarlane 7, Greenwell 6, Naehring 5, O'Leary 5, Tinsley 4, Haselman 3, McGee 1, Chamberlain 1, Jefferson 1, Hosey 1. **California (5)**—Phillips 2, Hudler 1, Martinez 1, Salmon 1. **Chicago (6)**—Karkovice 2, F. Thomas 2, Devereaux 1, Durham 1. **Cleveland (11)**—Belle 3, Sorrento 2, Baerga 2, Ramirez 2, Murray 1, Thome 1. **Detroit (6)**—Fielder 2, Fryman 2, Gomez 1, Higginson 1. **Kansas City (2)**—James 1, Lockhart 1. **Milwaukee (2)**—Vaughn 1, Valentin 1. **Minnesota (2)**—Puckett 1, Meares 1. **New York (2)**—Leyritz 1, Silvestri 1. **Oakland (8)**—McGwire 5, Henderson 1, Javier 1, Brosius 1. **Seattle (8)**—Buhner 2, E. Martinez 1, T. Martinez 1, Wilson 1, Newfield 1. **Texas (6)**—Gonzalez 2, Rodriguez 2, Pagliarulo 1, Tettleton 1. **Toronto (2)**—Molitor 1, Martinez 1.

AT CALIFORNIA (178):

Baltimore (11)—Palmeiro 3, Hoiles 3, Baines 2, Bonilla 1, Hammonds 1, Smith 1. **Boston (12)**—Canseco 3, Alicea 3, Vaughn 2, Naehring 1, Jefferson 1, Tinsley 1, Mahay 1. **California (90)**—Edmonds 16, Salmon 15, Snow 14, Phillips 13, Davis 11, G. Anderson 7, Myers 6, Hudler 4, Allanson 1, DiSarcina 1, Easley 1, Fabregas 1. **Chicago (6)**—F. Thomas 3, Raines 2, Ventura 1. **Cleveland (5)**—Thome 2, Alomar 1, Belle 1, Lofton 1. **Detroit (3)**—Samuel 1, Fielder 1, Bautista 1. **Kansas City (11)**—Vitiello 3, Gaetti 2, Nunnally 2, Samuel 1, Joyner 1, Grotewold 1, Lockhart 1. **Milwaukee (4)**—Surhoff 2, Oliver 1, Mieske 1. **Minnesota (9)**—Puckett 2, Leius 2, Clark 1, Knoblauch 1, Reboulet 1, Meares 1, Masteller 1. **New York (2)**—Kelly 1, B. Williams 1. **Oakland (6)**—McGwire 2, Steinbach 2, Berroa 2. **Seattle (9)**—E. Martinez 2, T. Martinez 2, Buhner 1, Griffey 1, Blowers 1, Sojo 1, Rodriguez 1. **Texas (6)**—Tettleton 2, Clark 1, Palmer 1, Frye 1, Greer 1. **Toronto (4)**—Carter 1, White 1, Alomar 1, Green 1.

AT CHICAGO (132):

Baltimore (3)—Hoiles 2, Baines 1. **Boston (4)**—Canseco 1, Macfarlane 1, Vaughn 1, Valentin 1. **California (11)**—Edmonds 3, Phillips 2, Davis 1, Gonzales 1, Myers 1, DiSarcina 1, Easley 1, Snow 1. **Chicago (59)**—F. Thomas 15, Ventura 8, Raines 6, Karkovice 5, Devereaux 4, Mouton 4, Lyons 3, Newson 3, Martinez 2, Kruk 2, Johnson 2, Guillen 1, Sabo 1, Martin 1, Durham 1, Snopek 1. **Cleveland (10)**—Belle 5, Lofton 2, Pena 1, Ripken 1, Baerga 1. **Detroit (6)**—Whitaker 1, Trammell 1, Stubbs 1, Fielder 1, Curtis 1, Flaherty 1. **Kansas City (5)**—Gaetti 2, Coleman 1, Miller 1, Vitiello 1. **Milwaukee (2)**—Vaughn 1, Mieske 1. **Minnesota (4)**—Clark 1, P. Munoz 1, Coomer 1, Cordova 1. **New York (4)**—Tartabull 2, O'Neill 1, G. Williams 1. **Oakland (8)**—McGwire 3, Henderson 1, Sierra 1, Berroa 1, Brosius 1, Williams 1. **Seattle (7)**—Wilson 2, Buhner 1, Blowers 1, T. Martinez 1, Newfield 1, Rodriguez 1. **Texas (6)**—Clark 1, Worthington 1, Gonzalez 1, Palmer 1, Rodriguez 1, Gil 1. **Toronto (3)**—Carter 2, White 1.

AT CLEVELAND (159):

Baltimore (2)—Baines 1, Palmeiro 1. **Boston (6)**—Greenwell 2, Vaughn 2, Donnels 1, Valentin 1. **California (4)**—Phillips 1, Snow 1, Edmonds 1, G. Anderson 1. **Chicago (7)**—Ventura 2, F. Thomas 2, Raines 1, Johnson 1, Devereaux 1. **Cleveland (99)**—Belle 25, Thome 13, Sorrento 12, Ramirez 12, Murray 8, Baerga 7, Lofton 5, Alomar 4, Vizquel 3, Perry 3, Winfield 1, Pena 1, Ripken 1, Amaro 1. **Detroit (4)**—Whitaker 1, Samuel 1, Fryman 1, Curtis 1. **Kansas City (3)**—Gaetti 1, Goodwin 1, Tucker 1. **Milwaukee (6)**—Jaha 2, Surhoff 1, Ward 1, Nilsson 1, Valentin 1. **Minnesota (8)**—Meares 2, Puckett 1, P. Munoz 1, Knoblauch 1, Brito 1, Stahoviak 1, Cordova 1. **New York (4)**—O'Neill 2, Fernandez 1, B. Williams 1. **Oakland (4)**—Henderson 1, Steinbach 1, Berroa 1, Brosius 1. **Seattle (6)**—Buhner 3, T. Martinez 2, E. Martinez 1. **Texas (1)**—Rodriguez 1. **Toronto (5)**—Carter 2, Green 2, Molitor 1.

AT DETROIT (185):

Baltimore (8)—Palmeiro 2, Baines 2, Bass 1, Bonilla 1, Anderson 1, Manto 1, Smith 1. **Boston (12)**—Vaughn 3, Valentin 3, Macfarlane 2, O'Leary 2, Greenwell 1, Whiten 1. **California (10)**—Edmonds 3, G. Anderson 3, Snow 2, DiSarcina 1, Salmon 1. **Chicago (15)**—Karkovice 4, Ventura 4, Raines 1, Martinez 1, Johnson 1, Grebeck 1, F. Thomas 1, Martin 1, Durham 1. **Cleveland (13)**—Ramirez 3, Belle 2, Sorrento 2, Thome 2, Murray 1, Alomar 1, Vizquel 1, Baerga 1. **Detroit (92)**—Fielder 16, Whitaker 11, Curtis 11, Higginson 10, Fryman 9, Gibson 7, Samuel 6, Flaherty 6, Gomez 5, Tingley 3, Bautista 3, Nevin 2, Trammell 1, Fletcher 1, Stubbs 1. **Kansas City (1)**—Nunnally 1. **Milwaukee (6)**—Vina 2, Jaha 1, Hulse 1, Mieske 1, Loretta 1. **Minnesota (6)**—Puckett 3, Hale 1, Cole 1, Knoblauch 1, Becker 1, Coomer 1. **New York (8)**—Stanley 3, B. Williams 2, O'Neill 1, Sierra 1, Leyritz 1. **Oakland (2)**—Javier 1, Gates 1. **Seattle (3)**—T. Martinez 2, Bragg 1. **Texas (6)**—Pagliarulo 2, Gonzalez 2, Rodriguez 1, Greer 1. **Toronto (3)**—Alomar 1, Sprague 1, Green 1.

AT KANSAS CITY (117):

Baltimore (5)—Baines 2, Gomez 1, Barberie 1, Zaun 1. **Boston (4)**—Vaughn 2, Canseco 1, Stairs 1. **California (10)**—Davis 2, Phillips 2, Salmon 2, Snow 2, Edmonds 2. **Chicago (7)**—F. Thomas 2, Lyons 1, Johnson 1, Ventura 1, Durham 1, Cameron 1. **Cleveland (6)**—Belle 2, Pena 1, Murray 1, Thome 1, Giles 1. **Detroit (2)**—Fryman 1, Curtis 1. **Kansas City (49)**—Gaetti 16, Joyner 6, Nunnally 6, Hamelin 3, Lockhart 3, Vitiello 3, Gagne 2, Coleman 2, Goodwin 2, Borders 1, Mayne 1, Hiatt 1, Randa 1, Tucker 1, Damon 1. **Milwaukee (1)**—Oliver 1. **Minnesota (3)**—Puckett 1, P. Munoz 1, Masteller 1. **New York (6)**—O'Neill 2, Leyritz 2, Fernandez 1, Velarde 1. **Oakland (8)**—Giambi 3, McGwire 1, Aldrete 1, Bordick 1, Tomberlin 1, Williams 1. **Seattle (2)**—E. Martinez 1, T. Martinez 1. **Texas (6)**—Palmer 2, Tettleton 1, Clark 1, Gonzalez 1, Rodriguez 1. **Toronto (8)**—Molitor 2, Green 2, Carter 2, Alomar 1, Olerud 1, Delgado 1.

AT MILWAUKEE (127):

Baltimore (9)—Baines 2, Ripken 2, Palmeiro 2, Bonilla 1, Huson 1, Hoiles 1. **Boston (9)**—Macfarlane 2, Vaughn 2, Naehring 1, Donnels 1, Jefferson 1, Valentin 1, Hosey 1. **California (4)**—Salmon 2, Davis 1, G. Anderson 1. **Chicago (5)**—F. Thomas 2, Karkovice 1, Ventura 1, Durham 1. **Cleveland (7)**—Belle 2, Baerga 2, Thome 2, Ramirez 1. **Detroit (6)**—Fielder 2, Whitaker 1, Tingley 1, Curtis 1, Higginson 1. **Kansas City (6)**—Gaetti 4, Borders 1, Nunnally 1. **Milwaukee (56)**—Vaughn 8, Jaha 8, Surhoff 7, Nilsson 7, Cirillo 6, Oliver 4, Hamilton 3, Ward 3, Valentin 3, Mieske 3, Seitzer 1, May 1, Hulse 1, Vina 1. **Minnesota (6)**—P. Munoz 2, Reboulet 2, Meares 1, Cordova 1. **New York (3)**—O'Neill 1, Velarde 1, B. Williams 1. **Oakland (2)**—Sierra 1, McGwire 1. **Seattle (2)**—Buhner 2. **Texas (4)**—Gonzalez 2, Tettleton 1, Greer 1. **Toronto (8)**—Olerud 2, Green 2, Molitor 1, Maldonado 1, White 1, Alomar 1.

AT MINNESOTA (179):

Baltimore (10)—Van Slyke 2, Palmeiro 2, Baines 1, Ripken 1, Nokes 1, Anderson 1, Hoiles 1, Hammonds 1. **Boston (9)**—O'Leary 3, Valentin 2, Canseco 1, Bell 1, Naehring 1, Vaughn 1. **California (15)**—Edmonds 3, Davis 2, Phillips 2, Allanson 2, Salmon 2, Owen 1, Myers 1, Easley 1, G. Anderson 1. **Chicago (8)**—F. Thomas 4, Ventura 2, Karkovice 1, Martinez 1. **Cleveland (16)**—Murray 5, Belle 3, Alomar 2, Ramirez 2, Espinoza 1, Baerga 1, Thome 1, Kirby 1. **Detroit (8)**—Samuel 2, Flaherty 2, Steverson 2, Fielder 1, Gomez 1. **Kansas City (13)**—Gaetti 4, Hiatt 3, Gagne 1, Joyner 1, Borders 1, Lockhart 1, Nunnally 1, Caceres 1. **Milwaukee (11)**—Jaha 3, Seitzer 2, Oliver 2, Hamilton 1, Nilsson 1, Mieske 1, Cirillo 1. **Minnesota (59)**—Cordova 16, Puckett 13, P. Munoz 10, Knoblauch 4, Meares 3, Leius 2, Coomer 2, Clark 1, Merullo 1, Maas 1, Reboulet 1, Walbeck 1, Stahoviak 1, Becker 1, Masteller 1, Lawton 1. **New York (1)**—B. Williams 1. **Oakland (11)**—Sierra 2, McGwire 2, Berroa 2, Paquette 2, Henderson 1, Javier 1, Steinbach 1. **Seattle (10)**—Buhner 5, Cora 1, Griffey 1, Blowers 1, T. Martinez 1, Newson 1. **Texas (5)**—Clark 2, Greer 2, Tettleton 1. **Toronto (3)**—Molitor 1, Sprague 1, Green 1.

AT NEW YORK (145):

Baltimore (5)—Anderson 2, Baines 1, Ripken 1, Palmeiro 1. **Boston (8)**—Vaughn 3, Valentin 2, Canseco 1, Macfarlane 1, Naehring 1. **California (4)**—Phillips 1, Easley 1, Salmon 1, Snow 1. **Chicago (3)**—Raines 1, Martinez 1, F. Thomas 1. **Cleveland (4)**—Belle 2, Sorrento 1, Ramirez 1. **Detroit (6)**—Gibson 1, Fielder 1, Fryman 1, Bautista 1, Higginson 1, Clark 1. **Kansas City (3)**—Gagne 1, James 1, Tucker 1. **Milwaukee (10)**—Vaughn 3, Seitzer 1, Surhoff 1, Nilsson 1, Jaha 1, Hulse 1, Valentin 1, Cirillo 1. **Minnesota (4)**—P. Munoz 2, Puckett 1, Knoblauch 1. **New York (69)**—Stanley 13, O'Neill 12, B. Williams 7, Mattingly 5, Sierra 5, Boggs 4, G. Williams 4, Fernandez 3, Strawberry 3, Leyritz 3, Tartabull 2, Polonia 2, Velarde 2, Davis 2, James 1, Kelly 1. **Oakland (11)**—Berroa 4, Sierra 3, McGwire 2, Henderson 1, Bordick 1. **Seattle (11)**—E. Martinez 3, T. Martinez 3, Buhner 1, Kreuter 1, Griffey 1, Sojo 1, Bragg 1. **Texas (1)**—Tettleton 1. **Toronto (6)**—Carter 3, Huff 1, Green 1, Gonzalez 1.

AT OAKLAND (155):

Baltimore (10)—Baines 3, Palmeiro 2, Manto 2, Ripken 1, Bass 1, Anderson 1. **Boston (10)**—Canseco 2, Macfarlane 2, Valentin 1, Greenwell 1, Haselman 1, Jefferson 1, Vaughn 1. **California (6)**—Snow 3, Salmon 1, Edmonds 1, G. Anderson 1. **Chicago (7)**—Ventura 3, F. Thomas 2, Durham 1, Mouton 1. **Cleveland (3)**—Pena 1, Belle 1, Ramirez 1. **Detroit (1)**—Gomez 1. **Kansas City (5)**—Gaetti 2, Samuel 1, Goodwin 1, Hamelin 1. **Milwaukee (7)**—Surhoff 2, Valentin 2, Oliver 1, Vaughn 1, Mieske 1. **Minnesota (2)**—Meares 1, Cordova 1. **New York (2)**—Mattingly 1, B. Williams 1. **Oakland (80)**—McGwire 15, Brosius 12, Berroa 10, Steinbach 9, Paquette 8, Henderson 3, Javier 3, Sierra 3, Gates 3, Tomberlin 3, Giambi 3, Aldrete 2, Bordick 2, Young 2, Tartabull 1, Williams 1. **Seattle (8)**—E. Martinez 2, T. Martinez 2, Buhner 1, Blowers 1, Sojo 1, Rodriguez 1. **Texas (5)**—Gil 2, Tettleton 1, Clark 1, Frye 1. **Toronto (9)**—Molitor 2, Carter 2, White 2, Alomar 1, Sprague 1, Gonzalez 1.

AT SEATTLE (174):

Baltimore (5)—Palmeiro 2, Anderson 1, Hoiles 1, Manto 1. **Boston (3)**—Valentin 2, Alicea 1. **California (8)**—Phillips 3, G. Anderson 2, Myers 1, DiSarcina 1, Edmonds 1. **Chicago (7)**—F. Thomas 2, Raines 1, Lyons 1, Johnson 1, Devereaux 1, Ventura 1. **Cleveland (5)**—Ramirez 2, Winfield 1, Belle 1, Sorrento 1. **Detroit (9)**—Curtis 3, Gomez 3, Bautista 2, Flaherty 1. **Kansas City (4)**—Joyner 1, Borders 1, Nunnally 1, Damon 1. **Milwaukee (3)**—Nilsson 1, Valentin 1, Mieske 1. **Minnesota (7)**—Meares 3, Puckett 2, Hale 1, Knoblauch 1. **New York (4)**—Boggs 1, James 1, Sierra 1, Velarde 1. **Oakland (8)**—McGwire 4, Javier 1, Tartabull 1, Sierra 1, Paquette 1. **Seattle (101)**—Buhner 21, Blowers 17, E. Martinez 16, T. Martinez 14, Griffey 13, Wilson 5, Sojo 4, Diaz 3, Coleman 1, Cora 1, Strange 1, Amaral 1, Newson 1, Bragg 1, Rodriguez 1, Widger 1. **Texas (6)**—Gonzalez 3, McLemore 1, Gil 1, Greer 1. **Toronto (4)**—Olerud 3, Alomar 1.

AT TEXAS (154):

Baltimore (3)—Palmeiro 2, Baines 1. **Boston (9)**—Canseco 3, Alicea 2, McGee 1, Naehring 1, Haselman 1, Tinsley 1. **California (6)**—Salmon 3, Edmonds 2, Perez 1. **Chicago (8)**—Johnson 2, Ventura 2, F. Thomas 2, LaValliere 1, Devereaux 1. **Cleveland (10)**—Sorrento 3, Alomar 2, Belle 2, Murray 1, Baerga 1, Ramirez 1. **Detroit (4)**—Fielder 3, Gibson 1. **Kansas City (5)**—Gaetti 1, Coleman 1, Joyner 1, Nunnally 1, Damon 1. **Milwaukee (3)**—Oliver 1, Vaughn 1, Jaha 1. **Minnesota (5)**—Puckett 1, Knoblauch 1, Stahoviak 1, Coomer 1, Cordova 1. **New York (2)**—O'Neill 1, Stanley 1. **Oakland (7)**—McGwire 3, Henderson 1, Javier 1, Bordick 1, Gates 1. **Seattle (4)**—Buhner 2, Griffey 1, Blowers 1. **Texas (81)**—Tettleton 22, Gonzalez 15, Clark 10, Greer 7, Palmer 5, Rodriguez 5, Gil 5, McLemore 3, Maldonado 2, Frye 2, Voigt 2, Pagliarulo 1, Worthington 1, Ortiz 1. **Toronto (7)**—Sprague 2, Cedeno 2, Molitor 1, White 1, Olerud 1.

AT TORONTO (152):

Baltimore (7)—Baines 1, Ripken 1, Bass 1, Hoiles 1, Alexander 1, Goodwin 1, Zaun 1. **Boston (8)**—Vaughn 3, Greenwell 2, Valentin 2, Jefferson 1. **California (5)**—Salmon 3, Davis 1, DiSarcina 1. **Chicago (4)**—Johnson 1, Ventura 1, F. Thomas 1, Durham 1. **Cleveland (12)**—Ramirez 4, Sorrento 3, Vizquel 2, Pena 1, Belle 1, Thome 1. **Detroit (8)**—Fielder 2, Curtis 2, Clark 2, Fryman 1, Flaherty 1. **Kansas City (7)**—Gagne 2, Joyner 2, Gaetti 1, Hamelin 1, Tucker 1. **Milwaukee (8)**—Valentin 2, Mieske 2, Hamilton 1, Oliver 1, Vaughn 1, Jaha 1. **Minnesota (3)**—Cordova 2, Knoblauch 1. **New York (7)**—Kelly 2, Mattingly 1, Tartabull 1, O'Neill 1, Velarde 1, B. Williams 1. **Oakland (4)**—Berroa 2, Aldrete 1, Brosius 1. **Seattle (4)**—T. Martinez 2, Blowers 1, Rodriguez 1. **Texas (2)**—McLemore 1, Gonzalez 1. **Toronto (73)**—Carter 13, Sprague 12, Gonzalez 8, Alomar 7, Molitor 6, Maldonado 5, Green 5, Parrish 4, White 4, Knorr 2, Delgado 2, Olerud 1, Cedeno 1, R. Perez 1, T. Perez 1, Martinez 1.

1995 N.L. STATISTICS

Batting

Pinch-hitting

Pitching

Fielding

Miscellaneous

BATTING

TEAM

Team	Avg.	G	TPA	AB	R	H	TB	2B	3B	HR	RBI	SH	SF	HP	BB	IBB	SO	SB	CS	GDP	LOB	ShO	Slg.	OBP
Colorado	.282	144	5647	4994	785	1406	2351	259	43	200	749	82	31	56	484	47	943	125	59	118	1008	11	.471	.350
Houston	.275	144	5857	5097	747	1403	2034	260	22	109	694	78	47	69	566	58	992	176	60	114	1134	4	.399	.353
San Diego	.272	144	5527	4950	668	1345	1964	231	20	116	618	56	38	35	447	45	872	124	46	125	979	6	.397	.334
Cincinnati	.270	144	5575	4903	747	1326	2156	277	35	161	694	62	50	40	519	42	946	190	68	92	993	3	.440	.342
New York	.267	144	5581	4958	657	1323	1984	218	34	125	617	92	43	42	446	44	994	58	39	105	1023	8	.400	.330
Chicago	.265	144	5543	4963	693	1315	2134	267	39	158	648	71	35	34	440	46	953	105	37	110	949	5	.430	.327
Los Angeles	.264	144	5544	4942	634	1303	1976	191	35	140	593	68	35	30	468	46	1023	127	45	99	1043	12	.400	.329
Philadelphia	.262	144	5613	4950	615	1296	1901	263	30	94	576	77	41	46	497	38	884	72	25	107	1101	9	.384	.332
Florida............	.262	143	5569	4886	673	1278	1982	214	29	144	636	69	48	49	517	36	916	131	53	105	1022	9	.406	.335
Pittsburgh.......	.259	144	5501	4937	629	1281	1955	245	27	125	587	51	33	24	456	45	972	84	55	88	1005	8	.396	.323
Montreal	.259	144	5452	4905	621	1268	1935	265	24	118	572	58	32	56	400	43	901	120	49	107	970	8	.394	.320
San Francisco ..	.253	144	5603	4971	652	1256	2007	229	33	152	610	79	24	57	472	55	1060	138	46	92	1035	8	.404	.323
Atlanta...........	.250	144	5464	4814	645	1202	1970	210	27	168	618	56	34	40	520	37	933	73	43	106	972	4	.409	.326
St. Louis	.247	143	5349	4779	563	1182	1789	238	24	107	533	48	40	46	436	31	920	79	46	110	942	19	.374	.314
Totals	.263	1007	77825	69049	9329	18184	28138	3367	418	1917	8745	947	531	624	6668	613	13309	1602	671	1478	14176	114	.408	.331

INDIVIDUAL

TOP QUALIFIERS FOR BATTING CHAMPIONSHIP

Minimum 446 plate appearances. *Lefthanded batter. †Switch-hitter.

Player, Team	Avg.	G	TPA	AB	R	H	TB	2B	3B	HR	RBI	SH	SF	HP	BB	IBB	SO	SB	CS	GDP	Slg.	OBP
Gwynn, Tony, San Diego*	.368	135	577	535	82	197	259	33	1	9	90	0	6	1	35	10	15	17	5	19	.484	.404
Piazza, Mike, Los Angeles........	.346	112	475	434	82	150	263	17	0	32	93	0	1	1	39	10	80	1	0	10	.606	.400
Bichette, Dante, Colorado	.340	139	612	579	102	197	359	38	2	40	128	0	7	4	22	5	96	13	9	16	.620	.364
Bell, Derek, Houston	.334	112	499	452	63	151	200	21	2	8	86	0	6	8	33	2	71	27	9	10	.442	.385
Grace, Mark, Chicago*	.326	143	627	552	97	180	285	51	3	16	92	1	7	2	65	9	46	6	2	10	.516	.395
Larkin, Barry, Cincinnati...........	.319	131	567	496	98	158	244	29	6	15	66	3	4	3	61	2	49	51	5	6	.492	.394
Castilla, Vinny, Colorado	.309	139	571	527	82	163	297	34	2	32	90	4	6	4	30	2	87	2	8	15	.564	.347
Segui, David, N.Y.-Mon.†	.309	130	511	456	68	141	210	25	4	12	68	8	3	3	40	5	47	2	7	10	.461	.367
Jefferies, Gregg, Philadelphia† ...	.306	114	521	480	69	147	215	31	2	11	56	0	6	0	35	5	26	9	5	14	.448	.349
Sanders, Reggie, Cincinnati	.306	133	567	484	91	148	280	36	6	28	99	0	6	8	69	4	122	36	12	9	.579	.397
Walker, Larry, Colorado*	.306	131	562	494	96	151	300	31	5	36	101	0	5	14	49	13	72	16	3	13	.607	.381
Caminiti, Ken, San Diego†	.302	143	602	526	74	159	270	33	0	26	94	0	6	1	69	8	94	12	5	11	.513	.380
Conine, Jeff, Florida	.302	133	562	483	72	146	251	26	2	25	105	0	12	1	66	5	94	2	0	13	.520	.379
Biggio, Craig, Houston..............	.302	141	673	553	123	167	267	30	2	22	77	11	7	22	80	1	85	33	8	6	.483	.406
Butler, Brett, N.Y.-L.A.*	.300	129	596	513	78	154	193	18	9	1	38	10	6	0	67	2	51	32	8	5	.376	.377

DEPARTMENTAL LEADERS: G—Bonds, S.F., McGriff, Atl., Sosa, Chi., 144; AB—McRae, Chi., 580; R—Biggio, Hou., 123; H—Bichette, Col., Gwynn, S.D., 197; TB—Bichette, Col., 359; 1B—Gwynn, S.D., 154; 2B—Grace, Chi., 51; 3B—Butler, N.Y.-L.A., Young, Col., 9; HR—Bichette, Col., 40; RBI—Bichette, Col., 128; SH—B. Jones, N.Y., 18; SF—Conine, Fla., 12; HP—Biggio, Hou., 22; BB—Bonds, S.F., 120; IBB—Bonds, S.F., 22; SO—Galarraga, Col., 146; SB—Veras, Fla., 56; CS—Veras, Fla., 21; GIDP—Hayes, Phi., 23; Slg. Pct.—Bichette, Col., .620; OB. Pct.—Bonds, S.F., .431.

ALL PLAYERS

*Lefthanded batter. †Switch-hitter.

Player, Team	Avg.	G	TPA	AB	R	H	TB	2B	3B	HR	RBI	SH	SF	HP	BB	IBB	SO	SB	CS	GDP	Slg.	OBP
Abbott, Kurt, Florida................	.255	120	468	420	60	107	190	18	7	17	60	2	5	5	36	4	110	4	3	6	.452	.318
Abbott, Kyle, Philadelphia*	.500	18	2	2	1	1	1	0	0	0	0	0	0	0	0	0	1	0	0	0	.500	.500
Acevedo, Juan, Colorado..........	.056	17	19	18	0	1	1	0	0	0	0	0	0	0	1	0	6	0	0	2	.056	.105
Alfonzo, Edgardo, New York......	.278	101	356	335	26	93	128	13	5	4	41	4	4	1	12	1	37	1	1	7	.382	.301
Alou, Moises, Montreal	.273	93	386	344	48	94	158	22	0	14	58	0	4	9	29	6	56	4	3	9	.459	.342
Alvarez, Tavo, Montreal	.000	8	14	12	1	0	0	0	0	0	0	2	0	0	0	0	4	0	0	0	.000	.000
Andrews, Shane, Montreal	.214	84	241	220	27	47	83	10	1	8	31	1	2	1	17	2	68	1	1	4	.377	.271
Anthony, Eric, Cincinnati*	.269	47	150	134	19	36	57	6	0	5	23	0	3	0	13	2	30	2	1	1	.425	.327
Aquino, Luis, Mon.-S.F.	.250	34	5	4	0	1	1	0	0	0	0	0	0	0	1	0	2	0	0	0	.250	.400
Arias, Alex, Florida	.269	94	246	216	22	58	80	9	2	3	26	3	3	2	22	1	20	1	0	8	.370	.337
Arocha, Rene, St. Louis	.000	41	1	1	0	0	0	0	0	0	0	0	0	0	0	0	1	0	0	0	.000	.000
Ashby, Andy, San Diego	.163	31	67	49	2	8	9	1	0	0	3	17	0	0	1	0	24	1	0	0	.184	.180
Ashley, Billy, Los Angeles.........	.237	81	244	215	17	51	80	5	0	8	27	0	2	2	25	4	88	0	0	3	.372	.320
Astacio, Pedro, Los Angeles	.125	48	27	24	0	3	4	1	0	0	0	2	0	0	1	0	9	0	0	1	.167	.160
Aude, Rich, Pittsburgh.............	.248	42	115	109	10	27	41	8	0	2	19	0	0	0	6	0	20	1	2	4	.376	.287
Aurilia, Rich, San Francisco	.474	9	22	19	4	9	18	3	0	2	4	1	1	0	1	0	2	1	0	1	.947	.476
Ausmus, Brad, San Diego	.293	103	369	328	44	96	135	16	4	5	34	4	4	2	31	3	56	16	5	6	.412	.353
Avery, Steve, Atlanta*	.208	29	63	53	4	11	20	1	1	2	4	8	1	0	1	0	17	0	0	0	.377	.218
Bagwell, Jeff, Houston	.290	114	539	448	88	130	222	29	0	21	87	0	6	6	79	12	102	12	5	9	.496	.399
Bailey, Roger, Colorado............	.125	39	20	16	2	2	2	0	0	0	1	3	0	0	1	0	3	0	0	0	.125	.174
Banks, Willie, Chi.-L.A.-Fla........	.269	28	29	26	2	7	8	1	0	0	1	1	0	1	1	0	9	0	0	0	.308	.321
Barber, Brian, St. Louis	.125	9	9	8	0	1	1	0	0	0	0	0	0	0	1	0	2	0	0	0	.125	.222
Barry, Jeff, New York†	.133	15	16	15	2	2	3	1	0	0	0	0	0	0	1	0	8	0	0	0	.200	.188
Barton, Shawn, San Fran..........	.000	52	1	0	0	0	0	0	0	0	0	0	0	0	0	0	0	0	0	0	.000	.000
Bates, Jason, Colorado†	.267	116	368	322	42	86	135	17	4	8	46	2	0	2	42	3	70	3	6	4	.419	.355
Battle, Allen, St. Louis	.271	61	137	118	13	32	37	5	0	0	2	3	0	1	15	0	26	3	3	0	.314	.358
Bautista, Jose, San Fran..........	.000	52	20	18	0	0	0	0	0	0	0	0	0	1	0	0	9	0	0	0	.000	.053
Bean, Billy, San Diego*	.000	4	8	7	1	0	0	0	0	0	0	0	0	0	1	0	4	0	0	0	.000	.125
Beck, Rod, San Francisco	.333	60	3	3	0	1	1	0	0	0	0	0	0	0	0	0	1	0	0	0	.333	.333

Player, Team	Avg.	G	TPA	AB	R	H	TB	2B	3B	HR	RBI	SH	SF	HP	BB	IBB	SO	SB	CS	GDP	Slg.	OBP
Bell, David, St. Louis	.250	39	151	144	13	36	53	7	2	2	19	0	1	2	4	0	25	1	2	0	.368	.278
Bell, Derek, Houston	.334	112	499	452	63	151	200	21	2	8	86	0	6	8	33	2	71	27	9	10	.442	.385
Bell, Jay, Pittsburgh	.262	138	593	530	79	139	214	28	4	13	55	3	1	4	55	1	110	2	5	13	.404	.336
Belliard, Rafael, Atlanta	.222	75	192	180	12	40	44	2	1	0	7	4	0	2	6	2	28	2	2	4	.244	.255
Benard, Marvin, San Fran.*	.382	13	35	34	5	13	18	2	0	1	4	0	0	0	1	0	7	1	0	1	.529	.400
Benes, Alan, St. Louis	.000	3	6	6	0	0	0	0	0	0	0	0	0	0	0	0	3	0	0	0	.000	.000
Benes, Andy, San Diego	.150	19	44	40	2	6	7	1	0	0	3	3	0	0	1	0	18	0	0	1	.175	.171
Benitez, Yamil, Montreal	.385	14	40	39	8	15	25	2	1	2	7	0	0	0	1	0	7	0	2	1	.641	.400
Benjamin, Mike, San Fran.	.220	68	202	186	19	41	56	6	0	3	12	7	0	1	8	3	51	11	1	3	.301	.256
Bennett, Gary, Philadelphia	.000	1	1	1	0	0	0	0	0	0	0	0	0	0	0	0	1	0	0	0	.000	.000
Benzinger, Todd, San Fran.†	.200	9	13	10	2	2	5	0	0	1	2	0	1	0	2	1	3	0	0	0	.500	.308
Berry, Sean, Montreal	.318	103	348	314	38	100	166	22	1	14	55	2	5	2	25	1	53	3	8	5	.529	.367
Berryhill, Damon, Cincinnati†	.183	34	97	82	6	15	24	3	0	2	11	1	4	0	10	2	19	0	0	3	.293	.260
Berumen, Andres, San Diego	.000	37	1	1	0	0	0	0	0	0	0	0	0	0	0	0	0	0	0	0	.000	.000
Bichette, Dante, Colorado	.340	139	612	579	102	197	359	38	2	40	128	0	7	4	22	5	96	13	9	16	.620	.364
Biggio, Craig, Houston	.302	141	673	553	123	167	267	30	2	22	77	11	7	22	80	1	85	33	8	6	.483	.406
Birkbeck, Mike, New York	.333	4	9	6	1	2	2	0	0	0	0	1	0	1	1	0	1	0	0	0	.333	.500
Blair, Willie, San Diego	.000	40	29	24	2	0	0	0	0	0	1	4	0	0	1	0	17	0	0	0	.000	.040
Blauser, Jeff, Atlanta	.211	115	504	431	60	91	147	16	2	12	31	2	2	12	57	2	107	8	5	6	.341	.319
Bochtler, Doug, San Diego	.000	34	2	2	0	0	0	0	0	0	0	0	0	0	0	0	0	0	0	0	.000	.000
Bogar, Tim, New York	.290	78	157	145	17	42	52	7	0	1	21	2	1	0	9	0	25	1	0	2	.359	.329
Bonds, Barry, San Francisco*	.294	144	635	506	109	149	292	30	7	33	104	0	4	5	120	22	83	31	10	12	.577	.431
Bonilla, Bobby, New York†	.325	80	351	317	49	103	190	25	4	18	53	0	2	1	31	10	48	0	3	11	.599	.385
Boone, Bret, Cincinnati	.267	138	571	513	63	137	220	34	2	15	68	5	5	6	41	0	84	5	1	14	.429	.326
Borbon, Pedro, Atlanta*	.000	41	1	1	0	0	0	0	0	0	0	0	0	0	0	0	0	0	0	0	.000	.000
Borders, Pat, Houston	.114	11	37	35	1	4	4	0	0	0	0	0	0	0	2	1	7	0	0	2	.114	.162
Borland, Toby, Philadelphia	.200	50	6	5	1	1	1	0	0	0	0	1	0	0	0	0	1	0	0	0	.200	.167
Bottalico, Ricky, Philadelphia*	.000	62	6	5	0	0	0	0	0	0	0	1	0	0	0	0	4	0	0	0	.000	.000
Bowen, Ryan, Florida	.333	4	6	6	1	2	2	0	0	0	0	0	0	0	0	0	2	0	0	0	.333	.333
Bradshaw, Terry, St. Louis*	.227	19	46	44	6	10	13	1	1	0	2	0	0	0	2	0	10	1	2	0	.295	.261
Branson, Jeff, Cincinnati*	.260	122	384	331	43	86	144	18	2	12	45	1	6	2	44	14	69	2	1	9	.435	.345
Brantley, Jeff, Cincinnati	.000	56	3	3	0	0	0	0	0	0	0	0	0	0	0	0	1	0	0	0	.000	.000
Brewington, Jamie, San Fran.	.217	14	27	23	3	5	5	0	0	0	1	4	0	0	0	0	7	0	0	0	.217	.217
Brito, Jorge, Colorado	.216	18	55	51	5	11	14	3	0	0	7	1	0	1	2	0	17	1	0	1	.275	.259
Brocail, Doug, Houston*	.250	37	20	16	3	4	6	0	1	0	1	4	0	0	0	0	5	0	0	0	.375	.250
Brogna, Rico, New York*	.289	134	540	495	72	143	240	27	2	22	76	2	2	2	39	7	111	0	0	10	.485	.342
Browne, Jerry, Florida†	.255	77	220	184	21	47	54	4	0	1	17	9	1	1	25	0	20	1	1	7	.293	.346
Brumfield, Jacob, Pittsburgh	.271	116	445	402	64	109	148	23	2	4	26	0	1	5	37	0	71	22	12	3	.368	.339
Brumley, Mike, Houston†	.056	18	18	18	1	1	4	0	0	1	2	0	0	0	0	0	6	1	0	0	.222	.056
Buechele, Steve, Chicago	.189	32	118	106	10	20	25	2	0	1	9	1	0	0	11	0	19	0	0	1	.236	.265
Buford, Damon, New York	.235	44	162	136	24	32	49	5	0	4	12	0	2	5	19	0	28	7	7	3	.360	.346
Bullett, Scott, Chicago*	.273	104	164	150	19	41	69	5	7	3	22	1	0	1	12	2	30	8	3	4	.460	.331
Bullinger, Jim, Chicago	.128	25	62	47	1	6	9	3	0	0	5	8	2	0	5	0	16	0	0	1	.191	.204
Burba, Dave, Cincinnati	.067	52	22	15	2	1	1	0	0	0	0	4	0	0	3	0	6	0	0	0	.067	.222
Burkett, John, Florida	.106	31	73	66	3	7	8	1	0	0	3	4	0	1	2	0	23	0	0	1	.121	.145
Burks, Ellis, Colorado	.266	103	321	278	41	74	138	10	6	14	49	1	1	2	39	0	72	7	3	7	.496	.359
Busch, Mike, Los Angeles	.235	13	17	17	3	4	13	0	0	3	6	0	0	0	0	0	7	0	0	0	.765	.235
Butler, Brett, N.Y.-L.A.*	.300	129	596	513	78	154	193	18	9	1	38	10	6	0	67	2	51	32	8	5	.376	.377
Byrd, Paul, New York	1.000	17	1	1	0	1	1	0	0	0	0	0	0	0	0	0	0	0	0	0	1.000	1.000
Caminiti, Ken, San Diego†	.302	143	602	526	74	159	270	33	0	26	94	0	6	1	69	8	94	12	5	11	.513	.380
Candiotti, Tom, Los Angeles	.109	30	63	55	2	6	6	0	0	0	2	5	0	0	3	0	16	0	0	1	.109	.155
Cangelosi, John, Houston†	.318	90	256	201	46	64	79	5	2	2	18	2	1	4	48	2	42	21	5	3	.393	.457
Caraballo, Ramon, St. Louis†	.202	34	110	99	10	20	32	4	1	2	3	2	0	0	33	3	2	1	3	.323	.269
Carr, Chuck, Florida	.227	105	365	308	54	70	96	20	0	2	20	7	2	2	46	1	49	25	11	2	.312	.330
Carrasco, Hector, Cincinnati	.000	64	7	7	0	0	0	0	0	0	0	0	0	0	0	0	4	0	0	0	.000	.000
Carreon, Mark, San Francisco	.301	117	426	396	53	119	194	24	0	17	65	0	3	4	23	1	37	0	1	7	.490	.343
Carter, Andy, Philadelphia*	1.000	4	1	1	0	1	1	0	0	0	0	0	0	0	0	0	0	0	0	0	1.000	1.000
Casian, Larry, Chicago	.000	42	2	2	0	0	0	0	0	0	0	0	0	0	0	0	1	0	0	0	.000	.000
Castellano, Pedro, Colorado	.000	4	7	5	0	0	0	0	0	0	0	0	0	0	2	0	3	0	0	0	.000	.286
Castilla, Vinny, Colorado	.309	139	571	527	82	163	297	34	2	32	90	4	6	4	30	2	87	2	8	15	.564	.347
Castillo, Alberto, New York	.103	13	33	29	2	3	3	0	0	0	0	0	0	1	3	0	9	1	0	1	.103	.212
Castillo, Frank, Chicago	.102	29	66	59	1	6	6	0	0	0	1	7	0	0	3	0	25	0	0	0	.102	.145
Castro, Juan, Los Angeles	.250	11	5	4	0	1	1	0	0	0	0	0	0	0	1	0	1	0	0	0	.250	.400
Cedeno, Andujar, San Diego	.210	120	424	390	42	82	120	16	2	6	31	0	1	5	28	7	92	5	3	12	.308	.271
Cedeno, Roger, Los Angeles†	.238	40	46	42	4	10	12	2	0	0	2	0	0	0	3	0	10	1	0	1	.286	.283
Charlton, Norm, Philadelphia†	1.000	25	1	1	0	1	2	1	0	0	1	0	0	0	0	0	0	0	0	0	2.000	1.000
Christiansen, Jason, Pittsburgh	.000	63	1	1	0	0	0	0	0	0	0	0	0	0	0	0	1	0	0	0	.000	.000
Cianfrocco, Archi, San Diego	.263	51	133	118	22	31	53	7	0	5	31	0	1	2	11	1	28	0	2	3	.449	.333
Clark, Dave, Pittsburgh*	.281	77	223	196	30	55	73	6	0	4	24	0	2	1	24	1	38	3	3	9	.372	.359
Clark, Phil, San Diego	.216	75	108	97	12	21	30	3	0	2	7	0	2	1	8	1	18	0	2	3	.309	.278
Clayton, Royce, San Fran.	.244	138	557	509	56	124	174	29	3	5	58	4	3	3	38	1	109	24	9	7	.342	.298
Clontz, Brad, Atlanta	.000	59	2	2	0	0	0	0	0	0	0	0	0	0	0	0	0	0	0	0	.000	.000
Colbrunn, Greg, Florida	.277	138	560	528	70	146	239	22	1	23	89	0	4	6	22	4	69	11	3	15	.453	.311
Coles, Darnell, St. Louis	.225	63	158	138	13	31	47	7	0	3	16	0	1	3	16	1	20	0	0	3	.341	.316
Conine, Jeff, Florida	.302	133	562	483	72	146	251	26	2	25	105	0	12	1	66	5	94	2	0	13	.520	.379
Cooper, Scott, St. Louis*	.230	118	430	374	29	86	117	18	2	3	40	0	4	3	49	3	85	0	3	7	.313	.321
Cordero, Wil, Montreal	.286	131	564	514	64	147	216	35	2	10	49	1	4	9	36	4	88	9	5	11	.420	.341
Cornelius, Reid, New York	.100	18	20	20	0	2	2	0	0	0	0	0	0	0	0	0	7	0	0	0	.100	.100
Counsell, Craig, Colorado*	.000	3	2	1	0	0	0	0	0	0	0	0	0	0	1	0	0	0	0	0	.000	.500
Cromer, Tripp, St. Louis	.226	105	369	345	36	78	112	19	0	5	18	1	5	4	14	2	66	0	0	14	.325	.261
Cummings, John, L.A.*	.000	35	3	3	0	0	0	0	0	0	0	0	0	0	0	0	1	0	0	0	.000	.000
Cummings, Midre, Pitts.*	.243	59	165	152	13	37	52	7	1	2	15	0	0	0	13	3	30	1	0	1	.342	.303
Daulton, Darren, Philadelphia*	.249	98	404	342	44	85	137	19	3	9	55	0	2	5	55	2	52	3	0	4	.401	.359

- 265 -

Player, Team	Avg.	G	TPA	AB	R	H	TB	2B	3B	HR	RBI	SH	SF	HP	BB	IBB	SO	SB	CS	GDP	Slg.	OBP
Dawson, Andre, Florida	.257	79	246	226	30	58	98	10	3	8	37	0	3	8	9	1	45	0	0	7	.434	.305
Decker, Steve, Florida	.226	51	154	133	12	30	43	2	1	3	13	0	2	0	19	1	22	1	0	1	.323	.318
DeLeon, Jose, Montreal	.000	7	2	0	0	0	0	0	0	0	0	1	0	0	1	0	0	0	0	0	.000	1.000
DeLucia, Rich, St. Louis	.200	56	12	10	1	2	2	0	0	0	0	1	0	0	1	0	3	0	0	1	.200	.273
Deshaies, Jim, Philadelphia*	.000	2	1	1	0	0	0	0	0	0	0	0	0	0	0	0	1	0	0	0	.000	.000
DeShields, Delino, L. A.*	.256	127	493	425	66	109	157	18	3	8	37	3	1	1	63	4	83	39	14	6	.369	.353
Devereaux, Mike, Atlanta	.255	29	57	55	7	14	20	3	0	1	8	0	0	0	2	0	11	2	0	1	.364	.281
Dewey, Mark, San Francisco	.000	27	1	1	0	0	0	0	0	0	0	0	0	0	0	0	1	0	0	0	.000	.000
Diaz, Mario, Florida	.230	49	89	87	5	20	26	3	0	1	6	1	0	0	1	0	12	0	0	4	.299	.239
DiPoto, Jerry, New York	.000	58	6	5	0	0	0	0	0	0	0	1	0	0	0	0	3	0	0	0	.000	.000
Dishman, Glenn, San Diego	.200	19	34	30	4	6	6	0	0	0	4	2	1	1	0	0	13	0	0	2	.200	.219
Donnels, Chris, Houston*	.300	19	33	30	4	9	9	0	0	0	2	0	0	0	3	2	6	0	0	1	.300	.364
Dougherty, Jim, Houston	.125	56	9	8	1	1	1	0	0	0	0	1	0	0	0	0	2	0	0	0	.125	.125
Drabek, Doug, Houston	.233	33	70	60	4	14	17	3	0	0	8	8	0	0	2	0	17	0	0	0	.283	.258
Duncan, Mariano, Phi.-Cin.	.287	81	277	265	36	76	112	14	2	6	36	1	5	1	5	0	62	1	3	7	.423	.297
Dunston, Shawon, Chicago	.296	127	503	477	58	141	225	30	6	14	69	7	3	6	10	3	75	10	5	8	.472	.317
Dyer, Mike, Pittsburgh	.571	55	8	7	1	4	4	0	0	0	1	1	0	0	0	0	2	0	0	0	.571	.571
Dykstra, Lenny, Philadelphia*	.264	62	292	254	37	67	90	15	1	2	18	0	2	3	33	2	28	10	5	1	.354	.353
Eischen, Joey, Los Angeles*	.000	17	1	1	0	0	0	0	0	0	0	0	0	0	0	0	1	0	0	0	.000	.000
Eisenreich, Jim, Philadelphia*	.316	129	423	377	46	119	175	22	2	10	55	2	5	1	38	4	44	10	0	7	.464	.375
Elster, Kevin, Philadelphia	.208	26	65	53	10	11	20	4	1	1	9	2	2	1	7	1	14	0	0	1	.377	.302
Encarnacion, Angelo, Pitts.	.226	58	175	159	18	36	53	7	2	2	10	3	0	0	13	5	28	1	1	3	.333	.285
Ericks, John, Pittsburgh	.097	19	37	31	2	3	4	1	0	0	1	6	0	0	0	0	12	0	0	0	.129	.097
Estes, Shawn, San Francisco	.000	3	5	5	0	0	0	0	0	0	0	0	0	0	0	0	2	0	0	1	.000	.000
Eusebio, Tony, Houston	.299	113	408	368	46	110	151	21	1	6	58	1	5	3	31	1	59	0	2	12	.410	.354
Everett, Carl, New York†	.260	79	331	289	48	75	126	13	1	12	54	1	0	2	39	2	67	2	5	11	.436	.352
Eversgerd, Bryan, Montreal	.000	25	1	1	0	0	0	0	0	0	0	0	0	0	0	0	0	0	0	0	.000	.000
Faneyte, Rikkert, San Fran.	.198	46	98	86	7	17	23	4	1	0	4	1	0	0	11	0	27	1	0	2	.267	.289
Fassero, Jeff, Montreal*	.070	30	70	57	6	4	4	0	0	0	1	8	0	0	5	0	29	0	0	0	.070	.145
Fernandez, Sid, Philadelphia*	.043	11	25	23	1	1	1	0	0	0	1	1	0	0	1	0	15	0	0	0	.043	.083
Finley, Steve, San Diego*	.297	139	630	562	104	167	236	23	8	10	44	4	2	3	59	5	62	36	12	8	.420	.366
Fletcher, Darrin, Montreal*	.286	110	389	350	42	100	156	21	1	11	45	1	2	4	32	1	23	0	1	15	.446	.351
Flora, Kevin, Philadelphia	.213	24	81	75	12	16	25	3	0	2	7	2	0	0	4	0	22	1	0	0	.333	.253
Florence, Don, New York	.000	14	1	1	0	0	0	0	0	0	0	0	0	0	0	0	1	0	0	0	.000	.000
Florie, Bryce, San Diego	.000	47	2	2	0	0	0	0	0	0	0	0	0	0	0	0	2	0	0	0	.000	.000
Floyd, Cliff, Montreal*	.130	29	77	69	6	9	13	1	0	1	8	0	0	1	7	0	22	3	0	1	.188	.221
Foley, Tom, Montreal*	.208	11	26	24	2	5	7	2	0	0	2	0	0	0	2	0	4	1	0	2	.292	.269
Fonville, Chad, Mon.-L.A.†	.278	102	350	320	43	89	97	6	1	0	16	6	0	1	23	1	42	20	7	3	.303	.328
Fordyce, Brook, New York	.500	4	3	2	1	1	2	1	0	0	0	0	0	0	1	0	0	0	0	0	1.000	.667
Foster, Kevin, Chicago	.250	33	68	60	7	15	21	1	1	1	9	5	0	0	3	0	16	2	0	0	.350	.286
Franco, Matt, Chicago*	.294	16	17	17	3	5	6	1	0	0	1	0	0	0	0	0	4	0	0	0	.353	.294
Frascatore, John, St. Louis	.000	14	9	7	0	0	0	0	0	0	0	1	0	0	1	0	6	0	0	0	.000	.125
Fraser, Willie, Montreal	.000	14	2	2	0	0	0	0	0	0	0	0	0	0	0	0	0	0	0	0	.000	.000
Frazier, Lou, Montreal†	.190	35	74	63	6	12	14	2	0	0	3	0	1	2	8	0	12	4	0	1	.222	.292
Freeman, Marvin, Colorado	.087	22	30	23	2	2	5	0	0	1	4	6	0	0	1	0	16	0	0	0	.217	.125
Frey, Steve, Philadelphia*	.000	18	1	1	0	0	0	0	0	0	0	0	0	0	0	0	1	0	0	0	.000	.000
Galarraga, Andres, Colorado	.280	143	604	554	89	155	283	29	3	31	106	0	5	13	32	6	146	12	2	14	.511	.331
Gallagher, Dave, Philadelphia	.318	62	176	157	12	50	65	12	0	1	12	2	1	0	16	0	20	0	0	5	.414	.379
Gant, Ron, Cincinnati	.276	119	493	410	79	113	227	19	4	29	88	1	5	3	74	5	108	23	8	11	.554	.386
Garces, Rich, Chicago	.000	18	1	1	0	0	0	0	0	0	0	0	0	0	0	0	0	0	0	0	.000	.000
Garcia, Carlos, Pittsburgh	.294	104	402	367	41	108	154	24	2	6	50	5	3	2	25	5	55	8	4	4	.420	.340
Garcia, Freddy, Pittsburgh	.140	42	66	57	5	8	11	1	1	0	1	1	0	0	8	0	17	0	1	0	.193	.246
Garcia, Karim, L.A.*	.200	13	20	20	1	4	4	0	0	0	0	0	0	0	0	0	4	0	0	0	.200	.200
Gardner, Mark, Florida	.190	39	25	21	1	4	4	0	0	0	1	4	0	0	0	0	6	0	0	0	.190	.190
Giannelli, Ray, St. Louis*	.091	9	14	11	0	1	1	0	0	0	0	0	0	0	3	0	4	0	0	0	.091	.286
Gibralter, Steve, Cincinnati	.333	4	3	3	0	1	1	0	0	0	0	0	0	0	0	0	1	0	0	0	.333	.333
Gilkey, Bernard, St. Louis	.298	121	531	480	73	143	235	33	4	17	69	1	3	5	42	3	70	12	6	17	.490	.358
Giovanola, Ed, Atlanta*	.071	13	17	14	2	1	1	0	0	0	0	0	0	0	3	0	5	0	0	1	.071	.235
Girardi, Joe, Colorado	.262	125	506	462	63	121	166	17	2	8	55	12	1	2	29	0	76	3	3	15	.359	.308
Glavine, Tom, Atlanta*	.222	29	74	63	6	14	18	1	0	1	8	8	0	1	2	0	15	0	0	1	.286	.258
Goff, Jerry, Houston*	.154	12	30	26	2	4	9	2	0	1	3	0	0	0	4	0	13	0	0	1	.346	.267
Gomez, Pat, San Francisco*	.000	18	1	1	0	0	0	0	0	0	0	0	0	0	0	0	1	0	0	0	.000	.000
Gonzalez, Luis, Hou.-Chi.*	.276	133	541	471	69	130	214	29	8	13	69	1	6	6	57	8	63	6	8	16	.454	.357
Gott, Jim, Pittsburgh	.000	25	1	1	0	0	0	0	0	0	0	0	0	0	0	0	0	0	0	0	.000	.000
Grace, Mark, Chicago*	.326	143	627	552	97	180	285	51	3	16	92	1	7	2	65	9	46	6	2	10	.516	.395
Grace, Mike, Philadelphia	.000	2	4	2	0	0	0	0	0	0	0	2	0	0	0	0	2	0	0	0	.000	.000
Grahe, Joe, Colorado	.417	17	18	12	1	5	6	1	0	0	2	6	0	0	0	0	3	0	0	0	.500	.417
Green, Tyler, Philadelphia	.182	27	52	44	2	8	16	5	0	1	5	8	0	0	0	0	16	0	1	0	.364	.182
Greene, Tommy, Philadelphia	.000	11	11	8	0	0	0	0	0	0	0	1	0	0	2	0	3	0	0	0	.000	.200
Greene, Willie, Cincinnati*	.105	8	22	19	1	2	2	0	0	0	0	0	0	0	3	0	7	0	0	1	.105	.227
Greer, Kenny, San Francisco	.000	8	1	1	0	0	0	0	0	0	0	0	0	0	0	0	1	0	0	0	.000	.000
Gregg, Tommy, Florida*	.237	72	176	156	20	37	60	5	0	6	20	0	2	2	16	1	33	3	1	3	.385	.313
Grissom, Marquis, Atlanta	.258	139	606	551	80	142	207	23	3	12	42	1	4	3	47	4	61	29	9	8	.376	.317
Grudzielanek, Mark, Montreal	.245	78	293	269	27	66	85	12	2	1	20	3	0	7	14	4	47	8	3	7	.316	.300
Gunderson, Eric, New York	.000	30	1	0	1	0	0	0	0	0	0	0	0	0	0	0	0	0	0	0	.000	1.000
Guthrie, Mark, Los Angeles	.000	24	1	1	0	0	0	0	0	0	0	0	0	0	0	0	1	0	0	0	.000	.000
Gutierrez, Ricky, Houston	.276	52	169	156	22	43	49	6	0	0	12	1	1	1	10	3	33	5	0	4	.314	.321
Gwynn, Chris, Los Angeles*	.214	67	92	84	8	18	28	3	2	1	10	0	1	1	6	1	23	0	0	5	.333	.272
Gwynn, Tony, San Diego*	.368	135	577	535	82	197	259	33	1	9	90	0	6	1	35	10	15	17	5	20	.484	.404
Habyan, John, St. Louis	.000	31	2	2	0	0	0	0	0	0	0	0	0	0	0	0	0	0	0	0	.000	.000
Hajek, Dave, Houston	.000	5	5	2	0	0	0	0	0	0	0	2	0	1	0	0	1	1	0	0	.000	.333
Hamilton, Joey, San Diego	.108	31	73	65	4	7	9	2	0	0	3	5	1	2	0	0	38	0	0	1	.138	.132
Hammond, Chris, Florida*	.271	25	60	48	7	13	18	2	0	1	4	5	0	0	7	0	16	0	0	1	.375	.364

Player, Team	Avg.	G	TPA	AB	R	H	TB	2B	3B	HR	RBI	SH	SF	HP	BB	IBB	SO	SB	CS	GDP	Slg.	OBP
Hampton, Mike, Houston	.146	24	57	48	7	7	7	0	0	0	0	4	0	1	4	0	14	0	0	0	.146	.226
Haney, Todd, Chicago	.411	25	81	73	11	30	44	8	0	2	6	1	0	0	7	0	11	0	0	0	.603	.463
Hansen, Dave, Los Angeles*	.287	100	211	181	19	52	65	10	0	1	14	0	1	1	28	4	28	0	0	4	.359	.384
Harnisch, Pete, New York	.091	18	36	33	0	3	3	0	0	0	0	3	0	0	0	0	6	0	0	0	.091	.091
Harris, Greg, Montreal†	.333	45	3	3	0	1	2	1	0	0	0	0	0	0	0	0	1	0	0	0	.667	.333
Harris, Lenny, Cincinnati*	.208	101	215	197	32	41	61	8	3	2	16	3	1	0	14	0	20	10	1	6	.310	.259
Hartgraves, Dean, Houston	.000	40	3	2	0	0	0	0	0	0	0	1	0	0	0	0	1	0	0	0	.000	.000
Hayes, Charlie, Philadelphia	.276	141	589	529	58	146	215	30	3	11	85	0	6	4	50	2	88	5	1	22	.406	.340
Hemond, Scott, St. Louis	.144	57	134	118	11	17	27	1	0	3	9	1	1	2	12	0	31	0	0	8	.229	.233
Henke, Tom, St. Louis	.000	52	1	1	0	0	0	0	0	0	0	0	0	0	0	0	0	0	0	0	.000	.000
Henry, Butch, Montreal*	.048	21	47	42	1	2	2	0	0	0	1	5	0	0	0	0	11	0	0	0	.048	.048
Henry, Doug, New York	1.000	51	2	1	1	1	1	0	0	0	0	1	0	0	0	0	0	0	0	0	1.000	1.000
Heredia, Gil, Montreal	.182	40	39	33	1	6	6	0	0	0	2	5	0	0	1	0	3	0	0	0	.182	.206
Hernandez, Carlos, L.A.	.149	45	103	94	3	14	21	1	0	2	8	1	0	1	7	0	25	0	0	5	.223	.216
Hernandez, Jeremy, Florida	.000	7	1	1	0	0	0	0	0	0	0	0	0	0	0	0	0	0	0	0	.000	.000
Hernandez, Jose, Chicago	.245	93	268	245	37	60	118	11	4	13	40	8	2	0	13	3	69	1	0	8	.482	.281
Hernandez, Xavier, Cincinnati*	.000	59	8	8	0	0	0	0	0	0	0	0	0	0	0	0	4	0	0	0	.000	.000
Hickerson, Bryan, Chi.-Col.*	.667	56	5	3	1	2	4	0	1	0	3	1	0	0	1	0	0	0	0	0	1.333	.750
Hill, Glenallen, San Francisco	.264	132	539	497	71	131	240	29	4	24	86	0	2	1	39	4	98	25	5	11	.483	.317
Hill, Ken, St. Louis	.194	18	39	31	1	6	6	0	0	0	3	5	1	0	2	0	10	0	0	3	.194	.235
Hoffman, Trevor, San Diego	.500	55	2	2	1	1	2	1	0	0	2	0	0	0	0	0	1	0	0	0	1.000	.500
Holbert, Ray, San Diego	.178	63	86	73	11	13	23	2	1	2	5	3	0	2	8	1	20	4	0	3	.315	.277
Hollandsworth, Todd, L.A.*	.233	41	115	103	16	24	41	2	0	5	13	0	1	1	10	2	29	2	1	1	.398	.304
Hollins, Dave, Philadelphia†	.229	65	267	205	46	47	84	12	2	7	25	0	4	5	53	4	38	1	1	4	.410	.393
Holmes, Darren, Colorado	.000	68	4	1	0	0	0	0	0	0	0	3	0	0	0	0	0	0	0	0	.000	.000
Hook, Chris, San Francisco	.000	45	3	3	0	0	0	0	0	0	0	0	0	0	0	0	2	0	0	0	.000	.000
Howard, Thomas, Cincinnati†	.302	113	304	281	42	85	113	15	2	3	26	1	1	1	20	0	37	17	8	3	.402	.350
Hubbard, Mike, Chicago	.174	15	25	23	2	4	4	0	0	0	1	0	0	0	2	0	2	0	0	1	.174	.240
Hubbard, Trent, Colorado	.310	24	67	58	13	18	31	4	0	3	9	1	0	0	8	0	6	2	1	2	.534	.394
Hudek, John, Houston†	1.000	19	1	1	0	1	1	0	0	0	2	0	0	0	0	0	0	0	0	0	1.000	1.000
Hulett, Tim, St. Louis	.182	4	11	11	0	2	2	0	0	0	0	0	0	0	0	0	3	0	0	0	.182	.182
Hundley, Todd, New York†	.280	90	326	275	39	77	133	11	0	15	51	1	3	5	42	5	64	1	0	4	.484	.382
Hunter, Brian R., Cincinnati	.215	40	93	79	9	17	26	6	0	1	9	0	2	1	11	1	21	2	1	2	.329	.312
Hunter, Brian L., Houston	.302	78	349	321	52	97	127	14	5	2	28	2	3	2	21	0	52	24	7	2	.396	.346
Huskey, Butch, New York	.189	28	102	90	8	17	27	1	0	3	11	1	1	0	10	0	16	1	0	3	.300	.267
Hyers, Tim, San Diego*	.000	6	5	5	0	0	0	0	0	0	0	0	0	0	0	0	1	0	0	1	.000	.000
Ingram, Garey, Los Angeles	.200	44	66	55	5	11	13	2	0	0	3	2	0	0	9	0	8	3	0	0	.236	.313
Isringhausen, Jason, N.Y.	.148	14	34	27	2	4	5	1	0	0	0	4	0	1	2	0	10	0	0	1	.185	.233
Jackson, Danny, St. Louis	.161	19	36	31	1	5	7	2	0	0	2	4	0	0	1	0	16	0	0	0	.226	.188
Jackson, Mike, Cincinnati	.250	40	4	4	0	1	1	0	0	0	0	0	0	0	0	0	1	0	0	0	.250	.250
Jacome, Jason, New York*	.000	8	7	0	0	0	0	0	0	0	0	1	0	0	0	0	6	0	0	0	.000	.000
Jarvis, Kevin, Cincinnati*	.143	19	23	21	2	3	4	1	0	0	0	1	0	1	0	0	9	0	0	0	.190	.182
Jefferies, Gregg, Philadelphia†	.306	114	521	480	69	147	215	31	2	11	56	0	6	0	35	5	26	9	5	15	.448	.349
Johnson, Brian, San Diego	.251	68	224	207	20	52	70	9	0	3	29	1	4	1	11	2	39	0	0	2	.338	.287
Johnson, Charles, Florida	.251	97	371	315	40	79	129	15	1	11	39	4	2	4	46	2	71	0	2	11	.410	.351
Johnson, Howard, Chicago†	.195	87	206	169	26	33	60	4	1	7	22	0	1	2	34	0	46	1	1	1	.355	.330
Johnson, Mark, Pittsburgh*	.208	79	261	221	32	46	93	6	1	13	28	0	1	2	37	2	66	5	2	2	.421	.326
Jones, Bobby, New York	.161	30	75	56	3	9	9	0	0	0	2	18	0	0	1	0	25	0	0	0	.161	.175
Jones, Chipper, Atlanta†	.265	140	602	524	87	139	236	22	3	23	86	1	4	0	73	1	99	8	4	10	.450	.353
Jones, Chris, New York	.280	79	201	182	33	51	85	6	2	8	31	2	3	1	13	1	45	2	1	2	.467	.327
Jones, Todd, Houston*	.200	68	5	5	1	1	2	1	0	0	0	0	0	0	0	0	1	0	0	0	.400	.200
Jordan, Brian, St. Louis	.296	131	525	490	83	145	239	20	4	22	81	0	2	11	22	4	79	24	9	5	.488	.339
Jordan, Kevin, Philadelphia	.185	24	57	54	6	10	17	1	0	2	6	0	0	1	2	1	9	0	0	1	.315	.228
Juden, Jeff, Philadelphia†	.056	13	21	18	1	1	4	0	0	1	4	3	0	0	0	0	12	0	0	0	.222	.056
Justice, Dave, Atlanta*	.253	120	491	411	73	104	197	17	2	24	78	0	5	2	73	5	68	4	2	5	.479	.365
Karros, Eric, Los Angeles	.298	143	620	551	83	164	295	29	3	32	105	0	4	4	61	4	115	4	4	14	.535	.369
Kelly, Mike, Atlanta	.190	97	153	137	26	26	43	6	1	3	17	2	1	2	11	0	49	7	3	2	.314	.258
Kelly, Roberto, Mon.-L.A.	.278	136	540	504	58	140	188	23	2	7	57	0	7	6	22	6	79	19	10	14	.373	.312
Kent, Jeff, New York	.278	125	514	472	65	131	219	22	3	20	65	1	4	8	29	3	89	3	3	9	.464	.327
Kile, Darryl, Houston	.111	25	45	36	1	4	5	1	0	0	6	5	0	0	4	0	20	0	0	1	.139	.200
King, Jeff, Pittsburgh	.265	122	509	445	61	118	203	27	2	18	87	0	8	1	55	5	63	7	4	10	.456	.342
Kingery, Mike, Colorado*	.269	119	402	350	66	94	144	18	4	8	37	6	1	0	45	1	40	13	5	7	.411	.351
Klesko, Ryan, Atlanta*	.310	107	381	329	48	102	200	25	2	23	70	0	3	2	47	10	72	5	4	8	.608	.396
Kmak, Joe, Chicago	.245	19	61	53	7	13	19	3	0	1	6	0	1	1	6	0	12	0	0	2	.358	.328
Kowitz, Brian, Atlanta*	.167	10	28	24	3	4	5	1	0	0	0	3	0	1	0	0	5	0	1	0	.208	.259
Laker, Tim, Montreal	.234	64	158	141	17	33	52	8	1	3	20	1	1	1	14	4	38	0	1	5	.369	.306
Lampkin, Tom, San Fran.*	.276	65	86	76	8	21	26	2	0	1	9	0	0	1	9	1	8	2	0	1	.342	.360
Lankford, Ray, St. Louis*	.277	132	553	483	81	134	248	35	2	25	82	0	5	2	63	6	110	24	8	10	.513	.360
Lansing, Mike, Montreal	.255	127	502	467	47	119	183	30	2	10	62	1	3	3	28	2	65	27	4	14	.392	.299
Larkin, Barry, Cincinnati	.319	131	567	496	98	158	244	29	6	15	66	3	4	3	61	2	49	51	5	6	.492	.394
Ledesma, Aaron, New York	.242	21	39	33	4	8	8	0	0	0	3	0	0	1	0	0	7	0	0	2	.242	.359
Lee, Manuel, St. Louis†	1.000	1	1	1	1	1	1	0	0	0	0	0	0	0	0	0	0	0	0	0	1.000	1.000
Leiper, Dave, Montreal*	.000	26	1	0	0	0	0	0	0	0	0	1	0	0	0	0	0	0	0	0	.000	.000
Leiter, Mark, San Francisco	.098	30	74	61	2	6	6	0	0	0	5	9	0	0	4	0	33	0	0	2	.098	.154
Lemke, Mark, Atlanta†	.253	116	453	399	42	101	142	16	5	5	38	7	3	0	44	4	40	2	2	17	.356	.325
Leonard, Mark, San Fran.*	.190	14	26	21	4	4	8	1	0	1	4	0	0	0	5	1	2	0	0	0	.381	.346
Leskanic, Curt, Colorado	.143	76	9	7	1	1	1	0	0	0	0	2	0	0	0	0	1	0	0	1	.143	.143
Lewis, Darren, S.F.-Cin.	.250	132	527	472	66	118	140	13	3	1	24	12	1	8	34	0	57	32	18	9	.297	.311
Lewis, Mark, Cincinnati	.339	81	194	171	25	58	82	13	1	3	30	0	2	0	21	2	33	0	3	1	.480	.407
Lewis, Richie, Florida	.000	21	2	1	0	0	0	0	0	0	0	0	0	0	1	0	1	0	0	0	.000	.500
Lieber, Jon, Pittsburgh*	.048	21	21	21	0	1	1	0	0	0	0	0	0	0	0	0	14	0	0	1	.048	.048
Lieberthal, Mike, Philadelphia	.255	16	54	47	1	12	14	2	0	0	4	0	2	0	5	0	5	0	0	1	.298	.327
Liriano, Nelson, Pittsburgh†	.286	107	289	259	29	74	103	12	1	5	38	1	3	2	24	3	34	2	2	2	.398	.347

Player, Team	Avg.	G	TPA	AB	R	H	TB	2B	3B	HR	RBI	SH	SF	HP	BB	IBB	SO	SB	CS	GDP	Slg.	OBP
Livingstone, Scott, San Diego*	.337	99	213	196	26	66	96	15	0	5	32	0	2	0	15	1	22	2	1	3	.490	.380
Loaiza, Esteban, Pittsburgh	.192	33	61	52	4	10	13	1	1	0	2	7	1	0	1	0	11	0	0	1	.250	.204
Lomon, Kevin, New York	.000	6	1	0	0	0	0	0	0	0	0	1	0	0	0	0	0	0	0	0	.000	.000
Longmire, Tony, Philadelphia*	.356	59	117	104	21	37	53	7	0	3	19	0	1	1	11	1	19	1	1	1	.510	.419
Lopez, Javy, Atlanta	.315	100	352	333	37	105	166	11	4	14	51	0	3	2	14	0	57	0	1	13	.498	.344
Mabry, John, St. Louis*	.307	129	418	388	35	119	157	21	1	5	41	0	4	2	24	5	45	0	3	6	.405	.347
Maddux, Greg, Atlanta	.153	28	81	72	8	11	13	2	0	0	6	6	0	0	3	0	22	0	0	0	.181	.187
Magadan, Dave, Houston*	.313	127	422	348	44	109	139	24	0	2	51	1	2	0	71	9	56	2	1	9	.399	.428
Manwaring, Kirt, San Fran.	.251	118	424	379	21	95	126	15	2	4	36	4	4	10	27	6	72	1	0	8	.332	.314
Manzanillo, Ravelo, Pitts.*	.000	5	1	1	0	0	0	0	0	0	0	0	0	0	0	0	1	0	0	0	.000	.000
Marsh, Tom, Philadelphia	.294	43	114	109	13	32	46	3	1	3	15	0	1	0	4	0	25	0	1	1	.422	.316
Martin, Al, Pittsburgh*	.282	124	486	439	70	124	194	25	3	13	41	1	0	2	44	6	92	20	11	5	.442	.351
Martinez, Pedro J., Montreal	.111	30	72	63	2	7	7	0	0	0	2	5	2	2	0	0	30	0	0	1	.111	.134
Martinez, Pedro A., Houston	.000	25	1	0	0	0	0	0	0	0	0	0	0	0	1	0	0	0	0	0	.000	1.000
Martinez, Ramon, L.A.*	.172	30	78	64	2	11	15	4	0	0	4	13	0	0	1	0	19	0	0	0	.234	.185
Mathews, T.J., St. Louis	.000	23	2	2	0	0	0	0	0	0	0	0	0	0	0	0	1	0	0	0	.000	.000
Mathews, Terry, Florida*	.462	57	13	13	2	6	8	2	0	0	3	0	0	0	0	0	4	0	0	1	.615	.462
Mauser, Tim, San Diego	.000	5	1	1	0	0	0	0	0	0	0	0	0	0	0	0	1	0	0	0	.000	.000
May, Derrick, Houston*	.301	78	229	206	29	62	103	15	1	8	41	0	3	1	19	0	24	5	0	4	.500	.358
McCarty, Dave, San Fran.	.250	12	22	20	1	5	6	1	0	0	2	0	0	0	2	0	4	1	0	0	.300	.318
McCracken, Quinton, Col.†	.000	3	1	1	0	0	0	0	0	0	0	0	0	0	0	0	1	0	0	0	.000	.000
McCurry, Jeff, Pittsburgh	.000	55	3	3	0	0	0	0	0	0	0	0	0	0	0	0	1	0	0	0	.000	.000
McDavid, Ray, San Diego*	.176	11	19	17	2	3	3	0	0	0	0	0	0	0	2	0	6	1	1	1	.176	.263
McElroy, Chuck, Cincinnati*	.000	44	3	3	0	0	0	0	0	0	0	0	0	0	0	0	0	0	0	0	.000	.000
McGriff, Fred, Atlanta*	.280	144	604	528	85	148	258	27	1	27	93	0	6	5	65	6	99	3	6	19	.489	.361
McMichael, Greg, Atlanta	.000	67	7	6	0	0	0	0	0	0	0	0	0	0	1	0	4	0	0	0	.000	.143
McMurtry, Craig, Houston	.000	11	1	1	0	0	0	0	0	0	0	0	0	0	0	0	0	0	0	0	.000	.000
McRae, Brian, Chicago†	.288	137	638	580	92	167	255	38	7	12	48	3	1	7	47	1	92	27	8	12	.440	.348
Mejia, Roberto, Colorado	.154	23	54	52	5	8	12	1	0	1	4	0	1	1	0	0	17	0	1	1	.231	.167
Merced, Orlando, Pittsburgh*	.300	132	545	487	75	146	228	29	4	15	83	0	5	1	52	9	74	7	2	9	.468	.365
Mercker, Kent, Atlanta*	.104	29	54	48	1	5	8	3	0	0	5	6	0	0	0	0	17	0	0	0	.167	.104
Miceli, Danny, Pittsburgh	.000	58	1	1	0	0	0	0	0	0	0	0	0	0	0	0	1	0	0	0	.000	.000
Miller, Orlando, Houston	.262	92	355	324	36	85	122	20	1	5	36	4	0	5	22	8	71	3	4	7	.377	.319
Mimbs, Michael, Phil.*	.143	35	43	35	2	5	6	1	0	0	2	8	0	0	0	0	12	0	0	1	.171	.143
Minor, Blas, New York	.000	35	2	2	0	0	0	0	0	0	0	0	0	0	0	0	0	0	0	0	.000	.000
Mintz, Steve, San Francisco*	.000	14	3	3	0	0	0	0	0	0	0	0	0	0	0	0	3	0	0	0	.000	.000
Mlicki, Dave, New York	.051	29	59	39	2	2	2	0	0	0	2	12	0	0	8	0	12	0	0	0	.051	.213
Mondesi, Raul, Los Angeles	.285	139	580	536	91	153	266	23	6	26	88	0	7	4	33	4	96	27	4	7	.496	.328
Morandini, Mickey, Phil.*	.283	127	550	494	65	140	206	34	7	6	49	4	1	9	42	3	80	9	6	11	.417	.350
Mordecai, Mike, Atlanta	.280	69	87	75	10	21	36	6	0	3	11	2	1	0	9	0	16	0	0	0	.480	.353
Morgan, Mike, Chi.-St.L.	.053	21	45	38	2	2	2	0	0	0	0	4	0	0	3	0	20	0	0	0	.053	.122
Morman, Russ, Florida	.278	34	76	72	9	20	33	2	1	3	7	0	1	0	3	0	12	0	0	5	.458	.316
Morris, Hal, Cincinnati*	.279	101	391	359	53	100	162	25	2	11	51	1	1	1	29	7	58	1	1	10	.451	.333
Mouton, James, Houston	.262	104	331	298	42	78	112	18	2	4	27	3	1	4	25	1	59	25	8	5	.376	.326
Mulholland, Terry, San Fran.	.102	30	54	49	3	5	11	1	1	1	3	3	1	0	1	0	22	0	0	1	.224	.118
Munoz, Bobby, Philadelphia	.000	3	5	5	0	0	0	0	0	0	0	0	0	0	0	0	2	0	0	0	.000	.000
Munoz, Mike, Colorado*	.500	64	4	2	1	1	2	1	0	0	1	0	0	0	2	0	1	0	0	0	1.000	.750
Munoz, Noe, Los Angeles	.000	2	1	1	0	0	0	0	0	0	0	0	0	0	0	0	0	0	0	0	.000	.000
Murphy, Rob, Los Angeles*	1.000	14	1	1	0	1	1	0	0	0	0	0	0	0	0	0	0	0	0	0	1.000	1.000
Murray, Matt, Atlanta*	.500	4	2	2	0	1	1	0	0	0	0	0	0	0	0	0	1	0	0	0	.500	.500
Myers, Randy, Chicago*	.000	57	1	0	0	0	0	0	0	0	0	1	0	0	0	0	1	0	0	0	.000	1.000
Nabholz, Chris, Chicago*	.000	34	1	1	0	0	0	0	0	0	0	0	0	0	0	0	0	0	0	0	.000	.000
Natal, Bob, Florida	.233	16	46	43	2	10	20	2	1	2	6	1	1	0	1	0	9	0	0	0	.465	.244
Navarro, Jaime, Chicago	.185	29	74	65	0	12	17	5	0	0	7	8	0	0	1	0	25	0	0	0	.262	.197
Neagle, Denny, Pittsburgh*	.122	32	83	74	5	9	15	3	0	1	8	5	0	0	4	0	26	0	0	0	.203	.167
Nevin, Phil, Houston	.117	18	69	60	4	7	8	1	0	0	1	0	1	1	7	1	13	1	0	2	.133	.221
Newfield, Marc, San Diego	.309	21	57	55	6	17	27	5	1	1	7	0	0	0	2	0	8	0	0	3	.491	.333
Nieves, Melvin, San Diego†	.205	98	262	234	32	48	98	6	1	14	38	1	3	5	19	0	88	2	3	9	.419	.276
Nitkowski, C.J., Cincinnati*	.200	9	10	10	1	2	2	0	0	0	1	0	0	0	0	0	6	0	0	0	.200	.200
Nokes, Matt, Colorado*	.182	10	12	11	1	2	3	1	0	0	0	0	0	0	1	1	4	0	0	1	.273	.250
Nomo, Hideo, Los Angeles	.091	28	72	66	2	6	6	0	0	0	4	5	1	0	0	0	33	0	0	1	.091	.090
O'Brien, Charlie, Atlanta	.227	67	233	198	18	45	79	7	0	9	23	0	0	6	29	2	40	0	1	8	.399	.343
Ochoa, Alex, New York	.297	11	39	37	7	11	12	1	0	0	0	0	0	0	2	0	10	1	0	1	.324	.333
Offerman, Jose, L.A.†	.287	119	511	429	69	123	161	14	6	4	33	10	0	3	69	0	67	2	7	5	.375	.389
Oliva, Jose, Atl.-St.L.	.142	70	198	183	15	26	52	5	0	7	20	0	1	2	12	0	46	0	0	5	.284	.202
Olivares, Omar, Col.-Phi.	.222	17	11	9	1	2	6	1	0	1	2	1	0	0	1	0	4	0	0	0	.667	.300
Oquendo, Jose, St. Louis†	.209	88	260	220	31	46	66	8	3	2	17	4	1	0	35	3	21	1	1	1	.300	.321
Orsulak, Joe, New York*	.283	108	317	290	41	82	108	19	2	1	37	1	6	1	19	2	35	1	3	3	.372	.323
Osborne, Donovan, St. Louis*	.161	19	38	31	1	5	8	3	0	0	4	3	0	1	3	0	15	0	0	0	.258	.257
Osuna, Antonio, Los Angeles	.000	39	2	2	0	0	0	0	0	0	0	0	0	0	0	0	0	0	0	0	.000	.000
Otero, Ricky, New York†	.137	35	55	51	5	7	9	2	0	0	1	1	0	0	3	0	10	2	1	1	.176	.185
Owens, Eric, Cincinnati	1.000	2	3	2	0	2	2	0	0	0	1	1	0	0	1	0	0	0	0	0	1.000	1.000
Owens, Jayhawk, Colorado	.244	18	49	45	7	11	25	2	0	4	12	0	1	1	2	0	15	0	0	0	.556	.286
Pagnozzi, Tom, St. Louis	.215	62	232	219	17	47	69	14	1	2	15	0	1	1	11	0	31	0	1	9	.315	.254
Painter, Lance, Colorado*	.111	33	11	9	0	1	2	1	0	0	0	1	0	0	1	0	4	0	0	0	.222	.200
Palacios, Vince, St. Louis	.167	20	7	6	1	1	1	0	0	0	0	1	0	0	0	0	4	0	0	0	.167	.167
Parent, Mark, Pit.-Chi.	.234	81	292	265	30	62	127	11	0	18	38	1	0	0	26	2	69	0	0	6	.479	.302
Park, Chan Ho, Los Angeles	.000	2	1	1	0	0	0	0	0	0	0	0	0	0	0	0	1	0	0	0	.000	.000
Parker, Rick, Los Angeles	.276	27	33	29	3	8	8	0	0	0	4	2	0	0	2	0	4	1	1	1	.276	.323
Parra, Jose, Los Angeles	.000	8	2	0	0	0	0	0	0	0	0	0	2	0	0	0	0	0	0	0	.000	.000
Parrett, Jeff, St. Louis	.500	59	2	2	0	1	1	0	0	0	0	0	0	0	0	0	1	0	0	0	.500	.500
Parris, Steve, Pittsburgh	.250	15	29	28	2	7	9	2	0	0	4	1	0	0	0	0	10	0	0	0	.321	.250
Patterson, John, San Fran.†	.205	95	237	205	27	42	56	5	3	1	14	6	0	12	14	1	41	4	2	7	.273	.294

Player, Team	Avg.	G	TPA	AB	R	H	TB	2B	3B	HR	RBI	SH	SF	HP	BB	IBB	SO	SB	CS	GDP	Slg.	OBP
Pegues, Steve, Pittsburgh	.246	82	179	171	17	42	68	8	0	6	16	0	3	1	4	0	36	1	2	3	.398	.263
Pena, Alejandro, Florida	.000	27	1	0	0	0	0	0	0	0	0	0	0	0	0	0	1	0	0	0	.000	.000
Pena, Geronimo, St. Louis†	.267	32	124	101	20	27	38	6	1	1	8	4	2	1	16	1	30	3	2	2	.376	.367
Pendleton, Terry, Florida†	.290	133	557	513	70	149	225	32	1	14	78	0	4	2	38	7	84	1	2	7	.439	.339
Pennington, Brad, Cincinnati*	.000	6	2	2	0	0	0	0	0	0	0	0	0	0	0	0	1	0	0	0	.000	.000
Perez, Carlos, Montreal*	.133	28	53	45	1	6	12	1	1	1	5	4	0	0	4	0	21	0	0	0	.267	.204
Perez, Eddie, Atlanta	.308	7	13	13	1	4	8	1	0	1	4	0	0	0	0	0	2	0	0	0	.615	.308
Perez, Mike, Chicago	.000	68	7	4	1	0	0	0	0	0	0	1	0	0	2	0	4	0	0	0	.000	.333
Perez, Yorkis, Florida*	.000	69	2	2	0	0	0	0	0	0	0	0	0	0	0	0	1	0	0	0	.000	.000
Perry, Gerald, St. Louis*	.165	65	85	79	4	13	17	4	0	0	5	0	0	0	6	0	12	0	0	2	.215	.224
Person, Robert, New York	.667	3	3	3	1	2	2	0	0	0	0	0	0	0	0	0	0	0	0	0	.667	.667
Petagine, Roberto, San Diego*	.234	89	152	124	15	29	46	8	0	3	17	2	0	0	26	2	41	0	0	2	.371	.367
Petkovsek, Mark, St. Louis	.081	26	46	37	4	3	3	0	0	0	2	3	1	0	5	0	11	0	0	3	.081	.186
Phillips, J.R., San Francisco*	.195	92	252	231	27	45	81	9	0	9	28	2	0	0	19	2	69	1	1	3	.351	.256
Piazza, Mike, Los Angeles	.346	112	475	434	82	150	263	17	0	32	93	0	1	1	39	10	80	1	0	10	.606	.400
Plantier, Phil, Hou.-S.D.*	.255	76	248	216	33	55	88	6	0	9	34	0	3	1	28	3	48	1	1	3	.407	.339
Plesac, Dan, Pittsburgh*	.250	58	4	4	0	1	1	0	0	0	0	0	0	0	0	0	3	0	0	0	.250	.250
Polonia, Luis, Atlanta*	.264	28	57	53	6	14	21	7	0	0	2	1	0	0	3	0	9	3	0	0	.396	.304
Portugal, Mark, S.F.-Cin.	.138	31	71	58	5	8	13	5	0	0	5	8	0	0	5	0	13	0	0	1	.224	.206
Powell, Ross, Pittsburgh*	.000	27	4	3	0	0	0	0	0	0	0	1	0	0	0	0	1	0	0	0	.000	.000
Pratt, Todd, Chicago	.133	25	67	60	3	8	10	2	0	0	4	0	1	0	6	1	21	0	0	1	.167	.209
Pride, Curtis, Montreal*	.175	48	69	63	10	11	12	1	0	0	2	1	0	0	5	0	16	3	2	2	.190	.235
Prince, Tom, Los Angeles	.200	18	44	40	3	8	15	2	1	1	4	0	0	0	4	0	10	0	0	0	.375	.273
Pugh, Tim, Cincinnati	.143	29	33	28	2	4	6	2	0	0	1	4	0	0	1	0	12	0	0	1	.214	.172
Pulliam, Harvey, Colorado	.400	5	5	5	1	2	6	1	0	1	3	0	0	0	0	0	2	0	0	0	1.200	.400
Pulsipher, Bill, New York*	.105	17	49	38	4	4	6	2	0	0	4	4	2	0	5	0	19	0	0	0	.158	.200
Pye, Eddie, Los Angeles	.000	7	8	8	0	0	0	0	0	0	0	0	0	0	0	0	4	0	0	0	.000	.000
Quantrill, Paul, Philadelphia*	.105	33	67	57	5	6	6	0	0	0	7	0	0	0	3	0	24	0	0	1	.105	.150
Rapp, Pat, Florida	.107	28	65	56	1	6	7	1	0	0	5	9	0	0	0	0	25	0	0	1	.125	.107
Ready, Randy Max, Phil.	.138	23	33	29	3	4	4	0	0	0	0	1	0	0	3	0	6	0	1	2	.138	.219
Reed, Jeff, San Francisco*	.265	66	134	113	12	30	32	2	0	0	9	1	0	0	20	3	17	0	0	3	.283	.376
Reed, Jody, San Diego	.256	131	515	445	58	114	146	18	1	4	40	3	3	5	59	1	38	6	4	9	.328	.348
Reed, Rick, Cincinnati	.000	4	5	3	0	0	0	0	0	0	0	2	0	0	0	0	0	0	0	0	.000	.000
Reed, Steve, Colorado	.333	71	3	3	0	1	1	0	0	0	0	0	0	0	0	0	1	0	0	0	.333	.333
Rekar, Bryan, Colorado	.038	15	33	26	1	1	1	0	0	0	0	4	0	0	3	0	15	0	1	2	.038	.138
Remlinger, Mike, New York*	.000	7	1	1	0	0	0	0	0	0	0	0	0	0	0	0	0	0	0	0	.000	.000
Reynolds, Shane, Houston	.127	31	74	63	4	8	9	1	0	0	1	10	0	0	1	0	30	0	0	2	.143	.141
Reynoso, Armando, Colorado	.133	20	33	30	1	4	4	0	0	0	0	2	0	0	1	0	11	0	0	2	.133	.161
Rhodes, Karl, Chicago*	.125	13	17	16	2	2	2	0	0	0	2	0	1	0	0	0	4	0	0	1	.125	.118
Rijo, Jose, Cincinnati	.136	14	24	22	1	3	4	1	0	0	3	2	0	0	0	0	3	0	0	0	.182	.136
Ritz, Kevin, Colorado	.188	31	63	48	3	9	10	1	0	0	2	11	0	2	2	0	20	1	1	1	.208	.250
Roberson, Kevin, Chicago†	.184	32	45	38	5	7	20	1	0	4	6	0	0	1	6	0	14	0	1	1	.526	.311
Roberts, Bip, San Diego†	.304	73	316	296	40	90	110	14	0	2	25	1	0	2	17	1	36	20	2	2	.372	.346
Rodriguez, Henry, L.A.-Mon.*	.239	45	150	138	13	33	45	4	1	2	15	0	1	0	11	2	28	0	1	5	.326	.293
Rojas, Mel, Montreal	.000	59	8	6	0	0	0	0	0	0	0	2	0	0	0	0	4	0	0	0	.000	.000
Roper, John, Cincinnati	.000	3	2	1	0	0	0	0	0	0	0	1	0	0	0	0	0	0	0	0	.000	.000
Rosselli, Joe, San Francisco	.200	9	11	10	1	2	2	0	0	0	1	1	0	0	0	0	3	0	0	0	.200	.200
Rueter, Kirk, Montreal*	.000	9	18	16	0	0	0	0	0	0	1	2	0	0	0	0	6	0	0	0	.000	.000
Ruffin, Bruce, Colorado†	.000	37	2	0	0	0	0	0	0	0	0	0	0	0	0	0	0	0	0	0	.000	.000
Ruffin, Johnny, Cincinnati	.000	10	2	2	0	0	0	0	0	0	0	0	0	0	0	0	0	0	0	0	.000	.000
Saberhagen, Bret, N.Y.-Col.	.102	25	56	49	3	5	6	1	0	0	0	5	0	0	2	0	12	0	0	0	.122	.137
Sabo, Chris, St. Louis	.154	5	14	13	0	2	3	1	0	0	3	0	0	1	0	2	1	0	1	.231	.214
Sager, A.J., Colorado	.000	10	3	3	0	0	0	0	0	0	0	0	0	0	0	0	1	0	0	0	.000	.000
Sanchez, Rey, Chicago	.278	114	453	428	57	119	154	22	2	3	27	8	2	1	14	2	48	6	4	9	.360	.301
Sanders, Deion, Cin.-S.F.*	.268	85	379	343	48	92	137	11	8	6	28	3	2	4	27	0	60	24	9	1	.399	.327
Sanders, Reggie, Cincinnati	.306	133	567	484	91	148	280	36	6	28	99	0	6	8	69	4	122	36	12	9	.579	.397
Sanders, Scott, San Diego	.296	17	31	27	2	8	9	1	0	0	4	3	0	0	1	0	3	1	0	0	.333	.321
Santangelo, F.P., Montreal†	.296	35	113	98	11	29	39	5	1	1	9	1	0	2	12	0	9	1	1	0	.398	.384
Santiago, Benito, Cincinnati	.286	81	296	266	40	76	129	20	0	11	44	0	2	4	24	1	48	2	2	7	.485	.351
Sasser, Mackey, Pittsburgh*	.154	14	26	26	1	4	5	1	0	0	0	0	0	0	0	0	0	0	0	0	.192	.154
Scarsone, Steve, San Fran.	.266	80	261	233	33	62	111	10	3	11	29	3	1	6	18	0	82	3	2	2	.476	.333
Schall, Gene, Philadelphia	.231	24	72	65	2	15	17	2	0	0	5	0	0	1	6	1	16	0	0	1	.262	.306
Scheid, Rich, Florida*	.000	6	1	1	0	0	0	0	0	0	0	0	0	0	0	0	0	0	0	0	.000	.000
Schilling, Curt, Philadelphia	.175	17	45	40	3	7	9	2	0	0	3	5	0	0	0	0	15	0	0	1	.225	.175
Schmidt, Jason, Atlanta	.200	9	7	5	0	1	1	0	0	0	0	1	0	0	1	0	2	0	0	0	.200	.333
Schofield, Dick, Los Angeles	.100	9	11	10	0	1	1	0	0	0	0	0	0	1	0	0	3	0	0	0	.100	.182
Schourek, Pete, Cincinnati*	.220	29	71	59	7	13	15	2	0	0	4	12	0	0	0	0	12	0	0	1	.254	.220
Scott, Tim, Montreal	.250	62	4	4	0	1	1	0	0	0	0	0	0	0	0	0	2	0	0	0	.250	.250
Seanez, Rudy, Los Angeles	.000	37	1	1	0	0	0	0	0	0	0	0	0	0	0	0	1	0	0	0	.000	.000
Sefcik, Kevin, Philadelphia	.000	5	4	4	1	0	0	0	0	0	0	0	0	0	0	0	2	0	0	0	.000	.000
Segui, David, N.Y.-Mon.†	.309	130	511	456	68	141	210	25	4	12	68	8	3	3	40	5	47	2	7	10	.461	.367
Servais, Scott, Hou.-Chi.	.265	80	304	264	38	70	131	22	0	13	47	2	3	3	32	4	52	2	2	9	.496	.348
Service, Scott, San Francisco	.000	28	1	1	0	0	0	0	0	0	0	0	0	0	0	0	1	0	0	0	.000	.000
Sharperson, Mike, Atlanta	.143	7	7	7	1	1	2	1	0	0	2	0	0	0	0	0	2	0	0	0	.286	.143
Shaw, Jeff, Montreal	.000	50	8	6	2	0	0	0	0	0	0	0	0	0	0	0	4	0	0	0	.000	.250
Sheaffer, Danny, St. Louis	.231	76	232	208	24	48	75	10	1	5	30	0	1	0	23	2	38	0	0	8	.361	.306
Sheffield, Gary, Florida	.324	63	274	213	46	69	125	8	0	16	46	0	2	4	55	8	45	19	4	3	.587	.467
Shipley, Craig, Houston	.263	92	245	232	23	61	80	8	1	3	24	1	2	2	8	3	28	6	1	13	.345	.291
Siddall, Joe, Montreal*	.300	7	14	10	4	3	3	0	0	0	1	0	0	1	3	0	3	0	0	0	.300	.500
Silvestri, Dave, Montreal	.264	39	83	72	12	19	31	6	0	2	7	1	1	0	9	0	27	2	0	2	.431	.341
Simms, Mike, Houston	.256	50	138	121	14	31	62	4	0	9	24	0	1	3	13	0	28	1	2	3	.512	.341
Slaught, Don, Pittsburgh	.304	35	123	112	13	34	40	6	0	0	13	1	0	1	9	2	8	0	0	5	.357	.361
Slocumb, Heathcliff, Phil.	.000	61	1	1	0	0	0	0	0	0	0	0	0	0	0	0	0	0	0	0	.000	.000

Player, Team	Avg.	G	TPA	AB	R	H	TB	2B	3B	HR	RBI	SH	SF	HP	BB	IBB	SO	SB	CS	GDP	Slg.	OBP
Smiley, John, Cincinnati*	.164	28	66	55	6	9	16	1	0	2	5	6	1	0	4	0	26	0	0	1	.291	.217
Smith, Dwight, Atlanta*	.252	103	147	131	16	33	54	8	2	3	21	0	1	2	13	1	35	0	3	2	.412	.327
Smith, Ozzie, St. Louis†	.199	44	182	156	16	31	38	5	1	0	11	5	2	2	17	0	12	4	3	6	.244	.282
Smith, Pete, Cincinnati	.000	11	5	3	0	0	0	0	0	0	0	0	0	0	2	0	2	0	0	0	.000	.400
Smoltz, John, Atlanta	.107	29	69	56	5	6	6	0	0	0	1	6	0	0	7	0	25	0	0	0	.107	.206
Sosa, Sammy, Chicago	.268	144	629	564	89	151	282	17	3	36	119	0	2	5	58	11	134	34	7	8	.500	.340
Spehr, Tim, Montreal	.257	41	44	35	4	9	17	5	0	1	3	3	0	0	6	0	7	0	0	0	.486	.366
Spiers, Bill, New York*	.208	63	87	72	5	15	19	2	1	0	11	1	2	0	12	1	15	0	1	0	.264	.314
Springer, Dennis, Philadelphia	.125	4	8	8	0	1	1	0	0	0	0	0	0	0	0	0	3	0	0	0	.125	.125
Springer, Russ, Philadelphia	.000	14	2	1	0	0	0	0	0	0	0	1	0	0	0	0	1	0	0	0	.000	.000
Stankiewicz, Andy, Houston	.115	43	65	52	6	6	7	1	0	0	7	1	0	0	12	2	19	4	2	1	.135	.281
Stinnett, Kelly, New York	.219	77	231	196	23	43	65	8	1	4	18	0	0	6	29	3	65	2	0	3	.332	.338
Stocker, Kevin, Philadelphia†	.218	125	477	412	42	90	113	14	3	1	32	10	3	9	43	9	75	6	1	7	.274	.304
Sullivan, Scott, Cincinnati	.000	3	1	1	0	0	0	0	0	0	0	0	0	0	0	0	1	0	0	0	.000	.000
Sweeney, Mark, St. Louis*	.273	37	90	77	5	21	29	2	0	2	13	1	2	0	10	0	15	1	1	3	.377	.348
Swift, Bill, Colorado	.194	19	43	36	5	7	11	1	0	1	4	5	0	0	2	0	5	1	0	0	.306	.237
Swindell, Greg, Houston	.240	34	59	50	4	12	15	3	0	0	5	6	0	0	3	0	9	0	0	1	.300	.283
Tabaka, Jeff, Houston	.000	34	2	1	0	0	0	0	0	0	0	1	0	0	0	0	0	0	0	0	.000	.000
Tapani, Kevin, Los Angeles	.176	13	20	17	0	3	4	1	0	0	2	3	0	0	0	0	7	0	0	0	.235	.176
Tarasco, Tony, Montreal*	.249	126	495	438	64	109	177	18	4	14	40	3	1	2	51	12	78	24	3	2	.404	.329
Tatum, Jimmy, Colorado	.235	34	35	34	4	8	11	1	1	0	4	0	0	0	1	0	7	0	0	1	.324	.257
Taubensee, Eddie, Cincinnati*	.284	80	244	218	32	62	107	14	2	9	44	1	1	2	22	2	52	2	2	2	.491	.354
Tavarez, Jesus, Florida†	.289	63	211	190	31	55	71	6	2	2	13	3	1	1	16	1	27	7	5	1	.374	.346
Telgheder, Dave, New York	.333	7	7	6	1	2	2	0	0	0	1	1	0	0	0	0	3	0	0	0	.333	.333
Thompson, Mark, Colorado	.385	21	14	13	2	5	5	0	0	0	1	0	0	0	0	0	7	0	0	0	.385	.385
Thompson, Milt, Houston*	.220	92	150	132	14	29	44	9	0	2	19	2	1	1	14	3	37	4	2	3	.333	.297
Thompson, Robby, San Fran.	.223	95	391	336	51	75	114	15	0	8	23	9	0	4	42	1	76	1	2	3	.339	.317
Thompson, Ryan, New York	.251	75	294	267	39	67	101	13	0	7	31	0	4	4	19	1	77	3	1	12	.378	.306
Timmons, Ozzie, Chicago	.263	77	185	171	30	45	81	10	1	8	28	0	1	0	13	2	32	3	0	8	.474	.314
Torres, Salomon, San Fran.	.000	4	1	1	0	0	0	0	0	0	0	0	0	0	0	0	0	0	0	0	.000	.000
Trachsel, Steve, Chicago	.265	30	58	49	3	13	15	2	0	0	4	6	1	0	2	0	17	0	0	0	.306	.288
Treadway, Jeff, L.A.-Mon.*	.209	58	72	67	6	14	18	2	1	0	13	0	0	0	5	1	4	0	1	0	.269	.264
Tucker, Scooter, Houston	.286	5	7	7	1	2	5	0	0	1	1	0	0	0	0	0	0	0	0	0	.714	.286
Urbani, Tom, St. Louis*	.316	24	24	19	3	6	10	1	0	1	3	2	0	0	3	0	6	0	0	0	.526	.409
Urbina, Ugueth, Montreal	.333	7	6	6	0	2	2	0	0	0	0	0	0	0	0	0	4	0	0	0	.333	.333
Valdes, Ismael, Los Angeles	.097	33	70	62	2	6	6	0	0	0	1	7	0	0	1	0	26	1	0	0	.097	.111
Valdes, Marc, Florida	.000	3	2	2	0	0	0	0	0	0	0	0	0	0	0	0	0	0	0	0	.000	.000
Valdez, Carlos, San Francisco	.000	11	1	1	0	0	0	0	0	0	0	0	0	0	0	0	1	0	0	0	.000	.000
Valdez, Sergio, San Francisco	.095	13	24	21	1	2	2	0	0	0	1	3	0	0	0	0	9	0	0	0	.095	.095
Valenzuela, Fernando, S.D.*	.250	29	35	32	3	8	15	1	0	2	8	3	0	0	0	0	6	0	0	0	.469	.250
Vander Wal, John, Colorado*	.347	105	118	101	15	35	60	8	1	5	21	0	1	0	16	5	23	1	1	2	.594	.432
VanLandingham, William, S.F.	.152	18	47	46	1	7	12	2	0	1	3	1	0	0	0	0	24	0	0	1	.261	.152
Van Slyke, Andy, Philadelphia*	.243	63	247	214	26	52	75	10	2	3	16	0	2	2	28	1	41	7	0	6	.350	.333
Varsho, Gary, Philadelphia*	.252	72	113	103	7	26	29	1	1	0	11	0	1	2	7	1	17	2	0	1	.282	.310
Veras, Quilvio, Florida†	.261	124	538	440	86	115	164	20	7	5	32	7	2	9	80	0	68	56	21	7	.373	.384
Veres, Dave, Houston	.000	72	6	5	0	0	0	0	0	0	0	1	0	0	0	0	4	0	0	0	.000	.000
Veres, Randy, Florida	.000	47	3	3	0	0	0	0	0	0	0	0	0	0	0	0	0	0	0	0	.000	.000
Villone, Ron, San Diego*	.000	19	1	1	0	0	0	0	0	0	0	0	0	0	0	0	0	0	0	0	.000	.000
Viola, Frank, Cincinnati*	.167	3	6	6	0	1	2	1	0	0	0	0	0	0	0	0	1	0	0	0	.333	.167
Vizcaino, Jose, New York†	.287	135	561	509	66	146	186	21	5	3	56	13	3	1	35	4	76	8	3	14	.365	.332
Wagner, Paul, Pittsburgh	.214	34	52	42	5	9	10	1	0	0	4	6	0	0	4	0	11	0	0	1	.238	.283
Walker, Larry, Colorado*	.306	131	562	494	96	151	300	31	5	36	101	0	5	14	49	13	72	16	3	13	.607	.381
Walker, Mike, Chicago	.000	42	3	3	0	0	0	0	0	0	0	0	0	0	0	0	1	0	0	0	.000	.000
Wall, Donnie, Houston	.000	6	8	5	0	0	0	0	0	0	0	3	0	0	0	0	2	0	0	0	.000	.000
Wallach, Tim, Los Angeles	.266	97	362	327	24	87	140	22	2	9	38	0	4	4	27	4	69	0	0	11	.428	.326
Walton, Jerome, Cincinnati	.290	102	188	162	32	47	85	12	1	8	22	3	2	4	17	0	25	10	7	0	.525	.368
Watson, Allen, St. Louis*	.417	21	41	36	5	15	19	4	0	0	5	3	0	0	2	0	7	0	0	1	.528	.447
Weathers, Dave, Florida	.154	28	31	26	1	4	4	0	0	0	1	5	0	0	0	0	17	0	0	0	.154	.154
Webster, Lenny, Philadelphia	.267	49	167	150	18	40	61	9	0	4	14	1	0	0	16	0	27	0	0	4	.407	.337
Webster, Mitch, Los Angeles†	.179	54	63	56	6	10	16	1	1	1	3	2	0	1	4	1	14	0	0	1	.286	.246
Wehner, John, Pittsburgh	.308	52	123	107	13	33	39	0	3	0	5	4	2	0	10	1	17	3	1	2	.364	.361
Weiss, Walt, Colorado†	.260	137	537	427	65	111	137	17	3	1	25	6	1	5	98	8	57	15	3	7	.321	.403
Wells, David, Cincinnati*	.143	11	29	28	2	4	4	0	0	0	0	1	0	0	0	0	6	0	0	0	.143	.143
Wendell, Turk, Chicago*	.000	43	8	7	0	0	0	0	0	0	0	1	0	0	0	0	5	0	0	0	.000	.125
West, David, Philadelphia*	.125	8	15	8	1	1	4	0	0	1	3	6	0	0	1	0	4	0	0	1	.500	.222
White, Gabe, Montreal*	.000	19	4	3	0	0	0	0	0	0	0	1	0	0	0	0	0	0	0	0	.000	.000
White, Rick, Pittsburgh	.067	15	17	15	1	1	2	1	0	0	1	2	0	0	0	0	3	0	0	0	.133	.067
White, Rondell, Montreal	.295	130	525	474	87	140	220	33	4	13	57	0	4	6	41	1	87	25	5	11	.464	.356
Whiten, Mark, Philadelphia†	.269	60	245	212	38	57	102	10	1	11	37	0	0	1	31	1	63	7	0	4	.481	.365
Whitmore, Darrell, Florida*	.190	27	65	58	6	11	16	2	0	1	2	1	1	0	5	0	15	0	0	1	.276	.250
Wilkins, Rick, Chi.-Hou.*	.203	65	251	202	30	41	65	3	0	7	19	0	2	1	46	2	61	0	0	9	.322	.351
Williams, Brian, San Diego	.071	44	14	14	1	1	2	1	0	0	0	0	0	0	0	0	4	0	0	1	.143	.071
Williams, Eddie, San Diego	.260	97	325	296	35	77	126	11	1	12	47	0	2	4	23	0	47	0	0	21	.426	.320
Williams, Matt, San Francisco	.336	76	318	283	53	95	183	17	1	23	65	0	3	2	30	8	58	2	0	8	.647	.399
Williams, Mike, Philadelphia†	.125	33	24	16	0	2	3	1	0	0	1	7	0	0	1	0	5	0	0	0	.188	.176
Williams, Reggie, Los Angeles†	.091	15	13	11	2	1	1	0	0	0	1	0	0	0	2	0	3	0	0	0	.091	.231
Williams, Todd, Los Angeles	.500	16	2	2	0	1	1	0	0	0	0	0	0	0	0	0	0	0	0	0	.500	.500
Wilson, Gary, Pittsburgh	.000	10	1	0	0	0	0	0	0	0	0	1	0	0	0	0	0	0	0	0	.000	.000
Wilson, Nigel, Cincinnati*	.000	5	7	7	0	0	0	0	0	0	0	0	0	0	0	0	4	0	0	0	.000	.000
Wilson, Trevor, San Fran.*	.233	19	33	30	1	7	8	1	0	0	3	3	0	0	0	0	8	0	0	0	.267	.233
Witt, Bobby, Florida	.063	21	38	32	0	2	3	1	0	0	2	4	1	0	1	0	10	0	0	0	.094	.088
Wohlers, Mark, Atlanta	.000	65	3	3	0	0	0	0	0	0	0	0	0	0	0	0	3	0	0	0	.000	.000
Woodall, Brad, Atlanta†	1.000	9	1	1	0	1	1	0	0	0	1	0	0	0	0	0	0	0	0	0	1.000	1.000

Player, Team	Avg.	G	TPA	AB	R	H	TB	2B	3B	HR	RBI	SH	SF	HP	BB	IBB	SO	SB	CS	GDP	Slg.	OBP
Worrell, Tim, San Diego	.000	9	1	1	0	0	0	0	0	0	0	0	0	0	0	0	0	0	0	0	.000	.000
Worrell, Todd, Los Angeles	.000	59	2	2	0	0	0	0	0	0	0	0	0	0	0	0	2	0	0	0	.000	.000
Worthington, Craig, Cincinnati	.278	10	20	18	1	5	9	1	0	1	2	0	0	0	2	0	1	0	0	0	.500	.350
Young, Anthony, Chicago	.667	32	3	3	2	2	2	0	0	0	0	0	0	0	0	0	0	0	0	0	.667	.667
Young, Eric, Colorado	.317	120	424	366	68	116	173	21	9	6	36	3	1	5	49	3	29	35	12	4	.473	.404
Young, Kevin, Pittsburgh	.232	56	195	181	13	42	69	9	0	6	22	1	3	2	8	0	53	1	3	5	.381	.268
Zeile, Todd, St.L.-Chi.	.246	113	473	426	50	105	169	22	0	14	52	4	5	4	34	1	76	1	0	13	.397	.305
Zosky, Eddie, Florida	.200	6	5	5	0	1	1	0	0	0	0	0	0	0	0	0	0	0	0	0	.200	.200

AWARDED FIRST BASE ON OBSTRUCTION OR CATCHER'S INTERFERENCE—Boone, Cincinnati (Castillo); Cianfrocco, San Diego (Encarnation); Kelly, Los Angeles (Taubensee); Segui, Montreal (Johnson); Van Slyke, Philadelphia (Piazza); Whiten, Philadelphia (Piazza).

PLAYERS WITH TWO OR MORE TEAMS

Player, Team	Avg.	G	TPA	AB	R	H	TB	2B	3B	HR	RBI	SH	SF	HP	BB	IBB	SO	SB	CS	GDP	Slg.	OBP
Aquino, Luis, Montreal	.333	29	4	3	0	1	1	0	0	0	0	0	0	0	1	0	1	0	0	0	.333	.500
Aquino, Luis, San Francisco	.000	5	1	1	0	0	0	0	0	0	0	0	0	0	0	1	0	1	0	0	.000	.000
Banks, Willie, Chicago	.000	10	1	1	0	0	0	0	0	0	0	0	0	0	0	1	0	0	0	0	.000	.000
Banks, Willie, Los Angeles	.125	6	11	8	1	1	1	0	0	0	0	1	0	1	1	0	4	0	0	0	.125	.300
Banks, Willie, Florida	.353	12	17	17	1	6	7	1	0	0	1	0	0	0	0	0	4	0	0	0	.412	.353
Butler, Brett, New York*	.311	90	418	367	54	114	144	13	7	1	25	6	2	0	43	2	42	21	7	4	.392	.381
Butler, Brett, Los Angeles*	.274	39	178	146	24	40	49	5	2	0	13	4	4	0	24	0	9	11	1	1	.336	.368
Duncan, Mariano, Philadelphia	.286	52	201	196	20	56	79	12	1	3	23	1	3	1	0	0	43	1	2	6	.403	.285
Duncan, Mariano, Cincinnati	.290	29	76	69	16	20	33	2	1	3	13	0	2	0	5	0	19	0	1	1	.478	.329
Fonville, Chad, Montreal†	.333	14	12	12	2	4	4	0	0	0	0	0	0	0	0	0	3	0	2	0	.333	.333
Fonville, Chad, Los Angeles†	.276	88	338	308	41	85	93	6	1	0	16	6	1	1	23	1	39	20	5	3	.302	.328
Gonzalez, Luis, Houston*	.258	56	234	209	35	54	90	10	4	6	35	1	3	3	18	3	30	1	3	8	.431	.322
Gonzalez, Luis, Chicago*	.290	77	307	262	34	76	124	19	4	7	34	0	3	3	39	5	33	5	5	8	.473	.384
Hickerson, Bryan, Chicago*	.500	38	3	2	1	1	1	0	0	0	1	0	0	1	0	0	0	0	0	0	.500	.667
Hickerson, Bryan, Colorado*	1.000	18	2	1	0	1	3	0	1	0	2	1	0	0	0	0	0	0	0	0	3.000	1.000
Kelly, Roberto, Montreal	.274	24	104	95	11	26	33	4	0	1	9	0	0	2	7	1	14	4	3	4	.347	.337
Kelly, Roberto, Los Angeles	.279	112	436	409	47	114	155	19	2	6	48	0	7	4	15	5	65	15	7	10	.379	.306
Lewis, Darren, San Francisco	.252	74	340	309	47	78	97	10	3	1	16	7	1	6	17	0	37	21	7	6	.314	.303
Lewis, Darren, Cincinnati	.245	58	187	163	19	40	43	3	0	0	8	5	0	2	17	0	20	11	11	3	.264	.324
Morgan, Mike, Chicago	.143	4	8	7	1	1	1	0	0	0	0	1	0	0	0	0	2	0	0	0	.143	.143
Morgan, Mike, St. Louis	.032	17	37	31	1	1	1	0	0	0	0	0	3	0	3	0	18	0	0	0	.032	.118
Oliva, Jose, Atlanta	.156	48	116	109	7	17	36	4	0	5	12	0	0	7	0	2	22	0	0	2	.330	.207
Oliva, Jose, St. Louis	.122	22	82	74	8	9	16	1	0	2	8	0	1	2	5	0	24	0	0	3	.216	.195
Olivares, Omar, Colorado	.143	12	9	7	0	1	2	1	0	0	0	1	0	0	1	0	3	0	0	0	.286	.250
Olivares, Omar, Philadelphia	.500	5	2	2	1	1	4	0	0	1	2	0	0	0	0	1	0	0	0	0	2.000	.500
Parent, Mark, Pittsburgh	.232	69	257	233	25	54	108	9	0	15	33	1	0	0	23	2	62	0	0	5	.464	.301
Parent, Mark, Chicago	.250	12	35	32	5	8	19	2	0	3	5	0	0	0	3	0	7	0	0	1	.594	.314
Plantier, Phil, Houston*	.250	22	83	68	12	17	31	2	0	4	15	0	3	1	11	1	19	0	0	0	.456	.349
Plantier, Phil, San Diego*	.257	54	165	148	21	38	57	4	0	5	19	0	0	0	17	2	29	1	1	3	.385	.333
Portugal, Mark, San Francisco	.103	17	38	29	1	3	5	2	0	0	1	7	0	0	2	0	6	0	0	1	.172	.161
Portugal, Mark, Cincinnati	.172	14	33	29	4	5	8	3	0	0	4	1	0	0	3	0	7	0	0	3	.276	.250
Rodriguez, Henry, L.A.*	.263	21	85	80	6	21	30	4	1	1	10	0	0	0	5	2	17	0	1	3	.375	.306
Rodriguez, Henry, Montreal*	.207	24	65	58	7	12	15	0	0	1	5	0	1	0	6	0	11	0	0	2	.259	.277
Saberhagen, Bret, New York	.114	16	41	35	2	4	5	1	0	0	0	5	0	0	1	0	8	0	0	0	.143	.139
Saberhagen, Bret, Colorado	.071	9	15	14	1	1	1	0	0	0	0	0	0	0	1	0	4	0	0	0	.071	.133
Sanders, Deion, Cincinnati*	.240	33	144	129	19	31	42	2	3	1	10	2	2	2	9	0	18	16	3	0	.326	.296
Sanders, Deion, San Fran.*	.285	52	235	214	29	61	95	9	5	5	18	1	0	2	18	0	42	8	6	1	.444	.346
Segui, David, New York*	.329	33	92	73	9	24	35	3	1	2	11	4	2	1	12	1	9	1	3	2	.479	.420
Segui, David, Montreal†	.305	97	419	383	59	117	175	22	3	10	57	4	1	2	28	4	38	1	4	8	.457	.355
Servais, Scott, Houston	.225	28	101	89	7	20	33	10	0	1	12	1	1	1	9	2	15	0	1	4	.371	.300
Servais, Scott, Chicago	.286	52	203	175	31	50	98	12	0	12	35	1	2	2	23	6	37	2	1	5	.560	.371
Treadway, Jeff, Los Angeles*	.118	17	17	17	2	2	4	0	1	0	3	0	0	0	0	0	2	0	0	0	.235	.118
Treadway, Jeff, Montreal*	.240	41	55	50	4	12	14	2	0	0	10	0	0	0	5	1	2	0	1	0	.280	.309
Wilkins, Rick, Chicago*	.191	50	200	162	24	31	51	2	0	6	14	0	1	1	36	1	51	0	0	8	.315	.340
Wilkins, Rick, Houston*	.250	15	51	40	6	10	14	1	0	1	5	0	1	0	10	1	10	0	0	1	.350	.392
Zeile, Todd, St. Louis	.291	34	148	127	16	37	58	6	0	5	22	0	2	1	18	1	23	1	0	2	.457	.378
Zeile, Todd, Chicago	.227	79	325	299	34	68	111	16	0	9	30	4	3	3	16	0	53	0	0	10	.371	.271

PINCH-HITTING

TEAM

Team	Avg.	G	TPA	AB	R	H	TB	2B	3B	HR	RBI	SH	SF	HP	BB	IBB	SO	SB	CS	GDP	Slg.	OBP
Colorado	.299	125	249	214	33	64	118	13	4	11	50	0	2	1	32	9	49	6	1	7	.551	.390
Houston	.297	122	300	249	41	74	121	15	1	10	54	4	3	3	41	6	57	9	1	4	.486	.399
New York	.274	117	240	208	30	57	86	12	1	5	35	3	5	3	21	2	51	1	1	3	.413	.342
Cincinnati	.271	117	251	218	28	59	89	11	2	5	38	1	2	0	30	2	46	4	1	3	.408	.356
Pittsburgh	.257	127	279	249	27	64	92	11	1	5	25	0	3	2	25	3	59	1	1	6	.369	.326
Chicago	.242	104	193	165	19	40	68	6	2	6	17	5	1	2	20	0	48	2	2	5	.412	.330
San Diego	.242	124	253	219	25	53	90	7	0	10	44	3	4	0	26	1	65	1	0	6	.411	.317
St. Louis	.237	123	247	215	22	51	74	11	0	4	22	2	1	1	28	2	46	1	1	6	.344	.327
Philadelphia	.233	119	240	215	24	50	82	9	1	7	37	1	1	2	21	4	55	1	2	1	.381	.305
Atlanta	.215	113	220	195	18	42	67	14	1	3	28	2	1	1	21	2	60	3	3	4	.344	.294
Florida	.213	110	226	202	15	43	48	5	0	0	14	4	2	3	15	0	41	1	1	12	.238	.275
San Francisco	.210	117	227	200	19	42	52	7	0	1	19	1	0	2	24	1	46	0	0	2	.260	.301
Montreal	.202	100	193	168	16	34	49	6	0	3	30	2	2	0	21	2	38	2	1	6	.292	.288
Los Angeles	.198	116	259	232	15	46	72	7	2	5	25	5	1	1	20	3	61	0	2	2	.310	.264
Totals	.244	1634	3377	2949	332	719	1108	134	15	75	438	33	28	21	345	37	722	32	17	67	.376	.325

TOP PINCH-HITTERS

Minimum 18 at-bats. *Lefthanded batter. †Switch-hitter.

Player, Team	Avg.	G	TPA	AB	R	H	TB	2B	3B	HR	RBI	SH	SF	HP	BB	IBB	SO	SB	CS	GDP	Slg.	OBP
Polonia, Luis, Atlanta*	.444	20	20	18	3	8	12	4	0	0	1	1	0	0	1	0	5	1	0	0	.667	.474
Jones, Chris, New York	.400	33	32	25	9	10	21	2	0	3	10	0	2	0	5	0	10	1	0	0	.840	.469
May, Derrick, Houston*	.391	27	27	23	4	9	19	4	0	2	12	0	1	0	3	0	4	1	0	0	.826	.444
Duncan, Mariano, Phi.-Cin.	.389	19	19	18	4	7	9	2	0	0	5	0	0	0	1	0	5	0	1	1	.500	.421
Eusebio, Tony, Houston	.389	21	21	18	1	7	11	1	0	1	6	0	1	1	1	0	2	0	0	1	.611	.429
Vander Wal, John, Colorado*	.389	92	85	72	12	28	49	7	1	4	17	0	1	0	12	5	12	1	1	2	.681	.471
Brumfield, Jacob, Pittsburgh	.389	20	20	18	3	7	9	2	0	0	1	0	0	0	2	0	4	0	0	0	.500	.450
Howard, Thomas, Cincinnati†	.361	42	41	36	8	13	20	4	0	1	7	0	0	0	5	0	9	0	0	0	.556	.439
Shipley, Craig, Houston	.360	28	28	25	4	9	15	1	1	1	5	0	0	0	3	1	5	1	0	0	.600	.429
Cummings, Midre, Pittsburgh*	.348	23	23	23	1	8	9	1	0	0	1	0	0	0	0	0	5	0	0	0	.391	.348
Clark, Dave, Pittsburgh*	.346	30	29	26	3	9	13	1	0	1	5	0	0	0	3	1	7	0	0	3	.500	.414
Livingstone, Scott, San Diego*	.326	49	47	43	3	14	19	2	0	1	8	0	2	0	2	0	9	0	0	1	.442	.340
Bullett, Scott, Chicago*	.324	45	43	37	4	12	21	2	2	1	2	1	0	0	5	0	12	2	1	0	.568	.405
Arias, Alex, Florida	.316	41	41	38	5	12	15	3	0	0	4	0	1	0	2	0	4	0	0	5	.395	.341
Orsulak, Joe, New York*	.314	40	39	35	7	11	17	3	0	1	8	0	1	1	2	0	11	0	0	0	.486	.359
Hansen, Dave, Los Angeles*	.314	49	42	35	0	11	14	3	0	0	5	0	0	0	7	2	9	0	0	1	.400	.429

ALL PINCH-HITTERS

*Lefthanded batter. †Switch-hitter.

Player, Team	Avg.	G	TPA	AB	R	H	TB	2B	3B	HR	RBI	SH	SF	HP	BB	IBB	SO	SB	CS	GDP	Slg.	OBP
Abbott, Kurt, Florida	.000	5	5	5	0	0	0	0	0	0	0	0	0	0	0	0	4	0	0	0	.000	.000
Alfonzo, Edgardo, New York	.200	11	11	10	0	2	2	0	0	0	0	0	0	1	0	0	2	0	0	0	.200	.273
Alou, Moises, Montreal	.000	1	1	0	0	0	0	0	0	0	0	0	0	0	1	1	0	0	0	0	.000	1.000
Andrews, Shane, Montreal	.091	14	13	11	1	1	4	0	0	1	4	0	0	0	2	0	5	1	0	0	.364	.231
Anthony, Eric, Cincinnati*	.333	9	9	9	2	3	6	0	0	1	4	0	0	0	0	0	1	0	0	0	.667	.333
Arias, Alex, Florida	.316	41	41	38	5	12	15	3	0	0	4	0	1	0	2	0	4	0	0	5	.395	.341
Ashley, Billy, Los Angeles	.143	15	15	14	0	2	2	0	0	0	1	0	0	1	0	0	9	0	0	0	.143	.200
Aude, Rich, Pittsburgh	.286	15	15	14	1	4	7	0	0	1	4	0	0	0	1	0	3	0	0	1	.500	.333
Aurilia, Rich, San Francisco	.000	2	2	2	0	0	0	0	0	0	0	0	0	0	0	0	0	0	0	0	.000	.000
Ausmus, Brad, San Diego	.000	1	1	1	0	0	0	0	0	0	0	0	0	0	0	0	1	0	0	0	.000	.000
Banks, Willie, Florida	.000	1	1	1	0	0	0	0	0	0	0	0	0	0	0	0	1	0	0	0	.000	.000
Barry, Jeff, New York†	.083	13	13	12	1	1	1	0	0	0	0	0	0	0	1	0	6	0	0	0	.083	.154
Bates, Jason, Colorado†	.333	9	9	9	1	3	3	0	0	0	2	0	0	0	0	0	3	0	0	0	.333	.333
Battle, Allen, St. Louis	.143	25	24	21	4	3	4	1	0	0	0	1	0	0	2	0	4	0	0	0	.190	.217
Bean, Billy, San Diego*	.000	1	1	1	0	0	0	0	0	0	0	0	0	0	0	0	0	0	0	0	.000	.000
Bell, Derek, Houston	.500	2	2	2	0	1	2	1	0	0	0	0	0	0	0	0	1	0	0	0	1.000	.500
Bell, Jay, Pittsburgh	.000	1	1	1	0	0	0	0	0	0	0	0	0	0	0	0	1	0	0	0	.000	.000
Benard, Marvin, San Francisco*	.200	5	5	5	0	1	1	0	0	0	1	0	0	0	0	0	1	0	0	0	.200	.200
Benitez, Yamil, Montreal	.000	2	2	2	0	0	0	0	0	0	0	0	0	0	0	0	1	0	0	0	.000	.000
Benjamin, Mike, San Francisco	.000	4	4	4	0	0	0	0	0	0	0	0	0	0	0	0	1	0	0	0	.000	.000
Bennett, Gary, Philadelphia	.000	1	1	1	0	0	0	0	0	0	0	0	0	0	0	0	0	0	0	0	.000	.000
Benzinger, Todd, San Francisco†.	.167	7	7	6	0	1	1	0	0	0	0	0	0	0	1	0	2	0	0	0	.167	.286
Berry, Sean, Montreal	.278	19	19	18	1	5	8	0	0	1	8	0	1	0	0	0	4	0	0	1	.444	.263
Berryhill, Damon, Cincinnati†	.167	8	8	6	2	1	4	0	0	1	3	0	0	0	2	0	2	0	0	0	.667	.375
Bichette, Dante, Colorado	.333	5	5	3	1	1	4	0	0	1	2	0	0	0	2	1	1	0	0	0	1.333	.600
Biggio, Craig, Houston	.000	1	1	1	0	0	0	0	0	0	0	0	0	0	0	0	0	0	0	0	.000	.000
Bogar, Tim, New York	.250	14	14	12	0	3	5	2	0	0	2	0	0	0	1	0	4	0	0	0	.417	.308
Bonds, Barry, San Francisco*	.000	1	1	1	0	0	0	0	0	0	0	0	0	0	0	0	1	0	0	0	.000	.000
Bonilla, Bobby, New York†	.000	1	1	1	0	0	0	0	0	0	0	0	0	0	0	0	1	0	0	0	.000	.000
Bradshaw, Terry, St. Louis*	.375	8	8	8	0	3	4	1	0	0	0	0	0	0	0	0	2	1	1	0	.500	.375
Branson, Jeff, Cincinnati*	.091	15	12	11	0	1	1	0	0	0	0	0	0	0	1	0	3	0	0	0	.091	.167
Brocail, Doug, Houston*	.000	1	1	1	0	0	0	0	0	0	0	0	0	0	0	0	0	0	0	0	.000	.000
Brogna, Rico, New York*	.222	11	11	9	1	2	3	1	0	0	1	0	0	0	2	1	3	0	0	0	.333	.364
Browne, Jerry, Florida†	.261	27	27	23	1	6	6	0	0	0	2	2	0	0	2	0	3	1	0	0	.261	.320
Brumfield, Jacob, Pittsburgh	.389	20	20	18	3	7	9	2	0	0	1	0	0	0	2	0	4	0	0	1	.500	.450

Player, Team	Avg.	G	TPA	AB	R	H	TB	2B	3B	HR	RBI	SH	SF	HP	BB	IBB	SO	SB	CS	GDP	Slg.	OBP
Brumley, Mike, Houston†	.125	8	8	8	1	1	4	0	0	1	1	0	0	0	0	0	2	0	0	0	.500	.125
Buford, Damon, New York	.500	4	4	4	1	2	2	0	0	0	0	0	0	0	0	0	1	0	0	0	.500	.500
Bullett, Scott, Chicago*	.324	45	43	37	4	12	21	2	2	1	2	1	0	0	5	0	12	2	1	0	.568	.405
Bullinger, Jim, Chicago	.000	1	1	1	0	0	0	0	0	0	0	0	0	0	0	0	1	0	0	0	.000	.000
Burkett, John, Florida	.000	1	1	0	0	0	0	0	0	0	0	1	0	0	0	0	0	0	0	0	.000	.000
Burks, Ellis, Colorado	.207	35	35	29	4	6	12	1	1	1	9	0	0	0	6	0	9	1	0	0	.414	.343
Busch, Mike, Los Angeles	.286	7	7	7	1	2	5	0	0	1	1	0	0	0	0	0	2	0	0	0	.714	.286
Butler, Brett, New York*	1.000	1	1	1	1	1	1	0	0	0	0	0	0	0	0	0	0	0	0	0	1.000	1.000
Cangelosi, John, Houston†	.276	38	39	29	10	8	12	1	0	1	5	1	0	1	8	0	10	4	1	1	.414	.447
Caraballo, Ramon, St. Louis†	.300	11	11	10	2	3	7	1	0	1	1	0	0	0	1	0	1	0	0	1	.700	.364
Carr, Chuck, Florida	.000	2	2	2	0	0	0	0	0	0	0	0	0	0	0	0	0	0	0	0	.000	.000
Carreon, Mark, San Francisco	.267	16	16	15	3	4	5	1	0	0	2	0	0	0	1	0	4	0	0	0	.333	.313
Castellano, Pedro, Colorado	.000	1	1	1	0	0	0	0	0	0	0	0	0	0	0	0	0	0	0	0	.000	.000
Castilla, Vinny, Colorado	.000	1	1	1	0	0	0	0	0	0	0	0	0	0	0	0	0	0	0	1	.000	.000
Cedeno, Andujar, San Diego	1.000	2	1	1	0	1	1	0	0	0	0	0	0	0	0	0	0	0	0	0	1.000	1.000
Cedeno, Roger, Los Angeles†	.200	5	5	5	0	1	2	1	0	0	0	0	0	0	0	0	3	0	0	0	.400	.200
Cianfrocco, Archi, San Diego	.400	12	11	10	4	4	13	0	0	3	10	0	0	0	0	0	2	0	0	0	1.300	.400
Clark, Dave, Pittsburgh*	.346	30	29	26	3	9	13	1	0	1	5	0	0	0	3	1	7	0	0	3	.500	.414
Clark, Phil, San Diego	.211	44	42	38	4	8	12	1	0	1	3	0	1	0	3	0	9	0	0	2	.316	.262
Clayton, Royce, San Francisco	.000	3	3	2	1	0	0	0	0	0	0	0	0	0	1	0	1	0	0	0	.000	.333
Colbrunn, Greg, Florida	.500	4	4	4	1	2	2	0	0	0	2	0	0	0	0	0	1	0	0	0	.500	.500
Coles, Darnell, St. Louis	.118	23	22	17	3	2	3	1	0	0	1	0	1	0	4	1	4	0	0	0	.176	.273
Conine, Jeff, Florida	.143	9	9	7	0	1	1	0	0	0	0	0	0	1	1	0	3	0	0	1	.143	.333
Cooper, Scott, St. Louis*	.250	13	12	8	2	2	3	1	0	0	0	0	0	1	3	0	3	0	0	0	.375	.500
Counsell, Craig, Colorado*	.000	1	1	0	0	0	0	0	0	0	0	0	0	0	1	0	0	0	0	0	.000	1.000
Cromer, Tripp, St. Louis	.000	2	2	2	0	0	0	0	0	0	0	0	0	0	0	0	0	0	0	0	.000	.000
Cummings, Midre, Pittsburgh*	.348	23	23	23	1	8	9	1	0	0	1	0	0	0	0	0	5	0	0	0	.391	.348
Daulton, Darren, Philadelphia*	.000	5	5	4	0	0	0	0	0	0	0	0	0	0	1	0	3	0	0	0	.000	.200
Dawson, Andre, Florida	.211	22	21	19	1	4	4	0	0	0	1	0	0	1	1	0	5	0	0	1	.211	.286
Decker, Steve, Florida	.200	6	6	5	0	1	1	0	0	0	0	0	0	0	1	0	2	0	0	0	.200	.333
DeShields, Delino, Los Angeles*	.300	14	14	10	1	3	3	0	0	0	1	1	0	0	3	0	3	0	2	0	.300	.462
Devereaux, Mike, Atlanta	.143	7	7	7	0	1	1	0	0	0	1	0	0	0	0	0	1	0	0	0	.143	.143
Diaz, Mario, Florida	.188	33	33	32	1	6	7	1	0	0	0	1	0	0	0	0	4	0	0	1	.219	.188
Donnels, Chris, Houston*	.556	11	10	9	2	5	5	0	0	0	0	0	0	0	1	1	0	0	0	0	.556	.600
Duncan, Mariano, Phi.-Cin.	.389	19	19	18	4	7	9	2	0	0	5	0	0	0	1	0	5	0	1	1	.500	.421
Dunston, Shawon, Chicago	.000	2	2	1	0	0	0	0	0	0	0	0	0	1	0	0	0	0	0	0	.000	.500
Dykstra, Lenny, Philadelphia*	.000	1	1	1	1	0	0	0	0	0	0	0	0	0	0	0	0	0	0	0	.000	.000
Eisenreich, Jim, Philadelphia*	.200	27	26	20	1	4	7	0	0	1	7	0	1	0	5	1	4	0	0	0	.350	.346
Elster, Kevin, Philadelphia	.333	3	3	3	1	1	1	0	0	0	0	0	0	0	0	0	0	0	0	0	.333	.333
Encarnacion, Angelo, Pittsburgh	.200	5	5	5	1	1	1	0	0	0	0	0	0	0	0	0	0	0	0	0	.200	.200
Eusebio, Tony, Houston	.389	21	21	18	1	7	11	1	0	1	6	0	1	1	1	0	2	0	0	1	.611	.429
Everett, Carl, New York†	.000	2	2	2	0	0	0	0	0	0	0	0	0	0	0	0	0	0	0	0	.000	.000
Faneyte, Rikkert, San Francisco	.200	13	13	10	0	2	2	0	0	0	2	1	0	0	2	0	5	0	0	0	.200	.333
Finley, Steve, San Diego*	1.000	1	1	1	1	1	1	0	0	0	0	0	0	0	0	0	0	0	0	0	1.000	1.000
Fletcher, Darrin, Montreal*	.364	14	13	11	0	4	5	1	0	0	4	0	0	0	2	0	1	0	0	0	.455	.462
Flora, Kevin, Philadelphia	.000	5	5	4	0	0	0	0	0	0	0	0	0	0	1	0	2	0	0	0	.000	.200
Floyd, Cliff, Montreal*	.000	8	9	8	1	0	0	0	0	0	0	0	0	0	1	0	2	0	0	0	.000	.111
Foley, Tom, Montreal*	.000	5	5	4	0	0	0	0	0	0	0	0	0	0	1	0	0	0	0	1	.000	.200
Fonville, Chad, Mon.-L.A.†	.250	16	16	16	1	4	4	0	0	0	0	0	0	0	0	0	3	0	1	0	.250	.250
Fordyce, Brook, New York	.500	3	3	2	1	1	2	1	0	0	0	0	0	0	1	0	0	0	0	0	1.000	.667
Franco, Matt, Chicago*	.273	11	11	11	1	3	4	1	0	0	0	0	0	0	0	0	1	0	0	0	.364	.273
Frazier, Lou, Montreal†	.000	10	10	10	0	0	0	0	0	0	0	0	0	0	0	0	2	0	0	0	.000	.000
Galarraga, Andres, Colorado	.000	2	2	1	0	0	0	0	0	0	0	0	0	0	1	0	0	0	0	0	.000	.500
Gallagher, Dave, Philadelphia	.600	10	10	10	2	6	10	4	0	0	2	0	0	0	0	0	1	0	0	0	1.000	.600
Gant, Ron, Cincinnati	.000	2	2	1	0	0	0	0	0	0	0	0	0	0	1	1	0	0	0	0	.000	.500
Garcia, Freddy, Pittsburgh	.100	25	24	20	2	2	4	0	1	0	1	0	0	0	4	0	7	0	0	0	.200	.250
Garcia, Karim, Los Angeles*	.250	8	8	8	0	2	2	0	0	0	0	0	0	0	0	0	3	0	0	0	.250	.250
Giannelli, Ray, St. Louis*	.250	6	6	4	0	1	1	0	0	0	0	0	0	0	2	0	1	0	0	0	.250	.500
Gibralter, Steve, Cincinnati	.500	2	2	2	0	1	1	0	0	0	0	0	0	0	0	0	0	0	0	0	.500	.500
Gilkey, Bernard, St. Louis	.333	3	3	3	0	1	1	0	0	0	2	0	0	0	0	0	0	0	0	0	.333	.333
Giovanola, Ed, Atlanta*	.000	3	3	2	1	0	0	0	0	0	0	0	0	0	1	0	0	0	0	0	.000	.333
Girardi, Joe, Colorado	.500	4	4	4	1	2	5	0	0	1	1	0	0	0	0	0	1	0	0	1	1.250	.500
Goff, Jerry, Houston*	.000	1	1	1	0	0	0	0	0	0	0	0	0	0	0	0	0	0	0	0	.000	.000
Gonzalez, Luis, Hou.-Chi.*	.750	5	5	4	0	3	3	0	0	0	1	0	0	0	1	0	1	0	0	0	.750	.800
Greene, Willie, Cincinnati*	.000	2	1	1	0	0	0	0	0	0	0	0	0	0	0	0	0	0	0	0	.000	.000
Gregg, Tommy, Florida*	.143	33	32	28	2	4	4	0	0	0	3	0	1	1	2	0	7	0	0	1	.143	.219
Grissom, Marquis, Atlanta	.000	4	4	4	0	0	0	0	0	0	0	0	0	0	0	0	1	0	0	0	.000	.000
Grudzielanek, Mark, Montreal	.000	3	3	3	0	0	0	0	0	0	0	0	0	0	0	0	0	0	0	0	.000	.000
Gutierrez, Ricky, Houston	.250	4	4	4	0	1	1	0	0	0	0	0	0	0	0	0	1	0	0	0	.250	.250
Gwynn, Chris, Los Angeles*	.233	51	48	43	5	10	17	2	1	1	7	0	1	0	3	1	12	0	0	1	.395	.292
Gwynn, Tony, San Diego*	.500	2	2	2	0	1	1	0	0	0	1	0	0	0	0	0	1	0	0	0	.500	.500
Hajek, Dave, Houston	.000	5	5	2	0	0	0	0	0	0	0	2	0	0	1	0	1	1	0	0	.000	.333
Haney, Todd, Chicago	.667	4	4	3	0	2	2	0	0	0	0	1	0	0	0	0	1	0	0	0	.667	.667
Hansen, Dave, Los Angeles*	.314	49	44	35	0	11	14	3	0	0	5	0	0	7	2	9	0	0	1	.400	.429
Harris, Lenny, Cincinnati*	.220	57	56	50	6	11	16	1	2	0	5	1	1	0	4	0	3	3	0	1	.320	.273
Hemond, Scott, St. Louis	.067	16	16	15	1	1	1	0	0	0	1	0	0	0	1	0	6	0	0	1	.067	.125
Hernandez, Carlos, Los Angeles	.400	6	6	5	1	2	5	0	0	1	3	0	0	0	1	0	1	0	0	0	1.000	.500
Hernandez, Jose, Chicago	.300	12	12	10	1	3	4	1	0	0	1	2	0	0	0	0	5	0	0	0	.400	.300
Hickerson, Bryan, Colorado*	1.000	1	1	1	0	1	3	0	1	0	2	0	0	0	0	0	0	0	0	0	3.000	1.000
Hill, Glenallen, San Francisco	.714	7	7	7	1	5	8	0	0	1	2	0	0	0	0	0	0	0	0	0	1.143	.714
Holbert, Ray, San Diego	.077	18	18	13	0	1	1	0	0	0	0	2	0	0	3	0	2	1	0	0	.077	.250
Hollandsworth, Todd, L.A.*	.000	4	4	4	0	0	0	0	0	0	0	0	0	0	1	0	1	0	0	0	.000	.000
Hollins, Dave, Philadelphia†	.000	5	5	5	0	0	0	0	0	0	0	0	0	0	2	0	0	0	0	0	.000	.000

Player, Team	Avg.	G	TPA	AB	R	H	TB	2B	3B	HR	RBI	SH	SF	HP	BB	IBB	SO	SB	CS	GDP	Slg.	OBP
Howard, Thomas, Cincinnati†	.361	42	41	36	8	13	20	4	0	1	7	0	0	0	5	0	9	0	0	0	.556	.439
Hubbard, Mike, Chicago	.167	7	7	6	1	1	1	0	0	0	0	0	0	0	1	0	1	0	0	0	.167	.286
Hubbard, Trent, Colorado	.300	10	10	10	1	3	3	0	0	0	0	0	0	0	0	0	2	0	0	1	.300	.300
Hulett, Tim, St. Louis	1.000	2	2	2	0	2	2	0	0	0	0	0	0	0	0	0	0	0	0	0	1.000	1.000
Hundley, Todd, New York†	.250	12	12	12	3	3	6	0	0	1	4	0	0	0	0	0	1	0	0	0	.500	.250
Hunter, Brian R., Cincinnati	.455	15	15	11	2	5	7	2	0	0	5	0	1	0	3	1	2	1	1	0	.636	.533
Hunter, Brian L., Houston	.667	4	3	3	0	2	3	1	0	0	0	0	0	0	0	0	1	0	0	0	1.000	.667
Hyers, Tim, San Diego*	.000	5	5	5	0	0	0	0	0	0	0	0	0	0	0	0	1	0	0	1	.000	.000
Ingram, Garey, Los Angeles	.143	17	17	14	1	2	2	0	0	0	0	1	0	0	2	0	2	0	0	0	.143	.250
Jefferies, Gregg, Philadelphia*	.000	1	1	1	0	0	0	0	0	0	0	0	0	0	0	0	0	0	0	0	.000	.000
Johnson, Brian, San Diego	.385	12	13	13	3	5	9	1	0	1	5	0	0	0	0	0	1	0	0	0	.692	.385
Johnson, Howard, Chicago†	.250	36	35	28	4	7	14	1	0	2	5	0	0	0	7	0	10	0	0	2	.500	.400
Johnson, Mark, Pittsburgh*	.167	14	14	12	2	2	5	0	0	1	3	0	0	0	2	0	4	0	0	0	.417	.286
Jones, Chipper, Atlanta†	.000	1	1	1	0	0	0	0	0	0	0	0	0	0	0	0	1	0	0	0	.000	.000
Jones, Chris, New York	.400	33	32	25	9	10	21	2	0	3	10	0	2	0	5	0	10	1	0	0	.840	.469
Jordan, Brian, St. Louis	.500	6	6	6	2	3	7	1	0	1	4	0	0	0	0	0	1	0	0	0	1.167	.500
Jordan, Kevin, Philadelphia	.100	14	13	10	2	1	4	0	0	1	3	0	0	1	2	1	4	0	0	0	.400	.308
Kelly, Mike, Atlanta	.214	16	15	14	1	3	5	2	0	0	1	0	0	0	1	0	4	1	0	0	.357	.267
Kelly, Roberto, Los Angeles	.333	3	3	3	0	1	1	0	0	0	0	0	0	0	0	0	1	0	0	0	.333	.333
Kent, Jeff, New York	.000	3	3	3	0	0	0	0	0	0	0	0	0	0	0	0	2	0	0	0	.000	.000
King, Jeff, Pittsburgh	.667	3	3	3	0	2	2	0	0	0	1	0	0	0	0	0	0	0	0	0	.667	.667
Kingery, Mike, Colorado*	.267	18	17	15	3	4	11	1	0	2	2	0	0	0	2	0	2	0	0	1	.733	.353
Klesko, Ryan, Atlanta*	.333	6	6	6	0	2	3	1	0	0	1	0	0	0	0	0	2	1	0	0	.500	.333
Kmak, Joe, Chicago	.500	3	3	2	1	1	1	0	0	0	0	0	0	0	1	0	0	0	0	0	.500	.667
Kowitz, Brian, Atlanta*	1.000	2	2	1	0	1	2	1	0	0	1	0	0	0	1	0	0	0	0	0	2.000	1.000
Laker, Tim, Montreal	.000	2	1	1	0	0	0	0	0	0	0	0	0	0	0	0	0	0	0	0	.000	.000
Lampkin, Tom, San Francisco*	.205	44	44	39	2	8	8	0	0	0	4	0	0	1	4	0	4	0	0	1	.205	.295
Lankford, Ray, St. Louis*	.333	4	4	3	0	1	1	0	0	0	0	0	0	0	1	0	2	0	0	0	.333	.500
Ledesma, Aaron, New York	.333	11	11	9	1	3	3	0	0	0	1	0	0	0	2	1	2	0	0	1	.333	.455
Lemke, Mark, Atlanta†	.000	1	1	1	0	0	0	0	0	0	0	0	0	0	0	0	0	0	0	0	.000	.000
Leonard, Mark, San Francisco*	.167	8	7	6	0	1	2	1	0	0	1	0	0	0	1	0	1	0	0	0	.333	.286
Lewis, Darren, S.F.-Cin.	.111	9	9	9	0	1	1	0	0	0	1	0	0	0	0	0	3	0	0	1	.111	.111
Lewis, Mark, Cincinnati	.235	24	24	17	1	4	6	2	0	0	3	0	0	0	7	0	6	0	0	0	.353	.458
Lieberthal, Mike, Philadelphia	.000	2	2	2	0	0	0	0	0	0	0	0	0	0	0	0	0	0	0	0	.000	.000
Liriano, Nelson, Pittsburgh†	.243	42	42	37	5	9	11	2	0	0	2	0	1	1	3	1	6	0	0	2	.297	.310
Livingstone, Scott, San Diego*	.326	49	47	43	3	14	19	2	0	1	8	0	2	0	2	0	9	0	0	1	.442	.340
Loaiza, Esteban, Pittsburgh	.000	1	1	1	0	0	0	0	0	0	0	0	0	0	0	0	0	0	0	0	.000	.000
Longmire, Tony, Philadelphia*	.303	38	37	33	4	10	20	1	0	3	11	0	0	0	4	1	8	0	1	0	.606	.378
Lopez, Javy, Atlanta	.091	11	11	11	0	1	1	0	0	0	0	0	0	0	0	0	4	0	0	2	.091	.091
Mabry, John, St. Louis*	.296	29	29	27	3	8	9	1	0	0	1	0	0	0	2	1	4	0	0	1	.333	.345
Magadan, Dave, Houston*	.300	29	29	20	3	6	6	0	0	0	5	0	0	0	9	3	3	0	0	0	.300	.517
Manwaring, Kirt, San Francisco	.000	1	1	1	0	0	0	0	0	0	0	0	0	0	0	0	0	0	0	0	.000	.000
Marsh, Tom, Philadelphia	.214	15	15	14	1	3	4	1	0	0	0	0	0	0	1	0	6	0	0	0	.286	.267
Martin, Al, Pittsburgh*	.167	16	16	12	2	2	5	0	0	1	2	0	0	0	4	1	3	0	1	0	.417	.375
Mathews, Terry, Florida*	.000	1	1	1	0	0	0	0	0	0	0	0	0	0	0	0	0	0	0	1	.000	.000
May, Derrick, Houston*	.391	27	27	23	4	9	19	4	0	2	12	0	1	0	3	0	4	1	0	0	.826	.444
McCarty, Dave, San Francisco	.333	9	8	6	0	2	3	1	0	0	1	0	0	0	2	0	1	0	0	0	.500	.500
McCracken, Quinton, Colorado†	.000	1	1	1	0	0	0	0	0	0	0	0	0	0	0	0	0	0	0	0	.000	.000
McDavid, Ray, San Diego*	.333	3	3	3	0	1	1	0	0	0	0	0	0	0	0	0	1	0	0	0	.333	.333
McRae, Brian, Chicago†	.000	1	1	1	0	0	0	0	0	0	0	0	0	0	0	0	0	0	0	0	.000	.000
Mejia, Roberto, Colorado	.250	4	4	4	0	1	1	0	0	0	1	0	0	0	0	0	3	0	0	0	.250	.250
Merced, Orlando, Pittsburgh*	.222	11	11	9	2	2	5	0	0	1	3	0	0	0	2	0	0	0	0	0	.556	.364
Miller, Orlando, Houston	.333	3	3	3	0	1	1	0	0	0	1	0	0	0	0	0	1	0	0	0	.333	.333
Mondesi, Raul, Los Angeles	.000	1	1	1	0	0	0	0	0	0	0	0	0	0	0	0	0	0	0	0	.000	.000
Morandini, Mickey, Philadelphia*	.111	9	9	9	1	1	4	0	0	1	2	0	0	0	0	0	6	0	0	0	.444	.111
Mordecai, Mike, Atlanta	.241	35	34	29	5	7	14	4	0	1	2	1	0	0	4	0	8	0	0	0	.483	.333
Morman, Russ, Florida	.308	14	14	13	1	4	4	0	0	0	1	0	0	0	1	0	2	0	0	1	.308	.357
Morris, Hal, Cincinnati*	.200	6	6	5	0	1	1	0	0	0	1	0	0	0	1	0	2	0	0	0	.200	.333
Mouton, James, Houston	.286	17	17	14	2	4	8	1	0	1	3	0	0	1	2	1	2	0	0	1	.571	.412
Natal, Bob, Florida	.000	3	3	3	0	0	0	0	0	0	0	0	0	0	0	0	1	0	0	0	.000	.000
Nevin, Phil, Houston	.000	1	1	1	0	0	0	0	0	0	0	0	0	0	0	0	0	0	0	0	.000	.000
Newfield, Marc, San Diego	.667	3	3	3	0	2	3	1	0	0	2	0	0	0	0	0	1	0	0	0	1.000	.667
Nieves, Melvin, San Diego†	.074	30	30	27	3	2	5	0	0	1	4	0	1	0	2	0	16	0	0	1	.185	.133
Nokes, Matt, Colorado*	.000	7	7	6	0	0	0	0	0	0	0	0	0	0	1	1	3	0	0	1	.000	.143
O'Brien, Charlie, Atlanta	.250	5	5	4	0	1	1	0	0	0	1	0	0	0	1	1	1	0	0	0	.250	.400
Ochoa, Alex, New York	1.000	1	1	1	1	1	1	0	0	0	0	0	0	0	0	0	0	0	0	0	1.000	1.000
Offerman, Jose, Los Angeles†	.000	5	5	3	1	0	0	0	0	0	0	0	0	0	1	0	0	0	0	0	.000	.250
Oliva, Jose, Atl.-St.L.	.091	25	25	22	0	2	2	0	0	0	2	0	0	0	3	0	7	0	0	1	.091	.200
Olivares, Omar, Philadelphia	1.000	1	1	1	1	1	4	0	0	1	2	0	0	0	0	0	0	0	0	0	4.000	1.000
Oquendo, Jose, St. Louis†	.250	4	4	4	1	1	4	0	0	1	1	0	0	0	0	0	0	0	0	0	1.000	.250
Orsulak, Joe, New York*	.314	40	39	35	7	11	17	3	0	1	8	0	1	1	2	0	11	0	0	0	.486	.359
Otero, Ricky, New York†	.273	11	11	11	0	3	4	1	0	0	0	0	0	0	0	0	1	0	0	1	.364	.273
Owens, Eric, Cincinnati	1.000	1	1	1	0	1	1	0	0	0	0	0	0	0	0	0	0	0	0	0	1.000	1.000
Owens, Jayhawk, Colorado	.500	2	2	2	1	1	1	0	0	0	1	0	0	0	0	0	1	0	0	0	.500	.500
Pagnozzi, Tom, St. Louis	.000	1	1	1	0	0	0	0	0	0	0	0	0	0	0	0	0	0	0	0	.000	.000
Painter, Lance, Colorado*	.000	1	1	0	0	0	0	0	0	0	0	0	0	0	1	0	0	0	0	0	.000	1.000
Parent, Mark, Pit.-Chi.	.286	7	7	7	0	2	3	1	0	0	0	0	0	0	0	0	3	0	0	1	.429	.286
Parker, Rick, Los Angeles	.000	5	5	4	0	0	0	0	0	0	0	0	0	0	1	0	1	0	0	0	.000	.200
Patterson, John, San Francisco†	.171	46	45	41	4	7	9	2	0	0	2	0	0	1	3	0	7	0	0	1	.220	.244
Pegues, Steve, Pittsburgh	.235	37	37	34	3	8	10	2	0	0	1	0	1	1	1	0	13	0	0	0	.294	.270
Pena, Geronimo, St. Louis†	.000	7	7	6	0	0	0	0	0	0	0	0	1	0	0	0	5	0	0	0	.000	.000
Pendleton, Terry, Florida†	.250	5	5	4	1	1	1	0	0	0	0	0	0	0	1	0	0	0	0	0	.250	.400
Perez, Eddie, Atlanta	.000	1	1	1	0	0	0	0	0	0	0	0	0	0	0	0	1	0	0	0	.000	.000

Player, Team	Avg.	G	TPA	AB	R	H	TB	2B	3B	HR	RBI	SH	SF	HP	BB	IBB	SO	SB	CS	GDP	Slg.	OBP
Perry, Gerald, St. Louis*	.220	56	56	50	4	11	15	4	0	0	4	0	0	0	6	0	6	0	0	1	.300	.304
Petagine, Roberto, San Diego*	.267	39	38	30	3	8	13	2	0	1	7	1	0	0	7	0	14	0	0	0	.433	.405
Phillips, J.R., San Francisco*	.214	16	16	14	2	3	4	1	0	0	2	0	0	0	2	0	6	0	0	0	.286	.313
Piazza, Mike, Los Angeles	.500	2	2	2	1	1	4	0	0	1	1	0	0	0	0	0	0	0	0	0	2.000	.500
Plantier, Phil, Hou.-S.D.*	.167	18	15	12	2	2	5	0	0	1	1	0	0	0	3	1	5	0	0	0	.417	.333
Polonia, Luis, Atlanta*	.444	20	20	18	3	8	12	4	0	0	1	1	0	0	1	0	5	1	0	0	.667	.474
Pratt, Todd, Chicago	.000	1	1	0	0	0	0	0	0	0	0	0	0	0	1	0	0	0	0	0	.000	1.000
Pride, Curtis, Montreal*	.111	20	19	18	1	2	2	0	0	0	1	0	0	0	1	0	7	1	0	2	.111	.158
Prince, Tom, Los Angeles	.000	2	2	2	0	0	0	0	0	0	0	0	0	0	0	0	0	0	0	0	.000	.000
Pugh, Tim, Cincinnati	.000	1	1	1	0	0	0	0	0	0	0	0	0	0	0	0	1	0	0	0	.000	.000
Pulliam, Harvey, Colorado	.500	4	4	4	1	2	6	1	0	1	3	0	0	0	0	0	1	0	0	0	1.500	.500
Pye, Eddie, Los Angeles	.000	5	5	5	0	0	0	0	0	0	0	0	0	0	0	0	2	0	0	0	.000	.000
Ready, Randy Max, Philadelphia	.125	19	19	16	2	2	2	0	0	0	0	0	1	0	2	0	3	0	0	1	.125	.222
Reed, Jeff, San Francisco*	.160	30	30	25	2	4	4	0	0	0	2	0	0	0	5	1	5	0	0	0	.160	.300
Reed, Jody, San Diego	.000	2	1	0	1	0	0	0	0	0	0	0	0	0	1	0	0	0	0	0	.000	1.000
Rhodes, Karl, Chicago*	.143	7	7	7	0	1	1	0	0	0	0	0	0	0	0	0	1	0	0	1	.143	.143
Roberson, Kevin, Chicago†	.200	23	23	20	3	4	11	1	0	2	3	0	0	1	2	0	6	0	1	0	.550	.304
Roberts, Bip, San Diego†	.500	4	4	2	0	1	1	0	0	0	1	0	0	0	2	0	0	0	0	0	.500	.750
Rodriguez, Henry, L.A.-Mon.*	.000	10	10	8	0	0	0	0	0	0	1	0	1	0	1	0	4	0	0	0	.000	.100
Sabo, Chris, St. Louis	.000	2	2	2	0	0	0	0	0	0	0	0	0	0	0	0	0	0	0	1	.000	.000
Sanchez, Rey, Chicago	.000	1	1	1	0	0	0	0	0	0	0	0	0	0	0	0	1	0	0	0	.000	.000
Sanders, Deion, Cincinnati*	1.000	1	1	1	0	1	1	0	0	0	0	0	0	0	0	0	0	0	0	0	1.000	1.000
Sanders, Reggie, Cincinnati	.000	3	3	3	0	0	0	0	0	0	0	0	0	0	0	0	1	0	0	0	.000	.000
Santangelo, F.P., Montreal†	.333	9	9	9	1	3	3	0	0	0	0	0	0	0	0	0	1	0	0	0	.333	.333
Santiago, Benito, Cincinnati	.429	7	7	7	0	3	4	1	0	0	2	0	0	0	0	0	1	0	0	0	.571	.429
Sasser, Mackey, Pittsburgh*	.286	7	7	7	0	2	3	1	0	0	0	0	0	0	0	0	0	0	0	0	.429	.286
Scarsone, Steve, San Francisco	.375	10	10	8	4	3	4	1	0	0	0	0	0	0	2	0	3	0	0	0	.500	.500
Schall, Gene, Philadelphia	.400	6	6	5	2	2	2	0	0	0	1	0	0	0	1	1	0	0	0	0	.400	.500
Schmidt, Jason, Atlanta	.000	1	1	0	0	0	0	0	0	0	0	0	0	0	1	0	0	0	0	0	.000	1.000
Schofield, Dick, Los Angeles	.167	6	6	6	0	1	1	0	0	0	0	0	0	0	0	0	2	0	0	0	.167	.167
Sefcik, Kevin, Philadelphia	.000	2	2	2	0	0	0	0	0	0	0	0	0	0	0	0	1	0	0	0	.000	.000
Segui, David, N.Y.-Mon.†	.444	10	10	9	1	4	6	2	0	0	3	1	0	0	0	0	0	0	0	1	.667	.444
Servais, Scott, Chicago	.000	2	2	2	0	0	0	0	0	0	0	0	0	0	0	0	1	0	0	0	.000	.000
Sharperson, Mike, Atlanta	.000	6	6	6	0	0	0	0	0	0	0	0	0	0	0	0	2	0	0	0	.000	.000
Sheaffer, Danny, St. Louis	.167	9	9	6	2	1	4	0	0	1	4	0	0	0	3	0	1	0	0	1	.667	.444
Sheffield, Gary, Florida	.000	2	2	0	0	0	0	0	0	0	0	0	0	0	2	0	0	0	0	0	.000	1.000
Shipley, Craig, Houston	.360	28	28	25	4	9	15	1	1	1	5	0	0	0	3	1	5	1	0	0	.600	.429
Siddall, Joe, Montreal*	.000	1	1	0	1	0	0	0	0	0	0	0	0	0	1	0	0	0	0	0	.000	1.000
Silvestri, Dave, Montreal	.385	17	17	13	3	5	6	1	0	0	2	1	0	0	3	0	6	0	0	1	.462	.500
Simms, Mike, Houston	.182	14	14	11	1	2	5	0	0	1	2	0	0	0	3	0	3	0	0	0	.455	.357
Slaught, Don, Pittsburgh	.500	4	4	4	1	2	3	1	0	0	0	0	0	0	0	0	0	0	0	0	.750	.500
Smith, Dwight, Atlanta*	.232	82	80	69	8	16	26	2	1	2	18	0	1	1	9	1	22	0	3	1	.377	.325
Smith, Ozzie, St. Louis†	.000	3	3	3	0	0	0	0	0	0	0	0	0	0	0	0	1	0	0	0	.000	.000
Sosa, Sammy, Chicago	.000	2	2	1	0	0	0	0	0	0	1	0	1	0	0	0	1	0	0	0	.000	.000
Spehr, Tim, Montreal	.500	4	4	2	1	1	4	0	0	1	2	1	0	0	1	0	0	0	0	0	2.000	.667
Spiers, Bill, New York*	.225	48	48	40	3	9	12	1	1	0	6	1	2	0	5	0	4	0	1	0	.300	.298
Stankiewicz, Andy, Houston	.250	13	13	12	3	3	4	1	0	0	2	1	0	0	0	0	6	0	0	0	.333	.250
Stinnett, Kelly, New York	.111	13	12	9	0	1	1	0	0	0	0	0	0	1	2	0	3	0	0	0	.111	.333
Sweeney, Mark, St. Louis*	.533	17	17	15	1	8	8	0	0	0	3	0	0	0	2	0	2	0	0	0	.533	.588
Swindell, Greg, Houston	.000	1	1	1	0	0	0	0	0	0	0	0	0	0	0	0	1	0	0	0	.000	.000
Tarasco, Tony, Montreal*	.250	10	8	8	0	2	2	0	0	0	1	0	0	0	0	0	0	0	0	0	.250	.250
Tatum, Jimmy, Colorado	.233	31	31	30	4	7	10	1	1	0	4	0	0	0	1	0	7	0	0	1	.333	.258
Taubensee, Eddie, Cincinnati*	.429	17	16	14	2	6	10	1	0	1	5	0	0	0	2	0	3	0	0	0	.714	.500
Tavarez, Jesus, Florida†	.000	2	2	2	0	0	0	0	0	0	0	0	0	0	0	0	0	0	0	0	.000	.000
Thompson, Milt, Houston*	.241	64	62	54	9	13	23	4	0	2	11	0	1	0	7	0	15	2	0	1	.426	.323
Thompson, Robby, San Fran.	.250	4	4	4	0	1	1	0	0	0	0	0	0	0	0	0	2	0	0	0	.250	.250
Thompson, Ryan, New York	1.000	1	1	1	1	1	1	0	0	0	0	0	0	0	0	0	0	0	0	0	1.000	1.000
Timmons, Ozzie, Chicago	.192	29	29	26	4	5	8	0	0	1	5	0	0	0	3	0	5	0	0	1	.308	.276
Treadway, Jeff, L.A.-Mon.*	.150	47	45	40	4	6	10	2	1	0	10	0	0	0	5	1	4	0	0	0	.250	.244
Tucker, Scooter, Houston	.000	3	3	3	0	0	0	0	0	0	0	0	0	0	0	0	0	0	0	0	.000	.000
Vander Wal, John, Colorado*	.389	92	85	72	12	28	49	7	1	4	17	0	1	0	12	5	12	1	1	2	.681	.471
Van Slyke, Andy, Philadelphia*	.000	8	8	8	0	0	0	0	0	0	0	0	0	0	0	0	2	0	0	0	.000	.000
Varsho, Gary, Philadelphia*	.261	53	51	46	4	12	15	1	1	0	5	0	0	1	4	0	7	1	0	0	.326	.333
Veras, Quilvio, Florida†	.000	3	3	2	0	0	0	0	0	0	0	0	0	0	1	0	0	0	1	0	.000	.333
Vizcaino, Jose, New York†	.000	1	1	1	0	0	0	0	0	0	0	0	0	0	0	0	1	0	0	0	.000	.000
Wagner, Paul, Pittsburgh	.000	1	1	1	0	0	0	0	0	0	0	0	0	0	0	0	0	0	0	0	.000	.000
Walker, Larry, Colorado*	1.000	2	2	1	1	1	4	0	0	1	3	0	0	1	0	0	0	0	0	0	4.000	1.000
Wallach, Tim, Los Angeles	.000	1	1	1	0	0	0	0	0	0	0	0	0	0	0	0	1	0	0	0	.000	.000
Walton, Jerome, Cincinnati	.176	19	19	17	2	3	6	0	0	1	1	0	0	0	2	0	3	0	0	0	.353	.263
Webster, Lenny, Philadelphia	.000	6	6	6	0	0	0	0	0	0	0	0	0	0	0	0	2	0	0	0	.000	.000
Webster, Mitch, Los Angeles†	.171	39	38	35	2	6	10	1	0	1	3	2	0	0	1	0	8	0	0	0	.286	.194
Wehner, John, Pittsburgh	.143	18	18	14	1	2	2	0	0	0	1	0	1	0	3	0	2	1	0	0	.143	.278
Weiss, Walt, Colorado†	.000	1	1	1	0	0	0	0	0	0	0	0	0	0	0	0	0	0	0	0	.000	.000
White, Rondell, Montreal	.222	11	11	9	2	2	3	1	0	0	0	0	0	0	2	0	1	0	0	1	.333	.364
Whiten, Mark, Philadelphia†	.333	6	6	6	1	2	2	0	0	0	0	0	0	0	0	0	1	0	0	0	.333	.333
Whitmore, Darrell, Florida*	.154	14	14	13	2	2	3	1	0	0	0	0	0	0	1	0	5	0	0	0	.231	.214
Wilkins, Rick, Chi.-Hou.*	.000	5	5	3	1	0	0	0	0	0	0	0	0	0	2	0	1	0	0	0	.000	.400
Williams, Eddie, San Diego	.125	19	19	16	1	2	5	0	0	1	2	0	0	0	3	0	3	0	0	1	.313	.263
Williams, Matt, San Francisco	.000	2	2	2	0	0	0	0	0	0	0	0	0	0	0	0	0	0	0	0	.000	.000
Williams, Reggie, Los Angeles†	.000	1	1	1	0	0	0	0	0	0	0	0	0	0	0	0	0	0	0	0	.000	.000
Wilson, Nigel, Cincinnati*	.000	3	3	3	0	0	0	0	0	0	0	0	0	0	0	0	2	0	0	0	.000	.000
Wilson, Trevor, San Francisco*	.000	1	1	1	0	0	0	0	0	0	0	0	0	0	0	0	1	0	0	0	.000	.000

Player, Team	Avg.	G	TPA	AB	R	H	TB	2B	3B	HR	RBI	SH	SF	HP	BB	IBB	SO	SB	CS	GDP	Slg.	OBP
Worthington, Craig, Cincinnati	.500	5	5	4	0	2	2	0	0	0	0	0	0	0	1	0	0	0	0	0	.500	.600
Young, Eric, Colorado	.211	25	25	19	3	4	6	2	0	0	4	0	1	0	5	1	3	4	0	0	.316	.360
Young, Kevin, Pittsburgh	.000	4	3	3	0	0	0	0	0	0	0	0	0	0	0	0	2	0	0	0	.000	.000
Zeile, Todd, St.L.-Chi.	.000	3	3	2	0	0	0	0	0	0	0	1	0	0	0	0	0	0	0	0	.000	.000

PINCH-HITTERS WITH TWO OR MORE TEAMS

Player, Team	Avg.	G	TPA	AB	R	H	TB	2B	3B	HR	RBI	SH	SF	HP	BB	IBB	SO	SB	CS	GDP	Slg.	OBP
Duncan, Mariano, Philadelphia	.625	8	8	8	1	5	7	2	0	0	4	0	0	0	0	0	2	0	1	0	.875	.625
Duncan, Mariano, Cincinnati	.200	11	11	10	3	2	2	0	0	0	1	0	0	0	1	0	3	0	0	1	.200	.273
Fonville, Chad, Montreal†	.400	10	10	10	1	4	4	0	0	0	0	0	0	0	0	0	2	0	1	0	.400	.400
Fonville, Chad, Los Angeles†	.000	6	6	6	0	0	0	0	0	0	0	0	0	0	0	0	1	0	0	0	.000	.000
Gonzalez, Luis, Houston*	1.000	3	3	2	0	2	2	0	0	0	1	0	0	0	1	0	0	0	0	0	1.000	1.000
Gonzalez, Luis, Chicago*	.500	2	2	2	0	1	1	0	0	0	0	0	0	0	0	0	1	0	0	0	.500	.500
Lewis, Darren, San Francisco	.000	1	1	1	0	0	0	0	0	0	0	0	0	0	0	0	0	0	0	0	.000	.000
Lewis, Darren, Cincinnati	.125	8	8	8	0	1	1	0	0	0	1	0	0	0	0	0	3	0	0	1	.125	.125
Oliva, Jose, Atlanta	.095	23	23	21	0	2	2	0	0	0	2	0	0	0	2	0	6	0	0	1	.095	.174
Oliva, Jose, St. Louis	.000	2	2	1	0	0	0	0	0	0	0	0	0	0	1	0	1	0	0	0	.000	.500
Parent, Mark, Pittsburgh	.400	5	5	5	0	2	3	1	0	0	0	0	0	0	0	0	2	0	0	0	.600	.400
Parent, Mark, Chicago	.000	2	2	2	0	0	0	0	0	0	0	0	0	0	0	0	1	0	0	1	.000	.000
Plantier, Phil, Houston*	.000	2	2	2	0	0	0	0	0	0	0	0	0	0	0	0	1	0	0	0	.000	.000
Plantier, Phil, San Diego*	.200	16	13	10	2	2	5	0	0	1	1	0	0	0	3	1	4	0	0	0	.500	.385
Rodriguez, Henry, Los Angeles*	.000	2	2	2	0	0	0	0	0	0	0	0	0	0	0	0	0	0	0	0	.000	.000
Rodriguez, Henry, Montreal*	.000	8	8	6	0	0	0	0	0	0	1	0	1	0	1	0	4	0	0	0	.000	.125
Segui, David, New York†	.375	9	9	8	0	3	4	1	0	0	3	1	0	0	0	0	0	0	0	1	.500	.375
Segui, David, Montreal†	1.000	1	1	1	1	1	2	1	0	0	0	0	0	0	0	0	0	0	0	0	2.000	1.000
Treadway, Jeff, Los Angeles*	.125	16	16	16	2	2	4	0	1	0	3	0	0	0	0	0	2	0	0	0	.250	.125
Treadway, Jeff, Montreal*	.167	31	29	24	2	4	6	2	0	0	7	0	0	0	5	1	2	0	0	0	.250	.310
Wilkins, Rick, Chicago*	.000	3	3	3	0	0	0	0	0	0	0	0	0	0	0	0	1	0	0	0	.000	.000
Wilkins, Rick, Houston*	.000	2	2	0	1	0	0	0	0	0	0	0	0	0	2	0	0	0	0	0	.000	1.000
Zeile, Todd, St. Louis	.000	1	1	1	0	0	0	0	0	0	0	0	0	0	0	0	0	0	0	0	.000	.000
Zeile, Todd, Chicago	.000	2	2	1	0	0	0	0	0	0	0	1	0	0	0	0	0	0	0	0	.000	.000

PITCHING

TEAM

Team	W	L	Pct.	ERA	G	ShO	GF	Sv.	IP	H	TBF	R	ER	HR	SH	SF	HB	BB	IBB	SO	WP	Bk.
Atlanta	90	54	.625	3.44	144	18	11	34	1291.2	1184	5410	540	494	107	63	34	32	436	46	1087	38	4
Los Angeles	78	66	.542	3.66	144	16	11	37	1295.0	1188	5481	609	526	125	59	33	37	462	45	1060	49	12
New York	69	75	.479	3.88	144	9	9	36	1291.0	1296	5483	618	556	133	62	40	35	401	48	901	39	12
Cincinnati	85	59	.590	4.03	144	8	10	38	1289.1	1270	5445	623	578	131	56	43	31	424	32	903	58	10
Houston	76	68	.528	4.06	144	6	8	32	1320.1	1357	5703	674	596	118	56	44	50	460	52	1056	53	6
St. Louis	62	81	.434	4.09	143	4	6	38	1265.2	1290	5420	658	575	135	83	35	40	445	37	842	51	6
Montreal	66	78	.458	4.11	144	7	9	42	1283.2	1286	5491	638	586	128	77	29	59	416	26	950	45	9
Chicago	73	71	.507	4.13	144	6	12	45	1301.0	1313	5664	671	597	162	63	40	34	518	68	926	38	6
San Diego	70	74	.486	4.13	144	6	10	35	1284.2	1242	5529	672	590	142	72	28	51	512	37	1047	60	5
Philadelphia	69	75	.479	4.21	144	8	8	41	1290.1	1241	5575	658	603	134	60	44	55	538	36	980	57	10
Florida	67	76	.469	4.27	143	12	7	29	1286.0	1299	5628	673	610	139	73	27	46	562	54	994	36	5
Pittsburgh	58	86	.403	4.70	144	11	7	29	1275.1	1407	5618	736	666	130	70	46	57	477	50	871	65	4
San Francisco	67	77	.465	4.86	144	12	5	34	1293.2	1368	5672	776	699	173	77	53	56	505	51	801	43	15
Colorado	77	67	.535	4.97	144	1	1	43	1288.1	1443	5706	783	711	160	76	35	41	512	31	891	62	13
Totals	1007	1007	.500	4.18	1007	124	114	513	18056.0	18184	77825	9329	8387	1917	947	531	624	6668	613	13309	694	117

NOTE—Totals for earned runs for several clubs do not agree with the composite total for all pitchers of each respective club due to instances in which provision 10.18(i) of the Scoring Rules were applied. The following differences are to be noted: Los Angeles pitchers add to 528; St. Louis pitchers add to 576; San Diego pitchers add to 592; Florida pitchers add to 611; Pittsburgh pitchers add to 667.

INDIVIDUAL

TOP QUALIFIERS FOR EARNED-RUN AVERAGE TITLE

Minimum 144 innings. *Throws lefthanded.

Pitcher, Team	W	L	Pct.	ERA	G	GS	CG	ShO	GF	Sv.	IP	H	TBF	R	ER	HR	SH	SF	HB	BB	IBB	SO	WP	Bk.
Maddux, Greg, Atlanta	19	2	.905	1.63	28	28	10	3	0	0	209.2	147	785	39	38	8	9	1	4	23	3	181	1	0
Nomo, Hideo, Los Angeles	13	6	.684	2.54	28	28	4	3	0	0	191.1	124	780	63	54	14	11	4	5	78	2	236	19	5
Ashby, Andy, San Diego	12	10	.545	2.94	31	31	2	2	0	0	192.2	180	800	79	63	17	10	4	11	62	3	150	7	0
Valdes, Ismael, Los Angeles	13	11	.542	3.05	33	27	6	2	1	1	197.2	168	804	76	67	17	10	5	1	51	5	150	1	3
Glavine, Tom, Atlanta*	16	7	.696	3.08	29	29	3	1	0	0	198.2	182	822	76	68	9	7	5	5	66	0	127	3	0
Hamilton, Joey, San Diego	6	9	.400	3.08	31	30	2	1	0	0	204.1	189	850	89	70	17	12	4	11	56	5	123	2	0
Smoltz, John, Atlanta	12	7	.632	3.18	29	29	2	1	0	0	192.2	166	808	76	68	15	13	5	4	72	8	193	13	0
Castillo, Frank, Chicago	11	10	.524	3.21	29	29	2	2	0	0	188.0	179	795	75	67	22	11	3	6	52	4	135	3	1
Schourek, Pete, Cincinnati*	18	7	.720	3.22	29	29	2	0	0	0	190.1	158	754	72	68	17	4	4	8	45	3	160	1	1
Navarro, Jaime, Chicago	14	6	.700	3.28	29	29	1	1	0	0	200.1	194	837	79	73	19	2	3	3	56	7	128	1	0
Hampton, Mike, Houston*	9	8	.529	3.35	24	24	0	0	0	0	150.2	141	641	73	56	11	5	4		49	3	115	3	1
Neagle, Denny, Pittsburgh*	13	8	.619	3.43	31	31	5	1	0	0	209.2	221	876	91	80	20	13	6	3	45	3	150	6	0
Rapp, Pat, Florida	14	7	.667	3.44	28	28	3	2	0	0	167.1	158	716	72	64	10	8	0	7	76	2	102	7	0
Smiley, John, Cincinnati*	12	5	.706	3.46	28	27	1	0	0	0	176.2	173	724	72	68	11	17	5	4	39	3	124	5	1
Reynolds, Shane, Houston	10	11	.476	3.47	30	30	3	2	0	0	189.1	196	792	87	73	15	8	0	2	37	6	175	7	1

DEPARTMENTAL LEADERS: W—Maddux, Atl., 19; L—Wagner, Pit., 16; G—Leskanic, Col., 76; GS—Ashby, S.D., Drabek, Hou., Loaiza, Pit., Neagle, Pit., Portugal, S.F.-Cin., 31; CG—Maddux, Atl., 10; ShO—Maddux, Atl., Nomo, L.A., 3; GF—Nen, Fla., Slocumb, Phi., 54; Sv.—Myers, Chi., 38; IP—Maddux, Atl., Neagle, Pit., 209.2; H—Neagle, Pit., 221; TBF—Neagle, Pit., 876; R—Loaiza, Pit., 115; ER—Loaiza, Pit., 99; HR—Foster, Chi., 32; SH—Fassero, Mon., 19; SF—Loaiza, Pit., 9; HB—Leiter, S.F., 17; BB—Martinez, L.A., 81; IBB—Jones, Hou., 17; SO—Nomo, L.A., 236; WP—Nomo, L.A., 19; Bk.—Nomo, L.A., 5.

ALL PITCHERS

*Throws lefthanded.

Pitcher, Team	W	L	Pct.	ERA	G	GS	CG	ShO	GF	Sv.	IP	H	TBF	R	ER	HR	SH	SF	HB	BB	IBB	SO	WP	Bk.
Abbott, Kyle, Philadelphia*	2	0	1.000	3.81	18	0	0	0	3	0	28.1	28	122	12	12	3	0	1	0	16	0	21	2	1
Acevedo, Juan, Colorado	4	6	.400	6.44	17	11	0	0	0	0	65.2	82	291	53	47	15	4	2	6	20	2	40	2	1
Adams, Terry, Chicago	1	1	.500	6.50	18	0	0	0	7	1	18.0	22	86	15	13	0	0	0	0	10	1	15	1	0
Alvarez, Tavo, Montreal	1	5	.167	6.75	8	8	0	0	0	0	37.1	46	173	30	28	2	1	0	3	14	0	17	1	0
Aquino, Luis, Mon.-S.F.	0	3	.000	5.10	34	0	0	0	9	2	42.1	57	199	34	24	6	1	1	3	13	2	26	3	0
Arocha, Rene, St. Louis	3	5	.375	3.99	41	0	0	0	13	0	49.2	55	216	24	22	6	8	2	3	18	4	25	2	0
Ashby, Andy, San Diego	12	10	.545	2.94	31	31	2	2	0	0	192.2	180	800	79	63	17	10	4	11	62	3	150	7	0
Astacio, Pedro, Los Angeles	7	8	.467	4.24	48	11	1	1	7	0	104.0	103	436	53	49	12	5	3	4	29	5	80	5	0
Avery, Steve, Atlanta*	7	13	.350	4.67	29	29	3	1	0	0	173.1	165	724	92	90	22	6	4	6	52	4	141	3	0
Bailey, Cory, St. Louis	0	0	.000	7.36	3	0	0	0	0	0	3.2	2	15	3	3	0	0	0	0	2	1	5	1	0
Bailey, Roger, Colorado	7	6	.538	4.98	39	6	0	0	9	0	81.1	88	360	49	45	9	7	2	1	39	3	33	7	1
Banks, Willie, Chi.-L.A.-Fla.	2	6	.250	5.66	25	15	0	0	2	0	90.2	106	430	71	57	14	6	3	2	58	7	62	9	1
Barber, Brian, St. Louis	2	1	.667	5.22	9	4	0	0	2	0	29.1	31	130	17	17	4	0	3	0	16	0	27	3	0
Barton, Shawn, San Fran.*	4	1	.800	4.26	52	0	0	0	11	1	44.1	37	181	22	21	3	1	3	2	19	1	22	0	1
Bautista, Jose, San Fran.	3	8	.273	6.44	52	6	0	0	19	0	100.2	120	451	77	72	24	8	5	5	26	3	45	1	2
Beck, Rod, San Francisco	5	6	.455	4.45	60	0	0	0	52	33	58.2	60	255	31	29	7	4	3	2	21	8	42	2	0
Bedrosian, Steve, Atlanta	1	2	.333	6.11	29	0	0	0	8	0	28.0	40	129	21	19	6	1	2	1	12	2	22	0	0
Benes, Alan, St. Louis	1	2	.333	8.44	3	3	0	0	0	0	16.0	24	76	15	15	2	1	0	1	4	0	20	3	0
Benes, Andy, San Diego	4	7	.364	4.17	19	19	1	1	0	0	118.2	121	518	65	55	10	3	4	4	45	3	126	3	0
Berumen, Andres, San Diego	2	3	.400	5.68	37	0	0	0	17	1	44.1	37	207	29	28	3	1	3	3	36	3	42	6	0
Birkbeck, Mike, New York	0	1	.000	1.63	4	4	0	0	0	0	27.2	22	104	5	5	2	2	0	0	2	0	20	1	0
Blair, Willie, San Diego	7	5	.583	4.34	40	12	0	0	11	0	114.0	112	485	60	55	11	8	2	2	45	3	83	4	0
Bochtler, Doug, San Diego	4	4	.500	3.57	34	0	0	0	11	1	45.1	38	181	18	18	5	2	1	0	19	0	45	1	0
Borbon, Pedro, Atlanta*	2	2	.500	3.09	41	0	0	0	19	2	32.0	29	143	12	11	2	3	1	1	17	4	33	0	1
Borland, Toby, Philadelphia*	1	3	.250	3.77	50	0	0	0	18	6	74.0	81	339	37	31	3	3	2	5	37	7	59	12	0
Bottalico, Ricky, Philadelphia	5	3	.625	2.46	62	0	0	0	20	1	87.2	50	350	25	24	7	3	1	4	42	3	87	1	0

1995 N.L. STATISTICS Pitching

Pitcher, Team	W	L	Pct.	ERA	G	GS	CG	ShO	GF	Sv.	IP	H	TBF	R	ER	HR	SH	SF	HB	BB	IBB	SO	WP	Bk.
Bowen, Ryan, Florida	2	0	1.000	3.78	4	3	0	0	0	0	16.2	23	85	11	7	3	1	2	0	12	2	15	0	0
Brantley, Jeff, Cincinnati	3	2	.600	2.82	56	0	0	0	49	28	70.1	53	283	22	22	11	2	3	1	20	3	62	2	2
Brewington, Jamie, San Fran.	6	4	.600	4.54	13	13	0	0	0	0	75.1	68	334	38	38	8	4	4	4	45	6	45	3	0
Brocail, Doug, Houston	6	4	.600	4.19	36	7	0	0	12	1	77.1	87	339	40	36	10	1	1	4	22	2	39	1	1
Bruske, Jim, Los Angeles	0	0	.000	4.50	9	0	0	0	3	1	10.0	12	45	7	5	0	0	0	1	4	0	5	1	0
Bullinger, Jim, Chicago	12	8	.600	4.14	24	24	1	1	0	0	150.0	152	665	80	69	14	12	5	9	65	7	93	5	1
Burba, Dave, S.F.-Cin.	10	4	.714	3.97	52	9	1	1	7	0	106.2	90	451	50	47	9	4	1	0	51	3	96	5	0
Burgos, Enrique, San Fran.*	0	0	.000	8.64	5	0	0	0	2	0	8.1	14	44	8	8	1	0	0	1	6	0	12	2	0
Burkett, John, Florida	14	14	.500	4.30	30	30	4	0	0	0	188.1	208	810	95	90	22	10	0	6	57	5	126	2	1
Byrd, Paul, New York	2	0	1.000	2.05	17	0	0	0	6	0	22.0	18	91	6	5	1	0	2	1	7	1	26	1	2
Candiotti, Tom, Los Angeles	7	14	.333	3.50	30	30	1	1	0	0	190.1	187	812	93	74	18	7	5	9	58	2	141	7	0
Cangelosi, John, Houston*	0	0	.000	0.00	1	0	0	0	1	0	1.0	0	4	0	0	0	0	0	0	1	0	0	0	0
Carrasco, Hector, Cincinnati	2	7	.222	4.12	64	0	0	0	28	5	87.1	86	391	45	40	1	2	6	2	46	5	64	15	0
Carter, Andy, Philadelphia*	0	0	.000	6.14	4	0	0	0	1	0	7.1	4	28	5	5	3	0	1	1	2	1	6	0	0
Casian, Larry, Chicago*	1	0	1.000	1.93	42	0	0	0	5	0	23.1	23	107	6	5	1	1	2	0	15	6	11	2	0
Castillo, Frank, Chicago	11	10	.524	3.21	29	29	2	2	0	0	188.0	179	795	75	67	22	11	3	6	52	4	135	3	1
Charlton, Norm, Philadelphia*	2	5	.286	7.36	25	0	0	0	5	0	22.0	23	102	19	18	2	1	1	3	15	3	12	1	0
Christiansen, Jason, Pitts.*	1	3	.250	4.15	63	0	0	0	13	0	56.1	49	255	28	26	5	6	3	3	34	9	53	4	1
Clark, Terry, Atlanta	0	0	.000	4.91	3	0	0	0	1	0	3.2	3	18	2	2	0	0	0	0	5	0	2	1	0
Clontz, Brad, Atlanta	8	1	.889	3.65	59	0	0	0	14	4	69.0	71	295	29	28	5	3	2	4	22	4	55	0	0
Cornelius, Reid, Mon.-N.Y.	3	7	.300	5.54	18	10	0	0	1	0	66.2	75	301	44	41	11	4	3	3	30	5	39	2	1
Courtright, John, Cincinnati*	0	0	.000	9.00	1	0	0	0	0	0	1.0	2	5	1	1	0	1	0	0	0	0	0	0	0
Creek, Doug, St. Louis*	0	0	.000	0.00	6	0	0	0	1	0	6.2	2	24	0	0	0	0	0	0	3	0	10	0	0
Cummings, John, L.A.*	3	1	.750	3.00	35	0	0	0	11	0	39.0	38	165	16	13	3	2	1	0	10	4	21	1	0
Daal, Omar, Los Angeles*	4	0	1.000	7.20	28	0	0	0	0	0	20.0	29	100	16	16	1	1	1	1	15	4	11	0	1
DeLeon, Jose, Montreal	0	1	.000	7.56	7	0	0	0	1	0	8.1	7	40	7	7	2	0	2	1	7	0	12	0	0
DeLucia, Rich, St. Louis	8	7	.533	3.39	56	1	0	0	8	0	82.1	63	342	38	31	9	5	2	3	36	2	76	5	0
Deshaies, Jim, Philadelphia*	0	1	.000	20.25	2	2	0	0	0	0	5.1	15	32	12	12	3	0	0	0	1	0	6	0	0
Dewey, Mark, San Francisco	1	0	1.000	3.13	27	0	0	0	5	0	31.2	30	137	12	11	2	1	1	0	17	6	32	1	0
DiPoto, Jerry, New York	4	6	.400	3.78	58	0	0	0	26	2	78.2	77	330	41	33	2	6	3	4	29	8	49	3	1
Dishman, Glenn, San Diego*	4	8	.333	5.01	19	16	0	0	1	0	97.0	104	421	60	54	11	6	3	4	34	1	43	3	1
Dougherty, Jim, Houston	8	4	.667	4.92	56	0	0	0	11	0	67.2	76	294	37	37	7	3	3	3	25	1	49	1	0
Drabek, Doug, Houston	10	9	.526	4.77	31	31	2	1	0	0	185.0	205	797	104	98	18	4	3	8	54	4	143	8	1
Dunbar, Matt, Florida*	0	1	.000	11.57	8	0	0	0	1	0	7.0	12	45	9	9	0	2	0	1	11	3	5	1	0
Dyer, Mike, Pittsburgh	4	5	.444	4.34	55	0	0	0	15	0	74.2	81	327	40	36	9	3	1	5	30	3	53	4	1
Edens, Tom, Chicago	1	0	1.000	6.00	5	0	0	0	1	0	3.0	6	18	3	2	0	0	0	0	3	0	2	0	0
Eischen, Joey, Los Angeles*	0	0	.000	3.10	17	0	0	0	8	0	20.1	19	95	9	7	1	0	0	2	11	1	15	1	0
Elliott, Donnie, San Diego	0	0	.000	0.00	1	0	0	0	1	0	2.0	2	9	0	0	0	0	0	0	1	0	3	0	0
Ericks, John, Pittsburgh	3	9	.250	4.58	19	18	1	0	0	0	106.0	108	472	59	54	7	5	5	2	50	4	80	11	1
Estes, Shawn, San Fran.*	0	3	.000	6.75	3	3	0	0	0	0	17.1	16	76	14	13	2	0	0	1	5	0	14	4	0
Eversgerd, Bryan, Montreal*	0	0	.000	5.14	25	0	0	0	5	0	21.0	22	95	13	12	2	1	2	1	9	2	8	1	0
Fassero, Jeff, Montreal*	13	14	.481	4.33	30	30	1	0	0	0	189.0	207	833	102	91	15	19	7	2	74	3	164	7	1
Fernandez, Sid, Philadelphia*	6	1	.857	3.34	11	11	0	0	0	0	64.2	48	263	25	24	11	1	0	1	21	0	79	0	1
Fletcher, Paul, Philadelphia	1	0	1.000	5.40	10	0	0	0	1	0	13.1	15	64	8	8	2	1	1	1	9	2	10	2	0
Florence, Don, New York*	3	0	1.000	1.50	14	0	0	0	3	0	12.0	17	57	3	2	0	1	0	0	6	0	5	0	0
Florie, Bryce, San Diego	2	2	.500	3.01	47	0	0	0	10	1	68.2	49	290	30	23	8	5	1	4	38	3	68	7	2
Fossas, Tony, St. Louis*	3	0	1.000	1.47	58	0	0	0	20	0	36.2	28	145	6	6	1	2	1	1	10	3	40	1	0
Foster, Kevin, Chicago	12	11	.522	4.51	30	28	0	0	1	0	167.2	149	703	90	84	32	4	6	6	65	4	146	2	2
Franco, John, New York*	5	3	.625	2.44	48	0	0	0	41	29	51.2	48	213	17	14	4	4	1	0	17	2	41	0	0
Frascatore, John, St. Louis	1	1	.500	4.41	14	4	0	0	3	0	32.2	39	151	19	16	3	1	1	2	16	1	21	0	0
Fraser, Willie, Montreal	2	1	.667	5.61	22	0	0	0	6	2	25.2	25	114	17	16	6	1	0	3	9	1	12	2	0
Freeman, Marvin, Colorado	3	7	.300	5.89	22	18	0	0	0	0	94.2	122	437	64	62	15	7	3	2	41	1	61	5	1
Frey, Steve, S.F.-Phi.*	0	1	.000	2.12	18	0	0	0	4	1	17.0	10	65	7	4	2	2	1	0	4	1	7	0	0
Garces, Rich, Chi.-Fla.	0	2	.000	4.44	18	0	0	0	7	0	24.1	25	108	15	12	1	1	0	0	11	2	22	0	0
Gardner, Mark, Florida	5	5	.500	4.49	39	11	1	1	7	1	102.1	109	456	60	51	14	7	0	5	43	5	87	3	1
Glavine, Tom, Atlanta*	16	7	.696	3.08	29	29	3	1	0	0	198.2	182	822	76	68	9	7	5	5	66	0	127	3	0
Gomez, Pat, San Francisco*	0	0	.000	5.14	18	0	0	0	3	0	14.0	16	70	8	8	2	0	0	0	12	1	15	0	1
Gott, Jim, Pittsburgh	2	4	.333	6.03	25	0	0	0	12	3	31.1	38	147	26	21	2	1	1	1	12	2	19	3	0
Grace, Mike, Philadelphia	1	1	.500	3.18	2	2	0	0	0	0	11.1	10	47	4	4	0	1	0	0	4	0	7	0	0
Grahe, Joe, Colorado	4	3	.571	5.08	17	9	0	0	0	0	56.2	69	265	42	32	6	3	3	3	27	2	27	3	2
Green, Tyler, Philadelphia	8	9	.471	5.31	26	25	4	2	0	0	140.2	157	623	86	83	15	5	6	4	66	3	85	9	2
Greene, Tommy, Philadelphia	0	5	.000	8.29	11	6	0	0	3	0	33.2	45	167	32	31	6	2	1	3	20	0	24	3	1
Greer, Kenny, San Francisco	0	2	.000	5.25	8	0	0	0	1	0	12.0	15	61	12	7	3	2	1	1	5	2	7	0	0
Groom, Buddy, Florida*	1	2	.333	7.20	14	0	0	0	5	0	15.0	26	71	12	12	2	0	0	0	6	0	12	0	0
Grott, Matt, Cincinnati*	0	0	.000	21.60	2	0	0	0	0	0	1.2	6	11	4	4	1	0	0	0	0	0	2	0	0
Gunderson, Eric, New York*	1	1	.500	3.70	30	0	0	0	7	0	24.1	25	103	10	10	2	0	1	1	8	3	19	1	0
Guthrie, Mark, Los Angeles*	0	2	.000	3.66	24	0	0	0	7	0	19.2	19	91	11	8	1	2	0	1	9	2	19	2	0
Habyan, John, St. Louis	3	2	.600	2.88	31	0	0	0	9	0	40.2	32	165	18	13	0	4	1	1	15	4	35	2	3
Hamilton, Joey, San Diego	6	9	.400	3.08	31	30	2	2	1	0	204.1	189	850	89	70	17	12	4	11	56	5	123	2	0
Hammond, Chris, Florida*	9	6	.600	3.80	25	24	3	2	0	0	161.0	157	683	73	68	17	7	7	9	47	2	126	3	1
Hampton, Mike, Houston*	9	8	.529	3.35	24	24	0	0	0	0	150.2	141	641	73	56	13	11	5	4	49	3	115	3	1
Hancock, Lee, Pittsburgh*	0	0	.000	1.93	11	0	0	0	3	0	14.0	10	54	3	3	0	0	0	0	2	0	6	2	0
Hansell, Greg, Los Angeles	0	1	.000	7.45	20	0	0	0	7	0	19.1	29	93	17	16	5	1	1	2	6	1	13	0	0
Harnisch, Pete, New York	2	8	.200	3.68	18	18	0	0	0	0	110.0	111	462	55	45	13	4	6	3	24	4	82	0	1
Harris, Gene, Philadelphia	2	2	.500	4.26	21	0	0	0	5	0	19.0	19	82	9	9	2	1	0	0	8	0	9	0	0
Harris, Greg, Montreal	2	3	.400	2.61	45	0	0	0	12	0	48.1	45	204	18	14	6	3	0	1	16	1	47	3	0
Hartgraves, Dean, Houston*	2	0	1.000	3.22	40	0	0	0	11	0	36.1	30	150	14	13	2	1	1	0	16	2	24	1	0
Harvey, Bryan, Florida	0	0	.000	0.00	1	0	0	0	0	0	0.0	2	3	3	3	1	0	0	0	1	0	0	0	0
Henke, Tom, St. Louis	1	1	.500	1.82	52	0	0	0	47	36	54.1	42	221	11	11	2	2	0	0	18	0	48	1	0
Henneman, Mike, Houston	0	1	.000	3.00	21	0	0	0	18	8	21.0	21	87	7	7	1	0	2	2	4	1	19	3	0
Henry, Butch, Montreal*	7	9	.438	2.84	21	21	1	1	0	0	126.2	133	524	47	40	11	7	3	2	28	3	60	0	1
Henry, Doug, New York	3	6	.333	2.96	51	0	0	0	20	4	67.0	48	273	23	22	7	3	2	1	25	6	62	6	1
Heredia, Gil, Montreal	5	6	.455	4.31	40	18	0	0	5	1	119.0	137	509	60	57	7	9	4	5	21	1	74	1	0

Pitcher, Team	W	L	Pct.	ERA	G	GS	CG	ShO	GF	Sv.	IP	H	TBF	R	ER	HR	SH	SF	HB	BB	IBB	SO	WP	Bk.
Hermanson, Dustin, S.D.	3	1	.750	6.82	26	0	0	0	6	0	31.2	35	151	26	24	8	3	0	1	22	1	19	3	0
Hernandez, Jeremy, Florida	0	0	.000	11.57	7	0	0	0	3	0	7.0	12	36	9	9	2	1	1	1	3	1	5	0	0
Hernandez, Xavier, Cincinnati	7	2	.778	4.60	59	0	0	0	19	3	90.0	95	391	47	46	8	6	2	4	31	1	84	7	0
Hickerson, Bryan, Chi.-Col.*	3	3	.500	8.57	56	0	0	0	13	1	48.1	69	239	52	46	8	2	0	1	28	5	40	5	1
Hill, Ken, St. Louis	6	7	.462	5.06	18	18	0	0	0	0	110.1	125	493	71	62	16	9	2	0	45	4	50	3	0
Hoffman, Trevor, San Diego	7	4	.636	3.88	55	0	0	0	51	31	53.1	48	218	25	23	10	0	0	0	14	3	52	1	0
Holmes, Darren, Colorado	6	1	.857	3.24	68	0	0	0	33	14	66.2	59	286	26	24	3	5	3	1	28	3	61	7	1
Hook, Chris, San Francisco	5	1	.833	5.50	45	0	0	0	14	0	52.1	55	239	33	32	7	3	3	3	29	3	40	2	0
Hope, John, Pittsburgh	0	0	.000	30.86	3	0	0	0	0	0	2.1	8	21	8	8	0	0	1	3	4	0	2	0	0
Hudek, John, Houston	2	2	.500	5.40	19	0	0	0	16	7	20.0	19	83	12	12	3	1	0	0	5	0	29	2	0
Isringhausen, Jason, N.Y.	9	2	.818	2.81	14	14	1	0	0	0	93.0	88	385	29	29	6	3	3	2	31	2	55	4	1
Jackson, Danny, St. Louis*	2	12	.143	5.90	19	19	2	1	0	0	100.2	120	467	82	66	10	10	7	6	48	1	52	6	0
Jackson, Mike, Cincinnati	6	1	.857	2.39	40	0	0	0	10	2	49.0	38	200	13	13	5	1	1	1	19	1	41	1	1
Jacome, Jason, New York*	0	4	.000	10.29	5	5	0	0	0	0	21.0	33	110	24	24	3	1	1	1	15	0	11	1	0
Jarvis, Kevin, Cincinnati	3	4	.429	5.70	19	11	1	1	2	0	79.0	91	354	56	50	13	2	5	3	32	2	33	2	0
Johnstone, John, Florida	0	0	.000	3.86	4	0	0	0	0	0	4.2	7	23	2	2	1	0	0	0	2	1	3	0	0
Jones, Bobby, New York	10	10	.500	4.19	30	30	3	1	0	0	195.2	209	839	107	91	20	11	6	7	53	6	127	2	1
Jones, Todd, Houston	6	5	.545	3.07	68	0	0	0	40	15	99.2	89	442	38	34	8	5	4	6	52	17	96	5	0
Juden, Jeff, Philadelphia	2	4	.333	4.02	13	10	1	0	0	0	62.2	53	271	31	28	6	5	4	5	31	0	47	4	1
Karp, Ryan, Philadelphia*	0	0	.000	4.50	1	0	0	0	0	0	2.0	1	10	1	1	0	0	0	0	3	0	2	1	0
Kile, Darryl, Houston	4	12	.250	4.96	25	21	0	0	1	0	127.0	114	570	81	70	5	7	3	12	73	2	113	11	1
Konuszewski, Dennis, Pitts.	0	0	.000	54.00	1	0	0	0	0	0	0.1	3	5	2	2	0	1	0	0	1	0	0	0	0
Kroon, Marc, San Diego	0	1	.000	10.80	2	0	0	0	1	0	1.2	1	7	2	2	0	0	0	0	2	0	2	0	0
Krueger, Bill, San Diego*	0	0	.000	7.04	6	0	0	0	0	0	7.2	13	41	6	6	1	2	0	0	4	1	6	2	0
Leiper, Dave, Montreal*	0	2	.000	2.86	26	0	0	0	7	2	22.0	16	88	8	7	2	2	0	0	6	0	12	0	1
Leiter, Mark, San Francisco	10	12	.455	3.82	30	29	7	1	0	0	195.2	185	817	91	83	19	10	6	17	55	4	129	9	3
Leskanic, Curt, Colorado	6	3	.667	3.40	76	0	0	0	27	10	98.0	83	406	38	37	7	3	2	0	33	1	107	6	1
Lewis, Richie, Florida	0	1	.000	3.75	21	1	0	0	6	0	36.0	30	152	15	15	9	2	0	1	15	5	32	1	2
Lieber, Jon, Pittsburgh	4	7	.364	6.32	21	12	0	0	3	0	72.2	103	327	56	51	7	5	6	4	14	0	45	3	0
Loaiza, Esteban, Pittsburgh	8	9	.471	5.16	32	31	1	0	0	0	172.2	205	762	115	99	21	10	9	5	55	3	85	6	1
Lomon, Kevin, New York	0	1	.000	6.75	6	0	0	0	1	0	9.1	17	47	8	7	0	0	0	0	5	1	6	0	0
Maddux, Greg, Atlanta	19	2	.905	1.63	28	28	10	3	0	0	209.2	147	785	39	38	8	9	1	4	23	3	181	1	0
Maddux, Mike, Pittsburgh	1	0	1.000	9.00	8	0	0	0	1	0	9.0	14	42	9	9	0	0	0	0	3	1	4	1	0
Mantei, Matt, Florida	0	1	.000	4.73	12	0	0	0	3	0	13.1	12	64	8	7	1	1	1	0	13	0	15	1	0
Manzanillo, Josias, New York	1	2	.333	7.88	12	0	0	0	4	0	16.0	18	73	15	14	3	0	1	0	6	2	14	5	0
Manzanillo, Ravelo, Pitts.*	0	0	.000	4.91	5	0	0	0	0	0	3.2	3	16	3	2	0	0	0	1	2	0	1	0	0
Martinez, Pedro J., Montreal	14	10	.583	3.51	30	30	2	2	0	0	194.2	158	784	79	76	21	7	3	11	66	1	174	5	2
Martinez, Pedro A., Houston*	0	0	.000	7.40	25	0	0	0	3	0	20.2	29	109	18	17	3	2	1	2	16	1	17	0	1
Martinez, Ramon, L.A.	17	7	.708	3.66	30	30	4	2	0	0	206.1	176	859	95	84	19	7	5	5	81	5	138	3	0
Mathews, T.J., St. Louis	1	1	.500	1.52	23	0	0	0	12	2	29.2	21	120	7	5	1	4	0	0	11	1	28	2	0
Mathews, Terry, Florida	4	4	.500	3.38	57	0	0	0	14	3	82.2	70	332	32	31	9	5	1	1	27	4	72	3	0
Mauser, Tim, San Diego	0	1	.000	9.53	5	0	0	0	1	0	5.2	4	30	6	6	0	0	0	0	9	0	9	0	0
May, Darrell, Atlanta*	0	0	.000	11.25	2	0	0	0	1	0	4.0	10	21	5	5	0	0	1	0	0	0	1	0	0
McCurry, Jeff, Pittsburgh	1	4	.200	5.02	55	0	0	0	10	1	61.0	82	282	38	34	9	4	0	5	30	4	27	2	0
McElroy, Chuck, Cincinnati*	3	4	.429	6.02	44	0	0	0	11	0	40.1	46	178	29	27	5	1	3	1	15	3	27	1	0
McMichael, Greg, Atlanta	7	2	.778	2.79	67	0	0	0	16	2	80.2	64	337	27	25	8	5	0	0	32	9	74	3	0
McMurtry, Craig, Houston	0	1	.000	7.84	11	0	0	0	3	0	10.1	15	56	11	9	0	2	2	1	9	1	4	2	0
Mercker, Kent, Atlanta*	7	8	.467	4.15	29	26	0	0	1	0	143.0	140	622	73	66	16	8	7	3	61	2	102	6	2
Miceli, Danny, Pittsburgh	4	4	.500	4.66	58	0	0	0	51	21	58.0	61	264	30	30	7	2	4	4	28	5	56	4	0
Mimbs, Michael, Philadelphia*	9	7	.563	4.15	35	19	2	1	6	1	136.2	127	603	70	63	10	6	8	6	75	2	93	9	0
Minor, Blas, New York	4	2	.667	3.66	35	0	0	0	10	1	46.2	44	192	21	19	6	4	0	1	13	1	43	3	0
Mintz, Steve, San Francisco	1	2	.333	7.45	14	0	0	0	3	0	19.1	26	96	16	16	4	2	1	2	12	3	7	0	0
Mlicki, Dave, New York	9	7	.563	4.26	29	25	0	0	1	0	160.2	160	696	82	76	23	8	5	4	54	2	123	5	1
Morel, Ramon, Pittsburgh	0	1	.000	2.84	5	0	0	0	0	0	6.1	6	23	2	2	0	1	0	0	2	1	3	0	0
Morgan, Mike, Chi.-St.L.	7	7	.500	3.56	21	21	1	0	0	0	131.1	133	548	56	52	12	12	5	6	34	2	61	6	0
Mulholland, Terry, San Fran.*	5	13	.278	5.80	29	24	2	0	2	0	149.0	190	666	112	96	25	11	6	4	38	1	65	4	0
Munoz, Bobby, Philadelphia	0	2	.000	5.74	3	3	0	0	0	0	15.2	15	70	13	10	2	0	2	3	9	0	6	0	0
Munoz, Mike, Colorado*	2	4	.333	7.42	64	0	0	0	19	2	43.2	54	208	38	36	9	2	2	1	27	0	37	5	0
Murphy, Rob, L.A.-Fla.*	1	2	.333	10.95	14	0	0	0	1	0	12.1	14	58	16	15	3	2	0	0	8	1	7	1	0
Murray, Matt, Atlanta	0	2	.000	6.75	4	1	0	0	1	0	10.2	10	46	8	8	3	1	0	1	5	0	3	0	0
Myers, Mike, Florida*	0	0	.000	0.00	2	0	0	0	2	0	2.0	1	9	0	0	0	0	0	0	3	0	0	0	0
Myers, Randy, Chicago*	1	2	.333	3.88	57	0	0	0	47	38	55.2	49	240	25	24	7	2	3	0	28	1	59	0	0
Nabholz, Chris, Chicago*	0	1	.000	5.40	34	0	0	0	4	0	23.1	22	104	15	14	4	1	2	0	14	3	21	2	0
Navarro, Jaime, Chicago	14	6	.700	3.28	29	29	1	1	0	0	200.1	194	837	79	73	19	2	3	3	56	7	128	1	0
Neagle, Denny, Pittsburgh*	13	8	.619	3.43	31	31	5	1	0	0	209.2	221	876	91	80	20	13	6	3	45	3	150	6	0
Nen, Robb, Florida	0	7	.000	3.29	62	0	0	0	54	23	65.2	62	279	26	24	6	0	1	1	23	3	68	2	0
Nichols, Rod, Atlanta	0	0	.000	5.40	5	0	0	0	0	0	6.2	14	38	11	4	3	0	0	0	5	1	3	0	0
Nied, Dave, Colorado	0	0	.000	20.77	2	0	0	0	0	0	4.1	11	27	10	10	2	0	0	0	3	0	3	0	0
Nitkowski, C.J., Cincinnati*	1	3	.250	6.12	9	7	0	0	0	0	32.1	41	154	25	22	4	2	1	2	15	1	18	1	2
Nomo, Hideo, Los Angeles	13	6	.684	2.54	28	28	4	3	0	0	191.1	124	780	63	54	14	11	4	5	78	2	236	19	5
Olivares, Omar, Col.-Phi.	1	4	.200	6.91	16	6	0	0	4	0	41.2	55	195	34	32	5	2	2	3	23	0	22	4	0
Osborne, Donovan, St. Louis*	4	6	.400	3.81	19	19	0	0	0	0	113.1	112	477	58	48	17	8	3	2	34	2	82	0	0
Osuna, Antonio, Los Angeles	2	4	.333	4.43	39	0	0	0	8	0	44.2	39	186	22	22	5	2	1	1	20	2	46	1	0
Painter, Lance, Colorado*	3	0	1.000	4.37	33	1	0	0	7	1	45.1	55	198	23	22	9	0	0	2	10	0	36	4	1
Palacios, Vince, St. Louis	2	3	.400	5.80	20	5	0	0	3	0	40.1	48	184	29	26	7	2	1	2	19	1	34	1	0
Park, Chan Ho, Los Angeles	0	0	.000	4.50	2	1	0	0	0	0	4.0	2	16	2	2	1	0	0	0	2	0	7	0	1
Parra, Jose, Los Angeles	0	0	.000	4.35	8	0	0	0	0	0	10.1	10	47	8	5	2	0	1	1	6	1	7	0	1
Parrett, Jeff, St. Louis	4	7	.364	3.64	59	0	0	0	17	0	76.2	71	328	33	31	8	5	2	1	28	5	71	7	0
Parris, Steve, Pittsburgh	6	6	.500	5.38	15	15	1	1	0	0	82.0	89	360	49	49	12	3	2	7	33	1	61	4	0
Pena, Alejandro, Fla.-Atl.	2	0	1.000	2.61	27	0	0	0	6	0	31.0	22	121	9	9	3	0	0	0	7	1	39	0	0
Pennington, Brad, Cincinnati*	0	0	.000	5.59	6	0	0	0	2	0	9.2	9	47	8	6	0	0	2	1	11	0	7	3	0
Perez, Carlos, Montreal*	10	8	.556	3.69	28	23	2	1	2	0	141.1	142	592	61	58	18	6	1	5	28	2	106	8	4
Perez, Mike, Chicago	2	6	.250	3.66	68	0	0	0	18	2	71.1	72	308	30	29	8	5	3	4	27	8	49	4	0

Pitcher, Team	W	L	Pct.	ERA	G	GS	CG	ShO	GF	Sv.	IP	H	TBF	R	ER	HR	SH	SF	HB	BB	IBB	SO	WP	Bk.
Perez, Yorkis, Florida*	2	6	.250	5.21	69	0	0	0	11	1	46.2	35	205	29	27	6	2	1	2	28	4	47	2	0
Person, Robert, New York	1	0	1.000	0.75	3	1	0	0	0	0	12.0	5	44	1	1	1	0	0	0	2	0	10	0	0
Petkovsek, Mark, St. Louis	6	6	.500	4.00	26	21	1	1	1	0	137.1	136	569	71	61	11	4	4	6	35	3	71	1	1
Plesac, Dan, Pittsburgh*	4	4	.500	3.58	58	0	0	0	16	3	60.1	53	259	26	24	3	4	3	1	27	7	57	1	0
Portugal, Mark, S.F.-Cin.	11	10	.524	4.01	31	31	1	0	0	0	181.2	185	775	91	81	17	9	1	4	56	2	96	7	0
Powell, Jay, Florida	0	0	.000	1.08	9	0	0	0	1	0	8.1	7	38	2	1	0	1	0	2	6	1	4	0	0
Powell, Ross, Hou.-Pit.*	0	2	.000	6.98	27	3	0	0	6	0	29.2	36	148	26	23	6	3	1	2	21	4	20	4	0
Pugh, Tim, Cincinnati	6	5	.545	3.84	28	12	0	0	4	0	98.1	100	413	46	42	13	2	2	1	32	2	38	3	1
Pulsipher, Bill, New York*	5	7	.417	3.98	17	17	2	0	0	0	126.2	122	530	58	56	11	2	1	4	45	0	81	2	1
Quantrill, Paul, Philadelphia	11	12	.478	4.67	33	29	0	0	1	0	179.1	212	784	102	93	20	9	6	6	44	3	103	0	3
Rapp, Pat, Florida	14	7	.667	3.44	28	28	3	2	0	0	167.1	158	716	72	64	10	8	0	7	76	2	102	7	0
Reed, Rick, Cincinnati	0	0	.000	5.82	4	3	0	0	1	0	17.0	18	70	12	11	5	1	0	0	3	0	10	0	0
Reed, Steve, Colorado	5	2	.714	2.14	71	0	0	0	15	3	84.0	61	327	24	20	8	3	1	1	21	3	79	0	2
Rekar, Bryan, Colorado	4	6	.400	4.98	15	14	1	0	0	0	85.0	95	375	51	47	11	7	4	3	24	2	60	3	2
Remlinger, Mike, N.Y.-Cin.*	0	1	.000	6.75	7	0	0	0	4	0	6.2	9	34	6	5	1	1	0	0	5	0	7	0	0
Reynolds, Shane, Houston	10	11	.476	3.47	30	30	3	2	0	0	189.1	196	792	87	73	15	8	0	2	37	6	175	7	1
Reynoso, Armando, Colorado	7	7	.500	5.32	20	18	0	0	0	0	93.0	116	418	61	55	12	8	2	5	36	3	40	2	0
Ricci, Chuck, Philadelphia	1	0	1.000	1.80	7	0	0	0	3	0	10.0	9	40	2	2	0	1	2	1	3	0	9	0	0
Rijo, Jose, Cincinnati	5	4	.556	4.17	14	14	0	0	0	0	69.0	76	295	33	32	6	3	3	0	22	1	62	3	0
Ritz, Kevin, Colorado	11	11	.500	4.21	31	28	0	0	3	2	173.1	171	743	91	81	16	8	5	6	65	3	120	6	0
Rivera, Roberto, Chicago*	0	0	.000	5.40	7	0	0	0	2	0	5.0	8	23	3	3	1	0	0	0	2	0	2	0	0
Rodriguez, Felix, Los Angeles	1	1	.500	2.53	11	0	0	0	5	0	10.2	11	45	3	3	2	0	0	0	5	0	5	0	0
Rodriguez, Rich, St. Louis*	0	0	.000	0.00	1	0	0	0	0	0	1.2	0	4	0	0	0	0	0	0	0	0	0	0	0
Rojas, Mel, Montreal	1	4	.200	4.12	59	0	0	0	48	30	67.2	69	302	32	31	2	2	1	7	29	4	61	6	0
Roper, John, Cin.-S.F.	0	0	.000	12.38	3	2	0	0	0	0	8.0	15	44	12	11	3	1	1	0	6	0	6	0	1
Rosselli, Joe, San Francisco*	2	1	.667	8.70	9	5	0	0	0	0	30.0	39	140	29	29	5	2	4	0	20	2	7	0	1
Rueter, Kirk, Montreal*	5	3	.625	3.23	9	9	1	1	0	0	47.1	38	184	17	17	3	4	0	1	9	0	28	0	0
Ruffin, Bruce, Colorado*	0	1	.000	2.12	37	0	0	0	19	11	34.0	26	140	8	8	1	4	0	0	19	1	23	1	0
Ruffin, Johnny, Cincinnati	0	0	.000	1.35	10	0	0	0	6	0	13.1	4	54	3	2	0	0	0	0	11	0	11	3	0
Saberhagen, Bret, N.Y.-Col.	7	6	.538	4.18	25	25	3	0	0	0	153.0	165	658	78	71	21	7	3	10	33	3	100	3	0
Sager, A.J., Colorado	0	0	.000	7.36	10	0	0	0	2	0	14.2	19	70	16	12	1	2	0	0	7	1	10	0	0
Sanders, Scott, San Diego	5	5	.500	4.30	17	15	1	0	0	0	90.0	79	383	46	43	14	2	2	2	31	4	88	6	1
Scheid, Rich, Florida*	0	0	.000	6.10	6	0	0	0	1	0	10.1	14	50	7	7	1	1	1	0	7	0	10	1	0
Schilling, Curt, Philadelphia	7	5	.583	3.57	17	17	1	0	0	0	116.0	96	473	52	46	12	5	2	3	26	2	114	0	1
Schmidt, Curt, Montreal	0	0	.000	6.97	11	0	0	0	0	0	10.1	15	54	8	8	1	1	0	2	9	0	7	0	0
Schmidt, Jason, Atlanta	2	2	.500	5.76	9	2	0	0	1	0	25.0	27	119	17	16	2	2	4	1	18	3	19	1	0
Schourek, Pete, Cincinnati*	18	7	.720	3.22	29	29	2	0	0	0	190.1	158	754	72	68	17	4	4	8	45	3	160	1	1
Scott, Tim, Montreal	2	0	1.000	3.98	62	0	0	0	15	2	63.1	52	268	30	28	6	4	1	6	23	2	57	4	0
Seanez, Rudy, Los Angeles	1	3	.250	6.75	37	0	0	0	12	3	34.2	39	159	27	26	5	3	0	1	18	3	29	0	0
Service, Scott, San Francisco	3	1	.750	3.19	28	0	0	0	6	0	31.0	18	129	11	11	4	3	2	2	20	4	30	3	0
Shaw, Jeff, Montreal	1	6	.143	4.62	50	0	0	0	17	3	62.1	58	268	35	32	4	6	1	3	26	4	45	0	0
Slocumb, Heathcliff, Phil.	5	6	.455	2.89	61	0	0	0	54	32	65.1	64	289	26	21	2	4	0	1	35	3	63	3	0
Small, Aaron, Florida	1	0	1.000	1.42	7	0	0	0	1	0	6.1	7	32	2	1	1	0	0	0	6	0	5	0	0
Smiley, John, Cincinnati*	12	5	.706	3.46	28	27	1	0	0	0	176.2	173	724	72	68	11	17	5	4	39	3	124	5	1
Smith, Pete, Cincinnati	1	2	.333	6.66	11	2	0	0	3	0	24.1	30	106	19	18	8	1	3	1	7	1	14	1	0
Smoltz, John, Atlanta	12	7	.632	3.18	29	29	2	1	0	0	192.2	166	808	76	68	15	13	5	4	72	8	193	13	0
Springer, Dennis, Phila.	0	3	.000	4.84	4	4	0	0	0	0	22.1	21	94	15	12	3	2	0	1	9	1	15	1	0
Springer, Russ, Philadelphia	0	0	.000	3.71	14	0	0	0	3	0	26.2	22	112	11	11	5	1	2	2	10	3	32	1	0
Stanton, Mike, Atlanta*	1	1	.500	5.59	26	0	0	0	10	1	19.1	31	94	14	12	3	2	1	1	6	2	13	1	1
Sturtze, Tanyon, Chicago	0	0	.000	9.00	2	0	0	0	0	0	2.0	2	9	2	2	1	0	0	0	1	0	0	0	0
Sullivan, Scott, Cincinnati	0	0	.000	4.91	3	0	0	0	1	0	3.2	4	17	2	2	0	1	0	0	2	0	2	0	0
Swartzbaugh, Dave, Chicago	0	0	.000	0.00	7	0	0	0	2	0	7.1	5	27	2	0	0	0	0	0	3	1	5	0	0
Swift, Bill, Colorado	9	3	.750	4.94	19	19	0	0	0	0	105.2	122	463	62	58	12	6	1	1	43	2	68	2	0
Swindell, Greg, Houston*	10	9	.526	4.47	33	26	1	1	3	0	153.0	180	659	86	76	21	4	8	2	39	2	96	3	0
Tabaka, Jeff, S.D.-Hou.*	1	0	1.000	3.23	34	0	0	0	6	0	30.2	27	128	11	11	2	0	0	0	17	1	25	1	0
Tapani, Kevin, Los Angeles	4	2	.667	5.05	13	11	0	0	0	0	57.0	72	255	37	32	8	3	2	1	14	2	43	1	0
Telgheder, Dave, New York	1	2	.333	5.61	7	4	0	0	2	0	25.2	34	118	18	16	4	3	1	0	7	3	16	0	1
Thobe, J.J., Montreal	0	0	.000	9.00	4	0	0	0	2	0	4.0	6	21	4	4	0	0	0	0	3	0	0	1	0
Thobe, Tom, Atlanta*	0	0	.000	10.80	3	0	0	0	1	0	3.1	7	17	4	4	0	0	0	0	0	0	2	0	0
Thompson, Mark, Colorado	2	3	.400	6.53	21	5	0	0	3	0	51.0	73	240	42	37	7	4	4	1	22	2	30	2	0
Torres, Salomon, San Fran.	0	1	.000	9.00	4	1	0	0	2	0	8.0	13	40	8	8	4	0	0	0	7	0	2	0	0
Trachsel, Steve, Chicago	7	13	.350	5.15	30	29	2	0	0	0	160.2	174	722	104	92	25	12	5	0	76	8	117	2	1
Urbani, Tom, St. Louis*	3	5	.375	3.70	24	13	0	0	2	0	82.2	99	354	40	34	11	6	0	2	21	4	52	5	0
Urbina, Ugueth, Montreal	2	2	.500	6.17	7	4	0	0	0	0	23.1	26	109	17	16	6	2	0	0	14	1	15	2	0
Valdes, Ismael, Los Angeles	13	11	.542	3.05	33	27	6	2	1	1	197.2	168	804	76	67	17	10	5	1	51	5	150	1	3
Valdes, Marc, Florida	0	0	.000	14.14	3	3	0	0	0	0	7.0	17	49	13	11	1	1	1	1	9	0	2	1	0
Valdez, Carlos, San Francisco	0	1	.000	6.14	11	0	0	0	3	0	14.2	19	69	10	10	1	0	1	1	8	1	7	1	1
Valdez, Sergio, San Fran.	4	5	.444	4.75	13	11	1	0	0	0	66.1	78	290	43	35	12	5	3	3	17	3	29	2	1
Valenzuela, Fernando, S.D.*	8	3	.727	4.98	29	15	0	0	5	0	90.1	101	395	53	50	16	10	2	0	34	2	57	4	0
VanLandingham, William, S.F.	6	3	.667	3.67	18	18	1	0	0	0	122.2	124	523	58	50	14	6	5	2	40	2	95	5	4
Veres, Dave, Houston	5	1	.833	2.26	72	0	0	0	15	1	103.1	89	418	29	26	5	6	8	4	30	6	94	4	0
Veres, Randy, Florida	4	4	.500	3.88	47	0	0	0	15	1	48.2	46	215	25	21	6	5	4	1	22	7	31	2	0
Villone, Ron, San Diego*	2	1	.667	4.21	19	0	0	0	8	1	25.2	24	111	12	12	5	0	1	0	11	0	37	2	0
Viola, Frank, Cincinnati*	0	1	.000	6.28	3	3	0	0	0	0	14.1	20	64	11	10	3	0	1	0	3	1	4	1	0
Wade, Terrell, Atlanta*	0	1	.000	4.50	3	0	0	0	0	0	4.0	3	18	2	2	1	0	0	0	4	0	3	1	0
Wagner, Billy, Houston*	0	0	.000	0.00	1	0	0	0	0	0	0.1	0	1	0	0	0	0	0	0	0	0	0	0	0
Wagner, Paul, Pittsburgh	5	16	.238	4.80	33	25	3	1	1	1	165.0	174	725	96	88	18	7	2	7	72	7	120	8	0
Walker, Mike, Chicago	1	3	.250	3.22	42	0	0	0	12	1	44.2	45	206	22	16	2	4	4	0	24	3	20	3	1
Walker, Pete, New York	1	0	1.000	4.58	13	0	0	0	10	0	17.2	24	79	9	9	3	0	1	0	5	0	5	0	0
Wall, Donnie, Houston	3	1	.750	5.55	6	5	0	0	0	0	24.1	33	110	19	15	5	0	2	0	5	0	16	1	0
Watson, Allen, St. Louis*	7	9	.438	4.96	21	19	0	0	1	0	114.1	126	491	68	63	17	2	1	5	41	0	49	2	2
Weathers, Dave, Florida	4	5	.444	5.98	28	15	0	0	0	0	90.1	104	419	68	60	8	7	3	5	52	3	60	3	0
Wells, David, Cincinnati*	6	5	.545	3.59	11	11	3	0	0	0	72.2	74	300	34	29	6	4	1	0	16	4	50	1	1

Pitcher, Team	W	L	Pct.	ERA	G	GS	CG	ShO	GF	Sv.	IP	H	TBF	R	ER	HR	SH	SF	HB	BB	IBB	SO	WP	Bk.
Wendell, Turk, Chicago	3	1	.750	4.92	43	0	0	0	17	0	60.1	71	270	35	33	11	3	3	2	24	4	50	1	0
West, David, Philadelphia*	3	2	.600	3.79	8	8	0	0	0	0	38.0	34	163	17	16	5	2	0	1	19	0	25	1	0
White, Gabe, Montreal*	1	2	.333	7.01	19	1	0	0	8	0	25.2	26	115	21	20	7	2	3	1	9	0	25	0	0
White, Rick, Pittsburgh	2	3	.400	4.75	15	9	0	0	2	0	55.0	66	247	33	29	3	3	3	2	18	0	29	2	0
Williams, Brian, San Diego	3	10	.231	6.00	44	6	0	0	7	0	72.0	79	337	54	48	3	7	1	8	38	4	75	7	1
Williams, Mike, Philadelphia	3	3	.500	3.29	33	8	0	0	7	0	87.2	78	367	37	32	10	5	3	3	29	2	57	7	0
Williams, Todd, Los Angeles	2	2	.500	5.12	16	0	0	0	5	0	19.1	19	83	11	11	3	3	1	0	7	2	8	0	0
Wilson, Gary, Pittsburgh	0	1	.000	5.02	10	0	0	0	1	0	14.1	14	61	8	8	2	0	0	2	5	0	8	1	0
Wilson, Trevor, San Fran.*	3	4	.429	3.92	17	17	0	0	0	0	82.2	82	354	42	36	8	5	2	4	38	1	38	0	1
Witt, Bobby, Florida	2	7	.222	3.90	19	19	1	0	0	0	110.2	104	472	52	48	8	5	3	2	47	1	95	2	0
Wohlers, Mark, Atlanta	7	3	.700	2.09	65	0	0	0	49	25	64.2	51	269	16	15	2	2	0	1	24	3	90	4	0
Woodall, Brad, Atlanta*	1	1	.500	6.10	9	0	0	0	3	0	10.1	13	52	10	7	1	1	1	0	8	1	5	1	0
Worrell, Tim, San Diego	1	0	1.000	4.73	9	0	0	0	4	0	13.1	16	63	7	7	2	1	0	1	6	0	13	1	0
Worrell, Todd, Los Angeles	4	1	.800	2.02	59	0	0	0	53	32	62.1	50	249	15	14	4	1	2	1	19	2	61	2	0
Young, Anthony, Chicago	3	4	.429	3.70	32	1	0	0	8	2	41.1	47	181	20	17	5	1	0	3	14	2	15	6	0

COMBINATION SHUTOUTS: **Atlanta (5)**—Maddux-McMichael, Mercker-Borbon-Wohlers, Maddux-McMichael-Schmidt, Schmidt-Wohlers, Maddux-Wohlers. **Chicago (8)**—Trachsel-Nabholz-Perez-Myers, Navarro-Myers, Morgan-Myers, Castillo-Perez, Trachsel-Perez-Hickerson, Foster-Myers, Castillo-Hickerson-Myers, Bullinger-Casian-Wendell-Nabholz-Myers. **Cincinnati (8)**—Schourek-Brantley 2, Rijo-Carrasco-Jackson-Pennington, Schourek-Carrasco-Brantley, Nitkowski-Brantley, Smiley-Carrasco-McElroy-Brantley, Burba-Jackson-Brantley, Schourek-Jackson. **Colorado (1)**—Rekar-Reed. **Florida (2)**—Burkett-Nen, Hammond-Veres-Nen. **Houston (4)**—Hampton-Martinez, Hampton-Jones-Hartgraves, Reynolds-Tabaka-Jones, Swindell-Jones-Veres-Henneman. **Los Angeles (2)**—Martinez-Seanez-Worrell, Valdes-Worrell. **Montreal (4)**—Martinez-Rojas, Henry-Rojas, Heredia-Scott-Shaw-Rojas, Rueter-Heredia. **New York (8)**—B. Jones-Franco, B. Jones-Henry, Harnisch-Henry, Pulsipher-Franco, Isringhausen-Florence-Franco, Isringhausen-Henry, Pulsipher-Franco, Isringhausen-Henry-Walker. **Philadelphia (5)**—Schilling-Harris, Fernandez-Borland, Quantrill-Slocumb, Fernandez-Bottalico-Slocumb, Grace-Bottalico-Slocumb. **Pittsburgh (4)**—Neagle-Gott-Miceli, Parris-Plesac-Miceli, Loaiza-Christiansen-Miceli, Ericks-Christiansen-Miceli. **St. Louis (3)**—Hill-Habyan, Urbani-DeLucia-Henke, Watson-Henke, Morgan-Parrett. **San Diego (5)**—Benes-Hoffman, Valenzuela-Florie-B. Williams-Hoffman, Blair-Florie-Hoffman, Ashby-Hoffman, Blair-Hoffman. **San Francisco (4)**—Leiter-Dewey-Bautista-Beck, Wilson-Dewey-Beck, Mulholland-Burba-Bautista, Brewington-Service-Barton-Beck.

PITCHERS WITH TWO OR MORE TEAMS

Pitcher, Team	W	L	Pct.	ERA	G	GS	CG	ShO	GF	Sv.	IP	H	TBF	R	ER	HR	SH	SF	HB	BB	IBB	SO	WP	Bk.
Aquino, Luis, Montreal	0	2	.000	3.86	29	0	0	0	8	2	37.1	47	171	24	16	4	0	1	3	11	1	22	3	0
Aquino, Luis, San Francisco	0	1	.000	14.40	5	0	0	0	1	0	5.0	10	28	10	8	2	1	0	0	2	1	4	0	0
Banks, Willie, Chicago	0	1	.000	15.43	10	0	0	0	2	0	11.2	27	73	23	20	5	1	1	0	12	4	9	3	0
Banks, Willie, Los Angeles	0	2	.000	4.03	6	6	0	0	0	0	29.0	36	138	21	13	2	1	1	1	16	2	23	4	1
Banks, Willie, Florida	2	3	.400	4.32	9	9	0	0	0	0	50.0	43	219	27	24	7	4	1	1	30	1	30	2	0
Burba, Dave, San Francisco	4	2	.667	4.98	37	0	0	0	7	0	43.1	38	191	26	24	5	3	1	0	25	2	46	2	0
Burba, Dave, Cincinnati	6	3	.750	3.27	15	9	1	1	0	0	63.1	52	260	24	23	4	1	0	0	26	1	50	3	0
Cornelius, Reid, Montreal	0	0	.000	8.00	8	0	0	0	1	0	9.0	11	43	8	8	3	0	0	2	5	0	4	1	0
Cornelius, Reid, New York	3	7	.300	5.15	10	10	0	0	0	0	57.2	64	258	36	33	8	4	3	1	25	5	35	1	1
Frey, Steve, San Francisco*	0	0	.000	4.26	9	0	0	0	1	0	6.1	7	29	6	3	1	1	0	2	0	5	0	0
Frey, Steve, Philadelphia*	0	0	.000	0.84	9	0	0	0	3	1	10.2	3	36	1	1	1	0	0	2	1	2	0	0
Garces, Rich, Chicago	0	0	.000	3.27	7	0	0	0	0	0	11.0	11	46	6	4	0	0	0	3	0	6	0	0
Garces, Rich, Florida	0	2	.000	5.40	11	0	0	0	3	0	13.1	14	62	9	8	1	0	0	8	2	16	0	0
Hickerson, Bryan, Chicago*	2	3	.400	6.82	38	0	0	0	8	1	31.2	36	144	28	24	3	2	0		15	4	28	3	0
Hickerson, Bryan, Colorado*	1	0	1.000	11.88	18	0	0	0	5	0	16.2	33	99	24	22	5	0	0		13	1	12	2	1
Morgan, Mike, Chicago	2	1	.667	2.19	4	4	0	0	0	0	24.2	19	100	8	6	2	2	0	1	9	1	15	0	0
Morgan, Mike, St. Louis	5	6	.455	3.88	17	17	1	0	0	0	106.2	114	448	48	46	10	10	5	5	25	1	46	6	0
Murphy, Rob, Los Angeles*	0	1	.000	12.60	6	0	0	0	1	0	5.0	6	23	7	7	2	0	0	3	0	2	1	0
Murphy, Rob, Florida*	1	1	.500	9.82	6	0	0	0	1	0	7.1	8	35	9	8	1	2	0	5	1	5	0	0
Olivares, Omar, Colorado	1	3	.250	7.39	11	6	0	0	1	0	31.2	44	151	28	26	4	1	1	2	21	1	15	4	0
Olivares, Omar, Philadelphia	0	1	.000	5.40	5	0	0	0	3	0	10.0	11	44	6	6	1	1	1	2	0	7	0	0
Pena, Alejandro, Florida	2	1	1.000	1.50	13	0	0	0	4	0	18.0	11	68	3	3	2	0	0	3	1	21	0	0
Pena, Alejandro, Atlanta	0	0	.000	4.15	14	0	0	0	2	0	13.0	11	53	6	6	1	0	0	4	0	18	0	0
Portugal, Mark, San Francisco	5	5	.500	4.15	17	17	1	0	0	0	104.0	106	445	56	48	10	5	0	2	34	2	63	2	0
Portugal, Mark, Cincinnati	6	5	.545	3.82	14	14	0	0	0	0	77.2	79	330	35	33	7	4	1	2	22	0	33	5	0
Powell, Ross, Houston*	0	0	.000	11.00	15	0	0	0	1	0	9.0	16	55	12	11	1	1	1	0	11	4	8	1	0
Powell, Ross, Pittsburgh*	0	2	.000	5.23	12	0	0	0	5	0	20.2	20	93	14	12	5	2	0	2	10	0	12	3	0
Remlinger, Mike, New York*	0	1	.000	6.35	5	0	0	0	4	0	5.2	7	27	5	4	1	1	0	0	2	0	6	0	0
Remlinger, Mike, Cincinnati*	0	0	.000	9.82	2	0	0	0	1	0	1.0	2	7	1	1	0	0	0	0	3	0	1	0	0
Roper, John, Cincinnati	0	0	.000	10.29	2	2	0	0	0	0	7.0	13	37	9	8	3	1	0	0	4	0	6	1	0
Roper, John, San Francisco	0	0	.000	27.00	1	0	0	0	1	0	1.0	2	7	3	3	0	0	1	0	2	0	0	0	0
Saberhagen, Bret, New York	5	5	.500	3.35	16	16	3	0	0	0	110.0	105	452	45	41	13	5	3	5	20	2	71	2	0
Saberhagen, Bret, Colorado	2	1	.667	6.28	9	9	0	0	0	0	43.0	60	206	33	30	8	2	0	5	13	1	29	1	0
Tabaka, Jeff, San Diego*	0	0	.000	7.11	10	0	0	0	3	0	6.1	10	32	5	5	1	0	0	0	5	1	6	1	0
Tabaka, Jeff, Houston*	1	0	1.000	2.22	24	0	0	0	6	0	24.1	17	96	6	6	1	0	0	0	12	0	19	0	0

FIELDING

TEAM

Team	Pct.	G	PO	A	E	TC	DP	PB
Cincinnati	.985	144	3868	1501	79	5448	138	11
Philadelphia	.982	144	3871	1515	97	5483	137	19
Atlanta	.982	144	3875	1564	100	5539	111	8
Colorado	.981	144	3865	1662	107	5634	141	10
San Francisco	.980	144	3881	1547	108	5536	134	7
San Diego	.980	144	3854	1534	108	5496	124	8
Montreal	.980	144	3851	1555	109	5515	112	6
St. Louis	.980	143	3797	1620	113	5530	147	9
New York	.979	144	3873	1602	115	5590	119	14
Chicago	.979	144	3903	1560	115	5578	107	19
Florida	.979	143	3858	1463	115	5436	135	8
Houston	.979	144	3961	1637	121	5719	114	14
Pittsburgh	.978	144	3826	1580	122	5528	137	12
Los Angeles	.976	144	3885	1488	130	5503	112	19
Totals	.980	1007	54168	21828	1539	77535	1768	164

TRIPLE PLAYS: Cincinnati 2.

INDIVIDUAL

FIRST BASEMEN

NOTE: All caps denotes fielding-percentage leader based on 72 games for catchers, 96 for all other non-pitchers and 144 innings for pitchers. *Throws lefthanded.

Player, Team	Pct.	G	PO	A	E	TC	DP
Andrews, Shane, Montreal	.977	29	160	11	4	175	11
Anthony, Eric, Cincinnati*	.966	17	102	10	4	116	11
Aude, Rich, Pittsburgh	.996	32	223	11	1	235	28
Ausmus, Brad, San Diego	.000	1	0	0	0	0	0
Bagwell, Jeff, Houston	.994	114	1004	129	7	1140	81
Benzinger, Todd, San Francisco	1.000	5	15	0	0	15	3
Berry, Sean, Montreal	1.000	3	22	4	0	26	0
Berryhill, Damon, Cincinnati	1.000	1	1	0	0	1	0
Bogar, Tim, New York	1.000	10	47	5	0	52	6
Bonilla, Bobby, New York	1.000	10	85	3	0	88	5
Branson, Jeff, Cincinnati	.000	1	0	0	0	0	0
BROGNA, RICO, New York*	.998	131	1112	93	3	1208	95
Brumley, Mike, Houston	1.000	1	1	1	0	2	0
Busch, Mike, Los Angeles	1.000	2	8	1	0	9	2
Carreon, Mark, San Francisco*	.993	81	703	44	5	752	65
Cianfrocco, Archi, San Diego	1.000	30	76	7	0	83	7
Clark, Phil, San Diego	1.000	2	7	0	0	7	1
Colbrunn, Greg, Florida	.996	134	1067	89	5	1161	108
Coles, Darnell, St. Louis	.992	18	122	7	1	130	7
Conine, Jeff, Florida	.991	14	97	11	1	109	10
Decker, Steve, Florida	1.000	2	3	0	0	3	0
Duncan, Mariano, Phi.-Cin.	.985	18	122	6	2	130	11
Elster, Kevin, Philadelphia	1.000	4	17	0	0	17	1
Floyd, Cliff, Montreal	.987	18	143	12	2	157	13
Foley, Tom, Montreal	1.000	4	21	2	0	23	1
Franco, Matt, Chicago	1.000	1	2	0	0	2	0
Galarraga, Andres, Colorado	.991	142	1299	120	13	1432	129
Giannelli, Ray, St. Louis	1.000	2	8	0	0	8	1
Grace, Mark, Chicago*	.995	143	1211	114	7	1332	93
Gregg, Tommy, Florida	1.000	2	17	1	0	18	2
Gwynn, Chris, Los Angeles*	1.000	2	5	1	0	6	2
Harris, Lenny, Cincinnati	1.000	23	127	13	0	140	10
Hollins, Dave, Philadelphia	.988	61	532	30	7	569	53
Hunter, Brian R., Cincinnati*	.983	23	164	12	3	179	20
Hyers, Tim, San Diego*	1.000	1	1	1	0	2	0
Jefferies, Gregg, Philadelphia	.994	59	492	33	3	528	53
Johnson, Brian, San Diego	.900	2	9	0	1	10	0
Johnson, Howard, Chicago	1.000	3	15	1	0	16	3
Johnson, Mark, Pittsburgh*	.986	70	527	36	8	571	53
Jones, Chris, New York	1.000	5	43	3	0	46	3
Karros, Eric, Los Angeles	.995	143	1234	109	7	1350	101
King, Jeff, Pittsburgh	.994	35	296	27	2	325	22
Kingery, Mike, Colorado*	.963	5	25	1	1	27	0
Klesko, Ryan, Atlanta*	.957	4	20	2	1	23	0
Ledesma, Aaron, New York	1.000	2	3	0	0	3	0
Livingstone, Scott, San Diego	.991	43	297	17	3	317	25
Mabry, John, St. Louis	.994	73	595	53	4	652	63
Magadan, Dave, Houston	1.000	11	66	4	0	70	5
May, Derrick, Houston	.000	1	0	0	0	0	0
McCarty, Dave, San Francisco*	1.000	2	14	0	0	14	0
McGriff, Fred, Atlanta*	.996	144	1285	96	5	1386	103
Merced, Orlando, Pittsburgh	.995	35	175	15	1	191	22
Mordecai, Mike, Atlanta	1.000	9	24	2	0	26	3
Morman, Russ, Florida	1.000	3	10	2	0	12	1
Morris, Hal, Cincinnati*	.994	99	757	73	5	835	78
Nieves, Melvin, San Diego	.917	2	11	0	1	12	1
Oliva, Jose, Atl.-St.L.	1.000	3	16	1	0	17	2
Orsulak, Joe, New York*	1.000	1	3	1	0	4	0
Perez, Eddie, Atlanta	1.000	1	3	0	0	3	1

Player, Team	Pct.	G	PO	A	E	TC	DP
Perry, Gerald, St. Louis	1.000	11	69	3	0	72	4
Petagine, Roberto, San Diego*	.996	51	262	22	1	285	21
Phillips, J.R., San Francisco*	.993	79	535	37	4	576	47
Ready, Randy, Philadelphia	.967	3	28	1	1	30	3
Rodriguez, Henry, L.A.-Mon.*	1.000	11	83	7	0	90	8
Sabo, Chris, St. Louis	.929	2	11	2	1	14	1
Santiago, Benito, Cincinnati	1.000	8	19	2	0	21	2
Scarsone, Steve, San Francisco	1.000	11	79	6	0	85	12
Schall, Gene, Philadelphia	.984	14	112	10	2	124	9
Segui, David, N.Y.-Mon.*	.997	104	881	73	3	957	72
Sheaffer, Danny, St. Louis	1.000	3	31	4	0	35	1
Shipley, Craig, Houston	1.000	1	1	0	0	1	0
Silvestri, Dave, Montreal	1.000	4	22	1	0	23	4
Simms, Mike, Houston	.995	25	204	17	1	222	17
Sweeney, Mark, St. Louis*	.994	19	153	11	1	165	20
Taubensee, Eddie, Cincinnati	1.000	3	12	1	0	13	2
Vander Wal, John, Colorado*	.957	10	42	3	2	47	3
Wallach, Tim, Los Angeles	1.000	1	11	0	0	11	0
Walton, Jerome, Cincinnati	1.000	3	3	0	0	3	0
Wilkins, Rick, Houston	1.000	2	6	2	0	8	1
Williams, Eddie, San Diego	.989	81	571	49	7	627	53
Worthington, Craig, Cincinnati	1.000	4	24	2	0	26	3
Young, Kevin, Pittsburgh	1.000	6	30	2	0	32	2
Zeile, Todd, St.L.-Chi.	.981	35	327	30	7	364	34

TRIPLE PLAYS: Morris, Cin. 2.

FIRST BASEMEN WITH TWO OR MORE TEAMS

Player, Team	Pct.	G	PO	A	E	TC	DP
Duncan, Mariano, Philadelphia	.980	12	90	6	2	98	10
Duncan, Mariano, Cincinnati	1.000	6	32	0	0	32	1
Oliva, Jose, Atlanta	.000	1	0	0	0	0	0
Oliva, Jose, St. Louis	1.000	2	16	1	0	17	2
Rodriguez, Henry, Los Angeles*	1.000	1	1	0	0	1	0
Rodriguez, Henry, Montreal*	1.000	10	82	7	0	89	8
Segui, David, New York*	1.000	7	41	3	0	44	4
Segui, David, Montreal*	.997	97	840	70	3	913	68
Zeile, Todd, St. Louis	.980	34	310	30	7	347	31
Zeile, Todd, Chicago	1.000	1	17	0	0	17	3

SECOND BASEMEN

Player, Team	Pct.	G	PO	A	E	TC	DP
Alfonzo, Edgardo, New York	.989	29	36	51	1	88	7
Arias, Alex, Florida	1.000	6	9	19	0	28	3
Bates, Jason, Colorado	.991	82	136	188	3	327	50
Bell, David, St. Louis	.967	37	75	103	6	184	27
Belliard, Rafael, Atlanta	1.000	32	41	91	0	132	11
Benjamin, Mike, San Francisco	1.000	8	7	14	0	21	0
Biggio, Craig, Houston	.986	141	299	419	10	728	78
Bogar, Tim, New York	.929	7	6	20	2	28	6
BOONE, BOB, Cincinnati	.994	138	311	362	4	677	106
Branson, Jeff, Cincinnati	1.000	6	1	1	0	2	0
Browne, Jerry, Florida	.992	27	62	66	1	129	13
Caraballo, Ramon, St. Louis	.956	24	56	73	6	135	20
Cianfrocco, Archi, San Diego	1.000	3	7	6	0	13	1
Cromer, Tripp, St. Louis	.969	11	15	16	1	32	4
DeShields, Delino, Los Angeles	.980	113	204	330	11	545	55
Diaz, Mario, Florida	.944	9	15	19	2	36	8
Donnels, Chris, Houston	1.000	1	0	1	0	1	0
Duncan, Mariano, Phi.-Cin.	.958	31	63	73	6	142	20
Foley, Tom, Montreal	1.000	3	2	5	0	7	2
Fonville, Chad, Mon.-L.A.	.966	38	71	98	6	175	14
Franco, Matt, Chicago	1.000	3	0	2	0	2	0
Frazier, Lou, Montreal	1.000	1	0	1	0	1	0
Garcia, Carlos, Pittsburgh	.982	92	217	264	9	490	70

Player, Team	Pct.	G	PO	A	E	TC	DP
Giovanola, Ed, Atlanta	1.000	7	9	5	0	14	1
Grudzielanek, Mark, Montreal	.963	13	26	26	2	54	5
Haney, Todd, Chicago	.978	17	31	57	2	90	12
Harris, Lenny, Cincinnati	1.000	1	2	0	0	2	0
Hemond, Scott, St. Louis	1.000	6	4	7	0	11	0
Hernandez, Jose, Chicago	.971	29	56	76	4	136	18
Holbert, Ray, San Diego	1.000	7	3	3	0	6	1
Hulett, Tim, St. Louis	.941	2	5	11	1	17	3
Ingram, Garey, Los Angeles	1.000	7	7	11	0	18	3
Johnson, Howard, Chicago	.889	8	7	9	2	18	2
Jordan, Kevin, Philadelphia	.984	9	28	33	1	62	8
Kent, Jeff, New York	.984	122	245	353	10	608	69
King, Jeff, Pittsburgh	1.000	8	8	14	0	22	4
Lansing, Mike, Montreal	.991	127	306	373	6	685	77
Lee, Manuel, St. Louis	.800	1	2	2	1	5	0
Lemke, Mark, Atlanta	.990	115	205	305	5	515	61
Lewis, Mark, Cincinnati	1.000	2	0	3	0	3	0
Liriano, Nelson, Pittsburgh	.981	67	130	132	5	267	31
Livingstone, Scott, San Diego	1.000	4	2	3	0	5	1
Mejia, Roberto, Colorado	.971	16	36	30	2	68	4
Morandini, Mickey, Philadelphia	.989	122	269	337	7	613	74
Mordecai, Mike, Atlanta	1.000	21	14	19	0	33	8
Oquendo, Jose, St. Louis	.981	62	114	148	5	267	37
Patterson, John, San Francisco	.983	53	114	112	4	230	34
Pena, Geronimo, St. Louis	.976	25	50	73	3	126	18
Ready, Randy, Philadelphia	1.000	1	1	1	0	2	0
Reed, Jody, San Diego	.994	130	303	362	4	669	79
Roberts, Bip, San Diego	.981	25	37	68	2	107	11
Sanchez, Rey, Chicago	.987	111	194	342	7	543	58
Santangelo, F.P., Montreal	1.000	5	1	0	0	1	0
Scarsone, Steve, San Francisco	.954	13	26	36	3	65	12
Shipley, Craig, Houston	1.000	4	5	10	0	15	1
Silvestri, Dave, Montreal	1.000	3	3	2	0	5	0
Spiers, Bill, New York	1.000	6	4	12	0	16	1
Stankiewicz, Andy, Houston	1.000	6	3	7	0	10	0
Thompson, Robby, San Fran.	.993	91	181	238	3	422	51
Treadway, Jeff, L.A.-Mon.	1.000	12	12	16	0	28	3
Veras, Quilvio, Florida	.986	122	297	315	9	621	85
Vizcaino, Jose, New York	1.000	1	0	1	0	1	0
Young, Eric, Colorado	.973	77	165	228	11	404	55
Zosky, Eddie, Florida	1.000	1	0	1	0	1	1

TRIPLE PLAYS: Boone, Cin. 2.

SECOND BASEMEN WITH TWO OR MORE TEAMS

Player, Team	Pct.	G	PO	A	E	TC	DP
Duncan, Mariano, Philadelphia	.957	24	50	60	5	115	17
Duncan, Mariano, Cincinnati	.963	7	13	13	1	27	3
Fonville, Chad, Montreal	.000	2	0	0	0	0	0
Fonville, Chad, Los Angeles	.966	36	71	98	6	175	14
Treadway, Jeff, Los Angeles	1.000	1	1	1	0	2	1
Treadway, Jeff, Montreal	1.000	11	11	15	0	26	2

THIRD BASEMEN

Player, Team	Pct.	G	PO	A	E	TC	DP
Alfonzo, Edgardo, New York	.962	58	40	111	6	157	9
Andrews, Shane, Montreal	.973	51	22	86	3	111	2
Arias, Alex, Florida	.939	21	8	23	2	33	3
Bates, Jason, Colorado	.973	15	10	26	1	37	1
Bell, David, St. Louis	.875	3	2	5	1	8	0
Bell, Jay, Pittsburgh	1.000	3	1	6	0	7	1
Benjamin, Mike, San Francisco	.964	43	29	77	4	110	3
Berry, Sean, Montreal	.947	83	54	162	12	228	19
Bogar, Tim, New York	.950	25	9	29	2	40	4
Bonilla, Bobby, New York	.882	46	24	73	13	110	8
Branson, Jeff, Cincinnati	.971	98	52	179	7	238	23
Browne, Jerry, Florida	1.000	7	1	10	0	11	0
Brumley, Mike, Houston	.000	1	0	0	1	1	0
Buechele, Steve, Chicago	.942	32	26	55	5	86	3
Busch, Mike, Los Angeles	.875	10	2	5	1	8	0
Caminiti, Ken, San Diego	.936	143	102	295	27	424	28
Castellano, Pedro, Colorado	1.000	3	1	0	0	1	0
Castilla, Vinny, Colorado	.958	137	84	256	15	355	21
Castro, Juan, Los Angeles	1.000	7	2	3	0	5	0
Cedeno, Andujar, San Diego	.500	1	0	1	1	2	0
Cianfrocco, Archi, San Diego	.000	3	0	0	0	0	0
Coles, Darnell, St. Louis	.951	22	13	26	2	41	1
Cooper, Scott, St. Louis	.945	110	65	243	18	326	24
Diaz, Mike, Florida	1.000	3	1	0	0	1	0
Donnels, Chris, Houston	.818	9	3	6	2	11	2
Duncan, Mariano, Cincinnati	1.000	1	2	2	0	4	0
Elster, Kevin, Philadelphia	1.000	2	2	2	0	4	0
Franco, Matt, Chicago	.000	1	0	0	0	0	0
Garcia, Freddy, Pittsburgh	.955	8	6	15	1	22	4
Giovanola, Ed, Atlanta	.000	3	0	0	0	0	0

Player, Team	Pct.	G	PO	A	E	TC	DP
Greene, Willie, Cincinnati	1.000	7	1	13	0	14	1
Grudzielanek, Mark, Montreal	.935	31	18	68	6	92	2
Gutierrez, Ricky, Houston	.000	2	0	0	0	0	0
Haney, Todd, Chicago	1.000	4	3	4	0	7	0
Hansen, Dave, Los Angeles	.933	58	27	70	7	104	6
Harris, Lenny, Cincinnati	.939	24	9	53	4	66	3
Hayes, Charlie, Philadelphia	.963	141	104	264	14	382	27
Hernandez, Jose, Chicago	1.000	20	12	36	0	48	1
Huskey, Butch, New York	.925	27	14	60	6	80	2
Ingram, Garey, Los Angeles	.750	12	9	15	8	32	0
Johnson, Howard, Chicago	.926	34	10	53	5	68	4
Jones, Chipper, Atlanta	.931	123	81	254	25	360	19
Jordan, Kevin, Philadelphia	1.000	1	1	2	0	3	0
King, Jeff, Pittsburgh	.942	84	48	164	13	225	14
Kmak, Joe, Chicago	1.000	1	0	1	0	1	0
Ledesma, Aaron, New York	.875	10	2	12	2	16	0
Lewis, Mark, Cincinnati	.968	72	19	103	4	126	4
Liriano, Nelson, Pittsburgh	1.000	5	0	5	0	5	0
Livingstone, Scott, San Diego	1.000	13	1	13	0	14	0
Magadan, Dave, Houston	.922	100	55	159	18	232	9
Mordecai, Mike, Atlanta	1.000	6	0	5	0	5	0
Nevin, Phil, Houston	.933	16	10	32	3	45	4
Oliva, Jose, Atl.-St.L.	.933	43	25	72	7	104	7
Oquendo, Jose, St. Louis	.000	2	0	0	0	0	0
Owens, Eric, Cincinnati	.000	2	0	0	0	0	0
Parker, Rick, Los Angeles	.000	2	0	0	0	0	0
Pendleton, Terry, Florida	.952	129	104	250	18	372	24
Pye, Eddie, Los Angeles	.000	2	0	0	0	0	0
Sabo, Chris, St. Louis	1.000	1	0	1	0	1	0
Scarsone, Steve, San Francisco	.927	50	30	71	8	109	8
Schofield, Dick, Los Angeles	.000	1	0	0	0	0	0
Sefcik, Kevin, Philadelphia	.000	2	0	1	0	1	1
Sharperson, Mike, Atlanta	.000	1	0	0	0	0	0
Sheaffer, Danny, St. Louis	1.000	1	0	2	0	2	0
Shipley, Craig, Houston	.982	65	27	82	2	111	5
Silvestri, Dave, Montreal	.938	8	2	13	1	16	0
Spiers, Bill, New York	.794	11	9	18	7	34	2
Stankiewicz, Andy, Houston	1.000	3	2	1	0	3	0
Treadway, Jeff, L.A.-Mon.	1.000	3	0	1	0	1	0
WALLACH, TIM, Los Angeles	.976	96	50	156	5	211	10
Wehner, John, Pittsburgh	1.000	19	11	26	0	37	1
Williams, Matt, San Francisco	.958	74	49	178	10	237	10
Worthington, Craig, Cincinnati	1.000	2	2	2	0	4	0
Young, Kevin, Pittsburgh	.919	48	28	108	12	148	7
Zeile, Todd, Chicago	.939	75	35	134	11	180	13

TRIPLE PLAY: Branson, Cin.

THIRD BASEMEN WITH TWO OR MORE TEAMS

Player, Team	Pct.	G	PO	A	E	TC	DP
Oliva, Jose, Atlanta	.902	25	14	41	6	61	3
Oliva, Jose, St. Louis	.977	18	11	31	1	43	4
Treadway, Jeff, Los Angeles	.000	2	0	0	0	0	0
Treadway, Jeff, Montreal	1.000	1	0	1	0	1	0

SHORTSTOPS

Player, Team	Pct.	G	PO	A	E	TC	DP
Abbott, Kurt, Florida	.959	115	149	290	19	458	66
Alfonzo, Edgardo, New York	1.000	6	5	9	0	14	3
Arias, Alex, Florida	.947	36	40	85	7	132	15
Aurilia, Rich, San Francisco	1.000	6	8	16	0	24	4
Bates, Jason, Colorado	.985	20	24	41	1	66	5
Bell, Jay, Pittsburgh	.978	136	205	409	14	628	88
Belliard, Rafael, Atlanta	.992	40	33	90	1	124	11
Benjamin, Mike, San Francisco	1.000	16	15	30	0	45	6
Blauser, Jeff, Atlanta	.970	115	151	337	15	503	62
Bogar, Tim, New York	.971	27	20	46	2	68	5
Branson, Jeff, Cincinnati	.980	32	31	65	2	98	15
Brumley, Mike, Houston	1.000	3	0	1	0	1	0
Castilla, Vinny, Colorado	1.000	5	2	8	0	10	1
Castro, Juan, Los Angeles	1.000	4	1	4	0	5	2
Cedeno, Andujar, San Diego	.965	116	139	304	16	459	58
Cianfrocco, Archi, San Diego	.945	15	17	35	3	55	7
Clayton, Royce, San Francisco	.969	136	223	411	20	654	93
Cordero, Wil, Montreal	.960	105	124	280	17	421	47
Counsell, Craig, Colorado	1.000	3	1	1	0	2	1
Cromer, Tripp, St. Louis	.960	95	111	276	16	403	57
Diaz, Mario, Florida	1.000	5	6	11	0	17	4
Duncan, Mariano, Phi.-Cin.	.966	20	22	64	3	89	11
Dunston, Shawon, Chicago	.969	125	187	336	17	540	51
Elster, Kevin, Philadelphia	.982	19	18	36	1	55	11
Fonville, Chad, Los Angeles	.971	38	38	95	4	137	13
Garcia, Carlos, Pittsburgh	.895	15	17	34	6	57	6
Giovanola, Ed, Atlanta	1.000	1	0	2	0	2	0
Grudzielanek, Mark, Montreal	.987	34	50	103	2	155	17

Player, Team	Pct.	G	PO	A	E	TC	DP
Gutierrez, Ricky, Houston	.956	44	64	108	8	180	17
Hernandez, Jose, Chicago	.961	43	45	77	5	127	18
Holbert, Ray, San Diego	.940	30	24	55	5	84	12
Hulett, Tim, St. Louis	.750	1	1	2	1	4	0
Johnson, Howard, Chicago	1.000	1	1	2	0	3	1
King, Jeff, Pittsburgh	.333	2	0	1	2	3	0
Lansing, Mike, Montreal	1.000	2	0	1	0	1	0
Larkin, Barry, Cincinnati	.980	130	192	341	11	544	72
Ledesma, Aaron, New York	.000	2	0	0	0	0	0
Lewis, Mark, Cincinnati	1.000	2	0	1	0	1	0
Liriano, Nelson, Pittsburgh	.000	1	0	0	0	0	0
Miller, Orlando, Houston	.964	89	131	270	15	416	52
Mordecai, Mike, Atlanta	1.000	6	1	5	0	6	1
Offerman, Jose, Los Angeles	.932	115	165	312	35	512	61
Oquendo, Jose, St. Louis	.988	24	20	61	1	82	14
Parker, Rick, Los Angeles	.000	2	0	0	0	0	0
Reed, Jody, San Diego	1.000	5	1	3	0	4	1
Roberts, Bip, San Diego	.960	7	6	18	1	25	4
Sanchez, Rey, Chicago	1.000	4	1	9	0	10	2
Schofield, Dick, Los Angeles	1.000	3	3	9	0	12	3
Shipley, Craig, Houston	.971	11	10	24	1	35	2
Silvestri, Dave, Montreal	1.000	9	8	20	0	28	1
Smith, Ozzie, St. Louis	.964	41	60	129	7	196	28
Stankiewicz, Andy, Houston	.985	14	15	51	1	67	6
Stocker, Kevin, Philadelphia	.969	125	147	383	17	547	72
VIZCAINO, JOSE, New York	.984	134	189	411	10	610	80
Wehner, John, Pittsburgh	1.000	1	0	2	0	2	0
Weiss, Walt, Colorado	.974	136	201	406	16	623	99
Zosky, Eddie, Florida	.667	4	1	1	1	3	0

TRIPLE PLAY: Larkin, Cin.

SHORTSTOPS WITH TWO OR MORE TEAMS

Player, Team	Pct.	G	PO	A	E	TC	DP
Duncan, Mariano, Philadelphia	.956	14	14	51	3	68	9
Duncan, Mariano, Cincinnati	1.000	6	8	13	0	21	2

OUTFIELDERS

Player, Team	Pct.	G	PO	A	E	TC	DP
Alou, Moises, Montreal	.981	92	147	5	3	155	2
Anthony, Eric, Cincinnati*	1.000	24	39	2	0	41	0
Ashley, Billy, Los Angeles	.972	69	102	2	3	107	0
Barry, Jeff, New York	1.000	2	2	0	0	2	0
Battle, Allen, St. Louis	.984	32	61	0	1	62	0
Bean, Billy, San Diego*	.750	4	3	0	1	4	0
Bell, David, Houston	.963	110	201	10	8	219	2
Benard, Marvin, San Francisco*	1.000	7	19	0	0	19	0
Benitez, Yamil, Montreal	.950	14	18	1	1	20	0
Bichette, Dante, Colorado	.986	136	208	9	3	220	0
Bogar, Tim, New York	.000	1	0	0	0	0	0
Bonds, Barry, San Francisco*	.980	143	279	12	6	297	2
Bonilla, Bobby, New York	.983	31	55	4	1	60	0
Bradshaw, Terry, St. Louis	.952	10	19	1	1	21	0
Browne, Jerry, Florida	.959	29	45	2	2	49	2
Brumfield, Jacob, Pittsburgh	.969	104	241	8	8	257	1
Brumley, Mike, Houston	1.000	3	2	0	0	2	0
Buford, Damon, New York	.972	39	67	2	2	71	0
Bullett, Scott, Chicago*	.968	64	59	1	2	62	0
Burks, Ellis, Colorado	.970	80	158	3	5	166	0
Butler, Brett, N.Y.-L.A.*	.993	128	282	6	2	290	1
Cangelosi, John, Houston*	.950	59	92	3	5	100	0
Carr, Chuck, Florida	.987	103	217	8	3	228	1
Carreon, Mark, San Francisco*	.938	22	29	1	2	32	0
Cedeno, Roger, Los Angeles	.977	36	43	0	1	44	0
Cianfrocco, Archi, San Diego	1.000	7	11	2	0	13	0
Clark, Dave, Pittsburgh	.961	61	98	1	4	103	0
Clark, Phil, San Diego	1.000	34	25	0	0	25	0
Coles, Darnell, St. Louis	1.000	1	1	0	0	1	0
Conine, Jeff, Florida	.976	118	195	7	5	207	2
Cordero, Wil, Montreal	.902	26	45	1	5	51	0
Cummings, Midre, Pittsburgh	.988	41	79	2	1	82	0
Dawson, Andre, Florida	.908	59	76	3	8	87	2
Devereaux, Mike, Atlanta	1.000	27	41	0	0	41	0
Duncan, Mariano, Cincinnati	1.000	3	6	0	0	6	0
Dykstra, Lenny, Philadelphia*	.987	61	153	2	2	157	1
EISENREICH, JIM, Philadelphia*	1.000	111	205	2	0	207	1
Everett, Carl, New York	.981	77	147	9	3	159	3
Faneyte, Rikkert, San Francisco	.981	34	49	3	1	53	0
Finley, Steve, San Diego*	.977	138	291	8	7	306	0
Flora, Kevin, Philadelphia	1.000	20	33	1	0	34	1
Floyd, Cliff, Montreal	.750	4	3	0	1	4	0
Fonville, Chad, Los Angeles	.947	11	16	2	1	19	1
Frazier, Lou, Montreal	.973	25	36	0	1	37	0
Gallagher, Dave, Philadelphia	1.000	55	89	1	0	90	0
Gant, Ron, Cincinnati	.985	117	191	7	3	201	0

Player, Team	Pct.	G	PO	A	E	TC	DP
Garcia, Freddy, Pittsburgh	1.000	10	13	0	0	13	0
Garcia, Karim, Los Angeles*	1.000	5	5	2	0	7	1
Giannelli, Ray, St. Louis	1.000	2	2	0	0	2	0
Gibralter, Steve, Cincinnati	1.000	2	1	0	0	1	0
Gilkey, Bernard, St. Louis	.986	118	206	10	3	219	4
Gonzalez, Luis, Hou.-Chi.	.978	131	266	7	6	279	1
Gregg, Tommy, Florida*	.984	38	63	0	1	64	0
Grissom, Marquis, Atlanta	.994	136	309	9	2	320	1
Gwynn, Chris, Los Angeles*	1.000	17	21	0	0	21	0
Gwynn, Tony, San Diego*	.992	133	245	8	2	255	1
Harris, Lenny, Cincinnati	1.000	8	9	2	0	11	0
Hill, Glenallen, San Francisco	.959	125	226	10	10	246	1
Holbert, Ray, San Diego	.000	1	0	0	0	0	0
Hollandsworth, Todd, L.A.*	.938	37	60	1	4	65	0
Howard, Thomas, Cincinnati	.985	82	126	2	2	130	1
Hubbard, Trent, Colorado	1.000	16	16	1	0	17	0
Hunter, Brian L., Houston	.955	74	182	8	9	199	2
Hunter, Brian R., Cincinnati*	1.000	4	7	1	0	8	0
Huskey, Butch, New York	1.000	1	2	0	0	2	0
Ingram, Garey, Los Angeles	1.000	4	1	0	0	1	0
Jefferies, Gregg, Philadelphia	1.000	55	87	3	0	90	1
Johnson, Howard, Chicago	1.000	13	12	0	0	12	0
Jones, Chipper, Atlanta	1.000	20	22	1	0	23	0
Jones, Chris, New York	.976	52	79	3	2	84	1
Jordan, Brian, St. Louis	.996	126	267	4	1	272	2
Justice, David, Atlanta*	.984	120	233	8	4	245	0
Kelly, Mike, Atlanta	.940	83	63	0	4	67	0
Kelly, Roberto, Mon.-L.A.	.974	134	225	3	6	234	1
Kingery, Mike, Colorado*	.979	108	180	4	4	188	0
Klesko, Ryan, Atlanta*	.942	102	111	2	7	120	0
Kowitz, Brian, Atlanta*	1.000	8	6	0	0	6	0
Lampkin, Tom, San Francisco	1.000	6	3	0	0	3	0
Lankford, Ray, St. Louis*	.990	129	300	7	3	310	2
Leonard, Mark, San Francisco	1.000	6	9	0	0	9	0
Lewis, Darren, S.F.-Cin.	.994	130	321	5	2	328	1
Longmire, Tony, Philadelphia	1.000	23	33	2	0	35	0
Mabry, John, St. Louis	1.000	39	57	5	0	62	2
Marsh, Tom, Philadelphia	.939	29	44	2	3	49	0
Martin, Al, Pittsburgh*	.977	121	206	8	5	219	2
May, Derrick, Houston	.974	55	74	0	2	76	0
McCarty, Dave, San Francisco*	.833	4	5	0	1	6	0
McCracken, Quinton, Colorado	.000	1	0	0	0	0	0
McDavid, Ray, San Diego	1.000	7	5	0	0	5	0
McRae, Brian, Chicago	.991	137	345	4	3	352	0
Merced, Orlando, Pittsburgh	.976	107	199	8	5	212	2
Mondesi, Raul, Los Angeles	.980	138	282	16	6	304	3
Mordecai, Mike, Atlanta	.000	1	0	0	0	0	0
Morman, Russ, Florida	.955	18	21	0	1	22	0
Mouton, James, Houston	1.000	94	136	4	0	140	0
Newfield, Marc, San Diego	1.000	19	24	1	0	25	0
Nieves, Melvin, San Diego	.990	79	95	5	1	101	1
Ochoa, Alex, New York	1.000	10	20	1	0	21	0
Oquendo, Jose, St. Louis	.000	1	0	0	0	0	0
Orsulak, Joe, New York*	.965	86	108	3	4	115	0
Otero, Ricky, New York*	1.000	23	31	1	0	32	0
Parker, Rick, Los Angeles	1.000	21	20	1	0	21	1
Pegues, Steve, Pittsburgh	.954	53	81	2	4	87	1
Petagine, Roberto, San Diego*	1.000	2	1	0	0	1	0
Phillips, J.R., San Francisco*	1.000	1	1	0	0	1	0
Plantier, Phil, Hou.-S.D.	.959	59	89	5	4	98	1
Polonia, Luis, Atlanta*	1.000	15	9	0	0	9	0
Pride, Curtis, Montreal	.920	24	23	0	2	25	0
Pulliam, Harvey, Colorado	.000	1	0	0	0	0	0
Rhodes, Karl, Chicago*	.889	11	8	0	1	9	0
Roberson, Kevin, Chicago	1.000	11	8	0	0	8	0
Roberts, Bip, San Diego	.989	50	92	2	1	95	0
Rodriguez, Henry, L.A.-Mon.*	.977	28	42	0	1	43	0
Sanders, Deion, Cin.-S.F.*	.977	85	215	2	5	222	1
Sanders, Reggie, Cincinnati	.983	130	269	12	5	286	2
Santangelo, F.P., Montreal	.979	25	46	0	1	47	0
Schall, Gene, Philadelphia	1.000	4	3	0	0	3	0
Segui, David, N.Y.-Mon.*	1.000	20	15	2	0	17	0
Sheffield, Gary, Florida	.942	61	109	5	7	121	1
Silvestri, Dave, Montreal	.000	3	0	0	0	0	0
Simms, Mike, Houston	1.000	12	17	0	0	17	0
Smith, Dwight, Atlanta	.923	25	24	0	2	26	0
Sosa, Sammy, Chicago	.962	143	320	13	13	346	4
Sweeney, Mark, St. Louis*	.000	1	0	0	1	1	0
Tarasco, Tony, Montreal	.979	116	230	7	5	242	3
Tatum, Jimmy, Colorado	1.000	2	1	0	0	1	0
Tavarez, Jesus, Florida	1.000	61	118	1	0	119	1
Thompson, Milt, Houston	.979	34	45	2	1	48	1
Thompson, Ryan, New York	.985	74	193	4	3	200	2

Player, Team	Pct.	G	PO	A	E	TC	DP
Timmons, Ozzie, Chicago	.970	55	63	1	2	66	1
Vander Wal, John, Colorado*	1.000	10	9	1	0	10	0
Van Slyke, Andy, Philadelphia	.984	56	117	5	2	124	1
Varsho, Gary, Philadelphia	.939	25	31	0	2	33	0
Veras, Quilvio, Florida	1.000	2	2	0	0	2	0
Walker, Larry, Colorado	.988	129	225	13	3	241	1
Walton, Jerome, Cincinnati	.982	89	107	2	2	111	0
Webster, Mitch, Los Angeles*	1.000	25	12	0	0	12	0
Wehner, John, Pittsburgh	1.000	23	22	1	0	23	1
White, Rondell, Montreal	.986	119	269	5	4	278	2
Whiten, Mark, Philadelphia	.965	55	105	4	4	113	0
Whitmore, Darrell, Florida	.960	16	24	0	1	25	0
Williams, Reggie, Los Angeles	1.000	14	6	0	0	6	0
Wilson, Nigel, Cincinnati*	1.000	2	2	0	0	2	0
Young, Eric, Colorado	1.000	19	15	3	0	18	0
Zeile, Todd, Chicago	.000	2	0	0	1	1	0

OUTFIELDERS WITH TWO OR MORE TEAMS

Player, Team	Pct.	G	PO	A	E	TC	DP
Butler, Brett, New York*	.995	90	207	6	1	214	1
Butler, Brett, Los Angeles*	.987	38	75	0	1	76	0
Gonzalez, Luis, Houston	.980	55	94	2	2	98	0
Gonzalez, Luis, Chicago	.978	76	172	5	4	181	1
Kelly, Roberto, Montreal	1.000	24	42	1	0	43	0
Kelly, Roberto, Los Angeles	.969	110	183	2	6	191	1
Lewis, Darren, San Francisco	.995	73	200	2	1	203	1
Lewis, Darren, Cincinnati	.992	57	121	3	1	125	0
Plantier, Phil, Houston	.962	20	25	0	1	26	0
Plantier, Phil, San Diego	.958	39	64	5	3	72	1
Rodriguez, Henry, Los Angeles*	1.000	20	36	0	0	36	0
Rodriguez, Henry, Montreal*	.857	8	6	0	1	7	0
Sanders, Deion, Cincinnati*	.968	33	88	2	3	93	1
Sanders, Deion, San Francisco*	.984	52	127	0	2	129	0
Segui, David, New York*	1.000	18	15	2	0	17	0
Segui, David, Montreal*	.000	2	0	0	0	0	0

CATCHERS

Player, Team	Pct.	G	PO	A	E	TC	DP	PB
Ausmus, Brad, San Diego	.992	100	656	63	6	725	14	3
Berryhill, Damon, Cincinnati	.988	29	152	12	2	166	1	1
Borders, Pat, Houston	.987	11	70	5	1	76	2	2
Brito, Jorge, Colorado	.991	18	109	6	1	116	0	4
Castillo, Alberto, New York	.974	12	66	9	2	77	0	2
Daulton, Darren, Philadelphia	.994	95	631	45	4	680	5	9
Decker, Steve, Florida	.985	46	296	24	5	325	3	3
Encarnacion, Angelo, Pitts.	.979	55	278	43	7	328	2	4
Eusebio, Tony, Houston	.993	103	645	49	5	699	9	11
Fletcher, Darrin, Montreal	.994	98	612	45	4	661	8	0
Girardi, Joe, Colorado	.988	122	730	61	10	801	7	5
Goff, Jerry, Houston	1.000	11	80	6	0	86	1	1
Hemond, Scott, St. Louis	.985	38	185	15	3	203	1	7
Hernandez, Carlos, L.A.	.983	41	210	25	4	239	4	5
Hubbard, Mike, Chicago	.971	9	33	0	1	34	0	0
Hundley, Todd, New York	.987	89	488	29	7	524	8	6
Johnson, Brian, San Diego	.993	55	394	32	3	429	2	5
Johnson, Charles, Florida	.992	97	641	63	6	710	9	5
Kmak, Joe, Chicago	1.000	18	93	8	0	101	0	1
Laker, Tim, Montreal	.977	61	265	27	7	299	1	4
Lampkin, Tom, San Fran.	1.000	17	59	5	0	64	1	1
Lieberthal, Mike, Phil.	.991	14	95	10	1	106	1	7
Lopez, Javy, Atlanta	.988	93	625	50	8	683	5	8
Manwaring, Kirt, San Fran.	.990	118	607	55	7	669	10	5
Munoz, Noe, Los Angeles	1.000	2	6	0	0	6	0	0
Natal, Bob, Florida	.988	13	80	3	1	84	1	0
Nokes, Matt, Colorado	.909	3	10	0	1	11	0	0
O'Brien, Charlie, Atlanta	.992	64	446	23	4	473	4	0
Owens, Jayhawk, Colorado	.988	16	79	6	1	86	2	1
Pagnozzi, Tom, St. Louis	.995	61	336	38	2	376	4	1
Parent, Mark, Pit.-Chi.	.992	77	430	44	4	478	1	9
Perez, Eddie, Atlanta	1.000	5	31	2	0	33	2	0
Piazza, Mike, Los Angeles	.990	112	805	52	9	866	8	12
Pratt, Todd, Chicago	.981	25	149	9	3	161	1	1
Prince, Tom, Los Angeles	.988	17	71	8	1	80	2	2
Reed, Jeff, San Francisco	.995	42	175	21	1	197	2	1
SANTIAGO, BENITO, Cin.	.996	75	461	33	2	496	4	6
Sasser, Mackey, Pittsburgh	1.000	11	35	3	0	38	0	0
Servais, Scott, Hou.-Chi.	.980	80	526	50	12	588	6	9
Sheaffer, Danny, St. Louis	.993	67	360	37	3	400	9	1
Siddall, Joe, Montreal	.882	7	14	1	2	17	0	2
Slaught, Don, Pittsburgh	.996	33	220	9	1	230	2	1
Spehr, Tim, Montreal	.990	38	92	11	1	105	3	0
Stinnett, Kelly, New York	.983	67	380	22	7	409	1	6
Tatum, Jimmy, Colorado	1.000	1	3	0	0	3	0	0
Taubensee, Eddie, Cincinnati	.983	65	326	21	6	353	0	4

Player, Team	Pct.	G	PO	A	E	TC	DP	PB
Tucker, Scooter, Houston	1.000	3	7	1	0	8	0	0
Webster, Lenny, Philadelphia	.990	43	274	18	3	295	1	3
Wehner, John, Pittsburgh	1.000	1	2	0	0	2	0	0
Wilkins, Rick, Chi.-Hou.	.990	62	375	33	4	412	7	6

CATCHERS WITH TWO OR MORE TEAMS

Player, Team	Pct.	G	PO	A	E	TC	DP	PB
Parent, Mark, Pittsburgh	.990	67	364	39	4	407	1	7
Parent, Mark, Chicago	1.000	10	66	5	0	71	0	2
Servais, Scott, Houston	.977	28	198	17	5	220	3	0
Servais, Scott, Chicago	.981	52	328	33	7	368	3	9
Wilkins, Rick, Chicago	.988	49	288	29	4	321	7	6
Wilkins, Rick, Houston	1.000	13	87	4	0	91	0	0

PITCHERS

Player, Team	Pct.	G	PO	A	E	TC	DP
Abbott, Kyle, Philadelphia*	.875	18	3	4	1	8	0
Acevedo, Juan, Colorado	.929	17	6	7	1	14	0
Adams, Terry, Chicago	1.000	18	2	1	0	3	0
Alvarez, Tavo, Montreal	.875	8	3	4	1	8	1
Aquino, Luis, Mon.-S.F.	1.000	34	3	4	0	7	2
Arocha, Rene, St. Louis	1.000	41	2	9	0	11	0
Ashby, Andy, San Diego	.964	31	6	21	1	28	0
Astacio, Pedro, Los Angeles	1.000	48	12	12	0	24	0
Avery, Steve, Atlanta*	.952	29	3	37	2	42	1
Bailey, Cory, St. Louis	1.000	3	0	1	0	1	0
Bailey, Roger, Colorado	.895	39	3	14	2	19	2
Banks, Willie, Chi.-L.A.-Fla.	.958	25	13	10	1	24	0
Barber, Brian, St. Louis	1.000	9	1	1	0	2	0
Barton, Shawn, San Francisco*	1.000	52	4	8	0	12	2
Bautista, Jose, San Francisco	.941	52	5	11	1	17	0
Beck, Rod, San Francisco	1.000	60	6	7	0	13	0
Bedrosian, Steve, Atlanta	.750	29	0	3	1	4	0
Benes, Alan, St. Louis	1.000	3	1	0	0	1	0
Benes, Andy, San Diego	.933	19	7	7	1	15	1
Berumen, Andres, San Diego	.833	37	4	1	1	6	0
Birkbeck, Mike, New York	1.000	4	0	5	0	5	0
Blair, Willie, San Diego	.905	40	6	13	2	21	1
Bochtler, Doug, San Diego	1.000	34	1	7	0	8	1
Borbon, Pedro, Atlanta*	1.000	41	1	6	0	7	1
Borland, Toby, Philadelphia	.857	50	2	10	2	14	0
Bottalico, Ricky, Philadelphia	1.000	62	6	7	0	13	1
Bowen, Ryan, Florida	1.000	4	0	2	0	2	0
Brantley, Jeff, Cincinnati	1.000	56	7	4	0	11	1
Brewington, Jamie, San Fran.	1.000	13	3	10	0	13	1
Brocail, Doug, Houston	1.000	36	11	9	0	20	0
Bruske, Jim, Los Angeles	1.000	9	1	0	0	1	0
Bullinger, Jim, Chicago	1.000	24	20	20	0	40	2
Burba, Dave, S.F.-Cin.	1.000	52	10	7	0	17	0
Burgos, Enrique, San Fran.*	.000	5	0	0	0	0	0
Burkett, John, Florida	1.000	30	18	26	0	44	0
Byrd, Paul, New York	.800	17	1	3	1	5	0
Candiotti, Tom, Los Angeles	.975	30	15	24	1	40	0
Cangelosi, John, Houston*	1.000	1	0	1	0	1	0
Carrasco, Hector, Cincinnati	.867	64	4	9	2	15	1
Carter, Andy, Philadelphia*	.000	4	0	0	0	0	0
Casian, Larry, Chicago*	1.000	42	2	4	0	6	0
Castillo, Frank, Chicago	.946	29	11	24	2	37	0
Charlton, Norm, Philadelphia*	.000	25	0	0	0	0	0
Christiansen, Jason, Pitts.*	.833	63	2	8	2	12	0
Clark, Terry, Atlanta	1.000	3	1	1	0	2	1
Clontz, Brad, Atlanta	1.000	59	7	8	0	15	1
Cornelius, Reid, Mon.-N.Y.	.950	18	7	12	1	20	2
Courtright, John, Cincinnati*	.000	1	0	0	0	0	0
Creek, Doug, St. Louis*	1.000	6	0	0	0	0	0
Cummings, John, L.A.*	1.000	35	2	4	0	6	1
Daal, Omar, Los Angeles*	1.000	28	0	2	0	2	0
DeLeon, Jose, Montreal	.000	7	0	0	0	0	0
DeLucia, Rich, St. Louis	.895	56	3	14	2	19	1
Deshaies, Jim, Philadelphia*	.000	2	0	0	0	0	0
Dewey, Mark, San Francisco	.800	27	1	3	1	5	1
DiPoto, Jerry, New York	.870	58	4	16	3	23	1
Dishman, Glenn, San Diego*	1.000	19	4	13	0	17	1
Dougherty, Jim, Houston	1.000	56	4	14	0	18	4
Drabek, Doug, Houston	.957	31	24	20	2	46	3
Dunbar, Matt, Florida*	1.000	3	0	3	0	3	1
Dyer, Mike, Pittsburgh	1.000	55	3	13	0	16	2
Edens, Tom, Chicago	1.000	5	1	0	0	1	0
Eischen, Joey, Los Angeles*	1.000	17	3	1	0	4	0
Elliott, Donnie, San Diego	.000	1	0	0	0	0	0
Ericks, John, Pittsburgh	.850	19	7	10	3	20	0
Estes, Shawn, San Francisco*	1.000	3	0	1	0	1	0
Eversgerd, Bryan, Montreal*	.800	25	2	2	1	5	0
Fassero, Jeff, Montreal*	.913	30	7	35	4	46	1

Player, Team	Pct.	G	PO	A	E	TC	DP
Fernandez, Sid, Philadelphia*	.667	11	0	2	1	3	0
Fletcher, Paul, Philadelphia	1.000	10	0	1	0	1	0
Florence, Don, New York*	1.000	14	0	4	0	4	0
Florie, Bryce, San Diego	.929	47	4	9	1	14	0
Fossas, Tony, St. Louis*	.800	58	1	3	1	5	1
Foster, Kevin, Chicago	1.000	30	7	14	0	21	0
Franco, John, New York*	1.000	48	2	9	0	11	1
Frascatore, John, St. Louis	1.000	14	3	2	0	5	0
Fraser, Willie, Montreal	1.000	22	1	4	0	5	0
Freeman, Marvin, Colorado	.870	22	9	11	3	23	0
Frey, Steve, S.F.-Phi.*	.667	18	0	2	1	3	0
Garces, Rich, Chi.-Fla.	1.000	18	2	1	0	3	0
Gardner, Mark, Florida	.875	39	4	10	2	16	1
Glavine, Tom, Atlanta*	.982	29	14	42	1	57	6
Gomez, Pat, San Francisco*	1.000	18	1	1	0	2	0
Gott, Jim, Pittsburgh	.900	25	2	7	1	10	0
Grace, Mark, Philadelphia	1.000	2	1	2	0	3	0
Grahe, Joe, Colorado	.944	17	5	12	1	18	1
Green, Tyler, Philadelphia	.963	26	9	17	1	27	2
Greene, Tommy, Philadelphia	1.000	11	3	3	0	6	0
Greer, Kenny, San Francisco	.750	8	0	3	1	4	0
Groom, Buddy, Florida*	1.000	14	0	3	0	3	0
Grott, Matt, Cincinnati*	1.000	2	0	1	0	1	0
Gunderson, Eric, New York*	1.000	30	3	5	0	8	0
Guthrie, Mark, Los Angeles	1.000	24	0	3	0	3	0
Habyan, John, St. Louis	1.000	31	5	7	0	12	0
Hamilton, Joey, San Diego	.875	31	12	30	6	48	1
Hammond, Chris, Florida*	.968	25	9	21	1	31	2
Hampton, Mike, Houston*	.917	24	10	23	3	36	2
Hancock, Lee, Pittsburgh*	1.000	11	1	1	0	2	1
Hansell, Greg, Los Angeles	1.000	20	2	1	0	3	0
Harnisch, Pete, New York	.917	18	10	12	2	24	1
Harris, Gene, Philadelphia	1.000	21	4	4	0	8	0
Harris, Greg A., Montreal	.800	45	3	5	2	10	0
Hartgraves, Dean, Houston*	1.000	40	3	5	0	8	0
Harvey, Bryan, Florida	.000	1	0	0	0	0	0
Henke, Tom, St. Louis	1.000	52	4	4	0	8	1
Henneman, Mike, Houston	1.000	21	1	1	0	2	0
Henry, Butch, Montreal*	1.000	21	11	25	0	36	3
Henry, Doug, New York	.929	51	4	9	1	14	0
Heredia, Gil, Montreal	1.000	40	9	21	0	30	0
Hermanson, Dustin, San Diego	1.000	26	4	4	0	8	2
Hernandez, Jeremy, Florida	.000	7	0	0	0	0	0
Hernandez, Xavier, Cincinnati	1.000	59	10	7	0	17	0
Hickerson, Bryan, Chi.-Col.*	1.000	56	3	3	0	6	1
Hill, Ken, St. Louis	.971	18	13	20	1	34	1
Hoffman, Trevor, San Diego	1.000	55	5	1	0	6	0
Holmes, Darren, Colorado	.950	68	6	13	1	20	0
Hook, Chris, San Francisco	1.000	45	5	4	0	9	1
Hope, John, Pittsburgh	.000	3	0	0	0	0	0
Hudek, John, Houston	1.000	19	1	5	0	6	0
Isringhausen, Jason, New York	.905	14	8	11	2	21	1
Jackson, Danny, St. Louis*	.864	19	7	12	3	22	0
Jackson, Mike, Cincinnati	1.000	40	2	3	0	5	0
Jacome, Jason, New York*	.800	5	0	4	1	5	0
Jarvis, Kevin, Cincinnati	.909	19	8	12	2	22	1
Johnstone, John, Florida	1.000	4	1	0	0	1	0
Jones, Bobby, New York	.872	30	11	30	6	47	1
Jones, Todd, Houston	.933	68	3	11	1	15	1
Juden, Jeff, Philadelphia	1.000	13	3	8	0	11	0
Karp, Ryan, Philadelphia*	.000	1	0	0	0	0	0
Kile, Darryl, Houston	.923	25	11	25	3	39	2
Konuszewski, Dennis, Pitts.	.000	1	0	0	0	0	0
Kroon, Marc, San Diego	.000	2	0	0	0	0	0
Krueger, Bill, San Diego*	1.000	6	0	1	0	1	0
Leiper, Dave, Montreal*	1.000	26	0	6	0	6	0
Leiter, Mark, San Francisco	.867	30	7	19	4	30	3
Leskanic, Curt, Colorado	1.000	76	9	17	0	26	1
Lewis, Richie, Florida	.818	21	7	2	2	11	0
Lieber, Jon, Pittsburgh	.947	21	2	16	1	19	0
Loaiza, Esteban, Pittsburgh	1.000	32	13	27	0	40	3
Lomon, Kevin, New York	.500	6	1	0	1	2	0
MADDUX, GREG, Atlanta	1.000	28	18	53	0	71	3
Maddux, Mike, Pittsburgh	1.000	8	0	1	0	1	0
Mantei, Matt, Florida	1.000	12	1	2	0	3	2
Manzanillo, Josias, New York	1.000	12	1	0	0	1	0
Manzanillo, Ravelo, Pitts.*	1.000	5	0	1	0	1	0
Martinez, Pedro A., Houston*	1.000	25	3	2	0	5	0
Martinez, Pedro J., Montreal	.949	30	14	23	2	39	0
Martinez, Ramon, Los Angeles	.935	30	16	27	3	46	2
Mathews, Terry, Florida	1.000	57	6	9	0	15	0
Mathews, T.J., St. Louis	.900	23	4	5	1	10	1
Mauser, Tim, San Diego	.000	5	0	0	0	0	0

Player, Team	Pct.	G	PO	A	E	TC	DP
May, Darrell, Atlanta*	1.000	2	0	1	0	1	0
McCurry, Jeff, Pittsburgh	1.000	55	1	12	0	13	0
McElroy, Chuck, Cincinnati*	1.000	44	2	4	0	6	1
McMichael, Greg, Atlanta	.909	67	4	6	1	11	0
McMurtry, Craig, Houston	1.000	11	1	3	0	4	0
Mercker, Kent, Atlanta*	.966	29	5	23	1	29	2
Miceli, Danny, Pittsburgh	1.000	58	2	5	0	7	0
Mimbs, Michael, Philadelphia*	.967	35	6	23	1	30	4
Minor, Blas, New York	1.000	35	3	7	0	10	0
Mintz, Steve, San Francisco	1.000	14	1	2	0	3	0
Mlicki, Dave, New York	.962	29	10	15	1	26	3
Morel, Ramon, Pittsburgh	1.000	5	1	2	0	3	0
Morgan, Mike, Chi.-St.L.	.977	21	13	29	1	43	2
Mulholland, Terry, San Fran.*	.903	29	5	23	3	31	2
Munoz, Bobby, Philadelphia	.750	3	0	3	1	4	0
Munoz, Mike, Colorado*	1.000	64	5	7	0	12	0
Murphy, Rob, L.A.-Fla.*	1.000	14	0	3	0	3	0
Murray, Matt, Atlanta	1.000	4	1	4	0	5	0
Myers, Mike, Florida*	.000	2	0	0	0	0	0
Myers, Randy, Chicago*	1.000	57	2	9	0	11	0
Nabholz, Chris, Chicago*	1.000	34	1	5	0	6	0
Navarro, Jaime, Chicago	.964	29	14	13	1	28	1
Neagle, Denny, Pittsburgh*	.979	31	13	33	1	47	4
Nen, Robb, Florida	1.000	62	3	9	0	12	1
Nichols, Rod, Atlanta	.667	5	0	2	1	3	0
Nied, David, Colorado	.000	2	0	0	0	0	0
Nitkowski, C.J., Cincinnati*	.833	9	3	2	1	6	0
Nomo, Hideo, Los Angeles	.857	28	6	12	3	21	2
Olivares, Omar, Col.-Phi.	1.000	16	4	8	0	12	1
Osborne, Donovan, St. Louis*	1.000	19	3	16	0	19	0
Osuna, Antonio, Los Angeles	1.000	39	0	7	0	7	2
Painter, Lance, Colorado*	1.000	33	3	6	0	9	0
Palacios, Vince, St. Louis	1.000	20	3	4	0	7	0
Park, Chan Ho, Los Angeles	.000	2	0	0	0	0	0
Parra, Jose, Los Angeles	1.000	8	0	1	0	1	0
Parrett, Jeff, St. Louis	.867	59	7	6	2	15	0
Parris, Steve, Pittsburgh	1.000	15	4	10	0	14	0
Pena, Alejandro, Fla.-Atl.	1.000	27	1	2	0	3	0
Pennington, Brad, Cincinnati*	.500	6	1	0	1	2	0
Perez, Carlos, Montreal*	.935	28	6	23	2	31	1
Perez, Mike, Chicago	.923	68	4	8	1	13	1
Perez, Yorkis, Florida*	1.000	69	1	4	0	5	0
Person, Robert, New York	.000	3	0	0	0	0	0
Petkovsek, Mark, St. Louis	1.000	26	8	17	0	25	2
Plesac, Dan, Pittsburgh*	1.000	58	1	8	0	9	1
Portugal, Mark, S.F.-Cin.	.968	31	9	21	1	31	2
Powell, Jay, Florida	1.000	9	1	3	0	4	0
Powell, Ross, Hou.-Pit.*	1.000	27	1	5	0	6	0
Pugh, Tim, Cincinnati	.950	28	10	9	1	20	0
Pulsipher, Bill, New York*	1.000	17	5	18	0	23	0
Quantrill, Paul, Philadelphia	.976	33	9	32	1	42	2
Rapp, Pat, Florida	.971	28	13	20	1	34	1
Reed, Rick, Cincinnati	1.000	4	2	1	0	3	0
Reed, Steve, Colorado	.952	71	4	16	1	21	1
Rekar, Bryan, Colorado	.962	15	9	16	1	26	0
Remlinger, Mike, N.Y.-Cin.*	.000	7	0	0	0	0	0
Reynolds, Shane, Houston	.981	30	13	39	1	53	0
Reynoso, Armando, Colorado	.946	20	7	28	2	37	2
Ricci, Chuck, Philadelphia	1.000	7	2	0	0	2	0
Rijo, Jose, Cincinnati	1.000	14	4	9	0	13	0
Ritz, Kevin, Colorado	1.000	31	10	39	0	49	1
Rivera, Roberto, Chicago*	1.000	7	0	1	0	1	0
Rodriguez, Felix, Los Angeles	1.000	11	0	1	0	1	1
Rodriguez, Rich, St. Louis*	1.000	1	0	0	0	0	0
Rojas, Mel, Montreal	1.000	59	4	7	0	11	1
Roper, John, Cin.-S.F.	1.000	3	0	1	0	1	0
Rosselli, Joe, San Francisco*	1.000	9	0	5	0	5	1
Rueter, Kirk, Montreal*	1.000	9	8	9	0	17	1
Ruffin, Bruce, Colorado*	1.000	37	0	8	0	8	0
Ruffin, Johnny, Cincinnati	1.000	10	2	1	0	3	1
Saberhagen, Bret, N.Y.-Col.	.977	25	8	34	1	43	3
Sager, A.J., Colorado	1.000	10	1	5	0	6	1
Sanders, Scott, San Diego	1.000	17	6	3	0	9	0
Scheid, Rich, Florida*	1.000	6	1	5	0	6	0
Schilling, Curt, Philadelphia	.909	17	2	8	1	11	1
Schmidt, Curt, Montreal	1.000	11	0	1	0	1	0
Schmidt, Jason, Atlanta	1.000	9	3	3	0	6	1
Schourek, Pete, Cincinnati*	.973	29	7	29	1	37	2
Scott, Tim, Montreal	1.000	62	3	4	0	7	1
Seanez, Rudy, Los Angeles	.857	37	3	3	1	7	0
Service, Scott, San Francisco	1.000	28	2	2	0	4	0
Shaw, Jeff, Montreal	1.000	50	6	11	0	17	0
Slocumb, Heathcliff, Phil.	.955	61	4	17	1	22	3

Player, Team	Pct.	G	PO	A	E	TC	DP
Small, Aaron, Florida	1.000	7	0	1	0	1	0
Smiley, John, Cincinnati*	1.000	28	3	27	0	30	3
Smith, Pete, Cincinnati	1.000	11	1	6	0	7	0
Smoltz, John, Atlanta	.938	29	12	18	2	32	0
Springer, Dennis, Philadelphia	.750	4	2	1	1	4	0
Springer, Russ, Philadelphia	1.000	14	3	4	0	7	1
Stanton, Mike, Atlanta*	.750	26	0	6	2	8	0
Sturtze, Tanyon, Chicago	.000	2	0	0	0	0	0
Sullivan, Scott, Cincinnati	1.000	3	0	1	0	1	0
Swartzbaugh, Dave, Chicago	.000	7	0	0	0	0	0
Swift, Bill, Colorado	.974	19	9	28	1	38	2
Swindell, Greg, Houston*	.976	33	9	31	1	41	1
Tabaka, Jeff, S.D.-Hou.*	1.000	34	1	3	0	4	0
Tapani, Kevin, Los Angeles	.933	13	4	10	1	15	0
Telgheder, Dave, New York	1.000	7	2	6	0	8	0
Thobe, J.J., Montreal	.000	4	0	0	1	1	0
Thobe, Tom, Atlanta*	.000	3	0	0	0	0	0
Thompson, Mark, Colorado	1.000	21	3	10	0	13	1
Torres, Salomon, San Fran.	1.000	4	1	1	0	2	1
Trachsel, Steve, Chicago	.952	30	7	13	1	21	0
Urbani, Tom, St. Louis*	1.000	24	4	19	0	23	0
Urbina, Ugueth, Montreal	1.000	7	5	4	0	9	0
Valdes, Ismael, Los Angeles	.979	33	16	31	1	48	0
Valdes, Marc, Florida	.000	3	0	0	0	0	0
Valdez, Carlos, San Francisco	1.000	11	1	2	0	3	0
Valdez, Sergio, San Francisco	.900	13	4	14	2	20	0
Valenzuela, Fernando, S.D.*	1.000	29	7	27	0	34	2
VanLandingham, William, S.F.	.963	18	7	19	1	27	2
Veres, Dave, Houston	.944	72	6	11	1	18	0
Veres, Randy, Florida	.833	47	2	3	1	6	0
Villone, Ron, San Diego*	1.000	19	0	2	0	2	0
Viola, Frank, Cincinnati	1.000	3	0	2	0	2	0
Wade, Terrell, Atlanta*	.000	3	0	0	0	0	0
Wagner, Billy, Houston*	.000	1	0	0	0	0	0
Wagner, Paul, Pittsburgh	1.000	33	12	24	0	36	1
Walker, Mike, Chicago	.917	42	4	7	1	12	0
Walker, Pete, New York	1.000	13	1	2	0	3	0
Wall, Donnie, Houston	.857	6	4	2	1	7	0
Watson, Allen, St. Louis*	1.000	21	7	21	0	28	0
Weathers, Dave, Florida	.882	28	3	12	2	17	0
Wells, David, Cincinnati*	1.000	11	4	6	0	10	1
Wendell, Turk, Chicago	.955	43	9	12	1	22	2
West, David, Philadelphia*	.800	8	1	3	1	5	0
White, Gabe, Montreal*	1.000	19	0	2	0	2	0
White, Rick, Pittsburgh	.917	15	2	9	1	12	1
Williams, Brian, San Diego	1.000	44	6	9	0	15	0
Williams, Mike, Philadelphia	.958	33	4	19	1	24	0
Williams, Todd, Los Angeles	1.000	16	2	5	0	7	1
Wilson, Gary, Pittsburgh	1.000	10	0	2	0	2	0
Wilson, Trevor, San Fran.*	.952	17	2	18	1	21	2
Witt, Bobby, Florida	1.000	19	7	15	0	22	0
Wohlers, Mark, Atlanta	1.000	65	4	3	0	7	0
Woodall, Brad, Atlanta*	1.000	9	0	2	0	2	1
Worrell, Tim, San Diego	1.000	9	0	2	0	2	0
Worrell, Todd, Los Angeles	1.000	59	6	11	0	17	2
Young, Anthony, Chicago	.800	32	5	3	2	10	1

PITCHERS WITH TWO OR MORE TEAMS

Player, Team	Pct.	G	PO	A	E	TC	DP
Aquino, Luis, Montreal	1.000	29	1	4	0	5	1
Aquino, Luis, San Francisco	1.000	5	2	0	0	2	1
Banks, Willie, Chicago	1.000	10	3	2	0	5	0
Banks, Willie, Los Angeles	1.000	6	4	3	0	7	0
Banks, Willie, Florida	.917	9	6	5	1	12	0
Burba, Dave, San Francisco	1.000	37	3	3	0	6	0
Burba, Dave, Cincinnati	1.000	15	7	4	0	11	0
Cornelius, Reid, Montreal	1.000	8	3	0	0	3	0
Cornelius, Reid, New York	.941	10	4	12	1	17	2
Frey, Steve, San Francisco*	.000	9	0	0	1	1	0
Frey, Steve, Philadelphia*	1.000	9	0	2	0	2	0
Garces, Rich, Chicago	1.000	7	1	1	0	2	0
Garces, Rich, Florida	1.000	11	1	0	0	1	0
Hickerson, Bryan, Chicago*	1.000	38	2	3	0	5	1
Hickerson, Bryan, Colorado*	1.000	18	1	0	0	1	0
Morgan, Mike, Chicago	1.000	4	5	5	0	10	0
Morgan, Mike, St. Louis	.970	17	8	24	1	33	2
Murphy, Rob, Los Angeles*	1.000	6	0	1	0	1	0
Murphy, Rob, Florida*	1.000	8	0	2	0	2	0
Olivares, Omar, Colorado	1.000	11	4	5	0	9	1
Olivares, Omar, Philadelphia	1.000	5	0	3	0	3	0
Pena, Alejandro, Florida	.000	13	0	0	0	0	0
Pena, Alejandro, Atlanta	1.000	14	1	2	0	3	0
Portugal, Mark, San Francisco	.947	17	5	13	1	19	1
Portugal, Mark, Cincinnati	1.000	14	4	8	0	12	1
Powell, Ross, Houston*	1.000	15	1	1	0	2	0
Powell, Ross, Pittsburgh*	1.000	12	0	4	0	4	0
Remlinger, Mike, New York*	.000	5	0	0	0	0	0
Remlinger, Mike, Cincinnati*	.000	2	0	0	0	0	0
Roper, John, Cincinnati	1.000	2	0	1	0	1	0
Roper, John, San Francisco	.000	1	0	0	0	0	0
Saberhagen, Bret, New York	1.000	16	6	26	0	32	3
Saberhagen, Bret, Colorado	.909	9	2	8	1	11	0
Tabaka, Jeff, San Diego*	.000	10	0	0	0	0	0
Tabaka, Jeff, Houston*	1.000	24	1	3	0	4	0

MISCELLANEOUS

SHUTOUT GAMES

Read across for wins, down for losses.

Team	Cin.	Atl.	Chi.	Hou.	S.D.	Mon.	N.Y.	L.A.	Phi.	Pit.	Fla.	S.F.	St.L.	Col.	W	L	Pct.
Cincinnati	..	0	0	1	0	0	0	1	2	0	2	1	1	2	10	3	.769
Atlanta	1	..	1	0	0	1	1	1	1	0	1	0	2	2	11	4	.733
Chicago	0	0	..	0	1	0	1	1	2	0	0	2	3	2	12	5	.706
Houston	0	1	1	..	0	0	0	1	0	2	0	0	3	0	8	4	.667
San Diego	0	0	1	0	..	1	0	0	1	2	0	1	3	1	10	6	.625
Montreal	0	1	1	1	1	..	1	0	0	1	1	1	1	0	9	8	.529
New York	1	1	0	1	2	2	..	0	1	0	1	0	0	0	9	8	.529
Los Angeles	0	1	1	0	0	1	2	..	0	1	1	2	1	1	11	12	.478
Philadelphia	1	0	0	0	1	0	0	4	..	0	0	1	1	0	8	9	.471
Pittsburgh	0	0	0	0	1	2	0	1	1	..	0	0	1	1	7	8	.467
Florida	0	0	0	0	0	0	2	1	0	0	..	0	3	1	7	9	.438
San Francisco	0	0	0	0	0	0	0	1	1	0	2	..	0	1	5	8	.385
St. Louis	0	0	0	1	0	1	1	1	0	1	1	0	..	0	6	19	.240
Colorado	0	0	0	0	0	0	0	0	0	1	0	0	0	..	1	11	.083
Lost	3	4	5	4	6	8	8	12	9	8	9	8	19	11	114	114	.500

HOME RECORD

Read across for home wins, down for road losses.

Team	Atl.	Cin.	Col.	N.Y.	S.D.	L.A.	St.L.	Fla.	S.F.	Hou.	Phi.	Chi.	Mon.	Pit.	W	L	Pct.
Atlanta	..	3	5	4	2	3	4	5	5	1	2	4	4	2	44	28	.611
Cincinnati	2	..	4	5	1	3	4	3	2	6	4	3	4	3	44	28	.611
Colorado	2	5	..	4	5	1	2	3	5	2	3	3	4	5	44	28	.611
New York	5	4	3	..	5	3	2	4	2	3	3	1	2	3	40	32	.556
San Diego	1	4	3	5	..	3	6	0	2	3	4	4	2	3	40	32	.556
Los Angeles	3	2	4	3	4	..	3	2	5	1	2	2	4	4	39	33	.542
St. Louis	3	3	3	3	5	2	..	3	4	3	2	2	2	4	39	33	.542
Florida	2	3	4	4	3	1	3	..	1	5	3	2	2	4	37	34	.521
San Francisco	1	1	3	4	2	4	5	2	..	2	5	2	2	4	37	35	.514
Houston	1	1	3	3	4	1	5	3	3	..	1	4	3	4	36	36	.500
Philadelphia	1	1	1	2	4	5	2	4	5	2	..	1	3	4	35	37	.486
Chicago	2	1	2	1	3	3	5	4	1	2	3	..	3	4	34	38	.472
Montreal	2	2	1	3	3	3	3	3	3	0	4	3	..	1	31	41	.431
Pittsburgh	1	1	3	2	1	1	4	6	4	2	2	2	2	..	31	41	.431
Lost on road	26	31	39	43	42	33	48	42	42	32	38	33	37	45	531	476	.527

ROAD RECORD

Read across for road wins, down for home losses.

Team	Atl.	Cin.	Hou.	Chi.	L.A.	Mon.	Phi.	Col.	S.D.	S.F.	Fla.	N.Y.	Pit.	St.L.	W	L	Pct.
Atlanta	..	5	5	4	2	5	5	4	3	2	5	1	2	3	46	26	.639
Cincinnati	3	..	6	4	1	4	5	1	2	1	3	2	5	4	41	31	.569
Houston	5	0	..	4	2	6	4	1	3	2	1	3	5	4	40	32	.556
Chicago	2	2	3	..	4	0	3	4	2	4	4	3	4	4	39	33	.542
Los Angeles	1	1	1	3	..	3	2	5	3	3	5	3	5	4	39	33	.542
Montreal	2	2	3	2	2	..	4	0	4	4	4	4	3	1	35	37	.486
Philadelphia	5	2	5	0	4	2	..	1	2	1	3	4	2	3	34	38	.472
Colorado	2	2	2	4	3	3	1	..	4	3	2	1	3	3	33	39	.458
San Diego	1	2	1	3	3	3	2	1	..	4	2	2	5	1	30	42	.417
San Francisco	0	2	1	5	1	4	1	2	5	..	1	4	2	2	30	42	.417
Florida	1	3	3	2	2	4	3	0	4	3	..	3	1	1	30	42	.417
New York	3	1	3	2	3	4	4	1	1	3	2	..	1	1	29	43	.403
Pittsburgh	1	4	2	2	3	2	1	1	3	2	2	1	..	2	27	45	.375
St. Louis	2	2	1	2	3	1	2	4	0	2	0	1	3	..	23	48	.324
Lost at home	28	28	36	38	33	41	37	28	32	35	34	32	41	33	476	531	.473

PITCHING AGAINST EACH CLUB

ATLANTA—90-54

Pitcher	Chi. W-L	Cin. W-L	Col. W-L	Fla. W-L	Hou. W-L	L.A. W-L	Mon. W-L	N.Y. W-L	Phi. W-L	Pit. W-L	St.L. W-L	S.D. W-L	S.F. W-L	Totals W-L
Avery	0-3	0-0	2-1	1-2	1-0	0-2	0-2	1-0	1-1	0-0	0-2	0-0	1-0	7-13
Bedrosian	1-0	0-1	0-0	0-0	0-0	0-0	0-0	0-0	0-1	0-0	0-0	0-0	0-0	1-2
Borbon	0-0	0-1	0-0	0-1	0-0	0-0	1-0	0-0	1-0	0-0	0-0	0-0	0-0	2-2
Clontz	0-0	0-1	0-0	1-0	0-0	1-0	0-0	0-0	0-0	3-0	0-0	1-0	1-0	8-1
Glavine	2-1	2-1	1-0	2-0	1-1	0-0	3-0	0-1	1-1	0-0	2-1	1-0	1-1	16-7
Maddux	1-0	2-1	0-1	1-0	2-0	0-0	2-0	2-0	2-0	1-0	3-0	1-0	2-0	19-2
McMichael	0-0	0-0	1-0	2-0	0-0	2-0	0-1	1-0	0-0	0-0	1-0	0-1	0-0	7-2
Mercker	1-0	0-0	2-1	0-0	2-0	0-2	1-1	0-1	1-1	0-0	0-1	0-1	0-0	7-8
Murray	0-0	0-0	0-0	0-0	0-1	0-0	0-0	0-0	0-0	0-0	0-0	0-0	0-0	0-2
Schmidt	1-0	0-0	1-0	0-0	0-0	0-0	0-0	0-2	0-0	0-0	0-0	0-0	0-0	2-2

Pitcher	Chi. W-L	Cin. W-L	Col. W-L	Fla. W-L	Hou. W-L	L.A. W-L	Mon. W-L	N.Y. W-L	Phi. W-L	Pit. W-L	St.L. W-L	S.D. W-L	S.F. W-L	Totals W-L
Smoltz	2-0	3-0	1-0	1-0	0-2	1-0	1-0	1-2	1-2	0-1	0-0	1-0	0-0	12-7
Stanton	0-0	0-0	0-0	0-0	0-1	0-0	0-0	0-0	0-0	0-0	0-0	0-0	1-0	1-1
Wade	0-0	0-0	0-0	0-0	0-0	0-0	0-0	0-1	0-0	0-0	0-0	0-0	0-0	0-1
Wohlers	0-0	1-0	1-0	1-0	0-1	1-0	0-0	0-1	0-0	0-1	1-0	1-0	1-0	7-3
Woodall	0-0	0-0	0-1	1-0	0-0	0-0	0-0	0-0	0-0	0-0	0-0	0-0	0-0	1-1
Totals	8-4	8-5	9-4	10-3	6-6	5-4	9-4	5-8	7-6	4-2	7-5	5-2	7-1	90-54

CHICAGO—73-71

Pitcher	Atl. W-L	Cin. W-L	Col. W-L	Fla. W-L	Hou. W-L	L.A. W-L	Mon. W-L	N.Y. W-L	Phi. W-L	Pit. W-L	St.L. W-L	S.D. W-L	S.F. W-L	Totals W-L
Adams	0-0	0-0	0-0	0-0	0-1	1-0	0-0	0-0	0-0	0-0	0-0	0-0	0-0	1-1
Banks	0-0	0-0	0-0	0-0	0-0	0-0	0-0	0-0	0-0	0-1	0-0	0-0	0-0	0-1
Bullinger	1-1	1-0	0-1	0-1	1-1	1-2	0-1	1-0	2-0	1-1	3-0	0-0	1-0	12-8
Casian	0-0	0-0	0-0	0-0	0-0	0-0	0-0	0-0	0-0	1-0	0-0	0-0	0-0	1-0
Castillo	0-2	0-0	3-0	1-1	0-2	1-0	0-2	0-0	1-0	0-0	1-1	3-1	1-1	11-10
Edens	0-0	1-0	0-0	0-0	0-0	0-0	0-0	0-0	0-0	0-0	0-0	0-0	0-0	1-0
Foster	0-1	1-1	1-1	3-0	1-0	1-0	1-1	1-0	0-0	2-0	1-2	0-3	0-2	12-11
Hickerson	0-1	0-0	0-0	0-0	0-0	0-0	0-0	0-1	0-0	1-0	0-0	0-0	0-0	2-3
Morgan	1-0	0-1	1-0	0-0	0-0	0-0	0-0	0-0	0-0	0-0	0-0	0-0	0-0	2-1
Myers	0-0	0-1	0-1	0-0	0-0	1-0	0-0	0-0	0-0	0-0	0-0	0-0	0-0	1-2
Nabholz	0-0	0-0	0-0	0-0	0-0	0-0	0-0	0-0	0-0	0-1	0-0	0-0	0-0	0-1
Navarro	2-0	0-1	0-1	2-0	1-0	0-1	2-1	1-0	1-0	2-0	0-0	1-0	2-2	14-6
Perez	0-1	0-1	0-1	0-1	1-1	0-0	0-0	0-0	0-0	1-0	0-1	0-0	0-0	2-6
Trachsel	0-2	0-1	0-1	1-0	0-1	0-1	0-0	1-1	0-1	0-2	3-0	1-2	1-1	7-13
Walker	0-0	0-0	0-0	0-0	0-2	1-0	0-0	0-1	0-0	0-0	0-0	0-0	0-0	1-3
Wendell	0-0	0-0	0-1	1-0	0-0	0-0	0-0	0-0	1-0	1-0	0-0	0-0	0-0	3-1
Young	0-0	0-1	1-0	0-0	1-0	0-1	0-0	0-0	1-0	0-1	0-0	0-0	0-1	3-4
Totals	4-8	3-7	6-7	8-4	5-8	7-5	3-5	4-3	6-1	8-5	9-4	5-7	5-7	73-71

NO-DECISIONS: Garces, Rivera, Sturtze, Swartzbaugh.

CINCINNATI—85-59

Pitcher	Atl. W-L	Chi. W-L	Col. W-L	Fla. W-L	Hou. W-L	L.A. W-L	Mon. W-L	N.Y. W-L	Phi. W-L	Pit. W-L	St.L. W-L	S.D. W-L	S.F. W-L	Totals W-L
Brantley	1-0	0-0	0-0	0-0	2-0	0-0	0-0	0-0	0-0	0-1	0-0	0-0	0-1	3-2
Burba	1-0	0-0	1-0	0-0	1-0	0-0	0-0	0-1	1-0	0-1	1-0	0-0	1-0	6-2
Carrasco	1-1	0-0	0-2	0-0	0-0	0-0	1-0	0-0	0-1	0-0	0-1	0-2	0-0	2-7
Hernandez	1-0	1-0	0-0	0-0	2-0	0-0	0-0	1-0	1-1	1-0	0-0	0-0	0-1	7-2
Jackson	0-0	2-0	0-0	1-0	0-0	0-0	1-0	0-0	1-0	0-0	0-1	1-0	0-0	6-1
Jarvis	0-0	0-0	1-1	1-1	0-0	0-0	0-0	0-1	0-0	0-1	1-0	0-0	0-0	3-4
McElroy	0-2	0-1	0-0	0-0	0-0	0-0	0-0	0-0	1-1	0-0	1-0	0-0	1-0	3-4
Nitkowski	0-1	0-0	0-0	0-0	0-0	0-1	0-0	0-0	1-0	0-0	0-0	0-1	0-0	1-3
Portugal	0-1	0-0	1-0	0-1	2-0	0-1	2-0	0-0	0-0	1-0	0-1	0-1	0-0	6-5
Pugh	0-0	0-1	0-1	1-0	1-0	0-0	1-0	1-1	0-0	0-0	2-0	0-1	0-0	6-5
Rijo	0-0	1-1	0-0	0-1	0-0	0-0	1-0	0-0	0-1	1-0	1-0	0-0	1-0	5-4
Schourek	0-1	2-0	1-1	2-1	1-0	2-0	2-0	1-1	2-0	3-0	1-1	0-1	1-1	18-7
Smiley	1-1	1-0	0-1	1-1	2-0	2-0	0-1	1-1	2-0	2-0	0-0	0-0	0-0	12-5
Smith	0-1	0-0	1-0	0-0	0-0	0-0	0-0	0-0	0-0	0-1	0-0	0-0	0-0	1-2
Viola	0-0	0-0	0-0	0-0	0-1	0-0	0-0	0-0	0-0	0-0	0-0	0-0	0-0	0-1
Wells	0-0	0-0	0-1	0-1	1-0	0-0	0-2	1-0	1-0	0-1	2-0	1-0	0-0	6-5
Totals	5-8	7-3	5-7	6-6	12-1	4-3	8-4	7-5	9-3	8-5	8-5	3-6	3-3	85-59

NO-DECISIONS: Courtright, Grott, Pennington, Reed, Remlinger, Roper, Ruffin, Sullivan.

COLORADO—77-67

Pitcher	Atl. W-L	Chi. W-L	Cin. W-L	Fla. W-L	Hou. W-L	L.A. W-L	Mon. W-L	N.Y. W-L	Phi. W-L	Pit. W-L	St.L. W-L	S.D. W-L	S.F. W-L	Totals W-L
Acevedo	0-2	0-1	1-0	0-0	0-0	0-1	1-0	0-0	0-0	0-1	1-1	0-0	1-0	4-6
Bailey	0-1	1-1	0-1	0-1	1-0	0-1	0-0	0-0	0-0	2-0	1-1	2-0	0-0	7-6
Freeman	0-1	0-1	0-1	0-0	0-0	0-1	1-1	0-0	0-0	1-0	1-0	0-1	0-0	3-7
Grahe	0-0	0-0	1-0	0-1	0-0	0-0	1-0	0-0	0-0	1-0	0-1	1-0	0-1	4-3
Hickerson	1-0	0-0	0-0	0-0	0-0	0-0	0-0	0-0	0-0	0-0	0-0	0-0	0-0	1-0
Holmes	1-1	1-0	0-0	0-0	0-0	0-0	0-0	0-0	0-0	1-0	1-0	1-0	1-0	6-1
Leskanic	1-0	1-0	1-0	0-0	1-1	0-0	0-0	1-0	0-0	0-0	1-1	0-0	0-1	6-3
Munoz	0-1	1-0	0-0	0-0	0-1	0-0	0-0	0-0	1-1	0-0	0-0	0-0	0-1	2-4
Olivares	0-1	0-0	0-0	0-0	1-1	0-1	0-1	0-0	0-0	0-0	0-0	0-0	0-0	1-3
Painter	1-0	0-0	0-0	0-0	0-0	0-0	0-0	0-0	0-0	1-0	0-0	0-0	1-0	3-0
Reed	0-0	0-0	1-0	2-1	0-0	0-1	1-0	0-0	1-0	0-0	0-0	1-0	0-0	5-2
Rekar	0-0	0-1	0-1	0-0	0-0	0-0	1-0	0-0	2-0	1-0	0-1	0-0	0-2	4-6
Reynoso	0-1	1-0	1-0	0-0	0-1	0-0	2-0	0-2	0-0	0-1	0-1	2-1	1-0	7-7
Ritz	0-0	1-1	1-2	1-2	1-0	1-2	1-0	1-1	0-1	1-1	0-0	1-1	2-0	11-11
Ruffin	0-0	0-0	0-0	0-0	0-0	0-0	0-0	0-0	0-0	0-0	0-1	0-0	0-0	0-1
Saberhagen	0-0	0-1	0-0	0-0	0-0	2-0	0-0	0-0	0-0	0-0	0-0	0-0	0-0	2-1
Swift	0-1	0-0	1-0	2-0	0-0	1-1	0-0	1-0	1-0	0-1	0-0	1-0	2-0	9-3
Thompson	0-0	1-0	0-0	0-0	0-0	0-1	0-0	1-1	0-0	0-0	0-0	0-1	0-0	2-3
Totals	4-9	7-6	7-5	5-7	4-4	4-9	7-1	5-4	4-2	8-4	5-7	9-4	8-5	77-67

NO-DECISIONS: Nied, Sager.

FLORIDA—67-76

Pitcher	Atl. W-L	Chi. W-L	Cin. W-L	Col. W-L	Hou. W-L	L.A. W-L	Mon. W-L	N.Y. W-L	Phi. W-L	Pit. W-L	St.L. W-L	S.D. W-L	S.F. W-L	Totals W-L
Banks	0-1	0-1	0-0	0-0	1-0	0-0	0-0	0-0	0-1	1-0	0-0	0-0	0-0	2-3
Bowen	0-0	0-0	0-0	0-0	0-0	0-0	0-0	1-0	1-0	0-0	0-0	0-0	0-0	2-0
Burkett	0-1	1-2	1-1	1-1	2-0	0-2	1-1	1-2	2-1	1-1	1-1	1-0	2-1	14-14
Dunbar	0-0	0-0	0-1	0-0	0-0	0-0	0-0	0-0	0-0	0-0	0-0	0-0	0-0	0-1
Garces	0-0	0-0	0-1	0-0	0-1	0-0	0-0	0-0	0-0	0-0	0-0	0-0	0-0	0-2
Gardner	0-1	0-0	1-0	0-1	1-0	0-1	0-1	0-0	0-0	0-1	1-0	2-0	0-0	5-5
Groom	0-0	0-0	0-0	1-0	0-0	0-0	0-0	0-0	0-0	0-2	0-0	0-0	0-0	1-2
Hammond	0-0	0-3	0-2	1-0	0-0	1-1	1-0	2-0	1-0	2-0	1-0	0-0	0-0	9-6
Lewis	0-0	0-0	0-0	0-0	0-0	0-0	0-0	0-0	0-1	0-0	0-0	0-0	0-0	0-1
Mantei	0-0	0-0	0-0	0-0	0-0	0-0	0-0	0-0	0-0	0-1	0-0	0-0	0-0	0-1
Mathews	1-0	0-0	0-0	1-1	0-0	0-1	0-1	0-1	0-0	1-0	0-0	0-0	1-0	4-4
Murphy	0-0	0-0	0-0	0-0	0-0	0-0	0-0	0-1	0-0	0-0	0-0	0-0	1-0	1-1
Nen	0-3	0-0	0-0	0-0	0-1	0-0	0-1	0-0	0-1	0-1	0-0	0-0	0-0	0-7
Pena	0-0	0-0	0-0	1-0	0-0	0-0	1-0	0-0	0-0	0-0	0-0	0-0	0-0	2-0
Perez	0-2	0-0	0-0	0-0	0-0	0-0	0-1	0-0	1-1	0-0	1-0	0-1	0-0	2-6
Rapp	2-0	2-0	2-1	1-2	1-0	1-1	2-1	2-1	1-0	0-0	0-0	0-0	0-1	14-7
Small	0-0	0-0	0-0	0-0	1-0	0-0	0-0	0-0	0-0	0-0	0-0	0-0	0-0	1-0
Veres	0-1	1-0	0-0	0-0	1-0	1-0	0-0	1-1	0-1	0-1	0-0	0-0	0-0	4-4
Weathers	0-0	0-2	2-0	0-0	1-0	0-0	1-1	0-0	0-1	0-0	0-0	0-1	0-0	4-5
Witt	0-1	0-0	0-0	1-0	0-1	0-1	0-0	0-0	0-0	0-2	0-1	0-0	1-1	2-7
Totals	3-10	4-8	6-6	7-5	8-4	3-7	6-7	7-6	6-7	5-8	4-3	3-2	5-3	67-76

NO-DECISIONS: Harvey, Hernandez, Johnstone, Myers, Powell, Scheid, Valdes.

HOUSTON—76-68

Pitcher	Atl. W-L	Chi. W-L	Cin. W-L	Col. W-L	Fla. W-L	L.A. W-L	Mon. W-L	N.Y. W-L	Phi. W-L	Pit. W-L	St.L. W-L	S.D. W-L	S.F. W-L	Totals W-L
Brocail	0-1	0-1	0-0	1-0	0-1	0-0	1-0	0-0	0-0	2-0	0-0	1-0	1-1	6-4
Dougherty	0-0	1-0	0-0	0-1	3-1	0-1	0-0	1-0	0-0	0-0	0-0	1-0	2-1	8-4
Drabek	1-1	0-1	1-0	0-0	0-2	1-0	1-1	1-1	1-1	0-0	1-2	2-0	1-0	10-9
Hampton	0-1	0-0	0-1	1-1	0-0	1-0	0-0	1-2	1-1	0-1	3-0	1-0	1-0	9-8
Hartgraves	0-0	0-0	0-0	0-0	0-0	0-0	0-0	0-0	1-0	0-0	1-0	0-0	0-0	2-0
Henneman	0-0	0-0	0-0	0-0	0-0	0-0	0-0	0-1	0-0	0-0	0-0	0-0	0-0	0-1
Hudek	1-0	0-0	0-0	0-0	0-1	0-0	1-0	0-1	0-0	0-0	0-0	0-0	0-0	2-2
Jones	1-0	1-1	0-1	1-0	0-0	0-0	0-0	0-1	0-1	1-1	1-0	1-0	0-0	6-5
Kile	0-1	1-1	0-2	1-2	0-0	0-0	1-0	0-0	1-1	0-2	0-0	0-2	0-1	4-12
McMurtry	0-1	0-0	0-0	0-0	0-0	0-0	0-0	0-0	0-0	0-0	0-0	0-0	0-0	0-1
Reynolds	2-0	2-0	0-4	0-0	0-2	1-0	1-1	1-2	0-0	2-0	1-0	0-2	0-0	10-11
Swindell	1-1	1-0	0-2	0-0	0-1	0-1	2-1	1-0	0-1	3-0	1-2	1-0	0-0	10-9
Tabaka	0-0	0-0	0-0	0-0	0-0	0-0	1-0	0-0	0-0	0-0	0-0	0-0	0-0	1-0
Veres	0-0	1-0	0-1	0-0	1-0	0-0	1-0	0-0	1-0	1-0	0-0	0-0	0-0	5-1
Wall	0-0	1-0	0-0	0-0	0-0	0-0	0-0	0-0	0-0	0-0	1-0	0-0	0-0	3-1
Totals	6-6	8-5	1-12	4-4	4-8	3-2	9-3	6-6	5-7	9-4	9-4	7-4	5-3	76-68

NO-DECISIONS: Cangelosi, Martinez, Powell, Wagner.

LOS ANGELES—78-66

Pitcher	Atl. W-L	Chi. W-L	Cin. W-L	Col. W-L	Fla. W-L	Hou. W-L	Mon. W-L	N.Y. W-L	Phi. W-L	Pit. W-L	St.L. W-L	S.D. W-L	S.F. W-L	Totals W-L
Astacio	0-1	0-0	0-0	0-0	1-1	1-0	0-0	1-1	0-2	1-1	2-2	1-0	0-0	7-8
Banks	0-0	0-0	0-1	0-0	0-0	0-1	0-0	0-0	0-0	0-0	0-0	0-0	0-0	0-2
Candiotti	0-0	0-1	0-1	0-2	2-1	0-1	0-0	1-2	1-2	0-0	2-0	0-2	1-2	7-14
Cummings	1-0	0-0	0-0	0-0	0-0	0-0	0-0	0-1	1-0	1-0	0-0	0-0	0-0	3-1
Daal	1-0	0-0	0-0	1-0	0-0	0-0	0-0	1-0	0-0	0-0	0-0	1-0	0-0	4-0
Guthrie	0-0	0-2	0-0	0-0	0-0	0-0	0-0	0-0	0-0	0-0	0-0	0-0	0-0	0-2
Hansell	0-0	0-0	0-0	0-0	0-0	0-0	0-0	0-0	0-0	0-0	0-0	0-1	0-0	0-1
Martinez	0-1	1-1	2-0	2-2	2-0	1-0	3-1	0-0	1-1	3-0	0-0	1-1	1-0	17-7
Murphy	0-1	0-0	0-0	0-0	0-0	0-0	0-0	0-0	0-0	0-0	0-0	0-0	0-0	0-1
Nomo	0-0	2-0	1-0	1-0	0-0	0-1	1-1	1-1	0-1	1-0	1-1	2-0	2-1	13-6
Osuna	0-0	0-0	0-0	0-0	0-0	0-0	0-0	0-0	0-0	0-2	0-2	2-0	0-0	2-4
F. Rodriguez	0-0	0-1	0-0	0-0	0-0	0-0	0-0	1-0	0-0	0-0	0-0	0-0	0-0	1-1
Seanez	0-1	0-1	0-0	0-0	0-0	0-0	0-0	0-0	0-1	0-0	0-0	1-0	0-0	1-3
Tapani	0-0	0-0	0-1	2-0	0-0	0-0	0-1	0-0	1-0	1-0	0-0	0-0	0-0	4-2
Valdes	2-1	2-1	0-1	1-0	1-1	0-0	2-2	0-0	0-2	2-1	1-0	1-1	1-1	13-11
T. Williams	0-0	0-0	0-0	1-0	0-0	0-0	0-0	0-0	0-0	0-2	1-0	0-0	0-0	2-2
Worrell	0-0	0-0	0-0	1-0	0-0	0-0	1-0	1-1	0-0	0-0	0-0	1-0	0-0	4-1
Totals	4-5	5-7	3-4	9-4	7-3	2-3	7-5	6-6	4-9	9-4	7-5	7-6	8-5	78-66

NO-DECISIONS: Bruske, Eischen, Park, Parra.

MONTREAL—66-78

Pitcher	Atl. W-L	Chi. W-L	Cin. W-L	Col. W-L	Fla. W-L	Hou. W-L	L.A. W-L	N.Y. W-L	Phi. W-L	Pit. W-L	St.L. W-L	S.D. W-L	S.F. W-L	Totals W-L
Alvarez	0-0	0-0	0-2	0-0	0-0	0-0	0-1	0-0	0-1	0-0	0-0	0-0	1-1	1-5
Aquino	0-1	0-0	0-1	0-0	0-0	0-0	0-0	0-0	0-0	0-0	0-0	0-0	0-0	0-2
DeLeon	0-0	0-0	0-0	0-0	0-0	0-0	0-0	0-0	0-0	0-0	0-0	0-1	0-0	0-1
Fassero	0-2	0-0	0-3	0-2	2-0	0-1	1-3	2-1	1-1	2-1	1-0	4-0	0-0	13-14
Fraser	0-0	0-0	0-0	0-0	1-0	0-0	0-1	0-0	0-0	0-0	0-0	1-0	0-0	2-1

Pitcher	Atl. W-L	Chi. W-L	Cin. W-L	Col. W-L	Fla. W-L	Hou. W-L	L.A. W-L	N.Y. W-L	Phi. W-L	Pit. W-L	St.L. W-L	S.D. W-L	S.F. W-L	Totals W-L
Harris	0-0	0-0	0-0	0-0	1-0	0-1	1-0	0-0	0-0	0-1	0-0	0-1	0-0	2-3
Henry	1-1	2-1	1-0	0-2	0-0	1-1	0-0	0-0	1-1	0-0	0-1	0-2	1-0	7-9
Heredia	0-0	1-0	0-0	0-1	0-1	1-1	1-1	0-0	1-1	0-0	0-0	0-1	1-0	5-6
Leiper	0-1	0-0	0-0	0-0	0-0	0-0	0-0	0-0	0-0	0-0	0-0	0-0	0-1	0-2
Martinez	1-2	1-1	0-1	1-1	0-0	1-3	0-0	3-0	2-0	1-1	1-0	1-1	2-0	14-10
Perez	2-1	0-0	1-0	0-0	1-2	0-1	1-1	0-2	2-1	1-0	2-0	0-0	0-0	10-8
Rojas	0-1	0-0	0-0	0-0	1-0	0-0	0-0	0-0	0-0	0-0	0-1	0-0	0-2	1-4
Rueter	0-0	0-1	2-0	0-0	1-1	0-0	1-0	0-1	0-0	0-0	0-0	0-0	1-0	5-3
Scott	0-0	0-0	0-0	0-0	0-0	0-0	0-0	1-0	1-0	0-0	0-0	0-0	0-0	2-0
Shaw	0-0	0-0	0-0	0-0	0-1	0-1	0-0	0-2	0-0	0-0	0-1	1-0	0-1	1-6
Urbina	0-0	1-0	0-0	0-1	0-0	0-0	0-0	1-0	0-0	0-1	0-0	0-0	0-0	2-2
G. White	0-0	0-0	0-1	0-0	0-1	0-0	0-0	0-0	0-0	0-0	0-0	0-0	1-0	1-2
Totals	4-9	5-3	4-8	1-7	7-6	3-9	5-7	7-6	8-5	4-4	4-3	7-5	7-6	66-78

NO-DECISIONS: Cornelius, Eversgerd, Schmidt, Thobe.

NEW YORK—69-75

Pitcher	Atl. W-L	Chi. W-L	Cin. W-L	Col. W-L	Fla. W-L	Hou. W-L	L.A. W-L	Mon. W-L	Phi. W-L	Pit. W-L	St.L. W-L	S.D. W-L	S.F. W-L	Totals W-L
Birkbeck	0-0	0-0	0-0	0-0	0-0	0-0	0-1	0-0	0-0	0-0	0-0	0-0	0-0	0-1
Byrd	0-0	0-0	0-0	0-0	0-0	0-0	0-0	1-0	0-0	0-0	0-0	0-0	1-0	2-0
Cornelius	0-0	0-0	1-1	0-0	0-1	0-2	0-0	0-0	2-0	0-0	0-0	0-1	0-2	3-7
DiPoto	0-0	1-0	0-0	0-0	0-0	0-0	1-2	0-1	0-0	1-0	1-1	0-2	0-0	4-6
Florence	0-0	0-0	0-0	0-0	0-0	0-0	0-0	0-0	1-0	0-0	0-0	1-0	1-0	3-0
Franco	0-0	1-0	0-0	1-0	0-0	0-0	0-0	1-0	1-1	0-0	1-0	0-2	0-0	5-3
Gunderson	0-0	0-0	0-0	0-0	0-0	0-1	0-0	0-0	1-0	0-0	0-0	0-0	0-0	1-1
Harnisch	0-1	0-1	0-2	1-0	0-0	0-0	0-1	0-2	0-0	0-0	1-1	0-0	0-0	2-8
Henry	1-0	0-0	0-1	0-1	0-0	1-0	1-1	0-0	0-0	0-0	0-1	0-1	0-1	3-6
Isringhausen	1-0	0-0	1-0	0-0	0-1	0-0	1-0	1-1	2-0	1-0	0-0	2-0	0-0	9-2
Jacome	0-0	0-0	0-1	0-0	0-0	0-1	0-0	0-2	0-0	0-0	0-0	0-0	0-0	0-4
B. Jones	2-1	1-0	1-2	1-1	1-2	2-0	0-0	1-0	0-2	0-0	0-1	0-1	1-0	10-10
Lomon	0-0	0-0	0-0	0-1	0-0	0-0	0-0	0-0	0-0	0-0	0-0	0-0	0-0	0-1
Manzanillo	0-1	0-0	0-0	0-0	0-0	0-0	0-0	1-1	0-0	0-0	0-0	0-0	0-0	1-2
Minor	1-0	0-0	1-0	0-0	1-0	0-0	0-0	0-0	0-0	0-0	1-0	0-1	0-1	4-2
Mlicki	1-1	0-0	0-0	0-0	1-2	2-1	3-0	0-0	0-1	0-0	1-1	0-0	1-1	9-7
Person	0-0	0-0	1-0	0-0	0-0	0-0	0-0	0-0	0-0	0-0	0-0	0-0	0-0	1-0
Pulsipher	0-0	0-2	0-0	1-0	1-1	0-1	0-0	1-1	0-1	1-1	0-0	1-0	0-0	5-7
Remlinger	0-0	0-0	0-0	0-1	0-0	0-0	0-0	0-0	0-0	0-0	0-0	0-0	0-0	0-1
Saberhagen	1-0	0-1	0-0	0-1	2-0	1-0	0-1	0-1	0-0	0-1	0-0	0-0	1-0	5-5
Telgheder	0-1	0-0	0-0	0-0	0-0	0-0	0-0	0-0	1-0	0-0	0-0	0-0	0-1	1-2
Walker	1-0	0-0	0-0	0-0	0-0	0-0	0-0	0-0	0-0	0-0	0-0	0-0	0-0	1-0
Totals	8-5	3-4	5-7	4-5	6-7	6-6	6-6	6-7	7-6	4-3	3-4	6-7	5-8	69-75

PHILADELPHIA—69-75

Pitcher	Atl. W-L	Chi. W-L	Cin. W-L	Col. W-L	Fla. W-L	Hou. W-L	L.A. W-L	Mon. W-L	N.Y. W-L	Pit. W-L	St.L. W-L	S.D. W-L	S.F. W-L	Totals W-L
Abbott	1-0	0-0	0-0	0-0	0-0	0-0	0-0	0-0	0-0	0-0	0-0	1-0	0-0	2-0
Borland	0-0	0-0	0-1	0-0	0-1	0-0	0-1	0-0	0-0	1-0	0-0	0-0	0-0	1-3
Bottalico	0-0	0-0	0-0	0-1	2-0	2-0	0-1	0-1	0-0	0-0	0-0	0-0	1-0	5-3
Charlton	0-0	1-0	0-1	0-0	0-0	0-1	0-0	0-0	0-0	0-1	0-1	0-1	1-0	2-5
Deshaies	0-0	0-1	0-0	0-0	0-0	0-0	0-0	0-0	0-0	0-0	0-0	0-0	0-0	0-1
Fernandez	1-0	0-0	0-0	0-0	0-0	0-0	1-0	2-1	0-0	0-0	1-0	1-0	0-0	6-1
Fletcher	0-0	0-0	0-0	0-0	0-0	1-0	0-0	0-0	0-0	0-0	0-0	0-0	0-0	1-0
Grace	0-0	0-0	0-0	0-0	0-0	0-0	1-0	0-0	0-0	0-0	0-1	0-0	0-0	1-1
Green	2-0	0-0	0-0	0-2	0-1	0-1	2-0	1-1	2-1	0-1	1-0	0-0	0-2	8-9
Greene	0-0	0-0	0-1	0-0	0-0	0-0	0-1	0-1	0-1	0-0	0-1	0-0	0-0	0-5
Harris	0-0	0-0	1-0	0-0	0-0	0-0	0-0	0-0	0-0	0-0	0-1	1-1	0-0	2-2
Juden	0-0	0-0	0-0	0-0	0-0	1-1	1-2	0-0	0-0	0-0	0-0	0-0	0-1	2-4
Mimbs	1-2	0-1	0-1	0-0	2-0	0-0	1-0	0-1	2-1	1-0	0-1	1-0	1-0	9-7
Munoz	0-1	0-1	0-0	0-0	0-0	0-0	0-0	0-0	0-0	0-0	0-0	0-0	0-0	0-2
Olivares	0-0	0-0	0-0	0-0	0-0	0-0	0-0	0-0	0-0	0-0	0-1	0-0	0-0	0-1
Quantrill	0-1	0-0	0-1	0-1	0-2	1-0	2-0	1-2	1-2	3-1	2-0	1-0	0-2	11-12
Ricci	0-0	0-0	1-0	0-0	0-0	0-0	0-0	0-0	0-0	0-0	0-0	0-0	0-0	1-0
Schilling	1-1	0-1	1-1	1-0	1-0	1-1	0-0	1-0	0-0	0-0	0-1	1-0	0-0	7-5
Slocumb	0-1	0-1	0-1	1-0	1-0	1-1	1-0	0-0	0-1	0-0	0-0	1-0	0-0	5-6
D. Springer	0-0	0-0	0-1	0-0	0-0	0-0	0-1	0-0	0-1	0-0	0-0	0-0	0-0	0-3
West	0-1	0-0	0-0	0-0	0-1	0-0	0-0	0-0	1-0	1-0	1-0	0-0	0-0	3-2
Williams	0-0	0-1	0-0	0-0	1-0	0-0	0-0	1-0	0-1	0-0	1-1	0-0	0-0	3-3
Totals	6-7	1-6	3-9	2-4	7-6	7-5	9-4	5-8	6-7	6-3	5-4	6-6	6-6	69-75

NO-DECISIONS: Carter, Frey, Karp, R. Springer.

PITTSBURGH—58-86

Pitcher	Atl. W-L	Chi. W-L	Cin. W-L	Col. W-L	Fla. W-L	Hou. W-L	L.A. W-L	Mon. W-L	N.Y. W-L	Phi. W-L	St.L. W-L	S.D. W-L	S.F. W-L	Totals W-L
Christiansen	0-0	0-0	0-0	0-0	0-0	0-1	1-0	0-0	0-0	0-0	0-0	0-1	0-1	1-3
Dyer	1-0	0-2	0-0	0-0	1-0	0-0	0-1	0-0	0-0	0-1	2-0	0-0	0-1	4-5
Ericks	0-0	0-2	0-0	0-1	0-0	1-0	0-1	0-2	1-0	1-1	0-0	0-2	0-0	3-9

1995 N.L. STATISTICS Miscellaneous

Pitcher	Atl. W-L	Chi. W-L	Cin. W-L	Col. W-L	Fla. W-L	Hou. W-L	L.A. W-L	Mon. W-L	N.Y. W-L	Phi. W-L	St.L. W-L	S.D. W-L	S.F. W-L	Totals W-L
Gott	0-1	0-1	0-0	0-0	0-0	0-1	0-0	1-0	1-0	0-0	0-0	0-1	0-0	2-4
Lieber	0-0	0-1	1-1	0-1	0-0	0-1	0-1	0-1	0-0	0-0	0-0	2-1	1-0	4-7
Loaiza	0-1	0-0	0-2	1-0	1-1	2-0	0-1	1-0	1-0	1-0	0-3	0-1	1-0	8-9
Maddux	0-0	1-0	0-0	0-0	0-0	0-0	0-0	0-0	0-0	0-0	0-0	0-0	0-0	1-0
McCurry	0-0	0-0	0-0	0-1	1-0	0-0	0-1	0-0	0-0	0-0	0-0	0-0	0-2	1-4
Miceli	0-0	1-1	0-1	0-0	2-0	1-0	0-0	0-0	0-1	0-0	0-0	0-0	0-1	4-4
Morel	0-0	0-0	0-0	0-0	0-0	0-0	0-0	0-0	0-0	0-1	0-0	0-0	0-0	0-1
Neagle	0-0	2-0	1-1	1-1	0-2	0-2	2-1	1-0	0-0	0-1	1-0	1-0	4-0	13-8
Parris	1-0	1-0	0-1	0-0	1-1	0-2	0-0	1-0	0-1	0-1	1-0	1-0	0-0	6-6
Plesac	0-2	0-0	1-0	0-0	1-0	0-0	1-0	0-0	0-0	1-1	0-0	0-1	0-0	4-4
Powell	0-0	0-0	0-0	0-1	0-0	0-0	0-0	0-0	0-1	0-0	0-0	0-0	0-0	0-2
Wagner	0-0	0-1	1-2	2-2	1-1	0-1	0-3	0-1	0-1	0-1	1-2	0-1	0-0	5-16
White	0-0	0-0	1-0	0-0	0-0	0-1	0-0	0-0	0-0	0-0	1-1	0-0	0-0	2-3
Wilson	0-0	0-0	0-0	0-0	0-0	0-0	0-0	0-0	0-0	0-0	0-0	0-0	0-1	0-1
Totals	2-4	5-8	5-8	4-8	8-5	4-9	4-9	4-4	3-4	3-6	6-7	4-8	6-6	58-86

NO-DECISIONS: Hancock, Hope, Konuszewski, Manzanillo.

ST. LOUIS—62-81

Pitcher	Atl. W-L	Chi. W-L	Cin. W-L	Col. W-L	Fla. W-L	Hou. W-L	L.A. W-L	Mon. W-L	N.Y. W-L	Phi. W-L	Pit. W-L	S.D. W-L	S.F. W-L	Totals W-L
Arocha	0-1	0-0	0-1	0-0	0-1	0-0	1-0	0-0	0-1	1-0	0-0	0-0	1-1	3-5
Barber	0-0	0-0	1-0	1-0	0-0	0-0	0-0	0-0	0-0	0-0	0-1	0-0	0-0	2-1
Benes	0-0	0-1	0-0	0-0	0-0	0-0	0-0	0-0	0-0	0-0	1-1	0-0	0-0	1-2
DeLucia	1-0	0-1	1-1	1-0	0-0	0-2	0-0	2-0	0-1	1-0	0-0	0-2	2-0	8-7
Fossas	0-0	0-0	0-0	1-0	0-0	0-0	0-0	0-0	1-0	0-0	0-0	1-0	0-0	3-0
Frascatore	0-1	0-0	0-0	0-0	0-0	0-0	1-0	0-0	0-0	0-0	0-0	0-0	0-0	1-1
Habyan	1-0	0-1	0-0	1-0	1-0	0-0	0-0	0-0	0-0	0-0	0-0	0-0	0-1	3-2
Henke	0-0	0-0	0-0	0-0	0-0	0-0	1-1	0-0	0-0	0-0	0-0	0-0	0-0	1-1
Hill	1-0	2-0	0-1	1-0	0-1	0-0	0-1	0-1	0-0	0-2	2-0	0-1	0-0	6-7
Jackson	0-1	0-1	0-1	0-1	1-0	0-2	0-1	0-1	0-0	1-1	0-1	0-2	0-0	2-12
Mathews	0-0	0-0	1-0	0-0	0-0	0-0	0-0	0-0	0-0	0-0	0-1	0-0	0-0	1-1
Morgan	0-1	0-1	1-0	1-0	0-0	0-1	0-1	1-0	0-0	1-0	1-0	0-0	0-2	5-6
Osborne	0-0	0-1	0-1	0-0	0-0	0-1	0-0	0-0	0-0	0-1	2-1	1-0	1-1	4-6
Palacios	0-0	0-0	0-1	0-0	0-0	1-0	0-1	0-0	0-1	0-0	0-0	0-0	1-0	2-3
Parrett	0-1	1-1	1-0	0-2	0-0	1-0	0-1	0-0	0-0	0-0	0-1	1-1	0-0	4-7
Petkovsek	0-1	0-0	0-0	1-1	0-1	0-2	2-0	0-0	1-0	0-0	0-0	1-0	1-1	6-6
Urbani	1-1	1-0	0-0	0-0	0-0	0-1	0-0	0-1	0-1	0-1	0-0	0-0	0-1	3-5
Watson	1-0	0-2	0-2	0-1	1-1	2-0	0-1	0-1	1-0	0-0	1-1	1-0	0-0	7-9
Totals	5-7	4-9	5-8	7-5	3-4	4-9	5-7	3-4	4-3	4-5	7-6	5-7	6-7	62-81

NO-DECISIONS: Bailey, Creek, Rodriguez.

SAN DIEGO—70-74

Pitcher	Atl. W-L	Chi. W-L	Cin. W-L	Col. W-L	Fla. W-L	Hou. W-L	L.A. W-L	Mon. W-L	N.Y. W-L	Phi. W-L	Pit. W-L	St.L. W-L	S.F. W-L	Totals W-L
Ashby	0-0	1-1	0-0	1-1	0-1	3-0	2-0	0-1	0-2	0-2	2-1	2-0	1-1	12-10
Benes	0-1	1-1	1-0	0-0	0-0	0-2	0-0	0-0	0-1	1-1	0-0	0-0	1-1	4-7
Berumen	0-0	0-1	1-0	0-1	0-0	0-0	0-0	0-2	0-0	0-0	0-0	0-0	0-0	2-3
Blair	0-1	1-0	1-1	1-0	1-0	0-0	0-1	1-0	1-1	0-0	0-1	0-0	1-0	7-5
Bochtler	1-0	0-1	0-0	0-0	0-0	0-0	0-2	0-0	1-0	0-0	1-0	1-1	0-0	4-4
Dishman	1-0	0-0	0-0	1-2	0-2	0-0	1-0	0-1	0-0	0-1	0-0	1-1	0-1	4-8
Florie	0-1	0-0	0-0	0-0	1-0	0-0	0-1	0-0	0-0	0-0	1-0	0-0	0-0	2-2
Hamilton	0-2	1-0	0-1	1-2	0-0	1-0	0-0	1-1	1-0	0-1	0-1	1-1	0-0	6-9
Hermanson	0-0	1-0	0-0	0-0	0-0	0-0	1-0	0-0	0-0	0-1	0-0	1-0	0-0	3-1
Hoffman	0-0	0-0	1-1	0-0	0-0	0-0	0-0	1-0	1-2	3-0	0-0	1-0	0-1	7-4
Kroon	0-0	0-0	0-0	0-0	0-0	0-1	0-0	0-0	0-0	0-0	0-0	0-0	0-0	0-1
Mauser	0-0	0-0	0-0	0-1	0-0	0-0	0-0	0-0	0-0	0-0	0-0	0-0	0-0	0-1
Sanders	0-0	0-1	1-0	0-1	0-0	0-0	1-0	2-0	1-1	0-0	0-0	0-1	0-1	5-5
Valenzuela	0-0	1-0	0-0	0-0	0-0	0-1	0-1	0-0	1-0	3-0	2-0	0-0	1-1	8-3
Villone	0-0	0-0	0-0	0-0	0-0	0-0	0-0	0-1	0-0	0-0	1-0	0-0	1-0	2-1
B. Williams	0-0	0-1	1-0	0-1	0-0	0-3	0-2	0-1	1-0	0-0	0-0	0-1	1-1	3-10
Worrell	0-0	0-0	0-0	0-0	0-0	0-0	1-0	0-0	0-0	0-0	0-0	0-0	0-0	1-0
Totals	2-5	7-5	6-3	4-9	2-3	4-7	6-7	5-7	7-6	6-6	8-4	7-5	6-7	70-74

NO-DECISIONS: Elliott, Krueger, Tabaka.

SAN FRANCISCO—67-77

Pitcher	Atl. W-L	Chi. W-L	Cin. W-L	Col. W-L	Fla. W-L	Hou. W-L	L.A. W-L	Mon. W-L	N.Y. W-L	Phi. W-L	Pit. W-L	St.L. W-L	S.D. W-L	Totals W-L
Aquino	0-0	0-0	0-1	0-0	0-0	0-0	0-0	0-0	0-0	0-0	0-0	0-0	0-0	0-1
Barton	0-0	0-0	1-0	1-0	0-0	0-0	0-0	1-0	1-0	0-0	0-0	0-0	0-1	4-1
Bautista	0-0	0-1	0-0	0-2	0-1	0-0	0-1	2-1	0-1	0-1	0-0	1-0	0-0	3-8
Beck	0-2	0-0	0-0	0-0	0-1	0-0	0-1	0-0	0-1	1-1	2-0	2-0	0-0	5-6
Brewington	1-0	0-0	0-0	2-0	1-0	0-0	0-1	1-0	0-0	0-1	0-1	1-1	0-0	6-4
Burba	0-1	0-0	1-0	0-0	0-0	0-0	0-1	1-0	1-0	0-0	1-0	0-0	0-0	4-2
Dewey	0-0	0-0	0-0	0-0	0-0	0-0	0-0	0-0	1-0	0-0	0-0	0-0	0-0	1-0
Estes	0-0	0-0	0-0	0-1	0-0	0-0	0-0	0-0	0-0	0-0	0-1	0-0	0-1	0-3
Frey	0-0	0-0	0-0	0-0	0-0	0-0	0-0	0-0	0-0	0-0	0-0	0-1	0-0	0-1

Pitcher	Atl. W-L	Chi. W-L	Cin. W-L	Col. W-L	Fla. W-L	Hou. W-L	L.A. W-L	Mon. W-L	N.Y. W-L	Phi. W-L	Pit. W-L	St.L. W-L	S.D. W-L	Totals W-L
Greer	0-1	0-0	0-0	0-0	0-0	0-1	0-0	0-0	0-0	0-0	0-0	0-0	0-0	0-2
Hook	0-0	0-0	0-0	0-0	0-0	2-0	1-0	0-0	1-0	0-1	0-0	0-0	1-0	5-1
Leiter	0-0	0-3	1-1	0-2	1-0	1-0	2-1	0-3	1-0	2-0	0-1	1-1	1-0	10-12
Mintz	0-0	1-0	0-0	0-0	0-0	0-0	0-0	0-1	0-0	0-0	0-1	0-0	0-0	1-2
Mulholland	0-2	1-1	0-1	0-2	0-1	0-1	1-1	0-1	1-1	1-0	0-0	0-1	1-1	5-13
Portugal	0-1	2-0	0-0	0-0	0-1	0-1	0-1	0-0	1-0	0-0	1-0	1-0	1-0	5-5
Rosselli	0-0	0-0	0-0	0-0	0-0	0-0	0-0	0-0	0-0	0-0	1-0	0-0	1-1	2-1
Service	0-0	0-0	0-0	1-0	0-0	0-1	0-0	1-0	0-0	0-0	1-0	0-0	0-0	3-1
Torres	0-0	0-0	0-0	0-0	0-1	0-0	0-0	0-0	0-0	0-0	0-0	0-0	0-0	0-1
C. Valdez	0-0	0-0	0-0	0-0	0-0	0-0	0-0	0-0	0-0	0-1	0-0	0-0	0-0	0-1
S. Valdez	0-0	2-0	0-0	1-0	0-0	0-0	0-0	0-0	0-0	0-1	0-1	0-1	0-2	4-5
VanLandingham	0-0	1-0	0-0	0-0	0-0	0-0	1-1	0-0	0-0	1-0	1-0	1-1	1-0	6-3
Wilson	0-0	0-0	0-0	0-1	1-0	0-1	0-0	0-0	0-1	1-1	0-0	1-0	0-0	3-4
Totals	1-7	7-5	3-3	5-8	3-5	3-5	5-8	6-7	8-5	6-6	6-6	7-6	7-6	67-77

NO-DECISIONS: Burgos, Gomez, Roper.

HOME RUNS BY PARKS

	At Atl.	At Chi.	At Cin.	At Col.	At Fla.	At Hou.	At L.A.	At Mon.	At N.Y.	At Phi.	At Pit.	At S.D.	At S.F.	At St.L.	Totals 1995	Totals 1994
Atlanta	94	5	13	8	6	6	4	4	7	5	2	5	4	5	168	137
Chicago	8	83	2	12	9	6	5	1	8	3	6	5	5	5	158	109
Cincinnati	8	7	76	6	3	9	4	6	9	9	6	6	5	7	161	124
Colorado	8	4	6	134	7	6	3	5	1	5	5	10	2	4	200	125
Florida	4	7	6	13	68	6	2	3	4	10	10	0	9	2	144	94
Houston	9	13	1	5	3	41	1	3	6	1	7	6	6	7	109	120
Los Angeles	2	11	1	11	6	0	62	8	6	9	8	6	3	7	140	115
Montreal	6	9	6	6	7	3	4	43	3	12	4	4	10	1	118	108
New York	3	2	6	5	6	3	4	7	63	4	3	5	7	7	125	117
Philadelphia	7	0	1	2	3	1	2	6	4	51	4	5	5	3	94	80
Pittsburgh	2	6	5	7	3	4	4	0	2	5	69	8	8	2	125	80
San Diego	1	6	1	9	5	2	8	4	5	6	3	55	7	4	116	92
San Francisco	5	5	3	14	1	2	2	7	8	9	6	8	76	6	152	123
St. Louis	3	8	7	9	0	1	3	5	3	0	3	4	7	54	107	108
1995 total	160	166	134	241	128	89	110	98	131	129	136	127	154	114	1917	....
1994 total	98	118	124	120	116	113	96	89	113	85	106	108	130	116	....	1532

AT ATLANTA (160):

Atlanta (94)—McGriff 15, Justice 15, Klesko 15, Jones 15, Lopez 8, Blauser 7, Grissom 5, O'Brien 4, Lemke 3, Avery 2, Devereaux 2, Glavine 1, Smith 1, Oliva 1, Mordecai 1. **Chicago (8)**—Sosa 2, Roberson 2, Dunston 1, McRae 1, Wilkins 1, Hernandez 1. **Cincinnati (8)**—Gant 3, Larkin 2, Santiago 1, M. Lewis 1, R. Sanders 1. **Colorado (8)**—Galarraga 2, Burks 2, Walker 2, Girardi 1, Castilla 1. **Florida (4)**—Dawson 2, Pendleton 2. **Houston (9)**—Bell 2, Biggio 1, May 1, Gonzalez 1, Simms 1, Bagwell 1, Eusebio 1, Hunter 1. **Los Angeles (2)**—Wallach 1, Offerman 1. **Montreal (6)**—Cordero 2, Segui 1, Alou 1, Lansing 1, R. White 1. **New York (3)**—Hundley 1, Brogna 1, Bogar 1. **Philadelphia (7)**—Hayes 3, Daulton 1, Duncan 1, Jefferies 1, Whiten 1. **Pittsburgh (2)**—Bell 1, Merced 1. **St. Louis (3)**—Lankford 1, Gilkey 1, Cromer 1. **San Diego (1)**—Cianfrocco 1. **San Francisco (5)**—Bonds 1, Thompson 1, Carreon 1, Clayton 1, Phillips 1.

AT CHICAGO (166):

Atlanta (5)—Blauser 1, Justice 1, Grissom 1, Jones 1, Mordecai 1. **Chicago (83)**—Sosa 19, Dunston 8, Servais 7, Johnson 6, Zeile 6, McRae 6, Hernandez 6, Gonzalez 5, Timmons 5, Grace 4, Wilkins 3, Parent 2, Bullett 2, Roberson 2, Haney 1, Kmak 1. **Cincinnati (7)**—Boone 3, R. Sanders 2, Larkin 1, Taubensee 1. **Colorado (4)**—Walker 1, Young 1, Hubbard 1, Bates 1. **Florida (7)**—Browne 1, Gregg 1, Sheffield 1, Decker 1, Arias 1, Abbott 1, Johnson 1. **Houston (13)**—Biggio 3, May 2, Bagwell 2, Thompson 1, Shipley 1, Brumley 1, Gonzalez 1, Wilkins 1, Mouton 1. **Los Angeles (11)**—Karros 3, Wallach 2, Ashley 2, Kelly 1, DeShields 1, Piazza 1, Mondesi 1. **Montreal (9)**—R. White 2, Kelly 1, Alou 1, Berry 1, Cordero 1, Lansing 1, Tarasco 1, Andrews 1. **New York (2)**—Bonilla 1, Hundley 1. **Pittsburgh (6)**—Parent 1, King 1, Merced 1, C. Garcia 1, Neagle 1, Young 1. **St. Louis (8)**—Cooper 2, Caraballo 2, Lankford 1, Gilkey 1, Jordan 1, Urbani 1. **San Diego (6)**—Cedeno 2, Caminiti 1, Cianfrocco 1, Nieves 1, Johnson 1. **San Francisco (5)**—Hill 2, Williams 1, Carreon 1, Benjamin 1.

AT CINCINNATI (134):

Atlanta (13)—McGriff 3, Justice 2, Jones 2, O'Brien 1, Lemke 1, Grissom 1, Klesko 1, Mordecai 1, Perez 1. **Chicago (2)**—Grace 2. **Cincinnati (76)**—Gant 12, R. Sanders 9, Branson 9, Larkin 8, Santiago 7, Morris 6, Boone 6, Walton 4, Taubensee 4, Anthony 3, Duncan 2, Berryhill 2, Smiley 1, D. Sanders 1, Howard 1, M. Lewis 1. **Colorado (6)**—Bichette 2, Galarraga 1, Kingery 1, Castilla 1, Vander Wal 1. **Florida (6)**—Dawson 1, Pendleton 1, Morman 1, Sheffield 1, Conine 1, Johnson 1. **Houston (1)**—Simms 1. **Los Angeles (1)**—Hernandez 1. **Montreal (6)**—Alou 2, Fletcher 1, Tarasco 1, R. White 1, Benitez 1. **New York (7)**—Bonilla 1, Vizcaino 1, Hundley 1, C. Jones 1, Brogna 1, Alfonzo 1. **Philadelphia (1)**—Duncan 1. **Pittsburgh (5)**—Johnson 2, King 1, Merced 1, C. Garcia 1. **St. Louis (7)**—Mabry 2, Lankford 1, Gilkey 1, Jordan 1, Oliva 1, Bell 1. **San Diego (1)**—E. Williams 1. **San Francisco (3)**—Bonds 2, Benjamin 1.

AT COLORADO (241):

Atlanta (8)—McGriff 2, O'Brien 1, Blauser 1, Justice 1, Grissom 1, Klesko 1, Jones 1. **Chicago (12)**—Sosa 4, Grace 2, Zeile 1, McRae 1, Gonzalez 1, Wilkins 1, Hernandez 1, Foster 1. **Cincinnati (6)**—Gant 2, R. Sanders 2, Taubensee 1, Branson 1. **Colorado (134)**—Bichette 31, Walker 24, Castilla 23, Galarraga 18, Burks 8, Girardi 6, Young 5, Kingery 4, Bates 4, Owens 3, Vander Wal 2, Hubbard 2, Swift 1, Freeman 1, Pulliam 1, Mejia 1. **Florida (13)**—Dawson 2, Pendleton 2, Sheffield 2, Conine 2, Johnson 2, Carr 1, Colbrunn 1, Tavarez 1. **Houston (5)**—Biggio 2, Bagwell 1, Bell 1, Mouton 1. **Los Angeles (11)**—Piazza 3, Mondesi 3, Karros 2, Webster 1, Kelly 1, Hollandsworth 1. **Montreal (6)**—Andrews 2, Fletcher 1, Berry 1, Cordero 1, Lansing 1. **New York (5)**—Bonilla 1, Hundley 1, C. Jones 1, Kent 1, Brogna 1. **Philadelphia (2)**—Jefferies 1, Morandini 1. **Pittsburgh (7)**—Bell 2, King 2, Parent 1, Merced 1, Martin 1. **St. Louis (9)**—Gilkey 3, Sheaffer 2, Lankford 1, Jordan 1, Mabry 1, Sweeney 1. **San Diego (9)**—Plantier 2, Caminiti 2, Finley 1, Cianfrocco 1, Nieves 1, Ausmus 1. **San Francisco (14)**—Williams 5, Bonds 2, Carreon 2, Phillips 2, Aurilia 2, Benard 1.

AT FLORIDA (128):

Atlanta (6)—McGriff 2, Grissom 1, Klesko 1, Oliva 1, Lopez 1. **Chicago (9)**—Sosa 2, Hernandez 2, Johnson 1, Dunston 1, Grace 1, Zeile 1, Sanchez 1. **Cincinnati (3)**—Santiago 1, Morris 1, R. Sanders 1. **Colorado (7)**—Castilla 3, Burks 2, Walker 2. **Florida (68)**—Conine 13, Colbrunn 12, Abbott 12, Pendleton 8, Sheffield 4, Johnson 3, Gregg 2, Decker 2, Arias 2, Natal 2, Veras 2, Dawson 1, Morman 1, Carr 1, Hammond 1, Whitmore 1, Tavarez 1. **Houston (3)**—Magadan 1, Biggio 1, Gonzalez 1. **Los Angeles (6)**—Piazza 2, Mondesi 1, Kelly 1, Hollandsworth 1. **Montreal (7)**—Cordero 3, Berry 1, Tarasco 1, Andrews 1. **New York (6)**—Bonilla 2, Kent 2, C. Jones 1, Stinnett 1. **Philadelphia (4)**—Eisenreich 1, Van Slyke 1, Webster 1, Morandini 1. **Pittsburgh (3)**—Parent 2, Martin 1. **San Diego (5)**—E. Williams 1, Caminiti 1, Clark 1, Nieves 1, Petagine 1. **San Francisco (1)**—Hill 1.

1995 N.L. STATISTICS · Miscellaneous

AT HOUSTON (89):

Atlanta (6)—McGriff 1, Blauser 1, Justice 1, Grissom 1, Jones 1, Kelly 1. **Chicago (6)**—Grace 2, Sosa 1, McRae 1, Servais 1, Timmons 1. **Cincinnati (9)**—Gant 4, Santiago 1, Walton 1, M. Lewis 1, R. Sanders 1, Boone 1. **Colorado (3)**—Bates 2, Bichette 1. **Florida (6)**—Sheffield 3, Colbrunn 2, Conine 1. **Houston (41)**—Bagwell 10, Biggio 6, Simms 5, Eusebio 5, May 3, Bell 3, Cangelosi 2, Mouton 2, Shipley 1, Goff 1, Gonzalez 1, Servais 1, Miller 1. **Montreal (3)**—Alou 2, Fletcher 1. **New York (3)**—Bonilla 1, Buford 1, Stinnett 1. **Philadelphia (3)**—Whiten 2, Jefferies 1. **Pittsburgh (4)**—Clark 1, Bell 1, Liriano 1, Johnson 1. **St. Louis (1)**—Lankford 1. **San Diego (2)**—Gwynn 1, E. Williams 1. **San Francisco (2)**—Bonds 1, Hill 1.

AT LOS ANGELES (110):

Atlanta (4)—Lopez 2, Justice 1, Oliva 1. **Chicago (5)**—Sosa 3, Dunston 1, Grace 1. **Cincinnati (4)**—Boone 2, Morris 1, Branson 1. **Colorado (6)**—Galarraga 2, Bichette 2, Walker 2. **Florida (2)**—Colbrunn 1, Johnson 1. **Houston (1)**—May 1. **Los Angeles (62)**—Karros 19, Mondesi 13, Piazza 9, Ashley 6, Wallach 4, Hollandsworth 3, Kelly 2, DeShields 2, Offerman 2, Gwynn 1, Hernandez 1. **Montreal (4)**—Fletcher 1, Segui 1, Berry 1, Tarasco 1. **New York (4)**—Bonilla 2, Kent 1, Brogna 1. **Philadelphia (1)**—Eisenreich 1. **Pittsburgh (4)**—Clark 1, Liriano 1, King 1, Aude 1. **St. Louis (3)**—Jordan 2, Sweeney 1. **San Diego (8)**—Caminiti 3, Gwynn 1, Plantier 1, Cedeno 1, Livingstone 1, Nieves 1. **San Francisco (2)**—Bonds 2.

AT MONTREAL (98):

Atlanta (4)—O'Brien 1, Klesko 1, Lopez 1, Kelly 1. **Chicago (1)**—Dunston 1. **Cincinnati (6)**—Walton 2, Morris 1, Taubensee 1, R. Sanders 1, Boone 1. **Colorado (5)**—Galarraga 1, Kingery 1, Bichette 1, Walker 1, Castilla 1. **Florida (3)**—Sheffield 1, Johnson 1, Veras 1. **Houston (3)**—Biggio 1, Simms 1, Bagwell 1. **Los Angeles (8)**—Piazza 4, Mondesi 2, Wallach 1, DeShields 1. **Montreal (43)**—Tarasco 7, R. White 6, Berry 5, Segui 4, Alou 4, Lansing 4, Fletcher 3, Cordero 2, Andrews 2, Rodriguez 1, Laker 1, Floyd 1, Grudzielanek 1, Santangelo 1, Benitez 1. **New York (7)**—Hundley 2, Kent 2, Everett 2, Thompson 1. **Philadelphia (2)**—Jefferies 1, Hollins 1. **St. Louis (5)**—Oquendo 1, Pagnozzi 1, Zeile 1, Lankford 1, Jordan 1. **San Diego (4)**—Livingstone 2, Caminiti 1, Finley 1. **San Francisco (7)**—Bonds 3, Williams 2, Scarsone 2.

AT NEW YORK (131):

Atlanta (7)—Jones 2, McGriff 1, O'Brien 1, Smith 1, Klesko 1, Oliva 1. **Chicago (8)**—McRae 2, Dunston 1, Grace 1, Zeile 1, Servais 1, Hernandez 1, Sanchez 1. **Cincinnati (9)**—Gant 2, Taubensee 2, Morris 1, Harris 1, Anthony 1, Howard 1, R. Sanders 1. **Colorado (1)**—Galarraga 1. **Florida (4)**—Conine 3, Colbrunn 1. **Houston (6)**—Biggio 2, May 1, Bagwell 1, Hunter 1, Miller 1. **Los Angeles (6)**—Karros 2, Wallach 1, Prince 1, DeShields 1, Mondesi 1. **Montreal (3)**—Lansing 2, Segui 1. **New York (63)**—Brogna 13, Kent 11, Everett 9, Bonilla 7, Hundley 6, C. Jones 4, Thompson 3, Vizcaino 2, Segui 2, Buford 2, Huskey 2, Orsulak 1, Stinnett 1. **Philadelphia (6)**—Marsh 2, Van Slyke 1, Hayes 1, Webster 1, Whiten 1. **Pittsburgh (2)**—Merced 1, Johnson 1. **St. Louis (3)**—Sheaffer 1, Lankford 1, Jordan 1. **San Diego (5)**—Finley 2, Nieves 2, E. Williams 1. **San Francisco (8)**—Hill 2, Bonds 1, Thompson 1, Williams 1, Sanders 1, Clayton 1, Scarsone 1.

AT PHILADELPHIA (129):

Atlanta (5)—Lemke 1, Justice 1, Grissom 1, Klesko 1, Jones 1. **Chicago (3)**—Grace 1, Servais 1, Sanchez 1. **Cincinnati (9)**—R. Sanders 2, Duncan 1, Smiley 1, Gant 1, Worthington 1, Harris 1, Anthony 1, Boone 1. **Colorado (5)**—Galarraga 1, Bichette 1, Girardi 1, Vander Wal 1, Bates 1. **Florida (10)**—Dawson 2, Sheffield 2, Gregg 1, Conine 1, Colbrunn 1, Abbott 1, Johnson 1, Veras 1. **Houston (1)**—Gonzalez 1. **Los Angeles (9)**—Piazza 4, DeShields 2, Karros 2, Mondesi 1. **Montreal (12)**—Alou 2, Laker 2, Fletcher 1, Segui 1, Spehr 1, Silvestri 1, Tarasco 1, R. White 1, Andrews 1, Perez 1. **New York (4)**—Brogna 2, Everett 1, Stinnett 1. **Philadelphia (51)**—Daulton 7, Hayes 6, Eisenreich 5, Hollins 5, Whiten 5, Jefferies 4, Morandini 3, Dykstra 2, Flora 2, Longmire 2, Duncan 1, Elster 1, Gallagher 1, Webster 1, Olivares 1, Juden 1, Marsh 1, Green 1, Stocker 1, Jordan 1. **Pittsburgh (5)**—Parent 1, Liriano 1, Merced 1, Martin 1, Johnson 1. **San Diego (6)**—Gwynn 1, E. Williams 1, Caminiti 1, Livingstone 1, Nieves 1, Johnson 1. **San Francisco (9)**—Bonds 3, Thompson 2, Williams 2, Mulholland 1, Sanders 1.

AT PITTSBURGH (136):

Atlanta (2)—Klesko 2. **Chicago (6)**—Hernandez 2, McRae 1, Gonzalez 1, Wilkins 1, Bullett 1. **Cincinnati (6)**—R. Sanders 4, Gant 1, Branson 1. **Colorado (5)**—Kingery 1, Burks 1, Walker 1, Castilla 1, Owens 1. **Florida (10)**—Colbrunn 2, Abbott 2, Pendleton 1, Morman 1, Gregg 1, Sheffield 1, Conine 1, Veras 1. **Houston (7)**—Miller 3, Plantier 1, Gonzalez 1, Bagwell 1, Bell 1. **Los Angeles (8)**—Piazza 4, Busch 2, Kelly 1, Mondesi 1. **Montreal (4)**—Fletcher 1, Segui 1, Alou 1, Andrews 1. **New York (3)**—Hundley 2, Bonilla 1. **Philadelphia (4)**—Eisenreich 2, Jefferies 1, West 1. **Pittsburgh (69)**—Bell 8, Merced 8, Martin 8, King 7, Johnson 7, Parent 5, Young 5, Pegues 5, C. Garcia 4, Brumfield 4, Clark 2, Liriano 2, Encarnacion 2, Cummings 1, Aude 1. **St. Louis (3)**—Gilkey 1, Lankford 1. **San Diego (3)**—Valenzuela 1, E. Williams 1, Finley 1. **San Francisco (6)**—Carreon 5, Hill 1.

AT ST. LOUIS (114):

Atlanta (5)—Justice 2, McGriff 1, Blauser 1, Kelly 1. **Chicago (5)**—Buechele 1, Sosa 1, Servais 1, Haney 1, Timmons 1. **Cincinnati (7)**—Gant 2, R. Sanders 2, Morris 1, Walton 1, Hunter 1. **Colorado (4)**—Kingery 1, Bichette 1, Walker 1, Castilla 1. **Florida (2)**—Gregg 1, Johnson 1. **Houston (3)**—Biggio 1, Plantier 2, Simms 1, Tucker 1. **Los Angeles (7)**—Piazza 3, DeShields 1, Hansen 1, Karros 1, Mondesi 1. **Montreal (1)**—Berry 1. **New York (7)**—Bonilla 2, Butler 1, C. Jones 1, Kent 1, Brogna 1, Alfonzo 1. **Philadelphia (3)**—Hayes 1, Hollins 1, Longmire 1. **Pittsburgh (2)**—King 1, Martin 1. **St. Louis (54)**—Lankford 16, Jordan 14, Gilkey 5, Coles 3, Hemond 3, Sheaffer 2, Zeile 2, Cromer 2, Mabry 2, Pagnozzi 1, Cooper 1, Pena 1, Oliva 1, Bell 1. **San Diego (4)**—Gwynn 1, E. Williams 1, Cianfrocco 1, Ausmus 1. **San Francisco (6)**—Williams 2, Bonds 1, Hill 1, Carreon 1, Scarsone 1.

AT SAN DIEGO (127):

Atlanta (5)—McGriff 1, O'Brien 1, Blauser 1, Smith 1, Lopez 1. **Chicago (5)**—Sosa 3, Parent 1, Timmons 1. **Cincinnati (6)**—Larkin 2, R. Sanders 2, Gant 1, Boone 1. **Colorado (10)**—Galarraga 5, Walker 2, Burks 1, Weiss 1, Castilla 1. **Houston (6)**—Thompson 1, Magadan 1, Biggio 1, Plantier 1, Bagwell 1, Bell 1. **Los Angeles (6)**—Piazza 2, Karros 1, H. Rodriguez 1, Mondesi 1, Busch 1. **Montreal (4)**—Berry 2, Fletcher 1, Alou 1. **New York (5)**—Hundley 1, Kent 1, Brogna 1, Thompson 1, Buford 1. **Philadelphia (5)**—Daulton 1, Van Slyke 1, Jefferies 1, Whiten 1, Morandini 1. **Pittsburgh (8)**—Parent 4, Bell 1, King 1, Martin 1, Johnson 1. **St. Louis (4)**—Oquendo 1, Zeile 1, Gilkey 1, Jordan 1. **San Diego (55)**—Caminiti 16, Gwynn 5, Nieves 5, E. Williams 4, Reed 4, Finley 4, Cedeno 3, Roberts 2, Ausmus 2, Petagine 2, Valenzuela 1, Plantier 1, Livingstone 1, Cianfrocco 1, Clark 1, Newfield 1, Johnson 1, Holbert 1. **San Francisco (8)**—Hill 3, Bonds 1, Williams 1, Sanders 1, Clayton 1, Phillips 1.

AT SAN FRANCISCO (154):

Atlanta (4)—McGriff 1, Grissom 1, Oliva 1, Lopez 1. **Chicago (5)**—Grace 2, Dunston 1, Sosa 1, Servais 1. **Cincinnati (5)**—Larkin 2, Santiago 1, Gant 1, Howard 1. **Colorado (2)**—Bichette 1, Vander Wal 1. **Florida (9)**—Conine 3, Colbrunn 3, Diaz 1, Sheffield 1, Abbott 1. **Houston (6)**—Bagwell 3, Biggio 2, Shipley 1. **Los Angeles (3)**—Karros 2, Offerman 1. **Montreal (10)**—Tarasco 2, R. White 2, Fletcher 1, Segui 1, Berry 1, Silvestri 1, Cordero 1, Lansing 1. **New York (7)**—Thompson 2, Alfonzo 2, Kent 1, Brogna 1, Huskey 1. **Philadelphia (5)**—Eisenreich 1, Jefferies 1, Webster 1, Whiten 1, Jordan 1. **Pittsburgh (8)**—King 4, Parent 1, Merced 1, Cummings 1, Pegues 1. **St. Louis (7)**—Gilkey 3, Cromer 2, Zeile 1, Lankford 1. **San Diego (7)**—Nieves 2, E. Williams 1, Caminiti 1, Finley 1, Ausmus 1, Holbert 1. **San Francisco (76)**—Bonds 16, Hill 13, Williams 9, Carreon 7, Scarsone 7, Phillips 5, Thompson 4, Manwaring 4, Sanders 2, Clayton 2, Benzinger 1, Lampkin 1, Benjamin 1, Leonard 1, Lewis 1, Patterson 1, VanLandingham 1.

HISTORY

All-time results

Award winners

Hall of Fame

Team by team

ALL-TIME RESULTS

AMERICAN LEAGUE CHAMPIONS

Year	Team	Manager	Year	Team	Manager
1901	Chicago	Clark Griffith	1950	New York	Casey Stengel
1902	Philadelphia	Connie Mack	1951	New York	Casey Stengel
1903	Boston	Jimmy Collins	1952	New York	Casey Stengel
1904	Boston	Jimmy Collins	1953	New York	Casey Stengel
1905	Philadelphia	Connie Mack	1954	Cleveland	Al Lopez
1906	Chicago	Fielder Jones	1955	New York	Casey Stengel
1907	Detroit	Hugh Jennings	1956	New York	Casey Stengel
1908	Detroit	Hugh Jennings	1957	New York	Casey Stengel
1909	Detroit	Hugh Jennings	1958	New York	Casey Stengel
1910	Philadelphia	Connie Mack	1959	Chicago	Al Lopez
1911	Philadelphia	Connie Mack	1960	New York	Casey Stengel
1912	Boston	Jake Stahl	1961	New York	Ralph Houk
1913	Philadelphia	Connie Mack	1962	New York	Ralph Houk
1914	Philadelphia	Connie Mack	1963	New York	Ralph Houk
1915	Boston	Bill Carrigan	1964	New York	Yogi Berra
1916	Boston	Bill Carrigan	1965	Minnesota	Sam Mele
1917	Chicago	Pants Rowland	1966	Baltimore	Hank Bauer
1918	Boston	Ed Barrow	1967	Boston	Dick Williams
1919	Chicago	Kid Gleason	1968	Detroit	Mayo Smith
1920	Cleveland	Tris Speaker	1969	Baltimore (East Division)	Earl Weaver
1921	New York	Miller Huggins	1970	Baltimore (East Division)	Earl Weaver
1922	New York	Miller Huggins	1971	Baltimore (East Division)	Earl Weaver
1923	New York	Miller Huggins	1972	Oakland (West Division)	Dick Williams
1924	Washington	Bucky Harris	1973	Oakland (West Division)	Dick Williams
1925	Washington	Bucky Harris	1974	Oakland (West Division)	Al Dark
1926	New York	Miller Huggins	1975	Boston (East Division)	Darrell Johnson
1927	New York	Miller Huggins	1976	New York (East Division)	Billy Martin
1928	New York	Miller Huggins	1977	New York (East Division)	Billy Martin
1929	Philadelphia	Connie Mack	1978	New York (East Division)	Billy Martin, Bob Lemon
1930	Philadelphia	Connie Mack	1979	Baltimore (East Division)	Earl Weaver
1931	Philadelphia	Connie Mack	1980	Kansas City (West Division)	Jim Frey
1932	New York	Joe McCarthy	1981	New York (East Division)	Gene Michael, Bob Lemon
1933	Washington	Joe Cronin	1982	Milwaukee (East Division)	Buck Rodgers, Harvey Kuenn
1934	Detroit	Mickey Cochrane	1983	Baltimore (East Division)	Joe Altobelli
1935	Detroit	Mickey Cochrane	1984	Detroit (East Division)	Sparky Anderson
1936	New York	Joe McCarthy	1985	Kansas City (West Division)	Dick Howser
1937	New York	Joe McCarthy	1986	Boston (East Division)	John McNamara
1938	New York	Joe McCarthy	1987	Minnesota (West Division)	Tom Kelly
1939	New York	Joe McCarthy	1988	Oakland (West Division)	Tony La Russa
1940	Detroit	Del Baker	1989	Oakland (West Division)	Tony La Russa
1941	New York	Joe McCarthy	1990	Oakland (West Division)	Tony La Russa
1942	New York	Joe McCarthy	1991	Minnesota (West Division)	Tom Kelly
1943	New York	Joe McCarthy	1992	Toronto (East Division)	Cito Gaston
1944	St. Louis	Luke Sewell	1993	Toronto (East Division)	Cito Gaston
1945	Detroit	Steve O'Neill	1994	None†	
1946	Boston	Joe Cronin	1995	Cleveland (Central Division)	Mike Hargrove
1947	New York	Bucky Harris			
1948	Cleveland*	Lou Boudreau			
1949	New York	Casey Stengel			

*Defeated Boston in one-game playoff. †New York finished the strike-shortened season with the league's best record.

NATIONAL LEAGUE CHAMPIONS

Year	Team	Manager	Year	Team	Manager
1876	Chicago	Albert Spalding	1899	Brooklyn	Edward Hanlon
1877	Boston	Harry Wright	1900	Brooklyn	Edward Hanlon
1878	Boston	Harry Wright	1901	Pittsburgh	Fred Clarke
1879	Providence	George Wright	1902	Pittsburgh	Fred Clarke
1880	Chicago	Adrian Anson	1903	Pittsburgh	Fred Clarke
1881	Chicago	Adrian Anson	1904	New York	John McGraw
1882	Chicago	Adrian Anson	1905	New York	John McGraw
1883	Boston	John Morrill	1906	Chicago	Frank Chance
1884	Providence	Frank Bancroft	1907	Chicago	Frank Chance
1885	Chicago	Adrian Anson	1908	Chicago	Frank Chance
1886	Chicago	Adrian Anson	1909	Pittsburgh	Fred Clarke
1887	Detroit	William Watkins	1910	Chicago	Frank Chance
1888	New York	James Mutrie	1911	New York	John McGraw
1889	New York	James Mutrie	1912	New York	John McGraw
1890	Brooklyn	William McGunnigle	1913	New York	John McGraw
1891	Boston	Frank Selee	1914	Boston	George Stallings
1892	Boston	Frank Selee	1915	Philadelphia	Pat Moran
1893	Boston	Frank Selee	1916	Brooklyn	Wilbert Robinson
1894	Baltimore	Edward Hanlon	1917	New York	John McGraw
1895	Baltimore	Edward Hanlon	1918	Chicago	Fred Mitchell
1896	Baltimore	Edward Hanlon	1919	Cincinnati	Pat Moran
1897	Boston	Frank Selee	1920	Brooklyn	Wilbert Robinson
1898	Boston	Frank Selee	1921	New York	John McGraw

Year	Team	Manager
1922	New York	John McGraw
1923	New York	John McGraw
1924	New York	John McGraw
1925	Pittsburgh	Bill McKechnie
1926	St. Louis	Rogers Hornsby
1927	Pittsburgh	Donie Bush
1928	St. Louis	Bill McKechnie
1929	Chicago	Joe McCarthy
1930	St. Louis	Gabby Street
1931	St. Louis	Gabby Street
1932	Chicago	Charlie Grimm
1933	New York	Bill Terry
1934	St. Louis	Frank Frisch
1935	Chicago	Charlie Grimm
1936	New York	Bill Terry
1937	New York	Bill Terry
1938	Chicago	Gabby Hartnett
1939	Cincinnati	Bill McKechnie
1940	Cincinnati	Bill McKechnie
1941	Brooklyn	Leo Durocher
1942	St. Louis	Billy Southworth
1943	St. Louis	Billy Southworth
1944	St. Louis	Billy Southworth
1945	Chicago	Charlie Grimm
1946	St. Louis*	Eddie Dyer
1947	Brooklyn	Burt Shotton
1948	Boston	Billy Southworth
1949	Brooklyn	Burt Shotton
1950	Philadelphia	Eddie Sawyer
1951	New York†	Leo Durocher
1952	Brooklyn	Charlie Dressen
1953	Brooklyn	Charlie Dressen
1954	New York	Leo Durocher
1955	Brooklyn	Walter Alston
1956	Brooklyn	Walter Alston
1957	Milwaukee	Fred Haney
1958	Milwaukee	Fred Haney
1959	Los Angeles‡	Walter Alston
1960	Pittsburgh	Danny Murtaugh
1961	Cincinnati	Fred Hutchinson

Year	Team	Manager
1962	San Francisco§	Al Dark
1963	Los Angeles	Walter Alston
1964	St. Louis	Johnny Keane
1965	Los Angeles	Walter Alston
1966	Los Angeles	Walter Alston
1967	St. Louis	Red Schoendienst
1968	St. Louis	Red Schoendienst
1969	New York (East Division)	Gil Hodges
1970	Cincinnati (West Division)	Sparky Anderson
1971	Pittsburgh (East Division)	Danny Murtaugh
1972	Cincinnati (West Division)	Sparky Anderson
1973	New York (East Division)	Yogi Berra
1974	Los Angeles (West Division)	Walter Alston
1975	Cincinnati (West Division)	Sparky Anderson
1976	Cincinnati (West Division)	Sparky Anderson
1977	Los Angeles (West Division)	Tommy Lasorda
1978	Los Angeles (West Division)	Tommy Lasorda
1979	Pittsburgh (East Division)	Chuck Tanner
1980	Philadelphia (East Division)	Dallas Green
1981	Los Angeles (West Division)	Tommy Lasorda
1982	St. Louis (East Division)	Whitey Herzog
1983	Philadelphia (East Division)	Pat Corrales, Paul Owens
1984	San Diego (West Division)	Dick Williams
1985	St. Loius (East Division)	Whitey Herzog
1986	New York (East Division)	Dave Johnson
1987	St. Louis (East Division)	Whitey Herzog
1988	Los Angeles (West Division)	Tommy Lasorda
1989	San Francisco (West Division)	Roger Craig
1990	Cincinnati (West Division)	Lou Piniella
1991	Atlanta (West Division)	Bobby Cox
1992	Atlanta (West Division)	Bobby Cox
1993	Philadelphia (East Division)	Jim Fregosi
1994	None∞	
1995	Atlanta (East Division)	Bobby Cox

*Defeated Brooklyn, two games to none, in playoff for pennant
†Defeated Brooklyn, two games to one, in playoff for pennant.
‡Defeated Milwaukee, two games to none, in playoff for pennant.
§Defeated Los Angeles, two games to one, in playoff for pennant.
∞Montreal finished the strike-shortened season with the league's best record.

WORLD SERIES

Year	Winner	Loser	Games
1903	Boston A.L.	Pittsburgh N.L.	5-3
1904	No Series		
1905	New York N.L.	Philadelphia A.L.	4-1
1906	Chicago A.L.	Chicago N.L.	4-2
1907	Chicago N.L.	Detroit A.L.	*4-0
1908	Chicago N.L.	Detroit A.L.	4-1
1909	Pittsburgh N.L.	Detroit A.L.	4-3
1910	Philadelphia A.L.	Chicago N.L.	4-1
1911	Philadelphia A.L.	New York N.L.	4-2
1912	Boston A.L.	New York N.L.	*4-3
1913	Philadelphia A.L.	New York N.L.	4-1
1914	Boston N.L.	Philadelphia A.L.	4-0
1915	Boston A.L.	Philadelphia N.L.	4-1
1916	Boston A.L.	Brooklyn N.L.	4-1
1917	Chicago A.L.	New York N.L.	4-2
1918	Boston A.L.	Chicago N.L.	4-2
1919	Cincinnati N.L.	Chicago A.L.	5-3
1920	Cleveland A.L.	Brooklyn N.L.	5-2
1921	New York N.L.	New York A.L.	5-3
1922	New York N.L.	New York A.L.	*4-0
1923	New York A.L.	New York N.L.	4-2
1924	Washington A.L.	New York N.L.	4-3
1925	Pittsburgh N.L.	Washington A.L.	4-3
1926	St. Louis N.L.	New York A.L.	4-3
1927	New York A.L.	Pittsburgh, N.L.	4-0
1928	New York A.L.	St. Louis N.L.	4-0
1929	Philadelphia A.L.	Chicago N.L.	4-1
1930	Philadelphia A.L.	St. Louis N.L.	4-2
1931	St. Louis N.L.	Philadelphia A.L.	4-3
1932	New York A.L.	Chicago N.L.	4-0
1933	New York N.L.	Washington A.L.	4-1
1934	St. Louis N.L.	Detroit A.L.	4-3
1935	Detroit A.L.	Chicago N.L.	4-2
1936	New York A.L.	New York N.L.	4-2
1937	New York A.L.	New York N.L.	4-1
1938	New York A.L.	Chicago N.L.	4-0

Year	Winner	Loser	Games
1939	New York A.L.	Cincinnati N.L.	4-0
1940	Cincinnati N.L.	Detroit A.L.	4-3
1941	New York A.L.	Brooklyn N.L.	4-1
1942	St. Louis N.L.	New York A.L.	4-1
1943	New York A.L.	St. Louis N.L.	4-1
1944	St. Louis N.L.	St. Louis A.L.	4-2
1945	Detroit A.L.	Chicago N.L.	4-3
1946	St. Louis N.L.	Boston A.L.	4-3
1947	New York A.L.	Brooklyn, N.L.	4-3
1948	Cleveland A.L.	Boston N.L.	4-2
1949	New York A.L.	Brooklyn N.L.	4-1
1950	New York A.L.	Philadelphia N.L.	4-0
1951	New York A.L.	New York N.L.	4-2
1952	New York A.L.	Brooklyn N.L.	4-3
1953	New York A.L.	Brooklyn N.L.	4-2
1954	New York N.L.	Cleveland A.L.	4-0
1955	Brooklyn N.L.	New York A.L.	4-3
1956	New York A.L.	Brooklyn N.L.	4-3
1957	Milwaukee N.L.	New York A.L.	4-3
1958	New York A.L.	Milwaukee N.L.	4-3
1959	Los Angeles N.L.	Chicago A.L.	4-2
1960	Pittsburgh N.L.	New York A.L.	4-3
1961	New York A.L.	Cincinnati N.L.	4-1
1962	New York A.L.	San Francisco N.L.	4-3
1963	Los Angeles N.L.	New York A.L.	4-0
1964	St. Louis N.L.	New York A.L.	4-3
1965	Los Angeles N.L.	Minnesota A.L.	4-3
1966	Baltimore A.L.	Los Angeles N.L.	4-0
1967	St. Louis N.L.	Boston A.L.	4-3
1968	Detroit A.L.	St. Louis N.L.	4-3
1969	New York N.L.	Baltimore A.L.	4-1
1970	Baltimore A.L.	Cincinnati N.L.	4-1
1971	Pittsburgh N.L.	Baltimore A.L.	4-3
1972	Oakland A.L.	Cincinnati N.L.	4-3
1973	Oakland A.L.	New York N.L.	4-3
1974	Oakland A.L.	Los Angeles N.L.	4-1

Year	Winner	Loser	Games
1975—Cincinnati N.L.	Boston A.L.		4-3
1976—Cincinnati N.L.	New York A.L.		4-0
1977—New York A.L.	Los Angeles N.L.		4-2
1978—New York A.L.	Los Angeles N.L.		4-2
1979—Pittsburgh N.L.	Baltimore A.L.		4-3
1980—Philadelphia N.L.	Kansas City A.L.		4-2
1981—Los Angeles N.L.	New York A.L.		4-2
1982—St. Louis N.L.	Milwaukee A.L.		4-3
1983—Baltimore A.L.	Philadelphia N.L.		4-1
1984—Detroit A.L.	San Diego N.L.		4-1
1985—Kansas City A.L.	St. Louis N.L.		4-3

Year	Winner	Loser	Games
1986—New York N.L.	Boston A.L.		4-3
1987—Minnesota A.L.	St. Louis N.L.		4-3
1988—Los Angeles N.L.	Oakland A.L.		4-1
1989—Oakland A.L.	San Francisco N.L.		4-0
1990—Cincinnati N.L.	Oakland A.L.		4-0
1991—Minnesota A.L.	Atlanta N.L.		4-3
1992—Toronto A.L.	Atlanta N.L.		4-2
1993—Toronto A.L.	Philadelphia N.L.		4-2
1994—No Series			
1995—Atlanta N.L.	Cleveland A.L.		4-2

*Includes tie game.

DIVISION SERIES

AMERICAN LEAGUE

Year	Winner (Division)	Loser (Division)	Games
1981—New York (East)	Milwaukee (East)		3-2
Oakland (West)	Kansas City (West)		3-0
1995—Cleveland (Central)	Boston (East)		3-0
Seattle (West)	New York* (East)		3-2

NATIONAL LEAGUE

Year	Winner (Division)	Loser (Division)	Games
1981—Montreal (East)	Philadelphia (East)		3-2
Los Angeles (West)	Houston (West)		3-2
1995—Atlanta (East)	Colorado* (West)		3-1
Cincinnati (Central)	Los Angeles (West)		3-0

*Wild-card team.

CHAMPIONSHIP SERIES

AMERICAN LEAGUE

Year	Winner (Division)	Loser (Division)	Games
1969—Baltimore (East)	Minnesota (West)		3-0
1970—Baltimore (East)	Minnesota (West)		3-0
1971—Baltimore (East)	Oakland (West)		3-0
1972—Oakland (West)	Detroit (East)		3-2
1973—Oakland (West)	Baltimore (East)		3-2
1974—Oakland (West)	Baltimore (East)		3-1
1975—Boston (East)	Oakland (West)		3-0
1976—New York (East)	Kansas City (West)		3-2
1977—New York (East)	Kansas City (West)		3-2
1978—New York (East)	Kansas City (West)		3-1
1979—Baltimore (East)	California (West)		3-1
1980—Kansas City (West)	New York (East)		3-0
1981—New York (East)	Oakland (West)		3-0
1982—Milwaukee (East)	California (West)		3-2
1983—Baltimore (East)	Chicago (West)		3-1
1984—Detroit (East)	Kansas City (West)		3-0
1985—Kansas City (West)	Toronto (East)		4-3
1986—Boston (East)	California (West)		4-3
1987—Minnesota (West)	Detroit (East)		4-1
1988—Oakland (West)	Boston (East)		4-0
1989—Oakland (West)	Toronto (East)		4-1
1990—Oakland (West)	Boston (East)		4-0
1991—Minnesota (West)	Toronto (East)		4-1
1992—Toronto (East)	Oakland (West)		4-2
1993—Toronto (East)	Chicago (West)		4-2
1994—No series			
1995—Cleveland (Central)	Seattle (West)		4-2

NATIONAL LEAGUE

Year	Winner (Division)	Loser (Division)	Games
1969—New York (East)	Atlanta (West)		3-0
1970—Cincinnati (West)	Pittsburgh (East)		3-0
1971—Pittsburgh (East)	San Francisco (West)		3-1
1972—Cincinnati (West)	Pittsburgh (East)		3-2
1973—New York (East)	Cincinnati (West)		3-2
1974—Los Angeles (West)	Pittsburgh (East)		3-1
1975—Cincinnati (West)	Pittsburgh (East)		3-0
1976—Cincinnati (West)	Philadelphia (East)		3-0
1977—Los Angeles (West)	Philadelphia (East)		3-1
1978—Los Angeles (West)	Philadelphia (East)		3-1
1979—Pittsburgh (East)	Cincinnati (West)		3-0
1980—Philadelphia (East)	Houston (West)		3-2
1981—Los Angeles (West)	Montreal (East)		3-2
1982—St. Louis (East)	Atlanta (West)		3-0
1983—Philadelphia (East)	Los Angeles (West)		3-1
1984—San Diego (West)	Chicago (East)		3-2
1985—St. Louis (East)	Los Angeles (West)		4-2
1986—New York (East)	Houston (West)		4-2
1987—St. Louis (East)	San Francisco (West)		4-3
1988—Los Angeles (West)	New York (East)		4-3
1989—San Francisco (West)	Chicago (East)		4-1
1990—Cincinnati (West)	Pittsburgh (East)		4-2
1991—Atlanta (West)	Pittsburgh (East)		4-3
1992—Atlanta (West)	Pittsburgh (East)		4-3
1993—Philadelphia (East)	Atlanta (West)		4-2
1994—No series			
1995—Atlanta (East)	Cincinnati (Central)		4-0

ALL-STAR GAME

Date	Site	Score (Winner)	Winning pitcher (Losing pitcher)	Winning manager (Losing manager)	Att.
7-6-33	Comiskey Park Chicago	4-2 (A.L.)	Lefty Gomez, Yankees (Bill Hallahan, Cardinals)	Connie Mack, Athletics (John McGraw, Giants)	47,595
7-10-34	Polo Grounds New York	9-7 (A.L.)	Mel Harder, Indians (Van Mungo, Dodgers)	Joe Cronin, Senators (Bill Terry, Giants)	48,363
7-8-35	Municipal Stadium Cleveland	4-1 (A.L.)	Lefty Gomez, Yankees (Bill Walker, Cardinals)	Mickey Cochrane, Tigers (Frankie Frisch, Cardinals)	69,831
7-7-36	Braves Field Boston	4-3 (N.L.)	Dizzy Dean, Cardinals (Lefty Grove, Red Sox)	Charlie Grimm, Cubs (Joe McCarthy, Yankees)	25,556
7-7-37	Griffith Stadium Washington	8-3 (A.L.)	Lefty Gomez, Yankees (Dizzy Dean, Cardinals)	Joe McCarthy, Yankees (Bill Terry, Giants)	31,391
7-6-38	Crosley Field Cincinnati	4-1 (N.L.)	Johnny Vander Meer, Reds (Lefty Gomez, Yankees)	Bill Terry, Giants (Joe McCarthy, Yankees)	27,067
7-11-39	Yankee Stadium New York	3-1 (A.L.)	Tommy Bridges, Tigers (Bill Lee, Cubs)	Joe McCarthy, Yankees (Gabby Hartnett, Cubs)	62,892
7-9-40	Sportsman's Park St. Louis	4-0 (N.L.)	Paul Derringer, Reds (Red Ruffing, Yankees)	Bill McKechnie, Reds (Joe Cronin, Red Sox)	32,373

Date	Site	Score (Winner)	Winning pitcher (Losing pitcher)	Winning manager (Losing manager)	Att.
7-8-41	Briggs Stadium	7-5	Ed Smith, White Sox	Del Baker, Tigers	54,674
	Detroit	(A.L.)	(Claude Passeau, Cubs)	(Bill McKechnie, Reds)	
7-6-42	Polo Grounds	3-1	Spud Chandler, Yankees	Joe McCarthy, Yankees	34,178
	New York	(A.L.)	(Mort Cooper, Cardinals)	(Leo Durocher, Dodgers)	
7-13-43	Shibe Park	5-3	Dutch Leonard, Senators	Joe McCarthy, Yankees	31,938
	Philadelphia	(A.L.)	(Mort Cooper, Cardinals)	(Billy Southworth, Cardinals)	
7-11-44	Forbes Field	7-1	Ken Raffensberger, Phillies	Billy Southworth, Cardinals	29,589
	Pittsburgh	(N.L.)	(Tex Hughson, Red Sox)	(Joe McCarthy, Yankees)	
1945	No game played.				
7-9-46	Fenway Park	12-0	Bob Feller, Indians	Steve O'Neill, Tigers	34,906
	Boston	(A.L.)	(Claude Passeau, Cubs)	(Charlie Grimm, Cubs)	
7-8-47	Wrigley Field	2-1	Frank Shea, Red Sox	Joe Cronin, Red Sox	41,123
	Chicago	(A.L.)	(Johnny Sain, Braves)	(Eddie Dyer, Cardinals)	
7-13-48	Sportsman's Park	5-2	Vic Raschi, Yankees	Bucky Harris, Yankees	34,009
	St. Louis	(A.L.)	(Johnny Schmitz, Cubs)	(Leo Durocher, Dodgers)	
7-12-49	Ebbets Field	11-7	Virgil Trucks, Tigers	Lou Boudreau, Indians	32,577
	Brooklyn	(A.L.)	(Don Newcombe, Dodgers)	(Billy Southworth, Braves)	
7-11-50	Comiskey Park	4-3*	Ewell Blackwell, Reds	Burt Shotton, Dodgers	46,127
	Chicago	(N.L.)	(Ted Gray, Tigers)	(Casey Stengel, Yankees)	
7-10-51	Briggs Stadium	8-3	Sal Maglie, Giants	Eddie Sawyer, Phillies	52,075
	Detroit	(N.L.)	(Ed Lopat, Yankees)	(Casey Stengel, Yankees)	
7-8-52	Shibe Park	3-2†	Bob Rush, Cubs	Leo Durocher, Giants	32,785
	Philadelphia	(N.L.)	(Bob Lemon, Indians)	(Casey Stengel, Yankees)	
7-14-53	Crosley Field	5-1	Warren Spahn, Braves	Chuck Dressen, Dodgers	30,846
	Cincinnati	(N.L.)	(Allie Reynolds, Yankees)	(Casey Stengel, Yankees)	
7-13-54	Municipal Stadium	11-9	Dean Stone, Senators	Casey Stengel, Yankees	68,751
	Cleveland	(A.L.)	(Gene Conley, Braves)	(Walter Alston, Dodgers)	
7-12-55	Milwaukee Co. Stadium	6-5‡	Gene Conley, Braves	Leo Durocher, Giants	45,643
	Milwaukee	(N.L.)	(Frank Sullivan, Red Sox)	(Al Lopez, Indians)	
7-10-56	Griffith Stadium	7-3	Bob Friend, Pirates	Walter Alston, Dodgers	28,843
	Washington	(N.L.)	(Billy Pierce, White Sox)	(Casey Stengel, Yankees)	
7-9-57	Busch Stadium	6-5	Jim Bunning, Tigers	Casey Stengel, Yankees	30,693
	St. Louis	(A.L.)	(Curt Simmons, Phillies)	(Walter Alston, Dodgers)	
7-8-58	Memorial Stadium	4-3	Early Wynn, White Sox	Casey Stengel, Yankees	48,829
	Baltimore	(A.L.)	(Bob Friend, Pirates)	(Fred Haney, Braves)	
7-7-59	Forbes Field	5-4	Johnny Antonelli, Giants	Fred Haney, Braves	35,277
	Pittsburgh	(N.L.)	(Whitey Ford, Yankees)	(Casey Stengel, Yankees)	
8-3-59	Memorial Coliseum	5-3	Jerry Walker, Orioles	Casey Stengel, Yankees	55,105
	Los Angeles	(A.L.)	(Don Drysdale, Dodgers)	(Fred Haney, Braves)	
7-11-60	Municipal Stadium	5-3	Bob Friend, Pirates	Walter Alston, Dodgers	30,619
	Kansas City	(N.L.)	(Bill Monbouquette, Red Sox)	(Al Lopez, White Sox)	
7-13-60	Yankee Stadium	6-0	Vernon Law, Pirates	Walter Alston, Dodgers	38,362
	New York	(N.L.)	(Whitey Ford, Yankees)	(Al Lopez, White Sox)	
7-11-61	Candlestick Park	5-4§	Stu Miller, Giants	Danny Murtaugh, Pirates	44,115
	San Francisco	(N.L.)	(Hoyt Wilhelm, Orioles)	(Paul Richards, Orioles)	
7-31-61	Fenway Park	1-1		Paul Richards, Orioles (A.L.)	31,851
	Boston	(tie)		Danny Murtaugh, Pirates (N.L.)	
7-10-62	District of Col. Stad.	3-1	Juan Marichal, Giants	Fred Hutchinson, Reds	45,480
	Washington	(N.L.)	(Camilo Pascual, Twins)	(Ralph Houk, Yankees)	
7-30-62	Wrigley Field	9-4	Ray Herbert, White Sox	Ralph Houk, Yankees	38,359
	Chicago	(A.L.)	(Art Mahaffey, Phillies)	(Fred Hutchinson, Reds)	
7-9-63	Municipal Stadium	5-3	Larry Jackson, Cubs	Alvin Dark, Giants	44,160
	Cleveland	(N.L.)	(Jim Bunning, Tigers)	(Ralph Houk, Yankees)	
7-7-64	Shea Stadium	7-4	Juan Marichal, Giants	Walter Alston, Dodgers	50,850
	New York	(N.L.)	(Dick Radatz, Red Sox)	(Al Lopez, White Sox)	
7-13-65	Metropolitan Stadium	6-5	Sandy Koufax, Dodgers	Gene Mauch, Phillies	46,706
	Bloomington, Minn.	(N.L.)	(Sam McDowell, Indians)	(Al Lopez, White Sox)	
7-12-66	Busch Stadium	2-1§	Gaylord Perry, Giants	Walter Alston, Dodgers	49,936
	St. Louis	(N.L.)	(Pete Richert, Senators)	(Sam Mele, Twins)	
7-11-67	Anaheim Stadium	2-1∞	Don Drysdale, Dodgers	Walter Alston, Dodgers	46,309
	Anaheim, Calif.	(N.L.)	(Jim Hunter, Athletics)	(Hank Bauer, Orioles)	
7-9-68	Astrodome	1-0	Don Drysdale, Dodgers	Red Schoendienst, Cardinals	48,321
	Houston	(N.L.)	(Luis Tiant, Indians)	(Dick Williams, Red Sox)	
7-23-69	R.F.K. Stadium	9-3	Steve Carlton, Cardinals	Red Schoendienst, Cardinals	45,259
	Washington	(N.L.)	(Mel Stottlemyre, Yankees)	(Mayo Smith, Tigers)	
7-14-70	Riverfront Stadium	5-4‡	Claude Osteen, Dodgers	Gil Hodges, Mets	51,838
	Cincinnati	(N.L.)	(Clyde Wright, Angels)	(Earl Weaver, Orioles)	
7-13-71	Tiger Stadium	6-4	Vida Blue, Athletics	Earl Weaver, Orioles	53,559
	Detroit	(A.L.)	(Dock Ellis, Pirates)	(Sparky Anderson, Reds)	
7-25-72	Atlanta Stadium	4-3∞	Tug McGraw, Mets	Danny Murtaugh, Pirates	53,107
	Atlanta	(N.L.)	(Dave McNally, Orioles)	(Earl Weaver, Orioles)	
7-24-73	Royals Stadium	7-1	Rick Wise, Cardinals	Sparky Anderson, Reds	40,849
	Kansas City	(N.L.)	(Bert Blyleven, Twins)	(Dick Williams, Athletics)	
7-23-74	Three Rivers Stadium	7-2	Ken Brett, Pirates	Yogi Berra, Mets	50,706
	Pittsburgh	(N.L.)	(Luis Tiant, Red Sox)	(Dick Williams, Athletics)	
7-15-75	Milwaukee Co. Stadium	6-3	Jon Matlack, Mets	Walter Alston, Dodgers	51,480
	Milwaukee	(N.L.)	(Jim Hunter, Yankees)	(Alvin Dark, Athletics)	

Date	Site	Score (Winner)	Winning pitcher (Losing pitcher)	Winning manager (Losing manager)	Att.
7-13-76	Veterans Stadium Philadelphia	7-1 (N.L)	Randy Jones, Padres (Mark Fidrych, Tigers)	Sparky Anderson, Reds (Darrell Johnson, Red Sox)	63,974
7-19-77	Yankee Stadium New York	7-5 (N.L.)	Don Sutton, Dodgers (Jim Palmer, Orioles)	Sparky Anderson, Reds (Billy Martin, Yankees)	56,683
7-11-78	San Diego Stadium San Diego	7-3 (N.L.)	Bruce Sutter, Cubs (Rich Gossage, Yankees)	Tommy Lasorda, Dodgers (Billy Martin, Yankees)	51,549
7-17-79	Kingdome Seattle	7-6 (N.L.)	Bruce Sutter, Cubs (Jim Kern, Rangers)	Tommy Lasorda, Dodgers (Bob Lemon, Yankees)	58,905
7-8-80	Dodger Stadium Los Angeles	4-2 (N.L.)	Jerry Reuss, Dodgers (Tommy John, Yankees)	Chuck Tanner, Pirates (Earl Weaver, Orioles)	56,088
8-9-81	Municipal Stadium Cleveland	5-4 (N.L.)	Vida Blue, Giants (Rollie Fingers, Brewers)	Dallas Green, Phillies (Jim Frey, Royals)	72,086
7-13-82	Olympic Stadium Montreal	4-1 (N.L.)	Steve Rogers, Expos (Dennis Eckersley, Red Sox)	Tommy Lasorda, Dodgers (Billy Martin, Athletics)	59,057
7-6-83	Comiskey Park Chicago	13-3 (A.L.)	Dave Stieb, Blue Jays (Mario Soto, Reds)	Harvey Kuenn, Brewers (Whitey Herzog, Cardinals)	43,801
7-10-84	Candlestick Park San Francisco	3-1 (N.L.)	Charlie Lea, Expos (Dave Stieb, Blue Jays)	Paul Owens, Phillies (Joe Altobelli, Orioles)	57,756
7-16-85	Metrodome Minneapolis	6-1 (N.L.)	LaMarr Hoyt, Padres (Jack Morris, Tigers)	Dick Williams, Padres (Sparky Anderson, Tigers)	54,960
7-15-86	Astrodome Houston	3-2 (A.L.)	Roger Clemens, Red Sox (Dwight Gooden, Mets)	Dick Howser, Royals (Whitey Herzog, Cardinals)	45,774
7-14-87	Oak.-Alameda Co. Col. Oakland	2-0▲ (N.L.)	Lee Smith, Cubs (Jay Howell, Athletics)	Dave Johnson, Mets (John McNamara, Red Sox)	49,671
7-12-88	Riverfront Stadium Cincinnati	2-1 (A.L.)	Frank Viola, Twins (Dwight Gooden, Mets)	Tom Kelly, Twins (Whitey Herzog, Cardinals)	55,837
7-11-89	Anaheim Stadium Anaheim, Calif.	5-3 (A.L.)	Nolan Ryan, Rangers (John Smoltz, Braves)	Tony La Russa, Athletics (Tommy Lasorda, Dodgers)	64,036
7-10-90	Wrigley Field Chicago	2-0 (A.L.)	Bret Saberhagen, Royals (Jeff Brantley, Giants)	Tony La Russa, Athletics (Roger Craig, Giants)	39,071
7-9-91	SkyDome Toronto	4-2 (A.L.)	Jimmy Key, Blue Jays (Dennis Martinez, Expos)	Tony La Russa, Athletics (Lou Piniella, Reds)	52,383
7-14-92	Jack Murphy Stadium San Diego	13-6 (A.L.)	Kevin Brown, Rangers (Tom Glavine, Braves)	Tom Kelly, Twins (Bobby Cox, Braves)	59,372
7-13-93	Oriole Park at Camden Yards, Baltimore	9-3 (A.L.)	Jack McDowell, White Sox (John Burkett, Giants)	Cito Gaston, Blue Jays (Bobby Cox, Braves)	48,147
7-12-94	Three Rivers Stadium Pittsburgh	8-7§ (N.L.)	Doug Jones, Phillies (Jason Bere, White Sox)	Jim Fregosi, Phillies (Cito Gaston, Blue Jays)	59,568
7-11-95	Ballpark in Arlington Arlington, Texas	3-2 (N.L.)	Heathcliff Slocumb, Phillies (Steve Ontiveros, A's)	Felipe Alou, Expos (Buck Showalter, Yankees)	50,920

*14 innings. †5 innings (rain). ‡12 innings. §10 innings. ∞15 innings. ▲13 innings.

AWARD WINNERS

MOST VALUABLE PLAYER

AMERICAN LEAGUE

Year	Player	Team	Pos.	Points
1929—Al Simmons	Philadelphia	OF	40
1930—Joe Cronin	Washington	SS	52
1931—Lou Gehrig	New York	1B	40
1932—Jimmie Foxx	Philadelphia	1B	46
1933—Jimmie Foxx	Philadelphia	1B	49
1934—Lou Gehrig	New York	1B	51
1935—Hank Greenberg	Detroit	1B	64
1936—Lou Gehrig	New York	1B	55
1937—Charley Gehringer	Detroit	2B	78
1938—Jimmie Foxx	Boston	1B	304
1939—Joe DiMaggio	New York	OF	280
1940—Hank Greenberg	Detroit	OF	292
1941—Joe DiMaggio	New York	OF	291
1942—Joe Gordon	New York	2B	270
1943—Spud Chandler	New York	P	246
1944—Bobby Doerr	Boston	2B	
1945—Eddie Mayo	Detroit	2B	

NATIONAL LEAGUE

Year	Player	Team	Pos.	Points
1929—No selection			
1930—Bill Terry	New York	1B	47
1931—Chuck Klein	Philadelphia	OF	40
1932—Chuck Klein	Philadelphia	OF	46
1933—Carl Hubbell	New York	P	64
1934—Dizzy Dean	St. Louis	P	57
1935—Arky Vaughan	Pittsburgh	SS	42
1936—Carl Hubbell	New York	P	61
1937—Joe Medwick	St. Louis	OF	70
1938—Ernie Lombardi	Cincinnati	C	229
1939—Bucky Walters	Cincinnati	P	303
1940—Frank McCormick	Cincinnati	1B	274
1941—Dolf Camilli	Brooklyn	1B	300
1942—Mort Cooper	St. Louis	P	263
1943—Stan Musial	St. Louis	OF	267
1944—Marty Marion	St. Louis	SS	
1945—Tommy Holmes	Boston	OF	

PLAYER AND PITCHER OF THE YEAR

AMERICAN LEAGUE

Year	Player	Team	Pos.
1944—Bobby Doerr	Boston	2B
Hal Newhouser	Detroit	P
1945—Eddie Mayo	Detroit	2B
Hal Newhouser	Detroit	P
1946—No selections		
1947—No selections		
1948—Lou Boudreau	Cleveland	SS
Bob Lemon	Cleveland	P
1949—Ted Williams	Boston	OF
Ellis Kinder	Boston	P
1950—Phil Rizzuto	New York	SS
Bob Lemon	Cleveland	P
1951—Ferris Fain	Philadelphia	1B
Bob Feller	Cleveland	P
1952—Luke Easter	Cleveland	1B
Bobby Shantz	Philadelphia	P
1953—Al Rosen	Cleveland	3B
Bob Porterfield	Washington	P
1954—Bobby Avila	Cleveland	2B
Bob Lemon	Cleveland	P
1955—Al Kaline	Detroit	OF
Whitey Ford	New York	P
1956—Mickey Mantle	New York	OF
Billy Pierce	Chicago	P
1957—Ted Williams	Boston	OF
Billy Pierce	Chicago	P
1958—Jackie Jensen	Boston	OF
Bob Turley	New York	P
1959—Nellie Fox	Chicago	2B
Early Wynn	Chicago	P
1960—Roger Maris	New York	OF
Chuck Estrada	Baltimore	P
1961—Roger Maris	New York	OF
Whitey Ford	New York	P
1962—Mickey Mantle	New York	OF
Dick Donovan	Cleveland	P
1963—Al Kaline	Detroit	OF
Whitey Ford	New York	P
1964—Brooks Robinson	Baltimore	3B
Dean Chance	Los Angeles	P
1965—Tony Oliva	Minnesota	OF
Jim Grant	Minnesota	P
1966—Frank Robinson	Baltimore	OF
Jim Kaat	Minnesota	P
1967—Carl Yastrzemski	Boston	OF
Jim Lonborg	Boston	P
1968—Ken Harrelson	Boston	OF
Denny McLain	Detroit	P
1969—Harmon Killebrew	Minnesota	1B-3B
Denny McLain	Detroit	P
1970—Harmon Killebrew	Minnesota	3B
Sam McDowell	Cleveland	P

NATIONAL LEAGUE

Year	Player	Team	Pos.
1944—Marty Marion	St. Louis	SS
Bill Voiselle	New York	P
1945—Tommy Holmes	Boston	OF
Hank Borowy	Chicago	P
1946—No selections		
1947—No selections		
1948—Stan Musial	St. Louis	OF-1B
Johnny Sain	Boston	P
1949—Enos Slaughter	St. Louis	OF
Howard Pollet	St. Louis	P
1950—Ralph Kiner	Pittsburgh	OF
Jim Konstanty	Philadelphia	P
1951—Stan Musial	St. Louis	OF
Preacher Roe	Brooklyn	P
1952—Hank Sauer	Chicago	OF
Robin Roberts	Philadelphia	P
1953—Roy Campanella	Brooklyn	C
Warren Spahn	Milwaukee	P
1954—Willie Mays	New York	OF
Johnny Antonelli	New York	P
1955—Duke Snider	Brooklyn	OF
Robin Roberts	Philadelphia	P
1956—Hank Aaron	Milwaukee	OF
Don Newcombe	Brooklyn	P
1957—Stan Musial	St. Louis	1B
Warren Spahn	Milwaukee	P
1958—Ernie Banks	Chicago	SS
Warren Spahn	Milwaukee	P
1959—Ernie Banks	Chicago	SS
Sam Jones	San Francisco	P
1960—Dick Groat	Pittsburgh	SS
Vern Law	Pittsburgh	P
1961—Frank Robinson	Cincinnati	OF
Warren Spahn	Milwaukee	P
1962—Maury Wills	Los Angeles	SS
Don Drysdale	Los Angeles	P
1963—Hank Aaron	Milwaukee	OF
Sandy Koufax	Los Angeles	P
1964—Ken Boyer	St. Louis	3B
Sandy Koufax	Los Angeles	P
1965—Willie Mays	San Francisco	OF
Sandy Koufax	Los Angeles	P
1966—Roberto Clemente	Pittsburgh	OF
Sandy Koufax	Los Angeles	P
1967—Orlando Cepeda	St. Louis	1B
Mike McCormick	San Francisco	P
1968—Pete Rose	Cincinnati	OF
Bob Gibson	St. Louis	P
1969—Willie McCovey	San Francisco	1B
Tom Seaver	New York	P
1970—Johnny Bench	Cincinnati	C
Bob Gibson	St. Louis	P

Year	Player	Team	Pos.	Year	Player	Team	Pos.
1971—	Tony Oliva	Minnesota	OF	1971—	Joe Torre	St. Louis	3B
	Vida Blue	Oakland	P		Ferguson Jenkins	Chicago	P
1972—	Dick Allen	Chicago	1B	1972—	Billy Williams	Chicago	OF
	Wilbur Wood	Chicago	P		Steve Carlton	Philadelphia	P
1973—	Reggie Jackson	Oakland	OF	1973—	Bobby Bonds	San Francisco	OF
	Jim Palmer	Baltimore	P		Ron Bryant	San Francisco	P
1974—	Jeff Burroughs	Texas	OF	1974—	Lou Brock	St. Louis	OF
	Jim Hunter	Oakland	P		Mike Marshall	Los Angeles	P
1975—	Fred Lynn	Boston	OF	1975—	Joe Morgan	Cincinnati	2B
	Jim Palmer	Baltimore	P		Tom Seaver	New York	P
1976—	Thurman Munson	New York	C	1976—	George Foster	Cincinnati	OF
	Jim Palmer	Baltimore	P		Randy Jones	San Diego	P
1977—	Rod Carew	Minnesota	1B	1977—	George Foster	Cincinnati	OF
	Nolan Ryan	California	P		Steve Carlton	Philadelphia	P
1978—	Jim Rice	Boston	OF	1978—	Dave Parker	Pittsburgh	OF
	Ron Guidry	New York	P		Vida Blue	San Francisco	P
1979—	Don Baylor	California	OF	1979—	Keith Hernandez	St. Louis	1B
	Mike Flanagan	Baltimore	P		Joe Niekro	Houston	P
1980—	George Brett	Kansas City	3B	1980—	Mike Schmidt	Philadelphia	3B
	Steve Stone	Baltimore	P		Steve Carlton	Philadelphia	P
1981—	Tony Armas	Oakland	OF	1981—	Andre Dawson	Montreal	OF
	Jack Morris	Detroit	P		Fernando Valenzuela	Los Angeles	P
1982—	Robin Yount	Milwaukee	SS	1982—	Dale Murphy	Atlanta	OF
	Dave Stieb	Toronto	P		Steve Carlton	Philadelphia	P
1983—	Cal Ripken Jr.	Baltimore	SS	1983—	Dale Murphy	Atlanta	OF
	LaMarr Hoyt	Chicago	P		John Denny	Philadelphia	P
1984—	Don Mattingly	New York	1B	1984—	Ryne Sandberg	Chicago	2B
	Willie Hernandez	Detroit	P		Rick Sutcliffe	Chicago	P
1985—	Don Mattingly	New York	1B	1985—	Willie McGee	St. Louis	OF
	Bret Saberhagen	Kansas City	P		Dwight Gooden	New York	P
1986—	Don Mattingly	New York	1B	1986—	Mike Schmidt	Philadelphia	3B
	Roger Clemens	Boston	P		Mike Scott	Houston	P
1987—	George Bell	Toronto	OF	1987—	Andre Dawson	Chicago	OF
	Jimmy Key	Toronto	P		Rick Sutcliffe	Chicago	P
1988—	Jose Canseco	Oakland	OF	1988—	Andy Van Slyke	Pittsburgh	OF
	Frank Viola	Minnesota	P		Orel Hershiser	Los Angeles	P
1989—	Ruben Sierra	Texas	OF	1989—	Kevin Mitchell	San Francisco	OF
	Bret Saberhagen	Kansas City	P		Mark Davis	San Diego	P
1990—	Cecil Fielder	Detroit	1B	1990—	Barry Bonds	Pittsburgh	OF
	Bob Welch	Oakland	P		Doug Drabek	Pittsburgh	P
1991—	Cal Ripken Jr.	Baltimore	SS	1991—	Barry Bonds	Pittsburgh	OF
	Roger Clemens	Boston	P		Tom Glavine	Atlanta	P

PITCHER OF THE YEAR

AMERICAN LEAGUE			NATIONAL LEAGUE		
Year	Pitcher	Team	Year	Pitcher	Team
1992—	Dennis Eckersley	Oakland	1992—	Greg Maddux	Chicago
1993—	Jack McDowell	Chicago	1993—	Greg Maddux	Atlanta
1994—	Jimmy Key	New York	1994—	Greg Maddux	Atlanta
1995—	Randy Johnson	Seattle	1995—	Greg Maddux	Atlanta

ROOKIE OF THE YEAR

1946—Combined selection—Del Ennis, Philadelphia N.L., OF
1947—Combined selection—Jackie Robinson, Brooklyn N.L., 1B
1948—Combined selection—Richie Ashburn, Philadelphia N.L., OF

AMERICAN LEAGUE				NATIONAL LEAGUE			
Year	Player	Team	Pos.	Year	Player	Team	Pos.
1949—	Roy Sievers	St. Louis	OF	1949—	Don Newcombe	Brooklyn	P
1950—	Whitey Ford	New York	P	1950—	Combined A.L.-N.L. selection		
1951—	Minnie Minoso	Chicago	OF	1951—	Willie Mays	New York	OF
1952—	Clint Courtney	St. Louis	C	1952—	Joe Black	Brooklyn	P
1953—	Harvey Kuenn	Detroit	SS	1953—	Jim Gilliam	Brooklyn	2B
1954—	Bob Grim	New York	P	1954—	Wally Moon	St. Louis	OF
1955—	Herb Score	Cleveland	P	1955—	Bill Virdon	St. Louis	OF
1956—	Luis Aparicio	Chicago	SS	1956—	Frank Robinson	Cincinnati	OF
1957—	Tony Kubek	New York	IF-OF	1957—	Ed Bouchee	Philadelphia	1B
	(No pitcher named)				Jack Sanford	Philadelphia	P
1958—	Albie Pearson	Washington	OF	1958—	Orlando Cepeda	San Francisco	1B
	Ryne Duren	New York	P		Carlton Willey	Milwaukee	P
1959—	Bob Allison	Washington	OF	1959—	Willie McCovey	San Francisco	1B
1960—	Ron Hansen	Baltimore	SS	1960—	Frank Howard	Los Angeles	OF
1961—	Dick Howser	Kansas City	SS	1961—	Billy Williams	Chicago	OF
	Don Schwall	Boston	P		Ken Hunt	Cincinnati	P
1962—	Tom Tresh	New York	OF-SS	1962—	Ken Hubbs	Chicago	2B
1963—	Pete Ward	Chicago	3B	1963—	Pete Rose	Cincinnati	2B
	Gary Peters	Chicago	P		Ray Culp	Philadelphia	P
1964—	Tony Oliva	Minnesota	OF	1964—	Dick Allen	Philadelphia	3B
	Wally Bunker	Baltimore	P		Billy McCool	Cincinnati	P

Year	Player	Team	Pos.		Year	Player	Team	Pos.
1965	Curt Blefary	Baltimore	OF		1965	Joe Morgan	Houston	2B
	Marcelino Lopez	California	P			Frank Linzy	San Francisco	P
1966	Tommie Agee	Chicago	OF		1966	Tommy Helms	Cincinnati	3B
	Jim Nash	Kansas City	P			Don Sutton	Los Angeles	P
1967	Rod Carew	Minnesota	2B		1967	Lee May	Cincinnati	1B
	Tom Phoebus	Baltimore	P			Dick Hughes	St. Louis	P
1968	Del Unser	Washington	OF		1968	Johnny Bench	Cincinnati	C
	Stan Bahnsen	New York	P			Jerry Koosman	New York	P
1969	Carlos May	Chicago	OF		1969	Coco Laboy	Montreal	3B
	Mike Nagy	Boston	P			Tom Griffin	Houston	P
1970	Roy Foster	Cleveland	OF		1970	Bernie Carbo	Cincinnati	OF
	Bert Blyleven	Minnesota	P			Carl Morton	Montreal	P
1971	Chris Chambliss	Cleveland	1B		1971	Earl Williams	Atlanta	C
	Bill Parsons	Milwaukee	P			Reggie Cleveland	St. Louis	P
1972	Carlton Fisk	Boston	C		1972	Dave Rader	San Francisco	C
	Dick Tidrow	Cleveland	P			Jon Matlack	New York	P
1973	Al Bumbry	Baltimore	OF		1973	Gary Matthews	San Francisco	OF
	Steve Busby	Kansas City	P			Steve Rogers	Montreal	P
1974	Mike Hargrove	Texas	1B		1974	Greg Gross	Houston	OF
	Frank Tanana	California	P			John D'Acquisto	San Francisco	P
1975	Fred Lynn	Boston	OF		1975	Gary Carter	Montreal	OF-C
	Dennis Eckersley	Cleveland	P			John Montefusco	San Francisco	P
1976	Butch Wynegar	Minnesota	C		1976	Larry Herndon	San Francisco	OF
	Mark Fidrych	Detroit	P			Butch Metzger	San Diego	P
1977	Mitchell Page	Oakland	OF		1977	Andre Dawson	Montreal	OF
	Dave Rozema	Detroit	P			Bob Owchinko	San Diego	P
1978	Paul Molitor	Milwaukee	2B		1978	Bob Horner	Atlanta	3B
	Rich Gale	Kansas City	P			Don Robinson	Pittsburgh	P
1979	Pat Putnam	Texas 1B			1979	Jeff Leonard	Houston	OF
	Mark Clear	California	P			Rick Sutcliffe	Los Angeles	P
1980	Joe Charboneau	Cleveland	OF		1980	Lonnie Smith	Philadelphia	OF
	Britt Burns	Chicago	P			Bill Gullickson	Montreal	P
1981	Rich Gedman	Boston	C		1981	Tim Raines	Montreal	OF
	Dave Righetti	New York	P			Fernando Valenzuela	Los Angeles	P
1982	Cal Ripken Jr.	Baltimore	SS-3B		1982	Johnny Ray	Pittsburgh	2B
	Ed Vande Berg	Seattle	P			Steve Bedrosian	Atlanta	P
1983	Ron Kittle	Chicago	OF		1983	Darryl Strawberry	New York	OF
	Mike Boddicker	Baltimore	P			Craig McMurtry	Atlanta	P
1984	Alvin Davis	Seattle	1B		1984	Juan Samuel	Philadelphia	2B
	Mark Langston	Seattle	P			Dwight Gooden	New York	P
1985	Ozzie Guillen	Chicago	SS		1985	Vince Coleman	St. Louis	OF
	Teddy Higuera	Milwaukee	P			Tom Browning	Cincinnati	P
1986	Jose Canseco	Oakland	OF		1986	Robby Thompson	San Francisco	2B
	Mark Eichhorn	Toronto	P			Todd Worrell	St. Louis	P
1987	Mark McGwire	Oakland	1B		1987	Benito Santiago	San Diego	C
	Mike Henneman	Detroit	P			Mike Dunne	Pittsburgh	P
1988	Walt Weiss	Oakland	SS		1988	Mark Grace	Chicago	1B
	Bryan Harvey	California	P			Tim Belcher	Los Angeles	P
1989	Craig Worthington	Baltimore	3B		1989	Jerome Walton	Chicago	OF
	Tom Gordon	Kansas City	P			Andy Benes	San Diego	P
1990	Sandy Alomar Jr.	Cleveland	C		1990	David Justice	Atlanta	OF
	Kevin Appier	Kansas City	P			Mike Harkey	Chicago	P
1991	Chuck Knoblauch	Minnesota	2B		1991	Jeff Bagwell	Houston	1B
	Juan Guzman	Toronto	P			Al Osuna	Houston	P
1992	Pat Listach	Milwaukee	SS		1992	Eric Karros	Los Angeles	1B
	Cal Eldred	Milwaukee	P			Tim Wakefield	Pittsburgh	P
1993	Tim Salmon	California	OF		1993	Mike Piazza	Los Angeles	C
	Aaron Sele	Boston	P			Kirk Rueter	Montreal	P
1994	Bob Hamelin	Kansas City	DH		1994	Raul Mondesi	Los Angeles	OF
	Brian Anderson	California	P			Steve Trachsel	Chicago	P
1995	Garret Anderson	California	OF		1995	Chipper Jones	Atlanta	3B
	Julian Tavarez	Cleveland	P			Hideo Nomo	Los Angeles	P

FIREMAN OF THE YEAR

AMERICAN LEAGUE			NATIONAL LEAGUE	
Year	Pitcher	Team	Pitcher	Team
1960	Mike Fornieles	Boston	Lindy McDaniel	St. Louis
1961	Luis Arroyo	New York	Stu Miller	San Francisco
1962	Dick Radatz	Boston	Roy Face	Pittsburgh
1963	Stu Miller	Baltimore	Lindy McDaniel	Chicago
1964	Dick Radatz	Boston	Al McBean	Pittsburgh
1965	Eddie Fisher	Chicago	Ted Abernathy	Chicago
1966	Jack Aker	Kansas City	Phil Regan	Los Angeles
1967	Minnie Rojas	California	Ted Abernathy	Cincinnati
1968	Wilbur Wood	Chicago	Phil Regan	L.A.-Chicago
1969	Ron Perranoski	Minnesota	Wayne Granger	Cincinnati
1970	Ron Perranoski	Minnesota	Wayne Granger	Cincinnati
1971	Ken Sanders	Milwaukee	Dave Giusti	Pittsburgh
1972	Sparky Lyle	New York	Clay Carroll	Cincinnati
1973	John Hiller	Detroit	Mike Marshall	Montreal
1974	Terry Forster	Chicago	Mike Marshall	Los Angeles

Year	Pitcher	Team	Year	Pitcher	Team
1975—Rich Gossage	Chicago		1975— Al Hrabosky	St. Louis	
1976—Bill Campbell	Minnesota		1976— Rawly Eastwick	Cincinnati	
1977—Bill Campbell	Boston		1977— Rollie Fingers	San Diego	
1978—Rich Gossage	New York		1978— Rollie Fingers	San Diego	
1979—Mike Marshall	Minnesota		1979— Bruce Sutter	Chicago	
Jim Kern	Texas				
1980—Dan Quisenberry	Kansas City		1980— Rollie Fingers	San Diego	
			Tom Hume	Cincinnati	
1981—Rollie Fingers	Milwaukee		1981— Bruce Sutter	St. Louis	
1982—Dan Quisenberry	Kansas City		1982— Bruce Sutter	St. Louis	
1983—Dan Quisenberry	Kansas City		1983— Al Holland	Philadelphia	
			Lee Smith	Chicago	
1984—Dan Quisenberry	Kansas City		1984— Bruce Sutter	St. Louis	
1985—Dan Quisenberry	Kansas City		1985— Jeff Reardon	Montreal	
1986—Dave Righetti	New York		1986— Todd Worrell	St. Louis	
1987—Dave Righetti	New York		1987— Steve Bedrosian	Philadelphia	
Jeff Reardon	Minnesota				
1988—Dennis Eckersley	Oakland		1988— John Franco	Cincinnati	
1989—Jeff Russell	Texas		1989— Mark Davis	San Diego	
1990—Bobby Thigpen	Chicago		1990— John Franco	New York	
1991—Dennis Eckersley	Oakland		1991— Lee Smith	St. Louis	
Bryan Harvey	California				
1992—Dennis Eckersley	Oakland		1992— Doug Jones	Houston	
			Lee Smith	St. Louis	
1993—Jeff Montgomery	Kansas City		1993— Randy Myers	Chicago	
1994—Lee Smith	Baltimore		1994— John Franco	New York	
1995—Jose Mesa	Cleveland		1995— Randy Myers	Chicago	

MAJOR LEAGUE PLAYER OF THE YEAR

Year	Player	Team	Year	Player	Team	Year	Player	Team
1936—Carl Hubbell	New York N.L.		1957—Ted Williams	Boston A.L.		1977—Rod Carew	Minnesota A.L.	
1937—Johnny Allen	Cleveland A.L.		1958—Bob Turley	New York A.L.		1978—Ron Guidry	New York A.L.	
1938—Johnny Vander Meer	Cincinnati N.L.		1959—Early Wynn	Chicago A.L.		1979—Willie Stargell	Pittsburgh N.L.	
1939—Joe DiMaggio	New York A.L.		1960—Bill Mazeroski	Pittsburgh N.L.		1980—George Brett	Kansas City A.L.	
1940—Bob Feller	Cleveland A.L.		1961—Roger Maris	New York A.L.		1981—Fernando Valenzuela	Los Angeles N.L.	
1941—Ted Williams	Boston A.L.		1962—Maury Wills	Los Angeles N.L.		1982—Robin Yount	Milwaukee A.L.	
1942—Ted Williams	Boston A.L.		Don Drysdale	Los Angeles N.L.		1983—Cal Ripken Jr.	Baltimore A.L.	
1943—Spud Chandler	New York A.L.		1963—Sandy Koufax	Los Angeles N.L.		1984—Ryne Sandberg	Chicago N.L.	
1944—Marty Marion	St. Louis N.L.		1964—Ken Boyer	St. Louis N.L.		1985—Don Mattingly	New York A.L.	
1945—Hal Newhouser	Detroit A.L.		1965—Sandy Koufax	Los Angeles N.L.		1986—Roger Clemens	Boston A.L.	
1946—Stan Musial	St. Louis N.L.		1966—Frank Robinson	Baltimore A.L.		1987—George Bell	Toronto A.L.	
1947—Ted Williams	Boston A.L.		1967—Carl Yastrzemski	Boston A.L.		1988—Orel Hershiser	Los Angeles N.L.	
1948—Lou Boudreau	Cleveland A.L.		1968—Denny McLain	Detroit A.L.		1989—Kevin Mitchell	San Francisco N.L.	
1949—Ted Williams	Boston A.L.		1969—Willie McCovey	San Francisco N.L.		1990—Barry Bonds	Pittsburgh N.L.	
1950—Phil Rizzuto	New York A.L.		1970—Johnny Bench	Cincinnati N.L.		1991—Cal Ripken Jr.	Baltimore A.L.	
1951—Stan Musial	St. Louis N.L.		1971—Joe Torre	St. Louis N.L.		1992—Gary Sheffield	San Diego N.L.	
1952—Robin Roberts	Philadelphia N.L.		1972—Billy Williams	Chicago N.L.		1993—Frank Thomas	Chicago A.L.	
1953—Al Rosen	Cleveland A.L.		1973—Reggie Jackson	Oakland A.L.		1994—Jeff Bagwell	Houston N.L.	
1954—Willie Mays	New York N.L.		1974—Lou Brock	St. Louis N.L.		1995—Albert Belle	Cleveland A.L.	
1955—Duke Snider	Brooklyn N.L.		1975—Joe Morgan	Cincinnati N.L.				
1956—Mickey Mantle	New York A.L.		1976—Joe Morgan	Cincinnati N.L.				

MAJOR LEAGUE MANAGER OF THE YEAR

Year	Manager	Team	Year	Manager	Team	Year	Manager	Team
1936—Joe McCarthy	New York A.L.		1960—Danny Murtaugh	Pittsburgh N.L.		1984—Jim Frey	Chicago N.L.	
1937—Bill McKechnie	Boston N.L.		1961—Ralph Houk	New York A.L.		1985—Bobby Cox	Toronto A.L.	
1938—Joe McCarthy	New York A.L.		1962—Bill Rigney	Los Angeles A.L.		1986—John McNamara	Boston A.L.	
1939—Leo Durocher	Brooklyn N.L.		1963—Walter Alston	Los Angeles N.L.		Hal Lanier	Houston N.L.	
1940—Bill McKechnie	Cincinnati N.L.		1964—Johnny Keane	St. Louis N.L.		1987—Sparky Anderson	Detroit A.L.	
1941—Billy Southworth	St. Louis N.L.		1965—Sam Mele	Minnesota A.L.		Buck Rodgers	Montreal N.L.	
1942—Billy Southworth	St. Louis N.L.		1966—Hank Bauer	Baltimore A.L.		1988—Tony La Russa	Oakland A.L.	
1943—Joe McCarthy	New York A.L.		1967—Dick Williams	Boston A.L.		Tom Lasorda	L.A. N.L. (tie)	
1944—Luke Sewell	St. Louis A.L.		1968—Mayo Smith	Detroit A.L.		Jim Leyland	Pit. N.L. (tie)	
1945—Ossie Bluege	Washington A.L.		1969—Gil Hodges	New York N.L.		1989—Frank Robinson	Baltimore A.L.	
1946—Eddie Dyer	St. Louis N.L.		1970—Danny Murtaugh	Pittsburgh N.L.		Don Zimmer	Chicago N.L.	
1947—Bucky Harris	New York A.L.		1971—Charlie Fox	San Francisco N.L.		1990—Jeff Torborg	Chicago A.L.	
1948—Bill Meyer	Pittsburgh N.L.		1972—Chuck Tanner	Chicago A.L.		Jim Leyland	Pittsburgh N.L.	
1949—Casey Stengel	New York A.L.		1973—Gene Mauch	Montreal N.L.		1991—Tom Kelly	Minnesota A.L.	
1950—Red Rolfe	Detroit A.L.		1974—Bill Virdon	New York A.L.		Bobby Cox	Atlanta N.L.	
1951—Leo Durocher	New York N.L.		1975—Darrell Johnson	Boston A.L.		1992—Tony La Russa	Oakland A.L.	
1952—Eddie Stanky	St. Louis N.L.		1976—Danny Ozark	Philadelphia N.L.		Jim Leyland	Pittsburgh N.L.	
1953—Casey Stengel	New York A.L.		1977—Earl Weaver	Baltimore A.L.		1993—Johnny Oates	Baltimore A.L.	
1954—Leo Durocher	New York N.L.		1978—George Bamberger	Milwaukee A.L.		Bobby Cox	Atlanta N.L.	
1955—Walter Alston	Brooklyn N.L.		1979—Earl Weaver	Baltimore A.L.		1994—Buck Showalter	New York A.L.	
1956—Birdie Tebbetts	Cincinnati N.L.		1980—Bill Virdon	Houston N.L.		Felipe Alou	Montreal N.L.	
1957—Fred Hutchinson	St. Louis N.L.		1981—Billy Martin	Oakland A.L.		1995—Mike Hargrove	Cleveland A.L.	
1958—Casey Stengel	New York A.L.		1982—Whitey Herzog	St. Louis N.L.		Don Baylor	Colorado N.L.	
1959—Walter A.L.ston	Los Angeles N.L.		1983—Tony La Russa	Chicago A.L.				

MAJOR LEAGUE EXECUTIVE OF THE YEAR

Year	Executive	Team	Year	Executive	Team	Year	Executive	Team
1936	Branch Rickey	St. Louis N.L.	1956	Gabe Paul	Cincinnati N.L.	1976	Joe Burke	Kansas City A.L.
1937	Ed Barrow	New York A.L.	1957	Frank Lane	St. Louis N.L.	1977	Bill Veeck	Chicago A.L.
1938	Warren Giles	Cincinnati N.L.	1958	Joe Brown	Pittsburgh N.L.	1978	Spec Richardson	San Francisco N.L.
1939	Larry MacPhail	Brooklyn N.L.	1959	Buzzie Bavasi	L.A. N.L.	1979	Hank Peters	Baltimore A.L.
1940	Walter Briggs Sr.	Detroit A.L.	1960	George Weiss	New York A.L.	1980	Tal Smith	Houston N.L.
1941	Ed Barrow	New York A.L.	1961	Dan Topping	New York A.L.	1981	John McHale	Montreal N.L.
1942	Branch Rickey	St. Louis N.L.	1962	Fred Haney	Los Angeles A.L.	1982	Harry Dalton	Milwaukee A.L.
1943	Clark Griffith	Washington A.L.	1963	Bing Devine	St. Louis N.L.	1983	Hank Peters	Baltimore A.L.
1944	Billy DeWitt	St. Louis A.L.	1964	Bing Devine	St. Louis N.L.	1984	Dallas Green	Chicago N.L.
1945	Phil Wrigley	Chicago N.L.	1965	Cal Griffith	Minnesota A.L.	1985	John Schuerholz	Kansas City A.L.
1946	Tom Yawkey	Boston A.L.	1966	Lee MacPhail	Commissioner's Office	1986	Frank Cashen	New York N.L.
1947	Branch Rickey	Brooklyn N.L.	1967	Dick O'Connell	Boston A.L.	1987	Al Rosen	San Francisco N.L.
1948	Bill Veeck	Cleveland A.L.	1968	Jim Campbell	Detroit A.L.	1988	Fred Claire	Los Angeles N.L.
1949	Bob Carpenter	Philadelphia N.L.	1969	John Murphy	New York N.L.	1989	Roland Hemond	Baltimore A.L.
1950	George Weiss	New York A.L.	1970	Harry Dalton	Baltimore A.L.	1990	Bob Quinn	Cincinnati N.L.
1951	George Weiss	New York A.L.	1971	Cedric Tallis	Kansas City A.L.	1991	Andy MacPhail	Minnesota A.L.
1952	George Weiss	New York A.L.	1972	Roland Hemond	Chicago A.L.	1992	Dan Duquette	Montreal N.L.
1953	Lou Perini	Milwaukee N.L.	1973	Bob Howsam	Cincinnati N.L.	1993	Lee Thomas	Philadelphia N.L.
1954	Horace Stoneham	New York N.L.	1974	Gabe Paul	New York A.L.	1994	John Hart	Cleveland A.L.
1955	Walter O'Malley	Brooklyn N.L.	1975	Dick O'Connell	Boston A.L.	1995	John Hart	Cleveland A.L.

HISTORY *Award winners*

GOLD GLOVE TEAMS

1957
MAJORS
- P— Bobby Shantz, New York A.L.
- C— Sherm Lollar, Chicago A.L.
- 1B— Gil Hodges, Brooklyn N.L.
- 2B— Nellie Fox, Chicago A.L.
- 3B— Frank Malzone, Boston A.L.
- SS— Roy McMillan, Cincinnati N.L.
- OF— Minnie Minoso, Chicago A.L.
- OF— Willie Mays, New York N.L.
- OF— Al Kaline, Detroit A.L.

1958
AMERICAN LEAGUE
- P— Bobby Shantz, New York
- C— Sherm Lollar, Chicago
- 1B— Vic Power, Cleveland
- 2B— Frank Bolling, Detroit
- 3B— Frank Malzone, Boston
- SS— Luis Aparicio, Chicago
- OF— Norm Siebern, New York
- OF— Jimmy Piersall, Boston
- OF— Al Kaline, Detroit

NATIONAL LEAGUE
- P— Harvey Haddix, Cincinnati
- C— Del Crandall, Milwaukee
- 1B— Gil Hodges, Los Angeles
- 2B— Bill Mazeroski, Pittsburgh
- 3B— Ken Boyer, St. Louis
- SS— Roy McMillan, Cincinnati
- OF— Frank Robinson, Cincinnati
- OF— Willie Mays, San Francisco
- OF— Hank Aaron, Milwaukee

1959
AMERICAN LEAGUE
- P— Bobby Shantz, New York
- C— Sherm Lollar, Chicago
- 1B— Vic Power, Cleveland
- 2B— Nellie Fox, Chicago
- 3B— Frank Malzone, Boston
- SS— Luis Aparicio, Chicago
- OF— Minnie Minoso, Cleveland
- OF— Al Kaline, Detroit
- OF— Jackie Jensen, Boston

NATIONAL LEAGUE
- P— Harvey Haddix, Pittsburgh
- C— Del Crandall, Milwaukee
- 1B— Gil Hodges, Los Angeles
- 2B— Charley Neal, Los Angeles
- 3B— Ken Boyer, St. Louis
- SS— Roy McMillan, Cincinnati
- OF— Jackie Brandt, San Francisco
- OF— Willie Mays, San Francisco
- OF— Hank Aaron, Milwaukee

1960
AMERICAN LEAGUE
- P— Bobby Shantz, New York
- C— Earl Battey, Washington
- 1B— Vic Power, Cleveland
- 2B— Nellie Fox, Chicago
- 3B— Brooks Robinson, Baltimore
- SS— Luis Aparicio, Chicago
- OF— Minnie Minoso, Chicago
- OF— Jim Landis, Chicago
- OF— Roger Maris, New York

NATIONAL LEAGUE
- P— Harvey Haddix, Pittsburgh
- C— Del Crandall, Milwaukee
- 1B— Bill White, St. Louis
- 2B— Bill Mazeroski, Pittsburgh
- 3B— Ken Boyer, St. Louis
- SS— Ernie Banks, Chicago
- OF— Wally Moon, Los Angeles
- OF— Willie Mays, San Francisco
- OF— Hank Aaron, Milwaukee

1961
AMERICAN LEAGUE
- P— Frank Lary, Detroit
- C— Earl Battey, Chicago
- 1B— Vic Power, Cleveland
- 2B— Bobby Richardson, New York
- 3B— Brooks Robinson, Baltimore
- SS— Luis Aparicio, Chicago
- OF— Al Kaline, Detroit
- OF— Jimmy Piersall, Cleveland
- OF— Jim Landis, Chicago

NATIONAL LEAGUE
- P— Bobby Shantz, Pittsburgh
- C— John Roseboro, Los Angeles
- 1B— Bill White, St. Louis
- 2B— Bill Mazeroski, Pittsburgh
- 3B— Ken Boyer, St. Louis
- SS— Maury Wills, Los Angeles
- OF— Willie Mays, San Francisco
- OF— Roberto Clemente, Pittsburgh
- OF— Vada Pinson, Cincinnati

1962
AMERICAN LEAGUE
- P— Jim Kaat, Minnesota
- C— Earl Battey, Minnesota
- 1B— Vic Power, Minnesota
- 2B— Bobby Richardson, New York
- 3B— Brooks Robinson, Baltimore
- SS— Luis Aparicio, Chicago
- OF— Jim Landis, Chicago
- OF— Mickey Mantle, New York
- OF— Al Kaline, Detroit

1960
NATIONAL LEAGUE
- P— Bobby Shantz, St. Louis
- C— Del Crandall, Milwaukee
- 1B— Bill White, St. Louis
- 2B— Ken Hubbs, Chicago
- 3B— Jim Davenport, San Francisco
- SS— Maury Wills, Los Angeles
- OF— Willie Mays, San Francisco
- OF— Roberto Clemente, Pittsburgh
- OF— Bill Virdon, Pittsburgh

1963
AMERICAN LEAGUE
- P— Jim Kaat, Minnesota
- C— Elston Howard, New York
- 1B— Vic Power, Minnesota
- 2B— Bobby Richardson, New York
- 3B— Brooks Robinson, Baltimore
- SS— Zoilo Versalles, Minnesota
- OF— Al Kaline, Detroit
- OF— Carl Yastrzemski, Boston
- OF— Jim Landis, Chicago

NATIONAL LEAGUE
- P— Bobby Shantz, St. Louis
- C— Johnny Edwards, Cincinnati
- 1B— Bill White, St. Louis
- 2B— Bill Mazeroski, Pittsburgh
- 3B— Ken Boyer, St. Louis
- SS— Bobby Wine, Philadelphia
- OF— Willie Mays, San Francisco
- OF— Roberto Clemente, Pittsburgh
- OF— Curt Flood, St. Louis

1964
AMERICAN LEAGUE
- P— Jim Kaat, Minnesota
- C— Elston Howard, New York
- 1B— Vic Power, Los Angeles
- 2B— Bobby Richardson, New York
- 3B— Brooks Robinson, Baltimore
- SS— Luis Aparicio, Baltimore
- OF— Al Kaline, Detroit
- OF— Jim Landis, Chicago
- OF— Vic Davalillo, Cleveland

NATIONAL LEAGUE
- P— Bobby Shantz, Philadelphia
- C— Johnny Edwards, Cincinnati
- 1B— Bill White, St. Louis
- 2B— Bill Mazeroski, Pittsburgh
- 3B— Ron Santo, Chicago
- SS— Ruben Amaro, Philadelphia
- OF— Willie Mays, San Francisco
- OF— Roberto Clemente, Pittsburgh
- OF— Curt Flood, St. Louis

- 305 -

1965

AMERICAN LEAGUE
P— Jim Kaat, Minnesota
C— Bill Freehan, Detroit
1B— Joe Pepitone, New York
2B— Bobby Richardson, New York
3B— Brooks Robinson, Baltimore
SS— Zoilo Versalles, Minnesota
OF— Al Kaline, Detroit
OF— Tom Tresh, New York
OF— Carl Yastrzemski, Boston

NATIONAL LEAGUE
P— Bob Gibson, St. Louis
C— Joe Torre, Atlanta
1B— Bill White, St. Louis
2B— Bill Mazeroski, Pittsburgh
3B— Ron Santo, Chicago
SS— Leo Cardenas, Cincinnati
OF— Willie Mays, San Francisco
OF— Roberto Clemente, Pittsburgh
OF— Curt Flood, St. Louis

1966

AMERICAN LEAGUE
P— Jim Kaat, Minnesota
C— Bill Freehan, Detroit
1B— Joe Pepitone, New York
2B— Bobby Knoop, California
3B— Brooks Robinson, Baltimore
SS— Luis Aparicio, Baltimore
OF— Al Kaline, Detroit
OF— Tommie Agee, Chicago
OF— Tony Oliva, Minnesota

NATIONAL LEAGUE
P— Bob Gibson, St. Louis
C— John Roseboro, Los Angeles
1B— Bill White, Philadelphia
2B— Bill Mazeroski, Pittsburgh
3B— Ron Santo, Chicago
SS— Gene Alley, Pittsburgh
OF— Willie Mays, San Francisco
OF— Curt Flood, St. Louis
OF— Roberto Clemente, Pittsburgh

1967

AMERICAN LEAGUE
P— Jim Kaat, Minnesota
C— Bill Freehan, Detroit
1B— George Scott, Boston
2B— Bobby Knoop, California
3B— Brooks Robinson, Baltimore
SS— Jim Fregosi, California
OF— Carl Yastrzemski, Boston
OF— Paul Blair, Baltimore
OF— Al Kaline, Detroit

NATIONAL LEAGUE
P— Bob Gibson, St. Louis
C— Randy Hundley, Chicago
1B— Wes Parker, Los Angeles
2B— Bill Mazeroski, Pittsburgh
3B— Ron Santo, Chicago
SS— Gene Alley, Pittsburgh
OF— Roberto Clemente, Pittsburgh
OF— Curt Flood, St. Louis
OF— Willie Mays, San Francisco

1968

AMERICAN LEAGUE
P— Jim Kaat, Minnesota
C— Bill Freehan, Detroit
1B— George Scott, Boston
2B— Bobby Knoop, California
3B— Brooks Robinson, Baltimore
SS— Luis Aparicio, Chicago
OF— Mickey Stanley, Detroit
OF— Carl Yastrzemski, Boston
OF— Reggie Smith, Boston

NATIONAL LEAGUE
P— Bob Gibson, St. Louis
C— Johnny Bench, Cincinnati
1B— Wes Parker, Los Angeles
2B— Glenn Beckert, Chicago
3B— Ron Santo, Chicago
SS— Dal Maxvill, St. Louis
OF— Willie Mays, San Francisco
OF— Roberto Clemente, Pittsburgh
OF— Curt Flood, St. Louis

1969

AMERICAN LEAGUE
P— Jim Kaat, Minnesota
C— Bill Freehan, Detroit
1B— Joe Pepitone, New York
2B— Dave Johnson, Baltimore
3B— Brooks Robinson, Baltimore
SS— Mark Belanger, Baltimore
OF— Paul Blair, Baltimore
OF— Mickey Stanley, Detroit
OF— Carl Yastrzemski, Boston

NATIONAL LEAGUE
P— Bob Gibson, St. Louis
C— Johnny Bench, Cincinnati
1B— Wes Parker, Los Angeles
2B— Felix Millan, Atlanta
3B— Clete Boyer, Atlanta
SS— Don Kessinger, Chicago
OF— Roberto Clemente, Pittsburgh
OF— Curt Flood, St. Louis
OF— Pete Rose, Cincinnati

1970

AMERICAN LEAGUE
P— Jim Kaat, Minnesota
C— Ray Fosse, Cleveland
1B— Jim Spencer, California
2B— Dave Johnson, Baltimore
3B— Brooks Robinson, Baltimore
SS— Luis Aparicio, Chicago
OF— Mickey Stanley, Detroit
OF— Paul Blair, Baltimore
OF— Ken Berry, Chicago

NATIONAL LEAGUE
P— Bob Gibson, St. Louis
C— Johnny Bench, Cincinnati
1B— Wes Parker, Los Angeles
2B— Tommy Helms, Cincinnati
3B— Doug Rader, Houston
SS— Don Kessinger, Chicago
OF— Roberto Clemente, Pittsburgh
OF— Tommie Agee, New York
OF— Pete Rose, Cincinnati

1971

AMERICAN LEAGUE
P— Jim Kaat, Minnesota
C— Ray Fosse, Cleveland
1B— George Scott, Boston
2B— Dave Johnson, Baltimore
3B— Brooks Robinson, Baltimore
SS— Mark Belanger, Baltimore
OF— Paul Blair, Baltimore
OF— Amos Otis, Kansas City
OF— Carl Yastrzemski, Boston

NATIONAL LEAGUE
P— Bob Gibson, St. Louis
C— Johnny Bench, Cincinnati
1B— Wes Parker, Los Angeles
2B— Tommy Helms, Cincinnati
3B— Doug Rader, Houston
SS— Bud Harrelson, New York
OF— Roberto Clemente, Pittsburgh
OF— Bobby Bonds, San Francisco
OF— Willie Davis, Los Angeles

1972

AMERICAN LEAGUE
P— Jim Kaat, Minnesota
C— Carlton Fisk, Boston
1B— George Scott, Milwaukee
2B— Doug Griffin, Boston
3B— Brooks Robinson, Baltimore
SS— Ed Brinkman, Detroit
OF— Paul Blair, Baltimore
OF— Bobby Murcer, New York
OF— Ken Berry, California

NATIONAL LEAGUE
P— Bob Gibson, St. Louis
C— Johnny Bench, Cincinnati
1B— Wes Parker, Los Angeles
2B— Felix Millan, Atlanta
3B— Doug Rader, Houston
SS— Larry Bowa, Philadelphia
OF— Roberto Clemente, Pittsburgh
OF— Cesar Cedeno, Houston
OF— Willie Davis, Los Angeles

1973

AMERICAN LEAGUE
P— Jim Kaat, Chicago
C— Thurman Munson, New York
1B— George Scott, Milwaukee
2B— Bobby Grich, Baltimore
3B— Brooks Robinson, Baltimore
SS— Mark Belanger, Baltimore
OF— Paul Blair, Baltimore
OF— Amos Otis, Kansas City
OF— Mickey Stanley, Detroit

NATIONAL LEAGUE
P— Bob Gibson, St. Louis
C— Johnny Bench, Cincinnati
1B— Mike Jorgensen, Montreal
2B— Joe Morgan, Cincinnati
3B— Doug Rader, Houston
SS— Roger Metzger, Houston
OF— Bobby Bonds, San Francisco
OF— Cesar Cedeno, Houston
OF— Willie Davis, Los Angeles

1974

AMERICAN LEAGUE
P— Jim Kaat, Chicago
C— Thurman Munson, New York
1B— George Scott, Milwaukee
2B— Bobby Grich, Baltimore
3B— Brooks Robinson, Baltimore
SS— Mark Belanger, Baltimore
OF— Paul Blair, Baltimore
OF— Amos Otis, Kansas City
OF— Joe Rudi, Oakland

NATIONAL LEAGUE
P— Andy Messersmith, Los Angeles
C— Johnny Bench, Cincinnati
1B— Steve Garvey, Los Angeles
2B— Joe Morgan, Cincinnati
3B— Doug Rader, Houston
SS— Dave Concepcion, Cincinnati
OF— Cesar Cedeno, Houston
OF— Cesar Geronimo, Cincinnati
OF— Bobby Bonds, San Francisco

1975

AMERICAN LEAGUE
P— Jim Kaat, Chicago
C— Thurman Munson, New York
1B— George Scott, Milwaukee
2B— Bobby Grich, Baltimore
3B— Brooks Robinson, Baltimore
SS— Mark Belanger, Baltimore
OF— Paul Blair, Baltimore
OF— Joe Rudi, Oakland
OF— Fred Lynn, Boston

NATIONAL LEAGUE
P— Andy Messersmith, Los Angeles
C— Johnny Bench, Cincinnati
1B— Steve Garvey, Los Angeles
2B— Joe Morgan, Cincinnati
3B— Ken Reitz, St. Louis
SS— Dave Concepcion, Cincinnati
OF— Cesar Cedeno, Houston
OF— Cesar Geronimo, Cincinnati
OF— Garry Maddox, Philadelphia

1976
AMERICAN LEAGUE
P— Jim Palmer, Baltimore
C— Jim Sundberg, Texas
1B— George Scott, Milwaukee
2B— Bobby Grich, Baltimore
3B— Aurelio Rodriguez, Detroit
SS— Mark Belanger, Baltimore
OF— Joe Rudi, Oakland
OF— Dwight Evans, Boston
OF— Rick Manning, Cleveland

NATIONAL LEAGUE
P— Jim Kaat, Philadelphia
C— Johnny Bench, Cincinnati
1B— Steve Garvey, Los Angeles
2B— Joe Morgan, Cincinnati
3B— Mike Schmidt, Philadelphia
SS— Dave Concepcion, Cincinnati
OF— Cesar Cedeno, Houston
OF— Cesar Geronimo, Cincinnati
OF— Garry Maddox, Philadelphia

1977
AMERICAN LEAGUE
P— Jim Palmer, Baltimore
C— Jim Sundberg, Texas
1B— Jim Spencer, Chicago
2B— Frank White, Kansas City
3B— Graig Nettles, New York
SS— Mark Belanger, Baltimore
OF— Juan Beniquez, Texas
OF— Carl Yastrzemski, Boston
OF— Al Cowens, Kansas City

NATIONAL LEAGUE
P— Jim Kaat, Philadelphia
C— Johnny Bench, Cincinnati
1B— Steve Garvey, Los Angeles
2B— Joe Morgan, Cincinnati
3B— Mike Schmidt, Philadelphia
SS— Dave Concepcion, Cincinnati
OF— Cesar Geronimo, Cincinnati
OF— Garry Maddox, Philadelphia
OF— Dave Parker, Pittsburgh

1978
AMERICAN LEAGUE
P— Jim Palmer, Baltimore
C— Jim Sundberg, Texas
1B— Chris Chambliss, New York
2B— Frank White, Kansas City
3B— Graig Nettles, New York
SS— Mark Belanger, Baltimore
OF— Fred Lynn, Boston
OF— Dwight Evans, Boston
OF— Rick Miller, California

NATIONAL LEAGUE
P— Phil Niekro, Atlanta
C— Bob Boone, Philadelphia
1B— Keith Hernandez, St. Louis
2B— Dave Lopes, Los Angeles
3B— Mike Schmidt, Philadelphia
SS— Larry Bowa, Philadelphia
OF— Garry Maddox, Philadelphia
OF— Dave Parker, Pittsburgh
OF— Ellis Valentine, Montreal

1979
AMERICAN LEAGUE
P— Jim Palmer, Baltimore
C— Jim Sundberg, Texas
1B— Cecil Cooper, Milwaukee
2B— Frank White, Kansas City
3B— Buddy Bell, Texas
SS— Rick Burleson, Boston
OF— Dwight Evans, Boston
OF— Sixto Lezcano, Milwaukee
OF— Fred Lynn, Boston

NATIONAL LEAGUE
P— Phil Niekro, Atlanta
C— Bob Boone, Philadelphia
1B— Keith Hernandez, St. Louis
2B— Manny Trillo, Philadelphia
3B— Mike Schmidt, Philadelphia
SS— Dave Concepcion, Cincinnati
OF— Garry Maddox, Philadelphia
OF— Dave Parker, Pittsburgh
OF— Dave Winfield, San Diego

1980
AMERICAN LEAGUE
P— Mike Norris, Oakland
C— Jim Sundberg, Texas
1B— Cecil Cooper, Milwaukee
2B— Frank White, Kansas City
3B— Buddy Bell, Texas
SS— Alan Trammell, Detroit
OF— Fred Lynn, Boston
OF— Dwayne Murphy, Oakland
OF— Willie Wilson, Kansas City

NATIONAL LEAGUE
P— Phil Niekro, Atlanta
C— Gary Carter, Montreal
1B— Keith Hernandez, St. Louis
2B— Doug Flynn, New York
3B— Mike Schmidt, Philadelphia
SS— Ozzie Smith, San Diego
OF— Andre Dawson, Montreal
OF— Garry Maddox, Philadelphia
OF— Dave Winfield, San Diego

1981
AMERICAN LEAGUE
P— Mike Norris, Oakland
C— Jim Sundberg, Texas
1B— Mike Squires, Chicago
2B— Frank White, Kansas City
3B— Buddy Bell, Texas
SS— Alan Trammell, Detroit
OF— Dwayne Murphy, Oakland
OF— Dwight Evans, Boston
OF— Rickey Henderson, Oakland

NATIONAL LEAGUE
P— Steve Carlton, Philadelphia
C— Gary Carter, Montreal
1B— Keith Hernandez, St. Louis
2B— Manny Trillo, Philadelphia
3B— Mike Schmidt, Philadelphia
SS— Ozzie Smith, San Diego
OF— Andre Dawson, Montreal
OF— Garry Maddox, Philadelphia
OF— Dusty Baker, Los Angeles

1982
AMERICAN LEAGUE
P— Ron Guidry, New York
C— Bob Boone, California
1B— Eddie Murray, Baltimore
2B— Frank White, Kansas City
3B— Buddy Bell, Texas
SS— Robin Yount, Milwaukee
OF— Dwight Evans, Boston
OF— Dave Winfield, New York
OF— Dwayne Murphy, Oakland

NATIONAL LEAGUE
P— Phil Niekro, Atlanta
C— Gary Carter, Montreal
1B— Keith Hernandez, St. Louis
2B— Manny Trillo, Philadelphia
3B— Mike Schmidt, Philadelphia
SS— Ozzie Smith, St. Louis
OF— Andre Dawson, Montreal
OF— Dale Murphy, Atlanta
OF— Garry Maddox, Philadelphia

1983
AMERICAN LEAGUE
P— Ron Guidry, New York
C— Lance Parrish, Detroit
1B— Eddie Murray, Baltimore
2B— Lou Whitaker, Detroit
3B— Buddy Bell, Texas
SS— Alan Trammell, Detroit
OF— Dwight Evans, Boston
OF— Dave Winfield, New York
OF— Dwayne Murphy, Oakland

NATIONAL LEAGUE
P— Phil Niekro, Atlanta
C— Tony Pena, Pittsburgh
1B— Keith Hernandez, St.L.-N.Y.
2B— Ryne Sandberg, Chicago
3B— Mike Schmidt, Philadelphia
SS— Ozzie Smith, St. Louis
OF— Andre Dawson, Montreal
OF— Dale Murphy, Atlanta
OF— Willie McGee, St. Louis

1984
AMERICAN LEAGUE
P— Ron Guidry, New York
C— Lance Parrish, Detroit
1B— Eddie Murray, Baltimore
2B— Lou Whitaker, Detroit
3B— Buddy Bell, Texas
SS— Alan Trammell, Detroit
OF— Dwight Evans, Boston
OF— Dave Winfield, New York
OF— Dwayne Murphy, Oakland

NATIONAL LEAGUE
P— Joaquin Andujar, St. Louis
C— Tony Pena, Pittsburgh
1B— Keith Hernandez, New York
2B— Ryne Sandberg, Chicago
3B— Mike Schmidt, Philadelphia
SS— Ozzie Smith, St. Louis
OF— Dale Murphy, Atlanta
OF— Bob Dernier, Chicago
OF— Andre Dawson, Montreal

1985
AMERICAN LEAGUE
P— Ron Guidry, New York
C— Lance Parrish, Detroit
1B— Don Mattingly, New York
2B— Lou Whitaker, Detroit
3B— George Brett, Kansas City
SS— Alfredo Griffin, Oakland
OF— Gary Pettis, California
OF— Dave Winfield, New York
OF— Dwight Evans, Boston (tie)
      Dwayne Murphy, Oakland (tie)

NATIONAL LEAGUE
P— Rick Reuschel, Pittsburgh
C— Tony Pena, Pittsburgh
1B— Keith Hernandez, New York
2B— Ryne Sandberg, Chicago
3B— Tim Wallach, Montreal
SS— Ozzie Smith, St. Louis
OF— Willie McGee, St. Louis
OF— Dale Murphy, Atlanta
OF— Andre Dawson, Montreal

1986
AMERICAN LEAGUE
P— Ron Guidry, New York
C— Bob Boone, California
1B— Don Mattingly, New York
2B— Frank White, Kansas City
3B— Gary Gaetti, Minnesota
SS— Tony Fernandez, Toronto
OF— Gary Pettis, California
OF— Jesse Barfield, Toronto
OF— Kirby Puckett, Minnesota

NATIONAL LEAGUE
P— Fernando Valenzuela, Los Angeles
C— Jody Davis, Chicago
1B— Keith Hernandez, New York
2B— Ryne Sandberg, Chicago
3B— Mike Schmidt, Philadelphia
SS— Ozzie Smith, St. Louis
OF— Tony Gwynn, San Diego
OF— Dale Murphy, Atlanta
OF— Willie McGee, St. Louis

1987
AMERICAN LEAGUE
P— Mark Langston, Seattle
C— Bob Boone, California
1B— Don Mattingly, New York
2B— Frank White, Kansas City
3B— Gary Gaetti, Minnesota
SS— Tony Fernandez, Toronto
OF— Jesse Barfield, Toronto
OF— Kirby Puckett, Minnesota
OF— Dave Winfield, New York

NATIONAL LEAGUE
P— Rick Reuschel, Pit.-S.F.
C— Mike LaValliere, Pittsburgh
1B— Keith Hernandez, New York
2B— Ryne Sandberg, Chicago
3B— Terry Pendleton, St. Louis
SS— Ozzie Smith, St. Louis
OF— Eric Davis, Cincinnati
OF— Tony Gwynn, San Diego
OF— Andre Dawson, Chicago

1988
AMERICAN LEAGUE
P— Mark Langston, Seattle
C— Bob Boone, California
1B— Don Mattingly, New York
2B— Harold Reynolds, Seattle
3B— Gary Gaetti, Minnesota
SS— Tony Fernandez, Toronto
OF— Kirby Puckett, Minnesota
OF— Devon White, California
OF— Gary Pettis, Detroit

NATIONAL LEAGUE
P— Orel Hershiser, Los Angeles
C— Benito Santiago, San Diego
1B— Keith Hernandez, New York
2B— Ryne Sandberg, Chicago
3B— Tim Wallach, Montreal
SS— Ozzie Smith, St. Louis
OF— Andy Van Slyke, Pittsburgh
OF— Eric Davis, Cincinnati
OF— Andre Dawson, Chicago

1989
AMERICAN LEAGUE
P— Bret Saberhagen, Kansas City
C— Bob Boone, Kansas City
1B— Don Mattingly, New York
2B— Harold Reynolds, Seattle
3B— Gary Gaetti, Minnesota
SS— Tony Fernandez, Toronto
OF— Kirby Puckett, Minnesota
OF— Devon White, California
OF— Gary Pettis, Detroit

NATIONAL LEAGUE
P— Ron Darling, New York
C— Benito Santiago, San Diego
1B— Andres Galarraga, Montreal
2B— Ryne Sandberg, Chicago
3B— Terry Pendleton, St. Louis
SS— Ozzie Smith, St. Louis
OF— Andy Van Slyke, Pittsburgh
OF— Tony Gwynn, San Diego
OF— Eric Davis, Cincinnati

1990
AMERICAN LEAGUE
P— Mike Boddicker, Boston
C— Sandy Alomar Jr., Cleveland
1B— Mark McGwire, Oakland
2B— Harold Reynolds, Seattle
3B— Kelly Gruber, Toronto
SS— Ozzie Guillen, Chicago
OF— Ken Griffey Jr., Seattle
OF— Ellis Burks, Boston
OF— Gary Pettis, Texas

NATIONAL LEAGUE
P— Greg Maddux, Chicago
C— Benito Santiago, San Diego
1B— Andres Galarraga, Montreal
2B— Ryne Sandberg, Chicago
3B— Tim Wallach, Montreal
SS— Ozzie Smith, St. Louis
OF— Barry Bonds, Pittsburgh
OF— Andy Van Slyke, Pittsburgh
OF— Tony Gwynn, San Diego

1991
AMERICAN LEAGUE
P— Mark Langston, California
C— Tony Pena, Boston
1B— Don Mattingly, New York
2B— Roberto Alomar, Toronto
3B— Robin Ventura, Chicago
SS— Cal Ripken, Baltimore
OF— Ken Griffey Jr., Seattle
OF— Kirby Puckett, Minnesota
OF— Devon White, Toronto

NATIONAL LEAGUE
P— Greg Maddux, Chicago
C— Tom Pagnozzi, St. Louis
1B— Will Clark, San Francisco
2B— Ryne Sandberg, Chicago
3B— Matt Williams, San Francisco
SS— Ozzie Smith, St. Louis
OF— Barry Bonds, Pittsburgh
OF— Andy Van Slyke, Pittsburgh
OF— Tony Gwynn, San Diego

1992
AMERICAN LEAGUE
P— Mark Langston, California
C— Ivan Rodriguez, Texas
1B— Don Mattingly, New York
2B— Roberto Alomar, Toronto
3B— Robin Ventura, Chicago
SS— Cal Ripken, Baltimore
OF— Ken Griffey Jr., Seattle
OF— Kirby Puckett, Minnesota
OF— Devon White, Toronto

NATIONAL LEAGUE
P— Greg Maddux, Chicago
C— Tom Pagnozzi, St. Louis
1B— Mark Grace, Chicago
2B— Jose Lind, Pittsburgh
3B— Terry Pendleton, Atlanta
SS— Ozzie Smith, St. Louis
OF— Barry Bonds, Pittsburgh
OF— Andy Van Slyke, Pittsburgh
OF— Larry Walker, Montreal

1993
AMERICAN LEAGUE
P— Mark Langston, California
C— Ivan Rodriguez, Texas
1B— Don Mattingly, New York
2B— Roberto Alomar, Toronto
3B— Robin Ventura, Chicago
SS— Omar Vizquel, Seattle
OF— Ken Griffey Jr., Seattle
OF— Kenny Lofton, Cleveland
OF— Devon White, Toronto

NATIONAL LEAGUE
P— Greg Maddux, Atlanta
C— Kirt Manwaring, San Francisco
1B— Mark Grace, Chicago
2B— Robby Thompson, San Fran.
3B— Matt Williams, San Francisco
SS— Jay Bell, Pittsburgh
OF— Barry Bonds, San Francisco
OF— Marquis Grissom, Montreal
OF— Larry Walker, Montreal

1994
AMERICAN LEAGUE
P— Mark Langston, California
C— Ivan Rodriguez, Texas
1B— Don Mattingly, New York
2B— Roberto Alomar, Toronto
3B— Wade Boggs, New York
SS— Omar Vizquel, Cleveland
OF— Ken Griffey Jr., Seattle
OF— Kenny Lofton, Cleveland
OF— Devon White, Toronto

NATIONAL LEAGUE
P— Greg Maddux, Atlanta
C— Tom Pagnozzi, St. Louis
1B— Jeff Bagwell, Houston
2B— Craig Biggio, Houston
3B— Matt Williams, San Francisco
SS— Barry Larkin, Cincinnati
OF— Barry Bonds, San Francisco
OF— Marquis Grissom, Montreal
OF— Darren Lewis, San Francisco

1995
AMERICAN LEAGUE
P— Mark Langston, California
C— Ivan Rodriguez, Texas
1B— J.T. Snow, California
2B— Roberto Alomar, Toronto
3B— Wade Boggs, New York
SS— Omar Vizquel, Cleveland
OF— Ken Griffey Jr., Seattle
OF— Kenny Lofton, Cleveland
OF— Devon White, Toronto

NATIONAL LEAGUE
P— Greg Maddux, Atlanta
C— Charles Johnson, Florida
1B— Mark Grace, Chicago
2B— Craig Biggio, Houston
3B— Ken Caminiti, San Diego
SS— Barry Larkin, Cincinnati
OF— Raul Mondesi, Los Angeles
OF— Marquis Grissom, Atlanta
OF— Steve Finley, San Diego

SILVER SLUGGER TEAMS

1980
AMERICAN LEAGUE
1B— Cecil Cooper, Milwaukee
2B— Willie Randolph, New York
3B— George Brett, Kansas City
SS— Robin Yount, Milwaukee
OF— Ben Oglivie, Milwaukee
OF— Al Oliver, Texas
OF— Willie Wilson, Kansas City
C— Lance Parrish, Detroit
DH— Reggie Jackson, New York

NATIONAL LEAGUE
1B— Keith Hernandez, St. Louis
2B— Manny Trillo, Philadelphia
3B— Mike Schmidt, Philadelphia
SS— Garry Templeton, St. Louis
OF— Dusty Baker, Los Angeles
OF— Andre Dawson, Montreal
OF— George Hendrick, St. Louis
C— Ted Simmons, St. Louis
P— Bob Forsch, St. Louis

1981
AMERICAN LEAGUE
1B— Cecil Cooper, Milwaukee
2B— Bobby Grich, California
3B— Carney Lansford, Boston
SS— Rick Burleson, California
OF— Rickey Henderson, Oakland
OF— Dwight Evans, Boston
OF— Dave Winfield, New York
C— Carlton Fisk, Chicago
DH— Al Oliver, Texas

NATIONAL LEAGUE
1B— Pete Rose, Philadelphia
2B— Manny Trillo, Philadelphia
3B— Mike Schmidt, Philadelphia
SS— Dave Concepcion, Cincinnati
OF— Andre Dawson, Montreal
OF— George Foster, Cincinnati
OF— Dusty Baker, Los Angeles
C— Gary Carter, Montreal
P— Fernando Valenzuela, Los Angeles

1982
AMERICAN LEAGUE
1B— Cecil Cooper, Milwaukee
2B— Damaso Garcia, Toronto
3B— Doug DeCinces, California
SS— Robin Yount, Milwaukee
OF— Dave Winfield, New York
OF— Willie Wilson, Kansas City
OF— Reggie Jackson, California
C— Lance Parrish, Detroit
DH— Hal McRae, Kansas City

NATIONAL LEAGUE
1B— Al Oliver, Montreal
2B— Joe Morgan, San Francisco
3B— Mike Schmidt, Philadelphia
SS— Dave Concepcion, Cincinnati
OF— Dale Murphy, Atlanta
OF— Pedro Guerrero, Los Angeles
OF— Leon Durham, Chicago
C— Gary Carter, Montreal
P— Don Robinson, Pittsburgh

1983
AMERICAN LEAGUE
1B— Eddie Murray, Baltimore
2B— Lou Whitaker, Detroit
3B— Wade Boggs, Boston
SS— Cal Ripken Jr., Baltimore
OF— Jim Rice, Boston
OF— Dave Winfield, New York
OF— Lloyd Moseby, Toronto
C— Lance Parrish, Detroit
DH— Don Baylor, New York

1984
AMERICAN LEAGUE
1B— Eddie Murray, Baltimore
2B— Lou Whitaker, Detroit
3B— Buddy Bell, Texas
SS— Cal Ripken Jr., Baltimore
OF— Tony Armas, Boston
OF— Jim Rice, Boston
OF— Dave Winfield, New York
C— Lance Parrish, Detroit
DH— Andre Thornton, Cleveland

NATIONAL LEAGUE
1B— George Hendrick, St. Louis
2B— Johnny Ray, Pittsburgh
3B— Mike Schmidt, Philadelphia
SS— Dickie Thon, Houston
OF— Andre Dawson, Montreal
OF— Dale Murphy, Atlanta
OF— Jose Cruz, Houston
C— Terry Kennedy, San Diego
P— Fernando Valenzuela, Los Angeles

NATIONAL LEAGUE
1B— Keith Hernandez, New York
2B— Ryne Sandberg, Chicago
3B— Mike Schmidt, Philadelphia
SS— Garry Templeton, San Diego
OF— Dale Murphy, Atlanta
OF— Jose Cruz, Houston
OF— Tony Gwynn, San Diego
C— Gary Carter, Montreal
P— Rick Rhoden, Pittsburgh

1985
AMERICAN LEAGUE
1B— Don Mattingly, New York
2B— Lou Whitaker, Detroit
3B— George Brett, Kansas City
SS— Cal Ripken Jr., Baltimore
OF— Rickey Henderson, New York
OF— Dave Winfield, New York
OF— George Bell, Toronto
C— Carlton Fisk, Chicago
DH— Don Baylor, New York

NATIONAL LEAGUE
1B— Jack Clark, St. Louis
2B— Ryne Sandberg, Chicago
3B— Tim Wallach, Montreal
SS— Hubie Brooks, Montreal
OF— Willie McGee, St. Louis
OF— Dale Murphy, Atlanta
OF— Dave Parker, Cincinnati
C— Gary Carter, New York
P— Rick Rhoden, Pittsburgh

1986
AMERICAN LEAGUE
1B— Don Mattingly, New York
2B— Frank White, Kansas City
3B— Wade Boggs, Boston
SS— Cal Ripken Jr., Baltimore
OF— George Bell, Toronto
OF— Kirby Puckett, Minnesota
OF— Jesse Barfield, Toronto
C— Lance Parrish, Detroit
DH— Don Baylor, Boston

NATIONAL LEAGUE
1B— Glenn Davis, Houston
2B— Steve Sax, Los Angeles
3B— Mike Schmidt, Philadelphia
SS— Hubie Brooks, Montreal
OF— Tony Gwynn, San Diego
OF— Tim Raines, Montreal
OF— Dave Parker, Cincinnati
C— Gary Carter, New York
P— Rick Rhoden, Pittsburgh

1987
AMERICAN LEAGUE
1B— Don Mattingly, New York
2B— Lou Whitaker, Detroit
3B— Wade Boggs, Boston
SS— Alan Trammell, Detroit
OF— George Bell, Toronto
OF— Dwight Evans, Boston
OF— Kirby Puckett, Minnesota
C— Matt Nokes, Detroit
DH— Paul Molitor, Milwaukee

NATIONAL LEAGUE
1B— Jack Clark, St. Louis
2B— Juan Samuel, Philadelphia
3B— Tim Wallach, Montreal
SS— Ozzie Smith, St. Louis
OF— Andre Dawson, Chicago
OF— Eric Davis, Cincinnati
OF— Tony Gwynn, San Diego
C— Benito Santiago, San Diego
P— Bob Forsch, St. Louis

1988
AMERICAN LEAGUE
1B— George Brett, Kansas City
2B— Julio Franco, Cleveland
3B— Wade Boggs, Boston
SS— Alan Trammell, Detroit
OF— Kirby Puckett, Minnesota
OF— Jose Canseco, Oakland
OF— Mike Greenwell, Boston
C— Carlton Fisk, Chicago
DH— Paul Molitor, Milwaukee

NATIONAL LEAGUE
1B— Andres Galarraga, Montreal
2B— Ryne Sandberg, Chicago
3B— Bobby Bonilla, Pittsburgh
SS— Barry Larkin, Cincinnati
OF— Darryl Strawberry, New York
OF— Andy Van Slyke, Pittsburgh
OF— Kirk Gibson, Los Angeles
C— Benito Santiago, San Diego
P— Tim Leary, Los Angeles

1989
AMERICAN LEAGUE
1B— Fred McGriff, Toronto
2B— Julio Franco, Texas
3B— Wade Boggs, Boston
SS— Cal Ripken Jr., Baltimore
OF— Kirby Puckett, Minnesota
OF— Ruben Sierra, Texas
OF— Robin Yount, Milwaukee
C— Mickey Tettleton, Baltimore
DH— Harold Baines, Chi.-Tex.

NATIONAL LEAGUE
1B— Will Clark, San Francisco
2B— Ryne Sandberg, Chicago
3B— Howard Johnson, New York
SS— Barry Larkin, Cincinnati
OF— Kevin Mitchell, San Francisco
OF— Tony Gwynn, San Diego
OF— Eric Davis, Cincinnati
C— Craig Biggio, Houston
P— Don Robinson, San Francisco

1990
AMERICAN LEAGUE
1B— Cecil Fielder, Detroit
2B— Julio Franco, Texas
3B— Kelly Gruber, Toronto
SS— Alan Trammell, Detroit
OF— Rickey Henderson, Oakland
OF— Jose Canseco, Oakland
OF— Ellis Burks, Boston
C— Lance Parrish, California
DH— Dave Parker, Milwaukee

NATIONAL LEAGUE
1B— Eddie Murray, Los Angeles
2B— Ryne Sandberg, Chicago
3B— Matt Williams, San Francisco
SS— Barry Larkin, Cincinnati
OF— Barry Bonds, Pittsburgh
OF— Bobby Bonilla, Pittsburgh
OF— Darryl Strawberry, New York
C— Benito Santiago, San Diego
P— Don Robinson, San Francisco

1991
AMERICAN LEAGUE
1B— Cecil Fielder, Detroit
2B— Julio Franco, Texas
3B— Wade Boggs, Boston
SS— Cal Ripken Jr., Baltimore
OF— Jose Canseco, Oakland
OF— Joe Carter, Toronto
OF— Ken Griffey Jr., Seattle
C— Mickey Tettleton, Detroit
DH— Frank Thomas, Chicago

NATIONAL LEAGUE
1B— Will Clark, San Francisco
2B— Ryne Sandberg, Chicago
3B— Howard Johnson, New York
SS— Barry Larkin, Cincinnati
OF— Barry Bonds, Pittsburgh
OF— Bobby Bonilla, Pittsburgh
OF— Ron Gant, Atlanta
C— Benito Santiago, San Diego
P— Tom Glavine, Atlanta

1992
AMERICAN LEAGUE
1B— Mark McGwire, Oakland
2B— Roberto Alomar, Toronto
3B— Edgar Martinez, Seattle
SS— Travis Fryman, Detroit
OF— Joe Carter, Toronto
OF— Juan Gonzalez, Texas
OF— Kirby Puckett, Minnesota
C— Mickey Tettleton, Detroit
DH— Dave Winfield, Toronto

NATIONAL LEAGUE
1B— Fred McGriff, San Diego
2B— Ryne Sandberg, Chicago
3B— Gary Sheffield, San Diego
SS— Barry Larkin, Cincinnati
OF— Barry Bonds, Pittsburgh
OF— Andy Van Slyke, Pittsburgh
OF— Larry Walker, Montreal
C— Darren Daulton, Philadelphia
P— Dwight Gooden, New York

1993
AMERICAN LEAGUE
1B— Frank Thomas, Chicago
2B— Carlos Baerga, Cleveland
3B— Wade Boggs, New York
SS— Cal Ripken Jr., Baltimore
OF— Albert Belle, Cleveland
OF— Juan Gonzalez, Texas
OF— Ken Griffey Jr., Seattle
C— Mike Stanley, New York
DH— Paul Molitor, Toronto

NATIONAL LEAGUE
1B— Fred McGriff, S.D.-Atl.
2B— Robby Thompson, San Fran.
3B— Matt Williams, San Francisco
SS— Jay Bell, Pittsburgh
OF— Barry Bonds, San Francisco
OF— Lenny Dykstra, Philadelphia
OF— David Justice, Atlanta
C— Mike Piazza, Los Angeles
P— Orel Hershiser, Los Angeles

1994
AMERICAN LEAGUE
1B— Frank Thomas, Chicago
2B— Carlos Baerga, Cleveland
3B— Wade Boggs, New York
SS— Cal Ripken Jr., Baltimore
OF— Albert Belle, Cleveland
OF— Ken Griffey Jr., Seattle
OF— Kirby Puckett, Minnesota
C— Ivan Rodriguez, Texas
DH— Julio Franco, Chicago

NATIONAL LEAGUE
1B— Jeff Bagwell, Houston
2B— Craig Biggio, Houston
3B— Matt Williams, San Francisco
SS— Wil Cordero, Montreal
OF— Moises Alou, Montreal
OF— Barry Bonds, San Francisco
OF— Tony Gwynn, San Diego
C— Mike Piazza, Los Angeles
P— Mark Portugal, San Francisco

1995
AMERICAN LEAGUE
1B— Mo Vaughn, Boston
2B— Chuck Knoblauch, Minnesota
3B— Gary Gaetti, Kansas City
SS— John Valentin, Boston
OF— Albert Belle, Cleveland
OF— Tim Salmon, California
OF— Manny Ramirez, Cleveland
C— Ivan Rodriguez, Texas
DH— Edgar Martinez, Seattle

NATIONAL LEAGUE
1B— Eric Karros, Los Angeles
2B— Craig Biggio, Houston
3B— Vinny Castilla, Colorado
SS— Barry Larkin, Cincinnati
OF— Dante Bichette, Colorado
OF— Tony Gwynn, San Diego
OF— Sammy Sosa, Chicago
C— Mike Piazza, Los Angeles
P— Tom Glavine, Atlanta

MAJOR LEAGUE ALL-STAR TEAMS

1925
1B— Jim Bottomley, St. Louis N.L.
2B— Rogers Hornsby, St. Louis N.L.
SS— Glenn Wright, Pittsburgh N.L.
3B— Pie Traynor, Pittsburgh N.L.
OF— Kiki Cuyler, Pittsburgh N.L.
OF— Max Carey, Pittsburgh N.L.
OF— Goose Goslin, Washington A.L.
C— Mickey Cochrane, Phil. A.L.
P— Walter Johnson, Washington A.L.
P— Ed Rommel, Philadelphia A.L.
P— Dazzy Vance, Brooklyn N.L.

1926
1B— George Burns, Cleveland A.L.
2B— Rogers Hornsby, St. Louis N.L.
SS— Joe Sewell, Cleveland A.L.
3B— Pie Traynor, Pittsburgh N.L.
OF— Goose Goslin, Washington A.L.
OF— John Mostil, Chicago A.L.
OF— Babe Ruth, New York A.L.
C— Bob O'Farrell, St. Louis N.L.
P— Herb Pennock, New York A.L.
P— George Uhle, Cleveland A.L.
P— Grover Alexander, St. Louis N.L.

1927
1B— Lou Gehrig, New York A.L.
2B— Rogers Hornsby, New York N.L.
SS— Travis Jackson, New York N.L.
3B— Pie Traynor, Pittsburgh N.L.
OF— Babe Ruth, New York A.L.
OF— Al Simmons, Philadelphia A.L.
OF— Paul Waner, Pittsburgh N.L.
C— Gabby Hartnett, Chicago N.L.
P— Charley Root, Chicago N.L.
P— Ted Lyons, Chicago A.L.

1928
1B— Lou Gehrig, New York A.L.
2B— Rogers Hornsby, Boston N.L.
SS— Travis Jackson, New York N.L.
3B— Fred Lindstrom, New York N.L.
OF— Babe Ruth, New York A.L.
OF— Heinie Manush, St. Louis A.L.
OF— Paul Waner, Pittsburgh N.L.
C— Mickey Cochrane, Phil. A.L.
P— Lefty Grove, Philadelphia A.L.
P— Waite Hoyt, New York A.L.

1929
1B— Jimmie Foxx, Philadelphia A.L.
2B— Rogers Hornsby, Chicago N.L.
SS— Travis Jackson, New York N.L.
3B— Pie Traynor, Pittsburgh, N.L.
OF— Al Simmons, Philadelphia A.L.
OF— Hack Wilson, Chicago N.L.
OF— Babe Ruth, New York A.L.
C— Mickey Cochrane, Phil. A.L.
P— Lefty Grove, Philadelphia A.L.
P— Burleigh Grimes, Pittsburgh N.L.

1930
1B— Bill Terry, New York N.L.
2B— Frank Frisch, St. Louis N.L.
SS— Joe Cronin, Washington A.L.
3B— Fred Lindstrom, New York N.L.
OF— Al Simmons, Philadelphia A.L.
OF— Hack Wilson, Chicago N.L.
OF— Babe Ruth, New York A.L.
C— Mickey Cochrane, Phil. A.L.
P— Lefty Grove, Philadelphia A.L.
P— Wes Ferrell, Cleveland A.L.

1931
1B— Lou Gehrig, New York A.L.
2B— Frank Frisch, St. Louis N.L.
SS— Joe Cronin, Washington A.L.
3B— Pie Traynor, Pittsburgh N.L.
OF— Al Simmons, Philadelphia A.L.
OF— Earl Averill, Cleveland A.L.
OF— Babe Ruth, New York A.L.
C— Mickey Cochrane, Phil. A.L.
P— Lefty Grove, Philadelphia A.L.
P— George Earnshaw, Phil. A.L.

1932
1B— Jimmie Foxx, Philadelphia A.L.
2B— Tony Lazzeri, New York A.L.
SS— Joe Cronin, Washington A.L.
3B— Pie Traynor, Pittsburgh N.L.
OF— Lefty O'Doul, Brooklyn N.L.
OF— Earl Averill, Cleveland A.L.
OF— Chuck Klein, Philadelphia N.L.
C— Bill Dickey, New York A.L.
P— Lefty Grove, Philadelphia A.L.
P— Lon Warneke, Chicago N.L.

1933
1B— Jimmie Foxx, Philadelphia A.L.
2B— Charley Gehringer, Detroit A.L.
SS— Joe Cronin, Washington A.L.
3B— Pie Traynor, Pittsburgh N.L.
OF— Al Simmons, Chicago A.L.
OF— Wally Berger, Boston N.L.
OF— Chuck Klein, Philadelphia N.L.
C— Bill Dickey, New York A.L.
P— Alvin Crowder, Washington A.L.
P— Carl Hubbell, New York N.L.

1934
1B— Lou Gehrig, New York A.L.
2B— Charley Gehringer, Detroit A.L.
SS— Joe Cronin, Washington A.L.
3B— Mike Higgins, Philadelphia A.L.
OF— Al Simmons, Chicago A.L.
OF— Earl Averill, Cleveland A.L.
OF— Mel Ott, New York N.L.
C— Mickey Cochrane, Detroit A.L.
P— Lefty Gomez, New York A.L.
P— Schoolboy Rowe, Detroit A.L.
P— Dizzy Dean, St. Louis N.L.

1935
1B— Hank Greenberg, Detroit A.L.
2B— Charley Gehringer, Detroit A.L.
SS— Arky Vaughan, Pittsburgh N.L.
3B— Pepper Martin, St. Louis N.L.
OF— Joe Medwick, St. Louis N.L.
OF— Doc Cramer, Philadelphia A.L.
OF— Mel Ott, New York N.L.
C— Mickey Cochrane, Detroit A.L.
P— Carl Hubbell, New York N.L.
P— Dizzy Dean, St. Louis N.L.

1936
1B— Lou Gehrig, New York A.L.
2B— Charley Gehringer, Detroit A.L.
SS— Luke Appling, Chicago A.L.
3B— Mike Higgins, Philadelphia A.L.
OF— Joe Medwick, St. Louis N.L.
OF— Earl Averill, Cleveland A.L.
OF— Mel Ott, New York N.L.
C— Bill Dickey, New York A.L.
P— Carl Hubbell, New York N.L.
P— Dizzy Dean, St. Louis N.L.

1937
1B— Lou Gehrig, New York A.L.
2B— Charley Gehringer, Detroit A.L.
SS— Dick Bartell, New York N.L.
3B— Red Rolfe, New York A.L.
OF— Joe Medwick, St. Louis N.L.
OF— Joe DiMaggio, New York A.L.
OF— Paul Waner, Pittsburgh N.L.
C— Gabby Hartnett, Chicago N.L.
P— Carl Hubbell, New York N.L.
P— Red Ruffing, New York A.L.

1938
1B— Jimmie Foxx, Boston A.L.
2B— Charley Gehringer, Detroit A.L.
SS— Joe Cronin, Boston A.L.
3B— Red Rolfe, New York A.L.
OF— Joe Medwick, St. Louis N.L.
OF— Joe DiMaggio, New York A.L.
OF— Mel Ott, New York N.L.
C— Bill Dickey, New York A.L.
P— Red Ruffing, New York A.L.
P— Lefty Gomez, New York A.L.
P— Johnny Vander Meer, Cin. N.L.

1939
1B— Jimmie Foxx, Boston A.L.
2B— Joe Gordon, New York A.L.
SS— Joe Cronin, Boston A.L.
3B— Red Rolfe, New York A.L.
OF— Joe Medwick, St. Louis N.L.
OF— Joe DiMaggio, New York A.L.
OF— Ted Williams, Boston A.L.
C— Bill Dickey, New York A.L.
P— Red Ruffing, New York A.L.
P— Bob Feller, Cleveland A.L.
P— Bucky Walters, Cincinnati N.L.

1940
1B— Frank McCormick, Cincinnati N.L.
2B— Joe Gordon, New York A.L.
SS— Luke Appling, Chicago A.L.
3B— Stan Hack, Chicago N.L.
OF— Hank Greenberg, Detroit A.L.
OF— Joe DiMaggio, New York A.L.
OF— Ted Williams, Boston A.L.
C— Harry Danning, New York N.L.
P— Bob Feller, Cleveland A.L.
P— Bucky Walters, Cincinnati N.L.
P— Paul Derringer, Cincinnati N.L.

1941
1B— Dolf Camilli, Brooklyn N.L.
2B— Joe Gordon, New York A.L.
SS— Cecil Travis, Washington A.L.
3B— Stan Hack, Chicago N.L.
OF— Ted Williams, Boston A.L.
OF— Joe DiMaggio, New York A.L.
OF— Pete Reiser, Brooklyn N.L.
C— Bill Dickey, New York A.L.
P— Bob Feller, Cleveland A.L.
P— Whitlow Wyatt, Brooklyn N.L.
P— Thornton Lee, Chicago A.L.

1942
1B— Johnny Mize, New York N.L.
2B— Joe Gordon, New York A.L.
SS— Johnny Pesky, Boston A.L.
3B— Stan Hack, Chicago N.L.
OF— Ted Williams, Boston A.L.
OF— Joe DiMaggio, New York A.L.
OF— Enos Slaughter, St. Louis N.L.
C— Mickey Owen, Brooklyn N.L.
P— Mort Cooper, St. Louis N.L.
P— Tiny Bonham, New York A.L.
P— Tex Hughson, Boston A.L.

1943
1B— Rudy York, Detroit A.L.
2B— Billy Herman, Brooklyn N.L.
SS— Luke Appling, Chicago A.L.
3B— Billy Johnson, New York A.L.
OF— Dick Wakefield, Detroit A.L.
OF— Stan Musial, St. Louis N.L.
OF— Bill Nicholson, Chicago N.L.
C— Walker Cooper, St. Louis N.L.
P— Spud Chandler, New York A.L.
P— Mort Cooper, St. Louis N.L.
P— Rip Sewell, Pittsburgh N.L.

1944
1B— Ray Sanders, St. Louis N.L.
2B— Bobby Doerr, Boston A.L.
SS— Marty Marion, St. Louis N.L.
3B— Bob Elliott, Pittsburgh N.L.
OF— Stan Musial, St. Louis N.L.
OF— Dick Wakefield, Detroit A.L.
OF— Dixie Walker, Brooklyn, N.L.
C— Walker Cooper, St. Louis N.L.
P— Hal Newhouser, Detroit A.L.
P— Mort Cooper, St. Louis N.L.
P— Dizzy Trout, Detroit A.L.

1945
1B— Phil Cavarretta, Chicago N.L.
2B— George Stirnweiss, N.Y. A.L.
SS— Marty Marion, St. Louis N.L.
3B— Whitey Kurowski, St. Louis N.L.
OF— Tommy Holmes, Boston N.L.
OF— Andy Pafko, Chicago N.L.
OF— Goody Rosen, Brooklyn N.L.
C— Paul Richards, Detroit A.L.
P— Hal Newhouser, Detroit A.L.
P— Boo Ferriss, Boston A.L.
P— Hank Borowy, Chicago N.L.

1946
1B— Stan Musial, St. Louis N.L.
2B— Bobby Doerr, Boston A.L.
SS— Johnny Pesky, Boston A.L.
3B— George Kell, Detroit A.L.
OF— Ted Williams, Boston A.L.
OF— Dom DiMaggio, Boston A.L.
OF— Enos Slaughter, St. Louis N.L.
C— Aaron Robinson, New York A.L.
P— Hal Newhouser, Detroit A.L.
P— Bob Feller, Cleveland A.L.
P— Boo Ferriss, Boston A.L.

1947
1B— Johnny Mize, New York N.L.
2B— Joe Gordon, Cleveland A.L.
SS— Lou Boudreau, Cleveland A.L.
3B— George Kell, Detroit A.L.
OF— Ted Williams, Boston A.L.
OF— Joe DiMaggio, New York A.L.
OF— Ralph Kiner, Pittsburgh N.L.
C— Walker Cooper, New York N.L.
P— Ewell Blackwell, Cincinnati N.L.
P— Bob Feller, Cleveland A.L.
P— Ralph Branca, Brooklyn N.L.

1948
1B— Johnny Mize, New York N.L.
2B— Joe Gordon, Cleveland A.L.
SS— Lou Boudreau, Cleveland A.L.
3B— Bob Elliott, Boston N.L.
OF— Ted Williams, Boston A.L.
OF— Joe DiMaggio, New York A.L.
OF— Stan Musial, St. Louis N.L.
C— Birdie Tebbetts, Boston A.L.
P— Johnny Sain, Boston N.L.
P— Bob Lemon, Cleveland A.L.
P— Harry Brecheen, St. Louis N.L.

1949
1B— Tommy Henrich, New York A.L.
2B— Jackie Robinson, Brooklyn N.L.
SS— Phil Rizzuto, New York A.L.
3B— George Kell, Detroit A.L.
OF— Ted Williams, Boston A.L.
OF— Stan Musial, St. Louis N.L.
OF— Ralph Kiner, Pittsburgh N.L.
C— Roy Campanella, Brooklyn N.L.
P— Mel Parnell, Boston A.L.
P— Ellis Kinder, Boston A.L.
P— Joe Page, New York A.L.

1950
1B— Walt Dropo, Boston A.L.
2B— Jackie Robinson, Brooklyn N.L.
SS— Phil Rizzuto, New York A.L.
3B— George Kell, Detroit A.L.
OF— Stan Musial, St. Louis N.L.
OF— Ralph Kiner, Pittsburgh N.L.
OF— Larry Doby, Cleveland A.L.
C— Yogi Berra, New York A.L.
P— Vic Raschi, New York A.L.
P— Bob Lemon, Cleveland A.L.
P— Jim Konstanty, Phil. N.L.

1951
1B— Ferris Fain, Philadelphia A.L.
2B— Jackie Robinson, Brooklyn N.L.
SS— Phil Rizzuto, New York A.L.
3B— George Kell, Detroit A.L.
OF— Stan Musial, St. Louis N.L.
OF— Ted Williams, Boston A.L.
OF— Ralph Kiner, Pittsburgh N.L.
C— Roy Campanella, Brooklyn N.L.
P— Sal Maglie, New York N.L.
P— Preacher Roe, Brooklyn N.L.
P— Allie Reynolds, New York A.L.

1952

1B— Ferris Fain, Philadelphia A.L.
2B— Jackie Robinson, Brooklyn N.L.
SS— Phil Rizzuto, New York A.L.
3B— George Kell, Boston A.L.
OF— Stan Musial, St. Louis N.L.
OF— Hank Sauer, Chicago N.L.
OF— Mickey Mantle, New York A.L.
C— Yogi Berra, New York A.L.
P— Robin Roberts, Philadelphia N.L.
P— Bobby Shantz, Philadelphia A.L.
P— Allie Reynolds, New York A.L.

1953

1B— Mickey Vernon, Washington A.L.
2B— Red Schoendienst, St. Louis N.L.
SS— Pee Wee Reese, Brooklyn N.L.
3B— Al Rosen, Cleveland A.L.
OF— Stan Musial, St. Louis N.L.
OF— Duke Snider, Brooklyn N.L.
OF— Carl Furillo, Brooklyn N.L.
C— Roy Campanella, Brooklyn N.L.
P— Robin Roberts, Philadelphia N.L.
P— Warren Spahn, Milwaukee N.L.
P— Bob Porterfield, Washington A.L.

1954

1B— Ted Kluszewski, Cincinnati N.L.
2B— Bobby Avila, Cleveland A.L.
SS— Alvin Dark, New York N.L.
3B— Al Rosen, Cleveland A.L.
OF— Willie Mays, New York N.L.
OF— Stan Musial, St. Louis N.L.
OF— Duke Snider, Brooklyn N.L.
C— Yogi Berra, New York A.L.
P— Bob Lemon, Cleveland A.L.
P— Johnny Antonelli, New York N.L.
P— Robin Roberts, Philadelphia N.L.

1955

1B— Ted Kluszewski, Cincinnati N.L.
2B— Nellie Fox, Chicago A.L.
SS— Ernie Banks, Chicago N.L.
3B— Ed Mathews, Milwaukee N.L.
OF— Duke Snider, Brooklyn N.L.
OF— Ted Williams, Boston A.L.
OF— Al Kaline, Detroit A.L.
C— Roy Campanella, Brooklyn N.L.
P— Robin Roberts, Philadelphia N.L.
P— Don Newcombe, Brooklyn N.L.
P— Whitey Ford, New York A.L.

1956

1B— Ted Kluszewski, Cincinnati N.L.
2B— Nellie Fox, Chicago A.L.
SS— Harvey Kuenn, Detroit A.L.
3B— Ken Boyer, St. Louis N.L.
OF— Mickey Mantle, New York A.L.
OF— Hank Aaron, Milwaukee N.L.
OF— Ted Williams, Boston A.L.
C— Yogi Berra, New York A.L.
P— Don Newcombe, Brooklyn N.L.
P— Whitey Ford, New York A.L.
P— Billy Pierce, Chicago A.L.

1957

1B— Stan Musial, St. Louis N.L.
2B— Red Schoendienst, N.Y.-Mil. N.L.
SS— Gil McDougald, New York A.L.
3B— Ed Mathews, Milwaukee N.L.
OF— Mickey Mantle, New York A.L.
OF— Ted Williams, Boston A.L.
OF— Willie Mays, New York N.L.
C— Yogi Berra, New York A.L.
P— Warren Spahn, Milwaukee N.L.
P— Billy Pierce, Chicago N.L.
P— Jim Bunning, Detroit A.L.

1958

1B— Stan Musial, St. Louis N.L.
2B— Nellie Fox, Chicago A.L.
SS— Ernie Banks, Chicago N.L.
3B— Frank Thomas, Pittsburgh N.L.
OF— Ted Williams, Boston A.L.
OF— Willie Mays, San Francisco N.L.
OF— Hank Aaron, Milwaukee N.L.
C— Del Crandall, Milwaukee N.L.
P— Bob Turley, New York A.L.
P— Warren Spahn, Milwaukee N.L.
P— Bob Friend, Pittsburgh N.L.

1959

1B— Orlando Cepeda, S.F. N.L.
2B— Nellie Fox, Chicago A.L.
SS— Ernie Banks, Chicago N.L.
3B— Ed Mathews, Milwaukee N.L.
OF— Minnie Minoso, Cleveland A.L.
OF— Willie Mays, San Francisco N.L.
OF— Hank Aaron, Milwaukee N.L.
C— Sherm Lollar, Chicago A.L.
P— Early Wynn, Chicago A.L.
P— Sam Jones, San Francisco N.L.
P— Johnny Antonelli, S.F. N.L.

1960

1B— Bill Skowron, New York A.L.
2B— Bill Mazeroski, Pittsburgh N.L.
SS— Ernie Banks, Chicago N.L.
3B— Ed Mathews, Milwaukee N.L.
OF— Minnie Minoso, Chicago A.L.
OF— Willie Mays, San Francisco N.L.
OF— Roger Maris, New York A.L.
C— Del Crandall, Milwaukee N.L.
P— Vernon Law, Pittsburgh N.L.
P— Warren Spahn, Milwaukee N.L.
P— Ernie Broglio, St. Louis N.L.

1961
AMERICAN LEAGUE

1B— Norm Cash, Detroit
2B— Bobby Richardson, New York
SS— Tony Kubek, New York
3B— Brooks Robinson, Baltimore
OF— Mickey Mantle, New York
OF— Roger Maris, New York
OF— Rocky Colavito, Detroit
C— Elston Howard, New York
P— Whitey Ford, New York
P— Frank Lary, Detroit

NATIONAL LEAGUE

1B— Orlando Cepeda, San Francisco
2B— Frank Bolling, Milwaukee
SS— Maury Wills, Los Angeles
3B— Ken Boyer, St. Louis
OF— Willie Mays, San Francisco
OF— Frank Robinson, Cincinnati
OF— Roberto Clemente, Pittsburgh
C— Smoky Burgess, Pittsburgh
P— Joey Jay, Cincinnati
P— Warren Spahn, Milwaukee

1962
AMERICAN LEAGUE

1B— Norm Siebern, Kansas City
2B— Bobby Richardson, New York
SS— Tom Tresh, New York
3B— Brooks Robinson, Baltimore
OF— Leon Wagner, Los Angeles
OF— Mickey Mantle, New York
OF— Al Kaline, Detroit
C— Earl Battey, Minnesota
P— Ralph Terry, New York
P— Dick Donovan, Cleveland

NATIONAL LEAGUE

1B— Orlando Cepeda, San Francisco
2B— Bill Mazeroski, Pittsburgh
SS— Maury Wills, Los Angeles
3B— Ken Boyer, St. Louis
OF— Tommy Davis, Los Angeles
OF— Willie Mays, San Francisco
OF— Frank Robinson, Cincinnati
C— Del Crandall, Milwaukee
P— Don Drysdale, Los Angeles
P— Bob Purkey, Cincinnati

1963
AMERICAN LEAGUE

1B— Joe Pepitone, New York
2B— Bobby Richardson, New York
SS— Luis Aparicio, Baltimore
3B— Frank Malzone, Boston
OF— Carl Yastrzemski, Boston
OF— Albie Pearson, Los Angeles
OF— Al Kaline, Detroit
C— Elston Howard, New York
P— Whitey Ford, New York
P— Gary Peters, Chicago

NATIONAL LEAGUE

1B— Bill White, St. Louis
2B— Jim Gilliam, Los Angeles
SS— Dick Groat, St. Louis
3B— Ken Boyer, St. Louis
OF— Tommy Davis, Los Angeles
OF— Willie Mays, San Francisco
OF— Hank Aaron, Milwaukee
C— John Edwards, Cincinnati
P— Sandy Koufax, Los Angeles
P— Juan Marichal, San Francisco

1964
AMERICAN LEAGUE

1B— Dick Stuart, Boston
2B— Bobby Richardson, New York
SS— Jim Fregosi, Los Angeles
3B— Brooks Robinson, Baltimore
OF— Harmon Killebrew, Minnesota
OF— Mickey Mantle, New York
OF— Tony Oliva, Minnesota
C— Elston Howard, New York
P— Dean Chance, Los Angeles
P— Gary Peters, Chicago

NATIONAL LEAGUE

1B— Bill White, St. Louis
2B— Ron Hunt, New York
SS— Dick Groat, St. Louis
3B— Ken Boyer, St. Louis
OF— Billy Williams, Chicago
OF— Willie Mays, San Francisco
OF— Roberto Clemente, Pittsburgh
C— Joe Torre, Milwaukee
P— Sandy Koufax, Los Angeles
P— Jim Bunning, Philadelphia

1965
AMERICAN LEAGUE

1B— Fred Whitfield, Cleveland
2B— Bobby Richardson, New York
SS— Zoilo Versalles, Minnesota
3B— Brooks Robinson, Baltimore
OF— Carl Yastrzemski, Boston
OF— Jimmie Hall, Minnesota
OF— Tony Oliva, Minnesota
C— Earl Battey, Minnesota
P— Jim Grant, Minnesota
P— Mel Stottlemyre, New York

NATIONAL LEAGUE
1B— Willie McCovey, San Francisco
2B— Pete Rose, Cincinnati
SS— Maury Wills, Los Angeles
3B— Deron Johnson, Cincinnati
OF— Willie Stargell, Pittsburgh
OF— Willie Mays, San Francisco
OF— Hank Aaron, Milwaukee
C— Joe Torre, Milwaukee
P— Sandy Koufax, Los Angeles
P— Juan Marichal, San Francisco

1966
AMERICAN LEAGUE
1B— Boog Powell, Baltimore
2B— Bobby Richardson, New York
SS— Luis Aparicio, Baltimore
3B— Brooks Robinson, Baltimore
OF— Frank Robinson, Baltimore
OF— Al Kaline, Detroit
OF— Tony Oliva, Minnesota
C— Paul Casanova, Washington
P— Jim Kaat, Minnesota
P— Earl Wilson, Detroit

NATIONAL LEAGUE
1B— Felipe Alou, Atlanta
2B— Pete Rose, Cincinnati
SS— Gene Alley, Pittsburgh
3B— Ron Santo, Chicago
OF— Willie Stargell, Pittsburgh
OF— Willie Mays, San Francisco
OF— Roberto Clemente, Pittsburgh
C— Joe Torre, Atlanta
P— Sandy Koufax, Los Angeles
P— Juan Marichal, San Francisco

1967
AMERICAN LEAGUE
1B— Harmon Killebrew, Minnesota
2B— Rod Carew, Minnesota
SS— Jim Fregosi, California
3B— Brooks Robinson, Baltimore
OF— Carl Yastrzemski, Boston
OF— Al Kaline, Detroit
OF— Frank Robinson, Baltimore
C— Bill Freehan, Detroit
P— Jim Lonborg, Boston
P— Earl Wilson, Detroit

NATIONAL LEAGUE
1B— Orlando Cepeda, St. Louis
2B— Bill Mazeroski, Pittsburgh
SS— Gene Alley, Pittsburgh
3B— Ron Santo, Chicago
OF— Hank Aaron, Atlanta
OF— Jim Wynn, Houston
OF— Roberto Clemente, Pittsburgh
C— Tim McCarver, St. Louis
P— Mike McCormick, San Francisco
P— Ferguson Jenkins, Chicago

1968
AMERICAN LEAGUE
1B— Boog Powell, Baltimore
2B— Rod Carew, Minnesota
SS— Luis Aparicio, Chicago
3B— Brooks Robinson, Baltimore
OF— Ken Harrelson, Boston
OF— Willie Horton, Detroit
OF— Frank Howard, Washington
C— Bill Freehan, Detroit
P— Dave McNally, Baltimore
P— Denny McLain, Detroit

NATIONAL LEAGUE
1B— Willie McCovey, San Francisco
2B— Tommy Helms, Cincinnati
SS— Don Kessinger, Chicago
3B— Ron Santo, Chicago
OF— Billy Williams, Chicago
OF— Curt Flood, St. Louis
OF— Pete Rose, Cincinnati
C— Johnny Bench, Cincinnati
P— Bob Gibson, St. Louis
P— Juan Marichal, San Francisco

1969
AMERICAN LEAGUE
1B— Boog Powell, Baltimore
2B— Rod Carew, Minnesota
SS— Rico Petrocelli, Boston
3B— Harmon Killebrew, Minnesota
OF— Frank Howard, Washington
OF— Paul Blair, Baltimore
OF— Reggie Jackson, Oakland
C— Bill Freehan, Detroit
RHP— Denny McLain, Detroit
LHP— Mike Cuellar, Baltimore

NATIONAL LEAGUE
1B— Willie McCovey, San Francisco
2B— Glenn Beckert, Chicago
SS— Don Kessinger, Chicago
3B— Ron Santo, Chicago
OF— Cleon Jones, New York
OF— Matty Alou, Pittsburgh
OF— Hank Aaron, Atlanta
C— Johnny Bench, Cincinnati
RHP— Tom Seaver, New York
LHP— Steve Carlton, St. Louis

1970
AMERICAN LEAGUE
1B— Boog Powell, Baltimore
2B— Dave Johnson, Baltimore
SS— Luis Aparicio, Chicago
3B— Harmon Killebrew, Minnesota
OF— Frank Howard, Washington
OF— Reggie Smith, Boston
OF— Tony Oliva, Minnesota
C— Ray Fosse, Cleveland
RHP— Jim Perry, Minnesota
LHP— Sam McDowell, Cleveland

NATIONAL LEAGUE
1B— Willie McCovey, San Francisco
2B— Glenn Beckert, Chicago
SS— Don Kessinger, Chicago
3B— Tony Perez, Cincinnati
OF— Billy Williams, Chicago
OF— Bobby Tolan, Cincinnati
OF— Hank Aaron, Atlanta
C— Johnny Bench, Cincinnati
RHP— Bob Gibson, St. Louis
LHP— Jim Merritt, Cincinnati

1971
AMERICAN LEAGUE
1B— Norm Cash, Detroit
2B— Cookie Rojas, Kansas City
SS— Leo Cardenas, Minnesota
3B— Brooks Robinson, Baltimore
OF— Merv Rettenmund, Baltimore
OF— Bobby Murcer, New York
OF— Tony Oliva, Minnesota
C— Bill Freehan, Detroit
RHP— Jim Palmer, Baltimore
LHP— Vida Blue, Oakland

NATIONAL LEAGUE
1B— Lee May, Cincinnati
2B— Glenn Beckett, Chicago
SS— Bud Harrelson, New York
3B— Joe Torre, St. Louis
OF— Willie Stargell, Pittsburgh
OF— Willie Davis, Los Angeles
OF— Hank Aaron, Atlanta
C— Manny Sanguillen, Pittsburgh
RHP— Ferguson Jenkins, Chicago
LHP— Steve Carlton, St. Louis

1972
AMERICAN LEAGUE
1B— Dick Allen, Chicago
2B— Rod Carew, Minnesota
SS— Luis Aparicio, Boston
3B— Brooks Robinson, Baltimore
OF— Joe Rudi, Oakland
OF— Bobby Murcer, New York
OF— Richie Scheinblum, Kansas City
C— Carlton Fisk, Boston
RHP— Gaylord Perry, Cleveland
LHP— Wilbur Wood, Chicago

NATIONAL LEAGUE
1B— Willie Stargell, Pittsburgh
2B— Joe Morgan, Cincinnati
SS— Chris Speier, San Francisco
3B— Ron Santo, Chicago
OF— Billy Williams, Chicago
OF— Cesar Cedeno, Houston
OF— Roberto Clemente, Pittsburgh
C— Johnny Bench, Cincinnati
RHP— Ferguson Jenkins, Chicago
LHP— Steve Carlton, Philadelphia

1973
AMERICAN LEAGUE
1B— John Mayberry, Kansas City
2B— Rod Carew, Minnesota
SS— Bert Campaneris, Oakland
3B— Sal Bando, Oakland
OF— Reggie Jackson, Oakland
OF— Amos Otis, Kansas City
OF— Bobby Murcer, New York
C— Thurman Munson, New York
RHP— Jim Palmer, Baltimore
LHP— Ken Holtzman, Oakland

NATIONAL LEAGUE
1B— Tony Perez, Cincinnati
2B— Dave Johnson, Atlanta
SS— Bill Russell, Los Angeles
3B— Darrell Evans, Atlanta
OF— Bobby Bonds, San Francisco
OF— Cesar Cedeno, Houston
OF— Pete Rose, Cincinnati
C— Johnny Bench, Cincinnati
RHP— Tom Seaver, New York
LHP— Ron Bryant, San Francisco

1974
AMERICAN LEAGUE
1B— Dick Allen, Chicago
2B— Rod Carew, Minnesota
SS— Bert Campaneris, Oakland
3B— Sal Bando, Oakland
OF— Joe Rudi, Oakland
OF— Paul Blair, Baltimore
OF— Jeff Burroughs, Texas
C— Thurman Munson, New York
DH— Tommy Davis, Baltimore
RHP— Jim Hunter, Oakland
LHP— Mike Cuellar, Baltimore

NATIONAL LEAGUE
1B— Steve Garvey, Los Angeles
2B— Joe Morgan, Cincinnati
SS— Dave Concepcion, Cincinnati
3B— Mike Schmidt, Philadelphia
OF— Lou Brock, St. Louis
OF— Jim Wynn, Los Angeles
OF— Richie Zisk, Pittsburgh
C— Johnny Bench, Cincinnati
RHP— Andy Messersmith, Los Angeles
LHP— Don Gullett, Cincinnati

1975
AMERICAN LEAGUE
1B— John Mayberry, Kansas City
2B— Rod Carew, Minnesota
SS— Toby Harrah, Texas
3B— Graig Nettles, New York
OF— Jim Rice, Boston
OF— Fred Lynn, Boston
OF— Reggie Jackson, Oakland
C— Thurman Munson, New York
DH— Willie Horton, Detroit
RHP— Jim Palmer, Baltimore
LHP— Jim Kaat, Chicago

NATIONAL LEAGUE
1B— Steve Garvey, Los Angeles
2B— Joe Morgan, Cincinnati
SS— Larry Bowa, Philadelphia
3B— Bill Madlock, Chicago
OF— Greg Luzinski, Philadelphia
OF— Al Oliver, Pittsburgh
OF— Dave Parker, Pittsburgh
C— Johnny Bench, Cincinnati
RHP— Tom Seaver, New York
LHP— Randy Jones, San Diego

1976
AMERICAN LEAGUE
1B— Chris Chambliss, New York
2B— Bobby Grich, Baltimore
3B— George Brett, Kansas City
SS— Mark Belanger, Baltimore
OF— Joe Rudi, Oakland
OF— Mickey Rivers, New York
OF— Reggie Jackson, Baltimore
C— Thurman Munson, New York
DH— Hal McRae, Kansas City
RHP— Jim Palmer, Baltimore
LHP— Frank Tanana, California

NATIONAL LEAGUE
1B— Willie Montanez, S.F.-Atl.
2B— Joe Morgan, Cincinnati
3B— Mike Schmidt, Philadelphia
SS— Dave Concepcion, Cincinnati
OF— George Foster, Cincinnati
OF— Cesar Cedeno, Houston
OF— Ken Griffey, Cincinnati
C— Bob Boone, Philadelphia
RHP— Don Sutton, Los Angeles
LHP— Randy Jones, San Diego

1977
AMERICAN LEAGUE
1B— Rod Carew, Minnesota
2B— Willie Randolph, New York
3B— Graig Nettles, New York
SS— Rick Burleson, Boston
OF— Jim Rice, Boston
OF— Larry Hisle, Minnesota
OF— Bobby Bonds, California
C— Carlton Fisk, Boston
DH— Hal McRae, Kansas City
RHP— Nolan Ryan, California
LHP— Frank Tanana, California

NATIONAL LEAGUE
1B— Steve Garvey, Los Angeles
2B— Joe Morgan, Cincinnati
3B— Mike Schmidt, Philadelphia
SS— Garry Templeton, St. Louis
OF— George Foster, Cincinnati
OF— Dave Parker, Pittsburgh
OF— Greg Luzinski, Philadelphia
C— Ted Simmons, St. Louis
RHP— Rick Reuschel, Chicago
LHP— Steve Carlton, Philadelphia

1978
AMERICAN LEAGUE
1B— Rod Carew, Minnesota
2B— Frank White, Kansas City
3B— Graig Nettles, New York
SS— Robin Yount, Milwaukee
OF— Jim Rice, Boston
OF— Larry Hisle, Milwaukee
OF— Fred Lynn, Boston
C— Jim Sundberg, Texas
DH— Rusty Staub, Detroit
RHP— Jim Palmer, Baltimore
LHP— Ron Guidry, New York

NATIONAL LEAGUE
1B— Steve Garvey, Los Angeles
2B— Dave Lopes, Los Angeles
3B— Pete Rose, Cincinnati
SS— Larry Bowa, Philadelphia
OF— George Foster, Cincinnati
OF— Dave Parker, Pittsburgh
OF— Jack Clark, San Francisco
C— Ted Simmons, St. Louis
RHP— Gaylord Perry, San Diego
LHP— Vida Blue, San Francisco

1979
AMERICAN LEAGUE
1B— Cecil Cooper, Milwaukee
2B— Bobby Grich, California
3B— George Brett, Kansas City
SS— Roy Smalley, Minnesota
OF— Jim Rice, Boston
OF— Fred Lynn, Boston
OF— Ken Singleton, Baltimore
C— Darrell Porter, Kansas City
DH— Don Baylor, California
RHP— Jim Kern, Texas
LHP— Mike Flanagan, Baltimore

NATIONAL LEAGUE
1B— Keith Hernandez, St. Louis
2B— Dave Lopes, Los Angeles
3B— Mike Schmidt, Philadelphia
SS— Garry Templeton, St. Louis
OF— Dave Kingman, Chicago
OF— Omar Moreno, Pittsburgh
OF— Dave Winfield, San Diego
C— Ted Simmons, St. Louis
RHP— Joe Niekro, Houston
LHP— Steve Carlton, Philadelphia

1980
AMERICAN LEAGUE
1B— Cecil Cooper, Milwaukee
2B— Willie Randolph, New York
3B— George Brett, Kansas City
SS— Robin Yount, Milwaukee
OF— Ben Oglivie, Milwaukee
OF— Al Bumbry, Baltimore
OF— Reggie Jackson, New York
DH— Reggie Jackson, New York
C— Rick Cerone, New York
RHP— Steve Stone, Baltimore
LHP— Tommy John, New York

NATIONAL LEAGUE
1B— Keith Hernandez, St. Louis
2B— Manny Trillo, Philadelphia
3B— Mike Schmidt, Philadelphia
SS— Garry Templeton, St. Louis
OF— Dusty Baker, Los Angeles
OF— Cesar Cedeno, Houston
OF— George Hendrick, St. Louis
C— Gary Carter, Montreal
RHP— Jim Bibby, Pittsburgh
LHP— Steve Carlton, Philadelphia

1981
AMERICAN LEAGUE
1B— Cecil Cooper, Milwaukee
2B— Bobby Grich, California
3B— Buddy Bell, Texas
SS— Rick Burleson, California
OF— Rickey Henderson, Oakland
OF— Dwayne Murphy, Oakland
OF— Tony Armas, Oakland
C— Jim Sundberg, Texas
DH— Richie Zisk, Seattle
RHP— Jack Morris, Detroit
LHP— Ron Guidry, New York

NATIONAL LEAGUE
1B— Pete Rose, Philadelphia
2B— Manny Trillo, Philadelphia
3B— Mike Schmidt, Philadelphia
SS— Dave Concepcion, Cincinnati
OF— George Foster, Cincinnati
OF— Andre Dawson, Montreal
OF— Pedro Guerrero, Los Angeles
C— Gary Carter, Montreal
RHP— Tom Seaver, Cincinnati
LHP— Fernando Valenzuela, Los Angeles

1982
AMERICAN LEAGUE
1B— Cecil Cooper, Milwaukee
2B— Damaso Garcia, Toronto
3B— Doug DeCinces, California
SS— Robin Yount, Milwaukee
OF— Dave Winfield, New York
OF— Gorman Thomas, Milwaukee
OF— Dwight Evans, Boston
C— Lance Parrish, Detroit
DH— Hal McRae, Kansas City
RHP— Dave Stieb, Toronto
LHP— Geoff Zahn, California

NATIONAL LEAGUE
1B— Al Oliver, Montreal
2B— Manny Trillo, Philadelphia
3B— Mike Schmidt, Philadelphia
SS— Ozzie Smith, St. Louis
OF— Lonnie Smith, St. Louis
OF— Dale Murphy, Atlanta
OF— Pedro Guerrero, Los Angeles
C— Gary Carter, Montreal
RHP— Steve Rogers, Montreal
LHP— Steve Carlton, Philadelphia

1983
AMERICAN LEAGUE
1B— Eddie Murray, Baltimore
2B— Lou Whitaker, Detroit
3B— Wade Boggs, Boston
SS— Cal Ripken, Baltimore
OF— Jim Rice, Boston
OF— Dave Winfield, New York
OF— Lloyd Moseby, Toronto
C— Carlton Fisk, Chicago
DH— Greg Luzinski, Chicago
RHP— LaMarr Hoyt, Chicago
LHP— Ron Guidry, New York

NATIONAL LEAGUE
1B— George Hendrick, St. Louis
2B— Glenn Hubbard, Atlanta
3B— Mike Schmidt, Philadelphia
SS— Dickie Thon, Houston
OF— Dale Murphy, Atlanta
OF— Andre Dawson, Montreal
OF— Tim Raines, Montreal
C— Tony Pena, Pittsburgh
RHP— John Denny, Philadelphia
LHP— Larry McWilliams, Pittsburgh

1984
AMERICAN LEAGUE
1B— Don Mattingly, New York
2B— Lou Whitaker, Detroit
3B— Buddy Bell, Texas
SS— Cal Ripken, Baltimore
OF— Tony Armas, Boston
OF— Dwight Evans, Boston
OF— Dave Winfield, New York
C— Lance Parrish, Detroit
DH— Dave Kingman, Oakland
RHP— Mike Boddicker, Baltimore
LHP— Willie Hernandez, Detroit

NATIONAL LEAGUE
1B— Keith Hernandez, New York
2B— Ryne Sandberg, Chicago
3B— Mike Schmidt, Philadelphia
SS— Ozzie Smith, St. Louis
OF— Dale Murphy, Atlanta
OF— Jose Cruz, Houston
OF— Tony Gwynn, San Diego
C— Gary Carter, Montreal
RHP— Rick Sutcliffe, Chicago
LHP— Mark Thurmond, San Diego

1985
AMERICAN LEAGUE
1B— Don Mattingly, New York
2B— Damaso Garcia, Toronto
3B— Wade Boggs, Boston
SS— Cal Ripken, Baltimore
OF— Rickey Henderson, New York
OF— Harold Baines, Chicago
OF— Phil Bradley, Seattle
C— Carlton Fisk, Chicago
DH— Don Baylor, New York
RHP— Bret Saberhagen, Kansas City
LHP— Ron Guidry, New York

NATIONAL LEAGUE
1B— Keith Hernandez, New York
2B— Tom Herr, St. Louis
3B— Tim Wallach, Montreal
SS— Ozzie Smith, St. Louis
OF— Dave Parker, Cincinnati
OF— Willie McGee, St. Louis
OF— Dale Murphy, Atlanta
C— Gary Carter, New York
RHP— Dwight Gooden, New York
LHP— John Tudor, St. Louis

1986
AMERICAN LEAGUE
1B— Don Mattingly, New York
2B— Tony Bernazard, Cleveland
3B— Wade Boggs, Boston
SS— Tony Fernandez, Toronto
OF— Jim Rice, Boston
OF— George Bell, Toronto
OF— Kirby Puckett, Minnesota
C— Rich Gedman, Boston
DH— Don Baylor, Boston
RHP— Roger Clemens, Boston
LHP— Teddy Higuera, Milwaukee

NATIONAL LEAGUE
1B— Keith Hernandez, New York
2B— Steve Sax, Los Angeles
3B— Mike Schmidt, Philadelphia
SS— Ozzie Smith, St. Louis
OF— Tim Raines, Montreal
OF— Tony Gwynn, San Diego
OF— Dave Parker, Cincinnati
C— Gary Carter, New York
RHP— Mike Scott, Houston
LHP— Fernando Valenzuela, Los Angeles

1987
AMERICAN LEAGUE
1B— Don Mattingly, New York
2B— Willie Randolph, New York
3B— Wade Boggs, Boston
SS— Alan Trammell, Detroit
OF— George Bell, Toronto
OF— Kirby Puckett, Minnesota
OF— Dwight Evans, Boston
C— Matt Nokes, Detroit
DH— Paul Molitor, Milwaukee
RHP— Roger Clemens, Boston
LHP— Jimmy Key, Toronto

NATIONAL LEAGUE
1B— Jack Clark, St. Louis
2B— Juan Samuel, Philadelphia
3B— Tim Wallach, Montreal
SS— Ozzie Smith, St. Louis
OF— Andre Dawson, Chicago
OF— Tony Gwynn, San Diego
OF— Eric Davis, Cincinnati
C— Benito Santiago, San Diego
RHP— Rick Sutcliffe, Chicago
LHP— Zane Smith, Atlanta

1988
AMERICAN LEAGUE
1B— George Brett, Kansas City
2B— Johnny Ray, California
3B— Wade Boggs, Boston
SS— Alan Trammell, Detroit
OF— Kirby Puckett, Minnesota
OF— Mike Greenwell, Boston
OF— Jose Canseco, Oakland
C— Ernie Whitt, Toronto
DH— Harold Baines, Chicago
RHP— Dave Stewart, Oakland
LHP— Frank Viola, Minnesota

NATIONAL LEAGUE
1B— Will Clark, San Francisco
2B— Ryne Sandberg, Chicago
3B— Bobby Bonilla, Pittsburgh
SS— Barry Larkin, Cincinnati
OF— Darryl Strawberry, New York
OF— Andy Van Slyke, Pittsburgh
OF— Kevin McReynolds, New York
C— Mike LaValliere, Pittsburgh
RHP— Orel Hershiser, Los Angeles
LHP— Danny Jackson, Cincinnati

1989
AMERICAN LEAGUE
1B— Fred McGriff, Toronto
2B— Julio Franco, Texas
3B— Carney Lansford, Oakland
SS— Cal Ripken, Baltimore
OF— Ruben Sierra, Texas
OF— Kirby Puckett, Minnesota
OF— Robin Yount, Milwaukee
C— Mickey Tettleton, Baltimore
DH— Harold Baines, Chi.-Tex.
RHP— Bret Saberhagen, Kansas City
LHP— Chuck Finley, California

NATIONAL LEAGUE
1B— Will Clark, San Francisco
2B— Ryne Sandberg, Chicago
3B— Howard Johnson, New York
SS— Shawon Dunston, Chicago
OF— Tony Gwynn, San Diego
OF— Kevin Mitchell, San Francisco
OF— Eric Davis, Cincinnati
C— Benito Santiago, San Diego
RHP— Mike Scott, Houston
LHP— Mark Davis, San Diego

1990
AMERICAN LEAGUE
1B— Cecil Fielder, Detroit
2B— Julio Franco, Texas
3B— Kelly Gruber, Toronto
SS— Alan Trammell, Detroit
OF— Rickey Henderson, Oakland
OF— Jose Canseco, Oakland
OF— Ellis Burks, Boston
C— Carlton Fisk, Chicago
DH— Dave Parker, Milwaukee
RHP— Bob Welch, Oakland
LHP— Chuck Finley, California

NATIONAL LEAGUE
1B— Eddie Murray, Los Angeles
2B— Ryne Sandberg, Chicago
3B— Matt Williams, San Francisco
SS— Barry Larkin, Cincinnati
OF— Barry Bonds, Pittsburgh
OF— Bobby Bonilla, Pittsburgh
OF— Darryl Strawberry, New York
C— Mike Scioscia, Los Angeles
RHP— Doug Drabek, Pittsburgh
LHP— Frank Viola, New York

1991
AMERICAN LEAGUE
1B— Cecil Fielder, Detroit
2B— Julio Franco, Texas
3B— Wade Boggs, Boston
SS— Cal Ripken, Baltimore
OF— Jose Canseco, Oakland
OF— Joe Carter, Toronto
OF— Ken Griffey Jr., Seattle
C— Mickey Tettleton, Detroit
RHP— Roger Clemens, Boston
LHP— Jim Abbott, California

NATIONAL LEAGUE
1B— Will Clark, San Francisco
2B— Ryne Sandberg, Chicago
3B— Terry Pendleton, Atlanta
SS— Barry Larkin, Cincinnati
OF— Barry Bonds, Pittsburgh
OF— Bobby Bonilla, Pittsburgh
OF— Ron Gant, Atlanta
C— Benito Santiago, San Diego
RHP— Jose Rijo, Cincinnati
LHP— Tom Glavine, Atlanta

1992
AMERICAN LEAGUE
1B— Mark McGwire, Oakland
2B— Roberto Alomar, Toronto
3B— Edgar Martinez, Seattle
SS— Travis Fryman, Detroit
OF— Joe Carter, Toronto
OF— Mike Devereaux, Baltimore
OF— Kirby Puckett, Minnesota
C— Mickey Tettleton, Detroit
RHP— Jack McDowell, Chicago
LHP— Dave Fleming, Seattle

NATIONAL LEAGUE
1B— Fred McGriff, San Diego
2B— Ryne Sandberg, Chicago
3B— Gary Sheffield, San Diego
SS— Barry Larkin, Cincinnati
OF— Barry Bonds, Pittsburgh
OF— Andy Van Slyke, Pittsburgh
OF— Larry Walker, Montreal
C— Darren Daulton, Philadelphia
RHP— Greg Maddux, Chicago
LHP— Tom Glavine, Atlanta

1993
AMERICAN LEAGUE
1B— Frank Thomas, Chicago
2B— Carlos Baerga, Cleveland
3B— Travis Fryman, Detroit
SS— Cal Ripken Jr., Baltimore
OF— Albert Belle, Cleveland
OF— Juan Gonzalez, Texas
OF— Ken Griffey Jr., Seattle
C— Mike Stanley, New York
DH— Paul Molitor, Toronto
RHP— Jack McDowell, Chicago
LHP— Jimmy Key, New York

NATIONAL LEAGUE
1B— Fred McGriff, S.D.-Atl.
2B— Robby Thompson, San Francisco
3B— Matt Williams, San Francisco
SS— Jay Bell, Pittsburgh
OF— Barry Bonds, San Francisco
OF— Lenny Dykstra, Philadelphia
OF— David Justice, Atlanta
C— Mike Piazza, Los Angeles
RHP— Greg Maddux, Atlanta
LHP— Steve Avery, Atlanta

1994
AMERICAN LEAGUE
1B— Frank Thomas, Chicago
2B— Chuck Knoblauch, Minnesota
3B— Wade Boggs, New York
SS— Cal Ripken Jr., Baltimore
OF— Albert Belle, Cleveland
OF— Ken Griffey Jr., Seattle
OF— Kirby Puckett, Minnesota
C— Ivan Rodriguez, Texas
DH— Paul Molitor, Toronto
RHP— David Cone, Kansas City
LHP— Jimmy Key, New York

NATIONAL LEAGUE
1B— Jeff Bagwell, Houston
2B— Craig Biggio, Houston
3B— Matt Williams, San Francisco
SS— Barry Larkin, Cincinnati
OF— Moises Alou, Montreal
OF— Barry Bonds, San Francisco
OF— Tony Gwynn, San Diego
C— Mike Piazza, Los Angeles
RHP— Greg Maddux, Atlanta
LHP— Danny Jackson, Philadelphia

1995
AMERICAN LEAGUE
1B— Mo Vaughn, Boston
2B— Carlos Baerga, Cleveland
3B— Jim Thome, Cleveland
SS— Cal Ripken Jr., Baltimore
OF— Albert Belle, Cleveland
OF— Tim Salmon, California
OF— Jim Edmonds, California
C— Ivan Rodriguez, Texas
DH— Edgar Martinez, Seattle
RHP— Mike Mussina, Baltimore
LHP— Randy Johnson, Seattle

NATIONAL LEAGUE
1B— Eric Karros, Los Angeles
2B— Craig Biggio, Houston
3B— Vinny Castilla, Colorado
SS— Barry Larkin, Cincinnati
OF— Reggie Sanders, Cincinnati
OF— Dante Bichette, Colorado
OF— Sammy Sosa, Chicago
C— Mike Piazza, Los Angeles
RHP— Greg Maddux, Atlanta
LHP— Pete Schourek, Cincinnati

MINOR LEAGUE PLAYER OF THE YEAR

Year   Player, Team, League
1936—John Vander Meer, Durham, Piedmont
1937—Charlie Keller, Newark, International
1938—Fred Hutchinson, Seattle, Pacific Coast
1939—Lou Novikoff, Tulsa, Texas; Los Angeles, Pacific Coast
1940—Phil Rizzuto, Kansas City, American Association
1941—John Lindell, Newark, International
1942—Dick Barrett, Seattle, Pacific Coast
1943—Chet Covington, Scranton, Eastern
1944—Rip Collins, Albany, Eastern
1945—Gil Coan, Chattanooga, Southern
1946—Sibby Sisti, Indianapolis, American Association
1947—Hank Sauer, Syracuse, International
1948—Gene Woodling, San Francisco, Pacific Coast
1949—Orie Arntzen, Albany, Eastern
1950—Frank Saucier, San Antonio, Texas
1951—Gene Conley, Hartford, Eastern
1952—Bill Skowron, Kansas City, American Association
1953—Gene Conley, Toledo, American Association
1954—Herb Score, Indianapolis, American Association
1955—John Murff, Dallas, Texas
1956—Steve Bilko, Los Angeles, Pacific Coast
1957—Norm Siebern, Denver, American Association
1958—Jim O'Toole, Nashville, Southern
1959—Frank Howard, Victoria-Spokane
1960—Willie Davis, Spokane, Pacific Coast
1961—Howie Koplitz, Birmingham, Southern
1962—Bob Bailey, Columbus, International
1963—Don Buford, Indianapolis, International
1964—Mel Stottlemyre, Richmond, International
1965—Joe Foy, Toronto, International
1966—Mike Epstein, Rochester, International

Year   Player, Team, League
1967—Johnny Bench, Buffalo, International
1968—Merv Rettenmund, Rochester, International
1969—Danny Walton, Oklahoma City, American Association
1970—Don Baylor, Rochester, International
1971—Bobby Grich, Rochester, International
1972—Tom Paciorek, Albuquerque, Pacific Coast
1973—Steve Ontiveros, Phoenix, Pacific Coast
1974—Jim Rice, Pawtucket, International
1975—Hector Cruz, Tulsa, American Association
1976—Pat Putnam, Asheville, Western Carolina
1977—Ken Landreaux, S.L.C., Pacific Coast; El Paso, Texas
1978—Champ Summers, Indianapolis, American Association
1979—Mark Bomback, Vancouver, Pacific Coast
1980—Tim Raines, Denver, American Association
1981—Mike Marshall, Albuquerque, Pacific Coast
1982—Ron Kittle, Edmonton, Pacific Coast
1983—Kevin McReynolds, Las Vegas, Pacific Coast
1984—Alan Knicely, Wichita, American Association
1985—Jose Canseco, Hunt., Southern-Tac., Pacific Coast
1986—Tim Pyznarski, Las Vegas, Pacific Coast
1987—Randy Milligan, Tidewater, International
1988—Sandy Alomar Jr., Las Vegas, Pacific Coast
         Gary Sheffield, Denver, American Association (tie)
1989—Sandy Alomar Jr., Las Vegas, Pacific Coast
1990—Jose Offerman, Albuquerque, Pacific Coast
1991—Pedro Martinez, Albuquerque, Pacific Coast
1992—Tim Salmon, Edmonton, Pacific Coast
1993—Cliff Floyd, Harrisburg, Eastern
1994—Derek Jeter, Tampa, Florida State; Albany, Eastern;
         Columbus, International
1995—Karim Garcia, Albuquerque, Pacific Coast

MINOR LEAGUE MANAGER OF THE YEAR

Year   Manager, Team, League
1936—Al Sothoron, Milwaukee, American Association
1937—Jake Flowers, Salisbury, Eastern Shore
1938—Paul Richards, Atlanta, Southern
1939—Bill Meyer, Kansas City, American Association

Year   Manager, Team, League
1940—Larry Gilbert, Nashville, Southern
1941—Burt Shotton, Columbus, American Association
1942—Eddie Dyer, Columbus, American Association
1943—Nick Cullop, Columbus, American Association

Year	Manager, Team, League	Year	Manager, Team, League
1944	Al Thomas, Baltimore, International	1970	Tom Lasorda, Spokane, Pacific Coast
1945	Lefty O'Doul, San Francisco, Pacific Coast	1971	Del Rice, Salt Lake City, Pacific Coast
1946	Clay Hopper, Montreal, International	1972	Hank Bauer, Tidewater, International
1947	Nick Cullop, Milwaukee, American Association	1973	Joe Morgan, Charleston, International
1948	Casey Stengel, Oakland, Pacific Coast	1974	Joe Altobelli, Rochester, International
1949	Fred Haney, Hollywood, Pacific Coast	1975	Joe Frazier, Tidewater, International
1950	Rollie Hemsley, Columbus, American Association	1976	Vern Rapp, Denver, American Association
1951	Charlie Grimm, Milwaukee, American Association	1977	Tommy Thompson, Arkan., Texas
1952	Luke Appling, Memphis, Southern	1978	Les Moss, Evansville, American Association
1953	Bobby Bragan, Hollywood, Pacific Coast	1979	Vern Benson, Syracuse, International
1954	Kerby Farrell, Indianapolis, American Association	1980	Hal Lanier, Springfield, American Association
1955	Bill Rigney, Minneapolis, American Association	1981	Del Crandall, Albuquerque, Pacific Coast
1956	Kerby Farrell, Indianapolis, American Association	1982	George Scherger, Indianapolis, American Association
1957	Ben Geraghty, Wichita, American Association	1983	Bill Dancy, Reading, Eastern
1958	Cal Ermer, Birmingham, Southern	1984	Bob Rodgers, Indianapolis, American Association
1959	Pete Reiser, Victoria, Texas	1985	Jim Fregosi, Louisville, American Association
1960	Mel McGaha, Toronto, International	1986	Joe Sparks, Indianapolis, American Association
1961	Kerby Farrell, Buffalo, International	1987	Terry Collins, Albuquerque, Pacific Coast
1962	Ben Geraghty, Jacksonville, International	1988	Joe Sparks, Indianapolis, American Association
1963	Rollie Hemsley, Indianapolis, International	1989	Bob Bailor, Syracuse, International
1964	Harry Walker, Jacksonville, International	1990	Sal Rende, Omaha, American Association
1965	Grady Hatton, Oklahoma City, Pacific Coast	1991	Chris Chambliss, Greenville, Southern
1966	Bob Lemon, Seattle, Pacific Coast	1992	Grady Little, Greenville, Southern
1967	Bob Skinner, San Diego, Pacific Coast	1993	Jim Tracy, Harrisburg, Eastern
1968	Jack Tighe, Toledo, International	1994	Mike Jirschele, Wilmington, Carolina
1969	Clyde McCullough, Tidewater, International	1995	Pete Mackanin, Ottawa, International

MINOR LEAGUE EXECUTIVE OF THE YEAR (HIGHER CLASSIFICATIONS, 1936-1992)

(Restricted to Class AAA starting in 1963)

Year	Executive, Team, League	Year	Executive, Team, League
1936	Earl Mann, Atlanta, Southern	1965	Harold Cooper, Columbus, International
1937	Robert LaMotte, Savannah, Sally	1966	John Quinn Jr., Hawaii, Pacific Coast
1938	Louis McKenna, St. Paul, American Association	1967	Hillman Lyons, Richmond, International
1939	Bruce Dudley, Louisville, American Association	1968	Gabe Paul Jr., Tulsa, Pacific Coast
1940	Roy Hamey, Kansas City, American Association	1969	Bill Gardner, Louisville, International
1941	Emil Sick, Seattle, Pacific Coast	1970	Dick King, Wichita, American Association
1942	Bill Veeck, Milwaukee, American Association	1971	Carl Steinfeldt Jr., Rochester, International
1943	Clarence Rowland, Los Angeles, Pacific Coast	1972	Don Labbruzzo, Evansville, American Association
1944	William Mulligan, Seattle, Pacific Coast	1973	Merle Miller, Tucson, Pacific Coast
1945	Bruce Dudley, Louisville, American Association	1974	John Carbray, Sacramento, Pacific Coast
1946	Earl Mann, Atlanta, Southern	1975	Stan Naccarato, Tacoma, Pacific Coast
1947	William Purnhage, Waterloo, I.I.I.	1976	Art Teece, Salt Lake City, Pacific Coast
1948	Edward Glennon, Birmingham, Southern	1977	George Sisler Jr., Columbus, International
1949	Ted Sullivan, Indianapolis, American Association	1978	Willie Sanchez, Albuquerque, Pacific Coast
1950	Clearnce (Brick) Laws, Oakland, Pacific Coast	1979	George Sisler Jr., Columbus, International
1951	Robert Howsam, Denver, West	1980	Jim Burris, Denver, American Association
1952	Jack Cooke, Toronto, International	1981	Pat McKernan, Albuquerque, Pacific Coast
1953	Richard Burnett, Dallas, Texas	1982	A. Ray Smith, Louisville, American Association
1954	Edward Stumpf, Indianapolis, American Association	1983	A. Ray Smith, Louisville, American Association
1955	Dewey Soriano, Seattle, Pacific Coast	1984	Mike Tamburro, Pawtucket, International
1956	Robert Howsam, Denver American Association	1985	Patty Cox Hampton, Oklahoma City, American Association
1957	John Stiglmeier, Buffalo, International	1986	Bob Goughan, Rochester, International
1958	Edward Glennon, Birmingham, Southern	1987	Stu Kehoe, Vancouver, Pacific Coast
1959	Edward Leishman, Salt Lake City, Pacific Coast	1988	Bob Rich, Buffalo, American Association
1960	Ray Winder, Little Rock, Southern	1989	Larry Schmittou, Nashville, American Association
1961	Elten Schiller, Omaha, American Association	1990	Greg Corns, Phoenix, Pacific Coast
1962	George Sisler Jr., Rochester, International	1991	Tom Maloney, Denver, American Association
1963	Lewis Matlin, Hawaii, Pacific Coast	1992	Lou Schwechheimer, Pawtucket, International
1964	Edward Leishman, San Diego, Pacific Coast		

MINOR LEAGUE EXECUTIVE OF THE YEAR (LOWER CLASSIFICATIONS, 1950-1990)

(Separate awards for Class AA and Class A started in 1963; for Short Class A in 1988)

Year	Executive, Team, League	Year	Executive, Team, League
1950	H. Cooper, Hutchinson, Western Association	1964	Glynn West, Birmingham, Southern
1951	O. W. (Bill) Hayes, Triple, B.S.		James Bayens, Rock Hill, W. Carolina
1952	Hillman Lyons, Danville, MOV	1965	Dick Butler, Dallas-Ft. Worth, Texas
1953	Carl Roth, Peoria, I.I.I.		Ken. Blackman, Quad Cities, Midwest
1954	James Meagham, Cedar Rapids, I.I.I.	1966	Tom Fleming, Evansville, Southern
1955	John Petrakis, Dubuque, MOV		Cappy Harada, Lodi, California
1956	Marvin Milkes, Fresno, California	1967	Robert Quinn, Reading, Eastern
1957	Richard Wagner, Lincoln, West.		Pat Williams, Spar'burg, W.C.
1958	Gerald Waring, Macon, Sally	1968	Phil Howser, Charlotte, Southern
1959	Clay Dennis, Des Moines, I.I.I.		Merle Miller, Burlington, Midwest
1960	Hubert Kittle, Yakima, Northwest	1969	Charlie Blaney, Albuquerque, Texas
1961	David Steele, Fresno, California		Bill Gorman, Visalia, California
1962	John Quinn Jr., San Jose, California	1970	Carl Sawatski, Arkansas, Texas
1963	Hugh Finnerty, Tulsa, Texas		Bob Williams, Bakersfield, California
	Ben Jewell, M. Valley, Pioneer	1971	Miles Wolff, Savannah, Dixie Association
			Ed Holtz, Appleton, Midwest

Year	Executive, Team, League
1972—	John Begzos, S. Antonio, Texas
	Bob Piccinini, Modesto, California
1973—	Dick Kravitz, Jacksonville, Southern
	Fritz Colschen, Clinton, Midwest
1974—	Jim Paul, El Paso, Texas
	Bing Russell, Portland, Northwest
1975—	Jim Paul, El Paso, Texas
	Cordy Jensen, Eugene, Northwest
1976—	Woodrow Reid, Chattanooga, Southern
	Don Buchheister, Cedar Rapids, Midwest
1977—	Jim Paul, El Paso, Texas
	Harry Pells, Quad Cities, Midwest
1978—	Larry Schmittou, Nashville, Southern
	Dave Hersh, Appleton, Midwest
1979—	Bill Rigney Jr., Midland, Texas
	Tom Romenesko, Greensboro, W.C.
1980—	Frances Crockett, Charlotte, Southern
	Tom Romenesko, Greensboro, W.C.
1981—	Allie Prescott, Memphis, Southern
	Dan Overstreet, Hagerstown, Caro.
1982—	Art Clarkson, Birmingham, Southern
	Bob Carruesco, Stockton, California

Year	Executive, Team, League
1983—	Edward Kenney, New Britain, Eastern
	Terry Reynolds, Vero Beach, Florida State
1984—	Bruce Baldwin, Greenville, Southern
	Dave Tarrolly, Beloit, Midwest
1985—	Ben Bernard, Albany-Colonie, Eastern
	Pete Vonachen, Peoria, Midwest
1986—	Bill Davidson, Midland, Texas
	Rob Dlugozima, Durham, Carolina
1987—	Joe Preseren, Tulsa, Texas
	Skip Weisman, Greensboro, South Atlantic
1988—	Bill Valentine, Arkansas, Texas
	Dennis Bastien, Charleston (W.Va.), South Atlantic
	Bob Beban, Eugene, Northwest
1989—	Chuck Domino, Reading, Eastern
	John Baxter, South Bend, Midwest
	Bill Pereira, Boise, Northwest
1990—	Joe Preseren, Tulsa, Texas
	Dan Chapman, Stockton, California
	Dave Baggott, Salt Lake City, Pioneer

MINOR LEAGUE EXECUTIVE OF THE YEAR

Year	Executive, Team, League
1993—	Todd Vander Woude, Harrisburg, Eastern (AA)
1994—	Scott Lane, West Michigan, Midwest (A)

Year	Executive, Team, League
1995—	Jack and Mary Cain, Portland, Northwest (A)

BASEBALL WRITERS' ASSOCIATION OF AMERICA

MOST VALUABLE PLAYER

AMERICAN LEAGUE

Year	Player	Team	Pos.	Points
1931—	Lefty Grove	Philadelphia	P	78
1932—	Jimmie Foxx	Philadelphia	1B	75
1933—	Jimmie Foxx	Philadelphia	1B	74
1934—	Mickey Cochrane	Detroit	C	67
1935—	Hank Greenberg	Detroit	1B	*80
1936—	Lou Gehrig	New York	1B	73
1937—	Charley Gehringer	Detroit	2B	78
1938—	Jimmie Foxx	Boston	1B	305
1939—	Joe DiMaggio	New York	OF	280
1940—	Hank Greenberg	Detroit	OF	292
1941—	Joe DiMaggio	New York	OF	291
1942—	Joe Gordon	New York	2B	270
1943—	Spud Chandler	New York	P	246
1944—	Hal Newhouser	Detroit	P	236
1945—	Hal Newhouser	Detroit	P	236
1946—	Ted Williams	Boston	OF	224
1947—	Joe DiMaggio	New York	OF	202
1948—	Lou Boudreau	Cleveland	SS	324
1949—	Ted Williams	Boston	OF	272
1950—	Phil Rizzuto	New York	SS	284
1951—	Yogi Berra	New York	C	184
1952—	Bobby Shantz	Philadelphia	P	280
1953—	Al Rosen	Cleveland	3B	*336
1954—	Yogi Berra	New York	C	230
1955—	Yogi Berra	New York	C	218
1956—	Mickey Mantle	New York	OF	*336
1957—	Mickey Mantle	New York	OF	233
1958—	Jackie Jensen	Boston	OF	233
1959—	Nellie Fox	Chicago	2B	295
1960—	Roger Maris	New York	OF	225
1961—	Roger Maris	New York	OF	202
1962—	Mickey Mantle	New York	OF	234
1963—	Elston Howard	New York	C	248
1964—	Brooks Robinson	Baltimore	3B	269
1965—	Zoilo Versalles	Minnesota	SS	275
1966—	Frank Robinson	Baltimore	OF	*280
1967—	Carl Yastrzemski	Boston	OF	275
1968—	Denny McLain	Detroit	P	*280
1969—	Harmon Killebrew	Minnesota	1B-3B	294
1970—	Boog Powell	Baltimore	1B	234
1971—	Vida Blue	Oakland	P	268
1972—	Dick Allen	Chicago	1B	321
1973—	Reggie Jackson	Oakland	OF	*336
1974—	Jeff Burroughs	Texas	OF	248
1975—	Fred Lynn	Boston	OF	326

NATIONAL LEAGUE

Year	Player	Team	Pos.	Points
1931—	Frank Frisch	St. Louis	2B	65
1932—	Chuck Klein	Philadelphia	OF	78
1933—	Carl Hubbell	New York	P	77
1934—	Dizzy Dean	St. Louis	P	78
1935—	Gabby Hartnett	Chicago	C	75
1936—	Carl Hubbell	New York	P	60
1937—	Joe Medwick	St. Louis	OF	70
1938—	Ernie Lombardi	Cincinnati	C	229
1939—	Bucky Walters	Cincinnati	P	303
1940—	Frank McCormick	Cincinnati	1B	274
1941—	Dolf Camilli	Brooklyn	1B	300
1942—	Mort Cooper	St. Louis	P	263
1943—	Stan Musial	St. Louis	OF	267
1944—	Marty Marion	St. Louis	SS	190
1945—	Phil Cavarretta	Chicago	1B	279
1946—	Stan Musial	St. Louis	1B	319
1947—	Bob Elliott	Boston	3B	205
1948—	Stan Musial	St. Louis	OF	303
1949—	Jackie Robinson	Brooklyn	2B	264
1950—	Jim Konstanty	Philadelphia	P	286
1951—	Roy Campanella	Brooklyn	C	243
1952—	Hank Sauer	Chicago	OF	226
1953—	Roy Campanella	Brooklyn	C	297
1954—	Willie Mays	New York	OF	283
1955—	Roy Campanella	Brooklyn	C	226
1956—	Don Newcombe	Brooklyn	P	223
1957—	Hank Aaron	Milwaukee	OF	239
1958—	Ernie Banks	Chicago	SS	283
1959—	Ernie Banks	Chicago	SS	2321/2
1960—	Dick Groat	Pittsburgh	SS	276
1961—	Frank Robinson	Cincinnati	OF	219
1962—	Maury Wills	Los Angeles	SS	209
1963—	Sandy Koufax	Los Angeles	P	237
1964—	Ken Boyer	St. Louis	3B	243
1965—	Willie Mays	San Francisco	OF	224
1966—	Roberto Clemente	Pittsburgh	OF	218
1967—	Orlando Cepeda	St. Louis	1B	*280
1968—	Bob Gibson	St. Louis	P	242
1969—	Willie McCovey	San Francisco	1B	265
1970—	Johnny Bench	Cincinnati	C	326
1971—	Joe Torre	St. Louis	3B	318
1972—	Johnny Bench	Cincinnati	C	263
1973—	Pete Rose	Cincinnati	OF	274
1974—	Steve Garvey	Los Angeles	1B	270
1975—	Joe Morgan	Cincinnati	2B	3211/2

Year	Player	Team	Pos.	Points	Year	Player	Team	Pos.	Points
1976—Thurman Munson	New York	C	304		1976—Joe Morgan	Cincinnati	2B	311	
1977—Rod Carew	Minnesota	1B	273		1977—George Foster	Cincinnati	OF	291	
1978—Jim Rice	Boston	OF	352		1978—Dave Parker	Pittsburgh	OF	320	
1979—Don Baylor	California	OF	347		1979—Willie Stargell	Pittsburgh	1B	216	
Keith Hernandez	St. Louis	1B	216						
1980—George Brett	Kansas City	3B	335		1980—Mike Schmidt	Philadelphia	3B	*336	
1981—Rollie Fingers	Milwaukee	P	319		1981—Mike Schmidt	Philadelphia	3B	321	
1982—Robin Yount	Milwaukee	SS	385		1982—Dale Murphy	Atlanta	OF	283	
1983—Cal Ripken Jr.	Baltimore	SS	322		1983—Dale Murphy	Atlanta	OF	318	
1984—Willie Hernandez	Detroit	P	306		1984—Ryne Sandberg	Chicago	2B	326	
1985—Don Mattingly	New York	1B	367		1985—Willie McGee	St. Louis	OF	280	
1986—Roger Clemens	Boston	P	339		1986—Mike Schmidt	Philadelphia	3B	287	
1987—George Bell	Toronto	OF	332		1987—Andre Dawson	Chicago	OF	269	
1988—Jose Canseco	Oakland	OF	*392		1988—Kirk Gibson	Los Angeles	OF	272	
1989—Robin Yount	Milwaukee	OF	256		1989—Kevin Mitchell	San Francisco	OF	314	
1990—Rickey Henderson	Oakland	OF	317		1990—Barry Bonds	Pittsburgh	OF	331	
1991—Cal Ripken Jr.	Baltimore	SS	318		1991—Terry Pendleton	Atlanta	3B	274	
1992—Dennis Eckersley	Oakland	P	306		1992—Barry Bonds	Pittsburgh	OF	304	
1993—Frank Thomas	Chicago	1B	*392		1993—Barry Bonds	San Francisco	OF	372	
1994—Frank Thomas	Chicago	1B	372		1994—Jeff Bagwell	Houston	1B	*392	
1995—Mo Vaughn	Boston	1B	308		1995—Barry Larkin	Cincinnati	SS	281	

*Unanimous selection.

CY YOUNG MEMORIAL AWARD

Year	Pitcher	Team	Votes	Year	Pitcher	Team	Votes
1956—Don Newcombe	Brooklyn	10		1979—A.L.—Mike Flanagan	Baltimore	136	
1957—Warren Spahn	Milwaukee	15		N.L.—Bruce Sutter	Chicago	72	
1958—Bob Turley	New York A.L.	5		1980—A.L.—Steve Stone	Baltimore	100	
1959—Early Wynn	Chicago A.L.	13		N.L.—Steve Carlton	Philadelphia	118	
1960—Vernon Law	Pittsburgh	8		1981—A.L.—Rollie Fingers	Milwaukee	126	
1961—Whitey Ford	New York A.L.	9		N.L.—Fernando Valenzuela	Los Angeles	70	
1962—Don Drysdale	Los Angeles N.L.	14		1982—A.L.—Pete Vuckovich	Milwaukee	87	
1963—Sandy Koufax	Los Angeles N.L.	*20		N.L.—Steve Carlton	Philadelphia	112	
1964—Dean Chance	Los Angeles A.L.	17		1983—A.L.—LaMarr Hoyt	Chicago	116	
1965—Sandy Koufax	Los Angeles N.L.	*20		N.L.—John Denny	Philadelphia	103	
1966—Sandy Koufax	Los Angeles N.L.	*20		1984—A.L.—Willie Hernandez	Detroit	88	
1967—A.L.—Jim Lonborg	Boston	18		N.L.—Rick Sutcliffe	Chicago	*120	
N.L.—Mike McCormick	San Francisco	18		1985—A.L.—Bret Saberhagen	Kansas City	127	
1968—A.L.—Denny McLain	Detroit	*20		N.L.—Dwight Gooden	New York	*120	
N.L.—Bob Gibson	St. Louis	*20		1986—A.L.—Roger Clemens	Boston	*140	
1969—A.L.—Denny McLain	Detroit	10		N.L.—Mike Scott	Houston	98	
Mike Cuellar	Baltimore	10		1987—A.L.—Roger Clemens	Boston	124	
N.L.—Tom Seaver	New York	23		N.L.—Steve Bedrosian	Philadelphia	57	
1970—A.L.—Jim Perry	Minnesota	55		1988—A.L.—Frank Viola	Minnesota	138	
N.L.—Bob Gibson	St. Louis	118		N.L.—Orel Hershiser	Los Angeles	*120	
1971—A.L.—Vida Blue	Oakland	98		1989—A.L.—Bret Saberhagen	Kansas City	138	
N.L.—Fergie Jenkins	Chicago	97		N.L.—Mark Davis	San Diego	107	
1972—A.L.—Gaylord Perry	Cleveland	64		1990—A.L.—Bob Welch	Oakland	107	
N.L.—Steve Carlton	Philadelphia	*120		N.L.—Doug Drabek	Pittsburgh	118	
1973—A.L.—Jim Palmer	Baltimore	88		1991—A.L.—Roger Clemens	Boston	119	
N.L.—Tom Seaver	New York	71		N.L.—Tom Glavine	Atlanta	110	
1974—A.L.—Jim Hunter	Oakland	90		1992—A.L.—Dennis Eckersley	Oakland	107	
N.L.—Mike Marshall	Los Angeles	96		N.L.—Greg Maddux	Chicago	112	
1975—A.L.—Jim Palmer	Baltimore	98		1993—A.L.—Jack McDowell	Chicago	124	
N.L.—Tom Seaver	New York	98		N.L.—Greg Maddux	Atlanta	119	
1976—A.L.—Jim Palmer	Baltimore	108		1994—A.L.—David Cone	Kansas City	108	
N.L.—Randy Jones	San Diego	96		N.L.—Greg Maddux	Atlanta	*140	
1977—A.L.—Sparky Lyle	New York	56½		1995—A.L.—Randy Johnson	Seattle	136	
N.L.—Steve Carlton	Philadelphia	*104		N.L.—Greg Maddux	Atlanta	*140	
1978—A.L.—Ron Guidry	New York	*140					
N.L.—Gaylord Perry	San Diego	116					

*Unanimous selection.

ROOKIE OF THE YEAR

1947—Combined selection—Jackie Robinson, Brooklyn N.L., 1B
1948—Combined selection—Alvin Dark, Boston N.L., SS

AMERICAN LEAGUE					NATIONAL LEAGUE				
Year	Player	Team	Pos.	Votes	Year	Player	Team	Pos.	Votes
1949—Roy Sievers	St. Louis	OF	10		1949—Don Newcombe	Brooklyn	P	21	
1950—Walt Dropo	Boston	1B	15		1950—Sam Jethroe	Boston	OF	11	
1951—Gil McDougald	New York	3B	13		1951—Willie Mays	New York	OF	18	
1952—Harry Byrd	Philadelphia	P	9		1952—Joe Black	Brooklyn	P	19	
1953—Harvey Kuenn	Detroit	SS	23		1953—Jim Gilliam	Brooklyn	2B	11	
1954—Bob Grim	New York	P	15		1954—Wally Moon	St. Louis	OF	17	
1955—Herb Score	Cleveland	P	18		1955—Bill Virdon	St. Louis	OF	15	
1956—Luis Aparicio	Chicago	SS	22		1956—Frank Robinson	Cincinnati	OF	*24	
1957—Tony Kubek	New York	IF-OF	23		1957—Jack Sanford	Philadelphia	P	16	
1958—Albie Pearson	Washington	OF	14		1958—Orlando Cepeda	San Francisco	1B	*21	
1959—Bob Allison	Washington	OF	18		1959—Willie McCovey	San Francisco	1B	*24	

HISTORY *Award winners*

Year	Player	Team	Pos.	Votes	Year	Player	Team	Pos.	Votes
1960—Ron Hansen	Baltimore	SS	22		1960—Frank Howard	Los Angeles	OF	12	
1961—Don Schwall	Boston	P	7		1961—Billy Williams	Chicago	OF	10	
1962—Tom Tresh	New York	OF-SS	13		1962—Ken Hubbs	Chicago	2B	19	
1963—Gary Peters	Chicago	P	10		1963—Pete Rose	Cincinnati	2B	17	
1964—Tony Oliva	Minnesota	OF	19		1964—Dick Allen	Philadelphia	3B	18	
1965—Curt Blefary	Baltimore	OF	12		1965—Jim Lefebvre	Los Angeles	2B	13	
1966—Tommie Agee	Chicago	OF	16		1966—Tommy Helms	Cincinnati	3B	12	
1967—Rod Carew	Minnesota	2B	19		1967—Tom Seaver	New York	P	11	
1968—Stan Bahnsen	New York	P	17		1968—Johnny Bench	Cincinnati	C	10½	
1969—Lou Piniella	Kansas City	OF	9		1969—Ted Sizemore	Los Angeles	2B	14	
1970—Thurman Munson	New York	C	23		1970—Carl Morton	Montreal	P	11	
1971—Chris Chambliss	Cleveland	1B	11		1971—Earl Williams	Atlanta	C	18	
1972—Carlton Fisk	Boston	C	*24		1972—Jon Matlack	New York	P	19	
1973—Al Bumbry	Baltimore	OF	13½		1973—Gary Matthews	San Francisco	OF	11	
1974—Mike Hargrove	Texas	1B	16½		1974—Bake McBride	St. Louis	OF	16	
1975—Fred Lynn	Boston	OF	23		1975—John Montefusco	San Francisco	P	12	
1976—Mark Fidrych	Detroit	P	22		1976—Butch Metzger	San Diego	P	11	
					Pat Zachry	Cincinnati	P	11	
1977—Eddie Murray	Baltimore	DH-1B	12½		1977—Andre Dawson	Montreal	OF	10	
1978—Lou Whitaker	Detroit	2B	21		1978—Bob Horner	Atlanta	3B	12½	
1979—John Castino	Minnesota	3B	7		1979—Rick Sutcliffe	Los Angeles	P	20	
Alfredo Griffin	Toronto	SS	7						
1980—Joe Charboneau	Cleveland	OF	103		1980—Steve Howe	Los Angeles	P	80	
1981—Dave Righetti	New York	P	127		1981—Fernando Valenzuela	Los Angeles	P	107	
1982—Cal Ripken	Baltimore	SS-3B	132		1982—Steve Sax	Los Angeles	2B	63	
1983—Ron Kittle	Chicago	OF	104		1983—Darryl Strawberry	New York	OF	109	
1984—Alvin Davis	Seattle	1B	134		1984—Dwight Gooden	New York	P	118	
1985—Ozzie Guillen	Chicago	SS	101		1985—Vince Coleman	St. Louis	OF	*120	
1986—Jose Canseco	Oakland	OF	110		1986—Todd Worrell	St. Louis	P	118	
1987—Mark McGwire	Oakland	1B	*140		1987—Benito Santiago	San Diego	C	*120	
1988—Walt Weiss	Oakland	SS	103		1988—Chris Sabo	Cincinnati	3B	79	
1989—Gregg Olson	Baltimore	P	136		1989—Jerome Walton	Chicago	OF	116	
1990—Sandy Alomar Jr.	Cleveland	C	*140		1990—Dave Justice	Atlanta	OF	118	
1991—Chuck Knoblauch	Minnesota	2B	136		1991—Jeff Bagwell	Houston	1B	118	
1992—Pat Listach	Milwaukee	SS	122		1992—Eric Karros	Los Angeles	1B	116	
1993—Tim Salmon	California	OF	*140		1993—Mike Piazza	Los Angeles	C	*140	
1994—Bob Hamelin	Kansas City	DH	134		1994—Raul Mondesi	Los Angeles	OF	*140	
1995—Marty Cordova	Minnesota	3B	105		1995—Hideo Nomo	Los Angeles	P	118	

*Unanimous selection. †Three writers did not vote.

MANAGER OF THE YEAR

AMERICAN LEAGUE

Year	Manager	Team	Points
1983—Tony La Russa	Chicago	17
1984—Sparky Anderson	Detroit	96
1985—Bobby Cox	Toronto	104
1986—John McNamara	Boston	95
1987—Sparky Anderson	Detroit	90
1988—Tony La Russa	Oakland	103
1989—Frank Robinson	Baltimore	125
1990—Jeff Torborg	Chicago	128
1991—Tom Kelly	Minnesota	138
1992—Tony La Russa	Oakland	132
1993—Gene Lamont	Chicago	72
1994—Buck Showalter	New York	132
1995—Lou Piniella	Seattle	86

NATIONAL LEAGUE

Year	Manager	Team	Points
1983—Tommy Lasorda	Los Angeles	10
1984—Jim Frey	Chicago	101
1985—Whitey Herzog	St. Louis	86
1986—Hal Lanier	Houston	108
1987—Buck Rodgers	Montreal	92
1988—Tommy Lasorda	Los Angeles	101
1989—Don Zimmer	Chicago	118
1990—Jim Leyland	Pittsburgh	99
1991—Bobby Cox	Atlanta	96
1992—Jim Leyland	Pittsburgh	109
1993—Dusty Baker	San Francisco	105
1994—Felipe Alou	Montreal	138
1995—Don Baylor	Colorado	122

EARLY MOST VALUABLE PLAYER AWARDS

CHALMERS AWARD

AMERICAN LEAGUE

Year	Player	Team	Pos.	Points
1911—Ty Cobb	Detroit	OF	64
1912—Tris Speaker	Boston	OF	59
1913—Walter Johnson	Washington	P	54
1914—Eddie Collins	Philadelphia	2B	63

NATIONAL LEAGUE

Year	Player	Team	Pos.	Points
1911—Frank Schulte	Chicago	OF	29
1912—Larry Doyle	New York	2B	48
1913—Jake Daubert	Brooklyn	1B	50
1914—Johnny Evers	Boston	2B	50

LEAGUE AWARDS

AMERICAN LEAGUE

Year	Player	Team	Pos.	Points
1922—George Sisler	St. Louis	1B	59
1923—Babe Ruth	New York	OF	64
1924—Walter Johnson	Washington	P	55
1925—Roger Peckinpaugh	Washington	SS	45
1926—George Burns	Cleveland	1B	63
1927—Lou Gehrig	New York	1B	56
1928—Mickey Cochrane	Philadelphia	C	53
1929—No selection			

NATIONAL LEAGUE

Year	Player	Team	Pos.	Points
1922—No selection			
1923—No selection			
1924—Dazzy Vance	Brooklyn	P	74
1925—Rogers Hornsby	St. Louis	2B	73
1926—Bob O'Farrell	St. Louis	C	79
1927—Paul Waner	Pittsburgh	OF	72
1928—Jim Bottomley	St. Louis	1B	76
1929—Rogers Hornsby	Chicago	2B	60

HALL OF FAME

Name	Des.*	Elec. year	Votes rec.†	Votes cast‡	% of vote	Teams as player
Aaron, Hank	P	1982	406	415	97.8	Milwaukee NL, Atlanta NL, Milwaukee AL
Alexander, Grover C.	P	1938	212	262	80.9	Philadelphia NL, Chicago NL, St. Louis NL
Alston, Walter	M	1983	CV	—	—	St. Louis NL
Anson, Cap	P	1939	C1	—	—	Chicago NL
Aparicio, Luis	P	1984	341	403	84.6	Chicago AL, Baltimore AL, Boston AL
Appling, Luke	P	1964	189	225	84	Chicago AL
Ashburn, Richie	P	1995	CV	—	—	Philadelphia NL, Chicago NL, New York NL
Averill, Earl	P	1975	CV	—	—	Cleveland AL, Detroit AL, Boston AL
Baker, Home Run	P	1955	CV	—	—	Philadelphia AL, New York AL
Bancroft, Dave	P	1971	CV	—	—	Philadelphia NL, New York NL, Boston NL, Brooklyn NL
Banks, Ernie	P	1977	321	383	83.8	Chicago NL
Barlick, Al	U	1989	CV	—	—	
Barrow, Ed	E	1953	CV	—	—	
Beckley, Jake	P	1971	CV	—	—	Pittsburgh NL, Pittsburgh PL, New York NL, Cincinnati NL, St. Louis NL
Bell, Cool Papa	P	1974	SCNL	—	—	Negro Leagues
Bench, Johnny	P	1989	431	447	96.4	Cincinnati NL
Bender, Chief	P	1953	CV	—	—	Philadelphia AL, Philadelphia NL, Chicago AL
Berra, Yogi	P	1972	339	396	85.6	New York AL, New York NL
Bottomley, Jim	P	1974	CV	—	—	St. Louis NL, Cincinnati NL, St. Louis AL
Boudreau, Lou	P	1970	232	300	77.3	Cleveland AL, Boston AL
Bresnahan, Roger	P	1945	C2	—	—	Washington NL, Chicago NL, Baltimore AL, New York NL, St. Louis NL
Brock, Lou	P	1985	315	395	79.7	Chicago NL, St. Louis NL
Brouthers, Dan	P	1945	C2	—	—	Troy NL, Buffalo NL, Detroit NL, Boston NL, Boston PL, Boston AA,Brooklyn NL, Baltimore NL,Louisville NL, Philadelphia NL, New York NL
Brown, Three Finger	P	1949	C2	—	—	St. Louis NL, Chicago NL, Cincinnati NL
Bulkeley, Morgan	E	1937	CC	—	—	
Burkett, Jesse	P	1946	C2	—	—	New York NL, Cleveland NL, St. Louis NL, St. Louis AL, Boston AL
Campanella, Roy	P	1969	270	340	79.4	Brooklyn NL
Carew, Rod	P	1991	401	447	89.7	Minnesota AL, California AL
Carey, Max	P	1961	CV	—	—	Pittsburgh NL, Brooklyn NL
Carlton, Steve	P	1994	436	455	95.8	St. Louis NL, Philadelphia NL, San Francisco NL, Chicago AL, Cleveland AL, Minnesota AL
Cartwright, Alexander	O	1938	CC	—	—	
Chadwick, Henry	O	1938	CC	—	—	
Chance, Frank	P	1946	C2	—	—	Chicago NL, New York AL
Chandler, Happy	E	1982	CV	—	—	
Charleston, Oscar	P	1976	SCNL	—	—	Negro Leagues
Chesbro, Jack	P	1946	C2	—	—	Pittsburgh NL, New York AL, Boston AL
Clarke, Fred	P	1945	C2	—	—	Louisville NL, Pittsburgh NL
Clarkson, John	P	1963	CV	—	—	Worcester NL, Chicago NL, Boston NL, Cleveland NL
Clemente, Roberto	P	1973	393	424	92.7	Pittsburgh NL
Cobb, Ty	P	1936	222	226	98.2	Detroit AL, Philadelphia AL
Cochrane, Mickey	P	1947	128	161	79.5	Philadelphia AL, Detroit AL
Collins, Eddie	P	1939	213	274	77.7	Philadelphia AL, Chicago AL
Collins, Jimmy	P	1945	C2	—	—	Boston NL, Louisville NL, Boston AL, Philadelphia AL
Combs, Earle	P	1970	CV	—	—	New York AL
Comiskey, Charley	F/P	1939	C1	—	—	St. Louis AA, Chicago PL, Cincinnati NL
Conlan, Jocko	U	1974	CV	—	—	Chicago AL
Connolly, Tommy	U	1953	CV	—	—	
Connor, Roger	P	1976	CV	—	—	Troy NL, New York NL, New York PL, Philadelphia NL, St. Louis NL
Coveleski, Stan	P	1969	CV	—	—	Philadelphia AL, Cleveland AL, Washington AL, New York AL
Crawford, Sam	P	1957	CV	—	—	Cincinnati NL, Detroit AL
Cronin, Joe	P	1956	152	193	78.8	Pittsburgh NL, Washington AL, Boston AL
Cummings, Candy	P	1939	C1	—	—	Hartford NL, Cincinnati NL
Cuyler, Kiki	P	1968	CV	—	—	Pittsburgh NL, Chicago NL, Cincinnati NL, Brooklyn NL
Dandridge, Ray	P	1987	CV	—	—	Negro Leagues
Day, Leon	P	1995	CV	—	—	Negro Leagues
Dean, Dizzy	P	1953	209	264	79.2	St. Louis NL, Chicago NL, St. Louis AL
Delahanty, Ed	P	1945	C2	—	—	Philadelphia NL, Cleveland PL, Washington AL
Dickey, Bill	P	1954	202	252	80.2	New York AL
Dihigo, Martin	P	1977	SCNL	—	—	Negro Leagues

HISTORY Hall of Fame

Name	Des.*	Elec. year	Votes rec.†	Votes cast‡	% of vote	Teams as player
DiMaggio, Joe	P	1955	223	251	88.8	New York AL
Doerr, Bobby	P	1986	CV	—	—	Boston AL
Drysdale, Don	P	1984	316	403	78.4	Brooklyn NL, Los Angeles NL
Duffy, Hugh	P	1945	C2	—	—	Chicago NL, Chicago PL, Boston AA, Boston NL, Milwaukee AL, Philadelphia NL
Durocher, Leo	M	1994	CV	—	—	New York AL, Cincinnati NL, St. Louis NL, Brooklyn NL
Evans, Billy	U	1973	CV	—	—	
Evers, Johnny	P	1946	C2	—	—	Chicago NL, Boston NL, Philadelphia NL, Chicago AL
Ewing, Buck	P	1939	C1	—	—	Troy NL, New York NL, New York PL, Cleveland NL, Cincinnati NL
Faber, Red	P	1964	CV	—	—	Chicago AL
Feller, Bob	P	1962	150	160	93.8	Cleveland AL
Ferrell, Rick	P	1984	CV	—	—	St. Louis AL, Boston AL, Washington AL
Fingers, Rollie	P	1992	349	430	81.2	Oakland AL, San Diego NL, Milwaukee AL
Flick, Elmer	P	1963	CV	—	—	Philadelphia NL, Philadelphia AL, Cleveland AL
Ford, Whitey	P	1974	284	365	77.8	New York AL
Foster, Rube	P	1981	CV	—	—	Negro Leagues
Foxx, Jimmie	P	1951	179	226	79.2	Philadelphia AL, Boston AL, Chicago NL, Philadelphia NL
Frick, Ford	E	1970	CV	—	—	
Frisch, Frank	P	1947	136	161	84.5	New York NL, St. Louis NL
Galvin, Pud	P	1965	CV	—	—	Buffalo NL, Pittsburgh AA, Pittsburgh NL, Pittsburgh PL, St. Louis NL
Gehrig, Lou	P	1939	SE	—	—	New York AL
Gehringer, Charley	P	1949	159	187	85.0	Detroit AL
Gibson, Bob	P	1981	337	401	84.0	St. Louis NL
Gibson, Josh	P	1972	SCNL	—	—	Negro Leagues
Giles, Warren	E	1979	CV	—	—	
Gomez, Lefty	P	1972	CV	—	—	New York AL, Washington AL
Goslin, Goose	P	1968	CV	—	—	Washington AL, St. Louis AL, Detroit AL
Greenberg, Hank	P	1956	164	193	85.0	Detroit AL, Pittsburgh NL
Griffith, Clark	M	1946	C2	—	—	St. Louis AA, Boston AA, Chicago NL, Chicago AL, New York AL, Cincinnati NL, Washington AL
Grimes, Burleigh	P	1964	CV	—	—	Pittsburgh NL, Brooklyn NL, New York NL, Boston NL, St. Louis NL, Chicago NL, New York AL
Grove, Lefty	P	1947	123	161	76.4	Philadelphia AL, Boston AL
Hafey, Chick	P	1971	CV	—	—	St. Louis NL, Cincinnati NL
Haines, Jesse	P	1970	CV	—	—	Cincinnati NL, St. Louis NL
Hamilton, Billy	P	1961	CV	—	—	Kansas City AA, Philadelphia NL, Boston NL
Harridge, Will	E	1972	CV	—	—	
Harris, Bucky	M	1975	CV	—	—	Washington AL, Detroit AL
Hartnett, Gabby	P	1955	195	251	77.7	Chicago NL, New York NL
Heilmann, Harry	P	1952	203	234	86.8	Detroit AL, Cincinnati NL
Herman, Billy	P	1975	CV	—	—	Chicago NL, Brooklyn NL, Boston NL, Pittsburgh NL
Hooper, Harry	P	1971	CV	—	—	Boston AL, Chicago AL
Hornsby, Rogers	P	1942	182	233	78.1	St. Louis NL, New York NL, Boston NL, Chicago NL, St. Louis AL
Hoyt, Waite	P	1969	CV	—	—	New York NL, Boston AL, New York AL, Detroit AL, Philadelphia AL, Brooklyn NL, Pittsburgh NL
Hubbard, Cal	U	1976	CV	—	—	
Hubbell, Carl	P	1947	140	161	87.0	New York NL
Huggins, Miller	M	1964	CV	—	—	Cincinnati NL, St. Louis NL
Hulbert, William	F	1995	CV	—	—	
Hunter, Catfish	P	1987	315	413	76.3	Kansas City AL, Oakland AL, New York AL
Irvin, Monte	P	1973	SCNL	—	—	New York NL, Chicago NL, Negro Leagues
Jackson, Reggie	P	1993	396	423	93.6	Kansas City AL, Oakland AL, Baltimore AL, New York AL, California AL
Jackson, Travis	P	1982	CV	—	—	New York NL
Jenkins, Ferguson	P	1991	334	447	74.7	Philadelphia NL, Chicago NL, Texas AL, Boston AL
Jennings, Hugh	P	1945	C2	—	—	Louisville AA, Louisville NL, Baltimore NL, Brooklyn NL, Philadelphia NL, Detroit AL
Johnson, Ban	E	1937	CC	—	—	
Johnson, Judy	P	1975	SCNL	—	—	Negro Leagues
Johnson, Walter	P	1936	189	226	83.6	Washington AL
Joss, Addie	P	1978	CV	—	—	Cleveland AL
Kaline, Al	P	1980	340	385	88.3	Detroit AL
Keefe, Tim	P	1964	CV	—	—	Troy NL, New York AA, New York NL, New York PL, Philadelphia NL
Keeler, Willie	P	1939	207	274	75.5	New York NL, Brooklyn, NL, Baltimore NL, New York AL
Kell, George	P	1983	CV	—	—	Philadelphia AL, Detroit AL, Boston AL, Chicago AL, Baltimore AL

Name	Des.*	Elec. year	Votes rec.†	Votes cast‡	% of vote	Teams as player
Kelley, Joe	P	1971	CV	—	—	Boston NL, Pittsburgh NL, Baltimore NL, Brooklyn NL, Baltimore AL, Cincinnati NL
Kelly, George	P	1973	CV	—	—	New York NL, Pittsburgh NL, Cincinnati NL, Chicago NL, Brooklyn NL
Kelly, Mike	P	1945	C2	—	—	Cincinnati NL, Chicago NL, Boston NL, Boston PL, Cincinnati AA, Boston AA, New York NL
Killebrew, Harmon	P	1984	335	403	83.1	Washington AL, Minnesota AL, Kansas City AL
Kiner, Ralph	P	1975	273	362	75.4	Pittsburgh NL, Chicago NL, Cleveland AL
Klein, Chuck	P	1980	CV	—	—	Philadelphia NL, Chicago NL, Pittsburgh NL
Klem, Bill	U	1953	CV	—	—	
Koufax, Sandy	P	1972	344	396	86.9	Brooklyn NL, Los Angeles NL
Lajoie, Nap	P	1937	168	201	83.6	Philadelphia NL, Philadelphia AL, Cleveland AL
Landis, Kenesaw M.	E	1944	C2	—	—	
Lazzeri, Tony	P	1991	CV	—	—	New York AL, Chicago NL, Brooklyn NL, New York NL
Lemon, Bob	P	1976	305	388	78.6	Cleveland AL
Leonard, Buck	P	1972	SCNL	—	—	Negro Leagues
Lindstrom, Fred	P	1976	CV	—	—	New York NL, Pittsburgh NL, Chicago NL, Brooklyn NL
Lloyd, John Henry	P	1977	SCNL	—	—	Negro Leagues
Lombardi, Ernie	P	1986	CV	—	—	Brooklyn NL, Cincinnati NL, Boston NL, New York NL
Lopez, Al	M	1977	CV	—	—	Brooklyn NL, Boston NL, Pittsburgh NL, Cleveland AL
Lyons, Ted	P	1955	217	251	86.5	Chicago AL
Mack, Connie	M	1937	CC	—	—	Washington NL, Buffalo PL, Pittsburgh NL
MacPhail, Larry	E	1978	CV	—	—	
Mantle, Mickey	P	1974	322	365	88.2	New York AL
Manush, Heinie	P	1964	CV	—	—	Detroit AL, St. Louis AL, Washington AL, Boston AL, Brooklyn NL, Pittsburgh NL
Maranville, Rabbit	P	1954	209	252	82.9	Boston NL, Pittsburgh NL, Chicago NL, Brooklyn NL, St. Louis NL
Marichal, Juan	P	1983	313	374	83.7	San Francisco NL, Boston AL, Los Angeles NL
Marquard, Rube	P	1971	CV	—	—	New York NL, Brooklyn NL, Cincinnati NL, Boston NL
Mathews, Eddie	P	1978	301	379	79.4	Boston NL, Milwaukee NL, Atlanta NL, Houston NL, Detroit AL
Mathewson, Christy	P	1936	205	226	90.7	New York NL, Cincinnati NL
Mays, Willie	P	1979	409	432	94.7	New York (Giants)NL, San Francisco NL, New York (Mets)NL
McCarthy, Joe	M	1957	CV	—	—	
McCarthy, Tommy	P	1946	C2	—	—	Boston UA, Boston NL, Philadelphia NL, St. Louis AA, Brooklyn NL
McCovey, Willie	P	1986	346	425	81.4	San Francisco NL, San Diego NL, Oakland AL
McGinnity, Joe	P	1946	C2	—	—	Baltimore NL, Brooklyn NL, Baltimore AL, New York NL
McGowan, Bill	U	1992	CV	—	—	
McGraw, John	M	1937	CC	—	—	Baltimore AA, Baltimore NL, St. Louis NL, Baltimore AL, New York NL
McKechnie, Bill	M	1962	CV	—	—	Pittsburgh NL, Boston NL, New York AL, New York NL, Cincinnati
Medwick, Joe	P	1968	240	283	84.8	St. Louis NL, Brooklyn NL, New York NL, Boston NL
Mize, Johnny	P	1981	CV	—	—	St. Louis NL, New York NL, New York AL
Morgan, Joe	P	1990	363	444	81.8	Houston NL, Cincinnati NL, San Francisco NL, Philadelphia NL, Oakland AL
Musial, Stan	P	1969	317	340	93.2	St. Louis NL
Newhouser, Hal	P	1992	CV	—	—	Detroit AL, Cleveland AL
Nichols, Kid	P	1949	C2	—	—	Boston NL, St. Louis NL, Philadelphia NL
O'Rourke, Jim	P	1945	C2	—	—	Boston NL, Providence NL, Buffalo NL, New York NL, Washington NL, New York PL
Ott, Mel	P	1951	197	226	87.2	New York NL
Paige, Satchel	P	1971	SCNL	—	—	Cleveland AL, St. Louis AL, Kansas City AL, Negro Leagues
Palmer, Jim	P	1990	411	444	92.6	Baltimore AL
Pennock, Herb	P	1948	94	121	77.7	Philadelphia AL, Boston AL, New York AL
Perry, Gaylord	P	1991	342	447	76.5	San Francisco NL, Cleveland AL, Texas AL, San Diego NL, New York AL, Atlanta NL, Seattle AL, Kansas City AL
Plank, Eddie	P	1946	C2	—	—	Philadelphia AL, St. Louis AL
Radbourn, Hoss	P	1939	C1	—	—	Buffalo NL, Providence NL, Boston NL, Boston PL, Cincinnati NL
Reese, Pee Wee	P	1984	CV	—	—	Brooklyn NL, Los Angeles NL
Rice, Sam	P	1963	CV	—	—	Washington AL, Cleveland AL
Rickey, Branch	E	1967	CV	—	—	St. Louis AL, New York AL
Rixey, Eppa	P	1963	CV	—	—	Philadelphia NL, Cincinnati NL
Rizzuto, Phil	P	1994	CV	—	—	New York AL
Roberts, Robin	P	1976	337	388	86.9	Philadelphia NL, Baltimore AL, Houston NL, Chicago NL

Name	Des.*	Elec. year	Votes rec.†	Votes cast‡	% of vote	Teams as player
Robinson, Brooks	P	1983	344	374	92.0	Baltimore AL
Robinson, Frank	P	1982	370	415	89.2	Cincinnati NL, Baltimore AL, Los Angeles NL, California AL, Cleveland AL
Robinson, Jackie	P	1962	124	160	77.5	Brooklyn NL
Robinson, Wilbert	M	1945	C2	—	—	Philadelphia AA, Baltimore AA, Baltimore NL, St. Louis NL, Baltimore AL
Roush, Edd	P	1962	CV	—	—	Chicago AL, New York NL, Cincinnati NL
Ruffing, Red	P	1967	266	306	86.9	Boston AL, New York AL, Chicago AL
Rusie, Amos	P	1977	CV	—	—	Indianapolis NL, New York NL, Cincinnati NL
Ruth, Babe	P	1936	215	˙226	95.1	Boston AL, New York AL, Boston NL
Schalk, Ray	P	1955	CV	—	—	Chicago AL, New York NL
Schmidt, Mike	P	1995	444	460	96.5	Philadelphia NL
Schoendienst, Red	P	1989	CV	—	—	St. Louis NL, New York (Giants) NL, Milwaukee NL
Seaver, Tom	P	1992	425	430	98.8	New York NL, Cincinnati NL, Chicago AL, Boston AL
Sewell, Joe	P	1977	CV	—	—	Cleveland AL, New York AL
Simmons, Al	P	1953	199	264	75.4	Philadelphia AL, Chicago AL, Detroit AL, Washington AL, Boston NL, Cincinnati NL, Boston AL
Sisler, George	P	1939	235	274	85.8	St. Louis AL, Washington AL, Boston NL
Slaughter, Enos	P	1985	CV	—	—	St. Louis NL, New York AL, Kansas City AL, Milwaukee NL
Snider, Duke	P	1980	333	385	86.5	Brooklyn NL, Los Angeles NL, New York NL, San Francisco NL
Spahn, Warren	P	1973	316	380	83.2	Boston NL, Milwaukee NL, New York NL, San Francisco NL
Spalding, Al	P	1939	C1	—	—	Chicago NL
Speaker, Tris	P	1937	165	201	82.1	Boston AL, Cleveland AL, Washington AL, Philadelphia AL
Stargell, Willie	P	1988	352	427	82.4	Pittsburgh NL
Stengel, Casey	M	1966	CV	—	—	Brooklyn NL, Pittsburgh NL, Philadelphia NL, New York NL, Boston NL
Terry, Bill	P	1954	195	252	77.4	New York NL
Thompson, Sam	P	1974	CV	—	—	Detroit NL, Philadelphia NL, Detroit AL
Tinker, Joe	P	1946	C2	—	—	Chicago NL, Cincinnati NL
Traynor, Pie	P	1948	93	121	76.9	Pittsburgh NL
Vance, Dazzy	P	1955	205	251	81.7	Pittsburgh NL, New York AL, Brooklyn NL, St. Louis NL, Cincinnati NL
Vaughan, Arky	P	1985	CV	—	—	Pittsburgh NL, Brooklyn NL
Veeck, Bill	E	1991	CV	—	—	
Waddell, Rube	P	1946	C2	—	—	Louisville NL, Pittsburgh NL, Chicago NL, Philadelphia AL, St. Louis AL
Wagner, Honus	P	1936	215	226	95.1	Louisville NL, Pittsburgh NL
Wallace, Bobby	P	1953	CV	—	—	Cleveland NL, St. Louis NL, St. Louis AL
Walsh, Ed	P	1946	C2	—	—	Chicago AL, Boston NL
Waner, Lloyd	P	1967	CV	—	—	Pittsburgh NL, Boston NL, Cincinnati NL, Philadelphia NL, Brooklyn NL
Waner, Paul	P	1952	195	234	83.3	Pittsburgh NL, Brooklyn NL, Boston NL, New York AL
Ward, John Montgomery	P	1964	CV	—	—	Providence NL, New York NL, Brooklyn PL, Brooklyn NL
Weiss, George	E	1971	CV	—	—	
Welch, Mickey	P	1973	CV	—	—	Troy NL, New York NL
Wheat, Zack	P	1959	CV	—	—	Brooklyn NL, Philadelphia AL
Wilhelm, Hoyt	P	1985	331	395	83.8	New York NL, St. Louis NL, Cleveland AL, Baltimore AL, Chicago AL California AL, Atlanta NL, Chicago NL, Los Angeles NL
Williams, Billy	P	1987	354	413	85.7	Chicago NL, Oakland AL
Williams, Ted	P	1966	282	302	93.4	Boston AL
Willis, Vic	P	1995	CV	—	—	Boston NL, Pittsburgh NL, St. Louis NL
Wilson, Hack	P	1979	CV	—	—	New York NL, Chicago NL, Brooklyn NL, Philadelphia NL
Wright, George	M	1937	CC	—	—	Boston NL, Providence NL
Wright, Harry	M	1953	CV	—	—	Boston NL
Wynn, Early	P	1972	301	396	76.0	Washington AL, Cleveland AL, Chicago AL
Yastrzemski, Carl	P	1989	423	447	94.6	Boston AL
Yawkey, Tom	E	1980	.CV	—	—	
Young, Cy	P	1937	153	201	76.1	Cleveland NL, St. Louis NL, Boston AL, Cleveland AL, Boston NL
Youngs, Ross	P	1972	CV	—	—	New York NL

*Designation for which he was honored. Abbreviations: E—executive; F—founder; M—manager; O—organizer; P—player; U—umpire.
†Where an abbreviation is listed rather than a vote total, the enshrinee was selected by one of the following groups: Centennial Commission (CC), committee of old-time players and writers (C1), committee on old-timers (C2), Committee on Veterans (CV), special election by Baseball Writers' Association of America (SE) or Special Committee on Negro Leagues (SCNL).
‡Votes cast by eligible members of the Baseball Writers' Association of America.
League abbreviations: AA—American Association; AL—American League; NL—National League; PL—Players League; UA—Union Association.

TEAM BY TEAM

AMERICAN LEAGUE

BALTIMORE ORIOLES

YEARLY FINISHES

Year	Position	W	L	Pct.	*GB	Manager	Attendance
1901†	8th	48	89	.350	35 1/2	Hugh Duffy	139,034
1902‡	2nd	78	58	.574	5	Jimmy McAleer	272,283
1903‡	6th	65	74	.468	26 1/2	Jimmy McAleer	380,405
1904‡	6th	65	87	.428	29	Jimmy McAleer	318,108
1905‡	8th	54	99	.354	40 1/2	Jimmy McAleer	339,112
1906‡	5th	76	73	.510	16	Jimmy McAleer	389,157
1907‡	6th	69	83	.454	24	Jimmy McAleer	419,025
1908‡	4th	83	69	.546	6 1/2	Jimmy McAleer	618,947
1909‡	7th	61	89	.407	36	Jimmy McAleer	366,274
1910‡	8th	47	107	.305	57	John O'Connor	249,889
1911‡	8th	45	107	.296	56 1/2	Bobby Wallace	207,984
1912‡	7th	53	101	.344	53	Bobby Wallace, George Stovall	214,070
1913‡	8th	57	96	.373	39	George Stovall, Branch Rickey	250,330
1914‡	5th	71	82	.464	28 1/2	Branch Rickey	244,714
1915‡	6th	63	91	.409	39 1/2	Branch Rickey	150,358
1916‡	5th	79	75	.513	12	Fielder Jones	335,740
1917‡	7th	57	97	.370	43	Fielder Jones	210,486
1918‡	5th	58	64	.475	15	Fielder Jones, Jimmy Austin, Jimmy Burke	122,076
1919‡	5th	67	72	.482	20 1/2	Jimmy Burke	349,350
1920‡	4th	76	77	.497	21 1/2	Jimmy Burke	419,311
1921‡	3rd	81	73	.526	17 1/2	Lee Fohl	355,978
1922‡	2nd	93	61	.604	1	Lee Fohl	712,918
1923‡	5th	74	78	.487	24	Lee Fohl, Jimmy Austin	430,296
1924‡	4th	74	78	.487	17	George Sisler	533,349
1925‡	3rd	82	71	.536	15	George Sisler	462,898
1926‡	7th	62	92	.403	29	George Sisler	283,986
1927‡	7th	59	94	.336	50 1/2	Dan Howley	247,879
1928‡	3rd	82	72	.532	19	Dan Howley	339,497
1929‡	4th	79	73	.520	26	Dan Howley	280,697
1930‡	6th	64	90	.416	38	Bill Killefer	152,088
1931‡	5th	63	91	.409	45	Bill Killefer	179,126
1932‡	6th	63	91	.409	44	Bill Killefer	112,558
1933‡	8th	55	96	.364	43 1/2	Bill Killefer, Allen Sothoron, Rogers Hornsby	88,113
1934‡	6th	67	85	.441	33	Rogers Hornsby	115,305
1935‡	7th	65	87	.428	28 1/2	Rogers Hornsby	80,922
1936‡	7th	57	95	.375	44 1/2	Rogers Hornsby	93,267
1937‡	8th	46	108	.299	56	Rogers Hornsby, Jim Bottomley	123,121
1938‡	7th	55	97	.362	44	Gabby Street	130,417
1939‡	8th	43	111	.279	64 1/2	Fred Haney	109,159
1940‡	6th	67	87	.435	23	Fred Haney	239,591
1941‡	6th (tied)	70	84	.455	31	Fred Haney, Luke Sewell	176,240
1942‡	3rd	82	69	.543	19 1/2	Luke Sewell	255,617
1943‡	6th	72	80	.474	25	Luke Sewell	214,392
1944‡	1st	89	65	.578	+1	Luke Sewell	508,644
1945‡	3rd	81	70	.536	6	Luke Sewell	482,986
1946‡	7th	66	88	.429	38	Luke Sewell, Zack Taylor	526,435
1947‡	8th	59	95	.383	38	Muddy Ruel	320,474
1948‡	6th	59	94	.386	37	Zack Taylor	335,546
1949‡	7th	53	101	.344	44	Zack Taylor	270,936
1950‡	7th	58	96	.377	40	Zack Taylor	247,131
1951‡	8th	52	102	.338	46	Zack Taylor	293,790
1952‡	7th	64	90	.416	31	Rogers Hornsby, Marty Marion	518,796
1953‡	8th	54	100	.351	46 1/2	Marty Marion	297,238
1954	7th	54	100	.351	57	Jimmie Dykes	1,060,910
1955	7th	57	97	.370	39	Paul Richards	852,039
1956	6th	69	85	.448	28	Paul Richards	901,201
1957	5th	76	76	.500	21	Paul Richards	1,029,581
1958	6th	74	79	.484	17 1/2	Paul Richards	829,991
1959	6th	74	80	.481	20	Paul Richards	891,926
1960	2nd	89	65	.578	8	Paul Richards	1,187,849
1961	3rd	95	67	.586	14	Paul Richards, Luman Harris	951,089
1962	7th	77	85	.475	19	Billy Hitchcock	790,254
1963	4th	86	76	.531	18 1/2	Billy Hitchcock	774,343
1964	3rd	97	65	.599	2	Hank Bauer	1,116,215
1965	3rd	94	68	.580	8	Hank Bauer	781,649
1966	1st	97	63	.606	+9	Hank Bauer	1,203,366

Year	Position	W	L	Pct.	*GB	Manager	Attendance
1967	6th (tied)	76	85	.472	15 1/2	Hank Bauer	955,053
1968	2nd	91	71	.562	12	Hank Bauer, Earl Weaver	943,977

EAST DIVISION

Year	Position	W	L	Pct.	*GB	Manager	Attendance
1969	1st§	109	53	.673	+19	Earl Weaver	1,058,168
1970	1st§	108	54	.667	+15	Earl Weaver	1,057,069
1971	1st§	101	57	.639	+12	Earl Weaver	1,023,037
1972	3rd	80	74	.519	5	Earl Weaver	899,950
1973	1st∞	97	65	.599	+8	Earl Weaver	958,667
1974	1st∞	91	71	.562	+2	Earl Weaver	962,572
1975	2nd	90	69	.566	4 1/2	Earl Weaver	1,002,157
1976	2nd	88	74	.543	10 1/2	Earl Weaver	1,058,609
1977	2nd (tied)	97	64	.602	2 1/2	Earl Weaver	1,195,769
1978	4th	90	71	.559	9	Earl Weaver	1,051,724
1979	1st§	102	57	.642	+8	Earl Weaver	1,681,009
1980	2nd	100	62	.617	3	Earl Weaver	1,797,438
1981	2nd/4th	59	46	.562	▲	Earl Weaver	1,024,652
1982	2nd	94	68	.580	1	Earl Weaver	1,613,031
1983	1st§	98	64	.605	+6	Joe Altobelli	2,042,071
1984	5th	85	77	.525	19	Joe Altobelli	2,045,784
1985	4th	83	78	.516	16	Joe Altobelli, Earl Weaver	2,132,387
1986	7th	73	89	.451	22 1/2	Earl Weaver	1,973,176
1987	6th	67	95	.414	31	Cal Ripken Sr.	1,835,692
1988	7th	54	107	.335	34 1/2	Cal Ripken Sr., Frank Robinson	1,660,738
1989	2nd	87	75	.537	2	Frank Robinson	2,535,208
1990	5th	76	85	.472	11 1/2	Frank Robinson	2,415,189
1991	6th	67	95	.414	24	Frank Robinson, Johnny Oates	2,552,753
1992	3rd	89	73	.549	7	Johnny Oates	3,567,819
1993	3rd (tied)	85	77	.525	10	Johnny Oates	3,644,965
1994	2nd	63	49	.563	6 1/2	Johnny Oates	2,535,359
1995	3rd	71	73	.493	15	Phil Regan	3,098,475

*Games behind winner. †Milwaukee Brewers. ‡St. Louis Browns. §Won championship series. ∞Lost championship series. ▲First half 31-23; second half 28-23.

MANAGERIAL RECORDS

Joe Altobelli 212-167, Jimmy Austin 29-38, Hank Bauer 407-318, Jim Bottomley 21-56, Jimmy Burke 172-180, Hugh Duffy 48-89, Jimmie Dykes 54-100, Lee Fohl 226-183, Fred Haney 125-227, Lum Harris 17-10, Billy Hitchcock 163-161, Rogers Hornsby 255-381, Dan Howley 220-239, Fielder Jones 158-196, Bill Killefer 224-329, Marty Marion 96-161, Jimmy McAleer 551-632, Johnny Oates 291-270, Jack O'Connor 47-107, Phil Regan 71-73, Paul Richards 517-539, Branch Rickey 139-179, Cal Ripken Sr. 67-101, Frank Robinson 230-285, Luke Sewell 432-410, George Sisler 218-241, Al Sothoron 2-6, George Stovall 91-158, Gabby Street 55-97, Zack Taylor 235-410, Bobby Wallace 57-134, Earl Weaver 1,481-1,060.

BOSTON RED SOX

YEARLY FINISHES

Year	Position	W	L	Pct.	*GB	Manager	Attendance
1901	2nd	79	57	.581	4	Jimmy Collins	289,448
1902	3rd	77	60	.562	6 1/2	Jimmy Collins	348,567
1903	1st	91	47	.659	+14 1/2	Jimmy Collins	379,338
1904	1st	95	59	.617	+1 1/2	Jimmy Collins	623,295
1905	4th	78	74	.513	16	Jimmy Collins	468,828
1906	8th	49	105	.318	45 1/2	Jimmy Collins, Chick Stahl	410,209
1907	7th	59	90	.396	32 1/2	George Huff, Bob Unglaub, Deacon McGuire	436,777
1908	5th	75	79	.487	15 1/2	Deacon McGuire, Fred Lake	473,048
1909	3rd	88	63	.583	9 1/2	Fred Lake	668,965
1910	4th	81	72	.529	22 1/2	Patsy Donovan	584,619
1911	5th	78	75	.510	24	Patsy Donovan	503,961
1912	1st	105	47	.691	+14	Jake Stahl	597,096
1913	4th	79	71	.527	15 1/2	Jake Stahl, Bill Carrigan	437,194
1914	2nd	91	62	.595	8 1/2	Bill Carrigan	481,359
1915	1st	101	50	.669	+2 1/2	Bill Carrigan	539,885
1916	1st	91	63	.591	+2	Bill Carrigan	496,397
1917	2nd	90	62	.592	9	Jack Barry	387,856
1918	1st	75	51	.595	+2 1/2	Ed Barrow	249,513
1919	6th	66	71	.482	20 1/2	Ed Barrow	417,291
1920	5th	72	81	.471	25 1/2	Ed Barrow	402,445
1921	5th	75	79	.487	23 1/2	Hugh Duffy	279,273
1922	8th	61	93	.396	33	Hugh Duffy	259,184
1923	8th	61	91	.401	37	Frank Chance	229,668
1924	7th	67	87	.435	25	Lee Fohl	448,556
1925	8th	47	105	.309	49 1/2	Lee Fohl	267,782
1926	8th	46	107	.301	44 1/2	Lee Fohl	285,155

Year	Position	W	L	Pct.	*GB	Manager	Attendance
1927	8th	51	103	.331	59	Bill Carrigan	305,275
1928	8th	57	96	.373	43 1/2	Bill Carrigan	396,920
1929	8th	58	96	.377	48	Bill Carrigan	394,620
1930	8th	52	102	.338	50	Heinie Wagner	444,045
1931	6th	62	90	.408	45	Shano Collins	350,975
1932	8th	43	111	.279	64	Shano Collins, Marty McManus	182,150
1933	7th	63	86	.423	34 1/2	Marty McManus	268,715
1934	4th	76	76	.500	24	Bucky Harris	610,640
1935	4th	78	75	.510	16	Joseph Cronin	558,568
1936	6th	74	80	.481	28 1/2	Joe Cronin	626,895
1937	5th	80	72	.526	21	Joe Cronin	559,659
1938	2nd	88	61	.591	9 1/2	Joe Cronin	646,459
1939	2nd	89	62	.589	17	Joe Cronin	573,070
1940	4th (tied)	82	72	.532	8	Joe Cronin	716,234
1941	2nd	84	70	.545	17	Joe Cronin	718,497
1942	2nd	93	59	.612	9	Joe Cronin	730,340
1943	7th	68	84	.447	29	Joe Cronin	358,275
1944	4th	77	77	.500	12	Joe Cronin	506,975
1945	7th	71	83	.461	17 1/2	Joe Cronin	603,794
1946	1st	104	50	.675	+12	Joe Cronin	1,416,944
1947	3rd	83	71	.539	14	Joe Cronin	1,427,315
1948	2nd†	96	59	.619	1	Joe McCarthy	1,558,798
1949	2nd	96	58	.623	1	Joe McCarthy	1,596,650
1950	3rd	94	60	.610	4	Joe McCarthy, Steve O'Neill	1,344,080
1951	3rd	87	67	.565	11	Steve O'Neill	1,312,282
1952	6th	76	78	.494	19	Lou Boudreau	1,115,750
1953	4th	84	69	.549	16	Lou Boudreau	1,026,133
1954	4th	69	85	.448	42	Lou Boudreau	931,127
1955	4th	84	70	.545	12	Pinky Higgins	1,203,200
1956	4th	84	70	.545	13	Pinky Higgins	1,137,158
1957	3rd	82	72	.532	16	Pinky Higgins	1,181,087
1958	3rd	79	75	.513	13	Pinky Higgins	1,077,047
1959	5th	75	79	.487	19	Pinky Higgins, Billy Jurges	984,102
1960	7th	65	89	.422	32	Billy Jurges, Pinky Higgins	1,129,866
1961	6th	76	86	.469	33	Pinky Higgins	850,589
1962	8th	76	84	.475	19	Pinky Higgins	733,080
1963	7th	76	85	.472	28	Johnny Pesky	942,642
1964	8th	72	90	.444	27	Johnny Pesky, Billy Herman	883,276
1965	9th	62	100	.383	40	Billy Herman	652,201
1966	9th	72	90	.444	26	Billy Herman, Pete Runnels	811,172
1967	1st	92	70	.568	+1	Dick Williams	1,727,832
1968	4th	86	76	.531	17	Dick Williams	1,940,788

EAST DIVISION

Year	Position	W	L	Pct.	*GB	Manager	Attendance
1969	3rd	87	75	.537	22	Dick Williams, Eddie Popowski	1,833,246
1970	3rd	87	75	.537	21	Eddie Kasko	1,595,278
1971	3rd	85	77	.525	18	Eddie Kasko	1,678,732
1972	2nd	85	70	.548	1/2	Eddie Kasko	1,441,718
1973	2nd	89	73	.549	8	Eddie Kasko	1,481,002
1974	3rd	84	78	.519	7	Darrell Johnson	1,556,411
1975	1st‡	95	65	.594	+4 1/2	Darrell Johnson	1,748,587
1976	3rd	83	79	.512	15 1/2	Darrell Johnson, Don Zimmer	1,895,846
1977	2nd (tied)	97	64	.602	2 1/2	Don Zimmer	2,074,549
1978	2nd§	99	64	.607	1	Don Zimmer	2,320,643
1979	3rd	91	69	.569	11 1/2	Don Zimmer	2,353,114
1980	4th	83	77	.519	19	Don Zimmer, Johnny Pesky	1,956,092
1981	5th/2nd (tied)	59	49	.546	∞	Ralph Houk	1,060,379
1982	3rd	89	73	.549	6	Ralph Houk	1,950,124
1983	6th	78	84	.481	20	Ralph Houk	1,782,285
1984	4th	86	76	.531	18	Ralph Houk	1,661,618
1985	5th	81	81	.500	18 1/2	John McNamara	1,786,633
1986	1st‡	95	66	.590	+5 1/2	John McNamara	2,147,641
1987	5th	78	84	.481	20	John McNamara	2,231,551
1988	1st▲	89	73	.549	+1	John McNamara, Joe Morgan	2,464,851
1989	3rd	83	79	.512	6	Joe Morgan	2,510,012
1990	1st▲	88	74	.543	+2	Joe Morgan	2,528,986
1991	2nd (tied)	84	78	.519	7	Joe Morgan	2,562,435
1992	7th	73	89	.451	23	Butch Hobson	2,468,574
1993	5th	80	82	.494	15	Butch Hobson	2,422,021
1994	4th	54	61	.470	17	Butch Hobson	1,775,818
1995	1st◆	86	58	.597	+7	Kevin Kennedy	2,164,410

*Games behind winner. †Lost pennant playoff. ‡Won championship series. §Lost division playoff. ∞First half 30-26; second half 29-23. ▲Lost championship series. ◆Lost division series.

MANAGERIAL RECORDS

Ed Barrow 213-203, Jack Barry 90-62, Lou Boudreau 229-232, Bill Carrigan 489-500, Frank Chance 61-91, Jimmy Collins 455-376, Shano Collins 73-134, Joe Cronin 1,071-916, Patsy Donovan 159-147, Hugh Duffy 136-172, Lee Fohl 160-299, Bucky Harris 76-76, Billy Herman 128-182, Pinky Higgins 560-556, Butch Hobson 207-232, Ralph Houk 312-282, George Huff 2-6, Darrell Johnson 220-188, Billy Jurges 59-63, Eddie Kasko 346-295, Kevin Kennedy 86-58, Fred Lake 110-80, Joe McCarthy 223-145, Deacon McGuire 98-123, Marty McManus 95-153, John McNamara 297-273, Joe Morgan 301-262, Steve O'Neill 150-99, Johnny Pesky 147-179, Eddie Popowski 5-4, Pete Runnels 8-8, Chick Stahl 14-26, Jake Stahl 144-88, Bob Unglaub 9-20, Heinie Wagner 52-102, Dick Williams 260-217, Don Zimmer 411-304.

CALIFORNIA ANGELS

YEARLY FINISHES

Year	Position	W	L	Pct.	*GB	Manager	Attendance
1961†	8th	70	91	.435	38 1/2	Bill Rigney	603,510
1962†	3rd	86	76	.531	10	Bill Rigney	1,144,063
1963†	9th	70	91	.435	34	Bill Rigney	821,015
1964†	5th	82	80	.506	17	Bill Rigney	760,439
1965†	7th	75	87	.463	27	Bill Rigney	566,727
1966	6th	80	82	.494	18	Bill Rigney	1,400,321
1967	5th	84	77	.522	7 1/2	Bill Rigney	1,317,713
1968	8th	67	95	.414	36	Bill Rigney	1,025,956

WEST DIVISION

Year	Position	W	L	Pct.	*GB	Manager	Attendance
1969	3rd	71	91	.438	26	Bill Rigney, Lefty Phillips	758,388
1970	3rd	86	76	.531	12	Lefty Phillips	1,077,741
1971	4th	76	86	.469	25 1/2	Lefty Phillips	926,373
1972	5th	75	80	.484	18	Del Rice	744,190
1973	4th	79	83	.488	15	Bobby Winkles	1,058,206
1974	6th	68	94	.420	22	Bobby Winkles, Dick Williams	917,269
1975	6th	72	89	.447	25 1/2	Dick Williams	1,058,163
1976	4th (tied)	76	86	.469	14	Dick Williams, Norm Sherry	1,006,774
1977	5th	74	88	.457	28	Norm Sherry, Dave Garcia	1,432,633
1978	2nd (tied)	87	75	.537	5	Dave Garcia, Jim Fregosi	1,755,386
1979	1st‡	88	74	.543	+3	Jim Fregosi	2,523,575
1980	6th	65	95	.406	31	Jim Fregosi	2,297,327
1981	4th/7th	51	59	.464	§	Jim Fregosi, Gene Mauch	1,441,545
1982	1st‡	93	69	.574	+3	Gene Mauch	2,807,360
1983	5th (tied)	70	92	.432	29	John McNamara	2,555,016
1984	2nd (tied)	81	81	.500	3	John McNamara	2,402,997
1985	2nd	90	72	.556	1	Gene Mauch	2,567,427
1986	1st‡	92	70	.568	+5	Gene Mauch	2,655,872
1987	6th (tied)	75	87	.463	10	Gene Mauch	2,696,299
1988	4th	75	87	.463	29	Cookie Rojas	2,340,925
1989	3rd	91	71	.562	8	Doug Rader	2,647,291
1990	4th	80	82	.494	23	Doug Rader	2,555,688
1991	7th	81	81	.500	14	Doug Rader, Buck Rodgers	2,416,236
1992	5th (tied)	72	90	.444	24	Buck Rodgers	2,065,444
1993	5th (tied)	71	91	.438	23	Buck Rodgers	2,057,460
1994	4th	47	68	.409	5 1/2	Buck Rodgers, Marcel Lachemann	1,512,622
1995	2nd	78	67	.538	1	Marcel Lachemann	1,748,680

*Games behind winner. †Los Angeles Angels through September 1, 1965. ‡Lost championship series. §First half 31-29; second half 20-30.

MANAGERIAL RECORDS

Jim Fregosi 237-249, Dave Garcia 60-66, Marcel Lachemann 109-111, Gene Mauch 379-332, John McNamara 151-173, Lefty Phillips 222-225, Doug Rader 232-216, Del Rice 75-80, Bill Rigney 625-707, Buck Rodgers 179-223, Cookie Rojas 75-87, Norm Sherry 76-71, Dick Williams 147-194, Bobby Winkles 109-127.

CHICAGO WHITE SOX

YEARLY FINISHES

Year	Position	W	L	Pct.	*GB	Manager	Attendance
1901	1st	83	53	.610	+4	Clark Griffith	354,350
1902	4th	74	60	.552	8	Clark Griffith	337,898
1903	7th	60	77	.438	30 1/2	Nixey Callahan	286,183
1904	3rd	89	65	.578	6	Nixey Callahan, Fielder Jones	557,123
1905	2nd	92	60	.605	2	Fielder Jones	687,419
1906	1st	93	58	.616	+3	Fielder Jones	585,202
1907	3rd	87	64	.576	5 1/2	Fielder Jones	666,307
1908	3rd	88	64	.579	1 1/2	Fielder Jones	636,096

Year	Position	W	L	Pct.	*GB	Manager	Attendance
1909	4th	78	74	.513	20	Billy Sullivan	478,400
1910	6th	68	85	.444	35 1/2	Hugh Duffy	552,084
1911	4th	77	74	.510	24	Hugh Duffy	583,208
1912	4th	78	76	.506	28	Nixey Callahan	602,241
1913	5th	78	74	.513	17 1/2	Nixey Callahan	644,501
1914	6th (tied)	70	84	.455	30	Nixey Callahan	469,290
1915	3rd	93	61	.604	9 1/2	Pants Rowland	539,461
1916	2nd	89	65	.578	2	Pants Rowland	679,923
1917	1st	100	54	.649	+9	Pants Rowland	684,521
1918	6th	57	67	.460	17	Pants Rowland	195,081
1919	1st	88	52	.629	+3 1/2	Kid Gleason	627,186
1920	2nd	96	58	.623	2	Kid Gleason	833,492
1921	7th	62	92	.403	36 1/2	Kid Gleason	543,650
1922	5th	77	77	.500	17	Kid Gleason	602,860
1923	7th	69	85	.448	30	Kid Gleason	573,778
1924	8th	66	87	.431	25 1/2	Johnny Evers	606,658
1925	5th	79	75	.513	18 1/2	Eddie Collins	832,231
1926	5th	81	72	.529	9 1/2	Eddie Collins	710,339
1927	5th	70	83	.458	29 1/2	Ray Schalk	614,423
1928	5th	72	82	.468	29	Ray Schalk, Lena Blackburne	494,152
1929	7th	59	93	.388	46	Lena Blackburne	426,795
1930	7th	62	92	.403	40	Donie Bush	406,123
1931	8th	56	97	.366	51	Donie Bush	403,550
1932	7th	49	102	.325	56 1/2	Lew Fonseca	233,198
1933	6th	67	83	.447	31	Lew Fonseca	397,789
1934	8th	53	99	.349	47	Lew Fonseca, Jimmie Dykes	236,559
1935	5th	74	78	.487	19 1/2	Jimmie Dykes	470,281
1936	3rd	81	70	.536	20	Jimmie Dykes	440,810
1937	3rd	86	68	.558	16	Jimmie Dykes	589,245
1938	6th	65	83	.439	32	Jimmie Dykes	338,278
1939	4th	85	69	.552	22 1/2	Jimmie Dykes	594,104
1940	4th (tied)	82	72	.532	8	Jimmie Dykes	660,336
1941	3rd	77	77	.500	24	Jimmie Dykes	677,077
1942	6th	66	82	.446	34	Jimmie Dykes	425,734
1943	4th	82	72	.532	16	Jimmie Dykes	508,962
1944	7th	71	83	.461	18	Jimmie Dykes	563,539
1945	6th	71	78	.477	15	Jimmie Dykes	657,981
1946	5th	74	80	.481	30	Jimmie Dykes, Ted Lyons	983,403
1947	6th	70	84	.455	27	Ted Lyons	876,948
1948	8th	51	101	.336	44 1/2	Ted Lyons	777,844
1949	6th	63	91	.409	34	Jack Onslow	937,151
1950	6th	60	94	.390	38	Jack Onslow, Red Corriden	781,330
1951	4th	81	73	.526	17	Paul Richards	1,328,234
1952	3rd	81	73	.526	14	Paul Richards	1,231,675
1953	3rd	89	65	.578	11 1/2	Paul Richards	1,191,353
1954	3rd	94	60	.610	17	Paul Richards, Marty Marion	1,231,629
1955	3rd	91	63	.591	5	Marty Marion	1,175,684
1956	3rd	85	69	.552	12	Marty Marion	1,000,090
1957	2nd	90	64	.584	8	Al Lopez	1,135,668
1958	2nd	82	72	.532	10	Al Lopez	797,451
1959	1st	94	60	.610	+5	Al Lopez	1,423,144
1960	3rd	87	67	.565	10	Al Lopez	1,644,460
1961	4th	86	76	.531	23	Al Lopez	1,146,019
1962	5th	85	77	.525	11	Al Lopez	1,131,562
1963	2nd	94	68	.580	10 1/2	Al Lopez	1,158,848
1964	2nd	98	64	.605	1	Al Lopez	1,250,053
1965	2nd	95	67	.586	7	Al Lopez	1,130,519
1966	4th	83	79	.512	15	Eddie Stanky	990,016
1967	4th	89	73	.549	3	Eddie Stanky	985,634
1968	8th (tied)	67	95	.414	36	Eddie Stanky, Al Lopez	803,775

WEST DIVISION

Year	Position	W	L	Pct.	*GB	Manager	Attendance
1969	5th	68	94	.420	29	Al Lopez, Don Gutteridge	589,546
1970	6th	56	106	.346	42	Don Gutteridge, Chuck Tanner	495,355
1971	3rd	79	83	.488	22 1/2	Chuck Tanner	833,891
1972	2nd	87	67	.565	5 1/2	Chuck Tanner	1,177,318
1973	5th	77	85	.475	17	Chuck Tanner	1,302,527
1974	4th	80	80	.500	9	Chuck Tanner	1,149,596
1975	5th	75	86	.466	22 1/2	Chuck Tanner	750,802
1976	6th	64	97	.398	25 1/2	Paul Richards	914,945
1977	3rd	90	72	.556	12	Bob Lemon	1,657,135
1978	5th	71	90	.441	20 1/2	Bob Lemon, Larry Doby	1,491,100
1979	5th	73	87	.456	14	Don Kessinger, Tony La Russa	1,280,702
1980	5th	70	90	.438	26	Tony La Russa	1,200,365
1981	3rd/6th	54	52	.509	†	Tony La Russa	946,651
1982	3rd	87	75	.537	6	Tony La Russa	1,567,787

Year	Position	W	L	Pct.	*GB	Manager	Attendance
1983	1st‡	99	63	.611	+20	Tony La Russa	2,132,821
1984	5th (tied)	74	88	.457	10	Tony La Russa	2,136,988
1985	3rd	85	77	.525	6	Tony La Russa	1,669,888
1986	5th	72	90	.444	20	Tony La Russa, Jim Fregosi	1,424,313
1987	5th	77	85	.475	8	Jim Fregosi	1,208,060
1988	5th	71	90	.441	32 1/2	Jim Fregosi	1,115,749
1989	7th	69	92	.429	29 1/2	Jeff Torborg	1,045,651
1990	2nd	94	68	.580	9	Jeff Torborg	2,002,357
1991	2nd	87	75	.537	8	Jeff Torborg	2,934,154
1992	3rd	86	76	.531	10	Gene Lamont	2,681,156
1993	1st‡	94	68	.580	+8	Gene Lamont	2,581,091

CENTRAL DIVISION

Year	Position	W	L	Pct.	*GB	Manager	Attendance
1994	1st	67	46	.593	+1	Gene Lamont	1,697,398
1995	3rd	68	76	.472	32	Gene Lamont, Terry Bevington	1,609,773

*Games behind winner. †First half 31-22; second half 23-30. ‡Lost championship series.

MANAGERIAL RECORDS

Terry Bevington 57-56, Lena Blackburne 99-133, Donie Bush 118-189, Nixey Callahan 309-329, Eddie Collins 160-147, Red Corriden 52-72, Larry Doby 37-50, Hugh Duffy 145-159, Jimmie Dykes 899-940, Johnny Evers 66-87, Lew Fonseca 120-196, Jim Fregosi 193-226, Kid Gleason 392-364, Clark Griffith 157-113, Don Gutteridge 109-172, Fielder Jones 426-293, Don Kessinger 46-60, Tony La Russa 522-510, Gene Lamont 258-210, Bob Lemon 124-112, Al Lopez 840-650, Ted Lyons 185-245, Marty Marion 179-138, Jack Onslow 71-133, Paul Richards 406-362, Pants Rowland 339-247, Ray Schalk 102-125, Eddie Stanky 206-197, Billy Sullivan 78-74, Chuck Tanner 401-414, Jeff Torborg 250-235.

CLEVELAND INDIANS

YEARLY FINISHES

Year	Position	W	L	Pct.	*GB	Manager	Attendance
1901	7th	54	82	.397	29	James McAleer	131,380
1902	5th	69	67	.507	14	Bill Armour	275,395
1903	3rd	77	63	.550	15	Bill Armour	311,280
1904	4th	86	65	.570	7 1/2	Bill Armour	264,749
1905	5th	76	78	.494	19	Nap Lajoie	316,306
1906	3rd	89	64	.582	5	Nap Lajoie	325,733
1907	4th	85	67	.559	8	Nap Lajoie	382,046
1908	2nd	90	64	.584	1/2	Nap Lajoie	422,242
1909	6th	71	82	.464	27 1/2	Nap Lajoie, Deacon McGuire	354,627
1910	5th	71	81	.467	32	Deacon McGuire	293,456
1911	3rd	80	73	.523	22	Deacon McGuire, George Stovall	406,296
1912	5th	75	78	.490	30 1/2	Harry Davis, J.L. Birmingham	336,844
1913	3rd	86	66	.566	9 1/2	J.L. Birmingham	541,000
1914	8th	51	102	.333	48 1/2	J.L. Birmingham	185,997
1915	7th	57	95	.375	44 1/2	J.L. Birmingham, Lee Fohl	159,285
1916	6th	77	77	.500	14	Lee Fohl	492,106
1917	3rd	88	66	.571	12	Lee Fohl	477,298
1918	2nd	73	54	.575	2 1/2	Lee Fohl	295,515
1919	2nd	84	55	.604	3 1/2	Lee Fohl, Tris Speaker	538,135
1920	1st	98	56	.636	+2	Tris Speaker	912,832
1921	2nd	94	60	.610	4 1/2	Tris Speaker	748,705
1922	4th	78	76	.507	16	Tris Speaker	528,145
1923	3rd	82	71	.536	16 1/2	Tris Speaker	558,856
1924	6th	67	86	.438	24 1/2	Tris Speaker	481,905
1925	6th	70	84	.455	27 1/2	Tris Speaker	419,005
1926	2nd	88	66	.571	3	Tris Speaker	627,426
1927	6th	66	87	.431	43 1/2	Jack McAllister	373,138
1928	7th	62	92	.403	39	Roger Peckinpaugh	375,907
1929	3rd	81	71	.533	24	Roger Peckinpaugh	536,210
1930	4th	81	73	.536	21	Roger Peckinpaugh	528,657
1931	4th	78	76	.506	30	Roger Peckinpaugh	483,027
1932	4th	87	65	.572	19	Roger Peckinpaugh	468,953
1933	4th	75	76	.497	23 1/2	Roger Peckinpaugh, Walter Johnson	387,936
1934	3rd	85	69	.552	16	Walter Johnson	391,338
1935	3rd	82	71	.536	12	Walter Johnson, Steve O'Neill	397,615
1936	5th	80	74	.519	22 1/2	Steve O'Neill	500,391
1937	4th	83	71	.539	19	Steve O'Neill	564,849
1938	3rd	86	66	.566	13	Ossie Vitt	652,006
1939	3rd	87	67	.565	20 1/2	Ossie Vitt	563,926
1940	2nd	89	65	.578	1	Ossie Vitt	902,576

Year	Position	W	L	Pct.	*GB	Manager	Attendance
1941	4th (tied)	75	79	.487	26	Roger Peckinpaugh	745,948
1942	4th	75	79	.487	28	Lou Boudreau	459,447
1943	3rd	82	71	.536	15 1/2	Lou Boudreau	438,894
1944	5th (tied)	72	82	.468	17	Lou Boudreau	475,272
1945	5th	73	72	.503	11	Lou Boudreau	558,182
1946	6th	68	86	.442	36	Lou Boudreau	1,057,289
1947	4th	80	74	.519	17	Lou Boudreau	1,521,978
1948	1st†	97	58	.626	+1	Lou Boudreau	2,620,627
1949	3rd	89	65	.578	8	Lou Boudreau	2,233,771
1950	4th	92	62	.597	6	Lou Boudreau	1,727,464
1951	2nd	93	61	.604	5	Al Lopez	1,704,984
1952	2nd	93	61	.604	2	Al Lopez	1,444,607
1953	2nd	92	62	.597	8 1/2	Al Lopez	1,069,176
1954	1st	111	43	.721	+8	Al Lopez	1,335,472
1955	2nd	93	61	.604	3	Al Lopez	1,221,780
1956	2nd	88	66	.571	9	Al Lopez	865,467
1957	6th	76	77	.497	21 1/2	Kerby Farrell	722,256
1958	4th	77	76	.503	14 1/2	Bobby Bragan, Joe Gordon	663,805
1959	2nd	89	65	.578	5	Joe Gordon	1,497,976
1960	4th	76	78	.494	21	Joe Gordon, Jimmie Dykes	950,985
1961	5th	78	83	.484	30 1/2	Jimmie Dykes	725,547
1962	6th	80	82	.494	16	Mel McGaha	716,076
1963	5th (tied)	79	83	.488	25 1/2	Birdie Tebbetts	562,507
1964	6th (tied)	79	83	.488	20	Birdie Tebbetts	653,293
1965	5th	87	75	.537	15	Birdie Tebbetts	934,786
1966	5th	81	81	.500	17	Birdie Tebbetts, George Strickland	903,359
1967	8th	75	87	.463	17	Joe Adcock	662,980
1968	3rd	86	75	.534	16 1/2	Alvin Dark	857,994

EAST DIVISION

Year	Position	W	L	Pct.	*GB	Manager	Attendance
1969	6th	62	99	.385	46 1/2	Alvin Dark	619,970
1970	5th	76	86	.469	32	Alvin Dark	729,752
1971	6th	60	102	.370	43	Alvin Dark, John Lipon	591,361
1972	5th	72	84	.462	14	Ken Aspromonte	626,354
1973	6th	71	91	.438	26	Ken Aspromonte	615,107
1974	4th	77	85	.475	14	Ken Aspromonte	1,114,262
1975	4th	79	80	.497	15 1/2	Frank Robinson	977,039
1976	4th	81	78	.509	16	Frank Robinson	948,776
1977	5th	71	90	.441	28 1/2	Frank Robinson, Jeff Torborg	900,365
1978	6th	69	90	.434	29	Jeff Torborg	800,584
1979	6th	81	80	.503	22	Jeff Torborg, Dave Garcia	1,011,644
1980	6th	79	81	.494	23	Dave Garcia	1,033,827
1981	6th/5th	52	51	.504	‡	Dave Garcia	661,395
1982	6th (tied)	78	84	.481	17	Dave Garcia	1,044,021
1983	7th	70	92	.432	28	Mike Ferraro, Pat Corrales	768,941
1984	6th	75	87	.463	29	Pat Corrales	734,079
1985	7th	60	102	.370	39 1/2	Pat Corrales	655,181
1986	5th	84	78	.519	11 1/2	Pat Corrales	1,471,805
1987	7th	61	101	.377	37	Pat Corrales, Doc Edwards	1,077,898
1988	6th	78	84	.481	11	Doc Edwards	1,411,610
1989	6th	73	89	.451	16	Doc Edwards, John Hart	1,285,542
1990	4th	77	85	.475	11	John McNamara	1,225,240
1991	7th	57	105	.352	34	John McNamara, Mike Hargrove	1,051,863
1992	4th (tied)	76	86	.469	20	Mike Hargrove	1,224,274
1993	6th	76	86	.469	19	Mike Hargrove	2,177,908

CENTRAL DIVISION

Year	Position	W	L	Pct.	*GB	Manager	Attendance
1994	2nd	66	47	.584	1	Mike Hargrove	1,995,174
1995	1st§∞	100	44	.694	+30	Mike Hargrove	2,842,745

*Games behind winner. †Won pennant playoff. ‡First half 26-24; second half 26-27. §Won division series. ∞Won championship series.

MANAGERIAL RECORDS

Joe Adcock 75-87, Bill Armour 232-195, Ken Aspromonte 220-260, Joe Birmingham 170-191, Lou Boudreau 728-649, Bobby Bragan 31-36, Pat Corrales 280-355, Alvin Dark 266-321, Harry Davis 54-71, Jimmie Dykes 103-115, Doc Edwards 173-207, Kerby Farrell 76-77, Mike Ferraro 40-60, Lee Fohl 327-310, Dave Garcia 247-244, Joe Gordon 184-151, Mike Hargrove 350-316, John Hart 8-11, Walter Johnson 179-168, Nap Lajoie 377-309, Johnny Lipon 18-41, Al Lopez 570-354, Jimmy McAleer 54-82, Jack McCallister 66-87, Mel McGaha 80-82, Deacon McGuire 91-117, John McNamara 102-137, Steve O'Neill 199-168, Roger Peckinpaugh 490-481, Frank Robinson 186-189, Tris Speaker 617-520, George Stovall 74-62, George Strickland 15-24, Birdie Tebbetts 269-298, Jeff Torborg 157-201, Oscar Vitt 262-198.

YEARLY FINISHES

Year	Position	W	L	Pct.	*GB	Manager	Attendance
1901	3rd	74	61	.548	8 1/2	George Stallings	259,430
1902	7th	52	83	.385	30 1/2	Frank Dwyer	189,469
1903	5th	65	71	.478	25	Ed Barrow	224,523
1904	7th	62	90	.408	32	Ed Barrow, Bobby Lowe	177,796
1905	3rd	79	74	.516	15 1/2	Bill Armour	193,384
1906	6th	71	78	.477	21	Bill Armour	174,043
1907	1st	92	58	.613	+1 1/2	Hughey Jennings	297,079
1908	1st	90	63	.588	+ 1/2	Hughey Jennings	436,199
1909	1st	98	54	.645	+3 1/2	Hughey Jennings	490,490
1910	3rd	86	68	.558	18	Hughey Jennings	391,288
1911	2nd	89	65	.578	13 1/2	Hughey Jennings	484,988
1912	6th	69	84	.451	36 1/2	Hughey Jennings	402,870
1913	6th	66	87	.431	30	Hughey Jennings	398,502
1914	4th	80	73	.523	19 1/2	Hughey Jennings	416,225
1915	2nd	100	54	.649	2 1/2	Hughey Jennings	476,105
1916	3rd	87	67	.565	4	Hughey Jennings	616,772
1917	4th	78	75	.510	21 1/2	Hughey Jennings	457,289
1918	7th	55	71	.437	20	Hughey Jennings	203,719
1919	4th	80	60	.571	8	Hughey Jennings	643,805
1920	7th	61	93	.396	37	Hughey Jennings	579,650
1921	6th	71	82	.464	27	Ty Cobb	661,527
1922	3rd	79	75	.513	15	Ty Cobb	861,206
1923	2nd	83	71	.539	16	Ty Cobb	911,377
1924	3rd	86	68	.558	6	Ty Cobb	1,015,136
1925	4th	81	73	.526	16 1/2	Ty Cobb	820,766
1926	6th	79	75	.513	12	Ty Cobb	711,914
1927	4th	82	71	.536	27 1/2	George Moriarty	773,716
1928	6th	68	86	.442	33	George Moriarty	474,323
1929	6th	70	84	.455	36	Bucky Harris	869,318
1930	5th	75	79	.487	27	Bucky Harris	649,450
1931	7th	61	93	.396	47	Bucky Harris	434,056
1932	5th	76	75	.503	29 1/2	Bucky Harris	397,157
1933	5th	75	79	.487	25	Del Baker	320,972
1934	1st	101	53	.656	+7	Mickey Cochrane	919,161
1935	1st	93	58	.616	+3	Mickey Cochrane	1,034,929
1936	2nd	83	71	.539	19 1/2	Mickey Cochrane	875,948
1937	2nd	89	65	.578	13	Mickey Cochrane	1,072,276
1938	4th	84	70	.545	16	Mickey Cochrane, Del Baker	799,557
1939	5th	81	73	.526	26 1/2	Del Baker	836,279
1940	1st	90	64	.584	+1	Del Baker	1,112,693
1941	4th (tied)	75	79	.487	26	Del Baker	684,915
1942	5th	73	81	.474	30	Del Baker	580,087
1943	5th	78	76	.506	20	Steve O'Neill	606,287
1944	2nd	88	66	.571	1	Steve O'Neill	923,176
1945	1st	88	65	.575	+1 1/2	Steve O'Neill	1,280,341
1946	2nd	92	62	.597	12	Steve O'Neill	1,722,590
1947	2nd	85	69	.552	12	Steve O'Neill	1,398,093
1948	5th	78	76	.506	18 1/2	Steve O'Neill	1,743,035
1949	4th	87	67	.565	10	Red Rolfe	1,821,204
1950	2nd	95	59	.617	3	Red Rolfe	1,951,474
1951	5th	73	81	.474	25	Red Rolfe	1,132,641
1952	8th	50	104	.325	45	Red Rolfe, Fred Hutchinson	1,026,846
1953	6th	60	94	.390	40 1/2	Fred Hutchinson	884,658
1954	5th	68	86	.442	43	Fred Hutchinson	1,079,847
1955	5th	79	75	.513	17	Bucky Harris	1,181,838
1956	5th	82	72	.532	15	Bucky Harris	1,051,182
1957	4th	78	76	.506	20	Jack Tighe	1,272,346
1958	5th	77	77	.500	15	Jack Tighe, Bill Norman	1,098,924
1959	4th	76	78	.494	18	Bill Norman, Jimmie Dykes	1,221,221
1960	6th	71	83	.461	26	Jimmie Dykes, Billy Hitchcock, Joe Gordon	1,167,669
1961	2nd	101	61	.623	8	Bob Scheffing	1,600,710
1962	4th	85	76	.528	10 1/2	Bob Scheffing	1,207,881
1963	5th (tied)	79	83	.488	25 1/2	Bob Scheffing, Charlie Dressen	821,952
1964	4th	85	77	.525	14	Charlie Dressen	816,139
1965	4th	89	73	.549	13	Charlie Dressen, Bob Swift	1,029,645
1966	3rd	88	74	.543	10	Charlie Dressen, Bob Swift, Frank Skaff	1,124,293
1967	2nd	91	71	.562	1	Mayo Smith	1,447,143
1968	1st	103	59	.636	+12	Mayo Smith	2,031,847

EAST DIVISION

Year	Position	W	L	Pct.	*GB	Manager	Attendance
1969	2nd	90	72	.556	19	Mayo Smith	1,577,481
1970	4th	79	83	.488	29	Mayo Smith	1,501,293
1971	2nd	91	71	.562	12	Billy Martin	1,591,073

HISTORY *Team by team*

Year	Position	W	L	Pct.	*GB	Manager	Attendance
1972	1st†	86	70	.551	+1/2	Billy Martin	1,892,386
1973	3rd	85	77	.525	12	Billy Martin, Joe Schultz	1,724,146
1974	6th	72	90	.444	19	Ralph Houk	1,243,080
1975	6th	57	102	.358	37 1/2	Ralph Houk	1,058,836
1976	5th	74	87	.460	24	Ralph Houk	1,467,020
1977	4th	74	88	.457	26	Ralph Houk	1,359,856
1978	5th	86	76	.531	13 1/2	Ralph Houk	1,714,893
1979	5th	85	76	.528	18	Les Moss, Dick Tracewski, Sparky Anderson	1,630,929
1980	5th	84	78	.519	19	Sparky Anderson	1,785,293
1981	4th/2nd (tied)	60	49	.550	‡	Sparky Anderson	1,149,144
1982	4th	83	79	.512	12	Sparky Anderson	1,636,058
1983	2nd	92	70	.568	6	Sparky Anderson	1,829,636
1984	1st§	104	58	.642	+15	Sparky Anderson	2,704,794
1985	3rd	84	77	.522	15	Sparky Anderson	2,286,609
1986	3rd	87	75	.537	8 1/2	Sparky Anderson	1,899,437
1987	1st†	98	64	.605	+2	Sparky Anderson	2,061,830
1988	2nd	88	74	.543	1	Sparky Anderson	2,081,162
1989	7th	59	103	.364	30	Sparky Anderson	1,543,656
1990	3rd	79	83	.488	9	Sparky Anderson	1,495,785
1991	2nd	84	78	.519	7	Sparky Anderson	1,641,661
1992	6th	75	87	.463	21	Sparky Anderson	1,423,963
1993	3rd (tied)	85	77	.525	10	Sparky Anderson	1,971,421
1994	5th	53	62	.461	18	Sparky Anderson	1,184,783
1995	4th	60	84	.417	26	Sparky Anderson	1,180,979

*Games behind winner. †Lost championship series. ‡First half 31-26; second half 29-23. §Won championship series.

MANAGERIAL RECORDS

Sparky Anderson 1,431-1,248, Bill Armour 150-152, Del Baker 392-336, Ed Barrow 97-117, Ty Cobb 479-444, Mickey Cochrane 379-278, Chuck Dressen 221-189, Frank Dwyer 52-83, Jimmie Dykes 118-115, Joe Gordon 26-31, Bucky Harris 516-557, Ralph Houk 366-443, Fred Hutchinson 155-235, Hugh Jennings 1,131-972, Bobby Lowe 30-44, Billy Martin 248-204, George Moriarty 150-157, Les Moss 27-26, Bill Norman 58-64, Steve O'Neill 509-414, Red Rolfe 278-256, Bob Scheffing 210-173, Joe Schultz 14-14, Frank Skaff 40-39, Mayo Smith 363-285, George Stallings 74-61, Bob Swift 56-43, Jack Tighe 99-104.

KANSAS CITY ROYALS

YEARLY FINISHES

WEST DIVISION

Year	Position	W	L	Pct.	*GB	Manager	Attendance
1969	4th	69	93	.429	28	Joe Gordon	902,414
1970	4th (tied)	65	97	.401	33	Charlie Metro, Bob Lemon	693,047
1971	2nd	85	76	.528	16	Bob Lemon	910,784
1972	4th	76	78	.494	16 1/2	Bob Lemon	707,656
1973	2nd	88	74	.543	6	Jack McKeon	1,345,341
1974	5th	77	85	.475	13	Jack McKeon	1,173,292
1975	2nd	91	71	.562	7	Jack McKeon, Whitey Herzog	1,151,836
1976	1st†	90	72	.556	+2 1/2	Whitey Herzog	1,680,265
1977	1st†	102	60	.630	+8	Whitey Herzog	1,852,603
1978	1st†	92	70	.568	+5	Whitey Herzog	2,255,493
1979	2nd	85	77	.525	3	Whitey Herzog	2,261,845
1980	1st‡	97	65	.599	+14	Jim Frey	2,288,714
1981	5th/1st∞	50	53	.485	§	Jim Frey, Dick Howser	1,279,403
1982	2nd	90	72	.556	3	Dick Howser	2,284,464
1983	2nd	79	83	.488	20	Dick Howser	1,963,875
1984	1st†	84	78	.519	+3	Dick Howser	1,810,018
1985	1st‡	91	71	.562	+1	Dick Howser	2,162,717
1986	3rd (tied)	76	86	.469	16	Dick Howser, Mike Ferraro	2,320,794
1987	2nd	83	79	.512	2	Billy Gardner, John Wathan	2,392,471
1988	3rd	84	77	.522	19 1/2	John Wathan	2,350,181
1989	2nd	92	70	.568	7	John Wathan	2,477,700
1990	6th	75	86	.466	27 1/2	John Wathan	2,244,956
1991	6th	82	80	.506	13	John Wathan, Hal McRae	2,161,537
1992	5th (tied)	72	90	.444	24	Hal McRae	1,867,689
1993	3rd	84	78	.519	10	Hal McRae	1,934,578

CENTRAL DIVISION

Year	Position	W	L	Pct.	*GB	Manager	Attendance
1994	3rd	64	51	.557	4	Hal McRae	1,400,494
1995	2nd	70	74	.486	30	Bob Boone	1,233,530

*Games behind winner. †Lost championship series. ‡Won championship series. §First half 20-30; second half 30-23. ∞Lost division series.

MANAGERIAL RECORDS

Bob Boone 70-74, Mike Ferraro 36-38, Jim Frey 127-105, Billy Gardner 62-64, Joe Gordon 69-93, Whitey Herzog 410-304, Dick Howser 404-365, Bob Lemon 207-218, Jack McKeon 215-205, Hal McRae 286-277, Charlie Metro 19-33, John Wathan 288-270.

YEARLY FINISHES

WEST DIVISION

Year	Position	W	L	Pct.	*GB	Manager	Attendance
1969†	6th	64	98	.395	33	Joe Schultz	677,944
1970	4th	65	97	.401	33	Dave Bristol	933,690
1971	6th	69	92	.429	32	Dave Bristol	731,531

EAST DIVISION

Year	Position	W	L	Pct.	*GB	Manager	Attendance
1972	6th	65	91	.417	21	Dave Bristol, Del Crandall	600,440
1973	5th	74	88	.457	23	Del Crandall	1,092,158
1974	5th	76	86	.469	15	Del Crandall	955,741
1975	5th	68	94	.420	28	Del Crandall	1,213,357
1976	6th	66	95	.410	32	Alex Grammas	1,012,164
1977	6th	67	95	.414	33	Alex Grammas	1,114,938
1978	3rd	93	69	.574	6 1/2	George Bamberger	1,601,406
1979	2nd	95	66	.590	8	George Bamberger	1,918,343
1980	3rd	86	76	.531	17	George Bamberger, Buck Rodgers	1,857,408
1981	3rd/1st§	62	47	.569	‡	Buck Rodgers	878,432
1982	1st∞	95	67	.586	+1	Buck Rodgers, Harvey Kuenn	1,978,896
1983	5th	87	75	.537	11	Harvey Kuenn	2,397,131
1984	7th	67	94	.416	36 1/2	Rene Lachemann	1,608,509
1985	6th	71	90	.441	28	George Bamberger	1,360,265
1986	6th	77	84	.478	18	George Bamberger, Tom Trebelhorn	1,265,041
1987	3rd	91	71	.562	7	Tom Trebelhorn	1,909,244
1988	3rd (tied)	87	75	.537	2	Tom Trebelhorn	1,923,238
1989	4th	81	81	.500	8	Tom Trebelhorn	1,970,735
1990	6th	74	88	.457	14	Tom Trebelhorn	1,752,900
1991	4th	83	79	.512	8	Tom Trebelhorn	1,478,729
1992	2nd	92	70	.568	4	Phil Garner	1,857,314
1993	7th	69	93	.426	26	Phil Garner	1,688,080

CENTRAL DIVISION

Year	Position	W	L	Pct.	*GB	Manager	Attendance
1994	5th	53	62	.461	15	Phil Garner	1,268,399
1995	4th	65	79	.451	35	Phil Garner	1,087,560

*Games behind winner. †Seattle Pilots. ‡First half 31-25; second half 31-22. §Lost division series. ∞Won championship series.

MANAGERIAL RECORDS

George Bamberger 377-351, Dave Bristol 144-209, Del Crandall 271-338, Phil Garner 279-304, Alex Grammas 133-190, Harvey Kuenn 160-118, Rene Lachemann 67-94, Buck Rodgers 124-102, Joe Schultz 64-98, Tom Trebelhorn 422-397.

YEARLY FINISHES

Year	Position	W	L	Pct.	*GB	Manager	Attendance
1901†	6th	61	72	.459	20 1/2	Jimmy Manning	161,661
1902†	6th	61	75	.449	22	Tom Loftus	188,158
1903†	8th	43	94	.314	47 1/2	Tom Loftus	128,878
1904†	8th	38	113	.251	55 1/2	Patsy Donovan	131,744
1905†	7th	64	87	.421	29 1/2	Jake Stahl	252,027
1906†	7th	55	95	.367	37 1/2	Jake Stahl	129,903
1907†	8th	49	102	.325	43 1/2	Joe Cantillon	221,929
1908†	7th	67	85	.441	22 1/2	Joe Cantillon	264,252
1909†	8th	42	110	.276	56	Joe Cantillon	205,199
1910†	7th	66	85	.437	36 1/2	Jimmy McAleer	254,591
1911†	7th	64	90	.416	38 1/2	Jimmy McAleer	244,884
1912†	2nd	91	61	.599	14	Clark Griffith	350,663
1913†	2nd	90	64	.584	6 1/2	Clark Griffith	325,831
1914†	3rd	81	73	.526	19	Clark Griffith	243,888
1915†	4th	85	68	.556	17	Clark Griffith	167,332
1916†	7th	76	77	.497	14 1/2	Clark Griffith	177,265
1917†	5th	74	79	.484	25 1/2	Clark Griffith	89,682
1918†	3rd	72	56	.563	4	Clark Griffith	182,122
1919†	7th	56	84	.400	32	Clark Griffith	234,096
1920†	6th	68	84	.447	29	Clark Griffith	359,260
1921†	4th	80	73	.523	18	George McBride	456,069
1922†	6th	69	85	.448	25	Clyde Milan	458,552
1923†	4th	75	78	.490	23 1/2	Donie Bush	357,406

Year	Position	W	L	Pct.	*GB	Manager	Attendance
1924†	1st	92	62	.597	+2	Bucky Harris	534,310
1925†	1st	96	55	.636	+8 1/2	Bucky Harris	817,199
1926†	4th	81	69	.540	8	Bucky Harris	551,580
1927†	3rd	85	69	.552	25	Bucky Harris	528,976
1928†	4th	75	79	.487	26	Bucky Harris	378,501
1929†	5th	71	81	.467	34	Walter Johnson	355,506
1930†	2nd	94	60	.610	8	Walter Johnson	614,474
1931†	3rd	92	62	.597	16	Walter Johnson	492,657
1932†	3rd	93	61	.604	14	Walter Johnson	371,396
1933†	1st	99	53	.651	+7	Joe Cronin	437,533
1934†	7th	66	86	.434	34	Joe Cronin	330,074
1935†	6th	67	86	.438	27	Bucky Harris	255,011
1936†	4th	82	71	.536	20	Bucky Harris	379,525
1937†	6th	73	80	.477	28 1/2	Bucky Harris	397,799
1938†	5th	75	76	.497	23 1/2	Bucky Harris	522,694
1939†	6th	65	87	.428	41 1/2	Bucky Harris	339,257
1940†	7th	64	90	.416	26	Bucky Harris	381,241
1941†	6th (tied)	70	84	.455	31	Bucky Harris	415,663
1942†	7th	62	89	.411	39 1/2	Bucky Harris	403,493
1943†	2nd	84	69	.549	13 1/2	Ossie Bluege	574,694
1944†	8th	64	90	.416	25	Ossie Bluege	525,235
1945†	2nd	87	67	.565	1 1/2	Ossie Bluege	652,660
1946†	4th	76	78	.494	28	Ossie Bluege	1,027,216
1947†	7th	64	90	.416	33	Ossie Bluege	850,758
1948†	7th	56	97	.366	40	Joe Kuhel	795,254
1949†	8th	50	104	.325	47	Joe Kuhel	770,745
1950†	5th	67	87	.435	31	Bucky Harris	699,697
1951†	7th	62	92	.403	36	Bucky Harris	695,167
1952†	5th	78	76	.506	17	Bucky Harris	699,457
1953†	5th	76	76	.500	23 1/2	Bucky Harris	595,594
1954†	6th	66	88	.429	45	Bucky Harris	503,542
1955†	8th	53	101	.344	43	Chuck Dressen	425,238
1956†	7th	59	95	.383	38	Chuck Dressen	431,647
1957†	8th	55	99	.357	43	Chuck Dressen, Cookie Lavagetto	457,079
1958†	8th	61	93	.396	31	Cookie Lavagetto	475,288
1959†	8th	63	91	.409	31	Cookie Lavagetto	615,372
1960†	5th	73	81	.474	24	Cookie Lavagetto	743,404
1961	7th	70	90	.438	38	Cookie Lavagetto, Sam Mele	1,256,723
1962	2nd	91	71	.562	5	Sam Mele	1,433,116
1963	3rd	91	70	.565	13	Sam Mele	1,406,652
1964	6th (tied)	79	83	.488	20	Sam Mele	1,207,514
1965	1st	102	60	.630	+7	Sam Mele	1,463,258
1966	2nd	89	73	.549	9	Sam Mele	1,259,374
1967	2nd (tied)	91	71	.562	1	Sam Mele, Cal Ermer	1,483,547
1968	7th	79	83	.488	24	Cal Ermer	1,143,257

WEST DIVISION

Year	Position	W	L	Pct.	*GB	Manager	Attendance
1969	1st‡	97	65	.599	+9	Billy Martin	1,349,328
1970	1st‡	98	64	.605	+9	Bill Rigney	1,261,887
1971	5th	74	86	.463	26 1/2	Bill Rigney	940,858
1972	3rd	77	77	.500	15 1/2	Bill Rigney, Frank Quilici	797,901
1973	3rd	81	81	.500	13	Frank Quilici	907,499
1974	3rd	82	80	.506	8	Frank Quilici	662,401
1975	4th	76	83	.478	20 1/2	Frank Quilici	737,156
1976	3rd	85	77	.525	5	Gene Mauch	715,394
1977	4th	84	77	.522	17 1/2	Gene Mauch	1,162,727
1978	4th	73	89	.451	19	Gene Mauch	787,878
1979	4th	82	80	.506	6	Gene Mauch	1,070,521
1980	3rd	77	84	.478	19 1/2	Gene Mauch, Johnny Goryl	769,206
1981	7th/4th	41	68	.376	§	Johnny Goryl, Billy Gardner	469,090
1982	7th	60	102	.370	33	Billy Gardner	921,186
1983	5th (tied)	70	92	.432	29	Billy Gardner	858,939
1984	2nd (tied)	81	81	.500	3	Billy Gardner	1,598,422
1985	4th (tied)	77	85	.475	14	Billy Gardner, Ray Miller	1,651,814
1986	6th	71	91	.438	21	Ray Miller, Tom Kelly	1,255,453
1987	1st∞	85	77	.525	+2	Tom Kelly	2,081,976
1988	2nd	91	71	.562	13	Tom Kelly	3,030,672
1989	5th	80	82	.494	19	Tom Kelly	2,277,438
1990	7th	74	88	.457	29	Tom Kelly	1,751,584
1991	1st∞	95	67	.586	+8	Tom Kelly	2,293,842
1992	2nd	90	72	.556	6	Tom Kelly	2,482,428
1993	5th (tied)	71	91	.438	23	Tom Kelly	2,048,673

Year	Position	W	L	Pct.	*GB	Manager	Attendance
1994	4th	53	60	.469	14	Tom Kelly	1,398,565
1995	5th	56	88	.389	44	Tom Kelly	1,057,667

*Games behind winner. †Washington Senators (original club). ‡Lost championship series. §First half 17-39; second half 24-29. ∞Won championship series.

MANAGERIAL RECORDS

Ossie Bluege 375-394, Donie Bush 75-78, Joe Cantillon 158-297, Joe Cronin 165-139, Patsy Donovan 38-113, Chuck Dressen 116-212, Cal Ermer 145-129, Billy Gardner 268-353, Johnny Goryl 34-38, Clark Griffith 693-646, Bucky Harris 1,336-1,416, Walter Johnson 350-264, Tom Kelly 707-707, Joe Kuhel 106-201, Cookie Lavagetto 271-384, Tom Loftus 104-169, Jimmy Manning 61-72, Billy Martin 97-65, Gene Mauch 378-394, Jimmy McAleer 130-175, George McBride 80-73, Sam Mele 524-436, Clyde Milan 69-85, Ray Miller 109-130, Frank Quilici 280-287, Bill Rigney 208-184, Jake Stahl 119-182.

NEW YORK YANKEES

YEARLY FINISHES

Year	Position	W	L	Pct.	*GB	Manager	Attendance
1901†	5th	68	65	.511	13 1/2	John McGraw	141,952
1902	8th	50	88	.362	34	John McGraw, Wilbert Robinson	174,606
1903	4th	72	62	.537	17	Clark Griffith	211,808
1904	2nd	92	59	.609	1 1/2	Clark Griffith	438,919
1905	6th	71	78	.477	21 1/2	Clark Griffith	309,100
1906	2nd	90	61	.596	3	Clark Griffith	434,709
1907	5th	70	78	.473	21	Clark Griffith	350,020
1908	8th	51	103	.331	39 1/2	Clark Griffith, Kid Elberfeld	305,500
1909	5th	74	77	.490	23 1/2	George Stallings	501,000
1910	2nd	88	63	.583	14 1/2	George Stallings, Hal Chase	355,857
1911	6th	76	76	.500	25 1/2	Hal Chase	302,444
1912	8th	50	102	.329	55	Harry Wolverton	242,194
1913	7th	57	94	.377	38	Frank Chance	357,551
1914	6th (tied)	70	84	.455	30	Frank Chance, Roger Peckinpaugh	359,477
1915	5th	69	83	.454	32 1/2	Bill Donovan	256,035
1916	4th	80	74	.519	11	Bill Donovan	469,211
1917	6th	71	82	.464	28 1/2	Bill Donovan	330,294
1918	4th	60	63	.488	13 1/2	Miller Huggins	282,047
1919	3rd	80	59	.576	7 1/2	Miller Huggins	619,164
1920	3rd	95	59	.617	3	Miller Huggins	1,289,422
1921	1st	98	55	.641	+4 1/2	Miller Huggins	1,230,696
1922	1st	94	60	.610	+1	Miller Huggins	1,026,134
1923	1st	98	54	.645	+16	Miller Huggins	1,007,066
1924	2nd	89	63	.586	2	Miller Huggins	1,053,533
1925	7th	69	85	.448	30	Miller Huggins	697,267
1926	1st	91	63	.591	+3	Miller Huggins	1,027,095
1927	1st	110	44	.714	+19	Miller Huggins	1,164,015
1928	1st	101	53	.656	+2 1/2	Miller Huggins	1,072,132
1929	2nd	88	66	.571	18	Miller Huggins, Art Fletcher	960,148
1930	3rd	86	68	.558	16	Bob Shawkey	1,169,230
1931	2nd	94	59	.614	13 1/2	Joe McCarthy	912,437
1932	1st	107	47	.695	+13	Joe McCarthy	962,320
1933	2nd	91	59	.607	7	Joe McCarthy	728,014
1934	2nd	94	60	.610	7	Joe McCarthy	854,682
1935	2nd	89	60	.597	3	Joe McCarthy	657,508
1936	1st	102	51	.667	+19 1/2	Joe McCarthy	976,913
1937	1st	102	52	.662	+13	Joe McCarthy	998,148
1938	1st	99	53	.651	+9 1/2	Joe McCarthy	970,916
1939	1st	106	45	.702	+17	Joe McCarthy	859,785
1940	3rd	88	66	.571	2	Joe McCarthy	988,975
1941	1st	101	53	.656	+17	Joe McCarthy	964,722
1942	1st	103	51	.669	+9	Joe McCarthy	988,251
1943	1st	98	56	.636	+13 1/2	Joe McCarthy	645,006
1944	3rd	83	71	.539	6	Joe McCarthy	822,864
1945	4th	81	71	.533	6 1/2	Joe McCarthy	881,846
1946	3rd	87	67	.565	17	Joe McCarthy, Bill Dickey, Johnny Neun	2,265,512
1947	1st	97	57	.630	+12	Bucky Harris	2,178,937
1948	3rd	94	60	.610	2 1/2	Bucky Harris	2,373,901
1949	1st	97	57	.630	+1	Casey Stengel	2,281,676
1950	1st	98	56	.636	+3	Casey Stengel	2,081,380
1951	1st	98	56	.636	+5	Casey Stengel	1,950,107
1952	1st	95	59	.617	+2	Casey Stengel	1,629,665
1953	1st	99	52	.656	+8 1/2	Casey Stengel	1,537,811
1954	2nd	103	51	.669	8	Casey Stengel	1,475,171
1955	1st	96	58	.623	+3	Casey Stengel	1,490,138

HISTORY Team by team

Year	Position	W	L	Pct.	*GB	Manager	Attendance
1956	1st	97	57	.630	+9	Casey Stengel	1,491,784
1957	1st	98	56	.636	+8	Casey Stengel	1,497,134
1958	1st	92	62	.597	+10	Casey Stengel	1,428,438
1959	3rd	79	75	.513	15	Casey Stengel	1,552,030
1960	1st	97	57	.630	+8	Casey Stengel	1,627,349
1961	1st	109	53	.673	+8	Ralph Houk	1,747,725
1962	1st	96	66	.593	+5	Ralph Houk	1,493,574
1963	1st	104	57	.646	+10 1/2	Ralph Houk	1,308,920
1964	1st	99	63	.611	+1	Yogi Berra	1,305,638
1965	6th	77	85	.475	25	Johnny Keane	1,213,552
1966	10th	70	89	.440	26 1/2	Johnny Keane, Ralph Houk	1,124,648
1967	9th	72	90	.444	20	Ralph Houk	1,259,514
1968	5th	83	79	.512	20	Ralph Houk	1,185,666

EAST DIVISION

Year	Position	W	L	Pct.	*GB	Manager	Attendance
1969	5th	80	81	.497	28 1/2	Ralph Houk	1,067,996
1970	2nd	93	69	.574	15	Ralph Houk	1,136,879
1971	4th	82	80	.506	21	Ralph Houk	1,070,771
1972	4th	79	76	.510	6 1/2	Ralph Houk	966,328
1973	4th	80	82	.494	17	Ralph Houk	1,262,103
1974	2nd	89	73	.549	2	Bill Virdon	1,273,075
1975	3rd	83	77	.519	12	Bill Virdon, Billy Martin	1,288,048
1976	1st‡	97	62	.610	+10 1/2	Billy Martin	2,012,434
1977	1st‡	100	62	.617	+2 1/2	Billy Martin	2,103,092
1978	1st§‡	100	63	.613	+1	Billy Martin, Bob Lemon	2,335,871
1979	4th	89	71	.556	13 1/2	Bob Lemon, Billy Martin	2,537,765
1980	1st∞	103	59	.636	+3	Dick Howser	2,627,417
1981	1st/6th◆‡	59	48	.551	▲	Gene Michael, Bob Lemon	1,614,533
1982	5th	79	83	.488	16	Bob Lemon, Gene Michael, Clyde King	2,041,219
1983	3rd	91	71	.562	7	Billy Martin	2,257,976
1984	3rd	87	75	.537	17	Yogi Berra	1,821,815
1985	2nd	97	64	.602	2	Yogi Berra, Billy Martin	2,214,587
1986	2nd	90	72	.556	5 1/2	Lou Piniella	2,268,030
1987	4th	89	73	.549	9	Lou Piniella	2,427,672
1988	5th	85	76	.528	3 1/2	Billy Martin, Lou Piniella	2,633,701
1989	5th	74	87	.460	14 1/2	Dallas Green, Bucky Dent	2,170,485
1990	7th	67	95	.414	21	Bucky Dent, Stump Merrill	2,006,436
1991	5th	71	91	.438	20	Stump Merrill	1,863,733
1992	4th (tied)	76	86	.469	20	Buck Showalter	1,748,733
1993	2nd	88	74	.543	7	Buck Showalter	2,416,965
1994	1st	70	43	.619	+6 1/2	Buck Showalter	1,675,556
1995	2nd■	79	65	.549	7	Buck Showalter	1,705,263

*Games behind winner. †Baltimore Orioles. ‡Won championship series. §Won pennant playoff. ∞Lost championship series. ▲First half 34-22; second half 25-26. ◆Won division series. ■Lost division series.

MANAGERIAL RECORDS

Yogi Berra 192-148, Frank Chance 117-168, Hal Chase 86-80, Bucky Dent 36-53, Bill Dickey 57-48, Bill Donovan 220-239, Kid Elberfeld 27-71, Art Fletcher 6-5, Dallas Green 56-65, Clark Griffith 419-370, Bucky Harris 191-117, Ralph Houk 944-806, Dick Howser 103-59, Miller Huggins 1,067-719, Johnny Keane 81-101, Clyde King 29-33, Bob Lemon 99-73, Billy Martin 501-385, Joe McCarthy 1,460-867, John McGraw 94-96, Stump Merrill 120-155, Gene Michael 92-76, Johnny Neun 8-6, Roger Peckinpaugh 10-10, Lou Piniella 224-193, Wilbert Robinson 24-57, Bob Shawkey 86-68, Buck Showalter 311-268, George Stallings 152-136, Casey Stengel 1,149-696, Bill Virdon 142-124, Harry Wolverton 50-102.

OAKLAND ATHLETICS

YEARLY FINISHES

Year	Position	W	L	Pct.	*GB	Manager	Attendance
1901†	4th	74	62	.544	9	Connie Mack	206,329
1902†	1st	83	53	.610	+5	Connie Mack	442,473
1903†	2nd	75	60	.556	14 1/2	Connie Mack	420,078
1904†	5th	81	70	.536	12 1/2	Connie Mack	512,294
1905†	1st	92	56	.622	+2	Connie Mack	554,576
1906†	4th	78	67	.538	12	Connie Mack	489,129
1907†	2nd	88	57	.607	1 1/2	Connie Mack	625,581
1908†	6th	68	85	.444	22	Connie Mack	455,062
1909†	2nd	95	58	.621	3 1/2	Connie Mack	674,915
1910†	1st	102	48	.680	+14 1/2	Connie Mack	588,905
1911†	1st	101	50	.669	+13 1/2	Connie Mack	605,749
1912†	3rd	90	62	.592	15	Connie Mack	517,653
1913†	1st	96	57	.627	+6 1/2	Connie Mack	571,896
1914†	1st	99	53	.651	+8 1/2	Connie Mack	346,641
1915†	8th	43	109	.283	58 1/2	Connie Mack	146,223
1916†	8th	36	117	.235	54 1/2	Connie Mack	184,471
1917†	8th	55	98	.359	44 1/2	Connie Mack	221,432

Year	Position	W	L	Pct.	*GB	Manager	Attendance
1918†	8th	52	76	.406	24	Connie Mack	177,926
1919†	8th	36	104	.257	52	Connie Mack	225,209
1920†	8th	48	106	.312	50	Connie Mack	287,888
1921†	8th	53	100	.346	45	Connie Mack	344,430
1922†	7th	65	89	.422	29	Connie Mack	425,356
1923†	6th	69	83	.454	29	Connie Mack	534,122
1924†	5th	71	81	.467	20	Connie Mack	531,992
1925†	2nd	88	64	.579	8 1/2	Connie Mack	869,703
1926†	3rd	83	67	.553	6	Connie Mack	714,308
1927†	2nd	91	63	.591	19	Connie Mack	605,529
1928†	2nd	98	55	.641	2 1/2	Connie Mack	689,756
1929†	1st	104	46	.693	+18	Connie Mack	839,176
1930†	1st	102	52	.662	+8	Connie Mack	721,663
1931†	1st	107	45	.704	+13 1/2	Connie Mack	627,464
1932†	2nd	94	60	.610	13	Connie Mack	405,500
1933†	3rd	79	72	.523	19 1/2	Connie Mack	297,138
1934†	5th	68	82	.453	31	Connie Mack	305,847
1935†	8th	58	91	.389	34	Connie Mack	233,173
1936†	8th	53	100	.346	49	Connie Mack	285,173
1937†	7th	54	97	.358	46 1/2	Connie Mack	430,733
1938†	8th	53	99	.349	46	Connie Mack	385,357
1939†	7th	55	97	.362	51 1/2	Connie Mack	395,022
1940†	8th	54	100	.351	36	Connie Mack	432,145
1941†	8th	64	90	.416	37	Connie Mack	528,894
1942†	8th	55	99	.357	48	Connie Mack	423,487
1943†	8th	49	105	.318	49	Connie Mack	376,735
1944†	5th (tied)	72	82	.468	17	Connie Mack	505,322
1945†	8th	52	98	.347	34 1/2	Connie Mack	462,631
1946†	8th	49	105	.318	55	Connie Mack	621,793
1947†	5th	78	76	.506	19	Connie Mack	911,566
1948†	4th	84	70	.545	12 1/2	Connie Mack	945,076
1949†	5th	81	73	.526	16	Connie Mack	816,514
1950†	8th	52	102	.338	46	Connie Mack	309,805
1951†	6th	70	84	.455	28	Jimmie Dykes	465,469
1952†	4th	79	75	.513	16	Jimmie Dykes	627,100
1953†	7th	59	95	.383	41 1/2	Jimmie Dykes	362,113
1954†	8th	51	103	.331	60	Ed Joost	304,666
1955‡	6th	63	91	.409	33	Lou Boudreau	1,393,054
1956‡	8th	52	102	.338	45	Lou Boudreau	1,015,154
1957‡	7th	59	94	.386	38 1/2	Lou Boudreau, Harry Craft	901,067
1958‡	7th	73	81	.474	19	Harry Craft	925,090
1959‡	7th	66	88	.429	28	Harry Craft	963,683
1960‡	8th	58	96	.377	39	Bob Elliot	774,944
1961‡	9th (tied)	61	100	.379	47 1/2	Joe Gordon, Hank Bauer	683,817
1962‡	9th	72	90	.444	24	Hank Bauer	635,675
1963‡	8th	73	89	.451	31 1/2	Ed Lopat	762,364
1964‡	10th	57	105	.352	42	Ed Lopat, Mel McGaha	642,478
1965‡	10th	59	103	.364	43	Mel McGaha, Haywood Sullivan	528,344
1966‡	7th	74	86	.463	23	Alvin Dark	773,929
1967‡	10th	62	99	.385	29 1/2	Alvin Dark, Luke Appling	726,639
1968	6th	82	80	.506	21	Bob Kennedy	837,466

WEST DIVISION

Year	Position	W	L	Pct.	*GB	Manager	Attendance
1969	2nd	88	74	.543	9	Hank Bauer, John McNamara	778,232
1970	2nd	89	73	.549	9	John McNamara	778,355
1971	1st§	101	60	.627	+16	Dick Williams	914,993
1972	1st∞	93	62	.600	+5 1/2	Dick Williams	921,323
1973	1st∞	94	68	.580	+6	Dick Williams	1,000,763
1974	1st∞	90	72	.556	+5	Alvin Dark	845,693
1975	1st§	98	64	.605	+7	Alvin Dark	1,075,518
1976	2nd	87	74	.540	2 1/2	Chuck Tanner	780,593
1977	7th	63	98	.391	38 1/2	Jack McKeon, Bobby Winkles	495,599
1978	6th	69	93	.426	23	Bobby Winkles, Jack McKeon	526,999
1979	7th	54	108	.333	34	Jim Marshall	306,763
1980	2nd	83	79	.512	14	Billy Martin	842,259
1981	1st/2nd◆§	64	45	.587	▲	Billy Martin	1,304,054
1982	5th	68	94	.420	25	Billy Martin	1,735,489
1983	4th	74	88	.457	25	Steve Boros	1,294,941
1984	4th	77	85	.475	7	Steve Boros, Jackie Moore	1,353,281
1985	4th (tied)	77	85	.475	14	Jackie Moore	1,334,599
1986	3rd (tied)	76	86	.469	16	Jackie Moore, Tony La Russa	1,314,646
1987	3rd	81	81	.500	4	Tony La Russa	1,678,921
1988	1st∞	104	58	.642	+13	Tony La Russa	2,287,335
1989	1st∞	99	63	.611	+7	Tony La Russa	2,667,225

HISTORY *Team by team*

Year	Position	W	L	Pct.	*GB	Manager	Attendance
1990	1st∞	103	59	.636	+9	Tony La Russa	2,900,217
1991	4th	84	78	.519	11	Tony La Russa	2,713,493
1992	1st§	96	66	.593	+6	Tony La Russa	2,494,160
1993	7th	68	94	.420	26	Tony La Russa	2,035,025
1994	2nd	51	63	.447	1	Tony La Russa	1,242,692
1995	4th	67	77	.465	11 1/2	Tony La Russa	1,174,310

*Games behind winner. †Philadelphia Athletics. ‡Kansas City Athletics. §Lost championship series. ∞Won championship series. ▲First half 37-23; second half 27-22. ◆Won division series.

MANAGERIAL RECORDS

Luke Appling 10-30, Hank Bauer 187-226, Steve Boros 94-112, Lou Boudreau 151-260, Harry Craft 162-196, Alvin Dark 314-291, Jimmie Dykes 198-254, Bob Elliott 58-96, Joe Gordon 26-33, Eddie Joost 51-103, Bob Kennedy 82-80, Tony La Russa 695-614, Eddie Lopat 90-124, Connie Mack 3,582-3,814, Jim Marshall 54-108, Billy Martin 215-218, Mel McGaha 45-91, Jack McKeon 71-105, John McNamara 97-78, Jackie Moore 163-190, Haywood Sullivan 54-82, Chuck Tanner 87-74, Dick Williams 288-190, Bobby Winkles 61-86.

SEATTLE MARINERS

YEARLY FINISHES

WEST DIVISION

Year	Position	W	L	Pct.	*GB	Manager	Attendance
1977	6th	64	98	.395	38	Darrell Johnson	1,338,511
1978	7th	56	104	.350	35	Darrell Johnson	877,440
1979	6th	67	95	.414	21	Darrell Johnson	844,447
1980	7th	59	103	.364	38	Darrell Johnson, Maury Wills	836,204
1981	6th/5th	44	65	.404	†	Maury Wills, Rene Lachemann	636,276
1982	4th	76	86	.469	17	Rene Lachemann	1,070,404
1983	7th	60	102	.370	39	Rene Lachemann, Del Crandall	813,537
1984	5th (tied)	74	88	.457	10	Del Crandall, Chuck Cottier	870,372
1985	6th	74	88	.457	17	Chuck Cottier	1,128,696
1986	7th	67	95	.414	25	Chuck Cottier, Marty Martinez, Dick Williams	1,029,045
1987	4th	78	84	.481	7	Dick Williams	1,134,255
1988	7th	68	93	.422	35 1/2	Dick Williams, Jim Snyder	1,022,398
1989	6th	73	89	.451	26	Jim Lefebvre	1,298,443
1990	5th	77	85	.475	26	Jim Lefebvre	1,509,727
1991	5th	83	79	.512	12	Jim Lefebvre	2,147,905
1992	7th	64	98	.395	32	Bill Plummer	1,651,398
1993	4th	82	80	.506	12	Lou Piniella	2,051,853
1994	3rd	49	63	.438	2	Lou Piniella	1,104,206
1995	1st‡§	79	66	.545	+1	Lou Piniella	1,643,203

*Games behind winner. †First half 21-36; second half 23-29. ‡Won division series. §Lost championship series.

MANAGERIAL RECORDS

Chuck Cottier 98-120, Del Crandall 93-141, Darrell Johnson 226-362, Rene Lachemann 140-180, Jim Lefebvre 233-253, Lou Piniella 210-209, Bill Plummer 64-98, Jimmy Snyder 45-60, Dick Williams 159-192, Maury Wills 26-56.

TEXAS RANGERS

YEARLY FINISHES

Year	Position	W	L	Pct.	*GB	Manager	Attendance
1961†	9th (tied)	61	100	.379	47 1/2	Mickey Vernon	597,287
1962†	10th	60	101	.373	35 1/2	Mickey Vernon	729,775
1963†	10th	56	106	.346	48 1/2	Mickey Vernon, Gil Hodges	535,604
1964†	9th	62	100	.383	37	Gil Hodges	600,106
1965†	8th	70	92	.432	32	Gil Hodges	560,083
1966†	8th	71	88	.447	25 1/2	Gil Hodges	576,260
1967†	6th (tied)	76	85	.472	15 1/2	Gil Hodges	770,863
1968†	10th	65	96	.404	37 1/2	Jim Lemon	546,661

EAST DIVISION

Year	Position	W	L	Pct.	*GB	Manager	Attendance
1969†	4th	86	76	.531	23	Ted Williams	918,106
1970†	6th	70	92	.432	38	Ted Williams	824,789
1971†	5th	63	96	.396	38 1/2	Ted Williams	655,156

WEST DIVISION

Year	Position	W	L	Pct.	*GB	Manager	Attendance
1972	6th	54	100	.351	38 1/2	Ted Williams	662,974
1973	6th	57	105	.352	37	Whitey Herzog, Del Wilber, Billy Martin	686,085
1974	2nd	84	76	.525	5	Billy Martin	1,193,902
1975	3rd	79	83	.488	19	Billy Martin, Frank Lucchesi	1,127,924

Year	Position	W	L	Pct.	*GB	Manager	Attendance
1976	4th (tied)	76	86	.469	14	Frank Lucchesi	1,164,982
1977	2nd	94	68	.580	8	Frank Lucchesi, Eddie Stanky, Connie Ryan, Billy Hunter	1,250,722
1978	2nd (tied)	87	75	.537	5	Billy Hunter, Pat Corrales	1,447,963
1979	3rd	83	79	.512	5	Pat Corrales	1,519,671
1980	4th	76	85	.472	20 1/2	Pat Corrales	1,198,175
1981	2nd/3rd	57	48	.543	‡	Don Zimmer	850,076
1982	6th	64	98	.395	29	Don Zimmer, Darrell Johnson	1,154,432
1983	3rd	77	85	.475	22	Doug Rader	1,363,469
1984	7th	69	92	.429	14 1/2	Doug Rader	1,102,471
1985	7th	62	99	.385	28 1/2	Doug Rader, Bobby Valentine	1,112,497
1986	2nd	87	75	.537	5	Bobby Valentine	1,692,002
1987	6th (tied)	75	87	.463	10	Bobby Valentine	1,763,053
1988	6th	70	91	.435	33 1/2	Bobby Valentine	1,581,901
1989	4th	83	79	.512	16	Bobby Valentine	2,043,993
1990	3rd	83	79	.512	20	Bobby Valentine	2,057,911
1991	3rd	85	77	.525	10	Bobby Valentine	2,297,720
1992	4th	77	85	.475	19	Bobby Valentine, Toby Harrah	2,198,231
1993	2nd	86	76	.531	8	Kevin Kennedy	2,244,616
1994	1st	52	62	.456	+1	Kevin Kennedy	2,503,198
1995	3rd	74	70	.514	4 1/2	Johnny Oates	1,985,910

*Games behind winner. †Washington Senators (second club). ‡First half 33-22; second half 24-26.

MANAGERIAL RECORDS

Pat Corrales 160-164, Toby Harrah 32-44, Whitey Herzog 47-91, Gil Hodges 321-444, Billy Hunter 146-108, Darrell Johnson 26-40, Kevin Kennedy 138-138, Jim Lemon 65-96, Frank Lucchesi 142-149, Billy Martin 137-141, Johnny Oates 74-70, Doug Rader 155-200, Connie Ryan 2-4, Eddie Stanky 1-0, Bobby Valentine 581-605, Mickey Vernon 135-227, Del Wilber 1-0, Ted Williams 273-364, Don Zimmer 95-106.

TORONTO BLUE JAYS

YEARLY FINISHES
EAST DIVISION

Year	Position	W	L	Pct.	*GB	Manager	Attendance
1977	7th	54	107	.335	45 1/2	Roy Hartsfield	1,701,052
1978	7th	59	102	.366	40	Roy Hartsfield	1,562,585
1979	7th	53	109	.327	50 1/2	Roy Hartsfield	1,431,651
1980	7th	67	95	.414	36	Bobby Mattick	1,400,327
1981	7th/7th	37	69	.349	†	Bobby Mattick	755,083
1982	6th (tied)	78	84	.481	17	Bobby Cox	1,275,978
1983	4th	89	73	.549	9	Bobby Cox	1,930,415
1984	2nd	89	73	.549	15	Bobby Cox	2,110,009
1985	1st‡	99	62	.615	+2	Bobby Cox	2,468,925
1986	4th	86	76	.531	9 1/2	Jimy Williams	2,455,477
1987	2nd	96	66	.593	2	Jimy Williams	2,778,429
1988	3rd (tied)	87	75	.537	2	Jimy Williams	2,595,175
1989	1st‡	89	73	.549	+2	Jimy Williams, Cito Gaston	3,375,883
1990	2nd	86	76	.531	2	Cito Gaston	3,885,284
1991	1st‡	91	71	.562	+7	Cito Gaston	4,001,527
1992	1st§	96	66	.593	+4	Cito Gaston	4,028,318
1993	1st§	95	67	.586	+7	Cito Gaston	4,057,947
1994	3rd	55	60	.478	16	Cito Gaston	2,907,933
1995	5th	56	88	.389	30	Cito Gaston	2,826,483

*Games behind winner. †First half 16-42; second half 21-27. ‡Lost championship series. §Won championship series.

MANAGERIAL RECORDS

Bobby Cox 355-292, Cito Gaston 556-477, Roy Hartsfield 166-318, Bobby Mattick 104-164, Jimy Williams 281-241.

NATIONAL LEAGUE

ATLANTA BRAVES

YEARLY FINISHES

Year	Position	W	L	Pct.	*GB	Manager	Attendance
1901†	5th	69	69	.500	20 1/2	Frank Selee	146,502
1902†	3rd	73	64	.533	29	Al Buckenberger	116,960
1903†	6th	58	80	.420	32	Al Buckenberger	143,155
1904†	7th	55	98	.359	51	Al Buckenberger	140,694
1905†	7th	51	103	.331	54 1/2	Fred Tenney	150,003
1906†	8th	49	102	.325	66 1/2	Fred Tenney	143,280
1907†	7th	58	90	.392	47	Fred Tenney	203,221

Year	Position	W	L	Pct.	*GB	Manager	Attendance
1908†	6th	63	91	.409	36	Joe Kelley	253,750
1909†	8th	45	108	.294	65 1/2	Frank Bowerman, Harry Smith	195,188
1910†	8th	53	100	.346	50 1/2	Fred Lake	149,027
1911†	8th	44	107	.291	54	Fred Tenney	116,000
1912†	8th	52	101	.340	52	Johnny Kling	121,000
1913†	5th	69	82	.457	31 1/2	George Stallings	208,000
1914†	1st	94	59	.614	+10 1/2	George Stallings	382,913
1915†	2nd	83	69	.546	7	George Stallings	376,283
1916†	3rd	89	63	.586	4	George Stallings	313,495
1917†	6th	72	81	.471	25 1/2	George Stallings	174,253
1918†	7th	53	71	.427	28 1/2	George Stallings	84,938
1919†	6th	57	82	.410	38 1/2	George Stallings	167,401
1920†	7th	62	90	.408	30	George Stallings	162,483
1921†	4th	79	74	.516	15	Fred Mitchell	318,627
1922†	8th	53	100	.346	39 1/2	Fred Mitchell	167,965
1923†	7th	54	100	.351	41 1/2	Fred Mitchell	227,802
1924†	8th	53	100	.346	40	Dave Bancroft	117,478
1925†	5th	70	83	.458	25	Dave Bancroft	313,528
1926†	7th	66	86	.434	22	Dave Bancroft	303,598
1927†	7th	60	94	.390	34	Dave Bancroft	288,685
1928†	7th	50	103	.327	44 1/2	Jack Slattery, Rogers Hornsby	227,001
1929†	8th	56	98	.364	43	Emil Fuchs	372,351
1930†	6th	70	84	.455	22	Bill McKechnie	464,835
1931†	7th	64	90	.416	37	Bill McKechnie	515,005
1932†	5th	77	77	.500	13	Bill McKechnie	507,606
1933†	4th	83	71	.539	9	Bill McKechnie	517,803
1934†	4th	78	73	.517	16	Bill McKechnie	303,205
1935†	8th	38	115	.248	61 1/2	Bill McKechnie	232,754
1936†	6th	71	83	.461	21	Bill McKechnie	340,585
1937†	5th	79	73	.520	16	Bill McKechnie	385,339
1938†	5th	77	75	.507	12	Casey Stengel	341,149
1939†	7th	63	88	.417	32 1/2	Casey Stengel	285,994
1940†	7th	65	87	.428	34 1/2	Casey Stengel	241,616
1941†	7th	62	92	.403	38	Casey Stengel	263,680
1942†	7th	59	89	.399	44	Casey Stengel	285,332
1943†	6th	68	85	.444	36 1/2	Casey Stengel	271,289
1944†	6th	65	89	.422	40	Bob Coleman	208,691
1945†	6th	67	85	.441	30	Bob Coleman, Del Bissonette	374,178
1946†	4th	81	72	.529	15 1/2	Billy Southworth	969,673
1947†	3rd	86	68	.558	8	Billy Southworth	1,277,361
1948†	1st	91	62	.595	+6 1/2	Billy Southworth	1,455,439
1949†	4th	75	79	.487	22	Billy Southworth	1,081,795
1950†	4th	83	71	.539	8	Billy Southworth	944,391
1951†	4th	76	78	.494	20 1/2	Billy Southworth, Tommy Holmes	487,475
1952†	7th	64	89	.418	32	Tommy Holmes, Charlie Grimm	281,278
1953‡	2nd	92	62	.597	13	Charlie Grimm	1,826,397
1954‡	3rd	89	65	.578	8	Charlie Grimm	2,131,388
1955‡	2nd	85	69	.552	13 1/2	Charlie Grimm	2,005,836
1956‡	2nd	92	62	.597	1	Charlie Grimm, Fred Haney	2,046,331
1957‡	1st	95	59	.617	+8	Fred Haney	2,215,404
1958‡	1st	92	62	.597	+8	Fred Haney	1,971,101
1959‡	2nd§	86	70	.551	2	Fred Haney	1,749,112
1960‡	2nd	88	66	.571	7	Chuck Dressen	1,497,799
1961‡	4th	83	71	.539	10	Chuck Dressen, Birdie Tebbetts	1,101,441
1962‡	5th	86	76	.531	15 1/2	Birdie Tebbetts	766,921
1963‡	6th	84	78	.519	15	Bobby Bragan	773,018
1964‡	5th	88	74	.543	5	Bobby Bragan	910,911
1965‡	5th	86	76	.531	11	Bobby Bragan	555,584
1966	5th	85	77	.525	10	Bobby Bragan, Billy Hitchcock	1,539,801
1967	7th	77	85	.475	24 1/2	Billy Hitchcock, Ken Silvestri	1,389,222
1968	5th	81	81	.500	16	Lum Harris	1,126,540

WEST DIVISION

Year	Position	W	L	Pct.	*GB	Manager	Attendance
1969	1st∞	93	69	.574	+3	Lum Harris	1,458,320
1970	5th	76	86	.469	26	Lum Harris	1,078,848
1971	3rd	82	80	.506	8	Lum Harris	1,006,320
1972	4th	70	84	.455	25	Lum Harris, Eddie Mathews	752,973
1973	5th	76	85	.472	22 1/2	Eddie Mathews	800,655
1974	3rd	88	74	.543	14	Eddie Mathews, Clyde King	981,085
1975	5th	67	94	.416	40 1/2	Clyde King, Connie Ryan	534,672
1976	6th	70	92	.432	32	Dave Bristol	818,179
1977	6th	61	101	.377	37	Dave Bristol, Ted Turner	872,464
1978	6th	69	93	.426	26	Bobby Cox	904,494
1979	6th	66	94	.413	23 1/2	Bobby Cox	769,465
1980	4th	81	80	.503	11	Bobby Cox	1,048,411

HISTORY *Team by team*

Year	Position	W	L	Pct.	*GB	Manager	Attendance
1981	4th/5th	50	56	.472	▲	Bobby Cox	535,418
1982	1st∞	89	73	.549	+1	Joe Torre	1,801,985
1983	2nd	88	74	.543	3	Joe Torre	2,119,935
1984	2nd (tied)	80	82	.494	12	Joe Torre	1,724,892
1985	5th	66	96	.407	29	Eddie Haas, Bobby Wine	1,350,137
1986	6th	72	89	.447	23 1/2	Chuck Tanner	1,387,181
1987	5th	69	92	.429	20 1/2	Chuck Tanner	1,217,402
1988	6th	54	106	.338	39 1/2	Chuck Tanner, Russ Nixon	848,089
1989	6th	63	97	.394	28	Russ Nixon	984,930
1990	6th	65	97	.401	26	Russ Nixon, Bobby Cox	980,129
1991	1st◆	94	68	.580	+1	Bobby Cox	2,140,217
1992	1st◆	98	64	.605	+8	Bobby Cox	3,077,400
1993	1st∞	104	58	.642	+1	Bobby Cox	3,884,725

EAST DIVISION

Year	Position	W	L	Pct.	*GB	Manager	Attendance
1994	2nd	68	46	.596	6	Bobby Cox	2,539,240
1995	1st■◆	90	54	.625	+21	Bobby Cox	2,561,831

*Games behind winner. †Boston Braves. ‡Milwaukee Braves. §Lost pennant playoff. ∞Lost championship series. ▲First half 25-29; second half 25-27. ◆Won championship series. ■Won division series.

MANAGERIAL RECORDS

Dave Bancroft 249-363, Del Bissonette 25-34, Frank Bowerman 23-55, Bobby Bragan 310-287, Dave Bristol 131-192, Al Buckenberger 186-242, Bob Coleman 107-140, Bobby Cox 760-670, Chuck Dressen 159-124, Emil Fuchs 56-98, Charlie Grimm 341-285, Eddie Haas 50-71, Fred Haney 341-231, Lum Harris 379-373, Billy Hitchcock 110-100, Tommy Holmes 61-69, Rogers Hornsby 39-83, Joe Kelley 63-91, Clyde King 96-101, Johnny Kling 52-101, Fred Lake 53-100, Eddie Mathews 149-161, Bill McKechnie 560-666, Fred Mitchell 186-274, Russ Nixon 130-216, Connie Ryan 9-18, Frank Selee 69-69, Ken Silvestri 0-3, Jack Slattery 11-20, Harry Smith 22-53, Billy Southworth 424-358, George Stallings 579-597, Casey Stengel 394-516, Chuck Tanner 153-208, Birdie Tebbetts 98-89, Fred Tenney 202-402, Joe Torre 257-229, Ted Turner 0-1, Bobby Wine 16-25.

CHICAGO CUBS

YEARLY FINISHES

Year	Position	W	L	Pct.	*GB	Manager	Attendance
1901	6th	53	86	.381	37	Tom Loftus	205,071
1902	5th	68	69	.496	34	Frank Selee	263,700
1903	3rd	82	56	.594	8	Frank Selee	386,205
1904	2nd	93	60	.608	13	Frank Selee	439,100
1905	3rd	92	61	.601	13	Frank Selee, Frank Chance	509,900
1906	1st	116	36	.763	+20	Frank Chance	654,300
1907	1st	107	45	.704	+17	Frank Chance	422,550
1908	1st	99	55	.643	+1	Frank Chance	665,325
1909	2nd	104	49	.680	6 1/2	Frank Chance	633,480
1910	1st	104	50	.675	+13	Frank Chance	526,152
1911	2nd	92	62	.597	7 1/2	Frank Chance	576,000
1912	3rd	91	59	.607	11 1/2	Frank Chance	514,000
1913	3rd	88	65	.575	13 1/2	Johnny Evers	419,000
1914	4th	78	76	.506	16 1/2	Hank O'Day	202,516
1915	4th	73	80	.477	17 1/2	Roger Bresnahan	217,058
1916	5th	67	86	.438	26 1/2	Joe Tinker	453,685
1917	5th	74	80	.481	24	Fred Mitchell	360,218
1918	1st	84	45	.651	+10 1/2	Fred Mitchell	337,256
1919	3rd	75	65	.536	21	Fred Mitchell	424,430
1950	5th (tied)	75	79	.487	18	Fred Mitchell	480,783
1921	7th	64	89	.418	30	Johnny Evers, Bill Killefer	410,107
1922	5th	80	74	.519	13	Bill Killefer	542,283
1923	4th	83	71	.539	12 1/2	Bill Killefer	703,705
1924	5th	81	72	.529	12	Bill Killefer	716,922
1925	8th	68	86	.442	27 1/2	Bill Killefer, Rabbit Maranville, George Gibson	622,610
1926	4th	82	72	.532	7	Joe McCarthy	885,063
1927	4th	85	68	.556	8 1/2	Joe McCarthy	1,159,168
1928	3rd	91	63	.591	4	Joe McCarthy	1,143,740
1929	1st	98	54	.645	+10 1/2	Joe McCarthy	1,485,166
1930	2nd	90	64	.584	2	Joe McCarthy, Rogers Hornsby	1,463,624
1931	3rd	84	70	.545	17	Rogers Hornsby	1,086,422
1932	1st	90	64	.584	+4	Rogers Hornsby, Charlie Grimm	974,688
1933	3rd	86	68	.558	6	Charlie Grimm	594,112
1934	3rd	86	65	.570	8	Charlie Grimm	707,525
1935	1st	100	54	.649	+4	Charlie Grimm	692,604
1936	2nd (tied)	87	67	.565	5	Charlie Grimm	699,370
1937	2nd	93	61	.604	3	Charlie Grimm	895,020
1938	1st	89	63	.586	+2	Charlie Grimm, Gabby Hartnett	951,640

Year	Position	W	L	Pct.	*GB	Manager	Attendance
1939	4th	84	70	.545	13	Gabby Hartnett	726,663
1940	5th	75	79	.487	25 1/2	Gabby Hartnett	534,878
1941	6th	70	84	.455	30	Jimmy Wilson	545,159
1942	6th	68	86	.442	38	Jimmy Wilson	590,872
1943	5th	74	79	.484	30 1/2	Jimmy Wilson	508,247
1944	4th	75	79	.487	30	Jimmy Wilson, Charlie Grimm	640,110
1945	1st	98	56	.636	+3	Charlie Grimm	1,036,386
1946	3rd	82	71	.536	14 1/2	Charlie Grimm	1,342,970
1947	6th	69	85	.448	25	Charlie Grimm	1,364,039
1948	8th	64	90	.416	27 1/2	Charlie Grimm	1,237,792
1949	8th	61	93	.396	36	Charlie Grimm, Frankie Frisch	1,143,139
1950	7th	64	89	.418	26 1/2	Frankie Frisch	1,165,944
1951	8th	62	92	.403	34 1/2	Frankie Frisch, Phil Cavarretta	894,415
1952	5th	77	77	.500	19 1/2	Phil Cavarretta	1,024,826
1953	7th	65	89	.422	40	Phil Cavarretta	763,658
1954	7th	64	90	.416	33	Stan Hack	748,183
1955	6th	72	81	.471	26	Stan Hack	875,800
1956	8th	60	94	.390	33	Stan Hack	720,118
1957	7th (tied)	62	92	.403	33	Bob Scheffing	670,629
1958	5th (tied)	72	82	.468	20	Bob Scheffing	979,904
1959	5th (tied)	74	80	.481	13	Bob Scheffing	858,255
1960	7th	60	94	.390	35	Charlie Grimm, Lou Boudreau	809,770
1961	7th	64	90	.416	29	Vedie Himsl, Harry Craft, Elvin Tappe, Lou Klein	673,057
1962	9th	59	103	.364	42 1/2	Charlie Metro, Elvin Tappe, Lou Klein	609,802
1963	7th	82	80	.506	17	Bob Kennedy	979,551
1964	8th	76	86	.469	17	Bob Kennedy	751,647
1965	8th	72	90	.444	25	Bob Kennedy, Lou Klein	641,361
1966	10th	59	103	.364	36	Leo Durocher	635,891
1967	3rd	87	74	.540	14	Leo Durocher	977,226
1968	3rd	84	78	.519	13	Leo Durocher	1,043,409

EAST DIVISION

Year	Position	W	L	Pct.	*GB	Manager	Attendance
1969	2nd	92	70	.568	8	Leo Durocher	1,674,993
1970	2nd	84	78	.519	5	Leo Durocher	1,642,705
1971	3rd (tied)	83	79	.512	14	Leo Durocher	1,653,007
1972	2nd	85	70	.548	11	Leo Durocher, Whitey Lockman	1,299,163
1973	5th	77	84	.478	5	Whitey Lockman	1,351,705
1974	6th	66	96	.407	22	Whitey Lockman, Jim Marshall	1,015,378
1975	5th (tied)	75	87	.463	17 1/2	Jim Marshall	1,034,819
1976	4th	75	87	.463	26	Jim Marshall	1,026,217
1977	4th	81	81	.500	20	Herman Franks	1,439,834
1978	3rd	79	83	.488	11	Herman Franks	1,525,311
1979	5th	80	82	.494	18	Herman Franks, Joe Amalfitano	1,648,587
1980	6th	64	98	.395	27	Preston Gomez, Joe Amalfitano	1,206,776
1981	6th/5th	38	65	.369	†	Joe Amalfitano	565,637
1982	5th	73	89	.451	19	Lee Elia	1,249,278
1983	5th	71	91	.438	19	Lee Elia, Charlie Fox	1,479,717
1984	1st‡	96	65	.596	+6 1/2	Jim Frey	2,104,219
1985	4th	77	84	.478	23 1/2	Jim Frey	2,161,534
1986	5th	70	90	.438	37	Jim Frey, John Vukovich, Gene Michael	1,859,102
1987	6th	76	85	.472	18 1/2	Gene Michael, Frank Lucchesi	2,035,130
1988	4th	77	85	.475	24	Don Zimmer	2,089,034
1989	1st‡	93	69	.574	+6	Don Zimmer	2,491,942
1990	4th	77	85	.475	18	Don Zimmer	2,243,791
1991	4th	77	83	.481	20	Don Zimmer, Joe Altobelli, Jim Essian	2,314,250
1992	4th	78	84	.481	18	Jim Lefebvre	2,126,720
1993	4th	84	78	.519	13	Jim Lefebvre	2,653,763

CENTRAL DIVISION

Year	Position	W	L	Pct.	*GB	Manager	Attendance
1994	5th	49	64	.434	16 1/2	Tom Trebelhorn	1,845,208
1995	3rd	73	71	.507	12	Jim Riggleman	1,918,265

*Games behind winner. †First half 15-37; second half 23-28. ‡Lost championship series.

MANAGERIAL RECORDS

Joe Amalfitano 66-116, Lou Boudreau 54-83, Roger Bresnahan 73-80, Phil Cavarretta 169-213, Frank Chance 753-379, Harry Craft 7-9, Leo Durocher 535-526, Lee Elia 127-158, Jim Essian 59-63, Johnny Evers 130-121, Charlie Fox 17-22, Herman Franks 238-241, Jim Frey 196-182, Frank Frisch 141-196, George Gibson 12-14, Preston Gomez 38-52, Charlie Grimm 946-784, Stan Hack 196-265, Gabby Hartnett 203-176, Vedie Himsl 10-21, Rogers Hornsby 141-114, Roy Johnson 0-1, Bob Kennedy 182-198, Bill Killefer 299-292, Lou Klein 65-83, Jim Lefebvre 162-162, Whitey Lockman 157-162, Tom Loftus 53-86, Frank Lucchesi 8-17, Rabbit Maranville 23-30, Jim Marshall 175-218, Joe McCarthy 442-321, Charlie Metro 43-69, Gene Michael 114-124, Fred Mitchell 308-269, Hank O'Day 78-76, Jim Riggleman 73-71, Bob Scheffing 208-254, Frank Selee 295-223, Elvin Tappe 46-69, Joe Tinker 67-86, Tom Trebelhorn 49-64, John Vukovich 1-1, Jimmy Wilson 213-258, Don Zimmer 265-259.

HISTORY Team by team

YEARLY FINISHES

Year	Position	W	L	Pct.	*GB	Manager	Attendance
1901	8th	52	87	.374	38	Bid McPhee	205,728
1902	4th	70	70	.500	33 1/2	Bid McPhee, Frank Bancroft, Joe Kelley	217,300
1903	4th	74	65	.532	16 1/2	Joe Kelley	351,680
1904	3rd	88	65	.575	18	Joe Kelley	391,915
1905	5th	79	74	.516	26	Joe Kelley	313,927
1906	6th	64	87	.424	51 1/2	Ned Hanlon	330,056
1907	6th	66	87	.431	41 1/2	Ned Hanlon	317,500
1908	5th	73	81	.474	26	John Ganzel	399,200
1909	4th	77	76	.503	33 1/2	Clark Griffith	424,643
1910	5th	75	79	.487	29	Clark Griffith	380,622
1911	6th	70	83	.458	29	Clark Griffith	300,000
1912	4th	75	78	.490	29	Hank O'Day	344,000
1913	7th	64	89	.418	37 1/2	Joe Tinker	258,000
1914	8th	60	94	.390	34 1/2	Buck Herzog	100,791
1915	7th	71	83	.461	20	Buck Herzog	218,878
1916	7th (tied)	60	93	.392	33 1/2	Buck Herzog, Christy Mathewson	255,846
1917	4th	78	76	.506	20	Christy Mathewson	269,056
1918	3rd	68	60	.531	15 1/2	Christy Mathewson, Heinie Groh	163,009
1919	1st	96	44	.686	+9	Pat Moran	532,501
1920	3rd	82	71	.536	10 1/2	Pat Moran	568,107
1921	6th	70	83	.458	24	Pat Moran	311,227
1922	2nd	86	68	.558	7	Pat Moran	493,754
1923	2nd	91	63	.591	4 1/2	Pat Moran	575,063
1924	4th	83	70	.542	10	Jack Hendricks	437,707
1925	3rd	80	73	.523	15	Jack Hendricks	464,920
1926	2nd	87	67	.565	2	Jack Hendricks	672,987
1927	5th	75	78	.490	18 1/2	Jack Hendricks	442,164
1928	5th	78	74	.513	16	Jack Hendricks	490,490
1929	7th	66	88	.429	33	Jack Hendricks	295,040
1930	7th	59	95	.383	33	Dan Howley	386,727
1931	8th	58	96	.377	43	Dan Howley	263,316
1932	8th	60	94	.390	30	Dan Howley	356,950
1933	8th	58	94	.382	33	Donie Bush	218,281
1934	8th	52	99	.344	42	Bob O'Farrell, Chuck Dressen	206,773
1935	6th	68	85	.444	31 1/2	Chuck Dressen	448,247
1936	5th	74	80	.481	18	Chuck Dressen	466,245
1937	8th	56	98	.364	40	Chuck Dressen, Bobby Wallace	411,221
1938	4th	82	68	.547	6	Bill McKechnie	706,756
1939	1st	97	57	.630	+4 1/2	Bill McKechnie	981,443
1940	1st	100	53	.654	+12	Bill McKechnie	850,180
1941	3rd	88	66	.571	12	Bill McKechnie	643,513
1942	4th	76	76	.500	29	Bill McKechnie	427,031
1943	2nd	87	67	.565	18	Bill McKechnie	379,122
1944	3rd	89	65	.578	16	Bill McKechnie	409,567
1945	7th	61	93	.396	37	Bill McKechnie	290,070
1946	6th	67	87	.435	30	Bill McKechnie	715,751
1947	5th	73	81	.474	21	Johnny Neun	899,975
1948	7th	64	89	.418	27	Johnny Neun, Bucky Walters	823,386
1949	7th	62	92	.403	35	Bucky Walters	707,782
1950	6th	66	87	.431	24 1/2	Luke Sewell	538,794
1951	6th	68	86	.442	28 1/2	Luke Sewell	588,268
1952	6th	69	85	.448	27 1/2	Luke Sewell, Rogers Hornsby	604,197
1953	6th	68	86	.442	37	Rogers Hornsby, Buster Mills	548,086
1954	5th	74	80	.481	23	Birdie Tebbetts	704,167
1955	5th	75	79	.487	23 1/2	Birdie Tebbetts	693,662
1956	3rd	91	63	.591	2	Birdie Tebbetts	1,125,928
1957	4th	80	74	.519	15	Birdie Tebbetts	1,070,850
1958	4th	76	78	.494	16	Birdie Tebbetts, Jimmie Dykes	788,582
1959	5th (tied)	74	80	.481	13	Mayo Smith, Fred Hutchinson	801,289
1960	6th	67	87	.435	28	Fred Hutchinson	663,486
1961	1st	93	61	.604	+4	Fred Hutchinson	1,117,603
1962	3rd	98	64	.605	3 1/2	Fred Hutchinson	982,085
1963	5th	86	76	.531	13	Fred Hutchinson	858,805
1964	2nd (tied)	92	70	.549	1	Fred Hutchinson, Dick Sisler	862,466
1965	4th	89	73	.549	8	Dick Sisler	1,047,824
1966	7th	76	84	.475	18	Don Heffner, Dave Bristol	742,958
1967	4th	87	75	.537	14 1/2	Dave Bristol	958,300
1968	4th	83	79	.512	14	Dave Bristol	733,354

HISTORY Team by team

Year	Position	W	L	Pct.	*GB	Manager	Attendance
1969	3rd	89	73	.549	4	Dave Bristol	987,991
1970	1st†	102	60	.630	+14 1/2	Sparky Anderson	1,803,568
1971	4th (tied)	79	83	.488	11	Sparky Anderson	1,501,122
1972	1st†	95	59	.617	+10 1/2	Sparky Anderson	1,611,459
1973	1st‡	99	63	.611	+3 1/2	Sparky Anderson	2,017,601
1974	2nd	98	64	.605	4	Sparky Anderson	2,164,307
1975	1st†	108	54	.667	+20	Sparky Anderson	2,315,603
1976	1st†	102	60	.630	+10	Sparky Anderson	2,629,708
1977	2nd	88	74	.543	10	Sparky Anderson	2,519,670
1978	2nd	92	69	.571	2 1/2	Sparky Anderson	2,532,497
1979	1st‡	90	71	.559	+1 1/2	John McNamara	2,356,933
1980	3rd	89	73	.549	3 1/2	John McNamara	2,022,450
1981	2nd/2nd	66	42	.611	§	John McNamara	1,093,730
1982	6th	61	101	.377	28	John McNamara, Russ Nixon	1,326,528
1983	6th	74	88	.457	17	Russ Nixon	1,190,419
1984	5th	70	92	.432	22	Vern Rapp, Pete Rose	1,275,887
1985	2nd	89	72	.553	5 1/2	Pete Rose	1,834,619
1986	2nd	86	76	.531	10	Pete Rose	1,692,432
1987	2nd	84	78	.519	6	Pete Rose	2,185,205
1988	2nd	87	74	.540	7	Pete Rose	2,072,528
1989	5th	75	87	.463	17	Pete Rose, Tommy Helms	1,979,320
1990	1st†	91	71	.562	+5	Lou Piniella	2,400,892
1991	5th	74	88	.457	20	Lou Piniella	2,372,377
1992	2nd	90	72	.556	8	Lou Piniella	2,315,946
1993	5th	73	89	.451	31	Tony Perez, Dave Johnson	2,453,232

CENTRAL DIVISION

Year	Position	W	L	Pct.	*GB	Manager	Attendance
1994	1st	66	48	.579	+ 1/2	Dave Johnson	1,897,681
1995	1st∞‡	85	59	.590	+9	Dave Johnson	1,837,649

*Games behind winner. †Won championship series. ‡Lost championship series. §First half 35-21; second half 31-21. ∞Won division series.

MANAGERIAL RECORDS

Sparky Anderson 863-586, Frank Bancroft 9-7, Dave Bristol 298-265, Donie Bush 58-94, Chuck Dressen 214-282, Jimmie Dykes 24-17, John Ganzel 73-81, Clark Griffith 222-238, Heinie Groh 7-3, Ned Hanlon 130-174, Don Heffner 37-46, Tommy Helms 14-21, Jack Hendricks 469-450, Buck Herzog 165-226, Rogers Hornsby 91-106, Dan Howley 177-285, Fred Hutchinson 443-372, Dave Johnson 204-172, Joe Kelley 275-230, Christy Mathewson 164-176, Bill McKechnie 747-632, John McNamara 279-244, Bid McPhee 79-124, Buster Mills 4-4, Pat Moran 425-329, Johnny Neun 117-137, Russ Nixon 101-131, Hank O'Day 75-78, Bob O'Farrell 30-60, Tony Perez 20-24, Lou Piniella 255-231, Vern Rapp 51-70, Pete Rose 426-388, Luke Sewell 176-234, Dick Sisler 121-94, Mayo Smith 35-45, Birdie Tebbetts 372-357, Joe Tinker 64-89, Bobby Wallace 5-20, Bucky Walters 81-123.

COLORADO ROCKIES

YEARLY FINISHES

WEST DIVISION

Year	Position	W	L	Pct.	*GB	Manager	Attendance
1993	6th	67	95	.414	37	Don Baylor	4,483,350
1994	3rd	53	64	.453	6 1/2	Don Baylor	3,281,511
1995	2nd†	77	67	.535	1	Don Baylor	3,390,037

*Games behind winner. †Lost division series.

MANAGERIAL RECORDS

Don Baylor 197-226.

FLORIDA MARLINS

YEARLY FINISHES

EAST DIVISION

Year	Position	W	L	Pct.	*GB	Manager	Attendance
1993	6th	64	98	.395	33	Rene Lachemann	3,064,847
1994	5th	51	64	.443	23 1/2	Rene Lachemann	1,937,467
1995	4th	67	76	.469	22 1/2	Rene Lachemann	1,700,466

*Games behind winner.

MANAGERIAL RECORDS

Rene Lachemann 182-238.

HISTORY *Team by team*

YEARLY FINISHES

Year	Position	W	L	Pct.	*GB	Manager	Attendance
1962†	8th	64	96	.400	36 1/2	Harry Craft	924,456
1963†	9th	66	96	.407	33	Harry Craft	719,502
1964†	9th	66	96	.407	27	Harry Craft, Luman Harris	725,773
1965	9th	65	97	.401	32	Luman Harris	2,151,470
1966	8th	72	90	.444	23	Grady Hatton	1,872,108
1967	9th	69	93	.426	32 1/2	Grady Hatton	1,348,303
1968	10th	72	90	.444	25	Grady Hatton, Harry Walker	1,312,887

WEST DIVISION

Year	Position	W	L	Pct.	*GB	Manager	Attendance
1969	5th	81	81	.500	12	Harry Walker	1,442,995
1970	4th	79	83	.488	23	Harry Walker	1,253,444
1971	4th (tied)	79	83	.488	11	Harry Walker	1,261,589
1972	2nd	84	69	.549	10 1/2	Harry Walker, Leo Durocher, Salty Parker	1,469,247
1973	4th	82	80	.506	17	Leo Durocher, Preston Gomez	1,394,004
1974	4th	81	81	.500	21	Preston Gomez	1,090,728
1975	6th	64	97	.398	43 1/2	Preston Gomez, Bill Virdon	858,002
1976	3rd	80	82	.494	22	Bill Virdon	886,146
1977	3rd	81	81	.500	17	Bill Virdon	1,109,560
1978	5th	74	88	.457	21	Bill Virdon	1,126,145
1979	2nd	89	73	.549	1 1/2	Bill Virdon	1,900,312
1980	1st‡§	93	70	.571	+1	Bill Virdon	2,278,217
1981	3rd/1st▲	61	49	.555	∞	Bill Virdon	1,321,282
1982	5th	77	85	.475	12	Bill Virdon, Bob Lillis	1,558,555
1983	3rd	85	77	.525	6	Bob Lillis	1,351,962
1984	2nd (tied)	80	82	.494	12	Bob Lillis	1,229,862
1985	3rd (tied)	83	79	.512	12	Bob Lillis	1,184,314
1986	1st§	96	66	.593	+10	Hal Lanier	1,734,276
1987	3rd	76	86	.469	14	Hal Lanier	1,909,902
1988	5th	82	80	.506	12 1/2	Hal Lanier	1,933,505
1989	3rd	86	76	.531	6	Art Howe	1,834,908
1990	4th (tied)	75	87	.463	16	Art Howe	1,310,927
1991	6th	65	97	.401	29	Art Howe	1,196,152
1992	4th	81	81	.500	17	Art Howe	1,211,412
1993	3rd	85	77	.525	19	Art Howe	2,084,546

CENTRAL DIVISION

Year	Position	W	L	Pct.	*GB	Manager	Attendance
1994	2nd	66	49	.574	1/2	Art Howe	1,561,136
1995	2nd	76	68	.528	9	Terry Collins	1,363,801

*Games behind winner. †Houston Colt .45s. ‡Won division playoff. §Lost championship series. ∞First half 28-29; second half 33-20. ▲Lost division series.

MANAGERIAL RECORDS

Terry Collins 142-117, Harry Craft 191-280, Leo Durocher 98-95, Preston Gomez 128-161, Lum Harris 70-105, Grady Hatton 164-221, Art Howe 392-418, Hal Lanier 254-232, Bob Lillis 276-261, Bill Virdon 544-522, Harry Walker 355-353.

YEARLY FINISHES

Year	Position	W	L	Pct.	*GB	Manager	Attendance
1901†	3rd	79	57	.581	9 1/2	Ned Hanlon	189,200
1902†	2nd	75	63	.543	27 1/2	Ned Hanlon	199,868
1903†	5th	70	66	.515	19	Ned Hanlon	224,670
1904†	6th	56	97	.366	50	Ned Hanlon	214,600
1905†	8th	48	104	.316	56 1/2	Ned Hanlon	227,924
1906†	5th	66	86	.434	50	Patsy Donovan	227,400
1907†	5th	65	83	.439	40	Patsy Donovan	312,500
1908†	7th	53	101	.344	46	Patsy Donovan	275,600
1909†	6th	55	98	.359	55 1/2	Harry Lumley	321,300
1910†	6th	64	90	.416	40	Bill Dahlen	279,321
1911†	7th	64	86	.427	33 1/2	Bill Dahlen	269,000
1912†	7th	58	95	.379	46	Bill Dahlen	243,000
1913†	6th	65	84	.436	34 1/2	Bill Dahlen	347,000
1914†	5th	75	79	.487	19 1/2	Wilbert Robinson	122,671
1915†	3rd	80	72	.526	10	Wilbert Robinson	297,766
1916†	1st	94	60	.610	+2 1/2	Wilbert Robinson	447,747
1917†	7th	70	81	.464	26 1/2	Wilbert Robinson	221,619
1918†	5th	57	69	.452	25 1/2	Wilbert Robinson	83,831

Year	Position	W	L	Pct.	*GB	Manager	Attendance
1919†	5th	69	71	.493	27	Wilbert Robinson	360,721
1920†	1st	93	61	.604	+7	Wilbert Robinson	808,722
1921†	5th	77	75	.507	16 1/2	Wilbert Robinson	613,245
1922†	6th	76	78	.494	17	Wilbert Robinson	498,856
1923†	6th	76	78	.494	19 1/2	Wilbert Robinson	564,666
1924†	2nd	92	62	.597	1 1/2	Wilbert Robinson	818,883
1925†	6th (tied)	68	85	.444	27	Wilbert Robinson	659,435
1926†	6th	71	82	.464	17 1/2	Wilbert Robinson	650,819
1927†	6th	65	88	.425	28 1/2	Wilbert Robinson	637,230
1928†	6th	77	76	.503	17 1/2	Wilbert Robinson	664,863
1929†	6th	70	83	.458	28 1/2	Wilbert Robinson	731,886
1930†	4th	86	68	.558	6	Wilbert Robinson	1,097,339
1931†	4th	79	73	.520	21	Wilbert Robinson	753,133
1932†	3rd	81	73	.526	9	Max Carey	681,827
1933†	6th	65	88	.425	26 1/2	Max Carey	526,815
1934†	6th	71	81	.467	23 1/2	Casey Stengel	434,188
1935†	5th	70	83	.458	29 1/2	Casey Stengel	470,517
1936†	7th	67	87	.435	25	Casey Stengel	489,618
1937†	6th	62	91	.405	33 1/2	Burleigh Grimes	482,481
1938†	7th	69	80	.463	18 1/2	Burleigh Grimes	663,087
1939†	3rd	84	69	.549	12 1/2	Leo Durocher	955,668
1940†	2nd	88	65	.575	12	Leo Durocher	975,978
1941†	1st	100	54	.649	+2 1/2	Leo Durocher	1,214,910
1942†	2nd	104	50	.675	2	Leo Durocher	1,037,765
1943†	3rd	81	72	.529	23 1/2	Leo Durocher	661,739
1944†	7th	63	91	.409	42	Leo Durocher	605,905
1945†	3rd	87	67	.565	11	Leo Durocher	1,059,220
1946†	2nd‡	96	60	.615	2	Leo Durocher	1,796,824
1947†	1st	94	60	.610	+5	Clyde Sukeforth, Burt Shotton	1,807,526
1948†	3rd	84	70	.545	7 1/2	Leo Durocher, Burt Shotton	1,398,967
1949†	1st	97	57	.630	+1	Burt Shotton	1,633,747
1950†	2nd	89	65	.578	2	Burt Shotton	1,185,896
1951†	2nd‡	97	60	.618	1	Chuck Dressen	1,282,628
1952†	1st	96	57	.627	+4 1/2	Chuck Dressen	1,088,704
1953†	1st	105	49	.682	+13	Chuck Dressen	1,163,419
1954†	2nd	92	62	.597	5	Walter Alston	1,020,531
1955†	1st	98	55	.641	+13 1/2	Walter Alston	1,033,589
1956†	1st	93	61	.604	+1	Walter Alston	1,213,562
1957†	3rd	84	70	.545	11	Walter Alston	1,028,258
1958	7th	71	83	.461	21	Walter Alston	1,845,556
1959	1st§	88	68	.564	+2	Walter Alston	2,071,045
1960	4th	82	72	.532	13	Walter Alston	2,253,887
1961	2nd	89	65	.578	4	Walter Alston	1,804,250
1962	2nd‡	102	63	.618	1	Walter Alston	2,755,184
1963	1st	99	63	.611	+6	Walter Alston	2,538,602
1964	6th (tied)	80	82	.494	13	Walter Alston	2,228,751
1965	1st	97	65	.599	+2	Walter Alston	2,553,577
1966	1st	95	67	.586	+1 1/2	Walter Alston	2,617,029
1967	8th	73	89	.451	28 1/2	Walter Alston	1,664,362
1968	7th	76	86	.469	21	Walter Alston	1,581,093

WEST DIVISION

Year	Position	W	L	Pct.	*GB	Manager	Attendance
1969	4th	85	77	.525	8	Walter Alston	1,784,527
1970	2nd	87	74	.540	14 1/2	Walter Alston	1,697,142
1971	2nd	89	73	.549	1	Walter Alston	2,064,594
1972	3rd	85	70	.548	10 1/2	Walter Alston	1,860,858
1973	2nd	95	66	.590	3 1/2	Walter Alston	2,136,192
1974	1st∞	102	60	.630	+4	Walter Alston	2,632,474
1975	2nd	88	74	.543	20	Walter Alston	2,539,349
1976	2nd	92	70	.568	10	Walter Alston, Tommy Lasorda	2,386,301
1977	1st∞	98	64	.605	+10	Tommy Lasorda	2,955,087
1978	1st∞	95	67	.586	+2 1/2	Tommy Lasorda	3,347,845
1979	3rd	79	83	.488	11 1/2	Tommy Lasorda	2,860,954
1980	2nd▲	92	71	.564	1	Tommy Lasorda	3,249,287
1981	1st/4th§∞	63	47	.573	◆	Tommy Lasorda	2,381,292
1982	2nd	88	74	.543	1	Tommy Lasorda	3,608,881
1983	1st▼	91	71	.652	+3	Tommy Lasorda	3,510,313
1984	4th	79	83	.488	13	Tommy Lasorda	3,134,824
1985	1st▼	95	67	.586	+5 1/2	Tommy Lasorda	3,264,593
1986	5th	73	89	.451	23	Tommy Lasorda	3,023,208
1987	4th	73	89	.451	17	Tommy Lasorda	2,797,409
1988	1st∞	94	67	.584	+7	Tommy Lasorda	2,980,262
1989	4th	77	83	.481	14	Tommy Lasorda	2,944,653
1990	2nd	86	76	.531	5	Tommy Lasorda	3,002,396

Year	Position	W	L	Pct.	*GB	Manager	Attendance
1991	2nd	93	69	.574	1	Tommy Lasorda	3,348,170
1992	6th	63	99	.389	35	Tommy Lasorda	2,473,266
1993	4th	81	81	.500	23	Tommy Lasorda	3,170,392
1994	1st	58	56	.509	+3 1/2	Tommy Lasorda	2,279,355
1995	1st	78	66	.542	+1	Tommy Lasorda	2,766,251

*Games behind winner. †Brooklyn Dodgers. ‡Lost pennant playoff. §Won pennant playoff. ∞Won championship series. ▲Lost division playoff. ◆First half 36-21; second half 27-26. ■Won division series. ▼Lost championship series.

MANAGERIAL RECORDS

Walter Alston 2,040-1,613, Max Carey 146-161, Bill Dahlen 251-355, Patsy Donovan 184-270, Chuck Dressen 298-166, Leo Durocher 738-565, Burleigh Grimes 131-171, Ned Hanlon 328-387, Tommy Lasorda 1,558-1,404, Harry Lumley 55-98, Wilbert Robinson 1,375-1,341, Burt Shotton 326-215, Casey Stengel 208-251, Clyde Sukeforth 2-0.

MONTREAL EXPOS

YEARLY FINISHES
EAST DIVISION

Year	Position	W	L	Pct.	*GB	Manager	Attendance
1969	6th	52	110	.321	48	Gene Mauch	1,212,608
1970	6th	73	89	.451	16	Gene Mauch	1,424,683
1971	5th	71	90	.441	25 1/2	Gene Mauch	1,290,963
1972	5th	70	86	.449	26 1/2	Gene Mauch	1,142,145
1973	4th	79	83	.488	3 1/2	Gene Mauch	1,246,863
1974	4th	79	82	.491	8 1/2	Gene Mauch	1,019,134
1975	5th (tied)	75	87	.463	17 1/2	Gene Mauch	908,292
1976	6th	55	107	.340	46	Karl Kuehl, Charlie Fox	646,704
1977	5th	75	87	.463	26	Dick Williams	1,433,757
1978	4th	76	86	.469	14	Dick Williams	1,427,007
1979	2nd	95	65	.594	2	Dick Williams	2,102,173
1980	2nd	90	72	.556	1	Dick Williams	2,208,175
1981	3rd/1st‡§	60	48	.556	†	Dick Williams, Jim Fanning	1,534,564
1982	3rd	86	76	.531	6	Jim Fanning	2,318,292
1983	3rd	82	80	.506	8	Bill Virdon	2,320,651
1984	5th	78	83	.484	18	Bill Virdon, Jim Fanning	1,606,531
1985	3rd	84	77	.522	16 1/2	Buck Rodgers	1,502,494
1986	4th	78	83	.484	29 1/2	Buck Rodgers	1,128,981
1987	3rd	91	71	.562	4	Buck Rodgers	1,850,324
1988	3rd	81	81	.500	20	Buck Rodgers	1,478,659
1989	4th	81	81	.500	12	Buck Rodgers	1,783,533
1990	3rd	85	77	.525	10	Buck Rodgers	1,373,087
1991	6th	71	90	.441	26 1/2	Buck Rodgers, Tom Runnells	934,742
1992	2nd	87	75	.537	9	Tom Runnells, Felipe Alou	1,669,077
1993	2nd	94	68	.580	3	Felipe Alou	1,641,437
1994	1st	74	40	.649	+6	Felipe Alou	1,276,250
1995	5th	66	78	.458	24	Felipe Alou	1,309,618

*Games behind winner. †First half 30-25; second half 30-23. ‡Won division series. §Lost championship series.

MANAGERIAL RECORDS

Felipe Alou 304-241, Jim Fanning 116-103, Charlie Fox 12-22, Karl Kuehl 43-85, Gene Mauch 499-627, Buck Rodgers 520-499, Tom Runnells 68-81, Bill Virdon 146-147, Dick Williams 380-347.

NEW YORK METS

YEARLY FINISHES

Year	Position	W	L	Pct.	*GB	Manager	Attendance
1962	10th	40	120	.250	60 1/2	Casey Stengel	922,530
1963	10th	51	111	.315	48	Casey Stengel	1,080,108
1964	10th	53	109	.327	40	Casey Stengel	1,732,597
1965	10th	50	112	.309	47	Casey Stengel, Wes Westrum	1,768,389
1966	9th	66	95	.410	28 1/2	Wes Westrum	1,932,693
1967	10th	61	101	.377	40 1/2	Wes Westrum, Salty Parker	1,565,492
1968	9th	73	89	.451	24	Gil Hodges	1,781,657

EAST DIVISION

Year	Position	W	L	Pct.	*GB	Manager	Attendance
1969	1st†	100	62	.617	+8	Gil Hodges	2,175,373
1970	3rd	83	79	.512	6	Gil Hodges	2,697,479
1971	3rd (tied)	83	79	.512	14	Gil Hodges	2,266,680
1972	3rd	83	73	.532	13 1/2	Yogi Berra	2,134,185
1973	1st†	82	79	.509	+1 1/2	Yogi Berra	1,912,390
1974	5th	71	91	.438	17	Yogi Berra	1,722,209

Year	Position	W	L	Pct.	*GB	Manager	Attendance
1975	3rd (tied)	82	80	.506	10 1/2	Yogi Berra, Roy McMillan	1,730,566
1976	3rd	86	76	.531	15	Joe Frazier	1,468,754
1977	6th	64	98	.395	37	Joe Frazier, Joe Torre	1,066,825
1978	6th	66	96	.407	24	Joe Torre	1,007,328
1979	6th	63	99	.389	35	Joe Torre	788,905
1980	5th	67	95	.414	24	Joe Torre	1,192,073
1981	5th/4th	41	62	.398	‡	Joe Torre	704,244
1982	6th	65	97	.401	27	George Bamberger	1,323,036
1983	6th	68	94	.420	22	George Bamberger, Frank Howard	1,112,774
1984	2nd	90	72	.556	6 1/2	Dave Johnson	1,842,695
1985	2nd	98	64	.605	3	Dave Johnson	2,761,601
1986	1st†	108	54	.667	+21 1/2	Dave Johnson	2,767,601
1987	2nd	92	70	.568	3	Dave Johnson	3,034,129
1988	1st§	100	60	.625	+15	Dave Johnson	3,055,445
1989	2nd	87	75	.537	6	Dave Johnson	2,918,710
1990	2nd	91	71	.562	4	Dave Johnson, Bud Harrelson	2,732,745
1991	5th	77	84	.478	20 1/2	Bud Harrelson, Mike Cubbage	2,284,484
1992	5th	72	90	.444	24	Jeff Torborg	1,779,534
1993	7th	59	103	.364	38	Jeff Torborg, Dallas Green	1,873,183
1994	3rd	55	58	.487	18 1/2	Dallas Green	1,151,471
1995	2nd (tied)	69	75	.479	21	Dallas Green	1,273,183

*Games behind winner. †Won championship series. ‡First half 17-34; second half 24-28. §Lost championship series.

MANAGERIAL RECORDS

George Bamberger 81-127, Yogi Berra 292-296, Mike Cubbage 3-4, Joe Frazier 101-106, Dallas Green 170-211, Bud Harrelson 145-129, Gil Hodges 339-309, Frank Howard 52-64, Davey Johnson 595-417, Roy McMillan 26-27, Salty Parker 4-7, Casey Stengel 175-404, Jeff Torborg 85-115, Joe Torre 286-420, Wes Westrum 142-237.

PHILADELPHIA PHILLIES

YEARLY FINISHES

Year	Position	W	L	Pct.	*GB	Manager	Attendance
1901	2nd	83	57	.593	7 1/2	Bill Shettsline	234,937
1902	7th	56	81	.409	46	Bill Shettsline	112,066
1903	7th	49	86	.363	39 1/2	Chief Zimmer	151,729
1904	8th	52	100	.342	53 1/2	Hugh Duffy	140,771
1905	4th	83	69	.546	21 1/2	Hugh Duffy	317,932
1906	4th	71	82	.464	45 1/2	Hugh Duffy	294,680
1907	3rd	83	64	.565	21 1/2	Bill Murray	341,216
1908	4th	83	71	.539	16	Bill Murray	420,660
1909	5th	74	79	.484	36 1/2	Bill Murray	303,177
1910	4th	78	75	.510	25 1/2	Red Dooin	296,597
1911	4th	79	73	.520	19 1/2	Red Dooin	416,000
1912	5th	73	79	.480	30 1/2	Red Dooin	250,000
1913	2nd	88	63	.583	12 1/2	Red Dooin	470,000
1914	6th	74	80	.481	20 1/2	Red Dooin	138,474
1915	1st	90	62	.592	+7	Pat Moran	449,898
1916	2nd	91	62	.595	2 1/2	Pat Moran	515,365
1917	2nd	87	65	.572	10	Pat Moran	354,428
1918	6th	55	68	.447	26	Pat Moran	122,266
1919	8th	47	90	.343	47 1/2	Jack Coombs, Gavvy Cravath	240,424
1920	8th	62	91	.405	30 1/2	Gavvy Cravath	330,998
1921	8th	51	103	.331	43 1/2	Bill Donovan, Kaiser Wilhelm	273,961
1922	7th	57	96	.373	35 1/2	Kaiser Wilhelm	232,471
1923	8th	50	104	.325	45 1/2	Art Fletcher	228,168
1924	7th	55	96	.364	37	Art Fletcher	299,818
1925	6th (tied)	68	85	.444	27	Art Fletcher	304,905
1926	8th	58	93	.384	29 1/2	Art Fletcher	240,600
1927	8th	51	103	.331	43	Stuffy McInnis	305,420
1928	8th	43	109	.283	51	Burt Shotton	182,168
1929	5th	71	82	.464	27 1/2	Burt Shotton	281,200
1930	8th	52	102	.338	40	Burt Shotton	299,007
1931	6th	66	88	.429	35	Burt Shotton	284,849
1932	4th	78	76	.506	12	Burt Shotton	268,914
1933	7th	60	92	.395	31	Burt Shotton	156,421
1934	7th	56	93	.376	37	Jimmy Wilson	169,885
1935	7th	64	89	.418	35 1/2	Jimmy Wilson	205,470
1936	8th	54	100	.351	38	Jimmy Wilson	249,219
1937	7th	61	92	.399	34 1/2	Jimmy Wilson	212,790
1938	8th	45	105	.300	43	Jimmy Wilson, Hans Lobert	166,111
1939	8th	45	106	.298	50 1/2	Doc Prothro	277,973
1940	8th	50	103	.327	50	Doc Prothro	207,177
1941	8th	43	111	.279	57	Doc Prothro	231,401
1942	8th	42	109	.278	62 1/2	Hans Lobert	230,183

Year	Position	W	L	Pct.	*GB	Manager	Attendance
1943	7th	64	90	.416	41	Bucky Harris, Fred Fitzsimmons	466,975
1944	8th	61	92	.399	43½	Fred Fitzsimmons	369,586
1945	8th	46	108	.299	52	Fred Fitzsimmons, Ben Chapman	285,057
1946	5th	69	85	.448	28	Ben Chapman	1,045,247
1947	7th (tied)	62	92	.403	32	Ben Chapman	907,332
1948	6th	66	88	.429	25½	Ben Chapman, Dusty Cooke, Eddie Sawyer	767,429
1949	3rd	81	73	.526	16	Eddie Sawyer	819,698
1950	1st	91	63	.591	+2	Eddie Sawyer	1,217,035
1951	5th	73	81	.474	23½	Eddie Sawyer	937,658
1952	4th	87	67	.565	9½	Eddie Sawyer, Steve O'Neill	775,417
1953	3rd (tied)	83	71	.539	22	Steve O'Neill	853,644
1954	4th	75	79	.487	22	Steve O'Neill, Terry Moore	738,991
1955	4th	77	77	.500	21½	Mayo Smith	922,886
1956	5th	71	83	.461	22	Mayo Smith	934,798
1957	5th	77	77	.500	19	Mayo Smith	1,146,230
1958	8th	69	85	.448	23	Mayo Smith, Eddie Sawyer	931,110
1959	8th	64	90	.416	23	Eddie Sawyer	802,815
1960	8th	59	95	.383	36	Eddie Sawyer, Andy Cohen, Gene Mauch	862,205
1961	8th	47	107	.305	46	Gene Mauch	590,039
1962	7th	81	80	.503	20	Gene Mauch	762,034
1963	4th	87	75	.537	12	Gene Mauch	907,141
1964	2nd (tied)	92	70	.568	1	Gene Mauch	1,425,891
1965	6th	85	76	.528	11½	Gene Mauch	1,166,376
1966	4th	87	75	.537	8	Gene Mauch	1,108,201
1967	5th	82	80	.506	19½	Gene Mauch	828,888
1968	7th (tied)	76	86	.469	21	Gene Mauch, George Myatt, Bob Skinner	664,546

EAST DIVISION

Year	Position	W	L	Pct.	*GB	Manager	Attendance
1969	5th	63	99	.389	37	Bob Skinner, George Myatt	519,414
1970	5th	73	88	.453	15½	Frank Lucchesi	708,247
1971	6th	67	95	.414	30	Frank Lucchesi	1,511,223
1972	6th	59	97	.378	37½	Frank Lucchesi, Paul Owens	1,343,329
1973	6th	71	91	.438	11½	Danny Ozark	1,475,934
1974	3rd	80	82	.494	8	Danny Ozark	1,808,648
1975	2nd	86	76	.531	6½	Danny Ozark	1,909,233
1976	1st†	101	61	.623	+9	Danny Ozark	2,480,150
1977	1st†	101	61	.623	+5	Danny Ozark	2,700,070
1978	1st†	90	72	.556	+1½	Danny Ozark	2,583,389
1979	4th	84	78	.519	14	Danny Ozark, Dallas Green	2,775,011
1980	1st‡	91	71	.562	+1	Dallas Green	2,651,650
1981	1st/3rd∞	59	48	.551	§	Dallas Green	1,638,752
1982	2nd	89	73	.549	3	Pat Corrales	2,376,394
1983	1st‡	90	72	.556	+6	Pat Corrales, Paul Owens	2,128,339
1984	4th	81	81	.500	15½	Paul Owens	2,062,693
1985	5th	75	87	.463	26	John Felske	1,830,350
1986	2nd	86	75	.534	21½	John Felske	1,933,335
1987	4th (tied)	80	82	.494	15	John Felske, Lee Elia	2,100,110
1988	6th	65	96	.404	35½	Lee Elia, John Vukovich	1,990,041
1989	6th	67	95	.414	26	Nick Leyva	1,861,985
1990	4th (tied)	77	85	.475	18	Nick Leyva	1,992,484
1991	3rd	78	84	.481	20	Nick Leyva, Jim Fregosi	2,050,012
1992	6th	70	92	.432	26	Jim Fregosi	1,927,448
1993	1st‡	97	65	.599	+3	Jim Fregosi	3,137,674
1994	4th	54	61	.470	20½	Jim Fregosi	2,290,971
1995	2nd (tied)	69	75	.479	21	Jim Fregosi	2,043,598

*Games behind winner. †Lost championship series. ‡Won championship series. §First half 34-21; second half 25-27. ∞Lost division series.

MANAGERIAL RECORDS

Ben Chapman 197-277, Andy Cohen 1-0, Dusty Cooke 6-6, Jack Coombs 18-44, Pat Corrales 132-115, Gavvy Cravath 91-137, Bill Donovan 31-71, Red Dooin 392-370, Hugh Duffy 206-251, Lee Elia 111-142, John Felske 190-194, Fred Fitzsimmons 102-179, Art Fletcher 231-378, Jim Fregosi 364-368, Dallas Green 169-130, Bucky Harris 40-53, Nick Leyva 148-189, Hans Lobert 42-111, Frank Lucchesi 166-233, Gene Mauch 645-684, Stuffy McInnis 51-103, Terry Moore 35-42, Pat Moran 323-257, Bill Murray 240-214, George Myatt 21-35, Steve O'Neill 182-140, Paul Owens 161-158, Danny Ozark 594-510, Doc Prothro 138-320, Eddie Sawyer 390-424, Bill Shettsline 139-138, Burt Shotton 370-549, Bob Skinner 92-123, Mayo Smith 264-281, John Vukovich 5-4, Kaiser Wilhelm 77-128, Jimmy Wilson 280-477, Chief Zimmer 49-86.

PITTSBURGH PIRATES

YEARLY FINISHES

Year	Position	W	L	Pct.	*GB	Manager	Attendance
1901	1st	90	49	.647	+7½	Fred Clarke	251,955
1902	1st	103	36	.741	+27½	Fred Clarke	243,826

Year	Position	W	L	Pct.	*GB	Manager	Attendance
1903	1st	91	49	.650	+6 1/2	Fred Clarke	326,855
1904	4th	87	66	.569	19	Fred Clarke	340,615
1905	2nd	96	57	.627	9	Fred Clarke	369,124
1906	3rd	93	60	.608	23 1/2	Fred Clarke	394,877
1907	2nd	91	63	.591	17	Fred Clarke	319,506
1908	2nd	98	56	.636	1	Fred Clarke	382,444
1909	1st	110	42	.724	+6 1/2	Fred Clarke	534,950
1910	3rd	86	67	.562	17 1/2	Fred Clarke	436,586
1911	3rd	85	69	.552	14 1/2	Fred Clarke	432,000
1912	2nd	93	58	.616	10	Fred Clarke	384,000
1913	4th	78	71	.523	21 1/2	Fred Clarke	296,000
1914	7th	69	85	.448	25 1/2	Fred Clarke	139,620
1915	5th	73	81	.474	18	Fred Clarke	225,743
1916	6th	65	89	.422	29	Jimmy Callahan	289,132
1917	8th	51	103	.331	47	Jimmy Callahan, Honus Wagner, Hugo Bezdek	192,807
1918	4th	65	60	.520	17	Hugo Bezdek	213,610
1919	4th	71	68	.511	24 1/2	Hugo Bezdek	276,810
1920	4th	79	75	.513	14	George Gibson	429,037
1921	2nd	90	63	.588	4	George Gibson	701,567
1922	3rd (tied)	85	69	.552	8	George Gibson, Bill McKechnie	523,675
1923	3rd	87	67	.565	8 1/2	Bill McKechnie	611,082
1924	3rd	90	63	.588	3	Bill McKechnie	736,883
1925	1st	95	58	.621	+8 1/2	Bill McKechnie	804,354
1926	3rd	84	69	.549	4 1/2	Bill McKechnie	798,542
1927	1st	94	60	.610	+1 1/2	Donie Bush	869,720
1928	4th	85	67	.559	9	Donie Bush	495,070
1929	2nd	88	65	.575	10 1/2	Donie Bush, Jewel Ens	491,377
1930	5th	80	74	.519	12	Jewel Ens	357,795
1931	5th	75	79	.487	26	Jewel Ens	260,392
1932	2nd	86	68	.558	4	George Gibson	287,262
1933	2nd	87	67	.565	5	George Gibson	288,747
1934	5th	74	76	.493	19 1/2	George Gibson, Pie Traynor	322,622
1935	4th	86	67	.562	13 1/2	Pie Traynor	352,885
1936	4th	84	70	.545	8	Pie Traynor	372,524
1937	3rd	86	68	.558	10	Pie Traynor	459,679
1938	2nd	86	64	.573	2	Pie Traynor	641,033
1939	6th	68	85	.444	28 1/2	Pie Traynor	376,734
1940	4th	78	76	.506	22 1/2	Frankie Frisch	507,934
1941	4th	81	73	.526	19	Frankie Frisch	482,241
1942	5th	66	81	.449	36 1/2	Frankie Frisch	448,897
1943	4th	80	74	.519	25	Frankie Frisch	604,278
1944	2nd	90	63	.588	14 1/2	Frankie Frisch	498,740
1945	4th	82	72	.532	16	Frankie Frisch	604,694
1946	7th	63	91	.409	34	Frankie Frisch, Spud Davis	749,962
1947	7th (tied)	62	92	.403	32	Billy Herman, Bill Burwell	1,283,531
1948	4th	83	71	.539	8 1/2	Billy Meyer	1,517,021
1949	6th	71	83	.461	26	Billy Meyer	1,499,435
1950	8th	57	96	.373	33 1/2	Billy Meyer	1,166,267
1951	7th	64	90	.416	32 1/2	Billy Meyer	980,590
1952	8th	42	112	.273	54 1/2	Billy Meyer	686,673
1953	8th	50	104	.325	55	Fred Haney	572,757
1954	8th	53	101	.344	44	Fred Haney	475,494
1955	8th	60	94	.390	38 1/2	Fred Haney	469,397
1956	7th	66	88	.429	27	Bobby Bragan	949,878
1957	7th (tied)	62	92	.403	33	Bobby Bragan, Danny Murtaugh	850,732
1958	2nd	84	70	.545	8	Danny Murtaugh	1,311,988
1959	4th	78	76	.506	9	Danny Murtaugh	1,359,917
1960	1st	95	59	.617	+7	Danny Murtaugh	1,705,828
1961	6th	75	79	.487	18	Danny Murtaugh	1,199,128
1962	4th	93	68	.578	8	Danny Murtaugh	1,090,648
1963	8th	74	88	.457	25	Danny Murtaugh	783,648
1964	6th (tied)	80	82	.494	13	Danny Murtaugh	759,496
1965	3rd	90	72	.556	7	Harry Walker	909,279
1966	3rd	92	70	.568	3	Harry Walker	1,196,618
1967	6th	81	81	.500	20 1/2	Harry Walker, Danny Murtaugh	907,012
1968	6th	80	82	.494	17	Larry Shepard	693,485

EAST DIVISION

Year	Position	W	L	Pct.	*GB	Manager	Attendance
1969	3rd	88	74	.543	12	Larry Shepard, Alex Grammas	769,369
1970	1st†	89	73	.549	+5	Danny Murtaugh	1,341,947
1971	1st‡	97	65	.599	+7	Danny Murtaugh	1,501,132
1972	1st†	96	59	.619	+11	Bill Virdon	1,427,460
1973	3rd	80	82	.494	2 1/2	Bill Virdon, Danny Murtaugh	1,319,913
1974	1st†	88	74	.543	+1 1/2	Danny Murtaugh	1,110,552

Year	Position	W	L	Pct.	*GB	Manager	Attendance
1975	1st†	92	69	.571	+6 1/2	Danny Murtaugh	1,270,018
1976	2nd	92	70	.568	9	Danny Murtaugh	1,025,945
1977	2nd	96	66	.593	5	Chuck Tanner	1,237,349
1978	2nd	88	73	.547	1 1/2	Chuck Tanner	964,106
1979	1st‡	98	64	.605	+2	Chuck Tanner	1,435,454
1980	3rd	83	79	.512	8	Chuck Tanner	1,646,757
1981	4th/6th	46	56	.451	§	Chuck Tanner	541,789
1982	4th	84	78	.519	8	Chuck Tanner	1,024,106
1983	2nd	84	78	.519	6	Chuck Tanner	1,225,916
1984	6th	75	87	.463	21 1/2	Chuck Tanner	773,500
1985	6th	57	104	.354	43 1/2	Chuck Tanner	735,900
1986	6th	64	98	.395	44	Jim Leyland	1,000,917
1987	4th (tied)	80	82	.494	15	Jim Leyland	1,161,193
1988	2nd	85	75	.531	15	Jim Leyland	1,866,713
1989	5th	74	88	.457	19	Jim Leyland	1,374,141
1990	1st†	95	67	.586	+4	Jim Leyland	2,049,908
1991	1st†	98	64	.605	+14	Jim Leyland	2,065,302
1992	1st†	96	66	.593	+9	Jim Leyland	1,829,395
1993	5th	75	87	.463	22	Jim Leyland	1,650,593

CENTRAL DIVISION

Year	Position	W	L	Pct.	*GB	Manager	Attendance
1994	3rd (tied)	53	61	.465	13	Jim Leyland	1,222,520
1995	5th	58	86	.403	27	Jim Leyland	905,517

*Games behind winner. †Lost championship series. ‡Won championship series. §First half 25-23; second half 21-33.

MANAGERIAL RECORDS

Hugo Bezdek 166-187, Bobby Bragan 102-155, Bill Burwell 1-0, Donie Bush 246-178, Jimmy Callahan 85-129, Fred Clarke 1,343-909, Spud Davis 1-2, Jewel Ens 176-167, Frank Frisch 539-528, George Gibson 401-330, Alex Grammas 4-1, Fred Haney 163-299, Billy Herman 61-92, Jim Leyland 778-774, Bill McKechnie 409-293, Billy Meyer 317-452, Danny Murtaugh 1,115-950, Larry Shepard 164-155, Chuck Tanner 711-685, Pie Traynor 457-406, Bill Virdon 163-128, Honus Wagner 1-4, Harry Walker 224-184.

ST. LOUIS CARDINALS

YEARLY FINISHES

Year	Position	W	L	Pct.	*GB	Manager	Attendance
1901	4th	76	64	.543	14 1/2	Patsy Donovan	379,988
1902	6th	56	78	.418	44 1/2	Patsy Donovan	226,417
1903	8th	43	94	.314	46 1/2	Patsy Donovan	226,538
1904	5th	75	79	.487	31 1/2	Kid Nichols	386,750
1905	6th	58	96	.377	47 1/2	Kid Nichols, Jimmy Burke, Matt Robison	292,800
1906	7th	52	98	.347	63	John McCloskey	283,770
1907	8th	52	101	.340	55 1/2	John McCloskey	185,377
1908	8th	49	105	.318	50	John McCloskey	205,129
1909	7th	54	98	.355	56	Roger Bresnahan	299,982
1910	7th	63	90	.412	40 1/2	Roger Bresnahan	355,668
1911	5th	75	74	.503	22	Roger Bresnahan	447,768
1912	6th	63	90	.412	41	Roger Bresnahan	241,759
1913	8th	51	99	.340	49	Miller Huggins	203,531
1914	3rd	81	72	.529	13	Miller Huggins	256,099
1915	6th	72	81	.471	18 1/2	Miller Huggins	252,666
1916	7th (tied)	60	93	.392	33 1/2	Miller Huggins	224,308
1917	3rd	82	70	.539	15	Miller Huggins	288,491
1918	8th	51	78	.395	33	Jack Hendricks	110,599
1919	7th	54	83	.394	40 1/2	Branch Rickey	167,059
1920	5th (tied)	75	79	.487	18	Branch Rickey	326,836
1921	3rd	87	66	.569	7	Branch Rickey	384,773
1922	3rd (tied)	85	69	.552	8	Branch Rickey	536,998
1923	5th	79	74	.516	16	Branch Rickey	338,551
1924	6th	65	89	.422	28 1/2	Branch Rickey	272,885
1925	4th	77	76	.503	18	Branch Rickey, Rogers Hornsby	404,959
1926	1st	89	65	.578	+2	Rogers Hornsby	668,428
1927	2nd	92	61	.601	1 1/2	Bob O'Farrell	749,340
1928	1st	95	59	.617	+2	Bill McKechnie	761,574
1929	4th	78	74	.513	20	Bill McKechnie, Billy Southworth	399,887
1930	1st	92	62	.597	+2	Gabby Street	508,501
1931	1st	101	53	.656	+13	Gabby Street	608,535
1932	6th (tied)	72	82	.468	18	Gabby Street	279,219
1933	5th	82	71	.536	9 1/2	Gabby Street, Frankie Frisch	256,171
1934	1st	95	58	.621	+2	Frankie Frisch	325,056
1935	2nd	96	58	.623	4	Frankie Frisch	506,084
1936	2nd (tied)	87	67	.565	5	Frankie Frisch	448,078
1937	4th	81	73	.526	15	Frankie Frisch	430,811

Year	Position	W	L	Pct.	*GB	Manager	Attendance
1938	6th	71	80	.470	17½	Frankie Frisch, Mike Gonzalez	291,418
1939	2nd	92	61	.601	4½	Ray Blades	400,245
1940	3rd	84	69	.549	16	Ray Blades, Mike Gonzalez, Billy Southworth	324,078
1941	2nd	97	56	.634	2½	Billy Southworth	633,645
1942	1st	106	48	.688	+2	Billy Southworth	553,552
1943	1st	105	49	.682	+18	Billy Southworth	517,135
1944	1st	105	49	.682	+14½	Billy Southworth	461,968
1945	2nd	95	59	.617	3	Billy Southworth	594,630
1946	1st†	98	58	.628	+2	Eddie Dyer	1,061,807
1947	2nd	89	65	.578	5	Eddie Dyer	1,247,913
1948	2nd	85	69	.552	6½	Eddie Dyer	1,111,440
1949	2nd	96	58	.623	1	Eddie Dyer	1,430,676
1950	5th	78	75	.510	12½	Eddie Dyer	1,093,411
1951	3rd	81	73	.526	15½	Marty Marion	1,013,429
1952	3rd	88	66	.571	8½	Eddie Stanky	913,113
1953	3rd (tied)	83	71	.539	22	Eddie Stanky	880,242
1954	6th	72	82	.468	25	Eddie Stanky	1,039,698
1955	7th	68	86	.442	30½	Eddie Stanky, Harry Walker	849,130
1956	4th	76	78	.494	17	Fred Hutchinson	1,029,773
1957	2nd	87	67	.565	8	Fred Hutchinson	1,183,575
1958	5th (tied)	72	82	.468	20	Fred Hutchinson, Stan Hack	1,063,730
1959	7th	71	83	.461	16	Solly Hemus	929,953
1960	3rd	86	68	.558	9	Solly Hemus	1,096,632
1961	5th	80	74	.519	13	Solly Hemus, Johnny Keane	855,305
1962	6th	84	78	.519	17½	Johnny Keane	953,895
1963	2nd	93	69	.574	6	Johnny Keane	1,170,546
1964	1st	93	69	.574	+1	Johnny Keane	1,143,294
1965	7th	80	81	.497	16½	Red Schoendienst	1,241,201
1966	6th	83	79	.512	12	Red Schoendienst	1,712,980
1967	1st	101	60	.627	+10½	Red Schoendienst	2,090,145
1968	1st	97	65	.599	+9	Red Schoendienst	2,011,167

EAST DIVISION

Year	Position	W	L	Pct.	*GB	Manager	Attendance
1969	4th	87	75	.537	13	Red Schoendienst	1,682,783
1970	4th	76	86	.469	13	Red Schoendienst	1,629,736
1971	2nd	90	72	.556	7	Red Schoendienst	1,604,671
1972	4th	75	81	.481	21½	Red Schoendienst	1,196,894
1973	2nd	81	81	.500	1½	Red Schoendienst	1,574,046
1974	2nd	86	75	.534	1½	Red Schoendienst	1,838,413
1975	3rd (tied)	82	80	.506	10½	Red Schoendienst	1,695,270
1976	5th	72	90	.444	29	Red Schoendienst	1,207,079
1977	3rd	83	79	.512	18	Vern Rapp	1,659,287
1978	5th	69	93	.426	21	Vern Rapp, Jack Krol, Ken Boyer	1,278,215
1979	3rd	86	76	.531	12	Ken Boyer	1,627,256
1980	4th	74	88	.457	17	Ken Boyer, Jack Krol, Whitey Herzog, Red Schoendienst	1,385,147
1981	2nd/2nd	59	43	.578	‡	Whitey Herzog	1,010,247
1982	1st§	92	70	.568	+3	Whitey Herzog	2,111,906
1983	4th	79	83	.488	11	Whitey Herzog	2,317,914
1984	3rd	84	78	.519	12½	Whitey Herzog	2,037,448
1985	1st§	101	61	.623	+3	Whitey Herzog	2,637,563
1986	3rd	79	82	.491	28½	Whitey Herzog	2,471,974
1987	1st§	95	67	.586	+3	Whitey Herzog	3,072,122
1988	5th	76	86	.469	25	Whitey Herzog	2,892,799
1989	3rd	86	76	.531	7	Whitey Herzog	3,080,980
1990	6th	70	92	.432	25	Whitey Herzog, Red Schoendienst, Joe Torre	2,573,225
1991	2nd	84	78	.519	14	Joe Torre	2,448,699
1992	3rd	83	79	.512	13	Joe Torre	2,418,483
1993	3rd	87	75	.537	10	Joe Torre	2,844,328

CENTRAL DIVISION

Year	Position	W	L	Pct.	*GB	Manager	Attendance
1994	3rd (tied)	53	61	.465	13	Joe Torre	1,866,544
1995	4th	62	81	.434	22½	Joe Torre, Mike Jorgensen	1,756,727

*Games behind winner. †Won pennant playoff. ‡First half 30-20; second half 29-23. §Won championship series.

MANAGERIAL RECORDS

Ray Blades 106-85, Ken Boyer 166-190, Roger Bresnahan 255-352, Jimmy Burke 17-32, Patsy Donovan 175-236, Eddie Dyer 446-325, Frank Frisch 458-354, Mike Gonzalez 9-13, Stan Hack 3-7, Solly Hemus 190-192, Jack Hendricks 51-78, Whitey Herzog 835-739, Rogers Hornsby 153-116, Miller Huggins 346-415, Fred Hutchinson 232-220, Mike Jorgensen 42-54, Johnny Keane 317-249, Marty Marion 81-73, John McCloskey 153-304, Bill McKechnie 129-88, Kid Nichols 94-108, Bob O'Farrell 92-61, Vern Rapp 89-90, Branch Rickey 458-485, Stanley Robison 22-35, Red Schoendienst 1,028-944, Billy Southworth 620-346, Eddie Stanky 260-238, Gabby Street 312-242, Joe Torre 351-354, Harry Walker 51-67.

SAN DIEGO PADRES

YEARLY FINISHES

Year	Position	W	L	Pct.	*GB	Manager	Attendance
1969	6th	52	110	.321	41	Preston Gomez	512,970
1970	6th	63	99	.389	39	Preston Gomez	643,679
1971	6th	61	100	.379	28 1/2	Preston Gomez	557,513
1972	6th	58	95	.379	36 1/2	Preston Gomez, Don Zimmer	644,273
1973	6th	60	102	.370	39	Don Zimmer	611,826
1974	6th	60	102	.370	42	John McNamara	1,075,399
1975	4th	71	91	.438	37	John McNamara	1,281,747
1976	5th	73	89	.451	29	John McNamara	1,458,478
1977	5th	69	93	.426	29	John McNamara, Bob Skinner, Alvin Dark	1,376,269
1978	4th	84	78	.519	11	Roger Craig	1,670,107
1979	5th	68	93	.422	22	Roger Craig	1,456,967
1980	6th	73	89	.451	19 1/2	Jerry Coleman	1,139,026
1981	6th/6th	41	69	.373	†	Frank Howard	519,161
1982	4th	81	81	.500	8	Dick Williams	1,607,516
1983	4th	81	81	.500	10	Dick Williams	1,539,815
1984	1st†	92	70	.568	+12	Dick Williams	1,983,904
1985	3rd (tied)	83	79	.512	12	Dick Williams	2,210,352
1986	4th	74	88	.457	22	Steve Boros	1,805,716
1987	6th	65	97	.401	25	Larry Bowa	1,454,061
1988	3rd	83	78	.516	11	Larry Bowa, Jack McKeon	1,506,896
1989	2nd	89	73	.549	3	Jack McKeon	2,009,031
1990	4th (tied)	75	87	.463	16	Jack McKeon, Greg Riddoch	1,856,396
1991	3rd	84	78	.519	10	Greg Riddoch	1,804,289
1992	3rd	82	80	.506	16	Greg Riddoch, Jim Riggleman	1,722,102
1993	7th	61	101	.377	43	Jim Riggleman	1,375,432
1994	4th	47	70	.402	12 1/2	Jim Riggleman	953,857
1995	3rd	70	74	.486	8	Bruce Bochy	1,041,805

*Games behind winner. †First half 23-33; second half 18-36. ‡Won championship series.

MANAGERIAL RECORDS

Bruce Bochy 70-74, Steve Boros 74-88, Larry Bowa 81-127, Jerry Coleman 73-89, Roger Craig 152-171, Alvin Dark 49-65, Preston Gomez 180-316, Frank Howard 41-69, Jack McKeon 193-164, John McNamara 224-310, Greg Riddoch 200-194, Jim Riggleman 112-179, Dick Williams 337-311, Don Zimmer 114-190.

SAN FRANCISCO GIANTS

YEARLY FINISHES

Year	Position	W	L	Pct.	*GB	Manager	Attendance
1901†	7th	52	85	.380	37	George Davis	297,650
1902†	8th	48	88	.353	53 1/2	Horace Fogel, Heinie Smith, John McGraw	302,875
1903†	2nd	84	55	.604	6 1/2	John McGraw	579,530
1904†	1st	106	47	.693	+13	John McGraw	609,826
1905†	1st	105	48	.686	+9	John McGraw	552,700
1906†	2nd	96	56	.632	20	John McGraw	402,850
1907†	4th	82	71	.536	25 1/2	John McGraw	538,350
1908†	2nd (tied)	98	56	.636	1	John McGraw	910,000
1909†	3rd	92	61	.601	18 1/2	John McGraw	783,700
1910†	2nd	91	63	.591	13	John McGraw	511,785
1911†	1st	99	54	.647	+7 1/2	John McGraw	675,000
1912†	1st	103	48	.682	+10	John McGraw	638,000
1913†	1st	101	51	.664	+12 1/2	John McGraw	630,000
1914†	2nd	84	70	.545	10 1/2	John McGraw	364,313
1915†	8th	69	83	.454	21	John McGraw	391,850
1916†	4th	86	66	.566	7	John McGraw	552,056
1917†	1st	98	56	.636	+10	John McGraw	500,264
1918†	2nd	71	53	.573	10 1/2	John McGraw	256,618
1919†	2nd	87	53	.621	9	John McGraw	708,857
1920†	2nd	86	68	.558	7	John McGraw	929,609
1921†	1st	94	59	.614	+4	John McGraw	773,247
1922†	1st	93	61	.604	+7	John McGraw	945,809
1923†	1st	95	58	.621	+4 1/2	John McGraw	820,780
1924†	1st	93	60	.608	+1 1/2	John McGraw	844,068
1925†	2nd	86	66	.566	8 1/2	John McGraw	778,993
1926†	5th	74	77	.490	13 1/2	John McGraw	700,362
1927†	3rd	92	62	.597	2	John McGraw	858,190
1928†	2nd	93	61	.604	2	John McGraw	916,191
1929†	3rd	84	67	.556	13 1/2	John McGraw	868,806
1930†	3rd	87	67	.565	5	John McGraw	868,714

Year	Position	W	L	Pct.	*GB	Manager	Attendance
1931†	2nd	87	65	.572	13	John McGraw	812,163
1932†	6th (tied)	72	82	.468	18	John McGraw, Bill Terry	484,868
1933†	1st	91	61	.599	+5	Bill Terry	604,471
1934†	2nd	93	60	.608	2	Bill Terry	730,851
1935†	3rd	91	62	.595	8 1/2	Bill Terry	748,748
1936†	1st	92	62	.597	+5	Bill Terry	837,952
1937†	1st	95	57	.625	+3	Bill Terry	926,887
1938†	3rd	83	67	.553	5	Bill Terry	799,633
1939†	5th	77	74	.510	18 1/2	Bill Terry	702,457
1940†	6th	72	80	.474	27 1/2	Bill Terry	747,852
1941†	5th	74	79	.484	25 1/2	Bill Terry	763,098
1942†	3rd	85	67	.559	20	Mel Ott	779,621
1943†	8th	55	98	.359	49 1/2	Mel Ott	466,095
1944†	5th	67	87	.435	38	Mel Ott	674,083
1945†	5th	78	74	.513	19	Mel Ott	1,016,468
1946†	8th	61	93	.396	36	Mel Ott	1,219,873
1947†	4th	81	73	.526	13	Mel Ott	1,600,793
1948†	5th	78	76	.506	13 1/2	Mel Ott, Leo Durocher	1,459,269
1949†	5th	73	81	.474	24	Leo Durocher	1,218,446
1950†	3rd	86	68	.558	5	Leo Durocher	1,008,876
1951†	1st‡	98	59	.624	+1	Leo Durocher	1,059,539
1952†	2nd	92	62	.597	4 1/2	Leo Durocher	984,940
1953†	5th	70	84	.455	35	Leo Durocher	811,518
1954†	1st	97	57	.630	+5	Leo Durocher	1,155,067
1955†	3rd	80	74	.519	18 1/2	Leo Durocher	824,112
1956†	6th	67	87	.435	26	Bill Rigney	629,179
1957†	6th	69	85	.448	26	Bill Rigney	653,923
1958	3rd	80	74	.519	12	Bill Rigney	1,272,625
1959	3rd	83	71	.539	4	Bill Rigney	1,422,130
1960	5th	79	75	.513	16	Bill Rigney, Tom Sheehan	1,795,356
1961	3rd	85	69	.552	8	Alvin Dark	1,390,679
1962	1st‡	103	62	.624	+1	Alvin Dark	1,592,594
1963	3rd	88	74	.543	11	Alvin Dark	1,571,306
1964	4th	90	72	.556	3	Alvin Dark	1,504,364
1965	2nd	95	67	.586	2	Herman Franks	1,546,075
1966	2nd	93	68	.578	1 1/2	Herman Franks	1,657,192
1967	2nd	91	71	.562	10 1/2	Herman Franks	1,242,480
1968	2nd	88	74	.543	9	Herman Franks	837,220

WEST DIVISION

Year	Position	W	L	Pct.	*GB	Manager	Attendance
1969	2nd	90	72	.556	3	Clyde King	873,603
1970	3rd	86	76	.531	16	Clyde King, Charlie Fox	740,720
1971	1st§	90	72	.556	+1	Charlie Fox	1,106,043
1972	5th	69	86	.445	26 1/2	Charlie Fox	647,744
1973	3rd	88	74	.543	11	Charlie Fox	834,193
1974	5th	72	90	.444	30	Charlie Fox, Wes Westrum	519,987
1975	3rd	80	81	.497	27 1/2	Wes Westrum	522,919
1976	4th	74	88	.457	28	Bill Rigney	626,868
1977	4th	75	87	.463	23	Joe Altobelli	700,056
1978	3rd	89	73	.549	6	Joe Altobelli	1,740,477
1979	4th	71	91	.438	19 1/2	Joe Altobelli, Dave Bristol	1,456,402
1980	5th	75	86	.466	17	Dave Bristol	1,096,115
1981	5th/3rd	56	55	.505	∞	Frank Robinson	632,274
1982	3rd	87	75	.537	2	Frank Robinson	1,200,948
1983	5th	79	83	.488	12	Frank Robinson	1,251,530
1984	6th	66	96	.407	26	Frank Robinson, Danny Ozark	1,001,545
1985	6th	62	100	.383	33	Jim Davenport, Roger Craig	818,697
1986	3rd	83	79	.512	13	Roger Craig	1,528,748
1987	1st§	90	72	.556	+6	Roger Craig	1,917,168
1988	4th	83	79	.512	11 1/2	Roger Craig	1,785,297
1989	1st▲	92	70	.568	+3	Roger Craig	2,059,701
1990	3rd	85	77	.525	6	Roger Craig	1,975,528
1991	4th	75	87	.463	19	Roger Craig	1,737,478
1992	5th	72	90	.444	26	Roger Craig	1,561,987
1993	2nd	103	59	.636	1	Dusty Baker	2,606,354
1994	2nd	55	60	.478	3 1/2	Dusty Baker	1,704,608
1995	4th	67	77	.465	11	Dusty Baker	1,241,500

*Games behind winner. †New York Giants. ‡Won pennant playoff. §Lost championship series. ∞First half 27-32; second half 29-23. ▲Won championship series.

MANAGERIAL RECORDS

Joe Altobelli 225-239, Dusty Baker 225-196, Dave Bristol 85-98, Roger Craig 586-566, Alvin Dark 366-277, Jim Davenport 56-88, George Davis 52-85, Leo Durocher 637-523, Horace Fogel 18-23, Charlie Fox 348-327, Herman Franks 367-280, Clyde King 109-95, John McGraw 2,604-1,801, Mel Ott 464-530, Danny Ozark 24-32, Bill Rigney 406-430, Frank Robinson 264-277, Tom Sheehan 46-50, Heinie Smith 5-27, Bill Terry 823-661, Wes Westrum 118-129.

HISTORY *Team by team*

MINOR LEAGUES

Farm systems

American Association

International League

Mexican League

Pacific Coast League

Eastern League

Southern League

Texas League

California League

Carolina League

Florida League

Midwest League

New York-Pennsylvania League

Northwest League

South Atlantic League

Appalachian League

Arizona League

Dominican Summer League

Gulf Coast League

Pioneer League

Minor league index

FARM SYSTEMS

AMERICAN LEAGUE

BALTIMORE (6): AAA—Rochester. AA—Bowie. A—High Desert, Frederick. Rookie—Bluefield, Gulf Coast Orioles.
BOSTON (6): AAA—Pawtucket. AA—Trenton. A—Sarasota, Michigan, Lowell. Rookie—Gulf Coast Red Sox.
CALIFORNIA (6): AAA—Vancouver. AA—Midland. A—Cedar Rapids, Lake Elsinore, Boise. Rookie—Mesa Angels.
CHICAGO (7): AAA—Nashville. AA—Birmingham. A—South Bend, Hickory, Prince William. Rookie—Bristol, Gulf Coast White Sox.
CLEVELAND (6): AAA—Buffalo. AA—Canton-Akron. A—Kinston, Columbus, Watertown. Rookie—Burlington.
DETROIT (6): AAA—Toledo. AA—Jacksonville. A—Lakeland, Fayetteville, Jamestown. Rookie—Gulf Coast Tigers.
KANSAS CITY (6): AAA—Omaha. AA—Wichita. A—Lansing, Wilmington, Spokane. Rookie—Gulf Coast Royals.
MILWAUKEE (5): AAA—New Orleans. AA—El Paso. A—Stockton, Beloit. Rookie—Helena.
MINNESOTA (6): AAA—Salt Lake. AA—Hardware City. A—Fort Myers, Fort Wayne. Rookie—Elizabethton, Gulf Coast Twins.
NEW YORK (6): AAA—Columbus. AA—Norwich. A—Tampa, Greensboro, Oneonta. Rookie—Gulf Coast Yankees.
OAKLAND (6): AAA—Edmonton. AA—Huntsville. A—Modesto, West Michigan, Southern Oregon. Rookie—Scottsdale A's.
SEATTLE (6): AAA—Tacoma. AA—Port City. A—Lancaster, Wisconsin, Everett. Rookie—Peoria Mariners.
TEXAS (6): AAA—Oklahoma City. AA—Tulsa. A—Charlotte, Charleston (SC), Hudson Valley. Rookie—Gulf Coast Rangers.
TORONTO (6): AAA—Syracuse. AA—Knoxville. A—Dunedin, Hagerstown, St. Catharines. Rookie—Medicine Hat.

NATIONAL LEAGUE

ATLANTA (7): AAA—Richmond. AA—Greenville. A—Durham, Macon, Eugene. Rookie—Danville, Gulf Coast Braves.
CHICAGO (6): AAA—Iowa. AA—Orlando. A—Daytona, Rockford, Williamsport. Rookie—Gulf Coast Cubs.
CINCINNATI (6): AAA—Indianapolis. AA—Chattanooga. A—Winston-Salem, Charleston (WV). Rookie—Billings, Princeton.
COLORADO (6): AAA—Colorado Springs. AA—New Haven. A—Salem, Asheville, Portland. Rookie—Mesa Rockies.
FLORIDA (6): AAA—Charlotte. AA—Portland. A—Brevard County, Kane County, Utica. Rookie—Gulf Coast Marlins.
HOUSTON (6): AAA—Tucson. AA—Jackson. A—Kissimmee, Quad City, Auburn. Rookie—Gulf Coast Astros.
LOS ANGELES (7): AAA—Albuquerque. AA—San Antonio. A—San Bernardino, Savannah, Vero Beach, Yakima. Rookie—Great Falls.
MONTREAL (6): AAA—Ottawa. AA—Harrisburg. A—West Palm Beach, Delmarva, Vermont. Rookie—Gulf Coast Expos.
NEW YORK (7): AAA—Norfolk. AA—Binghamton. A—St. Lucie, Capital City, Pittsfield. Rookie—Kingsport, Gulf Coast Mets.
PHILADELPHIA (6): AAA—Scranton/Wilkes-Barre. AA—Reading. A—Clearwater, Piedmont, Batavia. Rookie—Martinsville.
PITTSBURGH (6): AAA—Calgary. AA—Carolina. A—Lynchburg, Augusta, Erie. Rookie—Gulf Coast Pirates.
ST. LOUIS (6): AAA—Louisville. AA—Arkansas. A—St. Petersburg, Peoria (IL), New Jersey. Rookie—Johnson City.
SAN DIEGO (6): AAA—Las Vegas. AA—Memphis. A—Rancho Cucamonga, Clinton. Rookie—Idaho Falls, Peoria (AZ) Padres.
SAN FRANCISCO (5): AAA—Phoenix. AA—Shreveport. A—San Jose, Burlington, Bellingham.

AMERICAN ASSOCIATION

LEAGUE OFFICE

President
Branch Rickey

Address
6801 Miami Ave., Suite 3
Cincinnati, OH 45243

Phone
513-271-4800

TEAMS

BUFFALO BISONS

General manager
Mike Buczowski

Manager
Brian Graham

Ballpark (capacity, surface)
Pilot Field (21,050, grass)

Affiliation
Indians

Address
P.O. Box 450
Buffalo, NY 14203

Phone
716-846-2003

INDIANAPOLIS INDIANS

General manager
Max Schumacher

Manager
Dave Miley

Ballpark (capacity, surface)
Bush Stadium (12,000, grass)

Affiliation
Reds

Address
1501 W. 16th St.
Indianapolis, IN 46202

Phone
317-269-3545

IOWA CUBS

General manager
Sam Bernabe

Manager
Ron Clark

Ballpark (capacity, surface)
Sec Taylor Stadium (10,500, grass)

Affiliation
Cubs

Address
350 SW 1 St.
Des Moines, IA 50309

Phone
515-243-6111

LOUISVILLE REDBIRDS

General manager
Dale Owens

Manager
Joe Pettini

Ballpark (capacity, surface)
Cardinal Stadium (33,000, artificial)

Affiliation
Cardinals

Address
P.O. Box 36407
Louisville, KY 40233

Phone
502-367-9121

NASHVILLE SOUNDS

General manager
Larry Schmittou

Manager
Rick Renick

Ballpark (capacity, surface)
Greer Stadium (17,000, grass)

Affiliation
White Sox

Address
P.O. Box 23290
Nashville, TN 37202

Phone
615-242-4371

NEW ORLEANS ZEPHYRS

General manager
Jay Miller

Manager
Tim Ireland

Ballpark (capacity, surface)
Privateer Park (4,700, grass)

Affiliation
Brewers

Address
P.O. Box 24672
New Orleans, LA 70184

Phone
504-282-6777

OKLAHOMA CITY 89ERS

General Manager
Dorsena Picknell

Manager
Greg Biagini

Ballpark (capacity, surface)
All Sports Stadium (15,000, grass)

Affiliation
Rangers

Address
P.O. Box 75089
Oklahoma City, OK 73147

Phone
405-946-8989

OMAHA ROYALS

Vice president/general manager
Bill Gorman

Manager
Mike Jirschele

Ballpark (capacity, surface)
Rosenblatt Stadium (23,000, grass)

Affiliation
Royals

Address
P.O. Box 3665
Omaha, NE 68103

Phone
402-734-2550

1995 FINAL STANDINGS
COMPOSITE

Team	Ind.	Buf.	Oma.	Lou.	Iowa	Nash.	N.O.	O.C.	W	L	T	Pct.	GB
Indianapolis (Reds)	....	10	9	16	11	14	16	12	88	56	0	.611	....
Buffalo (Indians)	14	....	9	16	10	11	9	13	82	62	0	.569	6
Omaha (Royals)	9	9	....	7	14	9	10	18	76	68	0	.528	12
Louisville (Cardinals)	8	8	11	....	11	15	9	12	74	70	0	.514	14
Iowa (Cubs)	7	8	10	7	....	8	15	14	69	74	0	.483	18 1/2
Nashville (White Sox)	10	13	9	9	10	....	8	9	68	76	0	.472	20
New Orleans (Brewers)	2	9	14	9	8	10	....	11	63	79	0	.444	24
Oklahoma City (Rangers)	6	5	6	6	10	9	12	....	54	89	0	.378	33 1/2

Major league affiliations in parentheses.
Iowa club represented Des Moines, Iowa.

PLAYOFFS: Louisville defeated Indianapolis, three games to none; Buffalo defeated Omaha, three games to one; Louisville defeated Buffalo, three games to two, to win league championship.

REGULAR-SEASON ATTENDANCE: Buffalo, 900,782; Indianapolis, 366,254; Iowa, 466,320; Louisville, 556,211; Nashville, 355,133; New Orleans, 142,675; Oklahoma City, 259,198; Omaha, 417,761. Total—3,464,334. Playoffs (12 games)—72,847. Class AAA All-Star Game at Scranton/Wilkes-Barre—10,965.

MANAGERS: Buffalo, Brian Graham; Indianapolis, Marc Bombard; Iowa, Ron Clark; Louisville, Joe Pettini; Nashville, Rick Renick; New Orleans, Chris Bando; Oklahoma City, Greg Biagini; Omaha, Mike Jirschele.

ALL-STAR TEAM: 1B—Jeff Grotewald, Omaha; 2B—Eric Owens, Indianapolis; 3B—Tracy Woodson, Louisville; SS—Mark Loretta, New Orleans; OF—Steve Gibralter, Indianapolis; Brian Giles, Buffalo; Brooks Kieschnick, Iowa; C—John Marzano, Oklahoma City; DH—Drew Denson, Indianapolis; RHP—Joe Roa, Buffalo; LHP—Eric Bell, Buffalo; Relief Pitcher—Cory Bailey, Louisville; Most Valuable Player—Eric Owens, Indianapolis; Rookie of the Year—Eric Owens, Indianapolis; Manager of the Year—Marc Bombard, Indianapolis.

TEAM

Team	Avg.	G	TPA	AB	R	H	TB	2B	3B	HR	RBI	SH	SF	HP	BB	IBB	SO	SB	CS	GDP	LOB	SHO	Slg.	OBP
Buffalo	.276	144	5461	4847	708	1338	2068	261	41	129	658	35	55	63	461	31	660	63	28	119	1035	5	.427	.343
Indianapolis ...	.275	144	5500	4890	791	1344	2267	286	29	193	746	25	39	54	492	30	1001	93	50	109	961	3	.464	.345
Omaha	.273	144	5401	4772	698	1305	2065	266	31	144	643	57	45	52	473	37	859	69	49	101	1004	6	.433	.343
Iowa..............	.268	143	5282	4790	552	1285	1851	226	32	92	507	54	38	38	362	30	781	55	44	109	995	13	.386	.322
Nashville.......	.263	144	5452	4906	621	1288	1916	239	25	113	577	39	34	53	420	32	872	109	59	123	986	7	.391	.325
Louisville	.259	144	5299	4697	617	1217	1882	245	27	122	570	33	46	49	474	31	933	113	54	118	971	10	.401	.330
New Orleans ..	.253	142	5202	4611	572	1166	1687	206	30	85	520	45	45	58	442	24	862	107	66	98	969	14	.366	.323
Oklahoma City	.253	143	5215	4696	572	1186	1757	241	42	82	529	28	41	49	401	31	856	68	37	125	929	10	.374	.315

INDIVIDUAL

TOP QUALIFIERS FOR BATTING CHAMPIONSHIP

Minimum 389 plate appearances. *Lefthanded batter. †Switch-hitter.

Player, Team	Avg.	G	TPA	AB	R	H	TB	2B	3B	HR	RBI	SH	SF	HP	BB	IBB	SO	SB	CS	GDP	Slg.	OBP
Carter, Mike, Iowa.....................	.325	107	447	421	57	137	183	16	3	8	40	3	6	14	3	46	12	12	5	.435	.354
Snopek, Chris, Nashville...........	.323	113	456	393	56	127	194	23	4	12	55	6	3	4	50	1	72	2	5	5	.494	.402
Owens, Eric, Indianapolis........	.314	108	485	427	86	134	210	24	8	12	63	3	2	1	52	2	61	33	12	7	.492	.388
Ramsey, Fernando, Nashville...	.310	98	428	406	61	126	166	19	3	5	45	4	2	3	13	2	47	26	8	9	.409	.335
Giles, Brian, Buffalo*...............	.310	123	486	413	67	128	207	18	8	15	67	5	6	8	54	4	40	7	3	9	.501	.395
Marzano, John, Oklahoma City..	.309	120	474	427	55	132	206	41	3	9	56	0	6	8	33	2	54	3	4	17	.482	.365
Saenz, Olmedo, Nashville.........	.304	111	478	415	60	126	193	26	1	13	74	3	3	12	45	1	60	0	2	11	.465	.385
Brady, Doug, Nashville†	.298	125	488	450	71	134	176	15	6	5	27	4	3	0	31	3	76	32	6	4	.391	.341
Kieschnick, Brooks, Iowa*........	.295	138	570	505	61	149	250	30	1	23	73	0	3	4	58	7	91	2	3	11	.495	.370
Giannelli, Ray, Louisville*........	.295	119	441	390	56	115	184	19	1	16	70	0	4	3	44	5	85	3	7	6	.472	.367
Grotewold, Jeff, Omaha*...........	.294	105	441	350	70	103	173	19	0	17	60	3	1	5	82	5	88	0	2	14	.494	.434
Ripken, Billy, Buffalo*..............	.292	130	492	448	51	131	179	34	1	4	56	6	8	2	28	0	38	6	4	14	.400	.331
Martinez, Manny, Iowa	.290	122	429	397	63	115	172	17	8	8	49	7	2	3	20	0	64	11	8	3	.433	.327
Loretta, Mark, New Orleans......	.286	127	534	479	48	137	190	22	5	7	79	5	7	9	34	1	47	8	9	12	.397	.340
Burnitz, Jeromy, Buffalo*	.284	128	500	443	72	126	223	26	7	19	85	1	3	3	50	8	83	13	5	6	.503	.359

DEPARTMENTAL LEADERS: G—Robertson, 139; AB—Valrie, 544; R—Owens, 86; H—Kieschnick, 149; TB—Kieschnick, 250; 2B—Marzano, 41; 3B—Bradshaw, Giles, M. Martinez, Owens, 8; HR—Kieschnick, 23; RBI—Burnitz, 85; SH—Halter, 19; SF—Dorsett, Ripken, 8; HP—Denson, 19; BB—Grotewold, 82; IBB—Burnitz, 8; SO—Valrie, 107; SB—Owens, 33; CS—Singleton, Valrie, 15; GIDP—Kosco, 18; Slg.—Burnitz, .503; OBP—Grotewold, .434.

ALL PLAYERS

*Lefthanded batter. †Switch-hitter.

Player, Team	Avg.	G	TPA	AB	R	H	TB	2B	3B	HR	RBI	SH	SF	HP	BB	IBB	SO	SB	CS	GDP	Slg.	OBP
Abbott, Paul, Iowa.....................	.000	46	4	2	0	0	0	0	0	0	0	1	0	1	0	0	1	0	0	0	.000	.333
Amaro, Ruben, Buffalo†............	.305	54	242	213	42	65	104	15	3	6	22	3	1	7	18	1	29	6	1	5	.488	.377
Anderson, Mike, Iowa................	.000	27	14	11	0	0	0	0	0	0	0	2	0	0	1	0	5	0	0	0	.000	.083
Anthony, Eric, Indianapolis*.....	.292	7	30	24	7	7	19	0	0	4	8	0	0	0	6	3	4	2	0	2	.792	.433
Arias, Amador, Indianapolis†.....	.400	5	17	15	2	6	6	0	0	0	1	0	0	0	2	0	1	1	0	0	.400	.471
Aversa, Joe, Louisville†............	.220	45	172	141	23	31	37	6	0	0	9	3	2	0	26	2	29	7	3	1	.262	.337
Barber, Brian, Louisville...........	.400	20	6	5	1	2	3	1	0	0	2	0	0	0	1	0	3	0	0	0	.600	.500
Barker, Tim, New Orleans..........	.258	80	306	264	44	68	90	9	5	1	24	8	1	4	29	0	39	10	8	2	.341	.339
Basse, Mike, New Orleans*.......	.247	121	455	381	49	94	112	14	2	0	35	7	6	3	58	3	62	15	9	5	.294	.346
Batchelor, Richard, Louisville...	.000	50	3	1	0	0	0	0	0	0	0	0	1	0	0	1	0	0	0	0	.000	.500
Battle, Allen, Louisville	.280	47	198	164	28	46	69	12	1	3	18	5	0	1	28	0	32	7	1	3	.421	.389
Beatty, Blaine, Louisville*.........	.200	20	6	5	2	1	1	0	0	0	1	0	0	0	1	0	1	0	0	0	.200	.200
Belk, Tim, Indianapolis..............	.301	57	212	193	30	58	81	11	0	4	18	0	1	2	16	0	30	2	5	9	.420	.360
Bell, David, Buf.-Lou.	.273	88	366	330	43	90	135	14	2	9	43	2	3	7	24	1	47	4	3	6	.409	.332
Beltran, Rigo, Louisville*	.333	25	21	18	3	6	8	2	0	0	2	0	1	0	2	0	4	0	0	0	.444	.381
Benavides, Freddie, Iowa..........	.241	106	347	315	30	76	110	14	4	4	26	1	1	5	25	0	47	2	3	12	.349	.306
Benes, Alan, Louisville	.300	11	11	10	2	3	9	0	0	2	4	1	0	0	0	0	4	0	0	0	.900	.300
Bess, Johnny, Indianapolis†......	.000	2	5	5	0	0	0	0	0	0	0	0	0	0	0	0	2	0	0	0	.000	.000
Bolick, Frank, Buffalo†	.246	20	69	65	11	16	31	6	0	3	10	0	0	1	3	0	13	0	1	3	.477	.290
Borrelli, Dean, Oklahoma City....	.200	54	207	185	17	37	54	9	1	2	17	0	2	2	18	0	50	0	1	7	.292	.275
Bradshaw, Terry, Louisville*.....	.283	111	453	389	65	110	174	24	8	8	42	7	1	3	53	0	60	20	7	4	.447	.372
Brady, Doug, Nashville†............	.298	125	488	450	71	134	176	15	6	5	27	4	3	0	31	3	76	32	6	4	.391	.341
Bream, Scott, Iowa†..................	.159	29	96	82	10	13	20	1	0	2	9	3	0	0	11	0	20	1	0	1	.244	.258
Briley, Greg, Indianapolis*	.233	46	169	146	17	34	51	8	0	3	17	1	0	0	22	3	34	9	2	1	.349	.333
Brooks, Jerry, Indianapolis.......	.283	90	355	325	41	92	157	19	2	14	52	0	3	5	22	0	38	3	1	16	.483	.335
Brown, Chris, Indianapolis	.000	3	8	7	0	0	0	0	0	0	0	0	0	0	1	0	0	0	0	0	.000	.125
Brown, Kevin, Oklahoma City* ...	.400	3	12	10	1	4	5	1	0	0	0	0	0	0	2	0	4	0	0	0	.500	.500
Brown, Marty, Oklahoma City.....	.168	30	112	101	12	17	31	5	0	3	12	0	1	2	8	1	25	0	0	3	.307	.241
Bruett, J.T., Omaha*.................	.279	44	155	129	20	36	50	6	1	2	14	5	3	1	17	1	19	6	4	3	.388	.360
Buckels, Gary, Louisville	.000	13	1	1	0	0	0	0	0	0	0	0	0	0	0	0	1	0	0	0	.000	.000
Buckley, Travis, Indianapolis	.000	23	17	14	1	0	0	0	0	0	0	3	0	0	0	0	0	0	0	0	.000	.000
Buechele, Steve, Oklahoma City ..	.308	3	14	13	1	4	7	0	0	1	3	0	0	0	1	0	1	0	0	0	.538	.357
Burnitz, Jeromy, Buffalo*	.284	128	500	443	72	126	223	26	7	19	85	1	3	3	50	8	83	13	5	6	.503	.359
Burton, Darren, Omaha†............	.000	2	5	5	0	0	0	0	0	0	0	0	0	0	0	0	2	0	0	0	.000	.000
Busby, Mike, Louisville..............	.200	6	6	5	1	1	1	0	0	0	0	0	0	0	1	0	3	0	0	0	.200	.333
Byington, John, N.O.-O.C.	.259	122	473	437	49	113	142	16	3	2	32	4	6	5	21	2	41	7	2	16	.325	.296
Caceres, Edgar, Omaha†............	.206	37	117	107	13	22	27	3	1	0	12	1	1	0	8	3	10	3	1	2	.252	.259
Cadaret, Greg, Louisville*	.000	12	1	1	1	0	0	0	0	0	0	0	0	0	0	0	0	0	0	0	.000	.000
Cameron, Stanton, Okla. City.....	.167	5	16	12	2	2	3	1	0	0	0	0	0	0	4	0	3	0	0	0	.250	.375
Campbell, Mike, Iowa................	.000	21	8	8	0	0	0	0	0	0	0	0	0	0	0	0	4	0	0	0	.000	.000
Candaele, Casey, Buffalo†.........	.247	97	399	364	50	90	126	10	7	4	38	4	7	2	22	1	42	9	2	6	.346	.289
Cappuccio, Carmine, Nashville* ..	.273	66	248	216	30	59	88	14	0	5	24	1	1	1	29	4	26	0	2	6	.407	.360

Player, Team	Avg.	G	TPA	AB	R	H	TB	2B	3B	HR	RBI	SH	SF	HP	BB	IBB	SO	SB	CS	GDP	Slg.	OBP
Caraballo, Ramon, Louisville†	.318	69	276	245	38	78	114	10	1	8	25	4	4	4	19	1	42	14	4	5	.465	.371
Carpenter, Cris, Louisville	.000	49	1	1	0	0	0	0	0	0	0	0	0	0	0	0	1	0	0	0	.000	.000
Carter, Mike, Iowa	.325	107	447	421	57	137	183	16	3	8	40	3	3	6	14	3	46	12	12	5	.435	.354
Chamberlain, Wes, Omaha	.219	16	69	64	2	14	20	3	0	1	6	0	1	2	2	0	15	0	0	4	.313	.261
Chance, Tony, Oklahoma City	.214	63	213	196	19	42	60	12	0	2	20	1	1	0	15	0	55	1	1	5	.306	.269
Cholowsky, Dan, Louisville	.218	76	285	238	27	52	84	9	1	7	25	0	6	5	36	0	64	10	4	5	.353	.326
Clinton, Jim, Oklahoma City	.000	8	14	13	0	0	0	0	0	0	0	0	0	0	1	0	6	0	0	1	.000	.071
Coleman, Vince, Omaha†	.395	9	40	38	7	15	20	2	0	1	5	0	0	0	2	2	6	3	0	0	.526	.425
Colon, Cris, Iowa†	.260	106	391	366	35	95	127	18	1	4	36	3	1	4	17	4	51	1	0	5	.347	.299
Cookson, Brent, Omaha	.401	40	160	137	28	55	80	13	0	4	20	0	2	4	17	0	24	0	0	3	.584	.475
Costo, Tim, Buffalo	.247	105	369	324	41	80	128	11	2	11	60	3	7	8	27	0	65	2	0	7	.395	.314
Cotto, Henry, Nashville	.131	17	62	61	4	8	12	1	0	1	4	0	0	0	1	0	20	0	1	3	.197	.145
Coughlin, Kevin, Nashville*	.182	10	26	22	0	4	5	1	0	0	0	0	0	0	4	0	3	0	1	1	.227	.308
Courtright, John, Indianapolis*	.250	13	4	4	1	1	1	0	0	0	0	0	0	0	0	0	2	0	0	0	.250	.250
Cox, Darron, Iowa	.234	33	110	94	7	22	31	6	0	1	14	2	4	2	8	0	21	0	0	0	.330	.296
Creek, Doug, Louisville*	.000	26	1	1	0	0	0	0	0	0	0	0	0	0	0	0	0	0	0	0	.000	.000
Cron, Chris, Nashville	.217	21	78	69	3	15	23	2	0	2	10	1	0	0	8	2	20	0	0	2	.333	.299
Dabney, Fred, Iowa	.000	33	2	2	0	0	0	0	0	0	0	0	0	0	0	0	0	0	0	0	.000	.000
Deak, Brian, Louisville	.228	54	193	162	19	37	60	5	0	6	31	1	1	3	26	0	47	2	0	3	.370	.344
Deak, Darrel, Louisville†	.241	106	400	336	42	81	127	21	2	7	34	0	6	5	53	6	90	2	2	5	.378	.348
Denson, Drew, Indianapolis	.277	107	412	357	59	99	174	21	0	19	69	0	3	18	34	5	68	1	0	10	.487	.367
DeLaRosa, Francisco, Louisville†	.222	28	12	9	0	2	5	1	1	0	5	3	0	0	0	0	5	0	0	0	.556	.222
DiFelice, Mike, Louisville	.270	21	68	63	8	17	21	4	0	0	3	0	0	0	5	0	11	1	0	4	.333	.324
Diggs, Tony, Louisville†	.250	23	41	36	4	9	12	3	0	0	0	0	0	0	5	1	4	2	1	1	.333	.341
Dismuke, Jamie, Indianapolis*	.250	13	39	36	6	9	10	1	0	0	2	0	0	0	3	1	3	0	0	1	.278	.308
Dodson, Bo, New Orleans*	.281	62	244	203	29	57	91	5	1	9	34	0	5	0	36	6	27	0	0	4	.448	.381
Dorsett, Brian, Indianapolis	.262	91	350	313	40	82	157	25	1	16	58	0	8	4	25	0	47	1	1	11	.502	.317
Dostal, Bruce, Oklahoma City*	.212	88	331	293	35	62	100	14	6	4	31	4	1	3	30	0	49	11	3	7	.341	.291
Elster, Kevin, Omaha	.238	11	48	42	5	10	14	4	0	0	6	0	1	0	5	0	8	0	0	0	.333	.313
Fanning, Steve, Iowa	.000	4	6	5	0	0	0	0	0	0	0	0	0	0	1	0	4	0	0	0	.000	.167
Fariss, Monty, Iowa	.182	10	42	33	5	6	9	0	0	1	2	0	0	0	9	2	7	0	0	0	.273	.357
Figueroa, Bien, Oklahoma City	.100	9	22	20	1	2	2	0	0	0	2	1	1	0	0	0	2	1	0	0	.100	.095
Finn, John, New Orleans	.325	35	136	117	20	38	53	4	1	3	19	4	0	2	13	2	7	9	2	1	.453	.402
Flores, Miguel, Buffalo	.283	31	120	113	13	32	42	8	1	0	12	1	0	1	5	0	13	5	0	4	.372	.319
Fordyce, Brook, Buffalo	.250	58	195	176	18	44	57	13	0	0	9	3	0	2	14	0	20	1	0	2	.324	.313
Fox, Eric, Oklahoma City†	.278	92	388	349	52	97	147	22	5	6	50	4	3	2	30	7	68	5	5	7	.421	.336
Franco, Matt, Iowa*	.281	121	499	455	51	128	184	28	5	6	58	1	6	0	37	5	44	1	1	11	.404	.331
Fraraccio, Dan, Nashville	.250	10	30	28	2	7	7	0	0	0	3	1	0	0	1	0	6	2	0	1	.250	.276
Frascatore, John, Louisville	.000	28	2	2	0	0	0	0	0	0	0	0	0	0	0	0	0	0	0	0	.000	.000
Garber, Jeff, Omaha	.143	6	14	14	1	2	2	0	0	0	0	0	0	0	0	0	5	0	0	1	.143	.143
Gardner, Jeff, Iowa*	.323	65	262	235	35	76	96	11	0	3	24	2	1	1	23	0	27	1	2	5	.409	.385
Giannelli, Ray, Louisville*	.295	119	441	390	56	115	184	19	1	16	70	0	4	3	44	5	85	3	7	6	.472	.367
Gibralter, Steve, Indianapolis	.316	79	295	263	49	83	162	19	3	18	63	1	2	4	25	3	70	0	2	6	.616	.381
Giles, Brian, Buffalo*	.310	123	486	413	67	128	207	18	8	15	67	5	6	8	54	4	40	7	3	9	.501	.395
Gilkey, Bernard, Louisville	.333	2	7	6	3	2	6	1	0	1	1	0	0	0	1	0	0	0	0	0	1.000	.429
Glanville, Doug, Iowa	.270	112	449	419	48	113	145	16	2	4	37	7	4	3	16	0	64	13	9	4	.346	.299
Goldberg, Lonnie, Oklahoma City	.233	10	32	30	2	7	13	3	0	1	5	0	0	0	2	0	4	1	0	1	.433	.281
Gonzalez, Javier, New Orleans	.248	43	127	113	20	28	54	11	0	5	15	2	1	4	7	0	24	0	0	0	.478	.312
Gordon, Keith, Indianapolis	.264	89	281	265	36	70	104	14	1	6	38	1	0	0	15	0	94	3	4	3	.392	.304
Gousha, Sean, Iowa	.000	2	5	5	0	0	0	0	0	0	0	0	0	0	0	0	3	0	0	0	.000	.000
Gozzo, Mauro, Iowa	.000	6	1	1	0	0	0	0	0	0	0	0	0	0	0	0	1	0	0	0	.000	.000
Grant, Mark, Iowa	.000	11	10	10	0	0	0	0	0	0	0	0	0	0	0	0	7	0	0	0	.000	.000
Green, Gary, Omaha	.169	26	75	71	5	12	14	2	0	0	3	1	0	0	3	0	14	0	0	1	.197	.203
Greene, Willie, Indianapolis*	.243	91	370	325	57	79	152	12	2	19	45	0	4	3	38	2	67	3	3	6	.468	.324
Grotewold, Jeff, Omaha*	.294	105	441	350	70	103	173	19	0	17	60	3	1	5	82	5	88	0	2	14	.494	.434
Grott, Matt, Indianapolis*	.300	25	13	10	0	3	4	1	0	0	2	0	0	0	3	0	3	0	0	0	.400	.462
Gulan, Mike, Louisville	.236	58	210	195	21	46	79	10	4	5	27	0	2	3	10	1	53	2	2	6	.405	.281
Halter, Shane, Omaha	.230	124	452	392	42	90	139	19	3	8	39	19	1	0	40	0	97	2	3	6	.355	.300
Hamelin, Bob, Omaha*	.294	36	152	119	25	35	77	12	0	10	32	0	2	0	31	5	34	2	3	1	.647	.434
Haney, Todd, Iowa	.313	90	366	326	38	102	138	20	2	4	30	4	2	6	28	0	21	2	2	17	.423	.376
Hare, Shawn, Oklahoma City*	.265	68	267	238	27	63	94	13	3	4	30	1	1	4	23	2	47	3	1	9	.395	.338
Harris, Donald, Oklahoma City	.200	12	44	40	4	8	11	1	1	0	7	0	1	0	3	0	7	0	2	2	.275	.250
Harris, Mike, New Orleans*	.232	21	60	56	3	13	16	3	0	0	5	0	0	0	4	1	9	1	1	1	.286	.283
Hatcher, Billy, Omaha	.276	26	117	105	14	29	39	5	1	1	12	0	1	2	9	2	6	4	2	5	.371	.342
Hecht, Steve, Oklahoma City*	.261	67	261	238	26	62	83	6	3	3	14	3	1	3	16	3	45	9	5	1	.349	.314
Hemond, Scott, Louisville	.000	1	3	3	1	0	0	0	0	0	0	0	0	0	0	0	0	0	0	0	.000	.000
Hiatt, Phil, Omaha	.158	20	79	76	7	12	23	5	0	2	8	0	1	0	2	0	25	0	0	0	.303	.177
Hinzo, Tommy, Oklahoma City†	.252	82	277	254	33	64	76	10	1	0	20	3	3	4	13	1	38	8	3	3	.299	.296
Holbert, Aaron, Louisville	.257	112	434	401	57	103	154	16	4	9	40	3	5	5	20	1	60	14	6	10	.384	.297
Horn, Sam, Oklahoma City*	.308	46	182	156	26	48	93	9	0	12	42	0	1	0	25	3	49	0	2	4	.596	.401
Hosey, Dwayne, Omaha†	.295	75	304	271	59	80	145	21	4	12	50	1	2	1	29	2	45	15	6	1	.535	.363
Howard, Tim, Nashville*	.233	37	118	103	8	24	35	3	1	2	13	0	1	1	13	0	12	4	3	3	.340	.322
Howitt, Dann, Nas.-Buf.*	.262	86	284	252	35	66	109	14	4	7	33	0	2	0	30	6	62	0	3	7	.433	.338
Hubbard, Mike, Iowa	.260	75	289	254	28	66	93	6	3	5	23	6	3	0	26	1	60	6	1	5	.366	.325
Hughes, Keith, Omaha*	.289	103	378	342	51	99	158	22	2	11	46	1	4	1	30	3	41	4	2	4	.462	.345
Hulett, Tim, Lou.-O.C.	.219	42	160	151	15	33	45	7	1	1	10	0	0	0	9	1	33	0	1	1	.298	.263
Humphreys, Mike, Buffalo	.246	34	141	126	17	31	38	4	0	1	5	1	1	5	8	0	22	5	1	0	.302	.314
Hunter, Brian, Indianapolis	.361	9	42	36	7	13	30	5	0	4	11	0	0	0	6	1	11	0	1	0	.833	.452
Jaha, John, New Orleans	.400	3	12	10	2	4	8	1	0	1	3	0	0	0	2	1	1	0	0	1	.800	.500
James, Chris, Omaha	.167	3	13	12	3	2	6	1	0	1	3	0	0	0	1	0	2	0	0	0	.500	.231
Jarvis, Kevin, Indianapolis*	.571	10	8	7	1	4	4	0	0	0	3	0	0	0	1	0	1	0	0	0	.571	.625
Johns, Keith, Louisville	.000	5	10	10	0	0	0	0	0	0	0	0	0	0	0	0	2	0	0	0	.000	.000
Jose, Felix, Iowa†	.135	10	39	37	2	5	8	3	0	0	1	0	0	1	1	0	6	0	0	1	.216	.179

Player, Team	Avg.	G	TPA	AB	R	H	TB	2B	3B	HR	RBI	SH	SF	HP	BB	IBB	SO	SB	CS	GDP	Slg.	OBP
Kennedy, Darryl, Oklahoma City	.182	3	11	11	1	2	5	0	0	1	3	0	0	0	0	0	2	0	0	0	.455	.182
Kessinger, Keith, Iowa†	.229	68	245	210	21	48	65	11	0	2	20	7	2	1	25	2	23	1	1	6	.310	.311
Kieschnick, Brooks, Iowa*	.295	138	570	505	61	149	250	30	1	23	73	0	3	4	58	7	91	2	3	11	.495	.370
Kmak, Joe, Iowa	.173	34	109	98	6	17	26	3	0	2	7	3	2	0	6	0	24	0	0	4	.265	.217
Knapp, Mike, Indianapolis	.256	14	43	39	8	10	15	2	0	1	6	0	0	1	3	0	7	1	0	0	.385	.326
Kosco, Bryn, Iowa*	.251	119	399	363	50	91	166	24	3	15	52	2	3	1	30	5	85	2	2	18	.457	.307
Koslofski, Kevin, New Orleans*	.212	105	364	321	41	68	115	18	4	7	35	3	3	2	34	2	100	4	2	1	.358	.289
Kremblas, Frank, Indianapolis	.160	27	89	75	7	12	14	2	0	0	3	2	0	0	12	1	25	4	2	2	.187	.276
Lee, Manuel, Louisville†	.273	6	22	22	2	6	6	0	0	0	0	0	0	0	0	0	2	1	0	1	.273	.273
Levis, Jesse, Buffalo*	.311	66	231	196	26	61	89	16	0	4	20	1	0	2	32	0	11	0	3	7	.454	.413
Lindeman, Jim, Oklahoma City	.252	83	335	294	52	74	132	16	3	12	36	0	3	5	33	4	54	0	1	11	.449	.334
Lockhart, Keith, Omaha*	.378	44	166	148	24	56	80	7	1	5	19	1	0	1	16	3	10	1	3	0	.541	.442
Lofton, Rodney, New Orleans	.217	102	260	240	30	52	62	7	0	1	18	2	2	1	15	1	48	9	3	11	.258	.264
Long, Kevin, Omaha*	.250	22	70	64	7	16	19	3	0	0	1	0	0	0	5	0	8	1	2	3	.297	.304
Lopez, Luis, Buffalo	.262	123	499	455	62	119	193	21	1	17	66	0	7	8	29	3	47	1	1	15	.424	.313
Lopez, Pedro, New Orleans	.000	3	8	8	0	0	0	0	0	0	0	0	0	0	0	0	3	0	0	0	.000	.000
Loretta, Mark, New Orleans	.286	127	534	479	48	137	190	22	5	7	79	5	7	9	34	1	47	8	9	12	.397	.340
Lovullo, Torey, Buffalo†	.255	132	552	474	84	121	199	20	5	16	61	1	5	2	70	7	62	3	1	12	.420	.350
Luce, Roger, Oklahoma City	.000	1	3	3	0	0	0	0	0	0	0	0	0	0	0	0	2	0	0	0	.000	.000
Lyden, Mitch, Omaha	.253	71	259	237	26	60	106	8	1	12	44	3	6	2	11	2	66	0	0	5	.447	.285
Lyons, Barry, Nashville	.257	71	294	265	37	68	110	16	1	8	38	1	4	4	20	4	56	0	0	7	.415	.314
Mabry, John, Louisville*	.083	4	12	12	0	1	1	0	0	0	0	0	0	0	0	0	4	0	0	0	.083	.083
Machado, Robert, Nashville	.143	16	56	49	7	7	13	3	0	1	5	0	0	0	7	0	12	0	1	1	.265	.250
Magdaleno, Ricky, Indianapolis	.125	4	9	8	1	1	4	0	0	1	1	1	0	0	0	0	3	0	0	0	.500	.125
Marini, Marc, Buffalo*	.271	32	93	85	12	23	37	5	0	3	15	0	1	0	7	0	14	0	0	3	.435	.323
Martindale, Ryan, Buffalo	.161	11	31	31	4	5	6	1	0	0	0	0	0	0	0	0	9	1	0	1	.194	.161
Martinez, Carmelo, Buffalo	.278	11	43	36	8	10	17	1	0	2	9	0	0	0	7	0	10	0	0	1	.472	.395
Martinez, Domingo, Louisville	.261	64	245	222	26	58	100	15	0	9	31	0	4	4	15	2	49	0	0	7	.450	.314
Martinez, Frankie, Louisville	.000	38	1	1	0	0	0	0	0	0	0	0	0	0	0	0	1	0	0	0	.000	.000
Martinez, Manny, Iowa	.290	122	429	397	63	115	172	17	8	8	49	7	2	3	20	0	64	11	8	3	.433	.327
Marzano, John, Oklahoma City	.309	120	474	427	55	132	206	41	3	9	56	0	6	8	33	2	54	3	4	17	.482	.365
Massarelli, John, Buffalo	.000	3	2	1	0	0	0	0	0	0	0	0	0	0	1	0	0	0	0	0	.000	.000
Matheny, Mike, New Orleans	.353	6	20	17	3	6	17	2	0	3	4	0	0	3	0	0	5	0	0	0	1.000	.450
Mathile, Mike, Indianapolis	.000	14	1	1	0	0	0	0	0	0	0	0	0	0	0	0	1	0	0	0	.000	.000
McCarty, Dave, Indianapolis	.336	37	158	140	31	47	83	10	1	8	32	1	1	1	15	0	30	0	0	5	.593	.401
McClendon, Lloyd, Buffalo	.278	37	130	108	19	30	51	6	0	5	19	0	0	2	20	3	20	0	0	5	.472	.400
McCoy, Trey, Oklahoma City	.310	9	36	29	4	9	10	1	0	0	2	0	0	0	7	1	7	0	0	1	.345	.444
McNeely, Jeff, Louisville	.236	109	295	271	31	64	72	6	1	0	19	0	1	0	23	0	53	5	8	8	.266	.295
Mercedes, Henry, Omaha	.215	86	307	275	37	59	104	12	0	11	37	6	1	3	22	0	90	2	0	7	.378	.279
Miller, Keith, Omaha	.250	7	25	20	3	5	7	2	0	0	2	0	1	0	4	0	2	1	0	0	.350	.360
Milstien, Dave, Nashville	.235	11	37	34	1	8	9	1	0	0	2	0	0	0	3	0	4	0	0	1	.265	.297
Minchey, Nate, Louisville	.067	26	17	15	0	1	1	0	0	0	0	1	0	0	1	0	8	0	0	0	.067	.125
Mitchell, Keith, Indianapolis	.244	70	260	213	40	52	100	11	2	11	36	1	4	1	40	3	40	4	4	7	.469	.363
Morris, Hal, Indianapolis*	.400	2	6	5	2	2	2	0	0	0	1	0	0	0	1	0	0	0	0	0	.400	.500
Morton, Kevin, Iowa	.000	28	3	3	0	0	0	0	0	0	0	0	0	0	0	0	0	0	0	0	.000	.000
Mota, Jose, Omaha†	.322	27	100	87	6	28	32	4	0	0	10	4	2	1	6	0	9	1	2	3	.368	.365
Mottola, Chad, Indianapolis	.259	69	261	239	40	62	99	11	1	8	37	1	1	0	20	0	50	8	1	6	.414	.315
Mouton, Lyle, Nashville	.296	71	295	267	40	79	120	17	0	8	41	0	4	1	23	2	58	10	4	9	.449	.349
Nabholz, Chris, Iowa*	.000	6	3	3	0	0	0	0	0	0	0	0	0	0	0	0	0	0	0	0	.000	.000
Nilsson, Dave, New Orleans*	.444	3	11	9	1	4	7	0	0	1	4	0	0	0	2	0	0	0	0	0	.778	.545
Nitkowski, C.J., Indianapolis*	.000	6	3	2	0	0	0	0	0	0	0	1	0	0	0	0	2	0	0	0	.000	.000
Noriega, Rey, Nashville†	.164	20	60	55	6	9	16	4	0	1	3	1	1	0	3	0	20	0	0	0	.291	.203
Norman, Les, Omaha	.284	83	340	313	46	89	141	19	3	9	33	3	2	4	18	2	48	5	3	3	.450	.329
O'Halloran, Greg, Iowa*	.158	7	20	19	1	3	4	1	0	0	1	0	1	0	0	0	7	0	0	1	.211	.150
Oliver, Joe, New Orleans	.077	4	13	13	0	1	2	1	0	0	0	0	0	0	0	0	3	0	0	0	.154	.077
Ortiz, Javier, Nashville	.167	7	25	24	3	4	7	0	0	1	1	0	0	0	1	0	5	0	0	1	.292	.200
Ortiz, Junior, Nashville	.186	64	191	172	13	32	44	9	0	1	16	2	1	4	12	0	27	0	0	8	.256	.254
Ortiz, Luis, Nashville	.306	47	182	170	19	52	78	10	5	2	20	1	3	6	8	2	20	1	1	7	.459	.331
Osborne, Donovan, Louisville*	.000	1	2	2	0	0	0	0	0	0	0	0	0	0	0	0	1	0	0	0	.000	.000
Owens, Eric, Indianapolis	.314	108	485	427	86	134	210	24	8	12	63	3	2	1	52	2	61	33	12	7	.492	.388
Pagnozzi, Tom, Louisville	.500	5	17	16	4	8	13	2	0	1	3	0	0	0	1	0	0	0	0	1	.813	.529
Parra, Franklin, Oklahoma City†	.167	6	21	18	0	3	4	1	0	0	1	0	1	0	2	0	4	1	0	1	.222	.238
Pena, Geronimo, Louisville†	.381	6	24	21	5	8	15	1	0	2	6	0	0	3	2	1	9	0	0	0	.714	.458
Perez, Danny, New Orleans	.294	12	39	34	5	10	11	1	0	0	0	0	0	0	5	1	9	0	0	0	.324	.385
Perry, Herbert, Buffalo	.317	49	203	180	27	57	79	14	1	2	17	3	2	3	15	2	18	1	0	4	.439	.375
Petkovsek, Mark, Louisville	.091	8	11	11	0	1	2	1	0	0	0	0	0	0	0	0	1	0	0	0	.182	.091
Pledger, Kinnis, Iowa*	.083	9	26	24	1	2	2	0	0	0	2	0	0	0	2	0	12	0	0	1	.083	.154
Prager, Howard, Louisville*	.255	54	121	102	9	26	49	5	0	6	15	0	0	0	19	0	25	1	1	2	.480	.372
Pratt, Todd, Iowa	.328	23	62	58	3	19	20	1	0	0	5	0	0	0	4	1	17	0	0	6	.345	.371
Pugh, Tim, Indianapolis	.286	8	8	7	1	2	2	0	0	0	1	1	0	0	0	0	2	0	0	0	.286	.286
Raczka, Mike, Louisville*	.000	55	1	0	0	0	0	0	0	0	0	1	0	0	0	0	0	0	0	0	.000	.000
Ramsey, Fernando, Nashville	.310	98	428	406	61	126	166	19	3	5	45	4	2	3	13	2	47	26	8	9	.409	.335
Randa, Joe, Omaha	.275	64	259	233	33	64	102	10	2	8	33	1	1	2	22	0	33	2	2	9	.438	.341
Reed, Rick, Indianapolis	.182	22	13	11	2	2	3	1	0	0	1	2	0	0	0	0	0	0	0	0	.273	.182
Reese, Pokey, Indianapolis	.239	89	387	343	51	82	135	21	1	10	46	1	3	4	36	0	81	8	5	3	.394	.316
Remlinger, Mike, Indianapolis*	.500	41	2	2	0	1	2	1	0	0	0	0	0	0	0	0	0	0	0	0	1.000	.500
Reynolds, Harold, Omaha†	.202	38	124	109	12	22	33	6	1	1	11	0	2	0	13	1	10	2	3	2	.303	.282
Riles, Ernest, Nashville*	.278	6	23	18	5	5	8	0	0	1	7	0	1	1	3	0	4	0	0	2	.444	.391
Ripken, Billy, Buffalo	.292	130	492	448	51	131	179	34	1	4	56	6	8	2	28	0	38	6	4	14	.400	.333
Ritchie, Gregg, Oklahoma City*	.179	9	34	28	5	5	8	0	0	1	4	0	0	0	6	1	4	1	0	0	.286	.324
Rivera, Luis, Oklahoma City	.138	19	60	58	3	8	15	4	0	1	3	0	0	1	1	0	6	0	0	1	.259	.167
Robertson, Mike, Nashville*	.248	139	565	499	55	124	206	17	4	19	52	3	2	11	50	7	72	2	4	8	.413	.329
Rohrmeier, Dan, Indianapolis	.176	10	34	34	5	6	11	3	1	0	3	0	0	0	0	0	1	0	0	1	.324	.176

Player, Team	Avg.	G	TPA	AB	R	H	TB	2B	3B	HR	RBI	SH	SF	HP	BB	IBB	SO	SB	CS	GDP	Slg.	OBP
Rolls, David, Oklahoma City	.000	2	7	5	0	0	0	0	0	0	1	0	0	1	1	0	4	0	0	0	.000	.286
Ronan, Marc, Louisville*	.213	78	241	225	15	48	56	8	0	0	8	2	0	0	14	2	42	4	3	10	.249	.259
Roper, John, Indianapolis	.000	8	2	1	0	0	0	0	0	0	0	1	0	0	0	0	1	0	0	0	.000	.000
Ruffin, Johnny, Indianapolis	.000	36	1	1	0	0	0	0	0	0	0	0	0	0	0	0	0	0	0	0	.000	.000
Sabo, Chris, Louisville	.393	9	30	28	5	11	14	0	0	1	4	0	0	1	1	0	4	0	0	0	.500	.433
Saenz, Olmedo, Nashville	.304	111	478	415	60	126	193	26	1	13	74	3	3	12	45	1	60	0	2	11	.465	.385
Sagmoen, Marc, Oklahoma City*	.223	56	211	188	20	42	68	11	3	3	25	1	4	2	16	0	31	5	2	2	.362	.286
Salkeld, Roger, Indianapolis	.375	21	8	8	2	3	5	2	0	0	1	0	0	0	0	0	0	0	0	0	.625	.375
Sauveur, Rich, Indianapolis*	.000	52	1	1	0	0	0	0	0	0	0	0	0	0	0	0	1	0	0	0	.000	.000
Schu, Rick, Oklahoma City	.271	110	445	398	49	108	169	19	3	12	57	0	2	5	40	1	63	5	3	8	.425	.344
Scudder, Scott, Indianapolis	.500	7	2	2	0	1	2	1	0	0	0	0	0	0	0	0	0	0	0	0	1.000	.500
Sellers, Rick, Indianapolis	.263	5	20	19	3	5	15	1	0	3	7	0	0	1	0	0	3	0	0	0	.789	.300
Service, Scott, Indianapolis	.000	36	3	3	0	0	0	0	0	0	0	0	0	0	0	0	1	0	0	0	.000	.000
Shave, Jon, Oklahoma City	.205	32	92	83	10	17	18	1	0	0	5	1	0	1	7	0	28	1	0	1	.217	.275
Simmons, Scott, Louisville	.500	2	2	2	0	1	1	0	0	0	0	0	0	0	0	0	0	0	0	0	.500	.500
Singleton, Duane, New Orleans*	.268	106	401	355	48	95	125	10	4	4	29	3	1	3	39	2	63	31	15	7	.352	.344
Sisco, Steve, Omaha	.208	7	27	24	4	5	6	1	0	0	0	1	0	0	2	0	8	0	0	0	.250	.269
Smith, Ed, Buffalo	.323	13	35	31	4	10	21	0	1	3	9	0	1	0	3	0	5	0	1	0	.677	.371
Smith, Greg, N.O.-Ind.†	.212	63	208	184	19	39	44	3	1	0	9	2	1	2	19	1	25	11	7	6	.239	.291
Smith, Ottis, Iowa	.400	5	5	5	0	2	2	0	0	0	0	0	0	0	0	0	3	0	0	0	.400	.400
Snopek, Chris, Nashville	.323	113	456	393	56	127	194	23	4	12	55	6	3	4	50	1	72	2	5	5	.494	.402
Staton, Dave, New Orleans	.252	108	381	325	42	82	152	11	1	19	46	1	1	8	46	0	96	0	3	6	.468	.358
Steenstra, Kennie, Iowa	.000	29	16	16	0	0	0	0	0	0	0	0	0	0	0	0	9	0	0	0	.000	.000
Stefanski, Mike, New Orleans	.246	78	253	228	30	56	76	10	2	2	24	5	5	1	14	0	28	2	0	8	.333	.286
Stewart, Andy, Omaha	.301	44	176	156	24	47	67	11	0	3	21	0	0	8	12	1	18	0	1	4	.429	.381
Stillwell, Kurt, Indianapolis†	.264	100	390	341	50	90	131	14	3	7	30	0	3	1	45	1	51	4	3	6	.384	.349
Strickland, Chad, Omaha	.273	8	24	22	3	6	8	2	0	0	5	0	1	0	1	0	4	0	0	1	.364	.292
Sturtze, Tanyon, Iowa	.000	23	4	4	0	0	0	0	0	0	0	0	0	0	0	0	1	0	0	0	.000	.000
Stynes, Chris, Omaha	.275	83	349	306	51	84	133	12	5	9	42	4	5	5	27	0	24	4	5	7	.435	.338
Sutko, Glenn, New Orleans	.208	42	109	101	7	21	38	8	0	3	14	1	0	0	7	0	35	0	0	1	.376	.259
Swartzbaugh, Dave, Iowa	.000	30	1	1	0	0	0	0	0	0	0	0	0	0	0	0	1	0	0	0	.000	.000
Sweeney, Mark, Louisville*	.368	22	94	76	15	28	42	8	0	2	22	0	2	2	14	1	8	2	0	0	.553	.468
Talanoa, Scott, New Orleans	.143	31	107	98	9	14	21	4	0	1	3	0	1	2	6	0	26	0	0	5	.214	.206
Taylor, Rob, Iowa	.000	54	2	2	0	0	0	0	0	0	0	0	0	0	0	0	2	0	0	0	.000	.000
Thomas, Skeets, Louisville*	.249	84	292	273	29	68	112	15	1	9	34	0	0	1	18	0	76	0	0	14	.410	.298
Trafton, Todd, Indianapolis	.000	5	5	5	0	0	0	0	0	0	0	0	0	0	0	0	2	0	0	0	.000	.000
Tremie, Chris, Nashville	.200	67	209	190	13	38	48	4	0	2	16	4	0	2	13	0	37	0	0	6	.253	.259
Tucker, Michael, Omaha*	.305	71	307	275	37	84	122	18	4	4	28	2	2	4	24	5	39	11	4	3	.444	.367
Unroe, Tim, New Orleans	.261	102	402	371	43	97	140	21	2	6	45	1	5	7	18	1	94	4	3	9	.377	.304
Valrie, Kerry, Nashville	.250	138	593	544	75	136	193	30	3	7	55	2	4	3	40	0	107	22	15	15	.355	.303
Vargas, Hector, Oklahoma City	.275	98	343	305	38	84	98	10	2	0	27	4	2	2	30	1	54	6	1	9	.321	.342
Vasquez, Marcos, Indianapolis	.500	2	2	2	0	1	1	0	0	0	0	0	0	0	0	0	0	0	0	0	.500	.500
Viola, Frank, Indianapolis*	.333	6	4	3	0	1	1	0	0	0	0	1	0	0	0	0	0	0	0	0	.333	.333
Vitiello, Joe, Omaha	.279	59	249	229	33	64	118	14	2	12	42	0	2	6	12	0	50	0	1	9	.515	.329
Wachter, Derek, New Orleans	.257	112	432	384	44	98	147	23	1	8	45	0	3	5	40	2	69	2	2	11	.385	.331
Walker, Mike, Iowa	.000	16	1	1	0	0	0	0	0	0	0	0	0	0	0	0	1	0	0	0	.000	.000
Ward, Turner, New Orleans†	.242	11	37	33	3	8	14	1	1	1	3	0	0	0	4	0	10	0	0	1	.424	.324
Warren, Brian, Indianapolis	1.000	41	1	1	1	1	1	0	0	0	0	0	0	0	0	0	0	0	0	0	1.000	1.000
Watson, Allen, Louisville*	.000	4	3	2	0	0	0	0	0	0	0	0	0	0	1	0	0	0	0	0	.000	.333
Weger, Wes, New Orleans	.286	64	247	234	28	67	89	16	0	2	24	1	1	1	10	0	31	0	2	5	.380	.317
Wilson, Brandon, Nas.-Ind.	.278	31	104	97	11	27	35	5	0	1	10	1	0	0	6	0	12	3	1	3	.361	.320
Wilson, Nigel, Nashville*	.313	82	326	304	53	95	179	27	3	17	51	0	1	8	13	4	95	5	3	2	.589	.356
Wolak, Jerry, Nashville	.229	108	419	385	43	88	153	21	1	14	63	5	2	7	20	1	83	5	3	12	.397	.278
Woodson, Tracy, Louisville	.262	118	469	431	62	113	202	35	0	18	76	0	6	5	27	5	43	12	4	18	.469	.309
Worthington, Craig, Indianapolis	.318	81	313	277	48	88	134	19	0	9	41	1	4	0	31	1	51	1	1	5	.484	.381
Wrona, Rick, Buf.-Lou.	.226	47	135	124	10	28	40	7	1	1	12	2	2	2	5	0	25	0	1	8	.323	.263
Yelding, Eric, Buffalo	.346	29	88	81	13	28	38	7	0	1	9	0	1	0	6	0	12	3	1	0	.469	.386
Young, Dmitri, Louisville†	.286	2	8	7	3	2	2	0	0	0	0	0	0	1	0	1	0	0	0	0	.286	.375
Zeile, Todd, Louisville	.125	2	8	8	0	1	1	0	0	0	0	0	0	0	0	0	2	0	0	0	.125	.125
Zupcic, Bob, Nashville	.244	13	55	41	9	10	18	2	0	2	5	0	1	0	13	1	6	1	0	2	.439	.418

GRAND SLAMS: Burnitz, Gibralter, 3 each; Giannelli, Hamelin, McCarty, Mottola, Snopek, 2 each; Brooks, Bruett, Carter, Deak, Dodson, Dorsett, Dostal, Fox, Gordon, Grotewold, Horn, Hunter, Kosco, Koslofski, Mitchell, Pena, Ramsey, Weger, Worthington, 1 each.
AWARDED FIRST BASE ON CATCHER'S INTERFERENCE: Stynes 2 (Martindale, J. Ortiz); Koslofski (Tremie).

PLAYERS WITH TWO OR MORE TEAMS

Player, Team	Avg.	G	TPA	AB	R	H	TB	2B	3B	HR	RBI	SH	SF	HP	BB	IBB	SO	SB	CS	GDP	Slg.	OBP
Bell, David, Buffalo	.272	70	284	254	34	69	106	11	1	8	34	1	3	4	22	0	37	0	3	4	.417	.336
Bell, David, Louisville	.276	18	82	76	9	21	29	3	1	1	9	1	0	3	2	1	10	4	0	2	.382	.321
Byington, John, New Orleans	.255	13	52	47	5	12	16	1	0	1	3	0	2	1	2	0	4	1	0	1	.340	.288
Byington, John, Oklahoma City	.259	109	421	390	44	101	126	15	2	2	29	4	4	4	19	2	37	6	2	16	.323	.297
Duncan, Chip, Oklahoma City	.000	3	0	0	0	0	0	0	0	0	0	0	0	0	0	0	0	0	0	0	.000	.000
Duncan, Chip, New Orleans	.000	15	3	2	0	0	0	0	0	0	0	0	0	0	1	0	2	0	0	0	.000	.333
Howitt, Dann, Nashville*	.226	45	151	133	16	30	47	6	1	3	15	0	2	0	16	4	32	0	3	5	.353	.305
Howitt, Dann, Buffalo*	.303	41	133	119	19	36	62	8	3	4	18	0	0	0	14	2	30	0	0	2	.521	.376
Hulett, Tim, Louisville	.300	3	12	10	1	3	4	1	0	0	3	0	0	0	2	1	0	0	1	0	.400	.417
Hulett, Tim, Oklahoma City	.213	39	148	141	14	30	41	6	1	1	7	0	0	0	7	0	33	0	0	1	.291	.250
Smith, Greg, New Orleans†	.212	59	192	170	18	36	41	3	1	0	9	2	1	2	17	1	22	11	7	6	.241	.289
Smith, Greg, Indianapolis†	.214	4	16	14	1	3	3	0	0	0	0	0	0	0	2	0	3	0	0	0	.214	.313
Wilson, Brandon, Nashville	.294	27	90	85	8	25	33	5	0	1	10	1	0	0	4	0	11	3	1	3	.388	.326
Wilson, Brandon, Indianapolis	.167	4	14	12	3	2	2	0	0	0	0	0	0	0	2	0	1	0	0	0	.167	.286
Wrona, Rick, Buffalo	.226	31	101	93	9	21	27	6	0	0	10	2	1	2	3	0	19	0	1	7	.290	.263
Wrona, Rick, Louisville	.226	16	34	31	1	7	13	1	1	1	2	0	1	0	2	0	6	0	0	1	.419	.265

TEAM

Team	W	L	Pct.	ERA	G	CG	ShO	Sv.	IP	H	TBF	R	ER	HR	SH	SF	HB	BB	IBB	SO	WP	Bk.
Louisville	74	70	.514	3.79	144	10	8	42	1241.0	1208	5307	623	522	106	47	40	45	406	41	840	60	5
Buffalo	82	62	.569	3.91	144	13	8	45	1251.0	1278	5350	604	543	91	27	48	61	396	15	820	44	4
Indianapolis	88	56	.611	3.91	144	12	8	41	1262.0	1178	5348	642	548	111	33	46	40	434	33	883	67	5
New Orleans	63	79	.444	3.98	142	11	8	32	1213.2	1274	5221	606	537	113	29	32	50	445	29	806	67	10
Iowa	69	74	.483	4.03	143	13	8	32	1240.1	1224	5329	614	555	140	46	38	56	496	38	889	59	3
Nashville	68	76	.472	4.04	144	8	11	39	1276.2	1338	5502	673	573	145	44	50	40	405	40	931	49	9
Omaha	76	68	.528	4.26	144	12	10	36	1238.1	1301	5328	660	586	132	43	44	53	423	25	820	51	8
Oklahoma City	54	89	.378	4.56	143	11	7	26	1220.2	1328	5427	709	618	122	47	45	71	520	25	835	71	12

INDIVIDUAL

TOP QUALIFIERS FOR EARNED-RUN AVERAGE TITLE

Minimum 115 innings. *Lefthanded pitcher.

Pitcher, Team	W	L	Pct.	ERA	G	GS	CG	ShO	GF	Sv.	IP	H	TBF	R	ER	HR	SH	SF	HB	BB	IBB	SO	WP	Bk.
Bolton, Rodney, Nashville	14	3	.824	2.88	20	20	3	1	0	0	131.1	127	534	44	42	13	2	2	7	23	1	76	2	0
Reed, Rick, Indianapolis	11	4	.733	3.33	22	21	3	1	0	0	135.0	127	551	60	50	16	4	2	2	26	2	92	0	0
Anderson, Mike, Iowa	7	9	.438	3.46	27	27	3	1	0	0	171.2	156	715	71	66	23	3	3	12	69	3	123	7	1
Roa, Joe, Buffalo	17	3	.850	3.50	25	24	3	0	1	0	164.2	168	678	71	64	9	2	5	7	28	1	93	1	2
Taylor, Scott, N.O.-O.C.	8	8	.500	3.55	24	21	1	1	0	0	129.1	132	557	62	51	12	4	2	7	41	0	74	5	0
Abbott, Paul, Iowa	7	7	.500	3.67	46	11	0	0	7	0	115.1	104	498	50	47	12	4	1	0	64	4	127	12	0
Minchey, Nate, Louisville	8	7	.533	3.73	26	24	1	0	0	0	147.1	153	633	77	61	9	4	5	7	42	0	67	9	1
Steenstra, Kennie, Iowa	9	12	.429	3.89	29	26	6	2	1	0	171.1	174	722	85	74	15	6	6	8	48	3	96	6	0
Bell, Eric, Buffalo*	13	9	.591	3.90	28	24	3	1	1	0	161.1	177	687	76	70	18	1	4	7	47	0	86	3	0
DeLaRosa, Francisco, Louisville	2	5	.286	4.06	28	19	1	0	1	0	115.1	104	483	56	52	15	2	3	2	38	4	66	2	1
Salkeld, Roger, Indianapolis	12	2	.857	4.22	20	20	1	0	0	0	119.1	96	497	60	56	13	3	4	2	57	1	86	3	0
Farrell, John, Buffalo	11	9	.550	4.54	29	28	2	0	1	0	184.1	198	792	97	93	17	2	9	16	61	1	92	11	1
Farrell, Mike, New Orleans*	8	10	.444	4.57	25	24	0	0	0	0	141.2	173	619	84	72	19	2	5	4	38	3	74	2	1
Buckley, Travis, Indianapolis	10	9	.526	4.70	23	18	3	2	0	0	132.0	141	561	80	69	8	3	4	3	33	3	85	4	0
Beltran, Rigo, Louisville*	8	9	.471	5.21	24	24	0	0	0	0	129.2	156	575	81	75	12	2	8	5	34	0	92	4	2

DEPARTMENTAL LEADERS: W—Roa, 17; L—Perez, Steenstra, 12; Pct.—Salkeld, .857; G—Munoz, 57; GS—J. Farrell, 28; CG—Steenstra, 6; ShO—Buckley, Milacki, Nichting, Steenstra, 2; GF—Sauveur, 43; Sv.—Bailey, 25; IP—J. Farrell, 184.1; H—J. Farrell, 198; TBF—J. Farrell, 792; R—J. Farrell, 97; ER—J. Farrell, 93; HR—Baldwin, 27; SH—Raczka, 8; SF—J. Farrell, 9; HB—J. Farrell, 16; BB—M. Anderson, 69; IBB—Carpenter, 10; SO—Abbott, 127; WP—Jean, 14; Bk.—Baldwin, Jean, 3.

ALL PITCHERS

*Lefthanded pitcher.

Pitcher, Team	W	L	Pct.	ERA	G	GS	CG	ShO	GF	Sv.	IP	H	TBF	R	ER	HR	SH	SF	HB	BB	IBB	SO	WP	Bk.
Abbott, Paul, Iowa	7	7	.500	3.67	46	11	0	0	7	0	115.1	104	498	50	47	12	4	1	0	64	4	127	12	0
Adams, Terry, Iowa	0	0	.000	0.00	7	0	0	0	6	5	6.1	3	25	0	0	0	0	0	0	2	0	10	1	0
Alberro, Jose, Oklahoma City	4	2	.667	3.36	20	10	0	0	7	0	77.2	73	331	34	29	4	2	3	4	27	2	55	6	0
Anderson, Mike, Iowa	7	9	.438	3.46	27	27	3	1	0	0	171.2	156	715	71	66	23	3	3	12	69	3	123	7	1
Anderson, Scott, Omaha	3	6	.625	4.17	15	11	1	0	0	0	73.1	63	294	37	34	9	0	1	2	16	0	47	0	0
Archer, Kurt, New Orleans	2	6	.250	3.25	38	0	0	0	11	2	61.0	57	256	23	22	5	6	3	5	17	2	41	5	0
Austin, Jim, Buffalo	1	1	.500	12.00	2	1	0	0	0	0	3.0	7	19	6	4	1	0	0	0	2	0	1	1	0
Bailey, Cory, Louisville	5	3	.625	4.55	55	0	0	0	40	25	59.1	51	258	30	30	6	6	2	0	34	4	49	7	0
Baldwin, James, Nashville	5	9	.357	5.85	18	18	0	0	0	0	95.1	120	448	76	62	27	1	3	2	44	1	89	10	3
Barber, Brian, Louisville	6	5	.545	4.70	20	19	0	0	0	0	107.1	105	465	67	56	14	2	6	4	40	1	94	1	0
Barfield, John, Oklahoma City*	0	0	.000	0.00	4	0	0	0	1	0	7.1	4	26	2	0	0	0	0	0	1	0	2	0	0
Batchelor, Richard, Louisville	5	4	.556	3.28	50	6	0	0	7	0	85.0	85	352	39	31	5	4	3	7	16	2	61	0	0
Beatty, Blaine, Indianapolis*	7	1	.875	3.61	20	8	0	0	1	0	67.1	80	293	33	27	7	4	1	2	16	0	37	3	2
Belcher, Tim, Indianapolis	0	0	.000	1.80	2	2	0	0	0	0	10.0	6	36	2	2	0	0	1	1	0		8	0	0
Bell, Eric, Buffalo*	13	9	.591	3.90	28	24	3	1	1	0	161.1	177	687	76	70	18	1	4	7	47	0	86	3	0
Beltran, Rigo, Louisville*	8	9	.471	5.21	24	24	0	0	0	0	129.2	156	575	81	75	12	2	8	5	34	0	92	4	2
Benes, Alan, Louisville	4	2	.667	2.41	11	11	2	1	0	0	56.0	37	215	16	15	5	0	0	1	14	1	54	2	0
Bere, Jason, Nashville	1	0	1.000	3.38	1	1	0	0	0	0	5.1	6	24	2	2	0	0	0	0	2	0	7	0	0
Bertotti, Mike, Nashville*	2	3	.400	8.72	7	6	0	0	0	1	32.0	41	154	34	31	8	0	1	3	17	0	35	0	0
Bevil, Brian, Omaha	1	3	.250	9.41	6	6	0	0	0	0	22.0	40	119	31	23	7	1	0	3	14	1	10	2	0
Bluma, Jaime, Omaha	0	0	.000	3.04	18	0	0	0	10	4	23.2	21	101	13	8	1	3	3	0	14	4	13	3	0
Bolton, Rodney, Nashville	14	3	.824	2.88	20	20	3	1	0	0	131.1	127	534	44	42	13	2	2	7	23	1	76	2	0
Bolton, Tom, Nashville*	5	7	.417	4.43	19	17	1	1	1	0	101.2	106	433	52	50	10	0	3	1	31	0	82	3	2
Boze, Marshall, New Orleans	3	9	.250	4.27	23	19	1	0	1	1	111.2	134	495	65	53	10	2	2		45	1	47	6	1
Brandenburg, Mark, Okla. City	0	5	.000	2.02	35	0	0	0	15	4	58.0	52	235	16	13	2	3	1	2	15	5	51	0	2
Brewer, Billy, Omaha*	0	0	.000	0.00	6	0	0	0	6	0	7.0	7	25	0	0	0	0	0	0	7	0	5	2	1
Bronkey, Jeff, New Orleans	0	1	.000	2.25	2	0	0	0	0	0	8.0	8	29	2	2	0	1	0	0	1	0	2	1	0
Brown, Kevin, Omaha*	0	0	.000	7.62	7	1	0	0	0	0	13.0	20	71	13	11	0	3	2	0	12	1	5	1	0
Browning, Tom, Omaha*	2	1	.667	3.43	5	5	0	0	0	0	21.0	13	78	8	8	1	1	0	0	5	0	5	1	0
Brumley, Duff, Oklahoma City	1	1	.500	5.40	3	0	0	0	1	1	5.0	6	24	4	3	0	1	0	0	2	0	3	0	0
Buckels, Gary, Louisville	1	2	.333	5.51	13	0	0	0	6	5	16.1	18	80	11	10	3	2	1	0	13	2	8	3	0
Buckley, Travis, Indianapolis	10	9	.526	4.70	23	18	3	2	0	0	132.0	141	561	80	69	8	3	4	3	33	3	85	4	0
Bunch, Mel, Omaha	1	7	.125	4.57	12	11	1	0	0	0	65.0	63	272	37	33	10	3	4	0	20	2	50	8	1
Burrows, Terry, Oklahoma City*	0	1	.000	10.13	5	0	0	0	0	0	2.2	5	16	3	3	0	0	0		2	0	4	1	0
Busby, Mike, Louisville	2	2	.500	3.29	6	6	1	0	0	0	38.1	28	154	18	14	2	2	2	3	11	0	26	2	0
Bushing, Chris, Oklahoma City	0	0	.000	13.50	3	0	0	0	2	0	1.1	5	10	2	2	0	1	0	0	2	0	0	0	0
Caceres, Edgar, Omaha	0	0	.000	9.00	1	0	0	0	0	0	2.0	4	11	2	2	0	0	0	1	0		1	1	0
Cadaret, Greg, Louisville*	1	0	1.000	3.09	12	0	0	0	2	0	11.2	14	50	4	4	0	1	0	1	0		7	0	0
Campbell, Mike, Iowa	9	3	.750	2.45	21	15	0	0	2	0	102.2	93	419	31	28	10	4	3	3	29	5	88	2	0
Carpenter, Cris, Louisville	2	5	.286	2.43	49	0	0	0	20	5	66.2	59	273	18	18	6	6	2	1	20	10	41	3	0
Casian, Larry, Iowa*	0	0	.000	2.13	13	0	0	0	4	1	12.2	9	48	3	3	0	1	1	1	2	1	9	0	0

CLASS AAA American Association

Pitcher, Team	W	L	Pct.	ERA	G	GS	CG	ShO	GF	Sv.	IP	H	TBF	R	ER	HR	SH	SF	HB	BB	IBB	SO	WP	Bk.
Chapin, Darrin, Buffalo	0	1	.000	8.31	6	0	0	0	3	0	8.2	12	42	10	8	2	2	1	0	2	1	4	1	0
Cimorelli, Frank, Louisville	1	1	.500	9.00	6	0	0	0	2	0	5.0	12	26	7	5	2	0	0	0	0	0	3	0	0
Clark, Mark, Buffalo	4	0	1.000	3.57	5	5	0	0	0	0	35.1	39	151	14	14	0	1	2	2	10	0	17	0	0
Combs, Pat, New Orleans*	1	1	.500	5.40	12	2	0	0	5	0	15.0	19	78	11	9	1	0	1	1	13	0	10	5	0
Converse, Jim, Omaha	1	0	1.000	0.00	4	0	0	0	0	0	5.0	1	19	0	0	0	0	0	0	1	0	9	1	0
Costello, Fred, Nashville	0	2	.000	5.11	7	0	0	0	5	0	12.1	17	61	9	7	1	1	0	0	7	0	6	2	0
Courtright, John, Indianapolis*	2	1	.667	4.28	13	2	0	0	1	0	33.2	29	147	18	16	2	2	1	2	15	1	13	4	1
Crawford, Carlos, Buffalo	0	1	.000	5.64	13	3	0	0	3	1	30.1	36	137	22	19	2	2	0	0	12	0	15	0	0
Creek, Doug, Louisville*	3	2	.600	3.23	26	0	0	0	5	0	30.2	20	132	12	11	1	0	0	1	21	0	29	4	0
Curtis, Chris, Oklahoma City	3	5	.375	5.00	51	0	0	0	22	5	77.1	81	358	53	43	5	6	3	5	39	3	40	2	0
Dabney, Fred, Iowa*	4	6	.400	5.95	33	1	0	0	4	0	56.0	68	262	42	37	8	5	3	3	29	3	33	5	0
Darwin, Danny, Oklahoma City	0	0	.000	0.00	1	1	0	0	0	0	3.0	1	10	0	0	0	0	0	0	0	0	4	0	0
Davis, Clint, Louisville	0	0	.000	12.27	4	0	0	0	0	0	3.2	6	19	5	5	1	0	0	0	2	1	4	0	1
Davis, John, Nashville	1	1	.500	0.00	4	0	0	0	3	1	3.1	3	16	2	0	0	0	0	0	3	1	0	0	0
Davis, Storm, Indianapolis	0	0	.000	3.38	4	0	0	0	1	0	5.1	4	22	2	2	0	0	1	0	3	0	4	1	0
DeJesus, Jose, Omaha	3	6	.333	6.13	36	6	0	0	19	10	61.2	56	288	45	42	10	2	5	2	52	3	49	7	0
DeLaRosa, Francisco, Louisville	2	5	.286	4.06	28	19	1	0	1	0	115.1	104	483	56	52	15	2	3	2	38	4	66	2	1
DeLeon, Luis, Iowa	0	1	.000	13.50	2	0	0	0	1	0	2.0	6	12	3	3	0	0	0	0	0	0	3	0	1
Dettmer, John, Oklahoma City	0	0	.000	2.08	5	0	0	0	3	0	8.2	10	37	3	2	1	1	0	0	4	0	10	1	1
Dibble, Rob, New Orleans	0	1	.000	0.00	4	0	0	0	1	0	4.0	1	16	2	0	0	0	0	1	2	0	6	0	0
Dixon, Steve, Iowa*	6	3	.667	2.85	53	0	0	0	19	0	41.0	34	176	16	13	4	0	2	5	19	4	38	2	0
Donnelly, Brendan, Indianapolis	1	1	.500	23.63	3	0	0	0	0	0	2.2	7	18	8	7	2	0	1	1	2	0	1	2	0
Dorlarque, Aaron, Omaha	2	2	.500	4.24	24	1	0	0	13	4	40.1	38	166	19	19	7	1	3	3	15	1	24	1	0
Drahman, Brian, O.C.-Ind.	2	2	.500	2.83	24	0	0	0	15	4	35.0	39	157	11	11	3	1	1	2	15	3	22	0	0
Duncan, Chip, O.C.-N.O.	1	4	.200	5.90	17	5	0	0	6	0	39.2	50	183	28	26	7	2	3	2	19	2	26	5	1
Eddy, Chris, Omaha*	1	1	.500	7.27	14	0	0	0	6	0	17.1	20	84	15	14	1	1	2	2	12	2	12	0	0
Edens, Tom, Iowa	2	0	1.000	3.46	20	3	0	0	5	1	41.2	36	175	17	16	3	1	0	3	17	1	28	2	0
Ellis, Robert, Nashville	1	1	.500	2.18	4	4	0	0	0	0	20.2	16	85	7	5	2	0	1	1	10	0	9	1	0
Embree, Alan, Buffalo*	3	4	.429	0.89	30	0	0	0	19	5	40.2	31	170	10	4	0	1	2	1	19	2	56	0	0
Farrell, John, Buffalo	11	9	.550	4.54	29	28	2	0	1	0	184.1	198	792	97	93	17	2	9	16	61	1	92	11	1
Farrell, Mike, New Orleans*	8	10	.444	4.57	25	24	0	0	0	0	141.2	173	619	84	72	19	2	5	4	38	3	74	2	1
Ferry, Mike, Indianapolis	1	2	.333	5.19	3	3	0	0	0	0	17.1	21	76	15	10	3	0	2	0	3	0	3	0	0
Fleming, Dave, Omaha*	1	0	1.000	3.38	3	3	0	0	0	0	16.0	17	72	6	6	1	1	0	2	7	0	8	0	0
Franco, Matt, Iowa	0	0	.000	0.00	1	0	0	0	1	0	1.0	1	5	0	0	0	0	0	0	1	0	1	1	0
Frascatore, John, Louisville	2	8	.200	3.95	28	10	1	0	15	5	82.0	89	370	54	36	5	5	2	3	34	3	55	5	0
Fritz, John, New Orleans	6	3	.667	3.97	41	6	0	0	6	1	81.2	70	348	38	36	11	1	0	4	42	4	56	5	0
Frohwirth, Todd, Buffalo	0	1	.000	3.34	26	0	0	0	11	3	32.1	31	137	13	12	4	1	1	1	12	1	33	0	0
Fyhrie, Mike, Omaha	3	4	.429	4.45	14	11	0	0	2	0	60.2	71	259	34	30	7	0	2	4	14	0	39	0	0
Gajkowski, Steve, Nashville	0	1	.000	2.55	15	0	0	0	5	0	24.2	26	103	15	7	2	0	1	1	8	1	12	1	0
Ganote, Joe, New Orleans	7	4	.636	3.42	14	13	2	1	1	0	81.2	88	348	35	31	6	5	2	6	21	2	56	6	0
Garces, Rich, Iowa	0	2	.000	2.86	23	0	0	0	15	7	28.1	25	116	10	9	3	0	0	1	8	1	36	0	1
Garrelts, Scott, Omaha	1	2	.333	5.30	9	1	0	0	3	1	18.2	17	84	12	11	2	0	0	2	13	1	15	2	0
Geeve, Dave, Oklahoma City	2	5	.286	5.66	10	10	2	0	0	0	55.2	72	249	36	35	7	3	5	4	13	1	30	0	2
Givens, Brian, New Orleans*	7	4	.636	2.55	16	11	2	1	1	0	77.2	67	320	28	22	2	2	3	0	33	1	75	2	2
Goetz, Barry, Oklahoma City	4	6	.400	5.72	40	6	0	0	15	1	89.2	97	399	60	57	8	3	6	4	49	3	46	1	2
Gozzo, Mauro, Iowa	0	3	.000	4.15	6	6	0	0	0	0	30.1	37	131	22	14	4	2	0	0	11	1	11	3	0
Grant, Mark, Iowa	5	2	.714	3.13	11	11	2	0	0	0	69.0	58	276	28	24	6	0	2	2	10	0	39	1	0
Graves, Daniel, Buffalo	0	0	.000	3.00	3	0	0	0	3	0	3.0	5	16	4	1	0	0	0	0	1	0	2	1	0
Green, Gary, Omaha	0	0	.000	10.80	2	0	0	0	2	0	1.2	5	10	2	2	0	0	1	0	0	0	1	0	0
Grimsley, Jason, Buffalo	5	3	.625	2.91	10	10	2	0	0	0	68.0	61	285	26	22	4	2	3	3	19	0	40	4	0
Grott, Matt, Indianapolis*	7	3	.700	4.24	25	18	2	1	2	2	114.2	99	468	61	54	10	2	5	3	24	2	74	11	0
Hammaker, Atlee, Nashville*	1	2	.333	1.27	15	0	0	0	5	1	28.1	27	115	4	4	1	1	0	0	7	2	20	0	0
Harris, Pep, Buffalo	2	1	.667	2.48	14	0	0	0	3	0	32.2	32	141	11	9	2	0	0	0	15	0	18	0	0
Harris, Reggie, Omaha	0	1	.000	18.00	2	0	0	0	0	0	2.0	5	12	4	4	1	0	0	0	1	0	2	1	0
Harrison, Brian, Omaha	4	2	.667	6.13	16	8	1	0	1	0	54.1	76	248	39	37	7	3	3	1	10	0	12	1	0
Helling, Rick, Oklahoma City	4	8	.333	5.33	20	20	3	0	0	0	109.2	132	493	73	65	13	2	6	10	41	1	80	3	1
Heredia, Wilson, Oklahoma City	1	4	.200	6.82	8	7	0	0	0	0	31.2	40	158	26	24	3	1	1	5	25	1	21	1	0
Huisman, Rick, Omaha	0	0	.000	1.80	5	0	0	0	3	1	5.0	3	19	1	1	1	0	0	0	1	0	13	0	0
Hurst, James, O.C.-Ind.*	1	5	.167	7.20	31	7	0	0	13	5	50.0	73	249	42	40	7	2	0	3	26	0	43	4	0
Ignasiak, Mike, New Orleans	1	1	.500	2.50	4	2	0	0	1	0	18.0	9	71	5	5	2	0	0	0	8	0	19	1	0
Jackson, Danny, Louisville*	1	0	1.000	1.29	1	1	1	0	0	0	7.0	8	30	1	1	0	0	0	1	2	0	2	0	0
Jackson, Mike, Indianapolis	0	0	.000	0.00	2	1	0	0	1	0	2.0	0	6	0	0	0	0	0	0	0	0	1	0	0
Jarvis, Kevin, Indianapolis	4	2	.667	4.45	10	10	2	1	0	0	60.2	62	262	33	30	2	0	2	0	18	1	37	5	0
Jean, Domingo, O.C.-Ind.	4	8	.333	6.00	26	13	0	0	9	1	90.0	103	425	70	60	12	5	2	1	61	1	73	14	3
Johnson, Dane, Nashville	4	4	.500	2.41	46	0	0	0	28	15	56.0	48	240	24	15	2	5	1	1	28	6	51	3	1
Jones, Calvin, Nashville	0	0	.000	6.75	5	0	0	0	0	0	6.2	13	38	8	5	3	0	0	0	3	1	5	0	0
Jones, Stacy, New Orleans	3	2	.600	3.02	34	0	0	0	25	6	47.2	51	197	16	16	3	1	1	2	12	2	39	3	0
Karchner, Matt, Nashville	3	3	.500	1.45	28	0	0	0	21	9	37.1	39	156	7	6	3	5	0	0	10	5	29	2	0
Karl, Scott, New Orleans*	3	4	.429	3.30	8	6	1	1	1	0	46.1	47	191	18	17	3	0	1	2	12	2	29	1	0
Keyser, Brian, Nashville	2	4	.333	2.36	10	10	2	1	0	0	72.1	49	273	23	19	4	3	3	1	9	0	40	1	0
Kiefer, Mark, New Orleans	8	2	.800	2.82	12	12	1	0	0	0	70.1	60	290	22	22	5	1	0	5	19	0	52	6	0
Kilgo, Rusty, Indianapolis*	0	0	.000	4.50	2	0	0	0	0	0	2.0	4	10	2	1	0	0	0	0	1	0	1	0	0
Klink, Joe, Buffalo*	2	1	.667	3.00	45	0	0	0	21	8	39.0	31	161	13	13	0	3	5	1	15	0	32	3	0
Kutzler, Jerry, Omaha	8	5	.615	4.02	37	7	0	0	12	4	103.0	128	449	48	46	8	3	2	5	27	2	45	0	0
Lacy, Kerry, Oklahoma City	0	0	.000	0.00	1	0	0	0	1	1	2.1	0	7	0	0	0	0	0	0	0	0	1	0	0
Lancaster, Les, Buffalo	4	5	.444	4.31	45	3	1	0	10	0	87.2	90	372	45	42	6	2	1	2	19	5	68	4	0
Levine, Alan, Nashville	0	2	.000	5.14	3	3	0	0	0	0	14.0	20	69	10	8	1	0	0	0	7	0	14	3	0
Lewis, James, Buffalo	6	4	.600	3.64	18	16	1	0	2	1	94.0	101	405	42	38	7	1	3	9	25	0	50	4	0
Linton, Doug, Omaha	7	7	.500	4.40	18	18	2	1	0	0	108.1	129	472	60	53	9	5	3	7	24	2	85	3	1
Lopez, Albie, Buffalo	5	10	.333	4.44	18	18	1	1	0	0	101.1	101	448	57	50	10	0	5	2	51	0	82	8	0
Lorraine, Andrew, Nashville*	4	1	.800	6.00	7	7	0	0	0	0	39.0	51	184	29	26	4	1	3	1	12	0	26	2	0
Lynch, David, Buffalo*	1	2	.333	4.30	14	0	0	0	3	0	14.2	16	66	8	7	0	1	1	0	7	1	14	0	0
Magnante, Mike, Omaha*	5	1	.833	2.84	15	8	0	0	3	0	57.0	55	235	23	18	3	1	3	1	13	0	38	5	0

Pitcher, Team	W	L	Pct.	ERA	G	GS	CG	ShO	GF	Sv.	IP	H	TBF	R	ER	HR	SH	SF	HB	BB	IBB	SO	WP	Bk.
Mallicoat, Rob, Omaha*	0	1	.000	3.00	3	0	0	0	1	0	3.0	1	12	1	1	0	1	0	0	3	0	1	0	0
Marquez, Isidro, Nashville	7	4	.636	4.75	46	0	0	0	17	4	72.0	80	315	41	38	8	6	3	2	27	5	57	0	0
Martinez, Frankie, Louisville	2	1	.667	3.61	38	0	0	0	8	0	52.1	60	230	25	21	4	1	0	2	21	5	23	10	0
Mathews, T.J., Louisville	9	4	.692	2.70	32	7	0	0	10	1	66.2	60	298	35	20	2	0	3	3	27	2	50	1	0
Mathile, Mike, Indianapolis	0	2	.000	2.51	14	3	0	0	4	0	28.2	22	113	10	8	1	1	4	0	8	0	16	0	0
McAndrew, Jamie, New Orleans	7	5	.583	3.97	17	17	3	1	0	0	104.1	102	443	48	46	8	1	3	2	44	1	62	1	1
McClellan, Paul, New Orleans	0	3	.000	6.06	3	3	1	0	0	0	16.1	19	71	11	11	0	0	0	0	8	0	8	0	1
Meier, Kevin, Iowa	1	2	.333	8.44	3	2	0	0	0	0	10.2	18	51	10	10	6	0	0	0	3	0	7	1	0
Melendez, Jose, Omaha	3	4	.429	4.89	21	1	0	0	8	0	35.0	44	163	21	19	8	1	0	4	14	2	30	0	0
Milacki, Bob, Omaha	8	3	.727	3.33	15	15	2	2	0	0	105.1	90	421	42	39	8	1	0	2	31	0	63	3	0
Minchey, Nate, Louisville	8	7	.533	3.73	26	24	1	0	0	0	147.1	153	633	77	61	9	4	5	7	42	0	67	9	1
Mongiello, Mike, Nashville	3	3	.500	5.14	31	8	1	0	7	1	91.0	104	408	59	52	10	1	6	4	37	3	72	3	0
Moore, Marcus, Indianapolis	1	0	1.000	4.97	7	1	0	0	2	1	12.2	13	62	8	7	0	1	0	0	14	2	6	0	0
Morton, Kevin, Iowa*	1	7	.125	4.79	28	12	1	0	5	0	92.0	97	405	52	49	13	4	4	2	42	3	49	3	0
Munoz, J.J., Omaha*	2	3	.400	3.38	57	0	0	0	21	6	56.0	48	235	23	21	3	4	2	6	19	2	51	5	1
Myers, Rod, Omaha	4	5	.444	4.10	38	0	0	0	17	2	48.1	52	212	26	22	5	2	3	0	19	1	38	1	1
Nabholz, Chris, Iowa*	0	2	.000	6.41	6	5	0	0	0	0	19.2	27	98	17	14	3	0	3	12	0	16	3	0
Nichting, Chris, Oklahoma City	5	5	.500	2.13	23	7	3	2	8	1	67.2	58	275	19	16	4	2	2	19	0	72	2	0
Nitkowski, C.J., Indianapolis*	0	2	.000	5.20	6	6	0	0	0	0	27.2	28	120	16	16	3	0	2	1	10	0	21	0	1
Noriega, Rey, Nashville	0	0	.000	0.00	1	0	0	0	1	0	1.0	0	3	0	0	0	0	0	0	1	0	0	0	0
Novoa, Rafael, Nashville*	0	1	.000	10.80	3	3	0	0	0	0	10.0	17	58	13	12	0	0	1	2	9	0	3	0	0
Ogea, Chad, Buffalo	0	1	.000	4.58	4	4	0	0	0	0	17.2	16	79	12	9	1	0	0	2	8	0	11	0	0
Olsen, Steve, Nashville	1	7	.125	4.79	14	14	0	0	0	0	77.0	85	329	44	41	10	3	5	0	16	0	45	4	0
Olson, Gregg, Buf.-Oma.	0	0	.000	0.00	1	0	0	0	1	0	1.0	0	4	0	0	0	0	0	1	0	1	1	0
Osborne, Donovan, Louisville*	0	1	.000	3.86	1	1	0	0	0	0	7.0	8	30	3	3	0	1	0	0	0	3	0	0
Pall, Donn, Nashville	4	3	.571	3.98	44	0	0	0	13	3	86.0	89	365	40	38	10	5	3	4	20	7	79	3	0
Parker, Clay, New Orleans	0	0	.000	6.75	2	0	0	0	0	0	1.1	3	9	2	1	0	0	0	2	0	2	0	0
Patterson, Danny, Okla. City	0	1	1.000	1.65	14	0	0	0	3	2	27.1	23	111	8	5	0	3	2	1	9	2	9	4	0
Pennington, Brad, Indianapolis*	0	0	.000	10.29	11	2	0	0	1	0	14.0	17	79	19	16	3	0	1	0	21	1	11	2	0
Perez, David, Oklahoma City	5	12	.294	5.57	20	20	1	0	0	0	103.1	120	461	71	64	16	0	0	13	34	1	74	5	0
Perry, Pat, Omaha*	0	0	.000	5.79	5	0	0	0	4	3	4.2	5	21	3	3	0	0	0	2	1	4	0	0
Perschke, Greg, Buffalo	1	1	.500	5.74	3	3	0	0	0	0	15.2	13	65	10	10	2	0	1	0	6	0	11	0	0
Petkovsek, Mark, Louisville	4	1	.800	2.32	8	8	2	1	0	0	54.1	38	209	16	14	3	1	1	1	8	0	30	1	0
Pierce, Ed, Omaha*	0	0	.000	7.36	3	0	0	0	1	0	3.2	9	21	4	3	0	0	0	1	0	1	0	0
Pittsley, Jim, Omaha	4	1	.800	3.21	8	8	0	0	0	0	47.2	38	189	20	17	5	0	2	16	0	39	0	2
Poole, Jim, Buffalo*	0	0	.000	27.00	1	1	0	0	0	0	2.2	7	17	8	8	1	0	1	2	0	0	0	0
Popplewell, Tom, New Orleans	0	2	.000	6.75	10	0	0	0	1	0	13.1	13	64	11	10	0	0	2	1	11	1	16	2	0
Prager, Howard, Louisville*	0	0	.000	0.00	2	0	0	0	2	0	2.0	1	7	0	0	0	0	0	0	0	0	1	0	0
Pugh, Tim, Indianapolis	2	4	.333	4.68	6	6	1	1	0	0	42.1	42	184	24	22	4	1	4	5	14	1	20	1	0
Raczka, Mike, Louisville*	5	3	.625	3.86	55	0	0	0	16	1	49.0	49	216	23	21	7	8	2	3	20	6	43	3	0
Rambo, Dan, New Orleans	0	4	.000	5.20	7	6	0	0	1	0	36.1	39	155	23	21	6	2	0	2	9	1	22	1	0
Rasmussen, Dennis, Omaha*	6	3	.667	2.89	10	10	3	1	0	0	65.1	63	269	22	21	7	1	1	2	17	0	51	1	0
Reed, Rick, Indianapolis	11	4	.733	3.33	22	21	3	1	0	0	135.0	127	551	60	50	16	4	2	2	26	2	92	0	0
Remlinger, Mike, Indianapolis*	5	3	.625	4.05	41	1	0	0	7	0	46.2	40	210	24	21	4	2	1	2	32	4	58	8	0
Righetti, Dave, Nashville*	4	5	.444	3.23	16	15	1	1	0	0	83.2	81	344	40	30	9	3	4	1	20	0	44	2	2
Rightnowar, Ron, New Orleans	1	1	.500	2.67	25	0	0	0	20	10	30.1	37	135	16	9	3	2	1	2	9	1	22	3	0
Roa, Joe, Buffalo	17	3	.850	3.50	25	24	3	0	1	0	164.2	168	678	71	64	9	2	5	7	28	1	93	1	2
Roberson, Sid, New Orleans*	0	2	.000	7.62	4	3	0	0	0	0	13.0	20	69	11	11	1	0	2	1	10	0	8	0	0
Roper, John, Indianapolis	2	5	.286	4.97	8	8	0	0	0	0	41.2	47	186	26	23	9	0	0	1	16	1	23	4	0
Ruffcorn, Scott, Nashville	0	0	.000	108.00	2	2	0	0	0	0	0.1	3	9	4	4	0	0	0	2	3	0	1	0	0
Ruffin, Johnny, Indianapolis	3	1	.750	2.90	36	1	0	0	4	0	49.2	27	213	19	16	3	2	1	0	37	2	58	7	0
Salkeld, Roger, Indianapolis	12	2	.857	4.22	20	20	1	0	0	0	119.1	96	497	60	56	13	3	4	2	57	1	86	3	0
Santana, Julio, Oklahoma City	0	2	.000	39.00	2	2	0	0	0	0	3.0	9	25	14	13	3	0	0	7	0	6	1	1
Sauveur, Rich, Indianapolis*	5	2	.714	2.05	52	0	0	0	43	15	57.0	43	228	17	13	3	1	1	2	18	3	47	3	0
Scanlan, Bob, New Orleans	1	1	.500	5.40	3	3	0	0	0	0	11.2	17	51	7	7	0	0	1	3	0	5	1	0
Schuermann, Lance, Okla. City*	4	7	.364	4.67	33	13	0	0	6	0	88.2	101	398	51	46	12	1	4	2	40	0	44	8	0
Scudder, Scott, Indianapolis	1	4	.200	5.17	7	7	0	0	0	0	38.1	43	161	24	22	4	0	1	4	9	1	13	3	0
Seminara, Frank, New Orleans	2	3	.400	7.96	11	7	0	0	2	0	37.1	54	171	35	33	3	0	3	2	14	1	19	1	1
Service, Scott, Indianapolis	4	1	.800	2.18	36	0	0	0	32	18	41.1	33	175	13	10	4	2	1	3	15	2	48	1	0
Shifflett, Steve, Iowa	5	1	.833	5.33	26	0	0	0	8	0	27.0	30	116	18	16	2	3	4	1	6	1	10	0	0
Shinall, Zak, New Orleans	0	0	.000	7.62	9	0	0	0	1	0	13.0	15	58	11	11	4	0	0	1	7	1	5	2	0
Shuey, Paul, Buffalo	1	2	.333	2.63	25	0	0	0	19	11	27.1	21	108	9	8	2	3	0	0	7	0	27	2	0
Simas, Bill, Nashville	1	1	.500	3.86	7	0	0	0	3	0	11.2	12	50	5	5	0	1	0	0	3	1	12	0	0
Simmons, Scott, Louisville*	0	2	.000	8.00	2	2	0	0	0	0	9.0	11	40	9	8	3	0	0	1	1	0	2	0	0
Sirotka, Mike, Nashville*	1	5	.167	2.83	8	8	0	0	0	0	54.0	51	217	21	17	4	2	3	1	13	1	34	1	0
Slusarski, Joe, Buf.-N.O.	2	2	.500	2.39	37	2	0	0	23	11	64.0	55	255	22	17	6	1	2	1	15	2	39	0	0
Smith, Ottis, Iowa*	1	3	.250	10.45	5	5	0	0	0	0	20.2	34	108	25	24	3	1	1	13	0	12	0	0
Steenstra, Kennie, Iowa	9	12	.429	3.89	29	26	6	2	1	0	171.1	174	722	85	74	15	6	6	8	48	3	96	6	0
Strange, Don, Omaha	0	0	.000	7.47	9	0	0	0	3	1	15.2	24	75	13	13	2	0	1	0	6	0	11	0	0
Sturtze, Tanyon, Iowa	4	7	.364	6.80	23	17	1	1	0	0	86.0	108	398	66	65	18	5	2	5	42	1	48	5	0
Sullivan, Scott, Indianapolis	4	3	.571	3.53	44	0	0	0	21	1	58.2	51	253	31	23	2	3	4	2	24	4	54	3	0
Swartzbaugh, Dave, Iowa	3	0	1.000	1.53	30	0	0	0	9	0	47.0	33	187	10	8	1	2	0	1	18	1	38	1	0
Swingle, Paul, New Orleans	1	4	.200	4.57	35	0	0	0	8	0	43.1	42	185	25	22	7	1	0	1	15	2	41	5	0
Talanoa, Scott, New Orleans	0	0	.000	0.00	2	0	0	0	2	0	1.1	1	5	0	0	0	0	0	0	0	0	0	0	0
Taylor, Rob, Iowa	4	2	.667	2.81	54	0	0	0	40	18	57.2	42	241	20	18	3	5	3	2	28	2	48	4	0
Taylor, Scott, N.O.-O.C.	8	8	.500	3.55	24	21	1	1	0	0	129.1	132	557	62	51	12	4	2	7	41	0	74	5	0
Telford, Anthony, Buffalo	4	1	.800	3.46	16	2	0	0	4	0	39.0	35	161	15	15	1	1	4	2	10	3	24	1	0
Thomas, Mike, New Orleans*	0	1	.000	4.05	35	0	0	0	14	1	33.1	37	151	18	15	3	0	0	2	18	0	28	3	2
Torres, Dilson, New Orleans	3	1	.750	2.63	5	5	1	1	0	0	27.1	28	113	11	8	2	2	1	1	7	0	12	1	1
Toth, Robert, Omaha	1	2	.333	3.61	8	8	1	0	0	0	47.1	53	205	25	19	7	3	2	2	8	0	31	0	0
Turner, Matt, Buffalo	0	1	.000	5.23	13	0	0	0	10	3	10.1	16	54	7	6	0	0	1	5	0	10	0	1
Urbani, Tom, Louisville*	1	1	.500	2.93	2	2	0	0	0	0	15.1	16	65	6	5	0	0	0	5	0	11	0	0
Vasquez, Marcos, Indianapolis	0	0	.000	0.00	2	0	0	0	1	1	4.0	1	13	0	0	0	0	0	0	1	0	5	0	0

Pitcher, Team	W	L	Pct.	ERA	G	GS	CG	ShO	GF	Sv.	IP	H	TBF	R	ER	HR	SH	SF	HB	BB	IBB	SO	WP	Bk.
Vierra, Joey, Nashville*	2	2	.500	4.17	56	1	0	0	22	4	58.1	47	237	28	27	6	1	5	1	19	4	57	4	0
Viola, Frank, Indianapolis*	3	3	.500	4.09	6	6	0	0	0	0	33.0	33	138	17	15	3	0	2	2	6	0	25	0	0
Vosberg, Ed, Oklahoma City*	1	0	1.000	0.00	1	0	0	0	0	0	1.2	1	7	0	0	0	0	0	0	1	0	2	0	0
Walker, Mike, Iowa	1	1	.500	4.10	16	1	0	0	3	0	26.1	22	122	13	12	3	1	1	3	19	4	13	0	0
Warren, Brian, Indianapolis	2	1	.667	1.61	41	0	0	0	9	2	56.0	56	234	18	10	2	1	1	5	9	2	35	2	1
Watson, Allen, Louisville*	2	2	.500	2.63	4	4	1	1	0	0	24.0	20	97	10	7	1	0	0	0	6	0	19	3	0
Wilson, Steve, Nashville*	2	2	.500	4.56	20	7	0	0	4	1	51.1	60	234	32	26	7	3	4	3	17	1	26	1	1
Wishnevski, Rob, Okla. City	6	3	.667	3.47	41	8	0	0	12	3	109.0	101	466	51	42	9	5	7	53	2	78	13	0
Young, Anthony, Iowa	0	1	.000	11.25	3	1	0	0	0	0	4.0	9	23	5	5	0	0	1	0	4	0	6	0	0

COMBINATION SHUTOUTS: **Buffalo (6)**—Bell-Embree, Bell-Turner, Lewis-Embree-Olson, Grimsley-Frohwirth-Klink-Shuey, Grimsley-Klink-Shuey, Lewis-Klink-Frohwirth. **Indianapolis (2)**—Grott-Warren-Sauveur, Reed-Sullivan. **Iowa (4)**—Abbott-Morton-Taylor-Swartzbaugh, Campbell-Swartzbaugh-Dixon-Taylor, Edens-Swartzbaugh-Taylor, Sturtze-Garces. **Louisville (5)**—Beltran-Cimorelli, Beltran-Mathews-Raczka-Bailey, Benes-Batchelor-Raczka-Mathews, Benes-Batchelor-Carpenter-Raczka, Benes-Raczka-Buckels. **Nashville (7)**—Baldwin-Hammaker-Marquez, Bolton-Karchner, Bolton-Marquez, Bolton-Wilson, Ellis-Righetti-Karchner, Mongiello-Pall, Olsen-Karchner-Johnson-Gajkowski-Vierra-Pall. **New Orleans (4)**—Farrell-Archer-Thomas-Jones, Ganote-Swingle-Jones, Kiefer-Boze-Fritz, Kiefer-Jones. **Oklahoma City (4)**—Alberro-Schuermann-Goetz-Curtis, Perez-Nichting-Hurst, Schuermann-Goetz-Hurst-Curtis, Taylor-Wishnevski. **Omaha (5)**—Bevil-Anderson-Garretts, Brown-Kutzler-Perry-Dorlarque, Fleming-Converse-Huisman, Linton-Perry, Magnante-Harrison-Munoz-DeJesus.
NO-HIT GAMES: None.

PITCHERS WITH TWO OR MORE TEAMS

Pitcher, Team	W	L	Pct.	ERA	G	GS	CG	ShO	GF	Sv.	IP	H	TBF	R	ER	HR	SH	SF	HB	BB	IBB	SO	WP	Bk.
Drahman, Brian, Okla. City	2	2	.500	3.09	22	0	0	0	15	4	32.0	36	145	11	11	3	1	1	2	14	3	19	0	0
Drahman, Brian, Indianapolis	0	0	.000	0.00	2	0	0	0	1	0	3.0	3	12	0	0	0	0	0	0	1	0	3	0	0
Duncan, Chip, Oklahoma City	0	0	.000	3.38	3	0	0	0	1	0	5.1	6	22	2	2	0	1	0	1	0	0	3	0	0
Duncan, Chip, New Orleans	1	4	.200	6.29	14	5	0	0	5	0	34.1	44	161	26	24	7	1	2	2	18	2	23	5	1
Hurst, James, Okla. City*	1	5	.167	7.33	28	7	0	0	11	4	46.2	71	236	40	38	6	2	0	3	25	0	42	4	0
Hurst, James, Indianapolis*	0	0	.000	5.40	3	0	0	0	2	1	3.1	2	13	2	2	1	0	0	0	1	0	1	0	0
Jean, Domingo, Okla. City	3	8	.273	6.14	24	13	1	0	9	1	88.0	102	418	70	60	12	4	2	1	61	1	72	14	3
Jean, Domingo, Indianapolis	0	1	.000	0.00	2	0	0	0	0	0	2.0	1	7	0	0	0	1	0	0	1	0	0	0	0
Olson, Gregg, Buffalo	1	0	1.000	2.49	18	0	0	0	17	13	21.2	16	92	6	6	0	1	0	3	9	0	25	0	0
Olson, Gregg, Omaha	0	0	.000	0.00	1	0	0	0	1	0	1.0	0	4	0	0	0	0	0	0	1	0	1	1	0
Slusarski, Joe, Buffalo	1	1	.500	6.32	4	2	0	0	0	0	15.2	18	67	12	11	2	0	1	1	4	0	9	0	0
Slusarski, Joe, New Orleans	1	1	.500	1.12	33	0	0	0	23	11	48.1	37	188	10	6	4	1	1	0	11	2	30	0	0
Taylor, Scott, New Orleans	1	0	1.000	2.38	2	2	0	0	0	0	11.1	10	47	3	3	0	0	1	3	0	9	0	0
Taylor, Scott, Oklahoma City	7	8	.467	3.66	22	19	1	1	0	0	118.0	122	510	59	48	12	4	2	6	38	0	65	5	0

1995 FIELDING

TEAM

Team	Pct.	G	PO	A	E	TC	DP	PB	Team	Pct.	G	PO	A	E	TC	DP	PB
New Orleans	.980	142	3641	1572	107	5320	163	17	Louisville	.972	144	3723	1455	147	5325	107	15
Buffalo	.979	144	3753	1592	115	5460	137	10	Oklahoma City	.972	144	3662	1506	151	5319	156	19
Iowa	.978	143	3721	1503	120	5344	137	11	Nashville	.971	144	3830	1600	163	5593	144	16
Omaha	.975	144	3715	1479	134	5328	158	21	Indianapolis	.971	144	3786	1441	157	5384	114	20

TRIPLE PLAY: Iowa.

INDIVIDUAL

FIRST BASEMEN

NOTE: All caps denotes fielding-percentage leader based on 72 games for catchers, 96 for all other non-pitchers and 144 innings for pitchers. *Throws lefthanded.

Player, Team	Pct.	G	PO	A	E	TC	DP
Anthony, Eric, Indianapolis*	.909	2	9	1	1	11	1
Aversa, Joe, Louisville	1.000	1	1	0	0	1	0
Barker, Tim, New Orleans	1.000	10	62	4	0	66	7
Belk, Tim, Indianapolis	.989	50	428	20	5	453	24
Bolick, Frank, Buffalo	1.000	1	9	0	0	9	1
Borrelli, Dean, Oklahoma City	.972	3	33	2	1	36	4
Brooks, Jerry, Louisville	1.000	7	64	5	0	69	5
Brown, Marty, Oklahoma City	1.000	2	22	2	0	24	2
Byington, John, Oklahoma City	.994	22	151	9	1	161	13
Caceres, Edgar, Omaha	1.000	2	23	0	0	23	1
Cholowsky, Dan, Louisville	.961	6	48	1	2	51	3
Clinton, Jim, Oklahoma City	1.000	3	20	3	0	23	1
Colon, Cris, Iowa	.984	52	357	24	6	387	31
Costo, Tim, Buffalo	.991	66	584	47	6	637	56
Coughlin, Kevin, Nashville*	1.000	2	14	0	0	14	1
Cron, Chris, Nashville	1.000	2	9	0	0	9	2
Deak, Darrel, Louisville	.983	45	333	16	6	355	28
Denson, Drew, Indianapolis	.983	15	108	9	2	119	19
Dismuke, Jamie, Indianapolis	.981	11	91	10	2	103	9
Dodson, Bo, New Orleans*	.995	47	400	32	2	434	40
Fariss, Monty, Iowa	1.000	7	62	3	0	65	5
Franco, Matt, Iowa	.996	36	222	18	1	241	26
Giannelli, Ray, Louisville	.988	17	71	9	1	81	10
Grotewold, Jeff, Omaha*	.981	85	745	49	15	809	84
Hamelin, Bob, Omaha*	.967	19	157	19	6	182	21
Horn, Sam, Oklahoma City*	1.000	2	11	0	0	11	0

Player, Team	Pct.	G	PO	A	E	TC	DP
Hunter, Brian, Indianapolis*	1.000	4	35	1	0	36	0
Jaha, John, New Orleans	1.000	1	9	2	0	11	3
Kieschnick, Brooks, Iowa	1.000	7	13	3	0	16	2
Kosco, Bryn, Iowa	.993	70	548	43	4	595	57
Lindeman, Jim, Oklahoma City	.989	74	640	48	8	696	67
Lopez, Luis, Buffalo	.989	27	252	17	3	272	23
Lovullo, Torey, Buffalo	.974	11	70	6	2	78	6
Lyden, Mitch, Omaha	1.000	6	18	3	0	21	2
Lyons, Barry, Nashville	.993	17	128	7	1	136	10
Martinez, Carmelo, Buffalo	.500	1	0	1	1	2	0
Martinez, Domingo, Louisville	.988	35	299	30	4	333	24
McCarty, Dave, Indianapolis*	.994	37	335	14	2	351	27
McCoy, Trey, Oklahoma City	1.000	7	64	3	0	67	11
Morris, Hal, Indianapolis*	1.000	2	13	2	0	15	0
Norman, Les, Omaha	1.000	1	1	0	1	0	0
Ortiz, Luis, Oklahoma City	1.000	1	6	0	0	6	2
Perry, Herbert, Buffalo	.994	48	419	44	3	466	42
Prager, Howard, Louisville*	.980	33	188	13	4	205	13
Pratt, Todd, Iowa	.963	6	23	3	1	27	0
ROBERTSON, Mike, Nashville*	.992	137	1172	75	10	1257	111
Sabo, Chris, Louisville	1.000	7	32	4	0	36	2
Schu, Rick, Oklahoma City	1.000	18	130	11	0	141	17
Singleton, Duane, New Orleans	1.000	1	3	0	0	3	0
Smith, Ed, Buffalo	1.000	1	1	0	0	1	0
Staton, Dave, New Orleans	.993	54	419	33	3	455	45
Stefanski, Mike, New Orleans	1.000	1	8	0	0	8	3
Stewart, Andy, Omaha	1.000	11	72	13	0	85	5
Sweeney, Mark, Louisville*	.990	22	176	19	2	197	14
Talanoa, Scott, New Orleans	1.000	5	30	3	0	33	3
Unroe, Tim, New Orleans	1.000	47	321	23	0	344	46
Vargas, Hector, Oklahoma City	1.000	22	154	10	0	164	18

Player, Team	Pct.	G	PO	A	E	TC	DP
Vitiello, Joe, Omaha	.984	28	221	21	4	246	26
Wachter, Derek, New Orleans	1.000	1	1	0	0	1	0
Woodson, Tracy, Louisville	.965	12	102	9	4	115	4
Worthington, Craig, Indianapolis	.996	30	217	26	1	244	15
Zeile, Todd, Louisville	.923	2	11	1	1	13	0

TRIPLE PLAY: Kosco.

SECOND BASEMEN

Player, Team	Pct.	G	PO	A	E	TC	DP
Arias, Amador, Indianapolis	.938	5	10	20	2	32	7
Aversa, Joe, Louisville	.951	32	28	49	4	81	5
Barker, Tim, New Orleans	1.000	23	48	55	0	103	19
Bell, David, Buf.-Lou.	.991	21	43	62	1	106	11
Benavides, Freddie, Iowa	1.000	1	2	5	0	7	2
BRADY, Doug, Nashville	.975	116	238	304	14	556	88
Bream, Scott, Iowa	.980	25	43	57	2	102	17
Brown, Marty, Oklahoma City	.955	6	8	13	1	22	1
Byington, John, Oklahoma City...	.941	15	26	38	4	68	8
Caceres, Edgar, Omaha	.977	8	18	25	1	44	7
Candaele, Casey, Buffalo	.985	52	103	165	4	272	27
Caraballo, Ramon, Louisville	.981	58	126	178	6	310	39
Cholowsky, Dan, Louisville	.950	6	7	12	1	20	0
Clinton, Jim, Oklahoma City	1.000	1	1	1	0	2	0
Colon, Cris, Iowa	.990	23	39	61	1	101	16
Deak, Darrel, Louisville	.959	45	71	92	7	170	16
Finn, John, New Orleans	.961	14	17	32	2	51	5
Flores, Miguel, Buffalo	.980	29	53	92	3	148	22
Gardner, Jeff, Iowa	.988	49	103	153	3	259	39
Giannelli, Ray, Louisville	1.000	2	1	2	0	3	1
Halter, Shane, Omaha	.921	21	42	51	8	101	15
Haney, Todd, Iowa	.975	33	64	95	4	163	16
Hecht, Steve, Oklahoma City	.965	32	65	99	6	170	28
Hinzo, Tommy, Oklahoma City	.955	56	112	122	11	245	41
Howard, Tim, Nashville	.984	12	32	28	1	61	8
Hulett, Tim, Lou.-O.C.	1.000	7	11	12	0	23	2
Johns, Keith, Louisville	1.000	3	7	4	0	11	1
Kessinger, Keith, Iowa	1.000	23	44	70	0	114	16
Kremblas, Frank, Indianapolis	.966	7	13	15	1	29	3
Lofton, Rodney, New Orleans	.983	57	98	134	4	236	35
Loretta, Mark, New Orleans	1.000	1	1	1	0	2	1
Lovullo, Torey, Buffalo	.984	69	132	175	5	312	47
Milstien, Dave, Nashville	1.000	2	5	5	0	10	2
Mota, Jose, Omaha	1.000	9	13	23	0	36	6
Owens, Eric, Indianapolis	.967	105	219	274	17	510	63
Pena, Geronimo, Louisville	.926	5	9	16	2	27	3
Reynolds, Harold, Omaha	.966	33	63	80	5	148	22
Ripken, Bill, Buffalo	1.000	4	13	12	0	25	2
Schu, Rick, Oklahoma City	1.000	3	6	7	0	13	1
Shave, Jon, Oklahoma City	.964	28	43	64	4	111	16
Sisco, Steve, Omaha	.956	7	16	27	2	45	8
Smith, Greg, N.O.-Ind.	.968	23	41	49	3	93	11
Stillwell, Kurt, Indianapolis	.980	28	39	61	2	102	7
Stynes, Chris, Omaha	.966	69	136	176	11	323	51
Vargas, Hector, Oklahoma City	.958	13	33	35	3	71	8
Weger, Wes, New Orleans	.974	53	115	145	7	267	48
Wilson, Brandon, Nash.-Ind	.951	21	33	64	5	102	8

SECOND BASEMEN WITH TWO OR MORE TEAMS

Player, Team	Pct.	G	PO	A	E	TC	DP
Bell, David, Buffalo	1.000	3	4	8	0	12	4
Bell, David, Louisville	.989	18	39	54	1	94	7
Hulett, Tim, Louisville	1.000	3	6	5	0	11	0
Hulett, Tim, Oklahoma City	1.000	4	5	7	0	12	2
Smith, Greg, New Orleans	.973	19	31	40	2	73	8
Smith, Greg, Indianapolis	.950	4	10	9	1	20	3
Wilson, Brandon, Nashville	.950	20	32	63	5	100	8
Wilson, Brandon, Indianapolis	1.000	1	1	1	0	2	0

THIRD BASEMEN

Player, Team	Pct.	G	PO	A	E	TC	DP
Anderson, Charlie, Louisville	1.000	1	1	0	0	1	0
Aversa, Joe, Louisville	.957	16	3	19	1	23	2
Barker, Tim, New Orleans	.902	18	6	31	4	41	3
Bell, David, Buffalo	.954	66	37	151	9	197	9
Benavides, Freddie, Iowa	.903	17	7	21	3	31	3
Bolick, Frank, Buffalo	.943	17	8	25	2	35	1
Bream, Scott, Iowa	1.000	1	0	2	0	2	0
Brooks, Jerry, Indianapolis	1.000	2	1	7	0	8	1
Brown, Chris, Indianapolis	1.000	2	1	2	0	3	0
Brown, Marty, Oklahoma City	.938	20	12	48	4	64	6
Buechele, Steve, Oklahoma City..	.818	3	3	6	2	11	0
Byington, John, N.O.-O.C.	.945	77	66	163	15	244	25

Player, Team	Pct.	G	PO	A	E	TC	DP
Caceres, Edgar, Omaha	1.000	15	8	32	0	40	0
Candaele, Casey, Buffalo	1.000	1	0	4	0	4	0
Cholowsky, Dan, Louisville	1.000	1	1	0	0	1	0
Colon, Cris, Iowa	.945	21	8	44	3	55	5
Costo, Tim, Buffalo	.750	3	1	2	1	4	0
Cron, Chris, Nashville	.833	10	8	17	5	30	1
Deak, Darrel, Louisville	.929	9	5	8	1	14	0
Dodson, Bo, New Orleans*	1.000	1	0	1	0	1	0
Finn, John, New Orleans	.667	1	1	1	1	3	0
Franco, Matt, Iowa	.925	95	61	161	18	240	11
Garber, Jeff, Omaha	1.000	3	0	2	0	2	0
Gardner, Jeff, Iowa	.857	7	4	8	2	14	2
Giannelli, Ray, Louisville	.900	5	3	6	1	10	1
Green, Gary, Omaha	.846	5	3	8	2	13	0
Greene, Willie, Indianapolis	.952	62	41	118	8	167	6
Grotewold, Jeff, Omaha	1.000	3	5	3	0	8	1
Gulan, Mike, Louisville	.948	54	38	90	7	135	2
Haney, Todd, Iowa	.938	16	12	33	3	48	4
Howard, Tim, Nashville	.930	19	10	43	4	57	5
Hubbard, Mike, Iowa	1.000	1	1	1	0	2	0
Hulett, Tim, Oklahoma City	1.000	4	4	9	0	13	2
Kosco, Bryn, Iowa	.833	8	5	5	2	12	0
Kremblas, Frank, Indianapolis	.900	12	3	24	3	30	4
Lockhart, Keith, Omaha	.928	37	31	72	8	111	10
Lofton, Rodney, New Orleans	.963	31	20	57	3	80	8
Lopez, Luis, Buffalo	.958	11	3	20	1	24	2
Loretta, Mark, New Orleans	1.000	4	3	9	0	12	0
Lovullo, Torey, Buffalo	.930	58	30	116	11	157	13
McClendon, Lloyd, Buffalo	1.000	2	0	1	0	1	0
Mercedes, Henry, Omaha	.895	7	1	16	2	19	2
Milstien, Dave, Nashville	1.000	4	4	7	0	11	1
Ortiz, Luis, Oklahoma City	.931	38	29	93	9	131	7
Randa, Joe, Omaha	.958	64	42	96	6	144	8
Reynolds, Harold, Omaha	1.000	2	1	7	0	8	0
SAENZ, Olmedo, Nashville	.939	111	82	289	24	395	24
Schu, Rick, Oklahoma City	.889	21	9	31	5	45	4
Singleton, Duane, New Orleans ..	1.000	1	0	1	0	1	0
Smith, Ed, Buffalo	1.000	2	3	1	0	4	0
Smith, Greg, New Orleans	.913	30	19	54	7	80	8
Snopek, Chris, Nashville	.714	3	0	5	2	7	0
Staton, Dave, New Orleans	1.000	2	0	1	0	1	0
Stefanski, Mike, New Orleans	1.000	3	1	2	0	3	0
Stewart, Andy, Omaha	.000	1	0	0	2	2	0
Stillwell, Kurt, Indianapolis	.904	24	17	49	7	73	6
Stynes, Chris, Omaha	.947	13	8	28	2	38	5
Sutko, Glenn, New Orleans	.750	2	1	5	2	8	1
Unroe, Tim, New Orleans	.940	67	51	137	12	200	16
Vargas, Hector, Oklahoma City	1.000	2	0	3	0	3	0
Weger, Wes, New Orleans	.941	5	6	10	1	17	1
Wolak, Jerry, Nashville	.667	1	0	2	1	3	0
Woodson, Tracy, Louisville	.960	75	58	160	9	227	16
Worthington, Craig, Indianapolis	.947	52	28	114	8	150	11

THIRD BASEMEN WITH TWO OR MORE TEAMS

Player, Team	Pct.	G	PO	A	E	TC	DP
Byington, John, New Orleans...	.885	11	3	20	3	26	1
Byington, John, Oklahoma City...	.945	66	63	143	12	218	24

SHORTSTOPS

Player, Team	Pct.	G	PO	A	E	TC	DP
Aversa, Joe, Louisville	.985	35	43	87	2	132	14
Barker, Tim, New Orleans	1.000	2	4	9	0	13	2
Bell, David, Buffalo	.900	5	5	13	2	20	4
Benavides, Freddie, Iowa	.968	85	113	220	11	344	49
Brady, Doug, Nashville	.800	1	1	3	1	5	0
Bream, Scott, Iowa	.857	2	3	3	1	7	0
Brown, Marty, Oklahoma City	.778	1	1	6	2	9	1
Caceres, Edgar, Omaha	.913	6	9	12	2	23	6
Candaele, Casey, Buffalo	.881	19	20	32	7	59	8
Caraballo, Ramon, Louisville	.969	8	8	23	1	32	5
Clinton, Jim, Oklahoma City	1.000	3	3	0	0	3	0
Elster, Kevin, Omaha	1.000	11	22	30	0	52	12
Fanning, Steve, Iowa	1.000	1	0	2	0	2	0
Figueroa, Bien, Oklahoma City	.974	9	11	26	1	38	4
Fraraccio, Dan, Nashville	.933	8	17	39	4	60	8
Goldberg, Lonnie, Okla. City	.975	8	7	32	1	40	4
Green, Gary, Omaha	1.000	19	20	52	0	72	8
Greene, Willie, Indianapolis	.933	14	14	42	4	60	5
Halter, Shane, Omaha	.9779	103	183	304	11	498	75
Haney, Todd, Iowa	.975	22	26	53	2	81	13
Hinzo, Tommy, Oklahoma City	.957	26	27	63	4	94	14
Holbert, Aaron, Louisville	.936	109	153	302	31	486	53
Hulett, Tim, Oklahoma City	.921	27	45	72	10	127	19

Player, Team	Pct.	G	PO	A	E	TC	DP
Johns, Keith, Louisville	1.000	1	0	5	0	5	0
Kessinger, Keith, Iowa	.931	41	47	115	12	174	28
Lee, Manuel, Louisville	1.000	6	4	3	0	7	2
Lofton, Rodney, New Orleans	1.000	5	6	13	0	19	4
Loretta, Mark, New Orleans	.958	123	200	366	25	591	79
Lovullo, Torey, Buffalo	1.000	2	3	6	0	9	2
Magdaleno, Ricky, Indianapolis	.833	3	1	4	1	6	0
Milstien, Dave, Nashville	.947	5	4	14	1	19	1
Mota, Jose, Omaha	.918	13	17	28	4	49	5
Noriega, Rey, Nashville	.871	17	23	31	8	62	5
Parra, Franklin, Oklahoma City	.800	4	3	9	3	15	1
Reese, Pokey, Indianapolis	.935	88	131	258	27	416	37
RIPKEN, Bill, Buffalo	.9782	126	150	389	12	551	80
Rivera, Luis, Oklahoma City	.962	19	24	51	3	78	11
Schu, Rick, Oklahoma City	.961	63	85	162	10	257	34
Smith, Greg, New Orleans	.974	15	21	53	2	76	13
Snopek, Chris, Nashville	.942	110	133	353	30	516	71
Stillwell, Kurt, Indianapolis	.960	44	56	113	7	176	27
Weger, Wes, New Orleans	.909	2	3	7	1	11	2
Wilson, Brandon, Nash.-Ind.	.902	10	9	28	4	41	6

TRIPLE PLAY: Benavides.

SHORTSTOPS WITH TWO OR MORE TEAMS

Player, Team	Pct.	G	PO	A	E	TC	DP
Wilson, Brandon, Nashville	.933	7	6	22	2	30	6
Wilson, Brandon, Indianapolis	.818	3	3	6	2	11	0

OUTFIELDERS

Player, Team	Pct.	G	PO	A	E	TC	DP
Amaro, Ruben, Buffalo	.990	49	102	2	1	105	0
Anthony, Eric, Indianapolis*	1.000	2	2	0	0	2	0
Barker, Tim, New Orleans	1.000	34	41	2	0	43	0
Basse, Mike, New Orleans*	.988	91	150	8	2	160	0
Battle, Allen, Louisville	.982	47	106	1	2	109	0
Belk, Tim, Indianapolis	1.000	7	12	1	0	13	0
Bess, Johnny, Indianapolis	1.000	1	1	0	0	1	0
Bradshaw, Terry, Louisville	.969	107	248	1	8	257	0
Briley, Greg, Indianapolis	.972	44	69	1	2	72	0
Brooks, Jerry, Indianapolis	.932	32	39	2	3	44	0
Brown, Marty, Oklahoma City	1.000	1	1	0	0	1	0
Bruett, J.T., Omaha*	.977	39	84	0	2	86	0
Burnitz, Jeromy, Buffalo	.981	127	241	12	5	258	0
Burton, Darren, Omaha	1.000	2	6	0	0	6	0
Caceres, Edgar, Omaha	1.000	2	1	0	0	1	0
Cameron, Stanton, Okla. City	1.000	5	8	2	0	10	1
Candaele, Casey, Buffalo	.962	30	49	1	2	52	0
Cappuccio, Carmine, Nashville	.978	51	86	3	2	91	2
Carter, Mike, Iowa	.980	97	189	7	4	200	1
Chamberlain, Wes, Omaha	1.000	14	24	2	0	26	1
Chance, Tony, Oklahoma City	.990	58	90	6	1	97	1
Cholowsky, Dan, Louisville	.973	61	104	4	3	111	0
Coleman, Vince, Omaha	.950	9	19	0	1	20	0
Cookson, Brent, Omaha	1.000	26	56	3	0	59	1
Costo, Tim, Buffalo	.909	12	10	0	1	11	0
Cotto, Henry, Nashville	.833	5	5	0	1	6	0
Coughlin, Kevin, Nashville*	1.000	6	12	0	0	12	0
Diggs, Tony, Louisville	1.000	18	21	1	0	22	0
Dodson, Bo, New Orleans*	1.000	7	10	1	0	11	0
Dostal, Bruce, Oklahoma City*	.986	81	204	7	3	214	1
Finn, John, New Orleans	.972	23	33	2	1	36	0
Fox, Eric, Oklahoma City*	.982	87	157	4	3	164	0
Giannelli, Ray, Louisville	.983	95	164	9	3	176	2
Gibralter, Steve, Indianapolis	.977	78	207	2	5	214	0
Giles, Brian, Buffalo*	.981	118	248	4	5	257	0
Gilkey, Bernard, Louisville	1.000	2	2	0	0	2	0
Glanville, Doug, Iowa	.982	101	209	9	4	222	3
Gordon, Keith, Indianapolis	.988	80	155	3	2	160	2
Greene, Willie, Indianapolis	1.000	3	5	0	0	5	0
Haney, Todd, Iowa	.957	13	21	1	1	23	1
Hare, Shawn, Oklahoma City*	.966	63	110	4	4	118	2
Harris, Donald, Oklahoma City	1.000	10	23	1	0	24	0
Harris, Mike, New Orleans*	1.000	4	5	1	0	6	0
Hatcher, Billy, Omaha	.981	26	52	0	1	53	0
Hecht, Steve, Oklahoma City	.985	30	64	3	1	68	0
Hiatt, Phil, Omaha	.974	19	37	1	1	39	0
Hosey, Dwayne, Omaha	.971	62	125	10	4	139	2
Howitt, Dann, Nash.-Buf.	.973	45	67	4	2	73	0
Hughes, Keith, Omaha*	.965	74	130	9	5	144	2
Humphreys, Mike, Buffalo	1.000	33	80	4	0	84	1
Hunter, Brian, Indianapolis*	.889	7	7	1	1	9	0
Jose, Felix, Iowa	1.000	8	12	0	0	12	0
Kieschnick, Brooks, Iowa	.989	117	166	12	2	180	1
KOSLOFSKI, Kevin, New Orleans	.996	101	231	19	1	251	2

Player, Team	Pct.	G	PO	A	E	TC	DP
Kremblas, Frank, Indianapolis	1.000	2	6	0	0	6	0
Lindeman, Jim, Oklahoma City	1.000	1	1	0	0	1	0
Long, Kevin, Omaha*	1.000	18	32	0	0	32	0
Lopez, Luis, Buffalo	1.000	7	5	1	0	6	0
Mabry, John, Louisville	.889	4	8	0	1	9	0
Marini, Marc, Buffalo*	1.000	18	17	1	0	18	0
Martinez, Carmelo, Buffalo	1.000	2	2	0	0	2	0
Martinez, Manny, Iowa	.983	108	281	16	5	302	2
McClendon, Lloyd, Buffalo	.941	24	32	0	2	34	0
McNeely, Jeff, Louisville	.993	98	144	1	1	146	0
Miller, Keith, Omaha	1.000	1	2	0	0	2	0
Mitchell, Keith, Indianapolis	.979	65	136	4	3	143	1
Mota, Jose, Omaha	1.000	3	4	1	0	5	0
Mottola, Chad, Indianapolis	.976	69	151	11	4	166	2
Mouton, Lyle, Nashville	.978	62	123	8	3	134	1
Nilsson, Dave, New Orleans	1.000	1	2	0	0	2	0
Norman, Les, Omaha	.979	81	180	8	4	192	1
Pledger, Kinnis, Iowa	1.000	5	7	0	0	7	0
Ramsey, Fernando, Nashville	.973	87	211	4	6	221	1
Ritchie, Gregg, Oklahoma City*	1.000	6	11	0	0	11	0
Robertson, Mike, Nashville*	.889	5	8	0	1	9	0
Rohrmeier, Dan, Indianapolis	1.000	8	10	0	0	10	0
Sagmoen, Marc, Oklahoma City*	.980	54	97	3	2	102	0
Schu, Rick, Oklahoma City	.917	7	11	0	1	12	0
Singleton, Duane, New Orleans	.978	85	165	12	4	181	2
Smith, Ed, Buffalo	.750	9	9	0	3	12	0
Staton, Dave, New Orleans	1.000	2	1	0	0	1	0
Thomas, Skeets, Louisville	.969	57	87	7	3	97	1
Tucker, Michael, Omaha	.986	70	133	11	2	146	1
Unroe, Tim, New Orleans	1.000	1	1	0	0	1	0
Valrie, Kerry, Nashville	.972	124	265	11	8	284	6
Vargas, Hector, Oklahoma City	.971	47	62	6	2	70	2
Vitiello, Joe, Omaha	1.000	2	4	0	0	4	0
Wachter, Derek, New Orleans	.983	107	157	17	3	177	3
Ward, Turner, New Orleans	.900	9	9	0	1	10	0
Wilson, Nigel, Indianapolis*	.958	69	111	4	5	120	1
Wolak, Jerry, Nashville	.970	83	155	8	5	168	0
Yelding, Eric, Buffalo	.979	19	45	2	1	48	0
Young, Dmitri, Louisville	.750	2	3	0	1	4	0
Zupcic, Bob, Nashville	.923	9	9	3	1	13	0

TRIPLE PLAY: M. Martinez.

OUTFIELDERS WITH TWO OR MORE TEAMS

Player, Team	Pct.	G	PO	A	E	TC	DP
Howitt, Dann, Nashville	1.000	14	14	2	0	16	0
Howitt, Dann, Buffalo	.965	31	53	2	2	57	0

CATCHERS

Player, Team	Pct.	G	PO	A	E	TC	DP	PB
Borrelli, Dean, Oklahoma City	.997	49	282	24	1	307	1	4
Brooks, Jerry, Indianapolis	.986	52	323	22	5	350	1	12
Brown, Kevin, Oklahoma City	.750	2	6	0	2	8	0	0
Cox, Darron, Iowa	.986	28	187	18	3	208	4	1
Deak, Brian, Louisville	.993	51	247	18	2	267	0	4
DiFelice, Mike, Louisville	.984	21	111	10	2	123	2	2
Dorsett, Brian, Indianapolis	.982	87	506	34	10	550	4	5
Fordyce, Brook, Buffalo	.991	51	306	18	3	327	2	2
Gonzalez, Javier, New Orleans	.996	43	239	27	1	267	5	4
Gousha, Sean, Iowa	1.000	2	7	0	0	7	0	0
Hemond, Scott, Louisville	1.000	1	6	0	0	6	0	1
Hubbard, Mike, Iowa	.982	71	446	33	9	488	3	8
Kennedy, Darryl, Okla. City	.931	3	24	3	2	29	0	0
Kmak, Joe, Iowa	.992	33	209	26	2	237	3	1
Knapp, Mike, Indianapolis	1.000	13	60	3	0	63	0	1
Levis, Jesse, Buffalo	.994	60	338	20	2	360	5	3
Lopez, Luis, Buffalo	1.000	4	12	1	0	13	1	0
Lopez, Pedro, New Orleans	1.000	2	14	1	0	15	0	0
Luce, Roger, Oklahoma City	1.000	1	6	0	0	6	0	0
Lyden, Mitch, Omaha	.993	44	269	28	2	299	5	5
Lyons, Barry, Nashville	1.000	31	172	15	0	187	3	1
Machado, Robert, Nashville	.972	15	87	17	3	107	1	2
Martindale, Ryan, Buffalo	.978	11	41	4	1	46	0	1
Marzano, John, Okla. City	.992	93	551	64	5	620	12	4
Matheny, Mike, New Orleans	1.000	6	30	4	0	34	0	0
Mercedes, Henry, Omaha	.987	78	418	55	6	479	9	12
O'Halloran, Greg, Iowa	.935	5	28	1	2	31	0	1
Oliver, Joe, New Orleans	1.000	3	14	7	0	21	1	0
Ortiz, Junior, Nashville	.985	56	301	31	5	337	4	8
Pagnozzi, Tom, Louisville	1.000	5	19	0	0	19	0	0
Pratt, Todd, Iowa	.985	8	59	5	1	65	0	0
Rolls, David, Oklahoma City	1.000	2	15	1	0	16	0	1
RONAN, Marc, Louisville	.993	76	417	35	3	455	1	8
Sellers, Rick, Indianapolis	1.000	5	19	4	0	23	0	2

Player, Team	Pct.	G	PO	A	E	TC	DP	PB
Stefanski, Mike, New Orleans	.995	70	355	35	2	392	5	7
Stewart, Andy, Omaha	.981	25	140	16	3	159	2	3
Strickland, Chad, Omaha	1.000	8	32	3	0	35	0	1
Sutko, Glenn, New Orleans	.991	39	192	20	2	214	2	6
Tremie, Chris, Nashville	.998	67	394	30	1	425	5	5
Wrona, Rick, Buf.-Lou.	.992	44	224	20	2	246	4	4

CATCHERS WITH TWO OR MORE TEAMS

Player, Team	Pct.	G	PO	A	E	TC	DP	PB
Wrona, Rick, Buffalo	.995	31	167	16	1	184	3	4
Wrona, Rick, Louisville	.984	13	57	4	1	62	1	0

PITCHERS

Player, Team	Pct.	G	PO	A	E	TC	DP
Abbott, Paul, Iowa	.941	46	6	10	1	17	4
Adams, Terry, Iowa	1.000	7	1	2	0	3	0
Alberro, Jose, Okla. City	1.000	20	6	15	0	21	0
Anderson, Mike, Iowa	.971	27	17	17	1	35	0
Anderson, Scott, Omaha	.944	15	8	9	1	18	1
Archer, Kurt, New Orleans	1.000	38	1	7	0	8	0
Austin, Jim, Buffalo	.750	2	0	3	1	4	0
Bailey, Cory, Louisville	1.000	55	6	10	0	16	0
Baldwin, James, Nashville	.947	18	3	15	1	19	0
Barber, Brian, Louisville	.850	20	4	13	3	20	1
Barfield, John, Okla. City*	1.000	4	1	1	0	2	0
Batchelor, Richard, Louisville	.882	50	9	6	2	17	0
Beatty, Blaine, Indianapolis*	1.000	20	2	9	0	11	1
BELL, Eric, Buffalo*	1.000	28	11	27	0	38	3
Beltran, Rigo, Louisville*	.913	24	9	12	2	23	0
Benes, Alan, Louisville	1.000	11	6	5	0	11	1
Bere, Jason, Nashville	.500	1	0	1	1	2	0
Bertotti, Mike, Nashville*	1.000	7	1	1	0	2	0
Bevil, Brian, Omaha	1.000	6	0	1	0	1	0
Bluma, Jaime, Omaha	1.000	18	5	3	0	8	2
Bolton, Rodney, Nashville	1.000	20	12	20	0	32	6
Bolton, Tom, Nashville*	.944	19	3	14	1	18	0
Boze, Marshall, New Orleans	1.000	23	9	11	0	20	3
Brandenburg, Mark, Okla. City	.800	35	2	6	2	10	1
Brewer, Billy, Omaha*	1.000	6	1	1	0	2	0
Bronkey, Jeff, New Orleans	1.000	2	0	1	0	1	0
Brown, Kevin, Omaha	.800	7	1	3	1	5	0
Browning, Tom, Omaha*	1.000	5	3	1	0	4	0
Brumley, Duff, Okla. City	.500	3	0	1	1	2	0
Buckels, Gary, Louisville	.875	13	5	2	1	8	0
Buckley, Travis, Indianapolis	.938	23	10	20	2	32	1
Bunch, Mel, Omaha	1.000	12	6	7	0	13	1
Busby, Mike, Louisville	.833	6	4	1	1	6	0
Bushing, Chris, Okla. City	.000	3	0	0	1	1	0
Caceres, Edgar, Omaha	1.000	1	2	0	0	2	0
Cadaret, Greg, Louisville*	.750	12	0	3	1	4	0
Campbell, Mike, Iowa	1.000	21	5	15	0	20	0
Carpenter, Cris, Louisville	1.000	49	5	9	0	14	0
Casian, Larry, Iowa*	1.000	13	0	7	0	7	0
Chapin, Darrin, Buffalo	1.000	6	1	1	0	2	0
Cimorelli, Frank, Louisville	1.000	6	0	2	0	2	1
Clark, Mark, Buffalo	1.000	5	4	6	0	10	1
Combs, Pat, New Orleans*	1.000	12	0	1	0	1	0
Costello, Fred, Nashville	.667	7	1	1	1	3	0
Courtright, John, Indianapolis*	1.000	13	2	3	0	5	0
Crawford, Carlos, Buffalo	.833	13	0	5	1	6	1
Creek, Doug, Louisville*	1.000	26	4	3	0	7	0
Curtis, Chris, Okla. City	.750	51	2	10	4	16	0
Dabney, Fred, Iowa*	1.000	33	5	10	0	15	0
Davis, Storm, Indianapolis	1.000	4	1	1	0	2	1
DeJesus, Jose, Omaha	1.000	36	0	8	0	8	0
DeLaRosa, Francisco, Louisville	.947	28	8	10	1	19	0
Dettmer, John, Okla. City	1.000	5	0	1	0	1	0
Dibble, Rob, New Orleans	1.000	4	1	0	0	1	0
Dixon, Steve, Iowa*	.875	53	2	5	1	8	0
Dorlarque, Aaron, Omaha	.900	24	1	8	1	10	0
Drahman, Brian, O.C.-Ind.	1.000	24	2	3	0	5	0
Duncan, Chip, O.C.-N.O.	1.000	17	0	2	0	2	0
Eddy, Chris, Omaha*	1.000	14	0	1	0	1	0
Edens, Tom, Iowa	1.000	20	2	3	0	5	0
Ellis, Robert, Nashville	1.000	4	1	3	0	4	0
Embree, Alan, Buffalo*	1.000	30	2	3	0	5	0
Farrell, John, Buffalo	.911	29	14	27	4	45	1
Farrell, Mike, New Orleans*	1.000	25	9	17	0	26	4
Ferry, Mike, Indianapolis	1.000	3	0	2	0	2	0
Fleming, Dave, Omaha*	1.000	3	0	2	0	2	0
Frascatore, John, Louisville	.895	28	10	7	2	19	0
Fritz, John, New Orleans	.923	41	6	6	1	13	0
Frohwirth, Todd, Buffalo	1.000	26	1	5	0	6	0
Fyhrie, Mike, Omaha	1.000	14	7	6	0	13	1
Gajkowski, Steve, Nashville	1.000	15	4	2	0	6	0
Ganote, Joe, New Orleans	1.000	14	4	15	0	19	0
Garces, Rich, Iowa	1.000	23	3	2	0	5	0
Garrelts, Scott, Omaha	1.000	9	2	1	0	3	1
Geeve, Dave, Okla. City	1.000	10	3	7	0	10	0
Givens, Brian, New Orleans*	.867	16	3	10	2	15	0
Goetz, Barry, Oklahoma City	.895	40	5	12	2	19	4
Gozzo, Mauro, Iowa	.875	6	4	3	1	8	0
Grant, Mark, Iowa	1.000	11	7	7	0	14	1
Graves, Daniel, Buffalo	1.000	3	0	1	0	1	0
Grimsley, Jason, Buffalo	1.000	10	6	10	0	16	2
Grott, Matt, Indianapolis*	.833	25	4	6	2	12	0
Hammaker, Atlee, Nashville*	1.000	15	3	5	0	8	0
Harris, Pep, Buffalo	.875	14	3	4	1	8	1
Harrison, Brian, Omaha	1.000	16	2	6	0	8	0
Helling, Rick, Okla. City	1.000	20	4	14	0	18	0
Heredia, Wilson, Okla. City	1.000	8	3	0	0	3	0
Hurst, James, O.C.-Ind.*	1.000	31	2	2	0	4	0
Ignasiak, Mike, New Orleans	1.000	4	0	2	0	2	0
Jarvis, Kevin, Indianapolis	1.000	10	7	3	0	10	0
Jean, Domingo, O.C.-Ind.	.900	26	7	11	2	20	0
Johnson, Dane, New Orleans	.800	46	0	4	1	5	0
Jones, Calvin, Nashville	1.000	5	1	0	0	1	0
Jones, Stacy, New Orleans	1.000	34	4	3	0	7	0
Karchner, Matt, Nashville	.833	28	4	6	2	12	3
Karl, Scott, New Orleans*	.923	8	2	10	1	13	2
Keyser, Brian, Nashville	1.000	10	8	14	0	22	0
Kiefer, Mark, New Orleans	1.000	12	8	9	0	17	2
Kilgo, Rusty, Indianapolis*	1.000	2	0	1	0	1	0
Klink, Joe, Buffalo*	.889	45	2	6	1	9	1
KUTZLER, Jerry, Omaha	1.000	37	19	19	0	38	2
Lacy, Kerry, Oklahoma City	1.000	1	0	1	0	1	0
Lancaster, Les, Buffalo	.944	45	7	10	1	18	0
Levine, Alan, Nashville	1.000	3	1	0	0	1	0
Lewis, James, Buffalo	1.000	18	9	12	0	21	0
Linton, Doug, Omaha	.824	18	2	12	3	17	1
Lopez, Albie, Buffalo	.929	18	5	8	1	14	2
Lorraine, Andrew, Nashville*	1.000	7	0	2	0	2	0
Lynch, David, Buffalo*	1.000	14	5	1	0	6	0
Magnante, Mike, Omaha*	.941	15	4	12	1	17	1
Mallicoat, Rob, Omaha*	1.000	3	0	1	0	1	0
Marquez, Isidrio, Nashville	1.000	46	2	11	0	13	1
Martinez, Frankie, Louisville	1.000	38	4	11	0	15	0
Mathews, T.J., Louisville	1.000	32	5	5	0	10	0
Mathile, Mike, Indianapolis	1.000	14	5	2	0	7	2
McAndrew, Jamie, New Orleans...	.923	17	11	13	2	26	2
McClellan, Paul, New Orleans	1.000	3	1	3	0	4	0
Meier, Kevin, Iowa	1.000	3	0	3	0	3	1
Melendez, Jose, Omaha	1.000	21	1	4	0	5	0
Milacki, Bob, Omaha	.944	15	7	10	1	18	1
Minchey, Nate, Louisville	.920	26	7	16	2	25	1
Mongiello, Mike, Nashville	1.000	31	9	8	0	17	0
Moore, Marcus, Indianapolis	1.000	7	0	1	0	1	0
Morton, Kevin, Iowa*	.950	28	8	11	1	20	1
Munoz, J.J., Omaha*	.875	57	8	6	2	16	0
Myers, Rod, Omaha	1.000	38	4	7	0	11	0
Nabholz, Chris, Iowa*	1.000	6	0	2	0	2	0
Nichting, Chris, Okla. City	1.000	23	6	6	0	12	1
Nitkowski, C.J., Indianapolis*	1.000	6	1	5	0	6	0
Novoa, Rafael, Nashville*	1.000	3	1	1	0	2	0
Ogea, Chad, Buffalo	1.000	4	1	5	0	6	0
Olsen, Steve, Nashville	1.000	14	4	6	0	10	0
Olson, Gregg, Buf.-Oma.	1.000	19	1	6	0	7	0
Osborne, Donovan, Louisville*	1.000	1	2	1	0	3	0
Pall, Donn, New Orleans	1.000	44	5	14	0	19	0
Parker, Clay, New Orleans	1.000	2	1	0	0	1	0
Patterson, Danny, Okla. City	.818	14	5	4	2	11	1
Perez, David, Oklahoma City	.875	20	6	22	4	32	3
Perry, Pat, Omaha*	1.000	5	0	1	0	1	0
Perschke, Greg, Buffalo	1.000	3	1	3	0	4	0
Petkovsek, Mark, Louisville	.905	8	6	13	2	21	0
Pittsley, Jim, Omaha	1.000	8	1	4	0	5	0
Popplewell, Tom, New Orleans	1.000	10	0	2	0	2	0
Prager, Howard, Louisville*	1.000	2	1	0	0	1	0
Pugh, Tim, Indianapolis	.750	6	2	1	1	4	0
Raczka, Mike, Louisville*	.889	55	7	9	2	18	2
Rambo, Dan, New Orleans	1.000	7	5	3	0	8	0
Rasmussen, Dennis, Omaha*	1.000	10	1	14	0	15	1
Reed, Rick, Indianapolis	.964	22	7	20	1	28	1
Remlinger, Mike, Indianapolis*	.889	41	4	4	1	9	0
Righetti, Dave, Nashville*	.750	16	1	11	4	16	0
Rightnowar, Ron, New Orleans	1.000	25	4	7	0	11	1
Roa, Joe, Buffalo	.950	25	13	25	2	40	3

Player, Team	Pct.	G	PO	A	E	TC	DP
Roberson, Sid, New Orleans*	1.000	4	1	1	0	2	0
Roper, John, Indianapolis	1.000	8	3	7	0	10	0
Ruffin, Johnny, Indianapolis	.875	36	4	3	1	8	0
Salkeld, Roger, Indianapolis	.929	20	3	10	1	14	1
Sauveur, Rich, Indianapolis*	1.000	52	6	13	0	19	2
Scanlan, Bob, New Orleans	1.000	3	1	0	0	1	0
Schuermann, Lance, Okla. City*	1.000	33	3	8	0	11	0
Scudder, Scott, Indianapolis	.889	7	1	7	1	9	0
Seminara, Frank, New Orleans	.571	11	2	2	3	7	0
Service, Scott, Indianapolis	1.000	36	5	3	0	8	0
Shifflett, Steve, Iowa	.929	26	7	6	1	14	1
Shinall, Zak, New Orleans	1.000	9	1	2	0	3	0
Shuey, Paul, Buffalo	.667	25	0	2	1	3	0
Simas, Bill, Nashville	1.000	7	0	2	0	2	0
Simmons, Scott, Louisville*	1.000	2	1	3	0	4	0
Sirotka, Mike, Nashville*	.818	8	1	8	2	11	2
Slusarski, Joe, N.O.	1.000	37	4	6	0	10	0
Smith, Ottis, Iowa*	1.000	5	0	4	0	4	0
Steenstra, Kennie, Iowa	.978	29	14	31	1	46	2
Strange, Don, Omaha	1.000	9	1	3	0	4	0
Sturtze, Tanyon, Iowa	1.000	23	3	16	0	19	0
Sullivan, Scott, Indianapolis	.846	44	4	7	2	13	1
Swartzbaugh, Dave, Iowa	1.000	30	3	6	0	9	1
Swingle, Paul, New Orleans	1.000	35	4	1	0	5	0
Taylor, Rob, Iowa	.909	54	2	8	1	11	0
Taylor, Scott, N.O.-O.C.	1.000	24	12	17	0	29	1
Telford, Anthony, Buffalo	.933	16	9	5	1	15	0
Thomas, Mike, New Orleans*	1.000	35	1	2	0	3	0
Torres, Dilson, Omaha	.833	5	4	1	1	6	0
Toth, Robert, Omaha	.857	8	3	3	1	7	0
Turner, Matt, Buffalo	1.000	13	0	1	0	1	0
Urbani, Tom, Louisville*	1.000	2	1	1	0	2	0
Vasquez, Marcos, Indianapolis	1.000	2	2	0	0	2	0
Vierra, Joey, Nashville*	1.000	56	2	6	0	8	1
Viola, Frank, Indianapolis*	.857	6	4	2	1	7	1
Vosberg, Ed, Oklahoma City*	1.000	1	0	1	0	1	0
Walker, Mike, Iowa	1.000	16	4	4	0	8	1
Warren, Brian, Indianapolis	.933	41	2	12	1	15	1
Watson, Allen, Louisville*	1.000	4	3	5	0	8	1
Wilson, Steve, Nashville*	.900	20	3	6	1	10	0
Wishnevski, Rob, Okla. City	.963	41	16	10	1	27	2

PITCHERS WITH TWO OR MORE TEAMS

Player, Team	Pct.	G	PO	A	E	TC	DP
Drahman, Brian, Okla. City	1.000	22	2	3	0	5	0
Drahman, Brian, Indianapolis	.000	2	0	0	0	0	0
Duncan, Chip, Oklahoma City	.000	3	0	0	0	0	0
Duncan, Chip, New Orleans	1.000	14	0	2	0	2	0
Hurst, James, Okla. City*	1.000	28	2	2	0	4	0
Hurst, James, Indianapolis*	.000	3	0	0	0	0	0
Jean, Domingo, Okla. City	.889	24	7	9	2	18	0
Jean, Domingo, Indianapolis	1.000	2	0	2	0	2	0
Olson, Gregg, Buffalo	1.000	18	1	6	0	7	0
Olson, Gregg, Omaha	.000	1	0	0	0	0	0
Slusarski, Joe, Buffalo	1.000	4	1	1	0	2	0
Slusarski, Joe, New Orleans	1.000	33	3	5	0	8	0
Taylor, Scott, New Orleans	1.000	2	2	0	0	2	0
Taylor, Scott, Oklahoma City	1.000	22	10	17	0	27	1

The following players did not have any fielding statistics at the positions indicated or appeared only as a designated hitter, pinch-hitter or pinch-runner: Aversa, of; Belcher, p; Bolick, ss; Burrows, p; Converse, p; Darwin, p; C. Davis, p; J. Davis, p; DeLeon, p; Diggs, ss; Donnelly, p; Fordyce, of; Franco, c, p; Fraraccio, 3b; Goldberg, 3b; Green, p; M. Harris, 1b; R. Harris, p; Howard, ss, of; Howitt, 1b; Huisman, p; D. Jackson, p; M. Jackson, p; James, dh; Johns, 3b; Lofton, c; Magdaleno, 3b; Noriega, p; O'Halloran, of; J. Ortiz, dh, ph; Parra, of; Pennington, p; Dan. Perez, dh, ph, pr; Pierce, p; Poole, p; Riles, dh, ph; Ruffcorn, p; Santana, p; Stefanski, of; Stewart, of; Talanoa, p; Trafton, ph; B. Wilson, of; A. Young, p.

LEAGUE CHAMPIONS

Year	Team	Pct.
1902—	Indianapolis	.683
1903—	St. Paul	.657
1904—	St. Paul	.646
1905—	Columbus	.658
1906—	Columbus	.615
1907—	Columbus	.584
1908—	Indianapolis	.601
1909—	Louisville	.554
1910—	Minneapolis	.637
1911—	Minneapolis	.600
1912—	Minneapolis	.636
1913—	Milwaukee	.599
1914—	Milwaukee	.590
1915—	Minneapolis	.597
1916—	Louisville	.605
1917—	Indianapolis	.588
1918—	Kansas City	.589
1919—	St. Paul	.610
1920—	St. Paul	.701
1921—	Louisville	.583
1922—	St. Paul	.641
1923—	Kansas City	.675
1924—	St. Paul	.578
1925—	Louisville	.635
1926—	Louisville	.629
1927—	Toledo	.601
1928—	Indianapolis	.593
1929—	Kansas City	.665
1930—	Louisville	.608
1931—	St. Paul	.623
1932—	Minneapolis	.595
1933—	Columbus*	.604
	Minneapolis	.562
1934—	Minneapolis	.570
	Columbus*	.556
1935—	Minneapolis	.591
1936—	Milwaukee†	.584
1937—	Columbus†	.584
1938—	St. Paul	.596
	Kansas City (2nd)‡	.556
1939—	Kansas City	.695
	Louisville (4th)‡	.490
1940—	Kansas City	.625
	Louisville (4th)‡	.500
1941—	Columbus†	.621

Year	Team	Pct.
1942—	Kansas City	.549
	Columbus (3rd)‡	.532
1943—	Milwaukee	.596
	Columbus (3rd)‡	.532
1944—	Milwaukee	.667
	Louisville (3rd)‡	.574
1945—	Milwaukee	.604
	Louisville (3rd)‡	.545
1946—	Louisville†	.601
1947—	Kansas City	.608
	Milwaukee (3rd)†	.513
1948—	Indianapolis	.649
	St. Paul (3rd)‡	.558
1949—	St. Paul	.608
	Indianapolis (2nd)‡	.604
1950—	Minneapolis	.584
	Columbus (3rd)‡	.549
1951—	Milwaukee†	.623
1952—	Milwaukee	.656
	Kansas City (2nd)‡	.578
1953—	Toledo	.584
	Kansas City (2nd)‡	.571
1954—	Indianapolis	.625
	Louisville (2nd)‡	.556
1955—	Minneapolis†	.597
1956—	Indianapolis†	.597
1957—	Wichita	.604
	Denver (2nd)†	.584
1958—	Charleston	.589
	Minneapolis (3rd)‡	.536
1959—	Louisville§	.599
	Omaha§	.516
	Minneapolis (2nd)‡	.586
1960—	Denver	.571
	Louisville (2nd)‡	.556
1961—	Indianapolis	.573
	Louisville (2nd)‡	.553
1962—	Indianapolis	.605
	Louisville (4th)‡	.486
1963-1968—Did not operate.		
1969—	Omaha	.607
1970—	Omaha*	.529
	Denver	.504
1971—	Indianapolis	.604
	Denver*	.521
1972—	Wichita	.621
	Evansville*	.593

Year	Team	Pct.
1973—	Iowa	.610
	Tulsa*	.504
1974—	Indianapolis	.578
	Tulsa*	.567
1975—	Evansville*	.566
	Denver	.569
1976—	Denver*	.632
	Omaha	.574
1977—	Omaha	.563
	Denver*	.522
1978—	Indianapolis	.578
	Omaha*	.489
1979—	Evansville*	.574
	Oklahoma City	.533
1980—	Denver	.676
	Springfield*	.551
1981—	Omaha	.581
	Denver*	.559
1982—	Indianapolis*	.551
	Omaha	.518
1983—	Louisville	.578
	Denver‡	.545
1984—	Denver	.513
	Louisville‡	.510
1985—	Oklahoma City	.556
	Louisville*	.521
1986—	Indianapolis*	.563
	Denver	.535
1987—	Denver	.564
	Indianapolis‡	.536
1988—	Indianapolis	.627
	Omaha	.570
1989—	Indianapolis*	.596
	Omaha	.507
1990—	Omaha*	.589
	Nashville	.585
1991—	Buffalo	.566
	Denver*	.549
1992—	Buffalo	.604
	Oklahoma City*	.514
1993—	Iowa*	.590
	Nashville	.566
1994—	Indianapolis‡	.601
	Nashville	.576
1995—	Indianapolis	.611
	Louisville‡	.514

*Won playoff (East vs. West). †Won championship and four-team playoff. ‡Won four-team playoff. §Respective Eastern and Western division winners.

INTERNATIONAL LEAGUE

LEAGUE OFFICE

President
Randy Mobley

Address
55 S. High St., Suite 202
Dublin, OH 43017

Phone
614-791-9300

TEAMS

CHARLOTTE KNIGHTS

General manager
Bill Lavelle
Manager
Sal Rende
Ballpark (capacity, surface)
Knights Stadium (10,000, grass)
Affiliation
Marlins
Address
P.O. Box 1207
Fort Mill, SC 29716
Phone
803-548-8050

COLUMBUS CLIPPERS

General manager
Ken Schnacke
Manager
Stump Merrill
Ballpark (capacity, surface)
Cooper Stadium (15,000, artificial)
Affiliation
Yankees
Address
1155 W. Mound St.
Columbus, OH 43223
Phone
614-462-5250

NORFOLK TIDES

General manager
Dave Rosenfield
Manager
Bobby Valentine
Ballpark (capacity, surface)
Harbor Park (12,059, grass)
Affiliation
Mets
Address
150 Park Ave.
Norfolk, VA 23510
Phone
804-622-2222

OTTAWA LYNX

General manager
P.J. Loyello
Manager
Pete Mackanin
Ballpark (capacity, surface)
Ottawa Stadium (10,332, grass)
Affiliation
Expos
Address
300 Coventry Rd.
Ottawa, Ontario K1K 4P5
Phone
613-747-5969

PAWTUCKET RED SOX

General manager
Lou Schwechheimer
Manager
Buddy Bailey
Ballpark (capacity, surface)
McCoy Stadium (7,002, grass)
Affiliation
Red Sox
Address
P.O. Box 2365
Pawtucket, RI 02861
Phone
401-724-7300

RICHMOND BRAVES

General manager
Bruce Baldwin
Manager
Bill Dancy
Ballpark (capacity, surface)
The Diamond (12,156, grass)
Affiliation
Braves
Address
P.O. Box 6667
Richmond, VA 23230
Phone
804-359-4444

ROCHESTER RED WINGS

General manager
Joe Altobelli
Manager
Marv Foley
Ballpark (capacity, surface)
Silver Stadium (10,503, grass)
Affiliation
Orioles
Address
500 Norton St.
Rochester, NY 14621
Phone
716-467-3000

SCRANTON/WILKES-BARRE BARONS

General manager
Bill Terlecky
Manager
Butch Hobson
Ballpark (capacity, surface)
Lackawanna County Stadium (10,832, artificial)
Affiliation
Phillies
Address
P.O. Box 3449
Scranton, PA 18505
Phone
717-969-2255

SYRACUSE CHIEFS

General manager
Anthony "Tex" Simone
Manager
Richie Hebner
Ballpark (capacity, surface)
MacArthur Stadium (10,000, grass)
Affiliation
Blue Jays
Address
MacArthur Stadium
Syracuse, NY 13208
Phone
315-474-7833

TOLEDO MUD HENS

General manager
Gene Cook
Manager
Tom Runnells
Ballpark (capacity, surface)
Ned Skeldon Stadium (10,025, grass)
Affiliation
Tigers
Address
P.O. Box 6212
Toledo, OH 43614
Phone
419-893-9483

EAST DIVISION

Team	W	L	T	Pct.	GB
Rochester (Orioles)	73	69	0	.514	....
Ottawa (Expos)	72	70	0	.507	1
Pawtucket (Red Sox)	70	71	0	.496	2¹/₂
Scranton/Wilkes-Barre (Phillies)	70	72	0	.493	3
Syracuse (Blue Jays)	59	82	0	.418	13¹/₂

WEST DIVISION

Team	W	L	T	Pct.	GB
Norfolk (Mets)	86	56	0	.606	....
Richmond (Braves)	75	66	0	.532	10¹/₂
Columbus (Yankees)	71	68	0	.511	13¹/₂
Toledo (Tigers)	71	71	0	.500	15
Charlotte (Marlins)	59	81	0	.421	26

COMPOSITE

Team	Nor.	Rich.	Roc.	Col.	Ott.	Tol.	Paw.	SWB	Char.	Syr.	W	L	T	Pct.	GB
Norfolk (Mets)	....	11	7	8	9	12	10	6	13	10	86	56	0	.606	....
Richmond (Braves)	7	....	6	11	7	10	7	10	10	7	75	66	0	.532	10¹/₂
Rochester (Orioles)	7	8	....	9	7	5	10	9	9	9	73	69	0	.514	13
Columbus (Yankees)	10	7	5	....	8	10	7	6	10	8	71	68	0	.511	13¹/₂
Ottawa (Expos)	5	7	11	6	....	5	7	10	8	13	72	70	0	.507	14
Toledo (Tigers)	6	8	9	8	9	....	8	9	7	7	71	71	0	.500	15
Pawtucket (Red Sox)	4	7	8	6	11	6	....	10	7	11	70	71	0	.496	15¹/₂
Scranton/Wilkes-Barre (Phillies)	8	4	8	8	5	8	8	....	9	11	70	72	0	.493	16
Charlotte (Marlins)	5	8	5	6	6	11	7	5	....	6	59	81	0	.421	26
Syracuse (Blue Jays)	4	6	9	6	5	7	7	7	8	....	59	82	0	.418	26¹/₂

Major league affiliations in parentheses.

PLAYOFFS: Norfolk defeated Richmond, three games to two; Ottawa defeated Rochester, three games to two; Ottawa defeated Norfolk, three games to one, to win league championship.

REGULAR-SEASON ATTENDANCE: Charlotte, 336,001; Columbus, 541,451; Norfolk, 586,317; Ottawa, 511,865; Pawtucket, 486,029; Richmond, 524,210; Rochester, 402,127; Scranton/Wilkes-Barre, 489,040; Syracuse, 303,208; Toledo, 306,906. Total—4,487,154. Playoffs (14 games)—63,732. Class AAA All-Star Game at Scranton/Wilkes-Barre—10,965.

MANAGERS: Charlotte, Sal Rende; Columbus, Bill Evers; Norfolk, Toby Harrah; Ottawa, Pete Mackanin; Pawtucket, Buddy Bailey; Richmond, Grady Little; Rochester, Marv Foley; Scranton/Wilkes-Barre, Mike Quade; Syracuse, Bob Didier (April 6 through June 21), Hector Torres (June 22) and Richie Hebner (June 23 through end of season); Toledo, Tom Runnells. Managerial record of team with more than one manager: Syracuse, Didier, 25-43, Torres 1-0, Hebner 33-39.

ALL-STAR TEAM: 1B—Don Sparks, Columbus; 2B—Kevin Jordan, Scranton/Wilkes-Barre; 3B—Butch Huskey, Norfolk; SS—Derek Jeter, Columbus; OF—Alex Ochoa, Rochester-Norfolk; Robert Perez, Syracuse; Mark Smith, Rochester; C—Jorge Posada, Columbus; DH—Carlos Delgado, Syracuse; Starting Pitcher—Jason Isringhausen, Norfolk; Relief Pitcher—Rod Nichols, Richmond; Most Valuable Player—Butch Huskey, Norfolk; Most Valuable Pitcher—Jason Isringhausen, Norfolk; Rookie of the Year—Jason Isringhausen, Norfolk; Manager of the Year—Toby Harrah, Norfolk.

1995 BATTING

TEAM

Team	Avg.	G	TPA	AB	R	H	TB	2B	3B	HR	RBI	SH	SF	HP	BB	IBB	SO	SB	CS	GDP	LOB	ShO	Slg.	OBP
Scr./Wil.-Bar.	.272	142	5374	4734	645	1286	1849	248	48	73	602	58	50	72	459	19	777	95	55	129	1015	4	.391	.342
Columbus	.271	140	5308	4730	687	1281	1940	222	61	105	629	38	46	36	456	20	911	104	57	109	951	12	.410	.337
Pawtucket	.264	142	5302	4732	676	1249	1995	240	19	156	630	32	36	45	456	21	951	94	63	111	930	6	.422	.332
Rochester	.262	142	5303	4735	669	1242	1936	256	36	122	616	27	46	48	446	21	820	125	65	108	947	7	.409	.329
Charlotte	.260	140	5281	4695	620	1220	1775	218	17	101	582	42	35	48	464	15	729	119	70	97	951	9	.378	.328
Norfolk	.260	142	5269	4697	650	1219	1798	229	40	90	602	52	42	42	434	20	823	132	94	110	888	5	.383	.325
Richmond	.259	141	5272	4710	559	1222	1716	194	33	78	510	39	42	40	441	30	794	70	69	115	975	12	.364	.325
Syracuse	.258	141	5276	4764	615	1227	1936	243	41	128	561	18	39	39	416	21	885	76	58	104	940	11	.406	.320
Ottawa	.257	142	5242	4644	618	1195	1751	225	35	87	566	65	30	44	454	31	824	161	53	104	946	8	.377	.327
Toledo	.257	142	5337	4755	600	1222	1840	224	35	108	546	39	45	56	442	11	962	93	70	107	985	11	.387	.325

INDIVIDUAL

TOP QUALIFIERS FOR BATTING CHAMPIONSHIP

Minimum 383 plate appearances. *Lefthanded batter. †Switch-hitter.

Player, Team	Avg.	G	TPA	AB	R	H	TB	2B	3B	HR	RBI	SH	SF	HP	BB	IBB	SO	SB	CS	GDP	Slg.	OBP
Perez, Robert, Syracuse	.343	122	522	502	70	172	249	38	6	9	67	1	4	2	13	4	60	7	5	17	.496	.359
Giovanola, Ed, Richmond*	.321	99	385	321	45	103	137	18	2	4	36	4	4	1	55	3	37	8	7	10	.427	.417
Delgado, Carlos, Syracuse*	.318	91	387	333	59	106	203	23	4	22	74	0	4	5	45	7	78	0	4	8	.610	.403
Jeter, Derek, Columbus	.317	123	558	486	96	154	205	27	9	2	45	2	5	4	61	1	56	20	12	9	.422	.394
Schall, Gene, Scr./W.-B.	.313	92	383	320	52	100	169	25	4	12	63	0	4	10	49	2	54	3	3	14	.528	.415
Sparks, Don, Columbus	.312	137	585	545	67	170	237	26	10	7	90	1	9	1	29	3	75	2	0	17	.435	.342
Jordan, Kevin, Scr./W.-B.	.310	106	453	410	61	127	179	29	4	5	60	1	6	8	28	0	36	3	0	14	.437	.361
Garcia, Omar, Norfolk	.309	115	459	430	55	133	177	21	7	3	64	1	7	0	21	3	58	3	4	13	.412	.336
Castleberry, Kevin, Ottawa*	.294	118	489	428	65	126	173	18	4	7	56	5	4	0	52	3	59	9	7	5	.404	.368
Crespo, Felipe, Syracuse†	.294	88	392	347	56	102	171	20	5	13	41	1	1	2	41	4	56	12	7	5	.493	.371
Munoz, Jose, Richmond†	.290	135	588	520	65	151	188	18	5	3	45	5	6	4	53	4	65	7	10	18	.362	.357
Zuber, Jon, Scr./W.-B.*	.287	119	471	418	53	120	158	19	5	3	50	1	2	0	49	2	68	1	2	12	.378	.360
Huskey, Butch, Norfolk	.284	109	442	394	66	112	216	18	1	28	87	0	3	6	39	4	88	8	6	9	.548	.355
Ochoa, Alex, Roch.-Nor.	.283	125	505	459	58	130	192	24	4	10	61	1	3	2	41	1	62	24	10	12	.418	.341
Kowitz, Brian, Richmond*	.280	100	400	353	53	99	129	14	5	2	34	3	0	3	41	1	43	11	8	4	.365	.360
Yan, Julian, Ottawa	.280	114	392	372	49	104	198	22	3	22	79	2	1	2	15	2	90	5	1	10	.532	.310

DEPARTMENTAL LEADERS: G—Sparks, 137; AB—Sparks, 545; R—Jeter, 96; H—R. Perez, 172; TB—R. Perez, 249; 2B—R. Perez, 38; 3B—Sparks, 10; HR—Huskey, 28; RBI—Sparks, 90; SH—Buccheri, A. Rodriguez, 11; SF—Sparks, 9; HP—G. Murray, 11; BB—Tyler, 71; IBB—C. Delgado, 7; SO—Clark, 129; SB—Buccheri, 44; CS—Alicea, Ordonez, Otero, 13; GIDP—Munoz, 18; Slg.—C. Delgado, .610; OBP—Giovanola, .417.

CLASS AAA International League

ALL PLAYERS

*Lefthanded batter. †Switch-hitter.

Player, Team	Avg.	G	TPA	AB	R	H	TB	2B	3B	HR	RBI	SH	SF	HP	BB	IBB	SO	SB	CS	GDP	Slg.	OBP
Abbott, Kurt, Charlotte	.278	5	19	18	3	5	8	0	0	1	3	0	0	0	1	0	3	1	0	0	.444	.316
Abner, Shawn, Norfolk	.258	11	32	31	3	8	8	0	0	0	1	0	0	0	1	0	7	0	0	0	.258	.281
Acevedo, Juan, Norfolk	.000	2	1	0	0	0	0	0	0	0	0	0	0	0	1	0	0	0	0	0	.000	1.000
Adamson, Joel, Charlotte*	.071	19	14	14	0	1	1	0	0	0	0	0	0	0	0	0	5	0	0	0	.071	.071
Alfonzo, Edgar, Rochester	.185	18	60	54	5	10	16	3	0	1	6	3	1	0	2	0	10	0	0	3	.296	.211
Alicea, Ed, Norfolk†	.245	122	491	436	63	107	141	17	4	3	39	6	2	2	45	2	78	21	13	11	.323	.318
Alvarez, Clemente, Ottawa	.231	50	159	143	15	33	52	7	0	4	20	3	0	2	10	1	34	0	0	2	.364	.290
Alvarez, Jose, Richmond	.000	5	2	2	0	0	0	0	0	0	0	0	0	0	0	0	1	0	0	0	.000	.000
Azuaje, Jesus, Norfolk	.429	5	16	14	1	6	7	1	0	0	0	0	0	0	2	0	2	1	1	0	.500	.500
Baez, Kevin, Toledo	.231	116	411	376	30	87	116	13	2	4	37	10	2	1	22	1	57	1	6	13	.309	.274
Barbara, Don, Pawtucket*	.217	40	141	129	19	28	42	8	0	2	10	0	0	0	12	0	18	2	0	3	.326	.284
Bark, Brian, Rich.-Paw.*	.000	43	2	2	0	0	0	0	0	0	0	0	0	0	0	0	0	0	0	0	.000	.000
Barnwell, Rich, Columbus	.231	46	146	130	22	30	41	4	2	1	17	2	0	1	13	0	32	7	3	4	.315	.306
Barron, Tony, Ottawa	.245	50	164	147	20	36	76	10	0	10	22	0	1	2	14	1	22	0	2	3	.517	.311
Barry, Jeff, Norfolk†	.220	12	47	41	3	9	11	2	0	0	6	0	2	1	3	0	6	0	0	2	.268	.277
Bartee, Kimera, Rochester†	.154	15	55	52	5	8	12	2	1	0	3	2	1	0	0	0	16	0	0	0	.231	.151
Batista, Miguel, Charlotte	.083	34	13	12	0	1	1	0	0	0	0	0	0	0	1	0	6	0	0	0	.083	.154
Batiste, Kim, Scr./W.B.-Roc.	.264	98	397	382	41	101	143	17	2	7	47	1	1	3	10	0	41	5	8	13	.374	.288
Battle, Howard, Syracuse	.251	118	488	443	43	111	160	17	4	8	48	1	2	3	39	2	73	10	11	7	.361	.314
Bautista, Danny, Toledo	.241	18	63	58	6	14	17	3	0	0	4	1	0	3	1	0	10	1	2	1	.293	.259
Baxter, Robert, Ottawa*	.125	39	11	8	2	1	1	0	0	0	0	1	0	0	2	0	2	0	0	0	.125	.300
Bell, Juan, Pawtucket†	.263	68	284	262	42	69	107	18	1	6	23	1	0	0	21	0	46	4	5	7	.408	.318
Benitez, Yamil, Ottawa	.259	127	524	474	66	123	213	24	6	18	69	2	2	2	44	3	128	14	6	10	.449	.324
Bennett, Gary, Scr./W.-B.	.150	7	23	20	1	3	3	0	0	0	1	1	0	0	2	1	2	0	0	0	.150	.227
Benzinger, Todd, Columbus†	.280	12	52	50	4	14	20	3	0	1	4	0	0	0	2	1	10	0	0	2	.400	.308
Bieser, Steve, Scr./W.-B.†	.269	95	285	245	37	66	93	12	6	1	33	6	2	10	22	1	56	14	5	5	.380	.351
Birkbeck, Mike, Norfolk	.222	9	10	9	2	2	3	1	0	0	0	0	0	0	1	0	3	0	0	0	.333	.300
Blosser, Greg, Pawtucket*	.200	17	56	50	5	10	13	0	0	1	4	0	1	0	5	0	13	0	0	3	.260	.268
Boka, Ben, Norfolk	.143	19	22	21	0	3	3	0	0	0	1	1	0	0	0	0	8	0	0	0	.143	.143
Boston, Daryl, Charlotte*	.188	18	70	64	7	12	20	5	0	1	2	0	0	0	6	0	12	0	0	1	.313	.257
Boucher, Denis, Ottawa	.375	14	11	8	1	3	5	2	0	0	2	1	0	0	2	0	0	0	0	0	.625	.500
Bournigal, Rafael, Ottawa	.204	19	58	54	2	11	15	4	0	0	6	1	0	1	2	0	4	0	0	2	.278	.246
Bowers, Brent, Syracuse*	.252	111	318	305	38	77	118	16	5	5	26	1	1	1	10	0	57	5	1	3	.387	.278
Brewer, Rod, Charlotte*	.322	69	279	236	31	76	120	15	1	9	55	0	5	5	33	3	45	0	0	3	.508	.409
Briley, Greg, Toledo*	.238	31	90	84	8	20	29	4	1	1	7	0	0	0	6	0	25	0	2	3	.345	.289
Brito, Tilson, Syracuse	.242	90	363	327	49	79	122	16	3	7	32	2	1	4	29	0	69	17	8	6	.373	.310
Brock, Chris, Richmond	.000	23	9	8	0	0	0	0	0	0	0	0	0	0	0	0	3	0	0	1	.000	.111
Brock, Tarrik, Toledo*	.194	9	33	31	4	6	7	1	0	0	0	0	0	0	2	0	17	2	2	0	.226	.242
Brooks, Eric, Syracuse	.192	47	133	120	12	23	28	3	1	0	5	0	0	0	12	0	27	0	2	2	.233	.265
Brophy, E.J., Scr./W.-B.	.200	34	76	65	7	13	18	2	0	1	6	3	0	0	8	1	15	0	0	3	.277	.283
Brown, Jarvis, Nor.-Roch.	.294	62	251	218	41	64	90	16	5	0	21	4	0	1	28	0	49	7	4	5	.413	.377
Brown, Randy, Pawtucket	.250	74	232	212	27	53	67	6	1	2	12	4	2	4	10	0	53	5	1	4	.316	.294
Buccheri, Jim, Ottawa	.268	133	537	470	64	126	150	16	4	0	30	11	2	3	49	5	58	44	11	7	.319	.340
Buford, Damon, Rochester	.309	46	208	188	40	58	88	12	3	4	18	1	1	1	17	0	26	17	4	2	.468	.367
Butler, Rich, Syracuse*	.161	69	210	199	20	32	46	4	2	2	14	1	1	0	9	0	45	2	3	5	.231	.196
Butler, Robert, Scr./W.-B.*	.300	92	365	327	46	98	131	16	4	3	35	4	4	6	24	2	39	5	8	14	.401	.355
Byrd, Paul, Norfolk	.250	22	4	4	0	1	1	0	0	0	0	0	0	0	0	0	0	0	0	0	.250	.250
Cabrera, Francisco, Richmond	.231	36	111	104	7	24	32	5	0	1	14	0	2	0	5	2	22	0	1	3	.308	.261
Cairo, Sergio, Ottawa	.333	2	6	6	1	2	3	1	0	0	0	0	0	0	0	0	1	0	0	0	.500	.333
Canate, Willie, Syracuse	.238	114	382	345	48	82	112	17	2	3	30	3	2	9	23	0	62	8	5	9	.325	.301
Canseco, Jose, Pawtucket	.167	2	8	6	1	1	1	0	0	0	1	0	1	0	1	0	5	0	0	0	.167	.250
Capra, Nick, Charlotte	.256	119	465	406	60	104	150	17	1	9	51	2	2	1	54	0	45	22	12	5	.369	.343
Carey, Paul, Rochester*	.236	89	335	284	39	67	107	13	0	9	50	1	5	5	40	5	68	1	2	2	.377	.335
Carpenter, Bubba, Columbus*	.246	116	420	374	57	92	143	12	3	11	49	2	3	1	40	2	70	13	6	2	.382	.318
Carr, Chuck, Charlotte†	.217	7	25	23	5	5	10	0	1	1	2	0	0	0	2	1	1	2	0	0	.435	.280
Carter, Jeff, Charlotte†	.269	124	505	428	78	115	141	20	3	0	22	9	1	5	62	0	86	22	10	5	.329	.367
Carter, Steve, Charlotte*	.250	24	80	72	9	18	27	0	0	3	15	0	1	0	7	0	6	0	0	1	.375	.313
Castaldo, Vince, Charlotte*	.200	7	14	10	2	2	2	0	0	0	1	0	1	0	3	0	3	0	0	0	.200	.357
Castillo, Alberto, Norfolk	.267	69	249	217	23	58	85	13	1	4	31	3	2	1	26	0	32	2	3	6	.392	.346
Castleberry, Kevin, Ottawa*	.294	118	489	428	65	126	173	18	4	7	56	5	4	0	52	3	59	9	7	5	.404	.368
Chamberlain, Wes, Pawtucket	.350	48	190	183	28	64	119	17	1	12	40	0	1	3	3	0	45	5	3	3	.650	.368
Clark, Tony, Toledo†	.242	110	463	405	50	98	161	17	2	14	63	0	3	3	52	1	129	0	2	8	.398	.330
Clary, Marty, Charlotte	.500	9	4	2	0	1	1	0	0	0	0	0	0	2	0	0	0	0	0	0	.500	.500
Coffman, Kevin, Richmond	.000	2	1	0	0	0	0	0	0	0	0	0	0	0	1	0	0	0	0	0	.000	1.000
Combs, Pat, Scr./W.-B.*	.000	22	1	1	0	0	0	0	0	0	0	0	0	0	0	0	0	0	0	0	.000	.000
Cornelius, Reid, Ott.-Nor.	.063	14	19	16	0	1	1	0	0	0	0	0	0	0	0	0	10	0	0	3	.063	.063
Crawford, Joe, Norfolk*	.000	8	1	1	0	0	0	0	0	0	0	0	0	0	0	0	1	0	0	0	.000	.000
Crespo, Felipe, Syracuse†	.294	88	392	347	56	102	171	20	5	13	41	1	1	2	41	4	56	12	7	5	.493	.371
Crowley, Jim, Rochester	.173	34	110	98	7	17	23	3	0	1	6	1	0	4	7	0	21	0	1	2	.235	.257
Cruz, Ivan, Toledo*	.194	11	43	36	5	7	9	2	0	0	3	0	1	0	6	0	9	0	0	1	.250	.302
Cuyler, Milt, Toledo†	.305	54	232	203	33	62	98	10	4	6	28	0	4	5	20	0	40	6	7	1	.483	.375
Dascenzo, Doug, Charlotte†	.260	75	295	265	51	69	90	9	0	4	26	1	4	0	25	0	30	14	9	7	.340	.320
Daubach, Brian, Norfolk*	.000	9	7	7	0	0	0	0	0	0	0	0	0	0	0	0	2	1	0	0	.000	.000
Davis, Jay, Norfolk*	.192	10	26	26	1	5	8	1	1	0	3	0	0	0	0	0	2	0	1	1	.308	.192
Davis, Russ, Columbus	.250	20	95	76	12	19	31	4	1	2	15	0	1	1	17	3	23	0	0	0	.408	.389
DeBerry, Joe, Norfolk*	.292	10	25	24	3	7	13	2	2	0	4	0	0	0	1	0	6	0	0	1	.542	.320
Dejardin, Bobby, Rochester†	.314	9	40	35	6	11	13	2	0	0	3	0	2	0	3	0	3	1	0	0	.371	.350
Delgado, Alex, Pawtucket	.252	44	114	107	14	27	45	3	0	5	12	0	1	0	6	0	12	0	0	4	.421	.298
Delgado, Carlos, Syracuse*	.318	91	387	333	59	106	203	23	4	22	74	0	4	5	45	7	78	0	4	8	.610	.403
Delima, Rafael, Ottawa*	.259	10	33	27	4	7	7	0	0	0	3	1	0	0	5	0	3	2	0	2	.259	.375

Player, Team	Avg.	G	TPA	AB	R	H	TB	2B	3B	HR	RBI	SH	SF	HP	BB	IBB	SO	SB	CS	GDP	Slg.	OBP
Dellicarri, Joe, Toledo............	.250	4	15	12	4	3	6	0	0	1	1	0	0	2	1	0	2	1	0	0	.500	.400
Deshaies, Jim, Scr./W.-B.*....	.067	19	19	15	0	1	1	0	0	0	3	4	0	0	0	0	8	0	0	0	.067	.067
Devarez, Cesar, Rochester	.250	67	249	240	32	60	77	12	1	1	21	1	1	0	7	0	25	2	2	8	.321	.270
Diaz, Cesar, Norfolk...............	.182	3	11	11	2	2	2	0	0	0	0	0	0	0	0	0	2	0	0	0	.182	.182
Diaz, Edgar, Syracuse..........	.302	15	52	43	5	13	15	0	1	0	2	1	0	1	7	0	6	0	0	3	.349	.412
Diaz, Rafael, Ottawa.............	.000	32	4	2	0	0	0	0	0	0	0	0	0	0	2	0	1	0	0	0	.000	.500
Donnels, Chris, Pawtucket*...	.400	4	16	15	1	6	9	0	0	1	4	0	0	0	1	0	3	0	0	0	.600	.438
Eenhoorn, Robert, Columbus...	.252	92	349	318	36	80	112	11	3	5	32	6	2	3	20	0	54	2	4	5	.352	.300
Eischen, Joey, Ottawa*.........	.000	11	1	1	0	0	0	0	0	0	0	0	0	0	0	0	0	0	0	0	.000	.000
Elster, Kevin, Scr./W.-B.	.294	5	19	17	2	5	8	3	0	0	2	0	0	0	2	0	3	0	0	1	.471	.368
Engle, Tom, Norfolk	.000	1	1	1	0	0	0	0	0	0	0	0	0	0	0	0	0	0	0	0	.000	.000
Epps, Scott, Columbus	.143	4	8	7	0	1	1	0	0	0	0	1	0	0	0	0	1	0	0	0	.143	.143
Everett, Carl, Norfolk†...........	.300	67	286	260	52	78	120	16	4	6	35	1	1	4	20	1	47	12	6	2	.462	.358
Eversgerd, Bryan, Ottawa.......	.000	38	2	1	0	0	0	0	0	0	0	0	0	0	1	0	1	0	0	0	.000	.500
Felix, Junior, Ottawa†............	.225	51	179	160	22	36	58	7	3	3	24	1	0	3	15	1	48	1	2	6	.363	.303
Figga, Mike, Columbus	.280	8	29	25	2	7	11	1	0	1	3	1	0	0	3	0	5	0	0	0	.440	.357
Fleming, Carlton, Columbus†...	.221	32	95	86	9	19	25	6	0	0	5	1	0	0	8	0	6	0	2	3	.291	.287
Fletcher, Paul, Scr./W.-B.	.000	52	2	2	0	0	0	0	0	0	0	0	0	0	0	0	1	0	0	0	.000	.000
Florence, Don, Norfolk...........	.000	41	2	0	2	0	0	0	0	0	0	0	0	0	2	0	0	0	0	0	.000	1.000
Foley, Tom, Ottawa*.............	.306	23	72	62	13	19	24	5	0	0	7	2	0	0	8	0	7	1	0	4	.387	.386
Ford, Curt, Charlotte*...........	.305	57	179	167	18	51	70	10	0	3	17	0	0	3	9	1	29	2	4	4	.419	.352
Fox, Andy, Columbus*...........	.348	82	354	302	61	105	160	16	6	9	37	2	3	4	43	1	41	22	4	5	.530	.432
Fraser, Willie, Ottawa	.048	19	25	21	0	1	1	0	0	0	0	3	0	0	1	0	12	0	0	0	.048	.091
Frazier, Lou, Ottawa†...........	.218	31	126	110	11	24	30	3	0	1	10	1	1	1	13	0	20	10	1	2	.273	.304
Friedman, Jason, Paw.-Roch.*..	.339	39	123	112	15	38	63	7	0	6	18	1	1	1	8	1	11	0	0	3	.563	.385
Fulton, Ed, Pawtucket*.........	.294	9	21	17	0	5	7	2	0	0	2	0	0	0	3	1	6	0	0	0	.412	.400
Gaddy, Bob, Scr./W.-B.........	.000	17	12	9	0	0	0	0	0	0	0	2	0	0	1	0	2	0	0	0	.000	.100
Garcia, Omar, Norfolk...........	.309	115	459	430	55	133	177	21	7	3	64	1	7	0	21	3	58	3	4	13	.412	.336
Geisler, Phil, Scr./W.-B.*.......	.186	20	46	43	2	8	16	5	0	1	7	1	0	0	2	0	13	0	0	2	.372	.222
Gilbert, Shawn, Scr./W.-B.......	.263	136	614	536	84	141	177	26	2	2	42	4	4	6	64	0	102	16	11	8	.330	.346
Giovanola, Ed, Richmond*.....	.321	99	385	321	45	103	137	18	2	4	36	4	4	1	55	3	37	8	7	10	.427	.417
Givens, Jim, Toledo†............	.237	79	247	219	23	52	59	5	1	0	14	0	1	1	26	0	40	7	5	4	.269	.320
Gonzalez, Pete, Toledo	.211	6	23	19	0	4	5	1	0	0	2	0	0	1	3	0	6	0	0	0	.263	.348
Goodwin, Curtis, Rochester*...	.264	36	156	140	24	37	46	3	3	0	7	3	0	1	12	0	15	17	3	4	.329	.327
Grable, Rob, Scr./W.-B.	.229	26	92	83	7	19	32	4	0	3	11	1	0	1	7	0	34	3	0	1	.386	.297
Grace, Mike, Scr./W.-B.	.000	2	4	3	0	0	0	0	0	0	0	1	0	0	0	0	2	0	0	0	.000	.000
Graffanino, Tony, Richmond...	.190	50	198	179	20	34	52	6	0	4	17	1	2	1	15	0	49	2	2	4	.291	.254
Graham, Greg, Norfolk†.........	.197	47	141	122	14	24	29	5	0	0	9	2	1	1	15	1	23	1	2	5	.238	.288
Greene, Charlie, Norfolk.........	.193	27	92	88	6	17	20	3	0	0	4	1	0	0	3	0	28	0	1	1	.227	.220
Greene, Tommy, Scr./W.-B.	.125	4	10	8	0	1	1	0	0	0	0	1	0	0	1	0	3	0	0	0	.125	.222
Greenwell, Mike, Pawtucket*..	.500	1	5	4	0	2	4	2	0	0	0	0	0	0	1	0	0	0	0	0	1.000	.600
Gregg, Tommy, Charlotte*.....	.387	34	147	124	30	48	87	10	1	9	32	0	1	1	21	2	13	7	0	3	.702	.476
Gresham, Kris, Rochester......	.250	21	70	64	5	16	20	2	1	0	4	0	0	2	4	0	15	0	0	2	.313	.314
Grijak, Kevin, Richmond*......	.298	106	342	309	35	92	154	16	5	12	56	0	4	4	25	4	47	1	3	10	.498	.354
Grudzielanek, Mark, Ottawa ...	.298	49	201	181	26	54	68	9	1	1	22	2	4	4	10	0	17	12	1	6	.376	.342
Hall, Joe, Toledo...................	.320	91	360	319	52	102	158	19	2	11	47	1	2	2	36	1	50	4	1	7	.495	.390
Hardge, Mike, Pawtucket	.253	29	99	91	9	23	29	3	0	1	5	0	0	0	8	0	16	1	3	2	.319	.313
Hardtke, Jason, Norfolk†........	.286	4	9	7	1	2	3	1	0	0	0	0	0	0	2	0	0	1	1	0	.429	.444
Harris, Greg, Ottawa†...........	.000	11	1	1	0	0	0	0	0	0	0	0	0	0	0	0	0	0	0	0	.000	.000
Harrison, Tom, Richmond	.250	9	6	4	0	1	1	0	0	0	1	1	0	0	1	0	0	0	0	0	.250	.400
Hatteberg, Scott, Pawtucket*..	.271	85	299	251	36	68	106	15	1	7	27	1	3	4	40	2	39	2	0	8	.422	.376
Hayden, Dave, Scr./W.-B.	.293	20	47	41	6	12	19	1	0	2	3	0	0	0	6	0	13	0	2	1	.463	.383
Heble, Kurt, Syracuse	.000	4	1	1	0	0	0	0	0	0	0	0	0	0	0	0	1	0	0	0	.000	.000
Hecht, Steve, Toledo*...........	.236	25	84	72	14	17	24	5	1	0	6	1	2	2	7	0	6	5	0	0	.333	.313
Heffernan, Bert, Ottawa*........	.216	36	115	102	13	22	30	5	0	1	12	3	1	2	7	0	13	1	0	3	.294	.277
Hernandez, Jeremy, Charlotte...	.000	15	2	1	0	0	0	0	0	0	1	0	0	0	1	0	0	0	0	0	.000	.500
Hernandez, Kiki, Charlotte......	.240	60	170	150	13	36	65	8	0	7	28	0	3	1	16	1	26	0	0	5	.433	.312
Hill, Eric, Scr./W.-B...............	.000	21	1	0	0	0	0	0	0	0	0	0	0	0	1	0	0	0	0	0	.000	1.000
Hill, Lew, Columbus†............	.271	54	150	144	15	39	56	5	0	4	20	0	0	1	5	1	36	6	5	2	.389	.300
Holifield, Rick, Scr./W.-B.*......	.206	76	257	223	32	46	67	6	3	3	24	1	3	6	24	0	52	21	5	1	.300	.297
Houston, Tyler, Richmond*.....	.255	103	374	349	41	89	141	10	3	12	42	1	2	4	18	3	62	3	5	6	.404	.298
Howard, Tim, Pawtucket*.......	.311	38	99	90	13	28	35	5	1	0	11	1	0	1	7	0	11	7	3	3	.389	.360
Huskey, Butch, Norfolk..........	.284	109	442	394	66	112	216	18	1	28	87	0	3	6	39	4	88	8	6	9	.548	.355
Huson, Jeff, Rochester*........	.251	60	252	223	28	56	74	9	0	3	21	2	1	0	26	2	29	16	5	7	.332	.328
Ilsley, Blaise, Scr./W.-B.*.......	.357	30	22	14	1	5	7	2	0	0	2	3	0	0	5	0	2	0	0	1	.500	.526
Isringhausen, Jason, Norfolk...	.133	12	16	15	2	2	2	0	0	0	0	1	0	0	0	0	4	0	0	1	.133	.133
Jacobs, Frank, Nor.-Ott.†........	.246	19	69	57	11	14	24	3	2	1	10	0	0	1	11	0	7	0	1	2	.421	.377
Jacome, Jason, Norfolk*........	.000	8	7	7	0	0	0	0	0	0	0	0	0	0	0	0	0	0	0	0	.000	.000
Jeter, Derek, Columbus*........	.317	123	558	486	96	154	205	27	9	2	45	2	5	4	61	1	56	20	12	9	.422	.394
Johnson, Matt, Syracuse	.500	5	7	6	1	3	5	2	0	0	0	0	0	1	0	0	1	0	0	0	.833	.571
Jones, Chris, Norfolk	.333	33	129	114	20	38	61	12	1	3	19	0	3	1	11	1	20	5	2	2	.535	.388
Jordan, Kevin, Scr./W.-B.	.310	106	453	410	61	127	179	29	4	5	60	1	6	8	28	0	36	3	0	14	.437	.361
Jorgensen, Terry, Charlotte	.264	99	401	356	38	94	129	14	0	7	52	1	4	1	39	1	40	3	3	9	.362	.335
Juden, Jeff, Scr./W.-B.	.000	14	15	14	0	0	0	0	0	0	1	1	0	0	0	0	5	0	0	0	.000	.000
Karp, Ryan, Scr./W.-B.*	.071	13	18	14	1	1	1	0	0	0	2	3	1	0	0	0	2	0	0	0	.071	.067
Kelly, Mike, Richmond	.289	15	52	45	5	13	20	1	0	2	8	0	0	2	5	0	17	0	1	0	.444	.385
Kelly, Pat, Rich.-Syr............	.144	41	104	90	8	13	21	2	0	2	10	2	2	4	6	0	20	0	1	2	.233	.225
Kerley, Collin, Ottawa	.000	5	1	0	0	0	0	0	0	0	0	1	0	0	1	0	0	0	0	0	.000	.000
Knapp, Mike, Rochester	.183	40	140	126	10	23	29	1	1	1	12	0	1	1	12	0	26	1	1	3	.230	.257
Knorr, Randy, Syracuse.........	.269	18	73	67	6	18	28	5	1	1	6	0	1	0	5	0	14	0	0	1	.418	.315
Koelling, Brian, Scr./W.-B......	.264	16	55	53	5	14	15	1	0	0	3	0	1	0	1	0	14	3	1	1	.283	.273
Kowitz, Brian, Richmond*......	.280	100	400	353	53	99	129	14	5	2	34	3	0	3	41	1	43	11	8	4	.365	.360
Layana, Tim, Ottawa..............	.000	26	2	2	0	0	0	0	0	0	0	0	0	0	0	0	1	0	0	0	.000	.000

Player, Team	Avg.	G	TPA	AB	R	H	TB	2B	3B	HR	RBI	SH	SF	HP	BB	IBB	SO	SB	CS	GDP	Slg.	OBP
Leach, Jalal, Columbus*	.243	88	302	272	37	66	106	12	5	6	31	1	4	2	22	1	60	11	4	5	.390	.300
Ledesma, Aaron, Norfolk	.299	56	213	201	26	60	74	12	1	0	28	1	0	1	10	1	22	6	3	5	.368	.335
Lee, Derek, Norfolk*	.254	112	415	351	56	89	160	17	0	18	60	2	5	7	48	4	62	11	6	11	.456	.350
Leiper, Dave, Ottawa*	.000	2	1	1	0	0	0	0	0	0	0	0	0	0	0	0	1	0	0	0	.000	.000
Leiper, Tim, Toledo*	.212	18	71	66	3	14	15	1	0	0	6	0	1	0	4	0	8	0	0	3	.227	.254
Lemon, Don, Charlotte	.000	6	1	1	0	0	0	0	0	0	0	0	0	0	0	0	1	0	0	0	.000	.000
Lennon, Pat, Pawtucket	.273	40	146	128	20	35	54	6	2	3	20	0	1	1	16	0	42	6	4	6	.422	.356
Levangie, Dana, Pawtucket	.235	6	20	17	1	4	4	0	0	0	0	1	0	0	2	0	3	0	0	0	.235	.316
Lewis, Richie, Charlotte	.091	18	14	11	1	1	1	0	0	0	0	2	0	0	1	0	0	0	0	0	.091	.167
Lewis, T.R., Rochester	.295	22	87	78	12	23	42	7	0	4	19	0	1	1	7	0	14	1	1	2	.538	.356
Lieberthal, Mike, Scr./W.-B.	.281	85	340	278	44	78	120	20	2	6	42	2	7	9	44	2	26	1	4	14	.432	.388
Lis, Joe, Syracuse	.262	130	538	485	68	127	219	33	4	17	56	0	5	2	46	1	54	6	2	8	.452	.325
Livesey, Jeff, Columbus	.264	42	99	91	8	24	27	3	0	0	7	0	1	0	7	0	18	0	0	5	.297	.313
Lomon, Kevin, Richmond	.200	33	5	5	0	1	1	0	0	0	0	0	0	0	0	0	0	0	0	0	.200	.200
Long, Steve, Charlotte	.111	33	10	9	0	1	1	0	0	0	0	0	1	0	0	0	3	0	0	0	.111	.111
Ludwick, Eric, Norfolk	.250	4	4	4	1	1	1	0	0	0	0	0	0	0	0	0	2	0	0	0	.250	.250
Lukachyk, Rob, Toledo*	.254	104	387	346	43	88	147	24	7	7	26	3	3	2	33	0	75	8	5	5	.425	.320
Luke, Matt, Columbus*	.299	23	81	77	11	23	38	4	1	3	12	1	0	1	2	0	12	1	1	3	.494	.329
Lutz, Brent, Syracuse	.163	35	90	86	5	14	17	0	0	1	5	0	0	0	4	0	23	1	2	3	.198	.200
Maas, Kevin, Columbus*	.280	44	188	161	28	45	83	7	2	9	33	0	2	2	23	0	40	0	0	1	.516	.372
Magrane, Joe, Ottawa	.200	12	12	10	1	2	5	0	0	1	1	1	1	0	0	1	2	0	0	0	.500	.273
Mahay, Ron, Pawtucket*	.318	11	48	44	5	14	18	4	0	0	3	0	0	0	4	1	9	1	0	2	.409	.375
Malave, Jose, Pawtucket	.270	91	350	318	55	86	169	12	1	23	57	0	0	2	30	1	67	0	1	4	.531	.337
Malzone, John, Pawtucket*	.111	6	18	18	0	2	2	0	0	0	2	0	0	0	0	0	4	0	0	1	.111	.111
Manahan, Anthony, Scr./W.-B.	.288	90	333	299	36	86	108	11	1	3	32	2	0	4	28	4	39	6	1	7	.361	.356
Manuel, Barry, Ottawa	.077	35	18	13	3	1	1	0	0	0	0	2	0	0	3	0	4	0	0	0	.077	.250
Marsh, Tom, Scr./W.-B.	.307	78	315	296	46	91	153	22	5	10	47	0	2	4	13	1	39	9	3	10	.517	.343
Martin, Chris, Ottawa	.257	126	473	412	55	106	136	19	1	3	40	8	3	4	46	1	59	30	5	12	.330	.335
Martinez, Pablo, Toledo†	.229	14	50	48	5	11	15	0	2	0	4	0	0	0	2	0	7	1	1	3	.313	.260
Martinez, Ray, Ottawa	.250	39	119	108	17	27	33	6	0	0	9	3	1	0	6	0	17	3	0	3	.306	.287
Mashore, Justin, Toledo	.220	72	251	223	32	49	71	4	3	4	21	9	2	3	14	1	62	12	9	1	.318	.273
Massarelli, John, Charlotte	.244	65	284	254	37	62	79	7	2	2	8	1	1	2	26	0	55	14	10	2	.311	.318
Masse, Billy, Columbus	.224	49	195	165	19	37	59	6	2	4	24	0	2	4	24	1	31	3	3	7	.358	.333
May, Darrell, Richmond*	.000	10	8	5	1	0	0	0	0	0	0	1	0	0	2	0	4	0	0	0	.000	.286
McClain, Scott, Rochester	.251	61	226	199	32	50	85	9	1	8	22	1	2	1	23	0	34	0	1	5	.427	.329
McCoy, Trey, Norfolk	.209	25	74	67	6	14	28	5	0	3	7	0	0	2	5	0	11	0	0	2	.418	.284
McDowell, Oddibe, Columbus*	.217	14	54	46	5	10	15	0	1	1	2	2	0	0	6	0	9	0	1	1	.326	.308
McGee, Willie, Pawtucket†	.476	5	21	21	9	10	10	0	0	0	2	0	0	0	0	0	4	2	0	0	.476	.476
McGinnis, Russ, Rochester	.182	20	77	55	8	10	21	2	0	3	11	0	3	2	17	0	19	0	0	4	.382	.382
McGriff, Terry, Toledo	.271	58	208	188	14	51	71	8	0	4	23	0	0	0	20	0	29	0	0	9	.378	.341
McNair, Fred, Scr./W.-B.	.240	9	29	25	1	6	7	1	0	0	2	0	1	0	3	0	6	0	0	1	.280	.310
Melvin, Bob, Columbus	.288	19	69	66	7	19	27	5	0	1	4	0	0	0	3	1	12	0	0	3	.409	.319
Mendenhall, Kirk, Toledo	.200	11	36	30	2	6	10	1	0	1	4	1	0	0	5	0	1	2	0	1	.333	.314
Miller, Kurt, Charlotte	.167	22	28	24	1	4	4	0	0	0	0	3	0	0	1	0	8	0	0	0	.167	.200
Millette, Joe, Charlotte	.187	74	212	193	22	36	54	6	0	4	20	1	4	4	10	0	36	1	1	4	.280	.237
Milne, Darren, Toledo	.150	7	21	20	0	3	4	1	0	0	4	0	0	0	1	0	4	0	0	1	.200	.190
Minutelli, Gino, Richmond*	.000	5	2	2	0	0	0	0	0	0	0	0	0	0	0	0	1	0	0	0	.000	.000
Mitchell, John, Ottawa	.000	6	1	1	0	0	0	0	0	0	0	0	0	0	0	0	0	0	0	0	.000	.000
Montalvo, Rob, Syracuse*	.038	11	28	26	0	1	1	0	0	0	0	1	0	0	2	0	8	0	0	1	.038	.107
Montoya, Al, Syracuse*	.000	7	1	1	0	0	0	0	0	0	0	0	0	0	0	0	0	0	0	0	.000	.000
Montoyo, Charlie, Scr./W.-B.	.243	92	347	288	32	70	94	13	1	3	34	5	3	1	50	1	45	2	3	4	.326	.354
Moore, Bobby, Richmond	.258	108	365	329	45	85	116	18	2	3	27	3	2	4	27	1	27	9	7	6	.353	.320
Morgan, Kevin, Norfolk	.323	19	67	62	10	20	21	1	0	0	8	0	0	1	4	0	8	1	3	1	.339	.373
Morman, Russ, Charlotte	.314	44	187	169	28	53	80	7	1	6	36	0	3	1	14	3	22	2	2	4	.473	.364
Munoz, Jose, Richmond†	.290	135	588	520	65	151	188	18	5	3	45	5	6	4	53	4	65	7	10	18	.362	.357
Murray, Glenn, Pawtucket	.244	104	387	336	66	82	172	15	0	25	66	1	5	11	34	1	109	5	6	4	.512	.329
Murray, Matt, Richmond*	.200	19	19	15	2	3	3	0	0	0	3	1	0	0	3	0	2	0	0	0	.200	.333
Mutis, Jeff, Charlotte*	.000	27	3	3	0	0	0	0	0	0	0	0	0	0	0	0	1	0	0	0	.000	.000
Natal, Rob, Charlotte	.314	53	204	191	23	60	83	14	0	3	24	0	0	2	11	1	23	0	0	4	.435	.358
Nevin, Phil, Toledo	.304	7	24	23	3	7	12	2	0	1	3	0	0	1	0	0	5	0	0	2	.522	.333
Nichols, Rod, Richmond	.500	41	2	2	0	1	2	1	0	0	0	0	0	0	0	0	0	0	0	0	1.000	.500
Noboa, Junior, Rochester	.100	6	21	20	1	2	2	0	0	0	2	0	1	0	0	0	0	0	0	1	.100	.095
Obando, Sherman, Rochester	.296	85	360	324	42	96	161	26	6	9	53	0	4	3	29	3	57	1	1	11	.497	.350
Ochoa, Alex, Roch.-Nor.	.283	125	505	459	58	130	192	24	4	10	61	1	3	2	40	1	62	24	10	12	.418	.341
O'Connor, Kevin, Richmond*	.222	94	231	203	33	45	65	2	3	4	14	0	0	1	27	2	42	14	4	3	.320	.316
Olivares, Omar, Scr./W.-B.	.444	8	12	9	2	4	7	1	1	0	2	2	1	0	0	0	2	0	0	0	.778	.400
Olmeda, Jose, Richmond†	.253	80	263	241	22	61	81	11	3	1	24	3	2	1	16	2	41	2	1	5	.336	.300
Ordonez, Rey, Norfolk	.214	125	486	439	49	94	129	21	4	2	50	10	7	3	27	2	50	11	13	12	.294	.261
Orton, John, Rich.-Nor.	.264	73	243	220	26	58	81	11	0	4	26	1	1	4	17	0	67	3	5	5	.368	.324
Osuna, Al, Norfolk	.000	14	3	3	0	0	0	0	0	0	0	0	0	0	0	0	2	0	0	0	.000	.000
Otero, Ricky, Norfolk†	.268	72	325	295	37	79	102	8	6	1	23	2	0	1	27	0	33	16	13	2	.346	.331
Owens, Billy, Rochester†	.143	9	29	28	2	4	4	0	0	0	1	0	0	0	1	0	6	0	0	0	.143	.172
Pappas, Erik, Charlotte	.221	122	461	389	48	86	150	28	3	10	52	1	4	6	61	0	78	10	7	11	.386	.333
Payton, Jay, Norfolk	.240	50	215	196	33	47	78	11	4	4	30	4	2	2	11	0	22	11	3	5	.398	.284
Pecorilli, Aldo, Richmond	.260	49	150	127	16	33	54	3	0	6	17	2	0	2	19	2	20	0	0	5	.425	.360
Pemberton, Rudy, Toledo	.344	67	247	224	31	77	119	15	3	7	23	0	3	5	15	2	36	8	4	5	.531	.393
Penn, Shannon, Toledo†	.248	63	249	218	41	54	63	4	1	1	15	2	2	10	17	0	40	15	9	4	.289	.328
Perez, Eddie, Richmond	.265	92	341	324	31	86	120	19	0	5	40	1	2	2	12	0	58	1	2	12	.370	.294
Perez, Robert, Syracuse	.343	122	522	502	70	172	249	38	6	9	67	1	4	2	13	4	60	7	5	17	.496	.359
Perezchica, Tony, Columbus	.257	101	394	358	43	92	133	12	4	7	44	7	5	5	18	2	74	3	3	8	.372	.298
Person, Robert, Norfolk	.167	5	9	6	1	1	1	0	0	0	0	3	0	0	0	0	0	0	0	0	.167	.167
Posada, Jorge, Columbus†	.255	108	432	368	60	94	160	32	5	8	51	6	3	1	54	2	101	4	4	14	.435	.350
Potts, Mike, Richmond*	.000	38	4	4	0	0	0	0	0	0	0	0	0	0	0	0	3	0	0	0	.000	.000

Player, Team	Avg.	G	TPA	AB	R	H	TB	2B	3B	HR	RBI	SH	SF	HP	BB	IBB	SO	SB	CS	GDP	Slg.	OBP
Pough, Pork Chop, Pawtucket...	.232	30	108	99	12	23	48	8	1	5	23	0	1	1	7	1	27	0	0	2	.485	.287
Pride, Curtis, Ottawa*	.279	42	168	154	25	43	69	8	3	4	24	0	0	2	12	4	35	8	4	2	.448	.339
Pulsipher, Bill, Norfolk*	.091	13	13	11	1	1	1	0	0	0	1	0	1	0	1	0	2	0	0	0	.091	.154
Ramos, John, Syracuse	.252	116	463	413	59	104	190	24	1	20	75	1	5	6	38	1	83	2	2	11	.460	.320
Reed, Darren, Richmond.........	.265	57	151	136	11	36	58	7	0	5	22	0	3	1	11	0	28	0	0	4	.426	.318
Rhodes, Karl, Pawtucket*	.285	69	285	246	40	70	119	13	3	10	43	1	3	1	34	3	46	8	6	7	.484	.370
Rice, Lance, Toledo†	.268	15	46	41	2	11	15	1	0	1	6	1	0	0	4	0	6	0	3	0	.366	.333
Rivera, Ruben, Columbus	.270	48	204	174	37	47	104	8	2	15	35	0	1	3	26	0	62	8	4	5	.598	.373
Roa, Hector, Richmond†	.258	40	126	120	15	31	42	5	0	2	7	1	1	1	3	1	23	0	1	4	.350	.280
Roberts, Chris, Norfolk	.158	27	22	19	1	3	4	1	0	0	0	2	0	1	0	0	5	0	0	1	.211	.200
Robertson, Rod, Rochester†..	.278	101	370	338	54	94	164	21	2	15	58	4	2	4	22	1	63	8	7	8	.485	.328
Rodriguez, Carlos, Pawtucket†	.293	40	157	133	19	39	46	7	0	0	13	1	2	1	20	0	8	1	0	4	.346	.385
Rodriguez, Henry, Ottawa*	.200	4	16	15	0	3	4	1	0	0	2	0	0	0	1	0	4	0	0	0	.267	.250
Rodriguez, Steve, Pawtucket...	.241	82	358	324	39	78	103	16	3	1	24	2	3	4	25	1	34	12	10	7	.318	.301
Rodriguez, Tony, Pawtucket....	.268	96	353	317	37	85	104	15	2	0	21	11	4	6	15	0	39	11	5	8	.328	.310
Rodriguez, Victor, Pawtucket....	.276	31	122	116	10	32	37	5	0	0	8	3	1	0	2	0	13	1	1	3	.319	.286
Rogers, Bryan, Norfolk	.000	56	4	3	0	0	0	0	0	0	0	1	0	0	0	0	2	0	0	0	.000	.000
Rowland, Rich, Pawtucket	.258	34	133	124	20	32	63	7	0	8	24	0	1	1	7	1	24	0	1	2	.508	.301
Rudolph, Mason, Charlotte	.250	2	4	4	1	1	1	0	0	0	0	0	0	0	0	0	1	0	0	0	.250	.250
Rueter, Kirk, Ottawa*	.294	20	18	17	1	5	5	0	0	0	2	0	0	1	0	0	4	0	0	0	.294	.333
Rundels, Matt, Ottawa...........	.250	14	46	36	7	9	12	1	1	0	4	2	0	1	7	0	8	1	1	1	.333	.386
Sanders, Tracy, Norfolk*........	.227	64	148	110	21	25	43	6	0	4	14	0	0	4	34	0	34	3	1	2	.391	.426
Santangelo, F.P., Ottawa†	.255	95	315	267	37	68	95	15	3	2	25	6	4	6	32	3	22	7	4	2	.356	.343
Saunders, Chris, Norfolk........	.232	16	65	56	9	13	27	3	1	3	7	0	0	0	9	0	15	1	1	1	.482	.338
Sawkiw, Warren, Syracuse*....	.190	11	47	42	3	8	9	1	0	0	0	0	0	0	5	0	8	2	0	1	.214	.277
Schall, Gene, Scr./W.-B.	.313	92	383	320	52	100	169	25	4	12	63	0	4	10	49	2	54	3	3	14	.528	.415
Scheid, Rich, Charlotte*	.000	19	4	2	0	0	0	0	0	0	0	2	0	0	0	0	1	0	0	0	.000	.000
Schmidt, Curt, Ottawa	.000	43	1	1	0	0	0	0	0	0	0	0	0	0	0	0	0	0	0	0	.000	.000
Schmidt, Jason, Richmond......	.150	19	20	20	1	3	3	0	0	0	0	0	0	0	0	0	9	0	0	1	.150	.150
Schunk, Jerry, Charlotte.........	.224	101	372	343	36	77	108	13	0	6	33	4	4	2	19	2	31	8	0	16	.315	.266
Scott, Gary, Richmond	.151	27	98	86	7	13	14	1	0	0	2	0	1	1	10	0	13	0	1	0	.163	.245
Seefried, Tate, Columbus*	.164	29	113	110	7	18	27	6	0	1	12	0	2	0	1	0	34	0	0	2	.245	.168
Seelbach, Chris, Richmond.....	.000	14	11	9	0	0	0	0	0	0	0	2	0	0	0	0	4	0	0	0	.000	.000
Sefcik, Kevin, Scr./W.-B.	.346	7	30	26	5	9	17	6	1	0	6	0	1	0	3	0	1	0	0	1	.654	.400
Sharperson, Mike, Richmond...	.319	87	343	298	42	95	122	16	1	3	47	1	7	2	35	3	34	7	2	6	.409	.386
Shumpert, Terry, Pawtucket...	.271	37	150	133	17	36	49	7	0	2	11	2	0	1	14	0	27	10	4	3	.368	.345
Siddall, Joe, Ottawa*	.214	83	278	248	26	53	74	14	2	1	23	2	0	4	23	0	42	3	3	6	.298	.291
Small, Aaron, Syr.-Char..........	.000	34	2	2	0	0	0	0	0	0	0	0	0	0	0	0	2	0	0	0	.000	.000
Smith, Greg, Rochester†	.229	52	235	210	32	48	68	6	1	4	21	2	0	2	21	1	24	14	3	2	.324	.305
Smith, Mark, Rochester	.277	96	404	364	55	101	168	25	3	12	66	1	7	7	24	1	69	7	3	8	.462	.328
Smith, Pete, Charlotte	.125	10	9	8	0	1	1	0	0	0	0	0	0	0	0	0	4	0	0	1	.125	.222
Snyder, Cory, Pawtucket	.227	20	71	66	9	15	28	4	0	3	8	0	0	0	5	0	25	0	0	1	.424	.282
Sparks, Don, Columbus	.312	137	585	545	67	170	237	26	10	7	90	1	9	1	29	3	75	2	0	17	.435	.342
Spencer, Stan, Charlotte.........	.000	9	6	5	0	0	0	0	0	0	0	1	0	0	0	0	3	0	0	0	.000	.000
Spiers, Bill, Norfolk*	.220	12	51	41	4	9	11	2	0	0	4	1	1	0	8	0	6	0	1	4	.268	.340
Spradlin, Jerry, Charlotte†	.333	41	3	3	1	1	4	0	0	1	2	0	0	0	0	0	1	0	0	1	1.333	.333
Springer, Dennis, Scr./W.-B...	.048	30	26	21	1	1	1	0	0	0	0	5	0	0	0	0	12	0	0	0	.048	.048
Springer, Steve, Toledo	.265	25	108	102	14	27	42	7	1	2	10	0	2	0	4	1	18	1	1	3	.412	.287
Stairs, Matt, Pawtucket*	.284	75	305	271	40	77	133	17	0	13	56	1	3	1	29	3	41	3	3	10	.491	.352
Steverson, Todd, Toledo	.107	9	33	28	6	3	6	0	0	1	1	0	0	0	5	0	13	0	2	1	.214	.242
Stidham, Phil, Norfolk............	.000	34	5	5	0	0	0	0	0	0	0	0	0	0	0	0	1	0	0	0	.000	.000
Strawberry, Darryl, Columbus*..	.301	22	101	83	20	25	51	3	1	7	29	0	2	1	15	1	17	1	1	1	.614	.406
Swann, Pedro, Richmond*	.211	15	40	38	2	8	9	1	0	0	3	0	0	1	1	0	2	0	2	0	.237	.250
Tackett, Jeff, Toledo	.269	96	349	301	32	81	114	15	0	6	30	5	1	7	35	0	46	2	1	6	.379	.358
Tavarez, Jesus, Charlotte†	.300	39	151	140	15	42	55	6	2	1	8	0	2	0	9	0	19	7	7	1	.393	.338
Taylor, Sam, Scr./W.-B.*	.143	3	8	7	3	1	1	0	0	0	1	0	0	1	0	2	0	0	0	.143	.250
Telgheder, Dave, Norfolk	.000	29	13	12	0	0	0	0	0	0	0	1	0	0	0	0	8	0	0	0	.000	.000
Thobe, J.J, Ottawa	.333	55	3	3	0	1	1	0	0	0	0	0	0	0	0	0	0	0	0	0	.333	.333
Thobe, Tom, Richmond*	.250	48	5	4	0	1	2	1	0	0	0	1	0	0	0	0	2	0	0	0	.500	.250
Thomas, Royal, Richmond.....	.333	39	7	6	1	2	2	0	0	0	1	0	0	0	1	0	1	0	0	0	.333	.333
Thompson, Ryan, Norfolk.........	.340	15	61	53	7	18	27	3	0	2	11	0	4	0	4	0	15	4	1	0	.509	.361
Thoutsis, Paul, Columbus*	.215	52	137	130	10	28	34	4	1	0	15	1	1	1	4	0	16	1	0	4	.262	.243
Tokheim, David, Scr./W.-B.* ...	.271	127	483	450	64	122	189	18	8	11	66	3	7	5	18	2	55	6	7	11	.420	.302
Torres, Ricky, Ottawa	.250	32	9	8	2	2	3	1	0	0	1	1	0	0	0	0	4	0	0	0	.375	.250
Toth, David, Richmond	.231	7	14	13	1	3	3	0	0	0	1	0	0	0	1	0	2	0	1	1	.231	.286
Tovar, Raul, Ottawa	.304	20	64	56	8	17	19	2	0	0	7	0	0	0	8	0	5	0	0	3	.339	.391
Townley, Jason, Syracuse	.261	96	313	264	25	69	104	11	0	8	30	3	8	0	38	0	71	0	3	6	.394	.343
Tranberg, Mark, Scr./W.-B.......	.200	11	5	5	0	1	1	0	0	0	0	0	0	0	0	0	3	0	0	0	.200	.200
Tucker, Scooter, Richmond	.167	22	76	66	5	11	16	3	1	0	6	0	1	1	8	0	16	0	0	2	.242	.263
Twardoski, Mike, Richmond*	.138	19	69	58	7	8	9	1	0	0	5	1	0	0	10	2	13	1	0	0	.155	.265
Tyler, Brad, Rochester*	.258	114	441	361	60	93	167	17	3	17	52	0	5	4	71	4	63	10	5	3	.463	.381
Urbina, Ugueth, Ottawa..........	.000	13	16	16	1	0	0	0	0	0	0	0	0	0	0	0	9	0	0	0	.000	.000
Valdes, Marc, Charlotte	.125	27	29	24	1	3	5	2	0	0	3	5	0	0	0	0	7	0	0	0	.208	.125
Vatcher, Jim, Scr./W.-B.	.375	9	25	24	4	9	10	1	0	0	2	0	0	0	1	0	4	1	0	1	.417	.400
Velasquez, Guillermo, Ottawa*...	.250	45	120	112	11	28	36	5	0	1	9	0	0	0	8	1	14	1	2	3	.321	.300
Villanueva, Hector, Richmond...	.211	10	21	19	1	4	8	1	0	1	3	0	1	0	1	0	3	0	0	1	.421	.238
Wade, Scott, Pawtucket	.148	7	27	27	2	4	5	1	0	0	0	0	0	0	0	0	11	0	0	0	.185	.148
Wade, Terrell, Richmond*........	.207	24	32	29	2	6	8	2	0	0	4	2	0	0	1	0	9	0	0	0	.276	.233
Waggoner, Aubrey, Pawtucket*..	.188	16	59	48	3	9	10	1	0	0	8	1	0	0	10	1	22	2	2	0	.208	.328
Walker, Pete, Norfolk	.000	34	3	2	0	0	0	0	0	0	0	1	0	0	0	0	1	0	0	0	.000	.000
Warner, Mike, Richmond*	.206	28	110	97	10	20	32	4	1	2	8	2	0	1	10	0	21	0	3	0	.330	.287
Wawruck, Jim, Rochester*	.302	39	167	149	21	45	66	12	3	1	23	1	2	2	13	0	23	5	4	3	.443	.361
Weathers, David, Charlotte......	.000	1	1	1	0	0	0	0	0	0	0	0	0	0	0	0	0	0	0	0	.000	.000

Player, Team	Avg.	G	TPA	AB	R	H	TB	2B	3B	HR	RBI	SH	SF	HP	BB	IBB	SO	SB	CS	GDP	Slg.	OBP
Wedge, Eric, Pawtucket	.234	108	444	376	52	88	167	17	1	20	68	0	3	2	63	4	96	1	3	9	.444	.345
Weinke, Chris, Syracuse*	.226	113	388	341	42	77	123	12	2	10	41	0	2	1	44	2	74	4	3	10	.361	.314
West, David, Scr.W.-B.*	.000	1	2	1	0	0	0	0	0	0	0	1	0	0	0	0	0	0	0	0	.000	.000
White, Derrick, Toledo...........	.265	87	346	309	50	82	145	15	3	14	49	0	4	4	29	3	65	6	6	12	.469	.332
White, Gabe, Ottawa*	.000	12	3	3	0	0	0	0	0	0	0	0	0	0	0	0	2	0	0	0	.000	.000
Whiten, Mark, Pawtucket†	.284	28	121	102	19	29	46	3	1	4	13	0	0	0	19	0	30	4	2	3	.451	.397
Wiegandt, Scott, Scr.W.-B.*	.000	47	3	2	0	0	0	0	0	0	1	0	1	0	0	0	2	0	0	0	.000	.000
Williams, Jimmy, Nor.-Roch.*	.143	32	19	14	2	2	3	1	0	0	2	2	0	1	2	0	7	0	0	0	.214	.294
Williams, Juan, Richmond*	.264	45	147	129	18	34	54	5	0	5	11	0	1	0	17	0	38	1	3	5	.419	.347
Wilson, Craig, Toledo...........	.263	121	518	468	56	123	181	31	0	9	65	3	7	3	37	0	61	8	2	11	.387	.317
Wilson, Paul, Norfolk	.000	10	14	10	2	0	0	0	0	0	0	1	0	0	3	0	8	0	0	0	.000	.231
Wilson, Tom, Columbus	.258	22	73	62	11	16	21	3	1	0	9	2	0	0	9	0	10	0	0	0	.339	.352
Wilstead, Randy, Ottawa*	.292	9	34	24	6	7	11	2	1	0	3	0	2	2	6	0	3	0	0	1	.458	.441
Wood, Ted, Ottawa*	.267	98	369	326	35	87	129	16	1	8	49	1	3	2	37	6	63	9	2	8	.396	.342
Woodall, Brad, Richmond†	.222	14	12	9	2	2	3	1	0	0	1	0	0	0	2	0	3	0	0	0	.333	.364
Woods, Tyrone, Rochester	.261	70	265	238	30	62	105	17	1	8	31	0	2	1	24	1	68	2	3	6	.441	.328
Yan, Julian, Ottawa	.280	114	392	372	49	104	198	22	3	22	79	2	1	2	15	2	90	5	1	10	.532	.310
Zaun, Greg, Rochester†	.293	42	158	140	26	41	74	13	1	6	18	0	1	3	14	2	21	0	3	0	.529	.367
Zimmerman, Mike, Charlotte	.400	31	5	5	0	2	2	0	0	0	0	0	0	0	0	0	0	0	0	0	.400	.400
Zinter, Alan, Toledo†	.222	101	379	334	42	74	136	15	4	13	48	2	5	2	36	1	102	4	1	5	.407	.297
Zosky, Eddie, Charlotte	.247	92	326	312	27	77	105	15	2	3	42	5	1	1	7	0	48	2	3	8	.337	.265
Zuber, Jon, Scr.W.-B.*	.287	119	471	418	53	120	158	19	5	3	50	1	2	0	49	2	68	1	2	12	.378	.360
Zupcic, Bob, Charlotte...........	.295	72	283	254	34	75	120	12	0	11	47	1	4	0	24	0	35	2	2	3	.472	.351

GRAND SLAMS: Wedge, 2; Battle, Benitez, Bowers, Brewer, Ri. Butler, Capra, S. Carter, C. Delgado, Felix, Geisler, Hall, Houston, Leach, Lee, Lennon, Lewis, Lis, Malave, Morman, Perezchica, Ramos, Tyler, 1 each.

AWARDED FIRST BASE ON CATCHER'S INTERFERENCE: Buccheri 2 (Hernandez 2); Lee 2 (Alvarez, Gonzalez); Alvarez (Brooks); Fulton (Alvarez); Leach (Lutz); R. Martinez (Hernandez); Perezchica (Orton); Siddall (Tackett); M. Smith (Tackett); Zuber (Knorr).

PLAYERS WITH TWO OR MORE TEAMS

Player, Team	Avg.	G	TPA	AB	R	H	TB	2B	3B	HR	RBI	SH	SF	HP	BB	IBB	SO	SB	CS	GDP	Slg.	OBP
Bark, Brian, Richmond*	.000	13	2	2	0	0	0	0	0	0	0	0	0	0	0	0	0	0	0	0	.000	.000
Bark, Brian, Pawtucket*	.000	30	0	0	0	0	0	0	0	0	0	0	0	0	0	0	0	0	0	0	.000	.000
Batiste, Kim, Scr.W.-B.	.230	32	126	122	10	28	46	4	1	4	18	0	0	2	2	0	14	1	0	3	.377	.254
Batiste, Kim, Rochester........	.281	66	271	260	31	73	97	13	1	3	29	1	1	1	8	0	27	4	8	10	.373	.304
Brown, Jarvis, Norfolk	.284	45	169	148	29	42	60	12	3	0	17	2	0	1	18	0	29	6	3	3	.405	.365
Brown, Jarvis, Rochester........	.314	17	82	70	12	22	30	4	2	0	4	2	0	0	10	0	20	1	1	2	.429	.400
Cornelius, Reid, Ottawa........	.000	4	1	1	0	0	0	0	0	0	0	0	0	0	0	0	1	0	0	0	.000	.000
Cornelius, Reid, Norfolk........	.067	10	18	15	0	1	1	0	0	0	0	3	0	0	0	0	9	0	0	0	.067	.067
Friedman, Jason, Pawtucket*	.294	14	55	51	6	15	24	3	0	2	9	1	1	0	2	1	3	0	0	1	.471	.315
Friedman, Jason, Rochester*	.377	25	68	61	9	23	39	4	0	4	9	0	0	1	6	0	8	0	0	2	.639	.441
Jacobs, Frank, Norfolk*	.240	8	25	25	2	6	10	1	0	1	6	0	0	0	0	0	4	0	0	1	.400	.240
Jacobs, Frank, Ottawa*	.250	11	44	32	9	8	14	2	2	0	4	0	0	1	11	0	3	0	1	1	.438	.455
Kelly, Pat, Richmond	.182	11	24	22	2	4	5	1	0	0	2	0	0	2	0	0	5	0	1	1	.227	.250
Kelly, Pat, Syracuse...............	.132	30	80	68	6	9	16	1	0	2	8	2	2	2	6	0	15	0	1	1	.235	.218
Ochoa, Alex, Rochester........	.274	91	367	336	41	92	138	18	2	8	46	1	2	2	26	1	50	17	7	8	.411	.328
Ochoa, Alex, Norfolk	.309	34	138	123	17	38	54	6	2	2	15	0	1	0	14	0	12	7	3	4	.439	.377
Orton, John, Richmond...........	.180	17	56	50	6	9	15	3	0	1	6	1	1	1	3	0	22	2	2	1	.300	.236
Orton, John, Norfolk.............	.288	56	187	170	20	49	66	8	0	3	20	0	3	1	14	0	45	1	3	4	.388	.353
Small, Aaron, Syracuse........	.000	1	0	0	0	0	0	0	0	0	0	0	0	0	0	0	0	0	0	0	.000	.000
Small, Aaron, Charlotte	.000	33	2	2	0	0	0	0	0	0	0	0	0	0	0	0	2	0	0	0	.000	.000
Williams, Jimmy, Norfolk*	.143	27	19	14	2	2	3	1	0	0	2	2	0	1	2	0	7	0	0	0	.214	.294
Williams, Jimmy, Rochester*	.000	5	0	0	0	0	0	0	0	0	0	0	0	0	0	0	0	0	0	0	.000	.000

1995 PITCHING

TEAM

Team	W	L	Pct.	ERA	G	CG	ShO	Sv.	IP	H	TBF	R	ER	HR	SH	SF	HB	BB	IBB	SO	WP	Bk.
Norfolk	86	56	.606	3.01	142	15	18	35	1258.2	1153	5219	493	421	79	52	34	39	419	7	921	47	10
Richmond........	75	66	.532	3.46	141	4	14	41	1247.2	1289	5283	545	480	67	52	36	25	466	36	898	48	6
Toledo............	71	71	.500	3.47	142	10	10	39	1253.1	1241	5304	571	483	108	38	40	41	411	31	735	52	2
Rochester........	73	69	.514	3.80	142	9	5	36	1236.1	1263	5265	616	522	119	45	52	30	398	10	899	60	11
Ottawa............	72	70	.507	3.92	142	9	11	28	1224.1	1190	5174	601	533	87	51	48	50	410	13	761	53	6
Scr./W.-B.........	70	72	.493	4.03	142	12	8	39	1236.1	1211	5271	646	554	96	49	40	61	435	38	882	74	6
Columbus........	71	68	.511	4.07	140	5	8	33	1223.2	1220	5280	643	553	84	33	36	62	478	18	822	84	11
Pawtucket........	70	71	.496	4.54	142	6	1	33	1230.1	1310	5363	711	621	138	30	48	57	438	15	849	76	8
Syracuse........	59	82	.418	4.57	141	1	4	29	1229.2	1259	5437	768	624	137	32	40	35	530	30	946	67	7
Charlotte...........	59	81	.421	4.72	140	6	9	29	1225.1	1320	5363	735	642	133	28	47	57	483	11	763	90	8

INDIVIDUAL

TOP QUALIFIERS FOR EARNED-RUN AVERAGE TITLE

Minimum 114 innings. *Lefthanded pitcher.

Pitcher, Team	W	L	Pct.	ERA	G	GS	CG	ShO	GF	Sv.	IP	H	TBF	R	ER	HR	SH	SF	HB	BB	IBB	SO	WP	Bk.
Schmidt, Jason, Richmond....	8	6	.571	2.25	19	19	0	0	0	0	116.0	97	484	40	29	2	15	1	3	48	3	95	4	1
Murray, Matt, Richmond	10	3	.769	2.78	19	19	0	0	0	0	123.0	108	501	41	38	6	1	4	3	34	1	78	9	1
Weston, Mickey, Toledo........	11	7	.611	2.90	28	27	2	1	0	0	180.0	170	734	68	58	14	2	5	7	41	1	69	4	0
Rueter, Kirk, Ottawa*	9	7	.563	3.06	20	20	3	1	0	0	120.2	120	498	50	41	7	8	3	1	25	0	67	2	1
Adamson, Joel, Charlotte*	8	4	.667	3.29	19	18	2	0	0	0	115.0	113	471	51	42	12	0	3	6	20	0	80	4	2
Haynes, Jimmy, Rochester	12	8	.600	3.29	26	25	3	1	0	0	167.0	162	691	77	61	16	4	7	0	49	0	140	6	1

Pitcher, Team	W	L	Pct.	ERA	G	GS	CG	ShO	GF	Sv.	IP	H	TBF	R	ER	HR	SH	SF	HB	BB	IBB	SO	WP	Bk.
Deshaies, Jim, Scr./W.-B.*	7	8	.467	3.45	19	19	2	1	0	0	117.1	105	476	51	45	82		3	5	26	0	79	2	1
Williams, Jimmy, Nor.-Roc.*	12	6	.667	3.48	32	16	0	0	6	2	119.0	110	522	55	46	3	1	5	2	65	0	100	12	4
Ilsley, Blaise, Scr./W.-B.*	8	10	.444	3.88	29	29	2	1	0	0	185.1	210	786	96	80	17	8	4	5	34	2	102	6	0
Flener, Huck, Syracuse*	6	11	.353	3.94	30	23	1	0	3	0	134.2	131	572	70	59	20	1	6	6	41	2	83	2	2
Ojala, Kirt, Columbus*	8	7	.533	3.95	32	20	0	0	5	1	145.2	138	619	74	64	15	6	2	3	54	3	107	7	1
Carrara, Giovanni, Syracuse	7	7	.500	3.96	21	21	0	0	0	0	131.2	116	565	72	58	11	3	2	4	56	2	81	3	0
DeSilva, John, Rochester	11	9	.550	4.18	26	25	2	0	1	0	150.2	156	644	78	70	19	3	3	6	51	0	82	2	1
Carlyle, Ken, Toledo	8	8	.500	4.33	32	20	0	0	0	0	124.2	139	541	65	60	10	2	5	4	44	2	63	7	0
Bottenfield, Kent, Toledo	5	11	.313	4.54	27	19	2	1	3	1	136.2	148	601	80	69	15	6	4	4	55	4	68	6	**1**

DEPARTMENTAL LEADERS: W—Haynes, J. Williams, 12; L—Roberts, Valdes, 13; Pct.—Isringhausen, .900; G—Ricci, 68; GS—Ilsley, 29; CG—Pulsipher, Springer, Wilson, 4; ShO—Isringhausen, 3; GF—Ricci, 48; Sv.—Nichols, Ricci, 25; IP—Ilsley, 185.1; H—Ilsley, 210; TBF—Ilsley, 786; R—Springer, 101; ER—Roberts, Valdes, 92; HR—Roberts, 24; SH—J. Schmidt, 15; SF—Springer, 10; HB—Rumer, 16; BB—Rumer, 76; IBB—Wiegandt, 8; SO—Haynes, 140; WP—Long, 14; Bk.—J. Williams, 4.

ALL PITCHERS
*Lefthanded pitcher.

Pitcher, Team	W	L	Pct.	ERA	G	GS	CG	ShO	GF	Sv.	IP	H	TBF	R	ER	HR	SH	SF	HB	BB	IBB	SO	WP	Bk.
Acevedo, Juan, Norfolk	0	0	.000	0.00	2	2	0	0	0	0	3.0	0	9	0	0	0	0	1	1	0	0	2	0	0
Adamson, Joel, Charlotte*	8	4	.667	3.29	19	18	2	0	0	0	115.0	113	471	51	42	12	0	3	6	20	0	80	4	2
Ahearne, Pat, Toledo	7	9	.438	4.70	25	23	1	1	0	0	139.2	165	599	83	73	11	2	5	5	37	3	54	2	0
Alvarez, Jose, Richmond	1	3	.250	3.62	5	5	0	0	0	0	27.1	26	113	15	11	2	0	0	1	7	0	16	2	0
Alvarez, Tavo, Ottawa	2	1	.667	2.49	3	3	0	0	0	0	21.2	17	83	6	6	1	0	0	1	5	0	11	1	0
Ausanio, Joe, Columbus	1	0	1.000	7.50	11	0	0	0	9	3	12.0	12	53	10	10	1	1	2	1	5	0	20	1	0
Bakkum, Scott, Pawtucket	1	1	.500	1.71	15	0	0	0	4	2	26.1	21	114	13	5	3	0	1	2	7	0	15	4	0
Baptist, Travis, Syracuse*	3	4	.429	4.33	15	13	0	0	0	0	79.0	83	356	56	38	12	2	3	2	32	2	52	4	1
Bark, Brian, Rich.-Paw.*	5	3	.625	2.99	43	5	0	0	15	7	72.1	63	291	24	24	3	2	2	1	31	0	43	4	0
Barnes, Brian, Pawtucket*	7	5	.583	4.23	21	18	2	0	0	0	106.1	107	454	62	50	12	0	2	4	30	0	90	5	1
Barnwell, Rich, Columbus	0	0	.000	0.00	1	0	0	0	1	0	1.0	0	3	0	0	0	0	0	0	1	0	0	0	0
Batista, Miguel, Charlotte	6	12	.333	4.80	34	18	0	0	4	0	116.1	118	516	79	62	11	1	1	1	60	2	58	12	1
Bauer, Matt, Toledo*	2	1	.667	3.46	13	0	0	0	1	0	13.0	17	59	7	5	0	0	2	0	4	1	10	0	1
Baxter, Robert, Ottawa*	5	5	.500	3.92	39	13	0	0	10	0	101.0	125	426	51	44	6	4	5	0	25	1	39	3	0
Benitez, Armando, Charlotte	2	2	.500	1.25	17	0	0	0	17	8	21.2	10	81	4	3	2	0	0	0	7	0	37	1	0
Bennett, Joel, Pawtucket	2	4	.333	5.84	20	13	0	0	2	0	77.0	91	357	57	50	6	0	4	3	45	3	50	6	0
Bergman, Sean, Toledo	0	1	.000	6.00	1	1	0	0	0	0	3.0	4	13	2	2	1	0	0	1	0	0	4	0	0
Birkbeck, Mike, Norfolk	5	3	.625	2.36	9	9	0	0	0	0	53.1	52	215	20	14	2	3	0	1	13	0	39	1	0
Blair, Dirk, Richmond	1	1	.500	6.48	8	0	0	0	5	0	8.1	12	41	8	6	1	1	0	1	4	0	2	0	0
Blomdahl, Ben, Toledo	5	4	.556	3.54	41	0	0	0	23	3	56.0	55	232	24	22	6	1	1	2	13	4	39	3	0
Boehringer, Brian, Columbus	8	6	.571	2.77	17	17	3	0	0	0	104.0	101	439	39	32	6	3	3	4	31	1	58	9	0
Borland, Toby, Scr./W.-B.	0	0	.000	0.00	8	0	0	0	3	1	11.1	5	45	0	0	0	0	0	6	1	15	2	0	
Borowski, Joe, Rochester	1	3	.250	4.04	28	0	0	0	22	6	35.2	32	149	16	16	3	5	1	0	18	2	32	1	0
Bottenfield, Kent, Toledo	5	11	.313	4.54	27	19	2	1	3	1	136.2	148	601	80	69	15	6	4	4	55	4	68	6	1
Boucher, Denis, Ottawa*	2	3	.400	5.69	14	11	0	0	1	0	55.1	65	254	39	35	1	3	3	0	31	0	22	4	0
Bowen, Ryan, Charlotte	0	1	.000	9.64	1	1	0	0	0	0	4.2	5	22	5	5	1	0	0	0	4	0	3	0	0
Brock, Chris, Richmond	2	8	.200	5.40	22	9	0	0	5	0	60.0	68	270	37	36	2	3	3	1	27	2	43	1	2
Brow, Scott, Syracuse	1	5	.167	9.00	11	5	0	0	1	0	31.0	52	164	39	31	7	2	3	1	18	1	14	1	0
Brown, Chad, Syracuse*	1	1	.500	3.27	11	0	0	0	5	0	22.0	21	106	11	8	1	2	2	0	20	3	14	4	0
Brown, Jeff, Richmond*	1	2	.333	3.22	12	0	0	0	6	1	22.1	23	94	10	8	1	1	0	1	5	3	12	1	0
Brown, Keith, Charlotte	0	1	.000	2.45	4	0	0	0	2	0	7.1	6	31	3	2	1	0	0	1	2	0	3	1	0
Brown, Tim, Syracuse	3	8	.273	6.27	19	12	0	0	3	0	74.2	95	351	69	52	10	3	4	2	28	1	54	2	1
Buckels, Gary, Toledo	2	2	.500	2.15	31	0	0	0	7	0	46.0	37	193	14	11	2	1	1	0	20	2	38	10	0
Byrd, Paul, Norfolk	3	5	.375	2.79	22	10	1	0	10	6	87.0	71	341	29	27	6	0	1	5	21	0	61	1	0
Cain, Tim, Pawtucket	4	0	1.000	2.28	14	0	0	0	5	4	27.2	24	111	7	7	0	1	1	1	8	1	19	1	0
Capra, Nick, Charlotte	0	0	.000	0.00	1	0	0	0	1	0	0.1	1	3	0	0	0	0	0	0	1	0	0	0	0
Carlyle, Ken, Toledo	8	8	.500	4.33	32	20	0	0	0	0	124.2	139	541	65	60	10	2	5	4	44	2	63	7	0
Carper, Mark, Columbus	8	9	.471	4.82	33	14	0	0	3	1	106.1	114	478	61	57	10	2	2	7	55	0	61	10	0
Carrara, Giovanni, Syracuse	7	7	.500	3.96	21	21	0	0	0	0	131.2	116	565	72	58	11	3	2	4	56	2	81	3	0
Carter, Andy, Scr./W.-B.*	1	2	.333	4.35	14	1	0	0	5	0	20.2	17	91	10	10	2	0	1	3	13	2	18	1	1
Chavez, Carlos, Rochester	0	0	.000	10.80	1	0	0	0	0	0	1.2	3	11	2	2	0	0	1	0	3	0	1	2	0
Chitren, Steve, Rochester	0	0	.000	2.45	2	0	0	0	1	0	3.2	6	18	3	1	0	0	1	0	3	0	0	0	0
Christopher, Mike, Toledo	2	4	.333	2.23	36	0	0	0	35	21	36.1	38	160	14	9	1	3	3	1	8	4	32	1	0
Ciccarella, Joe, Pawtucket*	1	1	.500	3.86	11	5	0	0	2	0	25.2	22	112	15	11	2	3	0	4	10	1	13	4	0
Clark, Terry, Rochester	1	2	.333	2.70	9	0	0	0	7	5	10.0	5	37	3	3	2	0	1	0	2	1	10	0	1
Clary, Marty, Charlotte	2	2	.500	4.74	9	2	0	0	5	0	19.0	26	86	16	10	1	1	4	2	1	0	8	1	0
Clemens, Roger, Pawtucket	0	0	.000	0.00	1	1	0	0	0	0	5.0	1	19	0	0	0	0	0	0	3	0	5	0	0
Coffman, Kevin, Richmond	1	0	1.000	3.00	2	1	0	0	0	0	6.0	4	25	2	2	0	0	0	0	4	0	7	0	0
Combs, Pat, Scr./W.-B.*	4	4	.500	5.43	22	6	0	0	7	0	56.1	71	251	37	34	6	2	2	1	25	3	36	1	0
Cook, Andy, Columbus	2	3	.400	3.36	37	2	0	0	12	2	56.1	53	235	24	21	2	3	1	3	19	1	28	3	2
Coppinger, Rocky, Rochester	3	0	1.000	1.04	5	5	0	0	0	0	34.2	23	140	5	4	2	0	2	1	17	0	19	0	0
Cornelius, Reid, Ott.-Nor.	8	1	.889	1.67	14	13	1	0	0	0	81.0	73	341	22	15	3	3	2	8	24	0	50	3	0
Cornett, Brad, Syracuse	0	1	.000	4.91	3	3	0	0	0	0	11.0	13	49	6	6	1	0	1	0	4	0	8	1	0
Cox, Danny, Syracuse	0	0	.000	0.00	4	0	0	0	1	0	7.0	2	28	0	0	0	0	5	0	9	0	0		
Crabtree, Tim, Syracuse	0	2	.000	5.40	26	0	0	0	16	5	31.2	38	148	25	19	1	1	1	1	12	2	22	5	1
Crawford, Joe, Norfolk*	1	1	.500	1.93	8	0	0	0	1	0	18.2	9	70	5	4	1	0	1	0	4	0	13	0	0
Croghan, Andy, Columbus	1	1	.500	3.60	20	0	0	0	13	4	25.0	21	113	10	10	1	0	0	1	22	0	22	1	2
Crowley, Jim, Rochester	0	0	.000	13.50	1	0	0	0	1	0	2.0	4	11	3	3	0	0	0	0	1	0	3	0	0
Culberson, Calvin, Pawtucket	0	0	.000	6.39	6	0	0	0	1	0	12.2	18	65	12	9	0	0	3	0	11	0	4	1	0
Dascenzo, Doug, Charlotte*	0	0	.000	0.00	1	0	0	0	1	0	1.0	1	4	0	0	0	0	0	0	0	0	0	0	0
Davis, Mark, Charlotte*	0	0	.000	5.00	9	0	0	0	0	0	9.0	13	44	8	5	0	0	1	1	5	0	5	2	0
Dedrick, Jim, Rochester	0	0	1.000	1.77	24	2	0	0	4	1	45.2	45	190	9	9	0	2	1	4	1	31	4	0	
Deshaies, Jim, Scr./W.-B.*	7	8	.467	3.45	19	19	2	1	0	0	117.1	105	476	51	45	8	2	3	5	26	0	79	2	1
DeSilva, John, Rochester	11	9	.550	4.18	26	25	2	0	1	0	150.2	156	644	78	70	19	3	3	6	51	0	82	2	1
Dettmer, John, Rochester	4	7	.364	4.68	21	11	1	1	3	1	82.2	98	359	52	43	9	2	4	3	16	0	46	2	1
Diaz, Rafael, Ottawa	0	3	.000	6.56	32	2	0	0	7	0	48.0	51	218	38	35	6	2	4	4	25	2	31	4	1

Pitcher, Team	W	L	Pct.	ERA	G	GS	CG	ShO	GF	Sv.	IP	H	TBF	R	ER	HR	SH	SF	HB	BB	IBB	SO	WP	Bk.
Drahman, Brian, Charlotte	2	1	.667	6.30	21	0	0	0	15	4	20.0	28	99	14	14	1	2	1	0	11	1	17	3	0
Dunbar, Matt, Columbus*	2	3	.400	4.06	36	0	0	0	9	0	44.1	50	201	22	20	1	0	1	3	19	2	33	5	1
DuBois, Brian, Scr./W.-B.*	1	5	.167	4.56	49	0	0	0	19	1	51.1	58	230	31	26	4	3	2	1	25	5	48	5	0
Eiland, Dave, Columbus	8	7	.533	3.14	19	18	1	1	0	0	109.0	109	444	44	38	0	2	1	3	22	2	62	1	0
Eischen, Joey, Ottawa*	1	1	.500	1.72	11	0	0	0	3	0	15.2	9	61	4	3	0	1	0	0	8	1	13	0	0
Engle, Tom, Norfolk	0	1	.000	12.00	1	1	0	0	0	0	3.0	5	17	4	4	0	0	0	0	3	0	5	0	0
Eversgerd, Bryan, Ottawa*	6	2	.750	2.38	38	0	0	0	9	2	53.0	49	232	21	14	1	2	3	1	26	1	45	2	0
Fajardo, Hector, Ottawa	0	0	.000	4.11	11	0	0	0	5	0	15.1	18	69	7	7	2	1	0	0	6	0	9	1	0
Falteisek, Steve, Ottawa	2	0	1.000	1.17	3	3	1	1	0	0	23.0	17	86	4	3	0	0	0	1	5	0	18	0	1
Finnvold, Gar, Pawtucket	0	0	.000	0.00	1	1	0	0	0	0	3.2	1	15	1	0	0	0	0	0	1	0	3	0	0
Flener, Huck, Syracuse*	6	11	.353	3.94	30	23	1	0	3	0	134.2	131	572	70	59	20	1	6	6	41	2	83	2	2
Fletcher, Paul, Scr./W.-B.	4	1	.800	3.10	52	0	0	0	7	2	61.0	45	257	33	21	7	7	3	1	28	4	48	8	0
Florence, Don, Norfolk*	0	1	.000	0.96	41	0	0	0	16	4	47.0	37	191	6	5	0	5	1	1	17	3	29	2	0
Forney, Rick, Rochester	0	0	.000	3.94	3	3	0	0	0	0	16.0	19	72	9	7	2	2	1	0	6	0	12	2	0
Fraser, Willie, Ottawa	7	6	.538	3.19	19	19	1	1	0	0	107.1	94	434	44	38	11	3	3	3	18	0	84	2	0
Frazier, Ron, Columbus	1	2	.333	4.50	24	5	0	0	9	0	54.0	54	240	33	27	4	4	2	4	23	2	31	7	1
Frey, Steve, Scr./W.-B.*	0	0	.000	1.80	4	0	0	0	2	0	5.0	3	21	1	1	0	1	0	1	2	1	3	1	0
Fuller, Mark, Norfolk	0	0	.000	2.08	4	0	0	0	4	1	4.1	7	18	2	1	0	0	0	0	2	0	2	0	0
Gaddy, Bob, Scr./W.-B.*	5	7	.417	6.28	17	17	0	0	0	0	86.0	100	407	72	60	7	8	5	9	56	1	42	10	0
Gakeler, Dan, Pawtucket	0	2	.000	6.10	4	4	0	0	0	0	20.2	24	97	14	14	2	1	2	2	9	1	13	3	0
Ganote, Joe, Syracuse	0	0	.000	10.13	3	3	0	0	0	0	10.2	16	51	15	12	3	0	1	0	4	0	3	0	0
Garcia, Miguel, Ottawa*	0	0	.000	1.35	5	0	0	0	1	0	6.2	6	27	1	1	1	0	0	0	3	0	4	0	0
Gardiner, Mike, Toledo	0	1	.000	4.41	11	1	0	0	4	0	16.1	19	77	8	8	2	1	1	0	13	0	10	1	0
Gibson, Paul, Syracuse*	0	1	.000	4.81	26	0	0	0	8	3	24.1	24	106	16	13	0	1	0	2	6	2	28	1	0
Gohr, Greg, Toledo	0	2	.000	2.87	6	4	0	0	1	0	15.2	16	68	9	5	1	0	0	0	8	0	15	1	0
Gonzales, Frank, Toledo*	3	2	.600	3.31	49	0	0	0	6	0	51.2	43	217	23	19	4	2	0	3	17	1	54	2	0
Grace, Mike, Scr./W.-B.	2	0	1.000	1.59	2	2	1	0	0	0	17.0	17	68	3	3	0	0	0	0	2	0	13	2	0
Gray, Dennis, Syracuse*	2	2	.500	4.44	15	0	0	0	3	0	24.1	27	106	16	12	3	0	0	2	10	0	15	3	0
Greene, Tommy, Scr./W.-B.	3	0	1.000	2.22	4	4	0	0	0	0	28.1	18	105	8	7	1	1	1	0	6	0	19	5	0
Groom, Buddy, Toledo*	2	3	.400	1.91	6	5	1	0	0	0	33.0	31	132	14	7	4	1	0	0	4	0	24	0	0
Guzman, Juan, Syracuse	0	0	.000	0.00	1	1	0	0	0	0	5.0	1	18	0	0	0	0	0	0	3	0	5	1	0
Hammond, Chris, Charlotte*	0	0	.000	0.00	1	1	0	0	0	0	4.0	3	19	1	0	0	0	0	0	2	0	3	1	0
Hancock, Chris, Charlotte*	0	1	.000	13.50	3	0	0	0	1	0	3.1	6	20	6	5	0	0	1	0	4	0	2	0	0
Hansen, Brent, Pawtucket	7	5	.583	4.29	14	14	2	0	0	0	92.1	90	385	48	44	12	0	3	5	23	0	50	1	0
Harris, Greg, Ottawa	3	0	1.000	1.06	11	0	0	0	8	1	17.0	7	60	3	2	1	1	1	0	3	0	17	0	0
Harrison, Tom, Richmond	2	1	.667	3.21	9	6	0	0	1	1	42.0	34	182	17	15	2	4	3	2	20	1	16	0	1
Hartley, Mike, Paw.- Roc.	1	2	.333	3.43	34	1	0	0	16	1	57.2	51	235	22	22	7	1	2	3	14	1	51	2	2
Haynes, Jimmy, Rochester	12	8	.600	3.29	26	25	3	1	0	0	167.0	162	691	77	61	16	4	7	0	49	0	140	6	1
Heble, Kurt, Syracuse	0	0	.000	5.79	4	0	0	0	1	0	4.2	6	23	4	3	0	0	0	0	2	0	5	1	0
Heffernan, Bert, Ottawa	0	0	.000	0.00	1	0	0	0	0	0	0.1	1	3	0	0	0	0	0	0	1	0	1	0	0
Henry, Dwayne, Toledo	1	1	.500	3.35	41	0	0	0	28	11	48.1	43	212	21	18	3	1	3	3	24	0	52	5	0
Hernandez, Jeremy, Charlotte	0	2	.000	5.58	15	3	0	0	6	0	30.2	37	142	20	19	6	1	1	0	15	0	24	5	0
Hernandez, Willie, Columbus*	2	1	.667	7.67	22	0	0	0	10	0	27.0	43	134	24	23	3	0	3	2	12	0	16	2	1
Hill, Chris, Pawtucket*	2	3	.400	6.10	10	6	0	0	2	0	31.0	31	147	24	21	3	1	3	2	25	1	20	4	0
Hill, Eric, Scr./W.-B.	4	3	.571	4.30	21	0	0	0	7	2	23.0	24	99	13	11	4	1	0	0	9	0	16	2	0
Hoeme, Steve, Pawtucket	0	2	.000	4.62	15	2	0	0	5	1	39.0	40	165	21	20	2	0	1	1	15	0	21	1	0
Holman, Brad, Rochester	0	1	.000	0.00	1	1	0	0	0	0	1.2	5	12	4	0	0	0	0	1	2	0	0	1	0
Howard, Chris, Pawtucket*	3	1	.750	3.92	17	0	0	0	2	0	20.2	25	91	11	9	6	0	2	0	4	1	19	0	0
Hurst, James, Rochester*	1	1	.500	3.79	10	0	0	0	2	0	19.0	17	74	8	8	2	0	1	0	4	1	17	4	0
Hutton, Mark, Columbus	2	6	.250	8.43	11	11	0	0	0	0	52.1	64	243	51	49	7	0	3	4	24	1	23	2	0
Ilsley, Blaise, Scr./W.-B.*	8	10	.444	3.88	29	29	2	1	0	0	185.1	210	786	96	80	17	8	4	5	34	2	102	6	0
Innis, Jeff, Scr./W.-B.	0	2	.000	4.30	15	0	0	0	10	6	14.2	13	64	8	7	0	0	1	0	8	1	14	1	0
Isringhausen, Jason, Norfolk	9	1	.900	1.55	12	12	3	3	0	0	87.0	64	343	17	15	2	2	0	2	24	0	75	4	1
Jacome, Jason, Norfolk*	2	4	.333	3.92	8	8	0	0	0	0	43.2	40	181	21	19	5	4	1	1	13	0	31	1	0
Johnston, Joel, Pawtucket	1	2	.333	6.75	30	0	0	0	13	6	41.1	54	194	31	31	4	1	2	2	19	1	39	3	1
Jones, Calvin, Pawtucket	5	2	.714	4.03	33	0	0	0	27	8	38.0	37	165	23	17	5	3	2	0	15	1	36	6	0
Jordan, Ricardo, Syracuse*	0	0	.000	6.57	13	0	0	0	5	0	12.1	15	59	9	9	1	0	1	0	7	1	17	2	0
Juden, Jeff, Scr./W.-B.	6	4	.600	4.10	14	13	0	0	0	0	83.1	73	354	43	38	4	4	3	9	33	1	65	4	1
Juhl, Mike, Scr./W.-B.*	0	0	.000	0.00	1	0	0	0	1	0	0.1	0	1	0	0	0	0	0	0	0	0	0	1	0
Kamieniecki, Scott, Columbus	1	0	1.000	0.00	1	1	0	0	0	0	6.2	2	23	0	0	0	0	0	0	1	0	10	0	0
Karp, Ryan, Scr./W.-B.*	7	1	.875	4.20	13	13	0	0	0	0	81.1	81	357	43	38	6	2	4	8	31	0	73	2	0
Kerley, Collin, Ottawa	2	0	1.000	2.16	5	0	0	0	1	0	8.1	10	39	3	2	0	1	0	0	3	0	3	0	0
Kiely, John, Toledo	0	0	.000	1.46	14	0	0	0	5	0	12.1	13	56	4	2	1	0	0	0	6	2	8	0	0
King, Richard, Richmond	1	1	.500	2.57	14	0	0	0	5	0	14.0	13	63	8	4	1	0	0	0	6	0	3	0	0
Klingenbeck, Scott, Rochester	3	1	.750	2.72	8	7	0	0	0	0	43.0	46	177	14	13	2	3	2	1	10	0	29	2	0
Kramer, Tommy, Toledo	3	1	.750	4.61	6	5	0	0	0	0	27.1	23	116	15	14	6	0	2	0	16	0	15	0	0
Krivda, Rick, Rochester*	6	5	.545	3.19	16	16	1	0	0	0	101.2	96	429	44	36	11	6	4	2	32	0	74	3	3
Lane, Aaron, Rochester*	0	0	.000	6.30	9	0	0	0	2	0	10.0	11	47	11	7	2	0	0	2	5	0	9	2	0
Langbehn, Gregg, Pawtucket*	0	0	.000	0.00	7	0	0	0	0	0	2.0	0	12	0	0	0	0	0	0	1	0	6	1	0
Layana, Tim, Ottawa	1	1	.500	8.50	26	0	0	0	9	4	36.0	56	178	35	34	7	1	2	2	20	1	27	4	0
Lee, Mark, Rochester*	4	2	.667	1.57	25	0	0	0	8	3	28.2	18	108	6	5	0	1	0	0	5	0	35	1	0
Leiper, Dave, Ottawa*	0	0	.000	0.00	2	0	0	0	1	0	3.0	1	11	0	0	0	0	0	0	1	0	2	0	0
Lemon, Don, Charlotte	0	0	.000	5.40	6	0	0	0	2	0	11.2	11	50	7	7	2	0	0	0	3	0	8	0	0
Lemp, Chris, Rochester	0	0	.000	11.25	3	0	0	0	1	0	4.0	7	21	5	5	1	0	1	0	3	0	4	0	0
Lewis, Richie, Charlotte	5	2	.714	3.20	17	8	1	0	4	0	59.0	50	243	22	21	5	2	4	0	20	0	45	4	2
Lewis, Scott, Pawtucket	0	0	.000	3.86	3	0	0	0	1	0	4.2	7	19	2	2	2	0	0	0	0	0	1	1	0
Lima, Jose, Toledo	3	6	.625	3.01	11	11	1	0	0	0	74.2	69	301	26	25	9	3	4	1	14	2	40	2	0
Lomon, Kevin, Richmond	1	2	.333	3.00	32	3	0	0	8	1	60.0	62	261	23	20	9	4	4	0	32	4	52	4	0
Long, Steve, Charlotte	5	4	.556	5.96	33	6	0	0	10	4	74.0	71	344	57	49	7	1	2	8	46	1	46	14	0
Looney, Brian, Pawtucket*	4	7	.364	3.49	18	18	1	0	0	0	100.2	106	438	44	39	9	2	3	3	33	0	78	7	2
Ludwick, Eric, Norfolk	1	1	.500	5.85	4	3	0	0	0	0	20.0	22	88	15	13	3	0	0	1	7	0	9	1	0
MacDonald, Bob, Columbus*	2	1	.667	2.33	13	0	0	0	2	0	19.1	22	84	7	5	1	1	0	0	5	0	13	0	0
Magee, Bo, Rochester*	0	0	.000	13.50	2	0	0	0	0	0	2.0	4	11	3	3	0	0	0	0	1	0	1	0	0

Pitcher, Team	W	L	Pct.	ERA	G	GS	CG	ShO	GF	Sv.	IP	H	TBF	R	ER	HR	SH	SF	HB	BB	IBB	SO	WP	Bk.
Magrane, Joe, Ottawa*	3	6	.333	4.84	12	12	0	0	0	0	67.0	69	295	43	36	5	5	1	3	31	0	37	7	0
Mantei, Matt, Charlotte	0	1	.000	2.57	6	0	0	0	1	0	7.0	1	27	3	2	1	0	1	1	5	0	10	0	0
Manuel, Barry, Ottawa	5	12	.294	4.59	35	22	1	0	8	1	127.1	125	554	71	65	4	4	9	14	50	1	85	6	2
Marshall, Randy, Toledo*	7	3	.700	2.30	20	17	2	1	0	0	109.1	99	445	38	28	7	4	3	2	29	3	67	2	0
Martel, Ed, Toledo	0	1	.000	1.59	4	0	0	0	1	0	5.2	4	28	1	1	0	1	0	1	5	0	3	0	0
Martin, Tom, Richmond*	0	0	.000	9.00	7	0	0	0	2	0	9.0	10	45	9	9	4	0	0	0	10	2	3	0	0
Mathews, Terry, Charlotte	0	0	.000	4.91	2	0	0	0	0	0	3.2	5	15	2	2	0	0	0	0	0	0	5	0	0
Maxcy, Brian, Toledo	1	3	.250	5.26	20	0	0	0	9	2	25.2	32	120	20	15	3	4	0	1	11	1	11	3	0
May, Darrell, Richmond*	4	2	.667	3.71	9	9	0	0	0	0	51.0	53	216	21	21	1	1	3	0	16	1	42	2	0
McCready, Jim, Norfolk	0	1	.000	2.01	28	0	0	0	8	0	40.1	41	175	14	9	0	5	1	0	20	1	21	1	0
McDonald, Ben, Rochester	0	0	.000	2.45	1	1	0	0	0	0	3.2	1	17	2	1	0	0	0	0	4	0	1	1	0
McGehee, Kevin, Rochester	11	9	.550	5.83	27	20	0	0	0	0	126.2	150	554	89	82	18	3	7	5	33	0	84	5	1
Melendez, Jose, Scr./W.-B.	0	0	.000	6.00	2	0	0	0	0	0	3.0	6	19	4	2	0	1	1	1	2	0	1	0	0
Mendoza, Ramiro, Columbus	1	0	1.000	2.57	2	2	0	0	0	0	14.0	10	51	4	4	0	1	0	0	2	0	13	1	0
Menhart, Paul, Syracuse	2	4	.333	6.31	10	10	0	0	0	0	51.1	62	234	42	36	5	2	3	0	25	0	30	3	1
Miller, Kurt, Charlotte	8	11	.421	4.62	22	22	0	0	0	0	126.2	143	563	76	65	13	5	3	7	55	0	83	6	0
Mills, Alan, Rochester	0	1	.000	6.00	1	1	0	0	0	0	2.2	2	17	6	0	0	0	1	0	5	0	2	1	0
Minutelli, Gino, Richmond*	0	0	.000	4.41	5	3	0	0	0	0	16.1	20	70	8	8	0	1	1	0	3	0	8	0	0
Mitchell, John, Ottawa	0	1	.000	4.32	6	0	0	0	1	0	8.1	8	35	4	4	1	1	0	0	3	1	5	0	0
Montoya, Al, Syracuse*	0	0	.000	0.00	7	0	0	0	4	0	4.1	3	18	1	0	0	0	0	1	2	2	0	0	0
Munoz, Bobby, Scr./W.-B.	1	0	1.000	0.56	2	2	1	1	0	0	16.0	8	57	2	1	0	0	0	2	3	1	10	1	0
Murphy, Rob, Charlotte*	0	0	.000	0.00	3	0	0	0	3	2	3.0	2	11	0	0	0	0	0	0	1	1	1	0	0
Murray, Matt, Richmond	10	3	.769	2.78	19	19	0	0	0	0	123.0	108	501	41	38	6	1	4	3	34	1	78	9	1
Musset, Jose, Columbus	0	0	.000	6.23	5	0	0	0	1	0	4.1	4	19	4	3	2	0	0	0	2	0	4	1	0
Mutis, Jeff, Charlotte*	0	1	.000	3.72	27	0	0	0	5	2	36.1	31	153	18	15	2	2	4	1	14	2	21	1	0
Myers, Jimmy, Rochester	0	4	.000	3.06	55	0	0	0	28	6	64.2	72	289	28	22	2	3	2	1	29	1	31	1	0
Myers, Mike, Char.- Tol.*	0	5	.000	5.40	43	0	0	0	14	0	45.0	47	197	29	27	7	2	0	1	18	1	32	5	0
Newlin, Jim, Charlotte	0	0	.000	4.26	5	0	0	0	2	0	6.1	6	24	3	3	0	0	0	1	0	5	1	0
Nichols, Rod, Richmond	1	2	.333	2.53	41	3	0	0	37	25	57.0	54	232	16	16	5	0	1	2	6	1	57	1	0
Ojala, Kirt, Columbus*	8	7	.533	3.95	32	20	0	0	5	1	145.2	138	619	74	64	15	6	2	3	54	3	107	7	1
Olivares, Omar, Scr./W.-B.	0	3	.000	4.87	7	7	0	0	0	0	44.1	49	197	25	24	2	2	4	0	20	2	28	3	0
Oquist, Mike, Rochester	0	0	.000	5.25	7	0	0	0	3	2	12.0	17	56	8	7	0	0	0	5	1	11	0	0
Osuna, Al, Norfolk*	3	1	.750	3.00	14	4	0	0	2	0	42.0	39	175	14	14	5	0	3	1	12	0	31	1	0
Pacheco, Alex, Ottawa	1	0	1.000	6.23	4	0	0	0	0	0	8.2	8	35	6	6	2	0	0	0	5	0	4	0	0
Patterson, Jeff, Columbus	5	3	.625	3.61	33	0	0	0	8	0	62.1	56	268	30	25	0	3	3	0	30	2	36	9	0
Pavlas, Dave, Columbus	3	3	.500	2.61	48	0	0	0	32	18	58.2	43	233	19	17	2	4	1	1	20	2	51	4	0
Paxton, Darrin, Norfolk*	0	0	.000	9.00	1	0	0	0	0	0	2.0	3	10	2	2	0	0	0	0	2	0	0	0	0
Pena, Alejandro, Charlotte	0	0	.000	0.96	9	0	0	0	8	5	9.1	2	31	1	1	0	0	0	1	0	7	0	0
Pena, Jim, Ottawa*	0	0	.000	3.68	7	0	0	0	2	0	7.1	4	34	3	3	1	1	0	2	8	1	7	3	0
Perigny, Don, Ottawa	1	1	.500	5.14	6	0	0	0	3	0	7.0	8	30	6	4	1	0	1	1	1	0	10	2	0
Person, Robert, Norfolk	2	1	.667	4.50	5	4	0	0	0	0	32.0	30	138	17	16	2	1	1	0	13	0	33	4	0
Pettitte, Andy, Columbus*	0	0	.000	0.00	2	2	0	0	0	0	11.2	7	38	0	0	0	0	0	0	0	0	8	1	0
Pierce, Jeff, Pawtucket	4	2	.667	4.14	23	3	0	0	8	0	41.1	34	172	21	19	5	2	2	2	16	1	43	2	1
Plummer, Dale, Pawtucket	9	9	.500	5.19	34	10	1	0	9	0	100.2	140	457	73	58	13	5	5	6	18	2	47	0	1
Polley, Dale, Richmond*	3	2	.600	1.56	47	0	0	0	22	7	63.1	51	261	15	11	2	2	3	2	20	5	60	2	0
Potts, Mike, Richmond*	5	5	.500	3.79	38	1	0	0	17	1	73.2	79	320	35	31	4	3	1	0	37	4	52	6	0
Pulsipher, Bill, Norfolk*	6	4	.600	3.14	13	13	4	2	0	0	91.2	84	377	36	32	3	5	3	1	33	0	63	2	3
Quirico, Rafael, Columbus*	0	0	.000	4.70	20	0	0	0	8	0	23.0	15	96	14	12	1	0	1	3	14	0	21	5	2
Rapp, Pat, Charlotte	0	1	.000	6.00	1	1	0	0	0	0	6.0	6	23	4	4	0	0	0	1	0	5	2	0
Reed, Darren, Richmond	0	0	.000	0.00	1	0	0	0	1	0	1.0	1	5	0	0	0	0	0	1	0	1	0	0
Rhodes, Arthur, Rochester*	2	1	.667	2.70	4	4	1	0	0	0	30.0	27	125	12	9	2	3	0	1	8	0	33	1	0
Ricci, Chuck, Scr./W.-B.	4	3	.571	2.49	68	0	0	0	48	25	65.0	48	269	22	18	6	4	1	4	24	5	66	1	0
Rivera, Mariano, Columbus	2	2	.500	2.10	7	7	1	1	0	0	30.0	25	114	10	7	2	0	1	0	3	0	30	0	0
Roberts, Chris, Norfolk*	7	13	.350	5.52	25	25	2	0	0	0	150.0	197	676	99	92	24	6	4	8	58	0	88	5	0
Robertson, Rod, Rochester	0	0	.000	15.43	1	0	0	0	0	0	2.1	6	14	4	4	2	0	0	0	2	0	0	0	0
Robinson, Ken, Syracuse	5	3	.625	3.22	38	0	0	0	12	2	50.1	37	201	18	18	6	2	2	2	12	2	61	2	0
Rodriguez, Frank, Pawtucket	1	1	.500	4.00	13	2	0	0	8	2	27.0	19	109	12	12	2	0	0	3	8	0	18	1	0
Rogers, Bryan, Norfolk	8	3	.727	2.21	56	0	0	0	34	10	77.1	58	303	22	19	4	4	3	0	22	1	50	8	0
Rogers, Jimmy, Syracuse	3	4	.429	3.05	38	0	0	0	9	1	73.2	65	308	26	25	4	3	3	3	31	2	82	6	0
Rojas, Euclides, Charlotte	0	1	.000	3.00	2	0	0	0	1	0	3.0	2	13	1	1	0	0	0	0	2	0	2	0	0
Rueter, Kirk, Ottawa*	9	7	.563	3.06	20	20	3	1	0	0	120.2	120	498	50	41	7	8	3	1	25	0	67	2	1
Rumer, Tim, Columbus*	10	8	.556	5.22	28	25	0	0	1	0	141.1	156	654	98	82	13	7	5	16	76	1	110	5	1
Ryan, Ken, Pawtucket	0	1	.000	6.30	9	0	0	0	5	0	10.0	12	42	7	7	1	0	1	0	4	0	6	1	0
Ryan, Kevin, Rochester	0	3	.000	9.35	6	2	0	0	0	0	17.1	27	83	20	18	3	0	1	1	4	0	7	1	0
Sackinsky, Brian, Rochester	3	3	.500	4.60	14	11	0	0	0	0	62.2	70	260	33	32	6	1	4	1	10	0	42	4	0
Santos, Henry, Toledo*	0	1	.000	6.75	1	0	0	0	0	0	2.2	3	13	2	2	1	0	0	0	2	0	4	0	0
Satre, Jason, Pawtucket	1	5	.167	6.16	9	5	0	0	1	0	30.2	38	143	23	21	3	2	2	2	16	0	14	2	0
Scheid, Rich, Charlotte*	1	4	.200	5.93	19	8	0	0	1	0	54.2	74	246	40	36	10	1	4	2	15	0	37	1	0
Schmidt, Curt, Ottawa	5	0	1.000	2.22	43	0	0	0	38	15	52.2	40	206	14	13	1	0	1	4	18	0	38	2	0
Schmidt, Jason, Richmond	8	6	.571	2.25	19	19	0	0	0	0	116.0	97	484	40	29	2	15	1	3	48	3	95	4	1
Seelbach, Chris, Richmond	4	6	.400	4.66	14	14	1	0	0	0	73.1	64	314	39	38	7	0	3	2	39	0	65	3	0
Segura, Jose, Columbus	0	2	.000	8.71	11	0	0	0	8	4	10.1	18	59	12	10	0	0	0	8	0	8	2	0
Sele, Aaron, Pawtucket	0	0	.000	9.00	2	2	0	0	0	0	5.0	9	25	5	5	3	0	0	1	2	0	1	0	0
Seminara, Frank, Rochester	1	0	1.000	3.28	29	0	0	0	5	0	35.2	31	149	13	13	2	3	2	1	14	0	20	3	1
Senior, Shawn, Pawtucket*	0	1	.000	6.00	1	1	0	0	0	0	6.0	9	29	4	4	0	0	0	2	0	1	0	0
Shea, John, Rochester*	0	1	.000	2.95	38	0	0	0	19	4	39.2	38	172	16	13	8	1	1	1	17	2	37	2	0
Shepherd, Keith, Charlotte	1	1	.500	21.21	4	0	0	0	1	0	4.2	11	34	11	11	1	0	1	3	0	2	0	0
Small, Aaron, Syr.- Char.	2	1	.667	2.98	34	0	0	0	17	10	42.1	39	179	16	14	3	0	1	2	11	1	33	3	0
Smith, Daryl, Columbus	3	3	.500	4.00	13	7	0	0	2	0	51.1	54	225	31	23	5	0	3	4	20	1	23	5	0
Smith, Pete, Charlotte	2	1	.667	3.86	10	8	0	0	1	0	49.0	51	206	21	21	5	1	2	1	17	0	20	2	2
Smith, Zane, Pawtucket*	0	0	.000	0.00	1	1	0	0	0	0	7.0	5	23	0	0	0	0	0	0	0	5	0	0
Sodowsky, Clint, Toledo	5	1	.833	2.85	9	9	1	0	0	0	60.0	47	247	21	19	5	2	0	3	30	1	32	1	0
Spencer, Stan, Charlotte	1	4	.200	7.84	9	9	0	0	0	0	41.1	61	198	37	36	9	0	3	24	1	19	0	0

Pitcher, Team	W	L	Pct.	ERA	G	GS	CG	ShO	GF	Sv.	IP	H	TBF	R	ER	HR	SH	SF	HB	BB	IBB	SO	WP	Bk.
Spoljaric, Paul, Syracuse*	2	10	.167	4.93	43	9	0	0	27	10	87.2	69	382	51	48	133	1	2	54	3	108	8	0
Spradlin, Jerry, Charlotte	3	3	.500	3.03	41	0	0	0	14	1	59.1	59	244	26	20	6	2	3	3	15	1	38	5	0
Springer, Dennis, Scr./W.-B.	10	11	.476	4.68	30	23	4	0	3	0	171.0	163	715	101	89	19	0	10	7	47	1	115	8	0
Steed, Rick, Syracuse	4	3	.571	3.72	31	0	0	0	15	1	55.2	51	239	29	23	2	2	2	2	23	1	34	1	1
Stidham, Phil, Norfolk	6	2	.750	3.21	34	6	0	0	12	1	70.0	56	305	33	25	4	2	6	5	36	1	56	5	0
Stoddard, Bob, Norfolk	0	1	.000	6.75	3	0	0	0	1	0	2.2	5	14	2	2	0	0	0	1	0	1	1	1	1
Suppan, Jeff, Pawtucket	2	3	.400	5.32	7	7	0	0	0	0	45.2	50	191	29	27	9	0	1	1	9	0	32	2	0
Sutherland, John, Columbus	0	0	.000	9.00	3	0	0	0	2	0	3.0	5	14	3	3	0	0	0	0	0	0	2	0	0
Telgheder, Dave, Norfolk	5	4	.556	2.24	29	11	0	0	8	3	92.1	77	356	34	23	7	5	2	1	8	0	75	0	2
Thobe, J.J., Ottawa	5	8	.385	3.27	55	0	0	0	25	5	88.0	79	354	37	32	8	6	2	1	16	3	36	1	0
Thobe, Tom, Richmond*	7	0	1.000	1.84	48	2	1	1	15	5	88.0	65	350	27	18	2	3	1	1	26	5	57	5	0
Thomas, Royal, Richmond	7	7	.500	3.48	39	8	1	1	12	0	88.0	103	389	43	34	6	3	2	2	24	2	39	1	0
Tilmon, Pat, Syracuse	0	0	.000	1.50	4	0	0	0	0	0	6.0	8	28	3	1	0	0	0	4	0	2	0	0
Timlin, Mike, Syracuse	1	1	.500	1.04	8	0	0	0	2	0	17.1	13	70	6	2	2	0	0	4	0	13	0	0
Torres, Ricky, Ottawa	3	8	.273	5.01	32	11	1	0	4	0	91.2	90	391	58	51	9	3	4	6	26	1	58	5	0
Tranberg, Mark, Scr./W.-B.	1	4	.200	7.23	11	2	0	0	3	0	23.2	32	107	19	19	3	2	1	2	6	0	15	4	0
Tunnell, Lee, Toledo	0	1	.000	3.14	7	0	0	0	1	0	14.1	9	53	5	5	0	2	0	1	2	0	7	0	0
Urbina, Ugueth, Ottawa	6	2	.750	3.04	13	11	2	1	0	0	68.0	46	273	26	23	1	3	2	1	26	0	55	1	0
Valdes, Marc, Charlotte	9	13	.409	4.86	27	27	3	2	0	0	170.1	189	728	98	92	19	3	5	12	59	1	104	2	1
VanEgmond, Tim, Pawtucket	5	3	.625	3.92	12	12	0	0	0	0	66.2	66	279	32	29	10	1	2	4	21	1	47	5	0
Veres, Randy, Charlotte	1	0	1.000	2.70	6	0	0	0	6	1	6.2	3	29	2	2	1	1	0	0	5	0	5	1	0
Wade, Terrell, Richmond*	10	9	.526	4.56	24	23	1	0	0	0	142.0	137	600	76	72	10	3	5	1	63	1	124	5	1
Wainhouse, David, Syr.- Char.	3	2	.600	4.50	30	0	0	0	22	5	28.0	35	132	19	14	2	1	3	1	15	3	20	6	0
Wakefield, Tim, Pawtucket	2	1	.667	2.52	4	4	0	0	0	0	25.0	23	105	10	7	1	0	1	4	9	0	14	0	0
Walker, Pete, Norfolk	5	2	.714	3.91	34	1	0	0	25	8	48.1	51	207	24	21	4	3	1	1	16	1	39	2	1
Wallace, Kent, Columbus	4	1	.800	3.02	9	9	0	0	0	0	50.2	44	200	19	17	8	0	0	1	11	0	31	3	0
Ward, Duane, Syracuse	1	1	.500	15.00	6	0	0	0	4	0	6.0	14	33	10	10	1	0	0	2	1	4	0	0
Ware, Jeff, Syracuse	7	0	1.000	3.00	16	16	0	0	0	0	75.0	62	319	29	25	8	0	1	2	46	0	76	3	0
Weathers, David, Charlotte	0	0	.000	9.00	1	1	0	0	0	0	5.0	10	27	5	5	0	0	0	0	5	0	1	0
Weber, Ben, Syracuse	4	5	.444	5.40	25	15	0	0	3	1	91.2	111	403	62	55	10	2	1	3	27	1	38	5	0
Wegmann, Tom, Rochester	3	2	.600	3.44	9	5	1	0	2	0	34.0	30	140	15	13	3	3	1	3	9	0	23	0	0
Wengert, Bill, Pawtucket	1	0	1.000	5.40	7	0	0	0	1	0	11.2	17	53	7	7	1	0	0	0	4	0	10	0	0
Wertz, Bill, Pawtucket	4	5	.444	5.80	29	6	0	0	12	2	63.2	74	298	47	41	11	4	4	1	31	1	55	7	0
West, David, Scr./W.-B.*	1	0	1.000	0.00	1	1	1	1	0	0	7.0	2	22	0	0	0	0	0	0	0	0	6	0	0
Weston, Mickey, Toledo	11	7	.611	2.90	28	27	2	1	0	0	180.0	170	734	58	58	14	2	5	7	41	1	69	4	0
White, Gabe, Ottawa*	2	3	.400	3.90	12	12	0	0	0	0	62.1	58	264	31	27	10	1	4	4	17	0	37	2	1
Whitehurst, Wally, Paw.- Syr.	4	4	.500	5.17	12	10	0	0	0	0	55.2	68	242	37	32	7	2	0	0	12	0	34	4	0
Wickander, Kevin, Toledo*	2	1	.667	2.13	16	0	0	0	3	1	12.2	11	52	3	3	1	0	1	1	5	0	8	0	0
Wiegandt, Scott, Scr./W.-B.*	1	3	.250	2.98	47	0	0	0	15	2	54.1	55	234	19	18	0	1	0	2	27	8	41	5	2
Wiggs, Johnny, Pawtucket*	1	0	1.000	5.79	14	0	0	0	9	0	9.1	11	40	6	6	0	0	0	3	0	6	0	0
Williams, Jimmy, Nor.-Roc.*	12	6	.667	3.48	32	16	0	0	6	2	119.0	110	522	55	46	3	1	5	2	65	0	100	12	4
Williams, Mike, Scr./W.-B.	0	0	.000	4.66	3	3	1	0	0	0	9.2	8	39	5	5	0	0	0	0	2	0	7	0	0
Williams, Woody, Syracuse	0	0	.000	3.52	5	1	0	0	1	1	7.2	5	34	3	3	0	0	0	0	5	0	13	0	0
Wilson, Paul, Norfolk	5	3	.625	2.85	10	10	4	2	0	0	66.1	59	270	25	21	3	2	1	3	20	0	67	2	0
Woodall, Brad, Richmond*	4	4	.500	5.10	13	11	0	0	1	0	65.1	70	279	39	37	5	6	0	3	17	1	44	1	0
York, Mike, Syracuse	1	4	.200	7.00	20	5	0	0	3	0	45.0	55	227	50	35	11	0	2	1	27	0	37	5	0
Zimmerman, Mike, Charlotte	2	2	.500	5.30	31	7	0	0	9	0	69.2	84	319	46	41	6	3	3	4	41	0	30	10	0

COMBINATION SHUTOUTS: **Charlotte (7)**—Adamson-Hancock, Adamson-Lewis-Myers-Small, Lewis-Scheid-Spradlin, Long-Mutis, Miller-Myers, Miller-Small, Valdes-Myers. **Columbus (6)**—Boehringer-Pavlas, Eiland-Ausanio, Kamieniecki-Dunbar-Cook-Ausanio, Ojala-Carper, Ojala-Frazier, Pettitte-Ojala-Pavlas. **Norfolk (11)**—Cornelius-Byrd, Cornelius-Walker, Cornelius-Rogers-Florence-Byrd, Isringhausen-Florence-Walker, Jacome-Rogers-Florence-Byrd, Roberts-Stidham-Walker, Stidham-Crawford-McCready-Rogers-Walker, Stidham-Rogers-Walker, Telgheder-Stidham-Walker, Telgheder-Walker, Williams-Walker-Rogers. **Ottawa (7)**—Alvarez-Eversgerd, Fraser-Eversgerd-Thobe, Fraser-Pena-Layana, Fraser-Schmidt, Manuel-Eversgerd-Schmidt, Urbina-Layana-Eversgerd, Fraser-Urbina-Thobe-Schmidt. **Pawtucket (1)**—Hansen-Culberson-Wengert-Wiggs-Johnston. **Richmond (12)**—Murray-Nichols 2, Bark-Polley, May-Lomon-Polley, Murray-Brock-Nichols, Nichols-Thomas-Polley-Minutelli-Martin, Schmidt-Thobe-Lomon, Schmidt-Thobe-Nichols, Seelbach-Potts, Thobe-King-Brown, Wade-Lomon-Nichols, Woodall-Nichols. **Rochester (3)**—Coppinger-Oquist, Haynes-Benitez, Klingenbeck-Shea. **Scr./Wilkes-Barre (4)**—Ilsley-Ricci-Innis, Juden-DuBois-Fletcher, Juden-Wiegandt-DuBois, Springer-Wiegandt-Hill. **Syracuse (4)**—Brown-Montoya-Wainhouse, Flener-Steed, Ware-Crabtree, Whitehurst-Steed. **Toledo (6)**—Ahearne-Bauer-Christopher, Groom-Christopher, Marshall-Blomdahl-Maxcy-Christopher, Marshall-Buckels-Christopher, Sodowsky-Blomdahl-Gonzales-Buckels-Henry, Weston-Martel-Christopher.

NO-HIT GAMES: Rivera, Columbus, defeated Rochester, 3-0 (second game, five innings), June 26.

PITCHERS WITH TWO OR MORE TEAMS

Pitcher, Team	W	L	Pct.	ERA	G	GS	CG	ShO	GF	Sv.	IP	H	TBF	R	ER	HR	SH	SF	HB	BB	IBB	SO	WP	Bk.
Bark, Brian, Richmond*	2	2	.500	3.54	13	5	0	0	0	0	40.2	42	168	16	16	2	1	1	0	17	0	22	1	0
Bark, Brian, Pawtucket*	3	1	.750	2.27	30	0	0	0	15	7	31.2	21	123	8	8	1	1	1	1	14	0	21	3	0
Cornelius, Reid, Ottawa	1	1	.500	6.75	4	3	0	0	0	0	10.2	16	54	12	8	1	0	1	2	5	0	7	2	0
Cornelius, Reid, Norfolk	7	0	1.000	0.90	10	10	1	0	0	0	70.1	57	287	10	7	2	3	1	6	19	0	43	1	0
Hartley, Mike, Pawtucket	4	1	.500	4.05	26	1	0	0	10	1	46.2	47	196	21	21	7	1	2	3	12	0	39	2	2
Hartley, Mike, Rochester	0	1	.000	0.82	8	0	0	0	6	0	11.0	4	39	1	1	0	0	0	0	2	1	12	0	0
Myers, Mike, Charlotte*	0	5	.000	5.65	37	0	0	0	12	0	36.2	41	162	25	23	6	2	0	0	15	1	24	3	0
Myers, Mike, Toledo*	0	0	.000	4.32	6	0	0	0	2	0	8.1	6	35	4	4	1	0	0	1	3	0	8	2	0
Small, Aaron, Syracuse	0	0	.000	5.40	1	0	0	0	0	0	1.2	3	9	1	1	1	0	0	0	1	0	2	0	0
Small, Aaron, Charlotte	2	1	.667	2.88	33	0	0	0	17	10	40.2	36	170	15	13	2	0	1	2	10	1	31	3	0
Wainhouse, Dave, Syracuse	3	2	.600	3.70	26	0	0	0	21	5	24.1	29	111	13	10	1	1	2	1	11	3	18	4	0
Wainhouse, Dave, Charlotte	0	0	.000	9.82	4	0	0	0	1	0	3.2	6	21	6	4	1	0	1	0	4	0	2	2	0
Whitehurst, Wally, Pawtucket	1	3	.250	6.51	6	6	0	0	0	0	27.2	36	123	21	20	3	1	0	0	5	0	13	3	0
Whitehurst, Wally, Syracuse	3	1	.750	3.86	6	4	0	0	0	0	28.0	32	119	16	12	4	1	0	0	7	0	21	1	0
Williams, Jimmy, Norfolk*	11	4	.733	3.05	27	13	0	0	6	2	106.1	89	453	42	36	3	1	5	1	56	0	88	5	2
Williams, Jimmy, Rochester*	1	2	.333	7.11	5	3	0	0	0	0	12.2	21	69	13	10	0	0	0	1	9	0	12	7	2

TEAM

Team	Pct.	G	PO	A	E	TC	DP	PB	Team	Pct.	G	PO	A	E	TC	DP	PB
Ottawa	.976	142	3673	1644	131	5448	136	14	Charlotte	.973	140	3676	1630	145	5451	154	11
Richmond	.975	141	3743	1558	134	5435	122	10	Toledo	.972	142	3760	1735	157	5652	168	8
Scr./W-B	.975	142	3709	1467	133	5309	134	19	Rochester	.971	142	3709	1477	154	5340	127	11
Columbus	.975	140	3671	1606	137	5414	149	15	Pawtucket	.971	142	3691	1425	152	5268	104	21
Norfolk	.974	142	3776	1639	147	5562	147	8	Syracuse	.964	141	3689	1490	195	5374	116	13

TRIPLE PLAYS: Ottawa, Toledo.

INDIVIDUAL

FIRST BASEMEN

NOTE: All caps denotes fielding-percentage leader based on 71 games for catchers, 95 for all other non-pitchers and 142 innings for pitchers. *Throws lefthanded.

Player, Team	Pct.	G	PO	A	E	TC	DP
Barbara, Don, Pawtucket*	.985	29	235	20	4	259	15
Barry, Jeff, Norfolk	.984	12	117	9	2	128	10
Benzinger, Todd, Columbus	.986	12	131	8	2	141	12
Brewer, Rod, Charlotte*	.990	65	541	50	6	597	57
Cabrera, Francisco, Richmond	1.000	10	79	3	0	82	5
Capra, Nick, Charlotte	1.000	1	7	0	0	7	0
Carey, Paul, Rochester	.991	76	633	47	6	686	61
Carpenter, Bubba, Columbus*	1.000	3	20	1	0	21	3
Chamberlain, Wes, Pawtucket	1.000	1	1	0	0	1	0
Clark, Tony, Toledo	.981	62	615	51	13	679	73
Crowley, Jim, Rochester	1.000	2	21	0	0	21	1
Cruz, Ivan, Toledo*	.969	9	89	6	3	98	9
Daubach, Brian, Norfolk	1.000	2	21	3	0	24	3
Davis, Russ, Columbus	1.000	2	8	1	0	9	1
DeBerry, Joe, Columbus*	.974	5	36	2	1	39	1
Delgado, Alex, Pawtucket	1.000	5	16	2	0	18	1
Delgado, Carlos, Syracuse	.995	79	696	47	4	747	63
Friedman, Jason, Paw.-Roc.*	1.000	21	161	13	0	174	15
Garcia, Omar, Norfolk	.988	107	963	67	12	1042	89
Gregg, Tommy, Charlotte*	.993	13	123	12	1	136	14
Grijak, Kevin, Richmond	.992	51	355	25	3	383	26
Houston, Tyler, Richmond	.987	61	421	33	6	460	44
Huskey, Butch, Norfolk	.988	18	155	6	2	163	21
Jacobs, Frank, Nor.-Ott.*	1.000	3	21	0	0	21	2
Jorgensen, Terry, Charlotte	1.000	4	13	1	0	14	1
Ledesma, Aaron, Norfolk	1.000	3	33	0	0	33	4
Lis, Joe, Syracuse	1.000	2	16	0	0	16	1
Lukachyk, Rob, Toledo	.929	2	13	0	1	14	1
Lutz, Brent, Syracuse	1.000	1	2	0	0	2	1
Maas, Kevin, Columbus*	1.000	11	89	8	0	97	13
McCoy, Trey, Norfolk	.952	3	16	4	1	21	1
McGinnis, Russ, Rochester	1.000	4	29	1	0	30	2
McNair, Fred, Scr./W-B.	1.000	3	25	2	0	27	3
Melvin, Bob, Columbus	1.000	1	11	1	0	12	1
Montoyo, Charlie, Scr./W-B.	1.000	2	3	0	0	3	0
Morman, Russ, Charlotte	.998	40	407	23	1	431	42
Natal, Rob, Charlotte	1.000	1	8	2	0	10	1
Obando, Sherman, Rochester	.962	16	137	14	6	157	15
O'Connor, Kevin, Richmond	1.000	1	2	0	0	2	0
Owens, Billy, Rochester	.985	9	60	4	1	65	3
Pappas, Erik, Charlotte	.995	23	187	17	1	205	22
Pecorilli, Aldo, Richmond	1.000	27	170	11	0	181	16
Perez, Eddie, Richmond	1.000	2	1	0	0	1	0
Pough, Pork Chop, Pawtucket	.994	20	144	20	1	165	11
Ramos, John, Syracuse	.983	14	108	8	2	118	9
Robertson, Rod, Rochester	.944	4	17	0	1	18	1
Rodriguez, Tony, Pawtucket	1.000	1	2	0	0	2	0
Rodriguez, Victor, Pawtucket	.985	10	62	4	1	67	10
Rowland, Rich, Pawtucket	1.000	3	28	1	0	29	1
Sanders, Tracy, Norfolk	1.000	3	14	1	0	15	3
Schall, Gene, Scr./W-B.	.992	43	355	20	3	378	34
Seefried, Tate, Columbus	.993	28	271	25	2	298	27
Sharperson, Mike, Richmond	1.000	6	43	7	0	50	5
Snyder, Cory, Pawtucket	1.000	3	23	4	0	27	4
Son, Columbus	.994	80	762	55	5	822	76
Thoutsis, Paul, Columbus	1.000	5	28	3	0	31	4
Townley, Jason, Syracuse	.935	6	22	7	2	31	3
Twardoski, Mike, Richmond*	1.000	19	165	15	0	180	8
Velasquez, Guillermo, Ottawa	.996	29	216	16	1	233	14
Villanueva, Hector, Richmond	1.000	4	26	1	0	27	2
Wedge, Eric, Pawtucket	.995	74	554	40	3	597	49
Weinke, Chris, Syracuse	.991	50	379	46	4	429	28
White, Derrick, Toledo	.985	26	241	16	4	261	22
Wilstead, Randy, Ottawa*	1.000	3	35	2	0	37	3
Wood, Ted, Ottawa*	.986	33	260	20	4	284	21
Woods, Tyrone, Rochester	.988	30	227	18	3	248	22
YAN, Julian, Norfolk	.997	105	876	57	3	936	88
Zinter, Alan, Toledo	.992	48	476	32	4	512	48
Zuber, Jon, Scr./W-B.*	.996	104	825	63	4	892	86
Zupcic, Bob, Charlotte	1.000	4	21	1	0	22	1

TRIPLE PLAYS: Clark, Yan.

FIRST BASEMEN WITH TWO OR MORE TEAMS

Player, Team	Pct.	G	PO	A	E	TC	DP
Friedman, Jason, Pawtucket*	1.000	10	79	3	0	82	7
Friedman, Jason, Rochester*	1.000	11	82	10	0	92	8
Jacobs, Frank, Norfolk*	1.000	2	12	0	0	12	0
Jacobs, Frank, Ottawa*	1.000	1	9	0	0	9	2

SECOND BASEMEN

Player, Team	Pct.	G	PO	A	E	TC	DP
Alfonzo, Edgar, Rochester	1.000	1	1	3	0	4	0
Alicea, Ed, Norfolk	.965	114	224	325	20	569	75
Azuaje, Jesus, Norfolk	1.000	3	10	6	0	16	2
Bell, Juan, Pawtucket	.981	23	49	55	2	106	11
Bournigal, Rafael, Ottawa	1.000	1	0	2	0	2	0
Briley, Greg, Toledo	.957	8	13	31	2	46	6
Brito, Tilson, Syracuse	1.000	4	3	5	0	8	0
Brown, Randy, Pawtucket	1.000	2	3	6	0	9	0
Buccheri, Jim, Ottawa	.973	12	14	22	1	37	7
Capra, Nick, Charlotte	1.000	3	2	1	0	3	0
Carter, Jeff, Charlotte	.951	68	148	199	18	365	40
CASTLEBERRY, Kevin, Ottawa	.977	96	205	257	11	473	58
Crespo, Felipe, Syracuse	.938	86	160	220	25	405	38
Crowley, Jim, Rochester	.982	24	49	61	2	112	19
Dejardin, Bobby, Rochester	.974	8	15	23	1	39	5
Dellicarri, Joe, Toledo	.970	4	14	18	1	33	6
Diaz, Edgar, Syracuse	.667	2	0	2	1	3	0
Eenhoorn, Robert, Columbus	.979	82	162	219	8	389	63
Fleming, Carlton, Columbus	.934	20	37	62	7	106	12
Foley, Tom, Ottawa	.984	10	27	34	1	62	11
Fox, Andy, Columbus	1.000	4	2	5	0	7	2
Givens, Jim, Toledo	.972	39	56	116	5	177	29
Graffanino, Tony, Richmond	.983	50	102	127	4	233	30
Graham, Greg, Norfolk	.963	7	7	19	1	27	5
Hall, Joe, Toledo	1.000	1	0	1	0	1	0
Hardge, Mike, Pawtucket	.959	16	32	39	3	74	7
Hardtke, Jason, Norfolk	1.000	2	5	2	0	7	0
Hecht, Steve, Toledo	.989	15	43	51	1	95	16
Huson, Jeff, Pawtucket	1.000	8	25	28	0	53	9
Jordan, Kevin, Scr./W-B.	.976	102	217	279	12	508	70
Kelly, Pat, Rich.-Syr.	.957	12	18	26	2	46	4
Koelling, Brian, Scr./W-B.	.935	16	39	33	5	77	9
Leiper, Tim, Toledo	.933	6	17	11	2	30	2
Lis, Joe, Syracuse	.994	42	64	111	1	176	22
Manahan, Anthony, Scr./W-B.	.976	24	64	58	3	125	10
Martin, Chris, Ottawa	1.000	7	19	18	0	37	4
Martinez, Pablo, Richmond	.875	2	5	2	1	8	1
Millette, Joe, Charlotte	.951	47	75	139	11	225	32
Montalvo, Rob, Syracuse	.917	7	14	19	3	36	5
Montoyo, Charlie, Scr./W-B.	1.000	2	3	1	0	4	0
Morgan, Kevin, Norfolk	1.000	10	25	26	0	51	8
Munoz, Jose, Richmond	.988	51	111	146	3	260	36
Noboa, Junior, Rochester	.909	6	9	11	2	22	0
O'Connor, Kevin, Richmond	1.000	1	4	3	0	7	1
Olmeda, Jose, Richmond	.968	23	40	50	3	93	10
Penn, Shannon, Toledo	.962	58	106	173	11	290	37
Perezchica, Tony, Columbus	.981	48	75	128	4	207	28
Roa, Hector, Richmond	.969	13	23	40	2	65	5
Robertson, Rod, Rochester	.907	12	22	27	5	54	11
Rodriguez, Steve, Pawtucket	.975	80	167	191	9	367	37
Rodriguez, Tony, Pawtucket	.986	33	65	80	2	147	13

Player, Team	Pct.	G	PO	A	E	TC	DP
Rundels, Matt, Ottawa	.967	10	13	45	2	60	5
Santangelo, F.P., Ottawa	1.000	20	32	54	0	86	9
Schunk, Jerry, Charlotte	.978	32	50	82	3	135	27
Scott, Gary, Richmond	1.000	4	10	5	0	15	1
Sefcik, Kevin, Scr./W.-B.	1.000	7	13	16	0	29	4
Sharperson, Mike, Richmond	1.000	3	3	6	0	9	3
Shumpert, Terry, Pawtucket	1.000	3	2	1	0	3	0
Spiers, Bill, Norfolk	.936	8	19	25	3	47	7
Springer, Steve, Toledo	.976	22	46	75	3	124	19
Tyler, Brad, Rochester	.970	94	171	252	13	436	46
Wilson, Craig, Toledo	.966	7	8	20	1	29	4
Zosky, Eddie, Charlotte	.970	13	20	44	2	66	14

TRIPLE PLAY: Hecht.

SECOND BASEMEN WITH TWO OR MORE TEAMS

Player, Team	Pct.	G	PO	A	E	TC	DP
Kelly, Pat, Richmond	.833	1	3	2	1	6	1
Kelly, Pat, Syracuse	.975	11	15	24	1	40	3

THIRD BASEMEN

Player, Team	Pct.	G	PO	A	E	TC	DP
Alfonzo, Edgar, Rochester	.750	3	0	3	1	4	0
Alicea, Ed, Norfolk	.929	3	4	9	1	14	0
Azuaje, Jesus, Norfolk	1.000	2	1	6	0	7	0
Batiste, Kim, S/WB-Roc.	.940	91	75	160	15	250	16
Battle, Howard, Syracuse	.913	90	40	192	22	254	11
Bell, Juan, Pawtucket	.833	2	3	2	1	6	0
Bieser, Steve, Scr./W.-B.	.714	2	2	3	2	7	0
Bournigal, Rafael, Ottawa	1.000	1	0	1	0	1	0
Capra, Nick, Charlotte	.892	23	22	36	7	65	5
Castaldo, Vince, Charlotte	1.000	2	1	1	0	2	0
Castleberry, Kevin, Ottawa	.873	23	16	46	9	71	5
Crowley, Jim, Rochester	1.000	8	3	10	0	13	3
Davis, Russ, Columbus	.848	19	9	30	7	46	1
Dejardin, Bobby, Rochester	1.000	2	1	1	0	2	0
Delgado, Alex, Pawtucket	1.000	4	1	5	0	6	1
Donnels, Chris, Pawtucket	.833	3	2	3	1	6	0
Eenhoorn, Robert, Columbus	1.000	5	3	6	0	9	0
Epps, Scott, Columbus	1.000	1	1	0	0	1	0
Foley, Tom, Ottawa	1.000	5	5	9	0	14	0
Fox, Andy, Columbus	.968	69	59	184	8	251	22
Gilbert, Shawn, Scr./W.-B.	.929	3	2	11	1	14	2
Giovanola, Ed, Richmond	1.000	2	0	2	0	2	0
Givens, Jim, Toledo	.839	8	8	18	5	31	3
Grable, Rob, Scr./W.-B.	.846	4	4	7	2	13	2
Graham, Greg, Norfolk	.926	23	9	41	4	54	7
Hall, Joe, Toledo	.885	12	3	20	3	26	1
Hardge, Mike, Pawtucket	.906	13	8	21	3	32	0
Hayden, Dave, Scr./W.-B.	.917	13	7	15	2	24	2
Houston, Tyler, Richmond	.939	13	9	22	2	33	5
Huskey, Butch, Norfolk	.943	56	28	122	9	159	9
Johnson, Matt, Syracuse	1.000	1	0	1	0	1	0
JORGENSEN, Terry, Charlotte	.962	97	73	208	11	292	21
Kelly, Pat, Rich.-Syr.	1.000	6	1	9	0	10	1
Ledesma, Aaron, Norfolk	.929	48	39	91	10	140	8
Leiper, Tim, Toledo	1.000	2	3	6	0	9	0
Lieberthal, Mike, Scr./W.-B.	.500	1	0	1	1	2	0
Lis, Joe, Syracuse	.914	35	35	82	11	128	4
Lutz, Brent, Syracuse	.714	3	1	4	2	7	0
Malzone, John, Pawtucket	.833	5	2	8	2	12	1
Manahan, Anthony, Scr./W.-B.	.901	37	28	63	10	101	6
Martin, Chris, Ottawa	.921	46	36	115	13	164	12
Martinez, Ray, Ottawa	.944	31	16	68	5	89	3
McClain, Scott, Rochester	.940	61	41	130	11	182	9
McGriff, Terry, Toledo	.786	3	4	7	3	14	3
Millette, Joe, Charlotte	.857	1	1	5	1	7	1
Montalvo, Rob, Syracuse	1.000	2	1	2	0	3	1
Montoyo, Charlie, Scr./W.-B.	.952	71	46	114	8	168	9
Munoz, Jose, Richmond	.930	36	24	56	6	86	5
Natal, Rob, Charlotte	.909	4	4	6	1	11	0
Pecorilli, Aldo, Richmond	1.000	6	0	1	0	1	0
Perezchica, Tony, Columbus	.923	19	15	33	4	52	3
Pough, Pork Chop, Pawtucket	.778	1	1	6	2	9	1
Roa, Hector, Richmond	1.000	15	4	23	0	27	0
Robertson, Rod, Rochester	.935	10	5	24	2	31	5
Rodriguez, Tony, Pawtucket	.938	59	44	122	11	177	10
Rodriguez, Victor, Pawtucket	1.000	24	14	45	0	59	2
Rowland, Rich, Pawtucket	1.000	1	0	1	0	1	0
Rundels, Matt, Ottawa	1.000	2	2	4	0	6	0
Santangelo, F.P., Ottawa	.946	53	27	113	8	148	4
Saunders, Chris, Norfolk	.923	16	8	28	3	39	1
Sawkiw, Warren, Syracuse	.813	7	4	9	3	16	0
Schunk, Jerry, Charlotte	.914	15	9	23	3	35	0

Player, Team	Pct.	G	PO	A	E	TC	DP
Scott, Gary, Richmond	.909	23	14	46	6	66	4
Sharperson, Mike, Richmond	.969	69	32	125	5	162	9
Shumpert, Terry, Pawtucket	.896	30	27	68	11	106	12
Siddall, Joe, Ottawa	.750	1	2	1	1	4	0
Snyder, Cory, Pawtucket	.907	14	15	24	4	43	4
Sparks, Don, Columbus	.975	39	25	92	3	120	15
Spiers, Bill, Norfolk	.889	4	4	4	1	9	0
Springer, Steve, Toledo	.944	6	3	14	1	18	3
Tackett, Jeff, Toledo	1.000	1	2	2	0	4	0
Weinke, Chris, Syracuse	.875	18	9	19	4	32	1
Wilson, Craig, Toledo	.921	113	72	256	28	356	18
Zosky, Eddie, Charlotte	.975	13	16	23	1	40	8

TRIPLE PLAY: Wilson.

THIRD BASEMEN WITH TWO OR MORE TEAMS

Player, Team	Pct.	G	PO	A	E	TC	DP
Batiste, Kim, Scr./W.-B.	.952	28	24	56	4	84	7
Batiste, Kim, Rochester	.934	63	51	104	11	166	9
Kelly, Pat, Richmond	1.000	4	1	9	0	10	1
Kelly, Pat, Syracuse	.000	2	0	0	0	0	0

SHORTSTOPS

Player, Team	Pct.	G	PO	A	E	TC	DP
Abbott, Kurt, Charlotte	.909	5	5	15	2	22	3
Alfonzo, Edgar, Rochester	.971	9	13	21	1	35	5
BAEZ, Kevin, Toledo	.975	116	205	414	16	635	92
Batiste, Kim, Rochester	1.000	3	3	3	0	6	0
Battle, Howard, Syracuse	.923	34	42	89	11	142	11
Bell, Juan, Pawtucket	.929	43	56	87	11	154	11
Bournigal, Rafael, Ottawa	.984	15	15	48	1	64	10
Brito, Tilson, Syracuse	.952	88	120	235	18	373	48
Brown, Randy, Pawtucket	.949	67	102	161	14	277	33
Capra, Nick, Charlotte	1.000	1	1	0	0	1	0
Diaz, Edgar, Syracuse	.950	12	28	29	3	60	7
Eenhoorn, Robert, Columbus	1.000	5	3	6	0	9	2
Elster, Kevin, Scr./W.-B.	.947	5	6	12	1	19	4
Foley, Tom, Ottawa	1.000	6	13	19	0	32	4
Fox, Andy, Columbus	.970	10	10	22	1	33	3
Gilbert, Shawn, Scr./W.-B.	.953	107	156	347	25	528	71
Giovanola, Ed, Richmond	.965	90	125	284	15	424	52
Givens, Jim, Toledo	.952	28	37	83	6	126	17
Graham, Greg, Norfolk	.918	12	14	31	4	49	5
Grudzielanek, Mark, Ottawa	.939	49	58	156	14	228	29
Hayden, Dave, Scr./W.-B.	1.000	1	0	3	0	3	0
Huson, Jeff, Rochester	.974	54	85	175	7	267	43
Jeter, Derek, Columbus	.953	123	189	394	29	612	74
Johnson, Matt, Syracuse	1.000	5	2	7	0	9	1
Kelly, Pat, Syracuse	.950	15	19	38	3	60	9
Ledesma, Aaron, Norfolk	1.000	1	1	3	0	4	0
Lis, Joe, Syracuse	1.000	2	0	3	0	3	0
Manahan, Anthony, Scr./W.-B.	.925	17	31	43	6	80	12
Martin, Chris, Ottawa	.952	70	101	195	15	311	45
Martinez, Pablo, Richmond	.982	12	16	38	1	55	5
Martinez, Ray, Ottawa	.875	5	2	5	1	8	1
Mendenhall, Kirk, Toledo	.955	9	14	28	2	44	10
Millette, Joe, Charlotte	.934	19	25	46	5	76	10
Montalvo, Rob, Syracuse	1.000	1	2	5	0	7	1
Montoyo, Charlie, Scr./W.-B.	.947	16	23	31	3	57	3
Morgan, Kevin, Norfolk	.976	7	12	29	1	42	2
Munoz, Jose, Richmond	.916	36	44	119	15	178	9
Olmeda, Jose, Richmond	.824	3	6	8	3	17	4
Ordonez, Rey, Norfolk	.967	124	188	436	21	645	88
Perezchica, Tony, Columbus	.956	11	24	41	3	68	7
Roa, Hector, Richmond	.957	9	10	34	2	46	5
Robertson, Rod, Rochester	.926	33	40	86	10	136	16
Rodriguez, Carlos, Pawtucket	.962	38	51	99	6	156	13
Rodriguez, Tony, Pawtucket	.963	12	10	16	1	27	1
Santangelo, F.P., Ottawa	.958	5	7	16	1	24	5
Schunk, Jerry, Charlotte	.966	60	104	177	10	291	44
Smith, Dwight, Syracuse	.963	52	83	149	9	241	26
Zosky, Eddie, Charlotte	.966	63	125	212	12	349	52

TRIPLE PLAY: Martin.

OUTFIELDERS

Player, Team	Pct.	G	PO	A	E	TC	DP
Abner, Shawn, Norfolk	1.000	3	2	0	0	2	0
Barnwell, Rich, Columbus	.986	44	66	2	1	69	1
Barron, Tony, Ottawa	1.000	31	59	2	0	61	0
Bartee, Kimera, Rochester	1.000	15	37	2	0	39	0
Bautista, Danny, Toledo	.943	18	32	1	2	35	0
Benitez, Yamil, Ottawa	.964	116	177	10	7	194	2
Bieser, Steve, Scr./W.-B.	.988	39	82	1	1	84	0
Blosser, Greg, Pawtucket*	.886	16	30	1	4	35	0

Player, Team	Pct.	G	PO	A	E	TC	DP
Boston, Daryl, Charlotte*	1.000	8	12	1	0	13	0
Bowers, Brent, Syracuse	.945	94	150	5	9	164	0
Briley, Greg, Toledo	.973	16	36	0	1	37	0
Brock, Tarrik, Toledo*	.929	9	12	1	1	14	0
Brown, Jarvis, Nor.-Roc.	.955	60	126	2	6	134	1
Brown, Randy, Pawtucket	1.000	4	3	0	0	3	0
Bucceri, Jim, Ottawa	.984	116	235	7	4	246	0
Buford, Damon, Rochester	.983	46	115	2	2	119	0
Butler, Rich, Syracuse	.965	64	101	9	4	114	2
Butler, Robert, Scr./W.-B.*	.974	85	147	4	4	155	1
Cairo, Sergio, Ottawa	1.000	2	3	0	0	3	0
Canate, Willie, Syracuse	.963	112	223	14	9	246	4
Capra, Nick, Charlotte	.972	85	133	7	4	144	0
Carpenter, Bubba, Columbus*	.982	104	211	4	4	219	2
Carr, Chuck, Charlotte	1.000	7	9	0	0	9	0
Carter, Jeff, Charlotte	1.000	43	73	5	0	78	2
Carter, Steve, Charlotte	.900	12	15	3	2	20	0
Chamberlain, Wes, Pawtucket	.945	33	66	3	4	73	0
Cuyler, Milt, Toledo	.960	51	95	1	4	100	0
Dascenzo, Doug, Charlotte*	1.000	70	157	3	0	160	0
Davis, Jay, Norfolk*	1.000	8	11	0	0	11	0
Delgado, Carlos, Syracuse	1.000	14	28	2	0	30	0
Delima, Rafael, Ottawa*	1.000	8	6	2	0	8	0
Everett, Carl, Norfolk	1.000	64	133	7	0	140	0
Felix, Junior, Ottawa	1.000	33	60	0	0	60	0
Ford, Curt, Charlotte	.987	45	69	5	1	75	1
Fox, Andy, Columbus	1.000	8	13	0	0	13	0
Frazier, Lou, Ottawa	.974	30	73	3	2	78	0
Friedman, Jason, Rochester*	1.000	4	5	0	0	5	0
Geisler, Phil, Scr./W.-B.*	1.000	12	19	1	0	20	0
Gilbert, Shawn, Scr./W.-B.	.967	23	55	3	2	60	0
Goodwin, Curtis, Rochester*	.965	36	81	1	3	85	0
Grable, Rob, Scr./W.-B.	1.000	14	25	0	0	25	0
Gregg, Tommy, Charlotte*	1.000	13	17	1	0	18	0
Grijak, Kevin, Richmond	1.000	4	4	0	0	4	0
Hall, Joe, Toledo	.993	73	145	5	1	151	1
Hecht, Steve, Toledo	1.000	7	13	0	0	13	0
Heffernan, Bert, Ottawa	.800	1	4	0	1	5	0
Hill, Lew, Columbus	.984	37	62	0	1	63	0
Holifield, Rick, Scr./W.-B.*	.964	72	131	4	5	140	0
Houston, Tyler, Richmond	.963	15	25	1	1	27	0
Howard, Tim, Pawtucket	.965	31	55	0	2	57	0
Huskey, Butch, Norfolk	.972	41	65	4	2	71	0
Jones, Chris, Norfolk	.985	30	62	4	1	67	2
Kelly, Mike, Richmond	1.000	12	24	0	0	24	0
Kelly, Pat, Rich.-Syr.	1.000	8	12	1	0	13	0
Kowitz, Brian, Richmond*	.969	97	217	2	7	226	0
Leach, Jalal, Columbus*	.943	64	97	2	6	105	0
Lee, Derek, Norfolk	.959	65	86	8	4	98	1
Leiper, Tim, Toledo	1.000	4	11	0	0	11	0
Lennon, Pat, Pawtucket	.951	35	54	4	3	61	1
Lewis, T.R., Rochester	.905	10	19	0	2	21	0
Lis, Joe, Syracuse	.980	31	48	2	1	51	1
Lukachyk, Rob, Toledo	.988	96	157	2	2	161	1
Luke, Matt, Columbus*	.949	23	36	1	2	39	0
Lutz, Brent, Syracuse	.923	13	12	0	1	13	0
Maas, Kevin, Columbus*	1.000	22	26	0	0	26	0
Mahay, Ron, Pawtucket*	1.000	11	30	2	0	32	0
Malave, Jose, Pawtucket	.966	65	113	2	4	119	0
Marsh, Tom, Scr./W.-B.	.994	75	156	4	1	161	2
Mashore, Justin, Toledo	.986	68	140	6	2	148	1
Massarelli, John, Charlotte	.983	64	110	8	2	120	0
Masse, Billy, Columbus	.961	44	72	1	3	76	0
McCoy, Trey, Norfolk	1.000	2	4	0	0	4	0
McDowell, Oddibe, Columbus*	1.000	14	26	0	0	26	0
McGee, Willie, Pawtucket	.875	3	7	0	1	8	0
Milne, Darren, Toledo	1.000	6	3	1	0	4	0
MOORE, Bobby, Richmond	1.000	100	179	9	0	188	3
Morman, Russ, Charlotte	.900	3	9	0	1	10	0
Munoz, Jose, Richmond	.957	25	20	2	1	23	1
Murray, Glenn, Pawtucket	.975	95	227	5	6	238	0
Nevin, Phil, Toledo	1.000	4	2	0	0	2	0
Obando, Sherman, Rochester	.960	29	47	1	2	50	0
Ochoa, Alex, Roch.-Nor.	.974	124	249	10	7	266	1
O'Connor, Kevin, Richmond	.976	79	118	4	3	125	0
Olmeda, Jose, Richmond	.946	48	84	4	5	93	1
Otero, Ricky, Norfolk	.970	72	147	12	5	164	5
Pappas, Erik, Charlotte	.956	21	38	5	2	45	0
Payton, Jay, Norfolk	.982	49	106	3	2	111	0
Pecorilli, Aldo, Richmond	1.000	11	18	0	0	18	0
Pemberton, Rudy, Toledo	.953	43	59	2	3	64	2
Perez, Robert, Syracuse	.964	119	208	7	8	223	0
Perezchica, Tony, Columbus	.957	20	21	1	1	23	0
Pride, Curtis, Ottawa	.974	37	69	5	2	76	1
Ramos, John, Syracuse	.917	7	11	0	1	12	0
Reed, Darren, Richmond	1.000	30	52	1	0	53	0
Rhodes, Karl, Pawtucket*	.967	65	172	6	6	184	3
Rivera, Ruben, Columbus	.975	48	113	6	3	122	2
Robertson, Rod, Rochester	.909	39	57	3	6	66	0
Rundels, Matt, Ottawa	1.000	1	1	0	0	1	0
Sanders, Tracy, Norfolk	.980	27	47	1	1	49	0
Santangelo, F.P., Ottawa	.952	12	18	2	1	21	1
Sawkiw, Warren, Syracuse	.933	7	13	1	1	15	0
Schall, Gene, Scr./W.-B.	.988	45	76	5	1	82	0
Smith, Mark, Rochester	.961	95	167	4	7	178	1
Snyder, Cory, Pawtucket	1.000	2	2	0	0	2	0
Sparks, Don, Columbus	1.000	2	1	0	0	1	0
Stairs, Matt, Pawtucket	1.000	51	79	13	0	92	2
Steverson, Todd, Toledo	.818	7	8	1	2	11	0
Strawberry, Darryl, Columbus*	1.000	9	9	0	0	9	0
Swann, Pedro, Richmond	1.000	9	9	1	0	10	0
Tavarez, Jesus, Charlotte	.979	38	92	2	2	96	0
Taylor, Sam, Scr./W.-B.*	1.000	1	2	0	0	2	0
Thompson, Ryan, Norfolk	1.000	13	15	2	0	17	0
Thoutsis, Paul, Columbus	.953	31	41	0	2	43	0
Tokheim, David, Scr./W.-B.*	.982	92	158	8	3	169	2
Tovar, Raul, Ottawa	.963	14	26	0	1	27	0
Tyler, Brad, Rochester	.964	15	26	1	1	28	0
Vatcher, Jim, Scr./W.-B.	1.000	4	8	0	0	8	0
Wade, Scott, Pawtucket	1.000	7	15	1	0	16	0
Waggoner, Aubrey, Pawtucket	.939	13	31	0	2	33	0
Warner, Mike, Richmond*	.950	27	57	0	3	60	0
Wawruck, Jim, Rochester*	1.000	30	75	6	0	81	1
Weinke, Chris, Syracuse	.915	28	43	0	4	47	0
White, Derrick, Toledo	.947	48	86	4	5	95	0
Whiten, Mark, Pawtucket	.940	20	43	4	3	50	0
Williams, Juan, Richmond	.961	40	69	5	3	77	1
Wood, Ted, Ottawa*	.987	50	73	4	1	78	0
Woods, Tyrone, Rochester	.938	14	14	1	1	16	0
Yan, Julian, Ottawa	.600	3	3	0	2	5	0
Zinter, Alan, Toledo	.955	15	21	0	1	22	0
Zupcic, Bob, Charlotte	.977	54	81	4	2	87	0

OUTFIELDERS WITH TWO OR MORE TEAMS

Player, Team	Pct.	G	PO	A	E	TC	DP
Brown, Jarvis, Norfolk	.960	43	71	1	3	75	0
Brown, Jarvis, Rochester	.949	17	55	1	3	59	1
Kelly, Pat, Richmond	1.000	7	11	1	0	12	0
Kelly, Pat, Syracuse	1.000	1	1	0	0	1	0
Ochoa, Alex, Rochester	.975	91	183	9	5	197	1
Ochoa, Alex, Norfolk	.971	33	66	1	2	69	0

CATCHERS

Player, Team	Pct.	G	PO	A	E	TC	DP	PB
Alvarez, Clemente, Ottawa	.988	48	292	26	4	322	3	3
Bennett, Gary, Scr./W.-B.	1.000	7	38	4	0	42	0	1
Bieser, Steve, Scr./W.-B.	.973	39	230	25	7	262	3	7
Boka, Ben, Norfolk	.970	14	28	4	1	33	1	4
Brooks, Eric, Syracuse	.988	46	235	15	3	253	0	5
Brophy, E.J., Scr./W.-B.	.980	30	132	16	3	151	2	3
Cabrera, Francisco, Richmond	1.000	3	7	2	0	9	1	2
Castillo, Alberto, Norfolk	.987	67	469	44	7	520	4	1
Delgado, Alex, Pawtucket	.974	33	157	32	5	194	1	7
Devarez, Cesar, Rochester	.995	52	331	40	2	373	4	5
Diaz, Cesar, Norfolk	.938	3	13	2	1	16	1	0
Epps, Scott, Columbus	.941	4	15	1	1	17	0	0
Figga, Mike, Columbus	1.000	5	29	4	0	33	0	1
Fulton, Ed, Pawtucket	.971	7	31	2	1	34	1	2
Gonzalez, Pete, Toledo	.957	6	40	5	2	47	0	0
Greene, Charlie, Norfolk	1.000	27	157	25	0	182	1	0
Gresham, Kris, Rochester	.965	21	127	12	5	144	3	0
Hatteberg, Scott, Pawtucket	.984	77	446	45	8	499	5	7
Heffernan, Bert, Ottawa	.987	28	140	15	2	157	3	3
Hernandez, Kiki, Charlotte	.964	30	119	16	5	140	0	1
Houston, Tyler, Richmond	.986	21	124	13	2	139	2	1
Knapp, Mike, Rochester	.996	36	203	23	1	227	1	3
Knorr, Randy, Syracuse	.979	17	129	14	3	146	3	0
Levangie, Dana, Pawtucket	1.000	6	32	4	0	36	0	2
Lieberthal, Mike, Scr./W.-B.	.9927	83	503	45	4	552	2	8
Livesey, Jeff, Columbus	.984	26	113	7	2	122	0	0
Lutz, Brent, Syracuse	.975	19	71	8	2	81	0	2
Massarelli, John, Charlotte	1.000	2	11	0	0	11	0	1
McGinnis, Russ, Rochester	1.000	2	12	1	0	13	0	1
McGriff, Terry, Toledo	1.000	40	167	18	0	185	1	2
Melvin, Bob, Columbus	.971	12	66	2	2	70	0	0
Natal, Rob, Charlotte	.997	43	259	41	1	301	3	4

Player, Team	Pct.	G	PO	A	E	TC	DP	PB
Orton, John, Rich.-Nor.	.995	63	373	48	2	423	6	3
Pappas, Erik, Charlotte	.982	75	398	37	8	443	4	5
Pecorilli, Aldo, Richmond	1.000	2	1	2	0	3	0	0
Perez, Eddie, Richmond	.989	83	539	69	7	615	7	2
POSADA, Jorge, Columbus	.9928	93	500	58	4	562	7	14
Ramos, John, Syracuse	.959	10	68	2	3	73	0	0
Reed, Darren, Richmond	.978	7	41	3	1	45	0	1
Rice, Lance, Toledo	1.000	15	70	9	0	79	1	0
Robertson, Rod, Rochester	1.000	2	7	2	0	9	0	1
Rowland, Rich, Pawtucket	.984	27	177	8	3	188	0	3
Rudolph, Mason, Charlotte	1.000	2	6	0	0	6	0	0
Santangelo, F.P., Ottawa	1.000	1	5	0	0	5	0	0
Siddall, Joe, Ottawa	.990	78	346	56	4	406	6	8
Tackett, Jeff, Toledo	.987	93	485	58	7	550	5	6
Tijerina, Tony, Norfolk	1.000	1	1	0	0	1	0	0
Toth, David, Richmond	.947	5	15	3	1	19	0	0
Townley, Jason, Syracuse	.990	74	473	32	5	510	5	6
Tucker, Scooter, Richmond	.984	20	107	16	2	125	1	4
Villanueva, Hector, Richmond	1.000	2	5	1	0	6	0	0
Wedge, Eric, Pawtucket	1.000	9	42	6	0	48	0	2
Wilson, Tom, Columbus	.962	22	109	16	5	130	2	0
Zaun, Greg, Rochester	.989	34	243	18	3	264	1	1
Zinter, Alan, Toledo	1.000	3	5	1	0	6	0	0

CATCHERS WITH TWO OR MORE TEAMS

Player, Team	Pct.	G	PO	A	E	TC	DP	PB
Orton, John, Richmond	1.000	17	83	10	0	93	1	0
Orton, John, Norfolk	.994	46	290	38	2	330	5	3

PITCHERS

Player, Team	Pct.	G	PO	A	E	TC	DP
Adamson, Joel, Charlotte*	1.000	19	9	14	0	23	2
Ahearne, Pat, Toledo	1.000	25	10	16	0	26	0
Alvarez, Jose, Richmond	.800	5	0	4	1	5	0
Alvarez, Tavo, Ottawa	1.000	3	3	2	0	5	0
Ausanio, Joe, Columbus	1.000	11	0	3	0	3	0
Bakkum, Scott, Pawtucket	.667	15	2	0	1	3	0
Baptist, Travis, Syracuse*	1.000	15	4	10	0	14	1
Bark, Brian, Rich.-Paw.*	1.000	43	3	12	0	15	0
Barnes, Brian, Pawtucket*	.917	21	6	16	2	24	1
Batista, Miguel, Charlotte	.903	34	13	15	3	31	1
Bauer, Matt, Toledo*	.800	13	0	4	1	5	0
Baxter, Robert, Ottawa*	.957	39	8	14	1	23	2
Benitez, Armando, Rochester	1.000	17	1	2	0	3	0
Bennett, Joel, Pawtucket	1.000	20	6	12	0	18	1
Birkbeck, Mike, Norfolk	1.000	9	7	13	0	20	2
Blair, Dirk, Richmond	.667	8	1	1	1	3	0
Blomdahl, Ben, Toledo	1.000	41	3	7	0	10	0
Boehringer, Brian, Columbus	.842	17	4	12	3	19	1
Borland, Toby, Scr./W.-B.	.800	8	1	3	1	5	0
Borowski, Joe, Rochester	.750	28	1	2	1	4	0
Bottenfield, Kent, Toledo	.966	27	6	22	1	29	1
Boucher, Denis, Ottawa*	.909	14	4	6	1	11	3
Brock, Chris, Richmond	.929	22	5	8	1	14	0
Brow, Scott, Syracuse	.818	11	5	4	2	11	0
Brown, Chad, Syracuse*	1.000	11	1	8	0	9	1
Brown, Jeff, Richmond*	1.000	12	2	6	0	8	0
Brown, Keith, Charlotte	1.000	4	0	1	0	1	0
Brown, Tim, Syracuse	1.000	19	11	6	0	17	0
Buckels, Gary, Toledo	1.000	31	2	5	0	7	0
Byrd, Paul, Norfolk	.750	22	5	7	4	16	0
Cain, Tim, Pawtucket	1.000	14	3	3	0	6	0
Carlyle, Ken, Toledo	.967	32	8	21	1	30	4
Carper, Mark, Columbus	.909	33	7	13	2	22	2
Carrara, Giovanni, Syracuse	.900	21	17	19	4	40	2
Carter, Andy, Scr./W.-B.*	1.000	14	0	2	0	2	0
Chitren, Steve, Rochester	1.000	2	0	1	0	1	0
Christopher, Mike, Toledo	1.000	36	5	8	0	13	1
Ciccarella, Joe, Pawtucket*	1.000	11	3	4	0	7	1
Clark, Terry, Rochester	1.000	9	2	0	0	2	0
Clary, Marty, Charlotte	.714	9	1	4	2	7	0
Coffman, Kevin, Richmond	1.000	2	0	1	0	1	0
Combs, Pat, Scr./W.-B.*	.833	22	1	4	1	6	2
Cook, Andy, Columbus	.941	37	5	11	1	17	1
Coppinger, Rocky, Rochester	1.000	5	2	3	0	5	0
Cornelius, Reid, Ott.-Nor.	1.000	14	6	20	0	26	0
Cornett, Brad, Syracuse	1.000	3	2	2	0	4	0
Cox, Danny, Syracuse	1.000	4	0	2	0	2	0
Crabtree, Tim, Syracuse	.900	26	3	6	1	10	0
Crawford, Joe, Norfolk*	1.000	8	1	5	0	6	0
Croghan, Andy, Columbus	1.000	20	1	1	0	2	0
Culberson, Calvain, Pawtucket	1.000	6	0	2	0	2	0
Davis, Mark, Charlotte*	.750	9	1	2	1	4	0
Dedrick, Jim, Rochester	1.000	24	5	11	0	16	1
Deshaies, Jim, Scr./W.-B.*	.970	19	6	26	1	33	1
DeSilva, John, Rochester	.914	26	10	22	3	35	1
Dettmer, John, Rochester	.929	21	5	8	1	14	1
Diaz, Rafael, Ottawa	.867	32	6	7	2	15	0
Drahman, Brian, Charlotte	1.000	21	1	2	0	3	1
DuBois, Brian, Scr./W.-B.*	1.000	49	0	11	0	11	1
Dunbar, Matt, Columbus*	.857	36	1	5	1	7	0
Eiland, Dave, Columbus	1.000	19	10	22	0	32	3
Eischen, Joey, Ottawa*	1.000	11	3	1	0	4	0
Eversgerd, Bryan, Ottawa*	1.000	38	2	12	0	14	1
Fajardo, Hector, Ottawa	1.000	11	1	5	0	6	0
Falteisek, Steve, Ottawa	1.000	3	2	5	0	7	0
Flener, Huck, Syracuse*	.921	30	9	26	3	38	4
Fletcher, Paul, Scr./W.-B.	.714	52	2	3	2	7	0
Florence, Don, Norfolk*	.846	41	3	8	2	13	1
Forney, Rick, Rochester	.667	3	0	2	1	3	0
Fraser, Willie, Ottawa	.938	19	6	9	1	16	0
Frazier, Ron, Columbus	.769	24	2	8	3	13	0
Gaddy, Bob, Scr./W.-B.*	1.000	17	6	21	0	27	2
Gakeler, Dan, Pawtucket	1.000	4	2	2	0	4	0
Ganote, Joe, Syracuse	1.000	3	0	1	0	1	0
Garcia, Miguel, Ottawa*	1.000	5	1	4	0	5	1
Gardiner, Mike, Toledo	1.000	11	1	0	0	1	0
Gibson, Paul, Syracuse*	1.000	26	2	3	0	5	0
Gohr, Greg, Toledo	1.000	6	2	1	0	3	1
Gonzales, Frank, Toledo*	1.000	49	2	6	0	8	0
Grace, Mike, Scr./W.-B.	1.000	2	2	0	0	2	0
Gray, Dennis, Syracuse*	.875	15	2	5	1	8	0
Greene, Tommy, Scr./W.-B.	.833	4	0	5	1	6	0
Groom, Buddy, Toledo*	1.000	6	2	5	0	7	0
Guzman, Juan, Syracuse	1.000	1	0	1	0	1	0
Hammond, Chris, Charlotte*	1.000	1	0	1	0	1	0
Hancock, Chris, Charlotte*	1.000	3	1	1	0	2	0
Hansen, Brent, Pawtucket	1.000	14	9	7	0	16	1
Harris, Greg, Ottawa	1.000	11	2	5	0	7	1
Harrison, Tom, Richmond	.700	9	4	3	3	10	0
Hartley, Mike, Paw.-Roc.	1.000	34	1	5	0	6	0
Haynes, Jimmy, Rochester	.889	26	14	18	4	36	2
Heble, Kurt, Syracuse	1.000	4	1	1	0	2	0
Henry, Dwayne, Toledo	.857	41	3	3	1	7	1
Hernandez, Jeremy, Charlotte	1.000	15	3	2	0	5	0
Hernandez, Willie, Columbus*	1.000	22	2	4	0	6	1
Hill, Chris, Pawtucket*	1.000	10	1	1	0	2	0
Hill, Eric, Scr./W.-B.	1.000	21	3	2	0	5	0
Hoeme, Steve, Pawtucket	1.000	15	1	6	0	7	0
Holman, Brad, Rochester	.000	1	0	0	1	1	0
Howard, Chris, Pawtucket*	.800	17	3	1	1	5	0
Hurst, James, Rochester*	1.000	10	0	2	0	2	0
Hutton, Mark, Columbus	1.000	11	3	6	0	9	0
ILSLEY, Blaise, Scr./W.-B.*	1.000	29	13	36	0	49	6
Innis, Jeff, Scr./W.-B.	1.000	15	2	2	0	4	0
Isringhausen, Jason, Norfolk	.947	12	5	13	1	19	2
Jacome, Jason, Norfolk*	1.000	8	0	7	0	7	1
Johnston, Joel, Pawtucket	1.000	30	0	3	0	3	0
Jones, Calvin, Pawtucket	1.000	33	1	5	0	6	0
Jordan, Ricardo, Syracuse*	1.000	13	1	3	0	4	0
Juden, Jeff, Scr./W.-B.	.769	14	3	7	3	13	1
Karp, Ryan, Scr./W.-B.*	.875	13	2	5	1	8	1
Kerley, Collin, Ottawa	1.000	5	0	3	0	3	0
Kiely, John, Toledo	1.000	14	0	4	0	4	1
King, Richard, Rochester	1.000	14	3	1	0	4	0
Klingenbeck, Scott, Rochester	1.000	8	7	7	0	14	0
Kramer, Tommy, Toledo	1.000	6	2	0	0	2	0
Krivda, Rick, Rochester*	.917	16	2	9	1	12	0
Lane, Aaron, Rochester	1.000	9	0	2	0	2	0
Layana, Tim, Ottawa	1.000	26	0	2	0	2	1
Lee, Mark, Rochester*	1.000	25	1	1	0	2	0
Leiper, Dave, Ottawa*	1.000	2	0	1	0	1	0
Lemon, Don, Charlotte	1.000	6	0	1	0	1	0
Lewis, Richie, Charlotte	.889	17	1	7	1	9	0
Lima, Jose, Toledo	.929	11	4	9	1	14	1
Lomon, Kevin, Richmond	1.000	32	5	10	0	15	1
Long, Steve, Charlotte	.875	33	5	9	2	16	0
Looney, Brian, Pawtucket*	1.000	18	5	9	0	14	0
Ludwick, Eric, Norfolk	1.000	4	0	2	0	2	0
MacDonald, Bob, Columbus*	1.000	13	1	4	0	5	0
Magrane, Joe, Ottawa*	.929	12	2	11	1	14	0
Mantei, Matt, Charlotte	1.000	6	1	0	0	1	0
Manuel, Barry, Ottawa	1.000	35	5	9	0	14	1
Marshall, Randy, Toledo*	.920	20	4	19	2	25	1
Martel, Ed, Toledo	1.000	4	0	2	0	2	0
Martin, Tom, Richmond*	.667	7	0	2	1	3	0

Player, Team	Pct.	G	PO	A	E	TC	DP
Mathews, Terry, Charlotte	1.000	2	1	0	0	1	0
Maxcy, Brian, Toledo	.833	20	3	2	1	6	0
May, Darrell, Richmond*	.875	9	3	4	1	8	0
McCready, Jim, Norfolk	.917	28	1	10	1	12	1
McDonald, Ben, Rochester	1.000	1	1	1	0	2	0
McGehee, Kevin, Rochester	.885	27	16	7	3	26	1
Mendoza, Ramiro, Columbus	1.000	2	1	0	0	1	0
Menhart, Paul, Syracuse	1.000	10	3	7	0	10	0
Miller, Kurt, Charlotte	1.000	22	5	11	0	16	0
Minutelli, Gino, Richmond*	1.000	5	0	3	0	3	0
Mitchell, John, Ottawa	1.000	6	0	2	0	2	0
Montoya, Al, Syracuse*	1.000	7	3	3	0	6	1
Munoz, Bobby, Scr./W.-B.	1.000	2	1	2	0	3	0
Murphy, Rob, Charlotte*	1.000	3	0	1	0	1	0
Murray, Matt, Richmond	1.000	19	13	7	0	20	1
Mutis, Jeff, Charlotte*	.909	27	2	8	1	11	1
Myers, Jimmy, Rochester	.947	55	6	12	1	19	1
Myers, Mike, Char.-Tol.*	1.000	43	2	5	0	7	0
Newlin, Jim, Charlotte	1.000	5	0	2	0	2	1
Nichols, Rod, Columbus	.857	41	2	4	1	7	0
Ojala, Kirt, Columbus*	.971	32	10	23	1	34	2
Olivares, Omar, Scr./W.-B.	1.000	7	8	6	0	14	1
Oquist, Mike, Rochester	1.000	7	0	2	0	2	0
Osuna, Al, Norfolk*	1.000	14	4	5	0	9	0
Patterson, Jeff, Columbus	1.000	33	5	9	0	14	0
Pavlas, Dave, Columbus	.929	48	3	10	1	14	0
Pena, Jim, Ottawa*	1.000	7	0	2	0	2	0
Perigny, Don, Charlotte	1.000	6	0	1	0	1	0
Person, Robert, Norfolk	1.000	5	1	1	0	2	0
Pettitte, Andy, Columbus*	1.000	2	0	3	0	3	0
Pierce, Jeff, Pawtucket	1.000	23	0	5	0	5	0
Plummer, Dale, Pawtucket	.968	34	12	18	1	31	2
Polley, Dale, Richmond*	.789	47	2	13	4	19	0
Potts, Mike, Richmond*	1.000	38	8	13	0	21	2
Pulsipher, Bill, Norfolk*	.895	13	2	15	2	19	0
Quirico, Rafael, Columbus*	.800	20	1	3	1	5	0
Rapp, Pat, Charlotte	1.000	1	1	1	0	2	0
Rhodes, Arthur, Rochester*	1.000	4	0	6	0	6	1
Ricci, Chuck, Scr./W.-B.	1.000	68	6	12	0	18	1
Rivera, Mariano, Columbus	1.000	7	5	4	0	9	0
Roberts, Chris, Norfolk*	.968	25	7	23	1	31	2
Robinson, Ken, Syracuse	.750	38	0	3	1	4	0
Rodriguez, Frank, Pawtucket	.778	13	1	6	2	9	0
Rogers, Bryan, Norfolk	1.000	56	9	13	0	22	2
Rogers, Jimmy, Syracuse	1.000	38	1	9	0	10	0
Rojas, Euclides, Charlotte	1.000	2	0	1	0	1	0
Rueter, Kirk, Ottawa*	1.000	20	4	31	0	35	2
Rumer, Tim, Columbus*	.944	28	1	16	1	18	0
Ryan, Ken, Pawtucket	1.000	9	2	0	0	2	0
Ryan, Kevin, Rochester	1.000	6	3	3	0	6	0
Sackinsky, Brian, Rochester	1.000	14	3	4	0	7	0
Satre, Jason, Pawtucket	1.000	9	2	4	0	6	0
Scheid, Rich, Charlotte*	.875	19	2	12	2	16	0
Schmidt, Curt, Ottawa	1.000	43	6	8	0	14	1
Schmidt, Jason, Richmond	.950	19	4	15	1	20	0
Seelbach, Chris, Richmond	.917	14	5	6	1	12	2
Segura, Jose, Columbus	.667	11	1	1	1	3	0
Sele, Aaron, Pawtucket	1.000	2	1	1	0	2	0
Seminara, Frank, Rochester	.800	29	1	7	2	10	0
Senior, Shawn, Pawtucket*	1.000	1	2	3	0	5	0
Shea, John, Rochester*	1.000	38	1	4	0	5	0
Shepherd, Keith, Charlotte	1.000	4	1	0	0	1	0
Small, Aaron, Syr.-Char.	1.000	34	0	5	0	5	1
Smith, Daryl, Columbus	1.000	13	5	10	0	15	1
Smith, Pete, Charlotte	.933	10	4	10	1	15	2

Player, Team	Pct.	G	PO	A	E	TC	DP
Smith, Zane, Pawtucket*	1.000	1	0	2	0	2	1
Sodowsky, Clint, Toledo	1.000	9	5	8	0	13	0
Spencer, Stan, Charlotte	1.000	9	5	3	0	8	0
Spoljaric, Paul, Syracuse*	.882	43	6	9	2	17	1
Spradlin, Jerry, Charlotte	.769	41	4	6	3	13	0
Springer, Dennis, Scr./W.-B.	1.000	30	12	13	0	25	1
Steed, Rick, Syracuse	.875	31	2	5	1	8	0
Stidham, Phil, Norfolk	.762	34	7	9	5	21	1
Suppan, Jeff, Pawtucket	1.000	7	5	4	0	9	0
Sutherland, John, Columbus	1.000	3	1	0	0	1	0
Telgheder, Dave, Norfolk	1.000	29	6	16	0	22	1
Thobe, J.J., Ottawa	1.000	55	8	26	0	34	2
Thobe, Tom, Richmond*	1.000	48	5	11	0	16	0
Thomas, Royal, Richmond	.875	39	12	16	4	32	0
Tilmon, Pat, Syracuse	1.000	4	1	2	0	3	0
Timlin, Mike, Syracuse	1.000	8	0	4	0	4	0
Torres, Ricky, Ottawa	.813	32	4	9	3	16	1
Tranberg, Mark, Scr./W.-B.	1.000	11	3	2	0	5	0
Tunnell, Lee, Toledo	1.000	7	2	1	0	3	0
Urbina, Ugueth, Ottawa	1.000	13	6	8	0	14	0
Valdes, Marc, Charlotte	.972	27	8	27	1	36	1
VanEgmond, Tim, Pawtucket	.941	12	6	10	1	17	0
Wade, Terrell, Richmond*	1.000	24	5	20	0	25	0
Wainhouse, Dave, Syr.-Char.	.800	30	2	6	2	10	0
Wakefield, Tim, Pawtucket	1.000	4	0	4	0	4	0
Walker, Pete, Norfolk	.923	34	6	6	1	13	1
Wallace, Kent, Columbus	.929	9	6	7	1	14	0
Ward, Duane, Syracuse	1.000	6	0	1	0	1	0
Ware, Jeff, Syracuse	.917	16	2	9	1	12	0
Weathers, David, Charlotte	1.000	1	2	1	0	3	0
Weber, Ben, Syracuse	.958	25	12	11	1	24	1
Wegmann, Tom, Rochester	.909	9	1	9	1	11	0
Wengert, Bill, Pawtucket	1.000	7	1	2	0	3	1
Wertz, Bill, Pawtucket	1.000	29	5	8	0	13	1
West, David, Scr./W.-B.*	1.000	1	1	1	0	2	0
Weston, Mickey, Toledo	.978	28	19	25	1	45	0
White, Gabe, Ottawa*	1.000	12	2	4	0	6	0
Whitehurst, Wally, Paw.-Syr.	1.000	12	1	7	0	8	1
Wickander, Kevin, Toledo*	1.000	16	2	2	0	4	1
Wiegandt, Scott, Scr./W.-B.*	1.000	47	2	6	0	8	1
Wiggs, Johnny, Pawtucket*	1.000	14	0	1	0	1	0
Williams, Jimmy, Nor.-Roch.*	.733	32	2	9	4	15	0
Williams, Woody, Syracuse	1.000	5	0	1	0	1	0
Wilson, Paul, Norfolk	1.000	10	4	11	0	15	0
Woodall, Brad, Richmond*	.944	13	5	12	1	18	2
York, Mike, Syracuse	.667	20	2	4	3	9	0
Zimmerman, Mike, Charlotte	.960	31	7	17	1	25	1

PITCHERS WITH TWO OR MORE TEAMS

Player, Team	Pct.	G	PO	A	E	TC	DP
Bark, Brian, Richmond*	1.000	13	2	6	0	8	0
Bark, Brian, Pawtucket*	1.000	30	1	6	0	7	0
Cornelius, Reid, Ottawa	1.000	4	2	3	0	5	0
Cornelius, Reid, Norfolk	1.000	10	4	17	0	21	0
Hartley, Mike, Pawtucket	1.000	26	1	5	0	6	0
Hartley, Mike, Rochester	.000	8	0	0	0	0	0
Myers, Mike, Charlotte*	1.000	37	2	4	0	6	0
Myers, Mike, Toledo*	1.000	6	0	1	0	1	0
Small, Aaron, Syracuse	.000	1	0	0	0	0	0
Small, Aaron, Charlotte	1.000	33	0	5	0	5	1
Wainhouse, Dave, Syracuse	.889	26	2	6	1	9	0
Wainhouse, Dave, Charlotte	.000	4	0	0	1	1	0
Whitehurst, Wally, Pawtucket	1.000	6	0	3	0	3	0
Whitehurst, Wally, Syracuse	1.000	6	1	4	0	5	1
Williams, Jimmy, Norfolk*	.733	27	2	9	4	15	0
Williams, Jimmy, Rochester*	1.000	5	0	0	0	0	0

The following players did not have any fielding statistics at the positions indicated or appeared only as a designated hitter, pinch-hitter or pinch-runner: Acevedo, p; Barnwell, p; Bergman, p; Bowen, p; Brooks, of; Canseco, dh; Capra, p; Chavez, p; Clemens, p; Crowley, p; Dascenzo, p; E. Diaz, 3b; Engle, p; Finnvold, p; Frey, p; Fuller, p; Gonzales, of; Greenwell, dh; Heffernan, p; Juhl, p; Kamieniecki, p; Knapp, 3b; Langbehn, p; Lemp, p; S. Lewis, p; Livesey, 1b; Magee, p; Melendez, p; Mills, p; Montalvo, of; Musset, p; Pacheco, p; Paxton, p; A. Pena, p; Reed, p; Robertson, p; H. Rodriguez, dh; Santos, p; Schall, 3b; Shumpert, of; S. Springer, ss; Stoddard, p; Twardoski, of; Veres, p; M. Williams, p; Zupcic, 3b.

LEAGUE CHAMPIONS

Year	Team	Pct.	Year	Team	Pct.	Year	Team	Pct.
1884—	Trenton	.520	1892—	Providence	.615	1900—	Providence	.616
1885—	Syracuse	.584		Binghamton*	.667	1901—	Rochester	.642
1886—	Utica	.646	1893—	Erie	.606	1902—	Toronto	.669
1887—	Toronto	.644	1894—	Providence	.696	1903—	Jersey City	.742
1888—	Syracuse	.723	1895—	Springfield	.687	1904—	Buffalo	.657
1889—	Detroit	.649	1896—	Providence	.602	1905—	Providence	.638
1890—	Detroit	.617	1897—	Syracuse	.632	1906—	Buffalo	.607
1891—	Buffalo (reg. season)	.727	1898—	Montreal	.586	1907—	Toronto	.619
	Buffalo (supplemental)	.680	1899—	Rochester	.624	1908—	Baltimore	.593

Year	Team	Pct.	Year	Team	Pct.	Year	Team	Pct.
1909—	Rochester	.596	1946—	Montreal‡	.649	1972—	Louisville	.563
1910—	Rochester	.601	1947—	Jersey City	.610		Tidewater (3rd)†	.545
1911—	Rochester	.645		Syracuse (3rd)†	.575	1973—	Charleston	.586
1912—	Toronto	.595	1948—	Montreal‡	.614		Pawtucket▲†	.534
1913—	Newark	.625	1949—	Buffalo	.584	1974—	Memphis	.613
1914—	Providence	.617		Montreal (3rd)†	.545		Rochester ∞‡	.611
1915—	Buffalo	.632	1950—	Rochester	.609	1975—	Tidewater‡	.610
1916—	Buffalo	.586		Baltimore (3rd)†	.556	1976—	Rochester	.638
1917—	Toronto	.604	1951—	Montreal‡	.617		Syracuse (2nd)†	.590
1918—	Toronto	.693	1952—	Montreal	.629	1977—	Pawtucket	.571
1919—	Baltimore	.671		Rochester (3rd)†	.619		Charleston (2nd)‡	.557
1920—	Baltimore	.719	1953—	Rochester	.630	1978—	Charleston	.607
1921—	Baltimore	.717		Montreal (2nd)†	.586		Richmond (4th)†	.511
1922—	Baltimore	.689	1954—	Toronto	.630	1979—	Columbus‡	.612
1923—	Baltimore	.677		Syracuse (4th)§	.510	1980—	Columbus‡	.593
1924—	Baltimore	.709	1955—	Montreal	.617	1981—	Columbus‡	.633
1925—	Baltimore	.633		Rochester (4th)†	.497	1982—	Richmond	.590
1926—	Toronto	.657	1956—	Toronto	.566		Tidewater (3rd)†	.540
1927—	Buffalo	.667		Rochester (2nd)†	.553	1983—	Columbus	.593
1928—	Rochester	.549	1957—	Toronto	.575		Tidewater (4th)†	.511
1929—	Rochester	.613		Buffalo (2nd)†	.571	1984—	Columbus	.590
1930—	Rochester	.629	1958—	Montreal‡	.588		Pawtucket (4th)†	.536
1931—	Rochester	.601	1959—	Buffalo	.582	1985—	Syracuse	.564
1932—	Newark	.649		Havana (3rd)†	.523		Tidewater (4th)†	.540
1933—	Newark	.622	1960—	Toronto‡	.649	1986—	Richmond‡	.571
	Buffalo (4th)†	.494	1961—	Columbus	.597	1987—	Tidewater	.579
1934—	Newark	.608		Buffalo (3rd)†	.559		Columbus†	.550
	Toronto (3rd)†	.559	1962—	Jacksonville	.610	1988—	Rochester♦	.546
1935—	Montreal	.597		Atlanta (3rd)†	.539		Tidewater	.546
	Syracuse (2nd)†	.565	1963—	Syracuse∞	.533	1989—	Syracuse	.572
1936—	Buffalo‡	.610		Indianapolis‡	.562		Richmond♦	.555
1937—	Newark‡	.717	1964—	Jacksonville	.589	1990—	Rochester♦	.614
1938—	Newark‡	.684		Rochester (4th)†	.532		Columbus	.596
1939—	Jersey City	.582	1965—	Columbus	.582	1991—	Columbus♦	.590
	Rochester (2nd)†	.556		Toronto (3rd)†	.556		Pawtucket	.552
1940—	Rochester	.611	1966—	Rochester	.565	1992—	Columbus♦	.660
	Newark (2nd)†	.594		Toronto (2nd-tied)†	.558		Scr. W.B.	.592
1941—	Newark	.649	1967—	Richmond	.574	1993—	Charlotte♦	.610
	Montreal (2nd)†	.584		Toledo (3rd)†	.525		Rochester	.525
1942—	Newark	.601	1968—	Toledo	.565	1994—	Richmond♦	.567
	Syracuse (3rd)†	.513		Jacksonville (4th)†	.514		Pawtucket	.549
1943—	Toronto	.625	1969—	Tidewater	.563	1995—	Norfolk	.606
	Syracuse (3rd)†	.536		Syracuse (3rd)†	.536		Ottawa♦	.507
1944—	Baltimore‡	.553	1970—	Syracuse‡	.600			
1945—	Montreal	.621	1971—	Rochester‡	.614			
	Newark (2nd)†	.582						

*Won split-season playoff. †Won four-team playoff. ‡Won championship and four-team playoff. §Defeated Havana in game to decide fourth place, then won four-team playoff. ∞League was divided into Northern, Southern divisions. ▲League divided into American, National divisions. ♦League divided into Eastern, Western divisions; won playoffs. (NOTE—Known as Eastern League in 1884, New York State League in 1885, International League in 1886-87, International Association in 1888, International League in 1889-90, Eastern Association in 1891 and Eastern League from 1892 until 1912.)

MEXICAN LEAGUE

1995 FINAL STANDINGS

FIRST HALF

NORTHERN ZONE

Team	W	L	T	Pct.	GB
Reynosa	39	19	2	.672	......
Saltillo	34	25	0	.576	5½
Monterrey	31	27	1	.597	8
Aguascalientes	30	28	0	.517	9
Nuevo Laredo	27	32	0	.458	12½
Monclova	26	33	0	.441	13½
Torreon	22	36	1	.379	17
Jalisco	19	39	1	.328	20

SOUTHERN ZONE

Team	W	L	T	Pct.	GB
Mexico City Red Devils	39	18	1	.684	......
Mexico City Tigers	33	26	0	.559	7
Campeche	32	27	0	.542	8
Tabasco	30	27	2	.526	9
Puebla	29	29	1	.500	10½
Yucatan	28	30	1	.483	11½
Aguila	26	33	0	.441	14
Minatitlan	21	37	1	.362	18½

SECOND HALF

NORTHERN ZONE

Team	W	L	T	Pct.	GB
Reynosa	34	21	2	.618	......
Torreon	34	21	1	.618	......
Nuevo Laredo	35	22	0	.614	......
Monterrey	34	22	1	.607	½
Saltillo	29	28	0	.509	6
Aguascalientes	27	27	2	.500	6½
Monclova	20	36	1	.357	14½
Jalisco	11	43	1	.204	22½

SOUTHERN ZONE

Team	W	L	T	Pct.	GB
Mexico City Red Devils	41	15	0	.732	......
Tabasco	31	23	2	.574	9
Yucatan	31	25	0	.554	10
Campeche	28	27	1	.5090	12½
Mexico City Tigers	29	28	0	.5087	12½
Puebla	23	34	0	.404	18½
Minatitlan	20	36	1	.357	21
Aguila	19	38	0	.333	22½

COMPOSITE

NORTHERN ZONE

Team	W	L	T	Pct.	GB
Reynosa	73	40	3	.646	......
Monterrey	65	49	2	.570	8½
Saltillo	63	53	0	.543	11½
Nuevo Laredo	62	54	0	.534	12½
Aguascalientes	57	55	2	.509	15½
Torreon	56	57	2	.496	17
Monclova	46	69	1	.400	28
Jalisco	30	82	2	.268	42½

SOUTHERN ZONE

Team	W	L	T	Pct.	GB
Mexico City Red Devils	80	33	1	.708	......
Tabasco	61	50	4	.550	18
Mexico City Tigers	62	54	0	.534	19½
Campeche	60	54	1	.526	20½
Yucatan	59	55	1	.518	21½
Puebla	52	63	1	.452	29
Aguila	45	71	0	.388	36½
Minatitlan	41	73	2	.360	39½

PLAYOFFS—Reynosa defeated Nuevo Laredo, four games to three; Monterrey defeated Saltillo, four games to one, in Northern Zone first round. Mexico City Red Devils defeated Campeche, four games to two; Mexico City Tigers defeated Tabasco, four games to one, in Southern Zone first round. Monterrey defeated Reynosa, four games to two, in Northern Zone finals; Mexico City Red Devils defeated Mexico City Tigers, four games to two, in Southern Zone finals. Monterrey defeated Mexico City Red Devils, four games to none, in final series to capture league championship.

(Compiled by Ana Luisa Perea Talarico, League Statistician, Mexico, D.F.)

1995 BATTING

TEAM

Team	Avg.	G	TPA	AB	R	H	TB	2B	3B	HR	RBI	SH	SF	HP	BB	IBB	SO	SB	CS	GDP	LOB	ShO	Slg.	OBP
M.C. Red Devils	.317	114	4195	3683	660	1166	1680	173	22	99	609	40	38	27	407	42	397	84	45	81	804	4	.456	.385
Reynosa	.304	116	4424	3815	680	1160	1626	201	35	65	616	45	51	42	471	31	524	14	21	138	851	3	.426	.382
Monterrey	.301	116	4280	3720	566	1118	1597	193	38	70	524	52	29	24	455	28	516	100	61	124	849	6	.429	.378
Torreon	.295	115	4214	3669	588	1081	1571	160	36	86	520	78	31	37	396	25	516	47	33	109	803	7	.428	.367
Aguascalientes	.295	116	4177	3629	571	1072	1534	162	33	78	522	61	43	48	396	37	481	45	34	102	804	5	.423	.368
M.C. Tigers	.293	116	4261	3681	646	1080	1682	162	37	122	587	56	32	26	466	26	567	85	50	78	790	7	.457	.374
Puebla	.285	116	4074	3602	531	1025	1435	176	24	62	486	52	32	38	550	25	515	34	25	115	754	10	.398	.351
Saltillo	.278	116	4363	3725	578	1036	1544	178	39	84	524	63	31	30	514	33	604	56	34	98	887	3	.414	.367
Tabasco	.275	115	4088	3581	444	983	1333	157	26	47	403	72	25	30	380	40	484	45	39	117	827	12	.372	.347
Campeche	.273	115	4030	3459	464	944	1287	142	15	57	401	78	24	30	439	27	521	101	69	119	779	12	.372	.358
Monclova	.273	116	4161	3633	475	993	1350	137	35	50	443	66	40	28	394	22	446	49	45	100	804	13	.372	.346
Jalisco	.273	114	4065	3531	445	964	1288	166	13	44	392	48	39	37	410	24	530	45	51	133	792	7	.365	.351
Yucatan	.272	115	4204	3494	519	951	1326	139	22	64	474	84	29	38	559	32	462	45	25	120	875	6	.380	.376
Nuevo Laredo	.270	116	4280	3728	500	1005	1404	151	16	72	455	61	24	54	413	26	514	41	41	120	852	8	.377	.349
Aguila	.250	116	4089	3572	356	893	1134	120	17	29	303	83	29	32	373	32	472	55	26	88	802	19	.317	.324
Minatitlan	.249	116	4099	3627	343	904	1179	128	9	43	315	69	24	31	348	23	420	22	24	111	794	23	.325	.318

INDIVIDUAL

TOP QUALIFIERS FOR BATTING CHAMPIONSHIP

Minimum 313 plate appearances.

Player, Team	Avg.	G	TPA	AB	R	H	TB	2B	3B	HR	RBI	SH	SF	HP	BB	IBB	SO	SB	CS	GDP	Slg.	OBP
Gainey, Ty, MCRD	.411	86	352	285	69	117	221	19	2	27	115	0	2	1	64	13	44	4	0	6	.775	.517
Canizalez, Juan C., Mont.	.358	104	414	386	58	138	183	14	5	7	54	2	3	3	20	0	33	8	10	11	.474	.391
Mendez, Jesus, Agu.-Tab.	.356	113	460	399	54	142	181	21	3	4	54	5	1	0	55	13	17	2	2	12	.454	.433

Player, Team	Avg.	G	TPA	AB	R	H	TB	2B	3B	HR	RBI	SH	SF	HP	BB	IBB	SO	SB	CS	GDP	Slg.	OBP
Casillas, Adam, Rey............	.356	102	448	382	82	136	170	22	3	2	53	1	8	5	52	5	13	0	5	20	.445	.432
Garcia, Cornelio, Mont.	.348	104	451	391	83	136	188	24	11	2	47	4	3	1	52	2	51	34	17	6	.481	.423
Romero, Oscar, Tab.............	.344	115	482	410	72	141	195	24	0	10	47	11	1	2	58	5	42	10	6	19	.476	.427
Tolentino, Jose, Mont...........	.342	83	346	304	49	104	176	24	0	16	79	1	2	2	37	6	37	1	2	15	.579	.414
Gonzalez, Denio, Sal...........	.341	109	459	384	74	131	228	23	1	24	95	0	4	1	70	2	55	4	3	9	.594	.440
Rivera, German, Pue...........	.340	110	430	344	59	117	170	19	2	10	53	4	3	2	77	10	43	3	0	10	.494	.460
Arredondo, Luis A., MCRD.....	.340	112	485	421	90	143	192	19	3	8	58	4	5	1	54	3	49	15	7	7	.456	.412

DEPARTMENTAL LEADERS: G—Several players tied with 116; AB—Iturbe, 440; R—J. Robles, 93; H—Tellez, 144; 2B—A. Jimenez, 40; 3B—Co. Garcia, F. Villegas, 11; HR—Gainey, 27; RBI—Gainey, 115; SH—Luna, 21; SF—J. Castillo, 10; HP—G. Sanchez, 19; BB—R. Torres, 96; IBB—G. Wright, 14; SO—B. Castillo, 84; SB—Brinkley, 55; CS—Brinkley, 23; GIDP—Three players tied with 20; Slg.—Gainey, .775.

ALL PLAYERS

Player, Team	Avg.	G	TPA	AB	R	H	TB	2B	3B	HR	RBI	SH	SF	HP	BB	IBB	SO	SB	CS	GDP	Slg.	OBP
Abrego, Jesus, Jal.	.258	99	415	353	55	91	120	19	2	2	27	4	3	3	52	2	47	7	13	15	.340	.355
Aganza, Ruben, Monc.............	.296	116	476	412	66	122	201	24	2	17	66	2	5	2	55	4	31	0	1	12	.488	.378
Agramon, Antonio, Jal............	.244	41	145	131	16	32	54	7	0	5	21	3	1	1	9	1	36	1	0	5	.412	.296
Aguilar, Enrique, Ags............	.325	113	455	428	59	139	207	21	1	15	74	3	3	4	17	2	22	2	5	13	.484	.354
Aguilera, Armando, Sal.	.000	13	9	9	0	0	0	0	0	0	0	0	0	0	0	0	3	0	0	0	.000	.000
Almeida, Shammar, Sal...........	.272	97	350	287	43	78	128	6	1	14	42	3	4	7	49	6	79	0	2	5	.446	.386
Almendra, Gregorio, Tab.	.167	26	40	36	5	6	9	0	0	1	2	1	1	0	2	1	10	0	0	2	.250	.205
Alverez, Hector, Pue.............	.295	116	474	413	77	122	160	27	1	3	58	9	6	2	44	1	56	5	2	13	.387	.361
Alvarez, Ivan, Jal................	.250	2	4	4	0	1	1	0	0	0	0	0	0	0	0	0	2	0	0	0	.250	.250
Alvarez, Luis, Jal................	.372	24	84	78	11	29	39	8	1	0	7	0	0	0	6	0	8	1	1	1	.500	.417
Ansley, Willie, Agu.	.282	30	121	103	14	29	38	5	2	0	6	1	1	0	16	2	31	5	1	6	.369	.375
Arano, Wilfrido, N.L.	.333	13	16	12	5	4	7	1	1	0	2	0	0	1	3	0	2	2	0	0	.583	.500
Arauz, Ignacio, Monc.	.226	46	119	106	10	24	31	4	0	1	13	2	2	0	9	1	30	0	1	4	.292	.282
Arce, Francisco J., Min.	.304	90	331	303	18	92	115	17	0	2	28	4	3	1	20	2	21	0	0	14	.380	.346
Arevalo, Guadalupe, Ags.........	.321	66	181	162	27	52	64	8	2	0	13	2	0	0	17	2	14	2	1	3	.395	.385
Arias, Everardo, Pue.............	.205	49	154	127	17	26	34	4	2	0	12	4	2	0	21	0	31	1	0	1	.268	.313
Arredondo, Hernando, Pue.......	.291	77	171	158	16	46	52	4	1	0	12	2	1	1	9	1	25	1	2	4	.329	.331
Arredondo, Jesus A., Ags........	.322	113	486	388	79	125	157	16	8	0	49	10	3	13	72	0	37	7	4	10	.405	.441
Arredondo, Luis A., MCRD........	.340	112	485	421	90	143	192	19	3	8	58	4	5	1	54	3	49	15	7	7	.456	.412
Arvizu, Javier, Cam.	.307	100	348	287	35	88	116	18	2	2	27	3	2	2	54	2	45	4	6	9	.404	.417
Arzate, Martin, Jal...............	.230	80	209	178	17	41	48	5	1	0	20	5	6	1	19	0	19	1	3	12	.270	.299
Avila, Roberto, Min..............	.125	7	11	8	1	1	1	0	0	0	0	1	0	0	2	0	3	0	0	0	.125	.300
Avila, Ruben, Tor................	.270	114	456	403	58	109	175	19	1	15	63	6	6	3	38	2	70	3	2	9	.434	.333
Ayala, Armenta M., Monc.	.200	4	6	5	1	1	1	0	0	0	0	1	0	0	0	1	0	0	0	0	.200	.200
Balderas, S. Abelardo, Min.......	.183	61	121	104	12	19	20	1	0	0	10	2	3	0	12	0	20	0	0	3	.192	.261
Barrera, Jesus A., Min...........	.294	5	17	17	0	5	5	0	0	0	0	0	0	0	0	0	3	0	0	0	.294	.294
Barrera, Nelson, MCRD...........	.292	93	327	298	38	87	155	17	0	17	71	4	2	4	19	5	43	0	0	12	.520	.341
Bellazetin, Jose Juan, MCT	.192	9	38	26	8	5	5	0	0	0	2	0	1	0	11	0	3	0	1	0	.192	.421
Beltran, Gerardo, Min...........	.253	85	293	265	22	67	95	11	1	5	22	6	0	4	18	2	28	1	4	6	.358	.310
Brinkley, Darrell, Cam.	.338	106	446	397	79	134	203	26	2	13	50	3	4	5	37	4	38	55	23	10	.511	.397
Brumley, Duff, Mont.-Ags.	.000	1	0	0	0	0	0	0	0	0	0	0	0	0	0	0	0	0	0	0	.000	.000
Burguillos, Carlos M., Min.	.252	98	377	337	41	85	115	14	2	4	35	7	2	1	30	1	20	10	4	10	.341	.314
Cabreja, Alexis, Pue.............	.297	59	226	212	42	63	84	10	4	1	19	0	1	4	9	1	17	9	5	3	.396	.336
Cairo, Sergio, Yuc.	.313	58	221	195	26	61	81	2	0	6	35	5	3	0	18	1	21	3	1	6	.415	.366
Camacho, Adulfo, Yuc.	.245	113	478	372	69	91	118	14	2	3	34	20	2	8	76	0	47	4	7	9	.317	.382
Campos, Oscar, Agu.	.250	11	12	12	2	3	3	0	0	0	0	0	0	0	0	0	5	0	0	0	.250	.250
Canizalez, Juan C., Mont.	.358	104	414	386	58	138	183	14	5	7	54	2	3	3	20	0	33	8	10	11	.474	.391
Cano, Jose, Ags.................	.000	1	1	1	0	0	0	0	0	0	0	0	0	0	0	0	0	0	0	0	.000	.000
Cantu, Gerardo, Pue.............	.214	72	146	126	13	27	41	2	0	4	19	0	2	1	17	2	23	0	1	6	.325	.308
Caraballo, Gari, Mont.	.304	26	93	79	11	24	38	5	0	3	15	1	0	1	12	0	19	0	1	3	.481	.402
Carrasco, Ernesto, N.L.	.259	113	430	378	43	98	113	13	1	0	27	5	2	4	41	5	47	9	9	11	.299	.336
Carrillo, Matias, MCT	.331	97	398	338	81	112	194	14	4	20	78	2	3	3	52	7	43	20	7	8	.574	.422
Carter, Steve, Monc.	.273	14	50	44	5	12	16	1	0	1	7	0	0	0	6	0	1	0	0	1	.364	.360
Casillas, Adam, Rey.............	.356	102	448	382	82	136	170	22	3	2	53	1	8	5	52	5	13	0	5	20	.445	.432
Castaldo, Vince, Cam.	.250	40	155	132	21	33	56	6	1	5	22	0	0	1	22	1	23	3	2	4	.424	.361
Castaneda, Nick, Yuc.	.395	14	56	43	7	17	26	4	1	1	9	0	2	0	11	2	7	0	0	1	.605	.500
Castaneda, Rafael, N.L.	.278	116	468	406	52	113	150	16	3	5	43	8	3	2	49	3	42	5	6	20	.369	.357
Castillo, Braulio, Rey............	.312	95	416	356	77	111	200	30	7	15	81	0	4	4	52	1	84	3	1	16	.562	.401
Castillo, Juan, Ags..............	.335	106	456	376	73	126	179	16	8	7	58	10	10	2	58	5	58	6	3	14	.476	.417
Castro, Arnoldo, Min............	.253	109	438	380	39	96	119	9	1	4	32	19	0	3	36	0	24	2	2	11	.313	.322
Castro, Eddie, Min.-Sal.	.246	59	243	191	16	47	63	7	0	3	24	0	2	3	47	5	38	0	0	4	.330	.399
Castro, Leonel, Jal..............	.000	3	4	4	0	0	0	0	0	0	0	0	0	0	0	0	2	0	0	1	.000	.000
Cazarin, Manuel, Agu.	.244	113	422	386	28	94	130	22	1	4	38	7	4	4	21	4	16	2	1	13	.337	.287
Canedo, Alberto, Cam............	.179	36	48	39	7	7	12	2	0	1	4	2	0	1	6	0	12	0	1	1	.308	.304
Cecena, Manuel, Min............	.273	3	11	11	2	3	3	0	0	0	1	0	0	0	0	1	0	0	0	0	.273	.273
Cervera, Francisco, Jal...........	.263	95	342	274	47	72	103	13	3	4	31	3	5	10	50	5	59	4	5	6	.376	.389
Chan, Armando, Monc............	.274	81	228	201	31	55	70	8	2	1	19	3	1	0	23	1	35	0	1	5	.348	.347
Clement, Wes, Ags..............	.167	9	33	30	2	5	6	1	0	0	3	0	0	0	3	0	11	0	0	1	.200	.242
Cobos, Rogelio, MCRD...........	.200	7	6	5	1	1	1	0	0	0	0	0	0	0	1	0	2	0	1	0	.200	.333
Contreras, Cuitlahuac, Tor.-Monc...	.202	39	113	94	10	19	31	1	1	3	12	1	1	2	15	4	28	2	1	1	.330	.321
Cornejo, Edgar, Sal..............	.183	41	111	93	12	17	21	2	1	0	8	0	0	0	18	0	15	0	1	1	.226	.315
Corrales, Virgilio, N.L............	.111	5	20	18	2	2	4	2	0	0	3	0	0	0	2	0	5	0	0	1	.222	.200
Cruz, Luis Alfonso, Rey..........	.301	108	450	418	64	126	190	26	1	12	80	2	8	6	16	2	37	1	0	19	.455	.330
Cruz, Marco Antonio, N.L.........	.240	115	392	333	32	80	106	12	1	4	36	11	1	11	36	0	64	0	1	7	.318	.333
Cueto, Raul, Tab................	.100	5	11	10	2	1	1	0	0	0	0	0	0	0	1	0	2	0	0	1	.100	.182
Cuevas, Angelo, Tab.-Min.	.270	104	418	371	44	100	137	14	1	7	33	5	2	0	40	5	31	2	7	10	.369	.339
Dattola, Kevin, Tor..............	.265	29	130	117	15	31	41	2	1	2	13	1	0	1	11	1	15	3	1	4	.350	.333
Delgado, Tomas, Tab.	.284	28	79	67	13	19	28	1	1	2	6	1	0	0	11	0	8	0	1	2	.418	.385
DeLima, Rafael, Tab.............	.300	72	303	257	40	77	93	12	2	0	15	4	2	1	39	9	35	10	5	4	.362	.391

Player, Team	Avg.	G	TPA	AB	R	H	TB	2B	3B	HR	RBI	SH	SF	HP	BB	IBB	SO	SB	CS	GDP	Slg.	OBP
Diaz, Luis Fernando, MCT	.311	95	333	267	49	83	124	12	4	7	47	6	0	1	59	4	47	7	5	5	.464	.437
Diaz, Remigio, Mont.	.233	95	290	258	24	60	79	4	6	1	20	6	1	0	25	0	28	5	2	14	.306	.299
Dominguez, David, MCT-Min.	.297	88	332	263	36	78	118	11	1	9	37	4	3	0	62	0	46	1	3	6	.449	.427
Dominguez, Fausto, Tab.	.000	3	5	5	0	0	0	0	0	0	0	0	0	0	0	0	4	0	0	1	.000	.000
Duarte C., Rene, Min.	.264	74	213	197	23	52	65	7	0	2	16	4	1	3	8	0	23	2	1	6	.330	.301
Duran, Felipe, MCRD	.279	54	148	136	29	38	47	6	0	1	11	0	2	4	6	0	10	2	2	1	.346	.324
Elvira, Ramon H., Tab.	.000	2	2	2	0	0	0	0	0	0	0	0	0	0	0	0	1	0	0	0	.000	.000
Enriquez, Graciano, Ags.	.288	65	245	219	36	63	85	9	2	3	19	3	1	2	20	1	52	5	3	2	.388	.351
Enriquez, Martin, Ags.	.000	1	1	1	0	0	0	0	0	0	0	0	0	0	0	0	1	0	0	0	.000	.000
Escalante, Marcelo, Sal.	.245	83	240	220	19	54	77	10	2	3	29	5	3	2	10	1	63	1	0	7	.350	.281
Espinoza, Javier, Cam.	.247	83	257	198	24	49	61	7	1	1	19	8	3	2	46	5	24	2	3	4	.308	.393
Espinoza, Jose M., Monc.	.229	45	114	105	9	24	27	3	0	0	9	0	1	1	7	0	20	0	0	3	.257	.281
Esquer, Ramon, Rey.	.289	86	357	287	52	83	111	11	7	1	40	6	4	3	57	2	50	3	2	1	.387	.407
Estrada, Hector, Pue.	.313	116	450	418	51	131	187	23	0	11	78	1	7	2	22	3	47	1	4	17	.447	.345
Estrada, Ricardo, Min.-Agu.	.206	46	122	107	10	22	30	5	0	1	8	3	1	0	11	1	27	0	0	3	.280	.277
Estrada, Ruben, N.L.	.232	84	195	168	20	39	43	4	0	0	16	3	0	2	22	3	20	2	2	4	.256	.328
Fariss, Monty, Mont.	.259	43	144	112	20	29	45	7	0	3	14	0	0	1	31	1	26	1	0	3	.402	.424
Felix, Arturo, Yuc.	.246	107	391	333	42	82	102	14	3	0	32	6	2	3	47	1	50	7	1	13	.306	.343
Fentanes, Oscar, Tab.	.311	100	374	341	33	106	146	11	4	7	51	6	3	5	19	1	42	1	3	9	.428	.353
Fernandez, Carlos, Jal.	.260	13	54	50	5	13	21	2	0	2	7	0	0	1	3	0	16	0	0	0	.420	.315
Fernandez, Daniel, MCRD	.316	106	466	386	89	122	168	14	7	6	45	6	1	4	69	4	24	23	9	3	.435	.424
Fernandez, Fabian, Rey.	.200	6	11	10	2	2	3	1	0	0	0	0	0	0	1	0	1	0	0	1	.300	.273
Flores, Miguel, Mont.	.292	36	152	120	20	35	48	8	1	1	18	6	1	2	23	2	17	8	2	3	.400	.411
Franco, Manuel, Mont.	.280	72	245	225	29	63	94	14	4	3	41	1	5	3	11	0	49	7	6	9	.418	.316
Franklin, Jay, Mont.-Ags.	.000	1	0	0	1	0	0	0	0	0	0	0	0	0	0	0	0	0	0	0	.000	.000
Gainey, Ty, MCRD	.411	86	352	285	69	117	221	19	2	27	115	0	2	1	64	13	44	4	0	6	.775	.517
Gamboa, Jose A., Agu.	.234	81	235	205	20	48	64	6	2	2	15	4	1	5	20	1	24	2	2	5	.312	.316
Garcia, Carlos, Agu.	.207	97	297	246	31	51	62	8	0	1	14	11	1	2	37	1	48	3	3	3	.252	.315
Garcia, Cornelio, Mont.	.348	104	451	391	83	136	188	24	11	2	47	4	3	1	52	2	51	34	17	6	.481	.423
Garcia, Hector, Tor.	.294	109	464	405	60	119	144	11	7	0	42	13	3	4	39	0	43	11	6	18	.356	.359
Garcia, Heriberto, Agu.	.284	115	478	433	55	123	143	7	5	1	25	13	1	3	28	1	29	14	4	10	.330	.331
Garcia, Jose Luis, Mont.	.286	4	17	14	1	4	4	0	0	0	5	0	0	1	2	0	5	0	0	0	.286	.412
Garcia, Rosario, Rey.	.100	12	13	10	3	1	1	0	0	0	1	1	0	0	2	0	6	0	0	0	.100	.250
Garza, Gerardo, Tor.	.326	111	399	350	57	114	156	15	0	9	44	11	1	5	32	4	30	6	6	7	.446	.389
Garzon, Eliseo, Tab.	.223	100	350	292	31	65	97	11	0	7	37	9	3	3	43	3	49	0	2	3	.332	.326
Gastelum, Carlos, Min.	.239	59	178	163	11	39	42	3	0	0	1	5	0	2	8	0	25	1	0	2	.258	.283
Gastelum G., Sergio O., MCT	.000	3	4	3	0	0	0	0	0	0	0	1	0	0	0	0	2	0	0	0	.000	.000
Gavia, Jesus, Agu.-Min.	.237	52	141	131	10	31	42	2	0	3	12	0	1	2	7	0	21	0	0	5	.321	.284
Gil, Geronimo, MCRD	.286	4	7	7	1	2	2	0	0	0	0	0	0	0	0	0	1	0	0	0	.286	.286
Gonzalez, Denio, Sal.	.341	109	459	384	74	131	228	23	1	24	95	0	4	1	70	2	55	4	3	9	.594	.440
Gonzalez, Jesus, Jal.	.254	104	390	347	43	88	122	13	0	7	36	3	3	3	34	2	33	1	5	11	.352	.323
Gonzalez, Jose, Mont.	.313	103	427	368	74	115	188	23	4	14	67	1	4	2	52	3	61	19	7	15	.511	.397
Gonzalez, Pedro, Sal.	.217	33	93	69	19	15	32	2	3	3	9	2	0	3	19	1	20	4	0	2	.464	.407
Guerrero, Francisco, Tor.	.267	85	335	270	44	72	90	12	3	0	33	8	4	4	49	0	31	4	1	8	.333	.382
Guerrero, Jaime, Ags.	.235	72	232	217	23	51	74	9	1	4	22	4	0	1	10	0	50	2	2	5	.341	.272
Guerrero, Javier, Ags.	.251	75	240	203	30	51	85	9	2	7	27	4	0	1	32	4	51	3	1	5	.419	.356
Guizar, Hector, Cam.	.247	101	309	279	28	69	83	10	2	0	24	6	3	1	20	0	32	3	4	17	.297	.297
Gutierrez, Andres, Pue.	.196	54	108	97	16	19	25	4	1	0	6	3	0	0	8	0	16	1	0	1	.258	.257
Gutierrez, Arturo, Agu.	.000	1	0	0	0	0	0	0	0	0	0	0	0	0	0	0	0	0	0	0	.000	.000
Gutierrez, Felipe, Monc.	.205	20	49	44	6	9	17	2	0	2	7	0	2	1	2	0	8	0	0	1	.386	.245
Gutierrez, Jose Luis, Agu.	.247	90	263	227	18	56	65	6	0	1	21	4	3	7	22	1	34	0	1	7	.286	.328
Guzman, Marco A., Yuc.	.269	100	360	316	28	85	109	15	0	3	43	8	0	1	35	3	27	1	0	18	.345	.344
Harris, Donald, Agu.-Monc.	.271	53	216	188	26	51	90	7	4	8	31	2	2	4	20	0	45	5	3	4	.479	.350
Heath, Robert Lee, MCT	.321	99	329	305	40	98	126	12	5	2	30	1	3	4	16	0	52	10	7	4	.413	.360
Hecht, Steve, Monc.	.333	5	19	18	2	6	6	0	0	0	2	0	0	0	1	0	4	1	1	0	.333	.368
Hernandez, Miguel, Agu.	.257	59	178	152	10	39	42	3	0	0	9	11	1	1	13	0	14	1	0	2	.276	.317
Hernandez A., Martin, Cam.	.287	51	107	101	9	29	43	2	0	4	15	1	0	0	5	0	25	2	1	0	.426	.321
Hernandez B., Juan C., Pue.	.167	42	80	66	15	11	15	4	0	0	3	2	0	3	9	0	12	2	1	3	.227	.295
Hernandez W., Ger'do, Min.	.216	80	244	218	21	47	63	14	1	0	12	3	0	6	17	0	50	2	1	4	.289	.290
Herrera, Isidro, Cam.	.246	108	448	349	51	86	97	11	0	0	23	16	1	4	78	2	31	18	9	10	.278	.389
Horn, Sam, MCRD	.316	11	46	38	9	12	22	1	0	3	12	0	1	0	7	1	11	0	0	1	.579	.413
Housie, Wayne, Yuc.	.239	46	206	184	27	44	64	5	6	1	21	2	3	0	17	1	26	6	3	4	.348	.299
Howell, Patrick, MCT	.321	87	363	336	63	108	137	9	7	2	22	4	0	3	20	0	51	23	10	14	.408	.365
Hurst, Jonathan, Jal.-Mont.	.000	1	0	0	1	0	0	0	0	0	0	0	0	0	0	0	0	0	0	0	.000	.000
Hurtado, Hector, Mont.	.245	70	192	163	13	40	48	5	0	1	18	4	1	2	22	3	28	0	2	8	.294	.340
Infante, Alexis, Tab.	.299	95	394	354	52	106	122	10	3	0	26	8	4	4	24	1	25	3	3	15	.345	.347
Iturbe, Pedro, Pue.	.323	113	474	440	77	142	185	21	8	2	61	10	1	5	18	1	54	4	4	10	.420	.356
Jelks, Greg, Cam.	.211	54	206	175	20	37	66	6	1	7	29	1	1	3	26	1	32	5	5	9	.377	.322
Jeter, Shawn, Sal.	.337	24	96	89	17	30	43	4	3	1	7	1	0	0	6	0	15	4	3	1	.483	.379
Jimenez, Alfonso, Sal.	.337	112	475	398	79	134	200	40	4	6	59	7	5	1	64	2	47	6	2	6	.503	.425
Jimenez, Eduardo, Yuc.	.316	115	463	373	67	118	222	26	3	24	90	3	4	4	79	12	53	4	0	15	.595	.437
Jimenez, Ulises, Jal.	.233	30	93	86	7	20	22	2	0	0	7	4	0	0	3	0	12	1	2	2	.256	.258
Laurencio, Rodfer, Cam.	.182	10	22	22	2	4	4	0	0	0	0	0	0	0	0	0	5	0	0	2	.182	.182
Leal, Jose Guadalupe, Cam.	.269	100	344	308	37	83	111	12	2	4	51	6	3	0	27	2	62	1	7	5	.360	.325
Leyva, German, Monc.	.285	104	473	358	49	102	128	13	2	3	39	11	2	52	50	4	31	3	2	7	.358	.442
Lopez, Alfredo, Jal.	.293	26	104	92	11	27	34	4	0	1	11	1	2	2	7	0	12	2	1	2	.370	.350
Lopez, Fabian, MCRD	.214	9	15	14	2	3	3	0	0	0	1	0	0	0	1	0	1	0	0	1	.214	.267
Lopez, Gonzalo, Monc.	.323	101	393	362	35	117	160	18	5	5	66	4	8	2	17	4	22	1	4	15	.442	.350
Lopez, Miguel, Yuc.	.308	10	18	13	2	4	4	0	0	0	4	0	0	1	0	0	1	0	0	1	.308	.357
Lopez, Salvador, Rey.	.284	43	122	109	16	31	36	5	0	0	15	5	1	2	5	0	18	0	0	7	.330	.325
Lopez A., Victor M., Jal.	.286	79	271	255	24	73	91	13	1	1	31	5	2	2	7	0	37	5	3	6	.357	.308
Loredo, Jorge Luis, Cam.	.257	89	310	269	27	69	95	10	2	4	31	7	1	4	29	0	51	0	3	15	.353	.337
Luna, Jose Luis, Sal.	.224	93	296	254	21	57	71	12	1	0	26	21	0	2	19	0	27	0	3	8	.280	.284

Player, Team	Avg.	G	TPA	AB	R	H	TB	2B	3B	HR	RBI	SH	SF	HP	BB	IBB	SO	SB	CS	GDP	Slg.	OBP
Machiria, Pablo, Ags.	.333	112	454	406	61	135	194	21	1	12	72	6	8	5	29	5	35	3	2	13	.478	.377
Machorro, Roberto, Monc.	.171	22	43	41	1	7	11	2	1	0	5	0	0	0	2	0	2	1	0	1	.268	.209
Maclin, Lonnie, Agu.	.236	37	174	140	27	33	43	4	3	0	10	1	2	2	29	4	17	13	2	4	.307	.370
Magallanes, Ever, Mont.	.255	54	171	149	20	38	47	3	0	2	15	6	3	0	13	3	10	2	1	3	.315	.309
Magallanes, William, Tab.	.260	64	259	215	30	56	82	9	1	5	28	4	0	1	39	5	37	5	1	7	.381	.376
Magana, Gabriel, Yuc.	.222	24	43	36	7	8	9	1	0	0	2	0	0	3	4	0	4	0	0	1	.250	.349
Malpica, Enrique, Agu.	.239	79	201	176	16	42	43	1	0	0	14	6	3	0	16	1	34	1	1	3	.244	.297
Marrujo, Hector, Tab.	.233	95	327	292	29	68	84	8	4	0	18	8	1	3	23	1	44	2	1	13	.288	.295
Martinez, Carmelo, Monc.	.296	43	177	142	23	42	84	12	0	10	30	0	0	1	34	3	23	1	0	6	.592	.435
Martinez, Enrique, Mont.	.250	15	14	12	1	3	3	0	0	0	0	0	0	1	1	0	0	0	0	1	.250	.357
Martinez, Grimaldo, Monc.	.272	103	439	393	55	107	135	10	6	2	45	6	5	2	33	1	30	7	6	12	.344	.328
Martinez, Luis Carlos, Sal.	.227	46	72	66	10	15	19	4	0	0	4	6	0	0	0	0	5	0	0	3	.288	.227
Martinez, Raul, Sal.	.357	9	15	14	0	5	5	0	0	0	1	0	0	1	0	0	3	0	0	0	.357	.400
McCoy, Trey, N.L.	.321	9	35	28	7	9	15	0	0	2	3	0	0	0	7	0	4	0	1	1	.536	.457
Medina, Jose Ramon, Cam.	.224	56	111	98	15	22	25	1	1	0	6	3	1	2	7	1	23	0	0	3	.255	.287
Mendez, Jesus, Agu.-Tab.	.356	113	460	399	54	142	181	21	3	4	54	5	1	0	55	13	17	2	2	12	.454	.433
Mendez, Ramon, Ags.	.264	42	126	110	16	29	39	5	1	1	12	3	3	0	10	0	16	1	0	3	.355	.317
Mendez, Roberto C., MCRD	.304	99	360	309	50	94	132	8	3	8	47	8	5	4	34	4	29	9	7	7	.427	.375
Mendiola, Juan C., Agu.	.098	32	60	51	3	5	7	2	0	0	3	1	0	0	8	1	10	0	0	0	.137	.220
Mercedes, Luis, Yuc.	.316	52	224	196	35	62	74	5	2	1	10	2	0	2	24	1	26	7	5	7	.378	.396
Merchand, Mark, Rey.	.152	9	39	33	4	5	10	2	0	1	4	1	0	5	2	7	0	0	3	.303	.263
Mere, Pedro, MCT	.286	95	356	304	53	87	128	14	0	9	48	3	4	0	45	2	40	3	3	8	.421	.374
Meza, Alfredo, Mont.	.172	35	60	58	5	10	13	0	0	1	2	0	0	0	2	0	9	0	0	3	.224	.200
Michel, Domingo, Cam.	.323	44	164	127	30	41	76	8	0	9	32	2	2	0	33	0	25	2	1	2	.598	.457
Mitchell, Keith, Tab.	.333	24	100	81	15	27	53	6	1	6	26	0	1	0	18	0	10	0	6	1	.654	.450
Monroy, Francisco, Mont.	.333	4	3	3	0	1	1	0	0	0	0	0	0	0	0	0	0	0	1	0	.333	.333
Monroy, Victor Hugo, Rey.	.380	41	114	108	16	41	55	8	0	2	24	0	0	1	5	0	8	0	0	4	.509	.412
Montalvo, Ivan, MCT	.285	70	166	144	18	41	61	8	3	2	22	4	4	0	14	1	32	1	1	1	.424	.340
Mora, Andres, N.L.	.263	50	159	137	12	36	59	5	0	6	18	0	1	1	20	2	16	0	0	4	.431	.358
Morales, Alejandro, Tor.	.000	4	8	6	0	0	0	0	0	0	0	1	1	0	0	0	2	0	0	1	.000	.000
Morales, Florentino, N.L.	.254	99	397	342	49	87	113	19	2	1	21	5	2	6	42	2	54	2	1	10	.330	.344
Moreno, David, Sal.	.133	14	15	15	0	2	3	1	0	0	0	0	0	0	0	0	6	0	0	0	.200	.133
Morones, Martin, Monc.	.259	97	387	317	53	82	109	8	5	3	34	6	2	1	61	0	39	19	8	9	.344	.378
Motley, Darryl, Tor.-Agu.	.276	32	139	116	16	32	46	8	0	2	22	1	1	2	19	1	15	1	1	1	.397	.384
Munoz, Noe, Rey.	.314	36	141	121	23	38	49	8	0	1	22	0	1	0	19	1	17	0	0	7	.405	.404
Navarrete, Alejandro, Tab.	.000	1	1	1	0	0	0	0	0	0	0	0	0	0	0	0	1	0	0	0	.000	.000
Naveda, Edgar, Jal.	.290	103	402	352	45	102	135	25	1	2	37	1	3	1	45	6	30	8	6	19	.384	.369
Noris, Rogelio, N.L.	.205	65	140	122	15	25	34	4	1	1	13	3	1	0	14	1	32	0	2	5	.279	.285
Nunez Avina, Jose J., Jal.	.191	32	53	47	7	9	10	1	0	0	7	1	0	1	4	0	12	1	0	3	.213	.269
Nunez Garcia, Jose J., Jal.	.125	20	40	40	1	5	5	0	0	0	1	0	0	0	0	0	12	0	1	0	.125	.125
Ochoa, Marin Edgar, MCT	.228	52	104	92	10	21	36	6	0	3	12	3	1	1	7	0	20	0	0	6	.391	.287
Ojeda, Miguel, MCRD	.280	50	163	150	14	42	64	5	1	5	24	0	2	2	9	0	29	2	1	3	.427	.325
Olvera, Sergio, Monc.	.246	68	219	203	25	50	72	8	1	4	12	4	0	1	11	0	39	2	2	3	.355	.288
Orantes, Ramon, Mont.	.265	79	221	196	26	52	69	9	4	0	17	4	1	0	20	0	31	4	7	10	.352	.332
Ortega, Roberto, Tab.	.218	77	222	193	15	42	62	11	0	3	16	4	2	1	22	4	29	0	1	7	.321	.298
Ortiz, Alejandro, MCT	.282	97	384	330	53	93	151	13	0	15	64	1	3	3	47	2	44	4	5	13	.458	.373
Osuna, Hector, Yuc.	.185	13	68	54	7	10	10	0	0	0	11	2	0	2	10	1	11	0	0	1	.185	.333
Pacho, Juan Jose, Yuc.	.273	104	365	322	31	88	105	13	2	0	23	9	1	2	31	0	27	2	2	12	.326	.340
Paez, Raul, MCRD	.341	93	257	232	32	79	113	19	3	3	28	2	0	2	21	2	24	1	1	3	.487	.400
Palacios, Alfonso, P., Tab.	.167	5	6	6	1	1	1	0	0	0	0	0	0	0	0	0	1	0	0	0	.167	.167
Pardo, Victor, Manuel, Pue.	.260	104	334	288	36	75	109	12	2	6	27	5	1	2	38	2	42	2	1	10	.378	.350
Paredes, Johnny, Agu.	.179	7	31	28	4	5	5	0	0	0	1	0	0	0	3	0	3	0	1	1	.179	.258
Payro, Edison, Cam.	.233	28	33	30	2	7	8	1	0	0	7	0	0	1	2	0	6	0	0	1	.267	.303
Peralta, Amado, Yuc.-Jal.	.280	90	335	268	34	75	98	20	0	1	26	1	2	4	60	0	44	1	5	7	.366	.416
Perez, Alejandro, N.L.	.200	10	12	10	3	2	2	0	0	0	1	2	0	0	0	0	3	0	0	0	.200	.200
Perez, Alfredo, Pue.	.000	2	2	2	0	0	0	0	0	0	0	0	0	0	0	0	0	0	0	0	.000	.000
Perez, Francisco, Rey.	.281	51	106	96	13	27	40	3	2	2	21	0	3	1	6	1	34	0	1	1	.417	.321
Perez, Juan Luis, Tor.	.286	33	63	56	6	16	24	2	3	0	8	3	0	0	4	0	15	0	1	0	.429	.333
Pena, Carlos, Cam.	.250	14	34	28	3	7	8	1	0	0	5	3	0	0	3	0	10	0	0	0	.286	.333
Pena, Luis Alberto, Pue.	.310	108	364	326	36	101	152	18	0	11	61	2	3	2	31	3	59	1	1	11	.466	.370
Pena, M. Joel, Agu.	.000	9	10	9	1	0	0	0	0	0	0	0	0	0	1	0	2	0	0	1	.000	.100
Pierce, Dominique, Jal.	.160	7	29	25	0	4	5	1	0	0	0	0	0	4	1	6	0	0	2	.200	.276
Pledger, Kinnis E., Tor.	.234	14	54	47	7	11	16	0	1	1	5	0	0	1	6	0	14	0	0	0	.340	.333
Ponce, Hector, Cam.	.000	5	8	8	0	0	0	0	0	0	0	0	0	0	0	0	1	0	0	0	.000	.000
Precichi, Jorge, Sal.	.212	80	328	283	46	60	81	10	4	1	18	7	2	2	34	0	42	6	3	13	.286	.299
Pulido, Jesus, N.L.	.118	15	19	17	0	2	2	0	0	0	0	0	0	1	1	0	7	0	0	1	.118	.211
Quintana, Carlos, Min.-Yuc.	.325	78	329	268	47	87	112	9	2	4	37	6	1	3	51	2	23	2	1	19	.418	.437
Quintero, Guillermo, Mont.	.377	70	84	69	24	26	30	2	1	0	6	6	1	1	7	0	13	7	1	1	.435	.436
Quiroz, Jose Julian, Ags.	.239	60	179	155	21	37	57	9	1	3	28	0	2	1	21	5	28	1	0	5	.368	.330
Quinones, Luis, Yuc.	.235	44	190	153	31	36	50	5	0	3	19	5	4	0	28	2	17	4	1	2	.327	.346
Ramirez, Efren, Ags.	.252	84	284	246	27	62	86	6	3	4	23	8	1	11	18	0	42	0	6	6	.350	.330
Ramirez, Enrique, N.L.	.241	112	422	394	43	95	104	7	1	0	27	15	0	1	12	0	19	5	6	16	.264	.265
Ramirez G., Jesus A., MCRD	.175	47	42	40	13	7	8	1	0	0	4	1	0	0	1	0	3	2	2	0	.200	.195
Ramon, Reyes, Agu.	.077	5	13	13	0	1	1	0	0	0	0	0	0	0	0	0	6	0	0	0	.077	.077
Rendina, Mike, Monc.	.128	12	44	39	2	5	6	1	0	0	3	0	2	0	3	0	7	0	1	1	.154	.182
Renteria, Edison, Agu.-Cam.	.300	45	165	150	21	45	56	6	1	1	14	2	0	1	12	4	16	3	2	5	.373	.356
Reyes, Gilberto, Cam.	.277	111	406	361	37	100	131	10	0	7	36	8	1	3	33	4	56	2	2	15	.363	.342
Reyna, Luis, Monc.-Tab.	.272	50	194	173	23	47	64	5	0	4	31	1	4	1	15	2	17	6	3	5	.370	.326
Ritchie, Greg, Tab.	.345	17	66	55	7	19	28	3	3	0	8	1	0	2	8	0	8	2	2	4	.509	.446
Rivera, Alberto, Jal.	.263	55	162	133	18	35	39	2	1	0	9	3	3	4	19	1	20	4	0	8	.293	.365
Rivera, Eleazar, Monc.	.227	12	26	22	3	5	5	0	0	0	2	0	1	1	0	0	5	0	0	1	.227	.292
Rivera, German, Pue.	.340	110	430	344	59	117	170	19	2	10	53	4	3	2	77	10	43	3	0	10	.494	.460
Roa, Hector, MCT	.250	33	136	128	18	32	50	9	0	3	22	1	1	1	5	0	23	0	0	5	.391	.281

Player, Team	Avg.	G	TPA	AB	R	H	TB	2B	3B	HR	RBI	SH	SF	HP	BB	IBB	SO	SB	CS	GDP	Slg.	OBP
Robles, Javier, MCT	.311	113	474	409	93	127	218	24	8	17	53	13	5	3	44	1	61	7	6	6	.533	.377
Robles, Ricardo, Sal.	.222	12	12	9	2	2	2	0	0	0	1	0	0	0	3	2	5	0	0	0	.222	.417
Robles, Trinidad, MCT-Min.	.105	14	22	19	3	2	3	1	0	0	2	2	0	0	1	0	7	0	0	0	.158	.150
Rodriguez, Boi, N.L.	.307	82	340	293	54	90	178	18	2	22	77	0	5	1	41	4	47	5	3	4	.608	.388
Rodriguez, Fernando, Tor.	.320	105	397	347	49	111	168	17	2	12	49	4	2	8	36	4	43	3	5	12	.484	.394
Rodriguez, Genaro, N.L.	.267	75	210	187	12	50	64	4	2	2	25	5	1	2	15	1	28	1	3	7	.342	.327
Rodriguez, Hector, Rey.	.291	107	412	351	65	102	144	11	5	7	52	5	5	5	46	0	78	0	3	8	.410	.376
Rodriguez, Jose Luis, Agu.	.241	86	264	237	13	57	69	12	0	0	12	3	0	2	22	6	38	3	3	9	.291	.310
Rodriguez, Juan F., Rey.-Agu.	.178	52	209	174	18	31	33	2	0	0	12	7	1	1	26	0	7	0	1	3	.190	.287
Rodriguez, Ruben, Monc.	.258	19	66	62	8	16	20	4	0	0	4	1	0	2	1	0	4	1	0	0	.323	.292
Rodriguez, Serafin, Pue.	.286	5	15	14	2	4	4	0	0	0	0	1	0	0	0	0	1	0	0	0	.286	.286
Rodriguez S., Noel, Agu.	.316	10	21	19	3	6	6	0	0	0	1	2	0	0	0	0	4	1	1	1	.316	.316
Rojas, Francisco, Tab.	.169	32	71	65	6	11	13	2	0	0	5	1	0	1	4	0	11	0	0	1	.200	.229
Rojas, Homar, MCRD	.332	90	355	319	51	106	134	13	0	5	53	3	6	1	26	2	25	3	2	14	.420	.378
Romero, Marco A., MCT	.297	107	437	381	61	113	198	18	2	21	96	1	6	4	45	3	39	5	2	8	.520	.372
Romero, Oscar, Tab.	.344	115	482	410	72	141	195	24	0	10	47	11	1	2	58	5	42	10	6	19	.476	.427
Rubio, Marco A., Cam.-Min.	.224	80	264	232	10	52	62	7	0	1	14	8	4	1	19	2	19	1	1	11	.267	.281
Rubio, Sergio, Yuc.	.239	36	76	71	13	17	20	3	0	0	6	0	0	1	4	0	22	1	1	5	.282	.289
Ruiz, Demetrio, Jal.-Tab.	.214	36	96	84	4	18	21	1	1	0	7	4	2	0	6	0	4	0	0	2	.250	.261
Ruiz, Juan De Dios, Tor.	.306	105	409	360	70	110	176	16	10	10	67	5	6	1	37	4	38	9	2	13	.489	.366
Sabino, Miguel, Jal.	.167	7	23	18	1	3	3	0	0	0	3	0	0	0	5	2	4	0	1	2	.167	.348
Saenz, Ricardo, N.L.	.321	116	479	433	72	139	220	25	1	18	83	3	3	3	37	2	74	3	5	10	.508	.376
Saiz, Herminio, Tor.	.000	1	2	2	0	0	0	0	0	0	0	0	0	0	0	0	1	0	0	0	.000	.000
Salas, Heriberto, Tor.	.263	40	93	80	14	21	32	7	2	0	13	1	1	2	9	0	15	1	0	4	.400	.348
Salgado, Eduardo, MCT	.231	10	14	13	2	3	5	0	1	0	2	0	0	0	1	0	3	0	0	0	.385	.286
Samaniego, Manuel, Monc.	.327	68	198	171	19	56	74	9	3	1	30	3	1	4	19	0	15	1	2	5	.433	.405
Sanchez, Armando, Mont.	.293	92	334	290	35	85	100	13	1	0	29	5	1	0	38	2	22	2	0	5	.345	.374
Sanchez, Gerardo, N.L.	.323	116	490	400	72	129	184	20	1	11	59	1	5	19	65	3	38	5	3	20	.460	.436
Sanchez, Roque, Cam.	.266	56	115	109	9	29	33	4	0	0	9	5	1	0	0	1	9	1	0	5	.303	.264
Sandoval, Jose Luis, MCRD	.311	106	399	354	52	110	158	22	1	8	59	3	6	4	32	4	40	3	4	10	.446	.369
Santos, Julio, Jal.	.285	52	151	130	15	37	46	6	0	1	11	4	1	3	13	0	31	2	1	6	.354	.361
Santos, Luis Angel, Ags.	.250	3	4	4	3	1	1	0	0	0	1	0	0	0	0	0	1	0	0	0	.250	.250
Sasser, Mike, Min.	.286	15	59	56	4	16	23	1	0	2	11	0	0	0	3	0	6	0	0	0	.411	.322
Sievers, Carlos, Yuc.	.158	14	23	19	1	3	6	0	0	1	2	0	0	0	4	0	5	0	1	0	.316	.304
Snider, Van, Tor.	.325	81	336	302	61	98	192	22	0	24	67	0	2	1	31	5	57	0	0	8	.636	.387
Solis, Roberto, Pue.	.000	4	1	1	0	0	0	0	0	0	0	0	0	0	0	0	1	0	0	0	.000	.000
Sommers, Jesus, Pue.-Agu.	.224	96	351	317	12	71	87	11	1	1	20	2	1	2	29	1	36	1	0	11	.274	.292
Soriano, Ricardo, Tor.	.143	27	30	28	6	4	4	0	0	0	2	0	0	0	2	0	4	1	0	0	.143	.200
Soto, Emison, Pue.	.286	90	349	304	54	87	151	21	2	13	52	4	2	11	28	1	47	2	3	14	.497	.365
Sparks, Greg, MCT	.245	20	69	53	11	13	25	3	0	3	14	1	1	1	13	2	20	1	0	1	.472	.397
Stark, Matt, Rey.	.332	95	402	322	66	107	169	26	0	12	83	0	7	6	67	7	35	0	0	14	.525	.448
Tatis, Bernardo, MCRD	.303	84	358	304	69	92	121	13	2	4	45	2	2	0	50	4	27	17	3	4	.398	.399
Tatum, Willie, Yuc.	.000	3	10	9	0	0	0	0	0	0	0	0	0	0	1	0	3	0	0	0	.000	.100
Tejeda, Arturo, N.L.	.116	22	49	43	6	5	6	1	0	0	1	0	0	0	6	0	11	0	1	0	.140	.224
Tellez, Alonso, Rey.	.331	116	478	435	67	144	205	25	6	6	63	0	2	0	41	6	51	1	2	13	.471	.387
Tillman, Rusty, Agu.-Tab.	.248	63	256	202	30	50	90	7	0	11	34	1	5	2	46	4	69	6	2	2	.446	.384
Tiquet, Lazaro, Tab.	.281	101	387	352	35	99	146	29	3	4	52	6	4	4	21	2	51	4	6	14	.415	.325
Tolentino, Jose, Mont.	.342	83	346	304	49	104	176	24	0	16	79	1	2	37	6	37	1	2	15	.579	.414
Torres, Eduardo, Sal.	.222	104	398	338	46	75	129	13	4	11	52	4	3	0	53	3	74	6	5	10	.382	.325
Torres, Raymundo, Yuc.	.233	107	418	309	45	72	130	11	1	15	62	4	3	6	96	6	74	2	2	4	.421	.420
Tovar, Jose De Jesus, Sal.-Monc.	.228	56	185	167	15	38	40	2	0	0	15	5	1	2	10	0	26	1	2	1	.240	.278
Trafton, Todd, Tor.	.336	45	192	152	35	51	78	7	1	6	34	0	1	4	35	2	16	1	0	5	.513	.469
Trapaga, Miguel, MCT	.202	52	123	109	17	22	32	4	0	2	9	2	0	1	11	0	24	0	1	2	.294	.281
Trejo, David, Agu.	.000	1	4	4	1	0	0	0	0	0	0	0	0	0	0	0	0	0	0	0	.000	.000
Trevino, Alejandro, Mont.	.317	93	311	262	32	83	108	17	1	2	28	5	3	3	38	2	26	1	3	7	.412	.400
Valdez, Francisco J., Rey.	.267	81	261	217	36	58	75	12	1	1	30	4	3	4	33	4	27	0	1	11	.346	.370
Valdez, Jesus, Yuc.	.302	81	221	192	28	58	76	12	0	2	36	6	4	1	18	0	14	2	0	6	.396	.358
Valencia, Carlos, Ags.	.269	55	202	160	19	43	58	9	0	2	27	2	5	2	33	6	14	2	0	3	.363	.390
Valenzuela, Armando, Rey.	.256	97	424	367	62	94	110	10	3	0	31	16	3	2	36	0	38	4	4	7	.300	.324
Valenzuela, Eduardo, Sal.	.273	67	139	128	15	35	47	7	1	1	16	1	1	2	7	1	6	0	0	4	.367	.319
Valenzuela, Horacio, Min.-Jal.	.196	39	270	235	17	46	65	10	0	3	24	1	4	1	29	5	31	0	1	11	.277	.283
Valenzuela, Jose Luis, Ags.	.311	40	119	106	15	33	43	4	3	0	7	2	0	0	11	1	12	1	0	6	.406	.376
Valenzuela S., Joel, Tor.	.125	6	10	8	0	1	1	0	0	0	0	1	0	0	1	0	1	0	0	0	.125	.222
Valle, Jorge Luis, Tor.	.292	101	377	325	46	95	123	13	3	3	36	14	2	2	34	1	43	2	7	9	.378	.361
Valle, Jose Luis, Min.	.221	104	369	339	35	75	99	10	1	4	35	9	1	4	16	2	27	1	0	8	.292	.264
Valverde, Raul, Jal.	.302	75	251	242	23	73	103	13	1	5	33	2	1	0	6	0	33	1	3	9	.426	.317
Vargas, Trinidad, Pue.	.200	65	188	170	14	34	40	4	1	0	14	5	3	1	9	0	31	2	1	6	.235	.240
Vazquez, Felipe, MCRD	.333	26	28	27	3	9	11	2	0	0	1	0	0	0	1	0	5	0	0	2	.407	.357
Vega V., Edgar, MCT	.208	78	220	192	16	40	47	3	2	0	9	6	0	0	22	0	29	2	1	2	.245	.290
Velazquez, Armando, Agu.	.222	21	52	45	2	10	10	0	0	0	5	4	1	0	2	0	10	0	1	3	.222	.250
Velazquez, Guillermo, Mont.	.252	34	134	119	16	30	51	9	0	4	18	0	0	0	15	1	27	0	0	1	.429	.336
Verdugo, Guadalupe, Tor.	.222	28	58	45	7	10	12	2	0	0	5	3	0	0	10	0	10	1	0	1	.267	.364
Verdugo, Sostenes, Yuc.	.429	5	9	7	2	3	3	0	0	0	0	0	0	0	2	0	1	0	0	0	.429	.556
Verdugo, Vicente, MCRD	.285	106	381	358	48	102	128	14	0	4	35	7	4	0	12	0	30	2	6	8	.358	.305
Villaescusa, Fernando, Jal.	.352	60	203	179	26	63	72	7	1	0	14	4	2	2	16	2	4	4	1	5	.402	.407
Villanueva, Hector, MCT	.374	53	225	182	41	68	115	11	0	12	47	1	0	1	41	4	19	1	0	6	.632	.491
Villanueva, Luis, Ags.	.000	1	1	1	0	0	0	0	0	0	0	0	0	0	0	0	0	0	0	0	.000	.000
Villarreal, Alejandro, N.L.	.000	8	7	7	1	0	0	0	0	0	0	0	0	0	0	0	2	0	0	0	.000	.000
Villegas, Fernando, Sal.	.323	98	415	372	65	120	169	12	11	5	40	3	0	7	33	0	41	9	5	10	.454	.388
Villegas, Jose Angel, Ags.	.000	3	3	2	0	0	0	0	0	0	0	0	0	0	1	0	2	0	0	0	.000	.333
Vizcarra, Marco A., Rey.	.294	68	214	177	32	52	56	1	0	1	16	4	2	3	28	0	19	1	3	6	.316	.395
Vizcarra, Roberto, Ags.	.290	112	475	414	80	120	199	19	0	20	87	4	7	6	44	6	35	10	7	13	.481	.361
Wearing, Mel, Jal.-Sal.	.287	85	342	268	52	77	129	9	2	13	59	0	4	1	69	2	79	4	2	10	.481	.430

Player, Team	Avg.	G	TPA	AB	R	H	TB	2B	3B	HR	RBI	SH	SF	HP	BB	IBB	SO	SB	CS	GDP	Slg.	OBP
Wong Medrano, J., Monc.	.228	48	137	114	11	26	34	3	1	1	10	7	2	0	14	1	17	0	3	4	.298	.308
Wright, George, Sal.	.335	116	491	409	70	137	200	23	2	12	76	0	7	0	75	14	38	12	5	12	.489	.432
Wright, Tom, Jal.	.143	2	8	7	0	1	2	1	0	0	0	0	0	0	1	0	2	0	0	0	.286	.250
Yuriar, Jesus, Monc.	.278	101	365	313	40	87	104	9	4	0	35	8	2	3	39	0	43	2	6	12	.332	.361
Zambrano, Roberto, Pue.	.286	5	16	14	3	4	7	0	0	1	5	0	0	1	1	0	3	0	0	0	.500	.375
Zamudio, Rafael, Mont.-Agu.	.308	37	110	107	9	33	48	10	1	1	5	0	0	3	0		22	1	0	1	.449	.327
Zazueta, Juan Carlos, Tab.	.269	54	141	130	15	35	42	3	2	0	13	2	0	1	8	0	24	5	1	3	.323	.317
Zazueta, Mauricio, Tor.	.298	81	325	299	45	89	116	9	3	4	28	8	2	1	15	1	52	2	2	10	.388	.331
Zulueta, Felix, Tab.	.140	14	47	43	4	6	6	0	0	0	0	1	0	0	3	0	9	0	0	3	.140	.196

GRAND SLAMS: Ro. Mendez, R. Vizcarra, 2 each; Ru. Avila, Cairo, Camacho, Carter, B. Castillo, L. Cruz, Fentanes, Gainey, Jav. Guerrero, Horn, Machiria, W. Magallanes, C. Martinez, G. Martinez, Montalvo, Munoz, Saenz, Snider, Stark, Tellez, F. Valdez, M. Vizcarra, Wearing, Zambrano, 1 each.

AWARDED FIRST BASE ON CATCHER'S INTERFERENCE: Morones 3 (V. Lopez 2, Vega); Camacho (Cazarin); A. Castro (Cazarin); Jo. Espinoza (M. Cruz); Ru. Estrada (Machorro); D. Gonzalez (V. Lopez); Nunez Avina (M. Cruz); G. Sanchez (V. Lopez).

1995 PITCHING

TEAM

Team	W	L	Pct.	ERA	G	CG	ShO	Sv.	IP	H	TBF	R	ER	HR	SH	SF	HB	BB	IBB	SO	WP	Bk.
Tabasco	61	50	.550	3.31	115	28	12	23	944.1	947	3566	413	347	44	74	24	38	284	14	490	23	5
Campeche	60	54	.526	3.35	115	23	10	27	934.0	924	3513	442	348	58	73	32	31	409	48	374	30	3
Minatitlan	41	73	.360	3.60	116	12	5	21	973.0	1003	3649	451	389	59	67	25	27	430	51	431	20	3
M.C. Red Devils	80	33	.708	3.71	114	19	5	29	932.2	950	3501	442	384	64	56	35	20	421	9	621	53	3
Monterrey	65	49	.570	3.84	116	11	5	31	960.0	965	3628	473	410	56	64	27	31	408	22	546	52	2
Nuevo Laredo	62	54	.534	4.15	116	16	0	35	982.1	1018	3732	508	453	82	61	28	29	401	48	557	46	5
Saltillo	63	53	.543	4.18	116	13	3	24	969.0	1003	3644	523	450	63	56	31	45	478	14	538	43	5
Aguila	45	71	.388	4.19	116	13	3	24	964.2	1007	3630	500	449	69	58	30	46	417	24	459	22	5
Reynosa	73	40	.646	4.26	116	16	5	32	980.2	1066	3795	532	464	69	65	23	33	430	24	560	36	3
Puebla	52	63	.452	4.32	116	35	5	14	925.1	1030	3562	538	444	79	77	33	32	405	30	405	31	3
Yucatan	59	55	.518	4.41	115	18	5	23	938.0	1048	3627	530	460	62	80	23	27	426	26	480	65	2
Monclova	46	69	.400	4.41	116	16	1	30	949.2	1071	3692	547	465	70	49	41	30	430	35	539	56	2
Aguascalientes	57	55	.509	4.62	114	18	3	23	937.2	1056	3611	546	481	75	61	37	46	446	28	500	35	4
M.C. Tigers	62	54	.534	4.85	116	22	8	19	948.1	970	3609	575	511	72	49	36	44	513	30	539	56	1
Torreon	56	57	.496	4.98	115	23	3	26	943.2	1083	3654	599	522	83	52	48	36	432	38	473	50	2
Jalisco	30	82	.268	6.08	114	23	1	15	913.2	1234	3736	737	617	67	66	48	37	444	32	457	69	5

INDIVIDUAL

TOP QUALIFIERS FOR EARNED-RUN AVERAGE TITLE

Minimum 93 innings.

Pitcher, Team	W	L	Pct.	ERA	G	GS	CG	ShO	GF	Sv.	IP	H	TBF	R	ER	HR	SH	SF	HB	BB	IBB	SO	WP	Bk.
Ruiz, Cecilio, Tab.	13	5	.722	1.71	24	23	7	5	1	0	162.2	132	584	41	31	6	20	4	4	33	1	92	1	0
Solarte, Jose A., Min.	8	4	.667	1.72	45	6	3	1	39	4	115.0	93	397	23	22	2	9	3	1	42	9	64	1	0
Munoz, Ricardo, Tab.	12	6	.667	2.46	22	22	7	3	0	0	142.2	128	514	49	39	5	14	2	7	36	1	69	1	1
Ramirez, Roberto, MCRD	13	3	.813	2.56	20	20	8	3	0	0	137.1	125	502	50	39	9	5	3	5	35	0	70	3	2
Zappelli, Mark, Sal.	6	8	.429	2.63	33	9	2	0	24	6	106.0	109	396	40	31	2	9	0	6	47	0	45	3	0
Sierra, Abel, Cam.	11	9	.550	2.64	24	21	10	5	3	0	153.1	132	578	60	45	7	9	3	0	48	4	80	4	1
Vazquez, Adrian, Cam.	11	6	.647	2.64	21	21	3	0	0	0	136.1	118	487	48	40	8	10	1	5	72	3	39	4	1
Munoz, Miguel, Agu.-Rey.	11	3	.786	2.67	20	20	2	1	0	0	138.0	140	522	47	41	3	8	1	4	22	1	62	1	2
Cuervo, Bernardo, Cam.	12	4	.750	2.74	28	18	6	4	10	0	125.0	122	460	50	38	7	15	3	2	45	7	40	4	0
Martinez, Filiberto, Sal.	8	5	.615	2.76	19	19	3	2	0	0	107.2	98	399	38	33	2	5	2	7	57	0	57	3	1

DEPARTMENTAL LEADERS: W—A. Moreno, 16; L—Gomez Rios, F. Soto, 14; Pct.—Cordova, 1.000; G—J. Villegas, 52; GS—Soto, 25; CG—E. Lopez, Sierra, 10; ShO—Ruiz, Sierra, 5; GF—J. Villegas, 50; Sv.—Murillo, 30; IP—E. Lopez, 163.1; H—F. Soto, 182; TBF—; R—V. Gonzalez, 93; ER—Renteria, 74; HR—Rios, 17; SH—Ruiz, 20; SF—J. Moreno, 9; HB—J. Moreno, Palafox, 11; BB—Barraza, 73; IBB—Grajales, 13; SO—A. Moreno, A. Quiroz, 108; WP—Pina, Segura, 10; Bk.—L. Castro, 3.

ALL PITCHERS

Pitcher, Team	W	L	Pct.	ERA	G	GS	CG	ShO	GF	Sv.	IP	H	TBF	R	ER	HR	SH	SF	HB	BB	IBB	SO	WP	Bk.
Acosta, Aaron, Tor.	9	3	.750	4.08	21	21	4	1	0	0	128.0	138	477	66	58	9	6	4	3	56	1	76	8	0
Acosta, Francisco, Yuc.	0	0	.000	4.50	2	0	0	0	2	0	4.0	8	20	3	2	0	0	0	0	2	1	2	0	0
Acosta, Gerardo, MCRD	1	0	1.000	0.00	2	0	0	0	2	0	2.1	1	7	0	0	0	0	0	2	0	1	1	0	
Agosto, Juan, Mont.-Ags.	1	4	.200	6.15	17	6	0	0	11	4	45.1	62	187	37	31	6	3	2	5	15	0	18	4	0
Aguilar, Jose M., Min.-Tab.	4	10	.286	6.91	24	16	1	0	8	0	71.2	94	302	61	55	5	3	0	1	37	2	36	3	0
Aguirre, Gaudencio, Tab.	0	0	.000	11.81	3	0	0	0	3	0	5.1	11	26	7	7	1	0	0	1	4	0	2	0	0
Alicea, Miguel, Tor.	0	2	.000	3.46	28	0	0	0	28	15	26.0	31	107	18	10	4	3	2	0	8	1	11	0	0
Alvarez, Ivan, Jal.	0	4	.000	7.27	6	3	1	0	3	0	17.1	20	68	16	14	1	2	2	1	8	1	8	1	1
Alvarez, Juan Jesus, MCT	12	8	.600	3.70	23	23	4	0	0	0	153.1	158	578	71	63	10	9	2	8	59	3	65	6	0
Antunez, Martin, Jal.	3	8	.273	4.43	26	11	4	0	15	1	91.1	109	357	51	45	6	11	4	2	21	2	38	7	0
Arano, Ramon, Agu.	2	2	.500	6.86	5	5	1	1	0	0	21.0	28	89	17	16	2	1	1	1	6	0	7	0	0
Arce, Francisco J., Min.	0	0	.000	0.00	1	0	0	0	1	1	1.0	0	3	0	0	0	0	1	0	0	0	0	0	0
Arrington, Tom, Jal.	5	9	.357	5.26	16	16	4	0	0	0	92.1	129	371	65	54	6	8	3		32	4	47	3	0
Arzate, Martin, Jal.	0	0	.000	4.26	3	0	0	0	2	0	6.1	9	25	5	3	0	0	1	0	2	0	2	2	0
Austin, Jim, MCT	0	0	.000	5.40	3	0	0	0	3	0	1.2	2	7	2	1	0	0	0	2	0	0	2	0	
Ayrault, Bob, Monc.	0	0	.000	8.60	7	7	1	0	0	0	30.1	43	123	29	29	8	1	4	2	17	2	15	1	0
Baez, Sixto, Jal.	3	5	.375	5.29	28	13	0	0	15	2	78.1	89	294	50	46	4	3	4		46	3	22	2	1
Baller, Jay, MCRD	0	1	.000	2.37	16	0	0	0	6	0	19.0	10	62	8	5	1	1	2	1	17	0	13	3	0
Barfield, John David, N.L.	5	2	.714	2.70	34	1	1	0	33	24	63.1	50	219	19	19	2	4	0		13	4	36	4	0
Barraza, Ernesto, MCT	10	4	.714	3.15	24	17	4	0	0	0	125.2	111	454	58	44	1	6	3	1	73	3	78	7	0
Barron, Avelino, Sal.	1	4	.200	4.33	14	4	0	0	4	0	79.0	83	297	52	38	7	7	1	4	39	4	40	0	0

Pitcher, Team	W	L	Pct.	ERA	G	GS	CG	ShO	GF	Sv.	IP	H	TBF	R	ER	HR	SH	SF	HB	BB	IBB	SO	WP	Bk.
Bencomo, Omar, Sal.-Jal.	6	7	.462	4.33	35	1	0	0	34	2	70.2	73	268	37	34	3	5	3	1	27	2	56	5	0
Benitez, Francisco, Ags.-Jal.	0	2	.000	9.26	11	2	0	0	9	0	23.1	39	100	29	24	2	2	2	1	26	1	8	2	0
Browning, Mike, Cam.	1	3	.250	6.14	9	0	0	0	9	3	7.1	10	29	5	5	0	0	1	0	5	0	4	2	0
Brumley, Duff, Mont.-Ags.	1	3	.250	3.86	7	5	0	0	2	0	28.0	25	104	15	12	1	2	1	0	20	1	22	3	0
Burcham, Tim, Jal.	1	2	.333	3.18	6	6	2	1	0	0	28.1	25	105	10	10	1	2	0	0	9	1	17	4	0
Burlingame, Dennis, Monc.	0	1	.000	4.26	2	2	0	0	0	0	12.2	12	46	7	6	1	2	1	0	8	2	5	0	0
Cabrales, Gabriel, Tab.	3	2	.600	4.70	32	2	0	0	30	2	69.0	84	277	41	36	2	6	3	1	15	1	43	1	0
Calderon, Manaces, Min.	0	0	.000	1.59	3	0	0	0	3	0	5.2	2	19	2	1	0	0	0	0	4	0	3	1	0
Camacho, Adrian, Min.	2	2	.500	5.40	22	2	0	0	20	0	38.1	43	144	25	23	4	3	1	4	22	1	14	2	1
Camacho, Adulfo, Yuc.	0	0	.000	10.80	1	0	0	0	1	0	3.1	4	13	4	4	0	0	0	0	4	0	0	0	0
Campos, Francisco, Cam.	0	0	.000	1.93	5	1	0	0	4	0	9.1	9	35	2	2	0	0	1	0	3	0	2	1	0
Cano, Ezequiel, Jal.	3	12	.200	5.36	17	16	3	0	1	0	102.1	119	408	66	61	10	3	4	3	39	3	58	6	1
Cano, Jose, Ags.	9	7	.563	5.02	21	21	3	0	0	0	118.1	137	465	73	66	8	4	2	7	53	0	73	4	0
Cardenas, Benito, N.L.	0	0	.000	2.70	5	0	0	0	5	0	6.2	7	24	4	2	0	0	0	0	4	0	3	0	0
Carranza, Javier, Rey.	10	6	.625	4.86	21	20	2	0	1	0	113.0	128	451	67	61	8	6	2	4	45	2	72	7	0
Carrasco, Alejandro, MCRD	2	2	.500	4.91	30	2	0	0	28	1	47.2	54	175	29	26	4	1	3	0	18	1	13	5	0
Castaneda, Aurelio, Jal.	2	0	1.000	7.36	4	0	0	0	4	0	3.2	3	13	3	3	1	0	0	0	2	0	3	0	0
Castillo, Felipe, MCRD	3	1	.750	1.75	17	0	0	0	17	5	25.2	19	83	6	5	1	3	2	0	18	2	15	1	0
Castillo, Luis Trinidad, Monc.	1	1	.500	10.13	4	4	0	0	0	0	13.1	20	61	16	15	5	0	1	1	6	0	8	1	0
Castro, Gerardo, MCT	1	0	1.000	10.38	5	1	0	0	4	0	8.2	13	40	10	10	1	0	0	1	6	0	3	1	0
Castro, Leonel, Jal.	3	10	.231	6.04	19	19	2	0	0	0	107.1	141	444	91	72	7	9	3	4	45	3	49	6	3
Cazares, Juan, Jal.-Mont.	3	3	.500	4.81	35	1	0	0	34	2	33.2	43	137	19	18	2	0	0	1	20	2	18	4	0
Cazares, Rosario, Tab.	0	4	.000	3.47	34	1	0	0	33	3	46.2	37	170	21	18	4	4	3	2	16	2	22	0	1
Cazares, Tomas, MCRD-Rey.	1	0	1.000	5.96	15	1	0	0	14	0	22.2	31	92	16	15	2	2	1	1	10	0	10	0	0
Cecena, Jose Isabel, Sal.	4	4	.500	4.40	38	0	0	0	38	14	45.0	34	156	25	22	2	8	1	5	40	3	47	9	0
Cervantes, Lauro, Ags.-Agu.	3	5	.375	7.25	14	14	1	0	0	0	58.1	88	247	53	47	4	3	3	5	24	3	25	0	0
Chapin, Darrin, Rey.	1	1	.500	1.48	11	3	0	0	8	3	30.1	24	112	10	5	1	1	0	0	13	1	17	4	0
Cimorelli, Frank, Cam.	1	3	.250	3.26	19	0	0	0	19	4	30.1	38	118	15	11	0	4	2	0	13	2	13	2	0
Conde, Ricardo, Yuc.	0	0	.000	13.50	2	0	0	0	2	0	0.2	2	3	1	1	0	0	0	1	1	0	1	0	0
Contreras, Cuitlahuac, Tor.-Monc.	0	0	.000	0.00	1	0	0	0	1	0	3.1	6	15	1	0	0	0	0	0	2	0	0	0	0
Cordova, Francisco, MCRD	13	0	1.000	3.10	27	20	1	0	7	4	125.0	131	490	52	43	8	4	2	3	42	0	88	2	1
Cota, Guadalupe, N.L.	0	0	.000	6.75	1	0	0	0	1	0	1.1	2	5	1	1	0	0	0	0	1	0	0	0	0
Cota C., Armando, Tab.	0	2	.000	9.82	15	1	0	0	14	1	11.0	18	45	14	12	3	2	0	1	9	0	5	0	1
Couoh, Enrique, MCT	6	5	.545	3.70	39	10	4	2	29	8	97.1	82	348	45	40	8	3	8	4	65	4	67	8	0
Cruz, Andres, Yuc.	4	11	.267	4.73	23	21	4	0	2	0	125.2	146	485	74	66	8	14	6	5	48	5	61	8	0
Cruz, Javier, Rey.	8	5	.615	4.32	35	8	1	0	27	2	89.2	99	351	49	43	10	6	1	3	37	3	51	2	1
Cruz, Juan Alonso, Jal.	2	1	.667	5.77	26	1	0	0	25	0	53.0	76	228	38	34	3	1	0	4	29	1	31	2	0
Cruz, Juan Diego, Yuc.	0	2	.000	3.06	17	0	0	0	17	0	32.1	27	118	11	11	3	0	0	1	12	0	20	1	0
Cruz Soto, Antonio, Pue.	1	4	.200	3.73	14	5	1	0	9	0	41.0	35	151	23	17	6	4	2	2	39	4	23	0	0
Cuervo, Bernardo, Cam.	12	4	.750	2.74	28	18	6	4	10	0	125.0	122	460	50	38	7	15	3	2	45	7	40	4	0
Dehesa, Noel, Tab.	0	0	.000	6.10	6	0	0	0	6	0	10.1	14	46	9	7	2	0	0	1	2	0	2	0	0
Delfin, Adolfo, MCT	1	6	.143	5.19	37	0	0	0	37	3	69.1	81	278	45	40	6	3	5	8	30	3	30	3	0
Del Toro, Miguel, MCRD-Rey.	5	4	.556	2.25	37	0	0	0	37	16	68.0	54	253	23	17	2	5	2	4	43	1	49	4	0
Del Valle, Enrique, MCT-Agu.	1	0	1.000	14.59	11	1	0	0	10	0	12.1	29	61	21	20	0	1	2	1	13	0	7	1	0
Diaz, Alejandro, Agu.	2	4	.333	4.01	24	1	0	0	23	2	51.2	52	188	25	23	5	3	2	3	20	1	22	0	0
Diaz, Cesar, N.L.	4	3	.571	3.42	29	9	1	0	20	0	71.0	64	259	29	27	8	7	4	4	27	2	25	3	0
Diaz, Marcos, Mont.	4	2	.667	3.89	21	9	0	0	12	0	69.1	74	267	37	30	2	4	3	3	32	1	32	4	0
Diaz, Octavio, Ags.	0	0	.000	18.00	4	0	0	0	4	0	5.0	9	22	10	10	1	0	1	1	7	0	5	2	0
Dojaquez, Omar, Monc.	0	0	.000	13.50	1	0	0	0	1	0	0.2	2	5	1	1	0	0	0	0	0	0	1	1	0
Dominguez, Herminio, Cam.	4	2	.667	2.89	39	1	0	0	38	12	37.1	32	135	17	12	2	1	0	1	18	1	25	0	0
Draper, Mike, MCT	4	4	.500	3.62	22	0	0	0	22	5	32.1	26	117	13	13	2	4	0	1	16	3	11	1	0
Elvira, Narciso, Mont.	10	5	.667	5.13	18	18	1	1	0	0	93.0	98	363	59	53	12	1	0	3	40	0	70	3	0
Enriquez, Graciano, Ags.	0	1	.000	5.68	3	1	0	0	2	0	6.1	10	28	5	4	1	0	0	0	2	0	0	1	0
Enriquez, Martin, Ags.	8	8	.500	3.92	24	20	6	1	4	1	144.2	155	555	73	63	11	6	6	9	50	2	96	1	0
Espinoza, Mario, Yuc.	0	0	.000	....	1	0	0	0	1	0	0.0	2	2	2	2	0	0	0	0	0	0	0	0	0
Espinoza, Rogelio, Jal.	0	1	.000	9.00	7	0	0	0	7	1	6.0	14	29	6	6	0	1	0	1	5	1	3	0	0
Esquer, Mercedes, Yuc.-Mont.	7	3	.700	2.64	13	13	1	1	0	0	71.2	72	272	30	21	4	6	3	1	21	1	33	2	1
Farmer, Gorman, Pue.	0	1	.000	1.93	3	0	0	0	3	0	4.2	4	17	1	1	0	0	0	0	4	0	2	0	0
Felix, Arturo, Yuc.	0	0	.000	21.00	1	0	0	0	1	0	3.0	8	17	7	7	1	0	0	0	2	0	1	0	0
Figueroa, Fernando, Tor.	11	5	.688	4.72	17	17	2	0	0	0	114.1	124	443	69	60	8	0	3	1	46	2	54	7	0
Flores, Ignacio, Tor.	0	2	.000	6.44	21	1	0	0	20	0	29.1	42	124	27	21	7	1	1	1	19	1	12	0	0
Flynt, Will, MCRD	7	1	.875	2.24	10	9	3	0	1	0	56.1	51	210	18	14	0	2	2	0	27	0	49	5	0
Fonseca L., Pabel R., Min.	0	0	.000	0.00	1	0	0	0	1	0	0.2	1	3	0	0	0	0	0	0	1	0	0	0	0
Franklin, Jay, Mont.-Ags.	9	6	.600	3.52	22	21	3	2	1	0	122.2	127	459	65	48	4	8	3	7	57	2	60	6	0
Galvez, Rosario, N.L.	0	0	.000	15.00	6	0	0	0	6	0	6.0	13	29	10	10	0	0	1	0	5	0	4	2	1
Garcia, David, Monc.	0	0	.000	4.00	16	1	0	0	15	0	18.0	18	66	9	8	0	0	1	1	18	0	20	1	0
Garcia, Mike, Tab.	2	1	.667	1.94	26	2	1	0	24	14	46.1	36	165	10	10	0	6	3	0	6	1	30	1	0
Garcia Cruz, Jose Luis, MCT	4	6	.400	5.86	36	7	0	0	29	2	58.1	77	247	42	38	4	4	0	3	27	4	31	1	0
Garcia R., Miguel, Min.	4	3	.571	3.39	38	2	1	1	36	0	74.1	72	269	30	28	6	4	3	1	32	5	26	1	0
Garibay, Roberto, Pue.	4	3	.571	3.58	40	0	0	0	40	11	50.1	59	194	27	20	1	3	4	1	29	5	17	3	0
Garibay, Salvaror, Ags.	0	0	.000	3.00	23	1	0	0	22	0	54.0	60	197	20	18	1	4	5	2	24	1	31	2	0
Garibay Bravo, Daniel, MCT	2	0	1.000	6.40	21	5	0	0	16	0	45.0	49	176	32	32	3	1	0	4	29	3	26	2	0
Garza, Roberto, Rey.-N.L.	2	3	.400	6.71	19	7	0	0	12	0	51.0	54	194	40	38	9	3	4	0	31	7	20	3	1
Gomez, Jesus, A., Monc.	1	1	.500	4.70	10	3	0	0	7	0	23.0	28	93	16	12	2	2	0	1	19	2	15	2	0
Gomez Rios, Martin, Min.	4	14	.222	3.89	23	23	1	0	0	0	125.0	131	455	59	54	5	10	4	1	63	1	40	4	1
Gonzalez, Arturo, Mont.	7	8	.467	4.55	18	18	0	0	0	0	97.0	108	383	56	49	5	8	2	5	37	0	39	3	1
Gonzalez, Gilberto, Tor.	0	0	.000	40.50	3	0	0	0	3	0	0.2	4	6	3	3	1	0	0	0	3	0	0	2	0
Gonzalez, Victor Manuel, Jal.	1	6	.143	7.21	32	11	0	0	21	2	87.1	133	369	93	70	4	7	5	4	49	4	34	3	0
Grajales, Norberto, Tor.	4	1	.800	3.41	41	0	0	0	41	1	68.2	71	244	28	26	3	6	5	2	35	13	31	1	1
Green, Otis, Mont.	3	3	.500	1.95	21	0	0	0	21	4	32.1	19	106	7	7	2	2	1	0	15	0	39	1	0
Guerra, Esmili, Pue.	1	2	.333	3.86	8	3	0	0	5	0	18.2	26	71	13	8	0	3	0	1	8	0	7	1	0
Guerrero, Omar, Rey.	0	2	.000	11.12	7	2	0	0	5	0	11.1	23	51	14	14	1	1	0	1	9	2	6	1	0
Gutierrez, Arturo, Agu.	0	1	.000	4.19	8	2	0	0	6	0	19.1	19	69	9	9	0	0	2	1	13	0	6	0	0

Pitcher, Team	W	L	Pct.	ERA	G	GS	CG	ShO	GF	Sv.	IP	H	TBF	R	ER	HR	SH	SF	HB	BB	IBB	SO	WP	Bk.
Henry, John, Pue.	7	4	.636	4.10	15	10	5	1	5	0	68.0	67	254	31	31	5	4	2	4	24	1	37	3	1
Heredia, Hector, Mont.	9	9	.500	3.30	22	22	5	2	0	0	142.0	148	544	57	52	7	8	3	1	40	2	66	4	0
Hernandez, Dimas, C., Monc.	0	0	.000	4.81	13	0	0	0	13	0	24.1	21	88	17	13	4	0	3	0	19	1	12	4	0
Hernandez, Encarn'cn, Jal.-Monc.	2	1	.667	5.73	36	2	0	0	34	1	59.2	95	257	49	38	7	6	4	2	17	2	21	3	0
Hernandez, Jose Manuel, N.L.	7	4	.636	3.19	47	4	0	0	43	6	98.2	94	360	41	35	6	9	4	1	38	7	52	4	0
Hernandez, Julio, Agu.	5	11	.313	4.33	21	19	3	1	2	0	99.2	98	369	56	48	9	8	0	1	53	2	53	2	1
Hernandez, Manuel, A., MCRD	11	4	.733	3.18	23	23	5	2	0	0	141.2	142	531	54	50	9	10	1	2	54	0	98	4	0
Hernandez, Martin, Yuc.	11	3	.786	3.62	24	21	7	3	3	0	121.2	135	479	57	49	10	6	2	1	48	1	65	8	0
Hernandez, Ramon, Mont.	0	0	.000	10.53	13	0	0	0	13	0	19.2	28	88	25	23	1	1	1	0	18	0	11	6	0
Hernandez V., Manuel, Jal.	0	0	.000	7.71	1	0	0	0	1	0	2.1	4	9	2	2	1	0	1	0	1	0	0	0	0
Herrera, Calixto, Monc.	9	9	.500	3.69	50	3	1	1	47	0	92.2	82	332	42	38	3	11	3	9	59	11	69	8	0
Herrera, Enrique, Agu.	2	4	.333	2.64	34	3	0	0	31	1	71.2	83	275	25	21	6	2	3	3	23	1	35	4	0
Huerta, Luis Enrique, Pue.	9	7	.563	3.28	22	22	8	2	0	0	145.1	134	544	65	53	10	9	4	3	48	1	55	1	0
Hurst, Jonathan, Jal.-Mont.	4	1	.800	2.16	28	1	0	0	27	9	50.0	42	177	12	12	1	7	1	2	13	1	49	4	0
Inzunza, Jorge, Tab.	1	0	1.000	3.50	11	0	0	0	11	0	18.0	21	72	9	7	0	0	3	1	11	0	9	4	0
Iniguez, Dario, Jal.	2	7	.222	10.47	11	10	0	0	1	0	38.2	76	186	51	45	4	3	0	2	22	1	34	3	0
Jimenez, Cesar D., Monc.	3	6	.333	3.87	14	12	1	0	2	0	74.1	84	287	34	32	1	3	2	3	28	3	26	1	0
Jimenez, German, Yuc.-Ags.	6	4	.600	3.25	18	18	4	0	0	0	102.1	121	405	46	37	9	11	2	2	32	1	43	5	0
Jimenez, Issac, Yuc.	6	8	.429	3.20	19	19	3	0	0	0	112.2	117	422	46	40	3	8	0	9	56	1	54	5	0
Jones, Al, Tor.	4	9	.308	4.34	17	13	4	1	4	0	85.0	78	308	49	41	8	5	4	0	44	2	65	1	0
Juarez, Fernando, Tor.	1	0	1.000	4.26	10	0	0	0	10	0	6.1	7	26	3	3	0	0	1	1	3	0	1	0	0
Kelley, Drum Richard, Monc.	3	8	.273	3.10	12	12	0	0	0	0	72.2	68	267	33	25	2	5	1	2	39	3	48	8	0
Kiely, John, MCT	0	0	.000	0.00	1	0	0	0	1	0	0.1	0	0	0	0	0	0	0	0	0	0	0	0	0
Klvac, David John, Tor.	0	0	.000	10.80	3	0	0	0	3	1	5.0	5	19	6	6	0	0	0	0	6	0	4	0	0
Lara, Hugo, Cam.	8	5	.615	4.14	24	21	3	0	3	1	126.0	126	478	66	58	9	8	4	10	53	9	54	3	0
Lara, Jorge, Rey.	7	2	.778	2.33	39	1	0	0	37	4	73.1	53	261	28	19	2	4	3	0	38	3	45	1	0
Leal, Gerardo, Monc.	2	5	.286	7.13	25	6	0	0	19	0	70.2	109	299	62	56	8	3	4	1	30	0	28	8	0
Ledon, Juan Carlos, Jal.	0	2	.000	7.62	9	4	0	0	5	0	26.0	36	111	26	22	3	3	1	2	15	3	14	0	0
Leon, Danilo, Yuc.	1	3	.250	9.00	5	0	0	0	5	1	8.0	12	30	9	8	1	4	0	0	5	3	4	1	0
Lewis, Craig, Monc.	0	0	.000	6.28	3	3	0	0	0	0	14.1	19	58	12	10	0	0	1	0	11	1	10	2	0
Lewis, Scott, Mont.	2	1	.667	1.50	30	0	0	0	30	15	42.0	24	143	7	7	2	3	0	0	10	3	27	1	0
Leyva, Carlos Armando, MCT	0	1	1.000	7.30	26	0	0	0	26	0	24.2	33	100	24	20	0	3	2	1	27	3	9	7	0
Leyva, Filiberto, Agu.	1	2	.333	7.33	21	0	0	0	21	2	23.1	34	95	24	19	5	2	1	4	15	3	8	1	0
Lind, Orlando, Rey.	5	3	.625	2.60	12	12	3	1	0	0	72.2	72	263	24	21	5	11	0	2	32	0	42	1	0
Lizarraga, Andres, N.L.	0	0	.000	5.79	6	0	0	0	6	0	4.2	6	18	4	3	1	0	2	1	1	0	3	0	0
Lizarraga, Hugo, Cam.	3	4	.429	2.78	24	8	0	0	16	3	68.0	70	260	24	21	5	3	1	1	32	3	36	0	0
Llanes, Emeterio, Yuc.	1	0	1.000	6.89	11	1	0	0	10	0	15.2	19	62	12	12	1	0	0	3	7	0	5	1	0
Loaiza, Sabino, Cam.	0	5	.000	6.31	9	6	0	0	3	0	25.2	22	94	20	18	1	1	1	2	21	2	6	1	0
Lopez, Emigdio, Tab.	14	6	.700	3.09	25	23	10	3	2	0	163.1	169	630	62	56	11	4	4	7	38	2	82	3	0
Lopez, Gilberto, Agu.	0	0	.000	7.43	8	0	0	0	8	0	13.1	16	53	11	11	0	0	0	9	6	0	6	0	0
Lopez, Jesus Nain, Rey.	0	0	.000	18.00	1	0	0	0	1	0	1.0	4	5	2	2	1	0	0	3	0	0	0	0	0
Lopez, Jonas, Ags.	3	3	.500	4.06	20	7	0	0	13	0	44.1	55	179	23	20	5	2	2	4	9	1	19	1	0
Lopez, De La T., J.J., Min.	4	7	.364	2.57	36	0	0	0	36	16	56.0	46	201	19	16	3	1	1	2	23	6	37	3	0
Lozano, Miguel Angel, Min.	0	0	.000	12.27	3	0	0	0	3	0	3.2	8	16	5	5	0	0	1	0	4	0	1	0	0
Lucio, Martin, Pue.	0	0	.000	0.00	1	0	0	0	1	0	1.0	1	3	0	0	0	0	0	0	1	0	0	0	0
Luevano, Juan, Agu.	6	8	.429	3.30	41	4	0	0	37	12	84.2	71	303	33	31	3	8	3	3	24	1	50	2	0
Lynch, Dave, MCT	2	2	.500	2.75	8	4	2	0	4	0	36.0	32	131	11	11	1	2	1	2	15	1	31	1	0
Macias, Abraham, Agu.	0	1	.000	9.58	6	1	0	0	5	1	10.1	15	43	12	11	2	0	1	0	11	2	4	0	0
Mack, Tony Len, Tor.	0	2	.000	7.20	4	1	0	0	3	0	10.0	19	45	8	8	1	0	0	0	6	2	0	1	0
Maclin, Lonnie, Agu.	0	0	.000	0.00	1	0	0	0	1	0	1.0	1	4	0	0	0	0	0	0	0	0	1	0	0
Mansur, Jeff, Pue.	0	0	.000	4.50	13	1	0	0	12	1	12.0	16	45	8	6	1	4	0	0	10	1	4	1	0
Manzano, Adrian, MCT	0	0	.000	0.00	2	1	0	0	1	0	3.2	3	13	0	0	0	1	0	0	2	0	1	1	0
Marquez, Miguel, Mont.-Agu.	0	0	.000	18.00	1	0	0	0	1	0	1.0	5	8	2	2	0	0	0	0	1	0	0	0	0
Martin, Daniel, Yuc.	0	0	.000	9.00	5	0	0	0	5	0	3.0	7	14	3	3	0	1	0	0	4	0	2	1	0
Martin, Thomas, MCT	0	1	.000	27.00	1	1	0	0	0	0	1.1	5	9	5	4	0	0	0	1	0	0	1	0	0
Martinez, Filiberto, Sal.	8	5	.615	2.76	19	19	3	2	0	0	107.2	98	399	39	33	2	5	2	7	57	0	57	3	1
Martinez, Mauricio, Sal.	0	1	.000	4.87	11	1	0	0	10	0	20.1	20	77	13	11	1	0	0	0	16	1	12	0	0
Martinez, Ramon, Pue.	0	0	.000	12.27	7	0	0	0	7	0	3.2	12	23	5	5	0	0	0	0	3	0	2	0	0
Martinez, Sean, Pue.	0	0	.000	15.75	2	0	0	0	2	0	4.0	12	23	7	7	1	0	0	0	2	0	2	1	0
Medina, Jose Ramon, Cam.	0	0	.000	0.00	1	0	0	0	1	0	1.1	1	5	0	0	0	0	0	0	1	0	0	0	0
Mejia, Cesar, Cam.	4	6	.400	4.85	24	5	1	0	19	2	55.2	56	204	38	30	6	5	5	5	31	6	27	1	0
Mendez, Luis Fernando, Rey.	6	6	.500	4.57	21	21	3	0	0	0	106.1	129	413	62	54	7	7	2	5	41	1	68	4	0
Meza, Leobardo, Agu.	2	1	.667	0.69	7	5	0	0	0	0	26.0	15	85	3	2	1	2	2	0	5	0	13	0	0
Minutelli, Gino, MCT	2	3	.400	8.26	12	5	1	0	7	1	28.1	43	123	26	26	2	3	2	2	15	0	15	2	0
Miranda, Julio Cesar, Tor.	6	6	.500	6.44	41	1	0	0	40	8	58.2	67	229	43	42	7	7	3	2	20	9	25	7	0
Molina, Joaquin, Tor.	0	1	.000	5.34	17	0	0	0	17	1	30.1	29	111	19	18	3	2	3	2	17	0	17	3	0
Montano, Francisco, Monc.	8	9	.471	4.15	22	22	3	0	0	0	128.0	134	490	66	59	7	5	3	1	38	2	78	5	0
Mora, Eleazar, Agu.	6	10	.375	4.53	23	21	3	0	2	0	117.1	133	454	67	59	12	6	5	10	43	2	58	2	1
Moreno, Angel, N.L.	16	3	.842	3.20	22	22	8	0	0	0	160.1	136	586	61	57	9	5	2	4	44	2	108	0	0
Moreno, Claudio, MCRD	3	1	.750	5.19	27	1	0	0	26	1	59.0	66	224	39	34	5	5	2	3	35	2	36	5	0
Moreno, Jesus, Sal.	10	4	.714	4.95	22	22	1	0	0	0	131.0	147	549	80	72	12	2	9	11	50	0	60	1	0
Moreno, Leobardo, MCRD	6	1	.857	5.02	21	8	1	0	13	0	52.0	61	205	32	29	6	2	3	1	23	0	41	1	0
Moreno Alvarez, Ricardo, N.L.	0	0	.000	8.18	10	1	0	0	9	0	11.0	14	42	11	10	2	0	0	0	18	1	7	4	0
Moreno V., Ricardo, Jal.	0	2	.000	1.85	9	2	2	0	7	1	24.1	26	93	9	5	0	2	1	0	10	1	11	0	0
Murillo, Felipe, Monc.	1	1	.500	2.16	43	0	0	0	43	30	58.1	57	219	18	14	1	2	4	1	13	1	40	0	0
Munoz, Miguel, Agu.-Rey.	11	3	.786	2.67	20	20	2	1	0	0	138.0	140	522	47	41	3	8	1	4	22	1	62	1	2
Munoz, Pablo, Pue.	0	0	.000	6.35	10	0	0	0	10	0	5.2	8	22	4	4	1	1	0	0	3	0	3	0	0
Munoz, Ricardo, Tab.	12	6	.667	2.46	22	22	7	3	0	0	142.2	128	514	49	39	5	14	2	7	36	1	69	1	1
Navarro, Adolfo, Ags.	1	5	.167	7.22	9	7	1	0	2	0	33.2	39	128	29	27	2	3	4	3	24	0	12	0	0
Navarro, Luis A., Sal.	3	4	.429	5.61	19	8	0	0	11	0	51.1	53	200	36	32	6	1	5	2	29	0	24	2	0
Neri, Braulio, Yuc.-Tor.	1	1	.500	12.56	21	0	0	0	21	0	14.1	26	64	25	20	1	1	3	0	20	3	5	5	0
Neri, Eduardo, Agu.	4	5	.444	3.59	51	3	0	0	48	4	102.2	86	359	46	41	5	6	0	3	71	3	61	5	2
Nunez Avina, J.J., Jal.	0	1	.000	7.62	17	0	0	0	17	0	28.1	41	117	24	24	3	0	3	0	15	0	11	5	0

Pitcher, Team	W	L	Pct.	ERA	G	GS	CG	ShO	GF	Sv.	IP	H	TBF	R	ER	HR	SH	SF	HB	BB	IBB	SO	WP	Bk.
Ochoa, Porfirio, N.L.	0	1	.000	8.22	7	1	0	0	6	0	7.2	15	35	8	7	1	1	1	1	2	1	1	0	0
Olague, Jesus, Mont.	0	0	.000	4.58	7	2	0	0	5	0	19.2	20	69	10	10	0	1	4	2	14	0	9	2	1
Orozco, Jaime, Pue.	8	10	.444	4.24	23	22	5	0	1	0	140.0	154	541	80	66	9	12	6	6	48	1	67	5	1
Ortega, Pablo, N.L.	0	1	.000	5.93	5	2	1	0	3	0	13.2	11	52	9	9	2	0	0	2	5	0	7	1	0
Osuna, Ricardo, Tab.	2	4	.333	4.26	8	8	0	0	0	0	38.0	45	147	25	18	0	2	2	3	20	0	16	0	0
Osuna, Roberto, N.L.	6	13	.316	4.45	25	22	1	0	3	0	127.1	148	499	75	63	14	8	4	3	55	3	74	1	1
Palafox, Juan Manuel, Tor.	10	7	.588	4.73	21	21	9	1	0	0	139.0	155	537	82	73	13	7	3	11	44	1	63	5	1
Pelcastregui, Leonardo, Tor.	0	0	.000	13.50	5	0	0	0	5	0	2.0	2	7	3	3	0	1	0	0	3	0	1	1	0
Perez, Joaquin, Min.	0	0	.000	3.86	1	0	0	0	1	0	2.1	2	9	1	1	0	0	0	0	0	0	1	0	0
Perez, Leonardo, Mont.	8	4	.667	2.48	34	6	1	0	28	4	83.1	69	299	31	23	6	8	4	5	47	7	56	3	0
Perez, Vladimir, Rey.	1	1	.500	2.82	14	0	0	0	14	6	22.1	17	76	7	7	1	2	0	1	13	4	6	2	0
Perry, Jeff, N.L.	4	11	.267	4.86	25	19	1	0	6	0	109.1	113	418	62	59	9	11	1	3	63	8	61	5	1
Pena, Alejandro, Mont.	0	0	.000	0.00	2	0	0	0	2	1	2.2	1	9	0	0	0	0	0	0	0	0	2	0	0
Pimentel, Roberto, Tor.-Monc.	5	6	.455	5.51	39	5	0	0	34	0	47.1	59	187	32	29	4	8	2	3	32	1	20	2	1
Pina, Rafael, MCRD	6	3	.667	3.38	42	0	0	0	42	3	69.1	66	266	29	26	2	6	2	1	39	3	63	10	0
Pinero, Hugo Jose, Min.	0	0	.000	5.40	3	0	0	0	3	0	6.2	4	23	5	4	0	1	0	1	3	2	3	0	0
Pruneda, Armando, Monc.	2	4	.333	5.63	10	3	0	0	7	0	24.0	27	92	16	15	4	0	1	0	18	0	4	3	1
Puig, Benny, Ags.-Tor.	4	5	.444	3.23	16	15	4	0	1	0	97.2	94	363	41	35	7	7	3	5	46	0	38	6	0
Pulido, Raymundo, MCT	0	0	.000	11.81	2	2	0	0	0	0	5.1	5	19	7	7	2	0	0	0	7	0	4	3	0
Purata, Julio, Rey.	13	5	.722	3.60	22	22	5	3	0	0	132.2	126	493	61	53	11	7	1	2	50	1	74	0	0
Quijada, Mario, Tor.	0	0	.000	0.00	2	0	0	0	2	0	3.2	2	13	0	0	0	0	2	0	0	0	2	0	0
Quintanilla, Enrique, N.L.	2	2	.500	7.04	33	5	0	0	28	1	61.1	89	255	51	48	8	4	2	5	27	4	30	8	1
Quintero, Victor H., Tor.	1	0	1.000	6.75	5	0	0	0	5	0	8.0	10	36	11	6	2	0	0	1	3	0	5	1	0
Quiroz, Aaron, N.L.	11	7	.611	3.11	23	22	3	0	1	0	139.0	136	527	54	48	11	6	0	3	56	3	108	9	0
Quiroz, Jose J., Ags.	4	2	.667	3.67	23	0	0	0	23	1	34.1	28	119	14	14	2	4	2	0	20	3	27	1	0
Quinones, Enrique, Yuc.	1	4	.200	4.66	25	2	0	0	23	1	58.0	71	227	35	30	7	6	2	0	25	3	34	1	0
Ramirez, Martin, Ags.	1	0	1.000	10.80	5	0	0	0	5	0	8.1	13	36	10	10	0	1	1	1	2	0	4	1	0
Ramirez, Miguel, A., Jal.	0	1	.000	8.72	8	1	0	0	7	0	21.2	28	82	22	21	2	2	1	2	19	1	9	6	0
Ramirez, Roberto, MCRD	13	3	.813	2.56	20	20	8	3	0	0	137.1	125	502	50	39	9	5	3	5	35	0	70	3	2
Ramos, Jorge Luis, Pue.	1	4	.200	3.97	23	1	0	0	22	1	47.2	53	187	27	21	5	2	0	5	19	0	19	1	0
Raygoza, Martin, Monc.	7	10	.412	3.47	21	21	6	0	0	0	140.0	154	555	71	54	9	2	6	3	40	4	77	4	0
Renteria, Hilario, Tor.	5	10	.333	6.00	22	22	0	0	0	0	111.0	146	459	87	74	13	4	7	5	31	6	58	4	0
Retes, Lorenzo, Tab.-Min.	2	5	.286	5.24	24	17	0	0	7	0	87.2	119	359	61	51	6	11	4	0	40	2	38	1	0
Reyes, Dennis, MCRD	5	5	.500	6.60	17	15	1	0	2	0	58.2	76	228	49	43	4	7	5	0	41	0	44	2	0
Rincon, Ricardo, MCRD	6	6	.500	5.16	27	11	0	0	16	3	75.0	86	285	45	43	7	7	5	1	41	0	41	3	0
Rios, Jesus, MCT	10	6	.625	4.25	25	23	7	3	2	0	146.0	121	541	78	69	17	4	5	6	50	1	103	1	1
Rivera, Eleazar, Monc.	1	0	1.000	0.00	1	1	0	0	0	0	8.0	6	28	2	0	0	0	0	4	0	6	1	0
Rivera, Hector, Rey.-Agu.	6	8	.429	5.38	23	15	3	1	8	0	87.0	97	348	58	52	7	3	3	5	39	1	35	4	0
Rivera, Lino, Monc.	1	3	.250	8.42	5	5	0	0	0	0	25.2	41	111	29	24	4	1	1	1	13	0	17	3	0
Rivera, Paul, Ags.	2	1	.667	5.82	14	7	1	0	7	0	38.2	45	151	27	25	3	0	3	2	34	0	27	6	2
Rodriguez, Fernando, Pue.	0	0	.000	6.00	5	0	0	0	5	0	3.0	2	10	2	2	0	0	0	1	0	0	0	0	0
Rodriguez, Mario A., Rey.	0	1	.000	11.77	12	0	0	0	12	0	26.0	47	123	35	34	3	0	1	1	11	1	9	1	0
Rodriguez, Mario, Min.	3	9	.250	4.53	26	17	1	0	9	0	109.1	131	419	63	55	11	12	2	4	46	5	31	1	0
Rodriguez, Raul, Sal.	14	4	.778	3.30	23	22	3	1	1	0	144.2	126	527	59	53	6	6	3	4	55	0	106	2	1
Rodriguez, Rene, N.L.	3	3	.500	3.96	32	1	0	0	31	4	36.1	46	147	26	16	0	3	1	2	19	6	10	1	0
Rodriguez, Rosario, Mont.	0	0	.000	10.38	11	0	0	0	11	0	4.1	6	19	5	5	0	0	0	0	5	1	5	2	0
Rodriguez, Salvador, Yuc.	0	2	.000	6.08	10	3	0	0	7	1	26.2	28	102	19	18	3	1	0	0	20	0	14	2	1
Rojo, Oscar, Cam.-Rey.	3	1	.750	5.73	34	2	0	0	32	5	59.2	69	236	43	38	6	5	5	2	33	4	26	4	0
Romero, Juan, Tab.	3	5	.375	3.49	29	5	0	0	24	1	69.2	71	258	34	27	3	5	1	3	29	1	23	3	1
Romo, Guillermo, Tor.	1	3	.250	5.96	15	9	0	0	6	0	45.1	59	174	33	30	2	5	2	3	38	1	15	4	0
Ruiz, Cecilio, Tab.	13	5	.722	1.71	24	23	7	5	1	0	162.2	132	584	41	31	6	20	4	4	33	1	92	1	0
Sadecki, Steve, Jal.	0	5	.000	7.59	5	5	1	0	0	0	21.1	33	90	24	18	3	1	2	2	18	0	7	4	0
Saenz, Alfredo, Pue.	8	10	.444	3.60	26	20	9	1	6	1	132.1	143	507	73	53	13	12	3	6	52	4	71	6	1
Saldana, Edgardo, Agu.-Tab.	6	8	.429	3.22	23	20	4	1	3	0	117.1	121	451	47	42	6	8	3	4	42	1	70	4	1
Saldana, Gerardo, Pue.	0	1	.000	9.64	2	1	0	0	1	0	4.2	9	20	5	5	1	0	0	0	7	1	3	0	0
Salgado, Eduardo, MCT	0	0	.000	3.86	11	0	0	0	11	0	14.0	16	55	6	6	2	0	1	1	7	0	6	1	0
Sanchez, Hector, Agu.-Mont.	2	3	.400	5.44	24	0	0	0	24	1	44.2	60	180	30	27	8	2	2	4	11	3	16	2	0
Sanchez, Jose Luis, Jal.	1	4	.200	6.32	14	6	2	0	8	0	47.0	59	190	50	33	2	6	3	4	27	2	18	7	0
Sandoval, Carlos, Min.	0	1	.000	3.28	32	1	0	0	31	0	35.2	32	130	14	13	3	5	0	2	16	5	17	1	0
Sandoval, Guillermo, Mont.	2	4	.333	5.03	33	4	0	0	29	5	59.0	62	214	36	33	2	7	4	1	31	1	36	0	0
Segura, Jose, Yuc.	10	2	.833	2.13	38	0	0	0	38	14	54.1	47	199	29	27	3	7	0	0	27	3	38	10	0
Serna, Ramon, Ags.	4	3	.571	4.64	30	3	0	0	27	2	64.0	68	243	39	33	7	4	1	3	35	2	36	3	1
Sierra, Abel, Cam.	11	9	.550	2.64	24	21	10	5	3	0	153.1	132	578	60	45	7	9	0	3	48	4	80	4	1
Silverio, Victor, Agu.-Ags.	0	0	.000	6.75	2	0	0	0	2	0	1.1	2	6	1	1	0	0	0	0	5	0	1	0	0
Smith, Daryl, Sal.	3	2	.600	4.11	7	4	1	0	3	0	30.2	30	116	17	14	1	1	0	2	22	0	20	0	0
Solarte, Jose A., Min.	8	4	.667	1.72	45	6	3	1	39	4	115.0	93	397	23	22	2	9	3	1	42	9	64	1	0
Solis, Ricardo, Yuc.	9	9	.500	4.92	23	20	1	1	3	0	115.1	143	452	66	63	7	13	0	2	43	1	51	5	0
Sombra, Francisco, Sal.	2	3	.400	3.18	37	4	1	0	33	0	51.0	52	190	21	18	2	5	4	0	15	2	25	4	0
Soto, Fernando, Min.	7	14	.333	3.63	25	25	4	2	0	0	161.1	182	638	77	65	10	6	2	0	51	9	67	2	0
Soto, Ramon E., Agu.	0	0	.000	1.80	3	0	0	0	3	0	5.0	3	18	1	1	0	0	0	0	3	0	4	1	0
Strauss, Julio Cesar, Tab.	2	2	.500	2.13	12	0	0	0	12	2	12.2	9	41	3	3	0	2	0	0	10	4	9	0	0
Tapia, Jose, Cam.	0	0	.000	9.00	1	0	0	0	1	0	1.0	3	6	1	1	0	0	0	0	0	0	0	0	0
Tatum, Willie, Yuc.	0	0	.000	...	1	0	0	0	1	0	0.0	2	3	2	2	0	0	0	0	1	0	0	0	0
Tejeda, Juan, Cam.	3	4	.429	3.24	27	9	1	1	18	2	66.2	75	262	34	24	4	8	3	0	17	3	18	1	0
Tinoco, Ruben, Cam.	0	2	.000	4.34	25	1	0	0	24	0	56.0	70	223	35	27	6	3	4	3	21	5	16	4	1
Toledo, Mario, Cam.	2	2	.500	4.15	26	4	0	0	22	0	43.1	45	169	31	20	5	4	3	1	28	2	16	2	0
Tunnell, Lee, MCT	4	5	.444	5.91	14	4	0	0	10	0	35.0	34	132	27	23	4	1	1	1	14	1	25	2	0
Uribe, Juan Carlos, Yuc.	6	3	.667	1.93	43	1	1	1	42	6	70.0	52	244	19	15	1	5	3	30	5	43	5	0	
Valdez, Armando, Sal.-Pue.-Tor.	0	1	.000	24.16	10	0	0	0	10	0	6.1	26	44	18	17	3	1	0	1	8	1	5	0	1
Valdez, Jose Luis, N.L.	2	1	.667	3.80	15	1	0	0	14	0	21.1	28	90	11	9	1	2	0	5	1	11	2	0	
Valdez, Rafael, Rey.-Yuc.	8	1	.889	5.51	22	21	2	1	1	0	96.1	124	393	65	59	6	7	5	4	49	1	67	5	0
Valencia, Jorge, Sal.	6	5	.545	5.54	29	17	2	0	12	0	102.1	131	395	72	63	12	6	5	1	62	2	38	5	2
Valenzuela, Aurelio, Yuc.	1	0	1.000	6.23	7	1	0	0	6	0	13.0	15	54	16	9	1	0	2	0	7	0	3	0	0

Pitcher, Team	W	L	Pct.	ERA	G	GS	CG	ShO	GF	Sv.	IP	H	TBF	R	ER	HR	SH	SF	HB	BB	IBB	SO	WP	Bk.
Valenzuela, Jorge, Pue.	0	0	.000	22.50	6	0	0	0	6	0	4.0	10	22	10	10	3	0	0	0	5	0	3	1	0
Valenzuela, Saul, Pue.	10	8	.556	3.94	22	22	7	1	0	0	146.1	156	551	75	64	10	16	6	3	54	3	52	5	0
Vargas, Ignacio, Pue.	3	8	.273	6.08	18	8	0	0	10	0	53.1	67	207	44	36	6	5	2	0	31	1	17	1	0
Vargas, Joel, Tab.	0	0	.000	5.40	4	0	0	0	4	0	5.0	6	20	3	3	0	0	0	1	2	0	4	2	0
Vazquez, Adrian, Cam.	11	6	.647	2.64	21	21	3	0	0	0	136.1	118	487	48	40	8	10	1	5	72	3	39	4	1
Vazquez, Aguedo, Ags.	6	0	1.000	3.97	22	12	1	1	10	1	77.0	74	288	35	34	7	1	2	3	31	2	33	1	0
Vega, Obed, MCT	5	5	.500	5.75	18	14	0	0	4	0	76.2	78	289	58	49	10	5	3	1	58	2	41	6	1
Velazquez, Ernesto A., Tor.-Sal.	0	4	.000	8.65	19	7	0	0	12	0	42.2	63	179	43	41	8	2	3	2	33	0	10	4	0
Velazquez, Ildefonso, Yuc.	0	0	.000	10.13	3	0	0	0	3	0	2.2	4	13	4	3	1	1	0	0	3	0	1	1	0
Velazquez, Israel, Min.	4	12	.250	3.28	23	22	2	1	1	0	120.2	114	450	58	44	9	7	4	10	63	3	77	1	1
Veliz A., Francisco, Sal.-Monc.	0	0	.000	2.96	19	0	0	0	19	0	24.1	22	83	8	8	2	2	1	2	14	0	15	4	0
Verdugo, Orlando, Yuc.	0	0	.000	54.00	2	0	0	0	2	0	0.2	3	5	4	4	0	0	0	0	4	0	0	2	0
Villalobos, Noe, Mont.	0	0	.000	11.25	2	1	0	0	1	0	4.0	6	18	5	5	1	0	0	0	3	0	1	2	0
Villanueva, Luis, Ags.	2	2	.500	6.00	28	0	0	0	28	3	18.0	23	69	15	12	1	2	1	0	8	1	13	0	1
Villarreal, Antonio, Mont.-Yuc.	5	2	.714	2.95	34	2	0	0	32	1	76.1	78	288	33	25	4	7	3	2	35	5	43	7	0
Villegas, Jose Angel, Ags.	9	7	.563	3.70	52	2	0	0	50	7	82.2	86	310	38	34	7	9	2	2	46	7	35	5	0
Villegas, Ramon, Pue.	0	1	.000	5.97	17	1	0	0	16	0	37.2	50	153	28	25	5	1	2	1	14	2	16	1	0
Vizcarra A., Rodrigo, Ags.	0	0	.000	3.60	3	0	0	0	3	0	5.0	8	22	4	2	0	0	0	0	3	0	5	0	0
Wagner, Hector, Ags.	1	5	.167	6.03	15	3	0	0	12	5	31.1	46	130	21	21	2	4	0	0	21	5	18	1	0
Walker, Mike, MCRD	2	3	.400	4.01	19	5	0	0	14	4	42.2	41	152	21	19	5	1	2	2	20	1	23	4	0
Wayne, Gary, MCRD-Monc.	4	5	.444	3.41	22	6	2	0	16	2	58.0	60	220	26	22	6	5	2	1	14	1	51	7	0
Zappelli, Mark, Sal.	6	8	.429	2.63	33	9	2	0	24	6	106.0	109	396	40	31	2	9	6	4	47	0	45	3	0
Zavala, Marcos, MCT	0	0	.000	4.50	4	0	0	0	4	0	2.0	2	7	1	1	0	1	0	0	1	0	2	0	0

COMBINATION SHUTOUTS: A total of 70 combination shutouts were pitched in the Mexican League in 1995. Aguila led the league with 11.

NO-HIT GAMES: Ramirez, Mexico City Red Devils, defeated Tabasco, 2-0, June 6; Hernandez, Aguila, defeated Mexico City Red Devils, 1-0, June 20; Henry, Puebla, defeated Aguila, 3-0, July 1; Cuervo, Campeche, defeated Minatitlan, 4-0, July 2.

1995 FIELDING

TEAM

Team	Pct.	G	PO	A	E	TC	DP	PB	Team	Pct.	G	PO	A	E	TC	DP	PB
Aguascalientes	.981	114	2813	1272	80	4165	120	9	Monterrey	.975	116	2880	1269	105	4254	114	8
M.C. Red Devils	.979	114	2798	1292	86	4176	120	13	Saltillo	.972	116	2907	1358	123	4388	149	7
Minatitlan	.979	116	2919	1293	90	4302	131	11	Puebla	.971	116	2776	1312	122	4210	116	9
Nuevo Laredo	.978	116	2947	1291	96	4334	122	11	Tabasco	.969	115	2833	1289	131	4253	118	4
Mexico City Tigers	.977	116	2845	1240	96	4181	91	8	Campeche	.967	115	2802	1245	137	4184	120	8
Yucatan	.977	115	2814	1305	99	4218	107	12	Monclova	.966	116	2849	1236	145	4230	128	9
Torreon	.977	115	2831	1308	96	4235	134	12	Jalisco	.965	114	2741	1254	147	4142	126	10
Aguila	.976	116	2894	1363	106	4363	137	10									
Reynosa	.975	116	2942	1306	107	4355	128	4									

TRIPLE PLAYS: Aguila, Mexico City Tigers, Monclova, Nuevo Laredo, Torreon, Puebla.

INDIVIDUAL

FIRST BASEMEN

Player, Team	Pct.	G	PO	A	E	TC	DP
Estrada, Ruben, N.L.	1.000	66	381	29	0	410	45
Valdez, Jesus, Yuc.	1.000	41	273	21	0	294	26
Peralta, Amado, Yuc.-Jal.	1.000	29	256	11	0	267	23
Arce, Francisco J., Min.	1.000	23	179	11	0	190	23
Velazquez, Guillermo, Mont.	1.000	16	138	4	0	142	11
Sasser, Mike, Min.	1.000	15	150	7	0	157	15
Fariss, Monty, Mont.	1.000	13	100	3	0	103	12
Castaneda, Rafael, N.L.	1.000	12	76	6	0	82	4
Tillman, Rusty, Agu.-Tab.	1.000	11	91	4	0	95	10
Gonzalez, Denio, Sal.	1.000	11	85	7	0	92	10
Rendina, Mike, Monc.	1.000	11	81	9	0	90	8
Alvarez, Luis, Jal.	1.000	11	83	6	0	89	10
Carrillo, Matias, MCT	1.000	10	62	0	0	62	3
Guerrero, Javier, Ags.	.998	58	475	28	1	504	48
Romero, Marco Antonio, MCT	.996	105	929	61	4	994	78
Gavia, Jesus, Agu.-Min.	.996	29	209	13	1	223	22
Machaira, Pablo, Ags.	.996	26	215	21	1	237	31
Tolentino, Jose, Mont.	.995	76	691	41	4	736	67
Quintana, Carlos, Min.-Yuc.	.995	71	615	43	3	661	57
Valenzuela, Horacio, Min.-Jal.	.995	52	402	22	2	426	48
Pena, Luis Alberto, Pue.	.994	85	742	39	5	786	63
Paez, Raul, MCRD.	.994	84	507	34	3	544	58
Zulueta, Felix, Tab.	.992	13	115	8	1	124	8
Avila, Ruben, Tor.	.991	112	1022	71	10	1103	117
Casillas, Adam, Rey.	.991	90	785	76	8	869	80
Torres, Eduardo, Sal.	.991	15	108	4	1	113	10
Mendez, Jesus, Agu.-Tab.	.990	105	927	76	10	1013	102
Almeida, Shammar, Sal.	.990	93	757	57	8	822	101
Ortega, Roberto, Tab.	.990	49	376	35	4	415	54
Rodriguez, Genaro, N.L.	.989	56	329	21	4	354	43
Tejeda, Arturo, N.L.	.989	15	80	6	1	87	13
Aganza, Ruben, Monc.	.988	92	825	59	11	895	79
Naveda, Edgar, Jal.	.988	57	455	42	6	503	51
Quiroz, Jose Julian, Ags.	.988	16	80	4	1	85	9
Orantes, Ramon, Mont.	.988	11	80	4	1	85	8
Guerrero, Jaime, Ags.	.988	11	76	8	1	85	8
Stark, Matt, Rey.	.987	17	147	7	2	156	17

Player, Team	Pct.	G	PO	A	E	TC	DP
Barrera, Nelson, MCRD	.986	67	475	27	7	509	51
Castro, Eddie, Min.-Sal.	.986	32	262	19	4	285	38
Arvizu, Javier, Cam.	.985	92	798	47	13	858	83
Sommers, Jesus, Pue.-Agu.	.985	21	186	11	3	200	15
Michel, Domingo, Cam.	.985	18	129	5	2	136	11
Arevalo, Guadalupe, Ags.	.982	10	52	3	1	56	11
Chan, Armando, Monc.	.981	13	99	4	2	105	21
Zamudio, Rafael, Mont.-Agu.	.978	13	87	4	2	93	12
Estrada, Ricardo, Min.-Agu.	.976	38	316	15	8	339	32
Rivera, German, Pue.	.963	20	123	8	5	136	16
Reyna, Luis, Monc.-Tab.	.958	10	65	4	3	72	4
Hernandez A., Martin, Cam.	.948	17	53	2	3	58	5

FIRST BASEMEN WITH FEWER THAN 10 GAMES

Player, Team	Pct.	G	PO	A	E	TC	DP
Diaz, Luis Fernando, MCT	1.000	9	41	1	0	42	2
Infante, Alexis, Tab.	1.000	9	40	5	0	45	6
Rodriguez, Boi, N.L.	1.000	9	44	1	0	45	2
Merchand, Mark, Rey.	1.000	9	96	5	0	101	11
Cornejo, Edgar, Sal.	1.000	6	28	2	0	30	2
Mora, Andres, N.L.	1.000	6	46	2	0	48	8
Rubio, Marco A., Cam.-Min.	1.000	5	13	1	0	14	3
Ritchie, Greg, Tab.	1.000	4	31	3	0	34	3
Soto, Emison, Pue.	1.000	4	18	0	0	18	2
Leal, Jose Guadalupe, Cam.	1.000	4	26	1	0	27	5
Cobos, Rogelio, MCRD	1.000	3	11	2	0	13	0
Ojeda, Miguel, MCRD	1.000	3	17	2	0	19	1
Trevino, Alejandro, Mont.	1.000	3	10	0	0	10	0
Perez, Juan Luis, Tor.	1.000	3	18	2	0	20	2
Valverde, Raul, Jal.	1.000	3	17	2	0	19	4
Villanueva, Hector, MCT	1.000	2	12	0	0	12	0
Sparks, Greg, MCT	1.000	2	19	0	0	19	1
Pardo, Victor Manuel, Pue.	1.000	2	5	0	0	5	1
Canedo, Alberto, Cam.	1.000	2	8	0	0	8	1
Tatum, Willie, Yuc.	1.000	2	21	2	0	23	1
McCoy, Trey, N.L.	1.000	2	13	2	0	15	0
Motley, Darryl, Tor.-Agu.	1.000	2	8	1	0	9	0
Snider, Van, Tor.	1.000	2	8	2	0	10	1

Player, Team	Pct.	G	PO	A	E	TC	DP
Cervera, Francisco, Jal.	1.000	2	23	1	0	24	4
Nunez Avina, Jose Juan, Jal.	1.000	2	1	0	0	1	0
Mendez, Roberto C., MCRD	1.000	1	1	0	0	1	0
Mere, Pedro, MCT	1.000	1	0	1	0	1	0
Ortiz, Alejandro, MCT	1.000	1	1	0	0	1	0
Rojas, Francisco, Tab.	1.000	1	2	0	0	2	1
Valenzuela, Eduardo, Sal.	1.000	1	1	0	0	1	0
Martinez, Raul, Sal.	1.000	1	1	0	0	1	1
Robles, Ricardo, Sal.	1.000	1	3	0	0	3	2
Flores, Miguel, Mont.	1.000	1	10	0	0	10	0
Perez, Francisco, Rey.	1.000	1	1	0	0	1	0
Lopez, Gonzalo, Monc.	1.000	1	1	0	0	1	0
Enriquez, Graciano, Ags.	1.000	1	3	0	0	3	0
Lopez A., Victor M., Jal.	1.000	1	10	1	0	11	0
Alvarez, Ivan, Jal.	1.000	1	13	1	0	14	0
Clement, Wes, Ags.	.985	8	59	8	1	68	4
Guzman, Marco A., Yuc.	.977	6	40	3	1	44	5
Cantu, Gerardo, Pue.	.970	8	32	0	1	33	2
Garcia, Cornelio, Mont.	.969	5	29	2	1	32	6
Cruz, Luis Alfonso, Rey.	.958	6	39	7	2	48	8
Sabino, Miguel, Jal.	.955	5	39	3	2	44	7
Cuevas, Angelo, Tab.-Min.	.950	6	34	4	2	40	5
Payro, Edison, Cam.	.947	6	17	1	1	19	3
Cairo, Sergio, Yuc.	.900	2	15	3	2	20	2
Rivera, Alberto, Jal.	.750	1	3	0	1	4	0
Martinez, Grimaldo, Monc.	.667	1	1	1	1	3	1

TRIPLE PLAYS: Aganza, Avila, Ri. Estrada, Ru. Estrada, Romero, Sommers.

Player, Team	Pct.	G	PO	A	E	TC	DP
Vargas, Trinidad, Pue.	1.000	3	8	11	0	19	4
Perez, Alejandro, N.L.	1.000	3	4	1	0	5	0
Felix, Arturo, Yuc.	1.000	2	2	0	0	2	0
Malpica, Enrique, Agu.	1.000	2	3	5	0	8	1
Monroy, Francisco, Mont.	1.000	2	2	0	0	2	0
Ayala Armenta, Mario, Monc.	1.000	2	4	1	0	5	1
Roa, Hector, MCT.	1.000	1	4	3	0	7	0
Gastelum, G., Sergio, O., MCT.	1.000	1	0	3	0	3	0
Marrujo, Hector, Tab.	1.000	1	2	2	0	4	0
Perez, Alfredo, Pue.	1.000	1	1	1	0	2	0
Soto, Emison, Pue.	1.000	1	0	4	0	4	1
Brinkley, Darrell, Cam.	1.000	1	2	2	0	4	0
Diaz, Remigio, Mont.	1.000	1	1	1	0	2	1
Rodriguez, Genaro, N.L.	1.000	1	4	0	0	4	0
Rodriguez, Hector, Rey.	1.000	1	1	0	0	1	0
Contreras, Cuitlahuac, Tor.-Monc.	1.000	1	0	1	0	1	0
Olvera, Sergio, Monc.	1.000	1	1	1	0	2	1
Leyva, German, Monc.	1.000	1	3	4	0	7	0
Laurencio, Rodfer, Cam.	.975	9	16	23	1	40	1
Arredondo, Hernando, Pue.	.960	8	7	17	1	25	1
Cervera, Francisco, Jal.	.955	3	14	7	1	22	2
Canizalez, Juan Carlos, Mont.	.923	6	7	5	1	13	1
Montalvo, Ivan, MCT.	.909	7	7	13	2	22	1
Valenzuela S., Joel, Tor.	.889	6	3	5	1	9	0
Barrera, Jesus Antonio, Min.	.875	1	2	5	1	8	0
Valenzuela, Armando, Rey.	.833	1	1	4	1	6	0

TRIPLE PLAYS: Carrasco, Garcia, Mere.

SECOND BASEMEN

Player, Team	Pct.	G	PO	A	E	TC	DP
Balderas, S., Abelardo, Min.	1.000	12	16	24	0	40	4
Verdugo, Guadalupe, Tor.	1.000	11	26	23	0	49	6
Sanchez, Armando, Mont.	.994	64	151	164	2	317	45
Morales, Florentino, N.L.	.990	39	97	95	2	194	34
Camacho, Adulfo, Yuc.	.989	112	269	340	7	616	73
Esquer, Ramon, Rey.	.989	85	227	234	5	466	68
Zazueta, Mauricio, Tor.	.988	78	189	235	5	429	60
Ruiz, Juan De Dios, Tor.	.986	17	34	38	1	73	10
Rivera, Alberto, Jal.	.986	14	34	35	1	70	11
Renteria, Edison, Agu.-Cam.	.985	29	50	78	2	130	18
Zazueta, Juan Carlos, Tab.	.984	47	90	90	3	183	18
Martinez, Grimaldo, Monc.	.983	101	230	303	9	542	78
Vizcarra, Roberto, Ags.	.981	104	282	285	11	578	83
Rodriguez, Juan F., Rey.-Agu.	.981	49	119	144	5	268	38
Martinez, Luis Carlos, Sal.	.981	13	22	29	1	52	10
Castro, Arnoldo, Min.	.980	109	318	322	13	653	88
Verdugo, Vicente, MCRD	.979	105	213	306	11	530	76
Carrasco, Ernesto, N.L.	.979	93	225	235	10	470	67
Tovar, Jose De Jesus, Sal.-Monc.	.979	36	95	95	4	194	31
Mendiola, Juan Carlos, Agu.	.979	28	41	52	2	95	11
Garcia, Carlos, Agu.	.978	49	105	117	5	227	37
Mere, Pedro, MCT.	.977	89	205	271	11	487	57
Pardo, Victor Manuel, Pue.	.975	102	222	281	13	516	69
Flores, Miguel, Mont.	.975	34	103	91	5	199	23
Duran, Felipe, MCRD	.975	14	23	16	1	40	5
Gonzalez, Jesus, Jal.	.974	84	224	225	12	461	74
Trapaga, Miguel, Mont.	.970	31	39	59	3	101	7
Wong Medrano, Julian, Monc.	.969	10	14	17	1	32	7
Infante, Alexis, Tab.	.967	86	236	231	16	483	66
Hernandez B., Juan C., Pue.	.967	19	27	32	2	61	8
Loredo, Jorge Luis, Cam.	.966	68	137	180	11	328	47
Vizcarra, Marco, A., Rey.	.965	35	74	90	6	170	20
Precichi, Jorge, Sal.	.963	78	216	256	18	490	78
Magallanes, Ever, Mont.	.962	11	25	25	2	52	5
Salas, Heriberto, Tor.	.955	13	21	21	2	44	5
Sanchez, Roque, Cam.	.952	23	26	31	3	62	7
Santos, Julio, Jal.	.947	15	30	42	4	76	16
Arevalo, Guadalupe, Ags.	.941	10	7	25	2	34	5
Quintero, Guillermo, Mont.	.935	43	33	39	5	77	10
Rubio, Marco A., Cam.-Min.	.909	10	13	17	3	33	4

SECOND BASEMEN WITH FEWER THAN 10 GAMES

Player, Team	Pct.	G	PO	A	E	TC	DP
Lopez, Miguel, Yuc.	1.000	9	16	13	0	29	6
Paredes, Johnny, Agu.	1.000	7	19	18	0	37	5
Fernandez, Fabian, Rey.	1.000	6	6	4	0	10	4
Estrada, Ruben, N.L.	1.000	5	4	1	0	5	1
Gutierrez, Felipe, Monc.	1.000	5	12	10	0	22	4
Nunez Garcia, Jose J., Jal.	1.000	5	6	10	0	16	0
Ramirez, G., Jesus A., MCRD	1.000	4	1	8	0	9	1
Lopez, Fabian, MCRD	1.000	4	6	10	0	16	1
Arredondo, Jesus, A., Ags.	1.000	4	12	15	0	27	4
Robles, Trinidad, MCT-Min.	1.000	3	3	2	0	5	0

THIRD BASEMEN

Player, Team	Pct.	G	PO	A	E	TC	DP
Garcia, Carlos, Agu.	.990	46	27	69	1	97	10
Arevalo, Guadalupe, Ags.	.982	25	14	42	1	57	4
Sanchez, Roque, Cam.	.981	28	12	39	1	52	3
Balderas, S. Abelardo, Min.	.977	30	18	24	1	43	1
Castaneda, Rafael, N.L.	.973	107	112	245	10	367	33
Cornejo, Edgar, Sal.	.973	34	22	50	2	74	10
Roa, Hector, MCT.	.972	28	18	51	2	71	1
Aguilar, Enrique, Ags.	.968	61	47	103	5	155	9
Cruz, Luis Alfonso, Rey.	.967	11	6	23	1	30	2
Rivera, Alberto, Jal.	.964	19	15	39	2	56	3
Duran, Felipe, MCRD	.962	26	23	52	3	78	4
Valle, Jorge Luis, Tor.	.960	27	24	73	4	101	10
Ortiz, Alejandro, MCT.	.958	87	55	174	10	239	14
Orantes, Ramon, Mont.	.957	35	14	53	3	70	5
Peralta, Amado, Yuc.-Jal.	.955	54	46	101	7	154	15
Cazarin, Manuel, Agu.	.955	19	13	29	2	44	5
Tatis, Bernardo, MCRD	.949	83	71	190	14	275	15
Aganza, Ruben, Monc.	.947	22	28	44	4	76	11
Ruiz, Juan De Dios, Tor.	.945	86	73	183	15	271	20
Sanchez, Armando, Mont.	.945	28	14	38	3	55	3
Rivera, German, Pue.	.943	96	67	199	16	282	23
Arce, Francisco J., Min.	.943	55	37	112	9	158	15
Carrasco, Ernesto, N.L.	.943	12	9	24	2	35	3
Jimenez, Ulises, Jal.	.938	26	31	45	5	81	3
Leyva, German, Monc.	.934	93	84	170	18	272	23
Rubio, Marco A., Cam.-Min.	.933	63	48	120	12	180	13
Quinones, Luis, Yuc.	.933	42	32	107	10	149	13
Malpica, Enrique, Agu.	.929	57	37	119	12	168	13
Rodriguez, Hector, Rey.	.928	106	103	192	23	318	17
Guerrero, Jaime, Ags.	.927	34	29	60	7	96	10
Franco, Manuel, Mont.	.925	56	42	94	11	147	14
Gonzalez, Denio, Sal.	.922	90	78	160	20	258	22
Felix, Arturo, Yuc.	.922	69	59	131	16	206	10
Jelks, Greg, Cam.	.921	16	13	45	5	63	8
Barrera, Nelson, MCRD	.912	11	4	27	3	34	2
Loredo, Jorge Luis, Cam.	.909	13	6	24	3	33	2
Romero, Oscar, Tab.	.907	113	96	227	33	356	18
Santos, Julio, Jal.	.905	10	4	15	2	21	2
Arredondo, Hernando, Pue.	.900	33	13	50	7	70	3
Renteria, Edison, Agu.-Cam.	.900	17	18	27	5	50	0
Castaldo, Vince, Cam.	.894	39	26	67	11	104	8
Naveda, Edgar, Jal.	.825	10	9	24	7	40	3

THIRD BASEMEN WITH FEWER THAN 10 GAMES

Player, Team	Pct.	G	PO	A	E	TC	DP
Magallanes, Ever, Mont.	1.000	8	5	9	0	14	0
Vizcarra, Marco A., Rey.	1.000	8	0	3	0	3	0
Michel, Domingo, Cam.	1.000	7	4	10	0	14	2
Verdugo, Sostenes, Yuc.	1.000	5	2	6	0	8	1
Verdugo, Vicente, MCRD	1.000	4	0	2	0	2	0
Camacho, Adulfo, Yuc.	1.000	4	1	7	0	8	0
Estrada, Ricardo, Min.-Agu.	1.000	4	5	2	0	7	0
Barrera, Jesus Antonio, Min.	1.000	4	2	7	0	9	1

Player, Team	Pct.	G	PO	A	E	TC	DP
Villarreal, Alejandro, N.L.	1.000	4	0	1	0	1	0
Salas, Heriberto, Tor.	1.000	4	1	10	0	11	0
Trapaga, Miguel, MCT	1.000	3	0	2	0	2	0
Rojas, Francisco, Tab.	1.000	3	1	6	0	7	0
Romero, Marco A., MCT	1.000	2	1	5	0	6	0
Montalvo, Ivan, MCT	1.000	2	0	1	0	1	0
Arias, Everardo, Pue.	1.000	2	1	5	0	6	1
Vargas, Trinidad, Pue.	1.000	2	2	7	0	9	0
Fariss, Monty, Mont.	1.000	2	4	1	0	5	0
Hernandez B., Juan C., Pue.	1.000	1	1	2	0	3	1
Laurencio, Rodfer, Cam.	1.000	1	0	2	0	2	0
Jimenez, Alfonso, Sal.	1.000	1	3	1	0	4	0
Martinez, Luis Carlos, Sal.	1.000	1	0	1	0	1	0
Diaz, Remigio, Mont.	1.000	1	2	2	0	4	1
Contreras, Cuitlahuac, Tor.-Monc.	1.000	1	1	0	0	1	0
Rodriguez S., Noel, Agu.	.933	7	4	10	1	15	1
Valle, Jose Luis, Min.	.900	3	2	7	1	10	3
Castillo, Juan, Ags.	.875	2	3	4	1	8	1
Cervera, Francisco, Jal.	.818	3	3	6	2	11	0
Canizalez, Juan Carlos, Mont.	.800	4	2	6	2	10	1
Caraballo, Gari, Mont.	.778	9	3	18	6	27	1
Wong Medrano, Julian, Monc.	.700	5	2	5	3	10	1

TRIPLE PLAYS: Castaneda, Malpica, Ortiz.

Player, Team	Pct.	G	PO	A	E	TC	DP
Esquer, Ramon, Rey.	1.000	1	3	3	0	6	1
Rodriguez, Juan F., Rey.-Agu.	1.000	1	3	2	0	5	1
Rodriguez, Hector, Rey.	1.000	1	1	0	0	1	0
Martinez, Grimaldo, Monc.	1.000	1	1	1	0	2	1
Leyva, German, Monc.	1.000	1	3	2	0	5	0
Ayala Armenta, Mario, Monc.	1.000	1	1	6	0	7	1
Arevalo, Guadalupe, Ags.	1.000	1	1	1	0	2	0
Castillo, Juan, Ags.	1.000	1	2	0	0	2	0
Santos, Luis Angel, Ags.	1.000	1	1	2	0	3	1
Castro, Leonel, Jal.	1.000	1	1	1	0	2	0
Santos, Julio, Jal.	.963	6	8	18	1	27	5
Verdugo, Guadalupe, Tor.	.950	7	9	10	1	20	3
Zazueta, Juan Carlos, Tab.	.917	5	5	6	1	12	2
Infante, Alexis, Tab.	.913	6	7	14	2	23	3
Gutierrez, Felipe, Monc.	.900	3	5	4	1	10	1
Estrada, Ruben, N.L.	.857	2	3	3	1	7	0
Arredondo, Hernando, Pue.	.846	4	3	8	2	13	2
Tovar, Jose de Jesus, Sal.-Monc.	.833	9	11	29	8	48	10
Garcia, Carlos, Agu.	.750	4	0	3	1	4	0
Quinones, Luis, Yuc.	.714	1	2	3	2	7	0
Perez, Alfredo, Pue.	.667	1	1	1	1	3	0
Franco, Manuel, Mont.	.500	1	1	0	1	2	0

TRIPLE PLAYS: Arias, Olvera, Jor. Valle.

SHORTSTOPS

Player, Team	Pct.	G	PO	A	E	TC	DP
Quintero, Guillermo, Mont.	1.000	17	13	41	0	54	3
Trapaga, Miguel, MCT	1.000	11	11	20	0	31	5
Sandoval, Jose Luis, MCRD	.979	106	172	344	11	527	76
Arredondo, Jesus, A., Ags.	.976	108	211	387	15	613	84
Valle, Jose Luis, Min.	.975	101	181	328	13	522	67
Magana, Gabriel, Yuc.	.975	20	26	52	2	80	10
Diaz, Remigio, Mont.	.973	92	114	283	11	408	46
Loredo, Jorge Luis, Cam.	.973	13	13	23	1	37	2
Pacho, Juan Jose, Yuc.	.972	104	163	317	14	494	58
Garcia, Heriberto, Agu.	.971	115	240	420	20	680	86
Guerrero, Jaime, Ags.	.970	10	11	21	1	33	6
Guerrero, Francisco, Tor.	.966	83	153	520	14	687	49
Ramirez, Enrique, N.L.	.965	111	169	354	19	542	66
Jimenez, Alfonso, Sal.	.965	109	189	383	21	593	83
Robles, Javier, MCT	.963	112	189	330	20	539	61
Valenzuela, Armando, Rey.	.962	96	153	300	18	471	61
Vargas, Trinidad, Pue.	.960	60	79	158	10	247	22
Guizar, Hector, Cam.	.959	99	195	302	21	518	72
Cervera, Francisco, Jal.	.959	83	135	261	17	413	65
Nunez Garcia, Jose J., Jal.	.959	10	15	32	2	49	7
Rojas, Francisco, Tab.	.958	26	22	46	3	71	7
Magallanes, Ever, Mont.	.956	28	47	84	6	137	17
Hernandez B., Juan C., Pue.	.955	18	23	40	3	66	4
Marrujo, Hector, Tab.	.954	93	161	272	21	454	68
Martinez, Luis Carlos, Sal.	.954	25	19	43	3	65	11
Arias, Everardo, Pue.	.950	47	92	156	13	261	41
Carrasco, Ernesto, N.L.	.947	11	14	22	2	38	6
Wong Medrano, Julian, Monc.	.946	17	26	44	4	74	8
Valle, Jorge Luis, Tor.	.945	27	40	80	7	127	21
Balderas, S. Abelardo, Min.	.943	18	20	30	3	53	7
Vizcarra, Marco A., Rey.	.942	21	30	83	7	120	23
Duran, Felipe, MCRD	.941	15	21	27	3	51	6
Contreras, Cuitlahuac, Tor.-Monc.	.927	21	22	54	6	82	6
Nunez Avina, Jose Juan, Jal.	.927	11	12	26	3	41	6
Olvera, Sergio, Monc.	.919	68	86	175	23	284	37
Lopez, Gonzalo, Monc.	.909	13	12	28	4	44	5
Rivera, Alberto, Tor.	.906	18	17	41	6	64	11
Salas, Heriberto, Tor.	.880	10	9	13	3	25	4
Jelks, Greg, Cam.	.842	13	28	36	12	76	10

SHORTSTOPS WITH FEWER THAN 10 GAMES

Player, Team	Pct.	G	PO	A	E	TC	DP
Avila, Roberto, Min.	1.000	7	3	15	0	18	4
Rubio, Marco A., Cam.-Min.	1.000	6	10	24	0	34	5
Pardo, Victor Manuel, Pue.	1.000	3	0	7	0	7	0
Solis, Roberto, Pue.	1.000	3	2	2	0	4	0
Felix, Arturo, Yuc.	1.000	2	0	4	0	4	0
Escalante, Marcelo, Sal.	1.000	2	6	0	0	6	0
Perez, Alejandro, N.L.	1.000	2	0	2	0	2	0
Verdugo, Vicente, MCRD	1.000	1	1	2	0	3	0
Garzon, Eliseo, Tab.	1.000	1	2	4	0	6	0
Cantu, Gerardo, Pue.	1.000	1	0	1	0	1	0
Camacho, Adulfo, Yuc.	1.000	1	1	0	0	1	0
Gonzalez, Denio, Yuc.	1.000	1	0	4	0	4	0
Cornejo, Edgar, Sal.	1.000	1	0	2	0	2	0
Flores, Miguel, Mont.	1.000	1	2	3	0	5	0
Castaneda, Rafael, N.L.	1.000	1	2	4	0	6	1

OUTFIELDERS

Player, Team	Pct.	G	PO	A	E	TC	DP
Cruz, Luis Alfonso, Rey.	1.000	95	198	8	0	206	0
Cabreja, Alexis, Pue.	1.000	59	105	8	0	113	2
Valencia, Carlos, Ags.	1.000	49	89	7	0	96	0
Medina, Jose Ramon, Cam.	1.000	47	65	8	0	73	0
Tillman, Rusty, Agu.-Tab.	1.000	46	97	4	0	101	2
Espinoza, Jose M., Monc.	1.000	40	52	8	0	60	2
Maclin, Lonnie, Agu.	1.000	37	67	0	0	67	0
Valenzuela, Jose Luis, Agu.	1.000	33	56	2	0	58	1
Motley, Darryl, Tor.-Agu.	1.000	30	42	3	0	45	1
Soriano, Ricardo, Tor.	1.000	22	18	0	0	18	0
Ojeda, Miguel, MCRD	1.000	21	13	1	0	14	0
Valdez, Jesus, Yuc.	1.000	20	25	1	0	26	0
Santos, Julio, Jal.	1.000	15	31	2	0	33	0
Fariss, Monty, Mont.	1.000	14	22	2	0	24	0
Casillas, Adam, Rey.	1.000	13	18	1	0	19	1
Malpica, Enrique, Agu.	1.000	12	9	2	0	11	0
Moreno, David, Sal.	1.000	12	8	0	0	8	0
Quiroz, Jose Julian, Ags.	1.000	12	19	2	0	21	0
Ortega, Roberto, Tab.	1.000	11	11	0	0	11	0
Payro, Edison, Cam.	1.000	10	5	1	0	6	0
Michel, Domingo, Cam.	1.000	10	17	1	0	18	0
Contreras, Cuitlahuac, Tor.-Monc.	1.000	10	16	1	0	17	0
Tellez, Alonso, Rey.	.995	116	176	10	1	187	1
Arredondo, Luis A., MCRD	.995	111	184	15	1	200	3
Fernandez, Daniel, MCRD	.995	106	186	7	1	194	1
Diaz, Luis Fernando, MCT	.991	70	106	4	1	111	0
Villegas, Fernando, Sal.	.990	92	179	10	2	191	2
Cuevas, Angelo, Tab.-Min.	.990	66	100	3	1	104	0
Torres, Raymundo, Yuc.	.989	45	80	8	1	89	0
Lopez, Gonzalo, Monc.	.988	91	145	13	2	160	4
Noris, Rogelio, N.L.	.988	55	81	3	1	85	0
Valle, Jorge Luis, Tor.	.988	39	71	9	1	81	1
Mendez, Roberto C., MCRD	.987	98	146	5	2	153	0
Dattola, Kevin, Tor.	.987	28	73	4	1	78	1
Herrera, Isidro, Cam.	.984	96	179	2	3	184	1
Enriquez, Graciano, Ags.	.984	62	111	9	2	122	1
Canizalez, Juan Carlos, Mont.	.983	95	164	5	3	172	2
Iturbe, Pedro, Pue.	.982	113	207	13	4	224	0
Fentanes, Oscar, Tab.	.982	60	104	4	2	110	1
Harris, Donald, Agu.-Monc.	.982	51	106	4	2	112	1
Sanchez, Gerardo, N.L.	.981	113	201	6	4	211	0
Arzate, Martin, Jal.	.981	78	146	7	3	156	1
Rubio, Sergio, Yuc.	.981	30	47	5	1	53	0
Gutierrez, Andres, Pue.	.979	36	39	8	1	48	1
Burguillos, Carlos M., Min.	.976	98	193	10	5	208	2
Gutierrez, Jose Luis, Agu.	.976	62	75	5	2	82	0
Mercedes, Luis, Yuc.	.976	52	113	7	3	123	1
Valverde, Raul, Jal.	.976	37	79	1	2	82	0
Brinkley, Darrell, Cam.	.974	98	219	9	6	234	3
Heath, Robert Lee, MCT	.974	93	146	6	4	156	0
Magallanes, William, Tab.	.974	60	110	3	3	116	1
Zamudio, Rafael, Mont.-Agu.	.974	25	38	0	1	39	0
Garcia, Cornelio, Mont.	.973	99	140	5	4	149	1
Rodriguez, Fernando, Tor.	.972	73	99	6	3	108	0
Snider, Van, Tor.	.972	61	97	7	3	107	0
Yuriar, Jesus, Monc.	.971	99	227	9	7	243	5

Player, Team	Pct.	G	PO	A	E	TC	DP
Espinoza, Javier, Cam.	.971	69	130	5	4	139	2
Velazquez, Armando, Agu.	.971	21	34	0	1	35	0
Delgado, Tomas, Tab.	.971	20	29	4	1	34	1
Saenz, Ricardo, N.L.	.970	115	245	17	8	270	1
Castillo, Juan, Ags.	.970	104	216	9	7	232	2
Torres, Eduardo, Sal.	.970	86	122	9	4	135	0
Howell, Patrick, MCT	.970	84	148	11	5	164	0
Agramon, Antonio, Jal.	.970	39	62	3	2	67	0
Alvarez, Hector, Pue.	.969	116	240	14	8	262	3
Cairo, Sergio, Yuc.	.968	45	60	0	2	62	0
Jeter, Shawn, Sal.	.968	17	30	0	1	31	0
Reyna, Luis, Monc.-Tab.	.968	17	29	1	1	31	0
Hernandez, W. Gerardo, Min.	.967	75	165	11	6	182	0
Gamboa, Jose A., Agu.	.967	74	114	4	4	122	0
De Lima, Rafael, Tab.	.967	71	144	3	5	152	1
Garcia, Hector, Tor.	.966	105	185	12	7	204	1
Machiria, Pablo, Ags.	.966	84	134	6	5	145	0
Carrillo, Matias, MCT	.965	86	162	5	6	173	0
Felix, Arturo, Yuc.	.964	36	51	3	2	56	0
Leal, Jose Guadalupe, Cam.	.963	54	99	6	4	109	3
Beltran, Gerardo, Min.	.961	70	119	3	5	127	2
Dominguez, David, MCT-Min.	.961	63	95	4	4	103	0
Housie, Wayne, Yuc.	.960	46	92	3	4	90	0
Gonzalez, Jose, Mont.	.959	103	209	3	9	221	0
Soto, Emison, Pue.	.958	34	39	7	2	48	0
Escalante, Marcelo, Sal.	.957	57	84	4	4	92	1
Ansley, Willie, Agu.	.957	28	41	3	2	46	0
Lopez, Alfredo, Jal.	.957	25	44	0	2	46	0
Pledger, Kinnis E., Tor.	.957	13	21	1	1	23	0
Wright, George, Sal.	.956	110	201	17	10	228	1
Jimenez, Eduardo, Yuc.	.956	91	142	11	7	160	1
Naveda, Edgar, Jal.	.955	38	63	1	3	67	0
Morones, Martin, Monc.	.952	84	154	5	8	167	2
Montalvo, Ivan, MCT	.952	20	20	0	1	21	0
Castillo, Braulio, Rey.	.949	91	159	7	9	175	3
Rodriguez, Boi, N.L.	.946	80	134	6	8	148	0
Orantes, Ramon, Mont.	.946	26	51	2	3	56	1
Tiquet, Lazaro, Tab.	.943	54	78	5	5	88	0
Wearing, Mel, Jal.-Sal.	.943	45	78	5	5	88	1
Abrego, Jesus, Jal.	.941	54	87	9	6	102	0
Guerrero, Jaime, Ags.	.941	12	16	0	1	17	0
Ramirez G., Jesus A., MCRD	.938	33	13	2	1	16	0
Rodriguez, Jose Luis, Agu.	.935	62	99	2	7	108	0
Almendra, Gregorio, Tab.	.929	16	13	0	1	14	0
Ritchie, Greg, Tab.	.929	14	13	0	1	14	0
Trevino, Alejandro, Mont.	.923	21	35	1	3	39	1
Fernandez, Carlos, Jal.	.909	13	20	0	2	22	0
Lopez, Salvador, Rey.	.905	35	35	3	4	42	1
Mitchell, Keith, Tab.	.875	24	28	0	4	32	0
Martinez, Enrique, Mont.	.875	10	6	1	1	8	0

OUTFIELDERS WITH FEWER THAN 10 GAMES

Player, Team	Pct.	G	PO	A	E	TC	DP
Garcia, Rosario, Rey.	1.000	9	5	1	0	6	0
Salgado, Eduardo, MCT	1.000	8	8	0	0	8	0
Robles, Trinidad, MCT-Min.	1.000	7	9	2	0	11	0
Pena, M., Joel, Agu.	1.000	7	8	2	0	10	0
Nunez Avina, Jose Juan, Jal.	1.000	7	9	0	0	9	0
Tejeda, Arturo, N.L.	1.000	6	4	0	0	4	0
Ponce, Hector, Cam.	1.000	5	4	0	0	4	0
Reyes, Ramon, Agu.	1.000	5	4	0	0	4	0
Estrada, Ruben, N.L.	1.000	5	8	0	0	8	0
Arano, Wilfrido, N.L.	1.000	5	2	0	0	2	0
Perez, Francisco, Rey.	1.000	5	7	0	0	7	0
Tatis, Bernardo, MCRD	1.000	4	2	0	0	2	0
Palacios, Alfonso, P., Tab.	1.000	4	1	0	0	1	0
Zambrano, Roberto, Pue.	1.000	4	2	0	0	2	0
Sievers, Carlos, Yuc.	1.000	4	4	0	0	4	0
Morales, Alejandro, Tor.	1.000	4	8	0	0	8	0
Lopez A., Victor M., Jal.	1.000	4	7	0	0	7	0
Gil, Geronimo, MCRD	1.000	3	2	1	0	3	1
Sparks, Greg, MCT	1.000	3	0	1	0	1	0
Aguilera, Armando, Sal.	1.000	3	1	0	0	1	0
Tapia, Jose, Cam.	1.000	2	1	0	0	1	0
Salas, Heriberto, Tor.	1.000	2	2	0	0	2	0
Verdugo, Guadalupe, Tor.	1.000	2	0	1	0	1	0
Wright, Tom, Jal.	1.000	2	3	1	0	4	0
Pena, Luis Alberto, Pue.	1.000	1	3	0	0	3	0
Arvizu, Javier, Cam.	1.000	1	1	0	0	1	0
Jimenez, German, Yuc.-Ags.	1.000	1	2	0	0	2	0
Mendiola, Juan Carlos, Agu.	1.000	1	1	0	0	1	0
Estrada, Ricardo, Min.-Agu.	1.000	1	1	0	0	1	0
Trejo, David, Agu.	1.000	1	2	0	0	2	0
Balderas S., Abelardo, Min.	1.000	1	1	0	0	1	0
Stark, Matt, Rey.	1.000	1	2	0	0	2	0
Perez, Juan Luis, Tor.	1.000	1	1	0	0	1	0
Miranda, Julio Cesar, Tor.	1.000	1	3	1	0	4	0
Arevalo, Guadalupe, Ags.	1.000	1	0	1	0	1	0
Nunez Garcia, Jose J., Jal.	1.000	1	1	0	0	1	0
Quintana, Carlos, Min.-Yuc.	.947	8	17	1	1	19	0
Wong Medrano, Julian, Monc.	.929	8	13	0	1	14	0
Paez, Raul, MCRD	.889	7	7	1	1	9	0
Chan, Armando, Monc.	.889	7	8	0	1	9	0
Cecena, Manuel, Min.	.875	3	7	0	1	8	0
Rodriguez, Serafin, Pue.	.857	5	6	0	1	7	0
Alvarez, Luis, Jal.	.850	7	15	2	3	20	0
Hecht, Steve, Monc.	.750	2	3	0	1	4	0
Cervera, Francisco, Jal.	.333	1	0	1	2	3	1
Gainey, Ty, MCRD	.000	1	0	0	1	1	0

CATCHERS

Player, Team	Pct.	G	PO	A	E	TC	DP	PB
Meza, Alfredo, Mont.	1.000	32	89	12	0	101	1	1
Vazquez, Felipe, MCRD	1.000	26	62	6	0	68	0	3
Pena, Carlos, Yuc.	1.000	14	49	4	0	53	1	2
Campos, Oscar, Agu.	1.000	10	15	1	0	16	0	2
Mendez, Ramon, Ags.	.994	41	158	15	1	174	3	5
Ruiz, Demetrio, Jal.-Tab.	.993	34	122	24	1	147	2	1
Ojeda, Miguel, MCRD	.992	24	106	11	1	118	2	2
Hernandez, Miguel, Agu.	.991	49	187	35	2	224	6	1
Valdez, Francisco J., Rey.	.989	73	328	39	4	371	4	3
Gastelum, Carlos, Min.	.989	59	248	28	3	279	2	2
Duarte C., Rene, Min.	.988	63	209	35	3	247	4	8
Reyes, Gilberto, Cam.	.987	110	390	59	6	455	8	8
Abrego, Jesus, Jal.	.987	40	188	33	3	224	3	4
Vega V., Edgar, MCT	.986	77	330	37	5	372	2	3
Cazarin, Manuel, Agu.	.986	77	295	58	5	358	7	6
Villanueva, Hector, MCT	.986	27	136	9	2	147	1	4
Garzon, Eliseo, Tab.	.985	99	459	61	8	528	6	3
Ramirez, Efren, Ags.	.985	87	385	68	7	460	7	4
Cruz, Marco Antonio, N.L.	.984	115	572	54	10	636	6	8
Luna, Jose Luis, Sal.	.984	93	424	53	8	485	7	7
Samaniego, Manuel, Monc.	.984	53	218	27	4	249	3	2
Arauz, Ignacio, Monc.	.984	39	154	26	3	183	4	4
Rojas, Homar, MCRD	.983	89	489	39	9	537	2	8
Canedo, Alberto, Cam.	.983	31	53	6	1	60	1	0
Garza, Gerardo, Tor.	.982	108	470	73	10	553	9	9
Estrada, Hector, Pue.	.981	85	336	33	7	376	5	5
Trevino, Alejandro, Mont.	.981	66	262	44	6	312	6	2
Hurtado, Hector, Mont.	.981	55	228	24	5	257	4	4
Gavia, Jesus, Agu.-Min.	.980	14	38	10	1	49	1	1
Rivera, Eleazar, Monc.	.980	11	47	3	1	51	0	1
Ochoa, Marin Edgar, MCT	.979	46	128	15	3	146	2	1
Osuna, Hector, Yuc.	.977	30	111	15	3	129	2	1
Rodriguez, Ruben, Monc.	.973	19	98	12	3	113	2	1
Munoz, Noe, Rey.	.972	35	185	25	6	216	2	0
Monroy, Victor Hugo, Rey.	.971	24	86	15	3	104	0	1
Machorro, Roberto, Monc.	.969	16	56	7	2	65	0	1
Guzman, Marco A., Yuc.	.967	96	359	49	14	422	4	9
Perez, Juan Luis, Tor.	.962	21	44	7	2	53	1	2
Valenzuela, Eduardo, Sal.	.960	48	128	15	6	149	0	0
Lopez A., Victor M., Jal.	.957	63	240	33	12	285	5	5
Cantu, Gerardo, Pue.	.957	24	60	6	3	69	3	0
Pulido, Jesus, N.L.	.941	11	14	2	1	17	0	1
Soto, Emison, Pue.	.928	17	65	12	6	83	1	4
Corrales, Virgilio, N.L.	.895	12	15	2	2	19	0	2

CATCHERS WITH FEWER THAN 10 GAMES

Player, Team	Pct.	G	PO	A	E	TC	DP	PB
Aguilera, Armando, Sal.	1.000	8	5	0	0	5	0	0
Dominguez, Fausto, Tab.	1.000	3	6	0	0	6	0	1
Elvira, Ramon H., Tab.	1.000	2	2	0	0	2	0	0
Martinez, Raul, Sal.	1.000	1	1	0	0	1	0	0
Avila, Ruben, Sal.	1.000	1	2	0	0	2	0	0
Cueto, Raul, Tab.	.933	4	14	0	1	15	0	0

PITCHERS

Player, Team	Pct.	G	PO	A	E	TC	DP
Villegas, Jose Angel, Ags.	1.000	52	4	9	0	13	1
Herrera, Calixto, Monc.	1.000	50	2	20	0	22	1
Murillo, Felipe, Monc.	1.000	43	0	6	0	6	0
Pina, Rafael, MCRD	1.000	42	4	11	0	15	0
Miranda, Julio Cesar, Tor.	1.000	41	4	4	0	8	0
Grajales, Norberto, Tor.	1.000	41	5	21	0	26	3
Pimentel, Roberto, Tor.-Monc.	1.000	39	4	8	0	12	1

Player, Team	Pct.	G	PO	A	E	TC	DP
Segura, Jose, Yuc.	1.000	38	5	7	0	12	0
Garcia, R. Miguel, Min.	1.000	38	7	16	0	23	2
Cecena, Jose Isabel, Sal.	1.000	38	1	7	0	8	0
Del Toro, Miguel, MCRD-Rey.	1.000	37	6	9	0	15	0
Sombra, Francisco, Sal.	1.000	37	3	9	0	12	0
Garcia Cruz, Jose Luis, MCT	1.000	36	1	10	0	11	1
Lopez, De La T., Jose J., Min.	1.000	36	4	4	0	8	0
Hernandez, Encarn'cn, Jal.-Monc.	1.000	36	2	11	0	13	1
Bencomo, Omar, Sal.-Jal.	1.000	35	2	11	0	13	1
Barron, Avelino, Sal.	1.000	35	3	12	0	15	2
Cruz, Javier, Rey.	1.000	35	2	11	0	13	1
Cazares, Juan, Jal.-Mont.	1.000	35	1	7	0	8	0
Villarreal, Antonio, Mont.-Yuc.	1.000	34	2	19	0	21	1
Perez, Leonardo, Mont.	1.000	34	1	7	0	8	0
Zappelli, Mark, Sal.	1.000	33	12	17	0	29	0
Quintanilla, Enrique, N.L.	1.000	33	3	9	0	12	1
Cabrales, Gabriel, Tab.	1.000	32	1	18	0	19	1
Sandoval, Carlos, Min.	1.000	32	2	9	0	11	0
Carrasco, Alejandro, MCRD	1.000	30	2	5	0	7	1
Lewis, Scott, Mont.	1.000	30	0	6	0	6	0
Valencia, Jorge, Sal.	1.000	29	8	22	0	30	0
Alicea, Miguel, Tor.	1.000	28	2	4	0	6	1
Villanueva, Luis, Ags.	1.000	28	1	3	0	4	1
Rincon, Ricardo, MCRD	1.000	27	2	12	0	14	2
Leyva, Carlos Armando, MCT	1.000	26	1	4	0	5	0
Garcia, Mike, Tab.	1.000	26	4	9	0	13	0
Toledo, Mario, Cam.	1.000	26	1	6	0	7	0
Rodriguez, Mario A., Min.	1.000	26	4	16	0	20	2
Antunez, Martin, Jal.	1.000	26	6	11	0	17	0
Lopez, Emigdio, Tab.	1.000	25	18	32	0	50	1
Tinoco, Ruben, Cam.	1.000	25	0	16	0	16	2
Sierra, Abel, Cam.	1.000	24	3	9	0	12	1
Hernandez, Martin, Yuc.	1.000	24	3	12	0	15	2
Sanchez, Hector, Agu.-Mont.	1.000	24	5	7	0	12	1
Diaz, Alejandro, Agu.	1.000	24	7	12	0	19	3
Aguilar, Jose Miguel, Min.-Tab.	1.000	24	4	18	0	22	1
Enriquez, Martin, Agu.	1.000	24	5	18	0	23	0
Ramos, Jorge Luis, Pue.	1.000	23	2	7	0	9	0
Solis, Ricardo, Yuc.	1.000	23	6	24	0	30	2
Rivera, Hector, Rey.-Agu.	1.000	23	7	18	0	25	1
Garibay, Salvador, Ags.	1.000	23	4	7	0	11	1
Quiroz, Jose Julian, Ags.	1.000	23	4	4	0	8	2
Draper, Mike, MCT	1.000	22	4	3	0	7	0
Valenzuela, Saul, Pue.	1.000	22	9	35	0	44	1
Camacho, Adrian, Min.	1.000	22	1	7	0	8	0
Heredia, Hector, Mont.	1.000	22	8	24	0	32	1
Moreno, Angel, N.L.	1.000	22	11	33	0	44	3
Renteria, Hilario, Tor.	1.000	22	7	17	0	24	1
Vazquez, Aguedo, Ags.	1.000	22	9	10	0	19	1
Moreno, Leobardo, MCRD	1.000	21	1	8	0	9	0
Garibay, Bravo Daniel, MCT	1.000	21	0	5	0	5	1
Neri, Braulio, Yuc.-Tor.	1.000	21	2	3	0	5	0
Leyva, Filiberto, Mont.	1.000	21	0	1	0	1	0
Diaz, Marcos, Mont.	1.000	21	1	12	0	13	1
Green, Otis, Mont.	1.000	21	2	7	0	9	0
Mendez, Luis Fernando, Rey.	1.000	21	10	13	0	23	2
Palafox, Juan Manuel, Tor.	1.000	21	10	17	0	27	1
Flores, Ignacio, Tor.	1.000	21	1	2	0	3	0
Ramirez, Roberto, MCRD	1.000	20	6	35	0	41	7
Munoz, Miguel, Agu.-Rey.	1.000	20	6	31	0	37	3
Lopez, Jonas, Ags.	1.000	20	3	3	0	6	1
Cimorelli, Frank, Cam.	1.000	19	3	4	0	7	1
Garza, Roberto, Rey.-N.L.	1.000	19	3	6	0	9	0
Velazquez, Ernesto A., Tor.-Sal.	1.000	19	5	2	0	7	0
Vargas, Ignacio, Mont.	1.000	18	3	15	0	18	5
Jimenez, German, Yuc.-Ags.	1.000	18	3	15	0	18	0
Gonzalez, Arturo, Mont.	1.000	18	0	19	0	19	3
Elvira, Narciso, Mont.	1.000	18	3	12	0	15	2
Castillo, Felipe, MCRD	1.000	17	2	2	0	4	1
Villegas, Ramon, Pue.	1.000	17	2	2	0	4	0
Cruz, Juan Diego, Yuc.	1.000	17	1	3	0	4	0
Molina, Joaquin, Tor.	1.000	17	4	8	0	12	0
Figueroa, Fernando, Tor.	1.000	17	12	28	0	40	3
Nunez Avina, Jose Juan, Jal.	1.000	17	1	7	0	8	0
Garcia, David, Monc.	1.000	16	0	2	0	2	0
Arrington, Tom, Jal.	1.000	16	4	16	0	20	0
Cazares, Tomas, MCRD-Rey.	1.000	15	2	6	0	8	0
Cota, Armando, Tab.	1.000	15	0	5	0	5	1
Henry, John, Pue.	1.000	15	10	10	0	20	0
Valdez, Jose Luis, N.L.	1.000	15	0	3	0	3	0
Wagner, Hector, Ags.	1.000	15	1	8	0	9	0
Perez, Vladimir, Rey.	1.000	14	1	3	0	4	0
Mansur, Jeff, Pue.	1.000	13	1	5	0	6	0
Hernandez, Ramon, Mont.	1.000	13	1	2	0	3	0
Hernandez, Dimas C., Monc.	1.000	13	2	4	0	6	0
Strauss, Julio Cesar, Tab.	1.000	12	0	4	0	4	1
Salgado, Eduardo, MCT	1.000	11	1	1	0	2	0
Del Valle, Enrique, MCT-Agu.	1.000	11	1	2	0	3	1
Inzunza, Jorge, Tab.	1.000	11	1	1	0	2	0
Llanes, Emeterio, Yuc.	1.000	11	1	0	0	1	0
Rodriguez, Rosario, Mont.	1.000	11	0	1	0	1	0
Chapin, Darrin, Rey.	1.000	11	2	3	0	5	0
Moreno, Ricardo, MCT-N.L.	1.000	10	0	1	0	1	0
Juarez, Fernando, Tor.	1.000	10	0	4	0	4	0
Gomez, Jesus A., Monc.	1.000	10	0	3	0	3	0
Ruiz, Cecilio, Tab.	.978	24	6	39	1	46	2
Purata, Julio, Rey.	.974	22	4	33	1	38	2
Huerta, Luis Enrique, Pue.	.972	22	9	26	1	36	1
Jimenez, Issac, Yuc.	.971	19	6	28	1	35	1
Vazquez, Adrian, Cam.	.969	21	10	21	1	32	1
Carranza, Javier, Rey.	.967	21	9	20	1	30	0
Hernandez, Jose M., N.L.	.966	47	9	19	1	29	1
Moreno, Jesus, Sal.	.964	22	6	21	1	28	2
Acosta, Aaron, Tor.	.964	21	11	16	1	28	1
Soto, Fernando, Min.	.962	25	5	20	1	26	1
Cruz, Andres, Yuc.	.962	23	6	19	1	26	0
Herrera, Enrique, Agu.	.960	34	5	19	1	25	0
Kelley, Drum Richard, Monc.	.960	12	3	21	1	25	2
Orozco, Jaime, Pue.	.952	23	10	30	2	42	3
Osuna, Roberto, N.L.	.950	25	4	15	1	20	0
Vega, Obed, MCT	.950	18	6	13	1	20	2
Lara, Jorge, Rey.	.947	39	7	11	1	19	1
Romero, Juan, Tab.	.947	29	8	10	1	19	1
Hernandez, Manuel A., MCRD	.947	23	9	27	2	38	3
Jones, Al, Tor.	.947	17	4	14	1	19	4
Esquer, Mercedes, Yuc.-Mont.	.947	13	3	15	1	19	1
Lind, Orlando, Rey.	.947	12	6	12	1	19	1
Cuervo, Bernardo, Cam.	.946	28	7	28	2	37	1
Luevano, Juan, Agu.	.944	41	3	14	1	18	0
Couoh, Enrique, MCT	.944	39	7	10	1	18	0
Velazquez, Israel, Min.	.944	23	4	13	1	18	1
Cano, Ezequiel, Jal.	.944	17	2	15	1	18	0
Alvarez, Juan Jesus, MCT	.943	23	4	29	2	35	1
Barfield, John David, N.L.	.941	34	4	12	1	17	1
Cervantes, Lauro, Ags.-Agu.	.941	14	5	11	1	17	0
Saenz, Alfredo, Pue.	.939	26	6	25	2	33	0
Munoz, Ricardo, Tab.	.939	22	10	36	3	49	3
Raygoza, Martin, Monc.	.939	21	4	27	2	33	1
Barraza, Ernesto, MCT	.935	24	12	31	3	46	0
Cordova, Francisco, MCRD	.933	27	5	23	2	30	0
Valdez, Rafael, Rey.-Yuc.	.933	22	4	10	1	15	0
Cano, Jose, Ags.	.933	21	8	20	2	30	4
Rojo, Oscar, Cam.-Rey.	.929	34	3	10	1	14	1
Solarte, Jose A., Min.	.926	45	7	18	2	27	1
Puig, Benny, Ags.-Tor.	.926	16	3	22	2	27	3
Neri, Eduardo, Agu.	.923	51	5	31	3	39	5
Garibay, Roberto, Pue.	.923	40	5	7	1	13	0
Serna, Ramon, Ags.	.923	30	3	9	1	13	0
Rios, Jesus, MCT	.923	25	4	20	2	26	0
Saldana, Edgardo, Agu.-Tab.	.923	23	5	19	2	26	0
Gomez Rios, Martin, Min.	.923	23	9	15	2	26	1
Baez, Sixto, Agu.	.917	28	5	17	2	24	3
Quinones, Enrique, Yuc.	.917	25	1	10	1	12	2
Lara, Hugo, Cam.	.917	24	6	27	3	36	1
Reyes, Dennis, MCRD	.917	17	3	8	1	12	0
Romo, Guillermo, Tor.	.917	15	2	9	1	12	0
Cruz Soto, Antonio, Pue.	.917	14	1	10	1	12	1
Iniguez, Dario, Jal.	.917	11	4	7	1	12	0
Quiroz, Aaron, N.L.	.913	23	3	18	2	23	2
Lizarraga, Hugo, Cam.	.909	24	2	8	1	11	0
Wayne, Gary, MCRD-Monc.	.909	22	2	8	1	11	0
Martinez, Filiberto, Sal.	.909	19	3	18	2	23	1
Rodriguez, Raul, Sal.	.903	23	5	23	3	31	4
Dominguez, Herminio, Cam.	.900	39	0	9	1	10	1
Cazares, Rosario, Tab.	.900	34	4	5	1	10	0
Diaz, Cesar, N.L.	.900	29	3	6	1	10	0
Hurst, Jonathan, Jal.-Mont.	.900	28	5	4	1	10	1
Retes, Lorenzo, Tab.-Min.	.900	24	6	12	2	20	2
Walker, Mark, MCRD	.900	19	2	7	1	10	2
Franklin, Jay, Mont.-Ags.	.897	22	7	19	3	29	1
Mejia, Cesar, Cam.	.895	24	5	12	2	19	1
Perry, Jeff, N.L.	.889	25	6	10	2	18	0
Hernandez, Julio, Agu.	.886	21	9	22	4	35	3
Sandoval, Guillermo, Mont.	.882	33	2	13	2	17	0
Uribe, Juan Carlos, Yuc.	.875	43	2	5	1	8	0
Tejeda, Juan, Cam.	.875	27	2	12	2	16	1

Player, Team	Pct.	G	PO	A	E	TC	DP
Navarro, Luis A., Sal.	.875	19	4	3	1	8	0
Rodriguez, Mario A., Rey.	.875	12	4	3	1	8	0
Flynt, Will, MCRD	.875	10	2	5	1	8	0
Castro, Leonel, Jal.	.871	19	9	18	4	31	1
Mora, Eleazar, Agu.	.864	23	8	11	3	22	3
Veliz, A., Francisco, Sal.-Monc.	.857	19	1	5	1	7	2
Sanchez, Jose Luis, Jal.	.857	14	2	4	1	7	0
Jimenez, Cesar D., Monc.	.846	14	4	7	2	13	0
Delfin, Adolfo, MCT	.833	37	1	9	2	12	2
Cruz, Juan Alonso, Jal.	.833	26	0	5	1	6	0
Benitez, Francisco, Jal.-Jal.	.833	11	0	5	1	6	0
Rodriguez, Rene, N.L.	.818	32	2	7	2	11	0
Leal, Gerardo, Monc.	.818	25	3	6	2	11	0
Montano, Francisco, Monc.	.818	22	6	12	4	22	0
Moreno, Claudio, MCRD	.786	27	4	7	3	14	1
Tunnell, Lee, MCT	.778	14	0	7	2	9	0
Rivera, Paul, Ags.	.778	14	0	7	2	9	0
Agosto, Juan, Mont.-Ags.	.750	17	1	5	2	8	0
Martinez, Mauricio, Sal.	.750	11	0	3	1	4	0
Rodriguez, Salvador, Yuc.	.750	10	0	3	1	4	1
Pruneda, Armando, Monc.	.750	10	0	3	1	4	0
Gonzalez, Victor M., Jal.	.739	32	6	11	6	23	3
Minutelli, Gino, MCT	.667	12	1	3	2	6	0
Baller, Jay, MCRD	.600	16	0	3	2	5	0
Munoz, Pablo, Pue.	.000	10	0	0	1	1	0

PITCHERS WITH FEWER THAN 10 GAMES

Player, Team	Pct.	G	PO	A	E	TC	DP
Browning, Mike, Cam.	1.000	9	0	3	0	3	1
Loaiza, Sabino, Cam.	1.000	9	5	3	0	8	0
Navarro, Adolfo, Ags.	1.000	9	2	8	0	10	0
Moreno, Ricardo, Jal.	1.000	9	0	2	0	2	0
Lynch, Dave, MCT	1.000	8	1	9	0	10	1
Osuna, Ricardo, Tab.	1.000	8	2	9	0	11	2
Guerra, Esmili, Pue.	1.000	8	0	2	0	2	0
Gutierrez, Arturo, Agu.	1.000	8	0	6	0	6	1
Lopez, Gilberto, Agu.	1.000	8	2	3	0	5	0
Ramirez, Miguel A., Jal.	1.000	8	2	3	0	5	1
Martinez, Ramon, Pue.	1.000	7	0	1	0	1	0
Valenzuela, Aurelio, Yuc.	1.000	7	0	1	0	1	0

Player, Team	Pct.	G	PO	A	E	TC	DP
Meza, Leobardo, Agu.	1.000	7	2	4	0	6	1
Smith, Daryl, Sal.	1.000	7	0	5	0	5	0
Olague, Jesus, Mont.	1.000	7	0	3	0	3	0
Brumley, Duff, Mont.-Ags.	1.000	7	0	5	0	5	1
Ochoa, Porfirio, N.L.	1.000	7	0	2	0	2	0
Ayrault, Bob, Monc.	1.000	7	0	6	0	6	0
Espinoza, Rogelio, Jal.	1.000	7	0	1	0	1	0
Dehesa, Noel, Tab.	1.000	6	1	0	0	1	0
Valenzuela, Jorge, Pue.	1.000	6	1	0	0	1	0
Macias, Abraham, Agu.	1.000	6	2	2	0	4	0
Galvez, Rosario, N.L.	1.000	6	0	2	0	2	0
Burcham, Tim, Jal.	1.000	6	3	8	0	11	0
Campos, Francisco, Cam.	1.000	5	0	1	0	1	0
Leon, Danilo, N.L.	1.000	5	0	2	0	2	0
Martin, Daniel, Yuc.	1.000	5	0	1	0	1	0
Ortega, Pablo, N.L.	1.000	5	1	2	0	3	0
Quintero, Victor Hugo, Tor.	1.000	5	0	1	0	1	0
Rivera, Lino, Monc.	1.000	5	0	5	0	5	0
Ramirez, Martin, Ags.	1.000	5	0	1	0	1	0
Vargas, Joel, Jal.	1.000	4	1	0	0	1	0
Mack, Tony Len, Tor.	1.000	4	0	3	0	3	0
Castillo, Luis Trinidad, Monc.	1.000	4	1	1	0	2	0
Soto, Ramon E., Yuc.	1.000	3	0	1	0	1	0
Calderon, Manaces, Min.	1.000	3	0	1	0	1	0
Klvac, David John, Tor.	1.000	3	0	1	0	1	0
Lewis, Craig, Monc.	1.000	3	1	4	0	5	0
Pulido, Raymundo, MCT	1.000	2	0	1	0	1	0
Martinez, Sean, Pue.	1.000	2	1	0	0	1	0
Conde, Ricardo, Yuc.	1.000	2	1	1	0	2	0
Pena, Alejandro, Mont.	1.000	2	1	0	0	1	0
Burlingame, Dennis, Monc.	1.000	2	1	2	0	3	0
Camacho, Adulfo, Yuc.	1.000	1	1	0	0	1	0
Contreras, Cuitlahuac, Tor.-Monc.	1.000	1	0	1	0	1	0
Ledon, Juan Carlos, Jal.	.909	9	4	6	1	11	0
Sadecki, Steve, Jal.	.800	5	2	2	1	5	0
Alvarez, Ivan, Jal.	.750	6	2	1	1	4	0
Arano, Ramon, Agu.	.750	5	0	3	1	4	0
Pelcastregui, Leonardo, Tor.	.750	5	0	3	1	4	0
Cardenas, Benito, N.L.	.667	5	0	2	1	3	0
Pinero, Hugo Jose, Min.	.500	3	0	1	1	2	0

LEAGUE CHAMPIONS

Year	Team	Pct.
1955—	Mexico City Tigers*	.539
1956—	Mexico City Reds	.692
1957—	Yucatan	.567
	Mex. C. Reds (2nd)†	.550
1958—	Nuevo Laredo	.625
1959—	Poza Rica	.575
	Mex. C. Reds (3rd)†	.507
1960—	Mexico City Tigers	.538
1961—	Veracruz	.575
1962—	Monterrey	.592
1963—	Puebla	.606
1964—	Mexico City Reds	.586
1965—	Mexico City Tigers	.590
1966—	Mexico City Tigers‡	.614
	Mexico City Reds	.571
1967—	Jalisco	.607
1968—	Mexico City Reds	.586
1969—	Reynosa	.591
1970—	Aguila§	.580
	Mexico City Reds	.607
1971—	Jalisco§	.558
	Saltillo	.593
1972—	Saltillo	.636
	Cordoba§	.541

Year	Team	Pct.
1973—	Saltillo	.656
	Mexico City Reds∞	.590
1974—	Jalisco	.627
	Mexico City Reds∞	.551
1975—	Tampico∞	.541
	Cordoba	.649
1976—	Mexico City Reds∞	.543
	Union Laguna	.547
1977—	Mexico City Reds	.623
	Nuevo Laredo∞	.507
1978—	Aguascalientes∞	.589
	Union Laguna	.523
1979—	Saltillo	.704
	Puebla∞	.628
1980—	No champion▲	
1981—	Mexico City Reds	.615
	Reynosa	.492
1982—	Ciudad Juarez∞	.570
	Mexico City Tigers	.508
1983—	Campeche◆	.614
	Ciudad Juarez	.535
1984—	Yucatan◆	.560
	Ciudad Juarez	.509
1985—	Mexico City Reds◆	.606
	Nuevo Laredo	5275

Year	Team	Pct.
1986—	Puebla◆	.682
	Monclova	.598
1987—	Mexico City Reds◆	.605
	Monterrey	.536
1988—	Mexico City Reds◆	.646
	Nuevo Laredo	.602
1989—	Nuevo Laredo◆	.621
	Yucatan	.539
1990—	Nuevo Laredo	.618
	Leon◆	.565
1991—	Monterrey◆	.683
	Mexico City Reds	.627
1992—	Mexico City Tigers◆	.594
	Nuevo Laredo	.538
1993—	Nuevo Laredo	.589
	Tabasco◆	.528
1994—	Mexico City Red Devils◆	.646
	Monterrey Sultans	.608
1995—	Mexico City Red Devils	.708
	Monterrey Sultans◆	.570

*Defeated Nuevo Laredo, two games to none, in playoff for pennant. †Won four-team playoff. ‡Won split-season playoff. §League divided into Northern, Southern divisions; won two-team playoff. ∞League divided into Northern, Southern zones; sub-divided into Eastern, Western divisions, won eight-team playoff. ▲A players strike on July 1 forced the cancellation of the regular season and playoff schedule. ◆League divided into Northern, Southern zones; four clubs from each zone qualified for postseason play. Won final series for league championship.

CLASS AAA *Mexican League*

PACIFIC COAST LEAGUE

LEAGUE OFFICE

President/secretary-treasurer
Bill Cutler

Address
2345 S. Alma School Rd., Suite 110
Mesa, AZ 85210

Phone
602-838-2171

TEAMS

ALBUQUERQUE DUKES

General manager
Pat McKernan
Manager
Phil Regan
Ballpark (capacity, surface)
Albuquerque Sports Stadium (10,510, grass)
Affiliation
Dodgers
Address
1601 Stadium Blvd. SE
Albuquerque, NM 87106
Phone
505-243-1791

CALGARY CANNONS

General manager
Tom Valcke
Manager
Trent Jewitt
Ballpark (capacity, surface)
Name to be announced (7,500, grass)
Affiliation
Pirates
Address
P.O. Box 3690, Station B
Calgary, Alberta T2M 4M4
Phone
403-284-1111

COLORADO SPRINGS SKY SOX

General manager
Robert Goughan
Manager
Brad Mills
Ballpark (capacity, surface)
Sky Sox Stadium (8,500, grass)
Affiliation
Rockies
Address
4385 Tutt Blvd.
Colorado Springs, CO 80922
Phone
719-597-1449

EDMONTON TRAPPERS

President/general manager
Mel Kowalchuk
Manager
Gary Jones
Ballpark (capacity, surface)
John Ducey Park (10,000; artificial infield, grass outfield)
Affiliation
Athletics
Address
10233 96th Ave.
Edmonton, Alberta T5K 0A5
Phone
403-429-2934

LAS VEGAS STARS

General manager
Don Logan
Manager
Tim Flannery
Ballpark (capacity, surface)
Cashman Field (9,370, grass)
Affiliation
Padres
Address
850 Las Vegas Blvd. N
Las Vegas, NV 89101
Phone
702-386-7200

PHOENIX FIREBIRDS

Vice president/general manager
Craig Pletenik
Manager
Jim Davenport
Ballpark (capacity, surface)
Scottsdale Stadium (11,200, grass)
Affiliation
Giants
Address
P.O. Box 8528
Scottsdale, AZ 85252
Phone
602-275-0500

SALT LAKE BUZZ

Vice president/general manager
Tammy Felker-White
Manager
Phil Roof
Ballpark (capacity, surface)
Franklin-Quest Field (15,000, grass)
Affiliation
Twins

Address
P.O. Box 4108
Salt Lake City, UT 84110
Phone
801-485-3800

TACOMA RAINIERS

President/general manager
Dave Bean
Manager
Dave Myers
Ballpark (capacity, surface)
Cheney Stadium (10,106, grass)
Affiliation
Mariners
Address
P.O. Box 11087
Tacoma, WA 98411
Phone
206-752-7707

TUCSON TOROS

General manager
Mike Feder
Manager
Tim Tolman
Ballpark (capacity, surface)
Hi Corbett Field (8,000, grass)
Affiliation
Astros
Address
P.O. Box 27045
Tucson, AZ 85716
Phone
602-325-2621

VANCOUVER CANADIANS

Vice president/general manager
Brent Imlach
Manager
Don Long
Ballpark (capacity, surface)
Nat Bailey Stadium (6,500, grass)
Affiliation
Angels
Address
4601 Ontario St.
Vancouver, B.C. V5V 3H4
Phone
604-872-5232

CLASS AAA Pacific Coast League

1995 FINAL STANDINGS

FIRST HALF

NORTHERN DIVISION

Team	W	L	T	Pct.	GB
Vancouver (Angels)	45	27	0	.625	......
Salt Lake (Twins)	38	34	0	.528	7
Tacoma (Mariners)	37	35	0	.514	8
Edmonton (Athletics)	35	37	0	.486	10
Calgary (Pirates)	30	41	0	.423	14½

SOUTHERN DIVISION

Team	W	L	T	Pct.	GB
Colorado Springs (Rockies)	39	33	0	.542	......
Albuquerque (Dodgers)	38	34	0	.528	1
Tucson (Astros)	37	34	0	.521	1½
Phoenix (Giants)	34	38	0	.472	5
Las Vegas (Padres)	26	46	0	.361	13

SECOND HALF

NORTHERN DIVISION

Team	W	L	T	Pct.	GB
Salt Lake (Twins)	41	31	0	.569	....
Vancouver (Angels)	36	33	0	.522	3½
Edmonton (Athletics)	33	39	0	.458	8
Tacoma (Mariners)	31	41	0	.431	10
Calgary (Pirates)	28	42	0	.400	12

SOUTHERN DIVISION

Team	W	L	T	Pct.	GB
Tucson (Astros)	50	22	0	.694	....
Colorado Springs (Rockies)	38	33	0	.535	11½
Albuquerque (Dodgers)	37	35	0	.514	13
Las Vegas (Padres)	35	37	0	.486	15
Phoenix (Giants)	28	44	0	.389	22

COMPOSITE

Team	Tuc.	Van.	SLC	C.S.	Alb.	Tac.	Edm.	Phx.	L.V.	Cal.	W	L	T	Pct.	GB
Tucson (Astros)	....	8	9	8	4	12	10	14	10	12	87	56	0	.608	....
Vancouver (Angels)	8	....	8	6	8	12	8	12	9	10	81	60	0	.574	5
Salt Lake (Twins)	7	8	....	9	11	7	9	9	10	9	79	65	0	.549	8½
Colorado Springs (Rockies)	8	9	7	....	7	9	9	9	8	11	77	66	0	.538	10
Albuquerque (Dodgers)	12	8	5	9	....	7	7	9	8	10	75	69	0	.521	12½
Tacoma (Mariners)	4	4	9	7	9	....	11	7	11	6	68	76	0	.472	19½
Edmonton (Athletics)	6	8	7	7	9	5	....	9	8	9	68	76	0	.472	19½
Phoenix (Giants)	2	4	7	7	7	9	7	....	11	8	62	82	0	.431	25½
Las Vegas (Padres)	6	7	6	8	8	5	8	5	....	8	61	83	0	.424	26½
Calgary (Pirates)	3	4	7	5	6	10	7	8	8	....	58	83	0	.411	28

Major league affiliations in parentheses.

PLAYOFFS: Colorado Springs defeated Tucson, three games to one; Salt Lake defeated Vancouver, three games to one; Colorado Springs defeated Salt Lake, three games to two, to win league championship.

REGULAR-SEASON ATTENDANCE: Albuquerque, 340,050; Calgary, 279,054; Colorado Springs, 195,375; Edmonton, 426,012; Las Vegas, 330,869; Phoenix, 282,370; Salt Lake, 637,332; Tacoma, 316,103; Tucson, 301,963; Vancouver, 305,739. Total, 3,414,867. Playoffs (12 games)—43,642. Class AAA All-Star Game at Scranton/Wilkes-Barre—10,965.

MANAGERS: Albuquerque, Rick Dempsey; Calgary, Bobby Meacham; Colorado Springs, Brad Mills; Edmonton, Gary Jones; Las Vegas, Tim Flannery; Phoenix, Jim Davenport; Salt Lake, Phil Roof; Tacoma, Steve Smith; Tucson, Rick Sweet; Vancouver, Don Long.

ALL-STAR TEAM: 1B—Mike Busch, Albuquerque; 2B—Dave Hajek, Tucson; 3B—Ron Coomer, Albuquerque; SS—Fausto Cruz, Edmonton; OF—Trent Hubbard, Colorado Springs; Riccardo Ingram, Salt Lake; Karim Garcia, Albuquerque; C—George Williams, Edmonton; DH—Harvey Pulliam, Colorado Springs; RHP—Donne Wall, Tucson; LHP—Glenn Dishman, Las Vegas; Relief Pitcher—Scott Watkins, Salt Lake; Most Valuable Player—Donne Wall, Tucson; Manager of the Year—Don Long, Vancouver.

1995 BATTING

TEAM

Team	Avg.	G	TPA	AB	R	H	TB	2B	3B	HR	RBI	SH	SF	HP	BB	IBB	SO	SB	CS	GDP	LOB	ShO	Slg.	OBP
Salt Lake	.304	144	5589	4987	831	1516	2259	332	45	107	769	38	52	57	455	30	712	132	65	132	1025	6	.453	.365
Calgary	.302	141	5335	4812	743	1451	2145	306	35	106	697	37	50	38	398	39	704	98	58	110	987	10	.446	.356
Colo. Springs	.291	143	5395	4819	821	1403	2273	293	53	157	770	46	50	34	444	49	829	105	50	96	952	3	.472	.352
Tucson	.289	143	5514	4816	786	1393	2071	285	63	89	726	54	54	34	555	48	848	134	68	114	1034	4	.430	.363
Albuquerque	.285	144	5459	4901	754	1396	2110	277	52	111	691	46	27	32	452	38	821	92	71	134	968	10	.431	.347
Vancouver	.281	141	5359	4726	723	1328	1879	237	43	76	648	42	46	39	504	40	755	114	52	110	1007	14	.398	.352
Tacoma	.279	144	5429	4874	682	1358	2028	230	49	114	664	43	42	34	436	25	845	106	46	119	987	8	.416	.339
Edmonton	.278	144	5511	4816	759	1340	1979	295	43	86	685	49	61	44	541	35	811	80	45	126	1024	6	.411	.352
Las Vegas	.271	144	5363	4789	663	1300	1867	254	32	83	602	49	51	42	437	35	840	77	43	126	986	8	.390	.334
Phoenix	.265	144	5575	4871	658	1289	1878	258	44	81	604	63	62	54	525	38	791	66	58	115	1059	5	.386	.339

INDIVIDUAL

TOP QUALIFIERS FOR BATTING CHAMPIONSHIP

Minimum 389 plate appearances. *Lefthanded batter. †Switch-hitter.

Player, Team	Avg.	G	TPA	AB	R	H	TB	2B	3B	HR	RBI	SH	SF	HP	BB	IBB	SO	SB	CS	GDP	Slg.	OBP
Ingram, Riccardo, Salt Lake	.348	122	526	477	80	166	249	43	2	12	85	0	5	3	41	3	60	4	5	22	.522	.399
Hubbard, Trent, Colorado Springs	.340	123	553	480	102	163	242	29	7	12	66	2	5	5	61	5	59	37	14	2	.504	.416
Beamon, Trey, Calgary*	.334	118	498	452	74	151	205	29	5	5	62	2	3	2	39	4	55	18	8	7	.454	.387
Pulliam, Harvey, Colorado Springs	.327	115	465	407	90	133	250	30	6	25	91	0	6	3	49	10	59	6	2	11	.614	.398
Hajek, Dave, Tucson	.327	131	554	502	99	164	221	37	4	4	79	5	6	2	39	7	27	12	7	11	.440	.373
Simons, Mitch, Salt Lake	.325	130	543	480	87	156	207	34	4	3	46	4	2	10	47	2	45	32	16	9	.431	.395
Garcia, Karim, Albuquerque*	.319	124	519	474	88	151	257	26	10	20	91	2	3	2	38	5	102	12	6	12	.542	.369
Dunn, Steve, Salt Lake*	.316	109	439	402	57	127	196	31	1	12	83	0	6	1	30	4	63	3	2	6	.488	.360
Ramos, Ken, Tucson*	.315	112	391	327	57	103	152	24	8	3	47	4	5	3	51	3	27	14	5	3	.465	.407
Litton, Greg, Tacoma	.309	117	444	388	60	120	174	25	1	9	56	4	6	3	43	1	69	2	2	11	.448	.377
Palmeiro, Orlando, Vancouver*	.307	107	458	398	66	122	151	21	4	0	47	11	5	3	41	8	34	16	7	11	.379	.371
Cedeno, Roger, Albuquerque†	.305	99	429	367	67	112	155	19	9	2	44	4	3	2	53	2	56	23	18	5	.422	.393
Raabe, Brian, Salt Lake	.305	112	497	440	88	134	187	32	6	3	60	2	7	3	45	2	14	15	0	12	.425	.368
Benard, Marvin, Phoenix*	.304	111	441	378	70	115	159	14	6	6	32	5	3	5	50	3	66	10	13	2	.421	.390
Abreu, Bob, Tucson*	.304	114	491	415	72	126	214	24	17	10	75	0	8	1	67	9	120	16	14	6	.516	.395

DEPARTMENTAL LEADERS: G—Bowie, 141; AB—Bowie, 531; R—Hubbard, 102; H—R. Ingram, 166; TB—Garcia, 257; 2B—R. Ingram, 43; 3B—Abreu, 17; HR—Pulliam, 25; RBI—Garcia, Pulliam, 91; SH—Palmeiro, 11; SF—Wood, 12; HP—Quinlan, 15; BB—Leonard, 81; IBB—Pulliam, 10; SO—Quinlan, 124; SB—Hubbard, 37; CS—Cedeno, 18; GIDP—R. Ingram, 22; Slg.—Pulliam, .614; OBP—Hubbard, .416.

ALL PLAYERS

*Lefthanded batter. †Switch-hitter.

Player, Team	Avg.	G	TPA	AB	R	H	TB	2B	3B	HR	RBI	SH	SF	HP	BB	IBB	SO	SB	CS	GDP	Slg.	OBP
Abreu, Bob, Tucson*	.304	114	491	415	72	126	214	24	17	10	75	0	8	1	67	9	120	16	14	6	.516	.395
Acevedo, Juan, Colorado Springs	.000	3	5	4	0	0	0	0	0	0	0	1	0	0	0	0	2	0	0	0	.000	.000
Allensworth, Jermaine, Calgary	.316	51	209	190	46	60	90	13	4	3	11	1	0	5	13	0	30	13	4	3	.474	.375
Anderson, Garret, Vancouver*	.311	14	66	61	9	19	26	7	0	0	12	0	0	0	5	0	14	0	0	3	.426	.364
Aude, Rich, Calgary	.333	50	216	195	34	65	110	14	2	9	42	0	5	4	12	1	30	3	2	11	.564	.375
August, Don, Calgary	.000	2	2	2	0	0	0	0	0	0	0	0	0	0	0	0	1	0	0	0	.000	.000
Aurilia, Rich, Phoenix	.279	71	296	258	42	72	99	12	0	5	34	0	3	0	35	2	29	2	2	4	.384	.361
Backlund, Brett, Calgary	.143	12	7	7	1	1	2	1	0	0	0	0	0	0	0	0	2	0	0	0	.286	.143
Bailey, Roger, Colorado Springs	.250	3	5	4	1	1	2	1	0	0	0	0	0	0	1	0	1	0	0	0	.500	.400
Ball, Jeff, Tucson	.293	110	403	362	58	106	147	25	2	4	56	4	5	7	25	3	66	11	5	13	.406	.346
Barron, Tony, Tacoma	.200	9	28	25	4	5	5	0	0	0	2	0	1	2	0	3	0	0	0		.200	.286
Barton, Shawn, Phoenix	.000	15	2	2	0	0	0	0	0	0	0	0	0	0	0	0	1	0	0	0	.000	.000
Beamon, Trey, Las Vegas*	.334	118	498	452	74	151	205	29	5	5	62	2	3	2	39	4	55	18	8	7	.454	.387
Bean, Billy, Las Vegas*	.290	119	509	445	67	129	212	34	2	15	77	0	9	4	46	9	55	2	2	9	.476	.361
Beard, Garrett, Edmonton	.230	22	69	61	5	14	16	2	0	0	10	1	2	2	3	0	7	0	0	2	.262	.279
Beauchamp, Kash, Edmonton	.200	1	5	5	0	1	1	0	0	0	1	0	0	0	0	0	0	0	0	0	.200	.200
Becker, Rich, Salt Lake†	.309	36	152	123	26	38	63	7	0	6	28	0	2	1	26	0	24	6	1	1	.512	.428
Bellinger, Clay, Phoenix	.274	97	311	277	34	76	100	16	1	2	32	2	3	2	27	1	52	3	2	5	.361	.340
Benard, Marvin, Phoenix*	.304	111	441	378	70	115	159	14	6	6	32	5	3	5	50	3	66	10	13	6	.421	.390
Bennett, Chris, Calgary	.000	4	2	1	0	0	0	0	0	0	0	0	0	0	1	0	1	0	0	0	.000	.500
Bennett, Erik, Van.-Tuc.	.250	42	4	4	0	1	1	0	0	0	0	0	0	0	0	0	0	0	0	0	.250	.250
Blanco, Henry, Albuquerque	.227	29	110	97	11	22	34	4	1	2	13	1	2	0	10	1	23	0	0	5	.351	.294
Bochtler, Doug, Las Vegas	.000	18	2	2	0	0	0	0	0	0	0	0	0	0	0	0	2	0	0	0	.000	.000
Bolick, Frank, Colorado Springs†	.235	23	76	68	8	16	27	3	1	2	7	0	0	0	8	0	14	0	0	0	.397	.316
Bourgeois, Steve, Phoenix	.200	6	6	5	1	1	2	1	0	0	1	0	0	0	1	0	1	0	0	1	.400	.200
Bournigal, Rafael, Albuquerque	.129	15	33	31	2	4	5	1	0	0	1	0	1	0	1	1	2	0	0	0	.161	.182
Bowie, Jim, Edmonton*	.267	141	597	531	69	142	181	26	2	3	70	4	6	2	54	7	51	4	1	21	.341	.334
Bragg, Darren, Tacoma*	.307	53	236	212	24	65	96	13	3	4	31	0	1	0	23	1	39	10	3	3	.453	.373
Bream, Scott, Las Vegas†	.241	87	343	303	33	73	82	7	1	0	15	2	0	3	35	1	59	7	5	7	.271	.326
Brewer, Rod, Phoenix*	.244	15	55	45	8	11	18	4	0	1	8	0	2	5	3	0	10	1	1	1	.400	.345
Brink, Brad, Pho.-Edm.	.111	20	9	9	0	1	1	0	0	0	0	0	0	0	0	0	2	0	0	0	.111	.111
Brito, Bernardo, Salt Lake	.306	51	207	186	31	57	114	10	1	15	49	0	4		17	5	58	1	0	7	.613	.377
Brito, Jorge, Colorado Springs	.229	32	102	96	9	22	34	4	1	2	15	1	2	1	2	0	20	0	3		.354	.248
Brocail, Doug, Tucson*	1.000	3	2	1	0	1	1	0	0	0	1	0	0	0	0	0	0	0	0	0	1.000	1.000
Brosnan, Jason, Albuquerque*	.250	23	4	4	0	1	1	0	0	0	2	0	0	0	0	0	3	0	0	0	.250	.250
Brumley, Mike, Tucson†	.261	94	378	330	56	86	138	20	10	4	33	1	3	3	41	5	67	17	6	8	.418	.345
Bruno, Julio, Las Vegas	.245	38	148	139	13	34	42	6	1	0	6	0	1	0	8	0	24	1	3	6	.302	.284
Bruske, Jim, Albuquerque	.421	45	22	19	4	8	9	1	0	0	4	2	0	0	1	0	3	0	0	0	.474	.450
Bryant, Scott, Edmonton	.288	119	466	406	58	117	186	33	3	10	69	0	5	6	49	3	87	1	3	7	.458	.362
Bullock, Eric, Las Vegas*	.263	84	206	190	32	50	68	4	1	4	25	2	1	1	12	1	22	6	0	4	.358	.309
Burcham, Tim, Phoenix	.000	5	1	1	0	0	0	0	0	0	0	0	0	0	0	0	0	0	0	0	.000	.000
Burgos, Enrique, Phoenix*	.000	41	5	4	0	0	0	0	0	0	0	0	0	0	1	0	3	0	0	0	.000	.200
Burke, John, Colorado Springs†	.222	19	21	18	2	4	4	0	0	0	3	0	0	0	3	0	3	0	0	0	.222	.222
Burks, Ellis, Colorado Springs	.310	8	33	29	9	9	19	2	1	2	6	0	0		4	0	8	0	0	1	.655	.394
Busch, Mike, Albuquerque	.269	121	492	443	68	119	207	32	1	18	62	0	0	7	42	3	103	2	2	12	.467	.341
Bustillos, Albert, Colorado Springs	.167	28	28	24	1	4	4	0	0	0	2	1	0	0	3	0	6	0	0	0	.167	.259
Cadaret, Greg, Las Vegas*	.167	28	7	6	1	1	2	1	0	0	0	0	0	0	1	0	4	0	0	1	.333	.286
Cameron, Stanton, Calgary	.208	7	28	24	8	5	9	4	0	0	4	0	0	0	4	0	4	0	0	0	.375	.321
Candaele, Casey, Albuquerque†	.259	12	33	27	2	7	7	0	0	0	2	1	1	0	4	0	4	0	1	1	.259	.344
Cangelosi, John, Tucson†	.368	30	128	106	18	39	45	4	1	0	9	3	0	0	19	2	11	11	3	1	.425	.464
Carlson, Dan, Phoenix	.160	23	25	25	4	4	5	1	0	0	4	0	0	0	0	0	7	0	0	1	.200	.160
Carvajal, Jovino, Vancouver*	.325	41	168	163	25	53	65	3	3	1	10	1	0	1	3	0	18	10	7	6	.399	.341
Case, Mike, Colorado Springs	.286	7	14	14	2	4	5	1	0	0	4	0	0	0	0	0	4	1	1	0	.357	.286
Castellano, Pete, Colorado Springs	.266	99	368	334	40	89	143	23	2	9	47	3	5	2	24	1	56	2	0	10	.428	.315
Castillo, Juan, Tucson	.000	11	7	5	1	0	0	0	0	0	0	1	0	1	2	0	0	0	0	0	.000	.167
Castro, Juan, Albuquerque	.267	104	368	341	51	91	126	18	4	3	43	7	0	0	20	3	42	4	4	11	.370	.307
Cedeno, Roger, Albuquerque†	.305	99	429	367	67	112	155	19	9	2	44	4	3	2	53	2	56	23	18	5	.422	.393
Chavez, Raul, Tucson	.262	32	115	103	14	27	32	5	0	0	10	1	1	2	8	0	13	0	1	7	.311	.325
Chimelis, Joel, Phoenix	.259	118	442	398	48	103	158	30	1	7	66	3	8	5	28	4	53	1	2	7	.397	.306
Christopherson, Eric, Phoenix	.220	94	330	282	21	62	76	9	1	1	25	5	5	3	35	1	54	1	1	12	.270	.308
Cianfrocco, Archi, Las Vegas	.311	89	352	322	51	100	154	20	2	10	58	0	7	3	16	0	61	5	0	11	.478	.342
Clayton, Royal, Phoenix	.250	5	5	4	0	1	1	0	0	0	0	0	0	0	1	0	0	0	0	0	.250	.250
Cockrell, Alan, Colorado Springs	.313	106	388	355	58	111	171	22	1	12	58	1	0	2	30	3	65	0	3	8	.482	.370
Cohick, Emmitt, Vancouver*	.333	10	30	24	3	8	10	2	0	0	5	0	1	0	5	0	8	0	1	1	.417	.433
Colbert, Craig, Las Vegas	.249	74	264	241	30	60	73	8	1	1	24	1	1	0	21	0	44	1	0	14	.303	.308
Cole, Stu, Colorado Springs	.274	76	231	208	28	57	82	15	2	2	24	2	2	2	17	1	19	1	2	8	.394	.332
Cole, Victor, Las Vegas†	.000	4	6	5	0	0	0	0	0	0	0	0	0	0	1	0	1	0	0	0	.000	.167
Conroy, Brian, Colorado Springs†	.250	5	9	8	1	2	2	0	0	0	1	1	0	0	0	0	2	0	0	0	.250	.250
Cookson, Brent, Phoenix	.300	68	239	210	38	63	123	9	3	15	46	1	2	1	25	2	36	3	3	4	.586	.374
Coomer, Ron, Albuquerque	.322	85	347	323	54	104	179	23	2	16	76	0	4	2	18	1	28	5	2	16	.554	.357
Corbin, Archie, Calgary	.200	47	5	5	0	1	1	0	0	0	0	0	0	0	0	0	2	0	0	0	.200	.200
Corbin, Ted, Salt Lake†	.200	4	10	10	0	2	2	0	0	0	1	0	0	0	0	0	4	0	0	1	.200	.200
Correa, Ramser, Albuquerque	1.000	2	1	1	0	1	1	0	0	0	0	0	0	0	0	0	0	0	0	0	1.000	1.000
Correia, Rod, Vancouver	.303	73	298	264	42	80	99	6	5	1	39	4	4	0	26	3	33	8	4	7	.375	.361
Counsell, Craig, Colorado Springs*	.281	118	444	399	60	112	161	22	6	5	53	3	6	2	34	7	47	10	2	12	.404	.336
Cromwell, Nate, Las Vegas*	.333	9	3	3	1	1	2	1	0	0	2	0	0	0	0	0	1	0	0	0	.667	.333
Cruz, Fausto, Edmonton	.281	114	498	448	72	126	186	23	2	11	67	4	7	5	34	2	67	7	5	15	.415	.334
Cummings, Midre, Calgary*	.277	45	172	159	19	44	58	9	1	1	16	0	5	2	6	4	27	1	1	1	.365	.302
Czajkowski, Jim, Colorado Springs†	.000	60	2	1	0	0	0	0	0	0	0	0	1	0	0	0	0	0	0	0	.000	.000
Daal, Omar, Albuquerque*	.000	17	10	9	0	0	0	0	0	0	0	0	0	1	0	0	3	0	0	0	.000	.100

Player, Team	Avg.	G	TPA	AB	R	H	TB	2B	3B	HR	RBI	SH	SF	HP	BB	IBB	SO	SB	CS	GDP	Slg.	OBP
Dalesandro, Mark, Vancouver	.333	34	131	123	16	41	59	13	1	1	18	0	1	1	6	0	12	2	0	2	.480	.366
Daspit, Jim, Tuc.-Edm.	.200	38	6	5	0	1	1	0	0	0	0	1	0	0	0	0	2	0	0	0	.200	.200
Daugherty, Jack, Phoenix†	.152	10	36	33	4	5	6	1	0	0	3	0	1	0	2	1	4	0	0	1	.182	.194
Deer, Rob, Van.-L.V.	.290	89	353	303	54	88	173	23	4	18	65	0	3	0	47	6	89	2	2	4	.571	.382
DeLaRosa, Juan, Salt Lake	.224	31	54	49	7	11	13	2	0	0	5	3	1	0	1	1	6	0	0	2	.265	.235
DeLosSantos, Mariano, Calgary	.125	14	11	8	1	1	1	0	0	0	0	2	0	0	1	0	2	0	0	0	.125	.222
Demetral, Chris, Albuquerque*	.278	87	214	187	34	52	70	7	1	3	19	3	0	0	24	2	28	1	6	7	.374	.360
Diaz, Alex, Tacoma†	.250	10	42	40	3	10	11	1	0	0	4	0	0	0	2	0	5	1	2	0	.275	.286
Diaz, Eddy, Tacoma	.333	11	40	36	5	12	14	2	0	0	5	0	0	0	4	0	2	0	0	0	.389	.400
Dishman, Glenn, Las Vegas	.045	14	26	22	0	1	1	0	0	0	0	4	0	0	0	0	5	0	0	0	.045	.045
Dougherty, Jim, Tucson	.000	8	1	1	0	0	0	0	0	0	0	0	0	0	0	0	1	0	0	0	.000	.000
Duncan, Andres, Salt Lake†	.278	12	44	36	2	10	14	2	1	0	6	2	1	1	4	0	5	2	0	0	.389	.357
Dunn, Steve, Salt Lake*	.316	109	439	402	57	127	196	31	1	12	83	0	6	1	30	4	63	3	2	6	.488	.360
Durant, Mike, Salt Lake	.251	85	322	295	40	74	101	15	3	2	23	3	2	2	20	0	31	11	7	13	.342	.301
Durham, Leon, Vancouver*	.273	18	60	55	7	15	22	1	0	2	10	0	0	0	5	0	11	0	0	1	.400	.333
Ehmann, Kurt, Phoenix	.269	67	251	216	21	58	67	5	2	0	7	4	4	3	24	1	41	8	3	1	.310	.344
Eischen, Joey, Albuquerque*	.000	13	1	1	0	0	0	0	0	0	0	0	0	0	0	0	0	0	0	0	.000	.000
Encarnacion, Angelo, Calgary	.250	21	81	80	8	20	26	3	0	1	6	0	0	0	1	1	12	1	0	2	.325	.259
Ericks, John, Calgary	.143	5	8	7	0	1	1	0	0	0	0	1	0	0	0	0	2	0	0	0	.143	.143
Ettles, Mark, Las Vegas	.500	11	2	2	0	1	1	0	0	0	1	0	0	0	0	0	1	0	0	0	.500	.500
Fabregas, Jorge, Vancouver*	.247	21	83	73	9	18	33	3	0	4	10	0	1	0	9	3	12	0	0	1	.452	.325
Faneyte, Rikkert, Phoenix	.274	38	153	135	22	37	50	8	1	1	17	2	1	0	15	1	22	2	5	1	.370	.344
Faries, Paul, Edmonton	.300	117	472	424	67	127	146	15	2	0	46	7	5	2	34	1	47	14	8	14	.344	.351
Fermin, Felix, Tacoma	.333	1	3	3	0	1	1	0	0	0	0	0	0	0	0	0	0	0	0	0	.333	.333
Fesh, Sean, Tuc.-L.V.*	.000	40	1	1	0	0	0	0	0	0	0	0	0	0	0	0	0	0	0	0	.000	.000
Flora, Kevin, Vancouver	.298	38	142	124	22	37	53	7	0	3	14	1	1	0	16	0	33	7	4	2	.427	.376
Flynt, Bill, Calgary*	.000	12	2	1	1	0	0	0	0	0	0	0	0	0	1	0	1	0	0	0	.000	.500
Forbes, P.J., Vancouver	.274	109	411	369	47	101	132	22	3	1	52	7	10	2	21	0	46	4	6	4	.358	.308
Franklin, Micah, Calgary†	.293	110	411	358	64	105	196	28	0	21	71	0	5	1	47	8	95	3	3	7	.547	.372
Fredrickson, Scott, Col. Springs	.250	58	8	8	1	2	2	0	0	0	0	0	0	0	0	0	2	0	0	0	.250	.250
Gainer, Jay, Colorado Springs*	.291	112	410	358	57	104	194	19	1	23	86	0	6	0	42	9	64	2	3	7	.542	.360
Gallaher, Kevin, Tucson	.000	3	3	2	0	0	0	0	0	0	0	1	0	0	0	0	1	0	0	0	.000	.000
Gallego, Mike, Edmonton	.278	6	20	18	1	5	6	1	0	0	1	0	0	2	0	0	4	0	0	0	.333	.350
Gamez, Bob, Phoenix*	.167	36	13	12	1	2	4	0	1	0	2	0	0	0	1	0	2	0	0	0	.333	.231
Garcia, Karim, Albuquerque*	.319	124	519	474	88	151	257	26	10	20	91	2	3	2	38	5	102	12	6	12	.542	.369
Gardner, Chris, Tucson	1.000	16	2	2	1	2	3	1	0	0	1	0	0	0	0	0	0	0	0	0	1.500	1.000
Garrison, Webster, Col. Springs	.293	126	518	460	83	135	215	32	6	12	77	3	6	3	46	2	74	12	4	9	.467	.357
Giambi, Jason, Edmonton*	.342	55	229	190	34	65	102	26	1	3	41	0	3	2	34	4	26	0	0	4	.537	.441
Goff, Jerry, Tucson*	.222	68	238	207	23	46	77	11	1	6	34	0	2	0	29	3	56	0	0	3	.372	.315
Gonzales, Rene, Vancouver	.273	50	192	165	27	45	69	12	0	4	18	0	1	2	24	1	25	0	0	7	.418	.370
Grebeck, Brian, Vancouver	.245	81	292	241	41	59	89	11	2	5	30	5	3	5	38	1	38	4	0	6	.369	.355
Greene, Todd, Vancouver	.250	43	185	168	28	42	89	3	1	14	35	0	2	4	11	2	36	1	0	3	.530	.308
Greer, Ken, Phoenix	.000	38	4	3	0	0	0	0	0	0	0	1	0	0	0	0	2	0	0	0	.000	.000
Griffey, Ken, Tacoma*	.000	1	3	3	0	0	0	0	0	0	0	0	0	0	0	0	1	0	0	0	.000	.000
Guerrero, Juan, Tucson	.294	72	211	194	21	57	75	10	1	2	21	2	1	0	14	3	42	1	1	3	.387	.340
Guerrero, Wilton, Albuquerque	.327	14	52	49	10	16	19	1	1	0	2	2	0	0	1	1	7	2	3	1	.388	.340
Gutierrez, Ricky, Tucson	.301	64	270	236	46	71	94	12	4	1	26	1	2	3	28	4	28	9	7	6	.398	.379
Hajek, Dave, Tucson	.327	131	554	502	99	164	221	37	4	4	79	5	6	2	39	7	27	12	7	11	.440	.373
Hale, Chip, Salt Lake*	.286	16	56	49	5	14	18	4	0	0	2	0	0	0	7	1	5	0	1	2	.367	.375
Hall, Billy, Las Vegas†	.225	86	274	249	42	56	64	3	1	1	22	1	3	1	20	1	47	22	5	3	.257	.282
Hancock, Lee, Calgary*	.176	34	21	17	1	3	3	0	0	0	2	3	1	0	0	0	7	0	0	0	.176	.167
Hanel, Marcus, Calgary	.125	2	8	8	1	1	1	0	0	0	0	0	0	0	0	0	1	0	0	0	.125	.125
Hansell, Greg, Alb.-S.L.	.500	15	3	2	1	1	1	0	0	0	0	1	0	0	0	0	1	0	0	0	.500	.500
Hansen, Terrel, Tacoma	.220	20	54	50	5	11	21	1	0	3	10	0	1	1	2	0	12	0	0	5	.420	.259
Harriger, Denny, Las Vegas	.263	29	42	38	3	10	12	2	0	0	2	2	0	0	2	0	15	0	0	1	.316	.300
Hartgraves, Dean, Tucson	.000	14	2	2	0	0	0	0	0	0	0	0	0	0	0	0	0	0	0	0	.000	.000
Hatcher, Chris, Tucson	.286	94	339	290	59	83	148	19	2	14	50	1	2	4	42	2	107	7	3	9	.510	.382
Hathaway, Hilly, Las Vegas*	.214	15	16	14	2	3	3	0	0	0	2	2	0	0	0	0	2	1	0	3	.214	.214
Hawblitzel, Ryan, Col. Springs	.300	21	13	10	4	3	4	1	0	0	1	2	0	0	1	0	2	0	0	0	.400	.364
Hazlett, Steve, Salt Lake	.300	127	477	427	71	128	177	25	6	4	49	2	3	4	41	1	65	8	10	9	.415	.364
Helfand, Eric, Edmonton*	.214	19	71	56	5	12	23	4	2	1	12	5	1	0	9	1	10	0	1	3	.411	.318
Hernandez, Fernando, Las Vegas	.000	8	5	4	0	0	0	0	0	0	0	0	0	0	1	0	3	0	0	0	.000	.200
Hill, Milt, Calgary	.286	24	8	7	0	2	2	0	0	0	1	1	0	0	0	0	4	0	0	0	.286	.286
Hocking, Denny, Salt Lake†	.282	117	437	397	51	112	164	24	2	8	75	8	5	2	25	1	41	12	8	10	.413	.324
Holbert, Ray, Las Vegas	.115	9	31	26	3	3	4	1	0	0	3	0	0	0	5	0	10	1	1	1	.154	.258
Hollandsworth, Todd, Albuquerque*	.237	10	45	38	9	9	17	2	0	2	4	0	0	1	6	2	8	1	0	1	.447	.356
Holman, Shawn, Albuquerque	1.000	49	1	1	0	1	1	0	0	0	1	0	0	0	0	0	0	0	0	0	1.000	1.000
Holt, Chris, Tucson	.111	20	24	18	1	2	3	1	0	0	1	6	0	0	0	0	4	0	0	1	.167	.111
Hook, Chris, Phoenix†	.000	4	1	1	0	0	0	0	0	0	0	0	0	0	0	0	1	0	0	0	.000	.000
Hope, John, Calgary	.083	13	16	12	0	1	1	0	0	0	0	4	0	0	0	0	4	0	0	0	.083	.083
Horn, Jeff, Salt Lake	.500	3	10	10	0	5	6	1	0	0	2	0	0	0	0	0	1	0	0	0	.600	.500
Horn, Sam, Calgary*	.333	36	114	99	21	33	69	8	2	8	22	0	1	0	14	0	21	0	0	6	.697	.412
Hosey, Steve, Vancouver	.271	16	66	59	10	16	25	3	0	2	6	0	0	0	7	0	16	2	0	1	.424	.348
Howard, Chris, Tacoma	.243	83	294	268	33	65	91	14	0	4	31	4	2	2	18	2	70	0	1	9	.340	.293
Hubbard, Trent, Col. Springs	.340	123	553	480	102	163	242	29	7	12	66	2	5	5	61	5	59	37	14	2	.504	.416
Huckaby, Ken, Albuquerque	.324	89	298	278	30	90	113	16	2	1	40	3	1	4	12	1	26	3	1	16	.406	.359
Huisman, Rick, Tucson	.000	42	1	1	0	0	0	0	0	0	0	0	0	0	0	0	1	0	0	0	.000	.000
Humphreys, Mike, Tacoma	.200	18	39	35	3	7	9	2	0	0	1	0	1	0	3	0	11	0	0	0	.257	.256
Hunter, Brian, Tucson	.329	38	172	155	28	51	61	5	1	1	16	0	0	0	17	0	13	11	3	1	.394	.395
Hunter, Jim, Colorado Springs	.000	10	3	2	1	0	0	0	0	0	0	0	0	0	1	0	1	0	0	0	.000	.333
Hyers, Tim, Las Vegas*	.290	82	287	259	46	75	92	12	1	1	23	2	1	1	24	3	33	0	3	7	.355	.351
Ingram, Garey, Albuquerque	.246	63	259	232	28	57	79	11	4	1	30	0	3	3	21	1	40	10	4	4	.341	.313
Ingram, Riccardo, Salt Lake	.348	122	526	477	80	166	249	43	2	12	85	0	5	3	41	3	60	4	5	22	.522	.399

Player, Team	Avg.	G	TPA	AB	R	H	TB	2B	3B	HR	RBI	SH	SF	HP	BB	IBB	SO	SB	CS	GDP	Slg.	OBP
Jackson, John, Van.-S.L.*	.287	90	365	307	59	88	132	21	4	5	32	6	3	5	44	2	35	16	5	7	.430	.382
Jean, Domingo, Tucson	.000	3	3	3	0	0	0	0	0	0	0	0	0	0	0	0	3	0	0	0	.000	.000
Johnson, Erik, Calgary	.297	123	503	455	64	135	191	35	6	3	58	3	6	0	39	6	40	5	4	12	.420	.348
Johnson, Mark, Calgary*	.304	9	30	23	7	7	17	4	0	2	8	0	0	1	6	1	4	1	0	0	.739	.467
Johnston, Joel, Col. Springs	.000	18	2	2	0	0	0	0	0	0	0	0	0	0	0	0	1	0	0	0	.000	.000
Jones, Bobby, Col. Springs	.200	11	7	5	1	1	1	0	0	0	0	2	0	0	0	0	0	0	0	0	.200	.200
Jones, Dax, Phoenix	.267	112	444	404	47	108	141	21	3	2	45	2	5	2	31	3	52	11	10	8	.349	.319
Jones, Tim, Edmonton*	.500	2	6	6	1	3	4	1	0	0	1	0	0	0	0	0	0	0	0	0	.667	.500
Jordan, Ricky, Vancouver	.222	19	67	63	5	14	22	2	0	2	9	0	0	1	3	0	7	0	0	2	.349	.254
Keagle, Greg, Las Vegas	.000	14	8	6	0	0	0	0	0	0	0	2	0	0	0	0	2	0	0	0	.000	.000
Kellner, Frank, Tucson†	.180	28	106	89	11	16	21	3	1	0	7	1	1	0	15	0	12	1	0	2	.236	.295
Ketchen, Doug, Tucson	.063	19	17	16	1	1	1	0	0	0	0	0	0	0	1	0	2	0	0	0	.063	.118
Kile, Darryl, Tucson	.200	4	7	5	1	1	1	0	0	0	0	0	0	0	1	0	1	0	0	1	.200	.333
Kirkpatrick, Jay, Albuquerque*	.250	13	42	40	4	10	16	1	1	1	6	0	0	0	2	1	6	0	0	0	.400	.286
Knabenshue, Chris, Calgary*	.000	4	14	10	2	0	0	0	0	0	0	1	0	0	4	0	3	0	0	0	.000	.286
Knudsen, Kurt, Phoenix	.000	11	3	2	0	0	0	0	0	0	0	1	0	0	0	0	1	0	0	0	.000	.000
Kotarski, Mike, Col. Springs*	.000	22	5	4	0	0	0	0	0	0	0	1	0	0	0	0	2	0	0	0	.000	.000
Kreuter, Chad, Tacoma†	.292	15	56	48	6	14	22	5	0	1	11	0	0	0	8	0	11	0	0	3	.458	.393
Landrum, Ced, Col. Springs*	.259	82	185	166	31	43	58	5	2	2	19	5	2	1	11	1	29	12	5	2	.349	.306
Latham, Chris, Albuquerque†	.167	5	20	18	2	3	5	0	1	0	3	0	1	0	1	0	4	1	0	0	.278	.200
Lennon, Pat, Salt Lake	.400	34	129	115	26	46	79	15	0	6	29	0	1	1	12	2	29	2	1	1	.687	.457
Leonard, Mark, Phoenix*	.296	112	484	392	73	116	189	25	3	14	79	1	10	0	81	8	63	3	2	19	.482	.408
Lieber, Jon, Calgary*	.118	14	21	17	2	2	2	0	0	0	1	0	0	0	3	0	6	0	0	0	.118	.250
Lind, Jose, Vancouver	.222	10	37	36	2	8	10	2	0	0	5	0	0	0	1	0	4	1	0	0	.278	.243
Litton, Greg, Tacoma	.309	117	444	388	58	120	174	25	1	9	56	4	6	3	43	1	69	2	2	11	.448	.377
Loiselle, Rich, L.V.-Tuc.	.125	10	8	8	1	1	1	0	0	0	0	0	0	0	0	0	5	0	0	0	.125	.125
Lott, Billy, Albuquerque	.315	41	160	146	23	46	72	7	2	5	26	1	0	0	13	2	48	1	2	5	.493	.371
Lydy, Scott, Edmonton	.290	104	447	400	78	116	207	29	7	16	65	3	5	6	33	3	66	15	4	11	.518	.349
Mack, Quinn, Tacoma*	.265	70	230	204	30	54	68	11	0	1	17	1	0	1	24	5	21	9	2	6	.333	.345
Makarewicz, Scott, Tucson	.266	62	208	192	21	51	75	9	0	5	31	2	2	2	10	3	23	1	0	9	.391	.306
Maksudian, Mike, Edmonton*	.265	100	372	324	54	86	127	24	4	3	34	2	0	0	46	2	55	5	1	8	.392	.357
Marrero, Oreste, Albuquerque*	.348	7	24	23	5	8	16	2	0	2	6	0	0	0	1	0	5	0	0	0	.696	.375
Martin, Jim, Albuquerque*	.253	25	83	75	8	19	27	3	1	1	7	0	0	0	8	0	20	3	3	3	.360	.325
Martinez, Carlos, Vancouver	.247	25	106	97	17	24	30	3	0	1	6	0	0	2	7	2	17	1	2	4	.309	.311
Martinez, Chito, Col. Springs*	.155	42	122	110	18	17	37	8	0	4	6	0	0	0	12	0	32	0	2	0	.336	.238
Martinez, Jesus, Albuquerque*	.000	2	1	1	0	0	0	0	0	0	0	0	0	0	0	0	0	0	0	0	.000	.000
Martinez, Jose, Las Vegas	.045	27	26	22	0	1	2	1	0	0	0	3	0	1	0	0	9	0	0	1	.091	.087
Martinez, Pedro, Tucson*	.333	20	3	3	0	1	1	0	0	0	0	0	0	0	0	0	1	0	0	0	.333	.333
Marx, Tim, Calgary	.297	61	208	185	27	55	71	11	1	1	12	1	3	0	19	2	16	2	3	6	.384	.357
Mashore, Damon, Edmonton†	.300	117	390	337	50	101	133	19	5	1	37	3	3	5	42	0	77	17	5	9	.395	.382
Masteller, Dan, Salt Lake*	.303	48	174	152	25	46	82	10	7	4	18	1	3	3	15	3	17	4	1	3	.539	.370
Matos, Francisco, Calgary	.323	100	352	341	36	110	142	11	6	3	40	3	1	2	5	0	25	9	2	11	.416	.335
Maurer, Ron, Albuquerque.	.259	84	209	185	29	48	81	14	2	5	25	1	1	3	19	2	34	1	2	1	.438	.337
Mauser, Tim, Las Vegas	.000	35	1	1	0	0	0	0	0	0	0	0	0	0	0	0	0	0	0	0	.000	.000
Maynard, Scott, Tacoma	.000	1	1	1	0	0	0	0	0	0	0	0	0	0	0	0	0	0	0	1	.000	.000
Maysey, Matt, Calgary	.118	44	17	17	0	2	2	0	0	0	1	0	0	0	0	0	5	0	0	0	.118	.118
McCarthy, Tom, Albuquerque	.364	13	11	11	0	4	6	2	0	0	4	0	0	0	0	0	3	0	0	0	.545	.364
McCarty, Dave, Phoenix	.351	37	175	151	31	53	88	19	2	4	19	0	1	6	17	1	27	1	1	6	.583	.434
McCracken, Quinton, Col. Springs†	.361	61	270	244	55	88	123	14	6	3	28	2	0	1	23	3	30	17	6	4	.504	.418
McDavid, Ray, Las Vegas*	.271	52	201	166	28	45	70	8	1	5	27	0	1	4	30	0	35	7	1	2	.422	.393
McFarlin, Terric, Las Vegas†	.143	59	9	7	2	1	1	0	0	0	0	2	0	0	0	0	3	0	0	0	.143	.143
McMurtry, Craig, Tucson	.167	17	13	12	2	2	2	0	0	0	1	0	0	1	0	3	0	1	0	.167	.231
Mejia, Roberto, Col. Springs	.294	38	153	143	18	42	62	10	2	2	14	2	0	1	7	2	29	0	2	6	.434	.331
Menendez, Tony, Phoenix	.000	50	3	3	0	0	0	0	0	0	0	0	0	0	0	0	2	0	0	0	.000	.000
Mercedes, Luis, Calgary	.262	25	98	84	18	22	26	1	0	1	8	0	0	3	11	0	10	1	2	2	.310	.367
Milchin, Mike, Albuquerque*	.364	18	12	11	0	4	6	2	0	0	1	0	0	0	0	0	1	0	0	0	.545	.364
Miller, Barry, Phoenix*	.224	71	180	156	18	35	51	8	1	2	21	0	1	0	23	0	35	0	2	4	.327	.322
Miller, Damian, Salt Lake	.285	83	320	295	39	84	118	23	1	3	41	5	2	3	15	1	39	2	4	11	.400	.324
Miller, Roger, Phoenix	.212	43	150	137	14	29	38	4	1	1	10	4	0	0	9	0	15	0	0	3	.277	.260
Mimbs, Mark, Albuquerque*	.048	23	23	21	1	1	2	1	0	0	0	2	0	0	0	0	9	0	0	0	.095	.048
Mintz, Steve, Phoenix*	.000	31	3	2	0	0	0	0	0	0	0	1	0	0	0	0	1	0	0	0	.000	.000
Mirabelli, Doug, Phoenix	.167	23	81	66	3	11	13	0	1	0	7	0	2	1	12	1	10	1	0	5	.197	.296
Mlicki, Doug, Tucson	.444	6	11	9	2	4	4	0	0	0	2	1	0	0	1	0	1	0	0	0	.444	.500
Molina, Ben, Vancouver	.000	1	2	2	0	0	0	0	0	0	0	0	0	0	0	0	1	0	0	0	.000	.000
Molina, Izzy, Edmonton	.167	2	6	6	0	1	1	0	0	0	0	0	0	0	0	0	2	0	0	0	.167	.167
Montalvo, Rafael, Albuquerque.	.111	49	10	9	1	1	1	0	0	0	0	1	0	0	0	0	5	0	0	0	.111	.111
Montgomery, Ray, Tucson	.302	88	326	291	48	88	140	19	0	11	68	1	8	2	24	1	58	5	3	3	.481	.351
Monzon, Jose, Vancouver	.217	13	26	23	5	5	9	1	0	1	5	0	0	3	0	2	0	0	1	.391	.308
Moore, Kerwin, Edmonton†	.279	72	317	265	53	74	102	14	4	2	26	3	1	1	47	1	67	10	3	3	.385	.389
Mora, Melvin, Tucson	.600	2	7	5	3	3	5	0	1	0	1	0	0	0	2	1	0	1	0	0	1.000	.714
Mouton, James, Tucson	.455	3	11	11	1	5	8	0	0	1	1	0	0	0	0	0	2	0	1	0	.727	.455
Mueller, Bill, Phoenix†	.297	41	198	172	23	51	82	13	6	2	19	6	1	0	19	0	31	0	0	7	.477	.365
Mulligan, Sean, Las Vegas	.274	101	378	339	34	93	136	20	1	7	43	1	3	8	27	2	61	0	0	7	.401	.340
Munoz, Noe, Albuquerque	.224	23	60	58	1	13	14	1	0	0	3	0	0	0	2	0	8	0	0	3	.241	.250
Munoz, Orlando, Vancouver†	.100	4	10	10	0	1	1	0	0	0	0	0	0	0	0	0	3	0	1	1	.100	.100
Murray, Calvin, Phoenix	.180	13	56	50	8	9	22	1	0	4	10	1	1	0	4	0	6	2	2	2	.440	.236
Nevin, Phil, Tucson	.291	62	252	223	31	65	102	16	0	7	41	1	0	1	27	1	39	2	3	9	.457	.371
Newfield, Marc, Tac.-L.V.	.295	73	298	268	40	79	121	16	1	8	42	1	1	6	22	1	41	3	0	7	.451	.360
Nied, David, Colorado Springs.	.000	7	6	6	0	0	0	0	0	0	0	0	0	0	0	0	4	0	0	0	.000	.000
Nokes, Matt, Colorado Springs*	.216	12	43	37	7	8	22	2	0	4	10	0	3	1	2	0	4	0	0	1	.595	.256
Noland, J.D., Tacoma*	.275	76	271	251	27	69	100	10	3	5	28	4	3	0	13	1	37	14	6	7	.398	.307
Northrup, Kevin, Edmonton	.182	17	50	44	4	8	10	2	0	0	1	1	0	0	5	1	8	0	0	0	.227	.265
O'Donoghue, John, Albuquerque*	.091	25	13	11	0	1	1	0	0	0	1	1	0	0	1	0	0	0	0	0	.091	.167

Player, Team	Avg.	G	TPA	AB	R	H	TB	2B	3B	HR	RBI	SH	SF	HP	BB	IBB	SO	SB	CS	GDP	Slg.	OBP
Olivares, Omar, Col. Springs	.000	3	4	4	0	0	0	0	0	0	0	0	0	0	0	0	0	0	0	0	.000	.000
Ortiz, Ray, Phoenix*	.242	66	204	190	22	46	72	10	2	4	29	0	1	0	13	3	36	1	0	2	.379	.289
Osik, Keith, Calgary	.336	90	331	301	40	101	158	25	1	10	59	0	4	5	21	2	42	2	2	5	.525	.384
Owens, Jayhawk, Col. Springs	.294	70	251	221	47	65	124	13	5	12	48	1	2	7	20	2	61	2	1	2	.561	.368
Painter, Lance, Col. Springs*	.000	11	3	2	0	0	0	0	0	0	0	1	0	0	0	0	1	0	0	0	.000	.000
Palmeiro, Orlando, Vancouver*	.307	107	458	398	66	122	151	21	4	0	47	11	5	3	41	8	34	16	7	11	.379	.371
Park, Chan Ho, Albuquerque	.074	23	29	27	2	2	3	1	0	0	2	0	1	0	1	0	12	0	0	0	.111	.103
Parker, Rick, Albuquerque	.280	58	209	175	33	49	63	7	2	1	14	1	1	3	27	4	17	1	6	4	.360	.383
Parra, Jose, Albuquerque	.000	12	9	6	1	0	0	0	0	0	0	3	0	0	0	0	3	0	0	0	.000	.000
Patrick, Bronswell, Tucson	.400	43	10	5	1	2	2	0	0	0	2	2	0	1	2	0	1	0	0	0	.400	.625
Peever, Lloyd, Col. Springs	.222	8	11	9	2	2	3	1	0	0	0	1	0	0	1	0	3	0	0	0	.333	.300
Peguero, Jose, Vancouver	.254	17	59	59	6	15	21	6	0	0	3	0	0	0	0	0	8	1	0	2	.356	.254
Peguero, Julio, Tacoma†	.200	11	26	25	2	5	7	0	1	0	1	0	0	0	1	0	7	0	0	0	.280	.231
Perez, Eduardo, Vancouver	.325	69	278	246	39	80	124	12	7	6	37	1	4	2	25	0	34	6	2	5	.504	.386
Perez, Neifi, Colorado Springs†	.278	11	37	36	4	10	14	4	0	0	2	1	0	0	0	0	5	1	1	0	.389	.278
Petagine, Roberto, Las Vegas*	.214	19	70	56	8	12	19	2	1	1	5	1	0	0	13	1	17	1	0	0	.339	.362
Pevey, Marty, Tacoma*	.105	7	20	19	2	2	2	0	0	0	0	0	0	0	1	0	5	0	0	0	.105	.150
Phillips, Randy, Phoenix	.167	25	20	18	1	3	3	0	0	0	0	1	0	0	1	0	7	0	0	0	.167	.211
Phoenix, Steve, Edmonton	.000	41	2	1	0	0	0	0	0	0	0	0	0	0	1	0	1	0	0	0	.000	.500
Pirkl, Greg, Tacoma	.293	47	190	174	29	51	108	8	2	15	44	0	1	1	14	1	28	1	1	3	.621	.347
Plantier, Phil, Tucson*	.250	10	29	24	6	6	11	2	0	1	4	0	0	0	5	0	4	0	0	1	.458	.379
Polcovich, Kevin, Calgary	.282	62	237	213	31	60	79	8	1	3	27	2	3	8	11	0	32	5	6	7	.371	.336
Pose, Scott, Alb.-S.L.*	.301	77	257	219	46	66	78	10	1	0	20	3	3	1	31	2	28	15	4	2	.356	.386
Powell, Ross, Tucson*	.000	13	6	6	0	0	0	0	0	0	0	0	0	0	0	0	3	0	0	0	.000	.000
Pozo, Arquimedez, Tacoma	.300	122	484	450	57	135	196	19	6	10	62	1	4	3	26	1	31	3	3	15	.436	.340
Prince, Tom, Albuquerque	.318	61	222	192	30	61	97	15	0	7	36	1	0	2	27	2	41	0	0	6	.505	.407
Pritchett, Chris, Vancouver*	.276	123	498	434	66	120	179	27	4	8	53	2	1	5	56	6	79	2	3	7	.412	.365
Pulliam, Harvey, Col. Springs	.327	115	465	407	90	133	250	30	6	25	91	0	6	3	49	10	59	6	2	11	.614	.398
Pyc, Dave, Albuquerque*	.000	1	2	2	0	0	0	0	0	0	0	0	0	0	0	0	0	0	0	0	.000	.000
Pye, Eddie, Albuquerque	.295	84	337	302	49	89	120	20	1	3	32	2	2	1	30	2	36	11	2	7	.397	.358
Quinlan, Tom, Salt Lake	.279	130	527	466	78	130	215	22	6	17	88	1	6	15	39	2	124	6	3	12	.461	.350
Raabe, Brian, Salt Lake	.305	112	497	440	88	134	187	32	6	3	60	2	7	3	45	2	14	15	0	12	.425	.368
Ralph, Curtis, Calgary	.000	28	2	1	0	0	0	0	0	0	1	0	0	1	0	0	0	0	0	0	.000	.500
Ramirez, J.D., Vancouver	.000	1	4	4	0	0	0	0	0	0	0	0	0	0	0	0	1	0	0	0	.000	.000
Ramos, Ken, Tucson*	.315	112	391	327	57	103	152	24	8	3	47	4	5	3	51	3	27	14	5	3	.465	.407
Rath, Gary, Albuquerque*	.000	8	4	3	0	0	0	0	0	0	1	1	0	0	0	0	1	0	0	0	.000	.000
Ratliff, Daryl, Calgary	.343	95	310	286	41	98	111	11	1	0	37	4	0	2	18	2	30	9	6	7	.388	.386
Raven, Luis, Vancouver	.244	37	152	135	18	33	61	11	1	5	26	1	1	0	15	0	35	3	1	6	.452	.318
Rekar, Bryan, Col. Springs	.250	7	6	4	0	1	1	0	0	0	2	2	0	0	0	0	2	0	0	0	.250	.250
Relaford, Desi, Tacoma†	.239	30	128	113	20	27	40	5	1	2	7	0	2	0	13	2	24	6	0	2	.354	.313
Reynoso, Armando, Col. Springs	.000	5	3	3	0	0	0	0	0	0	0	0	0	0	0	0	0	0	0	0	.000	.000
Richardson, Jeff, Calgary	.333	7	24	18	4	6	6	0	0	0	3	3	1	0	2	0	1	0	0	1	.333	.381
Riley, Marquis, Vancouver	.262	120	533	477	70	125	143	6	6	0	43	2	4	1	49	3	69	29	10	11	.300	.330
Roberson, Kevin, Tacoma†	.236	42	180	157	17	37	63	6	1	6	17	0	2	2	19	1	51	1	1	4	.401	.322
Roberts, Bip, Las Vegas†	.333	3	13	12	1	4	4	0	0	0	2	0	1	0	0	0	3	1	0	0	.333	.308
Robinson, Scott, Phoenix	.346	32	30	26	3	9	15	1	1	1	3	3	0	0	1	0	7	1	0	1	.577	.370
Rodriguez, Alex, Tacoma	.360	54	237	214	37	77	140	12	3	15	45	1	2	2	18	1	44	2	4	2	.654	.411
Rodriguez, Boi, Calgary*	.256	11	42	39	10	10	18	2	0	2	10	0	0	0	3	1	5	1	0	0	.462	.310
Rodriguez, Felix, Albuquerque	.429	14	7	7	1	3	6	0	0	1	2	0	0	0	0	0	4	0	0	0	.857	.429
Rogers, Kevin, Phoenix†	.000	3	1	1	0	0	0	0	0	0	0	0	0	0	0	0	1	0	0	0	.000	.000
Rohde, Dave, Tucson†	.276	73	210	170	27	47	59	8	2	0	20	6	2	0	32	1	17	2	2	5	.347	.387
Romanoli, Paul, Col. Springs*	.000	31	1	0	0	0	0	0	0	0	0	0	0	0	1	0	0	0	0	0	.000	1.000
Roper, John, Phoenix	1.000	1	1	1	0	1	1	0	0	0	0	0	0	0	0	0	0	0	0	0	1.000	1.000
Rosselli, Joe, Phoenix	.000	14	15	12	0	0	0	0	0	0	0	3	0	0	0	0	0	0	0	0	.000	.000
Rossy, Rico, Las Vegas	.301	98	381	316	44	95	113	11	2	1	45	2	6	2	55	2	36	3	7	13	.358	.401
Russo, Paul, Las Vegas	.297	44	160	148	17	44	66	10	0	4	19	1	2	0	9	2	31	0	1	4	.446	.333
Sager, A.J., Colorado Springs	.286	23	23	21	2	6	6	0	0	0	1	0	0	0	2	0	7	0	0	1	.286	.348
St. Claire, Randy, Calgary	.000	54	2	2	0	0	0	0	0	0	0	0	0	0	0	0	2	0	0	0	.000	.000
Sanders, Scott, Las Vegas	.000	1	1	1	0	0	0	0	0	0	0	0	0	0	0	0	1	0	0	0	.000	.000
Saunders, Doug, Edm.-Tac.	.272	55	162	151	21	41	69	7	3	5	28	1	2	1	7	0	32	0	0	3	.457	.304
Schofield, Dick, Vancouver	.189	16	60	53	5	10	14	4	0	0	9	1	2	1	3	0	3	0	0	1	.264	.237
Scott, Darryl, Colorado Springs	.000	59	5	5	0	0	0	0	0	0	0	0	0	0	0	0	5	0	0	0	.000	.000
Scott, Gary, Phoenix	.265	68	253	219	33	58	93	16	2	5	26	0	1	7	26	5	39	2	2	3	.425	.360
Sealy, Scot, Tacoma	.300	4	10	10	1	3	3	0	0	0	0	0	0	0	0	0	0	0	0	0	.300	.300
See, Larry, Las Vegas	.307	38	122	114	11	35	51	8	1	2	20	0	2	1	5	0	12	0	0	5	.447	.336
Sepeda, Jamie, Tucson	.167	8	6	6	1	1	1	0	0	0	1	0	0	0	0	0	3	0	0	0	.167	.167
Sheets, Andy, Tacoma	.293	132	483	437	57	128	181	29	9	2	47	10	4	0	32	2	83	8	3	9	.414	.338
Sheldon, Scott, Edmonton	.258	45	150	128	21	33	54	7	1	4	12	4	1	2	15	0	15	4	2	0	.422	.342
Shelton, Ben, Salt Lake	.242	9	39	33	7	8	14	1	1	1	6	0	0	0	6	0	16	0	0	0	.424	.359
Sherman, Darrell, Tacoma*	.257	119	421	350	59	90	111	9	3	2	31	10	4	3	54	0	49	19	6	6	.317	.358
Shifflett, Steve, Col. Springs	.250	23	4	4	0	1	1	0	0	0	1	0	0	0	0	0	1	0	0	0	.250	.250
Shouse, Brian, Calgary*	.333	8	8	6	0	2	2	0	0	0	1	2	0	0	0	0	0	0	0	0	.333	.333
Simmons, Nelson, Calgary†	.281	107	333	299	44	84	128	17	0	9	58	0	4	0	30	3	45	1	1	5	.428	.342
Simms, Mike, Tucson	.295	85	361	319	56	94	175	26	8	13	66	0	4	3	35	0	65	10	2	6	.549	.366
Simons, Mitch, Salt Lake	.325	130	543	480	87	156	207	34	4	3	46	4	2	10	47	2	45	32	16	9	.431	.395
Small, Mark, Tucson	.600	51	5	5	2	3	3	0	0	0	2	0	0	0	0	0	1	0	0	0	.600	.600
Smiley, Reuben, Las Vegas*	.219	34	106	96	10	21	36	4	1	3	17	0	2	0	8	1	19	6	3	2	.375	.274
Smith, Ira, Las Vegas	.325	59	229	209	39	68	106	19	5	3	22	4	1	2	13	0	25	5	4	3	.507	.369
Snider, Van, Salt Lake*	.357	32	123	115	25	41	69	7	0	7	28	1	0	0	7	0	17	1	0	5	.600	.393
Snyder, Cory, Las Vegas	.265	8	35	34	4	9	10	1	0	0	5	0	0	0	1	0	10	0	0	2	.294	.286
Sojo, Luis, Tacoma	.176	4	17	17	1	3	6	0	0	1	1	0	0	0	0	0	2	0	0	0	.353	.176
Spearman, Vernon, Albuquerque*	.172	22	40	29	7	5	7	0	1	0	2	0	0	0	11	0	4	2	2	2	.241	.400
Springer, Steve, L.V.	.218	35	90	87	7	19	25	3	0	1	10	0	1	0	2	1	17	1	1	5	.287	.233

Player, Team	Avg.	G	TPA	AB	R	H	TB	2B	3B	HR	RBI	SH	SF	HP	BB	IBB	SO	SB	CS	GDP	Slg.	OBP
Stahoviak, Scott, Salt Lake*	.303	9	39	33	6	10	11	1	0	0	5	0	0	0	6	0	3	2	0	0	.333	.410
Stankiewicz, Andy, Tucson	.276	25	104	87	16	24	31	4	0	1	15	2	1	0	14	0	8	3	1	3	.356	.373
Strittmatter, Mark, Col. Springs	.294	5	17	17	1	5	7	2	0	0	3	0	0	0	0	0	3	0	0	0	.412	.294
Sveum, Dale, Calgary†	.284	118	462	408	71	116	188	34	1	12	70	1	5	0	48	2	78	2	2	9	.461	.356
Sweeney, Mark, Vancouver*	.345	69	275	226	48	78	117	14	2	7	59	1	1	2	43	4	33	3	1	6	.518	.452
Tatum, Jim, Colorado Springs	.323	27	102	93	17	30	55	7	0	6	18	0	2	1	6	0	21	0	1	2	.591	.363
Taylor, Kerry, Las Vegas	.273	8	11	11	1	3	4	1	0	0	1	0	0	0	0	0	6	0	0	0	.364	.273
Taylor, Scott, Calgary*	.111	27	27	27	1	3	3	0	0	0	0	0	0	0	0	0	9	0	0	0	.111	.111
Tejero, Fausto, Vancouver	.260	37	107	96	10	25	28	3	0	0	8	1	0	0	10	1	22	2	0	0	.292	.330
Thompson, Mark, Col. Springs	.300	11	12	10	3	3	6	0	0	1	1	2	0	0	0	0	4	0	0	0	.600	.300
Thurman, Gary, Tacoma	.300	93	392	363	65	109	158	10	12	5	46	3	1	5	20	0	62	22	8	2	.435	.344
Thurston, Jerrey, Las Vegas	.200	5	21	20	2	4	5	1	0	0	0	0	0	0	1	0	5	0	0	0	.250	.238
Tomberlin, Andy, Edmonton*	.250	14	59	52	9	13	22	3	0	2	7	1	0	1	5	0	15	0	0	1	.423	.328
Traxler, Brian, Albuquerque*	.283	110	378	353	46	100	159	24	1	11	50	1	0	0	24	3	27	1	3	11	.450	.329
Treadwell, Jody, Albuquerque	.400	30	20	15	2	6	6	0	0	0	5	3	1	0	1	0	3	0	0	0	.400	.412
Trlicek, Rick, Phoenix	.000	38	4	2	1	0	0	0	0	0	0	0	0	0	2	0	2	0	0	0	.000	.000
Turang, Brian, Tacoma	.240	59	215	196	22	47	56	4	1	1	18	3	3	0	13	0	35	7	4	7	.286	.283
Turner, Chris, Vancouver	.266	80	324	282	44	75	108	20	2	3	48	1	2	5	34	2	54	3	0	5	.383	.353
Valdez, Carlos, Phoenix	.000	18	2	2	0	0	0	0	0	0	0	0	0	0	0	0	1	0	0	0	.000	.000
Valdez, Sergio, Phoenix	.100	18	28	20	2	2	3	1	0	0	1	5	0	0	3	0	4	0	0	0	.150	.217
Van Burkleo, Ty, Col. Springs*	.286	76	264	231	43	66	126	14	2	14	57	1	2	1	29	2	57	2	1	1	.545	.365
Vanderweele, Doug, Phoenix	.000	11	2	2	0	0	0	0	0	0	0	0	0	0	0	0	2	0	0	0	.000	.000
Vatcher, Jim, Las Vegas	.292	101	399	356	56	104	162	31	3	7	43	2	5	3	33	6	46	3	4	6	.455	.353
Vaughn, Derek, Vancouver	.667	1	3	3	0	2	2	0	0	0	0	0	0	0	0	0	0	1	0	0	.667	.667
Velandia, Jorge, Las Vegas	.262	66	230	206	25	54	72	12	3	0	25	7	2	2	13	1	37	0	0	5	.350	.309
Wagner, Billy, Tucson*	.400	13	14	10	1	4	4	0	0	0	0	2	0	0	2	0	5	0	0	0	.400	.500
Wakamatsu, Don, Tacoma	.156	9	35	32	3	5	6	1	0	0	5	6	0	1	2	0	8	0	0	4	.188	.229
Wall, Donne, Tucson	.083	28	39	36	0	3	3	0	0	0	1	3	0	0	0	0	6	0	0	3	.083	.083
Wallach, Tim, Albuquerque	.333	1	3	3	1	1	1	0	0	0	1	0	0	0	0	0	2	0	0	0	.333	.333
Walters, Dan, Col. Springs	.284	52	165	155	15	44	66	9	2	3	23	1	1	1	7	1	20	0	0	6	.426	.317
Waring, Jim, Tucson*	.286	5	7	7	1	2	5	0	0	1	1	0	0	0	0	0	1	0	0	0	.714	.286
Weber, Wes, Tac.-L.V.	.167	29	7	6	1	1	1	0	0	0	0	0	0	0	1	0	3	0	0	0	.167	.286
Wehner, John, Calgary	.329	40	173	158	30	52	80	12	2	4	24	1	0	2	12	1	16	8	4	3	.506	.384
Westbrook, Destry, Tucson	.000	5	1	1	0	0	0	0	0	0	0	0	0	0	0	0	1	0	0	0	.000	.000
Whitaker, Steve, Phoenix*	.333	16	13	12	2	4	6	0	1	0	2	0	0	0	0	0	2	0	0	1	.500	.333
White, Chris, Tucson	.000	5	1	1	0	0	0	0	0	0	0	0	0	0	0	0	1	0	0	0	.000	.000
White, Rick, Calgary	.133	14	16	15	0	2	2	0	0	0	0	1	0	0	0	0	3	0	0	0	.133	.133
Whitehurst, Wally, Phoenix	.000	4	2	1	0	0	0	0	0	0	0	0	0	0	1	0	0	0	0	0	.000	.500
Widger, Chris, Tacoma	.276	50	184	174	29	48	88	11	1	9	21	1	0	0	9	0	29	0	0	4	.506	.311
Wilkerson, Curtis, Tacoma†	.222	5	19	18	1	4	4	0	0	0	3	0	0	1	0	0	3	0	0	0	.222	.263
Wilkins, Rick, Tucson*	.333	4	15	12	0	4	4	0	0	0	4	0	1	0	2	0	0	0	0	0	.333	.400
Willard, Jerry, Tacoma*	.268	85	279	228	33	61	104	16	0	9	47	0	3	3	45	6	43	0	0	7	.456	.391
Williams, George, Edmonton†	.310	81	347	290	53	90	149	20	0	13	55	3	2	2	50	6	52	0	4	9	.514	.413
Williams, Keith, Phoenix	.301	24	95	83	7	25	37	4	1	2	14	4	2	1	5	0	11	0	0	4	.446	.341
Williams, Reggie, Albuquerque†	.312	66	269	234	44	73	116	15	5	6	29	1	3	1	30	0	46	6	4	3	.496	.388
Williams, Todd, Albuquerque	.000	25	4	4	0	0	0	0	0	0	0	0	0	0	0	0	4	0	0	0	.000	.000
Willis, Travis, Calgary	1.000	22	1	1	0	1	1	0	0	0	1	0	0	0	0	0	0	0	0	0	1.000	1.000
Wilson, Gary, Calgary	.500	6	3	2	0	1	1	0	0	0	0	1	0	0	0	0	1	0	0	0	.500	.500
Wimmer, Chris, Phoenix	.263	132	503	449	55	118	155	23	4	2	44	5	5	13	31	1	49	13	7	10	.345	.325
Winston, Darrin, Calgary	.000	53	2	2	0	0	0	0	0	0	0	0	0	0	0	0	0	0	0	0	.000	.000
Wojciechowski, Steve, Edm.*	.000	14	1	1	0	0	0	0	0	0	0	0	0	0	0	0	0	0	0	0	.000	.000
Wolfe, Joel, Edmonton	.205	11	43	39	4	8	11	3	0	0	4	1	1	0	2	0	7	0	2	1	.282	.238
Womack, Tony, Calgary*	.280	30	119	107	12	30	35	3	1	0	6	0	0	0	12	1	11	7	5	1	.327	.353
Wood, Jason, Edmonton	.235	127	471	421	49	99	135	20	5	2	50	6	12	3	29	3	72	1	4	13	.321	.282
Worrell, Tim, Las Vegas	.000	10	4	4	0	0	0	0	0	0	0	0	0	0	0	0	3	0	0	0	.000	.000
Young, Ernie, Edmonton	.277	95	407	347	70	96	170	21	4	15	72	1	7	3	49	1	73	2	2	5	.490	.365
Young, Kevin, Calgary	.536	45	181	163	24	58	107	23	1	8	34	0	3	0	15	0	21	6	3	4	.656	.403

GRAND SLAMS: Deer, Gainer, Hajek, Pulliam, 2 each; Abreu, Bean, Burks, Cockrell, Coomer, Dalesandro, Demetral, Dunn, Garcia, Goff, Greene, Hocking, Makarewicz, McDavid, Murray, Pozo, A. Rodriguez, Russo, Saunders, Simms, Snider, Wehner, K. Williams, E. Young, 1 each.
AWARDED FIRST BASE ON CATCHER'S INTERFERENCE: Cianfrocco 2 (Chavez, Huckaby); Gainer 2 (Mulligan 2); Forbes (Geo. Williams); Parker (Geo. Williams); Ramos (Geo. Williams); Sweeney (Geo. Williams).

PLAYERS WITH TWO OR MORE TEAMS

Player, Team	Avg.	G	TPA	AB	R	H	TB	2B	3B	HR	RBI	SH	SF	HP	BB	IBB	SO	SB	CS	GDP	Slg.	OBP
Bennett, Erik, Vancouver	.000	28	0	0	0	0	0	0	0	0	0	0	0	0	0	0	0	0	0	0	.000	.000
Bennett, Erik, Tucson	.250	14	4	4	0	1	1	0	0	0	0	0	0	0	0	0	0	0	0	0	.250	.250
Brink, Brad, Phoenix	.111	11	9	9	0	1	1	0	0	0	0	0	0	0	0	0	2	0	0	0	.111	.111
Brink, Brad, Edmonton	.000	9	0	0	0	0	0	0	0	0	0	0	0	0	0	0	0	0	0	0	.000	.000
Daspit, Jim, Tucson	.200	36	6	5	0	1	1	0	0	0	0	1	0	0	0	0	2	0	0	0	.200	.200
Daspit, Jim, Edmonton	.000	2	0	0	0	0	0	0	0	0	0	0	0	0	0	0	0	0	0	0	.000	.000
Deer, Rob, Vancouver	.288	25	98	80	16	23	42	5	1	4	20	0	2	0	16	2	32	0	0	1	.525	.398
Deer, Rob, Las Vegas	.291	64	255	223	38	65	131	18	3	14	45	0	1	0	31	4	57	2	2	3	.587	.376
Fesh, Sean, Tucson*	.000	10	0	0	0	0	0	0	0	0	0	0	0	0	0	0	0	0	0	0	.000	.000
Fesh, Sean, Las Vegas*	.000	30	1	1	0	0	0	0	0	0	0	0	0	0	0	0	1	0	0	0	.000	.000
Hansell, Greg, Albuquerque	.500	8	3	2	1	1	1	0	0	0	0	1	0	0	0	0	0	0	0	0	.500	.500
Hansell, Greg, Salt Lake	.000	7	0	0	0	0	0	0	0	0	0	0	0	0	0	0	0	0	0	0	.000	.000
Jackson, John, Vancouver*	.301	35	140	113	20	34	46	7	1	1	11	3	0	2	22	2	15	8	3	3	.407	.423
Jackson, John, Salt Lake*	.278	55	225	194	39	54	86	14	3	4	21	3	3	3	22	0	20	8	2	4	.443	.356
Loiselle, Rich, Las Vegas	.125	8	8	8	1	1	1	0	0	0	0	0	0	0	0	0	5	0	0	0	.125	.125
Loiselle, Rich, Tucson	.000	2	0	0	0	0	0	0	0	0	0	0	0	0	0	0	0	0	0	0	.000	.000
Newfield, Marc, Tacoma	.278	53	222	198	30	55	81	11	0	5	30	0	0	5	19	1	30	1	0	6	.409	.356
Newfield, Marc, Las Vegas	.343	20	76	70	10	24	40	5	1	3	12	1	1	1	3	0	11	2	0	1	.571	.373

Player, Team	Avg.	G	TPA	AB	R	H	TB	2B	3B	HR	RBI	SH	SF	HP	BB	IBB	SO	SB	CS	GDP	Slg.	OBP
Pose, Scott, Albuquerque*	.188	7	18	16	5	3	4	1	0	0	1	0	0	0	2	0	0	2	0	0	.250	.278
Pose, Scott, Salt Lake*	.310	70	239	203	41	63	74	9	1	0	19	3	3	1	29	2	28	13	4	2	.365	.394
Saunders, Doug, Edmonton	.188	5	16	16	2	3	7	2	1	0	4	0	0	0	0	0	2	0	0	0	.438	.188
Saunders, Doug, Tacoma	.281	50	146	135	19	38	62	5	2	5	24	1	2	1	7	0	30	0	0	3	.459	.317
Weber, Wes, Tacoma	.000	20	0	0	0	0	0	0	0	0	0	0	0	0	0	0	0	0	0	0	.000	.000
Weber, Wes, Las Vegas	.167	9	7	6	1	1	1	0	0	0	0	0	0	0	1	0	3	0	0	0	.167	.286

1995 PITCHING

TEAM

Team	W	L	Pct.	ERA	G	CG	ShO	Sv.	IP	H	TBF	R	ER	HR	SH	SF	HB	BB	IBB	SO	WP	Bk.
Vancouver	81	60	.574	4.08	141	14	11	26	1215.2	1242	5223	620	551	99	44	44	46	421	25	782	63	3
Albuquerque	75	69	.521	4.12	144	6	7	42	1248.2	1340	5441	688	571	98	40	42	31	490	47	919	60	4
Tucson	87	56	.608	4.50	143	1	8	41	1244.2	1425	5468	698	623	63	51	51	52	427	17	859	66	8
Tacoma	68	76	.472	4.55	144	10	8	40	1249.0	1354	5469	734	631	105	33	57	43	471	45	771	47	18
Las Vegas	61	83	.424	4.75	144	15	8	29	1230.1	1337	5544	780	649	108	61	53	46	543	37	794	69	5
Phoenix	62	82	.431	4.86	144	8	5	28	1275.2	1436	5609	765	689	105	60	54	25	496	50	852	83	9
Colo. Springs	77	66	.538	4.91	143	4	11	32	1212.0	1359	5408	760	661	96	53	53	45	509	35	803	62	11
Salt Lake	79	65	.549	5.03	144	10	5	40	1249.2	1446	5512	773	698	116	39	44	34	448	39	754	60	11
Edmonton	68	76	.472	5.13	144	6	5	32	1239.1	1384	5499	790	706	109	39	55	43	541	55	703	90	12
Calgary	58	83	.411	5.32	141	7	6	26	1195.0	1451	5356	812	707	111	40	42	43	401	27	719	50	7

INDIVIDUAL

TOP QUALIFIERS FOR EARNED-RUN AVERAGE TITLE

Minimum 115 innings. *Lefthanded pitcher.

Pitcher, Team	W	L	Pct.	ERA	G	GS	CG	ShO	GF	Sv.	IP	H	TBF	R	ER	HR	SH	SF	HB	BB	IBB	SO	WP	Bk.
Wall, Donne, Tucson	17	6	.739	3.30	28	28	0	0	0	0	177.1	190	732	72	65	5	6	4	5	32	1	119	5	1
Williams, Shad, Vancouver	9	7	.563	3.37	25	25	3	1	0	0	149.2	142	627	65	56	16	3	3	4	48	2	114	7	1
Johns, Doug, Edmonton*	9	5	.643	3.41	23	21	0	0	1	0	132.0	148	567	55	50	8	3	1	3	43	3	70	6	3
Sager, A.J., Colorado Springs	8	5	.615	3.50	23	22	1	1	0	0	133.2	153	564	61	52	14	4	3	2	23	1	80	0	0
Hawkins, LaTroy, Salt Lake	9	7	.563	3.55	22	22	4	1	0	0	144.1	150	601	63	57	7	5	2	1	40	1	74	6	1
Treadwell, Jody, Albuquerque	7	5	.583	3.96	30	15	1	1	4	1	125.0	121	510	61	55	15	2	5	2	32	4	79	9	1
McFarlin, Terric, Las Vegas	7	6	.538	3.96	58	2	0	0	20	7	122.2	120	535	67	54	11	6	3	2	59	4	85	18	0
Harriger, Denny, Las Vegas	9	9	.500	4.07	29	28	7	2	0	0	177.0	187	776	94	80	12	6	5	4	60	2	97	4	1
Holt, Chris, Tucson	5	8	.385	4.10	20	19	0	0	0	0	118.2	155	524	65	54	5	7	3	7	32	1	69	6	0
Taylor, Scott, Calgary*	5	8	.385	4.11	27	25	1	0	0	0	140.0	144	578	73	64	10	3	4	3	35	2	83	3	0
Harikkala, Tim, Tacoma	5	12	.294	4.24	25	24	4	1	0	0	146.1	151	638	78	69	13	4	2	55	3	73	7	0
Carlson, Dan, Phoenix	9	5	.643	4.27	23	22	2	0	1	0	132.0	138	582	67	63	11	7	7	3	66	0	93	6	1
Bustillos, Albert, Col. Springs	8	4	.667	4.61	34	19	0	0	5	3	132.2	151	572	82	68	15	4	2	4	33	0	77	8	0
Robinson, Scott, Phoenix	5	7	.417	4.66	31	15	0	0	9	0	123.2	134	519	68	64	14	2	3	4	37	1	61	4	0
Weber, Wes, Las Vegas	6	11	.353	4.67	29	21	2	0	9	0	150.1	170	663	92	78	16	5	6	4	50	10	86	6	3

DEPARTMENTAL LEADERS: W—Wall, 17; L—Barcelo, R. Phillips, 13; Pct.—E. Bennett, .900; G—Czajkowski, 60; GS—Barcelo, Harriger, Wall, Wasdin, 28; CG—Harriger, 7; ShO—Harriger, 2; GF—Czajkowski, 44; Sv.—Watkins, 20; IP—Wall, 177.1; H—Barcelo, 214; TBF—Harriger, 776; R—Barcelo, 131; ER—Barcelo, 112; HR—Wasdin, 26; SH—Jo. Martinez, 9; SF—Mauser, 13; HB—Misuraca, 8; BB—Shaw, 88; IBB—Weber, 10; SO—Wall, 119; WP—McFarlin, 18; Bk.—Converse, Kubinski, 4.

ALL PITCHERS

*Lefthanded pitcher.

Pitcher, Team	W	L	Pct.	ERA	G	GS	CG	ShO	GF	Sv.	IP	H	TBF	R	ER	HR	SH	SF	HB	BB	IBB	SO	WP	Bk.
Acevedo, Juan, Col. Springs	5	5	.500	6.14	3	3	0	0	0	0	14.2	18	68	11	10	0	1	1	2	7	0	7	2	1
Adams, Willie, Edmonton	2	5	.286	4.37	11	10	1	0	1	0	68.0	73	288	35	33	2	2	6	15	5	40	3	0
Akerfelds, Darrel, Vancouver	3	3	.500	4.50	9	9	0	0	0	0	48.0	60	216	24	24	5	3	3	4	19	1	27	3	1
Alicea, Miguel, Albuquerque	1	1	.500	4.05	7	0	0	0	5	3	6.2	6	31	5	3	0	2	0	0	4	1	0	3	0
Apana, Matt, Tacoma	8	8	.500	4.95	21	20	0	0	0	0	103.2	121	481	72	57	9	3	6	5	61	0	58	6	0
Arvesen, Scott, Las Vegas	0	0	.000	15.00	2	0	0	0	2	0	3.0	4	16	5	5	1	0	0	1	2	0	2	0	0
August, Don, Calgary	0	2	.000	4.50	2	2	0	0	0	0	8.0	10	39	7	4	0	2	1	0	4	0	4	0	0
Ayrault, Bob, Calgary	0	0	.000	4.91	6	0	0	0	3	0	7.1	7	35	4	4	0	0	1	1	4	1	3	0	0
Backlund, Brett, Calgary	2	3	.400	5.22	12	8	0	0	1	0	50.0	59	213	29	29	6	1	2	0	9	0	29	0	0
Bailey, Roger, Col. Springs	3	0	1.000	2.70	3	3	0	0	0	0	16.2	15	71	9	5	0	0	8	0	7	0	0	0	0
Baker, Scott, Edmonton*	4	7	.364	5.28	22	20	1	0	0	0	107.1	123	474	69	63	9	2	2	3	46	4	56	4	0
Bankhead, Scott, Edmonton	1	3	.250	7.85	12	0	0	0	5	1	18.1	28	90	18	16	2	3	1	1	7	2	15	0	0
Barcelo, Marc, Salt Lake	8	13	.381	7.05	28	28	2	0	0	0	143.0	214	684	131	112	19	5	5	6	59	2	63	4	2
Barton, Shawn, Phoenix*	2	0	1.000	1.80	15	0	0	0	8	2	25.0	20	95	5	5	2	1	0	0	5	0	25	0	0
Bennett, Chris, Calgary	0	0	.000	5.14	4	0	0	0	1	0	7.0	11	35	7	4	0	0	2	0	1	0	7	0	0
Bennett, Erik, Van.-Tuc.	9	1	.900	4.42	42	1	0	0	16	3	73.1	71	316	41	36	6	0	5	5	32	4	63	4	1
Berumen, Andres, Las Vegas	0	0	.000	5.40	3	0	0	0	0	0	3.1	4	16	2	2	0	0	1	2	0	3	0	0
Bielecki, Mike, Vancouver	1	0	1.000	0.00	3	1	0	0	0	0	5.0	2	21	3	0	0	0	0	2	0	4	0	0
Bittiger, Jeff, Edmonton	2	0	1.000	5.28	6	1	0	0	0	0	15.1	17	70	10	9	1	1	2	0	7	0	10	3	0
Bochtler, Doug, Las Vegas	2	3	.400	4.25	18	2	0	0	7	1	36.0	31	161	18	17	5	1	2	1	26	6	32	2	0
Boskie, Shawn, Vancouver	1	0	1.000	3.00	1	1	0	0	0	0	6.0	4	25	2	2	1	0	0	0	4	0	1	0	0
Bourgeois, Steve, Phoenix	1	1	.500	3.38	6	5	0	0	0	0	34.2	38	153	18	13	2	0	0	2	13	0	23	4	1
Bowie, Jim, Edmonton*	0	0	.000	7.50	7	0	0	0	7	0	6.0	8	28	5	5	2	0	1	1	3	0	4	0	0
Bream, Scott, Las Vegas	0	1	.000	0.00	1	0	0	0	1	0	0.1	1	5	1	0	0	1	0	0	2	0	0	0	0
Brink, Brad, Pho.-Edm.	2	6	.250	6.29	20	12	0	0	4	0	68.2	79	327	55	48	5	1	5	4	46	3	48	2	0
Briscoe, John, Edmonton	0	0	.000	3.00	3	3	0	0	0	0	6.0	5	26	2	2	0	0	0	0	6	0	3	0	0
Brocail, Doug, Tucson	1	0	1.000	3.86	3	3	0	0	0	0	16.1	18	74	9	7	1	0	1	2	4	0	16	0	0

Pitcher, Team	W	L	Pct.	ERA	G	GS	CG	ShO	GF	Sv.	IP	H	TBF	R	ER	HR	SH	SF	HB	BB	IBB	SO	WP	Bk.
Brock, Russ, Edmonton	1	8	.111	6.87	18	8	0	0	2	1	55.0	75	266	44	42	6	0	3	3	31	4	44	2	1
Brosnan, Jason, Albuquerque*	2	0	1.000	4.35	23	1	0	0	11	2	31.0	30	128	16	15	3	0	2	0	9	1	18	0	1
Bruske, Jim, Albuquerque	7	5	.583	4.11	43	6	0	0	13	4	114.0	128	492	54	52	6	4	4	3	41	2	99	3	0
Bryant, Scott, Edmonton	0	0	.000	0.00	2	0	0	0	1	0	3.1	3	14	0	0	0	0	0	0	0	0	3	1	0
Bryant, Shawn, Salt Lake*	4	1	.800	4.88	31	0	0	0	8	0	48.0	62	221	31	26	1	3	0	2	16	2	27	1	2
Bullard, Jason, Col. Springs	0	0	.000	7.27	4	0	0	0	1	0	8.2	18	48	13	7	1	0	1	1	5	1	5	0	1
Burcham, Tim, Phoenix	1	0	1.000	5.06	5	0	0	0	1	0	10.2	18	50	7	6	1	0	1	0	2	0	6	3	0
Burgos, Enrique, Phoenix*	2	6	.250	6.14	41	2	0	0	13	2	58.2	63	273	44	40	7	5	3	0	40	5	77	4	1
Burke, John, Col. Springs	7	1	.875	4.55	19	17	0	0	1	1	87.0	79	376	46	44	7	2	3	1	48	0	65	5	1
Bustillos, Albert, Col. Springs	8	4	.667	4.61	34	19	0	0	5	3	132.2	151	572	82	68	15	4	2	4	33	0	77	8	0
Butler, Mike, Vancouver*	0	0	.000	0.00	3	0	0	0	0	0	6.0	4	25	3	3	0	2	0	1	2	0	3	0	0
Cadaret, Greg, Las Vegas*	3	5	.375	5.88	28	4	0	0	6	0	52.0	56	234	40	34	6	2	3	0	22	0	52	10	0
Campbell, Kevin, Tacoma	3	2	.600	3.67	31	0	0	0	8	1	49.0	50	211	28	20	6	0	2	5	14	3	34	3	1
Carlson, Dan, Phoenix	9	5	.643	4.27	23	22	2	0	1	0	132.2	138	582	67	63	11	7	7	3	66	0	93	6	1
Carmona, Rafael, Tacoma	4	3	.571	5.06	8	8	1	1	0	0	48.0	52	212	29	27	6	1	0	3	19	1	37	1	3
Castillo, Juan, Tucson	0	4	.000	10.93	11	10	0	0	1	0	40.1	66	206	51	49	4	1	3	5	27	0	21	5	0
Castro, Nelson, Albuquerque	0	0	.000	0.00	2	0	0	0	2	1	2.1	0	7	0	0	0	0	0	1	0	0	2	1	0
Chavez, Tony, Vancouver	2	0	1.000	1.50	8	0	0	0	5	1	12.0	7	46	4	2	0	1	0	0	4	0	8	0	0
Clayton, Royal, Phoenix	0	2	.000	5.87	5	5	0	0	0	0	23.0	35	108	18	15	1	2	0	0	6	2	13	0	0
Colbert, Craig, Las Vegas	0	0	.000	0.00	1	0	0	0	1	0	1.0	1	5	0	0	0	0	0	0	0	0	1	0	0
Cole, Victor, Las Vegas	0	2	.000	6.41	4	4	0	0	0	0	19.2	19	86	17	14	4	1	1	0	10	0	12	1	1
Conroy, Brian, Col. Springs	0	2	.000	6.11	5	5	0	0	0	0	28.0	36	128	19	19	0	0	0	0	11	1	9	0	0
Converse, Jim, Tacoma	4	7	.364	5.99	17	12	0	0	3	0	73.2	96	337	57	49	5	4	5	1	36	1	43	4	4
Corbin, Archie, Calgary	1	5	.167	8.56	47	1	0	0	13	1	61.0	76	309	63	58	6	0	5	3	55	0	54	7	0
Correa, Ramser, Albuquerque	0	0	.000	0.00	2	0	0	0	0	0	4.0	5	16	0	0	0	0	0	0	1	1	3	0	0
Corsi, Jim, Edmonton	0	0	.000	0.00	3	0	0	0	3	3	3.0	3	10	0	0	0	0	0	0	1	0	3	0	0
Courtright, John, Salt Lake*	3	7	.300	6.80	18	17	1	0	0	0	84.2	108	384	70	64	6	5	7	0	36	7	42	4	2
Cromwell, Nate, Las Vegas*	0	2	.000	13.50	9	3	0	0	3	0	15.1	35	94	27	23	5	1	0	1	14	1	11	0	0
Crowther, Brent, Col. Springs	0	1	.000	7.00	1	1	0	0	0	0	6.0	11	30	6	5	1	0	1	0	2	0	1	0	0
Cummings, John, Tacoma*	0	1	.000	7.71	1	1	0	0	0	0	2.1	6	16	4	2	1	0	0	0	3	0	3	0	0
Czajkowski, Jim, Col. Springs	3	10	.231	5.06	60	0	0	0	44	17	83.2	90	382	54	47	8	6	8	2	52	7	56	4	0
Daal, Omar, Albuquerque*	2	3	.400	3.88	17	9	0	0	3	1	53.1	56	232	28	23	3	0	0	1	26	2	46	1	0
Darwin, Jeff, Tacoma	7	2	.778	2.70	46	0	0	0	31	12	63.1	51	256	21	19	2	3	3	1	21	5	51	0	0
Daspit, Jim, Tuc.-Edm.	5	2	.714	4.10	38	0	0	0	11	1	68.0	69	294	36	31	5	2	5	2	24	1	54	7	1
Davis, Tim, Tacoma*	0	1	.000	5.40	2	2	0	0	0	0	13.1	15	57	8	8	2	0	0	0	4	0	13	0	0
Davison, Scott, Tacoma	1	1	.500	5.32	8	3	0	0	2	0	22.0	21	91	14	13	1	1	1	0	4	0	12	1	1
Deer, Rob, Las Vegas	0	0	.000	0.00	1	0	0	0	1	0	1.0	1	6	0	0	0	0	0	0	1	0	1	0	0
DeLosSantos, Mariano, Calgary	3	6	.333	6.15	14	14	0	0	0	0	71.2	85	321	57	49	4	4	4	3	22	0	36	2	1
Demetral, Chris, Albuquerque	0	0	.000	0.00	1	0	0	0	0	0	0.0	0	0	0	0	0	0	0	0	0	0	0	0	0
Dishman, Glenn, Las Vegas*	6	3	.667	2.55	14	14	3	1	0	0	106.0	91	430	37	30	12	4	1	0	20	2	64	3	1
Dougherty, Jim, Tucson	1	0	1.000	3.27	8	0	0	0	7	1	11.0	11	46	4	4	1	0	0	0	5	0	12	0	1
Edenfield, Ken, Vancouver	7	2	.778	3.45	33	0	0	0	4	0	60.0	56	259	24	23	2	3	3	5	25	2	44	5	0
Edwards, Wayne, Albuquerque*	1	2	.333	5.06	14	0	0	0	3	1	16.0	17	82	16	9	1	2	1	0	17	3	12	2	0
Eischen, Joey, Albuquerque*	3	0	1.000	0.00	13	0	0	0	6	2	16.1	8	59	0	0	0	0	0	1	3	0	14	1	0
Elliott, Donnie, Las Vegas	1	0	1.000	4.50	7	0	0	0	3	1	8.0	8	35	4	4	1	1	1	0	4	1	2	0	0
Ericks, John, Calgary	2	1	.667	2.48	5	5	0	0	0	0	29.0	20	116	8	8	2	1	0	0	13	0	25	3	0
Ettles, Mark, Las Vegas	0	0	.000	7.82	10	0	0	0	3	0	12.2	21	62	11	11	4	0	1	0	3	0	10	1	0
Evans, Dave, Tucson	0	0	.000	0.00	2	0	0	0	0	0	3.0	2	12	0	0	0	0	0	0	1	0	4	0	0
Fesh, Sean, Tuc.-L.V.*	3	1	.750	2.81	40	0	0	0	12	1	51.1	64	237	23	16	2	4	3	0	19	5	25	1	1
Flynt, Bill, Calgary*	1	0	1.000	5.40	12	1	0	0	3	0	21.2	27	103	15	13	4	1	1	0	12	0	12	1	0
Fortugno, Tim, Vancouver*	1	1	.500	1.54	10	0	0	0	7	1	11.2	8	45	2	2	1	0	0	0	4	1	7	0	0
Fredrickson, Scott, Col. Springs	11	3	.786	3.45	58	1	0	0	20	4	75.2	70	348	40	29	2	8	3	5	47	5	70	15	2
Gallaher, Kevin, Tucson	1	1	.500	6.43	3	3	0	0	0	0	14.0	19	70	11	10	1	0	2	2	9	0	11	2	0
Gamez, Bob, Phoenix*	3	5	.375	5.59	36	9	0	0	5	2	66.0	76	292	46	41	6	4	1	0	27	4	41	7	0
Gandarillas, Gus, Salt Lake	2	3	.400	6.44	22	0	0	0	13	2	29.1	34	135	23	21	5	3	1	1	19	4	17	5	0
Garcia, Jose, Albuquerque	1	3	.250	6.32	11	0	0	0	4	0	15.2	19	73	11	11	3	2	4	0	7	1	10	0	0
Gardella, Mike, Phoenix*	0	0	.000	13.50	3	0	0	0	1	0	4.0	9	21	6	6	0	0	0	0	1	0	3	0	0
Gardner, Chris, Tucson	1	4	.200	8.54	16	2	0	0	6	0	26.1	43	127	26	25	0	2	1	0	19	1	6	1	1
Gavaghan, Sean, Salt Lake	1	4	.200	5.51	35	0	0	0	15	5	47.1	53	221	32	29	3	6	1	3	31	3	28	3	0
Gibson, Paul, Calgary*	0	2	.000	3.72	19	0	0	0	9	1	19.1	21	86	11	8	1	0	2	1	9	1	17	3	0
Glinatsis, George, Tacoma	1	2	.333	7.34	8	8	0	0	0	0	30.2	39	138	25	25	4	0	2	1	13	0	13	0	0
Gomez, Pat, Phoenix*	0	0	.000	27.00	2	0	0	0	0	0	1.1	5	12	5	4	0	0	0	0	3	2	1	1	0
Gould, Clint, Tacoma	0	0	.000	0.00	1	0	0	0	0	0	0.1	0	1	0	0	0	0	0	0	0	0	0	0	0
Grahe, Joe, Col. Springs	1	1	.500	3.27	2	2	1	0	0	0	11.0	7	41	4	4	1	1	1	0	3	0	4	0	0
Graybill, Dave, Tacoma	0	0	.000	6.75	6	0	0	0	4	0	9.1	12	43	8	7	1	0	2	0	6	0	6	0	0
Green, Otis, Tacoma*	4	1	.800	5.76	18	0	0	0	3	0	25.0	26	113	19	16	1	1	1	0	12	2	17	3	0
Greer, Ken, Phoenix	5	2	.714	3.98	38	0	0	0	13	1	63.1	65	270	29	28	1	3	2	0	19	1	41	5	0
Grundt, Ken, Col. Springs*	0	0	.000	4.76	9	0	0	0	1	0	5.2	9	30	5	3	0	0	0	0	4	0	5	0	0
Guetterman, Lee, Tacoma*	1	2	.333	2.95	33	1	0	0	9	4	36.2	33	147	12	12	2	0	1	0	9	2	21	1	0
Hancock, Lee, Calgary*	6	10	.375	5.07	34	17	1	0	5	0	113.2	146	510	78	64	9	5	0	4	27	2	49	4	1
Hansell, Greg, Alb.-S.L.	4	2	.667	6.14	15	6	0	0	3	1	48.1	64	218	35	33	5	2	1	2	10	2	32	3	1
Harikkala, Tim, Tacoma	5	12	.294	4.24	25	24	4	1	0	0	146.1	151	638	78	69	13	3	4	2	55	3	73	7	0
Harriger, Denny, Las Vegas	9	9	.500	4.07	29	28	7	2	0	0	177.0	187	776	94	80	12	6	5	4	60	2	97	4	1
Hartgraves, Dean, Tucson*	3	2	.600	2.11	14	0	0	0	9	5	21.1	21	91	6	5	0	0	1	1	5	2	15	0	0
Hathaway, Hilly, Las Vegas*	4	6	.400	6.22	14	14	1	0	0	0	63.2	76	285	49	44	4	4	3	1	27	0	37	6	0
Hawblitzel, Ryan, Col. Springs	5	3	.625	4.55	21	14	0	0	1	0	83.0	88	352	47	42	7	3	5	3	17	1	40	2	0
Hawkins, LaTroy, Salt Lake	9	7	.563	3.55	22	22	4	1	0	0	144.1	150	601	63	57	7	5	2	1	40	1	74	6	1
Haynes, Heath, Edmonton	2	0	1.000	6.27	12	0	0	0	1	0	18.2	21	87	14	13	1	0	0	3	11	3	13	2	0
Henry, Jon, Salt Lake	1	0	1.000	6.75	3	2	0	0	0	0	12.0	15	53	9	9	3	1	0	0	2	0	3	0	0
Heredia, Julian, Vancouver	5	3	.625	3.63	51	0	0	0	37	10	74.1	69	319	34	30	8	5	1	5	23	3	65	9	0
Hermanson, Dustin, Las Vegas	0	1	.000	3.50	31	0	0	0	22	11	36.0	35	174	23	14	5	0	0	2	29	0	42	1	1
Hernandez, Fernando, Las Vegas	1	6	.143	7.65	8	8	0	0	0	0	37.2	43	186	32	32	3	0	2	3	31	3	40	4	0
Hill, Milt, Calgary	1	3	.250	4.90	24	5	0	0	8	3	60.2	69	260	38	33	8	3	3	1	14	2	31	2	1

Pitcher, Team	W	L	Pct.	ERA	G	GS	CG	ShO	GF	Sv.	IP	H	TBF	R	ER	HR	SH	SF	HB	BB	IBB	SO	WP	Bk.
Holridge, David, Vancouver	0	2	.000	4.61	11	0	0	0	6	1	13.2	18	68	10	7	0	2	0	1	7	1	13	3	0
Hollins, Stacy, Edmonton	0	7	.000	10.31	7	7	0	0	0	0	29.2	47	156	43	34	4	0	1	1	21	3	25	6	0
Holman, Brad, Tacoma	1	0	1.000	8.10	5	0	0	0	1	0	6.2	9	31	6	6	0	0	0	0	3	0	1	0	0
Holman, Shawn, Albuquerque	5	6	.455	5.13	49	1	0	0	22	5	79.0	107	386	58	45	3	5	5	5	39	7	60	7	0
Holt, Chris, Tucson	5	8	.385	4.10	20	19	0	0	0	0	118.2	155	524	65	54	5	7	3	7	32	1	69	6	0
Holzemer, Mark, Vancouver*	3	2	.600	2.47	28	4	0	0	11	2	54.2	45	228	18	15	2	5	0	3	24	4	35	2	0
Hook, Chris, Phoenix	0	0	.000	1.50	4	0	0	0	0	0	6.0	2	22	1	1	0	0	0	0	3	0	5	0	1
Hope, John, Calgary	7	1	.875	2.79	13	13	3	1	0	0	80.2	76	322	29	25	3	3	1	3	11	0	41	1	0
Horsman, Vince, Salt Lake*	1	0	1.000	10.38	16	0	0	0	7	0	13.0	23	64	15	15	3	0	0	0	4	2	10	1	0
Hostetler, Tom, Edmonton	0	0	.000	12.60	4	0	0	0	1	0	5.0	9	31	7	7	2	0	0	0	8	1	7	1	0
Huisman, Rick, Tucson	6	1	.857	4.45	42	0	0	0	28	6	54.2	58	246	33	27	1	0	3	1	28	3	47	3	1
Hunter, Jim, Col. Springs	2	2	.500	6.96	10	4	0	0	0	0	32.1	43	154	27	25	1	2	2	2	17	2	13	2	0
Janicki, Pete, Vancouver	1	4	.200	7.03	9	9	0	0	0	0	48.2	64	227	38	38	8	1	4	1	23	0	34	0	0
Jean, Domingo, Tucson	2	1	.667	6.59	3	3	0	0	0	0	13.2	15	62	10	10	1	0	0	0	7	0	14	3	0
Jimenez, Miguel, Edmonton	0	0	.000	12.27	6	3	0	0	2	0	7.1	12	43	10	10	0	0	1	0	10	0	4	0	0
Johns, Doug, Edmonton*	9	5	.643	3.41	23	21	0	0	1	0	132.0	148	567	55	50	8	3	1	3	43	3	70	6	3
Johnson, Judd, Salt Lake*	1	1	.500	3.43	17	0	0	0	7	1	21.0	27	103	11	8	1	1	4	0	12	5	11	2	1
Johnston, Joel, Col. Springs	2	2	.500	5.96	18	0	0	0	6	0	22.2	26	106	16	15	1	3	2	2	12	0	14	0	0
Jones, Bobby, Col. Springs*	1	2	.333	7.30	11	8	0	0	0	0	40.2	50	204	38	33	5	4	1	2	33	1	48	4	1
Jones, Stacy, Phoenix	0	1	.000	8.53	4	0	0	0	0	0	6.1	8	35	9	6	0	0	2	0	6	1	4	0	0
Keagle, Greg, Las Vegas	7	6	.538	4.28	14	13	0	0	1	0	75.2	76	351	47	36	3	6	5	6	42	2	49	2	0
Keling, Korey, Vancouver	0	2	.000	4.08	3	3	0	0	0	0	17.2	18	75	9	8	1	0	0	0	6	0	16	0	0
Ketchen, Doug, Tucson	3	6	.333	6.28	19	12	0	0	2	1	71.2	101	332	55	50	8	3	2	2	26	0	30	3	1
Kile, Darryl, Tucson	2	1	.667	8.51	4	4	0	0	0	0	24.1	29	113	23	23	0	1	0	4	12	0	15	5	0
King, Kevin, Tacoma*	0	0	.000	7.56	16	0	0	0	6	0	16.2	33	85	14	14	2	1	0	0	7	1	10	2	1
Knudsen, Kurt, Phoenix	0	1	.000	5.03	11	1	0	0	4	1	19.2	18	86	13	11	2	0	2	0	11	0	20	0	0
Kotarski, Mike, Col. Springs*	2	2	.500	10.80	22	0	0	0	11	0	30.0	48	162	37	36	5	1	2	2	20	1	21	4	0
Krueger, Bill, Tacoma*	5	3	.625	4.26	10	8	0	0	0	0	50.2	52	213	30	24	4	1	1	2	9	0	39	2	0
Kubinski, Tim, Edmonton*	1	2	.333	4.78	6	5	0	0	0	0	32.0	34	136	18	17	4	0	4	0	10	0	12	0	4
Leftwich, Phil, Vancouver	2	0	1.000	3.19	6	5	1	0	0	0	36.2	28	142	13	13	4	2	1	0	9	0	25	3	0
Leiper, Dave, Edmonton*	1	0	1.000	13.50	2	0	0	0	1	0	1.1	4	10	2	2	0	0	0	1	2	1	1	0	0
Lewis, Scott, Tacoma	1	1	.500	9.64	3	2	0	0	0	0	9.1	13	47	10	10	1	1	1	3	4	0	11	0	1
Lieber, Jon, Calgary	1	5	.167	7.01	14	14	0	0	0	0	77.0	122	365	69	60	6	1	0	0	19	0	34	0	0
Lilliquist, Derek, Albuquerque*	0	0	.000	2.70	13	0	0	0	12	5	13.1	18	55	4	4	1	0	0	3	2	9	0	0	0
Logsdon, Kevin, Col. Springs*	0	0	.000	24.00	2	0	0	0	1	0	3.0	8	21	8	8	1	0	0	0	5	0	2	0	1
Loiselle, Rich, L.V.-Tuc.	2	2	.500	5.97	10	8	1	1	0	0	37.2	44	175	31	25	5	1	0	2	13	0	20	0	1
Long, Joey, Las Vegas*	1	3	.250	4.60	25	0	0	0	9	0	31.1	38	143	22	16	1	0	4	0	16	2	13	0	0
Lorraine, Andrew, Vancouver*	6	6	.500	3.96	18	18	4	1	0	0	97.2	105	420	49	43	7	4	3	3	30	1	51	4	0
Mack, Tony, Vancouver	0	1	.000	4.50	4	3	0	0	0	0	20.0	19	83	10	10	4	1	1	0	6	0	15	1	0
Manzanillo, Ravelo, Calgary*	0	2	.000	12.75	8	1	0	0	0	0	12.0	23	65	18	17	4	0	1	1	10	0	2	1	3
Martinez, Jesus, Albuquerque*	1	1	.500	4.50	2	0	0	0	1	0	4.0	4	20	2	2	1	1	1	4	2	5	0	0
Martinez, Jose, Las Vegas	6	10	.375	4.75	27	25	2	1	0	0	151.2	156	646	86	80	9	9	5	7	44	2	64	5	0
Martinez, Pedro, Tucson*	1	1	.500	6.62	20	3	0	0	6	2	34.0	44	158	28	25	2	2	4	2	13	1	21	0	0
Maurer, Ron, Albuquerque	0	0	.000	0.00	1	0	0	0	1	0	1.0	0	3	0	0	0	0	0	0	0	0	1	0	0
Mauser, Tim, Las Vegas	3	4	.429	4.80	35	0	0	0	15	0	50.2	63	233	39	27	6	4	13	1	20	2	32	1	0
Maysey, Matt, Calgary	8	7	.533	5.50	44	12	0	0	4	1	103.0	122	468	67	63	9	2	3	7	44	3	71	7	0
McCarthy, Tom, Albuquerque	3	3	.500	6.00	13	8	0	0	1	0	48.0	61	223	41	32	4	1	2	1	22	2	28	2	0
McCurry, Jeff, Calgary	0	0	.000	1.80	3	0	0	0	0	0	5.0	3	22	1	1	0	0	2	2	0	2	0	0
McFarlin, Terric, Las Vegas	7	6	.538	3.96	58	2	0	0	20	7	122.2	120	535	67	54	11	6	3	2	59	4	85	18	0
McMurtry, Craig, Tucson	6	1	.857	1.29	13	13	1	0	0	0	69.2	54	275	11	10	2	3	1	4	19	1	41	5	0
Mecir, Jim, Tacoma	1	4	.200	3.10	40	0	0	0	22	8	69.2	63	298	29	24	3	3	1	1	28	7	46	5	0
Menendez, Tony, Phoenix	5	6	.455	3.92	50	0	0	0	31	13	64.1	67	288	34	28	6	5	4	2	32	9	61	3	0
Merriman, Brett, Las Vegas	2	2	.500	8.25	11	0	0	0	4	0	12.0	14	59	12	11	1	0	0	0	12	1	7	2	0
Milacki, Bob, Tacoma	6	4	.600	5.27	12	12	1	0	0	0	71.2	94	322	50	42	5	2	3	0	23	1	31	0	0
Milchin, Mike, Albuquerque*	8	4	.667	4.32	18	17	2	1	0	0	83.1	94	359	43	40	2	1	2	0	30	1	50	5	0
Mimbs, Mark, Albuquerque*	6	5	.545	2.97	23	16	1	0	2	0	106.0	105	433	40	35	7	3	3	1	22	0	96	7	1
Mintz, Steve, Phoenix	5	2	.714	2.39	31	0	0	0	19	7	49.0	42	205	16	13	4	3	0	2	21	4	36	4	0
Misuraca, Mike, Salt Lake	9	6	.600	5.34	31	19	1	0	2	0	143.1	174	628	93	85	15	0	6	8	36	1	67	7	0
Mlicki, Doug, Tucson	1	2	.333	5.56	6	6	0	0	0	0	34.0	44	155	27	21	3	2	1	2	6	0	22	1	0
Mohler, Mike, Edmonton*	2	1	.667	2.60	29	0	0	0	17	5	45.0	40	191	16	13	0	3	0	0	20	2	28	4	0
Montalvo, Rafael, Albuquerque	3	5	.375	2.65	49	0	0	0	19	4	98.1	105	430	44	29	5	2	3	4	34	7	65	1	0
Monteleone, Rich, Vancouver	1	0	1.000	3.24	7	1	0	0	1	1	16.2	19	73	7	6	1	0	1	0	3	0	7	0	0
Morman, Alvin, Tucson*	5	1	.833	3.91	45	0	0	0	10	3	48.1	50	211	26	21	6	5	8	0	20	1	36	2	0
Morrison, Keith, Vancouver	14	9	.609	4.93	28	26	4	1	1	0	160.2	178	685	97	88	16	2	11	6	40	0	84	4	0
Mulholland, Terry, Phoenix*	0	0	.000	2.25	1	1	0	0	0	0	4.0	4	18	3	1	0	0	0	1	0	4	0	0
Munoz, Oscar, Salt Lake	8	6	.571	4.95	19	19	1	1	0	0	112.2	121	486	67	62	9	0	7	3	35	1	74	7	0
Murphy, Dan, Edmonton	0	1	.000	5.40	1	0	0	0	0	0	1.2	1	8	1	1	0	0	0	0	3	0	2	0	0
Naulty, Dan, Salt Lake	2	6	.250	5.18	42	8	0	0	19	4	90.1	92	393	55	52	10	2	1	2	47	2	76	6	0
Nied, David, Colorado Springs	1	1	.500	4.99	7	7	0	0	0	0	30.2	31	141	18	17	0	4	0	2	25	2	21	2	0
O'Donoghue, John, Albuquerque*	5	6	.455	3.82	25	18	1	1	3	0	92.0	97	394	58	39	10	1	1	0	25	0	59	3	0
Olivares, Omar, Col. Springs	0	1	.000	5.40	3	2	0	0	0	0	11.2	14	52	7	7	1	1	1	2	6	0	0	0	0
Osik, Keith, Calgary	0	0	.000	4.50	2	0	0	0	0	0	2.0	1	8	1	1	0	0	0	1	0	3	0	0
Osuna, Antonio, Albuquerque	0	1	.000	4.42	19	0	0	0	17	11	18.1	15	76	9	9	2	1	0	1	9	0	19	2	0
Painter, Lance, Col. Springs*	0	3	.000	5.96	11	4	0	0	3	0	25.2	32	117	20	17	3	0	0	1	11	1	12	0	1
Park, Chan Ho, Albuquerque	6	7	.462	4.91	23	22	0	0	0	0	110.0	93	487	64	60	10	3	2	6	76	2	101	8	2
Parra, Jose, Albuquerque	3	2	.600	5.13	12	10	1	1	1	1	52.2	62	232	33	30	7	4	2	1	17	3	33	2	0
Patrick, Bronswell, Tucson	5	1	.833	4.19	43	4	0	0	10	1	81.2	91	352	42	38	3	2	3	1	21	1	62	4	0
Patterson, Ken, Vancouver*	0	0	.000	0.82	8	0	0	0	3	1	11.0	12	46	1	1	0	0	0	4	1	4	1	0
Peek, Tim, Edmonton	0	0	.000	4.57	12	0	0	0	3	1	21.2	20	87	11	11	3	0	1	0	7	0	6	2	0
Peever, Lloyd, Col. Springs	3	2	.600	5.36	8	8	0	0	0	0	42.0	45	185	26	25	5	0	3	1	16	0	25	3	0
Phillips, Randy, Phoenix	4	13	.235	5.11	25	24	2	1	0	0	132.0	155	574	83	75	11	4	6	4	40	2	66	8	2
Phillips, Tony, Tacoma	3	2	.600	4.12	47	1	0	0	19	1	87.1	98	370	44	40	6	3	7	6	14	7	44	0	2
Phoenix, Steve, Edmonton	4	3	.571	4.50	40	0	0	0	25	5	64.0	66	280	36	32	6	5	3	1	28	4	28	5	0

CLASS AAA Pacific Coast League

Pitcher, Team	W	L	Pct.	ERA	G	GS	CG	ShO	GF	Sv.	IP	H	TBF	R	ER	HR	SH	SF	HB	BB	IBB	SO	WP	Bk.
Piatt, Doug, Phoenix	0	1	.000	5.87	6	0	0	0	2	0	7.2	7	34	5	5	0	1	1	0	5	1	3	0	0
Plantenberg, Erik, Las Vegas*	0	0	.000	81.00	2	0	0	0	0	0	0.1	3	5	3	3	0	0	1	0	1	0	1	0	0
Pose, Scott, Salt Lake	0	0	.000	0.00	1	0	0	0	1	0	1.0	0	4	0	0	0	0	0	1	0	0	0	0	0
Powell, Ross, Tucson*	3	3	.500	3.08	13	4	0	0	5	1	38.0	37	169	16	13	3	5	0	1	15	0	34	1	0
Pulido, Carlos, Salt Lake*	8	1	.889	4.67	43	3	0	0	9	3	71.1	87	321	42	37	10	1	0	2	20	4	38	0	1
Pyc, Dave, Albuquerque*	0	1	.000	3.86	1	1	0	0	0	0	7.0	7	31	5	3	1	0	1	0	2	1	3	0	0
Ralph, Curtis, Calgary	1	4	.200	8.44	28	0	0	0	11	1	32.0	43	159	35	30	2	2	0	2	23	4	27	3	0
Ratekin, Mark, Vancouver	3	2	.600	5.33	19	3	0	0	3	0	50.2	62	223	35	30	7	6	3	1	18	2	14	3	0
Rath, Gary, Albuquerque*	3	5	.375	5.08	8	8	0	0	0	0	39.0	46	178	31	22	4	1	1	2	20	0	23	2	0
Rekar, Bryan, Colorado Springs	4	2	.667	1.49	7	7	2	1	0	0	48.1	29	182	10	8	0	1	0	2	13	0	39	3	0
Renko, Steve, Vancouver	2	5	.286	4.21	10	9	0	0	0	0	51.1	53	226	29	24	2	0	3	0	18	0	22	5	0
Revenig, Todd, Edmonton	4	5	.444	4.31	45	0	0	0	30	10	54.1	53	230	32	26	5	3	3	2	15	1	28	2	0
Reynoso, Armando, Col. Springs	2	1	.667	1.57	5	5	0	0	0	0	23.0	14	86	4	4	1	0	1	0	6	1	17	0	1
Risley, Bill, Tacoma	0	0	.000	0.00	1	0	0	0	0	0	1.0	0	4	0	0	0	0	0	0	1	0	2	0	0
Robertson, Rich, Salt Lake*	5	0	1.000	2.44	7	7	1	0	0	0	44.1	31	172	13	12	2	2	0	0	12	1	40	1	0
Robinson, Scott, Phoenix	5	7	.417	4.66	31	15	0	0	9	0	123.2	134	519	68	64	14	2	3	4	37	1	61	4	0
Rodriguez, Felix, Albuquerque	3	2	.600	4.24	14	11	0	0	0	0	51.0	52	224	29	24	5	4	1	0	26	0	46	0	1
Rogers, Kevin, Phoenix*	0	0	.000	4.15	3	1	0	0	0	0	4.1	9	22	2	2	0	0	0	0	2	0	1	2	0
Rohde, Dave, Tucson	0	0	.000	0.00	1	0	0	0	1	0	1.0	0	4	0	0	0	0	0	0	1	0	0	0	0
Romanoli, Paul, Col. Springs*	3	1	.750	4.50	31	0	0	0	9	3	20.0	27	99	13	10	2	1	1	1	10	2	23	1	0
Roper, John, Phoenix	0	1	.000	9.00	1	1	0	0	0	0	3.0	5	14	3	3	0	0	1	0	0	0	2	0	0
Rose, Scott, Edmonton	0	2	.000	6.30	5	1	0	0	2	0	10.0	13	45	7	7	0	1	0	0	7	0	0	0	0
Rosselli, Joe, Phoenix*	4	3	.571	4.99	13	13	1	0	0	0	79.1	94	332	47	44	8	2	4	0	12	0	34	2	0
Ryan, Matt, Calgary	0	0	.000	1.93	5	0	0	0	4	1	4.2	5	20	1	1	0	0	1	1	2	0	0	1	0
Rychel, Kevin, Calgary	0	1	.000	10.38	10	0	0	0	3	0	8.2	14	45	11	10	3	0	0	6	4	1	0	0
Sager, A.J., Col. Springs	8	5	.615	3.50	23	22	1	1	0	0	133.2	153	564	61	52	14	4	3	2	23	1	80	0	0
St. Claire, Randy, Calgary	3	5	.375	5.00	54	0	0	0	40	19	54.0	72	258	31	30	5	8	3	3	21	5	43	1	0
Salkeld, Roger, Tacoma	1	0	1.000	1.80	4	3	0	0	1	1	15.0	8	59	4	3	0	0	0	0	7	0	11	0	0
Sanchez, Alex, Edmonton	0	0	.000	5.19	8	0	0	0	0	0	17.1	18	75	12	10	0	0	2	0	10	0	8	2	0
Sanders, Scott, Las Vegas	0	0	.000	0.00	1	1	0	0	0	0	3.0	3	14	0	0	0	0	0	1	0	0	2	0	0
Sanford, Mo, Salt Lake	0	1	.000	6.35	4	0	0	0	0	0	5.2	6	27	4	4	1	0	0	0	4	0	8	0	0
Schmitt, Todd, Las Vegas	0	2	.000	7.82	12	0	0	0	8	2	12.2	16	61	11	11	0	0	1	2	9	0	6	2	0
Schullstrom, Erik, Salt Lake	2	0	1.000	4.66	10	0	0	0	7	2	9.2	12	43	5	5	1	0	0	0	4	0	8	0	0
Scott, Darryl, Col. Springs	4	10	.286	4.70	59	1	0	0	27	4	95.2	113	429	63	50	7	4	7	3	41	7	77	7	0
Sepeda, Jamie, Tucson	3	2	.600	4.91	8	8	0	0	0	0	40.1	52	178	22	22	1	4	0	2	12	0	19	1	2
Serafini, Dan, Salt Lake*	0	0	.000	6.75	1	0	0	0	1	1	4.0	4	17	3	3	2	0	0	1	0	4	0	0
Shaw, Curtis, Edmonton*	6	5	.545	4.67	42	3	0	0	11	2	98.1	91	454	60	51	4	5	6	6	88	8	52	17	1
Shifflett, Steve, Col. Springs	4	3	.571	6.87	23	0	0	0	9	0	38.0	61	184	33	29	6	1	4	0	13	2	21	0	2
Shouse, Brian, Calgary*	4	4	.500	6.18	8	8	1	0	0	0	39.1	62	185	35	27	2	1	1	1	7	0	17	3	0
Simas, Bill, Vancouver	6	3	.667	3.55	30	0	0	0	24	6	38.0	44	175	19	15	1	1	1	4	14	2	44	1	0
Small, Mark, Tucson	3	3	.500	4.09	51	0	0	0	40	19	66.0	74	285	32	30	5	1	2	1	19	2	51	8	0
Smith, Tim, Edmonton	3	2	.600	6.03	9	7	0	0	0	0	37.1	44	174	27	25	2	2	2	1	22	2	22	4	0
Springer, Russ, Vancouver	2	0	1.000	3.44	6	6	0	0	0	0	34.0	24	146	16	13	3	0	0	3	23	0	23	3	0
Stanhope, Chuck, Edmonton	1	1	.500	4.50	6	0	0	0	4	0	6.0	8	25	3	3	0	2	1	0	1	0	2	0	0
Stevens, Matt, Salt Lake	0	0	.000	3.52	7	0	0	0	3	1	7.2	9	34	4	3	1	0	1	1	2	0	5	0	0
Sveum, Dale, Calgary	0	0	.000	0.00	2	0	0	0	1	0	2.0	1	7	0	0	0	0	0	0	0	0	2	0	0
Swan, Russ, Edmonton*	3	3	.500	4.34	17	0	0	0	12	4	18.2	23	85	9	9	2	1	1	0	11	4	10	4	0
Tabaka, Jeff, Las Vegas*	0	1	.000	1.99	19	0	0	0	12	6	22.2	16	95	6	5	0	2	1	1	14	3	27	2	0
Taylor, Kerry, Las Vegas	2	2	.500	4.38	8	8	0	0	0	0	37.0	44	174	21	18	3	4	0	2	21	1	21	0	0
Taylor, Scott, Calgary*	5	8	.385	4.11	27	25	1	0	0	0	140.0	144	578	73	64	10	3	4	3	35	2	83	3	0
Telford, Anthony, Edmonton	3	2	.600	7.18	8	6	0	0	0	0	36.1	47	173	32	29	5	2	2	2	16	0	17	2	0
Thompson, John, Tacoma	0	1	.000	0.00	1	0	0	0	0	0	2.2	3	12	2	0	0	1	0	0	0	0	0	0	0
Thompson, Mark, Col. Springs	5	3	.625	6.10	11	10	0	0	0	0	62.0	73	276	43	42	2	2	6	25	0	38	0	0
Torres, Salomon, Pho.-Tac.	1	1	.500	3.00	6	4	0	0	1	0	30.0	22	122	10	10	2	2	1	2	13	1	24	2	1
Treadwell, Jody, Albuquerque	7	5	.583	3.96	30	15	1	1	4	1	125.0	121	510	60	55	15	2	5	2	32	4	79	9	1
Trlicek, Rick, Phoenix	5	4	.556	5.29	38	0	0	0	19	0	63.0	72	279	44	37	7	4	3	0	21	6	43	6	1
Trombley, Mike, Salt Lake	5	3	.625	3.62	12	12	0	0	0	0	69.2	71	301	32	28	3	0	5	2	26	1	59	4	1
Valdez, Carlos, Vancouver	1	0	1.000	2.76	18	0	0	0	12	2	29.1	29	131	9	9	2	2	0	0	13	2	30	3	0
Valdez, Sergio, Phoenix	6	7	.462	4.45	18	18	2	0	0	0	109.1	117	456	58	54	6	3	3	2	25	4	64	14	0
Valera, Julio, Vancouver	2	5	.286	5.70	13	13	2	0	0	0	71.0	85	314	54	45	2	0	2	21	0	43	1	0
Vanderweele, Doug, Phoenix	2	4	.333	6.10	11	4	1	0	1	0	38.1	57	178	29	26	9	2	3	1	11	3	20	1	1
VanRyn, Ben, Vancouver*	2	0	1.000	3.07	11	5	0	0	2	0	29.1	29	123	10	10	1	2	2	0	9	2	18	2	0
Villone, Ron, Tacoma*	1	0	1.000	0.61	22	0	0	0	16	13	29.2	9	117	6	2	1	2	0	19	0	43	1	0
Wagner, Billy, Tucson*	5	3	.625	3.18	13	13	0	0	0	0	76.1	70	325	28	27	3	4	2	1	32	0	80	4	0
Wagner, Matt, Tacoma	1	5	.167	6.27	6	6	1	0	0	0	33.0	43	157	29	23	3	0	1	1	17	1	33	2	0
Waldron, Joe, Tucson*	1	0	1.000	4.32	4	0	0	0	1	0	8.1	6	31	4	4	0	0	0	2	0	11	0	0
Wall, Donne, Tucson	17	6	.739	3.50	28	28	0	0	0	0	177.1	190	732	72	65	5	6	4	5	32	1	119	5	1
Waring, Jim, Tucson	2	2	.500	8.46	5	5	0	0	0	0	22.1	30	108	24	21	1	0	2	5	8	0	5	0	0
Wasdin, John, Edmonton	12	8	.600	5.52	29	28	2	1	0	0	174.1	193	744	117	107	26	3	11	4	38	3	111	10	1
Watkins, Scott, Salt Lake*	4	2	.667	2.88	45	0	0	0	33	20	54.2	45	217	18	17	4	1	3	1	13	1	57	1	0
Watson, Ron, Vancouver	0	1	.000	4.76	5	0	0	0	2	0	5.2	3	26	3	3	0	1	0	0	6	1	3	0	0
Weber, Wes, Tac.-L.V.	6	11	.353	4.67	29	21	2	0	3	0	150.1	170	663	92	78	16	5	6	4	50	10	86	6	3
Wengert, Don, Edmonton	1	1	.500	7.38	16	6	0	0	4	1	39.0	55	178	32	32	5	0	1	1	16	2	20	3	0
Westbrook, Destry, Tucson	0	0	.000	7.30	5	0	0	0	2	0	12.1	20	60	10	10	2	0	0	7	0	8	2	0
Whitaker, Steve, Phoenix*	0	5	.000	7.00	16	10	0	0	0	0	54.0	72	261	47	42	6	4	0	36	2	30	3	1
White, Chris, Tucson	1	1	.500	8.71	5	1	0	0	2	0	10.1	16	44	10	10	1	1	0	0	2	0	6	0	0
White, Rick, Calgary	6	4	.600	4.20	14	11	1	0	1	0	79.1	97	338	40	37	13	0	4	3	10	0	56	2	0
Whitehurst, Wally, Phoenix	0	1	.000	7.16	4	4	0	0	0	0	16.1	20	76	13	13	0	2	0	1	8	1	7	2	0
Williams, Jeff, Calgary	0	3	.000	8.22	8	3	0	0	4	0	23.0	31	109	21	21	1	3	2	12	0	8	0	0
Williams, Shad, Vancouver	9	7	.563	3.37	25	25	3	1	0	0	149.2	142	627	65	56	16	3	3	4	48	2	114	7	1
Williams, Todd, Albuquerque	4	1	.800	3.38	25	0	0	0	5	0	45.1	59	203	21	17	4	1	1	1	15	4	23	1	2
Willis, Carl, Vancouver	2	2	.500	4.11	20	0	0	0	7	0	35.0	40	154	17	16	2	0	2	0	11	2	17	2	0
Willis, Travis, Calgary	2	2	.500	7.15	22	0	0	0	7	0	39.0	57	188	35	31	4	2	0	4	15	4	13	2	0

Pitcher, Team	W	L	Pct.	ERA	G	GS	CG	ShO	GF	Sv.	IP	H	TBF	R	ER	HR	SH	SF	HB	BB	IBB	SO	WP	Bk.
Wilson, Gary, Calgary	1	2	.333	5.51	6	4	0	0	0	0	16.1	19	75	16	10	1	1	2	0	9	0	12	2	1
Winston, Darrin, Calgary*	4	6	.400	4.80	53	0	0	0	20	2	50.2	59	226	33	27	8	0	2	0	17	2	40	2	0
Wissler, Bill, Salt Lake	3	3	.500	4.62	37	2	0	0	9	1	60.1	69	262	32	31	7	3	0	1	24	1	26	5	0
Wojciechowski, Steve, Edm.*	6	3	.667	3.69	14	12	2	1	1	0	78.0	75	320	37	32	5	1	4	1	21	0	39	4	2
Wolcott, Bob, Tacoma	6	3	.667	4.08	13	13	2	1	0	0	79.1	94	347	49	36	10	1	4	5	16	0	43	2	1
Worrell, Tim, Las Vegas	0	2	.000	6.00	10	3	0	0	0	0	24.0	27	121	21	16	1	2	0	3	17	0	18	0	0

COMBINATION SHUTOUTS: **Albuquerque (3)**—McCarthy-Montalvo-Brosnan, Mimbs-Rodriguez-Montalvo, O'Donoghue-Bruske-Daal. **Calgary (5)**—DeLosSantos-Flynt-McCurry-St. Claire, Ericks-Backlund, Ericks-Corbin-Winston-St. Claire, Hope-Ralph-Winston, Taylor-Maysey-Ryan. **Colorado Springs (10)**—Peever-Bustillos 2, Fredrickson-Czajkowski, Nied-Sager-Scott, Rekar-Romanoli, Rekar-Scott, Reynoso-Hawblitzel-Czajkowski, Sager-Czajkowski, Sager-Scott, Sager-Shifflett. **Edmonton (3)**—Baker-Mohler, Johns-Mohler, Wojciechowski-Brock-Mohler. **Las Vegas (3)**—Harriger-McFarlin-Hermanson, Martinez-McFarlin-Tabaka, Taylor-Merriman-McFarlin-Hermanson. **Phoenix (4)**—Brink-Knudsen, Carlson-Rogers-Trlicek-Greer, Whitaker-Menendez, Whitehurst-Phillips-Burcham-Barton-Trlicek. **Salt Lake (3)**—Hawkins-Gavaghan, Munoz-Bryant-Schullstrom-Watkins, Trombley-Watkins. **Tacoma (5)**—Apana-Darwin, Apana-Mecir, Carmona-Darwin, Milacki-Phillips, Salkeld-Mecir. **Tucson (8)**—Jean-Small-Daspit, McMurtry-Ketchen-Huisman, McMurtry-Powell-Ketchen, Sepeda-Patrick-Hartgraves, Wall-Huisman, Wagner-Daspit-Bennett, Wagner-Morman-Huisman, Wagner-Small. **Vancouver (8)**—Akerfelds-Chavez, Holzemer-Patterson-Simas, Janicki-Edenfield-Holzemer, Morrison-Butler-Holdridge, Springer-Ratekin-Simas, VanRyn-Bennett-Simas, Williams-Heredia, Williams-Monteleone-Fortugno-Heredia.

NO-HIT GAMES: Milchin, Albuquerque, defeated Vancouver, 2-0 (second game), June 13.

PITCHERS WITH TWO OR MORE TEAMS

Pitcher, Team	W	L	Pct.	ERA	G	GS	CG	ShO	GF	Sv.	IP	H	TBF	R	ER	HR	SH	SF	HB	BB	IBB	SO	WP	Bk.
Bennett, Erik, Vancouver	6	0	1.000	4.26	28	0	0	0	12	2	50.2	44	206	24	24	5	0	2	3	18	2	39	4	1
Bennett, Erik, Tucson	3	1	.750	4.76	14	1	0	0	4	1	22.2	27	110	17	12	1	0	3	2	14	1	24	0	0
Brink, Brad, Phoenix	2	5	.286	7.05	11	9	0	0	0	0	44.2	55	215	35	35	3	1	4	2	30	0	33	1	0
Brink, Brad, Edmonton	0	1	.000	4.88	9	3	0	0	4	0	24.0	24	112	20	13	2	0	1	2	16	3	15	1	0
Daspit, Jim, Tucson	5	1	.833	3.57	36	0	0	0	11	1	63.0	63	272	30	25	3	2	5	2	22	1	49	5	0
Daspit, Jim, Edmonton	0	1	.000	10.80	2	0	0	0	0	0	5.0	6	22	6	6	2	0	0	0	2	0	5	2	0
Fesh, Sean, Tucson*	1	0	1.000	1.35	10	0	0	0	1	0	13.1	11	52	2	2	0	0	0	0	3	0	7	0	0
Fesh, Sean, Las Vegas*	2	1	.667	3.32	30	0	0	0	11	1	38.0	53	185	21	14	2	4	0	3	16	5	18	1	1
Hansell, Greg, Albuquerque	1	1	.500	8.44	8	1	0	0	3	1	16.0	25	77	15	15	2	1	0	1	6	1	15	0	0
Hansell, Greg, Salt Lake	3	1	.750	5.01	7	5	0	0	0	0	32.1	39	141	20	18	3	1	1	4	1	17	3	1
Loiselle, Rich, Las Vegas	2	2	.500	7.24	8	7	1	1	0	0	27.1	36	131	27	22	5	1	0	2	9	0	16	0	0
Loiselle, Rich, Tucson	0	0	.000	2.61	2	1	0	0	0	0	10.1	8	44	4	3	0	0	0	0	4	0	4	0	1
Torres, Salomon, Phoenix	0	0	.000	0.00	1	0	0	0	0	0	2.0	2	8	0	0	0	0	0	0	0	0	3	0	0
Torres, Salomon, Tacoma	1	1	.500	3.21	5	4	0	0	1	0	28.0	20	114	10	10	2	1	1	2	13	1	19	2	1
Weber, Weston, Tacoma	3	7	.300	4.60	20	13	1	0	3	0	101.2	111	443	55	52	12	3	4	2	41	10	54	5	3
Weber, Weston, Las Vegas	3	4	.429	4.81	9	8	1	0	0	0	48.2	59	220	37	26	4	2	2	2	9	0	32	1	0

1995 FIELDING

TEAM

Team	Pct.	G	PO	A	E	TC	DP	PB	Team	Pct.	G	PO	A	E	TC	DP	PB
Salt Lake	.981	144	3749	1647	103	5499	131	11	Edmonton	.973	144	3718	1678	148	5544	151	13
Vancouver	.978	141	3647	1459	117	5223	131	14	Tucson	.973	143	3734	1592	148	5474	146	19
Phoenix	.976	144	3827	1627	134	5588	165	11	Tacoma	.971	144	3747	1576	159	5482	130	16
Albuquerque	.974	144	3746	1663	144	5553	152	15	Calgary	.968	141	3585	1667	174	5426	150	15
Col. Springs	.974	143	3636	1532	139	5307	152	9	Las Vegas	.967	144	3691	1591	181	5463	133	20

TRIPLE PLAYS: Phoenix, Tacoma.

INDIVIDUAL

FIRST BASEMEN

NOTE: All caps denotes fielding-percentage leader based on 72 games for catchers, 96 for all other non-pitchers and 144 innings for pitchers. *Throws lefthanded.

Player, Team	Pct.	G	PO	A	E	TC	DP
Aude, Rich, Calgary	.988	49	447	31	6	484	58
Ball, Jeff, Tucson	.990	35	272	16	3	291	25
Barron, Tony, Tacoma	1.000	1	1	0	0	1	0
Bean, Billy, Las Vegas*	1.000	9	77	3	0	80	8
Bellinger, Clay, Phoenix	1.000	3	10	1	0	11	2
Blanco, Henry, Albuquerque	1.000	11	97	6	0	103	3
Bolick, Frank, C.S.	1.000	1	8	1	0	9	1
BOWIE, Jim, Edmonton*	.996	138	1215	126	6	1347	127
Brewer, Rod, Phoenix*	1.000	13	134	14	0	148	12
Brumley, Mike, Tucson	.667	2	3	0	0	3	0
Bryant, Scott, Edmonton	.980	10	45	4	1	50	5
Bullock, Eric, Las Vegas*	.667	1	2	0	1	3	0
Busch, Mike, Albuquerque	.994	40	303	21	2	326	30
Castellano, Pedro, C.S.	.995	26	186	9	1	196	24
Chimelis, Joel, Phoenix	.998	51	395	25	1	421	41
Cianfrocco, Archi, Las Vegas	.985	42	371	35	6	412	33
Colbert, Craig, Las Vegas	.857	2	6	0	1	7	0
Coomer, Ron, Albuquerque	.979	35	314	17	7	338	33
Dalesandro, Mark, Vancouver	1.000	1	9	0	0	9	0
Deer, Rob, Van.-L.V.	.976	17	113	11	3	127	10
Dunn, Steve, Salt Lake*	.991	102	916	59	9	984	75
Durant, Mike, Salt Lake	.917	1	11	0	1	12	0
Durham, Leon, Vancouver*	1.000	2	5	0	0	5	0
Gainer, Jay, C.S.*	.986	63	508	48	8	564	57
Giambi, Jason, Edmonton	1.000	3	7	0	0	7	1
Goff, Jerry, Tucson	.938	3	15	0	1	16	0
Gonzales, Rene, Vancouver	1.000	8	8	2	0	10	2

Player, Team	Pct.	G	PO	A	E	TC	DP
Hale, Chip, Salt Lake	1.000	3	25	2	0	27	5
Hansen, Terrel, Tacoma	1.000	9	71	6	0	77	5
Hatcher, Chris, Tucson	.977	73	590	40	15	645	62
Horn, Sam, Calgary*	.976	16	157	5	4	166	15
Huckaby, Ken, Albuquerque	1.000	1	3	0	0	3	0
Hyers, Tim, Las Vegas*	.998	54	450	24	1	475	40
Ingram, Riccardo, Salt Lake	1.000	1	1	0	0	1	0
Johnson, Mark, Calgary*	.972	8	65	5	2	72	4
Jordan, Ricky, Vancouver	1.000	1	4	0	0	4	0
Kirkpatrick, Jay, Albuquerque	1.000	6	51	4	0	55	1
Leonard, Mark, Phoenix	.989	13	89	1	1	91	11
Litton, Greg, Tacoma	.990	79	575	48	6	629	53
Maksudian, Mike, Edmonton	1.000	4	16	1	0	17	0
Marrero, Oreste, Albuquerque*	1.000	1	6	0	0	6	2
Martinez, Chito, C.S.*	.941	3	16	0	1	17	3
Masteller, Dan, Salt Lake*	.990	10	84	12	1	97	4
Maurer, Ron, Albuquerque	1.000	1	1	0	0	1	0
McCarty, Dave, Phoenix*	.994	35	327	31	2	360	39
Miller, Barry, Phoenix*	.994	38	290	17	2	309	31
Munoz, Orlando, Vancouver	1.000	1	1	0	0	1	0
Newfield, Marc, Las Vegas	1.000	1	10	1	0	11	1
Ortiz, Ray, Phoenix*	.990	13	91	5	1	97	15
Osik, Keith, Calgary	1.000	11	83	9	0	92	3
Perez, Eduardo, Vancouver	.986	8	67	4	1	72	3
Petagine, Roberto, Las Vegas*	.975	14	110	7	3	120	13
Pirkl, Greg, Tacoma	.983	33	276	19	5	300	31
Pritchett, Chris, Vancouver	.989	117	995	92	12	1099	99
Quinlan, Tom, Salt Lake	1.000	21	149	7	0	156	18
Raven, Luis, Vancouver	.971	3	32	1	1	34	6
Rodriguez, Boi, Calgary	.975	7	73	4	2	79	5
Saunders, Doug, Tacoma	1.000	4	35	3	0	38	2

Player, Team	Pct.	G	PO	A	E	TC	DP
See, Larry, Las Vegas	.995	24	195	15	1	211	18
Sheldon, Scott, Edmonton	1.000	3	21	2	0	23	2
Shelton, Ben, Salt Lake*	.970	7	59	5	2	66	10
Simmons, Nelson, Calgary	.956	9	62	3	3	68	7
Simms, Mike, Tucson	.985	48	376	24	6	406	43
Snider, Van, Salt Lake	.986	7	66	3	1	70	6
Springer, Steve, Las Vegas	1.000	3	32	3	0	35	2
Stahoviak, Scott, Salt Lake	1.000	5	32	1	0	33	2
Sveum, Dale, Calgary	.986	36	313	39	5	357	32
Sweeney, Mark, Vancouver*	.958	3	22	1	1	24	2
Traxler, Brian, Albuquerque*	.992	66	569	23	5	597	61
Turang, Brian, Tacoma	1.000	1	6	0	0	6	0
Turner, Chris, Vancouver	1.000	6	45	3	0	48	7
Van Burkleo, Ty, C.S.*	.982	65	521	29	10	560	53
Willard, Jerry, Tacoma	.976	46	324	35	9	368	26
Young, Kevin, Calgary	.978	12	124	11	3	138	11

TRIPLE PLAYS: Litton, McCarty.

FIRST BASEMEN WITH TWO OR MORE TEAMS

Player, Team	Pct.	G	PO	A	E	TC	DP
Deer, Rob, Vancouver	.977	5	40	2	1	43	4
Deer, Rob, Las Vegas	.976	12	73	9	2	84	6

SECOND BASEMEN

Player, Team	Pct.	G	PO	A	E	TC	DP
Abreu, Bob, Tucson	1.000	1	3	0	0	3	1
Bellinger, Clay, Phoenix	.956	16	15	28	2	45	3
Bream, Scott, Las Vegas	.975	65	134	177	8	319	42
Brumley, Mike, Tucson	.929	4	3	10	1	14	1
Candaele, Casey, Albuquerque	.958	6	23	23	2	48	8
Castro, Juan, Albuquerque	1.000	10	4	17	0	21	2
Chimelis, Joel, Phoenix	.958	20	34	34	3	71	15
Cole, Stu, C.S.	.987	14	34	41	1	76	15
Corbin, Ted, Salt Lake	.875	2	3	4	1	8	1
Correia, Rod, Vancouver	.944	8	15	19	2	36	5
Demetral, Chris, Albuquerque	.978	40	59	115	4	178	23
Diaz, Eddy, Tacoma	.966	7	10	18	1	29	4
Duncan, Andres, Salt Lake	1.000	1	4	0	0	4	1
Ehmann, Kurt, Phoenix	1.000	2	5	5	0	10	3
Faries, Paul, Edmonton	.984	105	230	261	8	499	75
FORBES, P.J., Vancouver	.986	103	180	257	6	443	63
Gallego, Mike, Edmonton	1.000	2	3	2	0	5	0
Garrison, Webster, C.S.	.971	100	193	307	15	515	66
Gonzales, Rene, Vancouver	.903	7	10	18	3	31	5
Grebeck, Brian, Vancouver	.973	16	37	34	2	73	11
Guerrero, Juan, Tucson	.947	5	10	8	1	19	0
Hajek, Dave, Tucson	.982	124	269	398	12	679	100
Hale, Chip, Salt Lake	1.000	5	3	13	0	16	2
Hall, Billy, Las Vegas	.928	69	108	149	20	277	32
Hocking, Denny, Salt Lake	1.000	1	2	3	0	5	0
Holbert, Ray, Las Vegas	.972	9	9	26	1	36	5
Ingram, Garey, Albuquerque	.975	48	90	144	6	240	38
Johnson, Erik, Calgary	.974	81	159	218	10	387	66
Jones, Tim, Edmonton	1.000	1	0	1	0	1	0
Kellner, Frank, Tucson	1.000	1	1	2	0	3	0
Lind, Jose, Vancouver	1.000	10	23	21	0	44	8
Matos, Francisco, Calgary	.967	48	84	123	7	214	29
Maurer, Ron, Albuquerque	.977	25	38	46	2	86	12
Mejia, Roberto, C.S.	.973	35	80	97	5	182	28
Mueller, Bill, Phoenix	1.000	1	3	3	0	6	1
Munoz, Orlando, Vancouver	1.000	3	3	5	0	8	1
Parker, Rick, Albuquerque	1.000	3	4	2	0	6	0
Pozo, Arquimedez, Tacoma	.971	81	162	245	12	419	49
Pye, Eddie, Albuquerque	.971	41	83	116	6	205	26
Raabe, Brian, Salt Lake	.989	56	98	169	3	270	37
Ramirez, J.D., Vancouver	1.000	1	1	5	0	6	0
Relaford, Desi, Tacoma	.958	29	50	88	6	144	18
Richardson, Jeff, Calgary	.963	5	11	15	1	27	7
Roberts, Bip, Las Vegas	1.000	1	0	2	0	2	0
Rohde, Dave, Tucson	.982	16	28	26	1	55	5
Rossy, Rico, Las Vegas	.973	14	30	43	2	75	12
Saunders, Doug, Edm.-Tac.	.986	11	33	37	1	71	11
Sheets, Andy, Tacoma	1.000	8	9	31	0	40	5
Sheldon, Scott, Edmonton	1.000	1	0	2	0	2	0
Simons, Mitch, Salt Lake	.984	90	195	244	7	446	63
Sojo, Luis, Tacoma	1.000	2	3	6	0	9	0
Stankiewicz, Andy, Tucson	.947	4	7	11	1	19	3
Turang, Brian, Tacoma	.947	12	25	29	3	57	5
Wehner, John, Calgary	.931	5	15	12	2	29	4
Wilkerson, Curtis, Tacoma	1.000	5	8	19	0	27	4
Wimmer, Chris, Phoenix	.983	127	224	371	10	605	96
Womack, Tony, Calgary	.967	15	15	44	2	61	4
Wood, Jason, Edmonton	.968	39	84	98	6	188	17

TRIPLE PLAYS: Pozo, Wimmer.

SECOND BASEMEN WITH TWO OR MORE TEAMS

Player, Team	Pct.	G	PO	A	E	TC	DP
Saunders, Doug, Edmonton	1.000	4	16	17	0	33	5
Saunders, Doug, Tacoma	.974	7	17	20	1	38	6

THIRD BASEMEN

Player, Team	Pct.	G	PO	A	E	TC	DP
Ball, Jeff, Tucson	.957	46	19	93	5	117	11
Bellinger, Clay, Phoenix	.981	27	15	37	1	53	5
Blanco, Henry, Albuquerque	.967	19	17	41	2	60	6
Bolick, Frank, C.S.	.927	17	12	26	3	41	1
Brumley, Mike, Tucson	.938	17	5	25	2	32	0
Bruno, Julio, Las Vegas	.925	38	25	99	10	134	10
Bryant, Scott, Edmonton	.700	2	4	3	3	10	1
Busch, Mike, Albuquerque	.941	75	31	143	11	185	14
Candaele, Casey, Albuquerque	1.000	1	0	1	0	1	0
Case, Mike, C.S.	.625	3	1	4	3	8	0
Castellano, Pedro, C.S.	.973	73	36	110	4	150	15
Chimelis, Joel, Phoenix	.938	24	15	45	4	64	4
Cianfrocco, Archi, Las Vegas	.880	31	17	64	11	92	3
Cole, Stu, C.S.	.912	18	8	23	3	34	3
Coomer, Ron, Albuquerque	.980	44	21	76	2	99	5
Correia, Rod, Vancouver	.875	6	4	10	2	16	1
Dalesandro, Mark, Vancouver	.846	7	4	7	2	13	0
Diaz, Eddy, Tacoma	1.000	4	2	5	0	7	1
Ehmann, Kurt, Phoenix	.913	13	7	14	2	23	2
Faries, Paul, Edmonton	.857	3	3	3	1	7	0
Gallego, Mike, Edmonton	1.000	1	0	2	0	2	1
Garrison, Webster, C.S.	.914	22	12	41	5	58	4
Giambi, Jason, Edmonton	.935	48	31	98	9	138	10
Gonzales, Rene, Vancouver	.966	11	10	18	1	29	2
Grebeck, Brian, Vancouver	.957	11	6	16	1	23	3
Guerrero, Juan, Tucson	.900	28	16	38	6	60	5
Hale, Chip, Salt Lake	1.000	9	5	11	0	16	2
Johnson, Erik, Calgary	1.000	11	7	25	0	32	0
Jones, Tim, Edmonton	1.000	1	1	4	0	5	0
Litton, Greg, Tacoma	.948	39	33	59	5	97	7
Maksudian, Mike, Edmonton	1.000	11	7	23	0	30	3
Martinez, Carlos, Vancouver	.970	24	17	48	2	67	3
Maurer, Ron, Albuquerque	.967	17	5	24	1	30	1
Mueller, Bill, Phoenix	.938	40	23	82	7	112	8
Munoz, Orlando, Vancouver	1.000	1	2	1	0	3	1
Nevin, Phil, Tucson	.923	57	39	128	14	181	17
Osik, Keith, Calgary	1.000	1	2	2	0	4	0
Parker, Rick, Albuquerque	1.000	3	1	4	0	5	0
Peguero, Jose, Vancouver	.929	17	6	33	3	42	2
Perez, Eduardo, Vancouver	.958	42	27	86	5	118	11
Pozo, Arquimedez, Tacoma	.946	33	29	59	5	93	2
Pye, Eddie, Albuquerque	1.000	3	1	2	0	3	0
QUINLAN, Tom, Salt Lake	.940	110	66	231	19	316	18
Raabe, Brian, Salt Lake	.975	31	16	63	2	81	1
Raven, Luis, Vancouver	.873	21	9	46	8	63	6
Rodriguez, Boi, Calgary	.625	2	0	5	3	8	1
Rohde, Dave, Tucson	.893	15	6	19	3	28	1
Rossy, Rico, Las Vegas	.894	27	20	56	9	85	3
Russo, Paul, Las Vegas	.960	43	30	91	5	126	10
Saunders, Doug, Tacoma	.947	34	18	54	4	76	9
Scott, Gary, Phoenix	.921	60	33	107	12	152	8
Sheets, Andy, Tacoma	.913	33	11	83	9	103	2
Sheldon, Scott, Edmonton	.959	32	20	74	4	98	8
Snyder, Cory, Las Vegas	.600	2	1	2	2	5	0
Springer, Steve, Las Vegas	.957	9	6	16	1	23	1
Stahoviak, Scott, Salt Lake	1.000	7	4	15	0	19	2
Stankiewicz, Andy, Tucson	1.000	2	2	8	0	10	1
Sveum, Dale, Calgary	.963	70	40	196	9	245	20
Tatum, Jim, C.S.	.945	23	13	39	3	55	6
Turang, Brian, Tacoma	.917	14	9	24	3	36	3
Turner, Chris, Vancouver	.909	14	7	23	3	33	2
Wallach, Tim, Albuquerque	1.000	1	0	1	0	1	0
Wehner, John, Calgary	.909	31	14	86	10	110	7
Wood, Jason, Edmonton	.939	59	48	136	12	196	15
Young, Kevin, Calgary	.913	31	20	74	9	103	4

SHORTSTOPS

Player, Team	Pct.	G	PO	A	E	TC	DP
Aurilia, Rich, Phoenix	.975	71	104	246	9	359	56
Bellinger, Clay, Phoenix	.960	29	42	79	5	126	19
Bournigal, Rafael, Albuquerque	.951	12	7	32	2	41	4
Bream, Scott, Las Vegas	.967	24	26	63	3	92	11
Brumley, Mike, Tucson	.961	24	22	52	3	77	9
Castro, Juan, Albuquerque	.971	92	148	327	14	489	67
Chimelis, Joel, Phoenix	.911	8	16	25	4	45	2
Cole, Stu, C.S.	.964	23	24	57	3	84	14

Player, Team	Pct.	G	PO	A	E	TC	DP
Corbin, Ted, Salt Lake	1.000	2	3	5	0	8	3
Correia, Rod, Vancouver	.961	60	106	193	12	311	35
Counsell, Craig, C.S.	.950	115	182	386	30	598	86
Cruz, Fausto, Edmonton	.958	113	196	355	24	575	72
Duncan, Andres, Salt Lake	.966	11	25	32	2	59	6
Ehmann, Kurt, Phoenix	.949	51	79	165	13	257	45
Faries, Paul, Edmonton	1.000	3	2	15	0	17	2
Forbes, P.J., Vancouver	1.000	6	10	14	0	24	1
Gallego, Mike, Edmonton	1.000	1	0	4	0	4	0
Gonzales, Rene, Vancouver	.947	26	25	82	6	113	18
Grebeck, Brian, Vancouver	.959	38	53	109	7	169	19
Guerrero, Juan, Tucson	1.000	2	0	1	0	1	1
Guerrero, Wilton, Albuquerque	.852	14	13	39	9	61	6
Gutierrez, Ricky, Tucson	.977	61	91	167	6	264	34
HOCKING, Denny, Salt Lake	.966	114	171	390	20	581	72
Johnson, Erik, Calgary	.920	26	32	71	9	112	9
Kellner, Frank, Tucson	.974	25	39	72	3	114	22
Litton, Greg, Tacoma	1.000	2	0	4	0	4	0
Matos, Francisco, Calgary	.944	45	56	145	12	213	32
Maurer, Ron, Albuquerque	1.000	13	12	33	0	45	3
Perez, Neifi, C.S.	.936	11	16	28	3	47	5
Polcovich, Kevin, Calgary	.959	61	90	215	13	318	49
Pye, Eddie, Albuquerque	.947	29	48	78	7	133	17
Raabe, Brian, Salt Lake	.958	9	6	17	1	24	4
Relaford, Desi, Las Vegas	1.000	2	2	5	0	7	0
Roberts, Bip, Las Vegas	.938	3	2	13	1	16	1
Rodriguez, Alex, Tacoma	.961	51	90	157	10	257	28
Rohde, Dave, Tucson	.948	32	30	62	5	97	11
Rossy, Rico, Las Vegas	.951	58	88	205	15	308	34
Schofield, Dick, Vancouver	.932	16	24	44	5	73	9
Sheets, Andy, Tacoma	.957	93	137	268	18	423	59
Sheldon, Scott, Edmonton	.933	3	3	11	1	15	2
Simons, Mitch, Salt Lake	.949	15	24	50	4	78	5
Sojo, Luis, Tacoma	1.000	1	1	3	0	4	1
Springer, Steve, Las Vegas	.920	4	4	19	2	25	3
Stankiewicz, Andy, Tucson	.978	20	27	62	2	91	9
Sveum, Dale, Calgary	.778	1	3	4	2	9	3
Velandia, Jorge, Las Vegas	.903	66	97	190	31	318	39
Womack, Tony, Calgary	.960	15	22	50	3	75	5
Wood, Jason, Edmonton	.945	30	41	97	8	146	20

OUTFIELDERS

Player, Team	Pct.	G	PO	A	E	TC	DP
Abreu, Bob, Tucson	.969	111	204	18	7	229	5
Allensworth, Jermaine, Calgary	.989	46	90	2	1	93	0
Anderson, Garret, Vancouver*	.957	11	22	0	1	23	0
Ball, Jeff, Tucson	1.000	15	19	0	0	19	0
Barron, Tony, Tacoma	1.000	5	11	0	0	11	0
Beamon, Trey, Calgary	.960	110	201	14	9	224	0
Bean, Billy, Las Vegas*	.983	110	219	6	4	229	2
Beauchamp, Kash, Edmonton	1.000	1	3	0	0	3	0
Becker, Rich, Salt Lake*	.991	36	108	5	1	114	0
Bellinger, Clay, Phoenix	1.000	23	32	0	0	32	0
Benard, Marvin, Phoenix*	.959	97	183	5	8	196	2
Blanco, Henry, Albuquerque	1.000	1	1	0	0	1	0
Bragg, Darren, Tacoma	.968	47	115	7	4	126	2
Brito, Bernardo, Salt Lake	1.000	4	15	0	0	15	0
Brumley, Mike, Tucson	.948	42	68	5	4	77	2
Bryant, Scott, Edmonton	.942	53	93	5	6	104	2
Bullock, Eric, Las Vegas*	.959	35	46	1	2	49	0
Burks, Ellis, C.S.	1.000	7	16	0	0	16	0
Busch, Mike, Albuquerque	.800	6	4	0	1	5	0
Cameron, Stanton, Calgary	1.000	7	10	0	0	10	0
Cangelosi, John, Tucson*	.986	29	67	2	1	70	0
Carvajal, Jovino, Vancouver	.980	38	92	5	2	99	0
Cedeno, Roger, Albuquerque	.985	94	189	3	3	195	0
Cianfrocco, Archi, Las Vegas	1.000	14	23	1	0	24	0
Cockrell, Alan, C.S.	.981	87	153	5	3	161	1
Cohick, Emmitt, Vancouver*	.905	7	19	0	2	21	0
Colbert, Craig, Las Vegas	1.000	2	3	1	0	4	0
Cookson, Brent, Phoenix	.967	56	86	2	3	91	1
Cummings, Midre, Calgary	.943	41	96	4	6	106	1
Dalesandro, Mark, Vancouver	1.000	18	33	1	0	34	0
Daugherty, Jack, Phoenix*	.909	7	10	0	1	11	0
Deer, Rob, Van.-L.V.	.963	49	77	0	3	80	0
Delarosa, Juan, Salt Lake	1.000	23	42	1	0	43	0
Demetral, Chris, Albuquerque	.952	16	18	2	1	21	1
Diaz, Alex, Tacoma	1.000	9	15	1	0	16	0
Durant, Mike, Salt Lake	1.000	3	5	0	0	5	0
Faneyte, Rikkert, Phoenix	.944	36	83	2	5	90	1
Flora, Kevin, Vancouver	.986	35	65	4	1	70	1
Franklin, Micah, Calgary	.965	100	162	3	6	171	0
Garcia, Karim, Albuquerque*	.932	122	185	7	14	206	0
Grebeck, Brian, Vancouver	1.000	12	11	0	0	11	0
Guerrero, Juan, Tucson	1.000	4	10	0	0	10	0
Hajek, Dave, Tucson	1.000	1	2	0	0	2	0
Hansen, Terrel, Tacoma	1.000	5	3	0	0	3	0
Hatcher, Chris, Tucson	1.000	6	9	0	0	9	0
Hazlett, Steve, Salt Lake	.986	124	273	13	4	290	0
Hollandsworth, Todd, Albuq.*	1.000	10	19	3	0	22	0
Hosey, Steve, Vancouver	.962	15	22	3	1	26	0
Hubbard, Trent, C.S.	.980	120	285	11	6	302	0
Humphreys, Mike, Tacoma	.955	15	21	0	1	22	0
Hunter, Brian, Tucson	1.000	37	91	1	0	92	0
Hyers, Tim, Las Vegas*	.953	23	40	1	2	43	0
Ingram, Garey, Albuquerque	1.000	19	25	0	0	25	0
Ingram, Riccardo, Salt Lake	.990	112	197	10	2	209	0
Jackson, John, Van.-S.L.*	.981	83	155	4	3	162	0
Jones, Dax, Phoenix	.980	105	284	9	6	299	0
Knabenshue, Chris, Calgary	1.000	2	1	0	0	1	0
Landrum, Ced, C.S.	.961	46	70	3	3	76	0
Latham, Chris, Albuquerque	1.000	5	7	0	0	7	0
Lennon, Pat, Salt Lake	1.000	6	10	0	0	10	0
Leonard, Mark, Phoenix	.976	89	154	9	4	167	3
Litton, Greg, Tacoma	1.000	3	2	1	0	3	0
Lott, Billy, Albuquerque	.988	40	76	4	1	81	3
Lydy, Scott, Edmonton	.968	92	202	12	7	221	1
Mack, Quinn, Tacoma*	.960	56	94	3	4	101	3
Maksudian, Mike, Edmonton	1.000	19	23	1	0	24	0
Marrero, Oreste, Albuquerque*	1.000	5	8	0	0	8	0
Martin, Jim, Albuquerque	.971	24	34	0	1	35	0
Martinez, Chito, C.S.*	.981	27	50	1	1	52	0
Mashore, Damon, Phoenix	.981	114	197	12	4	213	1
Masteller, Dan, Salt Lake*	1.000	31	53	2	0	55	0
Maurer, Ron, Albuquerque	1.000	8	12	0	0	12	0
McCarty, Dave, Phoenix*	1.000	3	3	1	0	4	0
McCracken, Quinton, C.S.	.991	57	104	5	1	110	1
McDavid, Ray, Las Vegas	1.000	49	134	0	0	134	0
Mercedes, Luis, Calgary	.940	25	43	4	3	50	2
Miller, Damian, Salt Lake	1.000	1	1	0	0	1	0
Montgomery, Ray, Tucson	.965	87	182	10	7	199	3
Moore, Kerwin, Edmonton	.974	63	147	5	4	156	2
Mora, Melvin, Tucson	1.000	2	2	0	0	2	0
Mouton, James, Tucson	.500	3	1	0	1	2	0
Murray, Calvin, Phoenix	1.000	13	19	2	0	21	0
Newfield, Marc, Tac.-L.V.	.971	49	99	2	3	104	0
Noland, J.D., Tacoma	.947	42	68	4	4	76	1
Northrup, Kevin, Edmonton	.933	10	12	2	1	15	0
Ortiz, Ray, Phoenix*	1.000	26	29	2	0	31	0
Osik, Keith, Calgary	1.000	3	1	0	0	1	0
PALMEIRO, Orlando, Vancouver	.995	103	192	4	1	197	2
Parker, Rick, Albuquerque	.975	44	78	1	2	81	0
Peguero, Julio, Tacoma	1.000	7	9	1	0	10	0
Plantier, Phil, Tucson	1.000	9	9	0	0	9	0
Pose, Scott, Alb.-S.L.	.980	66	92	8	2	102	0
Pritchett, Chris, Vancouver	1.000	1	4	0	0	4	0
Pulliam, Harvey, C.S.	.985	112	186	8	3	197	6
Ramos, Ken, Tucson*	.988	100	165	5	2	172	1
Ratliff, Daryl, Calgary	.978	79	177	4	4	185	0
Riley, Marquis, Vancouver	.994	119	326	2	2	330	0
Roberson, Kevin, Tacoma	.981	29	51	2	1	54	0
Shelton, Ben, Salt Lake*	1.000	2	3	0	0	3	0
Sherman, Darrell, Tacoma*	.974	112	252	12	7	271	1
Simmons, Nelson, Calgary	.965	35	51	4	2	57	2
Simms, Mike, Tucson	.964	34	48	6	2	56	1
Simons, Mitch, Salt Lake	1.000	12	12	0	0	12	0
Smiley, Reuben, Las Vegas*	.933	26	41	1	3	45	0
Smith, Ira, Las Vegas	.957	54	87	3	4	94	1
Snider, Van, Salt Lake	1.000	22	33	2	0	35	0
Snyder, Cory, Las Vegas	1.000	6	8	1	0	9	0
Spearman, Vernon, Albuquerque*	1.000	8	11	0	0	11	0
Springer, Steve, Las Vegas	.800	3	4	0	1	5	0
Sweeney, Mark, Vancouver*	.988	38	80	1	1	82	0
Thurman, Gary, Tacoma	.965	86	180	13	7	200	2
Tomberlin, Andy, Edmonton*	.929	12	25	1	2	28	0
Turang, Brian, Tacoma	.982	30	56	0	1	57	0
Turner, Chris, Vancouver	1.000	3	11	0	0	11	0
Vatcher, Jim, Las Vegas	.994	95	164	8	1	173	3
Vaughn, Derek, Vancouver	1.000	1	3	0	0	3	0
Wehner, John, Calgary	1.000	5	7	0	0	7	0
Widger, Chris, Tacoma	1.000	6	13	1	0	14	0
Williams, Keith, Phoenix	1.000	19	38	1	0	39	0
Williams, Reggie, Albuquerque	1.000	61	141	10	0	151	4
Wolfe, Joel, Edmonton	.923	11	12	0	1	13	0
Young, Ernie, Edmonton	.971	90	194	7	6	207	0

CLASS AAA Pacific Coast League

OUTFIELDERS WITH TWO OR MORE TEAMS

Player, Team	Pct.	G	PO	A	E	TC	DP
Deer, Rob, Vancouver	.917	9	11	0	1	12	0
Deer, Rob, Las Vegas	.971	40	66	0	2	68	0
Jackson, John, Vancouver*	1.000	31	56	3	0	59	0
Jackson, John, Salt Lake*	.971	52	99	1	3	103	0
Newfield, Marc, Tacoma	.966	30	55	1	2	58	0
Newfield, Marc, Las Vegas	.978	19	44	1	1	46	0
Pose, Scott, Albuquerque	1.000	4	2	0	0	2	0
Pose, Scott, Salt Lake	.980	62	90	8	2	100	0

CATCHERS

Player, Team	Pct.	G	PO	A	E	TC	DP	PB
Beard, Garrett, Edmonton	.977	17	75	10	2	87	1	0
Bellinger, Clay, Phoenix	1.000	1	2	0	0	2	0	0
Brito, Jorge, C.S.	.983	31	163	13	3	179	2	2
Chavez, Raul, Tucson	.980	32	203	39	5	247	3	4
Christopherson, Eric, Phoenix	.993	91	543	44	4	591	6	5
Cianfrocco, Archi, Las Vegas	1.000	1	1	0	0	1	0	0
Colbert, Craig, Las Vegas	.985	69	343	42	6	391	4	8
Dalesandro, Mark, Vancouver	1.000	4	10	0	0	10	0	0
Durant, Mike, Salt Lake	.990	70	354	30	4	388	3	2
Ehmann, Kurt, Phoenix	.750	1	3	0	1	4	0	2
Encarnacion, Angelo, Calgary	.984	21	113	14	2	129	1	3
Fabregas, Jorge, Vancouver	.969	21	112	12	4	128	2	0
Goff, Jerry, Tucson	.989	62	336	39	4	379	5	12
Greene, Todd, Vancouver	.995	30	175	17	1	193	1	5
Hanel, Marcus, Calgary	.923	2	12	0	1	13	0	1
Helfand, Eric, Edmonton	.968	16	79	11	3	93	2	1
Horn, Jeff, Salt Lake	1.000	3	18	1	0	19	0	2
Howard, Chris, Tacoma	.987	77	405	47	6	458	3	8
Huckaby, Ken, Albuquerque	.973	80	515	61	16	592	5	9
Kreuter, Chad, Tacoma	.988	14	70	10	1	81	3	1
Litton, Greg, Tacoma	1.000	2	2	0	0	2	0	0
Makarewicz, Scott, Tucson	.981	61	338	28	7	373	8	2
Maksudian, Mike, Edmonton	.989	54	241	33	3	277	2	8
Marx, Tim, Calgary	.977	54	268	27	7	302	5	5
Maurer, Ron, Albuquerque	1.000	5	18	3	0	21	0	0
Maynard, Scott, Tacoma	1.000	1	6	0	0	6	0	0
MILLER, Damian, Salt Lake	.998	76	394	52	1	447	5	7
Miller, Roger, Phoenix	.972	41	221	23	7	251	5	2
Mirabelli, Doug, Phoenix	.985	23	115	17	2	134	4	2
Molina, Ben, Vancouver	1.000	1	4	0	0	4	0	0
Molina, Izzy, Edmonton	1.000	2	9	1	0	10	0	0
Monzon, Jose, Vancouver	1.000	13	41	5	0	46	0	2
Mulligan, Sean, Las Vegas	.987	82	439	33	6	478	5	11
Munoz, Noe, Albuquerque	.991	19	89	16	1	106	1	3
Nokes, Matt, C.S.	.979	8	43	3	1	47	1	0
Osik, Keith, Calgary	.990	74	372	24	4	400	3	6
Owens, Jayhawk, C.S.	.989	68	390	46	5	441	8	4
Pevey, Marty, Tacoma	1.000	7	36	1	0	37	0	1
Prince, Tom, Albuquerque	.989	55	310	34	4	348	7	3
Sealy, Scot, Tacoma	.933	4	14	0	1	15	0	1
Strittmatter, Mark, C.S.	.973	5	32	4	1	37	0	0
Tatum, Jim, C.S.	.667	1	2	0	1	3	0	0
Tejero, Fausto, Vancouver	.995	37	186	29	1	216	3	2
Thurston, Jerry, Las Vegas	.976	5	36	4	1	41	0	1
Turner, Chris, Vancouver	.990	51	282	23	3	308	2	5
Wakamatsu, Don, Tacoma	.952	9	53	6	3	62	1	0
Walters, Dan, C.S.	.984	48	222	17	4	243	2	3
Widger, Chris, Tacoma	.980	37	176	21	4	201	3	4
Wilkins, Rick, Tucson	1.000	4	27	4	0	31	0	1
Willard, Jerry, Tacoma	1.000	12	38	0	0	38	0	1
Williams, George, Edmonton	.981	64	310	44	7	361	6	4

PITCHERS

Player, Team	Pct.	G	PO	A	E	TC	DP
Acevedo, Juan, C.S.	1.000	3	2	0	0	2	0
Adams, Willie, Edmonton	1.000	11	5	8	0	13	0
Akerfelds, Darrel, Vancouver	1.000	9	3	7	0	10	0
Alicea, Miguel, Albuquerque	1.000	7	1	2	0	3	0
Apana, Matt, Tacoma	.895	21	7	10	2	19	1
Arvesen, Scott, Las Vegas	1.000	2	0	2	0	2	0
August, Don, Calgary	1.000	2	1	0	0	1	0
Ayrault, Bob, Calgary	.500	6	0	1	1	2	0
Backlund, Brett, Calgary	1.000	12	4	4	0	8	0
Bailey, Roger, C.S.	1.000	3	0	1	0	1	0
Baker, Scott, Edmonton*	.955	22	4	17	1	22	0
Bankhead, Scott, Edmonton	1.000	12	1	2	0	3	0
Barcelo, Marc, Salt Lake	.938	28	8	22	2	32	0
Barton, Shawn, Phoenix*	.667	15	2	2	2	6	0
Bennett, Erik, Van.-Tuc.	1.000	42	3	7	0	10	0
Bittiger, Jeff, Edmonton	.833	6	3	2	1	6	0

Player, Team	Pct.	G	PO	A	E	TC	DP
Bochtler, Doug, Las Vegas	1.000	18	1	3	0	4	0
Bourgeois, Steve, Phoenix	1.000	6	4	2	0	6	0
Bowie, Jim, Edmonton*	1.000	7	0	3	0	3	2
Brink, Brad, Pho.-Edm.	1.000	20	6	12	0	18	0
Briscoe, John, Edmonton	1.000	3	1	0	0	1	0
Brocail, Doug, Tucson	.750	3	0	3	1	4	0
Brock, Russ, Edmonton	.875	18	2	5	1	8	1
Brosnan, Jason, Albuquerque*	1.000	23	1	0	0	1	0
Bruske, Jim, Albuquerque	.958	43	2	21	1	24	1
Bryant, Shawn, Salt Lake*	.875	31	1	6	1	8	0
Bullard, Jason, C.S.	1.000	4	0	1	0	1	0
Burcham, Tim, Phoenix	1.000	5	1	1	0	2	0
Burgos, Enrique, Phoenix*	.800	41	0	4	1	5	0
Burke, John, C.S.	.933	19	4	10	1	15	2
Bustillos, Albert, C.S.	.962	34	6	19	1	26	1
Butler, Mike, Vancouver*	1.000	3	0	3	0	3	0
Cadaret, Greg, Las Vegas*	.923	28	1	11	1	13	2
Campbell, Kevin, Tacoma	.909	31	3	7	1	11	1
Carlson, Dan, Phoenix	.960	23	11	13	1	25	1
Carmona, Rafael, Tacoma	.929	8	5	8	1	14	0
Castillo, Juan, Tucson	.750	11	4	2	2	8	0
Chavez, Tony, Vancouver	1.000	8	1	2	0	3	0
Clayton, Royal, Phoenix	1.000	5	5	12	0	17	1
Cole, Victor, Las Vegas	.750	4	2	1	1	4	0
Conroy, Brian, C.S.	1.000	5	3	2	0	5	0
Converse, Jim, Tacoma	1.000	17	3	7	0	10	2
Corbin, Archie, Calgary	.882	47	9	6	2	17	2
Courtright, John, Salt Lake*	.960	18	5	19	1	25	0
Cromwell, Nate, Las Vegas*	1.000	9	1	6	0	7	0
Crowther, Brent, C.S.	1.000	1	0	2	0	2	0
Czajkowski, Jim, C.S.	.941	60	6	10	1	17	1
Daal, Omar, Albuquerque*	.900	17	1	8	1	10	2
Darwin, Jeff, Tacoma	1.000	46	3	6	0	9	1
Daspit, Jim, Tuc.-Edm.	.909	38	3	7	1	11	0
Davis, Tim, Tacoma*	1.000	2	1	0	0	1	0
Davison, Scott, Tacoma	1.000	8	2	2	0	4	0
DeLosSantos, Mariano, Calgary	.882	14	6	9	2	17	0
Dishman, Glenn, Las Vegas*	1.000	14	6	21	0	27	0
Dougherty, Jim, Tucson	1.000	8	0	1	0	1	0
Edenfield, Ken, Vancouver	.857	33	2	10	2	14	3
Edwards, Wayne, Albuquerque*	.909	14	5	5	1	11	1
Eischen, Joey, Albuquerque*	1.000	13	1	0	0	1	0
Elliott, Donnie, Las Vegas	1.000	7	0	1	0	1	0
Ericks, John, Calgary	1.000	5	2	3	0	5	0
Ettles, Mark, Las Vegas	1.000	10	1	0	0	1	1
Evans, Dave, Tucson	1.000	2	0	1	0	1	0
Fesh, Sean, Tuc.-L.V.*	1.000	40	1	9	0	10	0
Flynt, Bill, Calgary*	1.000	12	0	3	0	3	0
Fortugno, Tim, Vancouver*	1.000	10	0	2	0	2	0
Fredrickson, Scott, C.S.	1.000	58	4	16	0	20	0
Gallaher, Kevin, Tucson	1.000	3	1	0	0	1	0
Gamez, Bob, Phoenix*	1.000	36	1	10	0	11	1
Gandarillas, Gus, Salt Lake	1.000	22	3	8	0	11	1
Garcia, Jose, Albuquerque	1.000	11	1	5	0	6	0
Gardner, Chris, Tucson	.857	16	0	6	1	7	1
Gavaghan, Sean, Salt Lake	.923	35	2	10	1	13	1
Gibson, Paul, Calgary*	.500	19	0	1	1	2	0
Glinatsis, George, Tacoma	1.000	8	2	7	0	9	1
Gomez, Pat, Phoenix*	.667	2	0	2	1	3	1
Grahe, Joe, C.S.	1.000	2	0	3	0	3	0
Graybill, Dave, Tacoma	1.000	6	1	0	0	1	0
Green, Otis, Tacoma*	1.000	18	2	5	0	7	0
Greer, Ken, Phoenix	1.000	38	3	8	0	11	0
Grundt, Ken, C.S.*	1.000	9	1	1	0	2	0
Guetterman, Lee, Tacoma*	1.000	33	7	9	0	16	0
Hancock, Lee, Calgary*	.964	34	5	22	1	28	2
Hansell, Greg, Alb.-S.L.	1.000	15	4	8	0	12	0
Harikkala, Tim, Tacoma	.926	25	11	14	2	27	3
Harriger, Denny, Las Vegas	.977	29	16	27	1	44	4
Hartgraves, Dean, Tucson*	1.000	14	0	1	0	1	0
Hathaway, Hilly, Las Vegas*	.944	14	4	13	1	18	1
Hawblitzel, Ryan, C.S.	.933	21	4	10	1	15	0
Hawkins, LaTroy, Salt Lake	.912	22	10	21	3	34	1
Haynes, Heath, Edmonton	1.000	12	1	4	0	5	1
Heredia, Julian, Vancouver	.900	51	3	6	1	10	0
Hermanson, Dustin, Las Vegas	1.000	31	0	2	0	2	0
Hernandez, Fernando, Las Vegas	1.000	8	2	0	0	2	0
Hill, Milt, Calgary	1.000	24	2	8	0	10	0
Holdridge, David, Vancouver	.800	11	1	3	1	5	0
Hollins, Stacy, Edmonton	1.000	7	2	5	0	7	0
Holman, Brad, Tacoma	.500	5	1	0	1	2	0
Holman, Shawn, Albuquerque	1.000	49	3	12	0	15	0

CLASS AAA Pacific Coast League

Player, Team	Pct.	G	PO	A	E	TC	DP
Holt, Chris, Tucson	.943	20	9	24	2	35	1
Holzemer, Mark, Vancouver*	.944	28	7	10	1	18	0
Hook, Chris, Phoenix	1.000	4	0	1	0	1	0
Hope, John, Calgary	1.000	13	14	17	0	31	2
Horsman, Vince, Salt Lake*	1.000	16	1	0	0	1	0
Hostetler, Tom, Edmonton	1.000	4	2	1	0	3	0
Huisman, Rick, Tucson	.818	42	5	4	2	11	1
Hunter, Jim, C.S.	1.000	10	0	8	0	8	0
Janicki, Pete, Vancouver	1.000	9	2	4	0	6	0
Johns, Doug, Edmonton*	.907	23	13	26	4	43	1
Johnson, Judd, Salt Lake*	1.000	17	1	6	0	7	0
Johnston, Joel, C.S.	1.000	18	0	2	0	2	0
Jones, Bobby, C.S.*	.889	11	2	6	1	9	0
Jones, Stacy, Phoenix	1.000	4	0	1	0	1	0
Keagle, Greg, Las Vegas	.933	14	5	9	1	15	0
Keling, Korey, Vancouver	1.000	3	0	3	0	3	0
Ketchen, Doug, Tucson	.824	19	6	8	3	17	1
Kile, Darryl, Tucson	1.000	4	2	5	0	7	0
King, Kevin, Tacoma*	.750	16	0	3	1	4	0
Knudsen, Kurt, Phoenix	1.000	11	0	3	0	3	0
Kotarski, Mike, C.S.*	1.000	22	1	2	0	3	0
Krueger, Bill, Calgary*	.917	10	1	10	1	12	0
Kubinski, Tim, Edmonton*	.889	6	2	6	1	9	0
Leftwich, Phil, Vancouver	1.000	6	4	7	0	11	0
Leiper, Dave, Edmonton*	1.000	2	1	0	0	1	0
Lewis, Scott, Tacoma	1.000	3	1	1	0	2	0
Lieber, Jon, Calgary	.867	14	7	6	2	15	0
Lilliquist, Derek, Albuquerque*	1.000	13	1	4	0	5	1
Logsdon, Kevin, C.S.*	1.000	2	1	0	0	1	0
Loiselle, Rich, L.V.-Tuc.	.800	10	2	2	1	5	0
Long, Joey, Las Vegas*	.833	25	1	4	1	6	0
Lorraine, Andrew, Vancouver*	1.000	18	7	15	0	22	2
Mack, Tony, Vancouver	1.000	4	1	5	0	6	0
Manzanillo, Ravelo, Calgary*	1.000	8	1	2	0	3	0
Martinez, Jose, Las Vegas	.970	27	11	21	1	33	1
Martinez, Pedro, Tucson*	.889	20	0	8	1	9	1
Mauser, Tim, Las Vegas	.778	35	1	6	2	9	0
Maysey, Matt, Calgary	.947	44	5	13	1	19	0
McCarthy, Tom, Albuquerque	.900	13	3	6	1	10	0
McCurry, Jeff, Calgary	1.000	3	0	2	0	2	0
McFarlin, Terric, Las Vegas	.949	58	11	26	2	39	1
McMurtry, Craig, Tucson	.938	13	5	10	1	16	1
Mecir, Jim, Tacoma	.933	40	6	8	1	15	0
Menendez, Tony, Phoenix	1.000	50	4	9	0	13	2
Merriman, Brett, Las Vegas	1.000	11	0	2	0	2	0
Milacki, Bob, Tacoma	.905	12	9	10	2	21	1
Milchin, Mike, Albuquerque*	1.000	18	2	13	0	15	0
Mimbs, Mark, Albuquerque*	1.000	23	4	15	0	19	1
Mintz, Steve, Phoenix	.800	31	1	3	1	5	0
Misuraca, Mike, Salt Lake	.973	31	8	28	1	37	3
Mlicki, Doug, Tucson	1.000	6	6	1	0	7	0
Mohler, Mike, Edmonton*	1.000	29	2	11	0	13	0
Montalvo, Rafael, Albuquerque	.833	49	7	18	5	30	1
Monteleone, Rich, Vancouver	1.000	7	1	4	0	5	0
Morman, Alvin, Tucson*	.917	45	3	8	1	12	0
Morrison, Keith, Vancouver	.974	28	14	23	1	38	0
Mulholland, Terry, Phoenix*	.000	1	0	0	1	1	0
Munoz, Oscar, Salt Lake	.909	19	8	12	2	22	2
Naulty, Dan, Salt Lake	1.000	42	3	5	0	8	1
Nied, David, C.S.	1.000	7	4	6	0	10	1
O'Donoghue, John, Albuquerque*	1.000	25	6	12	0	18	1
Olivares, Omar, C.S.*	1.000	3	0	2	0	2	0
Osuna, Antonio, Albuquerque	1.000	19	0	2	0	2	0
Painter, Lance, C.S.*	.875	11	1	6	1	8	0
Park, Chan Ho, Albuquerque	.958	23	7	16	1	24	1
Parra, Jose, Albuquerque	.667	12	3	3	3	9	0
Patrick, Bronswell, Tucson	1.000	43	7	4	0	11	0
Patterson, Ken, Vancouver*	1.000	8	1	0	0	1	0
Peek, Tim, Edmonton	1.000	12	2	3	0	5	0
Peever, Lloyd, C.S.	1.000	8	1	4	0	5	0
Phillips, Randy, Phoenix	.882	25	4	11	2	17	2
Phillips, Tony, Tacoma	.957	47	9	13	1	23	1
Phoenix, Steve, Phoenix	1.000	40	8	7	0	15	1
Piatt, Doug, Phoenix	1.000	6	1	2	0	3	0
Powell, Ross, Tucson*	.800	13	0	4	1	5	0
Pulido, Carlos, Salt Lake	1.000	43	1	11	0	12	1
Pyc, Dave, Albuquerque*	1.000	1	0	1	0	1	0
Ralph, Curtis, Calgary	1.000	28	2	5	0	7	0
Ratekin, Mark, Vancouver	1.000	19	2	8	0	10	0
Rath, Gary, Albuquerque*	1.000	8	0	4	0	4	0
Rekar, Bryan, C.S.	1.000	7	4	8	0	12	2
Renko, Steve, Vancouver	1.000	10	5	3	0	8	0
Revenig, Todd, Edmonton	.933	45	6	8	1	15	0
Reynoso, Armando, C.S.	.833	5	2	3	1	6	0
Robertson, Rich, Salt Lake*	1.000	7	2	6	0	8	1
Robinson, Scott, Phoenix	.974	31	12	26	1	39	3
Rodriguez, Felix, Albuquerque	1.000	14	3	8	0	11	1
Rogers, Kevin, Phoenix*	1.000	3	0	1	0	1	0
Rohde, Dave, Tucson	1.000	1	0	1	0	1	0
Romanoli, Paul, C.S.*	.750	31	1	2	1	4	0
Roper, John, Phoenix	1.000	1	0	1	0	1	0
Rose, Scott, Edmonton	1.000	5	1	1	0	2	0
Rosselli, Joe, Phoenix	1.000	13	1	7	0	8	1
Ryan, Matt, Calgary	1.000	5	0	1	0	1	0
Rychel, Kevin, Calgary	1.000	10	1	2	0	3	0
Sager, A.J., C.S.	.968	23	10	20	1	31	1
St. Claire, Randy, Calgary	.947	54	2	16	1	19	1
Salkeld, Roger, Tacoma	1.000	4	2	0	0	2	0
Sanchez, Alex, Edmonton	1.000	8	1	6	0	7	0
Schullstrom, Erik, Salt Lake	1.000	10	1	0	0	1	0
Scott, Darryl, C.S.	1.000	59	6	15	0	21	1
Sepeda, Jamie, Tucson	1.000	8	5	8	0	13	0
Shaw, Curtis, Edmonton*	.862	42	6	19	4	29	4
Shifflett, Steve, C.S.	1.000	23	4	6	0	10	0
Shouse, Brian, Calgary*	.833	8	2	3	1	6	0
Simas, Bill, Vancouver	.875	30	3	4	1	8	0
Small, Mark, Tucson	1.000	51	6	5	0	11	1
Smith, Tim, Edmonton	1.000	9	9	5	0	14	0
Springer, Russ, Vancouver	.857	6	3	3	1	7	0
Stanhope, Chuck, Edmonton	1.000	6	0	1	0	1	0
Stevens, Matt, Salt Lake	1.000	7	1	2	0	3	1
Sveum, Dale, Calgary	1.000	2	0	1	0	1	0
Swan, Russ, Edmonton*	.889	17	1	7	1	9	0
Tabaka, Jeff, Las Vegas*	1.000	19	1	1	0	2	0
Taylor, Kerry, Las Vegas	1.000	8	1	5	0	6	0
Taylor, Scott, Calgary*	1.000	27	8	27	0	35	6
Telford, Anthony, Edmonton	.857	8	5	7	2	14	0
Thompson, John, Tacoma	.000	1	0	0	1	1	0
Thompson, Mark, C.S.	1.000	11	3	5	0	8	1
Torres, Salomon, Pho.-Tac.	.900	6	3	6	1	10	1
Treadwell, Jody, Albuquerque	.826	30	1	18	4	23	2
Trlicek, Rick, Phoenix	.875	38	2	12	2	16	1
Trombley, Mike, Salt Lake	1.000	12	7	6	0	13	0
Valdez, Carlos, Phoenix	.800	18	0	4	1	5	0
Valdez, Sergio, Phoenix	1.000	18	9	14	0	23	2
Valera, Julio, Vancouver	.800	13	3	5	2	10	0
Vanderweele, Doug, Phoenix	.889	11	5	3	1	9	0
VanRyn, Ben, Vancouver*	1.000	11	3	3	0	6	0
Villone, Ron, Tacoma*	.800	22	0	4	1	5	0
Wagner, Billy, Tucson*	.933	13	2	12	1	15	0
Wagner, Matt, Tacoma	1.000	6	0	2	0	2	1
Waldron, Joe, Tucson*	1.000	4	0	1	0	1	0
WALL, Donne, Tucson	1.000	28	13	40	0	53	2
Waring, Jim, Tucson	1.000	5	1	2	0	3	0
Wasdin, John, Edmonton	.909	29	15	15	3	33	0
Watkins, Scott, Salt Lake*	.818	45	2	7	2	11	0
Watson, Ron, Vancouver	1.000	5	1	0	0	1	0
Weber, Weston, Tac.-L.V.	.971	29	17	17	1	35	1
Wengert, Don, Edmonton	1.000	16	2	5	0	7	1
Westbrook, Destry, Tucson	1.000	5	1	0	0	1	1
Whitaker, Steve, Phoenix*	1.000	16	1	14	0	15	1
White, Chris, Tucson	1.000	5	0	2	0	2	0
White, Rick, Calgary	1.000	14	5	4	0	9	0
Williams, Jeff, Tacoma	1.000	8	2	3	0	5	0
Williams, Shad, Vancouver	1.000	25	11	18	0	29	2
Williams, Todd, Albuquerque	.909	25	3	7	1	11	1
Willis, Carl, Vancouver	1.000	20	2	4	0	6	0
Willis, Travis, Calgary	1.000	22	8	7	0	15	0
Wilson, Gary, Calgary	1.000	6	1	6	0	7	0
Winston, Darrin, Calgary*	1.000	53	2	6	0	8	0
Wissler, Bill, Salt Lake	1.000	37	3	11	0	14	2
Wojciechowski, Steve, Edmonton*	1.000	14	6	17	0	23	0
Wolcott, Bob, Tacoma	1.000	13	3	8	0	11	0
Worrell, Tim, Las Vegas	1.000	10	0	4	0	4	0

PITCHERS WITH TWO OR MORE TEAMS

Player, Team	Pct.	G	PO	A	E	TC	DP
Bennett, Erik, Vancouver	1.000	28	3	4	0	7	0
Bennett, Erik, Tucson	1.000	14	0	3	0	3	0
Brink, Brad, Phoenix	1.000	11	4	8	0	12	0
Brink, Brad, Edmonton	1.000	9	2	4	0	6	0
Daspit, Jim, Tucson	.909	36	3	7	1	11	0
Daspit, Jim, Edmonton	1.000	2	0	0	0	0	0
Fesh, Sean, Tucson*	1.000	10	1	1	0	2	0
Fesh, Sean, Las Vegas*	1.000	30	0	8	0	8	0
Hansell, Greg, Albuquerque	1.000	8	0	4	0	4	0

Player, Team	Pct.	G	PO	A	E	TC	DP		Player, Team	Pct.	G	PO	A	E	TC	DP
Hansell, Greg, Salt Lake	1.000	7	4	4	0	8	0		Torres, Salomon, Tacoma	.889	5	3	5	1	9	1
Loiselle, Rich, Las Vegas	1.000	8	2	1	0	3	0		Weber, Weston, Tacoma	1.000	20	14	15	0	29	1
Loiselle, Rich, Tucson	.500	2	0	1	1	2	0		Weber, Weston, Las Vegas	.833	9	3	2	1	6	0
Torres, Salomon, Phoenix	1.000	1	0	1	0	1	0									

The following players did not have any fielding statistics at the positions indicated or appeared only as a designated hitter, pinch-hitter or pinch-runner: Ball, 2b; Beard, 1b; C. Bennett, p; Berumen, p; Bielecki, p; Boskie, p; Bream, of, p; Sc. Bryant, p; N. Castro, p; Colbert, 3b, p; Correa, p; Corsi, p; J. Cummings, p; Deer, p; Demetral, p; Fermin, ss; Gardella, p; Goff, 3b; Gould, p; Griffey, dh; W. Guerrero, of; Hall, of; Jean, p; Jimenez, p; Je. Martinez, p; Maurer, p; Murphy, p; Osik, p; Parker, ss; Plantenberg, p; Pose, p; Risley, p; Rohde, of; Sanders, p; Sanford, p; Saunders, ss; Schmitt, p; Serafini, p; I. Smith, 3b; Whitehurst, p; G. Williams, of.

LEAGUE CHAMPIONS

Year	Team	Pct.	Year	Team	Pct.	Year	Team	Pct.
1903—	Los Angeles	.630	1939—	Seattle	.589	1973—	Tucson	.583
1904—	Tacoma	.589		Sacramento (4th)†	.500		Spokane•	.563
	Tacoma§	.571	1940—	Seattle‡	.629	1974—	Spokane•	.549
	Los Angeles§	.571	1941—	Seattle‡	.598		Albuquerque	.535
1905—	Tacoma	.583	1942—	Sacramento	.590	1975—	Salt Lake City	.556
	Los Angeles*	.604		Seattle (3rd)†	.539		Hawaii•	.611
1906—	Portland	.657	1943—	Los Angeles	.710	1976—	Salt Lake City	.625
1907—	Los Angeles	.608		S. Francisco (2nd)†	.574		Hawaii•	.531
1908—	Los Angeles	.585	1944—	Los Angeles	.586	1977—	Phoenix•	.579
1909—	San Francisco	.623		S. Francisco (3rd)†	.509		Hawaii	.541
1910—	Portland	.567	1945—	Portland	.622	1978—	Tacoma††	.584
1911—	Portland	.589		S. Francisco (4th)†	.525		Albuquerque††	.557
1912—	Oakland	.591	1946—	San Francisco‡	.628	1979—	Albuquerque	.581
1913—	Portland	.559	1947—	Los Angeles▲	.567		Salt Lake City‡‡	.541
1914—	Portland	.574	1948—	Oakland‡	.606	1980—	Albuquerque	.578
1915—	San Francisco	.570	1949—	Hollywood‡	.583		Hawaii	.539
1916—	Los Angeles	.601	1950—	Oakland	.590	1981—	Albuquerque*	.712
1917—	San Francisco	.561	1951—	Seattle‡	.593		Tacoma	.561
1918—	Vernon	.569	1952—	Hollywood	.606	1982—	Albuquerque*	.594
	Los Angeles (2nd)◆	.548	1953—	Hollywood	.589		Spokane	.545
1919—	Vernon	.613	1954—	San Diego■	.604	1983—	Albuquerque	.594
1920—	Vernon	.556	1955—	Seattle	.552		Portland*	.528
1921—	Los Angeles	.574	1956—	Los Angeles	.637	1984—	Hawaii	.621
1922—	San Francisco	.638	1957—	San Francisco	.601		Edmonton*	.486
1923—	San Francisco	.617	1958—	Phoenix	.578	1985—	Vancouver*	.522
1924—	Seattle	.545	1959—	Salt Lake City	.552		Phoenix	.563
1925—	San Francisco	.643	1960—	Spokane	.601	1986—	Vancouver	.616
1926—	Los Angeles	.599	1961—	Tacoma	.630		Las Vegas*	.563
1927—	Oakland	.615	1962—	San Diego	.604	1987—	Calgary	.596
1928—	San Francisco*	.630	1963—	Spokane	.620		Albuquerque*	.542
	Sacramento∞	.626		Oklahoma City•	.632	1988—	Vancouver	.599
	San Francisco∞	.626	1964—	Arkansas	.609		Las Vegas*	.529
1929—	Mission	.643		San Diego•	.576	1989—	Albuquerque	.563
	Hollywood*	.592	1965—	Oklahoma City a	.628		Vancouver*	.514
1930—	Los Angeles*	.576		Portland	.547	1990—	Albuquerque*	.641
	Hollywood*	.650	1966—	Seattle•	.561		Edmonton	.553
1931—	Hollywood	.626		Tulsa	.578	1991—	Albuquerque	.580
	San Francisco*	.608	1967—	San Diego•	.574		Tucson*	.564
1932—	Portland	.587		Spokane	.541	1992—	Colorado Springs*	.596
1933—	Los Angeles	.610	1968—	Tulsa•	.642		Portland	.576
1934—	Los Angeles▼	.786		Spokane	.586	1993—	Portland	.608
	Los Angeles▼	.689	1969—	Tacoma•	.589		Tucson*	.580
1935—	Los Angeles	.648		Eugene	.603	1994—	Albuquerque*	.597
	San Francisco*	.608	1970—	Spokane•	.644		Vancouver	.542
1936—	Portland‡	.549		Hawaii	.671	1995—	Salt Lake	.549
1937—	Sacramento	.573	1971—	Salt Lake City	.534		Colorado Springs*	.538
	San Diego (3rd)†	.545		Tacoma	.545			
1938—	Los Angeles	.590	1972—	Albuquerque	.622			
	Sacramento (3rd)†	.537		Eugene	.534			

*Won split-season playoff. †Won four-team playoff. ‡Won pennant and four-team playoff. §Tied for second-half title with Tacoma winning playoff. ∞Tied for second-half title, with Sacramento winning playoff. ▲Ended regular season in tie with San Francisco and won one-game playoff for pennant, then won four-club playoff. ◆Won playoff from first-place Vernon and awarded championship. ■Defeated Hollywood in one-game playoff for pennant. ▼Won both halves, no playoff. •League was divided into Northern, Southern divisions in 1963, 1969-70-71, and Eastern, Western divisions in 1964 through 1968 and 1972 through 1977, won two-team playoff. ††League divided into Eastern and Western divisions, Tacoma and Albuquerque declared co-champions following cancellation of four-team playoff due to continuing rain and wet grounds. ‡‡Won second-half title and defeated Hawaii in four-team playoff.

EASTERN LEAGUE

President
John Levenda

Address
P.O. Box 60687
Harrisburg, PA 17106

Phone
717-233-4909

TEAMS

BINGHAMTON METS

General manager
R.C. Reuteman

Manager
John Tamargo

Ballpark (capacity, surface)
Binghamton Municipal Stadium (6,064, grass)

Affiliation
Mets

Address
P.O. Box 598
Binghamton, NY 13902

Phone
607-723-6387

BOWIE BAYSOX

General manager
Jon Danos

Manager
Jon Danos

Ballpark (capacity, surface)
Prince George's Stadium (10,000, grass)

Affiliation
Orioles

Address
P.O. Box 1661
Bowie, MD 20717

Phone
301-805-6000

CANTON/AKRON INDIANS

General manager
Jeff Auman

Manager
Jeff Datz

Ballpark (capacity, surface)
Thurman Munson Memorial Stadium (5,708, grass)

Affiliation
Indians

Address
2501 Allen Ave. SE
Canton, OH 44707

Phone
216-456-5100

HARDWARE CITY ROCK CATS

General manager
Gerry Berthiaume

Manager
Al Newman

Ballpark (capacity, surface)
Beehive Field (4,700, grass)

Affiliation
Twins

Address
P.O. Box 1718
New Britain, CT 06050

Phone
203-224-8383

HARRISBURG SENATORS

General manager
Todd Vander Woude

Manager
Pat Kelly

Ballpark (capacity, surface)
RiverSide Stadium (6,300, grass)

Affiliation
Expos

Address
P.O. Box 15757
Harrisburg, PA 17105

Phone
717-231-4444

NEW HAVEN RAVENS

General manager
Charles Dowd

Manager
Bill Hayes

Ballpark (capacity, surface)
Yale Field (6,200, grass)

Affiliation
Rockies

Address
63 Grove St.
New Haven, CT 06511

Phone
1-800-728-3671

NORWICH NAVIGATORS

General manager
George Brzezinski

Manager
Jim Essian

Ballpark (capacity, surface)
Name to be announced (7,000, grass)

Affiliation
Yankees

Address
P.O. Box 6003
Yantic, CT 06389

Phone
203-887-7962

PORTLAND SEA DOGS

General manager
Charles Eshbach

Manager
Carlos Tosca

Ballpark (capacity, surface)
Hadlock Field (6,000, grass)

Affiliation
Marlins

Address
P.O. Box 636
Portland, ME 04104

Phone
207-874-9300

READING PHILLIES

General manager
Chuck Domino

Manager
Bill Robinson

Ballpark (capacity, surface)
Municipal Memorial Stadium (8,000, grass)

Affiliation
Phillies

Address
P.O. Box 15050
Reading, PA 19610

Phone
610-375-8469

TRENTON THUNDER

General manager
Wayne Hodes

Manager
Ken Macha

Ballpark (capacity, surface)
Mercer County Waterfront Park (6,300, grass)

Affiliation
Red Sox

Address
One Thunder Road
Trenton, NJ 08611

Phone
609-394-8326

CLASS AA *Eastern League*

NORTHERN DIVISION

Team	W	L	T	Pct.	GB
Portland (Marlins)	86	56	0	.606	....
New Haven (Rockies)	79	63	0	.556	7
Norwich (Yankees)	70	71	0	.496	15½
Binghamton (Mets)	67	75	0	.472	19
New Britain (Twins)	65	77	0	.458	21

SOUTHERN DIVISION

Team	W	L	T	Pct.	GB
Trenton (Red Sox)	73	69	0	.514	....
Reading (Phillies)	73	69	0	.514	....
Bowie (Orioles)	68	74	0	.479	5
Canton/Akron (Indians)	67	75	0	.472	6
Harrisburg (Expos)	61	80	0	.433	11½

COMPOSITE

Team	Por.	N.H.	Tre.	Rea.	Nor.	Bow.	C.A.	Bin.	N.B.	Har.	W	L	T	Pct.	GB
Portland (Marlins)	....	10	5	9	13	10	10	10	10	9	86	56	0	.606	....
New Haven (Rockies)	8	....	6	8	7	9	10	11	10	10	79	63	0	.556	7
Trenton (Red Sox)	9	8	....	7	4	5	8	10	9	13	73	69	0	.514	13
Reading (Phillies)	5	6	11	....	7	9	9	8	10	10	73	69	0	.514	13
Norwich (Yankees)	5	11	10	7	....	6	10	6	10	5	70	71	0	.496	15½
Bowie (Orioles)	4	5	13	9	8	....	9	7	5	8	68	74	0	.479	18
Canton/Akron (Indians)	4	4	10	11	4	9	....	9	7	9	67	75	0	.472	19
Binghamton (Mets)	8	7	4	6	12	7	5	....	10	8	67	75	0	.472	19
New Britain (Twins)	8	8	5	4	8	9	7	8	....	8	65	77	0	.458	21
Harrisburg (Expos)	5	4	5	8	8	10	9	6	6	....	61	80	0	.433	24½

Major league affiliations in parentheses.

PLAYOFFS: Reading defeated Trenton, three games to none; New Haven defeated Portland, three games to one; Reading defeated New Haven, three game to two, to win league championship.

REGULAR-SEASON ATTENDANCE: Binghamton, 200,077; Bowie, 463,976; Canton/Akron, 195,049; Harrisburg, 240,488; New Britain, 124,560; New Haven, 283,766; Norwich, 281,473; Portland, 429,763; Reading, 383,984; Trenton, 453,915. Total—3,057,051. Playoffs (12 games)—45,913. Class AA All-Star Game at Shreveport—6,247.

MANAGERS: Binghamton, John Tamargo; Bowie, Bob Miscik; Canton/Akron, Ted Kubiak; Harrisburg, Pat Kelly; New Britain, Sal Butera; New Haven, Paul Zuvella; Norwich, Jimmy Johnson; Portland, Carlos Tosca; Reading, Bill Dancy; Trenton, Ken Macha.

ALL-STAR TEAM: 1B—David Kennedy, New Haven; 2B—Todd Walker, New Britain; 3B—Rob Grable, Reading; SS—Nomar Garciaparra, Trenton; OF—Angel Echevarria, New Haven; Billy McMillon, Portland; Jay Payton, Binghamton; C—Mike Figga, Norwich; DH—Clyde "Pork Chop" Pough, Trenton; P—Paul Wilson, Binghamton; Eric Ludwick, Binghamton; Jay Powell, Portland; Dan Serafini, New Britain; Most Valuable Player—Jay Payton, Binghamton; Pitcher of the Year—Paul Wilson, Binghamton; Rookie of the Year—Jay Payton, Binghamton; Manager of the Year—Bill Dancy, Reading.

1995 BATTING

TEAM

Team	Avg.	G	TPA	AB	R	H	TB	2B	3B	HR	RBI	SH	SF	HP	BB	IBB	SO	SB	CS	GDP	LOB	ShO	Slg.	OBP
Portland	.269	142	5541	4783	745	1286	1878	223	45	93	674	63	53	63	577	45	846	140	64	104	1067	4	.393	.352
New Haven	.261	142	5382	4771	699	1243	1784	226	27	87	641	47	38	52	471	20	951	145	57	100	990	7	.374	.331
Norwich	.258	141	5384	4666	635	1206	1802	237	46	89	600	38	50	71	559	33	1066	116	59	91	1053	12	.386	.343
Binghamton	.256	142	5466	4803	638	1231	1770	247	35	74	568	56	55	64	488	30	864	103	58	87	1046	9	.369	.330
Trenton	.256	142	5525	4829	649	1234	1848	239	33	103	584	51	52	64	529	35	935	135	84	99	1044	13	.383	.334
Bowie	.255	142	5370	4678	663	1193	1730	229	16	92	605	29	49	70	542	22	838	126	51	120	1011	11	.370	.338
Canton/Akron	.252	142	5239	4599	557	1158	1680	228	21	84	525	58	41	60	480	26	939	97	65	82	1018	9	.365	.328
Reading	.252	142	5367	4712	672	1186	1834	236	29	118	621	50	42	69	494	30	853	100	66	99	957	10	.389	.329
New Britain	.249	142	5335	4717	627	1175	1776	218	28	109	575	24	43	44	507	22	965	139	58	123	953	11	.377	.325
Harrisburg	.243	141	5215	4591	587	1116	1672	217	24	97	544	66	33	51	469	37	940	89	66	91	938	7	.364	.318

INDIVIDUAL

TOP QUALIFIERS FOR BATTING CHAMPIONSHIP

Minimum 383 plate appearances. *Lefthanded batter. †Switch-hitter.

Player, Team	Avg.	G	TPA	AB	R	H	TB	2B	3B	HR	RBI	SH	SF	HP	BB	IBB	SO	SB	CS	GDP	Slg.	OBP
Payton, Jay, Binghamton	.345	85	390	357	59	123	191	26	3	14	54	0	2	2	29	2	32	16	7	11	.535	.395
McGuire, Ryan, Trenton*	.333	109	477	414	59	138	190	29	1	7	59	4	1	0	58	5	51	11	8	10	.459	.414
McMillon, Billy, Portland*	.313	141	628	518	92	162	239	29	3	14	93	1	5	7	96	5	90	15	9	10	.461	.423
Jacobs, Frank, Bing.-Har.*	.312	101	402	337	56	105	166	22	0	13	60	0	2	5	58	7	56	1	3	5	.493	.418
Kennedy, David, New Haven	.306	128	541	484	75	148	240	22	2	22	96	0	4	5	48	1	131	4	1	12	.496	.372
Katzaroff, Rob, Portland	.304	116	505	441	87	134	188	16	4	10	49	4	4	7	49	3	33	18	10	4	.426	.379
Grable, Rob, Reading	.300	103	427	353	71	106	180	24	1	16	67	1	5	1	67	3	85	15	11	8	.510	.408
Echevarria, Angel, New Haven	.300	124	524	453	78	136	231	30	1	21	100	0	7	8	56	3	93	8	3	8	.510	.382
Horne, Tyrone, Har.-Nor.*	.291	133	554	460	82	134	225	33	5	16	69	3	6	1	84	3	101	18	10	7	.489	.397
Walker, Todd, New Britain*	.290	137	587	513	83	149	245	27	3	21	85	1	8	2	63	1	101	23	9	13	.478	.365
Renteria, Edgar, Portland	.289	135	558	508	70	147	197	15	7	7	68	8	2	2	32	2	85	30	11	10	.388	.329
Selby, Bill, Trenton*	.286	117	510	451	64	129	201	29	2	13	68	2	8	3	46	3	52	4	6	14	.446	.350
Hardtke, Jason, Binghamton†	.286	121	536	455	65	130	192	42	4	4	52	2	9	4	58	1	58	6	8	7	.422	.375
Ogden, Jamie, New Britain*	.284	117	438	384	54	109	172	22	1	13	61	0	5	1	48	5	90	6	5	10	.448	.361
Rogers, Lamarr, New Haven	.283	109	447	371	68	105	120	15	0	0	31	8	3	1	64	1	50	21	7	15	.323	.387

DEPARTMENTAL LEADERS: G—McMillon, 141; AB—Doster, 551; R—Milliard, 104; H—McMillon, 162; TB—Doster, 254; 2B—Hardtke, 42; 3B—Robertson, 10; HR—McNair, 23; RBI—Echevarria, 100; SH—Milliard, 13; SF—Barry, Hardtke, 9; HP—Delvecchio, 23; BB—McMillon, 96; IBB—Clark, 12; SO—Delvecchio, 133; SB—T. Jones, 51; CS—D. Jackson, 22; GIDP—Lucca, 18; Slg.—Pough, .543; OBP—McMillon, .423.

ALL PLAYERS

*Lefthanded batter. †Switch-hitter.

Player, Team	Avg.	G	TPA	AB	R	H	TB	2B	3B	HR	RBI	SH	SF	HP	BB	IBB	SO	SB	CS	GDP	Slg.	OBP
Abad, Andy, Trenton*	.240	89	335	287	29	69	101	14	3	4	32	6	3	3	36	2	58	5	7	6	.352	.328
Agbayani, Benny, Binghamton	.275	88	341	295	38	81	99	11	2	1	26	1	1	5	39	0	51	12	3	6	.336	.368
Alcantara, Israel, Harrisburg	.211	71	262	237	25	50	96	12	2	10	29	1	1	2	21	1	81	1	1	5	.405	.280
Alfonseca, Antonio, Portland	.059	19	18	17	1	1	4	0	0	1	2	1	0	0	0	0	8	0	0	1	.235	.059
Alfonzo, Edgar, Bowie	.304	28	123	112	14	34	43	6	0	1	19	0	1	0	10	1	16	1	2	2	.384	.358
Allen, Matt, Harrisburg	.143	5	16	14	2	2	2	0	0	0	1	0	0	0	2	0	2	0	0	1	.143	.250
Alomar, Sandy, Canton/Akron	.400	6	16	15	3	6	7	1	0	0	1	0	0	0	1	0	1	0	0	1	.467	.438
Alston, Garvin, New Haven	.000	47	5	5	0	0	0	0	0	0	0	0	0	0	0	0	1	0	0	1	.000	.000
Alvarez, Tavo, Harrisburg	1.000	3	4	3	1	3	3	0	0	0	1	1	0	0	0	0	0	0	0	0	1.000	1.000
Aminoff, Matt, New Haven	.000	6	1	1	0	0	0	0	0	0	0	0	0	0	0	0	0	0	0	0	.000	.000
Arnold, Ken, Bowie	.000	10	28	22	3	0	0	0	0	0	0	0	0	0	6	0	8	0	0	1	.000	.214
Arteaga, Ivan, New Haven*	.111	14	9	9	0	1	2	1	0	0	0	0	0	0	1	0	1	0	0	0	.222	.111
Aucoin, Derek, Harrisburg	.000	29	1	1	0	0	0	0	0	0	0	0	0	0	0	0	0	0	0	0	.000	.000
Avila, Rolando, Bowie	.233	16	51	43	8	10	12	2	0	0	4	1	1	0	6	0	8	2	2	0	.279	.320
Azuaje, Jesus, Binghamton	.198	24	102	86	10	17	22	5	0	0	8	3	0	2	11	0	25	1	1	1	.256	.303
Barron, Tony, Harrisburg	.291	29	116	103	20	30	65	5	0	10	23	0	0	2	10	0	21	0	0	8	.631	.365
Barry, Jeff, Binghamton†	.269	80	339	290	49	78	140	17	6	11	53	0	9	9	31	6	61	4	1	4	.483	.348
Bartee, Kimera, Bowie†	.284	53	247	218	45	62	82	9	1	3	19	3	2	1	23	1	45	22	7	1	.376	.352
Bates, Fletcher, Binghamton†..	.000	2	9	8	1	0	0	0	0	0	0	0	0	0	1	0	6	0	0	0	.000	.111
Batiste, Kim, Bowie	.358	24	102	95	16	34	51	5	0	4	27	0	1	0	6	0	14	2	0	5	.537	.392
Bautista, Juan, Bowie	.105	13	44	38	3	4	6	2	0	0	0	1	0	2	3	0	5	1	0	3	.158	.209
Beech, Matt, Reading*	.091	14	13	11	0	1	1	0	0	0	0	1	0	0	1	0	4	0	0	0	.091	.167
Benbow, Lou, Binghamton	1.000	3	2	1	0	1	1	0	0	0	0	0	0	0	1	0	0	0	0	0	1.000	1.000
Bennett, Gary, Reading	.236	86	301	271	27	64	87	11	0	4	40	3	2	3	22	1	36	0	0	12	.321	.299
Berrios, Harry, Bowie	.245	56	236	208	32	51	79	13	0	5	21	1	0	1	26	1	44	12	5	6	.380	.332
Biasucci, Joe, Canton/Akron	.244	41	159	135	19	33	47	8	0	2	16	1	1	2	20	0	35	0	0	2	.348	.348
Bigler, Jeff, Reading*	.091	13	53	44	4	4	5	1	0	0	2	1	1	1	6	2	10	0	0	1	.114	.212
Blasingame, Kent, Reading*	.205	86	236	195	38	40	51	4	2	1	17	5	2	5	29	0	43	9	7	3	.262	.320
Blazier, Ron, Reading	.000	57	8	8	0	0	0	0	0	0	0	0	0	0	0	0	2	0	0	0	.000	.000
Blosser, Greg, Trenton*	.246	49	196	179	25	44	90	13	0	11	34	1	3	0	13	0	42	3	2	4	.503	.292
Bournigal, Rafael, Harrisburg	.221	29	114	95	12	21	26	3	1	0	7	6	1	1	11	0	8	1	0	2	.274	.306
Brede, Brent, New Britain*	.274	134	532	449	71	123	164	28	2	3	39	6	5	3	69	2	82	14	6	13	.365	.371
Brito, Luis, Reading†	.333	2	3	3	1	1	1	0	0	0	1	0	0	0	0	0	1	0	0	0	.333	.333
Brophy, E.J., Reading	.500	2	4	4	0	2	3	1	0	0	0	0	0	0	0	0	1	0	0	0	.750	.500
Brown, Jarvis, Bowie	.279	58	259	219	50	61	93	12	1	6	23	2	1	4	33	0	49	12	3	5	.425	.381
Brown, Matt, Trenton	.182	4	12	11	1	2	2	0	0	0	0	0	0	0	1	0	2	0	0	0	.182	.250
Brownson, Mark, New Haven	.000	1	2	2	0	0	0	0	0	0	0	0	0	0	0	0	1	0	0	0	.000	.000
Bryant, Pat, Canton/Akron	.259	485	421	460	60	109	188	22	3	17	59	5	3	4	52	0	116	6	8	5	.447	.344
Buckley, Troy, Harrisburg	.291	48	169	158	16	46	62	10	0	2	15	1	1	0	9	2	19	0	1	2	.392	.327
Bullinger, Kirk, Harrisburg	.000	56	1	1	0	0	0	0	0	0	0	0	0	0	0	0	0	0	0	0	.000	.000
Bullock, Craig, Binghamton	.000	11	1	1	0	0	0	0	0	0	0	0	0	0	0	0	0	0	0	0	.000	.000
Burke, Alan, Reading	.200	11	25	20	5	4	9	2	0	1	3	1	0	3	1	1	6	0	0	0	.450	.333
Burnett, Roger, Norwich	.222	104	398	356	32	79	102	14	0	3	29	7	3	4	28	2	64	3	3	9	.287	.284
Byrd, Anthony, New Britain	.247	123	483	442	54	109	154	20	8	3	51	5	5	2	28	2	85	21	10	13	.348	.293
Byrne, Clayton, Bowie	.218	14	63	55	5	12	19	2	1	1	6	2	2	0	4	0	8	2	1	3	.345	.262
Cabreja, Alexis, Norwich	.091	6	14	11	1	1	1	0	0	0	1	0	0	1	0	0	3	1	0	0	.091	.286
Cabrera, Jolbert, Harrisburg	.286	9	38	35	4	10	12	2	0	0	1	2	0	0	1	0	3	3	1	1	.343	.306
Cairo, Sergio, Harrisburg	.000	4	15	13	0	0	0	0	0	0	0	0	0	1	1	0	2	0	0	1	.000	.133
Cameron, Stanton, Cant./Akron	.256	35	100	82	11	21	32	8	0	1	12	2	2	4	10	0	18	1	0	1	.390	.357
Campbell, Darrin, Cant./Akron	.000	2	7	7	1	0	0	0	0	0	0	0	0	0	0	0	0	0	0	0	.000	.000
Carey, Todd, Trenton*	.272	76	263	228	30	62	99	11	1	8	36	1	2	4	28	0	44	3	4	2	.434	.359
Case, Mike, New Haven	.245	102	364	310	55	76	126	16	2	10	46	3	4	4	43	4	72	6	2	6	.406	.341
Castaldo, Gregg, Bowie	.234	104	322	265	37	62	86	12	3	2	26	7	2	9	39	0	61	5	3	5	.325	.349
Castaneda, Hector, Bowie*	.154	34	76	65	3	10	12	2	0	0	6	0	1	0	10	0	10	0	0	1	.185	.263
Castillo, Ben, Canton/Akron	.224	32	129	116	15	26	43	7	2	2	15	0	1	1	11	0	23	1	2	2	.371	.295
Charbonnet, Mark, Harrisburg*	.251	120	443	407	34	102	148	14	4	8	57	4	6	4	26	3	104	5	4	12	.364	.287
Chavez, Eric, Bowie	.196	14	57	51	5	10	18	2	0	2	4	0	0	1	4	0	17	0	0	1	.353	.268
Chergey, Dan, Portland	.000	55	2	2	0	0	0	0	0	0	0	0	0	0	0	0	0	0	0	0	.000	.000
Chick, Bruce, Harrisburg	.268	12	41	41	4	11	15	2	1	0	6	0	0	0	0	0	9	0	0	1	.366	.268
Clapinski, Chris, Portland†	.236	87	248	208	32	49	76	9	3	4	30	5	5	2	28	2	44	5	2	4	.365	.325
Clark, Tim, Portland*	.271	134	568	499	62	135	197	34	2	8	88	0	7	3	59	12	86	0	5	13	.395	.347
Cosman, Jeff, Binghamton	.417	10	12	12	0	5	5	0	0	0	1	0	0	0	0	0	2	0	1	0	.417	.417
Cradle, Cobi, Binghamton*	.000	2	2	2	0	0	0	0	0	0	0	0	0	0	0	0	0	0	0	0	.000	.000
Crawford, Joe, Binghamton*	.667	42	4	3	1	2	3	1	0	0	2	1	0	0	0	0	0	0	0	1	1.000	.667
Crosby, Mike, Canton/Akron*	.165	75	245	224	18	37	59	5	1	5	20	7	1	3	10	0	60	1	1	4	.263	.210
Crowley, Jim, Bowie	.214	29	123	98	11	21	32	5	0	2	13	0	0	2	23	0	23	1	1	0	.327	.374
Cunnane, Will, Portland	.143	21	10	7	0	1	2	1	0	0	1	3	0	0	0	0	5	0	0	0	.286	.143
Daly, Bob, Binghamton	.000	1	5	4	1	0	0	0	0	0	0	0	0	1	1	0	1	0	0	0	.000	.000
Daubach, Brian, Binghamton*	.245	135	535	469	61	115	174	25	2	10	72	1	7	7	51	5	104	6	2	5	.371	.324
Dauphin, Phil, Harrisburg*	.244	111	454	398	53	97	136	20	2	5	38	3	7	2	43	8	61	17	7	1	.342	.316
Davenport, Adell, Canton/Akron	.276	9	33	29	2	8	9	1	0	0	4	0	0	1	3	0	5	0	0	0	.310	.364
Davis, Jay, Binghamton*	.255	116	484	443	64	113	151	17	6	3	50	1	6	8	26	1	68	11	5	7	.341	.304
Davis, Tommy, Bowie	.313	9	34	32	5	10	22	3	0	3	9	0	0	1	1	0	9	0	0	1	.688	.353
DeBerry, Joe, Norwich*	.000	2	4	4	0	0	0	0	0	0	0	0	0	0	0	0	2	0	0	0	.000	.000
DeHart, Rick, Harrisburg*	.167	35	12	12	0	2	2	0	0	0	0	0	0	0	0	0	2	0	0	0	.167	.167
Delgado, Alex, Trenton	.333	23	86	72	13	24	34	1	0	3	14	1	1	3	9	0	8	0	0	2	.472	.424
Delvecchio, Nick, Norwich*	.260	125	531	430	66	112	200	23	4	19	74	0	6	23	72	8	133	2	1	6	.465	.390
Diaz, Cesar, Binghamton	.170	13	53	47	5	8	10	2	0	0	5	0	0	0	6	0	20	0	1	3	.213	.264
Dixon, Colin, New Haven	.191	14	51	47	3	9	11	2	0	0	7	0	0	2	2	0	7	0	1	2	.234	.255
Doolan, Blake, Reading	.000	60	3	3	0	0	0	0	0	0	0	0	0	0	0	0	1	0	0	0	.000	.000

Player, Team	Avg.	G	TPA	AB	R	H	TB	2B	3B	HR	RBI	SH	SF	HP	BB	IBB	SO	SB	CS	GDP	Slg.	OBP
Doster, David, Reading............	.265	139	621	551	84	146	254	39	3	21	79	8	4	7	51	2	61	11	7	11	.461	.333
Duncan, Andres, New Britain† ...	.226	83	252	230	28	52	61	5	2	0	10	2	3	3	14	1	51	10	5	2	.265	.276
Eason, Tommy, Reading...........	.255	96	364	333	43	85	151	18	3	14	50	7	5	1	18	1	61	2	2	3	.453	.291
Echevarria, Angel, New Haven...	.300	124	524	453	78	136	231	30	1	21	100	0	7	8	56	3	93	8	3	8	.510	.382
Edmondson, Brian, Binghamton ..	.231	23	13	13	1	3	4	1	0	0	5	0	0	0	0	0	4	0	0	0	.308	.231
Engle, Tom, Binghamton.........	.000	13	3	2	0	0	0	0	0	0	0	0	0	0	1	0	2	0	0	0	.000	.333
Epperson, Chad, Binghamton† ...	.059	7	18	17	0	1	3	0	1	0	0	0	0	0	1	1	8	1	0	0	.176	.111
Epps, Scott, Norwich	.247	33	85	73	6	18	24	6	0	0	7	2	1	0	9	0	21	0	0	1	.329	.325
Estalella, Bobby, Reading	.235	10	39	34	5	8	15	1	0	2	9	0	1	4	1	0	7	0	0	1	.441	.333
Everson, Darin, Harrisburg*.....	.214	5	15	14	0	3	4	1	0	0	1	1	0	0	2	0	0	0	0	0	.286	.214
Falteisek, Steve, Harrisburg.....	.320	26	28	25	4	8	10	2	0	0	2	3	0	0	0	0	3	0	0	1	.400	.320
Farmer, Mike, New Haven†	.313	42	16	16	4	5	10	0	1	1	7	0	0	0	0	0	4	0	1	0	.625	.313
Fiegel, Todd, Binghamton*........	.000	4	1	1	0	0	0	0	0	0	0	0	0	0	0	0	1	0	0	0	.000	.000
Figga, Mike, Norwich	.271	109	451	399	59	108	177	22	4	13	61	2	6	1	43	3	90	1	0	10	.444	.339
Fisher, David, Reading...........	.230	79	227	204	18	47	70	18	1	1	20	2	4	3	14	0	29	4	4	0	.343	.284
Fitzpatrick, Robert, Harrisburg ...	.167	15	51	42	3	7	11	1	0	1	3	1	0	2	6	0	11	0	0	1	.262	.300
Fleming, Carlton, Norwich†......	.304	40	140	125	15	38	43	3	1	0	16	2	1	0	12	0	10	5	3	4	.344	.362
Foster, Mark, Reading*..........	.000	25	1	1	0	0	0	0	0	0	0	0	0	0	0	0	0	0	0	0	.000	.000
Fox, Andy, Norwich*	.206	44	196	175	23	36	64	3	5	5	17	1	1	0	19	0	36	8	1	3	.366	.282
Friedman, Jason, Bowie*.........	.232	63	248	228	22	53	73	11	0	3	27	1	1	2	16	2	23	1	1	7	.320	.287
Fuller, Aaron, Trenton†	.196	58	225	204	27	40	55	7	4	0	10	3	1	2	15	0	45	16	4	2	.270	.257
Fuller, Mark, Binghamton*	.400	47	5	5	2	2	3	1	0	0	0	0	0	0	0	0	3	0	0	0	.600	.400
Fully, Ed, Bing.-Bowie	.213	52	164	155	19	33	48	6	0	3	9	2	0	1	6	0	28	2	5	0	.310	.247
Garcia, Omar, Binghamton	.526	5	23	19	4	10	13	1	1	0	1	0	0	0	4	1	0	0	0	1	.684	.609
Garciaparra, Nomar, Trenton	.267	125	581	513	77	137	197	20	8	8	47	4	6	8	50	3	42	35	12	10	.384	.338
Garrow, David, New Britain	.143	6	16	14	0	2	2	0	0	0	1	0	0	0	2	0	2	0	0	1	.143	.250
Geisler, Phil, Reading*...........	.232	76	299	272	27	63	85	10	3	2	35	0	2	4	21	3	65	4	2	5	.313	.294
Gentile, Scott, Harrisburg........	.000	37	1	1	0	0	0	0	0	0	0	0	0	0	0	0	1	0	0	0	.000	.000
Gerald, Ed, New Britain†	.111	6	20	18	1	2	3	1	0	0	3	0	0	0	2	0	9	0	0	1	.167	.200
Gilmore, Joel, Reading	.000	18	4	4	0	0	0	0	0	0	0	0	0	0	0	0	1	0	0	0	.000	.000
Gomes, Wayne, Reading	.154	22	15	13	3	2	3	1	0	0	0	0	1	0	1	0	6	0	0	1	.231	.214
Gonzalez, Mauricio, New Haven†...	.268	73	173	164	20	44	55	5	3	0	12	1	0	1	7	0	29	0	1	1	.335	.302
Grable, Rob, Reading	.300	103	427	353	71	106	180	24	1	16	67	1	5	1	67	3	85	15	11	8	.510	.408
Grace, Mike, Reading	.111	24	20	18	1	2	2	0	0	0	2	2	0	0	0	0	8	0	0	0	.111	.111
Graham, Tim, Trenton*	.160	8	27	25	2	4	5	1	0	0	0	1	0	0	1	0	5	0	1	0	.200	.192
Greene, Charlie, Binghamton	.237	100	373	346	26	82	101	13	0	2	34	3	4	5	15	4	47	2	1	10	.292	.276
Gresham, Kris, Bowie............	.077	5	16	13	1	1	1	0	0	0	0	0	0	0	3	0	5	1	0	0	.077	.250
Grifol, Pedro, New Britain	.177	77	252	226	23	40	58	9	0	3	21	1	1	1	23	1	33	1	0	8	.257	.255
Grissom, Antonio, Harrisburg.....	.257	82	279	237	32	61	83	10	4	4	23	4	1	4	33	0	48	13	8	6	.350	.356
Grundt, Ken, New Haven*........	.000	28	1	0	0	0	0	0	0	0	0	0	0	0	0	0	0	0	0	0	.000	.000
Guerra, Mark, Binghamton	.250	6	4	4	1	1	1	0	0	0	0	0	0	0	0	0	2	0	0	0	.250	.250
Hagy, Gary, Canton/Akron	.294	6	18	17	2	5	7	2	0	0	3	0	0	1	0	0	2	0	0	0	.412	.333
Hammonds, Jeffrey, Bowie	.387	9	42	31	7	12	20	3	1	1	11	0	1	0	10	0	7	3	0	0	.645	.524
Hanselman, Carl, Reading*.......	.000	24	7	5	1	0	0	0	0	0	0	0	0	0	1	0	1	0	0	0	.000	.167
Hardge, Mike, Trenton	.244	40	141	127	18	31	37	4	1	0	12	1	2	0	11	0	26	3	4	7	.291	.300
Hardtke, Jason, Binghamton†.....	.286	121	536	455	65	130	192	42	4	4	52	2	9	4	66	1	58	6	8	7	.422	.375
Hartung, Andy, New Haven	.097	12	33	31	4	3	5	2	0	0	0	0	0	0	2	0	7	1	0	0	.161	.152
Harvey, Ray, Canton/Akron*......	.259	122	499	444	52	115	146	20	1	3	32	7	2	3	43	1	75	1	4	6	.329	.325
Hawkins, Kraig, Norwich†........	.222	12	54	45	5	10	10	0	0	0	3	2	0	0	7	0	11	7	2	0	.222	.327
Hayden, Dave, Reading	.234	68	221	192	22	45	60	6	0	3	11	0	2	1	26	3	39	0	3	6	.313	.326
Hecker, Doug, Trenton	.204	61	248	221	20	45	76	16	0	5	32	4	3	2	18	2	43	2	0	8	.344	.266
Held, Dan, Reading	.500	2	6	4	2	2	6	1	0	1	3	0	0	0	2	0	1	1	0	0	1.500	.667
Henderson, Rod, Harrisburg	.000	12	10	8	0	0	0	0	0	0	0	1	0	0	1	0	4	0	0	0	.000	.111
Heredia, Wilson, Portland	.222	4	10	9	1	2	2	0	0	0	0	1	0	0	0	0	2	0	0	1	.222	.222
Higgins, Mike, New Haven	.245	17	56	49	4	12	12	0	0	0	6	3	1	0	3	0	10	0	0	1	.245	.283
Hiljus, Erik, Binghamton..........	.091	10	14	11	1	1	1	0	0	0	1	2	0	0	1	0	2	0	0	0	.091	.167
Hill, Eric, Reading...............	.000	38	3	2	0	0	0	0	0	0	0	0	0	0	1	0	2	0	0	0	.000	.333
Hinds, Robert, Norwich	.252	132	516	445	71	112	125	8	1	1	37	6	3	12	50	0	102	27	10	4	.281	.341
Hinton, Steve, Harrisburg*.......	.222	10	25	18	4	4	4	0	0	0	0	0	0	0	7	0	5	0	0	0	.222	.440
Hodge, Roy, Bowie..............	.172	29	120	99	11	17	20	1	1	0	9	0	0	2	18	0	15	2	0	5	.202	.300
Holifield, Rick, Reading*	.247	30	118	93	18	23	31	3	1	1	5	2	0	1	22	3	18	5	2	0	.333	.397
Holman, Brad, New Haven	.000	7	1	0	0	0	0	0	0	0	0	0	0	0	0	0	0	0	0	0	.000	.000
Holman, Craig, Reading†	.000	33	5	3	0	0	0	0	0	0	0	0	2	0	0	0	4	0	0	1	.000	.000
Hood, Dennis, Canton/Akron	.217	8	26	23	6	5	6	1	0	0	2	0	0	0	2	0	7	1	0	0	.261	.280
Horne, Tyrone, Har.-Nor.*	.291	133	554	460	82	134	225	33	5	16	69	3	6	1	84	3	101	18	10	7	.489	.397
Howard, Matt, Bowie............	.303	70	289	251	42	76	91	8	2	1	15	3	1	5	29	1	27	22	4	6	.363	.385
Hughes, Troy, Norwich	.327	15	61	55	7	18	25	2	1	1	8	0	1	1	4	0	11	0	2	3	.455	.377
Hugo, Sean, Bowie*.............	.222	43	139	117	15	26	29	3	0	0	10	0	1	1	20	3	29	1	1	0	.248	.339
Hunter, Greg, New Britain*	.077	6	14	13	1	1	1	0	0	0	0	0	0	0	1	0	1	0	0	0	.077	.143
Hunter, Rich, Reading	.000	3	6	6	0	0	0	0	0	0	0	0	0	0	0	0	0	0	0	0	.000	.000
Hutchins, Jason, New Haven......	.000	12	1	1	0	0	0	0	0	0	0	0	0	0	0	0	0	0	0	0	.000	.000
Hymel, Lou, Harrisburg..........	.189	95	335	302	35	57	104	10	2	11	36	1	2	8	22	0	97	3	2	3	.344	.260
Isringhausen, Jason, Binghamton..	.357	6	15	14	1	5	7	2	0	0	1	0	0	0	0	0	2	0	0	0	.500	.357
Jackson, Damian, Cant./Akron	.248	131	565	484	67	120	153	20	2	3	34	7	0	9	65	0	103	40	22	6	.316	.343
Jackson, John, New Britain*	.298	16	69	57	8	17	30	2	1	3	8	0	0	1	11	0	7	3	4	0	.526	.420
Jacobs, Frank, Bing.-Har.*	.312	101	402	337	56	105	166	22	0	13	60	0	2	5	58	7	56	1	3	5	.493	.418
Johnson, Charles, Portland	.000	2	8	7	0	0	0	0	0	0	0	0	0	0	1	0	3	0	0	0	.000	.125
Johnson, J.J., Trenton...........	.500	2	6	6	1	3	3	0	0	0	1	0	0	0	0	0	0	0	0	0	.500	.500
Johnson, Jason, New Haven	.000	19	9	7	0	0	0	0	0	0	0	0	1	0	1	0	1	0	0	0	.000	.222
Jones, Bobby, New Haven	.286	27	10	7	1	2	2	0	0	0	0	1	0	0	2	0	3	0	0	0	.286	.444
Jones, Terry, New Haven†........	.269	124	521	472	78	127	144	12	1	1	26	3	3	3	39	0	104	51	19	6	.305	.327
Juday, Rob, Trenton†	.100	3	12	10	0	1	1	0	0	0	0	0	0	0	2	1	4	0	0	0	.100	.250
Juelsgaard, Jarod, Portland	.200	48	10	10	0	2	2	0	0	0	0	0	0	0	0	0	4	0	0	0	.200	.200

Player, Team	Avg.	G	TPA	AB	R	H	TB	2B	3B	HR	RBI	SH	SF	HP	BB	IBB	SO	SB	CS	GDP	Slg.	OBP
Karp, Ryan, Reading*	.333	7	4	3	1	1	1	0	0	0	0	0	0	0	1	0	0	0	0	1	.333	.500
Katzaroff, Rob, Portland	.304	116	505	441	87	134	188	16	4	10	49	4	4	7	49	3	33	18	10	4	.426	.379
Keister, Tripp, Binghamton*	.219	66	182	146	23	32	44	7	1	1	10	2	0	5	29	1	26	3	4	0	.301	.367
Kendrena, Ken, Harrisburg	.000	31	4	2	1	0	0	0	0	0	0	1	0	0	1	0	1	0	0	0	.000	.333
Kennedy, David, New Haven	.306	128	541	484	75	148	240	22	2	22	96	0	4	5	48	1	131	4	1	12	.496	.372
Kerley, Collin, Harrisburg	.000	2	2	0	1	0	0	0	0	0	0	0	2	0	0	0	0	0	0	0	.000	.000
Knackert, Brent, Binghamton	.167	48	8	6	0	1	1	0	0	0	0	1	0	0	1	1	1	0	0	0	.167	.286
Kontorinis, Andrew, New Britain*	.289	36	133	114	12	33	43	4	0	2	17	0	0	5	14	0	18	1	1	3	.377	.391
Kotarski, Mike, New Haven	.000	31	1	1	0	0	0	0	0	0	0	0	0	0	0	0	1	0	0	0	.000	.000
Kounas, Tony, Harrisburg	.235	66	218	196	15	46	54	5	0	1	22	0	1	2	19	1	27	1	1	7	.276	.307
Kremers, Jimmy, Portland*	.223	85	294	264	32	59	101	11	5	7	37	1	2	0	27	3	70	1	0	3	.383	.294
Lamb, David, Bowie†	.250	1	4	4	0	1	1	0	0	0	1	0	0	0	0	0	1	0	0	0	.250	.250
Lane, Dan, Harrisburg	.123	39	88	81	5	10	11	1	0	0	1	1	0	3	3	0	21	0	1	3	.136	.184
Lantigua, Eduardo, Cant./Akron	.196	13	49	46	5	9	14	2	0	1	4	1	0	1	1	0	14	0	0	2	.304	.229
Larkin, Andy, Portland	.000	9	6	6	0	0	0	0	0	0	0	0	0	0	0	0	5	0	0	0	.000	.000
Lawton, Matt, New Britain*	.269	114	485	412	75	111	179	19	5	13	54	2	3	12	56	1	70	26	9	8	.434	.371
Leahy, Pat, Portland	.000	13	6	3	1	0	0	0	0	0	0	1	0	1	2	0	1	1	0	0	.000	.500
LeGree, Keith, New Britain*	.200	43	131	110	10	22	24	2	0	0	6	0	0	0	21	0	33	3	1	3	.218	.328
Lemon, Don, Portland	.000	30	6	6	0	0	0	0	0	0	0	0	0	0	0	0	2	0	0	0	.000	.000
Lennon, Pat, Trenton	.398	27	113	98	19	39	49	7	0	1	8	0	1	0	14	0	22	7	2	3	.500	.478
Levangie, Dana, Trenton	.178	42	142	129	10	23	28	3	1	0	7	0	1	1	11	0	30	1	3	3	.217	.246
Lewis, T.R., Bowie	.294	86	357	309	57	91	127	19	1	5	44	1	6	1	40	2	43	12	3	8	.411	.371
List, Lou, New Haven	.278	82	234	212	26	59	95	10	4	6	44	0	1	1	20	0	43	2	2	4	.448	.342
Loewer, Carlton, Reading*	.200	8	13	10	3	2	2	0	0	0	0	1	0	0	2	0	5	0	0	0	.200	.333
Long, R.D., Norwich†	.212	9	40	33	4	7	10	3	0	0	5	0	0	0	7	0	11	2	1	1	.303	.350
Lopez, Rene, New Britain	.246	82	298	264	22	65	82	8	0	3	26	5	2	0	27	0	48	0	0	5	.311	.314
Lucca, Lou, Portland	.276	112	454	388	57	107	164	28	1	9	64	0	2	5	59	5	77	4	4	18	.423	.377
Ludwick, Eric, Binghamton	.071	23	18	14	2	1	2	1	0	0	1	3	0	0	1	0	3	0	0	0	.143	.133
Luke, Matt, Norwich*	.260	93	394	365	48	95	146	17	5	8	53	3	4	2	20	2	68	5	4	6	.400	.299
Magee, Wendell, Reading	.294	39	161	136	17	40	60	9	1	3	21	0	4	0	21	1	17	3	4	3	.441	.379
Mahalik, John, Binghamton	.225	67	213	187	19	42	65	6	1	5	19	5	1	1	19	1	34	1	1	6	.348	.298
Mahay, Ron, Trenton*	.235	93	363	310	37	73	106	12	3	5	28	2	4	3	44	3	90	5	6	5	.342	.332
Mantei, Matt, Portland	.000	8	1	1	0	0	0	0	0	0	0	0	0	0	0	0	1	0	0	0	.000	.000
Manto, Jeff, Bowie	.250	1	4	4	1	1	1	0	0	0	0	0	0	0	0	0	2	0	0	0	.250	.250
Marabella, Tony, Harrisburg*	.225	30	100	89	10	20	24	1	0	1	11	3	1	0	7	0	11	0	1	3	.270	.278
Marini, Marc, Canton/Akron*	.306	83	348	310	41	95	134	28	1	3	56	0	8	0	30	7	51	3	3	9	.432	.359
Martin, Jeff, Trenton	.217	78	284	254	25	55	79	10	1	4	30	6	3	5	16	0	83	3	3	10	.311	.273
Martindale, Ryan, Cant./Akron	.375	2	9	8	2	3	3	0	0	0	1	0	0	1	0	0	1	0	0	1	.375	.444
Martinez, Ray, Harrisburg	.237	48	173	152	18	36	45	6	0	1	13	0	0	1	20	2	24	3	2	6	.296	.329
Massarelli, John, Cant./Akron	.281	55	198	178	17	50	70	10	2	2	22	1	3	0	16	0	28	17	6	1	.393	.335
Maxwell, Pat, Canton/Akron*	.247	84	293	267	19	66	85	7	0	4	25	6	1	4	15	1	26	1	0	5	.318	.296
McCall, Rod, Canton/Akron*	.274	26	108	95	16	26	58	5	0	9	18	0	0	1	12	3	21	1	1	3	.611	.361
McClain, Scott, Bowie	.278	70	291	259	41	72	127	14	1	13	61	0	4	3	25	1	44	2	1	13	.490	.344
McConnell, Chad, Reading	.276	94	359	319	46	88	135	12	1	11	52	1	2	10	27	1	59	8	3	8	.423	.349
McCracken, Quinton, New Hav.†	.357	55	247	221	33	79	101	11	4	1	26	1	1	3	21	3	32	26	8	2	.457	.419
McDill, Allen, Binghamton*	.000	12	7	4	1	0	0	0	0	0	0	2	0	0	1	0	1	0	0	0	.000	.200
McGraw, Tom, Portland*	.125	51	9	8	0	1	1	0	0	0	0	1	0	0	0	0	1	0	0	0	.125	.125
McGuire, Ryan, Trenton*	.333	109	477	414	59	138	190	29	1	7	59	4	1	0	58	5	51	11	8	10	.459	.414
McKeel, Walt, Trenton	.238	29	94	84	11	20	31	3	1	2	11	0	2	0	8	0	15	2	1	1	.369	.298
McMillon, Billy, Portland*	.313	141	628	518	92	162	239	29	3	14	93	1	5	7	96	5	90	15	9	10	.461	.423
McNabb, Buck, Cant./Akron*	.167	19	57	48	3	8	8	0	0	0	1	2	0	1	6	0	14	0	1	0	.167	.273
McNair, Fred, Reading	.271	108	437	395	64	107	202	24	1	23	68	1	0	3	38	1	86	3	2	12	.511	.339
Mendoza, Reynol, Portland	.077	27	19	13	0	1	1	0	0	0	0	2	0	0	4	0	4	0	0	0	.077	.294
Mercedes, Feliciano, Bowie†	.150	28	89	80	10	12	13	1	0	0	7	1	1	1	6	0	14	2	3	2	.163	.216
Merloni, Lou, Trenton	.277	93	381	318	42	88	109	16	1	1	30	11	2	11	39	3	50	7	7	1	.343	.373
Michael, Jeff, Bowie	.167	4	16	12	2	2	2	0	0	0	0	0	0	0	4	0	4	0	0	0	.167	.375
Mikkelsen, Linc, Harrisburg†	.000	22	7	7	2	0	0	0	0	0	0	0	0	0	0	0	0	0	0	0	.000	.000
Millan, Adan, Reading	.350	10	26	20	3	7	13	3	0	1	7	0	1	1	4	0	3	0	0	1	.650	.462
Millares, Jose, Bowie	.248	120	459	411	50	102	150	30	3	4	50	2	6	19	20	0	62	7	6	14	.365	.309
Miller, Ryan, Binghamton	.053	9	22	19	3	1	1	0	0	0	1	0	0	2	4	1	0	0	0	0	.053	.143
Milliard, Ralph, Portland	.267	128	581	464	104	124	185	22	3	11	40	13	4	14	85	3	83	22	10	5	.399	.393
Mitchell, Larry, Reading	.000	25	13	12	0	0	0	0	0	0	0	1	0	0	0	0	8	0	0	0	.000	.000
Mix, Greg, Portland	.053	24	22	19	1	1	1	0	0	0	0	2	0	1	0	0	6	0	0	1	.053	.100
Moler, Jason, Reading	.265	22	96	83	17	22	31	3	0	2	14	0	1	0	12	2	13	2	2	1	.373	.354
Moore, Joel, New Haven*	.182	27	27	22	1	4	5	1	0	0	2	3	0	0	2	0	6	0	0	0	.227	.250
Moore, Tim, New Britain†	.241	90	343	311	39	75	123	19	1	9	45	0	2	6	24	4	86	4	2	7	.395	.306
Morgan, Kevin, Binghamton	.277	114	488	430	63	119	154	21	1	4	51	7	2	5	44	4	52	9	9	2	.358	.349
Mota, Gary, Reading	.227	33	119	110	13	25	36	4	2	1	9	1	0	0	8	2	23	0	2	2	.327	.280
Munoz, Bobby, Reading	.000	4	1	1	0	0	0	0	0	0	0	0	0	0	0	0	0	0	0	0	.000	.000
Murphy, Mike, Canton/Akron	.043	10	27	23	3	1	1	0	0	0	0	1	0	0	4	0	3	0	1	0	.043	.185
Murphy, Pat, Trenton*	.228	35	123	114	17	26	30	4	0	0	11	1	1	1	6	1	21	10	6	1	.263	.270
Myrow, John, New Haven	.246	96	394	353	52	87	116	18	1	3	50	3	3	8	25	2	67	16	5	13	.329	.308
Nava, Lipso, Trenton	.216	20	57	51	7	11	17	3	0	1	7	1	1	3	1	0	5	1	0	1	.333	.268
Neal, Mike, Canton/Akron	.267	134	511	419	64	112	155	24	2	5	46	4	8	9	71	3	79	5	6	7	.370	.379
Neier, Chris, New Haven	.143	38	15	14	0	2	2	0	0	0	1	0	0	1	0	0	1	0	0	1	.143	.200
Nixon, Trot, Trenton*	.160	25	105	94	9	15	26	3	1	2	8	2	2	0	7	0	20	2	1	0	.277	.214
Norman, Kenny, New Britain†	.290	12	36	31	4	9	10	1	0	0	1	0	0	0	5	0	9	0	1	1	.323	.389
Northrup, Kevin, Harrisburg	.309	40	163	152	23	47	64	14	0	1	27	0	1	0	10	1	16	0	1	3	.421	.350
Ogden, Jamie, New Britain*	.284	117	438	384	54	109	172	22	1	13	61	0	5	1	48	5	90	6	5	10	.448	.361
Owens, Billy, Bowie†	.269	122	505	453	57	122	200	27	0	17	91	0	8	1	43	6	87	2	1	13	.442	.329
Pacheco, Alex, Harrisburg	.000	45	4	4	0	0	0	0	0	0	0	0	0	0	0	0	3	0	0	0	.000	.000
Paniagua, Jose, Harrisburg	.250	25	15	12	1	3	5	2	0	0	2	0	0	0	1	0	7	0	0	0	.417	.308
Paxton, Darrin, Har.-Bing.*	.000	28	4	3	0	0	0	0	0	0	0	0	0	0	1	0	1	0	0	0	.000	.250

Player, Team	Avg.	G	TPA	AB	R	H	TB	2B	3B	HR	RBI	SH	SF	HP	BB	IBB	SO	SB	CS	GDP	Slg.	OBP
Payton, Jay, Binghamton	.345	85	390	357	59	123	191	20	3	14	54	0	2	2	29	2	32	16	7	11	.535	.395
Perez, Neifi, New Haven†	.253	116	458	427	59	108	157	28	3	5	43	4	1	2	24	2	52	5	2	6	.368	.295
Person, Robert, Binghamton	.000	26	4	4	0	0	0	0	0	0	0	0	0	0	0	0	2	0	0	0	.000	.000
Pettit, Doug, Portland*	.000	21	2	2	0	0	0	0	0	0	0	0	0	0	0	0	0	0	0	0	.000	.000
Phillips, Steve, Norwich*	.258	11	38	31	2	8	15	1	0	2	7	1	0	0	6	2	8	0	0	0	.484	.378
Pote, Lou, Harrisburg	.000	9	3	3	0	0	0	0	0	0	0	0	0	0	0	0	1	0	0	0	.000	.000
Pough, Pork Chop, Trenton	.278	97	424	363	68	101	197	23	5	21	69	0	4	7	50	8	101	11	5	1	.543	.373
Powell, Jay, Portland	.000	50	1	1	0	0	0	0	0	0	0	0	0	0	0	0	0	0	0	0	.000	.000
Ramirez, Alex, Canton/Akron	.248	33	140	133	15	33	47	3	4	1	11	1	1	0	5	1	24	3	5	5	.353	.273
Ramirez, Hector, Binghamton	.158	20	23	19	0	3	3	0	0	0	1	3	1	0	0	0	8	0	0	0	.158	.150
Ramirez, Omar, Canton/Akron	.324	10	38	34	6	11	11	0	0	0	3	1	0	0	3	0	3	0	0	0	.324	.378
Redmond, Mike, Portland	.255	105	365	333	37	85	107	11	1	3	39	4	3	3	22	2	27	2	2	9	.321	.305
Rekar, Bryan, New Haven	.091	12	16	11	0	1	1	0	0	0	2	5	0	0	0	0	5	0	0	0	.091	.091
Renteria, Dave, Norwich	.105	15	42	38	4	4	4	0	0	0	1	0	0	3	0	13	1	0	0	.105	.171
Renteria, Edgar, Portland	.289	135	558	508	70	147	197	15	7	7	68	8	8	2	32	2	85	30	11	10	.388	.329
Riggs, Kevin, Norwich*	.330	57	238	179	38	59	89	16	1	4	36	0	4	4	51	3	28	5	5	4	.497	.479
Rivera, Ruben, Norwich	.293	71	306	256	49	75	134	16	8	9	39	0	2	11	37	2	77	16	8	4	.523	.402
Robertson, Jason, Norwich*	.276	117	507	456	60	126	193	29	10	6	54	4	5	1	41	3	106	19	12	5	.423	.334
Rodriguez, Nerio, Bowie	.000	3	6	4	0	0	0	0	0	0	0	0	0	0	2	0	2	0	0	0	.000	.333
Rogers, Lamarr, New Haven	.283	109	447	371	68	105	120	15	0	0	31	8	3	1	64	1	50	21	7	15	.323	.387
Rojas, Euclides, Portland	.000	14	2	2	0	0	0	0	0	0	0	0	0	0	0	0	2	0	0	0	.000	.000
Rolen, Scott, Reading	.289	20	86	76	16	22	34	3	0	3	15	1	1	1	7	0	14	1	0	2	.447	.353
Romano, Scott, Norwich	.246	100	414	353	43	87	125	15	1	7	51	4	2	7	48	1	57	7	2	13	.354	.346
Roper, Chad, New Britain	.226	120	478	443	41	100	161	22	3	11	61	1	4	3	27	3	86	2	3	9	.363	.273
Rudolph, Mason, Portland	.197	41	80	76	9	15	33	4	1	4	16	0	1	2	1	0	29	0	1	2	.434	.225
Rundels, Matt, Harrisburg	.247	120	526	462	72	114	185	30	4	11	55	8	1	8	47	1	112	19	11	5	.400	.326
Saffer, Jon, Harrisburg*	.237	20	82	76	9	18	22	4	0	0	4	0	0	0	6	0	14	2	1	2	.289	.293
Salamon, John, New Haven	.000	6	3	2	0	0	0	0	0	0	0	1	0	0	0	0	2	0	0	0	.000	.000
Salcedo, Edwin, Norwich	.000	3	2	2	0	0	0	0	0	0	0	0	0	0	0	0	2	0	0	0	.000	.000
Sanders, Tracy, Binghamton*	.281	10	37	32	6	9	18	3	0	2	8	0	0	0	5	0	11	1	0	0	.563	.378
Saunders, Chris, Binghamton	.259	122	503	441	58	114	170	22	5	8	66	5	7	5	45	1	98	3	6	7	.385	.329
Scalzitti, Will, New Haven	.187	39	137	123	9	23	32	6	0	1	14	1	2	1	10	0	17	0	0	0	.260	.250
Schmidt, Tom, New Haven	.217	115	458	423	55	92	141	25	3	6	49	1	5	5	24	2	99	2	1	13	.333	.265
Schneider, Phil, New Haven*	.000	2	1	1	0	0	0	0	0	0	0	0	0	0	0	0	1	0	0	0	.000	.000
Schorr, Brad, Binghamton	.000	4	6	5	0	0	0	0	0	0	0	0	0	0	1	0	3	0	0	0	.000	.167
Seefried, Tate, Norwich*	.226	77	314	274	34	62	97	18	1	5	33	1	4	4	31	4	86	0	1	6	.354	.310
Sefcik, Kevin, Reading	.272	128	564	508	68	138	176	18	4	4	46	3	3	12	38	0	48	14	11	5	.346	.335
Selby, Bill, Trenton*	.286	117	510	451	64	129	201	29	2	13	68	2	8	3	46	3	52	4	6	14	.446	.350
Sexton, Chris, New Haven	.000	1	3	3	0	0	0	0	0	0	0	0	0	0	0	0	0	0	0	0	.000	.000
Shaw, Cedric, Harrisburg*	.000	5	2	1	0	0	0	0	0	0	0	0	0	1	0	0	1	0	0	0	.000	.500
Sheff, Chris, Portland	.276	131	557	471	85	130	205	25	7	12	91	1	8	5	72	6	84	23	6	10	.435	.372
Shelton, Ben, N.B.-Tre.	.218	91	370	294	60	64	122	7	0	17	43	0	3	6	67	4	89	5	1	10	.415	.370
Smith, Brandon, Binghamton	.000	2	2	2	0	0	0	0	0	0	0	0	0	0	0	0	0	0	0	0	.000	.000
Smith, Bubba, New Britain	.243	42	155	148	20	36	65	11	0	6	21	0	1	0	6	0	41	0	0	5	.439	.277
Smith, Ed, Canton/Akron	.241	103	412	365	41	88	143	18	2	11	52	7	3	1	36	4	93	0	2	6	.392	.309
Smith, Eric, Reading	.000	4	1	1	0	0	0	0	0	0	0	0	0	0	0	0	0	0	0	0	.000	.000
Smith, John, Binghamton	.083	9	15	12	2	1	2	1	0	0	1	0	0	1	2	0	6	0	0	0	.167	.267
Snyder, Randy, New Haven	.235	5	18	17	2	4	5	1	0	0	2	1	0	0	0	0	3	0	2	0	.294	.222
Soliz, Steve, Canton/Akron	.173	32	96	81	9	14	23	3	0	2	7	1	1	0	13	0	16	0	0	3	.284	.284
Solomon, Steve, Reading*	.228	119	420	356	50	81	121	19	6	3	42	3	2	11	48	3	82	17	4	11	.340	.336
Spencer, Stan, Portland	.000	8	7	4	0	0	0	0	0	0	0	1	0	0	2	0	0	0	0	1	.000	.333
Stidham, Phil, Binghamton	.000	7	1	1	0	0	0	0	0	0	0	0	0	0	0	0	0	0	0	0	.000	.000
Strittmatter, Mark, New Haven	.243	90	344	288	44	70	105	12	1	7	42	1	2	6	47	1	51	1	0	5	.365	.359
Stull, Everett, Harrisburg	.214	24	17	14	2	3	4	1	0	0	1	3	0	0	0	0	6	0	0	0	.286	.214
Tam, Jeff, Binghamton	.000	14	1	1	0	0	0	0	0	0	0	0	0	0	0	0	0	0	0	0	.000	.000
Taylor, Jamie, Canton/Akron*	.000	4	13	11	0	0	0	0	0	0	0	0	1	0	1	0	4	0	0	0	.000	.083
Tellers, Dave, New Haven	.000	33	5	4	0	0	0	0	0	0	0	0	1	0	0	0	3	0	0	0	.000	.000
Thompson, Ryan, Binghamton	.500	2	9	8	2	4	7	0	0	1	4	0	0	0	1	0	2	0	0	0	.875	.556
Thomson, John, New Haven	.000	26	19	12	0	0	0	0	0	0	0	5	0	0	2	0	5	0	0	0	.000	.143
Tijerina, Tony, Binghamton†	.178	32	124	118	3	21	26	5	0	0	9	0	2	3	1	0	22	0	0	2	.220	.202
Tinsley, Lee, Trenton*	.389	4	19	18	3	7	8	1	0	0	3	0	0	0	1	0	3	0	0	0	.444	.421
Tirpack, Ken, New Britain*	.250	7	21	16	4	4	12	2	0	2	3	0	0	0	5	1	3	1	0	1	.750	.429
Torres, Tony, Portland	.296	58	101	81	15	24	31	3	2	0	4	8	0	1	11	0	23	9	0	1	.383	.387
Tovar, Edgar, Harrisburg	.202	81	277	247	28	50	70	7	2	3	21	9	1	4	16	2	24	1	3	5	.283	.261
Townsend, Chad, Cant./Akron*	.262	116	447	404	39	106	157	22	1	9	50	1	3	8	31	4	90	3	2	6	.389	.323
Tranberg, Mark, Reading	.214	18	17	14	1	3	4	1	0	0	1	2	0	0	0	0	2	0	0	1	.286	.267
Trisler, John, Reading	.182	30	11	11	2	2	2	0	0	0	0	0	0	0	0	0	6	0	0	0	.182	.182
Turner, Brian, Norwich*	.296	86	343	311	39	92	131	21	3	4	43	2	4	1	25	2	72	3	2	5	.421	.346
Valette, Ramon, New Britain	.214	111	371	346	40	74	101	11	2	4	32	1	2	1	21	0	52	19	2	14	.292	.259
Van Slyke, Andy, Bowie*	.500	2	9	6	2	3	3	0	0	0	2	0	0	0	3	1	0	0	0	0	.500	.667
Ventress, Leroy, Harrisburg†	.220	11	46	41	4	9	9	0	0	0	3	0	0	0	5	0	19	3	0	0	.220	.304
Viano, Jake, New Haven	.000	57	3	3	0	0	0	0	0	0	0	0	0	0	0	0	1	0	0	0	.000	.000
Vidro, Jose, Harrisburg*	.260	64	274	246	33	64	96	16	2	4	38	4	3	1	20	2	37	3	7	5	.390	.315
Virgilio, George, Har.-Bowie†	.202	68	201	163	20	33	42	3	0	2	18	1	2	2	33	2	22	1	1	8	.258	.340
Waco, David, Reading	.300	5	10	10	1	3	3	0	0	0	1	0	0	0	0	0	2	0	0	0	.300	.300
Wakamatsu, Don, Cant./Akron	.266	51	171	143	16	38	60	10	0	4	23	3	2	6	17	2	21	0	0	7	.420	.363
Walker, Todd, New Britain	.290	137	587	513	83	149	245	27	3	21	85	1	8	2	63	1	101	23	9	13	.478	.365
Wallace, Derek, Binghamton	.000	15	1	1	0	0	0	0	0	0	0	0	0	0	0	0	0	0	0	0	.000	.000
Waller, Casey, Portland†	.222	14	42	36	4	8	12	2	1	0	5	0	0	0	6	0	4	1	0	2	.333	.333
Ward, Bryan, Portland*	.200	20	16	15	3	3	3	0	0	0	1	0	0	0	1	0	4	0	0	0	.200	.250
Waszgis, B.J., Bowie	.253	130	521	438	53	111	163	22	0	10	50	1	3	9	70	1	91	2	4	5	.372	.365
Wawruck, Jim, Bowie*	.278	56	239	212	29	59	86	7	1	6	30	1	3	3	20	2	31	7	3	7	.406	.345
Weber, Neil, Harrisburg*	.091	28	24	22	2	2	4	2	0	0	1	0	0	0	1	0	11	0	0	1	.182	.130

Player, Team	Avg.	G	TPA	AB	R	H	TB	2B	3B	HR	RBI	SH	SF	HP	BB	IBB	SO	SB	CS	GDP	Slg.	OBP
Wells, Forry, New Haven*	.214	4	16	14	3	3	3	0	0	0	1	0	0	1	1	1	2	0	0	1	.214	.313
Whisenant, Matt, Portland†	.000	23	19	16	1	0	0	0	0	0	0	1	2	0	0	1	0	8	0	0	.000	.059
White, Billy, New Haven	.232	58	208	181	25	42	62	9	1	3	34	0	0	0	27	0	44	2	2	3	.343	.332
White, Don, Binghamton	.236	94	365	314	48	74	104	17	2	3	20	6	3	2	40	0	56	25	6	10	.331	.323
Wilson, Paul, Binghamton	.200	16	20	15	0	3	5	2	0	0	1	5	0	0	0	0	5	0	0	1	.333	.200
Wilson, Pookie, Portland*	.273	107	386	348	51	95	127	13	5	3	44	5	4	11	18	2	51	9	4	9	.365	.325
Wilson, Thomas, Norwich	.143	28	101	84	6	12	16	4	0	0	4	0	0	0	17	0	22	0	0	3	.190	.287
Wipf, Mark, Binghamton†	.091	4	13	11	1	1	1	0	0	0	1	0	1	0	1	0	8	1	0	0	.091	.154
Yelding, Eric, Canton/Akron	.351	10	40	37	5	13	14	1	0	0	7	0	1	1	1	0	6	3	0	0	.378	.375
Zambrano, Eddie, Trenton	.147	19	76	68	5	10	14	1	0	1	7	0	1	1	6	1	25	0	0	1	.206	.224
Zambrano, Jose, Trenton	.242	22	76	62	7	15	27	6	0	2	7	0	0	3	11	0	15	2	1	3	.435	.382
Zolecki, Mike, New Haven	.111	9	10	9	0	1	1	0	0	0	0	1	0	0	0	0	3	0	0	1	.111	.111
Zuniga, David, Binghamton	.000	3	1	1	1	0	0	0	0	0	0	0	0	0	0	0	1	0	0	0	.000	.000

GRAND SLAMS: Estallela, Strittmatter, Townsend, 2 each; Alcantara, Barry, Blosser, Bryant, Carey, Clark, Echevarria, Garciaparra, Grissom, Holifield, Jacobs, Kennedy, List, Luke, Magee, Mahay, McClain, Ogden, Owens, E. Renteria, Rivera, Roper, Selby, Shelton, B. Smith, Solomon, 1 each.

AWARDED FIRST BASE ON CATCHER'S INTERFERENCE: Charbonnet 3 (Crosby, Grifol, Wakamatsu); Myrow 2 (Gresham, Kounas); Barron (Crosby); Chavez (Allen); Dauphin (Waszgis); Hood (Grifol); T. Jones (Epps); McMillon (Diaz); Millares (Kounas); Milliard (Strittmatter).

PLAYERS WITH TWO OR MORE TEAMS

Player, Team	Avg.	G	TPA	AB	R	H	TB	2B	3B	HR	RBI	SH	SF	HP	BB	IBB	SO	SB	CS	GDP	Slg.	OBP
Fully, Ed, Binghamton	.194	18	37	36	4	7	11	1	0	1	3	1	0	0	0	0	5	0	2	0	.306	.194
Fully, Ed, Bowie	.218	34	127	119	15	26	37	5	0	2	6	1	0	1	6	0	23	2	3	0	.311	.262
Horne, Tyrone, Harrisburg*	.296	87	359	294	59	87	154	17	4	14	47	3	3	1	58	2	65	14	8	3	.524	.410
Horne, Tyrone, Norwich*	.283	46	195	166	23	47	71	16	1	2	22	0	3	0	26	1	36	4	2	4	.428	.374
Jacobs, Frank, Binghamton*	.294	23	78	68	12	20	35	3	0	4	9	0	0	0	10	0	15	0	0	3	.515	.385
Jacobs, Frank, Harrisburg*	.316	78	324	269	44	85	131	19	0	9	51	0	2	5	48	7	41	1	3	2	.487	.426
Paxton, Darrin, Harrisburg*	.000	7	0	0	0	0	0	0	0	0	0	0	0	0	0	0	0	0	0	0	.000	.000
Paxton, Darrin, Binghamton*	.000	21	4	3	0	0	0	0	0	0	0	0	0	1	0	0	0	0	0	1	.000	.250
Shelton, Ben, New Britain	.239	56	221	176	37	42	86	5	0	13	30	0	2	3	40	0	58	4	0	6	.489	.385
Shelton, Ben, Trenton	.186	35	149	118	23	22	36	4	0	4	13	0	1	3	27	4	31	1	1	4	.305	.349
Virgilio, George, Harrisburg†	.143	27	77	56	9	8	11	0	0	1	5	0	1	0	20	2	11	1	1	2	.196	.364
Virgilio, George, Bowie†	.234	41	124	107	11	25	31	3	0	1	13	1	1	2	13	0	11	0	0	6	.290	.325

1995 PITCHING

TEAM

Team	W	L	Pct.	ERA	G	CG	ShO	Sv.	IP	H	TBF	R	ER	HR	SH	SF	HB	BB	IBB	SO	WP	Bk.
New Haven	79	63	.556	3.61	142	3	14	37	1239.2	1185	5332	592	497	68	51	42	53	521	29	951	53	18
Trenton	73	69	.514	3.78	142	15	8	35	1279.2	1197	5461	641	538	97	42	46	90	452	22	905	57	24
Portland	86	56	.606	3.79	142	6	9	40	1255.0	1184	5373	592	528	93	61	35	59	497	41	979	59	11
Binghamton	67	75	.472	3.91	142	15	10	28	1259.1	1162	5334	625	547	103	42	48	52	487	33	897	57	21
Reading	73	69	.514	3.99	142	7	8	31	1247.0	1211	5369	634	553	112	45	29	41	513	35	991	56	24
New Britain	65	77	.458	4.01	142	7	12	26	1246.2	1236	5430	653	555	81	58	54	51	500	18	935	64	10
Bowie	68	74	.479	4.13	142	7	10	32	1231.0	1225	5408	681	565	125	43	56	55	530	32	892	75	17
Canton/Akron	67	75	.472	4.24	142	9	9	33	1215.1	1187	5280	672	573	102	54	48	46	519	32	786	48	11
Harrisburg	61	80	.433	4.31	141	7	6	26	1219.2	1176	5354	682	584	94	50	45	80	543	28	981	58	10
Norwich	70	71	.496	4.32	141	6	7	39	1231.2	1265	5483	717	591	71	36	53	81	554	33	880	81	12

INDIVIDUAL

TOP QUALIFIERS FOR EARNED-RUN AVERAGE TITLE

Minimum 114 innings. *Lefthanded pitcher.

Pitcher, Team	W	L	Pct.	ERA	G	GS	CG	ShO	GF	Sv.	IP	H	TBF	R	ER	HR	SH	SF	HB	BB	IBB	SO	WP	Bk.
Wilson, Paul, Binghamton	6	3	.667	2.17	16	16	4	1	0	0	120.1	89	464	34	29	5	3	4	5	24	2	127	4	3
Falteisek, Steve, Harrisburg	9	6	.600	2.95	25	25	5	0	0	0	168.0	152	707	74	55	3	7	5	11	64	4	112	6	1
Ludwick, Eric, Binghamton	12	5	.706	2.95	23	22	3	2	0	0	143.1	108	590	52	47	9	4	6	2	68	1	131	6	0
Orellano, Rafael, Trenton*	11	7	.611	3.09	27	27	2	0	0	0	186.2	146	772	68	64	18	4	1	11	72	0	160	9	4
Moore, Joel, New Haven	14	6	.700	3.20	27	26	1	1	0	0	157.1	156	682	69	56	8	6	6	8	67	2	102	5	1
Whitten, Casey, Canton/Akron*	9	8	.529	3.31	20	20	2	1	0	0	114.1	100	469	49	42	10	1	2	3	38	0	91	5	2
Serafini, Dan, New Britain*	12	9	.571	3.38	27	27	1	1	0	0	162.2	155	692	74	61	7	3	4	12	72	0	123	3	4
Roberts, Brett, New Britain	11	9	.550	3.41	28	28	5	1	0	0	174.0	162	729	72	66	9	4	5		50	0	135	6	0
Mendoza, Reynol, Portland	9	10	.474	3.43	27	27	1	1	0	0	168.0	163	715	73	64	6	10	4	9	69	3	120	15	0
Whisenant, Matt, Portland*	10	6	.625	3.50	23	22	2	0	0	0	128.2	106	544	57	50	8	7	4	9	65	3	107	8	0
Grace, Mike, Reading	13	6	.684	3.54	24	24	2	0	0	0	147.1	137	606	65	58	13	5	0	6	35	0	118	3	2
Stephenson, Garrett, Bowie	7	10	.412	3.64	29	29	1	0	0	0	175.1	154	743	87	71	23	5	7	18	47	0	139	4	2
Cunnane, Will, Trenton	9	2	.818	3.67	21	21	1	1	0	0	117.2	120	497	48	48	10	3	0	5	34	1	83	2	0
Steph, Rod, Canton/Akron	8	10	.444	3.81	32	20	1	0	5	0	137.0	150	595	74	58	6	7	2	9	33	1	82	5	0
Brooks, Wes, Trenton	5	11	.313	4.12	29	23	5	0	0	0	161.2	149	670	87	74	17	4	7	11	43	0	85	5	6

DEPARTMENTAL LEADERS: W—Moore, 14; L—Buddie, Paniagua, Ramirez, Stull, 12; Pct.—Cunnane, .818; G—Doolan, 60; GS—Stephenson, 29; CG—Brooks, Falteisek, Roberts, 5; ShO—Tranberg, 3; GF—Viano, 49; Sv.—Powell, 24; IP—Orellano, 186.2; H—Miller, 172; TBF—Orellano, 772; R—Buddie, 102; ER—Weber, 85; HR—Stephenson, 23; SH—Norris, Weber, 11; SF—Senior, 11; HB—Stephenson, 18; BB—Weber, 90; IBB—Knackert, 8; SO—Orellano, 160; WP—Re. Mendoza, 15; Bk.—Brooks, Gomes, 6.

CLASS AA Eastern League

ALL PITCHERS

*Lefthanded pitcher.

Pitcher, Team	W	L	Pct.	ERA	G	GS	CG	ShO	GF	Sv.	IP	H	TBF	R	ER	HR	SH	SF	HB	BB	IBB	SO	WP	Bk.
Alfonseca, Antonio, Portland	9	3	.750	3.64	19	17	1	0	0	0	96.1	81	405	43	39	6	3	3	4	42	1	75	5	4
Alston, Garvin, New Haven	4	4	.500	2.84	47	0	0	0	20	6	66.2	47	271	24	21	1	4	2	3	26	3	73	4	0
Alvarez, Tavo, Harrisburg	2	1	.667	2.25	3	3	0	0	0	0	16.0	17	70	8	4	0	0	0	0	5	0	14	0	0
Aminoff, Matt, New Haven	0	2	.000	1.54	6	0	0	0	2	0	11.2	9	51	7	2	0	2	0	0	6	1	10	0	0
Amos, Chad, Trenton	0	0	.000	12.60	6	0	0	0	1	0	5.0	10	25	8	7	2	0	0	0	3	0	1	2	0
Andersen, Larry, Reading	0	0	.000	6.23	5	0	0	0	1	0	4.1	6	21	3	3	0	0	0	1	1	0	7	0	0
Antolick, Jeff, Norwich	1	1	.500	6.75	2	2	0	0	0	0	9.1	17	46	9	7	2	0	2	1	2	0	5	1	0
Arffa, Steve, Binghamton	0	0	.000	4.50	1	1	0	0	0	0	6.0	7	25	3	3	0	0	0	0	1	0	1	0	1
Arteaga, Ivan, New Haven	2	4	.333	5.56	14	11	0	0	0	0	34.0	36	162	26	21	3	1	2	5	21	0	18	1	3
Aucoin, Derek, Harrisburg	2	4	.333	4.96	29	0	0	0	10	1	52.2	52	242	34	29	3	0	5	8	28	2	48	2	0
Bakkum, Scott, Trenton	6	4	.600	1.34	28	0	0	0	10	0	47.0	31	181	12	7	4	1	1	2	9	2	24	1	0
Beech, Matt, Reading*	2	4	.333	2.96	14	13	0	0	0	0	79.0	67	345	33	26	7	6	2	6	33	1	70	4	1
Bennett, Shayne, Trenton	0	1	.000	5.06	10	0	0	0	6	3	10.2	16	48	6	6	0	3	1	0	3	0	6	1	0
Blais, Mike, Trenton	2	0	1.000	2.52	13	0	0	0	7	0	25.0	19	96	8	7	1	1	2	1	7	0	20	0	0
Blazier, Ron, Reading	4	5	.444	3.29	56	3	0	0	17	1	106.2	93	431	44	39	11	5	2	0	31	7	102	2	1
Bogott, Kurt, Trenton*	0	1	.000	2.70	2	0	0	0	2	0	3.1	3	13	1	1	1	0	0	0	1	0	2	0	0
Borowski, Joe, Bowie	2	2	.500	3.92	16	0	0	0	14	7	20.2	16	83	9	9	2	0	0	0	7	1	32	1	0
Botkin, Alan, Harrisburg*	0	0	.000	8.31	3	0	0	0	2	1	4.1	5	19	4	4	2	0	0	0	2	0	4	2	0
Brooks, Wes, Trenton	5	11	.313	4.12	29	23	5	0	0	0	161.2	149	670	87	74	17	4	7	11	43	0	85	5	6
Brown, Dan, Reading	1	0	1.000	7.71	2	0	0	0	1	0	2.1	4	12	4	2	1	0	0	0	0	0	2	0	0
Brown, Dickie, Canton/Akron	8	5	.615	4.67	37	9	0	0	11	3	98.1	88	449	56	51	9	7	3	4	67	7	51	9	0
Brownson, Mark, New Haven	0	0	.000	1.50	1	1	0	0	0	0	6.0	4	24	2	1	1	0	0	0	1	0	4	0	0
Buddie, Mike, Norwich	10	12	.455	4.81	29	27	2	0	1	1	149.2	155	689	102	80	4	6	8	15	81	2	106	13	1
Bullinger, Kirk, Harrisburg	5	3	.625	2.42	56	0	0	0	39	7	67.0	61	282	22	18	4	4	1	0	25	5	42	2	2
Bullock, Craig, Binghamton	0	3	.000	6.89	11	0	0	0	4	0	15.2	20	74	12	12	1	0	2	0	7	0	12	0	0
Cabrera, Jose, Canton/Akron	5	3	.625	3.28	24	11	1	1	4	0	85.0	83	350	32	31	7	1	6	1	21	1	61	0	2
Cain, Tim, Trenton	4	3	.571	3.73	29	1	0	0	8	4	50.2	46	215	25	21	1	4	0	6	17	3	45	3	0
Carper, Mark, Norwich	0	0	.000	10.80	1	1	0	0	0	0	5.0	9	26	6	6	2	0	1	2	1	0	3	2	0
Carter, Glenn, Trenton	1	1	.500	3.07	14	0	0	0	12	8	14.2	15	63	8	5	0	0	0	1	4	0	10	1	1
Carter, John, Canton/Akron	1	2	.333	3.95	5	5	0	0	0	0	27.1	27	118	13	12	0	0	0	3	13	2	14	1	0
Carter, Tom, Norwich*	3	7	.300	5.57	28	15	0	0	2	0	97.0	128	467	69	60	4	3	4	3	47	3	65	10	0
Caruso, Joe, Trenton	1	1	.500	11.37	11	0	0	0	5	0	12.2	21	64	16	16	1	0	0	2	8	0	8	2	0
Case, Mike, New Haven	0	0	.000	0.00	2	0	0	0	2	0	3.0	0	10	0	0	0	0	0	1	0	0	2	0	0
Cederblad, Brett, Trenton	3	2	.600	3.63	8	5	2	1	1	0	44.2	43	182	19	18	4	2	2	0	11	1	36	2	0
Chapin, Darrin, Canton/Akron	0	1	.000	4.50	4	0	0	0	2	0	8.0	12	38	7	4	0	1	0	0	2	0	6	0	1
Chavez, Carlos, Bowie	0	0	.000	0.00	1	0	0	0	0	0	2.0	0	6	0	0	0	0	0	0	1	0	2	0	0
Chergey, Dan, Portland	6	7	.462	3.47	55	0	0	0	27	5	80.1	62	331	35	31	7	7	2	3	26	6	75	2	0
Ciccarella, Joe, Trenton*	2	1	.667	2.73	22	2	0	0	6	0	33.0	31	138	13	10	3	1	3	0	12	0	33	0	0
Coleman, Billy, Norwich	6	4	.600	4.05	46	0	0	0	12	2	73.1	56	335	52	33	5	3	4	4	57	5	64	12	1
Conner, Scott, Bowie	5	1	.833	4.17	44	0	0	0	9	0	82.0	57	378	43	38	7	4	7	10	74	2	82	13	2
Coppinger, Rocky, Bowie	6	2	.750	2.69	13	13	2	2	0	0	83.2	58	352	33	25	7	0	4	3	43	0	62	4	1
Cosman, Jeff, Binghamton	2	4	.333	7.08	10	10	0	0	0	0	48.1	57	219	40	38	4	1	1	2	18	0	23	2	0
Crawford, Carlos, Cant./Akron	2	2	.500	2.61	8	8	2	0	0	0	51.2	47	212	19	15	1	1	0	1	15	0	36	2	0
Crawford, Joe, Binghamton*	7	2	.778	2.23	42	1	0	0	15	0	60.2	48	239	17	15	4	3	7	5	17	4	43	3	1
Cunnane, Will, Portland	9	2	.818	3.67	21	21	1	1	0	0	117.2	120	497	48	48	10	3	0	5	34	1	83	2	0
Dedrick, Jim, Bowie	4	2	.667	2.98	10	10	0	0	0	0	60.1	59	267	24	20	7	2	2	5	25	2	48	5	1
DeHart, Rick, Harrisburg	6	7	.462	4.84	35	12	0	0	4	0	93.0	94	417	62	50	13	4	6	5	39	3	64	4	4
DeJean, Mike, Norwich	5	5	.500	2.99	59	0	0	0	40	20	78.1	58	323	29	26	5	2	3	5	34	2	57	4	1
DeJesus, Javier, New Britain*	0	0	.000	1.59	4	0	0	0	2	0	5.2	8	26	2	1	0	0	1	0	1	0	3	1	0
DeLaMaza, Roland, Cant./Akron	2	1	.667	4.10	7	7	0	0	0	0	37.1	35	162	19	17	5	0	0	2	18	0	27	1	0
DeLaRosa, Maximo, Cant./Akron	0	0	.000	54.00	1	0	0	0	0	0	0.1	1	3	2	2	1	0	0	0	1	0	0	0	0
Devereux, Charles, Bowie	0	1	.000	5.21	12	0	0	0	3	0	19.0	24	100	13	11	2	0	2	0	17	3	27	1	0
Diaz, Ralph, Harrisburg	2	2	.500	5.59	11	1	0	0	2	0	19.1	17	83	13	12	3	2	0	1	9	2	16	1	0
Dodd, Robert, Reading*	0	0	.000	0.00	1	0	0	0	0	0	1.1	0	5	0	0	0	0	0	0	2	0	0	0	0
Doolan, Blake, Reading	11	5	.688	2.22	60	0	0	0	45	16	73.0	63	300	22	18	3	3	5	0	27	4	50	4	1
Driskill, Travis, Canton/Akron	3	4	.429	4.66	33	0	0	0	22	4	46.1	46	200	24	24	3	1	1	1	19	1	39	0	1
Edmondson, Brian, Binghamton	7	11	.389	4.76	23	22	2	1	0	0	134.1	150	601	82	71	17	5	5	6	59	2	69	7	0
Emerson, Scott, Bowie-Tre.*	0	2	.000	4.98	8	4	0	0	0	0	21.2	28	111	21	12	3	0	1	0	16	0	18	4	0
Engle, Tom, Binghamton	2	1	.667	5.40	13	2	0	0	5	0	28.1	28	118	19	17	5	2	0	3	7	0	15	2	0
Eshelman, Vaughn, Trenton*	0	1	.000	0.00	2	2	0	0	0	0	7.0	3	25	1	0	0	0	0	1	0	0	7	0	0
Faino, Jeff, Tre.-Bowie*	1	3	.250	2.66	36	0	0	0	15	0	50.2	43	207	21	15	3	3	3	2	16	1	22	2	0
Falteisek, Steve, Harrisburg	9	6	.600	2.95	25	25	5	0	0	0	168.0	152	707	74	55	3	7	5	11	64	4	112	6	1
Farmer, Mike, New Haven*	10	5	.667	4.89	40	12	0	0	7	0	110.1	117	475	63	60	8	6	2	5	35	4	77	5	3
Fernandez, Jared, Trenton	5	4	.556	3.90	11	10	1	0	0	0	67.0	64	290	32	29	4	3	1	5	28	1	40	2	0
Fernandez, Sid, Bowie*	1	0	1.000	0.75	2	2	1	1	0	0	12.0	4	41	2	1	0	0	0	0	3	0	10	1	0
Fiegel, Todd, Binghamton*	0	1	.000	15.00	4	0	0	0	1	0	3.0	4	21	5	5	1	0	1	4	3	0	3	1	1
Fisher, David, Reading	0	0	.000	0.00	2	0	0	0	2	0	2.1	1	8	0	0	0	0	0	1	0	0	1	0	0
Forney, Rick, Bowie	7	7	.500	5.75	23	19	1	1	2	0	97.0	110	437	69	62	14	2	6	3	42	0	73	7	1
Foster, Mark, Reading*	1	1	.500	5.66	25	0	0	0	4	1	20.2	25	106	15	13	1	2	1	1	17	3	15	2	4
Fronio, Jason, Canton/Akron	1	3	.250	7.22	8	5	1	0	1	0	28.2	32	137	25	23	2	0	3	4	16	0	23	5	0
Fuller, Mark, Binghamton	4	3	.571	2.95	47	1	0	0	12	1	79.1	83	330	33	26	7	2	3	5	22	5	34	0	4
Fultz, Aaron, New Britain*	0	2	.000	6.60	3	3	0	0	0	0	15.0	11	64	12	11	1	0	2	0	9	0	12	0	0
Gandarillas, Gus, New Britain	2	4	.333	6.12	25	0	0	0	18	7	32.1	38	152	26	22	1	2	0	3	16	0	25	3	0
Gavaghan, Sean, New Britain	2	1	.667	2.20	21	0	0	0	21	5	28.2	18	119	10	7	0	2	2	2	10	2	30	0	1
Gentile, Scott, Harrisburg	2	2	.500	3.44	37	0	0	0	26	11	49.2	36	202	19	19	3	2	1	4	15	2	48	1	0
Gilmore, Joel, Reading	2	0	1.000	6.25	18	3	0	0	4	0	36.0	45	168	27	25	6	1	2	3	18	2	27	3	1
Gomes, Wayne, Reading	7	4	.636	3.96	22	22	1	1	0	0	104.2	89	462	54	46	8	3	1	1	70	0	102	6	6
Grace, Mike, Reading	13	6	.684	3.54	24	24	2	0	0	0	147.1	137	606	65	58	13	5	0	6	35	0	118	3	2
Graves, Dan, Canton/Akron	1	0	1.000	0.00	17	0	0	0	17	10	23.1	10	82	1	0	0	4	0	1	2	0	11	0	0
Grundt, Ken, New Haven*	2	2	.500	2.13	28	0	0	0	8	3	38.0	26	146	14	9	1	2	0	1	10	2	27	2	0

Pitcher, Team	W	L	Pct.	ERA	G	GS	CG	ShO	GF	Sv.	IP	H	TBF	R	ER	HR	SH	SF	HB	BB	IBB	SO	WP	Bk.
Guerra, Mark, Binghamton	2	1	.667	5.79	6	5	1	0	0	0	32.2	35	139	24	21	6	1	0	0	9	1	24	0	0
Hancock, Chris, Portland*	0	0	.000	0.00	1	0	0	0	0	0	0.0	2	2	1	1	0	0	0	0	0	0	0	0	0
Hanselman, Carl, Reading	4	3	.571	6.37	24	1	0	0	4	2	41.0	45	186	29	29	7	1	1	4	17	1	35	2	0
Hansen, Brent, Trenton	4	5	.444	3.26	11	11	3	1	0	0	77.1	70	327	32	28	5	3	2	12	17	1	52	1	2
Harris, Doug, Bowie	3	5	.375	4.01	11	11	2	0	0	0	60.2	66	259	30	27	6	1	1	0	15	1	32	2	2
Harris, Pep, Canton/Akron	6	3	.667	2.39	32	7	0	0	20	10	83.0	78	346	34	22	4	8	4	4	23	3	40	2	2
Heflin, Bronson, Reading	0	0	.000	0.00	1	0	0	0	1	0	1.0	0	4	0	0	0	0	0	0	1	0	2	0	0
Henderson, Chris, New Haven	0	0	.000	0.00	3	0	0	0	3	0	4.0	1	15	0	0	0	1	0	0	2	0	2	1	0
Henderson, Rod, Harrisburg	3	6	.333	4.31	12	12	0	0	0	0	56.1	51	240	28	27	4	0	1	5	18	0	53	1	0
Heredia, Wilson, Portland	4	0	1.000	2.00	4	4	0	0	0	0	27.0	22	115	7	6	2	1	1	1	14	0	19	0	0
Hiljus, Erik, Binghamton	2	4	.333	5.86	10	10	0	0	0	0	55.1	60	252	38	36	8	2	1	1	32	1	40	4	2
Hill, Chris, Trenton*	0	0	.000	9.00	7	0	0	0	2	0	6.0	7	30	6	6	0	0	0	0	6	0	10	1	0
Hill, Eric, Reading	4	3	.571	2.90	38	0	0	0	16	4	59.0	55	251	23	19	1	3	3	0	27	6	52	2	1
Hines, Rich, Norwich*	3	5	.375	3.63	54	0	0	0	28	7	62.0	58	283	38	25	2	1	4	5	34	7	50	7	2
Hoeme, Steve, Trenton	2	0	1.000	3.33	20	0	0	0	14	6	24.1	23	108	9	9	1	2	2	3	8	0	17	3	0
Holman, Brad, New Haven	0	0	.000	3.38	7	1	0	0	4	0	16.0	8	58	6	6	0	0	1	0	5	0	9	1	1
Holman, Craig, Reading	1	1	.500	3.49	32	1	0	0	13	1	56.2	55	235	27	22	10	2	2	2	16	2	40	2	1
Hrusovsky, John, Cant./Akron	1	7	.125	7.11	35	4	0	0	11	1	69.2	77	323	64	55	12	4	6	2	35	3	59	1	0
Hubbard, Mark, Norwich*	4	4	.500	4.21	13	12	0	0	1	1	72.2	81	310	38	34	2	2	2	6	25	1	39	1	1
Hudson, Joe, Trenton	0	1	.000	1.71	22	0	0	0	17	8	31.2	20	133	8	6	0	1	0	1	17	3	24	2	1
Hunter, Rich, Reading	3	0	1.000	2.05	3	3	0	0	0	0	22.0	14	86	6	5	1	0	1	0	6	0	17	2	0
Hurst, James, Bowie*	0	0	.000	0.00	1	0	0	0	0	0	1.1	2	8	3	0	0	1	0	0	1	0	1	0	0
Hutchins, Jason, New Haven	0	0	.000	3.86	12	1	0	0	4	1	14.0	13	70	6	6	0	0	0	2	14	0	14	3	0
Ingram, Todd, Trenton	1	1	.500	5.84	18	0	0	0	7	0	24.2	27	125	19	16	2	2	2	1	21	4	16	1	1
Isringhausen, Jason, Bingham.	2	1	.667	2.85	6	6	1	0	0	0	41.0	26	164	15	13	1	0	0	3	12	0	59	6	0
Janzen, Marty, Norwich	1	2	.333	4.95	3	3	0	0	0	0	20.0	17	85	11	11	2	0	0	2	7	0	16	2	0
Jarvis, Matt, Bowie*	9	8	.529	5.11	26	21	0	0	1	0	118.0	154	531	71	67	11	4	4	4	42	1	60	5	3
Johnson, Dom, Trenton	1	2	.333	9.42	5	2	0	0	1	0	14.1	19	74	16	15	2	0	0	1	12	0	11	2	1
Johnson, Jason, New Haven	6	3	.667	5.32	19	12	0	0	1	0	67.2	77	297	43	40	2	1	4	3	29	1	37	6	0
Jones, Bobby, New Haven*	5	2	.714	2.58	27	8	0	0	9	3	73.1	61	315	27	21	4	3	3	8	36	2	70	7	0
Juelsgaard, Jarod, Portland	3	1	.750	3.89	48	0	0	0	13	2	71.2	65	313	35	31	3	1	2	2	44	2	44	5	0
Juhl, Mike, Reading*	1	8	.111	4.27	49	0	0	0	16	6	46.1	43	208	32	22	4	4	1	1	28	1	39	2	1
Karp, Ryan, Reading*	1	2	.333	3.06	7	7	0	0	0	0	47.0	44	190	18	16	4	3	0	0	15	0	37	1	2
Kendrena, Ken, Harrisburg	3	2	.600	2.51	30	0	0	0	8	1	64.2	58	277	27	18	5	2	1	4	25	2	46	3	0
Kerley, Collin, Harrisburg	0	0	.000	0.00	2	0	0	0	0	0	6.2	5	26	0	0	0	0	0	0	1	0	3	1	0
Kindell, Scott, Binghamton*	0	0	.000	0.00	1	0	0	0	0	0	1.0	2	5	0	0	0	0	0	0	0	0	0	0	0
Kirkreit, Daron, Cant./Akron	2	9	.182	5.69	14	14	1	0	0	0	80.2	74	360	54	51	13	5	5	6	46	1	67	2	0
Kline, Steve, Cant./Akron*	2	3	.400	2.42	14	14	0	0	0	0	89.1	86	377	34	24	6	4	1	1	30	3	45	1	1
Knackert, Brent, Binghamton	7	7	.500	2.30	48	0	0	0	28	11	82.1	53	324	23	21	4	5	2	3	26	8	69	3	0
Knowles, Greg, Bowie	5	2	.714	4.14	37	1	0	0	13	2	74.0	83	327	44	34	6	5	2	1	26	7	37	3	0
Koller, Rod, Canton/Akron	0	0	.000	7.23	9	1	0	0	2	1	18.2	26	89	17	15	2	0	1	2	4	0	3	0	0
Konieczki, Dom, New Britain*	0	1	.000	1.95	39	0	0	0	15	1	32.1	28	146	10	7	1	2	1	1	19	2	35	3	0
Kotarski, Mike, New Haven*	2	3	.400	3.24	31	0	0	0	10	2	50.0	43	234	25	18	4	4	2	1	36	4	54	3	5
Kozeniewski, Blaise, Norwich	1	0	1.000	4.91	29	0	0	0	13	0	55.0	53	250	35	30	2	1	2	6	27	0	33	3	0
Lane, Aaron, Bowie*	5	3	.625	4.17	40	0	0	0	18	2	45.1	45	200	23	21	2	5	0	1	21	3	31	3	1
Langbehn, Gregg, Trenton*	0	1	.000	5.40	14	0	0	0	2	1	13.1	9	57	9	8	0	0	0	1	9	0	11	0	0
Larkin, Andy, Portland	1	2	.333	3.38	9	9	0	0	0	0	40.0	29	160	16	15	5	4	0	6	11	2	23	1	0
Leahy, Pat, Portland	3	1	.750	4.50	13	6	0	0	1	0	42.0	32	175	24	21	5	5	1	1	20	3	37	2	0
Legault, Kevin, New Britain	6	1	.857	3.21	47	1	0	0	17	3	87.0	79	367	31	31	3	6	5	4	28	4	52	5	0
Lehman, Toby, Bowie	1	3	.250	7.94	4	4	0	0	0	0	17.0	20	77	15	15	4	0	0	0	11	0	14	0	0
Lemon, Don, Portland	1	6	.143	3.61	30	3	0	0	11	1	62.1	60	263	30	25	3	4	4	0	19	3	47	0	2
Lemp, Chris, Bowie	2	4	.333	5.40	18	0	0	0	16	4	20.0	28	94	13	12	0	1	2	2	7	3	14	3	0
Loewer, Carlton, Reading	4	1	.800	2.16	8	8	0	0	0	0	50.0	42	212	17	12	3	1	0	1	31	0	35	4	0
Long, Joe, Norwich	4	2	.667	4.85	43	1	0	0	15	2	81.2	103	391	54	44	4	2	6	6	48	3	34	3	0
Ludwick, Eric, Binghamton	12	5	.706	2.95	23	22	3	2	0	0	143.1	108	590	52	47	9	4	6	2	68	1	131	6	0
Maduro, Calvin, Bowie	0	6	.000	5.09	7	7	0	0	0	0	35.1	39	165	28	20	3	1	2	0	27	0	26	3	0
Magee, Bo, C-A/Bowie*	1	3	.250	6.63	26	1	0	0	11	1	38.0	43	185	34	28	2	0	2	0	34	2	32	5	0
Maldonado, Jay, New Britain	0	0	.000	11.81	5	0	0	0	1	0	5.1	7	28	8	7	0	1	0	0	3	0	4	0	3
Malloy, Chuck, Trenton	0	0	.000	4.76	1	1	0	0	0	0	5.2	9	28	5	3	0	0	2	2	1	0	1	1	0
Mansur, Jeff, New Britain*	0	0	.000	1.42	5	0	0	0	2	1	6.1	5	26	1	1	1	0	0	0	2	0	3	0	0
Mantei, Matt, Portland	1	0	1.000	2.38	8	0	0	0	4	1	11.1	10	48	3	3	0	1	0	1	5	0	15	0	0
Matthews, Mike, Cant./Akron*	5	8	.385	5.93	15	15	1	0	0	0	74.1	82	345	62	49	6	2	8	2	43	1	37	8	1
McCready, Jim, Binghamton	1	1	.500	3.23	32	0	0	0	16	4	39.0	42	178	21	14	4	3	2	2	14	1	17	5	0
McDill, Allen, Binghamton*	3	5	.375	4.56	12	12	1	0	0	0	73.0	69	324	42	37	5	1	4	3	38	2	44	3	1
McGraw, Tom, Portland*	5	0	1.000	1.81	51	0	0	0	11	2	74.2	69	322	21	15	2	7	3	4	31	3	60	4	0
Mendoza, Ramiro, Norwich	5	6	.455	3.21	19	19	2	1	0	0	89.2	87	380	39	32	4	1	1	2	33	0	68	2	1
Mendoza, Reynol, Portland	9	10	.474	3.43	27	27	1	1	0	0	168.0	163	715	73	64	6	10	4	9	69	3	120	15	0
Mikkelsen, Linc, Harrisburg	1	2	.333	5.37	21	5	0	0	5	0	53.2	57	243	33	32	1	5	2	4	24	0	39	1	1
Miller, Travis, New Britain*	7	9	.438	4.37	28	27	1	1	1	0	162.2	172	723	93	79	17	6	3	4	65	2	151	5	0
Mitchell, Larry, Reading	6	11	.353	5.54	25	24	1	1	1	0	128.1	136	584	85	79	13	2	2	4	72	4	107	7	1
Mix, Greg, Portland	6	4	.600	4.68	24	13	0	0	1	0	92.1	98	401	51	48	9	2	4	4	25	5	56	3	0
Moore, Joel, New Haven	14	6	.700	3.20	27	26	1	1	0	0	157.1	156	682	69	56	8	6	6	8	67	2	102	5	1
Moten, Scott, New Britain	8	5	.615	3.94	40	1	0	0	18	3	75.1	65	323	40	33	8	6	3	0	36	2	43	5	0
Munoz, Bobby, Reading	0	4	.000	10.80	4	4	0	0	0	0	15.0	28	74	19	18	4	0	0	0	3	0	8	1	0
Musselwhite, James, Norwich	5	9	.357	4.58	24	24	1	0	0	0	131.2	136	566	75	67	11	5	6	6	34	3	96	8	1
Musset, Jose, Norwich	4	1	.800	3.33	34	0	0	0	12	4	48.2	43	217	21	18	2	3	3	7	24	2	42	4	0
Neier, Chris, New Haven	10	4	.714	4.16	38	18	1	0	5	0	123.1	164	550	62	57	10	4	3	1	47	5	74	2	1
Newlin, Jim, Bowie	3	5	.375	3.68	40	1	0	0	26	11	63.2	69	283	35	26	6	3	5	2	22	3	51	9	1
Nied, David, New Haven	0	0	.000	8.10	1	1	0	0	0	0	3.1	4	14	3	3	2	0	0	0	0	0	0	0	0
Nieto, Tony, Bowie	0	0	.000	15.00	1	1	0	0	0	0	3.0	6	18	5	5	2	0	0	0	3	0	3	0	0
Norris, Joe, New Britain	5	6	.455	3.59	46	0	0	0	20	5	82.2	79	364	42	33	4	11	3	2	36	5	81	4	0
Novoa, Rafael, Binghamton*	0	1	.000	2.25	4	0	0	0	2	0	8.0	6	34	2	2	0	1	0	0	5	0	6	0	0
Ohme, Kevin, New Britain*	3	4	.429	3.46	35	11	0	0	7	0	101.1	89	427	51	39	5	7	7	3	45	1	52	7	0

Pitcher, Team	W	L	Pct.	ERA	G	GS	CG	ShO	GF	Sv.	IP	H	TBF	R	ER	HR	SH	SF	HB	BB	IBB	SO	WP	Bk.
Orellano, Rafael, Trenton*	11	7	.611	3.09	27	27	2	0	0	0	186.2	146	772	68	64	18	4	1	11	72	0	160	9	4
Pacheco, Alex, Harrisburg	9	7	.563	4.27	45	0	0	0	29	4	86.1	76	371	45	41	8	1	1	8	31	4	88	4	0
Paniagua, Jose, Harrisburg	7	12	.368	5.34	25	25	2	1	0	0	126.1	140	575	84	75	9	5	5	12	62	0	89	8	0
Pantoja, Johnny, Norwich	1	2	.333	6.48	11	2	0	0	2	0	25.0	29	119	23	18	1	1	1	2	14	0	19	0	0
Paxton, Darrin, Har.-Bing.*	1	2	.333	3.48	28	3	0	0	10	0	44.0	46	184	22	17	3	0	2	0	13	1	27	1	1
Percibal, Billy, Bowie	1	0	1.000	0.00	2	2	0	0	0	0	14.0	7	52	0	0	0	0	0	0	7	0	7	0	1
Perez, Melido, Norwich	1	0	1.000	0.00	2	2	0	0	0	0	9.0	7	35	0	0	0	0	0	0	3	0	9	0	1
Perschke, Greg, Cant./Akron	1	0	1.000	3.38	3	0	0	0	1	0	5.1	4	21	2	2	1	0	0	0	2	0	4	1	0
Person, Robert, Binghamton	5	4	.556	3.11	26	7	1	0	13	7	66.2	46	263	27	23	4	4	1	0	25	0	65	1	0
Peterson, Dean, Trenton	4	8	.333	5.38	20	14	1	0	2	0	88.2	96	389	57	53	7	3	3	4	27	3	47	3	4
Pettit, Doug, Portland	3	1	.750	3.69	21	0	0	0	9	2	31.2	30	129	13	13	1	2	0	2	6	3	24	0	0
Pierce, Ed, Bowie*	0	2	.000	6.43	7	4	0	0	1	1	21.0	32	102	16	15	2	1	2	0	9	0	16	2	0
Pollard, Damon, Harrisburg	0	0	.000	8.64	6	0	0	0	1	0	8.1	11	42	11	8	2	1	2	0	4	0	10	5	0
Popplewell, Tom, Cant./Akron	2	0	1.000	9.74	15	0	0	0	3	0	20.1	33	103	22	22	6	1	2	0	16	1	14	0	0
Pote, Lou, Harrisburg	0	1	.000	5.40	9	4	0	0	2	0	28.1	32	123	17	17	3	0	2	1	7	0	24	1	0
Powell, Jay, Portland	5	4	.556	1.87	50	0	0	0	44	24	53.0	42	213	12	11	2	3	1	2	15	1	53	2	1
Puig, Benny, Harrisburg*	0	0	.000	0.00	1	0	0	0	0	0	1.2	3	9	2	0	0	0	0	0	1	0	0	0	0
Ramirez, Hector, Binghamton	4	12	.250	4.60	20	20	2	0	0	0	123.1	127	534	69	63	12	2	2	3	48	2	63	3	5
Rekar, Bryan, New Haven	6	3	.667	2.13	12	12	1	1	0	0	80.1	65	325	28	19	4	3	0	3	16	1	80	0	0
Ricken, Ray, Norwich	4	2	.667	2.72	8	8	1	1	0	0	53.0	44	217	21	16	2	2	0	1	24	2	43	3	0
Riley, Ed, Trenton*	0	0	.000	2.76	16	0	0	0	7	1	16.1	14	74	6	5	1	0	2	4	9	1	10	0	0
Ritchie, Todd, New Britain	4	9	.308	5.73	24	21	0	0	0	0	113.0	135	515	78	72	12	4	5	6	54	0	60	8	0
Roberts, Brett, New Britain	11	9	.550	3.41	28	28	5	1	0	0	174.0	162	729	72	66	9	4	5	5	50	0	135	6	0
Rojas, Euclides, Portland	1	1	.500	7.77	14	1	0	0	5	1	22.0	27	104	20	19	3	0	0	1	13	1	22	2	1
Ruffin, Bruce, New Haven*	0	0	.000	0.00	2	2	0	0	0	0	2.0	1	7	0	0	0	0	0	0	0	0	2	0	0
Ryan, Ken, Trenton	0	2	.000	5.82	11	0	0	0	7	2	17.0	23	79	13	11	1	1	0	0	5	0	16	0	0
Ryan, Kevin, Bowie	4	3	.571	3.43	39	1	0	0	14	5	63.0	67	267	31	24	5	2	2	1	15	2	31	1	0
Saccavino, Craig, New Britain	1	6	.143	5.66	27	1	0	0	12	1	41.1	48	213	36	26	6	3	3	2	32	0	34	8	0
Salamon, John, New Haven	1	0	1.000	6.10	6	0	0	0	0	0	10.1	9	54	7	7	0	1	2	0	16	1	9	1	0
Schneider, Phil, New Haven*	0	1	.000	7.71	2	2	0	0	0	0	7.0	8	37	8	6	1	1	0	0	9	0	3	0	0
Schorr, Brad, Binghamton	0	2	.000	9.18	4	4	0	0	0	0	16.2	21	87	21	17	1	0	1	0	20	1	6	2	0
Sele, Aaron, Trenton	0	1	.000	3.38	2	2	0	0	0	0	8.0	8	33	3	3	0	0	1	2	2	0	9	0	0
Senior, Shawn, Trenton*	11	7	.611	4.52	27	27	0	0	0	0	151.1	154	673	91	76	15	5	11	9	68	2	90	10	4
Serafini, Dan, New Britain*	12	9	.571	3.38	27	27	1	1	0	0	162.2	155	692	74	61	7	3	4	12	72	0	123	3	4
Shaw, Cedric, Harrisburg*	0	1	.000	4.66	5	2	0	0	0	0	19.1	25	83	10	10	2	1	0	0	6	0	13	2	0
Shenk, Larry, Bowie	0	0	.000	6.52	6	0	0	0	1	0	9.2	6	45	8	7	1	1	0	1	8	0	8	2	0
Smith, Eric, Reading	0	1	.000	20.25	4	0	0	0	0	0	4.0	11	28	9	9	1	0	0	1	4	1	5	2	0
Spencer, Stan, Portland	1	4	.200	7.38	8	8	0	0	0	0	39.0	57	193	39	32	9	0	4	2	19	0	32	0	0
Standish, Scott, Norwich	4	3	.571	5.67	17	9	0	0	0	0	60.1	73	280	43	38	3	2	3	5	30	3	47	4	2
Steph, Rod, Canton/Akron	8	10	.444	3.81	32	20	1	0	5	0	137.0	150	595	74	58	6	7	2	9	33	1	82	5	0
Stephenson, Garrett, Bowie	7	10	.412	3.64	29	29	1	0	0	0	175.1	154	743	87	71	23	5	7	18	47	0	139	4	2
Stidham, Phil, Binghamton	0	0	.000	4.66	7	0	0	0	4	0	9.2	9	47	6	5	0	1	0	0	9	0	7	0	0
Stull, Everett, Harrisburg	3	12	.200	5.54	24	24	0	0	0	0	126.2	114	569	88	78	12	5	5	9	79	2	132	7	1
Sullivan, Grant, Norwich*	0	0	.000	54.00	1	0	0	0	0	0	0.2	4	6	4	4	1	0	0	0	0	0	0	0	0
Sullivan, Mike, Trenton	3	1	.750	1.37	15	0	0	0	9	2	19.2	17	79	5	3	1	1	0	2	3	0	16	0	0
Suppan, Jeff, Trenton	6	2	.750	2.36	15	15	1	1	0	0	99.0	86	409	35	26	5	1	3	8	26	1	88	4	0
Sutherland, John, Norwich	1	0	1.000	2.77	13	0	0	0	6	2	13.0	12	51	5	4	3	0	1	1	3	0	12	0	0
Tam, Jeff, Binghamton	0	2	.000	4.50	14	0	0	0	7	3	18.0	20	83	11	9	1	2	1	4	4	2	9	3	0
Taylor, Tommy, Canton/Akron	1	1	.500	3.72	5	0	0	0	3	0	9.2	9	41	4	4	2	1	1	0	6	0	3	0	0
Telford, Anthony, Canton/Akron	2	0	1.000	0.82	2	2	0	0	0	0	11.0	6	42	2	1	0	0	0	0	4	1	4	0	0
Tellers, Dave, New Haven	2	5	.286	2.87	33	3	0	0	4	1	69.0	60	278	29	22	3	2	3	4	14	1	63	3	0
Thomson, John, New Haven	7	8	.467	4.18	26	24	0	0	0	0	131.1	132	572	69	61	8	2	7	2	56	0	82	3	2
Tirado, Aris, Harrisburg	1	0	1.000	0.77	8	0	0	0	4	1	11.2	8	48	1	1	1	0	1	0	5	0	10	0	0
Tranberg, Mark, Reading	6	6	.500	3.73	18	18	3	3	0	0	111.0	110	458	50	46	7	3	3	3	30	0	62	5	0
Trinidad, Hector, New Britain	4	11	.267	4.61	23	22	0	0	1	0	121.0	137	516	67	62	6	1	10	7	22	0	92	6	2
Trisler, John, Reading	2	4	.333	5.16	30	10	0	0	10	0	82.0	96	366	51	47	6	1	3	6	26	1	50	2	2
Trlicek, Rick, Canton/Akron	5	3	.625	3.05	24	0	0	0	16	3	38.1	33	158	16	13	4	4	2	0	16	3	27	1	1
Turner, Brian, Norwich*	0	0	.000	9.00	2	0	0	0	2	0	2.0	2	12	2	2	1	0	0	1	2	0	0	0	0
Viano, Jake, New Haven	3	6	.333	3.38	57	0	0	0	49	19	72.0	51	304	31	27	5	7	3	2	38	1	85	2	0
Virgilio, George, Bowie	0	0	.000	0.00	1	0	0	0	0	0	1.0	0	4	0	0	0	0	0	0	0	0	0	0	0
Voisard, Mark, New Haven	2	0	1.000	3.23	27	0	0	0	10	2	30.2	31	132	12	11	1	0	1	2	14	0	22	4	0
Wainhouse, David, Portland	2	1	.667	7.20	17	0	0	0	5	0	25.0	39	122	22	20	3	0	1	1	8	1	16	1	0
Wallace, Derek, Binghamton	0	1	.000	5.28	15	0	0	0	11	2	15.1	11	62	9	9	1	0	3	1	9	1	8	1	2
Wallace, Kent, Norwich	7	6	.538	3.52	18	16	0	0	1	0	94.2	93	395	41	37	9	2	2	1	24	0	72	2	1
Ward, Bryan, Portland*	7	3	.700	4.50	20	11	1	1	5	2	72.0	70	321	42	36	9	1	1	2	31	3	71	7	3
Weber, Neil, Harrisburg*	6	11	.353	5.01	28	28	0	0	0	0	152.2	157	696	98	85	16	11	7	8	90	1	119	7	1
Wegmann, Tom, Bowie	2	3	.400	4.18	14	11	0	0	0	0	64.2	56	272	35	30	8	2	2	2	22	2	49	0	2
Welch, Mike, Binghamton	0	0	.000	0.00	1	0	0	0	1	0	1.0	0	3	0	0	0	0	0	0	0	0	2	0	0
West, David, Reading*	0	0	.000	1.50	1	1	0	0	0	0	6.0	2	23	1	1	1	0	0	0	3	0	8	0	0
Whisenant, Matt, Portland*	10	6	.625	3.50	23	22	2	0	0	0	128.2	106	544	57	50	8	7	4	9	65	3	107	8	0
Whitten, Casey, Canton/Akron*	9	8	.529	3.31	20	20	2	1	0	0	114.1	100	469	49	42	10	1	2	3	38	0	91	5	2
Williams, Greg, Canton/Akron*	0	0	.000	4.23	24	0	0	0	7	0	27.2	15	115	14	13	2	2	1	0	21	3	17	0	0
Wilson, Paul, Binghamton	6	3	.667	2.17	16	16	4	1	0	0	120.1	89	464	34	29	5	3	4	5	24	2	127	4	3
Wright, Jamey, New Haven	0	1	.000	9.00	1	1	0	0	0	0	3.0	6	20	6	3	0	0	0	1	3	0	0	0	0
Zolecki, Mike, New Haven	3	4	.429	3.25	9	7	0	0	1	0	55.1	56	229	25	20	2	1	1	1	20	1	32	0	2

COMBINATION SHUTOUTS: **Binghamton (6)**—Crawford-McCready-Paxton, Isringhausen-Knackert, Ludwick-Engle, Ludwick-Knackert, Ramirez-Person, Wilson-Knackert. **Bowie (6)**—Forney-Borowski, Forney-Newlin-Lane, Jarvis-Conner-Newlin, Percibal-Conner, Stephenson-Newlin, Wegmann-Conner-Lane-Lemp. **Canton/Akron (7)**—Brown-Harris-Graves, Crawford-Graves, Harris-Steph-Graves, Kline-Driskill, Kline-Steph-Trlicek, Whitten-Harris, Whitten-Brown-Magee-Hrusovsky. **Harrisburg (5)**—DeHart-Bullinger, Falteisek-Mikkelsen, Stull-DeHart-Pacheco, Stull-Pacheco, Weber-Aucoin. **New Britain (9)**—Serafini-Gandarillas 3, Legault-Moten, Miller-Gandarillas, Ohme-Gavaghan, Roberts-Gavaghan, Roberts-Norris, Serafini-Mansur-Norris. **New Haven (12)**—Arteaga-Grundt, Farmer-Kotarski-Henderson, Johnson-Kotarski, Johnson-Kotarski-Tellers-Viano, Jones-Voisard, Moore-Jones-Viano, Moore-Tellers-Voisard, Rekar-Alston-Hutchins, Rekar-Kotarski, Ruffin-Farmer, Thomson-Alston-Viano, Thomson-Aminoff-Hutchins. **Norwich (5)**—Buddie-DeJean, Hubbard-DeJean, Perez-Buddie, Standish-Coleman-Kozeniewski, Wallace-Musset-Long. **Portland (6)**—Alfonseca-Juelsgaard, Cunnane-Ward, Larkin-Pettit, Mendoza-McGraw, Mendoza-McGraw-Mantei, Mendoza-Powell-Chergey. **Reading (3)**—Gilmore-Hill, Mitchell-Hill, Mitchell-Holman. **Trenton (5)**—Brooks-Langbehn-Caruso, Orellano-Ciccarella, Senior-Cain, Senior-Caruso-Langbehn, Suppan-Hudson.

NO-HIT GAMES: None.

Pitcher, Team	W	L	Pct.	ERA	G	GS	CG	ShO	GF	Sv.	IP	H	TBF	R	ER	HR	SH	SF	HB	BB	IBB	SO	WP	Bk.
Emerson, Scott, Bowie*	0	2	.000	5.06	4	4	0	0	0	0	16.0	19	82	18	9	3	0	1	0	14	0	13	3	0
Emerson, Scott, Trenton*	0	0	.000	4.76	4	0	0	0	0	0	5.2	9	29	3	3	0	0	0	2	0	5	1	0
Faino, Jeff, Trenton*	1	1	.500	2.35	5	0	0	0	1	0	7.2	9	32	3	2	1	0	0	1	0	5	0	0
Faino, Jeff, Bowie*	0	2	.000	2.72	31	0	0	0	14	0	43.0	34	175	18	13	2	3	3	2	15	1	17	2	0
Magee, Bo, Canton/Akron*	0	2	.000	6.98	21	0	0	0	8	1	29.2	33	145	26	23	0	0	0	0	28	1	25	4	0
Magee, Bo, Bowie*	1	1	.500	5.40	5	1	0	0	3	0	8.1	10	40	8	5	2	0	2	0	6	1	7	1	0
Paxton, Darrin, Harrisburg*	0	1	.000	1.29	7	0	0	0	2	0	7.0	5	30	2	1	0	0	0	3	1	7	0	0
Paxton, Darrin, Binghamton*	1	1	.500	3.89	21	3	0	0	8	0	37.0	41	154	20	16	3	0	2	0	10	0	20	1	1

1995 FIELDING

TEAM

Team	Pct.	G	PO	A	E	TC	DP	PB	Team	Pct.	G	PO	A	E	TC	DP	PB
Binghamton	.978	142	3778	1545	117	5440	129	24	Canton/Akron	.968	142	3646	1512	173	5331	136	13
Reading	.977	142	3741	1481	122	5344	137	19	New Britain	.967	142	3740	1549	180	5469	120	17
Portland	.976	142	3765	1633	134	5532	116	15	Harrisburg	.967	141	3659	1438	175	5272	118	28
Trenton	.972	142	3839	1575	156	5570	108	23	Norwich	.965	141	3695	1525	188	5408	119	20
New Haven	.970	142	3719	1494	159	5372	130	13	Bowie	.965	142	3693	1485	188	5366	118	26

TRIPLE PLAYS: Bowie, New Britain.

INDIVIDUAL

FIRST BASEMEN

NOTE: All caps denotes fielding-percentage leader based on 71 games for catchers, 95 for all other non-pitchers and 142 innings for pitchers. *Throws lefthanded.

Player, Team	Pct.	G	PO	A	E	TC	DP
Arnold, Ken, Bowie	1.000	2	1	0	0	1	0
Barry, Jeff, Bowie	1.000	4	13	1	0	14	1
Bigler, Jeff, Reading*	.992	13	125	6	1	132	8
Brede, Brent, New Britain*	1.000	10	69	7	0	76	5
Cameron, Stanton, Cant./Akron	1.000	1	2	0	0	2	0
Carey, Todd, Trenton	1.000	8	49	4	0	53	3
Case, Mike, New Haven	.984	39	222	18	4	244	22
Charbonnet, Mark, Harrisburg*	.983	6	50	8	1	59	5
Chavez, Eric, Bowie	.981	12	99	7	2	108	8
Clapinski, Chris, Portland	.900	1	9	0	1	10	1
Clark, Tim, Portland*	.991	129	1158	98	11	1267	93
Daly, Bob, Binghamton	1.000	1	8	2	0	10	1
DAUBACH, Brian, Binghamton	.992	131	1137	98	10	1245	111
Davenport, Adell, Canton/Akron	1.000	6	45	2	0	47	3
Davis, Tommy, Bowie	1.000	3	28	2	0	30	4
Delvecchio, Nick, Norwich	.985	58	498	43	8	549	38
Eason, Tommy, Reading	.987	26	209	18	3	230	17
Epps, Scott, Norwich	1.000	1	7	0	0	7	0
Everson, Darin, Harrisburg	1.000	3	19	0	0	19	1
Fisher, David, Reading	1.000	1	6	0	0	6	0
Friedman, Jason, Bowie*	.987	44	359	35	5	399	31
Fully, Ed, Binghamton	1.000	1	1	0	0	1	1
Garcia, Omar, Binghamton	.978	4	43	2	1	46	3
Geisler, Phil, Reading*	.987	18	137	11	2	150	10
Hardge, Mike, Trenton	1.000	1	0	1	0	1	0
Hartung, Andy, New Haven	.966	3	26	2	1	29	1
Harvey, Ray, Canton/Akron*	.987	10	71	7	1	79	8
Hecker, Doug, Trenton	.994	30	283	26	2	311	16
Held, Dan, Reading	1.000	1	6	0	0	6	2
Hinton, Steve, Harrisburg*	.978	8	45	0	1	46	1
Hymel, Lou, Harrisburg	.985	25	186	17	3	206	19
Jacobs, Frank, Bing.-Har.*	.976	83	670	63	18	751	57
Kennedy, David, New Haven	.984	117	938	70	16	1024	105
Kontorinis, Andrew, New Britain	.991	14	107	8	1	116	5
Kounas, Tony, Harrisburg	.977	18	121	7	3	131	7
Kremers, Jimmy, Portland	.987	18	142	6	2	150	8
Lane, Dan, Harrisburg	1.000	1	2	0	0	2	0
Marabella, Tony, Harrisburg	1.000	7	42	4	0	46	5
Martinez, Ray, Harrisburg	.986	8	58	10	1	69	5
McCall, Rod, Canton/Akron	.992	12	111	7	1	119	15
McGuire, Ryan, Trenton*	.989	70	642	48	8	698	51
McKeel, Walt, Trenton	1.000	3	4	0	0	4	0
McNair, Fred, Reading	.987	88	765	46	11	822	73
Millan, Adan, Reading	1.000	1	8	0	0	8	1
Millares, Jose, Bowie	.966	3	24	4	1	29	3
Moler, Jason, Reading	1.000	1	9	1	0	10	0
Ogden, Jamie, New Britain*	.987	66	582	41	8	631	49
Owens, Billy, Bowie	.988	82	665	60	9	734	62
Pough, Pork Chop, Trenton	.980	32	262	31	6	299	17
Riggs, Kevin, Norwich	.966	3	27	1	1	29	1
Saunders, Chris, Binghamton	1.000	1	7	2	0	9	1
Seefried, Tate, Norwich	.989	58	497	39	6	542	52
Shelton, Ben, N.B.-Tre.*	.987	55	505	36	7	548	43

Player, Team	Pct.	G	PO	A	E	TC	DP
Smith, Bubba, New Britain	1.000	7	48	3	0	51	6
Smith, Ed, Canton/Akron	.987	12	70	4	1	75	6
Tirpack, Ken, New Britain	.953	5	38	3	2	43	3
Townsend, Chad, Canton/Akron*	.985	111	904	73	15	992	92
Turner, Brian, Norwich*	.990	26	197	11	2	210	20
Virgilio, George, Harrisburg	1.000	2	11	0	0	11	2
Waco, David, Reading	1.000	1	1	0	0	1	0
Waszgis, B.J., Bowie	1.000	1	1	0	0	1	0

TRIPLE PLAYS: Ogden, Owens.

FIRST BASEMEN WITH TWO OR MORE TEAMS

Player, Team	Pct.	G	PO	A	E	TC	DP
Jacobs, Frank, Binghamton*	.962	9	69	6	3	78	4
Jacobs, Frank, Harrisburg*	.978	74	601	57	15	673	53
Shelton, Ben, New Britain*	.988	49	446	36	6	488	40
Shelton, Ben, Trenton*	.983	6	59	0	1	60	3

SECOND BASEMEN

Player, Team	Pct.	G	PO	A	E	TC	DP
Alfonzo, Edgar, Bowie	1.000	19	36	38	0	74	10
Azuaje, Jesus, Binghamton	.989	20	31	63	1	95	16
Biasucci, Joe, Canton/Akron	1.000	4	11	11	0	22	1
Carey, Todd, Trenton	.973	21	46	63	3	112	15
Castaldo, Gregg, Bowie	.971	48	86	116	6	208	28
Clapinski, Chris, Portland	1.000	15	32	28	0	60	9
Crowley, Jim, Bowie	.976	8	19	21	1	41	6
Doster, David, Reading	.983	137	261	420	12	693	91
Duncan, Andres, New Britain	1.000	6	8	7	0	15	1
Fisher, David, Reading	1.000	9	5	18	0	23	2
Fleming, Carlton, Norwich	.950	32	57	75	7	139	14
Gonzalez, Mauricio, New Haven	.986	17	31	40	1	72	7
Hardge, Mike, Trenton	.951	13	17	41	3	61	7
Hardtke, Jason, Binghamton	.970	115	197	346	17	560	68
Hinds, Robert, Norwich	.960	111	248	322	24	594	73
Hunter, Greg, New Britain	1.000	2	1	1	0	2	0
Juday, Rob, Trenton	1.000	3	2	3	0	5	0
Lane, Dan, Harrisburg	1.000	10	21	16	0	37	1
Long, R.D., Norwich	1.000	2	1	4	0	5	0
Mahalik, John, Binghamton	.976	10	16	25	1	42	5
Marabella, Tony, Harrisburg	1.000	1	0	1	0	1	0
Martinez, Ray, Harrisburg	1.000	17	29	39	0	68	7
Maxwell, Pat, Canton/Akron	.960	20	40	57	4	101	10
Mercedes, Feliciano, Bowie	.982	26	44	67	2	113	11
Merloni, Lou, Trenton	.952	72	149	168	16	333	25
Millares, Jose, Bowie	.938	30	54	51	7	112	15
Miller, Ryan, Binghamton	1.000	2	1	4	0	5	0
Milliard, Ralph, Portland	.975	128	299	357	17	673	71
Murphy, Pat, Trenton	.951	7	17	22	2	41	7
Neal, Mike, Canton/Akron	.959	121	238	340	25	603	78
Renteria, Dave, Norwich	1.000	3	5	1	0	6	1
ROGERS, Lamarr, New Haven	.984	104	203	290	8	501	64
Rundels, Matt, Harrisburg	.993	93	196	241	21	458	64
Selby, Bill, Trenton	.966	35	70	70	5	145	14
Smith, Ed, Canton/Akron	1.000	1	0	1	0	1	1
Torres, Tony, Portland	.970	10	14	18	1	33	4
Valette, Ramon, New Britain	.963	26	38	91	5	134	26
Vidro, Jose, Harrisburg	.964	27	61	73	5	139	12
Virgilio, George, Bowie	.947	26	46	62	6	114	12

CLASS AA Eastern League

Player, Team	Pct.	G	PO	A	E	TC	DP
Walker, Todd, New Britain	.961	117	210	328	22	560	65
White, Billy, New Haven	.963	31	57	101	6	164	27
Zuniga, David, Binghamton	1.000	1	0	1	0	1	1

TRIPLE PLAY: Walker.

THIRD BASEMEN

Player, Team	Pct.	G	PO	A	E	TC	DP
Alcantara, Israel, Harrisburg	.892	68	48	118	20	186	9
Alfonzo, Edgar, Bowie	1.000	1	0	1	0	1	0
Azuaje, Jesus, Binghamton	.833	3	3	2	1	6	0
Batiste, Kim, Bowie	.881	23	14	38	7	59	1
Biasucci, Joe, Canton/Akron	.941	7	4	12	1	17	3
Burnett, Roger, Norwich	.915	21	7	47	5	59	3
Carey, Todd, Trenton	.925	27	16	46	5	67	3
Case, Mike, New Haven	1.000	12	8	8	0	16	1
Castaldo, Gregg, Bowie	1.000	2	2	0	0	2	0
Chavez, Eric, Bowie	.875	2	1	6	1	8	1
Clapinski, Chris, Portland	.978	30	24	64	2	90	4
Crowley, Jim, Bowie	.964	20	15	38	2	55	6
Dixon, Colin, New Haven	.815	12	9	13	5	27	0
Epps, Scott, Norwich	.500	3	0	1	1	2	0
Garrow, David, New Britain	1.000	3	2	5	0	7	1
Gonzalez, Mauricio, New Haven	1.000	5	1	3	0	4	0
Grable, Rob, Reading	.956	34	25	40	3	68	6
Hardge, Mike, Trenton	.920	9	7	16	2	25	2
Hardtke, Jason, Binghamton	.875	5	4	10	2	16	0
Hartung, Andy, New Haven	.923	5	6	6	1	13	1
Hayden, Dave, Reading	.924	58	33	89	10	132	7
Hinds, Robert, Norwich	.769	13	6	14	6	26	1
Hunter, Greg, New Britain	.667	1	0	2	1	3	0
Kontorinis, Andrew, New Britain	.750	3	1	2	1	4	0
Lane, Dan, Harrisburg	1.000	2	0	1	0	1	0
Lantigua, Eduardo, Cant./Akron	.811	13	8	22	7	37	1
Long, R.D., Norwich	.750	1	1	2	1	4	1
Lopez, Rene, New Britain	1.000	2	3	5	0	8	0
LUCCA, Lou, Portland	.952	111	56	261	16	333	23
Mahalik, John, Binghamton	.938	25	12	48	4	64	6
Marabella, Tony, Harrisburg	.904	17	16	31	5	52	1
Martinez, Ray, Harrisburg	.932	16	10	31	3	44	8
Maxwell, Pat, Canton/Akron	.944	42	20	82	6	108	6
McClain, Scott, Bowie	.933	70	57	165	16	238	15
Merloni, Lou, Trenton	.945	20	16	53	4	73	5
Millares, Jose, Bowie	.874	25	20	56	11	87	3
Moler, Jason, Reading	.967	21	15	43	2	60	4
Murphy, Pat, Trenton	.900	10	9	18	3	30	1
Nava, Lipso, Trenton	1.000	4	4	10	0	14	0
Neal, Mike, Canton/Akron	.947	6	6	12	1	19	1
Pough, Pork Chop, Trenton	.969	8	9	22	1	32	0
Redmond, Mike, Portland	1.000	1	1	0	0	1	0
Renteria, Dave, Norwich	1.000	6	5	10	0	15	0
Rolen, Scott, Reading	.934	20	10	47	4	61	3
Romano, Scott, Norwich	.913	99	70	236	29	335	19
Roper, Chad, New Britain	.938	117	69	248	21	338	21
Rundels, Matt, Harrisburg	.750	1	1	2	1	4	0
Saunders, Chris, Binghamton	.951	118	47	223	14	284	17
Schmidt, Tom, New Haven	.897	113	79	181	30	290	21
Sefcik, Kevin, Reading	1.000	21	9	33	0	42	5
Selby, Bill, Trenton	.885	74	49	136	24	209	11
Smith, Ed, Canton/Akron	.938	81	38	160	13	211	15
Taylor, Jamie, Canton/Akron	1.000	3	2	6	0	8	1
Torres, Tony, Portland	1.000	12	2	18	0	20	3
Tovar, Edgar, Harrisburg	.958	12	6	17	1	24	2
Vidro, Jose, Harrisburg	.963	19	8	44	2	54	4
Virgilio, George, Har.-Bowie	.930	17	10	30	3	43	2
Walker, Todd, New Britain	.865	21	5	27	5	37	1
Waller, Casey, Portland	1.000	1	0	6	0	6	1
White, Billy, New Haven	1.000	8	6	12	0	18	3
Wilson, Thomas, Norwich	.800	7	6	14	5	25	0

THIRD BASEMEN WITH TWO OR MORE TEAMS

Player, Team	Pct.	G	PO	A	E	TC	DP
Virgilio, George, Harrisburg	.921	16	9	26	3	38	2
Virgilio, George, Bowie	1.000	1	1	4	0	5	0

SHORTSTOPS

Player, Team	Pct.	G	PO	A	E	TC	DP
Alfonzo, Edgar, Bowie	.889	12	13	27	5	45	6
Arnold, Ken, Bowie	.964	7	6	21	1	28	5
Batiste, Kim, Bowie	.833	1	1	4	1	6	0
Bautista, Juan, Bowie	.907	12	21	28	5	54	8
Bournigal, Rafael, Harrisburg	.968	29	27	64	3	94	14
Brito, Luis, Reading	1.000	2	2	4	0	6	1

Player, Team	Pct.	G	PO	A	E	TC	DP
Burnett, Roger, Norwich	.931	75	116	194	23	333	39
Cabrera, Jolbert, Harrisburg	.935	9	11	18	2	31	5
Carey, Todd, Trenton	.985	14	20	45	1	66	7
Castaldo, Gregg, Bowie	.948	46	64	120	10	194	16
Clapinski, Chris, Portland	.971	10	9	25	1	35	2
Duncan, Andres, New Britain	.941	68	119	184	19	322	43
Fisher, David, Reading	.935	40	50	80	9	139	17
Fox, Andy, Norwich	.958	44	77	127	9	213	23
Garciaparra, Nomar, Trenton	.963	125	205	396	23	624	61
Garrow, David, New Britain	1.000	2	3	5	0	8	0
Gonzalez, Mauricio, New Haven	.933	22	22	61	6	89	13
Hagy, Gary, Canton/Akron	.963	5	8	18	1	27	3
Hardge, Mike, Trenton	.786	3	3	8	3	14	0
Hinds, Robert, Norwich	.926	13	22	28	4	54	9
Howard, Matt, Bowie	.972	67	86	196	8	290	38
Hunter, Greg, New Britain	.800	3	2	2	1	5	0
Jackson, Damian, Canton/Akron	.939	122	220	337	36	593	80
Lamb, David, Bowie	.800	1	1	3	1	5	2
Lane, Dan, Harrisburg	.935	20	11	32	3	46	4
Long, R.D., Norwich	.800	6	6	14	5	25	3
Mahalik, John, Binghamton	.944	27	30	72	6	108	11
Martinez, Ray, Harrisburg	1.000	3	3	11	0	14	1
Maxwell, Pat, Canton/Akron	.907	15	29	49	8	86	7
Merloni, Lou, Trenton	1.000	1	1	1	0	2	0
Michael, Jeff, Bowie	.750	4	8	7	5	20	2
Miller, Ryan, Binghamton	1.000	3	9	8	0	17	6
Morgan, Kevin, Binghamton	.962	114	192	340	21	553	73
Nava, Lipso, Trenton	1.000	3	6	5	0	11	1
Neal, Mike, Canton/Akron	.793	6	11	12	6	29	2
PEREZ, Neifi, New Haven	.967	114	175	358	18	551	80
Renteria, Dave, Norwich	.800	5	7	9	4	20	3
Renteria, Edgar, Portland	.944	134	179	379	33	591	55
Roper, Chad, New Britain	1.000	2	3	10	0	13	1
Rundels, Matt, Harrisburg	.875	9	11	24	5	40	4
Sefcik, Kevin, Reading	.963	112	157	316	18	491	63
Sexton, Chris, New Haven	1.000	1	0	3	0	3	0
Torres, Tony, Portland	.935	9	8	21	2	31	6
Tovar, Edgar, Harrisburg	.949	63	92	171	14	277	35
Valette, Ramon, New Britain	.927	84	90	215	24	329	34
Vidro, Jose, Harrisburg	.973	20	28	45	2	75	9
Virgilio, George, Harrisburg	.750	3	2	7	3	12	1
White, Billy, New Haven	.917	10	10	23	3	36	6

TRIPLE PLAYS: Bautista, Valette.

OUTFIELDERS

Player, Team	Pct.	G	PO	A	E	TC	DP
Abad, Andy, Trenton*	.987	86	143	9	2	154	1
Agbayani, Benny, Binghamton	.972	60	100	3	3	106	0
Avila, Rolando, Bowie	.935	13	28	1	2	31	0
Barron, Tony, Harrisburg	.975	22	37	2	1	40	0
Barry, Jeff, Binghamton	1.000	74	116	5	0	121	0
Bartee, Kimera, Bowie	.964	53	155	6	6	165	1
Bates, Fletcher, Binghamton	1.000	2	7	0	0	7	0
Berrios, Harry, Bowie	.979	54	94	1	2	97	0
Blasingame, Kent, Reading*	.904	46	64	2	7	73	0
Blosser, Greg, Trenton*	1.000	35	59	5	0	64	1
Brede, Brent, New Britain*	.962	120	238	12	10	260	3
Brown, Jarvis, Bowie	.972	58	135	4	4	143	1
Bryant, Pat, Canton/Akron	.975	120	302	8	8	318	1
Burke, Alan, Reading	.875	6	7	0	1	8	0
Byrd, Anthony, New Britain	.977	119	247	7	6	260	1
Byrne, Clayton, Bowie	1.000	14	27	2	0	29	1
Cabreja, Alexis, Norwich	.800	5	4	0	1	5	0
Cairo, Sergio, Harrisburg	1.000	3	4	0	0	4	0
Cameron, Stanton, Cant./Akron	.955	23	38	4	2	44	2
Case, Mike, New Haven	.979	52	86	8	2	96	1
Castillo, Ben, Canton/Akron	.941	31	59	5	4	68	0
Charbonnet, Mark, Harrisburg*	.995	91	182	3	1	186	1
Chick, Bruce, Harrisburg	.875	10	13	1	2	16	0
Clapinski, Chris, Portland	1.000	5	6	0	0	6	0
Dauphin, Phil, Harrisburg*	.977	104	207	4	5	216	0
Davis, Jay, Binghamton*	.965	112	210	9	8	227	1
Delvecchio, Nick, Norwich	.957	42	62	4	3	69	0
Duncan, Andres, New Britain	1.000	1	1	0	0	1	0
Echevarria, Angel, New Haven	.978	105	202	20	5	227	0
Epps, Scott, Norwich	1.000	1	1	0	0	1	0
Fleming, Carlton, Norwich	1.000	3	3	0	0	3	0
Friedman, Jason, Bowie*	1.000	2	2	0	0	2	0
Fuller, Aaron, Bowie	.972	56	135	6	4	145	2
Fully, Ed, Bing.-Bowie	.944	42	96	5	6	107	4
Geisler, Phil, Reading*	.984	58	121	6	2	129	2
Gerald, Ed, New Britain	.750	2	1	1	1	4	0

Player, Team	Pct.	G	PO	A	E	TC	DP
Grable, Rob, Reading	.980	72	94	2	2	98	0
Graham, Tim, Trenton	1.000	8	14	0	0	14	0
Grissom, Antonio, Harrisburg	.956	59	106	3	5	114	0
Hammonds, Jeffrey, Bowie	.923	7	12	0	1	13	0
Hardge, Mike, Trenton	.955	14	18	3	1	22	0
Harvey, Ray, Canton/Akron*	.977	51	85	0	2	87	0
Hawkins, Kraig, Norwich	1.000	12	28	0	0	28	0
Hayden, Dave, Reading	1.000	2	3	0	0	3	0
Hecker, Doug, Trenton	.929	18	24	2	2	28	0
Held, Dan, Reading	1.000	1	2	0	0	2	0
Hodge, Roy, Bowie	.968	27	54	6	2	62	0
Holifield, Rick, Reading*	.989	30	84	3	1	88	1
Hood, Dennis, Canton/Akron	1.000	8	10	1	0	11	1
Horne, Tyrone, Har.-Nor.	.955	90	164	7	8	179	0
Hughes, Troy, Norwich	.875	12	21	0	3	24	0
Hugo, Sean, Bowie*	1.000	34	64	2	0	66	0
Jackson, John, New Britain*	.880	13	21	1	3	25	1
Johnson, J.J., Trenton	1.000	2	1	0	0	1	0
Jones, Terry, New Haven	.966	121	264	18	10	292	0
Katzaroff, Rob, Portland	.985	99	193	1	3	197	0
Keister, Tripp, Binghamton*	.952	18	16	4	1	21	0
LAWTON, Matt, New Britain*	.991	110	221	12	2	235	2
LeGree, Keith, New Britain	.957	28	44	0	2	46	0
Lennon, Pat, Trenton	.919	22	32	2	3	37	0
Lewis, T.R., Bowie	.942	76	128	1	8	137	0
List, Lou, New Haven	.920	18	22	1	2	25	0
Luke, Matt, Norwich*	.979	93	178	12	4	194	1
Magee, Wendell, Reading	.932	39	65	4	5	74	0
Mahay, Ron, Trenton*	.970	91	187	9	6	202	2
Marabella, Tony, Harrisburg	1.000	1	2	0	0	2	0
Marini, Marc, Canton/Akron*	.994	83	150	3	1	154	0
Massarelli, John, Canton/Akron	.983	52	114	2	2	118	1
McConnell, Chad, Reading	.975	85	149	7	4	160	2
McCracken, Quinton, New Haven	.971	53	92	10	3	105	0
McGuire, Ryan, Trenton*	.973	37	66	7	2	75	1
McMillon, Billy, Portland*	.982	131	207	14	4	225	3
McNabb, Buck, Canton/Akron	1.000	18	31	0	0	31	0
Millares, Jose, Bowie	1.000	20	23	2	0	25	0
Moore, Tim, New Britain*	.882	15	15	0	2	17	0
Mota, Gary, Reading	.946	24	33	2	2	37	1
Murphy, Mike, Canton/Akron	1.000	9	18	1	0	19	1
Murphy, Pat, Trenton	.944	14	17	0	1	18	0
Myrow, John, New Haven	.977	94	161	11	4	176	0
Nava, Lipso, Trenton	1.000	11	18	0	0	18	0
Nixon, Trot, Trenton*	1.000	25	66	2	0	68	0
Norman, Kenny, New Britain	1.000	5	6	1	0	7	0
Northrup, Kevin, Harrisburg	.959	32	46	1	2	49	0
Ogden, Jamie, New Britain*	.988	40	78	3	1	82	0
Payton, Jay, Binghamton	.988	83	230	7	3	240	1
Phillips, Steve, Norwich*	1.000	11	21	0	0	21	0
Ramirez, Alex, Canton/Akron	.975	32	72	5	2	79	2
Ramirez, Omar, Canton/Akron	1.000	3	2	0	0	2	0
Rivera, Ruben, Norwich	.984	71	176	7	3	186	1
Robertson, Jason, Norwich*	.979	116	227	4	5	236	0
Rundels, Matt, Harrisburg	.978	20	44	1	1	46	0
Saffer, Jon, Harrisburg	.972	17	35	0	1	36	0
Sanders, Tracy, Binghamton	.909	7	10	0	1	11	0
Sheff, Chris, Portland	.985	113	191	4	3	198	0
Smith, Ed, Canton/Akron	.923	14	23	1	2	26	0
Smith, John, Binghamton	1.000	3	3	0	0	3	0
Solomon, Steve, Reading*	.990	97	197	8	2	207	0
Thompson, Ryan, Binghamton	1.000	2	2	0	0	2	0
Tinsley, Lee, Trenton	1.000	3	4	0	0	4	0
Tovar, Edgar, Harrisburg	1.000	1	1	0	0	1	0
Turner, Brian, Norwich*	.990	50	98	3	1	101	1
Van Slyke, Andy, Bowie	1.000	2	4	0	0	4	0
Ventress, Leroy, Harrisburg	1.000	9	18	2	0	20	2
Wawruck, Jim, Bowie*	.986	51	68	3	1	72	0
Wells, Forry, New Haven	1.000	4	5	0	0	5	0
White, Don, Binghamton	.984	78	180	7	3	190	0
Wilson, Pookie, Portland*	.988	88	159	3	2	164	1
Wipf, Mark, Binghamton	.750	4	6	0	2	8	0
Yelding, Eric, Canton/Akron	1.000	9	20	1	0	21	0
Zambrano, Eddie, Trenton	1.000	16	38	2	0	40	1
Zambrano, Jose, Trenton	.975	21	38	1	1	40	0

OUTFIELDERS WITH TWO OR MORE TEAMS

Player, Team	Pct.	G	PO	A	E	TC	DP
Fully, Ed, Binghamton	1.000	9	16	3	0	19	3
Fully, Ed, Bowie	.932	33	80	2	6	88	1
Horne, Tyrone, Harrisburg	.971	70	130	5	4	139	0
Horne, Tyrone, Norwich	.900	20	34	2	4	40	0

CATCHERS

Player, Team	Pct.	G	PO	A	E	TC	DP	PB
Allen, Matt, Harrisburg	.943	5	31	2	2	35	0	0
Alomar, Sandy, Canton/Akron	.958	5	23	0	1	24	0	0
Bennett, Gary, Reading	.994	82	551	65	4	620	13	6
Brophy, E.J., Reading	1.000	2	3	0	0	3	0	0
Brown, Matt, Trenton	1.000	4	19	1	0	20	0	0
Buckley, Troy, Harrisburg	.997	43	313	36	1	350	6	5
Campbell, Darrin, Cant./Akron	.923	2	11	1	1	13	0	0
Castaneda, Hector, Harrisburg	.984	32	113	12	2	127	2	3
Crosby, Mike, Canton/Akron	.984	73	389	53	7	449	7	5
Delgado, Alex, Trenton	.978	19	114	19	3	136	1	1
Diaz, Cesar, Binghamton	.987	13	72	2	1	75	0	5
Eason, Tommy, Reading	.990	58	368	32	4	404	7	10
Epperson, Chad, Binghamton	1.000	5	12	2	0	14	0	0
Epps, Scott, Trenton	.971	27	120	15	4	139	0	2
Estalella, Bobby, Reading	.986	10	60	9	1	70	1	3
Everson, Darin, Harrisburg	1.000	2	12	1	0	13	0	0
Figga, Mike, Norwich	.985	105	640	92	11	743	4	15
Fitzpatrick, Robert, Harrisburg	.991	14	98	9	1	108	3	3
GREENE, Charlie, Binghamton	.995	100	670	54	4	728	3	9
Gresham, Kris, Bowie	.971	5	33	1	1	35	0	0
Grifol, Pedro, New Britain	.980	74	442	42	10	494	2	12
Higgins, Mike, New Haven	.980	17	92	7	2	101	0	4
Hymel, Lou, Harrisburg	.986	49	324	30	5	359	0	16
Johnson, Charles, Portland	.958	2	23	1	1	24	0	0
Kounas, Tony, Harrisburg	.975	38	234	34	7	275	4	4
Kremers, Jimmy, Portland	.980	45	263	32	6	301	3	5
Levangie, Dana, Trenton	.996	42	248	26	1	275	3	5
Lopez, Rene, New Britain	.983	79	498	69	10	577	4	5
Martin, Jeff, Trenton	.989	75	484	43	6	533	4	13
Martindale, Ryan, Cant./Akron	1.000	2	13	0	0	13	0	0
McKeel, Walt, Trenton	.979	17	84	11	2	97	1	4
Millan, Adan, Reading	1.000	5	30	0	0	30	0	1
Redmond, Mike, Portland	.992	104	656	95	6	757	6	9
Rodriguez, Nerio, Bowie	1.000	3	13	1	0	14	0	0
Rudolph, Mason, Portland	1.000	16	44	2	0	46	0	1
Salcedo, Edwin, Norwich	1.000	3	8	0	0	8	0	0
Scalzitti, Will, New Haven	.996	39	220	28	1	249	0	4
Smith, Brandon, Binghamton	1.000	2	3	1	0	4	1	0
Snyder, Randy, New Haven	.941	5	30	2	2	34	0	1
Soliz, Steve, Canton/Akron	.979	32	161	24	4	189	1	3
Strittmatter, Mark, New Haven	.990	90	664	48	7	719	3	4
Tijerina, Tony, Binghamton	.991	32	199	14	2	215	1	10
Wakamatsu, Don, Cant./Akron	.992	47	219	22	2	243	2	5
Waszgis, B.J., Bowie	.982	125	782	89	16	887	6	23
Wilson, Thomas, Norwich	.993	19	129	12	1	142	0	3

TRIPLE PLAY: Waszgis.

PITCHERS

Player, Team	Pct.	G	PO	A	E	TC	DP
Alfonseca, Antonio, Portland	.889	19	9	15	3	27	0
Alston, Garvin, New Haven	.933	47	8	6	1	15	0
Alvarez, Tavo, Harrisburg	1.000	3	2	2	0	4	0
Aminoff, Matt, New Haven	.500	6	1	0	1	2	0
Amos, Chad, Trenton	1.000	6	1	0	0	1	0
Andersen, Larry, Reading	.500	5	0	1	1	2	0
Antolick, Jeff, Norwich	.833	2	2	3	1	6	0
Arffa, Steve, Binghamton*	.000	1	0	0	1	1	0
Arteaga, Ivan, New Haven	.917	14	3	8	1	12	1
Aucoin, Derek, Harrisburg	1.000	29	4	4	0	8	0
Bakkum, Scott, Trenton	.917	28	5	6	1	12	0
Beech, Matt, Reading*	1.000	14	2	9	0	11	0
Bennett, Shayne, Trenton	1.000	10	0	2	0	2	0
Blais, Mike, Trenton	1.000	13	0	1	0	1	0
Blazier, Ron, Reading	1.000	56	9	14	0	23	3
Borowski, Joe, Bowie	.750	16	0	3	1	4	1
Botkin, Alan, Harrisburg*	1.000	3	0	1	0	1	0
Brooks, Wes, Trenton	.929	29	11	28	3	42	1
Brown, Dan, Reading	.000	2	0	0	1	1	0
Brown, Dickie, Canton/Akron	.882	37	3	12	2	17	0
Buddie, Mike, Norwich	.941	29	10	22	2	34	1
Bullinger, Kirk, Harrisburg	.949	56	14	23	2	39	3
Bullock, Craig, Binghamton	1.000	11	3	5	0	8	0
Cabrera, Jose, Canton/Akron	1.000	24	5	4	0	9	0
Cain, Tim, Trenton	1.000	29	4	11	0	15	0
Carper, Mark, Norwich	1.000	1	1	1	0	2	0
Carter, Glenn, Trenton	.500	14	1	0	1	2	0
Carter, John, Canton/Akron	.857	5	2	4	1	7	0
Carter, Tom, Norwich*	.929	28	2	11	1	14	1
Caruso, Joe, Trenton	1.000	11	1	3	0	4	1
Case, Mike, New Haven	1.000	2	0	1	0	1	0
Cederblad, Brett, Trenton	1.000	8	6	7	0	13	0

Player, Team	Pct.	G	PO	A	E	TC	DP
Chapin, Darrin, Canton/Akron	1.000	4	0	2	0	2	0
Chergey, Dan, Portland	.867	55	4	9	2	15	2
Ciccarella, Joe, Trenton*	1.000	22	4	2	0	6	0
Coleman, Billy, Norwich	1.000	46	10	5	0	15	2
Conner, Scott, Bowie	.778	44	2	12	4	18	0
Coppinger, Rocky, Bowie	.938	13	11	4	1	16	1
Cosman, Jeff, Binghamton	1.000	10	5	9	0	14	0
Crawford, Carlos, Canton/Akron	1.000	8	5	8	0	13	1
Crawford, Joe, Binghamton*	1.000	42	2	12	0	14	1
CUNNANE, Will, Portland	1.000	21	14	20	0	34	2
Dedrick, Jim, Bowie	.966	10	10	18	1	29	3
DeHart, Rick, Harrisburg*	.789	35	6	9	4	19	2
DeJean, Mike, Norwich	.957	59	2	20	1	23	3
DeLaMaza, Roland, Cant./Akron	1.000	7	0	3	0	3	0
Diaz, Ralph, Harrisburg	.600	11	2	1	2	5	0
Doolan, Blake, Reading	.857	60	5	13	3	21	0
Driskill, Travis, Canton/Akron	1.000	33	1	2	0	3	0
Edmondson, Brian, Binghamton	.931	23	9	18	2	29	1
Emerson, Scott, Bowie-Tre.*	.571	8	2	2	3	7	1
Engle, Tom, Binghamton	1.000	13	2	2	0	4	0
Eshelman, Vaughn, Trenton*	1.000	2	0	3	0	3	0
Faino, Jeff, Tre.-Bowie*	.818	36	3	6	2	11	0
Falteisek, Steve, Harrisburg	.937	25	16	43	4	63	4
Farmer, Mike, New Haven*	.952	40	4	16	1	21	1
Fernandez, Jared, Trenton	1.000	11	2	12	0	14	0
Fernandez, Sid, Bowie*	1.000	2	0	2	0	2	1
Forney, Rick, Bowie	1.000	23	4	10	0	14	0
Foster, Mark, Reading*	1.000	25	1	3	0	4	0
Fronio, Jason, Canton/Akron	.833	8	2	3	1	6	0
Fuller, Mark, Binghamton	1.000	47	8	10	0	18	1
Fultz, Aaron, New Britain*	1.000	3	0	4	0	4	0
Gandarillas, Gus, New Britain	.800	25	2	2	1	5	0
Gavaghan, Sean, New Britain	1.000	21	2	6	0	8	1
Gentile, Scott, Harrisburg	1.000	37	2	7	0	9	0
Gilmore, Joel, Reading	1.000	18	4	7	0	11	0
Gomes, Wayne, Reading	.941	22	6	10	1	17	1
Grace, Mike, Reading	1.000	24	9	23	0	32	1
Graves, Dan, Canton/Akron	1.000	17	1	12	0	13	0
Grundt, Ken, New Haven*	.917	28	4	7	1	12	2
Guerra, Mark, Binghamton	1.000	6	4	4	0	8	0
Hanselman, Carl, Reading	.857	24	2	4	1	7	0
Hansen, Brent, Trenton	.938	11	6	9	1	16	0
Harris, Doug, Bowie	1.000	11	5	7	0	12	0
Harris, Pep, Canton/Akron	1.000	32	2	14	0	16	0
Henderson, Chris, New Haven	1.000	3	0	1	0	1	0
Henderson, Rod, Harrisburg*	.857	12	3	3	1	7	0
Heredia, Wilson, Portland	.800	4	0	4	1	5	0
Hiljus, Erik, Binghamton	.923	10	6	6	1	13	0
Hill, Chris, Trenton*	1.000	7	0	1	0	1	0
Hill, Eric, Reading	.889	38	3	5	1	9	1
Hines, Rich, Norwich*	.941	54	3	13	1	17	0
Hoeme, Steve, Trenton	1.000	20	1	3	0	4	0
Holman, Brad, New Haven	1.000	7	1	0	0	1	0
Holman, Craig, Reading	1.000	32	5	12	0	17	0
Hrusovsky, John, Canton/Akron.	.929	35	2	11	1	14	0
Hubbard, Mark, Norwich*	1.000	13	3	22	0	25	1
Hudson, Joe, Trenton	1.000	22	4	12	0	16	0
Hunter, Rich, Reading	1.000	3	1	2	0	3	1
Hurst, James, Bowie*	.000	1	0	0	1	1	0
Hutchins, Jason, New Haven	.750	12	1	2	1	4	0
Ingram, Todd, Trenton	1.000	18	1	1	0	2	0
Isringhausen, Jason, Binghamton.	.857	6	1	5	1	7	0
Janzen, Marty, Norwich	1.000	3	1	3	0	4	0
Jarvis, Matt, Bowie*	.970	26	10	22	1	33	1
Johnson, Dom, Trenton	.800	5	0	4	1	5	0
Johnson, Jason, New Haven	.846	19	5	6	2	13	0
Jones, Bobby, New Haven*	.882	27	5	10	2	17	0
Juelsgaard, Jarod, Portland	.880	48	4	18	3	25	2
Juhl, Mike, Reading*	.917	49	2	9	1	12	1
Karp, Ryan, Reading*	1.000	7	4	10	0	14	0
Kendrena, Ken, Harrisburg	1.000	30	6	14	0	20	0
Kerley, Collin, Harrisburg	1.000	2	0	1	0	1	0
Kindell, Scott, Binghamton*	1.000	1	0	1	0	1	0
Kirkreit, Daron, Canton/Akron	.933	14	6	8	1	15	1
Kline, Steve, Canton/Akron*	.960	14	7	17	1	25	0
Knackert, Brent, Binghamton	.957	48	7	15	1	23	0
Knowles, Greg, Bowie	1.000	37	8	16	0	24	1
Koller, Rod, Canton/Akron	1.000	9	6	5	0	11	0
Konieczki, Jose, New Britain*	1.000	39	4	7	0	11	0
Kotarski, Mike, New Haven*	.917	31	1	10	1	12	0
Kozeniewski, Blaise, Norwich	1.000	29	2	9	0	11	1
Lane, Aaron, Bowie*	1.000	40	4	7	0	11	1
Langbehn, Gregg, Trenton*	1.000	14	0	4	0	4	0
Larkin, Andy, Portland	1.000	9	3	10	0	13	0
Leahy, Pat, Portland	.818	13	0	9	2	11	0
Legault, Kevin, New Britain	1.000	47	6	20	0	26	1
Lehman, Toby, Bowie	.833	4	2	3	1	6	0
Lemon, Don, Portland	.923	30	5	7	1	13	0
Lemp, Chris, Bowie	1.000	18	2	4	0	6	0
Loewer, Carlton, Reading	1.000	8	3	4	0	7	0
Long, Joe, Norwich	.929	43	6	7	1	14	0
Ludwick, Eric, Binghamton	.966	23	11	17	1	29	1
Maduro, Calvin, Bowie	1.000	7	2	6	0	8	0
Magee, Bo, C-A/Bowie*	1.000	26	5	6	0	11	0
Maldonado, Jay, New Britain	1.000	5	1	1	0	2	0
Mansur, Jeff, New Britain*	1.000	5	1	1	0	2	0
Mantei, Matt, Portland	1.000	8	1	2	0	3	0
Matthews, Mike, Cant./Akron*	1.000	15	2	15	0	17	1
McCready, Jim, Binghamton	1.000	32	3	6	0	9	0
McDill, Allen, Binghamton*	1.000	12	7	9	0	16	0
McGraw, Tom, Portland*	1.000	51	10	13	0	23	3
Mendoza, Ramiro, Norwich	1.000	19	8	10	0	18	0
Mendoza, Reynol, Portland	.896	27	16	27	5	48	2
Mikkelsen, Linc, Harrisburg	.950	21	5	14	1	20	1
Miller, Travis, New Britain*	.815	28	10	12	5	27	0
Mitchell, Larry, Reading	.963	25	10	16	1	27	1
Mix, Greg, Portland	1.000	24	6	15	0	21	1
Moore, Joel, New Haven	.971	27	8	25	1	34	3
Moten, Scott, New Britain	.867	40	4	9	2	15	0
Munoz, Bobby, Reading	.667	4	1	1	1	3	0
Musselwhite, James, Norwich	1.000	24	12	19	0	31	0
Musset, Jose, Norwich	1.000	34	3	3	0	6	1
Neier, Chris, New Haven	1.000	38	13	10	0	23	1
Newlin, Jim, Bowie	.944	40	9	8	1	18	0
Nied, David, New Haven	1.000	1	1	0	0	1	0
Nieto, Tony, Bowie	1.000	1	1	0	0	1	0
Norris, Joe, New Britain	1.000	46	6	13	0	19	0
Novoa, Rafael, Binghamton*	1.000	4	2	0	0	2	0
Ohme, Kevin, New Britain*	.921	35	8	27	3	38	2
Orellano, Rafael, Trenton*	1.000	27	6	23	0	29	1
Pacheco, Alex, Harrisburg	.944	45	5	12	1	18	1
Paniagua, Jose, Harrisburg	.962	25	11	14	1	26	2
Pantoja, Johnny, Norwich	1.000	11	4	5	0	9	0
Paxton, Darrin, Har.-Bing.*	1.000	28	2	12	0	14	2
Percibal, Billy, Bowie	1.000	2	0	1	0	1	0
Perez, Melido, Norwich	1.000	2	0	2	0	2	0
Perschke, Greg, Canton/Akron	.500	3	0	1	1	2	0
Person, Robert, Binghamton	1.000	26	8	6	0	14	1
Peterson, Dean, Trenton	.952	20	7	13	1	21	0
Pettit, Doug, Portland	1.000	21	2	5	0	7	1
Pierce, Ed, Bowie*	.833	7	0	5	1	6	0
Pollard, Damon, Harrisburg	.500	6	0	1	1	2	0
Popplewell, Tom, Canton/Akron	1.000	15	0	2	0	2	0
Pote, Lou, Harrisburg	1.000	9	0	1	0	1	0
Powell, Jay, Portland	1.000	50	3	9	0	12	0
Puig, Benny, Harrisburg*	1.000	1	1	1	0	2	0
Ramirez, Hector, Binghamton	1.000	20	7	19	0	26	1
Rekar, Bryan, New Haven	.947	12	6	12	1	19	1
Ricken, Ray, Norwich	1.000	8	4	10	0	14	0
Riley, Ed, Trenton*	1.000	16	1	4	0	5	0
Ritchie, Todd, New Haven	.963	24	9	17	1	27	0
Roberts, Brett, New Britain	1.000	28	16	16	0	32	0
Rojas, Euclides, Portland	1.000	14	2	4	0	6	0
Ryan, Ken, Trenton	1.000	11	1	0	0	1	0
Ryan, Kevin, Bowie	1.000	39	9	9	0	18	1
Saccavino, Craig, New Britain	.889	27	3	5	1	9	0
Salamon, John, New Haven	.667	6	0	2	1	3	0
Schneider, Phil, New Haven*	1.000	2	0	2	0	2	0
Schorr, Brad, Binghamton	1.000	4	1	2	0	3	0
Sele, Aaron, Trenton	1.000	2	0	2	0	2	0
Senior, Shawn, Trenton*	1.000	27	8	24	0	32	2
Serafini, Dan, New Britain*	.864	27	4	15	3	22	0
Shaw, Cedric, Harrisburg*	.833	5	1	4	1	6	0
Shenk, Larry, Bowie	.667	6	1	1	1	3	0
Spencer, Stan, Portland	.500	8	0	1	1	2	0
Standish, Scott, Norwich	.909	17	7	3	1	11	0
Steph, Rod, Canton/Akron	.960	32	10	14	1	25	1
Stephenson, Garrett, Bowie	.800	29	14	22	9	45	1
Stidham, Phil, Binghamton	1.000	7	0	2	0	2	0
Stull, Everett, Harrisburg	.941	24	8	8	1	17	1
Sullivan, Mike, Trenton	1.000	15	4	5	0	9	0
Suppan, Jeff, Trenton	1.000	15	11	14	0	25	2
Sutherland, John, Norwich	1.000	13	1	2	0	3	0
Tam, Jeff, Binghamton	1.000	14	3	5	0	8	0
Taylor, Tommy, Canton/Akron	1.000	5	0	1	0	1	0
Telford, Anthony, Canton/Akron	1.000	2	1	2	0	3	0

Player, Team	Pct.	G	PO	A	E	TC	DP
Tellers, Dave, New Haven	.909	33	4	6	1	11	0
Thomson, John, New Haven	.885	26	12	11	3	26	0
Tirado, Aris, Harrisburg	1.000	8	3	1	0	4	0
Tranberg, Mark, Reading	1.000	18	6	15	0	21	2
Trinidad, Hector, New Britain	.958	23	7	16	1	24	1
Trisler, John, Reading	.933	30	3	11	1	15	0
Trlicek, Rick, Canton/Akron	1.000	24	1	6	0	7	0
Viano, Jake, New Haven	.846	57	5	6	2	13	0
Virgilio, George, Bowie	1.000	1	0	1	0	1	0
Voisard, Mark, New Haven	1.000	27	1	5	0	6	0
Wainhouse, David, Portland	.857	17	3	3	1	7	0
Wallace, Derek, Binghamton	1.000	15	6	1	0	7	0
Wallace, Kent, Norwich	1.000	18	4	13	0	17	0
Ward, Bryan, Portland*	.800	20	2	2	1	5	0
Weber, Neil, Harrisburg	.968	28	7	23	1	31	1
Wegmann, Tom, Bowie	1.000	14	5	6	0	11	0
West, David, Reading*	1.000	1	1	0	0	1	0
Whisenant, Matt, Portland*	.919	23	8	26	3	37	4
Whitten, Casey, Canton/Akron*	1.000	20	8	11	0	19	0
Williams, Greg, Canton/Akron*	1.000	24	1	8	0	9	0
Wilson, Paul, Binghamton	.964	16	10	17	1	28	1
Wright, Jamey, New Haven	.667	1	0	2	1	3	0
Zolecki, Mike, New Haven	.900	9	5	4	1	10	0

PITCHERS WITH TWO OR MORE TEAMS

Player, Team	Pct.	G	PO	A	E	TC	DP
Emerson, Scott, Bowie*	.667	4	2	2	2	6	1
Emerson, Scott, Trenton*	.000	4	0	0	1	1	0
Faino, Jeff, Trenton*	.000	5	0	0	1	1	0
Faino, Jeff, Bowie*	.900	31	3	6	1	10	0
Magee, Bo, Canton/Akron*	1.000	21	3	4	0	7	0
Magee, Bo, Bowie*	1.000	5	2	2	0	4	0
Paxton, Darrin, Harrisburg*	1.000	7	1	2	0	3	1
Paxton, Darrin, Binghamton*	1.000	21	1	10	0	11	1

The following players did not have any fielding statistics at the positions indicated or appeared only as a designated hitter, pinch-hitter or pinch-runner: Benbow, ph; Biasucci, of; Bogott, p; Brownson, p; Cameron, 3b; C. Chavez, p; Clark, of; Cradle, dh; Daubach, 3b; DeBerry, dh, ph; DeJesus, p; Delarosa, p; Delgado, 3b; Devereux, p; Dodd, p; Doster, of; Fiegel, p; Fisher, 3b, p; Hagy, 3b; Hancock, p; Hayden, ss; Heflin, p; Malloy, p; Manto, dh; Romano, of; Ruffin, p; Eric Smith, p; G. Sullivan, p; Turner, p; Valdez, of; Virgilio, of; Welch, p.

LEAGUE CHAMPIONS

Year	Team	Pct.	Year	Team	Pct.	Year	Team	Pct.
1923—	Williamsport	.661	1951—	Wilkes-Barre‡	.612	1975—	Reading	.613
1924—	Williamsport	.654		Scranton (2nd)†	.562		Bristol*	.587
1925—	York§	.583	1952—	Albany	.603	1976—	Three Rivers	.601
	Williamsport§	.583		Binghamton (2nd)‡	.562		West Haven††	.576
1926—	Scranton	.627	1953—	Reading	.682	1977—	West Haven‡‡	.623
1927—	Harrisburg	.630		Binghamton (2nd)‡	.636		Three Rivers	.551
1928—	Harrisburg	.603	1954—	Wilkes-Barre	.576	1978—	Reading	.642
1929—	Binghamton	.597		Albany (3rd)‡	.540		Bristol*	.580
1930—	Wilkes-Barre	.572	1955—	Reading	.613	1979—	West Haven§§	.597
1931—	Harrisburg	.597		Allentown (2nd)‡	.565	1980—	Holyoke*	.561
1932—	Wilkes-Barre	.561	1956—	Schenectady†	.609		Waterbury	.540
1933—	Binghamton	.690	1957—	Binghamton	.607	1981—	Glens Falls	.615
1934—	Binghamton	.694		Reading (3rd)‡	.529		Bristol*	.577
	Williamsport*	.603	1958—	Lancaster∞	.568	1982—	West Haven*	.614
1935—	Scranton	.657		Binghamton (6th)‡	.493		Lynn	.590
	Binghamton*	.580	1959—	Springfield†	.607	1983—	Lynn	.554
1936—	Scranton*	.609	1960—	Williamsport▲	.551		New Britain‡	.518
	Elmira	.629		Springfield (3rd)▲	.496	1984—	Waterbury	.543
1937—	Elmira†	.622	1961—	Springfield	.612		Vermont‡	.536
1938—	Elmira	.622	1962—	Williamsport	.593	1985—	Albany	.540
	Elmira (3rd)‡	.522		Elmira (2nd)‡	.514		Vermont‡	.514
1939—	Scranton†	.571	1963—	Charleston	.593	1986—	Reading	.566
1940—	Scranton	.568	1964—	Elmira	.586		Vermont‡	.554
	Binghamton (2nd)‡	.554	1965—	Pittsfield	.607	1987—	Pittsfield	.630
1941—	Wilkes-Barre	.630	1966—	Elmira	.633		Harrisburg‡	.550
	Elmira (3rd)‡	.514	1967—	Binghamton♦	.586	1988—	Glens Falls	.584
1942—	Albany	.600		Elmira	.532		Albany‡	.522
	Scranton (2nd)‡	.593	1968—	Pittsfield	.604	1989—	Albany‡	.657
1943—	Scranton	.630		Reading (2nd)‡	.579		Harrisburg	.522
	Elmira (2nd)‡	.568	1969—	York	.640	1990—	Albany	.568
1944—	Hartford	.723	1970—	Waterbury■	.560		London‡	.547
	Binghamton (4th)‡	.474		Reading■	.553	1991—	Harrisburg	.621
1945—	Utica	.615	1971—	Three Rivers	.569		Albany‡	.543
	Albany (3rd)‡	.564		Elmira▼	.561	1992—	Canton/Akron	.580
1946—	Scranton†	.691	1972—	West Haven▼	.600		Binghamton‡	.572
1947—	Utica†	.652		Three Rivers	.559	1993—	Harrisburg‡	.681
1948—	Scranton†	.636	1973—	Reading▼	.551		Canton/Akron	.543
1949—	Albany	.664		Pittsfield	.551	1994—	Harrisburg	.633
	Binghamton (4th)‡	.500	1974—	Thetford Miners (2nd)•	.536		Binghamton‡	.582
1950—	Wilkes-Barre‡	.652		Pittsfield (2nd)	.496	1995—	New Haven	.556
							Reading‡	.514

*Won split-season playoff. †Won championship and four-team playoff. ‡Won four-team playoff. §Tied for pennant, York winning playoff. ∞League was divided into Northern, Southern divisions and played a split season; Lancaster was overall season leader. ▲Playoff finals canceled after one game because of rain with Williamsport and Springfield declared playoff co-champions. ♦League was divided into Eastern, Western divisions; Binghamton won playoff. ■Tied for pennant, Waterbury winning playoff. ▼League was divided into American, National divisions; won playoff. •League was divided into American and National divisions; won four-team playoff. ††League was divided into Northern, Southern divisions, won playoff. ‡‡League was divided into New England and Canadian-American divisions; won playoff. §§Won both halves of split season (no playoffs). (NOTE—Known as New York-Pennsylvania League prior to 1938.)

CLASS AA *Eastern League*

SOUTHERN LEAGUE

LEAGUE OFFICE

President/secretary-treasurer
Arnold Fielkow

Address
1 Depot St., Suite 300
Marietta, GA 30060

Phone
770-428-4749

TEAMS

BIRMINGHAM BARONS

President/general manager
Bill Hardekopf

Manager
To be announced

Ballpark (capacity, surface)
Hoover Metropolitan Stadium (10,500, grass)

Affiliation
White Sox

Address
P.O. Box 360007
Birmingham, AL 35236

Phone
205-988-3200

CAROLINA MUDCATS

General manager
Joe Kremer

Manager
Marc Hill

Ballpark (capacity, surface)
Five County Stadium (6,000, grass)

Affiliation
Pirates

Address
P.O. Drawer 1218
Zebulon, NC 27597

Phone
919-269-2287

CHATTANOOGA LOOKOUTS

President/general manager
J. Frank Burke

Manager
Mark Berry

Ballpark (capacity, surface)
Historic Engel Stadium (7,500, grass)

Affiliation
Reds

Address
P.O. Box 11002
Chattanooga, TN 37401

Phone
615-267-2208

GREENVILLE BRAVES

General manager
Steve DeSalvo

Manager
Jeff Cox

Ballpark (capacity, surface)
Greenville Municipal Stadium (7,027, grass)

Affiliation
Braves

Address
P.O. Box 16683
Greenville, SC 29606

Phone
803-299-3456

HUNTSVILLE STARS

President/general manager
Don Mincher

Manager
Dick Scott

Ballpark (capacity, surface)
Joe W. Davis Stadium (10,400, grass)

Affiliation
Athletics

Address
P.O. Box 2769
Huntsville, AL 35804

Phone
205-882-2562

JACKSONVILLE SUNS

Vice president/general manager
Peter Bragan Jr.

Manager
To be announced

Ballpark (capacity, surface)
Wolfson Park (to be announced, grass)

Affiliation
Tigers

Address
P.O. Box 4756
Jacksonville, FL 32201

Phone
904-358-2846

KNOXVILLE SMOKIES

General manager
Dan Rajkowski

Manager
Omar Malave

Ballpark (capacity, surface)
Bill Meyer Stadium (6,412, grass)

Affiliation
Blue Jays

Address
633 Jessamine St.
Knoxville, TN 37917

Phone
615-637-9494

MEMPHIS CHICKS

President/general manager
David Hersh

Manager
Ed Romero

Ballpark (capacity, surface)
Tim McCarver Stadium (10,000, artificial infield, grass outfield)

Affiliation
Padres

Address
800 Home Run Lane
Memphis, TN 38104

Phone
901-272-1687

ORLANDO CUBS

General manager
Roger Wexelberg

Manager
Bruce Kimm

Ballpark (capacity, surface)
Tinker Field (6,000, grass)

Affiliation
Cubs

Address
287 S. Tampa Ave.
Orlando, FL 32805

Phone
407-245-2827

PORT CITY ROOSTERS

General manager
David Kotarba

Manager
Orlando Gomez

Ballpark (capacity, surface)
Brooks Field at UNC-Wilmington (3,500, grass)

Affiliation
Mariners

Address
P.O. Box 7217
Wilmington, NC 28406

Phone
910-350-7000

CLASS AA Southern League

FIRST HALF

EAST DIVISION

Team	W	L	T	Pct.	GB
Carolina (Pirates)	45	27	0	.625	....
Orlando (Cubs)	41	30	0	.577	3½
Greenville (Braves)	35	37	0	.486	10
Port City (Mariners)	32	39	0	.451	12½
Jacksonville (Tigers)	32	40	0	.444	13

WEST DIVISION

Team	W	L	T	Pct.	GB
Memphis (Padres)	40	32	0	.556	....
Chattanooga (Reds)	36	36	0	.500	4
Huntsville (Athletics)	35	37	0	.486	5
Birmingham (White Sox)	33	39	0	.458	7
Knoxville (Blue Jays)	30	42	0	.417	10

SECOND HALF

EAST DIVISION

Team	W	L	T	Pct.	GB
Carolina (Pirates)	44	28	0	.611	....
Jacksonville (Tigers)	43	29	0	.597	1
Orlando (Cubs)	35	37	0	.486	9
Port City (Mariners)	30	41	0	.423	13½
Greenville (Braves)	24	46	0	.343	19

WEST DIVISION

Team	W	L	T	Pct.	GB
Chattanooga (Reds)	47	24	0	.662	....
Birmingham (White Sox)	47	25	0	.653	½
Huntsville (Athletics)	35	37	0	.486	12½
Memphis (Padres)	28	42	0	.400	18½
Knoxville (Blue Jays)	24	48	0	.333	23½

COMPOSITE

Team	Caro.	Chat.	Bir.	Orl.	Jax.	Hun.	Mem.	P.C.	Grn.	Knx.	W	L	T	Pct.	GB
Carolina (Pirates)	....	5	5	12	15	6	4	18	10	14	89	55	0	.618	....
Chattanooga (Reds)	3	....	17	4	5	13	13	4	12	12	83	60	0	.580	5½
Birmingham (White Sox)	3	15	....	5	5	14	16	5	8	9	80	64	0	.556	9
Orlando (Cubs)	12	4	3	....	16	3	5	15	9	9	76	67	0	.531	12½
Jacksonville (Tigers)	9	3	3	16	....	5	7	13	9	10	75	69	0	.521	14
Huntsville (Athletics)	2	11	10	5	3	....	15	5	9	10	70	74	0	.486	19
Memphis (Padres)	4	11	8	3	1	17	....	5	10	9	68	74	0	.479	20
Port City (Mariners)	14	3	3	8	11	3	3	....	9	8	62	80	0	.437	26
Greenville (Braves)	6	4	8	7	7	7	4	7	....	9	59	83	0	.415	29
Knoxville (Blue Jays)	2	4	7	7	6	6	7	8	7	....	54	90	0	.375	35

Carolina's home games played in Zebulon, N.C.

Port City's home games played in Wilmington, N.C.

Major league affiliations in parentheses.

PLAYOFFS: Carolina defeated Orlando, three games to two; Chattanooga defeated Memphis, three games to two; Carolina defeated Chattanooga, three games to two, to win league championship.

REGULAR-SEASON ATTENDANCE: Birmingham, 303,066; Carolina, 317,802; Chattanooga, 290,002; Greenville, 223,225; Huntsville, 243,179; Jacksonville, 237,433; Knoxville, 123,428; Memphis, 221,302; Orlando, 191,080; Port City, 110,233. Total, 2,260,750. Playoffs (15 games)—26,846. Class AA All-Star Game at Shreveport—6,247.

MANAGERS: Birmingham, Terry Francona; Carolina, Trent Jewett; Chattanooga, Dave Miley; Greenville, Bruce Benedict; Huntsville, Dick Scott; Jacksonville, Bill Plummer; Knoxville, Garth Iorg; Memphis, Jerry Royster; Orlando, Bruce Kimm; Port City, Dave Myers.

ALL-STAR TEAM: 1B—Jim Bonnici, Port City; 2B—Brian Koelling, Chattanooga; 3B—Scott Spiezio, Huntsville; SS—Desi Relaford, Port City; Utility IF—Ruben Santana, Chattanooga; OF—Jermaine Dye, Greenville; Robin Jennings, Orlando; Charles Poe, Birmingham; Pedro Valdes, Orlando; C—Jason Kendall, Carolina; DH—Ivan Cruz, Jacksonville; RHP—(tie) Luis Andujar, Birmingham, and Elmer Dessens, Carolina; LHP—Matt Ruebel, Carolina; Most Valuable Player—Jason Kendall, Carolina; Most Outstanding Pitcher—Luis Andujar, Birmingham; Manager of the Year—Bruce Kimm, Orlando.

1995 BATTING

TEAM

Team	Avg.	G	TPA	AB	R	H	TB	2B	3B	HR	RBI	SH	SF	HP	BB	IBB	SO	SB	CS	GDP	LOB	ShO	Slg.	OBP
Chattanooga	.280	143	5506	4885	730	1366	2078	259	36	127	680	45	40	53	480	38	808	91	58	136	1037	7	.425	.348
Carolina	.270	144	5650	5023	689	1358	1935	257	31	86	629	67	48	67	445	42	826	129	72	116	1040	4	.385	.335
Greenville	.268	142	5337	4772	680	1278	1995	263	29	132	630	47	48	39	431	26	1006	90	87	98	918	6	.418	.330
Birmingham	.264	144	5449	4726	688	1249	1769	225	23	83	608	62	50	55	554	36	868	155	72	104	1038	12	.374	.345
Orlando	.261	143	5315	4736	617	1235	1770	233	28	82	560	50	39	34	454	30	786	83	73	127	940	4	.374	.327
Memphis	.258	142	5251	4753	624	1225	1856	205	39	116	573	32	34	36	389	26	1057	165	68	90	920	11	.390	.317
Port City	.253	142	5451	4814	604	1216	1772	229	24	93	540	35	37	58	500	35	948	107	74	117	1021	13	.368	.328
Huntsville	.251	144	5472	4779	643	1200	1819	202	30	119	592	34	45	59	552	22	1027	113	68	94	1076	9	.381	.333
Knoxville	.244	144	5203	4619	577	1125	1610	221	39	62	502	43	32	67	442	21	989	181	98	100	906	9	.349	.317
Jacksonville	.231	144	5385	4720	620	1091	1751	214	25	132	573	66	33	69	506	45	1055	103	61	97	913	9	.371	.313

INDIVIDUAL

TOP QUALIFIERS FOR BATTING CHAMPIONSHIP

Minimum 389 plate appearances. *Lefthanded batter. †Switch-hitter.

Player, Team	Avg.	G	TPA	AB	R	H	TB	2B	3B	HR	RBI	SH	SF	HP	BB	IBB	SO	SB	CS	GDP	Slg.	OBP
Coughlin, Kevin, Birmingham*	.385	96	376	327	56	126	168	29	2	3	49	8	2	5	34	7	43	5	2	3	.514	.448
Kendall, Jason, Carolina	.326	117	508	429	87	140	192	26	1	8	71	1	8	14	56	5	22	10	7	10	.448	.414
Rohrmeier, Dan, Chattanooga	.326	118	482	426	77	139	221	31	0	17	76	1	7	7	41	5	63	0	1	9	.519	.389
Swann, Pedro, Greenville*	.324	102	390	339	57	110	171	24	2	11	64	0	3	3	45	2	63	14	11	8	.504	.405
Valdes, Pedro, Orlando*	.300	114	474	426	57	128	183	28	3	7	68	0	6	5	37	3	77	3	6	7	.430	.359
Larregui, Ed, Carolina	.300	122	460	423	55	127	180	18	1	11	60	0	4	1	32	2	39	3	10	15	.426	.348
Koelling, Brian, Chattanooga	.296	107	486	432	71	128	172	21	7	3	44	8	3	3	40	1	63	30	12	9	.398	.358
Jennings, Robin, Orlando*	.296	132	543	490	71	145	237	27	7	17	79	0	5	4	44	5	61	7	14	11	.484	.355
Santana, Ruben, Chattanooga	.293	142	625	556	89	163	239	23	10	11	79	6	5	8	50	5	77	2	5	17	.430	.357

Player, Team	Avg.	G	TPA	AB	R	H	TB	2B	3B	HR	RBI	SH	SF	HP	BB	IBB	SO	SB	CS	GDP	Slg.	OBP
Ladell, Cleveland, Chattanooga.....	.292	135	565	517	76	151	208	28	7	5	43	4	2	2	39	1	88	28	15	12	.402	.343
Watkins, Pat, Chattanooga..........	.291	105	398	358	57	104	170	26	2	12	57	0	4	3	33	4	53	5	5	7	.475	.352
Wilson, Craig, Birmingham..........	.289	132	531	471	56	136	169	19	1	4	46	10	2	5	43	0	44	2	2	21	.359	.353
Canale, George, Carolina*..........	.287	130	545	487	71	140	245	30	6	21	102	0	8	4	46	6	83	1	3	15	.503	.349
Stewart, Shannon, Knoxville	.287	138	601	498	89	143	194	24	6	5	55	3	5	6	89	3	61	42	16	13	.390	.398
Relaford, Desmond, Port City† ...	.287	90	397	352	51	101	137	11	2	7	27	2	0	2	41	2	58	25	9	4	.389	.365

DEPARTMENTAL LEADERS: G—E. Burton, Coolbaugh, Santana, 142; AB—Santana, 556; R—E. Burton, 95; H—Santana, 163; TB—Bonnici, 246; 2B—Bonnici, 36; 3B—Delacruz, 12; HR—Cruz, 31; RBI—Canale, 102; SH—E. Burton, Sanchez, 15; SF—Spiezio, 14; HP—Delacruz, 15; BB—Stewart, 89; IBB—Bonnici, Cruz, 15; SO—Barker, 143; SB—E. Burton, 60; CS—E. Burton, 22; GIDP—C. Wilson, 21; Slg.—Cruz, .564; OBP—Kendall, .414.

ALL PLAYERS

*Lefthanded batter. †Switch-hitter.

Player, Team	Avg.	G	TPA	AB	R	H	TB	2B	3B	HR	RBI	SH	SF	HP	BB	IBB	SO	SB	CS	GDP	Slg.	OBP
Abbott, Jeff, Birmingham	.320	55	223	197	25	63	85	11	1	3	28	3	2	2	19	2	20	1	3	3	.431	.382
Adams, Tommy, Port City.........	.220	30	127	118	10	26	42	7	0	3	16	0	1	2	6	0	27	5	3	1	.356	.268
Adriana, Sharnol, Knoxville	.284	75	301	261	33	74	102	17	1	3	33	2	2	4	32	1	64	12	13	6	.391	.368
Allensworth, Jermaine, Carolina....	.269	56	251	219	37	59	80	14	2	1	14	2	0	5	25	0	34	13	8	4	.365	.357
Alvarez, Gabe, Memphis...........	.556	2	10	9	0	5	6	1	0	0	4	0	0	1	0	0	1	0	0	0	.667	.600
Arias, Amador, Chattanooga† ...	.222	71	115	108	17	24	29	3	1	0	4	1	0	0	6	0	15	3	2	4	.269	.263
Arnold, Jamie, Greenville	.091	10	12	11	0	1	3	0	1	0	1	1	0	0	0	0	2	0	0	1	.273	.091
Austin, Jake, Carolina*...........	.236	102	376	352	29	83	118	19	2	4	40	2	3	2	17	4	51	5	3	13	.335	.273
Ayrault, Joe, Greenville............	.245	89	328	302	27	74	115	20	0	7	42	7	3	3	13	5	70	2	4	8	.381	.280
Backlund, Brett, Carolina..........	.333	22	12	12	2	4	6	2	0	0	2	0	0	0	0	0	2	0	0	0	.500	.333
Baker, Jared, Memphis*...........	.500	4	2	2	0	1	1	0	0	0	1	0	0	0	0	0	1	0	0	0	.500	.500
Barker, Glen, Jacksonville..........	.239	133	562	507	74	121	185	26	4	10	49	12	1	9	33	0	143	39	16	1	.365	.296
Barnes, Jon, Memphis	.000	2	3	3	0	0	0	0	0	0	0	0	0	0	0	0	1	0	0	1	.000	.000
Batista, Tony, Huntsville..........	.255	120	459	419	55	107	180	23	1	16	61	6	3	2	29	0	98	7	8	8	.430	.305
Beard, Garrett, Huntsville	.190	43	144	126	18	24	29	2	0	1	8	0	2	1	15	1	21	2	3	4	.230	.278
Beasley, Tony, Carolina...........	.281	105	380	335	59	94	124	16	4	2	34	4	6	4	31	2	44	20	4	6	.370	.343
Beatty, Blaine, Chattanooga*	.125	8	8	8	0	1	1	0	0	0	0	0	0	0	0	0	2	0	0	0	.125	.125
Beckett, Robbie, Memphis	.000	36	8	8	0	0	0	0	0	0	0	0	0	0	0	0	6	0	0	0	.000	.000
Bennett, Chris, Carolina..........	.333	18	3	3	0	1	1	0	0	0	0	0	0	0	0	0	1	0	0	1	.333	.333
Blair, Dirk, Greenville	.000	40	2	2	0	0	0	0	0	0	0	0	0	0	0	0	1	0	0	0	.000	.000
Bonnici, James, Port City	.283	138	596	508	75	144	246	36	3	20	91	0	3	9	76	15	97	2	2	14	.484	.384
Boone, Aaron, Chattanooga.......	.227	23	74	66	6	15	18	3	0	0	3	1	2	0	5	0	12	2	0	5	.273	.274
Boston, D.J., Knoxville*..........	.244	132	533	479	51	117	179	27	1	11	71	2	3	2	47	1	100	12	8	12	.374	.313
Bradford, Troy, Orlando...........	.000	4	2	2	0	0	0	0	0	0	0	0	0	0	0	0	0	0	0	0	.000	.000
Briggs, Stoney, Memphis	.247	118	440	385	60	95	147	14	7	8	46	1	3	10	40	5	133	17	8	13	.382	.331
Briley, Greg, Jacksonville*.........	.087	8	26	23	2	2	5	0	0	1	4	0	1	0	2	0	6	0	1	0	.217	.154
Brock, Tarrik, Jacksonville*.......	.115	9	31	26	4	3	3	0	0	0	2	1	0	1	3	0	14	2	0	0	.115	.233
Brooks, Eric, Knoxville	.283	21	68	53	6	15	30	3	0	4	12	0	0	3	12	1	9	0	1	0	.566	.441
Brown, Adam, Chattanooga*.......	.266	77	259	233	24	62	95	14	2	5	32	0	1	1	24	4	36	0	1	9	.408	.336
Brown, Brant, Orlando*...........	.271	121	502	446	67	121	174	27	4	6	53	11	3	3	39	2	77	8	5	6	.390	.332
Brown, Chad, Knoxville*..........	.000	40	1	1	0	0	0	0	0	0	0	0	0	0	0	0	1	0	0	0	.000	.000
Brown, Michael, Carolina*........	.238	60	253	223	29	53	92	13	1	8	33	0	0	2	28	7	62	0	3	1	.413	.328
Brumfield, Jacob, Carolina........	.417	3	13	12	2	5	11	0	0	2	2	0	0	0	1	0	0	0	0	0	.917	.462
Brumley, Duff, Chattanooga	.000	25	2	2	0	0	0	0	0	0	0	0	0	0	0	0	0	0	0	1	.000	.000
Bruno, Julio, Memphis	.270	59	211	196	16	53	71	6	3	2	25	3	2	2	8	0	35	3	2	9	.362	.303
Buckley, Travis, Chattanooga.....	.000	3	3	2	0	0	0	0	0	0	0	0	0	0	1	0	0	0	0	0	.000	.333
Buckley, Troy, Chattanooga.......	.241	10	29	29	1	7	7	0	0	0	2	0	0	0	0	0	6	0	0	0	.241	.241
Bullinger, Jim, Orlando............	.000	1	2	0	0	0	0	0	0	0	0	0	0	0	0	0	0	0	0	0	.000	.000
Burgos, John, Chattanooga*......	.286	44	8	7	0	2	2	0	0	0	0	0	0	1	0	0	1	0	0	0	.286	.375
Burlingame, Ben, Orlando.........	.167	37	14	12	0	2	2	0	0	0	3	2	0	0	0	0	3	0	0	0	.167	.167
Burton, Darren, Orlando†..........	.306	62	249	222	40	68	100	16	2	4	21	0	0	0	27	2	42	7	4	5	.450	.382
Burton, Essex, Birmingham........	.255	142	656	554	95	141	163	15	2	1	43	15	2	5	80	4	79	60	22	9	.294	.353
Bush, Homer, Memphis............	.280	108	454	432	53	121	158	12	5	5	37	4	0	2	15	0	83	34	12	6	.366	.307
Butler, Rich, Knoxville*	.267	58	245	217	27	58	88	12	3	4	33	1	0	2	25	1	41	11	3	5	.406	.348
Cameron, Mike, Birmingham.......	.249	107	419	350	64	87	150	20	5	11	60	5	4	6	54	0	104	21	12	9	.429	.355
Canale, George, Carolina*.........	.287	130	545	487	71	140	245	30	6	21	102	0	8	4	46	6	83	1	3	15	.503	.349
Cappuccio, Carmine, Birming.*.....	.278	65	277	248	34	69	100	13	3	4	38	3	2	2	22	4	21	2	2	10	.403	.339
Cardenas, John, Port City........	.226	57	206	195	17	44	53	9	0	0	17	1	1	0	9	1	45	1	3	9	.272	.259
Casanova, Raul, Memphis........	.271	89	342	306	42	83	137	18	0	12	44	0	4	4	25	2	51	4	1	7	.448	.330
Catalanotto, Frank, Jacksonville*..	.226	134	559	491	66	111	164	19	5	8	48	6	4	9	49	4	56	13	8	9	.334	.306
Cole, Victor, Memphis†...........	.000	8	2	2	0	0	0	0	0	0	0	0	0	0	0	0	0	0	0	0	.000	.000
Coleman, Ken, Orlando†...........	.277	127	479	394	82	109	146	19	3	4	37	4	2	3	76	0	55	25	7	16	.371	.396
Colon, Felix, Jacksonville.........	.259	31	96	81	5	21	34	7	0	2	8	0	2	0	13	0	13	0	0	2	.420	.375
Conger, Jeff, Carolina*...........	.289	39	150	128	15	37	48	6	1	1	17	2	1	1	18	2	31	8	2	0	.375	.378
Coolbaugh, Mike, Knoxville	.240	142	555	500	71	120	183	32	2	9	56	4	3	11	37	3	110	7	11	13	.366	.305
Cooper, Gary, Jacksonville	.276	99	405	337	66	93	171	22	1	18	66	0	3	6	59	4	83	8	4	11	.507	.390
Cora, Manny, Port City†...........	.226	80	270	261	17	59	73	8	3	0	15	0	1	0	8	0	38	1	6	8	.280	.248
Cotton, John, Memphis*..........	.253	121	459	407	60	103	174	19	8	12	47	6	4	4	38	0	101	15	6	2	.428	.320
Coughlin, Kevin, Birmingham*....	.385	96	376	327	56	126	168	29	2	3	49	8	2	5	34	7	43	5	2	3	.514	.448
Cox, Darron, Orlando	.284	33	115	102	8	29	46	5	0	4	15	2	2	1	8	0	16	3	3	3	.451	.336
Cradle, Rickey, Knoxville	.179	41	139	117	17	21	40	5	1	4	13	1	1	3	17	0	29	3	3	3	.342	.293
Cranford, Jay, Carolina	.229	93	353	288	30	66	95	12	1	5	42	2	7	4	52	1	67	3	4	6	.330	.348
Cruz, Ivan, Jacksonville*.........	.282	108	460	397	65	112	224	17	1	31	93	0	3	0	60	15	94	0	0	7	.564	.374
Dabney, Fred, Orlando	.000	13	2	2	0	0	0	0	0	0	0	0	0	0	0	0	0	0	0	0	.000	.000
Danapilis, Eric, Jacksonville	.258	129	488	415	47	107	163	24	1	10	63	0	3	9	61	6	100	3	3	13	.393	.363
D'Andrea, Mike, Greenville	.500	40	11	8	2	4	4	0	0	0	1	0	0	0	2	0	0	0	0	0	.500	.600
Davis, Josh, Memphis	.500	1	3	2	0	1	1	0	0	0	0	0	0	0	1	0	0	0	0	0	.500	.667
DeLaCruz, Lorenzo, Knoxville	.274	140	560	508	63	139	207	20	12	8	61	1	0	15	36	3	129	11	11	14	.407	.340
DeLaNuez, Rex, Jacksonville	.263	111	399	331	47	87	138	22	1	9	41	8	3	8	49	3	74	10	6	5	.417	.368

Player, Team	Avg.	G	TPA	AB	R	H	TB	2B	3B	HR	RBI	SH	SF	HP	BB	IBB	SO	SB	CS	GDP	Slg.	OBP
DeLeon, Luis, Orlando	.000	5	2	1	1	0	0	0	0	0	0	1	0	0	0	0	1	0	0	0	.000	.000
DeLeon, Roberto, Memphis	.267	73	252	236	24	63	94	10	0	7	34	1	1	2	12	0	32	2	2	1	.398	.307
Delgado, Wilson, Port City†	.195	13	47	41	3	8	12	4	0	0	1	0	0	0	6	0	8	0	0	1	.293	.298
Dessens, Elmer, Carolina	.313	27	19	16	0	5	6	1	0	0	2	3	0	0	0	0	5	0	0	0	.375	.313
Diaz, Eddy, Port City	.261	110	474	421	66	110	180	22	0	16	47	1	4	8	40	3	39	9	7	9	.428	.334
DiSarcina, Glenn, Birmingham*	.269	9	28	26	4	7	8	1	0	0	2	0	0	0	2	0	3	0	0	0	.308	.321
Dismuke, Jamie, Chattanooga*	.285	99	402	347	56	99	170	11	0	20	69	0	1	10	44	10	45	0	0	11	.490	.381
Dotel, Mariano, Memphis†	.280	8	27	25	7	7	9	2	0	0	5	0	0	0	2	0	10	0	1	0	.360	.333
Dowler, Dee, Orlando	.226	9	33	31	6	7	9	2	0	0	1	0	0	0	2	0	5	1	0	0	.290	.273
Dreyer, Darren, Orlando	.000	14	1	1	0	0	0	0	0	0	0	0	0	0	0	0	1	0	0	0	.000	.000
Drinkwater, Sean, Memphis	.240	102	319	287	29	69	101	12	1	6	26	2	3	1	26	1	49	3	4	6	.352	.303
Duross, Gabe, Orlando*	.262	68	257	244	23	64	85	10	1	3	40	0	2	1	10	3	20	3	2	12	.348	.292
Dye, Jermaine, Greenville	.285	104	437	403	50	115	194	26	4	15	71	2	4	1	27	2	74	4	8	9	.481	.329
Edge, Tim, Carolina	.214	45	137	126	15	27	44	5	0	4	19	0	1	0	10	0	33	0	0	4	.349	.270
Erdman, Brad, Orlando	.111	14	39	36	4	4	4	0	0	0	0	0	0	2	1	0	6	0	0	4	.111	.179
Espinosa, Ramon, Carolina	.286	134	520	489	69	140	181	28	2	3	48	8	1	5	17	3	64	14	6	15	.370	.316
Etheridge, Roger, Greenville*	.214	32	14	14	1	3	5	0	1	0	0	0	0	0	0	0	2	0	0	1	.357	.214
Evans, Sean, Carolina	.000	29	1	1	0	0	0	0	0	0	0	0	0	0	0	0	0	0	0	0	.000	.000
Farmer, Howard, Chattanooga	.000	1	1	1	0	0	0	0	0	0	0	0	0	0	0	0	0	0	0	0	.000	.000
Farrell, Jon, Carolina	.220	94	339	314	34	69	112	13	0	10	47	3	3	4	15	0	82	3	4	9	.357	.262
Felix, Lauro, Huntsville	.111	10	29	27	3	3	6	0	0	1	1	0	0	0	2	0	8	0	0	1	.222	.172
Fermin, Carlos, Jacksonville	.173	59	132	127	10	22	29	4	0	1	9	0	0	0	5	0	16	0	2	2	.228	.205
Fernandez, Daniel, Jacksonville	.165	94	268	230	18	38	55	5	0	4	16	3	2	4	29	1	60	1	3	3	.239	.268
Ferry, Mike, Chattanooga	.190	24	28	21	2	4	4	0	0	0	1	5	0	0	2	0	6	0	0	0	.190	.261
Fox, Chad, Chattanooga	.200	20	11	10	0	2	2	0	0	0	1	1	0	0	0	0	3	0	0	0	.200	.200
Francisco, David, Huntsville	.279	129	534	477	75	133	167	17	1	5	48	5	3	11	38	0	92	30	8	10	.350	.344
Freitas, Mike, Memphis	.000	54	1	1	0	0	0	0	0	0	0	0	0	0	0	0	1	0	0	0	.000	.000
Fryman, Troy, Birmingham*	.222	112	416	356	48	79	122	13	3	8	41	2	3	6	49	6	97	9	1	4	.343	.324
Garcia, Luis, Jacksonville	.277	17	49	47	6	13	13	0	0	0	5	0	0	1	1	0	8	2	1	0	.277	.306
Gennaro, Brad, Memphis*	.267	104	428	397	46	106	142	19	1	5	60	3	5	2	21	2	62	11	8	9	.358	.304
Gipson, Charles, Port City	.223	112	437	391	36	87	102	11	2	0	29	7	1	8	30	0	66	10	12	13	.261	.291
Gomez, Fabio, Port City	.237	29	109	93	7	22	29	4	0	1	11	1	2	0	12	0	20	1	3	1	.312	.318
Gomez, Rudy, Orlando	.192	93	239	214	18	41	57	11	1	1	16	5	3	2	15	1	45	1	0	8	.266	.248
Gonzalez, Paul, Birmingham*	.269	8	28	26	4	7	14	1	0	2	4	0	0	0	2	0	7	0	1	0	.538	.321
Griffey, Craig, Port City	.177	96	365	299	43	53	66	11	1	0	24	3	3	9	46	0	77	13	3	5	.221	.303
Grijak, Kevin, Greenville*	.432	21	85	74	14	32	43	5	0	2	11	0	2	2	7	0	9	0	1	0	.581	.482
Gubanich, Creighton, Huntsville	.219	94	336	274	37	60	108	7	1	13	43	2	5	7	48	0	82	1	0	2	.394	.344
Haas, David, Orlando	.000	3	1	1	0	0	0	0	0	0	0	0	0	0	0	0	0	0	0	0	.000	.000
Hanel, Marcus, Carolina	.183	21	67	60	1	11	12	1	0	0	3	1	1	1	4	0	18	0	1	2	.200	.242
Hansen, Terrel, Jacksonville	.223	55	199	179	22	40	75	8	0	9	22	0	2	8	10	1	40	0	1	2	.419	.291
Hanson, Craig, Memphis	.000	25	2	2	0	0	0	0	0	0	0	0	0	0	0	0	1	0	0	0	.000	.000
Harley, Quentin, Memphis†	.245	50	174	159	21	39	59	5	3	3	14	0	1	1	13	1	34	7	1	2	.371	.305
Harmes, Kris, Knoxville*	.228	86	299	259	28	59	89	14	2	4	29	1	3	0	36	5	47	0	1	8	.344	.319
Harrah, Doug, Orlando	.000	44	2	2	0	0	0	0	0	0	0	0	0	0	0	0	1	0	0	0	.000	.000
Harrison, Brian, Memphis*	.000	38	1	1	0	0	0	0	0	0	0	0	0	0	0	0	0	0	0	0	.000	.000
Harrison, Tom, Greenville	.222	14	9	9	2	2	3	1	0	0	0	0	0	0	0	0	3	0	1	0	.333	.222
Hart, Chris, Huntsville	.262	36	120	103	11	27	40	3	2	2	20	3	2	2	10	1	30	1	3	1	.388	.333
Henry, Santiago, Knoxville	.220	138	481	454	47	100	139	25	4	2	30	7	5	5	10	0	91	16	6	7	.306	.243
Hernandez, Fernando, Memphis	.000	12	5	4	0	0	0	0	0	0	0	1	0	0	0	0	4	0	0	0	.000	.000
Herrera, Jose, Huntsville*	.282	92	389	358	37	101	138	11	4	6	45	0	2	2	27	2	58	9	8	8	.385	.334
Hickey, Mike, Port City†	.262	120	521	447	59	117	161	24	1	6	59	4	4	5	60	2	83	6	3	9	.360	.353
Hill, Milt, Carolina	.091	10	12	11	0	1	1	0	0	0	0	1	0	0	0	0	2	0	0	0	.091	.091
Hollinger, Adrian, Greenville*	.143	7	7	7	0	1	2	1	0	0	1	0	0	0	0	0	5	0	0	0	.286	.143
Hollins, Damon, Greenville	.247	129	520	466	64	115	199	26	2	18	77	0	6	4	44	6	120	6	6	7	.427	.313
Hostetler, Marcus, Greenville	.000	33	2	2	0	0	0	0	0	0	0	0	0	0	0	0	2	0	0	0	.000	.000
Hostetler, Mike, Greenville	.105	28	22	19	1	2	2	0	0	0	3	2	0	0	1	0	1	0	1	0	.105	.150
Hughes, Troy, Greenville	.255	73	221	200	24	51	78	7	1	6	25	0	2	2	17	0	52	3	6	1	.390	.317
Hurst, Jimmy, Birmingham	.189	91	339	301	47	57	104	11	0	12	34	0	2	1	33	0	95	12	5	5	.346	.270
Hutcheson, David, Orlando	.000	28	28	21	2	0	0	0	0	0	0	3	0	0	4	0	13	0	0	0	.000	.160
Hyzdu, Adam, Chattanooga	.263	102	364	312	55	82	137	14	1	13	48	2	1	4	45	2	56	3	2	4	.439	.362
Ingram, Todd, Knoxville	.000	21	1	1	0	0	0	0	0	0	0	0	0	0	0	0	1	0	0	0	.000	.000
Jenkins, Dee, Chattanooga*	.059	8	20	17	1	1	2	1	0	0	1	0	0	0	3	0	7	0	1	0	.118	.200
Jennings, Robin, Orlando*	.296	132	543	490	71	145	237	27	7	17	79	0	5	4	44	5	61	7	14	11	.484	.355
Johnson, Chris, Orlando	.000	46	2	2	0	0	0	0	0	0	0	0	0	0	0	0	2	0	0	0	.000	.000
Johnson, Earl, Memphis†	.200	2	11	10	0	2	2	0	0	0	0	0	0	0	1	0	0	0	1	0	.200	.273
Johnson, Jack, Orlando	.221	25	77	68	3	15	15	0	0	0	4	0	1	1	7	0	11	1	3	1	.221	.299
Johnson, Matt, Knoxville	.181	57	170	144	8	26	30	4	0	0	11	2	2	5	17	0	32	1	1	5	.208	.286
Kaufman, Brad, Memphis	.083	28	27	24	4	2	3	1	0	0	1	2	0	0	1	0	12	0	0	0	.125	.120
Keagle, Greg, Memphis	.143	15	9	7	2	1	1	0	0	0	0	1	0	0	1	0	0	0	0	0	.143	.250
Kelly, Pat, Knoxville	.242	47	180	161	22	39	53	6	1	2	14	5	0	1	13	1	30	1	1	1	.329	.303
Kendall, Jason, Carolina	.326	117	508	429	87	140	192	26	1	8	71	1	8	14	56	5	22	10	7	10	.448	.414
Kessinger, Keith, Orlando†	.258	18	71	62	8	16	21	5	0	0	5	2	0	1	6	0	3	0	0	1	.339	.333
Kilgo, Rusty, Chattanooga*	.000	54	2	2	0	0	0	0	0	0	0	0	0	0	0	0	1	0	0	0	.000	.000
Killeen, Tim, Memphis*	.235	77	258	230	27	54	95	14	0	9	40	0	1	0	27	6	71	2	0	5	.413	.314
Kimsey, Keith, Jacksonville	.161	34	128	118	8	19	28	4	1	1	10	0	1	2	7	0	39	1	1	6	.237	.219
Kingston, Mark, Orlando†	.266	66	226	199	17	53	81	13	0	5	24	2	2	1	22	5	41	0	1	4	.407	.339
Klesko, Ryan, Greenville*	.231	4	15	13	1	3	6	0	0	1	4	0	0	0	2	0	1	0	0	1	.462	.333
Koehler, Jim, Port City*	.000	2	2	2	0	0	0	0	0	0	0	0	0	0	0	0	1	0	0	0	.000	.000
Koelling, Brian, Chattanooga	.296	107	486	432	71	128	172	21	7	3	44	8	3	3	40	1	63	30	12	9	.398	.358
Koller, Jerry, Greenville	.200	25	27	25	0	5	5	0	0	0	1	2	0	0	0	0	6	0	0	1	.200	.200
Kopriva, Dan, Chattanooga	.281	51	138	121	14	34	45	8	0	1	11	2	0	2	11	0	14	1	1	5	.372	.351
Kramer, Tommy, Chattanooga†	.294	21	19	17	0	5	6	1	0	0	2	1	0	0	1	0	1	0	0	2	.353	.333
Kremblas, Frank, Chattanooga	.149	19	77	67	8	10	15	2	0	1	6	0	2	1	7	0	10	1	1	2	.224	.234

Player, Team	Avg.	G	TPA	AB	R	H	TB	2B	3B	HR	RBI	SH	SF	HP	BB	IBB	SO	SB	CS	GDP	Slg.	OBP
Krevokuch, Jim, Carolina	.282	70	197	174	20	49	65	13	0	1	11	4	2	5	12	1	20	1	1	6	.374	.342
Kroon, Marc, Memphis†	.000	22	15	13	1	0	0	0	0	0	1	1	0	0	1	0	4	0	0	0	.000	.071
Ladd, Jeff, Knoxville	.292	9	31	24	1	7	10	1	1	0	2	1	0	1	5	0	8	0	0	0	.417	.433
Ladell, Cleveland, Chattanooga	.292	135	565	517	76	151	208	28	7	5	43	4	2	2	39	1	88	28	15	12	.402	.343
LaRocca, Greg, Memphis	.143	2	7	7	0	1	1	0	0	0	0	0	0	0	0	0	1	0	1	1	.143	.143
Larregui, Ed, Orlando	.300	122	460	423	55	127	180	18	1	11	60	0	4	1	32	2	39	3	10	15	.426	.348
Lawrence, Sean, Carolina*	.000	12	1	1	0	0	0	0	0	0	0	0	0	0	0	0	1	0	0	0	.000	.000
Leary, Rob, Carolina*	.305	67	289	243	38	74	112	14	3	6	42	0	3	3	40	2	38	3	3	7	.461	.405
Lee, Derrek, Memphis	.111	2	9	9	0	1	1	0	0	0	1	0	0	0	0	0	2	0	0	0	.111	.111
Leiper, Tim, Jacksonville*	.259	110	435	375	60	97	142	19	1	8	46	3	6	3	48	6	30	3	3	11	.379	.343
Lesher, Brian, Huntsville	.261	127	538	471	78	123	207	23	2	19	71	0	1	2	64	2	110	7	8	7	.439	.351
Lidle, Kevin, Jacksonville	.163	36	82	80	12	13	23	7	0	1	5	1	0	0	1	0	31	1	0	1	.288	.173
Loiselle, Rich, Memphis	.125	13	9	8	1	1	2	1	0	0	1	0	0	0	1	0	3	0	0	0	.250	.222
Long, Joey, Memphis	.000	25	2	2	0	0	0	0	0	0	0	0	0	0	0	0	1	0	0	1	.000	.000
Luebbers, Larry, Chattanooga	.333	30	25	21	2	7	9	2	0	0	4	2	0	0	2	0	1	0	0	0	.429	.391
Lutz, Brent, Knoxville	.132	52	167	144	14	19	31	6	0	2	12	2	0	6	15	0	59	4	1	1	.215	.242
Mack, Quinn, Memphis*	.238	20	74	63	6	15	22	1	0	2	6	1	0	2	8	1	8	2	1	1	.349	.342
Madsen, Dan, Orlando†	.192	15	32	26	6	5	7	0	1	0	6	0	0	0	6	0	2	0	1	0	.269	.344
Magdaleno, Ricky, Chattanooga	.175	11	44	40	2	7	12	2	0	1	2	0	0	0	4	0	13	0	0	3	.300	.250
Malloy, Marty, Greenville*	.278	124	515	461	73	128	184	20	3	10	59	7	8	0	39	1	58	11	12	6	.399	.329
Manahan, Austin, Orlando†	.212	94	280	260	34	55	76	12	0	3	19	2	0	2	16	0	57	13	6	9	.292	.263
Manning, Henry, Birmingham	.300	11	34	30	3	9	16	1	0	2	11	0	3	0	1	0	6	0	0	1	.533	.294
Martinez, Angel, Knoxville*	.229	41	152	144	14	33	49	8	1	2	22	0	2	0	6	0	34	0	1	2	.340	.257
Martinez, Pablo, Greenville†	.255	120	510	462	70	118	163	22	4	5	29	8	1	2	37	0	89	12	12	7	.353	.314
Mashore, Justin, Jacksonville	.243	40	160	148	26	36	60	8	2	4	15	3	0	3	6	0	41	5	1	2	.405	.287
Mattson, Rob, Memphis*	.235	33	35	34	3	8	9	1	0	0	4	1	0	0	0	0	9	2	0	0	.265	.235
May, Darrell, Greenville*	.167	15	6	6	0	1	1	0	0	0	0	0	0	0	0	0	3	0	0	0	.167	.167
Meier, Kevin, Orlando	.167	11	7	6	0	1	2	1	0	0	1	0	0	0	1	0	2	0	0	0	.333	.286
Merchant, Mark, Chattanooga†	.208	25	60	53	4	11	14	0	0	1	6	0	0	0	7	1	15	0	0	4	.264	.300
Molina, Izzy, Huntsville	.259	83	337	301	38	78	120	16	1	8	26	0	2	8	26	0	62	3	4	6	.399	.332
Moore, Marcus, Chattanooga†	.000	36	3	3	0	0	0	0	0	0	0	0	0	0	0	0	3	0	0	0	.000	.000
Morales, Francisco, Orlando	.167	2	7	6	0	1	1	0	0	0	0	0	0	0	1	0	2	0	0	0	.167	.286
Morel, Ramon, Carolina	.000	10	12	12	1	0	0	0	0	0	0	0	0	0	0	0	2	0	0	0	.000	.000
Morland, Mike, Knoxville	.179	11	29	28	6	5	6	1	0	0	1	0	0	0	1	0	4	0	0	1	.214	.207
Mota, Domingo, Chattanooga	.000	5	6	6	0	0	0	0	0	0	0	0	0	0	0	0	1	0	0	1	.000	.000
Mottola, Chad, Chattanooga	.293	51	196	181	32	53	98	13	1	10	39	0	1	1	13	0	32	1	2	2	.541	.342
Moultrie, Pat, Knoxville*	.255	13	60	51	3	13	13	0	0	0	7	4	1	0	4	1	6	2	1	0	.255	.304
Munoz, Omer, Carolina	.265	67	249	234	29	62	80	10	1	2	25	5	2	3	5	0	23	2	0	7	.342	.287
Murray, Heath, Memphis*	.500	14	8	6	0	3	3	0	0	0	1	0	0	0	2	0	1	0	0	0	.500	.500
Murray, Matt, Greenville*	.250	5	4	4	0	1	1	0	0	0	0	0	0	0	0	0	0	0	0	0	.250	.250
Neill, Mike, Huntsville*	.299	33	120	107	11	32	46	6	1	2	16	0	1	0	12	1	29	1	0	1	.430	.367
Nitkowski, C.J., Chattanooga*	.000	8	8	7	1	0	0	0	0	0	0	1	0	0	0	0	4	0	0	0	.000	.000
Nix, Jim, Chattanooga	.000	40	5	5	0	0	0	0	0	0	0	0	0	0	0	0	1	0	0	0	.000	.000
Noriega, Rey, Birmingham†	.190	42	114	100	9	19	24	5	0	0	5	2	0	1	11	0	27	1	2	3	.240	.277
Norton, Greg, Birmingham†	.249	133	551	469	65	117	162	23	2	6	60	3	10	5	64	7	90	19	12	10	.345	.339
Nunez, Ramon, Greenville	.261	81	262	241	34	63	109	15	2	9	34	0	3	3	15	0	63	1	1	8	.452	.309
Olmeda, Jose, Greenville†	.250	31	115	108	16	27	46	5	1	4	10	0	0	7	0	0	18	1	0	4	.426	.296
Ortiz, Hector, Orlando	.234	96	325	299	13	70	82	12	0	0	18	1	4	1	20	0	39	0	5	10	.274	.281
Paige, Carey, Greenville	.167	7	6	6	0	1	2	1	0	0	0	0	0	0	0	0	2	0	0	0	.333	.167
Parris, Steve, Carolina	.083	14	15	12	1	1	1	0	0	0	0	3	0	0	0	0	3	0	0	0	.083	.083
Pearson, Eddie, Birmingham*	.224	50	211	201	20	45	64	13	0	2	25	0	2	1	7	0	36	1	0	9	.318	.251
Pecorilli, Aldo, Greenville	.385	70	298	265	51	102	144	17	2	7	42	1	4	6	22	2	39	2	8	4	.543	.438
Peguero, Julio, Port City†	.316	71	278	256	42	81	107	15	1	3	18	4	1	1	16	1	34	12	8	3	.418	.358
Perona, Joe, Jacksonville	.147	13	37	34	2	5	8	3	0	0	3	0	1	0	2	0	5	0	0	2	.235	.189
Peters, Chris, Carolina*	.000	2	3	2	0	0	0	0	0	0	0	1	0	0	0	0	1	0	0	0	.000	.000
Petersen, Chris, Orlando	.212	125	439	382	48	81	109	10	3	4	36	5	3	4	45	3	97	7	3	14	.285	.300
Petersen, Matt, Orlando	.154	24	14	13	1	2	2	0	0	0	0	1	0	0	0	0	3	0	0	0	.154	.154
Peterson, Charles, Carolina	.329	20	82	70	13	23	28	3	1	0	7	0	1	2	9	1	15	2	1	1	.400	.415
Pevey, Marty, Jacksonville*	.259	20	66	58	2	15	20	2	0	1	7	2	2	0	4	0	17	0	2	4	.345	.297
Pickett, Ricky, Chattanooga*	1.000	40	1	1	0	1	1	0	0	0	0	1	0	0	0	0	0	0	0	0	1.000	1.000
Pisciotta, Marc, Carolina	.000	56	2	2	0	0	0	0	0	0	0	0	0	0	0	0	0	0	0	0	.000	.000
Poe, Charles, Birmingham	.283	120	500	427	75	121	192	28	2	13	60	7	5	10	51	4	79	19	4	7	.450	.369
Polcovich, Kevin, Carolina	.317	64	244	221	27	70	87	8	0	3	18	3	1	5	14	1	29	10	5	3	.394	.369
Pratte, Evan, Jacksonville†	.250	18	61	52	2	13	15	2	0	0	1	0	0	2	7	3	9	0	3	2	.288	.361
Rackley, Keifer, Port City*	.256	114	484	430	55	110	149	17	2	6	40	6	5	4	39	2	96	8	4	11	.347	.320
Ralph, Curtis, Carolina	.000	18	1	1	0	0	0	0	0	0	0	0	0	0	0	0	1	0	0	0	.000	.000
Ramirez, Roberto, Port City	.278	129	540	490	67	136	223	24	6	17	82	3	6	6	35	4	98	11	10	14	.455	.330
Ratliff, Daryl, Carolina	.286	16	73	63	10	18	25	4	0	1	5	2	0	0	8	1	10	2	1	1	.397	.366
Ratliff, Jon, Orlando	.043	26	25	23	1	1	1	0	0	0	0	2	0	0	0	0	8	0	0	0	.043	.043
Relaford, Desmond, Port City†	.287	90	397	352	51	101	137	11	2	7	27	2	0	2	41	2	58	25	9	4	.389	.365
Rendina, Mike, Jacksonville*	.224	31	106	98	12	22	36	5	0	3	16	0	0	7	2	0	20	0	0	3	.367	.276
Rice, Lance, Jacksonville†	.123	65	167	154	8	19	31	1	1	3	11	2	0	0	11	0	23	0	0	5	.201	.182
Ripplemeyer, Brad, Greenville	.182	53	183	165	8	30	44	8	0	2	16	5	2	0	11	0	54	1	0	5	.267	.230
Rivera, Roberto, Orlando*	.400	50	6	5	1	2	6	1	0	1	4	1	0	0	0	0	0	0	0	0	1.200	.400
Roberts, Lonell, Knoxville†	.236	116	492	454	66	107	128	12	3	1	29	4	4	3	27	1	97	57	18	7	.282	.281
Robinson, Don, Greenville*	.214	13	34	28	2	6	9	1	1	0	3	1	1	0	4	0	4	1	0	0	.321	.303
Rodarte, Raul, Carolina	.370	16	66	54	8	20	27	5	1	0	11	2	0	0	10	3	14	2	2	2	.500	.469
Rohrmeier, Dan, Chattanooga	.326	118	482	426	77	139	221	31	0	17	76	1	7	7	41	5	63	0	1	9	.519	.389
Rose, Pete, Birmingham*	.385	5	16	13	1	5	6	1	0	0	2	0	0	0	3	0	3	0	0	0	.462	.500
Ruebel, Matt, Carolina*	.130	27	25	23	1	3	3	0	0	0	1	1	0	0	1	0	10	0	0	0	.130	.167
Rumfield, Toby, Chattanooga	.264	92	310	273	32	72	110	12	1	8	53	3	5	3	26	2	47	0	3	14	.403	.329
Russo, Paul, Memphis	.311	45	145	122	19	38	67	9	1	6	18	0	0	1	22	1	33	1	0	3	.549	.421
Ryan, Matt, Carolina	.000	44	1	1	0	0	0	0	0	0	0	0	0	0	0	0	0	0	0	0	.000	.000

Player, Team	Avg.	G	TPA	AB	R	H	TB	2B	3B	HR	RBI	SH	SF	HP	BB	IBB	SO	SB	CS	GDP	Slg.	OBP
Rychel, Kevin, Carolina.............	.000	40	4	3	0	0	0	0	0	0	0	1	0	0	0	0	1	0	0	0	.000	.000
Samuels, Scott, Orlando*.........	.286	5	24	21	3	6	10	1	0	1	4	0	0	0	3	0	4	2	0	0	.476	.375
Sanchez, Yuri, Jacksonville*....	.213	121	396	342	52	73	113	8	7	6	26	15	0	1	38	0	116	15	6	3	.330	.294
Sanders, Deion, Chattanooga*...	.571	2	7	7	1	4	7	0	0	1	2	0	0	0	0	0	1	1	0	0	1.000	.571
Sanford, Chance, Carolina*.......	.278	16	42	36	6	10	24	3	1	3	10	0	0	1	5	1	7	3	1	0	.667	.381
Santana, Ruben, Chattanooga.....	.293	142	625	556	89	163	239	23	10	11	79	6	5	8	50	5	77	2	5	17	.430	.357
Saunders, Doug, Port City.........	.263	28	128	114	13	30	53	9	1	4	16	0	2	2	10	1	28	2	0	4	.465	.328
Sawkiw, Warren, Knoxville†	.248	44	138	121	11	30	39	4	1	1	11	3	1	0	13	0	36	2	2	2	.322	.319
Schmitt, Todd, Memphis	.000	26	1	1	0	0	0	0	0	0	0	0	0	0	0	0	0	0	0	0	.000	.000
Schutz, Carl, Greenville*	1.000	51	1	1	0	1	1	0	0	0	0	0	0	0	0	0	0	0	0	0	1.000	1.000
Schwenke, Matt, Memphis	.242	23	69	62	7	15	18	3	0	0	4	1	1	1	3	0	16	0	0	0	.290	.284
Seelbach, Chris, Greenville........	.200	9	12	10	0	2	2	0	0	0	0	1	0	0	1	0	2	0	0	0	.200	.273
Sellers, Rick, Chattanooga	.238	89	337	281	40	67	110	13	3	8	41	2	4	5	45	3	66	2	1	8	.391	.349
Sheldon, Scott, Huntsville..........	.217	66	263	235	25	51	77	10	2	4	15	3	1	1	23	0	60	5	0	7	.328	.283
Shouse, Brian, Carolina*...........	.250	22	20	16	2	4	5	1	0	0	1	4	0	0	0	0	3	0	1	0	.313	.250
Simmons, John, Greenville*	.250	48	5	4	0	1	1	0	0	0	0	0	0	0	1	0	0	0	0	0	.250	.400
Slaught, Don, Carolina	.250	3	12	12	1	3	4	1	0	0	1	0	0	0	0	0	3	0	0	0	.333	.250
Smith, Ira, Memphis..................	.303	64	267	238	40	72	106	13	3	5	36	0	3	2	23	0	32	11	4	6	.445	.365
Smith, Ottis, Orlando................	.364	17	15	11	4	4	7	1	1	0	3	0	0	1	0	1	0	0	0	0	.636	.417
Smith, Robert, Greenville	.261	127	496	444	75	116	191	27	3	14	58	4	1	7	40	2	109	12	6	12	.430	.331
Snyder, Jared, Orlando	.500	1	4	4	2	2	2	0	0	0	0	0	0	0	0	0	0	0	0	0	.500	.500
Sobolewski, Mark, Huntsville	.205	83	340	307	35	63	100	14	1	7	34	2	1	8	22	1	62	2	1	11	.326	.275
Sparks, Greg, Greenville*..........	.214	65	168	145	15	31	52	6	0	5	21	2	2	2	17	1	41	0	0	3	.359	.301
Spiezio, Scott, Huntsville†.........	.282	141	616	528	78	149	237	33	8	13	86	2	14	4	67	2	78	10	3	10	.449	.359
Stewart, Shannon, Knoxville	.287	138	601	498	89	143	194	24	6	5	55	3	5	6	89	3	61	42	16	13	.390	.398
Sutherland, Alex, Port City	.205	13	49	44	1	9	12	3	0	0	3	0	0	0	5	0	7	1	0	3	.273	.286
Swann, Pedro, Greenville*.........	.324	102	390	339	57	110	171	24	2	11	64	0	3	3	45	2	63	14	11	8	.504	.405
Swartzbaugh, Dave, Orlando	.000	16	2	2	0	0	0	0	0	0	0	0	0	0	0	0	0	0	0	0	.000	.000
Telemaco, Amaury, Orlando	.250	22	17	16	2	4	4	0	0	0	1	0	0	0	0	0	3	0	0	0	.250	.250
Thomas, Keith, Memphis†...........	.253	109	378	356	66	90	141	13	4	10	33	1	0	1	20	0	85	43	11	6	.396	.294
Thompson, Jason, Memphis*......	.272	137	542	475	62	129	211	20	1	20	64	0	5	0	62	4	131	7	3	7	.444	.352
Tolar, Kevin, Carolina................	1.000	12	1	1	0	1	1	0	0	0	1	0	0	0	0	0	0	0	0	0	1.000	1.000
Torres, Paul, Orlando...............	.298	63	262	228	38	68	114	14	1	10	45	0	2	1	29	4	40	0	3	1	.500	.377
Tranbarger, Mark, Chattanooga*...	.000	48	2	2	0	0	0	0	0	0	0	0	0	0	0	0	1	0	0	0	.000	.000
Tredaway, Chad, Memphis†........	.267	10	33	30	5	8	9	1	0	0	4	0	0	3	1	0	5	1	0	0	.300	.333
Triessl, Mike, Memphis	.167	4	6	6	0	1	1	0	0	0	0	0	0	0	0	0	0	0	0	0	.167	.167
Tsamis, George, Car.-P.C.	.000	19	1	0	0	0	0	0	0	0	0	0	0	0	1	0	0	0	0	0	.000	1.000
Turnier, Aaron, Greenville*	.000	8	1	1	0	0	0	0	0	0	0	0	0	0	0	0	0	0	0	0	.000	.000
Tuttle, Dave, Chattanooga.........	.000	8	4	2	0	0	0	0	0	0	0	1	2	0	0	0	1	0	0	0	.000	.000
Valdes, Pedro, Orlando*...........	.300	114	474	426	57	128	183	28	3	7	68	0	6	5	37	3	77	3	6	7	.430	.359
VanRyn, Ben, Chattanooga*.......	.500	5	2	2	1	1	2	1	0	0	2	0	0	0	0	0	1	0	0	0	1.000	.500
Varitek, Jason, Port City†..........	.224	104	421	352	42	79	127	14	2	10	44	3	3	2	61	4	126	0	1	8	.361	.340
Vasquez, Chris, Chattanooga*....	.400	7	17	15	3	6	10	1	0	1	1	0	0	0	2	0	3	0	0	0	.667	.471
Vasquez, Marcos, Chattanooga...	.158	27	20	19	2	3	3	0	0	0	1	1	0	0	0	0	6	0	0	0	.158	.158
Velandia, Jorge, Memphis	.204	63	203	186	23	38	64	10	2	4	17	1	1	1	14	2	37	0	2	4	.344	.262
Viera, Jose, Orlando.................	.121	12	36	33	2	4	7	0	0	1	2	0	0	1	2	0	8	0	0	2	.212	.194
Vinas, Julio, Birmingham	.269	102	421	372	47	100	138	16	2	6	61	0	7	5	37	1	80	3	3	6	.371	.337
Vollmer, Scott, Birmingham	.236	81	309	258	35	61	84	5	0	6	39	4	4	1	42	1	39	0	1	5	.326	.341
Waggoner, Jim, Huntsville*.........	.200	51	149	110	18	22	29	5	1	0	15	3	0	2	34	0	29	1	2	1	.264	.397
Walker, Dane, Huntsville*...........	.232	110	436	370	46	86	109	13	2	2	35	2	3	2	57	6	84	9	7	9	.295	.336
Warner, Mike, Greenville*..........	.237	53	225	173	31	41	53	12	0	0	7	2	2	1	47	0	36	12	4	1	.306	.399
Watkins, Pat, Chattanooga	.291	105	398	358	57	104	170	26	2	12	57	0	4	3	33	4	53	5	5	7	.475	.352
White, Jason, Huntsville.............	.234	48	196	167	20	39	69	4	1	8	27	0	3	2	24	2	49	2	1	3	.413	.332
Wilkins, Marc, Carolina	.000	37	7	5	0	0	0	0	0	0	0	1	1	0	1	0	4	0	0	1	.000	.167
Williams, Juan, Greenville*	.313	62	214	192	40	60	123	14	2	15	39	0	3	0	19	3	44	4	3	5	.641	.369
Wilson, Brandon, Chattanooga....	.328	75	343	308	56	101	159	29	1	9	50	2	2	3	28	0	52	12	6	7	.516	.387
Wilson, Craig, Birmingham	.289	132	531	471	56	136	169	19	1	4	46	10	2	5	43	0	44	2	2	21	.359	.353
Wolfe, Joel, Huntsville...............	.256	108	466	399	58	102	157	15	2	12	41	6	2	5	54	4	75	23	12	5	.393	.350
Wollenburg, Doug, Greenville	.191	66	180	162	22	31	39	5	0	1	12	1	1	3	13	2	31	4	3	6	.241	.263
Womack, Tony, Carolina*..........	.256	82	364	332	52	85	105	9	4	1	19	11	0	2	19	2	36	27	10	2	.316	.300
Wooten, Shawn, Jacksonville......	.129	20	73	70	4	9	16	1	0	2	7	0	1	1	1	0	17	0	0	3	.229	.151

GRAND SLAMS: Cameron, 3; Danapilis, Killeen, Rohrmeier, Thompson, 2 each; Austin, Barker, Butler, Canale, Coolbaugh, Cooper, Cruz, Diaz, Dismuke, Gennaro, Gubanich, Hart, Hickey, Hollins, Kendall, Larregui, C. Petersen, Ramirez, Rendina, Rivera, Santana, Sellers, Spiezio, Swann, Watkins, Williams, 1 each.

AWARDED FIRST BASE ON CATCHER'S INTERFERENCE: Griffey 5 (Erdman, Kendall, Lutz, Molina, Ortiz); Casanova 3 (Brooks, Harmes, Pecorilli); Hurst 2 (Beard, Harmes); Kopriva 2 (A. Martinez 2); Torres 2 (Cardenas, Varitek); Walker 2 (A. Brown, Cox); Briggs (Vollmer); Bush (Pecorilli); F. Gomez (Perona); Hickey (Kendall); Ladell (Lidle); Rendina (Kendall); Schwenke (Vollmer); I. Smith (Pecorilli); Spiezio (Cox).

PLAYERS WITH TWO OR MORE TEAMS

Player, Team	Avg.	G	TPA	AB	R	H	TB	2B	3B	HR	RBI	SH	SF	HP	BB	IBB	SO	SB	CS	GDP	Slg.	OBP
Tsamis, George, Carolina..........	.000	12	1	0	0	0	0	0	0	0	0	0	0	0	1	0	0	0	0	0	.000	1.000
Tsamis, George, Port City........	.000	7	0	0	0	0	0	0	0	0	0	0	0	0	0	0	0	0	0	0	.000	.000

TEAM

Team	W	L	Pct.	ERA	G	CG	ShO	Sv.	IP	H	TBF	R	ER	HR	SH	SF	HB	BB	IBB	SO	WP	Bk.
Orlando	76	67	.531	3.41	143	6	14	43	1257.2	1174	5274	563	477	113	44	41	66	413	54	892	64	11
Carolina	89	55	.618	3.48	144	7	14	44	1322.1	1267	5603	611	511	86	57	34	63	418	40	979	71	5
Port City	62	80	.437	3.62	142	5	6	27	1264.0	1179	5382	617	508	89	52	33	78	475	18	989	79	13
Birmingham	80	64	.556	3.73	144	8	9	35	1248.1	1208	5282	599	517	94	36	44	39	413	18	962	67	10
Jacksonville	75	69	.521	3.73	144	13	8	36	1286.2	1303	5476	621	533	112	43	32	41	476	28	854	60	10
Chattanooga	83	60	.580	3.78	143	4	9	44	1258.1	1239	5439	633	528	85	60	49	39	488	29	1033	60	8
Huntsville	70	74	.486	4.03	144	1	7	39	1249.0	1230	5299	637	559	102	57	30	42	433	36	865	82	8
Memphis	68	74	.479	4.32	142	15	5	32	1236.0	1191	5513	704	593	103	31	43	88	652	51	1058	101	13
Greenville	59	83	.415	4.65	142	7	4	34	1234.2	1303	5401	726	638	134	52	46	44	477	35	819	66	8
Knoxville	54	90	.375	4.76	144	6	12	32	1222.1	1249	5350	761	646	114	39	54	37	508	12	919	84	7

INDIVIDUAL

TOP QUALIFIERS FOR EARNED-RUN AVERAGE TITLE

Minimum 115 innings. *Lefthanded pitcher.

Pitcher, Team	W	L	Pct.	ERA	G	GS	CG	ShO	GF	Sv.	IP	H	TBF	R	ER	HR	SH	SF	HB	BB	IBB	SO	WP	Bk.
Dessens, Elmer, Carolina	15	8	.652	2.49	27	27	1	0	0	0	152.0	170	638	62	42	10	11	4	3	21	3	68	7	2
Sodowsky, Clint, Jacksonville	5	5	.500	2.55	19	19	5	3	0	0	123.2	102	497	46	35	4	2	2	5	50	1	77	3	0
Miller, Trever, Jacksonville*	8	2	.800	2.72	31	16	3	2	4	0	122.1	122	512	46	37	5	4	2	5	34	0	77	1	0
Ruebel, Matt, Carolina*	13	5	.722	2.76	27	27	4	3	0	0	169.1	150	699	68	52	7	4	7	7	45	1	136	7	1
Wagner, Matt, Port City	5	8	.385	2.82	23	23	0	0	0	0	137.0	121	566	57	43	9	3	4	4	33	1	111	5	1
Andujar, Luis, Birmingham	14	8	.636	2.85	27	27	2	1	0	0	167.1	147	689	64	53	10	1	5	7	44	0	146	3	1
Telemaco, Amaury, Orlando	8	8	.500	3.29	22	22	3	1	0	0	147.2	112	587	60	54	13	8	3	4	42	3	151	7	1
Kramer, Tommy, Chattanooga	12	1	.923	3.33	21	18	2	0	1	0	127.0	117	513	54	47	8	5	5	2	28	4	126	4	0
Ratliff, Jon, Orlando	10	5	.667	3.47	26	25	1	1	1	0	140.0	143	599	67	54	9	2	8	10	42	1	94	13	0
Kroon, Marc, Memphis	7	5	.583	3.51	22	19	0	0	2	2	115.1	90	497	49	45	12	2	2	6	61	1	123	16	1
Fernandez, Osvaldo, Port City*	12	7	.632	3.57	27	26	0	0	0	0	156.1	139	654	78	62	6	4	1	5	60	1	160	12	1
Chouinard, Bobby, Huntsville	14	8	.636	3.62	29	29	1	1	0	0	166.2	155	694	81	67	10	9	1	4	50	5	106	4	0
Vasquez, Marcos, Chattanooga	7	6	.538	3.68	26	18	0	0	1	1	120.0	125	531	63	49	12	6	5	4	46	1	80	5	1
Moore, Tim, Birmingham	7	5	.583	3.68	29	19	0	0	3	0	120.0	118	521	58	49	10	7	6	4	40	1	78	6	2
Thompson, Justin, Jacksonville*	6	7	.462	3.73	18	18	3	0	0	0	110.0	102	502	55	51	7	4	2	3	38	2	98	3	0

DEPARTMENTAL LEADERS: W—Dessens, 15; L—Mattson, 13; Pct.—Kramer, .923; G—Kelly, 66; GS—Chouinard, 29; CG—Mattson, 11; ShO—Mattson, Ruebel, Sodowsky, 3; GF—Kelly, 58; Sv.—Kelly, Kilgo, 29; IP—Mattson, 201.2; H—Mattson, 199; TBF—Mattson, 862; R—Kaufman, 112; ER—Mi. Hostetler, Kaufman, 95; HR—Mi. Hostetler, 24; SH—Dessens, Franklin, 11; SF—Mattson, 15; HB—Mattson, 20; BB—Kaufman, 90; IBB—Veras, 11; SO—Fernandez, 160; WP—Beckett, 19; Bk.—Drumright, 5.

ALL PITCHERS

*Lefthanded pitcher.

Pitcher, Team	W	L	Pct.	ERA	G	GS	CG	ShO	GF	Sv.	IP	H	TBF	R	ER	HR	SH	SF	HB	BB	IBB	SO	WP	Bk.
Abbott, Todd, Huntsville	0	0	.000	4.05	4	0	0	0	1	0	6.2	6	28	3	3	1	1	0	0	3	0	4	1	0
Adam, Dave, Port City	6	10	.375	4.34	31	13	0	0	9	0	112.0	107	492	58	54	10	4	0	11	48	1	85	5	1
Adams, Terry, Orlando	2	3	.400	1.43	37	0	0	0	30	19	37.2	23	149	9	6	2	0	1	2	16	1	26	4	1
Adams, Willie, Huntsville	6	5	.545	3.01	13	13	0	0	0	0	80.2	75	330	33	27	8	2	1	2	17	0	72	1	0
Aldred, Scott, Jacksonville*	1	0	1.000	0.00	2	2	0	0	0	0	12.0	9	42	0	0	0	0	0	0	1	0	11	0	0
Almanzar, Carlos, Knoxville	3	12	.200	3.99	35	19	0	0	7	2	126.1	144	546	77	56	10	3	6	3	32	1	93	4	1
Andujar, Luis, Birmingham	14	8	.636	2.85	27	27	2	1	0	0	167.1	147	689	64	53	10	1	5	7	44	0	146	3	1
Apana, Matt, Port City	1	3	.250	4.32	6	6	0	0	0	0	33.1	34	154	24	16	4	1	0	2	24	1	28	2	0
Arnold, Jamie, Greenville	1	5	.167	6.35	10	10	0	0	0	0	56.2	76	266	42	40	8	0	2	7	25	1	19	6	0
Backlund, Brett, Carolina	5	6	.455	3.58	22	14	0	0	1	0	93.0	81	388	46	37	10	4	3	5	35	2	80	2	0
Baker, Jared, Memphis	1	0	1.000	14.73	4	0	0	0	1	0	7.1	10	39	12	12	1	0	1	0	8	0	6	1	0
Banks, Jim, Huntsville	3	2	.600	4.73	44	1	0	0	19	2	66.2	72	305	39	35	5	3	4	3	40	3	52	7	0
Barnes, Jon, Memphis	0	1	.000	3.24	2	1	0	0	0	0	8.1	9	34	3	3	0	0	0	2	0	2	1	0	
Bauer, Matt, Jacksonville*	1	1	.500	4.12	27	0	0	0	7	0	43.2	43	195	22	20	8	2	2	2	21	1	30	1	0
Beard, Garrett, Huntsville	0	0	.000	0.00	1	0	0	0	0	0	3.0	3	13	0	0	0	0	0	0	1	0	1	0	0
Beatty, Blaine, Chattanooga*	3	2	.600	3.46	8	8	1	0	0	0	52.0	60	220	22	20	2	3	3	1	17	2	34	2	1
Beckett, Robbie, Memphis*	3	4	.429	4.80	36	8	2	1	11	0	86.1	65	400	57	46	3	2	10	13	74	4	98	19	0
Beltran, Alonso, Knoxville	3	6	.333	5.69	28	6	0	0	7	1	87.0	111	399	60	55	8	3	4	5	32	0	54	6	2
Bene, Bill, Chattanooga	0	0	.000	13.50	4	0	0	0	1	0	4.0	7	27	6	6	2	0	0	0	9	0	4	1	0
Bennett, Bob, Huntsville	10	7	.588	4.22	23	21	0	0	0	0	117.1	119	482	62	55	13	4	3	3	28	0	70	3	1
Bennett, Chris, Carolina	0	1	.000	6.67	18	0	0	0	5	1	27.0	42	128	22	20	2	2	2	2	13	2	13	0	0
Berlin, Mike, Jacksonville*	0	0	.000	2.45	3	0	0	0	1	0	3.2	3	14	1	1	0	0	0	0	1	1	1	0	0
Bertotti, Mike, Birmingham*	2	7	.222	5.00	12	12	1	0	0	0	63.0	60	279	38	35	4	0	2	4	36	0	53	8	0
Blair, Dirk, Greenville	2	2	.500	4.21	40	0	0	0	19	2	62.0	69	261	29	29	7	3	0	3	11	2	38	1	0
Bradford, Troy, Greenville	1	1	.500	4.91	4	0	0	0	0	0	22.0	22	92	13	12	3	1	0	1	9	0	9	0	0
Brandow, Derek, Knoxville	5	6	.455	4.29	25	21	1	0	1	0	107.0	95	466	60	51	13	1	8	6	50	1	106	9	0
Brown, Chad, Knoxville*	1	3	.250	4.57	40	0	0	0	14	1	41.1	38	181	23	21	2	1	1	1	22	1	35	5	0
Brumley, Duff, Chattanooga	5	1	.833	1.68	25	0	0	0	9	0	48.1	31	193	11	9	0	3	2	2	16	2	60	3	2
Buckley, Travis, Chattanooga	2	2	.333	7.53	3	3	0	0	0	0	14.1	21	69	12	12	4	0	1	1	5	0	10	1	0
Bullinger, Jim, Orlando	0	0	.000	0.00	1	1	0	0	0	0	4.0	3	16	0	0	0	0	0	0	1	0	2	0	0
Burgess, Kurt, Greenville*	1	1	.500	7.20	8	0	0	0	3	0	10.0	16	48	8	8	0	1	1	0	2	0	3	1	0
Burgos, John, Chattanooga*	3	5	.375	2.78	44	0	0	0	13	0	100.1	95	424	42	31	7	5	3	4	19	4	82	2	1
Burlingame, Ben, Orlando	9	2	.818	3.53	37	10	0	0	10	1	97.0	93	415	39	38	7	3	6	4	38	6	73	4	0
Carmona, Rafael, Port City	0	1	.000	1.80	15	0	0	0	15	4	15.0	11	59	5	3	0	1	1	1	3	0	17	2	0
Carpenter, Chris, Knoxville	3	7	.300	5.18	12	12	0	0	0	0	64.1	71	287	47	37	3	1	4	1	31	1	53	9	0
Cedeno, Blas, Jacksonville	3	2	.600	3.46	48	5	0	0	13	0	80.2	71	329	34	31	7	1	4	1	36	1	53	2	1
Chouinard, Bobby, Huntsville	14	8	.636	3.62	29	29	1	1	0	0	166.2	155	694	81	67	10	9	1	4	50	5	106	4	0

Pitcher, Team	W	L	Pct.	ERA	G	GS	CG	ShO	GF	Sv.	IP	H	TBF	R	ER	HR	SH	SF	HB	BB	IBB	SO	WP	Bk.
Christman, Scott, Birmingham*	2	5	.286	6.39	12	12	0	0	0	0	62.0	76	284	49	44	6	2	4	3	24	1	37	6	0
Clark, Dera, Memphis	2	2	.500	2.39	23	0	0	0	13	5	26.1	18	111	7	7	1	0	0	0	14	3	29	5	0
Cole, Victor, Memphis	1	0	1.000	1.35	8	2	0	0	3	0	20.0	15	81	5	3	0	0	0	0	8	1	17	0	0
Connolly, Matt, Orlando	3	4	.429	4.08	21	4	0	0	11	2	39.2	34	165	18	18	5	0	0	2	11	3	43	1	0
Connors, Chad, Chattanooga	0	1	.000	2.79	10	0	0	0	8	0	9.2	9	46	3	3	1	0	1	0	9	1	15	1	0
Cooke, Steve, Carolina*	0	0	.000	7.20	1	1	0	0	0	0	5.0	5	27	4	4	0	0	0	0	5	0	4	1	0
Cullop, Glen, Chattanooga	0	0	.000	7.90	8	0	0	0	3	0	13.2	15	63	13	12	1	1	2	0	7	1	8	0	0
Dabney, Fred, Orlando*	2	1	.667	2.08	13	0	0	0	4	1	17.1	13	78	9	4	0	2	0	2	10	4	9	1	1
D'Andrea, Mike, Greenville	3	6	.333	4.88	40	7	0	0	11	2	99.2	110	447	65	54	5	4	9	3	53	8	61	7	1
Davison, Scott, Port City	2	0	1.000	0.89	34	0	0	0	28	10	40.2	22	156	4	4	1	6	2	1	16	1	50	2	0
DeLeon, Luis, Orlando	0	1	.000	2.00	4	0	0	0	2	0	9.0	7	35	2	2	1	2	0	0	2	1	3	0	0
DeLeon, Roberto, Memphis	0	0	.000	7.71	2	0	0	0	2	0	2.1	3	11	2	2	1	0	0	0	2	0	3	0	0
DeLosSantos, Mariano, Carolina	1	0	1.000	3.62	21	0	0	0	3	0	27.1	28	122	16	11	5	1	0	2	14	3	20	1	0
Dessens, Elmer, Carolina	15	8	.652	2.49	27	27	1	0	0	0	152.0	170	638	62	42	10	11	4	3	21	3	68	7	2
Dibble, Rob, Birmingham	0	1	.000	7.36	8	0	0	0	1	1	7.1	4	32	6	6	0	1	0	1	5	0	15	2	0
Doman, Roger, Knoxville	0	3	.000	5.87	14	0	0	0	6	0	30.2	42	140	25	20	2	1	1	1	11	0	16	3	0
Dressendorfer, Kirk, Huntsville	0	1	.000	3.15	9	4	0	0	1	0	20.0	13	79	7	7	1	0	0	2	5	0	18	1	0
Dreyer, Darren, Orlando	1	3	.250	4.18	14	0	0	0	5	0	23.2	24	98	11	11	1	3	1	3	3	1	10	0	0
Drinkwater, Sean, Memphis	0	1	.000	18.00	1	0	0	0	1	0	1.0	2	6	2	2	1	0	0	0	1	0	0	0	0
Drumright, Mike, Jacksonville	0	1	.000	3.69	5	5	0	0	0	0	31.2	30	137	13	13	4	0	0	2	15	1	34	1	5
Etheridge, Roger, Greenville*	2	10	.167	5.67	32	16	1	0	6	0	101.2	120	462	73	64	10	4	5	3	52	1	47	8	1
Evans, Sean, Carolina	5	2	.714	5.33	29	2	0	0	10	0	49.0	47	218	35	29	1	0	1	3	25	1	44	5	0
Farmer, Howard, Chattanooga	0	1	.000	6.75	1	1	0	0	0	0	4.0	5	21	6	3	1	0	0	0	1	0	2	0	0
Fermin, Ramon, Huntsville	6	7	.462	3.86	32	13	0	0	16	7	100.1	105	435	53	43	5	6	1	6	45	5	58	6	1
Fernandez, Osvaldo, Port City*	12	7	.632	3.57	27	26	0	0	0	0	156.1	139	654	78	62	6	4	1	5	60	1	160	12	1
Ferry, Mike, Chattanooga	9	5	.643	3.77	24	24	1	0	0	0	155.0	191	660	75	65	8	10	6	5	23	1	74	3	0
Figueroa, Fernando, Carolina*	0	0	.000	3.38	6	0	0	0	1	0	8.0	12	37	5	3	2	0	0	0	2	0	4	1	0
Fitzer, Doug, Port City*	0	0	.000	5.40	4	0	0	0	1	0	5.0	3	20	4	3	1	0	0	0	1	0	4	0	0
Flynt, Bill, Carolina*	0	0	.000	0.00	4	0	0	0	1	0	3.2	3	16	0	0	0	1	0	0	2	0	6	0	0
Fordham, Tom, Birmingham*	6	3	.667	3.38	14	14	2	1	0	0	82.2	79	348	35	31	9	2	2	0	28	2	61	3	0
Fox, Chad, Chattanooga	4	5	.444	5.06	20	17	0	0	1	0	80.0	76	363	49	45	2	2	2	3	52	1	56	14	0
Franklin, Ryan, Port City	6	10	.375	4.32	31	20	1	1	2	0	146.0	153	627	84	70	13	11	3	12	43	4	102	6	2
Freeman, Chris, Knoxville	2	3	.400	5.42	39	5	0	0	16	8	81.1	78	354	53	49	12	5	5	1	38	0	80	1	0
Freitas, Mike, Memphis	0	6	.000	3.66	54	0	0	0	16	2	59.0	55	246	26	24	3	2	3	2	26	8	36	3	1
Gaillard, Eddie, Jacksonville	0	1	.000	5.63	8	0	0	0	2	0	8.0	11	42	5	5	0	2	1	0	5	1	4	0	0
Gajkowski, Steve, Birmingham	4	4	.500	4.18	35	0	0	0	14	2	51.2	64	230	27	24	4	2	0	2	16	1	29	1	0
Glinatsis, George, Port City	6	7	.462	5.30	18	18	1	0	0	0	93.1	104	427	63	55	6	2	4	13	44	1	68	7	1
Goldsmith, Gary, Jacksonville	4	7	.364	4.61	15	15	0	0	0	0	82.0	78	347	52	42	14	1	4	2	31	1	42	5	0
Gray, Dennis, Knoxville*	0	3	.000	6.34	24	0	0	0	10	0	32.2	29	143	25	23	2	2	0	1	20	0	22	5	0
Greene, Rick, Jacksonville	6	2	.750	3.49	32	0	0	0	6	0	38.2	45	177	19	15	3	1	0	3	15	2	29	0	0
Grigsby, Benji, Huntsville	3	5	.375	4.01	30	6	0	0	8	3	76.1	66	306	40	34	7	0	3	1	20	1	55	6	0
Grimm, John, Jacksonville	2	1	.667	8.62	13	0	0	0	5	0	15.2	23	82	17	15	5	0	0	1	10	0	9	0	0
Guilfoyle, Michael, Jacksonville*	5	1	.833	2.88	56	0	0	0	14	3	59.1	55	256	23	19	2	2	2	0	31	3	50	1	0
Gutierrez, Jim, Jacksonville	8	4	.667	2.76	45	1	0	0	14	4	58.2	60	243	22	18	2	3	2	0	25	4	36	3	0
Haas, David, Orlando	0	3	.000	4.97	3	3	0	0	0	0	12.2	18	69	10	7	1	0	0	3	10	0	4	1	0
Hanson, Craig, Memphis	0	3	.000	6.43	25	3	0	0	8	1	49.0	64	247	36	35	8	0	3	2	39	4	33	5	0
Harrah, Doug, Orlando	5	2	.714	1.94	44	0	0	0	21	5	69.2	58	296	21	15	6	4	1	5	34	6	49	4	0
Harrison, Brian, Memphis*	2	1	.667	3.25	38	0	0	0	7	0	36.0	32	170	21	13	0	1	0	4	33	2	29	4	0
Harrison, Tom, Greenville	6	4	.600	4.38	14	14	1	0	0	0	88.1	87	370	50	43	9	7	1	2	27	3	57	5	0
Hart, Jason, Orlando	0	1	.000	2.12	14	0	0	0	10	3	17.0	14	69	5	4	0	1	3	1	4	0	20	1	0
Haught, Gary, Huntsville	1	1	.500	4.30	9	3	0	0	3	0	23.0	23	97	14	11	4	1	0	1	8	1	20	0	0
Heble, Kurt, Knoxville	3	7	.300	6.02	47	0	0	0	25	6	52.1	52	231	36	35	7	0	1	1	24	0	44	6	1
Hernandez, Fernando, Memphis	4	6	.400	5.16	12	12	0	0	0	0	66.1	72	303	46	38	4	0	0	3	42	1	74	8	1
Hickey, Mike, Port City	0	1	.000	18.00	1	0	0	0	1	0	1.0	2	6	2	2	0	0	0	1	0	0	0	0	0
Hill, Milt, Carolina	2	2	.500	4.02	10	10	0	0	0	0	56.0	53	226	27	25	6	4	1	2	6	0	46	0	0
Hollinger, Adrian, Greenville	1	4	.200	4.63	7	6	1	0	0	0	44.2	43	196	26	23	2	0	4	1	20	1	28	2	1
Hollins, Stacy, Huntsville	3	8	.273	5.33	15	15	0	0	0	0	82.2	80	364	52	49	10	4	2	4	42	6	62	8	2
Hostetler, Marcus, Greenville	5	2	.714	4.12	33	0	0	0	19	2	43.2	47	199	30	20	6	4	3	2	21	2	24	3	0
Hostetler, Mike, Greenville	10	10	.500	5.26	28	28	0	0	0	0	162.2	182	711	102	95	24	8	4	6	46	4	93	6	1
Huber, Jeff, Memphis*	0	0	.000	11.57	5	0	0	0	0	0	4.2	7	22	6	6	2	0	0	1	0	0	6	0	0
Hurtado, Edwin, Knoxville	2	4	.333	4.45	11	11	0	0	0	0	54.2	54	240	34	27	7	1	4	0	25	0	38	4	0
Hutcheson, David, Orlando	8	10	.444	4.01	28	27	1	1	1	0	168.1	178	708	84	75	23	5	3	8	45	3	103	6	0
Ingram, Todd, Knoxville	1	1	.500	3.71	20	0	0	0	9	3	34.0	26	143	17	14	3	1	2	0	16	0	19	1	0
Jackson, Mike, Chattanooga	0	0	.000	0.00	3	2	0	0	0	0	3.0	2	11	0	0	0	0	0	0	0	0	2	0	0
Janzen, Marty, Knoxville	5	1	.833	2.63	7	7	2	1	0	0	48.0	35	188	14	14	2	0	2	1	14	0	44	1	1
Jersild, Aaron, Knoxville*	2	2	.500	5.98	14	5	0	0	4	0	40.2	47	184	28	27	6	1	0	1	21	1	29	2	1
Jimenez, Miguel, Huntsville	3	2	.600	3.60	6	6	0	0	0	0	30.0	25	124	12	12	3	1	0	0	11	0	28	1	0
Johnson, Barry, Birmingham	7	4	.636	1.85	47	0	0	0	10	0	78.0	64	308	21	16	1	2	1	2	15	1	53	2	1
Johnson, Chris, Orlando	5	4	.556	3.45	46	0	0	0	21	5	70.1	68	296	34	27	6	4	3	1	24	7	49	3	0
Johnston, Sean, Birmingham*	5	2	.714	4.21	34	13	0	0	8	0	98.1	120	432	53	46	6	2	2	2	36	0	44	2	1
Kaufman, Brad, Memphis	11	10	.524	5.76	27	27	0	0	0	0	148.1	142	676	112	95	17	6	5	14	90	4	119	10	0
Keagle, Greg, Memphis	4	9	.308	5.11	15	15	1	0	0	0	81.0	82	365	52	46	11	1	3	6	41	2	82	8	3
Kelley, Rich, Jacksonville*	1	0	1.000	4.50	7	0	0	0	1	0	6.0	9	24	3	3	1	1	1	0	0	0	2	0	1
Kelly, John, Jacksonville	7	7	.500	2.09	66	0	0	0	58	29	77.1	76	322	24	18	4	6	2	0	21	5	47	3	1
Kilgo, Rusty, Chattanooga*	8	2	.800	2.32	54	0	0	0	47	29	66.0	67	273	21	17	0	2	0	0	13	5	61	4	0
King, Kevin, Port City*	1	2	.333	3.77	20	0	0	0	6	0	31.0	35	136	15	13	2	1	1	3	11	1	19	4	1
Koller, Jerry, Greenville	9	12	.429	4.94	25	25	3	0	0	0	147.2	163	629	86	81	16	5	7	2	37	4	84	5	1
Konuszewski, Dennis, Carolina	7	7	.500	3.65	48	0	0	0	18	2	61.2	63	278	33	25	3	3	1	1	26	5	48	5	1
Kotes, Chris, Knoxville	3	9	.250	4.91	36	11	1	0	9	1	106.1	109	470	66	58	7	4	3	4	45	2	74	9	1
Kramer, Tommy, Chattanooga	12	1	.923	3.33	21	18	2	0	1	0	127.0	117	513	54	47	8	5	5	2	28	4	126	4	0
Kroon, Marc, Memphis	7	5	.583	3.51	22	19	0	0	2	2	115.1	90	497	49	45	12	2	2	6	61	1	123	16	1
Lawrence, Sean, Carolina*	0	2	.000	5.48	12	3	0	0	3	0	21.1	27	96	13	13	2	0	0	1	8	1	19	0	0
Lemke, Steve, Huntsville	4	9	.308	4.38	25	19	0	0	1	0	125.1	144	544	72	61	5	7	3	8	29	4	65	9	0

Pitcher, Team	W	L	Pct.	ERA	G	GS	CG	ShO	GF	Sv.	IP	H	TBF	R	ER	HR	SH	SF	HB	BB	IBB	SO	WP	Bk.
Levine, Alan, Birmingham	4	3	.571	2.34	43	1	0	0	31	7	73.0	61	305	22	19	2	2	2	2	25	5	68	7	1
Loiselle, Rich, Memphis	6	3	.667	3.55	13	13	1	0	0	0	78.2	82	357	46	31	5	1	1	6	33	2	48	3	1
Long, Joey, Memphis*	0	2	.000	3.32	25	0	0	0	3	0	21.2	28	104	15	8	0	1	1	1	10	2	18	0	0
Lowe, Derek, Port City	1	6	.143	6.08	10	10	1	0	0	0	53.1	70	244	41	36	8	3	2	3	22	1	30	2	0
Luebbers, Larry, Chattanooga	10	6	.625	4.65	28	21	0	0	4	0	118.0	112	514	71	61	7	6	6	7	59	1	87	1	0
Manning, Derek, Huntsville*	1	2	.333	4.50	5	5	0	0	0	0	28.0	26	114	14	14	4	1	0	0	7	0	22	0	0
Mattson, Rob, Memphis	12	13	.480	4.11	30	28	11	3	1	0	201.2	199	862	109	92	20	7	15	20	73	2	139	4	4
Maurer, Mike, Huntsville	0	2	.000	6.53	17	0	0	0	14	6	20.2	34	100	18	15	0	2	1	0	5	2	19	2	0
May, Darrell, Greenville*	2	8	.200	3.55	15	15	0	0	0	0	91.1	81	377	44	36	18	2	5	3	20	0	79	4	0
McCarthy, Greg, Birmingham*	3	3	.500	5.04	38	0	0	0	13	3	44.2	37	195	28	25	4	4	2	2	29	3	48	3	1
Meier, Kevin, Orlando	4	1	.800	2.64	11	11	0	0	0	0	64.2	55	257	24	19	6	0	2	5	13	4	52	4	0
Meinershagen, Adam, Knoxville	1	1	.500	10.80	3	3	0	0	0	0	11.2	17	55	14	14	2	1	0	1	2	0	4	0	0
Michalak, Chris, Huntsville*	1	1	.500	11.12	7	0	0	0	4	1	5.2	10	32	7	7	1	1	0	1	5	0	4	2	0
Miller, Trever, Jacksonville*	8	2	.800	2.72	31	16	3	2	4	0	122.1	122	512	46	37	5	4	2	5	34	0	77	1	0
Moehler, Brian, Jacksonville	8	10	.444	4.82	28	27	0	0	1	0	162.1	176	696	94	87	14	3	5	6	52	1	89	15	0
Mongiello, Mike, Birmingham	3	1	.750	1.99	7	5	0	0	1	0	31.2	23	120	8	7	2	1	0	1	6	0	23	0	0
Moore, Marcus, Chattanooga	6	1	.857	4.98	36	0	0	0	8	2	43.1	31	192	24	24	6	2	2	2	34	1	57	3	1
Moore, Tim, Birmingham	7	5	.583	3.68	29	19	0	0	3	0	120.0	118	521	58	49	10	7	6	4	40	1	78	6	2
Morel, Ramon, Carolina	3	3	.500	3.52	10	10	0	0	0	0	69.0	71	281	31	27	4	1	2	2	10	0	34	2	0
Morgan, Mike, Orlando	0	2	.000	7.59	2	2	0	0	0	0	10.2	13	48	9	9	1	1	0	1	7	0	5	0	0
Murray, Heath, Memphis*	5	4	.556	3.38	14	14	0	0	0	0	77.1	83	363	36	29	1	3	3	4	42	1	71	7	1
Murray, Matt, Greenville	4	0	1.000	1.53	5	5	0	0	0	0	29.1	20	111	5	5	0	1	0	1	8	0	25	2	0
Nezelek, Andy, Carolina	1	0	1.000	5.14	6	0	0	0	1	1	14.0	16	64	9	8	3	0	0	0	3	0	14	0	0
Nickell, Jackie, Port City	5	8	.385	3.73	27	9	0	0	7	0	89.1	74	367	40	37	11	2	4	8	30	0	81	4	4
Nitkowski, C.J., Chattanooga*	4	2	.667	2.50	8	8	0	0	0	0	50.1	39	204	20	14	1	3	0	1	20	0	52	1	1
Nix, Jim, Chattanooga	3	5	.375	3.20	40	5	0	0	14	2	84.1	84	360	43	30	8	6	4	2	30	1	71	7	1
Norman, Scott, Jacksonville	1	3	.250	2.48	4	4	2	0	0	0	29.0	31	122	12	8	4	1	0	1	6	0	9	1	0
Olsen, Steve, Birmingham	8	3	.727	3.48	14	14	2	1	0	0	85.1	84	357	44	33	4	3	7	1	21	2	56	1	0
Pace, Scott, Knoxville*	6	8	.429	4.57	18	18	1	1	0	0	102.1	117	462	66	52	8	6	6	4	48	3	71	7	0
Paige, Carey, Greenville	1	4	.200	5.01	7	7	0	0	0	0	41.1	45	182	30	23	5	1	0	2	11	0	26	2	0
Parris, Steve, Carolina	9	1	.900	2.51	14	14	2	2	0	0	89.2	61	344	25	25	2	3	1	4	16	1	86	3	0
Peters, Chris, Carolina*	2	0	1.000	1.29	2	2	0	0	0	0	14.0	9	56	2	2	0	0	1	0	2	0	7	2	0
Petersen, Matt, Orlando	3	9	.250	5.87	24	15	1	1	2	0	89.0	107	414	66	58	15	5	4	7	39	5	59	2	2
Pett, Jose, Knoxville	8	9	.471	4.26	26	25	1	1	0	0	141.2	132	602	87	67	16	4	4	4	48	0	89	8	0
Pickett, Ricky, Chattanooga*	4	5	.444	3.28	40	0	0	0	19	9	46.2	22	203	20	17	3	2	0	0	44	3	69	1	0
Pierce, Rob, Huntsville	1	1	.500	9.87	15	0	0	0	5	0	17.1	26	92	21	19	2	0	1	1	14	1	16	8	1
Pierson, Jason, Birmingham*	0	2	.000	8.10	4	4	0	0	0	0	23.1	29	102	22	21	6	0	1	2	6	0	15	0	1
Pisciotta, Marc, Carolina	6	4	.600	4.15	56	0	0	0	27	9	69.1	60	313	37	32	2	7	3	6	45	8	57	4	0
Plantenberg, Erik, Memphis*	2	0	1.000	1.66	20	0	0	0	9	2	21.2	19	80	4	4	2	1	0	1	2	1	16	1	0
Plaster, Allen, Huntsville	1	0	1.000	3.18	43	0	0	0	14	2	68.0	63	290	26	24	4	4	2	0	26	0	47	7	0
Ralph, Curtis, Carolina	1	1	.500	2.42	18	1	0	0	2	1	26.0	23	105	8	7	3	0	0	0	10	0	17	1	0
Ratliff, Jon, Orlando	10	5	.667	3.47	26	25	1	1	1	0	140.0	143	599	67	54	9	2	8	10	42	1	94	13	0
Resendez, Oscar, Port City	0	2	.000	4.24	11	0	0	0	3	0	17.0	16	76	8	8	0	0	0	1	8	0	15	2	0
Rivera, Lino, Carolina	0	0	.000	6.00	4	0	0	0	1	0	6.0	10	31	6	4	0	0	0	0	3	0	4	0	0
Rivera, Roberto, Orlando*	6	2	.750	2.38	49	0	0	0	14	6	68.0	50	257	18	18	4	0	4	0	11	3	34	3	1
Roper, John, Chattanooga	0	0	.000	1.00	3	3	0	0	0	0	9.0	5	33	1	1	0	0	0	0	1	0	6	0	0
Rose, Scott, Huntsville	4	6	.400	2.59	38	5	0	0	23	13	80.0	70	316	24	23	2	5	3	2	23	5	35	6	0
Rosengren, John, Jacksonville*	2	7	.222	4.52	14	13	0	0	0	0	67.2	73	308	39	34	7	2	2	5	40	0	59	12	2
Ruebel, Matt, Carolina*	13	5	.722	2.76	27	27	4	3	0	0	169.1	150	699	68	52	7	4	7	7	45	1	136	7	1
Ruffcorn, Scott, Birmingham	0	2	.000	5.63	3	3	0	0	0	0	16.0	17	71	11	10	0	0	0	0	10	0	13	2	0
Russell, LaGrande, Port City	4	3	.571	3.24	39	0	0	0	13	1	72.1	68	329	32	26	7	4	3	1	43	3	54	9	0
Ryan, Matt, Carolina	2	1	.667	1.57	44	0	0	0	38	26	46.0	33	188	10	8	0	4	0	2	19	2	23	3	0
Rychel, Kevin, Carolina	3	2	.600	3.33	40	0	0	0	14	1	51.1	35	210	21	19	1	1	1	6	24	4	60	8	0
Sawkiw, Warren, Knoxville	0	0	.000	0.00	1	0	0	0	1	0	1.0	0	4	0	0	0	0	0	0	1	0	1	0	0
Schmitt, Todd, Memphis	0	0	.000	1.30	26	0	0	0	24	18	27.2	18	108	4	4	2	0	1	1	11	2	27	0	0
Schutz, Carl, Greenville*	3	7	.300	4.94	51	0	0	0	46	26	58.1	53	258	36	32	4	2	2	1	36	3	56	3	0
Seelbach, Chris, Greenville	6	0	1.000	1.64	9	9	1	1	0	0	60.1	38	249	15	11	2	5	3	4	30	0	65	3	1
Shafer, Bill, Greenville	2	2	.500	5.01	42	0	0	0	16	1	59.1	69	283	37	33	7	3	0	4	38	3	44	2	2
Shoemaker, Steve, Huntsville	4	4	.500	3.43	43	0	0	0	24	5	76.0	62	318	33	29	8	3	4	1	31	2	63	7	0
Shouse, Brian, Carolina*	7	6	.538	4.47	21	20	0	0	0	0	114.2	126	480	64	57	14	5	3	4	19	2	76	1	1
Silva, Jose, Knoxville	0	0	.000	9.00	3	0	0	0	0	0	2.0	3	15	2	2	0	1	1	0	6	0	2	0	0
Simmons, John, Greenville*	1	5	.167	4.62	48	0	0	0	15	1	60.1	67	266	35	31	9	1	0	0	22	2	54	3	0
Sirotka, Mike, Birmingham*	7	6	.538	3.20	16	16	1	0	0	0	101.1	95	412	42	36	11	3	3	2	22	0	79	4	1
Smith, Mike, Chattanooga	0	2	.000	17.47	3	2	0	0	0	0	5.2	11	37	13	11	0	0	0	1	5	0	5	1	0
Smith, Ottis, Orlando*	4	5	.444	3.07	17	17	0	0	0	0	108.1	109	461	50	37	9	2	1	4	38	4	51	5	4
Snyder, John, Birmingham	1	0	1.000	6.64	5	4	0	0	0	0	20.1	24	87	16	15	6	0	1	2	6	0	13	1	0
Sodowsky, Clint, Jacksonville	5	5	.500	2.55	19	19	5	3	0	0	123.2	102	497	46	35	4	2	2	5	50	1	77	3	0
Steed, Rick, Knoxville	2	4	.333	3.69	27	0	0	0	23	9	31.2	23	136	15	13	1	3	2	2	16	2	29	4	0
Swartzbaugh, Dave, Orlando	4	0	1.000	2.48	16	0	0	0	3	0	29.0	18	111	10	8	1	1	1	2	7	0	37	1	1
Taylor, Aaron, Huntsville	1	1	.500	2.13	5	4	0	0	0	0	25.1	26	106	7	6	3	1	1	1	6	0	24	1	1
Telemaco, Amaury, Orlando	8	8	.500	3.29	22	22	3	1	0	0	147.2	112	587	60	54	13	8	3	4	42	3	151	7	1
Thomas, Carlos, Hun.-Mem.	3	3	.500	7.62	18	0	0	0	7	0	26.0	28	127	24	22	3	3	1	1	19	1	24	2	1
Thomas, Larry, Birmingham*	4	1	.800	1.34	35	0	0	0	9	2	40.1	24	156	9	6	0	2	2	2	15	1	47	3	0
Thompson, Justin, Jacksonville*	6	7	.462	3.73	18	18	3	0	0	0	123.0	110	502	55	51	7	4	2	3	38	2	98	3	0
Tolar, Kevin, Carolina*	1	0	1.000	3.65	12	0	0	0	3	0	12.1	16	59	5	5	0	0	2	0	7	0	9	2	0
Tranbarger, Mark, Chattanooga*	3	1	.750	1.95	48	0	0	0	12	0	55.1	50	236	15	12	4	2	4	2	20	1	46	2	0
Tsamis, George, Car.-P.C.*	0	0	.000	3.38	19	0	0	0	6	0	21.1	23	97	9	8	1	1	0	1	16	3	10	2	0
Turnier, Aaron, Greenville*	0	1	.000	5.19	8	0	0	0	0	0	17.1	17	86	13	10	2	1	0	0	18	1	16	3	0
Tuttle, Dave, Chattanooga	1	6	.143	7.01	8	7	0	0	1	0	34.2	40	165	29	27	6	2	1	1	21	0	20	4	0
Urso, Sal, Port City*	2	0	1.000	2.17	51	0	0	0	8	1	45.2	41	185	13	11	0	0	0	0	21	0	44	7	1
VanRyn, Ben, Chattanooga*	0	1	.000	9.24	5	3	0	0	0	0	12.2	22	69	18	13	2	0	2	1	6	0	6	0	0
Vasquez, Chris, Chattanooga	0	0	.000	18.00	1	0	0	0	1	0	1.0	2	7	2	2	0	0	0	0	3	0	0	0	0
Vasquez, Marcos, Chattanooga	7	6	.538	3.68	26	18	0	0	1	1	120.0	125	531	63	49	12	6	5	4	46	1	80	5	1

Pitcher, Team	W	L	Pct.	ERA	G	GS	CG	ShO	GF	Sv.	IP	H	TBF	R	ER	HR	SH	SF	HB	BB	IBB	SO	WP	Bk.
Veras, Dario, Memphis	7	3	.700	3.81	58	0	0	0	22	1	82.2	81	360	38	35	8	3	1	7	27	11	70	5	1
Waggoner, Jim, Huntsville	0	0	.000	0.00	1	0	0	0	1	0	2.0	1	7	0	0	0	0	0	0	0	0	0	0	0
Wagner, Matt, Port City	5	8	.385	2.82	23	23	0	0	0	0	137.0	121	566	57	43	9	3	4	4	33	1	111	5	1
Walker, Dane, Huntsville	0	0	.000	0.00	1	0	0	0	0	0	0.2	0	4	0	0	0	0	0	2	0	0	0	0	0
Watkins, Jason, Birmingham	0	0	.000	3.95	10	0	0	0	3	0	13.2	18	64	7	6	1	0	0	1	3	0	10	1	1
Weber, Ben, Knoxville	4	1	.800	3.91	12	1	0	0	6	0	25.1	26	104	12	11	3	0	0	6	16	0	16	0	0
Wendell, Turk, Orlando	1	0	1.000	3.86	5	0	0	0	2	1	7.0	6	30	3	3	0	0	1	4	0	7	0	0	
Whiteside, Sean, Jacksonville*	2	0	1.000	3.78	27	1	0	0	4	0	33.1	34	148	17	14	4	2	3	0	20	4	17	4	0
Wilkins, Marc, Carolina	5	3	.625	3.99	37	12	0	0	1	0	99.1	91	436	47	44	8	5	3	11	44	2	80	9	0
Willis, Travis, Carolina	1	1	.500	2.91	16	0	0	0	6	3	21.2	23	101	10	7	0	1	1	3	10	2	12	2	0
Wilson, Gary, Carolina	0	0	.000	0.00	1	0	0	0	0	0	4.2	0	16	0	0	0	0	0	0	3	0	5	0	0
Withem, Shannon, Jacksonville	5	8	.385	5.75	19	18	0	0	1	0	108.0	142	481	77	69	17	5	1	5	24	1	80	4	0
Witte, Trey, Port City	3	2	.600	1.73	48	0	0	0	34	11	62.1	48	250	17	12	0	6	3	5	14	0	39	0	1
Wolcott, Bob, Port City	7	3	.700	2.20	12	12	2	1	0	0	86.0	60	320	26	21	6	0	3	3	13	0	53	2	0
Wolfe, Joel, Huntsville	0	0	.000	0.00	1	0	0	0	1	0	1.0	0	3	0	0	0	0	0	1	0	0	0	0	0
Woodfin, Chris, Birmingham	3	3	.500	4.50	48	0	0	0	41	20	64.0	59	269	34	32	6	2	2	1	24	1	72	10	0
Worley, Robert, Port City	1	7	.125	4.58	22	5	0	0	6	0	57.0	60	263	42	29	5	3	2	4	30	1	26	8	0
Worrell, Steve, Birmingham*	0	1	.000	8.31	4	0	0	0	2	0	4.1	5	21	5	4	2	0	0	0	2	0	2	2	0
Young, Anthony, Orlando	0	0	.000	0.00	2	0	0	0	0	0	5.0	6	24	1	0	0	0	0	3	0	5	0	0	
Zongor, Steve, Huntsville*	2	0	1.000	7.62	9	0	0	0	3	0	13.0	13	60	11	11	4	0	0	1	9	0	11	1	1

COMBINATION SHUTOUTS: **Birmingham (6)**—Andujar-McCarthy-Woodfin, Andujar-Thomas, Andujar-Thomas-Woodfin, Fordham-Gajkowski, Johnston-Johnson-Woodfin, Sirotka-Gajkowski-Woodfin. **Carolina (9)**—Dessens-Backlund-Konuszewski, Dessens-Konuszewski-Pisciotta, Parris-Figueroa-Rychel-Pisciotta, Parris-Rychel-Ryan, Ruebel-Konuszewski-Pisciotta, Ruebel-Ryan, Ruebel-Wilkins-Pisciotta-Ryan, Ruebel-Wilkins-Ryan, Wilson-Shouse-Ryan. **Chattanooga (9)**—Ferry-Brumley-Fox, Fox-Pickett, Kramer-Burgos, Luebbers-Brumley, Luebbers-Kilgo, Luebbers-Tranbarger-Burgos, Roper-Jackson-Kramer-Pickett, Vasquez-Pickett, Vasquez-Pickett-Kilgo. **Greenville (3)**—Murray-Schutz, Murray-Shafer-Schutz, Seelbach-Schutz. **Huntsville (6)**—Bennett-Banks, Chouinard-Plaster, Dressendorfer-Banks-Plaster-Rose, Fermin-Rose, Hollins-Shoemaker-Banks, Lemke-Pierce-Plaster-Banks. **Jacksonville (3)**—Gutierrez-Whiteside-Kelly, Sodowsky-Moehler, Thompson-Greene. **Knoxville (9)**—Almanzar-Freeman-Steed, Almanzar-Ingram-Steed, Beltran-Almanzar, Beltran-Brown, Brandow-Doman-Ingram, Carpenter-Beltran, Carpenter-Freeman, Kotes-Freeman, Pace-Ingram. **Memphis (1)**—Kaufman-Schmitt. **Orlando (10)**—Hutcheson-Johnson-Adams 2, Burlingame-Dabney-Hart, Burlingame-Rivera-Harrah, Burlingame-Rivera-Johnson, Bullinger-Ratliff, Ratliff-Rivera-Harrah-Adams, Ratliff-Rivera-Hart, Ratliff-Rivera-Wendell, Telemaco-Johnson-Adams. **Port City (4)**—Fernandez-Adam-Urso, Nickell-Franklin-Witte, Nickell-Witte, Wagner-King-Witte.

NO-HIT GAMES: Andujar, Birmingham, defeated Memphis, 1-0, August 8; Beckett, Memphis, lost to Chattanooga, 1-0 (second game), September 2.

PITCHERS WITH TWO OR MORE TEAMS

Pitcher, Team	W	L	Pct.	ERA	G	GS	CG	ShO	GF	Sv.	IP	H	TBF	R	ER	HR	SH	SF	HB	BB	IBB	SO	WP	Bk.
Thomas, Carlos, Huntsville	2	2	.500	4.97	7	0	0	0	3	0	12.2	13	56	8	7	2	2	0	1	5	1	12	1	1
Thomas, Carlos, Memphis	1	1	.500	10.13	11	0	0	0	4	0	13.1	15	71	16	15	1	1	1	0	14	0	12	1	0
Tsamis, George, Carolina*	0	0	.000	4.09	12	0	0	0	2	0	11.0	12	46	5	5	1	0	1	5	1	7	2	0	
Tsamis, George, Port City*	0	0	.000	2.61	7	0	0	0	4	0	10.1	11	51	4	3	0	1	0	0	11	2	3	0	0

1995 FIELDING

TEAM

Team	Pct.	G	PO	A	E	TC	DP	PB	Team	Pct.	G	PO	A	E	TC	DP	PB
Jacksonville	.976	144	3860	1779	139	5778	167	10	Memphis	.971	142	3708	1411	155	5274	122	27
Orlando	.973	143	3773	1531	146	5450	121	10	Birmingham	.970	144	3745	1507	165	5417	132	16
Huntsville	.971	144	3747	1663	161	5571	151	22	Chattanooga	.969	143	3775	1358	163	5296	122	19
Carolina	.971	144	3967	1639	168	5774	139	19	Greenville	.969	142	3704	1466	165	5335	111	7
Port City	.971	142	3792	1610	163	5565	161	31	Knoxville	.966	144	3667	1479	183	5329	129	19

TRIPLE PLAYS: Carolina, Chattanooga.

INDIVIDUAL

FIRST BASEMEN

NOTE: All caps denotes fielding-percentage leader based on 72 games for catchers, 96 for all other non-pitchers and 144 innings for pitchers. *Throws lefthanded.

Player, Team	Pct.	G	PO	A	E	TC	DP
Beard, Garrett, Huntsville	1.000	2	5	0	0	5	0
BONNICI, James, Port City	.995	137	1274	87	7	1368	136
Boston, D.J., Knoxville	.986	132	1129	91	17	1237	117
Brown, Brant, Orlando*	.990	107	917	92	10	1019	75
Brown, Michael, Carolina*	.991	56	503	36	5	544	33
Canale, George, Carolina	.994	38	294	22	2	318	34
Cardenas, John, Port City	1.000	5	25	0	0	25	2
Colon, Felix, Jacksonville	1.000	15	137	13	0	150	13
Coolbaugh, Mike, Knoxville	1.000	7	65	5	0	70	0
Cooper, Gary, Jacksonville	1.000	5	38	3	0	41	3
Cotton, John, Memphis	1.000	1	2	0	0	2	0
Coughlin, Kevin, Birmingham*	.989	26	160	13	2	175	15
Cruz, Ivan, Jacksonville*	.992	81	795	60	7	862	86
DeLeon, Roberto, Memphis	1.000	1	1	0	0	1	0
Dismuke, Jamie, Chattanooga	.989	95	647	69	8	724	64
Drinkwater, Sean, Memphis	.982	10	50	4	1	55	2
Duross, Gabe, Orlando*	.992	38	328	24	3	355	31
Farrell, Jon, Carolina	1.000	1	2	0	0	2	0
Fryman, Troy, Birmingham	.985	86	655	53	11	719	67
Gonzalez, Paul, Carolina	1.000	2	21	0	0	21	0
Grijak, Kevin, Greenville	.986	20	202	7	3	212	16
Gubanich, Creighton, Huntsville	.990	21	179	22	2	203	20
Hanel, Marcus, Carolina	1.000	1	2	0	0	2	1
Harmes, Kris, Knoxville	1.000	3	26	0	0	28	2
Hickey, Mike, Port City	1.000	7	44	4	0	48	7
Killeen, Tim, Memphis	1.000	1	1	0	0	1	0
Kingston, Mark, Orlando	1.000	4	10	0	0	10	1
Koehler, Jim, Port City*	1.000	1	1	0	0	1	0
Kopriva, Dan, Chattanooga	1.000	3	4	0	0	4	0
Leary, Rob, Carolina*	.985	59	557	36	9	602	51
Lee, Derrek, Memphis	1.000	2	16	3	0	19	1
Leiper, Tim, Jacksonville	.986	26	250	23	4	277	23
Lesher, Brian, Huntsville*	.941	3	14	2	1	17	2
Lutz, Brent, Knoxville	1.000	1	6	1	0	7	0
Merchant, Mark, Chattanooga	1.000	1	1	0	0	1	0
Molina, Izzy, Huntsville	.889	1	7	1	1	9	0
Munoz, Omer, Carolina	1.000	1	1	0	0	1	0
Nunez, Ramon, Greenville	.985	45	305	25	5	335	29
Olmeda, Jose, Greenville	1.000	1	5	1	0	6	0
Pearson, Eddie, Birmingham	.987	33	286	25	4	315	25
Pecorilli, Aldo, Greenville	.996	34	245	24	1	270	15
Perona, Joe, Jacksonville	1.000	1	1	0	0	1	0
Pevey, Marty, Jacksonville	1.000	4	27	2	0	29	2
Rendina, Mike, Jacksonville*	1.000	23	219	10	0	229	20
Rohrmeier, Dan, Chattanooga	.969	7	29	2	1	32	4
Rumfield, Toby, Chattanooga	.983	55	353	53	7	413	38
Russo, Paul, Memphis	1.000	1	12	2	0	14	0
Santana, Ruben, Chattanooga	1.000	1	8	4	0	12	0
Sawkiw, Warren, Knoxville	.947	3	16	2	1	19	1
Sheldon, Scott, Huntsville	.991	10	103	5	1	109	9
Sparks, Greg, Greenville*	.983	55	340	12	6	358	29
Spiezio, Scott, Huntsville	1.000	2	10	0	0	17	3
Swann, Pedro, Greenville	.954	7	59	3	3	65	6
Thompson, Jason, Memphis*	.994	135	1044	88	7	1139	102

CLASS AA *Southern League*

Player, Team	Pct.	G	PO	A	E	TC	DP
Torres, Paul, Orlando	1.000	2	15	0	0	15	0
Vinas, Julio, Birmingham	1.000	8	69	3	0	72	7
White, Jason, Huntsville*	.986	48	445	32	7	484	45
Wolfe, Joel, Huntsville	.992	62	592	48	5	645	60
Wollenburg, Doug, Greenville	.977	5	41	2	1	44	3

TRIPLE PLAYS: M. Brown, Rohrmeier.

SECOND BASEMEN

Player, Team	Pct.	G	PO	A	E	TC	DP
Alvarez, Gabe, Memphis	.833	2	0	5	1	6	1
Arias, Amador, Chattanooga	.966	40	40	45	3	88	10
Batista, Tony, Huntsville	.970	18	35	61	3	99	14
Beasley, Tony, Carolina	.968	80	146	217	12	375	44
Burton, Essex, Birmingham	.957	140	311	337	29	677	94
Bush, Homer, Memphis	.969	106	235	268	16	519	69
CATALANOTTO, Frank, Jacks'ville	.974	133	252	411	18	681	98
Coleman, Ken, Orlando	.974	79	121	180	8	309	33
Coolbaugh, Mike, Knoxville	1.000	6	8	12	0	20	2
Cora, Manny, Port City	.968	67	155	213	12	380	50
Cotton, John, Memphis	.800	2	3	1	1	5	1
DeLeon, Roberto, Memphis	1.000	3	2	3	0	5	1
Diaz, Eddy, Port City	.978	36	65	112	4	181	26
Drinkwater, Sean, Memphis	.974	6	13	24	1	38	4
Fermin, Carlos, Jacksonville	1.000	7	4	12	0	16	2
Gipson, Charles, Port City	.900	2	2	7	1	10	2
Gomez, Rudy, Orlando	.972	77	106	136	7	249	31
Harley, Quentin, Memphis	.970	26	41	55	3	99	9
Henry, Santiago, Knoxville	.972	106	209	269	14	492	69
Hickey, Mike, Port City	.945	34	74	99	10	183	23
Jenkins, Dee, Chattanooga	.917	7	11	11	2	24	3
Johnson, Matt, Knoxville	.988	28	27	58	1	86	13
Kelly, Pat, Knoxville	1.000	1	1	4	0	5	0
Kessinger, Keith, Orlando	.970	13	31	33	2	66	9
Koelling, Brian, Chattanooga	.980	56	132	117	5	254	23
Kremblas, Frank, Chattanooga	.956	19	44	42	4	90	12
Krevokuch, Jim, Carolina	.987	24	31	47	1	79	8
Leiper, Tim, Jacksonville	1.000	10	13	32	0	45	7
Malloy, Marty, Greenville	.973	124	246	321	16	583	69
Manahan, Austin, Orlando	.898	21	42	46	10	98	9
Munoz, Omer, Carolina	.987	48	103	130	3	236	28
Noriega, Rey, Birmingham	1.000	8	14	10	0	24	1
Nunez, Ramon, Greenville	.978	10	26	19	1	46	5
Olmeda, Jose, Greenville	1.000	3	10	13	0	23	2
Pratte, Evan, Jacksonville	1.000	4	14	15	0	29	7
Relaford, Desmond, Port City	.941	5	5	11	1	17	2
Rodarte, Raul, Carolina	.800	3	3	5	2	10	2
Sanchez, Yuri, Jacksonville	1.000	2	4	3	0	7	0
Santana, Ruben, Chattanooga	.945	50	76	114	11	201	21
Sawkiw, Warren, Knoxville	.974	11	15	23	1	39	5
Sheldon, Scott, Huntsville	.974	27	57	90	4	151	19
Sobolewski, Mark, Huntsville	.964	83	160	238	15	413	58
Spiezio, Scott, Huntsville	1.000	1	1	4	0	5	1
Tredaway, Chad, Memphis	.929	7	10	16	2	28	4
Waggoner, Jim, Huntsville	.979	21	39	55	2	96	12
Wollenburg, Doug, Greenville	.956	16	31	34	3	68	8
Womack, Tony, Carolina	.956	11	16	27	2	45	5

THIRD BASEMEN

Player, Team	Pct.	G	PO	A	E	TC	DP
Adriana, Sharnol, Knoxville	1.000	3	1	3	0	4	0
Beard, Garrett, Huntsville	1.000	1	0	1	0	1	0
Beasley, Tony, Carolina	1.000	2	0	2	0	2	0
Boone, Aaron, Chattanooga	.875	22	14	28	6	48	4
Bruno, Julio, Memphis	.934	52	32	109	10	151	15
Canale, George, Carolina	.942	26	18	31	3	52	2
Coleman, Ken, Orlando	.942	77	23	91	7	121	8
Coolbaugh, Mike, Knoxville	.935	126	83	279	25	387	30
Cooper, Gary, Jacksonville	.957	75	38	162	9	209	11
Cotton, John, Memphis	1.000	1	0	1	0	1	0
Cranford, Jay, Carolina	.914	86	69	177	23	269	14
DeLeon, Roberto, Memphis	.875	7	1	6	1	8	0
Diaz, Eddy, Port City	.932	29	25	44	5	74	6
Drinkwater, Sean, Memphis	.963	62	43	113	6	162	17
Fermin, Carlos, Jacksonville	.889	18	6	26	4	36	2
Gomez, Fabio, Port City	.914	17	13	40	5	58	6
Gonzalez, Paul, Birmingham	1.000	5	3	11	0	14	0
Gubanich, Creighton, Huntsville	.765	5	3	10	4	17	1
Harley, Quentin, Memphis	.737	7	4	10	5	19	2
Harmes, Kris, Knoxville	.667	3	2	2	2	6	0
Hickey, Mike, Port City	.927	73	35	142	14	191	10

Player, Team	Pct.	G	PO	A	E	TC	DP
Johnson, Matt, Knoxville	1.000	5	1	7	0	8	0
Kelly, Pat, Knoxville	1.000	9	5	25	0	30	1
Kessinger, Keith, Orlando	1.000	1	0	1	0	1	0
Kingston, Mark, Orlando	.946	58	38	85	7	130	6
Kopriva, Dan, Chattanooga	.848	33	19	48	12	79	2
Krevokuch, Jim, Carolina	.918	38	22	68	8	98	5
Leiper, Tim, Jacksonville	.944	33	21	80	6	107	12
Lidle, Kevin, Jacksonville	.786	6	2	9	3	14	2
Manahan, Austin, Orlando	.808	19	8	13	5	26	0
Noriega, Rey, Birmingham	.941	6	5	11	1	17	0
NORTON, Greg, Birmingham	.938	131	102	277	25	404	23
Nunez, Ramon, Greenville	.667	1	0	2	1	3	0
Olmeda, Jose, Greenville	1.000	1	0	5	0	5	0
Pecorilli, Aldo, Greenville	.867	3	2	11	2	15	0
Perona, Joe, Jacksonville	.900	7	2	7	1	10	1
Pratte, Evan, Jacksonville	.933	9	5	23	2	30	1
Rodarte, Raul, Carolina	.871	9	6	21	4	31	2
Rohrmeier, Dan, Chattanooga	.889	12	14	10	3	27	2
Rose, Pete, Birmingham	1.000	4	4	8	0	12	0
Russo, Paul, Memphis	.961	35	20	53	3	76	3
Santana, Ruben, Chattanooga	.929	98	64	160	17	241	14
Saunders, Doug, Port City	.963	28	14	63	3	80	7
Sawkiw, Warren, Knoxville	.833	5	1	14	3	18	1
Sheldon, Scott, Huntsville	1.000	2	3	5	0	8	2
Smith, Robert, Greenville	.937	126	120	265	26	411	25
Spiezio, Scott, Huntsville	.932	134	104	291	29	424	34
Torres, Paul, Orlando	.913	38	19	65	8	92	4
Tredaway, Chad, Memphis	1.000	2	0	1	0	1	0
Viera, Jose, Orlando	.913	9	7	14	2	23	1
Waggoner, Jim, Huntsville	1.000	6	5	6	0	11	1
Wollenburg, Doug, Greenville	.852	21	11	35	8	54	1
Wooten, Shawn, Jacksonville	.921	20	8	50	5	63	3

TRIPLE PLAY: Canale.

SHORTSTOPS

Player, Team	Pct.	G	PO	A	E	TC	DP
Adriana, Sharnol, Knoxville	.928	71	88	209	23	320	36
Alvarez, Gabe, Memphis	1.000	1	0	1	0	1	0
Arias, Amador, Chattanooga	.871	9	8	19	4	31	3
Batista, Tony, Huntsville	.945	102	133	310	26	469	59
Beasley, Tony, Carolina	.960	23	36	60	4	100	11
Coleman, Ken, Orlando	.917	4	7	4	1	12	2
Cora, Manny, Port City	.944	6	5	12	1	18	3
Cotton, John, Memphis	.941	24	30	34	4	68	7
Cranford, Jay, Carolina	.800	1	3	1	1	5	0
DeLeon, Roberto, Memphis	.941	54	73	134	13	220	19
Delgado, Wilson, Port City	.917	13	10	45	5	60	7
Diaz, Eddy, Port City	.940	46	75	129	13	217	30
DiSarcina, Glenn, Birmingham	1.000	3	5	4	0	9	2
Dotel, Mariano, Memphis	1.000	8	9	19	0	28	4
Drinkwater, Sean, Memphis	.935	14	18	25	3	46	4
Felix, Lauro, Huntsville	.964	9	7	20	1	28	6
Fermin, Carlos, Jacksonville	.939	32	53	85	9	147	25
Garcia, Luis, Jacksonville	.929	15	19	46	5	70	8
Gomez, Rudy, Orlando	.958	26	28	64	4	96	17
Harley, Quentin, Memphis	1.000	1	0	2	0	2	0
Henry, Santiago, Knoxville	.918	32	51	94	13	158	14
Johnson, Matt, Knoxville	.833	8	3	12	3	18	1
Kelly, Pat, Knoxville	.939	37	45	94	9	148	24
Kessinger, Keith, Orlando	.913	5	8	13	2	23	2
Koelling, Brian, Chattanooga	.932	51	87	117	15	219	28
Krevokuch, Jim, Carolina	1.000	1	1	0	0	1	0
LaRocca, Greg, Memphis	.889	2	6	2	1	9	1
Magdaleno, Ricky, Chattanooga	.839	11	20	32	10	62	6
MARTINEZ, Pablo, Greenville	.966	118	167	340	18	525	55
Noriega, Rey, Birmingham	.909	14	15	25	4	44	7
Olmeda, Jose, Greenville	.959	22	36	58	4	98	12
Petersen, Chris, Orlando	.964	125	212	357	21	590	66
Polcovich, Kevin, Carolina	.943	63	88	208	18	314	36
Pratte, Evan, Jacksonville	.857	4	3	3	1	7	0
Relaford, Desi, Port City	.929	84	129	265	30	424	62
Sanchez, Yuri, Jacksonville	.957	116	170	366	24	560	70
Sheldon, Scott, Huntsville	.948	25	40	88	7	135	23
Velandia, Jorge, Memphis	.952	60	88	152	12	252	29
Waggoner, Jim, Huntsville	.986	17	22	50	1	73	9
Wilson, Brandon, Chattanooga	.951	75	97	195	15	307	37
Wilson, Craig, Birmingham	.945	132	193	389	34	616	80
Wollenburg, Doug, Greenville	.909	6	8	12	2	22	6
Womack, Tony, Carolina	.953	68	110	214	16	340	49

TRIPLE PLAYS: Koelling, Womack.

OUTFIELDERS

Player, Team	Pct.	G	PO	A	E	TC	DP
Abbott, Jeff, Birmingham*	.966	42	55	1	2	58	0
Adams, Tommy, Port City	1.000	19	27	3	0	30	1
Allensworth, Jermaine, Carolina	.985	54	131	3	2	136	1
Austin, Jake, Carolina	.974	93	136	12	4	152	2
Barker, Glen, Jacksonville	.973	120	284	9	8	301	3
Beasley, Tony, Carolina	1.000	1	1	0	0	1	0
Briggs, Stoney, Memphis	.959	89	136	6	6	148	1
Briley, Greg, Jacksonville	1.000	7	11	0	0	11	0
Brock, Tarrik, Jacksonville*	.929	9	12	1	1	14	0
Brown, Brant, Orlando*	1.000	8	14	0	0	14	0
Brumfield, Jacob, Carolina	1.000	3	9	0	0	9	0
Burton, Darren, Orlando	.981	49	101	4	2	107	1
Butler, Rich, Knoxville	.974	48	106	5	3	114	1
Cameron, Mike, Birmingham	.985	107	250	7	4	261	1
Canale, George, Carolina	.962	30	45	5	2	52	0
Cappuccio, Carmine, Birmingham...	.985	65	119	9	2	130	0
Conger, Jeff, Carolina*	.969	39	90	3	3	96	3
Coolbaugh, Mike, Knoxville	1.000	2	3	0	0	3	0
Cotton, John, Memphis	.969	90	178	10	6	194	1
Coughlin, Kevin, Birmingham*	.971	73	128	7	4	139	3
Cradle, Rickey, Knoxville	.980	31	45	3	1	49	0
Danapilis, Eric, Jacksonville	.981	78	100	4	2	106	1
DeLaCruz, Lorenzo, Knoxville	.964	119	224	14	9	247	1
DeLaNuez, Rex, Jacksonville	.992	82	117	9	1	127	1
Dowler, Dee, Orlando	1.000	9	16	3	0	19	0
Drinkwater, Sean, Memphis	1.000	2	2	0	0	2	0
Duross, Gabe, Orlando*	1.000	1	1	0	0	1	0
Dye, Jermaine, Greenville	.981	103	234	22	5	261	2
Espinosa, Ramon, Carolina	.956	125	232	9	11	252	2
Farrell, Jon, Carolina	.957	79	147	10	7	164	2
Francisco, David, Huntsville	.979	128	267	15	6	288	4
Fryman, Troy, Birmingham	1.000	11	15	0	0	15	0
Gennaro, Brad, Memphis*	.984	102	172	10	3	185	1
Gipson, Charles, Port City	.980	110	233	12	5	250	4
Griffey, Craig, Port City	.982	92	152	8	3	163	1
Hansen, Terrel, Jacksonville	.986	44	69	3	1	73	1
Harley, Quentin, Memphis	1.000	5	7	0	0	7	0
Hart, Chris, Huntsville	.980	28	48	2	1	51	1
Herrera, Jose, Huntsville*	.958	90	176	6	8	190	0
Hollins, Damon, Greenville*	.978	129	330	18	8	356	3
Hughes, Troy, Greenville	.968	53	83	7	3	93	1
Hurst, Jimmy, Birmingham	.931	66	131	3	10	144	0
HYZDU, Adam, Chattanooga	.995	99	182	4	1	187	0
Jennings, Robin, Orlando*	.963	126	242	15	10	267	2
Johnson, Earl, Memphis	.800	2	4	0	1	5	0
Johnson, Matt, Knoxville	.750	2	3	0	1	4	0
Kimsey, Keith, Jacksonville	.984	30	57	5	1	63	1
Klesko, Ryan, Greenville*	1.000	2	2	0	0	2	0
Krevokuch, Jim, Carolina	1.000	1	2	0	0	2	0
Ladell, Cleveland, Chattanooga	.985	135	312	6	5	323	2
Larregui, Ed, Orlando	.976	92	156	6	4	166	2
Leary, Rob, Carolina*	1.000	2	5	0	0	5	0
Leiper, Tim, Jacksonville	.988	57	75	7	1	83	1
Lesher, Brian, Huntsville*	.974	114	184	5	5	194	2
Lidle, Kevin, Jacksonville	.500	1	1	0	1	2	0
Lutz, Brent, Knoxville	.923	8	11	1	1	13	0
Mack, Quinn, Memphis*	1.000	16	33	0	0	33	0
Madsen, Dan, Orlando*	1.000	9	16	1	0	17	0
Manahan, Austin, Orlando	.963	32	52	0	2	54	0
Mashore, Justin, Jacksonville	1.000	40	88	2	0	90	1
Merchant, Mark, Chattanooga	1.000	4	1	0	0	1	0
Mottola, Chad, Chattanooga	.974	50	106	6	3	115	2
Moultrie, Pat, Knoxville*	1.000	13	22	0	0	22	0
Neill, Mike, Huntsville*	1.000	13	24	0	0	24	0
Noriega, Rey, Birmingham	1.000	12	13	0	0	13	0
Pecorilli, Aldo, Greenville	.923	6	12	0	1	13	0
Peguero, Julio, Port City	.961	36	72	2	3	77	1
Peterson, Charles, Carolina	.977	20	40	2	1	43	0
Pevey, Marty, Jacksonville	1.000	6	8	0	0	8	0
Poe, Charles, Birmingham	.968	78	143	7	5	155	1
Rackley, Keifer, Port City	.960	78	116	4	5	125	0
Ramirez, Roberto, Port City	.961	102	165	8	7	180	3
Ratliff, Daryl, Carolina	.967	15	29	0	1	30	0
Roberts, Lonell, Knoxville	.947	81	159	3	9	171	0
Robinson, Don, Greenville	1.000	6	5	1	0	6	1
Rohrmeier, Dan, Chattanooga	1.000	56	103	7	0	110	2
Rumfield, Toby, Chattanooga	1.000	12	12	0	0	12	0
Samuels, Scott, Orlando	1.000	5	11	0	0	11	0
Sanders, Deion, Chattanooga*	1.000	1	3	1	0	4	1
Santana, Ruben, Chattanooga	1.000	1	2	0	0	2	0
Sawkiw, Warren, Knoxville	1.000	5	6	0	0	6	0
Smith, Ira, Memphis	.972	59	98	5	3	106	1
Stewart, Shannon, Knoxville	.980	132	283	6	6	295	1
Swann, Pedro, Greenville	.966	48	83	3	3	89	0
Thomas, Keith, Memphis	.982	88	160	7	3	170	1
Torres, Paul, Orlando	1.000	37	59	3	0	62	1
Valdes, Pedro, Orlando*	.979	106	172	11	4	187	6
Vasquez, Chris, Chattanooga	1.000	3	5	0	0	5	0
Walker, Dane, Huntsville	.944	50	65	2	4	71	0
Warner, Mike, Greenville*	.953	48	100	1	5	106	0
Watkins, Pat, Chattanooga	.960	104	185	8	8	201	1
Williams, Juan, Greenville	.991	51	104	2	1	107	0
Wolfe, Joel, Huntsville	1.000	24	44	2	0	46	0
Wollenburg, Doug, Greenville	1.000	1	1	0	0	1	0

TRIPLE PLAY: Farrell.

CATCHERS

Player, Team	Pct.	G	PO	A	E	TC	DP	PB
Ayrault, Joe, Greenville	.986	88	516	64	8	588	4	3
Beard, Garrett, Huntsville	.978	29	162	17	4	183	1	3
Brooks, Eric, Knoxville	.986	19	122	16	2	140	1	3
Brown, Adam, Chattanooga	.992	65	440	35	4	479	7	7
Buckley, Troy, Chattanooga	1.000	8	61	3	0	64	0	1
Cardenas, John, Port City	.989	48	328	34	4	366	5	10
Casanova, Raul, Memphis	.980	75	531	55	12	598	6	12
Cox, Darron, Orlando	.973	31	157	24	5	186	1	2
Davis, Josh, Memphis	1.000	1	6	0	0	6	0	0
Edge, Tim, Carolina	.983	34	198	31	4	233	3	2
Erdman, Brad, Orlando	.986	14	70	3	1	74	0	0
Fernandez, Daniel, Jacksonville	.991	93	464	61	5	530	7	5
Gubanich, Creighton, Huntsville...	.997	43	253	47	1	301	4	5
Hanel, Marcus, Carolina	1.000	18	103	13	0	116	4	6
Harmes, Kris, Knoxville	.974	43	275	24	8	307	3	2
Johnson, Jack, Orlando	.977	21	111	14	3	128	2	2
Kendall, Jason, Carolina	.989	98	692	54	8	754	7	11
Killeen, Tim, Memphis	.985	59	408	55	7	470	5	11
Kingston, Mark, Orlando	1.000	4	3	1	0	4	0	1
Ladd, Jeff, Knoxville	.977	7	38	4	1	43	0	0
Lidle, Kevin, Jacksonville	.990	20	90	10	1	101	1	0
Lutz, Brent, Knoxville	.971	39	217	19	7	243	1	9
Manning, Henry, Birmingham	.985	11	57	10	1	68	2	1
Martinez, Angel, Knoxville	.980	38	219	30	5	254	0	4
Molina, Izzy, Huntsville	.980	78	455	74	11	540	11	14
Morales, Francisco, Orlando	1.000	2	6	1	0	7	0	2
Morland, Mike, Knoxville	.985	9	60	5	1	66	0	1
Ortiz, Hector, Orlando	.991	94	567	72	6	645	5	3
Pecorilli, Aldo, Greenville	.913	6	39	3	4	46	0	0
Perona, Joe, Jacksonville	.909	6	17	3	2	22	0	0
Pevey, Marty, Jacksonville	.952	5	19	1	1	21	0	0
Rice, Lance, Jacksonville	.994	63	284	43	2	329	9	5
Ripplemeyer, Brad, Greenville	.972	53	287	28	9	324	3	4
Rumfield, Toby, Chattanooga	1.000	2	2	0	0	2	0	0
Schwenke, Matt, Memphis	.972	20	130	8	4	142	1	4
Sellers, Rick, Chattanooga	.987	88	567	55	8	630	7	11
Slaught, Don, Carolina	1.000	3	24	1	0	25	0	0
Snyder, Jared, Orlando	1.000	1	6	1	0	7	0	0
Sutherland, Alex, Port City	.990	13	91	10	1	102	0	0
Triessl, Mike, Memphis	.889	3	8	0	1	9	0	0
Varitek, Jason, Port City	.988	89	589	59	8	656	7	21
Vinas, Julio, Birmingham	.976	57	356	50	10	416	4	5
VOLLMER, Scott, Birmingham...	.992	79	554	70	5	629	8	10

PITCHERS

Player, Team	Pct.	G	PO	A	E	TC	DP
Abbott, Todd, Huntsville	1.000	4	0	1	0	1	0
Adam, Dave, Port City	.923	31	7	17	2	26	0
Adams, Terry, Orlando	.667	3	1	3	2	6	1
Adams, Willie, Huntsville	.857	13	4	8	2	14	0
Aldred, Scott, Jacksonville*	1.000	2	1	1	0	2	0
Almanzar, Carlos, Knoxville	.968	35	17	13	1	31	1
Andujar, Luis, Birmingham	.960	27	13	11	1	25	3
Apana, Matt, Port City	1.000	6	1	5	0	6	0
Arnold, Jamie, Greenville	1.000	10	2	5	0	7	0
Backlund, Brett, Carolina	1.000	22	4	14	0	18	0
Banks, Jim, Huntsville	.800	44	4	4	2	10	0
Barnes, Jon, Memphis	1.000	2	0	1	0	1	0
Bauer, Matt, Jacksonville*	1.000	27	4	5	0	9	0
Beatty, Blaine, Chattanooga*	.900	8	3	6	1	10	1
Beckett, Robbie, Memphis*	.500	36	1	2	3	6	0
Beltran, Alonso, Knoxville	.933	28	4	10	1	15	0
Bene, Bill, Chattanooga	1.000	4	1	0	0	1	0
Bennett, Bob, Huntsville	1.000	23	21	16	0	37	1
Bennett, Chris, Carolina	1.000	18	2	3	0	5	0
Berlin, Mike, Jacksonville	1.000	3	0	1	0	1	0

CLASS AA Southern League

Player, Team	Pct.	G	PO	A	E	TC	DP	Player, Team	Pct.	G	PO	A	E	TC	DP
Bertotti, Mike, Birmingham*	.824	12	2	12	3	17	0	King, Kevin, Port City*	.909	20	2	8	1	11	0
Blair, Dirk, Greenville	.875	40	2	5	1	8	1	Koller, Jerry, Greenville	1.000	25	8	17	0	25	0
Bradford, Troy, Orlando	1.000	4	0	1	0	1	0	Konuszewski, Dennis, Carolina	.923	48	5	7	1	13	1
Brandow, Derek, Knoxville	1.000	25	9	7	0	16	2	Kotes, Chris, Knoxville	.889	36	10	14	3	27	2
Brown, Chad, Knoxville*	.938	40	6	9	1	16	1	Kramer, Tommy, Chattanooga	1.000	21	9	15	0	24	0
Brumley, Duff, Chattanooga	.909	25	6	4	1	11	2	Kroon, Marc, Memphis	.800	22	4	4	2	10	1
Buckley, Travis, Chattanooga	1.000	3	1	0	0	1	0	Lawrence, Sean, Carolina*	1.000	12	1	2	0	3	0
Burgess, Kurt, Greenville	.667	8	0	2	1	3	0	Lemke, Steve, Huntsville	.968	25	10	20	1	31	2
Burgos, John, Chattanooga*	.947	44	9	9	1	19	0	Levine, Alan, Birmingham	1.000	43	3	17	0	20	1
Burlingame, Ben, Orlando	1.000	37	5	12	0	17	1	Loiselle, Rich, Memphis	.957	13	15	7	1	23	1
Carmona, Rafael, Port City	1.000	15	0	2	0	2	0	Long, Joey, Memphis*	1.000	25	1	6	0	7	0
Carpenter, Chris, Knoxville	.875	13	5	9	2	16	1	Lowe, Derek, Port City	1.000	10	2	8	0	10	0
Cedeno, Blas, Jacksonville	.952	48	5	15	1	21	1	LUEBBERS, Larry, Chattanooga	1.000	28	13	30	0	43	6
Chouinard, Bobby, Huntsville	.938	29	7	23	2	32	4	Manning, Derek, Huntsville*	1.000	5	0	5	0	5	0
Christman, Scott, Birmingham*	.941	12	4	12	1	17	0	Mattson, Rob, Memphis	.953	30	10	31	2	43	3
Clark, Dera, Memphis	1.000	23	2	3	0	5	0	Maurer, Mike, Huntsville	1.000	17	1	0	0	1	0
Cole, Victor, Memphis	1.000	8	1	3	0	4	1	May, Darrell, Greenville*	1.000	15	4	11	0	15	0
Connolly, Matt, Orlando	1.000	21	3	2	0	5	0	McCarthy, Greg, Birmingham*	1.000	38	2	8	0	10	1
Connors, Chad, Chattanooga	1.000	10	1	0	0	1	0	Meier, Kevin, Orlando	.882	11	3	12	2	17	0
Cooke, Steve, Carolina*	1.000	1	0	1	0	1	0	Meinershagen, Adam, Knoxville	1.000	3	0	2	0	2	0
Cullop, Glen, Chattanooga	.667	8	1	1	1	3	0	Michalak, Chris, Huntsville*	1.000	7	1	3	0	4	0
Dabney, Fred, Orlando*	.833	13	2	3	1	6	0	Miller, Trever, Jacksonville*	.971	31	8	25	1	34	2
D'Andrea, Mike, Greenville	.864	40	8	11	3	22	2	Moehler, Brian, Jacksonville	.977	28	19	24	1	44	1
Davison, Scott, Port City	.889	34	4	4	1	9	0	Mongiello, Mike, Birmingham	1.000	7	1	3	0	4	0
DeLeon, Luis, Orlando	1.000	4	2	3	0	5	0	Moore, Marcus, Chattanooga	.800	36	1	3	1	5	0
DeLosSantos, Mariano, Carolina	.889	21	3	5	1	9	0	Moore, Tim, Birmingham	1.000	29	11	11	0	22	0
Dessens, Elmer, Carolina	1.000	27	11	26	0	37	2	Morel, Ramon, Carolina	1.000	10	4	10	0	14	0
Doman, Roger, Knoxville	1.000	14	2	3	0	5	0	Morgan, Mike, Orlando	.833	2	1	4	1	6	1
Dressendorfer, Kirk, Huntsville	1.000	9	2	3	0	5	0	Murray, Heath, Memphis*	.867	14	6	7	2	15	0
Dreyer, Darren, Orlando	1.000	14	6	5	0	11	0	Murray, Matt, Greenville	1.000	5	1	2	0	3	0
Drinkwater, Sean, Memphis	1.000	1	0	1	0	1	0	Nezelek, Andy, Carolina	1.000	6	2	1	0	3	0
Drumright, Mike, Jacksonville	.875	5	2	5	1	8	0	Nickell, Jackie, Port City	.882	27	4	11	2	17	1
Etheridge, Roger, Greenville*	.962	32	2	23	1	26	0	Nitkowski, C.J., Chattanooga*	1.000	8	8	9	0	17	0
Evans, Sean, Carolina	.846	29	4	7	2	13	0	Nix, Jim, Chattanooga	.957	40	7	15	1	23	0
Farmer, Howard, Chattanooga	1.000	1	0	1	0	1	0	Norman, Scott, Jacksonville	1.000	4	1	4	0	5	0
Fermin, Ramon, Huntsville	.952	32	6	14	1	21	3	Olsen, Steve, Birmingham	1.000	14	6	7	0	13	1
Fernandez, Osvaldo, Port City*	1.000	27	8	28	0	36	4	Pace, Scott, Knoxville*	.889	18	4	12	2	18	0
Ferry, Mike, Chattanooga	1.000	24	19	10	0	29	1	Paige, Carey, Greenville	.857	7	1	5	1	7	0
Figueroa, Fernando, Carolina*	1.000	6	1	2	0	3	0	Parris, Steve, Carolina	.938	14	5	10	1	16	0
Fordham, Tom, Birmingham*	.750	14	2	10	4	16	0	Peters, Chris, Carolina*	1.000	2	1	1	0	2	0
Fox, Chad, Chattanooga	.765	20	9	4	4	17	2	Petersen, Matt, Orlando	1.000	24	4	13	0	17	0
Franklin, Ryan, Port City	.946	31	5	30	2	37	3	Pett, Jose, Knoxville	.950	26	5	14	1	20	0
Freeman, Chris, Knoxville	1.000	39	4	7	0	11	1	Pickett, Ricky, Chattanooga*	.875	4	1	6	1	8	0
Freitas, Mike, Memphis	1.000	54	2	9	0	11	3	Pierce, Rob, Huntsville	1.000	15	1	1	0	2	0
Gaillard, Eddie, Jacksonville	1.000	8	0	1	0	1	0	Pierson, Jason, Birmingham*	1.000	4	1	2	0	3	0
Gajkowski, Steve, Birmingham	1.000	35	4	12	0	16	1	Pisciotta, Marc, Carolina	.882	56	5	10	2	17	0
Glinatsis, George, Port City	1.000	18	4	12	0	16	3	Plantenberg, Erik, Memphis*	1.000	20	2	2	0	4	0
Goldsmith, Gary, Jacksonville	.833	15	5	10	3	18	1	Plaster, Allen, Huntsville	.846	43	2	9	2	13	1
Gray, Dennis, Knoxville*	.875	24	1	6	1	8	1	Ralph, Curtis, Carolina	1.000	18	1	2	0	3	0
Greene, Rick, Jacksonville	1.000	32	2	4	0	6	0	Ratliff, Jon, Orlando	.938	26	8	7	1	16	0
Grigsby, Benji, Huntsville	.875	30	8	6	2	16	0	Resendez, Oscar, Port City	1.000	11	1	2	0	3	0
Grimm, John, Jacksonville	.750	13	2	1	1	4	0	Rivera, Lino, Carolina	1.000	4	0	1	0	1	0
Guilfoyle, Michael, Jacksonville*	1.000	56	1	3	0	4	0	Rivera, Roberto, Orlando*	1.000	49	5	15	0	20	1
Gutierrez, Jim, Jacksonville	1.000	45	5	9	0	14	1	Roper, John, Chattanooga	1.000	3	3	0	0	3	0
Haas, David, Orlando	1.000	3	0	1	0	1	0	Rose, Scott, Huntsville	1.000	38	11	13	0	24	0
Hanson, Craig, Memphis	1.000	25	2	1	0	3	0	Rosengren, John, Jacksonville*	1.000	14	2	12	0	14	0
Harrah, Doug, Orlando	1.000	44	4	6	0	10	1	Ruebel, Matt, Carolina*	.949	27	10	27	2	39	2
Harrison, Brian, Memphis*	1.000	38	0	3	0	3	0	Ruffcorn, Scott, Birmingham	1.000	3	3	2	0	5	0
Harrison, Tom, Greenville	.944	14	9	8	1	18	0	Russell, LaGrande, Port City	.909	39	2	8	1	11	1
Hart, Jason, Orlando	1.000	14	1	3	0	4	0	Ryan, Matt, Carolina	.955	44	1	20	1	22	0
Haught, Gary, Huntsville	1.000	9	3	4	0	7	0	Rychel, Kevin, Carolina	1.000	40	3	6	0	9	2
Heble, Kurt, Knoxville	.875	47	2	5	1	8	0	Schmitt, Todd, Memphis	1.000	26	4	3	0	7	0
Hernandez, Fernando, Memphis	.750	12	1	2	1	4	1	Schutz, Carl, Greenville*	1.000	51	2	5	0	7	0
Hill, Milt, Carolina	1.000	10	0	8	0	8	0	Seelbach, Chris, Greenville	1.000	9	1	4	0	5	0
Hollinger, Adrian, Greenville	1.000	7	6	4	0	10	0	Shafer, Bill, Greenville	.333	42	0	1	2	3	0
Hollins, Stacy, Huntsville	1.000	15	4	9	0	13	0	Shoemaker, Steve, Huntsville	1.000	43	8	7	0	15	0
Hostetler, Marcus, Greenville	.833	32	1	4	1	6	0	Shouse, Brian, Carolina*	.950	21	5	14	1	20	1
Hostetler, Mike, Greenville	.846	28	5	17	4	26	0	Simmons, John, Greenville*	.571	48	1	3	3	7	0
Huber, Jeff, Memphis*	1.000	5	0	1	0	1	0	Sirotka, Mike, Birmingham*	.947	16	3	15	1	19	2
Hurtado, Edwin, Knoxville	.875	11	7	7	2	16	0	Smith, Mike, Chattanooga	1.000	3	1	0	0	1	0
Hutcheson, David, Orlando	.974	28	20	18	1	39	0	Smith, Ottis, Orlando*	.963	17	8	18	1	27	1
Ingram, Todd, Knoxville	1.000	20	3	3	0	6	0	Snyder, John, Birmingham	1.000	5	1	2	0	3	0
Janzen, Marty, Knoxville	1.000	7	1	10	0	11	1	Sodowsky, Clint, Jacksonville	.850	19	7	10	3	20	1
Jersild, Aaron, Knoxville*	1.000	14	0	7	0	7	1	Steed, Rick, Knoxville	.833	27	7	3	2	12	0
Jimenez, Miguel, Huntsville	1.000	6	2	0	0	2	0	Swartzbaugh, Dave, Orlando	.800	16	1	3	1	5	0
Johnson, Barry, Birmingham	1.000	47	6	15	0	21	0	Taylor, Aaron, Huntsville	1.000	5	1	5	0	6	1
Johnson, Chris, Orlando	1.000	46	4	9	0	13	1	Telemaco, Amaury, Orlando	.933	22	14	14	2	30	1
Johnston, Sean, Birmingham*	1.000	34	11	20	0	31	1	Thomas, Carlos, Hun.-Mem.	.750	18	2	4	2	8	0
Kaufman, Brad, Memphis	.886	27	12	19	4	35	1	Thomas, Larry, Birmingham*	1.000	35	3	6	0	9	0
Keagle, Greg, Memphis	1.000	15	8	10	0	18	0	Thompson, Justin, Jacksonville*	.920	18	4	19	2	25	0
Kelley, Rich, Jacksonville*	1.000	7	1	1	0	2	0	Tolar, Kevin, Carolina*	1.000	12	0	1	0	1	0
Kelly, John, Jacksonville	.933	66	3	11	1	15	1	Tranbarger, Mark, Chattanooga*	1.000	48	6	7	0	13	1
Kilgo, Rusty, Chattanooga*	1.000	54	8	16	0	24	1	Tsamis, George, Car.-P.C.*	1.000	19	1	2	0	3	0

Player, Team	Pct.	G	PO	A	E	TC	DP
Turnier, Aaron, Greenville*	1.000	8	1	0	0	1	0
Tuttle, Dave, Chattanooga	1.000	8	5	8	0	13	0
Urso, Sal, Port City*	1.000	51	3	18	0	21	2
VanRyn, Ben, Chattanooga*	1.000	5	2	3	0	5	0
Vasquez, Marcos, Chattanooga	1.000	26	12	20	0	32	2
Veras, Dario, Memphis	.875	58	8	6	2	16	0
Wagner, Matt, Port City	.862	23	9	16	4	29	2
Watkins, Jason, Birmingham	1.000	10	0	2	0	2	0
Weber, Ben, Knoxville	1.000	12	3	4	0	7	1
Wendell, Turk, Orlando	1.000	5	0	1	0	1	0
Whiteside, Sean, Jacksonville*	1.000	27	1	7	0	8	0
Wilkins, Marc, Carolina	1.000	37	1	12	0	13	1
Willis, Travis, Carolina	.833	16	3	2	1	6	0
Wilson, Gary, Carolina	1.000	1	0	2	0	2	0
Withem, Shannon, Jacksonville	1.000	19	10	12	0	22	2
Witte, Trey, Port City	.950	48	4	15	1	20	0
Wolcott, Bob, Port City	.941	12	9	7	1	17	1
Woodfin, Chris, Birmingham	.882	48	5	10	2	17	0
Worley, Robert, Port City	.857	22	2	4	1	7	0
Young, Anthony, Orlando	1.000	2	1	1	0	2	0
Zongor, Steve, Huntsville*	1.000	9	2	2	0	4	0

TRIPLE PLAY: Nitkowski.

PITCHERS WITH TWO OR MORE TEAMS

Player, Team	Pct.	G	PO	A	E	TC	DP
Thomas, Carlos, Huntsville	1.000	7	0	1	0	1	0
Thomas, Carlos, Memphis	.714	11	2	3	2	7	0
Tsamis, George, Carolina*	.000	12	0	0	0	0	0
Tsamis, George, Port City*	1.000	7	1	2	0	3	0

The following players did not have any fielding statistics at the positions indicated or appeared only as a designated hitter, pinch-hitter or pinch-runner: Baker, p; Beard, p; Briggs, 3b; A. Brown, 1b; Bullinger, p; Cooper, ss; R. DeLeon, p; Dibble, p; Felix, of; Fitzer, p; Flynt, p; Garcia, 3b; R. Gomez, 3b; Gubanich, of; Hickey, p; Jackson, p; Kaufman, of; Mashore, 2b; Mota, 2b, of; Munoz, 3b; Sanford, dh, ph, pr; Sawkiw, p; Silva, p; K. Thomas, 3b; C. Vazquez, p; Waggoner, p; Walker, p; Wolfe, p; Worrell, p.

LEAGUE CHAMPIONS

Year	Team	Pct.
1904—	Macon	.598
1905—	Macon	.625
1906—	Savannah	.637
1907—	Charleston	.620
1908—	Jacksonville	.694
1909—	Chattanooga*	.738
	Augusta	.702
1910—	Columbus	.588
1911—	Columbus*	.681
	Columbia	.710
1912—	Jacksonville*	.679
	Columbus	.632
1913—	Savannah	.754
	Savannah*	.593
1914—	Savannah*	.667
	Albany	.650
1915—	Macon	.588
	Columbus*	.686
1916—	Augusta*	.617
	Columbia	.631
1917—	Charleston	.741
	Columbia*	.667
1918—	Did not operate.	
1919—	Columbia	.585
1920—	Columbia	.633
1921—	Columbia	.642
1922—	Charleston	.625
1923—	Charlotte*	.653
	Macon	.580
1924—	Augusta	.612
1925—	Spartanburg	.620
1926—	Greenville	.662
1927—	Greenville	.622
1928—	Asheville	.664
1929—	Asheville	.605
	Knoxville*	.634
1930—	Greenville*	.620
	Macon	.643
1931-35—	Did not operate.	
1936—	Jacksonville	.652
	Columbus*	.650
1937—	Columbus	.572
	Savannah (3rd)†	.565
1938—	Savannah	.574
	Macon (2nd)†	.570
1939—	Columbus	.601
	Augusta (2nd)†	.597
1940—	Savannah	.627
	Columbus (2nd)†	.583
1941—	Macon	.643
	Columbia (2nd)†	.636
1942—	Charleston	.620
	Macon (2nd)†	.585
1943-45—	Did not operate.	
1946—	Columbus	.568
	Augusta (4th)†	.547
1947—	Columbus	.575
	Savannah (2nd)†	.563
1948—	Charleston	.572
	Greenville (3rd)†	.549
1949—	Macon‡	.623
1950—	Macon‡	.588
1951—	Montgomery	.607
1952—	Columbia	.649
	Montgomery (3rd)†	.558
1953—	Jacksonville	.679
	Savannah (2nd)†	.571
1954—	Jacksonville	.593
	Savannah (2nd)†	.571
1955—	Columbia	.636
	Augusta (3rd)†	.543
1956—	Jacksonville‡	.621
1957—	Augusta	.636
	Charlotte (2nd)†	.562
1958—	Augusta	.550
	Macon (3rd)†	.500
1959—	Knoxville	.557
	Gastonia (4th)†	.504
1960—	Columbia	.597
	Savannah (3rd)†	.561
1961—	Asheville	.635
1962—	Savannah	.662
	Macon (3rd)†	.576
1963—	Augusta*	.661
	Lynchburg	.662
1964—	Lynchburg	.579
1965—	Columbus	.572
1966—	Mobile	.629
1967—	Birmingham	.604
1968—	Asheville	.614
1969—	Charlotte	.579
1970—	Columbus	.569
1971—	Did not operate as league—clubs were members of Dixie Association.	
1972—	Asheville	.583
	Montgomery§	.561
1973—	Montgomery§	.580
	Jacksonville	.559
1974—	Jacksonville	.565
	Knoxville§	.533
1975—	Orlando	.587
	Montgomery§	.545
1976—	Montgomery∞	.591
	Orlando	.540
1977—	Montgomery∞	.628
	Jacksonville	.522
1978—	Knoxville∞	.611
	Savannah	.500
1979—	Columbus	.587
	Nashville∞	.576
1980—	Memphis	.576
	Charlotte∞	.500
1981—	Nashville	.566
	Orlando∞	.556
1982—	Jacksonville	.576
	Nashville∞	.535
1983—	Birmingham∞	.628
	Jacksonville	.531
1984—	Charlotte∞	.510
	Knoxville	.483
1985—	Charlotte	.545
	Huntsville∞	.542
1986—	Huntsville	.553
	Columbus∞	.500
1987—	Charlotte	.586
	Birmingham∞	.476
1988—	Greenville	.604
	Chattanooga∞	.566
1989—	Birmingham∞	.615
	Greenville	.504
1990—	Orlando	.590
	Memphis∞	.507
1991—	Greenville	.611
	Orlando∞	.535
1992—	Greenville∞	.699
	Chattanooga	.629
1993—	Birmingham∞	.549
	Knoxville	.500
1994—	Huntsville∞	.587
	Carolina	.529
1995—	Carolina∞	.618
	Chattanooga	.580

*Won split season playoff. †Won four-club playoff. ‡Won championship and four-club playoff. §League was divided into Eastern and Western divisions; won playoff. ∞League was divided into Eastern and Western divisions and played split season; won playoff.

CLASS AA Southern League

TEXAS LEAGUE

LEAGUE OFFICE

President/treasurer
Tom Kayser

Address
2442 Facet Oak
San Antonio, TX 78232

Phone
210-545-5297

TEAMS

ARKANSAS TRAVELERS

General manager
Bill Valentine
Manager
Rick Mahler
Ballpark (capacity, surface)
Ray Winder Field (6,783, grass)
Affiliation
Cardinals
Address
P.O. Box 5599
Little Rock, AR 72215
Phone
501-664-1555

EL PASO DIABLOS

General manager
Rick Parr
Manager
Dave Machemer
Ballpark (capacity, surface)
Cohen Stadium (9,765, grass)
Affiliation
Brewers
Address
P.O. Drawer 4797
El Paso, TX 79914
Phone
915-755-2000

JACKSON GENERALS

General manager
Bill Blackwell
Manager
Dave Engle
Ballpark (capacity, surface)
Smith-Wills Stadium (5,200, grass)
Affiliation
Astros

Address
P.O. Box 4209
Jackson, MS 39296
Phone
601-981-4664

MIDLAND ANGELS

General manager
Monty Hoppel
Manager
Mario Mendoza
Ballpark (capacity, surface)
Christensen Stadium (5,000, grass)
Affiliation
Angels
Address
P.O. Box 51187
Midland, TX 79710
Phone
915-683-4251

SAN ANTONIO MISSIONS

General manager
Burl Yarbrough
Manager
John Shelby
Ballpark (capacity, surface)
Nelson Wolf Stadium (6,300, grass)
Affiliation
Dodgers
Address
5757 Highway 90 West
San Antonio, TX 78227
Phone
210-675-7275

SHREVEPORT CAPTAINS

General manager
Gilbert Little
Manager
Frank Cacciatore

Ballpark (capacity, surface)
Fair Grounds Field (6,200, grass)
Affiliation
Giants
Address
P.O. Box 3448
Shreveport, LA 71133
Phone
318-636-5555

TULSA DRILLERS

Executive v.p./general manager
Chuck Lamson
Manager
Bobby Jones
Ballpark (capacity, surface)
Drillers Stadium (10,813, grass)
Affiliation
Rangers
Address
P.O. Box 4448
Tulsa, OK 74159
Phone
918-744-5998

WICHITA WRANGLERS

General manager
Steve Shaad
Manager
Ron Johnson
Ballpark (capacity, surface)
Lawrence-Dumont Stadium (6,067, artificial infield, grass outfield)
Affiliation
Royals
Address
P.O. Box 1420
Wichita, KS 67201
Phone
316-267-3372

1995 FINAL STANDINGS

FIRST HALF

EAST DIVISION

Team	W	L	T	Pct.	GB
Shreveport (Giants)	43	24	0	.642	......
Arkansas (Cardinals)	37	30	0	.552	6
Jackson (Astros)	32	35	0	.478	11
Tulsa (Rangers)	21	46	0	.313	22

WEST DIVISION

Team	W	L	T	Pct.	GB
Midland (Angels)	36	32	0	.529	......
San Antonio (Dodgers)	35	33	0	.515	1
El Paso (Brewers)	35	33	0	.515	1
Wichita (Royals)	31	37	0	.456	5

SECOND HALF

EAST DIVISION

Team	W	L	T	Pct.	GB
Shreveport (Giants)	45	23	0	.662	......
Arkansas (Cardinals)	33	35	0	.485	12
Tulsa (Rangers)	31	37	0	.456	14
Jackson (Astros)	30	38	0	.441	15

WEST DIVISION

Team	W	L	T	Pct.	GB
Wichita (Royals)	41	27	0	.603	......
El Paso (Brewers)	33	35	0	.485	8
Midland (Angels)	30	38	0	.441	11
San Antonio (Dodgers)	29	39	0	.426	12

COMPOSITE

Team	Shr.	Wch.	Ark.	E.P.	Mid.	S.A.	Jac.	Tul.	W	L	T	Pct.	GB
Shreveport (Giants)	...	7	18	7	7	7	22	20	88	47	0	.652	....
Wichita (Royals)	3	....	5	19	15	16	6	8	72	64	0	.529	16½
Arkansas (Cardinals)	14	5	....	6	3	7	16	19	70	65	0	.519	18
El Paso (Brewers)	3	13	4	....	17	19	4	8	68	68	0	.500	20½
Midland (Angels)	3	17	7	15	....	13	5	6	66	70	0	.485	22½
San Antonio (Dodgers)	3	16	3	13	19	....	4	6	64	72	0	.471	24½
Jackson (Astros)	9	4	6	6	5	6	....	16	62	73	0	.459	26
Tulsa (Rangers)	12	2	12	6	2	4	16	....	52	83	0	.385	36

Arkansas club represented Little Rock, Ark.

Major league affiliations in parentheses.

PLAYOFFS: Midland defeated Wichita, three games to two; Shreveport defeated Midland, four games to one, to win league championship.

REGULAR-SEASON ATTENDANCE: Arkansas, 248,340; El Paso, 329,233; Jackson, 171,508; Midland, 202,830; San Antonio, 387,090; Shreveport, 173,996; Tulsa, 321,662; Wichita, 203,134. Total—2,037,793. Playoffs (10 games)—28,569. Class AA All-Star Game at Shreveport—6,247. Texas League All-Star Game at El Paso—2,906.

MANAGERS: Arkansas, Mike Ramsey; El Paso, Tim Ireland; Jackson, Tim Tolman; Midland, Mario Mendoza; San Antonio, John Shelby; Shreveport, Ron Wotus; Tulsa, Bobby Jones; Wichita, Ron Johnson.

ALL-STAR TEAM: 1B—Todd Landry, El Paso; 2B—Jeff Berblinger, Arkansas; 3B—George Arias, Midland; SS—Wil Guerrero, San Antonio; OF—Brian Banks, El Paso; Jacob Cruz, Shreveport; Johnny Damon, Wichita; C—Todd Greene, Midland; DH—Oreste Marrero, San Antonio; Utility—Jay Canizaro, Shreveport; LHP—David Pyc, San Antonio; Gary Rath, San Antonio; Billy Wagner, Jackson; RHP—Steve Bourgeois, Shreveport; Edwin Corps, Shreveport; Steve Montgomery, Arkansas; Player of the Year—Johnny Damon, Wichita; Pitcher of the Year—Steve Bourgeois, Shreveport; Manager of the Year—Ron Johnson, Wichita.

1995 BATTING

TEAM

Team	Avg.	G	TPA	AB	R	H	TB	2B	3B	HR	RBI	SH	SF	HP	BB	IBB	SO	SB	CS	GDP	LOB	ShO	Slg.	OBP
El Paso	.286	136	5316	4656	733	1331	1993	274	68	84	665	32	48	53	527	22	888	84	54	130	990	1	.428	.362
Midland	.284	136	5292	4681	726	1328	2071	235	50	136	660	48	54	40	468	23	856	110	85	93	960	3	.442	.350
Wichita	.282	136	5278	4701	685	1328	1937	244	34	99	616	61	28	59	429	32	668	143	95	109	970	7	.412	.348
Shreveport ...	.280	135	5349	4644	733	1302	1894	267	35	85	663	57	48	54	546	40	742	108	66	114	1013	4	.408	.359
Arkansas	.268	135	5006	4387	617	1176	1739	199	32	100	570	52	26	47	492	31	787	86	63	116	938	3	.396	.346
San Antonio ...	.265	136	5115	4556	585	1209	1763	228	34	86	531	25	41	45	446	22	834	119	108	98	914	9	.387	.334
Jackson	.262	135	5058	4488	541	1174	1683	203	24	86	490	47	50	45	427	23	689	78	74	114	958	12	.375	.329
Tulsa	.257	135	5080	4513	540	1160	1648	202	35	72	501	53	42	46	424	18	683	54	50	121	949	12	.365	.324

INDIVIDUAL

TOP QUALIFIERS FOR BATTING CHAMPIONSHIP

Minimum 367 plate appearances. *Lefthanded batter. †Switch-hitter.

Player, Team	Avg.	G	TPA	AB	R	H	TB	2B	3B	HR	RBI	SH	SF	HP	BB	IBB	SO	SB	CS	GDP	Slg.	OBP
Guerrero, Wilton, San Antonio	.348	95	414	382	53	133	158	13	6	0	26	4	1	1	26	3	63	21	22	10	.414	.390
Damon, Johnny, Wichita*	.343	111	503	423	83	145	226	15	9	16	54	10	1	2	67	13	35	26	15	3	.534	.434
Berblinger, Jeff, Arkansas	.319	87	392	332	66	106	144	15	4	5	29	1	2	9	48	1	40	16	16	2	.434	.417
Carvajal, Jovino, Midland†	.313	79	374	348	58	109	138	13	5	2	23	5	2	1	18	2	42	39	21	3	.397	.347
Lopez, Roberto, El Paso†	.312	114	509	417	80	130	171	22	8	1	44	6	5	4	77	2	63	9	4	4	.410	.419
Mueller, Bill, Shreveport†	.309	88	393	330	56	102	125	16	2	1	39	1	5	4	53	2	36	6	5	9	.379	.406
Williamson, Antone, El Paso*	.309	104	446	392	62	121	184	30	6	7	90	0	4	3	47	3	57	3	1	10	.469	.383
Banks, Brian, El Paso†	.308	128	536	441	81	136	231	39	10	12	78	3	6	7	81	6	113	9	9	10	.524	.413
Myers, Rod, Wichita*	.307	131	548	499	71	153	208	22	6	7	62	8	3	4	34	3	77	29	16	7	.417	.354
Monell, Johnny, Tulsa†	.306	121	513	434	55	133	189	18	1	12	64	0	6	6	67	6	53	0	1	10	.435	.402
Wolff, Mike, Midland	.303	127	524	445	76	135	211	28	3	14	70	4	7	3	65	3	83	10	9	10	.474	.390
Romero, Mandy, Wichita†	.302	121	515	440	73	133	230	32	1	21	82	0	1	5	69	10	60	1	3	15	.523	.402
Bridges, Kary, Jackson*	.301	118	477	418	56	126	165	22	4	3	43	6	4	0	49	3	17	10	12	12	.395	.372
Mora, Melvin, Jackson	.298	123	522	467	63	139	180	32	0	3	45	7	7	9	32	1	57	22	11	11	.385	.350
Cruz, Jacob, Shreveport*	.297	127	529	458	88	136	210	33	1	13	77	4	2	8	57	6	72	9	8	15	.459	.383

DEPARTMENTAL LEADERS: G—Arias, 134; AB—Arias, 520; R—Arias, 91; H—Myers, 153; TB—Arias, 274; 2B—Banks, 39; 3B—Glenn, 11; HR—Arias, 30; RBI—Arias, 104; SH—R. Martinez, 18; SF—R. Martinez, 9; HP—Fasano, 16; BB—Banks, 81; IBB—Damon, 13; SO—Glenn, 126; SB—F. Martinez, 44; CS—W. Guerrero, 22; GIDP—Landry, 20; Slg.—Damon, .534; OBP—Damon, .434.

ALL PLAYERS

*Lefthanded batter. †Switch-hitter.

Player, Team	Avg.	G	TPA	AB	R	H	TB	2B	3B	HR	RBI	SH	SF	HP	BB	IBB	SO	SB	CS	GDP	Slg.	OBP
Alguacil, Jose, Shreveport*	.250	1	4	4	1	1	1	0	0	0	1	0	0	0	0	0	1	1	0	0	.250	.250
Allen, Ron, Jackson	.333	4	4	3	0	1	1	0	0	0	0	0	0	1	0	0	0	0	0	0	.333	.333
Anderson, Charlie, Arkansas	.283	77	262	240	31	68	99	15	2	4	29	0	1	0	21	1	55	1	2	10	.413	.340
Anderson, Paul, Arkansas	.250	38	5	4	0	1	3	0	1	0	1	0	0	0	0	0	0	0	1	.750	.250
Arias, George, Midland	.279	134	594	520	91	145	274	19	10	30	104	1	5	5	63	1	119	3	1	11	.527	.359
Arrandale, Matt, Arkansas	.000	47	2	2	0	0	0	0	0	0	0	0	0	0	0	0	1	0	0	0	.000	.000
Aurilia, Rich, Shreveport	.324	64	261	226	29	74	105	14	1	4	42	5	2	1	27	3	26	10	3	8	.465	.398
Badorek, Mike, Arkansas	.000	18	17	17	0	0	0	0	0	0	0	0	0	0	0	0	9	0	0	1	.000	.000
Bagwell, Jeff, Jackson	.167	4	16	12	0	2	2	0	0	0	0	0	0	1	3	1	2	0	0	0	.167	.375
Banks, Brian, El Paso†	.308	128	536	441	81	136	231	39	10	12	78	3	6	7	81	6	113	9	9	10	.524	.413
Berblinger, Jeff, Arkansas	.319	87	392	332	66	106	144	15	4	5	29	1	2	9	48	1	40	16	16	2	.434	.417
Bethea, Scott, Arkansas*	.176	11	39	34	6	6	7	1	0	0	4	2	1	0	2	0	5	1	0	0	.206	.216
Blanco, Henry, San Antonio	.255	88	335	302	37	77	139	18	4	12	48	0	2	3	27	2	52	1	1	4	.460	.328
Bourgeois, Steve, Shreveport	.323	24	35	31	6	10	17	2	1	1	8	2	0	0	0	0	7	0	0	0	.548	.364

Player, Team	Avg.	G	TPA	AB	R	H	TB	2B	3B	HR	RBI	SH	SF	HP	BB	IBB	SO	SB	CS	GDP	Slg.	OBP
Boykin, Tyrone, Midland	.271	62	235	210	34	57	95	11	3	7	25	1	3	0	21	1	36	2	1	3	.452	.333
Brannon, Cliff, Shreveport	.000	3	1	1	0	0	0	0	0	0	0	0	0	0	0	0	0	0	0	1	.000	.000
Brewington, Jamie, Shreveport	.143	16	18	14	1	2	2	0	0	0	2	1	0	0	3	0	3	0	0	0	.143	.294
Bridges, Kary, Jackson*	.301	118	477	418	56	126	165	22	4	3	43	6	4	0	49	3	17	10	12	12	.395	.372
Brosnan, Jason, San Antonio*	.000	19	1	1	0	0	0	0	0	0	0	0	0	0	0	0	1	0	0	0	.000	.000
Brunson, William, San Antonio*	.000	14	5	5	0	0	0	0	0	0	0	0	0	0	0	0	2	0	0	0	.000	.000
Burton, Darren, Wichita†	.239	41	185	163	13	39	53	9	1	1	20	9	0	1	12	0	27	6	6	2	.325	.295
Busby, Mike, Arkansas	.167	20	24	18	1	3	3	0	0	0	1	5	1	0	0	0	7	0	0	0	.167	.158
Butterfield, Chris, San Antonio†	.000	2	8	6	0	0	0	0	0	0	0	0	0	0	2	0	3	0	0	0	.000	.250
Cairo, Miguel, San Antonio	.278	107	474	435	53	121	146	20	1	1	41	4	4	5	26	0	32	33	16	6	.336	.323
Canizaro, Jay, Shreveport	.293	126	513	440	83	129	204	25	7	12	60	4	5	6	58	4	98	16	9	9	.464	.379
Carpenter, Brian, Arkansas	.000	17	6	6	0	0	0	0	0	0	0	0	0	0	0	0	2	0	0	0	.000	.000
Carpenter, Jerry, Midland	.000	2	2	2	1	0	0	0	0	0	0	0	0	0	0	0	1	0	0	0	.000	.000
Caruso, Gene, El Paso*	.000	46	1	1	0	0	0	0	0	0	0	0	0	0	0	0	0	0	0	0	.000	.000
Carvajal, Jovino, Midland†	.313	79	374	348	58	109	138	13	5	2	23	5	2	1	18	2	42	39	21	3	.397	.347
Castillo, Juan, Jackson	.091	12	13	11	2	1	1	0	0	0	0	1	0	0	1	0	3	0	0	0	.091	.167
Castillo, Mariano, Shreveport	.000	22	3	3	0	0	0	0	0	0	0	0	0	0	0	0	2	0	0	0	.000	.000
Castro, Nelson, San Antonio	.000	48	1	1	0	0	0	0	0	0	0	0	0	0	0	0	0	0	0	0	.000	.000
Centeno, Henri, Jackson†	.256	92	204	172	24	44	55	3	1	2	12	3	2	3	24	2	31	6	4	7	.320	.353
Charles, Frank, Tulsa	.253	126	510	479	51	121	190	24	3	13	72	1	4	4	22	0	92	1	0	19	.397	.289
Chavez, Raul, Jackson	.287	58	205	188	16	54	74	8	0	4	25	4	2	3	8	1	17	0	4	7	.394	.323
Cholowsky, Dan, Arkansas	.311	54	221	190	41	59	92	12	0	7	35	0	2	5	24	2	41	7	6	2	.484	.398
Christopher, Chris, Arkansas	.274	23	63	62	7	17	21	1	0	1	3	0	0	1	0	6	4	1	2	.339	.264
Clinton, Jim, Tulsa	.193	28	69	57	6	11	16	2	0	1	7	3	1	1	7	0	16	2	0	3	.281	.288
Cohick, Emmitt, Midland*	.229	56	193	153	25	35	58	13	2	2	23	2	3	2	33	1	45	3	2	0	.379	.366
Colon, Dennis, Jackson†	.224	106	415	379	33	85	110	10	0	5	31	2	6	4	24	2	38	3	6	8	.290	.274
Corps, Edwin, Shreveport	.360	27	32	25	3	9	10	1	0	0	4	2	0	0	5	0	5	0	0	0	.400	.467
Creek, Ryan, Jackson	.150	26	24	20	2	3	3	0	0	0	1	0	0	3	0	9	0	1	1	.150	.261
Cruz, Jacob, Shreveport*	.297	127	529	458	88	136	210	33	1	13	77	4	2	8	57	6	72	9	8	15	.459	.383
Damon, Johnny, Wichita*	.343	111	503	423	83	145	226	15	9	16	54	10	1	2	67	13	35	26	15	3	.534	.434
Dandridge, Brad, San Antonio	.417	3	12	12	1	5	5	0	0	0	1	0	0	0	0	0	1	0	1	0	.417	.417
Daniels, Moe, Midland	.202	25	100	84	9	17	25	5	0	1	4	0	0	2	14	0	22	2	4	0	.298	.324
Davis, Ray, Arkansas	.111	21	21	18	2	2	2	0	0	0	0	1	0	0	2	0	9	0	1	0	.111	.200
Diaz, Alfredo, Midland†	.240	8	27	25	3	6	9	3	0	0	4	2	0	0	0	0	12	0	0	1	.360	.240
Diaz, Lino, Wichita	.350	62	247	226	40	79	118	15	3	6	43	0	1	6	14	0	21	0	3	5	.522	.401
DiFelice, Mike, Arkansas	.267	62	205	176	14	47	62	10	1	1	24	2	1	3	23	0	29	0	2	13	.352	.360
Diggs, Tony, Arkansas†	.268	78	275	235	33	63	94	9	8	2	21	2	1	2	35	5	41	7	6	3	.400	.366
Dodson, Bo, El Paso*	.359	63	267	223	46	80	129	20	4	7	43	0	0	7	37	2	42	1	1	6	.578	.464
Donnels, Chris, Jackson*	.167	4	16	12	1	2	3	1	0	0	1	0	0	0	4	0	4	0	0	0	.250	.375
Dumas, Mike, El Paso	.217	12	27	23	5	5	7	0	1	0	4	0	1	0	3	0	0	2	1	0	.304	.296
Edwards, Mike, Tulsa	.216	38	130	111	11	24	38	3	1	3	13	1	1	2	15	0	13	0	0	5	.342	.318
Ehmann, Kurt, Shreveport	.231	38	163	130	24	30	38	5	0	1	17	4	2	5	22	1	15	1	2	5	.292	.358
Ellis, Paul, Arkansas*	.227	78	287	229	17	52	64	6	0	2	25	4	1	4	49	4	18	0	1	9	.279	.371
Estes, Shawn, Shreveport	.667	4	3	3	0	2	2	0	0	0	1	0	0	0	0	0	1	0	0	0	.667	.667
Estrada, Osmani, Tulsa	.266	120	463	410	44	109	147	23	3	3	43	5	4	9	35	2	49	0	2	9	.359	.334
Evans, Dave, Jackson	.000	49	2	2	0	0	0	0	0	0	0	0	0	0	0	0	0	0	0	0	.000	.000
Fasano, Sal, Wichita	.290	87	362	317	60	92	175	19	2	20	66	0	2	16	27	1	61	3	6	8	.552	.373
Felder, Ken, El Paso	.272	114	425	367	51	100	168	24	4	12	55	0	4	6	48	3	94	2	6	10	.458	.362
Felix, Lauro, El Paso	.277	83	276	220	51	61	85	13	1	3	25	5	2	4	45	0	44	6	1	4	.386	.406
Florez, Tim, Shreveport	.268	100	331	295	37	79	121	11	2	9	46	3	3	4	26	1	49	4	3	7	.410	.332
Forkner, Tim, Jackson*	.269	35	140	119	19	32	52	11	0	3	23	0	0	2	19	0	14	1	3	3	.437	.379
Frias, Hanley, Tulsa†	.281	93	416	360	44	101	127	18	4	0	27	8	2	1	45	0	53	14	12	6	.353	.360
Frontera, Chad, Shreveport	.077	20	17	13	0	1	1	0	0	0	0	2	0	0	2	0	5	0	0	0	.077	.200
Gallaher, Kevin, Jackson	.200	6	12	10	0	2	3	1	0	0	1	1	0	0	1	0	1	0	0	0	.300	.273
Gamez, Francisco, El Paso	.000	28	1	1	0	0	0	0	0	0	0	0	0	0	0	0	0	0	0	0	.000	.000
Garcia, Jose, San Antonio	.000	38	1	1	0	0	0	0	0	0	0	0	0	0	0	0	1	0	0	0	.000	.000
Gilmore, Tony, Jackson	.212	53	159	146	10	31	37	3	0	1	15	1	2	0	10	0	27	0	0	3	.253	.259
Glenn, Leon, Midland*	.254	120	475	433	68	110	202	19	11	17	65	3	3	2	34	1	126	16	11	9	.467	.309
Gonzales, Rene, Midland	.176	5	21	17	1	3	3	0	0	0	3	2	0	0	1	0	1	0	1	0	.176	.333
Gonzalez, Raul, Wichita	.291	22	87	79	14	23	36	3	2	2	11	0	0	0	8	0	13	4	0	1	.456	.356
Greene, Todd, Midland	.327	82	346	318	59	104	203	19	1	26	57	1	5	5	17	4	55	3	5	6	.638	.365
Griffin, Ty, Arkansas†	.274	94	302	263	38	72	117	16	1	9	44	0	3	0	36	2	59	17	2	5	.445	.358
Groppuso, Mike, Jackson	.215	24	97	79	5	17	25	3	1	1	5	0	1	1	16	3	17	2	1	1	.316	.351
Grzanich, Mike, Jackson	.000	50	4	3	0	0	0	0	0	0	0	0	0	0	1	0	0	0	0	0	.000	.250
Guerrero, Mike, El Paso†	.310	23	79	71	14	22	26	1	0	1	7	0	1	0	7	0	5	0	0	1	.366	.364
Guerrero, Pedro, Midland	.302	66	282	252	40	76	110	13	0	7	40	0	0	2	28	2	34	0	2	16	.437	.376
Guerrero, Wilton, San Antonio	.348	95	414	382	53	133	158	13	6	0	26	4	1	1	26	3	63	21	22	10	.414	.390
Gulan, Mike, Arkansas	.314	64	260	242	47	76	134	16	3	12	48	0	1	6	11	1	52	4	2	4	.554	.358
Harkrider, Timothy, Midland†	.291	124	529	460	66	134	170	22	4	2	39	14	4	2	48	3	36	3	5	7	.370	.358
Harris, Mike, El Paso*	.333	8	27	24	8	8	13	2	0	1	5	0	1	0	2	0	3	0	0	0	.542	.370
Hatcher, Chris, Jackson	.308	11	45	39	5	12	16	1	0	1	3	0	1	1	4	0	6	0	2	1	.410	.372
Hidalgo, Richard, Jackson	.266	133	530	489	59	130	212	28	6	14	59	0	7	2	32	1	76	8	9	11	.434	.309
Hingle, Larry, Jackson*	.000	9	1	0	0	0	0	0	0	0	0	1	0	0	0	0	0	0	0	0	.000	.000
Holt, Chris, Jackson	.333	5	6	3	0	1	1	0	0	0	0	2	0	0	1	0	1	0	0	0	.333	.500
Hosey, Steve, Midland	.239	30	103	88	16	21	31	4	0	2	16	0	1	2	12	1	31	5	4	2	.352	.340
Hubbs, Dan, San Antonio	.000	31	2	1	0	0	0	0	0	0	0	0	0	0	1	0	0	0	0	0	.000	.000
Hughes, Bobby, El Paso	.266	51	189	173	11	46	79	12	0	7	27	0	2	2	12	1	30	0	2	4	.457	.317
Hunter, Brian, Jackson	.500	2	7	6	1	3	3	0	0	0	0	0	0	0	1	0	0	0	0	1	.500	.571
Hyde, Rich, Shreveport	.000	33	6	6	0	0	0	0	0	0	0	0	0	0	0	0	2	0	0	0	.000	.000
Jaime, Angel, San Antonio	.364	9	24	22	5	8	11	0	0	1	2	0	0	0	2	0	3	2	1	1	.500	.417
Jenkins, Bernie, Shreveport	.167	5	14	12	1	2	5	0	0	1	1	0	0	0	2	0	5	0	0	1	.417	.286
Jenkins, Geoff, El Paso*	.278	22	88	79	12	22	33	4	2	1	13	0	1	0	8	0	23	3	1	1	.418	.341
Jennings, Lance, Wichita	.182	13	47	44	2	8	8	0	0	0	3	1	1	0	1	0	8	0	0	1	.182	.196

Player, Team	Avg.	G	TPA	AB	R	H	TB	2B	3B	HR	RBI	SH	SF	HP	BB	IBB	SO	SB	CS	GDP	Slg.	OBP
Jensen, Marcus, Shreveport†	.283	95	378	321	55	91	141	22	8	4	45	5	8	3	41	1	68	0	0	4	.439	.362
Johns, Keith, Arkansas	.280	111	466	396	69	111	134	13	2	2	28	11	2	2	55	0	53	14	7	11	.338	.369
Johnson, Russ, Jackson	.248	132	540	475	65	118	165	16	2	9	53	2	5	8	50	1	60	10	5	11	.347	.327
Jones, Keith, Arkansas*	.226	50	97	84	11	19	21	2	0	0	4	4	0	0	9	0	12	3	3	3	.250	.301
Kappesser, Bob, El Paso	.191	61	132	115	17	22	34	5	2	1	17	2	3	0	12	0	19	2	2	4	.296	.262
Kellner, Frank, Jackson†	.316	75	315	269	31	85	102	15	1	0	29	4	5	2	35	2	52	1	7	2	.379	.392
Kennedy, Darryl, Tulsa	.251	61	222	195	26	49	69	9	1	3	26	3	4	3	17	0	22	0	0	5	.354	.315
Ketchen, Doug, Jackson	.125	17	8	8	0	1	1	0	0	0	0	0	0	0	0	0	0	0	0	0	.125	.125
Landrum, Tito, San Antonio	.238	87	296	260	42	62	101	13	1	8	25	0	2	7	26	0	64	5	6	9	.388	.322
Landry, Todd, El Paso	.292	132	557	511	76	149	238	33	4	16	79	2	4	7	33	1	99	9	7	20	.466	.341
Latham, Chris, San Antonio†	.299	58	251	214	38	64	115	14	5	9	37	1	1	2	33	0	59	11	11	2	.537	.396
Lewis, Anthony, Arkansas*	.251	115	454	407	55	102	201	21	3	24	85	0	1	2	44	5	117	0	2	7	.494	.326
Lidle, Cory, El Paso	.000	45	1	1	0	0	0	0	0	0	0	0	0	0	0	0	0	0	0	0	.000	.000
Lister, Martin, Jackson*	.000	15	13	10	0	0	0	0	0	0	0	0	0	0	3	0	5	0	0	0	.000	.231
LoDuca, Paul, San Antonio	.246	61	227	199	27	49	60	8	0	1	8	0	0	2	26	0	25	5	5	12	.302	.339
Long, Kevin, Wichita*	.292	67	293	250	38	73	92	14	1	1	26	0	0	2	41	2	29	9	6	3	.368	.396
Long, Ryan, Wichita	.231	102	358	342	36	79	120	26	0	5	34	1	0	5	10	1	48	4	4	9	.351	.263
Long, Tony, Arkansas*	.000	32	3	3	0	0	0	0	0	0	0	0	0	0	0	0	1	0	0	0	.000	.000
Lopez, Pedro, El Paso	.312	84	243	218	32	68	99	15	2	4	28	3	0	4	18	1	45	0	3	8	.454	.375
Lopez, Roberto, El Paso†	.312	114	509	417	80	130	171	22	8	1	44	6	5	4	77	2	63	9	4	4	.410	.419
Lowe, Sean, Arkansas	.208	24	25	24	2	5	9	1	0	1	2	0	0	0	1	0	8	0	0	0	.375	.240
Luce, Roger, Jackson	.212	18	55	52	4	11	18	2	1	1	4	0	0	0	3	0	12	0	0	3	.346	.255
Luzinski, Ryan, San Antonio	.229	44	163	144	18	33	41	5	0	1	9	2	1	3	13	1	32	1	1	6	.285	.304
Maness, Dwight, San Antonio	.223	57	211	179	29	40	63	2	3	5	24	5	2	5	20	0	44	4	6	3	.352	.316
Marrero, Oreste, San Antonio*	.258	125	515	445	60	115	209	25	3	21	86	0	3	3	64	5	98	5	2	4	.470	.353
Marshall, Jason, Wichita	.226	60	156	146	14	33	36	1	1	0	9	5	0	1	4	0	23	0	0	8	.247	.252
Martin, Jim, San Antonio*	.235	95	372	327	43	77	115	20	3	4	36	0	4	5	36	2	83	18	10	4	.352	.317
Martinez, Felix, Wichita†	.263	127	468	426	53	112	142	15	3	3	30	4	1	6	31	0	71	44	20	5	.333	.321
Martinez, Francisco, Arkansas	.000	11	1	1	0	0	0	0	0	0	0	0	0	0	0	0	1	0	0	0	.000	.000
Martinez, Gabby, El Paso†	.278	44	141	133	13	37	44	3	2	0	11	3	1	2	2	0	22	5	1	2	.331	.297
Martinez, Jesus, San Antonio*	.083	24	14	12	1	1	2	1	0	0	0	1	0	0	0	0	7	0	0	0	.167	.083
Martinez, Ramon, Wichita	.275	103	466	393	58	108	141	20	2	3	51	18	9	4	42	1	50	11	8	11	.359	.344
Mayes, Craig, Shreveport*	.222	3	9	9	0	2	3	1	0	0	3	0	0	0	0	0	2	0	0	0	.333	.222
McEwing, Joe, Arkansas	.248	42	137	121	16	30	40	4	0	2	12	6	0	1	9	2	13	3	2	4	.331	.305
McFarlin, Jason, Shreveport*	.337	93	293	252	39	85	120	13	2	6	37	4	2	10	25	7	26	8	7	8	.476	.415
McLain, Mike, Shreveport*	.000	11	2	2	0	0	0	0	0	0	0	0	0	0	0	0	1	0	0	0	.000	.000
McNabb, Buck, Jackson*	.260	15	55	50	4	13	14	1	0	0	3	0	0	0	5	0	11	1	0	1	.280	.327
Medrano, Anthony, Wichita	.000	1	5	5	0	0	0	0	0	0	0	0	0	0	0	0	3	0	0	0	.000	.000
Melendez, Dan, San Antonio*	.261	128	522	464	46	121	172	28	1	7	59	0	6	1	51	5	66	0	3	11	.371	.331
Mercado, Hector, Jackson*	.000	8	8	7	1	0	0	0	0	0	0	0	0	0	1	0	5	0	0	1	.000	.125
Mercedes, Guillermo, Tulsa†	.119	15	47	42	4	5	6	1	0	0	1	1	0	0	4	0	6	0	0	2	.143	.196
Mesewicz, Mark, Arkansas*	.000	5	2	2	0	0	0	0	0	0	0	0	0	0	0	0	1	0	0	0	.000	.000
Metcalfe, Mike, San Antonio†	.244	10	50	41	10	10	11	1	0	0	2	1	1	0	7	0	2	1	2	0	.268	.347
Millan, Bernie, El Paso†	.242	13	35	33	2	8	12	1	0	1	3	0	1	1	0	0	3	0	0	6	.364	.257
Miller, Roger, Shreveport	.274	19	73	62	11	17	29	6	0	2	10	2	1	2	6	0	1	0	0	1	.468	.352
Mirabelli, Doug, Shreveport	.302	40	148	126	14	38	51	13	0	0	16	2	0	0	20	1	14	1	0	3	.405	.397
Mitchell, Tony, Jackson†	.266	96	371	331	45	88	166	17	2	19	61	0	3	1	35	1	83	1	2	10	.502	.335
Mlicki, Doug, Jackson	.000	16	13	9	0	0	0	0	0	0	0	3	0	0	1	0	2	0	0	0	.000	.100
Monell, Johnny, Tulsa†	.306	121	513	434	55	133	189	18	1	12	64	0	6	6	67	6	53	0	1	10	.435	.402
Montgomery, Ray, Jackson	.299	35	146	127	24	38	78	8	1	10	24	0	1	5	13	2	13	6	3	3	.614	.384
Montgomery, Steve, Arkansas	.000	55	1	1	0	0	0	0	0	0	0	0	0	0	0	0	0	0	0	0	.000	.000
Montoya, Norm, El Paso*	1.000	52	1	1	1	1	1	0	0	0	0	0	0	0	0	0	0	0	0	0	1.000	1.000
Monzon, Jose, Midland	.289	57	209	180	29	52	68	11	1	1	19	3	2	2	22	0	36	0	0	6	.378	.369
Mora, Melvin, Jackson	.298	123	522	467	63	139	180	32	0	3	45	7	7	9	32	1	57	22	11	11	.385	.350
Morrow, Chris, Shreveport*	.246	83	272	240	31	59	97	17	0	7	35	0	0	1	31	4	44	1	1	8	.404	.335
Mueller, Bill, Shreveport†	.309	88	393	330	56	102	125	16	2	1	39	1	5	4	53	2	36	6	5	9	.379	.406
Munoz, Orlando, Midland†	.314	87	355	309	39	97	127	19	4	1	44	5	6	2	33	2	33	9	5	4	.411	.377
Murphy, Steve, Wichita*	.333	18	46	39	9	13	15	2	0	0	4	2	1	0	4	1	5	0	1	2	.385	.386
Murray, Calvin, Shreveport	.236	110	509	441	77	104	133	17	3	2	29	5	1	3	59	2	70	26	10	5	.302	.329
Myers, Rod, Wichita*	.307	131	548	499	71	153	208	22	6	7	62	8	3	4	34	3	77	29	16	7	.417	.354
Narcisse, Tyrone, Jackson	.115	27	29	26	2	3	4	1	0	0	2	1	0	0	2	0	12	0	0	0	.154	.179
Nevers, Tom, Jac.-E.P.	.245	118	458	416	55	102	149	12	4	9	47	0	2	5	35	2	79	7	3	16	.358	.310
Nicholas, Darrell, El Paso	.205	15	40	39	4	8	10	0	1	0	2	1	0	0	0	0	11	4	0	0	.256	.205
Nilsson, Dave, El Paso*	.467	5	15	15	1	7	11	1	0	1	4	0	0	0	0	0	1	1	0	0	.733	.467
Norton, Chris, Arkansas	.240	10	37	25	6	6	8	2	0	0	6	0	1	0	11	2	5	0	0	0	.320	.459
Nunez, Rogelio, Tulsa†	.224	82	290	263	27	59	69	4	0	2	17	8	1	8	10	0	43	0	7	10	.262	.273
Odor, Rouglas, El Paso	.294	6	19	17	2	5	5	0	0	0	2	0	0	0	2	0	2	0	0	1	.294	.368
Oehrlein, Dave, Arkansas*	.182	23	13	11	2	2	3	1	0	0	0	1	0	0	1	0	4	0	0	1	.273	.250
Ortiz, Bo, Midland	.275	96	388	360	48	99	139	10	3	8	56	4	5	2	17	2	40	12	11	6	.386	.307
Osborne, Donovan, Arkansas*	.000	2	3	3	0	0	0	0	0	0	0	0	0	0	0	0	2	0	0	0	.000	.000
Otanez, Willis, San Antonio	.240	27	108	100	8	24	33	4	1	1	7	0	2	0	6	0	25	0	1	3	.330	.278
Parra, Franklin, Tulsa†	.245	71	283	261	27	64	83	9	2	2	26	5	5	0	12	0	51	7	9	5	.318	.273
Perez, Danny, El Paso	.276	22	82	76	16	21	24	1	1	0	7	0	1	1	4	0	14	1	0	0	.316	.317
Peterson, Mark, Shreveport*	.167	37	14	12	0	2	2	0	0	0	0	1	0	0	1	0	0	1	0	1	.167	.231
Pimentel, Wander, Arkansas	.000	2	2	2	0	0	0	0	0	0	0	0	0	0	0	0	0	0	0	0	.000	.000
Pote, Lou, Shreveport	.500	28	2	2	1	1	1	0	0	0	0	0	0	0	0	0	0	0	0	0	.500	.500
Prado, Jose, San Antonio	.125	28	10	8	1	1	1	0	0	0	0	2	0	0	0	0	2	0	0	0	.125	.125
Probst, Alan, Jackson	.236	28	99	89	11	21	29	5	0	1	8	0	2	1	7	0	25	0	0	3	.326	.293
Puchales, Javier, San Antonio*	.228	31	62	57	4	13	14	1	0	0	1	1	1	0	3	1	6	0	2	5	.246	.262
Pyc, Dave, San Antonio*	.333	26	13	12	0	4	4	0	0	0	1	1	0	0	0	0	1	0	0	0	.333	.333
Radziewicz, Doug, Arkansas*	.233	34	135	116	15	27	35	5	0	1	13	0	0	0	18	1	14	0	0	2	.302	.336
Ramirez, J.D., Midland	.271	80	285	251	34	68	116	16	1	10	36	2	5	5	22	0	49	1	1	5	.462	.336
Rath, Gary, San Antonio*	.154	18	13	13	0	2	2	0	0	0	1	0	0	0	0	0	4	0	0	1	.154	.154

Player, Team	Avg.	G	TPA	AB	R	H	TB	2B	3B	HR	RBI	SH	SF	HP	BB	IBB	SO	SB	CS	GDP	Slg.	OBP
Raven, Luis, Midland	.267	21	92	86	9	23	42	2	1	5	15	0	1	1	4	0	30	1	1	2	.488	.304
Redington, Tom, Midland	.250	9	38	32	5	8	10	2	0	0	3	0	0	0	6	0	5	0	0	1	.313	.368
Reid, Derek, Shreveport	.143	8	14	14	2	2	4	0	1	0	1	0	0	0	0	0	4	0	0	0	.286	.143
Richardson, Scott, El Paso	.254	82	279	256	29	65	89	9	6	1	29	2	0	5	16	0	42	8	6	13	.348	.310
Richey, Jeff, Shreveport	.000	8	2	1	0	0	0	0	0	0	0	0	1	0	0	0	1	0	0	0	.000	.000
Rios, Eddie, San Antonio	.285	98	392	365	43	104	149	22	4	5	53	1	5	1	20	2	47	2	4	8	.408	.320
Rodrigues, Cecil, El Paso	.266	72	264	244	36	65	94	9	7	2	24	0	4	1	15	0	51	5	2	2	.385	.307
Romero, Mandy, Wichita†	.302	121	515	440	73	133	230	32	1	21	82	0	1	5	69	10	60	1	3	15	.523	.402
Romero, Willie, San Antonio	.266	105	427	376	46	100	143	20	1	7	44	0	6	5	40	1	69	10	12	7	.380	.340
Rupp, Brian, Arkansas	.325	23	84	77	10	25	28	3	0	0	6	1	0	0	6	0	12	0	1	3	.364	.373
Sagmoen, Marc, Tulsa*	.231	63	272	242	36	56	92	8	5	6	22	1	2	4	23	0	23	5	4	2	.380	.306
Samples, Todd, El Paso	.000	2	5	4	1	0	0	0	0	0	0	0	0	1	0	1	0	0	0	0	.000	.200
Sepeda, Jaime, Jackson	.000	1	1	0	0	0	0	0	0	0	0	0	0	0	1	0	0	0	0	0	.000	1.000
Shabazz, Basil, El Paso	.216	47	122	102	19	22	30	2	3	0	7	4	2	0	14	1	23	9	5	2	.294	.305
Silvia, Brian, Arkansas	.241	12	34	29	4	7	8	1	0	0	3	0	0	1	4	0	9	0	0	1	.276	.353
Simmons, Scott, Arkansas	.056	22	25	18	0	1	1	0	0	0	1	4	1	1	1	0	3	0	0	0	.056	.143
Simonton, Benji, Wichita	.306	38	123	108	18	33	60	9	3	4	30	1	1	2	11	0	32	3	1	1	.556	.377
Sims, Wesley, Tulsa†	.233	12	49	43	4	10	13	1	1	0	5	0	0	0	6	0	3	0	1	1	.302	.327
Sisco, Steve, Wichita	.301	54	227	209	29	63	86	12	1	3	23	1	1	1	15	0	31	3	1	5	.411	.350
Smiley, Rueben, Wichita*	.240	41	114	104	16	25	36	3	1	2	13	0	2	0	8	0	20	1	3	3	.346	.289
Smith, Mike, Tulsa	.257	132	571	499	65	128	204	22	3	16	64	5	5	2	60	1	72	11	6	13	.409	.336
Soderstrom, Steve, Shreveport	.043	22	25	23	1	1	1	0	0	0	1	1	0	1	0	0	8	0	0	0	.043	.083
Steed, Dave, San Antonio	.252	40	137	123	13	31	52	10	1	3	16	0	2	1	11	0	32	0	1	2	.423	.314
Stefanski, Mike, El Paso	.407	6	27	27	5	11	17	3	0	1	6	0	0	0	0	0	3	1	0	0	.630	.407
Stewart, Andy, Wichita	.259	60	233	216	28	56	83	18	0	3	32	0	2	4	11	0	31	1	2	9	.384	.305
Strickland, Chad, Wichita	.224	51	191	183	16	41	51	7	0	1	21	2	1	0	5	0	22	0	0	9	.279	.243
Sutko, Glenn, El Paso	.277	44	141	119	18	33	56	9	1	4	20	0	2	0	20	1	34	1	0	5	.471	.376
Sutton, Larry, Wichita*	.269	53	227	197	31	53	81	11	1	5	32	0	2	2	26	0	33	1	1	3	.411	.357
Takayoshi, Todd, Midland*	.278	7	20	18	2	5	7	0	1	0	1	0	0	0	1	0	4	1	0	0	.389	.316
Talanoa, Scott, El Paso	.222	2	10	9	0	2	4	2	0	0	1	0	0	0	1	0	0	0	0	1	.444	.300
Taulbee, Andy, Shreveport	.077	14	15	13	2	1	4	0	0	1	3	1	0	1	0	0	3	0	0	0	.308	.143
Tejero, Fausto, Midland	.226	16	56	53	7	12	18	3	0	1	11	0	1	1	1	0	13	0	1	1	.340	.250
Texidor, Jose, Tulsa	.269	129	532	494	55	133	183	33	1	5	64	2	2	3	31	3	61	1	1	19	.370	.315
Thomas, Brian, Tulsa*	.269	131	522	458	61	123	177	24	9	4	35	5	5	2	50	6	87	8	4	8	.386	.340
Thompson, Fletcher, El Paso*	.192	11	27	26	3	5	5	0	0	0	3	0	0	1	0	0	9	0	0	1	.192	.222
Torres, Paul, Arkansas	.225	66	258	231	24	52	93	11	0	10	33	1	0	5	21	0	56	2	1	9	.403	.304
Troutman, Keith, San Antonio	.000	38	1	1	0	0	0	0	0	0	0	0	0	0	0	0	0	0	0	0	.000	.000
Turco, Frank, Tulsa	.208	53	173	149	23	31	39	5	1	1	12	5	0	1	18	0	34	4	3	2	.262	.304
Urso, Joe, Midland	.324	12	44	37	6	12	15	3	0	0	4	0	1	1	5	0	3	0	0	0	.405	.409
Valdez, Carlos, Shreveport	.000	22	6	6	0	0	0	0	0	0	0	0	0	0	0	0	1	0	0	0	.000	.000
Vanderweele, Doug, Shreveport	.214	13	17	14	0	3	3	0	0	0	0	0	2	0	1	0	2	0	0	0	.214	.267
Velez, Jose, Arkansas†	.296	107	307	287	37	85	121	13	1	7	41	2	2	2	13	1	36	5	4	8	.422	.329
Verduzco, Steven, Jackson	.241	18	29	29	4	7	13	3	0	1	1	0	0	0	0	0	8	0	1	1	.448	.241
Voigt, Jack, Tulsa	.188	4	18	16	1	3	6	0	0	1	3	0	0	0	2	0	5	1	0	2	.375	.278
Wagner, Billy, Jackson*	.286	12	17	14	1	4	6	0	1	0	1	2	0	0	1	0	3	0	0	0	.429	.333
Wagner, Bret, Arkansas*	.143	6	9	7	0	1	1	0	0	0	2	1	0	0	1	0	1	0	0	0	.143	.250
Waldron, Joe, Jackson*	.167	28	7	6	0	1	1	0	0	0	0	0	0	0	1	0	3	0	0	0	.167	.000
Walker, Jamie, Jackson*	.000	50	5	5	0	0	0	0	0	0	0	0	0	0	0	0	4	0	0	0	.000	.000
Waring, Jim, Jackson*	.200	18	7	5	1	1	2	1	0	0	2	0	0	0	1	0	1	0	0	0	.400	.200
Warner, Ron, Arkansas	.245	47	120	98	9	24	27	3	0	0	8	3	2	1	16	1	15	0	0	3	.276	.350
Weaver, Eric, San Antonio	.000	27	10	9	0	0	0	0	0	0	0	0	1	0	0	0	4	0	0	0	.000	.000
Weger, Wes, El Paso	.256	45	172	160	22	41	54	9	2	0	19	1	1	0	10	1	14	1	1	9	.338	.298
Wesson, Barry, Jackson	.667	4	3	3	2	2	4	0	1	0	1	0	0	0	0	0	0	0	0	0	1.333	.667
Whitaker, Steve, Shreveport*	.000	4	3	3	0	0	0	0	0	0	0	0	0	0	0	0	0	0	0	0	.000	.000
White, Chad, Jackson†	.273	32	88	77	11	21	25	4	0	0	3	3	0	0	8	1	9	2	1	3	.325	.341
White, Chris, Jackson	.375	39	8	8	2	3	3	0	0	0	2	0	0	0	0	0	1	0	0	0	.375	.375
White, Jimmy, Jackson*	.000	2	2	1	0	0	0	0	0	0	0	0	0	0	1	0	0	0	0	0	.000	.500
Wilkins, Rick, Jackson*	.000	4	14	11	0	0	0	0	0	0	0	0	0	0	3	0	2	0	0	0	.000	.214
Williams, Keith, Shreveport	.305	75	305	275	39	84	133	20	1	9	55	0	7	0	23	3	39	5	3	5	.484	.351
Williams, Ted, Wichita†	.000	1	0	0	1	0	0	0	0	0	0	0	0	0	0	0	0	0	0	0	.000	.000
Williamson, Antone, El Paso*	.309	104	446	392	62	121	184	30	6	7	90	0	4	3	47	3	57	3	1	10	.469	.383
Wilson, Desi, Shreveport*	.286	122	530	482	77	138	186	27	3	5	72	0	7	1	40	2	68	11	9	18	.386	.338
Witasick, Jay, Arkansas	.000	7	9	9	0	0	0	0	0	0	0	0	0	0	0	0	7	0	0	1	.000	.000
Witkowski, Matt, Shreveport	.289	17	50	38	7	11	12	1	0	0	5	2	1	1	8	1	7	0	0	0	.316	.417
Wolff, Mike, Midland	.303	127	524	445	76	135	211	28	3	14	70	4	7	3	65	3	83	10	9	10	.474	.390
Woods, Kenny, Shreveport	.254	89	236	209	30	53	73	11	0	3	23	2	1	1	23	2	29	4	5	4	.349	.329
Yard, Bruce, San Antonio*	.359	16	44	39	7	14	17	3	0	0	4	0	0	0	5	0	6	0	1	0	.436	.432
Young, Dmitri, Arkansas†	.292	97	403	367	54	107	167	18	6	10	62	0	3	3	30	3	46	2	4	11	.455	.347

GRAND SLAMS: Blanco, 3; Fasano, Glenn, Landry, 2 each; Charles, Chavez, Cohick, Cruz, Forkner, P. Guerrero, Johnson, Lewis, Marrero, McFarlin, Melendez, Simonton, Williamson, 1 each.

AWARDED FIRST BASE ON CATCHER'S INTERFERENCE: Thomas 2 (Ellis, Silvia); Harkrider (P. Lopez); Landrum (Monzon); J. Martinez (Jensen); Mitchell (Monzon); Radziewicz (Monzon); Velez (P. Lopez).

PLAYERS WITH TWO OR MORE TEAMS

Player, Team	Avg.	G	TPA	AB	R	H	TB	2B	3B	HR	RBI	SH	SF	HP	BB	IBB	SO	SB	CS	GDP	Slg.	OBP
Nevers, Tom, Jackson	.242	83	326	298	36	72	109	7	3	8	35	0	2	2	24	2	58	5	2	10	.366	.301
Nevers, Tom, El Paso	.254	35	132	118	19	30	40	5	1	1	12	0	0	3	11	0	21	2	1	6	.339	.333

TEAM

Team	W	L	Pct.	ERA	G	CG	ShO	Sv.	IP	H	TBF	R	ER	HR	SH	SF	HB	BB	IBB	SO	WP	Bk.
Shreveport	88	47	.652	3.28	135	6	14	44	1221.0	1181	5164	530	445	82	40	39	55	432	21	748	61	8
San Antonio	64	72	.471	3.77	136	6	5	38	1202.0	1214	5184	586	503	66	54	43	45	482	6	783	76	18
Jackson	62	73	.459	3.90	135	8	7	35	1185.2	1123	5083	607	514	85	57	44	59	495	36	815	81	9
Arkansas	70	65	.519	3.95	135	7	7	41	1154.0	1178	4953	602	506	71	60	37	40	374	21	751	53	5
Wichita	72	64	.529	4.30	136	3	5	45	1211.2	1243	5230	668	579	115	32	39	40	478	21	821	90	6
Tulsa	52	83	.385	4.54	135	9	6	24	1177.1	1318	5188	692	594	128	44	35	34	485	49	651	68	9
El Paso	68	68	.500	4.58	136	7	4	38	1199.1	1372	5438	764	610	90	48	54	59	558	38	867	86	4
Midland	66	70	.485	4.68	136	13	3	29	1196.1	1379	5254	711	622	111	40	46	57	455	19	711	93	12

INDIVIDUAL

TOP QUALIFIERS FOR EARNED-RUN AVERAGE TITLE

Minimum 109 innings. *Lefthanded pitcher.

Pitcher, Team	W	L	Pct.	ERA	G	GS	CG	ShO	GF	Sv.	IP	H	TBF	R	ER	HR	SH	SF	HB	BB	IBB	SO	WP	Bk.
Rath, Gary, San Antonio*	13	3	.813	2.77	18	18	3	1	0	0	117.0	96	483	42	36	6	3	2	4	48	0	81	4	2
Bourgeois, Steve, Shreveport	12	3	.800	2.85	22	22	2	2	0	0	145.1	140	604	50	46	8	4	5	4	53	1	91	11	1
Narcisse, Tyrone, Jackson	5	14	.263	3.24	27	27	2	0	0	0	163.2	140	686	76	59	8	10	8	10	60	5	93	8	0
Busby, Mike, Arkansas	7	6	.538	3.29	20	20	1	0	0	0	134.0	125	565	63	49	8	3	6	35	1	95	5	0	
Lidle, Cory, El Paso	5	4	.556	3.36	45	9	0	0	12	2	109.2	126	480	52	41	6	6	1	6	36	3	78	6	0
Pyc, Dave, San Antonio*	12	6	.667	3.38	26	26	1	0	0	0	157.0	170	676	72	59	6	6	4	3	49	1	78	3	1
Soderstrom, Steve, Shreveport	9	5	.643	3.41	22	22	0	0	0	0	116.0	106	508	53	44	6	5	2	10	51	0	91	12	2
Browne, Byron, El Paso	10	4	.714	3.43	25	20	2	1	3	0	126.0	106	541	55	48	7	3	9	6	78	2	110	7	0
Simmons, Scott, Arkansas*	11	9	.550	3.45	22	22	1	1	0	0	139.0	145	569	66	53	9	5	6	1	28	1	73	5	0
Keling, Korey, Midland	8	5	.615	3.46	29	12	1	1	7	1	122.1	113	518	53	47	7	0	1	1	52	3	101	9	2
Prado, Jose, San Antonio	7	11	.389	3.48	28	22	0	0	3	1	144.2	126	621	70	56	9	7	9	7	64	0	93	13	2
Martinez, Jesus, San Antonio*	6	9	.400	3.54	24	24	1	0	0	0	139.2	129	603	64	55	6	7	4	7	71	0	83	16	4
Creek, Ryan, Jackson	9	7	.563	3.63	26	24	1	1	1	0	143.2	137	622	74	58	11	6	8	6	64	0	120	12	2
Corps, Edwin, Shreveport	13	6	.684	3.86	27	27	2	0	0	0	165.2	195	712	80	71	16	2	6	8	41	2	53	4	2
Wiley, Chad, Tulsa	6	9	.400	3.89	26	23	0	2	0	0	159.2	165	672	78	69	19	5	3	6	52	3	69	6	4

DEPARTMENTAL LEADERS: W—Corps, Rath, 13; L—Narcisse, 14; Pct.—Rath, .813; G—Montgomery, 55; GS—Hancock, 28; CG—Hancock, 5; ShO—Badorek, Bourgeois, 2; GF—Montgomery, 53; Sv.—Montgomery, 36; IP—Hancock, 175.2; H—Hancock, 222; TBF—Hancock, 764; R—Hancock, 107; ER—Hancock, 89; HR—Wiley, 19; SH—Narcisse, 10; SF—Browne, Prado, Rodriguez, 9; HB—Several pitchers tied with 10; BB—Rodriguez, 80; IBB—Maloney, 9; SO—Rodriguez, 129; WP—Schmidt, 18; Bk.—J. Martinez, Wiley, 4.

ALL PITCHERS

*Lefthanded pitcher.

Pitcher, Team	W	L	Pct.	ERA	G	GS	CG	ShO	GF	Sv.	IP	H	TBF	R	ER	HR	SH	SF	HB	BB	IBB	SO	WP	Bk.
Akerfelds, Darrel, Midland	3	1	.750	3.44	29	1	0	0	5	0	55.0	46	235	21	21	3	1	2	6	26	3	16	2	0
Alkire, Jeff, Arkansas*	0	0	.000	3.00	2	0	0	0	0	0	3.0	4	13	1	1	0	1	0	0	0	0	2	1	0
Allen, Ron, Jackson	2	0	1.000	5.91	4	0	0	0	0	0	10.2	13	49	7	7	0	2	2	0	5	1	3	0	0
Anderson, Paul, Arkansas	1	0	1.000	3.26	38	1	0	0	15	0	58.0	60	243	27	21	1	4	2	1	11	1	31	5	1
Archer, Kurt, El Paso	0	0	.000	3.00	4	0	0	0	2	1	6.0	4	24	2	2	0	0	0	1	0	5	0	0	
Arrandale, Matt, Arkansas	3	5	.375	3.28	47	3	0	0	23	2	68.2	72	296	28	25	1	2	2	1	22	4	28	1	0
Atkinson, Neil, Wichita*	3	0	1.000	4.80	40	0	0	0	8	1	50.2	52	223	29	27	7	1	2	1	21	2	32	3	1
Badorek, Mike, Arkansas	7	5	.583	4.35	18	17	4	2	1	1	101.1	119	446	61	49	4	4	5	3	30	0	50	2	0
Bevil, Brian, Wichita	5	7	.417	5.84	15	15	0	0	0	0	74.0	85	334	51	48	7	0	3	3	35	0	57	7	0
Bluma, Jaime, Wichita	4	3	.571	3.09	42	0	0	0	40	22	55.1	38	214	19	19	9	3	1	1	9	2	31	1	0
Blyleven, Todd, Midland	3	1	.750	5.18	8	0	0	0	2	0	14.1	13	57	8	8	1	2	2	0	3	1	8	0	1
Bonanno, Rob, Midland	1	1	.500	9.45	3	3	0	0	0	0	13.1	24	68	16	14	5	0	1	0	6	0	6	0	0
Bourgeois, Steve, Shreveport	12	3	.800	2.85	22	22	2	2	0	0	145.1	140	604	50	46	8	4	5	4	53	1	91	11	1
Bovee, Mike, Wichita	8	6	.571	4.18	20	20	1	0	0	0	114.0	118	486	60	53	12	2	4	2	43	0	72	4	0
Brannon, Cliff, Shreveport	0	0	.000	5.40	3	1	0	0	0	0	10.0	13	47	7	6	0	1	0	0	4	0	7	2	2
Brewer, Nevin, Wichita	3	2	.600	3.96	19	4	1	1	4	0	50.0	54	218	31	22	6	0	1	1	21	1	21	9	1
Brewington, Jamie, Shreveport	8	3	.727	3.04	16	16	1	1	0	0	88.1	72	376	39	30	8	2	7	0	55	0	74	4	0
Bridges, Kary, Jackson	0	0	.000	9.00	1	0	0	0	1	0	1.0	1	4	1	1	1	0	0	0	0	0	1	0	0
Brosnan, Jason, San Antonio*	1	0	1.000	3.57	19	0	0	0	7	2	22.2	24	94	9	9	1	1	0	0	4	0	21	1	0
Brown, Willard, Midland	9	10	.474	5.18	27	27	2	0	0	0	147.2	188	651	92	85	17	9	3	9	47	1	80	9	0
Browne, Byron, El Paso	10	4	.714	3.43	25	20	2	1	3	0	126.0	106	541	55	48	7	3	9	6	78	2	110	7	0
Browning, Tom, Wichita*	1	0	1.000	7.50	1	1	0	0	0	0	6.0	10	28	5	5	0	0	2	0	1	0	5	0	0
Brunson, William, San Anton.*	4	5	.444	4.95	14	14	0	0	0	0	80.0	105	356	46	44	4	3	1	4	22	0	44	5	1
Busby, Mike, Arkansas	7	6	.538	3.29	20	20	1	0	0	0	134.0	125	565	63	49	8	3	6	35	1	95	5	0	
Butler, Mike, Midland*	1	1	.500	4.50	19	0	0	0	7	0	24.0	24	104	12	12	4	0	2	2	9	1	14	0	0
Camacho, Dan, San Antonio	1	1	.500	1.59	11	0	0	0	7	2	11.1	9	47	2	2	0	0	0	0	8	0	8	2	0
Carpenter, Brian, Arkansas	2	1	.667	4.96	17	4	0	0	1	0	52.2	57	232	32	29	6	6	2	3	21	1	35	1	1
Caruso, Gene, El Paso*	2	1	.667	6.08	46	1	0	0	19	2	71.0	87	331	55	48	6	3	2	3	36	3	53	4	0
Castillo, Felipe, Tulsa	2	2	.500	3.82	14	0	0	0	5	0	33.0	42	147	19	14	2	2	0	1	11	1	16	3	0
Castillo, Juan, Jackson	4	4	.500	4.01	12	12	0	0	0	0	67.1	68	301	39	30	5	2	1	7	27	0	38	4	0
Castillo, Mariano, Shreveport*	3	1	.750	3.13	22	0	0	0	4	0	37.1	38	161	17	13	4	4	0	0	13	3	31	0	0
Castro, Nelson, San Antonio	5	7	.417	5.20	48	1	0	0	14	3	81.1	98	360	51	47	5	4	3	1	30	1	51	5	0
Cather, Mike, Tulsa	2	0	1.000	3.32	18	0	0	0	12	0	21.2	20	90	11	8	4	1	1	7	5	15	0	0	
Chavez, Tony, Midland	0	1	.000	8.00	7	0	0	0	2	0	9.0	13	42	9	8	1	0	0	1	4	1	0		
Cimorelli, Frank, El Paso	0	0	.000	4.50	2	0	0	0	0	0	2.0	1	11	1	1	0	1	0	2	2	0	0	0	
Cole, Jim, El Paso	1	4	.200	8.75	6	6	0	0	0	0	23.2	42	121	28	23	3	0	3	0	11	0	14	1	1
Connolly, Chris, Wichita*	1	0	1.000	5.68	13	0	0	0	2	0	12.2	18	64	11	8	0	1	2	11	0	2	2	0	
Corona, John, Arkansas*	1	1	.500	7.20	5	0	0	0	2	0	5.0	7	28	5	4	0	1	0	1	6	1	3	0	0
Corps, Edwin, Shreveport	13	6	.684	3.86	27	27	2	0	0	0	165.2	195	712	80	71	16	2	6	8	41	2	53	4	2

Pitcher, Team	W	L	Pct.	ERA	G	GS	CG	ShO	GF	Sv.	IP	H	TBF	R	ER	HR	SH	SF	HB	BB	IBB	SO	WP	Bk.
Correa, Ramser, San Antonio	1	4	.200	4.53	42	0	0	0	32	17	49.2	54	221	29	25	5	0	2	0	21	0	34	4	0
Creek, Doug, Arkansas*	4	2	.667	2.88	26	0	0	0	11	1	34.1	24	143	12	11	4	3	0	3	16	2	50	1	0
Creek, Ryan, Jackson	9	7	.563	3.63	26	24	1	1	1	0	143.2	137	622	74	58	11	6	8	6	64	0	120	12	2
Cummings, John, San Antonio*	0	2	.000	3.95	6	5	0	0	0	0	27.1	28	113	13	12	0	2	1	1	7	0	13	3	2
Davidson, Jackie, Tulsa	0	2	.000	21.86	2	2	0	0	0	0	7.0	21	42	18	17	1	0	0	0	1	0	5	0	0
Davis, Jeff, Tulsa	1	0	1.000	0.00	1	1	0	0	0	0	7.0	2	24	0	0	0	0	0	0	1	0	4	1	0
Davis, Ray, Arkansas	7	6	.538	4.50	21	18	0	0	1	0	110.0	112	467	67	55	14	5	5	4	30	0	70	6	1
Dorlarque, Aaron, Wichita	1	1	.500	1.15	20	1	0	0	4	0	47.0	37	179	8	6	2	2	0	3	10	4	32	2	0
Dreyer, Steve, Tulsa	2	4	.333	2.89	10	10	1	0	0	0	62.1	56	252	22	20	6	2	1	2	19	1	48	4	0
Duda, Steve, El Paso	1	3	.250	4.87	24	4	0	0	7	1	44.1	58	212	33	24	0	2	2	5	16	1	29	0	0
Duey, Kyle, Jackson	0	2	.000	5.40	7	0	0	0	6	2	6.2	11	32	4	4	1	1	0	0	2	0	4	0	0
Duncan, Chip, Tulsa	2	1	.667	3.00	17	1	0	0	11	1	36.0	34	153	12	12	2	1	0	1	17	6	31	4	0
Eddy, Chris, Wichita*	1	0	1.000	4.00	9	0	0	0	5	1	9.0	8	38	4	4	1	0	0	1	3	0	10	0	0
Edsell, Geoff, Midland	2	3	.400	5.91	5	5	1	0	0	0	32.0	39	140	26	21	5	1	2	0	16	0	19	5	0
Escamilla, Jaime, Tulsa*	0	0	.000	1.80	4	0	0	0	0	0	5.0	6	23	4	1	1	0	0	0	2	0	5	1	0
Estes, Shawn, Shreveport*	2	0	1.000	2.01	4	4	0	0	0	0	22.1	14	90	5	5	1	0	1	3	10	0	18	3	0
Evans, Bart, Wichita	0	4	.000	10.48	7	7	0	0	0	0	22.1	22	123	28	26	3	1	0	1	45	0	13	7	1
Evans, Dave, Jackson	2	9	.182	3.33	49	0	0	0	37	18	67.2	50	278	29	25	2	5	3	4	28	6	54	0	1
Frontera, Chad, Shreveport	3	5	.375	4.17	20	13	0	0	2	1	82.0	88	368	45	38	9	2	3	6	39	0	52	2	0
Fyhrie, Mike, Wichita	3	2	.600	3.04	17	9	0	0	3	1	74.0	76	312	31	25	4	1	1	1	23	0	41	3	1
Gallaher, Kevin, Jackson	2	2	.500	3.40	6	6	1	0	0	0	42.1	31	179	18	16	1	3	1	0	23	1	28	4	0
Gamez, Francisco, El Paso	2	1	.667	5.29	27	8	0	0	6	2	68.0	79	316	46	40	8	5	2	4	39	5	33	6	0
Ganote, Joe, El Paso	5	1	.833	1.61	12	7	0	0	1	1	50.1	40	207	18	9	3	2	1	3	16	0	39	4	0
Garcia, Jose, San Antonio	2	6	.250	4.03	38	0	0	0	15	2	58.0	50	242	32	26	4	4	4	6	24	0	36	6	2
Geeve, Dave, Tulsa	3	8	.273	5.17	15	14	3	1	0	0	94.0	108	400	61	54	16	1	2	2	20	0	38	1	0
Gerstein, Ron, El Paso*	8	12	.400	4.55	28	22	1	0	2	1	126.2	155	584	90	64	14	4	6	2	58	3	69	4	1
Granger, Jeff, Wichita*	4	7	.364	5.93	18	18	0	0	0	0	95.2	122	439	76	63	9	3	4	1	40	0	81	10	0
Grundy, Phil, Wichita	1	1	.500	8.31	6	2	0	0	1	0	17.1	16	75	17	16	6	1	1	1	7	0	11	3	0
Grzanich, Mike, Jackson	5	3	.625	2.74	50	0	0	0	23	8	65.2	55	276	22	20	0	5	3	6	38	5	44	4	0
Guerrero, Mike, El Paso	0	0	.000	3.38	2	0	0	0	2	0	2.2	3	11	1	1	0	0	0	0	0	0	0	0	0
Hancock, Ryan, Midland	12	9	.571	4.56	28	28	5	1	0	0	175.2	222	764	107	89	17	5	4	8	45	1	79	7	3
Harris, Bryan, Midland*	6	5	.545	4.94	39	4	0	0	10	0	78.1	105	359	50	43	9	4	3	4	32	1	60	9	2
Harrison, Brian, Wichita	1	1	.500	4.73	15	0	0	0	5	2	26.2	35	120	18	14	1	1	1	1	7	1	11	0	0
Heredia, Wilson, Tulsa	4	2	.667	3.18	8	7	1	1	1	1	45.1	42	194	19	16	4	3	1	2	21	3	34	1	3
Herges, Matt, San Antonio	0	3	.000	4.88	19	0	0	0	13	8	27.2	34	130	16	15	2	3	0	0	16	1	18	3	0
Hingle, Larry, Jackson*	0	2	.000	11.12	9	0	0	0	1	0	11.1	11	58	15	14	1	2	1	0	15	1	5	7	1
Holdridge, David, Midland	1	0	1.000	1.78	14	0	0	0	11	1	25.1	20	100	8	5	1	1	0	1	8	0	23	2	0
Holt, Chris, Jackson	2	2	.500	1.67	5	5	1	1	0	0	32.1	27	126	8	6	2	1	0	0	5	1	24	1	0
Hubbs, Dan, San Antonio	2	1	.667	3.54	31	0	0	0	6	0	61.0	58	248	25	24	3	3	1	1	16	0	52	0	1
Humphrey, Rich, Jackson	1	1	.500	1.69	9	0	0	0	1	0	16.0	11	66	5	3	0	2	1	0	9	2	9	1	0
Hyde, Rich, Shreveport	5	1	.833	3.89	33	0	0	0	16	7	44.0	48	188	21	19	2	1	1	4	10	3	24	1	0
Jones, Stacy, El Paso	1	1	.500	2.03	8	0	0	0	5	3	13.1	12	58	7	3	0	1	0	0	4	0	14	1	0
Kappesser, Bob, El Paso	0	0	.000	9.28	8	0	0	0	7	0	10.2	18	56	11	11	3	0	1	1	5	0	2	0	1
Keling, Korey, Midland	8	5	.615	3.46	29	12	1	1	7	1	122.1	113	518	53	47	7	0	1	1	52	3	101	9	2
Kellner, Frank, Jackson	0	0	.000	4.50	1	0	0	0	0	0	2.0	3	10	1	1	0	0	0	0	1	0	1	0	0
Ketchen, Doug, Jackson	3	3	.500	3.59	15	5	0	0	5	1	52.2	55	216	23	21	5	0	0	1	15	0	45	8	0
Keusch, Joseph, Tulsa	0	0	.000	0.00	2	0	0	0	2	0	2.2	1	10	0	0	0	0	0	0	0	0	0	0	0
Kimel, Jack, Tulsa*	2	2	.500	7.32	17	2	0	0	5	0	35.2	52	181	33	29	7	1	3	0	23	2	10	0	0
Kloek, Kevin, El Paso	7	11	.389	4.93	28	27	3	1	0	0	157.0	196	699	103	86	6	2	5	10	48	0	121	12	0
Knox, Kerry, Tulsa*	2	2	.500	3.41	5	4	0	0	1	0	29.0	28	124	12	11	2	1	0	1	9	1	14	2	0
Kosenski, John, El Paso	3	1	.750	5.72	16	0	0	0	6	0	28.1	41	141	19	18	1	1	1	2	17	2	25	4	0
Lacy, Kerry, Tulsa	2	7	.222	4.28	28	7	0	0	16	9	82.0	94	363	47	39	5	3	3	3	39	7	49	7	0
Langbehn, Gregg, El Paso*	2	1	.667	5.24	16	0	0	0	3	0	22.1	19	97	16	13	6	0	2	1	12	1	20	2	0
Lidle, Cory, El Paso	5	4	.556	3.36	45	9	0	0	12	2	109.2	126	480	52	41	6	6	1	6	36	3	78	6	0
Linares, Yfrain, El Paso	1	1	.500	9.45	8	0	0	0	1	0	13.1	21	70	15	14	1	0	2	1	12	1	9	2	0
Lister, Martin, Jackson*	4	3	.571	4.00	15	13	1	1	1	0	69.2	80	299	35	31	2	3	2	1	24	0	27	6	0
Long, Tony, Arkansas*	4	4	.500	3.74	32	0	0	0	8	0	55.1	58	241	28	23	5	3	3	2	14	0	35	0	1
Lowe, Sean, Arkansas	9	8	.529	4.88	24	24	0	0	0	0	129.0	143	578	84	70	2	5	4	5	64	0	77	9	0
Mack, Tony, Midland	0	0	.000	0.00	3	0	0	0	0	0	5.2	3	21	0	0	0	1	0	0	1	0	5	0	0
Maloney, Sean, El Paso	7	5	.583	4.18	43	0	0	0	27	15	64.2	69	292	41	30	4	4	4	3	28	9	54	5	0
Marshall, Jason, Wichita	0	0	.000	9.00	1	0	0	0	1	0	1.0	4	6	1	1	1	0	0	0	0	0	0	0	0
Martin, Jerry, Tulsa	3	7	.300	5.18	22	17	0	0	1	0	88.2	100	405	55	51	12	4	3	2	51	1	46	7	0
Martinez, Francisco, Arkansas	1	1	.500	1.29	11	0	0	0	4	1	21.0	10	80	3	3	0	3	1	1	7	1	13	2	0
Martinez, Jesus, San Antonio*	6	9	.400	3.54	24	24	1	0	0	0	139.2	129	603	64	55	6	7	4	7	71	0	83	16	4
Martinez, Ramiro, Tulsa*	0	5	.000	5.17	13	5	0	0	0	0	47.0	53	220	29	27	5	0	3	1	34	2	37	3	0
Matranga, Jeff, Arkansas	0	0	.000	0.00	7	0	0	0	4	0	8.0	1	27	0	0	0	0	0	0	3	0	4	0	0
McDill, Allen, Wichita*	1	0	1.000	2.11	12	1	0	0	5	1	21.1	16	85	7	5	2	0	0	1	5	0	20	1	0
McLain, Mike, Shreveport	2	1	.667	3.12	11	0	0	0	4	1	17.1	13	66	7	6	1	1	0	1	3	0	11	0	0
Mercado, Hector, Jackson*	1	4	.200	7.80	8	7	0	0	0	0	30.0	36	157	33	26	5	2	1	2	32	1	20	4	0
Mesewicz, Mark, Arkansas*	0	1	.000	6.75	5	0	0	0	1	0	9.1	13	41	7	7	0	2	0	0	1	1	7	0	0
Mlicki, Doug, Jackson	8	3	.727	2.79	16	16	2	0	0	0	96.2	73	390	41	30	6	1	2	4	33	0	72	5	0
Montgomery, Steve, Arkansas	5	2	.714	3.25	55	0	0	0	53	36	61.0	52	259	22	22	6	7	1	4	22	6	56	5	1
Montoya, Norm, El Paso*	2	5	.286	3.42	51	0	0	0	9	2	76.1	88	330	36	29	3	5	2	2	18	5	43	4	0
Moody, Ritchie, Tulsa*	0	1	.000	6.97	11	0	0	0	5	0	20.2	24	94	18	16	2	1	1	1	18	1	9	2	0
Morones, Geno, Wichita	3	6	.333	4.10	17	16	0	0	0	0	79.0	85	353	49	36	5	4	6	3	39	0	32	3	0
Morvay, Joe, Tulsa	5	8	.385	5.21	37	0	0	0	28	8	65.2	82	305	45	38	4	6	1	4	28	6	30	4	0
Narcisse, Tyrone, Jackson	5	14	.263	3.24	27	27	2	0	0	0	163.2	140	686	76	59	8	10	8	10	60	5	93	8	0
Nieves, Ernesto, Midland	0	1	.000	4.05	6	1	0	0	1	0	13.1	15	62	7	6	1	2	1	1	10	1	3	1	0
Oehrlein, Dave, Arkansas*	4	7	.364	4.87	23	10	1	0	4	0	77.2	80	338	48	42	6	5	2	4	28	1	52	5	0
Oropesa, Eddie, San Antonio*	1	1	.500	3.12	16	0	0	0	7	1	17.1	22	87	8	6	2	1	2	3	12	1	16	0	1
Osborne, Donovan, Arkansas*	0	1	.000	2.45	2	2	0	0	0	0	11.0	12	46	4	3	0	0	0	1	2	0	6	0	0
Paskievitch, Tom, Wichita	1	1	.500	5.06	5	0	0	0	1	0	5.1	6	21	3	3	1	0	1	0	2	0	3	1	0
Patterson, Danny, Tulsa	2	2	.500	6.19	26	0	0	0	22	5	36.1	45	163	27	25	2	0	1	2	13	2	24	5	0

Pitcher, Team	W	L	Pct.	ERA	G	GS	CG	ShO	GF	Sv.	IP	H	TBF	R	ER	HR	SH	SF	HB	BB	IBB	SO	WP	Bk.
Perez, David, Tulsa	3	2	.600	5.24	8	7	0	0	0	0	46.1	49	204	30	27	5	5	0	1	18	2	25	1	0
Peterson, Mark, Shreveport*	4	3	.571	1.27	37	0	0	0	14	2	64.0	51	248	15	9	2	2	5	4	6	2	38	0	0
Pickett, Ricky, Shreveport*	2	0	1.000	1.71	14	0	0	0	9	3	21.0	9	82	5	4	1	0	1	0	9	0	23	2	0
Popplewell, Tom, El Paso	0	0	.000	15.00	4	0	0	0	0	0	3.0	7	21	5	5	0	0	0	1	6	0	1	2	0
Pote, Lou, Shreveport	2	2	.500	5.33	28	0	0	0	11	3	50.2	53	226	41	30	8	4	1	0	26	1	30	4	0
Powell, John, Tulsa	1	4	.200	3.89	7	7	0	0	0	0	39.1	45	174	21	17	9	0	1	2	16	0	27	1	1
Prado, Jose, San Antonio	7	11	.389	3.48	28	22	0	0	3	1	144.2	126	621	70	56	9	7	9	7	64	0	93	13	2
Pricher, John, Midland	0	0	.000	4.50	8	0	0	0	6	1	10.0	16	48	7	5	1	0	1	0	6	0	7	0	0
Purdy, Shawn, Shreveport	6	3	.667	3.75	52	1	0	0	40	21	62.1	61	260	31	26	7	1	3	1	18	2	33	3	0
Pyc, Dave, San Antonio*	12	6	.667	3.38	26	26	1	0	0	0	157.0	170	676	72	59	6	6	4	3	49	1	78	3	1
Ralston, Kris, Wichita	9	4	.692	3.56	18	16	0	0	0	0	93.2	85	389	40	37	10	3	2	7	28	0	84	6	0
Ratekin, Mark, Midland	0	0	.000	5.94	11	0	0	0	4	0	16.2	19	72	12	11	1	0	2	3	0	11	2	0
Rath, Gary, San Antonio*	13	3	.813	2.77	18	18	3	1	0	0	117.0	96	483	42	36	6	3	2	4	48	0	81	4	2
Rawitzer, Kevin, Wichita*	6	4	.600	5.25	28	3	0	0	7	1	48.0	48	209	30	28	4	0	2	1	19	0	42	1	0
Ray, Ken, Wichita	4	5	.444	5.97	14	14	0	0	0	0	75.1	83	342	55	50	7	1	0	1	46	0	53	8	1
Renko, Steve, Midland	3	5	.375	4.81	22	9	0	0	4	1	76.2	100	352	51	41	3	2	5	0	28	2	44	5	0
Richey, Jeff, Shreveport	1	2	.333	2.45	8	0	0	0	4	1	22.0	20	94	7	6	0	2	0	1	8	3	11	3	0
Rodriguez, Frankie, El Paso	9	8	.529	4.98	28	27	1	0	1	0	142.2	157	650	90	79	9	9	5	8	80	2	129	16	1
Santana, Julio, Tulsa	6	4	.600	3.15	15	15	3	0	0	0	103.0	91	438	40	36	8	2	4	0	52	2	71	8	1
Schmidt, Jeff, Midland	4	12	.250	5.83	20	20	0	0	0	0	100.1	127	466	75	65	12	2	4	5	48	1	46	18	1
Schooler, Mike, Midland	3	3	.500	1.79	54	0	0	0	47	20	65.1	49	257	16	13	5	3	4	0	19	3	55	5	0
Sebach, Kyle, Midland	1	1	.500	10.31	5	5	0	0	0	0	18.1	31	93	24	21	1	2	2	3	12	0	7	3	0
Sepeda, Jaime, Jackson	0	1	.000	9.00	1	1	0	0	0	0	4.0	7	21	4	4	0	0	1	0	2	0	1	0	0
Sheehan, Chris, Wichita	0	2	.000	5.51	31	0	0	0	10	2	50.2	51	221	35	31	5	4	2	16	6	31	5	0
Simmons, Scott, Arkansas*	11	9	.550	3.43	22	22	1	1	0	0	139.0	145	569	66	53	9	5	6	1	28	1	73	5	0
Smith, Scotty, Tulsa	5	8	.385	6.02	29	13	1	0	12	0	101.2	144	469	83	68	15	3	6	2	31	4	38	5	0
Snyder, John, Midland	8	9	.471	5.74	21	21	4	0	0	0	133.1	158	591	93	85	12	3	6	10	48	1	81	7	3
Soderstrom, Steve, Shreveport	9	5	.643	3.41	22	22	0	0	0	0	116.0	106	508	53	44	6	5	2	10	51	0	91	12	2
Strange, Don, Wichita	0	1	.000	1.50	24	0	0	0	17	8	36.0	28	136	7	6	2	0	1	0	7	0	36	5	0
Taulbee, Andy, Shreveport	1	1	.500	3.95	14	14	1	1	0	0	86.2	107	388	47	38	5	6	3	27	2	38	3	1
Thibert, John, Midland	0	0	.000	4.18	12	0	0	0	5	2	23.2	19	104	12	11	1	0	1	2	17	0	15	3	0
Toth, Robert, Wichita	8	4	.667	2.17	21	9	1	0	2	0	103.2	95	427	30	25	6	3	3	4	27	1	77	6	1
Troutman, Keith, San Antonio	1	2	.333	3.15	38	0	0	0	22	2	65.2	64	268	24	23	3	1	3	1	18	1	50	3	0
Valdez, Carlos, Shreveport	3	2	.600	1.27	22	3	0	0	8	5	64.0	40	240	11	9	0	1	0	3	14	2	51	1	0
Vanderweele, Doug, Shreveport	5	2	.714	2.52	13	9	0	0	0	0	64.1	61	253	18	18	3	1	0	2	13	0	22	3	0
VanRyn, Ben, Midland*	1	1	.500	2.78	19	0	0	0	8	1	32.1	33	133	10	10	4	0	2	2	12	0	24	2	0
Wagner, Billy, Jackson*	2	2	.500	2.57	12	12	0	0	0	0	70.0	49	288	25	20	7	1	4	36	1	77	4	1
Wagner, Bret, Arkansas*	1	2	.333	3.19	6	6	0	0	0	0	36.2	34	161	14	13	1	1	0	18	0	31	3	0
Wagner, Joe, El Paso	0	4	.000	9.95	5	5	0	0	0	0	19.0	32	109	31	21	7	0	0	2	22	0	8	4	0
Waldron, Joe, Jackson*	1	2	.333	3.71	28	0	0	0	12	5	51.0	57	215	22	21	5	4	2	4	11	1	39	2	1
Walker, Jamie, Jackson*	4	2	.667	4.50	50	0	0	0	19	2	58.0	59	250	29	29	6	3	2	2	24	5	38	4	1
Wallace, Derek, Wichita	4	3	.571	4.40	26	0	0	0	18	6	43.0	51	188	23	21	5	1	1	2	13	4	23	3	0
Wanke, Chuck, Shreveport*	2	3	.400	4.35	43	0	0	0	17	0	41.1	35	183	23	20	1	0	1	5	22	0	40	2	0
Waring, Jim, Jackson	1	4	.200	8.01	17	5	0	0	5	2	51.2	77	243	49	46	7	3	2	3	15	2	27	2	0
Watson, Allen, Arkansas*	1	0	1.000	0.00	1	1	0	0	0	0	5.0	4	19	1	0	0	0	0	0	0	0	7	0	0
Watson, Ron, Midland	0	0	.000	4.91	3	0	0	0	0	0	3.2	2	17	2	2	0	0	0	0	6	0	3	3	0
Weaver, Eric, San Antonio	8	11	.421	4.07	27	26	1	0	1	0	141.2	147	635	83	64	10	9	7	7	72	1	105	8	2
Webb, Doug, El Paso	2	1	.667	4.42	18	0	0	0	16	8	18.1	11	77	9	9	1	0	1	0	13	1	11	2	0
Wheeler, Earl, Tulsa	1	1	.500	5.40	5	0	0	0	3	0	8.1	14	41	8	5	1	0	1	0	2	0	6	2	0
Whitaker, Steve, Shreveport*	2	0	1.000	3.86	4	3	0	0	0	0	16.1	17	70	8	7	0	1	0	0	10	0	10	1	0
White, Chad, Jackson	0	0	.000	18.00	1	0	0	0	0	0	1.0	1	6	2	2	0	0	0	0	2	0	0	1	0
White, Chris, Jackson	6	3	.667	5.09	38	2	0	0	15	0	70.2	71	311	45	40	10	1	3	5	24	4	45	4	2
Wiley, Chad, Tulsa	6	9	.400	3.89	26	23	0	0	2	0	159.2	165	672	78	69	19	5	3	6	52	3	69	6	4
Witasick, Jay, Arkansas	2	4	.333	6.88	7	7	0	0	0	0	34.0	46	161	29	26	4	0	0	16	1	26	2	0

COMBINATION SHUTOUTS: **Arkansas (4)**—Lowe-Arrandale-Montgomery, Lowe-Long, Simmons-Montgomery, Witasick-Long-Anderson. **El Paso (2)**—Gamez-Browne, Lidle-Montoya-Duda. **Jackson (4)**—Gallaher-Walker, Lister-Grzanich-Evans, Wagner-Grzanich, Waring-Waldron-Evans. **Midland (1)**—Brown-Schooler. **San Antonio (4)**—Castro-Hubbs-Brosnan-Correa, Martinez-Castro-Correa, Martinez-Correa, Rath-Correa. **Shreveport (10)**—Corps-Hyde 2, Corps-Purdy 2, Bourgeois-Frontera, Brewington-Richey-Purdy, Corps-Valdez, Estes-Hyde-Purdy, Soderstrom-Castillo-Purdy, Soderstrom-Whitaker-Purdy. **Tulsa (4)**—Dreyer-Smith, Heredia-Morvay, Santana-Lacy, Smith-Cather. **Wichita (4)**—Morones-Atkinson-Wallace, Ralston-Fyhrie, Ralston-Strange, Ralston-Wallace.
NO-HIT GAMES: None.

1995 FIELDING

TEAM

Team	Pct.	G	PO	A	E	TC	DP	PB	Team	Pct.	G	PO	A	E	TC	DP	PB
Shreveport	.975	135	3663	1578	136	5377	150	17	Midland	.971	136	3589	1624	158	5371	169	20
Jackson	.973	135	3557	1538	144	5239	144	25	Tulsa	.969	135	3532	1549	162	5243	143	12
San Antonio	.972	136	3606	1568	148	5322	137	17	Wichita	.968	136	3635	1511	169	5315	125	11
Arkansas	.971	135	3462	1621	154	5237	125	7	El Paso	.960	136	3598	1552	213	5363	136	23

TRIPLE PLAYS: None.

INDIVIDUAL

FIRST BASEMEN

NOTE: All caps denotes fielding-percentage leader based on 68 games for catchers, 91 for all other non-pitchers and 136 innings for pitchers. *Throws lefthanded.

Player, Team	Pct.	G	PO	A	E	TC	DP
Anderson, Charlie, Arkansas	.986	13	65	6	1	72	5
Bagwell, Jeff, Jackson	1.000	3	24	6	0	30	3
Banks, Brian, El Paso	.975	5	37	2	1	40	1

Player, Team	Pct.	G	PO	A	E	TC	DP
Boykin, Tyrone, Midland	.980	19	131	17	3	151	14
Charles, Frank, Tulsa	.984	123	1108	73	19	1200	117
Cholowsky, Dan, Arkansas	.979	32	263	22	6	291	22
Clinton, Jim, Tulsa	.972	7	64	5	2	71	7
Colon, Dennis, Jackson	.985	101	892	79	15	986	89
Dodson, Bo, El Paso*	1.000	11	100	7	0	107	12
Fasano, Sal, Wichita	.982	35	303	30	6	339	36

Player, Team	Pct.	G	PO	A	E	TC	DP
Florez, Tim, Shreveport	.875	1	7	0	1	8	1
Glenn, Leon, Midland	.988	110	1009	60	13	1082	112
Greene, Todd, Midland	1.000	2	3	0	0	3	0
Groppuso, Mike, Jackson	1.000	8	56	4	0	60	4
Guerrero, Mike, El Paso	1.000	1	1	0	0	1	0
Guerrero, Pedro, Midland	.895	2	16	1	2	19	1
Hatcher, Chris, Jackson	1.000	3	28	4	0	32	1
Kellner, Frank, Jackson	1.000	23	200	17	0	217	20
Kennedy, Darryl, Tulsa	1.000	1	2	0	0	2	0
Landry, Todd, El Paso*	.989	121	1014	123	13	1150	101
Lewis, Anthony, Arkansas*	.917	3	20	2	2	24	1
LoDuca, Paul, San Antonio	1.000	2	7	0	0	7	1
Long, Kevin, Wichita*	.970	4	31	1	1	33	1
Lopez, Pedro, El Paso	.875	5	6	1	1	8	1
Luce, Roger, Jackson	1.000	1	9	1	0	10	0
Marrero, Oreste, San Antonio*	.994	19	154	13	1	168	17
Marshall, Jason, Wichita	.989	11	82	4	1	87	5
MELENDEZ, Dan, San Antonio*	.997	120	1068	98	3	1169	103
Millan, Bernie, El Paso	1.000	3	2	0	0	2	0
Mirabelli, Doug, Shreveport	1.000	3	27	0	0	27	2
Montgomery, Ray, Jackson	.980	5	43	5	1	49	2
Montoya, Norm, El Paso*	1.000	1	1	0	0	1	0
Morrow, Chris, Shreveport*	1.000	2	19	2	0	21	0
Munoz, Orlando, Midland	1.000	3	23	3	0	26	4
Myers, Rod, Wichita*	.857	2	6	0	1	7	0
Nevers, Tom, El Paso	1.000	3	10	0	0	10	3
Norton, Chris, Arkansas	.980	5	47	2	1	50	6
Radziewicz, Doug, Arkansas*	.994	33	330	27	2	359	37
Raven, Luis, Midland	1.000	6	45	5	0	50	10
Redington, Tom, Midland	1.000	7	62	6	0	68	8
Richardson, Scott, El Paso	.750	1	3	0	1	4	0
Romero, Mandy, Wichita	.933	2	13	1	1	15	3
Rupp, Brian, Arkansas	.963	12	70	7	3	80	4
Simonton, Benji, Shreveport	1.000	9	81	5	0	86	11
Stewart, Andy, Wichita	.994	41	328	28	2	358	33
Sutko, Glenn, El Paso	1.000	2	3	1	0	4	0
Sutton, Larry, Wichita*	.986	52	452	25	7	484	39
Torres, Paul, Arkansas	.987	54	560	34	8	602	37
Turco, Frank, Tulsa	.932	8	35	6	3	44	5
Voigt, Jack, Tulsa	1.000	1	8	1	0	9	0
Warner, Ron, Arkansas	1.000	1	1	0	0	1	0
Williamson, Antone, El Paso	1.000	6	32	1	0	33	8
Wilson, Desi, Shreveport*	.992	118	1113	72	9	1194	112
Witkowski, Matt, Shreveport	.960	8	45	3	2	50	8
Woods, Kenny, Shreveport	1.000	3	21	0	0	21	5

SECOND BASEMEN

Player, Team	Pct.	G	PO	A	E	TC	DP
Berblinger, Jeff, Arkansas	.968	87	183	270	15	468	61
Bridges, Kary, Jackson	.975	68	118	198	8	324	42
Cairo, Miguel, San Antonio	.963	80	159	227	15	401	50
Canizaro, Jay, Shreveport	.965	105	228	295	19	542	84
Centeno, Henri, Jackson	.966	58	82	116	7	205	41
Diaz, Alfredo, Midland	1.000	3	5	4	0	9	2
Diaz, Lino, Wichita	.833	2	1	4	1	6	1
Dumas, Mike, El Paso	.960	5	12	12	1	25	1
Estrada, Osmani, Tulsa	1.000	5	12	16	0	28	6
Felix, Lauro, El Paso	.957	20	40	49	4	93	18
Florez, Tim, Shreveport	.977	42	65	102	4	171	23
Gonzales, Rene, Midland	.964	5	11	16	1	28	6
Griffin, Ty, Arkansas	.978	40	84	136	5	225	24
Guerrero, Mike, El Paso	1.000	1	2	2	0	4	0
Kappesser, Bob, El Paso	1.000	8	2	6	0	8	2
Kellner, Frank, Jackson	1.000	20	30	59	0	89	18
Lopez, Roberto, El Paso	.972	110	229	295	15	539	69
Marshall, Jason, Wichita	1.000	16	19	28	0	47	3
MARTINEZ, Ramon, Wichita	.984	100	182	299	8	489	67
McEwing, Joe, Arkansas	1.000	4	7	11	0	18	1
Medrano, Anthony, Wichita	.909	1	3	7	1	11	0
Millan, Bernie, El Paso	1.000	5	3	10	0	13	2
Mueller, Bill, Shreveport	1.000	2	5	1	0	6	0
Munoz, Orlando, Midland	.994	69	131	185	2	318	50
Nevers, Tom, Jac.-E.P.	.938	14	28	33	4	64	8
Odor, Rouglas, El Paso	.833	1	1	4	1	6	1
Ortiz, Bo, Midland	1.000	1	0	3	0	3	0
Ramirez, J.D., Midland	.974	62	143	200	9	352	42
Richardson, Scott, El Paso	.000	2	0	0	1	1	0
Rios, Eddie, San Antonio	.974	62	107	156	7	270	34
Sims, Wesley, Tulsa	1.000	1	3	2	0	5	1
Sisco, Steve, Wichita	.993	29	59	80	1	140	15
Smith, Mike, Tulsa	.982	131	310	412	13	735	94
Thompson, Fletcher, El Paso	1.000	6	13	26	0	39	3
Urso, Joe, Midland	.956	9	17	26	2	45	11

Player, Team	Pct.	G	PO	A	E	TC	DP
Warner, Ron, Arkansas	1.000	7	17	7	0	24	4
Witkowski, Matt, Shreveport	.966	4	12	16	1	29	5
Woods, Kenny, Shreveport	.857	1	3	3	1	7	1
Yard, Bruce, San Antonio	1.000	1	2	3	0	5	1

SECOND BASEMEN WITH TWO OR MORE TEAMS

Player, Team	Pct.	G	PO	A	E	TC	DP
Nevers, Tom, Jackson	.938	13	27	33	4	64	8
Nevers, Tom, El Paso	1.000	1	1	0	0	1	0

THIRD BASEMEN

Player, Team	Pct.	G	PO	A	E	TC	DP
Anderson, Charlie, Arkansas	.921	48	21	108	11	140	6
ARIAS, George, Midland	.936	129	127	300	29	456	40
Banks, Brian, El Paso	1.000	2	1	1	0	2	0
Blanco, Henry, San Antonio	.963	88	79	210	11	300	21
Centeno, Henri, Jackson	1.000	2	0	1	0	1	0
Diaz, Alfredo, Midland	1.000	1	1	4	0	5	0
Diaz, Lino, Wichita	.965	61	40	124	6	170	13
Donnels, Chris, Jackson	.929	4	6	7	1	14	0
Dumas, Mike, El Paso	.833	3	3	7	2	12	0
Edwards, Mike, Tulsa	.911	25	28	44	7	79	6
Estrada, Osmani, Tulsa	.926	92	73	164	19	256	17
Felix, Lauro, El Paso	.951	16	5	34	2	41	4
Florez, Tim, Shreveport	.920	48	22	81	9	112	12
Forkner, Tim, Jackson	.900	34	27	63	10	100	8
Glenn, Leon, Midland	.889	3	3	5	1	9	0
Griffin, Ty, Arkansas	.818	17	7	29	8	44	0
Groppuso, Mike, Jackson	.965	15	14	41	2	57	3
Guerrero, Mike, El Paso	.333	2	0	1	2	3	0
Gulan, Mike, Arkansas	.929	63	33	150	14	197	12
Kappesser, Bob, El Paso	.882	11	4	11	2	17	0
Kellner, Frank, Jackson	.919	21	12	22	3	37	2
LoDuca, Paul, San Antonio	.833	2	0	5	1	6	0
Long, Ryan, Wichita	.912	69	43	134	17	194	6
Marshall, Jason, Wichita	.929	9	2	11	1	14	1
Millan, Bernie, El Paso	.833	2	2	3	1	6	0
Mora, Melvin, Jackson	.667	1	0	2	1	3	0
Mueller, Bill, Shreveport	.977	85	47	168	5	220	13
Munoz, Orlando, Midland	.778	3	1	6	2	9	1
Nevers, Tom, Jac.-E.P.	.881	100	77	204	38	319	16
Otanez, Willis, San Antonio	.957	27	18	48	3	69	4
Parra, Franklin, Tulsa	.944	22	18	33	3	54	4
Raven, Luis, Midland	.929	4	4	9	1	14	1
Rios, Eddie, San Antonio	1.000	26	15	65	0	80	8
Rupp, Brian, Arkansas	.905	6	4	15	2	21	1
Sisco, Steve, Wichita	1.000	6	1	15	0	16	1
Stefanski, Mike, El Paso	.842	6	2	14	3	19	2
Stewart, Andy, Wichita	1.000	2	0	2	0	2	0
Thompson, Fletcher, El Paso	.714	3	2	3	2	7	1
Verduzco, Steven, Jackson	1.000	3	2	0	0	2	0
Warner, Ron, Arkansas	1.000	9	6	11	0	17	1
Weger, Wes, El Paso	1.000	1	0	3	0	3	0
Williamson, Antone, El Paso	.862	76	47	134	29	210	6
Witkowski, Matt, Shreveport	.833	2	1	4	1	6	0
Woods, Kenny, Shreveport	.895	21	14	37	6	57	2

THIRD BASEMEN WITH TWO OR MORE TEAMS

Player, Team	Pct.	G	PO	A	E	TC	DP
Nevers, Tom, Jackson	.907	68	57	158	22	237	13
Nevers, Tom, El Paso	.805	32	20	46	16	82	3

SHORTSTOPS

Player, Team	Pct.	G	PO	A	E	TC	DP
Alguacil, Jose, Shreveport	.750	1	2	1	1	4	1
Arias, George, Midland	1.000	1	1	0	0	1	0
Aurilia, Rich, Shreveport	.962	63	122	237	14	373	52
Bethea, Scott, Arkansas	.943	10	13	37	3	53	8
Cairo, Miguel, San Antonio	.946	30	51	89	8	148	22
Canizaro, Jay, Shreveport	.941	19	26	38	4	68	10
Centeno, Henri, Jackson	1.000	1	0	1	0	1	0
Clinton, Jim, Tulsa	1.000	2	1	4	0	5	1
Diaz, Alfredo, Midland	1.000	4	5	6	0	11	2
Dumas, Mike, El Paso	.818	2	5	4	2	11	1
Ehmann, Kurt, Shreveport	.973	38	53	126	5	184	23
Estrada, Osmani, Tulsa	.966	18	30	56	3	89	13
Felix, Lauro, El Paso	.939	47	71	99	11	181	24
Florez, Tim, Shreveport	.941	6	6	10	1	17	3
Frias, Hanley, Tulsa	.948	93	137	301	24	462	65
Guerrero, Mike, El Paso	.938	18	35	40	5	80	7
Guerrero, Wilton, San Antonio	.953	88	121	263	19	403	46
Harkrider, Timothy, Midland	.948	124	177	402	32	611	95
Jaime, Angel, San Antonio	.944	4	4	13	1	18	1

CLASS AA Texas League

Player, Team	Pct.	G	PO	A	E	TC	DP
Johns, Keith, Arkansas	.952	111	159	354	26	539	66
JOHNSON, Russ, Jackson	.978	128	182	383	13	578	78
Kellner, Frank, Jackson	.933	7	12	16	2	30	4
Lopez, Roberto, El Paso	.909	6	4	6	1	11	0
Marshall, Jason, Wichita	.969	21	26	37	2	65	8
Martinez, Felix, Wichita	.922	125	222	371	50	643	76
Martinez, Gabby, El Paso	.949	43	65	103	9	177	27
Martinez, Ramon, Wichita	.941	2	4	12	1	17	1
Mercedes, Guillermo, Tulsa	.938	15	23	52	5	80	10
Metcalfe, Mike, San Antonio	.957	10	14	31	2	47	7
Munoz, Orlando, Midland	.949	13	16	40	3	59	6
Nevers, Tom, Jac.-E.P.	.947	7	7	11	1	19	3
Odor, Rouglas, El Paso	.962	5	11	14	1	26	6
Parra, Franklin, Tulsa	1.000	1	0	2	0	2	1
Pimentel, Wander, Arkansas	1.000	1	2	1	0	3	0
Sims, Wesley, Tulsa	.939	10	15	31	3	49	10
Warner, Ron, Arkansas	.939	22	31	62	6	99	14
Weger, Wes, El Paso	.931	37	62	100	12	174	16
Woods, Kenny, Shreveport	.906	21	32	55	9	96	12
Yard, Bruce, San Antonio	.950	9	19	19	2	40	6

SHORTSTOPS WITH TWO OR MORE TEAMS

Player, Team	Pct.	G	PO	A	E	TC	DP
Nevers, Tom, Jackson	1.000	5	5	8	0	13	1
Nevers, Tom, El Paso	.833	2	2	3	1	6	2

OUTFIELDERS

Player, Team	Pct.	G	PO	A	E	TC	DP
Anderson, Charlie, Arkansas	1.000	4	4	0	0	4	0
Banks, Brian, El Paso	.960	117	207	8	9	224	1
Boykin, Tyrone, Midland	.970	34	61	3	2	66	0
Bridges, Kary, Jackson	.955	28	39	3	2	44	0
Burton, Darren, Wichita	.963	41	73	4	3	80	1
Carvajal, Jovino, Midland	.983	79	161	10	3	174	2
Cholowsky, Dan, Arkansas	1.000	24	42	1	0	43	0
Christopher, Chris, Arkansas	.931	18	26	1	2	29	0
Clinton, Jim, Tulsa	1.000	14	13	1	0	14	1
Cohick, Emmitt, Midland*	.945	36	49	3	3	55	1
CRUZ, Jacob, Shreveport*	.996	114	235	16	1	252	2
Damon, Johnny, Wichita*	.984	108	296	11	5	312	2
Daniels, Moe, Midland	.962	24	46	4	2	52	2
Diggs, Tony, Arkansas	.972	71	164	8	5	177	0
Dodson, Bo, El Paso*	1.000	1	1	0	0	1	0
Felder, Ken, El Paso	.966	108	156	14	6	176	0
Glenn, Leon, Midland	1.000	5	9	1	0	10	0
Gonzalez, Raul, Wichita	.957	21	38	6	2	46	0
Hatcher, Chris, Jackson	.875	6	13	1	2	16	1
Hidalgo, Richard, Jackson	.981	129	238	14	5	257	3
Hosey, Steve, Midland	1.000	22	35	1	0	36	0
Hunter, Brian, Jackson	1.000	2	5	0	0	5	0
Jaime, Angel, San Antonio	1.000	4	3	0	0	3	0
Jenkins, Bernie, Shreveport	.833	4	5	0	1	6	0
Jenkins, Geoff, El Paso*	.857	21	41	1	7	49	0
Jones, Keith, Arkansas*	1.000	17	32	1	0	33	0
Landrum, Tito, San Antonio	.955	82	144	5	7	156	2
Landry, Todd, El Paso*	.875	17	13	1	2	16	0
Latham, Chris, San Antonio	.972	58	135	2	4	141	0
Lewis, Anthony, Arkansas*	1.000	77	105	4	0	109	0
Long, Kevin, Wichita*	.986	60	129	8	2	139	0
Long, Ryan, Wichita	1.000	22	40	1	0	41	0
Maness, Dwight, San Antonio	.952	55	156	1	8	165	1
Marrero, Oreste, San Antonio*	.984	34	60	0	1	61	0
Marshall, Jason, Wichita	1.000	3	3	0	0	3	0
Martin, Jim, San Antonio	.916	81	125	6	12	143	1
McEwing, Joe, San Antonio	1.000	30	54	1	0	55	1
McFarlin, Jason, Shreveport*	.956	64	84	3	4	91	1
McNabb, Buck, Jackson	1.000	13	23	0	0	23	0
Mitchell, Tony, Wichita	.933	73	118	7	9	134	2
Montgomery, Ray, Jackson	1.000	25	59	5	0	64	0
Mora, Melvin, Jackson	.981	119	244	14	5	263	6
Morrow, Chris, Shreveport*	1.000	56	90	4	0	94	1
Murphy, Steve, Wichita	.960	14	24	0	1	25	0
Murray, Calvin, Shreveport	.993	109	286	9	2	297	1
Myers, Rod, Wichita*	.967	129	256	8	9	273	2
Nicholas, Darrell, El Paso	.903	14	28	0	3	31	0
Nilsson, Dave, El Paso	1.000	5	4	0	0	4	0
Ortiz, Bo, Midland	.974	92	165	20	5	190	5
Parra, Franklin, Tulsa	.902	45	81	2	9	92	0
Puchales, Javier, San Antonio*	.963	18	22	4	1	27	0
Radziewicz, Doug, Arkansas*	1.000	3	4	1	0	5	0
Raven, Luis, Midland	.909	8	8	2	1	11	2
Reid, Derek, Shreveport	1.000	5	3	0	0	3	0
Richardson, Scott, El Paso	.958	75	109	5	5	119	3

Player, Team	Pct.	G	PO	A	E	TC	DP
Rodriques, Cecil, El Paso	.976	65	118	2	3	123	0
Romero, Willie, San Antonio	.966	103	215	14	8	237	6
Rupp, Brian, Arkansas	.929	7	13	0	1	14	0
Sagmoen, Marc, Tulsa*	.993	62	135	7	1	143	3
Samples, Todd, El Paso	1.000	1	3	0	0	3	0
Shabazz, Basil, El Paso	.938	40	53	8	4	65	1
Simonton, Benji, Shreveport	.938	18	29	1	2	32	1
Sisco, Steve, Wichita	1.000	2	2	0	0	2	0
Smiley, Rueben, Wichita*	.938	24	28	2	2	32	1
Stewart, Andy, Wichita	1.000	2	1	1	0	2	0
Strickland, Chad, Wichita	1.000	1	1	0	0	1	0
Texidor, Jose, Tulsa	.993	128	264	9	2	275	2
Thomas, Brian, Tulsa	.992	131	340	16	3	359	2
Torres, Paul, Arkansas	1.000	8	14	0	0	14	0
Turco, Frank, Tulsa	.987	36	66	8	1	75	2
Velez, Jose, Arkansas*	.972	95	130	8	4	142	2
Verduzco, Steven, Jackson	.818	6	9	0	2	11	0
Wesson, Barry, Jackson	1.000	2	3	0	0	3	0
White, Chad, Jackson	.981	30	51	1	1	53	0
Williams, Keith, Shreveport	.966	63	109	4	4	117	0
Wolff, Mike, Midland	.973	127	309	18	9	336	3
Woods, Kenny, Shreveport	.974	38	34	3	1	38	2
Young, Dmitri, Arkansas	.931	91	116	5	9	130	1

CATCHERS

Player, Team	Pct.	G	PO	A	E	TC	DP	PB
Banks, Brian, El Paso	.947	3	17	1	1	19	0	2
Blanco, Henry, San Antonio	1.000	1	2	0	0	2	0	0
Carpenter, Jerry, Midland	1.000	1	1	0	0	1	0	0
Chavez, Raul, Jackson	.987	55	316	52	5	373	8	7
Dandridge, Brad, San Antonio	1.000	2	9	0	0	9	0	1
DiFelice, Mike, Arkansas	.984	61	327	48	6	381	5	3
Ehmann, Kurt, Shreveport	.000	1	0	0	1	1	0	0
ELLIS, Paul, Arkansas	.998	76	408	39	1	448	5	4
Fasano, Sal, Wichita	.976	44	286	34	8	328	5	3
Gilmore, Tony, Jackson	.991	50	285	29	3	317	2	12
Glenn, Leon, Midland	1.000	1	6	1	0	7	0	0
Greene, Todd, Midland	.992	65	311	44	3	358	3	9
Hughes, Bobby, El Paso	.976	51	298	29	8	335	2	6
Jennings, Lance, Wichita	1.000	13	61	10	0	71	0	1
Jensen, Marcus, Shreveport	.991	89	471	70	5	546	5	11
Kappesser, Bob, El Paso	.975	35	157	37	5	199	0	7
Kennedy, Darryl, Tulsa	.979	59	280	43	7	330	6	5
LoDuca, Paul, San Antonio	.975	56	346	38	10	394	5	5
Lopez, Pedro, El Paso	.985	48	231	37	4	272	7	8
Luce, Roger, Jackson	.949	16	71	4	4	79	1	2
Luzinski, Ryan, San Antonio	.986	43	246	33	4	283	6	5
Mayes, Craig, Shreveport	1.000	3	11	4	0	15	0	0
Miller, Roger, Shreveport	.984	19	116	11	2	129	3	4
Mirabelli, Doug, Shreveport	.984	35	166	21	3	190	1	2
Monzon, Jose, Midland	.976	57	312	61	9	382	9	6
Nunez, Rogelio, Tulsa	.967	82	420	73	17	510	6	7
Probst, Alan, Jackson	.994	25	137	19	1	157	3	4
Romero, Mandy, Wichita	.982	26	146	17	3	166	1	1
Silvia, Brian, Arkansas	.936	11	39	5	3	47	0	0
Steed, Dave, San Antonio	.981	40	227	27	5	259	2	3
Stewart, Andy, Wichita	.964	17	74	6	3	83	1	1
Strickland, Chad, Wichita	.977	50	285	50	8	343	2	5
Sutko, Glenn, El Paso	.975	34	198	34	6	238	2	3
Takayoshi, Todd, Midland	1.000	6	28	2	0	30	0	0
Tejero, Fausto, Midland	.990	16	90	13	1	104	0	5
Wilkins, Rick, Jackson	1.000	4	23	1	0	24	0	0
Yard, Bruce, San Antonio	1.000	2	3	0	0	3	0	0

PITCHERS

Player, Team	Pct.	G	PO	A	E	TC	DP
Akerfelds, Darrel, Midland	.933	29	5	9	1	15	0
Alkire, Jeff, Arkansas*	1.000	2	0	2	0	2	0
Allen, Ron, Jackson	1.000	4	1	4	0	5	1
Anderson, Paul, Arkansas	.917	38	5	17	2	24	3
Archer, Kurt, El Paso	1.000	4	0	3	0	3	0
Arrandale, Matt, Arkansas	.909	47	3	17	2	22	0
Atkinson, Neil, Arkansas*	1.000	40	1	3	0	4	0
Badorek, Mike, Arkansas	1.000	18	4	13	0	17	2
Bevil, Brian, Wichita	1.000	15	6	6	0	12	1
Bluma, Jaime, Wichita	1.000	42	4	11	0	15	1
Blyleven, Todd, Midland	1.000	8	0	2	0	2	0
Bonanno, Rob, Midland	1.000	3	1	0	0	1	0
Bourgeois, Steve, Shreveport	.967	22	9	20	1	30	1
Bovee, Mike, Wichita	1.000	20	8	9	0	17	1
Brewer, Nevin, Wichita	.875	19	5	2	1	8	0
Brewington, Jamie, Shreveport	.941	16	7	9	1	17	2

Player, Team	Pct.	G	PO	A	E	TC	DP
Brosnan, Jason, San Antonio*	1.000	19	3	4	0	7	0
Brown, Willard, Midland	.882	27	5	10	2	17	0
Browne, Byron, El Paso	.966	25	10	18	1	29	6
Brunson, William, San Antonio*	.955	14	4	17	1	22	1
Busby, Mike, Arkansas*	.966	20	8	20	1	29	0
Butler, Mike, Midland*	1.000	19	1	0	0	1	0
Camacho, Dan, San Antonio	1.000	11	1	0	0	1	1
Carpenter, Brian, Arkansas	1.000	17	0	6	0	6	0
Caruso, Gene, El Paso*	1.000	46	6	9	0	15	1
Castillo, Felipe, Tulsa	.900	14	3	6	1	10	0
Castillo, Juan, Jackson	1.000	12	9	9	0	18	0
Castillo, Mariano, Shreveport	1.000	22	1	5	0	6	0
Castro, Nelson, San Antonio	.917	48	8	14	2	24	1
Cather, Mike, Tulsa	1.000	18	3	6	0	9	0
Chavez, Tony, Midland	1.000	7	1	1	0	2	0
Cimorelli, Frank, El Paso	1.000	2	0	2	0	2	0
Cole, Jim, El Paso	1.000	6	2	3	0	5	0
Connolly, Chris, Wichita*	1.000	13	0	4	0	4	0
Corona, John, Arkansas*	1.000	5	0	2	0	2	1
Corps, Edwin, Shreveport	.947	27	13	23	2	38	2
Correa, Ramser, San Antonio	1.000	42	5	4	0	9	0
Creek, Doug, Arkansas*	.833	26	1	4	1	6	0
Creek, Ryan, Jackson	.926	26	7	18	2	27	0
Cummings, John, San Antonio*	1.000	6	2	5	0	7	0
Davis, Jeff, Tulsa	1.000	1	1	1	0	2	0
Davis, Ray, Arkansas	1.000	21	6	16	0	22	1
Dorlarque, Aaron, Wichita	1.000	20	1	5	0	6	0
Dreyer, Steve, Tulsa	.929	10	3	10	1	14	0
Duda, Steve, El Paso	.909	24	4	6	1	11	0
Duey, Kyle, Jackson	1.000	7	1	2	0	3	0
Duncan, Chip, Tulsa	.900	17	2	7	1	10	0
Edsell, Geoff, Midland	1.000	5	3	7	0	10	1
Escamilla, Jaime, Tulsa*	1.000	4	0	2	0	2	0
Estes, Shawn, Shreveport*	.833	4	0	5	1	6	1
Evans, Bart, Wichita	.833	7	3	2	1	6	0
Evans, Dave, Jackson	.875	49	1	13	2	16	0
Frontera, Chad, Shreveport	1.000	20	7	18	0	25	3
Fyhrie, Mike, Wichita	1.000	17	9	14	0	23	2
Gallaher, Kevin, Jackson	1.000	6	6	6	0	12	0
Gamez, Francisco, El Paso	1.000	27	13	13	0	26	0
Ganote, Joe, El Paso	.889	12	8	8	2	18	0
Garcia, Jose, San Antonio	.950	38	9	10	1	20	1
Geeve, Dave, Tulsa	1.000	15	9	13	0	22	0
Gerstein, Ron, El Paso*	.961	28	13	36	2	51	3
Granger, Jeff, Wichita*	.870	18	4	16	3	23	0
Grundy, Phil, Wichita	1.000	6	1	1	0	2	0
Grzanich, Mike, Jackson	.929	50	7	6	1	14	0
Hancock, Ryan, Midland	.943	28	13	20	2	35	2
Harris, Bryan, Midland*	1.000	39	1	14	0	15	1
Harrison, Brian, Wichita	1.000	15	0	4	0	4	0
Heredia, Wilson, Tulsa	1.000	8	1	6	0	7	1
Herges, Matt, San Antonio	.889	19	2	6	1	9	1
Hingle, Larry, Jackson*	1.000	9	2	3	0	5	0
Holdridge, David, Midland	.750	14	2	1	1	4	0
Holt, Chris, Jackson	1.000	5	5	6	0	11	0
Hubbs, Dan, San Antonio	1.000	31	6	10	0	16	2
Humphrey, Rich, Jackson	1.000	9	1	2	0	3	0
Hyde, Rich, Shreveport	1.000	33	3	4	0	7	0
Jones, Stacy, El Paso	1.000	8	1	0	0	1	0
Kappesser, Bob, El Paso	1.000	8	0	1	0	1	0
Keling, Korey, Midland	.938	29	9	21	2	32	4
Ketchen, Doug, Jackson	1.000	15	6	7	0	13	0
Keusch, Joseph, Tulsa	.500	2	0	1	1	2	0
Kimel, Jack, Tulsa*	.909	17	2	8	1	11	1
Kloek, Kevin, El Paso	.950	28	17	21	2	40	4
Knox, Kerry, Tulsa*	1.000	5	2	8	0	10	0
Kosenski, John, El Paso	1.000	16	4	4	0	8	0
Lacy, Kerry, Tulsa	.929	28	7	19	2	28	4
Langbehn, Gregg, El Paso*	1.000	16	1	6	0	7	0
Lidle, Cory, El Paso	1.000	45	5	20	0	25	1
Linares, Yfrain, El Paso	1.000	8	0	1	0	1	0
Lister, Martin, Jackson*	.857	15	2	10	2	14	1
Long, Tony, Arkansas*	.917	32	2	9	1	12	0
Lowe, Sean, Arkansas	.914	24	13	19	3	35	0
Mack, Tony, Midland	1.000	3	0	1	0	1	0
Maloney, Sean, El Paso	1.000	43	6	18	0	24	1
Marshall, Jason, Wichita	1.000	1	0	2	0	2	1
Martin, Jerry, Tulsa	.818	22	4	5	2	11	0
Martinez, Francisco, Arkansas	1.000	11	3	3	0	6	0
Martinez, Jesus, San Antonio*	.903	24	5	23	3	31	0
Martinez, Ramiro, Tulsa*	1.000	13	0	3	0	3	0
Matranga, Jeff, Arkansas	1.000	7	0	1	0	1	0
McDill, Allen, Wichita*	.500	12	0	1	1	2	0
McLain, Mike, Shreveport	1.000	11	0	2	0	2	0
Mercado, Hector, Jackson*	1.000	8	1	5	0	6	0
Mesewicz, Mark, Arkansas*	1.000	5	0	2	0	2	0
Mlicki, Doug, Jackson	.895	16	8	9	2	19	1
Montgomery, Steve, Arkansas	1.000	55	2	7	0	9	0
Montoya, Norm, El Paso*	.900	51	11	7	2	20	1
Moody, Ritchie, Tulsa*	1.000	11	3	3	0	6	0
Morones, Geno, Wichita	.833	17	4	16	4	24	3
Morvay, Joe, Tulsa	.813	37	0	13	3	16	0
Narcisse, Tyrone, Jackson	.878	27	18	18	5	41	2
Nieves, Ernesto, Midland	1.000	6	0	3	0	3	0
Oehrlein, Dave, Arkansas*	1.000	23	4	12	0	16	0
Oropesa, Eddie, San Antonio*	1.000	16	1	0	0	1	0
Osborne, Donovan, Arkansas*	1.000	2	1	3	0	4	0
Patterson, Danny, Tulsa	.900	26	5	4	1	10	1
Perez, David, Tulsa	.786	8	0	11	3	14	1
Peterson, Mark, Shreveport*	.952	37	4	16	1	21	0
Pickett, Ricky, Shreveport*	.000	14	0	0	1	1	0
Pote, Lou, Shreveport	.800	28	2	10	3	15	1
Powell, John, Tulsa	1.000	7	0	5	0	5	0
Prado, Jose, San Antonio	.940	28	23	24	3	50	2
Pricher, John, Midland	1.000	8	1	1	0	2	0
Purdy, Shawn, Shreveport	1.000	52	1	8	0	9	0
Pyc, Dave, San Antonio*	1.000	26	6	42	0	48	4
Ralston, Kris, Wichita	.900	18	3	6	1	10	0
Ratekin, Mark, Midland	1.000	11	0	5	0	5	1
Rath, Gary, San Antonio*	1.000	18	1	15	0	16	0
Rawitzer, Kevin, Wichita*	.800	28	4	4	2	10	1
Ray, Ken, Wichita	.941	14	4	12	1	17	0
Renko, Steve, Midland	.857	22	4	8	2	14	2
Richey, Jeff, Shreveport	1.000	8	0	4	0	4	1
Rodriguez, Frankie, El Paso	.976	28	10	30	1	41	1
Santana, Julio, Tulsa	.957	15	7	15	1	23	2
Schmidt, Jeff, Midland	.636	20	2	5	4	11	0
Schooler, Mike, Midland	1.000	54	4	8	0	12	1
Sebach, Kyle, Midland	.833	5	2	3	1	6	2
Sepeda, Jaime, Jackson	1.000	1	0	1	0	1	0
Sheehan, Chris, Wichita	1.000	31	6	5	0	11	0
SIMMONS, Scott, Arkansas*	1.000	22	9	41	0	50	1
Smith, Scotty, Tulsa	1.000	29	5	14	0	19	0
Snyder, John, Midland	.833	21	8	17	5	30	1
Soderstrom, Steve, Shreveport	.895	22	8	9	2	19	1
Strange, Don, Wichita	1.000	24	3	2	0	5	0
Taulbee, Andy, Shreveport	.850	14	8	9	3	20	2
Thibert, John, Midland	1.000	12	1	2	0	3	0
Toth, Robert, Wichita	1.000	21	8	9	0	17	0
Troutman, Keith, San Antonio	1.000	38	4	7	0	11	1
Valdez, Carlos, Shreveport	.944	22	4	13	1	18	1
Vanderweele, Doug, Shreveport	1.000	13	6	11	0	17	5
VanRyn, Ben, Midland*	1.000	19	4	5	0	9	1
Wagner, Billy, Jackson*	.889	12	2	6	1	9	0
Wagner, Bret, Arkansas*	1.000	6	1	7	0	8	0
Wagner, Joe, El Paso	1.000	5	0	2	0	2	0
Waldron, Joe, Jackson*	1.000	28	3	4	0	7	1
Walker, Jamie, Jackson*	1.000	50	5	15	0	20	0
Wallace, Derek, Wichita	.778	26	1	6	2	9	0
Wanke, Chuck, Shreveport*	.778	43	0	7	2	9	1
Waring, Jim, Jackson	1.000	17	7	10	0	17	1
Watson, Allen, Arkansas*	1.000	1	0	1	0	1	0
Weaver, Eric, San Antonio	.889	27	15	17	4	36	0
Webb, Doug, El Paso	1.000	18	0	3	0	3	0
Whitaker, Steve, Shreveport*	1.000	4	0	3	0	3	0
White, Chris, Jackson	.938	38	5	10	1	16	0
Wiley, Chad, Tulsa	.902	26	9	28	4	41	2
Witasick, Jay, Arkansas	1.000	7	0	5	0	5	0

The following players did not have any fielding statistics at the positions indicated or appeared only as a designated hitter, pinch-hitter or pinch-runner: Brannon, p; Bridges, p; Browning, p; Butterfield, dh; Caruso, of; Charles, c; R. Chavez, 3b; Davidson, p; Eddy, p; Gamez, of; M. Guerrero, p; M. Harris, dh, ph; Kappesser, of; Kellner, p; Langbehn, of; Monell, dh, ph; Mora, 2b; Munoz, of; Paskievitch, p; Dan. Perez, dh, ph, pr; Popplewell, p; Ramirez, of; Redington, 3b; Richardson, 3b; Sparks, pr; Sutko, of; Talanoa, dh; Urso, 1b; Voigt, of; R. Watson, p; Wheeler, p; Chad White, p; J. White, ph; T. Williams, pr; Yard, 3b.

LEAGUE CHAMPIONS

Year	Team	Pct.
1888—	Dallas	.671
1889—	Houston	.551
1890—	Galveston	.705
1892—	Houston	.741
	Houston	.613
1895—	Dallas	.754
	Fort Worth*	.750
1896—	Fort Worth	.757
	Houston*	.679
	Galveston	.548
1897—	San Antonio†	.657
	Galveston†	.717
1898—	League disbanded.	
1899—	Galveston	.632
	Galveston	.762
1900-01—	Did not operate.	
1902—	Corsicana	.866
	Corsicana	.682
1903—	Paris-Waco	.615
	Dallas*	.648
1904—	Corsicana*	.615
	Fort Worth	.800
1905—	Fort Worth	.545
1906—	Fort Worth	.677
	Cleburne∞	.609
1907—	Austin	.629
1908—	San Antonio	.664
1909—	Houston	.601
1910—	Dallas†	.586
	Houston†	.586
1911—	Austin	.575
1912—	Houston	.626
1913—	Houston	.620
1914—	Houston†	.671
	Waco†	.671
1915—	Waco	.592
1916—	Waco	.587
1917—	Dallas	.600
1918—	Dallas	.584
1919—	Shreveport*	.677
	Fort Worth	.651
1920—	Fort Worth	.703
	Fort Worth	.750
1921—	Fort Worth	.691
	Fort Worth	.662
1922—	Fort Worth	.694
	Fort Worth	.711
1923—	Fort Worth	.632
	Fort Worth	.763
1924—	Fort Worth	.689
	Fort Worth	.763
1925—	Fort Worth	.711
	Fort Worth▲	.653
1926—	Dallas	.574
1927—	Wichita Falls	.654
1928—	Houston*	.679
	Wichita Falls	.731
1929—	Dallas*	.588
	Wichita Falls	.620
1930—	Wichita Falls	.697
	Fort Worth*	.632
1931—	Houston♦	.625
	Houston	.734
1932—	Beaumont*	.640
	Dallas	.727
1933—	Houston	.623
	San Antonio (4th)§	.523
1934—	Galveston‡	.579
1935—	Oklahoma City‡	.590
1936—	Dallas	.604
	Tulsa (3rd)§	.519
1937—	Oklahoma City	.635
	Fort Worth (3rd)§	.535
1938—	Beaumont	.635
1939—	Houston	.606
	Fort Worth (4th)§	.540
1940—	Houston‡	.652
1941—	Houston	.673
	Dallas (4th)§	.519
1942—	Beaumont	.605
	Shreveport (2nd)§	.576
1943-44-45—	Did not operate.	
1946—	Fort Worth	.656
	Dallas (2nd)§	.591
1947—	Houston‡	.623
1948—	Fort Worth‡	.601
1949—	Fort Worth	.649
	Tulsa (2nd)§	.584
1950—	Beaumont	.595
	San Antonio (4th)§	.513
1951—	Houston‡	.619
1952—	Dallas	.571
	Shreveport (3rd)§	.522
1953—	Dallas‡	.571
1954—	Shreveport	.559
	Houston (2nd)§	.553
1955—	Dallas	.581
	Shreveport (3rd)§	.540
1956—	Houston‡	.623
1957—	Dallas	.662
	Houston (2nd)§	.630
1958—	Fort Worth	.582
	Cor. Christi (3rd)§	.507
1959—	Victoria	.589
	Austin (2nd)§	.548
1960—	Rio Grande Valley	.590
	Tulsa (3rd)	.528
1961—	Amarillo	.643
	San Antonio (3rd)§	.532
1962—	El Paso	.571
	Tulsa (2nd)§	.550
1963—	San Antonio	.564
	Tulsa (3rd)§	.529
1964—	San Antonio‡	.607
1965—	Tulsa	.574
	Albuquerque■	.550
1966—	Arkansas	.579
1967—	Albuquerque	.557
1968—	Arkansas	.586
	El Paso■	.562
1969—	Amarillo	.593
	Memphis■	.504
1970—	Albuquerque♦	.615
	Memphis	.507
1971—	Did not operate as league—clubs were members of Dixie Association.	
1972—	Alexandria	.600
	El Paso■	.557
1973—	San Antonio	.590
	Memphis■	.558
1974—	Victoria■	.581
	El Paso	.555
1975—	Lafayette▼	.558
	Midland▼	.604
1976—	Amarillo■	.600
	Shreveport	.515
1977—	El Paso	.600
	Arkansas•	.485
1978—	El Paso•	.593
	Jackson	.567
1979—	Arkansas•	.571
	Midland	.563
1980—	Arkansas•	.596
	San Antonio	.544
1981—	San Antonio	.571
	Jackson•	.507
1982—	El Paso	.559
	Tulsa•	.515
1983—	Jackson	.507
	Beaumont•	.500
1984—	Beaumont	.654
	Jackson•	.610
1985—	El Paso	.632
	Jackson•	.537
1986—	El Paso•	.630
	Jackson	.533
1987—	Wichita•	.515
	Jackson	.515
1988—	El Paso	.552
	Tulsa•	.522
1989—	Arkansas•	.585
	Wichita	.537
1990—	San Antonio	.582
	Shreveport•	.489
1991—	Shreveport•	.632
	El Paso	.596
1992—	Shreveport	.566
	Wichita•	.515
1993—	El Paso	.563
	Jackson•	.541
1994—	El Paso•	.647
	Jackson	.548
1995—	Shreveport•	.652
	Midland	.485

*Won split-season playoff. †Won playoff for title. ‡Finished first and won four-club playoff. §Won four-club playoff. ∞Title to Cleburne by default. ▲Tied with Dallas in second half and won playoff for championship. ♦Tied with Beaumont at end of first half and won title in best-of-five series played as part of second-half schedule. ■League divided into Eastern, Western divisions; won two-team playoff. ▼League divided into Eastern, Western divisions; declared co-champions when playoffs were not completed. •League divided into Eastern and Western divisions and played split-season; won playoffs. NOTE—Championship awarded to winner of four-team playoff, 1933-51; first-place team and playoff winner co-champions, 1952-64.

CLASS AA Texas League

CALIFORNIA LEAGUE

LEAGUE OFFICE

President/treasurer
Joe Gagliardi
Address
2380 S. Bascom Ave., Suite 200
Campbell, CA 95008
Phone
408-369-8038

Teams (affiliation)
Bakersfield Blaze (independent)
High Desert Mavericks (Orioles)
Lake Elsinore Storm (Angels)
Modesto A's (A's)
Rancho Cucamonga Quakes (Padres)
Lancaster Jethawks (Mariners)

San Bernardino Stampede (Dodgers)
San Jose Giants (Giants)
Stockton Ports (Brewers)
Visalia Oaks (independent)

1995 FINAL STANDINGS

FIRST HALF

NORTHERN DIVISION

Team	W	L	T	Pct.	GB
Modesto (Athletics)	40	30	0	.571	....
San Jose (Giants)	36	34	0	.514	4
Stockton (Brewers)	35	34	0	.507	4½
Visalia (Co-op)	35	35	0	.500	5
Bakersfield (Co-op)	31	39	0	.443	9

SOUTHERN DIVISION

Team	W	L	T	Pct.	GB
San Bernardino (Dodgers)	44	25	0	.638	....
Lake Elsinore (Angels)	37	32	0	.536	7
Riverside (Mariners)	35	34	0	.507	9
Rancho Cucamonga (Padres)	32	36	0	.471	11½
High Desert (Orioles)	22	48	0	.314	22½

SECOND HALF

NORTHERN DIVISION

Team	W	L	T	Pct.	GB
San Jose (Giants)	41	29	0	.586	....
Stockton (Brewers)	39	31	0	.557	2
Modesto (Athletics)	38	32	0	.543	3
Bakersfield (Co-op)	27	43	0	.386	14
Visalia (Co-op)	23	47	0	.329	18

SOUTHERN DIVISION

Team	W	L	T	Pct.	GB
Lake Elsinore (Angels)	44	25	0	.638	....
San Bernardino (Dodgers)	40	29	0	.580	4
Riverside (Mariners)	37	33	0	.529	7½
Rancho Cucamonga (Padres)	36	34	0	.514	8½
High Desert (Orioles)	24	46	0	.343	20½

COMPOSITE

Team	S.B.	L.E.	Mod.	S.J.	Stk.	Riv.	R.C.	Vis.	Bak.	H.D.	W	L	T	Pct.	GB
San Bernardino (Dodgers)	...	11	7	10	4	8	14	9	5	17	85	54	0	.612	....
Lake Elsinore (Angels)	8	....	7	6	9	12	10	8	9	13	82	57	0	.590	3
Modesto (Athletics)	5	5	....	8	11	7	8	14	14	6	78	62	0	.557	7½
San Jose (Giants)	2	6	12	....	9	8	9	11	10	10	77	63	0	.550	8½
Stockton (Brewers)	8	3	9	11	....	6	4	10	12	11	74	66	0	.529	11½
Riverside (Mariners)	12	8	5	4	6	....	8	6	11	12	72	67	0	.518	13
Rancho Cucamonga (Padres)	6	10	4	3	8	11	....	6	7	13	68	71	0	.489	17
Visalia (Co-op)	3	4	6	9	10	6	6	....	7	7	58	82	0	.414	27½
Bakersfield (Co-op)	7	3	6	10	8	1	5	13	....	5	58	82	0	.414	27½
High Desert (Orioles)	3	7	6	2	1	8	7	5	7	....	46	94	0	.329	39½

Major league affiliations in parentheses.

High Desert played home games in Adelanto, Calif.

PLAYOFFS: San Jose defeated Stockton, two games to none; Lake Elsinore defeated Riverside, two games to one; San Jose defeated Modesto, three games to none; San Bernardino defeated Lake Elsinore, three games to none; San Bernardino defeated San Jose, three games to none, to win league championship.

REGULAR-SEASON ATTENDANCE: Bakersfield, 105,890; High Desert, 146,355; Lake Elsinore, 383,297; Modesto, 100,108; Rancho Cucamonga, 446,146; Riverside, 56,601; San Bernardino, 119,434; San Jose, 140,976; Stockton, 107,140; Visalia, 71,513. Total, 1,677,460. Playoffs (14 games)—31,796. All-Star Game at Lake Elsinore—5,870.

MANAGERS: Bakersfield, Greg Mahlberg; High Desert, Tim Blackwell; Lake Elsinore, Mitch Seoane; Modesto, Glenn Ezell; Rancho Cucamonga, Marty Barrett; Riverside, Dave Brundage; San Bernardino, Ron Roenicke; San Jose, Carlos Lezcano; Stockton, Bob Mariano; Visalia, Lyle Yates.

ALL-STAR TEAM: 1B—Steve Cox, Modesto; 2B—Adam Riggs, San Bernardino; 3B—Rick Ladjevich, Riverside; SS—Greg LaRocca, Rancho Cucamonga; OF—Alex Ramirez, Bakersfield; Armando Rios, San Jose; Greg Shockey, Lake Elsinore; C—Raul Ibanez, Riverside; DH—Rod McCall, Bakersfield; P—Matt Beaumont, Lake Elsinore; Carlos Castillo, Lake Elsinore; Keith Foulke, San Jose; Doug Webb, Stockton; Most Valuable Player—Adam Riggs, San Bernardino; Pitcher of the Year—Matt Beaumont, Lake Elsinore; Rookie of the Year—Adam Riggs, San Bernardino; Manager of the Year—Ron Roenicke, San Bernardino.

1995 BATTING

TEAM

Team	Avg.	G	TPA	AB	R	H	TB	2B	3B	HR	RBI	SH	SF	HP	BB	IBB	SO	SB	CS	GDP	LOB	ShO	Slg.	OBP
San Bernardino	.284	139	5466	4803	823	1362	2132	250	29	154	738	51	43	65	502	11	988	246	100	82	941	4	.444	.356
Stockton	.281	140	5406	4778	730	1341	1911	244	43	80	626	74	49	47	458	11	872	220	97	100	971	2	.400	.346
Lake Elsinore	.275	139	5492	4773	800	1312	2013	275	51	108	731	41	39	62	575	18	973	114	62	108	1045	4	.422	.358
Riverside	.274	139	5465	4813	799	1319	1875	213	44	85	698	30	54	86	482	12	914	153	72	81	992	5	.390	.347
R. Cucamonga	.272	139	5415	4733	742	1288	1850	220	30	94	676	36	50	73	522	14	980	169	62	104	1019	4	.391	.350
Modesto	.267	140	5534	4678	773	1251	1970	245	30	138	703	80	44	72	659	15	1064	137	79	104	1083	9	.421	.363
Bakersfield	.267	140	5327	4690	626	1250	1749	229	21	76	551	60	33	68	475	14	952	149	97	120	1003	11	.373	.340
San Jose	.260	140	5552	4835	695	1256	1801	227	54	70	602	66	43	68	528	19	1011	217	77	90	1069	10	.372	.338
High Desert	.259	140	5371	4710	669	1218	1871	215	39	120	601	44	41	91	484	5	1033	181	103	87	950	15	.397	.337
Visalia	.255	140	5358	4756	591	1211	1695	210	38	66	529	51	40	50	459	6	1025	116	83	105	1000	11	.356	.324

INDIVIDUAL

TOP QUALIFIERS FOR BATTING CHAMPIONSHIP

Minimum 378 plate appearances. *Lefthanded batter. †Switch-hitter.

Player, Team	Avg.	G	TPA	AB	R	H	TB	2B	3B	HR	RBI	SH	SF	HP	BB	IBB	SO	SB	CS	GDP	Slg.	OBP
Riggs, Adam, San Bernardino	.362	134	622	542	111	196	317	39	5	24	106	7	4	10	59	1	93	31	10	9	.585	.431
Hamlin, Jonas, Stockton.........	.332	99	416	388	65	129	219	32	5	16	69	1	6	4	17	2	86	5	4	7	.564	.361
Ibanez, Raul, Riverside*	.332	95	414	361	59	120	221	23	9	20	108	1	9	2	41	1	49	4	3	7	.612	.395
McCall, Rod, Bakersfield*........	.330	96	399	345	61	114	195	19	1	20	70	2	4	8	40	7	90	2	5	6	.565	.408
Shockey, Greg, Lake Elsinore*.....	.327	114	492	441	85	144	242	32	3	20	88	0	2	6	42	2	88	2	2	6	.549	.391
Ramirez, Alex, Bakersfield	.323	98	428	406	56	131	190	25	2	10	52	0	1	3	18	1	76	13	9	9	.468	.355
LaRocca, Greg, R.C...............	.322	125	524	466	77	150	220	36	5	8	74	0	2	12	44	0	77	15	4	13	.472	.393
Nicholas, Darrell, Stockton	.320	87	386	350	54	112	149	16	3	5	39	11	1	1	23	1	75	26	8	6	.426	.363
Barger, Mike, Riverside.........	.317	82	390	344	77	109	127	10	1	2	41	5	1	2	38	1	45	33	14	3	.369	.387
Ladjevich, Rick, Riverside	.309	122	525	470	74	145	192	26	0	7	71	3	4	22	26	2	65	3	2	8	.409	.370
Seitzer, Brad, Stockton	.308	127	507	428	66	132	184	28	3	6	56	2	2	3	72	2	68	7	4	10	.430	.410
Berry, Michael, Visalia	.307	98	434	368	69	113	176	28	4	9	61	1	3	5	57	1	70	12	6	9	.478	.404
Morillo, Cesar, Bakersfield†	.305	108	412	371	41	113	143	25	1	1	37	5	1	4	31	2	71	4	12	6	.385	.364
Sbrocco, Jon, San Jose*.........	.301	120	508	425	66	128	158	14	5	2	46	17	1	10	55	3	43	12	10	5	.372	.393
Lee, Derrek, R.C...............	.301	128	565	502	82	151	249	25	2	23	95	0	7	7	49	2	130	14	7	8	.496	.366
Ortega, Hector, Stockton.........	.301	137	601	539	81	162	221	27	4	8	76	6	7	10	39	0	109	26	13	8	.410	.355

DEPARTMENTAL LEADERS: G—H. Ortega, 137; AB—Riggs, 542; R—Riggs, 111; H—Riggs, 196; TB—Riggs, 317; 2B—Riggs, 39; 3B—D'Aquila, 11; HR—Cox, 30; RBI—Cox, 110; SH—Martins, 18; SF—Cox, 10; HP—Ladjevich, 22; BB—McDonald, 110; IBB—Redington, 8; SO—Hust, 169; SB—McDonald, 70; CS—Carr, 21; GIDP—Wingate, 25; Slg.—Ibanez, .612; OBP—Riggs, .431.

ALL PLAYERS

*Lefthanded batter. †Switch-hitter.

Player, Team	Avg.	G	TPA	AB	R	H	TB	2B	3B	HR	RBI	SH	SF	HP	BB	IBB	SO	SB	CS	GDP	Slg.	OBP
Adams, Tommy, Riverside.........	.287	69	290	251	46	72	121	17	4	8	40	1	3	7	28	0	40	12	4	5	.482	.370
Alguacil, Jose, San Jose*........	.236	58	253	225	30	53	69	10	3	0	17	8	2	4	14	0	44	11	6	2	.307	.290
Alimena, Charles, San Jose*	.205	54	184	171	17	35	45	3	2	1	18	0	1	1	11	0	44	1	0	8	.263	.255
Allanson, Andy, Lake Elsinore ...	.317	22	100	82	10	26	47	9	0	4	22	0	1	1	16	0	8	2	2	4	.573	.430
Alvarez, Gabe, R.C.............	.344	59	248	212	41	73	112	17	2	6	36	0	2	5	29	0	30	1	0	3	.528	.431
Asencio, Alex, San Bernardino* ..	.257	29	114	105	15	27	42	1	4	2	18	1	0	2	6	0	31	2	0	0	.400	.310
Avila, Rolando, High Desert......	.239	52	218	180	26	43	61	10	1	2	10	5	0	4	29	0	26	19	8	0	.339	.357
Banks, Tony, Modesto*	.198	28	99	81	10	16	22	3	0	1	10	4	1	0	13	0	17	3	0	0	.272	.305
Barger, Mike, Riverside.........	.317	82	390	344	77	109	127	10	1	2	41	5	1	2	38	1	45	33	14	3	.369	.387
Bautista, Juan, High Desert......	.262	99	408	374	54	98	152	13	4	11	51	6	3	7	18	0	74	22	9	8	.406	.306
Bellhorn, Mark, Modesto†........	.258	56	262	229	35	59	89	12	0	6	31	2	0	4	27	0	52	5	2	9	.389	.346
Bengoechea, Brandy, Modesto ...	.261	134	537	467	60	122	164	19	4	5	44	11	3	9	47	1	96	7	10	10	.351	.338
Berry, Michael, Visalia	.307	98	434	368	69	113	176	28	4	9	61	1	3	5	57	1	70	12	6	9	.478	.404
Bethea, Scott, Visalia...........	.241	105	433	370	51	89	112	17	3	0	27	9	3	4	47	1	35	14	9	4	.303	.330
Bishop, Steve, High Desert......	.116	12	48	43	5	5	8	1	1	0	3	0	0	1	4	0	12	1	0	1	.186	.208
Bogle, Bryan, High Desert........	.172	19	72	64	7	11	15	2	1	0	4	0	0	0	8	0	18	3	1	1	.234	.264
Bonds, Bobby, Visalia...........	.223	109	423	373	56	83	140	12	6	11	30	3	1	4	42	1	114	26	12	5	.375	.307
Bordick, Mike, Modesto	.000	1	3	2	0	0	0	0	0	0	0	0	0	1	0	0	0	0	1	0	.000	.333
Brakebill, Mark, Lake Elsinore	.143	2	8	7	0	1	1	0	0	0	0	0	0	1	0	0	2	0	0	0	.143	.250
Breuer, Jim, Bakersfield.........	.048	10	26	21	0	1	1	0	0	0	3	0	2	1	2	0	13	0	0	0	.048	.154
Brock, Tarrick, Visalia*..........	.225	45	161	138	21	31	43	5	2	1	15	2	0	4	17	0	52	11	1	2	.312	.327
Burke, Jamie, Lake Elsinore	.274	106	421	365	47	100	133	15	6	2	56	11	4	9	32	1	53	6	4	12	.364	.344
Byrne, Clayton, High Desert	.236	54	209	199	24	47	64	10	2	1	19	0	0	3	7	0	36	7	5	1	.322	.273
Cabrera, Jairo, High Desert	.205	14	46	39	2	8	8	0	0	0	3	2	1	1	3	0	7	1	0	2	.205	.273
Campillo, Rob, Stockton..........	.302	35	119	106	10	32	35	3	0	0	17	3	2	1	7	0	13	0	0	4	.330	.345
Carpenter, Jerry, Lake Elsinore....	.000	1	3	2	0	0	0	0	0	0	0	0	1	0	0	0	0	0	1	0	.000	.333
Carr, Jeremy, Bakersfield	.257	128	595	499	92	128	157	22	2	1	38	6	0	11	79	0	73	52	21	9	.315	.370
Carrasquel, Domingo, Stockton†..	.269	67	189	160	19	43	53	10	0	0	20	10	1	0	18	0	21	2	5	3	.331	.341
Cavanagh, Mike, San Jose	.125	6	20	16	2	2	4	0	1	0	3	2	0	0	2	0	8	0	0	0	.250	.222
Chavez, Eric, High Desert........	.232	74	288	254	38	59	116	15	0	14	37	0	2	4	27	0	74	4	2	4	.457	.314
Clark, Howie, High Desert*.......	.258	100	371	329	50	85	124	20	2	5	40	3	3	4	32	0	51	12	6	4	.377	.329
Claudio, Patricio, Bakersfield......	.281	32	145	128	19	36	54	9	3	1	9	2	0	2	13	0	26	5	7	3	.422	.357
Clyburn, Danny, High Desert......	.281	45	184	160	20	45	86	3	1	12	37	0	3	4	17	1	41	2	1	3	.538	.359
Conway, Jeff, R.C.*.............	.254	28	73	67	9	17	18	1	0	0	5	2	0	0	4	0	10	1	1	3	.269	.296
Cook, Jason, Riverside...........	.190	6	26	21	9	4	5	1	0	0	3	0	0	0	5	0	4	0	0	0	.238	.346
Corps, Erick, R.C.†..............	.191	73	213	183	21	35	44	6	0	1	13	4	2	2	22	0	54	1	1	5	.240	.282
Cox, Steve, Modesto*............	.298	132	591	483	95	144	269	29	3	30	110	0	10	14	84	6	88	5	4	12	.557	.409
Cromer, D.T., Modesto*..........	.259	108	430	378	59	98	168	18	5	14	52	6	4	6	36	1	66	5	7	10	.444	.325
Cruz, Jose, Riverside†...........	.257	35	170	144	34	37	67	7	1	7	29	0	2	0	24	1	50	3	1	1	.465	.359
Cuellar, Jose, Riverside	.111	19	57	45	7	5	5	0	0	0	2	0	0	0	12	0	9	0	0	1	.111	.298
Cuevas, Eduardo, R.C............	.243	43	150	140	14	34	46	5	2	1	24	0	3	0	7	1	16	5	1	6	.329	.273
Cunningham, Earl, Lake Elsinore ...	.239	78	308	284	50	68	130	13	2	15	55	0	2	6	15	0	97	8	3	7	.458	.290
Curtis, Kevin, High Desert	.293	112	470	399	70	117	208	26	1	21	70	0	5	12	54	1	83	8	6	7	.521	.389
Dandridge, Brad, San Bernardino ..	.320	82	342	322	56	103	154	14	2	11	61	1	2	3	14	0	34	16	5	11	.478	.352
Daniels, Moe, Lake Elsinore	.305	39	170	151	26	46	58	6	3	0	11	0	0	1	18	0	35	6	4	2	.384	.382
D'Aquila, Tom, High Desert	.264	110	438	386	48	102	167	10	11	11	63	0	3	4	45	1	111	8	7	11	.433	.345
Davis, Doug, Lake Elsinore.......	.333	1	4	3	0	1	1	0	0	0	0	0	0	1	0	1	0	0	0	0	.333	.500
Dean, Chris, Riverside†..........	.251	116	482	407	56	102	152	16	8	6	45	3	7	16	49	1	98	13	10	4	.373	.349
Delgado, Wilson, San Jose†.......	.000	1	2	2	1	0	0	0	0	0	0	0	0	0	0	0	0	0	0	0	.000	.000
Derotal, Francisco, R.C..........	.196	29	62	56	9	11	19	2	0	2	5	1	0	2	3	0	20	1	0	0	.339	.262
Diaz, Alfredo, Lake Elsinore†......	.235	49	169	149	25	35	54	12	2	1	25	3	6	0	11	0	54	1	1	6	.362	.277
Dobrolsky, Bill, Stockton	.270	88	290	252	28	68	94	14	3	2	30	2	5	6	25	0	37	3	4	4	.373	.344

Player, Team	Avg.	G	TPA	AB	R	H	TB	2B	3B	HR	RBI	SH	SF	HP	BB	IBB	SO	SB	CS	GDP	Slg.	OBP
Doty, Derrin, Lake Elsinore	.247	94	368	324	46	80	116	12	0	8	35	2	2	3	37	0	54	16	6	4	.358	.328
Dressendorfer, Kirk, Modesto	.000	27	1	1	0	0	0	0	0	0	0	0	0	0	0	0	1	0	0	0	.000	.000
Dumas, Mike, Stockton	.235	74	278	243	41	57	73	7	3	1	17	6	1	1	27	0	26	21	12	8	.300	.313
Dunn, Todd, Stockton	.293	67	272	249	44	73	118	20	2	7	40	1	1	2	19	2	67	14	3	5	.474	.347
Durkin, Chris, San Bernardino*	.268	57	197	164	24	44	80	10	1	8	31	1	3	1	28	0	48	9	6	3	.488	.372
Eaddy, Keith, High Desert	.244	99	395	336	58	82	143	17	4	12	42	3	3	10	43	0	107	20	9	8	.426	.344
Ealy, Tracey, San Jose†	.156	12	35	32	7	5	5	0	0	0	2	0	1	1	2	0	12	0	0	2	.156	.229
Erstad, Darin, Lake Elsinore*	.363	25	120	113	24	41	69	7	3	5	24	0	1	0	6	0	22	3	0	2	.611	.392
Faircloth, Kevin, San Bernardino	.185	56	176	146	23	27	30	3	0	0	6	4	2	10	14	0	40	7	3	2	.205	.297
Fernandez, Antonio, Visalia	.227	90	327	309	25	70	88	10	1	2	32	1	2	1	14	0	48	1	0	18	.285	.261
Fitzpatrick, Will, Stockton*	.207	13	37	29	5	6	10	1	0	1	4	0	0	0	8	0	16	0	0	0	.345	.378
Fuller, Aaron, Visalia†	.253	49	211	186	27	47	63	7	3	1	19	3	2	1	19	0	32	11	10	0	.339	.322
Fully, Ed, High Desert	.369	38	159	149	28	55	84	11	0	6	34	1	0	2	7	0	22	9	6	3	.564	.405
Galarza, Joel, San Jose	.292	58	235	209	28	61	97	13	1	7	44	4	5	2	11	0	35	6	2	4	.464	.326
Garcia, Manuel, Visalia	.100	12	44	40	3	4	8	2	1	0	4	0	1	2	1	0	18	3	0	0	.200	.159
Gargiulo, Mike, High Desert*	.206	14	36	34	2	7	8	1	0	0	4	1	0	0	1	0	9	0	1	1	.235	.229
Gibbs, Kevin, San Bernardino†	.231	5	13	13	1	3	4	1	0	0	0	0	0	0	0	0	2	1	0	0	.308	.231
Graham, John, Visalia*	.248	98	353	306	45	76	89	8	1	1	30	4	3	4	36	0	77	12	6	2	.291	.332
Grass, Darren, R.C.	.241	23	63	58	6	14	23	6	0	1	9	3	0	0	2	0	15	0	0	1	.397	.267
Gresham, Kris, High Desert	.257	47	160	140	25	36	59	8	0	5	15	2	4	12	1	1	31	1	3	6	.421	.329
Grieve, Ben, Modesto*	.262	28	124	107	17	28	39	5	0	2	14	0	2	0	15	1	22	2	0	3	.364	.347
Guevara, Giomar, Riverside†	.243	83	335	292	53	71	95	12	3	2	34	6	6	1	30	1	71	7	4	4	.325	.310
Guiel, Aaron, Lake Elsinore*	.269	113	493	409	73	110	170	25	7	7	58	4	4	7	69	0	96	7	6	7	.416	.380
Guillen, Jose, Modesto†	.257	41	129	113	16	29	36	2	1	1	11	5	0	0	11	0	24	9	3	3	.319	.323
Gulseth, Mark, San Jose*	.234	22	74	64	8	15	21	4	1	0	6	0	0	0	10	2	16	1	0	0	.328	.338
Hamlin, Jonas, Modesto	.332	99	416	388	65	129	219	32	5	16	69	1	6	4	17	2	86	5	4	7	.564	.361
Harmer, Frank, High Desert†	.250	6	17	12	3	3	7	1	0	1	1	0	0	0	5	0	5	0	0	0	.583	.471
Haught, Gary, Modesto†	.000	34	1	1	0	0	0	0	0	0	0	0	0	0	0	0	1	0	0	0	.000	.000
Hayashi, Hiroyasu, Visalia*	.268	40	169	138	19	37	43	6	0	0	15	4	0	1	26	1	27	2	3	4	.312	.388
Hecker, Doug, Visalia	.071	8	17	14	2	1	1	0	0	0	0	0	0	0	3	0	5	0	1	0	.071	.235
Hemphill, Bret, Lake Elsinore†	.199	45	170	146	12	29	39	7	0	1	17	0	3	3	18	0	36	2	1	4	.267	.294
Hence, Sam, Bakersfield	.125	4	9	8	1	1	1	0	0	0	0	0	1	0	0	0	1	0	0	0	.125	.125
Hilo, Johnny, San Bernardino†	.247	38	111	93	14	23	30	2	1	1	9	3	0	0	15	0	23	3	2	1	.323	.352
Hodge, Roy, High Desert	.300	42	180	140	31	42	61	8	1	3	15	0	1	3	36	0	24	8	7	3	.436	.450
Hollandsworth, Todd, San Bern.*	.500	1	2	2	0	1	1	0	0	0	0	0	0	0	0	0	1	0	1	0	.500	.500
Hostetler, Brian, Stockton*	.000	3	7	7	0	0	0	0	0	0	0	0	0	0	0	0	0	0	0	0	.000	.000
Hughes, Bobby, Stockton	.235	52	200	179	22	42	79	9	2	8	31	0	3	1	17	1	41	2	2	10	.441	.300
Hugo, Sean, High Desert*	.240	28	90	75	8	18	26	3	1	1	13	0	2	1	12	0	21	1	1	2	.347	.344
Hunter, Scott, San Bernardino	.285	113	428	379	68	108	166	19	3	11	59	4	1	6	36	1	83	27	8	0	.438	.355
Hust, Gary, Modesto	.238	128	539	467	85	111	216	20	2	27	87	4	3	4	61	3	169	10	4	4	.463	.329
Ibanez, Raul, Riverside*	.332	95	414	361	59	120	221	23	9	20	108	1	9	2	41	1	49	4	3	7	.612	.395
Ibarra, Jesse, San Jose†	.333	3	10	9	1	3	5	2	0	0	4	0	0	0	1	0	1	0	0	2	.556	.400
Jenkins, Geoff, Stockton*	.255	13	59	47	13	12	23	2	0	3	12	0	2	0	10	0	12	2	0	0	.489	.373
Jennings, Lance, Visalia	.301	85	356	316	31	95	130	15	1	6	41	0	2	2	36	2	56	0	2	8	.411	.374
Jimenez, Miguel, Modesto	.000	4	1	1	0	0	0	0	0	0	0	0	0	0	0	0	1	0	0	0	.000	.000
Johnson, Earl, R. Cucamonga†	.293	81	372	341	51	100	117	11	3	0	25	5	0	1	25	0	51	34	12	5	.343	.343
Johnson, Keith, San Bernardino	.242	111	451	417	64	101	180	26	1	17	68	11	2	4	17	0	83	20	12	4	.432	.277
Johnson, Todd, Bakersfield	.360	9	28	25	2	9	13	2	1	0	2	0	0	0	3	0	4	0	1	1	.520	.429
Jorgensen, Randy, Riverside*	.299	133	564	495	78	148	220	32	2	12	97	0	8	15	46	1	74	4	2	13	.444	.371
Keel, David, Modesto*	.200	9	29	25	4	5	8	0	0	1	3	1	0	0	3	0	7	0	0	0	.320	.286
Keene, Andre, San Jose*	.254	103	414	323	62	82	144	15	1	15	62	0	6	9	76	2	101	7	6	7	.446	.403
Keifer, Greg, San Jose	.212	28	75	66	9	14	22	2	0	2	12	0	0	0	9	0	31	2	0	0	.333	.307
King, Brett, San Jose	.274	107	451	394	61	108	154	29	4	3	41	5	6	5	41	1	86	28	8	8	.391	.345
Kirkpatrick, Jay, San Bernardino*	.270	71	309	267	38	72	136	19	0	15	50	0	2	0	40	3	75	3	0	3	.509	.362
Knapp, Mike, High Desert	.267	5	18	15	1	4	5	1	0	0	1	0	1	0	2	0	6	0	1	0	.333	.333
Konerko, Paul, San Bernardino	.277	118	519	448	77	124	204	21	1	19	77	2	6	4	59	2	88	3	1	12	.455	.362
Koscielniak, Dwain, R.C.	.222	7	13	9	1	2	5	0	0	1	2	0	1	0	3	0	2	0	0	0	.556	.385
Kruger, Andy, Visalia*	.253	100	391	356	46	90	125	9	7	4	32	3	1	2	28	0	65	10	15	4	.351	.310
Ladjevich, Rick, Riverside	.309	122	535	470	74	145	192	26	0	7	71	3	4	22	26	2	65	3	2	8	.409	.370
LaRocca, Greg, R.C.	.322	125	524	466	77	150	220	36	5	8	74	0	2	12	44	0	77	15	4	13	.472	.393
Lee, Derrek, R.C.	.301	128	565	502	82	151	249	25	2	23	95	0	7	7	49	0	130	14	7	8	.496	.366
Lemons, Rich, Bakersfield*	.282	36	139	124	18	35	52	5	0	4	16	1	0	1	13	1	42	4	2	2	.419	.355
Luuloa, Keith, Lake Elsinore	.263	102	418	380	50	100	151	22	7	5	53	7	1	6	24	0	47	1	5	9	.397	.316
Marnell, Anthony, R.C.	.043	16	24	23	3	1	1	0	0	0	1	0	0	0	0	0	13	0	0	1	.043	.083
Marquez, Jesus, Riverside*	.237	84	340	312	42	74	93	9	2	2	26	2	4	4	18	0	62	4	5	5	.298	.284
Martin, Lincoln, High Desert††	.240	54	184	150	27	36	50	7	2	1	12	4	2	0	28	0	37	7	4	2	.333	.356
Martinez, Gabby, Stockton†	.258	64	237	213	25	55	77	13	3	1	20	9	3	2	10	0	25	13	6	6	.362	.294
Martinez, Greg, Stockton†	.273	114	492	410	80	113	125	8	2	0	43	10	1	2	69	1	64	55	9	7	.305	.382
Martins, Eric, Modesto	.290	106	496	407	71	118	148	17	5	1	54	18	4	4	62	0	74	7	8	8	.364	.386
Marval, Raul, San Jose	.278	10	39	36	1	10	10	0	0	0	3	2	0	0	1	0	5	1	0	0	.278	.297
Mayes, Craig, San Jose*	.252	90	348	318	34	80	105	17	4	0	39	1	2	0	27	1	50	3	1	7	.330	.308
McCall, Rod, Bakersfield*	.330	96	399	345	61	114	195	19	1	20	70	2	4	8	40	7	90	2	5	6	.565	.408
McDonald, Jason, Modesto†	.262	133	619	493	109	129	186	25	7	6	50	8	2	6	110	0	84	70	20	6	.377	.401
McGonigle, Bill, Stockton	.262	78	248	210	33	55	65	8	1	0	21	8	3	4	23	0	35	3	4	3	.310	.342
McKinnis, Leroy, R.C.	.245	15	62	49	9	12	16	1	0	1	6	0	2	1	10	0	10	3	0	0	.327	.371
McNabb, Buck, Bakersfield*	.300	63	281	237	34	71	81	8	1	0	27	4	2	0	38	1	38	11	1	5	.342	.394
Meade, Paul, Bakersfield*	.000	24	1	1	0	0	0	0	0	0	0	0	0	0	0	0	1	0	0	0	.000	.000
Meilan, Tony, Bakersfield	.211	12	42	38	3	8	9	1	0	0	2	1	0	1	2	0	4	1	1	0	.237	.268
Mejia, Miguel, High Desert	.269	37	137	119	14	32	40	6	1	0	12	2	1	1	14	0	17	16	7	3	.336	.348
Mercedes, Feliciano, High Desert††	.243	45	113	107	10	25	31	4	1	0	10	1	0	0	5	0	24	5	0	1	.290	.268
Miller, Roy, Riverside	.183	65	194	175	21	32	39	4	0	1	18	1	1	5	12	0	49	3	4	4	.223	.254
Milstien, Dave, Stockton	.276	58	244	214	36	59	87	14	1	4	37	0	1	4	25	1	16	6	3	5	.407	.361
Moeder, Tony, Lake Elsinore	.238	68	283	252	39	60	98	18	1	6	26	0	1	3	27	2	61	2	3	7	.389	.318

Player, Team	Avg.	G	TPA	AB	R	H	TB	2B	3B	HR	RBI	SH	SF	HP	BB	IBB	SO	SB	CS	GDP	Slg.	OBP
Molina, Ben, Lake Elsinore	.385	27	112	96	21	37	54	7	2	2	12	3	1	4	8	1	7	0	0	2	.563	.450
Moore, Kerwin, Modesto†	.245	15	69	53	8	13	21	3	1	1	6	2	1	2	11	0	20	4	4	0	.396	.388
Moore, Mark, Modesto	.261	77	312	261	40	68	114	16	0	10	48	0	3	6	42	0	76	3	2	9	.437	.372
Moore, Vince, R.C.*	.227	84	337	299	50	68	126	11	1	15	57	0	1	2	35	0	102	10	5	5	.421	.312
Morales, William, Modesto	.277	109	460	419	49	116	160	32	0	4	60	2	4	7	28	1	75	1	4	13	.382	.330
Morillo, Cesar, Bakersfield†	.305	108	412	371	41	113	143	25	1	1	37	5	1	4	31	2	71	4	12	6	.385	.364
Morreale, John, Stockton	.239	30	98	88	13	21	25	2	1	0	8	1	1	0	8	0	16	0	3	4	.284	.299
Moschetti, Mike, Modesto	.351	23	87	77	5	27	33	6	0	0	9	3	1	0	6	0	16	0	2	2	.429	.393
Mowry, Dave, R.C.*	.239	50	164	142	19	34	53	10	0	3	23	0	1	0	21	1	38	0	0	3	.373	.335
Nadeau, Mike, High Desert	.246	22	71	57	5	14	14	0	0	0	4	3	0	5	6	0	12	3	2	1	.246	.368
Neill, Mike, Modesto*	.276	71	299	257	39	71	108	17	1	6	36	5	1	2	34	2	65	4	4	6	.420	.364
Nelson, Charles, San Bern.*	.250	1	4	4	0	1	1	0	0	0	0	0	0	0	0	0	0	0	0	0	.250	.250
Nevers, Tom, Stockton	.286	4	16	14	2	4	4	0	0	0	3	0	0	2	0	0	6	1	0	0	.286	.375
Newstrom, Doug, San Bern.*	.291	97	367	316	53	92	134	22	1	6	58	6	3	2	40	0	58	19	9	7	.424	.371
Nicholas, Darrell, Stockton	.320	87	386	350	54	112	149	16	3	5	39	11	1	1	23	1	75	26	8	6	.426	.363
Ohmura, Iwao, Visalia	.261	45	170	153	15	40	54	9	1	1	18	4	4	0	9	0	32	1	1	5	.353	.295
Ortega, Hector, Stockton	.301	137	601	539	81	162	221	27	4	8	76	6	7	10	39	0	109	26	13	8	.410	.355
Ortega, Randy, Modesto	.174	10	31	23	2	4	5	1	0	0	1	1	0	1	6	0	7	0	0	0	.217	.367
Owen, Spike, Lake Elsinore†	.200	3	12	10	1	2	3	1	0	0	0	0	0	0	2	0	2	0	0	0	.300	.333
Pagan, Angel, High Desert†	.157	35	125	115	12	18	26	3	1	1	10	2	1	3	4	0	29	3	2	4	.226	.203
Pagee, Shawn, Visalia†	.114	22	48	44	1	5	5	0	0	0	4	2	0	0	2	0	17	0	1	1	.114	.152
Parker, Alan, Visalia	.230	121	439	395	40	91	113	18	2	0	36	9	6	1	27	0	81	6	7	4	.286	.277
Patel, Manny, Riverside*	.285	83	314	274	45	78	98	8	6	0	32	1	1	5	33	0	30	9	4	5	.358	.371
Paulino, Arturo, Modesto	.111	5	14	9	2	1	1	0	0	0	0	1	0	0	4	0	4	1	0	1	.111	.385
Phillips, Gary, San Jose	.264	106	406	363	51	96	132	17	8	1	32	6	2	9	26	0	68	3	1	6	.364	.328
Pinoni, Scott, Visalia	.320	73	298	259	44	83	144	19	0	14	45	0	1	5	33	0	50	1	1	8	.556	.406
Powell, Chris, Lake Elsinore*	.200	13	56	40	7	8	15	2	1	1	2	0	0	3	13	0	10	0	2	1	.375	.429
Powell, Dante, San Jose	.248	135	559	505	74	125	194	23	8	10	70	1	4	3	46	2	131	43	12	8	.384	.312
Powell, Gordon, Stockton	.254	111	418	389	58	99	164	19	5	12	48	3	5	0	21	1	85	22	6	3	.422	.289
Priest, Chris, Visalia	.232	55	214	185	18	43	54	8	0	1	15	2	3	5	19	0	34	3	3	6	.292	.316
Prieto, Chris, R.C.*	.273	114	448	366	80	100	130	12	6	2	35	8	5	5	64	2	55	39	14	10	.355	.384
Prieto, Rick, Bakersfield†	.222	74	286	248	34	55	77	12	2	2	22	6	0	3	29	0	46	15	2	1	.310	.311
Ramirez, Alex, Bakersfield	.323	98	428	406	56	131	190	25	2	10	52	0	1	3	18	1	76	13	9	9	.468	.355
Rasmussen, Nate, Bakersfield*	.197	23	84	71	12	14	18	4	0	0	6	0	1	0	12	0	23	0	0	3	.254	.310
Raven, Luis, Lake Elsinore	.417	6	30	24	5	10	20	2	1	2	6	0	0	1	5	0	7	1	0	0	.833	.533
Redington, Tom, Lake Elsinore	.328	76	325	271	50	89	135	26	1	6	54	0	2	1	51	0	43	2	1	4	.498	.434
Reese, Matthew, Modesto*	.200	15	54	50	4	10	17	4	0	1	6	0	0	0	4	0	23	0	2	0	.340	.259
Richardson, Brian, San Bernardino	.284	127	513	462	68	131	187	18	1	12	58	6	3	7	35	2	122	17	16	11	.405	.341
Richardson, Scott, Stockton	.225	24	90	80	12	18	30	4	1	2	14	1	0	3	6	0	16	8	3	3	.375	.303
Riggs, Adam, San Bernardino	.362	134	622	542	111	196	317	39	5	24	106	7	4	10	59	1	93	31	10	9	.585	.431
Rios, Armando, San Jose*	.293	128	574	488	76	143	207	34	3	8	75	4	7	1	74	3	75	51	10	8	.424	.382
Rivera, Santiago, R. Cucamonga†	.215	61	147	130	11	28	35	5	1	0	10	2	1	1	13	0	36	2	0	3	.269	.290
Roberge, J.P., San Bernardino	.287	116	497	450	92	129	204	22	1	17	59	2	3	8	34	0	62	31	8	9	.453	.345
Roberts, Bip, R.C.†	.000	1	4	3	1	0	0	0	0	0	0	0	0	1	0	0	1	1	0	0	.000	.250
Roberts, John, R.C.	.278	98	389	327	59	91	131	16	3	6	51	2	2	14	44	2	86	27	8	9	.401	.385
Rodriguez, Miguel, Stockton	.300	12	12	10	2	3	6	1	1	0	1	0	0	1	1	0	4	0	0	0	.600	.417
Rodriguez, Nerio, High Desert	.236	58	166	144	20	34	53	7	0	4	12	2	1	1	18	0	50	5	3	0	.368	.323
Rodrigues, Cecil, Stockton	.266	45	190	173	21	46	70	6	3	4	20	1	3	0	13	0	31	4	4	3	.405	.312
Rossiter, Michael, Modesto	.000	18	1	1	0	0	0	0	0	0	0	0	0	0	0	0	0	0	0	0	.000	.000
Sbrocco, Jon, San Jose*	.301	120	508	425	66	128	158	14	5	2	46	17	1	10	55	3	43	12	10	5	.372	.393
Schaaf, Bob, San Bernardino	.252	52	165	151	18	38	60	7	0	5	21	0	0	2	12	0	32	4	4	4	.397	.315
Schneider, Dan, San Jose	.167	13	38	36	3	6	7	1	0	0	2	1	0	1	0	0	7	0	0	1	.194	.189
Schwenke, Matt, R.C.	.179	20	60	56	7	10	12	2	0	0	7	1	1	0	2	0	20	0	0	0	.214	.203
Sealy, Scot, Riverside	.243	58	225	206	23	50	61	5	0	2	30	1	1	1	16	0	36	2	2	4	.296	.299
See, Larry, R.C.	.345	49	191	171	34	59	111	10	0	14	50	0	2	4	14	1	31	0	2	4	.649	.403
Seitzer, Brad, Stockton	.308	127	507	428	66	132	184	28	3	6	56	2	2	3	72	2	68	7	4	10	.430	.410
Serra, Jose, High Desert	.261	76	262	234	30	61	69	6	1	0	22	3	1	6	18	0	30	11	5	2	.295	.328
Shepherd, Brian, San Jose	.156	13	46	32	2	5	5	0	0	0	1	2	0	1	11	0	6	0	0	2	.156	.386
Shockey, Greg, Lake Elsinore*	.327	114	492	441	85	144	242	32	3	20	88	0	2	6	42	2	88	2	2	6	.549	.391
Short, Rick, High Desert	.418	29	110	98	14	41	56	3	0	4	12	0	0	2	10	0	5	1	2	2	.571	.482
Simmons, Mark, Lake Elsinore†	.202	81	274	238	35	48	60	7	1	1	25	2	0	2	32	0	61	10	4	3	.252	.301
Simonton, Benji, San Jose	.289	61	279	225	38	65	110	9	6	8	37	0	4	10	40	2	78	7	0	5	.489	.412
Singleton, Chris, San Jose*	.277	94	441	405	55	112	141	13	5	2	31	5	1	5	17	1	49	33	13	5	.348	.313
Smith, Demond, Lake Elsinore†	.351	34	162	148	32	52	85	8	2	7	26	0	1	2	11	0	36	14	3	1	.574	.401
Smith, Frank, San Bernardino	.205	58	158	122	19	25	43	7	1	3	15	0	2	4	30	1	54	9	3	0	.352	.373
Smith, Joel, Vis.-L.E.	.266	97	387	350	44	93	151	16	3	12	62	2	6	3	26	0	80	0	1	13	.431	.317
Smith, Scott, Riverside	.235	56	200	179	28	42	54	6	0	2	20	0	0	0	21	1	60	2	1	7	.302	.315
Soliz, Steve, Bakersfield	.245	46	176	159	9	39	47	5	0	1	11	0	0	2	15	0	34	2	1	6	.296	.318
Spearman, Vernon, San Bern.*	.288	93	433	365	78	105	143	15	7	3	36	8	4	0	56	1	50	43	12	5	.392	.379
Stare, Lonny, Bakersfield	.272	104	422	372	54	101	153	21	2	9	59	8	2	7	33	1	65	14	10	4	.411	.341
Stuckenschneider, Eric, S.B.	.250	3	20	20	2	5	6	1	0	0	2	0	0	0	7	0	6	1	0	0	.300	.462
Sturdivant, Marcus, Riverside*	.274	99	393	347	60	95	121	13	5	1	34	2	4	1	39	1	41	31	13	3	.349	.345
Tachikawa, Takashi, Visalia	.176	47	128	119	10	21	28	2	1	1	14	0	1	0	8	0	28	1	1	7	.235	.227
Takayoshi, Todd, Lake Elsinore*	.242	60	201	157	19	38	55	6	3	3	30	2	0	2	42	1	30	1	1	5	.350	.402
Tejcek, John, Riverside	.260	105	458	416	72	108	166	22	3	10	54	4	2	4	32	1	116	23	3	5	.399	.317
Tejero, Fausto, Lake Elsinore	.238	8	27	21	5	5	6	1	0	0	3	0	0	1	5	0	6	1	0	1	.286	.370
Tena, Dario, R.C.†	.172	11	34	29	1	5	6	1	0	0	0	1	1	0	3	0	4	2	1	1	.207	.273
Thielen, D.J., San Jose	.213	91	328	282	38	60	99	13	1	8	34	3	2	3	38	1	81	4	5	5	.351	.311
Thurston, Jerrey, R.C.	.220	76	235	200	24	44	56	9	0	1	13	4	3	7	21	0	64	1	0	2	.280	.312
Tohyama, Shoji, Visalia*	.297	51	168	155	15	46	65	9	2	2	24	1	1	3	8	0	38	1	1	3	.419	.341
Tredaway, Chad, R. Cucamonga†	.277	109	449	408	53	113	152	17	2	6	57	1	3	8	29	3	43	4	2	10	.373	.324
Triessl, Mike, Riv.-R.C.	.292	71	238	212	28	62	81	10	0	3	38	1	2	5	17	1	47	1	0	6	.382	.356
Tyrus, Jason, Bakersfield	.173	25	91	81	12	14	26	0	0	4	12	1	0	2	7	0	28	4	2	1	.321	.253

Player, Team	Avg.	G	TPA	AB	R	H	TB	2B	3B	HR	RBI	SH	SF	HP	BB	IBB	SO	SB	CS	GDP	Slg.	OBP
Urbina, William, Modesto	.000	30	3	3	0	0	0	0	0	0	0	0	0	0	0	0	2	0	0	0	.000	.000
Urso, Joe, Lake Elsinore	.316	65	284	244	48	77	106	16	2	3	34	1	2	3	34	1	41	7	5	6	.434	.403
Vaughn, Derek, Lake Elsinore	.265	94	380	328	66	87	134	15	7	6	50	6	2	1	43	2	61	22	5	9	.409	.350
Wallace, Brian, San Jose	.222	25	93	81	15	18	25	1	0	2	8	2	0	1	9	1	18	3	0	2	.309	.308
Wallach, Tim, San Bernardino	.467	4	15	15	2	7	10	3	0	0	4	0	0	0	0	0	3	0	0	2	.667	.467
Walsh, Matthew, Modesto	.000	44	1	1	0	0	0	0	0	0	0	0	0	0	0	0	1	0	0	0	.000	.000
Whitaker, Ryan, Modesto	.000	32	2	1	0	0	0	0	0	0	0	0	0	0	1	0	1	0	0	0	.000	.500
White, Jason, Modesto	.307	76	339	267	63	82	166	16	1	22	71	7	3	8	54	0	71	1	2	9	.622	.434
Williams, Matt, San Jose	.182	4	12	11	2	2	5	0	0	1	2	0	0	1	0	0	3	0	0	0	.455	.250
Williamson, Joel, High Desert	.167	24	72	66	5	11	13	2	0	0	1	3	0	0	3	0	18	1	0	1	.197	.203
Wilson, Todd, San Jose	.239	37	128	117	14	28	37	7	1	0	13	3	0	2	6	0	19	1	0	5	.316	.288
Wingate, Ervan, Bakersfield	.234	121	501	445	51	104	153	23	1	8	59	4	4	6	42	0	86	5	8	25	.344	.306
Wittig, Paul, Bakersfield	.278	93	368	331	44	92	132	17	1	7	53	5	5	6	20	0	66	6	3	8	.399	.326
Wolff, Mike, High Desert*	.271	94	324	292	32	79	117	17	3	5	44	1	6	9	16	1	53	3	5	5	.401	.322
Woodridge, Dickie, R.C.*	.282	116	438	358	67	101	125	9	3	3	58	2	5	2	71	1	40	9	4	5	.349	.399
Wyngarden, Brett, Visalia	.263	76	289	270	21	71	94	14	0	3	24	1	3	3	12	0	81	1	2	6	.348	.299
Yard, Bruce, Bakersfield*	.230	59	228	191	19	44	57	8	1	1	17	7	2	1	27	0	22	2	5	10	.298	.326
Zahner, Kevin, Bakersfield	.233	82	282	257	25	60	77	7	2	2	31	6	5	2	10	0	37	4	1	10	.300	.268
Zellers, Kevin, Bakersfield	.241	96	384	332	39	80	113	16	1	5	27	2	3	8	39	1	106	5	6	6	.340	.332
Zongor, Steven, Modesto	.000	37	1	1	0	0	0	0	0	0	0	0	0	0	0	0	1	0	0	0	.000	.000

GRAND SLAMS: Adams, Alvarez, Riggs, 2 each; Asencio, Barger, Berry, Chavez, Dandridge, Dobrolsky, Guevara, Hunter, Hust, Ibanez, K. Johnson, Kirkpatrick, Ladjevich, Lee, Martins, McDonald, M. Moore, D. Powell, Redington, Shockey, Stare, Thielen, Treadway, White, 1 each.

AWARDED FIRST BASE ON CATCHER'S INTERFERENCE: Singleton 8 (Hughes 2, Triessl 2, Dandridge, Hemphill, M. Moore, Thurston); Galarza 4 (Dandridge, M. Rodriguez, Tejero, Wittig); Hunter 2 (Zahner 2); Chavez (Cuellar); Cunningham (Zahner); Kruger (Dobrolsky); Martins (Ibanez); Parker (Newstrom); Shockey (Harmer); Triessl (Newstrom); Wittig (Hemphill).

PLAYERS WITH TWO OR MORE TEAMS

Player, Team	Avg.	G	TPA	AB	R	H	TB	2B	3B	HR	RBI	SH	SF	HP	BB	IBB	SO	SB	CS	GDP	Slg.	OBP
Smith, Joel, Visalia	.286	67	285	262	32	75	120	12	3	9	43	2	3	3	15	0	65	0	1	9	.458	.329
Smith, Joel, Lake Elsinore	.205	30	102	88	12	18	31	4	0	3	19	0	3	0	11	0	15	0	0	4	.352	.284
Triessl, Mike, Riverside	.365	22	88	74	15	27	38	2	0	3	14	0	1	1	12	1	15	0	0	1	.514	.455
Triessl, Mike, R.C.	.254	49	150	138	13	35	43	8	0	0	20	1	1	4	5	0	32	1	0	5	.312	.297

1995 PITCHING

TEAM

Team	W	L	Pct.	ERA	G	CG	ShO	Sv.	IP	H	TBF	R	ER	HR	SH	SF	HB	BB	IBB	SO	WP	Bk.
San Jose	77	63	.550	3.05	140	5	17	35	1270.0	1147	5236	516	430	75	71	33	48	388	11	1013	56	14
Lake Elsinore	82	57	.590	3.73	139	5	9	36	1227.1	1246	5292	646	509	92	33	46	62	429	8	1022	58	10
Modesto	78	62	.557	4.13	140	0	5	41	1234.1	1260	5387	676	566	102	62	43	62	464	9	1077	98	15
San Bernardino	85	54	.612	4.25	139	3	8	41	1248.0	1311	5518	719	589	101	60	40	60	493	14	980	80	9
Stockton	74	66	.529	4.30	140	5	7	40	1239.2	1311	5523	694	592	93	68	38	85	555	19	880	68	24
R. Cucamonga	68	71	.489	4.45	139	0	4	40	1216.1	1212	5397	718	601	95	41	48	87	605	21	1074	100	17
Bakersfield	58	82	.414	4.53	140	3	4	33	1222.0	1299	5431	757	615	116	54	37	59	553	6	851	120	13
Riverside	72	67	.518	4.54	139	2	6	34	1226.1	1290	5483	767	618	83	55	52	67	577	21	981	90	17
Visalia	58	82	.414	4.66	140	11	9	24	1243.1	1322	5401	759	644	102	42	38	81	447	3	974	92	22
High Desert	46	94	.329	5.78	140	3	2	30	1227.2	1410	5718	996	789	132	47	61	71	633	13	960	115	31

INDIVIDUAL

TOP QUALIFIERS FOR EARNED-RUN AVERAGE TITLE

Minimum 112 innings. *Lefthanded pitcher.

Pitcher, Team	W	L	Pct.	ERA	G	GS	CG	ShO	GF	Sv.	IP	H	TBF	R	ER	HR	SH	SF	HB	BB	IBB	SO	WP	Bk.
Price, Tom, San Bernardino*	10	5	.667	2.20	42	13	2	0	9	3	151.2	145	605	49	37	5	5	1	3	14	4	82	5	0
Bonanno, Rob, Lake Elsinore	8	4	.667	3.05	17	17	4	2	0	0	112.0	112	455	49	38	10	2	4	3	16	0	72	0	0
Janicki, Pete, Lake Elsinore	9	4	.692	3.06	20	20	0	0	0	0	123.1	130	532	66	42	7	3	6	5	28	0	106	6	1
Moore, Trey, Riverside*	14	6	.700	3.09	24	24	0	0	0	0	148.1	122	605	65	51	6	2	5	2	58	1	134	6	1
Smith, Ryan, Riverside	10	7	.588	3.11	23	23	2	1	0	0	141.2	142	609	68	49	7	7	5	10	50	1	108	5	3
Percibal, Billy, High Desert	7	6	.538	3.23	21	20	2	0	0	0	128.0	123	547	63	46	10	2	2	3	55	0	105	7	4
Dixon, Bubba, R.C.*	10	7	.588	3.24	47	12	2	0	15	5	141.2	118	572	61	51	14	5	1	8	46	0	133	6	2
Beaumont, Matt, Lake Elsinore*	16	9	.640	3.29	27	26	0	0	0	0	175.1	162	724	80	64	15	1	6	7	57	1	149	1	1
Edwards, Wayne, Bakersfield*	9	8	.529	3.36	21	21	1	0	0	0	128.2	125	557	63	48	7	2	2	10	56	0	83	10	0
Foulke, Keith, San Jose	13	6	.684	3.50	28	26	2	1	0	0	177.1	166	723	85	69	16	10	3	7	32	0	168	6	2
DeClue, Jon, Vis.-L.E.*	11	6	.647	3.52	30	18	0	0	3	0	143.1	145	590	64	56	16	4	3	5	32	0	112	4	1
Howry, Bobby, San Jose	12	10	.545	3.54	27	25	1	0	1	0	165.1	171	695	79	65	6	12	4	8	54	0	107	7	3
Iglesias, Mike, Bak.-S.B.	8	12	.400	3.57	28	26	2	1	0	0	158.2	150	660	79	63	12	5	3	13	40	0	120	10	0
Edsell, Geoff, Lake Elsinore	8	12	.400	3.67	23	22	1	1	0	0	139.2	127	600	81	57	11	7	3	7	67	0	134	5	1
Endo, Masataka, Visalia	9	9	.500	3.76	28	27	6	1	0	0	186.2	162	763	87	78	13	7	2	7	62	1	178	17	8

DEPARTMENTAL LEADERS: W—Beaumont, 16; L—Griffin, 15; Pct.—Brunson, 1.000; G—Holtz, 56; GS—Clayton, LaChappa, 28; CG—Endo, 6; ShO—Bonanno, Murray, 2; GF—C. Castillo, R. Linares, 52; Sv.—C. Castillo, 32; IP—Endo, 186.2; H—Griffin, 182; TBF—Endo, 763; R—Griffin, 129; ER—Griffin, 108; HR—LaChappa, Macey, 17; SH—Howry, 12; SF—Griffin, 10; HB—Griffin, 17; BB—LaChappa, 88; IBB—Arroyo, 6; SO—Endo, 178; WP—Griffin, 21; Bk.—Endo, 8.

CLASS A California League

ALL PITCHERS

*Lefthanded pitcher.

Pitcher, Team	W	L	Pct.	ERA	G	GS	CG	ShO	GF	Sv.	IP	H	TBF	R	ER	HR	SH	SF	HB	BB	IBB	SO	WP	Bk.
Aguirre, Jose, Lake Elsinore*	0	1	.000	3.83	29	0	0	0	11	0	47.0	48	207	26	20	2	1	2	1	20	0	35	2	1
Anderson, Brian, Lake Elsinore*	1	1	.500	1.93	3	3	0	0	0	0	14.0	10	51	3	3	0	0	1	0	1	0	13	1	0
Andrakin, Rob, San Jose	2	1	.667	2.36	29	0	0	0	20	7	45.2	38	193	14	12	1	7	3	3	19	2	49	2	1
Aquino, Julio, San Bernardino	2	2	.500	7.84	25	3	0	0	6	0	59.2	96	293	59	52	5	2	2	1	23	0	42	5	1
Aquino, Luis, San Jose	0	0	.000	0.00	4	4	0	0	0	0	10.1	9	38	1	0	0	0	0	1	1	0	13	1	0
Arroyo, Luis, R.C.*	7	10	.412	5.25	26	24	0	0	0	0	128.2	158	599	97	75	9	8	6	12	62	6	102	7	3
Baker, Jared, R.C.	7	2	.778	4.44	31	15	1	1	3	1	101.1	98	442	57	50	9	3	4	8	49	1	98	3	1
Baldwin, Scott, Modesto*	0	1	.000	6.08	5	3	0	0	0	0	13.1	16	75	11	9	1	1	3	0	19	0	10	5	0
Barnes, Jon, R.C.	0	0	.000	1.69	5	1	0	0	3	0	10.2	6	39	3	2	0	0	0	0	2	0	10	0	0
Baron, Jim, R.C.*	0	0	.000	16.88	3	0	0	0	1	0	2.2	7	22	8	5	1	1	0	0	6	0	3	2	0
Barrett, Mark, R.C.*	1	0	1.000	3.58	32	0	0	0	11	1	32.2	39	149	18	13	2	2	1	2	11	1	29	0	0
Baxter, Herbert, Modesto*	4	7	.364	6.60	29	14	0	0	3	0	91.1	104	434	75	67	10	4	4	3	64	0	73	20	6
Beaumont, Matt, Lake Elsinore*	16	9	.640	3.29	27	26	0	0	0	0	175.1	162	724	80	64	15	1	6	7	57	1	149	1	1
Berumen, Andres, R.C.	0	0	.000	2.45	4	0	0	0	1	1	7.1	6	28	2	2	1	0	0	0	1	0	11	0	0
Bielecki, Mike, Lake Elsinore	0	0	.000	4.91	3	2	0	0	0	0	3.2	2	15	2	2	0	1	0	0	2	0	2	1	0
Bland, Nathan, Bakersfield*	4	9	.308	5.22	27	23	0	0	1	0	122.1	155	562	89	71	13	5	3	1	55	0	46	12	2
Blyleven, Todd, Lake Elsinore	0	1	.000	4.32	6	0	0	0	0	0	8.1	12	44	9	4	2	0	2	2	5	0	8	1	0
Bonanno, Rob, Lake Elsinore	8	4	.667	3.05	17	17	4	2	0	0	112.0	112	455	49	38	10	2	4	3	16	0	72	0	0
Boskie, Shawn, Lake Elsinore	0	0	.000	4.09	3	3	0	0	0	0	11.0	15	53	7	5	1	0	0	0	4	0	8	0	0
Brewer, Brian, High Desert*	1	9	.100	5.47	17	15	1	0	0	0	80.2	96	376	66	49	2	4	0	5	42	1	65	5	2
Briscoe, John, Modesto	0	0	.000	1.59	4	4	0	0	0	0	5.2	5	22	1	1	0	0	0	0	2	0	5	0	0
Brohawn, Troy, San Jose*	7	3	.700	1.65	11	10	0	0	1	0	65.1	45	246	14	12	4	1	1	1	20	0	57	5	1
Brown, Cory, High Desert	2	7	.222	5.36	30	10	0	0	8	3	94.0	104	417	66	56	15	5	5	6	32	0	80	3	1
Brown, Keith, Stockton*	1	0	1.000	1.62	12	0	0	0	3	0	16.2	11	65	4	3	1	0	0	1	6	2	8	1	0
Brunson, William, San Bern.*	10	0	1.000	2.05	13	13	0	0	0	0	83.1	68	334	24	19	4	3	5	5	21	0	70	3	0
Cafaro, Rocco, High Desert	4	5	.444	4.46	44	1	0	0	39	8	66.2	69	290	42	33	10	2	4	2	25	0	52	6	1
Camacho, Dan, San Bernardino	6	2	.750	3.95	43	1	0	0	27	9	68.1	66	295	32	30	7	5	1	1	30	3	79	5	1
Castillo, Carlos, Lake Elsinore	2	1	.667	2.41	52	0	0	0	52	32	52.1	55	223	18	14	2	1	0	5	15	0	40	2	1
Castillo, Mariano, San Jose	4	4	.500	1.59	21	0	0	0	8	3	56.2	49	226	14	10	1	2	0	2	13	0	51	1	0
Castro, Tony, Lake Elsinore	0	0	.000	5.56	8	0	0	0	2	0	11.1	15	57	9	7	1	1	1	0	8	0	9	2	0
Chavez, Tony, Lake Elsinore	4	2	.667	4.23	33	0	0	0	14	0	44.2	51	206	28	21	2	2	3	4	19	2	49	5	0
Clark, Howie, High Desert	0	0	.000	0.00	1	0	0	0	0	0	0.0	0	2	2	2	0	0	0	0	2	0	0	0	0
Clayton, Craig, Riverside	9	8	.529	5.00	28	28	0	0	0	0	160.1	171	738	102	89	16	11	6	7	83	3	156	7	1
Clement, Matt, R.C.	3	4	.429	4.24	12	12	0	0	0	0	57.1	61	267	37	27	1	2	4	5	49	0	33	12	0
Cole, Jim, Stockton	7	4	.636	3.48	14	13	1	0	0	0	85.1	88	359	43	33	7	1	2	5	20	0	52	1	1
Colon, Julio, San Bernardino	6	3	.667	4.33	49	0	0	0	30	12	79.0	68	343	47	38	7	1	1	2	37	2	75	12	0
Cope, Robin, Riverside	2	4	.333	7.39	11	5	0	0	0	0	31.2	50	162	31	26	2	0	1	0	18	1	13	3	2
Crills, Brad, High Desert	1	2	.333	5.51	5	3	0	0	1	0	16.1	19	78	15	10	0	0	1	1	8	0	10	3	2
Cromwell, Nate, R.C.*	0	1	.000	3.52	4	4	0	0	0	0	15.1	15	64	7	6	1	1	0	1	6	0	14	0	1
Crow, Dean, Riverside	3	4	.429	2.63	51	0	0	0	47	22	61.2	54	249	21	18	1	3	2	3	13	0	46	2	0
Dafun, George, Lake Elsinore	0	2	.000	5.54	3	3	0	0	0	0	13.0	8	53	8	8	0	0	0	1	11	0	13	2	1
Daigle, Tim, High Desert*	0	1	.000	4.95	19	0	0	0	9	4	43.2	46	203	33	24	7	1	1	0	20	0	36	4	0
Davis, Eddie, San Bernardino	0	0	.000	3.77	5	1	0	0	2	1	14.1	17	68	10	6	1	1	0	3	6	0	6	0	1
DeClue, Jon, Vis.-L.E.*	11	6	.647	3.52	30	18	0	0	3	0	143.1	145	590	64	56	16	4	3	5	32	0	112	4	1
Dennis, Shane, R.C.*	8	2	.800	2.51	11	11	2	1	0	0	79.0	63	316	27	22	8	3	2	0	22	1	77	1	0
Dixon, Bubba, R.C.*	10	7	.588	3.24	47	12	2	0	15	5	141.2	118	572	61	51	14	5	1	8	46	0	133	6	2
Dobrolsky, Bill, Stockton	0	0	.000	5.40	3	0	0	0	3	0	3.1	5	16	2	2	1	0	0	0	0	0	2	0	0
Dressendorfer, Kirk, Modesto	0	6	.000	4.62	27	16	0	0	2	0	37.0	39	171	24	19	5	2	2	2	18	0	50	6	0
Drewien, Dan, R.C.	1	2	.333	6.35	17	0	0	0	1	1	28.1	30	127	20	20	3	1	1	2	11	1	26	2	0
Drysdale, Brooks, Lake Elsinore	1	0	1.000	2.00	8	0	0	0	2	0	9.0	8	41	3	2	1	1	1	0	4	1	8	2	0
Duda, Steve, Stockton	3	6	.333	4.33	12	12	2	1	0	0	79.0	87	343	48	38	7	5	2	6	20	0	59	0	3
Dyess, Todd, High Desert	6	9	.400	5.10	23	22	0	0	0	0	125.1	145	573	94	71	9	5	5	9	58	0	118	17	5
Dykhoff, Radhames, High Desert*	1	5	.167	5.02	34	2	0	0	10	3	80.2	95	389	68	45	8	7	7	0	44	2	88	0	2
Eaddy, Brad, Bakersfield*	4	5	.444	2.95	42	1	0	0	19	5	79.1	66	328	29	26	4	4	0	0	36	1	68	3	0
Edsell, Geoff, Lake Elsinore	8	12	.400	3.67	23	22	1	1	0	0	139.2	127	600	81	57	11	7	3	7	67	0	134	6	1
Edwards, Wayne, Bakersfield*	9	8	.529	3.36	21	21	1	0	0	0	128.2	125	557	63	48	7	2	2	10	56	0	83	10	0
Endo, Masataka, Visalia	9	9	.500	3.76	28	27	6	1	0	0	186.2	162	763	87	78	13	7	2	7	62	1	178	17	8
Enoki, Yasuhiro, Visalia	4	7	.364	5.45	13	13	2	1	0	0	74.1	104	335	52	45	8	1	3	2	11	0	51	2	0
Erdos, Todd, R.C.	0	0	.000	13.50	1	0	0	0	0	0	2.2	5	13	4	4	0	0	1	0	0	0	4	0	0
Estes, Shawn, San Jose*	5	2	.714	2.17	9	8	0	0	0	0	49.2	32	191	13	12	1	0	3	1	17	0	61	7	0
Ettles, Mark, R.C.	0	0	.000	6.35	3	0	0	0	1	0	5.2	7	26	5	4	1	0	0	1	1	0	7	1	0
Felix, Ruben, Stockton*	0	2	.000	12.79	6	0	0	0	2	0	6.1	9	34	9	9	2	1	0	2	5	2	3	0	2
Fetchel, Tony, Visalia	0	1	.000	6.66	18	1	0	0	5	0	24.1	22	132	20	18	0	0	0	11	32	0	11	7	0
Fitzer, Douglas, Riverside*	0	0	.000	4.61	25	0	0	0	7	0	27.1	26	123	15	14	3	0	2	0	15	1	13	3	0
Foulke, Keith, San Jose	13	6	.684	3.50	28	26	2	1	0	0	177.1	166	723	85	69	16	10	3	7	32	0	168	6	2
Gambs, Chris, High Desert	0	0	.000	12.00	3	0	0	0	2	0	3.0	4	16	4	4	0	0	0	0	4	0	1	0	0
Gamez, Francisco, Stockton	2	1	.667	2.78	4	3	0	0	0	0	22.2	20	96	8	7	0	0	0	1	11	0	7	1	0
Garrett, Hal, R.C.	0	4	.000	2.79	23	1	0	0	5	0	42.0	40	196	21	13	2	2	5	2	25	0	43	7	1
Gates, Sean, R.C.	0	0	.000	0.00	1	0	0	0	0	0	2.2	1	10	0	0	0	0	0	1	0	0	2	0	0
Gomez, Dennys, San Jose	2	0	1.000	2.08	13	0	0	0	5	0	30.1	27	136	13	7	0	3	0	2	15	0	23	1	0
Gomez, Marcial, Lake Elsinore	1	0	1.000	5.84	7	0	0	0	0	0	12.1	11	56	10	8	0	0	1	1	10	0	10	2	1
Gomez, Pat, San Jose*	0	0	.000	1.42	3	2	0	0	0	0	6.1	5	29	2	1	0	1	0	0	5	0	5	1	1
Griffin, Ryan, High Desert	6	15	.286	6.80	31	25	0	0	4	3	143.0	182	686	129	108	14	4	10	17	80	0	96	21	2
Hackett, Jason, High Desert*	3	1	.750	5.18	18	2	0	0	9	1	40.0	43	195	30	23	6	2	1	2	31	2	29	6	0
Hanson, Craig, R.C.	3	4	.429	6.14	9	9	0	0	0	0	36.2	43	175	29	25	6	1	2	6	19	1	31	3	1
Hartmann, Pete, Stockton*	2	0	1.000	4.50	12	0	0	0	5	1	14.0	9	61	7	7	1	1	0	0	11	0	9	1	1
Hartvigson, Chad, San Jose*	4	4	.500	3.54	32	7	0	0	8	4	84.0	85	357	38	33	4	6	3	0	24	1	63	3	1
Hathaway, Hilly, R.C.*	0	1	.000	3.46	3	3	0	0	0	0	13.0	11	52	6	5	0	0	0	2	4	1	10	0	0
Haught, Gary, Modesto	9	5	.643	2.60	34	4	0	0	6	4	86.2	76	355	29	25	10	10	0	6	24	1	81	0	0
Hecker, Doug, Visalia	0	0	.000	0.00	2	0	0	0	2	0	2.0	1	9	1	0	0	0	1	1	1	0	2	1	0

Pitcher, Team	W	L	Pct.	ERA	G	GS	CG	ShO	GF	Sv.	IP	H	TBF	R	ER	HR	SH	SF	HB	BB	IBB	SO	WP	Bk.
Henrikson, Dan, San Jose*	0	1	.000	7.71	7	0	0	0	0	0	7.0	8	32	6	6	0	0	0	0	4	0	6	0	0
Herges, Matt, San Bernardino	5	2	.714	3.66	22	2	0	0	4	1	51.2	58	231	29	21	3	2	1	2	15	0	35	0	0
Hermanson, Mike, R.C.	4	6	.400	5.67	42	0	0	0	13	0	74.2	69	352	52	47	4	1	5	11	49	2	74	8	2
Hill, Chris, High Desert*	0	2	.000	9.00	5	1	0	0	2	0	13.0	20	66	13	13	5	0	3	1	7	0	10	1	0
Hinchliffe, Brett, Riverside	3	8	.273	6.61	15	15	0	0	0	0	77.2	110	373	69	57	10	5	3	8	35	3	68	4	0
Hinson, Dean, Vis.-L.E.	1	1	.500	4.17	28	0	0	0	18	3	41.0	38	186	27	19	2	3	1	5	22	0	39	10	2
Holdridge, David, Lake Elsinore	3	0	1.000	0.98	12	0	0	0	8	0	18.1	13	74	3	2	0	1	1	2	5	1	24	3	0
Holtz, Mike, Lake Elsinore*	4	4	.500	2.29	56	0	0	0	19	3	82.2	70	341	26	21	7	5	4	5	23	3	101	2	0
Howry, Bobby, San Jose	12	10	.545	3.54	27	25	1	0	1	0	165.1	171	695	79	65	6	12	4	8	54	0	107	7	3
Huber, Aaron, Modesto	0	0	.000	0.00	4	0	0	0	1	0	5.1	7	27	3	0	0	0	0	0	3	0	5	0	0
Hyde, Rich, San Jose	0	2	.000	2.00	16	0	0	0	15	7	18.0	19	77	6	4	1	2	0	0	5	1	13	3	0
Idemoto, Kenichiro, Visalia*	5	6	.455	4.10	31	8	2	0	5	2	101.0	104	428	54	46	11	4	2	4	27	0	83	1	0
Iglesias, Mike, Bak.-S.B.	8	12	.400	3.57	28	26	2	1	0	0	158.2	150	660	79	63	12	5	3	13	40	0	120	10	0
Ippolito, Rob, Riverside	1	3	.250	4.20	35	0	0	0	11	1	60.0	59	272	41	28	4	4	1	6	31	2	43	8	0
Isom, Jeff, R.C.*	1	0	1.000	9.00	4	0	0	0	3	0	4.0	6	21	4	4	1	0	1	1	0	0	2	0	0
Jacobsen, Joe, San Bernardino	0	0	.000	0.00	4	0	0	0	3	2	3.2	4	17	2	0	0	0	0	0	2	0	5	1	0
James, Mike, Lake Elsinore	0	0	.000	9.53	5	1	0	0	1	0	5.2	9	29	6	6	1	0	0	0	3	0	8	0	0
Janicki, Pete, Lake Elsinore	9	4	.692	3.06	20	20	0	0	0	0	123.1	130	532	66	42	7	3	6	5	28	0	106	6	1
Jaye, Jamie, Bakersfield*	1	2	.333	4.39	5	5	0	0	0	0	26.2	30	118	16	13	1	1	0	1	10	0	22	3	3
Jenkins, Jon, Visalia	1	1	.500	5.55	33	1	0	0	22	0	47.0	43	223	34	29	3	2	5	5	38	0	38	5	1
Jimenez, Miguel, Modesto	1	2	.333	6.00	4	4	0	0	0	0	18.0	14	83	13	12	5	0	1	2	14	0	11	4	0
Karns, Tim, High Desert	1	0	1.000	0.59	7	0	0	0	2	0	15.1	10	67	6	1	0	0	0	0	9	0	9	2	0
Keagle, Greg, R.C.	0	0	.000	4.50	2	2	0	0	0	0	14.0	14	59	9	7	1	0	1	2	2	0	11	1	0
Kenady, Jake, Bakersfield*	4	10	.286	6.72	23	16	0	0	1	0	87.0	107	419	76	65	7	1	3	3	68	0	69	10	1
Kramer, Jeff, Stockton	12	7	.632	4.47	32	24	0	0	2	1	149.0	174	662	87	74	9	8	4	12	58	0	108	9	6
Kubinski, Tim, Modesto*	6	10	.375	4.95	25	17	0	0	4	2	109.0	126	485	73	60	12	6	5	8	24	0	83	10	1
Kyslinger, Dan, Stockton	4	1	.800	3.59	37	0	0	0	11	1	52.2	58	253	24	21	2	4	2	2	37	1	44	6	2
LaChappa, Matt, R.C.*	11	7	.611	5.56	28	28	1	0	0	0	153.2	163	691	103	95	17	1	3	10	88	2	106	15	2
LaGarde, Joe, S.B-Bak.	4	10	.286	6.72	23	16	0	0	1	0	87.0	107	419	76	65	7	1	3	3	68	0	69	10	1
LaRocca, Todd, High Desert	0	7	.000	7.41	15	7	0	0	2	1	51.0	68	248	53	42	7	0	2	1	29	0	31	7	2
Linares, Rich, Bakersfield	4	4	.500	2.27	55	0	0	0	52	20	67.1	64	272	18	17	2	4	1	3	17	2	57	3	0
Linares, Yfrain, Stockton	2	0	1.000	1.17	7	3	0	0	1	0	23.0	20	98	7	3	1	1	0	0	16	1	17	3	0
Locklear, Dean, Visalia*	3	3	.500	3.93	9	9	0	0	0	0	52.2	50	225	29	23	4	1	1	5	21	0	27	6	0
Macey, Fausto, San Jose	8	9	.471	3.89	28	25	1	0	0	0	171.0	167	709	84	74	17	7	5	6	50	1	94	6	4
Magnelli, Anthony, Visalia	2	5	.286	4.24	29	0	0	0	25	11	40.1	40	161	20	19	2	4	1	0	6	0	30	5	1
Manning, Derek, Modesto*	10	1	.909	2.43	25	12	0	0	4	3	111.0	112	467	43	30	7	6	4	1	25	0	102	3	1
Martin, Jeff, San Jose	5	6	.455	3.30	36	0	0	0	28	5	71.0	60	305	34	26	5	5	2	3	25	3	63	1	0
Maurer, Mike, Modesto	2	2	.500	1.79	39	0	0	0	37	18	40.1	27	157	9	8	3	2	2	2	9	0	44	2	0
McGonigle, Bill, Stockton	0	0	.000	6.75	4	0	0	0	3	0	4.0	5	20	3	3	1	0	0	1	3	0	3	1	0
McLain, Mike, San Jose	0	1	.000	2.29	9	0	0	0	3	2	19.2	16	77	5	5	0	0	1	0	6	0	21	1	0
Meade, Paul, Bakersfield	2	2	.500	7.55	24	0	0	0	9	0	53.2	70	253	47	45	15	3	3	5	25	1	32	4	2
Meadows, Jimmy, Visalia	7	6	.538	4.37	27	21	1	1	2	0	125.2	136	543	71	61	14	3	5	11	51	1	94	12	2
Michalak, Chris, Modesto*	3	2	.600	2.62	44	0	0	0	16	2	65.1	56	266	26	19	3	4	3	4	27	1	49	2	1
Mitchell, Kendrick, Bakersfield*	1	2	.333	5.34	36	0	0	0	12	0	57.1	61	271	46	34	7	1	1	2	38	0	36	18	2
Montane, Ivan, Riverside	5	5	.500	5.63	24	16	0	0	6	0	92.2	101	442	67	58	3	3	6	10	71	0	79	19	0
Moore, Trey, Riverside*	14	6	.700	3.09	24	24	0	0	0	0	148.1	122	605	65	51	6	2	5	2	58	1	134	6	1
Murphy, Matt, Stockton*	2	1	.667	5.91	5	4	0	0	0	0	21.1	25	100	14	14	2	2	1	1	13	0	9	0	0
Murray, Heath, R.C.*	9	4	.692	3.12	14	14	4	2	0	0	92.1	80	381	37	32	5	3	2	4	38	1	81	6	3
Muto, Junichiro, Visalia	1	2	.333	3.52	17	0	0	0	10	5	38.1	33	149	16	15	1	1	1	2	5	0	35	1	0
Myers, Tom, Visalia*	3	8	.273	6.43	30	13	0	0	5	0	85.1	108	406	81	61	6	3	6	10	45	0	34	7	1
Nelson, Chris, Modesto	2	0	1.000	0.90	2	2	0	0	0	0	10.0	4	37	1	1	0	0	0	0	4	0	8	1	0
Newton, Geronimo, Riverside*	4	4	.500	3.15	46	0	0	0	11	2	71.1	74	307	35	25	1	3	3	4	24	3	42	2	4
Nomo, Hideo, Bakersfield	0	1	.000	3.38	1	1	0	0	0	0	5.1	6	24	2	2	0	0	0	1	1	0	6	1	0
Oropesa, Eddie, San Bernardino*	0	0	.000	0.00	1	0	0	0	1	1	1.0	0	3	0	0	0	0	0	0	0	0	0	0	0
Ortiz, Russell, San Jose	0	1	.000	1.50	5	0	0	0	5	0	6.0	4	24	1	1	0	0	1	0	2	0	7	0	0
Osuna, Antonio, San Bernardino	0	0	.000	1.29	5	0	0	0	2	0	7.0	3	31	1	1	1	1	0	2	5	0	11	3	1
Paluk, Jeff, San Bernardino	6	3	.667	5.71	41	0	0	0	19	1	52.0	65	255	34	33	2	4	3	7	30	2	52	1	0
Parra, Julio, San Bernardino	4	5	.444	5.19	14	13	0	0	0	0	69.1	76	310	45	40	7	2	2	3	29	0	65	2	3
Patterson, Ken, Lake Elsinore*	0	0	.000	0.00	6	0	0	0	2	1	9.2	7	35	0	0	0	0	0	0	1	0	9	1	0
Paul, Andy, Stockton	7	5	.583	4.06	38	13	0	0	11	1	106.1	116	473	59	48	7	5	1	8	42	4	87	6	3
Pearsall, J.J., San Bernardino*	0	1	.000	8.44	6	0	0	0	2	0	10.2	15	54	10	10	3	3	0	0	7	0	5	1	0
Pena, Alex, High Desert	3	4	.429	6.66	34	6	0	0	20	3	77.0	97	363	68	57	4	7	1	4	28	2	44	6	3
Percibal, Billy, High Desert	7	6	.538	3.23	21	20	2	0	0	0	128.0	123	547	63	46	10	2	2	3	55	0	105	7	4
Perisho, Matt, Lake Elsinore*	8	9	.471	6.32	24	22	0	0	0	0	115.1	137	541	91	81	10	0	8	6	60	0	68	7	0
Peters, Don, San Jose	3	3	.500	4.24	20	13	0	0	5	2	68.0	68	284	33	32	6	1	3	4	24	0	38	1	1
Pincavitch, Kevin, San Bern.	2	0	1.000	2.70	3	0	0	0	0	0	10.0	8	46	5	3	1	1	0	0	6	1	10	0	0
Pivaral, Hugo, San Bernardino	6	4	.600	4.63	24	24	0	0	0	0	103.0	106	460	61	53	14	6	2	7	43	0	89	13	0
Prater, Pete, San Jose	2	0	1.000	3.18	5	4	0	0	0	0	22.2	18	90	8	8	0	1	1	1	7	0	14	0	0
Price, Tom, San Bernardino*	10	5	.667	2.20	42	13	2	0	9	3	151.2	145	605	49	37	5	5	1	3	14	4	82	5	0
Pricher, John, Lake Elsinore	1	0	1.000	3.38	5	0	0	0	1	0	8.0	9	37	4	3	0	0	0	0	4	0	3	2	0
Ramos, Cesar, Bakersfield	6	3	.667	3.56	24	4	0	0	6	2	60.2	63	257	28	24	2	6	2	1	17	0	35	7	1
Ricabal, Dan, San Bernardino	4	1	.800	3.88	43	0	0	0	13	2	72.0	63	315	35	31	7	0	2	5	33	1	62	2	1
Rigby, Brad, Modesto	11	4	.733	3.84	31	23	0	0	4	2	154.2	135	653	79	66	5	2	7	12	48	0	145	8	2
Roach, Peter, San Bernardino*	1	2	.333	3.00	30	0	0	0	14	8	33.0	28	143	16	11	2	2	2	2	14	1	38	5	0
Rodriguez, Nerio, High Desert	0	0	.000	1.80	7	0	0	0	3	0	10.0	8	44	2	2	0	0	0	0	7	0	10	0	0
Rogers, Jason, High Desert*	1	3	.250	7.83	5	5	0	0	0	0	23.0	32	121	26	20	0	1	2	0	18	0	10	5	0
Rogers, Kevin, San Jose*	0	2	.000	1.80	4	4	0	0	0	0	10.0	10	38	2	2	0	0	0	0	1	0	5	0	0
Rolocut, Brian, San Bernardino	1	0	1.000	5.68	11	3	0	0	2	0	12.2	15	70	10	8	0	2	3	1	16	0	10	0	0
Rosenkranz, Terry, Stockton*	1	2	.333	6.20	35	1	0	0	14	0	49.1	44	234	34	34	4	5	4	1	49	2	43	4	0
Rossiter, Michael, Modesto	7	2	.778	4.19	18	7	0	0	3	0	68.2	68	290	33	32	5	2	2	2	19	0	70	1	1
Rowland, Thad, Visalia*	0	1	.000	4.91	7	0	0	0	3	0	11.0	18	53	8	6	1	0	0	1	4	0	5	1	0
Ryan, Reid, Visalia	0	6	.000	9.38	12	5	0	0	4	0	31.2	51	170	43	33	3	1	4	7	26	0	14	2	3
Sadler, Al, Stockton	4	9	.308	4.42	37	14	1	1	10	2	114.0	113	501	62	56	9	3	2	8	59	0	82	6	2

Pitcher, Team	W	L	Pct.	ERA	G	GS	CG	ShO	GF	Sv.	IP	H	TBF	R	ER	HR	SH	SF	HB	BB	IBB	SO	WP	Bk.
Salazar, Luis, Stockton	6	2	.750	2.32	52	0	0	0	26	10	89.1	66	350	28	23	6	5	3	7	18	5	71	0	1
Saneaux, Francisco, High Desert	0	8	.000	10.59	23	11	0	0	4	1	52.2	56	296	77	62	8	0	6	11	72	1	64	10	4
Santana, Marino, Riverside	3	5	.375	6.19	9	9	0	0	0	0	48.0	44	214	47	33	10	3	4	2	25	0	57	2	3
Sauritch, Chris, High Desert	1	0	1.000	6.14	7	0	0	0	4	0	14.2	20	68	10	10	3	0	0	0	8	1	10	1	0
Sawyer, Zach, Modesto	7	1	.875	5.40	55	0	0	0	16	3	70.0	88	328	45	42	8	5	0	5	28	0	72	15	0
Scafa, Bob, Bakersfield*	5	8	.385	4.23	42	5	0	0	13	4	78.2	92	349	56	37	13	2	3	4	26	1	61	4	0
Scheffler, Craig, Bakersfield*	3	8	.273	5.62	32	19	0	0	3	0	105.2	118	490	85	66	15	7	5	4	65	0	51	15	0
Schenbeck, T.J., Stockton	1	5	.167	7.05	31	1	0	0	11	2	44.2	66	222	41	35	3	5	3	4	16	1	32	4	0
Schlutt, Jason, R.C.*	0	1	.000	4.91	11	0	0	0	5	2	14.2	16	67	9	8	0	1	1	1	4	0	11	3	0
Schramm, Carl, San Jose	6	4	.600	2.54	37	0	0	0	19	5	71.0	57	297	23	20	4	8	2	2	24	3	68	5	0
Seanez, Rudy, San Bernardino	2	0	1.000	0.00	4	0	0	0	2	1	6.0	2	23	0	0	0	0	0	0	3	0	5	0	0
Sebach, Kyle, Lake Elsinore	7	2	.778	4.60	14	13	0	0	0	0	76.1	91	340	40	39	10	1	1	4	29	0	60	6	0
Seki, Kiyokazu, Visalia	5	6	.455	4.94	35	3	0	0	16	3	85.2	79	360	53	47	11	1	0	1	29	0	84	1	0
Shenk, Larry, High Desert	0	0	.000	16.88	2	0	0	0	1	1	2.2	6	16	5	5	2	0	0	0	3	0	2	0	0
Slade, Shawn, Lake Elsinore	1	0	1.000	5.14	15	0	0	0	6	0	14.0	15	65	11	8	1	2	5	1	5	0	15	0	2
Smith, Hut, High Desert	3	4	.429	9.13	11	9	0	0	1	0	46.1	58	216	54	47	10	2	5	8	15	0	38	4	1
Smith, Ryan, Riverside	10	7	.588	3.11	23	23	2	1	0	0	141.2	142	609	68	49	7	7	5	10	50	1	108	5	3
Spiller, Derron, Riverside*	5	8	.385	6.03	32	11	0	0	8	0	88.0	114	390	64	59	6	6	3	5	16	1	52	5	2
Stone, Ricky, San Bernardino	3	5	.375	6.52	12	12	0	0	0	0	58.0	79	273	50	42	7	6	3	2	25	0	31	5	0
Sullivan, Dan, Riverside	4	4	.500	4.13	53	0	0	0	26	8	85.0	98	383	49	39	3	2	4	3	38	3	59	4	0
Suzuki, Mac, Riverside	0	1	.000	4.70	6	0	0	0	1	0	7.2	10	39	4	4	0	0	1	0	6	0	6	2	0
Takayoshi, Todd, Lake Elsinore	0	0	.000	40.50	1	0	0	0	1	0	0.2	1	6	3	3	0	0	0	1	2	0	0	0	0
Tapia, Elias, Bakersfield	0	1	.000	3.90	17	0	0	0	10	1	32.1	35	152	22	14	3	1	1	2	14	0	14	4	1
Taulbee, Andy, San Jose	3	2	.600	3.02	10	9	1	1	0	0	62.2	50	251	27	21	7	4	0	4	22	0	33	2	0
Theron, Greg, Riverside	4	2	.667	5.03	40	0	0	0	20	1	68.0	72	299	44	38	8	4	2	7	23	0	45	8	0
Thomas, Robbie, Bakersfield*	1	6	.143	7.48	26	6	0	0	4	0	49.1	55	247	51	41	8	4	4	5	36	0	39	6	0
Trimarco, Mike, High Desert	6	6	.500	5.27	40	1	0	0	16	2	100.2	109	441	70	59	12	5	6	1	36	4	52	7	2
Urbina, William, Modesto	2	0	1.000	5.27	30	0	0	0	11	1	41.0	51	185	28	24	4	0	1	4	16	0	18	4	0
Vanhof, John, Riverside*	1	1	.500	10.59	4	4	0	0	0	0	17.0	26	88	25	20	3	1	2	0	12	0	12	2	1
VanLandingham, William, San Jose	1	0	1.000	0.00	1	1	0	0	0	0	6.2	4	26	0	0	0	0	0	0	2	0	5	0	0
Villano, Mike, San Jose	0	1	.000	1.65	21	0	0	0	16	1	32.2	27	137	7	6	2	0	1	3	11	0	42	3	0
Wada, Takashi, Visalia	1	0	1.000	4.62	17	1	0	0	5	0	37.0	44	173	20	19	3	0	2	2	18	0	43	4	1
Wagner, Joe, Stockton	7	6	.538	4.35	20	18	0	0	1	0	107.2	124	494	62	52	8	8	3	4	53	0	76	7	0
Walsh, Matthew, Modesto	2	7	.222	4.65	44	9	0	0	21	5	100.2	98	445	64	52	11	5	3	6	45	4	108	5	2
Watson, Ron, Lake Elsinore	1	0	1.000	4.76	10	0	0	0	6	0	11.1	6	50	6	6	1	0	2	6	8	1	1	1	1
Webb, Doug, Stockton	0	0	.000	1.70	32	0	0	0	31	22	37.0	17	140	7	7	3	1	0	1	8	0	34	0	0
Whitaker, Ryan, Modesto	5	10	.333	4.41	32	25	0	0	3	0	151.0	177	669	90	74	10	8	3	4	54	2	88	10	1
Whitaker, Steve, San Jose*	0	0	.000	4.50	2	0	0	0	1	1	6.0	7	26	3	3	0	0	0	2	2	0	2	0	0
White, Darell, R.C.	0	5	.000	6.22	42	0	0	0	17	0	59.1	69	285	49	41	3	3	2	3	43	3	49	8	0
Whitman, Ryan, R.C.	1	2	.333	4.96	14	0	0	0	5	0	16.1	23	79	13	9	0	1	0	2	13	0	13	0	1
Williams, Matt, Bakersfield*	2	0	1.000	2.36	7	7	0	0	0	0	34.1	34	150	9	9	1	3	2	3	14	0	30	1	1
Williard, Brian, Lake Elsinore	2	4	.333	4.26	29	3	0	0	5	0	61.1	64	252	32	29	3	2	0	2	13	0	44	1	0
Wilson, Trevor, San Jose*	0	1	.000	1.35	2	2	0	0	0	0	6.2	5	29	4	1	0	1	0	0	3	0	5	0	0
Wilstead, Judd, Stockton	8	9	.471	5.09	31	21	0	0	1	0	139.2	165	653	97	79	15	10	5	14	71	1	72	12	3
Winchester, Marty, Riverside*	3	1	.750	4.57	35	4	0	0	8	0	67	85	305	40	34	2	5	3	2	45	3	56	5	0
Wolff, Bryan, R.C.	2	7	.222	3.32	54	0	0	0	43	18	57.0	39	262	23	21	4	4	3	3	54	0	77	15	0
Worley, Robert, Riverside	6	4	.600	5.31	11	11	0	0	0	0	61.0	64	275	44	36	4	2	2	3	30	0	44	8	2
Worrell, Tim, R.C.	2	0	1.000	5.16	9	3	0	0	2	1	22.2	25	103	17	13	2	0	1	2	6	1	17	0	0
Wunsch, Kelly, Stockton*	5	6	.455	5.33	14	13	1	1	0	0	74.1	89	349	51	44	4	8	1	7	39	0	62	6	0
York, Charles, Bakersfield*	4	2	.667	5.82	31	5	0	0	7	1	68.0	75	298	47	44	6	5	4	3	24	1	69	7	0
Yoshida, Atsushi, R.C.	5	7	.417	3.60	13	13	0	0	0	0	75.0	88	310	37	30	4	2	0	0	12	0	68	3	0
Zerbe, Chad, San Bernardino*	11	7	.611	4.57	28	27	1	0	0	0	163.1	168	718	103	83	15	10	5	3	64	0	94	4	0
Zongor, Steven, Modesto*	7	2	.778	4.07	37	0	0	0	9	1	55.1	57	238	29	25	3	5	3	1	21	1	55	2	0

COMBINATION SHUTOUTS: **Bakersfield (3)**—Edwards-Linares, Iglesias-Linares, Thomas-Scafa. **High Desert (2)**—Percibal-Saneaux, Percibal-Trimarco. **Lake Elsinore (6)**—Beaumont-Aguirre-Watson, Bonanno-Holdridge, Janicki-Holtz, Perisho-Holtz-Castillo, Sebach-Aguirre, Sebach-Holtz-Castillo. **Modesto (5)**—Baxter-Walsh, Briscoe-Haught-Michalak-Zongor, Manning-Rigby, Rossiter-Sawyer-Maurer, Rossiter-Urbina-Sawyer. **Rancho Cucamonga (4)**—Clement-Dixon-Wolff, Dennis-Wolff, Dixon-White, LaChappa-Hermanson-Schlutt. **Riverside (5)**—Clayton-Newton-Crow, Clayton-Sullivan-Crow, Moore-Newton-Theron-Winchester, Smith-Sullivan-Crow, Winchester-Ippolito-Fitzer. **San Bernardino (8)**—Brunson-Price-Camacho-Colon-Paluk-Roach, Brunson-Roach-Camacho, Brunson-Camacho-Ricabal, Herges-Camacho, Lagarde-Camacho, Pivaral-Herges-Colon, Price-Camacho, Stone-Ricabal-Roach. **San Jose (15)**—Aquino-Howry, Brohawn-Andrakin, Brohawn-Villano, Estes-Martin, Estes-Peters, Foulke-Castillo, Foulke-Peters, Howry-Andrakin-Hartvigson, Howry-Schramm, Howry-Schramm-Hyde, Macey-Andrakin-Peters, Peters-Castillo, Prater-Hartvigson-Andrakin, VanLandingham-McLain, Wilson-Martin-Schramm-Ortiz. **Stockton (4)**—Kramer-Salazar, Linares-Paul-Webb, Paul-Sadler, Rosenkranz-Paul-Sadler-Schenbeck. **Visalia (6)**—Endo-Magnelli, Meadows-DeClue-Jenkins, Meadows-Seki, Myers-Muto, Spiller-Wada, Yoshida-DeClue.

NO-HIT GAMES: None.

PITCHERS WITH TWO OR MORE TEAMS

Pitcher, Team	W	L	Pct.	ERA	G	GS	CG	ShO	GF	Sv.	IP	H	TBF	R	ER	HR	SH	SF	HB	BB	IBB	SO	WP	Bk.
DeClue, Jon, Visalia*	6	5	.545	3.50	21	14	0	0	3	0	103.0	95	421	48	40	11	3	2	7	27	0	90	3	1
DeClue, Jon, Lake Elsinore*	5	1	.833	3.57	9	4	0	0	0	0	40.1	50	169	16	16	5	1	1	2	5	0	22	1	0
Hinson, Dean, Visalia	1	1	.500	3.93	23	0	0	0	14	3	34.1	30	150	18	15	1	3	0	4	16	0	35	9	2
Hinson, Dean, Lake Elsinore	0	0	.000	5.40	5	0	0	0	4	0	6.2	8	36	4	4	1	0	1	1	6	0	4	1	0
Iglesias, Mike, Bakersfield	7	10	.412	3.26	24	23	2	1	0	0	143.2	124	586	65	52	11	5	3	11	38	0	108	7	0
Iglesias, Mike, San Bernardino	1	2	.333	6.60	4	3	0	0	0	0	15.0	26	74	14	11	1	0	0	2	2	0	12	3	0
LaGarde, Joe, San Bernardino	5	10	.333	4.60	24	24	0	0	0	0	123.1	135	557	83	63	9	4	7	9	68	0	102	10	1
LaGarde, Joe, Bakersfield	1	1	.500	2.91	4	4	0	0	0	0	21.2	19	98	8	7	1	0	0	0	13	0	25	5	0

1995 FIELDING

TEAM

Team	Pct.	G	PO	A	E	TC	DP	PB
San Jose	.968	140	3810	1446	174	5430	120	16
San Bernardino	.968	139	3744	1562	177	5483	94	29
Stockton	.965	140	3719	1564	192	5475	120	22
Visalia	.964	140	3730	1530	199	5459	143	29
Lake Elsinore	.964	139	3682	1493	196	5371	124	22
Rancho Cucamonga	.963	139	3649	1463	199	5311	128	29
Riverside	.960	139	3679	1534	217	5430	124	46
Bakersfield	.959	140	3666	1639	224	5529	142	23
Modesto	.959	140	3703	1511	222	5436	112	16
High Desert	.950	140	3683	1508	275	5466	112	36

TRIPLE PLAY: Rancho Cucamonga.

INDIVIDUAL

FIRST BASEMEN

NOTE: All caps denotes fielding-percentage leader based on 70 games for catchers, 93 for all other non-pitchers and 140 innings for pitchers. *Throws lefthanded.

Player, Team	Pct.	G	PO	A	E	TC	DP
Alguacil, Jose, San Jose	1.000	1	1	0	0	1	0
Alimena, Charles, San Jose*	.987	35	280	15	4	299	22
Bengoechea, Brandy, Modesto	.927	4	37	1	3	41	3
Brakebill, Mark, Lake Elsinore	1.000	1	9	1	0	10	0
Breuer, Jim, Bakersfield	1.000	2	16	1	0	17	0
Burke, Jamie, Lake Elsinore	.987	21	152	5	2	159	15
Chavez, Eric, High Desert	.974	4	35	3	1	39	0
Cox, Steve, Modesto*	.984	114	991	77	17	1085	85
Cromer, D.T., Modesto*	1.000	4	34	8	0	42	2
Curtis, Kevin, High Desert	.983	70	576	53	11	640	52
Diaz, Alfredo, Lake Elsinore	1.000	1	4	0	0	4	0
Fernandez, Antonio, Visalia	.982	13	99	8	2	109	15
Galarza, Joel, San Jose	1.000	5	40	2	0	42	2
Gulseth, Mark, San Jose	1.000	16	112	11	0	123	6
Hamlin, Jonas, Stockton	.984	98	851	65	15	931	81
Hecker, Doug, Visalia	.974	6	35	3	1	39	2
Hughes, Bobby, Stockton	1.000	1	1	0	0	1	0
Ibanez, Raul, Riverside	.959	9	66	5	3	74	7
JORGENSEN, Randy, Riverside*	.989	131	1081	116	13	1210	101
Keene, Andre, San Jose*	.974	50	431	22	12	465	35
Kirkpatrick, Jay, San Bernardino	.994	52	462	39	3	504	33
Ladjevich, Rick, Riverside	1.000	6	40	4	0	44	8
Lee, Derrek, R.C.	.983	121	970	86	18	1074	96
McCall, Rod, Bakersfield	.979	52	490	26	11	527	52
Moeder, Tony, Lake Elsinore	.974	61	508	44	15	567	50
Morales, William, Modesto	.964	3	25	2	1	28	3
Mowry, Dave, R.C.*	1.000	8	38	2	0	40	3
Newstrom, Doug, San Bern.	.988	51	467	47	6	520	29
Ortega, Hector, Stockton	1.000	2	7	1	0	8	0
Ortega, Randy, Modesto	1.000	1	1	0	0	1	1
Pagee, Shawn, Visalia	.900	1	9	0	1	10	1
Pinoni, Scott, Visalia	.993	68	631	35	5	671	50
Powell, Gordon, Stockton	1.000	4	28	4	0	32	2
Rasmussen, Nate, Bakersfield*	.994	19	167	3	1	171	17
Redington, Tom, Lake Elsinore	.990	56	456	30	5	491	45
Richardson, Brian, San Bern.	1.000	6	41	4	0	45	2
Roberge, J.P., San Bernardino	.995	35	339	30	2	371	21
Sealy, Scot, Riverside	1.000	1	10	1	0	11	1
See, Larry, R.C.	.966	11	75	10	3	88	6
Seitzer, Brad, Stockton	.992	47	348	38	3	389	27
Shockey, Greg, Lake Elsinore*	1.000	1	5	0	0	5	0
Simonton, Benji, San Jose	.991	35	309	19	3	331	27
Smith, Frank, San Bernardino	1.000	1	2	0	0	2	0
Smith, Joel, Vis.-L.E.	.978	15	124	8	3	135	13
Smith, Scott, Riverside	1.000	2	5	1	0	6	0
Takayoshi, Todd, Lake Elsinore	.974	6	38	0	1	39	2
Tohyama, Shoji, Visalia*	.988	46	308	31	4	343	33
Triessl, Mike, R.C.	1.000	4	31	0	0	31	1
Wallace, Brian, San Jose	1.000	1	6	0	0	6	1
White, Jason, Modesto*	1.000	16	132	7	0	139	11
Wilson, Todd, San Jose	1.000	6	47	3	0	50	7
Wingate, Ervan, Bakersfield*	.991	56	508	35	5	548	50
Wittig, Paul, Bakersfield	.964	2	25	2	1	28	2
Wolff, Mike, High Desert*	.988	79	576	71	8	655	49
Wyngarden, Brett, Visalia	.939	7	58	4	4	66	8
Zahner, Kevin, Bakersfield	.962	15	87	13	4	104	9

FIRST BASEMEN WITH TWO OR MORE TEAMS

Player, Team	Pct.	G	PO	A	E	TC	DP
Smith, Joel, Visalia	1.000	12	105	8	0	113	9
Smith, Joel, Lake Elsinore	.864	3	19	0	3	22	4

SECOND BASEMEN

Player, Team	Pct.	G	PO	A	E	TC	DP
Alguacil, Jose, San Jose	.990	25	44	58	1	103	17
Bengoechea, Brandy, Modesto	1.000	4	8	9	0	17	1
Berry, Michael, Visalia	.980	46	68	77	3	148	18
Bethea, Scott, Visalia	.969	74	163	184	11	358	53
Carr, Jeremy, Bakersfield	.970	121	325	346	21	692	102
Carrasquel, Domingo, Stockton	.957	31	48	84	6	138	18
Clark, Howie, High Desert	.938	9	16	14	2	32	1
Corps, Erick, R.C.	1.000	5	11	23	0	34	5
Cuevas, Eduardo, R.C.	.931	14	29	25	4	58	9
Dean, Chris, Riverside	.939	115	207	304	33	544	68
Diaz, Alfredo, Lake Elsinore	1.000	2	4	3	0	7	1
Dumas, Mike, Stockton	.967	34	79	69	5	153	14
Faircloth, Kevin, San Bernardino	.944	12	11	23	2	36	3
Fernandez, Antonio, Visalia	.957	13	15	30	2	47	4
Fuller, Aaron, Visalia	.833	1	3	2	1	6	0
Garcia, Manuel, Visalia	.980	11	19	30	1	50	8
Guiel, Aaron, Lake Elsinore	.958	108	214	294	22	530	72
Guillen, Jose, Modesto	.962	12	18	33	2	53	4
LaRocca, Greg, R.C.	.929	24	42	63	8	113	12
Martin, Lincoln, High Desert	.937	36	53	81	9	143	19
Martins, Eric, Modesto	.956	98	188	242	20	450	51
Marval, Raul, San Jose	1.000	4	4	10	0	14	1
McDonald, Jason, Modesto	.943	14	22	28	3	53	4
Mercedes, Feliciano, High Desert	.976	24	28	52	2	82	8
Morillo, Cesar, Bakersfield	.944	10	20	31	3	54	12
Morreale, John, Stockton	.982	11	24	32	1	57	7
Moschetti, Mike, Modesto	.940	20	38	56	6	100	11
Nadeau, Mike, High Desert	.947	20	30	42	4	76	5
Nevers, Tom, Stockton	.833	2	3	2	1	6	1
Owen, Spike, Lake Elsinore	1.000	1	0	1	0	1	0
Pagan, Angel, High Desert	.913	11	15	27	4	46	5
Patel, Manny, Riverside	.984	27	46	81	2	129	18
Phillips, Gary, San Jose	1.000	1	2	2	0	4	1
Powell, Gordon, Stockton	.959	73	130	217	15	362	43
Priest, Chris, Visalia	1.000	1	0	8	0	8	0
Richardson, Scott, Stockton	1.000	1	1	2	0	3	1
Riggs, Adam, San Bernardino	.928	121	223	303	41	567	47
Rivera, Santiago, R.C.	1.000	1	1	0	0	1	0
Roberge, J.P., San Bernardino	1.000	5	4	6	0	10	3
Sbrocco, Jon, San Jose	.962	114	226	311	21	558	60
Schaaf, Bob, San Bernardino	1.000	9	19	27	0	46	6
Serra, Jose, High Desert	.904	40	75	123	21	219	19
Short, Rick, High Desert	.939	25	48	59	7	114	12
Simmons, Mark, Lake Elsinore	.967	16	28	30	2	60	5
Tredaway, Chad, R.C.	1.000	4	8	10	0	18	1
Urso, Joe, Lake Elsinore	.969	22	40	54	3	97	15
Wallace, Brian, San Jose	.889	3	6	10	2	18	1
Wingate, Ervan, Bakersfield	.982	9	19	36	1	56	5
WOODRIDGE, Dickie, R.C.	.988	97	178	235	5	418	64

THIRD BASEMEN

Player, Team	Pct.	G	PO	A	E	TC	DP
Alguacil, Jose, San Jose	.950	14	19	19	2	40	2
Alvarez, Gabe, R.C.	.960	9	5	19	1	25	0
Bengoechea, Brandy, Modesto	.895	129	82	226	36	344	13
Berry, Michael, Visalia	.885	48	25	98	16	139	10
Bogle, Bryan, High Desert	.927	16	12	26	3	41	2
Brakebill, Mark, Lake Elsinore	1.000	1	0	1	0	1	0
Burke, Jamie, Lake Elsinore	.927	89	68	186	20	274	20
Chavez, Eric, High Desert	.882	37	18	49	9	76	3
Clark, Howie, High Desert	.917	82	60	151	19	230	12
Corps, Erick, R.C.	.704	9	3	16	8	27	1
Diaz, Alfredo, Lake Elsinore	.922	30	26	69	8	103	7
Fernandez, Antonio, Visalia	.922	60	42	111	13	166	14
Fuller, Aaron, Visalia	.800	2	1	3	1	5	0
Guillen, Jose, Modesto	.950	7	6	13	1	20	1

Player, Team	Pct.	G	PO	A	E	TC	DP
Johnson, Keith, San Bernardino....	.857	5	4	8	2	14	1
Koscielniak, Dwain, R.C.	.833	4	1	4	1	6	1
LADJEVICH, Rick, Riverside....	.936	94	72	176	17	265	21
LaRocca, Greg, R.C.	.933	11	5	23	2	30	2
Martins, Eric, Modesto	.967	11	5	24	1	30	2
Miller, Roy, Riverside	.900	21	11	25	4	40	4
Milstien, Dave, Stockton	1.000	1	0	1	0	1	0
Morales, William, Modesto	1.000	1	0	3	0	3	0
Morillo, Cesar, Bakersfield....	.938	18	11	50	4	65	2
Morreale, John, Stockton	.933	8	3	11	1	15	1
Nadeau, Mike, High Desert	1.000	2	0	1	0	1	0
Nevers, Tom, Stockton	1.000	1	1	1	0	2	0
Ortega, Hector, Stockton	.911	72	75	120	19	214	10
Ortega, Randy, Modesto	1.000	2	1	2	0	3	0
Owen, Spike, Lake Elsinore	1.000	1	0	2	0	2	0
Pagan, Angel, High Desert	.818	10	5	22	6	33	1
Parker, Alan, Visalia	1.000	2	1	3	0	4	0
Patel, Manny, Riverside	.904	34	21	73	10	104	6
Phillips, Gary, San Jose	.906	103	66	194	27	287	18
Priest, Chris, Visalia	.889	35	30	58	11	99	7
Raven, Luis, Lake Elsinore	1.000	5	5	15	0	20	3
Redington, Tom, Lake Elsinore	.500	1	1	0	1	2	0
Richardson, Brian, San Bernardino....	.926	122	82	254	27	363	18
Rivera, Santiago, R.C.	.909	24	9	21	3	33	4
Roberge, J.P., San Bernardino	1.000	1	0	1	0	1	0
Schaaf, Bob, San Bernardino	.923	18	6	30	3	39	2
Seitzer, Brad, Stockton	.925	67	47	150	16	213	15
Serra, Jose, High Desert	1.000	2	1	0	0	1	0
Short, Rick, High Desert	1.000	5	3	8	0	11	0
Simmons, Mark, Lake Elsinore	.935	23	13	30	3	46	4
Smith, Scott, Riverside	1.000	4	4	8	0	12	0
Tredaway, Chad, R.C.	.923	97	73	202	23	298	24
Urso, Joe, Lake Elsinore	.500	1	1	0	1	2	0
Wallace, Brian, San Jose	.929	5	3	10	1	14	1
Wallach, Tim, San Jose	.909	4	2	8	1	11	1
Williams, Matt, San Jose	1.000	4	0	4	0	4	0
Wilson, Todd, San Jose	.960	25	17	55	3	75	5
Wingate, Ervan, Bakersfield....	.905	33	27	59	9	95	4
Zellers, Kevin, Bakersfield	.912	94	68	223	28	319	21

SHORTSTOPS

Player, Team	Pct.	G	PO	A	E	TC	DP
Alguacil, Jose, San Jose	.969	19	28	35	2	65	7
Alvarez, Gabe, R.C.	.884	43	47	113	21	181	13
Bautista, Juan, High Desert	.911	96	154	253	40	447	46
Bellhorn, Mark, Modesto	.927	55	94	172	21	287	29
Bengoechea, Brandy, Modesto	1.000	1	2	4	0	6	1
Bethea, Scott, Visalia	.938	27	34	72	7	113	11
Bordick, Mike, Modesto	1.000	1	2	1	0	3	0
Carrasquel, Domingo, Stockton	.943	30	31	68	6	105	14
Cook, Jason, Riverside	.897	5	12	14	3	29	4
Corps, Erick, R.C.	.846	6	5	6	2	13	1
Delgado, Wilson, San Jose	1.000	1	1	2	0	3	1
Diaz, Alfredo, Lake Elsinore	.957	12	17	27	2	46	3
Dumas, Mike, Stockton	1.000	1	1	3	0	4	0
Faircloth, Kevin, San Bernardino	.961	42	47	102	6	155	11
Guevara, Giomar, Riverside	.929	83	123	231	27	381	47
Guillen, Jose, Riverside	1.000	5	3	5	0	8	2
JOHNSON, Keith, San Bernardino....	.963	105	170	319	19	508	42
King, Brett, San Jose	.950	107	165	269	23	457	52
LaRocca, Greg, R.C.	.931	87	131	220	26	377	49
Luuloa, Keith, Lake Elsinore	.921	101	155	290	38	483	54
Martinez, Gabby, Stockton	.924	64	96	158	21	275	33
Marval, Raul, San Jose	.871	7	17	10	4	31	2
McDonald, Jason, Modesto	.885	78	119	213	43	375	44
Meilan, Tony, Bakersfield	.891	12	10	31	5	46	5
Mercedes, Feliciano, High Desert	.839	8	12	14	5	31	2
Miller, Roy, Riverside	.929	38	60	96	12	168	21
Milstien, Dave, Stockton	.954	56	104	168	13	285	28
Morillo, Cesar, Bakersfield....	.917	73	109	222	30	361	42
Nevers, Tom, Stockton	.800	1	2	2	1	5	0
Pagan, Angel, High Desert	.944	14	19	32	3	54	8
Parker, Alan, Visalia	.949	118	202	352	30	584	81
Patel, Manny, Riverside	.923	21	33	51	7	91	9
Paulino, Arturo, Modesto	1.000	4	3	10	0	13	1
Phillips, Gary, San Jose	1.000	1	0	1	0	1	0
Prieto, Rick, Bakersfield	1.000	2	3	7	0	10	1
Rivera, Santiago, R.C.	.891	15	24	25	6	55	6
Schaaf, Bob, San Bernardino	.933	4	6	8	1	15	3
Serra, Jose, High Desert	.887	35	38	64	13	115	17
Simmons, Mark, Lake Elsinore	.923	8	6	18	2	26	3
Stare, Lonny, Bakersfield	.500	1	0	1	1	2	0

Player, Team	Pct.	G	PO	A	E	TC	DP
Urso, Joe, Lake Elsinore	.938	24	30	61	6	97	11
Wallace, Brian, San Jose	.908	16	34	45	8	87	10
Wingate, Ervan, Bakersfield	.929	2	5	8	1	14	0
Yard, Bruce, Bakersfield	.957	53	77	192	12	281	49

TRIPLE PLAY: Alvarez (unassisted).

OUTFIELDERS

Player, Team	Pct.	G	PO	A	E	TC	DP
Adams, Tommy, Riverside	.979	48	91	2	2	95	0
Alguacil, Jose, San Jose	.857	4	6	0	1	7	0
Alimena, Charles, San Jose*	1.000	3	1	0	0	1	0
Asencio, Alex, San Bernardino*	.942	29	48	1	3	52	0
Avila, Rolando, High Desert	.955	49	105	2	5	112	1
Banks, Tony, Modesto*	.977	25	41	1	1	43	0
Barger, Mike, Riverside	.982	78	160	6	3	169	0
Bishop, Steve, High Desert	.917	9	9	2	1	12	0
Bogle, Bryan, High Desert	1.000	1	1	0	0	1	0
Bonds, Bobby, Visalia	.947	103	225	9	13	247	2
Breuer, Jim, Bakersfield	1.000	7	7	0	0	7	0
Brock, Tarrick, Visalia*	.949	39	90	4	5	99	1
Byrne, Clayton, High Desert	.945	51	113	7	7	127	3
Carr, Jeremy, Bakersfield	1.000	1	1	0	0	1	0
Chavez, Eric, High Desert	1.000	8	9	2	0	11	1
Claudio, Patricio, Bakersfield	.960	32	67	5	3	75	0
Clyburn, Danny, High Desert	.932	42	63	6	5	74	0
Conway, Jeff, R.C.*	1.000	25	33	2	0	35	2
Corps, Erick, R.C.	.982	34	50	4	1	55	0
Cromer, D.T., Modesto*	.944	95	126	8	8	142	0
Cruz, Jose, Riverside	.961	33	70	4	3	77	1
Cunningham, Earl, Lake Elsinore	1.000	8	5	0	0	5	0
Curtis, Kevin, High Desert	1.000	2	2	0	0	2	0
Dandridge, Brad, San Bernardino....	.976	23	39	1	1	41	0
Daniels, Moe, Lake Elsinore	.990	38	91	4	1	96	0
D'Aquila, Tom, High Desert	.917	73	120	2	11	133	0
Derotal, Francisco, R.C.	.960	27	23	1	1	25	0
Doty, Derrin, Lake Elsinore	.971	91	128	4	4	136	0
Dumas, Mike, Stockton	.985	34	62	2	1	65	0
Dunn, Todd, Stockton	.968	63	116	6	4	126	1
Durkin, Chris, San Bernardino*	.946	53	83	4	5	92	0
Eaddy, Keith, High Desert	.957	84	151	4	7	162	0
Ealy, Tracey, San Jose	1.000	3	5	0	0	5	0
Erstad, Darin, Lake Elsinore*	.985	25	65	2	1	68	0
Fuller, Aaron, Visalia	.967	47	114	5	4	123	3
Fully, Ed, High Desert	.963	34	76	3	3	82	0
Gibbs, Kevin, San Bernardino	1.000	5	5	0	0	5	0
Graham, John, Visalia*	.972	65	97	7	3	107	0
Grieve, Ben, Modesto	.951	27	37	2	2	41	0
Guillen, Jose, Modesto	1.000	2	1	0	0	1	0
Hayashi, Hiroyasu, Visalia*	.967	26	55	3	2	60	0
Hence, Sam, Bakersfield	1.000	2	1	1	0	2	0
Hilo, Johnny, San Bernardino*	.930	34	39	1	3	43	0
Hodge, Roy, High Desert	.922	36	55	4	5	64	0
Hugo, Sean, High Desert*	.941	24	45	3	3	51	0
Hunter, Scott, San Bernardino	.953	111	177	7	9	193	0
Hust, Gary, Modesto	.974	128	214	11	6	231	3
Jenkins, Geoff, Stockton*	.895	13	14	3	2	19	0
Johnson, Earl, R.C.	.972	81	225	16	7	248	2
Keel, David, Modesto	1.000	9	12	0	0	12	0
Keifer, Greg, San Jose	1.000	22	20	0	0	20	0
Kruger, Andy, Visalia*	.940	71	123	2	8	133	1
Lemons, Rich, Bakersfield	.942	35	46	3	3	52	0
Marquez, Jesus, Riverside*	.971	68	123	9	4	136	0
Martin, Lincoln, High Desert	1.000	4	1	0	0	1	0
Martinez, Greg, Stockton	.985	109	253	4	4	264	0
McDonald, Jason, Modesto	.965	43	106	5	4	115	1
McGonigle, Bill, Stockton	.976	60	114	10	3	127	3
McNabb, Buck, Bakersfield	.991	63	101	8	1	110	1
Mejia, Miguel, High Desert	.952	34	58	2	3	63	0
Miller, Roy, Riverside	1.000	1	1	0	0	1	0
Moore, Kerwin, Modesto	.966	15	27	1	1	29	0
Moore, Vince, R.C.*	.960	84	154	15	7	176	3
Neill, Mike, Modesto*	.968	59	113	7	4	124	0
Nelson, Charles, San Bernardino*	1.000	1	2	0	0	2	0
Newstrom, Doug, San Bernardino....	1.000	10	4	2	0	6	0
Nicholas, Darrell, Stockton	.936	53	97	6	7	110	0
Ohmura, Iwao, Visalia	.969	42	58	5	2	65	2
Ortega, Hector, Stockton	.988	46	79	6	1	86	1
Powell, Chris, Lake Elsinore*	.957	13	21	1	1	23	0
Powell, Dante, San Jose	.967	130	308	18	11	337	3
Priest, Chris, Visalia	1.000	15	14	2	0	16	1
Prieto, Chris, R.C.*	.957	89	146	10	7	163	2
Prieto, Rick, Bakersfield	.970	68	156	4	5	165	2

Player, Team	Pct.	G	PO	A	E	TC	DP
Ramirez, Alex, Bakersfield	.941	84	150	9	10	169	2
Reese, Matthew, Modesto*	1.000	6	11	0	0	11	0
Richardson, Scott, Stockton	.900	20	26	1	3	30	0
Rios, Armando, San Jose*	.963	118	220	16	9	245	5
Rivera, Santiago, R.C.	1.000	9	9	0	0	9	0
Roberge, J.P., San Bernardino	.986	46	67	2	1	70	1
Roberts, John, R.C.	.978	95	165	13	4	182	2
Rodriques, Cecil, Stockton	.952	45	94	5	5	104	2
Schaaf, Bob, San Bernardino	1.000	5	4	1	0	5	0
Shockey, Greg, Lake Elsinore*	.976	107	187	16	5	208	1
Simmons, Mark, Lake Elsinore	.959	34	46	1	2	49	0
Singleton, Chris, San Jose*	.955	91	142	6	7	155	0
Smith, Demond, Lake Elsinore	.929	34	62	3	5	70	0
Smith, Frank, San Bernardino	.971	51	63	5	2	70	1
Smith, Scott, Riverside	.938	32	59	1	4	64	0
SPEARMAN, Vernon, San Bern.*	.987	93	224	9	3	236	2
Stare, Lonny, Bakersfield	.964	99	170	16	7	193	0
Stuckenschneider, Eric, San Bern.	1.000	2	3	0	0	3	0
Sturdivant, Marcus, Riverside*	.958	78	130	7	6	143	0
Tachikawa, Takashi, Visalia	.973	36	65	6	2	73	3
Tejcek, John, Riverside	.955	92	183	9	9	201	1
Tena, Dario, R.C.	.889	11	8	0	1	9	0
Thielen, D.J., San Jose	.974	79	144	7	4	155	4
Tyrus, Jason, Bakersfield	.942	24	47	2	3	52	0
Vaughn, Derek, Lake Elsinore	.969	92	181	9	6	196	1
White, Jason, Modesto*	.927	26	36	2	3	41	0
Wingate, Ervan, Bakersfield	1.000	18	26	0	0	26	0
Woodridge, Dickie, R.C.	1.000	4	3	0	0	3	0

CATCHERS

Player, Team	Pct.	G	PO	A	E	TC	DP	PB
Allanson, Andy, Lake Elsinore	.993	22	122	11	1	134	1	3
Cabrera, Jairo, High Desert	.969	14	78	16	3	97	0	1
Campillo, Rob, Stockton	.978	35	192	30	5	227	1	7
Carpenter, Jerry, Lake Elsinore	1.000	1	9	3	0	12	0	0
Cavanagh, Mike, San Jose	1.000	6	45	3	0	48	0	1
Chavez, Eric, High Desert	.941	12	42	6	3	51	0	2
Cuellar, Jose, Riverside	.972	19	92	11	3	106	1	6
Dandridge, Brad, San Bern.	.984	43	267	34	5	306	3	10
Dobrolsky, Bill, Stockton	.984	79	431	73	8	512	3	9
Galarza, Joel, San Jose	.983	37	267	28	5	300	3	3
Gargiulo, Mike, High Desert	1.000	14	76	8	0	84	2	3
Grass, Darren, R.C.	.994	21	138	23	1	162	1	2
Gresham, Kris, High Desert	.975	47	270	46	8	324	1	11
Harmer, Frank, High Desert	.962	5	22	3	1	26	0	1
Hemphill, Bret, Lake Elsinore	.976	45	354	47	10	411	1	6
Hughes, Bobby, Stockton	.987	45	251	50	4	305	4	5
Ibanez, Raul, Riverside	.980	63	399	49	9	457	3	25
Jennings, Lance, Visalia	.988	76	501	71	7	579	10	9
Johnson, Todd, Bakersfield	1.000	7	36	4	0	40	0	1
Knapp, Mike, High Desert	.949	5	32	5	2	39	1	1
Konerko, Paul, San Bernardino	.985	95	676	68	11	755	0	18
Ladjevich, Rick, Riverside	1.000	4	15	0	0	15	0	0
Marnell, Anthony, R.C.	.968	16	82	8	3	93	0	1
MAYES, Craig, San Jose	.992	84	576	61	5	642	9	9
McKinnis, Leroy, R.C.	1.000	10	88	15	0	103	3	4
Molina, Ben, Lake Elsinore	.995	27	195	16	1	212	0	4
Moore, Mark, Modesto	.970	37	269	18	9	296	2	7
Morales, William, Modesto	.991	101	772	100	8	880	9	8
Newstrom, Doug, San Bern.	.962	14	49	2	2	53	0	1
Ortega, Randy, Modesto	1.000	7	57	2	0	59	0	1
Pagee, Shawn, Visalia	.964	17	92	15	4	111	2	2
Rodriguez, Miguel, Stockton	.957	11	21	1	1	23	0	1
Rodriguez, Nerio, High Desert	.978	50	324	33	8	365	3	10
Schneider, Dan, San Jose	.989	12	80	6	1	87	0	0
Schwenke, Matt, R.C.	.981	22	135	16	3	154	0	4
Sealy, Scot, Riverside	.981	54	408	50	9	467	1	8
See, Larry, R.C.	1.000	1	1	0	0	1	0	0
Shepherd, Brian, San Jose	.978	13	76	14	2	92	0	3
Smith, Joel, Vis.-L.E.	.991	45	297	45	3	345	5	6
Soliz, Steve, Bakersfield	.989	44	237	43	3	283	2	4
Takayoshi, Todd, Lake Elsinore	.987	35	198	23	3	224	2	5
Tejero, Fausto, Lake Elsinore	.982	8	48	8	1	57	2	1
Thurston, Jerrey, R.C.	.980	75	489	57	11	557	5	9
Triessl, Mike, Riv.-R.C.	.971	40	208	25	7	240	6	16
Williamson, Joel, High Desert	.962	24	136	16	6	158	1	7
Wittig, Paul, Bakersfield	.974	61	368	48	11	427	4	14
Wyngarden, Brett, Visalia	.977	36	189	19	5	213	3	15
Zahner, Kevin, Bakersfield	.969	47	231	21	8	260	2	4

CATCHERS WITH TWO OR MORE TEAMS

Player, Team	Pct.	G	PO	A	E	TC	DP	PB
Smith, Joel, Visalia	.991	28	192	30	2	224	4	3
Smith, Joel, Lake Elsinore	.992	17	105	15	1	121	1	3
Triessl, Mike, Riverside	.962	11	68	7	3	78	2	7
Triessl, Mike, R.C.	.975	29	140	18	4	162	4	9

PITCHERS

Player, Team	Pct.	G	PO	A	E	TC	DP
Aguirre, Jose, Lake Elsinore*	.800	29	0	4	1	5	0
Anderson, Brian, Lake Elsinore*	1.000	3	1	4	0	5	0
Andrakin, Rob, San Jose	.900	29	6	3	1	10	0
Aquino, Julio, San Bernardino	.875	25	8	6	2	16	0
Arroyo, Luis, R.C.*	.943	26	11	22	2	35	0
Baker, Jared, R.C.	1.000	31	8	9	0	17	0
Baldwin, Scott, Modesto*	.833	5	1	4	1	6	1
Barnes, Jon, R.C.	1.000	5	5	0	0	5	0
Baron, Jim, R.C.*	.500	3	0	1	1	2	0
Barrett, Mark, R.C.*	1.000	32	0	3	0	3	0
Baxter, Herbert, Modesto*	.893	29	4	21	3	28	1
Beaumont, Matt, Lake Elsinore*	.962	27	9	41	2	52	2
Berumen, Andres, R.C.	1.000	4	1	0	0	1	0
Bielecki, Mike, Lake Elsinore	1.000	3	0	1	0	1	0
Bland, Nathan, Bakersfield*	.900	27	3	24	3	30	0
Blyleven, Todd, Lake Elsinore	1.000	6	0	3	0	3	0
Bonanno, Rob, Lake Elsinore	.926	17	8	17	2	27	1
Brewer, Brian, High Desert	.920	17	3	20	2	25	0
Briscoe, John, Modesto	1.000	4	1	0	0	1	0
Brohawn, Troy, San Jose*	1.000	11	4	10	0	14	0
Brown, Cory, High Desert	.950	30	9	10	1	20	0
Brown, Keith, Stockton*	1.000	12	1	5	0	6	0
Brunson, William, San Bernardino*	.962	13	4	21	1	26	0
Cafaro, Rocco, High Desert	.909	44	3	7	1	11	0
Camacho, Dan, San Bernardino	1.000	43	5	10	0	15	1
Castillo, Carlos, Lake Elsinore	1.000	52	5	6	0	11	2
Castillo, Mariano, San Jose	.833	21	1	4	1	6	0
Castro, Tony, Lake Elsinore	1.000	8	0	2	0	2	0
Chavez, Tony, Lake Elsinore	1.000	33	1	5	0	6	0
Clayton, Craig, Riverside	.960	28	12	12	1	25	0
Clement, Matt, R.C.	.923	12	3	9	1	13	1
Cole, Jim, Stockton	.882	14	1	14	2	17	2
Colon, Julio, San Bernardino	1.000	49	9	13	0	22	1
Cope, Robin, Riverside	.625	11	2	3	3	8	0
Crills, Brad, High Desert	1.000	5	1	3	0	4	0
Cromwell, Nate, R.C.*	1.000	4	1	5	0	6	0
Crow, Dean, Riverside	1.000	51	2	8	0	10	1
Dafun, George, Lake Elsinore	1.000	3	0	1	0	1	0
Daigle, Tim, High Desert*	.944	19	9	8	1	18	0
Davis, Eddie, San Bernardino	1.000	5	1	2	0	3	0
DeClue, Jon, Vis.-L.E.*	.931	30	5	22	2	29	0
Dennis, Shane, R.C.*	.938	11	4	11	1	16	0
Dixon, Bubba, R.C.*	.897	47	8	27	4	39	1
Dressendorfer, Kirk, Modesto	.875	27	1	6	1	8	1
Drewien, Dan, R.C.	1.000	17	0	4	0	4	0
Drysdale, Brooks, Lake Elsinore	1.000	8	1	1	0	2	0
Duda, Steve, Stockton	.941	12	3	13	1	17	1
Dyess, Todd, High Desert	.909	23	17	23	4	44	1
Dykhoff, Radhames, High Desert*	.941	34	6	10	1	17	0
Eaddy, Brad, Bakersfield*	.810	42	4	13	4	21	0
Edsell, Geoff, Lake Elsinore	.875	23	4	24	4	32	0
Edwards, Wayne, Bakersfield*	.882	21	2	13	2	17	0
Endo, Masataka, Visalia	.943	28	13	37	3	53	4
Enoki, Yasuhiro, Visalia	1.000	13	5	6	0	11	0
Estes, Shawn, San Jose*	.818	9	2	7	2	11	0
Ettles, Mark, R.C.	1.000	3	1	2	0	3	1
Felix, Ruben, Stockton*	1.000	6	1	1	0	2	0
Fetchel, Tony, Visalia	.900	18	1	8	1	10	0
Fitzer, Douglas, Riverside*	.714	25	3	2	2	7	1
Foulke, Keith, San Jose	.972	28	10	25	1	36	2
Gamez, Francisco, Stockton	1.000	4	3	4	0	7	0
Garrett, Hal, R.C.	.778	23	3	4	2	9	0
Gates, Sean, R.C.	1.000	1	0	1	0	1	0
Gomez, Dennys, San Jose	1.000	13	1	4	0	5	0
Gomez, Marcial, Lake Elsinore	1.000	7	2	1	0	3	0
Gomez, Pat, San Jose*	1.000	3	0	1	0	1	0
Griffin, Ryan, High Desert	.878	31	13	23	5	41	0
Hackett, Jason, High Desert*	1.000	18	2	5	0	7	0
Hanson, Craig, R.C.	.750	9	2	1	1	4	0
Hartmann, Pete, Stockton*	1.000	12	2	2	0	4	0
Hartvigson, Chad, San Jose*	.917	32	0	11	1	12	0

Player, Team	Pct.	G	PO	A	E	TC	DP
Hathaway, Hilly, R.C.*	1.000	3	1	3	0	4	0
Haught, Gary, Modesto	.893	34	3	22	3	28	1
Hecker, Doug, Visalia	1.000	2	0	1	0	1	0
Herges, Matt, San Bernardino	.857	22	3	9	2	14	0
Hermanson, Mike, R.C.	1.000	42	3	6	0	9	0
Hill, Chris, High Desert*	1.000	5	0	1	0	1	0
Hinchliffe, Brett, Riverside	.875	15	2	12	2	16	0
Hinson, Dean, Vis.-L.E.	.909	28	4	6	1	11	1
Holdridge, David, Lake Elsinore	1.000	12	4	1	0	5	1
Holtz, Mike, Lake Elsinore*	.733	56	5	6	4	15	1
Howry, Bobby, San Jose	.969	27	14	17	1	32	3
Hyde, Rich, San Jose	1.000	16	1	1	0	2	0
Idemoto, Kenichiro, Visalia*	.846	31	3	19	4	26	2
Iglesias, Mike, Bak.-S.B.	.960	28	5	19	1	25	0
Ippolito, Rob, Riverside	1.000	35	4	7	0	11	0
Isom, Jeff, R.C.*	1.000	4	0	1	0	1	0
Jacobsen, Joe, San Bernardino	1.000	4	1	0	0	1	0
James, Mike, Lake Elsinore	.000	5	0	0	1	1	0
Janicki, Pete, Lake Elsinore	.833	20	6	14	4	24	1
Jaye, Jamie, Bakersfield*	1.000	5	0	4	0	4	0
Jenkins, Jon, Visalia	.833	33	1	9	2	12	0
Jimenez, Miguel, Modesto	1.000	4	2	2	0	4	0
Karns, Tim, High Desert	1.000	7	1	0	0	1	0
Keagle, Greg, R.C.	1.000	2	1	0	0	1	0
Kenady, Jake, Bakersfield*	.813	3	3	10	3	16	1
Kramer, Jeff, Stockton	.927	32	19	19	3	41	1
Kubinski, Tim, Modesto*	1.000	25	6	22	0	28	2
Kyslinger, Dan, Stockton	.857	37	3	3	1	7	0
LaChappa, Matt, R.C.*	.964	28	12	15	1	28	0
LaGarde, Joe, S.B.-Bak.	.943	28	19	31	3	53	3
LaRocca, Todd, High Desert	.889	15	13	11	3	27	1
Linares, Rich, Bakersfield	.944	55	6	11	1	18	0
Linares, Yfrain, Stockton	.714	7	3	2	2	7	1
Locklear, Dean, Visalia*	1.000	9	2	10	0	12	0
Macey, Fausto, San Jose	.922	28	9	38	4	51	3
Magnelli, Anthony, Visalia	.923	29	3	9	1	13	0
Manning, Derek, Modesto*	.923	25	7	17	2	26	2
Martin, Jeff, San Jose	.857	36	2	4	1	7	0
Maurer, Mike, Modesto	1.000	39	0	3	0	3	0
McLain, Mike, San Jose	.833	9	2	3	1	6	0
Meade, Paul, Bakersfield	1.000	24	4	6	0	10	0
Meadows, Jimmy, Visalia	.902	27	16	30	5	51	3
Michalak, Chris, Modesto*	.946	44	5	30	2	37	0
Mitchell, Kendrick, Bakersfield*	.727	36	5	3	3	11	0
Montane, Ivan, Riverside	.771	24	8	19	8	35	2
Moore, Trey, Riverside*	.970	24	5	27	1	33	2
Murphy, Matt, Stockton*	1.000	5	0	2	0	2	0
Murray, Heath, R.C.*	.950	14	3	16	1	20	1
Muto, Junichiro, Visalia	1.000	17	2	4	0	6	1
Myers, Tom, Visalia*	.813	30	4	22	6	32	1
Nelson, Chris, Modesto	1.000	2	0	1	0	1	0
Newton, Geronimo, Riverside*	1.000	46	5	25	0	30	2
Ortiz, Russell, San Jose	.000	5	0	0	1	1	0
Osuna, Antonio, San Bernardino	1.000	5	0	3	0	3	0
Paluk, Jeff, San Bernardino	.909	41	2	8	1	11	0
Parra, Julio, San Bernardino	.909	14	3	7	1	11	0
Patterson, Ken, Lake Elsinore*	1.000	6	1	0	0	1	0
Paul, Andy, Stockton	.955	38	6	15	1	22	0
Pearsall, J.J., San Bernardino*	1.000	6	0	1	0	1	0
Pena, Alex, High Desert	1.000	34	12	17	0	29	1
Percibal, Billy, High Desert	1.000	21	13	19	0	32	3
Perisho, Matt, Lake Elsinore*	.944	24	3	14	1	18	0
Peters, Don, San Jose	.917	20	0	11	1	12	1
Pincavitch, Kevin, San Bernardino	.500	3	1	0	1	2	0
Pivaral, Hugo, San Jose	.813	24	6	7	3	16	1
Prater, Pete, San Jose	1.000	5	0	5	0	5	0
Price, Tom, San Bernardino*	.978	42	14	30	1	45	2
Ramos, Cesar, Bakersfield	.864	24	8	11	3	22	0
Ricabal, Dan, San Bernardino	.933	43	8	6	1	15	1
Rigby, Brad, Modesto	.938	31	12	18	2	32	3
Roach, Peter, San Bernardino*	.909	30	2	8	1	11	2
Rodriguez, Nerio, High Desert	1.000	7	1	1	0	2	0
Rogers, Jason, High Desert*	.875	5	2	5	1	8	0
Rogers, Kevin, San Jose*	1.000	4	0	2	0	2	0
Rolocut, Brian, San Bernardino	1.000	11	1	2	0	3	1
Rosenkranz, Terry, Stockton*	.857	35	4	2	1	7	0
Rossiter, Michael, Modesto	1.000	18	3	7	0	10	0
Rowland, Thad, Visalia*	1.000	7	1	1	0	2	0
Ryan, Reid, Visalia	.875	12	1	6	1	8	0
Sadler, Al, Stockton	1.000	37	11	13	0	24	0
Salazar, Luis, Stockton	.933	52	6	22	2	30	1
Saneaux, Francisco, High Desert	.625	23	2	3	3	8	0
Santana, Marino, Riverside	.889	9	5	3	1	9	0
Saurtich, Chris, High Desert	1.000	7	2	1	0	3	0
Sawyer, Zach, Modesto	.733	55	7	4	4	15	0
Scafa, Bob, Bakersfield*	.885	42	1	22	3	26	0
Scheffler, Craig, Bakersfield*	.852	32	3	20	4	27	1
Schenbeck, T.J., Stockton	.929	31	6	7	1	14	0
Schlutt, Jason, R.C.*	1.000	11	1	2	0	3	0
Schramm, Carl, San Jose	1.000	37	6	17	0	23	0
Seanez, Rudy, San Bernardino	1.000	4	0	1	0	1	0
Sebach, Kyle, Lake Elsinore	1.000	14	5	11	0	16	0
Seki, Kiyokazu, Visalia	.941	35	5	11	1	17	1
Shenk, Larry, High Desert	1.000	2	1	0	0	1	0
Slade, Shawn, Lake Elsinore	1.000	15	1	2	0	3	0
Smith, Hut, High Desert	.833	11	4	11	3	18	1
Smith, Ryan, Riverside	.977	23	21	21	1	43	3
Spiller, Derron, Visalia*	.900	32	0	9	1	10	0
Stone, Ricky, San Bernardino	.882	12	9	6	2	17	0
Sullivan, Dan, Riverside	.913	53	8	13	2	23	1
Suzuki, Mac, Riverside	.500	6	1	0	1	2	0
Tapia, Elias, Bakersfield	.867	17	3	10	2	15	0
Taulbee, Andy, San Jose	.923	11	1	11	1	13	0
Theron, Greg, Riverside	.941	40	4	12	1	17	1
Thomas, Robbie, Bakersfield*	.667	26	2	4	3	9	0
Trimarco, Mike, High Desert	.917	40	7	15	2	24	1
Urbina, William, Modesto	1.000	30	1	10	0	11	1
Vanhof, John, Riverside*	.857	4	0	6	1	7	0
Villano, Mike, San Jose	1.000	21	3	3	0	6	0
Wada, Takashi, Visalia	1.000	17	1	9	0	10	2
Wagner, Ron, Stockton	.826	20	4	15	4	23	0
Walsh, Matthew, Modesto	1.000	44	3	10	0	13	2
Watson, Ron, Lake Elsinore	1.000	10	1	0	0	1	0
Webb, Doug, Stockton	.889	32	5	3	1	9	0
Whitaker, Ryan, Modesto	.936	32	12	32	3	47	0
Whitaker, Steve, San Jose*	1.000	2	0	2	0	2	0
White, Darell, R.C.	.941	42	7	9	1	17	0
Whitman, Ryan, R.C.	.750	14	1	2	1	4	1
Williams, Matt, Bakersfield*	1.000	7	3	4	0	7	0
Williard, Brian, Lake Elsinore	.941	29	7	9	1	17	2
Wilson, Trevor, San Jose*	1.000	2	0	1	0	1	0
Wilstead, Judd, Stockton	.960	31	8	16	1	25	1
Winchester, Marty, Riverside*	.950	35	2	17	1	20	1
Wolff, Bryan, R.C.	.833	54	1	4	1	6	0
Worley, Robert, Riverside	.647	11	5	6	6	17	0
Worrell, Tim, R.C.	.857	9	2	4	1	7	0
Wunsch, Kelly, Stockton*	.929	14	3	10	1	14	0
York, Charles, Bakersfield*	.938	31	2	13	1	16	0
Yoshida, Atsushi, Visalia	.952	13	2	18	1	21	1
ZERBE, Chad, San Bernardino*...	1.000	28	14	47	0	61	1
Zongor, Steven, Modesto*	.917	37	2	9	1	12	1

PITCHERS WITH TWO OR MORE TEAMS

Player, Team	Pct.	G	PO	A	E	TC	DP
DeClue, Jon, Visalia*	.923	21	3	21	2	26	0
DeClue, Jon, Lake Elsinore*	1.000	9	2	1	0	3	0
Hinson, Dean, Visalia	.900	23	4	5	1	10	0
Hinson, Dean, Lake Elsinore	1.000	5	0	1	0	1	1
Iglesias, Mike, Bakersfield	.958	24	4	19	1	24	0
Iglesias, Mike, San Bernardino	1.000	4	1	0	0	1	0
LaGarde, Joe, San Bernardino	.939	24	17	29	3	49	3
LaGarde, Joe, Bakersfield	1.000	4	2	2	0	4	0

The following players did not have any fielding statistics at the positions indicated or appeared only as a designated hitter, pinch-hitter or pinch-runner: L. Aquino, p; Boskie, p; Carrasquel, 3b; Clark, 1b, ss, of, c, p; Cook, 3b; Cuevas, of; D. Davis, dh; Dobrolsky, p; Erdos, p; Fitzpatrick, dh, ph; Gambs, p; Henrikson, p; Hollandsworth, of; Hostetler, dh, ph; Huber, p; Ibarra, dh, ph; Keene, of; McGonigle, p; Mowry, of; Nomo, p; Oropesa, p; Paulino, 3b; Pricher, p; Rivera, 1b; L. Roberts, dh; Short, ss; Sturdivant, 1b; Takayoshi, p; Thielen, 3b; VanLandingham, p; Zahner, of.

LEAGUE CHAMPIONS

Year	Team	Pct.
1914—	Fresno	.571
1915—	Modesto	.857
1916-40—Did not operate.		
1941—	Fresno	.643
	Santa Barbara (2nd)*	.597
1942—	Santa Barbara†	.642
1943-44-45—Did not operate.		
1946—	Stockton‡	.600
1947—	Stockton‡	.679
1948—	Fresno‡	.607
	Santa Barbara (3rd)*	.529
1949—	Bakersfield	.612
	San Jose (4th)*	.543
1950—	Ventura	.607
	Modesto (2nd)*	.586
1951—	Santa Barbara‡	.599
1952—	Fresno†	.629
1953—	San Jose‡	.664
1954—	Modesto‡	.623
1955—	Stockton	.733
	Fresno§	.718
1956—	Fresno§	.650
1957—	Visalia∞	.622
	Salinas (4th)*	.504
1958—	Fresno*	.639
	Bakersfield	.672
1959—	Bakersfield	.592
	Modesto§	.643
1960—	Reno	.614
	Reno	.657
1961—	Reno	.743
	Reno	.643
1962—	San Jose§	.686
	Reno	.587

Year	Team	Pct.
1963—	Modesto	.589
	Stockton§	.687
1964—	Fresno	.638
	Fresno	.600
1965—	San Jose	.586
	Stockton§	.614
1966—	Modesto	.577
	Modesto	.671
1967—	San Jose§	.676
	Modesto	.586
1968—	San Jose	.629
	Fresno§	.623
1969—	Stockton§	.600
	Visalia	.614
1970—	Bakersfield	.667
	Bakersfield	.671
1971—	Visalia§	.583
	Fresno	.500
1972—	Modesto§	.547
	Bakersfield	.629
1973—	Lodi§	.657
	Bakersfield	.571
1974—	Fresno§	.607
	San Jose	.579
1975—	Reno	.614
	Reno	.614
1976—	Salinas	.650
	Reno§	.547
1977—	Salinas	.564
	Lodi§	.579
1978—	Visalia§	.698
	Lodi	.607
1979—	San Jose§	.636
	Reno	.525

Year	Team	Pct.
1980—	Stockton§	.638
	Visalia	.507
1981—	Visalia	.621
	Lodi§	.521
1982—	Modesto§	.671
	Visalia	.586
1983—	Visalia	.621
	Redwood§	.529
1984—	Modesto§	.597
	Bakersfield	.486
1985—	Fresno§	.575
	Stockton	.566
1986—	Palm Springs	.613
	Stockton§	.585
1987—	Fresno§	.559
	Reno	.535
1988—	Stockton	.657
	Riverside§	.599
1989—	Stockton	.627
	Bakersfield§	.577
1990—	Visalia	.638
	Stockton§	.582
1991—	San Jose	.676
	High Desert§	.537
1992—	Stockton§	.610
	Visalia	.551
1993—	High Desert§	.620
	Modesto	.529
1994—	Modesto	.706
	Rancho Cucamonga§	.566
1995—	San Bernardino§	.612
	San Jose	.550

*Won four-club playoff. †League disbanded June 28. ‡Won championship and four-club playoff. §Won split-season playoff. ∞Won both halves of split season.

CAROLINA LEAGUE

LEAGUE OFFICE

President/treasurer
John Hopkins
Address
P.O. Box 9503
Greensboro, NC 27429
Phone
910-691-9030

Teams (affiliation)
Durham Bulls (Braves)
Frederick Keys (Orioles)
Kinston Indians (Indians)
Lynchburg Hillcats (Pirates)
Prince William Cannons (White Sox)
Salem Avalanche (Rockies)

Wilmington Blue Rocks (Royals)
Winston-Salem Warthogs (Reds)

1995 FINAL STANDINGS

FIRST HALF

NORTHERN DIVISION

Team	W	L	T	Pct.	GB
Prince William (White Sox)	37	33	0	.529	......
Wilmington (Royals)	35	34	0	.507	1½
Lynchburg (Pirates)	33	36	0	.478	3½
Frederick (Orioles)	27	41	0	.397	9

SOUTHERN DIVISION

Team	W	L	T	Pct.	GB
Kinston (Indians)	45	24	0	.652	......
Winston-Salem (Reds)	36	34	0	.514	9½
Salem (Rockies)	34	36	0	.486	11½
Durham (Braves)	30	39	0	.435	15

SECOND HALF

NORTHERN DIVISION

Team	W	L	T	Pct.	GB
Wilmington (Royals)	48	21	0	.696	......
Lynchburg (Pirates)	34	35	0	.493	14
Frederick (Orioles)	31	38	0	.449	17
Prince William (White Sox)	27	43	0	.386	21½

SOUTHERN DIVISION

Team	W	L	T	Pct.	GB
Kinston (Indians)	36	32	0	.529	......
Winston-Salem (Reds)	33	34	0	.493	2½
Salem (Rockies)	34	36	0	.486	3
Durham (Braves)	33	37	0	.471	4

COMPOSITE

Team	Wil.	Kin.	W.S.	Sal.	Lyn.	P.W.	Dur.	Fre.	W	L	T	Pct.	GB
Wilmington (Royals)	....	9	10	11	11	15	13	14	83	55	0	.601	......
Kinston (Indians)	11	....	9	15	10	10	13	13	81	56	0	.591	1½
Winston-Salem (Reds)	10	9	....	8	10	12	13	7	69	68	0	.504	13½
Salem (Rockies)	9	5	12	....	13	7	9	13	68	72	0	.486	16
Lynchburg (Pirates)	8	10	10	7	....	12	12	8	67	71	0	.486	16
Prince William (White Sox)	5	10	8	13	8	....	8	12	64	76	0	.457	20
Durham (Braves)	7	7	7	11	7	12	....	12	63	76	0	.453	20½
Frederick (Orioles)	5	6	12	7	12	8	8	....	58	79	0	.423	24½

Major league affiliations in parentheses.

PLAYOFFS: Wilmington defeated Prince William, two games to none; Kinston defeated Wilmington, three games to none, to win league championship.

REGULAR-SEASON ATTENDANCE: Durham, 390,486; Frederick, 300,968; Kinston, 140,116; Lynchburg, 111,654; Prince William, 215,250; Salem, 140,111; Wilmington, 358,766; Winston-Salem, 158,842. Total, 1,816,193. Playoffs (5 games)—15,694. All-Star Game at Lynchburg—5,690.

MANAGERS: Durham, Matt West; Frederick, Mike O'Berry; Kinston, Gordy MacKenzie; Lynchburg, Marc Hill; Prince William, Dave Huppert; Salem, Bill Hayes; Wilmington, John Mizerock; Winston-Salem, Mark Berry.

ALL-STAR TEAM: 1B—Richie Sexson, Kinston; 2B—Ricky Gutierrez, Kinston; 3B—Aaron Boone, Winston-Salem; SS—Enrique Wilson, Kinston; Utility IF—Anthony Medrano, Wilmington; Edgard Velasquez, Salem; OF—James Betzsold, Kinston; Charles Peterson, Lynchburg; Utility OF—Bruce Aven, Kinston; C—Mike Sweeney, Wilmington; DH—Reed Secrist, Lynchburg; Starting Pitcher—Bartolo Colon, Kinston; Relief Pitcher—Dan Graves, Kinston; Most Valuable Player—Richie Sexson, Kinston; Pitcher of the Year—Bartolo Colon, Kinston; Manager of the Year—John Mizerock, Wilmington.

1995 BATTING

TEAM

Team	Avg.	G	TPA	AB	R	H	TB	2B	3B	HR	RBI	SH	SF	HP	BB	IBB	SO	SB	CS	GDP	LOB	ShO	Slg.	OBP
Lynchburg	.264	138	5128	4483	655	1185	1774	214	27	107	577	45	40	59	501	31	880	156	107	102	915	8	.396	.343
Wilmington	.255	138	5144	4591	550	1173	1668	204	33	75	485	70	33	57	393	24	771	135	87	89	938	4	.363	.320
Kinston	.254	137	5114	4509	605	1145	1786	222	31	119	555	35	48	63	459	30	900	139	85	63	912	8	.396	.328
Salem	.252	140	5347	4699	619	1186	1802	231	29	109	562	42	33	55	516	35	991	69	51	101	1015	13	.383	.331
Durham	.249	139	4981	4447	566	1109	1661	197	14	109	519	32	25	77	399	32	1007	150	100	101	838	16	.374	.320
Prince William	.247	140	5169	4576	572	1130	1666	210	28	90	520	24	35	57	477	26	878	96	48	135	963	9	.364	.323
Winston-Salem	.246	137	5094	4508	601	1110	1752	204	21	132	562	40	35	53	458	43	961	105	72	83	895	8	.389	.321
Frederick	.234	137	4999	4430	497	1038	1488	197	26	67	424	47	31	64	426	29	979	110	78	96	892	12	.336	.309

INDIVIDUAL

TOP QUALIFIERS FOR BATTING CHAMPIONSHIP

Minimum 378 plate appearances. *Lefthanded batter. †Switch-hitter.

Player, Team	Avg.	G	TPA	AB	R	H	TB	2B	3B	HR	RBI	SH	SF	HP	BB	IBB	SO	SB	CS	GDP	Slg.	OBP
Sweeney, Mike, Wilmington	.310	99	407	332	61	103	182	23	1	18	53	1	5	9	60	7	39	6	1	4	.548	.424
Sexson, Richie, Kinston	.306	131	554	494	80	151	251	34	0	22	85	0	7	10	43	5	115	4	6	8	.508	.368
Velazquez, Edgard, Salem	.300	131	553	497	74	149	225	25	6	13	69	3	7	4	40	4	102	7	10	17	.453	.352

Player, Team	Avg.	G	TPA	AB	R	H	TB	2B	3B	HR	RBI	SH	SF	HP	BB	IBB	SO	SB	CS	GDP	Slg.	OBP
Zapata, Ramon, Lynchburg	.298	119	469	416	59	124	179	27	2	8	45	9	0	2	42	0	58	6	8	13	.430	.365
Rodarte, Raul, Lynchburg	.286	104	388	346	57	99	157	18	2	12	48	2	1	4	35	2	49	19	13	8	.454	.358
Medrano, Anthony, Wilmington	.285	123	518	460	69	131	172	20	6	3	43	15	4	5	34	2	42	11	6	10	.374	.338
Williams, Harold, Prince William*	.282	129	534	472	56	133	207	30	1	14	72	1	2	11	48	11	98	4	2	16	.439	.360
Secrist, Reed, Lynchburg*	.282	112	442	380	60	107	188	18	3	19	75	1	4	3	54	7	88	3	4	6	.495	.372
Culp, Brian, Salem	.279	128	539	459	69	128	187	33	1	8	63	0	5	4	71	4	80	8	3	8	.407	.377
Collier, Lou, Lynchburg	.276	114	463	399	68	110	147	19	3	4	38	3	3	7	51	4	60	31	11	13	.368	.365
Peterson, Charles, Lynchburg	.274	107	447	391	61	107	145	9	4	7	51	6	5	2	43	1	73	31	17	11	.371	.345
Mendez, Carlos, Wilmington	.273	107	420	396	46	108	152	19	2	7	61	1	5	0	18	1	36	0	4	17	.384	.301
Betts, Todd, Kinston*	.272	109	430	331	52	90	138	15	3	9	44	1	4	6	88	2	56	2	3	5	.417	.429
Lopez, Mendy, Wilmington	.271	130	470	428	42	116	157	29	3	2	36	7	2	5	28	0	73	18	10	12	.367	.322
Sexton, Chris, W-S/Salem	.271	127	587	476	84	129	172	16	6	5	37	12	1	1	97	2	55	14	11	11	.361	.395

DEPARTMENTAL LEADERS: G—Menechino, 137; AB—Velazquez, 497; R—Sexton, 84; H—Sexson, 151; TB—Sexson, 251; 2B—Sexson, 34; 3B—Delaney, Gutierrez, E. Wilson, 7; HR—J. Thomas, 26; RBI—Sexson, 85; SH—Medrano, 15; SF—E. Wilson, 10; HP—Knott, 15; BB—Sexton, 97; IBB—Simon, 14; SO—J. Thomas, 156; SB—Gutierrez, 43; CS—Pagano, Valdez, 21; GIDP—Polidor, 18; Slg.—Sweeney, .548; OBP—Betts, .429.

ALL PLAYERS

*Lefthanded batter. †Switch-hitter.

Player, Team	Avg.	G	TPA	AB	R	H	TB	2B	3B	HR	RBI	SH	SF	HP	BB	IBB	SO	SB	CS	GDP	Slg.	OBP
Abbott, Jeff, Prince William	.348	70	298	264	41	92	120	16	0	4	47	1	5	2	26	0	25	7	1	8	.455	.404
Akers, Chad, Winston-Salem	.260	103	399	361	41	94	116	14	1	0	29	7	3	1	27	1	49	25	8	7	.321	.311
Anderson, Milt, Kinston†	.000	4	5	5	1	0	0	0	0	0	0	0	0	0	0	0	0	0	0	0	.000	.000
Arnold, Jamie, Durham	.000	15	2	2	1	0	0	0	0	0	0	0	0	0	0	0	0	0	0	0	.000	.000
Austin, Jake, Lynchburg*	.270	18	79	74	7	20	29	6	0	1	11	0	2	0	3	0	8	0	3	1	.392	.291
Aven, Bruce, Kinston	.261	130	534	479	70	125	227	23	5	23	69	0	1	13	41	3	109	15	9	7	.474	.335
Avila, Rolando, Frederick	.263	52	197	175	26	46	59	8	1	1	13	5	0	3	14	0	27	15	5	2	.337	.328
Bako, Paul, Winston-Salem*	.285	82	299	249	29	71	107	11	2	7	27	6	1	1	42	6	66	3	1	6	.430	.389
Benbow, Lou, Durham	.220	82	262	245	20	54	73	7	0	4	17	3	0	3	11	0	53	2	3	8	.298	.263
Bernhardt, Steven, Salem	.217	59	200	180	18	39	58	3	2	4	16	5	2	5	8	0	38	2	3	5	.322	.267
Berrios, Harry, Frederick	.208	71	278	240	33	50	89	5	2	10	28	0	2	4	32	3	66	10	6	3	.371	.309
Bess, Johnny, Winston-Salem†	.187	88	286	246	35	46	72	10	2	4	21	2	0	8	30	4	83	12	4	4	.293	.296
Betts, Todd, Kinston*	.272	109	430	331	52	90	138	15	3	9	44	1	4	6	88	2	56	2	3	5	.417	.429
Betzsold, James, Kinston	.268	126	524	455	77	122	223	22	2	25	71	0	4	10	55	3	137	3	5	4	.490	.357
Bonifay, Ken, Lynchburg*	.245	116	453	375	57	92	148	22	2	10	54	0	4	11	63	4	88	3	5	6	.395	.366
Boone, Aaron, Winston-Salem	.261	108	453	395	61	103	166	19	1	14	50	4	2	9	43	7	77	11	7	4	.420	.345
Bridgers, Brandon, Frederick	.161	10	44	31	3	5	8	3	0	0	5	1	1	0	11	0	5	1	1	0	.258	.372
Broach, Donald, Winston-Salem	.261	117	522	460	74	120	175	23	4	8	34	5	2	5	50	2	73	16	14	9	.380	.338
Brooks, Eddie, Lynchburg	.118	27	79	68	6	8	9	1	0	0	2	1	1	1	8	0	21	0	1	1	.132	.218
Brooks, Ramy, Wilmington	.218	94	359	326	41	71	111	16	0	8	30	1	1	6	25	1	82	2	1	7	.340	.285
Brown, Adrian, Lynchburg†	.242	54	233	215	30	52	64	5	2	1	14	4	1	1	12	0	20	11	6	3	.298	.284
Brown, Ray, Winston-Salem*	.265	122	512	445	63	118	201	26	0	19	77	0	4	11	52	12	85	3	2	8	.452	.354
Brown, Todd, Frederick†	.237	32	69	59	6	14	18	4	0	0	2	4	0	1	5	0	21	6	2	1	.305	.308
Buchanan, Shawn, Prince William	.000	4	1	1	2	0	0	0	0	0	0	0	0	0	0	0	0	0	0	0	.000	.000
Byington, Jimmie, Wilmington	.223	92	295	273	24	61	69	6	1	0	23	3	2	4	13	0	33	12	6	3	.253	.267
Byrne, Clayton, Frederick	.228	35	142	136	16	31	47	7	0	3	13	0	0	0	5	0	29	3	4	4	.346	.255
Cabrera, Jairo, Frederick	.183	25	70	60	7	11	12	1	0	0	1	2	0	1	7	0	13	0	1	1	.200	.279
Canetto, John, Lynchburg†	.250	13	32	28	5	7	9	2	0	0	2	0	1	0	3	0	13	0	0	0	.321	.313
Carpenter, Matt, Salem	.000	1	1	0	0	0	0	0	0	0	0	0	0	1	0	0	0	0	0	0	.000	1.000
Carr, Jeremy, Wilmington	.231	5	14	13	1	3	4	1	0	0	0	0	0	0	1	0	3	0	1	0	.308	.286
Carranza, Pete, Salem	.216	18	60	51	9	11	25	2	0	4	8	0	0	0	9	0	8	2	0	0	.490	.333
Castaneda, Hector, Frederick*	.213	17	56	47	6	10	13	1	1	0	4	2	1	0	6	0	9	0	0	2	.277	.296
Cawhorn, Gerad, Kinston	.210	85	300	262	23	55	70	12	0	1	22	5	2	2	29	2	60	4	1	7	.267	.292
Claudio, Patricio, Kinston	.265	89	330	298	37	79	109	7	4	5	27	5	1	0	26	2	73	27	11	2	.366	.323
Clyburn, Danny, W-S/Fre.	.250	74	297	272	31	68	119	14	2	11	45	0	2	6	17	1	77	3	5	5	.438	.306
Collier, Lou, Lynchburg	.276	114	463	399	68	110	147	19	3	4	38	3	3	7	51	4	60	31	11	13	.368	.365
Conger, Jeff, Lynchburg*	.264	90	369	318	44	84	116	13	5	3	23	7	3	6	35	1	74	26	16	1	.365	.345
Cornelius, Brian, Lynchburg*	.154	12	44	39	2	6	9	3	0	0	4	1	0	0	4	0	11	0	1	1	.231	.233
Correa, Miguel, Durham†	.236	118	425	398	43	94	172	19	1	19	70	2	3	3	19	2	95	9	13	6	.432	.274
Cradle, Cobi, Winston-Salem*	.183	23	94	71	14	13	15	2	0	0	2	1	1	0	21	0	8	9	2	0	.211	.393
Culp, Brian, Salem	.279	128	539	459	69	128	187	33	1	8	63	0	5	4	71	4	80	8	3	8	.407	.377
Daniel, Mike, Salem	.284	50	202	169	31	48	91	11	1	10	35	2	1	1	29	4	36	0	2	7	.538	.390
Davis, Tommy, Frederick	.268	130	545	496	62	133	210	26	3	15	57	1	3	4	41	7	105	7	1	14	.423	.323
Delaney, Donovan, Wilmington	.250	114	395	360	22	90	126	13	7	3	39	4	2	4	25	0	82	6	9	8	.350	.304
Dellucci, David, Frederick*	.281	28	111	96	16	27	33	3	0	1	10	0	0	3	12	1	10	1	2	3	.344	.378
Diaz, Einar, Kinston	.263	104	398	373	46	98	137	21	0	6	43	1	4	8	12	2	29	3	6	6	.367	.290
Diaz, Lino, Wilmington	.301	51	190	173	20	52	68	6	2	2	23	2	0	4	11	0	9	0	5	2	.393	.356
Dixon, Colin, Salem	.291	57	240	220	25	64	94	13	1	5	30	0	2	5	13	1	30	0	0	10	.427	.342
Durso, Joe, Prince William	.213	58	198	178	16	38	57	3	2	4	22	1	1	2	16	1	31	0	0	2	.320	.284
Evans, Michael, Wilmington*	.218	96	351	317	26	69	110	15	4	3	36	4	1	2	27	3	79	0	2	8	.347	.282
Fasano, Sal, Wilmington	.227	23	94	88	12	20	30	2	1	2	7	0	0	1	5	0	16	0	0	4	.341	.277
Foster, Jim, Frederick	.261	128	493	429	44	112	163	27	3	6	56	0	5	8	51	5	63	2	3	10	.380	.345
Fraraccio, Dan, Prince William	.230	24	83	74	11	17	28	5	0	2	6	1	0	0	8	0	12	0	0	1	.378	.305
French, Anton, Durham†	.269	7	30	26	3	7	8	1	0	0	2	0	0	1	3	0	2	4	1	0	.308	.367
Frye, Dan, Winston-Salem	.182	7	16	11	3	2	6	1	0	1	2	0	0	0	5	0	4	0	0	0	.545	.438
Gann, Steve, Winston-Salem	.244	15	48	41	5	10	12	2	0	0	5	2	1	0	5	0	13	5	0	1	.293	.304
Garcia, Adrian, Durham	.250	5	16	12	2	3	4	1	0	0	2	0	0	0	4	0	4	0	0	0	.333	.438
Garcia, Guillermo, Winston-Salem	.237	78	278	245	26	58	81	10	2	3	29	2	2	1	28	0	32	2	2	0	.331	.315
Garcia, Jesse, Frederick	.225	124	432	365	52	82	107	13	3	3	27	7	2	9	49	0	75	5	10	3	.296	.329
Garcia, Vincente, Salem	.243	119	518	457	62	111	169	26	1	10	41	5	2	1	53	3	73	5	0	10	.370	.322
Gargiulo, Mike, Frederick*	.273	6	12	11	1	3	3	0	0	0	0	0	0	1	0	0	4	0	0	0	.273	.333
Giudice, John, Salem	.258	99	387	356	49	92	142	21	4	7	48	0	3	4	24	2	81	7	4	7	.399	.310
Goligoski, Jason, Prince William*	.217	95	360	300	42	65	76	7	2	0	24	2	3	4	52	0	47	16	5	4	.253	.335

Player, Team	Avg.	G	TPA	AB	R	H	TB	2B	3B	HR	RBI	SH	SF	HP	BB	IBB	SO	SB	CS	GDP	Slg.	OBP
Gonzalez, Paul, Prince William*	.207	92	328	290	25	60	91	10	0	7	34	1	3	3	31	3	85	1	1	7	.314	.287
Gonzalez, Raul, Wilmington	.292	86	334	308	36	90	148	19	3	11	49	3	7	2	14	3	34	6	4	3	.481	.320
Grunewald, Keith, Salem†	.265	118	473	412	48	109	151	22	1	6	45	2	3	10	46	8	84	8	4	8	.367	.350
Gutierrez, Ricky, Kinston	.262	117	521	439	63	115	162	21	7	4	46	7	4	4	67	3	62	43	16	3	.369	.362
Hagy, Gary, Kinston	.134	52	162	142	12	19	31	3	0	3	9	5	2	1	12	1	34	3	2	1	.218	.204
Hanel, Marcus, Lynchburg	.185	40	142	135	14	25	40	4	1	3	8	2	0	1	4	0	33	0	1	1	.296	.214
Harriss, Robin, Kinston	.245	15	54	49	8	12	23	3	1	2	6	1	1	0	3	0	8	0	0	1	.469	.283
Hawkins, Wes, Frederick	.211	78	219	199	13	42	56	10	2	0	16	4	1	4	11	0	49	4	1	9	.281	.265
Hendricks, Ryan, Frederick*	.133	5	17	15	1	2	6	1	0	1	3	0	0	0	2	0	6	0	0	1	.400	.235
Hicks, Jamie, Durham	.219	41	111	105	9	23	29	6	0	0	14	0	1	0	5	2	18	0	2	5	.276	.252
Higgins, Mike, Salem	.241	53	182	158	9	38	47	9	0	0	18	2	4	1	17	1	30	1	3	0	.297	.311
Hodge, Roy, Frederick	.256	48	191	172	19	44	61	12	1	1	17	0	2	1	16	0	31	4	3	8	.355	.319
Holdren, Nate, Salem	.245	119	464	420	48	103	168	16	2	15	69	2	2	6	34	0	126	6	3	7	.400	.310
House, Mitch, Lynchburg	.180	16	61	50	7	9	15	3	0	1	6	0	1	1	9	1	13	0	1	2	.300	.311
Hugo, Sean, Frederick*	.281	29	112	89	13	25	41	4	0	4	13	0	2	0	21	1	24	0	0	4	.461	.411
Hunter, Lanier, Frederick†	.143	7	15	14	1	2	3	1	0	0	0	0	0	0	1	0	7	0	0	0	.214	.200
Izquierdo, Sergio, Prince William	.188	10	36	32	6	6	8	2	0	0	2	0	0	2	2	0	3	0	0	2	.250	.278
Jacobs, Ryan, Durham	.000	29	1	1	0	0	0	0	0	0	0	0	0	0	0	0	0	0	0	0	.000	.000
Jenkins, Demetrish, Winst.-Salem*	.289	50	168	149	25	43	64	7	1	4	14	0	1	0	18	0	25	0	6	1	.430	.363
Jimenez, Manny, Durham	.245	121	400	375	40	92	118	16	2	2	23	3	0	5	17	1	71	8	6	11	.315	.287
Jimenez, Oscar, Wilmington	.251	121	446	374	42	94	123	18	4	1	31	6	3	10	53	2	92	11	8	3	.329	.357
Johnson, Todd, Kinston	.232	21	58	56	4	13	17	2	1	0	9	2	0	0	0	0	13	0	0	3	.304	.232
Jones, Pookie, Salem	.208	16	58	53	9	11	17	3	0	1	3	1	0	1	3	0	16	1	1	4	.321	.263
King, Andre, Dur.-P.W.	.245	120	519	453	63	111	169	23	4	9	36	6	4	10	45	1	135	16	13	7	.373	.324
Kirgan, Chris, Frederick*	.201	124	410	378	25	76	131	18	2	11	47	1	3	3	25	3	107	3	2	7	.347	.254
Knoblauh, Jay, Lynchburg	.277	87	292	264	40	73	117	16	2	8	47	1	5	6	16	0	62	3	2	3	.443	.326
Knott, John, Durham	.267	112	426	344	55	92	145	14	3	11	46	2	2	15	63	2	100	11	13	5	.422	.401
Knowles, Brian, Wilmington	.000	9	27	25	1	0	0	0	0	0	1	2	0	0	0	0	5	0	0	2	.000	.074
Kopriva, Dan, Winston-Salem	.345	17	64	58	4	20	26	4	1	0	5	0	1	1	4	0	6	1	0	2	.448	.391
Lamb, David, Frederick†	.222	124	497	436	39	97	121	14	2	2	34	8	5	10	38	5	81	6	7	10	.278	.279
Larkin, Stephen, Winston-Salem*	.220	13	54	50	2	11	12	1	0	0	4	0	1	0	3	1	12	2	2	0	.240	.259
Leary, Rob, Lynchburg*	.260	63	259	208	42	54	87	9	0	8	31	0	2	5	44	4	43	9	4	3	.418	.398
LeCronier, Jason, Frederick*	.282	40	143	131	17	37	65	8	1	6	19	0	0	2	12	2	40	1	0	3	.496	.343
Lemons, Rich, Kinston*	.250	5	14	12	1	3	4	1	0	0	0	0	0	0	2	0	4	1	0	1	.333	.357
Lezeau, James, Salem*	.000	4	6	5	0	0	0	0	0	0	0	0	0	0	1	0	3	0	0	1	.000	.167
Lofton, James, Winston-Salem†	.220	38	134	123	15	27	34	5	1	0	14	2	0	1	8	1	22	1	4	0	.276	.273
Lopez, Mendy, Wilmington	.271	130	470	428	42	116	157	29	3	2	36	7	2	5	28	0	73	18	10	12	.367	.322
Machado, Robert, Prince William	.254	83	322	272	37	69	101	14	0	6	31	2	1	7	40	5	47	0	0	6	.371	.363
Mader, Chris, Kinston	.074	11	30	27	1	2	2	0	0	0	2	1	0	1	1	0	5	0	0	0	.074	.138
Magdaleno, Ricky, Winston-Salem..	.223	91	332	309	30	69	105	13	1	7	40	3	3	2	15	0	69	3	1	4	.340	.261
Magee, Danny, Durham	.256	76	290	266	38	68	93	11	1	4	29	1	0	12	11	0	46	7	5	5	.350	.315
Manto, Jeff, Frederick	.375	2	8	8	1	3	6	0	0	1	3	0	0	0	0	1	0	0	0	0	.750	.375
McBride, Gator, Durham	.236	102	422	360	60	85	141	15	1	13	59	1	2	5	54	1	109	11	4	5	.392	.342
McKinnon, Sandy, Prince William	.253	125	540	494	64	125	160	19	5	2	23	3	1	3	39	0	93	35	17	6	.324	.311
Medrano, Anthony, Wilmington	.285	123	518	460	69	131	172	20	6	3	43	15	4	5	34	2	42	11	6	10	.374	.338
Meggers, Mike, Winston-Salem	.246	76	309	272	45	67	147	18	1	20	54	0	4	1	32	5	69	7	3	5	.540	.324
Meluskey, Mitch, Kinston†	.241	8	31	29	5	7	12	5	0	0	2	0	0	0	2	0	9	0	0	1	.414	.290
Mendez, Carlos, Wilmington	.273	107	420	396	46	108	152	19	2	7	61	1	5	0	18	1	36	0	4	17	.384	.301
Mendez, Sergio, Lynchburg	.246	65	252	236	30	58	95	13	0	8	35	2	2	3	9	1	49	9	4	9	.403	.280
Menechino, Frank, Prince William	.261	137	594	476	65	124	179	31	3	6	58	3	8	11	96	2	75	6	2	17	.376	.391
Michael, Jeff, Frederick	.246	66	236	203	19	50	62	12	0	0	17	5	3	1	24	1	46	3	4	4	.305	.325
Monds, Wonderful, Durham	.279	81	317	297	44	83	118	17	0	6	33	1	1	1	17	1	63	28	7	7	.397	.320
Montilla, Julio, Wilmington†	.222	8	32	27	0	6	6	0	0	0	1	1	0	0	4	0	6	0	0	0	.222	.323
Murphy, Mike, Kinston	.232	67	197	177	26	41	50	6	0	1	15	1	1	3	15	1	30	13	4	2	.282	.301
Newell, Brett, Durham	.215	33	87	79	10	17	18	1	0	0	3	2	1	1	4	0	20	0	1	2	.228	.259
Newhouse, Andre, Prince William	.213	78	278	258	28	55	73	10	1	2	21	1	2	1	16	0	59	7	2	6	.283	.260
Nunez, Ramon, Durham	.370	17	64	54	13	20	39	4	0	5	15	1	1	0	8	0	9	0	0	4	.722	.444
Nunez, Sergio, Wilmington	.237	124	528	460	63	109	135	10	2	4	25	13	1	3	51	4	66	33	19	8	.293	.317
Oglesby, Luke, Wilmington*	.200	53	69	60	18	12	12	0	0	0	1	4	0	1	4	0	21	19	6	0	.200	.262
Ordonez, Magglio, Prince William	.238	131	535	487	61	116	180	24	2	12	65	0	4	3	41	0	71	11	5	16	.370	.299
Oyas, Danny, Winston-Salem	.214	50	190	173	19	37	67	6	0	8	31	3	2	2	10	0	45	1	1	6	.387	.262
Pagan, Angel, Frederick	.194	31	78	72	8	14	22	3	1	1	6	1	0	0	5	0	19	0	1	2	.306	.247
Pagano, Scott, Durham†	.266	110	405	354	47	94	111	12	1	1	26	7	1	5	38	5	75	41	21	8	.314	.344
Paul, Kortney, Wilmington	.111	8	11	9	1	1	1	0	0	0	0	1	0	0	1	0	2	0	0	1	.111	.200
Peterson, Charles, Lynchburg	.274	107	447	391	61	107	145	9	4	7	51	6	5	2	43	1	73	31	17	11	.371	.345
Polidor, Wil, Prince William†	.249	95	362	346	34	86	108	14	4	0	24	5	2	0	9	0	33	2	6	18	.312	.266
Pozo, Yohel, Salem	.170	43	142	135	7	23	27	4	0	0	3	4	0	1	2	0	21	0	1	4	.200	.188
Prieto, Rick, Kinston†	.193	26	102	88	12	17	24	2	1	1	10	1	0	0	13	0	20	3	1	2	.273	.297
Quillin, Ty, Frederick*	.122	16	45	41	4	5	5	0	0	0	3	0	0	0	4	0	15	0	1	0	.122	.200
Reynolds, Chance, Lynchburg†	.200	5	20	15	0	3	3	0	0	0	2	0	0	2	3	0	2	1	0	1	.200	.400
Richardson, Eric, Prince William	.167	9	19	18	2	3	3	0	0	0	1	0	0	0	1	0	3	0	1	2	.167	.211
Riemer, Matt, Frederick	.182	27	81	77	6	14	19	2	0	1	10	0	0	0	4	0	22	0	1	1	.247	.222
Robertson, Robbie, Winst.-Salem*	.216	91	304	278	34	60	95	11	0	8	32	1	2	1	22	3	77	2	4	7	.342	.274
Robertson, Tommy, Lynchburg*	.273	61	185	161	16	44	54	7	0	1	23	1	2	1	20	2	41	3	7	2	.335	.353
Rodarte, Raul, Lynchburg	.286	104	388	346	57	99	157	18	2	12	48	2	1	4	35	2	49	19	13	8	.454	.358
Rodriguez, Roman, Lynchburg	.254	44	143	130	11	33	37	4	0	0	9	3	1	2	7	0	25	1	0	9	.285	.300
Sanford, Chance, Lynchburg*	.333	16	74	66	8	22	35	4	3	1	14	0	1	0	7	0	13	1	0	1	.530	.392
Sauritch, Chris, Frederick†	.067	9	23	15	2	1	1	0	0	0	1	0	0	3	5	0	6	2	1	0	.067	.391
Scalzitti, Will, Salem	.200	11	41	35	4	7	8	1	0	0	1	0	1	4	1	5	0	1	1	.229	.300
Secrist, Reed, Lynchburg*	.282	112	442	380	60	107	188	18	3	19	75	1	4	3	54	7	88	3	4	6	.495	.372
Sexson, Richie, Kinston	.306	131	554	494	80	151	251	34	0	22	85	0	7	10	43	5	115	4	6	8	.508	.368
Sexton, Chris, W-S/Salem	.271	127	587	476	84	129	172	16	6	5	37	12	1	1	97	2	55	14	11	11	.361	.395
Short, Rick, Frederick	.077	5	14	13	1	1	1	0	0	0	2	0	0	0	1	0	2	1	0	0	.077	.143

Player, Team	Avg.	G	TPA	AB	R	H	TB	2B	3B	HR	RBI	SH	SF	HP	BB	IBB	SO	SB	CS	GDP	Slg.	OBP
Simon, Randall, Durham*	.264	122	466	420	56	111	185	18	1	18	79	0	5	5	36	14	63	6	5	15	.440	.326
Smith, Jason, Salem	.093	30	99	86	4	8	14	1	1	1	5	1	0	1	11	0	38	0	0	1	.163	.204
Smith, Sean, Durham*	.280	32	103	93	10	26	43	8	0	3	13	1	0	0	9	1	22	1	0	3	.462	.343
Snyder, Randy, Salem	.289	23	95	76	19	22	36	5	0	3	14	0	0	1	18	0	13	2	1	3	.474	.432
Spinello, Joe, Prince William	.133	10	32	30	1	4	5	1	0	0	2	1	0	1	0	0	9	0	0	2	.167	.161
Sweeney, Mike, Wilmington	.310	99	407	332	61	103	182	23	1	18	53	1	5	9	60	7	39	6	1	4	.548	.424
Teeters, Brian, Wilmington*	.228	64	184	162	25	37	62	7	0	6	26	2	0	1	19	1	51	11	5	3	.383	.313
Thomas, Greg, Kinston*	.219	102	365	329	32	72	126	21	0	11	43	1	7	3	25	4	98	0	2	2	.383	.275
Thomas, Juan, Prince William	.235	132	515	464	64	109	215	20	4	26	69	1	2	8	40	4	156	4	5	16	.463	.305
Thomas, Rod, Winston-Salem	.222	20	63	54	7	12	20	2	0	2	7	0	0	1	8	0	22	2	3	0	.370	.333
Toth, Dave, Durham	.245	85	289	257	20	63	87	6	0	6	26	0	1	6	25	1	42	3	3	6	.339	.325
Valdez, Trovin, Frederick†	.245	112	405	375	51	92	112	12	4	0	13	6	1	5	18	0	77	34	21	3	.299	.288
Van Slyke, Andy, Frederick*	.000	1	5	2	1	0	0	0	0	0	0	0	0	1	2	1	1	1	0	0	.000	.600
Velazquez, Edgard, Salem	.300	131	553	497	74	149	225	25	6	13	69	3	7	4	40	4	102	7	10	17	.453	.352
Walker, Joe, Prince William†	.333	1	4	3	1	1	3	0	1	0	2	0	0	0	1	0	1	0	0	0	1.000	.500
Warner, Ken, Durham	.226	51	154	137	12	31	50	11	1	2	13	3	2	0	1	0	32	1	2	1	.365	.285
Watkins, Pat, Winston-Salem	.206	27	120	107	14	22	39	3	1	4	13	1	2	0	10	0	24	1	0	5	.364	.269
Watson, Marty, Prince William	.259	23	91	85	12	22	44	3	2	5	14	0	1	0	5	0	21	2	1	4	.518	.297
Weaver, Colby, Durham	.278	8	22	18	2	5	7	2	0	0	2	0	0	0	4	0	6	0	0	0	.389	.409
Webb, Kevin, Durham	.182	43	144	121	17	22	41	4	0	5	11	0	1	4	18	0	39	2	0	5	.339	.306
Wells, Forry, Salem*	.254	119	469	402	60	102	187	23	4	18	67	3	1	7	56	6	105	6	3	2	.465	.354
Wells, Mark, Salem*	.195	66	252	236	24	46	84	8	0	10	31	1	1	1	13	3	83	0	3	2	.356	.239
White, Jimmy, Winston-Salem*	.261	31	119	111	15	29	57	5	1	7	18	1	1	2	4	0	33	1	1	1	.514	.297
Wieser, Mike, Durham	.210	28	65	62	5	13	18	2	0	1	3	0	0	1	2	0	12	0	1	0	.290	.246
Williams, Harold, Prince William*	.282	129	534	472	56	133	207	30	1	14	72	1	2	11	48	11	98	4	2	16	.439	.360
Wilson, Brian, Wilmington	.224	20	65	58	10	13	20	1	0	2	8	0	0	0	7	0	16	1	2	2	.345	.308
Wilson, Enrique, Kinston†	.267	117	505	464	55	124	180	24	7	6	52	4	10	2	25	2	38	18	19	10	.388	.305
Zapata, Ramon, Lynchburg	.298	119	469	416	59	124	179	27	2	8	45	9	0	2	42	0	58	6	8	13	.430	.365

GRAND SLAMS: Correa, Secrist, 3 each; Betts, Betzsold, Cawhorn, Collier, Davis, G. Garcia, P. Gonzalez, Gutierrez, Holdren, Magdaleno, McBride, Meggers, Menechino, Ordonez, R. Robertson, Simon, Sweeney, G. Thomas, F. Wells, M. Wells, White, 1 each.
AWARDED FIRST BASE ON CATCHER'S INTERFERENCE: Velazquez 2 (R. Brooks, S. Smith); Byrne (Johnson); King (Higgins).

PLAYERS WITH TWO OR MORE TEAMS

Player, Team	Avg.	G	TPA	AB	R	H	TB	2B	3B	HR	RBI	SH	SF	HP	BB	IBB	SO	SB	CS	GDP	Slg.	OBP
Clyburn, Danny, Winston-Salem	.260	59	246	227	27	59	106	10	2	11	41	0	2	4	13	1	59	2	4	5	.467	.309
Clyburn, Danny, Frederick	.200	15	51	45	4	9	13	4	0	0	4	0	0	2	4	0	18	1	1	0	.289	.294
King, Andre, Durham	.252	111	480	421	59	106	161	22	3	9	33	5	4	10	39	1	126	15	13	5	.382	.327
King, Andre, Prince William	.156	9	39	32	4	5	8	1	1	0	3	1	0	0	6	0	9	1	0	2	.250	.289
Sexton, Chris, Winston-Salem	.400	4	19	15	3	6	9	0	0	1	5	0	0	0	4	0	0	0	0	0	.600	.526
Sexton, Chris, Salem	.267	123	568	461	81	123	163	16	6	4	32	12	1	1	93	2	55	14	11	11	.354	.390

1995 PITCHING

TEAM

Team	W	L	Pct.	ERA	G	CG	ShO	Sv.	IP	H	TBF	R	ER	HR	SH	SF	HB	BB	IBB	SO	WP	Bk.
Wilmington	83	55	.601	2.84	138	2	17	46	1232.2	1017	5054	459	389	63	35	29	57	405	33	1005	86	13
Kinston	81	56	.591	3.24	137	8	10	37	1214.0	1056	5006	500	437	98	44	35	74	408	23	943	69	7
Winston-Salem	69	68	.504	3.33	137	12	11	30	1198.0	1065	4983	538	443	102	34	24	60	427	19	850	57	14
Prince William	64	76	.457	3.41	140	12	11	32	1206.0	1176	5147	594	524	114	40	44	58	432	28	962	81	6
Frederick	58	79	.423	3.92	137	10	11	32	1190.2	1123	5130	617	518	101	45	38	68	487	25	1018	103	16
Salem	68	72	.486	4.10	140	8	6	34	1237.0	1238	5355	667	563	115	42	34	57	536	54	871	114	22
Lynchburg	67	71	.486	4.16	138	5	9	27	1182.2	1213	5091	640	547	106	44	36	51	393	34	893	83	16
Durham	63	76	.453	4.25	139	6	3	39	1186.2	1188	5210	650	560	109	51	40	60	541	34	825	74	9

INDIVIDUAL

TOP QUALIFIERS FOR EARNED-RUN AVERAGE TITLE

Minimum 112 innings. *Lefthanded pitcher.

Pitcher, Team	W	L	Pct.	ERA	G	GS	CG	ShO	GF	Sv.	IP	H	TBF	R	ER	HR	SH	SF	HB	BB	IBB	SO	WP	Bk.
Rusch, Glendon, Wilmington*	14	6	.700	1.74	26	26	1	1	0	0	165.2	110	629	41	32	5	4	3	4	34	3	147	3	1
Colon, Bartolo, Kinston	13	3	.813	1.96	21	21	0	0	0	0	128.2	91	493	31	28	8	1	2	0	39	0	152	4	3
Byrdak, Tim, Wilmington*	11	5	.688	2.16	27	26	0	0	0	0	166.1	118	657	46	40	7	3	3	10	45	2	127	1	0
Peters, Chris, Lynchburg*	11	5	.688	2.43	24	24	3	3	0	0	144.2	126	586	57	39	5	7	4	5	35	2	132	12	1
Wright, Jamey, Salem	10	8	.556	2.47	26	26	2	1	0	0	171.0	160	732	74	47	7	3	6	13	72	3	95	16	2
Maduro, Calvin, Frederick	8	5	.615	2.94	20	20	2	2	0	0	122.1	109	493	43	40	16	3	2	6	34	0	120	2	0
Lyons, Curt, Winston-Salem	9	9	.500	2.98	26	26	0	0	0	0	160.1	139	672	66	53	10	6	2	15	67	3	122	9	3
Robbins, Jason, Winston-Salem	9	6	.600	3.06	23	23	3	1	0	0	141.0	113	571	62	48	16	0	5	7	42	1	106	5	1
Rosado, Jose, Wilmington*	10	7	.588	3.13	25	25	0	0	0	0	138.0	128	562	53	48	9	2	7	3	30	6	117	1	5
Pratt, Rich, Prince William*	5	11	.313	3.14	25	25	2	1	0	0	152.0	139	619	66	53	12	2	5	4	42	0	120	10	2
Pfaff, Jason, Lynchburg	5	6	.455	3.23	35	10	0	0	8	0	114.1	115	488	56	41	6	5	2	8	31	3	95	8	0
Reed, Chris, Winston-Salem	10	7	.588	3.32	24	24	3	1	0	0	149.0	116	613	63	55	11	3	1	4	68	1	104	3	1
Vaught, Jay, Kinston	8	12	.400	3.37	27	26	4	1	0	0	171.0	184	717	80	64	19	8	5	15	28	3	82	6	1
Jacobs, Ryan, Durham*	11	6	.647	3.51	29	25	1	0	3	0	148.2	145	640	72	58	12	6	5	3	57	3	99	10	0
Mathews, Del, Durham	7	8	.467	3.54	33	16	1	0	8	1	112.0	117	478	53	44	6	4	1	10	38	2	77	6	0

DEPARTMENTAL LEADERS: W—Rusch, 14; L—Woods, 15; Pct.—Colon, .813; G—Byrd, 60; GS—Pool, 28; CG—Vaught, 4; ShO—Peters, 3; GF—Byrd, 53; Sv.—Byrd, 27; IP—Vaught, Wright, 171.0; H—Pool, 191; TBF—Wright, 732; R—Pool, 90; ER—Pool, 88; HR—Vaught, 19; SH—Bowie, 13; SF—Marenghi, 8; HB—Lyons, Vaught, 15; BB—Green, Million, 79; IBB—Bock, Rizzo, 8; SO—Colon, 152; WP—Heathcott, 18; Bk.—Dillinger, 7.

ALL PITCHERS

*Lefthanded pitcher.

Pitcher, Team	W	L	Pct.	ERA	G	GS	CG	ShO	GF	Sv.	IP	H	TBF	R	ER	HR	SH	SF	HB	BB	IBB	SO	WP	Bk.
Abramavicius, Jason, Lynchburg*	1	0	1.000	7.30	9	0	0	0	2	0	12.1	22	64	13	10	0	0	0	0	5	1	11	1	0
Aminoff, Matt, Salem	4	6	.400	3.21	39	0	0	0	32	16	53.1	53	237	28	19	3	7	3	4	22	4	31	6	0
Anderson, Eric, Wilmington	3	1	.750	2.93	16	0	0	0	10	2	27.2	28	109	9	9	1	0	0	0	4	0	19	4	1
Anderson, Jimmy, Lynchburg*	1	5	.167	4.13	10	9	0	0	1	0	52.1	56	231	29	24	1	4	1	5	21	1	32	7	3
Arnold, Jamie, Durham	4	8	.333	3.94	15	14	1	0	0	0	80.0	86	347	42	35	5	4	1	9	21	0	44	4	0
Atkinson, Neil, Wilmington*	1	1	.500	2.86	8	0	0	0	5	3	22.0	21	93	7	7	1	2	0	1	6	3	20	3	0
Barnes, Keith, Salem*	4	5	.444	5.35	15	15	1	0	0	0	79.0	90	335	52	47	11	1	3	3	24	0	43	4	0
Binkley, Brett, Durham*	2	2	.500	5.97	24	0	0	0	6	0	28.2	34	138	20	19	2	2	1	1	21	1	20	4	1
Bliss, Bill, Salem	3	2	.600	4.23	34	0	0	0	17	4	44.2	38	193	24	21	4	2	1	1	25	6	23	9	2
Bock, Jeff, Durham	5	1	.833	3.36	32	0	0	0	11	2	67.0	58	282	31	25	9	4	3	1	31	8	45	3	0
Bowie, Micah, Durham*	4	11	.267	3.59	23	23	1	0	0	0	130.1	119	561	65	52	8	13	3	8	61	3	91	4	3
Brabant, Dan, Kinston	7	4	.636	4.23	47	0	0	0	12	1	93.2	81	405	47	44	9	3	4	6	49	3	89	9	0
Brewer, Brian, Frederick*	2	4	.333	2.53	14	8	0	0	3	1	67.2	49	263	22	19	2	3	2	3	19	1	48	5	2
Brewer, Nevin, Wilmington	1	1	.500	0.93	17	0	0	0	13	8	29.0	19	120	4	3	0	0	0	1	15	2	20	3	0
Brownson, Mark, Salem	2	1	.667	4.02	9	1	0	0	5	1	15.2	16	71	8	7	0	3	0	0	10	4	9	4	0
Burgess, Kurt, Durham*	2	4	.333	7.83	34	0	0	0	11	0	43.2	48	219	44	38	3	2	3	8	34	2	25	4	1
Byrd, Matt, Durham	5	4	.556	2.97	60	0	0	0	53	27	69.2	52	296	24	23	8	0	3	3	32	4	79	9	0
Byrdak, Tim, Wilmington*	11	5	.688	2.16	27	26	0	0	0	0	166.1	118	657	46	40	7	3	3	10	45	2	127	1	0
Call, Mike, Prince William	4	7	.364	5.42	28	9	3	1	8	1	104.2	114	462	66	63	14	3	3	7	37	1	62	5	0
Callistro, Rob, Prince William	1	1	.500	4.00	8	0	0	0	1	0	18.0	19	79	8	8	3	1	0	0	7	0	18	1	1
Caruso, Joe, Lynchburg	4	0	1.000	2.95	29	0	0	0	14	4	39.2	36	168	13	13	0	4	4	3	16	4	27	2	1
Chaves, Rafael, Lynchburg	1	3	.250	2.66	42	0	0	0	41	22	35.0	41	191	17	14	3	4	0	1	13	3	45	5	1
Chavez, Carlos, Frederick	5	5	.500	2.55	43	1	0	0	16	6	81.1	62	342	38	23	4	1	0	2	40	2	107	16	1
Christman, Scott, Prince William*	4	4	.500	3.59	13	13	1	0	0	0	85.1	83	346	38	34	7	1	6	2	19	2	56	3	0
Christmas, Maurice, Durham	2	7	.222	4.83	31	18	0	0	2	0	113.2	135	493	68	61	15	2	3	4	19	2	68	2	0
Clemons, Chris, Prince William	7	12	.368	4.73	27	27	1	0	0	0	137.0	136	606	78	72	18	4	4	11	64	2	92	2	0
Colon, Bartolo, Kinston	13	3	.813	1.96	21	21	0	0	0	0	128.2	91	493	31	28	8	1	2	0	39	0	152	4	3
Conley, Curt, Salem*	4	1	.800	3.61	39	0	0	0	20	3	47.1	42	211	22	19	4	2	3	2	27	3	35	4	2
Connolly, Chris, Wilmington*	5	2	.714	3.48	27	0	0	0	13	1	44.0	38	196	23	17	2	1	5	23	2	29	10	1
Connors, Chad, Winston-Salem	2	2	.500	6.86	16	0	0	0	8	2	19.2	28	95	16	15	3	0	0	3	11	1	13	2	0
Coppinger, Rocky, Frederick	7	1	.875	1.57	11	11	2	1	0	0	68.2	46	272	16	12	3	3	1	0	24	0	91	1	0
Crills, Brad, Frederick	2	5	.286	3.06	9	9	3	1	0	0	61.2	63	259	26	21	2	3	2	3	12	1	33	2	2
Crowther, Brent, Salem	3	6	.333	2.76	12	12	3	1	0	0	78.1	70	322	31	24	4	5	0	2	25	5	60	7	2
Cruz, Nelson, Prince William	2	1	.667	0.47	9	0	0	0	7	1	19.1	12	75	1	1	0	2	0	0	6	0	18	0	0
Cullop, Glen, Winston-Salem	0	1	.000	0.90	6	0	0	0	5	0	10.0	7	39	1	1	0	0	1	0	5	0	9	2	0
Daigle, Tim, Frederick*	0	2	.000	8.53	6	0	0	0	0	0	6.1	9	38	12	6	1	0	2	1	5	0	9	2	0
Daniels, Lee, Durham	1	4	.200	4.24	21	0	0	0	7	4	23.1	26	113	13	11	1	0	3	1	14	1	24	4	2
Dawley, Joey, Frederick	1	2	.333	6.34	24	0	0	0	8	1	32.2	41	163	28	23	4	1	1	3	22	1	29	5	1
DeLaMaza, Roland, Kinston	6	0	1.000	2.37	26	12	0	0	5	1	110.1	99	445	31	29	13	7	0	3	28	3	100	3	0
DeLaRosa, Maximo, Kinston	5	2	.714	2.19	43	0	0	0	21	8	61.2	46	266	23	15	0	5	2	4	37	3	61	7	1
DeLeon, Elcilio, Lynchburg	2	0	1.000	4.24	13	0	0	0	3	0	17.0	12	74	9	8	2	1	1	3	11	0	9	0	0
Dickens, John, Wilmington*	3	1	.750	1.77	48	0	0	0	27	9	76.1	57	296	17	15	1	2	3	3	17	3	59	5	0
Dietrich, Jason, Salem	1	0	1.000	8.59	6	0	0	0	1	0	7.1	9	39	7	7	2	0	0	1	8	0	9	0	0
Dillinger, John, Lynchburg	6	6	.500	4.02	27	22	0	0	1	0	123.0	111	540	62	55	10	5	5	7	67	4	97	9	7
Donnelly, Brendan, Winston-Salem	1	2	.333	1.02	23	0	0	0	14	3	35.1	20	138	6	4	2	2	2	2	14	2	32	0	1
Doorneweerd, Dave, Lynchburg	0	1	.000	6.75	5	0	0	0	2	0	8.0	8	38	6	6	0	0	1	5	0	9	1	0	
Downs, John, Wilmington	1	0	1.000	5.40	8	0	0	0	5	0	11.2	9	55	7	7	2	0	1	0	2	1	7	2	0
Doyle, Tom, Winston-Salem*	3	1	.750	3.45	21	3	0	0	3	1	31.1	32	140	18	12	2	1	0	3	12	0	22	5	0
Driskill, Travis, Kinston	0	2	.000	2.74	15	0	0	0	9	0	23.0	17	90	7	7	2	0	3	1	5	1	24	1	0
Dyess, Todd, Frederick	0	2	.000	6.59	3	3	0	0	0	0	13.2	17	61	10	10	1	0	1	1	5	0	8	3	0
Etler, Todd, Winston-Salem	6	12	.333	3.69	24	23	3	0	0	0	153.2	148	643	71	63	13	4	5	2	49	2	78	3	2
Evans, Bart, Wilmington	4	1	.800	2.89	16	0	0	0	4	2	46.2	30	215	21	15	0	0	1	5	44	0	47	7	0
Faino, Jeff, Frederick*	0	0	.000	4.76	4	0	0	0	2	0	5.2	7	26	5	3	0	1	0	0	2	0	8	1	0
Farson, Bryan, Lynchburg*	7	3	.700	5.82	27	6	0	0	7	0	51.0	51	228	41	33	13	1	2	2	19	4	35	3	0
Flury, Pat, Wilmington	1	0	1.000	2.45	15	0	0	0	6	1	22.0	18	89	6	6	2	0	1	1	9	1	14	1	1
Fordham, Tom, Prince William*	9	0	1.000	2.04	13	13	1	1	0	0	84.0	66	340	20	19	7	2	1	2	35	2	78	1	0
Gamboa, Javier, Wilmington	3	4	.429	4.04	8	8	0	0	0	0	49.0	42	202	23	22	6	3	0	1	13	0	33	2	0
Garrett, Neil, Salem	1	0	1.000	12.27	5	0	0	0	1	0	3.2	5	24	8	5	0	1	0	1	5	0	3	3	0
Giron, Emiliano, Winston-Salem	2	0	1.000	2.30	17	0	0	0	11	0	27.1	23	121	15	7	1	0	0	3	10	0	29	2	2
Goldman, Barry, Salem	0	3	.000	5.79	8	0	0	0	6	0	9.1	8	41	7	6	0	0	0	0	7	1	6	2	0
Graves, Dan, Kinston	3	1	.750	0.82	38	0	0	0	37	21	44.0	30	177	11	4	0	1	0	0	12	2	46	0	0
Green, Jason, Durham	2	4	.333	5.58	39	1	0	0	14	3	50.0	31	248	31	31	1	2	4	1	79	1	59	13	1
Grundy, Phillip, Wilmington	6	6	.500	3.31	20	16	0	0	3	1	106.0	106	445	46	39	7	4	1	5	32	2	90	7	0
Hagan, Danny, Winston-Salem*	1	0	1.000	1.80	1	1	0	0	0	0	5.0	5	21	1	1	0	0	0	4	0	2	0	0	
Hale, Shane, Frederick*	0	2	.000	10.93	6	2	0	0	0	0	14.0	21	69	18	17	1	3	1	3	6	2	6	1	0
Hanson, Kris, Kinston	5	6	.455	5.04	20	18	1	0	0	0	96.1	102	404	56	54	11	1	3	5	24	1	53	3	0
Harrison, Tom, Durham	3	1	.750	0.96	7	6	0	0	0	0	37.2	22	145	5	4	1	0	0	1	13	1	25	0	0
Hartzog, Cullen, Lynchburg	6	4	.600	3.34	43	1	0	0	17	0	59.1	49	254	23	22	5	1	1	2	30	2	45	8	0
Harvell, Pete, Winston-Salem*	0	1	.000	12.60	4	0	0	0	1	0	5.0	9	28	7	7	1	0	1	0	4	0	1	1	0
Heathcott, Mike, Prince William	4	9	.308	4.67	27	14	1	0	4	3	88.2	96	387	56	46	8	2	7	2	36	3	68	18	0
Heiserman, Rick, Frederick	9	3	.750	3.74	19	19	1	0	0	0	113.0	97	470	55	47	13	3	4	9	42	1	86	6	1
Hernandez, Francisco, Frederick	0	1	.000	6.00	3	0	0	0	3	0	3.0	3	15	2	2	1	0	1	0	3	0	3	0	0
Hodges, Kevin, Wilmington	2	3	.400	4.53	12	10	0	0	1	0	53.2	53	232	31	27	1	1	1	3	25	1	27	4	0
Hostetler, Marcus, Durham	1	1	.500	6.61	12	0	0	0	3	0	16.1	23	80	13	12	1	2	0	1	7	0	6	0	0
Huber, Jeff, Frederick*	2	0	1.000	5.21	21	0	0	0	9	0	19.0	29	92	16	11	5	1	2	0	5	1	11	2	0
Jacobs, Ryan, Durham*	11	6	.647	3.51	29	25	1	0	0	0	148.2	145	640	72	58	12	6	5	3	57	3	99	10	0
Jesperson, Bob, Winston-Salem	2	1	.667	4.26	5	0	0	0	4	0	6.1	5	26	3	3	0	0	0	0	4	1	9	1	0
Johnson, Jason, Lynchburg	1	4	.200	4.91	10	10	0	0	0	0	55.0	58	236	37	30	9	0	3	2	20	0	41	2	0
Johnson, Jason, Salem	1	2	.333	2.05	5	4	0	0	0	0	22.0	23	94	6	5	0	1	0	1	5	0	9	1	0
Kirkreit, Daron, Kinston	0	1	.000	5.93	3	3	0	0	0	0	13.2	14	63	9	9	1	1	0	2	6	0	14	1	0

Pitcher, Team	W	L	Pct.	ERA	G	GS	CG	ShO	GF	Sv.	IP	H	TBF	R	ER	HR	SH	SF	HB	BB	IBB	SO	WP	Bk.
Kitchen, Ron, Frederick	2	2	.500	7.23	30	0	0	0	11	0	37.1	55	179	35	30	6	3	2	1	10	3	10	1	1
Kummerfeldt, Jason, Winst.-Sal.	4	6	.400	3.48	37	3	0	0	14	3	77.2	78	326	37	30	7	1	7	19	5	51	1	0
Kusiewicz, Michael, Salem*	0	0	.000	1.50	1	1	0	0	0	0	6.0	7	26	1	1	0	0	0	2	0	0	7	0	1
Larock, Scott, Salem	5	4	.556	3.90	52	1	0	0	18	6	101.2	96	423	52	44	10	4	2	0	27	7	92	5	3
Lavenia, Mark, Durham*	0	1	.000	5.56	6	0	0	0	1	0	11.1	14	51	8	7	1	0	1	0	5	0	9	3	0
Lawrence, Sean, Lynchburg*	5	8	.385	4.22	20	19	0	0	0	0	111.0	115	465	56	52	16	3	3	1	25	0	82	3	0
LaPlante, Michel, Lynchburg	1	1	.500	8.22	5	2	0	0	0	0	15.1	21	73	14	14	4	0	1	1	3	0	13	2	0
LaRocca, Todd, Frederick	3	1	.750	1.76	5	5	0	0	0	0	30.2	22	132	7	6	0	2	0	2	16	0	24	4	0
Lehman, Toby, Frederick	0	5	.000	4.25	19	10	1	0	2	0	55.0	44	237	30	26	9	3	1	3	27	1	48	6	0
Lemp, Chris, Frederick	2	3	.400	2.38	41	0	0	0	36	19	45.1	44	194	16	12	4	3	2	0	17	2	50	8	0
Leroy, John, Durham	6	9	.400	5.44	24	22	1	0	0	0	125.2	128	545	82	76	17	2	5	5	57	1	77	5	1
Lindemann, Wayne, Prince William*	2	0	1.000	5.86	19	0	0	0	14	1	43.0	54	196	30	28	7	1	5	2	20	2	32	3	0
Locklear, Jeff, Salem*	0	0	.000	12.79	6	0	0	0	2	0	6.1	10	33	9	9	2	0	2	0	4	0	3	0	0
Lombardi, John, Frederick	0	4	.000	7.16	6	3	0	0	0	0	16.1	22	75	13	13	2	0	1	2	6	0	13	2	0
Lyons, Curt, Winston-Salem	9	9	.500	2.98	26	26	0	0	0	0	160.1	139	672	66	53	10	6	2	15	67	3	122	9	3
Maberry, Louis, Winston-Salem	1	0	1.000	4.34	20	0	0	0	12	0	37.1	40	154	20	18	5	1	0	2	7	0	19	7	0
Maduro, Calvin, Frederick	8	5	.615	2.94	20	20	2	2	0	0	122.1	109	499	43	40	16	3	2	6	34	0	120	2	0
Magee, Bo, Frederick*	2	1	.667	4.05	5	5	0	0	0	0	26.2	28	111	15	12	4	2	0	2	5	0	28	2	0
Magre, Pete, Winston-Salem	1	1	.500	3.09	17	0	0	0	4	2	32.0	39	150	14	11	3	2	0	3	15	1	27	3	3
Maine, Dalton, Frederick	1	1	.500	3.68	19	0	0	0	10	0	22.0	20	98	10	9	2	0	1	2	11	0	21	5	0
Mansur, Jeff, Frederick*	0	0	.000	4.70	12	0	0	0	6	0	15.1	20	70	8	8	1	1	1	2	5	1	12	0	0
Marenghi, Matt, Frederick	4	13	.235	5.08	30	16	0	0	8	0	113.1	108	475	73	64	14	1	8	9	41	2	85	6	1
Martinez, Johnny, Kinston	3	0	1.000	1.64	6	0	0	0	5	2	11.0	9	44	2	2	0	0	1	4	0	13	1	0
Mathews, Del, Durham*	7	8	.467	3.54	33	16	1	0	8	1	112.0	117	478	53	44	6	4	1	10	38	2	77	6	0
Mattson, Craig, Lynchburg	2	0	1.000	3.09	11	0	0	0	5	0	11.2	11	46	5	4	1	0	1	0	0	5	0	0
Mayse, Robert, Frederick	1	0	1.000	3.72	6	0	0	0	1	0	9.2	9	42	5	4	0	0	1	8	0	7	0	0
McKenzie, Scott, Winston-Salem	3	4	.429	2.75	49	0	0	0	41	20	72.0	42	294	27	22	7	5	0	5	30	2	55	7	0
Mesa, Rafael, Kinston	4	3	.571	2.94	35	1	0	0	24	0	52.0	34	206	19	17	5	4	3	4	20	2	29	4	0
Mesewicz, Mark, Lynchburg*	0	1	.000	23.14	6	0	0	0	1	0	4.2	13	29	12	12	2	0	0	2	0	3	1	0
Million, Doug, Salem*	5	7	.417	4.62	24	23	0	0	0	0	111.0	111	513	71	57	6	6	1	9	79	4	85	9	4
Montoya, Wilmer, Kinston	1	0	1.000	5.40	1	0	0	0	0	0	3.1	4	15	2	2	0	1	0	0	1	0	2	0	0
Morel, Ramon, Lynchburg	3	7	.300	3.47	12	12	1	1	0	0	72.2	80	304	35	28	2	2	3	3	13	2	44	2	0
Murphy, Chris, Winston-Salem*	2	1	.667	2.70	4	3	0	0	1	0	20.0	13	75	7	6	2	1	1	0	5	0	22	1	0
Najera, Noe, Kinston*	0	1	.000	2.25	8	3	0	0	2	0	20.0	10	78	6	5	0	1	0	2	9	1	14	0	0
Nelson, Earl, Durham*	0	1	.000	4.95	15	0	0	0	9	2	20.0	27	105	17	11	4	1	1	3	17	2	17	2	0
Nieto, Tony, Frederick	1	4	.200	3.92	21	0	0	0	6	0	39.0	38	162	19	17	4	2	1	5	9	2	14	1	1
Oropeza, Igor, Kinston	2	3	.400	4.50	20	2	0	0	2	1	38.0	24	164	19	19	4	3	2	3	29	2	31	3	0
Paige, Carey, Durham	5	3	.625	3.38	10	10	1	0	0	0	64.0	53	252	24	24	8	2	3	1	15	1	37	1	0
Perkins, Paul, Lynchburg	0	3	.000	3.94	25	0	0	0	14	1	29.2	34	135	15	13	1	0	2	10	3	28	1	0
Peters, Chris, Lynchburg*	11	5	.688	2.43	24	24	3	3	0	0	144.2	126	586	57	39	5	7	4	5	35	2	132	12	1
Pfaff, Jason, Lynchburg	5	6	.455	3.23	35	10	0	0	4	0	114.1	115	488	56	41	6	5	2	8	31	3	95	8	0
Pickford, Kevin, Lynchburg*	0	3	.000	4.94	4	4	0	0	0	0	27.1	31	110	15	15	5	0	1	0	6	0	15	2	1
Pierson, Jason, Prince William*	5	4	.556	4.42	21	12	0	0	5	0	91.2	91	382	48	45	9	1	4	2	22	0	69	1	0
Place, Mike, Durham	2	1	.667	10.57	7	0	0	0	1	0	7.2	11	36	11	9	0	0	0	6	0	2	0	0
Pontbriant, Matt, Lynchburg*	7	7	.500	5.05	27	17	1	1	4	0	108.2	137	476	67	61	16	5	2	1	28	3	60	2	1
Pool, Matt, Salem	9	9	.500	4.80	28	28	2	0	0	0	165.0	191	705	90	88	18	5	2	6	50	5	95	16	1
Pratt, Rich, Prince William*	5	11	.313	3.14	25	25	2	1	0	0	152.0	139	619	66	53	12	2	5	4	42	0	120	10	2
Priest, Eddie, Winston-Salem*	5	5	.500	3.63	12	12	1	1	0	0	67.0	60	275	32	27	7	2	2	0	22	0	60	2	0
Raines, Ken, Durham*	1	0	1.000	4.94	19	0	0	0	3	0	23.2	38	118	19	13	3	2	1	0	12	2	15	0	0
Ramos, Cesar, Kinston	1	2	.333	3.65	8	0	0	0	2	0	12.1	16	56	6	5	0	2	0	2	3	1	4	0	0
Rawitzer, Kevin, Wilmington*	2	0	1.000	2.33	15	1	0	0	7	3	27.0	21	111	8	7	0	1	0	3	8	1	22	1	0
Ray, Ken, Wilmington	4	6	.400	2.69	13	13	1	0	0	0	77.0	74	320	32	23	3	3	1	22	2	63	17	2
Reed, Chris, Winston-Salem	10	7	.588	3.32	24	24	3	1	0	0	149.0	116	613	63	55	11	3	1	4	68	1	104	3	1
Rhodes, Joe, Frederick	0	1	.000	4.50	2	1	0	0	1	0	6.0	8	28	3	3	0	1	0	0	2	1	0
Riemer, Matt, Frederick	0	0	.000	0.00	1	0	0	0	1	0	1.0	1	5	0	0	0	1	0	0	0	0
Rizzo, Todd, Prince William*	3	5	.375	2.78	36	0	0	0	10	1	68.0	68	307	30	21	2	2	1	3	39	8	59	13	0
Robbins, Jason, Winston-Salem	9	6	.600	3.06	23	23	3	1	0	0	141.0	113	571	62	48	16	0	5	7	42	1	106	5	1
Roberts, Ray, Wilmington*	2	4	.333	3.32	13	0	0	0	6	4	19.0	18	79	7	7	2	0	1	0	2	0	16	0	0
Rogers, Jason, Frederick*	1	3	.250	4.32	15	14	1	0	0	0	66.2	64	309	38	32	1	2	2	3	45	1	39	6	2
Rosado, Jose, Wilmington*	10	7	.588	3.13	25	25	0	0	0	0	138.0	128	562	53	48	9	2	7	3	30	6	117	1	5
Runion, Tony, Kinston	7	11	.389	4.09	28	24	0	0	2	0	143.0	131	599	70	65	9	2	6	13	57	0	84	10	0
Rusch, Glendon, Wilmington*	14	6	.700	1.74	26	26	1	1	0	0	165.2	110	629	41	32	5	4	3	4	34	3	147	3	1
Ruyak, Todd, Winston-Salem*	5	6	.455	3.99	34	9	0	0	7	0	85.2	99	369	44	38	8	6	3	1	20	0	48	2	1
Saipe, Mike, Salem	4	5	.444	3.48	21	9	0	0	7	3	85.1	68	347	35	33	7	1	1	2	32	4	90	9	1
Salamon, John, Salem	1	0	1.000	6.14	8	0	0	0	4	1	14.2	13	60	10	10	5	0	0	5	0	9	0	0
Sauritch, Chris, Frederick	0	0	.000	9.00	1	0	0	0	1	0	1.0	1	4	1	1	1	0	0	0	0	1	0	0
Sexton, Jeff, Kinston	5	1	.833	2.53	8	8	2	1	0	0	57.0	52	226	17	16	3	0	0	2	7	0	41	6	1
Sheehan, Chris, Wilmington	2	1	.667	1.86	13	0	0	0	5	3	19.1	7	67	5	4	0	2	0	2	2	0	27	1	0
Sinnes, David, Wilmington	0	2	.000	3.04	18	0	0	0	11	3	23.2	15	115	12	8	0	1	1	5	24	1	34	6	0
Smith, Hut, Frederick	3	2	.600	6.47	20	2	0	0	7	2	32.0	39	162	23	23	4	2	1	4	31	1	28	7	1
Smith, Toby, Wilmington	5	7	.417	3.08	30	7	0	0	13	4	79.0	67	320	32	27	9	2	1	3	20	2	65	6	2
Sobkoviak, Jeff, Salem	5	3	.625	4.80	40	5	0	0	10	2	86.1	96	371	52	46	13	3	4	5	37	5	44	7	0
Sosa, Jose, Lynchburg	0	0	.000	6.88	10	0	0	0	4	0	17.0	27	82	14	13	1	1	0	0	6	1	12	4	1
Stewart, Chris, Salem	0	2	.000	8.53	10	0	0	0	4	0	12.2	18	64	15	12	3	0	1	0	11	2	10	3	2
Stewart, Rachaad, Frederick*	8	8	.500	3.64	28	26	1	1	0	0	150.2	126	635	71	61	8	5	1	10	66	1	140	12	4
Tagle, Hank, Prince William*	3	2	.600	3.09	33	0	0	0	16	2	70.0	58	275	28	24	4	2	5	15	1	66	3	0
Tolar, Kevin, Lynchburg*	2	0	1.000	2.79	18	0	0	0	7	0	19.1	13	77	7	6	1	0	1	5	6	0	19	3	0
Towns, Ryan, Wilmington	1	0	1.000	5.63	12	0	0	0	2	0	16.0	12	75	11	10	0	0	0	18	0	8	1	0
Tuttle, Dave, Winston-Salem	3	3	.500	3.18	10	10	2	1	0	0	62.1	49	248	28	22	5	0	2	3	19	0	54	3	0
Vaught, Jay, Kinston	8	12	.400	3.37	27	26	4	1	0	0	171.0	184	717	80	64	19	8	5	15	28	3	82	6	1
Vazquez, Archie, Prince William	3	4	.429	3.59	47	0	0	0	45	20	57.2	53	261	26	23	5	9	1	1	30	4	70	8	0
Voisard, Mark, Salem	0	0	.000	7.36	6	0	0	0	2	0	7.1	8	33	6	6	4	0	1	1	5	0	3	1	0
Waldron, Joe, Salem*	1	2	.333	2.51	9	0	0	0	3	0	14.1	23	64	5	4	0	0	0	1	0	17	0	0

Pitcher, Team	W	L	Pct.	ERA	G	GS	CG	ShO	GF	Sv.	IP	H	TBF	R	ER	HR	SH	SF	HB	BB	IBB	SO	WP	Bk.
Walker, James, Frederick	2	2	.500	3.48	9	0	0	0	1	0	20.2	15	90	12	8	0	1	0	1	9	1	19	2	0
Walls, Doug, Salem	5	5	.500	3.84	15	15	0	0	1	0	79.2	61	344	39	34	10	1	3	3	49	1	79	5	2
Wells, David, Durham	0	0	.000	4.73	7	0	0	0	1	0	13.1	21	63	8	7	2	0	1	0	2	0	6	0	0
White, Gary, Frederick*	1	0	1.000	3.00	1	1	0	0	0	0	6.0	3	23	2	2	1	0	0	0	2	0	4	0	0
Williams, Greg, Kinston*	2	1	.667	2.45	30	0	0	0	8	3	22.0	15	88	9	6	1	0	2	0	8	0	18	5	0
Winkle, Ken, Wilmington	1	1	.500	10.54	11	0	0	0	5	1	13.2	16	67	18	16	5	1	1	1	10	1	14	1	0
Woods, Brian, Prince William	9	15	.375	5.17	27	27	3	0	0	0	139.1	155	632	89	80	14	5	4	14	53	1	102	12	3
Worrell, Steve, Prince William*	3	1	.750	1.52	29	0	0	0	18	3	47.1	32	180	10	8	3	3	1	1	7	2	52	1	0
Wright, Jamey, Salem	10	8	.556	2.47	26	26	2	1	0	0	171.0	160	732	74	47	7	3	6	13	72	3	95	16	2
Young, Danny, Lynchburg*	2	4	.333	7.40	24	2	0	0	7	0	41.1	52	196	37	34	3	1	2	2	27	1	34	5	0
Zolecki, Mike, Salem	0	1	.000	7.20	9	0	0	0	1	0	15.0	22	73	15	12	2	0	1	0	7	0	12	4	0

COMBINATION SHUTOUTS: **Durham (3)**—Harrison-Nelson, Jacobs-Bock, Jacobs-Byrd. **Frederick (6)**—Brewer-Marenghi, Coppinger-Smith-Lemp, Dyess-Mayse-Maine-Smith, Maduro-Chavez-Lemp, Magee-Marenghi, Rogers-Kitchen-Lemp-Maine. **Kinston (8)**—Colon-DeLaMaza, Colon-Oropeza-Williams-Brabant, DeLaMaza-Martinez, Mesa-Delarosa-Graves, Najera-Martinez, Runion-Delarosa, Runion-Williams-Delarosa, Vaught-Mesa. **Lynchburg (4)**—Anderson-Farson, Dillinger-Pfaff, Farson-Caruso-Perkins, Lawrence-Chaves. **Prince William (8)**—Fordham-Vazquez 2, Christman-Cruz, Christman-Worrell, Fordham-Heathcott-Call, Heathcott-Tagle-Vazquez, Pratt-Vazquez, Woods-Vazquez. **Salem (4)**—Barnes-Larock-Sobkoviak-Goldman, Pool-Aminoff, Saipe-Aminoff-Bliss, Walls-Aminoff. **Wilmington (16)**—Rusch-Brewer 2, Byrdak-Anderson, Byrdak-Brewer, Byrdak-Dickens, Gamboa-Evans, Grundy-Anderson, Grundy-Dickens, Hodges-Smith, Ray-Dickens, Ray-Sheehan-Rawitzer-Sinnes, Rosado-Atkinson, Rosado-Flury, Rosado-Sinnes-Connolly, Rusch-Smith-Connolly, Smith-Sinnes-Roberts-Flury. **Winston-Salem (7)**—Doyle-Kummerfeldt-Donnelly-McKenzie, Etler-McKenzie, Lyons-McKenzie, Lyons-Ruyak-Giron, Priest-Kummerfeldt, Robbins-Doyle-McKenzie, Robbins-Kummerfeldt-Ruyak-Harvell.

NO-HIT GAMES: Woods-Vazquez, Prince William, defeated Salem, 8-0, April 8; Rosado-Flury, Wilmington, defeated Winston-Salem, 3-0, April 15; Harrison-Nelson, Durham, defeated Prince William, 4-0, April 30; Pratt, Prince William, defeated Frederick, 3-0 (second game), May 19.

1995 FIELDING

TEAM

Team	Pct.	G	PO	A	E	TC	DP	PB	Team	Pct.	G	PO	A	E	TC	DP	PB
Kinston	.978	137	3642	1555	119	5316	136	17	Winston-Salem	.969	137	3594	1543	165	5302	127	29
Wilmington	.974	138	3698	1533	139	5370	107	14	Durham	.968	139	3560	1353	160	5073	134	23
Prince William	.970	140	3618	1525	157	5300	99	12	Lynchburg	.967	138	3548	1569	175	5292	130	16
Salem	.970	140	3711	1667	166	5544	134	23	Frederick	.966	137	3572	1461	179	5212	105	23

TRIPLE PLAYS: Lynchburg, Wilmington.

INDIVIDUAL

FIRST BASEMEN

NOTE: All caps denotes fielding-percentage leader based on 70 games for catchers, 93 for all other non-pitchers and 140 innings for pitchers. *Throws lefthanded.

Player, Team	Pct.	G	PO	A	E	TC	DP
Bernhardt, Steven, Salem	1.000	2	9	0	0	9	1
Bess, Johnny, Winston-Salem	.977	19	115	11	3	129	16
Bonifay, Ken, Lynchburg	.995	57	541	25	3	569	53
Brown, Ray, Winston-Salem	.981	100	919	52	19	990	81
Byington, Jimmie, Wilmington	1.000	8	63	6	0	69	9
Cawhorn, Gerad, Kinston	1.000	4	22	3	0	25	4
Culp, Brian, Salem	1.000	2	11	1	0	12	2
Daniel, Mike, Lynchburg	.967	8	80	7	3	90	9
Dixon, Colin, Salem	.993	38	377	24	3	404	37
Evans, Michael, Wilmington	.971	43	315	22	10	347	21
Fasano, Sal, Wilmington	1.000	2	17	2	0	19	1
Garcia, Guillermo, Winst.-Salem	.990	10	95	8	1	104	7
Hagy, Gary, Kinston	1.000	1	2	0	0	2	0
Hanel, Marcus, Lynchburg	1.000	1	1	0	0	1	0
Hendricks, Ryan, Frederick	1.000	2	12	1	0	13	1
Holdren, Nate, Salem	.982	90	764	63	15	842	74
House, Mitch, Lynchburg	.992	12	114	7	1	122	16
Hugo, Sean, Frederick*	.893	4	22	3	3	28	2
Kirgan, Chris, Frederick*	.989	115	872	50	10	932	68
Knoblauh, Jay, Lynchburg	.966	4	26	2	1	29	1
Knott, John, Durham	.987	20	153	4	2	159	13
Larkin, Stephen, Winston-Salem*	.917	3	21	1	2	24	3
Leary, Rob, Lynchburg*	.983	23	168	6	3	177	12
MENDEZ, Carlos, Wilmington	.993	95	831	57	6	894	67
Michael, Jeff, Frederick	1.000	28	174	11	0	185	16
Nunez, Ramon, Durham	.983	7	53	4	1	58	3
Riemer, Matt, Frederick	1.000	12	74	8	0	82	4
Robertson, Robbie, Winst.-Sal.*	.980	12	96	4	2	102	9
Rodarte, Raul, Lynchburg	.957	2	21	1	1	23	1
Secrist, Reed, Lynchburg	.995	38	370	9	2	381	27
Sexson, Richie, Kinston	.990	125	1135	79	12	1226	109
Simon, Randall, Durham*	.989	113	864	51	10	925	89
Smith, Jason, Salem	1.000	1	7	1	0	8	0
Thomas, Greg, Kinston*	.990	12	94	5	1	100	9
Thomas, Juan, Prince William	.994	68	619	36	4	659	49
Webb, Kevin, Durham	.980	7	47	2	1	50	7
Wells, Forry, Salem	.981	19	147	11	3	161	11
Wieser, Mike, Durham	1.000	2	9	1	0	10	2
Williams, Harold, Prince William*	.985	72	617	40	10	667	40

TRIPLE PLAYS: Mendez, Secrist.

SECOND BASEMEN

Player, Team	Pct.	G	PO	A	E	TC	DP
Akers, Chad, Winston-Salem	.978	75	169	225	9	403	52
Benbow, Lou, Durham	.938	7	5	10	1	16	0
Bernhardt, Steven, Salem	.977	25	59	66	3	128	20
Brooks, Eddie, Lynchburg	.972	18	35	34	2	71	7
Byington, Jimmie, Wilmington	.862	9	16	9	4	29	1
Carr, Jeremy, Wilmington	1.000	1	1	3	0	4	1
Cawhorn, Gerad, Kinston	1.000	13	29	20	0	49	4
Gann, Steve, Winston-Salem	1.000	1	2	3	0	5	1
Garcia, Jesse, Frederick	.952	123	283	278	28	589	69
Garcia, Vincente, Salem	.984	114	252	295	9	556	70
Grunewald, Keith, Salem	1.000	2	3	8	0	11	1
GUTIERREZ, Ricky, Kinston	.986	116	250	318	8	576	90
Hagy, Gary, Kinston	.936	14	17	27	3	47	4
Jenkins, Demetrish, Winst.-Salem	.981	31	72	82	3	157	25
Jimenez, Manny, Durham	.976	95	204	200	10	414	65
Lofton, James, Winston-Salem	.932	36	74	76	11	161	17
Medrano, Anthony, Wilmington	1.000	12	20	29	0	49	5
Menechino, Frank, Prince William	.975	137	293	295	15	603	76
Michael, Jeff, Frederick	.891	12	19	22	5	46	6
Montilla, Julio, Wilmington	1.000	5	5	6	0	11	1
Newell, Brett, Durham	1.000	3	4	3	0	7	0
Nunez, Sergio, Wilmington	.954	124	231	313	26	570	70
Pagan, Angel, Frederick	.975	13	19	20	1	40	1
Polidor, Wil, Prince William	.929	5	3	10	1	14	1
Prieto, Rick, Kinston	1.000	1	3	2	0	5	1
Rodarte, Raul, Lynchburg	1.000	5	7	6	0	13	2
Rodriguez, Roman, Lynchburg	.979	13	22	25	1	48	6
Sanford, Chance, Lynchburg	.961	16	34	39	3	76	9
Sauritch, Chris, Frederick	1.000	1	2	3	0	5	1
Sexton, Chris, Salem	1.000	3	6	9	0	15	2
Warner, Ken, Durham	.957	47	71	84	7	162	25
Wieser, Mike, Durham	.500	1	1	1	2	4	0
Zapata, Ramon, Lynchburg	.976	98	209	246	11	466	68

TRIPLE PLAY: Medrano.

THIRD BASEMEN

Player, Team	Pct.	G	PO	A	E	TC	DP
Benbow, Lou, Durham	.894	18	12	30	5	47	6
Bernhardt, Steven, Salem	.909	21	15	55	7	77	1
Betts, Todd, Kinston	.929	92	50	184	18	252	19
Bonifay, Ken, Lynchburg	.931	24	25	56	6	87	6
BOONE, Aaron, Winston-Salem	.940	108	59	272	21	352	21
Brooks, Eddie, Lynchburg	1.000	5	0	9	0	9	0

Player, Team	Pct.	G	PO	A	E	TC	DP
Byington, Jimmie, Wilmington	.947	12	8	28	2	38	1
Carranza, Pete, Salem	.842	13	5	27	6	38	2
Cawhorn, Gerad, Kinston	.961	50	32	117	6	155	11
Davis, Tommy, Frederick	.897	120	83	240	37	360	13
Diaz, Einar, Kinston	.800	2	0	4	1	5	0
Diaz, Lino, Wilmington	.969	32	23	70	3	96	4
Fraraccio, Dan, Prince William	.945	24	13	56	4	73	3
Frye, Dan, Winston-Salem	.929	5	2	11	1	14	1
Gann, Steve, Winston-Salem	.926	7	3	22	2	27	1
Garcia, Guillermo, Winst.-Salem	.933	6	0	14	1	15	2
Goligoski, Jason, Prince William	.907	38	18	99	12	129	10
Gonzalez, Paul, Prince William	.931	84	58	210	20	288	12
Grunewald, Keith, Salem	.944	87	65	224	17	306	23
Hagy, Gary, Kinston	.933	6	5	9	1	15	1
Holdren, Nate, Salem	.500	1	1	0	1	2	0
Jimenez, Manny, Durham	.966	21	16	41	2	59	3
Knott, John, Durham	.912	55	40	94	13	147	7
Kopriva, Dan, Winston-Salem	.956	16	9	34	2	45	1
Lopez, Mendy, Wilmington	.939	108	55	271	21	347	11
Manto, Jeff, Frederick	1.000	1	0	2	0	2	0
Michael, Jeff, Frederick	.956	15	11	32	2	45	7
Montilla, Julio, Wilmington	1.000	1	1	2	0	3	1
Newell, Brett, Durham	.917	26	20	35	5	60	3
Newhouse, Andre, Prince William	1.000	1	0	3	0	3	0
Pagan, Angel, Frederick	1.000	9	0	11	0	11	0
Polidor, Wil, Prince William	1.000	1	0	3	0	3	0
Riemer, Matt, Frederick	1.000	1	0	4	0	4	1
Rodarte, Raul, Lynchburg	.920	95	56	267	28	351	27
Rodriguez, Roman, Lynchburg	1.000	11	6	35	0	41	3
Secrist, Reed, Lynchburg	.915	18	7	36	4	47	2
Short, Rick, Frederick	.800	1	0	4	1	5	0
Webb, Kevin, Durham	.849	32	23	39	11	73	3
Wells, Forry, Salem	.853	26	19	45	11	75	2
Wieser, Mike, Durham	.889	16	13	19	4	36	2

SHORTSTOPS

Player, Team	Pct.	G	PO	A	E	TC	DP
Akers, Chad, Winston-Salem	.948	24	37	55	5	97	13
Benbow, Lou, Durham	.948	57	71	165	13	249	35
Brooks, Eddie, Lynchburg	.923	8	7	17	2	26	1
Byington, Jimmie, Wilmington	.932	13	12	29	3	44	4
Collier, Lou, Lynchburg	.937	112	156	361	35	552	68
Fraraccio, Dan, Prince William	1.000	2	1	2	0	3	0
Frye, Dan, Winston-Salem	.000	1	0	0	1	1	0
Gann, Steve, Winston-Salem	.933	3	5	9	1	15	3
Garcia, Guillermo, Winst.-Sal	1.000	1	6	7	0	13	0
Goligoski, Jason, Prince William	.953	56	77	167	12	256	24
Grunewald, Keith, Salem	.957	26	37	73	5	115	17
Hagy, Gary, Kinston	.983	24	41	76	2	119	19
Jimenez, Manny, Durham	.917	9	13	20	3	36	5
Lamb, David, Frederick	.954	120	151	348	24	523	53
Lopez, Mendy, Wilmington	.959	22	29	64	4	97	13
Magdaleno, Ricky, Winst.-Sal.	.929	91	145	274	32	451	57
Magee, Danny, Durham	.934	73	94	176	19	289	39
Medrano, Anthony, Wilmington	.963	113	160	308	18	486	54
Michael, Jeff, Frederick	.963	15	18	34	2	54	7
Montilla, Julio, Wilmington	1.000	3	2	4	0	6	1
Newell, Brett, Durham	.933	4	6	8	1	15	3
Pagan, Angel, Frederick	.952	5	4	16	1	21	4
Polidor, Wil, Prince William	.950	89	106	271	20	397	31
Rodriguez, Roman, Lynchburg	.909	18	18	52	7	77	4
Sauritch, Chris, Frederick	1.000	1	0	6	0	6	0
SEXTON, Chris, W-S/Salem	.966	120	201	423	22	646	73
Wieser, Mike, Durham	.857	9	5	13	3	21	3
Wilson, Brian, Winston-Salem	.926	20	20	55	6	81	9
Wilson, Enrique, Kinston	.964	114	181	375	21	577	68
Zapata, Ramon, Lynchburg	.936	13	11	33	3	47	3

TRIPLE PLAYS: Collier, Lopez.

SHORTSTOPS WITH TWO OR MORE TEAMS

Player, Team	Pct.	G	PO	A	E	TC	DP
Sexton, Chris, Winston-Salem	1.000	4	6	17	0	23	2
Sexton, Chris, Salem	.965	116	195	406	22	623	71

OUTFIELDERS

Player, Team	Pct.	G	PO	A	E	TC	DP
Abbott, Jeff, Prince William*	.958	62	88	3	4	95	0
Austin, Jake, Lynchburg	.971	18	30	3	1	34	0
Aven, Bruce, Kinston	.983	110	158	11	3	172	1
Avila, Rolando, Frederick	.991	51	106	7	1	114	0
Bernhardt, Steven, Salem	1.000	3	2	1	0	3	0
Berrios, Harry, Frederick	.973	46	71	1	2	74	0
Bess, Johnny, Winston-Salem	1.000	21	28	3	0	31	0
Betzsold, James, Kinston	.959	123	196	13	9	218	3
Bonifay, Ken, Lynchburg	.964	17	26	1	1	28	0
Bridgers, Brandon, Frederick	1.000	10	23	0	0	23	0
Broach, Donald, Winston-Salem	.985	116	258	11	4	273	2
Brown, Adrian, Lynchburg	.983	54	110	6	2	118	0
Brown, Todd, Frederick	.970	27	31	1	1	33	1
Byington, Jimmie, Wilmington	.989	48	86	0	1	87	0
Byrne, Clayton, Frederick	.948	34	85	7	5	97	2
Carr, Jeremy, Wilmington	1.000	1	1	0	0	1	0
Claudio, Patricio, Kinston	.988	89	233	5	3	241	2
Clyburn, Danny, W-S/Fre.	.945	59	79	6	5	90	1
Conger, Jeff, Lynchburg*	.953	85	156	5	8	169	1
Cornelius, Brian, Lynchburg	.941	12	15	1	1	17	0
Correa, Miguel, Durham	.972	92	198	12	6	216	1
Cradle, Cobi, Winston-Salem*	1.000	21	38	2	0	40	0
Culp, Brian, Salem	.970	106	153	9	5	167	1
Daniel, Mike, Lynchburg	1.000	2	1	1	0	2	0
Delaney, Donovan, Wilmington	.950	110	138	14	8	160	2
Dellucci, David, Frederick*	.966	23	26	2	1	29	0
Evans, Michael, Wilmington	1.000	15	23	1	0	24	0
French, Anton, Durham	1.000	7	19	0	0	19	0
Giudice, John, Salem	.981	98	193	13	4	210	4
Gonzalez, Raul, Wilmington	.966	76	137	5	5	147	1
Hawkins, Wes, Frederick	.980	41	49	0	1	50	0
Hodge, Roy, Frederick	.981	47	99	4	2	105	0
Hugo, Sean, Frederick*	1.000	19	22	0	0	22	0
Hunter, Lanier, Frederick	1.000	3	7	0	0	7	0
Jimenez, Oscar, Wilmington	.969	119	239	12	8	259	1
KING, Andre, Dur.-P.W.	1.000	106	279	9	0	288	3
Knoblauh, Jay, Lynchburg	.985	54	61	3	1	65	0
Knott, John, Durham	1.000	32	37	4	0	41	0
Knowles, Brian, Wilmington	1.000	7	12	3	0	15	0
Larkin, Stephen, Winston-Salem*	1.000	10	19	0	0	19	0
Leary, Rob, Lynchburg*	.889	34	31	1	4	36	0
LeCronier, Jason, Frederick	.957	27	43	1	2	46	0
Lemons, Rich, Kinston	.750	2	3	0	1	4	0
Lezeau, James, Salem	1.000	3	5	0	0	5	0
McBride, Gator, Durham	.930	78	123	10	10	143	1
McKinnon, Sandy, Prince William	.978	123	263	6	6	275	4
Meggers, Mike, Winston-Salem	.976	67	116	6	3	125	1
Monds, Wonderful, Durham	.984	51	112	9	2	123	2
Murphy, Mike, Kinston	.977	57	78	7	2	87	0
Newhouse, Andre, Prince William	.964	72	103	5	4	112	1
Oglesby, Luke, Wilmington	.957	39	45	0	2	47	0
Ordonez, Magglio, Prince William	.978	130	256	5	6	267	1
Oyas, Danny, Winston-Salem	.973	42	70	3	2	75	1
Pagano, Scott, Durham	.976	84	154	12	4	170	3
Peterson, Charles, Lynchburg	.962	104	192	11	8	211	1
Prieto, Rick, Kinston	.982	25	52	3	1	56	1
Quillin, Ty, Frederick	.900	8	9	0	1	10	0
Richardson, Eric, Prince William	1.000	6	6	1	0	7	0
Riemer, Matt, Frederick	1.000	7	9	2	0	11	0
Robertson, Robbie, Winst.-Sal.*	.977	54	80	6	2	88	0
Robertson, Tommy, Lynchburg	.952	42	38	2	2	42	1
Secrist, Reed, Lynchburg	.976	25	39	1	1	41	1
Sexton, Chris, Salem	1.000	3	3	0	0	3	0
Teeters, Brian, Wilmington*	1.000	51	99	1	0	100	0
Thomas, Greg, Kinston*	.943	20	31	2	2	35	0
Thomas, Rod, Winston-Salem	.964	18	24	3	1	28	0
Valdez, Trovin, Frederick	.934	106	167	16	13	196	4
Van Slyke, Andy, Frederick	1.000	1	3	0	0	3	0
Velazquez, Edgard, Salem	.976	131	273	16	7	296	1
Watkins, Pat, Winston-Salem	.982	26	51	5	1	57	0
Watson, Marty, Prince William	.933	22	41	1	3	45	0
Wells, Forry, Salem	.969	39	62	1	2	65	1
Wells, Mark, Salem	.963	56	73	6	3	82	1

OUTFIELDERS WITH TWO OR MORE TEAMS

Player, Team	Pct.	G	PO	A	E	TC	DP
Clyburn, Danny, Winst.-Salem	.947	49	66	6	4	76	1
Clyburn, Danny, Frederick	.929	10	13	0	1	14	0
King, Andre, Durham	1.000	97	261	9	0	270	3
King, Andre, Prince William	1.000	9	18	0	0	18	0

CATCHERS

Player, Team	Pct.	G	PO	A	E	TC	DP	PB
Bako, Paul, Winston-Salem	.989	78	478	49	6	533	3	15
Bess, Johnny, Winston-Salem	.993	20	122	14	1	137	1	3
Brooks, Ramy, Wilmington	.992	53	326	36	3	365	4	4
Cabrera, Jairo, Frederick	.976	25	136	29	4	169	1	6
Canetto, John, Lynchburg	1.000	11	50	8	0	58	0	2

Player, Team	Pct.	G	PO	A	E	TC	DP	PB
Castaneda, Hector, Frederick	.984	10	55	6	1	62	0	1
Daniel, Mike, Lynchburg	.992	19	115	7	1	123	1	1
DIAZ, Einar, Kinston	.9924	103	676	107	6	789	7	13
Dixon, Colin, Salem	1.000	2	4	0	0	4	0	0
Durso, Joe, Prince William	.974	50	310	25	9	344	2	4
Fasano, Sal, Wilmington	1.000	17	115	10	0	125	2	1
Foster, Jim, Frederick	.988	112	804	89	11	904	4	15
Garcia, Adrian, Durham	.966	5	24	4	1	29	0	1
Garcia, Guillermo, Winst.-Sal.	.983	54	301	38	6	345	2	11
Gargiulo, Mike, Frederick	1.000	3	20	4	0	24	0	1
Hanel, Marcus, Lynchburg	.993	40	241	38	2	281	4	4
Harriss, Robin, Kinston	1.000	15	94	11	0	105	0	1
Hicks, Jamie, Durham	.991	39	199	14	2	215	0	8
Higgins, Mike, Salem	.978	51	359	48	9	416	5	6
Izquierdo, Sergio, Prince William	.972	10	61	8	2	71	0	3
Johnson, Todd, Kinston	.971	21	117	16	4	137	2	1
Machado, Robert, Prince William	.9921	76	548	78	5	631	2	5
Mader, Chris, Kinston	.923	1	11	1	1	13	0	1
Meluskey, Mitch, Kinston	.985	7	58	6	1	65	1	1
Mendez, Carlos, Wilmington	1.000	1	3	1	0	4	0	1
Mendez, Sergio, Lynchburg	.985	60	409	55	7	471	3	8
Paul, Kortney, Wilmington	.962	7	23	2	1	26	0	0
Pozo, Yohel, Salem	.976	42	205	37	6	248	2	7
Reynolds, Chance, Lynchburg	1.000	5	32	4	0	36	0	0
Rodarte, Raul, Lynchburg	1.000	2	5	0	0	5	0	0
Scalzitti, Will, Salem	1.000	11	55	11	0	66	0	5
Secrist, Reed, Lynchburg	.979	14	44	2	1	47	0	1
Smith, Jason, Salem	.966	24	125	19	5	149	3	2
Smith, Sean, Durham	.989	27	152	25	2	179	2	1
Snyder, Randy, Salem	1.000	23	149	23	0	172	0	3
Spinello, Joe, Prince William	1.000	9	61	4	0	65	0	0
Sweeney, Mike, Wilmington	.989	72	575	45	7	627	5	8
Toth, Dave, Durham	.989	82	472	57	6	535	10	11
Walker, Joe, Prince William	.889	1	8	0	1	9	0	0
Weaver, Colby, Durham	.964	5	24	3	1	28	0	2
Webb, Kevin, Durham	.500	1	1	0	1	2	0	0

PITCHERS

Player, Team	Pct.	G	PO	A	E	TC	DP
Abramavicius, Jason, Lynchburg*	1.000	9	0	1	0	1	0
Aminoff, Matt, Salem	.882	39	4	11	2	17	4
Anderson, Eric, Wilmington	1.000	16	2	7	0	9	2
Anderson, Jimmy, Lynchburg*	1.000	10	4	6	0	10	0
Arnold, Jamie, Durham	.957	15	8	14	1	23	1
Atkinson, Neil, Wilmington*	1.000	8	0	5	0	5	0
Barnes, Keith, Salem*	.870	15	1	19	3	23	0
Binkley, Brett, Durham*	1.000	24	1	12	0	13	1
Bliss, Bill, Salem	1.000	34	1	6	0	7	0
Bock, Jeff, Durham	.900	32	2	7	1	10	1
Bowie, Micah, Durham*	.850	23	5	12	3	20	1
Brabant, Dan, Kinston	.952	47	7	13	1	21	2
Brewer, Brian, Frederick*	.917	14	3	8	1	12	0
Brewer, Nevin, Wilmington	1.000	17	4	5	0	9	1
Brownson, Mark, Salem	1.000	9	3	3	0	6	0
Burgess, Kurt, Durham*	.929	34	3	10	1	14	1
Byrd, Matt, Durham	1.000	60	2	7	0	9	0
Byrdak, Tim, Wilmington*	.977	27	15	27	1	43	2
Call, Mike, Prince William	1.000	28	1	13	0	14	0
Callistro, Rob, Prince William	1.000	8	1	1	0	2	0
Caruso, Joe, Lynchburg	1.000	29	1	4	0	5	0
Chaves, Rafael, Lynchburg	.842	40	8	8	0	8	0
Chavez, Carlos, Frederick	.875	43	3	11	2	16	2
Christman, Scott, Prince Will.*	.893	13	6	19	3	28	0
Christmas, Maurice, Durham	1.000	31	6	16	0	22	2
Clemons, Chris, Prince William	.971	27	11	23	1	35	0
Colon, Bartolo, Kinston	.952	21	7	13	1	21	1
Conley, Curt, Salem*	1.000	39	2	6	0	8	0
Connolly, Chris, Wilmington*	1.000	27	3	7	0	10	0
Connors, Chad, Winst.-Salem	1.000	16	1	2	0	3	0
Coppinger, Rocky, Frederick	1.000	11	0	5	0	5	1
Crills, Brad, Frederick*	1.000	9	4	13	0	17	0
Crowther, Brent, Salem	.895	12	6	11	2	19	0
Cruz, Nelson, Prince William	1.000	9	1	2	0	3	0
Cullop, Glen, Winston-Salem	1.000	6	0	1	0	1	1
Daniels, Lee, Durham	1.000	21	1	4	0	5	0
Dawley, Joe, Frederick	1.000	24	3	6	0	9	0
DeLaMaza, Roland, Kinston	1.000	26	5	18	0	23	1
DeLaRosa, Maximo, Kinston	.833	43	5	10	3	18	1
DeLeon, Elcilio, Lynchburg	1.000	13	1	0	0	1	0
Dickens, John, Wilmington*	.941	48	3	13	1	17	1
Dillinger, John, Lynchburg	.786	27	2	9	3	14	0
Donnelly, Brendan, Winst.-Sal.	.857	23	2	4	1	7	0

Player, Team	Pct.	G	PO	A	E	TC	DP
Doorneweerd, Dave, Lynchburg	1.000	5	0	1	0	1	0
Downs, John, Wilmington	1.000	8	1	2	0	3	0
Doyle, Tom, Winston-Salem*	1.000	21	1	4	0	5	0
Dyess, Todd, Frederick	1.000	3	1	2	0	3	0
Etler, Todd, Winston-Salem	1.000	24	19	19	0	38	4
Evans, Bart, Wilmington	.889	16	6	2	1	9	0
Faino, Jeff, Frederick*	1.000	4	0	1	0	1	0
Farson, Bryan, Lynchburg*	.750	27	0	3	1	4	0
Flury, Pat, Wilmington	1.000	15	0	4	0	4	0
Fordham, Tom, Prince William*	.857	13	3	15	3	21	0
Gamboa, Javier, Wilmington	1.000	8	5	4	0	9	0
Garrett, Neil, Salem	.000	5	0	0	2	2	0
Goldman, Barry, Salem	1.000	8	1	2	0	3	0
Graves, Dan, Kinston	1.000	38	5	9	0	14	0
Green, Jason, Durham	.900	39	3	6	1	10	0
Grundy, Phillip, Wilmington	.909	20	12	8	2	22	0
Hagan, Danny, Winston-Salem*	1.000	1	0	3	0	3	1
Hale, Shane, Frederick*	.800	6	0	4	1	5	1
Hanson, Kris, Kinston	.962	20	7	18	1	26	0
Harrison, Tom, Durham	1.000	7	3	8	0	11	1
Hartzog, Cullen, Lynchburg	.727	43	2	6	3	11	0
Harvell, Pete, Winston-Salem*	1.000	4	1	0	0	1	0
Heathcott, Mike, Prince William	1.000	27	3	15	0	18	0
Heiserman, Rick, Kinston	1.000	19	4	10	0	14	0
Hernandez, Francisco, Frederick	1.000	3	0	2	0	2	0
Hodges, Kevin, Wilmington	.857	12	0	6	1	7	1
Hostetler, Marcus, Durham	.500	12	0	1	1	2	0
Huber, Jeff, Frederick*	1.000	21	1	2	0	3	0
Jacobs, Ryan, Durham*	.976	29	8	32	1	41	2
Jesperson, Bob, Winston-Salem	1.000	5	1	1	0	2	0
Johnson, Jason M., Lynchburg	.765	10	3	10	4	17	1
Johnson, Jason S., Salem	1.000	5	0	1	0	1	0
Kirkreit, Daron, Kinston	1.000	3	1	3	0	4	0
Kitchen, Ron, Frederick	.895	30	4	13	2	19	0
Kummerfeldt, Jason, Winst.-Sal.	1.000	37	5	12	0	17	1
Kusiewicz, Michael, Salem*	1.000	1	0	2	0	2	0
LaPlante, Michel, Lynchburg	1.000	5	0	1	0	1	0
LaRocca, Todd, Frederick	1.000	5	4	8	0	12	0
Larock, Scott, Salem	.842	52	5	11	3	19	0
Lavenia, Mark, Durham*	1.000	6	0	1	0	1	0
Lawrence, Sean, Lynchburg*	.895	20	4	13	2	19	0
Lehman, Toby, Frederick	1.000	19	2	7	0	9	1
Lemp, Chris, Frederick	1.000	41	2	5	0	7	1
Leroy, John, Durham	1.000	24	5	14	0	19	1
Lindemann, Wayne, Prince Will.*	.909	19	1	9	1	11	1
Lombardi, John, Frederick	1.000	6	0	2	0	2	0
Lyons, Curt, Winston-Salem	.923	26	13	23	3	39	0
Maberry, Louis, Winston-Salem	.900	20	3	6	1	10	0
Maduro, Calvin, Frederick	.972	20	2	33	1	36	1
Magee, Bo, Frederick*	1.000	5	2	4	0	6	0
Magre, Pete, Winston-Salem	.833	17	1	4	1	6	0
Maine, Dalton, Frederick	1.000	19	1	1	0	2	0
Mansur, Jeff, Frederick*	1.000	12	1	4	0	5	0
Marenghi, Matt, Frederick	.850	30	5	12	3	20	0
Martinez, Johnny, Kinston	1.000	6	0	1	0	1	1
Mathews, Del, Durham*	.962	33	6	19	1	26	1
Mattson, Craig, Lynchburg	.500	11	1	0	1	2	0
Mayse, Robert, Frederick	1.000	6	1	0	0	1	0
McKenzie, Scott, Winst.-Salem	.929	49	2	11	1	14	1
Mesa, Rafael, Kinston	.900	35	2	7	1	10	1
Million, Doug, Salem*	.957	24	4	18	1	23	0
Montoya, Wilmer, Kinston	1.000	1	2	1	0	3	0
Morel, Ramon, Lynchburg	1.000	12	5	9	0	14	2
Murphy, Chris, Winston-Salem*	1.000	4	0	3	0	3	0
Najera, Noe, Kinston*	1.000	8	2	2	0	4	0
Nelson, Earl, Durham*	.800	15	0	4	1	5	0
Nieto, Tony, Frederick	.875	21	2	12	2	16	1
Oropeza, Igor, Kinston	.857	20	3	3	1	7	0
Paige, Carey, Durham	1.000	10	5	11	0	16	0
Perkins, Paul, Lynchburg	1.000	25	1	1	0	2	0
Peters, Chris, Lynchburg	.968	24	1	29	1	31	3
Pfaff, Jason, Lynchburg	.968	35	6	24	1	31	2
Pickford, Kevin, Lynchburg*	1.000	4	1	2	0	3	0
Pierson, Jason, Prince William*	1.000	21	4	18	0	22	0
Place, Mike, Durham	.800	7	1	3	1	5	1
Pontbriant, Matt, Lynchburg*	.900	27	3	15	2	20	2
Pool, Matt, Salem	.955	28	20	22	2	44	1
Pratt, Rich, Prince William*	.939	25	1	30	2	33	1
Priest, Eddie, Winston-Salem*	.938	12	1	14	1	16	0
Raines, Ken, Durham*	1.000	19	1	11	0	12	1
Ramos, Cesar, Kinston	.800	8	2	2	1	5	0
Rawitzer, Kevin, Wilmington*	1.000	15	3	5	0	8	1

Player, Team	Pct.	G	PO	A	E	TC	DP	Player, Team	Pct.	G	PO	A	E	TC	DP
Ray, Ken, Wilmington	.952	13	3	17	1	21	1	Stewart, Chris, Salem	1.000	10	1	0	0	1	0
Reed, Chris, Winston-Salem	.977	24	17	25	1	43	1	Stewart, Rachaad, Frederick*	1.000	26	2	23	0	25	0
Rhodes, Joe, Frederick	.500	2	0	1	1	2	0	Tagle, Hank, Prince William*	.952	33	6	14	1	21	0
Rizzo, Todd, Prince William*	.800	36	0	8	2	10	0	Tolar, Kevin, Lynchburg*	1.000	18	2	0	0	2	0
Robbins, Jason, Winston-Salem	.931	23	12	15	2	29	0	Towns, Ryan, Wilmington	1.000	12	3	2	0	5	0
Roberts, Ray, Wilmington*	1.000	13	0	3	0	3	0	Tuttle, Dave, Winston-Salem	.923	10	3	9	1	13	0
Rogers, Jason, Frederick*	.889	15	5	11	2	18	1	Vaught, Jay, Kinston	.943	27	11	22	2	35	0
Rosado, Jose, Wilmington*	1.000	25	8	14	0	22	1	Vazquez, Archie, Prince William	.800	47	1	7	2	10	0
Runion, Tony, Kinston	.875	28	5	9	2	16	0	Voisard, Mark, Salem	.667	6	1	1	1	3	0
RUSCH, Glendon, Wilmington*	1.000	26	10	29	0	39	5	Waldron, Joe, Salem*	1.000	9	2	1	0	3	1
Ruyak, Todd, Winston-Salem*	.938	34	6	9	1	16	0	Walker, James, Frederick	1.000	9	2	6	0	8	0
Saipe, Mike, Salem	.875	21	4	10	2	16	2	Walls, Doug, Salem	.833	15	4	6	2	12	0
Salamon, John, Salem	.750	8	0	3	1	4	0	Wells, David, Durham	1.000	7	0	2	0	2	0
Sexton, Jeff, Kinston	1.000	8	4	9	0	13	1	Williams, Greg, Kinston*	1.000	30	2	4	0	6	0
Sheehan, Chris, Wilmington	1.000	13	0	3	0	3	0	Winkle, Ken, Wilmington	1.000	11	1	3	0	4	0
Sinnes, David, Wilmington	1.000	18	2	2	0	4	0	Woods, Brian, Prince William	.867	27	10	16	4	30	0
Smith, Hut, Frederick	.429	20	0	3	4	7	0	Worrell, Steve, Prince William*	1.000	29	1	7	0	8	0
Smith, Toby, Wilmington	1.000	30	6	12	0	18	0	Wright, Jamey, Salem	.959	26	16	31	2	49	2
Sobkoviak, Jeff, Salem	1.000	40	3	6	0	9	0	Young, Danny, Lynchburg*	.833	24	1	4	1	6	0
Sosa, Jose, Lynchburg	1.000	10	1	1	0	2	0	Zolecki, Mike, Salem	1.000	9	0	5	0	5	0

The following players did not have any fielding statistics at the positions indicated or appeared only as a designated hitter, pinch-hitter or pinch-runner: M. Anderson, of; Bess, ss; Buchanan, dh, pr; Carpenter, ph; Carranza, of; Daigle, p; Davis, of; Dietrich, p; Dixon, 3b; Driskill, p; M. Evans, c; Foster, 3b; Giron, p; P. Gonzalez, of; Grunewald, 1b; Gutierrez, ss; Jones, dh, ph; Knott, 2b; Lamb, 2b; Locklear, p; Mader, 3b; Mesewicz, p; Riemer, p; Sauritch, 3b, p; S. Smith, 3b; Sweeney, 3b; Toth, of; G. White, p; J. White, dh, ph; E. Wilson, 2b.

LEAGUE CHAMPIONS

Year	Team	Pct.	Year	Team	Pct.	Year	Team	Pct.
1945—	Danville	.681	1964—	Kinston§	.572	1980—	Peninsula‡	.714
1946—	Greensboro	.599		Winston-Salem§†	.590		Durham	.600
	Raleigh (2nd)†	.563	1965—	Peninsula§	.597	1981—	Peninsula	.522
1947—	Burlington	.613		Durham§	.580		Hagerstown‡	.507
	Raleigh (3rd)†	.574		Tidewater†	.528	1982—	Alexandria‡	.597
1948—	Raleigh	.592	1966—	Kinston§	.547		Durham	.588
	Martinsville (2nd)†	.570		Winston-Salem§	.586	1983—	Lynchburg‡	.691
1949—	Danville	.601		Rocky Mount†	.533		Winston-Salem	.529
	Burlington (4th)†	.500	1967—	Durham∞(West.)	.536	1984—	Lynchburg‡	.645
1950—	Winston-Salem*	.693		Raleigh (East.)	.542		Durham	.486
1951—	Durham	.600	1968—	Salem (West.)	.607	1985—	Lynchburg	.679
	Wins-Salem (2nd)†	.583		Ral-Dur (East.)	.597		Winston-Salem‡	.417
1952—	Raleigh	.581		HP-Thom.▲(W.)	.493	1986—	Hagerstown	.655
	Reidsville (4th)†	.536	1969—	Rocky M (East.)	.569		Winston-Salem‡	.594
1953—	Raleigh	.593		Salem (West.)	.542	1987—	Salem‡	.576
	Danville (2nd)†	.572		Ral-Dur◆(East.)	.560		Kinston	.536
1954—	Fayetteville*	.628	1970—	Winston-Salem‡	.586	1988—	Kinston§	.629
1955—	HP-Thomasville	.580		Burlington	.597		Lynchburg	.486
	Danville (2nd)†	.533	1971—	Peninsula‡	.647	1989—	Durham	.609
1956—	HP-Thomasville	.591		Kinston	.623		Prince William‡	.522
	Fayetteville (4th)§	.523	1972—	Salem‡	.657	1990—	Kinston	.652
1957—	Durham	.632		Burlington	.632		Frederick‡	.544
	HP-Thomasville	.622	1973—	Lynchburg	.588	1991—	Kinston‡	.645
1958—	Danville	.576		Winston-Salem‡	.557		Lynchburg	.482
	Burlington (4th)†	.511	1974—	Salem	.671	1992—	Lynchburg	.570
1959—	Raleigh	.600		Salem	.582		Peninsula‡	.536
	Wilson (2nd)†	.550	1975—	Rocky Mount	.667	1993—	Wilmington	.532
1960—	Greensboro‡	.636		Rocky Mount	.614		Winston-Salem‡	.514
	Burlington	.586	1976—	Winston-Salem	.618	1994—	Wilmington†	.681
1961—	Wilson	.594		Winston-Salem	.551		Winston-Salem	.555
1962—	Durham	.636	1977—	Lynchburg	.591	1995—	Wilmington	.601
	Wilson	.600		Peninsula‡	.556		Kinston‡	.591
	Kinston (2nd)†	.593	1978—	Peninsula	.696			
1963—	Kinston§	.538		Lynchburg‡	.614			
	Greensboro§	.590	1979—	Winston-Salem■	.607			
	Wilson (2nd)†	.535						

*Won championship and four-club playoff. †Won four-club playoff. ‡Won split-season playoff. §League was divided into Eastern, Western divisions. ∞Won eight-club, two-division playoff. ▲Won eight-club, two-division playoff against Raleigh-Durham. ◆Won eight-club, two-division playoff against Burlington. ■Won both halves of split season (no playoffs).

FLORIDA STATE LEAGUE

LEAGUE OFFICE

President
Chuck Murphy

Address
P.O. Box 349
Daytona Beach, FL 32115

Phone
904-252-7479

Teams (affiliation)
Brevard County Manatees (Marlins)
Charlotte Rangers (Rangers)
Clearwater Phillies (Phillies)
Daytona Cubs (Cubs)
Dunedin Blue Jays (Blue Jays)
Fort Myers Miracle (Twins)
Kissimmee Cobras (Astros)

Lakeland Tigers (Tigers)
St. Lucie Mets (Mets)
St. Petersburg Cardinals (Cardinals)
Sarasota Red Sox (Red Sox)
Tampa Yankees (Yankees)
Vero Beach Dodgers (Dodgers)
West Palm Beach Expos (Expos)

1995 FINAL STANDINGS

FIRST HALF

EAST DIVISION

Team	W	L	T	Pct.	GB
Daytona (Cubs)	41	28	0	.594	......
Vero Beach (Dodgers)	39	31	0	.557	2$\frac{1}{2}$
St. Lucie (Mets)	33	35	0	.485	7$\frac{1}{2}$
Brevard County (Marlins)	30	38	0	.441	10$\frac{1}{2}$
Kissimmee (Astros)	28	41	0	.406	13
West Palm Beach (Expos)	25	44	0	.362	16

WEST DIVISION

Team	W	L	T	Pct.	GB
Tampa (Yankees)	41	29	0	.586	......
Clearwater (Phillies)	38	32	0	.543	3
Lakeland (Tigers)	36	33	0	.522	4$\frac{1}{2}$
Dunedin (Blue Jays)	35	33	0	.515	5
Charlotte (Rangers)	35	33	0	.515	5
Fort Myers (Twins)	34	34	0	.500	6
Sarasota (Red Sox)	34	34	0	.500	6
St. Petersburg (Cardinals)	32	36	0	.471	8

SECOND HALF

EAST DIVISION

Team	W	L	T	Pct.	GB
Daytona (Cubs)	46	20	0	.697	......
Vero Beach (Dodgers)	35	28	0	.556	9$\frac{1}{2}$
Brevard County (Marlins)	31	36	0	.463	15$\frac{1}{2}$
West Palm Beach (Expos)	29	37	1	.439	17
St. Lucie (Mets)	28	38	1	.424	18
Kissimmee (Astros)	27	40	0	.403	19$\frac{1}{2}$

WEST DIVISION

Team	W	L	T	Pct.	GB
Fort Myers (Twins)	41	21	1	.661	......
Clearwater (Phillies)	41	27	0	.603	3
St. Petersburg (Cardinals)	32	31	0	.508	9$\frac{1}{2}$
Sarasota (Red Sox)	31	34	1	.477	11$\frac{1}{2}$
Tampa (Yankees)	31	35	0	.470	12
Charlotte (Rangers)	30	34	1	.469	12
Lakeland (Tigers)	28	36	1	.438	14
Dunedin (Blue Jays)	28	41	0	.406	16$\frac{1}{2}$

COMPOSITE

Team	Day.	Ft.M.	Clw.	V.B.	Tam.	Char.	Sar.	St.P.	Lak.	Dun.	StL	B.C.	Kis.	WPB	W	L	T	Pct.	GB
Daytona (Cubs)	....	5	4	6	8	6	2	6	4	6	8	10	10	12	87	48	0	.644	......
Fort Myers (Twins)	1	....	8	3	6	8	11	6	9	6	2	6	4	5	75	55	1	.577	9$\frac{1}{2}$
Clearwater (Phillies)	4	4	....	6	5	10	8	5	7	10	3	7	6	4	79	59	0	.572	9$\frac{1}{2}$
Vero Beach (Dodgers)	6	5	2	....	5	5	3	5	2	5	9	8	9	10	74	59	0	.556	12
Tampa (Yankees)	0	6	5	2	....	7	10	10	7	7	5	4	5	4	72	64	0	.529	15$\frac{1}{2}$
Charlotte (Rangers)	2	6	2	2	5	....	4	6	9	8	5	5	4	7	65	67	1	.492	20$\frac{1}{2}$
Sarasota (Red Sox)	4	5	4	3	2	8	....	4	9	6	5	5	5	5	65	68	1	.489	21
St. Petersburg (Cardinals)	2	6	11	2	6	4	7	....	4	5	4	5	4	4	64	67	0	.489	21
Lakeland (Tigers)	4	1	5	6	5	6	6	8	....	7	5	1	5	6	64	69	1	.481	22
Dunedin (Blue Jays)	2	6	6	3	9	2	6	7	4	....	7	3	4	4	63	74	0	.460	25
St. Lucie (Mets)	8	4	5	7	3	3	3	2	3	1	....	7	7	8	61	73	1	.455	25$\frac{1}{2}$
Brevard County (Marlins)	6	1	1	8	3	3	1	3	6	5	9	....	9	6	61	74	0	.452	26
Kissimmee (Astros)	5	4	2	5	3	4	3	4	3	4	4	7	....	7	55	81	0	.404	32$\frac{1}{2}$
West Palm Beach (Expos)	4	2	4	6	4	1	2	3	2	4	7	6	9	....	54	81	1	.400	33

Brevard County played home games in Melbourne, Fla.

Charlotte played home games in Port Charlotte, Fla.

Major league affiliations in parentheses.

PLAYOFFS: Fort Myers defeated Tampa, two games to one; Daytona defeated Fort Myers, three games to two, to win league championship.

REGULAR-SEASON ATTENDANCE: Brevard County, 140,109; Charlotte, 60,000; Clearwater, 71,761; Daytona, 90,071; Dunedin, 65,764; Fort Myers, 78,431; Kissimmee, 41,091; Lakeland, 21,635; St. Lucie, 80,734; St. Petersburg, 100,055; Sarasota, 65,223; Tampa, 48,598; Vero Beach, 42,702; West Palm Beach, 71,446. Total, 977,620. Playoffs (8 games), 4,392. All-Star Game, 3,587.

MANAGERS: Brevard County, Fredi Gonzalez; Charlotte, Butch Wynegar; Clearwater, Don McCormack; Daytona, Dave Trembley; Dunedin, Jim Nettles; Fort Myers, Al Newman; Kissimmee, Dave Engle; Lakeland, Dave Anderson; St. Lucie, Rafael Landestoy; St. Petersburg, Chris Maloney; Sarasota, Tommy Barrett; Tampa, Jake Gibbs; Vero Beach, Jon Debus; West Palm Beach, Gomer Hodge (April 6 through June 3) and Rick Sofield (June 4 through end of season). Managerial records of team with more than one manager: West Palm Beach, Hodge 19-36, Sofield 35-45.

ALL-STAR TEAM: 1B—Dan Held, Clearwater; 2B—Bobby Morris, Daytona; 3B—Gary Caraballo, Fort Myers; SS—Jason Maxwell, Daytona; Utility IF—Michael Metcalfe, Vero Beach; LF—Shane Spencer, Tampa; CF—Wendell Magee, Clearwater; RF—Scott Samuels, Daytona; Utility OF—Chris Latham, Vero Beach; C—Bobby Estalella, Clearwater, and Kevin Brown, Charlotte; DH—Bubba Trammell, Lakeland; RHP—Matt Drews, Tampa; Shane Bowers, Fort Myers; LHP—Benj Sampson, Fort Myers; Troy Carrasco, Fort Myers; Relievers—Joe Jacobsen, Vero Beach; Jason Hart, Daytona; Most Valuable Player—Shane Spencer, Tampa; Manager of the Year—Dave Trembley, Daytona.

(left margin) **CLASS A** *Florida State League*

TEAM

Team	Avg.	G	TPA	AB	R	H	TB	2B	3B	HR	RBI	SH	SF	HP	BB	IBB	SO	SB	CS	GDP	LOB	ShO	Slg.	OBP
Vero Beach	.261	133	4883	4280	583	1119	1540	182	22	65	507	41	42	68	451	23	755	184	87	99	918	11	.360	.338
Clearwater	.261	138	5209	4565	653	1192	1747	219	33	90	576	35	38	86	484	11	822	119	67	129	986	9	.383	.341
Lakeland	.261	135	4944	4460	553	1162	1623	190	38	65	493	29	33	33	388	13	935	133	68	83	920	10	.364	.322
Sarasota	.260	134	4923	4400	571	1146	1591	198	26	65	499	30	30	52	407	7	927	126	105	80	886	10	.362	.328
Daytona	.256	135	4995	4355	638	1114	1524	187	32	53	549	35	49	78	471	21	759	161	78	98	890	4	.350	.336
Charlotte	.253	133	4969	4375	543	1106	1548	210	32	56	483	34	33	78	449	12	839	96	96	94	956	11	.354	.331
Dunedin	.250	138	5238	4616	621	1156	1682	218	37	78	556	30	38	50	504	20	930	79	44	86	994	8	.364	.328
Brevard County	.248	135	5138	4492	556	1113	1530	197	23	58	490	39	52	52	502	11	891	83	53	118	998	8	.341	.327
Fort Myers	.248	131	4825	4220	552	1045	1447	196	22	54	471	62	32	70	440	20	784	84	73	99	883	9	.343	.327
Tampa	.247	136	5137	4438	580	1098	1570	191	31	73	512	44	35	56	557	15	911	98	56	84	1015	7	.354	.336
West Palm Bch.	.242	136	4861	4324	510	1045	1396	182	29	37	443	41	37	40	419	13	851	123	72	81	880	13	.323	.312
Kissimmee	.241	134	5051	4452	508	1073	1464	205	21	48	432	27	46	75	450	14	855	141	66	109	945	13	.329	.318
St. Lucie	.240	135	4875	4313	484	1034	1394	154	40	42	414	61	31	53	413	18	908	133	89	83	889	8	.323	.312
St. Petersburg	.234	131	4726	4175	468	975	1326	173	20	46	408	35	35	37	440	14	813	69	39	107	883	16	.318	.310

INDIVIDUAL

TOP QUALIFIERS FOR BATTING CHAMPIONSHIP

Minimum 378 plate appearances. *Lefthanded batter. †Switch-hitter.

Player, Team	Avg.	G	TPA	AB	R	H	TB	2B	3B	HR	RBI	SH	SF	HP	BB	IBB	SO	SB	CS	GDP	Slg.	OBP
Magee, Wendell, Clearwater	.353	96	432	388	67	137	189	24	5	6	46	1	5	4	33	3	40	7	10	15	.487	.405
Samuels, Scott, Daytona*	.327	112	473	388	92	127	186	29	12	2	42	3	4	8	69	7	63	38	14	8	.479	.435
Nelson, Bry, Kissimmee†	.327	105	423	395	47	129	182	34	5	3	52	1	6	1	20	0	37	14	10	8	.461	.355
Saffer, Jon, West Palm Beach*	.318	92	384	324	60	103	137	10	6	4	35	4	1	2	53	1	49	18	9	7	.423	.416
Morris, Bobby, Daytona*	.308	95	397	344	44	106	134	18	2	2	55	2	5	8	38	6	46	22	8	5	.390	.385
Roberts, David, Lakeland*	.303	92	401	357	67	108	137	10	5	3	30	2	2	1	39	2	43	30	8	7	.384	.371
Metcalfe, Mike, Vero Beach†	.301	120	509	435	86	131	159	13	3	3	35	6	5	3	60	2	37	60	27	8	.366	.386
Spencer, Shane, Tampa	.300	134	573	500	87	150	235	31	3	16	88	2	3	7	61	2	60	14	8	7	.470	.382
Berg, David, Brevard County	.298	114	474	382	71	114	143	18	1	3	39	7	9	8	68	1	61	9	4	5	.374	.407
Fick, Chris, St. Petersburg*	.293	113	399	348	56	102	172	25	3	13	52	0	3	10	38	2	79	1	2	9	.494	.376
Facione, Chris, Lakeland	.293	110	444	400	44	117	161	17	6	5	56	2	4	2	35	3	76	20	10	13	.403	.349
Tebbs, Nathan, Sarasota†	.291	118	487	440	58	128	157	15	4	2	52	4	1	3	39	0	80	25	15	7	.357	.362
Freeman, Sean, Lakeland*	.290	119	472	414	42	120	163	21	2	6	65	0	7	2	49	3	98	3	4	3	.394	.362
Millar, Kevin, Brevard County	.288	129	515	459	53	132	207	32	2	13	68	0	10	12	70	2	66	4	4	8	.451	.388
Cabrera, Jolbert, W. Palm Beach	.286	103	413	357	62	102	132	23	2	1	25	6	4	8	30	0	61	19	12	3	.370	.364

DEPARTMENTAL LEADERS: G—Held, Spencer, 134; AB—A. Ramirez, 541; R—Samuels, 92; H—Spencer, 150; TB—Spencer, 235; 2B—Held, 35; 3B—Samuels, 12; HR—Held, 21; RBI—Spencer, 88; SH—B. Jones, 16; SF—Millar, 10; HP—Cooney, 23; BB—Patzke, 85; IBB—Patzke, 8; SO—S. Smith, 136; SB—Metcalfe, 60; CS—Metcalfe, 27; GIDP—Kingman, 21; Slg.—Fick, .494; OBP—Samuels, .435.

ALL PLAYERS

*Lefthanded batter. †Switch-hitter.

Player, Team	Avg.	G	TPA	AB	R	H	TB	2B	3B	HR	RBI	SH	SF	HP	BB	IBB	SO	SB	CS	GDP	Slg.	OBP
Abad, Andy, Sarasota*	.288	18	65	59	5	17	20	3	0	0	10	0	0	0	6	0	13	4	3	0	.339	.354
Adolfo, Carlos, West Palm Beach	.185	28	86	81	6	15	19	1	0	1	7	0	0	0	5	0	22	1	0	1	.235	.233
Agbayani, Benny, St. Lucie	.310	44	191	155	24	48	69	9	3	2	29	1	4	5	26	1	27	8	3	4	.445	.416
Alcantara, Israel, W. Palm Beach	.276	39	148	134	16	37	57	7	2	3	22	2	1	2	9	0	35	3	0	0	.425	.329
Almanzar, Richard, Lakeland	.307	42	167	140	29	43	55	9	0	1	14	5	0	4	18	0	20	11	9	5	.393	.401
Alvarado, Basilio, W. Palm Beach	.222	9	19	18	0	4	4	0	0	0	0	0	0	0	1	0	5	0	0	1	.222	.263
Amador, Manuel, Clearwater†	.279	96	359	330	45	92	137	19	4	6	47	1	0	6	22	0	38	5	2	6	.415	.335
Anderson, Cliff, Vero Beach*	.271	113	391	365	48	99	141	20	2	6	44	6	2	8	10	1	58	1	4	4	.386	.304
Angeli, Doug, Clearwater	.191	16	54	47	4	9	12	3	0	0	3	2	1	1	3	0	13	0	1	0	.255	.250
Arano, Eloy, Lakeland†	.283	102	366	353	35	100	111	9	1	0	33	3	1	0	9	1	55	5	6	7	.314	.319
Asencio, Alex, Vero Beach*	.266	58	196	184	24	49	69	8	3	2	21	1	4	1	6	0	22	4	3	0	.375	.287
Aybar, Ramon, Lakeland*	.125	3	9	8	1	1	1	0	0	0	0	0	0	0	1	0	5	0	0	0	.125	.222
Azuaje, Jesus, St. Lucie	.239	91	362	306	35	73	86	5	1	2	20	11	0	7	36	1	55	14	9	5	.281	.331
Babin, Brady, Brevard County	.248	32	118	105	15	26	39	3	2	2	19	1	2	1	9	0	20	0	1	4	.371	.308
Baker, Jason, Fort Myers*	.239	91	324	276	35	66	75	9	0	0	26	8	3	7	30	1	38	8	8	5	.272	.323
Basey, Marsalis, Kissimmee	.230	91	344	317	37	73	79	6	0	0	16	2	3	4	18	1	35	12	5	6	.249	.278
Baugh, Gavin, Brevard County†	.188	81	286	250	24	47	65	11	2	1	21	2	3	4	26	0	70	10	3	3	.260	.272
Bell, Mike, Charlotte	.260	129	523	470	49	122	159	20	1	5	52	3	2	0	48	0	72	9	8	11	.338	.327
Bellum, Donnie, St. Petersburg	.195	64	136	118	16	23	26	0	0	0	9	4	2	0	12	0	23	0	2	5	.220	.265
Benbow, Lou, St. Lucie	.364	12	36	33	4	12	14	2	0	0	2	1	0	1	1	0	7	0	1	0	.424	.400
Benz, Jake, West Palm Beach*	.000	1	1	1	0	0	0	0	0	0	0	0	0	0	0	0	0	0	0	0	.000	.000
Berg, David, Brevard County	.298	114	474	382	71	114	143	18	1	3	39	7	9	8	68	1	61	9	4	5	.374	.407
Berry, Michael, W. Palm Beach	.165	24	92	79	16	13	21	3	1	1	2	0	0	0	13	0	16	0	1	1	.266	.283
Beyna, Terry, Kissimmee	.167	15	45	42	4	7	8	1	0	0	2	0	0	1	2	0	12	0	0	4	.190	.222
Bierek, Kurt, Tampa*	.248	126	517	447	60	111	143	16	2	4	53	2	2	4	61	3	73	3	4	11	.320	.342
Biltimier, Mike, Vero Beach*	.225	127	482	422	62	95	151	14	0	14	50	3	4	5	48	1	109	0	1	8	.358	.309
Blair, Mike, Charlotte*	.223	69	302	264	34	59	70	5	3	0	9	2	1	1	34	3	42	14	6	4	.265	.313
Blum, Geoffrey, W. Palm Beach†	.263	125	502	457	54	120	147	20	2	1	62	1	7	3	34	1	61	6	5	12	.322	.313
Bokemeier, Matt, Charlotte†	.236	105	417	385	42	91	133	16	1	8	34	4	0	2	26	1	76	7	7	11	.345	.288
Borel, Jamie, Lakeland	.122	16	48	41	8	5	6	1	0	0	1	0	0	1	6	0	6	2	1	2	.146	.250
Borrero, Rikchy, Sarasota	.204	34	108	98	9	20	25	5	0	0	4	1	2	2	5	0	22	0	1	1	.255	.252
Boyd, Quincy, Vero Beach	.152	31	75	66	4	10	12	2	0	0	1	0	0		9	0	20	0	0	2	.182	.253
Braddy, Junior, Sarasota	.264	114	455	413	41	109	137	12	5	2	36	2	4	5	31	0	99	13	12	10	.332	.320

Player, Team	Avg.	G	TPA	AB	R	H	TB	2B	3B	HR	RBI	SH	SF	HP	BB	IBB	SO	SB	CS	GDP	Slg.	OBP
Brito, Domingo, Clearwater	.000	1	1	1	0	0	0	0	0	0	0	0	0	0	0	0	1	0	0	0	.000	.000
Brito, Luis, Clearwater†	.274	109	409	383	42	105	134	14	3	3	41	5	3	1	17	0	35	12	5	14	.350	.304
Brock, Tarrick, Lakeland*	.209	28	104	91	12	19	22	3	0	0	5	1	0	0	12	0	32	5	3	2	.242	.301
Brown, Armann, Fort Myers	.190	23	68	63	6	12	20	2	3	0	9	0	1	1	3	0	15	1	0	1	.317	.235
Brown, Kevin, Charlotte	.265	107	419	355	48	94	154	25	1	11	57	1	4	9	50	0	96	2	3	9	.434	.366
Brown, Ron, Brevard County	.260	121	448	404	48	105	140	22	2	3	51	1	9	3	31	0	79	6	12	14	.347	.311
Brown, Shawn, Lakeland	.167	10	29	24	2	4	5	1	0	0	0	0	0	1	4	0	5	0	0	0	.208	.310
Brown, Willie, Brevard County*	.222	63	215	189	26	42	68	6	1	6	23	0	0	1	25	3	74	4	3	1	.360	.316
Browne, Jerry, Brevard County†	.286	3	9	7	0	2	2	0	0	0	2	0	1	0	1	0	1	0	0	0	.286	.333
Brunson, Matt, Lakeland†	.129	45	162	132	10	17	21	2	1	0	7	4	0	0	26	0	41	9	2	4	.159	.272
Burke, Alan, Clearwater	.222	3	9	9	2	2	5	0	0	1	2	0	0	0	0	0	2	0	0	1	.556	.222
Cabrera, Alex, Daytona	.294	54	229	214	26	63	83	14	0	2	35	0	2	4	9	0	36	2	4	8	.388	.332
Cabrera, Jolbert, W. Palm Beach	.286	103	413	357	62	102	132	23	2	1	25	6	4	8	38	0	61	19	12	3	.370	.364
Cabrera, Orlando, W. Palm Beach	.200	3	5	5	0	1	1	0	0	0	0	0	0	0	0	0	1	0	0	0	.200	.200
Campos, Jesus, W. Palm Beach	.221	107	361	326	32	72	82	6	2	0	21	6	2	2	25	0	40	18	7	5	.252	.279
Candelaria, Ben, Dunedin*	.259	125	532	471	66	122	168	21	5	5	49	3	5	0	53	1	98	11	4	11	.357	.331
Caraballo, Gary, Fort Myers	.307	85	351	309	51	95	144	24	2	7	55	0	3	5	34	3	44	5	6	10	.466	.382
Carey, Todd, Sarasota*	.306	25	94	85	15	26	44	6	0	4	19	0	0	0	9	0	17	2	1	3	.518	.372
Castro, Ramon, Kissimmee	.208	36	128	120	6	25	30	5	0	0	8	0	1	1	6	0	21	0	0	1	.250	.250
Champion, Jim, Fort Myers*	.227	99	354	308	38	70	101	14	4	3	33	5	3	12	26	0	88	3	1	3	.328	.309
Chick, Bruce, West Palm Beach	.100	3	11	10	0	1	1	0	0	0	1	0	0	0	1	0	3	0	0	1	.100	.182
Christmon, Drew, Lakeland*	.220	79	294	273	34	60	107	8	6	9	39	1	2	4	14	1	96	7	2	4	.392	.266
Clark, Kevin, Sarasota	.225	84	317	293	23	66	89	11	0	4	31	1	0	2	21	0	63	2	5	9	.304	.282
Collier, Dan, Sarasota	.256	67	270	242	30	62	112	12	1	12	44	0	3	5	20	0	83	5	9	3	.463	.322
Cooney, Kyle, Vero Beach	.278	105	400	356	44	99	132	11	2	6	54	1	2	23	17	1	50	4	3	15	.371	.349
Cooper, Tim, Tampa	.176	63	201	170	16	30	44	3	1	3	13	0	2	5	24	0	48	1	1	3	.259	.294
Cossins, Tim, Charlotte	.059	7	21	17	1	1	1	0	0	0	0	0	0	0	4	1	5	0	1	0	.059	.238
Costello, Brian, Clearwater	.249	112	445	406	52	101	151	19	2	9	56	0	0	2	37	0	88	14	9	9	.372	.315
Cradle, Cobi, St. Lucie*	.233	78	302	257	34	60	70	5	1	1	12	4	3	1	37	0	45	19	3	1	.272	.329
Cradle, Rickey, Dunedin	.275	50	211	178	33	49	86	10	3	7	27	1	2	2	28	0	49	6	2	2	.483	.376
Crespo, Mike, Charlotte†	.162	28	80	74	6	12	14	2	0	0	3	0	0	0	6	0	23	0	0	3	.189	.225
Cromer, Brandon, Dunedin*	.237	106	385	329	40	78	113	11	3	6	43	5	3	5	43	3	84	0	5	6	.343	.332
Dalton, Dee, St. Petersburg	.205	118	438	385	36	79	103	16	1	2	30	2	3	3	45	0	81	10	4	7	.268	.291
Davenport, Jeff, Sarasota	.000	10	28	22	1	0	0	0	0	0	3	0	2	0	1	0	8	0	0	0	.000	.040
Davila, Vic, Dunedin*	.257	109	370	331	48	85	127	14	5	6	45	3	4	8	24	2	66	1	3	4	.384	.319
Dawson, Andre, Brevard County	.100	3	10	10	0	1	1	0	0	0	0	0	0	0	0	0	2	0	0	1	.100	.100
Deares, Greg, St. Petersburg*	.235	20	54	51	3	12	13	1	0	0	4	0	0	0	2	0	8	0	0	0	.255	.264
DeBerry, Joe, Tampa*	.224	58	216	196	16	44	62	9	3	1	18	0	1	0	19	3	45	1	0	3	.316	.292
DeJesus, Malvin, Lakeland	.301	73	273	239	39	72	98	7	5	3	23	2	1	4	27	0	51	7	6	1	.410	.380
DeLaCruz, Carlos, Lakeland	.000	2	3	3	0	0	0	0	0	0	0	0	0	0	0	0	2	0	0	0	.000	.000
Delafield, Wil, Tampa	.269	7	29	26	4	7	11	1	0	1	6	0	0	1	2	0	11	1	0	0	.423	.345
Diaz, Cesar, St. Lucie	.233	102	386	361	33	84	123	17	2	6	40	3	1	2	19	1	91	0	5	13	.341	.274
Diaz, Edwin, Charlotte	.284	115	495	450	48	128	188	26	5	8	56	3	2	7	33	0	94	8	13	10	.418	.341
Diaz, Linardo, Clearwater	.212	11	37	33	1	7	8	1	0	0	1	0	1	0	3	0	7	0	0	1	.242	.270
Donato, Daniel, Tampa*	.250	3	9	8	1	2	5	0	0	1	1	0	0	1	0	0	2	0	0	0	.625	.333
Dowler, Dee, Daytona	.251	112	479	415	70	104	129	12	2	3	59	7	4	8	45	0	51	26	15	11	.311	.333
Driskell, Jeff, Lakeland	.262	23	67	61	8	16	26	4	0	2	8	0	1	0	5	0	17	0	0	1	.426	.313
Duross, Gabe, Daytona*	.241	60	240	224	20	54	72	9	0	3	34	0	3	2	11	2	12	4	4	6	.321	.279
Ellis, Kevin, Daytona	.270	120	471	430	57	116	163	17	6	6	66	0	4	10	26	1	73	6	3	11	.379	.323
Epperson, Chad, St. Lucie†	.190	42	141	121	7	23	35	7	1	1	14	1	2	0	17	2	32	1	0	7	.289	.286
Erdman, Brad, Daytona	.154	8	31	26	4	4	5	1	0	0	3	1	0	0	4	0	6	0	0	0	.192	.267
Estalella, Bobby, Clearwater	.260	117	469	404	51	105	176	24	1	15	58	3	4	2	56	2	76	0	3	12	.436	.350
Evans, Stan, Clearwater*	.248	89	322	286	34	71	82	5	3	0	32	4	3	0	29	0	33	10	5	6	.287	.314
Evans, Tom, Dunedin	.279	130	513	444	63	124	186	29	3	9	66	3	7	8	51	0	80	7	2	10	.419	.359
Everson, Darin, W. Palm Beach*	.219	38	124	105	7	23	28	2	0	1	13	0	1	6	12	2	22	0	0	3	.267	.331
Facione, Chris, Lakeland	.293	110	444	400	44	117	161	17	6	5	56	2	4	2	35	3	76	20	10	13	.403	.349
Ferrier, Ross, St. Lucie	.201	68	258	234	27	47	78	6	2	7	23	1	2	3	18	1	69	2	5	6	.333	.265
Fick, Chris, St. Petersburg*	.293	113	399	348	56	102	172	25	3	13	52	0	3	10	38	2	79	1	2	9	.494	.376
Fithian, Grant, Tampa	.250	3	4	4	0	1	1	0	0	0	1	0	0	0	0	0	0	0	0	0	.250	.250
Fitzpatrick, Robert, W. Palm Beach	.209	17	53	43	3	9	13	1	0	1	5	0	1	0	9	0	12	3	3	0	.302	.340
Flores, Jose, Clearwater	.222	49	212	185	25	41	54	4	3	1	19	7	1	4	15	0	27	12	5	4	.292	.293
Forkerway, Trey, Daytona	.202	75	214	188	22	38	45	4	0	1	11	4	1	1	20	0	29	10	1	5	.239	.281
Forkner, Tim, Kissimmee*	.284	89	367	296	42	84	115	20	4	1	34	2	4	5	60	2	40	4	2	11	.389	.408
Foster, Jeff, West Palm Beach*	.207	65	194	179	22	37	62	7	3	4	26	3	1	1	10	1	42	10	3	4	.346	.251
Freeman, Sean, Lakeland*	.290	119	472	414	42	120	163	21	2	6	65	0	7	2	49	3	98	3	4	3	.394	.362
Frias, Hanley, Charlotte†	.333	33	140	120	23	40	52	6	3	0	14	3	1	1	15	0	11	8	6	0	.433	.409
Froschauer, Trevor, Kissimmee	.197	102	390	325	32	64	110	8	1	12	40	0	3	13	49	0	121	2	0	10	.338	.323
Gallone, Santy, Clearwater	.244	90	357	283	45	69	104	15	1	6	40	2	7	18	47	1	39	5	3	11	.367	.377
Garcia, Luis, Lakeland	.280	102	378	361	39	101	125	10	4	2	35	4	4	1	8	0	42	9	10	6	.346	.294
Garcia, Osmel, St. Petersburg	.175	105	356	315	37	55	59	4	0	0	13	7	0	6	28	0	66	24	11	8	.187	.255
Gibbs, Kevin, Vero Beach	.250	7	20	20	1	5	6	1	0	0	2	0	0	0	0	0	0	1	0	0	.300	.250
Gonzalez, Alex, Brevard County	.203	17	61	59	6	12	16	2	1	0	8	0	0	1	1	0	14	1	1	2	.271	.230
Gousha, Sean, Daytona	.250	5	9	8	1	2	4	2	0	0	0	0	0	0	0	0	0	0	0	1	.500	.333
Grissom, Antonio, W. Palm Beach	.200	8	24	20	3	4	5	1	0	0	1	0	0	0	4	0	6	2	1	0	.250	.333
Gross, Rafael, Vero Beach	.252	35	124	115	18	29	35	4	1	0	8	1	2	3	3	0	15	5	4	1	.304	.285
Gyselman, Jeff, Clearwater	.172	26	70	64	8	11	11	0	0	0	3	0	0	0	6	0	14	0	0	4	.172	.243
Halemanu, Joshua, Kissimmee*	.133	6	16	15	1	2	2	0	0	0	3	0	0	0	1	0	7	0	0	0	.133	.188
Hammell, Al, St. Lucie	.157	34	88	70	7	11	15	1	0	1	3	1	0	1	16	0	19	2	1	2	.214	.322
Hansen, Elston, Tampa	.193	61	222	187	28	36	56	12	1	2	19	5	3	4	23	0	45	0	1	4	.299	.290
Hare, Rich, Lakeland	.150	9	21	20	3	3	3	0	0	0	2	0	0	1	0	0	4	0	0	0	.150	.190
Hastings, Lionel, Brevard County	.273	120	523	469	60	128	169	20	0	7	45	5	2	3	44	0	64	3	3	14	.360	.338
Hawkins, Kraig, Tampa†	.243	111	512	432	56	105	123	9	3	1	19	11	1	2	66	0	95	28	14	6	.285	.345
Haws, Scott, Clearwater*	.000	2	1	1	0	0	0	0	0	0	0	0	0	0	0	0	1	0	0	0	.000	.500

Player, Team	Avg.	G	TPA	AB	R	H	TB	2B	3B	HR	RBI	SH	SF	HP	BB	IBB	SO	SB	CS	GDP	Slg.	OBP
Held, Daniel, Clearwater	.272	134	569	489	82	133	233	35	1	21	82	1	4	19	56	1	127	2	1	13	.476	.366
Henry, Antoine, Sarasota	.226	16	70	62	14	14	22	0	1	2	8	0	0	0	8	0	7	5	2	1	.355	.314
Hernaiz, Juan, Vero Beach	.212	50	170	156	17	33	42	1	1	2	9	4	0	1	9	1	39	5	1	4	.269	.259
Hilt, Scott, Fort Myers*	.167	19	46	42	3	7	10	0	0	1	3	0	0	1	3	0	12	0	0	4	.238	.239
Hollis, Ronald, Vero Beach*	.000	43	1	1	0	0	0	0	0	0	0	0	0	0	0	0	1	0	0	0	.000	.000
Horn, Jeff, Fort Myers	.266	66	245	199	25	53	60	5	1	0	20	1	3	4	38	1	30	2	3	4	.302	.389
Hunter, Torii, Fort Myers	.246	113	447	391	64	96	136	15	2	7	36	5	1	12	38	1	77	7	4	8	.348	.330
Jackson, Gavin, Sarasota	.266	100	402	342	61	91	112	19	1	0	36	8	4	6	40	3	43	11	12	8	.327	.349
Johnson, Andre, Daytona	.071	5	14	14	2	1	1	0	0	0	2	0	0	0	0	0	4	0	0	0	.071	.071
Johnson, Jack, Daytona	.375	4	9	8	1	3	6	0	0	1	2	0	0	0	1	0	4	0	0	0	.750	.444
Johnson, J.J., Sarasota	.276	107	427	391	49	108	162	16	4	10	43	2	2	6	26	0	74	7	8	9	.414	.329
Jones, Ben, Fort Myers	.239	109	399	335	60	80	94	10	2	0	31	16	1	6	41	2	53	19	6	10	.281	.332
Jones, Ryan, Dunedin	.249	127	531	478	65	119	201	28	0	18	78	0	5	7	41	3	92	1	1	7	.421	.315
Keister, Tripp, St. Lucie*	.330	28	111	94	15	31	40	5	2	0	14	0	1	2	14	0	11	5	4	1	.426	.423
Kelly, Pat, Tampa	.235	3	17	17	0	4	5	1	0	0	2	0	0	0	0	0	1	0	0	0	.294	.235
Kendall, Jeremey, Clearwater	.215	36	158	135	18	29	43	1	2	3	10	1	2	6	14	0	40	15	5	2	.319	.312
Kimsey, Keith, Lakeland	.217	54	197	175	30	38	68	8	2	6	16	0	0	0	22	0	58	1	1	4	.389	.305
Kingman, Brendan, Brevard County	.253	95	384	348	37	88	139	19	4	8	47	0	4	1	31	3	45	1	0	21	.399	.313
Kingston, Mark, Daytona†	.235	49	188	170	23	40	54	8	0	2	23	0	3	1	14	2	33	1	1	5	.318	.293
Knauss, Tom, Fort Myers	.237	99	353	316	37	75	99	19	1	1	26	1	2	6	28	1	72	2	8	4	.313	.310
Knowles, Eric, Tampa	.271	115	444	391	45	106	141	24	4	1	33	3	2	3	45	0	58	7	3	8	.361	.349
Koeyers, Ramsey, W. Palm Beach	.189	77	261	244	19	46	54	6	1	0	18	5	3	0	9	0	64	2	1	10	.221	.215
Landaker, Dave, Kissimmee	.206	96	348	287	30	59	70	7	2	0	18	4	5	10	42	0	47	8	10	6	.244	.323
Landry, Lonny, Lakeland	.161	19	59	56	2	9	10	1	0	0	4	1	0	0	2	0	16	0	0	0	.179	.190
Latham, Chris, Vero Beach†	.286	71	322	259	53	74	113	13	4	6	39	2	3	2	56	4	54	42	11	2	.436	.413
Lee, Manuel, St. Petersburg†	.353	6	19	17	2	6	7	1	0	0	3	0	0	0	2	0	3	0	0	0	.412	.421
Lewis, Tyrone, Vero Beach	.000	1	1	1	0	0	0	0	0	0	0	0	0	0	0	0	1	0	0	0	.000	.000
Little, Mark, Charlotte	.256	115	507	438	75	112	186	31	8	9	50	2	2	14	51	1	108	20	14	4	.425	.350
Loeb, Marc, Dunedin	.223	64	222	193	17	43	58	12	0	1	23	3	0	2	24	0	46	1	1	3	.301	.315
Lombardi, John, Sarasota	.263	7	20	19	2	5	7	2	0	0	1	0	0	1	0	0	4	0	0	0	.368	.300
Long, Justin, Brevard County	.118	9	18	17	3	2	2	0	0	0	1	0	0	0	1	0	11	0	0	0	.118	.167
Long, R.D., Tampa†	.250	110	475	384	70	96	143	15	10	4	36	9	2	2	72	1	100	28	13	4	.372	.370
Lopez, Jose, St. Lucie	1.000	1	4	2	0	2	2	0	0	0	1	0	0	0	2	0	0	0	0	0	1.000	1.000
Lowery, Terrell, Charlotte	.257	11	42	35	4	9	15	2	2	0	4	0	0	1	6	0	6	1	0	2	.429	.381
Luzinski, Ryan, Vero Beach	.336	38	144	134	15	45	72	12	0	5	23	0	1	0	9	3	21	1	0	4	.537	.375
Macon, Leland, Charlotte	.259	119	477	405	52	105	132	15	3	2	38	2	7	22	41	1	85	14	12	10	.326	.354
Madonna, Chris, St. Lucie*	.000	3	5	5	0	0	0	0	0	0	0	0	0	0	0	0	1	0	0	0	.000	.000
Madsen, Dan, Daytona†	.194	13	41	36	7	7	11	1	0	1	3	1	0	1	3	0	11	4	2	0	.306	.275
Madsen, Dave, St. Petersburg	.281	121	469	388	48	109	147	20	3	4	64	0	9	2	70	1	62	1	0	14	.379	.386
Magee, Wendell, Clearwater	.353	96	432	388	67	137	189	24	5	6	46	1	5	4	33	3	40	7	10	15	.487	.405
Majeski, Brian, Vero Beach	.224	69	178	147	22	33	44	3	1	2	11	3	0	2	26	2	34	9	8	0	.299	.349
Malone, Scott, Charlotte*	.236	100	369	314	33	74	96	14	1	2	40	5	3	2	45	1	41	5	2	8	.306	.332
Maness, Dwight, V.B.-St.L.	.225	57	219	187	20	42	58	7	0	3	28	3	5	6	18	0	35	14	7	2	.310	.306
Mangham, Rodney, Kissimmee†	.209	42	160	134	19	28	37	7	1	0	12	3	1	0	22	0	31	5	3	1	.276	.318
Marabella, Tony, W. Palm Beach*	.259	60	217	201	22	52	60	6	1	0	21	0	3	0	13	0	23	1	1	4	.299	.300
Marine, Del, Lakeland	.241	77	278	257	27	62	88	14	0	4	25	0	3	5	13	0	63	5	1	3	.342	.288
Marrero, Elieser, St. Petersburg	.211	107	415	383	43	81	129	16	1	10	55	0	7	1	23	2	55	9	4	10	.337	.254
Marsh, Roy, Kissimmee	.216	114	437	393	51	85	121	18	3	4	23	2	0	4	38	0	95	22	11	6	.308	.292
Martin, Mike, Lakeland	.176	6	21	17	1	3	3	0	0	0	1	1	0	0	3	0	1	0	0	1	.176	.300
Martinez, Dalvis, Lakeland	.189	38	126	111	12	21	26	5	0	0	5	2	0	1	12	0	26	0	1	6	.234	.274
Martinez, Ramon, Brevard County†	.263	99	410	372	47	98	115	7	2	2	24	4	1	4	29	2	84	21	4	0	.309	.323
Matvey, Mike, St. Petersburg	.273	87	350	304	32	83	106	15	4	0	20	2	1	3	40	1	67	1	5	2	.349	.362
Maxwell, Jason, Daytona	.263	117	466	388	66	102	151	13	3	10	58	1	8	6	63	1	68	12	7	6	.389	.368
McCalmont, Jim, Fort Myers	.228	92	323	285	30	65	94	13	2	4	21	3	4	8	23	1	54	2	7	8	.330	.300
McEwing, Joe, St. Petersburg	.228	75	317	281	33	64	80	13	0	1	23	6	4	1	25	3	49	2	3	5	.285	.289
McKeel, Walt, Sarasota	.333	62	231	198	26	66	104	14	0	8	35	0	5	3	25	0	28	6	3	4	.525	.407
McKinnon, Tom, St. Petersburg*	.267	53	178	172	15	46	68	16	0	2	10	0	1	0	5	2	39	1	1	4	.395	.287
McMullen, Jon, Clearwater*	.237	30	138	118	17	28	38	7	0	1	14	0	0	0	20	2	19	0	0	6	.322	.348
Melhuse, Adam, Dunedin†	.215	123	495	428	43	92	124	20	0	4	41	1	4	1	61	1	87	6	1	7	.290	.312
Meluskey, Mitch, Kissimmee†	.215	78	295	261	23	56	85	18	1	3	31	2	4	1	27	2	33	3	0	12	.326	.287
Mercedes, Guillermo, Charlotte†	.218	33	121	110	10	24	26	2	0	0	5	2	1	1	7	0	12	1	2	1	.236	.269
Metcalfe, Mike, Vero Beach†	.301	120	509	435	86	131	159	13	3	3	35	6	5	3	60	2	37	60	27	8	.366	.386
Micucci, Mike, Daytona*	.195	23	47	41	4	8	10	2	0	0	3	2	0	0	4	0	9	0	0	0	.244	.267
Mientkiewicz, Doug, Fort Myers*	.245	38	131	110	9	27	38	6	1	1	15	2	0	1	18	1	19	2	2	1	.345	.357
Millar, Kevin, Brevard County	.288	129	551	459	53	132	207	32	2	13	68	0	10	12	70	2	66	4	4	8	.451	.388
Miller, Ryan, St. Lucie	.244	89	309	279	32	68	90	10	3	2	23	8	2	7	13	0	42	5	3	7	.323	.292
Mitchell, Mike, Tampa*	.266	102	406	368	40	98	140	16	1	8	61	1	6	2	29	1	52	1	0	10	.380	.319
Molina, Jose, Daytona	.236	82	273	233	27	55	69	9	1	1	19	2	2	7	29	0	53	1	0	7	.296	.336
Moore, Mike, Vero Beach	.273	7	28	22	3	6	7	1	0	0	1	0	0	0	6	0	8	0	1	1	.318	.429
Morales, Francisco, Day.-St.P.	.229	64	221	188	27	43	78	11	0	8	33	0	2	4	27	0	57	2	1	5	.415	.335
Morris, Bobby, Daytona*	.308	95	397	344	44	106	134	18	2	2	55	2	5	8	38	6	46	22	8	5	.390	.385
Mota, Santo, St. Petersburg†	.156	64	190	173	27	27	38	8	0	1	11	2	0	0	15	0	40	6	0	2	.220	.223
Motes, Jeff, St. Lucie	.200	12	38	35	7	7	7	0	0	0	4	1	0	1	1	0	7	0	0	1	.200	.243
Motte, James, Fort Myers	.235	119	432	392	47	92	125	17	2	4	37	5	2	2	31	1	78	8	10	13	.319	.293
Motuzas, Jeff, Tampa	.159	28	76	69	6	11	14	0	0	1	8	1	0	2	4	0	24	1	0	0	.203	.227
Moultrie, Pat, Dunedin*	.246	92	385	349	40	86	105	8	4	1	29	3	3	3	27	1	65	15	4	5	.301	.304
Murphy, Jeffrey, St. Petersburg†	.180	50	143	122	9	22	33	3	1	2	14	0	0	2	19	0	36	0	0	5	.270	.301
Murphy, Pat, Sarasota*	.201	54	200	189	18	38	48	4	0	2	15	2	0	1	8	0	26	12	5	2	.254	.237
Nava, Lipso, Sarasota	.258	21	73	62	11	16	26	4	0	2	10	0	0	4	7	0	7	1	0	3	.419	.370
Nava, Marlon, Fort Myers	.242	112	413	376	47	91	112	18	0	1	37	11	2	2	22	1	45	5	9	6	.298	.286
Nelson, Bry, Kissimmee†	.327	105	423	395	47	129	182	34	5	3	52	1	6	1	20	0	37	14	10	8	.461	.355
Nelson, Charles, Vero Beach*	.271	80	327	277	37	75	92	13	2	0	30	3	1	0	46	2	50	33	13	7	.332	.373
Niethammer, Marc, W. Palm Beach*	.187	96	353	315	34	59	106	11	3	10	31	1	2	4	31	3	105	4	6	2	.337	.267

Player, Team	Avg.	G	TPA	AB	R	H	TB	2B	3B	HR	RBI	SH	SF	HP	BB	IBB	SO	SB	CS	GDP	Slg.	OBP
Nihart, Tim, Fort Myers	.200	4	11	10	1	2	4	2	0	0	2	0	0	0	1	0	3	0	0	0	.400	.273
Nixon, Trot, Sarasota*	.303	73	312	264	43	80	114	11	4	5	39	0	2	1	45	3	46	7	5	5	.432	.404
Northeimer, Jamie, Clearwater	.316	6	24	19	1	6	7	1	0	0	5	0	0	2	3	0	4	0	0	0	.368	.458
Northrup, Kevin, St. Lucie	.297	17	70	64	7	19	22	1	1	0	12	0	2	0	4	0	6	2	1	2	.344	.329
Nuneviller, Tom, Clearwater	.233	12	49	43	2	10	12	2	0	0	6	0	2	0	4	0	6	0	0	1	.279	.286
O'Brien, Joe, Clearwater	.140	13	54	50	6	7	11	1	0	1	7	0	0	1	3	0	13	1	0	4	.220	.204
Orie, Kevin, Daytona	.244	119	474	409	54	100	152	17	4	9	51	0	6	15	42	2	71	5	4	11	.372	.333
Ortiz, Nick, Sarasota	.247	91	337	304	38	75	112	20	1	5	38	1	1	4	27	0	68	6	4	3	.368	.315
Otanez, Willis, Vero Beach	.260	92	389	354	39	92	146	24	0	10	53	0	5	2	28	3	59	1	1	15	.412	.314
Ottavinia, Paul, W. Palm Beach*	.235	112	438	395	35	93	120	20	2	1	37	5	2	2	34	2	44	13	6	10	.304	.298
Pachot, John, West Palm Beach	.251	67	245	227	17	57	67	10	0	0	23	3	1	2	12	0	38	1	2	4	.295	.293
Parra, Julio, Vero Beach	.000	22	1	0	0	0	0	0	0	0	0	1	0	0	0	0	0	0	0	0	.000	.000
Patton, Greg, Sarasota	.217	8	25	23	1	5	5	0	0	0	0	0	0	0	2	0	8	0	0	0	.217	.280
Patzke, Jeff, Dunedin†	.264	129	560	470	68	124	201	32	6	11	75	1	2	2	85	8	81	5	3	10	.428	.377
Perez, Jhonny, Kissimmee	.271	65	244	214	24	58	82	12	0	4	31	0	0	7	22	1	37	23	7	5	.383	.358
Perez, Joe, Charlotte*	.257	24	86	74	8	19	26	4	0	1	9	0	1	2	9	0	12	1	1	0	.351	.349
Perez, Richard, Daytona	.220	85	289	255	31	56	64	8	0	0	26	4	1	1	28	0	41	4	2	5	.251	.298
Peterson, Nate, Kissimmee*	.280	76	283	257	34	72	101	17	0	4	22	0	1	4	21	2	42	3	1	5	.393	.343
Petrulis, Paul, St. Lucie	.227	104	347	291	33	66	79	10	0	1	16	8	1	2	45	0	51	3	11	8	.271	.333
Pichardo, Sandy, St. Lucie†	.274	125	522	478	55	131	153	10	6	0	27	12	1	3	28	3	64	29	17	6	.320	.318
Pico, Brandon, Daytona*	.245	16	58	49	4	12	14	2	0	0	4	2	0	0	7	0	8	1	1	0	.286	.339
Porter, Bo, Daytona	.217	113	377	336	54	73	98	12	2	3	19	4	3	2	32	0	104	22	10	5	.292	.287
Post, David, Vero Beach	.237	52	143	114	16	27	31	2	1	0	11	3	1	2	23	0	11	3	0	5	.272	.371
Prater, Andrew, Brevard County	.150	73	204	173	18	26	37	5	0	2	16	5	4	4	18	0	49	0	0	3	.214	.241
Querecuto, Juan, Dunedin	.179	53	151	140	16	25	34	4	1	1	10	0	0	3	8	1	31	0	0	5	.243	.238
Radmanovich, Ryan, Fort Myers*	.317	12	44	41	3	13	15	2	0	0	5	0	0	1	2	0	8	0	0	0	.366	.364
Raifstanger, John, Sarasota	.270	102	367	326	52	88	115	19	1	2	24	2	2	3	34	1	63	6	1	5	.353	.342
Raleigh, Matt, West Palm Beach	.207	66	243	179	29	37	54	11	0	2	18	1	3	6	54	1	64	4	2	4	.302	.401
Ramirez, Angel, Dunedin	.275	131	569	541	78	149	202	19	5	8	52	0	2	5	21	0	99	17	12	12	.373	.308
Ramirez, Hiram, Sarasota	.186	40	146	140	13	26	34	2	0	2	12	2	1	0	3	0	29	3	2	2	.243	.201
Ramos, Eddie, Kissimmee	.114	30	112	105	5	12	17	3	1	0	8	0	3	0	4	1	27	0	0	5	.162	.143
Reeves, Glen, Brevard County	.270	117	504	415	68	112	141	22	2	1	33	2	3	6	78	0	78	6	7	12	.340	.390
Renteria, David, Tampa	.217	33	78	69	6	15	23	3	1	1	4	2	2	1	4	0	16	1	1	1	.333	.263
Rijo, Rafael, Charlotte	.304	16	52	46	3	14	16	2	0	0	5	1	0	0	5	1	11	2	0	0	.348	.373
Roberge, John, Vero Beach	.000	3	9	9	1	0	0	0	0	0	0	0	0	0	0	0	2	0	0	0	.000	.000
Roberts, David, Lakeland*	.303	92	401	357	67	108	137	10	5	3	30	2	2	1	39	2	43	30	8	7	.384	.371
Robinson, Dan, Brevard County*	.237	105	395	354	38	84	128	17	3	7	52	2	3	1	35	0	81	10	6	14	.362	.305
Roche, Marlon, Kissimmee	.227	26	102	97	10	22	29	7	0	0	7	1	1	0	3	0	24	3	2	2	.299	.248
Rodriguez, Adam, Lakeland	.250	30	96	88	8	22	29	4	0	1	10	0	0	0	8	0	17	1	0	1	.330	.313
Rojas, Roberto, Lakeland*	.250	4	13	12	1	3	3	0	0	0	2	0	0	0	1	1	4	1	0	0	.250	.308
Rolen, Scott, Clearwater	.290	66	283	238	45	69	116	13	2	10	39	0	3	5	37	1	46	4	0	4	.487	.392
Rupp, Brian, St. Petersburg	.277	90	357	325	30	90	106	12	2	0	23	4	0	1	27	1	43	0	0	14	.326	.334
Rupp, Chad, Fort Myers	.266	107	420	376	44	100	161	23	1	12	50	0	3	2	38	1	77	14	3	10	.428	.334
Sabo, Chris, St. Petersburg	.231	14	51	39	10	9	15	0	0	2	7	0	0	1	10	0	6	1	0	2	.385	.400
Saffer, Jon, West Palm Beach*	.318	92	384	324	60	103	137	10	6	4	35	4	1	2	53	1	49	18	9	7	.423	.416
Samuels, Scott, Daytona*	.327	112	473	388	92	127	186	29	12	2	42	3	4	8	69	7	63	38	14	8	.479	.435
Sanchez, Omar, Dunedin	.250	39	147	120	25	30	35	5	0	0	8	2	1	3	21	0	22	6	4	0	.292	.372
Sanchez, Victor, Kissimmee	.268	78	308	272	34	73	105	11	0	7	38	1	4	8	23	1	69	6	3	6	.386	.339
Santucci, Steven, St. Petersburg	.236	106	324	292	25	69	92	5	3	4	25	2	3	0	27	0	60	9	3	8	.315	.298
Sauve, Erik, Charlotte	.143	31	79	70	9	10	13	3	0	0	4	4	0	0	9	0	13	0	2	1	.186	.241
Saylor, Jamie, Kissimmee*	.228	89	319	289	38	66	78	4	1	2	19	0	2	6	22	1	58	13	6	5	.270	.295
Schaaf, Rob, Vero Beach	.217	21	61	60	7	13	17	1	0	1	5	0	0	1	0	0	13	0	0	2	.283	.230
Schmitz, Mike, Tampa	.231	4	13	13	2	3	4	1	0	0	0	0	0	0	0	0	1	0	0	1	.308	.231
Scolaro, Donnie, Kissimmee	.302	23	74	63	9	19	22	3	0	0	3	2	2	0	7	0	12	1	0	1	.349	.361
Sell, Donald, Vero Beach*	.270	80	248	222	21	60	71	6	1	1	23	2	2	4	18	0	33	1	3	5	.320	.333
Sheffield, Tony, Sarasota*	.238	103	350	315	45	75	101	17	3	1	25	4	1	2	28	0	109	9	11	4	.321	.303
Shirley, Al, St. Lucie	.186	59	212	183	27	34	61	6	3	5	18	0	1	5	23	1	94	8	4	2	.333	.292
Shores, Scott, Clearwater	.254	133	530	460	74	117	171	23	5	7	52	3	2	10	55	1	127	30	16	11	.372	.345
Shugars, Shawn, Charlotte*	.348	27	23	4	8	11	1	1	0	3	0	0	1	3	0	4	0	0	2	.478	.444
Sims, Michael, Brevard County	.185	89	283	260	24	48	57	6	0	1	20	5	1	2	15	0	52	4	2	14	.219	.234
Sims, Wes, Charlotte†	.273	5	13	11	2	3	4	1	0	0	1	0	0	0	2	0	5	0	0	0	.364	.385
Smith, Bubba, Fort Myers	.330	60	195	176	27	58	112	15	0	13	51	0	3	0	16	4	38	1	2	8	.636	.379
Smith, Dave, Sarasota	.299	23	80	67	12	20	27	5	1	0	6	1	0	3	9	0	10	1	5	1	.403	.405
Smith, Sloan, Tampa†	.260	124	494	412	61	107	171	23	1	13	64	1	3	4	74	3	136	6	8	8	.415	.375
Snyder, Jared, Daytona	.167	18	42	36	2	6	6	0	0	0	4	2	1	1	2	0	4	0	1	2	.167	.225
Solano, Fausto, Dunedin	.208	41	167	144	19	30	42	5	2	1	10	5	0	1	17	0	30	3	2	4	.292	.296
Sosa, Juan, Vero Beach	.222	8	27	27	2	6	12	1	1	1	6	0	0	0	0	0	4	0	2	0	.444	.222
Southard, Scott, Brevard County	.210	68	245	219	18	46	61	7	1	2	21	5	0	1	20	0	40	4	3	2	.279	.279
Sowards, Ryan, Vero Beach*	.286	75	252	196	36	56	78	13	0	3	34	2	4	3	47	2	32	1	0	6	.398	.424
Spencer, Shane, Tampa	.300	134	570	500	87	150	235	31	3	16	88	2	3	7	61	2	60	14	8	7	.470	.382
Steed, David, Vero Beach	.251	59	218	195	11	49	65	16	0	0	24	1	1	3	18	0	53	0	0	5	.333	.323
Stewart, Tom, Kissimmee†	.251	52	191	167	9	42	51	4	1	1	15	3	1	3	17	0	48	0	2	3	.305	.330
Stovall, Darond, W. Palm Beach†	.232	121	510	461	52	107	145	22	2	4	51	2	3	0	44	2	117	18	12	4	.315	.297
Strawberry, Darryl, Tampa†	.222	2	10	9	1	2	6	1	0	1	2	0	0	0	1	0	2	0	0	1	.667	.300
Stricklin, Scott, Fort Myers*	.187	65	212	166	20	31	32	1	0	0	8	5	0	0	41	2	25	4	4	3	.193	.348
Subero, Carlos, Charlotte†	.136	17	45	44	3	6	7	1	0	0	4	1	0	0	0	0	10	0	0	1	.159	.136
Suplee, Ray, Tampa	.233	98	364	317	33	74	106	9	1	7	37	3	4	7	33	1	94	4	2	2	.334	.316
Taylor, Mike, St. Petersburg*	.239	70	192	159	13	38	49	3	1	2	15	4	1	0	28	0	24	0	2	2	.308	.351
Tebbs, Nathan, Sarasota†	.291	118	487	440	58	128	157	15	4	2	52	4	1	3	39	0	80	25	15	7	.357	.352
Terrell, Matt, St. Lucie	.197	86	216	193	24	38	48	6	2	0	9	3	1	1	18	0	53	11	2	3	.249	.268
Thompson, Billy, Lakeland	.242	73	243	223	26	54	84	13	1	5	28	1	3	1	15	0	45	4	0	2	.377	.289
Torborg, Dale, St.L-Tampa	.100	7	10	10	0	1	1	0	0	0	1	0	0	0	0	0	5	0	1	0	.100	.100
Torres, Jaime, Tampa	.239	107	408	364	45	87	128	17	0	8	45	3	3	10	28	1	29	1	1	14	.352	.309

Player, Team	Avg.	G	TPA	AB	R	H	TB	2B	3B	HR	RBI	SH	SF	HP	BB	IBB	SO	SB	CS	GDP	Slg.	OBP
Trammell, Bubba, Lakeland	.284	122	510	454	61	129	215	32	3	16	72	0	4	4	48	2	80	13	3	9	.474	.355
Troilo, Jason, Tampa	.000	1	3	2	0	0	0	0	0	0	0	0	0	1	0	0	2	0	0	0	.000	.333
Twitty, Sean, Tampa	.250	1	4	4	0	1	1	0	0	0	0	0	0	0	0	0	1	0	0	1	.250	.250
Ugueto, Jesus, St. Petersburg	.130	37	83	77	3	10	11	1	0	0	3	1	1	1	3	0	18	0	1	4	.143	.171
Unrat, Chris, Charlotte*	.250	66	201	172	22	43	56	8	1	1	17	4	2	0	23	1	38	1	2	6	.326	.335
Varriano, Mark, Sarasota	.000	8	17	16	0	0	0	0	0	0	0	0	0	0	1	0	9	0	0	0	.000	.059
Venezia, Danny, Fort Myers	.245	16	57	49	5	12	15	1	1	0	4	0	1	0	7	0	8	1	0	1	.306	.333
Verduzco, Steve, Kissimmee	.250	98	399	348	47	87	125	17	0	7	50	3	5	6	37	3	50	18	4	10	.359	.328
Vessel, Andrew, Charlotte	.265	129	553	498	67	132	189	26	2	9	78	1	7	15	32	2	75	3	17	11	.380	.324
Vidro, Jose, West Palm Beach†	.325	44	177	163	20	53	81	15	2	3	24	2	2	2	8	0	21	0	1	5	.497	.360
Waco, David, Clearwater	.223	59	226	193	22	43	53	8	1	0	13	5	0	5	23	0	27	2	2	5	.275	.321
Warner, Randy, St. Lucie	.260	122	480	446	43	116	181	23	6	10	70	0	4	3	27	0	86	6	7	9	.406	.304
Whatley, Gabe, Daytona*	.262	15	51	42	8	11	17	3	0	1	5	0	0	0	5	0	7	5	2	0	.405	.367
White, Jimmy, Kissimmee*	.182	16	66	55	6	10	15	3	1	0	3	1	0	1	9	0	9	4	0	2	.273	.308
Whitehurst, Todd, St. Lucie†	.222	58	216	189	13	42	51	7	1	0	18	1	1	4	21	2	37	2	3	1	.270	.312
Williams, Ed, Lakeland†	.267	4	15	15	1	4	7	1	1	0	1	0	0	0	0	0	4	0	0	0	.467	.267
Wilson, Tom, Tampa	.167	17	61	48	3	8	8	0	0	0	2	2	1	1	10	1	13	1	0	0	.167	.317
Wipf, Mark, St. Lucie†	.246	123	490	435	52	107	151	20	6	4	53	4	5	5	39	6	95	15	7	4	.347	.312
Wooten, Shawn, Lakeland	.230	38	148	135	11	31	49	10	1	2	11	0	1	2	10	0	28	0	1	2	.363	.291
Wyrick, Chris, St. Petersburg	.237	55	156	139	20	33	44	6	1	1	15	1	0	5	10	0	25	3	1	3	.317	.312
Zambrano, Jose, Sarasota	.367	10	43	30	4	11	18	1	0	2	8	0	0	1	12	0	11	1	1	0	.600	.558
Zuniga, David, St. Lucie	.172	10	30	29	1	5	5	0	0	0	0	0	0	0	1	0	6	0	1	1	.172	.200

GRAND SLAMS: Alcantara, Bierek, Collier, L. Garcia, Malone, Morales, Morris, M. Nava, Rolen, C. Rupp, B. Smith, Spencer, Torres, Vessel, 1 each.

AWARDED FIRST BASE ON CATCHER'S INTERFERENCE: R.D. Long 6 (Melhuse 2, Marine, Meluskey, Rodriguez, Thompson); Davenport 3 (K. Brown 2, Marine); Orie 3 (Stricklin 2, C. Diaz); Azuaje 2 (Luzinski 2); Whatley 2 (V. Sanchez 2); Wipf 2 (K. Brown, M. Sims); Baugh (Luzinski); Bierek (Melhuse); Cooney (Melhuse); Deares (Castro); Ellis (Melhuse); Facione (Marrero); Jackson (Castro); Magee (Marine); Marrero (C. Diaz); Jh. Perez (Melhuse); C. Rupp (Luzinski); Sabo (Torres); Samuels (Torres); Wyrick (Thompson).

PLAYERS WITH TWO OR MORE TEAMS

Player, Team	Avg.	G	TPA	AB	R	H	TB	2B	3B	HR	RBI	SH	SF	HP	BB	IBB	SO	SB	CS	GDP	Slg.	OBP
Maness, Dwight, Vero Beach	.231	43	167	143	16	33	45	3	0	3	23	2	5	6	11	0	29	13	5	2	.315	.303
Maness, Dwight, St. Lucie	.205	14	52	44	4	9	13	4	0	0	5	1	0	0	7	0	6	1	2	0	.295	.314
Morales, Francisco, Daytona	.257	36	122	101	17	26	50	6	0	6	23	0	2	3	16	0	28	1	1	2	.495	.369
Morales, Francisco, St. Petersburg	.195	28	99	87	10	17	28	5	0	2	10	0	0	1	11	0	29	1	0	3	.322	.293
Torborg, Dale, St. Lucie	.111	5	9	9	0	1	1	0	0	0	0	1	0	0	0	0	4	0	0	0	.111	.111
Torborg, Dale, Tampa	.000	2	1	1	0	0	0	0	0	0	0	0	0	0	0	0	1	0	0	0	.000	.000

1995 PITCHING

TEAM

Team	W	L	Pct.	ERA	G	CG	ShO	Sv.	IP	H	TBF	R	ER	HR	SH	SF	HB	BB	IBB	SO	WP	Bk.
Tampa	72	64	.529	2.81	136	7	13	44	1187.2	1054	4992	513	371	42	35	32	58	439	17	939	67	19
Daytona	87	48	.644	2.82	135	3	13	49	1173.0	1020	4853	484	368	60	33	20	49	382	12	980	77	11
Fort Myers	75	55	.577	2.85	131	10	12	31	1136.0	978	4719	450	360	60	36	44	62	409	13	823	66	9
St. Petersburg	64	67	.489	3.03	131	7	12	34	1121.1	947	4667	475	378	56	32	34	40	416	16	925	63	13
St. Lucie	61	73	.455	3.25	135	18	16	27	1161.2	1085	4875	504	419	50	44	33	50	412	24	793	71	22
Vero Beach	74	59	.556	3.40	133	3	7	40	1137.0	990	4889	521	429	64	43	38	35	563	14	939	115	23
Brevard County	61	74	.452	3.44	135	5	14	29	1191.1	1123	5109	582	456	65	44	40	79	462	20	828	57	12
West Palm Beach	54	81	.400	3.49	136	8	7	29	1146.1	1110	4960	550	445	43	41	53	70	478	18	745	92	17
Charlotte	65	67	.492	3.50	133	7	8	35	1154.1	1120	4916	538	449	77	38	33	50	394	9	758	55	23
Clearwater	79	59	.572	3.55	138	8	10	36	1201.2	1202	5151	583	474	59	49	43	40	416	20	891	67	29
Sarasota	65	68	.489	3.81	134	6	10	34	1153.0	1142	5027	606	488	57	35	33	66	466	28	819	82	25
Lakeland	64	69	.481	3.87	135	5	7	44	1156.2	1181	5015	617	498	56	36	46	72	450	28	887	75	19
Dunedin	63	74	.460	4.02	138	4	5	30	1200.0	1205	5286	668	536	93	37	33	79	541	8	840	77	22
Kissimmee	55	81	.404	4.19	136	5	7	30	1183.2	1221	5315	729	551	48	40	49	78	547	5	813	96	26

INDIVIDUAL

TOP QUALIFIERS FOR EARNED-RUN AVERAGE TITLE

Minimum 112 innings. *Lefthanded pitcher.

Pitcher, Team	W	L	Pct.	ERA	G	GS	CG	ShO	GF	Sv.	IP	H	TBF	R	ER	HR	SH	SF	HB	BB	IBB	SO	WP	Bk.
Pincavitch, Kevin, Vero Beach	10	7	.588	1.66	32	13	2	1	5	2	124.2	83	504	37	23	7	5	1	5	48	0	103	12	1
Bowers, Shane, Fort Myers	13	5	.722	2.16	23	23	1	0	0	0	145.2	119	580	43	35	6	2	4	12	32	1	103	6	1
Drews, Matthew, Tampa	15	7	.682	2.27	28	28	3	0	0	0	182.0	142	748	73	46	5	5	1	7	58	0	140	8	2
Nunez, Clemente, Brevard County	12	6	.667	2.48	19	19	4	2	0	0	123.1	99	490	48	34	3	2	2	5	22	1	79	3	5
Larson, Toby, St. Lucie	6	7	.462	2.52	19	18	3	1	0	0	121.2	122	508	44	34	5	4	0	7	30	2	82	7	1
Walker, Wade, Daytona	8	6	.571	2.53	25	24	2	1	0	0	135.0	113	541	50	38	5	3	2	2	36	0	117	8	1
King, Curtis, St. Petersburg	7	8	.467	2.58	28	21	3	0	1	0	136.0	117	567	49	39	3	4	2	11	49	2	65	6	0
Janzen, Marty, Tampa	10	3	.769	2.61	18	18	1	0	0	0	113.2	102	461	38	33	4	1	2	4	30	0	104	3	4
Guerra, Mark, St. Lucie	9	9	.500	2.64	23	23	4	3	0	0	160.0	148	644	55	47	5	4	4		33	1	110	2	3
Winslett, Dax, V.B.-Day.	12	6	.667	2.78	26	25	0	0	0	0	152.0	148	627	59	47	11	4	2	2	39	0	111	13	2
Davis, Jeff, Charlotte	12	7	.632	2.89	26	26	0	0	0	0	165.1	149	691	74	53	10	6	2	11	37	0	105	6	2
Box, Shawn, Daytona	8	6	.571	3.05	25	23	0	0	0	0	124.0	114	511	50	42	5	3	0	3	35	1	90	5	1
Yan, Esteban, W. Palm Beach	6	8	.429	3.07	24	21	1	0	1	0	137.2	139	580	63	47	3	7	5	10	33	0	89	8	3
Carrasco, Troy, Fort Myers*	12	4	.750	3.13	25	25	2	0	0	0	138.0	131	596	62	48	4	7	8		63	0	96	11	2
Dodd, Robert, Clearwater*	8	7	.533	3.16	26	26	0	0	0	0	151.0	144	636	64	53	4	3	6	1	58	0	110	3	7

DEPARTMENTAL LEADERS: W—Drews, 15; L—Granger, 12; Pct.—Debrino, .786; G—Metheney, 59; GS—Drews, 28; CG—Cosman, 6; ShO—Guerra, 3; GF—Rios, 52; Sv.—Jacobsen, 32; IP—Drews, 182.0; H—Granger, 176; TBF—Drews, 748; R—Brower, Granger, 93; ER—Granger, 79; HR—Brower, 16; SH—Lewis, Sampson, 8; SF—DaSilva, Norman, Walter, 9; HB—O'Malley, 18; BB—Forster, 80; IBB—McLaughlin, 7; SO—Detmers, 150; WP—Ashworth, 24; Bk.—Dodd, McCommon, 7.

ALL PITCHERS

*Lefthanded pitcher.

Pitcher, Team	W	L	Pct.	ERA	G	GS	CG	ShO	GF	Sv.	IP	H	TBF	R	ER	HR	SH	SF	HB	BB	IBB	SO	WP	Bk.
Adkins, Tim, Dunedin*	7	4	.636	3.75	45	0	0	0	37	17	48.0	54	215	29	20	2	3	2	1	33	0	49	7	0
Agostinelli, Peter, Clearwater*	4	4	.500	4.34	57	0	0	0	23	6	45.2	54	207	26	22	1	2	0	2	22	5	32	3	1
Albaladejo, Randy, Kissimmee	0	0	.000	11.42	7	0	0	0	4	0	8.2	13	51	13	11	0	1	1	3	10	0	5	2	0
Aldred, Scott, Lakeland*	4	2	.667	3.19	13	7	0	0	3	2	67.2	57	275	25	24	3	2	1	3	19	0	64	2	0
Andersen, Mark, Brevard County	0	1	.000	3.96	20	0	0	0	9	0	36.1	42	169	25	16	2	1	1	2	17	0	21	3	0
Antoszek, Chris, Sarasota	1	2	.333	4.15	3	3	0	0	0	0	17.1	21	77	10	8	0	0	1	0	4	0	9	2	2
Aquino, Julio, Vero Beach	0	0	.000	0.00	3	0	0	0	2	1	3.0	1	14	0	0	0	0	0	0	3	0	0	0	0
Arffa, Steve, St. Lucie*	5	5	.500	4.30	32	10	1	1	2	2	88.0	99	373	46	42	8	0	4	3	22	3	46	8	1
Ashworth, Kym, Vero Beach*	7	4	.636	3.53	24	24	1	1	0	0	120.0	111	515	56	47	8	6	5	1	64	0	97	24	3
Aybar, Manuel, St. Petersburg	2	5	.286	3.35	9	9	0	0	0	0	48.1	42	202	27	18	4	0	1	1	16	0	43	7	1
Baine, David, Charlotte*	1	3	.250	4.10	21	3	0	0	9	1	48.1	47	212	23	22	4	0	2	0	24	0	29	3	1
Barkley, Brian, Sarasota*	8	10	.444	3.25	24	24	2	2	0	0	146.2	147	611	66	53	5	2	3	5	37	3	70	4	1
Beech, Matt, Clearwater*	9	4	.692	4.19	15	15	0	0	0	0	86.0	87	363	45	40	5	3	2	3	30	0	85	6	0
Belinda, Stan, Sarasota	0	0	.000	4.50	1	1	0	0	0	0	2.0	2	7	1	1	0	0	0	0	0	0	2	0	0
Bennett, Shayne, Sarasota	2	5	.286	2.56	52	0	0	0	43	24	59.2	50	255	23	17	3	4	2	4	21	4	69	5	1
Benz, Jake, West Palm Beach*	0	2	.000	1.17	44	0	0	0	38	22	54.0	44	220	13	7	0	3	2	3	18	3	48	4	1
Berlin, Mike, Lakeland	2	1	.667	3.06	16	0	0	0	4	1	32.1	25	139	13	11	0	0	2	2	21	0	23	4	0
Berry, Jason, Tampa	2	0	1.000	0.92	7	0	0	0	1	0	19.2	14	78	3	2	0	0	1	1	10	0	14	1	0
Biehl, Rod, Fort Myers*	2	0	1.000	4.05	12	0	0	0	4	0	20.0	15	81	9	9	1	0	1	1	8	1	20	5	0
Blake, Todd, St. Petersburg*	2	2	.500	2.59	42	0	0	0	20	0	55.2	58	244	25	16	3	3	3	0	17	2	35	2	0
Bogott, Kurt, Sarasota*	6	4	.600	3.05	41	9	0	0	15	0	88.2	89	388	44	30	3	4	1	4	41	0	62	8	3
Borkowski, David, Lakeland	1	0	1.000	0.00	1	1	0	0	0	0	5.0	2	17	0	0	0	0	0	0	1	0	3	0	0
Bowen, Mitchel, Brevard County	0	2	.000	2.56	41	3	0	0	17	3	88.0	87	381	36	25	3	5	1	3	32	2	51	6	0
Bowen, Ryan, Brevard County	0	2	.000	2.45	3	3	0	0	0	0	11.0	6	43	3	3	1	0	0	0	6	0	10	0	0
Bowers, Shane, Fort Myers	13	5	.722	2.16	23	23	1	0	0	0	145.2	119	580	43	35	6	2	4	12	32	1	103	6	1
Box, Shawn, Daytona	8	6	.571	3.05	25	23	0	0	0	0	124.0	114	511	50	42	5	3	0	3	35	1	90	5	1
Breitenstein, Keith, Kissimmee*	0	1	.000	3.00	4	0	0	0	1	0	6.0	7	29	2	2	0	1	1	0	3	1	4	0	0
Briscoe, Janos, Charlotte	0	0	.000	0.00	1	0	0	0	1	0	2.0	3	10	0	0	0	0	0	0	0	0	1	0	0
Brower, Jim, Charlotte	7	10	.412	3.89	27	27	2	1	0	0	173.2	170	740	93	75	16	3	3	8	62	1	110	11	0
Brown, Alvin, Lakeland	2	3	.400	4.24	9	9	0	0	0	0	46.2	35	202	23	22	1	1	1	4	33	0	35	9	1
Brown, Brett, Kissimmee*	0	0	.000	0.00	1	0	0	0	1	0	0.2	1	3	0	0	0	0	0	0	0	0	0	0	0
Buckles, Bucky, Charlotte	2	9	.182	3.13	48	0	0	0	43	16	69.0	70	293	29	24	5	5	2	0	21	3	43	4	2
Bullock, Craig, St. Lucie	4	5	.444	2.52	40	0	0	0	28	5	50.0	47	203	15	14	2	6	2	1	13	3	27	1	2
Cain, Chance, St. Petersburg	1	0	1.000	3.27	7	0	0	0	2	0	11.0	18	51	6	4	0	0	1	0	2	0	4	0	1
Caridad, Ron, Fort Myers	2	3	.400	2.40	17	0	0	0	9	0	41.1	27	171	15	11	1	1	2	3	18	0	38	4	0
Carl, Todd, Brevard County	3	4	.429	3.96	15	7	0	0	3	1	52.1	44	224	26	23	3	1	2	2	27	0	19	3	0
Carpenter, Brian, St. Petersburg	5	3	.625	2.14	16	7	0	0	2	0	59.0	40	226	17	14	4	1	1	0	11	0	51	4	0
Carpenter, Chris, Dunedin	3	5	.375	2.17	15	15	0	0	0	0	99.1	83	420	29	24	3	2	0	4	50	0	56	9	3
Carrasco, Troy, Fort Myers*	12	4	.750	3.13	25	25	2	0	0	0	138.0	131	596	62	48	6	4	7	8	63	0	96	11	2
Cederblad, Brett, Sarasota	7	6	.538	4.09	24	12	0	0	2	0	92.1	98	384	50	42	4	0	4	6	21	0	71	7	2
Challinor, John, Vero Beach	2	6	.250	3.86	37	1	0	0	15	1	74.2	62	318	36	32	6	1	4	0	35	1	59	5	1
Cindrich, Jeff, Tampa	1	4	.200	4.35	24	0	0	0	9	0	39.1	50	177	28	19	4	0	3	0	17	1	32	5	0
Clelland, Rick, West Palm Beach	2	4	.333	2.69	35	5	0	0	10	0	70.1	59	316	30	21	3	3	5	8	46	1	66	10	0
Clemens, Roger, Sarasota	0	0	.000	0.00	1	1	0	0	0	0	4.0	0	14	0	0	0	0	0	0	2	0	7	0	0
Connolly, Matt, Daytona	7	1	.875	0.98	18	2	0	0	7	2	55.1	37	216	14	6	0	3	0	2	9	2	77	6	0
Corn, Chris, Tampa	0	1	.000	3.18	4	0	0	0	1	0	5.2	3	25	2	2	0	0	0	2	3	0	9	2	0
Cosman, Jeff, St. Lucie	4	9	.308	3.12	15	15	6	2	0	0	101.0	96	412	43	35	2	3	1	3	27	3	72	5	1
Costa, Tony, Clearwater	9	10	.474	3.85	25	25	2	1	0	0	145.0	155	631	75	62	5	6	5	10	39	0	71	11	4
Croushore, Rick, St. Petersburg	6	4	.600	3.51	12	11	0	0	0	0	59.0	44	251	25	23	2	3	1	4	32	0	57	5	0
Culberson, Don, Daytona	1	1	.500	4.56	12	0	0	0	6	0	23.2	27	113	15	12	2	0	2	4	15	0	15	2	1
Cumberland, Chris, Tampa*	1	2	.333	1.82	5	5	0	0	0	0	24.2	28	104	10	5	1	1	0	1	5	0	10	1	0
Dace, Derek, Kissimmee*	0	1	.000	16.88	1	1	0	0	0	0	2.2	4	17	5	5	0	1	0	0	5	0	1	0	0
DaSilva, Fernando, W. Palm Beach	7	10	.412	3.70	27	20	2	0	1	0	124.0	136	530	61	51	3	2	9	11	31	1	54	5	1
Dault, Donnie, Kissimmee	4	7	.364	3.08	41	5	0	0	16	6	108.0	95	445	52	37	2	4	0	5	36	0	95	8	5
Davis, Jeff, Charlotte	12	7	.632	2.89	26	26	0	0	0	0	165.1	159	691	74	53	10	6	2	11	37	0	105	6	2
Davis, Mark, Brevard County*	0	0	.000	0.00	3	0	0	0	1	0	5.0	2	16	0	0	0	0	0	0	0	0	4	0	0
DeBrino, Rob, Fort Myers	11	3	.786	3.14	41	0	0	0	18	0	48.2	38	206	24	17	2	0	2	5	25	3	30	2	0
DeLaHoya, Javier, Brevard County	1	0	1.000	1.74	5	0	0	0	1	0	10.1	6	40	2	2	1	0	0	2	2	0	8	0	0
Delgado, Ernie, Brevard County	1	6	.143	7.07	18	10	0	0	4	0	62.1	74	308	51	49	4	1	4	7	59	0	36	7	2
Detmers, Kris, St. Petersburg*	10	9	.526	3.25	25	25	1	0	0	0	146.2	120	606	64	53	12	3	7	2	57	0	150	3	2
DeVries, Andrew, Daytona*	1	0	1.000	3.57	21	1	0	0	9	0	45.1	45	203	21	18	2	2	2	5	22	0	21	6	0
Dodd, Robert, Clearwater*	8	7	.533	3.16	26	26	0	0	0	0	151.0	144	636	64	53	4	3	6	1	58	0	110	3	7
Dotel, Octavio, St. Lucie	1	0	1.000	5.63	3	0	0	0	2	0	8.0	10	38	5	5	1	1	2	0	4	0	9	2	0
Drews, Matthew, Tampa	15	7	.682	2.27	28	28	3	0	0	0	182.0	142	748	73	46	5	5	5	17	58	0	140	8	2
Dreyer, Darren, Daytona	3	5	.375	1.94	29	0	0	0	19	7	55.2	42	214	18	12	3	1	2	1	9	0	45	0	0
Drumheller, Al, Tampa*	3	3	.500	1.34	32	0	0	0	10	2	40.1	24	158	11	6	1	2	1	2	14	2	45	1	0
Drumright, Mike, Lakeland	1	1	.500	4.29	5	5	0	0	0	0	21.0	19	87	11	10	2	1	0	0	9	0	19	1	2
Duran, Roberto, Vero Beach*	7	4	.636	3.38	23	22	0	0	0	0	101.1	82	446	42	38	8	3	1	1	70	0	114	12	2
Ehler, Daniel, Brevard County	5	6	.455	3.57	16	15	0	0	0	0	88.1	88	380	46	35	2	4	3	8	26	1	66	0	1
Emerson, Scott, Sarasota*	2	5	.286	4.77	16	11	1	0	1	0	60.1	66	273	38	32	2	2	2	6	29	2	47	6	0
Engle, Tom, St. Lucie	3	3	.500	1.80	9	9	1	0	0	0	50.0	34	203	16	10	1	0	3	5	15	1	41	0	0
Evans, Stan, Clearwater	0	0	.000	0.00	1	0	0	0	0	0	2.0	2	11	2	0	0	0	0	0	2	0	1	0	0
Ferran, Alex, Sarasota*	0	0	.000	0.00	1	0	0	0	1	0	1.0	1	6	1	0	0	0	0	0	2	0	0	2	0
Fiore, Tony, Clearwater	6	2	.750	3.71	24	10	0	0	3	2	70.1	70	323	41	29	4	3	5	2	44	2	45	9	3
Forster, Scott, West Palm Beach*	6	11	.353	4.05	26	26	1	0	0	0	146.2	129	643	78	66	6	5	4	7	80	1	92	16	0
Foster, Mark, Clearwater*	0	1	.000	5.40	24	0	0	0	6	1	23.1	30	108	17	14	1	1	0	4	10	0	13	1	1
Franek, Tom, Clearwater	0	0	.000	3.55	9	0	0	0	5	0	12.2	12	54	6	5	2	0	0	0	3	1	9	0	1
Fultz, Aaron, Fort Myers*	3	6	.333	3.25	21	21	2	0	0	0	122.0	115	516	52	44	10	4	3	8	41	1	127	7	1
Gaillard, Eddy, Lakeland	2	4	.333	1.31	43	0	0	0	38	25	55.0	48	227	13	8	1	1	3	0	23	2	51	2	1
Gallaher, Kevin, Kissimmee	1	1	.500	5.71	7	7	0	0	0	0	17.1	8	86	11	11	0	0	0	3	24	0	21	2	0

Pitcher, Team	W	L	Pct.	ERA	G	GS	CG	ShO	GF	Sv.	IP	H	TBF	R	ER	HR	SH	SF	HB	BB	IBB	SO	WP	Bk.
Gallone, Santy, Clearwater	0	0	.000	0.00	1	0	0	0	1	0	1.0	1	4	0	0	0	0	0	0	0	0	2	0	0
Gandolph, Dave, Kissimmee*	0	2	.000	5.28	12	4	0	0	3	0	15.1	15	77	11	9	0	0	3	0	20	0	8	3	0
Garcia, Frank, St. Petersburg	0	1	.000	10.26	16	0	0	0	8	1	16.2	27	98	22	19	1	0	1	1	18	0	8	3	0
Gardner, Scott, Lakeland	0	0	.000	2.77	5	0	0	0	2	0	13.0	10	54	6	4	1	0	0	0	7	0	14	0	0
Gaspar, Cade, Lakeland	7	6	.538	3.90	23	23	0	0	0	0	99.1	95	422	48	43	5	1	3	9	44	0	97	13	3
Gonzalez, Generoso, Lakeland	0	0	.000	0.00	1	0	0	0	0	0	2.2	1	8	0	0	0	0	0	0	1	0	1	1	0
Gonzalez, Geremis, Daytona	5	1	.833	1.22	19	2	0	0	7	4	44.1	34	178	15	6	0	1	2	1	13	1	30	4	2
Gordon, Mike, Tampa-Dun.	5	8	.385	3.69	28	27	1	0	0	0	161.0	155	700	86	66	12	5	1	7	73	0	132	11	2
Gorecki, Rick, Vero Beach	1	2	.333	0.67	6	5	0	0	0	0	27.0	19	110	6	2	0	1	1	4	9	0	24	1	0
Granger, Greg, Lakeland	9	12	.429	5.01	27	25	1	1	0	0	142.0	176	639	93	79	7	6	7	15	46	0	91	8	2
Grasser, Craig, St. Petersburg	4	2	.667	1.36	26	0	0	0	7	0	33.0	26	133	5	5	2	0	0	2	12	1	27	2	0
Greene, Tommy, Clearwater	0	3	.000	3.15	3	3	0	0	0	0	20.0	12	77	7	7	2	0	0	2	7	0	20	1	0
Grennan, Steve, St. Lucie*	0	0	.000	2.16	9	0	0	0	3	0	8.1	8	38	3	2	0	0	0	1	4	0	10	0	0
Groot, Franz, Vero Beach	0	0	.000	5.83	14	1	0	0	10	1	29.1	28	127	21	19	4	2	5	3	18	0	15	2	1
Guerra, Mark, St. Lucie	9	9	.500	2.64	23	23	4	3	0	0	160.0	148	644	55	47	5	4	4	4	33	1	110	2	3
Gunderson, Mike, Kissimmee	0	0	.000	0.00	1	0	0	0	0	0	2.1	1	8	0	0	0	0	0	0	0	0	0	0	0
Halperin, Mike, Dunedin*	3	5	.375	3.62	14	12	0	0	0	0	69.2	70	298	36	28	4	1	0	3	29	1	63	2	0
Hammond, Chris, Brevard County*	0	0	.000	0.00	1	1	0	0	0	0	4.0	3	16	1	0	0	1	0	0	0	0	4	0	0
Harris, D.J., Dunedin	3	3	.500	3.22	42	0	0	0	16	2	67.0	54	294	29	24	6	3	3	6	41	1	56	2	0
Harris, Greg, Fort Myers	1	1	.500	0.95	3	3	1	0	0	0	19.0	12	69	3	2	1	1	0	0	4	0	11	1	1
Hart, Jason, Daytona	0	3	.000	2.21	37	0	0	0	34	24	40.2	29	172	15	10	2	2	0	1	18	2	50	0	0
Hartgrove, Lyle, Sarasota	3	1	.750	3.98	47	1	0	0	15	2	74.2	73	316	36	33	3	2	3	4	21	2	52	1	2
Hartmann, Pete, Charlotte*	2	4	.333	7.32	15	2	0	0	9	2	35.2	46	180	34	29	7	4	2	0	26	0	30	3	4
Hartmann, Rich, St. Petersburg	0	0	.000	1.65	13	0	0	0	1	0	16.1	13	65	5	3	2	0	0	0	3	0	12	3	0
Hartnett, Bill, Kissimmee	1	1	.500	4.01	32	2	0	0	7	2	74.0	87	346	52	33	3	1	2	4	32	1	61	6	1
Hecker, Doug, Sarasota	1	2	.333	3.43	10	1	0	0	2	1	21.0	24	96	9	8	0	1	1	1	7	0	16	4	1
Heflin, Bronson, Clearwater	2	3	.400	2.95	57	0	0	0	44	21	61.0	52	256	25	20	3	6	1	0	21	5	84	4	0
Heiserman, Rick, St. Petersburg	2	3	.400	5.46	6	5	0	0	1	0	28.0	28	118	18	17	2	0	2	1	11	0	18	4	0
Henderson, Ryan, Vero Beach	11	5	.688	3.88	39	6	0	0	10	2	104.1	98	453	53	45	1	6	1	5	58	3	86	9	2
Henriquez, Oscar, Kissimmee	3	4	.429	5.04	20	0	0	0	7	1	44.2	40	207	29	25	2	2	2	6	30	0	36	3	0
Heredia, Felix, Brevard County*	6	4	.600	3.57	34	8	0	0	3	1	95.2	101	420	52	38	6	0	7	4	36	1	76	6	1
Hernandez, Jeremy, Brevard County	0	0	.000	2.35	4	2	0	0	0	0	7.2	5	29	2	2	0	0	0	0	2	0	5	2	0
Herrmann, Gary, Clearwater*	7	2	.778	3.60	42	3	0	0	10	3	70.0	64	295	31	28	3	3	3	0	28	1	56	1	0
Hiljus, Erik, St. Lucie	8	4	.667	2.99	17	17	0	0	0	0	111.1	85	453	46	37	4	6	5	3	50	2	98	10	6
Hill, Shawn, Daytona	5	3	.625	3.68	37	0	0	0	22	3	58.2	48	241	31	24	6	1	0	2	17	3	71	0	1
Hingle, Larry, Kissimmee*	0	0	.000	18.78	10	0	0	0	6	0	7.2	15	48	18	16	1	0	0	0	11	0	2	1	0
Hmielewski, Chris, W. Palm Beach*	1	3	.250	3.59	36	2	0	0	15	0	57.2	57	259	31	23	4	3	2	2	28	4	41	6	0
Hollinger, Adrian, Brevard County	0	2	.000	5.40	11	4	0	0	4	2	25.0	26	118	17	15	1	0	1	1	18	0	18	1	1
Hollis, Ronald, Vero Beach	2	5	.286	2.47	43	0	0	0	13	0	73.0	55	306	22	20	1	3	2	2	38	6	56	1	0
Housely, Adam, Lakeland	0	1	.000	6.00	19	1	0	0	3	1	30.0	39	141	23	20	0	1	0	3	11	0	23	1	2
Howard, Chris, Sarasota*	0	2	.000	5.23	6	5	0	0	0	0	10.1	10	45	6	6	1	1	2	0	4	0	7	1	3
Hubbard, Mark, Tampa*	4	3	.571	1.84	13	11	1	0	0	0	68.1	52	269	22	14	2	1	2	4	21	0	40	2	0
Huffman, Jeff, Sarasota	4	4	.500	4.58	15	11	0	0	1	0	76.2	72	335	43	39	3	3	1	4	36	1	55	8	1
Humphrey, Rich, Kissimmee	3	1	.750	1.96	46	0	0	0	39	14	55.0	45	233	16	12	1	5	2	3	20	0	33	2	1
Hunter, Rich, Clearwater	6	0	1.000	2.93	9	9	0	0	0	0	58.1	62	242	23	19	3	3	2	5	7	0	46	3	3
Hurst, William, Brevard County	1	4	.200	3.02	39	4	0	0	29	12	50.2	33	228	20	17	1	3	1	8	41	4	35	4	0
Jacobsen, Joe, Vero Beach	1	3	.250	3.67	47	0	0	0	44	32	49.0	42	215	22	20	2	5	2	2	23	2	54	10	1
Janzen, Marty, Tampa	10	3	.769	2.61	18	18	1	0	0	0	113.2	102	461	38	33	4	1	2	4	30	0	104	3	4
Jersild, Aaron, Dunedin*	2	6	.250	4.81	22	3	0	0	10	1	48.2	54	219	30	26	1	2	2	6	17	0	39	2	5
Jerzembeck, Michael, Tampa	0	1	.000	9.00	2	0	0	0	0	0	3.0	5	17	4	3	1	0	0	0	2	0	1	1	0
Johnson, Jonathan, Charlotte	1	5	.167	2.70	8	7	1	0	1	0	43.1	34	178	14	13	2	2	0	1	16	0	25	3	3
Jordan, Jason, Lakeland	1	3	.250	5.95	4	4	0	0	0	0	19.2	32	94	20	13	1	0	4	1	7	0	8	1	0
Kamieniecki, Scott, Tampa	1	0	1.000	1.80	1	1	0	0	0	0	5.0	6	22	2	1	0	0	0	0	1	0	2	1	0
Kell, Rob, Charlotte*	1	0	1.000	3.05	11	0	0	0	5	1	20.2	16	93	9	7	1	0	0	2	15	0	21	2	0
Kendrena, Ken, W. Palm Beach	3	3	.500	3.04	16	0	0	0	5	2	23.2	23	102	9	8	2	1	1	0	11	2	19	3	0
Kenny, Sean, St. Lucie	4	9	.308	2.70	46	0	0	0	15	2	56.2	51	229	22	17	1	4	1	3	15	1	26	2	2
Kerley, Collin, West Palm Beach	1	3	.250	3.95	19	0	0	0	8	0	27.1	28	119	16	12	0	0	0	1	11	1	17	2	0
Keusch, Joseph, Charlotte	9	4	.692	1.82	40	0	0	0	27	8	64.1	56	257	19	13	3	2	3	2	14	2	36	3	1
Khoury, Tony, Daytona	2	0	1.000	4.05	7	0	0	0	5	0	6.2	10	30	3	3	1	0	1	0	2	0	4	0	0
King, Curtis, St. Petersburg	7	8	.467	2.58	28	21	3	0	1	0	136.0	117	567	49	39	3	4	2	11	49	2	65	6	0
Knieper, Aaron, W. Palm Beach	2	4	.333	3.95	32	6	0	0	10	0	70.2	67	317	38	31	0	3	4	4	46	2	48	12	4
Kostich, Bill, Lakeland*	1	0	1.000	0.00	4	0	0	0	2	0	6.0	2	21	0	0	0	1	0	1	2	0	2	0	0
Kozeniewski, Blaise, Tampa	3	1	.750	0.95	11	0	0	0	0	0	19.0	11	69	3	2	1	0	0	0	3	0	17	1	1
Kramer, Dan, Sarasota*	2	0	1.000	6.14	21	0	0	0	4	0	14.2	18	69	12	10	1	0	2	0	7	0	13	1	2
Lankford, Frank, Tampa	4	6	.400	2.59	55	0	0	0	36	15	73.0	64	305	29	21	0	7	0	2	22	6	58	1	0
Largusa, Levon, Dunedin*	4	4	.500	4.10	16	7	1	1	1	0	59.1	68	268	32	27	2	1	1	0	28	0	37	1	0
Larson, Toby, St. Lucie	6	7	.462	2.52	19	18	3	1	0	0	121.2	122	508	44	34	5	4	0	7	30	2	82	7	1
Leahy, Pat, Brevard County	4	4	.500	3.88	11	11	0	0	0	0	46.1	41	200	29	20	6	1	2	5	22	1	43	2	0
Lehoisky, Russ, Fort Myers	0	5	.000	3.29	26	0	0	0	10	0	52.0	45	240	25	19	0	7	2	4	38	3	29	5	0
Leshnock, Donnie, Tampa	10	6	.625	3.08	28	10	0	0	2	2	87.2	78	378	41	30	2	1	5	4	45	0	67	7	2
Lewis, Michael, Brevard County*	4	5	.444	2.32	43	0	0	0	8	1	62.0	48	251	22	16	5	8	0	2	22	3	44	1	0
Lima, Jose, Lakeland	3	1	.750	2.57	4	4	0	0	0	0	21.0	23	86	11	6	2	0	0	0	0	0	20	1	0
Linebarger, Keith, Fort Myers	7	4	.636	2.10	29	10	1	1	12	4	103.0	74	418	30	24	6	3	2	9	35	1	73	4	0
Liquet, Wilton, Vero Beach	0	0	.000	4.05	4	1	0	0	1	0	6.2	5	29	3	3	0	1	0	0	5	0	3	1	0
Loewer, Carlton, Clearwater	7	5	.583	3.30	20	20	1	0	0	0	114.2	124	502	59	42	6	3	5	5	36	0	83	7	3
Loiz, Niuman, Kissimmee	0	8	.000	5.56	13	13	0	0	0	0	56.2	71	271	48	35	2	2	3	2	30	0	33	10	0
Lopez, Johann, Kissimmee	5	5	.500	2.61	18	12	0	0	3	1	69.0	55	283	30	20	3	1	2	3	25	0	67	5	3
Lopez, Orlando, Daytona*	7	2	.778	2.68	44	0	0	0	15	8	80.2	75	342	30	24	6	5	1	3	32	1	76	6	2
Lovingier, Kevin, St. Petersburg*	1	0	1.000	1.66	22	0	0	0	6	0	21.2	9	82	4	4	0	1	1	2	10	1	14	1	0
Lukasiewicz, Mark, Dunedin*	3	6	.333	5.60	31	13	0	0	11	1	88.1	80	383	62	55	13	1	2	7	42	0	71	7	0
Maldonado, Jay, Fort Myers	0	1	.000	6.23	5	0	0	0	1	0	4.1	6	23	4	3	0	0	0	0	4	1	4	1	1
Mallory, Trevor, Dunedin	0	5	.000	5.01	37	3	0	0	10	0	70.0	80	326	53	39	4	1	3	3	41	0	46	7	0
Malloy, Charles, Sarasota	6	4	.600	3.54	16	12	2	1	2	0	86.1	72	354	38	34	5	2	2	0	39	2	51	6	1

Pitcher, Team	W	L	Pct.	ERA	G	GS	CG	ShO	GF	Sv.	IP	H	TBF	R	ER	HR	SH	SF	HB	BB	IBB	SO	WP	Bk.
Manning, David, Charlotte	9	5	.643	3.50	26	20	0	0	2	0	128.2	127	545	56	50	7	3	3	3	46	0	66	0	5
Markham, Andy, W. Palm Beach	7	11	.389	3.94	24	23	1	0	0	0	121.0	129	532	62	53	8	4	6	9	44	1	58	4	1
Marquardt, Scott, St. Petersburg	3	4	.429	3.78	9	9	0	0	0	0	52.1	55	222	24	22	4	1	1	3	15	0	39	4	4
Marquez, Ihosvany, Sarasota	1	1	.500	3.00	12	0	0	0	4	1	15.0	10	70	6	5	1	1	0	2	13	1	18	0	0
Marrero, Kenny, Lakeland	1	4	.200	3.72	37	0	0	0	18	5	55.2	54	239	28	23	5	1	2	0	28	1	46	6	1
Martinez, Cesar, Sarasota*	6	6	.500	3.75	34	10	0	0	2	0	110.1	108	477	62	46	6	3	2	4	40	2	61	9	1
Martinez, Ramiro, Charlotte*	2	2	.500	4.08	14	6	0	0	6	2	46.1	45	192	21	21	3	3	3	0	15	0	30	3	0
Matranga, Jeff, St. Petersburg	3	4	.429	2.74	53	0	0	0	17	3	65.2	49	272	27	20	2	3	3	9	20	3	71	2	0
Matulevich, Jeff, St. Petersburg	1	5	.167	2.76	51	0	0	0	48	30	58.2	50	253	20	18	3	2	1	0	30	3	61	4	0
McCommon, Jason, W. Palm Bch.	7	11	.389	3.75	26	26	3	1	0	0	156.0	153	650	75	65	13	7	6	10	38	0	94	6	7
McDill, Allen, St. Lucie*	4	2	.667	1.64	7	7	1	1	0	0	49.1	36	190	11	9	2	1	0	1	13	0	28	3	0
McLain, Mike, Lakeland	1	1	.500	3.58	21	0	0	0	11	1	27.2	33	118	13	11	3	1	0	1	7	0	27	3	0
McLaughlin, Denis, Sarasota	3	2	.600	3.26	54	0	0	0	30	6	66.1	57	305	31	24	3	4	1	7	46	7	79	5	3
Medina, Rafael, Tampa	2	2	.500	2.37	6	6	0	0	0	0	30.1	29	131	12	8	0	0	0	1	12	0	25	0	2
Meinershagen, Adam, Dunedin	5	9	.357	3.75	21	13	1	0	2	0	98.1	115	430	59	41	13	3	8	6	23	1	53	3	0
Mercado, Hector, Kissimmee*	6	8	.429	3.46	19	17	2	0	0	0	104.0	96	433	50	40	2	2	3	3	37	0	75	4	1
Merrill, Ethan, Sarasota*	11	7	.611	3.78	27	25	1	1	2	0	150.0	155	672	86	63	11	3	5	11	67	2	78	7	0
Metheney, Nelson, Clearwater	5	5	.500	3.00	59	0	0	0	11	1	72.0	65	310	32	24	2	7	4	0	25	3	38	3	2
Meyer, David, Tampa*	3	4	.429	6.52	12	11	0	0	0	0	58.0	84	281	49	42	3	2	3	4	29	0	29	6	4
Militello, Sam, Brevard County	0	1	.000	7.84	4	4	0	0	0	0	10.1	7	58	10	9	1	0	0	1	20	0	18	6	0
Miller, Shawn, Fort Myers	4	4	.500	1.90	30	2	0	0	16	4	71.0	68	288	16	15	4	2	2	2	13	1	35	2	0
Mix, Greg, Brevard County	3	1	.750	3.94	5	4	1	0	0	0	29.2	27	119	13	13	1	0	0	3	10	0	17	1	1
Moody, Eric, Charlotte	5	5	.500	2.75	13	13	2	2	0	0	88.1	84	353	30	27	2	3	1	5	13	0	57	0	0
Moody, Ritchie, Charlotte*	0	1	.000	6.23	1	1	0	0	0	0	4.1	3	22	3	3	0	1	0	0	8	0	0	0	0
Moraga, David, W. Palm Beach*	1	1	.500	3.94	3	3	0	0	0	0	16.0	20	75	7	7	0	0	0	0	10	0	10	0	0
Morris, Matt, St. Petersburg	3	2	.600	2.38	6	6	1	1	0	0	34.0	22	134	16	9	1	2	0	0	11	0	31	0	2
Morse, Paul, Fort Myers	3	1	.750	3.82	35	0	0	0	29	15	61.1	57	247	30	26	3	1	4	3	12	0	56	4	1
Mysel, David, Lakeland	1	1	.500	5.83	20	0	0	0	8	2	29.1	36	141	22	19	3	3	0	3	14	0	32	2	0
Newell, Brandon, St. Lucie	2	2	.500	2.96	39	0	0	0	16	3	48.2	42	211	18	16	1	5	2	3	29	2	39	4	0
Norman, Scott, Lakeland	7	7	.500	4.07	22	21	3	0	0	0	128.1	141	571	86	58	4	2	9	6	38	1	63	4	2
Nunez, Clemente, Brevard County	12	6	.667	2.48	19	19	4	2	0	0	123.1	99	490	48	34	3	2	2	5	22	1	79	3	5
Nye, Ryan, Clearwater	12	7	.632	3.40	27	27	5	1	0	0	167.0	164	681	71	63	8	5	5	6	33	1	116	4	3
O'Brien, Brian, Fort Myers*	0	3	.000	2.88	24	0	0	0	17	0	34.1	31	147	20	11	2	2	1	0	15	1	20	4	0
O'Malley, Paul, Kissimmee	8	10	.444	3.61	27	27	0	0	0	0	147.0	148	661	86	59	7	3	3	18	62	0	80	13	2
Oropesa, Eddie, Vero Beach*	3	1	.750	3.81	19	1	0	0	7	1	28.1	25	120	12	12	0	1	2	3	10	0	23	4	2
Pack, Steve, St. Lucie	0	0	.000	4.82	5	0	0	0	2	0	9.1	15	48	6	5	0	1	0	1	1	0	6	0	0
Paluk, Jeff, Vero Beach	1	0	1.000	6.75	2	0	0	0	0	0	4.0	5	19	3	3	0	0	0	0	2	0	4	0	0
Parra, Julio, Vero Beach	7	3	.700	2.85	22	1	0	0	12	0	41.0	39	176	21	13	2	1	2	1	20	1	36	4	1
Pena, Juan, Sarasota	1	1	.500	4.91	2	2	0	0	0	0	7.1	8	35	4	4	0	0	0	2	3	0	5	1	1
Perkins, Ron, Clearwater	1	1	.500	2.84	6	0	0	0	3	0	6.1	6	30	3	2	1	0	0	1	5	0	3	1	0
Perpetuo, Nelson, Charlotte*	0	0	.000	7.71	5	0	0	0	1	0	7.0	5	33	7	6	0	1	0	1	5	0	7	0	0
Petcka, Joe, St. Lucie	1	1	.500	5.98	30	1	0	0	12	0	46.2	39	213	35	31	1	2	0	3	35	0	28	7	0
Petersen, Matt, Daytona	2	1	.667	4.15	3	3	0	0	0	0	17.1	13	66	8	8	2	0	1	0	3	0	13	0	0
Peterson, Dean, Sarasota	1	3	.250	6.75	4	4	0	0	0	0	17.1	25	90	17	13	2	1	1	3	10	0	15	1	0
Pettit, Doug, Brevard County	2	5	.286	2.83	27	0	0	0	14	4	35.0	37	158	18	11	3	2	3	0	13	4	22	1	0
Phelps, Tommy, W. Palm Beach*	0	2	.000	16.20	2	2	0	0	0	0	5.0	10	33	10	9	0	0	0	0	11	0	5	2	0
Pincavitch, Kevin, Vero Beach	10	7	.588	1.66	32	13	2	1	5	2	124.2	83	504	37	23	7	5	1	5	48	0	103	12	1
Pisciotta, Scott, W. Palm Beach	5	4	.556	2.52	53	0	0	0	29	2	60.2	55	271	26	17	1	1	4	0	36	2	38	11	0
Pollard, Damon, W. Palm Beach	4	3	.571	3.35	28	0	0	0	6	1	51.0	38	208	21	19	0	1	4	2	26	0	43	3	0
Powell, John, Charlotte	4	1	.800	3.00	19	2	0	0	9	2	48.0	44	201	18	16	2	2	2	3	13	1	47	1	1
Querecuto, Juan, Dunedin	0	0	.000	0.00	1	0	0	0	1	0	2.0	1	9	0	0	0	0	0	0	1	0	2	0	0
Raggio, Brady, St. Petersburg	2	3	.400	3.80	20	3	0	0	4	0	47.1	43	195	24	20	2	3	1	1	13	2	35	2	1
Rama, Shelby, Clearwater	0	0	.000	4.32	4	0	0	0	1	0	8.1	12	36	4	4	0	0	0	0	1	0	2	1	0
Ramos, Edgar, Kissimmee	4	0	1.000	0.41	4	4	0	0	0	0	22.0	11	80	4	1	1	0	0	0	1	0	16	0	0
Rathbun, Jason, Tampa	1	0	1.000	4.05	10	5	0	0	3	0	26.2	27	118	17	12	2	1	0	2	10	0	14	2	0
Redman, Mark, Fort Myers*	2	1	.667	2.76	8	5	0	0	0	0	32.2	28	134	13	10	4	1	2	1	13	0	26	2	0
Reed, Jason, Vero Beach*	0	0	.000	3.42	21	0	0	0	9	0	23.2	18	102	9	9	3	0	0	1	11	1	17	0	0
Resz, Greg, Tampa	0	1	.000	3.38	12	0	0	0	3	1	13.1	10	61	9	5	0	0	0	1	9	2	16	3	0
Reyes, Dennis, Vero Beach*	1	0	1.000	1.80	3	2	0	0	0	0	10.0	8	43	2	2	0	1	0	0	6	0	9	0	1
Reyes, Jose, Charlotte	1	3	.250	4.40	30	2	0	0	11	3	61.1	67	274	38	30	7	0	3	4	22	0	41	5	0
Ricken, Ray, Tampa	3	4	.429	2.15	11	11	1	0	0	0	75.1	47	291	25	18	3	2	1	1	27	0	58	1	2
Rios, Dan, Tampa	0	4	.000	2.00	57	0	0	0	52	24	67.1	67	296	24	15	1	5	2	8	20	4	72	2	0
Rodriguez, Chris, Daytona	1	0	1.000	5.91	5	0	0	0	1	0	10.2	14	46	7	7	2	0	0	2	2	0	6	0	0
Rodriguez, Salvador, Tampa	0	1	.000	11.05	6	0	0	0	0	0	7.1	13	40	10	9	1	0	0	1	4	0	7	1	0
Rojano, Rafael, Tampa	0	2	.000	6.23	3	0	0	0	0	0	4.1	4	19	3	3	0	1	0	0	2	1	1	0	0
Roman, Dan, Charlotte*	2	2	.500	7.71	7	5	0	0	1	0	25.2	30	126	22	22	2	1	2	6	19	1	21	2	2
Romano, Michael, Dunedin	11	7	.611	4.13	28	26	1	1	1	0	150.1	141	654	79	69	15	4	3	11	75	0	102	5	3
Root, Derek, Kissimmee*	0	0	.000	4.50	5	0	0	0	1	0	6.0	10	29	3	3	0	0	0	0	2	0	3	0	0
Roque, Rafael, St. Lucie*	6	9	.400	3.56	24	24	2	1	0	0	136.2	114	582	65	54	7	2	4	4	72	1	81	11	4
Rosengren, John, Lakeland*	3	3	.500	3.99	13	8	0	0	1	0	56.1	46	253	33	25	6	2	2	7	36	0	35	2	0
Rushworth, Jim, W. Palm Beach	1	0	1.000	3.65	10	0	0	0	4	1	12.1	11	54	5	5	0	1	1	1	6	0	9	0	0
Ryan, Jason, Daytona	11	5	.688	3.48	26	26	0	0	0	0	134.2	128	579	61	52	10	3	2	9	54	0	98	13	1
Sacharko, Mark, Kissimmee	0	1	.000	6.59	6	1	0	0	2	0	13.2	16	68	10	10	0	0	2	2	11	0	6	2	0
Salazar, Mike, Lakeland*	7	3	.700	3.19	42	3	0	0	18	5	87.1	86	371	37	31	4	4	1	6	21	1	52	2	1
Sampson, Benj, Fort Myers*	11	9	.550	3.49	28	27	3	2	1	0	160.0	148	664	71	62	11	8	8	4	52	0	95	5	0
Sanchez, Victor, Kissimmee	0	0	.000	3.00	3	0	0	0	3	0	3.0	2	14	1	1	0	0	0	0	3	0	1	0	0
Santana, Julio, Charlotte	0	3	.000	3.73	5	5	1	0	0	0	31.1	32	136	16	13	1	1	1	0	16	0	27	7	2
Santiago, Sandi, Tampa	3	2	.600	3.90	34	3	0	0	12	0	57.2	54	251	28	25	1	1	3	0	29	1	55	6	0
Santos, Henry, Lakeland*	5	6	.455	4.24	35	10	0	0	7	0	97.2	111	434	59	46	3	5	4	6	40	0	80	10	0
Sauerbeck, Scott, St. Lucie*	0	1	.000	2.03	20	1	0	0	4	0	26.2	26	116	10	6	0	0	2	0	14	1	25	2	2
Saunders, Tony, Brevard County*	6	5	.545	3.04	13	13	0	0	0	0	71.0	60	275	29	24	6	1	4	7	15	0	54	3	0
Schlomann, Brett, Tampa	2	0	1.000	1.64	2	2	0	0	0	0	11.0	10	44	6	2	2	0	0	0	0	0	5	0	0
Schneider, Tom, W. Palm Beach*	0	1	.000	10.80	4	0	0	0	1	0	3.1	8	21	5	4	0	0	0	1	2	0	3	0	0

Pitcher, Team	W	L	Pct.	ERA	G	GS	CG	ShO	GF	Sv.	IP	H	TBF	R	ER	HR	SH	SF	HB	BB	IBB	SO	WP	Bk.
Seip, Rod, Charlotte	1	2	.333	2.00	6	4	0	0	1	0	27.0	26	116	9	6	1	0	2	1	6	1	23	1	0
Sele, Aaron, Sarasota	0	0	.000	0.00	2	2	0	0	0	0	7.0	6	27	0	0	0	0	0	0	1	0	8	0	0
Serna, Joe, Lakeland	0	1	.000	2.00	5	0	0	0	3	1	9.0	10	44	4	2	1	2	0	1	5	2	3	1	2
Shoemaker, Stephen, Tampa	0	1	.000	1.08	3	2	0	0	0	0	16.2	9	73	5	2	1	2	1	0	13	0	12	2	0
Shrum, Dennis, Kissimmee	7	6	.538	3.24	38	0	0	0	15	5	91.2	96	408	44	33	7	5	1	5	28	0	69	5	5
Sikes, Ken, Vero Beach	3	4	.429	5.06	14	12	0	0	1	0	64.0	64	291	44	36	4	0	2	2	36	0	50	4	1
Siler, Jeff, Lakeland*	2	2	.500	2.28	27	0	0	0	10	1	27.2	21	100	9	7	2	2	0	0	7	1	26	0	1
Sinacori, Chris, Dunedin	0	1	.000	6.75	12	0	0	0	11	2	12.0	13	53	9	9	1	0	0	3	4	1	11	1	0
Sinclair, Steve, Dunedin*	5	3	.625	2.59	46	0	0	0	18	2	73.0	69	297	26	21	4	1	1	3	17	1	52	2	3
Smith, Dan, Charlotte	5	1	.833	2.95	9	9	1	1	0	0	58.0	53	242	23	19	4	1	2	3	16	0	34	1	0
Smith, Eric, Clearwater	0	0	.000	0.00	8	0	0	0	7	4	8.0	3	27	0	0	0	0	0	0	1	0	7	0	0
Smith, Keilan, Dunedin	11	6	.647	4.11	26	24	1	0	1	0	149.0	164	663	83	68	11	6	2	15	53	1	85	16	3
Southard, Scott, Brevard County	0	0	.000	0.00	1	0	0	0	1	0	1.0	0	3	0	0	0	0	0	0	0	0	1	0	0
Spring, Josh, Dunedin	1	0	1.000	1.05	18	0	0	0	6	2	25.2	16	110	6	3	1	1	0	1	17	1	23	3	0
Standish, Scott, Tampa	0	0	.000	2.57	4	2	0	0	0	0	14.0	10	55	5	4	1	0	1	0	4	0	10	1	0
Stanifer, Robert, Brevard County	3	6	.333	4.14	18	13	0	0	0	0	82.2	97	360	47	38	4	4	5	7	15	0	45	2	0
Steinert, Robert, Dunedin	3	4	.429	4.70	17	11	0	0	1	0	74.2	82	329	48	39	4	4	4	3	29	0	41	6	4
Steinke, Brock, Kissimmee	0	3	.000	6.61	8	5	0	0	0	0	32.2	48	160	28	24	0	0	4	1	16	0	15	5	1
Stentz, Brent, Lakeland	0	0	.000	0.00	2	0	0	0	1	0	2.0	0	6	0	0	0	0	0	0	0	0	4	0	0
Stephenson, Brian, Daytona	10	9	.526	3.96	26	26	0	0	0	0	150.0	145	640	79	66	7	6	3	7	58	2	109	14	2
Stevenson, Jason, Daytona	2	0	1.000	2.95	8	0	0	0	3	1	18.1	11	71	6	6	0	1	0	1	6	0	15	1	0
Stewart, Chris, St. Petersburg	0	1	.000	5.35	30	0	0	0	7	0	33.2	29	150	22	20	2	2	2	1	25	1	36	2	1
Swan, Tyrone, Clearwater	2	3	.400	3.40	37	0	0	0	10	0	47.2	50	208	25	18	5	2	2	1	19	1	46	6	0
Tatar, Jason, Fort Myers	4	5	.444	2.61	21	15	0	0	4	1	82.2	64	339	33	24	3	0	4	2	36	0	60	3	2
Telgheder, Jim, Sarasota	0	3	.000	6.48	22	0	0	0	5	0	25.0	30	122	20	18	3	2	0	2	15	2	24	4	1
Tewksbury, Bob, Charlotte	1	0	1.000	0.00	1	1	0	0	0	0	6.0	3	22	0	0	0	0	0	0	0	0	4	0	0
Thompson, Justin, Lakeland*	2	1	.667	4.88	6	6	0	0	0	0	24.0	30	107	13	13	1	0	2	2	8	0	20	0	0
Thornton, Paul, Brevard County	4	5	.444	3.27	42	1	0	0	27	4	71.2	66	311	34	26	5	5	1	8	27	2	56	3	0
Tidwell, Jason, Brevard County	0	0	.000	0.00	4	1	0	0	0	0	7.0	5	31	3	0	0	0	0	0	3	0	3	0	0
Toney, Mike, Dunedin	1	2	.333	8.03	12	0	0	0	8	3	12.1	19	67	14	11	0	1	1	1	13	1	6	2	0
Tucker, Julien, Kissimmee	2	11	.154	5.00	19	15	0	0	0	0	68.1	86	327	61	38	3	1	6	5	27	0	28	5	3
Turrentine, Rich, St. Lucie	0	3	.000	6.05	4	4	0	0	0	0	19.1	17	92	14	13	3	1	0	2	17	0	14	3	0
Tuttle, Dave, Lakeland	1	4	.200	2.90	6	4	1	0	1	0	31.0	31	132	11	10	1	0	3	2	12	0	28	1	0
Twiggs, Greg, Daytona*	8	3	.727	1.41	18	13	1	0	1	0	89.1	64	355	30	14	3	1	1	5	28	0	80	4	0
Urbina, Dan, Vero Beach	5	7	.417	4.32	18	16	0	0	0	0	91.2	90	412	56	44	4	0	5	3	52	0	68	13	4
Urbina, Ugueth, W. Palm Beach	1	0	1.000	0.00	2	2	0	0	0	0	9.0	4	30	0	0	0	0	0	1	1	0	11	0	0
Valley, Jason, Clearwater	0	0	.000	12.46	4	0	0	0	0	0	4.1	9	23	6	6	0	1	0	0	4	0	4	1	0
Vandemark, John, Clearwater*	1	2	.333	5.67	24	0	0	0	6	0	27.0	24	127	21	17	4	1	1	0	21	1	18	2	1
Viola, Frank, Dunedin*	0	1	.000	3.97	3	3	0	0	0	0	11.1	12	53	9	5	2	0	1	1	3	0	8	0	0
Wagner, Bret, St. Petersburg*	5	4	.556	2.12	17	17	1	0	0	0	93.1	77	373	36	22	3	3	2	2	28	0	59	4	0
Walker, Wade, Daytona	8	6	.571	2.53	25	24	2	1	0	0	135.0	113	541	50	38	5	3	2	2	36	0	117	8	1
Walter, Michael, Kissimmee	4	3	.571	5.55	41	0	0	0	21	0	71.1	78	338	58	44	4	5	9	10	42	1	42	9	2
Ward, Bryan, Brevard County*	5	1	.833	2.88	11	11	0	0	0	0	72.0	68	296	27	23	5	4	0	2	17	0	65	1	1
Ward, Duane, Dunedin	0	1	.000	6.23	3	2	0	0	0	0	4.1	4	19	3	3	1	1	0	2	1	0	4	0	1
Waring, Jim, Kissimmee	2	1	.667	1.78	5	5	1	0	0	0	30.1	23	120	10	6	1	1	1	3	11	0	16	4	1
Watts, Brandon, Vero Beach*	5	3	.625	4.04	13	8	0	0	1	0	49.0	46	215	29	22	5	0	2	1	22	0	42	4	1
Weathers, Dave, Brevard County	0	0	.000	0.00	1	1	0	0	0	0	4.0	4	15	0	0	0	0	0	0	1	0	3	0	0
Welch, Mike, St. Lucie	4	4	.500	5.40	44	6	0	0	33	15	70.0	96	322	50	42	7	4	3	6	18	4	51	4	0
Wendell, Turk, Daytona	0	0	.000	1.17	4	2	0	0	0	0	7.2	5	30	2	1	0	1	0	0	1	0	8	1	0
Westbrook, Destry, Kissimmee	0	1	.000	10.07	10	0	0	0	2	1	19.2	34	106	24	22	2	1	0	0	13	1	22	2	0
Whiteman, Greg, Lakeland*	1	2	.333	6.05	4	4	0	0	0	0	19.1	18	87	16	13	0	0	2	0	15	0	20	1	1
Whitten, Michael, Brevard County*	1	4	.200	3.96	22	0	0	0	9	1	38.2	47	170	21	17	2	1	3	2	9	1	25	2	0
Williams, Matt, Kissimmee*	4	6	.400	4.63	19	18	2	0	0	0	101.0	115	446	60	52	7	5	3	2	44	1	71	5	1
Winslett, Dax, V.B.-Day.	12	6	.667	2.78	26	25	0	0	0	0	152.0	148	627	59	47	11	4	2	2	39	0	111	13	2
Witasick, Jay, St. Petersburg	7	7	.500	2.74	18	18	1	1	0	0	105.0	80	425	39	32	4	1	4	0	36	1	109	5	1
Wright, Howard, Kissimmee	1	0	1.000	3.60	2	0	0	0	0	0	5.0	1	21	3	2	0	0	0	0	4	0	3	0	0
Yan, Esteban, West Palm Beach	6	8	.429	3.07	24	21	1	0	1	1	137.2	139	580	63	47	3	7	5	10	33	0	89	8	3
Yocum, David, Vero Beach*	2	1	.667	2.96	8	7	0	0	0	0	27.1	22	116	12	9	2	3	2	0	12	0	20	3	1
Young, Anthony, Daytona	0	0	.000	5.63	6	1	0	0	3	0	8.0	5	36	5	5	0	0	0	0	4	0	3	0	0

COMBINATION SHUTOUTS: **Brevard County (12)**—Ward-Hurst 2, Carl-Lewis-Bowen-Hurst, Ehler-Heredia-Davis-Lewis-Hurst, Ehler-Lewis, Hollinger-Lewis-Carl-Andersen, Leahy-Heredia-Hurst, Nunez-Lewis, Nunez-Whitten, Saunders-Pettit, Saunders-Pettit-Hurst, Stanifer-Ehler-Pettit. **Charlotte (4)**—Davis-Buckels, Moody-Keusch-Buckles, Roman-Manning-Buckles, Seip-Buckels. **Clearwater (8)**—Beech-Swan-Foster, Costa-Herrmann-Franek, Dodd-Metheney-Agostinelli, Fiore-Metheney-Swan, Hunter-Agostinelli-Heflin, Loewer-Herrmann-Metheney-Agostinelli, Nye-Heflin-Perkins, Nye-Metheney-Heflin. **Daytona (12)**—Box-Connolly-Hart, Box-Stevenson, Gonzalez-Dreyer, Gonzalez-Lopez-Hart, Ryan-Rodriguez-Hart, Stephenson-Young-Hart, Twiggs-Hill, Walker-Gonzalez, Walker-Lopez, Walker-Lopez-Hart, Winslett-DeVries-Dreyer, Winslett-Lopez. **Dunedin (3)**—Carpenter-Sinclair, Largusa-Adkins, Smith-Harris-Sinacori. **Fort Myers (7)**—Bowers-Linebarger, Linebarger-DeBrino, Sampson-DeBrino-Morse, Sampson-Maldonado-Biehl, Tatar-Caridad-Linebarger, Tatar-DeBrino, Tatar-O'Brien-DeBrino. **Kissimmee (7)**—Gallaher-Lopez 2, Lopez-Dault, Mercado-Hartnett, Mercado-Shrum-Humphrey, Ramos-Shrum-Dault, Tucker-Wright-Shrum. **Lakeland (6)**—Borkowski-Stentz-Gaillard, Drumright-Gaillard, Gaspar-Salazar, Gaspar-Salazar-Housely-Marrero, Lima-Aldred, Thompson-Santos. **St. Lucie (7)**—Engle-Bullock-Welch, Engle-Kenny-Welch, Larsen-Kenny-Welch, McDill-Newell-Arffa, McDill-Petcka-Kenny, Roque-Bullock, Roque-Newell-Kenny. **St. Petersburg (10)**—Aybar-Lovingier-Matranga-Matulevich, Carpenter-Grasser, Croushore-Lovingier-Matranga, Croushore-King-Blake-Garcia, Croushore-Matranga-Matulevich, Detmers-Garcia, Detmers-Lovingier-Matulevich, Detmers-Stewart-Grasser-Matranga, King-Matranga-Matulevich, Wagner-Lovingier-Matulevich. **Sarasota (6)**—Barkley-Bogott-McLaughlin-Bennett, Cederblad-Bennett, Cederblad-Kramer-Telgheder-Martinez, Howard-Merrill, Malloy-Bogott-Bennett, Peterson-Bennett. **Tampa (13)**—Drews-Lankford 2, Janzen-Rios 2, Drews-Rios, Drews-Santiago-Cindrich, Hubbard-Rodriguez-Lankford, Hubbard-Kozeniewski-Santiago, Janzen-Rodriguez-Rios, Leshnock-Corn-Rios, Medina-Lankford-Resz-Santiago, Rathbun-Rios, Santiago-Berry-Lankford-Rios. **Vero Beach (5)**—Duran-Hollis-Jacobsen, Duran-Parra-Henderson-Jacobsen, Pincavitch-Jacobsen, Urbina-Hollis-Jacobsen, Watts-Aquino. **West Palm Beach (6)**—Yan-Benz 2, DaSilva-Benz-Pisciotta, Markham-Pollard-Pisciotta, McCommon-Benz, Urbina-Yan.

NO-HIT GAMES: Moody, Charlotte, defeated Sarasota, 11-0, April 20; Nunez, Brevard County, defeated West Palm Beach, 2-0, May 28; Roque, St. Lucie, defeated Dunedin, 6-1, June 28; Duran-Hollis-Jacobsen, Vero Beach, defeated West Palm Beach, 3-0 (second game), June 28.

PITCHERS WITH TWO OR MORE TEAMS

Pitcher, Team	W	L	Pct.	ERA	G	GS	CG	ShO	GF	Sv.	IP	H	TBF	R	ER	HR	SH	SF	HB	BB	IBB	SO	WP	Bk.
Gordon, Mike, Tampa	4	6	.400	3.04	21	21	1	0	0	0	124.1	111	521	54	42	6	3	1	4	49	0	96	9	2
Gordon, Mike, Dunedin	1	2	.333	5.89	7	6	0	0	0	0	36.2	44	179	32	24	6	2	0	3	24	0	36	2	0
Winslett, Dax, Vero Beach	6	4	.600	3.18	14	13	0	0	0	0	85.0	87	358	35	30	7	4	1	1	21	0	59	6	2
Winslett, Dax, Daytona	6	2	.750	2.28	12	12	0	0	0	0	67.0	61	269	24	17	4	0	1	1	18	0	52	7	0

TEAM

Team	Pct.	G	PO	A	E	TC	DP	PB		Team	Pct.	G	PO	A	E	TC	DP	PB
Fort Myers	.974	131	3408	1382	129	4919	135	9		Vero Beach	.967	133	3411	1415	165	4991	102	25
St. Petersburg	.971	131	3364	1219	138	4721	89	14		Brevard County	.967	135	3574	1628	179	5381	148	22
St. Lucie	.971	135	3485	1504	151	5140	137	18		Lakeland	.966	135	3470	1522	177	5169	117	18
Daytona	.969	135	3519	1384	158	5061	120	11		W. Palm Beach	.963	136	3439	1446	186	5071	110	20
Charlotte	.969	133	3463	1404	158	5025	109	19		Dunedin	.963	138	3600	1482	194	5276	122	24
Tampa	.967	136	3563	1497	170	5230	106	24		Sarasota	.961	134	3459	1475	198	5132	124	38
Clearwater	.967	138	3605	1425	169	5199	102	21		Kissimmee	.955	136	3551	1520	240	5311	119	32

TRIPLE PLAY: Daytona.

INDIVIDUAL

FIRST BASEMEN

NOTE: All caps denotes fielding-percentage leader based on 69 games for catchers, 92 for all other non-pitchers and 138 innings for pitchers. *Throws lefthanded.

Player, Team	Pct.	G	PO	A	E	TC	DP
Abad, Andy, Sarasota*	.978	12	84	6	2	92	10
Baugh, Gavin, Brevard County	1.000	1	2	0	0	2	0
Beyna, Terry, Kissimmee	1.000	4	40	2	0	42	2
Biltimier, Mike, Vero Beach*	.991	127	1025	103	10	1138	89
Blair, Brian, Charlotte*	.982	8	56	0	1	57	6
Bokemeier, Matt, Charlotte	.983	13	107	7	2	116	10
Boyd, Quincy, Vero Beach	.941	5	31	1	2	34	3
Braddy, Junior, Sarasota	1.000	1	6	0	0	6	0
Brown, Kevin, Charlotte	1.000	1	12	0	0	12	1
Cabrera, Alex, Daytona	.989	39	335	16	4	355	31
Caraballo, Gary, Fort Myers	1.000	1	5	0	0	5	2
Carey, Todd, Sarasota	1.000	12	93	11	0	104	10
Champion, Jim, Fort Myers*	.990	57	442	43	5	490	46
Clark, Kevin, Sarasota	.975	46	411	18	11	440	36
Cooper, Tim, Tampa	.989	32	255	16	3	274	13
Davila, Vic, Dunedin	1.000	1	1	0	0	1	0
DeBerry, Joe, Tampa*	.984	49	414	26	7	447	36
Duross, Gabe, Daytona*	.988	60	526	28	7	561	48
Ellis, Kevin, Daytona	1.000	5	7	2	0	9	1
Epperson, Chad, St. Lucie	.972	15	123	17	4	144	16
Everson, Darin, W. Palm Beach	.994	21	158	15	1	174	12
FREEMAN, Sean, Lakeland*	.993	118	980	89	7	1076	91
Froschauer, Trevor, Kissimmee	.980	64	549	47	12	608	52
Halemanu, Joshua, Kissimmee*	1.000	1	10	0	0	10	0
Held, Daniel, Clearwater	.990	132	1115	72	12	1199	87
Johnson, Jack, Daytona	1.000	2	6	2	0	8	0
Jones, Ryan, Dunedin	.977	119	1041	67	26	1134	90
Kingman, Brendan, Brev. County	1.000	3	16	2	0	18	0
Kingston, Mark, Daytona	.986	37	320	33	5	358	33
Koeyers, Ramsey, W. Palm Beach	1.000	1	6	1	0	7	1
Landaker, Dave, Kissimmee	.981	10	94	9	2	105	9
Loeb, Marc, Dunedin	1.000	1	1	0	0	1	1
Long, R.D., Tampa	1.000	1	17	0	0	17	0
Madsen, Dave, St. Petersburg	.996	55	415	33	2	450	34
Malone, Scott, Charlotte	.990	99	830	68	9	907	73
Marabella, Tony, W. Palm Beach	.988	19	157	7	2	166	13
Marine, Del, Lakeland	.979	15	84	8	2	94	4
McKeel, Walt, Sarasota	1.000	2	15	0	0	15	0
Melhuse, Adam, Dunedin	1.000	3	18	5	0	23	1
Mientkiewicz, Doug, Fort Myers	.994	24	160	12	1	173	22
Millar, Kevin, Brevard County	.991	125	1213	95	12	1320	134
Mitchell, Mike, Tampa	.993	57	518	47	4	569	43
Murphy, Jeffrey, St. Petersburg	1.000	1	9	1	0	10	0
Niethammer, Marc, W. Palm Bch.	.976	73	575	38	15	628	56
Ottavinia, Paul, W. Palm Beach*	.981	11	95	6	2	103	5
Patton, Greg, Sarasota	1.000	2	8	0	0	8	0
Querecuto, Juan, Dunedin	.983	21	161	12	3	176	18
Raifstanger, John, Sarasota	.991	49	435	20	4	459	41
Raleigh, Matt, W. Palm Beach	.989	20	172	12	2	186	14
Ramirez, Hiram, Sarasota	.989	18	174	7	2	183	16
Ramos, Eddie, Kissimmee	.996	29	264	10	1	275	22
Roberge, John, Vero Beach	1.000	1	10	2	0	12	1
Robinson, Dan, Brevard County	.989	13	86	4	1	91	5
Rodriguez, Adam, Lakeland	.981	13	91	10	2	103	7
Rupp, Brian, St. Petersburg	.990	59	463	27	5	495	31
Rupp, Chad, Fort Myers	.994	55	468	24	3	495	41
Sabo, Chris, St. Petersburg	1.000	10	58	6	0	64	5
Sanchez, Victor, Kissimmee	.968	37	284	21	10	315	24
Sauve, Erik, Charlotte	1.000	13	65	3	0	68	5
Schaaf, Rob, Vero Beach	1.000	2	20	0	0	20	0
Schmitz, Mike, Tampa	1.000	3	21	5	0	26	1
Sell, Donald, Vero Beach	1.000	3	25	1	0	26	1

Player, Team	Pct.	G	PO	A	E	TC	DP
Smith, Bubba, Fort Myers	1.000	8	34	1	0	35	5
Sowards, Ryan, Vero Beach	.909	4	9	1	1	11	0
Taylor, Mike, St. Petersburg*	.982	20	101	7	2	110	7
Torborg, Dale, St.L.-Tampa	1.000	6	29	1	0	30	2
Unrat, Chris, Charlotte	.978	12	83	8	2	93	6
Waco, David, Clearwater	1.000	8	63	2	0	65	8
Warner, Randy, St. Lucie	.988	104	894	70	12	976	97
Whatley, Gabe, Daytona	1.000	1	1	0	0	2	1
Whitehurst, Todd, St. Lucie	.988	20	152	7	2	161	11

TRIPLE PLAY: Cabrera.

FIRST BASEMEN WITH TWO OR MORE TEAMS

Player, Team	Pct.	G	PO	A	E	TC	DP
Torborg, Dale, St. Lucie	1.000	5	29	1	0	30	2
Torborg, Dale, Tampa	.000	1	0	0	0	0	0

SECOND BASEMEN

Player, Team	Pct.	G	PO	A	E	TC	DP
Almanzar, Richard, Lakeland	.984	36	92	92	3	187	16
Amador, Manuel, Clearwater	.955	47	90	124	10	224	26
Anderson, Cliff, Vero Beach	.965	97	149	234	14	397	45
Arano, Eloy, Lakeland	.949	17	27	47	4	78	9
Aybar, Ramon, Lakeland	1.000	3	3	4	0	7	0
Azuaje, Jesus, St. Lucie	.955	50	123	133	12	268	40
Basey, Marsalis, Kissimmee	.971	73	159	213	11	383	49
Baugh, Gavin, Brevard County	.813	3	7	6	3	16	1
Berg, David, Brevard County	1.000	7	22	25	0	47	8
Berry, Michael, W. Palm Beach	.975	10	20	19	1	40	3
Blum, Geoffrey, W. Palm Beach	.982	60	102	167	5	274	33
Bokemeier, Matt, Charlotte	1.000	10	15	32	0	47	2
Brito, Luis, Clearwater	1.000	3	9	8	0	17	2
Brunson, Matt, Lakeland	.953	30	63	78	7	148	14
Cabrera, Jolbert, W. Palm Beach	.967	14	22	37	2	61	2
Dalton, Dee, St. Petersburg	.934	22	30	27	4	61	4
Davila, Vic, Dunedin	.967	24	33	56	3	92	14
DeJesus, Malvin, Lakeland	.952	45	98	118	11	227	35
Diaz, Edwin, Charlotte	.968	110	213	277	16	506	67
Flores, Jose, Clearwater	.955	9	21	21	2	44	6
Forkerway, Ryan, Lakeland	.976	40	62	99	4	165	29
Foster, Jeff, West Palm Beach	.958	19	38	30	3	71	5
Gallone, Santy, Clearwater	.946	42	78	96	10	184	22
Garcia, Luis, Lakeland	.932	9	21	20	3	44	5
Hansen, Elston, Tampa	.947	42	65	97	9	171	19
Hastings, Lionel, Brevard County	.9767	118	251	378	15	644	93
Kelly, Pat, Tampa	1.000	3	8	14	0	22	3
Landaker, Dave, Kissimmee	.600	1	2	1	2	5	0
Lee, Manuel, St. Petersburg	1.000	1	0	2	0	2	0
Long, R.D., Tampa	.965	94	195	272	17	484	45
Marabella, Tony, W. Palm Beach	.857	2	5	1	1	7	1
Martin, Mike, Lakeland	.929	6	11	15	2	28	3
McCalmont, Jim, Fort Myers	.982	71	132	147	5	284	46
McEwing, Joe, St. Petersburg	.954	72	133	176	15	324	35
Miller, Ryan, St. Lucie	.950	6	5	14	1	20	1
Morris, Bobby, Daytona	.910	64	109	133	24	266	33
Mota, Santo, St. Petersburg	.948	43	69	77	8	154	15
Murphy, Pat, Sarasota	.992	22	65	57	1	123	16
Nava, Marlon, Fort Myers	.953	61	85	116	10	211	24
Nelson, Bry, Kissimmee	.972	6	14	21	1	36	8
Ortiz, Nick, Sarasota	1.000	1	0	1	0	1	0
PATZKE, Jeff, Dunedin	.9774	117	255	307	13	575	59
Perez, Richard, Daytona	.953	47	64	98	8	170	18
Pichardo, Sandy, St. Lucie	.969	79	177	223	13	413	52
Post, David, Vero Beach	.975	39	74	82	4	160	20
Raifstanger, John, Sarasota	.957	33	67	67	6	140	20
Raleigh, Matt, W. Palm Beach	.750	3	1	5	2	8	0
Renteria, David, Tampa	1.000	8	6	16	0	22	3
Sauve, Erik, Charlotte	1.000	12	21	23	0	44	5

Player, Team	Pct.	G	PO	A	E	TC	DP
Saylor, Jamie, Kissimmee	.971	57	89	149	7	245	31
Schaaf, Rob, Vero Beach	.972	11	10	25	1	36	5
Scolaro, Donnie, Kissimmee	.968	8	9	21	1	31	2
Sims, Wes, Charlotte	.875	2	4	3	1	8	0
Smith, Dave, Sarasota	.929	19	35	57	7	99	15
Sosa, Juan, Vero Beach	1.000	5	8	13	0	21	2
Southard, Scott, Brevard County	.934	15	24	33	4	61	9
Sowards, Ryan, Vero Beach	.500	1	0	1	1	2	0
Subero, Carlos, Charlotte	1.000	9	13	21	0	34	6
Tebbs, Nathan, Sarasota	.977	71	153	185	8	346	43
Ugueto, Jesus, St. Petersburg	1.000	4	8	5	0	13	1
Venezia, Danny, Fort Myers	.941	15	30	50	5	85	10
Vidro, Jose, West Palm Beach	.979	35	91	93	4	188	35
Waco, David, Clearwater	.982	47	86	128	4	218	20
Zuniga, David, St. Lucie	1.000	6	12	11	0	23	4

Player, Team	Pct.	G	PO	A	E	TC	DP
Sims, Wes, Charlotte	1.000	1	0	3	0	3	0
Smith, Bubba, Fort Myers	.950	6	6	13	1	20	2
Southard, Scott, Brevard County	.884	15	10	28	5	43	5
Sowards, Ryan, Vero Beach	.895	12	5	12	2	19	2
Stewart, Tom, Kissimmee	.857	7	5	7	2	14	1
Tebbs, Nathan, Sarasota	.889	16	6	26	4	36	5
Ugueto, Jesus, St. Petersburg	.857	10	3	3	1	7	0
Verduzco, Steve, Kissimmee	.750	2	2	1	1	4	0
Vidro, Jose, West Palm Beach	1.000	3	2	5	0	7	0
Waco, David, Clearwater	.667	4	4	4	4	12	0
Whatley, Gabe, Daytona	1.000	1	2	2	0	4	0
Whitehurst, Todd, St. Lucie	.915	39	26	82	10	118	7
Wooten, Shawn, Lakeland	.942	38	23	90	7	120	5
Wyrick, Chris, St. Petersburg	.917	13	11	22	3	36	2

THIRD BASEMEN

Player, Team	Pct.	G	PO	A	E	TC	DP
Alcantara, Israel, W. Palm Beach	.906	29	30	57	9	96	3
Almanzar, Richard, Lakeland	.818	4	3	6	2	11	1
Amador, Manuel, Clearwater	.875	2	5	1	1	8	0
Anderson, Cliff, Vero Beach	1.000	1	0	3	0	3	0
Arano, Eloy, Lakeland	.968	55	36	116	5	157	8
Azuaje, Jesus, St. Lucie	.970	26	12	52	2	66	6
Baugh, Gavin, Brevard County	.921	72	51	181	20	252	31
Bell, Mike, Charlotte	.914	126	91	280	35	406	19
Benbow, Lou, St. Lucie	1.000	2	1	1	0	2	0
Berg, David, Brevard County	.943	52	39	144	11	194	13
Berry, Michael, W. Palm Beach	.846	11	7	15	4	26	4
Beyna, Teddy, Kissimmee	.833	3	1	4	1	6	1
Bierek, Kurt, Tampa	.916	122	85	219	28	332	17
Blum, Geoffrey, W. Palm Beach	.921	13	14	21	3	38	5
Bokemeier, Matt, Charlotte	.850	6	3	14	3	20	1
Brito, Luis, Clearwater	1.000	11	11	19	0	30	1
Brown, Shawn, Lakeland	.826	9	4	15	4	23	1
Browne, Jerry, Brevard County	.667	1	1	1	1	3	0
Cabrera, Jolbert, W. Palm Beach	.931	10	10	17	2	29	1
Caraballo, Gary, Fort Myers	.934	83	74	197	19	290	22
Carey, Todd, Sarasota	.800	6	3	13	4	20	5
Cooper, Tim, Tampa	.818	16	8	28	8	44	0
DALTON, Dee, St. Petersburg	.931	100	66	191	19	276	15
Davila, Vic, Dunedin	.897	12	9	17	3	29	0
Donato, Daniel, Tampa	1.000	1	2	1	0	3	1
Evans, Tom, Dunedin	.922	129	92	309	34	435	16
Flores, Jose, Clearwater	.927	30	18	71	7	96	2
Forkner, Tim, Kissimmee	.916	89	66	196	24	286	15
Foster, Jeff, W. Palm Beach	.917	15	12	43	5	60	0
Gallone, Santy, Clearwater	.946	15	7	28	2	37	2
Gross, Rafael, Vero Beach	.947	35	21	69	5	95	6
Hansen, Elston, Tampa	.000	1	0	0	1	1	0
Jackson, Gavin, Sarasota	1.000	1	1	2	0	3	0
Landaker, Dave, Kissimmee	.915	36	28	80	10	118	3
Lopez, Jose, St. Lucie	1.000	1	0	2	0	2	0
Madsen, Dave, St. Petersburg	.941	11	7	9	1	17	0
Marabella, Tony, W. Palm Beach	.938	31	36	54	6	96	6
Martinez, Dalvis, Lakeland	.872	38	16	79	14	109	6
McCalmont, Jim, Fort Myers	.889	13	6	26	4	36	2
Mota, Santo, St. Petersburg	1.000	1	0	1	0	1	0
Motes, Jeff, St. Lucie	.926	9	5	20	2	27	0
Murphy, Pat, Sarasota	.965	21	19	36	2	57	3
Nava, Lipso, Sarasota	.927	14	5	33	3	41	2
Nava, Marlon, Fort Myers	.932	35	30	66	7	103	7
Nelson, Bry, Kissimmee	1.000	6	3	7	0	10	0
O'Brien, Joe, Clearwater	.973	12	6	30	1	37	1
Orie, Kevin, Daytona	.916	106	80	204	26	310	20
Ortiz, Nick, Sarasota	.887	76	50	186	30	266	25
Otanez, Willis, Vero Beach	.925	89	59	186	20	265	18
Patton, Greg, Sarasota	1.000	1	1	2	0	3	0
Perez, Jhonny, Kissimmee	1.000	1	2	0	0	2	0
Perez, Richard, Daytona	.922	37	26	68	8	102	6
Petrulis, Paul, St. Lucie	.984	69	41	140	3	184	13
Querecuto, Juan, Dunedin	.750	2	1	2	1	4	0
Radmanovich, Ryan, Ft. Myers	.806	11	7	22	7	36	0
Raifstanger, John, Sarasota	.880	8	4	18	3	25	3
Raleigh, Matt, W. Palm Beach	.900	29	20	52	8	80	4
Renteria, David, Tampa	1.000	1	1	1	0	2	0
Rolen, Scott, Clearwater	.899	65	43	135	20	198	13
Rupp, Brian, St. Petersburg	.879	13	12	17	4	33	2
Sabo, Chris, St. Petersburg	.750	2	0	3	1	4	0
Sauve, Erik, Charlotte	.800	2	2	2	1	5	0
Scolaro, Donnie, Kissimmee	1.000	3	0	5	0	5	0

SHORTSTOPS

Player, Team	Pct.	G	PO	A	E	TC	DP
Amador, Manuel, Clearwater	.966	23	37	47	3	87	11
Anderson, Cliff, Vero Beach	.961	17	21	53	3	77	9
Angeli, Doug, Clearwater	.957	16	17	49	3	69	12
Arano, Eloy, Lakeland	.945	27	38	66	6	110	14
Azuaje, Jesus, St. Lucie	.959	16	24	46	3	73	11
Babin, Brady, Brevard County	.914	32	55	73	12	140	17
Benbow, Lou, St. Lucie	.886	10	14	25	5	44	3
Berg, David, Brevard County	.948	56	96	179	15	290	34
Berry, Michael, W. Palm Beach	1.000	1	0	1	0	1	0
Blum, Geoffrey, W. Palm Beach	.941	38	50	110	10	170	17
Bokemeier, Matt, Charlotte	.954	62	99	173	13	285	35
Brito, Luis, Clearwater	.939	96	117	266	25	408	46
Brunson, Matt, Lakeland	.900	15	22	50	8	80	14
Cabrera, Jolbert, W. Palm Beach	.934	80	116	240	25	381	38
Cabrera, Orlando, W. Palm Beach	.833	2	2	3	1	6	0
Carey, Todd, Sarasota	.938	3	5	10	1	16	0
Cromer, Brandon, Dunedin	.964	94	146	259	15	420	57
DeJesus, Malvin, Lakeland	.957	4	3	19	1	23	0
Flores, Jose, Clearwater	.943	10	15	35	3	53	4
Forkerway, Trey, Daytona	.935	30	26	61	6	93	10
Foster, Jeff, W. Palm Beach	.937	19	45	44	6	95	14
Frias, Hanley, Charlotte	.932	33	45	106	11	162	25
Garcia, Luis, Lakeland	.932	92	146	282	31	459	45
Gonzalez, Alex, Brevard County	.906	17	26	51	8	85	12
Jackson, Gavin, Sarasota	.956	94	121	331	21	473	47
Knowles, Eric, Tampa	.939	115	191	382	37	610	53
Landaker, Dave, Kissimmee	.857	4	4	8	2	14	0
Lee, Manuel, St. Petersburg	.833	5	2	8	2	12	0
Long, R.D., Tampa	.943	7	12	21	2	35	4
Matvey, Mike, St. Petersburg	.968	87	116	218	11	345	28
MAXWELL, Jason, Daytona	.969	116	181	325	16	522	65
Mercedes, Guillermo, Charlotte	.977	33	42	83	3	128	12
Metcalfe, Mike, Vero Beach	.919	120	153	301	40	494	50
Miller, Ryan, St. Lucie	.954	82	124	225	17	366	49
Mota, Santo, St. Petersburg	.805	10	16	17	8	41	5
Motes, Jeff, St. Lucie	1.000	3	3	2	0	5	0
Motte, James, Fort Myers	.955	116	155	336	23	514	70
Murphy, Pat, Sarasota	.889	1	1	7	1	9	1
Nava, Lipso, Sarasota	1.000	6	6	13	0	19	3
Nava, Marlon, Fort Myers	.953	22	29	53	4	86	10
Nelson, Bry, Kissimmee	.905	59	89	159	26	274	35
Ortiz, Nick, Sarasota	.938	13	17	28	3	48	6
Patton, Greg, Sarasota	.923	4	3	9	1	13	1
Patzke, Jeff, Dunedin	.932	13	19	22	3	44	5
Perez, Jhonny, Kissimmee	.901	33	47	116	18	181	20
Perez, Richard, Daytona	.500	1	0	1	1	2	1
Petrulis, Paul, St. Lucie	.959	33	46	95	6	147	20
Renteria, David, Tampa	.920	20	27	53	7	87	12
Saylor, Jamie, Kissimmee	.917	22	35	75	10	120	17
Scolaro, Donnie, Kissimmee	.804	9	14	23	9	46	4
Sims, Wes, Charlotte	.857	1	2	4	1	7	2
Smith, Dave, Sarasota	.818	2	2	7	2	11	0
Solano, Fausto, Dunedin	.932	38	75	116	14	205	32
Sosa, Juan, Vero Beach	.909	2	2	8	1	11	2
Southard, Scott, Brevard County	.927	39	57	120	14	191	21
Stewart, Tom, Kissimmee	.877	19	26	38	9	73	8
Subero, Carlos, Charlotte	.964	6	8	19	1	28	2
Tebbs, Nathan, Sarasota	.897	23	26	52	9	87	8
Ugueto, Jesus, St. Petersburg	.982	20	23	32	1	56	8
Vidro, Jose, West Palm Beach	1.000	6	8	12	0	20	1
Wyrick, Chris, St. Petersburg	.920	30	30	62	8	100	12
Zuniga, David, St. Lucie	1.000	4	2	7	0	9	1

TRIPLE PLAY: Forkerway.

OUTFIELDERS

Player, Team	Pct.	G	PO	A	E	TC	DP
Abad, Andy, Sarasota*	1.000	8	6	0	0	6	0
Adolfo, Carlos, W. Palm Beach	.939	22	29	2	2	33	0
Agbayani, Benny, St. Lucie	.950	19	37	1	2	40	0
Alcantara, Israel, W. Palm Beach	1.000	3	4	1	0	5	0
Arano, Eloy, Lakeland	1.000	2	1	0	0	1	0
Asencio, Alex, Vero Beach*	.982	58	101	10	2	113	2
Baker, Jason, Fort Myers*	.979	84	136	1	3	140	0
Basey, Marsalis, Kissimmee	.943	18	31	2	2	35	0
Bellum, Donnie, St. Petersburg	1.000	59	77	1	0	78	0
Berry, Michael, W. Palm Beach	1.000	1	1	1	0	2	0
Beyna, Terry, Kissimmee	1.000	3	3	1	0	4	0
Blair, Brian, Charlotte*	.981	49	96	5	2	103	0
Borel, Jamie, Lakeland	1.000	12	26	1	0	27	0
Braddy, Junior, Sarasota	.951	99	167	7	9	183	0
Brock, Tarrick, Lakeland*	.966	28	56	1	2	59	0
Brown, Armann, Fort Myers	.970	19	32	0	1	33	0
Brown, Ron, Brevard County	.989	112	163	12	2	177	2
Brown, Willie, Brevard County	1.000	49	87	3	0	90	0
Browne, Jerry, Brevard County	1.000	1	2	0	0	2	0
Burke, Alan, Clearwater	1.000	1	5	0	0	5	0
Campos, Jesus, W. Palm Beach	.960	96	196	19	9	224	4
Candelaria, Ben, Dunedin	.971	121	189	10	6	205	0
Champion, Jim, Fort Myers*	1.000	31	42	3	0	45	1
Chick, Bruce, W. Palm Beach	1.000	2	3	0	0	3	0
Christmon, Drew, Lakeland	.946	54	77	10	5	92	0
Collier, Dan, Sarasota	.825	24	32	1	7	40	0
Cooney, Kyle, Vero Beach	1.000	1	1	0	0	1	0
Cooper, Tim, Tampa	1.000	2	1	0	0	1	0
Costello, Brian, Clearwater	.965	99	212	7	8	227	0
Cradle, Cobi, St. Lucie*	.976	57	120	3	3	126	0
Cradle, Rickey, Dunedin	1.000	48	94	4	0	98	1
Davila, Vic, Dunedin	.929	12	13	0	1	14	0
Deares, Greg, St. Petersburg	1.000	17	24	2	0	26	0
DeLaCruz, Carlos, Lakeland	1.000	2	3	0	0	3	0
Delafield, Wil, Tampa	1.000	3	3	0	0	3	0
Diaz, Linardo, Clearwater	1.000	11	17	2	0	19	0
Dowler, Dee, Daytona	.996	109	243	9	1	253	4
Ellis, Kevin, Daytona	.927	69	98	4	8	110	0
Evans, Stan, Clearwater	.973	72	135	9	4	148	1
Facione, Chris, Lakeland	.990	105	195	6	2	203	0
Ferrier, Ross, St. Lucie	.971	44	64	3	2	69	1
Fick, Chris, St. Petersburg	.956	105	145	7	7	159	1
Gallone, Santy, Clearwater	1.000	4	9	0	0	9	0
Garcia, Osmel, St. Petersburg	.982	102	211	11	4	226	1
Gibbs, Kevin, Vero Beach	1.000	7	12	0	0	12	0
Grissom, Antonio, W. Palm Bch.	1.000	4	6	0	0	6	0
Halemanu, Joshua, Kissimmee*	1.000	2	3	0	0	3	0
Hare, Rich, Lakeland	.889	7	16	0	2	18	0
Hawkins, Kraig, Tampa	.991	111	224	9	2	235	0
Henry, Antoine, Sarasota	1.000	12	28	1	0	29	1
Hernaiz, Juan, Vero Beach	.964	46	78	2	3	83	0
Hunter, Torii, Fort Myers	.973	103	242	15	7	264	7
Johnson, J.J., Sarasota	.954	97	159	8	8	175	1
JONES, Ben, Fort Myers	1.000	103	221	10	0	231	3
Keister, Tripp, St. Lucie*	1.000	16	27	3	0	30	0
Kendall, Jeremey, Clearwater	.945	36	83	3	5	91	0
Kimsey, Keith, Lakeland	.986	49	68	2	1	71	1
Knauss, Tom, Fort Myers	.976	88	152	9	4	165	2
Landaker, Dave, Kissimmee	.976	44	75	5	2	82	0
Landry, Lonny, Lakeland	.972	19	35	0	1	36	0
Latham, Chris, Vero Beach	.949	59	125	5	7	137	0
Little, Mark, Charlotte	.966	96	274	8	10	292	1
Long, Justin, Brevard County	1.000	6	7	0	0	7	0
Lowery, Terrell, Charlotte	1.000	11	18	0	0	18	0
Macon, Leland, Charlotte	.958	107	217	11	10	238	3
Madsen, Dan, Daytona*	1.000	13	15	1	0	16	0
Magee, Wendell, Clearwater	.973	93	166	12	5	183	0
Majeski, Brian, Vero Beach	.971	58	99	3	3	105	0
Maness, Dwight, V.B.-St.L.	.992	52	121	7	1	129	1
Mangham, Rodney, Kissimmee*	.959	42	90	4	4	98	0
Marsh, Roy, Sarasota	.971	112	257	10	8	275	1
Martinez, Ramon, Brevard County	.958	93	178	5	8	191	0
McEwing, Joe, St. Petersburg	1.000	2	6	0	0	6	0
McKinnon, Tom, St. Petersburg	.948	52	87	4	5	96	1
Mota, Santo, St. Petersburg	1.000	3	7	1	0	8	0
Moultrie, Pat, Dunedin*	.966	77	132	9	5	146	0
Murphy, Pat, Sarasota	1.000	2	6	0	0	6	0
Nelson, Bry, Kissimmee	1.000	20	38	1	0	39	0
Nelson, Charles, Vero Beach*	.971	76	96	3	3	102	0
Nixon, Trot, Sarasota*	.986	69	140	4	2	146	1
Northrup, Kevin, St. Lucie	1.000	14	24	1	0	25	0
Nuneviller, Tom, Clearwater	.900	8	8	1	1	10	0
Ottavinia, Paul, W. Palm Beach*	.972	100	170	5	5	180	0
Perez, Joe, Charlotte*	1.000	15	30	2	0	32	0
Peterson, Nate, Kissimmee	.949	46	71	4	4	79	0
Pichardo, Sandy, St. Lucie	.970	22	31	1	1	33	0
Pico, Brandon, Daytona*	.895	11	17	0	2	19	0
Porter, Bo, Daytona	.980	110	183	10	4	197	3
Post, David, Vero Beach	1.000	4	3	0	0	3	0
Raifstanger, John, Sarasota	1.000	10	5	0	0	5	0
Ramirez, Angel, Dunedin	.968	130	320	17	11	348	0
Reeves, Glen, Brevard County	.969	111	172	13	6	191	2
Rijo, Rafael, Charlotte	1.000	10	13	0	0	13	0
Roberge, John, Vero Beach	1.000	1	2	0	0	2	0
Roberts, David, Lakeland	.985	31	61	3	1	65	0
Robinson, Dan, Brevard County	.964	51	75	6	3	84	0
Roche, Marlon, Kissimmee	.976	26	38	2	1	41	0
Rojas, Roberto, Lakeland*	1.000	4	6	0	0	6	0
Rupp, Brian, St. Petersburg	.967	19	28	1	1	30	0
Saffer, Jon, West Palm Beach	.976	77	118	3	3	124	1
Samuels, Scott, Daytona	.989	106	170	6	2	178	2
Sanchez, Omar, Dunedin	.970	34	59	6	2	67	2
Santucci, Steven, St. Petersburg	.984	96	184	6	3	193	3
Schaaf, Rob, Vero Beach	1.000	6	9	0	0	9	0
Scolaro, Donnie, Kissimmee	1.000	2	0	1	0	1	0
Sell, Donald, Vero Beach	.990	67	98	1	1	100	0
Sheffield, Tony, Sarasota*	.971	95	198	5	6	209	3
Shirley, Al, St. Lucie	1.000	56	123	1	0	124	0
Shores, Scott, Clearwater	.965	103	236	11	9	256	2
Shugars, Shawn, Charlotte*	.909	6	10	0	1	11	0
Smith, Sloan, Tampa	.982	124	206	11	4	221	2
Sowards, Ryan, Vero Beach	.957	17	22	0	1	23	0
Spencer, Shane, Tampa	.966	109	166	6	6	178	0
Stewart, Tom, Kissimmee	.959	29	44	3	2	49	0
Stovall, Darond, W. Palm Beach*	.990	114	283	13	3	299	3
Suplee, Ray, Tampa	.919	66	96	6	9	111	1
Tebbs, Nathan, Sarasota	1.000	2	1	0	0	1	0
Terrell, Matt, St. Lucie	.977	70	124	3	3	130	0
Trammell, Bubba, Lakeland	.973	113	176	7	5	188	0
Verduzco, Steve, Kissimmee	.963	94	147	9	6	162	1
Vessel, Andrew, Charlotte	.974	110	218	9	6	233	1
Warner, Randy, St. Lucie	.500	4	2	0	2	4	0
Whatley, Gabe, Daytona	1.000	10	5	2	0	7	0
White, Jimmy, Kissimmee	1.000	5	5	2	0	7	0
Wipf, Mark, St. Lucie	.969	114	237	11	8	256	4
Zambrano, Jose, Sarasota	.917	6	10	1	1	12	0

OUTFIELDERS WITH TWO OR MORE TEAMS

Player, Team	Pct.	G	PO	A	E	TC	DP
Maness, Dwight, Vero Beach	.991	43	106	6	1	113	0
Maness, Dwight, St. Lucie	1.000	9	15	1	0	16	1

CATCHERS

Player, Team	Pct.	G	PO	A	E	TC	DP	PB
Alvarado, Basilio, W. Palm Bch	.968	6	25	5	1	31	0	0
Borrero, Rikchy, Sarasota	.980	30	189	9	4	202	0	14
Boyd, Quincy, Vero Beach	.982	13	54	2	1	57	0	1
Brown, Kevin, Charlotte	.985	96	523	60	9	592	3	11
Castro, Ramon, Kissimmee	.967	34	184	18	7	209	0	3
Clark, Kevin, Sarasota	.979	30	167	18	4	189	0	10
Cooney, Kyle, Vero Beach	.982	59	394	52	8	454	3	18
Cossins, Tim, Charlotte	1.000	3	12	2	0	14	0	1
Crespo, Mike, Charlotte	1.000	19	87	12	0	99	0	3
Davenport, Jeff, Sarasota	.975	9	36	3	1	40	0	1
Diaz, Cesar, St. Lucie	.982	96	569	85	12	666	7	8
Driskell, Jeff, Lakeland	1.000	13	50	7	0	57	1	0
Epperson, Chad, St. Lucie	.981	17	81	24	2	107	0	4
Erdman, Brad, Daytona	1.000	5	35	3	0	38	0	0
Estalella, Bobby, Clearwater	.987	114	771	82	11	864	1	17
Everson, Darin, W. Palm Beach	.957	5	19	3	1	23	1	0
Fithian, Grant, Tampa	1.000	3	6	3	0	9	0	1
Fitzpatrick, Robert, W. Palm Bch.	.986	12	62	8	1	71	0	0
Froschauer, Trevor, Kissimmee	.964	33	162	28	7	197	3	21
Gousha, Sean, Daytona	1.000	5	24	2	0	26	0	1
Gyselman, Jeff, Clearwater	.993	26	112	22	1	135	0	4
Hammell, Al, St. Lucie	.989	34	145	27	2	174	3	6
Hilt, Scott, Fort Myers	.983	13	56	3	1	60	0	1
Horn, Jeff, Fort Myers	.989	65	424	40	5	469	5	3
Johnson, Jack, Daytona	1.000	2	17	1	0	18	0	0
Kingston, Mark, Daytona	1.000	1	1	1	0	2	0	0
Koeyers, Ramsey, W. Palm Beach	.980	63	362	38	8	408	2	9
Loeb, Marc, Dunedin	.988	40	225	22	3	250	0	7
Lombardi, John, Sarasota	1.000	7	26	8	0	34	0	0
Luzinski, Ryan, Vero Beach	.955	23	148	23	8	179	2	1
Madonna, Chris, St. Lucie	.667	2	2	0	1	3	0	0

CLASS A Florida State League

Player, Team	Pct.	G	PO	A	E	TC	DP	PB
Marine, Del, Lakeland	.970	58	312	47	11	370	3	5
Marrero, Elieser, St. Petersburg	.984	81	574	52	10	636	6	5
McKeel, Walt, Sarasota	.977	56	326	51	9	386	2	10
Melhuse, Adam, Dunedin	.980	94	574	55	13	642	8	14
Meluskey, Mitch, Kissimmee	.980	75	443	40	10	493	3	5
Micucci, Mike, Daytona	1.000	22	92	4	0	96	0	1
Molina, Jose, Daytona	.987	82	501	91	8	600	4	7
Morales, Francisco, Day.-St.P.	.988	51	364	38	5	407	3	7
Motuzas, Jeff, Tampa	1.000	28	122	13	0	135	1	2
Murphy, Jeffrey, St. Petersburg	.996	40	241	31	1	273	5	4
Nihart, Tim, Fort Myers	1.000	4	21	3	0	24	0	0
Northeimer, Jamie, Clearwater	1.000	6	47	6	0	53	0	0
Pachot, John, W. Palm Beach	.984	60	310	60	6	376	1	11
Prater, Andrew, Brevard County	.975	73	344	46	10	400	3	7
Querecuto, Juan, Dunedin	1.000	14	70	11	0	81	0	3
Ramirez, Hiram, Sarasota	.989	14	81	10	1	92	1	2
Rodriguez, Adam, Lakeland	.983	15	104	9	2	115	1	1
Sanchez, Victor, Kissimmee	.943	9	43	7	3	53	1	3
SIMS, Michael, Brevard County	.9911	89	505	53	5	563	3	15
Snyder, Jared, Daytona	.968	18	86	5	3	94	1	0
Steed, David, Vero Beach	.987	52	345	39	5	389	0	5
Stricklin, Scott, Fort Myers	.990	65	352	54	4	410	7	5
Thompson, Billy, Lakeland	.973	66	447	52	14	513	3	12
Torres, Jaime, Tampa	.9905	105	741	95	8	844	4	19
Troilo, Jason, Tampa	1.000	1	5	0	0	5	0	1
Unrat, Chris, Charlotte	.965	33	179	16	7	202	0	4
Varriano, Mark, Sarasota	.952	7	20	0	1	21	0	1
Williams, Ed, Lakeland	1.000	1	4	1	0	5	0	0
Wilson, Tom, Tampa	1.000	13	85	7	0	92	0	1

CATCHERS WITH TWO OR MORE TEAMS

Player, Team	Pct.	G	PO	A	E	TC	DP	PB
Morales, Francisco, Daytona	.988	29	222	22	3	247	1	2
Morales, Francisco, St. P'burg	.988	22	142	16	2	160	2	5

PITCHERS

Player, Team	Pct.	G	PO	A	E	TC	DP
Adkins, Tim, Dunedin*	.900	45	2	7	1	10	1
Agostinelli, Peter, Clearwater*	.875	57	9	5	2	16	0
Albaladejo, Randy, Kissimmee	1.000	7	1	0	0	1	0
Aldred, Scott, Lakeland*	.955	13	3	18	1	22	0
Andersen, Mark, Brevard County	.833	20	3	2	1	6	1
Antoszek, Chris, Sarasota	.750	3	0	3	1	4	0
Arffa, Steve, St. Lucie*	.938	32	5	10	1	16	1
Ashworth, Kym, Vero Beach*	.950	24	8	30	2	40	1
Aybar, Manuel, St. Petersburg	1.000	9	6	5	0	11	0
Baine, David, Charlotte*	.857	21	1	5	1	7	0
Barkley, Brian, Sarasota*	.941	24	6	26	2	34	1
Beech, Matt, Clearwater*	.769	15	5	5	3	13	1
Belinda, Stan, Sarasota	1.000	1	0	1	0	1	0
Bennett, Shayne, Sarasota	.750	52	1	5	2	8	0
Benz, Jake, W. Palm Beach*	.941	44	2	14	1	17	1
Berlin, Mike, Lakeland	1.000	16	2	6	0	8	1
Berry, Jason, Tampa	.750	7	0	3	1	4	1
Biehl, Rod, Fort Myers*	1.000	12	1	2	0	3	0
Blake, Todd, St. Petersburg*	1.000	42	1	3	0	4	0
Bogott, Kurt, Sarasota*	.895	41	5	12	2	19	1
Borkowski, David, Lakeland	1.000	1	0	3	0	3	1
Bowen, Mitchel, Brevard County	.960	41	9	15	1	25	1
Bowen, Ryan, Brevard County	.500	3	1	0	1	2	0
Bowers, Shane, Fort Myers	1.000	23	6	23	0	29	2
Box, Shawn, Daytona	.933	25	10	18	2	30	0
Breitenstein, Keith, Kissimmee*	1.000	4	0	1	0	1	0
Brower, Jim, Charlotte	.946	27	11	24	2	37	3
Brown, Alvin, Lakeland	1.000	9	5	10	0	15	1
Buckles, Bucky, Charlotte	1.000	48	7	14	0	21	0
Bullock, Craig, St. Lucie	.944	40	1	16	1	18	3
Cain, Chance, St. Petersburg	1.000	7	1	2	0	3	0
Caridad, Ron, Fort Myers	1.000	17	4	8	0	12	0
Carl, Todd, Brevard County	.800	15	2	6	2	10	0
Carpenter, Brian, Fort Myers*	1.000	16	3	4	0	7	0
Carpenter, Chris, Dunedin	.771	15	10	17	8	35	3
Carrasco, Troy, Fort Myers*	.917	25	4	18	2	24	1
Cederblad, Brett, Sarasota	1.000	24	4	13	0	17	0
Challinor, John, Vero Beach	1.000	37	2	7	0	9	0
Cindrich, Jeff, Tampa	1.000	24	1	3	0	4	0
Clelland, Rick, W. Palm Beach	.833	35	2	3	1	6	0
Connolly, Matt, Daytona	.750	18	1	2	1	4	0
Corn, Chris, Tampa	1.000	4	0	1	0	1	0
Cosman, Jeff, St. Lucie	.889	15	11	13	3	27	2
Costa, Tony, Clearwater	.900	25	10	17	3	30	3
Croushore, Rick, St. Petersburg	.875	12	2	5	1	8	0
Culberson, Don, Daytona	.500	12	0	2	2	4	0
Cumberland, Chris, Tampa*	.875	5	1	6	1	8	0
DaSilva, Fernando, W. Palm Beach	.947	27	7	11	1	19	1
Dault, Donnie, Kissimmee	.967	41	9	20	1	30	0
Davis, Jeff, Charlotte	.971	26	13	21	1	35	2
DeBrino, Rob, Fort Myers	1.000	41	2	3	0	5	1
DeLaHoya, Javier, Brevard County	1.000	5	1	1	0	2	0
Delgado, Ernie, Brevard County	1.000	18	4	8	0	12	0
Detmers, Kris, St. Petersburg*	.960	25	1	23	1	25	0
DeVries, Andrew, Daytona*	1.000	21	4	7	0	11	0
Dodd, Robert, Clearwater*	.950	26	3	16	1	20	1
Dotel, Octavio, St. Lucie	1.000	3	0	1	0	1	0
Drews, Matthew, Tampa	.944	28	18	16	2	36	5
Dreyer, Darren, Daytona	1.000	29	5	8	0	13	0
Drumheller, Al, Tampa*	1.000	32	3	5	0	8	1
Drumright, Mike, Lakeland	1.000	5	2	3	0	5	1
Duran, Roberto, Vero Beach*	.875	23	2	5	1	8	0
Ehler, Daniel, Brevard County	.895	16	4	13	2	19	1
Emerson, Scott, Sarasota*	.615	16	1	7	5	13	0
Engle, Tom, St. Lucie	1.000	9	5	4	0	9	0
Fiore, Tony, Clearwater	.960	24	9	15	1	25	3
Forster, Scott, W. Palm Beach*	.829	26	6	28	7	41	1
Foster, Mark, Clearwater*	1.000	24	1	3	0	4	0
Franek, Tom, Clearwater	1.000	9	1	1	0	2	0
Fultz, Aaron, Fort Myers*	1.000	21	7	18	0	25	0
Gaillard, Eddy, Lakeland	1.000	43	3	4	0	7	1
Gallaher, Kevin, Kissimmee	.667	7	1	1	1	3	1
Gallone, Santy, Clearwater	1.000	1	0	1	0	1	0
Gandolph, Dave, Kissimmee*	.500	12	0	1	1	2	0
Garcia, Frank, St. Petersburg	1.000	16	0	1	0	1	0
Gardner, Scott, Lakeland	.750	5	0	3	1	4	1
Gaspar, Cade, Lakeland	1.000	23	10	13	0	23	0
Gonzalez, Geremis, Daytona	.800	19	3	5	2	10	0
Gordon, Mike, Tampa-Dun.	.880	28	14	30	6	50	0
Gorecki, Rick, Vero Beach	1.000	6	2	3	0	5	0
Granger, Greg, Lakeland	1.000	27	7	14	0	21	0
Grasser, Craig, St. Petersburg	1.000	26	1	2	0	3	0
Greene, Tommy, Clearwater	1.000	3	1	1	0	2	0
Grennan, Steve, St. Lucie*	1.000	9	0	2	0	2	0
Groot, Franz, Vero Beach	1.000	14	3	2	0	5	0
Guerra, Mark, St. Lucie	.953	23	14	27	2	43	5
Gunderson, Mike, Kissimmee	1.000	13	1	0	0	1	0
Halperin, Mike, Dunedin*	.946	14	6	29	2	37	0
Hammond, Chris, Brev. County*	1.000	1	0	2	0	2	0
Harris, D.J., Dunedin	.905	42	7	12	2	21	0
Harris, Greg, Fort Myers	1.000	3	1	2	0	3	0
Hart, Jason, Daytona	1.000	37	2	6	0	8	1
Hartgrove, Lyle, Sarasota	1.000	47	5	9	0	14	1
Hartmann, Pete, Charlotte*	.667	15	0	6	3	9	0
Hartnett, Bill, Kissimmee	.923	32	4	8	1	13	0
Hecker, Doug, Sarasota	1.000	10	0	3	0	3	0
Heflin, Bronson, Clearwater	.923	57	3	9	1	13	0
Heiserman, Rick, St. Petersburg	1.000	6	2	3	0	5	0
Henderson, Ryan, Vero Beach	.962	39	8	17	1	26	4
Henriquez, Oscar, Kissimmee	1.000	20	4	6	0	10	1
Heredia, Felix, Brevard County*	.950	34	3	16	1	20	2
Hernandez, Jeremy, Brev. County	1.000	4	1	0	0	1	0
Herrmann, Gary, Clearwater*	.929	42	4	9	1	14	2
Hiljus, Erik, St. Lucie	.889	17	5	11	2	18	0
Hill, Shawn, Daytona	.875	37	3	4	1	8	0
Hingle, Larry, Kissimmee*	1.000	10	1	2	0	3	1
Hmielewski, Chris, W. Palm Bch.*	.933	36	1	13	1	15	0
Hollinger, Adrian, Brevard County	1.000	11	2	4	0	6	1
Hollis, Ronald, Vero Beach	1.000	43	13	14	0	27	3
Housely, Adam, Lakeland	1.000	19	4	6	0	10	0
Howard, Chris, Sarasota*	1.000	6	0	4	0	4	0
Hubbard, Mark, Tampa*	.958	13	5	18	1	24	1
Huffman, Jeff, Sarasota	.952	15	9	11	1	21	1
Humphrey, Rich, Kissimmee	1.000	46	5	18	0	23	0
Hunter, Rich, Clearwater	1.000	9	2	7	0	9	1
Hurst, William, Brevard County	.857	39	3	9	2	14	1
Jacobsen, Joe, Vero Beach	.929	47	3	10	1	14	1
Janzen, Marty, Tampa	.857	18	6	6	2	14	0
Jersild, Aaron, Dunedin*	.636	22	0	7	4	11	1
Johnson, Jonathan, Charlotte	1.000	8	5	9	0	14	1
Jordan, Jason, Lakeland	1.000	4	1	2	0	3	0
Kamieniecki, Scott, Tampa	1.000	1	2	1	0	3	0
Kell, Rob, Charlotte*	1.000	11	2	2	0	4	0
Kendrena, Ken, W. Palm Beach	.900	16	4	5	1	10	0
Kenny, Sean, St. Lucie	.923	46	0	12	1	13	0
Kerley, Collin, W. Palm Beach	.875	19	2	5	1	8	1
Keusch, Joseph, Charlotte	1.000	40	7	9	0	16	1
King, Curtis, St. Petersburg	.936	28	17	27	3	47	5
Knieper, Aaron, W. Palm Beach	.889	32	2	14	2	18	1

Player, Team	Pct.	G	PO	A	E	TC	DP
Kostich, Bill, Lakeland*	1.000	4	0	2	0	2	0
Kozeniewski, Blaise, Tampa	1.000	11	0	1	0	1	0
Lankford, Frank, Tampa	1.000	55	7	11	0	18	1
Largusa, Levon, Dunedin*	1.000	16	2	5	0	7	0
Larson, Toby, St. Lucie	.929	19	13	13	2	28	0
Leahy, Pat, Brevard County	.933	11	8	6	1	15	1
Lehoisky, Russ, Fort Myers	.818	26	4	5	2	11	0
Leshnock, Donnie, Tampa	.813	28	3	10	3	16	1
Lewis, Michael, Brevard County*	1.000	43	5	11	0	16	0
Lima, Jose, Lakeland	1.000	4	2	1	0	3	0
Linebarger, Keith, Fort Myers	.947	29	10	8	1	19	0
Liquet, Wilton, Vero Beach	1.000	4	1	2	0	3	0
Loewer, Carlton, Clearwater	.778	20	2	5	2	9	0
Loiz, Niuman, Kissimmee	.889	13	4	4	1	9	1
Lopez, Johann, Kissimmee	1.000	18	6	5	0	11	1
Lopez, Orlando, Daytona*	.909	44	6	14	2	22	2
Lovingier, Kevin, St. Petersburg*	1.000	22	2	5	0	7	1
Lukasiewicz, Mark, Dunedin*	.800	31	4	8	3	15	0
Mallory, Trevor, Dunedin	1.000	37	2	6	0	8	1
Malloy, Charles, Sarasota	1.000	16	4	6	0	10	1
Manning, David, Charlotte	1.000	26	7	18	0	25	3
Markham, Andy, W. Palm Beach	.913	24	6	15	2	23	0
Marquardt, Scott, St. Petersburg	1.000	9	4	6	0	10	0
Marrero, Kenny, Lakeland	.857	37	1	5	1	7	0
Martinez, Cesar, Sarasota*	1.000	34	2	12	0	14	0
Martinez, Ramiro, Charlotte*	1.000	14	3	6	0	9	0
Matranga, Jeff, St. Petersburg	.889	53	6	10	2	18	0
Matulevich, Jeff, St. Petersburg	1.000	51	2	5	0	7	0
McCommon, Jason, W. Palm Bch.	.974	26	8	30	1	39	2
McDill, Allen, St. Lucie*	.800	7	1	3	1	5	0
McLain, Mike, Lakeland	.667	21	1	3	2	6	0
McLaughlin, Denis, Sarasota	.800	54	3	9	3	15	0
Medina, Rafael, Tampa	.800	6	1	3	1	5	0
Meinershagen, Adam, Dunedin	.765	21	5	8	4	17	0
Mercado, Hector, Kissimmee*	.842	19	1	15	3	19	0
Merrill, Ethan, Sarasota*	.862	27	4	21	4	29	1
Metheney, Nelson, Clearwater	.813	59	2	11	3	16	0
Meyer, David, Tampa*	1.000	12	6	12	0	18	1
Militello, Sam, Brevard County	1.000	4	0	1	0	1	0
Miller, Shawn, Fort Myers	.818	30	5	4	2	11	1
Mix, Greg, Brevard County	.800	5	2	6	2	10	1
Moody, Eric, Charlotte	1.000	13	9	15	0	24	5
Moody, Ritchie, Charlotte*	1.000	1	0	3	0	3	0
Moraga, David, W. Palm Beach*	1.000	3	0	2	0	2	0
Morris, Matt, St. Petersburg	1.000	6	3	3	0	6	0
Morse, Paul, Fort Myers	1.000	35	10	8	0	18	1
Mysel, David, Lakeland	1.000	20	2	3	0	5	0
Newell, Brandon, St. Lucie	1.000	39	3	15	0	18	2
Norman, Scott, Lakeland	.810	22	8	9	4	21	1
Nunez, Clemente, Brevard County	.773	19	6	11	5	22	0
Nye, Ryan, Clearwater	1.000	27	10	15	0	25	1
O'Brien, Brian, Fort Myers*	.833	24	4	6	2	12	0
O'Malley, Paul, Kissimmee	.864	27	16	22	6	44	0
Oropesa, Eddie, Vero Beach*	1.000	19	6	5	0	11	0
Pack, Steve, St. Lucie	1.000	5	1	2	0	3	0
Paluk, Jeff, Vero Beach	1.000	2	0	2	0	2	0
Parra, Julio, Vero Beach	.750	22	3	3	2	8	3
Perkins, Ron, Clearwater	1.000	6	0	1	0	1	0
Perpetuo, Nelson, Charlotte*	.000	5	0	0	1	1	0
Petcka, Joe, St. Lucie	.909	30	3	7	1	11	0
Petersen, Matt, Daytona	1.000	3	0	2	0	2	0
Peterson, Dean, Sarasota	1.000	4	2	2	0	4	0
Pettit, Doug, Brevard County	1.000	27	4	4	0	8	1
Phelps, Tommy, W. Palm Beach*	1.000	2	0	1	0	1	0
Pincavitch, Kevin, Vero Beach	.844	32	8	19	5	32	1
Pisciotta, Scott, W. Palm Beach	.727	53	4	4	3	11	0
Pollard, Damon, W. Palm Beach	.923	28	4	8	1	13	2
Powell, John, Charlotte	1.000	19	2	1	0	3	0
Raggio, Brady, St. Petersburg	1.000	20	4	7	0	11	0
Rama, Shelby, Clearwater	1.000	4	1	1	0	2	0
Ramos, Edgar, Kissimmee	1.000	4	0	2	0	2	0
Rathbun, Jason, Tampa	.857	10	3	3	1	7	0
Redman, Mark, Fort Myers*	.875	8	2	5	1	8	0
Reed, Jason, Vero Beach*	1.000	21	0	4	0	4	0
Resz, Greg, Tampa	1.000	12	0	1	0	1	0
Reyes, Dennis, Vero Beach*	1.000	3	2	2	0	4	0
Reyes, Jose, Charlotte	.846	30	2	9	2	13	0
Ricken, Ray, Tampa	.933	11	2	12	1	15	0
Rios, Dan, Tampa	.933	57	5	9	1	15	2
Rodriguez, Chris, Daytona	1.000	5	0	2	0	2	1
Rodriguez, Salvador, Tampa	1.000	6	1	0	0	1	0
Rojano, Rafael, Tampa	1.000	3	1	1	0	2	0
Roman, Dan, Charlotte*	.833	7	1	4	1	6	0
Romano, Michael, Dunedin	.872	28	11	23	5	39	1
Root, Derek, Kissimmee*	.500	5	0	1	1	2	0
Roque, Rafael, St. Lucie*	.840	24	4	17	4	25	0
Rosengren, John, Lakeland*	.923	13	2	10	1	13	0
Rushworth, Jim, W. Palm Beach	1.000	10	0	3	0	3	0
Ryan, Jason, Daytona	.879	26	7	22	4	33	0
Sacharko, Mark, Kissimmee	1.000	6	2	1	0	3	0
Salazar, Mike, Lakeland*	.900	42	6	12	2	20	0
Sampson, Benj, Fort Myers*	1.000	28	6	17	0	23	1
Sanchez, Victor, Kissimmee	1.000	3	0	1	0	1	0
Santana, Julio, Charlotte	1.000	5	2	0	0	2	0
Santiago, Sandi, Tampa	1.000	34	6	2	0	8	0
Santos, Henry, Lakeland*	1.000	35	2	8	0	10	0
Sauerbeck, Scott, St. Lucie*	1.000	20	0	3	0	3	0
Saunders, Tony, Brevard County*	1.000	13	8	10	0	18	1
Schneider, Tom, W. Palm Beach*	1.000	4	0	1	0	1	0
Seip, Rod, Charlotte	.800	6	2	2	1	5	0
Serna, Joe, Lakeland	1.000	5	1	4	0	5	0
Shoemaker, Stephen, Tampa	1.000	3	0	2	0	2	0
Shrum, Dennis, Kissimmee	.867	38	5	21	4	30	0
Sikes, Ken, Vero Beach	.950	14	10	9	1	20	0
Siler, Jeff, Lakeland*	1.000	27	2	16	0	18	0
Sinacori, Chris, Dunedin	1.000	12	1	0	0	1	0
Sinclair, Steve, Dunedin*	.952	46	6	14	1	21	2
Smith, Dan, Charlotte	.833	9	0	5	1	6	0
Smith, Eric, Clearwater	1.000	8	0	1	0	1	0
Smith, Keilan, Dunedin	.926	26	7	18	2	27	1
Spring, Josh, Dunedin	.857	18	2	4	1	7	1
Stanifer, Robert, Brevard County	.920	18	7	16	2	25	2
Steinert, Robert, Dunedin	.786	17	2	9	3	14	2
Steinke, Brock, Kissimmee	1.000	8	2	1	0	3	0
Stephenson, Brian, Daytona	.882	26	4	11	2	17	1
Stevenson, Jason, Daytona	1.000	8	1	2	0	3	0
Stewart, Chris, St. Petersburg	1.000	30	1	3	0	4	0
Swan, Tyrone, Clearwater	1.000	37	0	2	0	2	0
Tatar, Jason, Fort Myers	1.000	21	1	11	0	12	3
Telgheder, Jim, Sarasota	1.000	22	0	3	0	3	1
Tewksbury, Bob, Charlotte	.500	1	1	0	1	2	0
Thompson, Justin, Lakeland*	1.000	6	2	6	0	8	0
Thornton, Paul, Brevard County	.957	42	7	15	1	23	0
Tidwell, Jason, Brevard County	1.000	4	0	2	0	2	0
Toney, Mike, Dunedin	1.000	12	2	1	0	3	0
Tucker, Julien, Kissimmee	.824	19	6	8	3	17	1
Turrentine, Rich, St. Lucie	1.000	4	2	4	0	6	0
Tuttle, Dave, Lakeland	1.000	6	6	6	0	12	2
Twiggs, Greg, Daytona*	.929	18	3	10	1	14	0
Urbina, Dan, Vero Beach	.852	18	6	17	4	27	0
Valley, Jason, Clearwater	1.000	4	1	0	0	1	0
Vandemark, John, Clearwater*	.857	24	1	5	1	7	0
Wagner, Bret, St. Petersburg*	.958	17	5	18	1	24	1
WALKER, Wade, Daytona	1.000	25	8	22	0	30	1
Walter, Michael, Kissimmee	.955	41	8	13	1	22	0
Ward, Bryan, Brevard County*	.769	11	0	10	3	13	0
Ward, Duane, Dunedin	1.000	3	1	1	0	2	0
Waring, Jim, Kissimmee	.889	5	3	5	1	9	0
Watts, Brandon, Vero Beach*	.857	13	1	5	1	7	1
Weathers, Dave, Brevard County	1.000	1	0	1	0	1	0
Welch, Mike, St. Lucie	.769	44	3	7	3	13	1
Wendell, Turk, Daytona	1.000	4	2	3	0	5	0
Westbrook, Destry, Kissimmee	.667	10	0	2	1	3	0
Whiteman, Greg, Lakeland*	1.000	4	0	5	0	5	0
Whitten, Michael, Bre. County*	1.000	22	3	3	0	6	0
Williams, Matt, Kissimmee*	1.000	19	3	11	0	14	0
Winslett, Dax, V.B.-Day.	.975	26	20	19	1	40	1
Witasick, Jay, St. Petersburg	.889	18	5	11	2	18	1
Yan, Esteban, W. Palm Beach	.854	24	9	26	6	41	0
Yocum, David, Vero Beach*	1.000	8	2	8	0	10	0
Young, Anthony, Daytona	1.000	6	2	1	0	3	0

PITCHERS WITH TWO OR MORE TEAMS

Player, Team	Pct.	G	PO	A	E	TC	DP
Gordon, Mike, Tampa	.897	21	12	23	4	39	0
Gordon, Mike, Dunedin	.818	7	2	7	2	11	0
Winslett, Dax, Vero Beach	1.000	14	16	10	0	26	1
Winslett, Dax, Daytona	.929	12	4	9	1	14	0

The following players did not have any fielding statistics at the positions indicated or appeared only as a designated hitter, pinch-hitter or pinch-runner: Aquino, p; Basey, 3b; Briscoe, p; D. Brito, 2b; B. Brown, p; Clemens, p; Dace, p; M. Davis, p; Dawson, dh; E. Diaz, ss; Donato, of; Epperson, 3b; S. Evans, p; Ferran, p; Forkerway, of; Gen. Gonzalez, p; R. Hartmann, p; Haws, ph; Jerzembeck, p; A. Johnson, of; Khoury, p; Kingman, c; Kramer, p; T. Lewis, ph; Maldonado, p; Malone, of; Marquez, p; McMullen, dh; Melhuse, of; Moore, dh; M. Nava, of; Pena, p; Querecuto, of; Raleigh, ss, c; A. Rodriguez, 3b; Sabo, of; Schlomann, p; Sele, p; Southard, p; Standish, p; Stentz, p; Strawberry, dh; Taylor, of; Twitty, dh; Unrat, ss; U. Urbina, p; Viola, p; Waco, of; Wright, p; Wyrick, 2b.

CLASS A *Florida State League*

Year	Team	Pct.
1919—	Sanford*	.605
	Orlando*	.703
1920—	Tampa	.654
	Tampa	.722
1921—	Orlando	.635
1922—	St. Petersburg	.503
	St. Petersburg	.618
1923—	Orlando	.667
	Orlando	.678
1924—	Lakeland	.695
	Lakeland	.683
1925—	St. Petersburg	.667
	Tampa†	.696
1926—	Sanford	.647
	Sanford	.623
1927—	Orlando†	.600
	Miami	.661
1928-35—	Did not operate.	
1936—	Gainesville	.542
	St. Augustine (4th)†	.492
1937—	Gainesville§	.616
1938—	Leesburg	.626
	Gainesville (2nd)‡	.615
1939—	Sanford§	.787
1940—	Daytona Beach	.619
	Orlando (4th)‡	.507
1941—	St. Augustine	.659
	Leesburg (4th)‡	.488
1942-45—	Did not operate.	
1946—	Orlando§	.681
1947—	St. Augustine	.625
	Gainesville (2nd)‡	.584
1948—	Orlando	.643
	Daytona Beach (2nd)‡	.616
1949—	Gainesville	.635
	St. Augustine (3rd)‡	.556
1950—	Orlando	.629
	DeLand (3rd)‡	.590
1951—	DeLand§	.643
1952—	DeLand∞	.704
	Palatka (3rd)‡	.569
1953—	Daytona Beach†	.657
	DeLand	.703
1954—	Jacksonville Beach	.629
	Lakeland†	.594
1955—	Orlando	.671
	Orlando	.643
1956—	Cocoa	.614
	Cocoa	.671
1957—	Palatka	.629
	Tampa†	.681
1958—	St. Petersburg	.732
	St. Petersburg	.681
1959—	Tampa	.591
	St. Petersburg†	.612
1960—	Lakeland	.731
	Palatka†	.614
1961—	Tampa†	.710
	Sarasota	.696
1962—	Sarasota	.689
	Fort Lauderdale†	.623
1963—	Sarasota	.645
	Sarasota	.667
1964—	Fort Lauderdale†	.629
	St. Petersburg	.594
1965—	Fort Lauderdale	.627
	Fort Lauderdale	.634
1966—	Leesburg†	.781
	St. Petersburg	.700
1967—	St. Petersburg▲	.691
	Orlando	.638
1968—	Miami	.613
	Orlando♦	.579
1969—	Miami■	.606
	Orlando	.606
1970—	Miami▼	.662
	St. Petersburg	.600
1971—	Miami▼	.667
	Daytona Beach	.586
1972—	Miami•	.562
	Daytona Beach	.606
1973—	St. Petersburg††	.575
	West Palm Beach	.580
1974—	West Palm Beach††	.598
	Fort Lauderdale	.626
1975—	St. Petersburg††	.652
	Miami	.581
1976—	Tampa	.559
	Lakeland††	.536
1977—	Lakeland††	.616
	West Palm Beach	.583
1978—	Lakeland§	.565
	Miami§	.539
1979—	Fort Lauderdale	.643
	Winter Haven‡‡	.577
1980—	Daytona Beach	.628
	Fort Lauderdale††	.606
1981—	Fort Myers	.554
	Daytona Beach§§	.504
1982—	Fort Lauderdale§§	.621
	Tampa	.546
1983—	Daytona Beach	.634
	Vero Beach§§	.515
1984—	Tampa	.532
	Fort Lauderdale§§	.521
1985—	Fort Myers∞∞∞	.590
	Fort Lauderdale	.550
1986—	St. Petersburg∞∞∞	.647
	West Palm Beach	.593
1987—	Fort Lauderdale∞∞∞	.616
	Osceola	.576
1988—	Osceola	.606
	St. Lucie▲▲	.532
1989—	Port Charlotte▲▲	.540
	St. Petersburg	.540
1990—	West Palm Beach	.697
	Vero Beach▲▲	.585
1991—	Clearwater	.623
	West Palm Beach▲▲	.550
1992—	Sarasota	.639
	Lakeland♦♦	.530
1993—	St. Lucie	.600
	Clearwater§§	.556
1994—	Tampa§§	.606
	Brevard County	.561
1995—	Daytona§§	.644
	Fort Myers	.577

*Split-season playoff abandoned after each team won three games. †Won split-season playoff. ‡Won four-club playoff. §Won championship and four-club playoff. ∞Won both halves of split season. ▲League divided into Eastern and Western divisions with split season. St. Petersburg and Orlando won both halves of split season; St. Petersburg won playoff. ♦League divided into Eastern and Western divisions. Miami won regular-season pennant on basis of highest won-lost percentage. Orlando won four-club playoff involving first two teams in each division. ■League divided into Southern and Central divisions. Miami won playoff between division leaders. (NOTE—Pennant awarded to playoff winner in 1936.) ▼League divided into Eastern and Western divisions. Miami won regular-season pennant on basis of highest won-loss percentage, and also won four-club playoff involving first two teams in each division. •League divided into Eastern and Western divisions. Won four-club playoff involving first two teams in each division. ††League divided into Northern and Southern divisions. Same two clubs won both halves; won playoffs. §§Won split-season playoff. ∞∞∞League divided into Western, Central and Southern divisions. Won four-club playoff. ▲▲League divided into Eastern, Western and Central divisions; played split-season. Won six-club playoff. ♦♦League divided into Eastern, Western and Central divisions; played split-season. Won eight-club playoff.

MIDWEST LEAGUE

LEAGUE OFFICE

President
George H. Spelius
Address
P.O. Box 936
Beloit, WI 53512
Phone
608-364-1188

Teams (affiliation)
Beloit Snappers (Brewers)
Burlington Bees (Giants)
Cedar Rapids Kernels (Angels)
Clinton Lumber Kings (Padres)
Fort Wayne Wizards (Twins)
Kane County Cougars (Marlins)
Lansing Lugnuts (Royals)

Michigan Battle Cats (Red Sox)
Peoria Chiefs (Cardinals)
Quad City River Bandits (Astros)
Rockford Cubbies (Cubs)
South Bend Silver Hawks (White Sox)
West Michigan Whitecaps (A's)
Wisconsin Timber Rattlers (Mariners)

1995 FINAL STANDINGS

FIRST HALF

EASTERN DIVISION

Team	W	L	T	Pct.	GB
Michigan (Red Sox)	36	32	0	.529	....
West Michigan (Athletics)	35	33	0	.515	1
Fort Wayne (Twins)	35	35	0	.500	2
South Bend (White Sox)	31	36	0	.463	4½

CENTRAL DIVISION

Team	W	L	T	Pct.	GB
Beloit (Brewers)	45	25	0	.643	....
Kane County (Marlins)	39	31	0	.557	6
Rockford (Cubs)	34	36	0	.486	11
Wisconsin (Mariners)	30	38	0	.441	14

WESTERN DIVISION

Team	W	L	T	Pct.	GB
Quad City (Astros)	40	27	0	.597	....
Springfield (Royals)	38	31	0	.551	3
Cedar Rapids (Angels)	38	31	0	.551	3
Peoria (Cardinals)	32	35	0	.478	8
Burlington (Giants)	29	38	0	.433	11
Clinton (Padres)	17	51	0	.250	23½

SECOND HALF

EASTERN DIVISION

Team	W	L	T	Pct.	GB
Fort Wayne (Twins)	40	30	0	.571	....
Michigan (Red Sox)	39	31	0	.557	1
South Bend (White Sox)	35	33	0	.515	4
West Michigan (Athletics)	32	36	0	.471	7

CENTRAL DIVISION

Team	W	L	T	Pct.	GB
Beloit (Brewers)	43	26	0	.623	....
Rockford (Cubs)	41	29	0	.586	2½
Wisconsin (Mariners)	33	37	0	.471	10½
Kane County (Marlins)	30	38	0	.441	12½

WESTERN DIVISION

Team	W	L	T	Pct.	GB
Cedar Rapids (Angels)	38	31	0	.551	....
Quad City (Astros)	36	34	0	.514	2½
Clinton (Padres)	34	35	0	.493	4
Peoria (Cardinals)	30	37	0	.448	7
Springfield (Royals)	27	43	0	.386	11½
Burlington (Giants)	25	43	0	.368	12½

COMPOSITE

Team	Bel.	Q.C.	C.R.	Mch.	Rck.	F.W.	K.C.	W.M.	S.B.	Spr.	Peo.	Wis.	Bur.	Cln.	W	L	T	Pct.	GB
Beloit (Brewers)	...	4	5	7	11	6	11	6	6	5	3	14	5	5	88	51	0	.633	....
Quad City (Astros)	4	....	7	3	5	4	4	6	2	11	11	3	9	7	76	61	0	.555	11
Cedar Rapids (Angels)	3	9	....	3	4	5	6	3	3	6	10	3	11	10	76	62	0	.551	11½
Michigan (Red Sox)	1	3	5	....	3	10	6	7	14	5	5	7	3	6	75	63	0	.543	12½
Rockford (Cubs)	9	3	4	5	....	6	6	4	5	6	7	8	6	6	75	65	0	.536	13½
Fort Wayne (Twins)	2	4	3	10	2	...	5	14	10	7	4	4	3	7	75	65	0	.536	13½
Kane County (Marlins)	9	4	2	2	14	3	...	4	3	6	4	9	5	4	69	69	0	.500	18½
West Michigan (Athletics)	1	2	4	13	4	6	4	...	11	5	5	2	4	6	67	69	0	.493	19½
South Bend (White Sox)	2	6	5	6	3	10	3	8	...	2	4	5	7	5	66	69	0	.489	20
Springfield (Royals)	3	5	10	3	2	1	2	2	6	....	6	6	8	11	65	74	0	.468	23
Peoria (Cubs)	5	5	6	3	1	4	4	3	2	6	....	4	9	10	62	72	0	.463	24½
Wisconsin (Mariners)	6	4	5	1	12	4	11	6	3	2	3	...	2	4	63	75	0	.457	24½
Burlington (Giants)	3	3	4	5	2	5	3	4	1	8	5	6	....	5	54	81	0	.400	32
Clinton (Padres)	3	9	2	2	2	1	4	2	3	5	5	4	9	....	51	86	0	.372	36

Kane County's home games played in Geneva, Ill.

Michigan's home games played in Battle Creek, Mich.

Quad City's home games played in Davenport, Ia.

West Michigan's home games played in Comstock Park, Mich.

Major league affiliations in parentheses.

PLAYOFFS: Beloit defeated Rockford, two games to none; Michigan defeated Fort Wayne, two games to none; Quad City defeated Cedar Rapids, two games to one; West Michigan defeated Kane County, two games to one; Beloit defeated Quad City, two games to one; Michigan defeated West Michigan, two games to one; Beloit defeated Michigan, three games to none, to win league championship.

REGULAR-SEASON ATTENDANCE: Beloit, 60,816; Burlington, 69,412; Cedar Rapids, 135,840; Clinton, 50,126; Fort Wayne, 253,568; Kane County, 477,550; Michigan, 171,794; Peoria, 195,056; Quad City, 257,501; Rockford, 110,052; South Bend, 225,999; Springfield, 39,467; West Michigan, 507,989; Wisconsin, 209,159. Total, 2,764,329. Playoffs (19 games), 38,047. All-Star Game at West Michigan—8,483.

MANAGERS: Beloit, Dub Kilgo; Burlington, Mike Hart; Cedar Rapids, Tom Lawless; Clinton, Ed Romero; Fort Wayne, Dan Rohn; Kane County, Lynn Jones; Michigan, Demarlo Hale; Peoria, Roy Silver; Quad City, Jim Pankovits; Rockford, Steve Roadcap; South Bend, Fred Kendall; Springfield, Brian Poldberg; West Michigan, Jim Colborn; Wisconsin, Mike Goff.

ALL-STAR TEAM: 1B—Jesus Ibarra, Burlington; 2B—Luis Castillo, Kane County; 3B—Sean McNally, Springfield; SS—Donnie Sadler, Michigan; OF—Demond Smith, Cedar Rapids-West Michigan; Todd Dunwoody, Kane County; Ryan Jackson, Kane County; C—Jose Valentin, Fort Wayne; DH—Derek Hacopian, Beloit; LHP—Tony Mounce, Quad City; RHP—Jeff D'Amico, Beloit; LH Reliever—Jeff Keith, Burlington; RH Reliever—Travis Welch, Peoria; Most Valuable Player—Jesus Ibarra, Burlington; Prospect of the Year—Jose Valentin, Fort Wayne; Manager of the Year—Demarlo Hale, Michigan.

1995 BATTING

TEAM

Team	Avg.	G	TPA	AB	R	H	TB	2B	3B	HR	RBI	SH	SF	HP	BB	IBB	SO	SB	CS	GDP	LOB	ShO	Slg.	OBP
Quad City	.269	137	5036	4447	660	1195	1721	226	33	78	585	40	46	59	438	8	767	206	95	94	907	11	.387	.339
Kane County	.264	138	5240	4550	706	1201	1758	235	38	82	616	43	47	60	535	21	935	171	70	78	997	3	.386	.346
Cedar Rapids	.263	138	5180	4497	697	1184	1777	234	28	101	597	47	43	65	525	16	880	195	82	83	954	6	.395	.346
Beloit	.263	139	5227	4491	723	1181	1761	234	35	92	620	44	37	90	560	24	860	194	99	84	975	6	.392	.354
Rockford	.263	140	5368	4678	764	1229	1813	275	30	83	662	26	40	98	524	19	894	184	71	91	1015	7	.388	.347
Fort Wayne	.261	140	5397	4786	661	1251	1859	253	38	93	601	30	37	66	476	22	926	135	72	84	1034	8	.388	.334
South Bend	.257	135	5172	4507	630	1158	1628	198	40	64	563	41	55	57	511	18	857	143	72	80	983	4	.361	.336
Michigan	.252	138	5299	4601	684	1158	1780	233	34	107	607	38	39	86	534	16	1058	175	60	75	1004	3	.387	.338
Peoria	.249	134	4762	4271	534	1065	1473	175	37	53	454	50	29	52	356	16	738	131	72	94	839	7	.345	.313
Wisconsin	.245	138	5100	4444	593	1089	1546	230	31	55	529	46	48	89	452	24	926	166	59	81	962	8	.348	.324
Springfield	.245	139	5073	4503	638	1101	1670	217	41	90	563	39	38	68	425	15	980	187	59	92	900	6	.371	.317
Burlington	.240	135	4808	4255	569	1022	1563	166	18	113	497	37	24	61	429	8	960	103	46	98	879	7	.367	.317
Clinton	.234	137	4936	4316	521	1011	1343	188	18	36	451	39	31	38	510	13	910	160	72	75	951	18	.311	.313
West Michigan	.232	136	5104	4304	650	1000	1411	192	24	57	533	72	40	82	606	23	996	226	96	84	919	5	.328	.335

INDIVIDUAL

TOP QUALIFIERS FOR BATTING CHAMPIONSHIP

Minimum 378 plate appearances. *Lefthanded batter. †Switch-hitter.

Player, Team	Avg.	G	TPA	AB	R	H	TB	2B	3B	HR	RBI	SH	SF	HP	BB	IBB	SO	SB	CS	GDP	Slg.	OBP
Smith, Demond, C.R.-W.M.†	.338	87	397	349	70	118	187	26	8	9	44	6	1	7	34	3	69	40	14	3	.536	.407
Ibarra, Jesus, Burlington†	.330	129	519	437	72	144	278	30	1	34	96	0	1	4	77	6	94	1	2	8	.636	.434
Mitchell, Donovan, Quad City*	.329	111	422	383	72	126	163	23	1	4	42	5	3	2	29	0	38	21	15	10	.426	.376
Castillo, Luis, Kane County	.326	89	400	340	71	111	123	4	4	0	23	4	1	0	55	1	50	41	18	1	.362	.419
Hacopian, Derek, Beloit	.324	123	508	442	75	143	244	30	1	23	92	0	2	8	56	5	35	4	5	20	.552	.407
Valentin, Jose, Fort Wayne†	.321	112	433	383	59	123	216	26	5	19	65	1	0	2	47	7	75	0	5	7	.564	.398
Rodriguez, Noel, Quad City	.311	109	422	386	48	120	180	26	5	8	71	0	4	4	28	1	49	4	5	11	.466	.360
Koskie, Corey, Fort Wayne*	.310	123	515	462	64	143	238	37	5	16	78	1	5	9	38	3	79	2	4	10	.515	.370
Freire, Alejandro, Quad City	.305	125	482	417	71	127	197	23	1	15	65	2	7	6	50	1	83	9	5	9	.472	.381
Pico, Brandon, Rockford*	.300	96	428	383	59	115	162	27	4	4	47	4	3	2	34	0	53	7	7	7	.423	.358
Delgado, Wilson, Wis.-Bur.†	.299	112	477	435	65	130	174	23	3	5	44	4	1	2	35	1	72	12	9	12	.400	.353
Trammell, Gary, Quad City*	.298	103	378	336	44	100	124	12	3	2	33	5	3	1	33	0	62	14	8	4	.369	.369
Belliard, Ron, Beloit	.297	130	507	461	76	137	214	28	5	13	76	2	1	7	36	2	67	16	12	10	.464	.356
Roskos, John, Kane County	.297	114	472	418	74	124	202	36	3	12	88	0	6	6	42	1	86	2	0	6	.483	.364
Jackson, Ryan, Kane County*	.293	132	547	471	78	138	219	39	6	10	82	0	5	4	67	7	74	13	8	9	.465	.382
Betances, Junior, Beloit	.293	122	504	427	66	125	165	21	8	1	52	7	7	2	61	1	67	21	9	9	.386	.378

DEPARTMENTAL LEADERS: G—Robledo, Williams, 135; AB—Robledo, 537; R—Sadler, 103; H—Robledo, 153; TB—Ibarra, 278; 2B—Jackson, 39; 3B—R. Mendez, 11; HR—Ibarra, 34; RBI—Robledo, 108; SH—F. Soriano, 18; SF—Robledo, 16; HP—Dennis, 16; BB—Carone, 84; IBB—Several batters tied with 7; SO—Denbow, 143; SB—Hernandez, 58; CS—Hernandez, 21; GIDP—Hacopian, 20; Slg.—Ibarra, .636; OBP—Ibarra, .434.

ALL PLAYERS

*Lefthanded batter. †Switch-hitter.

Player, Team	Avg.	G	TPA	AB	R	H	TB	2B	3B	HR	RBI	SH	SF	HP	BB	IBB	SO	SB	CS	GDP	Slg.	OBP
Alexander, Chad, Quad City	.286	2	7	7	2	2	2	0	0	0	1	0	0	0	0	0	0	0	0	0	.286	.286
Alguacil, Jose, Burlington†	.221	38	148	136	15	30	32	2	0	0	5	3	0	2	7	0	27	13	1	2	.235	.269
Allen, Dustin, Clinton	.266	36	152	139	25	37	66	12	1	5	31	0	0	1	12	1	29	1	0	3	.475	.329
Allison, Chris, Michigan	.315	87	361	298	46	94	110	8	4	0	22	4	0	7	52	1	39	36	4	5	.369	.429
Altman, Heath, Burlington†	.125	20	29	24	4	3	6	0	0	1	2	0	0	1	4	0	15	1	0	0	.250	.276
Alvarez, Luis, Cedar Rapids*	.195	42	137	123	14	24	39	7	1	2	13	0	1	1	12	3	15	2	2	3	.317	.270
Alvarez, Rafael, Fort Wayne*	.283	99	416	374	62	106	148	17	5	5	36	2	4	2	34	1	53	15	11	5	.396	.343
Amerson, Gordon, Clinton*	.157	48	169	134	15	21	26	2	0	1	8	0	0	0	35	2	41	5	5	2	.194	.331
Amezcua, Adan, Quad City	.246	46	150	142	13	35	59	8	2	4	12	1	1	1	5	0	28	2	3	4	.415	.275
Andreopouls, Alex, Beloit*	.301	60	208	163	32	49	61	9	0	1	20	3	1	3	35	1	16	5	3	2	.374	.431
Augustine, Andy, Wisconsin	.171	56	160	129	17	22	25	0	0	1	6	4	0	8	19	0	43	3	1	5	.194	.314
Avalos, Gilbert, Rockford	.237	104	402	350	57	83	106	15	1	2	34	7	2	4	39	0	74	18	4	8	.303	.319
Ballara, Juan, Peoria	.255	86	262	243	33	62	110	12	6	8	27	0	0	2	17	1	53	5	3	5	.453	.309
Barnes, Kelvin, Rockford	.167	5	14	12	1	2	2	0	0	0	0	0	0	1	1	0	3	0	0	0	.167	.286
Barton, Scott, Rockford*	.231	14	30	26	2	6	9	3	0	0	2	1	0	0	3	0	6	0	1	0	.346	.310
Bautista, Juan, Peoria	.222	84	201	189	31	42	54	4	1	2	22	3	3	2	4	0	43	18	8	1	.286	.242
Bazzani, Matt, Michigan	.116	29	86	69	8	8	13	5	0	0	6	4	0	2	11	0	28	1	0	0	.188	.256
Belliard, Ron, Beloit	.297	130	507	461	76	137	214	28	5	13	76	2	1	7	36	2	67	16	12	10	.464	.356
Betances, Junior, Beloit	.293	122	504	427	66	125	165	21	8	1	52	7	7	2	61	1	67	21	9	9	.386	.378
Betten, Randy, Cedar Rapids	.233	36	74	60	8	14	16	2	0	0	4	0	1	0	13	0	8	6	2	0	.267	.365
Biermann, Steve, Peoria†	.238	59	143	122	10	29	32	3	0	0	10	2	0	4	15	1	16	4	3	5	.262	.340
Bogle, Bryan, Rockford	.206	36	106	97	13	20	29	3	0	2	11	0	1	0	8	0	20	4	1	2	.299	.264
Booty, Josh, Kane County	.101	31	121	109	6	11	16	2	0	1	6	0	1	0	11	0	45	1	0	1	.147	.182
Borrero, Rikchy, Michigan	.229	23	80	70	8	16	28	4	1	2	6	0	0	4	6	0	17	0	1	2	.400	.293
Boulware, Benjamin, S. Bend	.258	129	521	476	68	123	158	19	5	2	60	2	3	8	32	2	78	24	13	10	.332	.314
Bowers, R.J., Quad City	.242	110	426	372	52	90	147	19	1	12	58	6	6	13	35	1	119	10	9	7	.395	.324
Bowles, John, Michigan*	.241	106	415	352	48	85	115	18	0	4	46	5	3	9	46	1	70	5	8	13	.327	.341
Brandon, Jelani, Springfield	.243	74	272	230	32	56	79	12	1	3	37	2	3	2	35	0	37	6	2	4	.343	.344
Bray, Notorris, Burlington	.200	15	56	45	8	9	11	0	1	0	2	1	0	2	8	0	12	3	0	1	.244	.345
Brown, Armann, Fort Wayne	.233	78	293	253	35	59	75	9	2	1	25	2	0	8	30	0	57	26	7	8	.296	.333
Brown, Emil, West Michigan	.251	124	528	459	63	115	147	11	3	4	67	0	6	11	52	0	77	35	19	17	.320	.337

Player, Team	Avg.	G	TPA	AB	R	H	TB	2B	3B	HR	RBI	SH	SF	HP	BB	IBB	SO	SB	CS	GDP	Slg.	OBP
Buchanan, Shawn, S. Bend	.269	103	410	350	45	94	124	16	4	2	35	1	3	10	46	0	72	10	8	10	.354	.367
Buhner, Shawn, Wisconsin	.240	87	318	292	24	70	96	14	3	2	36	0	4	6	16	2	65	0	2	9	.329	.289
Burchel, Brad, Beloit	.147	13	39	34	4	5	6	1	0	0	3	0	0	2	3	0	11	0	3	0	.176	.256
Burgos, Carlos, Springfield	.181	27	83	72	8	13	15	2	0	0	8	0	1	3	7	0	11	0	0	2	.208	.277
Burt, Chris, Beloit	.000	37	1	1	0	0	0	0	0	0	0	0	0	0	0	0	0	0	0	0	.000	.000
Bustos, Saul, Rockford	.253	95	323	289	46	73	119	12	2	10	47	2	8	2	22	0	66	5	2	8	.412	.302
Cady, Todd, Kane County†	.251	115	448	387	47	97	155	23	1	11	66	0	4	9	47	3	104	1	0	4	.401	.342
Campillo, Rob, Beloit	.211	47	144	123	17	26	30	4	0	0	13	7	2	5	7	1	20	0	0	2	.244	.277
Carmona, Cesarin, Clinton†	.178	42	146	129	13	23	27	2	1	0	5	1	0	1	15	0	35	10	7	2	.209	.269
Carone, Richard, South Bend	.254	111	447	347	56	88	133	16	1	9	51	5	2	9	84	0	91	0	3	7	.383	.410
Carpenter, Jerry, Cedar Rapids	.100	11	34	30	2	3	3	0	0	0	2	0	0	0	4	0	9	0	0	0	.100	.206
Carroll, Doug, Wisconsin*	.225	90	311	276	29	62	95	18	0	5	40	0	3	14	18	3	60	3	0	7	.344	.302
Castillo, Alberto, Burlington*	.165	34	110	103	7	17	33	4	0	4	13	0	0	0	7	0	43	2	0	2	.320	.218
Castillo, Luis, Kane County	.326	89	400	340	71	111	123	4	4	0	23	4	1	0	55	1	50	41	18	1	.362	.419
Castro, Dennis, Kane County*	.246	46	156	138	12	34	58	9	0	5	21	2	1	0	15	1	33	1	0	4	.420	.318
Castro, Jose, West Michigan†	.240	113	509	409	76	98	128	20	2	2	40	13	0	11	76	2	94	51	20	2	.313	.373
Cedeno, Edwardo, Springfield	.224	81	234	210	30	47	79	7	2	7	27	3	2	5	14	0	67	7	3	1	.376	.286
Cephas, Ruben, Beloit*	.170	76	105	94	17	16	16	0	0	0	1	3	0	1	7	0	25	13	3	0	.170	.235
Chevalier, Virgil, Michigan	.667	2	7	6	2	4	5	1	0	0	0	0	0	0	1	0	0	1	0	0	.833	.714
Choi, Kyung, Cedar Rapids*	.228	36	136	123	14	28	39	4	2	1	14	1	2	1	9	0	12	4	1	4	.317	.281
Clifford, James, Wisconsin*	.244	101	371	307	46	75	137	26	3	10	44	1	5	13	40	2	87	8	4	3	.446	.351
Cline, Pat, Rockford	.272	112	464	390	65	106	172	27	0	13	77	0	5	11	58	3	93	6	1	6	.441	.377
Coe, Ryan, Quad City	.261	38	111	92	16	24	46	7	0	5	18	0	1	3	13	0	20	1	2	4	.500	.367
Cole, Abdul, Kane County	.123	56	150	122	10	15	21	3	0	1	7	3	2	6	17	0	48	3	1	4	.172	.259
Coleman, Michael, Michigan	.268	112	477	422	70	113	166	16	2	11	61	6	3	6	40	1	93	29	5	7	.393	.338
Contreras, Efrain, Peoria*	.258	98	305	271	35	70	113	9	2	10	48	1	3	3	27	3	45	1	3	12	.417	.329
Cook, Hayward, Kane County	.280	78	277	261	50	73	104	5	1	8	23	2	1	1	12	0	61	23	4	4	.398	.313
Cook, Jason, Wisconsin	.269	117	491	405	61	109	152	24	2	5	64	3	6	12	64	7	44	12	5	8	.375	.380
Cordero, Pablo, Burlington	.242	59	210	190	21	46	65	9	2	2	21	3	1	2	14	0	38	2	1	4	.342	.300
Corujo, Rey, Burlington	.133	14	47	45	2	6	7	1	0	0	0	0	0	0	2	0	8	1	1	2	.156	.170
Cruz, Deivi, Burlington	.138	16	63	58	2	8	12	1	0	1	9	1	0	0	4	0	7	1	1	1	.207	.194
Cuevas, Eduardo, Clinton	.259	69	276	263	39	68	87	11	1	2	31	1	3	0	9	1	31	17	3	5	.331	.280
D'Amico, Jeff, West Michigan	.226	125	511	434	56	98	145	24	1	7	55	4	7	10	56	2	94	8	5	12	.334	.323
Dantzler, Eric, Burlington	.167	30	100	84	6	14	18	1	0	1	7	1	3	0	12	0	24	2	0	5	.214	.263
Darcuiel, Faruq, Wisconsin*	.259	83	315	282	29	73	92	10	3	1	20	4	2	5	22	0	50	27	6	1	.326	.322
Darden, Tony, Kane County	.287	86	337	286	42	82	116	15	5	3	31	1	2	8	40	1	40	5	5	6	.406	.387
DaSilva, Manny, West Michigan	.316	7	25	19	5	6	13	2	1	1	3	1	0	1	4	0	4	0	0	1	.684	.458
Davalillo, David, Cedar Rapids	.270	44	153	141	17	38	47	7	1	0	16	4	1	0	7	0	32	1	0	3	.333	.302
Davis, Josh, Clinton	.200	8	16	15	2	3	3	0	0	0	2	0	0	0	1	0	5	0	0	0	.200	.250
Dean, Mark, Peoria†	.205	75	216	190	19	39	45	2	2	0	12	5	0	7	14	0	42	4	3	3	.237	.284
DeBoer, Rob, West Michigan	.242	104	406	339	57	82	129	25	2	6	50	1	4	4	58	1	110	11	6	6	.381	.356
Delaney, Sean, Springfield	.298	62	214	188	24	56	83	8	2	5	22	1	1	5	19	1	27	5	1	5	.441	.376
DeLeon, Raymond, Clinton*	.267	9	34	30	3	8	9	1	0	0	4	0	1	1	2	0	3	0	1	1	.300	.324
DeLeon, Santo, Wisconsin*	.105	9	24	19	0	2	2	0	0	0	0	2	0	0	3	0	5	1	0	0	.105	.227
Delgado, Wilson, Wis.-Bur.†	.299	112	477	435	65	130	174	23	3	5	44	4	1	2	35	1	72	12	9	12	.400	.353
Denbow, Don, Burlington	.178	105	374	326	42	58	103	7	1	12	33	1	0	5	42	0	143	14	2	2	.316	.282
Dennis, Brian, Rockford	.206	51	135	102	10	21	30	3	0	2	16	1	3	16	13	0	28	1	1	3	.294	.373
DePastino, Joe, Michigan	.277	98	368	325	47	90	148	20	4	10	53	0	5	8	30	1	70	3	3	5	.455	.348
Derosso, Tony, Michigan	.233	106	434	382	57	89	150	20	1	13	50	1	2	11	38	2	93	9	1	5	.393	.319
Donati, John, Cedar Rapids.	.286	116	453	381	63	109	185	24	2	16	75	1	4	10	57	1	92	5	3	4	.486	.389
Dumas, Mike, Beloit	.254	20	83	71	11	18	23	1	2	0	4	1	0	0	11	0	11	9	6	0	.324	.354
Dunwoody, Todd, K. C.*	.283	132	565	494	89	140	218	20	8	14	89	2	9	8	52	7	105	39	11	7	.441	.355
Ebbert, Chad, Clinton	.000	2	5	5	0	0	0	0	0	0	0	0	0	0	0	0	1	0	0	0	.000	.000
Encarnacion, Anito, Ced. Rapids.	.209	42	89	86	4	18	21	3	0	0	6	1	0	0	2	0	12	0	0	4	.244	.227
Espinal, Juan, Clinton	.208	116	400	336	28	70	102	11	0	7	46	6	7	4	47	2	79	3	3	8	.304	.307
Espiritu, Michael, Cedar Rapids	.167	9	31	24	1	4	4	0	0	0	2	0	0	0	7	1	3	1	1	2	.167	.355
Evans, Jason, South Bend†	.280	101	432	336	70	94	137	17	4	6	36	8	3	6	79	1	74	11	4	3	.408	.422
Faggett, Ethan, Michigan*	.243	115	445	399	56	97	146	11	7	8	47	3	2	4	37	3	112	23	7	9	.366	.312
Failla, Paul, Cedar Rapids†	.253	129	537	459	77	116	153	23	4	2	48	7	3	2	66	0	102	30	19	5	.333	.347
Fitzpatrick, Will, Beloit*	.200	55	158	115	18	23	36	5	1	2	14	0	1	4	38	1	35	5	3	0	.313	.411
Fortin, Troy, Kane County*	.258	112	458	407	49	105	149	21	1	7	48	0	3	8	38	1	69	4	5	7	.366	.331
Francisco, Vicente, W. Mich.†	.245	85	321	277	41	68	83	8	2	1	25	12	1	1	30	0	48	4	8	4	.300	.320
Fraser, Joe, Fort Wayne	.200	5	16	15	0	3	3	0	0	0	2	0	1	0	0	0	5	1	0	0	.200	.188
Freeman, Richard, Rockford	.273	131	535	466	89	127	203	33	5	11	67	0	1	7	61	3	57	8	3	11	.436	.364
Freire, Alejandro, Quad City	.305	125	482	417	71	127	197	23	1	15	65	2	7	6	50	1	83	9	5	9	.472	.381
French, Anton, Peoria†	.273	116	467	417	71	114	173	19	5	10	37	7	0	6	37	2	98	57	16	6	.415	.341
Fric, Sean, Rockford	.235	7	21	17	3	4	5	1	0	0	2	0	0	0	4	0	2	0	0	1	.294	.381
Garcia, Amaury, Kane County.	.241	26	77	58	19	14	23	4	1	1	5	0	0	1	18	0	12	5	2	1	.397	.429
Garcia, Carlos, Fort Wayne	.189	34	105	95	13	18	23	5	0	0	10	3	0	0	7	0	13	11	0	0	.242	.245
Garcia, Franklin, Beloit	.230	26	68	61	7	14	16	2	0	0	6	1	1	0	5	0	14	5	2	2	.262	.284
Gazarek, Marty, Rockford	.261	107	439	399	57	104	139	24	1	3	53	2	3	8	27	1	58	7	5	8	.348	.318
Gerteisen, Aaron, Peoria*	.216	73	247	218	24	47	61	6	1	2	17	3	1	0	25	0	29	7	5	4	.280	.295
Gibralter, David, Michigan	.252	121	492	456	48	115	199	34	1	16	82	3	4	8	20	2	79	3	4	7	.436	.293
Glenn, Darrin, Burlington	.214	62	211	182	35	39	72	4	1	9	27	0	1	5	23	0	59	4	3	8	.396	.318
Gonzalez, Jimmy, Quad City	.244	35	88	78	4	19	27	3	1	1	10	0	1	1	8	0	13	1	2	2	.346	.318
Goodell, Steve, Kane County	.286	9	7	7	0	2	2	0	0	0	1	0	0	0	2	0	2	0	0	0	.286	.444
Gordon, Adrian, Fort Wayne	.240	75	253	217	34	52	70	10	1	2	18	1	3	6	26	1	63	16	7	3	.323	.333
Grandizio, Steve, Peoria	.280	117	438	379	65	106	135	18	4	1	33	2	5	10	42	1	63	21	8	10	.356	.362
Grieve, Ben, W. Michigan*	.261	102	445	371	53	97	127	16	1	4	62	0	6	8	60	6	75	11	3	10	.342	.371
Gugino, Mark, Kane County	.244	58	208	164	29	40	66	13	2	3	20	3	2	4	35	0	29	5	3	4	.402	.385
Gulseth, Mark, Burlington*	.277	41	159	137	15	38	57	7	0	4	19	0	2	2	18	0	30	3	3	4	.416	.365
Gunderson, Shane, Ft. Wayne	.253	26	103	87	17	22	35	7	0	2	12	4	0	2	10	1	17	2	1	0	.402	.343
Hacopian, Derek, Beloit	.324	123	508	442	75	143	244	30	1	23	92	0	2	8	56	5	35	4	5	20	.552	.407

– 503 –

Player, Team	Avg.	G	TPA	AB	R	H	TB	2B	3B	HR	RBI	SH	SF	HP	BB	IBB	SO	SB	CS	GDP	Slg.	OBP
Hall, Ryan, Peoria*	.271	108	378	317	38	86	131	24	0	7	44	3	5	4	49	2	70	1	2	7	.413	.371
Hamburg, Leon, W. Mich.	.183	85	317	268	40	49	75	16	2	2	32	2	1	4	42	0	78	12	3	5	.280	.302
Hamilton, Joe, Michigan*	.217	119	491	405	65	88	155	15	2	16	59	2	6	5	73	3	124	8	7	1	.383	.339
Hansen, Jed, Springfield	.258	122	506	414	86	107	175	27	7	9	50	6	1	7	78	0	73	44	10	8	.423	.384
Harris, Eric, West Michigan	.168	70	237	202	29	34	68	9	2	7	29	0	2	7	26	0	73	5	0	5	.337	.283
Harris, Mike, Beloit*	.341	12	45	41	8	14	17	1	1	0	5	0	0	0	4	0	5	7	1	0	.415	.400
Harvey, Aaron, Kane County*	.292	100	376	336	58	98	150	25	3	7	54	4	4	5	25	0	70	11	7	4	.446	.346
Hause, Brendan, W. Michigan*	.000	32	1	1	0	0	0	0	0	0	0	0	0	0	0	0	0	0	0	0	.000	.000
Heath, Jason, Wisconsin	.268	70	272	235	29	63	99	20	2	4	32	7	4	7	19	2	60	3	3	4	.421	.336
Hemphill, Bret, Cedar Rapids†	.252	72	264	234	36	59	96	11	1	8	28	1	4	4	21	0	54	0	2	7	.410	.319
Henderson, Juan, Ced. Rapids	.229	123	453	402	61	92	112	12	1	2	28	10	2	3	36	0	79	47	12	6	.279	.296
Hernandez, Carlos, Quad City	.260	126	530	470	74	122	165	19	6	4	40	9	1	11	39	1	68	58	21	4	.351	.330
Herrick, Jason, Cedar Rapids*	.285	104	404	358	54	102	164	21	4	11	57	3	3	2	38	2	84	19	3	7	.458	.354
Hightower, Vee, Rockford†	.265	64	284	238	51	63	97	11	1	7	36	0	1	6	39	1	52	23	6	6	.408	.380
Hilt, Scott, Fort Wayne*	.185	30	105	92	13	17	27	5	1	1	15	0	0	2	11	0	28	0	0	3	.293	.286
Hinds, Collin, Wisconsin	.071	5	16	14	0	1	1	0	0	0	1	0	0	0	2	0	8	1	0	0	.071	.188
Iatarola, Aaron, Cedar Rapids*	.260	115	445	388	62	101	171	20	1	16	69	1	7	5	44	1	92	7	4	2	.441	.338
Ibarra, Jesus, Burlington†	.330	129	519	437	72	144	278	30	1	34	96	0	1	4	77	6	94	1	2	8	.636	.434
Jackson, Ryan, Kane County*	.293	132	547	471	78	138	219	39	6	10	82	0	5	4	67	7	74	13	8	9	.465	.382
Jaha, John, Beloit	.000	1	4	4	1	0	0	0	0	0	0	0	0	0	0	0	1	0	0	0	.000	.000
Johnson, Jack, Rockford	.214	24	79	70	5	15	23	2	0	2	14	0	1	0	8	2	17	0	0	1	.329	.291
Johnson, James, Clinton	.118	8	19	17	0	2	2	0	0	0	0	1	0	0	1	0	3	0	1	1	.118	.167
Jones, Ken, Clinton	.184	31	84	76	8	14	16	2	0	0	7	1	0	1	6	0	20	1	0	1	.211	.253
Jumonville, Joe, Peoria	.228	113	393	378	37	86	124	18	4	4	45	1	4	1	9	0	47	2	1	12	.328	.245
Keefe, Jamie, Clinton	.240	67	203	175	28	42	50	3	1	1	10	3	0	2	23	0	42	12	3	2	.286	.331
Keifer, Greg, Burlington	.143	6	16	14	3	2	3	1	0	0	2	0	0	0	2	0	4	1	0	0	.214	.250
Kimbler, Doug, Rockford	.286	102	401	353	69	101	174	33	2	12	67	3	2	4	39	0	61	7	3	8	.493	.362
King, Bill, West Michigan	.000	30	2	2	0	0	0	0	0	0	0	0	0	0	0	0	1	0	0	0	.000	.000
Klassen, Danny, Beloit	.275	59	241	218	27	60	85	15	2	2	25	0	3	4	16	0	43	12	4	4	.390	.332
Kominek, Toby, Beloit	.278	55	218	187	38	52	91	14	2	7	30	0	2	10	18	1	56	12	2	1	.487	.369
Koskie, Corey, Fort Wayne*	.310	123	515	462	64	143	238	37	5	16	78	1	5	9	38	3	79	2	4	10	.515	.370
Krause, Scott, Beloit	.247	134	553	481	83	119	196	30	4	13	76	3	7	12	50	5	126	24	10	7	.407	.329
Kuilan, Hector, Kane County	.000	2	7	7	0	0	0	0	0	0	0	0	0	0	0	0	1	0	0	0	.000	.000
Kurek, Chris, Michigan	.193	52	166	145	14	28	40	8	2	0	18	1	2	5	13	0	47	0	0	2	.276	.279
Lane, Ryan, Fort Wayne	.266	115	514	432	69	115	172	37	1	6	56	6	4	7	65	0	92	17	9	9	.398	.368
Lanza, Mike, Wisconsin	.204	101	365	333	28	68	89	13	1	2	29	6	2	2	22	0	67	10	5	7	.267	.256
LaValliere, Mike, South Bend	.600	2	6	5	1	3	4	1	0	0	1	0	0	0	1	0	0	0	0	0	.800	.667
Levias, Andres, South Bend†	.234	25	87	77	13	18	19	1	0	0	12	1	3	0	6	1	14	7	3	2	.247	.279
Lewis, Marc, Beloit	.152	36	103	92	14	14	21	2	1	1	5	2	0	0	9	0	16	10	3	1	.228	.228
Linares, Yfrain, Beloit	.000	20	1	1	0	0	0	0	0	0	0	0	0	0	0	0	0	0	0	0	.000	.000
Livsey, Shane, Rockford†	.283	57	250	226	39	64	82	10	1	2	27	0	0	2	22	3	30	21	7	0	.363	.352
Llanos, Victor, Peoria	.277	21	50	47	7	13	15	2	0	0	3	0	0	0	3	0	7	0	1	0	.319	.320
Logan, Chris, Clinton	.000	53	1	1	0	0	0	0	0	0	0	0	0	0	0	0	1	0	0	0	.000	.000
Lowry, Curt, Clinton	.214	57	211	182	33	39	44	1	2	0	16	0	1	1	26	1	51	7	6	2	.242	.314
Lugo, Jesus, Peoria	.265	65	234	219	26	58	79	11	2	2	29	0	0	2	12	3	31	1	1	8	.361	.304
Madsen, Dan, Rockford†	.261	29	110	88	18	23	33	6	2	0	11	0	2	6	14	0	15	14	4	6	.375	.391
Martin, Mike, Clinton*	.189	51	158	127	10	24	27	3	0	0	14	2	4	1	24	0	24	2	0	2	.213	.314
Martinez, Erik, Clinton	.102	29	64	59	4	6	6	0	0	0	2	1	0	1	3	0	10	2	0	0	.102	.152
Marval, Raul, Burlington	.267	88	316	296	42	79	94	8	2	1	19	3	1	6	10	0	32	4	6	9	.318	.304
Mathews, Byron, S. Bend†	.199	97	378	332	40	66	88	11	4	1	34	7	4	3	32	2	70	16	11	6	.265	.272
Mathis, Joe, Wisconsin*	.266	117	427	376	59	100	141	17	3	6	43	5	2	0	43	1	91	26	6	7	.375	.340
Matthews, Gary, Clinton†	.238	128	501	421	57	100	132	18	4	2	40	3	3	6	68	1	109	28	8	8	.314	.349
McCalmont, Jim, Ft. Wayne	.333	7	36	33	5	11	23	3	0	3	7	0	0	0	3	0	3	2	0	1	.697	.389
McDonald, Keith, Peoria	.268	65	213	179	22	48	57	6	0	1	20	4	0	6	22	0	38	0	1	2	.318	.354
McNally, Sean, Springfield	.271	132	528	479	60	130	210	28	8	12	79	0	6	8	35	6	119	6	3	10	.438	.322
Mealing, Al, Beloit*	.220	19	44	41	4	9	11	2	0	0	2	0	0	3	0	0	17	2	1	0	.268	.273
Medina, Alger, Rockford	.194	26	71	62	8	12	16	1	0	1	8	0	0	2	7	0	15	6	1	2	.258	.296
Melo, Juan, Clinton†	.282	134	524	479	65	135	184	32	1	5	46	5	2	5	33	0	88	12	10	11	.384	.333
Mendez, Emilio, Beloit	.059	7	19	17	1	1	1	0	0	0	0	1	0	0	1	0	9	0	0	0	.059	.111
Mendez, Rudolfo, Springfield	.276	129	500	449	70	124	204	28	11	10	72	2	7	8	34	2	121	40	10	13	.454	.333
Mendoza, Francisco, Springfield	.253	96	339	308	38	78	131	18	1	11	49	0	5	2	24	1	65	4	1	7	.425	.307
Milstien, Dave, Beloit	.327	53	226	196	47	64	84	12	1	2	21	1	0	6	23	1	15	8	4	6	.429	.413
Miranda, Alex, W. Michigan*	.232	124	479	393	53	91	140	21	2	8	60	2	4	5	75	6	78	6	8	3	.356	.356
Mitchell, Donavon, Quad City*	.329	111	422	383	72	126	163	23	1	4	42	5	3	2	29	0	38	21	15	10	.426	.376
Moeder, Tony, Cedar Rapids	.268	48	194	168	32	45	103	11	1	15	47	0	3	4	19	0	36	2	2	2	.613	.351
Molina, Ben, Cedar Rapids	.293	39	151	133	15	39	60	9	0	4	17	1	1	1	15	0	11	1	1	4	.451	.367
Molina, Luis, Wisconsin	.255	109	401	337	45	86	115	18	1	3	42	7	7	8	42	3	72	7	9	5	.341	.345
Monahan, Shane, Wisconsin	.283	59	256	233	34	66	90	9	6	1	32	7	3	2	11	0	40	9	2	4	.386	.317
Montiel, David, Beloit†	.160	74	126	100	20	16	17	1	0	0	11	4	3	8	11	0	19	19	10	0	.170	.281
Moore, Brandon, S. Bend	.257	132	573	510	75	131	146	3	0	0	37	7	5	3	48	1	49	34	8	15	.286	.322
Moriarty, Mike, Fort Wayne	.227	62	237	203	26	46	70	6	3	4	26	2	3	2	27	1	44	8	0	1	.345	.319
Morris, Gregory, Ced. Rapids	.287	103	425	355	65	102	162	18	0	14	57	0	3	6	61	4	59	8	2	6	.456	.398
Moschetti, Mike, W. Michigan	.318	8	26	22	6	7	9	2	0	0	3	1	0	0	3	0	8	1	0	0	.409	.400
Mucker, Kelcey, Ft. Wayne*	.230	109	439	405	48	93	132	16	1	7	47	1	2	4	27	1	59	12	4	8	.326	.283
Mullins, Greg, Beloit*	.000	15	1	1	0	0	0	0	0	0	0	0	0	0	0	0	0	0	0	0	.000	.000
Nelson, Bryant, Quad City†	.038	6	26	26	1	1	2	1	0	0	2	0	0	0	0	0	3	0	0	2	.077	.038
Newhan, David, W. Michigan*	.219	25	112	96	9	21	35	5	0	3	8	1	1	1	13	1	26	3	2	2	.365	.315
Newman, Damon, W. Mich.	.000	21	1	1	0	0	0	0	0	0	0	0	0	0	0	0	1	0	0	0	.000	.000
Nilsson, Dave, Beloit*	.545	3	13	11	2	6	12	3	0	1	7	0	0	0	2	0	0	0	0	0	1.091	.615
Nunez, Isaias, Peoria*	.217	120	410	378	37	82	119	19	6	2	43	1	5	1	25	1	66	1	6	4	.315	.264
Oglesby, Luke, Springfield*	.197	50	149	122	27	24	30	0	0	2	6	3	0	5	19	0	26	24	5	0	.246	.329
Olinde, Chad, Rockford*	.238	54	196	164	21	39	53	11	0	1	26	3	1	5	23	0	42	3	2	0	.323	.347
Olmstead, Nate, Ced. Rapids†	.232	59	182	155	20	36	47	3	0	1	15	2	1	2	20	1	37	1	0	7	.303	.326

Player, Team	Avg.	G	TPA	AB	R	H	TB	2B	3B	HR	RBI	SH	SF	HP	BB	IBB	SO	SB	CS	GDP	Slg.	OBP
Ortega, Randy, W. Mich.	.216	48	177	162	8	35	39	4	0	0	13	1	0	1	13	0	27	0	2	8	.241	.278
Paez, Israel, Fort Wayne	.260	113	428	388	47	101	123	12	2	2	45	3	1	1	35	1	55	12	11	8	.317	.322
Patterson, Jake, Ft. Wayne*	.264	116	484	435	56	115	190	23	5	14	68	0	5	9	35	4	118	0	2	5	.437	.329
Patton, Greg, Michigan	.248	69	263	226	34	56	96	13	0	9	27	2	2	2	31	2	58	4	3	2	.425	.341
Pearce, Jeff, Wisconsin*	.000	28	1	1	0	0	0	0	0	0	0	0	0	0	0	0	0	0	0	0	.000	.000
Pearson, Kevin, Fort Wayne	.141	29	88	78	10	11	17	1	1	1	7	1	0	3	6	0	30	1	0	2	.218	.230
Perez, Mike, Rockford	.245	39	124	106	12	26	31	3	1	0	11	2	1	2	13	0	24	3	3	5	.292	.336
Pico, Brandon, Rockford*	.300	96	428	383	59	115	162	27	4	4	47	4	3	2	34	0	53	7	7	7	.423	.358
Pierzynski, A.J., Ft. Wayne*	.310	22	87	84	10	26	39	5	1	2	14	0	1	0	2	0	10	0	0	1	.464	.322
Polanco, Placido, Peoria	.266	103	394	361	43	96	117	7	4	2	41	11	2	2	18	0	30	7	6	8	.324	.303
Poor, Jeff, Burlington	.242	101	361	322	33	78	115	23	1	4	38	2	3	7	27	1	68	1	0	9	.357	.312
Powell, Chris, Cedar Rapids*	.159	25	76	63	11	10	15	3	1	0	4	0	1	1	11	1	17	6	0	2	.238	.289
Pratt, Wes, Quad City	.227	14	51	44	5	10	19	1	1	2	10	0	0	0	7	0	11	2	0	2	.432	.333
Price, Christopher, Springfield	.264	52	186	159	22	42	60	7	1	3	14	1	1	2	23	0	32	6	2	5	.377	.362
Prieto, Alejandro, Springfield†	.251	124	491	431	61	108	129	9	3	2	44	12	2	6	40	1	69	11	7	10	.299	.322
Probst, Alan, Quad City	.258	52	167	151	23	39	74	12	1	7	27	1	1	1	13	0	28	2	0	3	.490	.319
Rajotte, Jason, W. Michigan*	.000	44	2	1	1	0	0	0	0	0	0	0	0	0	1	0	0	0	0	0	.000	.500
Ramirez, Joel, Wisconsin	.083	7	24	24	1	2	3	1	0	0	1	0	0	0	0	0	4	1	0	0	.125	.083
Ramos, Jeff, Springfield*	.219	39	111	96	14	21	41	8	0	4	20	0	5	1	9	0	25	0	0	3	.427	.279
Reid, Derek, Burlington	.285	95	393	354	74	101	163	15	4	13	55	3	1	4	31	0	55	22	4	7	.460	.349
Rennhack, Mike, Quad City†	.271	100	351	299	46	81	100	14	1	1	47	4	8	1	39	1	37	15	4	3	.334	.349
Reyes, Michael, Kane County	.189	14	45	37	8	7	10	3	0	0	4	0	0	1	7	0	11	0	2	0	.270	.333
Richardson, Eric, South Bend	.231	63	223	199	32	46	59	11	1	0	19	2	1	1	19	0	39	23	6	3	.296	.300
Rincones, Wuarnner, S. Bend	.214	20	66	56	4	12	13	1	0	0	7	0	3	1	6	0	13	0	1	0	.232	.288
Robbins, Lance, Cedar Rapids	.235	38	93	81	18	19	23	4	0	0	6	0	1	2	9	0	16	1	3	0	.284	.323
Robinson, Darek, Peoria†	.240	113	411	363	36	87	108	15	0	2	23	7	1	2	37	2	60	2	5	7	.298	.313
Robledo, Nilson, S. Bend	.285	135	587	537	71	153	243	24	3	20	108	1	16	3	30	4	100	0	2	8	.453	.317
Rocha, Juan, Springfield	.233	94	314	292	33	68	121	21	1	10	41	1	1	4	16	0	65	5	2	4	.414	.281
Rodriguez, Maximo, K.C.	.191	72	260	236	18	45	69	7	1	5	30	1	2	2	18	0	65	0	1	7	.292	.252
Rodriguez, Noel, Quad City	.311	109	422	386	48	120	180	26	5	8	71	0	4	4	28	1	49	4	5	11	.466	.360
Rodriguez, Victor, K.C.	.235	127	535	472	65	111	122	9	1	0	43	16	4	2	40	0	47	18	6	17	.258	.295
Rondon, Alex, W. Michigan	.216	25	82	74	11	16	25	3	0	2	5	0	0	1	7	0	13	1	0	2	.338	.293
Root, Mitch, Clinton	.275	89	350	309	37	85	116	20	1	3	42	0	2	2	37	1	52	3	1	8	.375	.354
Rosario, Melvin, S. Bend†	.273	118	488	450	58	123	210	30	6	15	57	1	3	4	30	7	109	1	8	0	.467	.322
Rose, Pete, South Bend*	.277	116	491	423	56	117	165	24	6	4	65	2	7	5	54	0	45	2	0	6	.390	.360
Roskos, John, Kane County	.297	114	472	418	74	124	202	36	3	12	88	0	6	6	42	1	86	2	0	6	.483	.364
Ross, Tony, Quad City	.257	107	378	339	46	87	115	11	4	3	41	2	3	3	31	0	57	21	5	4	.339	.322
Ryder, Derek, Cedar Rapids	.095	17	29	21	1	2	2	0	0	0	2	3	0	0	5	0	7	0	1	1	.095	.269
Sadler, Donnie, Michigan	.283	118	529	438	103	124	192	25	8	9	55	3	3	6	79	0	85	41	13	5	.438	.397
Salzano, Jerry, Rockford	.286	6	22	21	0	6	9	1	1	0	2	0	0	0	1	0	1	0	1	1	.429	.318
Sanchez, Marcos, Clinton†	.111	6	19	18	0	2	3	1	0	0	0	0	0	0	1	0	6	0	0	2	.167	.158
Sanchez, Victor, Quad City	.235	13	40	34	3	8	8	0	0	0	1	0	0	0	6	0	10	1	0	2	.235	.350
Sanders, Pat, W. Michigan*	.208	11	29	24	4	5	5	0	0	0	3	0	1	0	4	0	6	0	0	0	.208	.310
Santana, Jose, Quad City†	.227	88	267	229	36	52	69	10	2	1	21	4	2	8	24	0	40	6	4	7	.301	.319
Schneider, Dan, Burlington	.213	51	157	141	13	30	40	4	0	2	12	3	0	3	10	0	27	1	1	6	.284	.279
Schwenke, Matt, Clinton	.190	36	107	100	3	19	29	5	1	1	8	2	1	1	2	0	34	0	0	3	.290	.212
Smith, Dave, Michigan	.219	61	217	187	18	41	55	11	0	1	23	1	4	5	20	0	46	1	1	3	.294	.306
Smith, Demond, C.R.-W.M.†	.338	87	397	349	70	118	187	26	8	9	44	6	1	7	34	3	69	40	14	3	.536	.407
Smith, John, Beloit	.211	76	288	261	38	55	109	16	4	10	44	1	2	4	20	1	88	8	2	4	.418	.275
Smith, Matt, Springfield*	.226	117	439	412	49	93	131	18	1	6	46	1	1	1	24	4	96	8	5	11	.318	.269
Smith, Scott, Wisconsin	.327	34	122	107	13	35	58	12	1	3	17	1	1	2	11	0	21	0	1	7	.542	.397
Snook, Robert, Beloit	.000	3	8	6	0	0	0	0	0	0	0	0	0	0	2	0	3	0	0	0	.000	.250
Snyder, Jarod, Rockford	.185	24	76	65	7	12	17	2	0	1	6	1	0	4	6	0	15	0	0	1	.262	.293
Soriano, Fred, W. Michigan†	.262	107	384	305	68	80	102	7	3	3	32	18	2	8	51	1	72	40	6	0	.334	.380
Soriano, Jose, W. Michigan	.213	123	474	413	64	88	122	12	2	6	43	15	5	8	33	3	103	35	12	7	.295	.281
Sparks, Rodney, Springfield	.219	43	105	96	11	21	28	4	0	1	7	1	0	0	8	0	14	0	0	0	.292	.279
Spinello, Joe, South Bend	.214	7	16	14	2	3	3	0	0	0	1	0	0	0	2	0	3	0	0	1	.214	.313
Stasio, Chris, Michigan	.305	87	348	315	44	96	141	22	1	7	47	1	3	4	25	0	78	1	0	7	.448	.360
Sutherland, Alex, Wisconsin	.224	90	327	303	36	68	92	17	2	1	35	2	1	2	19	2	56	2	0	5	.304	.274
Swift, Scott, Burlington†	.191	68	256	209	29	40	45	3	1	0	17	5	3	0	37	0	33	9	5	4	.215	.309
Tena, Dario, Clinton†	.183	99	328	295	30	54	60	6	0	0	19	5	2	1	25	0	41	33	10	3	.203	.248
Topham, Ryan, S. Bend*	.250	14	53	48	4	12	15	3	0	0	2	1	0	0	4	0	12	0	0	0	.313	.308
Totman, Jason, Clinton	.288	61	262	229	32	66	91	19	3	0	32	1	2	4	26	0	27	6	1	2	.397	.368
Towner, Kyle, Wisconsin†	.226	104	376	301	64	68	83	12	0	1	24	5	3	4	63	1	59	34	11	1	.276	.364
Trammell, Gary, Quad City*	.298	103	378	336	44	100	124	12	3	2	33	5	3	1	33	0	62	14	8	4	.369	.359
Treanor, Matt, Springfield	.185	75	240	211	17	39	58	6	2	3	19	2	2	4	21	0	59	1	1	1	.275	.269
Truby, Chris, Quad City	.233	118	451	400	68	93	151	23	4	9	64	3	3	3	41	0	66	27	8	11	.378	.306
Tyler, Josh, Beloit	.237	77	234	186	24	44	55	5	0	2	27	7	3	2	36	0	40	3	6	4	.296	.361
Tyrus, Jason, Clinton	.226	65	173	159	15	36	49	5	1	2	17	3	0	1	10	0	53	4	5	0	.308	.276
Ullan, Dave, Clinton	.208	43	122	96	8	20	24	1	0	1	11	2	1	3	20	1	16	0	2	1	.250	.358
Valentin, Jose, Fort Wayne†	.321	112	433	383	59	123	216	26	5	19	65	1	0	2	47	7	75	0	5	7	.564	.398
Villalobos, Carlos, Wisconsin	.260	110	436	389	64	101	152	16	4	9	53	4	5	3	35	1	76	16	4	3	.391	.322
Vizcaino, Romulo, Ft. Wayne†	.248	103	387	343	44	85	109	13	4	1	22	3	5	1	35	1	56	6	6	6	.318	.315
Walker, Joe, South Bend†	.000	6	10	6	0	0	0	0	0	0	0	0	0	0	4	0	4	0	0	0	.000	.400
Walker, Steve, Rockford†	.289	103	462	415	78	120	167	24	7	3	44	0	0	10	37	3	104	40	16	1	.402	.361
Wallace, Brian, Burlington	.213	97	390	338	48	72	111	12	0	9	38	7	5	6	34	0	65	7	5	7	.328	.292
Walls, Eric, Springfield*	.227	101	322	299	53	68	90	14	1	2	21	4	0	2	17	0	65	20	7	8	.301	.274
Wambach, James, S. Bend*	.214	9	30	28	1	6	6	0	0	0	2	0	0	0	2	0	6	0	0	1	.214	.267
Ward, Turner, Beloit†	.000	2	8	5	0	0	0	0	0	0	0	0	0	0	3	0	1	0	0	0	.000	.375
Wathan, Dusty, Wisconsin†	.091	5	12	11	1	1	4	0	0	1	3	0	0	1	0	0	3	0	0	0	.364	.167
Watson, Kevin, Burlington	.186	80	271	247	29	46	74	5	1	7	25	2	1	3	18	0	88	1	2	4	.300	.249
Welch, Coby, Springfield	.171	19	40	35	3	6	6	0	0	0	1	0	0	3	2	0	9	0	0	0	.171	.275
Whatley, Gabe, Rockford*	.257	95	396	339	54	87	135	23	2	7	54	0	6	6	45	3	58	11	3	6	.398	.348

Player, Team	Avg.	G	TPA	AB	R	H	TB	2B	3B	HR	RBI	SH	SF	HP	BB	IBB	SO	SB	CS	GDP	Slg.	OBP
White, Chad, Quad City†	.244	75	289	242	36	59	73	14	0	0	18	4	2	1	37	3	35	12	4	5	.302	.344
White, Walter, Kane County	.285	63	250	207	30	59	84	18	2	1	23	5	3	3	32	0	52	3	2	3	.406	.384
Whittaker, Jay, South Bend	.220	67	259	227	29	50	85	14	3	5	31	1	2	3	26	0	58	14	5	5	.374	.306
Williams, Drew, Beloit*	.267	135	517	427	66	114	181	21	2	14	66	1	2	6	81	4	76	8	8	9	.424	.390
Wilson, Chris, Beloit	.190	28	68	63	12	12	15	1	1	0	6	0	0	2	3	0	14	5	1	0	.238	.250
Wilson, Todd, Burlington	.257	30	115	105	8	27	38	5	0	2	11	0	0	4	6	0	12	1	0	1	.362	.322
Winget, Jeremy, Clinton*	.269	120	445	375	49	101	139	23	0	5	44	1	1	1	67	3	75	4	4	7	.371	.381
Wojtkowski, Steve, Michigan*	.000	6	17	14	2	0	0	0	0	0	0	0	0	0	3	0	3	0	0	1	.000	.176
Woodard, Steve, Beloit*	.000	22	1	1	0	0	0	0	0	0	0	1	0	0	0	0	0	0	0	0	.000	.000
Wulfert, Mark, Clinton	.245	48	167	147	17	36	51	10	1	1	16	1	1	1	17	0	34	9	2	1	.347	.325
Young, Kevin, Cedar Rapids	.291	119	459	395	58	115	147	22	2	2	46	7	4	15	37	0	42	17	12	7	.372	.370
Zaletel, Brian, Burlington	.227	27	105	97	9	22	32	4	0	2	5	0	1	3	4	0	19	0	0	5	.330	.276
Zerpa, Mauro, South Bend	.221	41	95	86	5	19	20	1	0	0	5	2	0	1	6	0	20	1	0	3	.233	.280
Zwisler, Josh, Beloit	.234	98	287	252	29	59	76	12	1	1	18	2	0	4	28	1	46	8	4	4	.302	.320

GRAND SLAMS: Carone, Donati, E. Harris, Moeder, 2 each; Bautista, Delgado, Faggett, Freeman, Freire, Hacopian, Hamilton, Herrick, Jackson, Livsey, Melo, Nilsson, Pratt, Robledo, Rocha, N. Rodriguez, Sadler, J. Soriano, Towner, Truby, Watson, Whittaker, 1 each.

AWARDED FIRST BASE ON CATCHER'S INTERFERENCE: Clifford 5 (Amezcua, Andreopoulos, Coe, Fortin, Welch); Andreopoulos 3 (Cline, Hilt, Valentin); C. White 3 (Valentin 3); Coe 2 (Ballara, Cline); Harvey 2 (Ballara, Cline); McDonald 2 (Espiritu, Roskos); Olmstead 2 (Rosario, Zwisler); Pico 2 (Schneider, Sutherland); Swift 2 (Cline, Rosario); Cady (Poor); J. Cook (DePastino); Fortin (B. Molina); Gibralter (Cline); Kominek (M. Rodriguez); Lowry (Valentin); Lugo (Rosario); Mathis (Valentin); Richardson (Ortega); Robinson (Rosario); M. Rodriguez (Barton); V. Rodriguez (Encarnacion); Schwenke (Campillo); Swift (Cline); Truby (Sutherland); Young (Cline); Zwisler (Cline).

PLAYERS WITH TWO OR MORE TEAMS

Player, Team	Avg.	G	TPA	AB	R	H	TB	2B	3B	HR	RBI	SH	SF	HP	BB	IBB	SO	SB	CS	GDP	Slg.	OBP
Delgado, Wilson, Wisconsin†	.243	19	75	70	13	17	20	3	0	0	7	2	0	0	3	0	15	3	0	5	.286	.274
Delgado, Wilson, Burlington†	.310	93	402	365	52	113	154	20	3	5	37	2	1	2	32	1	57	9	9	7	.422	.368
Smith, Demond, Cedar Rapids†	.341	79	361	317	64	108	168	25	7	7	41	5	1	6	32	2	61	37	12	3	.530	.410
Smith, Demond, West Michigan†	.313	8	36	32	6	10	19	1	1	2	3	1	0	1	2	1	8	3	2	0	.594	.371

1995 PITCHING

TEAM

Team	W	L	Pct.	ERA	G	CG	ShO	Sv.	IP	H	TBF	R	ER	HR	SH	SF	HB	BB	IBB	SO	WP	Bk.
Quad City	76	61	.555	3.19	137	7	11	35	1166.1	1011	4930	533	414	73	38	31	59	427	11	922	63	10
Wisconsin	63	75	.457	3.75	138	14	8	35	1180.0	1055	5062	599	492	74	36	36	60	501	28	917	82	13
South Bend	66	69	.489	3.76	135	13	8	27	1183.2	1169	5119	620	495	74	55	40	71	459	6	843	87	30
Peoria	62	72	.463	3.80	134	6	9	36	1131.0	1039	4864	605	478	72	41	33	39	466	6	937	55	15
Beloit	88	51	.633	3.93	139	8	9	49	1195.2	1114	5142	618	522	83	40	35	59	503	12	1064	89	28
West Michigan	67	69	.493	3.95	136	1	9	36	1174.2	1146	5209	664	515	62	36	30	81	550	11	893	83	26
Fort Wayne	75	65	.536	4.03	140	4	8	41	1236.1	1187	5365	660	554	83	50	42	74	515	13	1029	120	20
Michigan	75	63	.543	4.05	138	9	5	31	1208.2	1130	5227	665	544	81	50	55	71	502	13	975	82	13
Cedar Rapids	76	62	.551	4.08	138	16	6	40	1184.2	1184	5160	655	534	79	48	31	4	425	23	907	81	21
Rockford	75	65	.536	4.12	140	4	5	29	1201.0	1136	5226	663	550	76	36	52	73	508	8	829	123	16
Kane County	69	69	.500	4.20	138	5	8	26	1181.2	1168	5230	668	551	79	49	41	99	495	28	879	87	10
Springfield	65	74	.468	4.32	139	4	5	22	1175.1	1248	5161	680	564	103	41	45	54	429	3	729	95	7
Clinton	51	86	.372	4.32	137	19	4	25	1129.0	1146	5035	690	542	70	44	38	71	504	43	865	93	17
Burlington	54	81	.400	4.45	135	6	4	35	1103.0	1112	4972	710	545	95	42	45	56	597	38	898	114	13

INDIVIDUAL

TOP QUALIFIERS FOR EARNED-RUN AVERAGE TITLE

Minimum 112 innings. *Lefthanded pitcher.

Pitcher, Team	W	L	Pct.	ERA	G	GS	CG	ShO	GF	Sv.	IP	H	TBF	R	ER	HR	SH	SF	HB	BB	IBB	SO	WP	Bk.
Corrigan, Cory, Peoria	4	7	.364	2.32	47	10	0	0	5	0	112.2	90	450	36	29	3	5	5	2	23	0	84	4	1
D'Amico, Jeff, Beloit	13	3	.813	2.39	21	20	3	1	0	0	132.0	102	523	40	35	7	3	2	4	31	2	119	6	1
Mounce, Tony, Quad City*	16	8	.667	2.43	25	25	3	1	0	0	159.0	118	649	55	43	6	6	6	3	57	2	143	6	2
Smith, Charles, South Bend	10	10	.500	2.69	26	25	4	2	1	0	167.0	128	688	70	50	8	7	2	16	61	0	145	21	14
Walters, Brett, Clinton	8	7	.533	2.71	32	19	4	0	4	1	146.0	133	598	58	44	9	6	1	10	27	3	122	4	2
Dickson, Jason, Cedar Rapids	14	6	.700	2.86	25	25	9	1	0	0	173.0	151	708	71	55	12	4	3	8	45	0	134	7	2
Dale, Carl, Peoria	9	9	.500	2.94	24	24	2	1	0	0	143.2	124	613	66	47	8	3	2	1	62	0	104	4	1
Kester, Tim, Quad City	12	5	.706	2.97	28	23	2	0	3	0	160.2	158	665	80	53	8	5	6	10	20	1	111	4	0
Bieniasz, Derek, Wisconsin	11	10	.524	3.13	27	27	4	2	0	0	175.1	145	717	76	61	7	8	6	10	54	3	99	4	3
Cloude, Ken, Wisconsin	9	8	.529	3.24	25	25	4	0	0	0	161.0	137	677	64	58	8	1	7	8	63	4	140	10	1
Parisi, Michael, Kane County*	9	8	.529	3.29	26	26	2	1	0	0	164.1	152	687	73	60	7	2	6	9	42	1	113	11	0
Bigham, Dave, South Bend*	8	7	.533	3.29	25	23	1	1	1	0	153.0	176	651	62	56	9	10	5	11	35	0	101	10	2
King, Bill, West Michigan	9	7	.563	3.34	30	18	0	0	3	2	148.1	152	633	75	55	6	5	1	5	41	0	95	6	5
Isom, Jeff, Clinton*	8	8	.500	3.40	35	15	2	1	8	2	116.1	123	501	56	44	7	7	5	6	42	5	94	5	1
Tollberg, Brian, Beloit	13	4	.765	3.41	22	22	1	1	0	0	132.0	119	529	59	50	10	2	5	6	27	0	110	5	4

DEPARTMENTAL LEADERS: W—Mounce, 16; L—Lock, 15; Pct.—D'Amico, .813; G—Reed, 63; GS—Several pitchers tied with 27; CG—Dickson, 9; ShO—C. Beck, Bieniasz, Raggio, C. Smith, 2; GF—Rain, 51; Sv.—Welch, 31; IP—Al. Garcia, 177.0; H—R. Smith, 179; TBF—Al. Garcia, 755; R—R. Smith, 100; ER—R. Smith, 89; HR—Mercado, 18; SH—Bigham, 10; SF—Barksdale, Faulkner, 9; HB—Al. Garcia, 15; BB—Miranda, 88; IBB—B. Smith, 7; SO—C. Smith, 145; WP—Mix, 29; Bk.—C. Smith, 11.

ALL PITCHERS

*Lefthanded pitcher.

Pitcher, Team	W	L	Pct.	ERA	G	GS	CG	ShO	GF	Sv.	IP	H	TBF	R	ER	HR	SH	SF	HB	BB	IBB	SO	WP	Bk.
Abreu, Jose, Burlington	1	0	1.000	3.46	8	0	0	0	1	0	13.0	9	61	8	5	0	1	1	1	12	0	14	0	2
Abreu, Juan, Burlington*	0	0	.000	0.00	2	0	0	0	1	0	2.0	1	11	3	0	0	0	1	0	4	1	0	0	0
Aguirre, Jose, Cedar Rapids*	0	0	.000	3.86	6	2	0	0	0	0	14.0	12	61	6	6	1	0	1	0	10	0	12	2	0
Alejo, Nigel, Kane County	4	1	.800	2.39	48	0	0	0	38	7	52.2	48	233	17	14	5	2	0	2	25	2	47	5	0
Ali, Sam, Burlington	0	0	.000	2.25	3	0	0	0	2	0	4.0	4	16	1	1	0	0	0	0	0	0	2	0	0
Altman, Heath, Burlington	0	0	.000	2.45	3	0	0	0	1	0	3.2	3	20	2	1	0	0	0	0	6	0	5	1	0
Alvarado, Luis, Fort Wayne	1	1	.500	2.92	16	1	0	0	6	2	37.0	41	165	18	12	2	0	1	1	14	1	24	1	0
Alvarez, Ivan, Burlington*	1	2	.333	4.85	4	2	0	0	0	0	13.0	17	59	12	7	2	1	0	0	5	0	12	3	0
Ambrose, John, South Bend	1	1	.500	5.40	3	3	1	0	0	0	16.2	18	77	13	10	2	1	0	0	10	0	15	2	0
Andersen, Mark, Kane County	1	2	.333	3.46	15	0	0	0	5	1	26.0	29	116	13	10	3	1	1	1	13	1	15	2	0
Anderson, Eric, Springfield	9	5	.643	3.40	21	14	1	1	2	1	92.2	89	391	39	35	4	0	2	4	34	1	52	8	0
Bair, Dennis, Rockford	4	2	.667	1.51	9	7	0	1	0	0	53.2	41	209	10	9	2	1	1	1	6	0	40	4	1
Barker, Richard, Rockford	2	0	1.000	3.71	32	0	0	0	15	1	43.2	45	196	20	18	2	1	0	2	20	1	23	5	0
Barksdale, Joe, Michigan	9	8	.529	4.53	24	24	1	0	0	0	141.0	139	643	91	71	7	6	9	14	78	1	93	11	3
Baron, Jim, Clinton*	0	8	.000	6.22	11	9	1	0	1	0	50.2	65	232	42	35	4	3	2	1	16	2	31	4	0
Barrios, Manuel, Quad City	1	5	.167	2.25	50	0	0	0	48	23	52.0	44	219	16	13	1	2	1	4	17	1	55	1	0
Beck, Chris, Wisconsin	12	8	.600	3.88	28	19	2	2	6	2	130.0	113	553	62	56	13	3	3	4	61	2	119	10	1
Beck, Greg, Beloit	5	2	.714	4.72	35	5	0	0	12	2	74.1	73	331	46	39	2	1	6	2	35	2	91	7	2
Bedinger, Doug, Fort Wayne	6	6	.500	4.61	46	0	0	0	35	9	66.1	74	301	37	34	8	7	5	4	28	3	62	5	0
Bell, Jason, Fort Wayne	3	1	.750	1.31	9	6	0	0	2	0	34.1	26	139	11	5	0	3	0	1	6	0	40	6	2
Bernal, Manuel, Springfield	1	5	.167	7.38	8	8	0	0	0	0	42.2	55	193	37	35	9	1	0	3	9	0	17	1	0
Betances, Junior, Beloit	0	0	.000	0.00	1	0	0	0	1	0	0.1	1	2	0	0	0	0	0	0	0	0	0	0	1
Betti, Rich, Michigan*	0	0	.000	0.00	1	0	0	0	0	0	2.0	0	7	0	0	0	0	0	0	1	0	1	0	0
Beverlin, Jason, West Michigan	3	9	.250	4.04	22	14	0	0	1	0	89.0	76	392	51	40	4	3	3	8	40	1	84	5	5
Bieniasz, Derek, Wisconsin	11	10	.524	3.13	27	27	4	2	0	0	175.1	145	717	76	61	7	8	6	10	54	3	99	4	3
Bigham, Dave, South Bend*	8	7	.533	3.29	25	23	1	1	1	0	153.0	176	651	62	56	9	10	5	11	35	0	101	10	2
Blais, Mike, Michigan	2	1	.667	1.96	32	0	0	0	26	10	46.0	34	184	12	10	0	3	4	1	11	3	35	4	0
Blanco, Alberto, Quad City*	3	3	.500	3.13	11	11	1	1	0	0	54.2	47	231	22	19	2	0	3	1	19	0	58	3	0
Bogle, Sean, Rockford	1	0	1.000	1.21	13	0	0	0	3	0	22.1	17	84	3	3	0	2	1	0	9	0	15	1	0
Bonilla, Welnis, Michigan	1	1	.500	6.17	12	0	0	0	8	1	11.2	12	58	12	8	1	1	0	1	10	0	7	0	1
Brewer, Billy, Springfield*	0	0	.000	0.00	1	0	0	0	1	1	2.0	2	9	1	0	0	0	0	1	0	2	0	0	
Brixey, Dustin, Springfield	4	5	.444	3.79	36	8	0	0	6	2	102.0	101	438	51	43	3	6	7	40	0	44	6	0	
Bronkey, Jeff, Beloit	0	1	.000	3.68	3	3	0	0	0	0	7.1	5	32	5	3	1	0	0	1	3	0	8	1	0
Broome, Curtis, South Bend	5	8	.385	4.48	29	4	1	0	10	1	90.1	101	399	53	45	9	3	2	3	39	0	62	5	1
Bryant, Chris, Rockford*	2	2	.500	6.43	21	0	0	0	9	0	35.0	32	152	26	25	5	0	1	3	17	1	29	3	0
Burt, Chris, Beloit	1	3	.250	3.80	36	0	0	0	32	27	42.2	34	176	19	18	2	4	2	1	17	1	42	2	0
Bush, Craig, Michigan	7	3	.700	3.82	34	2	0	0	18	6	75.1	68	320	37	32	8	2	3	0	30	0	78	4	0
Bushart, John, Cedar Rapids*	2	2	.500	7.36	19	3	0	0	7	0	36.2	47	179	34	30	6	0	0	4	17	0	24	3	0
Bussa, Todd, Kane County	0	1	.000	0.86	36	0	0	0	33	14	42.0	20	162	4	4	1	1	6	15	5	38	3	0	
Byrne, Earl, Rockford*	4	3	.571	4.65	13	11	0	0	0	0	60.0	54	269	36	31	2	3	6	3	38	0	51	8	1
Cardona, Isbell, Burlington	0	4	.000	7.00	6	4	0	0	0	0	18.0	19	94	21	14	4	1	2	1	20	1	12	2	1
Carl, Todd, Kane County	0	5	.000	8.54	12	7	0	0	2	0	39.0	69	192	37	37	8	0	1	5	11	0	22	7	0
Carroll, David, Peoria*	2	2	.500	4.38	24	6	0	0	5	0	51.1	53	230	33	25	3	2	0	3	24	0	41	6	1
Carter, Lance, Springfield	9	5	.643	3.99	27	24	1	1	0	0	137.2	151	584	77	61	14	2	4	8	22	0	118	11	1
Casey, Ryan, Rockford	0	2	.000	6.05	16	0	0	0	8	1	19.1	19	89	15	13	1	1	1	1	11	0	12	3	1
Castro, Dennis, Kane County	0	0	.000	0.00	1	0	0	0	1	0	1.0	2	7	1	0	0	0	0	0	1	0	0	0	0
Chapman, Walker, Fort Wayne	2	6	.250	6.24	14	11	0	0	2	1	53.1	59	249	41	37	4	2	3	2	36	0	31	3	1
Charlton, Aaron, Burlington	0	1	.000	4.13	16	0	0	0	6	0	24.0	18	105	13	11	2	0	1	4	13	0	16	4	0
Cintron, Jose, Cedar Rapids	5	3	.625	3.84	13	9	1	1	0	0	68.0	65	280	36	29	4	2	2	9	0	38	2	1	
Cloude, Ken, Wisconsin	9	8	.529	3.24	25	25	4	0	0	0	161.0	137	677	64	58	8	1	7	8	63	4	140	10	1
Cobb, Trevor, Fort Wayne*	4	4	.500	3.88	11	10	0	0	0	0	53.1	51	226	26	23	3	1	0	3	18	0	46	6	0
Cochrane, Chris, West Michigan	6	4	.600	3.07	41	4	0	0	29	9	85.0	79	357	37	29	7	4	1	5	28	3	48	3	1
Cook, Jake, Michigan	5	3	.625	4.83	21	11	1	0	3	0	76.1	68	333	48	41	3	5	1	2	39	0	50	12	2
Corrigan, Cory, Peoria	4	7	.364	2.32	47	10	0	0	5	0	112.2	90	450	36	29	3	5	5	2	23	0	84	4	1
Crossley, Chad, Cedar Rapids	0	0	.000	7.71	12	0	0	0	7	1	16.1	18	85	16	14	2	2	2	8	15	0	9	5	1
Crump, Jody, Peoria*	1	1	.500	6.19	25	0	0	0	7	0	36.1	40	167	25	25	3	1	1	0	26	0	16	3	1
Curran, Tighe, Peoria*	3	0	1.000	2.90	24	0	0	0	7	0	40.1	35	174	18	13	0	2	0	2	21	0	21	2	1
Dafun, George, Cedar Rapids	0	1	.000	3.27	5	1	0	0	2	0	11.0	15	56	5	4	1	0	1	0	10	1	13	1	0
Dale, Carl, Peoria	9	9	.500	2.94	24	24	2	1	0	0	143.2	124	613	66	47	8	3	2	1	62	0	104	4	1
Dalton, Brian, Beloit	4	3	.571	2.74	34	4	0	0	13	4	82.0	70	345	31	25	0	4	2	2	44	0	75	5	4
D'Amico, Jeff, Beloit	13	3	.813	2.39	21	20	3	1	0	0	132.0	102	523	40	35	7	3	2	4	31	2	119	6	1
Daniels, John, Wisconsin	4	5	.444	2.66	39	0	0	0	19	7	74.1	63	315	28	22	5	0	2	6	22	2	60	2	0
Davalillo, David, Cedar Rapids	0	0	.000	0.00	1	0	0	0	1	0	2.0	0	7	0	0	0	0	0	0	1	0	3	0	1
Davis, Keith, Clinton	2	5	.286	5.22	36	8	0	0	15	2	70.2	64	313	41	41	2	0	5	3	45	0	54	7	1
Deakman, Josh, Cedar Rapids	4	2	.667	3.59	13	13	0	0	0	0	72.2	67	301	33	29	5	3	2	7	24	0	53	5	0
Dean, Mark, Peoria	0	0	.000	0.00	2	0	0	0	2	0	2.0	0	7	0	0	0	0	0	0	1	0	1	0	0
Delvalle, Henry, West Michigan*	1	1	.500	3.38	3	0	0	0	0	0	5.1	4	24	4	2	0	0	0	0	4	0	8	1	0
Dennis, Brian, Rockford	0	0	.000	3.60	3	0	0	0	2	1	5.0	6	21	2	2	0	0	0	0	4	0	4	0	0
Dennis, Shane, Clinton*	3	9	.250	3.87	14	14	3	0	0	0	86.0	68	364	51	37	5	4	0	2	35	3	80	5	0
DeWitt, Scott, Kane County*	0	0	.000	0.00	1	0	0	0	1	0	3.0	10	0	0	0	0	0	0	1	0	2	0	0	
Dickson, Jason, Cedar Rapids	14	6	.700	2.86	25	25	9	1	0	0	173.0	151	708	71	55	12	4	3	8	45	0	134	7	2
Diorio, Mike, Quad City	6	4	.600	3.24	33	11	0	0	4	1	91.2	82	391	39	33	6	4	0	4	36	1	81	13	2
Dixon, Jim, South Bend	1	2	.333	4.86	10	1	0	0	6	0	16.2	25	81	16	9	2	1	1	3	4	1	11	3	1
Domenico, Brian, Michigan	0	2	.000	2.89	6	1	0	0	1	0	9.1	11	48	12	3	3	3	0	0	11	1	5	0	0
Doughty, Brian, Wisconsin	5	7	.417	3.95	32	3	0	0	12	4	84.1	83	360	50	37	4	8	6	26	3	54	5	0	
Dowhower, Deron, Fort Wayne*	3	0	1.000	3.27	35	0	0	0	13	5	77.0	53	331	32	28	4	4	4	49	0	97	13	0	
Droll, Jeff, South Bend	0	1	.000	3.21	8	0	0	0	4	1	14.0	25	72	11	5	0	0	1	4	1	9	0	0	
Duncan, Sean, South Bend*	0	0	.000	0.79	12	0	0	0	7	0	11.1	8	44	2	1	0	0	0	3	0	8	0	0	
Dutch, John, Michigan	2	4	.333	7.94	32	0	0	0	16	1	51.0	80	257	50	45	5	3	6	3	20	1	23	3	1
Elarton, Scott, Quad City	13	7	.650	4.45	26	26	0	0	0	0	149.2	149	668	86	74	12	8	4	8	71	2	112	12	0

Pitcher, Team	W	L	Pct.	ERA	G	GS	CG	ShO	GF	Sv.	IP	H	TBF	R	ER	HR	SH	SF	HB	BB	IBB	SO	WP	Bk.
Epstein, Ian, West Michigan*	5	0	1.000	5.89	18	0	0	0	7	0	18.1	24	89	14	12	2	1	1	2	10	0	16	3	0
Erdos, Todd, Clinton	0	0	.000	5.40	5	1	0	0	1	0	5.0	4	27	4	3	0	0	0	0	8	1	1	2	0
Estes, Shawn, Wis.-Bur.*	0	0	.000	2.84	6	6	0	0	0	0	25.1	18	110	9	8	2	0	1	2	17	0	33	4	1
Farmer, Jon, Kane County*	1	4	.200	6.98	29	11	0	0	4	0	78.2	97	369	65	61	9	1	5	8	32	1	60	7	2
Farrell, Jim, Michigan	3	2	.600	3.65	13	13	1	0	0	0	69.0	62	291	34	28	10	1	1	5	23	0	70	3	1
Faulkner, Neal, Rockford	2	3	.400	3.90	40	0	0	0	17	1	67.0	61	290	36	29	3	3	9	3	29	1	47	10	1
Felix, Ruben, Beloit*	4	3	.571	5.40	45	0	0	0	9	0	48.1	49	233	33	29	6	5	1	2	36	2	60	4	1
Fennell, Barry, Rockford*	2	1	.667	2.35	4	4	0	0	0	0	23.0	19	94	8	6	2	0	2	1	8	0	13	1	1
Fidge, Darren, Fort Wayne	6	5	.545	3.68	39	17	1	0	20	13	134.1	126	572	62	55	11	4	2	9	37	1	106	15	1
Filbeck, Ryan, Kane County	5	0	1.000	3.67	25	0	0	0	6	1	41.2	40	182	19	17	0	2	3	3	17	3	28	7	0
Fitzpatrick, Kenneth, Springfield	2	2	.500	3.92	12	7	0	0	1	0	43.2	36	187	26	19	3	1	1	1	17	0	29	4	1
Fitzpatrick, Will, Beloit	0	0	.000	2.45	3	0	0	0	3	0	3.2	3	17	1	1	1	0	0	1	2	0	2	0	0
Fletcher, Paul, South Bend*	4	4	.500	2.98	36	0	0	0	24	5	57.1	55	250	21	19	2	5	1	3	24	1	49	5	1
Flury, Pat, Springfield	2	6	.250	4.31	34	0	0	0	19	1	54.1	65	246	32	26	5	4	1	1	24	0	35	2	0
Foderaro, Kevin, Peoria	3	8	.273	6.20	15	14	0	0	0	0	69.2	80	316	58	48	4	3	5	1	24	1	36	3	0
Freehill, Michael, Cedar Rapids	4	5	.444	2.62	54	0	0	0	49	28	55.0	54	234	25	16	4	3	0	7	12	5	47	10	1
Gamboa, Javier, Springfield	6	6	.500	3.15	19	19	1	0	0	0	105.2	83	429	45	37	10	3	2	0	32	0	66	4	0
Garcia, Alfredo, Rockford	14	9	.609	3.76	27	27	1	1	0	0	177.0	176	755	94	74	13	4	4	15	43	0	120	10	0
Garcia, Ariel, South Bend	4	2	.667	3.14	10	10	0	0	0	0	57.1	54	246	23	20	3	3	2	8	19	0	46	4	2
Garrett, Hal, Clinton	3	8	.273	5.59	11	11	1	0	0	0	58.0	58	268	43	36	4	5	2	4	34	3	41	5	0
Gates, Sean, Clinton	0	2	.000	4.99	29	0	0	0	12	1	39.2	39	178	23	22	3	2	2	5	19	3	27	1	0
Gautreau, Mike, Peoria	4	3	.571	4.55	45	0	0	0	9	0	63.1	62	278	42	32	3	3	1	2	29	1	55	2	2
Gomez, Augustine, S. Bend	7	6	.538	4.13	25	25	1	0	0	0	144.0	120	615	85	66	7	4	7	8	68	0	99	9	6
Gomez, Dennys, Burlington	1	1	.500	3.74	14	0	0	0	9	0	21.2	25	97	11	9	2	1	0	0	11	1	26	6	0
Gonzalez, Gabe, Kane County*	4	4	.500	2.28	32	0	0	0	10	1	43.1	32	181	18	11	0	2	1	2	14	2	41	1	0
Gonzalez, Geremis, Rockford	4	4	.500	5.10	12	12	1	0	0	0	65.1	63	297	43	37	4	1	4	8	28	0	36	8	1
Gonzalez, Juan, Beloit	11	5	.688	4.16	42	6	0	0	17	6	88.2	86	386	50	41	4	3	4	6	37	1	53	16	0
Gooda, David, Beloit*	0	0	.000	3.77	3	3	0	0	0	0	14.1	13	61	8	6	1	1	0	1	7	0	9	0	0
Gould, Clint, Wisconsin	0	0	.000	5.77	25	0	0	0	15	0	34.1	34	164	24	22	4	1	0	2	28	1	20	1	0
Gourdin, Tom, Fort Wayne	6	6	.500	4.42	41	0	0	0	19	6	89.2	90	384	49	44	10	3	3	9	32	0	74	11	2
Green, Chris, Wisconsin	1	5	.167	3.67	35	0	0	0	18	2	56.1	55	244	31	23	3	3	3	5	21	6	43	3	3
Grenert, Geoff, Cedar Rapids	3	4	.429	4.13	27	4	0	0	7	1	72.0	76	319	43	33	4	1	4	9	23	1	55	3	1
Grote, Jason, Burlington	0	1	.000	9.35	6	0	0	0	2	1	8.2	10	41	10	9	2	0	0	2	5	0	5	1	0
Gunderson, Mike, Quad City	3	2	.600	2.74	44	0	0	0	10	1	65.2	46	270	25	20	1	0	0	5	27	0	48	4	2
Gunther, Kevin, W. Michigan	1	3	.250	3.71	17	0	0	0	7	2	26.2	28	117	16	11	1	0	2	2	3	1	17	2	1
Halama, John, Quad City*	1	2	.333	2.02	55	0	0	0	26	2	62.1	48	241	16	14	7	2	1	3	22	1	56	1	0
Hale, Chad, Michigan*	6	3	.667	2.48	42	0	0	0	14	2	69.0	68	280	27	19	4	2	5	2	13	1	49	3	0
Hall, Billy, Quad City	4	2	.667	2.15	36	0	0	0	20	7	50.1	29	199	18	12	3	0	0	2	18	2	36	3	1
Hall, Yates, Peoria	2	5	.286	4.53	9	8	0	0	0	0	45.2	45	197	25	23	4	0	1	0	24	0	47	5	0
Hammerschmidt, Andy, Clinton*	5	5	.500	3.87	14	14	1	0	0	0	86.0	89	355	40	37	7	3	3	6	18	2	51	0	2
Hause, Brendan, W. Michigan*	8	7	.533	3.87	31	18	0	0	4	0	137.1	136	595	75	59	10	5	5	4	57	0	106	6	0
Hebbert, Allan, Kane County	0	1	.000	12.38	5	2	0	0	2	0	8.0	9	46	12	11	1	0	1	2	15	0	3	2	0
Herbert, Russell, South Bend	2	4	.333	3.52	9	9	0	0	0	0	53.2	46	224	25	21	3	1	0	3	27	0	48	1	2
Hernandez, Santos, Burlington	5	8	.385	2.66	44	0	0	0	28	9	64.1	54	274	27	19	3	4	4	2	20	2	85	1	0
Hill, Jason, Cedar Rapids*	2	1	.667	4.55	48	0	0	0	17	2	59.1	59	276	38	30	4	8	1	5	41	6	49	2	1
Huntsman, Scott, Beloit	4	3	.571	2.72	43	0	0	0	14	1	49.2	42	229	17	15	3	2	1	5	34	2	49	5	0
Hutzler, Jeff, Burlington	3	5	.375	3.48	9	9	0	0	0	0	51.2	51	223	34	20	4	3	2	2	17	1	44	4	1
Ignasiak, Mike, Beloit	0	0	.000	0.00	1	1	0	0	0	0	3.0	0	11	0	0	0	0	0	0	2	0	4	0	0
Isom, Jeff, Clinton*	8	8	.500	3.40	35	15	2	1	8	2	116.1	123	501	56	44	7	7	5	6	42	5	94	5	1
Jenkins, A.J., Clinton	1	12	.077	6.60	33	13	2	0	5	0	91.1	109	437	80	67	10	3	6	5	55	5	54	10	0
Johnson, Ron, Peoria*	5	7	.417	3.17	22	19	0	0	0	0	102.1	105	449	56	36	9	4	4	4	36	0	61	1	0
Jones, Scott, Michigan	2	0	1.000	5.68	5	0	0	0	3	0	6.1	3	31	5	4	2	0	0	0	8	0	13	2	0
Keith, Jeffrey, Burlington*	1	3	.250	2.98	47	0	0	0	38	23	66.1	35	275	26	22	1	4	3	6	42	4	74	4	0
Kester, Tim, Quad City	12	5	.706	2.97	28	23	2	0	3	0	160.2	158	665	80	53	8	5	6	10	20	1	111	4	0
Khoury, Tony, Rockford	2	2	.500	4.60	28	1	0	0	13	0	45.0	49	213	37	23	4	2	2	5	26	1	38	6	0
King, Bill, West Michigan	9	7	.563	3.34	30	18	0	0	3	2	148.1	152	633	75	55	6	5	1	5	41	0	95	6	5
Knox, Jeffery, Cedar Rapids	7	6	.538	4.92	25	17	0	0	1	0	108.0	125	479	69	59	4	4	3	13	24	0	56	6	6
Krause, Kevin, Rockford	6	7	.462	3.81	30	13	0	0	5	0	99.1	96	431	53	42	7	2	1	5	41	0	58	10	1
Krueger, Robert, Wisconsin*	0	0	.000	4.50	19	0	0	0	5	0	22.0	21	99	12	11	0	0	0	2	11	0	20	4	0
Kurek, Chris, Michigan	0	0	.000	9.00	1	0	0	0	1	0	1.0	1	4	1	1	1	0	0	0	0	0	0	0	0
Lake, Kevin, Burlington*	10	7	.588	4.45	28	21	0	0	2	0	119.1	136	544	75	59	10	2	3	6	61	3	85	9	0
Leach, Jumaane, Clinton*	1	3	.250	3.71	19	0	0	0	7	0	26.2	30	123	17	11	1	1	0	2	7	2	12	2	0
Leibee, Skye, West Michigan*	0	1	.000	11.74	9	0	0	0	1	0	7.2	9	48	13	10	0	0	1	3	13	0	5	2	0
Leiber, Zane, South Bend	0	0	.000	6.91	14	0	0	0	8	1	28.2	35	134	26	22	3	1	1	2	9	0	21	2	3
Linares, Yfrain, Beloit	3	3	.500	4.29	19	12	0	0	3	0	71.1	75	324	42	34	2	1	3	5	43	0	63	5	3
Lindemann, Wayne, S. Bend	0	4	.000	7.36	7	6	0	0	1	0	22.0	32	117	21	18	5	1	1	2	16	0	15	0	0
Lintern, Cory, Burlington	1	0	1.000	6.00	8	0	0	0	4	0	15.0	19	67	10	10	4	1	0	1	5	1	8	1	0
Lock, Dan, Quad City*	8	15	.348	4.15	27	27	1	0	0	0	143.0	152	642	94	66	13	8	4	10	58	0	90	5	0
Logan, Chris, Clinton	4	6	.400	2.18	53	0	0	0	42	17	62.0	62	284	29	15	0	1	0	2	27	4	61	7	0
Lowe, Jason, West Michigan	0	0	.000	11.00	7	0	0	0	4	0	9.0	17	50	14	11	4	0	0	0	6	0	7	2	0
Lundquist, David, South Bend	8	4	.667	3.58	18	18	5	1	0	0	118.0	107	492	54	47	4	7	3	5	38	0	60	3	0
MacDonald, Mike, Springfield	6	5	.545	3.30	55	0	0	0	48	12	62.2	49	261	24	23	8	4	2	3	27	0	49	3	1
Mamott, Joe, Michigan	3	6	.333	5.96	14	13	1	0	0	0	77.0	76	352	56	51	4	1	7	8	50	0	66	5	3
Marquez, Ihosvany, Michigan	1	0	1.000	7.71	3	0	0	0	0	0	4.2	3	21	4	4	0	0	0	0	4	0	7	0	0
Martinez, Javier, Rockford	6	6	.500	3.96	18	18	1	0	0	0	104.2	100	455	56	46	6	5	4	12	39	0	53	15	2
Martinez, Uriel, Clinton	0	0	.000	5.19	11	0	0	0	2	0	17.1	27	84	15	10	2	0	1	0	3	0	8	5	2
May, Scott, Rockford	3	0	1.000	1.71	8	3	0	0	0	0	26.1	20	108	7	5	0	1	0	1	9	0	24	0	0
Mays, Marcus, Kane County*	1	2	.333	6.17	8	0	0	0	5	0	11.2	15	56	8	8	1	2	0	0	7	1	6	1	0
McCormack, Andy, South Bend*	1	2	.333	4.63	6	4	0	0	2	0	23.1	26	105	14	12	3	2	1	1	11	0	10	1	0
McMillan, Leonard, Burlington	1	0	1.000	5.27	8	0	0	0	1	0	13.2	15	65	8	8	2	0	0	1	10	1	4	3	0
McMullen, Mike, Burlington	4	10	.286	5.49	29	11	2	0	6	0	83.2	98	410	76	51	5	2	4	9	54	3	53	9	2
Meadows, Brian, Kane County	9	9	.500	4.22	26	26	1	1	0	0	147.0	163	646	90	69	11	8	4	12	41	0	103	3	2
Mercado, Gabby, Beloit	11	6	.647	5.36	24	23	0	0	1	0	129.1	138	565	89	77	18	3	3	5	50	1	89	6	3

Pitcher, Team	W	L	Pct.	ERA	G	GS	CG	ShO	GF	Sv.	IP	H	TBF	R	ER	HR	SH	SF	HB	BB	IBB	SO	WP	Bk.
Meyhoff, Jason, Fort Wayne*	2	1	.667	6.59	17	10	0	0	3	0	54.2	70	258	52	40	5	1	5	2	30	0	35	5	3
Micknich, Steve, Kane County	1	0	1.000	2.31	9	0	0	0	3	0	11.2	13	58	3	3	0	0	1	4	6	0	10	4	1
Miles, Chad, Kane County*	1	1	.500	7.24	19	0	0	0	4	0	27.1	35	145	33	22	3	4	4	4	23	1	14	2	1
Miranda, Walter, Kane County	8	7	.533	4.08	25	25	1	0	0	0	128.0	102	562	68	58	9	7	4	9	88	2	106	11	2
Mitchell, Alvin, Michigan	6	8	.429	5.31	30	17	0	0	4	1	115.1	120	513	75	68	9	7	8	7	64	1	74	10	1
Mix, Derek, Clinton	1	0	1.000	5.14	35	0	0	0	18	1	49.0	34	247	42	28	1	2	3	12	54	2	40	29	0
Montelongo, Joseph, Rockford	10	7	.588	4.26	20	20	1	0	0	0	118.1	109	512	62	56	8	4	5	6	49	0	82	8	1
Morgan, Eric, Wisconsin	0	0	.000	1.35	7	0	0	0	4	1	13.1	5	54	6	2	1	1	1	2	7	0	7	1	0
Morrison, Chris, West Michigan	4	1	.800	4.98	13	0	0	0	4	0	21.2	28	97	13	12	1	1	1	0	4	0	13	2	1
Mosman, Marc, Burlington	0	0	.000	0.00	8	0	0	0	5	0	9.0	5	34	0	0	0	0	0	0	4	0	6	1	0
Mott, Tom, Fort Wayne	13	4	.765	4.03	25	25	1	0	0	0	129.2	123	557	67	58	6	6	3	10	48	0	64	14	0
Mounce, Tony, Quad City*	16	8	.667	2.43	25	25	3	1	0	0	159.0	118	649	55	43	6	6	6	3	57	2	143	6	2
Mull, Blaine, Springfield	4	10	.286	4.88	25	25	0	0	0	0	125.1	142	564	79	68	12	9	7	6	50	1	71	14	0
Mullins, Greg, Beloit*	3	1	.750	3.96	15	4	0	0	6	2	36.1	26	151	16	16	2	0	1	5	14	0	48	2	3
Myers, Jason, Burlington*	2	9	.182	5.02	16	16	1	0	0	0	95.0	109	413	64	53	14	3	5	2	26	0	85	4	0
Nartker, Mike, Fort Wayne	5	5	.500	3.10	17	16	1	1	0	0	95.2	87	387	36	33	5	2	5	1	20	1	79	3	2
Nate, Scott, Beloit*	1	0	1.000	2.77	20	0	0	0	8	2	26.0	26	118	12	8	2	0	0	1	13	0	29	2	0
Nelson, Rodney, Springfield	6	10	.375	5.46	25	21	1	0	2	0	115.1	131	541	82	70	7	3	8	7	73	0	58	14	0
Newman, Damon, W. Michigan	3	4	.429	3.74	21	9	0	0	5	1	67.1	57	306	32	28	4	1	1	6	50	1	52	7	2
Newman, Eric, Clinton	1	7	.125	7.65	11	10	1	0	0	0	42.1	52	212	41	36	5	1	2	2	38	2	31	3	3
Ormonde, Troy, Rockford	0	3	.000	8.14	7	5	0	0	0	0	24.1	29	131	29	22	2	1	2	4	28	0	13	8	0
Padilla, Roy, Michigan*	0	1	.000	6.48	4	1	0	0	2	0	8.1	10	46	9	6	0	0	1	3	7	0	7	2	0
Parisi, Michael, Kane County	11	8	.579	3.29	26	26	2	1	0	0	164.1	152	687	73	60	7	2	6	9	42	1	113	11	0
Pavano, Carl, Michigan	6	6	.500	3.44	22	22	1	0	0	0	141.1	118	591	63	54	7	6	7	6	52	0	138	9	0
Pavicich, Paul, Fort Wayne*	4	3	.571	3.01	39	0	0	0	15	5	86.2	75	360	39	29	9	3	2	1	28	3	100	3	0
Pearce, Jeff, Wisconsin*	0	1	.000	7.03	27	0	0	0	9	0	24.1	21	122	21	19	1	1	1	6	25	0	19	1	1
Perez, Jayson, Clinton	0	1	.000	6.53	13	1	0	0	2	0	20.2	31	110	28	15	2	0	2	2	15	2	17	1	0
Perez, Juan, West Michigan*	11	8	.579	3.64	30	19	1	0	3	1	141.0	129	610	73	57	4	1	2	8	55	0	117	5	1
Perkins, Dan, Fort Wayne	7	12	.368	5.49	29	22	0	0	2	0	121.1	133	562	86	74	3	3	4	13	69	1	89	22	2
Peters, Brannon, Fort Wayne*	1	1	.500	4.38	11	1	0	0	5	0	24.2	29	115	17	12	1	2	0	1	16	1	24	3	0
Peterson, Jayson, Rockford	4	7	.364	6.47	13	13	0	0	0	0	65.1	67	312	56	47	5	1	2	0	47	0	45	9	1
Petroff, Daniel, Cedar Rapids	9	10	.474	4.62	27	27	2	0	0	0	146.0	153	635	86	75	9	5	4	14	47	0	98	9	2
Phillips, Marc, Springfield*	6	2	.750	3.05	38	2	0	0	14	3	85.2	88	387	47	29	5	3	5	3	38	0	41	10	0
Pineda, Leonel, Kane County	2	2	.500	3.51	5	5	1	0	0	0	33.1	44	142	14	13	0	2	2	0	6	1	10	3	0
Place, Mike, South Bend	4	5	.444	3.95	28	2	0	0	13	3	54.2	56	235	30	24	3	4	4	4	19	2	34	7	0
Pontes, Dan, Peoria	2	5	.286	1.60	34	6	0	0	9	1	67.2	47	267	19	12	1	4	1	4	15	1	88	1	0
Portillo, Alex, South Bend*	0	1	.000	4.91	2	0	0	0	1	0	3.2	5	15	2	2	0	0	0	0	0	0	4	0	0
Prater, Pete, Burlington	7	5	.583	3.69	21	20	2	0	1	0	114.2	112	499	58	47	13	4	6	2	56	3	80	13	2
Press, Greg, Kane County	10	8	.556	3.60	29	21	0	0	1	0	132.1	127	571	72	53	8	5	3	5	37	1	82	10	0
Putrich, Josh, Rockford	0	2	.000	7.45	6	1	0	0	3	0	9.2	10	41	8	8	1	0	1	0	5	1	6	1	0
Quirk, John, South Bend*	3	2	.600	3.96	22	1	0	0	9	0	52.1	52	245	32	23	4	1	6	1	36	0	30	4	0
Radinsky, Scott, South Bend*	0	0	.000	0.00	6	0	0	0	5	2	9.2	5	33	0	0	0	0	0	0	0	0	11	0	0
Radlosky, Robert, Fort Wayne	11	8	.579	4.03	30	18	1	0	5	0	120.2	111	522	64	54	11	7	5	11	55	2	102	5	2
Raggio, Brady, Peoria	3	0	1.000	1.85	8	8	3	2	0	0	48.2	42	181	13	10	1	1	1	0	2	0	34	0	0
Rain, Steve, Rockford	5	2	.714	1.21	53	0	0	0	51	23	59.1	38	234	12	8	0	3	2	2	23	3	66	8	0
Rajotte, Jason, W. Michigan*	2	2	.500	3.12	44	0	0	0	37	13	52.0	51	242	27	18	1	3	1	3	38	3	52	3	0
Ramos, Edgar, Quad City	0	1	.000	15.43	2	2	0	0	0	0	4.2	5	27	9	8	0	0	0	1	7	0	5	1	0
Rantz, Ron, Beloit*	0	1	.000	16.20	10	0	0	0	1	0	8.1	12	54	15	15	0	0	0	2	15	0	12	6	1
Ratliff, Chris, Burlington	2	6	.250	6.34	15	14	1	1	0	0	61.0	74	281	49	43	7	1	2	1	32	5	33	5	0
Rector, Bobby, Burlington	9	11	.450	4.11	27	24	0	0	0	0	135.2	135	589	78	62	7	4	5	6	59	3	102	9	2
Reed, Brian, Peoria	11	3	.786	1.79	63	0	0	0	30	4	90.1	55	357	29	18	5	5	3	6	25	2	119	3	1
Renfroe, Chad, Michigan	1	3	.250	3.13	12	3	0	0	6	2	31.2	28	138	16	11	1	0	1	2	15	2	25	4	0
Ritter, Jason, Springfield	1	0	1.000	12.34	7	0	0	0	2	0	11.2	19	65	20	16	1	0	1	2	6	0	12	3	0
Rivette, Scott, West Michigan	1	0	1.000	2.93	8	0	0	0	4	2	15.1	12	65	5	5	0	0	2	0	7	0	15	1	0
Robbins, Michael, Springfield*	2	3	.400	4.50	8	8	0	0	0	0	40.0	47	172	22	20	4	0	1	1	10	0	26	2	2
Roberts, Ray, Springfield*	2	5	.286	4.52	38	0	0	0	12	1	65.2	86	292	38	33	6	4	3	3	17	0	43	5	0
Roettgen, Mark, Peoria	0	4	.000	10.29	4	4	0	0	0	0	14.0	24	76	20	16	1	1	0	0	15	0	14	3	3
Rose, Brian, Michigan	8	5	.615	3.44	21	20	2	0	0	0	136.0	127	561	63	52	5	3	1	9	31	0	105	4	0
Rosenbohm, Jim, Burlington	0	0	.000	19.80	3	0	0	0	1	0	5.0	9	36	11	11	1	0	1	1	11	0	3	5	0
Rosenkranz, Terry, Beloit*	0	0	.000	0.00	4	0	0	0	2	0	8.0	2	30	2	0	0	0	0	0	2	0	4	0	0
Ruch, Rob, Fort Wayne	0	1	.000	2.73	9	3	0	0	1	1	26.1	17	108	8	8	1	0	0	2	16	0	27	1	0
Runyan, Sean, Quad City*	4	6	.400	3.66	22	11	0	0	2	0	76.1	67	327	37	31	10	1	2	3	29	0	65	4	0
Rushing, William, Ft. Wayne*	1	1	.500	1.78	13	0	0	0	5	1	25.1	15	100	11	5	0	0	0	0	10	0	25	4	2
Sak, James, Clinton	6	1	.857	1.98	7	7	3	0	0	0	50.0	42	200	12	11	2	1	2	0	14	0	37	0	3
Salmon, Fabian, South Bend	4	1	.800	3.80	15	0	0	0	8	3	23.2	18	103	15	10	1	0	0	1	11	0	15	2	0
Santana, Marino, Wisconsin	8	3	.727	1.77	15	15	2	1	0	0	96.2	57	368	26	19	5	2	2	1	25	0	110	6	0
Scheffer, Aaron, Wisconsin	0	1	.000	6.59	9	0	0	0	6	0	13.2	17	65	14	10	2	1	0	0	5	1	8	2	0
Schenbeck, T.J., Beloit	4	2	.667	3.62	18	1	0	0	9	5	37.1	35	171	18	15	3	3	3	2	23	1	37	5	0
Schiefelbein, Mike, Burlington	0	0	.000	0.00	1	0	0	0	0	0	0.0	0	1	0	0	0	0	0	0	1	0	0	0	0
Scott, Ron, Peoria*	0	2	.000	8.47	21	1	0	0	8	0	34.0	37	168	36	32	4	1	4	5	30	0	21	9	2
Shaver, Tony, Quad City	2	0	1.000	1.61	35	0	0	0	9	1	56.0	35	222	15	10	2	2	0	2	19	1	40	2	1
Sick, David, Cedar Rapids	6	5	.545	3.67	50	0	0	0	12	3	73.2	72	331	41	30	5	5	2	10	27	3	64	5	1
Sikorski, Brian, Quad City	1	0	1.000	0.00	2	0	0	0	1	0	3.0	1	11	1	0	0	0	0	0	0	0	4	0	0
Silva, Luis, West Michigan	1	0	1.000	6.75	10	1	0	0	1	0	21.1	31	102	16	16	2	1	1	2	7	0	24	2	3
Skuse, Nicholas, Cedar Rapids	13	7	.650	4.04	26	25	3	1	1	0	147.0	155	650	84	66	10	3	3	9	61	1	116	12	3
Slade, Shawn, Cedar Rapids	3	1	.750	4.25	30	0	0	0	14	3	42.1	42	186	24	20	1	3	2	2	19	2	35	4	1
Slininger, Dennis, Peoria	0	3	.000	10.97	3	3	0	0	0	0	10.2	16	54	13	13	5	0	0	0	7	0	12	0	0
Smith, Andy, West Michigan	4	10	.286	3.89	30	22	0	0	4	2	122.2	117	554	71	53	3	2	3	10	72	1	68	6	1
Smith, Brook, Burlington*	3	2	.600	5.01	39	4	0	0	12	1	88.0	85	414	67	49	7	7	3	3	72	7	70	19	2
Smith, Charles, South Bend	10	10	.500	2.69	26	25	4	2	1	0	167.0	128	688	70	50	8	7	2	13	61	0	145	21	11
Smith, John, West Michigan*	1	0	1.000	4.05	25	0	0	0	11	1	33.1	32	149	21	15	4	2	0	3	18	0	33	2	1
Smith, Mason, Burlington	0	4	.000	6.94	8	4	0	0	2	0	23.1	26	109	18	18	1	0	1	0	12	1	19	2	1
Smith, Roy, Wisconsin	7	14	.333	5.38	27	27	1	0	0	0	149.0	179	669	100	89	9	5	2	3	54	2	109	10	2

Pitcher, Team	W	L	Pct.	ERA	G	GS	CG	ShO	GF	Sv.	IP	H	TBF	R	ER	HR	SH	SF	HB	BB	IBB	SO	WP	Bk.
Smith, Shad, Burlington	0	1	.000	6.23	2	2	0	0	0	0	8.2	10	42	8	6	1	1	0	0	6	1	4	1	0
Sosa, Helpis, West Michigan	3	5	.375	4.70	21	6	0	0	5	2	53.2	59	255	47	28	5	3	4	4	26	0	37	5	1
Stark, Zachary, Kane County*	1	1	.500	15.51	5	4	0	0	0	0	15.2	27	94	30	27	2	1	0	2	17	0	5	1	0
Steed, Sam, Springfield*	2	0	1.000	2.45	8	0	0	0	6	0	14.2	14	64	4	4	0	1	0	0	6	0	14	2	0
Stein, Blake, Peoria	10	6	.625	3.80	27	27	1	0	0	0	139.2	122	596	69	59	12	1	4	5	61	0	133	2	1
Steinke, Brock, Quad City	2	1	.667	4.34	21	1	0	0	7	0	37.1	30	168	20	18	2	0	4	3	27	0	18	4	2
Stevenson, Jason, Rockford	4	3	.571	5.59	33	5	0	0	9	2	77.1	85	333	50	48	9	1	4	1	31	0	54	5	5
Surratt, Jamie, South Bend	3	3	.500	3.12	26	0	0	0	22	11	40.1	32	163	15	14	5	3	2	2	12	1	34	3	1
Telgheder, Jim, Michigan	5	1	.833	1.80	22	1	0	0	18	4	35.0	29	142	8	7	0	2	2	1	8	2	39	3	0
Theodile, Robert, South Bend	1	2	.333	7.62	7	4	0	0	0	0	26.0	45	130	30	22	1	1	1	1	13	0	16	5	0
Thomas, Carlos, Clinton	2	0	1.000	2.45	13	0	0	0	1	1	18.1	19	86	9	5	1	2	0	1	10	1	14	0	0
Thompson, John, Wisconsin	2	8	.200	4.13	38	7	0	0	29	19	69.2	65	314	41	32	8	2	2	2	43	2	69	13	1
Thurmond, Travis, Ced. Rapids	2	5	.286	5.31	14	2	0	0	4	2	39.0	36	172	25	23	4	2	0	1	20	4	55	3	0
Tidwell, Jason, Kane County	1	4	.200	8.62	6	4	0	0	0	0	15.2	19	80	17	15	2	1	0	4	14	0	13	3	0
Tillmon, Darrell, Michigan*	6	3	.667	2.24	13	10	2	0	2	0	76.1	56	293	25	19	8	2	0	0	12	0	53	1	0
Tollberg, Brian, Beloit	13	4	.765	3.41	22	22	1	1	0	0	132.0	119	529	59	50	10	2	5	6	27	0	110	5	4
Torres, Luis, Clinton	0	0	.000	13.50	3	0	0	0	0	0	2.0	5	16	3	3	0	0	0	1	5	0	1	0	2
Towns, Ryan, Springfield	0	1	.000	5.58	18	1	0	0	7	0	30.2	33	141	24	19	6	1	0	2	17	0	31	4	1
Tyrrell, Jim, Michigan*	2	3	.400	3.60	16	0	0	0	7	4	25.0	17	114	17	10	3	2	4	4	15	1	37	2	1
Upchurch, Wayne, Springfield	2	3	.400	4.25	18	2	0	0	11	1	29.2	40	137	19	14	3	2	2	2	4	1	13	0	1
Vandeweg, Ryan, Clinton	6	4	.600	4.15	15	15	1	0	0	0	91.0	92	400	56	42	5	3	2	7	32	3	89	3	1
Vanhof, Dave, Wisconsin*	4	5	.444	4.16	15	13	1	0	1	0	62.2	52	291	42	29	4	4	3	3	50	2	27	8	0
Vardijan, Daniel, Kane County	0	0	.000	6.00	1	1	0	0	0	0	3.0	5	17	3	2	0	0	0	1	2	0	2	1	0
Villano, Mike, Burlington	3	1	.750	2.84	16	0	0	0	7	1	25.1	20	120	12	8	1	2	1	4	21	0	29	5	0
Walls, Eric, Springfield*	0	0	.000	0.00	1	0	0	0	1	0	1.0	1	4	0	0	0	0	0	0	0	0	0	0	0
Walters, Brett, Clinton	8	7	.533	2.71	32	19	4	0	4	1	146.0	133	598	58	44	9	6	1	10	27	3	122	4	2
Warren, Deshawn, Ced. Rapids*	2	3	.400	3.26	7	7	1	1	0	0	30.1	20	122	12	11	2	1	0	2	13	0	26	1	0
Washburn, Jarrod, Ced. Rapids*	0	1	.000	3.44	3	3	0	0	0	0	18.1	17	79	7	7	1	2	1	3	7	0	20	1	0
Weinberg, Todd, W. Michigan*	5	4	.444	4.76	36	9	0	0	5	1	87.0	86	392	52	46	3	2	1	13	56	2	54	19	2
Welch, Travis, Peoria	3	4	.429	4.50	46	0	0	0	46	31	46.0	40	203	26	23	6	5	0	3	18	1	45	5	1
West, Adam, Peoria*	0	3	.000	12.08	4	4	0	0	0	0	12.2	22	81	21	17	0	0	1	0	24	0	5	2	0
Wiesner, Chad, Wisconsin	0	0	.000	3.00	1	0	0	0	0	0	3.0	3	12	1	1	0	0	0	0	1	0	2	0	0
Williams, Juan, Fort Wayne*	0	0	.000	4.50	3	0	0	0	3	0	6.0	7	29	4	3	0	2	0	0	3	0	4	0	3
Winkle, Ken, Springfield	1	1	.500	9.49	9	0	0	0	3	0	12.1	16	56	13	13	3	0	0	1	2	0	8	2	0
Woodard, Steve, Beloit	7	4	.636	4.54	21	21	1	0	0	0	115.0	113	490	68	58	12	6	2	5	31	0	94	6	5
Wunsch, Kelly, Beloit*	4	7	.364	4.20	14	14	3	1	0	0	85.2	90	364	47	40	7	2	0	3	37	0	66	6	0
Ybarra, Jamie, Kane County	5	5	.500	3.00	50	2	0	0	16	2	96.0	62	398	37	32	7	5	2	13	40	4	104	2	2
Zancanaro, Dave, W. Michigan*	0	2	.000	2.20	16	16	0	0	0	0	32.2	19	132	8	8	1	2	0	3	15	0	42	1	2
Zanolla, Dan, Kane County	4	4	.500	3.58	28	3	0	0	3	0	60.1	58	276	34	24	2	3	2	6	28	3	54	1	0

COMBINATION SHUTOUTS: **Beloit (6)**—Beck-Linares, D'Amico-Dalton-Burt, D'Amico-Mullins, Gonzalez-Dalton-Burt, Linares-Dalton, Tollberg-Huntsman. **Burlington (3)**—Lake-Keith, Prater-Hernandez, Rector-Hernandez. **Cedar Rapids (2)**—Skuse-Sick-Freehill, Warren-Sick. **Clinton (3)**—Dennis-Isom, Hammerschmidt-Isom, Isom-Davis. **Fort Wayne (7)**—Bell-Pavicich-Rushing-Fidge, Cobb-Rushing, Fidge-Bedinger, Nartker-Fidge, Perkins-Pavicich, Ruch-Pavicich-Fidge, Ruch-Perkins-Rushing. **Kane County (6)**—Meadows-Gonzalez-Alejo, Miranda-Alejo, Press-Andersen, Zanolla-Ybarra, Meadows-Zanolla-Bussa, Press-Miles-Bussa. **Michigan (5)**—Mitchell-Bush-Telgheder, Mitchell-Hale, Rose-Blais, Rose-Bush, Rose-Tillmon. **Peoria (6)**—Corrigan-Pontes-Welch, Dale-Corrigan, Foderaro-Corrigan-Carroll, Stein-Pontes-Reed, Stein-Reed, Stein-Welch. **Quad City (9)**—Blanco-Hall, Elarton-Halama-Barrios, Lock-Diorio, Mounce-Barrios, Mounce-Halama-Barrios, Mounce-Hall, Mounce-Kester, Runyan-Gunderson, Steinke-Halama-Barrios. **Rockford (4)**—Bair-Bogle, Garcia-Casey, Krause-Faulkner-Barker, Martinez-Rain. **South Bend (4)**—Bigham-Salmon, Garcia-Leiber, Gomez-Surratt, Herbert-Radinsky. **Springfield (3)**—Anderson-Roberts-MacDonald, Carter-Anderson-Brixey-MacDonald, Gamboa-Brixey. **West Michigan (9)**—Hause-Rajotte, King-Cochrane, King-Epstein-Hause-Rajotte, Newman-Weinberg-Beverlin-Sosa, Perez-Epstein-Smith, Perez-Gunther-Rajotte, Weinberg-Morrison-Rajotte, Zancanaro-Hause, Zancanaro-Perez-Gunther. **Wisconsin (3)**—Bieniasz-Daniels-Morgan-Green, Smith-Doughty, Smith-Krueger.

NO-HIT GAMES: None.

PITCHERS WITH TWO OR MORE TEAMS

Pitcher, Team	W	L	Pct.	ERA	G	GS	CG	ShO	GF	Sv.	IP	H	TBF	R	ER	HR	SH	SF	HB	BB	IBB	SO	WP	Bk.
Estes, Shawn, Wisconsin*	0	0	.000	0.90	2	2	0	0	0	0	10.0	5	38	1	1	0	0	1	0	5	0	11	2	1
Estes, Shawn, Burlington*	0	0	.000	4.11	4	4	0	0	0	0	15.1	13	72	8	7	2	0	0	2	12	0	22	2	0

1995 FIELDING

TEAM

Team	Pct.	G	PO	A	E	TC	DP	PB	Team	Pct.	G	PO	A	E	TC	DP	PB
Beloit	.968	139	3587	1508	168	5263	112	22	Kane County	.962	138	3545	1412	196	5153	118	21
Michigan	.968	138	3626	1428	169	5223	106	32	Quad City	.962	137	3499	1546	200	5245	106	18
Cedar Rapids	.966	138	3554	1517	176	5247	114	19	Fort Wayne	.962	140	3709	1542	210	5461	115	31
Wisconsin	.965	138	3540	1555	184	5279	114	27	Burlington	.961	135	3309	1451	194	4954	111	34
South Bend	.964	135	3551	1488	186	5225	107	23	Springfield	.960	139	3526	1579	215	5320	105	30
Peoria	.964	134	3393	1403	178	4974	103	25	West Michigan	.956	136	3524	1511	231	5266	119	19
Rockford	.964	140	3603	1552	193	5348	104	27	Clinton	.950	137	3387	1405	252	5044	102	25

TRIPLE PLAYS: South Bend, West Michigan.

INDIVIDUAL

FIRST BASEMEN

NOTE: All caps denotes fielding-percentage leader based on 70 games for catchers, 93 for all other non-pitchers and 144 innings for pitchers. *Throws lefthanded.

Player, Team	Pct.	G	PO	A	E	TC	DP
Allen, Dustin, Clinton	.967	23	137	10	5	152	17
Altman, Heath, Burlington	1.000	1	1	0	0	1	0
Ballara, Juan, Peoria	1.000	2	11	1	0	12	1

Player, Team	Pct.	G	PO	A	E	TC	DP
Bazzani, Matt, Michigan	.750	1	3	0	1	4	1
Bowles, John, Michigan	1.000	3	9	1	0	10	1
Buhner, Shawn, Wisconsin	.985	62	543	38	9	590	42
Burchel, Brad, Beloit	1.000	1	5	0	0	5	1
Burgos, Carlos, Springfield	1.000	8	81	2	0	83	6
Cady, Todd, Kane County	.982	88	724	46	14	784	62
Castillo, Alberto, Burlington*	.985	33	238	21	4	263	18
Castro, Dennis, Kane County	.857	1	12	0	2	14	2

Player, Team	Pct.	G	PO	A	E	TC	DP
Chevalier, Virgil, Michigan	1.000	1	4	2	0	6	1
Clifford, James, Wisconsin*	.985	81	729	49	12	790	59
Coe, Ryan, Quad City	1.000	2	9	0	0	9	0
Dantzler, Eric, Burlington	.973	12	69	3	2	74	8
DeLeon, Raymond, Clinton*	1.000	3	21	2	0	23	2
Dennis, Brian, Rockford	.900	9	16	2	2	20	0
DePastino, Joe, Michigan	1.000	9	75	3	0	78	10
Donati, John, Cedar Rapids	.976	72	658	30	17	705	43
Fitzpatrick, Will, Beloit	1.000	13	59	4	0	63	4
Fortin, Troy, Fort Wayne	.991	80	737	44	7	788	53
Francisco, Vicente, W. Michigan	.966	3	26	2	1	29	0
FREEMAN, Richard, Rockford	.9953	131	1181	82	6	1269	81
Freire, Alejandro, Quad City	.993	101	931	70	7	1008	73
Gibralter, David, Michigan	.988	92	788	54	10	852	61
Glenn, Darrin, Burlington	.967	5	29	0	1	30	1
Grandizio, Steve, Peoria	1.000	1	4	0	0	4	0
Gulseth, Mark, Burlington	.991	40	315	25	3	343	25
Gunderson, Shane, Ft. Wayne	1.000	4	34	3	0	37	4
Hacopian, Derek, Beloit	.988	27	160	11	2	173	13
Hall, Ryan, Peoria	.993	18	129	11	1	141	6
Harris, Eric, West Michigan	.989	24	164	10	2	176	11
Heath, Jason, Wisconsin	1.000	1	1	0	0	1	0
Ibarra, Jesus, Burlington	.976	56	457	35	12	504	45
Jackson, Ryan, Kane County*	.988	52	475	31	6	512	42
Johnson, Jack, Rockford	1.000	4	28	3	0	31	3
Kimbler, Doug, Rockford	1.000	1	2	0	0	2	0
Krause, Scott, Beloit	1.000	1	1	0	0	1	1
Llanos, Victor, Peoria	.965	9	53	2	2	57	6
Martin, Mike, Clinton	1.000	1	2	1	0	3	1
McNally, Sean, Springfield	1.000	1	11	1	0	12	0
Mendoza, Francisco, Springfield	.977	20	154	13	4	171	16
Milstien, Dave, Beloit	1.000	1	1	0	0	1	0
Miranda, Alex, W. Michigan*	.986	118	972	79	15	1066	89
Moeder, Tony, Cedar Rapids	1.000	40	396	19	0	415	30
Nunez, Isaias, Peoria*	.981	119	966	80	20	1066	78
Olmstead, Nate, Cedar Rapids	.979	33	256	24	6	286	24
Patterson, Jake, Fort Wayne*	.980	56	478	23	10	511	38
Patton, Greg, Michigan	1.000	2	8	0	0	8	0
Pearson, Kevin, Fort Wayne	.958	8	42	4	2	48	4
Robbins, Lance, Ced. Rapids	1.000	1	2	0	0	2	0
Robledo, Nilson, South Bend	.983	135	1224	82	22	1328	91
Rodriguez, Noel, Quad City	.990	46	382	14	4	400	24
Root, Mitch, Clinton	.981	56	498	25	10	533	40
Rose, Pete, South Bend	1.000	1	3	0	0	3	1
Salzano, Jerry, Rockford	1.000	3	22	0	0	22	2
Sanchez, Victor, Quad City	1.000	2	15	0	0	15	1
Sanders, Pat, W. Michigan*	1.000	6	19	3	0	22	0
Schwenke, Matt, Clinton	1.000	6	35	1	0	36	1
Smith, Matt, Springfield*	.988	116	1081	78	14	1173	72
Stasio, Chris, Michigan	.997	40	334	21	1	356	21
Tyler, Josh, Beloit	1.000	6	14	1	0	15	0
Whatley, Gabe, Rockford	.985	7	61	3	1	65	6
Williams, Drew, Beloit	.9946	124	1050	57	6	1113	79
Winget, Jeremy, Clinton*	.981	61	483	43	10	536	36
Zwisler, Josh, Beloit	1.000	2	6	0	0	6	0

TRIPLE PLAYS: Miranda, Robledo.

SECOND BASEMEN

Player, Team	Pct.	G	PO	A	E	TC	DP
Allison, Chris, Michigan	.969	83	160	211	12	383	53
Avalos, Gilbert, Rockford	.980	32	52	92	3	147	16
Belliard, Ron, Beloit	.955	119	219	314	25	558	69
Betances, Junior, Beloit	1.000	7	9	11	0	20	3
Betten, Randy, Cedar Rapids	.963	20	18	34	2	54	6
Biermann, Steve, Peoria	.941	9	3	13	1	17	1
Boulware, Benjamin, S. Bend	.962	129	244	332	23	599	72
Bowles, John, Michigan	.921	28	30	52	7	89	8
Carmona, Cesarin, Clinton	.928	36	50	78	10	138	16
Castillo, Luis, Kane County	.962	89	193	241	17	451	55
Castro, Jose, West Michigan	.954	99	230	247	23	500	53
Cedeno, Edwardo, Springfield	.944	7	2	15	1	18	0
Cook, Jason, Wisconsin	.989	59	104	174	3	281	31
Cruz, Deivi, Burlington	.962	14	16	35	2	53	6
Cuevas, Eduardo, Clinton	.900	6	7	11	2	20	3
Darden, Tony, Kane County	.979	10	21	25	1	47	7
Davalillo, David, Cedar Rapids	1.000	8	8	19	0	27	6
Dean, Mark, Peoria	.959	25	50	44	4	98	8
Dumas, Mike, Beloit	1.000	1	2	1	0	3	1
Francisco, Vicente, W. Michigan	.964	41	81	79	6	166	23
Fraser, Joe, Fort Wayne	.947	4	8	10	1	19	2
Garcia, Amaury, Kane County	.818	4	4	5	2	11	1
Garcia, Carlos, Fort Wayne	.974	9	19	18	1	38	4
Garcia, Franklin, Beloit	.943	20	27	39	4	70	10

Player, Team	Pct.	G	PO	A	E	TC	DP
Hamburg, Leon, W. Michigan	.938	8	16	14	2	32	3
Hansen, Jed, Springfield	.963	120	220	345	22	587	63
HENDERSON, Juan, Ced. Rapids	.974	114	251	304	15	570	72
Hernandez, Carlos, Quad City	.964	98	157	276	16	449	50
Keefe, Jamie, Clinton	.962	40	65	87	6	158	20
Kimbler, Doug, Rockford	1.000	5	4	4	0	8	1
Krause, Scott, Beloit	1.000	1	1	0	0	1	0
Lane, Ryan, Fort Wayne	.969	42	65	92	5	162	13
Lanza, Mike, Wisconsin	.963	39	76	105	7	188	18
Livsey, Shane, Rockford	.941	52	83	109	12	204	20
Martinez, Erik, Clinton	.913	8	6	15	2	23	4
Marval, Raul, Burlington	.962	79	149	182	13	344	51
McCalmont, Jim, Fort Wayne	.973	6	16	20	1	37	9
Milstien, Dave, Beloit	.923	2	7	5	1	13	2
Mitchell, Donovan, Quad City	.968	50	67	115	6	188	19
Molina, Luis, Wisconsin	.971	43	66	100	5	171	19
Moschetti, Mike, W. Michigan	.909	6	10	20	3	33	0
Olinde, Chad, Rockford	.943	39	42	91	8	141	11
Paez, Israel, Fort Wayne	.955	91	178	247	20	445	44
Patton, Greg, Michigan	1.000	7	11	15	0	26	3
Perez, Mike, Rockford	.967	37	37	82	4	123	15
Polanco, Placido, Peoria	1.000	1	2	3	0	5	1
Ramirez, Joel, Wisconsin	.912	5	9	22	3	34	4
Robbins, Lance, Cedar Rapids	.964	12	22	32	2	56	3
Robinson, Darek, Peoria	.960	111	208	276	20	504	59
Smith, Dave, Michigan	.951	36	47	70	6	123	14
Sparks, Rodney, Springfield	.923	23	30	42	6	78	7
Swift, Scott, Burlington	.948	53	84	99	10	193	16
Totman, Jason, Clinton	.949	57	106	137	13	256	30
Tyler, Josh, Beloit	1.000	1	1	0	0	1	0
White, Walter, Kane County	.943	44	89	110	12	211	24
Wojtkowski, Steve, Michigan	1.000	2	1	2	0	3	1
Zerpa, Mauro, South Bend	.923	8	10	14	2	26	1

TRIPLE PLAYS: Boulware, Castro.

THIRD BASEMEN

Player, Team	Pct.	G	PO	A	E	TC	DP
Avalos, Gilbert, Rockford	.885	72	51	157	27	235	4
Barnes, Kelvin, Rockford	.900	4	3	6	1	10	0
Belliard, Ron, Beloit	.971	15	2	32	1	35	2
BETANCES, Junior, Beloit	.932	102	59	216	20	295	18
Betten, Randy, Cedar Rapids	1.000	2	2	4	0	6	0
Biermann, Steve, Peoria	1.000	3	0	1	0	1	1
Booty, Josh, Kane County	.913	31	23	71	9	103	4
Bowles, John, Michigan	.931	19	17	50	5	72	6
Burchel, Brad, Beloit	1.000	1	1	0	0	1	0
Castro, Dennis, Kane County	.925	42	31	93	10	134	8
Cedeno, Edwardo, Springfield	.882	6	2	13	2	17	0
Cook, Jason, Wisconsin	.956	35	23	85	5	113	6
Cruz, Deivi, Burlington	1.000	2	4	6	0	10	1
Cuevas, Eduardo, Clinton	.907	30	11	57	7	75	0
D'Amico, Jeff, West Michigan	.916	108	93	247	31	371	25
Darden, Tony, Kane County	.888	47	30	97	16	143	10
Davalillo, David, Cedar Rapids	.938	30	12	63	5	80	1
Dean, Mark, Peoria	.899	34	19	52	8	79	6
Derosso, Tony, Michigan	.928	80	63	155	17	235	6
Donati, John, Cedar Rapids	1.000	2	0	2	0	2	0
Dumas, Mike, Beloit	1.000	3	0	14	0	14	0
Espinal, Juan, Clinton	.889	107	73	182	32	287	8
Francisco, Vicente, W. Michigan	.884	36	21	63	11	95	4
Garcia, Amaury, Kane County	.750	20	7	26	11	44	1
Garcia, Carlos, Fort Wayne	.862	14	9	16	4	29	1
Gibralter, David, Michigan	.900	16	17	28	5	50	5
Glenn, Darrin, Burlington	.758	11	2	23	8	33	1
Gugino, Mark, Kane County	.500	1	1	0	1	2	0
Jumonville, Joe, Peoria	.924	112	72	219	24	315	22
Keefe, Jamie, Clinton	1.000	4	4	4	0	8	1
Kimbler, Doug, Rockford	.952	49	46	92	7	145	11
Klassen, Danny, Beloit	1.000	2	3	5	0	8	1
Kominek, Toby, Beloit	1.000	3	1	1	0	2	0
Koskie, Corey, Fort Wayne	.900	109	80	244	36	360	23
Martinez, Erik, Clinton	.500	2	0	1	1	2	1
McCalmont, Jim, Fort Wayne	.889	2	2	6	1	9	1
McNally, Sean, Springfield	.927	128	91	278	29	398	12
Mendoza, Francisco, Springfield	.829	12	14	20	7	41	3
Mitchell, Donovan, Quad City	.909	4	3	7	1	11	0
Molina, Luis, Wisconsin	1.000	5	2	7	0	9	1
Morris, Gregory, Cedar Rapids	.909	102	65	226	29	320	15
Nelson, Bryant, Quad City	1.000	1	0	2	0	2	0
Olinde, Chad, Rockford	.870	17	15	32	7	54	2
Ortega, Randy, West Michigan	.857	2	2	4	1	7	0
Paez, Israel, Fort Wayne	.875	19	15	41	8	64	3
Patton, Greg, Michigan	.956	24	19	46	3	68	1

Player, Team	Pct.	G	PO	A	E	TC	DP
Rincones, Wuarnner, S. Bend	.912	20	25	37	6	68	8
Robbins, Lance, Cedar Rapids	.875	15	6	22	4	32	1
Root, Mitch, Clinton	1.000	2	0	5	0	5	0
Rose, Pete, South Bend	.921	113	124	249	32	405	23
Salzano, Jerry, Rockford	.429	3	1	2	4	7	0
Smith, Dave, Michigan	.875	2	1	6	1	8	0
Sparks, Rodney, Springfield	.833	4	0	5	1	6	1
Trammell, Gary, Quad City	.833	21	9	46	11	66	8
Truby, Chris, Quad City	.903	118	73	279	38	390	26
Tyler, Josh, Beloit	.957	40	28	60	4	92	4
Valentin, Jose, Fort Wayne	1.000	9	6	14	0	20	2
Villalobos, Carlos, Wisconsin	.878	104	76	234	43	353	16
Wallace, Brian, Burlington	.911	97	62	225	28	315	19
Whatley, Gabe, Rockford	.826	10	4	15	4	23	0
White, Walter, Kane County	.800	8	2	14	4	20	0
Wilson, Todd, Burlington	.920	29	12	57	6	75	1
Wojtkowski, Steve, Michigan	1.000	2	1	5	0	6	0
Zerpa, Mauro, South Bend	.882	15	9	21	4	34	2

TRIPLE PLAY: Francisco.

SHORTSTOPS

Player, Team	Pct.	G	PO	A	E	TC	DP
Alguacil, Jose, Burlington	.910	36	66	95	16	177	17
Allison, Chris, Michigan	1.000	1	2	2	0	4	1
Betances, Junior, Beloit	.920	23	24	57	7	88	10
Betten, Randy, Cedar Rapids	.750	2	1	2	1	4	1
Biermann, Steve, Peoria	.932	40	36	87	9	132	15
Burchel, Brad, Beloit	.844	9	5	22	5	32	4
BUSTOS, Saul, Rockford	.969	94	117	289	13	419	36
Castro, Jose, West Michigan	.896	14	17	26	5	48	4
Cedeno, Edwardo, Springfield	.910	26	26	55	8	89	5
Cruz, Deivi, Burlington	1.000	1	0	1	0	1	0
D'Amico, Jeff, West Michigan	.933	21	27	57	6	90	5
Darden, Tony, Kane County	1.000	1	0	1	0	1	0
Davalillo, David, Cedar Rapids	.923	4	4	8	1	13	2
Dean, Mark, Peoria	.917	11	7	26	3	36	4
Delgado, Wilson, Wis.-Bur.	.953	112	156	350	25	531	63
Dumas, Mike, Beloit	.930	9	12	28	3	43	4
Failla, Paul, Cedar Rapids	.935	129	162	343	35	540	65
Francisco, Vicente, W. Michigan	.769	11	9	21	9	39	4
Garcia, Franklin, Beloit	.333	2	1	0	2	3	0
Goodell, Steve, Kane County	.923	2	6	6	1	13	2
Henderson, Juan, Cedar Rapids	.952	7	5	15	1	21	0
Hernandez, Carlos, Quad City	.954	30	31	73	5	109	9
Keefe, Jamie, Clinton	.903	9	9	19	3	31	2
Kimbler, Doug, Rockford	.943	54	113	154	16	283	36
Klassen, Danny, Beloit	.917	56	70	128	18	216	23
Lane, Ryan, Fort Wayne	.943	75	111	222	20	353	38
Lanza, Mike, Wisconsin	.931	58	82	160	18	260	28
Martinez, Erik, Clinton	.913	7	8	13	2	23	1
Marval, Raul, Burlington	.949	12	14	23	2	39	5
Melo, Juan, Clinton	.922	132	183	372	47	602	70
Mendez, Emilio, Beloit	.895	7	6	11	2	19	2
Milstien, Dave, Beloit	.940	49	69	149	14	232	21
Mitchell, Donovan, Quad City	.925	42	46	103	12	161	8
Molina, Luis, Wisconsin	.957	63	106	180	13	299	32
Moore, Brandon, South Bend	.956	132	193	398	27	618	64
Moriarty, Mike, Fort Wayne	.956	62	96	165	12	273	22
Nelson, Bryant, Quad City	.750	1	1	2	1	4	1
Paez, Israel, Fort Wayne	1.000	8	8	13	0	21	2
Patton, Greg, Michigan	.958	19	24	45	3	72	8
Polanco, Placido, Peoria	.950	101	112	283	21	416	40
Prieto, Alejandro, Springfield	.936	123	199	358	38	595	70
Ramirez, Joel, Wisconsin	1.000	2	3	2	0	5	0
Robbins, Lance, Cedar Rapids	.500	2	0	2	2	4	1
Rodriguez, Victor, Kane County	.959	127	151	312	20	483	56
Sadler, Donnie, Michigan	.944	112	168	307	28	503	59
Santana, Jose, Quad City	.920	80	101	223	28	352	43
Smith, Dave, Michigan	.913	12	10	32	4	46	3
Soriano, Fred, West Michigan	.938	106	140	298	29	467	52
Sparks, Rodney, Springfield	.968	6	6	24	1	31	3
White, Walter, Kane County	.912	13	21	31	5	57	8
Zerpa, Mauro, South Bend	.960	12	6	18	1	25	1

TRIPLE PLAYS: D'Amico, Zerpa.

SHORTSTOPS WITH TWO OR MORE TEAMS

Player, Team	Pct.	G	PO	A	E	TC	DP
Delgado, Wilson, Wisconsin	.940	19	29	65	6	100	14
Delgado, Wilson, Burlington	.956	93	127	285	19	431	49

OUTFIELDERS

Player, Team	Pct.	G	PO	A	E	TC	DP
Alexander, Chad, Quad City	1.000	2	3	0	0	3	0
Allen, Dustin, Clinton	.902	18	34	3	4	41	1
Altman, Heath, Burlington	1.000	13	15	1	0	16	0
Alvarez, Luis, Cedar Rapids*	.667	3	2	0	1	3	0
Alvarez, Rafael, Fort Wayne	.961	96	189	7	8	204	0
Amerson, Gordon, Clinton*	.864	47	49	2	8	59	0
Bautista, Juan, Peoria	.936	63	86	2	6	94	0
Bogle, Bryan, Rockford	.904	33	45	2	5	52	1
Bowers, R.J., Quad City	.957	107	148	7	7	162	0
Bowles, John, Michigan	.937	38	56	3	4	63	0
Brandon, Jelani, Springfield	.967	57	80	7	3	90	0
Bray, Notorris, Burlington	.974	15	37	1	1	39	0
Brown, Armann, Fort Wayne	.973	76	138	5	4	147	0
Brown, Emil, West Michigan	.957	109	165	12	8	185	4
Buchanan, Shawn, South Bend	.983	94	171	6	3	180	1
Carroll, Doug, Wisconsin	.918	47	59	8	6	73	0
Castro, Jose, West Michigan	1.000	2	3	1	0	4	0
Cedeno, Edwardo, Springfield	.980	29	45	5	1	51	0
Cephas, Ruben, Beloit	.929	63	50	2	4	56	0
Choi, Kyung, Cedar Rapids*	.960	33	42	6	2	50	1
Cole, Abdul, Kane County	.955	50	82	2	4	88	2
Coleman, Michael, Michigan	.981	111	251	5	5	261	0
Contreras, Efrain, Peoria	.951	77	112	5	6	123	2
Cook, Hayward, Kane County	.984	65	123	4	2	129	1
Cook, Jason, Wisconsin	.966	20	25	3	1	29	0
Cordero, Pablo, Burlington	.912	57	79	4	8	91	0
Corujo, Rey, Burlington	.846	13	11	0	2	13	0
Dantzler, Eric, Burlington	1.000	9	9	0	0	9	0
Darcuiel, Faruq, Wisconsin*	.925	76	119	5	10	134	1
Darden, Tony, Kane County	.975	26	37	2	1	40	1
DeLeon, Santo, Wisconsin	.909	9	10	0	1	11	0
Denbow, Don, Burlington	.973	105	176	7	5	188	0
Donati, John, Cedar Rapids	1.000	1	3	0	0	3	0
Dumas, Mike, Beloit	1.000	7	9	1	0	10	0
Dunwoody, Todd, Kane County*	.983	129	284	6	5	295	1
Evans, Jason, South Bend	.964	87	152	11	6	169	3
Faggett, Ethan, Michigan*	.966	107	168	5	6	179	0
Freire, Alejandro, Quad City	1.000	3	1	0	0	1	0
French, Anton, Peoria	.939	113	164	6	11	181	1
Fric, Sean, Rockford	.800	5	4	0	1	5	0
Garcia, Carlos, Fort Wayne	1.000	7	13	0	0	13	0
Gazarek, Marty, Rockford	.949	70	120	11	7	138	3
Gerteisen, Aaron, Peoria	.975	66	117	1	3	121	0
Glenn, Darrin, Burlington	1.000	14	22	2	0	24	0
Gordon, Adrian, Fort Wayne	.956	41	40	3	2	45	1
Grandizio, Steve, Peoria	.981	93	153	3	3	159	1
Grieve, Ben, West Michigan	.942	92	125	6	8	139	0
Gugino, Mark, Kane County	.951	36	58	0	3	61	0
Gunderson, Shane, Ft. Wayne	1.000	21	20	2	0	22	1
Hacopian, Derek, Beloit	.969	74	90	3	3	96	1
Hamburg, Leon, W. Michigan	.943	61	90	9	6	105	0
Hamilton, Joe, Michigan	.973	115	204	11	6	221	2
Harris, Eric, West Michigan	1.000	6	3	0	0	3	0
Harvey, Aaron, Kane County	.976	57	82	0	2	84	0
Herrick, Jason, Cedar Rapids*	.952	100	148	9	8	165	2
Hightower, Vee, Rockford	.968	17	29	1	1	31	0
Hinds, Collin, Wisconsin	1.000	4	5	0	0	5	0
Iatarola, Aaron, Cedar Rapids*	.955	72	83	2	4	89	0
Jackson, Ryan, Kane County*	.990	59	96	1	1	98	1
Johnson, James, Clinton	.917	7	10	1	1	12	0
Keifer, Greg, Burlington	.875	5	7	0	1	8	0
Kominek, Toby, Beloit	.976	51	80	2	2	84	0
KRAUSE, Scott, Beloit	.985	131	177	14	3	194	3
Levias, Andres, South Bend	.971	23	32	2	1	35	0
Lewis, Marc, Michigan	.981	31	48	3	1	52	0
Linares, Yfrain, Beloit	1.000	1	1	0	0	1	0
Lowry, Curt, Clinton	.957	56	103	7	5	115	2
Lugo, Jesus, Peoria	.984	36	58	2	1	61	1
Madsen, Dan, Rockford*	.984	29	61	0	1	62	0
Martinez, Erik, Clinton	.800	7	4	0	1	5	0
Mathews, Byron, South Bend	.959	89	201	7	9	217	2
Mathis, Joe, Wisconsin	.983	112	165	10	3	178	1
Matthews, Gary, Clinton	.966	127	245	9	9	263	3
Mealing, Al, Beloit	.857	14	11	1	2	14	0
Medina, Alger, Rockford	.941	20	16	0	1	17	0
Mendez, Rudolfo, Springfield	.932	124	185	20	15	220	3
Moeder, Tony, Cedar Rapids	1.000	7	13	0	0	13	0
Monahan, Shane, Wisconsin	.971	59	100	0	3	103	0

Player, Team	Pct.	G	PO	A	E	TC	DP
Montiel, David, Beloit	.981	55	49	2	1	52	0
Mucker, Kelcey, Fort Wayne	.957	105	147	10	7	164	2
Nelson, Bryant, Quad City	.909	5	9	1	1	11	1
Newhan, David, W. Michigan	.976	23	37	3	1	41	0
Oglesby, Luke, Springfield	1.000	42	81	1	0	82	0
Olmsted, Nate, Cedar Rapids	1.000	6	4	1	0	5	0
Pearson, Kevin, Fort Wayne	1.000	14	11	0	0	11	0
Pico, Brandon, Rockford*	.977	94	159	12	4	175	1
Powell, Chris, Cedar Rapids*	.977	23	41	1	1	43	0
Pratt, Wes, Quad City	1.000	14	25	0	0	25	0
Price, Christopher, Springfield	.957	48	88	1	4	93	0
Reid, Derek, Burlington	.975	95	187	7	5	199	1
Rennhack, Mike, Quad City*	.973	93	143	2	4	149	0
Reyes, Michael, Kane County	.875	13	20	1	3	24	0
Richardson, Eric, South Bend	.976	49	78	2	2	82	0
Robbins, Lance, Cedar Rapids	.833	5	4	1	1	6	1
Rocha, Juan, Springfield	.945	75	113	7	7	127	1
Ross, Tony, Quad City	.968	96	148	5	5	158	1
Salzano, Jerry, Rockford	1.000	1	1	0	0	1	0
Smith, Demond, C.R.-W.M.	.968	86	177	3	6	186	0
Smith, John, Beloit	1.000	73	126	5	0	131	0
Smith, Scott, Wisconsin	1.000	28	36	5	0	41	1
Soriano, Jose, West Michigan	.964	121	257	13	10	280	3
Stasio, Chris, Michigan	.925	33	37	0	3	40	0
Swift, Scott, Burlington	1.000	12	15	4	0	19	1
Tena, Dario, Clinton	.970	90	154	8	5	167	3
Topham, Ryan, South Bend*	.941	13	16	0	1	17	0
Towner, Kyle, Wisconsin	.983	98	165	10	3	178	2
Trammell, Gary, Quad City	.932	37	49	6	4	59	2
Tyler, Josh, Beloit	1.000	4	3	0	0	3	0
Tyrus, Jason, Clinton	.968	53	86	6	3	95	0
Vizcaino, Romulo, Fort Wayne	.968	98	137	13	5	155	0
Walker, Steve, Rockford	.974	99	254	12	7	273	2
Walls, Eric, Springfield*	.965	83	162	3	6	171	0
Ward, Turner, Beloit	1.000	2	1	0	0	1	0
Watson, Kevin, Burlington	.961	73	94	5	4	103	0
Whatley, Gabe, Rockford	.983	74	106	7	2	115	0
White, Chad, Quad City	.975	73	149	6	4	159	0
Whittaker, Jay, South Bend	.964	61	129	3	5	137	1
Williams, Drew, Beloit	.857	5	6	0	1	7	0
Wilson, Chris, Beloit	1.000	20	27	2	0	29	1
Wulfert, Mark, Clinton	.922	46	56	3	5	64	0
Young, Kevin, Cedar Rapids	.984	116	175	12	3	190	3
Zaletel, Brian, Burlington	1.000	21	19	0	0	19	0
Zwisler, Josh, Beloit	1.000	19	16	1	0	17	0

OUTFIELDERS WITH TWO OR MORE TEAMS

Player, Team	Pct.	G	PO	A	E	TC	DP
Smith, Demond, Cedar Rapids	.971	79	165	2	5	172	0
Smith, Demond, W. Michigan	.929	7	12	1	1	14	0

CATCHERS

Player, Team	Pct.	G	PO	A	E	TC	DP	PB
Amezcua, Adan, Quad City	.979	46	285	34	7	326	4	11
Andreopouls, Alex, Beloit	.978	55	361	45	9	415	1	3
Augustine, Andy, Wisconsin	.997	55	274	34	1	309	3	12
Ballara, Juan, Peoria	.986	52	310	35	5	350	3	10
Barton, Scott, Rockford	.960	5	20	4	1	25	1	1
Bazzani, Matt, Michigan	.986	23	126	11	2	139	2	10
Borrero, Rikchy, Michigan	.962	16	95	5	4	104	1	0
Burgos, Carlos, Springfield	.985	12	62	3	1	66	0	1
Cady, Todd, Kane County	1.000	7	33	6	0	39	1	2
Campillo, Rob, Beloit	.992	45	303	49	3	355	0	4
CARONE, Richard, S. Bend	.988	83	563	76	8	647	6	11
Carpenter, Jerry, Ced. Rapids	1.000	11	52	8	0	60	0	1
Chevalier, Virgil, Michigan	1.000	1	5	1	0	6	0	0
Cline, Pat, Rockford	.973	91	549	64	17	630	2	18
Coe, Ryan, Quad City	.988	30	150	17	2	169	0	1
DaSilva, Manny, W. Michigan	.951	5	36	3	2	41	0	2
Davis, Josh, Clinton	.952	8	37	3	2	42	1	1
DeBoer, Rob, W. Michigan	.982	83	494	54	10	558	2	13
Delaney, Sean, Springfield	.974	45	187	36	6	229	8	8
Dennis, Brian, Rockford	.986	17	65	6	1	72	2	14
DePastino, Joe, Michigan	.991	68	451	71	5	527	1	4
Ebbert, Chad, Clinton	1.000	2	10	1	0	11	0	1
Encarnacion, Anito, C. Rapids	.928	14	54	10	5	69	0	4
Espiritu, Michael, Ced. Rapids	.944	9	59	8	4	71	1	1
Fortin, Troy, Fort Wayne	.800	4	7	1	2	10	1	0
Glenn, Darrin, Burlington	1.000	4	6	0	0	6	0	0
Gonzalez, Jimmy, Quad City	.987	30	136	13	2	151	0	3
Hall, Ryan, Peoria	.992	39	228	27	2	257	2	11
Hamburg, Leon, W. Michigan	1.000	2	3	0	0	3	0	0
Heath, Jason, Wisconsin	.977	13	76	10	2	88	0	5

Player, Team	Pct.	G	PO	A	E	TC	DP	PB
Hemphill, Bret, Ced. Rapids	.992	68	429	69	4	502	6	7
Hilt, Scott, Fort Wayne	.975	30	181	15	5	201	1	10
Ibarra, Jesus, Burlington	.943	22	121	12	8	141	0	11
Johnson, Jack, Rockford	.976	19	107	16	3	126	1	1
Jones, Ken, Clinton	.971	31	181	19	6	206	2	4
Kuilan, Hector, Kane Co.	.944	2	12	5	1	18	0	0
Kurek, Chris, Michigan	.975	49	303	43	9	355	2	9
LaValliere, Mike, S. Bend	1.000	2	3	0	0	3	0	0
Martin, Mike, Clinton	.978	50	281	35	7	323	3	7
McDonald, Keith, Peoria	.991	62	411	54	4	469	5	4
Molina, Ben, Cedar Rapids	.978	39	283	32	7	322	5	5
Ortega, Randy, W. Michigan	.984	42	278	22	5	305	3	5
Pierzynski, A.J., Ft. Wayne	.939	20	119	34	10	163	0	4
Poor, Jeff, Burlington	.985	74	469	54	8	531	3	18
Probst, Alan, Quad City	.992	52	318	42	3	363	1	1
Ramos, Jeff, Springfield	1.000	12	50	4	0	54	0	2
Rodriguez, Maximo, K. C.	.976	65	414	39	11	464	4	12
Rondon, Alex, W. Michigan	.958	21	124	14	6	144	2	5
Rosario, Melvin, S. Bend	.962	49	271	58	13	342	5	10
Roskos, John, Kane County	.986	71	431	47	7	485	5	7
Ryder, Derek, Cedar Rapids	.983	16	50	8	1	59	1	1
Sanchez, Marcos, Clinton	.973	6	32	4	1	37	0	4
Sanchez, Victor, Quad City	.980	6	43	5	1	49	0	2
Schneider, Dan, Burlington	.984	51	328	45	6	379	4	5
Schwenke, Matt, Clinton	.962	31	153	23	7	183	4	5
Snook, Robert, Beloit	1.000	3	19	2	0	21	0	0
Snyder, Jarod, Rockford	.962	24	112	13	5	130	0	3
Spinello, Joe, South Bend	.929	4	13	0	1	14	0	0
Sutherland, Alex, Wisconsin	.986	85	554	66	9	629	5	10
Treanor, Matt, Springfield	.976	74	390	66	11	467	4	10
Tyler, Josh, Beloit	1.000	2	8	0	0	8	0	1
Ullan, Dave, Clinton	.956	37	199	20	10	229	0	2
Valentin, Jose, Fort Wayne	.973	101	730	108	23	861	11	17
Walker, Joe, South Bend	1.000	6	20	1	0	21	0	2
Wathan, Dusty, Wisconsin	1.000	5	21	5	0	26	0	0
Welch, Coby, Springfield	.969	18	85	9	3	97	1	3
Williams, Drew, Beloit	1.000	2	6	0	0	6	0	0
Zwisler, Josh, Beloit	.974	67	325	45	10	380	1	14

PITCHERS

Player, Team	Pct.	G	PO	A	E	TC	DP
Aguirre, Jose, Cedar Rapids*	1.000	6	0	1	0	1	0
Alejo, Nigel, Kane County	.857	48	2	4	1	7	0
Ali, Sam, Burlington	1.000	3	0	2	0	2	0
Altman, Heath, Burlington	1.000	3	0	1	0	1	1
Alvarado, Luis, Fort Wayne	.800	16	1	3	1	5	1
Alvarez, Ivan, Burlington*	1.000	4	0	3	0	3	0
Ambrose, John, South Bend	.800	3	2	2	1	5	0
Andersen, Mark, Kane County	1.000	15	5	2	0	7	1
Anderson, Eric, Springfield	.923	21	4	8	1	13	0
Bair, Dennis, Rockford	1.000	9	1	8	0	9	0
Barker, Richard, Rockford	1.000	32	5	7	0	12	0
Barksdale, Joe, Michigan	.923	24	10	14	2	26	0
Baron, Jim, Clinton*	.875	11	0	7	1	8	0
Barrios, Manuel, Quad City	.778	50	1	6	2	9	0
Beck, Chris, Wisconsin	.923	28	10	14	2	26	0
Beck, Greg, Beloit	.833	35	9	6	3	18	0
Bedinger, Doug, Fort Wayne	.882	46	4	11	2	17	0
Bell, Jason, Fort Wayne	1.000	9	3	12	0	15	2
Bernal, Manuel, Springfield	.917	8	2	9	1	12	1
Betances, Junior, Beloit	1.000	1	0	1	0	1	0
Betti, Rich, Michigan*	1.000	1	1	0	0	1	0
Beverlin, Jason, W. Michigan	1.000	22	4	14	0	18	0
Bieniasz, Derek, Wisconsin	.933	27	13	29	3	45	1
Bigham, Dave, South Bend*	.923	25	5	31	3	39	0
Blais, Mike, Michigan	1.000	32	3	10	0	13	1
Blanco, Alberto, Quad City*	.833	11	2	8	2	12	0
Bogle, Sean, Rockford	1.000	13	4	5	0	9	0
Bonilla, Welnis, Michigan	1.000	12	0	3	0	3	0
Brixey, Dustin, Springfield	.923	36	6	18	2	26	0
Bronkey, Jeff, Beloit	1.000	3	0	1	0	1	0
Broome, Curtis, South Bend	1.000	29	9	16	0	25	1
Bryant, Chris, Rockford*	.900	21	0	9	1	10	0
Burt, Chris, Beloit	1.000	36	3	5	0	8	1
Bush, Craig, Michigan	.875	34	0	7	1	8	0
Bushart, John, Cedar Rapids*	1.000	19	2	4	0	6	0
Bussa, Todd, Kane County	1.000	36	2	5	0	7	0
Byrne, Earl, Rockford*	.905	13	1	18	2	21	1
Cardona, Isbell, Burlington	.000	6	0	0	1	1	0
Carl, Todd, Kane County	1.000	12	0	2	0	2	0
Carroll, David, Peoria*	.923	24	6	6	1	13	1
Carter, Lance, Springfield	.967	27	13	16	1	30	0

CLASS A *Midwest League*

CLASS A *Midwest League*

Player, Team	Pct.	G	PO	A	E	TC	DP
Casey, Ryan, Rockford	1.000	16	1	2	0	3	0
Chapman, Walker, Fort Wayne*	1.000	14	2	5	0	7	1
Charlton, Aaron, Burlington	.750	16	1	2	1	4	0
Cintron, Jose, Cedar Rapids	1.000	13	4	12	0	16	1
Cloude, Ken, Wisconsin	.886	25	8	23	4	35	1
Cobb, Trevor, Fort Wayne*	.833	11	2	3	1	6	0
Cochrane, Chris, W. Michigan	1.000	41	9	24	0	33	3
Cook, Jake, Michigan	.897	21	9	17	3	29	1
Corrigan, Cory, Peoria	.967	47	10	19	1	30	2
Crossley, Chad, Cedar Rapids	1.000	12	0	1	0	1	0
Crump, Jody, Peoria*	1.000	25	3	6	0	9	0
Curran, Tighe, Peoria*	.952	24	7	13	1	21	1
Dafun, George, Cedar Rapids	1.000	5	1	1	0	2	0
Dale, Carl, Peoria	.943	24	9	24	2	35	2
Dalton, Brian, Beloit	1.000	34	5	7	0	12	1
D'Amico, Jeff, Beloit	.958	21	10	13	1	24	0
Daniels, John, Wisconsin	.895	39	6	11	2	19	1
Davis, Keith, Clinton	.857	36	6	6	2	14	0
Deakman, Josh, Ced. Rapids	.923	13	2	10	1	13	1
Dennis, Brian, Rockford	1.000	3	0	1	0	1	0
Dennis, Shane, Clinton*	.852	14	3	20	4	27	0
DeWitt, Scott, Kane County*	1.000	1	1	0	0	1	0
Dickson, Jason, Ced. Rapids	.980	25	14	35	1	50	2
Diorio, Mike, Quad City	.857	33	6	12	3	21	1
Dixon, Jim, South Bend	1.000	10	2	3	0	5	0
Domenico, Brian, Michigan	.750	6	2	1	1	4	0
Doughty, Brian, Wisconsin	.944	32	3	14	1	18	1
Dowhower, Deron, F.t Wayne	.917	35	4	7	1	12	0
Droll, Jeff, South Bend	1.000	8	0	2	0	2	0
Duncan, Sean, South Bend*	.667	12	0	2	1	3	0
Dutch, John, Michigan	1.000	32	3	5	0	8	0
Elarton, Scott, Quad City	.958	26	7	16	1	24	2
Epstein, Ian, West Michigan*	1.000	18	1	0	0	1	0
Erdos, Todd, Clinton	1.000	5	0	1	0	1	0
Estes, Shawn, Wis.-Bur.*	.875	6	2	5	1	8	1
Farmer, Jon, Kane County*	.917	29	4	7	1	12	1
Farrell, Jim, Michigan	1.000	13	3	4	0	7	0
Faulkner, Neal, Rockford	.900	40	4	5	1	10	0
Felix, Ruben, Beloit*	.833	45	0	5	1	6	0
Fennell, Barry, Rockford*	1.000	4	0	4	0	4	1
Fidge, Darren, Fort Wayne	.943	39	8	25	2	35	1
Filbeck, Ryan, Kane County	.857	25	3	9	2	14	0
Fitzpatrick, Kenneth, Springfield	1.000	12	3	7	0	10	0
Fitzpatrick, Will, Beloit	1.000	3	0	1	0	1	0
Fletcher, Paul, South Bend*	1.000	36	1	9	0	10	2
Flury, Pat, Springfield	1.000	34	3	13	0	16	1
Foderaro, Kevin, Peoria	.933	15	6	8	1	15	0
Freehill, Michael, Cedar Rapids	1.000	54	4	12	0	16	1
Gamboa, Javier, Springfield	.833	19	6	14	4	24	0
GARCIA, Alfredo, Rockford	1.000	27	12	29	0	41	3
Garcia, Ariel, South Bend	1.000	10	2	7	0	9	0
Garrett, Hal, Clinton	.933	11	4	10	1	15	0
Gates, Sean, Clinton	.714	29	3	2	2	7	0
Gautreau, Mike, Peoria	.813	45	4	9	3	16	0
Gomez, Augustine, S. Bend	.826	25	8	11	4	23	0
Gomez, Dennys, Burlington	1.000	14	1	3	0	4	0
Gonzalez, Gabe, Kane County*	.929	32	6	7	1	14	0
Gonzalez, Geremis, Rockford	.739	12	7	10	6	23	1
Gonzalez, Juan, Beloit	.909	42	8	12	2	22	0
Gooda, David, Beloit*	1.000	3	0	6	0	6	0
Gould, Clint, Wisconsin	1.000	25	3	6	0	9	0
Gourdin, Tom, Fort Wayne	.963	41	7	19	1	27	0
Green, Chris, Wisconsin	1.000	35	9	16	0	25	2
Grenert, Geoff, Cedar Rapids	.944	27	5	12	1	18	1
Grote, Jason, Burlington	1.000	6	0	2	0	2	0
Gunderson, Mike, Quad City	.938	44	3	12	1	16	0
Gunther, Kevin, W. Michigan	1.000	17	1	2	0	3	0
Halama, John, Quad City*	.920	55	3	20	2	25	1
Hale, Chad, Michigan*	1.000	42	2	13	0	15	0
Hall, Billy, Quad City	1.000	36	2	14	0	16	2
Hall, Yates, Peoria	1.000	9	1	4	0	5	0
Hammerschmidt, Andy, Clinton*	.935	14	2	27	2	31	3
Hause, Brendan, W. Michigan	.911	31	10	31	4	45	1
Hebbert, Allan, Kane County	.667	5	1	3	2	6	0
Herbert, Russell, South Bend	.900	9	1	8	1	10	0
Hernandez, Santos, Burlington	1.000	44	1	10	0	11	1
Hill, Jason, Cedar Rapids*	1.000	48	4	12	0	16	1
Huntsman, Scott, Beloit	1.000	43	2	3	0	5	0
Hutzler, Jeff, Burlington	.900	9	2	7	1	10	0
Isom, Jeff, Clinton*	1.000	35	2	19	0	21	0
Jenkins, A.J., Clinton	.800	33	3	9	3	15	0
Johnson, Ron, Peoria*	.964	22	5	22	1	28	0
Keith, Jeffrey, Burlington*	.957	47	9	13	1	23	0
Kester, Tim, Quad City	.895	28	11	23	4	38	0
Khoury, Tony, Rockford	1.000	28	3	5	0	8	0
King, Bill, West Michigan	.892	30	14	19	4	37	0
Knox, Jeffery, Cedar Rapids	.885	25	10	13	3	26	1
Krause, Kevin, Rockford	.917	30	8	14	2	24	1
Krueger, Robert, Wisconsin*	1.000	19	2	2	0	4	0
Lake, Kevin, Burlington*	.923	28	8	28	3	39	1
Leach, Jumaane, Clinton*	1.000	19	0	7	0	7	0
Leibee, Skye, West Michigan*	1.000	9	2	1	0	3	0
Leiber, Zane, South Bend	.800	14	3	1	1	5	0
Linares, Yfrain, Beloit	.833	19	4	6	2	12	0
Lindemann, Wayne, S. Bend*	1.000	7	0	4	0	4	1
Lintern, Cory, Burlington	1.000	8	2	1	0	3	0
Lock, Dan, Quad City*	.849	27	9	36	8	53	4
Logan, Chris, Clinton	.889	53	4	12	2	18	0
Lowe, Jason, West Michigan	.667	7	0	2	1	3	0
Lundquist, David, South Bend	1.000	18	5	10	0	15	1
MacDonald, Mike, Springfield	.929	55	4	9	1	14	1
Mamott, Joe, Michigan	.889	14	4	12	2	18	0
Martinez, Javier, Rockford	.917	18	3	19	2	24	1
Martinez, Uriel, Clinton	1.000	11	2	4	0	6	0
May, Scott, Rockford	1.000	8	0	3	0	3	0
Mays, Marcus, Kane County*	1.000	8	0	2	0	2	0
McCormack, Andy, S. Bend*	1.000	6	1	3	0	4	0
McMillan, Leonard, Burlington	1.000	8	3	3	0	6	1
McMullen, Mike, Burlington	.895	29	6	11	2	19	1
Meadows, Brian, Kane County	.944	26	12	22	2	36	2
Mercado, Gabby, Beloit	.926	24	6	19	2	27	0
Meyhoff, Jason, Fort Wayne*	1.000	17	2	6	0	8	2
Micknich, Steve, Kane County	1.000	9	0	1	0	1	0
Miles, Chad, Kane County*	1.000	19	1	5	0	6	0
Miranda, Walter, Kane County	.932	25	15	26	3	44	2
Mitchell, Alvin, Michigan	.960	30	9	15	1	25	4
Mix, Derek, Clinton	.846	35	1	10	2	13	0
Montelongo, Joseph, Rockford	.889	20	11	21	4	36	1
Morgan, Eric, Wisconsin	.857	7	1	5	1	7	0
Morrison, Chris, W. Michigan	1.000	13	2	1	0	3	0
Mosman, Marc, Burlington	1.000	8	1	4	0	5	1
Mott, Tom, Fort Wayne	.914	25	14	18	3	35	3
Mounce, Tony, Quad City*	.907	25	9	30	4	43	1
Mull, Blaine, Springfield	.947	25	12	24	2	38	0
Mullins, Greg, Beloit*	.933	15	4	10	1	15	1
Myers, Jason, Burlington*	.938	16	3	12	1	16	0
Nartker, Mike, Fort Wayne	1.000	17	4	11	0	15	0
Nate, Scott, Beloit*	1.000	20	2	5	0	7	1
Nelson, Rodney, Springfield	.778	25	8	13	6	27	0
Newman, Damon, W. Michigan	.923	21	5	7	1	13	1
Newman, Eric, Clinton	1.000	11	2	11	0	13	2
Ormonde, Troy, Rockford	1.000	7	4	7	0	11	0
Padilla, Roy, Michigan*	.750	4	0	3	1	4	0
Parisi, Michael, Kane County	.886	26	10	21	4	35	1
Pavano, Carl, Michigan	.943	22	16	17	2	35	0
Pavicich, Paul, Fort Wayne*	1.000	39	1	11	0	12	0
Pearce, Jeff, Wisconsin*	1.000	27	0	5	0	5	0
Perez, Jayson, Clinton	.636	13	2	5	4	11	0
Perez, Juan, West Michigan*	.943	30	4	29	2	35	2
Perkins, Dan, Fort Wayne	.875	29	7	14	3	24	0
Peters, Brannon, Ft. Wayne*	1.000	11	1	2	0	3	0
Peterson, Jayson, Rockford	.778	13	3	4	2	9	0
Petroff, Daniel, Cedar Rapids	.953	28	13	28	2	43	1
Phillips, Marc, Springfield*	.826	38	6	13	4	23	2
Pineda, Leonel, Kane County	1.000	5	4	10	0	14	0
Place, Mike, South Bend	1.000	28	2	5	0	7	0
Pontes, Dan, Peoria	.833	34	5	10	3	18	2
Portillo, Alex, South Bend*	1.000	2	0	1	0	1	0
Prater, Pete, Burlington	.957	21	7	15	1	23	1
Press, Greg, Kane County	.905	29	8	30	4	42	1
Putrich, Josh, Rockford	1.000	6	2	0	0	2	0
Quirk, John, South Bend*	.800	22	0	8	2	10	0
Radinsky, Scott, S. Bend*	1.000	6	0	1	0	1	0
Radlosky, Robert, Ft. Wayne	.913	30	9	12	2	23	1
Raggio, Brady, Peoria	1.000	8	6	11	0	17	2
Rain, Steve, Rockford	.909	53	1	9	1	11	1
Rajotte, Jason, W. Michigan*	.944	44	4	13	1	18	2
Ramos, Edgar, Quad City	1.000	2	0	1	0	1	0
Ratliff, Chris, Burlington	.944	15	4	13	1	18	0
Rector, Bobby, Burlington	.929	27	7	19	2	28	1
Reed, Brian, Peoria	.833	64	4	11	3	18	1
Renfroe, Chad, Michigan	.909	12	5	5	1	11	0
Ritter, Jason, Springfield	1.000	7	1	0	0	1	0
Rivette, Scott, West Michigan	1.000	8	0	3	0	3	0
Robbins, Michael, Springfield*	.889	8	1	7	1	9	1
Roberts, Ray, Springfield*	1.000	38	2	9	0	11	0

Player, Team	Pct.	G	PO	A	E	TC	DP
Roettgen, Mark, Peoria	1.000	4	0	2	0	2	0
Rose, Brian, Michigan	.925	21	13	24	3	40	0
Rosenkranz, Terry, Beloit*	1.000	4	0	1	0	1	0
Ruch, Rob, Fort Wayne	1.000	9	3	1	0	4	0
Runyan, Sean, Quad City*	.895	22	7	10	2	19	0
Rushing, William, Ft. Wayne*	1.000	13	0	4	0	4	1
Sak, James, Clinton	1.000	7	3	6	0	9	0
Salmon, Fabian, South Bend	1.000	15	4	2	0	6	0
Santana, Marino, Wisconsin	.913	15	5	16	2	23	0
Scheffer, Aaron, Wisconsin	1.000	9	0	4	0	4	0
Schenbeck, T.J., Beloit	1.000	18	4	10	0	14	0
Scott, Ron, Peoria*	.800	21	3	1	1	5	0
Shaver, Tony, Quad City	.923	35	5	7	1	13	2
Sick, David, Cedar Rapids	.938	50	3	12	1	16	0
Sikorski, Brian, Quad City	1.000	2	0	1	0	1	0
Silva, Luis, West Michigan	.857	10	1	5	1	7	0
Skuse, Nicholas, Ced. Rapids	.972	27	12	23	1	36	1
Slade, Shawn, Cedar Rapids	1.000	30	1	7	0	8	0
Slininger, Dennis, Peoria	1.000	3	0	2	0	2	0
Smith, Andy, West Michigan	.771	30	8	19	8	35	1
Smith, Brook, Burlington*	.952	39	9	31	2	42	0
Smith, Charles, South Bend	.896	26	10	33	5	48	1
Smith, John, West Michigan*	.800	25	1	7	2	10	1
Smith, Mason, Burlington	1.000	8	0	6	0	6	0
Smith, Roy, Wisconsin	.960	27	10	14	1	25	0
Smith, Shad, Burlington	.600	2	2	1	2	5	0
Sosa, Helpis, West Michigan	.714	21	1	4	2	7	0
Stark, Zachary, Kane County*	.750	5	0	6	2	8	0
Steed, Sam, Springfield*	1.000	8	3	5	0	8	0
Stein, Blake, Peoria	.778	27	9	12	6	27	0
Steinke, Brock, Quad City	.800	21	2	2	1	5	0
Stevenson, Jason, Rockford	.941	33	7	9	1	17	2
Surratt, Jamie, South Bend	.917	26	5	6	1	12	0

Player, Team	Pct.	G	PO	A	E	TC	DP
Telgheder, Jim, Michigan	.857	22	2	4	1	7	0
Theodile, Robert, South Bend	.909	7	4	6	1	11	0
Thomas, Carlos, Clinton	1.000	13	5	1	0	6	0
Thompson, John, Wisconsin	.900	38	4	5	1	10	0
Thurmond, Travis, Ced. Rapids	1.000	14	2	6	0	8	0
Tidwell, Jason, Kane County	1.000	6	0	5	0	5	0
Tillmon, Darrell, Michigan*	.800	13	7	5	3	15	0
Tollberg, Brian, Beloit	.971	22	10	23	1	34	2
Towns, Ryan, Springfield	.750	18	1	2	1	4	0
Tyrrell, Jim, Michigan*	1.000	16	1	4	0	5	1
Upchurch, Wayne, Springfield	.875	18	6	1	1	8	1
Vanhof, Dave, Wisconsin*	.810	15	5	12	4	21	0
Vandeweg, Ryan, Clinton	.909	15	6	14	2	22	1
Villano, Mike, Burlington	.875	16	3	4	1	8	1
Walters, Brett, Clinton	.919	32	7	27	3	37	2
Warren, Deshawn, Ced. Rapids*	1.000	7	0	7	0	7	0
Washburn, Jarrod, Ced. Rapids*	1.000	3	2	3	0	5	0
Weinberg, Todd, W. Michigan*	.875	36	3	18	3	24	1
Welch, Travis, Peoria	1.000	46	4	8	0	12	0
West, Adam, Peoria*	.667	4	0	2	1	3	0
Wiesner, Chad, Wisconsin	1.000	1	1	0	0	1	0
Williams, Juan, Fort Wayne*	1.000	3	1	0	0	1	0
Woodard, Steve, Beloit	1.000	21	7	17	0	24	1
Wunsch, Kelly, Beloit*	.864	14	2	17	3	22	2
Ybarra, Jamie, Kane County	.917	50	9	13	2	24	1
Zancanaro, Dave, W. Michigan*	.800	16	0	4	1	5	0
Zanolla, Dan, Kane County	.909	28	3	7	1	11	0

PITCHERS WITH TWO OR MORE TEAMS

Player, Team	Pct.	G	PO	A	E	TC	DP
Estes, Shawn, Wisconsin*	1.000	2	2	2	0	4	1
Estes, Shawn, Burlington*	.750	4	0	3	1	4	0

The following players did not have any fielding statistics at the positions indicated or appeared only as a designated hitter, pinch-hitter or pinch-runner: Jose Abreu, p; Juan Abreu, p; Avalos, of; Betances, of; Boulware, of; Brewer, p; Buchanan, 3b; Bustos, 3b; D. Castro, p; Contreras, ss; Jason Cook, ss; Davalillo, p; Dean, of, c, p; Delvalle, p; Fraser, 3b; M. Harris, dh, ph, pr; Ignasiak, p; Jaha, dh; S. Jones, p; Keefe, of; Kurek, p; Lanza, 3b; Llanos, 3b; Marquez, p; Milstien, of; Nilsson, dh; Rantz, p; Root, 2b; Rosenbohm, p; Schiefelbein, p; Torres, p; Truby, of; Vardijan, p; Walls, p; Wambach, dh, ph; D. Williams, 3b; Winkle, p.

LEAGUE CHAMPIONS

Year	Team	Pct.	Year	Team	Pct.	Year	Team	Pct.
1947—	Belleville	.667	1965—	Burlington	.667	1981—	Wausau■	.636
	Belleville	.672		Burlington	.677		Quad Cities	.570
1948—	West Frankfort*	.708	1966—	Fox Cities◆	.689	1982—	Madison	.626
1949—	Centralia	.627		Cedar Rapids	.762		Appleton▼	.579
	Paducah (4th)†	.454	1967—	Wisconsin Rapids	.685	1983—	Appleton•	.635
1950—	Centralia‡	.675		Appleton◆	.587		Springfield	.576
1951—	Paris§	.700	1968—	Decatur	.656	1984—	Appleton•	.640
	Danville (4th)†	.432		Quad Cities◆	.648		Springfield	.504
1952—	Danville∞	.685	1969—	Appleton	.648	1985—	Kenosha▼	.568
	Decatur (3rd)†	.584		Appleton	.690		Peoria	.536
1953—	Decatur*	.576	1970—	Quincy◆	.691	1986—	Springfield	.621
1954—	Decatur	.587		Quad Cities	.581		Waterloo▼	.557
	Danville (2nd)‡	.528	1971—	Appleton	.642	1987—	Springfield	.671
1955—	Dubuque*	.587		Quad Cities■	.548		Kenosha▼	.586
1956—	Paris▲	.656	1972—	Appleton	.598	1988—	Cedar Rapids■	.621
	Dubuque	.603		Danville■	.584		Kenosha	.579
1957—	Decatur▲	.683	1973—	Wisconsin Rapids■	.562	1989—	South Bend■	.644
	Clinton	.623		Danville	.537		Springfield	.541
1958—	Michigan City	.623	1974—	Appleton	.593	1990—	Cedar Rapids	.657
	Waterloo◆	.613		Danville■	.517		Quad City■	.579
1959—	Waterloo	.613	1975—	Waterloo■	.727	1991—	Clinton■	.583
	Waterloo	.613		Quad Cities	.624		Madison	.558
1960—	Waterloo	.629	1976—	Waterloo■	.600	1992—	Quad City	.664
	Waterloo	.677		Cedar Rapids	.595		Cedar Rapids■	.594
1961—	Waterloo	.613	1977—	Waterloo	.580	1993—	Clinton	.597
	Quincy◆	.594		Burlington■	.511		South Bend■	.566
1962—	Dubuque◆	.667	1978—	Appleton■	.708	1994—	Rockford	.640
	Waterloo	.625		Burlington	.500		Cedar Rapids■	.554
1963—	Clinton	.710	1979—	Waterloo	.600	1995—	Beloit††	.633
	Clinton	.629		Quad Cities■	.579		Michigan	.543
1964—	Clinton	.667	1980—	Waterloo■	.610			
	Fox Cities◆	.667		Quad Cities	.532			

*Won championship and four-club playoff. †Won four-club playoff. ‡Playoff finals canceled because of bad weather. §Won both halves of split season. ∞Won first half of split season and tied Paris for second-half title. ▲Won first-half title and four-team playoff. ◆Won split season playoff. ■League divided into Northern and Southern divisions and played split season. Playoff winner. ▼League divided into Northern, Central and Southern divisions. Playoff winner. •League divided into Northern, Central and Southern divisions; regular season and playoff winner. ††League divided into Eastern, Central and Western divisions; regular season and playoff winner. (NOTE—Known as Illinois State League in 1947-48 and Mississippi-Ohio Valley League from 1949 through 1955.)

NEW YORK-PENN LEAGUE

LEAGUE OFFICE

President
Bob Julian

Address
1629 Oneida St.
Utica, NY 13501

Phone
315-733-8036

Teams (affiliation)
Auburn Doubledays (Astros)
Batavia Clippers (Phillies)
Elmira Pioneers (Marlins)
Erie SeaWolves (Pirates)
Hudson Valley Renegades (Rangers)
Jamestown Jammers (Tigers)
New Jersey Cardinals (Cardinals)

Oneonta Yankees (Yankees)
Pittsfield Mets (Mets)
St. Catharines Blue Jays (Blue Jays)
Utica Blue Sox (Red Sox)
Vermont Expos (Expos)
Watertown Indians (Indians)
Williamsport Cubs (Cubs)

1995 FINAL STANDINGS

McNAMARA DIVISION

Team	W	L	T	Pct.	GB
Vermont (Expos)	49	27	0	.645	......
Hudson Valley (Rangers)	47	27	0	.635	1
New Jersey (Cardinals)	35	41	0	.461	14
Pittsfield (Mets)	34	42	0	.447	15

PINCKNEY DIVISION

Team	W	L	T	Pct.	GB
Batavia (Phillies)	41	34	0	.547	......
St. Catharines (Blue Jays)	38	37	0	.507	3
Erie (Pirates)	34	41	0	.453	7
Jamestown (Tigers)	32	44	0	.421	9½

STEDLER DIVISION

Team	W	L	T	Pct.	GB
Watertown (Indians)	46	27	0	.630	......
Auburn (Astros)	40	34	0	.541	6½
Williamsport (Cubs)	37	39	0	.487	10½
Oneonta (Yankees)	34	41	0	.453	13
Utica (Red Sox)	33	40	0	.452	13
Elmira (Marlins)	25	51	0	.329	22½

COMPOSITE

Team	Ver.	H.V.	Wat.	Bat.	Aub.	St.C.	Wpt.	N.J.	One.	Erie	Uti.	Pit.	Jam.	Elm.	W	L	T	Pct.	GB
Vermont (Expos)	....	7	4	3	2	3	2	7	2	2	2	9	4	2	49	27	0	.645	......
Hudson Valley (Rangers)	5	....	2	4	2	1	2	8	4	4	2	9	2	2	47	27	0	.635	1
Watertown (Indians)	0	1	....	2	5	3	4	4	7	4	6	1	3	6	46	27	0	.630	1½
Batavia (Phillies)	1	0	2	....	1	6	2	3	2	7	2	3	9	3	41	34	0	.547	7½
Auburn (Astros)	2	2	5	3	....	3	4	2	2	3	4	2	2	6	40	34	0	.541	8
St. Catharines (Blue Jays)	1	3	1	5	1	....	4	2	3	6	3	1	4	4	38	37	0	.507	10½
Williamsport (Cubs)	2	2	4	2	4	0	....	2	2	2	6	2	2	7	37	39	0	.487	12
New Jersey (Cardinals)	5	4	0	1	2	2	2	....	2	3	2	6	2	4	35	41	0	.461	14
Oneonta (Yankees)	2	0	1	2	6	1	6	2	....	1	4	1	3	5	34	41	0	.453	14½
Erie (Pirates)	2	0	0	5	1	6	2	1	3	....	1	3	7	3	34	41	0	.453	14½
Utica (Red Sox)	2	1	2	2	4	1	2	2	7	2	....	2	1	5	33	40	0	.452	14½
Pittsfield (Mets)	3	3	3	1	2	3	2	6	3	1	2	....	3	2	34	42	0	.447	15
Jamestown (Tigers)	0	2	1	3	2	8	2	2	1	5	3	1	....	2	32	44	0	.421	17
Elmira (Marlins)	2	2	2	1	2	0	5	0	3	1	3	2	2	....	25	51	0	.329	24

Major league affiliations in parentheses.

Hudson Valley home games played in Fishkill, N.Y.

New Jersey home games played in Augusta, N.J.

Vermont home games played in Winooski, Vt.

PLAYOFFS: Vermont defeated Hudson Valley, two games to none; Watertown defeated Batavia, two games to one; Watertown defeated Vermont, two games to one, to win league championship.

REGULAR-SEASON ATTENDANCE: Auburn, 58,972; Batavia, 38,313; Elmira, 43,759; Erie, 181,815; Hudson Valley, 161,673; Jamestown, 48,938; New Jersey, 176,788; Oneonta, 53,990; Pittsfield, 73,273; St. Catharines, 50,528; Utica, 64,487; Vermont, 120,917; Watertown, 45,202; Williamsport, 63,192. Total—1,181,847. Playoffs (8 games)—14,684.

MANAGERS: Auburn, Manny Acta; Batavia, Al LeBoeuf; Elmira, Paul Kirsch; Erie, Scott Little; Hudson Valley, Bump Wills; Jamestown, Bruce Fields; New Jersey, Luis Melendez; Oneonta, Rob Thomson; Pittsfield, Ron Gideon; St. Catharines, J.J. Cannon; Utica, Bob Geren; Vermont, Jim Gabella; Watertown, Joel Skinner; Williamsport, Oneri Fleita.

ALL-STAR TEAM: 1B—Steve Carver, Batavia; 2B—Marlon Anderson, Batavia; 3B—Clifford Brumbaugh, Hudson Valley; SS—Oscar Robles, Auburn; Utility IF—Jose Fernandez, Vermont; OF—Ed Bady, Pittsfield; Fletcher Bates, Pittsfield; Jose Guillen, Erie; Luke Wilcox, Oneonta; C—Ramon Castro, Auburn; Scott Vieira, Williamsport; DH—Virgil Chevalier, Utica; RHP—Chris Weidert, Vermont; Scott Mudd, Hudson Valley; LHP—Bryan Link, Hudson Valley; Michael Venafro, Hudson Valley; Most Valuable Player—Clifford Brumbaugh, Hudson Valley; Manager of the Year—Joel Skinner, Watertown.

1995 BATTING

TEAM

Team	Avg.	G	TPA	AB	R	H	TB	2B	3B	HR	RBI	SH	SF	HP	BB	IBB	SO	SB	CS	GDP	LOB	ShO	Slg.	OBP
Auburn	.267	74	2765	2444	383	653	897	112	18	32	331	10	24	29	258	5	410	71	27	69	533	1	.367	.341
Hudson Valley	.267	74	2859	2512	376	670	897	105	25	24	306	13	31	50	252	13	465	107	51	72	533	5	.357	.342
Erie	.264	75	2829	2503	368	661	941	92	25	46	307	23	20	50	232	3	502	81	50	62	498	5	.376	.336
Batavia	.262	75	2918	2592	389	680	941	106	31	31	336	22	17	50	236	5	474	88	35	49	536	1	.363	.334
St. Catharines	.257	75	2918	2557	344	658	911	119	25	28	289	40	20	53	248	9	570	96	45	25	565	8	.356	.333
Vermont	.257	76	2842	2505	354	643	865	94	28	24	287	17	27	36	257	9	457	152	72	36	515	2	.345	.331
Watertown	.257	73	2834	2456	360	630	896	127	26	29	306	21	24	34	299	11	529	49	23	61	564	3	.365	.342
Utica	.256	74	2708	2425	358	622	865	98	23	33	304	21	30	41	191	2	453	125	55	49	431	1	.357	.318
Williamsport	.255	76	2919	2561	379	654	907	122	34	21	324	12	24	47	275	7	523	85	44	51	543	6	.354	.336
Jamestown	.254	76	2963	2544	368	646	926	117	29	35	312	19	21	40	338	9	526	104	48	50	577	9	.364	.348

Team	Avg.	G	TPA	AB	R	H	TB	2B	3B	HR	RBI	SH	SF	HP	BB	IBB	SO	SB	CS	GDP	LOB	ShO	Slg.	OBP
New Jersey	.250	76	2979	2603	370	651	849	105	27	13	314	29	14	53	280	6	477	93	43	54	550	3	.326	.334
Pittsfield	.249	76	2858	2498	325	623	830	101	32	14	270	26	23	36	274	7	487	103	50	36	545	6	.332	.330
Elmira	.243	76	2860	2534	316	616	884	106	30	34	261	14	17	42	253	11	552	111	52	61	532	6	.349	.320
Oneonta	.243	75	2812	2489	312	604	843	125	30	18	261	9	27	28	259	4	553	87	33	42	548	6	.339	.318

INDIVIDUAL

TOP QUALIFIERS FOR BATTING CHAMPIONSHIP

Minimum 205 plate appearances. *Lefthanded batter. †Switch-hitter.

Player, Team	Avg.	G	TPA	AB	R	H	TB	2B	3B	HR	RBI	SH	SF	HP	BB	IBB	SO	SB	CS	GDP	Slg.	OBP
Brumbaugh, Clifford, Hud. Valley....	.358	74	325	282	44	101	134	19	4	2	45	0	2	2	39	4	51	15	3	11	.475	.437
Bady, Edward, Vermont†	.329	72	326	295	51	97	124	15	3	2	25	2	0	5	24	3	52	34	19	3	.420	.389
Casey, Sean, Watertown*	.329	55	229	207	26	68	92	18	0	2	37	0	3	1	18	4	21	3	0	6	.444	.380
Wilcox, Chris, Oneonta*	.327	59	246	223	25	73	106	16	7	1	28	0	2	1	20	3	28	9	3	4	.475	.382
Bates, Fletcher, Pittsfield†	.326	75	325	276	52	90	140	14	9	6	37	1	3	4	41	0	72	17	9	1	.507	.417
Jorgensen, Tim, Watertown*	.325	73	331	295	44	96	157	19	9	8	52	1	1	2	32	4	63	4	1	4	.532	.394
Vieira, Scott, Williamsport	.318	61	252	214	35	68	98	8	2	6	46	0	4	9	25	1	37	3	1	3	.458	.405
Rice, Charles, Erie†	.316	70	298	269	44	85	128	15	2	8	33	0	1	8	19	0	59	7	5	5	.476	.377
Dawkins, Walter, Batavia	.315	58	239	203	46	64	86	11	4	1	31	2	3	4	27	0	36	15	6	6	.424	.401
Winn, Randy, Elmira.................	.315	51	233	213	38	67	82	7	4	0	22	0	2	3	15	0	31	19	7	1	.385	.365
Guillen, Jose, Erie	.314	66	281	258	41	81	136	17	1	12	46	0	1	12	10	0	44	1	5	5	.527	.367
Bovender, Andy, Auburn	.313	71	278	243	42	76	114	15	4	5	41	0	1	4	30	2	70	1	2	7	.469	.396
Hall, Andy, New Jersey†	.310	64	279	252	30	78	101	10	5	1	34	4	0	4	19	2	44	19	6	2	.401	.367
Miyake, Chris, Erie	.308	61	246	227	34	70	92	6	5	2	25	1	1	5	12	0	31	14	6	3	.405	.355
Chevalier, Virgil, Utica	.308	64	267	250	34	77	114	12	2	7	46	0	3	3	11	0	35	15	6	6	.456	.341

DEPARTMENTAL LEADERS: G—Daly, 76; AB—Anderson, 312; R—Sanchez, 62; H—Brumbaugh, 101; TB—Jorgensen, 157; 2B—Daly, 22; 3B—Joseph, 10; HR—Guillen, 12; RBI—Daly, 60; SH—Several players tied with 7; SF—Daly, Olsen, 7; HP—Goodell, 14; BB—M. Miller, 60; IBB—Weaver, 5; SO—Landers, 86; SB—Am. Garcia, 41; CS—Bady, 19; GIDP—Booty, 12; Slg.—Jorgensen, .532; OBP—Brumbaugh, .437.

ALL PLAYERS

*Lefthanded batter. †Switch-hitter.

Player, Team	Avg.	G	TPA	AB	R	H	TB	2B	3B	HR	RBI	SH	SF	HP	BB	IBB	SO	SB	CS	GDP	Slg.	OBP
Adams, Jason, Auburn.................	.215	51	212	181	28	39	45	6	0	0	18	1	0	3	27	1	19	3	1	5	.249	.327
Adamson, Jason, Erie	.286	2	7	7	0	2	2	0	0	0	2	0	0	0	0	0	1	0	0	0	.286	.286
Afenir, Tom, Watertown	.200	6	17	15	2	3	5	2	0	0	3	1	0	1	0	0	3	0	0	1	.333	.250
Alexander, Chad, Auburn..............	.291	71	316	278	45	81	121	15	5	5	43	1	5	7	25	1	37	7	1	11	.435	.359
Anderson, Marlon, Batavia*	.295	74	337	312	52	92	122	13	4	3	40	2	4	4	15	2	20	22	8	2	.391	.331
Antrim, Patrick, Oneonta†	.192	26	82	78	6	15	16	1	0	0	5	1	1	1	1	0	23	3	1	1	.205	.210
Arvelo, Tom, Pittsfield	.305	67	303	279	41	85	107	8	7	0	17	2	1	5	16	0	63	24	6	0	.384	.352
Austin, Lakevie, Utica	.242	34	101	91	10	22	28	3	0	1	6	1	0	1	8	0	38	5	2	1	.308	.310
Babin, Brady, Elmira..................	.350	6	24	20	4	7	10	1	1	0	2	1	0	0	3	0	1	0	0	0	.500	.435
Bady, Edward, Vermont†..............	.329	72	326	295	51	97	124	15	3	2	25	2	0	5	24	3	52	34	19	3	.420	.389
Barrett, Michael, Vermont	.100	3	12	10	0	1	1	0	0	0	1	0	1	0	1	0	1	0	0	0	.100	.167
Barton, Scott, Williamsport*	.222	16	51	45	3	10	19	3	0	2	13	1	1	0	4	0	13	0	1	2	.422	.280
Bates, Fletcher, Pittsfield†	.326	75	325	276	52	90	140	14	9	6	37	1	3	4	41	0	72	17	9	1	.507	.417
Bazzani, Matt, Utica	.243	29	87	74	15	18	37	4	3	3	17	3	0	6	4	0	17	1	0	0	.500	.333
Bentley, Kevin, Williamsport	.217	50	130	115	14	25	41	4	3	2	13	1	0	0	14	0	48	1	3	1	.357	.302
Betts, Darrell, New Jersey†	.152	54	193	151	22	23	27	4	0	0	11	7	0	3	32	0	38	3	6	2	.179	.312
Blakeney, Mo, Vermont	.265	39	144	132	17	35	51	8	1	2	17	0	0	4	8	0	23	12	2	3	.386	.326
Booty, Josh, Elmira	.220	74	313	287	33	63	101	18	1	6	37	0	2	5	19	0	85	4	4	12	.352	.278
Borges, Mariano, Erie	.111	17	50	45	4	5	5	0	0	0	2	0	0	2	3	0	11	1	1	2	.111	.200
Boryczewski, Marty, Erie	.094	10	33	32	0	3	3	0	0	0	0	0	0	0	1	0	6	0	0	2	.094	.121
Bourne, Charles, St. Catharines	.199	55	203	176	24	35	49	11	0	1	17	4	2	3	18	0	50	12	3	2	.278	.281
Bovender, Andy, Auburn	.313	71	278	243	42	76	114	15	4	5	41	0	1	4	30	2	70	1	2	7	.469	.396
Brannon, Tony, Utica	.216	42	139	125	11	27	37	5	1	1	18	1	2	2	9	0	26	5	2	5	.296	.275
Brinkley, Josh, Vermont	.221	38	144	122	14	27	29	2	0	0	11	0	2	6	14	0	26	6	1	4	.238	.326
Briones, Christopher, Hud. Valley. ...	.221	48	174	163	18	36	65	12	1	5	26	1	3	3	4	0	53	0	0	2	.399	.249
Brito, Domingo, Batavia	.125	11	41	32	1	4	4	0	0	0	2	0	0	0	9	0	9	0	0	2	.125	.317
Brumbaugh, Clifford, Hud. Valley	.358	74	325	282	44	101	134	19	4	2	45	0	2	2	39	4	51	15	3	11	.475	.437
Brunner, Michael, Auburn	.193	26	88	83	7	16	28	6	0	2	11	0	0	0	5	0	25	2	1	3	.337	.239
Budzinski, Mark, Watertown*	.253	70	318	253	50	64	101	12	8	3	25	3	2	8	52	1	49	15	5	3	.399	.394
Caballero, Manuel, Jamestown*.......	.197	52	177	142	23	28	49	4	1	5	20	0	2	1	32	0	42	3	2	10	.345	.345
Cabrera, Orlando, Vermont	.282	65	271	248	37	70	101	12	5	3	33	2	4	1	16	0	28	15	8	3	.407	.323
Cameron, Ken, New Jersey*	.239	39	154	138	18	33	44	9	1	0	12	0	2	0	12	0	20	5	0	2	.319	.309
Camfield, Eric, Oneonta*	.270	73	323	296	45	80	100	11	3	1	42	2	2	1	22	0	41	17	7	1	.338	.327
Camilli, Jason, Vermont	.243	63	280	243	37	59	76	10	2	1	21	3	2	2	30	1	52	17	10	4	.313	.329
Canetto, John, Erie†	.160	11	32	25	5	4	4	0	0	0	0	0	0	0	7	0	7	0	0	1	.160	.344
Cardona, Ruben, New Jersey*.........	.251	49	221	195	36	49	62	5	4	0	24	3	1	1	21	0	24	7	2	3	.318	.326
Carpenter, Matt, Watertown	.323	12	35	31	4	10	13	3	0	0	4	0	0	0	4	0	7	0	0	1	.419	.400
Carver, Steve, Batavia*	.304	56	236	217	35	66	104	13	2	7	41	1	1	0	17	1	29	2	1	3	.479	.353
Casey, Sean, Watertown*	.329	55	229	207	26	68	92	18	0	2	37	0	3	1	18	4	21	3	0	6	.444	.380
Castro, Ramon, Auburn	.299	63	254	224	40	67	111	17	0	9	49	0	6	0	24	0	27	2	3	6	.496	.358
Chamblee, James, Utica	.255	62	231	200	36	51	68	9	1	2	16	1	1	6	23	0	45	9	7	5	.340	.348
Chevalier, Virgil, Utica	.308	64	267	250	34	77	114	12	2	7	46	0	3	3	11	0	35	15	6	6	.456	.341
Choate, Jonathan, Watertown*	.219	59	223	196	28	43	63	10	2	2	24	0	2	1	24	0	36	2	3	5	.321	.305
Coats, Nathan, Watertown	.276	12	33	29	2	8	12	2	1	0	3	0	0	0	4	0	11	0	0	0	.414	.364
Conley, Brian, Williamsport	.251	69	292	259	42	65	88	18	1	1	23	2	3	4	24	0	49	7	3	4	.340	.321
Cornelius, Jonathon, Batavia.........	.262	68	295	263	29	69	97	11	4	3	41	3	2	5	22	0	59	4	2	4	.369	.329
Cox, Charles, Batavia	.218	38	135	124	13	27	35	4	2	0	11	0	0	0	11	0	41	2	0	5	.282	.281
Crane, Todd, Batavia	.246	27	84	69	15	17	20	3	0	0	1	1	0	13	0	0	25	2	0	2	.290	.373

Player, Team	Avg.	G	TPA	AB	R	H	TB	2B	3B	HR	RBI	SH	SF	HP	BB	IBB	SO	SB	CS	GDP	Slg.	OBP
Culp, Matt, Watertown*	.129	33	102	85	7	11	17	3	0	1	8	0	0	3	14	0	26	1	0	1	.200	.275
Culp, Randy, Vermont	.000	1	3	3	0	0	0	0	0	0	0	0	0	0	0	0	0	0	0	0	.000	.000
Daly, Rob, Pittsfield	.294	76	333	303	43	89	126	22	3	3	60	0	7	1	22	1	28	4	1	5	.416	.336
Davis, Albert, Erie	.230	44	178	152	31	35	53	12	0	2	12	2	3	2	19	0	26	8	2	3	.349	.318
Dawkins, Walter, Batavia	.315	58	239	203	46	64	86	11	4	1	31	2	3	4	27	0	36	15	6	6	.424	.401
DeLaRosa, Elvis, Jamestown	.238	14	44	42	3	10	12	2	0	0	5	0	1	0	1	0	15	1	1	1	.286	.250
Deluca, Nic, New Jersey	.250	3	8	8	1	2	2	0	0	0	0	0	0	0	0	0	2	0	0	0	.250	.250
Deman, Lou, New Jersey	.220	52	205	186	22	41	55	8	0	2	24	1	1	5	12	0	60	2	3	3	.296	.284
Denning, Wes, Vermont*	.196	56	202	168	30	33	37	0	2	0	17	4	3	4	23	0	45	16	5	1	.220	.303
Dennis, Les, Oneonta	.264	48	167	148	24	39	52	6	2	1	13	0	2	3	14	0	40	5	2	4	.351	.335
Deshenes, Marc, Watertown	.208	42	174	144	18	30	39	4	1	1	14	5	4	3	18	0	45	6	2	3	.271	.302
Diaz, Linardo, Batavia	.240	22	88	75	13	18	27	4	1	1	7	4	0	6	3	0	17	4	1	1	.360	.321
Dieguez, Mike, Pittsfield	.215	59	225	181	31	39	48	7	1	0	17	1	0	12	31	0	29	0	5	5	.265	.366
Doezie, Troy, New Jersey	.190	23	95	84	15	16	28	5	2	1	12	0	0	1	10	0	18	0	1	5	.333	.284
Echols, Mandell, Hudson Valley	.284	58	235	215	31	61	78	8	3	1	21	0	1	5	14	0	48	15	13	5	.363	.340
Edwards, Aaron, Erie	.264	15	60	53	10	14	14	0	0	0	3	1	0	0	6	1	10	7	2	2	.264	.339
Ellison, Tony, Williamsport	.222	5	21	18	5	4	7	0	0	1	2	0	0	1	2	0	5	0	0	0	.389	.333
Emmons, Scott, Oneonta	.198	67	277	242	25	48	75	15	3	2	32	2	5	3	25	0	62	1	1	5	.310	.276
Engleka, Douglas, Jamestown	.283	44	194	166	32	47	65	8	2	2	20	1	3	4	20	0	28	11	5	5	.392	.368
Erwin, Mat, Elmira	.262	68	290	260	22	68	96	12	2	4	39	0	2	6	22	2	36	2	1	10	.369	.331
Evans, Kyle, Hudson Valley*	.238	57	225	189	31	45	70	11	1	4	25	0	2	7	27	1	39	4	1	3	.370	.351
Fana, Alberto, Batavia	.262	20	64	61	5	16	17	1	0	0	4	1	0	0	2	0	11	0	0	1	.279	.294
Fernandez, Jose, Vermont	.274	66	287	270	38	74	106	6	7	4	41	1	2	1	13	2	51	29	4	2	.393	.308
Flanigan, Steven, Erie	.271	25	87	85	8	23	32	4	1	1	10	0	0	1	1	0	23	1	0	1	.376	.287
Freel, Ryan, St. Catharines	.280	65	284	243	30	68	97	10	5	3	29	7	5	7	22	0	49	12	7	3	.399	.354
Freitas, Joe, New Jersey	.191	14	55	47	8	9	15	6	0	0	9	0	2	1	5	0	18	2	0	1	.319	.273
Fuller, Brian, Jamestown	.270	40	159	137	28	37	66	9	1	6	24	0	0	3	19	1	26	4	2	0	.482	.371
Funaro, Joe, Elmira	.265	56	209	189	24	50	72	10	3	2	16	1	2	0	17	1	21	5	2	3	.381	.322
Gallagher, Shawn, Hudson Valley	.150	5	22	20	1	3	5	2	0	0	4	0	0	1	1	0	4	0	0	2	.250	.227
Garcia, Amaury, Elmira	.273	62	272	231	40	63	76	7	3	0	17	3	0	4	34	2	50	41	12	1	.329	.375
Garcia, Apostol, Jamestown	.235	60	221	200	25	47	61	8	3	0	21	7	1	3	10	0	36	10	6	3	.305	.280
Garcia, Jaime, Vermont	.242	50	183	149	22	36	53	7	2	2	16	2	1	4	27	2	30	1	1	1	.356	.370
Garman, Sean, New Jersey*	.195	50	159	133	20	26	31	5	0	0	8	3	1	1	21	0	25	1	0	4	.233	.308
Garrett, Jason, Elmira	.221	41	146	131	15	29	38	4	1	1	11	1	0	3	11	0	31	2	1	5	.290	.297
Gipner, Marcus, Oneonta†	.099	25	96	81	0	8	9	1	0	0	0	0	0	0	15	0	20	1	1	4	.111	.240
Gonzalez, Rich, Watertown	.266	55	207	184	24	49	58	4	1	1	17	4	2	0	17	0	19	1	0	7	.315	.325
Goodell, Steve, Elmira	.253	69	306	253	42	64	107	14	4	7	30	1	2	14	36	0	50	4	5	8	.423	.374
Goodwin, Joseph, Hudson Valley	.282	57	211	181	29	51	60	6	0	1	27	2	2	6	20	0	20	2	1	7	.331	.368
Goodwin, Keith, Utica	.260	39	164	146	26	38	50	4	1	2	16	3	1	0	14	0	22	10	1	5	.342	.323
Gorecki, Ryan, Hudson Valley*	.296	59	213	189	24	56	60	4	0	0	20	2	2	3	17	1	10	8	6	9	.317	.360
Gray, Ricky, Jamestown*	.152	25	97	79	15	12	23	3	1	2	8	0	0	1	17	1	30	4	0	2	.291	.309
Guillen, Jose, Erie	.314	66	281	258	41	81	136	17	1	12	46	0	1	12	10	0	44	1	5	5	.527	.367
Halemanu, Joshua, Auburn*	.197	52	193	157	25	31	58	6	0	7	25	0	4	3	29	0	60	2	2	0	.369	.326
Hall, Andy, New Jersey†	.310	64	279	252	30	78	101	10	5	1	34	4	0	4	19	2	44	19	6	2	.401	.367
Hare, Rich, Jamestown	.193	27	60	57	6	11	15	4	0	0	3	0	0	1	2	0	13	4	1	0	.263	.233
Hayes, Chris, St. Catharines	.306	70	304	271	39	83	112	17	3	2	36	1	1	7	24	0	50	8	7	2	.413	.364
Hayes, Heath, Watertown	.212	15	60	52	4	11	14	3	0	0	6	0	1	0	7	0	14	1	1	1	.269	.300
Hermansen, Chad, Erie	.273	44	189	165	30	45	77	8	3	6	25	0	2	4	18	0	39	4	2	6	.467	.354
Hernandez, Rob, Elmira†	.040	8	31	25	0	1	1	0	0	0	0	1	0	0	5	0	7	1	0	0	.040	.200
Holley, Jack, St. Catharines	.240	65	280	246	33	59	72	2	1	3	26	7	0	5	22	0	47	3	3	4	.293	.315
Horton, Eric, St. Catharines	.000	21	1	1	0	0	0	0	0	0	0	0	0	0	0	0	1	0	0	0	.000	.000
Imersek, Jason, Oneonta	.077	6	14	13	1	1	1	0	0	0	1	0	0	0	1	0	2	0	0	0	.077	.143
Insunza, Miguel, New Jersey	.242	55	240	207	30	50	56	6	0	0	21	3	1	5	24	0	8	11	8	8	.271	.333
Jaroncyk, Ryan, Pittsfield	.231	4	17	13	5	3	3	0	0	0	0	0	0	1	3	0	5	5	0	0	.231	.412
Jasco, Elinton, Williamsport	.320	6	26	25	2	8	10	2	0	0	4	1	0	0	0	0	5	2	0	0	.400	.320
Jefferson, Joe, Elmira	.077	5	14	13	1	1	1	0	0	0	0	0	0	0	1	0	3	2	0	3	.077	.143
Johnson, Damon, St. Catharines	.216	63	248	232	26	50	72	9	5	1	25	3	1	4	8	1	73	9	2	4	.310	.253
Johnson, Jason, Hudson Valley	.240	46	169	150	27	36	64	7	3	5	16	0	2	5	12	0	38	10	6	2	.427	.314
Jones, Jaime, Elmira*	.284	125	116	21	33	55	6	2	4	11	0	0	0	9	0	30	5	4	2	.474	.336
Jorgensen, Tim, Watertown*	.325	73	331	295	44	96	157	19	9	8	52	1	1	2	32	4	63	4	1	4	.532	.394
Joseph, Terry, Williamsport	.292	70	298	260	49	76	107	8	10	1	34	1	0	7	30	1	33	18	6	5	.412	.380
Kapler, Gabriel, Jamestown	.288	65	265	236	38	68	107	19	4	4	34	0	4	2	23	0	37	1	2	4	.453	.351
Kimm, Tyson, Batavia†	.270	14	44	37	8	10	12	2	0	0	6	0	0	1	6	0	6	0	0	0	.324	.386
Koonce, Graham, Jamestown*	.280	73	327	289	37	81	108	16	1	3	34	0	1	2	35	0	63	8	3	1	.374	.361
Lackey, Steve, Pittsfield	.240	21	80	75	7	18	23	5	0	0	6	1	1	1	2	0	16	1	0	1	.307	.266
Landers, Mark, St. Catharines*	.232	74	324	271	43	63	104	11	0	10	52	0	4	4	45	4	86	1	2	0	.384	.346
Lariviere, Jason, New Jersey	.280	33	116	100	13	28	33	3	1	0	9	2	0	4	14	0	10	8	2	2	.330	.370
Lauterhahn, Mike, Williamsport	.143	5	19	14	5	2	3	1	0	0	0	0	0	0	5	0	5	1	1	0	.214	.368
Leaman, Jeff, Batavia	.264	62	244	220	30	58	82	10	1	4	22	2	0	2	20	0	55	2	4	3	.373	.324
Lebron, Ruben, Utica†	.287	52	169	150	30	43	58	6	3	1	15	4	2	2	11	0	28	16	7	0	.387	.339
LeClair, Paul, Pittsfield	.180	11	111	100	10	18	21	3	0	0	6	1	1	1	7	0	35	0	1	0	.210	.239
Lemonis, Chris, Jamestown*	.236	57	216	191	19	45	56	7	2	0	21	3	1	2	18	0	32	5	1	4	.293	.307
Lewis, Marc, Utica	.301	69	294	272	47	82	122	15	5	5	39	2	3	0	17	0	32	24	9	6	.449	.339
Lobaton, Jose, Oneonta	.221	41	161	145	23	32	52	11	3	1	11	1	0	2	13	0	30	4	1	2	.359	.294
Long, Garrett, Erie	.278	29	126	108	17	30	40	4	0	2	16	0	2	1	15	0	25	2	2	6	.370	.356
Long, Justin, Elmira	.210	56	206	186	25	39	62	6	4	3	17	1	1	1	17	0	54	13	3	3	.333	.278
Long, Terrence, Pittsfield*	.257	51	208	187	24	48	77	9	4	4	31	1	1	1	18	2	36	11	4	2	.412	.324
Lowell, Mike, Oneonta	.260	72	313	281	36	73	94	18	0	1	27	0	6	3	23	0	34	3	1	5	.335	.316
Lugo, Julio, Auburn	.291	59	260	230	36	67	82	6	3	1	16	2	0	2	26	0	31	17	7	7	.357	.368
Macias, Jose, Vermont†	.239	53	199	176	24	42	50	4	2	0	9	2	0	2	19	0	19	11	7	3	.284	.320
Mackert, Jamie, Erie	.218	35	125	101	18	22	40	4	4	2	17	1	0	1	22	0	46	0	4	2	.396	.363
Maleski, Tom, Williamsport	.232	40	136	112	13	26	36	8	1	0	14	1	2	2	19	0	25	1	1	2	.321	.348
Martinez, Dave, Hudson Valley*	.250	44	142	124	19	31	37	6	0	0	17	0	2	3	13	1	25	1	1	1	.298	.331

Player, Team	Avg.	G	TPA	AB	R	H	TB	2B	3B	HR	RBI	SH	SF	HP	BB	IBB	SO	SB	CS	GDP	Slg.	OBP
Martinez, Roger, Pittsfield	.101	23	76	69	1	7	10	3	0	0	3	0	1	1	5	0	20	1	0	1	.145	.171
May, Freddie, Erie*	.267	27	98	90	10	24	32	3	1	1	12	1	1	1	5	0	23	5	5	2	.356	.309
Maynor, Tonka, Erie*	.129	11	37	31	2	4	8	1	0	1	3	0	0	2	4	0	2	0	0	0	.258	.270
McAulay, John, Hudson Valley	.212	24	66	52	7	11	11	0	0	0	4	1	3	2	8	0	9	1	1	1	.212	.323
McCartney, Sommer, Elmira	.179	33	120	112	11	20	27	4	0	1	5	0	0	2	6	0	29	1	3	1	.241	.233
McClendon, Travis, New Jersey	.286	50	178	161	25	46	60	9	1	1	18	1	1	5	10	1	25	6	3	5	.373	.345
McCormick, Cody, Oneonta	.276	74	305	268	33	74	112	16	2	6	32	1	2	4	30	1	60	4	2	2	.418	.355
McDonald, Ashanti, Williamsport*	.249	59	213	193	26	48	57	4	1	1	20	2	1	4	13	0	46	4	5	5	.295	.308
McHugh, Ryan, New Jersey	.194	26	109	98	7	19	26	4	0	1	14	1	1	1	8	0	39	2	0	3	.265	.259
McLendon, Craig, Hudson Valley	.000	4	6	6	0	0	0	0	0	0	0	0	0	0	0	0	3	0	0	0	.000	.000
McNally, Shawn, New Jersey	.256	24	104	90	11	23	31	5	0	1	10	1	0	5	8	0	18	5	1	1	.344	.350
Miller, Kumandac, Elmira	.201	47	169	154	9	31	41	4	3	0	15	2	3	2	8	0	40	2	4	4	.266	.246
Miller, Michael, Jamestown	.228	64	267	197	39	45	65	9	1	3	27	0	0	10	60	0	66	10	7	6	.330	.431
Milord, Clausel, Jamestown	.207	34	110	87	13	18	26	3	1	1	12	0	2	1	20	0	21	6	4	1	.299	.355
Minici, Jason, Watertown	.208	66	263	231	28	48	71	5	0	6	27	2	1	4	25	1	65	4	3	3	.307	.295
Mitchell, Rivers, Jamestown	.282	60	257	234	28	66	86	8	6	0	17	7	0	3	13	0	35	15	7	2	.368	.328
Miyake, Chris, Erie	.308	61	246	227	34	70	92	6	5	2	25	1	1	5	12	0	31	14	6	3	.405	.355
Morales, Eric, Pittsfield	.241	66	267	237	18	57	68	6	1	1	28	6	3	1	20	2	36	2	2	4	.287	.299
Morenz, Shea, Oneonta*	.276	33	135	116	11	32	46	5	3	1	20	0	1	3	15	0	27	1	4	4	.397	.370
Morgan, Scott, Watertown	.262	66	282	244	42	64	88	18	0	2	33	0	4	8	26	0	63	6	5	11	.361	.348
Mota, Gleydel, Pittsfield*	.162	14	42	37	4	6	6	0	0	0	2	1	0	0	4	0	11	2	2	0	.162	.244
Motes, Jeff, Pittsfield	.231	52	198	169	14	39	52	7	3	0	15	4	3	1	21	0	33	1	1	5	.308	.314
Mueller, Bret, New Jersey	.262	70	292	267	39	70	97	5	8	2	39	0	1	4	20	0	61	7	3	6	.363	.322
Nelson, Tray, Oneonta	.146	16	54	48	5	7	10	3	0	0	8	0	2	0	4	0	21	0	0	0	.208	.204
Nieves, Jose, Williamsport	.214	69	306	276	46	59	86	13	1	4	44	0	3	6	21	1	39	11	10	4	.312	.281
Norman, Ty, Utica	.252	49	175	159	23	40	54	5	0	3	15	2	4	2	8	0	28	8	4	5	.340	.289
Nova, Jose Feliz, Williamsport	.221	52	197	172	25	38	47	7	1	0	13	1	2	1	21	0	48	2	1	6	.273	.306
Olsen, Donald, Vermont	.256	70	300	270	33	69	108	16	1	7	44	0	7	3	20	0	52	3	4	5	.400	.307
Owens, Walter, Watertown	.273	23	52	44	9	12	13	1	0	0	3	2	0	0	6	0	12	1	1	1	.295	.360
Palmer, Jim, Oneonta	.070	15	51	43	4	3	3	0	0	0	4	0	0	1	7	0	16	0	0	0	.070	.216
Parker, Michael, Pittsfield	.500	3	2	2	0	1	1	0	0	0	0	0	0	0	0	0	1	0	0	0	.500	.500
Parsons, Jeff, Pittsfield	.227	49	212	172	31	39	43	4	0	0	10	3	0	0	37	0	33	25	7	1	.250	.364
Pelis, Andy, Pittsfield	.053	8	23	19	3	1	1	0	0	0	0	0	0	0	4	0	7	0	0	2	.053	.217
Perez, Mike, Williamsport	.294	7	24	17	2	5	7	0	1	0	3	0	1	3	3	0	3	0	0	0	.412	.458
Pettiford, Torrey, Batavia	.311	41	164	151	21	47	56	5	2	0	17	3	0	5	5	0	18	12	2	4	.371	.354
Pierce, Kirk, Batavia	.218	30	118	101	18	22	29	5	1	0	7	1	0	6	10	0	23	0	0	4	.287	.325
Pileski, Mark, Pittsfield	.161	8	33	31	2	5	6	1	0	0	4	1	0	0	1	0	2	1	0	2	.194	.188
Podsednik, Scott, Hudson Valley*	.266	65	291	252	42	67	70	3	0	0	20	1	2	1	35	3	31	20	6	9	.278	.355
Pollock, Elton, Erie	.299	43	189	174	29	52	67	7	1	2	21	1	1	1	12	1	30	12	5	4	.385	.346
Pratt, Wes, Auburn	.266	66	281	256	42	68	85	11	0	2	44	0	1	4	20	0	43	6	3	9	.332	.327
Prodanov, Peter, Utica	.244	55	192	172	26	42	61	10	0	3	22	1	3	0	16	1	31	12	2	2	.355	.304
Putko, James, Williamsport*	.270	47	159	141	18	38	59	12	0	3	23	0	0	2	16	1	34	0	1	3	.418	.352
Rascon, Rene, Elmira*	.219	34	137	114	12	25	31	4	1	0	11	2	1	0	20	3	34	3	3	3	.272	.333
Rathmell, Lance, Utica	.285	66	261	228	34	65	80	10	1	1	30	0	4	1	28	0	25	4	5	7	.351	.360
Raynor, Mark, Batavia	.262	66	309	267	49	70	101	10	6	3	37	1	1	2	38	1	42	13	4	1	.378	.357
Reed, Billy, Hudson Valley	.216	45	158	134	16	29	38	4	1	1	11	6	0	1	17	0	24	3	2	5	.284	.309
Reilly, John, St. Catharines	.260	32	96	77	8	20	29	2	2	1	10	2	1	10	6	0	20	0	0	0	.377	.383
Reynolds, Paul, Erie†	.242	37	142	120	17	29	31	2	0	0	18	1	4	3	14	0	18	0	2	5	.258	.326
Rice, Charles, Erie†	.316	70	298	269	44	85	128	15	2	8	33	0	1	8	19	0	59	7	5	5	.476	.377
Richard, Chris, New Jersey*	.282	75	339	284	36	80	109	14	3	3	43	0	2	6	47	3	31	6	6	3	.384	.392
Rivera, Wilfredo, Utica	.210	44	150	138	14	29	40	2	3	1	15	0	2	5	5	0	35	3	1	3	.290	.260
Robinson, David, Batavia*	.219	56	226	201	27	44	65	9	3	2	26	0	2	2	20	0	45	9	3	2	.323	.293
Robinson, Hassan, Auburn	.265	65	259	245	32	65	75	8	1	0	18	2	1	2	9	0	25	12	2	9	.306	.296
Robles, Oscar, Auburn*	.287	58	257	216	49	62	73	9	1	0	19	1	1	0	39	1	15	8	2	5	.338	.395
Rodriguez, Luis, St. Catharines	.276	66	271	257	22	71	94	16	2	1	20	2	1	1	10	1	49	2	4	7	.366	.305
Rojas, Ron, Jamestown*	.213	17	59	47	8	10	14	1	0	1	8	1	1	2	8	1	9	4	0	0	.298	.345
Rosado, Juan, Vermont*	.245	48	177	155	20	38	49	4	2	1	24	0	3	1	18	1	16	4	5	2	.316	.322
Rosario, Felix, St. Catharines	.226	64	244	217	24	49	58	6	0	1	21	5	3	1	18	1	44	9	3	1	.267	.285
Russell, Jason, Batavia	.191	40	161	141	9	27	38	3	1	2	18	1	3	5	11	0	25	0	2	4	.270	.269
Sagers, Kory, Utica†	.182	25	72	66	11	12	15	1	1	0	7	1	0	0	5	0	18	1	1	1	.227	.239
Salzano, Jerry, Williamsport	.298	62	245	218	28	65	82	13	2	0	23	0	1	4	22	0	28	4	3	6	.376	.371
Samuel, Cody, Oneonta	.274	37	139	124	15	34	55	7	1	4	17	0	3	2	10	0	42	2	0	3	.444	.333
Sanchez, Omar, St. Catharines	.301	74	341	292	62	88	125	16	6	3	23	2	0	8	39	1	50	26	16	0	.428	.398
Sapp, Damien, Utica	.198	37	133	111	19	22	32	5	1	1	14	2	1	5	14	0	34	0	2	0	.288	.313
Schreiber, Stan, Erie	.286	3	8	7	1	2	6	0	2	0	2	0	0	0	1	0	2	0	0	0	.857	.375
Schreimann, Eric, Batavia	.269	15	61	52	9	14	27	1	0	4	13	0	1	7	1	1	7	0	1	1	.519	.361
Scolaro, Donald, Auburn	.239	49	176	159	14	38	44	6	0	0	25	2	2	2	11	0	27	1	3	6	.277	.293
Segura, Juan, Erie	.257	26	110	105	10	27	41	2	3	2	9	2	0	0	3	1	24	1	1	1	.390	.278
Seidel, Ryan, Williamsport	.296	64	225	203	27	60	78	8	5	0	20	1	3	1	17	2	37	13	2	3	.384	.348
Shanahan, Jason, Elmira†	.239	64	265	230	19	55	84	9	4	4	28	1	2	2	30	3	50	7	3	5	.365	.330
Shumpert, Derek, Oneonta†	.209	62	229	196	25	41	54	7	3	0	11	2	0	2	29	0	58	13	3	6	.276	.317
Smith, Akili, Erie	.125	14	46	40	6	5	8	0	0	1	1	1	0	1	4	0	13	1	0	1	.200	.222
Smith, Rod, Oneonta†	.235	49	220	187	34	44	58	8	3	0	10	0	1	2	30	0	49	24	7	1	.310	.345
Snusz, Chris, Batavia	.227	21	72	66	9	15	19	1	0	1	5	0	0	0	6	0	11	1	4	2	.288	.292
Solano, Fausto, St. Catharines	.285	57	245	207	28	59	84	17	1	2	24	4	1	3	30	1	28	14	4	2	.406	.382
Soriano, Carlos, Pittsfield	.176	5	18	17	1	3	5	2	0	0	1	0	0	0	1	0	2	1	0	1	.294	.222
Speed, Dorian, Williamsport	.216	60	237	204	30	44	64	8	3	2	23	1	3	1	28	0	56	18	5	3	.314	.309
Springfield, Bo, Erie*	.263	25	92	76	11	20	28	1	2	1	6	2	1	0	13	0	20	8	4	2	.368	.367
Stadler, Mike, Watertown	.238	6	22	21	2	5	6	1	0	0	2	0	0	0	0	0	6	0	0	0	.286	.227
Steinkemper, Jacob, Vermont	.164	21	72	61	4	10	13	3	0	0	5	0	1	0	10	0	15	1	3	0	.213	.292
Stratton, Kelly, Hudson Valley*	.207	30	67	58	10	12	17	2	0	1	8	0	0	2	7	1	6	1	1	2	.293	.313
Taylor, Jerry, Watertown	.286	5	22	21	3	6	7	1	0	0	1	0	1	0	0	0	1	0	0	1	.333	.318
Thornhill, Chad, Watertown*	.250	55	204	164	34	41	51	8	1	0	16	1	1	1	37	1	31	0	0	5	.311	.389

– 519 –

Player, Team	Avg.	G	TPA	AB	R	H	TB	2B	3B	HR	RBI	SH	SF	HP	BB	IBB	SO	SB	CS	GDP	Slg.	OBP
Tippin, Greg, Utica*	.228	68	260	232	20	53	68	7	1	2	27	0	4	8	16	1	68	12	6	1	.293	.296
Tribolet, Scott, Auburn	.250	50	191	172	23	43	61	7	4	1	22	1	3	2	13	0	31	12	2	1	.355	.305
Turner, Rocky, Pittsfield	.259	33	128	116	9	30	34	4	0	0	10	1	1	3	7	0	17	8	7	0	.293	.315
Ugueto, Hector, New Jersey	.287	54	232	202	37	58	72	7	2	1	28	1	3	9	17	0	36	9	2	4	.356	.364
Valera, Willy, Watertown	.254	65	260	240	33	61	89	13	3	3	29	2	2	2	14	0	57	4	2	6	.371	.298
Varriano, Mark, Utica	.091	4	13	11	2	1	1	0	0	0	1	0	0	0	2	0	3	0	0	0	.091	.231
Vasquez, Danny, Hudson Valley	.267	69	263	240	38	64	93	9	4	4	31	0	4	3	15	1	58	16	5	4	.388	.313
Venezia, Richard, Erie	.204	38	127	108	11	22	27	2	0	1	10	4	2	0	13	0	24	5	1	1	.250	.285
Vieira, Scott, Williamsport	.318	61	252	214	35	68	98	8	2	6	46	0	4	9	25	1	37	3	1	3	.458	.405
Viruel, Willie, Pittsfield	.188	11	40	32	4	6	6	0	0	0	5	2	0	2	4	0	7	0	0	0	.188	.316
Vopata, Nathan, Hudson Valley*	.281	68	265	231	37	65	93	12	8	0	30	0	5	6	23	1	36	10	5	7	.403	.355
Waggoner, James, Jamestown*	.245	63	231	204	21	50	72	5	4	3	24	0	3	2	22	1	40	2	3	2	.353	.320
Walker, Rodney, Hudson Valley	.077	13	27	26	2	2	2	0	0	0	1	0	1	0	0	0	10	1	0	2	.077	.074
Weaver, Scott, Jamestown*	.301	65	279	236	33	71	101	11	2	5	34	0	2	3	38	5	33	16	4	9	.428	.401
Whipple, Boomer, Erie	.253	67	268	225	29	57	67	4	0	2	33	6	1	6	30	0	18	4	3	8	.298	.355
Wilcox, Chris, Oneonta*	.327	59	246	223	25	73	106	16	7	1	28	0	2	1	20	3	28	9	3	4	.475	.382
Williams, Brian, St. Catharines	.194	24	77	67	5	13	15	2	0	0	6	3	1	0	6	0	23	0	0	0	.224	.257
Winn, Randy, Elmira	.315	51	233	213	38	67	82	7	4	0	22	0	2	3	15	0	31	19	7	1	.385	.365
Wolger, Michael, Vermont*	.256	60	242	203	27	52	67	7	1	2	23	1	2	2	34	0	47	3	3	5	.330	.365
Yoder, Paul, Pittsfield*	.213	55	217	183	25	39	53	6	4	0	18	1	1	2	30	2	34	0	5	6	.290	.329
Zuleta, Julio, Williamsport	.173	30	88	75	9	13	18	3	1	0	6	0	0	2	11	1	21	0	1	4	.240	.295

GRAND SLAMS: Caballero, Engleka, Fuller, Nieves, Prodanov, Raynor, Speed, Tippin, Waggoner, 1 each.
AWARDED FIRST BASE ON CATCHER'S INTERFERENCE: LeClair (McAulay); Lemonis (Reynolds); Rice (Rodriguez); D. Robinson (Stadler); Vasquez (Morales).

1995 PITCHING

TEAM

Team	W	L	Pct.	ERA	G	CG	ShO	Sv.	IP	H	TBF	R	ER	HR	SH	SF	HB	BB	IBB	SO	WP	Bk.
Vermont	49	27	.645	2.86	76	1	9	30	667.2	558	2793	282	212	19	18	18	54	251	5	479	63	16
Watertown	46	27	.630	3.10	73	1	7	23	645.1	580	2695	268	222	27	11	21	30	228	18	508	41	19
Williamsport	37	39	.487	3.38	76	0	2	20	665.1	678	2905	362	250	25	23	19	44	193	3	494	34	18
Oneonta	34	41	.453	3.51	75	0	2	20	646.2	611	2869	368	252	12	19	23	39	287	4	595	68	11
Erie	34	41	.453	3.51	75	5	5	16	653.0	648	2861	350	255	31	27	17	35	256	12	434	48	9
Hudson Valley	47	27	.635	3.57	74	4	3	24	660.0	637	2817	325	262	25	27	16	38	236	12	536	98	24
St. Catharines	38	37	.507	3.71	75	1	3	19	669.2	652	2887	341	276	38	23	22	41	292	0	461	59	14
Pittsfield	34	42	.447	3.85	76	3	4	22	659.0	671	2876	369	282	18	18	22	31	265	4	451	56	14
New Jersey	35	41	.461	3.85	76	0	5	17	682.0	649	3002	372	292	28	19	35	52	303	9	607	61	25
Batavia	41	34	.547	3.93	75	4	8	14	666.0	716	2882	369	291	28	21	20	42	194	6	507	71	18
Utica	33	40	.452	4.00	73	7	2	19	631.1	643	2840	379	283	20	11	31	41	300	10	500	68	7
Auburn	40	34	.541	4.50	74	6	5	24	621.2	620	2764	366	311	28	15	24	42	300	7	431	52	7
Elmira	25	51	.329	4.55	76	0	2	16	658.0	675	2937	424	333	30	19	22	46	293	7	507	71	30
Jamestown	32	44	.421	4.59	76	1	1	15	666.2	673	2936	427	340	46	25	29	54	254	4	494	61	24

INDIVIDUAL

TOP QUALIFIERS FOR EARNED-RUN AVERAGE TITLE

Minimum 61 innings. *Lefthanded pitcher.

Pitcher, Team	W	L	Pct.	ERA	G	GS	CG	ShO	GF	Sv.	IP	H	TBF	R	ER	HR	SH	SF	HB	BB	IBB	SO	WP	Bk.
Weidert, Chris, Vermont	11	1	.917	1.79	15	15	1	1	0	0	95.1	67	378	31	19	4	0	2	4	21	0	52	8	0
Dixon, Timothy, Vermont*	7	2	.778	1.83	18	9	0	0	2	1	69.0	58	287	20	14	0	3	0	8	16	0	58	5	7
McNeese, John, Williamsport*	5	3	.625	1.86	13	12	0	0	0	0	72.2	73	297	24	15	2	1	1	2	10	1	47	2	2
Young, Joe, St. Catharines	6	5	.545	2.04	15	15	0	0	0	0	83.2	72	349	29	19	4	3	4	5	35	0	73	5	3
Mudd, Scott, Hudson Valley	7	1	.875	2.24	15	15	3	1	0	0	100.2	91	402	37	25	2	2	3	2	18	0	62	10	1
Bullock, Derek, Erie	4	4	.500	2.35	11	11	1	1	0	0	65.0	65	270	21	17	0	1	0	2	15	0	27	1	0
Yeager, Gary, Batavia	9	4	.692	2.56	19	8	1	0	4	0	81.0	74	327	33	23	2	0	0	3	16	0	57	7	4
Trumpour, Andy, Pittsfield	7	6	.538	2.57	15	15	2	1	0	0	105.0	95	427	44	30	2	3	3	5	32	0	75	7	0
Stephens, Shannon, Elmira	8	5	.615	2.58	17	12	0	0	2	0	90.2	72	364	38	26	4	3	3	3	17	1	74	6	2
Hamilton, Bo, Batavia	7	2	.778	2.58	14	13	1	0	0	0	83.2	73	348	30	24	2	3	0	5	23	0	62	10	1
Munro, Peter, Utica	4	4	.556	2.60	14	14	0	0	0	0	90.0	79	389	38	26	3	3	7	3	1	74	4	0	
Jacobs, Mike, Utica	8	3	.727	2.71	13	13	2	1	0	0	86.1	83	371	35	26	1	2	0	1	37	2	51	8	0
Young, Ryan, Erie	5	2	.714	2.79	16	10	1	0	2	1	67.2	62	288	34	21	5	5	1	3	17	0	38	0	1
St. Pierre, Bob, Oneonta	3	3	.625	2.83	15	15	0	0	0	0	89.0	83	368	39	28	4	1	4	2	24	0	91	4	2
Horton, Eric, St. Catharines	6	2	.750	2.84	21	7	0	0	9	3	69.2	50	276	28	22	4	1	3	3	26	0	51	4	2

DEPARTMENTAL LEADERS: W—Weidert, 11; L—Bettencourt, 8; Pct.—Weidert, .917; G—Donnelly, 36; GS—Several pitchers tied with 15; CG—Mudd, 3; ShO—Several pitchers tied with 1; GF—Tessmer, 33; Sv.—R. Marquez, 21; IP—Trumpour, 105.0; H—Cordero, 96; TBF—Trumpour, 427; R—Cordero, 62; ER—Cordero, 51; HR—Martinez, 10; SH—Farrow, 6; SF—Miedreich, 11; HB—Mamott, 11; BB—Fuller, 51; IBB—Kahlon, 5; SO—St. Pierre, 91; WP—Bauer, Goedde, 13; Bk.—Dixon, Pailthorpe, 7.

ALL PITCHERS

*Lefthanded pitcher.

Pitcher, Team	W	L	Pct.	ERA	G	GS	CG	ShO	GF	Sv.	IP	H	TBF	R	ER	HR	SH	SF	HB	BB	IBB	SO	WP	Bk.
Adge, Jason, Watertown	5	1	.833	1.58	19	0	0	0	8	1	45.2	40	179	10	8	0	1	1	1	9	1	26	5	0
Albaladejo, Randy, Auburn	0	0	.000	5.23	9	0	0	0	6	2	10.1	12	48	6	6	0	0	2	2	5	0	7	2	0
Antonini, Adrian, Batavia	0	1	.000	9.53	3	3	0	0	0	0	5.2	12	30	6	6	0	0	0	1	0	8	0	0	
Arellano, Carlos, Watertown	0	0	.000	3.60	2	2	0	0	0	0	5.0	3	21	2	2	1	0	0	0	4	0	4	1	0
Atkins, Dannon, Watertown	5	2	.714	3.26	13	10	0	0	1	1	60.2	52	255	28	22	2	1	2	2	26	0	46	5	2
Atwater, Joe, Pittsfield	1	0	1.000	2.25	1	1	0	0	0	0	8.0	8	33	2	2	0	0	0	0	3	0	6	0	0
Bair, Dennis, Williamsport	2	3	.400	1.60	7	7	0	0	0	0	39.1	33	161	13	7	0	1	1	2	13	0	31	1	3
Bajda, Mike, Jamestown	2	2	.500	7.99	13	3	0	0	0	0	23.2	35	123	26	21	2	2	1	3	17	0	14	3	3

Pitcher, Team	W	L	Pct.	ERA	G	GS	CG	ShO	GF	Sv.	IP	H	TBF	R	ER	HR	SH	SF	HB	BB	IBB	SO	WP	Bk.
Baker, Jason, Vermont	6	5	.545	4.13	14	14	0	0	0	0	72.0	59	317	40	33	2	1	0	5	47	1	57	11	0
Ballew, Preston, Pittsfield*	1	0	1.000	0.00	1	1	0	0	0	0	5.0	2	20	0	0	0	0	0	0	3	0	4	1	0
Barker, Jeff, Jamestown	2	2	.500	3.94	14	0	0	0	2	0	16.0	15	70	10	7	2	2	0	2	8	0	14	0	0
Barnes, Monte, Oneonta*	0	0	.000	3.86	3	0	0	0	2	0	4.2	5	23	2	2	0	0	0	0	4	0	3	0	0
Barnett, Marty, Batavia	1	6	.143	6.20	10	10	0	0	0	0	49.1	67	228	45	34	3	2	4	5	10	1	32	9	3
Bauer, Charles, Hudson Valley	4	3	.571	3.17	15	15	0	0	0	0	82.1	81	357	42	29	0	1	1	8	32	0	62	13	6
Bazzani, Matt, Utica	0	0	.000	0.00	1	0	0	0	1	0	0.1	2	3	0	0	0	0	0	0	1	0	0	0	0
Beach, Scott, Erie	1	0	1.000	7.50	14	0	0	0	4	0	18.0	24	97	21	15	3	0	0	2	17	1	8	1	0
Beagle, Chad, Elmira*	1	3	.250	5.73	5	5	0	0	0	0	22.0	25	101	16	14	0	0	0	13	0	0	21	4	1
Becker, Tom, Oneonta	6	6	.500	5.33	15	15	0	0	0	0	77.2	83	353	55	46	0	4	4	2	40	0	65	12	2
Bell, Mike, Vermont*	0	0	.000	0.54	7	0	0	0	4	1	16.2	7	59	5	1	0	1	0	1	5	2	12	0	0
Benes, Adam, New Jersey	5	3	.625	3.36	19	10	0	0	3	0	75.0	71	311	30	28	3	0	4	3	23	0	47	5	2
Bennett, Jason, Watertown	3	3	.500	3.76	16	12	0	0	2	0	79.0	86	333	36	33	5	2	0	9	20	3	53	2	1
Bennett, Matt, New Jersey	3	0	1.000	3.42	23	0	0	0	7	0	47.1	49	203	30	18	0	2	2	2	13	1	34	3	5
Berry, Jason, Oneonta	2	0	1.000	0.00	8	0	0	0	0	0	12.2	9	50	1	0	0	1	0	0	4	0	19	1	0
Bettencourt, Justin, Jamestown*	2	8	.200	4.84	14	14	0	0	0	0	74.1	73	332	53	40	7	0	5	4	41	0	63	9	3
Betti, Rich, Utica*	2	1	.667	1.02	12	0	0	0	5	2	17.2	9	65	2	2	1	0	0	0	2	0	25	1	0
Bigler, Cory, Erie	0	6	.000	4.66	10	4	0	0	3	0	29.0	34	135	21	15	2	2	1	2	13	1	13	1	1
Boardman, Eric, Oneonta	3	4	.429	3.82	11	6	0	0	0	0	33.0	30	149	24	14	1	1	1	2	21	0	23	3	0
Bogle, Sean, Williamsport	1	2	.000	2.05	12	0	0	0	5	1	22.0	22	99	12	5	0	2	1	1	8	0	15	2	1
Bowman, Paul, Pittsfield	0	1	.000	9.64	2	0	0	0	2	0	4.2	7	25	6	5	0	0	0	0	5	0	3	2	0
Brandt, Dale, Oneonta*	1	2	.333	3.73	23	0	0	0	14	0	31.1	36	143	21	13	0	1	1	1	15	1	24	0	0
Brown, Shawn, Jamestown	1	2	.333	6.05	18	0	0	0	11	0	19.1	27	97	16	13	1	0	1	3	6	0	10	2	1
Bullock, Derek, Erie	4	4	.500	2.35	11	11	1	1	0	0	65.0	65	270	21	17	0	1	0	2	15	0	27	1	0
Burgus, Travis, Jamestown	7	5	.583	3.48	15	15	0	0	0	0	88.0	84	369	45	34	7	3	3	4	29	0	68	4	1
Cannon, Kevan, Utica*	3	4	.429	3.39	9	9	1	0	0	0	61.0	59	260	33	23	2	0	3	5	23	1	51	2	2
Centeno, Jose, Vermont*	0	0	.000	0.90	6	0	0	0	4	1	10.0	8	39	2	1	1	0	0	0	6	0	6	1	0
Chew, Greg, Erie	2	3	.400	3.23	24	0	0	0	13	3	30.2	37	141	18	11	1	1	0	1	2	15	4	23	4	1
Choi, Chang Yang, Batavia	1	3	.250	4.96	7	7	0	0	0	0	32.2	35	146	20	18	1	1	1	2	14	0	32	7	4
Civit, Xavier, Vermont	3	3	.500	2.85	19	0	0	0	6	1	53.2	44	222	21	17	0	1	2	3	21	0	44	5	0
Codd, Tim, Hudson Valley	3	0	1.000	3.08	25	0	0	0	5	0	38.0	36	170	15	13	2	1	0	2	21	0	38	12	0
Collie, Tim, Erie	3	6	.333	2.00	29	0	0	0	22	11	36.0	32	149	18	8	1	2	0	9	2	27	0	1
Conley, Brian, Williamsport	0	0	.000	18.00	1	0	0	0	1	0	1.0	4	10	5	2	0	0	0	0	2	0	1	0	0
Cordero, Francisco, Jamestown	4	7	.364	5.22	15	14	0	0	0	0	88.0	96	392	62	51	3	3	3	8	37	0	54	11	0
Corey, Bryan, Jamestown	2	2	.500	3.86	29	0	0	0	28	10	28.0	21	116	14	12	2	0	1	1	12	1	41	4	0
Corominus, Mike, Auburn*	2	1	.667	6.94	13	0	0	0	5	0	23.1	22	111	20	18	2	0	1	1	24	0	14	3	1
Coronado, Osvaldo, Pittsfield	5	4	.444	3.87	15	15	0	0	0	0	90.2	91	381	52	39	2	2	3	4	26	0	57	6	2
Crowell, Jim, Watertown	5	2	.714	2.86	12	9	0	0	0	0	56.2	50	241	22	18	1	0	2	1	27	1	48	2	1
Crowther, John, St. Catharines	3	6	.333	5.40	15	14	0	0	0	0	68.1	87	305	43	41	7	1	2	3	34	0	44	9	4
Cummins, Brian, Jamestown*	2	1	.667	3.38	18	0	0	0	2	1	34.2	37	152	22	13	1	2	4	1	9	0	24	3	0
Davey, Tom, St. Catharines	4	3	.571	3.32	7	7	0	0	0	0	38.0	27	160	19	14	2	0	2	3	21	0	29	3	1
DeLaCruz, Narciso, St. Cath.*	1	1	.500	7.20	21	0	0	0	10	0	35.0	39	170	31	28	5	2	3	4	22	0	19	5	0
Dempster, Ryan, Hudson Valley	1	0	1.000	3.18	1	1	0	0	0	0	5.2	7	24	2	2	0	1	0	0	1	0	6	0	0
Diaz, Jairo, Williamsport	1	7	.125	2.98	30	0	0	0	6	0	45.1	39	188	21	15	2	5	0	3	10	1	55	4	1
Dixon, Timothy, Vermont*	7	2	.778	1.83	18	9	0	0	2	1	69.0	58	287	20	14	0	3	0	8	16	0	58	5	7
Donnelly, Robert, New Jersey	1	3	.250	3.54	36	0	0	0	13	0	48.1	37	210	21	19	1	4	1	3	30	4	63	5	0
Draeger, Mark, Hudson Valley	3	4	.429	5.40	21	2	0	0	4	0	40.0	40	193	33	24	0	1	2	4	26	2	33	10	0
Duffy, Ryan, Erie	1	2	.333	4.76	19	8	0	0	4	0	51.0	59	223	33	27	1	0	1	14	0	31	2	0
Durkovic, Peter, Jamestown*	0	0	.000	5.92	14	1	0	0	4	1	24.1	28	115	17	16	4	0	4	1	10	0	10	2	1
Eby, Michael, Jamestown*	2	1	.667	1.52	23	0	0	0	9	2	29.2	20	118	7	5	1	3	0	1	5	0	33	1	4
Einertson, Darrel, Oneonta	0	4	.000	1.88	25	0	0	0	8	0	38.1	32	167	20	8	1	1	0	3	15	1	35	0	1
Enard, Tony, Elmira	0	5	.000	7.63	15	5	0	0	8	0	30.2	33	149	36	26	1	0	5	4	22	0	27	10	4
Farr, Mark, Elmira	3	1	.750	6.08	9	9	0	0	0	0	40.0	45	200	34	27	3	1	1	4	31	1	24	5	2
Farrow, Jason, Erie	3	1	.750	2.23	20	4	0	0	2	0	48.1	44	213	18	12	0	6	2	6	20	2	50	4	2
Ferguson, Tim, Vermont*	0	0	.000	7.71	3	0	0	0	1	0	4.2	2	20	4	4	0	0	0	0	2	0	2	0	0
Fernandes, Jamie, Utica	0	1	.000	4.66	3	1	0	0	1	1	9.2	9	41	5	5	0	0	1	0	3	0	7	1	0
Fernandez, Jared, Utica	3	2	.600	1.89	5	5	1	0	0	0	38.0	30	148	11	8	2	0	1	1	9	1	23	1	0
Ferullo, Matt, Pittsfield	1	0	1.000	0.00	2	0	0	0	1	0	5.0	3	19	0	0	0	0	0	0	6	0	0	0
Fitterer, Scott, St. Catharines	0	0	.000	1.14	22	0	0	0	17	9	23.2	18	101	7	3	1	1	0	1	13	0	22	2	0
Foran, John, Jamestown	1	2	.333	5.82	14	0	0	0	4	1	17.0	17	79	15	11	1	0	1	1	6	0	18	3	0
Ford, Ben, Oneonta	5	0	1.000	0.87	29	0	0	0	10	0	52.0	39	224	23	5	1	0	2	5	16	0	50	5	0
Ford, Brian, Batavia*	3	1	.750	1.18	29	0	0	0	26	10	38.0	24	143	8	5	1	2	2	0	5	0	44	2	0
Frascatore, Steve, New Jersey	4	6	.400	4.68	16	15	0	0	1	0	82.2	86	370	56	43	2	1	3	6	30	0	43	6	2
Fuller, Stephen, Auburn	6	5	.545	4.86	14	14	0	0	0	0	66.2	70	317	51	36	2	1	5	3	51	0	29	9	1
Gaiko, Robert, Batavia	1	1	.500	8.18	20	0	0	0	10	0	33.0	50	165	34	30	3	1	1	4	11	3	25	7	0
Gambs, Chris, Batavia	3	2	.600	5.50	7	7	0	0	0	0	34.1	31	148	21	21	0	1	0	1	22	0	21	4	0
Garcia, Rick, Elmira	1	7	.125	5.97	15	15	0	0	0	0	75.1	80	341	56	50	3	1	2	5	46	0	53	5	2
Glynn, Ryan, Hudson Valley	3	3	.500	4.70	9	8	0	0	0	0	44.0	56	192	27	23	0	0	3	16	1	21	10	3
Goedde, Roger, Erie	1	3	.250	7.97	5	5	0	0	0	0	20.1	31	110	23	18	1	2	4	0	17	0	8	13	0
Green, Jason, Auburn	8	2	.800	3.81	14	14	2	1	0	0	82.2	80	365	48	35	1	4	0	10	29	0	48	5	0
Greene, Brian, Williamsport	3	2	.600	3.33	18	5	0	0	3	0	46.0	52	203	28	17	1	2	1	2	16	0	25	4	1
Grife, Richard, Watertown	1	2	.333	2.53	5	0	0	0	2	0	10.2	10	44	5	3	0	1	0	0	5	0	8	1	0
Groves, Brian, Jamestown*	0	1	.000	4.44	16	0	0	0	6	0	24.1	21	111	17	12	0	0	2	17	0	15	5	0
Gulin, Lindsey, Pittsfield*	1	0	1.000	3.86	1	1	0	0	0	0	7.0	4	29	4	3	1	0	0	3	0	3	1	1
Hall, Yates, New Jersey	3	0	1.000	1.37	5	5	0	0	0	0	26.1	19	109	7	4	0	0	1	1	10	0	22	4	1
Hamilton, Bo, Batavia	7	2	.778	2.58	14	13	0	0	0	0	83.2	73	348	30	24	2	3	6	23	0	62	10	1
Hammack, Brandon, Williamspt	1	5	.167	4.18	27	0	0	0	17	6	32.1	32	151	20	15	3	2	1	2	14	1	40	2	0
Hartshorn, Tyson, St. Cath.	3	4	.429	4.26	13	13	1	1	0	0	69.2	83	307	45	33	6	3	1	3	25	0	25	6	1
Harvey, Terry, Watertown	6	2	.750	1.82	8	8	0	0	0	0	54.1	36	205	13	11	1	0	3	1	6	1	33	0	0
Helvey, Rob, New Jersey*	2	1	.667	0.73	11	0	0	0	8	2	12.1	7	45	1	1	0	1	0	5	0	15	0	0
Hernandez, Elvin, Erie	6	1	.857	2.89	14	14	2	1	0	0	90.1	82	377	40	29	8	5	3	4	22	0	54	2	1
Herr, David, Vermont	6	3	.667	3.76	18	8	0	0	0	0	55.0	53	229	26	23	0	1	2	4	18	1	35	5	0
Horn, Keith, Watertown	3	2	.600	2.86	8	8	0	0	0	0	44.0	39	180	18	14	4	0	1	0	12	0	36	0	2

Pitcher, Team	W	L	Pct.	ERA	G	GS	CG	ShO	GF	Sv.	IP	H	TBF	R	ER	HR	SH	SF	HB	BB	IBB	SO	WP	Bk.
Horton, Aaron, Oneonta*	0	2	.000	3.22	6	3	0	0	1	0	22.1	19	96	13	8	0	2	0	3	4	0	12	0	1
Horton, Eric, St. Catharines	6	2	.750	2.84	21	7	0	0	9	3	69.2	50	276	28	22	4	1	3	3	26	0	51	4	2
Howard, Tom, Elmira*	0	0	.000	7.43	10	0	0	0	5	0	13.1	9	69	13	11	0	0	1	0	21	0	7	6	0
Howatt, Jeff, Pittsfield	1	2	.333	4.15	17	0	0	0	5	1	39.0	37	167	22	18	2	1	3	0	15	0	26	3	3
Hoy, Wayne, St. Catharines	5	3	.625	2.21	24	1	0	0	9	3	57.0	39	228	20	14	0	1	0	3	23	0	34	5	1
Hritz, Derrick, Watertown*	0	1	.000	2.10	18	0	0	0	10	1	30.0	28	130	9	7	0	2	1	1	16	2	23	4	1
Imersek, Jason, Oneonta	0	0	.000	0.00	1	0	0	0	1	0	0.1	0	1	0	0	0	0	0	0	0	0	0	0	0
Jacobs, Mike, Utica	8	3	.727	2.71	13	13	2	1	0	0	86.1	83	371	35	26	1	2	0	1	37	2	51	8	0
Johnson, Scott, Elmira	0	0	.000	4.32	4	0	0	0	1	0	8.1	10	37	4	4	0	0	1	1	0	4	0	0	1
Jones, Scott, Utica	0	1	.000	1.35	20	0	0	0	20	13	20.0	11	78	3	3	0	1	2	0	9	1	26	3	0
Kahlon, Bobby, Hudson Valley	5	5	.500	2.32	30	0	0	0	16	3	54.1	35	220	16	14	3	5	0	1	21	5	76	10	1
Kast, Nick, New Jersey*	5	1	.833	1.38	29	0	0	0	7	0	45.2	29	188	11	7	0	1	2	7	21	1	64	3	4
Kawabata, Kyle, Batavia	2	0	1.000	3.58	18	0	0	0	4	0	32.2	34	140	16	13	3	2	1	3	5	1	30	2	1
Kelley, Jason, Williamsport	1	1	.500	1.62	3	3	0	0	0	0	16.2	14	70	3	3	0	0	0	1	7	0	6	1	0
Kendrick, Scott, Williamsport	2	1	.667	3.33	5	5	0	0	0	0	27.0	26	117	14	10	2	1	2	3	8	0	15	3	0
Kindell, Scott, Pittsfield*	4	1	.800	2.36	20	0	0	0	9	0	26.2	25	109	11	7	1	2	2	1	6	0	14	2	0
Koenig, Matthew, Pittsfield	4	5	.444	4.27	15	12	0	0	1	0	78.0	81	334	47	37	6	1	1	3	23	0	43	6	0
Lail, Jerry, Oneonta	5	6	.455	3.97	13	13	0	0	0	0	68.0	66	309	38	30	3	1	4	5	31	0	59	1	0
Link, Bryan, Hudson Valley*	5	3	.625	3.49	15	15	1	0	0	0	90.1	79	370	39	35	5	5	2	3	25	0	88	7	1
Lisio, Joseph, Pittsfield	2	2	.500	1.62	28	0	0	0	23	12	33.1	27	141	8	6	0	2	5	1	14	1	24	2	0
Loiz, Niuman, Auburn	1	1	.500	2.63	3	3	1	1	0	0	13.2	7	56	5	4	0	0	0	0	8	0	11	2	1
Long, Justin, Elmira	0	0	.000	0.00	1	0	0	0	1	0	1.0	0	3	0	0	0	0	0	0	0	0	2	0	0
Lowe, Ben, St. Catharines*	4	5	.444	4.35	15	15	0	0	0	0	78.2	89	358	43	38	3	3	3	9	40	0	61	10	1
Mamott, Joe, Utica	0	4	.000	6.68	9	6	0	0	1	0	32.1	40	173	35	24	1	0	3	11	28	0	36	10	0
Marquez, Ihosvany, Utica	0	0	.000	2.70	12	0	0	0	3	0	20.0	13	84	8	6	0	0	1	4	13	0	23	4	0
Marquez, Robert, Vermont	1	1	.500	0.84	29	0	0	0	29	21	32.0	15	122	5	3	0	1	0	1	11	0	32	1	0
Martineau, Brian, Hud. Valley	5	2	.714	1.30	30	0	0	0	26	18	41.2	30	166	10	6	1	5	0	3	10	1	39	4	5
Martinez, Osvaldo, Jamestown	4	4	.500	3.77	15	15	1	0	0	0	90.2	85	384	46	38	10	3	1	6	30	1	56	2	4
Mathis, Sammie, Watertown	4	1	.800	4.36	18	0	0	0	4	0	33.0	39	153	22	16	1	0	3	4	15	1	21	1	2
Mattes, Troy, Vermont	3	4	.429	3.72	10	10	0	0	0	0	46.0	51	209	34	19	3	5	4	5	20	0	23	7	0
McClurg, Clinton, Batavia	2	2	.500	4.30	10	5	1	0	1	0	37.2	41	171	26	18	2	3	2	4	21	0	14	4	0
McEntire, Ethan, Pittsfield*	4	2	.667	5.06	13	13	0	0	0	0	69.1	81	325	43	39	2	1	2	5	46	0	41	7	0
McHugh, Michael, Hud. Valley*	0	0	.000	8.40	10	0	0	0	3	0	15.0	26	85	17	14	0	0	0	2	14	0	9	4	0
McNeese, John, Williamsport*	5	3	.625	1.86	13	12	0	0	0	0	72.2	73	297	24	15	2	1	1	2	10	1	47	2	2
McNichol, Brian, Williamsport*	3	1	.750	3.08	9	9	0	0	0	0	49.2	57	215	28	17	1	1	1	2	8	0	35	1	1
Mejia, Carlos, Utica*	1	1	.500	4.73	10	0	0	0	5	1	13.1	15	62	8	7	0	1	1	0	5	0	14	4	2
Mendes, Jaime, Batavia	1	1	.500	3.92	30	0	0	0	14	3	41.1	50	177	23	18	3	2	2	6	35	0	35	4	0
Mensink, Brian, Batavia	4	1	.800	2.98	11	8	0	0	1	0	48.1	56	207	23	16	0	2	1	5	10	0	37	3	2
Merrick, Brett, Watertown*	2	1	.667	1.93	22	0	0	0	11	4	37.1	15	142	10	8	2	0	1	0	18	3	44	3	0
Micknich, Steve, Elmira	0	0	.000	0.00	4	0	0	0	4	2	5.1	1	20	0	0	0	0	0	1	2	0	6	0	0
Miedreich, Kevin, New Jersey	2	6	.250	4.70	15	15	0	0	0	0	74.2	84	340	47	39	2	2	7	8	33	0	39	5	1
Miles, Chad, Elmira*	1	1	.500	6.65	14	0	0	0	4	0	21.2	29	105	18	16	2	1	1	1	10	0	10	5	1
Miller, David, Elmira	1	1	.500	4.32	9	0	0	0	4	1	16.2	17	73	8	8	1	1	0	2	7	1	11	1	2
Mitchell, Courtney, Batavia*	0	5	.000	4.89	28	0	0	0	9	1	42.1	46	194	28	23	2	1	2	3	23	1	40	4	1
Mitchell, Scott, Vermont	3	1	.750	2.23	18	1	0	0	5	1	40.1	35	171	18	10	1	2	2	4	15	0	30	2	1
Moore, Robert, Hudson Valley	2	3	.400	5.43	13	13	0	0	0	0	63.0	77	280	45	38	5	2	5	4	13	0	45	10	3
Moore, Sam, Elmira	2	4	.333	1.84	15	0	0	0	9	3	29.1	23	112	8	6	1	1	0	1	4	0	22	3	1
Morris, Chad, Vermont	1	0	1.000	2.40	9	0	0	0	6	0	15.0	11	65	4	4	1	0	1	9	0	19	5	3
Morris, Matt, New Jersey	2	0	1.000	1.64	2	2	0	0	0	0	11.0	12	45	3	2	1	0	0	3	0	13	0	3
Mosley, Tim, Williamsport	2	0	1.000	4.28	23	0	0	0	6	1	33.2	40	161	23	16	0	2	2	4	16	0	26	2	0
Mudd, Scott, Hudson Valley	7	1	.875	2.24	15	15	3	1	0	0	100.2	91	402	37	25	2	3	2	18	0	62	10	1
Munro, Peter, Utica	5	4	.556	2.54	14	14	0	0	0	0	90.0	79	389	38	26	3	3	3	7	33	1	74	4	0
Murray, Dan, Pittsfield	0	6	.000	1.97	22	0	0	0	19	6	32.0	24	145	17	7	1	2	0	1	16	3	34	3	0
Neese, Josh, Jamestown	3	1	.750	3.72	20	2	0	0	5	0	36.1	29	153	15	15	2	4	3	4	14	2	38	4	4
Negrette, Richard, Watertown	3	3	.500	5.52	18	5	0	0	6	3	45.2	42	203	30	28	5	2	2	7	23	2	35	6	1
Noffke, Andrew, Utica	0	2	.000	7.71	23	0	0	0	9	0	25.2	34	137	30	22	1	0	2	3	24	0	24	5	0
Noone, Bill, Batavia	1	0	1.000	14.29	6	0	0	0	2	0	5.2	14	35	11	9	1	0	1	0	3	0	2	1	0
Nunez, Maximo, St. Catharines	1	0	1.000	9.39	7	0	0	0	4	0	7.2	11	42	10	8	1	1	0	1	7	0	6	1	0
Nuttle, Jamison, Erie	0	1	.000	3.07	13	0	0	0	9	1	14.2	8	59	8	5	1	0	1	0	7	0	13	0	0
Oakley, Matt, Jamestown	0	0	.000	18.00	1	0	0	0	1	0	1.0	3	7	2	2	0	0	0	1	0	0	0	0
Olivier, Rich, Oneonta	3	3	.500	3.73	12	12	0	0	0	0	60.1	63	264	36	25	2	3	2	4	21	0	50	8	0
Ormonde, Troy, Williamsport	2	4	.333	4.29	14	14	0	0	0	0	71.1	61	324	50	34	2	4	3	5	39	0	41	3	2
Pailthorpe, Bob, Elmira	2	7	.222	4.88	13	12	0	0	0	0	51.2	69	241	41	28	2	1	3	1	17	0	38	2	7
Patterson, Casey, Pittsfield	0	4	.000	9.53	12	4	0	0	3	0	34.0	47	181	43	36	4	1	1	6	28	0	18	4	2
Peguero, Jose, St. Catharines	2	1	.667	4.50	17	0	0	0	7	0	34.0	31	148	19	17	1	4	2	1	19	0	19	0	0
Pena, Jesus, Erie*	0	3	.000	12.66	3	3	0	0	0	0	10.2	18	56	16	15	1	1	0	2	7	0	5	0	1
Perez, Gil, Erie	2	2	.500	2.79	18	1	0	0	1	0	38.2	39	172	19	12	1	2	2	4	15	0	27	8	0
Perez, Hilario, Utica	2	2	.500	4.81	20	3	0	0	7	1	43.0	50	203	38	23	4	0	5	1	22	2	22	1	0
Peterman, Ernie, St. Catharines	1	1	.500	5.94	4	3	0	0	0	0	16.2	18	71	11	11	1	1	1	4	2	0	8	0	1
Peterson, Jayson, Williamsport	2	0	1.000	3.71	3	3	0	0	0	0	17.0	15	73	7	7	1	0	0	1	5	0	14	1	0
Phillips, Jon, Auburn*	2	0	1.000	0.00	2	0	0	0	1	0	5.1	6	23	0	0	0	0	0	1	1	0	5	0	0
Pinango, Simon, Utica*	2	4	.333	6.91	20	0	0	0	6	0	28.2	30	135	27	22	2	0	3	1	16	1	27	4	0
Powell, Brian, Jamestown	2	1	.667	3.08	5	5	0	0	0	0	26.1	19	108	12	9	1	0	1	5	8	0	15	3	0
Powell, Jeremy, Vermont	5	5	.500	4.34	15	15	0	0	0	0	87.0	88	373	48	42	5	2	2	6	34	1	47	6	2
Pyrtle, Joe, Pittsfield	0	1	.000	3.48	17	0	0	0	7	2	31.0	32	140	18	12	1	1	1	0	12	0	17	2	3
Rakers, Jason, Watertown	4	3	.571	3.00	14	14	1	1	0	0	75.0	72	315	27	25	3	0	2	0	24	1	73	6	2
Randolph, Steve, Oneonta*	0	3	.000	7.48	6	6	0	0	0	0	21.2	19	109	22	18	0	0	2	1	23	0	31	5	0
Reames, Britt, New Jersey	2	1	.667	1.52	5	5	0	0	0	0	29.2	19	121	7	5	1	1	0	3	12	0	42	5	0
Reichstein, Derek, Elmira	4	4	.200	5.23	22	2	0	0	8	1	51.2	52	234	37	30	2	2	4	5	27	1	37	5	4
Reid, Rayon, Erie	3	3	.500	2.45	8	7	0	0	0	0	47.2	37	189	16	13	2	0	3	11	0	47	4	1
Reilly, John, St. Catharines	0	1	.000	0.00	1	1	0	0	0	0	0.2	1	6	2	0	0	0	0	0	0	0	0	0	0
Reinfelder, David, Jamestown*	2	5	.286	4.60	16	14	0	0	0	0	78.1	85	334	48	40	6	5	3	6	17	0	55	5	0
Reyes, Jose, Erie	2	3	.400	3.39	19	7	1	0	1	0	58.1	53	253	25	22	2	1	0	1	29	1	44	3	0

Pitcher, Team	W	L	Pct.	ERA	G	GS	CG	ShO	GF	Sv.	IP	H	TBF	R	ER	HR	SH	SF	HB	BB	IBB	SO	WP	Bk.
Ricketts, Chad, Williamsport	4	5	.444	4.19	12	12	0	0	0	0	68.2	89	312	46	32	4	0	3	8	16	0	37	1	3
Robbins, Jake, Oneonta	0	0	.000	0.00	1	0	0	0	1	0	1.0	0	3	0	0	0	0	0	0	0	0	1	0	0
Romboli, Curtis, Utica*	2	3	.400	4.56	14	6	2	0	3	0	51.1	60	225	32	26	1	1	1	1	16	0	34	4	1
Root, Derek, Auburn*	2	0	1.000	3.29	17	3	0	0	5	1	38.1	28	165	14	14	0	2	1	2	24	0	37	4	1
Rosenbohm, Jim, Auburn	2	4	.333	3.66	22	1	0	0	6	1	51.2	48	236	23	21	0	1	0	10	32	3	50	5	0
Ross, Jeremy, Elmira	1	0	1.000	3.00	20	0	0	0	3	2	42.0	38	184	17	14	0	1	2	2	20	1	40	6	3
Sagedal, Brent, Hudson Valley	0	2	.000	7.08	14	5	0	0	4	1	34.1	42	158	29	27	7	2	1	1	18	1	25	7	1
St. Pierre, Bob, Oneonta	5	3	.625	2.83	15	15	0	0	0	0	89.0	83	368	39	28	4	1	4	2	24	0	91	4	2
Santiago, Antonio, Utica*	0	3	.000	5.30	4	4	0	0	0	0	18.2	24	91	17	11	0	1	1	0	13	0	11	7	0
Santoro, Gary, Elmira	1	4	.200	3.75	24	0	0	0	20	6	36.0	45	164	21	15	1	2	0	6	10	1	34	6	0
Santos, Rafael, Erie	0	0	.000	0.00	2	0	0	0	0	0	1.0	0	5	0	0	0	0	0	0	2	0	1	0	0
Sauve, Jeff, Utica	1	1	.500	4.70	11	0	0	0	5	1	15.1	19	72	12	8	1	1	1	1	8	1	16	2	1
Schulte, Troy, Auburn	1	2	.333	4.88	23	0	0	0	17	6	31.1	30	130	20	17	5	2	0	1	9	0	22	1	0
Schultz, Scott, Watertown	1	3	.250	4.70	9	5	0	0	3	2	30.2	39	141	24	16	2	0	1	2	11	0	20	2	3
Scolaro, Donald, Auburn	0	0	.000	54.00	1	0	0	0	1	0	0.1	2	3	2	2	2	0	0	0	0	0	0	0	0
Severino, Jose, New Jersey	3	3	.500	5.29	17	10	0	0	1	0	66.1	65	303	48	39	8	1	4	2	37	2	68	9	3
Short, Barry, Pittsfield	0	0	.000	4.50	2	0	0	0	1	1	2.0	4	10	1	1	0	0	0	0	4	0	3	1	0
Shumaker, Anthony, Batavia*	2	2	.500	1.62	9	4	1	1	0	0	39.0	38	157	10	7	0	0	0	4	0	0	31	2	0
Sikorski, Brian, Auburn	1	2	.333	2.10	23	0	0	0	19	12	34.1	22	137	8	8	1	0	1	0	14	2	35	1	0
Smart, J.D., Vermont	0	1	.000	2.28	5	5	0	0	0	0	27.2	29	118	9	7	1	1	3	3	7	0	21	0	0
Smith, Eric, Auburn	2	6	.250	3.93	14	14	0	0	0	0	71.0	70	314	37	31	4	0	4	5	30	0	56	5	3
Smith, Justin, Batavia	4	3	.571	4.26	15	10	0	0	0	0	61.1	71	266	35	29	5	1	2	5	20	0	37	5	2
Smith, Randy, St. Catharines	0	2	.000	3.27	18	0	0	0	9	2	33.0	34	141	14	12	0	0	1	9	0	0	26	1	0
Smyth, Gregg, Auburn*	6	6	.500	4.56	14	14	1	1	0	0	75.0	87	332	48	38	2	2	6	2	25	0	48	6	0
Spaulding, Scott, New Jersey	1	0	1.000	2.59	35	0	0	0	11	2	48.2	36	200	17	14	4	1	0	6	14	0	40	2	1
Speier, Justin, Williamsport	2	1	.667	1.49	30	0	0	0	22	12	36.1	27	142	6	6	1	2	2	1	4	0	39	0	0
Stachler, Eric, Auburn	1	2	.333	8.42	18	0	0	0	5	2	36.1	47	179	35	34	2	2	1	27	2	32	4	0	
Steinke, Brock, Auburn	1	0	1.000	2.08	6	0	0	0	3	0	8.2	11	38	2	2	1	0	0	0	3	0	6	0	0
Stephens, Bill, Vermont	3	1	.750	1.65	13	0	0	0	8	3	27.1	17	111	5	5	0	0	0	5	7	0	30	5	0
Stephens, Shannon, Elmira	8	5	.615	2.58	17	12	0	0	2	0	90.2	72	364	38	26	4	3	0	4	17	1	74	6	2
Stern, Marty, Vermont	0	0	.000	3.38	8	0	0	0	4	0	13.1	12	57	5	5	1	0	0	1	6	0	10	1	0
Swenson, Mike, New Jersey*	2	4	.333	4.82	19	6	0	0	3	0	52.1	53	246	35	28	1	0	3	7	32	0	54	5	0
Tatis, Ramon, Pittsfield*	4	5	.444	3.63	13	13	1	1	0	0	79.1	88	341	40	32	2	1	1	3	27	0	69	8	3
Tessmer, Jay, Oneonta	2	0	1.000	0.95	34	0	0	0	33	20	38.0	27	156	8	4	0	0	0	3	12	2	52	3	2
Thomas, Rob, Erie*	1	1	.500	4.60	15	0	0	0	7	0	15.2	9	71	10	8	2	0	2	1	17	1	9	4	0
Tickell, Brian, Auburn	5	3	.625	5.57	13	11	2	0	0	0	72.2	79	310	47	45	6	1	2	4	18	0	31	5	0
Treend, Pat, Elmira	0	2	.000	6.29	17	1	0	0	6	0	34.1	43	171	32	24	3	2	0	5	16	0	29	3	0
Trumpour, Andy, Pittsfield	7	6	.538	2.57	15	15	2	1	0	0	105.0	95	427	44	30	2	3	3	5	32	0	75	7	0
Venafro, Michael, Hud. Valley*	9	1	.900	2.13	32	0	0	0	12	2	50.2	37	200	13	12	0	2	1	5	21	2	32	1	3
Viegas, Randy, Elmira*	0	0	.000	6.30	8	1	0	0	2	0	10.0	14	53	9	7	0	0	0	2	9	0	9	1	0
Villafana, Jose, New Jersey	0	6	.000	4.91	27	0	0	0	21	13	29.1	35	141	17	16	0	4	2	0	21	1	28	4	2
Volkert, Oreste, St. Catharines	2	3	.400	2.67	12	0	0	0	8	2	54.0	53	225	20	16	3	1	1	0	14	0	44	8	0
Ward, Jon, New Jersey	0	7	.000	8.07	9	8	0	0	1	0	32.1	47	170	42	29	5	1	5	4	18	0	35	5	1
Weber, David, Williamsport	2	3	.400	7.94	22	2	0	0	9	0	34.0	51	165	38	30	3	1	0	2	15	0	28	2	2
Weber, Eric, Jamestown	2	2	.500	5.23	15	3	0	0	4	0	32.2	35	142	25	19	2	0	0	2	11	0	22	3	0
Weber, Lenny, Watertown	1	0	1.000	2.00	5	0	0	0	3	0	9.0	5	37	2	2	0	1	0	0	5	1	5	0	0
Weidert, Chris, Vermont	11	1	.917	1.79	15	15	1	1	0	0	95.1	67	378	31	19	4	0	2	4	21	0	52	8	0
Welch, Robb, Utica	4	4	.500	5.68	12	12	1	0	0	0	65.0	76	303	45	41	1	1	3	5	39	0	35	7	1
Whitworth, Clint, Oneonta	0	2	.000	5.93	12	1	0	0	2	0	27.1	31	136	23	18	0	0	2	5	15	0	15	9	0
Wilkinson, Arrow, Oneonta	1	0	1.000	4.13	14	0	0	0	2	0	28.1	28	135	19	13	0	3	1	1	23	0	24	4	1
Wilson, Mike, Oneonta	2	4	.333	4.20	14	4	0	0	0	0	40.2	41	183	24	19	0	1	0	2	19	0	41	8	2
Wilson, Mike, Jamestown	1	3	.250	6.55	5	5	0	0	0	0	22.0	27	103	20	16	1	1	1	4	6	0	11	0	0
Winchester, Scott, Watertown	3	1	.750	2.83	23	0	0	0	22	11	28.2	24	116	10	9	0	1	2	6	2	2	27	2	2
Wolff, Thomas, Pittsfield	0	2	.000	8.00	4	1	0	0	2	0	9.0	15	49	11	8	1	0	0	2	5	0	8	1	0
Wolger, Michael, Vermont*	0	0	.000	16.88	2	0	0	0	2	0	2.2	2	16	5	5	0	0	0	1	7	0	1	1	0
Wood, Kerry,, Williamsport	0	0	.000	10.38	2	2	0	0	0	0	4.1	5	23	8	5	0	0	0	0	5	0	5	1	0
Wyatt, Cortez, Williamsport	4	3	.571	2.63	22	2	0	0	7	0	48.0	38	194	16	14	3	0	1	6	8	0	35	3	0
Yeager, Gary, Batavia	9	4	.692	2.56	19	8	1	0	4	0	81.0	74	327	33	23	2	0	3	0	16	0	57	7	4
Young, Joe, St. Catharines	6	5	.545	2.04	15	15	0	0	0	0	83.2	72	349	29	19	4	3	4	5	35	0	73	5	3
Young, Ryan, Erie	5	2	.714	2.79	16	10	1	0	2	1	67.2	62	288	34	21	5	5	1	3	17	0	38	0	1

COMBINATION SHUTOUTS: **Auburn (2)**—Rosenbohm-Root, Smith-Rosenbohm-Stachler-Albaladejo. **Batavia (7)**—Gambs-Ford, Gambs-McClurg-Mendes-Ford, Gambs-Mensink-Ford, Hamilton-Ford, Mensink-Mendes-Ford, Smith-Mendes, Yeager-Mitchell. **Elmira (2)**—Stephens-Miller-Santoro, Stephens-Reichstein. **Erie (3)**—Bullock-Perez-Viegas, Bullock-Reyes-Chew, Reid-Perez-Reyes-Nuttle. **Hudson Valley (2)**—Link-Venafro-Martineau, Mudd-Kahlon-Martineau. **Jamestown (1)**—Neese-Eby-Corey. **New Jersey (5)**—Frascatore-Spaulding-Donnelly, Hall-Donnelly-Spaulding, Miedreich-Kast-Donnelly-Helvey, Morris-Donnelly-Spaulding-Villafana, Reames-Bennett-Benes. **Oneonta (2)**—Becker-Einertson-Tessmer 2. **Pittsfield (2)**—Ballew-Pyrtle-Lisio, Coronado-Kindell-Lisio. **St. Catharines (2)**—Crowther-Hoy-Fitterer, Davey-Hoy. **Utica (1)**—Jacobs-Sauve. **Vermont (8)**—Baker-Civit-Marquez, Baker-Dixon-Marquez, Baker-Mitchell-Marquez, Baker-Stephens-Morris, Dixon-Civit, Dixon-Herr-Marquez, Herr-Stephens, Mattes-Civit-Marquez. **Watertown (6)**—Atkins-Merrick-Winchester, Atkins-Schultz, Atkins-Weber, Crowell-Atkins, Harvey-Hritz, Horn-Merrick. **Williamsport (2)**—Kelley-Mosley-Weber, Wood-Hammack-Mosley-Diaz-Speier.

NO-HIT GAMES: Hernandez, Erie, defeated Oneonta, 7-0, August 24.

1995 FIELDING

TEAM

Team	Pct.	G	PO	A	E	TC	DP	PB	Team	Pct.	G	PO	A	E	TC	DP	PB
Watertown	.972	73	1936	894	83	2913	72	16	Jamestown	.957	76	2000	896	131	3027	63	13
Vermont	.962	76	2003	858	113	2974	79	26	Elmira	.956	76	1974	894	133	3001	64	16
Hudson Valley	.960	74	1980	864	120	2964	64	18	Pittsfield	.955	76	1977	880	135	2992	67	15
St. Catharines	.959	75	2009	917	126	3052	72	13	Utica	.952	73	1909	827	138	2874	62	29
Batavia	.959	75	1998	877	124	2999	90	10	Erie	.950	75	1959	897	150	3006	72	14
Auburn	.958	74	1865	832	119	2816	71	15	Williamsport	.947	76	1996	828	158	2982	57	29
New Jersey	.957	76	2046	739	124	2909	55	16	Oneonta	.944	75	1940	827	165	2932	50	24

TRIPLE PLAYS: Auburn, Elmira, Erie, Hudson Valley, Oneonta, St. Catharines.

INDIVIDUAL

FIRST BASEMEN

NOTE: All caps denotes fielding-percentage leader based on 38 games for catchers, 51 for all other non-pitchers and 76 innings for pitchers. *Throws lefthanded.

Player, Team	Pct.	G	PO	A	E	TC	DP
Adams, Jason, Auburn	1.000	1	2	0	0	2	0
Brumbaugh, Clifford, Hud. Valley	1.000	2	6	0	0	6	1
Carver, Steve, Batavia	.983	50	451	17	8	476	46
Casey, Sean, Watertown	.985	52	510	24	8	542	37
Chevalier, Virgil, Utica	.994	19	166	10	1	177	14
Culp, Matt, Watertown	.987	9	72	5	1	78	9
Daly, Rob, Pittsfield	.989	76	724	60	9	793	58
Emmons, Scott, Oneonta	.966	13	136	7	5	148	9
EVANS, Kyle, Hudson Valley*	.996	53	467	24	2	493	35
Fana, Alberto, Batavia	.981	13	96	9	2	107	12
Gallagher, Shawn, Hud. Valley	.978	5	44	1	1	46	2
Garman, Sean, New Jersey	.917	5	11	0	1	12	0
Garrett, Jason, Elmira	1.000	19	177	8	0	185	10
Gipner, Marcus, Oneonta	.972	23	195	14	6	215	12
Halemanu, Joshua, Auburn*	.978	52	463	32	11	506	42
Hayes, Chris, St. Catharines	1.000	2	14	0	0	14	0
Hayes, Heath, Watertown	.993	13	131	9	1	141	13
Johnson, Jason, Hud. Valley	.500	1	1	0	1	2	0
Koonce, Graham, Jamestown*	.985	72	694	70	12	776	49
Landers, Mark, St. Catharines*	.988	74	704	41	9	754	61
Leaman, Jeff, Batavia	.964	19	145	17	6	168	16
Lewis, Marc, Utica	1.000	1	20	2	0	22	0
Long, Garrett, Erie	.977	17	161	12	4	177	14
Mackert, Jamie, Erie	.985	22	184	9	3	196	13
Maleski, Tom, Williamsport	1.000	3	16	2	0	18	0
Martinez, Dave, Hudson Valley*	1.000	24	173	11	0	184	18
Maynor, Tonka, Erie	.988	8	77	3	1	81	8
McCartney, Sommer, Elmira	1.000	1	7	1	0	8	1
Morales, Eric, Pittsfield	1.000	1	4	0	0	4	0
Olsen, Donald, Vermont	1.000	48	462	26	0	488	48
Palmer, Jim, Oneonta	.955	7	64	0	3	67	1
Prodanov, Peter, Utica	.833	4	9	1	2	12	2
Putko, James, Williamsport	.969	36	262	19	9	290	18
Rathmell, Lance, Utica	.917	2	10	1	1	12	2
Rice, Charles, Erie	.960	31	275	13	12	300	21
Richard, Chris, New Jersey*	.984	75	620	43	11	674	51
Salzano, Jerry, Williamsport	.986	53	403	27	6	436	33
Samuel, Cory, Oneonta	.974	37	319	12	9	340	20
Sapp, Damien, Utica	1.000	1	1	0	0	1	0
Scolaro, Donald, Auburn	1.000	24	207	14	0	221	22
Seidel, Ryan, Williamsport	1.000	2	14	2	0	16	0
Shanahan, Jason, Elmira	.995	57	563	51	3	617	49
Smith, Akili, Erie	.958	2	21	2	1	24	6
Thornhill, Chad, Watertown	.939	6	28	3	2	33	4
Tippin, Greg, Utica*	.984	56	453	32	8	493	35
Vieira, Scott, Williamsport	1.000	1	3	0	0	3	0
Waggoner, James, Jamestown	.979	5	43	4	1	48	4
Walker, Rodney, Hudson Valley	.778	2	7	0	2	9	0
Wolger, Michael, Vermont*	.990	28	267	17	3	287	21

TRIPLE PLAYS: Landers, Rice, Scolaro.

SECOND BASEMEN

Player, Team	Pct.	G	PO	A	E	TC	DP
Adams, Jason, Auburn	.949	47	73	151	12	236	35
ANDERSON, Marlon, Batavia	.9648	73	153	231	14	398	67
Antrim, Patrick, Oneonta	.500	1	0	1	1	2	0
Arvelo, Tom, Pittsfield	.944	67	133	173	18	324	38
Brinkley, Josh, Vermont	1.000	2	6	6	0	12	0
Brito, Domingo, Batavia	1.000	3	0	2	0	2	0
Cabrera, Orlando, Vermont	.964	53	115	152	10	277	38
Cardona, Ruben, New Jersey	.967	48	98	135	8	241	33
Conley, Brian, Williamsport	.930	50	100	125	17	242	22
DeLuca, Nic, New Jersey	1.000	1	0	1	0	1	0
Dennis, Les, Oneonta	.922	31	48	70	10	128	13
Deshenes, Marc, Watertown	.970	35	59	100	5	164	21
Engleka, Douglas, Jamestown	.957	21	33	56	4	93	9
Freel, Ryan, St. Catharines	.940	65	118	181	19	318	32
Funaro, Joe, Elmira	.963	17	30	49	3	82	13
Garcia, Amaury, Elmira	.944	60	128	178	18	324	33
Garcia, Apostol, Jamestown	.000	1	0	0	1	1	0
Gorecki, Ryan, Hudson Valley	.9647	53	92	154	9	255	35
Hall, Andy, New Jersey	1.000	4	6	10	0	16	1
Holley, Jack, St. Catharines	1.000	8	15	15	0	30	2
Insunza, Miguel, New Jersey	.939	25	45	63	7	115	8
Jasco, Elinton, Williamsport	1.000	6	11	17	0	28	1
Lebron, Ruben, Utica	.968	48	84	128	7	219	21
Lemonis, Chris, Jamestown	.960	51	99	140	10	249	29

Player, Team	Pct.	G	PO	A	E	TC	DP
Lugo, Julio, Auburn	.937	20	42	62	7	111	12
Macias, Jose, Vermont	.949	21	49	62	6	117	15
McDonald, Ashanti, Williamsport	.885	8	6	17	3	26	3
Miyake, Chris, Erie	.9647	38	89	130	8	227	25
Nieves, Jose, Williamsport	.960	9	21	27	2	50	8
Parsons, Jeff, Pittsfield	1.000	1	2	0	0	3	0
Perez, Mike, Williamsport	1.000	7	15	21	0	36	7
Pettiford, Torrey, Batavia	.947	3	7	11	1	19	1
Pollock, Elton, Erie	1.000	3	5	3	0	8	1
Rathmell, Lance, Utica	.911	20	31	41	7	79	11
Rojas, Ron, Jamestown	.942	10	26	23	3	52	6
Sagers, Kory, Utica	.962	15	31	45	3	79	8
Sanchez, Omar, St. Catharines	.911	7	18	23	4	45	7
Schreiber, Stan, Erie	.867	2	8	5	2	15	4
Scolaro, Donald, Auburn	.953	8	18	23	2	43	4
Segura, Juan, Erie	.944	12	25	43	4	72	7
Smith, Rod, Oneonta	.939	49	74	125	13	212	23
Soriano, Carlos, Pittsfield	1.000	2	2	7	0	9	0
Thornhill, Chad, Watertown	.978	48	107	112	5	224	32
Turner, Rocky, Pittsfield	.857	1	2	4	1	7	1
Venezia, Richard, Erie	.958	22	35	56	4	95	13
Viruet, Willie, Pittsfield	.957	9	21	24	2	47	6
Vopata, Nathan, Hudson Valley	.946	27	54	51	6	111	10
Walker, Rodney, Hudson Valley	1.000	1	2	0	0	2	0
Whipple, Boomer, Erie	1.000	2	3	1	0	4	0

TRIPLE PLAYS: Adams, Dennis, Am. Garcia, Holley.

THIRD BASEMEN

Player, Team	Pct.	G	PO	A	E	TC	DP
Adams, Jason, Auburn	.000	1	0	0	1	1	0
Booty, Josh, Elmira	.898	73	56	173	26	255	20
Bovender, Andy, Auburn	.900	58	42	102	16	160	12
Brannon, Tony, Utica	.879	41	31	85	16	132	6
Brinkley, Josh, Vermont	.933	7	6	8	1	15	0
Brumbaugh, Clifford, Hud. Valley	.914	73	54	149	19	222	11
Cox, Charles, Batavia	.400	1	1	1	3	5	0
DeLuca, Nic, New Jersey	1.000	2	1	3	0	4	0
DIEGUEZ, Mike, Pittsfield	.954	52	42	104	7	153	9
Engleka, Douglas, Jamestown	.917	6	1	10	1	12	3
Fernandez, Jose, Vermont	.907	63	48	157	21	226	13
Funaro, Joe, Elmira	1.000	1	1	2	0	3	0
Garman, Sean, New Jersey	.919	44	45	68	10	123	7
Hall, Andy, New Jersey	.773	38	19	39	17	75	2
Hayes, Chris, St. Catharines	.954	28	26	77	5	108	8
Holley, Jack, St. Catharines	.914	46	40	108	14	162	8
Insunza, Miguel, New Jersey	.800	3	2	2	1	5	0
Jorgensen, Tim, Watertown	.936	73	42	205	17	264	24
Leaman, Jeff, Batavia	.926	38	17	83	8	108	9
Lemonis, Chris, Jamestown	.900	4	4	5	1	10	0
Lowell, Mike, Oneonta	.911	72	59	188	24	271	8
Macias, Jose, Vermont	.950	9	5	14	1	20	1
Mackert, Jamie, Erie	.882	12	2	28	4	34	3
Maleski, Tom, Williamsport	.857	3	2	4	1	7	0
McDonald, Ashanti, Williamsport	.934	25	12	59	5	76	3
Miller, Michael, Jamestown	.908	64	36	141	18	195	8
Motes, Jeff, Pittsfield	.908	24	13	46	6	65	3
Nova, Jose Feliz, Williamsport	.853	52	24	86	19	129	4
Palmer, Jim, Oneonta	1.000	3	3	6	0	9	0
Prodanov, Peter, Utica	.923	22	12	48	5	65	4
Rathmell, Lance, Utica	.966	22	11	46	2	59	3
Rodriguez, Luis, St. Catharines	1.000	2	1	3	0	4	0
Rojas, Ron, Jamestown	.917	6	4	7	1	12	0
Russell, Jason, Batavia	.884	40	29	78	14	121	8
Scolaro, Donald, Auburn	.923	16	8	28	3	39	2
Segura, Juan, Erie	.750	2	0	3	1	4	0
Shanahan, Jason, Elmira	1.000	2	2	5	0	7	1
Soriano, Carlos, Pittsfield	.700	3	1	6	3	10	1
Venezia, Richard, Erie	1.000	3	2	3	0	5	1
Vieira, Scott, Williamsport	.833	2	1	4	1	6	1
Viruet, Willie, Pittsfield	1.000	1	2	2	0	4	0
Vopata, Nathan, Hudson Valley	1.000	5	0	4	0	4	0
Waggoner, James, Jamestown	1.000	3	0	5	0	5	0
Walker, Rodney, Hudson Valley	1.000	1	0	1	0	1	0
Whipple, Boomer, Erie	.947	64	67	146	12	225	14

TRIPLE PLAYS: Booty, Whipple.

SHORTSTOPS

Player, Team	Pct.	G	PO	A	E	TC	DP
Antrim, Patrick, Oneonta	.804	23	25	65	22	112	7
Arvelo, Tom, Pittsfield	1.000	1	1	3	0	4	0
Babin, Brady, Elmira	.963	5	5	21	1	27	2

Player, Team	Pct.	G	PO	A	E	TC	DP
Barrett, Michael, Vermont	1.000	1	1	3	0	4	0
Betts, Darrell, New Jersey	.900	51	73	117	21	211	23
Brinkley, Josh, Vermont	.900	1	2	7	1	10	2
Brito, Domingo, Batavia	.964	9	6	21	1	28	2
Cabrera, Orlando, Vermont	.891	12	20	37	7	64	4
Camilli, Jason, Vermont	.939	62	87	191	18	296	45
Chamblee, James, Utica	.892	62	87	162	30	279	33
Conley, Brian, Williamsport	.750	3	7	2	3	12	0
Dennis, Les, Oneonta	.958	17	19	50	3	72	10
Deshenes, Marc, Watertown	.897	12	10	25	4	39	4
Engleka, Douglas, Jamestown	.930	22	37	43	6	86	9
Funaro, Joe, Elmira	.917	3	5	6	1	12	1
Garcia, Apostol, Jamestown	.904	60	66	189	27	282	28
Goodell, Steve, Elmira	.899	66	85	209	33	327	34
Hayes, Chris, St. Catharines	.928	14	36	41	6	83	9
Hermansen, Chad, Erie	.839	39	52	104	30	186	15
Holley, Jack, St. Catharines	.926	5	11	14	2	27	4
Insunza, Miguel, New Jersey	.886	28	30	63	12	105	12
Jaroncyk, Ryan, Pittsfield	.900	4	4	14	2	20	0
Kimm, Tyson, Batavia	.800	1	1	3	1	5	0
Lackey, Steve, Pittsfield	.956	21	29	79	5	113	16
Leaman, Jeff, Batavia	1.000	2	1	4	0	5	1
Lobaton, Jose, Oneonta	.892	41	46	111	19	176	19
Lugo, Julio, Auburn	.947	19	36	54	5	95	10
McDonald, Ashanti, Williamsport	.941	23	43	84	8	135	15
Miyake, Chris, Erie	.941	18	26	69	6	101	12
Motes, Jeff, Pittsfield	.941	9	9	23	2	34	3
Nieves, Jose, Williamsport	.881	54	64	166	31	261	21
Parsons, Jeff, Pittsfield	.870	40	63	125	28	216	23
Pileski, Mark, Pittsfield	.900	3	5	13	2	20	1
Prodanov, Peter, Utica	.957	11	11	33	2	46	1
Rathmell, Lance, Utica	1.000	1	4	3	0	7	0
Raynor, Mark, Batavia	.950	66	109	231	18	358	56
Reed, Billy, Hudson Valley	.884	42	53	115	22	190	13
Robles, Oscar, Auburn	.949	55	105	190	16	311	39
Rojas, Ron, Jamestown	1.000	1	0	3	0	3	0
Sagers, Kory, Utica	.800	7	3	13	4	20	3
Segura, Juan, Erie	.975	12	24	53	2	79	12
Shanahan, Jason, Elmira	.889	2	1	7	1	9	0
SOLANO, Fausto, St. Catharines	.955	57	115	183	14	312	41
Thornhill, Chad, Watertown	1.000	1	0	4	0	4	0
Valera, Willy, Watertown	.953	65	96	211	15	322	32
Venezia, Richard, Erie	.977	8	15	27	1	43	5
Vopata, Nathan, Hudson Valley	.923	37	59	96	13	168	20
Walker, Rodney, Hudson Valley	.917	7	7	15	2	24	2

TRIPLE PLAYS: Lobaton, Lugo, Reed.

OUTFIELDERS

Player, Team	Pct.	G	PO	A	E	TC	DP
Adamson, Jason, Erie	1.000	2	2	0	0	2	0
Alexander, Chad, Auburn	.965	68	129	8	5	142	1
Austin, Lakevie, Utica	.886	29	37	2	5	44	0
Bady, Edward, Vermont	.962	71	166	11	7	184	4
Bates, Fletcher, Pittsfield	.912	70	119	6	12	137	1
Bazzani, Matt, Utica	1.000	1	1	0	0	1	0
Bentley, Kevin, Williamsport	.962	43	47	4	2	53	1
Blakeney, Mo, Vermont	.958	38	42	4	2	48	0
Borges, Mariano, Erie	.875	16	20	1	3	24	1
Bourne, Charles, St. Catharines	.896	53	91	12	12	115	1
Budzinski, Mark, Watertown*	.959	70	113	5	5	123	2
Cameron, Ken, New Jersey*	.986	28	69	3	1	73	0
Camfield, Eric, Oneonta*	.945	67	94	9	6	109	1
Chevalier, Virgil, Utica	1.000	1	4	0	0	4	0
Choate, Jonathan, Watertown	.946	40	50	3	3	56	0
Cornelius, Jonathon, Batavia	.927	63	105	10	9	124	3
Cox, Charles, Batavia	1.000	2	3	0	0	3	0
Crane, Todd, Batavia	.972	21	34	1	1	36	0
Culp, Matt, Watertown	1.000	4	1	0	0	1	0
Davis, Albert, Erie	.973	44	67	5	2	74	1
Dawkins, Walter, Batavia	.984	51	120	3	2	125	0
Denning, Wes, Vermont	.936	55	80	8	6	94	0
Diaz, Linardo, Batavia	.959	21	44	3	2	49	2
Echols, Mandell, Hudson Valley	.959	56	114	4	5	123	1
Edwards, Aaron, Erie	.917	13	21	1	2	24	0
Ellison, Tony, Williamsport	.857	3	5	1	1	7	0
Freitas, Joe, New Jersey	.970	14	32	0	1	33	0
Funaro, Joe, Elmira	.953	33	37	4	2	43	0
Goodwin, Keith, Utica	.900	36	60	3	7	70	0
Gray, Ricky, Jamestown*	.977	27	42	1	1	44	1
Guillen, Jose, Erie	.900	64	107	10	13	130	5
Hare, Rich, Jamestown	1.000	15	12	1	0	13	0
Hayes, Chris, St. Catharines	1.000	3	2	1	0	3	0
Jefferson, Dave, Elmira	.833	5	4	1	1	6	0
Johnson, Damon, St. Catharines	.957	60	84	5	4	93	0
Johnson, Jason, Hudson Valley	.944	36	48	3	3	54	0
Jones, Jaime, Elmira*	.907	30	38	1	4	43	0
Joseph, Terry, Williamsport	.955	66	103	3	5	111	1
Kapler, Gabriel, Jamestown	.926	61	103	9	9	121	3
Lariviere, Jason, New Jersey	.960	33	43	5	2	50	0
Lauterhahn, Mike, Williamsport	1.000	4	5	1	0	6	0
Leaman, Jeff, Batavia	.900	5	8	1	1	10	0
LeClair, Paul, Pittsfield	.981	29	50	2	1	53	2
Lewis, Marc, Utica	.969	66	115	9	4	128	3
Long, Garrett, Erie	.950	9	17	2	1	20	0
Long, Justin, Elmira	.979	52	87	7	2	96	1
LONG, Terrence, Pittsfield*	.9913	51	111	3	1	115	0
Lugo, Julio, Auburn	1.000	3	7	0	0	7	0
Macias, Jose, Vermont	.951	23	39	0	2	41	0
May, Freddie, Erie*	1.000	25	42	2	0	44	0
McHugh, Ryan, New Jersey	.980	24	45	3	1	49	0
McNally, Shawn, New Jersey	.976	24	39	2	1	42	1
Miller, Kumandac, Elmira	.928	42	63	1	5	69	0
Milord, Clausel, Jamestown	1.000	28	56	0	0	56	0
Minici, Jason, Watertown	.9908	63	106	2	1	109	1
Mitchell, Rivers, Jamestown	.935	52	92	9	7	108	2
Morenz, Shea, Oneonta	.964	31	26	1	1	28	0
Morgan, Scott, Watertown	.946	40	50	3	3	56	0
Mota, Gleydel, Pittsfield*	.941	11	16	0	1	17	0
Mueller, Bret, New Jersey	.945	66	134	3	8	145	0
Nelson, Tray, Oneonta	.824	13	14	0	3	17	0
Norman, Ty, Utica	.982	47	102	8	2	112	2
Owens, Walter, Watertown	1.000	18	18	1	0	19	0
Pettiford, Torrey, Batavia	.000	1	0	0	1	1	0
Podsednik, Scott, Hud.Valley*	.978	65	125	6	3	134	2
Pollock, Elton, Erie	.976	41	79	2	2	83	1
Pratt, Wes, Auburn	.955	54	122	5	6	133	3
Prodanov, Peter, Utica	1.000	14	16	3	0	19	1
Rascon, Rene, Elmira*	.933	26	28	0	2	30	0
Rivera, Wilfredo, Utica	.937	43	69	5	5	79	1
Robinson, David, Batavia*	.967	54	86	1	3	90	1
Robinson, Hassan, Auburn	.936	59	66	7	5	78	0
Rosado, Juan, Vermont*	1.000	48	77	7	0	84	1
Rosario, Felix, St. Catharines	.961	55	93	5	4	102	2
Salzano, Jerry, Williamsport	.933	17	27	1	2	30	0
Sanchez, Omar, St. Catharines	.969	60	117	9	4	130	0
Schreimann, Eric, Batavia	.917	14	22	0	2	24	0
Seidel, Ryan, Williamsport	.963	59	100	3	4	107	2
Shumpert, Derek, Oneonta	.964	60	101	6	4	111	2
Smith, Akili, Erie	.692	7	6	3	4	13	0
Speed, Dorian, Williamsport	.968	58	146	5	5	156	4
Springfield, Bo, Erie	.903	17	27	1	3	31	0
Stratton, Kelly, Hudson Valley*	.900	18	16	2	2	20	0
Tippin, Greg, Utica*	.750	6	5	1	2	8	0
Tribolet, Scott, Auburn	.916	40	74	2	7	83	0
Rocky, Pittsfield	.934	27	56	1	4	61	0
Ugueto, Hector, New Jersey	.990	53	96	5	1	102	0
Vasquez, Danny, Hudson Valley	.966	67	102	12	4	118	0
Vieira, Scott, Williamsport	.500	5	1	0	1	2	0
Waggoner, James, Jamestown	1.000	3	1	0	0	1	0
Weaver, Scott, Jamestown*	.943	62	81	2	5	88	0
Wilcox, Chris, Oneonta	.947	59	84	6	5	95	0
Winn, Randy, Elmira	.954	51	103	1	5	109	0
Yoder, Paul, Pittsfield	.938	46	68	7	5	80	1

TRIPLE PLAY: Johnson.

CATCHERS

Player, Team	Pct.	G	PO	A	E	TC	DP	PB
Afenir, Tom, Watertown	.955	6	39	3	2	44	0	1
Barton, Scott, Williamsport	.987	14	71	4	1	76	1	9
Bazzani, Matt, Utica	.979	23	121	17	3	141	2	4
Boryczewski, Marty, Erie	.945	10	64	5	4	73	1	3
Brinkley, Josh, Vermont	.981	16	87	14	2	103	2	15
Briones, Christopher, H. V.	1.000	5	7	2	0	9	0	1
Brunner, Michael, Auburn	.969	24	137	19	5	161	0	5
Caballero, Manuel, Jamestown	.984	37	229	24	4	257	2	4
Canetto, John, Erie	.967	10	55	3	2	60	1	3
Carpenter, Matt, Watertown	1.000	4	18	3	0	21	0	1
Castro, Ramon, Auburn	.994	54	297	46	2	345	4	10
Chevalier, Virgil, Utica	.992	21	112	12	1	125	0	5
Coats, Nathan, Watertown	1.000	12	45	8	0	53	2	4
Cox, Charles, Batavia	.980	34	225	21	5	251	2	3
DeLaRosa, Elvis, Jamestown	.956	14	96	12	5	113	0	3
Deman, Lou, New Jersey	1.000	22	173	27	0	200	0	5
Doezie, Troy, New Jersey	.947	14	94	13	6	113	0	3
Emmons, Scott, Oneonta	.975	37	315	32	9	356	1	10
Erwin, Mat, Elmira	.978	57	367	69	10	446	3	9

Player, Team	Pct.	G	PO	A	E	TC	DP	PB
Flanigan, Steven, Erie	.986	22	128	16	2	146	3	3
Fuller, Brian, Jamestown	.986	31	183	28	3	214	3	6
Garcia, Jaime, Vermont	.983	50	316	41	6	363	2	8
GONZALEZ, Rich, Watertown	1.000	55	371	41	0	412	4	6
Goodwin, Joseph, H.V.	.973	57	368	62	12	442	5	10
Hernandez, Rob, Elmira	.975	6	36	3	1	40	0	2
Imersek, Jason, Oneonta	1.000	1	1	0	0	1	0	0
Maleski, Tom, Williamsport	.957	28	154	22	8	184	1	10
Martinez, Roger, Pittsfield	.968	17	77	13	3	93	2	3
McAulay, John, Hud. Valley	.974	24	129	21	4	154	3	7
McCartney, Sommer, Elmira	.982	15	103	8	2	113	0	5
McClendon, Travis, N. Jersey	.993	46	341	61	3	405	4	8
McCormick, Cody, Oneonta	.987	38	283	26	4	313	2	14
McLendon, Craig, Hud. Valley	.958	4	22	1	1	24	0	0
Morales, Eric, Pittsfield	.973	57	340	63	11	414	2	11
Parker, Michael, Pittsfield	1.000	3	5	1	0	6	0	0
Pelis, Andy, Pittsfield	.976	8	34	6	1	41	0	1
Pierce, Kirk, Batavia	.974	27	167	24	5	196	4	0
Reilly, John, St. Catharines	.958	4	16	7	1	24	1	0
Reynolds, Paul, Erie	.972	36	204	37	7	248	0	5
Rodriguez, Luis, St. Catharines	.975	62	383	80	12	475	7	11
Sapp, Damien, Utica	.982	35	234	37	5	276	2	17
Schreimann, Eric, Batavia	1.000	1	7	2	0	9	0	1
Snusz, Chris, Batavia	.964	18	121	14	5	140	2	6
Stadler, Mike, Watertown	.955	5	38	4	2	44	2	4
Steinkemper, Jacob, Vermont	.954	15	75	8	4	87	0	3
Varriano, Mark, Utica	.939	4	29	2	2	33	0	3
Vieira, Scott, Williamsport	.976	27	157	9	4	170	1	5
Williams, Brian, St. Catharines	.989	16	80	12	1	93	0	2
Zuleta, Julio, Williamsport	.966	25	131	12	5	148	1	5

TRIPLE PLAY: Goodwin.

PITCHERS

Player, Team	Pct.	G	PO	A	E	TC	DP
Adge, Jason, Watertown	1.000	19	0	5	0	5	1
Antonini, Adrian, Batavia	.500	3	0	1	1	2	0
Arellano, Carlos, Watertown	1.000	2	2	1	0	3	0
Atkins, Dannon, Watertown	.905	13	7	12	2	21	1
Atwater, Joe, Pittsfield*	1.000	1	0	1	0	1	0
Bair, Dennis, Williamsport	1.000	7	1	8	0	9	1
Bajda, Mike, Jamestown	1.000	13	3	4	0	7	0
Baker, Jason, Vermont	.824	14	5	9	3	17	0
Ballew, Preston, Pittsfield*	1.000	1	1	3	0	4	0
Barker, Jeff, Jamestown	.667	14	0	2	1	3	0
Barnett, Marty, Batavia	.941	10	2	14	1	17	0
BAUER, Charles, Hudson Valley	1.000	15	3	18	0	21	1
Beach, Scott, Erie	1.000	14	2	4	0	6	1
Beagle, Chad, Elmira*	1.000	5	2	4	0	6	0
Becker, Tom, Oneonta	.963	15	7	19	1	27	3
Bell, Mike, Vermont*	1.000	7	2	3	0	5	1
Benes, Adam, New Jersey	1.000	19	5	7	0	12	1
Bennett, Jason, Watertown	.972	16	2	33	1	36	4
Bennett, Matt, New Jersey	.929	23	4	9	1	14	0
Berry, Jason, Oneonta	1.000	8	0	1	0	1	0
Bettencourt, Justin, Jamestown*	.950	14	6	13	1	20	1
Betti, Rich, Utica*	1.000	12	2	0	0	2	0
Bigler, Cory, Erie	.857	10	3	3	1	7	0
Boardman, Eric, Oneonta	1.000	11	4	10	0	14	1
Bogle, Sean, Williamsport	.625	12	1	4	3	8	0
Bowman, Paul, Pittsfield	1.000	2	1	0	0	1	0
Brandt, Dale, Oneonta*	.857	23	0	6	1	7	0
Brown, Shawn, Jamestown	1.000	18	2	4	0	6	0
Bullock, Derek, Erie	1.000	11	3	11	0	14	0
Burgus, Travis, Elmira	.950	15	2	17	1	20	0
Cannon, Kevan, Utica*	1.000	9	4	15	0	19	2
Centeno, Jose, Vermont*	1.000	6	0	1	0	1	0
Choi, Chang Yang, Batavia	1.000	7	0	1	0	1	0
Civit, Xavier, Vermont	.800	19	5	7	3	15	0
Codd, Tim, Hudson Valley	1.000	25	0	5	0	5	0
Collie, Tim, Erie	1.000	29	1	5	0	6	1
Cordero, Francisco, Jamestown	.850	15	12	22	6	40	0
Corey, Bryan, Jamestown	1.000	29	4	4	0	8	0
Corominus, Mike, Auburn*	1.000	13	3	3	0	6	0
Coronado, Osvaldo, Pittsfield	.880	15	9	13	3	25	2
Crowell, Jim, Watertown*	.933	12	1	13	1	15	0
Crowther, John, St. Catharines	.875	15	4	10	2	16	0
Cummins, Brian, Jamestown*	1.000	18	2	11	0	13	1
Davey, Tom, St. Catharines	.875	7	1	6	1	8	0
DeLaCruz, Narcisco, St. Cath.*	1.000	21	3	7	0	10	1
Dempster, Ryan, Hudson Valley	1.000	9	1	0	0	1	0
Diaz, Jairo, Williamsport	.867	30	2	11	2	15	0
Dixon, Timothy, Vermont*	.867	18	3	10	2	15	0
Donnelly, Robert, New Jersey	1.000	36	1	5	0	6	0
Draeger, Mark, Hudson Valley	.917	21	1	10	1	12	0
Duffy, Ryan, Erie	.929	19	3	10	1	14	0
Durkovic, Peter, Jamestown*	1.000	14	2	4	0	6	0
Eby, Michael, Jamestown*	1.000	23	8	4	0	12	0
Einertson, Darrel, Oneonta	.667	25	1	3	2	6	1
Enard, Tony, Elmira	.857	15	1	5	1	7	0
Farr, Mark, Elmira	1.000	9	5	6	0	11	0
Farrow, Jason, Erie	1.000	20	2	10	0	12	1
Fernandes, Jamie, Utica	1.000	3	0	2	0	2	0
Fernandez, Jared, Utica	1.000	5	0	4	0	4	0
Ferullo, Matt, Pittsfield	1.000	2	0	1	0	1	0
Fitterer, Scott, St. Catharines	.750	22	0	3	1	4	0
Foran, John, Jamestown	1.000	14	2	2	0	4	0
Ford, Ben, Oneonta	.545	29	1	5	5	11	0
Ford, Brian, Batavia*	1.000	29	2	5	0	7	0
Frascatore, Steve, New Jersey	.688	16	1	10	5	16	0
Fuller, Stephen, Auburn	.875	14	3	11	2	16	0
Gaiko, Robert, Batavia	.800	20	1	7	2	10	0
Gambs, Chris, Batavia	1.000	7	2	3	0	5	0
Garcia, Rick, Elmira	.846	15	7	15	4	26	0
Garcia, Jason, Auburn	.800	14	4	16	5	25	0
Goedde, Roger, Erie	.750	5	2	1	1	4	0
Green, Jason, Auburn	.800	14	4	16	5	25	0
Greene, Brian, Williamsport	.889	18	5	3	1	9	0
Grife, Richard, Watertown	1.000	5	0	2	0	2	0
Groves, Brian, Jamestown*	1.000	16	2	4	0	6	0
Gulin, Lindsey, Pittsfield*	1.000	1	0	2	0	2	0
Hall, Yates, New Jersey	.500	5	1	0	1	2	0
Hamilton, Bo, Batavia	.952	14	7	13	1	21	0
Hammack, Brandon, Williamspt.	1.000	27	3	5	0	8	0
Hartshorn, Tyson, St. Catharines	.800	13	4	8	3	15	1
Harvey, Terry, Watertown	.895	8	7	10	2	19	0
Hernandez, Elvin, Erie	.864	14	7	12	3	22	0
Herr, David, Vermont	.778	18	1	6	2	9	1
Horn, Keith, Watertown	1.000	8	2	1	0	3	0
Horton, Aaron, Oneonta*	1.000	6	2	4	0	6	0
Horton, Eric, St. Catharines	.955	21	6	15	1	22	1
Howard, Tom, Elmira*	.800	11	1	3	1	5	0
Howatt, Jeff, Pittsfield	.800	17	3	1	1	5	0
Hoy, Wayne, St. Catharines	.944	24	4	13	1	18	1
Hritz, Derrick, Watertown*	1.000	18	2	6	0	8	0
Jacobs, Mike, Utica	.944	13	7	10	1	18	0
Johnson, Scott, Elmira	1.000	4	0	1	0	1	0
Jones, Scott, Utica	1.000	20	1	1	0	2	0
Kahlon, Bobby, Hudson Valley	1.000	30	0	15	0	15	0
Kast, Nick, New Jersey*	1.000	29	0	6	0	6	0
Kawabata, Kyle, Batavia	1.000	18	2	6	0	8	1
Kelley, Jason, Williamsport	1.000	3	0	1	0	1	0
Kendrick, Scott, Williamsport	.667	5	2	0	1	3	0
Kindell, Scott, Pittsfield*	.909	20	2	8	1	11	0
Koenig, Matthew, Pittsfield	.955	15	7	14	1	22	1
Lail, Jerry, Oneonta	.667	13	3	5	4	12	0
Link, Bryan, Hudson Valley*	.929	15	7	19	2	28	1
Lisio, Joseph, Pittsfield	1.000	28	3	2	0	5	1
Loiz, Niuman, Auburn	1.000	3	0	1	0	1	0
Lowe, Ben, St. Catharines*	.909	15	2	8	1	11	0
Mamott, Joe, Utica	.600	9	1	5	4	10	0
Marquez, Ihosvany, Utica	1.000	12	1	2	0	3	0
Marquez, Robert, Vermont	.857	29	3	3	1	7	0
Martineau, Brian, Hud. Valley	.917	30	1	10	1	12	0
Martinez, Osvaldo, Jamestown	.882	15	5	10	2	17	0
Mathis, Sammie, Watertown	1.000	18	2	6	0	8	0
Mattes, Troy, Vermont	1.000	10	0	8	0	8	0
McClurg, Clinton, Batavia	1.000	10	5	3	0	8	1
McEntire, Ethan, Pittsfield*	1.000	13	2	12	0	14	1
McHugh, Michael, Hud. Valley*	1.000	10	0	2	0	2	0
McNeese, John, Williamsport*	.952	13	0	20	1	21	0
McNichol, Brian, Williamsport*	1.000	9	3	7	0	10	0
Mejia, Carlos, Utica*	1.000	10	0	1	0	1	0
Mendes, Jaime, Batavia	1.000	30	1	3	0	4	0
Mensink, Brian, Batavia	.857	11	3	9	2	14	1
Merrick, Brett, Watertown*	.800	22	1	3	1	5	1
Miedreich, Kevin, New Jersey	1.000	15	6	9	0	15	0
Miles, Chad, Elmira*	1.000	14	1	1	0	2	0
Miller, David, Elmira	1.000	9	0	1	0	1	0
Mitchell, Courtney, Batavia*	.769	28	3	7	3	13	1
Mitchell, Scott, Vermont	.889	18	4	4	1	9	0
Moore, Robert, Hudson Valley	1.000	13	4	10	0	14	1
Moore, Sam, Elmira	.750	15	2	1	1	4	0
Morris, Chad, Vermont	1.000	9	0	1	0	1	0
Mosley, Tim, Williamsport	1.000	23	0	2	0	2	0
Mudd, Scott, Hudson Valley	.867	15	5	8	2	15	0
Munro, Peter, Utica	.957	14	9	13	1	23	0

Player, Team	Pct.	G	PO	A	E	TC	DP
Murray, Dan, Pittsfield	1.000	22	0	5	0	5	0
Neese, Josh, Jamestown	1.000	20	4	4	0	8	0
Negrette, Richard, Watertown	.889	18	1	7	1	9	0
Noffke, Andrew, Utica	.667	23	2	0	1	3	0
Noone, Bill, Batavia	1.000	6	1	0	0	1	0
Nunez, Maximo, St. Catharines	1.000	7	2	0	0	2	0
Nuttle, Jamison, Erie	1.000	13	1	1	0	2	0
Olivier, Rich, Oneonta	.909	12	2	8	1	11	0
Ormonde, Troy, Williamsport	.960	14	13	11	1	25	1
Pailthorpe, Bob, Elmira	1.000	13	9	8	0	17	3
Patterson, Casey, Pittsfield	1.000	12	1	4	0	5	0
Peguero, Jose, St. Catharines	.667	17	2	4	3	9	0
Pena, Jesus, Erie*	1.000	3	2	4	0	6	0
Perez, Gil, Erie	.938	18	3	12	1	16	1
Perez, Hilario, Utica	.909	20	3	7	1	11	0
Peterman, Ernie, St. Catharines	1.000	4	5	4	0	9	2
Peterson, Jayson, Williamsport	.667	3	2	0	1	3	0
Phillips, Jon, Auburn*	1.000	2	1	1	0	2	0
Pinango, Simon, Utica*	1.000	20	2	3	0	5	0
Powell, Brian, Jamestown	1.000	5	1	3	0	4	0
Powell, Jeremy, Vermont	.867	15	14	12	4	30	4
Pyrtle, Joe, Pittsfield	1.000	17	0	1	0	1	0
Rakers, Jason, Watertown	1.000	14	2	11	0	13	0
Randolph, Steve, Oneonta*	1.000	6	1	1	0	2	0
Reames, Britt, New Jersey	1.000	5	0	4	0	4	0
Reichstein, Derek, Elmira	1.000	22	4	5	0	9	0
Reid, Rayon, Erie	1.000	8	4	4	0	8	1
Reinfelder, David, Jamestown*	.905	16	4	15	2	21	1
Reyes, Jose, Erie	1.000	19	8	6	0	14	0
Ricketts, Chad, Williamsport	.727	12	3	5	3	11	0
Romboli, Curtis, Utica*	.778	14	3	4	2	9	2
Root, Derek, Auburn*	.929	17	7	6	1	14	0
Rosenbohm, Jim, Auburn	1.000	22	2	10	0	12	1
Ross, Jeremy, Elmira	1.000	20	0	1	0	1	0
Sagedal, Brent, Hudson Valley	1.000	14	1	6	0	7	0
Santiago, Antonio, Utica*	.800	4	0	4	1	5	0
Santoro, Gary, Elmira	.800	24	3	5	2	10	0
Santos, Rafael, Erie	1.000	2	0	1	0	1	0
Schulte, Troy, Auburn	.875	23	3	4	1	8	1
Schultz, Scott, Watertown	.889	9	0	8	1	9	0
Severino, Jose, New Jersey	.818	17	3	6	2	11	0
Shumaker, Anthony, Batavia*	1.000	9	3	5	0	8	1
Sikorski, Brian, Auburn	1.000	23	2	3	0	5	0
Smart, J.D., Vermont	1.000	5	2	3	0	5	0
Smith, Eric, Auburn	.870	14	5	15	3	23	2
Smith, Justin, Batavia	.875	15	2	5	1	8	0
Smith, Randy, St. Catharines	1.000	18	6	4	0	10	0
Smyth, Gregg, Auburn*	.769	14	3	7	3	13	0
Spaulding, Scott, New Jersey	1.000	35	6	5	0	11	0
Speier, Justin, Williamsport	1.000	30	2	6	0	8	0
St. Pierre, Bob, Oneonta	.913	15	7	14	2	23	0
Stachler, Eric, Auburn	1.000	18	1	3	0	4	0
Steinke, Brock, Auburn	1.000	6	0	2	0	2	0
Stephens, Bill, Vermont	1.000	13	3	5	0	8	0
Stephens, Shannon, Elmira	.926	17	10	15	2	27	0
Stern, Marty, Vermont	1.000	8	2	0	0	2	0
Swenson, Mike, New Jersey*	.889	19	2	6	1	9	2
Tatis, Ramon, Pittsfield*	.938	13	5	10	1	16	1
Tessmer, Jay, Oneonta	.909	34	3	7	1	11	0
Thomas, Rob, Erie*	.833	15	1	4	1	6	0
Tickell, Brian, Auburn	.909	13	3	7	1	11	0
Treend, Pat, Elmira	.667	17	1	1	1	3	0
Trumpour, Andy, Pittsfield	.917	15	8	14	2	24	0
Venafro, Michael, Hud. Valley*	.957	32	5	17	1	23	3
Villafana, Jose, New Jersey	.857	27	1	5	1	7	0
Volkert, Oreste, St. Catharines	.875	22	3	11	2	16	1
Ward, Jon, New Jersey	.500	9	0	1	1	2	0
Weber, David, Williamsport	.846	22	2	9	2	13	1
Weber, Eric, Jamestown	1.000	15	2	4	0	6	0
Weber, Lenny, Watertown	1.000	5	2	0	0	2	0
WEIDERT, Chris, Vermont	1.000	15	9	12	0	21	1
Welch, Robb, Utica	.800	12	5	7	3	15	0
Whitworth, Clint, Oneonta	1.000	12	0	1	0	1	0
Wilkinson, Arrow, Oneonta	.900	14	1	8	1	10	0
Wilson, Mike L., Oneonta	1.000	14	1	7	0	8	0
Wilson, Mike R., Jamestown	1.000	5	3	4	0	7	0
Winchester, Scott, Watertown	1.000	23	3	3	0	6	0
Wolff, Thomas, Pittsfield	.714	4	3	2	2	7	0
Wolger, Michael, Vermont*	1.000	2	0	1	0	1	1
Wyatt, Cortez, Williamsport	1.000	22	6	9	0	15	0
Yeager, Gary, Batavia	.929	19	6	7	1	14	2
Young, Joe, St. Catharines	1.000	15	3	7	0	10	0
Young, Ryan, Erie	.900	16	7	11	2	20	1

The following players did not have any fielding statistics at the positions indicated or appeared only as a designated hitter, pinch-hitter or pinch-runner: Albaladejo, p; Barnes, p; Bazzani, p; Chew, p; Conley, p; R. Culp, dh; Ferguson, p; Gorecki, 3b; Helvey, p; Imersek, p; Lebron, ss; J. Long, p; Micknich, p; M. Morris, p; Oakley, p; Pierce, 1b; Prodanov, 2b; Reilly, of, p; Robbins, p; Salzano, 3b; Sauve, p; Scolaro, p; Short, p; Taylor, dh; Viegas, p; Wood, p.

LEAGUE CHAMPIONS

Year	Team	Pct.	Year	Team	Pct.	Year	Team	Pct.
1939—	Olean*	.631	1961—	Geneva	.616	1981—	Oneonta▲	.658
1940—	Olean*	.625		Olean (4th)†	.512		Jamestown	.649
1941—	Jamestown	.618	1962—	Jamestown	.580	1982—	Oneonta	.566
	Bradford (2nd)†	.549		Auburn (3rd)†	.521		Niagara Falls▲	.553
1942—	Jamestown*	.672	1963—	Auburn	.585	1983—	Utica▲	.649
1943—	Lockport	.591		Batavia (3rd)†	.485		Newark	.649
	Wellsville (3rd)†	.532	1964—	Auburn§	.622	1984—	Newark	.622
1944—	Lockport	.608	1965—	Binghamton	.677		Little Falls▲	.587
	Jamestown (2nd)†	.565		Binghamton	.607	1985—	Oneonta*	.705
1945—	Batavia*	.677	1966—	Auburn∞	.620		Auburn	.603
1946—	Jamestown‡	.672		Binghamton	.646	1986—	Oneonta	.766
	Batavia‡	.672	1967—	Auburn	.667		St. Catharines◆	.632
1947—	Jamestown*	.690	1968—	Auburn	.645	1987—	Geneva▲	.632
1948—	Lockport*	.603		Oneonta (2nd)*	.558		Watertown	.579
1949—	Bradford*	.635	1969—	Oneonta	.662	1988—	Oneonta▲	.632
1950—	Hornell	.653	1970—	Auburn	.623		Jamestown	.618
	Olean (2nd)†	.568	1971—	Oneonta	.662	1989—	Pittsfield	.697
1951—	Olean	.622	1972—	Niagara Falls	.686		Jamestown▲	.579
	Hornell (3rd)†	.568	1973—	Auburn	.667	1990—	Oneonta■	.667
1952—	Hamilton	.659	1974—	Oneonta	.768		Geneva	.662
	Jamestown (2nd)†	.643	1975—	Newark	.688	1991—	Pittsfield	.662
1953—	Jamestown*	.704		Newark	.714		Jamestown■	.654
1954—	Corning*	.621	1976—	Elmira	.727	1992—	Hamilton	.737
1955—	Hamilton*	.656		Elmira	.703		Geneva▼	.547
1956—	Wellsville*	.617	1977—	Oneonta▲	.671	1993—	Niagara Falls▼	.603
1957—	Wellsville	.632		Batavia	.600		Pittsfield	.533
	Erie (2nd)†	.598	1978—	Oneonta	.729	1994—	Auburn	.592
1958—	Wellsville	.556		Geneva◆	.718		New Jersey▼	.573
	Geneva (2nd)†	.548	1979—	Geneva	.725	1995—	Vermont	.645
1959—	Wellsville†	.635		Oneonta◆	.618		Watertown▼	.630
1960—	Erie	.643	1980—	Oneonta▲	.662			
	Wellsville (2nd)†	.535		Geneva	.649			

*Won championship and four-club playoff. †Won four-club playoff. ‡Jamestown and Batavia declared co-champions; Batavia defeated Jamestown in final of four-club playoff. §Won championship and two-club playoff. ∞Won split-season playoff. ▲League divided into Eastern and Western divisions; won playoff. ◆League divided into Wrigley and Yawkey divisions; won playoff. ■League divided into Eastern, Western and Stedler divisions; won playoff. ▼League divided into McNamara, Pinckney and Stedler divisions; won playoff. (NOTE—Known as Pennsylvania-Ontario-New York League from 1939 through 1956.)

NORTHWEST LEAGUE

LEAGUE OFFICE

President/treasurer
Bob Richmond
Address
P.O. Box 4941
Scottsdale, AZ 85261
Phone
602-483-8224

Teams (affiliation)
Bellingham Giants (Giants)
Boise Hawks (Angels)
Eugene Emeralds (Braves)
Everett AquaSox (Mariners)
Portland Rockies (Rockies)
Southern Oregon Timberjacks (A's)

Spokane Indians (Royals)
Yakima Bears (Dodgers)

1995 FINAL STANDINGS

NORTH DIVISION

Team	W	L	T	Pct.	GB
Bellingham (Giants)	43	33	0	.566	......
Everett (Mariners)	37	39	0	.487	6
Spokane (Royals)	36	40	0	.474	7
Yakima (Dodgers)	28	48	0	.368	15

SOUTH DIVISION

Team	W	L	T	Pct.	GB
Boise (Angels)	48	27	0	.640	......
Portland (Rockies)	41	34	0	.547	7
Eugene (Braves)	37	39	0	.487	11½
Southern Oregon (Athletics)	33	43	0	.434	15½

COMPOSITE

Team	Boi.	Bell.	Port.	Ever.	Eug.	Spo.	S.O.	Yak.	W	L	T	Pct.	GB
Boise (Angels)	....	7	8	7	5	7	6	8	48	27	0	.640	......
Bellingham (Giants)	3	....	4	6	6	7	9	8	43	33	0	.566	5½
Portland (Rockies)	3	6	....	6	7	4	10	5	41	34	0	.547	7
Everett (Mariners)	3	6	4	....	4	5	5	10	37	39	0	.487	11½
Eugene (Braves)	7	4	5	6	....	5	5	5	37	39	0	.487	11½
Spokane (Royals)	3	5	6	7	5	....	4	6	36	40	0	.474	12½
Southern Oregon (Athletics)	6	1	2	5	7	6	....	6	33	43	0	.434	15½
Yakima (Dodgers)	2	4	5	2	5	6	4	....	28	48	0	.368	20½

Southern Oregon played home games in Medford, Ore.

Major league affiliations in parentheses.

PLAYOFFS: Boise defeated Bellingham, two games to one, to win league championship.

REGULAR-SEASON ATTENDANCE: Bellingham, 54,104; Boise, 165,255; Eugene, 134,878; Everett, 89,950; Portland, 249,696; Southern Oregon, 84,682; Spokane, 162,344; Yakima, 81,570. Total—1,022,479. Playoffs (3 games)—7,181.

MANAGERS: Bellingham, Glenn Tufts; Boise, Tom Kotchman; Eugene, Paul Runge; Everett, Orlando Gomez; Portland, P.J. Carey; Southern Oregon, Tony DeFrancesco; Spokane, Al Pedrique; Yakima, Joe Vavra.

ALL-STAR TEAM: 1B—Danny Buxbaum, Boise; 2B—Jonathan Watson, Bellingham; 3B—Ryan Kane, Boise; SS—Miguel Tejada, Southern Oregon; OF—Kevin Gibbs, Yakima; Kevin Ham, Boise; Joe Trippy, Eugene; C—Patrick Hallmark, Spokane; DH—James Vida, Spokane; RHP—Travis Thurmond, Boise; LHP—Marc D'Alessandro, Portland; RH Reliever—Grant Vermillion, Boise; LH Reliever—Adam Butler, Eugene; Most Valuable Player—Danny Buxbaum, Boise; Manager of the Year—Glenn Tufts, Bellingham.

1995 BATTING

TEAM

Team	Avg.	G	TPA	AB	R	H	TB	2B	3B	HR	RBI	SH	SF	HP	BB	IBB	SO	SB	CS	GDP	LOB	ShO	Slg.	OBP
Boise	.265	75	2963	2523	411	669	965	117	16	49	358	24	19	44	350	16	506	68	30	59	621	1	.382	.362
Eugene	.249	76	2864	2534	364	630	926	104	24	48	307	19	20	58	233	7	578	137	62	34	492	3	.365	.324
Yakima	.244	76	2897	2560	288	624	853	116	25	21	240	20	26	24	260	13	545	122	36	53	575	5	.333	.317
Spokane	.242	76	2933	2575	333	623	845	110	11	30	281	19	18	50	271	9	546	54	36	65	556	3	.328	.324
Everett	.241	76	2996	2591	369	625	959	116	16	62	316	21	16	50	318	12	650	113	45	48	586	5	.370	.334
Bellingham	.239	76	2923	2563	334	613	878	111	11	44	290	20	24	40	276	25	654	79	42	44	544	5	.343	.320
Southern Oregon	.237	76	2970	2488	372	589	846	109	20	36	311	26	31	40	385	8	509	107	44	53	576	6	.340	.344
Portland	.223	75	2806	2407	316	536	729	92	19	21	255	19	19	48	307	10	542	126	54	46	517	4	.303	.320

INDIVIDUAL

TOP QUALIFIERS FOR BATTING CHAMPIONSHIP

Minimum 205 plate appearances. *Lefthanded batter. †Switch-hitter.

Player, Team	Avg.	G	TPA	AB	R	H	TB	2B	3B	HR	RBI	SH	SF	HP	BB	IBB	SO	SB	CS	GDP	Slg.	OBP
Buxbaum, Danny, Boise	.329	68	289	231	46	76	115	15	0	8	51	0	5	4	49	5	31	1	0	3	.498	.446
Vida, James, Spokane*	.323	74	311	291	38	94	121	13	1	4	39	0	0	1	19	5	32	0	0	5	.416	.367
Bilderback, Ty, Boise*	.322	61	210	177	35	57	81	11	2	3	25	0	1	3	29	0	29	10	5	4	.458	.424
Ham, Kevin, Boise	.315	69	287	238	39	75	109	7	3	7	43	0	1	8	40	2	57	2	2	9	.458	.429
Gibbs, Kevin, Yakima†	.313	52	228	182	36	57	74	6	4	1	18	2	3	5	36	1	46	38	5	3	.407	.434
Trippy, Joe, Eugene*	.309	75	300	259	48	80	102	16	0	2	38	2	2	13	24	0	31	29	13	1	.394	.393
Hallmark, Patrick, Spokane	.304	56	246	227	36	69	92	11	0	4	25	2	2	2	13	0	37	5	3	5	.405	.344
Watson, Jonathan, Bellingham	.299	65	262	231	42	69	84	9	0	2	27	4	3	4	20	2	41	16	9	3	.364	.360
Cruz, Deivi, Bellingham	.296	62	245	223	32	66	92	17	0	3	28	1	2	0	19	3	21	6	3	5	.413	.348
Hodges, Randy, Eugene*	.291	61	229	206	29	60	83	7	5	2	28	3	1	7	12	1	35	10	6	3	.403	.350
Tinoco, Luis, Everett	.286	62	242	203	34	58	99	10	2	9	31	0	1	3	35	1	41	9	3	6	.488	.397

Player, Team	Avg.	G	TPA	AB	R	H	TB	2B	3B	HR	RBI	SH	SF	HP	BB	IBB	SO	SB	CS	GDP	Slg.	OBP
Sheffer, Chad, Everett†	.280	56	232	193	31	54	65	9	1	0	18	6	4	2	27	0	38	28	8	3	.337	.367
Kane, Ryan, Boise	.276	74	318	283	39	78	138	14	2	14	59	0	5	5	25	4	57	0	0	10	.488	.340
Filchner, Duane, S. Oregon*	.275	62	231	189	34	52	74	4	0	6	34	1	3	3	35	2	28	12	8	4	.392	.391
Wathan, Dusty, Everett†	.271	53	206	181	32	49	78	9	1	6	25	1	0	7	17	0	26	2	1	4	.431	.356
Miranda, Tony, Spokane	.271	71	306	266	53	72	95	17	0	2	22	3	2	7	28	1	36	15	10	8	.357	.353

DEPARTMENTAL LEADERS: G—Trippy, 75; AB—Vida, 291; R—Miranda, 53; H—Vida, 94; TB—Kane, 138; 2B—Morales, 18; 3B—Hodges, Tejada, 5; HR—Kane, 14; RBI—Kane, 59; SH—Vallone, 8; SF—Amado, Buxbaum, Kane, 5; HP—Trippy, Whitley, 13; BB—Drizos, 54; IBB—Amado, Calderon, 6; SO—Vickers, 102; SB—Gibbs, 38; CS—Lombard, Trippy, 13; GIDP—Roland, 13; Slg.—Buxbaum, .498; OBP—Buxbaum, .446.

ALL PLAYERS

*Lefthanded batter. †Switch-hitter.

Player, Team	Avg.	G	TPA	AB	R	H	TB	2B	3B	HR	RBI	SH	SF	HP	BB	IBB	SO	SB	CS	GDP	Slg.	OBP
Alzualde, Daniel, Boise	.284	24	74	67	3	19	25	3	0	1	8	1	0	1	5	0	19	0	0	2	.373	.342
Amado, Jose, Everett	.265	57	250	215	33	57	98	15	1	8	33	0	5	6	24	6	19	15	5	4	.456	.348
Ardoin, Danny, S. Oregon	.234	58	224	175	28	41	58	9	1	2	23	5	4	9	31	0	50	2	1	2	.331	.370
Arias, Rogelio, Portland	.279	13	45	43	4	12	13	1	0	0	3	0	1	0	1	0	3	3	1	2	.302	.289
Backowski, Lance, Yakima	.193	34	125	114	8	22	25	1	1	0	8	2	1	0	8	1	16	4	1	7	.219	.244
Barthol, Blake, Portland	.236	56	221	191	20	45	62	10	2	1	25	1	3	4	22	0	32	5	2	5	.325	.323
Baughman, Justin, Boise	.233	58	243	215	26	50	63	4	3	1	20	4	1	2	18	0	38	19	4	2	.293	.297
Benner, Brian, Bellingham	.125	2	9	8	0	1	2	1	0	0	1	0	0	0	1	0	4	0	0	0	.250	.222
Betten, Randy, Boise	.375	2	9	8	2	3	3	0	0	0	2	0	0	0	1	0	2	0	0	0	.375	.444
Bilderback, Ty, Boise*	.322	61	210	177	35	57	81	11	2	3	25	0	1	3	29	0	29	10	5	4	.458	.424
Bray, Notorris, Bellingham	.500	2	7	4	3	2	2	0	0	0	0	0	0	0	3	0	1	0	1	0	.500	.714
Brown, Roosevelt, Eugene*	.309	57	183	165	28	51	92	12	4	7	32	0	2	3	13	2	30	6	3	1	.558	.366
Bryan, Leonardo, Boise	.200	42	96	80	8	16	21	3	1	0	6	0	0	0	16	0	18	3	2	3	.263	.333
Brzozoski, Marc, Portland	.233	66	272	240	22	56	72	6	2	2	25	1	2	4	25	3	71	6	4	4	.300	.314
Burrows, Mike, Everett*	.206	67	272	223	28	46	78	5	3	7	33	2	2	3	42	1	72	13	8	1	.350	.337
Buxbaum, Danny, Boise	.329	68	289	231	46	76	115	15	0	8	51	0	5	4	49	5	31	1	0	3	.498	.446
Calderon, Ricardo, Bellingham*	.227	67	245	216	23	49	76	9	0	6	35	1	2	4	22	6	73	1	2	5	.352	.307
Carpentier, Mike, Yakima	.255	53	208	188	20	48	76	8	4	4	28	3	3	1	13	0	23	4	5	2	.404	.302
Castillo, Alberto, Bellingham*	.213	74	302	263	19	56	82	11	0	5	23	0	3	1	35	4	99	0	1	2	.312	.305
Choi, Kyung, Boise*	.299	21	77	67	14	20	22	2	0	0	5	0	1	0	9	1	5	3	1	0	.328	.377
Christenson, Ryan, S. Oregon	.190	49	183	158	14	30	39	4	1	1	16	1	2	0	22	0	33	5	5	3	.247	.286
Corujo, Rey, Bellingham	.221	60	237	208	23	46	81	15	1	6	34	1	4	1	23	0	27	6	4	8	.389	.297
Cruz, Deivi, Bellingham	.296	62	245	223	32	66	92	17	0	3	28	1	2	0	19	3	21	8	3	5	.413	.348
Cruz, Jose, Everett†	.455	3	14	11	6	5	5	0	0	0	2	0	0	0	3	0	3	1	0	0	.455	.571
Cuevas, Trent, Yakima	.203	38	139	123	13	25	35	7	0	1	8	1	1	0	14	0	22	3	4	3	.285	.283
Dalton, Jed, Boise*	.262	48	135	126	10	33	43	8	1	0	10	1	0	0	8	1	20	1	1	2	.341	.306
Dantzler, Eric, Bellingham	.118	6	17	17	2	2	6	1	0	1	1	0	0	0	0	0	5	0	0	1	.353	.118
DaSilva, Manny, S. Oregon	.246	55	231	195	31	48	79	14	4	3	33	1	3	6	26	1	25	3	1	9	.405	.348
Daugherty, Keith, Eugene	.125	2	8	8	0	1	1	0	0	0	0	0	0	0	0	0	3	0	0	0	.125	.125
Davalillo, David, Boise	.223	36	120	112	17	25	39	9	1	1	12	1	0	1	6	0	21	1	0	4	.348	.269
Davanon, Jeff, S. Oregon†	.251	57	207	167	29	42	55	6	2	1	17	5	1	0	34	0	49	6	5	1	.329	.376
DeLeon, Reymundo, Eugene	.189	50	142	127	14	24	33	2	2	1	11	0	1	1	13	0	48	2	3	3	.260	.268
Drizos, Justin, Portland*	.205	71	283	224	37	46	72	15	1	3	24	1	1	3	54	1	55	7	1	3	.321	.365
Durrington, Trent, Boise	.171	50	163	140	23	24	39	4	1	3	19	2	2	2	17	0	35	2	0	4	.279	.267
Elam, Brett, Portland	.143	33	105	84	11	12	12	0	0	0	8	2	1	1	17	0	17	3	2	3	.143	.291
Ellison, Skeeter, Eugene†	.133	19	21	15	5	2	2	0	0	0	1	0	1	0	5	0	7	4	2	0	.133	.333
Escandon, Emiliano, Spokane†	.318	13	51	44	7	14	20	1	1	1	12	0	1	0	6	0	11	1	0	0	.455	.412
Felix, Pedro, Bellingham	.274	43	124	113	14	31	35	2	1	0	16	2	2	0	7	0	33	1	1	2	.310	.311
Feuerstein, David, Portland	.268	70	300	269	40	72	103	10	3	5	44	3	3	2	23	2	41	20	8	9	.383	.327
Filchner, Duane, S. Oregon*	.275	62	231	189	34	52	74	4	0	6	34	1	3	3	35	2	28	12	8	4	.392	.391
Finnieston, Adam, Spokane	.237	10	42	38	4	9	9	0	0	0	4	1	1	1	1	0	9	0	1	0	.237	.268
Foote, Derek, Eugene*	.000	1	1	0	0	0	0	0	0	0	0	0	0	0	1	0	0	0	0	0	.000	1.000
Frazier, Tyrone, Spokane	.170	51	168	147	15	25	28	3	0	0	9	5	0	5	11	0	46	8	4	3	.190	.252
Gibbs, Kevin, Yakima†	.313	52	228	182	36	57	74	6	4	1	18	2	3	5	36	1	46	38	5	3	.407	.434
Granzow, Judd, Yakima*	.224	50	175	156	12	35	56	5	2	4	13	0	1	3	15	4	53	3	1	3	.359	.303
Graves, Bryan, Boise	.208	32	70	53	9	11	16	2	0	1	5	0	0	0	17	0	12	0	0	0	.302	.400
Griffin, Chad, Everett*	.183	36	99	82	11	15	20	2	0	1	5	1	0	0	16	1	36	1	0	0	.244	.316
Groseclose, Harold, Portland	.333	5	17	12	2	4	5	1	0	0	2	0	1	2	2	0	2	0	1	0	.417	.471
Gross, Rafael, Yakima	.254	40	158	142	17	36	51	4	1	3	15	1	1	1	13	1	17	12	2	3	.359	.318
Hacker, Steve, Yakima	.211	16	61	57	4	12	21	3	0	2	9	0	1	2	1	0	13	0	0	1	.368	.246
Hallead, John, Portland*	.168	45	164	143	17	24	36	5	2	1	16	2	2	2	15	0	49	9	5	1	.252	.253
Hallmark, Patrick, Spokane	.304	56	246	227	36	69	92	11	0	4	25	2	2	2	13	0	37	5	3	5	.405	.344
Ham, Kevin, Boise	.315	69	287	238	39	75	109	7	3	7	43	0	1	8	40	2	57	2	2	9	.458	.429
Harmon, Brian, Yakima	.254	22	73	59	4	15	18	3	0	0	8	0	2	0	12	0	9	0	0	0	.305	.370
Harris, Robert, S. Oregon	.252	63	272	230	31	58	77	14	1	1	16	3	4	3	32	0	32	9	5	5	.335	.346
Heams, Shane, Everett	.197	27	65	61	5	12	19	4	0	1	4	0	0	1	3	0	28	2	0	2	.311	.246
Hernaiz, Juan, Yakima	.278	50	167	158	23	44	57	9	2	0	16	1	1	1	6	0	30	9	3	1	.361	.307
Hilo, Johnny, Yakima*	.250	50	194	168	18	42	61	10	0	3	22	0	0	3	23	2	33	5	2	4	.363	.351
Hines, Pooh, Everett	.242	44	152	124	26	30	49	7	3	2	13	4	1	3	20	1	27	13	2	3	.395	.358
Hodges, Randy, Eugene*	.291	61	229	206	29	60	83	7	5	0	28	1	3	7	12	1	35	10	6	5	.403	.350
Hutchins, Norm, Boise†	.250	45	198	176	34	44	60	6	2	2	11	4	1	2	15	0	44	10	6	2	.341	.314
Jimenez, Elvis, Portland	.179	37	132	123	8	22	29	0	2	1	9	1	0	0	8	0	36	7	4	4	.236	.237
Kane, Ryan, Boise	.276	74	318	283	39	78	138	14	2	14	59	0	5	5	25	4	57	0	0	10	.488	.340
Keifer, Greg, Bellingham	.278	10	42	36	6	10	18	1	2	1	3	0	1	1	4	1	14	0	1	0	.500	.357
Klostermeyer, Mike, S. Oregon*	.237	64	223	186	31	44	60	7	0	3	19	2	1	3	31	1	36	4	2	4	.323	.353
Knight, Bill, Southern Oregon	.206	48	163	136	21	28	43	7	1	2	19	3	2	1	21	0	43	5	4	3	.316	.313
Kortmeyer, Scott, Spokane	.141	21	74	64	6	9	11	2	0	0	2	0	2	3	5	0	26	0	0	2	.172	.230
Lewis, Dwayne, Spokane*	.208	46	183	149	24	31	38	2	1	1	9	3	0	1	30	0	55	8	8	2	.255	.352
Lombard, George, Eugene*	.252	68	293	262	38	66	92	5	3	5	19	2	1	5	23	0	91	35	13	6	.351	.323

CLASS A *Northwest League*

Player, Team	Avg.	G	TPA	AB	R	H	TB	2B	3B	HR	RBI	SH	SF	HP	BB	IBB	SO	SB	CS	GDP	Slg.	OBP
Lunar, Fernando, Eugene..............	.244	38	142	131	13	32	44	6	0	2	16	2	0	0	9	0	28	0	1	2	.336	.293
Mahoney, Mike, Eugene..............	.241	43	132	112	14	27	36	6	0	1	15	1	1	3	15	1	17	6	2	5	.321	.344
Malave, Joshua, Yakima..............	.270	44	147	137	12	37	57	13	2	1	15	1	2	1	6	0	41	1	1	1	.416	.301
Markert, Jason, Yakima..............	.272	34	96	81	10	22	28	4	1	0	10	0	0	1	14	0	17	1	1	2	.346	.385
Mayber, Chan, Portland..............	.205	27	95	78	13	16	20	2	1	0	8	2	0	2	13	0	22	6	3	0	.256	.333
McAninch, John, Boise	.250	42	126	112	16	28	43	9	0	2	12	1	0	2	11	0	24	0	0	6	.384	.328
McClain, Terrance, Yakima	.204	33	70	54	12	11	13	2	0	0	2	1	0	3	12	0	23	7	3	1	.241	.377
Medrano, Teodoro, Everett..........	.333	1	3	3	0	1	1	0	0	0	0	0	0	0	0	0	1	0	0	0	.333	.333
Melito, Mark, Spokane	.250	61	240	200	24	50	68	7	1	3	20	5	2	6	27	0	30	2	2	3	.340	.353
Meskauskas, John, Portland	.345	9	38	29	4	10	16	3	0	1	9	0	0	1	8	1	7	2	2	0	.552	.500
Meyer, Travis, Yakima..............	.205	36	97	83	9	17	24	7	0	0	5	0	2	1	11	0	22	0	1	4	.289	.299
Miranda, Tony, Spokane	.271	71	306	266	53	72	95	17	0	2	22	3	2	7	28	1	36	15	10	8	.357	.353
Morales, Julio, Bellingham..........	.254	66	294	248	43	63	105	18	3	6	25	0	1	11	34	0	60	26	9	1	.423	.367
Moreno, Victor, Spokane............	.167	7	27	24	3	4	5	1	0	0	0	0	0	1	2	0	10	0	0	0	.208	.259
Morimoto, Ken, Yakima..............	.270	55	202	178	27	48	56	4	2	0	14	3	2	0	19	1	40	19	4	1	.315	.337
Moschetti, Mike, S. Oregon..........	.241	39	168	141	21	34	40	4	1	0	15	0	1	6	20	0	27	13	1	4	.284	.357
Mota, Alfonso, Boise*	.288	51	128	104	25	30	41	5	0	2	16	2	0	1	21	1	11	4	0	1	.394	.413
Myers, Aaron, Portland	.201	57	209	184	25	37	60	5	0	6	24	0	0	2	23	1	44	1	3	6	.326	.294
Nathan, Joe, Bellingham	.232	56	208	177	23	41	61	7	2	3	20	5	2	2	22	1	48	3	2	5	.345	.320
Nations, Joel, Spokane.............	.214	40	161	140	15	30	38	6	1	0	16	0	0	1	20	0	26	1	1	2	.271	.317
Neubart, Garrett, Portland	.266	39	158	128	23	34	42	8	0	0	8	0	2	7	21	0	24	12	3	0	.328	.392
Newhan, David, S. Oregon*	.269	42	179	145	25	39	67	8	1	6	21	1	3	1	29	1	30	10	5	2	.462	.388
Norton, Andy, Bellingham	.218	25	67	55	3	12	13	1	0	0	5	2	0	2	8	2	15	0	0	3	.236	.314
Owen, Andy, Yakima*	.242	56	184	165	16	40	54	12	1	0	17	1	2	3	9	0	35	6	1	4	.327	.291
Paulin, Randy, Spokane............	.204	54	210	191	14	39	54	6	0	3	22	0	2	3	14	0	49	0	1	8	.283	.267
Pena, Elvis, Portland†	.251	58	245	215	29	54	66	6	3	0	18	3	0	1	26	0	45	28	7	2	.307	.333
Person, Wilton, Eugene.............	.264	62	226	197	25	52	62	8	1	0	23	1	1	7	20	0	21	7	6	4	.315	.351
Pinoni, Scott, Spokane	.184	11	44	38	4	7	9	2	0	0	4	0	0	1	5	0	9	0	0	1	.237	.295
Pomierski, Joe, Everett*	.221	59	247	217	31	48	102	15	3	11	38	0	0	4	26	0	58	4	2	2	.470	.316
Prospero, Teodoro, Bellingham	.138	41	122	109	7	15	20	2	0	1	6	3	2	2	6	0	45	0	1	1	.183	.193
Quinn, Mark, Spokane	.284	44	185	162	28	46	80	12	2	6	37	0	3	5	15	0	28	0	1	5	.494	.357
Ramirez, Joel, Everett	.251	70	291	243	31	61	76	12	0	1	31	2	0	9	37	0	39	9	6	3	.313	.370
Rand, Ian, Bellingham	.128	23	53	47	4	6	6	0	0	0	1	0	1	0	2	0	25	0	0	0	.128	.226
Rasmussen, Nate, Yakima*	.234	44	133	128	12	30	35	3	1	0	5	0	0	1	4	0	43	1	1	4	.273	.263
Reynolds, Paul, Portland	.207	45	154	135	15	28	40	7	1	1	6	0	1	3	5	1	43	9	3	0	.296	.250
Robles, Juan, Spokane.............	.000	4	10	9	0	0	0	0	0	0	0	0	0	0	1	0	5	0	0	0	.000	.100
Rodriguez, Javier, Everett..........	.133	20	68	60	2	8	9	1	0	0	1	0	0	1	7	0	13	0	0	1	.150	.235
Roland, William, Spokane	.218	70	296	262	26	57	87	16	1	4	30	1	3	4	26	3	53	1	1	13	.332	.295
Rondon, Alex, S. Oregon...........	.359	14	49	39	7	14	18	4	0	0	7	1	1	4	4	0	12	0	1	0	.462	.458
Rust, Brian, Eugene...............	.204	53	170	157	18	32	53	7	1	4	19	2	2	2	7	0	43	2	1	2	.338	.244
Sachse, Matthew, Everett*	.230	59	227	191	34	44	53	6	0	1	14	2	1	4	29	1	76	5	4	3	.277	.342
Sasser, Rob, Eugene	.269	57	244	216	40	58	96	9	1	9	32	0	2	3	23	1	51	14	4	2	.444	.344
Saturnino, Sherton, Eugene	.238	8	22	21	4	5	8	0	0	1	1	0	0	0	1	0	7	2	0	0	.381	.273
Schafer, Brett, Spokane	.195	62	248	205	23	40	50	7	0	1	19	1	1	2	39	0	42	11	1	4	.244	.328
Sheffer, Chad, Everett††	.280	56	232	193	31	54	65	9	1	0	18	6	4	2	27	0	38	28	8	3	.337	.367
Shy, Jason, Eugene	.241	20	55	54	6	13	21	2	0	2	6	0	0	0	1	0	12	0	0	1	.389	.253
Simonton, Cy Leon, Everett*	.206	48	174	155	17	32	36	2	1	0	15	3	1	1	14	0	36	8	4	3	.232	.275
Slemmer, David, S. Oregon	.224	66	284	246	36	55	69	5	3	1	20	1	1	0	36	1	42	16	4	9	.280	.322
Sosa, Juan, Spokane	.235	61	239	217	26	51	78	10	4	3	16	4	2	1	15	2	39	8	1	4	.359	.285
Spiegel, Rich, Eugene	.143	7	17	14	0	2	2	0	0	0	0	0	0	1	2	0	3	0	0	1	.143	.294
Taylor, Matthew, Eugene*	.000	10	30	24	1	0	0	0	0	0	0	0	0	1	5	0	8	0	1	1	.000	.200
Tejada, Miguel, S. Oregon	.245	74	315	269	45	66	115	15	5	8	44	0	3	2	41	2	54	19	2	3	.428	.344
Thomasson, Shane, Everett.........	.210	40	106	100	10	21	23	0	1	0	3	2	0	2	2	0	23	7	2	1	.230	.240
Thompson, Bruce, Bellingham*	.232	66	285	241	49	56	73	7	2	2	13	1	0	0	43	1	75	18	6	1	.303	.349
Thompson, Karl, Everett............	.246	54	211	187	29	46	76	13	1	5	26	2	2	4	16	0	39	4	0	9	.406	.316
Tinoco, Luis, Everett..............	.286	62	242	203	34	58	99	10	2	9	31	0	1	3	35	1	41	9	3	6	.488	.397
Tocco, Todd, Eugene*	.197	59	140	117	12	23	29	3	0	1	8	2	2	2	17	0	32	0	1	1	.248	.304
Topping, Dan, Bellingham	.267	57	203	180	15	48	68	5	0	5	31	0	1	8	14	4	24	0	0	6	.378	.324
Torrealba, Yolvit, Bellingham	.155	26	75	71	2	11	14	3	0	0	8	0	1	1	2	0	14	0	1	1	.197	.187
Trippy, Joe, Eugene*	.309	75	300	259	48	80	102	16	0	2	38	2	2	13	24	1	31	29	13	1	.394	.393
Tucker, Jonathan, Yakima*	.165	41	130	115	6	19	25	3	0	1	5	0	1	1	13	0	35	0	0	2	.217	.254
Twist, Jeffrey, Portland†	.139	27	90	79	6	11	14	3	0	0	6	0	1	1	9	0	18	0	2	2	.177	.233
Valenti, Jon, Southern Oregon	.209	35	122	110	13	23	34	5	0	2	16	1	2	1	8	0	19	1	0	3	.309	.264
Vallone, Gar, Boise†	.242	37	131	99	21	24	30	6	0	0	16	8	1	3	20	1	33	4	2	3	.303	.382
Vandergriend, Jon, Boise*	.287	56	186	157	30	45	62	8	0	3	24	0	0	3	26	1	32	7	3	3	.395	.398
Vickers, Randy, Everett	.256	68	289	266	35	68	121	13	2	12	37	0	0	3	20	2	102	5	2	6	.455	.315
Vida, James, Spokane*	.323	74	311	291	38	94	121	13	1	4	39	0	0	1	19	5	32	0	0	5	.416	.367
Wagner, Kyle, Boise..............	.141	36	103	78	14	11	15	1	0	1	14	0	1	7	17	0	18	1	4	1	.192	.340
Walkanoff, A.J., Yakima...........	.223	38	135	112	7	25	30	5	0	0	15	0	2	0	17	0	21	1	0	1	.268	.321
Wathan, Dusty, Everett††	.271	53	206	181	32	49	78	9	1	6	25	1	0	7	17	0	26	2	1	4	.431	.356
Watson, Jonathan, Bellingham......	.299	65	262	231	42	69	84	9	0	2	27	4	3	4	20	2	41	16	9	3	.364	.360
Weathersby, Leon, Spokane........	.229	37	131	118	13	27	40	4	3	1	12	0	0	4	9	0	42	2	1	4	.339	.305
Weaver, Terry, Bellingham	.250	37	126	116	24	29	40	2	0	3	13	0	0	1	9	1	30	2	1	0	.345	.310
Welch, Brandon, S. Oregon*	.147	39	119	102	6	15	18	3	0	0	11	1	0	1	15	0	30	1	0	3	.176	.263
Whitley, Bill, Portland	.230	64	282	230	40	53	67	10	2	0	20	3	1	13	35	1	33	8	3	5	.291	.362
Williams, Glenn, Eugene†	.224	71	296	268	39	60	100	11	4	7	36	0	2	5	21	1	71	7	4	4	.373	.291

GRAND SLAMS: Buxbaum, 3; Quinn, 2; Burrows, Calderon, Carpentier, Kane, Lombard, Myers, Pomierski, K. Thompson, Weathersby, Williams, 1 each.
AWARDED FIRST BASE ON CATCHER'S INTERFERENCE: Reynolds 6 (Lunar 2, Graves, Hallmark, Rondon, Walkanoff); Baughman 3 (Lunar 2, K. Thompson); Owen 3 (Arias, Mahoney, Rondon); Walkanoff 2 (Ardoin, Norton).

1995 PITCHING

TEAM

Team	W	L	Pct.	ERA	G	CG	ShO	Sv.	IP	H	TBF	R	ER	HR	SH	SF	HB	BB	IBB	SO	WP	Bk.
Bellingham	43	33	.566	3.05	76	0	8	21	685.1	618	2931	297	232	34	22	15	29	285	2	591	43	13
Portland	41	34	.547	3.06	75	4	4	23	662.1	531	2779	284	225	27	21	20	40	277	13	561	58	19
Eugene	37	39	.487	3.56	76	0	2	19	667.0	606	2955	372	264	39	26	21	44	313	19	635	53	11
Everett	37	39	.487	3.63	76	5	4	15	680.0	622	2919	346	274	55	15	14	44	294	14	572	54	15
Spokane	36	40	.474	3.65	76	1	4	20	680.2	653	2952	345	276	38	20	21	52	269	11	522	44	9
Southern Oregon	33	43	.434	3.72	76	0	3	13	669.1	667	2941	374	277	40	28	28	59	237	16	542	51	13
Boise	48	27	.640	3.90	75	4	5	20	653.2	575	2836	343	283	44	17	17	48	329	13	590	69	9
Yakima	28	48	.368	4.54	76	0	2	17	667.2	637	3039	426	337	34	19	37	40	396	12	537	95	16

INDIVIDUAL

TOP QUALIFIERS FOR EARNED-RUN AVERAGE TITLE

Minimum 61 innings. *Lefthanded pitcher.

Pitcher, Team	W	L	Pct.	ERA	G	GS	CG	ShO	GF	Sv.	IP	H	TBF	R	ER	HR	SH	SF	HB	BB	IBB	SO	WP	Bk.
Randall, Scott, Portland	7	3	.700	1.99	15	15	1	0	0	0	95.0	76	391	35	21	2	2	2	8	28	1	78	7	2
Blood, Darin, Bellingham	6	3	.667	2.54	14	13	0	0	0	0	74.1	63	315	26	21	2	4	0	3	32	1	78	6	1
Cruz, Charlie, Eugene*	6	7	.462	2.55	15	15	0	0	0	0	81.1	68	348	34	23	2	2	3	4	36	2	90	2	1
Niemeier, Todd, Everett*	4	3	.571	2.81	15	15	0	0	0	0	80.0	74	338	33	25	4	4	2	3	26	0	80	5	2
Villarreal, Modesto, Spokane	8	2	.800	2.90	16	11	0	0	1	0	80.2	73	330	30	26	4	2	3	3	23	2	57	5	2
McKnight, Chris, Eugene*	5	2	.714	2.92	13	13	0	0	0	0	64.2	63	282	31	21	4	6	4	1	21	1	30	6	0
D'Alessandro, Marc, Portland*	9	3	.750	2.96	16	15	2	0	0	0	97.1	85	397	41	32	9	0	4	3	28	0	64	2	3
Thurmond, Travis, Boise	9	3	.750	3.11	16	15	4	1	1	0	101.1	75	401	36	35	7	0	3	3	31	0	93	7	0
Kurtz, Danny, Everett	5	2	.714	3.12	14	12	1	0	0	0	69.1	60	293	27	24	6	1	2	6	32	1	43	4	2
Trawick, Tim, Everett	6	2	.750	3.14	16	13	3	1	1	0	86.0	66	350	34	30	11	0		9	30	1	63	1	2
Prihoda, Stephen, Spokane*	1	6	.143	3.25	14	13	1	0	0	0	69.1	65	293	36	25	7	3	1	5	18	0	63	4	0
Soden, Chad, Everett*	4	3	.571	3.38	13	12	0	0	0	0	61.1	55	256	30	23	3	0	0	1	17	1	52	3	1
Silva, Luis, Southern Oregon	4	3	.571	3.81	19	14	0	0	3	1	78.0	79	337	43	33	8	3	3	7	20	0	76	5	0
Garcia, Jose, Eugene	3	3	.500	3.86	14	14	0	0	0	0	70.0	64	307	43	30	7	1	0	0	35	0	62	2	2
Cooper, Brian, Boise	3	2	.600	3.92	13	11	0	0	1	1	62.0	60	264	31	27	5	4	1	6	22	1	66	4	1

DEPARTMENTAL LEADERS: W—Vermillion, 12; L—Wuestenhoefer, 9; Pct.—Vermillion, Villarreal, .800; G—Chrismon, 32; GS—Several pitchers tied with 15; GS—Several pitchers tied with 15; CG—Thurmond, 4; ShO—Thurmond, Trawick, 1; GF—Emiliano, 22; Sv.—Scutero, 12; IP—Thurmond, 101.1; H—Wuestenhoefer, 88; TBF—Thurmond, 401; R—Blythe, 55; ER—Blythe, 41; HR—Trawick, 11; SH—McKnight, 4; SF—Hodge, 6; HB—Holden, 17; BB—S. Soto, 54; IBB—Butler, 5; SO—Thurmond, 93; WP—Several pitchers tied with 12; Bk.—Gonzalez, McNeely, Mitchell, 5.

ALL PITCHERS

*Lefthanded pitcher.

Pitcher, Team	W	L	Pct.	ERA	G	GS	CG	ShO	GF	Sv.	IP	H	TBF	R	ER	HR	SH	SF	HB	BB	IBB	SO	WP	Bk.
Abbott, Todd, S. Oregon	2	3	.400	2.96	17	5	0	0	2	1	48.2	39	199	22	16	3	1	1	0	18	0	41	2	1
Abreu, Jose, Bellingham	1	2	.333	4.63	13	0	0	0	5	1	23.1	17	99	12	12	0	1	0	1	12	0	29	2	0
Adam, Justin, Spokane	3	4	.429	5.29	15	8	0	0	2	1	49.1	45	220	34	29	2	0	0	4	31	0	35	2	0
Agosto, Stevenson, Boise*	6	2	.750	2.92	13	11	0	0	1	0	52.1	39	224	20	17	1	0	3	5	30	2	34	12	0
Albrecht, Jon, Spokane*	2	2	.500	3.38	17	0	0	0	13	6	21.1	14	89	8	8	1	0	0	3	12	1	15	2	0
Ali, Sam, Bellingham	0	2	.000	7.88	5	0	0	0	4	0	8.0	10	38	7	7	1	1	0	0	4	0	3	2	1
Alvarez, Juan, Boise*	0	0	.000	0.77	9	0	0	0	2	0	11.2	12	47	1	1	0	0	0	1	2	0	11	0	0
Avila, Edwin, Boise	1	1	.500	10.35	14	1	0	0	6	0	20.0	27	100	27	23	6	0	0	1	14	0	17	2	2
Babineaux, Darrin, Yakima	1	6	.143	3.64	12	10	0	0	2	0	59.1	53	251	33	24	3	1	3	4	18	1	36	0	1
Bailey, Philip, Bellingham*	6	1	.857	1.36	19	4	0	0	0	0	59.2	51	237	15	9	3	0	0	3	15	0	39	1	1
Barcelo, Lorenzo, Bellingham	3	2	.600	3.45	12	11	0	0	0	0	47.0	43	198	23	18	3	0	1	2	19	0	34	1	1
Batchelder, Bill, S. Oregon	1	4	.200	5.52	18	5	0	0	4	0	44.0	56	195	30	27	3	0	1	1	13	1	20	1	0
Bermudez, Manuel, Bellingham	1	2	.333	3.81	13	13	0	0	0	0	56.2	51	244	28	24	3	2	2	2	25	0	39	4	1
Bevel, Bobby, Portland*	2	3	.400	3.54	25	0	0	0	8	1	28.0	24	128	13	11	0	3	2	1	18	4	25	5	0
Blasingim, Joseph, Bellingham	1	1	.500	4.26	13	1	0	0	3	0	25.1	31	118	14	12	0	1	2	1	14	0	22	3	0
Blood, Darin, Bellingham*	6	3	.667	2.54	14	13	0	0	0	0	74.1	63	315	26	21	2	4	0	3	32	1	78	6	1
Blythe, Billy, Eugene	1	6	.143	9.80	14	10	0	0	2	1	37.2	45	213	55	41	4	0	2	7	49	1	24	12	0
Bost, Allen, Portland	1	0	1.000	3.38	10	0	0	0	1	0	16.0	15	63	6	6	1	0	0	0	6	0	25	1	0
Brester, Jason, Bellingham*	1	0	1.000	4.13	8	6	0	0	0	0	24.0	23	104	11	11	3	0	0	1	12	0	17	0	0
Brizek, Seth, Everett	0	2	.000	6.97	8	0	0	0	1	0	10.1	13	55	10	8	1	0	0	2	8	0	16	1	0
Brooks, Antone, Eugene*	2	0	1.000	0.53	15	0	0	0	5	0	17.0	9	67	5	1	1	0	0	8	1	26	0	0	
Brown, Darold, Eugene*	0	3	.000	4.24	3	3	0	0	0	0	17.0	18	77	16	8	3	1	0	0	6	1	13	1	0
Butler, Adam, Eugene*	4	1	.800	2.49	23	0	0	0	18	8	25.1	15	109	9	7	0	1	0	3	12	5	50	1	0
Cervantes, Peter, Yakima	3	5	.375	4.65	13	10	0	0	1	0	50.1	55	226	32	26	3	1	2	3	16	0	35	1	0
Chambers, Scott, Yakima*	1	2	.333	5.34	20	1	0	0	6	1	28.2	31	130	20	17	4	1	1	0	13	0	37	4	0
Charles, Israel, Spokane	1	0	1.000	4.50	4	0	0	0	1	0	6.0	6	28	3	3	0	0	0	0	3	0	5	1	1
Chrismon, Thad, Eugene	2	2	.500	2.61	32	0	0	0	13	0	38.0	31	165	15	11	3	0	4	5	21	1	28	5	0
Clifford, Eric, Everett	3	2	.600	2.40	28	0	0	0	11	4	45.0	39	183	17	12	2	2	3	2	11	1	39	4	1
Coe, Keith, Boise	2	5	.286	4.69	13	12	0	0	0	0	55.2	49	250	35	29	4	2	0	5	38	1	42	5	1
Collett, Andy, Everett	0	0	.000	0.00	1	0	0	0	0	0	0.1	1	4	0	0	0	0	0	0	2	0	1	0	0
Connelly, Steven, S. Oregon	2	4	.333	3.81	17	0	0	0	4	0	28.1	29	133	17	12	1	3	2	4	14	4	19	6	0
Conway, Robert, Everett	1	0	1.000	4.00	6	0	0	0	0	0	9.0	6	42	6	4	0	0	0	0	11	1	3	4	1
Cooper, Brian, Boise	3	2	.600	3.92	13	11	0	0	1	1	62.0	60	264	31	27	5	4	1	6	22	1	66	4	1
Cooper, David, Everett	1	2	.333	7.36	17	2	0	0	0	0	33.0	36	166	31	27	5	1	0	3	31	0	20	8	0
Costello, T.J., S. Oregon*	0	0	.000	6.23	3	0	0	0	0	0	4.1	8	25	4	3	0	0	0	1	2	0	5	0	0
Coyle, Bryan, Yakima	2	0	1.000	1.40	6	1	0	0	1	0	19.1	14	78	3	3	1	1	0	0	8	0	17	1	0
Crossley, Chad, Boise	0	0	.000	20.25	2	0	0	0	1	0	1.1	3	9	4	3	0	1	0	2	3	0	4	2	0
Cruz, Charlie, Eugene*	6	7	.462	2.55	15	15	0	0	0	0	81.1	68	348	34	23	2	2	3	4	36	2	90	2	1

Pitcher, Team	W	L	Pct.	ERA	G	GS	CG	ShO	GF	Sv.	IP	H	TBF	R	ER	HR	SH	SF	HB	BB	IBB	SO	WP	Bk.
Dafun, George, Boise	4	4	.500	5.31	16	12	0	0	2	1	59.1	57	271	40	35	5	4	1	8	33	1	61	4	0
D'Alessandro, Marc, Portland*	9	3	.750	2.96	16	15	2	0	0	0	97.1	85	397	41	32	9	0	4	3	28	0	64	2	3
Davis, Eddie, Yakima	2	3	.400	4.89	20	4	0	0	5	1	53.1	61	248	33	29	2	1	3	5	32	2	36	5	0
Deakman, Josh, Boise	1	1	.500	1.54	3	3	0	0	0	0	11.2	11	49	8	2	0	0	1	0	4	0	8	0	0
DeLaCruz, Fernando, Boise	0	0	.000	13.50	1	0	0	0	0	0	1.1	3	11	6	2	1	0	0	1	2	0	4	0	0
Dietrich, Jason, Portland	0	0	.000	0.00	10	1	0	0	5	4	13.1	5	48	0	0	0	0	0	0	5	0	24	0	0
Emiliano, James, Portland	4	1	.800	3.49	28	0	0	0	22	11	38.2	31	165	18	15	0	2	1	4	16	2	41	5	0
Epstein, Ian, Southern Oregon*	2	2	.500	2.90	23	0	0	0	19	1	40.1	32	163	17	13	1	2	5	2	9	2	36	2	1
Farfan, David, Boise	1	0	1.000	2.53	14	0	0	0	4	0	21.1	19	94	9	6	0	0	0	0	12	0	17	2	2
Fontenot, Joe, Bellingham	0	3	.000	1.93	6	6	0	0	0	0	18.2	14	77	5	4	0	0	0	0	10	0	14	0	2
Foster, Kris, Yakima	2	3	.400	2.89	15	10	0	0	5	3	56.0	38	241	27	18	2	2	4	2	38	3	55	8	1
French, Jon, Southern Oregon	1	2	.333	6.41	20	0	0	0	12	0	26.2	34	132	21	19	3	1	0	5	17	1	18	3	0
Garcia, Jose, Eugene	3	3	.500	3.86	14	14	0	0	0	0	70.0	64	307	43	30	7	1	0	0	35	0	62	2	2
Gerland, Greg, Eugene*	4	2	.667	2.16	19	2	0	0	2	1	41.2	39	180	18	10	1	3	1	1	15	1	33	2	1
Giard, Ken, Eugene	3	0	1.000	2.38	25	0	0	0	7	2	34.0	31	137	9	9	3	2	0	1	5	1	44	3	0
Gomez, Dennys, Bellingham	0	1	.000	7.50	4	0	0	0	2	1	6.0	8	31	6	5	2	0	0	0	3	0	6	1	0
Gonzalez, Laril, Portland	3	4	.429	4.06	15	11	0	0	2	2	57.2	44	258	31	26	4	1	1	7	43	0	48	9	5
Gryboski, Kevin, Everett	1	5	.167	3.50	25	0	0	0	14	2	36.0	27	156	18	14	2	3	1	3	18	2	25	3	0
Gunther, Kevin, S. Oregon	1	1	.500	1.42	5	5	0	0	0	0	19.0	14	71	6	3	0	0	0	0	2	0	11	2	0
Herrera, Ivan, Bellingham	0	0	.000	0.00	1	0	0	0	0	0	2.0	0	7	0	0	0	0	0	0	1	0	1	0	0
Hilton, Willy, Southern Oregon*	1	4	.200	4.40	16	1	0	0	6	1	30.2	37	143	22	15	1	3	2	0	12	1	31	4	1
Hodge, Hal, Everett	3	1	.750	4.26	16	15	0	0	0	0	69.2	81	308	39	33	5	2	6	7	20	0	45	3	2
Holden, Jason, S. Oregon	2	6	.250	4.72	19	8	0	0	6	0	61.0	64	290	42	32	2	4	4	17	23	0	30	10	4
Hutzler, Jeff, Bellingham	2	2	.500	1.72	7	7	0	0	0	0	31.1	35	130	7	6	0	1	0	0	8	0	19	2	2
Iddon, Brent, Everett	3	5	.375	4.36	14	14	1	0	0	0	74.1	86	326	49	36	8	1	0	6	25	0	67	3	0
Judice, Bryan, Spokane	0	1	.000	7.91	14	0	0	0	4	1	19.1	29	101	18	17	0	1	1	4	10	2	14	4	0
Kammerer, James, Portland*	2	1	.667	1.53	11	5	0	0	0	0	35.1	24	135	8	6	0	1	1	0	11	0	17	1	0
Kaysner, Brent, Spokane	0	2	.000	1.56	19	0	0	0	11	4	34.2	15	147	7	6	1	1	0	7	24	0	37	4	0
Keehn, Drew, Portland	2	4	.333	3.80	20	0	0	0	6	0	42.2	38	182	22	18	3	4	1	1	17	1	30	1	1
Keppen, Jeffrey, Yakima	2	2	.500	5.66	20	3	0	0	6	0	41.1	46	210	35	26	1	1	5	6	32	0	32	7	1
Kjos, Ryan, Southern Oregon	2	0	1.000	2.45	9	0	0	0	4	2	11.0	9	47	4	3	2	0	0	0	5	0	16	2	0
Knoll, Brian, Bellingham	5	2	.714	2.05	22	2	0	0	5	0	57.0	44	232	22	13	1	4	1	3	17	0	35	2	1
Koehler, P.K., Eugene*	0	2	.000	22.50	2	2	0	0	0	0	4.0	4	27	10	10	1	0	0	1	12	0	5	0	1
Kurtz, Danny, Everett	5	2	.714	3.12	14	12	1	0	1	0	69.1	60	293	27	24	6	1	2	6	32	1	43	4	2
Leibee, Skye, S. Oregon*	0	0	.000	3.86	2	0	0	0	1	0	2.1	1	10	1	1	0	0	0	1	1	1	3	0	0
Lintern, Cory, Bellingham	2	0	1.000	0.87	3	0	0	0	1	1	10.1	6	41	2	1	0	1	0	2	0	0	6	0	0
Liz, Jesus, Spokane*	0	0	.000	7.11	9	0	0	0	4	0	12.2	19	70	15	10	0	2	0	12	0	11	3	0
Macca, Christopher, Portland	3	2	.600	3.28	24	0	0	0	16	5	35.2	25	152	15	13	1	2	2	6	17	1	41	6	0
Marte, Damaso, Everett*	2	2	.500	2.21	11	5	0	0	1	0	36.2	25	141	11	9	2	1	1	1	10	0	39	3	3
Martin, Chandler, Portland	4	1	.800	1.66	7	7	0	0	0	0	38.0	20	153	10	7	0	2	0	2	21	0	34	3	3
Masaoka, Onan, Yakima*	2	4	.333	3.65	15	7	0	0	5	0	49.1	28	225	25	20	2	1	0	4	47	0	75	12	4
Mayber, Chan, Portland	0	0	.000	0.00	1	0	0	0	1	0	1.0	0	4	0	0	0	0	0	0	0	0	0	0	0
Mayer, Aaron, Boise	3	1	.750	5.40	20	1	0	0	1	0	35.0	38	159	29	21	4	1	0	2	22	0	32	11	0
Mayhew, Keith, Eugene	0	1	.000	4.54	24	1	0	0	3	1	39.2	46	185	29	20	2	2	1	3	17	0	35	4	2
Mazzone, Tony, Eugene	3	1	.750	3.89	25	0	0	0	7	2	44.0	50	200	24	19	3	2	4	7	12	1	38	1	0
McDonald, Matt, S. Oregon*	3	2	.600	3.14	13	9	0	0	0	0	51.2	42	211	22	18	4	2	1	2	18	0	47	2	1
McKnight, Chris, Eugene*	5	2	.714	2.92	13	13	0	0	0	0	64.2	63	282	31	21	4	6	4	1	21	1	30	6	0
McMullen, Jerry, Eugene*	1	1	.500	1.47	22	0	0	0	8	1	30.2	28	128	7	5	0	4	0	1	8	2	35	4	0
McNeely, Mitch, Yakima*	3	4	.429	4.25	24	3	0	0	8	1	53.0	53	226	30	25	1	2	0	15	2	31	6	5
McWilliams, Matt, Eugene	2	3	.400	2.01	24	4	0	0	10	0	49.1	34	208	21	11	1	1	0	7	16	2	42	4	2
Medero, Gadiel, Bellingham	0	0	.000	6.35	4	0	0	0	0	0	5.2	10	33	7	4	1	0	0	0	4	0	4	3	0
Mimnaugh, Scott, S. Oregon	0	2	.000	3.24	3	3	0	0	0	0	8.1	10	43	8	3	1	1	0	2	4	0	8	0	1
Mitchell, Kelvin, Everett*	3	2	.600	4.62	25	0	0	0	6	1	37.0	41	171	26	19	2	0	3	2	23	4	24	6	5
Mlodik, Kevin, S. Oregon	2	2	.500	3.15	20	10	0	0	1	0	60.0	62	273	35	21	3	0	3	8	20	0	43	4	2
Morrison, Chris, S. Oregon	2	1	.667	2.40	6	0	0	0	2	0	15.0	14	56	4	4	0	0	0	1	1	0	11	1	0
Mosman, Marc, Bellingham	0	0	.000	5.81	12	3	0	0	1	0	26.1	38	122	21	17	4	1	0	8	0	21	2	0
Murphy, Sean, Portland	2	0	1.000	1.59	21	0	0	0	7	0	39.2	21	156	11	7	1	0	1	1	16	2	39	3	1
Nelson, Chris, S. Oregon	2	3	.400	3.48	16	6	0	0	3	1	54.1	43	218	25	21	5	3	3	3	13	1	52	1	1
Newman, Damon, S. Oregon	3	3	.500	3.61	14	7	0	0	1	1	47.1	51	221	32	19	1	1	0	4	24	0	35	4	1
Nied, David, Portland	0	0	.000	0.00	1	1	0	0	0	0	3.0	1	10	0	0	0	0	0	0	1	0	5	0	0
Niemeier, Todd, Everett*	4	3	.571	3.25	15	15	0	0	0	0	80.0	74	338	33	25	4	4	3	2	36	0	80	5	2
O'Quinn, James, Boise*	0	0	.000	4.84	23	0	0	0	9	0	22.1	22	106	12	12	1	1	2	3	18	2	26	6	0
Ortiz, Russell, Bellingham	2	0	1.000	0.52	25	0	0	0	20	11	34.1	19	131	4	2	0	1	2	3	13	0	55	2	1
Pearsall, J.J., Yakima*	2	3	.400	3.26	20	1	0	0	8	1	38.2	39	167	18	14	1	1	2	14	0	26	5	0
Petri, Tom, Boise	1	0	1.000	4.18	10	1	0	0	1	0	23.2	27	105	12	11	0	1	4	1	13	0	9	5	1
Prihoda, Stephen, Spokane*	1	6	.143	3.25	14	13	1	0	0	0	69.1	65	293	36	25	7	3	1	5	18	0	63	4	0
Randall, Scott, Portland	7	3	.700	1.99	15	15	1	0	0	0	95.0	76	391	35	21	2	2	2	8	28	1	78	7	2
Reitzenstein, Brad, Portland	0	1	.000	10.13	7	0	0	0	2	0	8.0	2	44	10	9	0	1	2	16	1	10	10	2
Renko, Todd, Boise	0	0	.000	7.36	5	0	0	0	2	0	3.2	6	20	8	3	3	0	0	0	3	0	2	1	0
Ritter, Jason, Spokane	3	1	.750	3.21	10	4	0	0	0	0	33.2	25	135	12	12	1	0	1	3	15	0	29	1	1
Rivette, Scott, Southern Oregon	2	0	1.000	0.95	9	1	0	0	3	2	19.0	16	83	5	2	0	1	1	1	11	2	22	1	0
Robbins, Mike, Spokane*	1	3	.250	2.33	5	5	0	0	0	0	27.0	23	109	9	7	1	0	2	6	0	16	1	1
Rocker, John, Eugene*	1	5	.167	5.16	12	12	0	0	0	0	59.1	45	260	40	34	4	1	1	2	36	0	74	7	2
Rodriguez, Luis, Bellingham*	0	0	.000	6.00	4	0	0	0	1	0	6.0	6	33	5	4	0	0	0	2	8	1	0	0
Rolish, Chad, Southern Oregon*	1	0	1.000	3.00	4	0	0	0	0	0	6.0	6	26	3	2	0	0	4	2	1	4	0	0
Romine, Jason, Portland	0	1	.000	6.39	4	3	0	0	0	0	12.2	14	58	9	9	2	0	2	0	7	0	5	0	0
Rose, Brian, Portland	1	1	.500	5.19	5	0	0	0	1	0	8.2	10	40	5	5	1	2	1	2	6	1	11	0	0
Ruskey, Jason, Everett*	0	3	.000	6.08	8	3	0	0	0	0	13.1	15	62	13	9	3	0	0	1	9	0	7	2	0
Saier, Matthew, Spokane	2	4	.333	3.31	16	0	0	0	9	4	35.1	24	138	14	13	2	2	1	2	12	0	41	4	0
Sanchez, Mike, Yakima	1	2	.333	0.95	18	1	0	0	11	5	28.1	16	121	4	3	0	2	1	4	20	2	27	5	1
Sanders, Allen, Spokane	4	5	.444	4.47	14	10	0	0	2	0	56.1	67	257	43	28	2	3	1	2	18	1	36	3	0
Sanders, Craig, Spokane	3	1	.750	1.94	22	0	0	0	12	3	46.1	32	197	11	10	2	2	1	2	24	0	32	2	1
Santiago, Jose, Spokane	2	4	.333	3.14	22	0	0	0	10	1	48.2	60	227	26	17	1	1	2	5	20	4	32	3	0

Pitcher, Team	W	L	Pct.	ERA	G	GS	CG	ShO	GF	Sv.	IP	H	TBF	R	ER	HR	SH	SF	HB	BB	IBB	SO	WP	Bk.
Scheer, Greg, Everett*	0	1	.000	4.15	18	0	0	0	5	1	21.2	16	102	12	10	0	1	2	3	19	2	23	2	0
Scheffer, Aaron, Everett	2	5	.286	3.74	24	0	0	0	9	1	43.1	44	185	23	18	4	1	0	2	16	1	38	2	1
Schiefelbein, Mike, Bellingham	0	0	.000	0.00	3	0	0	0	1	0	0.2	1	6	0	0	0	0	0	0	3	0	1	0	0
Scutero, Brian, Boise	1	2	.333	4.91	22	0	0	0	20	12	22.0	17	101	13	12	1	2	0	1	16	1	17	1	0
Silva, Luis, Southern Oregon	4	3	.571	3.81	19	14	0	0	3	1	78.0	79	337	43	33	8	3	7	20	0	76	5	0
Soden, Chad, Everett*	4	3	.571	3.38	13	12	0	0	0	0	61.1	55	256	30	23	3	0	0	1	17	1	52	3	1
Sosa, Helpis, Southern Oregon	0	1	.000	6.75	6	2	0	0	2	0	13.1	21	65	11	10	2	0	2	1	6	1	17	1	0
Soto, Daniel, Spokane	0	3	.000	5.06	3	2	0	0	1	0	10.2	11	45	6	6	1	0	1	1	4	0	10	0	0
Soto, Seferino, Yakima	0	2	.000	7.75	15	6	0	0	1	0	36.0	30	189	37	31	1	0	2	1	54	2	34	9	2
South, Carl, Yakima	3	6	.333	6.14	13	10	0	0	1	0	55.2	72	257	47	38	4	1	3	1	19	0	30	12	0
Stone, Ricky, Yakima	4	4	.500	5.25	16	6	0	0	7	2	48.0	54	213	31	28	5	2	2	2	20	0	28	4	1
Stoops, Jim, Bellingham	6	5	.545	3.43	24	0	0	0	14	4	42.0	32	178	23	16	1	2	1	5	17	0	58	2	0
Sumter, Kevin, Boise	0	1	.000	2.27	21	0	0	0	5	0	31.2	15	141	8	8	1	0	0	2	31	1	38	5	1
Szimanski, Tom, Everett	2	0	1.000	1.69	16	0	0	0	11	5	21.1	13	79	4	4	1	0	0	0	6	0	32	0	0
Takahashi, Kurt, Bellingham	1	2	.333	5.61	17	0	0	0	5	0	25.2	28	116	18	16	2	0	0	2	14	0	20	4	0
Tapia, Elias, Yakima	0	1	.000	5.40	13	1	0	0	3	0	23.1	23	111	20	14	3	1	1	2	13	0	15	8	0
Thomas, Robbie, Yakima*	0	1	.000	3.60	7	2	0	0	1	0	20.0	15	89	11	8	0	1	2	1	11	0	17	2	0
Thomasson, Shane, Everett	0	0	.000	9.00	2	0	0	0	2	0	2.0	5	10	2	2	1	0	0	0	0	0	1	2	0
Thurmond, Travis, Boise	9	3	.750	3.11	16	15	4	1	1	0	101.1	75	401	36	35	7	0	3	3	31	0	93	7	0
Trawick, Tim, Everett	6	2	.750	3.14	16	13	3	1	1	0	86.0	66	350	34	30	11	0	9	30	1	63	1	2
Tucker, Benjamin, Bellingham	2	1	.667	1.91	12	10	0	0	1	0	56.2	53	249	21	12	4	2	4	19	0	48	2	1
Upchurch, Wayne, Spokane	1	1	.500	6.39	7	0	0	0	5	0	12.2	22	64	12	9	2	2	0	5	1	7	2	0
Valdez, Ken, Boise	1	0	1.000	4.63	5	0	0	0	5	0	11.2	11	55	8	6	1	0	2	7	0	9	2	0
Vavrek, Mike, Portland*	0	0	.000	0.00	3	3	0	0	0	0	14.0	8	52	0	0	0	0	3	0	14	0	0
Vermillion, Grant, Boise	12	3	.800	1.96	30	0	0	0	15	6	59.2	49	244	19	13	2	2	1	5	16	4	50	2	1
Villarreal, Modesto, Spokane	8	2	.800	2.90	16	11	0	0	1	0	80.2	73	330	30	26	4	2	3	3	23	2	57	5	2
Vukson, John, Boise	0	0	.000	16.71	11	0	0	0	5	0	7.0	9	57	20	13	1	0	4	3	26	0	6	6	0
Washburn, Jarrod, Boise*	3	2	.600	3.33	8	8	0	0	0	0	46.0	35	185	17	17	1	0	1	2	14	0	54	1	0
Williamson, Jeremy, Spokane*	3	1	.750	1.43	11	7	0	0	0	0	44.0	32	171	12	7	4	0	1	1	9	0	35	0	1
Winders, Brian, Spokane	0	1	.000	30.00	2	1	0	0	0	0	3.0	10	23	10	10	2	0	1	3	0	2	0	0
Woodrow, James, Bellingham	4	4	.500	3.65	27	0	0	0	14	3	44.1	35	192	18	18	3	2	3	2	25	2	34	3	1
Wuestenhoefer, Brady, Portland	1	9	.100	4.64	14	14	1	0	0	0	77.2	88	343	50	40	5	1	2	3	23	0	50	5	2
Zedalis, Craig, Eugene	0	0	.000	2.70	8	0	0	0	1	0	13.1	16	62	6	4	0	0	1	4	0	10	0	0

COMBINATION SHUTOUTS: **Bellingham (8)**—Barcelo-Knoll-Takahashi-Ortiz, Barcelo-Woodrow, Bermudez-Knoll-Ortiz, Blood-Woodrow, Brester-Bailey-Stoops, Brester-Bailey-Woodrow, Tucker-Abreu-Takahashi-Ortiz, Tucker-Ortiz. **Boise (4)**—Cooper-Sumter, Dafun-Sumter-O'Quinn-Mayer-Scutero, Deakman-Farfan-O'Quinn-Scutero, Thurmond-Vermillion. **Eugene (2)**—Gerland-McMullen-Butler, McKnight-Giard-Butler. **Everett (3)**—Kurtz-Marte-Gryboski-Scheer-Scheffer, Soden-Cooper-Clifford-Scheer, Trawick-Cooper-Scheer-Clifford. **Portland (4)**—Kammerer-Macca-Emiliano, Martin-Gonzalez, Randall-Macca-Dietrich, Randall-Rose-Dietrich. **Southern Oregon (3)**—Mlodik-Newman, Newman-Rivette-French, Silva-Abbott. **Spokane (4)**—Hodge-Albrecht, Hodge-Sanders, Villarreal-Adam, Villarreal-Adam-Kaysner. **Yakima (2)**—Babineaux-Chambers-Davis, Coyle-Foster.
NO-HIT GAMES: None.

1995 FIELDING

TEAM

Team	Pct.	G	PO	A	E	TC	DP	PB	Team	Pct.	G	PO	A	E	TC	DP	PB
Portland	.967	75	1987	909	100	2996	68	27	Bellingham	.958	76	2056	860	129	3045	55	21
Boise	.965	75	1961	808	99	2868	66	9	Southern Oregon	.954	76	2008	915	140	3063	54	22
Everett	.963	76	2040	874	112	3026	63	22	Yakima	.954	76	2003	878	139	3020	63	21
Spokane	.962	76	2042	920	117	3079	73	25	Eugene	.946	76	2001	844	161	3006	54	23

TRIPLE PLAYS: None.

INDIVIDUAL

FIRST BASEMEN

NOTE: All caps denotes fielding-percentage leader based on 38 games for catchers, 51 for all other non-pitchers and 76 innings for pitchers. *Throws lefthanded.

Player, Team	Pct.	G	PO	A	E	TC	DP
Amado, Jose, Everett	1.000	3	17	3	0	20	0
Buxbaum, Danny, Boise	.985	56	497	20	8	525	40
Calderon, Ricardo, Bellingham*	1.000	1	5	0	0	5	0
Castillo, Alberto, Bellingham*	.978	74	650	54	16	720	46
Dalton, Jed, Boise	.750	1	3	0	1	4	0
Dantzler, Eric, Bellingham	.917	3	10	1	1	12	1
DaSilva, Manny, S. Oregon	1.000	12	91	15	0	106	6
Daugherty, Keith, Eugene	.941	2	14	2	1	17	2
DRIZOS, Justin, Portland*	.992	71	668	45	6	719	57
Felix, Pedro, Bellingham	1.000	4	19	0	0	19	2
Filchner, Duane, S. Oregon*	.950	3	17	2	1	20	1
Hacker, Steve, Eugene	.966	12	81	5	3	89	8
Hallmark, Patrick, Spokane	1.000	2	18	2	0	20	4
Harmon, Brian, Yakima	.958	4	22	1	1	24	6
Klostermeyer, Mike, S. Oregon*	.989	57	474	45	6	525	28
Malave, Joshua, Yakima	.981	14	94	8	2	104	7
McAninch, John, Boise	.986	11	65	4	1	70	9
Moreno, Victor, Spokane	1.000	3	14	2	0	16	1
Paulin, Randy, Spokane	.986	14	129	15	2	146	18
Person, Wilton, Eugene	.980	50	423	27	9	459	27
Pinoni, Scott, Spokane	.979	4	46	1	1	48	0
Pomierski, Joe, Everett	.985	58	486	42	8	536	38
Rasmussen, Nate, Yakima*	.975	40	292	16	8	316	15

Player, Team	Pct.	G	PO	A	E	TC	DP
Rondon, Alex, S. Oregon	.900	2	8	1	1	10	1
Slemmer, David, S. Oregon	1.000	2	11	3	0	14	2
Spiegel, Rich, Eugene	1.000	1	2	1	0	3	0
Tinoco, Luis, Everett	1.000	4	8	0	0	8	1
Tocco, Todd, Eugene	.987	29	145	12	2	159	8
Tucker, Jonathan, Yakima*	.979	38	302	26	7	335	22
Twist, Jeffrey, Portland	.986	8	62	6	1	69	4
Valenti, Jon, Southern Oregon	.977	16	117	11	3	131	11
Vandergriend, Jon, Boise	.993	16	131	11	1	143	14
Vickers, Randy, Everett	.990	13	94	8	1	103	10
Vida, James, Spokane*	.987	57	545	42	8	595	46
Wathan, Dusty, Everett	.973	7	68	3	2	73	4

SECOND BASEMEN

Player, Team	Pct.	G	PO	A	E	TC	DP
Amado, Jose, Everett	.875	4	6	8	2	16	2
Backowski, Lance, Yakima	.947	16	26	46	4	76	11
Betten, Randy, Boise	.833	2	1	4	1	6	0
Carpentier, Mike, Yakima	.959	11	25	45	3	73	7
Cruz, Michael, Bellingham	1.000	6	8	11	0	19	0
Davalillo, David, Boise	.950	24	33	62	5	100	13
Durrington, Trent, Boise	.979	37	52	90	3	145	19
Elam, Brett, Portland	.952	4	3	17	1	21	3
Ellison, Skeeter, Eugene	1.000	4	3	4	0	7	0
Griffin, Chad, Everett	.911	20	20	31	5	56	4
Groseclose, Harold, Portland	1.000	4	7	16	0	23	4

Player, Team	Pct.	G	PO	A	E	TC	DP
Harris, Robert, S. Oregon	.936	39	47	99	10	156	14
Hines, Pooh, Eugene	.954	29	42	61	5	108	10
Hodges, Randy, Eugene	.957	46	88	111	9	208	22
Lewis, Dwayne, Spokane	.892	13	27	39	8	74	6
Mayber, Chan, Portland	.966	17	32	52	3	87	15
Moschetti, Mike, So. Oregon	.931	29	45	89	10	144	12
Mota, Alfonso, Boise	1.000	9	7	11	0	18	0
Nations, Joel, Spokane	.971	37	67	103	5	175	23
Pena, Elvis, Portland	.954	52	92	137	11	240	24
Prospero, Teodoro, Bellingham	.944	36	65	88	9	162	16
RAMIREZ, Joel, Everett	.959		142	163	13	318	36
Schafer, Brett, Spokane	.945	28	63	74	8	145	21
Slemmer, David, S. Oregon	.964	13	19	35	2	56	8
Sosa, Juan, Yakima	.9586	51	85	147	10	242	23
Taylor, Matthew, Eugene	1.000	6	10	16	0	26	3
Vallone, Gar, Boise	.987	21	29	46	1	76	14
Vickers, Randy, Everett	.500	3	1	0	1	2	0
Watson, Jonathan, Bellingham	.968	44	92	122	7	221	24
Whitley, Bill, Portland	1.000	4	9	15	0	24	4

THIRD BASEMEN

Player, Team	Pct.	G	PO	A	E	TC	DP
Amado, Jose, Everett	.919	44	44	104	13	161	14
Backowski, Lance, Yakima	.913	16	5	37	4	46	2
CRUZ, Deivi, Bellingham	.941	54	47	113	10	170	12
Dalton, Jed, Boise	.667	2	0	2	1	3	0
DaSilva, Manny, S. Oregon	.833	4	2	8	2	12	1
Davalillo, David, Boise	1.000	10	7	16	0	23	1
Elam, Brett, Portland	.914	14	9	23	3	35	3
Escandon, Emiliano, Spokane	.667	2	2	2	2	6	0
Felix, Pedro, Bellingham	.960	25	11	37	2	50	4
Griffin, Chad, Everett	1.000	4	1	6	0	7	1
Gross, Rafael, Yakima	.926	40	28	97	10	135	5
Harris, Robert, S. Oregon	.929	15	7	32	3	42	1
Hines, Pooh, Eugene	1.000	1	0	3	0	3	0
Hodges, Randy, Eugene	.800	10	6	10	4	20	1
Kane, Ryan, Boise	.917	69	42	135	16	193	19
Malave, Joshua, Yakima	.854	23	10	31	7	48	2
Mayber, Chan, Portland	.962	9	6	19	1	26	0
Myers, Aaron, Portland	.914	51	28	89	11	128	8
Pomierski, Joe, Everett	1.000	1	0	2	0	2	0
Quinn, Mark, Spokane	.837	13	8	33	8	49	3
Reynolds, Paul, Portland	.893	16	9	16	3	28	0
Roland, William, Spokane	.932	58	30	149	13	192	14
Rust, Brian, Eugene	.841	51	26	80	20	126	9
Sasser, Rob, Eugene	.833	4	3	7	2	12	0
Schafer, Brett, Spokane	.882	6	3	12	2	17	1
Slemmer, David, S. Oregon	.927	51	37	116	12	165	7
Sosa, Juan, Yakima	.810	7	3	14	4	21	1
Thomasson, Shane, Everett	.625	5	0	5	3	8	0
Tocco, Todd, Eugene	.846	28	14	52	12	78	3
Valenti, Jon, Southern Oregon	.942	16	11	38	3	52	1
Vickers, Randy, Everett	.874	32	20	70	13	103	6
Watson, Jonathan, Bellingham	.727	7	0	8	3	11	0

SHORTSTOPS

Player, Team	Pct.	G	PO	A	E	TC	DP
Baughman, Justin, Boise	.915	57	68	157	21	246	36
Carpentier, Mike, Yakima	.929	41	53	117	13	183	21
Cuevas, Trent, Yakima	.917	35	46	98	13	157	17
Durrington, Trent, Boise	.904	12	18	29	5	52	3
Elam, Brett, Portland	.909	15	14	56	7	77	11
Escandon, Emiliano, Spokane	.965	10	21	34	2	57	6
Groseclose, Harold, Portland	1.000	1	2	4	0	6	1
Harris, Robert, S. Oregon	.800	4	2	10	3	15	2
Hines, Pooh, Eugene	.881	12	23	29	7	59	4
Lewis, Dwayne, Spokane	.907	9	10	39	5	54	8
Mayber, Chan, Portland	.875	1	3	4	1	8	1
MELITO, Mark, Spokane	.967	61	100	189	10	299	36
Nathan, Joe, Bellingham	.897	54	76	150	26	252	23
Ramirez, Joel, Everett	.917	9	5	17	2	24	1
Rust, Brian, Eugene	1.000	2	0	1	0	1	0
Sasser, Rob, Eugene	.890	54	71	164	29	264	21
Sheffer, Chad, Everett	.948	53	81	139	12	232	19
Slemmer, David, S. Oregon	1.000	4	3	9	0	12	1
Sosa, Juan, Yakima	.900	3	5	13	2	20	2
Taylor, Matthew, Eugene	.952	4	10	10	1	21	4
Tejada, Miguel, S. Oregon	.930	72	129	214	26	369	39
Thomasson, Shane, Everett	.936	28	40	62	7	109	6
Vallone, Gar, Boise	.974	14	16	21	1	38	1
Weaver, Terry, Bellingham	.907	24	31	57	9	97	8
Whitley, Bill, Portland	.942	58	83	210	18	311	40
Williams, Glenn, Eugene	.905	9	15	23	4	42	5

OUTFIELDERS

Player, Team	Pct.	G	PO	A	E	TC	DP
BILDERBACK, Ty, Boise*	1.000	58	73	2	0	75	0
Bray, Notorris, Bellingham	1.000	1	3	0	0	3	0
Brown, Roosevelt, Eugene	.857	44	45	3	8	56	0
Bryan, Leonardo, Boise	.909	36	34	6	4	44	0
Brzozoski, Marc, Portland	.971	52	63	4	2	69	0
Burrows, Mike, Everett*	.992	67	127	4	1	132	1
Calderon, Ricardo, Bellingham*	.942	52	92	6	6	104	0
Choi, Kyung, Boise*	.920	20	22	1	2	25	0
Christenson, Ryan, S. Oregon	.978	48	84	3	2	89	1
Corujo, Rey, Bellingham	.946	35	49	4	3	56	0
Cruz, Jose, Everett	1.000	3	7	0	0	7	0
Dalton, Jed, Boise	.970	33	30	2	1	33	0
Davanon, Jeff, S. Oregon	.864	40	47	4	8	59	0
DeLeon, Reymundo, Eugene	.878	46	62	3	9	74	0
Ellison, Skeeter, Eugene	1.000	7	8	0	0	8	0
Feuerstein, David, Portland	.974	64	104	8	3	115	3
Filchner, Duane, S. Oregon*	.988	56	81	4	1	86	2
Finnieston, Adam, Spokane	.947	9	15	3	1	19	1
Frazier, Tyrone, Spokane	.963	50	73	4	3	80	1
Gibbs, Kevin, Yakima	.973	36	71	1	2	74	0
Granzow, Judd, Yakima	.944	36	47	4	3	54	3
Gross, Rafael, Yakima	1.000	1	1	0	0	1	0
Hallead, John, Portland*	.955	38	80	4	4	88	1
Ham, Kevin, Boise	.966	59	77	9	3	89	1
Heams, Shane, Everett	.895	22	13	4	2	19	0
Hernaiz, Juan, Yakima	.914	39	52	1	5	58	0
Hilo, Johnny, Yakima	.974	40	72	3	2	77	0
Hodges, Randy, Eugene	.667	5	2	0	1	3	0
Hutchins, Norm, Boise*	.979	45	92	3	2	97	0
Jimenez, Elvis, Portland	.971	27	32	2	1	35	0
Keifer, Greg, Bellingham	.833	6	9	1	2	12	0
Klostermeyer, Mike, S. Oregon*	1.000	1	1	0	0	1	0
Knight, Bill, Southern Oregon	.926	45	60	3	5	68	0
Kortmeyer, Scott, Spokane	.941	21	30	2	2	34	0
Lewis, Dwayne, Spokane	.971	22	33	0	1	34	0
Lombard, George, Eugene	.962	65	71	5	3	79	2
McClain, Terrance, Yakima	.923	21	30	6	3	39	1
Miranda, Tony, Boise	.980	60	94	3	2	99	0
Morales, Julio, Bellingham	.953	64	138	5	7	150	1
Moreno, Victor, Spokane	1.000	5	6	1	0	7	0
Morimoto, Ken, Yakima	.982	48	107	3	2	112	0
Neubart, Garrett, Portland	1.000	23	39	2	0	41	1
Newhan, David, S. Oregon	.964	39	50	4	2	56	0
Owen, Andy, Portland*	.978	34	39	5	1	45	0
Person, Wilton, Eugene	1.000	10	9	0	0	9	0
Quinn, Mark, Spokane	.963	19	24	2	1	27	0
Rand, Ian, Bellingham	.962	22	25	0	1	26	0
Reynolds, Paul, Portland	.957	25	18	4	1	23	1
Sachse, Matthew, Everett*	.978	50	85	3	2	90	1
Saturnino, Sherton, Eugene	.778	6	7	0	2	9	0
Schafer, Brett, Spokane	.968	29	59	1	2	62	1
Shy, Jason, Eugene	.955	12	21	0	1	22	0
Simonton, Cy Leon, Everett*	.971	45	61	6	2	69	0
Thompson, Bruce, Bellingham	.952	64	96	3	5	104	0
Tinoco, Luis, Everett	.937	58	67	7	5	79	2
Trippy, Joe, Eugene*	.970	74	126	5	4	135	0
Valenti, Jon, Southern Oregon	1.000	2	1	0	0	1	0
Vandergriend, Jon, Boise	1.000	19	30	3	0	33	0
Vickers, Randy, Everett	1.000	10	9	2	0	11	0
Weathersby, Leon, Spokane	.961	34	45	4	2	51	0
Welch, Brandon, S. Oregon	.912	26	30	1	3	34	0

CATCHERS

Player, Team	Pct.	G	PO	A	E	TC	DP	PB
Alzualde, Daniel, Boise	.988	21	146	18	2	166	1	2
Ardoin, Danny, S. Oregon	.971	57	402	61	14	477	0	13
Arias, Rogelio, Portland	.990	13	92	11	1	104	1	8
Barthol, Blake, Portland	.986	47	333	26	5	364	2	12
DaSilva, Manny, S. Oregon	.964	16	99	9	4	112	1	6
Foote, Derek, Eugene	1.000	1	1	0	0	1	0	0
Graves, Bryan, Boise	.969	27	117	8	4	129	1	3
Hallmark, Patrick, Spokane	.970	51	334	51	12	397	2	20
Lunar, Fernando, Eugene	.977	37	298	41	8	347	2	7
Mahoney, Mike, Eugene	.981	41	265	38	6	309	3	13
Malave, Joshua, Yakima	1.000	3	1	0	0	1	0	0
Markert, Jason, Yakima	.994	30	156	15	1	172	2	1
McAninch, John, Boise	.993	20	117	20	1	138	0	1
Medrano, Teodoro, Everett	1.000	1	8	2	0	10	0	0
Meskauskas, John, Portland	1.000	7	57	6	0	63	0	2
Meyer, Travis, Yakima	.982	32	147	19	3	169	1	12
Norton, Andy, Bellingham	.970	24	136	23	5	164	1	5
Paulin, Randy, Spokane	.973	24	172	10	5	187	2	4

Player, Team	Pct.	G	PO	A	E	TC	DP	PB
Robles, Juan, Spokane	1.000	4	27	3	0	30	0	1
Rondon, Alex, S. Oregon	.938	10	54	7	4	65	0	3
Shy, Jason, Eugene	.933	9	40	2	3	45	0	2
Spiegel, Rich, Eugene	1.000	4	24	3	0	27	2	1
Thompson, Karl, Everett	.997	37	275	28	1	304	2	10
TOPPING, Dan, Bellingham	.988	47	291	46	4	341	2	10
Torrealba, Yolvit, Bellingham	.973	26	152	26	5	183	1	6
Twist, Jeffrey, Portland	.961	14	91	8	4	103	0	5
Wagner, Kyle, Boise	.996	36	221	27	1	249	1	1
Walkanoff, A.J., Yakima	.986	36	241	31	4	276	6	8
Wathan, Dusty, Everett	.984	41	307	53	6	366	4	12

PITCHERS

Player, Team	Pct.	G	PO	A	E	TC	DP
Abbott, Todd, S. Oregon	1.000	17	2	7	0	9	1
Abreu, Jose, Bellingham	.667	13	0	2	1	3	1
Adam, Justin, Spokane	.706	15	8	4	5	17	1
Agosto, Stevenson, Boise*	.857	13	2	10	2	14	0
Albrecht, Jon, Spokane*	1.000	17	5	2	0	7	0
Ali, Sam, Bellingham	1.000	5	0	3	0	3	0
Alvarez, Juan, Boise*	1.000	9	1	1	0	2	0
Avila, Edwin, Boise	1.000	14	0	2	0	2	0
Babineaux, Darrin, Yakima	.941	12	8	8	1	17	0
BAILEY, Philip, Bellingham*	1.000	19	2	21	0	23	2
Barcelo, Lorenzo, Bellingham	1.000	12	2	6	0	8	0
Batchelder, Bill, S. Oregon	1.000	18	9	5	0	14	0
Bermudez, Manuel, Bellingham	.947	14	7	11	1	19	0
Bevel, Bobby, Portland*	1.000	25	1	7	0	8	0
Blasingim, Joseph, Bellingham	1.000	13	3	4	0	7	0
Blood, Darin, Bellingham	.955	14	7	14	1	22	1
Blythe, Billy, Eugene	1.000	14	9	11	0	20	1
Bost, Allen, Portland	1.000	10	2	2	0	4	0
Brester, Jason, Bellingham*	1.000	8	1	5	0	6	0
Brizek, Seth, Everett	1.000	8	1	1	0	2	0
Brooks, Antone, Eugene*	.857	15	0	6	1	7	2
Brown, Darold, Eugene*	.900	3	1	8	1	10	0
Butler, Adam, Eugene*	1.000	23	1	1	0	2	0
Cervantes, Peter, Yakima	.800	13	10	6	4	20	1
Chambers, Scott, Yakima*	1.000	20	1	1	0	2	0
Charles, Israel, Spokane	1.000	4	1	1	0	2	0
Chrismon, Thad, Eugene	1.000	32	3	5	0	8	1
Clifford, Eric, Everett	1.000	28	3	9	0	12	1
Coe, Keith, Boise	.917	13	1	10	1	12	2
Connelly, Steven, S. Oregon	.889	17	4	4	1	9	0
Conway, Robert, Everett	.667	6	1	1	1	3	0
Cooper, Brian, Boise	.867	13	3	10	2	15	0
Cooper, David, Everett	.750	17	2	4	2	8	0
Coyle, Bryan, Yakima	.750	6	0	3	1	4	0
Cruz, Charlie, Eugene*	.962	15	6	19	1	26	0
Dafun, George, Boise	.842	16	6	10	3	19	0
D'Alessandro, Marc, Portland*	.971	16	11	23	1	35	1
Davis, Eddie, Yakima	1.000	20	3	8	0	11	0
Deakman, Josh, Boise	1.000	3	1	5	0	6	0
Dietrich, Jason, Portland	1.000	10	0	2	0	2	0
Emiliano, James, Portland	.889	28	4	4	1	9	0
Epstein, Ian, S. Oregon*	1.000	23	2	5	0	7	0
Farfan, David, Boise	1.000	14	1	4	0	5	0
Fontenot, Joe, Bellingham	.800	6	2	2	1	5	0
Foster, Kris, Yakima	.667	15	2	6	4	12	0
French, Jon, Southern Oregon	1.000	20	6	2	0	8	0
Garcia, Jose, Eugene	1.000	14	6	13	0	19	1
Gerland, Greg, Eugene*	1.000	19	2	8	0	10	1
Giard, Ken, Eugene	.857	25	1	5	1	7	0
Gonzalez, Laril, Portland	.929	15	2	11	1	14	0
Gryboski, Kevin, Everett	1.000	25	4	6	0	10	2
Gunther, Kevin, S. Oregon	1.000	5	2	2	0	4	0
Hilton, Will, Southern Oregon	.667	16	6	0	3	9	0
Hodge, Hal, Spokane*	.929	16	1	12	1	14	0
Holden, Jason, S. Oregon	.950	19	5	14	1	20	0
Hutzler, Jeff, Bellingham	1.000	7	4	6	0	10	2
Iddon, Brent, Everett	1.000	14	6	7	0	13	1
Judice, Bryan, Spokane	1.000	14	3	2	0	5	0
Kammerer, James, Portland*	1.000	11	2	11	0	13	1
Kaysner, Brent, Spokane	1.000	19	1	5	0	6	0
Keehn, Drew, Portland	.692	20	3	6	4	13	1
Keppen, Jeffrey, Yakima	.500	20	0	3	3	6	0
Kjos, Ryan, Southern Oregon	1.000	9	0	1	0	1	0
Knoll, Brian, Bellingham	.889	22	2	6	1	9	0

Player, Team	Pct.	G	PO	A	E	TC	DP
Kurtz, Danny, Everett	1.000	14	6	7	0	13	0
Leibee, Skye, Southern Oregon*	1.000	2	0	1	0	1	0
Lintern, Cory, Bellingham	1.000	3	4	4	0	8	0
Liz, Jesus, Spokane*	.500	9	0	1	1	2	0
Macca, Christopher, Portland	1.000	24	3	6	0	9	0
Marte, Damaso, Everett*	.714	11	3	7	4	14	1
Martin, Chandler, Portland	1.000	7	2	8	0	10	1
Masaoka, Onan, Yakima*	.750	15	1	5	2	8	0
Mayer, Aaron, Boise	.900	20	3	6	1	10	0
Mayhew, Keith, Eugene	1.000	24	1	9	0	10	1
Mazzone, Tony, Eugene	.875	25	3	4	1	8	1
McDonald, Matt, S. Oregon*	1.000	13	6	10	0	16	2
McKnight, Chris, Eugene*	.929	13	3	10	1	14	2
McMullen, Jerry, Eugene*	1.000	22	1	9	0	10	0
McNeely, Mitch, Yakima*	.889	24	4	12	2	18	0
McWilliams, Matt, Eugene	.923	24	3	9	1	13	1
Medero, Gadiel, Bellingham	.000	4	0	0	1	1	0
Mimnaugh, Scott, S. Oregon	.667	3	0	2	1	3	0
Mitchell, Kelvin, Everett*	.818	25	1	8	2	11	0
Mlodik, Kevin, S. Oregon	.813	20	8	5	3	16	1
Morrison, Chris, S. Oregon	1.000	6	4	3	0	7	0
Mosman, Marc, Bellingham	.750	12	3	0	1	4	0
Murphy, Sean, Portland	.938	21	7	8	1	16	2
Nelson, Chris, S. Oregon	.769	16	6	4	3	13	1
Newman, Damon, S. Oregon	.895	14	6	11	2	19	0
Nied, David, Portland	1.000	1	0	1	0	1	0
Niemeier, Todd, Everett*	1.000	15	2	14	0	16	0
O'Quinn, James, Boise*	.750	23	0	3	1	4	0
Ortiz, Russell, Bellingham	1.000	25	3	6	0	9	1
Pearsall, J.J., Yakima*	.846	20	5	6	2	13	0
Petri, Tom, Boise	1.000	10	1	3	0	4	0
Prihoda, Stephen, Spokane*	1.000	14	2	12	0	14	0
Randall, Scott, Portland	.912	15	11	20	3	34	1
Reitzenstein, Brad, Portland	1.000	7	0	3	0	3	0
Ritter, Jason, Spokane	1.000	10	3	5	0	8	1
Rivette, Scott, S. Oregon	1.000	9	1	3	0	4	0
Robbins, Mike, Spokane*	1.000	5	2	4	0	6	0
Rocker, John, Eugene*	.900	12	3	6	1	10	0
Rolish, Chad, S. Oregon*	.750	4	0	3	1	4	0
Romine, Jason, Portland	1.000	4	0	1	0	1	0
Rose, Brian, Portland	1.000	5	0	2	0	2	0
Ruskey, Jason, Everett*	1.000	3	1	1	0	2	0
Saier, Matthew, Spokane	1.000	16	3	2	0	5	0
Sanchez, Mike, Yakima	1.000	18	0	6	0	6	1
Sanders, Allen, Spokane	.909	14	2	8	1	11	0
Sanders, Craig, Spokane	1.000	22	3	7	0	10	0
Santiago, Jose, Spokane	.750	22	3	6	3	12	1
Scheer, Greg, Everett*	1.000	18	3	8	0	11	0
Scheffer, Aaron, Everett	.818	24	0	9	2	11	1
Scutero, Brian, Boise	.900	22	4	5	1	10	0
Silva, Luis, Southern Oregon	1.000	19	8	9	0	17	0
Soden, Chad, Everett*	1.000	13	4	8	0	12	1
Sosa, Helpis, S. Oregon	1.000	6	4	1	0	5	0
Soto, Daniel, Spokane	1.000	3	0	2	0	2	1
Soto, Seferino, Yakima	1.000	15	3	4	0	7	0
South, Carl, Yakima	.889	13	3	13	2	18	1
Stone, Ricky, Yakima	.778	16	3	4	2	9	1
Stoops, Jim, Bellingham	1.000	24	2	5	0	7	0
Sumter, Kevin, Boise	1.000	21	0	3	0	3	0
Szimanski, Tom, Everett	1.000	16	3	3	0	6	0
Takahashi, Kurt, Bellingham	1.000	17	2	2	0	4	0
Tapia, Elias, Yakima	.833	13	0	5	1	6	0
Thomas, Robbie, Yakima*	1.000	7	0	3	0	3	0
Thurmond, Travis, Boise	.952	16	7	13	1	21	0
Trawick, Tim, Everett	1.000	16	8	9	0	17	3
Tucker, Benjamin, Bellingham	1.000	11	2	4	0	6	1
Upchurch, Wayne, Spokane	1.000	7	1	1	0	2	0
Valdez, Ken, Boise	1.000	5	1	0	0	1	0
Vavrek, Mike, Portland*	.750	3	0	3	1	4	0
Vermillion, Grant, Boise	.857	30	2	10	2	14	0
Villarreal, Modesto, Spokane	.963	16	6	20	1	27	2
Vukson, John, Yakima	.500	11	0	1	1	2	0
Washburn, Jarrod, Boise*	1.000	8	0	6	0	6	0
Williamson, Jeremy, Spokane*	1.000	11	3	5	0	8	0
Winders, Brian, Spokane	1.000	2	0	1	0	1	0
Woodrow, James, Bellingham	.900	27	5	4	1	10	0
Wuestenhoefer, Brady, Portland	.909	14	3	7	1	11	0
Zedalis, Craig, Eugene	1.000	8	3	3	0	6	0

The following players did not have any fielding statistics at the positions indicated or appeared only as a designated hitter, pinch-hitter or pinch-runner: Backowski, of; Benner, dh; R. Brown, 2b; Bryan, c; Collett, p; Costello, p; Crossley, p; Davalillo, of; DeLaCruz, p; Ellison, 1b; Gomez, p; Griffin, ss; Heams, 3b; Herrera, p; Koehler, p; Lombard, c; Mayber, p; Meyer, of; Morimoto, ss; Mota, 3b, ss; Myers, 2b; Person, 3b, ss; Renko, p; J. Rodriguez, dh, ph; L. Rodriguez, p; Schiefelbein, p; Sheffer, 3b; Thomasson, 2b, of, p; Vallone, 3b; Vandergriend, c.

CLASS A *Northwest League*

Year	Team	Pct.	Year	Team	Pct.	Year	Team	Pct.
1901—	Portland	.675	1952—	Victoria	.631	1976—	Portland	.556
1902—	Butte	.608	1953—	Salem	.635		Walla Walla◆	.639
1903—	Butte	.578		Spokane*	.590	1977—	Bellingham■	.618
1904—	Boise	.625	1954—	Vancouver*	.636		Portland	.667
1905—	Vancouver	.586		Lewiston	.629	1978—	Grays Harbor▼	.671
	Everett*	.667	1955—	Salem	.646		Eugene	.514
1906—	Tacoma	.600		Eugene*	.639	1979—	Central Oregon◆	.606
1907—	Aberdeen	.625	1956—	Yakima	.691		Walla Walla	.571
1908—	Vancouver	.578		Yakima	.619	1980—	Bellingham•	.643
1909—	Seattle	.653	1957—	Eugene	.576		Eugene•	.529
1910—	Spokane	.596		Wenatchee*	.647	1981—	Medford◆	.600
1911—	Vancouver	.628	1958—	Lewiston	.621		Bellingham	.557
1912—	Seattle	.600		Yakima*	.594	1982—	Medford	.757
1913—	Vancouver	.600	1959—	Salem	.623		Salem◆	.486
1914—	Vancouver	.632		Yakima*	.563	1983—	Medford††	.735
1915—	Seattle	.564	1960—	Yakima	.638		Bellingham	.588
1916—	Spokane	.622		Yakima	.562	1984—	Tri-Cities††	.622
1917—	Great Falls	.592	1961—	Lewiston*	.621		Medford	.608
1918—	Seattle	.588		Yakima	.600	1985—	Everett††	.541
1919—	Seattle	.590	1962—	Wenatchee*	.574		Eugene	.541
1920—	Victoria	.600		Tri-City	.580	1986—	Bellingham††	.608
1921—	Yakima	.710	1963—	Lewiston	.594		Eugene	.608
	Yakima	.660		Yakima*	.613	1987—	Spokane▲	.711
1922—	Calgary‡	.600	1964—	Eugene	.636		Everett	.653
1923-36—	Did not operate.			Yakima*	.611	1988—	Southern Oregon	.605
1937—	Wenatchee	.603	1965—	Lewiston	.667		Spokane◆	.553
	Tacoma*	.627		Tri-City*	.681	1989—	Southern Oregon	.600
1938—	Yakima	.583	1966—	Tri-City	.679		Spokane◆	.547
	Bellingham (2nd)†	.511	1967—	Medford	.607	1990—	Boise	.697
1939—	Wenatchee	.601	1968—	Tri-City	.600		Spokane◆	.645
	Tacoma (2nd)†	.533	1969—	Rogue Valley	.633	1991—	Boise◆	.658
1940—	Spokane	.587	1970—	Lewiston§	.538		Yakima	.579
	Tacoma (4th)†	.500		Coos Bay-No. Bend	.563	1992—	Bellingham◆	.566
1941—	Spokane	.669	1971—	Tri-City§	.625		Bend	.566
1942—	Vancouver	.594		Bend	.538	1993—	Bellingham	.579
1943-45—	Did not operate.		1972—	Lewiston§	.675		Boise◆	.539
1946—	Wenatchee	.622		Walla Walla	.513	1994—	Yakima	.645
1947—	Vancouver	.566	1973—	Walla Walla∞	.638		Boise◆	.579
1948—	Spokane	.614		Portland	.563	1995—	Boise◆	.640
1949—	Yakima	.660	1974—	Bellingham	.619		Bellingham	.566
	Vancouver (2nd)†	.615		Eugene▲	.571			
1950—	Yakima	.613	1975—	Portland	.545			
1951—	Spokane	.655		Eugene◆	.684			

*Won split-season playoff. †Won four-club playoff. ‡League disbanded June 18. §League divided into Northern and Southern divisions, declared champion under league rules. ∞League divided into Eastern and Western divisions, declared champion under league rules. ▲League divided into Eastern and Western divisions; won two-team playoff. ◆League divided into North and South divisions; won two-team playoff. ■League divided into Affiliate and Independent divisions; won two-team playoff. ▼Declared league champion after winning one-game playoff. Balance of playoff canceled due to rain and wet grounds. •Declared co-champion after winning one game. Balance of playoff canceled due to rain and wet grounds. ††League divided into Washington and Oregon divisions; won two-team playoff. (NOTE—Known as Pacific Northwest League 1901-02, Pacific National League 1903-04, Northwestern League 1905-18, Pacific Coast International League 1919-22 and Western International League 1937-54.)

SOUTH ATLANTIC LEAGUE

LEAGUE OFFICE

President/secretary-treasurer
John Moss
Address
P.O. Box 38
Kings Mountain, NC 28086
Phone
704-739-3466

Teams (affiliation)
Asheville Tourists (Rockies)
Augusta Greenjackets (Pirates)
Capital City Bombers (Mets)
Charleston (S.C.) Riverdogs (Rangers)
Charleston (W.Va.) Alley Cats (Reds)
Columbus Redstixx (Indians)
Delmarva Shorebirds (Expos)

Fayetteville Generals (Tigers)
Greensboro Bats (Yankees)
Hagerstown Suns (Blue Jays)
Hickory Crawdads (White Sox)
Macon Braves (Braves)
Piedmont Bollweevils (Phillies)
Savannah Cardinals (Cardinals)

1995 FINAL STANDINGS

FIRST HALF

NORTHERN DIVISION

Team	W	L	T	Pct.	GB
Piedmont (Phillies)	45	25	0	.643	......
Fayetteville (Tigers)	42	27	0	.618	2
Hagerstown (Blue Jays)	36	33	0	.522	8 1/2
Greensboro (Yankees)	35	34	0	.507	9 1/2
Charleston (W.Va.) (Reds)	34	36	0	.486	11
Asheville (Rockies)	32	36	0	.471	12
Hickory (White Sox)	21	47	0	.309	23

SOUTHERN DIVISION

Team	W	L	T	Pct.	GB
Augusta (Pirates)	43	25	0	.627	......
Columbia (Mets)	38	32	0	.543	5 1/2
Columbus (Indians)	37	33	0	.522	7
Macon (Braves)	35	34	0	.507	8
Savannah (Cardinals)	32	37	0	.464	11
Albany (Expos)	31	39	0	.443	12 1/2
Charleston (SC) (Rangers)	24	47	0	.343	19 1/2

SECOND HALF

NORTHERN DIVISION

Team	W	L	T	Pct.	GB
Asheville (Rockies)	44	27	0	.620	......
Fayetteville (Tigers)	44	28	0	.611	1/2
Charleston (W.Va.) (Reds)	43	29	0	.597	1 1/2
Piedmont (Phillies)	37	33	0	.529	6 1/2
Hagerstown (Blue Jays)	37	35	0	.514	7 1/2
Greensboro (Yankees)	35	36	0	.493	9
Hickory (White Sox)	28	42	0	.400	15 1/2

SOUTHERN DIVISION

Team	W	L	T	Pct.	GB
Columbus (Indians)	43	29	0	.597	......
Macon (Braves)	36	36	0	.500	7
Columbia (Mets)	34	36	0	.486	8
Augusta (Pirates)	33	37	0	.471	9
Albany (Expos)	31	39	0	.443	11
Charleston (SC) (Rangers)	26	42	0	.382	15
Savannah (Cardinals)	24	46	0	.343	18

COMPOSITE

Team	Fay.	Pie.	C'us	Aug.	Ash.	CWV	Hag.	C'ia	Mac.	Gbr.	Alb.	Sav.	CSC	Hck.	W	L	T	Pct.	GB
Fayetteville (Tigers)	....	7	7	2	9	11	10	5	3	10	6	5	4	7	86	55	0	.610	......
Piedmont (Phillies)	7	....	3	4	8	9	8	5	4	8	5	7	2	12	82	58	0	.586	3 1/2
Columbus (Indians)	1	5	....	8	3	4	3	8	6	4	13	9	11	5	80	62	0	.563	6 1/2
Augusta (Pirates)	6	4	6	....	3	3	3	8	12	6	5	7	8	5	76	62	0	.551	8 1/2
Asheville (Rockies)	5	5	5	5	....	6	10	5	2	9	5	4	5	10	76	63	0	.547	9
Charleston (W.Va.) (Reds)	3	5	4	5	8	....	9	3	6	3	6	7	7	11	77	65	0	.542	9 1/2
Hagerstown (Blue Jays)	4	6	5	4	4	7	....	6	5	10	4	6	4	8	73	68	0	.518	13
Columbia (Mets)	3	5	6	6	3	5	2	....	6	5	6	8	15	2	72	68	0	.514	13 1/2
Macon (Braves)	5	4	8	4	6	2	3	8	....	6	8	2	9	6	71	70	0	.504	15
Greensboro (Yankees)	6	6	4	2	4	11	4	2	2	....	6	7	4	12	70	70	0	.500	15 1/2
Albany (Expos)	2	3	3	9	3	2	4	7	6	2	....	10	7	4	62	78	0	.443	23 1/2
Savannah (Cardinals)	3	1	5	6	4	1	2	6	11	1	4	....	9	3	56	83	0	.403	29
Charleston (SC) (Rangers)	4	1	3	4	3	1	4	3	5	4	7	7	....	4	50	89	0	.360	35
Hickory (White Sox)	6	6	3	3	5	3	6	2	2	2	3	4	4	....	49	89	0	.355	35 1/2

Major league affiliations in parentheses.

PLAYOFFS: Augusta defeated Columbus, two games to none; Piedmont defeated Asheville, two games to one; Augusta defeated Piedmont, three games to none, to win league championship.

REGULAR-SEASON ATTENDANCE: Albany, 91,289; Asheville, 138,148; Augusta, 171,166; Charleston (S.C.), 101,280; Charleston (W.Va.), 106,530; Columbia, 152,207; Columbus, 128,816; Fayetteville, 121,051; Greensboro, 170,444; Hagerstown, 113,438; Hickory, 265,017; Macon, 113,825; Piedmont, 115,649; Savannah, 113,849. Total—1,902,709. Playoffs (8 games)—15,267. All-Star Game at Albany—4,102.

MANAGERS: Albany, Doug Sisson; Asheville, Bill McGuire; Augusta, Jeff Banister; Charleston (S.C.), Mike Berger; Charleston (W.Va.), Razor Shines; Columbia, Howie Freiling; Columbus, Jeff Datz; Fayetteville, Dwight Lowry; Greensboro, Trey Hillman; Hagerstown, Omar Malave; Hickory, Mike Rojas; Macon, Nelson Norman; Piedmont, Roy Majtyka; Savannah, Scott Melvin.

ALL-STAR TEAM: 1B—Daryle Ward, Fayetteville; 2B—Julio Zorrilla, Columbia; 3B—Wes Helms, Macon; SS—Hiram Bocachica, Albany; Utility IF—Dan Donato, Greensboro; OF—Derrick Gibson, Asheville; Vladimir Guerrero, Albany; Andruw Jones, Macon; Utility OF—Gus Kennedy, Macon; C—Julio Mosquera, Hagerstown; DH—Jeff Ladd, Hagerstown; RHP—Brent Crowther, Asheville; LHP—Larry Wimberly, Piedmont; Most Valuable Player—Andruw Jones, Macon; Most Outstanding Pitcher—Larry Wimberly, Piedmont; Most Outstanding Major League Prospect—Andruw Jones, Macon; Manager of the Year—Roy Majtyka, Piedmont.

1995 BATTING

TEAM

Team	Avg.	G	TPA	AB	R	H	TB	2B	3B	HR	RBI	SH	SF	HP	BB	IBB	SO	SB	CS	GDP	LOB	ShO	Slg.	OBP
Augusta	.256	138	5070	4531	628	1158	1579	203	37	48	539	33	32	60	411	23	940	215	108	74	871	11	.348	.324
Hagerstown	.255	141	5293	4678	638	1191	1788	244	34	95	557	29	34	90	461	15	1173	100	56	95	1014	7	.382	.331
Columbus	.254	142	5343	4748	630	1207	1797	221	45	93	551	31	32	50	480	24	918	134	65	102	1016	5	.378	.327
Albany	.254	140	5415	4757	633	1206	1743	251	44	66	550	23	39	84	510	24	1099	136	105	75	1026	7	.366	.334

Team	Avg.	G	TPA	AB	R	H	TB	2B	3B	HR	RBI	SH	SF	HP	BB	IBB	SO	SB	CS	GDP	LOB	ShO	Slg.	OBP
Fayetteville	.252	141	5270	4633	660	1169	1718	234	30	85	585	37	38	73	489	15	1025	158	79	84	955	6	.371	.331
Piedmont	.249	140	5307	4595	683	1146	1601	213	46	50	573	54	49	89	519	23	938	123	75	106	996	9	.348	.334
Greensboro	.249	140	5284	4632	645	1154	1687	223	26	86	557	49	28	49	525	30	1077	127	80	108	972	11	.364	.330
Charleston (W.Va.)	.249	142	5208	4551	633	1133	1588	206	57	45	549	44	41	56	513	17	1002	230	101	82	961	12	.349	.330
Macon	.245	141	5579	4876	739	1197	1871	231	31	127	651	24	34	73	571	26	1225	172	54	79	1030	7	.384	.331
Asheville	.243	139	5067	4477	578	1086	1587	210	24	81	488	45	37	65	438	19	928	130	82	78	876	9	.354	.317
Columbia	.241	140	5156	4619	571	1111	1581	183	34	73	481	54	36	57	387	27	1118	187	85	86	889	12	.342	.305
Charleston (S.C.)	.234	139	5147	4509	546	1054	1452	220	20	46	450	39	45	40	514	14	939	218	135	64	932	9	.322	.315
Hickory	.227	138	5061	4538	459	1030	1457	198	29	57	387	28	27	71	397	14	1047	118	101	92	883	13	.321	.298
Savannah	.215	139	5214	4534	448	977	1321	188	36	50	362	46	29	60	544	18	1243	124	71	102	1036	16	.291	.306

INDIVIDUAL
TOP QUALIFIERS FOR BATTING CHAMPIONSHIP
Minimum 383 plate appearances. *Lefthanded batter. †Switch-hitter.

Player, Team	Avg.	G	TPA	AB	R	H	TB	2B	3B	HR	RBI	SH	SF	HP	BB	IBB	SO	SB	CS	GDP	Slg.	OBP
Guerrero, Vladimir, Albany	.333	110	464	421	77	140	229	21	10	16	63	0	4	7	30	3	45	12	7	8	.544	.383
Fullmer, Brad, Albany*	.323	123	527	468	69	151	221	38	4	8	67	0	6	17	36	4	33	10	10	9	.472	.387
Donato, Dan, Greensboro*	.318	108	431	387	55	123	176	30	1	7	69	0	3	4	37	5	46	7	6	12	.455	.381
White, Eric, Columbus	.317	112	423	369	49	117	165	24	3	6	46	1	1	1	51	5	45	11	7	12	.447	.400
Ladd, Jeff, Hagerstown	.305	94	401	311	54	95	175	17	3	19	58	0	3	9	78	5	94	6	3	2	.563	.454
Tatis, Fernando, Cha. (S.C.)†	.303	131	556	499	74	151	247	43	4	15	84	1	4	7	45	4	94	22	19	5	.495	.366
Hall, Ronnie, Asheville	.299	130	518	448	64	134	174	20	4	4	46	1	4	17	44	4	78	26	13	7	.388	.380
Millan, Adam, Piedmont	.294	107	449	394	69	116	175	25	2	10	64	1	3	7	44	3	45	1	4	15	.444	.373
Rivers, Jonathon, Hagerstown	.294	123	480	429	54	126	172	16	6	6	48	1	4	6	40	0	104	18	5	9	.401	.359
Gibson, Derrick, Asheville	.292	135	561	506	91	148	280	16	10	32	115	1	6	19	29	5	136	31	13	10	.553	.350
Staton, T.J., Augusta*	.292	112	421	391	43	114	160	21	5	5	53	0	1	2	27	5	97	27	13	6	.409	.340
Northeimer, Jamie, Piedmont	.291	115	471	392	56	114	149	24	4	1	54	4	2	20	53	1	72	9	4	13	.380	.400
Mosquera, Julio, Hagerstown	.291	108	456	406	64	118	159	22	5	3	46	3	5	13	29	2	53	5	5	13	.392	.353
Cardenas, Epi, Columbus	.290	125	556	513	69	149	206	28	4	7	56	6	5	2	30	0	64	11	7	4	.402	.329
Darr, Mike, Fayetteville*	.289	112	463	395	58	114	154	21	2	5	66	0	6	4	58	2	88	5	2	5	.390	.380
Glass, Chip, Columbus*	.289	115	449	402	70	116	158	17	5	5	45	5	0	5	37	1	47	37	8	5	.393	.356

DEPARTMENTAL LEADERS: G—A. Jones, Morrow, 139; AB—Helms, 539; R—A. Jones, 104; H—Fulmer, Tatis, 151; TB—Gibson, 280; 2B—Tatis, 43; 3B—Guiliano, 12; HR—Gibson, R. Wright, 32; RBI—Gibson, 115; SH—Lobaton, 11; SF—A. Jones, 9; HP—Northeimer, 20; BB—Kennedy, 95; IBB—Ward, 11; SO—Schwab, 173; SB—A. Jones, 56; CS—Rutz, 26; GIDP—Friedrich, 16; Slg.—Ladd, .563; OBP—Ladd, .454.

ALL PLAYERS
*Lefthanded batter. †Switch-hitter.

Player, Team	Avg.	G	TPA	AB	R	H	TB	2B	3B	HR	RBI	SH	SF	HP	BB	IBB	SO	SB	CS	GDP	Slg.	OBP
Abell, Tony, Savannah	.122	17	55	49	1	6	7	1	0	0	2	1	0	1	4	0	18	1	1	0	.143	.204
Acosta, Ed, Albany	.152	51	122	105	9	16	17	1	0	0	9	2	2	5	8	0	30	1	3	2	.162	.242
Adolfo, Carlos, Albany	.243	57	234	214	31	52	87	13	5	4	33	1	0	2	17	0	65	5	6	4	.407	.305
Afenir, Tom, Columbus	.077	5	13	13	1	1	1	0	0	0	0	0	0	0	0	0	5	0	0	1	.077	.077
Aguila, Hector, Cha. (S.C.)	.152	13	39	33	4	5	6	1	0	0	3	1	0	0	5	0	13	0	1	2	.182	.263
Albert, Rashad, Hickory	.213	88	366	328	34	70	105	16	2	5	20	4	1	14	19	1	108	22	12	4	.320	.285
Alderman, Kurt, Albany*	.248	55	173	161	21	40	56	8	1	2	17	0	0	1	11	0	40	2	1	1	.348	.301
Allen, Marlon, Cha. (W.Va.)	.270	117	457	396	47	107	160	26	0	9	76	0	6	13	42	3	108	2	2	10	.404	.354
Almanzar, Richard, Fayetteville*	.247	80	353	308	47	76	90	12	1	0	16	9	0	7	29	0	32	39	15	5	.292	.326
Almond, Greg, Savannah	.161	18	65	56	2	9	11	2	0	0	3	0	0	1	8	0	16	0	1	0	.196	.277
Amador, Manny, Piedmont†	.000	1	5	4	0	0	0	0	0	0	0	0	0	1	0	0	0	0	0	1	.000	.200
Ambrosina, Pete, Savannah†	.239	129	550	464	55	111	128	10	2	1	36	4	2	11	69	3	100	20	12	6	.276	.350
Antczak, Chuck, Hickory	.200	6	5	5	0	1	1	0	0	0	1	0	0	0	0	0	2	0	0	0	.200	.200
Arias, Rogelio, Asheville	.160	67	227	213	9	34	38	4	0	0	4	6	0	1	7	0	25	0	3	2	.178	.190
Arvelo, Tom, Columbia†	.125	8	19	16	4	2	2	0	0	0	0	0	0	0	3	0	7	2	0	0	.125	.263
Asche, Mike, Augusta	.266	106	423	376	62	100	147	17	6	6	59	3	3	5	35	1	60	21	5	6	.391	.334
Ashby, Chris, Greensboro	.274	88	359	288	45	79	131	23	1	9	45	2	2	6	61	2	68	3	3	9	.455	.409
Balfe, Ryan, Fayetteville†	.261	113	456	398	53	104	158	20	2	10	49	0	1	9	48	0	85	1	1	11	.397	.353
Balint, Rob, Fayetteville	.242	13	34	33	4	8	13	2	0	1	4	0	0	0	1	0	15	0	0	0	.394	.265
Barkett, Andy, Cha. (S.C.)*	.218	21	91	78	7	17	23	6	0	0	12	0	3	0	10	0	21	0	0	3	.295	.297
Bass, Jayson, Fayetteville*	.215	108	410	368	47	79	136	15	6	10	48	1	1	3	37	1	111	14	3	3	.370	.291
Bearden, Doug, Hickory	.156	44	149	141	9	22	35	5	1	2	12	2	0	1	5	1	44	1	1	6	.248	.190
Beeney, Ryan, Greensboro	.278	57	265	227	32	63	69	6	0	0	21	2	3	4	29	0	48	9	8	3	.304	.365
Bocachica, Hiram, Albany	.284	96	444	380	65	108	154	20	10	2	30	3	1	8	52	3	78	47	17	4	.405	.381
Boka, Ben, Columbia	.083	8	14	12	1	1	1	0	0	0	0	1	0	1	0	0	4	0	0	1	.083	.143
Borel, Jamie, Fayetteville	.244	86	325	279	60	68	83	9	3	0	20	1	2	2	41	0	43	36	14	2	.297	.343
Bowen, Glenn, Savannah	.231	16	52	52	1	12	15	3	0	0	2	0	0	0	0	0	17	0	1	0	.288	.231
Bragga, Matt, Cha. (W.Va.)*	.248	88	293	258	35	64	85	11	5	0	26	0	3	4	28	2	62	6	5	2	.329	.326
Branyan, Russell, Columbus†	.256	76	310	277	46	71	148	8	6	19	55	0	3	3	27	2	120	1	1	5	.534	.326
Brewer, Brett, Macon	.241	128	530	452	78	109	174	25	8	8	60	3	5	10	60	0	113	15	5	6	.385	.340
Brinkley, Josh, Albany	.174	22	75	69	8	12	18	3	0	1	5	0	0	3	5	0	11	2	2	1	.261	.240
Brooks, Eddie, Macon	.273	67	272	238	40	65	94	13	5	2	37	2	3	1	28	0	61	3	5	2	.395	.348
Brown, Adrian, Augusta†	.300	76	326	287	64	86	121	15	4	4	31	3	2	1	33	0	23	25	14	2	.422	.372
Brown, Nate, Albany*	.254	117	441	397	34	101	142	23	3	4	49	4	3	5	32	1	112	4	8	6	.358	.316
Brown, Ray, Cha. (W.Va.)*	.118	6	21	17	3	2	3	1	0	0	0	0	0	0	4	0	3	0	0	0	.176	.286
Brown, Vick, Greensboro	.227	118	491	432	66	98	116	10	1	2	36	8	1	6	44	0	93	24	9	11	.269	.306
Brunson, Matt, Fayetteville†	.222	43	168	144	18	32	44	3	3	1	8	1	0	1	22	0	34	16	6	1	.306	.329
Buchanan, Brian, Greensboro	.302	23	106	96	19	29	41	3	0	3	12	0	0	1	9	1	17	7	1	1	.427	.368
Camilli, Jason, Albany	.188	53	224	181	28	34	48	5	0	3	16	0	2	3	38	0	50	13	10	0	.265	.335
Cancel, David, Hickory†	.288	76	254	240	24	69	82	3	2	2	13	2	1	0	11	0	37	11	10	3	.342	.317
Cardenas, Epi, Columbus	.290	125	556	513	69	149	206	28	4	7	56	6	5	2	30	0	64	11	7	4	.402	.329
Cardona, Javier, Fayetteville	.206	52	179	165	18	34	51	8	0	3	15	2	1	0	13	0	30	1	0	5	.309	.268
Carpenter, Matt, Ash.-C'bus	.143	11	30	28	2	4	9	2	0	1	6	0	0	1	1	0	4	0	0	0	.321	.200

Player, Team	Avg.	G	TPA	AB	R	H	TB	2B	3B	HR	RBI	SH	SF	HP	BB	IBB	SO	SB	CS	GDP	Slg.	OBP
Carranza, Pete, Asheville	.254	111	488	433	67	110	161	32	2	5	29	2	5	3	45	2	49	10	9	4	.372	.325
Caruthers, Clayton, Cha. (W.Va.)†	.000	29	0	0	1	0	0	0	0	0	0	0	0	0	0	0	0	0	0	0	.000	.000
Carvajal, Jhonny, Cha. (W.Va.)	.263	135	558	486	78	128	156	18	5	0	42	4	4	6	58	0	77	44	19	4	.321	.347
Chambers, Mack, Columbus	.000	2	5	4	0	0	0	0	0	0	0	0	0	0	1	0	1	0	1	0	.000	.200
Chapman, Eric, Columbus	.241	54	220	199	27	48	63	9	3	0	8	2	0	0	19	1	42	23	6	4	.317	.307
Coach, Calvin, Savannah*	.197	65	241	218	15	43	47	2	1	0	10	2	0	1	20	1	58	8	4	3	.216	.268
Collum, Gary, Columbia	.250	9	28	24	2	6	8	0	1	0	7	0	2	0	2	0	7	2	0	0	.333	.286
Colombino, Carlo, Columbus	.000	1	2	2	0	0	0	0	0	0	0	0	0	0	0	0	1	0	0	0	.000	.000
Comeaux, Edward, Cha. (S.C.)	.210	90	290	243	38	51	60	7	1	0	19	3	3	2	39	0	58	10	7	3	.247	.321
Conner, Decomba, Cha. (W.Va.)	.263	91	360	308	55	81	120	10	7	5	40	4	6	3	39	1	77	22	5	6	.390	.346
Cooney, James, Cha. (S.C.)	.087	18	49	46	2	4	7	0	0	1	2	0	0	0	3	0	14	1	0	1	.152	.143
Cooper, Steve, Savannah	.250	48	180	156	13	39	46	7	0	0	12	0	1	1	22	0	51	2	0	4	.295	.344
Coquillette, Trace, Albany	.269	128	541	458	67	123	167	27	4	3	57	4	6	9	64	2	91	17	16	8	.365	.365
Cossins, Tim, Cha. (S.C.)	.203	22	69	59	8	12	20	5	0	1	8	0	0	1	9	0	13	2	0	2	.339	.319
Darr, Mike, Fayetteville*	.289	112	463	395	58	114	154	21	2	5	66	0	6	4	58	2	88	5	2	5	.390	.380
Dawson, Charles, Macon	.246	42	142	122	19	30	45	6	0	3	13	0	2	0	18	0	27	1	0	3	.369	.338
DeBerry, Joe, Greensboro*	.400	12	54	45	14	18	36	3	0	5	11	0	0	0	9	3	6	0	0	1	.800	.500
Delafield, Wil, Greensboro	.208	107	407	384	37	80	106	14	0	4	29	5	1	1	16	0	107	3	7	12	.276	.241
Delgado, Jose, Macon†	.237	45	186	169	19	40	60	5	3	3	16	4	2	0	11	0	28	3	4	2	.355	.280
Diaz, Linardo, Piedmont	.083	9	12	12	0	1	2	1	0	0	0	0	0	0	0	0	2	0	0	0	.167	.083
Dishington, Nate, Savannah*	.214	124	529	444	56	95	155	17	5	11	44	0	6	17	62	4	154	13	7	14	.349	.329
Donato, Dan, Greensboro*	.318	108	431	387	55	123	176	30	1	7	69	0	3	4	37	5	46	7	6	12	.455	.381
Drent, Brian, Hickory	.188	24	80	69	8	13	23	5	1	1	5	0	1	4	6	0	28	0	4	0	.333	.288
Dukart, Derek, Greensboro*	.256	86	341	305	35	78	121	21	2	6	40	2	4	2	28	4	59	2	3	11	.397	.319
Eaglin, Mike, Macon	.266	129	607	530	82	141	170	15	4	2	30	5	1	7	64	0	94	41	13	8	.321	.352
Ealy, Tracey, Savannah†	.243	101	419	370	38	90	131	18	1	7	35	3	3	2	41	3	103	8	5	10	.354	.320
Eddie, Steve, Cha. (W.Va.)	.275	115	371	331	45	91	131	16	3	6	47	3	6	7	24	0	46	10	3	9	.396	.332
Edwards, Aaron, Augusta	.263	47	174	160	29	42	50	4	2	0	9	1	1	1	11	0	39	10	4	2	.313	.312
Elam, Brett, Asheville	.000	1	2	2	0	0	0	0	0	0	0	0	0	0	0	0	1	0	0	0	.000	.000
Encarnacion, Juan, Fayetteville	.282	124	498	457	62	129	222	31	7	16	72	1	2	8	30	0	113	5	6	10	.486	.336
Estrada, Josue, Albany	.213	70	264	235	27	50	69	11	1	2	17	3	0	2	24	3	70	2	3	7	.294	.291
Falciglia, Tony, Savannah	.169	23	82	71	4	12	14	2	0	0	5	0	1	1	9	0	17	1	1	1	.197	.268
Fantauzzi, John, Asheville*	.213	107	387	329	38	70	114	20	0	8	44	1	2	3	51	2	79	1	1	6	.347	.322
Ferrier, Ross, Columbia	.186	23	79	70	6	13	20	1	0	2	5	0	0	1	8	0	20	5	0	4	.286	.278
Figueroa, Danny, Asheville	.233	80	267	227	34	53	86	22	1	3	22	7	3	6	24	0	73	3	7	2	.379	.319
Fithian, Grant, Greensboro	.225	51	177	151	16	34	50	8	1	2	12	3	3	1	19	0	45	5	4	5	.331	.310
Flores, Jose, Piedmont	.263	61	222	186	22	49	56	7	0	0	19	5	4	3	24	0	29	11	8	6	.301	.350
Friedrich, Steve, Hickory	.252	136	559	532	56	134	188	24	6	6	50	2	4	5	16	0	107	19	16	16	.353	.278
Fullmer, Brad, Albany*	.323	123	527	468	69	151	221	38	4	8	67	0	6	17	36	4	33	10	10	9	.472	.387
Fussell, Denny, Cha. (W.Va.)*	.250	20	49	44	4	11	13	2	0	0	7	0	1	0	4	1	10	1	0	0	.295	.306
Gainey, Bryon, Columbia*	.243	124	489	448	49	109	181	20	5	14	64	0	2	9	30	1	157	1	3	7	.404	.303
Gambill, Chad, Asheville	.256	106	392	367	34	94	145	25	1	8	57	3	4	2	16	2	92	6	4	9	.395	.288
Gann, Steve, Cha. (W.Va.)	.208	15	55	48	3	10	11	1	0	0	4	0	1	0	6	0	7	1	1	1	.229	.291
Garcia, Neil, Fayetteville†	.231	88	326	251	46	58	93	12	1	7	33	2	4	10	59	0	49	3	6	5	.371	.392
Gatti, Dom, Cha. (S.C.)	.230	96	399	335	50	77	93	8	4	0	32	3	4	4	53	0	38	39	15	5	.278	.338
Giardi, Mike, Greensboro	.168	46	120	101	10	17	24	4	0	1	5	0	1	3	15	0	17	3	4	2	.238	.292
Gibson, Derrick, Asheville	.292	135	561	506	91	148	280	16	10	32	115	1	6	19	29	5	136	31	13	10	.553	.350
Gipner, Marcus, Greensboro†	.150	7	22	20	0	3	4	1	0	0	2	0	1	0	1	0	6	0	0	2	.200	.182
Glass, Chip, Columbus*	.289	115	449	402	70	116	158	17	5	5	45	5	0	5	37	1	47	37	8	4	.393	.356
Goldberg, Lonnie, Cha. (S.C.)	.218	100	375	340	29	74	94	12	1	2	31	2	4	1	26	1	54	17	11	3	.276	.272
Gomez, Paul, Columbia	.204	68	221	181	19	37	61	10	1	4	20	1	2	4	33	0	65	0	3	4	.337	.336
Gomez, Ramon, Hickory	.229	76	254	231	26	53	59	6	0	0	9	3	0	2	18	0	64	17	9	5	.255	.291
Gonzalez, Jhonny, Asheville*	.000	21	1	1	0	0	0	0	0	0	0	0	0	0	0	0	0	0	0	0	.000	.000
Gonzalez, Mario, Cha. (S.C.)†	.207	11	33	29	3	6	7	1	0	0	1	0	1	0	3	0	4	2	1	0	.241	.273
Gonzalez, Wikleman, Augusta	.241	84	313	278	41	67	93	17	0	3	36	2	5	2	26	0	32	5	4	7	.335	.305
Green, Bert, Savannah	.228	132	497	429	48	98	120	7	6	1	25	9	1	3	55	0	101	26	9	6	.280	.320
Guerrero, Rafael, Columbia	.277	116	448	415	47	115	160	18	3	7	56	2	6	0	25	1	63	13	8	15	.386	.314
Guerrero, Vladimir, Albany	.333	110	464	421	77	140	229	21	10	16	63	0	4	7	30	3	45	12	7	8	.544	.383
Guiliano, Matt, Piedmont	.226	129	524	451	67	102	160	22	12	4	59	9	6	7	51	1	114	6	8	7	.355	.311
Guillen, Jose, Augusta	.235	10	38	34	6	8	17	1	1	2	6	0	0	2	2	0	9	0	0	1	.500	.316
Haas, Matt, Albany*	.235	52	190	166	18	39	46	7	0	0	15	3	1	2	18	1	30	1	5	1	.277	.316
Hall, Ronnie, Asheville	.299	130	518	448	64	134	174	20	4	4	46	1	4	17	44	4	78	26	13	7	.388	.380
Hammell, Al, Columbia	.000	3	9	6	0	0	0	0	0	0	0	1	0	0	2	0	4	0	0	0	.000	.250
Hampton, Mike, Cha. (W.Va.)	.245	96	364	302	46	74	99	16	3	1	32	2	1	6	53	1	70	17	4	6	.328	.367
Harper, Rantie, Savannah	.208	91	359	318	34	66	91	12	2	3	31	2	3	2	34	0	114	13	3	6	.286	.286
Harris, G.G., Augusta	.245	100	395	368	38	90	119	23	0	2	46	2	4	4	17	1	50	2	6	9	.323	.282
Harriss, Robin, Columbus	.223	51	196	179	18	40	52	6	0	2	18	3	0	3	11	0	30	0	3	8	.291	.280
Hayes, Darren, Hickory	.245	58	220	196	18	48	73	12	2	3	19	1	1	6	16	1	53	7	2	6	.372	.320
Heller, Bradley, Cha. (S.C.)	.224	76	242	214	27	48	73	13	0	4	15	6	1	0	21	0	37	3	1	4	.341	.292
Helms, Wes, Macon	.276	136	602	539	89	149	216	32	1	11	85	0	3	10	50	0	107	2	2	8	.401	.347
Helton, Todd, Asheville*	.254	54	227	201	24	51	67	11	1	1	15	0	0	1	25	1	32	1	1	7	.333	.339
Henley, Bob, Albany	.281	102	432	335	45	94	125	20	1	3	46	1	2	11	83	3	57	1	2	11	.373	.436
Herider, Jeremy, Cha. (W.Va.)†	.133	8	17	15	2	2	2	0	0	0	0	0	0	0	2	0	6	0	0	0	.133	.235
Holley, Jack, Hagerstown	.203	23	84	79	6	16	20	4	0	0	7	1	0	1	3	0	18	0	2	4	.253	.241
Hooker, Kevin, Piedmont	.174	16	59	46	4	8	10	2	0	0	6	0	1	3	9	0	13	1	0	0	.217	.339
Houser, Kyle, Asheville	.211	112	404	361	43	76	93	11	0	2	32	6	2	1	34	0	43	5	4	7	.258	.279
Huff, Larry, Piedmont	.272	130	576	481	86	131	168	26	4	1	51	7	4	10	74	5	64	26	8	9	.349	.378
Hunter, Scott, Columbia	.250	12	45	40	2	10	10	0	0	0	1	1	1	1	2	0	13	2	1	2	.250	.295
Izquierdo, Sergio, Hickory	.146	45	135	123	6	18	20	2	0	0	4	3	1	0	8	0	20	0	0	4	.163	.197
Jarrett, Linc, Asheville†	.235	116	480	404	46	95	106	11	0	0	20	10	2	2	62	1	60	12	10	5	.262	.338
Jenkins, Dee, Cha. (W.Va.)*	.244	31	102	86	14	21	24	1	1	0	5	1	0	0	15	0	19	5	0	2	.279	.356
Johnson, Jeff, Hickory	.229	53	188	170	15	39	54	9	0	2	14	3	1	1	13	1	40	2	2	2	.318	.286
Johnson, Mark, Hickory*	.182	107	385	319	31	58	73	9	0	2	17	2	2	3	59	1	52	3	5	4	.229	.313

Player, Team	Avg.	G	TPA	AB	R	H	TB	2B	3B	HR	RBI	SH	SF	HP	BB	IBB	SO	SB	CS	GDP	Slg.	OBP
Jones, Andruw, Macon	.277	139	632	537	104	149	275	41	5	25	100	0	9	16	70	7	122	56	11	9	.512	.372
Jones, Pookie, Asheville	.349	16	65	63	16	22	32	6	2	0	8	0	0	0	2	0	14	3	0	1	.508	.369
Kelley, Erskine, Augusta	.218	105	380	349	47	76	111	13	5	4	32	1	1	7	22	2	86	24	7	10	.318	.277
Kennedy, Gus, Macon	.253	128	539	439	83	111	222	29	5	24	76	0	3	2	95	10	151	20	6	7	.506	.386
Key, Jeff, Piedmont*	.258	111	426	384	55	99	159	18	6	10	54	2	5	9	26	4	100	5	7	6	.414	.316
Koerick, Thomas, Hickory	.185	73	223	200	15	37	55	10	1	2	20	0	1	7	15	0	85	2	2	2	.275	.265
Lackey, Steve, Columbia	.191	67	199	178	21	34	45	8	0	1	21	5	3	2	11	1	42	9	2	2	.253	.242
Ladd, Jeff, Hagerstown	.305	94	401	311	54	95	175	17	3	19	58	0	3	9	78	5	94	6	3	2	.563	.454
Landry, Dan, Macon	.226	13	63	53	4	12	13	1	0	0	6	0	1	3	6	0	16	2	0	0	.245	.333
Lantigua, Eduardo, Columbus	.241	23	94	87	13	21	29	5	0	1	10	0	1	2	4	1	20	2	1	2	.333	.272
Larkin, Stephen, Cha. (S.C.)*	.255	113	432	369	50	94	130	19	1	5	45	3	5	1	54	2	80	18	10	7	.352	.347
Ledee, Ricky, Greensboro*	.269	89	390	335	65	90	160	16	6	14	49	0	1	2	51	6	66	10	4	3	.478	.368
Lee, Carlos, Hickory	.248	63	227	218	18	54	77	9	1	4	30	0	1	8	2	34	1	5	7	.353	.278
Leon, Geraldo, Savannah	.165	41	145	133	15	22	28	4	1	0	11	1	0	1	10	1	46	0	1	6	.211	.229
Lewis, Andreaus, Columbus†	.261	76	287	245	35	64	88	8	5	2	23	1	2	3	36	2	86	18	7	3	.359	.360
Lewis, Rob, Columbus	.152	20	77	66	6	10	17	1	0	2	8	0	1	1	9	0	18	0	1	3	.258	.260
Lidle, Kevin, Fayetteville	.142	36	135	113	15	16	34	4	1	4	13	3	2	1	16	0	44	0	1	1	.301	.250
Light, Tal, Asheville	.270	23	84	63	13	17	33	4	0	4	13	0	3	0	18	0	17	0	0	0	.524	.417
Llanos, Aurelio, Hagerstown	.251	106	421	378	54	95	173	25	1	17	63	0	3	11	29	2	115	9	7	5	.458	.321
Lobaton, Jose, Greensboro	.243	60	222	185	26	45	61	6	5	0	23	11	2	2	22	0	58	11	6	3	.330	.327
Lofton, James, Cha. (W.Va.)	.208	65	215	192	20	40	52	10	1	0	14	2	0	3	18	1	43	8	5	2	.271	.286
Lombard, George, Macon*	.206	49	214	180	32	37	54	6	1	3	16	1	0	5	27	3	44	16	4	4	.300	.325
Long, Terrence, Columbia*	.197	55	208	178	27	35	46	1	2	2	13	1	0	1	28	4	43	8	5	3	.258	.309
Lopez, Jose, Columbia	.232	82	328	280	37	65	105	17	4	5	38	2	7	4	35	3	76	7	2	7	.375	.319
Lopez, Victor, Cha. (S.C.)	.289	12	43	38	4	11	14	3	0	0	2	0	0	1	4	0	3	3	0	1	.368	.372
Luciano, Virgilio, Cha. (S.C.)*	.218	104	321	285	30	62	84	14	1	2	31	3	4	3	26	2	76	18	9	2	.295	.286
Lunar, Fernando, Macon	.179	39	150	134	13	24	26	2	0	0	9	3	0	3	10	0	38	1	0	3	.194	.252
Martinez, Dalvis, Fayetteville	.255	36	119	102	17	26	42	7	0	3	15	1	0	0	16	0	35	1	0	0	.412	.356
Matos, Julius, Columbus	.245	52	170	155	16	38	51	7	3	0	13	1	0	3	11	1	21	2	2	8	.329	.308
Matos, Pasqual, Macon	.185	72	250	238	23	44	72	11	1	5	26	0	0	1	11	0	86	2	2	4	.303	.224
Mayber, Chan, Asheville	.193	34	96	88	11	17	21	4	0	0	3	1	0	0	7	0	19	7	0	1	.239	.253
McClure, Craig, Hickory	.169	49	172	154	13	26	37	3	1	2	8	1	0	0	17	0	56	6	2	4	.240	.251
McDougal, Mike, Savannah	.080	15	52	50	2	4	4	0	0	0	4	0	0	0	2	0	17	1	1	1	.080	.115
McLamb, Brian, Greensboro†	.226	81	285	252	34	57	86	11	0	6	32	2	0	6	25	2	61	11	4	9	.341	.311
McMillan, Tom, Savannah	.214	85	304	262	21	56	87	8	1	7	21	3	2	2	35	2	91	5	4	3	.332	.309
McNally, Shawn, Savannah	.219	94	197	169	21	37	52	8	2	1	14	2	1	1	24	0	48	8	2	2	.308	.313
Mendoza, Jesus, Hickory	.251	116	485	434	49	109	161	24	2	8	49	2	4	9	36	3	53	2	7	11	.371	.319
Mercedes, Guillermo, Columbus†	.191	55	205	183	23	35	48	5	1	2	8	1	0	3	18	0	19	6	3	5	.262	.275
Meskauskas, John, Asheville	.278	30	86	79	11	22	35	4	0	3	13	0	2	1	4	0	16	0	1	4	.443	.314
Millan, Adam, Piedmont	.294	107	449	394	69	116	175	25	2	10	64	1	3	7	44	3	45	1	4	15	.444	.373
Millican, Kevin, Cha. (S.C.)	.215	88	306	270	27	58	90	17	0	5	28	1	2	2	31	1	81	2	4	3	.333	.298
Mobilia, Bill, Piedmont	.240	55	173	150	17	36	45	5	2	0	17	7	1	2	13	0	39	1	0	1	.300	.307
Monroe, Darryl, Fayetteville	.259	104	432	382	55	99	133	21	2	3	28	8	3	16	23	1	76	23	12	7	.348	.325
Morales, Eric, Columbia	.275	38	125	109	12	30	34	4	0	0	11	3	0	1	12	0	18	2	1	1	.312	.352
Morales, Francisco, Savannah	.147	19	81	75	3	11	20	3	0	2	4	0	1	1	4	0	23	0	2	2	.267	.198
Morgan, Dave, Hagerstown	.265	67	272	249	26	66	94	14	1	4	26	1	2	2	18	1	53	1	0	4	.378	.317
Morillo, Donald, Cha. (S.C.)	.000	19	1	1	0	0	0	0	0	0	0	0	0	0	0	0	0	0	0	0	.000	.000
Morrow, Nick, Cha. (W.Va.)	.251	139	549	467	67	117	188	28	8	9	54	2	1	2	77	2	123	41	17	5	.403	.358
Mosquera, Julio, Hagerstown	.291	108	456	406	64	118	159	22	5	3	46	3	5	13	29	2	53	5	5	13	.392	.353
Mota, Guillermo, Columbia	.243	123	443	400	45	97	139	24	3	4	45	6	1	4	32	1	127	8	3	5	.348	.304
Moyle, Mike, Columbus	.203	73	272	227	19	46	71	7	0	6	31	3	6	1	35	0	46	2	3	3	.313	.305
Mummau, Rob, Hagerstown	.257	107	431	366	63	94	132	17	3	5	42	6	3	14	42	1	74	6	1	7	.361	.353
Myers, Aaron, Asheville	.138	20	70	65	1	9	12	3	0	0	6	1	0	1	3	0	27	0	0	1	.185	.188
Navas, Jesus, Hickory†	.228	79	241	202	23	46	56	7	0	1	16	3	3	5	28	0	36	3	6	4	.277	.332
Newell, Brett, Macon	.256	76	322	285	39	73	84	9	1	0	29	5	1	7	24	0	72	5	1	5	.295	.328
Nitschke, Bear, Piedmont*	.000	2	4	4	0	0	0	0	0	0	0	0	0	0	0	0	3	0	0	0	.000	.000
Northeimer, Jamie, Piedmont	.291	115	471	392	56	114	149	24	4	1	54	4	2	20	53	1	72	9	4	13	.380	.400
Oakland, Mike, Asheville	.208	18	60	48	4	10	11	1	0	0	2	1	0	1	10	0	6	0	0	1	.229	.356
O'Brien, Joe, Piedmont	.217	60	217	189	27	41	50	4	1	1	31	1	2	6	19	0	38	2	5	6	.265	.306
Ocasio, Fred, Asheville	.308	14	42	39	3	12	12	0	0	0	2	0	0	0	3	0	7	0	2	0	.308	.357
Oram, Jon, Columbus	.217	64	220	198	20	43	61	6	3	2	19	1	4	4	13	1	40	2	5	9	.308	.274
Ordaz, Luis, Cha. (W.Va.)	.231	112	390	359	43	83	117	14	7	2	42	8	4	6	13	1	47	12	5	10	.326	.267
Ortman, Ben, Asheville	.158	14	43	38	7	6	10	1	0	1	4	0	1	0	4	0	9	1	1	0	.263	.233
Ozario, Yudith, Columbia	.217	123	504	456	59	99	121	12	2	2	33	9	2	3	34	3	113	40	15	8	.265	.275
Pearson, Cory, Cha. (S.C.)	.208	61	206	183	21	38	49	8	0	1	13	0	0	5	18	1	53	13	6	5	.268	.296
Pena, Elvis, Asheville†	.228	48	180	145	27	33	35	2	0	0	4	3	0	4	28	0	32	23	6	1	.241	.367
Perez, Joe, Cha. (S.C.)*	.272	67	266	243	24	66	93	14	2	3	29	0	2	3	18	2	55	10	3	2	.383	.327
Perez, Santiago, Fayetteville†	.238	130	470	425	54	101	130	15	1	4	44	7	7	1	30	0	98	10	9	6	.306	.283
Perry, Chan, Columbus	.285	113	472	411	66	117	182	30	4	9	50	2	4	2	53	1	49	7	2	6	.443	.366
Petillo, Bruce, Piedmont	.111	2	9	9	0	1	1	0	0	0	2	0	0	0	0	0	3	0	0	0	.111	.111
Pollock, Elton, Augusta	.234	26	105	94	8	22	29	5	1	0	10	2	2	0	7	0	23	8	3	5	.309	.282
Pond, Simon, Albany*	.213	23	86	80	4	17	22	5	0	0	7	0	0	2	4	0	25	1	0	3	.275	.267
Pozo, Yohel, Asheville	.216	40	145	139	7	30	36	3	0	1	15	1	1	0	4	0	32	0	3	7	.259	.236
Prensi, Dagoberto, Hagerstown	.208	104	387	361	40	75	115	18	5	4	33	1	1	5	18	0	106	10	6	10	.319	.255
Preston, Doyle, Cha. (W.Va.)*	.125	7	20	16	1	2	3	1	0	0	2	0	0	0	4	0	5	0	2	1	.188	.300
Prieto, Ricky, Columbus	.222	4	18	18	1	4	7	0	0	1	2	0	0	0	0	0	3	0	0	0	.389	.222
Pullen, Shane, Piedmont*	.251	118	479	435	65	109	164	26	4	7	57	2	5	3	34	3	70	4	2	12	.377	.306
Reilly, John, Hagerstown	.000	1	3	2	1	0	0	0	0	0	0	0	0	1	0	0	1	0	0	0	.000	.000
Resetar, Gary, Asheville*	.000	2	2	2	0	0	0	0	0	0	0	0	0	0	0	0	0	0	0	1	.000	.000
Reyes, Winston, Piedmont	.176	6	18	17	1	3	5	0	1	0	5	0	0	1	0	0	8	0	1	0	.294	.222
Reynolds, Chance, Augusta†	.215	24	81	65	8	14	19	2	0	1	6	0	0	4	12	1	11	0	2	1	.292	.370
Rice, Charles, Augusta†	.222	14	58	54	8	12	18	3	0	1	8	0	0	2	2	0	14	0	0	0	.333	.276
Rivera, Miguel, Savannah	.253	128	550	514	44	130	162	14	3	4	41	6	4	5	21	1	76	10	6	15	.315	.287

Player, Team	Avg.	G	TPA	AB	R	H	TB	2B	3B	HR	RBI	SH	SF	HP	BB	IBB	SO	SB	CS	GDP	Slg.	OBP
Rivers, Jonathon, Hagerstown	.294	123	480	429	54	126	172	16	6	6	48	1	4	6	40	0	104	18	5	9	.401	.359
Rives, Sherron, Fayetteville	.227	56	169	150	15	34	42	8	0	0	19	2	3	3	11	0	36	3	1	5	.280	.287
Robinson, Tony, Augusta	.229	96	348	297	34	68	83	9	0	2	37	1	1	11	38	1	60	21	11	4	.279	.337
Robles, Rafael, Savannah†	.197	56	185	142	15	28	32	2	1	0	7	3	0	1	39	2	43	2	4	2	.225	.374
Rodriguez, Adam, Fayetteville	.302	39	151	139	16	42	70	14	1	4	25	1	0	2	9	0	25	0	1	5	.504	.353
Rosado, Juan, Albany*	.182	5	11	11	0	2	3	1	0	0	3	0	0	0	0	0	4	1	0	0	.273	.182
Royster, Aaron, Piedmont	.264	126	539	489	73	129	182	23	3	8	58	0	4	7	39	1	106	22	9	16	.372	.325
Rutz, Ryan, (S.C.)	.220	133	557	491	60	108	133	20	1	1	22	7	2	2	55	0	88	36	26	6	.271	.300
Sanders, Anthony, Hagerstown	.232	133	583	512	72	119	173	28	1	8	48	9	5	5	52	0	103	26	14	8	.338	.307
Sanders, Rod, Cha. (W.Va.)	.204	81	168	152	22	31	45	7	2	1	11	3	0	1	12	0	45	4	8	3	.296	.267
Sanderson, David, Columbia*	.237	121	411	363	53	86	122	11	5	5	36	7	0	3	38	8	81	20	10	6	.336	.314
Santa, Roberto, Cha. (S.C.)*	.261	99	361	295	35	77	105	11	1	5	46	1	8	2	55	1	37	0	6	4	.356	.372
Saturnino, Sherton, Macon	.188	42	123	117	6	22	30	2	0	2	13	1	0	2	3	1	36	1	2	1	.256	.221
Schreimann, Eric, Piedmont	.174	7	25	23	1	4	5	1	0	0	1	0	1	0	1	1	4	0	0	0	.217	.200
Schwab, Chris, Albany	.227	122	537	484	60	110	153	22	3	5	43	0	4	1	48	1	173	4	6	4	.316	.296
Seguignol, Fernando, Albany†	.208	121	498	457	59	95	157	22	2	12	66	1	6	6	28	3	141	12	8	6	.344	.260
Segura, Juan, Augusta	.225	25	86	80	3	18	20	2	0	0	4	4	1	0	1	0	21	0	2	3	.250	.232
Sharp, Scott, Cha. (W.Va.)	.211	55	174	161	7	34	40	2	2	0	16	4	1	1	7	0	63	1	2	4	.248	.247
Shugars, Shawn, Cha. (S.C.)*	.227	8	24	22	2	5	6	1	0	0	3	0	0	1	1	0	3	0	2	0	.273	.292
Shumpert, Derek, Greensboro†	.216	56	180	153	21	33	38	3	1	0	14	7	0	2	18	0	41	4	2	2	.248	.306
Silvia, Brian, Savannah	.247	59	240	198	25	49	91	14	2	8	33	0	3	8	31	1	39	4	2	9	.460	.367
Simmons, Brian, Hickory†	.190	41	184	163	13	31	45	6	1	2	11	0	0	2	19	0	44	4	4	2	.276	.283
Smith, Jason, Asheville	.100	24	90	80	7	8	14	3	0	1	8	0	0	2	8	0	40	0	1	1	.175	.200
Smith, Rod, Greensboro†	.243	62	273	235	31	57	74	5	6	0	9	2	0	2	34	1	41	17	12	4	.315	.343
Staton, T.J., Augusta*	.292	112	421	391	43	114	160	21	5	5	53	0	1	2	27	5	97	27	13	6	.409	.340
Stingley, Derek, Piedmont	.179	39	96	84	20	15	20	2	0	1	5	1	1	4	6	0	24	13	2	2	.238	.263
Stone, Craig, Hagerstown	.276	96	402	355	47	98	150	20	4	8	52	0	5	8	34	0	104	3	2	6	.423	.348
Strange, Mike, Hagerstown	.234	96	357	290	51	68	84	9	2	1	27	2	0	4	61	0	92	13	3	7	.290	.375
Stumberger, Darren, Columbus	.270	127	520	448	62	121	181	27	0	11	57	0	5	9	56	2	72	3	3	13	.404	.359
Subero, Carlos, Augusta†	.186	31	102	97	8	18	20	2	0	0	6	3	0	0	2	0	24	1	0	2	.206	.202
Swafford, Derek, Augusta*	.253	119	497	447	69	113	147	15	5	3	48	6	2	8	33	1	101	52	16	4	.329	.314
Sweet, Jonathan, Augusta*	.285	87	295	267	28	76	90	9	1	1	22	2	2	5	18	2	31	5	4	6	.337	.339
Tatis, Fernando, Cha. (S.C.)†	.303	131	556	499	74	151	247	43	4	15	84	1	4	7	45	4	94	22	19	5	.495	.366
Taylor, Byron, Savannah*	.103	14	31	29	2	3	3	0	0	0	0	0	0	1	1	0	10	0	0	0	.103	.161
Thobe, Steve, Augusta	.299	84	325	291	43	87	121	12	2	6	38	0	0	5	29	6	71	1	3	2	.416	.372
Thomas, Rod, Cha. (W.Va.)	.146	29	91	82	8	12	18	3	0	1	6	0	2	0	7	1	25	3	0	3	.220	.209
Thompson, Andy, Hagerstown	.239	124	502	461	48	110	151	19	2	6	57	1	3	8	29	2	108	2	3	15	.328	.293
Thompson, Leroy, Columbus*	.214	82	294	248	34	53	95	15	3	7	35	1	0	5	40	4	78	1	2	4	.383	.334
Tidick, Michael, Hickory*	.212	56	160	132	17	28	47	9	2	2	9	0	2	5	21	2	41	5	4	1	.356	.338
Torborg, Dale, Greensboro	.198	33	89	81	10	16	23	4	0	1	11	0	0	1	7	0	28	1	0	0	.284	.270
Torok, John, Piedmont*	.188	91	255	202	26	38	55	4	5	1	22	6	1	1	45	1	39	11	7	2	.272	.337
Towle, Justin, Cha. (W.Va.)	.268	107	395	343	54	92	142	22	2	8	60	1	3	1	44	0	95	3	6	6	.414	.350
Trimble, Rob, Greensboro*	.133	33	88	83	5	11	13	2	0	0	5	1	0	0	4	0	22	0	1	0	.157	.172
Troilo, Jason, Greensboro	.288	19	66	59	6	17	30	4	0	3	9	3	1	0	3	0	19	0	1	0	.508	.317
Turner, Rocky, Columbia	.176	12	21	17	2	3	3	0	0	0	1	2	0	0	2	0	5	0	2	0	.176	.263
Turrentine, Rich, Columbia	.000	26	1	1	0	0	0	0	0	0	0	0	0	0	0	0	1	0	0	0	.000	.000
Twitty, Sean, Greensboro	.283	80	330	293	49	83	140	25	1	10	58	0	2	6	29	1	83	6	2	9	.478	.358
Utting, Ben, Macon*	.218	21	62	55	5	12	14	2	0	0	6	0	0	0	7	0	13	1	1	0	.255	.306
Valdez, Mario, Hickory*	.272	130	516	441	65	120	193	30	5	11	56	0	3	5	67	2	107	9	7	5	.438	.372
Valera, Willy, Columbus	.163	31	108	104	8	17	28	3	1	2	6	0	0	0	4	0	35	0	1	3	.269	.194
Van Overen, Ryan, Albany†	.163	49	152	135	11	22	29	4	0	1	7	1	2	0	14	0	44	1	1	0	.215	.238
Vaske, Terry, Macon*	.169	53	166	148	14	25	47	7	0	5	18	0	0	0	18	2	58	0	1	1	.318	.259
Vasquez, Danilo, Cha. (S.C.)	.214	44	143	131	12	28	41	6	2	1	7	1	1	4	6	0	42	6	3	4	.313	.268
Veras, Juan, Cha. (S.C.)	.203	102	346	305	39	62	77	11	2	0	17	7	1	1	32	0	69	16	8	1	.252	.280
Waldrop, Tom, Macon*	.237	60	212	194	19	46	68	11	1	3	24	1	1	2	14	2	52	1	1	3	.351	.294
Walker, Shon, Augusta*	.229	110	431	358	49	82	120	20	0	6	51	1	4	0	68	3	127	10	9	3	.335	.349
Wampler, Sam, Piedmont†	.000	1	3	3	0	0	0	0	0	0	0	0	0	0	0	0	0	0	0	0	.000	.000
Ward, Daryle, Fayetteville*	.284	137	582	524	75	149	223	32	0	14	106	0	7	5	46	11	111	1	2	13	.426	.344
Warner, Bryan, Columbus*	.239	119	424	393	47	94	140	14	4	8	58	4	0	2	25	3	73	8	2	5	.356	.288
Watts, Josh, Piedmont*	.234	111	414	355	50	83	111	13	0	5	43	3	7	4	45	3	96	8	5	6	.313	.321
Weaver, Colby, Macon	.243	14	44	37	4	9	12	0	0	1	6	0	0	2	5	0	8	1	0	1	.324	.364
Wells, Mark, Asheville*	.287	40	128	115	21	33	69	6	3	8	23	1	1	2	9	2	38	1	3	1	.600	.339
White, Eric, Columbus	.317	112	423	369	49	117	165	24	3	6	46	1	1	5	51	5	45	11	7	12	.447	.400
White, Jimmy, Cha. (W.Va.)*	.169	20	74	65	7	11	19	3	1	1	8	1	1	1	6	0	27	1	1	0	.292	.247
Whitehurst, Todd, Columbia†	.164	21	77	61	10	10	16	3	0	1	1	1	0	4	11	0	19	2	1	0	.262	.329
Wilhelm, Brent, Hickory	.225	67	258	240	19	54	73	9	2	2	24	0	2	1	15	0	36	4	3	6	.304	.271
Williams, Curtis, Savannah*	.187	51	159	134	14	25	32	2	1	1	9	5	0	0	20	0	44	2	5	2	.239	.292
Williams, Glenn, Macon†	.175	38	141	120	13	21	25	4	0	0	14	1	3	1	16	0	42	2	1	3	.208	.271
Williams, Mark, Savannah	.154	64	240	201	19	31	45	2	0	4	13	5	1	0	33	0	57	0	0	10	.224	.272
Williamson, Matt, Piedmont	.235	88	330	285	44	67	84	10	2	1	25	6	2	2	35	0	67	3	4	5	.295	.321
Wilson, Brian, Cha. (W.Va.)	.308	5	15	13	3	4	5	1	0	0	1	2	0	0	0	0	1	3	0	0	.385	.308
Wilson, Preston, Columbia	.269	111	474	442	70	119	215	26	5	20	61	1	3	9	19	2	114	20	6	4	.486	.311
Wilson, Vance, Columbia	.250	91	354	324	34	81	110	11	0	6	32	1	2	8	19	1	45	4	3	6	.340	.306
Winterlee, Scott, Columbia	.429	4	9	7	0	3	3	0	0	0	0	0	0	0	2	0	1	0	0	0	.429	.556
Witt, Kevin, Hagerstown*	.232	119	514	479	58	111	190	35	1	14	50	3	0	4	28	2	148	1	5	5	.397	.280
Wright, Ron, Macon	.271	135	594	527	93	143	264	23	1	32	104	0	3	2	62	1	118	2	0	11	.501	.348
Wright, Terry, Cha. (W.Va.)	.283	125	470	410	68	116	155	13	10	2	56	7	1	2	50	4	43	46	16	8	.378	.363
Wuerch, Jason, Greensboro*	.188	31	98	85	4	16	18	2	0	0	8	1	1	0	11	0	20	2	2	5	.212	.278
Yedo, Carlos, Greensboro*	.246	117	490	435	65	107	170	22	1	13	57	0	2	0	53	5	126	2	1	4	.391	.327
Zorrilla, Julio, Columbia†	.276	133	563	518	65	143	164	15	3	0	31	10	4	3	27	2	75	42	18	9	.317	.315
Zuniga, David, Columbia	.178	36	84	73	6	13	15	2	0	0	4	1	0	3	7	0	19	0	2	2	.205	.277

GRAND SLAMS: Gainey, Gibson, 2 each; A. Brown, Darr, Encarnacion, R. Guerrero, Hayes, A. Jones, Kennedy, A. Lewis, Luciano, McLamb, Mendoza, T. Sanders, Thobe, R. Wright, 1 each.
AWARDED FIRST BASE ON CATCHER'S INTERFERENCE: Hall 4 (W. Gonzalez, Lunar, Mosquera, Northeimer); Towle 3 (Morgan 2, P. Gomez); Goldberg 2 (Cardona, Dawson); V. Guerrero 2 (Fithian, M. Williams); Stumberger 2 (W. Gonzalez, Lunar); Asche (Boka); Fantauzzi (N. Garcia); Ledee (M. Johnson); Lombard (Henley); Prensi (V. Wilson); Swafford (Moyle); Sweet (Towle).

Player, Team	Avg.	G	TPA	AB	R	H	TB	2B	3B	HR	RBI	SH	SF	HP	BB	IBB	SO	SB	CS	GDP	Slg.	OBP
Carpenter, Matt, Asheville........	.095	9	22	21	0	2	3	1	0	0	3	0	0	0	1	0	2	0	0	0	.143	.136
Carpenter, Matt, Columbus......	.286	2	8	7	2	2	6	1	0	1	3	0	0	1	0	0	2	0	0	0	.857	.375

1995 PITCHING

TEAM

Team	W	L	Pct.	ERA	G	CG	ShO	Sv.	IP	H	TBF	R	ER	HR	SH	SF	HB	BB	IBB	SO	WP	Bk.
Asheville................	76	63	.547	3.14	139	7	13	42	1212.0	1060	5056	505	423	69	27	19	64	450	7	1011	104	30
Augusta................	76	62	.551	3.14	138	4	8	36	1199.1	1059	5109	533	419	60	40	28	57	460	18	1000	93	10
Columbia................	72	68	.514	3.16	140	13	11	30	1235.2	1067	5182	542	434	65	35	37	58	488	14	1045	99	20
Fayetteville............	86	55	.610	3.22	141	3	10	54	1231.2	1035	5205	571	440	55	34	33	81	524	6	1183	105	17
Piedmont...............	82	58	.586	3.27	140	7	12	38	1218.1	1087	5150	574	442	62	38	37	59	460	7	1074	93	19
Columbus...............	80	62	.563	3.41	142	3	17	48	1242.1	1085	5300	598	471	66	38	29	78	569	39	1103	74	20
Hagerstown...........	73	68	.518	3.52	141	11	8	41	1216.0	1178	5152	599	476	76	39	31	56	391	9	906	97	11
Greensboro...........	70	70	.500	3.58	140	5	11	38	1226.0	1137	5204	595	488	79	34	40	52	450	19	1130	91	11
Charleston (W.Va.) ..	77	65	.542	3.60	142	10	11	42	1209.0	1166	5154	559	483	59	41	35	83	443	47	930	90	18
Savannah...............	56	83	.403	3.65	139	3	6	36	1228.2	1121	5307	608	498	79	38	43	54	492	25	1118	120	11
Albany	62	78	.443	3.90	140	6	5	31	1242.1	1282	5465	713	538	59	46	47	62	460	16	1016	82	12
Macon................	71	70	.504	3.90	141	2	9	31	1269.2	1127	5548	699	550	89	39	32	79	627	9	1136	122	24
Hickory................	49	89	.355	3.98	138	7	9	27	1222.0	1236	5315	712	541	106	48	45	62	436	46	988	89	26
Charleston (S.C.)....	50	89	.360	4.11	139	7	4	23	1201.1	1179	5264	683	548	78	39	45	72	509	27	1032	104	19

INDIVIDUAL

TOP QUALIFIERS FOR EARNED-RUN AVERAGE TITLE

Minimum 114 innings. *Lefthanded pitcher.

Pitcher, Team	W	L	Pct.	ERA	G	GS	CG	ShO	GF	Sv.	IP	H	TBF	R	ER	HR	SH	SF	HB	BB	IBB	SO	WP	Bk.
Kusiewicz, Michael, Asheville*......	8	4	.667	2.06	21	21	0	0	0	0	122.1	92	484	40	28	6	2	0	6	34	0	103	9	1
Jordan, Jason, Fayetteville	10	4	.714	2.28	24	24	0	0	0	0	138.0	128	575	48	35	5	0	3	8	43	0	103	13	1
Manning, Len, Piedmont*...........	10	10	.500	2.64	27	26	1	0	0	0	160.0	130	658	68	47	10	7	5	7	58	0	154	4	2
Wimberly, Larry, Piedmont*........	10	3	.769	2.67	24	24	0	0	0	0	135.0	99	542	48	40	9	1	3	9	44	0	139	8	4
Herbert, Russell, Hickory	3	8	.273	2.67	18	18	1	1	0	0	114.2	83	474	48	34	9	3	3	8	46	0	115	5	2
Moraga, David, Albany*	8	8	.500	2.68	25	24	1	0	0	0	147.2	136	620	63	44	6	6	4	1	46	0	109	10	0
Atwater, Joe, Columbia*	9	6	.600	2.69	27	18	3	2	6	1	147.1	106	567	52	44	10	4	6	2	28	1	127	5	2
Allen, Cedric, Cha. (W.Va.)*	13	7	.650	2.85	27	27	5	2	0	0	170.1	143	690	64	54	8	6	4	14	46	4	108	6	4
Sievert, Mark, Hagerstown	12	6	.667	2.91	27	27	3	0	0	0	160.2	126	644	59	52	14	5	1	2	46	0	140	2	0
Gooch, Arnold, Ash.-C'bia	5	8	.385	2.94	21	21	1	1	0	0	128.2	111	541	51	42	8	3	3	4	57	0	117	13	0
O'Flynn, Gardner, Cha. (S.C.)*.....	9	10	.474	2.96	30	24	2	1	1	0	167.0	156	698	70	55	11	4	3	6	61	0	110	7	4
Meiners, Doug, Hagerstown	8	4	.667	2.99	18	18	3	0	0	0	117.1	121	477	52	39	5	2	2	3	14	0	73	4	1
Briggs, Anthony, Macon	8	5	.615	2.99	29	24	1	1	0	0	147.1	145	635	76	49	12	2	1	4	56	1	114	9	0
Wright, Jaret, Columbus	5	6	.455	3.00	24	24	0	0	0	0	129.0	93	554	55	43	9	3	6	13	79	0	113	11	3
Johnston, Sean, Columbia*.........	11	6	.647	3.03	23	22	2	0	0	0	148.1	132	621	60	50	6	4	4	11	63	2	105	15	1

DEPARTMENTAL LEADERS: W—Ebert, 14; L—Ramirez, 15; Pct.—B. Smith, .900; G—Golden, 64; GS—C. Smith, 29; CG—Allen, 5; ShO—B. Crowther, 3; GF—Reed, 53; Sv.—Reed, 41; IP—Ebert, 182.0; H—Ebert, 184; TBF—Ebert, 766; R—Hackman, 95; ER—Hackman, 85; HR—John Kelly, 16; SH—Culp, J. Ford, 8; SF—Durocher, 11; HB—C. Smith, 18; BB—Shumate, C. Smith, 87; IBB—Welch, 10; SO—Moss, Sanchez, 177; WP—C. Smith, 21; Bk.—Hackman, 7.

ALL PITCHERS

*Lefthanded pitcher.

Pitcher, Team	W	L	Pct.	ERA	G	GS	CG	ShO	GF	Sv.	IP	H	TBF	R	ER	HR	SH	SF	HB	BB	IBB	SO	WP	Bk.
Adair, Scott, Columbia................	0	1	.000	10.38	3	0	0	0	0	0	4.1	10	26	8	5	0	0	1	1	0	0	4	0	0
Alazaun, Shawn, Greensboro*......	3	1	.750	5.54	33	0	0	0	6	1	39.0	43	179	25	24	5	2	3	1	18	0	40	0	1
Allen, Cedric, Cha. (W.Va.)*	13	7	.650	2.85	27	27	5	2	0	0	170.1	143	690	64	54	8	6	4	14	46	4	108	6	4
Almanza, Armando, Savannah*	3	9	.250	3.92	20	20	0	0	0	0	108.0	108	476	62	47	13	5	4	3	40	1	72	6	1
Ambrose, John, Hickory	4	8	.333	3.95	14	14	0	0	0	0	73.0	65	314	41	32	6	2	3	3	35	0	49	9	2
Anderson, Jimmy, Augusta*	4	2	.667	1.53	14	14	0	0	0	0	76.2	51	305	15	13	1	1	0	4	31	0	75	9	1
Anez, Maycoll, Hickory	0	0	.000	2.25	2	0	0	0	1	0	4.0	3	19	2	1	0	0	0	0	4	0	4	1	0
Antonini, Adrian, Piedmont	2	0	1.000	3.80	6	5	0	0	1	0	21.1	19	85	10	9	1	0	0	2	2	0	26	1	1
Arias, Alfredo, Hagerstown	4	6	.400	4.16	35	1	0	0	17	1	71.1	67	308	37	33	6	6	2	3	35	2	59	8	1
Atwater, Joe, Columbia*	9	6	.600	2.69	27	18	3	2	6	1	147.1	106	567	52	44	10	4	6	2	28	1	127	5	2
Avrard, Corey, Savannah	1	6	.143	3.98	13	13	0	0	0	0	54.1	38	228	25	24	4	1	4	0	33	2	51	6	0
Aybar, Manuel, Savannah	3	8	.273	3.04	18	18	2	1	0	0	112.2	82	461	46	38	8	7	4	2	36	0	99	8	1
Bajda, Mike, Fayetteville	0	0	.000	3.00	4	0	0	0	1	0	9.0	8	41	5	3	1	0	0	0	4	2	0	1	0
Baker, Derek, Columbia	2	8	.200	3.30	36	0	0	0	24	6	62.2	52	267	25	23	5	2	0	6	35	0	44	5	1
Barbao, Joe, Piedmont	8	4	.667	3.38	43	3	0	0	14	1	66.2	70	288	34	25	2	4	5	7	12	1	24	2	1
Barnes, Keith, Savannah*	2	1	1.000	1.98	10	6	0	0	1	1	36.1	25	142	10	8	2	2	0	0	15	0	21	4	0
Beirne, Kevin, Hickory	0	0	.000	4.50	3	0	0	0	1	0	4.0	7	16	2	2	0	0	0	0	0	0	4	0	0
Bell, Mike, Albany*	3	3	.500	2.61	12	0	0	0	4	0	20.2	13	81	8	6	0	2	0	1	8	0	14	0	0
Benson, Jeremy, Greensboro*	0	1	.000	0.00	3	0	0	0	3	0	4.0	1	14	0	0	0	0	0	0	2	0	4	0	0
Beverlin, Jason, Greensboro	2	4	.333	2.65	7	7	1	1	0	0	51.0	49	198	15	15	1	0	0	0	6	0	31	4	0
Binversie, Brian, Greensboro......	0	4	.000	4.96	31	0	0	0	12	0	45.1	53	206	30	25	7	0	5	2	18	1	32	2	0
Bledsoe, Randy, Savannah	2	1	.667	6.42	28	0	0	0	7	0	33.2	41	167	25	24	0	1	3	4	21	1	28	4	0
Blythe, Billy, Macon	0	2	.000	10.34	7	2	0	0	2	1	15.2	15	79	20	18	0	1	4	14	0	15	5	2
Bost, Heath, Asheville	4	1	.800	1.52	9	2	0	0	4	0	23.2	20	90	6	4	1	0	0	1	3	0	17	1	2
Bowie, Micah, Macon*	4	1	.800	2.28	5	5	0	0	0	0	27.2	9	104	8	7	1	0	0	3	11	0	36	1	0
Boyd, Jason, Piedmont	6	8	.429	3.58	26	24	1	0	1	0	151.0	151	638	77	60	8	5	3	4	44	0	129	18	2
Briggs, Anthony, Macon	8	5	.615	2.99	29	24	1	1	0	0	147.1	145	635	76	49	12	2	1	4	56	1	114	9	0
Broome, John, Hickory	0	1	.000	9.64	4	0	0	0	3	0	4.2	8	25	5	5	1	0	1	0	4	0	3	0	0
Brown, Charlie, Greensboro	4	4	.500	4.42	45	2	0	0	22	4	57.0	57	252	31	28	6	3	3	2	23	5	69	11	1

Pitcher, Team	W	L	Pct.	ERA	G	GS	CG	ShO	GF	Sv.	IP	H	TBF	R	ER	HR	SH	SF	HB	BB	IBB	SO	WP	Bk.
Brown, Darold, Macon*	3	1	.750	3.29	31	0	0	0	20	5	54.2	39	230	22	20	1	3	4	4	32	1	55	7	2
Brownson, Mark, Asheville	6	7	.462	4.01	23	12	0	0	4	1	98.2	106	422	52	44	12	2	2	4	29	0	94	4	2
Burdick, Morgan, Asheville	0	1	.000	4.39	17	0	0	0	7	0	26.2	26	110	13	13	1	0	0	0	10	1	19	2	0
Buteaux, Shane, Hickory	2	7	.222	7.29	13	13	0	0	0	0	66.2	90	316	63	54	10	4	5	3	32	2	30	2	1
Cain, Travis, Macon	1	2	.333	7.52	14	2	0	0	4	0	26.1	25	136	23	22	2	0	0	6	31	0	32	7	0
Caldwell, David, Columbus*	11	10	.524	4.40	27	27	0	0	0	0	151.1	162	655	87	74	12	4	2	4	58	0	104	6	2
Callahan, Damon, Cha. (W.Va.)	2	1	.667	6.12	6	6	0	0	0	0	25.0	33	120	22	17	1	0	1	2	14	2	17	4	0
Carlson, Garret, Hickory	0	0	.000	32.40	3	0	0	0	1	0	1.2	2	11	6	6	1	0	0	0	4	0	2	0	0
Caruthers, Clayton, Cha. (W.Va.)	11	7	.611	3.70	27	27	0	0	0	0	138.2	149	600	67	57	6	5	4	14	50	1	105	13	2
Castillo, Carlos, Hickory	5	6	.455	3.73	14	12	2	0	2	1	79.2	85	343	42	33	11	1	3	3	18	0	67	3	6
Censale, Silvio, Piedmont*	10	6	.625	3.15	22	21	0	0	0	0	120.0	96	507	54	42	6	5	4	5	54	0	123	10	3
Chavarria, David, Cha. (S.C.)	3	5	.375	3.92	52	0	0	0	22	6	62.0	55	277	33	27	5	2	5	1	38	3	68	16	0
Chaves, Rafael, Augusta	1	0	1.000	2.08	7	0	0	0	2	2	8.2	2	36	3	2	0	2	0	0	6	0	9	0	0
Civit, Xavier, Albany	2	3	.400	7.62	12	1	0	0	0	0	26.0	34	135	30	22	0	2	0	2	18	4	29	2	2
Clark, Doug, Fayetteville	0	1	.000	11.57	4	0	0	0	2	0	4.2	10	27	11	6	2	0	0	0	3	0	3	0	1
Cole, Jason, Albany	3	3	.500	4.37	32	4	0	0	11	1	57.2	67	257	33	28	3	2	2	4	22	2	51	2	1
Collins, Zach, Macon*	0	0	.000	5.40	4	0	0	0	2	0	3.1	7	20	4	2	0	0	0	1	2	0	3	0	0
Colmenares, Luis, Asheville	2	2	.500	2.29	45	0	0	0	38	21	55.0	37	223	15	14	1	2	2	1	29	1	74	11	2
Conway, Keith, Savannah*	7	2	.778	1.46	60	0	0	0	26	10	74.0	49	297	14	12	1	5	3	3	26	3	87	3	0
Cook, Rodney, Cha. (S.C.)	3	8	.273	2.53	60	0	0	0	36	11	96.0	83	415	32	27	3	5	4	9	39	5	88	8	1
Cooke, Steve, Augusta*	1	0	1.000	0.00	1	1	0	0	0	0	5.0	2	19	0	0	0	0	0	0	1	0	6	0	0
Cooney, James, Cha. (S.C.)	0	0	.000	0.00	1	0	0	0	0	0	0.0	0	0	0	0	0	0	0	0	0	0	0	0	0
Cooper, Steve, Savannah	0	1	.000	6.75	2	0	0	0	2	0	1.1	2	8	1	1	0	0	0	1	1	1	0	1	0
Cordero, Francisco, Fayetteville	0	3	.000	6.30	4	4	0	0	0	0	20.0	26	92	16	14	1	2	2	0	12	0	19	4	0
Corn, Chris, Greensboro	8	7	.533	1.76	49	0	0	0	39	24	82.0	54	317	20	16	3	1	2	2	22	0	101	5	1
Crine, Dennis, Hickory	3	6	.333	6.12	15	11	0	0	1	1	60.1	74	276	52	41	7	2	4	5	20	2	20	5	1
Crowther, Brent, Asheville	12	3	.800	2.28	15	15	3	3	0	0	98.2	79	393	31	25	4	0	1	3	25	0	72	11	1
Crowther, John, Hagerstown	1	3	.250	5.45	11	11	0	0	0	0	38.0	52	189	36	23	3	0	0	3	27	0	21	10	2
Cruise, Mark, Savannah	0	0	.000	3.68	6	0	0	0	0	0	7.1	8	37	5	3	1	0	0	0	1	0	5	1	1
Cruz, Nelson, Hickory	2	7	.222	2.70	44	0	0	0	29	9	66.2	65	285	31	20	6	3	1	4	15	2	68	5	0
Cubillan, Darwin, Greensboro	5	5	.500	3.62	22	14	1	1	3	0	97.0	86	409	50	39	5	3	1	4	38	1	78	5	0
Culp, Wes, Macon	4	6	.400	3.53	39	5	0	0	14	3	104.2	100	456	56	41	7	8	5	6	44	2	56	9	1
Davenport, Joe, Hagerstown	0	1	.000	6.11	13	0	0	0	2	0	17.2	22	91	19	12	3	0	0	1	13	0	13	6	0
Davey, Tom, Hagerstown	4	1	.800	3.38	8	8	0	0	0	0	37.1	29	167	23	14	2	1	1	2	31	0	25	9	0
Davis, Kane, Augusta	12	6	.667	3.75	26	25	1	0	0	0	139.1	136	602	73	58	4	3	4	9	43	0	78	10	1
Dinnen, Kevin, Columbus	2	7	.222	4.14	49	0	0	0	24	1	58.2	47	255	34	27	4	4	4	3	34	9	43	1	0
Dinyar, Eric, Fayetteville	4	3	.571	2.49	42	0	0	0	16	5	86.2	77	356	34	24	1	1	4	8	25	0	71	2	1
Dixon, Jim, Hickory	4	1	.800	1.93	35	0	0	0	17	5	51.1	43	220	23	11	1	4	2	1	16	5	56	6	1
Doman, Roger, Hagerstown	2	2	.500	4.41	14	6	0	0	3	1	51.0	65	233	32	25	0	0	1	3	13	0	24	4	0
Done, J.J., Columbus	0	3	.000	9.00	4	3	0	0	0	0	12.0	21	65	15	12	1	0	1	1	9	1	8	3	1
Donnelly, Brendan, Cha. (W.Va.)	1	1	.500	1.19	24	0	0	0	22	12	30.1	14	112	4	4	0	1	2	1	7	1	33	1	0
Donovan, Scot, Columbus	0	6	.000	4.81	40	0	0	0	31	10	48.2	53	238	38	26	6	3	0	3	36	4	38	6	1
Dougherty, Tony, Columbus	4	4	.500	4.72	27	10	0	0	3	0	87.2	85	405	61	46	5	2	4	8	50	4	78	4	1
Doyle, Tom, Cha. (W.Va.)*	6	4	.600	4.35	14	12	1	0	0	0	62.0	57	272	34	30	3	2	1	7	30	3	66	9	0
Durocher, Jayson, Albany	3	7	.300	3.91	24	22	1	0	1	0	122.0	105	526	67	53	5	4	11	5	56	1	88	11	1
Ebert, Derrin, Macon*	14	5	.737	3.31	28	28	0	0	0	0	182.0	184	766	87	67	12	5	4	7	46	0	124	3	2
Eden, Bill, Asheville	5	3	.625	2.14	33	0	0	0	17	9	67.1	55	269	22	16	4	1	0	1	14	0	80	7	2
Escamilla, Jaime, Cha. (S.C.)*	3	4	.429	4.42	32	5	0	0	10	2	71.1	59	305	38	35	8	3	3	2	38	1	76	8	1
Estavil, Mauricio, Piedmont*	3	5	.375	3.68	42	0	0	0	18	1	44.0	33	202	20	18	0	0	0	2	37	1	58	6	0
Evangelista, Alberto, Macon	4	4	.500	3.50	24	2	1	0	12	0	54.0	42	224	29	21	4	4	3	2	16	0	51	6	2
Fantauzzi, John, Asheville*	0	0	.000	18.00	1	0	0	0	1	0	1.0	2	8	2	2	0	0	0	0	4	0	1	0	0
Fereira, Marcos, Hickory	0	2	.000	16.88	4	0	0	0	1	0	2.2	6	20	6	5	0	2	1	1	4	2	1	2	3
Forbes, Adam, Hickory*	0	0	.000	9.82	2	0	0	0	1	0	3.2	5	19	5	4	1	0	1	2	0	0	1	1	0
Ford, Ben, Greensboro	0	0	.000	5.14	7	0	0	0	2	0	7.0	4	31	4	4	1	1	0	0	5	1	8	2	0
Ford, Jack, Hickory*	8	14	.364	3.89	27	27	3	0	0	0	173.2	174	738	86	75	14	8	5	6	66	3	157	5	0
France, Aaron, Augusta	6	6	.500	2.47	18	15	0	0	0	0	94.2	80	388	29	26	4	3	3	5	26	0	77	6	2
Franklin, Joel, Cha. (W.Va.)	3	3	.500	4.97	24	1	0	0	4	2	50.2	49	221	28	28	2	2	3	4	22	2	58	6	0
Gambs, Chris, Piedmont	0	0	.000	6.86	9	0	0	0	2	0	19.2	24	95	17	15	2	0	2	1	14	0	15	3	0
Garcia, Frank, Savannah	0	3	.000	3.16	34	0	0	0	32	24	37.0	26	156	17	13	3	0	1	2	15	0	41	8	0
Garcia-Luna, Francisco, Augusta	2	1	.667	2.86	14	10	1	0	0	0	63.0	57	263	31	20	3	1	2	3	17	0	48	5	0
Gardner, Scott, Fayetteville	6	3	.667	2.06	49	1	0	0	22	4	87.1	62	351	26	20	5	1	0	2	24	1	112	8	2
Genke, Todd, Piedmont	3	2	.600	3.91	31	1	0	0	4	1	53.0	50	227	30	23	3	3	1	2	18	3	37	4	0
Giard, Kenneth, Macon	1	0	1.000	0.68	5	0	0	0	3	0	13.1	7	51	1	1	0	1	0	0	5	0	19	2	0
Giron, Emiliano, Cha. (W.Va.)	0	0	.000	0.94	30	0	0	0	28	20	28.2	12	108	3	3	0	1	0	1	8	0	39	1	2
Glauber, Keith, Savannah	2	1	.667	3.73	40	0	0	0	3	0	62.2	50	277	29	26	2	2	3	5	36	3	62	9	1
Gogolewski, Chris, Cha. (S.C.)*	5	13	.278	4.23	30	19	2	0	5	0	140.1	169	627	93	66	5	4	5	12	38	1	84	12	2
Golden, Matthew, Savannah	7	3	.700	2.00	64	0	0	0	24	1	90.0	71	355	22	20	2	2	2	0	21	4	94	4	2
Gonzalez, Jhonny, Asheville*	4	3	.571	2.48	21	0	0	0	10	3	32.2	23	136	13	9	3	2	1	1	15	1	31	1	1
Gooch, Arnold, Ash.-C'bia	5	8	.385	2.94	21	21	1	1	0	0	128.2	111	541	51	42	8	3	3	4	57	0	117	13	0
Graham, Steve, Macon	1	1	.500	9.35	5	0	0	0	2	0	8.2	17	53	12	9	2	1	0	1	5	0	7	1	1
Granata, Chris, Columbus	11	5	.688	2.47	33	12	0	0	6	0	113.0	94	477	43	31	2	6	3	4	53	7	93	8	1
Grebe, Brett, Augusta	2	2	.500	3.62	32	0	0	0	15	2	37.1	42	165	19	15	3	1	2	0	16	1	36	2	1
Grundt, Ken, Asheville*	0	0	.000	0.30	20	0	0	0	11	1	30.1	18	111	1	1	0	1	1	1	7	1	38	2	0
Hackman, Luther, Asheville	11	11	.500	4.64	28	28	2	0	0	0	165.0	162	710	95	85	11	3	3	14	65	0	108	9	7
Halley, Allen, Hickory	2	1	.667	2.55	13	9	0	0	2	1	60.0	46	234	21	17	6	1	0	2	12	2	58	2	1
Hamilton, Paul, Piedmont	1	0	1.000	4.71	15	1	0	0	4	0	21.0	24	90	11	11	0	0	1	2	7	0	10	2	0
Hampton, Mark, Augusta	5	5	.500	4.13	39	0	0	0	15	0	56.2	46	255	32	26	8	4	1	1	38	2	45	6	0
Handy, Russell, Albany	2	7	.222	4.27	30	5	0	0	6	2	71.2	78	340	50	34	4	6	3	6	37	1	57	14	1
Hartmann, Rich, Savannah	1	2	.333	5.05	31	0	0	0	10	0	41.0	35	182	26	23	8	2	1	3	20	2	52	3	0
Hartshorn, Tyson, Hagerstown	3	4	.429	5.36	12	7	0	0	1	0	48.2	59	224	37	29	8	1	1	5	20	0	28	6	0
Harvell, Pete, Cha. (W.Va.)*	0	0	.000	2.93	27	0	0	0	9	0	27.2	25	114	11	9	2	1	1	3	10	1	17	5	0
Hausmann, Isaac, Cha. (S.C.)	0	0	.000	9.45	5	0	0	0	4	0	6.2	10	35	10	7	2	1	0	2	1	0	6	0	1
Helvey, Rob, Savannah*	2	1	.667	7.97	18	0	0	0	7	0	20.1	28	107	22	18	1	2	0	3	16	0	25	5	0

Pitcher, Team	W	L	Pct.	ERA	G	GS	CG	ShO	GF	Sv.	IP	H	TBF	R	ER	HR	SH	SF	HB	BB	IBB	SO	WP	Bk.
Henderson, Chris, Asheville	1	1	.500	1.63	17	0	0	0	10	1	27.2	20	119	6	5	1	0	1	4	18	0	28	4	0
Herbert, Russell, Hickory	3	8	.273	2.67	18	18	1	1	0	0	114.2	83	474	48	34	9	3	3	8	46	0	115	5	2
Hibbard, Billy, Hagerstown	2	1	.667	3.89	16	0	0	0	5	0	34.2	42	149	16	15	1	0	1	1	6	1	20	2	0
Housley, Adam, Fayetteville	3	1	.750	2.37	19	0	0	0	6	1	38.0	26	156	14	10	0	0	1	1	11	1	43	1	0
Hower, Dan, Cha. (S.C.)*	4	7	.364	7.29	22	17	0	0	3	1	82.2	96	404	88	67	5	4	3	5	59	1	55	13	0
Humphry, Trevor, Piedmont	5	7	.417	3.62	28	20	2	0	4	0	119.1	122	532	67	48	7	2	4	6	63	0	102	13	0
Hunter, Rich, Piedmont	10	2	.833	2.77	15	15	3	2	0	0	104.0	79	404	37	32	9	1	1	2	19	0	80	0	0
Jacobson, Kelton, Fayetteville	5	7	.417	5.82	25	12	0	0	5	0	68.0	72	317	52	44	3	2	3	6	44	1	64	9	2
Jarvis, Jason, Gre.-Hag.	12	10	.545	3.19	30	24	0	0	2	0	160.2	152	678	74	57	8	6	9	4	51	4	124	20	2
Johnson, Jason, Augusta	3	5	.375	4.36	11	11	1	0	0	0	53.2	57	233	32	26	2	1	1	4	17	0	42	3	0
Johnston, Sean, Columbia*	11	6	.647	3.03	23	22	2	0	0	0	148.1	132	621	60	50	6	4	4	11	63	2	105	15	1
Jordan, Jason, Fayetteville	10	4	.714	2.28	24	24	0	0	0	0	138.0	128	575	48	35	5	0	3	8	43	0	103	13	1
Judd, Mike, Greensboro	0	0	.000	0.00	1	0	0	0	1	0	2.2	2	11	0	0	0	0	0	0	0	0	1	0	0
Karvala, Kyle, Piedmont*	5	1	.833	3.44	20	0	0	0	10	2	18.1	13	75	9	7	0	0	2	0	7	0	17	1	0
Kell, Rob, Cha. (S.C.)*	1	4	.200	3.48	7	7	0	0	0	0	44.0	38	184	20	17	2	3	1	2	9	0	47	3	0
Kelly, Jeff, Augusta*	6	11	.353	3.47	26	26	0	0	0	0	142.2	134	608	68	55	6	5	5	4	51	0	114	12	0
Kelly, John, Columbia	8	8	.500	3.88	28	28	3	0	0	0	167.0	148	691	80	72	16	2	5	10	65	0	124	11	2
Kindell, Scott, Columbia*	0	0	.000	0.00	1	0	0	0	1	0	0.1	0	1	0	0	0	0	0	0	0	0	0	0	0
Knight, Brandon, Cha. (S.C.)	4	2	.667	3.13	9	9	0	0	0	0	54.2	37	218	22	19	5	0	4	0	21	0	52	4	1
Knighton, Toure, Cha. (S.C.)	1	9	.100	4.88	22	19	1	0	1	0	107.0	121	482	64	58	5	2	3	8	46	0	100	8	1
Koppe, Clint, Cha. (W.Va.)	7	13	.350	3.37	30	22	2	0	1	0	157.2	144	653	66	59	10	4	5	6	47	5	119	8	1
Kosek, Kory, Piedmont	1	2	.333	0.00	15	0	0	0	7	3	20.1	13	83	8	0	1	2	0	3	5	2	24	0	0
Kramer, Scott, Columbus	2	2	.500	2.08	19	1	0	0	6	2	52.0	45	213	19	12	3	0	0	6	14	1	53	4	0
Kusiewicz, Michael, Asheville*	8	4	.667	2.06	21	21	0	0	0	0	122.1	92	484	40	28	6	2	0	6	34	0	103	9	1
LaPoint, Jason, Albany*	5	2	.714	3.52	33	0	0	0	12	0	61.1	72	272	34	24	1	1	2	1	15	0	52	3	0
Larson, Toby, Columbia	3	3	.500	2.63	8	8	0	0	0	0	51.1	43	224	24	15	2	1	2	1	19	0	53	5	1
Lasbury, Robert, Asheville	0	2	.000	8.64	6	0	0	0	1	0	8.1	10	43	11	8	1	0	0	0	6	0	5	1	0
Lavenia, Mark, Macon*	4	3	.571	2.14	24	3	0	0	16	4	46.1	38	195	17	11	2	3	0	1	14	1	45	1	1
Lee, Jeremy, Hagerstown	7	11	.389	4.20	26	26	1	0	0	0	148.0	160	626	82	69	11	1	8	8	29	0	118	4	0
Legrow, Brett, Piedmont	0	1	.000	5.14	8	2	0	0	4	1	14.0	16	64	10	8	2	0	0	0	5	0	8	2	0
Leiber, Zane, Hickory	1	0	1.000	5.60	14	0	0	0	7	0	17.2	19	78	13	11	3	0	1	0	5	0	13	5	1
Logan, Marcus, Savannah	3	6	.333	3.32	34	7	0	0	2	0	86.2	73	373	42	32	3	1	5	2	38	0	83	11	1
Lott, Brian, Cha. (W.Va.)	8	7	.533	3.46	28	20	0	0	3	1	138.0	155	586	56	53	9	4	1	6	33	3	96	3	3
Lovingier, Kevin, Savannah*	6	3	.667	1.34	38	0	0	0	18	1	47.0	35	195	14	7	1	3	1	1	21	5	54	3	0
Maberry, Louis, Cha. (W.Va.)	0	1	.000	0.00	4	0	0	0	2	0	5.0	2	21	1	0	0	1	0	0	3	1	0	0	0
Magre, Pete, Cha. (W.Va.)	2	1	.667	5.08	21	0	0	0	2	0	28.1	34	119	16	16	2	1	2	2	8	2	19	3	0
Manning, Len, Piedmont*	10	10	.500	2.64	27	26	1	0	0	0	160.0	130	658	68	47	10	7	5	7	58	0	154	4	2
Martin, Chandler, Asheville	4	3	.571	3.83	8	8	0	0	0	0	49.1	48	216	23	21	0	2	0	3	27	0	32	6	1
Martinez, Johnny, Columbus	6	1	.857	1.83	16	2	0	0	2	0	54.0	37	210	15	11	0	2	1	4	14	0	43	3	0
Martinez, Osvaldo, Fayetteville	0	0	.000	4.15	6	0	0	0	2	0	13.0	11	49	6	6	2	1	1	0	1	0	15	0	1
Maskivish, Joe, Augusta	2	1	.667	2.12	26	0	0	0	26	20	29.2	23	122	9	7	0	1	0	3	9	4	33	2	0
Mattes, Troy, Albany	0	2	.000	5.03	4	4	0	0	0	0	19.2	21	90	12	11	0	2	0	0	12	1	15	1	1
McAdams, Denny, Asheville	0	0	.000	3.86	5	0	0	0	3	0	7.0	7	29	4	3	1	0	0	0	2	0	7	0	0
McBride, Chris, Hagerstown	5	10	.333	4.29	19	19	2	0	0	0	107.0	121	461	61	51	4	5	3	5	27	1	52	3	1
McClinton, Patrick, Asheville*	1	2	.333	3.51	18	0	0	0	7	2	33.1	27	140	16	13	2	3	3	4	9	1	22	3	3
McEntire, Ethan, Columbia*	3	2	.600	3.34	6	6	1	1	0	0	32.1	26	146	14	12	4	3	0	0	23	0	31	3	0
McNeill, Kevin, Savannah*	3	7	.300	4.96	29	21	0	0	2	0	110.2	131	502	74	61	5	1	0	3	47	1	87	14	0
Medina, Rafael, Greensboro	4	4	.500	4.01	19	19	1	0	0	0	98.2	86	418	48	44	8	0	5	6	38	0	108	6	3
Meiners, Doug, Hagerstown	8	4	.667	2.99	18	18	3	0	0	0	117.1	121	477	52	39	5	2	2	3	14	0	73	4	1
Mejias, Fernando, Hickory	2	9	.182	4.59	30	16	0	0	4	0	111.2	128	497	78	57	6	3	3	5	38	4	76	11	2
Meyer, David, Greensboro*	8	4	.667	4.86	14	14	1	1	0	0	87.0	104	377	52	47	5	3	2	3	28	0	54	5	1
Mikkelsen, Lincoln, Albany	0	1	.000	1.93	12	0	0	0	5	5	23.1	24	107	14	5	0	1	0	3	8	0	17	1	0
Millwood, Kevin, Macon	5	6	.455	4.63	29	12	0	0	5	0	103.0	86	458	65	53	10	3	1	5	57	0	89	10	0
Minor, Tom, Savannah	1	1	.500	4.91	8	0	0	0	3	0	7.1	10	33	7	4	1	0	1	0	2	0	9	0	0
Mitchell, Courtney, Piedmont*	0	1	.000	10.38	5	0	0	0	2	0	4.1	7	22	5	5	0	0	0	0	5	0	3	1	0
Mittauer, Casey, Greensboro	3	6	.333	1.94	49	0	0	0	22	8	74.1	60	294	26	16	3	6	4	3	14	4	59	5	0
Montoya, Wilmer, Columbus	3	3	.500	3.12	51	0	0	0	41	31	80.2	65	337	33	28	4	1	0	2	36	1	91	6	2
Moore, David, Hickory	1	0	1.000	6.18	20	0	0	0	12	0	27.2	41	128	20	19	5	0	2	3	7	1	15	2	0
Moraga, David, Albany*	8	8	.500	2.68	25	24	1	0	0	0	147.2	136	620	63	44	6	6	4	1	46	0	109	10	0
Morillo, Donald, Cha. (S.C.)	1	4	.200	2.10	18	0	0	0	13	1	25.2	22	115	7	6	1	0	0	3	17	2	28	1	0
Mortimer, Mick, Cha. (S.C.)	0	0	.000	0.00	5	0	0	0	1	0	13.1	10	52	2	0	0	0	2	1	6	0	11	2	0
Moss, Damian, Macon*	9	10	.474	3.56	27	27	0	0	0	0	149.1	134	653	73	59	13	0	2	12	70	0	177	14	5
Najera, Noe, Columbus*	3	1	.750	3.38	43	0	0	0	15	1	42.2	34	189	20	16	3	2	1	6	24	3	53	4	2
Newton, Chris, Fayetteville*	0	0	.000	5.79	2	0	0	0	1	0	4.2	6	20	3	3	0	0	1	0	1	0	3	0	0
Nieto, Tony, Cha. (W.Va.)	3	4	.429	3.44	13	8	2	2	0	0	55.0	55	246	37	21	1	6	1	8	21	6	35	1	0
Nunez, Maximo, Hagerstown	1	1	.500	5.54	22	0	0	0	11	0	37.1	40	172	29	23	4	3	2	3	20	0	21	8	0
Nuttle, Jamison, Augusta	0	0	.000	1.17	6	0	0	0	0	0	7.2	5	38	3	1	0	0	0	0	8	0	10	0	0
Nyari, Pete, Piedmont	5	1	.833	4.52	35	1	0	0	12	1	61.2	58	279	40	31	0	3	2	5	39	0	49	8	6
Nygaard, Chris, Albany*	6	4	.600	2.86	41	0	0	0	18	1	56.2	60	241	25	18	5	3	0	2	8	0	43	3	0
Ocasio, Fred, Asheville	0	0	.000	0.00	1	0	0	0	1	0	0.2	0	2	0	0	0	0	0	0	0	0	0	0	0
O'Flynn, Gardner, Cha. (S.C.)*	9	10	.474	2.96	30	24	2	1	1	0	167.0	156	698	70	55	11	4	3	6	61	0	110	7	4
Olszewski, Eric, Macon	2	5	.286	3.76	35	1	0	0	15	5	81.1	54	351	37	34	3	1	1	8	50	1	103	11	3
Oropeza, Igor, Columbus	4	1	.800	1.48	9	8	0	0	0	0	48.2	39	200	13	8	1	2	0	3	13	0	46	2	2
Pace, Scott, Hagerstown*	4	2	.667	1.09	11	6	2	1	2	1	57.2	32	211	8	7	2	1	0	2	12	0	57	4	0
Pack, Steve, Columbia	2	7	.222	3.70	36	0	0	0	22	12	56.0	63	254	33	23	1	3	0	1	20	5	35	0	3
Parotte, Frisco, Greensboro	3	1	.750	2.80	22	0	0	0	8	0	35.1	40	161	20	11	3	2	1	2	16	1	35	3	0
Paugh, Rick, Augusta*	6	2	.750	2.59	52	0	0	0	25	2	59.0	60	252	23	17	3	4	1	0	17	5	61	6	1
Pauls, Matthew, Cha. (S.C.)	3	3	.500	4.22	16	0	0	0	14	2	21.1	22	103	20	10	0	3	2	2	10	4	19	2	0
Pelka, Brian, Augusta	1	3	.250	5.98	26	0	0	0	7	0	40.2	46	193	31	27	3	4	2	5	20	1	29	4	1
Perez, Joe, Cha. (S.C.)*	0	0	.000	0.00	1	0	0	0	1	0	1.0	0	3	0	0	0	0	0	0	0	0	0	0	0
Perez, Julio, Columbus	8	5	.615	4.02	22	17	0	0	5	1	109.2	109	461	53	49	4	2	3	4	39	5	100	5	5
Perpetuo, Nelson, Cha. (S.C.)*	6	4	.600	3.21	32	10	1	0	13	0	103.2	80	439	47	37	11	3	2	5	51	5	125	5	1
Peterman, Ernie, Hagerstown	0	1	.000	12.60	2	0	0	0	2	0	5.0	9	25	7	7	2	0	0	0	1	0	4	0	0

Pitcher, Team	W	L	Pct.	ERA	G	GS	CG	ShO	GF	Sv.	IP	H	TBF	R	ER	HR	SH	SF	HB	BB	IBB	SO	WP	Bk.
Phelps, Tommy, Albany*	10	9	.526	3.33	24	24	1	0	0	0	135.1	142	597	76	50	6	0	4	5	45	0	119	5	1
Phillips, Jason, Augusta	4	3	.571	3.60	30	6	0	0	3	0	80.0	76	354	46	32	2	2	2	0	53	1	65	10	0
Phipps, Chris, Piedmont	0	2	.000	1.96	11	0	0	0	3	0	23.0	24	101	9	5	0	0	2	2	8	0	10	3	0
Pickford, Kevin, Augusta*	7	3	.700	2.00	16	16	0	0	0	0	85.2	85	354	28	19	5	2	1	5	16	1	59	2	0
Portillo, Alex, Hickory*	0	3	.000	2.25	33	0	0	0	15	2	56.0	57	243	24	14	1	3	0	6	10	5	36	0	0
Powell, Brian, Fayetteville	4	0	1.000	1.61	5	5	0	0	0	0	28.0	15	111	5	5	0	1	1	2	11	0	37	2	0
Powell, Jeremy, Albany	1	0	1.000	1.59	1	1	0	0	0	0	5.2	4	20	1	1	0	0	0	1	0	0	6	1	0
Presley, Kirk, Columbia	1	2	.333	5.14	4	4	0	0	0	0	21.0	30	100	17	12	0	1	0	0	13	0	8	1	0
Raines, Ken, Macon*	1	1	.500	1.93	14	0	0	0	12	8	18.2	11	70	4	4	0	0	0	0	5	1	22	1	1
Ramirez, Rafael, Savannah	6	15	.286	3.91	26	25	0	0	0	0	147.1	160	645	81	64	8	4	9	7	42	1	91	9	2
Reames, Britt, Savannah	3	5	.375	3.46	10	10	1	0	0	0	54.2	41	227	23	21	7	0	0	5	15	0	63	9	1
Reed, Brandon, Fayetteville	3	0	1.000	0.97	55	0	0	0	53	41	64.2	40	252	11	7	1	1	0	3	18	1	78	8	0
Reid, Rayon, Augusta	2	5	.286	4.38	12	11	1	0	0	0	61.2	52	268	36	30	6	1	1	5	28	0	47	4	1
Reyes, Jose, Cha. (S.C.)	0	0	.000	18.00	4	0	0	0	2	0	4.0	10	25	8	8	2	0	0	0	3	0	5	1	0
Reynolds, Chance, Augusta	0	0	.000	0.00	1	0	0	0	1	0	0.1	1	2	0	0	0	0	0	0	0	0	0	0	0
Rhine, Kendall, Hagerstown	3	3	.500	2.60	42	0	0	0	36	13	55.1	41	230	20	16	2	4	0	3	28	1	49	8	0
Rhodriguez, Rory, Albany	3	4	.429	3.50	37	7	0	0	10	2	90.0	80	379	44	35	8	3	3	2	34	0	83	3	0
Ricken, Ray, Greensboro	3	2	.600	2.23	10	10	0	0	0	0	64.2	42	245	20	16	2	1	1	0	16	1	77	3	0
Roberts, Willis, Fayetteville	3	4	.667	2.70	17	15	0	0	0	0	80.0	72	339	33	24	2	1	2	6	40	0	52	15	3
Robinson, Martin, Greensboro*	1	0	1.000	7.56	2	1	0	0	0	0	8.1	8	44	7	7	0	1	0	0	12	0	5	1	0
Rocker, John, Macon*	4	4	.500	4.50	16	16	0	0	0	0	86.0	86	375	50	43	5	1	1	4	52	0	61	5	1
Rojano, Rafael, Greensboro	0	0	.000	6.58	19	1	0	0	9	1	26.0	35	134	24	19	5	0	0	7	13	0	38	5	2
Rose, Brian, Asheville	1	0	1.000	4.91	10	1	0	0	5	0	14.2	14	62	8	8	0	0	0	4	2	0	15	1	0
Ruiz, Rafael, Hickory*	1	0	1.000	15.75	5	0	0	0	1	0	4.0	7	25	8	7	0	0	0	1	5	0	5	2	0
Runion, Jeff, Cha. (S.C.)	1	1	.500	3.18	2	2	0	0	0	0	11.1	12	54	8	4	0	2	0	1	6	0	6	2	0
Runyan, Paul, Cha. (W.Va.)	6	2	.750	4.13	15	5	0	0	2	0	52.1	56	227	29	24	3	0	1	2	17	5	28	5	0
Rushworth, Jim, Albany	1	2	.333	8.31	6	0	0	0	4	1	8.2	10	44	9	8	0	1	0	1	6	3	5	3	0
Ryan, Reid, Cha. (S.C.)	0	4	.000	9.38	22	5	0	0	6	0	47.0	64	250	57	49	3	1	1	6	40	2	39	4	0
Sanchez, Jesus, Columbia*	9	7	.563	3.13	27	27	4	0	0	0	169.2	154	705	76	59	9	2	5	7	58	0	177	10	4
Sanders, Frankie, Columbus	1	1	.500	3.00	2	0	0	0	1	0	9.0	9	39	3	3	0	1	0	1	4	0	9	1	0
Sauerbeck, Scott, Columbia*	5	4	.556	3.27	19	0	0	0	13	2	33.0	28	139	14	12	2	2	0	1	14	1	33	3	1
Schaffner, Eric, Greensboro	0	1	.000	5.06	1	1	0	0	0	0	5.1	5	28	8	3	0	1	0	5	0	0	2	0
Schlomann, Brett, Greensboro	10	7	.588	3.90	25	25	1	0	0	0	147.2	144	639	76	64	10	2	1	9	54	1	140	8	1
Schneider, Jeff, Hagerstown	1	0	1.000	27.00	2	0	0	0	1	0	0.2	1	8	2	2	0	0	0	1	4	0	0	0	1
Serna, Joe, Fayetteville	4	0	1.000	2.36	12	0	0	0	4	0	26.2	14	105	13	7	1	3	0	2	10	0	21	2	0
Sexton, Jeff, Columbus	6	2	.750	2.19	14	13	2	2	0	0	82.1	66	318	27	20	2	1	1	3	16	0	71	1	0
Sharp, Scott, Cha. (W.Va.)	0	0	.000	27.00	1	0	0	0	1	0	1.0	7	13	3	3	0	0	1	0	3	0	0	2	0
Shelby, Anthony, Greensboro*	3	8	.273	4.01	27	13	0	0	3	0	89.2	87	381	54	40	5	2	4	6	28	0	81	6	0
Shoemaker, Steve, Greensboro	4	4	.500	3.11	17	17	0	0	0	0	81.0	62	347	33	28	3	2	4	52	0	82	4	0
Short, Barry, Columbus	4	3	.571	1.97	40	1	0	0	15	4	77.2	63	319	22	17	1	2	0	2	22	2	56	5	2
Shumate, Jacob, Macon	0	8	.000	7.23	17	14	0	0	0	0	56.0	38	296	56	45	7	1	3	9	87	0	57	19	2
Sievert, Mark, Hagerstown	12	6	.667	2.91	27	27	3	0	0	0	160.2	126	644	59	52	14	5	1	2	46	0	140	2	0
Siler, Jeff, Fayetteville*	1	1	.500	4.09	21	0	0	0	4	1	22.2	16	86	2	1	0	2	0	1	11	0	25	1	1
Silva, Theodore, Cha. (S.C.)	5	4	.556	3.38	11	11	0	0	0	0	66.2	59	276	26	25	4	1	3	7	12	2	66	5	2
Skrmetta, Matt, Fayetteville	9	4	.692	2.71	44	2	0	0	15	2	89.2	66	371	36	27	9	6	1	3	35	2	105	2	0
Slamka, John, Asheville*	1	1	.500	4.09	6	1	0	0	2	0	11.0	9	46	5	5	0	0	1	1	4	0	7	1	1
Smith, Brian, Hagerstown	9	1	.900	0.87	47	0	0	0	36	21	104.0	77	402	18	10	1	5	0	5	16	1	101	2	2
Smith, Cam, Fayetteville	13	8	.619	3.81	29	29	2	2	0	0	149.0	110	652	75	63	6	3	18	87	0	166	21	1
Smith, Justin, Cha. (W.Va.)	4	5	.444	3.61	44	0	0	0	14	1	62.1	66	275	28	25	3	4	1	2	24	5	43	3	1
Sobik, Trad, Fayetteville	8	5	.615	4.16	18	18	0	0	0	0	101.2	100	430	68	47	4	2	6	3	43	0	58	1	2
Solomon, David, Cha. (W.Va.)*	1	2	.333	3.40	43	0	0	0	27	6	39.2	38	175	19	15	3	2	2	5	23	2	29	6	2
Spade, Matt, Augusta	6	5	.545	2.92	51	1	0	0	21	5	71.0	50	289	23	23	4	1	0	6	19	3	71	5	1
Spring, Josh, Hagerstown	1	4	.200	4.17	19	4	0	0	4	0	45.1	44	198	23	21	5	2	3	19	0	33	4	0
Stephens, Bill, Albany	1	3	.250	5.75	13	1	0	0	6	0	20.1	25	95	16	13	2	1	3	1	9	0	16	3	0
Stewart, Scott, Cha. (S.C.)*	1	7	.125	3.69	11	11	1	0	0	0	75.2	76	302	38	31	6	1	4	0	14	1	47	3	5
Stubbs, Jerry, Albany	3	2	.600	3.22	47	1	0	0	17	3	100.2	106	438	51	36	4	6	3	10	30	2	80	8	1
Stumpf, Brian, Piedmont	3	3	.500	2.34	55	0	0	0	47	28	61.2	59	258	20	16	2	5	2	0	19	0	66	7	0
Surratt, Jamie, Hickory	0	1	.000	1.76	12	0	0	0	9	3	15.1	13	69	8	3	1	1	1	0	8	4	19	1	0
Swanson, David, C'bia-Ash.*	8	1	.889	2.02	37	4	0	0	18	4	80.1	62	332	21	18	3	2	3	5	38	2	67	7	2
Tatis, Ramon, Columbia*	2	3	.400	5.63	18	2	0	0	9	0	32.0	34	141	27	20	1	2	1	1	14	0	27	5	0
Temple, Jason, Augusta	5	2	.714	2.26	51	0	0	0	18	5	71.2	45	297	26	18	6	4	3	28	0	84	5	1
Theodile, Robert, Hickory	6	9	.400	3.79	20	17	1	1	1	0	107.0	103	470	61	45	8	3	5	5	53	2	77	13	4
Thompson, Mark, Macon	3	2	.600	4.71	13	0	0	0	8	2	21.0	13	82	12	11	1	2	4	1	4	1	15	0	1
Thurman, Michael, Albany	3	8	.273	5.47	22	22	2	0	0	0	110.1	133	482	79	67	4	3	7	4	32	0	77	7	0
Tomko, Brett, Cha. (W.Va.)	4	2	.667	1.84	9	7	0	0	0	0	49.0	41	192	12	10	1	1	2	1	9	1	46	4	2
Toney, Mike, Hagerstown	3	3	.500	2.48	20	0	0	0	10	4	29.0	21	127	11	8	0	1	3	0	17	2	26	6	2
Trimble, Rob, Greensboro	1	1	.500	3.65	6	0	0	0	3	0	12.1	12	51	5	5	0	0	0	4	0	5	1	0
Turrentine, Rich, Columbia	4	4	.500	2.51	26	14	0	0	8	2	104.0	70	437	38	29	3	6	4	6	60	1	111	16	1
Tweedle, Brad, Cha. (W.Va.)	2	4	.333	6.16	19	7	0	0	4	0	49.2	46	226	36	34	3	0	4	3	34	0	40	5	1
Tyner, Mark, Macon	2	2	.500	3.28	29	0	0	0	16	3	46.2	48	204	31	17	5	2	2	0	17	1	38	9	0
Van Overen, Ryan, Albany	0	1	.000	9.00	1	0	0	0	1	0	1.0	1	5	1	1	0	0	0	0	1	0	1	0	0
Vaske, Terry, Macon	0	1	.000	36.00	1	0	0	0	1	0	1.0	4	8	4	4	0	0	0	1	0	0	0	0	0
Vavrek, Mike, Asheville*	5	4	.556	2.00	12	12	1	0	0	0	76.2	64	322	24	17	3	0	1	5	25	0	54	4	5
Vazquez, Javier, Albany	6	6	.500	5.08	21	21	1	0	0	0	102.2	109	459	67	58	8	1	2	9	47	0	87	2	2
Vejil, Aaron, Cha. (W.Va.)*	2	0	1.000	6.00	6	0	0	0	3	0	3.1	2	15	0	0	0	0	0	3	1	5	0	0
Waldrep, Art, Asheville	3	0	.000	5.68	15	3	0	0	5	1	31.2	48	153	23	20	3	2	3	10	2	21	3	1
Warrecker, Teddy, Columbus	10	5	.667	4.13	24	24	1	1	0	0	130.2	104	559	76	60	10	3	3	13	80	1	125	6	0
Weber, Lenny, Columbus	4	0	1.000	1.84	17	0	0	0	5	2	29.1	19	113	6	6	2	0	0	10	3	32	3	0
Wehn, Kevin, Asheville	2	0	.000	6.30	5	0	0	0	3	1	10.0	9	42	7	7	1	0	0	0	4	0	5	1	0
Weidert, Chris, Albany	1	2	.333	7.84	3	1	0	0	0	0	10.1	16	55	14	9	3	0	1	0	5	0	17	0	0
Weiss, Marc, Cha. (W.Va.)	1	0	1.000	5.12	11	0	0	0	2	0	14.2	23	78	10	9	2	0	0	13	2	12	1	0
Welch, David, Hickory*	4	5	.444	2.67	60	0	0	0	19	5	77.2	68	328	39	23	5	6	2	3	21	10	82	7	1
Wells, David, Hickory	1	5	.500	5.17	17	1	0	0	4	0	38.1	44	167	28	22	4	2	2	1	13	2	30	2	1

Pitcher, Team	W	L	Pct.	ERA	G	GS	CG	ShO	GF	Sv.	IP	H	TBF	R	ER	HR	SH	SF	HB	BB	IBB	SO	WP	Bk.
Whiteman, Greg, Fayetteville*	6	8	.429	4.23	23	23	1	1	0	0	125.2	108	547	68	59	9	5	4	9	58	0	145	4	1
Whiteman, Tony, Fayetteville*	0	1	.000	3.96	28	0	0	0	4	0	25.0	25	117	16	11	1	2	1	2	18	0	23	2	0
Wilkerson, Steven, Cha. (W.Va.).....	1	1	.500	5.49	16	0	0	0	8	0	19.2	21	97	13	12	0	0	0	2	18	0	15	4	0
Wilson, Mike, Fayetteville	4	3	.571	4.38	17	8	0	0	3	0	49.1	43	211	29	24	2	1	0	7	19	0	36	8	1
Wimberly, Larry, Piedmont*	10	3	.769	2.67	24	24	0	0	0	0	135.0	99	542	48	40	9	1	3	9	44	0	139	8	4
Windham, Mike, Savannah	6	9	.400	4.07	26	25	0	0	0	0	132.2	133	581	73	60	11	2	2	10	60	1	115	16	1
Wolff, Tom, Columbia................	0	0	.000	4.37	15	0	0	0	13	0	22.2	21	99	13	11	0	0	1	3	8	0	16	3	0
Woodring, Jason, Albany	1	1	.500	2.66	48	0	0	0	39	16	50.2	46	222	19	15	0	2	2	5	20	2	50	3	2
Wright, Jaret, Columbus	5	6	.455	3.00	24	24	0	0	0	0	129.0	93	554	55	43	9	3	6	13	79	0	113	11	3
Young, Danny, Augusta*	1	0	1.000	2.51	6	2	0	0	1	0	14.1	9	66	6	4	0	0	1	0	16	0	11	2	0
Zedalis, Craig, Macon..............	1	1	.500	4.76	12	0	0	0	6	0	22.2	25	102	12	12	2	1	1	1	8	0	17	2	0
Zolecki, Mike, Asheville............	3	2	.600	3.80	9	9	0	0	0	0	42.2	34	187	20	18	3	1	0	3	29	0	33	6	1
Zubiri, Jon, Columbus	0	0	.000	0.00	1	1	0	0	0	0	3.0	3	12	0	0	0	0	0	0	0	0	3	0	0

COMBINATION SHUTOUTS: **Albany (5)**—Moraga-Nygaard, Moraga-Woodring, Phelps-Handy-Woodring, Vazquez-Mikkelson, Vazquez-Rushworth. **Asheville (9)**—Barnes-Colmenares, Crowther-Grundt-Colmenares, Gooch-McClinton, Hackman-Bost, Kusiewicz-Barnes-Rose, Kusiewicz-Colmenares, Kusiewicz-Eden-Colmenares, Kusiewicz-Gonzalez-Colmenares, Vavrek-Colmenares. **Augusta (8)**—Anderson-Hampton, Anderson-Phillips-Hampton-Spade-Paugh, France-Grebe-Paugh, France-Paugh-Temple, Johnson-Temple-Paugh, Kelly-Temple-Maskivish, Pickford-Pelka-Phillips-Paugh, Pickford-Spade-Maskivish. **Charleston (S.C.) (3)**—Hower-Cook, O'Flynn-Cook, Silva-Hower. **Charleston (W.Va.) (7)**—Allen-Magre-Giron, Caruthers-Koppe-Solomon, Caruthers-Smith, Lott-Solomon, Runyan-Franklin, Tomco-Smith-Harvell-Magre, Tweedlie-Tomko-Giron. **Columbia (8)**—Atwater-Pack, Kelly-Baker, Johnston-Short-Baker, Kelly-Atwater-Baker, Sanchez-Atwater, Sanchez-Baker, Sanchez-Turrentine, Short-Sauerbeck. **Columbus (14)**—Granata-Montoya 2, Caldwell-Kramer-Donovan, Caldwell-Weber-Najera-Montoya, Granata-Donovan-Najera-Montoya, Oropeza-Najera-Montoya, Oropeza-Weber, Oropeza-Weber-Najera-Montoya, Perez-Najera, Sexton-Dinnen-Montoya, Warrecker-Najera-Montoya, Wright-Granata-Najera-Montoya, Wright-Kramer-Donovan, Wright-Perez. **Fayetteville (7)**—Jordan-Reed, Jordan-Whiteman-Dinyar-Gardner-Reed, Powell-Housley-Siler-Reed, Smith-Reed, Whiteman-Dinyar, Whiteman-Dinyar-Gardner, Whiteman-Skrmetta-Reed. **Greensboro (8)**—Jarvis-Mittauer, Medina-Shelby-Brown, Ricken-Binversie, Ricken-Binversie-Parotte-Brown, Ricken-Corn, Shelby-Parotte-Ford-Rojano-Benson, Shoemaker-Jarvis-Corn, Shoemaker-Mittauer-Corn. **Hagerstown (7)**—Davey-Smith, Meiners-Smith, Pace-Hartshorn-Smith, Pace-Hibbard-Rhine, Sievert-Davenport, Sievert-Pace, Sievert-Toney. **Hickory (7)**—Ambrose-Welch, Castillo-Dixon-Portillo, Crine-Cruz-Welch-Dixon, Crine-Portillo, Crine-Welch-Portillo, Herbert-Cruz, Theodile-Dixon. **Macon (8)**—Ebert-Raines 2, Bowie-Evangelista, Lavenia-Brown, Millwood-Olszewski, Moss-Shumate-Culp, Moss-Thompson, Moss-Zedalis. **Piedmont (10)**—Wimberly-Stumpf 2, Censale-Genke-Humphry, Censale-Stumpf, Hunter-Stumpf, Manning-Barbao-Gambs, Wimberly-Barbao, Wimberly-Genke-Stumpf, Wimberly-Kosek, Wimberly-Nyari-Stumpf. **Savannah (5)**—Almanza-Conway-Garcia, Almanza-Golden-Conway, Aybar-Glauber-Lovingier-Golden-Conway-Garcia, Reames-Conway, Windham-Lovingier-Garcia.
NO-HIT GAMES: None.

PITCHERS WITH TWO OR MORE TEAMS

Pitcher, Team	W	L	Pct.	ERA	G	GS	CG	ShO	GF	Sv.	IP	H	TBF	R	ER	HR	SH	SF	HB	BB	IBB	SO	WP	Bk.
Gooch, Arnold, Asheville	5	8	.385	2.94	21	21	1	1	0	0	128.2	111	541	51	42	8	3	3	4	57	0	117	13	0
Gooch, Arnold, Columbia	2	3	.400	4.46	6	6	0	0	0	0	38.1	39	169	25	19	3	0	1	2	15	0	34	5	0
Jarvis, Jason, Greensboro	8	7	.533	3.01	22	16	0	0	2	0	110.2	103	468	47	37	5	4	5	1	38	3	82	13	1
Jarvis, Jason, Hagerstown	4	3	.571	3.60	8	8	0	0	0	0	50.0	49	210	27	20	3	2	4	3	13	1	42	7	1
Swanson, David, Columbia*	7	1	.875	1.46	29	4	0	0	16	3	67.2	48	276	14	11	2	1	3	4	31	2	60	7	2
Swanson, David, Asheville*	1	0	1.000	4.97	8	0	0	0	2	1	12.2	14	56	7	7	1	1	0	1	7	0	7	0	0

1995 FIELDING

TEAM

Team	Pct.	G	PO	A	E	TC	DP	PB	Team	Pct.	G	PO	A	E	TC	DP	PB
Asheville..............	.971	139	3636	1584	156	5376	137	31	Piedmont	.961	140	3655	1467	208	5330	113	32
Charleston (W.Va.)	.968	142	3627	1525	169	5321	112	26	Charleston (S.C.) ...	.961	139	3604	1480	207	5291	120	31
Columbus.............	.966	142	3727	1575	184	5486	146	31	Macon................	.960	141	3809	1586	226	5621	122	23
Greensboro	.965	140	3678	1432	185	5295	100	31	Fayetteville	.960	141	3695	1508	218	5421	107	27
Columbia.............	.962	140	3707	1525	206	5438	126	22	Hickory	.957	138	3666	1517	231	5414	104	21
Savannah.............	.962	139	3686	1397	202	5285	105	35	Augusta...............	.955	138	3598	1484	239	5321	114	15
Hagerstown..........	.961	141	3648	1517	208	5373	103	34	Albany.................	.945	140	3727	1519	303	5549	118	25

TRIPLE PLAY: Charleston (W.Va.).

INDIVIDUAL

FIRST BASEMEN

NOTE: All caps denotes fielding-percentage leader based on 71 games for catchers, 94 for all other non-pitchers and 142 innings for pitchers. *Throws lefthanded.

Player, Team	Pct.	G	PO	A	E	TC	DP
Allen, Marlon, Charleston (W.Va.)	.974	64	489	32	14	535	38
Balint, Rob, Fayetteville	1.000	5	32	1	0	33	1
Barkett, Andy, Charleston (S.C.)*	.986	16	127	10	2	139	11
Boka, Ben, Columbia	1.000	1	1	0	0	1	1
Bragga, Matt, Charleston (W.Va.)	.973	26	168	12	5	185	13
Brown, Nate, Albany*	.971	102	861	77	28	966	74
Brown, Ray, Charleston (W.Va.)	1.000	2	20	4	0	24	2
Carranza, Pete, Asheville	1.000	2	4	1	0	5	1
Cooney, James, Charleston (S.C.)	1.000	7	50	0	0	50	9
Cooper, Steve, Savannah	.997	36	306	16	1	323	27
DeBerry, Joe, Greensboro*	1.000	12	99	9	0	108	9
Dishington, Nate, Savannah	.986	85	713	44	11	768	48
Donato, Dan, Greensboro	1.000	6	40	5	0	45	4
Eddie, Steve, Charleston (W.Va.).......	.995	76	504	56	3	563	47
Fantauzzi, John, Asheville*	.984	85	838	74	15	927	79
Friedrich, Steve, Hickory	1.000	1	1	0	0	1	0
Fullmer, Brad, Albany	.974	32	248	13	7	268	16
Fussell, Denny, Charleston (W.Va.)* ..	1.000	1	10	0	0	10	0
Gainey, Bryon, Columbia	.979	118	998	57	23	1078	90
Garcia, Neil, Fayetteville	1.000	6	41	1	0	42	3
Giardi, Steve, Hickory	1.000	1	7	0	0	7	0
Gipner, Marcus, Greensboro	1.000	1	1	0	0	1	0
Goldberg, Lonnie, Charleston (S.C.) ..	.969	4	28	3	1	32	3
Gomez, Paul, Columbia	.957	6	21	1	1	23	2
Guerrero, Rafael, Columbia	.996	26	213	13	1	227	17
Haas, Matt, Albany	.958	12	109	6	5	120	14
Harris, G.G., Augusta	.985	70	600	40	10	650	49
Heller, Bradley, Charleston (S.C.)	1.000	1	12	1	0	13	0
Helton, Todd, Asheville*	.990	44	388	21	4	413	31
Izquierdo, Sergio, Hickory...............	1.000	1	1	0	0	1	0
Koerick, Thomas, Hickory	.986	26	205	14	3	222	12
Ladd, Jeff, Hagerstown	.987	15	146	11	2	159	12
Lantigua, Eduardo, Columbus	.970	4	31	1	1	33	2
Larkin, Stephen, Charleston (S.C.)* ...	.980	55	371	29	8	408	35
Lidle, Kevin, Fayetteville	1.000	1	11	2	0	13	1
Llanos, Aurelio, Hagerstown	.968	17	145	8	5	158	11
McDougal, Mike, Savannah	.970	12	93	4	3	100	8
McMillan, Tom, Savannah	1.000	1	1	0	0	1	0
Millan, Adam, Piedmont	.991	75	627	41	6	674	50
Millican, Kevin, Charleston (S.C.)	.935	8	54	4	4	62	1
Mobilia, Bill, Piedmont	1.000	15	94	5	0	99	6
Morgan, Dave, Hagerstown	.981	19	148	8	3	159	6
Mosquera, Julio, Hagerstown	1.000	1	4	0	0	4	0
Mota, Guillermo, Columbia	1.000	1	3	0	0	3	0
Moyle, Mike, Columbus	.947	2	17	1	1	19	2
Mummau, Rob, Hagerstown	1.000	1	1	0	0	1	1
Oakland, Mike, Asheville	.986	7	68	4	1	73	5
Perry, Chan, Columbus	.997	64	570	37	2	609	65
Pullen, Shane, Piedmont	.988	59	472	40	6	518	37
Reyes, Winston, Piedmont	1.000	3	19	1	0	20	2
Rice, Charles, Augusta	.971	10	92	8	3	103	9
Rives, Sherron, Fayetteville	.944	3	16	1	1	18	1

Player, Team	Pct.	G	PO	A	E	TC	DP
Robles, Rafael, Savannah	1.000	2	4	0	0	4	0
Rodriguez, Adam, Fayetteville	.990	13	86	10	1	97	7
Santa, Roberto, Charleston (S.C.)*	.993	64	521	42	4	567	46
Silvia, Brian, Savannah	.986	8	70	2	1	73	2
Smith, Jason, Asheville	.957	5	43	1	2	46	5
STONE, Craig, Hagerstown	.991	95	829	64	8	901	59
Stumberger, Darren, Columbus	.991	76	620	53	6	679	65
Thobe, Steve, Augusta	.979	61	562	33	13	608	39
Torborg, Dale, Greensboro	.967	14	59	0	2	61	2
Valdez, Mario, Hickory	.989	120	1040	67	12	1119	77
Vaske, Terry, Macon	.969	21	177	10	6	193	17
Ward, Daryle, Fayetteville*	.987	121	1009	77	14	1100	77
Whitehurst, Todd, Columbia	1.000	2	5	0	0	5	0
Wright, Ron, Macon	.984	120	1035	99	18	1152	85
Wuerch, Jason, Greensboro	.980	5	46	2	1	49	6
Yedo, Carlos, Greensboro*	.985	111	930	84	15	1029	68

TRIPLE PLAY: Eddie.

SECOND BASEMEN

Player, Team	Pct.	G	PO	A	E	TC	DP
Acosta, Ed, Albany	.920	13	20	26	4	50	4
Aguila, Hector, Charleston (S.C.)	1.000	1	2	2	0	4	1
Almanzar, Richard, Fayetteville	.971	79	170	226	12	408	40
Amador, Manny, Piedmont	1.000	1	0	6	0	6	1
Ambrosina, Pete, Savannah	.957	121	224	286	23	533	65
Arvelo, Tom, Columbia	.889	4	1	7	1	9	0
Bocachica, Hiram, Albany	1.000	2	4	3	0	7	1
Brinkley, Josh, Albany	1.000	1	1	2	0	3	0
Brooks, Eddie, Augusta	.931	24	40	54	7	101	12
Brown, Vick, Greensboro	.948	117	226	269	27	522	55
Brunson, Matt, Fayetteville	.973	33	71	71	4	146	15
Camilli, Jason, Albany	.951	18	38	39	4	81	5
CARDENAS, Epi, Columbus	.978	124	267	353	14	634	92
Carranza, Pete, Asheville	1.000	1	2	2	0	4	0
Carvajal, Jhonny, Charleston (W.Va.)	.969	106	206	270	15	491	60
Chambers, Mack, Columbus	1.000	1	2	2	0	4	1
Coquillette, Trace, Albany	.975	110	252	292	14	558	62
Delgado, Jose, Macon	.958	4	10	13	1	24	4
Eaglin, Mike, Macon	.954	128	274	354	30	658	74
Eddie, Steve, Charleston (W.Va.)	1.000	4	3	5	0	8	0
Flores, Jose, Piedmont	.931	9	13	14	2	29	4
Friedrich, Steve, Hickory	.963	89	180	238	16	434	29
Garcia, Neil, Fayetteville	1.000	2	2	1	0	3	0
Giardi, Mike, Greensboro	1.000	12	19	25	0	44	2
Goldberg, Lonnie, Charleston (S.C.)	.935	13	18	25	3	46	4
Herider, Jeremy, Charleston (W.Va.)	.500	1	0	1	1	2	1
Holley, Jack, Hagerstown	1.000	1	2	3	0	5	1
Hooker, Kevin, Piedmont	1.000	2	2	3	0	5	0
Huff, Larry, Piedmont	.953	127	252	292	27	571	78
Jarrett, Linc, Asheville	.991	80	128	185	3	316	44
Jenkins, Dee, Charleston (W.Va.)	.959	24	39	54	4	97	10
Lackey, Steve, Columbia	.909	4	4	6	1	11	0
Landry, Dan, Macon	1.000	2	5	4	0	9	0
Lofton, James, Charleston (W.Va.)	.986	22	22	47	1	70	10
Matos, Julius, Columbus	.963	6	14	12	1	27	4
Mayber, Chan, Asheville	1.000	7	8	25	0	33	6
McLamb, Brian, Greensboro	.952	21	37	43	4	84	9
Mendoza, Jesus, Hickory	.967	46	83	124	7	214	29
Mobilia, Bill, Piedmont	1.000	1	1	1	0	2	0
Mummau, Rob, Hagerstown	.980	54	103	144	5	252	18
Navas, Jesus, Hickory	.939	18	27	35	4	66	9
Newell, Brett, Macon	.976	9	19	22	1	42	8
Ocasio, Fred, Asheville	.976	10	19	22	1	42	4
Oram, Jon, Columbus	.957	9	23	21	2	46	6
Pena, Elvis, Savannah	.954	48	86	140	11	237	39
Rivera, Miguel, Savannah	1.000	1	2	1	0	3	0
Rives, Sherron, Fayetteville	.957	36	68	64	6	138	15
Robles, Rafael, Savannah	.959	18	32	38	3	73	8
Rutz, Ryan, Charleston (S.C.)	.963	131	274	330	23	627	77
Segura, Juan, Augusta	1.000	5	11	11	0	22	2
Smith, Rod, Greensboro	1.000	1	1	2	0	3	1
Strange, Mike, Hagerstown	.939	93	134	237	24	395	45
Subero, Carlos, Augusta	1.000	1	2	0	0	2	0
Swafford, Derek, Augusta	.941	115	207	290	31	528	53
Utting, Ben, Macon	1.000	1	0	1	0	1	0
Van Overen, Ryan, Albany	.900	6	10	8	2	20	2
Veras, Juan, Charleston (S.C.)	1.000	2	4	2	0	6	1
White, Eric, Columbus	.895	4	8	9	2	19	2
Williamson, Matt, Piedmont	.962	7	9	16	1	26	3
Zorrilla, Julio, Columbus	.961	128	257	285	22	564	68
Zuniga, David, Columbia	1.000	8	9	17	0	26	4

TRIPLE PLAY: Carvajal.

THIRD BASEMEN

Player, Team	Pct.	G	PO	A	E	TC	DP
Acosta, Ed, Albany	.769	26	11	29	12	52	4
Adolfo, Carlos, Albany	.000	1	0	0	1	1	0
Aguila, Hector, Charleston (S.C.)	.923	7	5	19	2	26	2
Ambrosina, Pete, Savannah	1.000	1	0	2	0	2	0
Asche, Mike, Augusta	.857	97	61	172	39	272	7
Balfe, Ryan, Fayetteville	.906	104	55	206	27	288	22
Balint, Rob, Fayetteville	1.000	2	2	6	0	8	0
Branyan, Russell, Columbus	.856	62	34	120	26	180	9
Brinkley, Josh, Albany	.815	20	12	32	10	54	4
Brooks, Eddie, Augusta	.882	27	14	46	8	68	3
CARRANZA, Pete, Asheville	.936	102	69	266	23	358	16
Colombino, Carlo, Columbus	1.000	1	0	1	0	1	0
Coquillette, Trace, Albany	.824	18	14	28	9	51	2
Donato, Dan, Greensboro	.965	54	31	106	5	142	9
Dukart, Derek, Greensboro	.945	73	60	130	11	201	11
Eddie, Steve, Charleston (W.Va.)	.953	31	18	43	3	64	5
Flores, Jose, Piedmont	.937	44	34	84	8	126	8
Friedrich, Steve, Hickory	.890	30	28	53	10	91	3
Fullmer, Brad, Albany	.763	41	21	53	23	97	3
Gann, Steve, Charleston (W.Va.)	.897	14	5	21	3	29	3
Garcia, Neil, Fayetteville	.833	3	1	4	1	6	2
Giardi, Mike, Greensboro	1.000	5	3	7	0	10	1
Goldberg, Lonnie, Charleston (S.C.)	.857	15	10	26	6	42	3
Gomez, Paul, Columbia	1.000	1	0	2	0	2	0
Haas, Matt, Albany	.800	2	2	2	1	5	0
Hampton, Mike, Charleston (W.Va.)	.885	94	56	167	29	252	14
Harper, Rantie, Savannah	1.000	1	1	2	0	3	0
Helms, Wes, Macon	.900	133	91	269	40	400	25
Holley, Jack, Hagerstown	.951	12	5	34	2	41	1
Hooker, Kevin, Piedmont	.852	10	3	20	4	27	2
Huff, Larry, Piedmont	1.000	1	1	0	0	1	0
Koerick, Thomas, Hickory	.774	13	3	21	7	31	1
Lackey, Steve, Columbia	.848	38	14	64	14	92	4
Landry, Dan, Macon	.667	2	1	3	2	6	0
Lantigua, Eduardo, Columbus	.962	9	6	19	1	26	2
Lee, Carlos, Hickory	.848	44	30	76	19	125	4
Leon, Geraldo, Savannah	.810	20	8	26	8	42	3
Lidle, Kevin, Fayetteville	.857	9	4	20	4	28	3
Lofton, James, Charleston (W.Va.)	1.000	9	3	17	0	20	0
Lopez, Jose, Columbia	.907	79	44	171	22	237	16
Martinez, Dalvis, Fayetteville	.942	26	20	45	4	69	7
Matos, Julius, Columbus	1.000	1	1	0	0	1	0
Mayber, Chan, Asheville	.912	22	14	38	5	57	3
McLamb, Brian, Greensboro	.875	13	5	16	3	24	0
Meskauskas, John, Asheville	1.000	1	0	2	0	2	0
Mobilia, Bill, Piedmont	.774	18	12	29	12	53	2
Mummau, Rob, Hagerstown	.939	12	8	23	2	33	1
Myers, Aaron, Asheville	.886	20	12	50	8	70	6
Newell, Brett, Macon	.880	8	7	15	3	25	1
O'Brien, Joe, Piedmont	.791	14	9	25	9	43	4
Ocasio, Fred, Asheville	1.000	3	0	2	0	2	0
Oram, Jon, Columbus	.850	15	13	21	6	40	1
Pond, Simon, Albany	.789	22	11	49	16	76	3
Preston, Doyle, Charleston (W.Va.)	.833	7	0	15	3	18	1
Reyes, Winston, Piedmont	.786	2	2	9	3	14	0
Rivera, Miguel, Savannah	.905	117	86	255	36	377	16
Rives, Sherron, Fayetteville	.778	10	2	12	4	18	2
Robles, Rafael, Savannah	.950	6	5	14	1	20	0
Segura, Juan, Augusta	.900	3	0	9	1	10	0
Tatis, Fernando, Charleston (S.C.)	.900	124	98	235	37	370	24
Thobe, Steve, Augusta	.917	15	5	28	3	36	2
Thompson, Andy, Hagerstown	.869	119	86	200	43	329	13
Van Overen, Ryan, Albany	.908	31	19	70	9	98	7
Vaske, Terry, Macon	.750	3	1	2	1	4	0
White, Eric, Columbus	.920	68	43	141	16	200	16
Whitehurst, Todd, Columbia	.970	20	19	46	2	67	1
Wilhelm, Brent, Hickory	.899	67	32	138	19	189	5
Williamson, Matt, Piedmont	.903	68	63	132	21	216	8
Wuerch, Jason, Greensboro	.818	3	2	7	2	11	0
Zuniga, David, Columbia	.854	20	4	31	6	41	2

SHORTSTOPS

Player, Team	Pct.	G	PO	A	E	TC	DP
Acosta, Ed, Albany	.786	6	5	6	3	14	0
Aguila, Hector, Charleston (S.C.)	1.000	2	0	4	0	4	0
Arvelo, Tom, Columbia	1.000	2	3	4	0	7	1
Bearden, Doug, Hickory	.880	44	47	114	22	183	20
Beeney, Ryan, Greensboro	.900	56	76	150	25	251	20
Bocachica, Hiram, Albany	.880	94	161	263	58	482	55
Brinkley, Josh, Albany	1.000	1	1	2	0	3	0

CLASS A — *South Atlantic League*

Player, Team	Pct.	G	PO	A	E	TC	DP
Brooks, Eddie, Augusta	.769	5	1	9	3	13	1
Brown, Vick, Greensboro	1.000	1	0	1	0	1	0
Brunson, Matt, Fayetteville	.943	10	5	28	2	35	1
Camilli, Jason, Albany	.902	37	48	99	16	163	19
Carvajal, Jhonny, Charleston (W.Va.)	.968	35	36	86	4	126	11
Chambers, Mack, Columbus	.750	1	2	1	1	4	1
Delgado, Jose, Macon	.924	41	59	112	14	185	18
Dukart, Derek, Greensboro	.800	1	3	1	1	5	0
Flores, Jose, Piedmont	.943	8	10	23	2	35	3
Giardi, Mike, Greensboro	1.000	2	0	3	0	3	0
Goldberg, Lonnie, Charleston (S.C.)	.922	46	53	124	15	192	20
Gonzalez, Mario, Charleston (S.C.)	.897	7	14	12	3	29	7
Green, Bert, Savannah	.917	132	205	358	51	614	58
Guiliano, Matt, Piedmont	.936	129	146	382	36	564	65
Herider, Jeremy, Charleston (W.Va.)	.813	5	2	11	3	16	3
HOUSER, Kyle, Asheville	.973	110	151	318	13	482	64
Jarrett, Linc, Asheville	.980	32	47	100	3	150	25
Johnson, Jeff, Hickory	.937	50	59	134	13	206	20
Lackey, Steve, Columbia	.976	25	27	54	2	83	13
Landry, Dan, Macon	.974	8	12	26	1	39	4
Lobaton, Jose, Greensboro	.928	58	62	170	18	250	33
Matos, Julius, Columbus	.914	30	43	96	13	152	18
Mayber, Chan, Asheville	.800	2	4	4	2	10	0
McLamb, Brian, Greensboro	.929	27	30	61	7	98	11
Mercedes, Guillermo, Columbus	.966	54	70	155	8	233	29
Mobilia, Bill, Piedmont	1.000	1	1	3	0	4	0
Mota, Guillermo, Columbia	.935	122	202	373	40	615	66
Mummau, Rob, Hagerstown	.960	26	49	72	5	126	15
Navas, Jesus, Hickory	.914	56	79	145	21	245	28
Newell, Brett, Macon	.933	47	69	155	16	240	32
Oram, Jon, Columbus	.921	33	37	91	11	139	18
Ordaz, Luis, Charleston (W.Va.)	.954	111	164	290	22	476	52
Perez, Santiago, Fayetteville	.916	129	176	327	46	549	58
Rives, Sherron, Fayetteville	.862	8	7	18	4	29	2
Robinson, Tony, Augusta	.930	93	131	281	31	443	53
Robles, Rafael, Savannah	.814	10	13	22	8	43	0
Rutz, Ryan, Charleston (S.C.)	.750	1	0	3	1	4	0
Segura, Juan, Augusta	.975	18	27	50	2	79	9
Subero, Carlos, Augusta	.948	29	53	93	8	154	21
Utting, Ben, Macon	.888	20	22	49	9	80	9
Valera, Willy, Columbus	.919	31	43	94	12	149	31
Van Overen, Ryan, Albany	1.000	12	7	26	0	33	6
Veras, Juan, Charleston (S.C.)	.951	94	126	245	19	390	45
Wilhelm, Brent, Hickory	.800	1	3	1	1	5	0
Williams, Glenn, Macon	.867	32	37	87	19	143	11
Williamson, Matt, Piedmont	.789	4	3	12	4	19	3
Wilson, Brian, Charleston (W.Va.)	1.000	5	8	13	0	21	2
Witt, Kevin, Hagerstown	.919	117	203	338	48	589	61
Zuniga, David, Columbia	1.000	1	1	0	0	1	0

TRIPLE PLAY: Ordaz.

OUTFIELDERS

Player, Team	Pct.	G	PO	A	E	TC	DP
Abell, Tony, Savannah	.826	17	17	2	4	23	0
Acosta, Ed, Albany	1.000	7	6	0	0	6	0
Adolfo, Carlos, Albany	1.000	50	96	6	0	102	2
Aguila, Hector, Charleston (S.C.)	1.000	1	0	1	0	1	0
Albert, Rashad, Hickory	.976	85	194	7	5	206	3
Barkett, Andy, Charleston (S.C.)*	1.000	5	8	1	0	9	0
Bass, Jayson, Fayetteville*	.932	95	133	4	10	147	1
Borel, Jamie, Fayetteville	.993	70	143	4	1	148	2
Bragga, Matt, Charleston (W.Va.)	.971	24	32	1	1	34	0
Brewer, Brett, Macon	.961	112	170	7	3	180	1
Brooks, Eddie, Augusta	1.000	1	1	0	0	1	0
Brown, Adrian, Augusta	.950	68	124	8	7	139	1
Brown, Nate, Albany*	.917	11	21	1	2	24	0
Buchanan, Brian, Greensboro	.970	23	31	1	1	33	0
Cancel, David, Hickory	.938	66	115	5	8	128	0
Carranza, Pete, Asheville	1.000	3	2	0	0	2	0
Carvajal, Jhonny, Charleston (W.Va.)	1.000	1	1	0	0	1	0
Chapman, Eric, Columbus	.967	51	88	1	3	92	0
Coach, Calvin, Savannah*	.985	63	121	7	2	130	1
Collum, Gary, Columbia*	1.000	5	5	0	0	5	0
Comeaux, Edward, Charleston (S.C.)	.966	80	137	7	5	149	1
Conner, Decomba, Charleston (W.Va.)	.989	90	184	3	2	189	2
Coquillette, Trace, Albany	1.000	5	3	0	0	3	0
Darr, Mike, Fayetteville	.939	97	123	15	9	147	2
Delafield, Wil, Greensboro	.965	105	208	11	8	227	3
Diaz, Linardo, Piedmont	.938	9	15	0	1	16	0
Donato, Dan, Greensboro	1.000	8	13	0	0	13	0
Drent, Brian, Hickory	.900	23	26	1	3	30	0

Player, Team	Pct.	G	PO	A	E	TC	DP
Ealy, Tracey, Savannah	.972	97	167	5	5	177	0
Eddie, Steve, Charleston (W.Va.)	.813	10	13	0	3	16	0
Edwards, Aaron, Augusta	.964	43	78	3	3	84	0
Encarnacion, Juan, Fayetteville	.956	102	143	10	7	160	0
Estrada, Josue, Albany	.989	61	87	5	1	93	0
Ferrier, Ross, Columbia	.955	13	19	2	1	22	0
Figueroa, Danny, Asheville	.968	49	87	4	3	94	1
Friedrich, Steve, Hickory	1.000	3	9	0	0	9	0
Gambill, Chad, Asheville	1.000	90	138	7	0	145	3
Gatti, Dom, Charleston (S.C.)	.978	96	176	2	4	182	0
Giardi, Mike, Greensboro	1.000	11	18	2	0	20	1
Gibson, Derrick, Asheville	.957	125	190	11	9	210	2
Glass, Chip, Columbus*	.984	111	178	11	3	192	2
Goldberg, Lonnie, Charleston (S.C.)	.909	16	18	2	2	22	0
Gomez, Ramon, Hickory	.976	72	147	13	4	164	1
Guerrero, Rafael, Columbia	.990	59	92	12	1	105	1
Guerrero, Vladimir, Albany	.953	94	207	15	11	233	4
Guillen, Jose, Augusta	1.000	6	5	0	0	5	0
Haas, Matt, Albany	1.000	1	1	0	0	1	0
Hall, Ronnie, Asheville	.948	130	209	11	12	232	3
Harper, Rantie, Savannah	.980	85	140	4	3	147	1
Hayes, Darren, Hickory	.946	56	81	6	5	92	0
Holley, Jack, Hagerstown	.857	2	5	1	1	7	0
Hunter, Scott, Columbia	.957	12	21	1	1	23	0
Jones, Andruw, Macon	.988	130	332	10	4	346	4
Kelley, Erskine, Augusta	.975	96	143	13	4	160	2
Kennedy, Gus, Macon	.978	109	169	10	4	183	0
Key, Jeff, Piedmont	.963	61	102	3	4	109	0
Lantigua, Eduardo, Columbus	.750	7	6	0	2	8	0
Larkin, Stephen, Charleston (S.C.)*	.903	28	53	3	6	62	1
Ledee, Ricky, Greensboro*	.982	87	160	7	3	170	2
Leon, Geraldo, Savannah	1.000	1	1	0	0	1	0
Lewis, Andreaus, Columbus	.973	75	103	4	3	110	0
Lidle, Kevin, Fayetteville	1.000	1	2	0	0	2	0
Llanos, Aurelio, Hagerstown	.958	70	133	5	6	144	3
Lofton, James, Charleston (W.Va.)	.913	20	18	3	2	23	0
Lombard, George, Macon	.958	35	44	2	2	48	1
Long, Terrence, Columbia*	.937	49	69	5	5	79	0
Luciano, Virgilio, Charleston (S.C.)*	.976	81	107	14	3	124	3
Martinez, Dalvis, Fayetteville	1.000	1	1	0	0	1	0
Matos, Julius, Columbus	1.000	14	18	0	0	18	0
McClure, Craig, Hickory	.963	46	74	4	3	81	0
McLamb, Brian, Greensboro	1.000	8	13	0	0	13	0
McMillan, Tom, Savannah	.938	67	103	3	7	113	1
McNally, Shawn, Savannah	.989	49	87	3	1	91	1
Millican, Kevin, Charleston (S.C.)	1.000	3	1	0	0	1	0
Monroe, Darryl, Fayetteville	.992	70	116	4	1	121	0
Morrow, Nick, Charleston (W.Va.)	.975	138	292	17	8	317	3
O'Brien, Joe, Piedmont	.978	31	43	1	1	45	0
Oram, Jon, Columbus	1.000	4	3	0	0	3	0
Ortman, Ben, Asheville	1.000	10	9	1	0	10	0
Ozario, Yudith, Columbia	.969	115	213	9	7	229	1
Pearson, Cory, Charleston (S.C.)	.953	50	77	4	4	85	1
Perez, Joe, Charleston (S.C.)*	.980	57	92	4	2	98	0
Perry, Chan, Columbus	1.000	17	28	0	0	28	0
Pollock, Elton, Augusta	.926	26	50	0	4	54	0
Prensi, Dagoberto, Hagerstown	.973	103	168	9	5	182	1
Prieto, Ricky, Columbus	1.000	4	11	0	0	11	0
Pullen, Shane, Piedmont	1.000	19	27	2	0	29	1
Rivers, Jonathon, Hagerstown	.958	122	212	14	10	236	1
Rives, Sherron, Fayetteville	1.000	1	1	0	0	1	0
Robles, Rafael, Savannah	.909	5	10	0	1	11	0
Rosado, Juan, Albany*	1.000	5	5	0	0	5	0
ROYSTER, Aaron, Piedmont	.991	123	204	8	2	212	2
Sanders, Anthony, Hagerstown	.990	133	274	15	3	292	5
Sanders, Rod, Charleston (W.Va.)	.979	62	85	10	2	97	2
Sanderson, David, Columbia*	.976	74	118	5	3	126	0
Saturnino, Sherton, Macon	.769	25	18	2	6	26	1
Schreimann, Eric, Piedmont	1.000	2	2	0	0	2	0
Schwab, Chris, Albany*	.949	106	142	6	8	156	1
Seguignol, Fernando, Albany	.964	110	205	7	8	220	1
Shumpert, Derek, Greensboro	1.000	51	77	1	0	78	0
Simmons, Brian, Hickory	.988	41	77	2	1	80	1
Smith, Rod, Greensboro	.948	62	89	3	5	97	1
Staton, T.J., Augusta*	.948	100	153	10	9	172	1
Stingley, Derek, Piedmont	.978	30	43	1	1	45	1
Taylor, Byron, Savannah	1.000	4	2	0	0	2	0
Thomas, Rod, Charleston (W.Va.)	.944	18	32	2	2	36	1
Thompson, Leroy, Columbus*	.976	37	37	4	1	42	1
Tidick, Michael, Hickory	.967	47	57	2	2	61	1

Player, Team	Pct.	G	PO	A	E	TC	DP
Torok, John, Piedmont	.966	89	130	11	5	146	1
Turner, Rocky, Columbia	1.000	8	12	0	0	12	0
Twitty, Sean, Greensboro	.918	66	116	7	11	134	0
Vasquez, Danilo, Charleston (S.C.)	.962	42	64	11	3	78	3
Waldrop, Tom, Macon*	1.000	24	38	1	0	39	0
Walker, Shon, Augusta*	.944	96	151	19	10	180	5
Warner, Bryan, Columbus*	.978	110	170	12	4	186	3
Watts, Josh, Piedmont	.987	106	144	11	2	157	2
Wells, Mark, Asheville	1.000	28	38	4	0	42	1
White, Eric, Columbus	.986	38	66	6	1	73	0
Williams, Curtis, Savannah*	.958	47	69	0	3	72	0
Williams, Mark, Savannah	.500	1	1	0	1	2	0
Wilson, Preston, Columbia	.961	104	189	10	8	207	3
Wright, Terry, Charleston (W.Va.)*	.985	115	180	13	3	196	3
Wuerch, Jason, Greensboro	.952	14	18	2	1	21	1

CATCHERS

Player, Team	Pct.	G	PO	A	E	TC	DP	PB
Afenir, Tom, Columbus	1.000	5	23	7	0	30	0	2
Alderman, Kurt, Albany	.954	23	136	9	7	152	1	5
Almond, Greg, Savannah	1.000	11	112	9	0	121	0	3
Arias, Rogelio, Asheville	.986	67	440	49	7	496	5	20
Ashby, Chris, Greensboro	.983	62	456	65	9	530	2	11
Balint, Rob, Fayetteville	1.000	2	16	0	0	16	0	1
Boka, Ben, Columbia	.903	7	27	1	3	31	0	1
Bowen, Glenn, Savannah	.982	16	100	8	2	110	1	6
Cardona, Javier, Fayetteville	.990	48	339	48	4	391	4	7
Carpenter, Matt, Ash.-C'bus	.960	11	38	10	2	50	0	0
Cooney, James, Charleston (S.C.)	1.000	4	15	0	0	15	0	0
Cossins, Tim, Charleston (S.C.)	.966	19	130	13	5	148	1	1
Dawson, Charles, Macon	.983	38	257	32	5	294	3	1
Donato, Dan, Greensboro	1.000	1	2	0	0	2	0	0
Eddie, Steve, Charleston (W.Va.)	1.000	2	3	0	0	3	0	0
Falciglia, Tony, Savannah	1.000	18	116	13	0	129	1	4
Fithian, Grant, Greensboro	.985	51	352	49	6	407	3	14
Garcia, Neil, Fayetteville	.981	52	386	38	8	432	0	16
Gomez, Paul, Columbia	.970	26	142	20	5	167	0	3
Gonzalez, Wikleman, Augusta	.985	49	345	43	6	394	5	6
Haas, Matt, Albany	.987	31	197	23	3	223	0	6
Hammell, Al, Columbia	.967	3	25	4	1	30	0	1
Harriss, Robin, Columbus	.981	51	397	68	9	474	6	9
Heller, Bradley, Charleston (S.C.)	.978	65	405	37	10	452	2	8
Henley, Bob, Albany	.983	94	684	111	14	809	9	14
Izquierdo, Sergio, Hickory	.979	44	276	50	7	333	4	9
Johnson, Mark, Hickory	.986	100	681	67	11	759	3	10
Koerick, Thomas, Hickory	.982	12	48	7	1	56	0	2
Ladd, Jeff, Hagerstown	.984	26	163	24	3	190	3	9
Lewis, Rob, Columbia	.990	20	178	18	2	198	2	3
Lidle, Kevin, Fayetteville	.985	23	219	36	4	259	0	3
Lopez, Victor, Charleston (S.C.)	1.000	12	95	8	0	103	1	3
Lunar, Fernando, Macon	.967	32	261	35	10	306	7	6
Matos, Pasqual, Macon	.985	72	498	76	9	583	1	16
Meskauskas, John, Asheville	.979	29	171	16	4	191	0	4
Millan, Adam, Piedmont	.989	31	243	26	3	272	0	4
Millican, Kevin, Charleston (S.C.)	.985	62	395	50	7	452	5	19
Morales, Eric, Columbia	.987	35	264	41	4	309	1	3
Morales, Francisco, Savannah	1.000	18	123	15	0	138	7	4
Morgan, Dave, Hagerstown	.969	23	112	15	4	131	0	9
MOSQUERA, Julio, Hagerstown	.991	98	637	103	7	747	6	16
Moyle, Mike, Columbus	.979	67	494	66	12	572	8	17
Nitschke, Bear, Piedmont	1.000	2	5	3	0	8	0	0
Northeimer, Jamie, Piedmont	.987	108	812	92	12	916	6	27
Petillo, Bruce, Piedmont	.900	1	9	0	1	10	0	1
Pozo, Yohel, Asheville	.970	40	322	39	11	372	2	6
Reynolds, Chance, Augusta	1.000	22	143	22	0	165	2	2
Rodriguez, Adam, Fayetteville	.988	24	214	39	3	256	1	0
Schreimann, Eric, Piedmont	.973	5	32	4	1	37	0	1
Sharp, Scott, Charleston (W.Va.)	.982	53	319	54	7	380	3	10
Silvia, Brian, Savannah	.976	24	185	19	5	209	3	4
Smith, Jason, Asheville	1.000	8	37	5	0	42	1	1
Sweet, Jonathan, Augusta	.985	77	534	51	9	594	4	7
Towle, Justin, Charleston (W.Va.)	.984	100	622	103	12	737	3	16
Trimble, Rob, Greensboro	.987	24	206	15	3	224	1	1
Troilo, Jason, Greensboro	1.000	16	98	13	0	111	0	5
Vaske, Terry, Macon	1.000	1	2	0	0	2	0	0
Weaver, Colby, Macon	.983	14	104	14	2	120	2	6
Williams, Mark, Savannah	.991	62	491	62	5	558	6	16
Wilson, Vance, Columbia	.981	85	605	99	14	718	4	12
Winterlee, Scott, Columbia	1.000	1	2	1	0	3	0	1

CATCHERS WITH TWO OR MORE TEAMS

Player, Team	Pct.	G	PO	A	E	TC	DP	PB
Carpenter, Matt, Asheville	.956	9	33	10	2	45	0	0
Carpenter, Matt, Columbus	1.000	2	5	0	0	5	0	0

PITCHERS

Player, Team	Pct.	G	PO	A	E	TC	DP
Adair, Scott, Columbia	.500	3	0	1	1	2	0
Alazaus, Shawn, Greensboro*	1.000	33	2	3	0	5	0
Allen, Cedric, Charleston (W.Va.)*	.980	27	17	31	1	49	2
Almanza, Armando, Savannah*	1.000	20	0	17	0	17	0
Ambrose, John, Hickory	.857	14	5	13	3	21	1
Anderson, Jimmy, Augusta*	.968	14	5	25	1	31	6
Anez, Maycoll, Hickory	1.000	2	0	1	0	1	0
Antonini, Adrian, Piedmont	.667	6	1	3	2	6	0
Arias, Alfredo, Hagerstown	.727	35	0	8	3	11	0
Atwater, Joe, Columbia*	.947	27	8	10	1	19	2
Avrard, Corey, Savannah	1.000	13	2	7	0	9	0
Aybar, Manuel, Savannah	1.000	18	16	17	0	33	1
Bajda, Mike, Fayetteville	1.000	4	2	0	0	2	0
Baker, Derek, Columbia	1.000	36	4	6	0	10	1
Barbao, Joe, Piedmont	.786	43	4	7	3	14	0
Barnes, Keith, Asheville*	1.000	10	4	5	0	9	0
Bell, Mike, Albany*	1.000	12	0	5	0	5	1
Benson, Jeremy, Greensboro*	1.000	3	0	1	0	1	0
Beverlin, Jason, Greensboro	1.000	7	2	7	0	9	1
Binversie, Brian, Greensboro	1.000	31	3	2	0	5	1
Bledsoe, Randy, Savannah	.833	28	1	4	1	6	0
Blythe, Billy, Macon	1.000	7	3	2	0	5	0
Bost, Heath, Asheville	.875	9	3	4	1	8	0
Bowie, Micah, Macon*	1.000	5	1	2	0	3	0
Boyd, Jason, Piedmont	.912	26	14	17	3	34	1
Briggs, Anthony, Macon	.935	29	19	10	2	31	0
Brown, Charlie, Greensboro	.909	45	4	6	1	11	0
Brown, Darold, Macon*	.882	31	5	10	2	17	0
Brownson, Mark, Asheville	.913	23	6	15	2	23	1
Burdick, Morgan, Asheville	.833	17	2	3	1	6	1
Buteaux, Shane, Hickory	.963	13	7	19	1	27	1
Cain, Travis, Macon	1.000	14	3	1	0	4	0
CALDWELL, David, Columbus*	1.000	27	6	28	0	34	2
Callahan, Damon, Charleston (W.Va.)	.714	6	2	3	2	7	0
Carlson, Garret, Hickory	1.000	3	0	1	0	1	0
Caruthers, Clayton, Char. (W.Va.)	.964	27	11	16	1	28	1
Castillo, Carlos, Hickory	.900	14	5	13	2	20	0
Censale, Silvio, Piedmont*	.810	22	5	12	4	21	1
Chavarria, David, Charleston (S.C.)	.923	52	3	9	1	13	0
Chaves, Rafael, Augusta	.000	7	0	1	1	1	0
Civit, Xavier, Albany	.889	12	3	5	1	9	0
Clark, Doug, Fayetteville	1.000	4	0	2	0	2	0
Cole, Jason, Albany	.800	32	2	10	3	15	0
Collins, Zach, Macon*	1.000	4	0	2	0	2	1
Colmenares, Luis, Asheville	.875	45	1	6	1	8	1
Conway, Keith, Savannah*	.909	60	3	7	1	11	1
Cook, Rodney, Charleston (S.C.)	.912	60	6	25	3	34	2
Cooke, Steve, Augusta*	1.000	1	0	1	0	1	0
Cordero, Francisco, Fayetteville	.625	4	2	3	3	8	0
Corn, Chris, Greensboro	.857	49	6	12	3	21	1
Crine, Dennis, Hickory	.857	15	3	9	2	14	1
Crowther, Brent, Asheville	.944	15	14	20	2	36	3
Crowther, John, Hagerstown	.667	11	1	5	3	9	0
Cruise, Mark, Savannah	1.000	6	2	3	0	5	0
Cruz, Nelson, Hickory	.909	44	1	9	1	11	0
Cubillan, Darwin, Greensboro	.933	22	3	11	1	15	1
Culp, Wes, Piedmont	1.000	39	7	17	0	24	0
Davenport, Joe, Hagerstown	.500	13	0	1	1	2	0
Davey, Tom, Hagerstown	1.000	8	5	4	0	9	1
Davis, Kane, Augusta	.929	26	9	30	3	42	3
Dinnen, Kevin, Columbus	1.000	49	4	10	0	14	0
Dinyar, Eric, Fayetteville	.893	42	3	22	3	28	3
Dixon, Jim, Hickory	1.000	35	5	7	0	12	0
Doman, Roger, Hagerstown	.933	13	3	11	1	15	0
Done, J.J., Columbus	1.000	4	0	2	0	2	0
Donnelly, Brendan, Char. (W.Va.)	.667	24	3	3	3	9	0
Donovan, Scot, Columbus	.833	40	3	7	2	12	0
Dougherty, Tony, Columbus	.800	27	3	5	2	10	0
Doyle, Tom, Charleston (W.Va.)*	.947	14	5	13	1	19	1
Durocher, Jayson, Albany	.970	24	13	19	1	33	2
Ebert, Derrin, Macon*	.946	28	9	44	3	56	3
Eden, Bill, Asheville*	.857	33	1	5	1	7	0
Escamilla, Jaime, Char. (S.C.)*	1.000	32	4	11	0	15	0
Estavil, Mauricio, Piedmont*	1.000	42	2	6	0	8	0
Evangelista, Alberto, Macon	.727	24	5	3	3	11	0

Player, Team	Pct.	G	PO	A	E	TC	DP
Fereira, Marcos, Hickory	1.000	4	0	1	0	1	0
Ford, Ben, Greensboro	1.000	7	0	2	0	2	0
Ford, Jack, Hickory*	.919	27	6	28	3	37	0
France, Aaron, Augusta	.957	18	6	16	1	23	0
Franklin, Joel, Charleston (W.Va.)	1.000	24	1	8	0	9	1
Gambs, Chris, Piedmont	.800	9	1	3	1	5	0
Garcia, Frank, Savannah	1.000	34	1	3	0	4	0
Garcia-Luna, Francisco, Augusta	.889	14	0	8	1	9	1
Gardner, Scott, Fayetteville	.923	49	8	16	2	26	0
Genke, Todd, Piedmont	1.000	31	3	7	0	10	0
Giard, Kenneth, Macon	1.000	5	2	1	0	3	0
Giron, Emiliano, Char. (W.Va.)	1.000	30	2	0	0	2	0
Glauber, Keith, Savannah	1.000	40	9	10	0	19	1
Gogolewski, Chris, Char. (S.C.)*	.892	30	7	26	4	37	4
Golden, Matthew, Savannah	.850	64	7	10	3	20	0
Gonzalez, Jhonny, Asheville*	1.000	21	0	6	0	6	0
Gooch, Arnold, Ash.-C'bia	.962	27	9	16	1	26	1
Graham, Steve, Macon	.750	5	0	3	1	4	0
Granata, Chris, Columbus	.944	33	7	10	1	18	2
Grebe, Brett, Augusta	.909	32	7	3	1	11	0
Grundt, Ken, Asheville*	1.000	20	1	2	0	3	0
Hackman, Luther, Asheville	.976	28	13	27	1	41	2
Halley, Allen, Hickory	.846	13	4	7	2	13	0
Hamilton, Paul, Piedmont	.800	15	2	2	1	5	1
Hampton, Mark, Augusta	1.000	39	6	10	0	16	0
Handy, Russell, Albany	.846	30	10	12	4	26	0
Hartmann, Rich, Savannah	.909	31	3	7	1	11	0
Hartshorn, Tyson, Hagerstown	.867	12	4	9	2	15	0
Harvell, Pete, Charleston (W.Va.)*	1.000	27	1	7	0	8	1
Helvey, Rob, Savannah*	.857	18	5	1	1	7	0
Henderson, Chris, Asheville	1.000	17	2	2	0	4	1
Herbert, Russell, Hickory	.852	18	6	17	4	27	0
Hibbard, Billy, Hagerstown	.900	16	5	4	1	10	0
Housley, Adam, Fayetteville	.917	19	6	5	1	12	0
Hower, Dan, Charleston (S.C.)*	.818	22	6	12	4	22	1
Humphry, Trevor, Piedmont	.941	28	3	13	1	17	0
Hunter, Rich, Piedmont	.943	15	6	27	2	35	2
Jacobson, Kelton, Fayetteville	.941	25	7	9	1	17	1
Jarvis, Jason, Gre.-Hag.	.951	30	14	25	2	41	1
Johnson, Jason, Augusta	1.000	11	1	6	0	7	0
Johnston, Sean, Columbia*	.974	23	9	29	1	39	5
Jordan, Jason, Fayetteville	.857	24	6	12	3	21	1
Karvala, Kyle, Piedmont*	1.000	20	0	1	0	1	0
Kell, Rob, Charleston (S.C.)*	1.000	7	2	6	0	8	0
Kelly, Jeff, Augusta*	.871	26	7	20	4	31	4
Kelly, John, Columbia	.875	28	9	19	4	32	0
Knight, Brandon, Charleston (S.C.)	.833	9	3	7	2	12	0
Knighton, Toure, Charleston (S.C.)	.933	22	4	10	1	15	1
Koppe, Clint, Charleston (W.Va.)	.958	30	9	14	1	24	1
Kosek, Kory, Piedmont	1.000	15	1	5	0	6	0
Kramer, Scott, Columbus	.846	19	6	5	2	13	1
Kusiewicz, Michael, Asheville*	.848	21	8	20	5	33	1
LaPoint, Jason, Albany*	.769	33	2	8	3	13	0
Larson, Toby, Columbia	.923	8	8	4	1	13	1
Lasbury, Robert, Asheville	1.000	6	1	2	0	3	0
Lavenia, Mark, Macon*	1.000	24	3	4	0	7	1
Lee, Jeremy, Hagerstown	1.000	26	10	12	0	22	0
Legrow, Brett, Piedmont	1.000	8	1	0	0	1	0
Logan, Marcus, Savannah	.933	34	4	10	1	15	0
Lott, Brian, Charleston (W.Va.)	.971	28	15	19	1	35	0
Lovingier, Kevin, Savannah*	.909	38	2	8	1	11	0
Maberry, Louis, Charleston (W.Va.)	1.000	4	1	1	0	2	0
Magre, Pete, Charleston (W.Va.)	1.000	21	2	2	0	4	0
Manning, Len, Piedmont*	.791	27	8	26	9	43	2
Martin, Chandler, Asheville	1.000	8	1	10	0	11	0
Martinez, Johnny, Columbus	.923	16	2	10	1	13	2
Martinez, Osvaldo, Fayetteville	1.000	6	2	3	0	5	1
Maskivish, Joe, Augusta	.714	26	2	3	2	7	1
Mattes, Troy, Albany	1.000	4	1	4	0	5	1
McAdams, Denny, Asheville	1.000	5	0	2	0	2	0
McBride, Chris, Hagerstown	.967	19	10	19	1	30	1
McClinton, Patrick, Asheville*	1.000	18	0	7	0	7	1
McEntire, Ethan, Columbia*	.938	6	5	10	1	16	0
McNeill, Kevin, Savannah*	.949	29	5	32	2	39	3
Medina, Rafael, Greensboro	.846	19	3	8	2	13	1
Meiners, Doug, Hagerstown	.931	18	7	20	2	29	0
Mejias, Fernando, Hickory	.840	30	6	15	4	25	3
Meyer, David, Greensboro*	.960	14	6	18	1	25	0
Mikkelsen, Lincoln, Albany	1.000	12	2	6	0	8	0
Millwood, Kevin, Macon	1.000	29	10	11	0	21	0
Minor, Tom, Savannah	.500	8	1	0	1	2	0
Mitchell, Courtney, Piedmont*	1.000	5	0	1	0	1	0
Mittauer, Casey, Greensboro	.920	49	8	15	2	25	1
Montoya, Wilmer, Columbus	.889	51	7	9	2	18	3
Moore, David, Hickory	1.000	20	0	2	0	2	0
Moraga, David, Albany*	.971	25	8	26	1	35	1
Morillo, Donald, Charleston (S.C.)	.750	18	1	2	1	4	0
Mortimer, Mick, Charleston (S.C.)	1.000	5	2	2	0	4	2
Moss, Damian, Macon*	.889	27	7	25	4	36	0
Najera, Noe, Columbus*	.833	43	0	5	1	6	0
Newton, Chris, Fayetteville*	1.000	2	0	2	0	2	0
Nieto, Tony, Charleston (W.Va.)	.882	13	2	13	2	17	3
Nunez, Maximo, Hagerstown	.900	22	1	8	1	10	0
Nuttle, Jamison, Augusta	1.000	6	0	1	0	1	0
Nyari, Pete, Piedmont	.846	35	6	5	2	13	1
Nygaard, Chris, Albany*	.867	41	2	11	2	15	0
O'Flynn, Gardner, Char. (S.C.)*	.930	30	11	42	4	57	1
Olszewski, Eric, Macon	.941	35	11	5	1	17	0
Oropeza, Igor, Columbus	.857	9	1	5	1	7	0
Pace, Scott, Hagerstown*	1.000	11	3	14	0	17	0
Pack, Steve, Columbia	.929	36	5	8	1	14	0
Parotte, Frisco, Greensboro	.900	22	1	8	1	10	1
Paugh, Rick, Augusta*	.818	52	2	7	2	11	0
Pauls, Matthew, Charleston (S.C.)	1.000	16	0	2	0	2	0
Pelka, Brian, Augusta	.875	26	1	6	1	8	1
Perez, Julio, Columbus	.963	22	11	15	1	27	1
Perpetuo, Nelson, Char. (S.C.)*	.941	32	2	14	1	17	0
Peterman, Ernie, Hagerstown	1.000	2	3	0	0	3	0
Phelps, Tommy, Albany*	.903	24	3	25	3	31	1
Phillips, Jason, Augusta	.929	30	5	8	1	14	0
Phipps, Chris, Piedmont	1.000	11	9	2	0	11	0
Pickford, Kevin, Augusta*	.957	16	3	19	1	23	0
Portillo, Alex, Hickory*	1.000	33	3	9	0	12	1
Powell, Brian, Fayetteville	1.000	5	2	2	0	4	0
Powell, Jeremy, Albany	1.000	1	0	1	0	1	0
Presley, Kirk, Columbia	.800	4	1	3	1	5	1
Raines, Ken, Macon*	1.000	14	1	5	0	6	0
Ramirez, Rafael, Savannah	.958	26	8	15	1	24	0
Reames, Britt, Savannah	.778	10	0	7	2	9	1
Reed, Brandon, Fayetteville	.750	55	1	5	2	8	0
Reid, Rayon, Augusta	.867	12	6	7	2	15	0
Reyes, Jose, Charleston (S.C.)	1.000	4	2	0	0	2	0
Rhine, Kendall, Hagerstown	.944	42	4	13	1	18	3
Rhodriguez, Rory, Albany	.857	37	5	7	2	14	0
Ricken, Ray, Greensboro	.941	10	8	8	1	17	0
Roberts, Willis, Fayetteville	.857	17	3	15	3	21	1
Robinson, Martin, Greensboro*	1.000	2	0	3	0	3	0
Rocker, John, Macon*	1.000	16	4	18	0	22	2
Rojano, Rafael, Greensboro	1.000	19	6	3	0	9	0
Rose, Brian, Asheville	1.000	10	1	2	0	3	0
Ruiz, Rafael, Hickory*	1.000	5	0	2	0	2	0
Runion, Jeff, Charleston (S.C.)	.857	2	2	4	1	7	0
Runyan, Paul, Charleston (W.Va.)	1.000	15	4	8	0	12	1
Rushworth, Jim, Albany	1.000	6	1	4	0	5	0
Ryan, Reid, Charleston (S.C.)	.643	22	2	7	5	14	0
Sanchez, Jesus, Columbia*	.978	27	9	35	1	45	2
Sanders, Frankie, Columbus	1.000	2	1	1	0	2	0
Sauerbeck, Scott, Columbia*	1.000	19	1	6	0	7	1
Schaffner, Eric, Greensboro	1.000	1	1	1	0	2	0
Schlomann, Brett, Greensboro	.875	25	4	10	2	16	0
Serna, Joe, Fayetteville	.875	12	1	6	1	8	0
Sexton, Jeff, Columbus	.913	14	12	9	2	23	0
Shelby, Anthony, Greensboro*	.957	27	5	17	1	23	1
Shoemaker, Steve, Greensboro	.944	17	6	11	1	18	2
Short, Barry, Columbia	.957	40	6	16	1	23	1
Shumate, Jacob, Macon	1.000	17	3	7	0	10	1
Sievert, Mark, Hagerstown	.973	27	9	27	1	37	2
Siler, Jeff, Fayetteville*	.889	21	0	8	1	9	0
Silva, Theodore, Char. (S.C.)	1.000	11	5	10	0	15	1
Skrmetta, Matt, Fayetteville	.941	44	4	12	1	17	0
Slamka, John, Asheville*	1.000	6	0	1	0	1	0
Smith, Brian, Hagerstown	.885	47	6	17	3	26	1
Smith, Cam, Fayetteville	.789	29	14	16	8	38	1
Smith, Justin, Charleston (W.Va.)	1.000	44	8	9	0	17	0
Sobik, Trad, Fayetteville	.805	18	10	23	8	41	2
Solomon, David, Charleston (W.Va.)*	.875	43	5	9	2	16	0
Spade, Matt, Augusta	.929	51	1	12	1	14	0
Spring, Josh, Hagerstown	1.000	19	4	5	0	9	1
Stephens, Bill, Albany	.800	13	0	4	1	5	0
Stewart, Scott, Charleston (S.C.)*	.952	11	2	18	1	21	0
Stubbs, Jerry, Albany	.935	47	5	24	2	31	1
Stumpf, Brian, Piedmont	.850	55	4	13	3	20	0
Surratt, Jamie, Hickory	1.000	12	1	2	0	3	0
Swanson, David, C'bia-Ash.*	1.000	8	2	1	0	3	0

Player, Team	Pct.	G	PO	A	E	TC	DP
Tatis, Ramon, Columbia*	.500	18	1	1	2	4	0
Temple, Jason, Augusta	.625	51	4	6	6	16	0
Theodile, Robert, Hickory	.900	20	7	20	3	30	1
Thompson, Mark, Macon	1.000	13	0	2	0	2	0
Thurman, Michael, Albany	1.000	22	10	14	0	24	1
Tomko, Brett, Charleston (W.Va.)	1.000	9	1	3	0	4	0
Toney, Mike, Hagerstown	.909	20	5	5	1	11	0
Trimble, Rob, Greensboro	1.000	6	3	1	0	4	0
Turrentine, Rich, Columbia	.920	26	8	15	2	25	2
Tweedlie, Brad, Charleston (W.Va.)	.833	19	1	9	2	12	0
Tyner, Mark, Macon	1.000	29	1	3	0	4	0
Vavrek, Mike, Asheville*	.917	12	3	8	1	12	0
Vazquez, Javier, Albany	.852	21	10	13	4	27	1
Waldrep, Art, Asheville	1.000	15	2	2	0	4	0
Warrecker, Teddy, Columbus	.800	24	6	10	4	20	2
Weber, Lenny, Columbus	1.000	17	2	5	0	7	0
Wehn, Kevin, Asheville	1.000	5	2	3	0	5	1
Weidert, Chris, Albany	1.000	3	1	1	0	2	0
Weiss, Marc, Charleston (W.Va.)	1.000	11	0	4	0	4	0
Welch, David, Hickory*	.889	60	2	14	2	18	0
Wells, David, Hickory	1.000	17	2	4	0	6	0
Whiteman, Greg, Fayetteville*	.952	23	4	16	1	21	1
Whiteman, Tony, Fayetteville*	.846	28	5	6	2	13	0
Wilkerson, Steven, Char. (W.Va.)	.857	16	3	3	1	7	0
Wilson, Mike, Fayetteville	.889	17	1	7	1	9	0
Wimberly, Larry, Piedmont*	.870	24	1	19	3	23	0
Windham, Mike, Savannah	.933	26	9	19	2	30	1
Wolff, Tom, Columbia	1.000	15	0	2	0	2	0
Woodring, Jason, Albany	1.000	48	4	12	0	16	1
Wright, Jaret, Columbus	.913	24	7	14	2	23	0
Young, Danny, Augusta*	1.000	6	0	3	0	3	0
Zedalis, Craig, Macon	1.000	12	3	5	0	8	0
Zolecki, Mike, Asheville	.818	9	3	6	2	11	0

PITCHERS WITH TWO OR MORE TEAMS

Player, Team	Pct.	G	PO	A	E	TC	DP
Gooch, Arnold, Asheville	1.000	21	9	13	0	22	1
Gooch, Arnold, Columbia	.750	6	0	3	1	4	0
Jarvis, Jason, Greensboro	.969	22	13	18	1	32	1
Jarvis, Jason, Hagerstown	.889	8	1	7	1	9	0
Swanson, David, Columbia*	1.000	29	4	16	0	20	2
Swanson, David, Asheville*	1.000	8	2	1	0	3	0

The following players did not have any fielding statistics at the positions indicated or appeared only as a designated hitter, pinch-hitter or pinch-runner: Antczak, of, c; Beirne, p; Broome, p; Cardona, of; Cooney, p; Cooper, p; Eddie, ss; Elam, 3b; Fantauzzi, p; Figueroa, 1b; Forbes, p; R. Gomez, 1b; Hausmann, p; R. Jones, dh; Judd, p; Key, 1b; Kindell, p; Lackey, 1b; C. Lee, ss; Leiber, p; Light, dh, ph; D. Martinez, ss; O'Brien, 1b; Ocasio, p; Oram, 1b; Jo. Perez, p; Reilly, dh; Resetar, ph; Reynolds, p; Rodriguez, of; Schneider, p; Sharp, p; Shugars, of; Silvia, of; Towle, 1b; Van Oeveren, p; Vaske, p; Vejil, p; Wampler, dh; J. White, dh; Zubiri, p.

LEAGUE CHAMPIONS

Year	Team	Pct.	Year	Team	Pct.	Year	Team	Pct.
1948—	Lincolnton*	.627	1969—	Greenwood‡	.587	1983—	Columbia	.620
1949—	Newton-Conover	.667		Shelby	.565		Gastonia‡	.587
	Rutherford Co. (2nd)†	.627	1970—	Greenville	.576	1984—	Charleston	.549
1950—	Newton-Conover	.627		Greenville	.619		Asheville‡	.510
	Lenoir (2nd)†	.626	1971—	Greenwood	.631	1985—	Florence‡	.599
1951—	Morganton	.645		Greenwood	.759		Greensboro	.540
	Shelby (2nd)†	.604	1972—	Spartanburg‡	.788	1986—	Columbia‡	.682
1952—	Lincolnton	.649		Greenville	.652		Asheville	.643
	Shelby (2nd)†	.645	1973—	Spartanburg‡	.646	1987—	Asheville	.655
1953-59—League inactive.				Gastonia	.619		Myrtle Beach‡	.597
1960—	Lexington	.707	1974—	Gastonia	.606	1988—	Charleston (S.C.)	.616
	Salisbury (2nd)†	.650		Gastonia	.672		Spartanburg‡	.500
1961—	Salisbury	.627	1975—	Spartanburg	.543	1989—	Gastonia	.657
	Shelby (4th)†	.481		Spartanburg	.614		Augusta‡	.535
1962—	Statesville	.563	1976—	Asheville	.544	1990—	Columbia	.580
	Statesville	.700		Greenwood‡	.600		Charleston (W.Va.)‡	.538
1963—	Greenville†	.576	1977—	Greenwood	.557	1991—	Charleston (W.Va.)	.648
	Salisbury	.631		Gastonia‡	.590		Columbia‡	.614
1964—	Rock Hill	.672	1978—	Greenwood	.614	1992—	Columbia	.572
	Salisbury‡	.631		Greenwood	.565		Myrtle Beach‡	.522
1965—	Salisbury	.641	1979—	Greenwood‡	.565	1993—	Savannah‡	.662
	Rock Hill‡	.603		Spartanburg	.525		Greensboro	.603
1966—	Spartanburg	.682	1980—	Greensboro	.590	1994—	Columbus	.630
	Spartanburg	.767		Charleston	.561		Savannah‡	.599
1967—	Spartanburg	.730	1981—	Greensboro‡	.695	1995—	Piedmont	.586
	Spartanburg	.567		Greenwood	.549		Augusta‡	.551
1968—	Spartanburg	.597	1982—	Greensboro‡	.681			
	Greenwood‡	.597		Florence	.546			

*Won championship and four-club playoff. †Won four-club playoff. ‡Won split-season playoff. (NOTE—Known as Western Carolina League from 1948 through 1962 and known as Western Carolinas League through 1979.)

APPALACHIAN LEAGUE

LEAGUE OFFICE

President
Lee Landers
Address
20360 Carson Lane
Bristol, VA 24202
Phone
703-669-3644

Teams (affiliation)
Bluefield Orioles (Orioles)
Bristol White Sox (White Sox)
Burlington Indians (Indians)
Danville Braves (Braves)
Elizabethton Twins (Twins)
Johnson City Cardinals (Cardinals)

Kingsport Mets (Mets)
Martinsville Phillies (Phillies)
Princeton Reds (Reds)

1995 FINAL STANDINGS

NORTH DIVISION

Team	W	L	T	Pct.	GB
Bluefield (Orioles)	49	16	0	.754	....
Princeton (Reds)	31	32	0	.492	17
Martinsville (Phillies)	30	37	0	.448	20
Burlington (Indians)	26	38	0	.406	22 1/2
Danville (Braves)	27	40	0	.403	23

SOUTH DIVISION

Team	W	L	T	Pct.	GB
Kingsport (Mets)	48	18	0	.727	....
Elizabethton (Twins)	33	31	0	.516	14
Johnson City (Cardinals)	35	33	0	.515	14
Bristol (White Sox)	28	39	0	.418	20 1/2
Huntington (Co-op)	22	45	0	.328	26 1/2

COMPOSITE

Team	Blu.	Kng.	Elz.	J.C.	Pri.	Mar.	Brs.	Bur.	Dan.	Hun.	W	L	T	Pct.	GB
Bluefield (Orioles)	....	1	5	3	6	6	4	8	8	8	49	16	0	.754	....
Kingsport (Mets)	2	....	6	6	6	4	7	3	5	9	48	18	0	.727	1 1/2
Elizabethton (Twins)	0	4	....	7	3	3	5	2	4	5	33	31	0	.516	15 1/2
Johnson City (Cardinals)	1	4	3	....	2	5	6	3	3	8	35	33	0	.515	15 1/2
Princeton (Reds)	3	3	1	2	....	4	3	5	6	4	31	32	0	.492	17
Martinsville (Phillies)	4	1	1	5	5	....	2	3	6	3	30	37	0	.448	20
Bristol (White Sox)	1	3	4	4	2	2	....	6	1	5	28	39	0	.418	22
Burlington (Indians)	1	1	2	2	3	7	4	....	5	1	26	38	0	.406	22 1/2
Danville (Braves)	2	0	5	2	4	4	3	5	....	2	27	40	0	.403	23
Huntington (Co-op)	2	1	4	2	1	2	5	3	2	....	22	45	0	.328	28

Major league affiliations in parentheses.

PLAYOFFS: Kingsport defeated Bluefield, two games to one, to win league championship.

REGULAR-SEASON ATTENDANCE: Bluefield, 45,127; Bristol, 29,691; Burlington, 32,648; Danville, 63,905; Elizabethton, 18,982; Huntington, 20,631; Johnson City, 41,449; Kingsport, 35,891; Martinsville, 46,155; Princeton, 29,021. Total—363,500. Playoffs (3 games)—2,524.

MANAGERS: Bluefield, Andy Etchebarren; Bristol, Chris Cron; Burlington, Harry Spilman; Danville, Max Venable; Elizabethton, John Russell; Huntington, Phillip Wellman; Johnson City, Steve Turco; Kingsport, John Gibbons; Martinsville, Ramon Henderson; Princeton, Brad Kelly.

ALL-STAR TEAM: 1B—Jarrod Patterson, Kingsport; 2B—Kevin Hooker, Martinsville; 3B—Carlos Lee, Bristol; SS—Eddy Martinez, Bluefield; Utility IF—Zach Elliott, Martinsville; OF—Johnny Isom, Bluefield; Jeramie Simpson, Kingsport; Darron Ingram, Princeton; Utility OF—Eugene Kingsale, Bluefield; C—A.J. Pierzynski, Elizabethton; DH—Tony Boyette, Princeton; RHP—Chris Fussell, Bluefield; LHP—Chris Murphy, Johnson City; Relief Pitcher—Manuel Mendez, Johnson City; Most Valuable Player—Jarrod Patterson, Kingsport; Manager of the Year—John Gibbons, Kingsport.

1995 BATTING

TEAM

Team	Avg.	G	TPA	AB	R	H	TB	2B	3B	HR	RBI	SH	SF	HP	BB	IBB	SO	SB	CS	GDP	LOB	ShO	Slg.	OBP
Bluefield	.293	65	2493	2174	437	637	927	120	22	42	370	24	27	27	241	7	416	128	46	43	427	0	.426	.367
Elizabethton	.263	64	2466	2172	363	572	879	108	11	59	315	9	15	27	243	4	493	78	36	36	458	1	.405	.343
Kingsport	.263	66	2520	2199	402	578	819	98	22	33	327	23	18	33	247	7	458	113	39	29	440	3	.372	.344
Danville	.258	67	2526	2230	326	576	823	100	21	35	274	6	20	28	241	10	546	128	58	37	470	4	.369	.335
Bristol	.253	67	2495	2209	296	559	773	91	18	29	251	18	19	38	210	6	546	95	39	38	478	2	.350	.326
Johnson City	.249	68	2632	2261	357	562	811	119	23	28	300	14	20	33	304	4	583	70	51	37	506	4	.359	.343
Martinsville	.247	67	2477	2131	325	526	739	98	17	27	279	13	17	58	257	6	531	91	32	53	471	4	.347	.341
Burlington	.238	64	2384	2133	298	508	750	92	15	40	236	6	15	31	194	3	598	104	39	29	420	5	.352	.309
Princeton	.237	63	2362	2098	330	497	782	100	13	53	286	15	14	25	210	3	546	71	26	25	396	5	.373	.312
Huntington	.237	67	2461	2134	307	505	741	96	22	32	255	23	19	30	255	5	552	108	44	37	438	7	.347	.324

INDIVIDUAL

TOP QUALIFIERS FOR BATTING CHAMPIONSHIP

Minimum 184 plate appearances. *Lefthanded batter. †Switch-hitter.

Player, Team	Avg.	G	TPA	AB	R	H	TB	2B	3B	HR	RBI	SH	SF	HP	BB	IBB	SO	SB	CS	GDP	Slg.	OBP
Elliott, Zach, Martinsville	.358	45	193	151	46	54	78	10	4	2	19	1	2	7	32	1	30	13	5	3	.517	.484
Munoz, Juan, Johnson City*	.347	57	219	190	43	66	101	12	1	7	31	0	2	0	27	0	17	13	2	1	.532	.425
Lee, Carlos, Bristol	.346	67	282	269	43	93	133	17	1	7	45	0	3	2	8	3	34	17	7	6	.494	.365
Isom, Johnny, Bluefield	.344	59	247	212	47	73	113	14	4	6	56	2	7	1	25	0	27	9	2	5	.533	.404
Hooker, Kevin, Martinsville	.335	49	210	179	38	60	105	16	1	9	46	0	3	7	21	0	34	2	3	1	.587	.419
Pierzynski, A.J., Elizabethton*	.332	56	220	205	29	68	104	13	1	7	45	0	1	0	14	1	23	0	2	6	.507	.373
Mendoza, Carlos, Kingsport*	.328	51	228	192	56	63	75	9	0	1	24	4	2	3	27	0	24	28	6	3	.391	.415
Simpson, Jeramie, Kingsport*	.323	59	259	229	50	74	105	11	10	0	28	1	3	6	20	0	37	25	5	2	.459	.388
Rincones, Wuarnner, Bristol	.317	61	227	189	25	60	81	10	4	1	25	0	2	4	32	0	29	2	0	5	.429	.423
Kingsale, Eugene, Bluefield†	.316	47	209	171	45	54	69	11	2	0	16	4	2	5	27	0	31	20	8	0	.404	.420

Player, Team	Avg.	G	TPA	AB	R	H	TB	2B	3B	HR	RBI	SH	SF	HP	BB	IBB	SO	SB	CS	GDP	Slg.	OBP
Russin, Tom, Bluefield	.312	57	238	215	42	67	105	21	1	5	41	0	1	4	18	2	27	1	1	3	.488	.374
Martinez, Eddy, Bluefield	.308	57	215	185	42	57	77	11	3	1	35	1	1	5	23	0	42	5	5	1	.416	.397
Almonte, Wady, Bluefield	.307	51	201	189	37	58	90	12	1	6	30	0	2	1	9	2	49	6	5	4	.476	.338
Garcia, Carlos, Elizabethton	.306	62	262	235	42	72	104	15	1	5	34	3	4	4	16	0	41	27	8	5	.443	.355
Cross, Adam, Danville	.304	50	195	181	21	55	73	15	0	1	16	0	1	2	11	0	16	15	11	7	.403	.349

DEPARTMENTAL LEADERS: G—Haas, C. Lee, 67; AB—C. Lee, 269; R—Mendoza, 56; H—C. Lee, 93; TB—C. Lee, 133; 2B—Russin, 21; 3B—Simpson, 10; HR—Ingram, 14; RBI—Patterson, 57; SH—Mastrullo, 10; SF—Isom, 7; HP—Schreimann, 13; BB—Haas, 52; IBB—Hendricks, C. Lee, 3; SO—Haas, 93; SB—M. Anderson, 38; CS—Cross, 11; GIDP—Bryant, 10; Slg.—Hooker, .587; OBP—Elliott, .484.

ALL PLAYERS

*Lefthanded batter. †Switch-hitter.

Player, Team	Avg.	G	TPA	AB	R	H	TB	2B	3B	HR	RBI	SH	SF	HP	BB	IBB	SO	SB	CS	GDP	Slg.	OBP
Abell, Antonio, Johnson City	.258	55	222	190	27	49	63	10	2	0	16	2	3	5	22	1	76	8	8	0	.332	.345
Albert, Chernan, Bristol	.270	38	165	152	27	41	67	5	3	5	14	1	0	3	9	1	37	12	8	2	.441	.323
Almonte, Wady, Bluefield	.307	51	201	189	37	58	90	12	1	6	30	0	2	1	9	2	49	6	5	4	.476	.338
Anderson, Frank, Bristol	.222	46	163	153	10	34	49	7	1	2	16	0	2	0	7	0	52	2	3	0	.320	.253
Anderson, Milton, Burlington†	.257	58	256	210	45	54	76	7	3	3	19	0	1	4	41	1	44	38	6	2	.362	.387
Andino, Luis, Martinsville	.192	27	80	73	13	14	24	5	1	1	11	1	1	1	4	0	27	1	2	1	.329	.241
Andrews, Jeff, Huntington	.107	34	121	112	10	12	15	0	0	1	12	0	1	2	6	0	31	1	1	1	.134	.165
Anglen, Toby, Danville*	.253	63	249	221	32	56	76	11	0	3	35	0	3	1	24	1	33	14	4	5	.344	.325
Antczak, Chuck, Bristol	.305	24	73	59	11	18	25	4	0	1	10	0	1	7	6	0	16	2	0	1	.424	.425
Bagley, Sean, Bristol	.203	35	75	64	8	13	16	1	1	0	5	2	0	1	8	0	25	9	3	1	.250	.301
Bass, Jayson, Danville†	.224	64	302	268	38	60	85	17	4	0	17	0	2	4	28	2	61	24	8	2	.317	.305
Bates, Shawn, Bluefield*	.000	14	1	1	0	0	0	0	0	0	0	0	0	0	0	0	0	0	0	1	.000	.000
Bearden, Doug, Bristol	.234	46	181	167	26	39	60	10	1	3	22	3	2	3	6	0	40	5	0	1	.359	.290
Black, Brandon, Kingsport*	.292	31	118	106	17	31	45	5	0	3	20	0	1	3	8	0	23	7	1	3	.425	.356
Bogle, Bryan, Bristol	.452	10	38	31	11	14	19	2	0	1	4	0	1	2	4	0	2	1	0	1	.613	.526
Bowness, Brian, Bristol	.223	54	217	202	20	45	52	4	0	1	23	0	1	2	12	0	37	0	1	0	.257	.272
Boyette, Tony, Princeton	.293	61	249	222	41	65	112	15	1	10	49	0	3	3	21	0	41	2	0	3	.505	.357
Bracho, Darwin, Princeton†	.207	31	87	82	5	17	22	5	0	0	7	0	0	1	4	0	16	0	2	2	.268	.253
Brito, Domingo, Martinsville	.148	29	93	81	8	12	12	0	0	0	3	1	0	0	11	0	32	1	0	0	.148	.250
Brown, Jerome, Elizabethton†	.183	17	71	71	10	13	15	2	0	0	1	0	0	1	5	0	25	5	0	2	.211	.247
Bryant, Chris, Bluefield	.287	58	227	195	39	56	83	10	1	5	37	1	3	3	25	0	30	6	4	10	.426	.372
Buckles, Matt, Martinsville*	.190	22	63	58	6	11	13	2	0	0	4	1	0	2	2	1	17	2	0	2	.224	.242
Cardona, Alex, Johnson City	.217	22	58	46	9	10	13	3	0	0	7	1	0	0	11	1	4	0	1	0	.283	.368
Cloud, Tony, Princeton	.000	12	1	1	0	0	0	0	0	0	0	0	0	0	0	0	1	0	0	0	.000	.000
Coats, Nathan, Burlington	.313	20	72	64	8	20	28	5	0	1	5	1	0	3	4	0	15	1	0	1	.438	.380
Coburn, Todd, Huntington	.281	62	251	228	37	64	94	12	3	4	39	0	0	1	22	1	47	7	1	5	.412	.347
Colburn, Brian, Elizabethton*	.175	11	45	40	3	7	7	0	0	0	4	0	0	2	3	0	8	2	0	1	.175	.267
Concepcion, David, Princeton†	.236	60	249	203	44	48	80	10	2	6	24	2	1	1	42	1	44	10	0	2	.394	.368
Conner, Decomba, Princeton	.125	6	20	16	2	2	4	2	0	0	5	0	1	0	3	0	3	2	0	0	.250	.250
Cox, Robert, Kingsport	.197	57	224	188	29	37	55	9	0	3	25	1	0	5	30	1	59	1	3	2	.293	.323
Cross, Adam, Danville	.304	50	195	181	21	55	73	15	0	1	16	0	1	2	11	0	16	15	11	7	.403	.349
Current, Jeremy, Johnson City	.254	23	76	63	5	16	19	3	0	0	6	1	1	3	8	0	23	0	0	0	.302	.360
Cushman, Dwayne, Princeton	.000	26	1	1	0	0	0	0	0	0	0	0	0	0	0	0	1	0	0	0	.000	.000
Daedlow, Craig, Bluefield	.000	5	18	13	1	0	0	0	0	0	1	0	1	0	4	0	3	0	1	0	.000	.222
Davidson, Cleatus, Elizabethton†	.296	39	166	152	27	45	64	6	2	3	27	0	3		11	0	31	10	4	2	.421	.355
Davis, James, Princeton	.276	58	243	225	40	62	89	12	0	1	29	1	2	1	14	0	33	8	0	2	.396	.318
Deck, Billy, Johnson City*	.259	59	245	205	27	53	68	12	0	1	30	1	2	7	30	0	52	4	6	1	.332	.369
Dellucci, David, Bluefield*	.333	20	77	69	11	23	36	5	1	2	12	0	1	1	6	1	7	3	1	1	.522	.390
Diaz, Ivan, Johnson City	.214	6	14	14	0	3	3	0	0	0	2	0	0	0	0	0	3	0	0	0	.214	.214
Dougherty, Keith, Danville	.294	25	90	85	14	25	47	5	1	5	14	0	1	1	3	1	24	1	1	2	.553	.322
Drent, Brian, Bristol	.242	49	206	161	31	39	67	13	0	5	26	0	3	3	39	1	58	16	2	5	.416	.393
Duncan, Robert, Danville*	.232	49	178	142	23	33	38	3	1	0	8	1	1	5	29	0	45	5	3	1	.268	.379
Edmondson, Tracy, Kingsport	.265	44	187	155	36	41	61	11	0	3	25	2	1	2	27	1	34	8	1	0	.394	.378
Edwards, Donald, Burlington	.169	43	149	130	20	22	24	2	0	0	5	0	0	2	17	0	35	5	2	2	.185	.275
Elliott, Zach, Martinsville	.358	45	193	151	46	54	78	10	4	2	19	1	2	7	32	1	30	13	5	3	.517	.484
Ennis, Wayne, Princeton	.048	10	22	21	4	1	1	0	0	0	2	1	0	0	0	0	8	0	1	0	.048	.048
Erickson, Corey, Kingsport	.333	2	9	9	1	3	6	0	0	1	4	0	0	0	0	0	3	0	0	0	.667	.333
Espada, Angel, Danville	.301	33	126	113	17	34	39	0	1	1	16	0	0	0	12	0	16	16	4	3	.345	.368
Falciglia, Tony, Johnson City	.314	33	134	118	18	37	63	14	0	4	26	0	3	1	12	0	34	0	1	4	.534	.373
Fernandez, Randy, Huntington*	.308	15	46	39	2	12	12	0	0	0	3	2	0	0	5	0	16	2	4	0	.308	.386
Foote, Derek, Danville*	.362	17	62	58	10	21	34	4	0	3	9	0	0	1	3	0	21	0	0	0	.586	.403
Franklin, James, Danville	.243	51	178	148	30	36	45	5	2	0	17	1	1	0	28	1	51	9	5	4	.304	.362
Fraser, Joseph, Elizabethton	.261	46	210	184	29	48	64	4	0	4	21	2	2	2	20	0	22	5	4	5	.348	.337
Frost, Robert, Kingsport	.333	11	33	30	7	10	13	2	0	0	1	0	0	1	1	0	5	1	0	0	.400	.375
Gabriel, Denio, Bluefield†	.289	53	213	180	39	52	59	4	0	1	24	6	1	1	25	0	36	31	8	1	.328	.377
Garcia, Carlos, Elizabethton	.306	62	262	235	42	72	104	15	1	5	34	3	4	4	16	0	41	27	8	5	.443	.355
Gargiulo, Mike, Bluefield*	.289	48	192	180	24	52	76	7	4	3	21	1	1	0	10	1	35	1	2	6	.422	.325
Gill, Sean, Kingsport	.000	8	19	18	2	0	0	0	0	0	0	0	0	0	0	0	10	0	1	0	.000	.053
Glavine, Mike, Burlington*	.245	46	180	155	38	38	81	10	0	11	28	0	1		22	0	37	1	0	0	.523	.339
Gunderson, Shane, Elizabethton	.309	37	162	139	32	43	79	11	2	7	30	0	1	2	20	0	24	4	0	3	.568	.401
Guthrie, David, Princeton†	.204	55	207	181	28	37	48	11	0	0	13	4	1	3	18	1	41	7	1	4	.265	.286
Haas, Chris, Johnson City*	.269	67	295	242	43	65	107	15	3	7	50	0	0	1	52	0	93	1	3	8	.442	.400
Hall, Darran, Princeton*	.120	9	32	25	3	3	3	0	0	0	1	1	0	1	5	0	10	1	2	0	.120	.258
Hardy, Brian, Burlington*	.200	29	91	80	15	16	35	4	0	5	12	0	1	0	10	0	40	1	0	1	.438	.297
Harmer, Francis, Bluefield†	.190	18	69	58	5	11	14	3	0	0	10	0	2	0	9	0	14	1	0	0	.241	.290
Harris, Rodger, Johnson City†	.182	45	143	121	26	22	29	5	1	0	7	1	0	2	19	0	44	5	2	3	.240	.303
Helms, Ryan, Bristol†	.164	48	162	146	16	24	28	2	1	0	9	2	1	2	11	0	33	3	1	3	.192	.231
Hendricks, Ryan, Huntington*	.258	58	226	178	38	46	91	12	0	11	36	0	2	0	46	3	50	8	1	2	.511	.407
Herdman, Eli, Elizabethton*	.212	62	254	217	36	46	86	10	0	10	36	0	2	1	34	1	60	1	2	4	.396	.319
Herrera, Jesus, Princeton†	.242	46	162	149	18	36	47	8	0	1	9	1	1	4	7	0	38	6	5	1	.315	.292

Player, Team	Avg.	G	TPA	AB	R	H	TB	2B	3B	HR	RBI	SH	SF	HP	BB	IBB	SO	SB	CS	GDP	Slg.	OBP
Higman, Joel, Blu.-Hun.	.246	24	76	69	6	17	18	1	0	0	7	0	0	1	6	0	26	3	0	4	.261	.316
Hobbie, Matt, Huntington*	.227	60	240	211	25	48	76	12	5	2	24	0	5	1	23	0	49	17	5	1	.360	.300
Hodges, Randy, Danville*	.250	2	9	8	1	2	5	0	0	1	1	0	0	1	0	0	2	0	1	1	.625	.333
Hollins, Darontaye, Bristol	.248	62	250	222	24	55	66	7	2	0	14	2	2	4	20	1	75	14	5	5	.297	.319
Hooker, Kevin, Martinsville	.335	49	210	179	38	60	105	16	1	9	46	0	3	7	21	0	34	2	3	1	.587	.419
Hoover, Will, Kingsport	.190	11	23	21	1	4	5	1	0	0	3	0	0	0	2	0	10	0	0	0	.238	.261
Hunter, Lanier, Huntington†	.250	62	260	216	36	54	82	12	2	4	18	2	2	8	32	0	64	15	10	2	.380	.364
Ingram, Darron, Princeton	.275	60	247	233	37	64	118	6	3	14	53	0	2	1	11	0	78	3	1	5	.506	.308
Isom, Johnny, Bluefield	.344	59	247	212	47	73	113	14	4	6	56	2	7	1	25	0	27	9	2	5	.533	.404
Janke, Jared, Martinsville	.242	46	178	149	24	36	56	11	0	3	27	0	0	3	26	0	25	5	1	6	.376	.365
Jensen, Blair, Burlington	.191	21	54	47	3	9	10	1	0	0	2	1	0	0	6	0	21	2	0	3	.213	.283
Jimenez, Ruben, Johnson City†	.164	41	139	116	13	19	27	0	4	0	20	1	3	3	16	0	27	5	6	2	.233	.275
Johnson, Heath, Elizabethton*	.209	59	246	201	31	42	55	10	0	1	16	0	1	3	41	1	51	4	5	3	.274	.350
Johnson, Travis, Elizabethton*	.341	14	49	44	6	15	28	5	1	2	4	0	0	0	5	0	10	2	1	0	.636	.408
Jones, Ivory, Elizabethton*	.199	47	161	136	21	27	39	4	1	2	11	3	0	0	22	0	43	6	5	0	.287	.310
Juarez, Raul, Elizabethton	.283	40	144	120	25	34	50	7	0	3	16	0	1	0	23	1	50	10	3	0	.417	.396
Kearney, Chad, Martinsville	.225	29	91	80	9	18	22	1	0	1	5	0	0	1	10	0	32	1	2	1	.275	.319
Kennedy, Justin, Martinsville*	.199	43	156	146	11	29	38	7	1	0	15	0	2	1	7	0	36	11	0	2	.260	.237
Kerr, Brian, Bluefield†	.167	3	6	6	0	1	2	1	0	0	1	0	0	0	0	0	2	0	0	0	.333	.167
Kingsale, Eugene, Bluefield†	.316	47	209	171	45	54	69	11	2	0	16	4	2	5	27	0	31	20	8	0	.404	.420
Lakovic, Greg, Elizabethton	.244	14	48	41	7	10	12	2	0	0	8	1	0	3	3	0	8	0	1	1	.293	.340
Langford, Derrick, Danville	.341	27	96	85	7	29	35	3	0	1	16	0	1	1	9	0	18	1	2	2	.412	.406
Lantigua, Miguel, Kingsport†	.125	6	18	16	0	2	2	0	0	0	1	0	1	0	1	1	6	0	0	1	.125	.167
LeCronier, Jason, Bluefield*	.246	21	81	69	11	17	29	4	1	2	10	0	1	0	11	1	17	1	1	1	.420	.346
Lee, Carlos, Bristol	.346	67	282	269	43	93	133	17	1	7	45	0	3	2	8	3	34	17	7	6	.494	.365
Lee, Jason, Johnson City*	.105	28	86	76	10	8	9	1	0	0	4	1	0	1	8	0	38	2	4	0	.118	.200
Livingston, Clyde, Martinsville*.	.212	33	113	104	15	22	37	5	2	2	25	0	1	0	8	0	22	1	0	4	.356	.265
Lugo, Ursino, Burlington†	.245	32	98	94	13	23	23	0	0	0	5	1	0	0	3	0	29	9	4	6	.245	.268
Malin, Edgar, Huntington	.175	21	73	63	12	11	15	1	0	1	8	0	0	0	10	0	27	3	2	3	.238	.288
Mapp, Eric, Princeton†	.224	61	233	210	32	47	73	11	0	5	23	2	0	3	18	0	58	10	1	1	.348	.294
Martin, Ryan, Danville	.214	5	18	14	2	3	4	1	0	0	2	0	0	0	3	0	5	0	1	0	.286	.353
Martinez, Eddy, Bluefield	.308	57	215	185	42	57	77	11	3	1	35	1	1	5	23	0	42	5	5	1	.416	.397
Martinez, Tony, Johnson City	.234	24	105	77	18	18	26	0	1	2	8	1	0	1	26	0	14	3	2	2	.338	.433
Mason, Lamont, Princeton	.167	26	94	78	11	13	18	3	1	0	3	0	0	0	16	0	21	6	4	2	.231	.309
Mastrullo, Mike, Huntington	.179	46	176	134	20	24	33	5	2	0	14	10	4	3	25	0	43	5	4	4	.246	.313
Mata, Manuel, Martinsville*	.400	1	5	5	1	2	2	0	0	0	2	0	0	0	0	0	0	0	0	0	.400	.400
McCarthy, Kevin, Kingsport*	.132	26	109	91	11	12	19	2	1	1	4	0	0	1	17	1	18	1	2	0	.209	.275
McClure, Craig, Bristol	.233	64	253	223	26	52	74	6	2	4	26	4	1	3	22	0	65	7	8	3	.332	.309
McCroskey, Jackie, Huntington*	.288	49	186	156	26	45	73	12	5	2	27	0	1	3	26	1	31	12	3	0	.468	.398
McDougal, Mike, Johnson City ..	.175	32	103	97	8	17	31	3	1	3	12	0	0	0	6	0	27	0	2	2	.320	.223
McNeal, Pepe, Bur.-J.C.	.226	54	210	186	13	42	56	8	0	2	27	0	2	3	19	1	48	4	0	4	.301	.305
McWhite, Ray, Danville†	.260	64	253	231	37	60	114	16	1	12	53	1	2	3	16	0	76	8	4	5	.494	.313
Mejia, Miguel, Bluefield	.298	51	208	181	50	54	75	6	3	3	30	6	2	1	18	0	30	36	5	5	.414	.361
Mendoza, Carlos, Kingsport*	.328	51	228	192	56	63	75	9	0	1	24	4	3	2	27	0	24	28	6	3	.391	.415
Mepri, Sal, Princeton	.200	6	5	5	0	1	1	0	0	0	0	0	0	0	0	0	3	0	0	0	.200	.200
Messner, Jake, Burlington*	.222	46	164	144	17	32	42	2	4	0	9	0	1	1	14	0	40	8	5	0	.292	.294
Mifflin, Brian, Kingsport	.250	1	5	4	1	1	1	0	0	0	0	0	0	0	1	0	0	0	0	0	.250	.400
Milledge, Tony, Johnson City	.276	31	95	87	14	24	42	7	1	3	12	0	0	1	7	0	15	1	0	2	.483	.337
Mota, Christian, Burlington†	.282	59	244	234	37	66	95	17	3	2	36	0	2	2	6	1	55	7	3	4	.406	.303
Mota, Gleydel, Kingsport*	.000	1	4	3	1	0	0	0	0	0	0	0	0	0	1	0	2	0	0	0	.000	.250
Mullen, Adam, Danville	.137	17	57	51	2	7	9	0	1	0	3	1	1	0	4	0	17	1	1	0	.176	.196
Munoz, Juan, Johnson City*	.347	57	219	190	43	66	101	12	1	7	31	0	2	0	27	0	17	13	2	1	.532	.425
Murphy, Quinn, Burlington*	.175	40	142	126	12	22	33	5	0	2	9	1	0	1	14	0	56	2	5	0	.262	.262
Naples, Brandon, Kingsport	.275	32	122	109	22	30	36	1	1	1	23	0	1	1	11	0	11	2	0	0	.330	.344
Nolte, Bruce, Huntington	.220	61	238	209	30	46	65	6	2	3	21	5	1	2	21	0	46	16	5	3	.311	.296
O'Connor, Richard, Martinsville	.224	53	208	174	27	39	45	4	1	0	11	4	0	4	26	1	52	13	8	1	.259	.338
Oliveros, Leonardo, Martinsville	.284	48	173	155	17	44	59	9	0	2	18	0	2	3	14	1	18	0	0	8	.381	.347
Patellis, Anthony, Princeton	.253	46	181	166	21	42	84	7	1	11	32	0	1	3	11	1	58	4	2	1	.506	.309
Patterson, Jarrod, Kingsport*	.279	64	271	240	45	67	129	17	3	13	57	0	3	0	28	2	50	3	1	2	.538	.351
Pena, Francisco, Elizabethton	.190	10	23	21	4	4	6	2	0	0	2	0	0	0	2	0	9	0	0	0	.286	.261
Pena, Jose, Burlington	.200	23	71	70	7	14	22	2	0	2	6	0	1	1	0	0	21	0	1	2	.314	.208
Pennyfeather, William, Princeton ..	.000	1	3	3	0	0	0	0	0	0	0	0	0	0	0	0	1	0	0	0	.000	.000
Pickett, Eric, Danville*	.220	61	242	218	20	48	63	5	5	0	26	0	3	2	19	2	67	9	4	2	.289	.285
Pierzynski, A.J., Elizabethton*	.332	56	220	205	29	68	104	13	1	7	45	0	1	0	13	1	23	0	2	6	.507	.373
Pointer, Corey, Danville	.278	46	184	158	33	44	79	5	3	8	27	0	2	5	19	1	60	8	4	1	.500	.370
Polanco, Enohel, Kingsport	.229	62	231	205	28	47	62	5	2	2	21	3	3	2	18	0	60	7	6	5	.302	.294
Raio, Domenick, Martinsville	.214	6	16	14	1	3	3	0	0	0	1	0	0	0	1	0	4	0	0	0	.214	.267
Ramirez, Alonso, Burlington	.167	10	22	18	3	3	3	0	0	0	0	1	0	1	3	0	6	0	0	0	.167	.273
Ramirez, Daniel, Kingsport	.248	62	251	226	30	56	72	6	2	2	32	9	0	1	15	1	44	21	10	5	.319	.298
Ramos, Noel, Bluefield	.196	31	119	107	18	21	43	5	1	5	18	0	0	2	10	0	43	1	0	0	.402	.277
Raymondi, Mike, Huntington	.220	28	89	82	8	18	24	3	0	1	8	0	0	2	5	0	27	1	0	3	.293	.281
Reyes, Freddy, Elizabethton	.277	40	140	130	17	36	63	10	1	5	21	0	1	1	6	0	28	0	0	4	.485	.321
Reyes, Winston, Huntington	.265	20	72	68	5	18	22	4	0	0	8	1	0	0	3	0	17	3	2	4	.324	.296
Rincones, Wuarnner, Bristol	.317	61	227	189	25	60	81	10	4	1	25	0	2	4	32	0	29	2	0	5	.429	.423
Roberson, Gerald, Danville	.213	52	210	188	43	40	62	11	1	3	14	2	2	5	13	0	31	12	4	3	.330	.279
Robinson, Kerry, Johnson City*	.296	60	271	250	44	74	105	12	8	1	26	3	2	0	16	1	30	14	10	3	.420	.336
Russin, Tom, Bluefield	.312	57	238	215	42	67	105	21	1	5	41	0	1	4	18	2	27	1	1	3	.488	.374
Salano, Manuel, Princeton	.216	30	83	74	12	16	23	4	0	1	14	1	0	1	7	0	20	2	2	0	.311	.293
Santiago, Arnold, Burlington	.285	35	129	123	15	35	42	1	5	0	11	0	2	0	4	0	22	3	1	1	.341	.302
Sasser, Rob, Danville	.319	12	52	47	8	15	19	2	1	0	7	0	1	0	4	1	7	5	1	1	.404	.365
Schofield, Andy, Johnson City	.227	40	141	119	22	27	35	8	0	0	11	0	0	3	19	0	30	6	1	0	.294	.348
Schreimann, Eric, Martinsville	.299	38	153	127	12	38	52	8	0	2	18	2	1	13	10	2	20	2	1	4	.409	.404
Schroeder, John, Elizabethton*	.263	62	259	236	44	62	103	7	2	10	39	0	2	3	18	0	59	2	1	0	.436	.320

Player, Team	Avg.	G	TPA	AB	R	H	TB	2B	3B	HR	RBI	SH	SF	HP	BB	IBB	SO	SB	CS	GDP	Slg.	OBP
Serafin, Ricardo, Martinsville	.189	22	56	53	8	10	14	1	0	1	4	0	0	2	1	0	20	4	0	2	.264	.232
Serbio, Carmen, Martinsville	.229	28	109	83	15	19	33	6	1	2	12	2	0	4	20	0	23	0	1	5	.398	.402
Short, Richard, Bluefield	.282	11	43	39	9	11	19	2	0	2	12	0	1	1	2	0	1	2	1	2	.487	.326
Shy, Jason, Danville	.231	8	15	13	1	3	3	0	0	0	0	0	0	0	2	0	3	0	0	0	.231	.333
Simpson, Jeramie, Kingsport*	.323	59	259	229	50	74	105	11	10	0	28	1	3	6	20	0	37	25	5	2	.459	.388
Smalley, Jevon, Princeton*	.258	39	115	97	17	25	38	5	1	2	14	0	0	2	16	0	31	3	2	1	.392	.374
Soriano, Juan, Kingsport	.262	40	130	107	29	28	35	5	1	0	12	0	1	2	20	0	21	7	2	1	.327	.385
Spry, Shane, Bristol*	.233	15	54	43	5	10	12	2	0	0	6	0	1	0	10	0	7	0	0	0	.279	.370
Stone, Matthew, Martinsville*	.252	40	143	111	15	28	36	8	0	0	13	0	1	2	29	0	37	3	0	5	.324	.413
Strasser, John, Bristol	.226	46	187	159	24	36	43	3	2	0	10	4	0	4	20	0	38	6	1	1	.270	.328
Sturges, Brian, Johnson City	.143	17	48	42	5	6	7	1	0	0	6	1	0	3	2	0	7	0	0	3	.167	.234
Taylor, Jerry, Burlington	.296	10	37	27	7	8	17	1	1	2	8	0	1	1	8	0	6	1	0	0	.630	.459
Taylor, Reggie, Martinsville*	.222	64	272	239	36	53	75	4	6	2	32	0	4	6	·23	0	58	18	7	5	.314	.301
Terry, Tony, Princeton†	.170	47	128	106	15	18	21	3	0	0	8	2	1	2	17	0	40	7	4	0	.198	.294
Tiller, Brad, Burlington	.236	55	213	195	24	46	61	10	1	1	23	2	2	3	11	0	49	11	5	2	.313	.284
Torbett, Hanes, Kingsport	.261	19	56	46	10	12	17	1	2	0	5	0	1	0	9	0	8	0	0	0	.370	.375
Townsend, Terric, Martinsville	.286	5	18	14	4	4	4	0	0	0	1	0	0	1	3	0	2	1	0	0	.286	.444
Utting, Ben, Danville*	.238	55	220	189	30	45	55	8	1	0	15	1	1	2	27	2	34	12	4	1	.291	.338
Valera, Yojanny, Kingsport	.294	56	223	204	30	60	82	13	0	3	36	2	1	5	11	0	33	2	1	6	.402	.344
Wampler, Sam, Martinsville†	.136	11	25	22	0	3	3	0	0	0	1	0	0	0	3	0	10	0	0	2	.136	.240
Whitaker, Chad, Burlington*	.238	47	197	181	20	43	73	13	1	5	27	0	1	1	14	1	59	2	3	1	.403	.294
Williams, Errick, Martinsville	.239	36	122	113	19	27	28	1	0	0	11	0	0	2	6	0	32	13	2	1	.248	.289
Williams, Jewell, Burlington	.219	46	167	146	20	32	52	6	1	4	15	0	0	8	13	0	52	11	4	3	.356	.317
Winn, Wess, Bluefield†	.224	24	64	49	4	11	13	2	0	0	9	3	0	0	12	0	12	2	2	0	.265	.377
Wood, Tony, Huntington	.268	56	224	205	26	55	64	5	2	0	19	1	1	2	15	0	55	5	2	4	.312	.323
Woolf, Jason, Johnson City†	.279	31	124	111	16	31	40	7	1	0	14	1	3	1	8	0	21	6	3	0	.360	.325

GRAND SLAMS: Ingram, 3; Coburn, McWhite, 2 each; Drent, Gargiulo, Gunderson, Jones, Munoz, Patellis, Pierzynski, Valera, 1 each.
AWARDED FIRST BASE ON CATCHER'S INTERFERENCE: Messner 4 (Foote 2, Antczak, Gargiulo); F. Anderson (Coats); Martin (Gunderson); J. Pena (McNeal); E. Williams (Boyette).

PLAYERS WITH TWO OR MORE TEAMS

Player, Team	Avg.	G	TPA	AB	R	H	TB	2B	3B	HR	RBI	SH	SF	HP	BB	IBB	SO	SB	CS	GDP	Slg.	OBP
Higman, Joel, Bluefield	.208	11	27	24	2	5	5	0	0	0	3	0	0	0	3	0	8	2	0	2	.208	.296
Higman, Joel, Huntington	.267	13	49	45	4	12	13	1	0	0	4	0	0	1	3	0	18	1	0	2	.289	.327
McNeal, Pepe, Burlington	.281	27	96	89	4	25	33	2	0	2	15	0	1	2	4	0	20	2	0	1	.371	.323
McNeal, Pepe, Johnson City	.175	27	114	97	9	17	23	6	0	0	12	0	1	1	15	1	28	2	0	3	.237	.289

1995 PITCHING

TEAM

Team	W	L	Pct.	ERA	G	CG	ShO	Sv.	IP	H	TBF	R	ER	HR	SH	SF	HB	BB	IBB	SO	WP	Bk.
Bluefield	49	16	.754	3.22	65	2	3	28	561.0	511	2381	269	201	41	14	10	36	227	4	531	50	10
Elizabethton	33	31	.516	3.41	64	4	5	13	551.0	550	2396	299	209	29	21	14	23	183	7	535	53	18
Kingsport	48	18	.727	3.49	66	5	6	20	574.1	480	2414	263	223	38	18	10	35	226	5	532	52	4
Princeton	31	32	.492	4.19	63	1	4	15	543.1	538	2434	339	253	29	6	18	24	267	16	506	73	13
Bristol	28	39	.418	4.24	67	2	2	10	566.1	552	2493	347	267	40	18	22	27	224	2	532	52	16
Danville	27	40	.403	4.35	67	2	2	18	570.2	540	2515	378	276	31	17	37	33	243	3	536	74	14
Martinsville	30	37	.448	4.58	67	0	1	17	557.2	582	2475	349	284	38	10	17	35	247	4	511	77	13
Johnson City	35	33	.515	4.75	68	4	3	20	589.0	599	2666	399	311	50	21	20	36	279	5	539	55	27
Burlington	26	38	.406	4.88	64	4	4	12	550.0	535	2491	373	298	38	12	12	35	272	7	582	57	9
Huntington	22	45	.328	5.49	67	6	1	11	560.1	630	2551	425	342	44	14	24	46	234	2	465	79	14

INDIVIDUAL

TOP QUALIFIERS FOR EARNED-RUN AVERAGE TITLE

Minimum 54 innings. *Lefthanded pitcher.

Pitcher, Team	W	L	Pct.	ERA	G	GS	CG	ShO	GF	Sv.	IP	H	TBF	R	ER	HR	SH	SF	HB	BB	IBB	SO	WP	Bk.
Garber, Joel, Bristol*	5	1	.833	1.20	19	6	0	0	4	0	60.0	37	229	13	8	3	1	2	1	12	0	66	4	1
Murphy, Chris, Princeton*	7	1	.875	1.55	10	10	1	1	0	0	63.2	51	266	23	11	4	0	2	2	19	0	52	6	0
Fussell, Chris, Bluefield	9	1	.900	2.19	12	12	1	1	0	0	65.2	37	265	18	16	4	1	1	7	32	0	98	3	1
Abreu, Winston, Danville	6	3	.667	2.31	13	13	1	0	0	0	74.0	54	277	29	19	5	0	4	1	13	0	90	2	0
Ojeda, Erick, Kingsport*	6	2	.750	2.40	14	5	0	0	3	0	60.0	47	240	18	16	3	2	0	1	12	0	60	4	1
Olson, Phillip, Kingsport	6	2	.750	2.42	10	10	2	1	1	1	67.0	47	271	24	18	1	1	1	8	23	0	45	4	1
Feliz, Bienvenido, Burlington	4	2	.667	2.71	12	12	1	1	0	0	73.0	55	296	29	22	8	1	1	0	20	0	78	2	2
Sanders, Frankie, Burlington	3	5	.375	2.96	12	12	3	0	0	0	70.0	48	292	31	23	2	1	0	3	32	0	80	2	1
Figueroa, Nelson, Kingsport	7	3	.700	3.07	12	12	2	2	0	0	76.1	57	304	36	26	3	3	2	5	22	1	79	5	0
Roberts, Randolph, Princeton	4	5	.444	3.16	15	9	0	0	2	0	62.2	51	281	35	22	3	1		6	33	3	74	14	2
Wagner, Ken, Burlington	5	5	.500	3.16	13	12	0	0	0	0	68.1	54	285	34	24	7	1	2	1	23	0	80	7	1
Splittorff, James, Elizabethton	5	4	.556	3.24	13	12	1	1	1	0	72.1	64	319	40	26	5	0	2	7	29	0	72	11	2
Mear, Rich, Johnson City*	7	3	.700	3.35	14	14	0	0	0	0	78.0	68	338	37	29	4	3	1	4	40	1	75	11	1
Mahaffey, Alan, Elizabethton*	5	6	.455	3.47	13	12	1	0	0	0	70.0	66	308	42	27	4	2		3	21	0	73	4	8
Jimenez, Jose, Johnson City	5	7	.417	3.49	14	14	1	1	1	0	90.1	81	380	48	35	3	5	1	5	25	0	85	7	1

DEPARTMENTAL LEADERS: W—Fussell, 9; L—Adair, 9; Pct.—Fussell, .900; G—S. Reed, 31; GS—Jimenez, Mear, Young, 14; CG—Sanders, 3; ShO—Figueroa, 2; GF—Mendez, 28; Sv.—Mendez, 19; IP—Jimenez, 90.1; H—Adair, 96; TBF—Jimenez, 380; R—Secoda, 57; ER—M. DeWitt, 49; HR—Roettgen, 11; SH—Mahaffey, 6; SF—Adair, Guiliano, Schnur, 5; HB—Oldham, Young, 9; BB—Pumphrey, 42; IBB—Roberts, 3; SO—Fussell, 98; WP—Roberts, Shumate, 14; Bk.—Mahaffey, 8.

Pitcher, Team	W	L	Pct.	ERA	G	GS	CG	ShO	GF	Sv.	IP	H	TBF	R	ER	HR	SH	SF	HB	BB	IBB	SO	WP	Bk.
Abreu, Winston, Danville	6	3	.667	2.31	13	13	1	0	0	0	74.0	54	277	29	19	5	0	4	1	13	0	90	2	0
Adair, Scott, Huntington	2	9	.182	4.70	13	13	1	0	0	0	74.2	96	317	47	39	3	2	5	2	13	0	28	2	0
Aguiar, Douglas, Martinsville	2	2	.500	5.56	15	7	0	0	4	0	45.1	46	195	28	28	3	0	1	3	21	0	42	5	1
Alexis, Julio, Huntington	1	6	.143	4.74	14	13	0	0	0	0	81.2	89	352	55	43	9	2	2	3	21	0	65	5	1
Alvarado, Luis, Huntington	3	4	.429	3.68	11	5	1	0	1	0	44.0	43	195	28	18	4	1	1	1	12	0	43	4	0
Anderson, Eric, Elizabethton*	3	2	.600	2.95	21	2	0	0	5	0	39.2	48	185	21	13	0	4	0	2	19	1	31	1	1
Anderson, Gary, Burlington	1	2	.333	6.35	14	0	0	0	12	3	17.0	18	81	12	12	2	0	0	4	8	0	22	3	0
Anez, Maycoll, Bristol	0	2	.000	5.74	7	2	0	0	1	1	15.2	24	78	14	10	1	1	1	0	8	0	11	0	0
Angerhofer, Chad, Princeton*	2	4	.333	7.22	13	7	0	0	2	0	38.2	52	189	37	31	5	0	2	1	17	0	38	6	1
Barfield, Rodney, Johnson City	2	7	.222	9.82	10	10	0	0	0	0	36.2	52	199	50	40	3	3	2	8	30	0	18	4	2
Bartels, Todd, Elizabethton	6	2	.750	4.11	13	9	2	0	1	0	57.0	66	239	27	26	4	1	2	1	3	0	45	0	1
Bates, Shawn, Bluefield*	2	0	1.000	2.45	14	2	0	0	5	3	25.2	22	113	13	7	1	1	0	2	16	0	31	5	1
Beebe, Joey, Kingsport*	5	1	.833	3.25	9	7	0	0	1	0	44.1	43	182	16	16	3	2	1	1	12	0	34	5	0
Beirne, Kevin, Bristol	1	0	1.000	0.00	9	0	0	0	7	2	9.0	4	35	0	0	0	0	0	0	4	0	12	0	0
Blang, Michael, Kingsport	0	0	.000	3.18	23	0	0	0	15	7	28.1	19	111	10	10	3	0	1	1	7	1	18	3	1
Blank, John, Elizabethton*	3	0	1.000	4.54	15	5	0	0	2	0	35.2	40	159	21	18	3	0	0	0	16	1	32	5	2
Boggs, Harold, Elizabethton	3	5	.375	5.82	12	12	0	0	0	0	60.1	77	276	53	39	2	2	4	2	20	0	55	6	0
Bowser, Robert, Martinsville	2	2	.500	3.90	17	0	0	0	8	1	32.1	30	136	15	14	1	1	1	4	9	2	35	0	2
Burger, Rob, Martinsville	2	4	.333	4.65	9	9	0	0	0	0	40.2	47	188	25	21	1	0	2	3	23	0	54	5	0
Buteaux, Shane, Bristol	7	6	.538	4.26	13	13	1	0	0	0	74.0	72	337	45	35	9	0	4	8	41	0	49	9	4
Chapman, Walker, Elizabethton	0	1	.000	5.63	4	1	0	0	1	0	8.0	9	34	6	5	1	0	1	1	0	0	7	2	1
Chen, Bruce, Danville*	4	4	.500	3.97	14	13	1	0	0	0	70.1	78	310	42	31	3	1	4	3	19	1	56	4	1
Cloud, Tony, Princeton	4	5	.444	4.20	12	12	0	0	0	0	55.2	47	232	34	26	1	0	3	1	26	1	46	8	0
Cochrane, Andrew, Danville*	1	1	.500	4.63	6	0	0	0	1	0	11.2	14	57	11	6	0	0	1	0	6	0	10	2	0
Coggin, David, Martinsville	5	3	.625	3.00	11	11	0	0	0	0	48.0	45	209	25	16	1	1	1	5	31	0	37	8	1
Collins, Ken, Danville	1	0	1.000	4.18	18	1	0	0	10	0	32.1	36	153	31	15	2	2	2	4	15	0	29	7	0
Cooper, Chadwick, Kingsport	0	0	.000	3.03	22	1	0	0	14	6	29.2	21	123	12	10	3	0	0	2	12	0	38	1	0
Cooper, Keith, Danville	1	0	1.000	1.65	17	0	0	0	14	4	27.1	20	106	9	5	1	1	1	1	5	0	23	3	0
Cope, Craig, Kingsport*	0	0	.000	8.44	12	0	0	0	7	0	10.2	9	54	12	10	0	0	1	1	12	0	10	5	0
Corey, Mark, Princeton	1	1	.500	3.68	4	3	0	0	0	0	14.2	12	61	7	6	1	0	0	0	6	0	8	0	0
Crills, Brad, Bluefield	3	0	1.000	0.90	4	4	0	0	0	0	20.0	15	78	3	2	0	0	5	5	0	0	15	1	0
Cruz, Nelson, Bristol	0	0	.000	9.00	1	0	0	0	1	0	1.0	2	6	1	1	0	0	1	0	0	0	0	0	0
Cushman, Dwayne, Princeton	2	3	.400	3.09	26	0	0	0	21	8	35.0	33	159	21	12	1	0	1	1	15	2	40	2	0
Davis, Lance, Princeton*	3	7	.300	3.88	15	9	0	0	0	0	58.0	77	271	39	25	2	2	1	3	25	2	43	6	2
Dean, Greg, Bluefield	6	2	.750	3.89	10	6	0	0	3	1	37.0	34	159	22	16	3	1	1	2	17	0	33	4	1
Desrosiers, Erik, Bristol	0	2	.000	3.09	22	0	0	0	15	2	32.0	22	129	13	11	1	2	2	3	7	1	47	1	0
DeWitt, Chris, Kingsport	1	0	1.000	3.86	23	0	0	0	10	5	28.0	31	123	18	12	3	0	1	1	7	1	16	2	0
DeWitt, Matt, Johnson City	2	6	.250	7.04	13	12	0	0	0	0	62.2	84	305	56	49	10	0	3	1	32	0	45	5	6
Dunne, Brian, Martinsville*	2	3	.400	4.28	16	6	0	0	1	1	48.1	67	229	39	23	7	1	2	2	10	0	33	3	2
Edwards, Jon, Burlington	3	2	.600	5.30	19	1	0	0	5	1	37.1	44	172	28	22	2	0	0	1	16	1	31	3	0
Eibey, Scott, Bluefield	3	1	.750	5.56	14	6	0	0	3	2	43.2	51	196	32	27	4	2	0	2	24	0	26	6	1
Feingold, Leon, Burlington	0	0	.000	216.00	1	0	0	0	0	0	0.1	2	11	8	8	0	0	0	8	0	1	0	0	0
Feliz, Bienvenido, Burlington	4	2	.667	2.71	12	12	1	1	0	0	73.0	55	296	29	22	8	1	0	1	20	0	78	2	2
Fereira, Marcos, Huntington	0	1	.000	15.63	5	1	0	0	3	0	6.1	9	45	16	11	0	0	2	2	14	0	3	3	1
Figueroa, Nelson, Kingsport	7	3	.700	3.07	12	12	2	2	0	0	76.1	57	304	31	26	3	3	2	5	22	1	79	5	0
Fleetwood, Tony, Martinsville*	2	2	.500	4.71	18	0	0	0	9	0	28.2	25	131	18	15	5	0	1	2	14	0	34	2	1
Fonceca, Chad, Princeton	0	0	.000	7.25	11	1	0	0	3	0	22.1	27	107	19	18	4	0	1	1	10	2	21	2	0
Frace, Ryan, Martinsville	3	2	.600	2.17	14	0	0	0	7	1	29.0	20	121	14	7	1	0	0	1	9	1	31	4	1
Fussell, Chris, Bluefield	9	1	.900	2.19	12	12	1	1	0	0	65.2	37	265	18	16	4	1	1	7	32	0	98	3	1
Garber, Joel, Bristol*	5	1	.833	1.20	19	6	0	0	4	0	60.0	37	229	13	8	3	1	2	1	12	0	66	4	1
Giron, Roberto, Princeton	1	1	.500	5.50	24	0	0	0	12	4	36.0	33	159	23	22	3	1	3	4	14	1	41	6	1
Giuliano, Joe, Danville	2	5	.286	7.25	11	11	0	0	0	0	49.2	71	236	45	40	7	1	5	1	19	0	48	7	2
Gobert, Chris, Danville*	0	0	.000	0.00	3	0	0	0	1	0	5.2	1	23	0	0	0	0	0	0	3	0	3	1	0
Grife, Richard, Burlington	2	0	1.000	2.32	16	0	0	0	5	1	31.0	20	126	12	8	0	1	0	1	10	0	31	2	0
Hackett, Jason, Bluefield*	3	1	.750	3.02	13	6	0	0	4	1	50.2	45	226	28	17	3	1	1	3	28	2	54	13	1
Halley, Allen, Bristol	1	0	1.000	12.00	2	0	0	0	1	0	3.0	5	15	4	4	0	1	0	0	1	0	3	0	0
Harris, Jeffrey, Elizabethton	1	3	.250	3.82	21	0	0	0	10	0	33.0	42	154	15	14	2	1	0	4	13	1	27	6	1
Harrison, Scott, Burlington	0	1	.000	9.00	5	0	0	0	0	0	5.0	9	32	16	5	3	2	2	1	13	0	13	1	0
Hasselhoff, Derek, Bristol	7	3	.700	3.66	12	11	0	0	1	0	66.1	66	281	32	27	4	1	1	2	14	0	46	2	2
Herbison, Brett, Kingsport	1	0	1.000	7.20	1	1	0	0	0	0	5.0	6	23	4	4	2	0	0	0	4	0	1	0	0
Hoalton, Brandon, Huntington	1	3	.250	5.34	6	6	0	0	0	0	28.2	31	127	23	17	4	1	1	2	11	0	26	5	0
Hunt, Jon, Bristol*	2	4	.333	4.47	13	13	0	0	0	0	58.1	52	262	39	29	2	1	3	4	34	0	54	11	2
Jimenez, Jose, Johnson City	5	7	.417	3.49	14	14	1	1	0	0	90.1	81	380	48	35	3	3	1	5	25	0	85	7	1
Kershner, Jason, Martinsville*	4	2	.667	5.14	13	13	0	0	0	0	63.0	67	278	42	36	10	0	2	5	29	0	64	6	0
Kessel, Kyle, Kingsport*	4	0	1.000	1.80	5	5	0	0	0	0	30.0	33	134	11	6	1	0	0	4	10	1	23	0	0
King, Matt, Johnson City	0	0	.000	67.50	1	0	0	0	0	0	0.2	2	8	5	5	0	0	0	0	2	0	1	0	0
Knoll, Randy, Martinsville	0	3	.000	8.83	6	6	0	0	0	0	17.1	21	83	18	17	1	0	1	0	9	0	22	8	0
Knowland, Sam, Danville	4	2	.667	2.86	20	0	0	0	5	1	34.2	37	155	23	11	3	3	4	2	10	1	21	2	3
Koehler, P.K., Danville*	2	1	.667	3.54	11	6	0	0	2	1	40.2	39	178	25	16	2	1	2	1	16	0	46	4	1
Kosek, Kory, Martinsville	1	0	1.000	2.37	9	0	0	0	7	2	19.0	10	69	5	5	1	0	0	4	0	0	17	2	0
Kown, John, Johnson City	4	2	.667	2.65	16	4	1	0	1	0	51.0	41	220	31	15	2	2	2	18	1	42	7	4
Kraus, Tim, Bristol	0	1	.000	2.35	5	0	0	0	4	1	7.2	3	33	3	2	0	1	1	0	7	0	9	3	1
Kruse, Kelly, Bristol	0	1	.000	12.32	15	0	0	0	8	0	19.0	29	107	32	26	5	2	0	4	16	0	21	2	3
LaRocca, Todd, Bluefield	4	1	.800	3.05	8	6	1	1	0	0	44.1	38	181	17	15	5	0	3	14	0	38	1	0
Loewe, Kevin, Danville*	1	3	.250	3.79	20	0	0	0	9	5	38.0	24	151	20	16	1	2	0	1	10	0	43	3	0
Loudermilk, Darren, Burlington	2	2	.500	5.05	21	1	0	0	6	0	41.0	40	195	27	23	1	0	1	6	23	1	38	8	0
Lowry, Elliott, Burlington*	0	0	.000	5.85	10	0	0	0	0	0	20.0	26	95	15	13	1	1	0	0	10	0	13	5	0
Mahaffey, Alan, Elizabethton*	5	6	.455	3.47	13	12	1	0	0	0	70.0	66	308	42	27	4	6	2	3	21	0	73	4	8
Maine, Dalton, Bluefield	0	1	.000	11.25	1	0	0	0	1	0	4.0	7	18	5	5	2	0	0	1	0	0	2	0	0
Manon, Julio, Huntington	3	4	.429	3.65	16	8	2	0	3	1	74.0	75	319	34	30	4	0	3	2	30	2	77	10	0

Pitcher, Team	W	L	Pct.	ERA	G	GS	CG	ShO	GF	Sv.	IP	H	TBF	R	ER	HR	SH	SF	HB	BB	IBB	SO	WP	Bk.
Martinez, Dennis, Burlington	0	1	.000	7.90	15	2	0	0	6	0	27.1	35	139	31	24	1	0	1	2	18	1	22	7	1
Martinez, Willie, Burlington	0	7	.000	9.45	11	11	0	0	0	0	40.0	64	208	50	42	1	2	2	4	25	0	36	6	3
Mattox, Gene, Princeton	0	0	.000	11.32	11	0	0	0	4	0	10.1	13	56	13	13	0	0	0	1	12	1	10	3	2
McCaffrey, Dennis, Johnson City	2	0	1.000	4.78	24	0	0	0	7	0	32.0	36	148	24	17	3	0	1	2	17	1	24	7	1
McDougal, Mike, Johnson City	0	0	.000	0.00	1	0	0	0	0	0	0.0	0	1	0	0	0	0	0	0	1	0	0	0	0
McKnight, Chris, Danville*	0	1	.000	3.00	1	1	0	0	0	0	3.0	1	12	2	1	0	0	0	0	1	0	6	0	0
Mear, Rich, Johnson City*	7	3	.700	3.35	14	14	0	0	0	0	78.0	68	338	37	29	4	3	1	3	40	1	75	11	1
Mendez, Manuel, Johnson City*	3	0	1.000	3.08	30	0	0	0	28	19	38.0	33	158	13	13	2	1	0	1	12	0	61	2	3
Mercedes, Carlos, Bluefield	0	0	.000	9.00	1	0	0	0	1	0	1.0	2	6	1	1	0	0	0	0	1	0	1	0	0
Milledge, Tony, Johnson City	0	0	.000	18.00	2	0	0	0	1	0	2.0	5	11	4	4	1	0	0	0	0	0	1	0	0
Miller, Brian, Martinsville	6	4	.600	5.16	23	0	0	0	8	3	45.1	46	194	28	26	3	1	1	2	15	0	35	6	3
Montgomery, Joe, Princeton	3	0	1.000	2.38	13	3	0	0	4	0	45.1	45	190	19	12	1	0	1	2	14	0	27	5	3
Moore, David, Bristol	1	0	1.000	5.16	15	0	0	0	5	0	29.2	34	136	22	17	3	0	1	0	11	0	37	3	0
Moreno, Julio, Bluefield	4	3	.571	4.20	9	8	0	0	1	0	49.1	61	214	31	23	3	1	3	0	12	0	36	3	1
Morseman, Robert, Bluefield*	1	0	1.000	2.02	18	1	0	0	12	6	35.2	22	142	9	8	2	1	1	1	14	1	38	1	0
Mosquea, Alberto, Martinsville	0	0	.000	4.58	9	3	0	0	0	0	19.2	13	98	10	10	0	0	1	3	25	0	15	6	1
Murphy, Chris, Princeton*	7	1	.875	1.55	15	10	1	1	0	0	63.2	51	266	23	11	4	0	2	2	19	0	52	6	0
Niedermaier, Brad, Elizabethton	2	0	1.000	2.21	7	7	0	0	0	0	40.2	33	171	14	10	1	0	1	0	17	0	47	9	0
Noone, Bill, Martinsville	0	0	.000	2.08	1	1	0	0	0	0	4.1	3	17	1	1	0	0	0	0	1	0	5	0	0
Ojeda, Erick, Kingsport*	6	2	.750	2.40	14	5	0	0	3	0	60.0	47	240	18	16	3	2	0	1	12	0	60	4	1
Oldham, Bob, Burlington	3	6	.333	5.50	18	8	0	0	4	0	52.1	55	249	43	32	3	2	1	9	32	2	55	4	0
Olson, Phillip, Kingsport	6	2	.750	2.42	12	10	2	1	1	0	67.0	47	271	24	18	1	1	1	8	23	0	45	4	1
Olszewski, Tim, Bluefield	3	2	.600	3.06	16	0	0	0	9	3	35.1	34	155	19	12	2	3	1	4	19	0	29	4	1
Ortiz, Steve, Burlington*	1	3	.250	4.55	22	0	0	0	19	7	27.2	30	130	16	14	2	1	1	0	20	2	46	2	0
Osting, James, Danville*	2	7	.222	7.15	11	10	0	0	0	0	39.0	46	190	34	31	1	1	0	1	25	0	43	12	0
Peters, Tim, Elizabethton*	2	3	.400	1.65	27	0	0	0	7	0	32.2	27	134	16	6	1	0	0	0	5	2	36	4	0
Pierce, Drew, Huntington	2	4	.333	6.21	22	0	0	0	17	2	33.1	46	159	29	23	2	3	2	4	10	0	42	9	1
Pizarro, Melvin, Martinsville*	0	0	.000	6.23	10	0	0	0	4	0	17.1	20	79	13	12	1	0	3	4	5	0	17	0	2
Ponson, Sidney, Bluefield	6	3	.667	4.17	13	13	0	0	0	0	77.2	79	324	44	36	7	1	2	1	16	0	56	4	3
Poupart, Melvin, Kingsport	1	1	.500	5.06	18	0	0	0	4	1	26.2	27	119	17	15	5	1	0	1	10	1	32	4	1
Prejean, Alex, Huntington	3	2	.600	9.38	14	3	0	0	2	0	31.2	37	164	36	33	2	0	3	3	31	0	23	11	1
Pumphrey, Kenny, Kingsport	7	3	.700	3.86	12	12	0	0	0	0	65.1	50	283	32	28	3	3	0	6	42	0	76	7	0
Quintana, Urbano, Huntington	1	2	.333	5.71	19	1	0	0	11	3	34.2	43	162	26	22	4	1	1	5	12	0	35	6	5
Raines, Ken, Danville*	0	0	.000	0.71	11	0	0	0	11	6	12.2	8	47	4	1	0	0	2	1	0	0	14	0	1
Rath, Fred, Elizabethton	1	1	.500	1.35	27	0	0	0	25	12	33.1	20	134	8	5	2	0	1	1	11	1	50	3	0
Reed, Dan, Bluefield*	1	0	1.000	2.57	6	1	0	0	1	1	14.0	10	53	5	4	1	0	0	0	5	0	11	0	0
Reed, Kenny, Martinsville	0	1	.000	7.43	13	0	0	0	6	0	23.0	29	119	22	19	3	0	2	21	0	15	13	0	
Reed, Steven, Johnson City	2	2	.500	4.43	31	0	0	0	19	1	42.2	48	194	24	21	2	0	1	0	15	0	41	3	2
Reynolds, Walker, Danville	1	3	.250	3.99	20	0	0	0	7	1	38.1	26	166	19	17	3	1	2	6	19	1	30	3	0
Richardson, Kasey, Elizabethton*	1	0	1.000	2.33	3	3	0	0	0	0	19.1	12	79	8	5	0	3	1	1	13	1	11	1	0
Roberts, Randolph, Princeton	4	5	.444	3.16	15	9	0	0	2	0	62.2	51	281	35	22	3	1	2	6	33	3	74	14	2
Roettgen, Mark, Johnson City	4	5	.444	5.59	13	13	0	0	0	0	66.0	63	302	48	41	11	4	3	6	40	0	60	4	4
Rogan, Sean, Johnson City*	1	0	1.000	5.65	12	0	0	0	6	0	28.2	30	134	22	18	4	2	3	1	17	2	22	2	0
Roque, Jorge, Johnson City	2	0	1.000	5.12	14	0	0	0	3	0	19.1	15	81	11	11	4	1	1	2	9	1	22	0	3
Ruiz, Rafael, Bristol*	1	2	.333	2.15	22	0	0	0	6	1	37.2	26	154	14	9	1	3	0	0	15	0	57	2	0
Sanders, Frankie, Burlington	3	5	.375	2.96	12	12	3	0	0	0	70.0	48	292	31	23	2	1	0	3	32	0	80	4	1
Santamaria, Bill, Kingsport	5	3	.625	4.18	13	13	1	0	0	0	71.0	62	303	37	33	8	1	3	3	29	0	55	3	0
Santos, Juan, Bluefield	0	0	.000	0.00	1	0	0	0	0	0	3.0	1	10	0	0	0	0	0	0	2	0	1	0	0
Sauritch, Chris, Bluefield	4	1	.800	3.72	13	0	0	0	3	0	19.1	18	91	13	8	3	2	0	2	11	1	16	2	0
Schleuss, Will, Princeton*	3	0	.000	4.50	23	0	0	0	5	1	32.0	29	142	20	16	1	1	1	22	2	34	9	0	
Schnur, Curt, Danville	1	4	.200	5.74	18	0	0	0	7	0	31.1	34	159	24	20	0	3	5	4	22	0	31	5	3
Secoda, Jason, Bristol	2	8	.200	5.35	13	12	0	0	0	0	65.2	78	307	57	39	3	1	3	1	33	0	63	8	1
Sellner, Aaron, Elizabethton	2	3	.333	2.14	19	1	0	0	5	0	33.2	30	137	15	8	1	0	1	0	10	0	32	1	1
Shumaker, Anthony, Martinsville*	1	3	.250	4.50	6	4	0	0	2	0	28.0	31	120	16	14	1	2	0	1	8	0	26	3	0
Shumate, Jacob, Danville	1	2	.333	10.80	7	2	0	0	2	0	13.1	6	80	21	16	1	0	2	3	32	0	16	14	0
Sikes, Jason, Martinsville	0	3	.000	5.94	4	3	0	0	0	0	16.2	23	81	13	11	1	2	1	0	9	0	10	4	0
Snyder, Matt, Bluefield	0	0	.000	1.04	17	0	0	0	15	8	34.2	35	150	9	4	1	0	0	3	13	0	46	1	0
Spang, R.J., Huntington	1	2	.333	4.60	18	0	0	0	10	3	31.1	31	138	21	16	3	1	5	9	0	31	2	3	
Sparks, Jeff, Princeton	2	0	1.000	3.23	16	2	0	0	7	2	39.0	32	172	19	14	2	0	1	0	27	2	49	2	1
Splittorff, James, Elizabethton	5	4	.556	3.24	13	12	1	1	0	0	72.1	64	319	40	26	5	0	2	7	29	0	72	11	2
Starling, Marcus, Huntington*	0	2	.000	15.19	13	3	0	0	4	0	21.1	36	130	39	36	2	0	1	6	25	0	22	11	0
Tanksley, William, Elizabethton	0	1	.000	4.11	11	0	0	0	4	1	15.1	16	67	13	7	3	2	0	1	5	0	17	0	1
Tebbetts, Scott, Martinsville	1	3	.250	2.25	22	0	0	0	20	9	32.0	31	133	15	8	0	1	0	0	7	1	30	1	0
Vejil, Aaron, Huntington*	1	0	1.000	5.95	14	0	0	0	5	0	19.2	19	91	15	13	2	1	1	2	10	0	21	5	1
Vicentino, Andy, Princeton*	2	2	.500	7.50	10	7	0	0	2	0	30.0	36	149	30	25	1	1	0	1	27	0	23	4	1
Villafuerte, Brandon, Kingsport	5	1	.833	5.63	20	0	0	0	6	0	32.0	28	144	21	20	0	1	1	1	26	0	42	8	0
Virchis, Adam, Bristol	0	7	.000	5.30	10	10	1	0	0	0	56.0	65	239	39	33	5	4	3	4	19	1	41	2	0
Vota, Michael, Bristol	2	4	.333	4.60	22	0	0	0	12	3	31.1	33	145	19	16	3	2	3	1	14	1	24	5	0
Wagner, Ken, Burlington	5	5	.500	3.16	13	12	0	0	0	0	68.1	54	285	34	24	7	1	2	1	23	0	80	7	1
West, Adam, Johnson City*	1	1	.500	2.85	18	1	0	0	1	0	41.0	41	187	26	13	1	4	3	19	1	41	2	0	
Wise, James, Danville*	0	1	.000	15.43	2	0	0	0	1	0	2.1	3	14	4	4	0	0	0	0	4	0	3	1	1
Wise, William, Danville	0	3	.000	5.63	10	10	0	0	0	0	46.1	42	201	33	29	2	2	2	7	23	0	24	3	0
Yoder, Jason, Martinsville	2	3	.333	5.40	8	0	0	0	3	0	28.1	33	126	20	17	2	1	0	11	0	23	3	0	
Young, Ty, Huntington	4	6	.400	4.67	14	14	2	1	0	0	79.0	75	352	56	41	5	0	1	9	36	0	49	6	1

COMBINATION SHUTOUTS: **Bluefield (1)**—Crills-Morseman. **Bristol (2)**—Garber-Desrosiers, Hunt-Desrosiers-Beirne. **Burlington (3)**—Feliz-Loudermilk-Ortiz, Oldham-Grife. Sanders-Edwards. **Danville (2)**—Abreu-Cochran-Loewe-Reynolds, Osting-Koehler. **Elizabethton (4)**—Blank-Sellner-Anderson, Niedermaier-Peters-Rath, Niedermaier-Splittorff, Splittorff-Chapman-Anderson-Harris. **Huntington (0)**—None. **Johnson City (2)**—Jimenez-Reed-Roque-Mendez, Mear-Mendez. **Kingsport (3)**—Beebe-Blang, Ojeda-Blang, Pumphrey-Blang. **Martinsville (1)**—Burger-Dunne-Miller-Tebbetts. **Princeton (3)**—Corey-Schleuss, Davis-Cushman, Montgomery-Giron.
NO-HIT GAMES: Abreu, Danville, defeated Burlington, 7-1 (seven innings), July 2; Young, Huntington, defeated Elizabethton, 4-0 (seven innings), August 3.

1995 FIELDING

TEAM

Team	Pct.	G	PO	A	E	TC	DP	PB	Team	Pct.	G	PO	A	E	TC	DP	PB
Kingsport	.962	66	1723	687	94	2504	45	11	Burlington	.947	64	1650	613	127	2390	42	21
Bluefield	.956	65	1683	651	107	2441	56	18	Johnson City	.946	68	1767	685	141	2593	38	15
Martinsville	.953	67	1673	682	115	2470	50	11	Princeton	.944	63	1630	657	136	2423	47	17
Danville	.949	67	1712	650	126	2488	49	29	Bristol	.941	67	1699	691	151	2541	43	11
Huntington	.948	67	1681	704	131	2516	40	16	Elizabethton	.934	64	1653	741	168	2562	51	13

TRIPLE PLAY: Bristol.

INDIVIDUAL

FIRST BASEMEN

NOTE: All caps denotes fielding-percentage leader based on 34 games for catchers, 45 for all other non-pitchers and 68 innings for pitchers. *Throws lefthanded.

Player, Team	Pct.	G	PO	A	E	TC	DP
Anglen, Toby, Danville	1.000	1	1	0	0	1	0
Bowness, Brian, Bristol	.982	54	441	44	9	494	29
Boyette, Tony, Princeton	.971	39	313	22	10	345	24
Cardona, Alex, Johnson City	.500	2	1	0	1	2	0
Coburn, Todd, Huntington	.985	14	119	10	2	131	8
Davis, James, Princeton	.971	4	31	3	1	35	2
Deck, Billy, Johnson City*	.985	58	492	38	8	538	25
Dougherty, Keith, Danville	.972	19	125	15	4	144	8
Ennis, Wayne, Princeton	.958	8	44	2	2	48	8
Foote, Derek, Danville	1.000	1	7	0	0	7	0
Glavine, Mike, Burlington*	.990	38	278	19	3	300	15
Gunderson, Shane, Elizabethton	1.000	1	9	1	0	10	0
Hardy, Brian, Burlington	1.000	2	10	0	0	10	0
Hendricks, Ryan, Huntington	.985	52	434	35	7	476	27
Janke, Jared, Martinsville	.972	36	259	20	8	287	18
Lakovic, Greg, Elizabethton	.929	1	11	2	1	14	1
Lantigua, Miguel, Kingsport	1.000	1	2	0	0	2	0
Lee, Carlos, Bristol	1.000	5	26	3	0	29	2
Mastrullo, Mike, Huntington	1.000	1	5	0	0	5	0
Mata, Manuel, Martinsville*	.857	1	6	0	1	7	1
McDougal, Mike, Johnson City	.969	11	89	6	3	98	4
McWhite, Ray, Danville	.976	51	416	23	11	450	34
Naples, Brandon, Kingsport*	.982	15	103	7	2	112	8
PATTERSON, Jarrod, Kingsport	.992	54	463	35	4	502	28
Pierzynski, A.J., Elizabethton	1.000	1	4	1	0	5	0
Ramos, Noel, Bluefield	.996	27	231	19	1	251	18
Raymondi, Mike, Huntington	.933	2	14	0	1	15	1
Reyes, Freddy, Elizabethton	.981	18	147	12	3	162	9
Rincones, Wuarnner, Bristol	.929	13	80	11	7	98	5
Russin, Tom, Bluefield	.974	40	304	29	9	342	33
Santiago, Arnold, Burlington	1.000	31	222	15	0	237	17
Schroeder, John, Elizabethton	.958	47	440	36	21	497	36
Smalley, Jevon, Princeton	.972	20	135	6	4	145	9
Stone, Matthew, Martinsville*	.976	35	266	17	7	290	23
Torbett, Hanes, Kingsport	.857	1	5	1	1	7	1

TRIPLE PLAY: Bowness.

SECOND BASEMEN

Player, Team	Pct.	G	PO	A	E	TC	DP
Anglen, Toby, Danville	.978	11	16	29	1	46	6
Bracho, Darwin, Princeton	.938	6	4	11	1	16	2
Brito, Domingo, Martinsville	.778	2	2	5	2	9	0
Brown, Jerome, Elizabethton	1.000	3	5	0	0	8	1
Concepcion, David, Princeton	.941	36	65	110	11	186	16
Cross, Adam, Danville	.970	27	49	48	3	100	10
Daedlow, Craig, Bluefield	1.000	2	5	4	0	9	2
Diaz, Ivan, Johnson City	1.000	4	2	4	0	6	0
Edmonston, Tracy, Kingsport	.958	41	56	105	7	168	15
Erickson, Corey, Kingsport	1.000	1	6	2	0	8	2
Espada, Angel, Danville	.966	31	57	84	5	146	16
Fraser, Joseph, Elizabethton	.920	45	67	140	18	225	23
GABRIEL, Denio, Bluefield	.965	50	73	122	7	202	24
Garcia, Carlos, Elizabethton	.944	20	30	54	5	89	12
Guthrie, David, Princeton	.944	4	6	11	1	18	1
Harris, Rodger, Johnson City	.926	42	66	96	13	175	11
Helms, Ryan, Bristol	.922	47	79	111	16	206	19
Hodges, Randy, Danville	1.000	2	1	4	0	5	1
Hooker, Kevin, Martinsville	.963	43	67	88	6	161	21
Jimenez, Ruben, Johnson City	.956	22	38	49	4	91	13
Mason, Lamont, Princeton	.940	25	52	73	8	133	20
Mastrullo, Mike, Huntington	.950	24	36	60	5	101	4
Milledge, Tony, Johnson City	1.000	9	18	17	0	35	1
Murphy, Quinn, Burlington	.911	35	50	94	14	158	14
O'Connor, Richard, Martinsville	.964	23	40	68	4	112	11

Player, Team	Pct.	G	PO	A	E	TC	DP
Rincones, Wuarnner, Bristol	.957	5	6	16	1	23	3
Roberson, Gerald, Huntington	.952	39	47	110	8	165	16
Short, Richard, Bluefield	.962	7	9	16	1	26	3
Simpson, Jeramie, Kingsport	.800	4	1	3	1	5	0
Soriano, Juan, Kingsport	.943	21	36	46	5	87	10
Strasser, John, Bristol	.933	20	36	47	6	89	7
Sturges, Brian, Johnson City	1.000	1	0	3	0	3	0
Tiller, Brad, Burlington	.919	32	49	87	12	148	12
Torbett, Hanes, Kingsport	1.000	6	8	14	0	22	0
Winn, Wess, Bluefield	.956	15	21	22	2	45	7
Wood, Tony, Huntington	.969	6	10	21	1	32	7

THIRD BASEMEN

Player, Team	Pct.	G	PO	A	E	TC	DP
Anglen, Toby, Danville	.950	45	25	90	6	121	7
Bearden, Doug, Bristol	.800	3	1	3	1	5	0
Bogle, Bryan, Bluefield	.900	6	8	10	2	20	1
Brito, Domingo, Martinsville	.909	17	7	33	4	44	0
BRYANT, Chris, Bluefield	.923	58	48	96	12	156	9
Concepcion, David, Princeton	.854	20	9	32	7	48	3
Cox, Robert, Kingsport	.904	57	35	107	15	157	5
Cross, Adam, Danville	1.000	4	2	4	0	6	0
Daedlow, Craig, Bluefield	.667	1	1	1	1	3	0
Dougherty, Keith, Danville	.750	2	1	2	1	4	0
Elliott, Zach, Martinsville	1.000	1	3	1	0	4	0
Garcia, Carlos, Elizabethton	.917	5	2	9	1	12	0
Guthrie, David, Princeton	.857	8	3	9	2	14	2
Haas, Chris, Johnson City	.893	64	51	116	20	187	9
Herdman, Eli, Elizabethton	.850	58	39	114	27	180	8
Hooker, Kevin, Martinsville	.944	6	6	11	1	18	0
Jensen, Blair, Burlington	.750	11	2	10	4	16	0
Jimenez, Ruben, Johnson City	1.000	1	0	3	0	3	0
Lee, Carlos, Bristol	.900	58	58	104	18	180	10
Mastrullo, Mike, Huntington	.862	13	9	16	4	29	0
McWhite, Ray, Danville	.970	9	10	22	1	33	1
Milledge, Tony, Johnson City	.810	8	5	12	4	21	1
Mota, Christian, Burlington	.917	59	45	99	13	157	8
Murphy, Quinn, Burlington	.667	3	2	4	3	9	0
O'Connor, Richard, Martinsville	.916	25	23	53	7	83	5
Patellis, Anthony, Princeton	.868	41	31	61	14	106	4
Reyes, Freddy, Elizabethton	.600	2	1	2	2	5	1
Reyes, Winston, Huntington	.906	18	12	36	5	53	4
Rincones, Wuarnner, Bristol	.970	11	7	25	1	33	1
Sasser, Rob, Danville	.852	11	7	16	4	27	1
Serbio, Carmen, Martinsville	.873	19	16	32	7	55	1
Short, Richard, Bluefield	.941	4	3	13	1	17	2
Soriano, Juan, Kingsport	.970	14	6	26	1	33	4
Torbett, Hanes, Kingsport	1.000	3	2	5	0	7	1
Townsend, Terric, Martinsville	.857	2	1	5	1	7	1
Wood, Tony, Huntington	.869	40	19	67	13	99	3

TRIPLE PLAY: Lee.

SHORTSTOPS

Player, Team	Pct.	G	PO	A	E	TC	DP
Anglen, Toby, Danville	.950	6	5	14	1	20	1
Bearden, Doug, Bristol	.850	43	54	116	30	200	16
Brito, Domingo, Martinsville	1.000	10	14	30	0	44	7
Brown, Jerome, Elizabethton	.615	6	5	11	10	26	2
Cross, Adam, Danville	.786	10	8	14	6	28	2
Daedlow, Craig, Bluefield	1.000	2	1	4	0	5	1
Davidson, Cleatus, Elizabethton	.884	38	54	113	22	189	20
Edwards, Donald, Burlington	.897	42	60	97	18	175	16
Elliott, Zach, Martinsville	.937	43	63	115	12	190	27
Gabriel, Denio, Bluefield	1.000	3	5	8	0	13	2
Garcia, Carlos, Elizabethton	.876	24	29	63	13	105	6
Guthrie, David, Princeton	.902	47	65	119	20	204	19
Jimenez, Ruben, Johnson City	.838	19	16	41	11	68	3
Martinez, Eddy, Bluefield	.904	56	71	135	22	228	31

Player, Team	Pct.	G	PO	A	E	TC	DP
Martinez, Tony, Johnson City	.919	23	19	60	7	86	4
Milledge, Tony, Johnson City	.917	2	5	6	1	12	1
Nolte, Bruce, Huntington	.913	60	90	163	24	277	25
O'Connor, Richard, Martinsville	.773	7	6	11	5	22	1
POLANCO, Enohel, Kingsport	.922	61	81	155	20	256	28
Roberson, Gerald, Huntington	.857	2	3	3	1	7	0
Salano, Manuel, Princeton	.847	27	34	49	15	98	12
Serbio, Carmen, Martinsville	.958	8	6	17	1	24	1
Soriano, Juan, Kingsport	1.000	7	3	16	0	19	3
Strasser, John, Bristol	.887	29	35	59	12	106	8
Tiller, Brad, Burlington	.897	24	32	46	9	87	11
Townsend, Terric, Martinsville	.875	3	5	9	2	16	1
Utting, Ben, Danville	.894	55	68	151	26	245	29
Winn, Wess, Bluefield	.964	8	15	12	1	28	3
Wood, Tony, Huntington	1.000	9	15	16	0	31	2
Woolf, Jason, Johnson City	.810	28	49	62	26	137	15

OUTFIELDERS

Player, Team	Pct.	G	PO	A	E	TC	DP
Abell, Antonio, Johnson City	.918	52	87	2	8	97	1
Albert, Chernan, Bristol	.903	35	63	2	7	72	0
Almonte, Wady, Bluefield	.918	47	52	4	5	61	1
Anderson, Milton, Burlington	.938	57	102	3	7	112	1
Andino, Luis, Martinsville	.886	20	27	4	4	35	0
Bagley, Sean, Bristol	.750	11	6	0	2	8	0
Bass, Jayson, Danville	.966	62	141	2	5	148	0
Black, Brandon, Kingsport	.938	26	43	2	3	48	0
Bracho, Darwin, Princeton	.000	3	0	0	1	1	0
Brown, Jerome, Elizabethton	.909	8	9	1	1	11	0
Buckles, Matt, Martinsville	.931	15	26	1	2	29	0
Coburn, Todd, Huntington	1.000	1	1	0	0	1	0
Colburn, Brian, Elizabethton*	.900	10	9	0	1	10	0
Conner, Decomba, Princeton	1.000	6	18	2	0	20	0
Current, Jeremy, Johnson City	.960	20	22	2	1	25	0
Dellucci, David, Bluefield*	.846	12	11	0	2	13	0
Drent, Brian, Bristol	.909	44	57	3	6	66	1
Duncan, Robert, Danville*	.937	43	58	1	4	63	0
Fernandez, Randy, Huntington*	.778	11	14	0	4	18	0
Franklin, James, Danville	.922	34	45	2	4	51	0
Garcia, Carlos, Elizabethton	.957	17	21	1	1	23	0
Gunderson, Shane, Elizabethton	.862	25	23	2	4	29	0
Hall, Darran, Princeton*	1.000	9	18	0	0	18	0
Herrera, Jesus, Princeton	.872	37	39	2	6	47	0
Higman, Joel, Blu.-Hun.	.897	21	22	4	3	29	0
HOBBIE, Matt, Elizabethton*	.984	58	122	1	2	125	0
Hollins, Darontaye, Bristol	.980	56	95	5	2	102	2
Hunter, Lanier, Huntington	.936	59	96	7	7	110	2
Ingram, Darron, Princeton	.952	57	98	2	5	105	0
Isom, Johnny, Bluefield	.974	48	71	5	2	78	0
Johnson, Heath, Elizabethton	.892	56	70	4	9	83	1
Johnson, Travis, Elizabethton	1.000	13	12	2	0	14	0
Jones, Ivory, Elizabethton*	.985	41	58	6	1	65	1
Juarez, Raul, Elizabethton	.961	35	47	2	2	51	0
Kearney, Chad, Martinsville	.893	23	23	2	3	28	2
Kennedy, Justin, Martinsville*	.932	41	63	5	5	73	1
Kerr, Brian, Bluefield	1.000	1	2	0	0	2	0
Kingsale, Eugene, Bluefield	.899	44	95	3	11	109	1
Langford, Derrick, Danville	1.000	9	8	0	0	8	0
LeCronier, Jason, Bluefield	1.000	5	8	0	0	8	0
Lee, Jason, Johnson City	.905	19	19	0	2	21	0
Lugo, Ursino, Burlington	.897	22	25	1	3	29	1
Malin, Edgar, Huntington	.750	17	18	0	6	24	0
Mapp, Eric, Princeton	.959	61	115	3	5	123	0
Mastrullo, Mike, Huntington	1.000	1	2	0	0	2	0
McCarthy, Kevin, Kingsport*	.919	25	34	0	3	37	0
McClure, Craig, Bristol	.944	59	80	4	5	89	1
McCroskey, Jackie, Huntington*	.939	41	75	2	5	82	0
Mejia, Miguel, Bluefield	.940	45	74	5	5	84	1
Mendoza, Carlos, Kingsport*	.951	33	54	4	3	61	0
Messner, Jake, Burlington*	.985	43	63	3	1	67	1
Mifflin, Brian, Kingsport	1.000	1	1	0	0	1	0
Mota, Christian, Burlington	1.000	1	2	0	0	2	0
Mota, Gleydel, Kingsport	.750	1	3	0	1	4	0
Munoz, Juan, Johnson City*	.983	55	101	14	2	117	0
Naples, Brandon, Kingsport*	.846	11	11	0	2	13	0
Pennyfeather, William, Princeton	1.000	1	3	0	0	3	0
Pickett, Eric, Danville	.956	57	103	6	5	114	1
Ramirez, Daniel, Kingsport	.947	62	122	3	7	132	0
Roberson, Gerald, Huntington	.929	9	23	3	2	28	0
Robinson, Kerry, Johnson City*	.938	51	86	5	6	97	1
Schofield, Andy, Johnson City	.933	25	26	2	2	30	0
Schreimann, Eric, Martinsville	1.000	3	4	1	0	5	0
Serafin, Ricardo, Martinsville	.909	19	28	2	3	33	0

Player, Team	Pct.	G	PO	A	E	TC	DP
Simpson, Jeramie, Kingsport	.976	46	80	2	2	84	0
Spry, Shane, Bristol*	1.000	2	1	0	0	1	0
Taylor, Reggie, Martinsville	.940	63	116	9	8	133	3
Terry, Tony, Princeton	.964	36	26	1	1	28	0
Whitaker, Chad, Burlington	.920	39	44	2	4	50	0
Williams, Errick, Martinsville	.949	33	51	5	3	59	0
Williams, Jewell, Burlington	.942	42	48	1	3	52	0

OUTFIELDERS WITH TWO OR MORE TEAMS

Player, Team	Pct.	G	PO	A	E	TC	DP
Higman, Joel, Bluefield	.800	8	3	1	1	5	0
Higman, Joel, Huntington	.917	13	19	3	2	24	0

CATCHERS

Player, Team	Pct.	G	PO	A	E	TC	DP	PB
Anderson, Frank, Bristol	.983	46	350	64	7	421	2	6
Andrews, Jeff, Huntington	.968	34	202	39	8	249	3	9
Antczak, Chuck, Bristol	.972	23	131	10	4	145	0	3
Bagley, Sean, Bristol	.977	12	37	5	1	43	0	2
Boyette, Tony, Princeton	.990	12	89	8	1	98	0	4
Bracho, Darwin, Princeton	.991	18	97	14	1	112	0	4
Cardona, Alex, Johnson City	.987	19	130	17	2	149	3	4
Coats, Nathan, Burlington	.982	19	145	16	3	164	1	6
Coburn, Todd, Huntington	.970	27	198	32	7	237	1	5
Davis, James, Princeton	.980	40	296	50	7	353	1	9
Falciglia, Tony, Johnson City	.981	20	130	24	3	157	1	3
Foote, Derek, Danville	.969	14	117	6	4	127	2	1
Frost, Robert, Kingsport	1.000	8	59	7	0	66	1	2
Gargiulo, Mike, Bluefield	.973	48	384	51	12	447	3	11
Gunderson, Shane, Elizabethton	.967	10	83	4	3	90	0	0
Harmer, Francis, Bluefield	.994	18	150	13	1	164	1	7
Hoover, Will, Kingsport	1.000	8	22	6	0	28	0	5
Lakovic, Greg, Elizabethton	1.000	4	27	2	0	29	0	1
Lantigua, Miguel, Kingsport	.974	3	36	2	1	39	0	0
Livingston, Clyde, Martinsville	.976	9	76	4	2	82	0	1
Martin, Ryan, Danville	1.000	3	25	4	0	29	0	1
McNeal, Pepe, Bur.-J.C.	.986	53	438	40	7	485	3	12
Mepri, Sal, Princeton	1.000	5	5	0	0	5	0	0
Mullen, Adam, Danville	.969	16	110	13	4	127	2	7
OLIVEROS, Leonardo, Martins.	1.000	40	270	52	0	322	3	7
Pena, Francisco, Elizabethton	1.000	7	38	6	0	44	0	1
Pena, Jose, Burlington	.979	21	175	10	4	189	0	8
Pierzynski, A.J., Elizabethton	.974	49	372	71	12	455	3	11
Pointer, Corey, Danville	.958	35	241	34	12	287	4	19
Raio, Domenick, Martinsville	1.000	3	20	2	0	22	1	0
Ramirez, Alonso, Burlington	.977	9	42	1	1	44	1	1
Raymondi, Mike, Huntington	.983	11	54	4	1	59	0	2
Schreimann, Eric, Martinsville	.982	14	98	11	2	111	1	3
Shy, Jason, Danville	.881	8	34	3	5	42	0	1
Sturges, Brian, Johnson City	.988	13	70	10	1	81	0	2
Valera, Yojanny, Kingsport	.989	53	409	58	5	472	4	4
Wampler, Sam, Martinsville	.975	9	37	2	1	40	0	0

CATCHERS WITH TWO OR MORE TEAMS

Player, Team	Pct.	G	PO	A	E	TC	DP	PB
McNeal, Pepe, Burlington	.992	27	229	21	2	252	2	6
McNeal, Pepe, Johnson City	.996	26	209	19	5	233	1	6

PITCHERS

Player, Team	Pct.	G	PO	A	E	TC	DP
Abreu, Winston, Danville	1.000	13	5	5	0	10	0
ADAIR, Scott, Huntington	1.000	13	7	13	0	20	0
Aguiar, Douglas, Martinsville	1.000	15	3	4	0	7	0
Alexis, Julio, Huntington	.810	14	9	8	4	21	0
Alvarado, Luis, Huntington	1.000	11	1	4	0	5	0
Anderson, Eric, Elizabethton*	.909	21	3	7	1	11	0
Anderson, Gary, Burlington	1.000	14	0	1	0	1	1
Anez, Maycoll, Bristol	1.000	7	2	3	0	5	0
Angerhofer, Chad, Princeton*	.800	13	2	2	1	5	0
Barfield, Rodney, Johnson City	1.000	10	0	2	0	2	0
Bartels, Todd, Huntington	.938	13	9	6	1	16	0
Bates, Shawn, Bluefield*	.875	14	1	6	1	8	1
Beebe, Joey, Kingsport*	.800	9	2	2	1	5	1
Beirne, Kevin, Bristol	1.000	9	1	2	0	3	0
Blang, Michael, Kingsport	1.000	23	7	6	0	13	1
Blank, John, Elizabethton*	.900	15	3	6	1	10	0
Boggs, Harold, Elizabethton	.875	12	3	4	1	8	0
Bowser, Robert, Martinsville	1.000	17	2	7	0	9	0
Burger, Rob, Martinsville	.500	9	1	1	2	4	0
Buteaux, Shane, Bristol	.857	13	4	2	1	7	0
Chapman, Walker, Elizabethton	1.000	4	3	2	0	5	1
Chen, Bruce, Danville*	1.000	14	1	9	0	10	0
Cloud, Tony, Princeton	1.000	12	5	9	0	14	0
Cochrane, Andrew, Danville*	.500	6	0	1	1	2	0

Player, Team	Pct.	G	PO	A	E	TC	DP
Coggin, David, Martinsville	.857	11	6	6	2	14	1
Collins, Ken, Danville	1.000	18	2	1	0	3	0
Cooper, Chadwick, Kingsport	1.000	22	0	3	0	3	0
Cooper, Keith, Danville	.800	17	1	3	1	5	0
Corey, Mark, Princeton	.750	4	2	1	1	4	0
Crills, Brad, Bluefield	1.000	4	1	5	0	6	1
Cushman, Dwayne, Princeton	.857	26	1	5	1	7	0
Davis, Lance, Princeton*	.857	15	5	7	2	14	0
Dean, Greg, Bluefield	1.000	10	2	3	0	5	0
Desrosiers, Erik, Bristol	.800	22	3	1	1	5	0
DeWitt, Chris, Kingsport	.833	23	5	5	2	12	0
DeWitt, Matt, Johnson City	.929	13	5	8	1	14	0
Dunne, Brian, Martinsville*	1.000	16	3	8	0	11	1
Edwards, Jon, Burlington	.889	19	3	5	1	9	0
Eibey, Scott, Bluefield*	.900	14	3	6	1	10	1
Feliz, Bienvenido, Burlington	.778	12	7	7	4	18	1
Fereira, Marcos, Huntington	.500	5	0	1	1	2	0
Figueroa, Nelson, Kingsport	.889	12	3	13	2	18	2
Fleetwood, Tony, Burlington*	.714	18	1	4	2	7	0
Fonceca, Chad, Princeton	1.000	11	3	0	0	3	0
Frace, Ryan, Martinsville	1.000	14	3	2	0	5	0
Fussell, Chris, Bluefield	.857	12	1	5	1	7	1
Garber, Joel, Bristol*	.944	19	7	10	1	18	0
Giron, Roberto, Princeton	.875	24	3	4	1	8	0
Giuliano, Joe, Danville	.800	11	1	3	1	5	1
Gobert, Chris, Danville*	1.000	3	1	1	0	2	0
Grife, Richard, Burlington	1.000	16	2	4	0	6	0
Hackett, Jason, Bluefield*	.917	13	5	6	1	12	1
Halley, Allen, Bristol	1.000	2	1	1	0	2	0
Harris, Jeffrey, Elizabethton	1.000	21	3	5	0	8	1
Harrison, Scott, Burlington	1.000	5	0	5	0	5	0
Hasselhoff, Derek, Bristol	.833	12	10	10	4	24	0
Hoalton, Brandon, Huntington	1.000	6	1	8	0	9	0
Hunt, Jon, Bristol*	.667	13	4	6	5	15	0
Jimenez, Jose, Johnson City	.943	14	12	21	2	35	1
Kershner, Jason, Martinsville*	.882	13	5	10	2	17	0
Kessel, Kyle, Kingsport*	1.000	5	1	5	0	6	1
Knoll, Randy, Martinsville	.571	6	1	3	3	7	0
Knowland, Sam, Danville	1.000	20	5	6	0	11	0
Koehler, P.K., Danville*	.750	11	1	2	1	4	0
Kosek, Kory, Martinsville	1.000	9	0	4	0	4	0
Kown, John, Johnson City	1.000	16	4	6	0	10	0
Kraus, Tim, Bristol	1.000	5	2	3	0	5	0
Kruse, Kelly, Bristol	1.000	15	0	2	0	2	0
LaRocca, Todd, Bluefield	1.000	8	4	11	0	15	1
Loewe, Kevin, Danville*	.917	20	5	6	1	12	0
Loudermilk, Darren, Burlington	.846	21	5	6	2	13	0
Lowry, Elliott, Burlington*	.875	10	0	7	1	8	0
Mahaffey, Alan, Elizabethton*	.833	13	0	10	2	12	0
Maine, Dalton, Bluefield	1.000	1	1	1	0	2	1
Manon, Julio, Huntington	.929	16	5	8	1	14	2
Martinez, Dennis, Burlington	.875	15	2	5	1	8	1
Martinez, Willie, Burlington	.692	11	1	8	4	13	1
Mattox, Gene, Princeton	1.000	11	0	1	0	1	0
McCaffrey, Dennis, Johnson City	1.000	24	3	0	0	3	0
McKnight, Chris, Danville*	1.000	1	0	1	0	1	0
Mear, Rich, Johnson City*	.905	14	4	15	2	21	1
Mendez, Manuel, Johnson City*	1.000	30	1	3	0	4	0
Miller, Brian, Martinsville	.900	23	5	4	1	10	0
Montgomery, Joe, Princeton	1.000	13	3	2	0	5	0

Player, Team	Pct.	G	PO	A	E	TC	DP
Moore, David, Bristol	1.000	15	2	4	0	6	1
Moreno, Julio, Bluefield	.625	9	4	1	3	8	0
Morseman, Robert, Bluefield*	1.000	18	0	8	0	8	0
Mosquea, Alberto, Martinsville	.750	9	2	1	1	4	0
Murphy, Chris, Princeton*	.895	10	3	14	2	19	0
Niedermaier, Brad, Elizabethton	1.000	7	4	5	0	9	1
Noone, Bill, Martinsville	1.000	1	2	0	0	2	0
Ojeda, Erick, Kingsport*	.944	14	6	11	1	18	1
Oldham, Bob, Burlington	.688	18	1	10	5	16	0
Olson, Phillip, Kingsport	.950	12	5	14	1	20	0
Olszewski, Tim, Bluefield	.833	16	1	4	1	6	1
Ortiz, Steve, Burlington	1.000	22	0	1	0	1	0
Osting, James, Danville*	1.000	11	1	5	0	6	0
Peters, Tim, Elizabethton*	1.000	27	4	7	0	11	1
Pierce, Drew, Huntington	1.000	22	3	6	0	9	0
Pizarro, Melvin, Martinsville*	1.000	10	1	1	0	2	0
PONSON, Sidney, Bluefield	1.000	13	10	10	0	20	0
Poupart, Melvin, Kingsport	.500	18	1	0	1	2	0
Prejean, Alex, Huntington	.833	14	3	2	1	6	0
Pumphrey, Kenny, Kingsport	.933	12	5	9	1	15	0
Quintana, Urbano, Huntington	1.000	19	2	1	0	3	0
Raines, Ken, Danville*	1.000	11	1	3	0	4	0
Rath, Fred, Elizabethton	.833	27	2	3	1	6	1
Reed, Dan, Bluefield*	1.000	6	2	3	0	5	0
Reed, Steven, Johnson City	.750	31	0	3	1	4	0
Reynolds, Walker, Danville	.600	20	2	1	2	5	0
Richardson, Kasey, Elizabethton*	1.000	3	0	5	0	5	0
Roberts, Randolph, Princeton	.789	15	5	10	4	19	0
Roettgen, Mark, Johnson City	.917	13	2	9	1	12	0
Rogan, Sean, Johnson City*	.333	12	0	1	2	3	0
Roque, Jorge, Johnson City	1.000	14	1	4	0	5	0
Ruiz, Rafael, Bristol*	.667	22	2	2	2	6	0
Sanders, Frankie, Burlington	.938	12	2	13	1	16	1
Santamaria, Bill, Kingsport	.833	13	3	7	2	12	0
Sauritch, Chris, Bluefield	.875	13	3	4	1	8	0
Schleuss, Will, Princeton*	1.000	23	0	6	0	6	0
Schnur, Curt, Danville	.600	18	1	5	4	10	0
Secoda, Jason, Bristol	.846	13	8	3	2	13	0
Sellner, Aaron, Elizabethton	.833	19	1	4	1	6	0
Shumaker, Anthony, Martinsville*	1.000	6	3	3	0	6	0
Shumate, Jacob, Danville	.500	7	0	1	1	2	0
Sikes, Jason, Martinsville	.833	4	1	4	1	6	0
Snyder, Matt, Bluefield	1.000	17	0	5	0	5	0
Spang, R.J., Huntington	.750	18	4	5	3	12	0
Sparks, Jeff, Princeton	1.000	16	2	1	0	3	0
Splittorff, James, Elizabethton	.900	13	6	12	2	20	2
Starling, Marcus, Elizabethton	.875	13	1	6	1	8	1
Tanksley, William, Elizabethton	.750	11	1	2	1	4	0
Tebbetts, Scott, Martinsville	.900	22	4	5	1	10	0
Vejil, Aaron, Huntington*	1.000	14	1	2	0	3	0
Vicentino, Andy, Princeton*	.833	10	0	5	1	6	0
Villafuerte, Brandon, Kingsport	1.000	20	4	6	0	10	1
Virchis, Adam, Bristol	1.000	10	7	8	0	15	1
Vota, Michael, Bristol	1.000	22	3	2	0	5	0
Wagner, Ken, Burlington	.818	13	1	8	2	11	1
West, Adam, Johnson City*	.818	18	4	5	2	11	0
Wise, William, Danville	.882	10	5	10	2	17	0
Yoder, Jason, Martinsville	.857	8	2	4	1	7	0
Young, Ty, Huntington	.792	14	7	12	5	24	0

The following players did not have any fielding statistics at the positions indicated or appeared only as a designated hitter, pinch-hitter or pinch-runner: Andino, 3b; Cope, p; Cruz, p; Feingold, p; Gill, of; Herbison, p; King, p; McDougal, p; Mercedes, p; Milledge, p; C. Mota, ss; Raio, of; K. Reed, p; Santos, p; Schroeder, of; Serbio, 2b; J. Taylor, dh, ph; Torbett, of; J. Wise, p.

LEAGUE CHAMPIONS

Year	Team	Pct.
1921—	Greenville	.608
	Johnson City*	.627
1922—	Bristol	.557
1923—	Knoxville	.635
1924—	Knoxville*	.642
	Bristol	.607
1925—	Greenville	.667
1926-36—	Did not operate.	
1937—	Elizabethton	.559
	Pennington Gap*	.580
1938—	Elizabethton	.664
	Greenville (3rd)†	.571
1939—	Elizabethton‡	.597
1940—	Johnson City§	.726
	Elizabethton	.750

Year	Team	Pct.
1941—	Johnson City	.614
	Elizabethton*	.661
1942—	Bristol	.667
	Bristol∞	.660
1943—	Bristol	.755
	Bristol▲	.617
1944—	Kingsport‡	.575
1945—	Kingsport‡	.670
1946—	New River‡	.675
1947—	Pulaski	.648
	New River (3rd)†	.516
1948—	Pulaski‡	.680
1949—	Bluefield‡	.721
1950—	Bluefield	.600
	Bluefield◆	.745

Year	Team	Pct.
1951—	Kingsport‡	.659
1952—	Johnson City	.595
	Welch (3rd)†	.509
1953—	Welch*	.705
	Johnson City	.672
1954—	Bluefield‡	.619
1955—	Salem■	.689
1956—	Did not operate.	
1957—	Bluefield	.701
1958—	Johnson City	.662
1959—	Morristown	.603
1960—	Wytheville	.614
1961—	Middlesboro	.591
1962—	Bluefield	.671
1963—	Bluefield	.652

Year	Team	Pct.	Year	Team	Pct.	Year	Team	Pct.
1964—	Johnson City	.662	1976—	Johnson City▼	.714	1988—	Kingsport•	.644
1965—	Salem	.614		Bluefield	.600		Burlington	.529
1966—	Marion	.623	1977—	Kingsport	.623	1989—	Elizabethton•	.691
1967—	Bluefield	.627	1978—	Elizabethton	.594		Pulaski	.618
1968—	Marion	.583	1979—	Paintsville	.800	1990—	Elizabethton	.761
1969—	Pulaski▼	.576	1980—	Paintsville	.657	1991—	Pulaski•	.662
	Johnson City	.544	1981—	Paintsville	.657		Burlington	.597
1970—	Bluefield	.638	1982—	Bluefield▼	.681	1992—	Elizabethton	.742
1971—	Bluefield▼	.609		Johnson City	.478		Bluefield•	.597
	Kingsport	.559	1983—	Paintsville	.653	1993—	Burlington•	.647
1972—	Bristol▼	.588	1984—	Elizabethton•	.580		Elizabethton	.552
	Covington	.586		Pulaski	.536	1994—	Princeton•	.621
1973—	Kingsport	.757	1985—	Bristol††	.638		Johnson City	.618
1974—	Bristol▼	.754	1986—	Johnson City	.667	1995—	Bluefield	.754
	Bluefield	.536		Pulaski•	.621		Kingsport•	.727
1975—	Marion	.515	1987—	Burlington•	.729			
	Johnson City▼	.603		Johnson City	.609			

*Won split-season playoff. †Won four-team playoff. ‡Won championship and four-team playoff. §Johnson City, first-half winner, won playoff involving six clubs. ∞Won both halves and defeated second-place Elizabethton in playoff. ▲Won both halves, but Erwin won four-team playoff. ◆Won both halves, but Bristol won two-club playoff. ■Salem and Johnson City declared playoff co-champions when weather forced cancellation of final series. ▼League was divided into Northern, Southern divisions; declared league champion based on highest won-lost percentage. •League was divided into North and South divisions; won playoff. ††Bristol declared league champion based on regular-season record.

ARIZONA LEAGUE

LEAGUE OFFICE

President/treasurer
Bob Richmond
Address
P.O. Box 4941
Scottsdale, AZ 85261
Phone
602-483-8224

Teams*
Angels
Athletics
Diamondbacks
Mariners
Padres
Rockies

*Teams play their games in Chandler, Mesa, Peoria, Scottsdale and other Arizona sites to be announced.

1995 FINAL STANDINGS

COMPOSITE

Team	Ath.	Ang.	Brw.	Pad.	Mar.	Rck.	W	L	T	Pct.	GB
Athletics	....	6	8	5	7	11	37	19	0	.661	....
Angels	5	....	6	10	6	8	35	21	0	.625	2
Brewers	4	6	....	8	7	9	34	22	0	.607	3
Padres	5	2	3	....	6	8	24	31	0	.436	12$\frac{1}{2}$
Mariners	5	4	4	5	....	6	24	32	0	.429	13
Rockies	0	3	1	3	6	....	13	42	0	.236	23$\frac{1}{2}$

Games played in Chandler, Mesa, Peoria and Scottsdale.

Club names are major league affiliations.

PLAYOFFS: No playoffs scheduled.

REGULAR-SEASON ATTENDANCE: No total official attendance figures reported.

MANAGERS: Angels, Bruce Hines; Athletics, Juan Navarette; Brewers, Ralph Dickenson; Mariners, Tommy LeVasseur; Padres, Dan Norman; Rockies, Jim Eppard.

ALL-STAR TEAM: 1B—David Arias, Mariners; 2B—Dionys Cesar, Athletics; 3B—Juan Polanco, Athletics; SS—Edward Lara, Athletics; OF—Richard Stuart, Angels; Juan Rodriguez, Angels; Salvadore Duverge, Rockies; C—Ramon Hernandez, Athletics; DH—Daryl Rutherford, Padres; LHP—Keith Volkman, Angels; RHP—Jose Paulino, Athletics; LH Reliever—Keith Volkman, Angels; RH Reliever—Robert Kazmirski, Athletics; Most Valuable Player—Ramon Hernandez, Athletics; Manager of the Year—Juan Navarette, Athletics.

1995 BATTING

TEAM

Team	Avg.	G	TPA	AB	R	H	TB	2B	3B	HR	RBI	SH	SF	HP	BB	IBB	SO	SB	CS	GDP	LOB	ShO	Slg.	OBP
Brewers	.265	56	2173	1899	315	504	643	68	28	5	254	13	19	38	203	2	376	106	45	40	391	2	.339	.345
Angels	.263	56	2121	1832	287	482	639	60	35	9	223	23	18	34	214	3	386	92	47	32	393	0	.349	.348
Mariners	.260	56	2241	1959	304	510	698	93	28	13	228	8	18	32	224	1	477	71	47	32	443	2	.356	.343
Padres	.257	55	2041	1822	254	469	655	78	27	18	212	9	12	21	177	4	482	69	45	36	372	3	.359	.348
Athletics	.256	56	2177	1847	329	473	682	61	44	20	253	8	28	31	262	5	481	134	65	27	395	3	.369	.353
Rockies	.230	55	2083	1819	237	418	536	60	17	8	182	8	18	42	194	1	503	63	33	46	385	5	.295	.315

INDIVIDUAL

TOP QUALIFIERS FOR BATTING CHAMPIONSHIP

Minimum 151 plate appearances. *Lefthanded batter. †Switch-hitter.

Player, Team	Avg.	G	TPA	AB	R	H	TB	2B	3B	HR	RBI	SH	SF	HP	BB	IBB	SO	SB	CS	GDP	Slg.	OBP
Hernandez, Ramon, Athletics	.364	48	194	143	37	52	85	9	6	4	37	0	4	8	39	1	16	6	2	3	.594	.510
Johnson, Duan, Mariners	.351	43	186	174	33	61	76	9	3	0	28	0	2	2	8	0	14	3	2	5	.437	.382
Rutherford, Daryl, Padres	.333	47	200	186	29	62	97	12	4	5	27	0	3	0	11	1	28	13	7	3	.522	.365
Arias, David, Mariners*	.332	48	211	184	30	61	99	18	4	4	37	0	3	1	23	1	52	2	0	2	.538	.403
Wilkerson, Adrian, Brewers	.331	54	184	160	22	53	56	1	1	0	28	3	3	2	16	0	28	18	7	82	.350	.392
Cesar, Dionys, Athletics†	.322	48	201	171	41	55	80	11	4	2	21	3	2	2	23	0	29	17	10	6	.468	.404
Rodriguez, Miguel, Brewers	.313	49	180	163	24	51	68	12	1	1	18	1	1	4	11	0	34	9	2	4	.417	.369
Barnes, Larry, Angels*	.310	56	232	197	42	61	84	8	3	3	37	1	2	5	27	0	40	12	5	1	.426	.403
Cruz, Cirilo, Mariners	.308	39	167	146	22	45	53	8	0	0	20	2	0	3	16	0	37	0	2	2	.363	.388
Stuart, Rich, Angels	.299	56	236	204	42	61	89	10	6	2	33	2	2	3	25	1	42	20	8	5	.436	.380
Rodriguez, Juan, Angels†	.298	54	228	215	27	64	91	8	8	1	31	1	2	3	7	0	49	4	7	1	.423	.324
Polanco, Juan, Athletics	.296	48	204	179	41	53	80	11	5	2	23	1	4	2	17	0	35	18	8	2	.447	.356
Harrison, Adonis, Mariners*	.290	45	199	155	31	45	65	7	5	1	14	0	4	3	37	0	37	7	9	0	.419	.427
Lara, Edward, Athletics†	.288	47	211	184	42	53	74	6	6	1	26	1	2	2	22	0	19	23	9	4	.402	.367
Vidal, Carlos, Rockies	.287	39	163	136	19	39	55	11	1	1	20	0	3	1	23	0	20	3	3	9	.404	.387
Duverge, Salvador, Rockies	.287	46	193	164	22	47	65	9	3	1	18	0	3	6	20	1	36	11	4	5	.396	.378

DEPARTMENTAL LEADERS: G—Barnes, Stuart, 56; AB—Ju. Rodriguez, 215; R—Barnes, Lara, Stuart, 42; H—Ju. Rodriguez, 64; TB—Arias, 99; 2B—Arias, 18; 3B—Ju. Rodriguez, 8; HR—Paciorek, Rutherford, 5; RBI—Arias, Barnes, R. Hernandez, 37; SH—Wardrop, 3; SF—Martinez, 7; HP—R. Hernandez, 8; BB—R. Hernandez, 39; IBB—Jacobo, 2; SO—Paciorek, 58; SB—R. Harris, 26; CS—Cesar, R. Harris, 10; GIDP—Vidal, 9; Slg.—R. Hernandez, .594; OBP—R. Hernandez, .510.

ALL PLAYERS

*Lefthanded batter. †Switch-hitter.

Player, Team	Avg.	G	TPA	AB	R	H	TB	2B	3B	HR	RBI	SH	SF	HP	BB	IBB	SO	SB	CS	GDP	Slg.	OBP
Acevedo, Juan, Rockies	.211	29	103	90	10	19	23	2	1	0	8	2	1	1	9	0	25	2	4	3	.256	.287
Alamo, Efrain, Rockies	.252	39	161	147	14	37	49	4	4	0	14	0	2	5	7	0	36	4	2	2	.333	.304
Allen, Tony, Brewers	.221	46	133	113	19	25	35	0	5	0	14	2	2	2	14	0	35	7	2	2	.310	.313
Arias, David, Mariners*	.332	48	211	184	30	61	99	18	4	4	37	0	3	1	23	1	52	2	0	2	.538	.403

Player, Team	Avg.	G	TPA	AB	R	H	TB	2B	3B	HR	RBI	SH	SF	HP	BB	IBB	SO	SB	CS	GDP	Slg.	OBP
Balcazar, Carlos, Angels*	.301	35	107	93	11	28	38	5	1	1	11	0	0	2	12	1	20	2	0	1	.409	.393
Barnes, Larry, Angels*	.310	56	232	197	42	61	84	8	3	3	37	1	2	5	27	0	40	12	5	1	.426	.403
Barrios, Esteban, Angels*	.211	28	90	71	11	15	18	1	1	0	2	1	0	1	17	0	9	3	1	4	.254	.360
Campusano, Carlos, Brewers	.249	54	194	173	25	43	52	4	1	1	15	1	1	5	14	1	27	7	3	6	.301	.321
Carmona, Cesarin, Padres†	.255	15	57	51	7	13	22	2	2	1	4	1	0	0	5	0	10	3	3	0	.431	.321
Castro, Nelson, Angels†	.195	55	226	190	34	37	42	1	2	0	22	4	1	4	27	0	50	15	7	2	.221	.306
Cesar, Dionys, Athletics†	.322	48	201	171	41	55	80	11	4	2	21	3	2	2	23	0	29	17	10	0	.468	.404
Cespedes, Angel, Rockies†	.211	19	68	57	11	12	15	1	1	0	11	0	1	3	7	0	12	1	4	4	.263	.324
Chambers, Victor, Athletics*	.309	34	126	110	11	34	42	2	3	0	16	0	1	1	14	1	17	12	4	3	.382	.389
Chavez, Steven, Padres*	.259	55	228	197	30	51	68	7	5	0	24	1	1	5	24	0	48	5	6	4	.345	.352
Clark, John, Rockies	.203	52	214	192	22	39	46	5	1	0	12	1	3	4	14	0	52	6	1	4	.240	.268
Cowsill, Brendon, Angels	.257	34	135	113	18	29	40	5	3	0	13	2	2	0	18	0	28	7	0	1	.354	.353
Cruz, Cirilo, Mariners	.308	39	167	146	22	45	53	8	0	0	20	2	0	3	16	0	37	0	2	2	.363	.388
Cruz, Francisco, Padres	.000	1	3	2	0	0	0	0	0	0	0	0	0	0	1	0	1	1	0	0	.000	.333
Darrell, Thomas, Angels	.000	18	1	1	0	0	0	0	0	0	0	0	0	0	0	0	1	0	0	0	.000	.000
Davis, Josh, Padres	.203	37	147	128	20	26	32	4	1	0	7	2	0	3	14	0	35	3	3	1	.250	.297
Delacruz, Jesus, Angels	.241	31	87	79	6	19	25	4	1	0	10	2	0	3	3	1	17	1	2	2	.316	.294
Delgado, Ariel, Angels*	.206	53	211	189	26	39	50	5	3	0	19	1	1	5	15	0	36	5	3	7	.265	.281
Ducasse, Luis, Athletics	.063	6	22	16	1	1	1	0	0	0	1	0	1	0	5	0	8	0	0	2	.063	.273
Duverge, Salvador, Rockies	.287	46	193	164	22	47	65	9	3	1	18	0	3	6	20	1	36	11	4	5	.396	.378
Ebbert, Chad, Padres	.315	35	138	127	18	40	57	5	3	2	21	0	1	1	9	0	29	2	2	4	.449	.362
Erstad, Darin, Angels*	.556	4	19	18	2	10	11	1	0	0	1	0	0	0	1	0	1	1	0	0	.611	.579
Figueroa, Luis, Mariners	.292	32	135	120	14	35	37	2	0	0	11	0	1	2	12	0	9	1	2	4	.308	.363
Fowler, Marvin, Mariners*	.258	26	108	97	13	25	35	4	3	0	8	0	4	0	7	0	29	4	4	0	.361	.333
Freeman, Terrance, Athletics†	.242	34	109	95	14	23	25	0	1	0	5	1	0	3	10	0	25	3	3	3	.263	.333
Gordon, Garfield, Rockies	.252	36	160	135	20	34	38	2	1	0	8	0	0	3	22	0	37	20	7	1	.281	.369
Groseclose, Harold, Rockies	.252	31	136	119	19	30	36	4	1	0	8	0	0	0	15	0	26	4	0	3	.303	.336
Guerrero, Diogene, Athletics	.228	41	168	136	27	31	48	4	5	1	13	0	1	2	29	1	48	11	7	0	.353	.369
Harris, Mike, Brewers*	.304	6	25	23	5	7	11	2	1	0	4	0	0	0	2	0	7	0	1	0	.478	.360
Harris, Rico, Brewers†	.279	48	214	172	40	48	60	6	3	0	22	0	1	4	37	1	22	26	10	2	.349	.416
Harrison, Adonis, Mariners*	.290	45	199	155	31	45	65	7	5	1	14	0	4	3	37	0	37	7	9	0	.419	.427
Hernandez, Ramon, Athletics	.364	48	194	143	37	52	85	9	6	4	37	0	4	8	39	1	16	6	2	3	.594	.510
Hernandez, Victor, Athletics	.152	21	52	46	5	7	7	0	0	0	3	0	0	1	5	0	21	0	2	1	.152	.250
Hunter, Andy, Padres	.208	35	124	106	14	22	28	2	2	0	11	0	0	1	17	0	39	2	1	2	.264	.323
Hutchins, Norm, Angels†	.271	14	67	59	9	16	19	1	1	0	7	2	1	1	4	0	10	8	4	1	.322	.323
Iapoce, Anthony, Brewers	.333	3	4	3	2	1	1	0	0	0	0	0	0	0	1	0	1	1	0	0	.333	.500
Isom, Daleon, Mariners	.258	28	111	89	17	23	32	4	1	1	8	1	1	2	18	0	19	11	8	2	.360	.391
Jackson, Rod, Padres	.253	45	162	150	16	38	44	6	0	0	6	1	0	2	9	0	39	11	3	3	.293	.304
Jacobo, Roberto, Padres†	.241	46	179	166	18	40	48	2	3	0	15	0	0	1	12	2	49	10	7	3	.289	.296
Jacobus, Brian, Padres*	.194	44	155	144	12	28	35	7	0	0	11	0	1	2	8	0	32	0	1	7	.243	.245
Johnson, Duan, Mariners	.351	43	186	174	33	61	76	9	3	0	28	0	2	2	8	0	21	6	2	5	.437	.382
Johnson, Jace, Athletics	.132	17	43	38	4	5	9	1	0	1	4	0	0	1	4	0	16	1	1	0	.237	.233
Jones, Ken, Padres	.500	1	4	4	0	2	3	1	0	0	1	0	0	0	0	0	1	0	0	1	.750	.500
Jones, Timothy, Athletics*	.198	32	103	96	7	19	25	2	2	0	10	1	0	0	6	0	36	5	3	1	.260	.245
Judge, Mike, Brewers	.293	16	52	41	8	12	16	2	1	0	6	0	0	3	8	0	9	2	1	2	.390	.442
Kirkpatrick, Brian, Rockies	.139	38	136	122	11	17	21	1	0	1	7	2	1	0	11	0	54	4	1	4	.172	.209
Lara, Edward, Athletics†	.288	47	211	184	42	53	74	6	6	1	26	1	2	2	22	0	19	23	9	4	.402	.367
Law, Khris, Athletics	.165	36	120	103	17	17	24	1	0	2	11	0	0	2	15	1	37	5	3	2	.233	.283
Lawrence, Mike, Angels†	.162	18	46	37	5	6	7	1	0	0	5	0	1	1	7	0	11	1	0	1	.189	.304
Lindsey, John, Rockies	.235	48	198	179	23	42	58	10	0	2	22	0	1	7	11	0	48	0	2	4	.324	.303
Llanos, Alexis, Angels†	.283	26	57	53	6	15	20	1	2	0	3	1	0	0	3	0	11	0	0	1	.377	.321
Marnell, Anthony, Padres	.400	1	5	5	1	2	3	1	0	0	3	0	0	0	0	0	2	0	0	1	.600	.400
Martinez, Hipolito, Athletics	.221	46	173	149	23	33	51	4	4	2	27	0	7	1	16	1	47	8	4	1	.342	.289
Maynard, Scott, Mariners	.236	21	84	72	6	17	22	2	0	1	12	1	2	0	9	0	21	0	0	0	.306	.313
McDavid, Ray, Padres*	.464	9	36	28	13	13	20	2	1	1	6	0	0	0	8	0	7	3	1	0	.714	.583
McDougali, Matt, Mariners	.238	27	114	101	17	24	27	3	0	0	9	0	0	1	12	0	21	9	4	0	.267	.325
McGuire, Brandon, Angels†	.250	4	5	4	0	1	1	0	0	0	1	0	0	0	1	0	1	0	0	0	.250	.400
McNally, Jason, Rockies	.213	41	165	141	18	30	38	2	0	2	18	1	1	4	18	0	39	2	1	3	.270	.317
Medrano, Teodoro, Mariners	.000	1	3	3	0	0	0	0	0	0	0	0	0	0	0	0	0	0	0	0	.000	.000
Moore, Donald, Brewers	.239	38	82	71	10	17	20	0	0	1	6	0	0	2	8	0	27	3	1	0	.282	.333
Moore, James, Padres	.320	15	57	50	7	16	25	4	1	1	9	1	1	1	4	0	17	1	2	2	.500	.382
Needham, Scott, Mariners	.177	21	79	62	12	11	18	5	1	0	10	0	1	2	14	0	22	0	1	0	.290	.342
Niles, David, Rockies*	.198	40	140	116	21	23	26	3	0	0	9	1	0	1	22	0	50	3	0	0	.224	.331
Paciorek, Peter, Padres†	.257	54	218	183	32	47	79	11	3	5	24	1	0	1	33	1	58	6	4	1	.432	.373
Paulino, Arturo, Athletics	.256	31	133	117	18	30	40	2	4	0	13	0	0	2	14	0	36	14	2	2	.342	.346
Pernell, Brandon, Padres	.247	48	196	174	22	43	62	11	1	2	29	2	3	1	16	0	54	8	2	2	.356	.309
Peters, Tony, Brewers	.244	51	204	172	25	42	60	8	2	2	24	1	0	2	29	0	55	9	3	2	.349	.360
Polanco, Juan, Athletics	.296	48	204	179	41	53	80	11	5	2	23	1	4	2	17	0	35	18	8	2	.447	.356
Randolph, Edward, Mariners†	.281	41	153	135	22	38	66	11	4	3	25	1	2	3	12	0	30	5	5	3	.489	.349
Rauer, Troy, Athletics	.160	30	115	100	13	16	25	2	2	1	12	0	2	1	12	0	43	3	3	1	.250	.252
Rendon, Miguel, Brewers	.259	48	181	162	23	42	51	5	2	0	25	0	5	5	9	0	18	4	2	5	.315	.309
Ritter, Ryan, Brewers	.200	4	15	15	1	3	6	3	0	0	2	0	0	0	0	0	0	0	0	1	.400	.200
Roche, Michael, Brewers	.255	47	191	161	33	41	56	11	2	0	31	2	3	7	18	0	42	9	3	3	.348	.349
Rodriguez, Franklin, Mariners	.298	16	66	57	14	17	19	0	1	0	1	1	0	0	8	0	18	3	0	1	.333	.385
Rodriguez, John, Padres	.202	31	99	94	12	19	25	1	1	1	10	0	0	2	1	0	27	0	3	0	.266	.222
Rodriguez, Juan, Angels†	.298	54	228	215	27	64	91	8	8	1	31	1	2	3	7	0	49	4	7	1	.423	.326
Rodriguez, Miguel, Brewers	.313	49	180	163	24	51	68	12	1	1	18	1	1	4	11	0	34	9	2	4	.417	.369
Rogue, Francisco, Brewers	.226	19	63	62	10	14	19	3	1	0	10	0	0	0	1	0	9	0	0	2	.306	.238
Rosario, Eliezer, Padres	.259	7	33	27	3	7	7	0	0	0	3	0	0	1	5	0	6	1	0	0	.259	.394
Rose, Carlos, Mariners	.152	27	97	92	10	14	18	1	0	1	6	0	0	2	3	0	33	4	1	5	.196	.196
Rowson, James, Mariners	.189	30	117	106	9	20	28	6	1	0	9	1	1	3	6	0	38	9	2	1	.264	.250
Rushdan, Rasheed, Rockies	.000	6	20	18	1	0	0	0	0	0	3	0	0	0	2	0	5	0	0	2	.000	.100
Rutherford, Daryl, Padres	.333	47	200	186	29	62	97	12	4	5	27	0	3	0	11	1	28	13	7	3	.522	.365

Player, Team	Avg.	G	TPA	AB	R	H	TB	2B	3B	HR	RBI	SH	SF	HP	BB	IBB	SO	SB	CS	GDP	Slg.	OBP
Saucedo, Robert, Angels	.280	30	90	75	13	21	27	1	1	1	9	0	2	1	12	0	11	3	1	1	.360	.378
Schaub, Greg, Brewers	.274	33	102	95	12	26	36	4	3	0	11	1	1	0	5	0	20	5	4	1	.379	.307
Scheker, Luis, Athletics	.250	16	74	60	9	15	23	3	1	1	11	0	3	0	11	0	16	1	1	2	.383	.351
Selga, Andres, Rockies	.179	21	75	67	7	12	14	2	0	0	5	1	1	1	5	0	29	1	1	0	.209	.243
Silverio, Richard, Rockies*	.272	35	151	136	19	37	52	4	4	1	19	0	1	6	8	0	34	2	3	0	.382	.338
Singleton, Samuel, Brewers*	.245	47	163	139	28	34	44	4	3	0	19	1	2	1	20	0	33	2	3	3	.317	.340
Soriano, Jacobo, Angels	1.000	12	1	1	0	1	1	0	0	0	0	0	0	0	0	0	0	0	0	0	1.000	1.000
Stewart, Keith, Mariners*	.196	15	58	46	12	9	14	0	1	1	6	1	0	0	11	0	23	3	0	0	.304	.351
Stuart, Rich, Angels	.299	56	236	204	42	61	89	10	6	2	33	2	2	3	25	1	42	20	8	5	.436	.380
Tolbert, Ernest, Angels	.176	26	102	91	16	16	26	3	2	1	7	0	0	2	9	0	24	2	2	1	.286	.265
Vazquez, Ramon, Mariners*	.206	39	162	141	20	29	34	3	1	0	11	0	0	2	19	0	27	4	3	2	.241	.309
Ventura, Wilfredo, Athletics	.279	34	129	104	19	29	43	3	1	3	20	1	1	3	20	0	32	7	3	0	.413	.406
Veras, Illuminado, Angels	.253	32	95	87	9	22	31	4	1	1	9	1	2	0	5	0	13	2	2	2	.356	.287
Vidal, Carlos, Rockies	.287	39	163	136	19	39	55	11	1	1	20	0	3	1	23	0	20	3	3	9	.404	.387
Walther, Christopher, Brewers	.259	50	186	174	28	45	52	3	2	0	19	1	0	1	10	0	9	4	3	5	.299	.303
Wardrop, Adam, Angels†	.253	49	188	146	26	37	45	4	2	0	10	5	1	6	30	0	36	8	7	2	.308	.399
Wilkerson, Adrian, Brewers	.331	54	184	160	22	53	56	1	1	0	28	3	3	2	16	0	28	18	7	82	.350	.392
Williams, Marcus, Mariners	.227	22	89	88	6	20	29	7	1	0	6	0	1	0	0	0	23	4	2	4	.330	.225

GRAND SLAMS: Balcarzar, Paciorek, 1 each.

AWARDED FIRST BASE ON CATCHER'S INTERFERENCE: Groseclose 2 (Saucedo, Veras); D. Moore (Randolph); Polanco (Randolph).

1995 PITCHING

TEAM

Team	W	L	Pct.	ERA	G	CG	ShO	Sv.	IP	H	TBF	R	ER	HR	SH	SF	HB	BB	IBB	SO	WP	Bk.
Angels	35	21	.625	2.94	56	5	6	17	489.0	422	2073	222	160	5	10	14	47	193	7	429	57	21
Brewers	34	22	.607	3.28	56	2	16	493.2	444	2122	238	180	11	16	21	26	199	5	536	60	20	
Athletics	37	19	.661	3.37	56	1	3	15	491.1	436	2073	238	184	17	7	10	26	190	2	496	42	25
Padres	24	31	.436	3.76	55	3	2	12	469.1	457	2083	292	196	14	11	18	43	205	0	406	49	20
Mariners	24	32	.429	4.30	56	1	10	493.2	528	2228	326	230	13	9	27	25	244	1	448	62	18	
Rockies	13	42	.236	5.82	55	0	0	5	473.1	569	2257	410	306	13	16	23	31	243	1	390	72	28

INDIVIDUAL

TOP QUALIFIERS FOR EARNED-RUN AVERAGE TITLE

Minimum 45 innings. *Lefthanded pitcher.

Pitcher, Team	W	L	Pct.	ERA	G	GS	CG	ShO	GF	Sv.	IP	H	TBF	R	ER	HR	SH	SF	HB	BB	IBB	SO	WP	Bk.
Darrell, Thomas, Angels	4	3	.571	1.71	18	5	0	0	7	2	63.0	51	254	18	12	1	1	3	4	14	0	49	3	1
Plant, David, Athletics	4	2	.667	1.76	14	6	0	0	4	2	51.0	34	198	11	10	1	0	0	2	12	0	51	2	1
Clark, Chris, Padres	5	5	.500	2.10	13	12	1	0	0	0	73.0	52	313	30	17	1	1	1	7	38	0	82	5	0
Bishop, Joshua, Brewers	8	2	.800	2.16	14	13	3	1	0	0	96.0	64	382	34	23	4	3	1	1	29	0	134	9	3
DeLosSantos, Valerio, Brewers*	4	6	.400	2.20	14	12	0	0	1	0	82.0	81	341	34	20	3	5	4	6	12	2	57	6	2
Romero, John, Angels	7	3	.700	2.41	18	6	2	1	4	1	71.0	57	291	29	19	0	0	2	5	18	1	64	8	4
Blevins, Jeremy, Angels	5	1	.833	2.45	11	9	0	0	0	0	51.1	39	224	20	14	0	2	0	4	32	0	48	4	1
Volkman, Keith, Angels*	5	2	.714	2.53	11	10	0	0	0	0	67.2	61	279	30	19	0	1	4	25	0	49	5	1
Jacob, Russell, Mariners	6	2	.750	2.88	12	11	0	0	1	0	56.1	47	248	29	18	0	0	1	3	31	0	54	6	2
Walker, Kevin, Padres*	5	5	.500	3.01	13	12	0	0	0	0	71.2	74	295	34	24	1	1	3	2	12	0	69	1	3
Desabrias, Mark, Padres	2	1	.667	3.11	19	2	0	0	13	0	55.0	52	234	28	19	2	1	1	7	20	0	28	3	0
Duncan, Devohn, Padres	4	5	.444	3.12	11	10	0	0	0	0	52.0	47	231	39	18	2	1	3	4	22	0	40	12	5
Paulino, Jose, Athletics	9	2	.818	3.19	15	13	0	0	2	0	87.1	74	343	35	31	5	2	2	2	17	0	72	2	3
Baez, Benito, Athletics*	5	1	.833	3.34	14	11	1	0	0	0	70.0	64	303	35	26	2	2	2	4	28	0	83	2	0
Stahl, Anders, Rockies	3	5	.375	3.46	12	12	0	0	0	0	52.0	42	223	31	20	1	3	1	3	19	0	44	9	2

DEPARTMENTAL LEADERS: W—Ishee, Paulino, 9; L—Rosa, 9; Pct.—Ishee, Paulino, .818; G—Kazmirski, 28; GS—Bishop, Druckrey, Paulino, 13; CG—Bishop, 3; ShO—Bishop, Kolb, Romero, Stockstill, 1; GF—Kazmirski, 25; Sv.—Kazmirski, Pavlovich, 10; IP—Bishop, 96.0; H—DeLosSantos, 81; TBF—Bishop, 382; R—Podjan, 58; ER—Podjan, 45; HR—Paulino, 5; SH—DeLosSantos, 5; SF—Blanco, Ishee, 6; HB—Druckrey, 8; BB—Ishee, 41; IBB—DeLosSantos, Kazmirski, Soriano, 2; SO—Bishop 134; WP—Podjan, 14; Bk.—Douglas, 11.

ALL PITCHERS

*Lefthanded pitcher.

Pitcher, Team	W	L	Pct.	ERA	G	GS	CG	ShO	GF	Sv.	IP	H	TBF	R	ER	HR	SH	SF	HB	BB	IBB	SO	WP	Bk.
Abreu, Oscar, Athletics	1	2	.333	7.96	20	1	0	0	7	0	26.0	33	146	30	23	0	0	1	2	35	0	29	11	2
Agosto, Stevenson, Angels*	0	1	.000	5.40	1	1	0	0	0	0	5.0	3	22	5	3	0	2	1	1	2	0	2	3	0
Ashley, Antonio, Angels	0	0	.000	2.25	5	0	0	0	2	0	8.0	6	31	3	2	0	0	0	1	0	0	4	0	1
Baez, Benito, Athletics*	5	1	.833	3.34	14	11	1	0	0	0	70.0	64	303	35	26	2	2	2	4	28	0	83	2	0
Barnes, Larry, Brewers	0	1	.000	1.77	6	5	0	0	0	0	20.1	16	84	4	4	0	0	0	0	14	0	31	1	1
Bennett, Tom, Athletics	1	1	.500	2.72	11	6	0	0	0	0	36.1	20	150	16	11	1	1	1	2	16	0	46	4	0
Bishop, Joshua, Brewers	8	2	.800	2.16	14	13	3	1	0	0	96.0	64	382	34	23	4	3	1	1	29	0	134	9	3
Blanco, Roger, Mariners	1	6	.143	5.50	12	12	0	0	0	0	54.0	60	247	43	33	2	1	6	7	24	0	27	5	2
Blevins, Jeremy, Angels	5	1	.833	2.45	11	9	0	0	0	0	51.1	39	224	20	14	0	2	0	4	32	0	48	4	1
Bonilla, Denis, Mariners*	1	1	.500	3.06	21	0	0	0	10	2	35.1	39	151	21	12	0	0	3	1	9	0	39	2	0
Bowles, Matt, Brewers	0	1	.000	6.60	7	0	0	0	0	0	15.0	20	69	12	11	0	0	2	1	3	0	4	3	1
Burton, Isaac, Mariners	0	0	.000	3.00	2	0	0	0	0	0	3.0	1	15	2	1	0	0	1	0	2	0	1	0	0
Cesar, Dionys, Athletics	0	0	.000	0.00	1	0	0	0	0	0	2.0	0	6	0	0	0	0	0	0	1	0	2	0	0
Clark, Chris, Padres	5	5	.500	2.10	13	12	1	0	0	0	73.0	52	313	30	17	1	1	1	7	38	0	82	5	0
Contreras, Orlando, Rockies	2	2	.500	6.04	16	0	0	0	5	1	28.1	40	144	27	19	0	1	2	0	17	0	18	0	0
Costello, Terrance, Athletics*	2	3	.400	3.74	12	6	0	0	2	0	43.1	46	180	22	18	2	0	0	2	9	0	41	5	1
Craig, Casey, Mariners	1	0	1.000	6.00	2	0	0	0	0	0	3.0	5	14	2	2	0	0	0	2	0	0	1	0	0
Darrell, Thomas, Angels	4	3	.571	1.71	18	5	0	0	7	2	63.0	51	254	18	12	1	1	3	4	14	0	49	3	1
DeLosSantos, Valerio, Brewers*	4	6	.400	2.20	14	12	0	0	1	0	82.0	81	341	34	20	3	5	4	6	12	2	57	6	2

Pitcher, Team	W	L	Pct.	ERA	G	GS	CG	ShO	GF	Sv.	IP	H	TBF	R	ER	HR	SH	SF	HB	BB	IBB	SO	WP	Bk.
Derenches, Albert, Mariners*	1	2	.333	3.31	19	0	0	0	3	0	35.1	36	155	15	13	1	0	1	1	21	0	40	5	0
Desabrias, Mark, Padres	2	1	.667	3.11	19	2	0	0	13	0	55.0	52	234	28	19	2	1	1	7	20	0	28	3	0
Douglas, Reggie, Rockies	0	1	.000	9.33	15	0	0	0	9	1	27.0	37	135	29	28	1	2	0	2	19	0	17	11	11
Drewien, Dan, Padres	0	0	.000	0.00	1	0	0	0	0	0	2.2	2	11	1	0	0	0	0	1	0	0	2	0	0
Druckrey, Chris, Rockies	0	8	.000	5.04	14	13	0	0	1	0	69.2	75	330	54	39	1	0	1	8	38	0	65	13	3
Drysdale, Brooks, Angels	0	0	.000	8.10	4	0	0	0	3	1	3.1	4	16	4	3	0	0	0	0	1	1	7	0	0
Duncan, Devohn, Padres	4	5	.444	3.12	11	10	0	0	0	0	52.0	47	231	39	18	2	1	3	4	22	0	40	12	5
Estrada, Horacio, Brewers*	0	1	.000	3.71	8	1	0	0	3	2	17.0	13	73	9	7	1	1	1	0	8	0	21	4	2
Ettles, Mark, Padres	0	0	.000	5.79	3	0	0	0	0	0	4.2	6	24	6	3	1	0	0	1	4	0	2	2	1
Florentino, Osmil, Rockies	0	2	.000	6.85	19	0	0	0	11	2	43.1	55	208	42	33	2	3	3	2	17	0	27	1	5
Foster, Cliff, Athletics	0	0	.000	27.00	1	1	0	0	0	0	1.0	4	8	4	3	0	0	0	0	0	0	0	0	0
Glick, Dave, Brewers*	2	0	1.000	4.26	18	0	0	0	4	0	25.1	24	115	13	12	0	1	0	1	14	0	29	4	4
Gomez, Alex, Angels	4	3	.571	5.58	13	3	0	0	2	0	30.2	30	143	21	19	0	1	1	4	23	1	31	8	0
Gonzalez, Jose, Mariners	4	4	.500	5.30	12	10	0	0	0	0	56.0	56	250	40	33	1	1	2	2	31	0	66	8	5
Guerrero, Diogene, Athletics	0	0	.000	0.00	1	0	0	0	0	0	1.0	0	4	0	0	0	0	0	1	0	0	0	0	1
Gutierrez, Alfredo, Brewers	0	0	.000	6.48	7	0	0	0	4	0	8.1	10	44	9	6	0	0	1	2	8	0	7	1	0
Gutierrez, Javier, Mariners	1	4	.200	5.88	14	4	1	0	4	0	33.2	43	159	31	22	4	1	2	1	19	0	38	8	1
Guzman, Jonathan, Brewers*	0	0	.000	10.38	11	0	0	0	4	0	13.0	18	71	16	15	1	0	2	3	8	0	4	2	3
Hamada, Nori, Angels	0	0	.000	13.50	1	0	0	0	0	0	0.2	1	4	1	1	0	0	0	0	1	0	0	2	0
Henderson, James, Padres	0	1	.000	8.22	3	1	0	0	0	0	7.2	12	40	8	7	0	0	0	1	6	0	12	1	3
Hernandez, Victor, Athletics	0	0	.000	18.00	1	0	0	0	0	0	1.0	2	6	2	2	0	0	0	0	1	0	0	0	0
Hill, Tyrone, Brewers*	0	0	.000	3.18	4	4	0	0	0	0	11.1	8	48	4	4	0	0	0	0	5	0	9	1	0
Ishee, Gabe, Brewers	9	2	.818	3.63	15	12	2	0	1	0	79.1	78	344	41	32	0	1	6	5	41	1	90	12	2
Jacob, Russell, Mariners	6	2	.750	2.88	12	11	0	0	1	0	56.1	47	248	29	18	0	0	1	3	31	0	54	6	2
Jimenez, Jhonny, Mariners	1	2	.333	4.45	19	0	0	0	6	0	32.1	39	147	23	16	1	0	3	2	14	0	28	2	4
Johnson, Shelby, Mariners	1	1	.500	5.29	9	0	0	0	3	0	17.0	12	84	15	10	0	1	1	2	9	0	14	2	0
Kammerer, James, Rockies*	1	0	1.000	0.96	6	0	0	0	5	0	9.1	11	43	5	1	0	0	0	3	0	14	1	0
Kaye, Justin, Mariners	0	1	.000	10.71	12	0	0	0	4	0	19.1	33	111	28	23	1	0	2	1	19	0	13	4	0
Kazmirski, Robert, Athletics	4	0	1.000	2.13	28	0	0	0	25	10	38.0	36	155	13	9	0	0	1	6	2	32	2	7
Kjos, Ryan, Athletics	0	0	.000	19.64	3	0	0	0	0	0	3.2	9	23	10	8	1	0	0	1	1	0	5	2	0
Knickerbocker, Thomas, A's*	4	3	.571	3.92	17	7	0	0	1	1	43.2	39	193	27	19	0	0	5	25	0	40	7	0
Kolb, Brandon, Padres	1	1	.500	1.17	4	4	1	1	0	0	23.0	13	100	10	3	0	0	3	13	0	21	4	0
Law, Khris, Athletics	0	1	.000	6.00	2	0	0	0	0	0	3.0	2	15	3	2	0	0	0	3	0	3	0	0
Leftwich, Phil, Angels	1	1	.500	0.45	4	4	0	0	0	0	20.0	13	76	4	1	0	0	2	0	2	0	32	0	0
Lenhardt, Bruce, Brewers	1	0	1.000	3.86	2	0	0	0	0	0	4.2	8	23	2	2	0	2	1	0	3	1	0
Lopez, Jose, Angels	2	2	.500	2.40	11	7	0	0	0	0	41.1	45	178	18	11	0	0	6	13	0	36	5	2
Lopez, Rodrigo, Padres	1	1	.500	5.45	11	7	0	0	0	0	34.2	41	162	29	21	0	1	2	2	14	0	33	3	1
Lowe, Derek, Mariners	1	0	1.000	0.93	2	2	0	0	0	0	9.2	5	35	1	1	0	0	0	2	0	11	0	0
Mahlberg, John, Rockies	2	3	.400	4.38	10	7	0	0	0	0	39.0	44	178	27	19	3	2	1	21	0	52	3	1
Martinez, Hipolito, Athletics	0	0	.000	.000	1	0	0	0	1	0	0.2	1	2	0	0	0	0	0	0	0	0	0	0	0
Martino, Wil, Rockies*	3	1	.750	5.32	16	3	0	0	6	0	44.0	48	203	27	26	2	0	4	23	0	44	7	2
Matlack, Dan, Padres	0	2	.000	3.58	16	0	0	0	5	0	27.2	20	122	15	11	1	2	3	14	0	16	0	1
Mays, Joseph, Mariners	2	3	.400	3.25	10	10	0	0	0	0	44.1	41	189	24	16	0	2	2	1	18	0	44	7	1
McDonald, Matt, Athletics*	1	0	1.000	2.20	5	1	0	0	2	0	16.1	16	71	7	4	1	0	2	1	9	0	23	1	1
McGuire, Brandon, Angels	1	0	1.000	3.38	2	0	0	0	0	0	5.1	3	20	3	2	0	0	0	3	0	6	1	0
Moreno, Juan, Athletics*	6	2	.750	1.21	20	0	0	0	8	0	44.2	36	181	10	6	1	1	1	0	20	0	49	2	5
Nash, Damond, Padres	1	3	.250	7.31	15	3	1	0	2	0	44.1	55	212	42	36	2	2	3	27	0	32	4	0
Neiman, Joshua, Padres	0	1	.000	4.24	10	0	0	0	4	1	17.0	20	74	9	8	2	0	1	3	0	18	2	1
Nivar, Amaury, Rockies	0	1	.000	4.50	2	0	0	0	2	0	2.0	2	8	1	1	0	0	0	0	0	1	0	0
Nivar, Amaury, Rockies	0	0	.000	11.12	6	0	0	0	1	0	11.1	14	63	18	14	0	0	1	2	14	0	10	4	1
Nix, Wayne, Athletics	0	2	.000	5.79	6	3	0	0	0	0	14.0	15	57	10	9	3	1	0	1	4	0	14	1	0
Nogowski, Brandon, Mariners*	0	2	.000	2.70	20	0	0	0	17	7	26.2	30	123	10	8	0	0	1	0	13	1	27	4	0
Norris, McKenzie, Brewers	1	0	1.000	0.61	2	2	0	0	0	0	14.2	7	60	4	1	0	0	0	0	6	1	14	3	0
Osteen, Gavin, Athletics*	0	1	.000	0.00	1	1	0	0	0	0	2.0	1	7	0	0	0	0	0	1	0	1	0	0
Palki, Jeromy, Mariners	0	0	.000	7.94	4	0	0	0	1	0	5.2	7	29	7	5	0	1	0	5	0	2	1	0
Patterson, Ken, Angels*	0	0	.000	0.00	1	1	0	0	0	0	3.0	0	10	0	0	0	0	0	1	0	3	0	0
Paulino, Jose, Athletics	9	2	.818	3.19	15	13	0	0	2	0	87.1	74	343	35	31	5	2	2	2	17	0	72	2	3
Pavlovich, Tony, Brewers	0	2	.000	4.00	19	0	0	0	18	10	18.0	20	78	10	8	0	2	1	0	3	0	20	1	0
Perez, Jayson, Padres	0	0	.000	9.00	2	0	0	0	1	1	2.0	3	11	2	2	0	0	0	2	0	1	1	0
Perez, Jesse, Brewers	2	2	.500	2.70	16	0	0	0	9	4	20.0	16	84	6	6	1	0	1	2	4	1	20	3	1
Plant, David, Brewers	4	2	.667	1.16	14	6	0	0	4	2	51.0	34	198	11	10	1	0	0	2	12	0	51	2	1
Podjan, James, Rockies	2	7	.222	9.00	17	5	0	0	3	0	45.0	71	231	58	45	3	2	3	3	27	0	30	14	1
Polanco, Juan, Athletics	0	0	.000	18.00	1	0	0	0	0	0	1.0	1	5	2	2	0	0	0	1	0	1	3
Prempas, Lyle, Brewers*	6	5	.545	4.09	13	6	0	0	2	0	50.2	49	226	33	23	1	2	2	1	28	0	67	4	0
Preston, George, Brewers	0	0	1.000	0.00	2	0	0	0	1	0	7.2	5	30	1	0	0	0	0	0	3	0	15	1	1
Quinteros, Steve, Angels	0	0	.000	4.38	7	1	0	0	1	0	12.1	19	63	10	6	1	0	0	4	3	1	13	2	2
Richmond, Terrance, Angels	0	0	.000	9.00	1	0	0	0	0	0	1.0	1	5	1	1	1	0	0	0	1	0	0	0	0
Riley, Brian, Angels	0	1	.000	3.00	17	0	0	0	17	9	15.0	11	63	5	5	0	1	0	1	10	0	16	2	1
Rodriguez, Hector, Angels	2	2	.500	2.92	9	2	1	0	2	0	24.2	21	99	9	8	1	1	1	2	9	0	21	8	0
Rojas, Miguel, Angels	1	0	1.000	4.66	9	0	0	0	4	0	9.2	10	47	6	5	0	0	2	6	5	0	7	3	4
Romero, John, Angels	7	3	.700	2.41	18	6	2	1	4	1	71.0	57	291	29	19	0	0	2	5	18	1	64	8	4
Rosa, Cristy, Rockies	0	9	.000	5.37	12	12	0	0	0	0	58.2	77	273	56	35	0	2	4	2	16	0	42	8	2
Schroeder, Scott, Padres	0	1	.000	7.36	2	2	0	0	0	0	7.1	12	38	7	6	0	0	0	2	2	0	8	1	0
Segura, Juan, Rockies*	0	1	.000	5.22	20	0	0	0	12	1	29.1	32	140	19	17	0	1	4	3	19	1	20	1	0
Smith, Josh, Padres*	1	2	.333	1.69	8	0	0	0	4	1	10.2	12	53	8	2	0	1	0	1	8	0	8	6	1
Soriano, Jacobo, Angels	0	1	.000	3.09	11	0	0	0	9	4	11.2	9	53	6	4	0	0	3	7	2	10	0	2
Stahl, Anders, Rockies	3	5	.375	3.46	12	12	0	0	0	0	52.0	42	223	31	20	1	3	1	3	19	0	44	9	2
Stockstill, Jason, Angels*	3	1	.750	5.08	12	7	2	1	0	0	44.1	38	195	29	25	1	1	2	3	22	1	31	3	2
Suazo, Rigoberto, Athletics	1	0	1.000	1.69	2	0	0	0	1	1	5.1	3	20	1	1	0	0	0	1	2	0	5	0	1
Suzuki, Mac, Mariners	1	0	1.000	6.75	4	3	0	0	0	0	4.0	5	19	4	3	1	0	0	0	3	0	0	0
Szimanski, Tom, Mariners	0	0	.000	4.15	4	0	0	0	2	0	4.1	2	18	2	2	0	0	0	0	3	0	5	1	1
Tijerina, Tano, Brewers	0	0	.000	4.50	1	1	0	0	0	0	2.0	3	10	1	1	0	0	0	0	2	0	1	1	0
Tisdale, Warren, Mariners	1	1	.500	1.64	13	0	0	0	3	1	22.0	17	88	5	4	0	0	1	0	10	0	9	3	0

Pitcher, Team	W	L	Pct.	ERA	G	GS	CG	ShO	GF	Sv.	IP	H	TBF	R	ER	HR	SH	SF	HB	BB	IBB	SO	WP	Bk.
Torres, Derek, Brewers	0	0	.000	1.69	6	0	0	0	3	0	5.1	2	21	1	1	0	0	0	2	2	0	7	1	0
Torres, Luis, Padres	4	3	.571	4.75	22	2	0	0	20	8	36.0	36	163	24	19	2	2	3	5	20	1	34	4	4
Updike, Jon, Brewers	0	0	.000	12.00	4	0	0	0	1	0	3.0	2	19	4	4	0	0	0		8	0	3	2	0
Volkman, Keith, Angels*	5	2	.714	2.53	13	10	0	0	0	0	67.2	61	279	30	19	0	1	0	4	25	0	49	5	1
Walker, Kevin, Padres*	5	5	.500	3.01	13	12	0	0	0	0	71.2	74	295	34	24	1	1	3	2	12	0	69	1	3
Weymouth, Martin, Mariners	2	3	.400	3.98	9	4	0	0	1	0	31.2	37	144	23	14	2	1	1	2	10	0	26	3	1
Williams, Patrick, Rockies	0	2	.000	5.65	5	3	0	0	0	0	14.1	21	78	16	9	0	0	0	1	10	0	6	0	0

COMBINATION SHUTOUTS: **Angels (4)**—Darrell-Rodriguez-Riley, Lopez-Romero-Riley, Volkman-Gomez-Soriano, Volkman-Romero. **Athletics (3)**—Baez-Costello, Osteen-Plant-Costello-Kazmirski, Paulino-Kazmirski. **Brewers (1)**—Ishee-DeLosSantos. **Mariners (1)**—Jacob-Johnson-Derenches-Kaye. **Padres (1)**—Clark-Smith-Torres. **Rockies (0)**—None.

NO-HIT GAMES: Stockstill, Angels, defeated Brewers, 3-0, July 11.

1995 FIELDING

TEAM

Team	Pct.	G	PO	A	E	TC	DP	PB	Team	Pct.	G	PO	A	E	TC	DP	PB
Angels	.955	56	1467	654	100	2221	53	20	Brewers	.944	56	1481	621	125	2227	37	22
Athletics	.949	56	1474	602	111	2187	54	17	Padres	.935	55	1408	571	137	2116	43	15
Mariners	.945	56	1481	649	123	2253	49	28	Rockies	.933	55	1420	628	146	2194	43	15

TRIPLE PLAYS: None.

INDIVIDUAL

FIRST BASEMEN

NOTE: All caps denotes fielding-percentage leader based on 28 games for catchers, 37 for all other non-pitchers and 56 innings for pitchers. *Throws lefthanded.

Player, Team	Pct.	G	PO	A	E	TC	DP
ARIAS, David, Mariners*	.989	46	436	27	5	468	36
Balcazar, Carlos, Angels	1.000	4	23	2	0	25	0
Barnes, Larry, Angels*	.987	55	494	19	7	520	49
Cruz, Cirilo, Mariners	1.000	1	16	0	0	16	0
Hernandez, Ramon, Athletics	.966	13	81	3	3	87	10
Jacobo, Roberto, Padres*	.980	4	47	2	1	50	4
Johnson, Jace, Athletics	1.000	1	5	1	0	6	0
Jones, Timothy, Athletics	1.000	1	1	0	0	1	0
Judge, Mike, Brewers	.947	5	32	4	2	38	2
Lindsey, John, Rockies	.964	26	209	8	8	225	15
McNally, Jason, Rockies	1.000	1	10	1	0	11	1
Niles, David, Rockies*	.983	34	267	24	5	296	17
Paciorek, Peter, Padres*	.988	53	462	26	6	494	37
Paulino, Arturo, Athletics	1.000	4	32	2	0	34	3
Peters, Tony, Brewers	.985	24	184	17	3	204	13
Polanco, Juan, Athletics	.989	11	89	3	1	93	5
Rauer, Troy, Athletics	.941	10	92	3	6	101	7
Rendon, Miguel, Brewers	.929	4	25	1	2	28	0
Rodriguez, Juan, Padres	1.000	2	3	0	0	3	0
Rogue, Francisco, Brewers	1.000	4	12	1	0	13	1
Scheker, Luis, Athletics	.970	16	123	8	4	135	19
Ventura, Wilfredo, Athletics	.979	5	43	3	1	47	1
Walther, Christopher, Brewers	.978	26	235	26	6	267	14
Williams, Marcus, Mariners	.950	11	92	4	5	101	6

SECOND BASEMEN

Player, Team	Pct.	G	PO	A	E	TC	DP
Campusano, Carlos, Brewers	.750	4	1	2	1	4	1
Cesar, Dionys, Athletics	.930	34	67	65	10	142	15
Cespedes, Angel, Rockies	.916	15	24	52	7	83	6
Clark, John, Rockies	.951	17	44	53	5	102	13
Davis, Josh, Padres	1.000	3	7	7	0	14	1
Delacruz, Jesus, Angels	.890	21	21	44	8	73	9
Figueroa, Luis, Mariners	1.000	2	1	3	0	4	0
Freeman, Terrance, Athletics	.925	25	43	43	7	93	8
Groseclose, Harold, Rockies	.934	23	44	69	8	121	9
Guerrero, Diogene, Athletics	1.000	1	1	0	0	1	0
Harris, Rico, Brewers	.936	40	82	79	11	172	12
Harrison, Adonis, Mariners	.950	43	83	88	9	180	23
Jackson, Rod, Padres	.916	44	79	117	18	214	23
Kirkpatrick, Brian, Rockies	1.000	3	5	6	0	11	1
Lara, Edward, Athletics	1.000	1	1	1	0	2	0
Llanos, Alexis, Angels	.913	10	9	12	2	23	2
Paulino, Arturo, Athletics	.750	2	3	3	2	8	1
Polanco, Juan, Athletics	1.000	2	5	5	0	10	2
Roche, Michael, Brewers	.918	20	33	57	8	98	9
Rodriguez, Franklin, Mariners	.889	14	23	33	7	63	4
Rodriguez, John, Padres	.960	7	12	12	1	25	3
Rosario, Eliezer, Padres	.786	2	4	7	3	14	2
Rutherford, Daryl, Padres	.889	3	4	4	1	9	1
Vazquez, Ramon, Mariners	1.000	1	5	2	0	7	2
WARDROP, Adam, Angels	.960	37	74	96	7	177	23

THIRD BASEMEN

Player, Team	Pct.	G	PO	A	E	TC	DP
Acevedo, Juan, Rockies	.804	15	8	33	10	51	4
Campusano, Carlos, Brewers	.854	36	17	65	14	96	1
Cesar, Dionys, Athletics	1.000	4	2	7	0	9	0
CHAVEZ, Steven, Padres	.871	51	44	111	23	178	13
Clark, John, Rockies	1.000	3	5	2	0	7	1
Cowsill, Brendon, Angels	.927	33	19	96	9	124	8
Cruz, Cirilo, Mariners	.864	22	13	38	8	59	3
Delacruz, Jesus, Angels	.867	5	2	11	2	15	1
Figueroa, Luis, Mariners	.921	24	9	61	6	76	3
Hernandez, Ramon, Athletics	.813	6	6	7	3	16	0
Johnson, Duan, Mariners	.923	8	9	15	2	26	1
Kirkpatrick, Brian, Rockies	.780	23	16	30	13	59	3
Lara, Edward, Athletics	.667	2	2	0	1	3	0
Lawrence, Mike, Angels	.900	17	10	26	4	40	3
McNally, Jason, Rockies	.870	17	8	32	6	46	0
Paulino, Arturo, Athletics	.881	16	16	36	7	59	0
Polanco, Juan, Athletics	.880	34	31	72	14	117	10
Roche, Michael, Brewers	.714	18	8	17	10	35	1
Rodriguez, Franklin, Mariners	1.000	2	0	2	0	2	0
Rodriguez, John, Padres	.556	4	1	4	4	9	0
Rutherford, Daryl, Padres	1.000	2	2	2	0	4	0
Schaub, Greg, Brewers	.933	11	6	8	1	15	1
Vazquez, Ramon, Mariners	.900	3	4	5	1	10	0
Wardrop, Adam, Angels	.852	10	7	16	4	27	2

SHORTSTOPS

Player, Team	Pct.	G	PO	A	E	TC	DP
Campusano, Carlos, Brewers	.921	19	15	43	5	63	5
Carmona, Cesarin, Padres	.865	14	17	28	7	52	7
Castro, Nelson, Angels	.939	55	106	173	18	297	32
Cesar, Dionys, Athletics	.920	8	8	15	2	25	6
Cespedes, Angel, Rockies	.889	4	5	11	2	18	3
Clark, John, Rockies	.883	32	51	92	19	162	12
Figueroa, Luis, Mariners	.857	1	0	6	1	7	1
Groseclose, Harold, Rockies	.955	8	15	27	2	44	7
Harrison, Adonis, Mariners	1.000	1	1	1	0	2	0
Johnson, Duan, Mariners	.897	20	29	67	11	107	11
Kirkpatrick, Brian, Rockies	.867	12	15	24	6	45	4
LARA, Edward, Athletics	.963	45	80	127	8	215	25
Llanos, Alexis, Angels	1.000	4	1	2	0	3	1
Paulino, Arturo, Athletics	.926	7	8	17	2	27	4
Polanco, Juan, Athletics	1.000	1	4	4	0	8	0
Ritter, Ryan, Brewers	.786	3	5	6	3	14	0
Rodriguez, John, Padres	.841	18	17	41	11	69	6
Rosario, Eliezer, Padres	.957	5	8	14	1	23	3
Rutherford, Daryl, Padres	.898	25	32	47	9	88	5
Singleton, Samuel, Brewers	.924	46	66	104	14	184	18
Vazquez, Ramon, Mariners	.940	35	51	107	10	168	20
Wardrop, Adam, Angels	.667	3	0	2	1	3	0

OUTFIELDERS

Player, Team	Pct.	G	PO	A	E	TC	DP
Acevedo, Juan, Rockies	.882	12	15	0	2	17	0
Alamo, Efrain, Rockies	.900	36	60	3	7	70	1
Allen, Tony, Brewers	.957	43	43	1	2	46	0
Barnes, Larry, Angels*	.750	2	2	1	1	4	0

Player, Team	Pct.	G	PO	A	E	TC	DP
Barrios, Esteban, Angels*	1.000	13	17	1	0	18	0
Chambers, Victor, Athletics	.893	29	23	2	3	28	0
Cruz, Cirilo, Mariners	.882	9	14	1	2	17	0
Cruz, Francisco, Padres	.000	1	0	0	1	1	0
Delgado, Ariel, Angels*	.949	51	69	6	4	79	1
Ducasse, Luis, Athletics	1.000	6	8	0	0	8	0
Duverge, Salvador, Rockies	.896	39	55	5	7	67	1
Erstad, Darin, Angels*	1.000	3	3	0	0	3	0
Fowler, Marvin, Mariners	.886	26	28	3	4	35	1
Gordon, Garfield, Rockies	.915	32	54	0	5	59	0
Guerrero, Diogene, Athletics	.935	38	51	7	4	62	0
Hernandez, Victor, Athletics	1.000	13	12	3	0	15	1
Hunter, Andy, Padres	.980	32	47	3	1	51	0
Hutchins, Norm, Angels*	.895	14	17	0	2	19	0
Iapoce, Anthony, Brewers*	1.000	2	3	0	0	3	0
Isom, Daleon, Mariners	.875	26	35	0	5	40	0
Jacobo, Roberto, Padres*	.797	39	50	5	14	69	0
Jacobus, Brian, Padres*	.915	41	58	7	6	71	0
Jones, Timothy, Athletics	.978	22	42	3	1	46	1
Law, Khris, Athletics	.976	32	37	4	1	42	1
Martinez, Hipolito, Athletics	.964	40	48	6	2	56	0
McDavid, Ray, Padres	1.000	1	1	0	0	1	0
McDougall, Matt, Mariners	.921	25	33	2	3	38	1
Moore, Donald, Brewers	.964	35	26	1	1	28	0
Moore, James, Padres	.944	13	17	0	1	18	0
Niles, David, Rockies*	.800	1	3	1	1	5	1
Pernell, Brandon, Padres	.950	44	69	7	4	80	2
Peters, Tony, Brewers	.970	26	32	0	1	33	0
Rauer, Troy, Athletics	1.000	8	7	1	0	8	0
Rendon, Miguel, Brewers	.944	18	16	1	1	18	1
Rodriguez, Juan, Angels	.959	40	68	3	3	74	1
Rose, Carlos, Mariners	.842	25	30	2	6	38	0
Rowson, James, Mariners	.947	28	36	0	2	38	0
Rushdan, Rasheed, Rockies	1.000	5	12	3	0	15	1
Schaub, Greg, Brewers	.955	20	21	0	1	22	0
Selga, Andres, Rockies	1.000	13	28	3	0	31	1
Silverio, Richard, Rockies*	.964	31	49	5	2	56	1
Stewart, Keith, Mariners	1.000	11	15	1	0	16	1
STUART, Rich, Angels	.976	51	76	5	2	83	0
Tolbert, Ernest, Mariners	.976	24	39	2	1	42	1
Walther, Christopher, Brewers	.963	23	26	0	1	27	0
Wilkerson, Adrian, Brewers	.973	53	64	8	2	74	1
Williams, Marcus, Mariners	.941	10	15	1	1	17	0

CATCHERS

Player, Team	Pct.	G	PO	A	E	TC	DP	PB
Balcazar, Carlos, Angels	.979	20	123	17	3	143	2	4
Davis, Josh, Padres	.963	24	194	15	8	217	0	7
Ebbert, Chad, Padres	.980	29	208	40	5	253	0	6
HERNANDEZ, Ramon, Athletics	.982	31	271	51	6	328	2	12
Jones, Ken, Padres	1.000	1	6	0	0	6	0	1
Marnell, Anthony, Padres	1.000	1	2	2	0	4	0	1
Maynard, Scott, Mariners	.978	21	152	25	4	181	0	12
McDougall, Matt, Mariners	1.000	3	8	3	0	11	0	0
McNally, Jason, Rockies	.970	23	138	24	5	167	1	7
Medrano, Teodoro, Mariners	1.000	1	4	1	0	5	0	0
Randolph, Edward, Mariners	.962	40	263	67	13	343	2	16
Rodriguez, Miguel, Brewers	.968	45	378	73	15	466	3	17
Rogue, Francisco, Brewers	.966	16	121	20	5	146	4	5
Saucedo, Robert, Angels	.972	20	89	17	3	109	0	11
Ventura, Wilfredo, Athletics	.979	29	216	19	5	240	2	5
Veras, Illuminado, Angels	.972	30	218	28	7	253	1	5
Vidal, Carlos, Rockies	.961	34	251	47	12	310	7	8

PITCHERS

Player, Team	Pct.	G	PO	A	E	TC	DP
Abreu, Oscar, Athletics	.000	20	0	0	1	1	0
Baez, Benito, Athletics*	.833	14	1	14	3	18	0
Barnes, Larry, Brewers	1.000	6	0	2	0	2	0
Bennett, Tom, Athletics	.875	11	1	13	2	16	0
Bishop, Joshua, Brewers	.962	14	3	22	1	26	0
Blanco, Roger, Mariners	.933	12	4	10	1	15	0
Blevins, Jeremy, Angels	.857	11	2	4	1	7	0
Bonilla, Denis, Mariners*	.889	21	4	4	1	9	0
Bowles, Matt, Brewers	.800	7	3	1	1	5	0
Burton, Isaac, Mariners	.500	2	1	0	1	2	0
Cesar, Dionys, Athletics	1.000	2	0	1	0	1	1
Clark, Chris, Padres	.778	13	1	6	2	9	0
Contreras, Orlando, Rockies	.833	16	2	3	1	6	0

Player, Team	Pct.	G	PO	A	E	TC	DP
Costello, Terrance, Athletics*	1.000	12	0	11	0	11	0
Craig, Casey, Mariners	1.000	2	0	1	0	1	1
Darrell, Thomas, Angels	.900	18	2	16	2	20	0
DeLosSantos, Valerio, Brewers*	.867	14	4	9	2	15	1
Derenches, Albert, Mariners*	.750	20	2	4	2	8	0
Desabrias, Mark, Padres	.846	19	0	11	2	13	0
Douglas, Reggie, Rockies	.857	15	2	4	1	7	0
Druckrey, Chris, Rockies	1.000	14	5	10	0	15	0
Drysdale, Brooks, Angels	.500	4	0	1	1	2	0
Duncan, Devohn, Padres	.909	11	3	7	1	11	0
Estrada, Horacio, Brewers*	.667	8	0	2	1	3	0
Florentino, Osmil, Rockies	.727	19	4	4	3	11	0
Foster, Cliff, Athletics	1.000	1	1	0	0	1	0
Glick, Dave, Athletics*	.875	18	0	7	1	8	0
Gomez, Alex, Angels	.500	13	0	1	1	2	0
Gonzalez, Jose, Mariners	.941	12	3	13	1	17	1
Gutierrez, Javier, Mariners	.889	14	3	5	1	9	0
Guzman, Jonathan, Brewers*	.750	11	1	2	1	4	0
Henderson, James, Padres	1.000	3	0	1	0	1	0
Hill, Tyrone, Brewers*	1.000	4	0	3	0	3	0
Ishee, Gabe, Brewers	.967	15	8	21	1	30	0
Jacob, Russell, Mariners	.875	12	5	9	2	16	2
Jimenez, Jhonny, Mariners	1.000	19	2	3	0	5	1
Johnson, Shelby, Mariners	.800	9	1	3	1	5	1
Kaye, Justin, Mariners	.333	12	0	1	2	3	0
Kazmirski, Robert, Athletics	1.000	28	1	5	0	6	0
Kjos, Ryan, Athletics	.000	3	0	0	1	1	0
Knickerbocker, Thomas, A's*	.714	17	0	5	2	7	0
Kolb, Brandon, Padres	1.000	4	2	3	0	5	0
Law, Khris, Athletics	1.000	2	0	1	0	1	0
Leftwich, Phil, Angels	.500	4	0	1	1	2	0
Lenhardt, Bruce, Brewers	1.000	2	0	1	0	1	0
Lopez, Jose, Angels	.889	11	2	6	1	9	0
Lopez, Rodrigo, Padres	.900	11	1	8	1	10	0
Lowe, Derek, Mariners	1.000	2	0	2	0	2	0
Mahlberg, John, Rockies	1.000	10	3	5	0	8	0
Martino, Wil, Rockies*	.833	16	0	5	1	6	0
Matlack, Dan, Brewers	.800	16	1	3	1	5	0
Mays, Joseph, Mariners	.833	10	3	12	3	18	2
McDonald, Matt, Athletics*	.750	5	0	3	1	4	0
Moreno, Juan, Athletics*	.688	20	2	9	5	16	1
Nash, Damond, Padres	1.000	15	5	8	0	13	0
Neiman, Joshua, Padres	1.000	10	1	1	0	2	1
Niles, David, Rockies*	1.000	2	0	1	0	1	0
Nivar, Amaury, Rockies	1.000	6	1	0	0	1	0
Nix, Wayne, Athletics	1.000	6	1	0	0	1	0
Nogowski, Brandon, Mariners*	1.000	20	1	2	0	3	0
Norris, McKenzie, Brewers	.500	2	0	1	1	2	0
Palki, Jeromy, Mariners	1.000	4	1	1	0	2	0
Patterson, Ken, Angels*	1.000	1	2	0	0	2	0
Paulino, Jose, Athletics	.750	15	2	7	3	12	0
Pavlovich, Tony, Brewers	1.000	19	1	4	0	5	0
Perez, Jesse, Brewers	.889	16	4	4	1	9	0
PLANT, David, Athletics	1.000	14	6	12	0	18	0
Podjan, James, Rockies	.778	17	2	12	4	18	0
Polanco, Juan, Brewers	1.000	1	1	0	0	1	0
Prempas, Lyle, Brewers*	.750	13	5	7	4	16	0
Preston, George, Brewers	.333	2	0	1	2	3	0
Quinteros, Steve, Angels	1.000	7	0	2	0	2	1
Riley, Brian, Angels	1.000	17	1	2	0	3	0
Rodriguez, Hector, Angels	.625	9	1	4	3	8	0
Rojas, Miguel, Angels	1.000	9	0	1	0	1	0
ROMERO, John, Angels	1.000	18	3	15	0	18	2
Rosa, Cristy, Rockies	.850	12	5	12	3	20	0
Schroeder, Scott, Padres	.500	2	0	1	1	2	0
Segura, Juan, Rockies*	1.000	20	0	4	0	4	0
Smith, Josh, Padres*	1.000	8	0	2	0	2	0
Soriano, Jacobo, Angels	1.000	11	0	2	0	2	1
Stahl, Anders, Rockies	.938	12	3	12	1	16	0
Stockstill, Jason, Angels*	.875	12	1	6	1	8	0
Suzuki, Mac, Mariners	1.000	4	1	0	0	1	0
Szimanski, Tom, Mariners	1.000	4	1	2	0	3	0
Tisdale, Warren, Mariners	1.000	13	3	4	0	7	0
Torres, Derek, Brewers	1.000	6	1	0	0	1	0
Torres, Luis, Padres	.833	22	3	7	2	12	0
Volkman, Keith, Angels*	.900	13	2	16	2	20	0
Walker, Kevin, Padres*	.882	13	3	12	2	17	1
Weymouth, Martin, Mariners	.800	9	2	6	2	10	0
Williams, Patrick, Rockies	1.000	5	2	1	0	3	0

The following players did not have any fielding statistics at the positions indicated or appeared only as a designated hitter, pinch-hitter or pinch-runner: Agosto, p; Ashley, p; C. Cruz, 2b; Drewien, p; Ducasse, 2b; Ettles, p; Guerrero, 3b, p; A. Gutierrez, p; Hamada, p; M. Harris, dh; R. Harris, of; V. Hernandez, p; D. Johnson, 1b; Kammerer, p; Martinez, p; McGuire, p; Needham, dh, ph; Osteen, p; Ja. Perez, p; Randolph, of; Richmond, p; Suazo, p; Tijerina, p; Updike, p.

LEAGUE CHAMPIONS

Year	Team	Pct.
1988—	Peoria Brewers	.690
1989—	Peoria Brewers	.732
1990—	Peoria Brewers	.679

Year	Team	Pct.
1991—	Scottsdale A's	.650
1992—	Scottsdale A's	.607
1993—	Scottsdale A's	.636

Year	Team	Pct.
1994—	Chandler Cardinals	.607
1995—	Scottsdale A's	.661

SUMMER CLASS A *Arizona League*

DOMINICAN SUMMER LEAGUE

1995 FINAL STANDINGS

WEST DIVISION

Team	W	L	T	Pct.	GB
Toronto	44	24	0	.647	......
New York Mets	41	27	0	.603	3
New York Yankees	31	37	0	.456	13
Pittsburgh	30	36	0	.455	13
Kansas City/Colorado	24	40	1	.375	18

CENTRAL DIVISION

Team	W	L	T	Pct.	GB
Cleveland	48	20	1	.706	......
Oakland	44	21	1	.677	2½
Texas	39	28	0	.582	8½
Florida	26	42	0	.382	22
Chicago (N.L.)/San Diego	22	45	1	.328	25½

EAST DIVISION

Team	W	L	T	Pct.	GB
Seattle	45	21	0	.682	......
Detroit	34	34	1	.500	12
Dodgers I	28	36	0	.438	16
Philadelphia/St. Louis	25	44	0	.362	21½
Montreal	21	47	1	.309	25

SAN PEDRO DE MACORIS DIVISION

Team	W	L	T	Pct.	GB
Toyo Carp	58	13	0	.817	......
Dodgers II	44	25	0	.638	13
California	31	39	1	.443	26½
Baltimore/Chicago (A.L.)	30	40	0	.429	27½
Houston/Milwaukee	28	39	1	.418	28
San Francisco	27	44	0	.380	31
Atlanta	26	44	0	.371	31½

Club names are major league affiliations.

PLAYOFFS—Toyo Carp defeated Toronto, two games to one; Cleveland defeated Seattle, two games to one; Toyo Carp defeated Cleveland, two games to none, to win league championship.

MANAGERS—Atlanta, Pedro Gonzalez; Baltimore/Chicago (A.L.), Carlos Bernhardt; California, Charles Romero; Chicago (N.L.)/San Diego, Julio Valdez; Cleveland, Alejandro Taveras; Detroit, Felix Nivar; Dodgers I, Antonio Bautista; Dodgers II, Victor Horacio Nazario; Florida, Hilario Soriano; Houston/Milwaukee, Ricardo Aponte; Kansas City/Colorado, Oscar Martinez; Montreal, Arturo De Freitas; New York Mets, Luis Natera; New York Yankees, Rafael Concepcion; Oakland, Luis Martinez; Philadelphia/St. Louis, Wilfredo Tejeda; Pittsburgh, Ramon Sambo; San Francisco, Mateos Rojas Alou; Seattle, Ramon De Los Santos; Texas, Manuel Batista; Toronto, Ignacio Javier-Mike Guerrero; Toyo Carp, Manuel Castillo.

ALL-STAR TEAM: 1B—Pablo Sencion, Toronto; 2B—Edwin Perez, Cleveland; 3B—Marco Scuttaro, Cleveland; SS—Alfonso Guilleard, Toyo Carp; OF—Jesus Hernandez, Cleveland; Juan Moreno, N.Y. Mets; Charlie Pena, Toyo Carp; C—Ignacio Suero, Toronto; DH—Ramon Pena, Toronto; RHP—Luis Vizcaino, Oakland; LHP—Ismel Zabala, Seattle; Player of the Year—Jesus Hernandez, Cleveland; Pitcher of the Year—Luis Vizcaino, Oakland; Manager of the Year—Manuel Castillo, Toyo Carp.

1995 BATTING

TEAM

Team	Avg.	G	TPA	AB	R	H	TB	2B	3B	HR	RBI	SH	SF	HP	BB	IBB	SO	SB	CS	GDP	LOB	ShO	Slg.	OBP
Toyo Carp	.296	71	2958	2439	587	721	1023	124	30	39	469	12	48	50	409	7	346	105	31	56	559	...	.419	...
Toronto	.293	68	2666	2294	409	671	955	103	11	53	339	19	19	43	291	15	391	143	72	60	517	...	.416	...
Cleveland	.291	69	2753	2399	461	699	956	130	38	17	366	21	27	51	255	11	305	124	44	58	517	...	.398	...
Seattle	.290	68	2592	2181	427	633	963	100	19	64	370	20	18	35	338	19	390	77	61	60	514	...	.442	...
Texas	.277	67	2613	2171	419	601	835	94	22	32	330	11	23	41	367	7	407	87	63	57	536	...	.385	...
N.Y. Mets	.271	68	2656	2260	420	613	957	102	10	74	345	12	25	39	320	6	433	85	53	45	517	...	.423	...
Dodgers II	.265	69	2719	2265	454	600	813	96	30	19	353	24	25	55	350	13	337	114	48	66	517	...	.359	...
N.Y. Yankees	.263	68	2577	2219	345	583	832	105	18	36	281	7	22	39	290	6	365	86	50	72	485	...	.375	...
Pittsburgh	.262	66	2529	2190	342	573	798	81	18	36	278	13	18	48	260	3	433	65	59	57	496	...	.364	...
Phil./St.L.	.258	69	2625	2306	372	595	815	108	29	18	283	13	30	31	245	9	439	114	68	60	462	...	.353	...
Oakland	.257	66	2553	2138	388	549	796	97	21	36	313	18	26	28	343	8	416	87	50	51	488	...	.372	...
Bal./Chi. AL	.256	70	2733	2323	376	595	810	82	18	33	299	21	22	40	327	5	491	145	63	50	511	...	.349	...
Dodgers I	.255	64	2502	2100	351	536	754	91	20	29	288	18	19	36	329	12	378	44	29	55	514	...	.359	...
Chi. NL/S.D.	.251	68	2576	2177	344	547	725	83	16	21	266	15	21	33	330	5	393	52	50	76	519	...	.333	...
Montreal	.248	69	2678	2306	319	573	757	95	16	19	260	19	27	50	276	15	367	117	63	59	531	...	.328	...
Florida	.243	68	2523	2186	295	532	721	83	14	26	238	25	16	34	260	6	516	91	51	49	486	...	.330	...
San Francisco	.243	71	2553	2224	333	540	726	94	16	29	266	15	8	57	249	5	412	114	44	69	488	...	.326	...
Hou./Mil.	.242	68	2659	2270	359	549	756	99	15	26	324	26	43	42	296	12	383	169	59	43	482	...	.333	...
K.C./Colo.	.240	65	2441	2121	312	508	667	63	19	16	234	11	21	29	259	7	357	72	69	65	413	...	.310	...
Atlanta	.238	70	2753	2245	360	534	725	93	22	18	288	28	25	64	391	6	449	128	48	59	574	...	.323	...
Detroit	.236	69	2742	2199	373	519	725	80	30	22	299	31	27	60	425	18	467	91	64	65	569	...	.330	...
California	.234	71	2708	2282	325	535	706	90	18	15	254	13	15	39	359	13	401	93	41	52	576	...	.309	...

INDIVIDUAL

TOP QUALIFIERS FOR BATTING CHAMPIONSHIP

Minimum 192 plate appearances.

Player, Team	Avg.	G	TPA	AB	R	H	TB	2B	3B	HR	RBI	SH	SF	HP	BB	IBB	SO	SB	CS	GDP	Slg.	OBP
Hernandez, Jesus, Cleveland	.406	66	294	251	60	102	138	22	7	0	53	0	4	2	37	2	15	20	3	2	.550	.480
Scuttaro, Marco, Cleveland	.393	66	296	262	71	103	133	18	6	0	38	2	4	8	20	1	11	32	11	4	.508	.446
Guilleard, Alfonso, Toyo Carp	.366	63	272	227	52	83	113	12	3	4	55	1	8	6	30	1	19	8	2	1	.498	.439
Pena, Ramon, Toronto	.366	59	242	213	22	78	95	11	0	2	34	0	5	8	16	3	20	3	4	6	.446	.421
Guerrero, Wascar, Seattle	.364	48	194	173	37	63	109	14	1	10	43	0	1	2	18	2	40	1	0	4	.630	.428
Moreno, Juan, N.Y. Mets	.360	58	264	228	59	82	137	14	1	13	36	1	1	2	32	1	24	15	10	2	.601	.441
Guzman, Martin, Toyo Carp	.349	58	270	229	58	80	119	16	1	7	54	0	7	5	29	0	29	0	1	3	.520	.422
Valera, Ramon, Seattle	.347	59	261	202	50	70	88	6	3	2	20	7	2	3	47	0	23	46	20	3	.436	.472
Encarnacion, Mario, Oakland	.345	64	278	229	56	79	124	11	5	8	44	1	4	4	40	0	36	17	8	3	.541	.444
Pena, Charlies, Toyo Carp	.336	68	321	241	80	81	132	27	0	8	66	0	5	9	66	2	30	17	2	4	.548	.486

ALL PLAYERS

Player, Team	Avg.	G	TPA	AB	R	H	TB	2B	3B	HR	RBI	SH	SF	HP	BB	IBB	SO	SB	CS	GDP	Slg.	OBP
Abreu, Dennis, Chi. (NL)/S.D.	.285	64	280	242	44	69	75	6	0	0	23	1	1	3	33	1	26	11	12	9	.310	.376
Abreu, Miguel, Florida	.171	60	239	210	26	36	43	4	0	1	11	2	1	5	21	1	45	4	2	8	.205	.262
Aguilar, Jose, Oakland	.357	6	16	14	2	5	6	1	0	0	2	0	0	0	2	0	2	0	0	1	.429	.438
Agustin, Filiberto, Houston	.244	42	188	168	26	41	59	13	1	1	23	1	3	1	15	2	32	18	4	1	.351	.305
Alcala, Juan F., Seattle	.164	25	71	61	5	10	13	1	1	0	7	0	1	0	9	0	18	0	1	1	.213	.268
Alfonzo, Iran, Toronto	.165	30	89	79	8	13	15	2	0	0	6	2	1	1	6	0	14	0	3	4	.190	.230
Almonte, Hector, Florida	.000	0	1	1	0	0	0	0	0	0	0	0	0	0	0	0	1	0	0	0	.000	.000
Alvarez, Carlos, Cleveland	.236	28	86	72	18	17	22	3	1	0	6	0	1	5	8	2	14	7	0	0	.306	.349
Amador, Juan, Atlanta	.130	36	89	77	9	10	11	1	0	0	2	0	0	0	12	0	21	2	1	3	.143	.247
Andujar, Eliezer, Atlanta	.228	62	264	206	35	47	54	7	0	0	33	2	7	2	47	0	29	23	5	9	.262	.366
Andujar, Juan, Florida	.253	44	169	154	15	39	46	1	0	2	16	2	1	3	9	0	37	1	1	5	.299	.305
Antonio, Junior, Houston	.259	22	29	27	2	7	11	1	0	1	3	1	0	1	0	0	10	0	1	1	.407	.286
Antunez, Javier, Montreal	.208	20	55	48	3	10	11	1	0	0	1	0	1	2	4	0	11	1	0	0	.229	.283
Araujo, Danilo, Phi./St.L.	.296	47	202	159	41	47	62	5	5	0	28	1	3	6	33	0	25	18	6	1	.390	.428
Arbornoz, Hernan, Montreal	.243	27	85	74	12	18	21	3	0	0	8	1	0	0	10	0	10	2	2	2	.284	.333
Arias, Jorge, Phi./St.L.	.188	28	85	80	6	15	19	2	1	0	6	0	1	0	4	0	11	1	0	4	.238	.224
Baez, Juan, Toronto	.250	4	5	4	0	1	1	0	0	0	1	0	0	0	1	0	2	0	0	0	.250	.400
Banci, Aaron, Florida	.200	50	186	170	18	34	54	9	1	3	19	0	1	1	14	0	37	2	4	2	.318	.263
Barreras, Rafael, Texas	.291	29	62	55	15	16	16	0	0	0	5	1	1	0	5	0	13	5	4	2	.291	.344
Basabe, Jesus, Oakland	.227	40	132	110	25	25	35	5	1	1	13	0	0	1	21	0	22	4	0	4	.318	.356
Bautista, Francisco, K.C./Colo.	.208	23	90	72	13	15	20	2	0	1	9	0	1	1	16	0	23	5	1	3	.278	.356
Bello, Gilberto, Bal./Chi.(AL)	.296	60	241	199	32	59	89	14	2	4	38	3	4	3	32	0	30	6	7	9	.447	.395
Belmonte, Jose, California	.182	36	106	88	12	16	18	2	0	0	9	0	0	4	14	0	25	3	4	3	.205	.321
Beltre, Adrian, Dodgers I	.307	62	279	218	56	67	112	15	3	8	40	0	2	5	54	2	26	2	1	8	.514	.452
Beltres, Manuel, N.Y. Yankees	.215	56	179	158	21	34	48	6	1	2	14	0	1	1	19	0	38	2	5	2	.304	.302
Benitez, Miguel, K.C./Colo.	.203	25	68	59	7	12	13	1	0	0	5	0	1	1	7	0	18	0	0	3	.220	.294
Betancourt, Romulo, Bal./Chi.(AL)	.245	34	115	94	21	23	27	4	0	0	9	0	1	3	17	0	28	11	3	1	.287	.374
Blanco, Billy, Oakland	.050	14	24	20	1	1	1	0	0	0	0	0	0	0	4	0	8	0	0	1	.050	.208
Blanco, Daniel, San Francisco	.216	28	97	88	4	19	22	3	0	0	7	0	0	3	6	0	14	0	1	3	.250	.289
Blanco, Danny, Cleveland	.155	35	99	84	9	13	18	5	0	0	7	0	1	0	14	0	10	1	0	4	.214	.273
Bracho, Didimo, Montreal	.248	61	233	202	23	50	70	12	1	2	30	0	1	2	28	3	34	8	9	4	.347	.343
Bravo, Eulis, Cleveland	.212	48	132	118	20	25	29	4	0	0	8	3	0	2	9	0	8	4	3	7	.246	.279
Brea, Rafael, Florida	.242	65	275	247	48	60	77	8	5	3	15	9	1	4	54	0	49	23	5	1	.372	.406
Briceno, Freddy, Montreal	.171	42	101	76	12	13	13	0	0	0	5	1	1	6	17	0	10	4	3	6	.171	.360
Brito, Felix, N.Y. Yankees	.209	21	57	43	7	9	15	1	1	1	6	0	0	2	12	0	6	0	0	2	.349	.404
Brito, Johan, San Francisco	.222	55	225	176	31	39	46	4	0	1	14	1	0	10	38	0	24	30	6	6	.261	.383
Cabrera, Danny, N.Y. Mets	.296	45	173	142	25	42	66	12	0	4	25	1	2	0	28	2	26	1	3	2	.465	.407
Cadet, Javier, Chi. (NL)/S.D.	.000	1	3	3	0	0	0	0	0	0	0	0	0	0	0	0	0	0	0	1	.000	.000
Caines, Franklin, Phi./St.L.	.285	62	264	246	38	70	104	14	4	4	38	0	1	0	17	2	52	6	3	9	.423	.330
Camacaro, Pedro, Texas	.159	14	51	44	7	7	9	0	1	0	3	0	0	0	7	0	9	0	0	0	.205	.275
Camacho, Wandy, California	.190	51	162	142	11	27	35	8	0	0	20	1	2	0	17	3	39	0	1	6	.246	.273
Carmona, Antonio, Bal./Chi.(AL)	.217	49	162	138	21	30	44	2	0	4	18	0	3	3	18	0	18	6	2	4	.319	.315
Carvajal, Hugo, Dodgers II	.078	28	65	51	4	4	4	0	0	0	2	1	0	1	12	0	6	0	1	3	.078	.266
Casimiro, Claudio, Bal./Chi.(AL)	.259	31	137	108	17	28	49	7	1	4	19	2	1	2	24	0	36	10	4	0	.454	.400
Castillo, Alex, Houston	.271	42	153	129	30	35	56	7	1	4	16	1	0	3	20	0	21	10	1	3	.434	.382
Castillo, Daniel A., Dodgers I	.000	7	0	0	1	0	0	0	0	0	0	0	0	0	0	0	0	0	0	0	.000	.000
Castillo, Geramel, Texas	.335	51	188	161	27	54	70	7	3	1	14	0	1	3	23	0	20	11	5	3	.435	.426
Castro, Cesar, California	.375	9	19	16	2	4	6	2	0	0	3	0	0	0	3	1	2	1	0	1	.375	.368
Castro, Jesus, Toronto	1.000	1	1	1	0	1	1	0	0	0	0	0	0	0	0	0	0	0	0	0	1.000	1.000
Castro, Jorge, Dodgers II	.238	39	129	105	14	25	31	3	0	1	16	1	2	2	19	1	19	1	3	4	.295	.359
Castro, Martirez, Texas	.307	67	273	225	35	69	102	14	2	5	44	0	4	6	38	1	44	3	10	7	.453	.414
Castro, Rafael, Phi./St.L.	.236	18	56	55	3	13	15	2	0	0	5	0	0	0	1	0	11	0	1	5	.273	.250
Cedeno, Ruddy, Houston	.317	51	197	161	41	51	65	10	2	0	14	0	3	0	33	1	14	12	7	1	.404	.426
Celedonio, Carlos, San Francisco	.262	55	215	183	33	48	70	13	0	3	14	1	0	5	26	0	38	11	4	5	.295	.369
Chavel, Ali, California	.250	5	14	12	2	3	6	0	0	1	3	0	0	0	2	0	5	0	1	1	.500	.357
Ciociola, Miguel, Dodgers I	.263	33	105	80	14	21	28	5	1	0	5	3	0	6	16	0	22	3	2	0	.350	.422
Collado, Hugo, Dodgers I	.283	38	135	106	21	30	34	2	1	0	17	1	1	1	26	1	15	5	3	2	.321	.425
Collado, Juan, N.Y. Yankees	.272	29	90	81	14	22	39	6	1	3	11	0	1	2	6	0	17	1	0	2	.481	.333
Compres, Miguel, N.Y. Yankees	.167	23	56	54	6	9	14	2	0	1	5	0	0	1	1	0	10	0	0	3	.259	.196
Cordero, Willie, Texas	.254	45	146	122	25	31	34	1	1	0	19	0	1	3	20	0	15	4	1	4	.279	.370
Corporan, Manuel, Bal./Chi.(AL)	.207	31	99	87	15	18	19	1	0	0	6	2	0	1	9	0	25	3	2	2	.218	.289
Cruz, Charlie, Dodgers I	.179	14	29	28	2	5	7	0	1	0	1	0	0	0	1	0	13	0	0	0	.250	.207
Cruz, Luis, Toyo Carp	.325	50	321	271	75	88	123	14	3	5	51	0	5	5	40	0	34	18	5	7	.454	.414
Cruz, Radhames, K.C./Colo.	.225	43	125	111	12	25	34	4	1	1	15	1	2	3	8	0	22	0	4	5	.306	.290
Cruz, Silvio, K.C./Colo.	.255	63	253	212	43	54	80	11	3	3	24	3	2	4	32	0	22	11	6	4	.377	.360
Dacosta, Samuel, Montreal	.269	27	65	52	5	14	17	3	0	0	11	0	1	1	11	0	6	0	0	1	.327	.400
DeJesus, Eddy, California	.242	50	175	153	22	37	55	12	0	2	20	2	0	2	18	0	36	6	3	3	.359	.329
DeJesus, Wilmer, Montreal	.178	38	102	90	6	16	20	1	0	1	9	1	0	2	9	0	18	0	0	4	.222	.267
DeLaCruz, Antonio, N.Y. Mets	.263	35	115	95	21	25	33	3	1	1	12	0	0	2	18	0	25	5	4	0	.347	.391
DeLaCruz, Henry, Chi. (NL)/S.D.	.181	38	123	94	12	17	25	5	0	1	10	0	1	1	27	0	44	2	3	2	.266	.366
DeLaCruz, Jose, Oakland	.248	41	154	125	26	31	43	6	0	2	12	0	1	2	26	0	29	4	0	2	.344	.383
DeLaCruz, Juan, San Francisco	.260	58	189	177	20	46	61	6	0	3	25	2	0	3	7	0	27	17	4	7	.345	.299
DeLaCruz, Pedro, Toronto	.205	15	40	39	5	8	12	2	1	0	2	0	1	0	0	0	8	1	1	1	.308	.200
DeLaCruz, Rafael, San Francisco	.175	24	60	57	2	10	12	2	0	0	2	1	0	1	1	0	15	0	2	3	.211	.203
DeLaCruz, Raul, Pittsburgh	.223	60	247	229	27	51	74	12	1	3	20	1	1	6	10	0	53	8	4	9	.323	.272
DeLaEspada, Miguel, Houston	.247	43	177	158	24	39	73	10	3	6	35	0	2	2	15	2	34	8	2	3	.462	.316
DeLaRosa, Erasmo, Houston	.206	33	115	102	13	21	31	3	2	1	13	1	1	2	9	0	25	5	5	2	.304	.281
DeLaRosa, Miguel, Texas	.259	56	209	158	36	41	66	7	0	6	26	4	2	3	42	0	57	10	11	1	.418	.420
DeLeon, Jose, Detroit	.280	35	117	100	12	28	30	2	0	0	14	0	2	2	13	2	22	4	2	3	.300	.368
DeLeon, Ricardo, Atlanta	.260	36	139	123	11	32	41	4	1	1	25	1	0	0	15	1	23	1	2	2	.333	.341
Delgado, Ramon, Seattle	.306	62	249	206	46	63	109	10	3	10	45	0	1	3	39	6	46	1	2	6	.529	.422

Player, Team	Avg.	G	TPA	AB	R	H	TB	2B	3B	HR	RBI	SH	SF	HP	BB	IBB	SO	SB	CS	GDP	Slg.	OBP
DeLosSantos, Aurelio, Phi./St.L.	.179	27	84	78	6	14	17	3	0	0	7	0	0	0	6	1	16	2	2	3	.218	.238
Del Valle, Carlos, Detroit	.266	66	275	222	35	59	78	12	2	1	28	2	1	0	50	4	26	2	1	9	.351	.399
Diaz, Emenegildo, San Francisco	.295	55	209	176	32	52	95	12	2	9	45	0	2	5	26	2	24	3	3	7	.540	.397
Diaz, Ivan, Phi./St.L.	.292	12	51	48	4	14	15	1	0	0	10	1	1	0	1	0	4	0	1	2	.313	.300
Diaz, Miguel, California	.217	53	212	198	28	43	58	12	0	1	23	1	1	5	7	0	37	5	2	5	.293	.261
Diaz, Welvis, Oakland	.274	57	228	168	31	46	65	7	3	2	19	2	1	3	54	2	49	3	5	4	.387	.456
D'Leon, Sandy, Seattle	.239	43	104	88	12	21	30	2	2	1	11	3	2	2	9	0	13	0	0	3	.341	.317
Dominguez, Enrique, Montreal	.202	50	126	109	18	22	24	2	0	0	10	1	1	7	8	0	16	9	3	4	.220	.296
Duncan, Jan Carlos, Phi./St.L.	.231	51	211	182	27	42	57	7	4	0	25	1	7	1	20	1	44	8	7	3	.313	.300
Duverge, Salvador, K.C./Colo.	.304	6	25	23	5	7	19	1	1	3	8	0	0	1	1	0	2	0	1	0	.826	.360
Ellis, Franklin, Houston	.239	29	103	92	10	22	30	5	0	1	13	2	4	0	5	0	19	5	1	1	.326	.267
Encarnacion, Edgardo, California	.226	51	174	159	22	36	48	8	2	0	15	1	1	1	12	0	16	4	2	7	.302	.283
Encarnacion, Mario, Oakland	.345	64	278	229	56	79	124	11	5	8	44	1	4	4	40	0	36	17	8	3	.541	.444
Encarnacion, Pedro, Bal./Chi.(AL)	.329	37	168	140	31	46	69	7	2	4	30	0	2	2	24	0	25	9	1	4	.493	.429
Encarnacion, Sonder, Seattle	.286	54	204	168	33	48	76	7	0	7	35	1	5	5	25	1	16	6	7	6	.452	.384
Espino, Fernando, Seattle	.335	62	242	203	41	68	103	15	1	6	33	0	1	6	32	5	23	3	7	7	.507	.438
Espino, Jose, Toyo Carp	.265	58	225	204	34	54	72	9	3	1	34	1	3	5	12	0	46	5	3	7	.353	.317
Estevez, Domingo, Toronto	.220	45	164	141	23	31	46	6	0	3	15	3	2	2	16	1	26	7	4	3	.326	.304
Eusebio, Ruben, Houston	.235	34	111	98	14	23	23	0	0	0	2	2	0	4	7	0	10	3	6	3	.235	.312
Fajardo, Alejandro, Phi./St.L.	.329	52	221	183	31	60	80	11	3	1	21	1	2	3	32	0	24	17	7	10	.437	.432
Farraez, Adel, Houston	.207	35	102	87	11	18	20	2	0	0	11	0	1	4	10	0	17	9	3	5	.230	.314
Farraez, Jesus, Houston	.227	40	139	119	15	27	35	5	0	1	12	0	0	0	20	0	17	18	2	0	.294	.338
Felix, Edgar, California	.230	35	147	135	13	31	43	3	0	3	11	0	0	2	10	0	32	0	1	4	.319	.293
Fernandez, Juan, Dodgers I	.233	41	108	86	13	20	28	2	3	0	8	1	0	0	21	0	18	3	3	0	.326	.383
Fernandez, Robert, Cleveland	.227	14	51	44	9	10	13	0	0	1	6	0	1	1	5	0	10	3	0	1	.295	.314
Fernandez, Winston, Texas	.229	50	156	109	41	25	36	3	4	0	19	1	1	3	42	0	11	21	7	2	.330	.452
Ferreiras, Luis, Cleveland	.230	27	65	61	3	14	23	3	0	2	14	0	0	0	4	1	15	0	1	4	.377	.277
Figueroa, Jose, Oakland	.212	39	134	113	19	24	41	8	0	3	17	2	3	2	14	1	21	2	0	3	.363	.303
Fischer, Carlos, California	.329	48	194	155	25	51	54	3	0	0	13	0	1	1	37	0	16	10	5	2	.348	.459
Flores, Carlos, Houston	.200	5	15	15	0	3	5	1	0	0	2	0	0	0	0	0	4	0	1	1	.333	.200
Flores, Julio, Montreal	.306	58	228	196	29	60	79	10	3	1	29	2	3	3	24	3	16	16	7	5	.403	.385
Font, Franklin, Chi. (NL)/S.D.	.312	64	285	237	50	74	90	8	4	0	30	2	1	2	43	1	25	8	7	6	.380	.420
Francisco, Frank, Atlanta	.236	64	266	229	29	54	77	10	5	1	23	1	1	4	31	0	73	18	6	2	.336	.336
Franco, Deyvi, Detroit	.256	23	56	43	9	11	12	1	0	0	6	0	0	3	10	0	13	3	2	3	.279	.429
Franco, Jorge, Montreal	.227	29	100	88	11	20	25	3	1	0	7	2	2	2	6	0	9	2	1	7	.284	.286
Galban, Elvis, Montreal	.307	64	268	231	42	71	97	14	3	2	37	0	6	6	25	1	20	24	8	6	.420	.381
Garcia, Eduardo, California	.276	17	71	58	11	16	22	4	1	0	8	1	0	0	12	0	13	2	1	0	.379	.400
Garcia, Juan, Atlanta	.292	64	295	240	54	70	102	15	7	1	40	0	4	5	46	1	45	16	8	4	.425	.410
Garcia, Juan, Detroit	.179	22	32	28	4	5	7	2	0	0	3	0	0	1	3	0	14	1	0	0	.250	.281
Garcia, Julio, N.Y. Yankees	.333	4	13	12	2	4	4	0	0	0	1	0	0	0	1	0	1	1	0	1	.333	.385
Garcia, Leoncio, California	.242	46	165	124	14	30	39	2	2	1	17	0	3	5	33	1	30	3	0	0	.315	.412
Garcia, Luis, Dodgers II	.297	53	240	185	56	55	83	8	7	2	24	2	0	5	48	2	29	10	7	3	.449	.454
German, Aris, N.Y. Mets	.256	52	52	43	6	11	13	2	0	0	2	1	0	2	6	0	10	1	0	1	.302	.373
German, Julian, Detroit	.214	59	195	154	26	33	42	4	1	1	14	1	0	6	34	1	34	13	11	5	.273	.376
Germosen, Julio, Pittsburgh	.231	62	268	238	32	55	79	9	3	3	38	4	1	4	21	1	61	3	3	7	.332	.303
Geronimo, Cesar, California	.246	61	245	211	29	52	71	9	2	2	24	3	2	2	27	1	16	8	5	7	.336	.335
Gil, Alberto, Cleveland	.306	61	233	196	36	60	90	7	7	3	30	1	4	2	30	2	32	7	4	1	.459	.397
Giron, Edilberto, Pittsburgh	.190	18	51	42	7	8	9	1	0	0	4	0	0	1	8	0	18	1	0	0	.214	.333
Giron, Isabel, Toronto	.250	36	124	120	14	30	42	4	1	2	13	0	0	1	3	0	34	2	3	5	.350	.274
Giron, Juan, Atlanta	.292	56	226	171	33	50	62	9	0	1	25	1	1	16	37	1	27	6	5	7	.363	.458
Gomera, Rafael, Dodgers I	.242	60	240	215	37	52	75	7	2	4	28	1	2	1	21	2	59	3	3	1	.349	.310
Gomez, Luis, Houston	.155	29	72	58	6	9	15	3	0	1	6	0	3	3	8	1	10	3	1	0	.259	.278
Gonzalez, Adalberto, Montreal	.214	24	59	42	7	9	10	1	0	0	0	1	0	2	14	1	11	5	1	0	.238	.431
Gonzalez, Cesar, Montreal	.194	23	75	62	7	12	14	2	0	0	9	3	1	2	7	0	9	4	4	1	.226	.292
Gonzalez, Franklin, Chi. (NL)/S.D.	.260	24	90	77	14	20	23	1	1	0	8	4	0	0	9	0	13	1	3	3	.299	.337
Gonzalez, Santo, Chi. (NL)/S.D.	.222	59	221	180	29	40	60	8	3	2	19	1	1	2	37	0	32	6	6	3	.333	.359
Guerra, Carlos, Cleveland	.150	10	22	20	2	3	4	1	0	0	1	0	0	1	1	0	2	0	0	1	.200	.227
Guerra, Hubert, California	.171	50	172	146	20	25	36	6	1	1	16	1	1	0	24	1	27	13	2	3	.247	.287
Guerrero, Frank, Houston	.187	39	136	123	16	23	28	3	1	0	15	1	1	2	9	0	24	2	2	4	.228	.252
Guerrero, Hamlet, N.Y. Mets	.285	61	249	214	37	61	110	10	0	13	43	0	4	4	27	1	30	7	2	3	.514	.369
Guerrero, Wascar, Seattle	.364	48	194	173	37	63	109	14	1	10	43	0	1	2	18	2	40	1	0	4	.630	.428
Guilleard, Alfonso, Toyo Carp	.366	63	272	227	52	83	113	12	3	4	55	1	8	6	30	1	19	8	2	1	.498	.439
Gutierrez, Victor, Pittsburgh	.247	51	170	150	19	37	51	3	1	3	20	0	2	1	17	0	21	6	3	5	.340	.324
Guzman, Carlos, Detroit	.202	31	101	84	13	17	23	2	2	0	12	0	2	2	13	0	14	5	3	2	.274	.317
Guzman, Cristian, N.Y. Yankees	.269	46	180	160	24	43	68	6	5	3	20	2	1	5	12	1	23	11	7	2	.425	.337
Guzman, Juan, Bal./Chi.(AL)	.200	37	128	120	12	24	30	6	0	0	12	1	0	1	6	0	20	2	2	1	.250	.244
Guzman, Juan, Phi./St.L.	.187	50	175	155	25	29	40	4	2	1	16	3	1	1	15	0	37	6	5	1	.258	.262
Guzman, Martin, Toyo Carp	.349	58	270	229	58	80	119	16	1	7	54	0	7	5	29	0	29	0	1	3	.520	.422
Guzman, Santos, Pittsburgh	.328	37	142	131	16	43	59	5	1	3	16	0	1	1	9	0	27	1	1	1	.450	.373
Haad, Yamid, Pittsburgh	.254	36	132	118	17	30	31	1	0	0	8	2	1	2	9	0	17	1	9	2	.263	.315
Heredia, Andres, K.C./Colo.	.150	25	62	60	2	9	9	0	0	0	4	0	0	0	2	0	15	0	1	2	.150	.177
Heredia, Rafael, Chi. (NL)/S.D.	.298	61	248	215	38	64	117	15	4	10	41	0	5	7	21	1	38	6	1	5	.544	.371
Hernandez, Darwin, Pittsburgh	.255	57	251	204	37	52	73	7	4	2	24	2	1	4	40	0	40	8	9	6	.358	.386
Hernandez, Jesus, Cleveland	.406	66	294	251	60	102	138	22	7	0	53	0	4	2	37	2	15	20	3	2	.550	.480
Hernandez, Jorgelio, Toyo Carp	.246	18	66	61	9	15	17	2	0	0	6	0	0	0	5	0	4	3	2	4	.279	.303
Hernandez, Leonardo, N.Y. Mets	.209	41	99	91	4	19	22	1	1	0	10	0	1	2	4	0	21	4	2	0	.242	.255
Hernandez, Rafael, Montreal	.317	56	245	218	34	69	103	16	3	4	32	1	5	1	20	1	30	7	3	5	.472	.369
Herrera, Alvaro, California	.228	61	236	184	34	42	55	7	3	0	16	0	2	12	38	4	36	10	2	2	.299	.390
Infante, Danny, Texas	.303	63	250	234	31	71	96	13	0	4	39	1	2	0	13	1	49	2	5	1	.410	.337
Infante, Julio, Dodgers I	.207	24	64	58	4	12	14	2	0	0	5	0	0	1	5	0	14	0	1	2	.241	.281
Iquerey, Rodney, Cleveland	.205	43	107	88	13	18	20	2	0	0	7	1	0	4	14	0	14	2	3	3	.227	.340
Jadagui, Carlos, Chi. (NL)/S.D.	.204	32	110	93	14	19	24	2	0	1	6	0	0	2	15	0	22	0	0	7	.258	.327
Javier, Jesus, Dodgers I	.246	46	165	126	20	31	36	5	0	0	11	3	0	1	35	0	30	1	2	2	.286	.414

Player, Team	Avg.	G	TPA	AB	R	H	TB	2B	3B	HR	RBI	SH	SF	HP	BB	IBB	SO	SB	CS	GDP	Slg.	OBP
Jimenez, Felipe, Chi. (NL)/S.D.	.209	45	174	148	23	31	36	2	0	1	18	2	1	4	19	1	28	9	6	8	.243	.314
Jimenez, Miguel, Seattle	.327	62	265	226	50	74	108	11	1	7	51	1	1	5	32	2	33	9	4	4	.478	.420
Jimenez, Ramon, N.Y. Yankees	.241	39	90	79	21	19	28	3	0	2	13	0	0	0	11	0	22	10	2	1	.354	.333
Jose, Leonardo, Oakland	.250	18	71	60	7	15	17	0	1	0	3	0	1	3	7	0	21	10	6	0	.283	.352
King, Cesar, Texas	.302	54	209	182	33	55	73	9	0	3	22	0	0	5	22	1	34	3	2	9	.401	.392
King, Daniel, Oakland	.238	27	100	80	13	19	26	4	0	1	16	1	0	2	17	0	18	1	0	1	.325	.384
Langagney, Shelwin, Toronto	.335	65	270	221	45	74	92	15	0	1	39	1	2	3	43	3	29	16	8	7	.416	.446
Lara, Balnes, Detroit	.213	57	203	160	26	34	50	6	2	2	22	3	5	5	30	1	65	5	2	5	.313	.345
Lara, Felix, Pittsburgh	.185	46	154	135	19	25	34	2	2	1	9	0	0	4	15	1	53	2	4	3	.252	.282
Ledesma, Felipe, Dodgers II	.306	63	261	235	43	72	90	10	4	0	53	0	5	4	17	1	15	12	6	8	.383	.356
Leidens, Misael, Montreal	.257	34	122	109	20	28	36	3	1	1	8	0	1	2	10	0	18	4	4	2	.330	.328
Lima, Jose, K.C./Colo.	.217	8	27	23	4	5	8	1	1	0	2	0	0	0	4	0	4	2	0	0	.348	.333
Lina, Donald, K.C./Colo.	.179	39	128	112	17	20	22	0	1	0	5	1	0	1	14	0	12	3	1	5	.196	.276
Linares, Rafael, Bal./Chi.(AL)	.194	45	120	98	18	19	20	1	0	0	3	1	0	5	16	0	23	8	3	1	.204	.336
Linares, Sendry, Houston	.254	29	82	71	10	18	23	2	0	1	10	4	0	0	7	0	4	10	5	1	.324	.321
Loaisiga, Stanley, Montreal	.289	65	251	232	22	67	93	10	2	4	30	1	3	4	11	5	35	6	2	3	.401	.328
Lopez, Luis, San Francisco	.269	58	241	219	41	59	87	9	2	5	33	0	0	5	17	0	35	9	3	14	.352	.336
Lorenzo, Julio, Detroit	.173	46	103	81	9	14	21	3	2	0	6	1	1	2	18	0	19	0	2	2	.259	.333
Loyo, Oscar, Florida	.327	14	56	52	4	17	31	5	0	3	14	0	0	0	4	0	8	0	0	1	.596	.375
Maldonado, Franklin, Chi. (NL)/S.D.	.241	52	184	162	23	39	49	7	0	1	23	2	0	4	16	0	28	2	2	4	.302	.324
Marcano, Dennys, Chi. (NL)/S.D.	.250	46	176	152	28	38	50	9	0	1	15	0	1	4	19	1	37	4	0	2	.329	.347
Marte, Julian, Dodgers II	.307	49	195	163	23	50	57	3	2	0	33	1	3	4	24	0	13	3	5	5	.350	.402
Marte, Nestor, Detroit	.259	43	88	58	14	15	19	2	1	0	11	1	1	1	27	0	8	3	2	4	.328	.494
Martich, Juan, Dodgers I	.000	5	13	12	1	0	0	0	0	0	0	0	0	1	0	0	3	0	0	0	.000	.077
Martinez, Andres, N.Y. Mets	.240	48	147	129	21	31	48	7	2	2	11	2	1	2	13	0	45	2	3	0	.372	.317
Martinez, Claudio, Dodgers II	.000	6	0	0	0	0	0	0	0	0	0	0	0	0	0	0	0	0	0	0	.000	.000
Martinez, David, Toronto	.312	58	233	199	34	62	76	6	1	2	29	2	2	3	27	0	39	8	3	6	.382	.398
Martinez, Fausto, N.Y. Mets	.195	27	50	41	8	8	10	0	1	0	2	0	1	2	6	0	16	0	1	1	.244	.320
Martinez, Gregorio, Dodgers II	.189	60	211	159	36	30	40	6	2	0	15	2	1	1	48	0	54	13	4	3	.252	.378
Martinez, Jose, Cleveland	.317	61	244	218	35	69	92	20	0	1	38	1	1	11	13	0	25	2	1	13	.422	.383
Martinez, Winston, Detroit	.179	35	75	56	9	10	13	0	0	1	5	0	1	7	11	0	21	0	1	1	.232	.373
Mata, Felix, Toyo Carp	.000	7	7	5	1	0	0	0	0	0	1	0	1	0	1	0	2	0	0	0	.000	.143
Mateo, Amaury, Texas	.301	48	201	176	30	53	80	9	3	4	42	1	2	2	20	1	23	1	2	3	.455	.355
Mateo, Freddy, Dodgers II	.283	66	282	240	50	68	106	13	2	7	45	0	5	13	24	2	49	8	2	5	.442	.372
Mateo, Victor, N.Y. Yankees	.333	46	273	248	34	83	114	17	4	2	37	0	2	3	20	0	19	5	4	8	.460	.388
Matos, Wellington, N.Y. Yankees	.282	59	243	209	36	59	96	8	1	9	39	0	1	2	31	2	32	2	1	7	.459	.379
McDonald, Gabriel, San Fran.	.236	58	225	178	31	42	60	8	5	0	24	1	2	11	33	1	49	11	2	5	.337	.384
McFarlane, Ivan, K.C./Colo.	.261	37	99	88	15	23	28	5	0	0	5	0	0	1	10	0	26	2	2	3	.318	.343
McLean, Guillermo, Dodgers II	.232	26	69	56	12	13	16	1	1	0	7	0	0	4	9	0	12	2	0	2	.286	.377
Medina, Richy, Detroit	.182	42	113	88	15	16	23	2	1	1	6	5	0	1	19	1	24	8	2	2	.261	.333
Mejia, Jose, Atlanta	.238	35	102	84	13	20	26	6	0	0	7	2	2	5	9	0	16	6	1	5	.310	.340
Mejia, Juan, Phi./St.L.	.284	54	235	218	30	62	85	12	1	3	26	1	6	3	7	0	43	14	4	6	.390	.308
Mejia, Luis, Houston	.275	28	108	80	22	22	32	2	1	2	15	0	2	1	25	0	18	8	3	0	.400	.444
Mejia, Oliver, Pittsburgh	.313	52	200	179	30	56	71	9	3	0	25	0	1	2	18	0	27	4	4	7	.397	.380
Mejia, Renato, Florida	.329	65	271	240	36	79	109	13	1	5	29	0	2	2	27	0	53	10	7	2	.454	.399
Mendez, Claudio R., Seattle	.174	26	54	46	8	8	9	1	0	0	5	0	0	2	6	0	9	0	1	0	.196	.296
Mento, Alfredo, N.Y. Mets	.228	51	188	158	29	36	67	11	1	6	24	0	0	3	27	0	42	4	3	2	.424	.351
Meran, Jorge, Detroit	.270	67	276	237	36	64	96	8	3	6	41	1	3	6	29	3	52	12	8	6	.405	.360
Mercado, Henry, Cleveland	.231	32	61	52	10	12	14	2	0	0	3	0	0	4	5	0	18	4	2	0	.269	.344
Mercedes, Luis, San Francisco	.142	37	127	113	14	16	23	1	0	2	8	1	0	0	13	0	28	2	1	2	.204	.230
Mercedes, Matias, Detroit	.283	58	251	198	48	56	78	3	2	5	27	5	1	7	40	1	24	12	11	3	.394	.419
Mijares, Robert, Dodgers II	.173	34	89	75	14	13	17	2	1	0	6	0	0	0	14	0	15	5	0	5	.227	.303
Molina, Alfredo, Dodgers II	.216	34	90	74	14	16	17	1	0	0	6	3	0	1	12	0	8	1	2	4	.230	.333
Morales, Anaximando, Atlanta	.207	38	147	116	23	24	40	4	0	4	12	4	0	8	19	0	31	1	1	4	.345	.357
Morales, Cesar, San Francisco	.250	33	102	92	10	23	35	4	1	2	8	2	1	1	6	1	16	0	0	1	.380	.300
Morales, Domingo, Bal./Chi.(AL)	.311	38	114	106	15	33	42	4	1	1	14	0	0	1	7	0	7	12	4	1	.396	.360
Morelo, Fulvio, N.Y. Yankees	.207	51	122	111	13	23	33	5	1	1	12	2	3	1	5	0	9	1	1	9	.297	.242
Moreno, Antony, Houston	.226	32	116	93	10	21	26	5	0	0	6	6	0	5	12	0	11	4	3	0	.280	.345
Moreno, Johnny, Bal./Chi.(AL)	.283	55	201	184	25	52	79	11	2	4	27	1	3	1	12	1	45	10	4	3	.424	.325
Moreno, Jose, Seattle	.237	53	181	152	28	36	48	10	1	0	24	1	0	2	26	0	13	4	6	5	.316	.356
Moreno, Juan, N.Y. Mets	.360	58	264	228	59	82	137	14	1	13	36	1	1	2	32	1	24	15	10	2	.601	.441
Moreno, Willy, N.Y. Yankees	.275	21	51	7	14	20	3	0	1	7	0	0	0	20	1	15	2	0	1	.392	.479	
Moreta, Ramon, Dodgers II	.304	67	302	253	57	77	95	8	5	0	39	5	4	2	38	1	25	31	9	6	.375	.394
Mota, Pedro, San Francisco	.236	36	128	110	11	26	34	4	2	0	13	1	1	1	15	0	24	4	1	3	.309	.331
Mota, Victor, Detroit	.193	45	136	109	14	21	36	6	3	1	29	0	1	2	24	1	33	0	3	4	.330	.346
Mundo, Alberto, Atlanta	.239	66	308	230	51	55	62	3	2	0	11	2	3	4	69	0	43	25	9	6	.270	.418
Munoz, Eduardo, Seattle	.170	20	55	47	5	8	9	1	0	0	4	2	0	2	4	0	13	1	0	5	.191	.264
Nina, Amaury, Texas	.289	37	128	114	27	33	46	7	3	0	15	0	2	3	9	1	28	5	2	1	.404	.352
Nina, Jose, Toronto	.297	43	141	118	17	35	41	2	2	0	15	2	0	1	20	0	28	7	9	3	.347	.403
Nova, Joselin, Florida	.250	60	239	224	18	56	69	11	1	0	21	1	1	2	11	1	30	0	2	8	.308	.290
Nova, Kelvin, Oakland	.209	47	179	153	29	32	45	8	1	1	14	1	3	1	21	1	23	9	4	4	.294	.303
Nunez, Abraham, Toronto	.301	54	219	186	49	56	84	10	3	4	25	1	0	2	30	1	27	24	6	4	.452	.404
Nunez, Bienvenido, San Fran.	.284	29	87	74	7	21	30	4	1	1	12	0	0	3	10	1	15	1	1	2	.405	.391
Nunez, Euripides, Bal./Chi.(AL)	.207	46	132	111	8	23	25	0	1	0	12	2	1	0	18	0	35	7	5	2	.225	.315
Nunez, Jorge, Toronto	.133	13	16	15	1	2	5	0	0	1	4	0	0	0	1	0	5	0	0	0	.333	.188
Nunez, Jose, K.C./Colo.	.236	64	239	203	29	48	61	4	3	1	30	0	3	1	32	0	33	5	4	3	.300	.339
Nunez, Jose, Oakland	.225	51	176	151	26	34	58	7	1	5	29	0	2	3	20	0	62	2	2	3	.384	.324
Oliva, Osvaldo, Atlanta	.213	67	297	240	37	51	95	14	0	10	58	0	5	7	45	0	69	7	4	6	.396	.334
Olivares, Melvin, N.Y. Mets	.326	64	260	236	39	77	121	12	1	10	54	1	5	3	15	0	21	3	4	6	.513	.367
Olivero, Ricardo, Montreal	.214	40	117	98	8	21	25	4	0	0	7	2	1	0	16	1	15	2	2	1	.255	.322
Oramas, Victor, Houston	.250	20	55	48	6	12	12	0	0	0	1	0	0	0	7	1	6	1	0	1	.250	.345
Ortiz, Jose, Oakland	.300	61	254	217	45	65	108	12	2	9	41	2	3	0	32	0	32	14	7	7	.498	.385
Otano, Delvin, Toyo Carp	.306	63	290	245	51	75	112	13	3	6	60	0	2	1	42	2	30	2	3	9	.461	.407

Player, Team	Avg.	G	TPA	AB	R	H	TB	2B	3B	HR	RBI	SH	SF	HP	BB	IBB	SO	SB	CS	GDP	Slg.	OBP
Ovalle, Jesus, Texas	.230	41	105	87	11	20	23	3	0	0	8	1	1	0	16	0	6	2	3	5	.264	.346
Ovalle, Albin, K.C./Colo.	.223	53	177	139	27	31	35	4	0	0	13	0	1	5	32	1	18	4	10	6	.252	.384
Ozuna, Pedro, N.Y. Yankees	.335	57	227	182	42	61	77	10	3	0	21	0	3	2	40	1	12	6	8	10	.423	.454
Paz, Richard, Bal./Chi.(AL)	.287	67	293	230	46	66	82	8	1	2	27	1	3	4	55	3	28	18	4	7	.357	.428
Pena, Charlies, Toyo Carp	.336	68	321	241	80	81	132	27	0	8	66	0	5	9	66	2	30	17	2	4	.548	.486
Pena, Elvi, Seattle	.258	41	115	97	16	25	36	2	0	3	13	1	2	0	15	0	16	1	2	2	.371	.351
Pena, Onesimo, N.Y. Mets	.215	50	127	107	31	23	42	1	0	6	21	1	1	4	14	0	34	8	1	4	.393	.325
Pena, Ramon, Toronto	.366	59	242	213	22	78	95	11	0	2	34	0	5	8	16	3	20	3	4	6	.446	.421
Pena, Reynaldo, Detroit	.255	69	307	255	50	65	101	13	7	3	28	6	2	9	35	2	27	14	11	5	.396	.362
Pena, Victor, Phi./St.L.	.148	28	88	81	12	12	22	4	0	2	4	0	0	1	6	0	29	4	2	1	.272	.216
Pena, Warren, N.Y. Yankees	.197	41	141	117	17	23	29	6	0	0	9	0	2	3	19	1	12	1	2	2	.248	.319
Penalver, Juan, N.Y. Mets	.295	65	270	200	58	59	74	4	1	3	16	1	0	3	66	0	25	15	7	6	.370	.476
Peralta, Santiago, Toyo Carp	.276	58	261	225	46	62	90	4	9	2	46	1	3	3	29	1	35	11	4	9	.400	.362
Perdomo, Roberto, San Francisco	.139	23	82	72	10	10	12	2	0	0	4	1	0	3	6	0	16	6	2	1	.167	.235
Perez, Angelo, Toronto	.306	67	280	255	39	78	115	7	0	10	35	4	2	4	15	0	43	26	12	6	.451	.351
Perez, David, Atlanta	.166	47	164	151	5	25	28	3	0	0	17	6	1	1	5	0	35	0	0	5	.185	.196
Perez, Edwin, Cleveland	.322	63	268	239	58	77	109	9	7	3	37	2	1	3	23	2	24	14	4	4	.456	.387
Perez, Jose, Cleveland	.111	7	19	18	0	2	2	0	0	0	4	0	1	0	0	0	8	1	0	1	.111	.105
Perez, Manuel, Phi./St.L.	.273	38	102	77	21	21	24	1	1	0	3	0	1	2	22	0	12	8	7	1	.312	.441
Perez, Richard, Bal./Chi.(AL)	.307	60	264	218	48	67	90	6	4	3	21	4	2	8	32	0	32	28	14	7	.413	.412
Perez, Stiwar, Dodgers I	.306	61	257	219	32	67	103	10	1	8	42	4	3	8	23	1	44	5	1	4	.470	.387
Perez, Wegner, Cleveland	.200	26	49	45	9	9	15	3	0	1	4	0	0	3	1	0	6	0	0	2	.333	.265
Perez, Wilman, Florida	.209	36	106	91	16	19	23	4	0	0	6	1	0	1	13	0	27	7	1	0	.253	.314
Pimentel, Jose, Dodgers II	.278	66	269	223	56	62	97	17	3	4	38	2	4	8	32	3	21	24	5	8	.435	.382
Pimentel, Marino, Florida	.278	46	196	169	23	47	55	8	0	0	18	6	0	2	19	2	42	18	7	3	.325	.358
Pinales, Victor, Houston	.208	24	89	77	13	16	22	1	1	1	7	1	0	5	6	1	17	7	1	0	.286	.307
Pineda, Luis, Texas	.000	1	0	0	0	0	0	0	0	0	0	0	0	0	0	0	0	0	0	0	.000	.000
Pinedo, Hector, Phi./St.L.	.186	36	126	113	15	21	24	0	0	1	9	1	2	0	10	0	31	3	2	2	.212	.248
Polanco, Julio, Texas	.182	12	25	22	2	4	4	0	0	0	3	0	1	2	1	6	0	0	2	.182	.280	
Polanco, Raul, Chi. (NL)/S.D.	.274	56	236	197	23	54	75	11	2	2	26	0	5	2	32	1	33	1	4	5	.381	.373
Polonia, Israel, Florida	.188	66	241	191	29	36	50	6	1	2	19	1	4	3	42	2	68	8	11	6	.262	.338
Polonio, Enrique, Pittsburgh	.312	63	282	237	48	74	91	8	0	3	24	0	5	9	31	0	24	20	13	7	.384	.404
Preciado, Victor, N.Y. Yankees	.290	57	232	210	30	61	79	15	0	1	29	1	6	1	14	0	29	1	1	10	.376	.329
Pringle, Juan, N.Y. Yankees	.248	34	107	101	13	25	34	6	0	1	15	0	0	2	4	0	24	0	0	1	.337	.290
Pujols, Rafael, Oakland	.250	49	189	168	26	42	50	6	1	0	19	3	2	3	13	1	13	3	2	4	.298	.312
Quero, Pedro, Montreal	.183	37	115	109	9	20	28	2	0	2	7	1	1	0	4	0	19	1	0	7	.257	.211
Quezada, Adalberto, San Fran.	.289	34	107	90	24	26	26	0	0	0	4	0	0	0	17	0	24	14	7	2	.289	.402
Ramirez, Aramis, Pittsburgh	.294	64	271	214	41	63	109	13	0	11	54	1	4	10	42	0	26	2	4	3	.509	.426
Ramirez, David, Texas	.148	33	72	61	6	9	10	1	0	0	3	0	1	2	8	0	14	0	2	4	.164	.264
Ramirez, Jordy, Toyo Carp	.266	41	131	109	26	29	32	3	0	0	9	3	1	4	14	0	26	5	1	2	.294	.367
Ramirez, Juan, K.C./Colo.	.210	62	247	229	22	48	56	6	1	0	27	1	3	3	11	0	20	3	2	13	.245	.252
Ramirez, Narciso, Montreal	.150	54	172	140	26	21	28	4	0	1	9	0	0	5	27	0	68	12	8	0	.200	.308
Ramirez, Rafael, Detroit	.190	48	149	116	18	22	34	7	1	1	19	2	2	3	26	0	32	2	2	1	.293	.347
Ramos, Kelly, N.Y. Mets	.253	54	175	158	18	40	56	7	0	3	24	1	4	3	9	0	28	3	3	1	.354	.299
Rebolledo, Jairo, Chi. (NL)/S.D.	.225	53	202	173	23	39	45	4	1	0	19	1	2	2	24	0	23	4	3	12	.260	.323
Renteria, Everth, Atlanta	.260	52	215	181	26	47	52	5	0	0	14	4	0	5	25	0	12	14	2	4	.287	.365
Reyes, Cristian, Oakland	.045	11	31	22	3	1	1	0	0	0	2	1	0	0	8	0	3	1	0	0	.045	.300
Reynoso, Ismael, Florida	.247	21	95	85	16	21	25	2	1	0	12	0	1	0	9	0	12	2	2	3	.294	.316
Ricardo, Alfredo, Oakland	.255	51	188	165	22	42	54	3	0	3	30	3	2	2	16	1	28	6	4	6	.327	.324
Ricardo, Luis, Dodgers I	.200	30	100	95	10	19	22	3	0	0	9	0	0	2	3	0	11	1	4	7	.232	.240
Richardson, Elbin, Texas	.283	26	67	60	9	17	25	3	1	1	10	0	0	2	5	0	11	1	0	1	.417	.358
Rios, Carlos, Houston	.261	56	215	176	25	46	65	11	1	2	25	1	2	0	36	4	26	4	5	6	.369	.383
Rivera, Juan C., Chi. (NL)/S.D.	.174	13	55	46	3	8	10	2	0	0	7	1	1	0	7	0	11	0	2	2	.217	.278
Rivera, Santo, San Francisco	.244	64	255	234	37	57	81	13	1	3	30	1	0	5	15	0	36	4	3	6	.346	.303
Rivera, Yorki, Dodgers I	.201	53	214	169	33	34	45	7	2	0	13	3	2	1	39	0	32	10	1	3	.266	.351
Robles, Victor, Bal./Chi.(AL)	.208	40	117	101	17	21	32	1	2	2	13	1	0	3	12	0	39	2	1	0	.317	.310
Rodriguez, Alfredo, Dodgers II	.321	35	121	106	19	34	49	6	0	3	31	0	0	4	11	0	22	0	1	2	.462	.405
Rodriguez, Felipe, Toronto	.267	52	213	165	48	44	51	3	2	0	5	2	1	7	38	0	36	42	11	0	.309	.422
Rodriguez, Geremias, Toyo Carp	.243	66	312	235	71	57	78	9	3	2	25	5	5	8	59	0	22	16	2	5	.332	.404
Rodriguez, Jose, Florida	.201	46	152	134	18	27	41	3	1	3	13	2	0	3	13	0	56	8	0	2	.306	.287
Rodriguez, Juan, Pittsburgh	.270	58	214	178	36	48	74	8	3	4	25	3	1	2	30	1	34	9	4	3	.416	.379
Rodriguez, Miguel, Phi./St.L.	.375	48	170	144	31	54	75	13	1	2	28	1	3	2	20	1	16	11	5	1	.521	.450
Rodriguez, Nelson, Dodgers I	.197	49	157	127	23	25	33	4	2	0	11	1	0	2	27	0	23	5	2	10	.260	.346
Romero, Mario, Houston	.207	13	35	29	4	6	8	2	0	0	1	1	0	2	3	0	11	2	2	1	.276	.324
Romero, Robinson, N.Y. Yankees	.257	47	117	101	11	26	42	1	0	5	19	0	1	3	12	0	19	1	0	5	.416	.350
Rondon, Jhonny, Seattle	.309	40	72	55	20	17	25	4	2	0	5	0	0	1	16	1	15	2	2	2	.455	.472
Rosario, Carlos, K.C./Colo.	.313	61	249	217	31	68	85	8	3	1	32	0	1	1	30	6	43	6	10	4	.392	.398
Rosario, Ramon, Houston	.241	28	96	83	10	20	29	3	0	2	13	0	2	3	8	0	12	4	0	5	.349	.323
Ruiz, Francis, Toyo Carp	.257	60	265	218	52	56	75	9	2	2	38	1	2	2	42	0	38	15	3	4	.344	.379
Ruiz, Jose, Seattle	.260	54	177	150	28	39	69	7	1	7	27	2	1	1	23	0	50	2	4	4	.460	.360
Salazar, Oscar, Oakland	.271	53	194	166	29	45	57	10	1	0	23	2	3	1	22	0	23	5	5	4	.343	.354
Samuel, Yojairo, Texas	.000	1	1	1	0	0	0	0	0	0	0	0	0	0	0	0	0	0	0	0	.000	.000
Sanchez, Jose, Detroit	.171	25	43	35	6	6	8	0	1	0	2	1	0	1	6	0	9	0	0	1	.229	.310
Sanchez, Manuel, Atlanta	.249	57	241	197	34	49	75	12	7	0	21	5	1	7	31	1	25	9	4	2	.381	.369
Sanchez, Willington, Toronto	.100	12	22	20	3	2	2	0	0	0	0	0	0	0	2	0	4	2	1	1	.100	.182
Sanquintin, Alexis, Cleveland	.107	12	31	28	2	3	3	0	0	0	1	0	0	0	3	0	0	0	0	1	.107	.194
Santana, Juan, Dodgers II	.213	50	193	164	24	35	47	7	1	1	16	5	0	5	19	0	20	4	2	4	.287	.314
Santana, Luis, Dodgers II	.231	34	105	91	15	21	27	6	0	0	10	1	1	1	11	1	20	0	0	3	.297	.317
Santana, Mario, California	.240	57	230	183	22	44	51	2	1	1	24	0	2	45	1	16	9	3	4	.279	.396	
Santana, Pedro, Houston	.288	52	221	184	39	53	67	6	1	2	14	2	1	3	31	0	29	34	4	1	.364	.397
Santana, Ramon, K.C./Colo.	.209	52	178	148	25	31	33	2	0	0	15	1	0	2	27	0	23	13	9	4	.223	.339
Santana, Richard, K.C./Colo.	.212	49	154	137	13	29	35	3	0	1	14	3	4	0	10	0	19	4	4	3	.255	.258
Santelise, Osvaldo, Bal./Chi.(AL)	.232	51	175	155	18	36	60	5	2	5	28	0	0	1	19	1	47	0	0	0	.381	.320

Player, Team	Avg.	G	TPA	AB	R	H	TB	2B	3B	HR	RBI	SH	SF	HP	BB	IBB	SO	SB	CS	GDP	Slg.	OBP
Santos, Jose, California	.320	12	27	25	5	8	11	0	0	1	5	0	0	0	2	0	9	0	0	0	.440	.370
Santos, Jose, Texas	.304	56	249	184	53	56	96	10	3	8	39	0	2	6	57	0	41	9	5	4	.522	.478
Saturria, Arturo, Phi./St.L.	.318	66	283	245	48	78	114	16	7	2	33	0	2	2	34	1	26	12	7	5	.465	.403
Scuttaro, Marco, Cleveland	.393	66	296	262	71	103	133	18	6	0	38	2	4	8	20	1	11	32	11	4	.508	.446
Segura, Winston, Texas	.292	37	103	89	14	26	31	5	0	0	11	0	1	1	12	1	13	8	3	4	.348	.379
Sencion, Pablo, Toronto	.297	68	299	249	58	74	137	22	1	13	53	0	3	0	47	4	49	3	2	6	.550	.415
Severino, Danny, Florida	.275	68	295	258	28	71	98	9	3	4	45	1	4	8	24	0	51	8	9	8	.380	.350
Shinozuka, Takeiro, Montreal	.286	4	14	14	1	4	4	0	0	0	0	0	0	0	0	0	0	0	0	0	.286	.286
Sierra, Henry, N.Y. Mets	.193	42	132	119	17	23	32	3	0	2	8	1	0	0	12	1	23	4	2	5	.269	.267
Silverio, Richard, K.C./Colo.	.211	5	19	19	2	4	6	0	1	0	1	0	0	0	0	0	4	1	0	0	.316	.211
Silvestre, Juan, Seattle	.287	59	234	209	38	60	103	4	3	11	43	0	1	1	23	2	46	0	3	7	.493	.359
Smith, Nestor, N.Y. Yankees	.220	56	240	182	31	40	44	4	0	0	12	1	0	11	46	0	51	42	17	4	.242	.406
Solano, Joel, Toronto	.042	20	30	24	6	1	1	0	0	0	2	1	1	1	3	0	6	0	2	0	.042	.172
Sosa, Henry, Florida	.000	1	0	0	0	0	0	0	0	0	0	0	0	0	0	0	0	0	0	0	.000	.000
Sosa, Jorge, K.C./Colo.	.253	32	100	91	10	23	26	3	0	0	1	0	0	1	8	0	26	1	6	4	.286	.320
Sosa, Leonel, Dodgers I	.253	31	82	79	10	20	22	2	0	0	9	0	0	0	3	1	8	1	1	0	.278	.280
Soto, Luis, Chi. (NL)/S.D.	.222	50	189	158	20	35	46	3	1	2	21	1	2	0	28	0	32	0	1	7	.291	.335
Suero, Ignacio, Toronto	.333	65	275	243	37	81	139	13	0	15	61	1	2	7	22	3	20	2	3	8	.572	.401
Suriel, Miguel, Dodgers I	.295	57	242	210	28	62	89	11	2	4	47	0	8	1	23	0	17	2	1	8	.424	.355
Tavarez, Carlos, Seattle	.235	41	114	98	10	23	28	5	0	0	4	2	0	0	14	0	16	1	2	1	.286	.330
Taveras, Frank, Cleveland	.254	65	270	236	42	60	88	11	7	1	45	6	4	1	23	1	46	9	6	0	.373	.318
Taveras, Jose, K.C./Colo.	.315	54	201	178	35	56	87	8	4	5	24	1	3	4	15	0	27	12	8	3	.489	.375
Taveras, Luis, Texas	.161	37	118	87	17	14	18	2	1	0	8	2	2	1	26	0	13	2	1	4	.207	.353
Thomas, Wilson, N.Y. Yankees	.233	41	139	120	16	28	48	6	1	4	11	1	1	0	17	0	26	0	1	3	.400	.326
Tobias, Enrique, Dodgers I	.235	28	95	85	9	20	29	6	0	1	6	1	1	4	4	0	20	0	0	3	.341	.298
Tolentino, Juan, California	.270	48	164	137	27	37	53	5	1	3	11	1	3	3	22	0	30	5	5	2	.387	.380
Torres, Jairo, Bal./Chi.(AL)	.229	13	44	35	4	8	8	0	0	0	3	0	1	1	7	0	4	0	0	3	.229	.364
Toussent, Andres, Toronto	.000	3	2	2	0	0	0	0	0	0	0	0	0	0	1	0	1	0	0	0	.000	.333
Trinidad, Cesar, San Francisco	.258	44	141	128	19	33	45	8	2	0	19	3	2	1	7	0	17	1	2	2	.344	.297
Ubiera, Nadin, Toyo Carp	.243	56	217	169	32	41	59	6	3	2	24	0	6	2	40	1	31	5	3	1	.349	.382
Ubiera, Vinicio, Dodgers II	.294	30	98	85	15	25	37	5	2	1	12	1	0	0	12	2	9	0	1	1	.435	.381
Urquiola, Edgar, Montreal	.241	47	145	116	24	28	39	4	2	1	11	0	0	4	25	0	14	11	5	1	.336	.393
Valderrama, Carlos, San Fran.	.228	22	63	57	7	13	14	1	0	0	4	0	0	0	6	0	10	1	2	0	.246	.302
Valdez, Alvaro, Cleveland	.273	42	146	132	23	36	44	4	2	0	17	3	0	0	11	0	11	4	1	4	.333	.329
Valdez, Jose, Phi./St.L.	.157	35	123	102	24	16	19	3	0	0	5	1	0	9	11	0	26	4	4	1	.186	.295
Valdez, Socrates, Dodgers I	.273	51	217	187	37	51	77	10	2	4	36	0	0	3	27	5	23	3	4	5	.412	.373
Valera, Ramon, Seattle	.347	59	261	202	50	70	88	6	3	2	20	7	2	3	47	0	23	46	20	3	.436	.472
Vals, Lucrecio, Bal./Chi.(AL)	.211	58	223	199	28	42	47	5	0	0	19	3	1	1	19	0	49	13	6	5	.236	.282
Vargas, Iankel, Detroit	.246	58	222	175	29	43	54	7	2	0	26	3	5	2	37	2	30	7	1	7	.309	.374
Vasquez, Alejandro, Houston	.174	31	105	92	12	16	21	5	0	0	8	0	1	2	10	0	12	2	0	3	.228	.267
Vasquez, Arnulfo, Cleveland	.333	17	62	51	8	17	27	4	0	2	13	1	1	1	8	0	14	1	0	1	.529	.426
Vasquez, Jose, Oakland	.243	56	205	177	28	43	65	9	5	1	29	0	1	1	26	2	36	6	7	4	.367	.341
Vasquez, Moises, Cleveland	.203	23	63	59	3	12	20	1	2	1	3	0	0	0	4	1	14	3	0	0	.339	.254
Velasquez, Geovanny, California	.221	32	117	95	18	21	28	3	2	0	12	1	0	0	21	0	8	4	1	5	.295	.362
Ventura, Frank, Cleveland	.266	59	218	184	33	49	72	12	1	3	34	1	4	3	26	0	22	13	5	5	.391	.359
Ventura, Jose, California	.232	24	67	56	12	13	19	1	1	1	5	0	0	1	10	0	16	3	2	1	.339	.358
Vilomar, Henry, N.Y. Mets	.250	54	221	188	33	47	83	7	1	9	38	2	3	3	25	1	43	11	7	7	.441	.342
Virgil, Marcus, California	.222	30	95	81	6	18	21	3	0	0	7	1	1	1	11	0	10	4	2	0	.259	.319
Williams, Johanny, Phi./St.L.	.193	44	149	140	10	27	43	10	0	2	19	2	0	1	6	2	32	0	5	5	.307	.231
Zamora, Junior, N.Y. Mets	.261	33	135	111	14	29	43	8	0	2	19	0	2	4	18	0	20	2	1	3	.387	.378

1995 PITCHING

TEAM

Team	W	L	Pct.	ERA	G	CG	ShO	Sv.	IP	H	TBF	R	ER	HR	SH	SF	HB	BB	IBB	SO	WP	Bk.
Cleveland	48	20	.706	2.84	69	2	5	23	605.1	512	2528	293	191	16	19	19	29	221	5	417	48	4
Toyo Carp	58	13	.817	2.95	71	19	5	20	617.0	524	2679	288	202	23	14	17	45	278	2	408	40	13
Oakland	44	21	.677	3.17	66	11	5	15	572.2	536	2493	286	202	22	20	21	20	250	6	393	55	5
Toronto	44	24	.647	3.54	68	2	2	25	589.1	533	2559	308	232	33	13	13	37	305	6	476	35	7
California	31	39	.443	3.62	71	15	0	13	604.1	543	2714	372	243	24	15	21	45	313	5	421	45	12
Detroit	34	34	.500	3.80	69	5	3	14	600.0	626	2711	353	253	22	25	20	37	292	27	448	55	12
Dodgers II	44	25	.638	3.81	69	5	5	14	592.1	564	2680	355	251	22	15	25	48	311	10	380	51	18
Texas	39	28	.582	3.94	67	5	4	14	556.2	542	2492	311	244	34	22	21	30	278	12	327	41	5
Seattle	45	21	.682	4.07	66	2	4	20	562.1	503	2513	329	254	47	18	26	47	386	7	477	55	12
Florida	26	42	.382	4.24	68	1	0	11	573.2	579	2630	372	270	30	18	18	57	352	4	411	91	12
N.Y. Mets	41	27	.603	4.26	68	5	1	19	581.1	646	2564	355	275	69	14	15	36	201	10	426	44	10
N.Y. Yankees	31	37	.456	4.31	68	1	2	11	580.2	522	2645	360	278	39	10	13	52	393	1	482	56	11
Hou./Mil.	28	39	.418	4.35	68	2	1	12	594.1	533	2728	390	287	16	25	19	55	395	15	430	99	30
Bal./Chi. (AL)	29	41	.414	4.59	70	10	0	9	594.1	594	2630	432	303	53	17	22	49	336	2	403	55	9
Pittsburgh	30	36	.455	4.82	66	12	3	9	557.0	578	2538	373	298	46	9	21	34	294	7	485	75	13
K.C./Colo.	24	40	.375	4.96	65	2	2	14	566.0	646	2616	446	312	27	15	30	46	236	12	281	77	8
Dodgers I	28	36	.438	4.99	64	1	2	10	542.2	613	2582	395	301	19	21	23	43	360	27	322	70	8
Montreal	21	47	.309	5.08	69	6	0	10	597.0	604	2769	435	337	38	14	30	51	398	16	429	54	10
Phil./St.L.	25	44	.362	5.10	69	1	0	14	586.1	680	2745	486	332	17	14	36	43	291	5	339	81	5
San Francisco	27	44	.380	5.23	71	6	0	10	588.1	650	2922	497	342	18	22	22	62	385	12	360	96	14
Atlanta	26	44	.371	5.30	70	6	1	14	600.1	664	2879	492	354	27	25	25	58	386	15	427	70	10
Chi. (NL)/S.D.	22	45	.328	5.72	68	4	1	9	561.1	651	2653	475	357	40	21	33	35	331	2	344	76	10

INDIVIDUAL

TOP QUALIFIERS FOR EARNED-RUN AVERAGE TITLE

Pitcher, Team	W	L	Pct.	ERA	G	GS	CG	ShO	GF	Sv.	IP	H	TBF	R	ER	HR	SH	SF	HB	BB	IBB	SO	WP	Bk.
Patino, Leonardo, California	5	4	.556	1.35	21	6	2	0	12	3	73.1	56	303	26	11	2	3	1	2	28	2	63	4	3
Guzman, Wilson, Pittsburgh	5	0	1.000	1.47	16	6	1	0	9	4	55.0	52	231	17	9	3	0	1	1	17	2	48	2	1
DeLaCruz, Francisco, Toyo Carp	11	1	.917	1.56	16	13	9	2	1	1	103.2	73	419	26	18	0	0	1	7	31	0	80	5	1
Petique, Marino, Toyo Carp	10	1	.909	1.61	16	12	3	1	2	2	84.0	65	350	29	15	2	4	4	3	32	0	41	1	4
Henriquez, Roman, Dodgers I	8	4	.667	1.81	37	0	0	0	33	8	59.2	56	271	21	12	0	8	3	8	31	5	40	3	1
Mota, Henry, Texas	6	3	.667	1.85	29	4	0	0	23	8	63.1	48	249	19	13	1	4	4	5	12	0	57	4	0
Baez, Miguel, Cleveland	7	2	.778	1.99	15	15	1	1	0	0	95.0	64	369	34	21	0	3	0	6	24	0	74	5	0
Garcia, Jose, Cleveland	6	2	.750	2.02	19	10	0	0	6	2	71.1	60	289	27	16	1	3	1	4	16	1	67	7	0
Ortiz, Ramon, California	8	6	.571	2.23	16	16	7	0	0	0	97.0	79	466	44	24	2	1	2	3	54	0	100	6	2
Zapata, Juan, Houston	5	4	.556	2.31	13	13	1	1	0	0	81.2	60	353	40	21	1	1	1	4	43	1	60	10	0

ALL PITCHERS

Pitcher, Team	W	L	Pct.	ERA	G	GS	CG	ShO	GF	Sv.	IP	H	TBF	R	ER	HR	SH	SF	HB	BB	IBB	SO	WP	Bk.
Aguilar, Henry, California	3	8	.273	3.77	17	15	2	0	2	2	88.1	85	391	64	37	4	3	3	10	40	1	49	3	3
Almonte, Aquiles, Oakland	0	0	.000	0.00	3	0	0	0	3	1	6.0	3	22	0	0	0	0	0	0	3	0	6	0	0
Almonte, Hector, Florida	1	2	.333	4.26	20	1	0	0	16	9	31.2	28	129	17	15	0	1	2	6	11	0	27	3	0
Alvino, Roger, Chi. (NL)/S.D.	2	5	.286	6.02	25	3	0	0	15	8	52.1	46	240	47	35	6	3	5	3	36	1	48	14	0
Andrade, Jensy, Bal./Chi.(AL)	2	1	.667	4.66	6	3	0	0	3	1	19.1	20	91	11	10	1	2	0	1	13	0	15	3	3
Andujar, Elias, Atlanta	2	7	.222	6.28	16	10	2	0	5	0	67.1	85	325	61	47	8	1	4	7	32	0	36	9	2
Aquino, Cleto, Seattle	1	2	.333	11.57	11	2	0	0	4	0	14.0	19	83	21	18	1	0	0	1	24	0	9	4	0
Aracena, Juan, Cleveland	6	2	.750	2.06	24	3	0	0	15	5	56.2	39	224	19	13	0	0	3	4	18	0	31	5	0
Aracena, Ramon, Toyo Carp	7	3	.700	3.68	24	7	2	0	16	6	63.2	66	289	33	26	5	2	1	1	31	1	58	5	1
Arias, Cesarin, Chi. (NL)/S.D.	3	3	.500	5.15	12	12	2	0	0	0	57.2	68	257	44	33	3	2	3	3	14	0	33	1	1
Arias, Jose, Phi./St.L.	7	7	.500	5.31	18	17	1	0	0	0	81.1	98	383	73	48	0	1	2	5	49	0	42	10	0
Arias, Jose, N.Y. Yankees	0	1	.000	13.51	6	1	0	0	2	0	7.1	6	42	13	11	1	0	0	1	16	0	4	3	0
Arias, Kelvin, N.Y. Mets	1	2	.333	5.28	13	4	0	0	3	1	30.2	32	134	21	18	5	1	0	2	12	0	18	4	2
Arias, Miguel, Dodgers II	3	1	.750	1.82	10	8	0	1	0	0	49.1	36	207	12	10	0	1	0	6	22	0	34	3	0
Arias, Rafael, Chi. (NL)/S.D.	0	3	.000	13.74	8	4	0	0	0	0	19.0	35	114	39	29	3	3	2	1	20	0	6	2	0
Arias, Rafael, San Francisco	6	2	.750	3.79	16	10	1	0	1	0	73.2	73	336	49	31	3	2	4	10	31	1	38	8	1
Arias, Roberto, N.Y. Mets	5	2	.714	5.12	13	13	1	0	0	0	63.1	76	279	40	36	9	0	1	4	23	0	43	8	0
Asencio, Eddy, Detroit	3	3	.500	3.06	19	7	1	0	9	1	70.2	76	309	36	24	7	4	2	2	19	3	49	4	1
Avila, Jose, Pittsburgh	6	4	.600	3.09	14	14	4	2	0	0	90.1	73	364	35	31	4	0	1	5	27	0	95	8	0
Baez, Jose, Pittsburgh	0	3	.000	6.62	17	1	0	0	6	0	34.0	47	171	35	25	3	1	0	2	16	2	25	4	3
Baez, Miguel, Cleveland	7	2	.778	1.99	15	15	1	1	0	0	95.0	64	369	34	21	0	3	0	6	24	0	74	5	0
Balbuena, Martin, K.C./Colo.	5	6	.455	3.66	19	9	1	1	3	0	83.2	95	367	51	34	2	3	1	3	34	5	46	8	1
Baruch, Jaime, Montreal	0	2	.000	5.65	8	2	0	0	4	0	14.1	10	70	10	9	0	2	0	2	16	0	11	2	1
Belliard, Carlos, Dodgers II	7	3	.700	3.08	15	13	1	3	2	0	79.0	68	327	35	27	6	2	1	1	31	0	54	4	2
Bello, Emerson, Seattle	7	2	.778	2.80	13	13	1	0	0	0	83.2	72	353	33	26	4	3	2	2	33	1	76	5	1
Betancourt, William, Cleveland	6	2	.750	3.21	13	13	0	0	0	0	67.1	61	285	35	24	1	1	0	1	28	0	48	5	1
Bezhodashvila, N., California	0	1	.000	11.77	8	1	0	0	4	1	13.0	19	74	20	17	1	0	3	1	25	0	12	4	2
Blanco, Daniel, San Francisco	0	0	.000	0.00	1	0	0	0	1	0	1.0	0	6	0	0	0	0	0	0	3	0	1	0	0
Blanco, Fabian, Dodgers II	4	3	.571	4.02	14	13	1	0	1	0	62.2	59	288	45	28	2	0	4	6	38	1	56	10	3
Blanco, Pablo, Florida	3	5	.375	5.36	11	8	0	0	0	0	50.1	48	235	40	30	2	2	4	6	39	0	32	14	1
Blanco Veras, Johanny, Cleveland	3	1	.750	2.91	21	0	0	0	11	6	43.1	36	179	19	14	3	1	1	1	14	1	32	8	0
Bracho, Alejandro, N.Y. Yankees	6	2	.750	2.83	11	11	0	0	0	0	60.1	48	247	22	19	5	1	1	1	30	0	49	0	1
Brand, Fausto, Atlanta	1	7	.125	6.79	12	10	2	0	0	0	51.2	62	258	59	39	0	0	2	6	31	1	38	4	3
Bravo, Luis, Cleveland	1	0	1.000	2.25	1	0	0	0	0	0	4.0	4	15	1	1	0	0	0	0	1	0	3	0	0
Brazoban, Melvin, Texas	3	2	.600	5.57	7	7	0	0	0	0	32.1	30	145	25	20	1	2	2	1	20	0	27	1	0
Brea, Ramsey, Detroit	2	2	.500	4.71	7	7	0	0	0	0	36.1	32	167	29	19	0	1	0	2	27	0	25	5	2
Brito, Jose, California	0	0	.000	6.75	3	1	0	0	0	0	8.0	8	40	8	6	2	0	0	1	3	0	6	4	0
Cabral, Martires, Toronto	2	0	1.000	2.61	15	0	0	0	8	0	20.2	15	89	9	6	1	0	1	2	13	0	20	0	1
Caceres, Antonio, Toronto	3	6	.333	4.72	13	13	0	0	0	0	68.2	75	311	45	36	7	2	6	2	30	0	32	6	0
Cadet, Javier, Chi. (NL)/S.D.	1	0	1.000	5.11	18	1	0	0	12	1	24.2	29	121	17	14	0	0	2	0	21	0	12	4	0
Calderon, Ramon, San Francisco	2	5	.286	3.51	19	7	1	0	3	1	59.0	66	274	40	23	0	4	1	6	25	2	19	6	1
Carela, Jesus, Oakland	0	0	.000	0.00	1	0	0	0	0	0	1.2	1	8	1	0	0	0	0	1	1	0	3	0	0
Cariolan, Roberto, N.Y. Yankees	3	4	.429	5.01	16	7	0	0	4	1	41.1	31	194	28	23	4	1	0	5	39	0	53	6	2
Carjaval, Tomas, California	1	0	1.000	1.80	3	0	0	0	3	1	5.0	3	18	1	1	1	1	0	0	2	0	2	0	0
Carrasquel, Alejandro, Montreal	0	4	.000	8.07	24	0	0	0	15	3	35.2	41	185	40	32	4	3	0	2	40	2	22	8	1
Carrion, Jorge, Houston	1	1	.500	9.52	5	0	0	0	3	0	5.2	6	28	6	6	0	1	0	1	5	1	5	1	0
Carty, Henry, Texas	0	0	.000	0.00	1	0	0	0	0	0	0.2	0	2	0	0	0	0	0	0	0	0	1	0	0
Castillo, Daniel A., Dodgers I	0	1	.000	3.68	3	3	0	0	0	0	7.1	11	36	7	3	0	0	0	0	2	0	1	0	0
Castillo, Jose, Detroit	2	1	.667	3.68	21	0	0	0	12	3	36.2	38	163	18	15	1	2	4	3	15	1	18	1	1
Castillo, Victor, Toronto	0	0	.000	4.50	1	0	0	0	1	0	2.0	3	11	3	1	0	0	0	1	0	0	2	0	0
Castro, Eleuterio, Toyo Carp	0	0	.000	3.86	5	0	0	0	3	2	9.1	8	42	4	4	2	0	0	1	5	0	4	0	0
Celta, Nicolas, Houston	3	8	.273	5.66	16	14	0	0	0	0	70.0	60	318	56	44	2	3	5	5	53	0	61	17	7
Cera, Aquiles, Dodgers II	3	1	.750	4.30	16	3	1	0	7	2	52.1	58	249	36	25	2	3	4	8	24	2	39	1	1
Coco, Pascual, Toronto	7	1	.875	2.78	11	11	0	0	0	0	58.1	51	265	30	18	2	0	1	8	36	0	38	2	1
Collado, Hugo, Dodgers I	0	0	.000	1.29	6	0	0	0	1	0	7.0	7	34	3	1	0	1	0	0	4	0	4	1	0
Contreras, Angel, Pittsburgh	1	2	.333	6.75	9	0	0	0	3	0	14.2	16	75	13	11	1	2	1	1	15	1	9	8	0
Corniell, Henry, Cleveland	0	0	.000	13.50	2	1	0	0	0	0	4.0	7	23	6	6	0	0	1	0	4	0	1	0	0
Cornielle, Alex, Toyo Carp	1	0	1.000	6.41	15	0	0	0	7	2	26.2	39	138	24	19	1	1	3	1	13	0	9	1	2
Cota, Marino, Dodgers II	4	3	.571	4.24	22	0	0	0	8	0	34.0	30	154	21	16	0	4	3	2	10	1	23	0	1
Cruz, Charlie, Dodgers I	0	0	.000	7.59	7	1	0	0	3	0	10.2	11	57	11	9	0	0	2	1	13	0	2	3	0
Cruz, Raul, Oakland	1	1	.500	1.93	10	0	0	0	5	0	18.2	9	82	6	4	0	2	0	2	13	1	12	5	0
Cueto, Jose, Seattle	6	1	.857	3.06	13	13	4	0	0	0	67.2	56	292	36	23	4	2	5	8	31	0	56	4	3
Dacosta, Samuel, Cleveland	0	1	.000	7.15	5	0	0	0	3	0	11.1	15	57	12	9	1	0	1	0	11	0	5	0	0
Davis, Melvin, San Francisco	0	2	.000	4.82	7	0	0	0	1	0	9.1	6	53	8	5	0	1	0	2	14	0	15	1	0
DeLaCruz, Fernando, California	3	5	.375	7.09	10	8	0	0	1	0	39.1	36	198	43	31	0	0	1	1	45	1	49	4	1

SUMMER CLASS A   Dominican Summer League

Pitcher, Team	W	L	Pct.	ERA	G	GS	CG	ShO	GF	Sv.	IP	H	TBF	R	ER	HR	SH	SF	HB	BB	IBB	SO	WP	Bk.
DeLaCruz, Francisco, Toyo Carp	11	1	.917	1.56	16	13	9	2	1	1	103.2	73	419	26	18	0	0	1	7	31	0	80	5	1
DeLaCruz, Inocencio, N.Y. Mets	5	1	.833	3.38	14	13	3	0	0	0	69.1	69	299	36	26	9	1	1	4	24	1	60	4	3
DeLeon, Jose, Detroit	0	1	.000	9.00	1	0	0	0	0	0	2.0	3	11	3	2	0	0	0	0	2	0	1	3	0
DeLeon, Jose, Phi./St.L.	2	3	.400	4.19	24	4	0	0	4	1	73.0	95	337	53	34	3	3	5	2	19	0	40	7	1
DeLeon, Julio, N.Y. Yankees	4	5	.444	5.61	12	12	1	0	0	0	59.1	63	271	47	37	5	1	1	5	31	0	43	6	1
Delgado, Manuel, Toronto	4	4	.500	2.36	25	2	0	0	17	9	53.1	34	212	19	14	2	1	1	2	15	1	60	2	0
Deliza, Angel, Chi. (NL)/S.D.	1	4	.200	6.47	14	0	0	0	7	0	32.0	45	157	29	23	3	0	3	3	18	0	17	5	1
Del Orbe, Wellington, Cleveland	3	2	.600	4.30	14	0	0	0	4	0	23.0	21	102	15	11	1	0	0	1	10	0	8	1	0
DeLosSantos, A., K.C./Colo.	2	3	.400	6.38	22	9	0	0	2	1	66.1	71	309	58	47	6	0	1	7	32	0	38	5	2
DeLosSantos, D., K.C./Colo.	3	4	.429	7.44	26	1	0	0	13	0	42.1	67	207	45	35	2	1	4	2	14	0	19	5	0
DeLosSantos, Luis, N.Y. Yankees	3	4	.429	3.92	12	11	0	0	0	0	64.1	64	288	41	28	1	1	3	5	27	0	40	6	1
Diaz, Esteban, Dodgers I	0	3	.000	4.31	12	10	0	0	2	0	48.0	47	213	28	23	1	2	0	1	31	1	28	2	2
Diese, Jose, Toyo Carp	6	1	.857	2.33	12	10	0	1	1	0	54.0	39	241	27	14	1	1	1	3	36	0	51	11	4
Disla, Francisco, N.Y. Yankees	2	3	.400	2.62	9	9	0	0	0	0	34.1	19	150	15	10	1	1	0	3	31	0	32	0	0
D'LaCruz, Ignacio, San Francisco	1	3	.250	8.33	20	3	0	0	7	0	31.1	39	160	33	29	1	0	2	2	29	1	15	4	2
Dotel, Melido, Dodgers II	4	5	.444	4.91	13	13	1	0	0	0	58.2	52	263	42	32	2	2	2	5	43	0	25	6	0
Ernesto, Hector, Florida	1	1	.500	5.59	16	1	0	0	6	0	46.2	60	217	35	29	5	1	1	6	19	0	22	5	1
Escarlante, Simon, Phi./St.L.	1	9	.100	5.35	19	11	0	0	7	1	72.1	86	345	74	43	4	4	4	1	41	1	39	18	0
Escobar, Kelvin, Toronto	0	1	.000	1.72	3	2	0	0	0	0	15.2	14	62	3	3	0	0	0	0	5	1	20	0	0
Espinal, Orlando, Montreal	0	3	.000	5.59	14	6	0	0	3	0	37.0	30	181	28	23	0	0	1	9	33	0	20	3	2
Esquea, Alvin, Texas	0	0	.000	....	1	0	0	0	0	0	0.0	0	3	2	2	0	0	0	0	3	0	0	0	0
Estrella, Leoncio, N.Y. Mets	2	4	.333	5.44	12	8	0	0	1	0	43.0	61	202	37	26	5	0	4	4	13	0	32	6	2
Felix, Miguel, Bal./Chi.(AL)	3	5	.375	4.94	15	14	1	0	1	0	82.0	77	380	61	45	4	2	4	13	49	0	47	10	0
Felix, Osvaldo, K.C./Colo.	0	0	.000	9.00	5	0	0	0	1	0	5.0	10	29	7	5	1	0	1	0	2	0	3	0	0
Fernandez, Robert, Cleveland	2	0	1.000	3.94	6	3	0	0	1	0	16.0	9	71	10	7	0	0	0	2	16	0	14	2	0
Fernandez, Winston, Texas	0	0	.000	0.00	1	0	0	0	1	0	0.1	1	3	1	0	0	0	0	0	0	0	0	1	0
Florentino, Osmil, K.C./Colo.	0	0	.000	7.36	2	0	0	0	0	0	3.2	5	18	5	3	0	1	0	0	3	0	2	2	0
Francisco, Norberto, Bal./Chi.(AL)	0	0	.000	4.82	5	1	0	0	0	0	9.1	8	48	8	5	1	0	1	2	12	0	6	1	0
Frias, Jovanny, Bal./Chi.(AL)	1	6	.143	4.67	13	12	0	0	1	0	71.1	86	318	52	37	7	1	0	4	28	0	34	0	2
Fructuoso, Jose, Seattle	2	2	.500	3.13	7	6	0	0	1	1	23.0	16	96	9	8	3	0	0	1	12	0	17	1	1
Galvez, Randy, Dodgers I	5	5	.500	4.27	32	0	0	0	13	2	65.1	67	285	38	31	3	1	4	3	31	6	48	4	4
Garcia, Espedy, Oakland	1	2	.333	9.15	8	5	0	0	3	0	19.2	16	102	26	20	2	1	1	1	24	0	28	4	0
Garcia, Jhoan, Seattle	1	2	.333	5.96	20	1	0	0	4	1	25.2	23	127	23	17	1	1	4	4	27	0	19	2	1
Garcia, Jose, Cleveland	6	2	.750	2.02	19	10	0	0	6	2	71.1	60	289	27	16	1	3	1	4	16	1	67	7	0
Garcia, Rafael, Seattle	3	1	.750	4.84	18	5	0	0	1	0	48.1	35	216	32	26	6	2	3	4	42	0	40	3	0
Genao, Henry, Cleveland	0	0	.000	8.38	8	0	0	0	4	0	9.2	13	58	14	9	1	0	0	1	16	0	5	1	0
Genao, Martin, Dodgers II	4	2	.667	3.29	17	3	0	0	8	2	52.0	58	233	26	19	0	0	0	5	19	1	30	3	2
German, John, N.Y. Mets	6	2	.750	4.99	18	9	0	0	3	2	52.1	65	243	34	29	8	0	2	5	23	1	32	4	0
German, Julio, Detroit	0	0	.000	0.00	1	0	0	0	0	0	1.0	0	4	0	0	0	0	1	0	1	0	0	0	0
Glaterol, Becker, Toronto	4	3	.571	4.00	23	6	0	0	14	10	65.1	61	274	33	29	2	1	0	2	23	1	69	3	0
Gomez, Domingo, California	0	1	.000	3.35	18	0	0	0	13	5	48.1	39	163	23	18	1	1	6	2	17	0	8	0	2
Gomez, Jose, Seattle	4	3	.571	4.60	23	1	0	0	4	0	45.0	37	208	36	23	6	1	2	5	35	0	19	5	3
Gomez, Luis, Detroit	2	1	.667	4.68	17	0	0	0	8	0	25.0	22	126	23	13	0	3	2	3	26	2	17	7	0
Gomez, Luis, Houston	0	0	.000	3.86	7	0	0	0	3	0	9.1	8	42	7	4	1	0	0	2	2	0	3	0	0
Gomez, Manuel, Detroit	3	4	.429	3.30	21	4	0	0	9	6	46.1	43	206	22	17	2	3	1	2	23	7	49	2	1
Gomez, Miguel, Toronto	2	0	1.000	1.23	3	3	2	0	0	0	22.0	14	81	6	3	2	0	0	2	5	0	19	1	0
Gomez, Rafael, N.Y. Mets	3	4	.429	4.01	17	2	0	0	8	2	42.2	49	177	21	19	3	0	2	3	6	1	39	2	0
Gomez, Ricardo, Pittsburgh	2	3	.400	8.14	11	3	0	0	3	1	24.1	32	115	24	22	4	1	1	1	15	0	20	6	0
Gondola, Roberto, N.Y. Yankees	1	2	.333	3.37	15	0	0	0	3	1	34.2	37	155	19	13	1	0	2	1	19	0	38	6	1
Gonzalez, Edwin, K.C./Colo.	3	1	.750	2.66	35	0	0	0	28	10	50.2	55	232	27	15	2	1	5	4	19	3	40	10	0
Gonzalez, Elin, K.C./Colo.	0	0	.000	32.34	1	1	0	0	0	0	1.2	7	15	6	6	1	0	0	0	4	0	0	0	0
Guerra, Robert, California	0	0	.000	0.00	2	0	0	0	2	0	0.2	1	2	0	0	0	0	0	0	0	0	0	0	0
Guerrero, Jose, Seattle	4	1	.800	2.09	29	0	0	0	28	15	38.2	23	155	12	9	3	3	0	2	17	2	57	1	0
Guevara, Carlos, Pittsburgh	1	2	.333	5.79	5	0	0	0	2	0	9.1	11	43	8	6	1	0	0	1	4	0	10	0	0
Guillen, Angel, San Francisco	3	4	.429	5.23	28	0	0	0	20	6	43.0	41	190	31	25	2	4	1	4	25	3	21	8	6
Guzman, Ambiorix, Texas	2	3	.400	5.21	19	1	0	0	11	3	38.0	37	176	25	22	3	3	4	4	19	3	17	1	1
Guzman, Leybi, Dodgers I	1	2	.333	6.59	9	8	0	0	0	0	27.1	38	137	28	20	0	0	2	0	17	0	13	10	0
Guzman, Toribio A., Phi./St.L.	3	3	.500	4.03	18	7	0	0	3	0	58.0	55	265	37	26	1	1	3	4	35	0	46	9	0
Guzman, Wilson, Pittsburgh	5	0	1.000	1.47	16	6	1	0	9	4	55.0	52	231	17	9	3	0	1	1	17	2	48	2	1
Henriquez, Hector, Florida	1	3	.250	3.16	13	13	0	0	0	0	57.0	50	257	26	20	2	3	0	5	46	0	51	6	2
Henriquez, Jovanny, Texas	1	4	.200	3.74	15	9	0	0	4	1	53.0	45	244	32	22	3	2	1	1	39	1	34	7	0
Henriquez, Roman, Dodgers I	8	4	.667	1.81	37	0	0	0	33	8	59.2	56	271	21	12	0	8	3	8	31	5	40	3	1
Heredia, Maximo, Bal./Chi.(AL)	4	7	.364	3.86	16	15	3	0	1	0	93.1	89	323	68	40	5	3	3	12	43	0	46	3	1
Heredia, Ruddy, Toronto	1	0	1.000	0.00	1	0	0	0	0	0	1.0	1	5	0	0	0	0	0	0	1	0	0	0	0
Heredia, Willy, Atlanta	2	2	.500	11.44	11	1	0	0	3	0	19.2	31	120	34	25	0	0	4	3	25	1	11	8	1
Hernandez, German, Texas	1	0	1.000	2.53	3	2	0	0	0	0	10.2	10	46	3	3	0	0	0	0	8	0	3	0	1
Hernandez, Jose, Montreal	5	2	.714	3.90	15	15	1	0	0	0	99.1	99	442	59	43	7	0	2	4	39	2	98	4	0
Hernandez, Julio, California	0	2	.000	7.71	3	2	0	0	0	0	14.0	16	68	13	12	0	0	2	0	10	0	9	2	1
Hernandez, Pedro, Dodgers II	5	4	.556	3.73	14	14	1	1	0	0	79.2	87	356	47	33	5	1	3	5	20	0	46	8	4
Herrera, Misael, Chi. (NL)/S.D.	4	6	.400	4.66	15	13	1	0	1	0	73.1	70	317	51	38	2	0	2	5	29	0	43	6	3
Hiraldo, Juan, Cleveland	4	2	.667	4.44	14	9	0	0	0	0	50.2	48	221	34	25	1	4	5	3	27	0	35	1	0
Javier, Elias, K.C./Colo.	0	0	.000	33.71	2	0	0	0	1	0	2.2	7	22	10	10	1	0	0	0	6	0	1	5	0
Javier, Frank, Florida	2	2	.500	3.05	15	0	0	0	6	0	20.2	18	93	12	7	1	2	0	1	14	0	12	2	0
Jimenez, Alejandro, Texas	0	3	.000	12.97	5	2	0	0	0	0	8.1	9	52	19	12	1	0	0	0	20	0	7	2	0
Jimenez, Denny, Oakland	8	3	.727	2.67	15	11	3	2	3	1	84.1	92	358	37	25	1	4	5	2	19	0	48	3	0
Jimenez, Jhonatan, Texas	0	0	.000	6.00	1	0	0	0	1	1	3.0	2	14	2	2	0	0	1	0	3	0	2	1	0
Jimenez, Johnn, Dodgers I	3	0	1.000	4.54	13	0	0	0	1	0	35.2	39	164	29	18	0	1	2	3	20	3	22	4	0
Jimenez, Kelly, K.C./Colo.	4	2	.667	3.62	16	13	0	0	0	0	77.0	75	311	38	31	3	1	2	2	5	0	32	4	0
Jimenez, Ricardo, Bal./Chi.(AL)	2	3	.400	7.43	15	7	0	0	5	2	40.0	45	207	41	33	4	0	5	3	40	0	27	1	0
Lara, Nelson, Florida	0	3	.000	8.10	5	5	0	0	0	0	20.0	26	103	24	18	2	0	2	3	17	0	8	2	0
LaReal, Guillermo, San Francisco	2	0	1.000	4.12	13	0	0	0	6	1	19.2	26	92	12	9	0	0	0	2	6	0	8	1	1
Lechler, Luis, Dodgers II	4	2	.667	4.94	16	1	0	0	3	0	27.1	22	134	20	15	1	0	1	3	31	2	20	5	1
Leon, Rafael, Florida	2	6	.250	3.31	17	5	0	0	7	1	49.0	52	231	34	18	4	3	1	3	28	1	45	8	2

Pitcher, Team	W	L	Pct.	ERA	G	GS	CG	ShO	GF	Sv.	IP	H	TBF	R	ER	HR	SH	SF	HB	BB	IBB	SO	WP	Bk.
Leyva, Edgar, California	4	2	.667	2.78	11	9	1	0	1	0	68.0	57	289	27	21	3	2	0	9	28	0	42	0	2
Linares, Edwin, Atlanta	1	3	.250	4.11	15	15	1	0	0	0	85.1	84	395	59	39	2	8	4	2	66	2	78	13	2
Linares, Mario, Toyo Carp	8	3	.727	4.02	15	13	3	0	0	0	87.1	87	397	54	39	4	1	1	16	36	0	45	8	0
Lizardo, Julio, San Francisco	4	5	.444	4.82	13	10	0	0	0	0	56.0	57	375	38	30	1	2	3	14	37	0	41	5	0
Lora, Edison, K.C./Colo.	1	6	.143	4.91	17	10	0	0	2	0	51.1	54	243	43	28	2	2	1	6	28	0	19	7	1
Lora, Freddy, Pittsburgh	3	6	.333	3.93	15	9	1	0	2	0	66.1	58	288	36	29	4	0	2	0	32	0	61	9	2
Lorenzo, Martin, Houston	2	7	.222	5.59	18	10	0	0	1	0	66.0	61	319	55	41	1	1	3	12	43	0	33	7	9
Luis, Cristain, Houston	0	0	.000	6.23	14	1	0	0	4	0	17.1	21	85	13	12	2	0	2	3	12	0	8	4	0
Maria, Alcibiades, Texas	2	1	.667	4.94	11	2	0	0	4	0	27.1	40	136	18	15	5	0	2	2	11	1	9	3	0
Marshall, Victor, N.Y. Yankees	4	3	.571	5.87	22	1	0	0	15	5	23.0	17	111	17	15	1	1	2	4	20	0	27	4	1
Marte, Julian, Dodgers II	1	0	1.000	0.00	4	0	0	0	2	0	8.0	6	35	3	0	0	0	0	4	0	1	2	0
Marte, Luis, K.C./Colo.	1	5	.167	2.82	11	6	0	0	2	0	38.1	33	173	27	12	1	1	1	4	15	1	27	4	0
Martinez, Claudio, Dodgers II	0	0	.000	5.58	6	0	0	0	2	0	9.2	8	46	10	6	1	0	0	0	8	0	5	2	1
Martinez, Frank, Houston	2	1	.667	3.90	17	9	0	0	2	0	60.0	56	267	35	26	1	1	3	33	0	31	10	2
Martinez, Gabriel, Chi. (NL)/S.D.	0	1	.000	8.10	7	1	0	0	4	0	10.0	12	50	9	9	1	0	1	0	12	0	5	7	0
Martinez, Jhonny, K.C./Colo.	0	0	.000	4.16	3	0	0	0	1	0	4.1	6	21	3	2	0	0	1	2	1	1	1	0
Martinez, Jose, Texas	6	3	.667	3.47	16	7	1	0	7	0	62.1	60	267	28	24	4	5	1	1	19	2	39	3	1
Martinez, Juan R., Texas	0	0	.000	9.00	1	0	0	0	1	0	1.0	2	5	1	1	0	0	0	0	0	0	0	0	0
Martinez, Romulo, Detroit	0	0	.000	7.73	1	1	0	0	0	0	2.1	3	12	3	2	0	0	0	0	3	0	2	0	0
Martinez, Sandy, Houston	1	2	.333	5.40	19	0	0	0	4	0	38.1	51	193	33	23	1	4	2	4	27	1	24	5	1
Martinez, Wander, California	3	5	.375	2.55	11	9	3	0	0	0	67.0	62	297	34	19	2	1	1	4	17	0	44	5	1
Matias, Hansell, Atlanta	5	5	.500	4.81	21	2	1	0	9	1	76.2	101	359	63	41	6	4	4	5	24	0	47	2	0
Matos, Dauris, N.Y. Mets	0	0	.000	4.43	21	1	0	0	11	2	40.2	44	187	24	20	8	2	0	2	25	0	25	2	0
McWellyng, Venien, California	0	0	.000	16.17	3	0	0	0	2	0	1.2	3	9	3	3	0	0	0	0	2	0	2	0	0
Medina, Carlos, Florida	2	3	.400	7.18	12	11	1	0	0	0	62.0	59	266	29	15	2	2	0	30	0	47	9	0
Medina, Edward, Detroit	2	0	.000	7.00	12	1	0	0	2	0	9.0	7	58	13	7	0	2	1	3	19	0	1	1	0
Mejia, Luis, N.Y. Yankees	2	2	.500	2.60	15	0	0	0	7	0	27.2	13	125	15	8	0	0	0	3	28	0	38	1	1
Melian, Jhonathan, Seattle	1	0	1.000	3.60	17	0	0	0	4	0	20.0	16	103	11	8	3	1	1	3	23	1	12	5	0
Mena, Eddy, Detroit	0	0	.000	0.00	1	0	0	0	0	0	3.2	7	18	1	0	0	0	0	0	0	0	1	0	0
Mendez, Lenin, Seattle	0	0	.000	5.68	8	0	0	0	3	0	12.2	11	62	12	8	1	0	2	2	10	1	6	0	0
Mercedes, Carlos, Bal./Chi.(AL)	2	4	.333	4.74	12	0	0	0	10	2	24.2	29	115	19	13	1	1	1	1	7	0	25	1	0
Mercedes, Daniel, Pittsburgh	0	0	.000	11.57	6	0	0	0	2	0	7.0	10	42	10	9	0	0	1	2	12	0	3	5	0
Mercedes, Jose, Oakland	2	6	.250	5.03	15	13	1	0	1	1	73.1	87	352	63	41	5	5	5	2	48	0	36	10	0
Mercedes, Matias, Detroit	0	0	.000	13.43	1	0	0	0	0	0	2.0	3	11	0	0	0	0	0	2	0	0	0	0
Mercedes, Tomas, Toronto	4	2	.667	4.24	13	3	0	0	5	0	40.1	38	186	24	19	3	2	2	5	25	0	25	5	1
Mesa, Willy, K.C./Colo.	0	0	.000	4.91	6	0	0	0	0	0	7.1	7	35	5	4	0	0	0	0	6	0	5	4	0
Mesina, Juan, Florida	4	1	.800	3.13	20	0	0	0	10	0	31.2	24	142	14	11	1	1	0	3	20	3	28	3	0
Minaya, Pablo, Florida	1	4	.200	5.23	14	11	0	0	0	0	51.2	54	254	36	30	1	0	3	9	50	0	28	16	2
Monero, Pablo, California	2	1	.667	4.91	19	1	0	0	8	0	36.2	36	181	32	20	3	0	1	10	12	0	21	6	4
Montanez, Johan, Toronto	6	2	.750	3.51	13	12	0	0	0	0	77.0	82	337	34	30	6	0	1	1	45	1	42	2	0
Montero, Agustin, Oakland	0	1	.000	11.59	1	0	0	0	0	0	2.1	7	17	6	3	1	0	1	0	2	0	2	3	0
Montero, Francisco, Phi./St.L.	4	2	.667	3.69	29	0	0	0	15	2	53.2	50	247	26	22	0	0	2	8	29	2	34	1	1
Morel, Jose, Pittsburgh	4	2	.667	4.36	9	7	0	0	0	0	41.1	47	185	26	20	2	0	4	0	14	0	31	7	0
Moreno, Willy, N.Y. Yankees	0	0	.000	0.00	1	0	0	0	1	0	1.0	0	4	0	0	0	0	0	1	0	1	1	0
Moris, Miguel, N.Y. Mets	0	2	.000	3.47	13	3	0	0	3	0	33.2	33	149	23	13	4	2	1	4	10	0	19	4	0
Morrobel, Juan, Pittsburgh	0	1	.000	7.20	7	2	0	0	1	0	15.0	18	84	13	12	3	0	2	0	21	0	15	1	0
Mota, Henry, Texas	6	3	.667	1.85	29	4	0	0	23	8	63.1	48	249	19	13	1	4	4	5	12	0	57	4	0
Mota, Leonardo, San Francisco	0	1	.000	5.86	23	2	0	0	4	0	43.0	47	211	41	28	6	2	0	6	41	1	21	9	1
Nina, Jose, Bal./Chi.(AL)	2	0	1.000	9.88	8	0	0	0	2	0	13.2	21	70	16	15	6	0	1	1	11	0	4	4	1
Nivar, Amaury, K.C./Colo.	1	0	1.000	7.73	3	0	0	0	0	0	2.1	3	15	7	2	0	0	1	0	5	0	2	2	0
Nunez, Enrique, Phi./St.L.	2	7	.222	4.59	15	15	0	0	0	0	80.1	87	362	62	41	2	0	8	10	29	0	44	4	1
Nunez, Franklin, Dodgers II	1	0	1.000	7.36	12	1	0	0	4	0	22.0	27	118	25	18	0	1	3	20	0	17	2	0
Oliver, Jose, Oakland	4	2	.667	3.10	19	3	0	0	11	2	49.1	51	214	24	17	4	4	2	1	13	1	36	6	1
Olivo, Gary, San Francisco	0	2	.000	11.17	8	7	0	0	0	0	19.1	20	113	32	24	0	1	1	0	33	1	7	12	1
Olivo, Juan, Toyo Carp	3	0	1.000	2.89	19	2	0	0	8	5	46.2	44	192	17	15	2	1	0	17	0	27	4	1
Orta, Carlos, Montreal	2	6	.250	6.71	22	5	0	0	6	0	61.2	83	317	57	46	5	1	7	10	55	4	38	8	1
Ortiz, Eusebio, Phi./St.L.	0	1	.000	7.49	16	1	0	0	6	0	39.2	58	206	46	33	2	2	4	2	19	1	16	6	0
Ortiz, Pedro, Dodgers I	0	0	.000	9.52	8	0	0	0	2	0	5.2	11	37	9	6	3	1	0	0	8	1	2	3	0
Ortiz, Ramon, California	8	6	.571	2.23	16	16	7	0	0	0	97.0	79	466	44	24	2	1	2	3	54	0	100	6	2
Oviedo, Alexander, Oakland	8	1	.889	3.25	14	13	2	1	0	0	82.1	73	346	37	27	1	0	4	2	34	0	65	6	0
Ozorio, Douglas, N.Y. Yankees	0	1	.000	8.31	5	0	0	0	4	1	4.1	6	23	5	4	1	1	0	2	4	1	2	1	0
Ozorio, Eric, Atlanta	1	6	.143	9.08	20	5	0	0	15	3	37.2	53	200	50	38	1	3	1	3	34	0	24	6	0
Ozuna, Carlos, Oakland	2	0	1.000	2.61	12	1	0	0	5	1	41.1	37	179	15	12	2	0	1	2	26	0	19	1	0
Padua, Gerardo, N.Y. Yankees	1	1	.500	3.79	14	0	0	0	8	0	19.0	16	88	9	8	2	0	0	3	13	0	12	4	0
Paniagua, Freddy, Florida	4	2	.667	3.46	21	0	0	0	14	1	26.0	26	120	15	10	1	1	3	16	2	15	5	1
Paraqueima, Jesus, N.Y. Yankees	1	2	.333	6.67	11	6	0	0	0	0	27.0	27	130	23	20	3	0	0	3	27	0	22	4	1
Paredes, Roberto, Cleveland	3	2	.600	1.99	29	0	0	0	19	7	45.1	36	184	14	10	3	2	3	15	2	30	1	1
Parra, Catalino, N.Y. Yankees	2	1	.667	3.60	15	1	0	0	3	0	45.0	45	199	22	18	1	1	0	4	23	0	31	3	0
Parra, Jesus, Houston	4	4	.500	3.13	12	12	0	0	0	0	68.1	49	298	30	23	0	5	1	6	41	2	74	6	2
Parra, Jorge, Texas	0	1	.000	4.78	21	1	0	0	5	0	37.2	44	177	23	20	4	1	2	2	20	2	17	0	0
Parra, Klisber, Florida	4	5	.444	4.23	12	11	0	0	1	0	66.0	61	281	41	31	5	1	0	3	20	0	46	8	2
Pascual, Roberto, Chi. (NL)/S.D.	0	0	.000	0.00	1	0	0	0	1	0	0.2	0	3	1	0	0	0	0	1	0	1	1	0
Pascual, Ubaldo, Chi. (NL)/S.D.	5	1	.167	4.35	23	0	0	0	13	0	51.2	50	241	40	25	4	0	6	4	31	0	36	7	0
Patino, Leonardo, California	5	4	.556	1.35	21	6	2	0	12	3	73.1	56	303	26	11	2	3	1	2	28	2	63	4	3
Paulino, Arison, Pittsburgh	0	0	.000	10.29	7	0	0	0	2	0	7.0	15	47	11	8	0	0	3	1	8	1	6	0	3
Paulino, Manuel, Oakland	5	1	.833	1.09	17	0	0	0	17	8	33.0	25	133	6	4	0	1	0	7	3	28	2	0
Peguero, Americo, Bal./Chi.(AL)	8	3	.727	2.48	15	13	6	0	1	1	101.2	64	417	38	28	5	3	1	8	47	0	120	11	0
Pena, Domingo, Pittsburgh	0	2	.000	8.03	11	0	0	0	7	0	12.1	8	62	13	11	0	0	1	18	0	10	7	0
Perdomo, Roberto, San Francisco	1	1	.500	4.11	9	0	0	0	3	0	15.1	16	65	8	7	0	0	0	2	5	0	7	1	0
Perez, Jorge, N.Y. Yankees	0	1	.000	4.96	8	1	0	0	3	0	16.1	14	74	12	9	2	0	0	1	16	0	10	2	0
Perez, Samuel, Cleveland	4	2	.667	2.61	18	6	0	0	2	1	62.0	51	265	30	18	3	4	1	2	26	0	46	9	1
Perozo, Alberto, Atlanta	4	3	.571	4.03	25	0	0	0	23	9	38.0	46	179	22	17	1	1	0	4	22	1	20	5	0
Petique, Marino, Toyo Carp	10	1	.909	1.61	16	12	3	1	2	2	84.0	65	350	29	15	2	4	4	3	32	0	41	1	4

Pitcher, Team	W	L	Pct.	ERA	G	GS	CG	ShO	GF	Sv.	IP	H	TBF	R	ER	HR	SH	SF	HB	BB	IBB	SO	WP	Bk.
Pinales, Demetrio, Texas	0	1	.000	3.15	7	2	0	0	0	0	20.0	18	93	9	7	1	1	0	1	11	0	14	1	0
Pinales, Otilio, Seattle	0	1	.000	9.58	14	2	0	0	3	0	20.2	20	118	27	22	1	1	0	4	38	0	17	7	0
Pineda, Luis, Texas	6	1	.857	3.00	12	5	0	0	1	0	39.0	36	186	17	13	0	2	0	4	31	2	19	6	1
Polanco, Elvis, Chi. (NL)/S.D.	1	5	.167	8.12	15	13	1	0	0	0	57.2	90	307	65	52	5	2	2	8	43	0	60	9	0
Polanco, Julio, Texas	0	0	.000	6.75	3	1	0	0	0	0	5.1	2	30	6	4	0	0	1	0	12	0	0	6	1
Presinal, Gilberto, Chi. (NL)/S.D.	1	1	.500	5.18	12	0	0	0	3	0	24.1	24	115	16	14	4	0	1	0	20	0	15	0	3
Quezada, Anulfo, California	2	4	.333	4.00	14	3	0	0	5	1	36.1	36	171	27	16	3	2	1	2	16	0	12	4	1
Quezada, Edward, Montreal	0	1	.000	6.77	1	0	0	0	0	0	1.1	2	8	3	1	1	1	1	0	2	0	0	0	0
Quiroz, Misael, Pittsburgh	2	6	.250	4.00	15	14	3	0	1	0	81.0	83	368	49	36	9	2	2	6	34	0	64	13	2
Racero, Aramis, Toronto	1	1	.500	6.46	8	8	0	0	0	0	30.2	38	148	29	22	5	0	0	3	26	0	19	3	0
Rafael, Jorge, Toronto	5	1	.833	3.59	11	8	0	0	1	0	47.2	33	201	24	19	1	2	0	7	31	0	36	5	4
Ramirez, Antonio, Montreal	2	1	.667	3.95	11	7	0	0	1	0	43.1	41	184	22	19	6	1	1	1	18	0	44	0	0
Ramirez, Jose, Detroit	7	5	.583	2.49	17	14	1	0	1	1	94.0	100	405	45	26	1	2	2	4	36	1	82	5	1
Ramos, Fernando, Phi./St.L.	2	5	.286	6.27	15	8	0	0	3	0	56.0	75	254	49	39	4	0	2	6	16	0	31	5	0
Ramos, Jose, Dodgers I	3	2	.600	5.10	26	2	0	0	2	0	67.0	82	319	51	38	2	5	3	9	32	4	35	9	0
Ramos, Juan C., Montreal	3	6	.333	5.09	16	15	4	0	1	1	88.1	99	386	56	50	6	0	5	6	29	2	66	2	1
Ravelo, Carlos, San Francisco	0	0	.000	13.03	9	0	0	0	4	0	9.2	19	67	25	14	0	0	3	1	14	0	5	9	0
Regalado, Frank, Toyo Carp	3	1	.750	10.64	8	0	0	0	2	0	11.0	14	56	15	13	2	0	0	0	9	0	8	1	0
Regalado, Maximo, Dodgers I	0	2	.000	7.86	11	3	0	0	0	0	18.1	21	93	20	16	3	0	1	2	14	1	13	2	0
Reyes, Bernardo, Dodgers II	0	0	.000	4.82	6	0	0	0	1	0	9.1	6	51	8	5	0	0	1	3	13	0	1	1	0
Reyes, Jose Luis, N.Y. Mets	3	3	.500	5.44	21	0	0	0	13	4	48.0	64	217	38	29	6	4	1	2	11	1	45	3	0
Reyes, Juan, Montreal	1	9	.100	5.40	15	9	1	0	2	0	61.2	68	289	52	37	1	0	4	5	42	2	36	5	2
Reyes, Pedro, N.Y. Yankees	0	1	.000	5.04	14	0	0	0	5	0	25.0	27	127	18	14	3	0	1	5	14	0	12	2	1
Reyes, Santos, Detroit	2	1	.667	3.66	10	0	0	0	5	1	19.2	19	84	10	8	1	2	1	2	9	0	9	1	0
Richardson, Roberto, Phi./St.L.	0	2	.000	14.29	12	2	0	0	5	0	17.0	31	102	33	27	0	0	2	3	19	0	8	8	0
Rijo, Fernando, Dodgers I	3	6	.333	7.07	16	11	1	0	0	0	56.0	71	279	51	44	0	0	3	1	45	2	28	3	0
Rijo, Francisco, Toyo Carp	2	1	.667	3.06	15	1	0	0	10	1	35.1	20	146	15	12	2	2	0	3	19	1	26	1	0
Rijo, Jose, Houston	3	5	.375	3.92	28	0	0	0	24	7	43.2	40	187	22	19	1	0	0	4	25	3	37	8	0
Rincones, Gabriel, Seattle	4	3	.571	5.98	13	12	1	0	0	0	58.2	62	270	44	39	10	1	3	5	32	0	41	7	0
Rivera, Homero, Detroit	0	0	.000	4.44	16	2	0	0	7	0	26.1	26	119	14	13	1	0	0	4	12	1	21	1	0
Rivera, Juan C., Chi. (NL)/S.D.	0	0	.000	11.59	2	0	0	0	2	0	2.1	6	14	3	3	1	0	0	0	2	0	3	1	0
Rodriguez, Aron, Bal./Chi.(AL)	0	2	.000	6.75	10	0	0	0	4	0	17.1	17	88	22	13	2	0	0	0	19	0	3	2	1
Rodriguez, Franklin, Toronto	2	1	.667	2.82	19	0	0	0	5	0	38.1	37	170	24	12	2	3	1	2	24	0	39	3	0
Rodriguez, Henry, Bal./Chi.(AL)	3	5	.375	3.65	21	0	0	0	15	1	49.1	55	229	35	20	10	1	0	0	23	1	33	9	0
Rodriguez, Marcell, Oakland	1	0	1.000	9.00	2	0	0	0	1	0	2.0	2	10	2	2	0	0	0	0	2	0	1	0	0
Rodriguez, Nelson, Dodgers I	0	0	.000	0.00	1	0	0	0	1	0	0.2	1	4	0	0	0	0	0	0	1	0	0	1	0
Rodriguez, Pedro, Seattle	3	2	.600	3.57	13	11	0	0	0	0	53.0	39	241	24	21	4	1	2	5	45	0	25	6	3
Rodriguez, Rodney, Atlanta	0	0	.000	18.57	4	0	0	0	0	0	5.1	9	39	14	11	0	0	1	5	7	0	0	4	0
Rojas, Cesar, Texas	5	3	.625	4.30	13	10	2	0	1	1	67.0	74	292	38	32	7	1	2	5	14	0	29	2	0
Rojas, Francisco, Dodgers II	2	1	.667	3.21	16	0	0	0	7	2	28.0	29	130	14	10	0	1	1	1	23	3	20	2	3
Rojas, Juan P., Atlanta	4	2	.667	4.06	14	14	0	0	0	0	68.2	72	324	44	31	2	0	1	5	47	2	36	3	0
Romano, Manuel, San Francisco	3	5	.375	5.11	10	9	1	0	0	0	56.1	60	270	51	32	1	0	1	4	38	2	49	7	1
Romero, Mario, Houston	0	0	.000	9.00	11	0	0	0	5	0	12.0	16	67	13	12	0	0	1	4	11	0	8	7	0
Romero, Raumer, Montreal	5	4	.556	3.36	32	0	0	0	20	5	67.0	54	285	34	25	4	3	3	3	40	4	49	11	0
Rondon, Gabriel, Houston	2	2	.500	5.21	18	0	0	0	9	3	38.0	33	178	27	22	2	2	0	2	26	2	32	5	4
Rosario, Rafael, Detroit	0	3	.000	7.48	19	2	0	0	4	1	33.2	48	179	37	28	1	0	2	3	27	2	14	4	1
Rosario, Ramon, Oakland	2	2	.500	2.75	13	4	0	0	5	1	39.1	33	170	16	12	3	2	0	1	25	1	19	5	2
Rosario, Reynaldo, Detroit	2	3	.400	4.73	10	9	0	0	1	0	45.2	43	197	26	24	4	2	1	0	23	4	47	2	0
Rosario, Ruben, Phi./St.L.	1	1	.500	4.15	3	3	0	0	0	0	13.0	14	62	10	6	1	0	0	0	6	0	9	2	0
Samuel, Yojairo, Texas	6	3	.667	3.16	15	14	2	1	1	0	79.2	76	337	39	28	3	1	1	4	31	1	47	2	0
Sanchez, Jose, Detroit	0	0	.000	9.00	2	0	0	0	2	0	1.0	5	8	1	1	0	0	0	0	0	0	1	0	0
Sanchez, Jossys, Montreal	0	0	.000	2.45	8	0	0	0	3	1	11.0	5	51	4	3	0	2	1	3	8	0	12	1	0
Sanchez, Martin, Atlanta	4	4	.500	3.87	16	16	2	0	0	0	102.1	88	450	58	44	6	2	2	12	41	0	110	12	2
Sanchez, Wellington, Chi. (NL)/S.D.	3	5	.375	4.91	15	10	0	0	1	0	58.2	63	266	47	32	2	3	2	2	26	0	21	2	2
Santamaria, Juan, Detroit	0	1	.000	9.00	1	1	0	0	0	0	3.0	4	16	3	3	0	0	0	0	3	0	3	1	0
Santana, Alfredo, Detroit	4	3	.571	2.66	13	9	0	0	2	1	67.2	65	298	25	20	0	4	2	8	29	6	34	10	4
Santana, Aris, Bal./Chi.(AL)	1	4	.200	6.17	16	5	0	0	4	1	42.1	44	201	40	29	0	4	4	3	33	1	34	9	1
Santana, Humberto, N.Y. Mets	6	2	.750	3.16	11	10	1	1	1	0	57.0	46	233	26	20	4	2	1	2	13	1	41	1	2
Santana, Luis, Dodgers II	2	0	1.000	3.10	9	0	0	0	9	0	20.1	18	89	11	7	3	0	4	0	5	0	9	2	0
Santana, Orlando, Bal./Chi.(AL)	0	0	.000	4.67	11	0	0	0	7	1	17.1	25	90	11	9	7	0	0	1	6	0	5	1	0
Santiago, Cesar, Florida	1	4	.200	6.25	15	2	0	0	1	0	36.0	48	175	33	25	2	2	1	3	17	0	30	6	1
Santos, Ricardo, N.Y. Yankees	0	1	.000	3.97	12	0	0	0	8	1	22.2	20	101	11	10	4	1	1	1	13	0	19	2	0
Santos, Victor, Detroit	7	5	.583	3.72	15	12	3	2	2	0	77.1	88	339	46	32	4	0	1	1	18	0	75	11	1
Segura, Yodys, Dodgers I	3	3	.500	3.88	14	11	0	0	1	0	55.2	62	266	33	24	3	1	0	3	41	2	36	8	0
Selmo, Alexandre, Atlanta	2	5	.286	4.15	20	0	0	0	9	1	47.2	33	230	28	22	1	6	2	6	57	4	27	4	0
Serrano, Wascar, Chi. (NL)/S.D.	3	3	.500	3.11	12	7	0	0	1	0	46.1	63	210	24	16	2	5	2	0	15	0	23	9	0
Sido, Wilson, Toyo Carp	1	0	1.000	2.88	11	0	0	0	2	1	25.0	19	108	10	8	1	2	2	1	15	0	22	1	0
Sierra, Luis, Toronto	2	2	.500	3.57	21	0	0	0	10	3	40.1	28	172	20	16	0	1	0	1	21	2	46	2	0
Silva, Luis, Toronto	1	0	1.000	4.50	5	0	0	0	5	3	8.0	9	35	5	4	0	1	0	0	4	0	9	1	0
Solano, Darling, Dodgers I	0	2	.000	13.20	11	3	0	0	1	0	15.0	18	93	28	22	2	0	3	3	33	0	9	7	1
Soler, Miguel, N.Y. Yankees	0	1	.000	4.28	12	5	0	0	1	0	33.2	27	148	21	16	1	1	1	1	21	0	27	2	1
Soriano, Gabriel, Dodgers I	2	6	.250	4.83	15	12	0	0	2	0	63.1	71	294	38	34	2	1	0	9	37	2	41	10	0
Sosa, Henry, Florida	0	1	.000	3.96	16	0	0	0	6	0	25.0	25	127	16	11	2	1	1	6	22	1	20	4	0
Soto, Angel, K.C./Colo.	1	1	.500	6.50	14	0	0	0	2	0	18.0	19	98	20	13	1	2	2	3	20	0	7	8	0
Soto, Carlos, N.Y. Mets	6	1	.857	1.96	19	0	0	0	14	7	36.2	27	148	10	8	1	0	1	2	16	4	27	4	0
Suarez, Ramon, K.C./Colo.	1	4	.200	5.14	18	4	0	0	6	3	42.0	50	201	36	24	1	3	5	6	18	2	14	4	1
Tavares, Heriberto, Pittsburgh	3	1	.750	3.78	17	0	0	0	13	4	16.2	14	79	9	7	2	1	1	2	17	1	20	2	0
Terrero, Ruben, N.Y. Mets	1	2	.333	4.55	15	3	0	0	3	0	31.2	35	148	22	16	3	0	1	1	19	0	25	2	1
Tineo, Marcos, Phi./St.L.	3	3	.500	2.48	28	1	0	0	25	10	40.0	28	171	20	11	0	3	4	2	27	1	29	8	2
Torres, Jairo, Bal./Chi.(AL)	1	1	.500	4.26	8	0	0	0	6	0	12.2	14	53	10	6	0	0	2	0	5	0	4	0	0
Trejo, Ulises, Houston	2	3	.400	5.06	12	8	0	0	0	0	42.2	37	200	37	24	3	3	2	1	42	0	30	11	3
Urena, Pedro, Texas	1	0	1.000	4.69	5	0	0	0	2	0	7.2	8	35	4	4	1	0	0	0	5	0	5	1	0
Uribe, Maximo, California	0	0	.000	8.21	7	0	0	0	3	0	7.2	7	44	7	7	0	1	0	0	14	1	2	3	0

Pitcher, Team	W	L	Pct.	ERA	G	GS	CG	ShO	GF	Sv.	IP	H	TBF	R	ER	HR	SH	SF	HB	BB	IBB	SO	WP	Bk.
Valdez, Juan, Pittsburgh	0	1	.000	6.57	6	1	0	0	1	0	12.1	9	66	12	9	0	1	1	2	18	0	5	2	0
Valdez, Orlando, San Francisco	3	7	.300	4.37	24	8	1	0	15	2	82.1	92	385	65	40	1	4	3	6	44	1	49	5	0
Valdez, Wolkin, N.Y. Yankees	2	2	.500	3.93	14	3	0	0	1	1	34.1	42	168	22	15	3	0	1	4	20	0	22	3	0
Valenzuela, Jose, Chi. (NL)/S.D.	2	4	.333	6.04	17	4	0	0	4	0	50.2	48	237	41	34	4	3	2	5	43	1	21	9	0
Vanderhorst, F., K.C./Colo.	2	8	.200	5.32	17	12	1	0	2	0	69.1	82	320	58	41	4	0	5	8	23	0	25	8	3
Vargas, Francisco, Cleveland	3	3	.500	3.25	16	10	1	1	4	2	61.0	70	266	41	22	2	0	6	1	10	1	24	3	1
Vargas, Jose, Toyo Carp	6	2	.750	2.43	13	13	2	1	0	0	70.1	50	301	34	19	1	1	3	9	34	0	37	2	0
Vasquez, Cesar, Houston	3	2	.600	2.18	22	1	0	0	11	2	41.1	35	193	16	10	1	4	1	4	32	5	24	8	2
Vasquez, Luis, N.Y. Mets	3	2	.600	4.18	16	2	0	0	3	1	32.1	45	148	23	15	4	2	0	1	6	1	20	0	0
Vega, Juan, San Francisco	2	7	.222	5.84	15	15	2	0	0	0	69.1	88	325	64	45	3	2	3	3	40	0	65	19	0
Veras, Carlos, Pittsburgh	0	0	.000	24.91	8	0	0	0	2	0	8.2	19	56	25	24	5	0	0	1	12	0	3	0	1
Villar, Maximo, Pittsburgh	3	3	.500	4.23	9	9	3	0	0	0	61.2	66	262	37	29	5	1	2	6	14	0	60	1	1
Vizcaino, Luis, Oakland	10	2	.833	2.27	16	15	5	1	0	0	115.0	93	477	41	29	3	1	3	3	29	0	89	10	2
Zabala, Ismel J., Seattle	9	1	.900	1.05	30	0	0	0	12	3	51.1	25	189	9	6	0	2	2	1	17	2	83	5	0
Zapata, Juan, Houston	5	4	.556	2.31	13	13	1	1	0	0	81.2	60	353	40	21	1	1	1	4	43	1	60	10	0
Zapata, Rolando, Montreal	3	8	.273	5.54	19	10	0	0	3	0	65.0	67	314	58	40	3	1	4	6	65	0	28	10	1

1995 FIELDING

TEAM

Team	Pct.	G	PO	A	E	TC	DP	PB	Team	Pct.	G	PO	A	E	TC	DP	PB
Toronto	.956	68	1768	809	118	2695	51	4	Oakland	.939	66	1718	778	163	2659	70	20
N.Y. Mets	.950	68	1744	725	130	2599	47	16	Dodgers I	.937	64	1628	769	161	2558	69	18
Cleveland	.948	69	1816	838	145	2799	66	26	Bal./Chi.(AL)	.933	70	1676	698	170	2544	71	6
Detroit	.948	69	1800	785	143	2728	74	19	Hou./Mil.	.932	68	1783	823	191	2797	55	53
Seattle	.948	66	1687	692	131	2510	69	19	California	.931	71	1629	752	177	2558	57	10
Texas	.947	66	1670	703	133	2506	50	10	San Francisco	.930	71	1671	737	180	2588	61	8
Toyo Carp	.947	71	1851	692	143	2686	48	16	Chi.(NL)/S.D.	.929	68	1684	696	183	2563	55	12
Montreal	.946	69	1791	765	145	2701	62	18	Florida	.927	68	1721	776	197	2694	58	16
N.Y. Yankees	.945	68	1742	799	149	2690	66	23	K.C./Colo.	.922	65	1698	737	206	2641	53	23
Pittsburgh	.942	66	1671	685	144	2500	52	17	Atlanta	.915	70	1801	731	235	2767	56	27
Dodgers II	.939	69	1777	718	161	2656	50	32	Phil./St.L.	.911	69	1759	744	244	2747	50	36

INDIVIDUAL

Player, Team	Pos.	Pct.	PO	A	E	DP	PB	Player, Team	Pos.	Pct.	PO	A	E	DP	PB
Abreu, Dennis, Chi. (NL)/S.D.	2B	.895	141	133	32	11	0	Beltres, Manuel, N.Y. Yankees	2B	.902	83	119	22	12	0
Abreu, Miguel, Florida	OF	.972	65	4	2	2	0	Benitez, Miguel, K.C./Colo.	C	.941	91	5	6	0	2
Aguilar, Henry, California	P	.800	1	3	1	0	0	Betancourt, Romulo, Bal./Chi.(AL)	OF	.873	42	6	7	3	0
Aguilar, Jose, Oakland	DH	1.000	6	1	0	0	0	Betancourt, William, Cleveland	P	.929	1	12	1	0	0
Agustin, Filiberto, Houston	OF	.970	60	4	2	1	0	Bezhodashvila, Nina, California	P	1.000	0	1	0	0	0
Alcala, Juan F. Seattle	C	.966	100	14	4	2	2	Blanco, Billy, Oakland	C	.971	29	4	1	0	0
Alfonzo, Iran, Toronto	C	.987	56	20	1	0	1	Blanco, Daniel, San Francisco	C	.963	159	21	7	0	5
Almonte, Hector, Florida	P	.750	1	5	2	0	0	Blanco, Danny, Cleveland	DH	.951	39	0	2	0	0
Alvarez, Carlos, Cleveland	OF	.914	29	3	3	2	0	Blanco, Fabian, Dodgers II	P	.727	3	5	3	0	0
Alvino, Roger, Chi. (NL)/S.D.	P	.778	6	8	4	0	0	Blanco, Pablo, Florida	P	.684	1	12	6	0	0
Amador, Juan, Atlanta	IF	.764	22	62	26	9	0	Blanco Veras, Johanny, Clev.	P	.900	1	8	1	0	0
Andujar, Elias, Atlanta	P	.842	5	11	3	1	0	Bracho, Eulis, Cleveland	SS	.927	50	114	13	12	0
Andujar, Eliezer, Atlanta	OF	.921	110	7	10	1	0	Bracho, Didimo, Montreal	OF	.917	74	3	7	1	0
Andujar, Juan, Florida	1B	.981	237	17	5	0	0	Brand, Fausto, Atlanta	P	.857	2	4	1	0	0
Antonio, Junior, Houston	C	1.000	8	0	0	0	2	Bravo, Eulis, Cleveland	P	1.000	0	6	0	0	0
Antunez, Javier, Montreal	OF	.951	36	3	2	1	0	Bravo, Luis, Cleveland	P	1.000	0	4	0	0	0
Aracena, Juan, Cleveland	P	.938	6	9	1	2	0	Brazoban, Melvin, Texas	P	1.000	0	6	0	0	0
Aracena, Ramon, Toyo Carp	P	.909	2	8	1	0	0	Brea, Rafael, Florida	2B	.964	126	114	9	10	0
Araujo, Danilo, Phi./St.L.	DH	.876	30	62	13	1	0	Brea, Ramsey, Detroit	P	.636	1	6	4	0	0
Arbornoz, Hernan, Montreal	2B	.952	30	29	3	3	0	Briceno, Freddy, Montreal	SS	.939	54	85	9	11	0
Arias, Cesarin, Chi. (NL)/S.D.	P	.857	4	8	2	1	0	Brito, Felix, N.Y. Yankees	C	.981	93	10	2	0	5
Arias, Jorge, Phi./St.L.	C	.955	108	19	6	0	0	Brito, Johan, San Francisco	IF	.938	117	111	15	8	0
Arias, Jose, Phi./St.L.	P	.656	8	13	11	0	0	Cabral, Martires, Toronto	P	1.000	0	2	0	0	0
Arias, Jose, N.Y. Yankees	P	1.000	1	2	0	0	0	Cabrera, Danny, N.Y. Mets	1B	.991	292	21	3	0	0
Arias, Kelvin, N.Y. Mets	P	1.000	1	2	0	0	0	Caceres, Antonio, Toronto	P	.750	2	7	3	0	0
Arias, Miguel, Dodgers II	P	.929	3	10	1	0	0	Cadet, Javier, Chi. (NL)/S.D.	P	.750	0	3	1	0	0
Arias, Rafael, Chi. (NL)/S.D.	P	1.000	0	5	0	0	0	Caines, Franklin, Phi./St.L.	1B	.959	419	29	19	0	0
Arias, Rafael, San Francisco	P	.875	0	7	1	0	0	Calderon, Ramon, San Francisco	P	.923	1	11	1	0	0
Arias, Roberto, N.Y. Mets	P	.625	1	4	3	0	0	Camacaro, Pedro, Texas	2B	.923	36	12	4	2	0
Asencio, Eddy, Detroit	P	1.000	0	10	0	0	0	Camacho, Wandy, California	IF	.953	114	8	6	0	0
Avila, Jose, Pittsburgh	P	.913	6	15	2	1	0	Carela, Jesus, Oakland	P	.000	0	0	1	0	0
Baez, Jose, Pittsburgh	P	.750	2	4	2	0	0	Cariolan, Roberto, N.Y. Yankees	P	.800	1	3	1	0	0
Baez, Miguel, Cleveland	P	.968	5	25	1	6	0	Carjaval, Tomas, California	P	1.000	1	0	0	0	0
Balbuena, Martin, K.C./Colo.	P	.774	6	18	7	2	0	Carmona, Antonio, Bal./Chi.(AL)	C/IF	.976	140	23	4	0	0
Banci, Aaron, Florida	2B	.953	227	59	14	3	0	Carrasquel, Alejandro, Montreal	P	.692	1	8	4	0	0
Barreras, Rafael, Texas	OF	.925	37	0	3	0	0	Carrion, Jorge, Houston	P	1.000	0	3	0	0	0
Baruch, Jaime, Montreal	P	1.000	2	5	0	0	0	Carvajal, Hugo, Dodgers II	C	.976	111	9	3	1	3
Basabe, Jesus, Oakland	OF	.979	45	1	1	0	0	Casimiro, Claudio, Bal./Chi.(AL)	IF	.911	63	90	15	8	0
Bautista, Francisco, K.C./Colo.	OF	.935	35	3	4	0	0	Castillo, Alex, Houston	3B	.902	41	124	18	10	0
Belliard, Carlos, Dodgers II	P	1.000	5	9	0	1	0	Castillo, Daniel A., Dodgers I	P	.500	1	0	1	0	0
Bello, Emerson, Seattle	P	.857	3	15	3	0	0	Castillo, Geramel, Texas	2B	.913	110	79	18	6	0
Bello, Gilberto, Bal./Chi.(AL)	IF	.972	424	30	13	1	0	Castillo, Jose, Detroit	P	.833	1	4	1	0	0
Belmonte, Jose, California	IF	.775	19	60	23	6	0	Castro, Cesar, California	C/IF	.970	29	3	1	0	2
Beltre, Adrian, Dodgers I	3B	.899	88	187	31	19	0	Castro, Eleuterio, Toyo Carp	P	.500	0	1	1	0	0

Player, Team	Pos.	Pct.	PO	A	E	DP	PB
Castro, Jesus, Toronto	OF	1.000	5	0	0	0	0
Castro, Jorge, Dodgers II	C	.966	203	25	8	0	18
Castro, Martirez, Texas	OF	.944	110	7	7	1	0
Castro, Rafael, Phi./St.L.	C	.933	64	19	6	0	0
Cedeno, Ruddy, Houston	SS	.872	67	103	25	9	0
Celedonio, Carlos, San Fran.	IF	.838	47	77	24	6	0
Celta, Nicolas, Houston	P	.864	4	15	3	1	0
Cera, Aquiles, Dodgers II	P	1.000	1	5	0	0	0
Chavel, Ali, California	OF	.846	9	2	2	0	0
Ciociola, Miguel, Dodgers I	OF	.951	35	4	2	1	0
Coco, Pascual, Toronto	P	1.000	0	6	0	0	0
Collado, Hugo, Dodgers I	OF-P	.944	47	4	3	0	0
Collado, Juan, N.Y. Yankees	OF	.971	33	0	1	0	0
Compres, Miguel, N.Y. Yankees	C	.962	90	11	4	0	5
Contreras, Angel, Pittsburgh	P	1.000	2	2	0	0	0
Cordero, Willie, Texas	SS	.876	43	106	21	4	0
Corniell, Henry, Oakland	P	1.000	1	2	0	0	0
Cornielle, Alex, Toyo Carp	P	.875	2	5	1	0	0
Corporan, Manuel, Bal./Chi.(AL)	IF	.936	70	64	9	4	0
Cota, Marino, Dodgers II	P	1.000	0	7	0	0	0
Cruz, Charlie, Dodgers I	1B	.950	52	5	3	0	0
Cruz, Luis, Toyo Carp	OF/IF	.949	97	51	8	3	0
Cruz, Radhames, K.C./Colo.	C	.947	138	24	9	0	16
Cruz, Raul, Oakland	P	.833	0	5	1	0	0
Cruz, Silvio, K.C./Colo.	2B	.932	131	129	19	12	0
Cueto, Jose, Seattle	P	.857	4	8	2	2	0
Dacosta, Samuel, Montreal	1B-P	.981	92	8	2	1	0
Davis, Melvin, San Francisco	P	1.000	0	3	0	0	0
DeJesus, Eddy, California	OF	.933	67	3	5	0	0
DeJesus, Wilmer, Montreal	C	.969	185	36	7	2	0
DeLaCruz, Antonio, N.Y. Mets	SS	.868	36	56	14	5	0
DeLaCruz, Fernando, California	P	.833	1	4	1	0	0
DeLaCruz, Fernando, Toyo Carp	P	.909	3	17	2	3	0
DeLaCruz, Henry, Chi. (NL)/S.D.	OF	.933	37	5	3	1	0
DeLaCruz, Inocencio, N.Y. Mets	P	.875	3	11	2	1	0
DeLaCruz, Jose, Oakland	3B	.872	75	61	20	11	0
DeLaCruz, Juan, San Francisco	IF	.880	68	5	10	4	0
DeLaCruz, Pedro, Toronto	OF	.923	12	0	1	0	0
DeLaCruz, Rafael, San Francisco	1B	.935	91	9	7	2	0
DeLaCruz, Raul, Pittsburgh	OF	.975	75	3	2	0	0
DeLaEspada, Miguel, Houston	OF	.931	53	1	4	0	0
DeLaRosa, Erasmo, Houston	OF	.888	31	1	4	1	0
DeLaRosa, Miguel, Texas	DH	.947	71	1	4	0	0
DeLeon, Jose, Detroit	OF	.941	12	4	1	0	0
DeLeon, Jose, Phi./St.L.	P	.917	2	9	1	0	0
DeLeon, Julio, N.Y. Yankees	P	.905	4	15	2	0	0
DeLeon, Ricardo, Atlanta	C	.986	63	6	1	0	3
Delgado, Manuel, Toronto	P	.750	1	2	1	0	0
Delgado, Ramon, Seattle	1B	.987	286	12	4	4	0
Deliza, Angel, Chi. (NL)/S.D.	P	1.000	1	2	0	0	0
Del Orbe, Wellington, Cleveland	P	.800	1	3	1	0	0
DeLosSantos, Americo, K.C./Colo.	P	.810	2	15	4	0	0
DeLosSantos, Aurelio, Phi./St.L.	C	.930	115	31	11	0	0
DeLosSantos, Domingo, K.C./Colo.	P	.500	2	1	3	0	0
DeLosSantos, Luis, N.Y. Yankees	P	.950	4	15	1	1	0
Del Valle, Carlos, Detroit	1B	.975	601	23	16	4	0
Diaz, Emergildo, San Francisco	IF	.981	442	21	9	2	0
Diaz, Esteban, Dodgers I	P	.833	1	9	2	0	0
Diaz, Ivan, Phi./St.L.	DH	.902	33	4	4	0	0
Diaz, Miguel, California	OF	.905	81	5	9	0	0
Diaz, Welvis, Oakland	OF	.935	67	5	5	0	0
Diese, Jose, Toyo Carp	P	.929	2	11	1	0	0
Disla, Francisco, N.Y. Yankees	P	1.000	0	8	0	0	0
D'LaCruz, Ignacio, San Fran.	P	.571	0	4	3	0	0
D'Leon, Sandy, Seattle	C	.972	174	31	6	1	2
Dominguez, Enrique, Montreal	OF	.971	65	3	2	1	0
Dotel, Melido, Dodgers II	P	.722	2	11	5	0	0
Duncan, Jan Carlos, Phi./St.L.	3B	.841	52	96	28	11	0
Duverge, Salvador, K.C./Colo.	DH	.667	2	0	1	0	0
Ellis, Franklin, Houston	OF	.923	29	7	3	1	0
Encarnacion, Edgardo, California	IF	.854	60	98	27	10	0
Encarnacion, Mario, Oakland	OF	.945	112	9	7	4	0
Encarnacion, Pedro, Bal./Chi.(AL)	P	.957	63	3	3	0	0
Encarnacion, Sonder, Seattle	2B	.940	63	77	9	5	0
Ernesto, Hector, Florida	P	.571	3	1	3	0	0
Escarlante, Simon, Phi./St.L.	P	.667	0	6	3	0	0
Escobar, Kelvin, Toronto	P	1.000	2	6	0	0	0
Espinal, Orlando, Montreal	P	.800	1	3	1	0	0
Espino, Fernando, Seattle	OF	.946	80	8	5	5	0
Espino, Jose, Toyo Carp	OF	.911	93	9	10	2	0
Estevez, Domingo, Toronto	OF	.917	42	2	4	0	0
Estrella, Leoncio, N.Y. Mets	P	1.000	4	3	0	0	0
Eusebio, Ruben, Houston	2B	.956	62	68	6	3	0
Fajardo, Alejandro, Phi./St.L.	OF	.930	102	4	8	1	0
Farraez, Adel, Houston	OF	.895	32	2	4	0	0
Farraez, Jesus, Houston	OF	.915	70	5	7	2	0
Felix, Edgar, Pittsburgh	SS	.887	39	87	16	5	0
Felix, Miguel, Bal./Chi.(AL)	P	.706	1	11	5	0	0
Felix, Osvaldo, K.C./Colo.	P	1.000	1	1	0	1	0
Fernandez, Juan, Dodgers I	SS	.820	26	83	24	7	0
Fernandez, Robert, Cleveland	OF-P	.938	24	5	2	1	0
Fernandez, Winston, Texas	P	.969	91	2	3	0	0
Ferreiras, Luis, Cleveland	C	.959	61	10	3	0	11
Figueroa, Jose, Oakland	C	.974	171	15	5	2	3
Fischer, Carlos, California	IF	.916	69	137	19	13	0
Florentino, Osmil, K.C./Colo.	P	1.000	0	1	0	0	0
Flores, Carlos, Houston	OF	1.000	3	1	0	0	0
Flores, Julio, Montreal	OF	.922	67	4	6	0	0
Font, Franklin, Chi. (NL)/S.D.	3B	.937	114	153	18	14	0
Francisco, Frank, Atlanta	OF	.884	104	10	15	2	0
Francisco, Norberto, Bal./Chi.(AL)	P	1.000	1	2	0	1	0
Franco, Deyvi, Detroit	DH	.667	2	0	1	0	0
Franco, Jorge, Montreal	C	.993	120	26	1	0	0
Frias, Jovanny, Bal./Chi.(AL)	P	1.000	0	8	0	0	0
Fructuoso, Jose, Seattle	P	1.000	0	5	0	0	0
Galban, Elvis, Montreal	2B	.928	96	109	16	7	0
Galvez, Randy, Dodgers I	P	.917	3	8	1	0	0
Garcia, Eduardo, California	IF	.926	21	29	4	1	0
Garcia, Jhoan, Seattle	P	.556	2	3	4	0	0
Garcia, Jose, Cleveland	P	.882	3	12	2	0	0
Garcia, Juan, Atlanta	OF	.954	122	3	6	1	0
Garcia, Juan, Detroit	OF	1.000	3	0	0	0	0
Garcia, Julio, N.Y. Yankees	2B	.818	5	4	2	0	0
Garcia, Leoncio, California	C	.964	121	14	5	0	5
Garcia, Luis, Dodgers II	OF	.944	48	3	3	1	0
Garcia, Rafael, Seattle	P	.833	1	4	1	0	0
Genao, Martin, Dodgers II	P	.875	4	3	1	0	0
German, Aris, N.Y. Mets	C	.985	59	8	1	0	4
German, John, N.Y. Mets	P	.857	1	5	1	1	0
German, Julian, Detroit	2B	.968	65	84	5	8	0
Germosen, Julio, Pittsburgh	2B	.951	109	163	14	14	0
Geronimo, Cesar, California	P	.958	111	4	5	0	0
Gil, Alberto, Cleveland	OF	.967	84	3	3	1	0
Giron, Edilberto, Pittsburgh	DH	.800	4	0	1	0	0
Giron, Isabel, Toronto	SS	.927	38	102	11	7	0
Giron, Juan, Atlanta	3B	.801	51	78	32	4	0
Glaterol, Becker, Toronto	P	1.000	5	8	0	0	0
Gomera, Rafael, Dodgers I	OF	.926	116	22	11	5	0
Gomez, Domingo, California	P	.875	1	6	1	1	0
Gomez, Jose, Seattle	P	.750	3	9	4	1	0
Gomez, Luis, Detroit	P	1.000	0	4	0	0	0
Gomez, Luis, Houston	C	.952	127	14	7	0	10
Gomez, Manuel, Detroit	P	1.000	1	6	0	0	0
Gomez, Miguel, Toronto	P	1.000	2	4	0	1	0
Gomez, Rafael, N.Y. Mets	P	.875	3	4	1	0	0
Gomez, Ricardo, Pittsburgh	P	1.000	0	1	0	0	0
Gondola, Roberto, N.Y. Yankees	P	1.000	1	4	0	0	0
Gonzalez, Adalberto, Montreal	SS	.929	19	46	5	2	0
Gonzalez, Cesar, Montreal	3B	.918	20	36	5	0	0
Gonzalez, Edwin, K.C./Colo.	P	1.000	3	7	0	0	0
Gonzalez, Franklin, Chi. (NL)/S.D.	P	.923	57	3	5	0	0
Gonzalez, Santo, Chi. (NL)/S.D	SS	.934	83	142	16	11	0
Guerra, Carlos, Cleveland	SS	.939	12	19	2	2	0
Guerra, Robert, California	IF	.895	56	115	20	9	0
Guerrero, Frank, Houston	3B	.816	29	92	27	9	0
Guerrero, Hamlet, N.Y. Mets	OF	.979	87	7	2	0	0
Guerrero, Jose, Seattle	P	1.000	0	4	0	0	0
Guerrero, Wascar, Seattle	1B	.984	303	13	5	4	0
Guevara, Carlos, Pittsburgh	P	1.000	1	2	0	0	0
Guilleard, Alfonso, Toyo Carp	SS	.892	103	118	34	15	0
Guillen, Angel, San Francisco	P	.889	0	8	1	0	0
Gutierrez, Victor, Pittsburgh	2B	.923	73	95	14	10	0
Guzman, Ambiorix, Texas	P	.857	2	4	1	1	0
Guzman, Carlos, Detroit	OF	.944	30	4	2	0	0
Guzman, Cristian, N.Y. Yankees	SS	.882	58	159	29	13	0
Guzman, Juan, Bal./Chi.(AL)	C/1B	.974	191	35	6	0	3
Guzman, Juan, Phi./St.L.	OF	.954	98	6	5	0	0
Guzman, Leybi, Dodgers I	P	.750	0	3	1	0	0
Guzman, Martin, Toyo Carp	C/1B	.973	365	25	11	1	7
Guzman, Santos, Pittsburgh	C	.969	231	18	8	0	12
Guzman, Toribio A., Phi./St.L.	P	.643	3	6	5	0	0
Guzman, Wilson, Dodgers I	P	.875	2	12	2	1	0
Haad, Yamid, Pittsburgh	C	.980	265	31	6	1	5
Henriquez, Hector, Florida	P	.647	2	20	12	1	0
Henriquez, Jovanny, Texas	P	.714	0	5	2	0	0
Henriquez, Roman, Dodgers I	P	.773	2	15	5	0	0

Player, Team	Pos.	Pct.	PO	A	E	DP	PB
Heredia, Andres, K.C./Colo.	C	.935	72	14	6	0	5
Heredia, Maximo, Bal./Chi.(AL)	P	1.000	1	11	0	0	0
Heredia, Rafael, Chi. (NL)/S.D.	1B	.956	229	11	11	2	0
Heredia, Ruddy, Toronto	P	1.000	1	0	0	0	0
Heredia, Willy, Atlanta	P	.667	3	1	2	0	0
Hernandez, Darwin, Pittsburgh	1B	.982	448	46	9	5	0
Hernandez, German, Texas	P	1.000	0	3	0	0	0
Hernandez, Jesus, Cleveland	OF	.943	95	4	6	0	0
Hernandez, Jorgelio, Toyo Carp	OF	.952	19	1	1	0	0
Hernandez, Jose, Montreal	P	.952	12	8	1	0	0
Hernandez, Julio, California	P	.600	0	3	2	0	0
Hernandez, Leonardo, N.Y. Mets	OF	.962	44	7	2	2	0
Hernandez, Pedro, Dodgers II	P	.826	3	16	4	1	0
Hernandez, Rafael, Montreal	3B	.923	53	78	11	10	0
Herrera, Alvaro, California	1B	.980	366	21	8	1	0
Herrera, Misael, Chi. (NL)/S.D.	P	.800	1	11	3	0	0
Hiraldo, Juan, Cleveland	P	.545	0	6	5	0	0
Infante, Danny, Texas	1B	.983	343	52	7	9	0
Infante, Julio, Dodgers I	OF	.962	21	4	1	1	0
Iquerey, Rodney, Cleveland	3B	.962	109	41	6	3	0
Jadagui, Carlos, Chi. (NL)/S.D.	C	.927	118	22	11	2	4
Javier, Frank, Florida	P	.909	5	5	1	1	0
Javier, Jesus, Dodgers I	SS	.934	57	98	11	11	0
Jimenez, Alejandro, Texas	P	.800	0	4	1	0	0
Jimenez, Denny, Oakland	P	.929	4	9	1	1	0
Jimenez, Felipe, Chi. (NL)/S.D.	OF	.925	83	3	7	1	0
Jimenez, Johnn, Dodgers I	P	.636	3	4	4	0	0
Jimenez, Kelly, K.C./Colo.	P	.857	5	13	3	1	0
Jimenez, Miguel, Seattle	3B	.908	62	145	21	16	0
Jimenez, Ramon, N.Y. Yankees	OF	.956	43	0	2	0	0
Jimenez, Ricardo, Bal./Chi.(AL)	P	1.000	0	4	0	0	0
Jose, Leonardo, Oakland	3B	.915	36	29	6	2	0
King, Cesar, Texas	C	.967	277	43	11	0	5
King, Daniel, Oakland	1B	.979	223	10	5	1	0
Langagney, Shelwin, Toronto	P	.954	116	8	6	2	0
Lara, Balnes, Detroit	OF	.941	91	5	6	2	0
Lara, Felix, Pittsburgh	P	.909	57	3	6	0	0
Lara, Nelson, Florida	P	.667	2	4	3	0	0
LaReal, Guillermo, San Francisco	P	1.000	0	6	0	0	0
Lechler, Luis, Dodgers I	P	.800	2	2	1	0	0
Ledesma, Felipe, Dodgers II	3B	.909	54	115	17	7	0
Leidens, Misael, Montreal	SS	.896	47	82	15	8	0
Leon, Rafael, Florida	P	.733	4	7	4	2	0
Leyva, Edgar, California	P	1.000	0	13	0	0	0
Lima, Jose, K.C./Colo.	2B	.852	9	14	4	1	0
Lina, Donald, K.C./Colo.	SS	.814	29	50	18	3	0
Linares, Edwin, Atlanta	P	.929	4	35	3	0	0
Linares, Mario, Toyo Carp	P	.929	3	10	1	0	0
Linares, Rafael, Bal./Chi.(AL)	OF	.962	44	8	2	1	0
Linares, Sendry, Houston	C	.973	120	25	4	0	16
Lizardo, Julio, San Francisco	P	.900	0	9	1	2	0
Loaisiga, Stanley, Montreal	1B	.990	467	37	5	7	0
Lopez, Luis, San Francisco	OF	.944	78	7	5	3	0
Lora, Edison, K.C./Colo.	P	.889	3	13	2	1	0
Lora, Freddy, Pittsburgh	P	.571	1	3	3	0	0
Lorenzo, Julio, Detroit	OF	.945	62	7	4	2	0
Lorenzo, Martin, Houston	P	1.000	4	10	0	0	0
Loyo, Oscar, Florida	3B	.881	10	27	5	1	0
Luis, Cristian, Houston	P	1.000	1	2	0	0	0
Maldonado, Franklin, Chi. (NL)/S.D.	OF	.944	88	14	6	3	0
Marcano, Dennys, Chi. (NL)/S.D.	3B	.852	78	37	20	1	0
Maria, Alcibiades, Texas	P	.444	0	4	5	0	0
Marshall, Victor, N.Y. Yankees	P	.800	2	2	1	0	0
Marte, Julian, Dodgers II	IF	.938	74	107	12	9	0
Marte, Luis, K.C./Colo.	P	.600	2	4	4	0	0
Marte, Nestor, Detroit	OF	.931	25	2	2	1	0
Martinez, Andres, N.Y. Mets	DH	.900	29	34	7	2	0
Martinez, Claudio, Dodgers II	P	.500	2	0	2	0	0
Martinez, David, Toronto	3B	.888	45	129	22	8	0
Martinez, Fausto, N.Y. Mets	OF	.917	22	0	2	0	0
Martinez, Frank, Houston	P	.750	2	10	4	0	0
Martinez, Gabriel, Chi. (NL)/S.D.	P	1.000	0	2	0	0	0
Martinez, Gregorio, Dodgers II	SS	.844	92	162	47	11	0
Martinez, Jose, Cleveland	1B	.978	437	14	10	2	0
Martinez, Jose, Texas	P	.917	4	7	1	0	0
Martinez, Sandy, Houston	P	.750	1	5	2	0	0
Martinez, Wander, California	P	1.000	5	5	0	0	0
Martinez, Winston, Detroit	3B	.903	26	30	6	5	0
Mateo, Amaury, Texas	OF	.982	55	1	1	0	0
Mateo, Freddy, Dodgers II	1B	.975	487	28	13	0	0
Mateo, Victor, N.Y. Yankees	3B	.933	80	129	15	9	0
Matias, Hansell, Atlanta	P	.857	2	16	3	1	0
Matos, Dauris, N.Y. Mets	P	.909	4	6	1	0	0
Matos, Wellington, N.Y. Yankees	1B	.976	494	27	13	1	0
McDonald, Gabriel, San Fran.	OF	.838	55	2	11	0	0
McFarlane, Ivan, K.C./Colo.	OF	.828	22	2	5	0	0
McLean, Guillermo, Dodgers II	OF	.833	12	3	3	1	0
McWellyng, Venzen, California	P	1.000	0	1	0	0	0
Medina, Carlos, Florida	P	.778	2	12	4	0	0
Medina, Edward, Detroit	P	1.000	1	0	0	0	0
Medina, Richy, Detroit	3B	.825	28	52	17	5	0
Mejia, Jose, Atlanta	C	.938	158	37	13	2	10
Mejia, Juan, Phi./St.L.	SS	.910	62	121	18	12	0
Mejia, Luis, Houston	OF	.846	21	1	4	0	0
Mejia, Luis, N.Y. Yankees	P	.750	0	3	1	0	0
Mejia, Oliver, Pittsburgh	SS	.935	94	64	11	6	0
Mejia, Renato, Florida	OF	.943	144	6	9	2	0
Melian, Jhonathan, Seattle	P	.750	0	3	1	0	0
Mena, Eddy, Detroit	P	1.000	1	0	0	0	0
Mendez, Claudio R., Seattle	OF	.950	18	1	1	0	0
Mendez, Lenin, Seattle	P	1.000	0	2	0	0	0
Mento, Alfredo, N.Y. Mets	3B	.897	114	77	22	3	0
Meran, Jorge, Detroit	C	.964	294	54	13	1	0
Mercado, Henry, Cleveland	DH	.889	15	1	2	0	0
Mercedes, Carlos, Bal./Chi.(AL)	P	1.000	0	3	0	0	0
Mercedes, Daniel, Pittsburgh	P	.667	1	1	1	0	0
Mercedes, Jose, Oakland	P	.769	0	10	3	0	0
Mercedes, Luis, San Francisco	IF	.960	38	105	6	7	0
Mercedes, Matias, Detroit	2B-P	.929	89	134	17	18	0
Mercedes, Tomas, Toronto	P	1.000	3	4	0	0	0
Mesa, Willy, K.C./Colo.	P	1.000	2	0	0	0	0
Mesina, Juan, Florida	P	.750	1	5	2	0	0
Mijares, Robert, Dodgers II	OF	1.000	35	3	0	1	0
Minaya, Pablo, Florida	P	.941	2	14	1	0	0
Molina, Alfredo, Dodgers II	IF	.938	33	58	6	5	0
Monero, Pablo, California	P	.600	0	3	2	0	0
Montanez, Johan, Toronto	P	.941	2	14	1	1	0
Montero, Francisco, Phi./St.L.	P	.857	5	13	3	0	0
Morales, Anaximando, Atlanta	3B	.778	40	30	20	1	0
Morales, Cesar, San Francisco	P	.932	157	22	13	0	0
Morales, Domingo, Bal./Chi.(AL)	OF	.938	29	1	2	0	0
Morel, Jose, Pittsburgh	P	.750	0	6	2	0	0
Morelo, Fulvio, N.Y. Yankees	3B	.935	31	55	6	7	0
Moreno, Antony, Houston	SS	.888	41	94	17	9	0
Moreno, Johnny, Bal./Chi.(AL)	OF	.944	145	7	9	2	0
Moreno, Jose, Seattle	2B	.932	89	102	14	9	0
Moreno, Juan, N.Y. Mets	OF	.977	77	8	2	2	0
Moreno, Willy, N.Y. Yankees	OF	.846	10	1	2	0	0
Moreta, Ramon, Dodgers II	OF	.960	141	4	6	0	0
Moris, Miguel, N.Y. Mets	P	.818	1	8	2	0	0
Morrobel, Juan, Pittsburgh	P	.500	0	1	1	0	0
Mota, Henry, Texas	P	.917	0	11	1	0	0
Mota, Leonardo, San Francisco	P	.583	1	6	5	0	0
Mota, Pedro, San Francisco	OF	.929	24	2	2	1	0
Mota, Victor, Detroit	P	.971	59	9	2	1	0
Mundo, Alberto, Atlanta	OF/IF	.888	119	119	30	17	0
Munoz, Eduardo, Seattle	DH	1.000	18	2	0	1	0
Nina, Amaury, Texas	OF	.977	43	0	1	0	0
Nina, Jose, Toronto	SS	.929	67	128	15	10	0
Nova, Joselin, Florida	C	.977	359	75	10	0	14
Nova, Kelvin, Oakland	2B	.970	84	79	5	7	0
Nunez, Abraham, Toronto	2B	.962	80	97	7	6	0
Nunez, Bienvenido, San Francisco	C	.943	57	9	4	0	3
Nunez, Enrique, Phi./St.L.	P	.818	5	4	2	0	0
Nunez, Euripides, Bal./Chi.(AL)	IF	.867	13	65	12	8	0
Nunez, Franklin, Dodgers II	P	.500	0	1	1	0	0
Nunez, Jorge, Toronto	SS	1.000	1	0	0	0	0
Nunez, Jose, K.C./Colo.	3B	.902	58	162	24	12	0
Nunez, Jose, Oakland	C	.990	181	23	2	0	9
Oliva, Osvaldo, Atlanta	1B	.973	506	32	15	2	0
Olivares, Melvin, N.Y. Mets	SS	.936	82	167	17	18	0
Oliver, Jose, Oakland	P	.750	1	2	1	1	0
Olivero, Andres, Montreal	C	.968	160	21	6	0	0
Olivo, Gary, San Francisco	P	.800	0	4	1	0	0
Olivo, Juan, Toyo Carp	P	.889	3	5	1	0	0
Oramas, Victor, Houston	C	.980	84	13	2	0	4
Orta, Carlos, Montreal	P	.913	5	16	2	0	0
Ortiz, Eusebio, Phi./St.L.	P	.667	3	3	3	0	0
Ortiz, Jose, Oakland	SS	.885	110	182	38	17	0
Ortiz, Pedro, Dodgers I	P	1.000	1	2	0	0	0
Ortiz, Ramon, California	P	.944	3	14	1	1	0
Otano, Delvin, Toyo Carp	3B	.893	58	151	25	11	0
Ovalle, Jesus, Texas	SS	.926	52	85	11	11	0
Ovalles, Albin, K.C./Colo.	SS	.900	73	143	24	10	0
Oviedo, Alexander, Oakland	P	.958	5	18	1	2	0
Ozorio, Douglas, N.Y. Yankees	P	1.000	1	2	0	1	0

Player, Team	Pos.	Pct.	PO	A	E	DP	PB
Ozorio, Eric, Atlanta	P	.833	1	9	2	0	0
Ozuna, Carlos, Oakland	P	1.000	2	7	0	0	0
Ozuna, Pedro, N.Y. Yankees	2B	.923	64	91	13	11	0
Padua, Gerardo, N.Y. Yankees	P	.750	2	4	2	0	0
Paniagua, Freddy, Florida	P	.875	0	7	1	0	0
Paraqueima, Jesus, N.Y. Yankees	P	1.000	1	5	0	1	0
Paredes, Roberto, Cleveland	P	.800	3	5	2	0	0
Parra, Catalino, N.Y. Yankees	P	.875	2	12	2	0	0
Parra, Jesus, Houston	P	.857	2	10	2	1	0
Parra, Jorge, Texas	P	1.000	0	5	0	0	0
Parra, Klisber, Florida	P	.846	3	8	2	0	0
Pascual, Ubaldo, Chi. (NL)/S.D.	P	.750	1	2	1	0	0
Patino, Leonardo, California	P	.842	2	14	3	0	0
Paulino, Arison, Pittsburgh	P	1.000	0	1	0	0	0
Paulino, Manuel, Oakland	P	1.000	1	9	0	1	0
Paz, Richard, Bal./Chi.(AL)	SS	.949	89	211	16	23	0
Peguero, Americo, Bal./Chi.(AL)	P	1.000	4	10	0	0	0
Pena, Charlies, Toyo Carp	OF	.994	165	2	1	1	0
Pena, Domingo, Pittsburgh	P	.667	0	2	1	1	0
Pena, Elvi, Seattle	C	.978	187	33	5	0	7
Pena, Onesimo, N.Y. Mets	OF	.947	85	5	5	0	0
Pena, Ramon, Toronto	DH	1.000	26	4	0	1	1
Pena, Reynaldo, Detroit	SS	.946	140	229	21	25	0
Pena, Victor, Phi./St.L.	SS	.837	36	46	16	6	0
Pena, Warren, N.Y. Yankees	OF	.967	54	5	2	1	0
Penalver, Juan, N.Y. Mets	2B	.966	130	129	9	5	0
Peralta, Santiago, Toyo Carp	1B	.981	451	18	9	2	0
Perdomo, Roberto, San Fran.	OF	.943	30	3	2	1	0
Perez, Angelo, Toronto	OF	.958	120	16	6	4	0
Perez, David, Atlanta	C	.994	294	54	2	1	14
Perez, Edwin, Cleveland	2B	.963	170	139	12	11	0
Perez, Jorge, N.Y. Yankees	P	.750	0	4	1	0	0
Perez, Jose, Cleveland	C	.974	32	6	1	0	4
Perez, Manuel, Phi./St.L.	2B	.921	30	28	5	2	0
Perez, Richard, Bal./Chi.(AL)	OF	.900	77	4	9	0	0
Perez, Samuel, Cleveland	P	.880	7	15	3	1	0
Perez, Stiwar, Dodgers I	1B	.977	533	24	13	0	0
Perez, Wegner, Cleveland	SS	.847	20	30	9	4	0
Perez, Wilman, Florida	1B	.941	171	38	13	4	0
Perozo, Alberto, Atlanta	P	.833	1	4	1	1	0
Petique, Marino, Toyo Carp	P	.909	3	7	1	0	0
Pimentel, Jose, Dodgers II	OF	.974	110	3	3	1	0
Pimentel, Marino, Florida	OF	.897	91	5	11	0	0
Pinales, Demetrio, Texas	P	1.000	1	4	0	0	0
Pinales, Otilio, Seattle	P	.667	0	2	1	0	0
Pinales, Victor, Houston	C	.929	76	15	7	1	17
Pineda, Luis, Texas	P	1.000	0	9	0	0	0
Pinedo, Hector, Phi./St.L.	2B	.926	74	88	13	8	0
Polanco, Elvis, Chi. (NL)/S.D.	P	.773	3	14	5	1	0
Polanco, Julio, Texas	1B-P	.980	49	0	1	0	0
Polanco, Raul, Chi. (NL)/S.D.	OF	.915	80	6	8	1	0
Polonia, Israel, Florida	SS	.903	99	179	30	22	0
Polonio, Enrique, Pittsburgh	OF	.897	73	5	9	0	0
Preciado, Victor, N.Y. Yankees	OF	.953	121	21	7	3	0
Presinal, Gilberto, Chi. (NL)/S.D.	P	.833	1	4	1	0	0
Pringle, Juan, N.Y. Yankees	DH	.934	76	9	6	1	3
Pujols, Rafael, Oakland	3B	.966	176	49	8	2	0
Quero, Pedro, Montreal	OF	.865	30	2	5	0	0
Quezada, Adalberto, San Fran.	OF	.978	41	4	1	1	0
Quezada, Anulfo, California	P	.800	4	4	2	0	0
Quezada, Edward, Montreal	P	1.000	0	1	0	0	0
Quiroz, Misael, Pittsburgh	P	.842	6	10	3	0	0
Racero, Aramis, Toronto	P	.857	2	4	1	0	0
Rafael, Jorge, Toronto	P	.857	2	4	1	0	0
Ramirez, Antonio, Montreal	P	.900	3	6	1	0	0
Ramirez, Aramis, Pittsburgh	3B	.886	65	82	19	4	0
Ramirez, David, Texas	3B	.913	40	23	6	3	0
Ramirez, Jordy, Toyo Carp	IF	.867	34	51	13	4	0
Ramirez, Jose, Detroit	P	.882	1	14	2	0	0
Ramirez, Juan, K.C./Colo.	1B	.980	568	30	12	3	0
Ramirez, Narciso, Montreal	OF	.902	84	8	10	1	0
Ramirez, Rafael, Detroit	OF	.957	39	5	2	0	0
Ramos, Fernando, Phi./St.L.	P	.789	5	10	4	0	0
Ramos, Jose, Dodgers I	P	.870	4	16	3	0	0
Ramos, Juan C., Montreal	P	.813	6	7	3	0	0
Ramos, Kelly, N.Y. Mets	C	.994	296	43	2	0	4
Rebolledo, Jairo, Chi. (NL)/S.D.	1B	.975	328	16	9	0	0
Regalado, Frank, Toyo Carp	P	1.000	0	1	0	0	0
Regalado, Maximo, Dodgers I	P	.667	0	2	1	0	0
Renteria, Everth, Atlanta	2B	.889	72	56	16	4	0
Reyes, Bernardo, Dodgers II	P	1.000	0	2	0	0	0
Reyes, Cristian, Oakland	SS	.891	22	19	5	2	0
Reyes, Jose Luis, N.Y. Mets	P	.917	4	7	1	1	0
Reyes, Juan, Montreal	P	1.000	3	6	0	0	0
Reyes, Pedro, N.Y. Yankees	P	1.000	1	1	0	0	0
Reyes, Santos, Detroit	P	1.000	2	2	0	0	0
Reynoso, Ismael, Florida	SS	.888	32	55	11	5	0
Ricardo, Alfredo, Detroit	C	.977	171	39	5	0	8
Ricardo, Luis, Dodgers I	OF	.935	25	4	2	0	0
Richardson, Elbin, Texas	DH	.966	14	14	1	0	0
Richardson, Roberto, Phi./St.L.	P	1.000	0	1	0	0	0
Rijo, Fernando, Dodgers I	P	1.000	2	10	0	0	0
Rijo, Francisco, Toyo Carp	P	1.000	1	5	0	1	0
Rijo, Jose, Houston	P	.800	3	1	1	0	0
Rincones, Gabriel, Seattle	P	1.000	1	2	0	0	0
Rios, Carlos, Houston	1B	.984	470	23	8	0	0
Rivera, Homero, Detroit	P	1.000	0	4	0	0	0
Rivera, Juan C., Chi. (NL)/S.D.	3B-P	.833	9	21	6	4	0
Rivera, Santo, San Francisco	IF	.955	169	127	14	5	0
Rivera, Yorki, Dodgers I	OF	.939	70	7	5	3	0
Robles, Victor, Bal./Chi.(AL)	OF	.852	40	6	8	3	0
Rodriguez, Alfredo, Dodgers II	C	.990	182	13	2	0	11
Rodriguez, Aron, Bal./Chi.(AL)	P	.000	0	0	1	0	0
Rodriguez, Felipe, Toronto	2B	.957	112	113	10	6	0
Rodriguez, Franklin, Toronto	P	.778	0	7	2	0	0
Rodriguez, Geremias, Toyo Carp	2B	.959	92	93	8	4	0
Rodriguez, Henry, Bal./Chi.(AL)	P	1.000	6	0	0	1	0
Rodriguez, Jose, Florida	3B	.891	36	79	14	4	0
Rodriguez, Juan, Pittsburgh	OF	.940	115	11	8	3	0
Rodriguez, Miguel, Phi./St.L.	2B	.873	63	68	19	3	0
Rodriguez, Nelson, Dodgers I	2B-P	.954	114	113	11	11	0
Rodriguez, Pedro, Seattle	P	.889	1	7	1	0	0
Rodriguez, Rodney, Atlanta	P	1.000	1	1	0	0	0
Rojas, Cesar, Texas	P	1.000	4	8	0	0	0
Rojas, Francisco, Dodgers II	P	.889	2	6	1	0	0
Rojas, Juan P., Atlanta	P	.909	2	8	1	1	0
Romano, Manuel, San Francisco	P	.857	5	13	3	2	0
Romero, Mario, Houston	OF	.850	16	1	3	0	0
Romero, Raumer, Montreal	P	.765	4	9	4	0	0
Romero, Robinson, N.Y. Yankees	C	.982	230	38	5	2	10
Rondon, Gabriel, Houston	P	.714	4	2	0	0	0
Rondon, Jhonny, Seattle	2B	.828	20	28	10	3	0
Rosario, Carlos, K.C./Colo.	OF	.934	120	7	9	2	0
Rosario, Rafael, Detroit	P	1.000	3	2	0	0	0
Rosario, Ramon, Houston	1B/C	1.000	150	13	0	1	2
Rosario, Ramon, Oakland	P	.947	2	16	1	1	0
Rosario, Reynaldo, Detroit	P	.833	1	4	1	0	0
Rosario, Ruben, Phi./St.L.	P	1.000	1	4	0	0	0
Ruiz, Francis, Toyo Carp	C	.975	284	26	8	0	9
Ruiz, Jose, Seattle	OF	.987	72	5	1	0	0
Salazar, Oscar, Oakland	SS	.888	94	159	32	16	0
Samuel, Yojairo, Texas	P	.938	4	11	1	2	0
Sanchez, Jose, Detroit	3B	.877	30	20	7	0	0
Sanchez, Jossys, Montreal	P	.800	0	4	1	0	0
Sanchez, Manuel, Atlanta	IF	.900	112	122	26	8	0
Sanchez, Martin, Atlanta	P	.833	3	17	4	0	0
Sanchez, Wellington, Chi. (NL)/S.D.	P	.950	5	14	1	0	0
Sanchez, Willington, Toronto	2B	.846	3	8	2	1	0
Sanquintin, Alexis, Cleveland	C	.958	39	7	2	0	3
Santamaria, Juan, Detroit	P	1.000	1	1	0	0	0
Santana, Alfredo, Detroit	P	.750	4	11	5	0	0
Santana, Aris, Bal./Chi.(AL)	P	.636	2	5	4	0	0
Santana, Humberto, N.Y. Mets	P	.813	6	7	3	0	0
Santana, Juan, Dodgers II	2B	.920	84	101	16	8	0
Santana, Luis, Dodgers II	OF	.986	66	6	1	2	0
Santana, Mario, California	C	.979	285	48	7	0	3
Santana, Pedro, Houston	2B	.933	110	126	17	4	0
Santana, Ramon, K.C./Colo.	OF	.885	112	3	15	0	0
Santana, Richard, K.C./Colo.	OF	.976	77	4	2	1	0
Santelise, Osvaldo, Bal./Chi.(AL)	1B	.955	162	7	8	1	0
Santiago, Cesar, Florida	P	1.000	1	6	0	0	0
Santos, Jose, California	C	.833	4	1	1	0	0
Santos, Jose, Texas	3B	.961	74	122	8	7	0
Santos, Ricardo, N.Y. Yankees	P	1.000	1	1	0	0	0
Santos, Victor, Detroit	P	.947	3	15	1	0	0
Saturria, Arturo, Phi./St.L.	OF	.864	126	14	22	3	0
Scuttaro, Marco, Cleveland	3B	.931	57	211	20	17	0
Segura, Winston, Texas	2B	.911	46	46	9	4	0
Segura, Yodys, Dodgers I	P	.833	7	13	4	0	0
Selmo, Alexandre, Atlanta	P	.813	4	9	3	0	0
Sencion, Pablo, Toronto	1B	.988	611	29	8	2	0
Serrano, Wascar, Chi. (NL)/S.D.	P	.846	1	10	2	0	0
Severino, Danny, Florida	OF	.862	96	10	17	1	0
Shinozuka, Takeiro, Montreal	SS	.909	10	10	2	1	0
Sido, Wilson, Toyo Carp	P	1.000	1	2	0	0	0
Sierra, Henry, N.Y. Mets	C	.980	211	31	5	0	8

Player, Team	Pos.	Pct.	PO	A	E	DP	PB
Sierra, Luis, Toronto	P	1.000	1	4	0	0	0
Silva, Luis, Toronto	P	1.000	0	1	0	0	0
Silverio, Richard, K.C./Colo.	OF	.909	10	0	1	0	0
Silvestre, Juan, Seattle	OF	.939	44	2	3	0	0
Smith, Nestor, N.Y. Yankees	OF	.968	86	5	3	2	0
Solano, Darling, Dodgers I	P	.667	1	1	1	0	0
Solano, Joel, Toronto	OF	.750	2	1	1	1	0
Soler, Miguel, N.Y. Yankees	P	1.000	1	7	0	0	0
Soriano, Gabriel, Dodgers I	P	.692	1	8	4	0	0
Sosa, Henry, Florida	P	.333	1	2	6	0	0
Sosa, Jorge, K.C./Colo.	SS	.797	13	46	15	3	0
Sosa, Leonel, Dodgers I	C	.982	96	13	2	0	0
Soto, Angel, K.C./Colo.	P	1.000	0	3	0	0	0
Soto, Carlos, N.Y. Mets	P	.750	1	8	3	0	0
Soto, Luis, Chi. (NL)/S.D.	C	.973	214	40	7	2	5
Suarez, Ramon, K.C./Colo.	P	.813	2	11	3	0	0
Suero, Ignacio, Toronto	C	.970	410	77	15	1	2
Suriel, Miguel, Dodgers I	DH	.972	143	29	5	3	0
Tavares, Heriberto, Pittsburgh	P	1.000	0	3	0	0	0
Tavarez, Carlos, Seattle	OF	.904	47	0	5	0	0
Taveras, Frank, Cleveland	DH	.922	162	52	18	2	0
Taveras, Jose, K.C./Colo.	OF	.991	103	4	1	1	0
Taveras, Luis, Texas	C	.975	163	29	5	0	5
Terrero, Ruben, N.Y. Mets	P	.500	1	1	2	0	0
Thomas, Wilson, N.Y. Yankees	DH	.959	69	2	3	1	0
Tineo, Marcos, Phi./St.L.	P	.889	3	5	1	0	0
Tobias, Enrique, Dodgers I	C	.974	127	22	4	0	0
Tolentino, Juan, California	OF	.921	31	4	3	1	0
Torres, Jairo, Bal./Chi.(AL)	IF	.824	9	33	9	4	0
Toussent, Andres, Toronto	3B	1.000	0	1	0	0	0
Trejo, Ulises, Houston	P	.765	1	12	4	1	0
Trinidad, Cesar, San Francisco	IF	.856	56	123	30	16	0
Ubiera, Nadin, Toyo Carp	OF	.930	68	7	5	1	0
Ubiera, Vinicio, Dodgers II	OF	.905	18	1	2	1	0
Urena, Pedro, Texas	P	1.000	1	0	0	0	0
Urquiola, Edgar, Montreal	2B	.942	41	56	6	3	0
Valderrama, Carlos, San Fran.	OF	1.000	32	0	0	0	0
Valdez, Alvaro, Cleveland	C	.989	217	60	3	3	5
Valdez, Jose, Phi./St.L.	OF	.892	50	8	7	0	0
Valdez, Juan, Pittsburgh	P	.750	0	3	1	0	0
Valdez, Orlando, San Francisco	P	.867	1	12	2	1	0
Valdez, Socrates, Dodgers I	2B	.949	52	59	6	3	0
Valdez, Wolkin, N.Y. Yankees	P	.800	0	4	1	0	0
Valenzuela, Jose, Chi. (NL)/S.D.	P	.692	2	7	4	0	0
Valera, Ramon, Seattle	SS	.928	108	148	20	16	0
Vals, Lucrecio, Bal./Chi.(AL)	IF	.799	60	51	28	10	0
Vanderhorst, Francisco, K.C./Colo.	P	.773	7	10	5	0	0
Vargas, Francisco, Cleveland	P	.857	4	8	2	1	0
Vargas, Iankel, Detroit	C	.970	185	39	7	2	0
Vargas, Jose, Toyo Carp	P	.909	2	8	1	0	0
Vasquez, Alejandro, Houston	OF	.955	60	3	3	1	0
Vasquez, Arnulfo, Cleveland	C	.960	64	8	3	0	3
Vasquez, Cesar, Houston	P	.900	3	6	1	1	0
Vasquez, Jose, Oakland	OF	.949	92	1	5	0	0
Vasquez, Luis, N.Y. Mets	P	.857	2	4	1	0	0
Vasquez, Moises, California	OF	.909	26	4	3	1	0
Vega, Juan, San Francisco	P	.800	2	6	2	0	0
Velasquez, Geovanny, California	IF	.946	74	85	9	10	0
Ventura, Frank, Cleveland	OF	.924	69	4	6	2	0
Ventura, Jose, California	OF	.857	14	4	3	0	0
Veras, Carlos, Pittsburgh	P	.500	0	1	1	0	0
Villar, Maximo, Pittsburgh	P	.857	2	10	2	1	0
Vilomar, Henry, N.Y. Mets	OF	.920	76	5	7	0	0
Virgil, Marcus, California	IF	.957	54	36	4	3	0
Vizcaino, Luis, Oakland	P	.846	8	14	4	0	0
Williams, Johanny, Phi./St.L.	1B	.964	262	29	11	1	0
Zabala, Ismel J., Seattle	P	1.000	1	8	0	0	0
Zamora, Junior, N.Y. Mets	3B	.919	57	56	10	7	0
Zapata, Juan, Houston	P	1.000	2	9	0	0	0
Zapata, Rolando, Montreal	P	.824	4	10	3	0	0

GULF COAST LEAGUE

LEAGUE OFFICE

President
Tom Saffell

Address
1503 Clower Creek Dr., H-262
Sarasota, FL 34231

Phone
813-966-6407

Teams*
Astros
Blue Jays
Braves
Cubs
Expos
Marlins
Mets
Orioles
Pirates
Rangers
Red Sox
Royals
Twins
White Sox
Yankees

*Teams play their games in Bradenton, Dunedin, Fort Myers, Kissimmee, Melbourne, Port Charlotte, Port St. Lucie, Sarasota, Tampa and West Palm Beach, Fla.

1995 FINAL STANDINGS

EASTERN DIVISION

Team	W	L	T	Pct.	GB
Marlins	40	16	0	.714	......
Mets	38	19	0	.667	2½
Expos	21	35	0	.375	19
Braves	14	43	0	.246	26½

NORTHERN DIVISION

Team	W	L	T	Pct.	GB
Tigers	33	24	0	.579	......
Yankees	32	26	0	.552	1½
Astros	32	26	0	.552	1½
Blue Jays	19	40	0	.322	15

NORTHWEST DIVISION

Team	W	L	T	Pct.	GB
White Sox	36	22	0	.621	......
Orioles	34	25	0	.576	2½
Rangers	24	34	0	.414	12
Pirates	23	36	0	.390	13½

SOUTHWEST DIVISION

Team	W	L	T	Pct.	GB
Royals	37	20	0	.649	......
Cubs	35	22	0	.614	2
Red Sox	21	36	0	.368	16
Twins	20	35	0	.364	16

COMPOSITE

Team	Mrl.	Mets	Ryl.	W.S.	Cubs	Tig.	Ori.	Yan.	Ast.	Rng.	Pir.	Exp.	R.S.	Twi.	B.J.	Brv.	W	L	T	Pct.	GB
Marlins	....	11	0	0	0	0	0	0	0	0	0	13	0	0	0	16	40	16	0	.714	......
Mets	8	....	0	0	0	0	0	0	0	0	0	13	0	0	0	17	38	19	0	.667	2½
Royals	0	0	....	0	7	0	2	0	0	2	1	0	12	13	0	0	37	20	0	.649	3½
White Sox	0	0	2	....	2	0	8	0	0	8	14	0	1	1	0	0	36	22	0	.621	5
Cubs	0	0	9	0	....	0	2	0	0	2	1	0	10	11	0	0	35	22	0	.614	5½
Tigers	0	0	0	0	0	....	0	10	10	0	0	0	0	0	13	0	33	24	0	.579	7½
Orioles	0	0	0	9	0	0	....	0	0	11	11	0	2	1	0	0	34	25	0	.576	7½
Yankees	0	0	0	0	0	9	0	....	7	0	0	0	0	0	16	0	32	26	0	.552	9
Astros	0	0	0	0	0	9	0	12	....	0	0	0	0	0	11	0	32	26	0	.552	9
Rangers	0	0	0	9	0	0	6	0	0	....	7	0	2	0	0	0	24	34	0	.414	17
Pirates	0	0	1	3	1	0	6	0	0	10	....	0	1	1	0	0	23	36	0	.390	18½
Expos	5	6	0	0	0	0	0	0	0	0	0	....	0	0	0	0	21	35	0	.375	19
Red Sox	0	0	4	1	7	0	0	0	0	0	1	0	....	8	0	0	21	36	0	.368	19½
Twins	0	0	4	5	0	1	0	0	1	1	1	0	8	....	0	0	20	35	0	.364	19½
Blue Jays	0	0	0	0	0	6	0	4	9	0	0	0	0	0	....	0	19	40	0	.322	22½
Braves	3	2	0	0	0	0	0	0	0	0	0	9	0	0	0	....	14	43	0	.246	26½

Games played in Bradenton, Dunedin, Fort Myers, Melbourne, Osceola, Port Charlotte, St. Lucie County, Sarasota, Tampa and West Palm Beach, Fla.

Club names are major league affiliations.

PLAYOFFS: Tigers defeated Marlins, one game to none; Royals defeated White Sox, one game to none; Royals defeated Tigers, two games to none, to win league championship.

REGULAR-SEASON ATTENDANCE: No official attendance figures reported.

MANAGERS: Astros, Bobby Ramos; Blue Jays, Rocket Wheeler; Braves, Jim Saul; Cubs, Sandy Alomar; Expos, Luis Dorante; Marlins, Juan Bustabad; Mets, John Stephenson; Orioles, Julio Garcia; Pirates, Woody Huyke; Rangers, Chino Cadahia; Red Sox, Felix Maldonado; Royals, Bob Herold; Tigers, Kevin Bradshaw; Twins, Mike Boulanger; White Sox, Mike Gellinger; Yankees, Hector Lopez.

ALL-STAR TEAM: 1B—Gary Coffee, Royals; 2B—Elinton Jasco, Cubs; 3B—Jose Cepeda, Royals; SS—Alex Gonzalez, Marlins; OF—Jose Camilo, Marlins; Carlos Delacruz, Tigers; Thomas Peck, Blue Jays; C—Brian Downs, White Sox; Starting Pitcher—Octavio Dotel, Mets; Relief Pitcher—Brent Stentz, Tigers; Manager of the Year—Bob Herold, Royals.

1995 BATTING

TEAM

Team	Avg.	G	TPA	AB	R	H	TB	2B	3B	HR	RBI	SH	SF	HP	BB	IBB	SO	SB	CS	GDP	LOB	ShO	Slg.	OBP
Marlins	.260	56	2105	1835	289	478	629	72	23	11	212	10	19	28	213	5	306	95	26	33	403	3	.343	.343
Mets	.260	57	2157	1875	306	487	706	92	26	25	256	12	35	30	205	8	360	63	23	33	417	3	.377	.337
Pirates	.256	59	2098	1899	245	487	661	72	21	20	211	8	13	15	163	3	331	39	19	47	371	6	.348	.318
Royals	.256	57	2100	1834	294	470	696	82	18	36	238	5	20	26	214	1	366	43	25	32	389	3	.379	.339
Cubs	.255	57	2055	1793	276	457	655	73	28	23	226	18	21	23	199	3	397	128	47	39	343	4	.365	.333
Astros	.252	56	2028	1784	268	449	600	69	19	15	205	26	13	31	173	4	381	114	58	37	342	6	.336	.326
Yankees	.246	58	2149	1883	285	463	636	74	21	19	229	20	14	28	202	10	409	52	22	36	404	5	.338	.326
Orioles	.241	59	2127	1856	260	448	601	85	13	14	198	10	20	28	212	1	375	59	31	44	410	5	.324	.325
White Sox	.241	58	2118	1858	271	448	628	83	14	23	218	12	12	33	203	11	418	48	26	36	411	4	.338	.325

Team	Avg.	G	TPA	AB	R	H	TB	2B	3B	HR	RBI	SH	SF	HP	BB	IBB	SO	SB	CS	GDP	LOB	ShO	Slg.	OBP
Tigers............	.240	57	1970	1715	237	411	566	50	24	19	185	18	12	36	189	2	467	122	39	27	359	6	.330	.326
Rangers	.232	58	2005	1783	230	414	567	68	20	15	188	10	17	25	170	1	417	135	40	30	334	6	.318	.305
Twins	.222	55	1920	1709	169	380	500	71	8	11	138	15	15	35	145	4	363	73	31	28	365	6	.293	.294
Red Sox	.221	57	2041	1785	223	395	505	59	6	13	169	24	15	40	175	1	382	73	29	31	370	5	.283	.303
Blue Jays	.221	59	2171	1819	259	402	577	82	21	17	215	19	16	52	258	5	467	47	22	45	440	5	.317	.332
Expos............	.217	56	1951	1727	195	375	504	75	15	8	137	16	9	24	175	1	425	62	57	25	332	4	.292	.297
Braves..........	.189	57	1920	1721	141	326	425	53	2	14	116	13	6	19	161	2	401	36	33	39	333	6	.247	.265

INDIVIDUAL

TOP QUALIFIERS FOR BATTING CHAMPIONSHIP

Minimum 162 plate appearances. *Lefthanded batter. †Switch-hitter.

Player, Team	Avg.	G	TPA	AB	R	H	TB	2B	3B	HR	RBI	SH	SF	HP	BB	IBB	SO	SB	CS	GDP	Slg.	OBP
Cepeda, Jose, Royals............	.348	54	209	187	32	65	79	6	4	0	21	1	4	2	15	0	5	2	2	0	.422	.394
Gallagher, Shawn, Rangers	.338	58	233	210	34	71	111	13	3	7	40	0	3	1	19	0	44	17	4	7	.529	.391
Camilo, Jose, Marlins*	.335	48	200	155	37	52	79	5	3	4	22	2	1	1	41	1	28	19	6	2	.510	.475
DelaCruz, Carlos, Tigers........	.329	47	175	155	24	51	66	7	1	2	17	0	0	0	20	1	45	28	4	1	.426	.406
Coffee, Gary, Royals..............	.328	52	217	189	30	62	110	9	3	11	45	0	0	0	28	0	38	2	0	3	.582	.415
Samboy, Nelson, Astros	.313	55	226	192	39	60	79	12	2	1	22	4	1	3	26	0	19	21	8	4	.411	.401
Barrett, Michael, Expos	.311	50	199	183	22	57	78	13	4	0	19	0	1	0	15	1	19	7	6	1	.426	.362
Mifflin, Brian, Mets	.306	51	206	193	29	59	89	13	1	5	40	0	7	1	5	0	43	1	1	7	.461	.316
Bunkley, Antuan, Twins	.298	49	205	181	24	54	81	9	0	6	23	0	0	9	15	0	35	11	4	3	.448	.380
Gonzalez, Alex, Marlins	.294	53	213	187	30	55	76	7	4	2	30	1	4	2	19	0	27	11	2	2	.406	.358
Saffer, Jeffrey, Yankees	.293	50	202	184	30	54	78	10	1	4	33	0	0	1	17	0	55	0	2	1	.424	.356
Rivera, Roberto, Orioles	.293	42	164	150	21	44	66	7	3	3	26	0	2	2	10	0	38	6	3	5	.440	.341
Velazquez, Jose, Yankees*.....	.287	58	245	209	33	60	82	9	2	3	34	0	3	1	30	2	20	3	4	3	.392	.374
Barnes, Kelvin, Cubs	.286	49	195	168	28	48	84	6	6	6	37	0	2	1	24	0	37	11	4	4	.500	.374
Kopacz, Derek, Tigers	.285	53	194	165	24	47	71	12	3	2	30	0	3	1	25	0	40	11	3	2	.430	.376

DEPARTMENTAL LEADERS: G—Peck, 59; AB—Peck, 215; R—Peck, 42; H—Gallagher, 71; TB—Gallagher, 111; 2B—Kehoe, 17; 3B—Jimenez, 8; HR—Coffee, 11; RBI—Coffee, 45; SH—Butler, 8; SF—Mifflin, 7; HP—Douglas, 18; BB—Camilo, Whitlock, 41; IBB—Strawberry, 5; SO—Barksdale, 61; SB—Jasco, 29; CS—Barksdale, 11; GIDP—Ad. Pena, 9; Slg.—Coffee, .582; OBP—Camilo, .475.

ALL PLAYERS

*Lefthanded batter. †Switch-hitter.

Player, Team	Avg.	G	TPA	AB	R	H	TB	2B	3B	HR	RBI	SH	SF	HP	BB	IBB	SO	SB	CS	GDP	Slg.	OBP
Abreu, Nelson, Cubs	.214	57	201	173	21	37	50	3	2	2	24	6	3	0	19	1	37	12	8	8	.289	.287
Adamson, Jason, Pirates	.255	42	165	145	20	37	49	9	0	1	16	0	0	3	17	0	21	1	1	6	.338	.345
Agnoly, Earl, Marlins	.272	55	234	213	39	58	65	5	1	0	20	0	2	3	16	0	18	19	5	3	.305	.329
Aguila, Hector, Rangers	.192	53	200	182	20	35	52	7	5	0	17	1	2	3	12	0	27	6	2	8	.286	.251
Akins, Carlos, Orioles	.283	42	165	138	35	39	59	9	1	3	20	0	2	3	22	0	28	9	3	1	.428	.388
Alayon, Elvis, Red Sox*	.200	25	91	85	7	17	20	3	0	0	5	0	1	2	3	0	10	4	1	2	.235	.242
Alfonzo, Edgar, Orioles	.167	6	19	18	1	3	3	0	0	0	1	0	0	1	0	0	1	0	0	0	.167	.211
Alley, William, Orioles†	.300	12	44	30	10	9	13	4	0	0	3	0	2	1	11	0	4	0	0	1	.433	.477
Alleyne, Roberto, Astros	.218	35	120	110	12	24	29	2	0	1	11	1	0	1	8	1	27	5	5	4	.264	.277
Alvarado, Basilio, Expos	.297	28	81	74	8	22	33	6	1	1	12	3	0	0	4	0	11	1	1	3	.446	.333
Amaya, Edilberto, White Sox ..	.192	26	82	78	9	15	21	3	0	1	9	0	0	1	3	0	20	0	1	0	.269	.232
Antigua, Nilson, Pirates..........	.242	27	102	99	6	24	29	3	1	0	9	0	1	0	2	0	19	0	1	5	.293	.255
Antrim, Patrick, Yankees†	.250	16	59	52	9	13	17	2	1	0	4	2	0	1	4	0	13	3	0	1	.327	.316
Astacio, Onofre, Twins†	.224	47	189	165	21	37	42	3	1	0	8	1	1	5	17	0	42	26	6	3	.255	.314
Aybar, Ramon, Tigers*	.241	38	141	112	22	27	31	2	1	0	10	4	2	5	18	0	38	16	5	2	.277	.365
Ayuso, Julio, Twins	.169	25	80	71	5	12	12	0	0	0	3	0	0	1	7	1	20	0	1	3	.169	.253
Bales, Taylor, Royals..............	.000	8	20	14	2	0	0	0	0	0	0	0	0	0	4	0	6	0	0	0	.000	.263
Balint, Rob, Tigers..................	.200	1	5	5	1	1	4	0	0	1	1	0	0	0	0	0	2	0	0	0	.800	.200
Barksdale, Shane, Astros*	.258	47	182	159	19	41	61	9	1	3	25	0	0	3	20	1	61	7	11	3	.384	.352
Barnes, Kelvin, Cubs	.286	49	195	168	28	48	84	6	6	6	37	0	2	1	24	0	37	11	4	4	.500	.374
Barrett, Michael, Expos	.311	50	199	183	22	57	78	13	4	0	19	0	1	0	15	1	19	7	6	1	.426	.362
Bartee, Kimera, Orioles†	.238	5	24	21	5	5	8	0	0	1	3	0	0	0	3	0	2	1	1	0	.381	.333
Bautista, Jorge, Marlins	.206	42	140	126	16	26	34	6	1	0	4	1	0	1	12	0	23	0	0	1	.270	.281
Beaumont, Hamil, Yankees......	.104	18	54	48	6	5	8	0	0	1	3	0	0	1	5	0	22	1	0	1	.167	.204
Bejarano, Brian, Blue Jays	.254	52	187	173	20	44	67	6	4	3	25	0	1	2	10	0	53	1	1	3	.387	.305
Beltran, Carlos, Royals†	.278	52	200	180	29	50	59	9	0	0	23	1	3	3	13	0	30	5	3	1	.328	.332
Betancourt, Rafael, Red Sox	.256	51	189	168	18	43	48	5	0	0	19	4	3	1	13	0	31	8	5	3	.286	.308
Bishop, Tim, Mets..................	.237	47	175	156	31	37	59	6	0	2	15	0	3	3	13	0	38	4	2	0	.378	.303
Black, Brandon, Mets*	.352	30	117	105	16	37	58	12	3	1	25	0	1	0	10	0	11	1	1	2	.552	.410
Blosser, Douglas, Royals*.......	.255	50	196	161	18	41	74	10	1	7	33	0	2	1	32	0	39	0	0	3	.460	.378
Borges, Victor, Cubs*	.213	35	116	94	20	20	22	0	1	0	6	2	0	1	17	0	18	8	2	1	.234	.339
Bowers, Kevin, Mets	.220	36	146	123	20	27	39	4	1	2	19	0	1	1	21	1	38	1	0	2	.317	.336
Brown, Derek, Orioles	.233	49	171	146	15	34	39	5	0	0	11	0	1	1	23	0	32	3	3	5	.267	.339
Bunkley, Antuan, Twins	.298	49	205	181	24	54	81	9	0	6	23	0	0	9	15	0	35	11	4	3	.448	.380
Burns, Kevin, Astros*	.250	42	149	136	17	34	49	4	1	3	23	0	1	0	12	1	24	8	3	5	.360	.309
Butler, Garrett, Yankees†	.232	48	215	185	40	43	55	4	4	0	16	8	1	5	16	0	45	11	0	1	.297	.309
Camilo, Jose, Marlins*	.335	48	200	155	37	52	79	5	3	4	22	2	1	1	41	1	28	19	6	2	.510	.475
Campos, Miguel, Cubs	.209	36	128	115	21	24	39	6	0	3	13	2	0	3	8	0	37	5	1	2	.339	.278
Capallen, Rene, Tigers	.317	33	120	101	17	32	37	3	1	0	13	4	0	2	13	0	14	6	4	0	.366	.405
Cardona, Luis, Red Sox	.213	42	150	136	14	29	38	6	0	1	15	0	1	5	8	0	35	0	1	5	.279	.283
Carubelli, Gustavo, Braves	.196	49	174	148	13	29	43	8	0	2	6	1	0	1	24	0	31	3	3	6	.291	.312
Casimiro, Carlos, Orioles	.252	32	121	107	14	27	41	4	2	2	11	1	2	1	10	0	22	1	3	3	.383	.317
Cedeno, Jesus, Tigers	.255	40	132	110	20	28	43	2	2	3	14	1	1	4	16	0	26	2	2	1	.391	.366
Cepeda, Jose, Royals..............	.348	54	209	187	32	65	79	6	4	0	21	1	4	2	15	0	5	2	2	0	.422	.394
Chapman, Scott, Astros	.286	14	33	28	3	8	9	1	0	0	1	1	0	0	4	0	4	1	1	2	.321	.375

Player, Team	Avg.	G	TPA	AB	R	H	TB	2B	3B	HR	RBI	SH	SF	HP	BB	IBB	SO	SB	CS	GDP	Slg.	OBP
Charles, Curtis, Orioles	.159	25	72	63	6	10	12	2	0	0	3	0	0	0	9	0	29	1	1	0	.190	.264
Charles, Steve, Blue Jays*	.214	48	179	145	17	31	39	4	2	0	15	1	1	4	24	1	47	7	1	4	.269	.339
Chastain, Dan, Marlins	.200	4	10	10	0	2	2	0	0	0	0	0	0	0	0	0	1	1	0	1	.200	.200
Chick, Bruce, Expos	.235	15	57	51	4	12	20	5	0	1	9	0	0	1	5	0	8	1	2	1	.392	.316
Cisar, Ryan, Blue Jays	.153	35	95	72	10	11	12	1	0	0	5	1	0	2	20	0	24	0	0	1	.167	.351
Coffee, Gary, Royals	.328	52	217	189	30	62	110	9	3	11	45	0	0	0	28	0	38	2	0	3	.582	.415
Cole, Eric, Astros	.270	39	134	122	17	33	38	3	1	0	12	3	0	2	7	0	21	7	5	0	.311	.321
Colon, Ariel, Braves	.202	30	98	84	6	17	19	2	0	0	7	2	0	3	9	0	25	1	0	0	.226	.302
Colon, Jose, Cubs	.227	40	134	119	14	27	37	4	0	2	11	1	1	3	10	0	30	8	5	4	.311	.301
Colson, Jeremiah, Expos*	.063	23	52	48	4	3	5	0	1	0	4	1	0	1	2	0	24	1	2	0	.104	.118
Connell, Jerry, Cubs	.211	22	82	76	6	16	24	5	0	1	6	0	0	0	6	0	12	1	1	3	.316	.268
Cordero, Edward, Tigers	.214	49	145	126	17	27	33	2	2	0	11	2	1	4	12	0	23	11	5	2	.262	.301
Corzo, Beau, Braves	.207	27	95	87	7	18	30	3	0	3	7	0	1	2	5	0	22	0	0	1	.345	.263
Cossins, Tim, Rangers	.000	2	4	4	0	0	0	0	0	0	0	0	0	0	0	0	1	0	0	0	.000	.000
Crutchfield, David, Cubs*	.231	31	121	104	19	24	37	5	4	0	8	3	1	2	11	0	33	13	1	1	.356	.314
Cruz, Andres, Twins	.241	32	123	112	10	27	34	5	1	0	9	0	1	1	7	1	19	1	0	4	.304	.289
Culp, Randy, Expos	.152	10	34	33	2	5	7	2	0	0	1	0	0	0	1	0	9	0	1	0	.212	.176
Daedelow, Craig, Orioles	.259	49	198	170	35	44	56	9	0	1	11	1	0	3	24	0	19	7	2	5	.329	.360
Daniels, Ronny, Expos	.162	20	78	74	6	12	20	4	2	0	3	0	0	0	4	0	27	3	1	1	.270	.205
Dasher, Melvin, Royals	.200	16	36	35	3	7	12	2	0	1	5	0	0	0	1	0	15	0	0	1	.343	.222
Davenport, Jeff, Red Sox	.077	5	16	13	0	1	1	0	0	0	0	1	0	0	0	0	3	0	0	0	.077	.077
Davidson, Cleatus, Twins†	.200	21	85	75	11	15	19	2	1	0	5	0	0	0	10	0	17	8	3	0	.253	.294
Davis, Albert, Pirates	.302	10	44	43	8	13	25	3	0	3	9	0	0	0	1	0	6	1	0	0	.581	.318
Davis, Torrance, Expos	.273	45	162	139	19	38	41	1	1	0	5	6	1	4	12	0	25	13	7	2	.295	.346
DeLaCruz, Carlos, Tigers	.329	47	175	155	24	51	66	7	1	2	17	0	0	0	20	1	45	28	4	1	.426	.406
DeLaCruz, Wilfredo, Yankees	.195	43	138	118	17	23	24	1	0	0	7	1	0	4	15	0	36	6	2	2	.203	.307
Delgado, Daniel, Pirates	.179	33	122	106	15	19	21	2	0	0	7	0	0	1	15	0	16	6	0	1	.198	.287
Dent, Darrell, Orioles*	.280	36	149	125	24	35	48	7	3	0	6	0	1	2	21	0	22	6	2	2	.384	.389
Deshazer, Jeremy, Astros†	.245	38	119	106	13	26	34	6	1	0	11	0	1	4	8	0	19	6	1	2	.321	.319
DiSalle, Javier, Orioles	.333	4	12	12	0	4	4	0	0	0	1	0	0	0	0	0	1	1	1	0	.333	.333
DiSarcina, Glenn, White Sox*	.194	9	37	36	6	7	12	3	1	0	3	0	0	1	0	0	4	1	0	3	.333	.216
Domingo, Tyrone, Tigers	.206	35	115	107	18	22	27	1	2	0	1	0	0	3	5	0	25	20	4	1	.252	.261
Douglas, John, Blue Jays	.235	55	228	179	21	42	54	6	0	2	26	3	4	18	24	1	35	6	4	4	.302	.373
Downs, Brian, White Sox	.285	37	139	130	22	37	51	8	0	2	18	0	0	2	7	0	27	0	1	2	.392	.331
Elliott, Dawan, Pirates*	.220	34	115	109	8	24	29	1	2	0	9	0	0	0	6	0	30	2	0	2	.266	.261
Ellison, Skeeter, Braves†	.226	20	68	62	4	14	20	4	1	0	4	0	0	0	6	0	27	1	4	0	.323	.294
Encarnacion, Pedro, White Sox	.333	10	26	24	1	8	8	0	0	0	1	1	0	0	1	0	4	2	1	0	.333	.360
Engle, Beau, Mets	.179	10	31	28	3	5	9	2	1	0	1	1	0	0	2	0	3	0	0	2	.321	.233
Erickson, Corey, Mets	.281	53	224	178	38	50	79	6	1	7	35	0	5	4	37	3	40	10	3	2	.444	.406
Fagley, Daniel, Marlins	.182	16	38	33	4	6	6	0	0	0	4	0	0	1	4	0	8	0	0	0	.182	.289
Fauske, Joshua, White Sox	.257	33	121	105	18	27	46	7	0	4	18	1	1	3	11	1	22	1	0	1	.438	.342
Febles, Carlos, Royals	.282	54	219	188	40	53	85	13	5	3	20	1	0	4	26	0	30	16	8	5	.452	.381
Feliz, Edgar, Pirates†	.236	17	58	55	4	13	17	4	0	0	8	0	1	0	2	0	14	0	2	1	.309	.259
Ferguson, Dwight, Red Sox*	.194	22	83	62	10	12	15	3	0	0	6	0	0	4	17	0	24	4	3	0	.242	.398
Fitzpatrick, Rob, Expos	.200	9	32	25	5	5	8	3	0	0	4	0	0	0	7	0	4	0	0	1	.320	.375
Flores, Oswaldo, Red Sox†	.273	14	36	33	8	9	12	0	0	1	6	0	0	0	3	0	11	1	1	0	.364	.333
Fortin, Blaine, Blue Jays	.205	42	122	112	13	23	32	4	1	1	14	0	2	3	5	0	16	0	2	3	.286	.254
Franco, Raul, Marlins	.277	49	205	184	30	51	63	12	0	0	22	1	2	2	16	0	14	9	3	5	.342	.338
Frias, Ovidio, Pirates	.283	29	109	99	16	28	37	5	2	0	7	0	0	3	7	0	10	1	0	1	.374	.349
Gallagher, Shawn, Rangers	.338	58	233	210	34	71	111	13	3	7	40	0	3	1	19	0	44	17	4	7	.529	.391
Garcia, Julio, Yankees	.154	4	15	13	1	2	2	0	0	0	3	0	1	0	1	0	3	2	0	0	.154	.200
Garcia, Luis, White Sox	.230	45	187	161	33	37	46	5	2	0	12	3	3	0	20	0	29	9	3	3	.286	.310
Gil, Daniel, Cubs	.167	9	7	6	0	1	1	0	0	0	0	0	0	0	1	0	0	0	0	0	.167	.286
Gomez, Ramon, White Sox	.262	30	118	103	16	27	33	3	0	1	6	0	0	3	12	0	22	12	4	2	.320	.356
Gonzalez, Alex, Marlins	.294	53	213	187	30	55	76	7	4	2	30	1	4	2	19	0	27	11	2	2	.406	.358
Goodwin, Rawlin, Red Sox	.429	18	72	63	15	27	29	2	0	0	11	3	1	2	3	0	8	10	1	1	.460	.464
Gordon, Buck, Cubs	.100	4	12	10	0	1	1	0	0	0	2	0	0	0	2	0	2	0	0	1	.100	.250
Green, Raymond, Marlins	.000	3	6	5	0	0	0	0	0	0	0	0	0	1	0	0	0	0	0	2	.000	.167
Green, Ronald, Cubs	.319	34	141	119	28	38	59	7	4	2	12	1	2	1	18	0	33	13	7	0	.496	.407
Griffin, Juan, Astros	.172	26	76	64	11	11	14	1	1	0	10	3	0	3	6	0	22	5	1	2	.219	.274
Gruber, Nick, Red Sox	.111	13	29	27	1	3	3	0	0	0	1	0	0	0	2	0	5	0	0	1	.111	.172
Guillen, Carlos, Astros	.295	30	118	105	17	31	45	4	2	2	15	1	2	1	9	1	17	17	1	0	.429	.350
Hagge, Kirk, Tigers†	.177	43	112	96	8	17	17	0	0	0	3	0	0	0	16	1	32	3	2	5	.177	.295
Harrison, Jamal, Twins	.143	5	16	14	0	2	3	1	0	0	2	0	0	0	2	0	1	0	0	0	.214	.250
Hayes, Darren, White Sox	.300	6	23	20	2	6	6	0	0	0	2	0	0	1	2	0	1	0	0	0	.300	.391
Hermansen, Chad, Pirates	.304	24	102	92	14	28	49	10	1	3	17	0	1	0	9	1	19	0	0	2	.533	.363
Hernandez, Alexander, Pirates*	.269	49	207	186	24	50	64	5	3	1	17	1	2	1	17	1	33	4	4	3	.344	.330
Higman, Joel, Orioles	.143	6	24	21	2	3	3	0	0	0	1	0	1	0	2	0	7	1	0	1	.143	.208
Horn, Marvin, White Sox*	.240	38	144	129	13	31	45	7	2	1	14	1	2	1	11	2	38	0	1	3	.349	.301
Imrisek, Jason, Yankees	.283	15	57	53	5	15	21	3	0	1	8	0	0	2	2	0	12	2	2	1	.396	.333
James, Kennouth, Expos†	.212	43	179	156	20	33	34	1	0	0	3	0	0	3	20	0	43	11	8	1	.218	.313
Jaroncyk, Ryan, Mets	.276	44	193	174	31	48	59	5	3	0	14	3	2	1	13	1	28	7	2	3	.339	.326
Jasco, Elinton, Cubs	.379	34	148	124	28	47	62	6	3	1	17	2	4	2	16	1	18	29	9	1	.500	.445
Jelsovsky, Craig, Mets	.233	18	52	43	6	10	12	2	0	0	6	2	1	3	3	0	4	0	2	0	.279	.320
Jenkins, Corey, Red Sox	.145	35	137	124	12	18	22	1	0	1	6	0	0	2	11	0	43	5	2	1	.177	.226
Jimenez, D'Angelo, Yankees†	.280	57	245	214	41	60	96	14	8	2	28	3	4	1	23	1	31	6	3	4	.449	.347
Johnson, Carlisle, Twins	.180	19	62	50	2	9	10	1	0	0	4	0	0	1	11	0	13	1	1	1	.200	.339
Johnson, Rontrez, Red Sox	.254	52	228	193	37	49	57	4	2	0	11	3	1	1	30	0	30	25	5	1	.295	.356
Johnson, Travis, Twins*	.316	24	95	76	14	24	32	5	0	1	10	1	0	7	11	0	9	5	4	1	.421	.447
Jones, Bryan, Tigers	.247	33	107	93	13	23	25	2	0	0	7	2	1	0	11	0	34	7	1	2	.269	.324
Jones, Jamie, Marlins*	.222	5	23	18	2	4	4	0	0	0	3	0	0	0	5	1	4	0	0	0	.222	.391
Juarez, Raul, Twins	.346	7	27	26	3	9	15	1	1	1	6	0	1	0	0	0	5	0	0	1	.577	.333
Katayama, Daiki, Tigers	.180	28	54	50	5	9	16	1	0	2	4	1	0	0	3	0	13	0	0	1	.320	.226

Player, Team	Avg.	G	TPA	AB	R	H	TB	2B	3B	HR	RBI	SH	SF	HP	BB	IBB	SO	SB	CS	GDP	Slg.	OBP
Keech, Erik, Yankees*	.225	37	134	120	6	27	37	7	0	1	19	0	1	1	12	1	18	0	1	6	.308	.299
Kehoe, John, Blue Jays	.274	57	241	201	32	55	88	17	5	2	32	1	2	2	35	0	52	8	0	8	.438	.383
Kelly, Pat, Yankees	.000	1	5	2	0	0	0	0	0	0	1	0	0	2	1	0	0	0	0	0	.000	.600
Kerr, Brian, Orioles	.184	10	44	38	4	7	14	2	1	1	7	1	1	2	2	0	10	1	0	1	.368	.233
Kerr, James, Yankees	.241	26	93	83	12	20	22	2	0	0	6	2	1	2	5	0	24	0	0	2	.265	.297
King, Brian, Orioles	.277	17	50	47	4	13	15	2	0	0	4	0	1	0	2	0	12	1	0	0	.319	.300
King, Kevin, Expos	.263	14	41	38	6	10	13	3	0	0	0	0	0	1	2	0	19	3	0	0	.342	.317
Kinnie, Donald, Cubs	.250	35	136	120	20	30	44	6	4	0	14	0	1	3	12	0	36	12	1	1	.367	.331
Klee, Charles, White Sox	.213	44	178	155	24	33	41	8	0	0	19	0	2	2	19	0	41	3	2	3	.265	.303
Knabenshue, Chris, Pirates*	.176	4	17	17	1	3	6	0	0	1	2	0	0	0	0	0	1	0	0	2	.353	.176
Kofler, Eric, Yankees*	.246	19	73	69	11	17	33	3	2	3	13	0	0	1	3	0	8	1	1	2	.478	.288
Kopacz, Derek, Tigers	.285	53	194	165	24	47	71	12	3	2	30	0	3	1	25	0	40	11	3	2	.430	.376
Kuilan, Hector, Marlins	.248	48	175	153	14	38	46	8	0	0	27	2	2	1	17	1	20	4	1	4	.301	.324
LaForest, Pierre, Expos*	.000	2	8	6	1	0	0	0	0	0	0	0	0	0	2	0	4	0	0	0	.000	.250
Landry, Dan, Braves	.238	38	139	122	16	29	40	5	0	2	7	3	0	3	11	0	25	4	1	2	.328	.316
Lantigua, Miguel, Mets	.262	27	93	84	11	22	28	6	0	0	7	1	1	3	4	0	16	4	2	3	.333	.315
Lebron, Juan, Royals	.177	47	163	147	17	26	41	5	2	2	13	0	4	2	10	0	38	0	3	6	.279	.233
Leon, Donny, Yankees*	.171	16	44	41	3	7	8	1	0	0	5	0	0	3	0	0	14	0	1	0	.195	.227
Lignitz, Jeremiah, Tigers*	.232	30	94	82	9	19	25	1	1	1	7	0	0	3	9	0	27	1	3	1	.305	.330
Lima, Estivinson, Rangers	.180	31	101	89	10	16	24	5	0	1	7	0	0	4	8	0	19	0	1	3	.270	.277
Liniak, Cole, Red Sox	.266	23	86	79	9	21	31	7	0	1	8	2	0	1	4	0	8	2	0	2	.392	.310
Llanos, Francisco, Expos	.149	37	125	114	15	17	26	9	0	0	5	0	0	1	10	0	40	3	2	1	.228	.224
Llibre, Brian, Rangers	.269	14	71	67	4	18	20	2	0	0	8	0	2	0	2	0	21	1	0	0	.299	.282
Lomasney, Steven, Red Sox*	.163	29	106	92	10	15	21	6	0	0	7	1	0	5	8	1	16	2	1	0	.228	.267
Long, Garrett, Pirates	.349	20	80	63	13	22	29	2	1	1	8	0	0	0	17	0	10	0	1	3	.460	.488
Longueira, Tony, Royals	.242	41	108	95	12	23	31	5	0	1	13	1	2	1	9	0	11	3	0	1	.326	.308
Lopez, Edgar, Braves	.214	38	138	117	14	25	29	4	0	0	5	1	0	0	20	0	13	5	5	3	.248	.328
Lorenzo, Juan, Twins†	.217	14	51	46	3	10	10	0	0	0	2	0	1	0	4	0	6	0	0	0	.217	.275
Lowery, Terrell, Rangers	.265	10	40	34	10	9	23	3	1	3	7	0	0	0	6	0	7	1	0	1	.676	.375
Lutz, Manuel, White Sox*	.281	46	183	160	23	45	70	10	3	3	31	0	2	2	19	2	42	0	0	3	.438	.361
Maas, Kevin, Yankees*	.444	2	9	9	1	4	7	0	0	1	3	0	0	0	0	0	0	0	0	0	.778	.444
Macero, Victor, Cubs	.234	41	146	128	17	30	41	5	0	2	11	1	2	1	14	0	25	4	2	2	.320	.310
Maloney, Jeff, Blue Jays	.163	29	101	92	9	15	20	5	0	0	12	0	1	2	6	0	24	2	1	4	.217	.228
Mateo, Henry, Expos†	.148	38	147	122	11	18	18	0	0	0	6	5	1	5	14	0	47	2	7	2	.148	.261
May, Freddie, Pirates*	.333	29	115	96	18	32	47	5	2	2	13	0	1	0	18	0	16	2	4	2	.490	.435
Maysonet, Jose, Blue Jays	.145	29	87	69	14	10	12	2	0	0	1	2	0	2	14	0	11	1	2	3	.174	.306
McCarthy, Kevin, Mets*	.133	22	80	75	5	10	14	1	0	1	5	0	2	1	2	0	13	0	0	2	.187	.163
McDonald, Donzell, Yankees†	.236	28	129	110	23	26	33	5	1	0	9	0	1	2	16	0	24	11	2	1	.300	.341
McHenry, Joseph, Twins*	.219	34	126	114	9	25	33	8	0	0	7	2	1	0	9	0	38	2	3	1	.289	.274
McLendon, Craig, Rangers	.242	25	72	66	7	16	18	2	0	0	4	0	0	1	5	0	10	1	0	2	.273	.306
McSparin, Paul, Pirates	.292	28	78	72	14	21	35	5	0	3	13	0	1	1	4	0	19	1	1	2	.486	.333
Medina, Alger, Cubs	.224	23	88	76	10	17	24	5	1	0	11	0	1	1	10	0	4	7	4	4	.316	.318
Medina, Robert, Blue Jays	.177	30	72	62	5	11	20	1	1	2	8	0	0	4	0	0	23	1	1	1	.323	.227
Mejia, Marlon, Astros	.235	34	114	98	19	23	24	1	0	0	5	6	0	2	8	0	21	2	3	5	.245	.306
Mercado, Julio, Rangers	.167	55	168	156	13	26	31	5	0	0	12	1	1	0	10	0	49	9	2	1	.199	.216
Mifflin, Brian, Mets	.306	51	206	193	29	59	89	13	1	5	40	0	7	1	5	0	43	1	1	7	.461	.316
Miles, Aaron, Astros*	.257	47	190	171	32	44	59	9	3	0	18	4	1	0	14	0	14	9	6	3	.345	.312
Millwood, Terry, Twins	.217	47	183	161	15	35	46	5	3	0	11	0	1	4	17	0	29	5	2	1	.286	.306
Miyauchi, Hector, Expos	.233	16	53	43	9	10	15	2	0	1	2	0	0	3	7	0	8	3	1	0	.349	.377
Monds, Wonderful, Braves	.133	4	16	15	1	2	2	0	0	0	1	0	0	0	1	0	8	2	1	0	.133	.188
Monroe, Craig, Rangers	.249	54	216	193	22	48	58	6	2	0	33	1	2	2	18	0	25	13	2	1	.301	.316
Montas, Ricardo, Royals	.071	22	32	28	2	2	5	0	0	1	3	0	0	1	3	0	6	0	0	1	.179	.188
Montilla, Julio, Royals†	.239	17	56	46	6	11	11	0	0	0	3	0	1	0	9	0	5	0	0	1	.239	.357
Morrison, Ryan, Mets*	.255	38	134	110	20	28	38	7	0	1	11	0	3	4	17	1	21	3	0	0	.345	.366
Mota, Gleydel, Mets*	.320	34	149	122	32	39	49	6	2	0	18	3	4	1	19	1	27	21	5	1	.402	.404
Nelson, Kevin, Twins	.145	45	152	138	7	20	31	8	0	1	11	1	2	0	11	1	36	1	1	3	.225	.205
Nobles, Ivan, Blue Jays	.143	36	125	105	14	15	20	3	1	0	12	2	1	4	13	0	40	2	1	1	.190	.260
Nova, Fernando, White Sox	.208	36	147	125	17	26	32	6	0	0	7	1	1	4	16	2	46	1	3	4	.256	.315
Nova, Geraldo, White Sox†	.077	21	33	26	1	2	2	0	0	0	3	1	1	1	4	0	7	0	0	0	.077	.219
Nunez, Juan, Rangers†	.241	43	157	137	16	33	40	2	1	1	7	3	0	2	15	0	46	26	9	0	.292	.325
Olmeda, Jose, Red Sox†	.217	42	150	129	15	28	46	4	1	4	14	5	2	3	11	0	42	3	3	5	.357	.290
Orndorff, Dave, Twins	.209	23	82	67	12	14	17	0	0	1	3	0	0	2	13	0	11	5	0	1	.254	.354
Oropeza, William, Expos	.231	45	156	143	14	33	52	8	1	3	27	0	4	0	9	0	28	2	5	3	.364	.269
Ortiz, Asbel, Rangers†	.305	43	142	128	18	39	60	10	1	3	23	2	1	3	8	0	26	4	2	0	.469	.357
Ortiz, Pedro, Orioles	.217	14	49	46	1	10	12	2	0	0	3	0	0	0	3	0	13	1	0	2	.261	.265
Otero, Oscar, Braves	.128	29	91	86	3	11	11	0	0	0	2	0	1	1	3	0	16	1	1	3	.128	.165
Ovalle, Bonelly, Rangers	.000	18	0	0	0	0	0	0	0	0	0	0	0	0	0	0	0	1	0	0	.000	.000
Ovalles, Homy, Expos	.234	30	68	64	7	15	20	3	1	0	2	0	0	0	4	0	18	1	1	1	.313	.279
Owen, Tom, Marlins	.227	28	81	66	13	15	18	3	0	0	10	2	1	0	12	0	6	0	2	7	.273	.342
Parra, Jose, Rangers†	.156	45	165	135	16	21	29	4	2	0	7	2	0	4	24	0	41	12	6	1	.215	.301
Pascual, Edison, Pirates*	.228	45	151	136	19	31	47	3	2	3	18	2	3	0	10	0	26	3	0	1	.346	.275
Paxton, Chris, Orioles*	.226	11	34	31	1	7	10	1	1	0	6	0	0	2	1	0	4	0	0	0	.323	.294
Payano, Alexi, Cubs†	.297	29	108	91	20	27	39	4	1	2	14	0	1	5	11	1	16	1	0	1	.429	.398
Pearson, Eddie, White Sox**	.300	6	23	20	7	6	11	2	0	1	6	0	0	0	3	0	6	0	0	0	.550	.391
Peck, Thomas, Blue Jays*	.270	59	265	215	42	58	80	12	2	2	22	4	2	4	40	0	39	10	6	3	.372	.391
Pena, Adelis, Pirates	.282	54	210	202	27	57	68	7	2	0	23	1	1	3	3	1	26	6	1	9	.337	.301
Pena, Alex, Pirates	.238	48	179	172	15	41	57	7	3	1	20	1	0	0	6	0	26	3	3	4	.331	.264
Pena, Frank, Twins	.188	21	76	69	7	13	19	6	0	0	5	1	1	0	5	1	18	0	0	0	.275	.240
Pena, Jose, Rangers	.242	50	169	153	25	37	49	4	4	0	10	0	3	1	12	1	29	22	5	2	.320	.296
Pendergrass, Tyrone, Braves†	.181	52	204	188	19	34	41	4	0	1	7	0	0	1	15	0	51	8	4	5	.218	.246
Peniche, Fray, Tigers	.157	28	88	83	8	13	17	1	0	1	4	0	1	2	2	0	31	2	0	1	.205	.193
Phillips, Darren, Blue Jays†	.136	20	49	44	3	6	6	0	0	0	3	1	0	0	4	0	21	0	1	0	.136	.208
Pickering, Calvin, Orioles	.500	15	63	60	8	30	43	10	0	1	22	0	1	0	2	0	6	0	0	3	.717	.508

Player, Team	Avg.	G	TPA	AB	R	H	TB	2B	3B	HR	RBI	SH	SF	HP	BB	IBB	SO	SB	CS	GDP	Slg.	OBP
Pinto, Rene, Yankees	.184	15	58	49	2	9	11	0	1	0	4	0	1	1	7	0	11	0	0	3	.224	.293
Pitts, Shedrick, Royals†	.253	36	96	79	25	20	27	1	0	2	6	1	1	2	13	0	23	11	1	0	.342	.368
Pond, Simon, Expos*	.150	45	156	133	13	20	28	6	1	0	12	0	0	1	22	0	34	2	3	3	.211	.276
Porter, Kedric, Orioles	.218	47	173	147	20	32	41	4	1	1	12	1	0	4	21	0	17	11	3	2	.279	.331
Prada, Nelson, Twins	.269	24	88	78	5	21	27	4	1	0	13	0	3	4	3	0	12	0	0	2	.346	.318
Pressley, Kasey, Cubs*	.236	39	153	140	12	33	39	4	1	0	16	0	2	0	11	0	47	1	1	5	.279	.288
Quezado, Dalmiro, Twins	.155	32	110	103	5	16	22	6	0	0	6	4	1	1	1	0	17	1	1	4	.214	.170
Radcliff, Victor, Royals	.260	38	143	123	25	32	56	8	2	4	15	0	1	7	12	0	24	3	6	3	.455	.357
Ramirez, Francisco, Tigers	.217	41	155	143	15	31	51	4	5	2	22	2	0	3	7	0	38	6	4	3	.357	.268
Ramirez, Julio, Marlins*	.284	48	219	204	35	58	81	9	4	2	13	1	0	1	13	0	42	17	6	2	.397	.330
Ramos, Jeff, Royals*	.227	28	85	75	10	17	30	4	0	3	7	0	1	2	7	0	16	0	1	1	.400	.306
Ramos, Noel, Orioles	.200	4	18	15	1	3	4	1	0	0	5	0	1	0	2	0	6	0	1	1	.267	.278
Rengifo, Daliene, White Sox	.208	27	86	72	7	15	17	2	0	0	5	1	0	3	10	0	21	5	2	1	.236	.329
Reyes, Freddy, Twins	.238	6	24	21	2	5	9	1	0	1	4	0	2	0	1	0	6	0	0	0	.429	.250
Reynoso, Ismael, Marlins	.221	25	81	68	12	15	15	0	0	0	8	0	0	1	12	0	18	1	0	0	.221	.346
Ribaudo, Mike, Orioles	.244	16	46	41	3	10	11	1	0	0	4	0	1	1	3	0	10	0	0	1	.268	.304
Rivera, Juan, Rangers	.186	28	83	70	8	13	15	2	0	0	6	0	0	0	13	0	29	5	1	1	.214	.313
Rivera, Roberto, Orioles	.293	42	164	150	21	44	66	7	3	3	26	0	2	2	10	0	38	6	3	5	.440	.341
Robertson, Dean, Orioles	.156	28	109	90	18	14	18	4	0	0	6	0	1	2	14	1	18	4	4	2	.200	.280
Robles, Juan, Royals	.162	29	84	74	9	12	15	3	0	0	7	0	1	0	9	0	9	0	0	1	.203	.250
Roche, Marlon, Astros	.326	29	108	92	20	30	35	5	0	0	11	1	3	2	10	0	19	9	8	1	.380	.393
Rodriguez, Carlos, Red Sox†	.214	13	52	42	12	9	12	3	0	0	0	1	0	0	9	0	3	0	1	0	.286	.353
Rodriguez, Liubiemithz, W.S.†..	.227	36	144	119	18	27	38	6	1	1	11	2	0	0	23	0	19	4	2	2	.319	.352
Rodriguez, Sammy, Mets	.278	6	20	18	1	5	5	0	0	0	1	0	0	0	2	0	4	0	1	0	.278	.350
Rojas, Moises, Red Sox	.207	42	171	140	22	29	37	5	0	1	16	2	3	5	20	0	34	5	3	3	.264	.321
Rolison, Nate, Marlins*	.276	37	158	134	22	37	54	10	2	1	19	0	1	8	15	1	34	0	0	1	.403	.380
Roman, Felipe, Red Sox	.227	50	187	176	14	40	55	8	2	1	17	1	1	2	7	0	38	1	0	3	.313	.263
Rosado, Luis, Yankees	.256	52	194	168	25	43	56	7	0	2	16	2	0	2	22	1	31	2	1	4	.333	.349
Rosario, Juan, Marlins	.000	5	11	7	1	0	0	0	0	0	0	0	0	0	4	0	2	1	0	1	.000	.364
Rose, Damian, Rangers	.097	13	38	31	5	3	3	0	0	0	2	0	0	3	4	0	16	3	1	2	.097	.263
Rose, Michael, Astros	.258	35	103	89	13	23	30	2	1	1	9	0	0	3	11	0	18	2	1	1	.337	.359
Ruiz, Cesar, Tigers†	.288	45	149	132	17	38	57	6	5	1	19	1	2	3	11	0	35	4	2	0	.432	.351
Saffer, Jeffrey, Yankees	.293	50	202	184	30	54	78	10	1	4	33	0	0	1	17	0	55	0	2	1	.424	.356
Salazar, Juan, Cubs*	.285	36	140	130	12	37	52	7	1	2	24	0	1	0	9	0	12	3	1	4	.400	.329
Samboy, Nelson, Astros	.313	55	226	192	39	60	79	12	2	1	22	4	1	3	26	0	19	21	8	4	.411	.401
Sanford, Chance, Pirates*	.211	6	21	19	2	4	7	0	0	1	1	0	0	0	2	0	2	0	0	0	.368	.286
Santos, Edgardo, Expos*	.221	23	73	68	4	15	19	2	1	0	4	1	1	0	3	0	6	2	2	2	.279	.250
Scharrer, Jim, Braves	.180	48	186	172	10	31	41	4	0	2	22	0	0	1	13	0	43	1	3	3	.238	.242
Schneider, Brian, Expos*	.227	30	112	97	7	22	25	3	0	0	4	0	0	1	14	0	23	2	4	1	.258	.330
Schreiber, Stan, Pirates	.258	38	155	128	16	33	38	1	2	0	10	3	1	2	21	0	23	8	1	1	.297	.368
Selivanov, Andrei, Braves*	.154	23	59	52	4	8	11	3	0	0	4	0	0	0	7	0	7	0	0	4	.212	.254
Serra, Joaquin, Orioles	.141	29	94	85	7	12	12	0	0	0	3	3	0	0	6	0	12	2	2	2	.141	.198
Shelton, Barry, White Sox	.282	33	121	103	10	29	40	5	0	2	13	1	0	7	10	0	16	0	1	2	.388	.383
Shipman, Thomas, Tigers†	.183	30	73	60	8	11	16	2	0	1	10	0	0	3	10	0	21	4	0	0	.267	.329
Shipp, Skip, Pirates	.130	18	61	54	4	7	7	0	0	0	4	0	1	1	5	0	13	0	0	2	.130	.213
Shirley, Al, Mets	.333	4	18	15	4	5	7	2	0	0	0	0	0	0	3	0	4	3	1	0	.467	.444
Sime, Rafael, Marlins*	.240	55	230	204	26	49	74	7	6	2	22	0	3	3	20	1	48	7	1	3	.363	.313
Simmons, Brian, White Sox† ..	.176	5	23	17	5	3	7	1	0	1	5	0	0	0	6	0	1	0	0	1	.412	.391
Smith, John, Astros	.149	23	75	67	9	10	20	3	2	1	5	0	2	3	3	0	23	2	2	0	.299	.213
Smith, Phillip, Braves	.123	38	120	114	5	14	15	1	0	0	5	2	0	0	4	0	37	0	1	2	.132	.153
Solano, Angel, White Sox	.232	44	161	151	20	35	45	5	1	1	13	0	1	0	9	1	23	7	3	0	.298	.273
Solano, Fausto, Blue Jays	.295	11	53	44	12	13	24	5	0	2	7	3	1	2	3	0	6	2	1	4	.545	.360
Soriano, Carlos, Mets	.263	47	187	167	25	44	76	11	3	5	24	1	2	2	15	0	24	1	2	4	.455	.328
Soriano, Juan, Mets	.219	10	36	32	5	7	12	2	0	1	3	0	0	0	4	0	9	3	0	1	.375	.306
Spencer, Jeffrey, Braves	.234	48	189	171	17	40	62	8	1	4	21	1	3	2	12	2	42	7	2	1	.363	.287
Springfield, Bo, Pirates*	.000	3	7	6	1	0	0	0	0	0	0	0	0	0	1	0	1	1	0	0	.000	.143
Stafford, Kimani, Royals	.164	39	79	67	13	11	14	1	1	0	4	0	0	0	12	0	30	0	0	1	.209	.291
Stephens, Joel, Orioles	.232	23	91	82	8	19	24	3	1	0	10	1	0	3	5	0	25	2	1	3	.293	.300
Stevens, Clayton, White Sox	.224	42	167	143	19	32	56	1	4	5	21	1	0	3	20	3	40	3	2	6	.392	.331
Stevenson, Chad, Tigers	.158	32	111	95	11	15	30	4	1	3	12	1	1	3	11	0	23	1	0	5	.316	.255
Strawberry, Darryl, Yankees*	.250	7	30	20	3	5	7	2	0	0	4	0	1	0	9	5	5	2	0	1	.350	.467
Suero, Rey, Rangers	.216	39	129	111	19	24	29	3	1	0	5	0	3	1	14	0	23	12	5	1	.261	.302
Sullivan, Davey, Orioles	.232	38	140	125	13	29	38	6	0	1	12	2	2	1	10	0	23	1	1	1	.304	.291
Tardiff, Jeremy, Red Sox	.130	10	24	23	2	3	8	0	1	1	4	0	0	0	1	0	2	0	0	1	.348	.167
Taylor, Avery, Orioles	.033	13	33	30	2	1	1	0	0	0	2	0	0	0	3	0	12	0	0	2	.033	.121
Taylor, Matthew, Braves*	.161	35	126	112	9	18	20	2	0	0	6	2	0	2	10	0	11	1	4	4	.179	.242
Terry, Reggie, Rangers	.294	5	17	17	3	5	5	0	0	0	0	0	0	0	0	0	4	2	0	0	.294	.294
Tessmar, Timothy, Mets*	.209	56	232	196	20	41	54	5	4	0	28	0	2	4	30	1	27	4	1	2	.276	.323
Tillero, Adrian, Royals	.252	36	111	103	14	26	33	4	0	1	11	0	0	8	1	0	33	1	1	3	.320	.355
Torrealba, Steve, Braves	.207	30	106	92	3	19	23	4	0	0	10	0	1	2	11	0	20	0	0	3	.250	.302
Truitt, Theron, Marlins	.179	24	80	67	8	12	12	0	0	0	8	0	3	3	7	0	13	6	0	0	.179	.275
Ubaldo, Nelson, Astros	.243	34	116	103	12	25	36	4	2	1	9	1	1	3	8	0	32	9	2	3	.350	.304
Valencia, Enrique, Red Sox*	.000	1	1	1	0	0	0	0	0	0	0	0	0	0	0	0	1	0	0	0	.000	.000
Valencia, Victor, Yankees	.241	25	64	58	5	14	18	1	0	1	8	0	0	0	6	0	22	0	0	1	.310	.313
Varriano, Mark, Red Sox	.163	18	57	49	4	8	9	1	0	0	6	0	0	2	6	0	10	0	0	1	.184	.281
Vecchioni, Gerald, Braves	.172	33	111	99	10	17	18	1	0	0	2	1	0	1	10	0	23	2	3	2	.182	.255
Velazquez, Jose, Yankees*	.287	58	245	209	33	60	82	9	2	3	34	0	3	1	30	2	20	3	4	3	.392	.374
Veras, Wilton, Red Sox	.264	31	101	91	7	24	25	1	0	0	5	0	0	3	7	0	9	1	2	2	.275	.337
Vilchez, Jose, Twins†	.225	45	147	142	14	32	38	6	0	0	6	4	0	0	1	0	29	7	5	0	.268	.231
Villa, Willie, Blue Jays	.181	40	154	138	20	25	35	6	2	0	11	1	0	1	14	0	28	2	1	2	.254	.261
Ware, Jeremy, Expos	.241	38	138	116	18	28	42	4	2	2	15	0	1	3	18	0	28	5	4	2	.362	.355
Weisner, Randy, White Sox*	.286	5	8	7	1	2	3	1	0	0	4	0	0	0	0	0	0	0	0	0	.429	.375
Welch, Coby, Royals	.279	16	46	43	7	12	14	2	0	0	6	0	0	0	3	0	8	0	1	0	.326	.326

Player, Team	Avg.	G	TPA	AB	R	H	TB	2B	3B	HR	RBI	SH	SF	HP	BB	IBB	SO	SB	CS	GDP	Slg.	OBP
Wesson, Barry, Astros............	.188	45	160	138	14	26	38	2	2	2	18	1	1	1	19	0	40	4	0	2	.275	.289
West, Kenyon, Marlins............	.000	13	1	1	0	0	0	0	0	0	0	0	0	0	0	0	0	0	0	0	.000	.000
White, Mickey, Astros............	.000	1	4	4	1	0	0	0	0	0	0	0	0	0	0	0	0	0	0	0	.000	.000
Whitlock, Mike, Blue Jays*.....	.256	54	216	168	27	43	68	10	3	3	22	0	1	6	41	3	48	5	0	4	.405	.417
Winn, Wess, Orioles†	.222	5	21	18	2	4	6	2	0	0	5	0	0	0	3	0	3	0	0	1	.333	.333
Zambrano, Eddie, Red Sox	.000	1	5	5	0	0	0	0	0	0	0	0	0	0	0	0	2	0	0	0	.000	.000
Zambrano, Jose, Red Sox	.286	10	38	28	5	8	14	0	0	2	9	0	1	1	8	0	10	2	0	0	.500	.447
Zambrano, Victor, Yankees†	.205	27	86	78	10	16	21	3	1	0	5	2	0	1	5	0	15	2	3	2	.269	.262
Zamora, Junior, Mets............	.232	20	64	56	9	13	19	2	2	0	4	1	1	1	5	0	10	0	0	2	.339	.302

GRAND SLAMS: Barnes, 2; Adamson, Coffee, Daedelow, Erickson, Fauske, Gallagher, Tardiff, 1 each.
AWARDED FIRST BASE ON CATCHER'S INTERFERENCE: R. Medina 4 (Keech 2, Stevenson 2); S. Charles 3 (Griffin 2, Keech); Velazquez 2 (Griffin, Stevenson); T. Bales (Campos); Borges (F. Pena); Cruz (Cardona); Je. Davenport (T. Bales); Robertson (Weisner); M. Rojas (Payano).

1995 PITCHING

TEAM

Team	W	L	Pct.	ERA	G	CG	ShO	Sv.	IP	H	TBF	R	ER	HR	SH	SF	HB	BB	IBB	SO	WP	Bk.
Cubs..............	35	22	.614	2.07	57	0	5	11	483.0	369	2015	184	111	11	20	22	29	189	6	344	31	15
Marlins...........	40	16	.714	2.30	56	2	4	16	481.2	367	1966	167	123	15	21	13	27	158	9	401	40	8
Mets..............	38	19	.667	2.53	57	3	4	17	490.2	381	2012	175	138	14	7	12	21	173	4	439	57	12
Orioles...........	34	25	.576	2.66	59	6	7	17	490.1	407	2073	223	145	16	9	19	21	190	5	377	28	10
Royals............	37	20	.649	2.76	57	1	5	15	483.0	406	2011	223	148	16	15	16	45	142	1	423	46	9
Yankees..........	32	26	.552	2.89	58	2	8	13	489.1	372	2052	215	157	16	19	9	43	241	3	483	79	21
White Sox........	36	22	.621	2.91	58	3	5	13	482.2	438	2021	217	156	21	6	17	18	155	3	400	34	14
Twins.............	20	35	.364	3.12	55	5	6	9	453.1	406	1982	244	157	16	18	16	32	232	1	357	52	16
Astros............	32	26	.552	3.21	58	2	4	12	476.1	429	2066	228	170	16	23	12	29	199	6	492	59	13
Tigers	33	24	.579	3.39	57	3	5	23	462.0	406	2003	243	174	16	22	16	32	177	10	399	57	20
Rangers...........	24	34	.414	3.68	58	3	5	13	477.1	456	2082	274	195	18	8	18	32	196	3	385	51	7
Red Sox	21	36	.368	3.93	57	7	3	9	476.2	494	2084	287	208	37	12	14	18	181	4	400	42	7
Expos.............	21	35	.375	3.99	56	1	6	12	466.1	470	2056	275	207	18	13	24	26	179	2	310	51	16
Pirates	23	36	.390	4.22	59	2	3	9	488.0	523	2196	316	229	20	14	11	30	196	2	363	49	9
Braves	14	43	.246	4.34	57	2	2	7	467.0	448	2099	314	225	11	10	20	27	244	1	342	72	19
Blue Jays.........	19	40	.322	4.88	59	3	5	7	480.0	518	2196	363	260	22	19	18	43	205	2	350	86	20

INDIVIDUAL

TOP QUALIFIERS FOR EARNED-RUN AVERAGE TITLE
Minimum 48 innings. *Lefthanded pitcher.

Pitcher, Team	W	L	Pct.	ERA	G	GS	CG	ShO	GF	Sv.	IP	H	TBF	R	ER	HR	SH	SF	HB	BB	IBB	SO	WP	Bk.
Martin, Jeffrey, Royals	3	1	.750	1.47	11	10	1	1	0	0	55.0	35	216	12	9	1	0	2	7	11	0	53	2	3
Alicea, Patrick, Tigers............	5	2	.714	1.93	12	8	2	1	2	1	51.1	45	211	21	11	1	1	2	3	14	0	43	5	1
Dace, Derek, Astros*	3	4	.429	1.95	11	10	2	1	1	0	69.1	60	274	20	15	2	3	1	1	6	0	77	5	2
Pena, Juan, Red Sox	3	2	.600	1.95	13	4	2	1	6	1	55.1	41	217	17	12	2	1	2	1	6	0	47	2	1
DeWitt, Scott, Marlins*	5	3	.625	1.98	11	10	1	0	0	0	63.2	48	245	15	14	1	3	2	2	9	0	70	1	1
White, Gary, Orioles*	5	4	.556	2.17	12	10	2	1	1	0	66.1	52	262	26	16	1	1	2	1	16	1	56	5	1
Dotel, Octavio, Mets	7	4	.636	2.18	13	12	2	0	1	0	74.1	48	293	23	18	0	1	0	5	17	1	86	9	0
Kolb, Daniel, Rangers...........	1	7	.125	2.21	12	11	0	0	0	0	53.0	38	219	22	13	0	0	2	3	28	0	46	8	2
Perez, Odaliz, Braves*	3	5	.375	2.22	12	12	1	1	0	0	65.0	48	264	22	16	0	3	0	3	18	0	62	7	3
Robinson, Martin, Yankees*	6	1	.857	2.48	11	8	2	2	0	0	61.2	54	236	20	17	4	2	0	3	13	0	56	7	2
Santiago, Derek, Marlins........	5	1	.833	2.48	11	10	0	0	1	0	58.0	55	245	20	16	1	1	2	3	17	0	59	8	1
Pacheco, Delvis, Braves.........	1	8	.111	2.55	13	13	0	0	0	0	60.0	47	260	26	17	1	0	1	3	38	0	52	5	2
Prestash, J.D., Astros*	4	3	.571	2.63	11	11	0	0	0	0	51.1	48	225	18	15	0	2	1	5	24	0	56	4	6
Birsner, Roark, Cubs	3	2	.600	2.70	12	12	0	0	0	0	60.0	40	209	18	15	2	0	1	4	22	0	42	3	1
Nichols, James, White Sox	7	2	.778	2.89	11	10	0	0	1	0	65.1	64	257	31	21	4	0	2	2	12	0	38	3	0

DEPARTMENTAL LEADERS: W—Dotel, Nichols, 7; L—Pacheco, 8; Pct.—Carmano, Robinson, .857; G—Hernandez, Severino, Stentz, 24; GS—Pacheco, 13; CG—Black, 3; ShO—K. Richardson, Robinson, 2; GF—Stentz, 24; Sv.—Stentz, 16; IP—Dotel, 74.1; H—Black, 83; TBF—Rhodes, 311; R—R. Santos, 49; ER—R. Santos, 36; HR—Asher, Santana, 6; SH—Several pitchers tied with 5; SF—Villegas, 6; HB—Glover, 11; BB—Taylor, 54; IBB—Austin, R. Martinez, 3; SO—Dotel, 86; WP—T. Smith, 17; Bk.—Mejia, Prestash, 6.

ALL PITCHERS
*Lefthanded pitcher.

Pitcher, Team	W	L	Pct.	ERA	G	GS	CG	ShO	GF	Sv.	IP	H	TBF	R	ER	HR	SH	SF	HB	BB	IBB	SO	WP	Bk.
Aguilar, Alonzo, Royals...........	0	1	.000	3.76	15	1	0	0	5	1	26.1	26	116	14	11	2	0	3	7	10	0	24	4	0
Aguilar, Carlo, Yankees	6	0	1.000	2.08	18	0	0	0	6	1	39.0	36	159	11	9	0	3	0	0	13	1	34	8	1
Alicea, Patrick, Tigers	5	2	.714	1.93	12	8	2	1	2	1	51.1	45	211	21	11	1	1	2	3	14	0	43	5	1
Alvarado, Carlos, Pirates	0	0	.000	6.00	2	0	0	0	1	0	3.0	1	15	2	2	0	0	0	5	0	2	3	0
Alvarado, David, Pirates	1	0	1.000	4.80	9	2	0	0	4	1	15.0	15	66	8	8	1	0	0	2	4	0	15	3	2
Anderson, John, Astros	0	2	.000	3.00	2	0	0	0	1	0	3.0	3	13	3	1	0	0	0	0	1	0	5	2	0
Anez, Maycoll, White Sox	4	1	.800	0.93	7	1	0	0	3	1	29.0	19	109	6	3	0	0	1	4	0	21	3	0
Armas, Antonio, Yankees..........	0	1	.000	0.64	5	4	0	0	0	0	14.0	12	61	9	1	1	1	1	6	0	13	3	1
Arroyo, Bronson, Pirates	5	4	.556	4.26	13	9	0	0	3	1	61.1	72	275	39	29	4	2	0	4	9	0	48	5	0
Asher, Ray, Red Sox	3	0	.000	6.92	10	3	0	0	4	0	26.0	32	139	29	20	6	1	2	2	26	2	21	4	0
Austin, Swan, Marlins............	0	2	.000	3.10	15	0	0	0	4	0	20.1	22	91	9	7	0	2	0	0	12	3	15	2	0
Bair, Wayne, Marlins*	2	2	.500	2.96	6	6	0	0	0	0	24.1	21	97	10	8	1	2	0	1	7	0	22	0	2
Bales, Joseph, White Sox	3	1	.750	3.97	11	9	1	0	0	0	45.1	44	213	27	20	0	1	2	3	31	0	44	3	1
Ballew, Preston, Mets*	3	0	1.000	1.75	14	2	0	0	6	4	36.0	27	143	8	7	0	1	0	2	8	0	42	5	1
Batista, Mario, Pirates	0	1	.000	5.40	1	1	0	0	0	0	5.0	7	23	4	3	1	0	0	0	3	0	2	2	0

Pitcher, Team	W	L	Pct.	ERA	G	GS	CG	ShO	GF	Sv.	IP	H	TBF	R	ER	HR	SH	SF	HB	BB	IBB	SO	WP	Bk.
Battaglia, Chuck, Rangers	4	3	.571	4.97	10	8	0	0	1	0	41.2	46	186	31	23	2	0	2	1	13	0	35	5	0
Bauldree, Joe, Braves	0	0	.000	7.09	12	0	0	0	3	0	26.2	26	129	21	21	1	0	0	4	26	0	19	2	0
Beckerman, Andy, Astros	0	0	.000	0.00	2	0	0	0	0	0	3.0	1	12	0	0	0	0	0	0	0	0	3	0	0
Beirne, Kevin, White Sox	0	0	.000	2.45	2	0	0	0	2	2	3.2	2	15	2	1	0	0	0	1	1	0	3	0	0
Bell, Rob, Braves	1	6	.143	6.88	10	8	0	0	0	0	34.0	38	154	29	26	2	0	2	2	14	0	33	7	0
Bernal, Manuel, Royals	3	0	1.000	1.36	6	6	0	0	0	0	33.0	29	130	9	5	1	0	1	1	4	0	25	3	0
Betti, Rich, Red Sox*	1	0	1.000	2.45	3	1	0	0	2	1	7.1	7	30	3	2	0	0	0	1	3	0	13	1	0
Birrell, Simon, Braves	2	3	.400	5.97	13	3	0	0	6	1	37.2	47	184	37	25	2	3	2	4	23	0	18	4	1
Birsner, Roark, Cubs	3	2	.600	2.70	12	12	0	0	0	0	50.0	40	209	18	15	2	0	1	4	22	0	42	3	1
Black, Jayson, Red Sox	4	5	.444	4.43	12	9	3	1	0	0	65.0	83	293	42	32	3	2	1	7	14	0	50	7	0
Boike, Todd, Expos	2	4	.333	3.94	23	1	0	0	13	2	48.0	54	220	32	21	1	1	2	6	13	1	35	6	2
Bonilla, Miguel, Pirates	0	0	.000	1.93	2	0	0	0	2	0	4.2	5	20	1	1	0	0	0	0	1	0	2	0	0
Booker, Chris, Cubs	3	2	.600	2.76	13	7	0	0	2	1	42.1	36	173	22	13	0	0	2	0	16	0	43	4	1
Borkowski, David, Tigers	3	2	.600	2.96	10	10	1	0	0	0	51.2	45	212	24	17	2	1	0	5	8	0	36	1	2
Borkowski, Robert, Mets	0	0	.000	2.25	5	0	0	0	1	1	8.0	6	31	2	2	0	0	0	3	1	1	2	0	0
Bowles, Brian, Blue Jays	0	1	.000	2.40	8	0	0	0	2	0	15.0	18	70	12	4	2	0	1	1	3	0	11	2	1
Boyd, Bradley, Expos	1	1	.500	5.01	17	0	0	0	9	1	23.1	27	111	17	13	0	1	2	1	13	0	10	5	1
Brand, Scott, Yankees	0	0	.000	0.90	4	0	0	0	0	0	10.0	5	37	1	1	1	0	0	0	3	0	8	1	0
Bray, Christopher, Orioles	3	2	.600	3.68	12	2	0	0	1	0	29.1	27	135	20	12	1	0	0	3	16	1	22	5	3
Brito, Juan, Mets*	3	2	.600	3.89	13	4	0	0	7	2	37.0	42	162	20	16	1	0	1	1	10	0	33	4	1
Brown, Brett, Astros*	0	0	.000	3.18	12	0	0	0	9	1	11.1	12	52	7	4	0	1	0	0	6	1	12	0	0
Brown, Tighe, White Sox	0	0	.000	1.17	3	0	0	0	1	0	7.2	3	28	1	1	0	0	1	0	2	0	12	1	0
Bruner, Clayton, Tigers	0	1	.000	3.94	5	4	0	0	0	0	16.0	15	77	12	7	1	3	0	3	10	0	15	1	0
Bryant, Chris, Cubs*	0	0	.000	4.91	6	0	0	0	0	0	11.0	11	49	6	6	0	1	2	0	5	1	13	0	0
Bryant, Scooter, Rangers	0	0	.000	0.00	1	0	0	0	1	0	1.0	0	4	0	0	0	0	0	0	1	0	1	0	0
Buckman, Thomas, W. Sox	1	2	.333	3.08	18	0	0	0	15	7	26.1	26	113	15	9	1	1	1	1	6	0	18	1	2
Burchart, Kyle, Blue Jays	1	3	.250	7.64	13	2	0	0	2	0	35.1	55	186	45	30	2	1	4	4	20	0	27	11	5
Burke, Ethan, Mets	1	1	.333	4.34	13	0	0	0	12	5	18.2	19	83	9	9	0	0	1	0	5	0	14	2	0
Burnett, Allan, Mets	2	3	.400	4.28	9	8	1	0	1	0	33.2	27	144	16	16	2	0	2	2	23	0	26	7	4
Burton, Jamie, Royals*	0	0	.000	8.25	6	1	0	0	1	0	12.0	13	60	11	11	0	1	1	0	10	0	14	5	1
Butler, Robert, Red Sox	1	4	.200	5.01	14	8	0	0	2	0	46.2	48	216	36	26	5	1	0	1	32	1	58	8	0
Cannon, Kevan, Red Sox*	2	1	.667	0.68	5	3	1	0	0	0	26.2	14	107	6	2	1	0	0	0	9	0	38	0	1
Carlson, Garret, White Sox	2	0	1.000	0.00	2	0	0	0	1	0	5.0	2	17	0	0	0	0	0	0	0	0	3	0	0
Carmano, Kevin, Royals	6	1	.857	2.12	15	0	0	0	7	2	34.0	25	140	18	8	0	5	0	8	9	0	16	4	1
Centeno, Jose, Expos*	1	0	1.000	2.45	15	0	0	0	7	1	25.2	18	105	7	7	1	1	1	2	6	0	17	1	1
Chantres, Carlos, White Sox	2	3	.400	3.21	11	11	2	0	0	0	61.2	65	257	32	22	2	1	1	1	14	0	47	1	2
Cobb, Trevor, Twins*	2	0	1.000	0.95	3	3	0	0	0	0	19.0	11	74	5	2	0	1	0	7	0	15	2	0
Coe, Brent, Blue Jays*	0	1	.000	3.38	2	2	0	0	0	0	8.0	8	35	4	3	0	1	0	0	3	0	6	2	0
Collins, Zach, Braves*	0	0	.000	2.57	3	0	0	0	3	1	7.0	6	27	2	2	0	1	0	0	1	0	2	0	0
Cook, O.J., Pirates	0	4	.000	3.63	12	7	0	0	4	2	34.2	33	154	24	14	1	0	1	1	22	0	25	4	0
Cooper, Keith, Braves	1	0	1.000	3.00	2	0	0	0	1	0	3.0	2	12	1	1	0	0	0	0	1	0	3	0	0
Corba, Lisandro, Braves	0	2	.000	1.06	6	3	0	0	0	0	17.0	9	63	5	2	0	0	0	1	1	0	18	1	4
Corrales, Rafael, Cubs	1	1	.500	2.42	12	0	0	0	5	2	22.1	23	97	8	6	2	1	0	1	8	0	10	3	1
Crawford, Christopher, Astros	1	0	1.000	3.62	10	5	0	0	0	0	32.1	29	147	15	13	0	2	1	3	25	0	22	3	0
Crawford, Paxton, Red Sox	2	4	.333	2.74	12	7	1	0	4	2	46.0	38	184	17	14	2	0	0	1	12	0	44	6	0
Cumberland, Chris, Yankees	0	1	.000	1.29	4	4	0	0	0	0	7.0	3	26	1	1	0	0	0	0	1	0	7	0	0
Dace, Derek, Astros*	3	4	.429	1.95	11	10	2	1	1	0	69.1	60	274	20	15	2	3	1	1	6	0	77	5	2
Davenport, Joe, Blue Jays	2	3	.400	5.66	15	10	1	0	1	1	55.2	67	267	47	35	2	3	2	3	30	0	29	9	3
DeLaRosa, Raul, White Sox	4	1	.800	1.67	11	2	0	0	5	0	27.0	22	116	9	5	0	1	2	1	16	1	22	4	0
DeLosSantos, Luis, Yankees	0	0	.000	0.00	2	0	0	0	0	1	5.0	5	23	2	0	0	0	1	2	0	6	0	0	
Demorejon, Pedro, W. Sox	3	4	.429	3.60	12	0	0	0	5	1	30.0	28	125	14	12	3	1	0	2	5	1	34	1	4
Dempster, Ryan, Rangers	3	1	.750	2.36	8	6	1	0	0	0	34.1	34	154	21	9	1	0	1	2	17	0	37	2	1
Dessellier, Chris, Tigers	0	0	.000	0.00	1	0	0	0	1	1	1.0	0	5	0	0	0	0	0	0	1	0	3	0	0
Deutsch, Curry, Pirates*	2	4	.333	2.83	14	0	0	0	10	1	35.0	40	149	17	11	1	3	2	0	11	1	19	3	0
DeWitt, Scott, Marlins*	5	3	.625	1.98	11	10	1	0	0	0	63.2	48	245	15	14	1	3	2	2	9	0	70	1	1
Dickson, Lance, Cubs	0	0	1.000	0.00	2	1	0	0	0	0	3.0	2	14	0	0	0	0	0	3	0	3	0	0	
Dotel, Octavio, Mets	7	4	.636	2.18	13	12	2	0	1	0	74.1	48	293	23	18	0	1	6	5	17	1	86	9	0
Dreyer, Steve, Rangers	0	1	.000	1.00	2	2	0	0	0	0	9.0	6	34	1	1	0	0	1	0	2	0	7	0	0
Duncan, Sean, White Sox*	0	0	.000	0.00	3	0	0	0	1	1	6.0	5	25	3	0	0	0	0	0	1	0	6	1	0
Dunn, Cordell, Pirates	1	1	.500	5.40	5	0	0	0	2	0	10.0	13	46	9	6	0	0	0	4	0	5	2	0	
Duvall, Michael, Marlins*	5	0	1.000	2.22	16	1	0	0	10	1	28.1	15	120	8	7	1	0	0	2	12	1	34	4	2
Ellison, Austin, Twins	0	0	.000	3.78	11	0	0	0	6	2	16.2	17	78	10	7	0	0	0	1	15	0	11	3	1
Enloe, Mark, Mets*	2	1	.667	3.12	11	2	0	0	0	0	26.0	24	114	14	9	0	0	0	0	16	0	25	4	1
Espina, Randy, Twins*	0	1	.000	0.90	4	2	0	0	0	0	10.0	11	50	10	1	0	1	0	0	6	0	3	3	2
Eyre, Scott, White Sox*	0	2	.000	2.30	9	9	0	0	0	0	27.1	16	106	7	7	0	0	1	1	12	0	40	2	0
Farnsworth, Kyle, Cubs	3	2	.600	0.87	16	0	0	0	6	1	31.0	22	120	8	3	0	4	0	1	11	0	18	1	1
Farrell, Jim, Red Sox	1	0	1.000	1.50	1	1	0	0	0	0	6.0	2	20	1	1	0	0	0	1	0	3	1	0	
Feliz, Jose, Cubs	3	2	.600	1.75	13	5	0	0	6	1	36.0	29	158	20	7	0	2	1	4	10	0	27	2	0
Fereira, Marcos, White Sox	0	1	.000	14.73	7	0	0	0	4	0	7.1	11	40	14	12	2	0	0	0	8	0	4	4	1
Figueroa, Julio, Expos	2	3	.400	3.08	10	10	0	0	0	0	49.2	44	211	27	17	5	4	2	0	20	0	37	2	1
Fisher, Louis, Orioles	4	3	.571	1.85	9	7	2	1	0	0	39.0	27	167	23	8	0	0	3	0	24	0	29	4	2
Fisher, Ryan, Pirates*	0	0	.000	0.00	1	0	0	0	1	0	1.0	1	4	0	0	0	0	0	1	0	0	0	0	
Fleming, Dave, Royals*	0	0	.000	0.00	1	1	0	0	0	0	3.0	2	11	1	0	0	0	0	0	1	0	0	0	0
Forster, Peter, Twins*	2	5	.286	3.71	10	7	2	0	1	0	43.2	37	191	21	18	1	4	0	4	27	0	36	6	1
Fortune, Peter, Expos*	3	5	.375	4.69	11	11	1	0	0	0	48.0	46	209	33	25	1	2	1	2	18	0	27	3	0
Fowler, Benjamin, Braves	1	2	.333	1.09	12	0	0	0	6	1	24.2	17	106	13	3	0	0	0	13	0	23	4	0	
Fuduric, Tony, Tigers	5	2	.714	2.97	16	0	0	0	7	0	30.1	25	136	13	10	1	2	2	1	21	0	21	4	3
Gaerte, Travis, Pirates	0	0	.000	6.00	6	0	0	0	1	0	12.0	14	57	9	8	2	0	0	3	2	0	5	1	1
Garcia, Freddy, Astros	6	3	.667	4.47	11	11	0	0	0	0	58.1	60	256	32	29	2	3	3	6	14	0	58	5	0
Garff, Jeffery, Twins	4	2	.667	1.75	16	6	0	0	6	1	45.2	34	175	12	9	3	1	0	4	5	0	30	1	0
Garsky, Brian, Expos	2	3	.400	3.12	14	6	0	0	2	1	43.1	48	199	25	15	1	3	2	0	19	0	43	6	3
Gaston, Ryan, Rangers	0	0	.000	1.99	10	1	0	0	5	2	22.2	19	95	9	5	0	0	2	2	6	0	9	1	0
Geraldo, Antonio, Blue Jays	0	0	.000	1.50	2	2	0	0	0	0	6.0	6	24	1	1	0	0	0	0	1	0	6	2	0

Pitcher, Team	W	L	Pct.	ERA	G	GS	CG	ShO	GF	Sv.	IP	H	TBF	R	ER	HR	SH	SF	HB	BB	IBB	SO	WP	Bk.
Gerland, Greg, Braves*	1	0	1.000	0.00	2	0	0	0	2	0	4.0	1	14	0	0	0	0	0	0	1	0	3	0	0
Getz, Rod, Marlins	1	1	.500	3.38	6	6	0	0	0	0	29.1	25	112	12	11	2	0	1	1	4	0	30	3	0
Gil, Daniel, Cubs	1	1	.500	3.46	7	0	0	0	2	2	13.0	9	59	7	5	0	0	1	2	8	0	9	4	0
Gillispie, Ryan, Pirates	0	1	.000	2.45	4	0	0	0	4	0	7.1	8	37	4	2	0	0	1	1	6	0	4	1	0
Glover, John, Blue Jays	3	7	.300	4.91	12	10	2	0	0	0	62.1	62	279	48	34	4	4	3	11	26	0	46	8	0
Goedde, Roger, Pirates	1	1	.500	2.61	6	6	1	0	0	0	31.0	31	130	12	9	0	1	0	2	7	0	25	0	0
Gonzalez, Generoso, Tigers	5	3	.625	3.89	16	4	0	0	2	1	39.1	29	163	19	17	1	2	1	1	16	0	45	8	1
Gosch, Grant, Astros*	0	0	.000	0.00	1	0	0	0	1	0	0.2	0	3	0	0	0	0	0	0	1	0	1	0	0
Gray, Jason, White Sox	4	2	.667	2.02	14	4	0	0	6	1	35.2	35	150	10	8	1	0	0	9	1	37	2	0
Gulin, Lindsey, Mets*	6	0	1.000	1.71	10	4	0	0	3	0	47.1	36	182	11	9	4	0	1	1	13	0	48	2	2
Guzman, Jose, Cubs	0	0	.000	1.50	2	2	0	0	0	0	6.0	5	24	1	1	1	0	0	0	0	0	3	0	0
Hacen, Abraham, Orioles	2	3	.400	2.54	13	8	0	0	2	2	46.0	34	201	21	13	2	1	3	4	32	0	37	3	1
Hale, Shane, Orioles	0	0	.000	1.29	2	0	0	0	1	0	7.0	6	32	2	1	0	0	0	0	4	0	6	0	0
Halladay, Roy, Blue Jays	3	5	.375	3.40	10	8	0	0	1	0	50.1	35	203	25	19	4	2	0	1	16	0	48	9	2
Hammons, Matt, Cubs	3	1	.750	2.35	10	8	0	0	1	0	46.0	35	186	14	12	1	1	3	2	16	0	32	2	1
Harris, Doug, Orioles	1	0	1.000	0.00	1	0	0	0	1	0	1.0	2	4	0	0	0	0	0	0	0	0	0	0	0
Hausmann, Isaac, Rangers	1	2	.333	2.67	18	0	0	0	15	6	30.1	24	128	11	9	0	1	1	2	9	0	23	0	0
Hecker, Doug, Red Sox	0	0	.000	5.40	2	0	0	0	1	0	1.2	4	11	2	1	0	0	0	0	0	0	4	0	0
Herbison, Brett, Mets	3	0	1.000	2.20	9	9	0	0	0	0	41.0	31	170	13	10	3	1	2	0	16	0	31	4	0
Hernandez, Francisco, Orioles	2	2	.500	1.32	24	0	0	0	20	11	27.1	18	105	4	4	1	0	1	1	6	0	23	2	1
Holobinko, Mike, Cubs*	3	2	.600	1.74	8	1	0	0	3	0	20.2	16	86	8	4	1	1	2	3	8	0	11	1	0
Hook, Jeff, Astros	1	0	1.000	0.00	2	0	0	0	0	0	6.0	4	24	0	0	0	0	0	0	2	0	4	0	0
Horton, Aaron, Yankees*	2	1	.667	1.57	8	6	0	0	0	0	23.0	17	93	7	4	0	0	1	5	6	0	21	3	1
Hundley, Chanin, White Sox	0	0	.000	6.23	3	0	0	0	0	0	4.1	7	22	5	3	1	0	3	0	2	0	2	0	0
Huntsman, Brandon, Orioles	6	3	.667	3.86	13	12	1	0	0	0	65.1	53	286	38	28	4	2	2	3	33	0	64	4	0
Hurtado, Victor, Marlins	3	1	.750	0.81	7	7	1	0	0	0	33.1	14	134	5	3	0	2	1	2	16	0	28	2	0
Izquierdo, Hansel, Marlins	0	0	.000	0.00	1	0	0	0	0	0	2.0	3	10	3	0	0	1	0	0	2	0	0	1	0
Jelsovsky, Craig, Mets	0	0	.000	0.00	1	0	0	0	1	1	1.0	0	3	0	0	0	0	0	0	0	0	0	0	0
Johnson, Joaquin, Braves*	0	0	.000	5.00	11	2	0	0	6	0	27.0	25	125	17	15	2	2	3	1	16	0	15	8	1
Johnson, Mike, Blue Jays	0	2	.000	7.20	3	3	0	0	0	0	15.0	20	74	15	12	1	0	0	3	8	0	13	7	0
Jolliffee, Brian, Braves*	0	2	.000	6.65	11	0	0	0	5	1	23.0	36	112	24	17	0	0	2	1	9	0	15	6	3
Judd, Mike, Yankees	1	1	.500	1.11	21	0	0	0	18	8	32.1	18	123	5	4	0	0	0	4	6	0	30	4	0
Kauflin, David, Tigers	2	1	.667	4.86	5	3	0	0	0	0	16.2	11	69	11	9	0	1	0	7	0	13	4	0
Kelley, Jason, Cubs	1	1	.500	0.70	7	5	0	0	1	0	25.2	10	110	11	2	0	0	5	19	0	20	2	2
Kessel, Kyle, Mets*	3	0	1.000	1.80	7	7	0	0	0	0	40.0	29	160	12	8	1	4	1	2	11	0	47	3	0
Key, Francis, Royals	1	2	.333	2.57	16	0	0	0	11	2	28.0	17	118	13	8	0	4	0	4	12	1	34	3	1
Kinney, Matt, Red Sox	1	3	.250	2.93	8	2	0	0	4	2	27.2	29	119	13	9	0	1	2	2	10	0	11	5	0
Knight, Brandon, Rangers	2	1	.667	5.25	3	2	0	0	0	0	12.0	12	54	7	7	0	0	1	0	6	0	11	2	0
Kolb, Daniel, Rangers	1	7	.125	2.21	12	11	0	0	0	0	53.0	38	219	22	13	0	0	2	3	28	0	46	8	2
Kruse, Kelly, White Sox	1	0	1.000	4.50	3	0	0	0	2	0	4.0	4	17	2	2	0	0	0	1	0	2	0	1	1
Lacey, James, Expos	1	1	.500	8.34	12	1	0	0	6	0	22.2	35	120	29	21	2	0	4	14	0	10	3	2
Lakman, Jason, White Sox	3	0	1.000	3.27	9	5	0	0	1	0	41.1	44	181	17	15	2	0	2	5	12	0	23	2	2
LaPlante, Michael, Pirates	0	0	.000	0.00	2	0	0	0	0	0	3.0	1	12	0	0	0	0	0	0	0	0	4	0	0
Lara, Nelson, Marlins	1	1	.500	3.74	11	0	0	0	4	1	21.2	21	101	13	9	1	0	1	2	11	1	9	2	1
Lara, Yovanny, Expos	1	2	.333	5.10	11	4	0	0	1	0	30.0	35	139	21	17	4	0	3	2	19	0	16	0	1
Lawrence, Clint, Blue Jays*	1	5	.167	4.57	12	9	0	0	3	0	45.1	40	202	33	23	1	0	1	1	26	0	40	9	1
Lawrie, Jason, Tigers	0	1	.000	4.50	4	4	0	0	0	0	12.0	10	59	8	6	0	0	0	1	12	2	12	0	0
Lebron, Jose, Expos	0	0	.000	0.00	2	0	0	0	1	0	2.0	0	9	0	0	0	0	0	0	3	0	0	0	0
Licciardi, Ronald, Cubs*	4	3	.571	2.43	17	1	0	0	7	0	33.1	24	141	13	9	1	1	0	1	16	2	22	3	4
Lynch, James, Astros	2	1	.667	1.56	17	1	0	0	12	4	34.2	14	148	12	6	1	0	0	26	0	49	10	2
Macero, Victor, Cubs	0	1	.000	5.40	1	1	0	0	0	0	5.0	3	19	3	3	1	0	0	1	0	5	0	0
Maine, Dalton, Orioles	1	0	1.000	2.08	18	0	0	0	6	2	30.1	24	122	7	7	0	0	1	0	9	1	32	1	0
Malko, Bryan, Twins	1	2	.333	2.73	10	4	0	0	3	1	33.0	23	142	14	10	1	3	1	4	23	0	29	5	0
Manley, Kevin, Mets	0	0	.000	6.75	2	0	0	0	1	0	1.1	1	8	1	1	0	0	0	3	0	0	1	0
Manser, Chris, Tigers	3	2	.600	2.45	6	5	0	0	1	0	29.1	24	120	10	8	1	1	2	0	5	0	26	6	0
Mansur, Jeff, Orioles*	0	0	.000	3.38	3	0	0	0	1	0	5.1	11	27	5	2	1	0	1	1	0	2	0	0
Markey, Barret, Cubs	4	1	.800	1.76	17	1	0	0	9	1	41.0	43	168	11	8	0	1	0	0	7	0	24	1	1
Marquez, Ralph, Twins	0	4	.000	4.09	11	0	0	0	11	1	22.0	19	103	13	10	1	1	1	0	18	1	19	2	3
Marriott, Michael, Marlins	0	0	.000	1.13	2	2	0	0	0	0	8.0	2	32	2	1	0	0	1	7	0	6	1	0
Marshall, Lee, Twins	0	1	.000	4.91	6	1	0	0	1	0	11.0	16	57	10	6	1	1	2	8	0	7	2	0
Martin, Cleburne, Expos	2	5	.286	4.85	17	4	0	0	5	2	42.2	43	187	26	23	1	0	4	0	22	1	26	10	1
Martin, Jeffrey, Royals	3	1	.750	1.47	11	10	1	1	0	0	55.0	35	216	12	9	1	0	2	7	11	0	53	2	3
Martinez, Humberto, R. Sox	0	3	.000	3.62	14	0	0	0	6	1	27.1	25	119	14	11	3	0	2	17	0	19	2	0
Martinez, Juan, Rangers	2	3	.400	5.40	12	6	0	0	5	0	38.1	43	166	28	23	5	0	0	11	1	27	1	0
Martinez, Ramulo, Tigers	0	0	.000	7.50	16	0	0	0	3	1	24.0	27	115	22	20	0	1	0	13	3	14	3	5
Martino, Jason, Cubs	0	0	.000	0.00	8	0	0	0	5	0	10.2	4	42	2	0	0	0	0	5	1	4	1	0
Mason, Roger, Pirates	1	0	1.000	0.00	1	0	0	0	0	0	1.0	2	5	0	0	0	0	0	0	0	0	1	0	0
Mattes, Troy, Expos	2	0	1.000	0.00	2	2	0	0	0	0	12.0	7	43	0	0	0	0	0	3	0	8	0	0
Maysonet, Jose, Blue Jays	0	0	.000	0.00	1	0	0	0	0	0	1.0	1	6	0	0	0	0	0	2	0	1	0	0
McBride, Rodney, Twins	3	7	.300	3.08	12	11	1	1	1	1	61.1	63	275	38	21	3	4	5	3	34	0	36	8	1
McCarter, Jason, Astros	1	0	1.000	2.86	16	0	0	0	9	2	22.0	16	97	8	7	2	5	0	2	16	0	21	6	0
McCaskey, Thomas, W. Sox	1	1	.500	3.00	6	1	0	0	0	0	18.0	17	77	6	6	1	0	0	7	0	16	4	1
McCormack, Andy, W. Sox*	1	0	1.000	1.50	1	1	0	0	0	0	6.0	4	21	1	1	1	0	0	0	0	0	3	0	0
McFarlane, Joseph, Tigers	0	0	.000	0.00	1	0	0	0	0	0	1.1	1	5	0	0	0	0	0	0	0	1	0	0
McFerrin, Chris, Astros	4	4	.500	2.86	20	0	0	0	12	5	34.2	28	153	20	11	0	0	5	17	2	39	6	1
McKnight, Tony, Astros	1	1	.500	3.86	3	3	0	0	0	0	11.2	14	48	5	5	0	0	0	2	0	8	1	0
Meady, Todd, Royals	3	3	.500	2.63	12	6	0	0	2	2	37.2	33	156	21	11	1	0	1	2	6	0	26	2	0
Medina, Tomas, Astros	1	0	1.000	8.46	11	1	0	0	0	0	22.1	37	115	26	21	0	1	0	1	14	0	23	7	0
Mejia, Felix, Yankees	2	0	1.000	3.45	9	0	0	0	3	0	15.2	11	68	6	6	0	0	2	13	0	21	6	6
Mendoza, David, Blue Jays	2	5	.286	4.99	12	10	0	0	0	0	48.2	58	225	37	27	0	2	1	4	14	0	39	4	3
Mendoza, Geronimo, W. Sox	0	1	.000	4.30	10	0	0	0	8	0	14.2	8	59	9	7	3	0	2	1	7	0	11	1	0
Mercedes, Carlos, Orioles	2	1	.667	2.55	10	1	0	0	2	0	24.2	22	96	8	7	2	0	0	0	2	0	10	0	0
Mesewicz, Mark, Pirates*	0	0	.000	3.86	3	0	0	0	0	0	4.2	5	21	2	2	0	0	0	0	1	0	6	0	0

Pitcher, Team	W	L	Pct.	ERA	G	GS	CG	ShO	GF	Sv.	IP	H	TBF	R	ER	HR	SH	SF	HB	BB	IBB	SO	WP	Bk.
Meyhoff, Jason, Twins*	0	0	.000	4.50	2	0	0	0	1	0	2.0	3	9	3	1	0	1	0	0	0	0	3	1	0
Mills, Al, Orioles	0	0	.000	0.00	1	1	0	0	0	0	2.0	3	11	0	0	0	0	0	0	2	0	1	0	1
Moody, Ritchie, Rangers	0	0	.000	2.70	2	2	0	0	0	0	10.0	10	46	3	3	0	0	0	0	6	0	10	1	0
Moore, David, Royals	2	2	.500	4.18	14	1	0	0	8	2	28.0	28	124	17	13	3	0	1	1	12	0	12	3	0
Moreno, Julio, Orioles	3	2	.600	1.59	5	5	1	1	0	0	34.0	17	131	9	6	0	1	2	1	7	0	29	1	1
Moreno, Orber, Royals	1	1	.500	2.45	8	3	0	0	1	0	22.0	15	89	9	6	0	0	2	7	0	21	2	0
Moreno, Ricardo, Rangers	1	0	1.000	1.80	4	1	1	0	2	1	15.0	13	56	3	3	1	2	0	1	0	8	0	1
Mota, Daniel, Yankees	2	3	.400	2.20	14	0	0	0	9	0	32.2	27	133	9	8	2	4	0	2	4	0	35	6	3
Mullis, Steven, Royals*	2	1	.667	2.92	8	1	0	0	3	1	12.1	7	52	6	4	0	0	1	0	7	0	13	2	0
Newell, Brandon, Mets	0	0	.000	0.00	1	0	0	0	1	0	1.0	1	7	2	0	0	0	1	0	2	1	2	0	0
Nezelek, Andy, Pirates	1	1	.500	7.71	4	0	0	0	4	1	7.0	12	34	7	6	0	1	0	0	2	1	6	2	0
Nichols, James, White Sox	7	2	.778	2.89	11	10	0	0	1	0	65.1	64	257	31	21	4	0	2	2	12	0	38	3	0
Ocando, Stewart, Twins	0	1	.000	5.96	14	0	0	0	8	0	22.2	26	118	25	15	2	1	4	4	22	0	20	7	4
O'Conner, Brian, Pirates*	2	2	.500	1.88	14	5	0	0	5	1	43.0	33	183	22	9	1	0	1	0	13	0	43	4	2
Olson, Philip, Mets	0	0	.000	4.50	1	0	0	0	0	0	2.0	1	10	1	1	0	0	0	0	3	0	3	0	0
Ovalle, Bonelly, Rangers	4	2	.667	3.72	17	5	1	1	3	1	58.0	51	243	29	24	1	2	3	6	20	1	58	5	0
Pacheco, Delvis, Braves	1	8	.111	2.55	13	13	0	0	0	0	60.0	47	260	26	17	1	0	1	3	38	0	52	5	2
Paredes, Carlos, Royals	4	2	.667	3.53	10	10	0	0	0	0	51.0	56	221	28	20	2	2	2	2	17	0	37	4	0
Parotte, Frisco, Yankees	0	0	.000	2.79	9	0	0	0	7	1	9.2	9	43	3	3	0	1	0	0	6	0	8	2	0
Pena, Jesus, Pirates*	0	0	.000	2.57	7	6	0	0	0	0	35.0	20	138	11	10	0	0	0	19	0	36	4	0
Pena, Juan, Red Sox	3	2	.600	1.95	13	4	2	1	6	1	55.1	41	217	17	12	2	1	2	1	6	0	47	2	1
Penny, Tony, Royals	2	0	1.000	5.06	10	0	0	0	4	0	16.0	17	66	9	9	4	0	0	4	0	7	0	0
Peraza, Jose, Cubs*	0	0	.000	0.00	3	0	0	0	1	0	2.1	0	8	0	0	0	1	0	1	0	2	0	0
Perez, Leonardo, Orioles	1	1	.500	4.41	8	0	0	0	4	0	16.1	14	76	13	8	1	0	3	3	7	0	7	0	0
Perez, Odaliz, Braves*	3	5	.375	2.22	12	12	1	1	0	0	65.0	48	264	22	16	0	3	0	3	18	0	62	7	3
Persails, Mark, Tigers	1	4	.200	4.41	11	10	0	0	1	0	51.0	50	237	37	25	4	5	3	4	25	0	30	8	1
Petcka, Joe, Mets	0	0	.000	0.00	1	0	0	0	1	0	2.0	1	7	0	0	0	0	0	0	0	0	0	0	0
Prestash, J.D., Astros*	4	3	.571	2.63	11	11	0	0	0	0	51.1	48	225	18	15	0	2	1	5	24	0	56	4	6
Puffer, Brandon, Twins	0	3	.000	2.88	14	5	0	0	6	1	40.2	29	175	21	13	0	0	2	21	0	35	5	0
Quezada, Edward, Expos	0	7	.000	4.99	12	10	0	0	2	0	52.1	52	221	36	29	2	1	1	5	10	0	36	10	1
Ramos, Edgar, Astros	0	1	.000	1.84	5	5	0	0	0	0	14.2	14	62	6	3	0	1	0	2	5	0	16	1	0
Randolph, Stephen, Yankees*	4	0	1.000	2.22	8	3	0	0	1	0	24.1	11	94	7	6	1	0	0	1	16	0	34	3	1
Rangel, Julio, Yankees	1	3	.250	4.40	14	0	0	0	5	2	28.2	20	123	18	14	2	1	0	4	16	1	30	2	0
Rauch, Robert, Red Sox	0	1	.000	4.76	7	0	0	0	6	2	5.2	8	27	4	3	0	2	0	0	2	1	6	0	0
Reilly, Sean, Twins*	0	1	.000	5.27	6	0	0	0	1	0	13.2	19	65	12	8	1	0	0	6	0	11	0	0
Reynolds, Mark, Rangers	0	2	.000	5.40	7	1	0	0	2	0	10.0	8	50	10	6	1	0	0	0	11	0	10	2	1
Rhodes, Joe, Orioles	4	2	.667	3.04	13	11	0	0	0	0	71.0	72	311	36	24	0	3	1	2	28	1	43	2	0
Richardson, David, Marlins	0	2	.000	2.30	9	0	0	0	6	1	15.2	8	62	5	4	1	0	1	2	5	0	8	1	0
Richardson, Kasey, Twins*	5	2	.714	1.15	7	7	2	2	0	0	47.0	38	190	10	6	1	0	3	11	0	35	1	0
Ricketts, Chad, Cubs	1	0	1.000	0.00	2	2	0	0	0	0	9.0	1	32	1	0	0	0	0	1	1	0	5	0	0
Ritter, Jason, Royals	0	0	.000	0.00	2	0	0	0	1	1	3.2	3	16	1	0	0	1	0	0	1	0	2	1	0
Robbins, Jake, Yankees	2	3	.400	5.54	14	3	0	0	3	0	37.1	32	159	26	23	2	2	1	1	18	1	17	4	0
Roberts, Franklin, Rangers	0	0	.000	27.00	1	0	0	0	0	0	0.2	1	7	2	2	0	0	0	4	0	0	0	0
Roberts, Grant, Mets	2	1	.667	2.15	11	3	0	0	4	0	29.1	19	121	13	7	1	1	3	14	1	24	4	1
Robinson, Martin, Yankees*	6	1	.857	2.48	11	8	2	2	0	0	61.2	54	236	20	17	4	2	0	3	13	0	56	7	2
Rodriguez, Tomas, Tigers	0	0	.000	2.53	14	0	0	0	8	1	21.1	14	93	13	6	0	1	5	8	0	21	5	1
Rojas, Euclides, Marlins	2	0	1.000	0.90	2	2	0	0	0	0	10.0	6	35	1	1	0	1	0	0	1	0	7	0	1
Romo, Greg, Tigers	3	1	.750	2.63	5	5	0	0	0	0	27.1	25	110	9	8	0	0	2	0	5	0	25	3	0
Rosario, Juan, Marlins	0	0	.000	13.50	1	0	0	0	0	0	1.1	4	10	2	2	0	0	0	1	0	3	1	0
Ross, Jeremy, Marlins	2	0	1.000	0.00	3	0	0	0	3	1	8.0	8	33	1	0	0	0	1	1	11	1	0
Ruch, Rob, Twins	1	3	.250	3.86	7	2	0	0	4	2	23.1	16	98	13	10	0	1	0	16	0	30	3	0
Ruffcorn, Scott, White Sox	0	0	.000	0.90	3	3	0	0	0	0	10.0	7	46	4	1	0	1	0	5	0	7	1	0
Ryan, Michael-Sean, Rangers	2	5	.286	2.35	17	0	0	0	8	2	38.1	36	159	15	10	1	1	2	8	1	22	0	0
Sacharko, Mark, Astros	1	2	.333	3.75	12	0	0	0	8	0	24.0	23	105	14	10	5	0	2	2	12	1	22	0	0
Samboy, Javier, Mets*	5	3	.625	2.98	12	4	0	0	4	1	48.1	40	196	17	16	0	0	2	3	17	0	31	3	0
Sanchez, Bienvenido, Expos	1	2	.333	1.46	16	1	0	0	9	5	37.0	27	153	7	6	0	2	0	3	12	0	29	4	3
Sanders, Allen, Royals	0	0	.000	0.00	1	0	0	0	1	1	2.0	1	6	0	0	0	0	0	0	0	3	0	0
Santamaria, Juan, Tigers	2	0	1.000	5.40	12	0	0	0	2	1	20.0	26	104	17	12	2	1	1	4	11	1	17	4	3
Santana, Pedro, Red Sox	4	2	.333	6.41	12	6	0	0	2	0	39.1	51	182	40	28	6	2	3	0	20	0	14	3	1
Santiago, Antonio, Red Sox*	2	2	.500	4.32	6	3	0	0	2	0	25.0	30	107	17	12	1	0	0	3	0	24	2	1
Santiago, Derek, Marlins	5	1	.833	2.48	11	11	0	0	0	0	58.0	55	245	20	16	1	1	2	3	17	0	59	8	1
Santos, Juan, Orioles	0	2	.000	3.20	21	0	0	0	15	2	25.1	25	107	11	9	3	1	0	2	4	1	16	1	0
Santos, Rafael, Pirates	2	5	.286	6.31	11	10	1	0	1	0	51.1	63	246	49	36	1	4	2	6	27	0	26	1	0
Schaffner, Eric, Yankees	2	2	.500	1.65	11	7	0	0	1	0	43.2	31	182	17	8	1	4	1	4	16	0	48	4	2
Schneider, Jeff, Blue Jays	0	2	.000	15.43	3	2	0	0	0	0	4.2	9	33	10	8	0	0	1	2	7	0	2	1	0
Schrenk, Steve, White Sox	0	1	.000	0.00	2	1	0	0	0	0	7.0	5	27	2	0	0	0	0	0	0	6	0	0
Scofield, Josh, Pirates*	0	0	.000	9.00	2	0	0	0	0	0	2.0	3	13	2	2	0	0	0	4	0	4	0	0
Seabury, Jaron, Blue Jays	3	0	1.000	3.18	15	0	0	0	5	1	39.2	35	164	16	14	2	2	1	7	17	0	18	6	1
Settle, Brian, Pirates	2	0	1.000	8.27	11	0	0	0	5	0	20.2	25	105	22	19	4	2	3	1	20	0	11	4	1
Severino, Edy, Blue Jays	1	3	.250	5.63	24	0	0	0	12	1	24.0	31	121	25	15	0	2	2	13	0	13	8	2
Shannon, Bobby, Royals*	1	1	.500	3.25	16	0	0	0	9	2	27.2	28	112	11	10	0	1	2	3	3	0	26	4	0
Shiell, Jason, Braves	1	3	.250	4.43	12	0	0	0	9	2	22.1	23	101	16	11	0	0	2	10	1	13	3	0
Shurman, Ryan, Braves	1	6	.143	6.75	10	7	0	0	0	0	34.2	37	158	31	26	1	0	0	2	21	0	26	9	3
Simmons, Carlos, Rangers	4	3	.571	3.28	14	9	0	0	3	0	57.2	57	255	33	21	1	2	9	22	0	44	4	0
Smart, J.D., Expos	2	0	1.000	1.69	2	2	0	0	0	0	10.2	10	43	2	2	0	0	1	2	1	6	0	0
Smith, Dan, Rangers	0	3	.000	4.26	4	3	0	0	0	0	19.0	19	81	9	9	0	0	1	2	5	0	12	0	0
Smith, Tom, Rangers	0	0	.000	27.00	5	0	0	0	1	0	3.0	6	33	14	9	0	0	0	17	0	4	17	2
Sorzano, Ronnie, Expos	1	2	.333	5.21	4	4	0	0	0	0	19.0	24	86	13	11	0	0	1	1	4	0	16	1	0
Stading, Kris, Cubs*	0	0	.000	0.66	11	0	0	0	5	0	13.2	8	66	4	1	0	0	1	14	0	12	1	1
Stallings, Ben, Red Sox	1	1	.500	7.82	8	0	0	0	0	0	12.2	14	61	11	11	2	0	0	0	11	0	7	1	0
Stark, Zac, Marlins	3	1	.750	1.73	11	1	0	0	3	2	26.0	18	102	7	5	0	2	1	0	6	0	16	1	0
Stentz, Brent, Tigers	2	1	.667	2.36	24	0	0	0	24	16	26.2	21	107	7	7	1	1	1	12	2	28	4	1
Stewart, Scott, Twins	0	0	.000	6.35	3	1	0	0	0	0	5.2	7	29	4	4	0	0	0	1	4	0	9	0	1

Pitcher, Team	W	L	Pct.	ERA	G	GS	CG	ShO	GF	Sv.	IP	H	TBF	R	ER	HR	SH	SF	HB	BB	IBB	SO	WP	Bk.
Styles, Bobby, Rangers............	0	0	.000	6.55	12	1	0	0	7	1	22.0	31	106	24	16	4	0	3	9	0	21	3	0
Suero, Rey, Rangers................	0	1	.000	13.50	2	0	0	0	2	0	1.1	2	6	2	2	1	0	0	0	0	0	0	0
Symmonds, Mike, Pirates.......	1	1	.500	4.70	6	0	0	0	5	0	7.2	3	39	5	4	0	0	0	4	9	0	9	6	0
Tam, Jeff, Mets	0	0	.000	3.00	2	1	0	0	0	0	3.0	2	13	1	1	0	1	0	1	1	0	2	1	0
Taylor, Brien, Yankees*..........	2	5	.286	6.08	11	11	0	0	0	0	40.0	29	199	37	27	1	0	1	10	54	0	38	16	1
Tejera, Michael, Marlins*........	3	1	.750	2.65	11	3	0	0	4	2	34.0	28	142	13	10	2	4	1	2	16	1	28	3	0
Tessmar, Timothy, Mets*........	1	0	1.000	0.00	1	0	0	0	0	0	1.1	1	7	0	0	0	0	0	1	0	1	1	0
Thorn, Todd, Royals*.............	4	2	.667	3.23	11	10	0	0	0	0	47.1	43	201	23	17	1	1	1	6	14	0	58	4	1
Tillmon, Darrell, Red Sox*.......	1	0	1.000	1.13	3	1	0	0	0	0	8.0	4	29	2	1	0	0	0	0	5	0	5	0	0
Torres, Eric, Mets	0	2	.000	0.44	11	0	0	0	6	3	20.2	11	83	5	1	1	1	0	1	6	0	8	4	2
Trimble, Rob, Yankees	0	0	.000	0.57	11	0	0	0	2	1	15.2	12	62	2	1	0	0	1	0	4	0	14	0	0
Turley, Jason, Astros	5	0	1.000	5.63	11	0	0	0	2	0	16.0	14	79	13	10	0	0	1	2	13	1	13	1	2
Valencia, Enrique, Red Sox*....	1	2	.333	4.76	14	4	0	0	7	0	34.0	51	154	25	18	3	0	1	0	9	0	19	0	2
Vanderbush, Matt, Twins*.......	2	3	.400	4.00	8	6	0	0	1	0	36.0	37	153	23	16	2	1	2	3	9	0	28	3	3
Vaninetti, Gene, Blue Jays	0	2	.000	4.98	20	0	0	0	9	0	21.2	25	98	14	12	3	1	0	0	6	1	7	1	2
Vardijan, Daniel, Marlins	5	0	1.000	1.64	9	8	0	0	1	0	44.0	21	164	11	8	2	0	1	5	10	0	34	2	0
Veniard, Jay, Blue Jays*.........	2	0	1.000	0.82	3	1	0	0	2	0	11.0	4	39	2	1	0	0	0	1	2	0	18	2	0
Verdin, Cesar, Yankees*.........	2	2	.500	3.46	11	5	0	0	0	0	26.0	26	114	15	10	1	1	0	0	10	0	35	1	0
Viegas, Randy, Pirates*..........	3	2	.600	2.54	6	4	0	0	2	0	28.1	28	119	13	8	0	0	1	5	0	0	24	0	0
Villar, Maximo, Pirates...........	1	1	.500	7.20	6	3	0	0	1	1	20.0	29	101	21	16	2	0	3	9	0	13	1	2
Villegas, Ismael, Cubs	3	2	.600	2.40	11	10	0	0	0	0	41.1	33	168	17	11	1	2	6	2	11	0	26	3	2
Vizcaino, Edward, Cubs	1	1	.500	2.70	14	0	0	0	6	1	16.2	15	77	10	5	1	5	2	2	6	2	11	0	0
Wallace, Jeff, Royals*............	5	3	.625	1.23	14	12	0	0	3	1	44.0	28	177	30	6	0	1	1	1	15	0	51	3	2
Ward, Kerry, Pirates.............	2	6	.250	4.87	11	6	0	0	2	0	44.1	59	204	33	24	2	1	1	0	13	0	27	3	1
West, Kenyon, Marlins............	2	1	.667	2.45	13	0	0	0	7	3	29.1	32	125	17	8	2	2	0	1	6	2	9	0	0
White, Eric, Braves	1	1	.500	6.75	13	1	0	0	8	0	32.0	39	161	37	24	1	1	3	1	22	0	10	9	0
White, Gary, Orioles*.............	5	4	.556	2.17	12	10	2	1	1	0	66.1	52	262	26	16	1	1	2	1	16	1	56	5	1
Wicks, Ross, Mets................	0	1	.000	3.38	12	1	0	0	6	0	18.2	15	75	7	7	1	0	0	6	0	15	1	0
Widerski, Jonathan, Marlins	1	0	1.000	3.33	14	0	0	0	3	1	24.1	16	106	13	9	1	1	2	1	18	0	12	7	0
Williams, Bradford, Yankees*....	0	3	.000	5.32	11	7	0	0	0	0	23.2	14	117	19	14	0	1	2	4	34	0	28	9	3
Wise, Willie, Braves*..............	2	0	1.000	6.75	4	0	0	0	3	0	6.2	11	35	8	5	0	0	1	0	3	0	6	1	0
Wood, Kerry, Cubs	0	0	.000	0.00	1	1	0	0	0	0	3.0	9	9	0	0	0	0	0	0	1	0	2	0	0
Wyatt, Ben, Braves*..............	1	3	.250	2.98	12	8	1	0	3	1	42.1	36	194	25	14	1	0	4	3	27	0	24	6	2
Yanez, Luis, Astros	2	5	.286	2.95	11	11	0	0	0	0	61.0	52	253	29	20	4	2	1	0	15	1	63	8	0
Yonemura, Kazuki, Tigers	2	4	.333	2.32	14	4	0	0	4	1	42.2	38	180	20	11	2	4	0	3	9	2	49	1	2
Yount, Andrew, Red Sox..........	0	1	.000	2.76	5	5	0	0	0	0	16.1	13	69	8	5	1	1	0	2	6	0	17	1	1
Zavershnik, Mike, Blue Jays* ..	1	1	.500	5.45	19	0	0	0	8	2	36.1	44	170	29	22	1	1	2	3	11	1	26	5	0

COMBINATION SHUTOUTS: **Astros (3)**—Prestash-McCarter, Prestash-McFarrin, Yanez-Lynch. **Blue Jays (4)**—Halladay-Zavershnik 2, Lawrence-Severino-Vaninetti, Mendoza-Seabury-Vaninetti. **Braves (1)**—Shurman-Perille. **Cubs (5)**—Birsner-Markey, Hammons-Farnsworth-Licciardi, Hammons-Stading-Farnsworth, Ricketts-Farnsworth-Markey, Villegas-Stading-Licciardi. **Expos (6)**—Figueroa-Centeno-Boyd, Fortune-Garsky-Centeno, Garsky-Lacey-Boike, Mattes-Boike, Mattes-Garsky, Sanchez-Garsky. **Marlins (4)**—Duvall-Lara, Hurtado-Duvall-Stark, Rojas-Widerski-Austin, Vardijan-Richardson. **Mets (4)**—Dotel-Burke, Dotel-Samboy, Gulin-Ballew, Gulin-Wicks. **Orioles (4)**—Huntsman-Hacen-Bray-Santos, Mercedes-Hernandez, Rhodes-Hernandez, White-Huntsman-Hernandez-Santos. **Pirates (3)**—Goedde-Cook, Goedde-Viegas, Villar-Alvarado. **Rangers (4)**—Dempster-Ovalle-Kolb-Hausman, Knight-Ovalle, Reynolds-Ryan-Hausmann, Smith-Knight-Hausman. **Red Sox (1)**—Yount-Crawford. **Royals (4)**—Bernal-Meady-Key, Meady-Aguilar-Moore, Moreno-Key, Paredes-Carmano. **Tigers (4)**—Alicea-Yonemura-Stentz, Manser-Gonzalez-Rodriguez, Persails-Stentz, Romo-Yonemura-Gonzalez-Stentz. **Twins (3)**—Cobb-Ruch-Puffer, McBride-Malko, Richardson-Ruch. **White Sox (5)**—DeLaRosa-Mendoza, Eyre-Carlson, Nichols-Buckman, Nichols-Demorejon-Fereira, Ruffcorn-Demorejon-Buckman. **Yankees (6)**—Cumberland-Schaffner-Judd, Randolph-Judd-Parotte, Schaffner-Trimble-Mota-Rangel, Verdin-Brand-Robbins-Judd, Williams-Aguilar-Judd, Williams-Verdin-Horton-Trimble.
NO-HIT GAMES: None.

1995 FIELDING

TEAM

Team	Pct.	G	PO	A	E	TC	DP	PB	Team	Pct.	G	PO	A	E	TC	DP	PB
Mets	.966	57	1472	633	75	2180	28	6	Tigers	.949	57	1386	574	105	2065	42	20
Marlins	.961	56	1445	606	84	2135	39	5	Red Sox	.948	57	1430	573	109	2112	40	31
Rangers..........	.957	58	1432	589	91	2112	47	25	Cubs...............	.947	57	1449	551	111	2111	40	17
Yankees	.956	58	1468	641	96	2205	57	15	Orioles	.947	59	1471	640	118	2229	46	13
White Sox........	.955	58	1448	606	97	2151	49	12	Twins	.946	55	1360	621	113	2094	45	26
Astros.............	.955	58	1429	600	96	2125	35	15	Pirates	.946	59	1464	638	120	2222	46	17
Royals	.954	57	1449	615	100	2164	54	18	Braves	.942	57	1401	604	124	2129	41	15
Expos	.952	56	1399	622	101	2122	44	5	Blue Jays.........	.939	59	1440	664	137	2241	47	26

TRIPLE PLAY: None.

INDIVIDUAL

FIRST BASEMEN

NOTE: All caps denotes fielding-percentage leader based on 30 games for catchers, 40 for all other non-pitchers and 59 innings for pitchers. *Throws lefthanded.

Player, Team	Pct.	G	PO	A	E	TC	DP
Agnoly, Earl, Marlins..................	.996	26	217	10	1	228	13
Alleyne, Roberto, Astros............	.994	22	157	15	1	173	16
Amaya, Edilberto, White Sox	.991	25	208	13	2	223	20
Antigua, Nilson, Pirates............	1.000	1	2	0	0	2	0
Balint, Rob, Tigers	1.000	1	8	2	0	10	1
Bejarano, Brian, Blue Jays	.981	15	138	14	3	155	11
Blosser, Douglas, Royals...........	.970	20	149	10	5	164	15
Brown, Derek, Orioles..............	.978	16	130	3	3	136	12
Bunkley, Antuan, Twins............	.970	29	247	16	8	271	22
Burns, Kevin, Astros*..............	.982	39	301	21	6	328	14

Player, Team	Pct.	G	PO	A	E	TC	DP
Cardona, Luis, Red Sox	.906	3	28	1	3	32	4
Chastain, Dan, Marlins................	1.000	1	5	1	0	6	0
Coffee, Gary, Royals	.983	34	285	10	5	300	25
Colon, Ariel, Braves	.979	23	173	13	4	190	14
Cruz, Andres, Twins	.988	21	163	6	2	171	15
Culp, Randy, Expos....................	1.000	5	49	2	0	51	7
Erickson, Corey, Mets	1.000	1	2	0	0	2	0
Gallagher, Shawn, Rangers	.986	57	478	19	7	504	42
Hagge, Kirk, Tigers....................	.981	42	284	26	6	316	25
Harrison, Jamal, Twins...............	1.000	4	28	3	0	31	2
Hernandez, Alexander, Pirates*...	.952	9	77	3	4	84	6
Horn, Marvin, White Sox*	.986	36	272	14	4	290	21
Jelsovsky, Craig, Mets...............	1.000	2	5	0	0	5	0
Katayama, Daiki, Tigers..............	.917	4	20	2	2	24	1
Landry, Dan, Braves..................	1.000	1	9	0	0	9	0

Player, Team	Pct.	G	PO	A	E	TC	DP
Lima, Estivinson, Rangers	1.000	1	14	0	0	14	0
Llanos, Francisco, Expos	.966	32	265	16	10	291	22
Long, Garrett, Pirates	.986	14	134	6	2	142	12
Macero, Victor, Cubs	.971	28	222	9	7	238	15
Mifflin, Brian, Mets	.957	3	22	0	1	23	0
Montilla, Julio, Royals	.983	10	56	3	1	60	3
Oropeza, William, Expos	1.000	5	16	0	0	16	2
Pascual, Edison, Pirates*	.952	37	278	22	15	315	25
Pearson, Eddie, White Sox	1.000	2	12	0	0	12	2
Phillips, Darren, Blue Jays	1.000	2	15	1	0	16	1
Pickering, Calvin, Orioles	.968	11	86	6	3	95	2
Pressley, Kasey, Cubs	.955	23	166	2	8	176	15
Ramos, Jeff, Royals	1.000	3	6	0	0	6	2
Ramos, Noel, Orioles	1.000	4	30	3	0	33	2
Reyes, Freddy, Twins	1.000	5	42	4	0	46	1
Ribaudo, Mike, Orioles	1.000	4	16	0	0	16	1
Robertson, Dean, Orioles	.986	28	259	25	4	288	22
Rolison, Nate, Marlins	.984	30	283	20	5	308	20
Roman, Felipe, Red Sox	.974	48	358	21	10	389	27
Rose, Michael, Astros	.750	1	2	1	1	4	0
Ruiz, Cesar, Tigers	.985	26	184	13	3	200	11
Salazar, Juan, Cubs	.981	7	49	2	1	52	3
Santos, Edgardo, Expos*	.995	22	180	9	1	190	11
Scharrer, Jim, Braves	.973	36	304	25	9	338	23
Serra, Joaquin, Orioles	1.000	1	3	0	0	3	2
Shelton, Barry, White Sox	1.000	1	8	0	0	8	1
Smith, John, Astros	1.000	1	9	0	0	9	0
Soriano, Carlos, Mets	1.000	1	1	0	0	1	1
TESSMAR, Timothy, Mets*	.996	56	478	35	2	515	25
Velazquez, Jose, Yankees	.986	58	519	46	8	573	48
Veras, Wilton, Red Sox	.986	9	69	2	1	72	3
Welch, Coby, Royals	1.000	1	3	0	0	3	0
Whitlock, Mike, Blue Jays	.957	45	400	41	20	461	31

SECOND BASEMEN

Player, Team	Pct.	G	PO	A	E	TC	DP
Alayon, Elvis, Red Sox	.927	20	41	48	7	96	11
Alfonzo, Edgar, Orioles	.857	2	3	9	2	14	2
Antrim, Patrick, Yankees	.929	13	18	34	4	56	7
Astacio, Onofre, Twins	.953	17	38	43	4	85	14
Aybar, Ramon, Tigers	.959	33	38	80	5	123	10
Bautista, Jorge, Marlins	.971	11	14	19	1	34	3
Betancourt, Rafael, Red Sox	.950	22	46	49	5	100	12
Brown, Derek, Orioles	1.000	2	2	1	0	3	0
Campos, Miguel, Cubs	.875	9	13	15	4	32	4
Casimiro, Carlos, Orioles	.957	22	37	51	4	92	10
Cepeda, Jose, Royals	1.000	4	6	10	0	16	1
Daedelow, Craig, Orioles	1.000	1	3	3	0	6	1
Davidson, Cleatus, Twins	1.000	7	19	25	0	44	5
Delgado, Daniel, Pirates	.915	9	15	28	4	47	5
Douglas, John, Blue Jays	1.000	2	4	5	0	9	1
ERICKSON, Corey, Mets	.961	45	81	116	8	205	8
Febles, Carlos, Royals	.948	54	117	101	12	230	39
Franco, Raul, Marlins	.933	49	91	104	14	209	21
Frias, Ovidio, Pirates	.941	14	22	26	3	51	6
Garcia, Julio, Yankees	.955	4	13	8	1	22	4
Jasco, Elinton, Cubs	.937	34	77	57	9	143	13
Jelsovsky, Craig, Mets	1.000	1	2	3	0	5	0
Jones, Bryan, Tigers	.949	25	28	65	5	98	14
Kehoe, John, Blue Jays	.952	49	66	132	10	208	20
Kelly, Pat, Yankees	1.000	1	3	3	0	6	3
Kerr, Brian, Orioles	.932	9	19	22	3	44	6
Kerr, James, Yankees	.961	20	38	35	3	76	11
Kopacz, Derek, Tigers	1.000	3	5	8	0	13	2
Landry, Dan, Braves	1.000	3	1	5	0	6	0
Longueira, Tony, Royals	1.000	3	6	6	0	12	0
Lopez, Edgar, Braves	.955	36	66	103	8	177	19
Mateo, Henry, Expos	.949	37	69	98	9	176	22
Maysonet, Jose, Blue Jays	.981	12	25	27	1	53	2
Medina, Alger, Cubs	.971	17	35	31	2	68	7
Miles, Aaron, Astros	.934	21	35	50	6	91	9
Montas, Ricardo, Royals	.900	5	7	2	1	10	1
Montilla, Julio, Royals	1.000	2	5	4	0	9	2
Nova, Geraldo, Red Sox	.925	12	19	18	3	40	4
Nunez, Juan, Rangers	.953	31	57	84	7	148	16
Otero, Oscar, Braves	.813	4	7	6	3	16	2
Ovalles, Homy, Expos	.951	17	25	33	3	61	2
Pond, Simon, Expos	.944	12	14	20	2	36	4
Quezado, Dalmiro, Twins	.970	31	78	83	5	166	14
Reynoso, Ismael, Marlins	1.000	4	5	10	0	15	0
Rodriguez, Carlos, Red Sox	.933	8	14	14	2	30	3
Rodriguez, Liubiemithz, W. Sox	.971	36	63	102	5	170	19
Ruiz, Cesar, Tigers	.889	2	2	6	1	9	0

Player, Team	Pct.	G	PO	A	E	TC	DP
Samboy, Nelson, Astros	.977	39	86	85	4	175	15
Sanford, Chance, Pirates	.944	4	8	9	1	18	3
Schreiber, Stan, Pirates	.969	35	80	74	5	159	14
Serra, Joaquin, Orioles	.948	24	42	49	5	96	11
Solano, Angel, White Sox	.956	25	46	63	5	114	11
Soriano, Carlos, Mets	1.000	7	11	9	0	20	3
Soriano, Juan, Mets	1.000	8	14	30	0	44	5
Suero, Rey, Rangers	.968	27	59	61	4	124	15
Taylor, Avery, Orioles	.909	7	10	10	2	22	2
Taylor, Matthew, Braves	.976	20	36	44	2	82	7
Winn, Wess, Orioles	1.000	2	3	6	0	9	1
Zambrano, Victor, Yankees	.958	23	36	55	4	95	15

THIRD BASEMEN

Player, Team	Pct.	G	PO	A	E	TC	DP
Aguila, Hector, Rangers	.925	52	36	113	12	161	10
Alfonzo, Edgar, Orioles	1.000	1	0	1	0	1	0
Barnes, Kelvin, Cubs	.888	46	34	109	18	161	6
Barrett, Michael, Expos	1.000	1	0	2	0	2	0
Bautista, Jorge, Marlins	.855	31	15	50	11	76	2
Bejarano, Brian, Blue Jays	.771	12	10	17	8	35	2
Betancourt, Rafael, Red Sox	.940	19	14	33	3	50	0
Brown, Derek, Orioles	.909	33	23	77	10	110	8
Bunkley, Antuan, Twins	.904	24	18	48	7	73	0
Campos, Miguel, Cubs	.920	7	8	15	2	25	1
Capallen, Rene, Tigers	.667	3	0	2	1	3	0
CEPEDA, Jose, Royals	.955	52	45	123	8	176	14
Cole, Eric, Astros	.857	32	18	54	12	84	3
Culp, Randy, Expos	.333	1	1	0	2	3	0
Douglas, John, Blue Jays	.850	42	22	63	15	100	6
Frias, Ovidio, Pirates	.933	4	5	9	1	15	1
Jelsovsky, Craig, Mets	.800	4	1	3	1	5	0
Kehoe, John, Blue Jays	.889	9	6	18	3	27	0
King, Brian, Orioles	.737	17	5	23	10	38	1
Kopacz, Derek, Tigers	.838	47	32	87	23	142	10
Landry, Dan, Braves	.929	8	4	9	1	14	0
Leon, Donny, Yankees	.939	10	7	24	2	33	4
Liniak, Cole, Red Sox	.974	21	21	53	2	76	1
Long, Garrett, Pirates	.667	1	0	2	1	3	0
Longueira, Tony, Royals	.667	3	0	2	1	3	0
Lutz, Manuel, White Sox	.915	35	17	58	7	82	4
Medina, Alger, Cubs	.818	5	4	14	4	22	0
Montas, Ricardo, Royals	.828	9	11	13	5	29	2
Montilla, Julio, Royals	1.000	1	1	1	0	2	1
Nelson, Kevin, Twins	.890	36	18	63	10	91	6
Oropeza, William, Expos	.883	30	31	52	11	94	7
Ortiz, Asbel, Rangers	.792	10	7	12	5	24	3
Otero, Oscar, Braves	.750	6	6	9	5	20	1
Ovalles, Homy, Expos	1.000	1	0	1	0	1	0
Owen, Tom, Marlins	.833	20	12	33	9	54	1
Pena, Adelis, Pirates	.883	54	42	117	21	180	10
Pena, Alex, Pirates	1.000	1	2	2	0	4	2
Phillips, Darren, Blue Jays	.750	4	1	5	2	8	1
Pond, Simon, Expos	.908	31	18	81	10	109	1
Quezado, Dalmiro, Twins	1.000	1	1	2	0	3	0
Radcliff, Victor, Royals	.842	8	5	11	3	19	0
Reynoso, Ismael, Marlins	.893	14	6	19	3	28	2
Ribaudo, Mike, Orioles	.760	9	5	14	6	25	1
Rosado, Luis, Yankees	.935	51	16	84	7	107	12
Ruiz, Cesar, Tigers	.886	16	10	21	4	35	1
Samboy, Nelson, Astros	.886	14	13	26	5	44	1
Serra, Joaquin, Orioles	1.000	2	0	2	0	2	0
Shelton, Barry, White Sox	.795	26	9	53	16	78	4
Smith, John, Astros	.745	17	11	27	13	51	1
Solano, Angel, White Sox	1.000	1	2	2	0	4	0
Soriano, Carlos, Mets	.906	38	28	88	12	128	3
Spencer, Jeffrey, Braves	.839	42	38	82	23	143	6
Taylor, Avery, Orioles	1.000	1	1	1	0	2	0
Taylor, Matthew, Braves	1.000	2	0	2	0	2	0
Veras, Wilton, Red Sox	.885	22	11	35	6	52	1
Winn, Wess, Orioles	1.000	4	1	8	0	9	0
Zamora, Junior, Mets	.943	20	19	31	3	53	5

SHORTSTOPS

Player, Team	Pct.	G	PO	A	E	TC	DP
Abreu, Nelson, Cubs	.916	57	91	161	23	275	24
Alfonzo, Edgar, Orioles	1.000	1	1	2	0	3	1
Antrim, Patrick, Yankees	1.000	1	2	3	0	5	0
Astacio, Onofre, Twins	.890	30	30	75	13	118	10
Barrett, Michael, Expos	.892	48	65	141	25	231	26
Betancourt, Rafael, Red Sox	.960	13	16	32	2	50	6
Campos, Miguel, Cubs	.500	2	0	1	1	2	0
Capallen, Rene, Tigers	.899	21	28	43	8	79	8

Player, Team	Pct.	G	PO	A	E	TC	DP
Casimiro, Carlos, Orioles	.820	13	11	30	9	50	4
Cepeda, Jose, Royals	1.000	4	8	12	0	20	5
Cole, Eric, Astros	.842	4	13	3	3	19	1
Cordero, Edward, Tigers	.950	47	71	80	8	159	16
Daedelow, Craig, Orioles	.930	49	60	152	16	228	28
Davidson, Cleatus, Twins	.907	14	19	49	7	75	10
Delgado, Daniel, Pirates	.898	22	28	69	11	108	11
DiSarcina, Glenn, White Sox	.875	2	3	4	1	8	0
Douglas, John, Blue Jays	.857	8	14	16	5	35	3
Erickson, Corey, Mets	.903	6	8	20	3	31	4
Feliz, Edgar, Pirates	.885	16	12	34	6	52	3
Frias, Ovidio, Pirates	.941	6	9	23	2	34	3
Gonzalez, Alex, Marlins	.932	52	65	168	17	250	26
Hermansen, Chad, Pirates	.884	16	20	56	10	86	9
JARONCYK, Ryan, Mets	.952	43	59	121	9	189	8
Jelsovsky, Craig, Mets	.854	12	15	20	6	41	5
Jimenez, D'Angelo, Yankees	.927	56	95	173	21	289	31
Klee, Charles, White Sox	.935	42	46	126	12	184	26
Landry, Dan, Braves	.910	14	26	35	6	67	8
Longueira, Tony, Royals	.898	37	24	82	12	118	13
Lopez, Edgar, Braves	1.000	1	1	2	0	3	0
Lorenzo, Juan, Twins	.862	14	15	41	9	65	7
Maloney, Jeff, Blue Jays	.840	27	37	68	20	125	13
Mateo, Henry, Expos	1.000	2	2	7	0	9	0
Maysonet, Jose, Blue Jays	.907	15	34	34	7	75	7
Mejia, Marlon, Astros	.914	33	32	74	10	116	17
Miles, Aaron, Astros	.895	25	18	50	8	76	7
Montas, Ricardo, Royals	.750	6	1	8	3	12	2
Montilla, Julio, Royals	.905	5	9	10	2	21	3
Nova, Geraldo, Red Sox	.800	1	1	3	1	5	1
Olmeda, Jose, Red Sox	.900	42	60	111	19	190	23
Ortiz, Asbel, Rangers	.864	17	18	39	9	66	5
Otero, Oscar, Braves	.364	2	0	4	7	11	0
Ovalles, Homy, Expos	.942	11	15	34	3	52	5
Parra, Jose, Rangers	.939	43	58	141	13	212	20
Pena, Adelis, Pirates	1.000	1	1	0	0	1	0
Radcliff, Victor, Royals	.856	26	25	64	15	104	5
Reynoso, Ismael, Marlins	.944	8	12	22	2	36	6
Rodriguez, Carlos, Red Sox	1.000	3	6	10	0	16	2
Serra, Joaquin, Orioles	.800	2	3	1	1	5	0
Solano, Angel, White Sox	.908	16	26	43	7	76	9
Solano, Fausto, Blue Jays	.955	11	28	36	3	67	9
Soriano, Juan, Mets	1.000	1	1	1	0	2	0
Taylor, Matthew, Braves	.894	13	20	39	7	66	8
Vecchioni, Gerald, Braves	.929	30	36	68	8	112	10
Zambrano, Victor, Yankees	1.000	3	1	1	0	2	0

OUTFIELDERS

Player, Team	Pct.	G	PO	A	E	TC	DP
Adamson, Jason, Pirates	.966	28	54	2	2	58	0
Agnoly, Earl, Marlins	.966	20	26	2	1	29	0
Akins, Carlos, Orioles	.955	39	55	8	3	66	1
Alleyne, Roberto, Astros	1.000	13	22	1	0	23	0
Ayuso, Julio, Twins	1.000	15	15	2	0	17	0
Barksdale, Shane, Astros	.889	46	58	6	8	72	0
Barnes, Kelvin, Cubs	1.000	2	7	2	0	9	1
Bartee, Kimera, Orioles	1.000	5	15	0	0	15	0
Beaumont, Hamil, Yankees	1.000	10	12	1	0	13	0
Bejarano, Brian, Blue Jays	1.000	8	17	1	0	18	0
Beltran, Carlos, Royals	.977	51	79	6	2	87	0
Bishop, Tim, Mets	.973	47	71	2	2	75	0
Black, Brandon, Mets	.984	30	59	2	1	62	0
Borges, Victor, Cubs*	1.000	27	57	1	0	58	0
Butler, Garrett, Yankees	.933	48	67	3	5	75	1
Camilo, Jose, Marlins*	.984	34	63	0	1	64	0
Campos, Miguel, Cubs	.000	1	0	0	1	1	0
Capallen, Rene, Tigers	.955	13	20	1	1	22	0
Carubelli, Gustavo, Braves	.963	49	98	6	4	108	2
Cedeno, Jesus, Tigers	1.000	33	42	3	0	45	1
Charles, Curtis, Orioles	1.000	8	10	1	0	11	0
Charles, Steve, Blue Jays	.974	47	69	6	2	77	1
Chick, Bruce, Expos	.941	11	15	1	1	17	0
Coffee, Gary, Royals	1.000	2	2	0	0	2	0
Colon, Jose, Cubs	.987	38	73	4	1	78	3
Colson, Jeremiah, Expos*	.966	18	26	2	1	29	0
Connell, Jerry, Cubs	1.000	20	52	2	0	54	0
Crutchfield, David, Cubs	.959	28	66	4	3	73	1
Dasher, Melvin, Royals	.929	12	13	0	1	14	0
Davis, Albert, Pirates	1.000	9	8	1	0	9	0
Davis, Torrance, Expos	.986	41	67	6	1	74	1
DeLaCruz, Carlos, Tigers	.949	33	55	1	3	59	0
DeLaCruz, Wilfredo, Yankees	.976	34	40	1	1	42	0
Dent, Darrell, Orioles*	.975	31	75	2	2	79	0

Player, Team	Pct.	G	PO	A	E	TC	DP
Deshazer, Jeremy, Astros	.966	27	25	3	1	29	0
Domingo, Tyrone, Tigers	.980	29	49	1	1	51	0
Elliott, Dawan, Pirates*	.913	30	41	1	4	46	0
Ellison, Skeeter, Braves	.917	18	20	2	2	24	0
Encarnacion, Pedro, White Sox	1.000	10	14	0	0	14	0
Ferguson, Dwight, Red Sox*	.938	20	29	1	2	32	0
Flores, Oswaldo, Red Sox	1.000	13	15	2	0	17	0
Garcia, Luis, White Sox	.958	41	65	4	3	72	0
Gil, Daniel, Cubs	1.000	1	1	0	0	1	0
Gomez, Ramon, White Sox	.914	26	30	2	3	35	0
Goodwin, Rawlin, Red Sox	1.000	15	21	4	0	25	2
Green, Ronald, Cubs	.955	33	60	4	3	67	0
Hayes, Darren, White Sox	1.000	5	5	3	0	8	1
Hernandez, Alexander, Pirates*	.987	36	71	4	1	76	1
Higman, Joel, Orioles	.875	4	6	1	1	8	0
James, Kennouth, Expos	.976	41	80	3	2	85	1
Jenkins, Corey, Red Sox	.985	32	62	3	1	66	0
Johnson, Carlisle, Twins	.800	12	11	1	3	15	0
Johnson, Rontrez, Red Sox	.960	49	90	7	4	101	0
Johnson, Travis, Twins	.944	22	31	3	2	36	0
Jones, Jamie, Marlins*	1.000	4	3	0	0	3	0
Juarez, Raul, Twins	.941	7	16	0	1	17	0
Kerr, Brian, Orioles	1.000	1	1	0	0	1	0
King, Kevin, Expos	.963	14	26	0	1	27	0
Kinnie, Donald, Cubs	.984	30	59	4	1	64	0
Knabenshue, Chris, Pirates	1.000	3	6	2	0	8	0
Kofler, Eric, Yankees*	.885	18	21	2	3	26	1
Landry, Dan, Braves	.938	9	13	2	1	16	0
Lebron, Juan, Royals	.915	46	54	0	5	59	0
Lima, Estivinson, Rangers	.875	10	13	1	2	16	0
Lowery, Terrell, Rangers	1.000	3	7	0	0	7	0
Maas, Kevin, Yankees*	1.000	2	3	0	0	3	0
Macero, Victor, Cubs	1.000	1	1	0	0	1	0
May, Freddie, Pirates*	.963	25	50	2	2	54	0
McCarthy, Kevin, Mets*	.967	22	28	1	1	30	0
McDonald, Donzell, Yankees	.936	28	44	0	3	47	0
McHenry, Joseph, Twins	.920	33	42	4	4	50	3
Medina, Alger, Cubs	1.000	3	4	0	0	4	0
Mercado, Julio, Rangers	.973	55	102	6	3	111	4
Mifflin, Brian, Mets	.941	16	16	0	1	17	0
Millwood, Terry, Twins	.967	44	55	4	2	61	0
Miyauchi, Hector, Expos	.966	16	27	1	1	29	0
Monds, Wonderful, Braves	1.000	4	8	0	0	8	0
Monroe, Craig, Rangers	.962	53	94	7	4	105	1
Morrison, Ryan, Mets	.938	34	44	1	3	48	0
Mota, Gleydel, Mets*	.964	33	52	2	2	56	0
Nobles, Ivan, Blue Jays	.868	32	32	1	5	38	0
Nova, Fernando, White Sox	.958	30	67	2	3	72	0
Nunez, Juan, Rangers	1.000	1	2	0	0	2	0
Ortiz, Asbel, Rangers	1.000	4	4	0	0	4	0
Ortiz, Pedro, Orioles	1.000	5	1	0	0	1	0
Otero, Oscar, Braves	1.000	4	3	0	0	3	0
Pascual, Edison, Pirates*	1.000	3	5	0	0	5	0
PECK, Thomas, Blue Jays	1.000	58	107	6	0	113	0
Pena, Alex, Pirates	.968	45	86	6	3	95	0
Pena, Jose, Rangers	.944	47	62	5	4	71	0
Pendergrass, Tyrone, Braves	1.000	52	101	2	0	103	0
Peniche, Fray, Tigers	1.000	28	29	1	0	30	0
Pitts, Shedrick, Royals	1.000	32	35	3	0	38	0
Pond, Simon, Expos	1.000	3	1	0	0	1	0
Porter, Kedric, Orioles	.975	42	76	2	2	80	1
Ramirez, Francisco, Tigers	.902	26	36	1	4	41	0
Ramirez, Julio, Marlins	.983	46	109	7	2	118	1
Rengifo, Daliene, White Sox	.974	24	37	1	1	39	0
Rivera, Roberto, White Sox	.929	32	49	3	4	56	2
Roche, Marlon, Astros	.976	27	38	2	1	41	1
Rojas, Moises, Red Sox	.949	37	70	4	4	78	0
Rose, Damian, Rangers	.778	12	7	0	2	9	0
Saffer, Jeffrey, Yankees	.915	40	43	0	4	47	0
Selivanov, Andrei, Braves	.714	4	5	0	2	7	0
Shipman, Thomas, Tigers	.875	26	27	1	4	32	0
Shirley, Al, Mets	1.000	4	5	0	0	5	0
Sime, Rafael, Marlins*	.964	52	78	3	3	84	1
Simmons, Brian, White Sox	1.000	5	13	1	0	14	0
Smith, Phillip, Braves	.981	37	49	3	1	53	0
Springfield, Bo, Pirates	1.000	2	2	0	0	2	0
Stafford, Kimani, Royals	1.000	33	28	0	0	28	0
Stephens, Joel, Orioles	.958	16	23	0	1	24	0
Stevens, Clayton, White Sox	.986	36	69	1	1	71	1
Strawberry, Darryl, Yankees*	1.000	3	4	0	0	4	0
Suero, Rey, Rangers	1.000	2	2	0	0	2	0
Tardiff, Jeremy, Red Sox	.909	9	8	2	1	11	1
Terry, Reggie, Rangers	1.000	4	5	0	0	5	0

SUMMER CLASS A *Gulf Coast League*

Player, Team	Pct.	G	PO	A	E	TC	DP
Tillero, Adrian, Royals	.971	36	31	2	1	34	0
Truitt, Theron, Marlins	1.000	15	13	0	0	13	0
Ubaldo, Nelson, Astros	.963	30	26	0	1	27	0
Vilchez, Jose, Twins	.964	44	73	8	3	84	0
Villa, Willie, Blue Jays	.962	36	47	3	2	52	1
Ware, Jeremy, Expos	1.000	37	57	8	0	65	2
Wesson, Barry, Astros	1.000	44	71	9	0	80	1
White, Mickey, Astros	1.000	1	1	0	0	1	0
Zambrano, Jose, Red Sox	1.000	8	13	1	0	14	0

CATCHERS

Player, Team	Pct.	G	PO	A	E	TC	DP	PB
Alley, William, Orioles	.971	12	61	6	2	69	0	1
Alvarado, Basilio, Expos	.987	28	143	13	2	158	0	0
Antigua, Nilson, Pirates	.980	25	159	33	4	196	1	4
Bales, Taylor, Royals	.973	8	30	6	1	37	0	5
Bowers, Kevin, Mets	.982	21	145	17	3	165	0	3
Campos, Miguel, Cubs	.963	20	117	14	5	136	4	8
Cardona, Luis, Red Sox	.943	20	124	8	8	140	0	15
Chapman, Scott, Astros	1.000	13	71	9	0	80	0	3
Chastain, Dan, Marlins	.938	2	12	3	1	16	0	0
Cisar, Ryan, Blue Jays	.974	20	62	13	2	77	1	5
Corzo, Beau, Braves	.981	25	128	27	3	158	2	7
Cossins, Tim, Rangers	.909	2	10	0	1	11	0	0
Davenport, Jeff, Red Sox	1.000	5	29	1	0	30	0	0
DiSalle, Javier, Orioles	.950	4	17	2	1	20	0	0
Downs, Brian, White Sox	.983	37	268	30	5	303	3	3
Engle, Beau, Mets	.985	10	55	10	1	66	0	1
Fagley, Daniel, Marlins	.965	15	75	8	3	86	4	1
Fauske, Joshua, White Sox	.951	25	131	6	7	144	2	9
Fitzpatrick, Rob, Expos	.923	2	11	1	1	13	0	0
Fortin, Blaine, Blue Jays	.993	31	109	30	1	140	2	10
Gordon, Buck, Cubs	1.000	2	4	1	0	5	0	0
Green, Raymond, Marlins	1.000	2	8	1	0	9	0	0
Griffin, Juan, Astros	.972	26	181	29	6	216	1	9
Gruber, Nick, Red Sox	.968	13	53	8	2	63	1	3
Imrisek, Jason, Yankees	.961	14	108	14	5	127	1	4
Katayama, Daiki, Tigers	.985	24	115	16	2	133	2	1
Keech, Erik, Yankees	.964	18	134	25	6	165	1	3
Kuilan, Hector, Marlins	.994	47	309	52	2	363	1	4
Lantigua, Miguel, Mets	.987	26	186	41	3	230	2	1
Leon, Donny, Yankees	.818	3	8	1	2	11	0	1
Lignitz, Jeremiah, Tigers	.968	22	105	16	4	125	0	11
Lima, Estivinson, Rangers	1.000	3	14	0	0	14	0	1
Llibre, Brian, Rangers	.986	11	63	8	1	72	0	11
Lomasney, Steven, Red Sox	.972	23	146	29	5	180	1	11
McLendon, Craig, Rangers	.981	25	144	15	3	162	1	4
McSparin, Paul, Pirates	.959	19	105	13	5	123	1	2
Medina, Robert, Blue Jays	.951	26	93	23	6	122	0	11
Orndorff, Dave, Twins	.966	20	133	11	5	149	1	8
Oropeza, William, Expos	.974	6	32	6	1	39	1	2
Paxton, Chris, Orioles	.957	11	56	10	3	69	2	2
Payano, Alexi, Cubs	.978	19	124	11	3	138	0	3
Pena, Frank, Twins	.960	14	106	15	5	126	1	5
Phillips, Darren, Blue Jays	.971	15	59	8	2	69	0	0
Pinto, Rene, Yankees	1.000	10	62	16	0	78	0	2
Prada, Nelson, Twins	.975	24	135	19	4	158	1	13
Ramos, Jeff, Royals	.980	25	134	15	3	152	1	3
Rivera, Juan, Rangers	.983	28	160	18	3	181	1	9
Robles, Juan, Royals	.985	28	177	24	3	204	2	8
Rodriguez, Sammy, Mets	.977	6	34	8	1	43	0	1
ROSE, Michael, Astros	1.000	33	214	44	0	258	0	3
Salazar, Juan, Cubs	.993	20	114	23	1	138	1	6
Schneider, Brian, Expos	.982	27	138	26	3	167	0	3
Selivanov, Andrei, Braves	.970	10	29	3	1	33	0	1
Shipp, Skip, Pirates	.984	18	109	15	2	126	2	11
Stevenson, Chad, Tigers	.969	28	165	20	6	191	3	8
Sullivan, Davey, Orioles	.968	38	249	25	9	283	1	10
Torrealba, Steve, Braves	.982	30	185	33	4	222	2	7
Valencia, Victor, Yankees	.978	25	148	27	4	179	0	5
Varriano, Mark, Red Sox	.948	12	44	11	3	58	3	2
Weisner, Randy, White Sox	.909	5	9	1	1	11	0	0
Welch, Coby, Royals	.976	14	78	4	2	84	0	2

PITCHERS

Player, Team	Pct.	G	PO	A	E	TC	DP
Aguilar, Carlo, Yankees	.889	18	3	5	1	9	1
Alicea, Patrick, Tigers	1.000	12	1	13	0	14	4
Alvarado, Carlos, Pirates	1.000	2	0	1	0	1	0
Alvarado, David, Pirates	1.000	9	1	2	0	3	0
Anderson, John, Astros	1.000	2	1	1	0	2	0
Anez, Maycoll, White Sox	.818	7	3	6	2	11	0

Player, Team	Pct.	G	PO	A	E	TC	DP
Armas, Antonio, Yankees	1.000	5	0	3	0	3	0
Arroyo, Bronson, Pirates	.857	13	3	9	2	14	2
Asher, Ray, Red Sox	.750	10	0	3	1	4	0
Austin, Swan, Marlins	1.000	15	1	0	0	1	0
Bair, Wayne, Marlins*	1.000	6	0	9	0	9	0
Bales, Joseph, White Sox	.833	11	2	8	2	12	1
Ballew, Preston, Mets*	1.000	14	1	4	0	5	0
Batista, Mario, Pirates	1.000	1	1	1	0	2	0
Battaglia, Chuck, Rangers	.778	10	1	6	2	9	0
Bauldree, Joe, Braves	.833	12	1	4	1	6	0
Beckerman, Andy, Astros	1.000	2	0	2	0	2	0
Beirne, Kevin, White Sox	1.000	2	0	1	0	1	0
Bell, Rob, Braves	.857	10	3	3	1	7	0
Bernal, Manuel, Royals	1.000	6	2	7	0	9	0
Betti, Rich, Red Sox*	1.000	3	0	1	0	1	0
Birrell, Simon, Braves	.875	13	4	3	1	8	0
Birsner, Roark, Cubs	1.000	12	1	8	0	9	1
Black, Jayson, Red Sox	.923	12	2	10	1	13	0
Boike, Todd, Expos	.917	23	5	6	1	12	0
Bonilla, Miguel, Pirates	1.000	2	0	1	0	1	0
Booker, Chris, Cubs	.667	13	0	2	1	3	0
Borkowski, David, Tigers	.905	10	5	14	2	21	0
Bowles, Brian, Blue Jays	.750	8	1	2	1	4	0
Boyd, Bradley, Expos	.800	17	0	4	1	5	1
Brand, Scott, Yankees	1.000	4	0	1	0	1	0
Bray, Christopher, Orioles	.875	12	1	6	1	8	0
Brito, Juan, Mets*	.750	13	1	5	2	8	0
Bruner, Clayton, Tigers	.833	5	1	4	1	6	0
Bryant, Chris, Cubs*	1.000	6	0	1	0	1	0
Buckman, Thomas, White Sox	.667	18	1	1	1	3	0
Burchart, Kyle, Blue Jays	.933	13	2	12	1	15	0
Burke, Ethan, Mets	1.000	13	1	1	0	2	0
Burnett, Allan, Mets	1.000	9	2	5	0	7	1
Burton, Jamie, Royals*	1.000	6	1	2	0	3	0
Butler, Robert, Red Sox	.846	14	4	7	2	13	0
Cannon, Kevan, Red Sox*	.625	5	2	3	3	8	0
Carlson, Garret, White Sox	1.000	2	0	1	0	1	0
Carmano, Kevin, Royals	.857	15	2	4	1	7	1
Centeno, Jose, Expos*	1.000	15	2	4	0	6	0
Chantres, Carlos, White Sox	.909	11	4	16	2	22	0
Cobb, Trevor, Twins*	1.000	3	3	5	0	8	1
Coe, Brent, Blue Jays*	1.000	2	1	0	0	1	0
Collins, Zach, Braves*	1.000	3	0	1	0	1	0
Cook, O.J., Pirates	1.000	12	3	4	0	7	0
Cooper, Keith, Braves	1.000	2	0	1	0	1	0
Corba, Lisandro, Braves	.750	6	1	5	2	8	0
Corrales, Rafael, Cubs	1.000	12	0	2	0	2	0
Crawford, Christopher, Astros	.818	10	6	3	2	11	0
Crawford, Paxton, Red Sox	.800	12	2	6	2	10	0
Cumberland, Chris, Yankees*	1.000	4	0	1	0	1	0
Dace, Derek, Astros*	1.000	11	4	17	0	21	0
Davenport, Joe, Blue Jays	.733	15	7	4	4	15	0
DeLaRosa, Raul, White Sox	1.000	11	1	5	0	6	0
DeLosSantos, Luis, Yankees	.250	2	1	0	3	4	0
Demorejon, Pedro, White Sox	.833	12	2	3	1	6	0
Dempster, Ryan, Rangers	.750	8	1	2	1	4	0
Deutsch, Curry, Pirates*	.933	14	7	7	1	15	0
DeWitt, Scott, Marlins*	1.000	11	3	15	0	18	0
Dickson, Lance, Cubs*	1.000	2	0	1	0	1	0
Dotel, Octavio, Mets	.944	13	7	10	1	18	0
Dreyer, Steve, Rangers	1.000	2	0	2	0	2	0
Duncan, Adam, White Sox*	1.000	3	2	1	0	3	0
Dunn, Cordell, Pirates	1.000	5	1	2	0	3	0
Duvall, Michael, Marlins*	1.000	16	1	3	0	4	0
Ellison, Austin, Twins	.000	11	0	0	1	1	0
Enloe, Mark, Mets*	.875	11	1	6	1	8	0
Espina, Randy, Twins*	1.000	4	1	1	0	2	0
Eyre, Scott, White Sox*	1.000	9	1	2	0	3	0
Farnsworth, Kyle, Cubs	1.000	16	0	9	0	9	0
Farrell, Jim, Red Sox	1.000	1	1	1	0	2	0
Feliz, Jose, Cubs	.667	13	0	2	1	3	0
Fereira, Marcos, White Sox	.333	7	0	1	2	3	1
Figueroa, Julio, Expos	1.000	10	3	9	0	12	0
Fisher, Louis, Orioles	.833	9	1	4	1	6	0
Fleming, Dave, Royals*	1.000	1	0	2	0	2	0
Forster, Peter, Twins*	.850	10	2	15	3	20	0
Fortune, Peter, Expos*	.833	11	2	3	1	6	0
Fowler, Benjamin, Braves	.444	12	3	1	5	9	1
Fuduric, Tony, Tigers	1.000	16	1	9	0	10	1
Gaerte, Travis, Pirates	1.000	6	0	3	0	3	0
Garcia, Freddy, Astros	1.000	11	9	12	0	21	1
Garff, Jeffery, Twins	.900	15	0	9	1	10	0
Garsky, Brian, Expos	1.000	14	2	4	0	6	0

Player, Team	Pct.	G	PO	A	E	TC	DP
Gaston, Ryan, Rangers	.667	10	1	3	2	6	0
Geraldo, Antonio, Blue Jays	1.000	2	2	1	0	3	0
Gerland, Greg, Braves*	1.000	2	1	2	0	3	0
Getz, Rod, Marlins	.750	6	2	1	1	4	0
Gil, Daniel, Cubs	.667	7	1	1	1	3	0
Gillispie, Ryan, Pirates	1.000	4	1	1	0	2	0
Glover, John, Blue Jays	.769	12	5	15	6	26	1
Goedde, Roger, Pirates	.900	6	3	6	1	10	0
Gonzalez, Generoso, Tigers	1.000	16	3	1	0	4	0
Gray, Jason, White Sox	.714	14	1	4	2	7	1
Gulin, Lindsey, Mets*	.900	10	1	8	1	10	0
Guzman, Jose, Cubs	1.000	2	1	1	0	2	0
Hacen, Abraham, Orioles	.800	13	1	7	2	10	0
Halladay, Roy, Blue Jays	.944	10	4	13	1	18	1
Hammons, Matt, Cubs	.933	10	3	11	1	15	0
Harris, Doug, Orioles	1.000	1	1	0	0	1	0
Hausmann, Isaac, Rangers	1.000	18	0	5	0	5	0
Herbison, Brett, Mets	1.000	9	4	7	0	11	0
Hernandez, Francisco, Orioles	.800	24	3	1	1	5	0
Holobinko, Mike, Cubs*	.500	8	0	3	3	6	0
Horton, Aaron, Yankees*	1.000	8	2	5	0	7	1
Hundley, Chanin, White Sox	1.000	3	0	1	0	1	0
Huntsman, Brandon, Orioles	.895	13	4	13	2	19	0
Hurtado, Victor, Marlins	1.000	7	2	4	0	6	1
Izquierdo, Hansel, Marlins	.000	1	0	0	1	1	0
Johnson, Joaquin, Braves*	.857	11	1	5	1	7	0
Johnson, Mike, Blue Jays	.750	3	1	2	1	4	0
Jolliffe, Brian, Braves*	.818	11	2	7	2	11	1
Judd, Mike, Yankees	1.000	21	4	7	0	11	2
Kauflin, David, Tigers	.667	5	0	2	1	3	0
Kelley, Jason, Cubs	.333	7	0	1	2	3	0
Kessel, Kyle, Mets*	.889	7	1	7	1	9	1
Key, Francis, Royals	1.000	16	0	3	0	3	0
Kinney, Matt, Red Sox	1.000	8	2	1	0	3	0
Knight, Brandon, Rangers	1.000	3	1	2	0	3	1
Kolb, Daniel, Rangers	1.000	12	0	6	0	6	1
Lacey, James, Expos	1.000	12	1	1	0	2	0
Lakman, Jason, White Sox	1.000	9	3	2	0	5	0
LaPlante, Michael, Pirates	1.000	2	1	0	0	1	0
Lara, Nelson, Marlins	1.000	11	2	4	0	6	0
Lara, Yovanny, Expos	.667	11	1	3	2	6	0
Lawrence, Clint, Blue Jays*	.867	12	3	10	2	15	0
Lawrie, Jason, Tigers	1.000	4	1	1	0	2	0
Lebron, Jose, Expos	1.000	2	0	1	0	1	0
Licciardi, Ronald, Cubs*	1.000	17	0	6	0	6	1
Lynch, James, Astros	1.000	17	1	5	0	6	0
Maine, Dalton, Orioles	1.000	18	3	2	0	5	0
Malko, Bryan, Twins	.750	10	5	4	3	12	0
Manser, Chris, Tigers	.800	6	2	2	1	5	0
Mansur, Jeff, Orioles*	1.000	3	0	2	0	2	0
Markey, Barret, Cubs	.833	17	0	5	1	6	1
Marquez, Ralph, Twins	.875	11	3	4	1	8	0
Marriott, Michael, Marlins	.500	2	0	1	1	2	1
Marshall, Lee, Twins	.333	6	0	1	2	3	0
Martin, Cleburne, Expos	.818	17	2	7	2	11	2
Martin, Jeffrey, Royals	.833	11	1	9	2	12	0
Martinez, Humberto, Red Sox	.900	14	3	6	1	10	0
Martinez, Juan, Rangers	1.000	12	1	3	0	4	1
Martinez, Ramulo, Tigers	1.000	16	4	2	0	6	0
Martino, Jason, Cubs	1.000	8	0	1	0	1	0
Mattes, Troy, Expos	1.000	2	0	1	0	1	0
McBride, Rodney, Twins	.938	12	3	12	1	16	0
McCarter, Jason, Astros	1.000	16	1	5	0	6	0
McCaskey, Thomas, W. Sox.	1.000	6	2	3	0	5	0
McCormack, Andy, W. Sox*	1.000	1	0	1	0	1	0
McFerrin, Chris, Astros	1.000	20	4	11	0	15	0
McKnight, Tony, Astros	1.000	3	1	0	0	1	0
Meady, Todd, Royals	1.000	12	0	3	0	3	0
Medina, Tomas, Astros	.833	11	1	4	1	6	0
Mejia, Felix, Yankees	1.000	9	0	1	0	1	0
Mendoza, David, Blue Jays	.882	12	10	5	2	17	0
Mendoza, Geronimo, W. Sox	.500	10	0	1	1	2	0
Mercedes, Carlos, Orioles	.667	10	0	2	1	3	0
Moore, David, Royals	1.000	14	3	10	0	13	1
Moreno, Julio, Orioles	1.000	5	2	4	0	6	0
Moreno, Orber, Royals	1.000	8	0	2	0	2	0
Moreno, Ricardo, Rangers	1.000	4	2	4	0	6	0
Mota, Daniel, Yankees	.714	14	1	4	2	7	0
Nezelek, Andy, Pirates	.750	4	1	2	1	4	0
Nichols, James, White Sox	.957	11	5	17	1	23	3
Ocando, Stewart, Twins	1.000	14	1	6	0	7	1
O'Conner, Brian, Pirates*	.900	14	1	8	1	10	1
Ovalle, Bonelly, Rangers	.833	17	3	7	2	12	1
Pacheco, Delvis, Braves	.917	13	4	7	1	12	0
Paredes, Carlos, Royals	.900	10	3	15	2	20	0
Parotte, Frisco, Yankees	1.000	9	3	2	0	5	1
Pena, Jesus, Pirates*	.833	7	0	5	1	6	0
Pena, Juan, Red Sox	1.000	13	2	6	0	8	1
Penny, Tony, Royals	1.000	10	1	2	0	3	0
Perez, Leonardo, Orioles	1.000	8	0	2	0	2	0
Perez, Odaliz, Braves*	.880	12	4	18	3	25	0
Persails, Mark, Tigers	.842	11	5	11	3	19	0
Prestash, J.D., Astros*	.786	11	4	7	3	14	0
Puffer, Brandon, Twins	1.000	14	4	5	0	9	0
Quezada, Edward, Expos	.786	12	3	8	3	14	0
Ramos, Edgar, Astros	.800	5	0	4	1	5	0
Randolph, Stephen, Yankees*	.714	8	1	4	2	7	0
Rangel, Julio, Yankees	1.000	14	2	2	0	4	0
Reilly, Sean, Twins*	1.000	6	1	1	0	2	0
Rhodes, Joe, Orioles	1.000	13	2	17	0	19	2
Richardson, David, Marlins	.833	9	2	3	1	6	0
Richardson, Kasey, Twins*	.880	7	2	20	3	25	0
Ricketts, Chad, Cubs	1.000	2	0	1	0	1	0
Ritter, Jason, Royals	1.000	2	1	1	0	2	0
Robbins, Jake, Yankees	.900	14	1	8	1	10	0
Roberts, Grant, Mets	.917	11	3	8	1	12	1
ROBINSON, Martin, Yankees*	1.000	11	2	20	0	22	2
Rodriguez, Tomas, Tigers	.667	14	1	1	1	3	0
Rojas, Euclides, Marlins	1.000	2	0	3	0	3	0
Romo, Greg, Tigers	1.000	5	2	2	0	4	0
Ruch, Rob, Twins	.750	7	1	5	2	8	0
Ruffcorn, Scott, White Sox	1.000	3	1	2	0	3	0
Ryan, Michael-Sean, Rangers	.833	17	0	10	2	12	0
Sacharko, Mark, Astros	.667	12	0	2	1	3	0
Samboy, Javier, Mets*	.800	12	5	3	2	10	0
Sanchez, Bienvenido, Expos	1.000	16	3	5	0	8	0
Sanders, Allen, Royals	1.000	1	0	1	0	1	1
Santamaria, Juan, Tigers	.800	12	2	2	1	5	0
Santana, Pedro, Red Sox	.429	12	1	2	4	7	0
Santiago, Antonio, Red Sox*	.833	6	0	5	1	6	0
Santiago, Derek, Marlins	1.000	11	3	6	0	9	0
Santos, Juan, Orioles	.667	21	0	2	1	3	0
Santos, Rafael, Pirates	.929	11	2	11	1	14	1
Schaffner, Eric, Yankees	.857	11	2	10	2	14	0
Schrenk, Steve, White Sox	1.000	2	0	1	0	1	0
Seabury, Jaron, Blue Jays	1.000	15	4	13	0	17	1
Settle, Brian, Pirates	.667	11	0	2	1	3	0
Severino, Edy, Blue Jays	.800	24	4	4	2	10	0
Shannon, Bobby, Royals*	1.000	16	2	3	0	5	0
Shiell, Jason, Braves	.917	12	5	6	1	12	0
Shurman, Ryan, Braves	.833	10	0	10	2	12	1
Simmons, Carlos, Rangers	.917	14	5	6	1	12	1
Smart, J.D., Expos	.667	2	1	1	1	3	0
Smith, Dan, Rangers	1.000	4	0	1	0	1	0
Smith, Tom, Rangers	1.000	5	0	1	0	1	0
Sorzano, Ronnie, Expos	1.000	4	1	2	0	3	1
Stading, Kris, Cubs*	.000	11	0	0	1	1	0
Stallings, Ben, Red Sox	1.000	8	1	0	0	1	0
Stark, Zac, Marlins*	1.000	11	1	4	0	5	0
Stentz, Brent, Tigers	1.000	24	1	3	0	4	1
Stewart, Scott, Twins*	1.000	3	0	2	0	2	0
Styles, Bobby, Rangers	.750	12	1	2	1	4	0
Symmonds, Mike, Pirates*	.000	6	0	0	1	1	0
Tam, Jeff, Mets	1.000	2	0	2	0	2	0
Taylor, Brien, Yankees*	1.000	11	2	4	0	6	1
Tejera, Michael, Marlins*	1.000	11	0	7	0	7	0
Thorn, Todd, Royals*	1.000	11	0	8	0	8	0
Tillmon, Darrell, Red Sox*	1.000	3	0	3	0	3	0
Torres, Eric, Mets	.857	11	2	4	1	7	0
Trimble, Rob, Yankees	1.000	11	2	3	0	5	0
Turley, Jason, Astros	1.000	11	2	2	0	4	0
Valencia, Enrique, Red Sox*	1.000	14	1	7	0	8	0
Vanderbush, Matt, Twins*	.778	8	1	6	2	9	0
Vaninetti, Gene, Blue Jays	1.000	20	0	4	0	4	0
Vardijan, Daniel, Marlins	.867	9	2	11	2	15	1
Veniard, Jay, Blue Jays*	1.000	3	0	3	0	3	1
Verdin, Cesar, Yankees*	1.000	11	1	2	0	3	0
Viegas, Randy, Pirates*	1.000	6	2	5	0	7	0
Villar, Maximo, Pirates	.800	6	1	3	1	5	1
Villegas, Ismael, Cubs	.846	11	4	7	2	13	0
Vizcaino, Edward, Cubs	.750	14	1	2	1	4	0
Wallace, Jeff, Royals*	.778	12	3	11	4	18	0
Ward, Kerry, Pirates	1.000	11	5	6	0	11	1
West, Kenyon, Marlins	.714	13	4	1	2	7	0
White, Eric, Braves	.800	13	2	2	1	5	0
White, Gary, Orioles*	.893	12	6	19	3	28	2

Player, Team	Pct.	G	PO	A	E	TC	DP
Wicks, Ross, Mets	.600	12	1	2	2	5	0
Widerski, Jonathan, Marlins	1.000	14	1	2	0	3	0
Williams, Bradford, Yankees*	.500	11	0	2	2	4	0
Wood, Kerry, Cubs	1.000	1	0	1	0	1	0
Wyatt, Ben, Braves*	.818	12	4	5	2	11	0

Player, Team	Pct.	G	PO	A	E	TC	DP
Yanez, Luis, Astros	.818	11	4	5	2	11	0
Yonemura, Kazuki, Tigers	.789	14	4	11	4	19	1
Yount, Andrew, Red Sox	1.000	5	1	1	0	2	0
Zavershnik, Mike, Blue Jays*	1.000	19	1	8	0	9	1

The following players did not have any fielding statistics at the positions indicated or appeared only as a designated hitter, pinch-hitter or pinch-runner: Aguila, of; A. Aguilar, p; Bejarano, ss; R. Borkowski, p; B. Brown, p; T. Brown, p; B. Bryant, p; Cisar, of; Daniels, dh, pr; Dessellier, p; DiSarcina, of; Erickson, 3b; E. Feliz, 3b; R. Fisher, p; Gil, 3b; Gosch, p; Guillen, dh, ph; Hale, p; Hecker, p; Hook, p; Jelsovsky, p; Kruse, p; LaForest, 3b; Lantigua, 1b; Llanos, of; Libre, 3b; Macero, p; Manley, p; Mason, p; Maysonet, p; McFarlane, p; Mesewicz, p; Meyhoff, p; Mills, p; Moody, p; Morrison, 3b; Mullis, p; Newell, p; Olson, p; A. Ortiz, 2b; Peraza, p; Petcka, p; Radcliff, of; Rauch, p; Reynolds, p; F. Roberts, p; Rosario, of, p; Ross, p; J. Schneider, p; Scofield, p; Shelton, c; Stafford, 2b; Suero, p; Tessmar, p; Wise, p; E. Zambrano, dh.

LEAGUE CHAMPIONS

Year	Team	Pct.	Year	Team	Pct.	Year	Team	Pct.
1964—	Sarasota Braves	.610	1978—	Texas	.600	1988—	Yankees†	.714
1965—	Bradenton Astros	.632	1979—	Houston	.635		Royals	.619
1966—	New York AL	.667	1980—	Kansas City-Blue	.635	1989—	Yankees‡	.651
1967—	Kansas City	.614	1981—	Kansas City-Gold	.688		Dodgers	.635
1968—	Oakland	.650	1982—	New York AL	.667	1990—	Expos	.635
1969—	Montreal	.585	1983—	Texas	.645		Dodgers‡	.603
1970—	Chicago AL	.600		Los Angeles†	.617	1991—	Orioles	.593
1971—	Kansas City	.755	1984—	White Sox	.651		Expos∞	.533
1972—	Chicago NL*	.651		Rangers†	.571	1992—	Royals∞	.695
	Kansas City*	.651	1985—	Yankees§	.705		Expos	.593
1973—	Texas	.732		Rangers	.532	1993—	Rangers▲	.667
1974—	Chicago NL	.702	1986—	Reds	.548		Astros	.593
1975—	Texas	.774		Dodgers†	.541	1994—	Royals◆	.797
1976—	Texas	.704	1987—	Dodgers†	.683		Astros	.695
1977—	Chicago AL	.731		Royals	.635	1995—	Royals■	.649
							Tigers	.579

*Declared co-champions; no playoff. †League divided into Northern and Southern divisions; won one-game playoff for league championship. ‡League divided into Northern and Southern divisions; won best-of-three playoff for league championship. §Yankees declared champion based on winning percentage when one-game playoff against Rangers was rained out. ∞League divided into Northern, Southern and Central divisions; won best-of-three playoff for league championship. ▲League divided into Eastern, Central and Western divisions; won three-team playoff. ◆League divided into Eastern, Northern and Western divisions; won three-team playoff. ■League divided into Eastern, Northern, Northwest and Southwest divisions; won four-team playoff. (Note— Known as Sarasota Rookie League in 1964 and Florida Rookie League in 1965.)

SUMMER CLASS A *Gulf Coast League*

PIONEER LEAGUE

LEAGUE OFFICE

President
Jim McCurdy

Address
P.O. Box 2564
Spokane, WA 99220

Phone
509-456-7615

Teams (affiliation)
Billings Mustangs (Reds)
Butte Copper Kings (Tampa Bay Devil Rays)
Great Falls Dodgers (Dodgers)
Helena Brewers (Brewers)
Idaho Falls Braves (Braves)

Lethbridge Black Diamonds (Arizona Diamondbacks)
Medicine Hat Blue Jays (Blue Jays)
Ogden Raptors (Brewers)

1995 FINAL STANDINGS

FIRST HALF

NORTHERN DIVISION

Team	W	L	T	Pct.	GB
Billings (Reds)	25	8	0	.758	....
Great Falls (Dodgers)	18	15	0	.545	7
Medicine Hat (Blue Jays)	16	20	0	.444	10½
Lethbridge (Co-op)	15	21	0	.417	11½

SOUTHERN DIVISION

Team	W	L	T	Pct.	GB
Idaho Falls (Padres)	22	13	0	.629	....
Helena (Brewers)	20	15	0	.571	2
Ogden (Co-op)	14	20	0	.412	7½
Butte (Co-op)	8	26	0	.235	13½

SECOND HALF

NORTHERN DIVISION

Team	W	L	T	Pct.	GB
Billings (Reds)	24	12	0	.667	....
Medicine Hat (Blue Jays)	19	17	0	.528	5
Great Falls (Dodgers)	13	23	0	.361	11
Lethbridge (Co-op)	10	26	0	.278	14

SOUTHERN DIVISION

Team	W	L	T	Pct.	GB
Helena (Brewers)	29	7	0	.806	....
Idaho Falls (Padres)	20	16	0	.556	9
Ogden (Co-op)	18	18	0	.500	11
Butte (Co-op)	11	25	0	.306	18

COMPOSITE

Team	Bil.	Hel.	I.F.	M.H.	Ogd.	G.F.	Let.	But.	W	L	T	Pct.	GB
Billings (Reds)	....	4	3	10	3	10	15	4	49	20	0	.710	....
Helena (Brewers)	2	....	10	5	11	2	6	13	49	22	0	.690	1
Idaho Falls (Padres)	3	5	....	4	10	3	3	14	42	29	0	.592	8
Medicine Hat (Blue Jays)	6	1	2	....	3	9	10	4	35	37	0	.486	15½
Ogden (Co-op)	3	5	6	3	....	5	3	7	32	38	0	.457	17½
Great Falls (Dodgers)	3	4	3	7	1	....	7	6	31	38	0	.449	18
Lethbridge (Co-op)	1	0	3	6	3	9	....	3	25	47	0	.347	25½
Butte (Co-op)	2	3	2	2	7	0	3	....	19	51	0	.271	30

Major league affiliations in parentheses.

PLAYOFFS: Helena defeated Idaho Falls, two games to one; Medicine Hat defeated Billings, two games to one; Helena defeated Medicine Hat, two games to none, to win league championship.

REGULAR-SEASON ATTENDANCE: Billings, 103,758; Butte, 19,658; Great Falls, 62,312; Helena, 36,224; Idaho Falls, 57,620; Lethbridge, 47,607; Medicine Hat, 19,603; Ogden, 56,630. Total, 766,912. Playoffs (7 games), 7,480.

MANAGERS: Billings, Donnie Scott; Butte, Billy Gardner; Great Falls, John Shoemaker; Helena, Alex Morales; Idaho Falls, Mike Basso; Lethbridge, Dan Simonds; Medicine Hat, Darren Balsley; Ogden, Willie Ambos.

ALL-STAR TEAM: 1B—Sean Watkins, Idaho Falls; 2B—Ricardo Gama, Idaho Falls; 3B—Mike Kinkade, Helena; SS—Mickey Lopez, Helena; OF—Jamie Lopiccolo, Ogden; Christian Rojas, Billings; Manuel Gonzalez, Great Falls; C—Ben Davis, Idaho Falls; DH—(tie) Shane Jones, Ogden, and Gerry Parent, Helena; RHP—Damon Callahan, Billings; LHP—Justin Atchley, Billings; Relief Pitcher—John Mitchell, Medicine Hat; Player of the Year—Jamie Lopiccolo, Ogden; Manager of the Year—Mike Basso, Idaho Falls.

1995 BATTING

TEAM

Team	Avg.	G	TPA	AB	R	H	TB	2B	3B	HR	RBI	SH	SF	HP	BB	IBB	SO	SB	CS	GDP	LOB	ShO	Slg.	OBP
Helena	.304	71	2911	2428	558	739	1092	160	14	55	458	20	31	45	387	12	424	119	68	49	542	1	.450	.405
Idaho Falls	.293	71	2987	2525	519	741	1091	133	26	55	467	18	32	50	361	10	485	83	38	53	588	1	.432	.388
Ogden	.291	70	2866	2430	444	708	982	131	10	41	379	34	24	42	336	9	462	55	45	65	562	1	.404	.383
Billings	.289	69	2845	2426	463	702	1017	138	21	45	389	15	27	38	339	15	514	80	51	51	583	1	.419	.381
Great Falls	.272	69	2679	2326	399	632	915	118	33	33	335	12	32	40	268	8	536	97	49	51	484	4	.393	.353
Butte	.266	70	2778	2394	372	638	890	113	35	23	322	6	21	47	309	4	521	88	38	55	564	4	.372	.359
Medicine Hat	.261	72	2828	2434	415	636	939	130	19	45	351	13	27	36	317	16	611	84	35	58	539	1	.386	.351
Lethbridge	.241	72	2784	2404	340	580	788	92	28	20	261	22	19	49	290	13	531	98	46	62	517	4	.328	.333

INDIVIDUAL

TOP QUALIFIERS FOR BATTING CHAMPIONSHIP

Minimum 194 plate appearances. *Lefthanded batter. †Switch-hitter.

Player, Team	Avg.	G	TPA	AB	R	H	TB	2B	3B	HR	RBI	SH	SF	HP	BB	IBB	SO	SB	CS	GDP	Slg.	OBP
Lopiccolo, Jamie, Ogden	.388	70	326	260	74	101	154	11	3	12	55	0	3	8	55	4	40	15	7	7	.592	.503
Watkins, Sean, Idaho Falls*	.372	67	302	247	51	92	153	20	1	13	67	0	2	10	43	6	55	0	1	13	.619	.480

Player, Team	Avg.	G	TPA	AB	R	H	TB	2B	3B	HR	RBI	SH	SF	HP	BB	IBB	SO	SB	CS	GDP	Slg.	OBP
Gonzalez, Manuel, G. Falls†	.360	59	210	197	35	71	98	9	3	4	30	1	3	0	9	1	27	16	7	2	.497	.383
Lopez, Louis, Ogden	.357	46	205	182	36	65	101	15	0	7	39	3	2	2	16	0	20	1	1	5	.555	.411
Parent, Gerald, Helena*	.355	57	256	203	50	72	109	16	0	7	63	0	3	0	50	2	30	1	7	6	.537	.477
Kinkade, Mike, Helena	.353	69	325	266	76	94	127	19	1	4	39	0	6	10	43	2	38	26	9	6	.477	.452
Scott, Thomas, Billings	.353	67	304	252	68	89	142	24	4	7	43	2	3	3	44	0	65	17	9	0	.563	.450
Mealing, Al, Helena*	.349	55	195	169	35	59	90	11	4	4	31	2	0	1	23	1	43	17	7	3	.533	.430
Goodhart, Steven, Billings	.340	65	288	250	48	85	105	12	4	0	45	3	5	2	28	1	34	9	4	1	.420	.404
Barkett, Andy, Butte*	.333	45	202	162	33	54	90	11	5	5	51	0	4	3	33	2	39	1	0	1	.556	.446
Ozuna, Rafael, Great Falls†	.327	62	268	245	45	80	114	15	5	3	34	2	2	2	17	2	36	5	6	8	.465	.372
Lopez, Mickey, Helena†	.324	57	274	225	60	73	99	19	2	1	41	2	4	5	38	3	20	12	8	1	.440	.426
Jones, Shane, Ogden	.323	70	323	297	46	96	145	21	2	8	69	2	7	0	17	0	55	3	3	6	.488	.352
Gama, Ricardo, Idaho Falls	.320	70	336	266	71	85	129	16	2	8	58	3	10	2	55	1	29	17	4	2	.485	.426
Curl, John, Medicine Hat*	.319	69	304	270	47	86	135	26	1	7	63	0	3	0	31	8	61	5	1	11	.500	.385

DEPARTMENTAL LEADERS: G—Peeples, Woodward, 72; AB—Jones, 297; R—Kinkade, 76; H—Lopiccolo, 101; TB—Lopiccolo, 154; 2B—Curl, 26; 3B—Cropper, Kernan, 7; HR—Watkins, 13; RBI—Jones, 69; SH—Several players tied with 6; SF—Gama, 10; HP—Bray, J. Larue, 12; BB—McCormick, 64; IBB—Curl, 8; SO—Hinds, 87; SB—Hutchison, Levias, 33; CS—Coca, 13; GIDP—Peeples, 14; Slg.—Watkins, .619; OBP—Lopiccolo, .503.

ALL PLAYERS

*Lefthanded batter. †Switch-hitter.

Player, Team	Avg.	G	TPA	AB	R	H	TB	2B	3B	HR	RBI	SH	SF	HP	BB	IBB	SO	SB	CS	GDP	Slg.	OBP
Abernathy, George, Id. Falls*	.293	63	291	256	52	75	124	12	5	9	45	1	3	5	26	1	64	6	4	2	.484	.366
Allen, Dustin, Idaho Falls	.327	29	127	104	21	34	53	7	0	4	24	0	2	0	21	0	19	1	2	2	.510	.433
Amerson, Gordon, Id. Falls*	.305	46	208	167	40	51	80	16	5	1	22	0	0	2	39	0	33	8	7	4	.479	.442
Andreopoulos, Alex, Helena*	.556	3	13	9	3	5	11	0	0	2	7	0	0	0	4	0	0	0	0	0	1.222	.692
Arevalos, Ryan, Helena	.241	47	182	137	40	33	53	11	0	3	18	2	0	4	39	0	38	5	4	2	.387	.422
Arrollado, Courtney, Butte	.269	62	241	216	34	58	69	11	0	0	21	2	2	2	19	0	38	9	2	4	.319	.331
Aviles, Ronnel, Lethbridge†	.078	43	90	77	6	6	8	2	0	0	0	1	0	3	9	0	22	0	1	4	.104	.202
Baker, Jason, Great Falls	.260	55	122	104	17	27	42	3	0	4	22	0	0	7	11	0	23	2	1	3	.404	.369
Barkett, Andy, Butte*	.333	45	202	162	33	54	90	11	5	5	51	0	4	3	33	2	39	1	0	1	.556	.446
Barlock, Todd, Great Falls	.274	59	221	190	43	52	77	12	5	1	31	0	1	1	29	0	45	10	3	1	.405	.371
Benner, Brian, Butte	.302	67	296	245	42	74	105	15	5	2	40	0	3	4	44	1	83	5	2	3	.429	.412
Bethea, Larry, Great Falls	.172	21	31	29	2	5	5	0	0	0	3	0	0	1	1	0	7	0	0	2	.172	.226
Bledsoe, Jim, Ogden	.359	38	150	131	17	47	70	14	0	3	22	0	0	0	19	0	27	3	1	3	.534	.440
Bogle, Bryan, Butte	.333	2	10	9	0	3	4	1	0	0	2	0	0	1	0	0	4	0	0	0	.444	.400
Bramlett, Jeff, Great Falls	.145	32	70	55	5	8	12	2	1	0	5	0	2	1	12	0	23	1	2	1	.218	.300
Bray, Notorris, Butte	.255	60	248	188	50	48	62	9	1	1	14	1	1	12	46	0	35	27	10	4	.330	.429
Brown, Eric, Great Falls	.255	54	172	145	26	37	66	10	5	3	36	0	5	0	22	2	56	6	3	4	.455	.343
Bucci, Carmen, Idaho Falls	.186	50	134	113	22	21	23	2	0	0	7	0	2	5	14	0	32	7	2	1	.204	.299
Burks, Donny, Lethbridge	.155	62	221	181	19	28	35	3	2	0	6	2	0	4	34	0	40	4	2	6	.193	.301
Burress, Andrew, Billings	.262	35	113	103	17	27	46	9	2	2	18	0	1	3	6	0	16	0	2	4	.447	.319
Cancel, Robinson, Helena	.240	46	168	154	18	37	46	9	0	0	24	1	2	2	9	0	20	8	3	3	.299	.287
Carpentier, Mike, Great Falls	.263	6	20	19	4	5	7	2	0	0	2	0	0	0	1	0	3	0	0	0	.368	.300
Claybrook, Stephen, Billings*	.287	63	240	188	45	54	66	9	0	1	14	3	1	3	45	1	52	21	6	2	.351	.430
Coca, Mark, Ogden	.296	70	338	277	61	82	95	11	1	0	36	4	1	2	54	1	43	11	13	7	.343	.413
Cook, John, Lethbridge	.264	58	245	220	26	58	75	10	2	1	29	4	2	1	18	1	32	4	3	6	.341	.320
Cornish, Tim, Butte	.119	13	46	42	3	5	6	1	0	0	2	0	0	0	4	0	19	1	0	0	.143	.196
Cropper, Roger, Lethbridge†	.284	65	281	243	38	69	97	11	7	1	24	6	4	4	24	1	53	16	5	4	.399	.353
Curl, John, Medicine Hat*	.319	69	304	270	47	86	135	26	1	7	63	0	3	0	31	8	61	5	1	11	.500	.385
Davis, Ben, Idaho Falls†	.279	52	219	197	36	55	84	8	3	5	46	3	1	1	17	1	36	0	0	3	.426	.338
Davis, Josh, Idaho Falls	.222	4	19	18	3	4	5	1	0	0	1	0	0	0	1	0	2	0	0	1	.278	.263
Demetral, Scott, Ogden*	.273	60	262	231	37	63	79	11	1	1	27	0	0	3	22	1	42	3	4	6	.342	.344
DeSensi, Craig, Butte	.208	29	82	72	10	15	19	2	1	0	5	0	0	4	6	0	14	2	0	3	.264	.305
Dillingham, Daniel, Lethbridge	.174	51	182	161	21	28	44	7	0	3	16	2	2	2	15	2	49	4	2	0	.273	.250
Ebbert, Chad, Idaho Falls	.333	1	4	3	0	1	1	0	0	0	0	0	0	0	1	0	1	0	0	1	.333	.500
Elliott, David, Helena	.262	54	213	172	35	45	79	11	1	7	37	1	4	3	33	1	29	3	5	3	.459	.382
Farner, Matt, Medicine Hat*	.275	45	169	142	28	39	54	3	3	2	24	0	0	1	26	3	48	9	5	3	.380	.391
Fehrenbach, Todd, Billings*	.094	15	37	32	2	3	3	0	0	0	0	0	0	0	5	0	13	1	0	0	.094	.216
Flores, Eric, Idaho Falls	.229	40	100	83	12	19	26	5	1	0	9	1	0	0	16	0	28	3	1	1	.313	.354
Gama, Ricardo, Idaho Falls	.320	70	336	266	71	85	129	16	2	8	58	3	10	2	55	1	29	17	4	2	.485	.426
Garcia, Miguel, Great Falls†	.222	59	197	171	32	38	52	7	2	1	20	2	1	5	18	0	47	22	4	2	.304	.313
Gavello, Tim, Ogden*	.269	8	34	26	3	7	10	3	0	0	4	0	0	0	8	0	5	0	0	0	.385	.441
Giallella, Brian, Butte†	.240	33	113	100	12	24	33	3	0	2	20	0	2	0	11	0	14	0	1	1	.330	.310
Gonzalez, Manuel, G. Falls†	.360	59	210	197	35	71	98	9	3	4	30	1	3	0	9	1	27	16	7	2	.497	.383
Goodhart, Steven, Billings	.340	65	288	250	48	85	105	12	4	0	45	3	5	2	28	1	34	9	4	1	.420	.404
Goodman, Herbert, Billings	.203	37	89	79	10	16	19	3	0	0	4	0	0	1	9	0	24	3	1	1	.241	.292
Gordon, Herman, Med. Hat†	.232	51	197	181	26	42	61	2	1	5	20	1	4	1	10	0	57	2	1	0	.337	.270
Gronowski, Craig, Ogden*	.333	10	48	36	11	12	13	1	0	0	3	0	0	0	12	1	5	4	2	0	.361	.500
Guerrero, Sergio, Helena	.302	41	148	129	26	39	63	10	1	4	17	3	1	2	13	0	12	5	1	6	.488	.372
Hall, Darran, Billings*	.148	15	35	27	11	4	6	0	1	0	2	0	0	0	8	0	3	1	1	2	.222	.343
Hampton, Robbie, Med. Hat	.235	55	206	187	28	44	81	14	1	7	27	0	2	6	10	0	73	2	3	2	.433	.296
Hills, Richard, Idaho Falls	.308	61	271	224	49	69	106	14	1	7	48	0	5	11	31	0	27	4	1	5	.473	.410
Hinds, Collin, Lethbridge	.186	69	246	220	26	41	60	7	0	4	27	0	1	4	21	1	87	5	5	9	.273	.268
Hokanson, Don, Lethbridge	.000	9	1	1	0	0	0	0	0	0	0	0	0	0	0	0	0	0	0	0	.000	.000
Hunt, Kenya, Idaho Falls	.219	32	90	73	13	16	24	2	0	2	15	0	0	1	16	1	32	1	0	0	.329	.367
Hutchison, Tom, Lethbridge	.276	62	257	217	43	60	76	7	3	1	17	4	0	4	32	1	21	33	6	3	.350	.379
Iapoce, Anthony, Helena	.301	39	180	146	43	44	51	7	0	0	13	2	2	2	28	0	24	19	3	2	.349	.416
Illig, Brett, Great Falls	.167	23	46	42	4	7	8	1	0	0	1	1	0	0	3	0	14	0	0	2	.190	.222
Jenkins, Geoff, Helena*	.321	7	32	28	2	9	11	0	1	0	9	0	1	0	3	0	11	0	2	0	.393	.375
Johnson, Anthony, Lethbridge	.297	61	256	229	30	68	94	10	3	2	41	1	2	6	18	2	33	6	8	9	.393	.361
Johnson, Brian, Helena	.247	32	100	85	24	21	29	2	0	2	8	0	3	2	9	0	17	3	4	1	.341	.327
Johnson, Ledowick, Helena*	.253	35	120	95	18	24	30	3	0	1	18	1	2	2	20	0	25	5	6	0	.316	.387

Player, Team	Avg.	G	TPA	AB	R	H	TB	2B	3B	HR	RBI	SH	SF	HP	BB	IBB	SO	SB	CS	GDP	Slg.	OBP
Jones, Shane, Ogden	.323	70	323	297	46	96	145	21	2	8	69	2	7	0	17	0	55	3	3	6	.488	.352
Judge, Mike, Helena	.348	30	130	112	28	39	54	13	1	0	25	1	0	6	11	0	12	1	2	4	.482	.434
Keighley, Chris, Ogden	.188	47	179	133	21	25	36	5	0	2	21	5	4	1	36	1	31	1	1	4	.271	.356
Kernan, Phil, Butte*	.275	59	232	200	24	55	90	9	7	4	39	0	2	4	26	0	57	0	2	5	.450	.366
King, Brian, Ogden*	.257	9	40	35	4	9	14	3	1	0	5	0	0	1	4	0	10	0	1	1	.400	.350
Kinkade, Mike, Helena	.353	69	325	266	76	94	127	19	1	4	39	0	6	10	43	2	38	26	9	6	.477	.452
Knight, Brook, Helena	.235	16	42	34	4	8	9	1	0	0	4	0	0	0	8	0	2	1	0	3	.265	.381
Kominek, Tobias, Helena	.333	13	53	48	7	16	28	1	1	3	18	0	1	1	3	0	9	2	1	0	.583	.377
Langdon, Trajan, Idaho Falls	.174	11	28	23	4	4	7	0	0	1	3	2	0	0	3	0	9	0	1	0	.304	.269
Larue, Michael, Billings	.273	58	215	183	35	50	75	8	1	5	31	2	2	12	16	2	28	3	5	2	.410	.366
LaRue, Shaun, Lethbridge*	.333	29	6	6	0	2	2	0	0	0	0	0	0	0	0	0	1	0	0	0	.333	.333
Levias, Andres, Butte†	.294	57	263	228	47	67	89	7	6	1	26	1	1	2	30	0	35	33	12	3	.390	.379
Lewis, Dwayne, Lethbridge*	.255	16	63	47	8	12	19	3	2	0	8	0	0	1	15	0	9	0	1	0	.404	.444
Lindsey, Rodney, Idaho Falls	.265	35	173	155	30	41	53	4	4	0	14	0	1	4	13	0	37	21	7	1	.342	.335
Lopez, Louis, Ogden	.357	46	205	182	36	65	101	15	0	7	39	3	2	2	16	0	20	1	1	5	.555	.411
Lopez, Mickey, Helena†	.324	57	274	225	66	73	99	19	2	1	41	2	4	5	38	3	20	12	8	1	.440	.426
Lopiccolo, Jamie, Ogden	.388	70	326	260	74	101	154	11	3	12	55	0	3	8	55	4	40	15	7	7	.592	.503
Manfredi, Joel, Great Falls	.219	33	79	73	6	16	21	2	0	1	10	0	0	0	6	0	14	0	0	3	.288	.278
Marnell, Anthony, Idaho Falls	.125	3	10	8	0	1	2	1	0	0	1	0	0	0	2	0	1	0	1	0	.250	.300
Martinez, Erik, Ogden	.259	34	140	116	21	30	42	9	0	1	13	6	1	6	11	0	26	1	0	4	.362	.351
Martinez, Matt, Ogden	.200	4	13	10	3	2	2	0	0	0	0	1	0	1	1	0	2	0	0	0	.200	.333
Martinez, Obed, Idaho Falls	.275	53	212	193	31	53	65	7	1	1	31	1	0	3	15	0	33	3	3	8	.337	.336
Martinez, Rafael, Great Falls*	.273	58	213	183	30	50	81	13	3	4	30	0	3	3	23	0	36	6	3	6	.443	.358
Mateo, Jose, Great Falls†	.245	40	128	110	20	27	29	2	0	0	3	3	0	2	13	0	30	4	3	2	.264	.334
Mauch, Dennis, Great Falls	.253	28	97	79	10	20	22	2	0	0	9	1	1	6	10	0	19	4	2	1	.278	.375
McCarty, Matt, G.F.-Let.	.294	54	180	163	30	48	62	3	4	1	15	0	1	3	13	0	35	6	3	5	.380	.356
McCormick, Andrew, Med. Hat	.295	69	328	258	64	76	113	18	2	5	37	1	1	3	64	0	67	15	5	3	.438	.439
Mealing, Al, Helena*	.349	55	195	169	35	59	90	11	4	4	31	2	0	1	23	1	43	17	7	3	.533	.430
Merila, Mark, Idaho Falls†	.284	56	255	197	42	56	63	7	0	0	39	6	3	5	43	0	21	5	3	5	.320	.419
Messick, J.T., But.-Let.	.215	46	176	149	18	32	41	7	1	0	20	1	3	0	23	0	27	0	0	6	.275	.314
Meyer, Bobby, Great Falls	.150	25	45	40	4	6	8	0	1	0	4	1	1	0	3	0	14	0	0	1	.200	.205
Montgomery, Andre, Billings	.254	44	134	122	18	31	38	2	1	1	9	1	2	1	8	0	20	4	4	0	.311	.301
Moore, James, Idaho Falls	.255	15	56	47	10	12	19	5	1	0	6	0	1	1	7	0	9	1	0	1	.404	.357
Moreno, Victor, Lethbridge	.280	46	180	157	25	44	72	10	3	4	24	0	1	4	18	2	43	7	2	2	.459	.367
Morrison, Gregory, G. Falls*	.323	55	183	164	29	53	71	8	2	2	30	0	5	2	12	1	15	1	3	4	.433	.366
O'Hearn, Paul, Ogden†	1.000	1	3	2	1	2	2	0	0	0	0	0	0	0	1	0	0	0	0	0	1.000	1.000
O'Neal, Troy, Let.-Hel.	.242	47	184	149	22	36	41	3	1	0	16	0	4	9	22	1	21	3	3	6	.275	.364
Ozuna, Rafael, Great Falls†	.327	62	268	245	45	80	114	15	5	3	34	2	2	2	17	2	36	5	6	8	.465	.372
Padilla, Roy, Butte*	.000	16	1	1	0	0	0	0	0	0	0	0	0	0	0	0	0	0	0	0	.000	.000
Parent, Gerald, Helena*	.355	57	256	203	50	72	109	16	0	7	63	0	0	3	50	2	30	1	7	6	.537	.477
Parsons, Jason, Billings	.315	60	264	222	47	70	105	20	0	5	48	1	4	5	32	0	41	3	1	2	.473	.407
Paul, Kortney, Lethbridge	.239	58	229	201	28	48	68	11	0	3	24	0	2	1	25	2	48	3	2	0	.338	.323
Peeples, Michael, Med. Hat	.312	72	330	285	55	89	120	14	4	3	50	2	5	3	35	1	46	27	5	14	.421	.393
Pena, Angel, Great Falls	.290	49	165	138	24	40	65	11	1	4	15	0	3	3	21	2	32	2	1	5	.471	.388
Perez, Nelson, Butte	.223	61	227	215	24	48	69	5	5	2	20	1	0	2	9	0	44	2	2	9	.321	.261
Phair, Kelly, Ogden	.250	62	230	188	35	47	58	7	2	0	25	5	4	7	26	0	28	8	5	5	.309	.356
Preston, Doyle, Billings*	.285	65	289	242	40	69	101	12	1	6	43	0	3	2	42	3	60	1	2	7	.417	.391
Prokopec, Luke, Great Falls*	.244	43	132	119	16	29	45	6	2	2	24	0	4	1	8	0	37	5	2	1	.378	.288
Ritter, Ryan, Helena	.281	47	184	167	32	47	83	7	1	9	38	2	0	1	14	0	50	10	2	3	.497	.331
Roche, Michael, Helena	.118	4	20	17	4	2	2	0	0	0	1	0	0	1	2	0	4	1	0	0	.118	.250
Rodriguez, Sammy, Butte	.246	17	61	57	7	14	18	1	0	1	6	0	0	0	4	0	13	2	1	0	.316	.295
Rojas, Christian, Billings	.263	68	308	270	48	71	125	11	5	11	56	0	1	2	35	5	57	6	6	3	.463	.351
Rosario, Eliezer, Idaho Falls	.246	20	74	69	9	17	22	3	1	0	7	1	1	0	3	0	9	4	2	1	.319	.274
Sanchez, Ismael, Ogden	.283	20	81	60	16	17	19	2	0	0	8	0	0	5	16	0	13	2	1	0	.317	.469
Sanchez, Marcos, Idaho Falls†	.327	42	178	165	35	54	78	8	2	4	33	1	1	0	11	0	36	5	0	3	.473	.367
Scheffer, Lawrence, Ogden	.283	61	250	233	34	66	98	11	0	7	41	0	2	5	10	1	43	1	3	8	.421	.324
Schock, Jared, Ogden	.091	7	12	11	1	1	1	0	0	0	0	0	0	0	0	0	3	0	0	2	.091	.167
Schultea, Matt, Ogden	.000	34	1	1	0	0	0	0	0	0	0	0	0	0	0	0	1	0	0	0	.000	.000
Scott, Thomas, Billings	.353	67	304	252	68	89	142	24	4	7	43	2	3	3	44	0	65	17	9	0	.563	.450
Shanks, Cliff, Butte	.279	42	158	147	19	41	57	8	1	2	22	0	0	6	5	0	37	0	1	7	.388	.329
Shapiro, Tony, Butte	.289	40	134	121	13	35	55	9	1	3	15	0	0	4	9	0	34	2	0	2	.455	.358
Shatley, Andy, Medicine Hat	.226	70	298	261	32	59	81	12	2	2	30	0	4	4	29	2	66	1	3	9	.310	.309
Smith, Ramon, Med. Hat†	.000	20	2	2	0	0	0	0	0	0	0	0	0	0	0	0	1	0	0	0	.000	.000
Smith, Rick, Helena*	.307	61	261	218	42	67	112	19	1	8	44	0	3	4	36	3	40	0	4	6	.514	.410
Snelling, Allen, Medicine Hat	.226	35	127	115	9	26	31	2	0	1	11	2	0	3	7	0	31	1	2	1	.270	.288
Sorg, Jay, Billings*	.296	67	277	247	42	73	110	14	1	7	40	0	1	3	26	3	52	4	3	5	.445	.368
Srebroski, Andrew, Ogden	.067	18	30	30	3	2	2	0	0	0	0	0	0	0	1	0	12	0	1	1	.067	.063
Stewart, Paxton, Med. Hat*	.248	50	186	161	30	40	57	13	2	0	17	1	1	0	23	0	34	4	2	6	.354	.341
Stuckenschneider, Eric, G.F.	.314	40	156	118	32	37	61	8	2	4	16	0	1	5	32	0	26	10	7	2	.517	.474
Timmons, Shayne, Med. Hat	.167	24	51	42	5	7	8	1	0	0	3	0	1	2	6	0	11	0	1	1	.190	.294
Underwood, Devin, Butte†	.237	55	226	190	22	45	57	12	0	0	17	0	2	4	30	0	31	0	4	6	.300	.350
Valdespino, Jose, Med. Hat*	.190	35	127	105	14	20	36	3	2	3	13	1	1	2	18	0	34	1	1	6	.343	.317
Vallero, Rich, Lethbridge	.228	46	145	127	17	29	35	6	0	0	9	2	0	0	16	0	35	1	2	4	.276	.315
Walker, Rodney, Lethbridge	.264	39	151	125	21	33	39	4	1	0	8	2	0	4	20	0	31	7	4	5	.312	.383
Ward, Jason, Lethbridge	.125	11	30	24	3	3	3	0	0	0	2	0	0	0	6	0	6	0	0	2	.125	.300
Watkins, Sean, Idaho Falls*	.372	67	302	247	51	92	153	20	1	13	67	0	2	10	43	6	55	0	1	13	.619	.480
Whitson, Eric, Ogden†	.000	22	2	2	0	0	0	0	0	0	0	0	0	0	0	0	0	0	0	0	.000	.000
Wilson, Brian, Billings	.287	62	252	209	32	60	76	14	1	0	36	3	4	1	35	0	49	7	7	2	.364	.386
Wilson, Craig, Med. Hat	.283	49	215	184	33	52	89	14	1	7	35	0	4	6	24	1	41	8	4	1	.484	.367
Woodward, Chris, Med. Hat	.232	72	288	241	44	56	73	8	0	3	21	5	3	6	33	1	41	9	4	1	.303	.336
Zumwalt, Rusty, Butte*	.274	41	129	113	19	31	40	5	2	0	10	1	0	1	15	1	20	5	1	2	.354	.357

GRAND SLAMS: Allen, Keighley, McCormick, Ritter, 2 each; Abernathy, Andreopoulos, Baker, Hills, Kernan, Lopiccolo, Moreno, Ozuna, Scheffer, Stuckenschneider, C. Wilson, 1 each.
AWARDED FIRST BASE ON CATCHER'S INTERFERENCE: Levias (C. Wilson); R. Martinez (Valdespino); McCormick (Vallero); Merila (C. Wilson).

Player, Team	Avg.	G	TPA	AB	R	H	TB	2B	3B	HR	RBI	SH	SF	HP	BB	IBB	SO	SB	CS	GDP	Slg.	OBP
McCarty, Matt, Great Falls	.227	16	24	22	3	5	5	0	0	0	1	0	0	1	1	0	4	0	1	0	.227	.292
McCarty, Matt, Lethbridge	.305	38	156	141	27	43	57	3	4	1	14	0	1	2	12	0	31	6	2	5	.404	.365
Messick, J.T., Butte	.200	40	155	130	16	26	33	5	1	0	14	1	3	0	21	0	23	0	0	5	.254	.305
Messick, J.T., Lethbridge	.316	6	21	19	2	6	8	2	0	0	6	0	0	2	4	0	4	0	0	1	.421	.381
O'Neal, Troy, Lethbridge	.230	43	169	135	17	31	35	2	1	0	15	0	4	9	21	1	21	3	3	6	.259	.361
O'Neal, Troy, Helena	.357	4	15	14	5	5	6	1	0	0	1	0	0	0	1	0	0	0	0	0	.429	.400

1995 PITCHING

TEAM

Team	W	L	Pct.	ERA	G	CG	ShO	Sv.	IP	H	TBF	R	ER	HR	SH	SF	HB	BB	IBB	SO	WP	Bk.
Billings	49	20	.710	3.58	69	0	4	23	613.0	613	2670	316	244	20	12	20	29	239	22	474	48	14
Medicine Hat	35	37	.486	4.44	72	5	3	17	624.2	613	2816	422	308	46	27	26	44	312	5	510	70	14
Great Falls	31	38	.449	4.68	69	0	0	9	594.1	635	2748	426	309	37	13	29	37	309	16	485	61	12
Helena	49	22	.690	4.69	71	0	3	17	616.0	608	2854	388	321	44	16	16	61	411	4	559	69	21
Lethbridge	25	47	.347	4.90	72	5	2	14	632.0	710	2890	446	344	48	18	30	35	297	8	595	51	15
Idaho Falls	42	29	.592	5.25	71	1	3	17	634.2	669	2877	455	370	30	24	27	50	344	7	564	84	9
Ogden	32	38	.457	5.84	70	4	1	9	617.2	759	2893	506	401	51	15	30	53	313	10	443	57	16
Butte	19	51	.271	6.69	70	0	0	12	597.1	769	2930	551	444	41	15	35	38	382	15	454	76	23

INDIVIDUAL

TOP QUALIFIERS FOR EARNED-RUN AVERAGE TITLE

Minimum 58 innings. *Lefthanded pitcher.

Pitcher, Team	W	L	Pct.	ERA	G	GS	CG	ShO	GF	Sv.	IP	H	TBF	R	ER	HR	SH	SF	HB	BB	IBB	SO	WP	Bk.
Veniard, Jay, Medicine Hat	4	1	.800	2.71	11	0	0	0	0	0	63.0	67	280	34	19	2	2	3	3	21	0	43	6	2
Callahan, Damon, Billings	9	2	.818	2.91	14	14	0	0	0	0	80.1	82	347	36	26	1	2	3	4	30	2	50	7	0
Bailey, Ben, Billings	6	4	.600	2.96	13	13	0	0	0	0	79.0	74	340	32	26	2	2	3	3	29	2	68	11	0
Atchley, Justin, Billings*	10	0	1.000	3.51	13	13	0	0	0	0	77.0	91	327	33	30	4	2	1	2	20	2	65	2	1
Neal, Billy, G.F.-Let.	3	3	.500	3.72	16	9	1	0	3	0	65.1	74	290	42	27	1	1	2	4	24	1	55	6	3
Lapka, Rick, Billings	8	4	.667	3.76	14	14	0	0	0	0	79.0	66	334	36	33	2	2	2	6	43	3	46	7	2
Rodriguez, Victor, Med. Hat	4	1	.800	3.88	17	2	0	0	9	0	58.0	42	255	31	25	5	3	2	9	40	0	45	11	0
Novak, Troy, Ogden	5	1	.833	3.88	15	15	2	1	0	0	97.1	101	416	50	42	5	1	3	3	41	0	71	5	0
Reed, Jason, Great Falls*	2	5	.286	4.09	15	12	0	0	1	1	72.2	79	323	42	33	2	1	2	5	28	1	45	0	1
Gooda, David, Helena*	4	4	.500	4.17	10	10	0	0	0	0	58.1	54	267	32	27	3	4	2	7	33	1	33	1	5
Mann, James, Medicine Hat	5	4	.556	4.29	14	14	1	1	0	0	77.2	78	347	47	37	5	3	2	7	37	0	66	6	0
Clement, Matt, Idaho Falls	6	3	.667	4.33	14	14	0	0	0	0	81.0	61	349	53	39	3	6	3	13	42	0	65	19	2
Newman, Eric, Idaho Falls	8	4	.667	4.41	15	14	0	0	0	0	81.2	91	365	49	40	3	5	4	7	35	0	65	3	1
Kirkman, Casey, Lethbridge	5	6	.455	4.55	15	15	1	0	0	0	95.0	94	404	56	48	4	2	4	3	39	0	91	1	1
Flores, Ignacio, Great Falls	6	4	.600	4.72	16	12	0	0	1	0	68.2	66	301	42	36	3	0	1	4	38	0	76	4	2

DEPARTMENTAL LEADERS: W—Atchley, 10; L—Corral, Friedman, Justiniano, 8; Pct.—Atchley. 1.000; G—Schultea, 34; GS—Kirkman, Novak, Remington, D. Richardson, 15; CG—Corral, Novak, Porzio, 2; ShO—Several pitchers tied with 1; GF—Bryant, 26; Sv.—Bryant, Guzman, Mitchell, 11; IP—Novak, 97.1; H—Remington, D. Richardson, 106; TBF—Novak, 416; R—Corral, Spear, 65; ER—Justiniano, Remington, 50; HR—Martinez, 10; SH—Clement, 6; SF—Corral, 7; HB—O'Hearn, 14; BB—Collins, 63; IBB—Several pitchers tied with 4; SO—Kirkman, 91; WP—Clement, 19; Bk.—Justiniano, 7.

ALL PITCHERS

*Lefthanded pitcher.

Pitcher, Team	W	L	Pct.	ERA	G	GS	CG	ShO	GF	Sv.	IP	H	TBF	R	ER	HR	SH	SF	HB	BB	IBB	SO	WP	Bk.
Abreu, Juan, Butte*	1	4	.200	8.74	8	5	0	0	2	0	22.2	27	124	31	22	1	2	0	2	28	0	21	11	0
Alexander, Donald, Ogden	2	4	.333	6.40	19	1	0	0	6	0	32.1	43	164	32	23	0	4	1	3	26	1	30	7	3
Atchley, Justin, Billings*	10	0	1.000	3.51	13	13	0	0	0	0	77.0	91	327	33	30	4	2	1	2	20	2	65	2	1
Bailey, Ben, Billings	6	4	.600	2.96	13	13	0	0	0	0	79.0	74	340	32	26	2	2	3	3	29	2	68	11	0
Bales, Daniel, Idaho Falls	0	1	.000	10.67	10	1	0	0	3	1	14.1	26	85	24	17	0	0	0	2	13	0	8	3	0
Barnes, Larry, Helena	2	0	1.000	2.25	3	2	0	0	0	0	12.0	5	49	5	3	0	0	1	1	6	0	15	6	0
Baron, Jim, Idaho Falls*	2	3	.400	5.65	27	1	0	0	5	0	43.0	51	201	31	27	2	0	2	1	19	1	43	8	0
Battaglia, Chuck, Lethbridge	0	3	.000	3.98	4	3	0	0	0	0	20.1	24	90	11	9	2	1	1	0	6	0	9	1	0
Benny, Peter, Helena	5	0	1.000	3.88	11	7	0	0	1	0	46.1	48	205	25	20	2	0		4	24	0	47	4	1
Berninger, Darren, Helena	3	1	.750	7.71	21	0	0	0	4	0	28.0	45	159	28	24	4	1	1	2	34	2	11	2	0
Besser, Mike, Ogden*	1	1	.500	5.14	4	0	0	0	1	0	7.0	10	27	4	4	1	0	1	2	2	0	1	0	0
Bonilla, Welnis, Butte	2	2	.500	4.38	27	2	0	0	13	5	39.0	46	202	34	19	4	0	0	3	33	2	30	3	4
Bourbakis, Michael, G. Falls	1	2	.333	5.14	11	1	0	0	6	0	14.0	16	69	10	8	0	0	3	1	8	0	13	0	0
Bowles, Matt, Helena	1	0	1.000	15.19	6	3	0	0	0	0	10.2	17	66	18	18	2	0	0	5	18	0	10	7	0
Brabec, William, Med. Hat.	0	1	.000	7.03	19	0	0	0	7	0	24.1	31	136	33	19	2	1	0	7	20	0	25	9	1
Bryant, Adam, Billings	4	2	.667	3.13	29	0	0	0	26	11	37.1	39	157	13	13	3	0	1	2	5	1	30	4	4
Bucci, Carmen, Idaho Falls	0	0	.000	27.00	1	0	0	0	1	0	1.0	3	7	3	3	0	0	0	0	1	0	0	0	0
Burge, Jason, Lethbridge*	2	4	.333	3.44	23	0	0	0	15	5	34.0	27	151	17	13	2	2	1	4	13	0	49	0	1
Callahan, Damon, Billings	9	2	.818	2.91	14	14	0	0	0	0	80.1	82	347	36	26	1	2	3	4	30	2	50	7	0
Camp, Jared, Helena	1	4	.200	8.65	8	8	0	0	0	0	34.1	44	166	39	33	1	1	3	3	20	0	26	6	2
Campbell, Tim, Idaho Falls	1	1	.500	5.20	18	0	0	0	5	1	36.1	37	162	21	21	0	1	1	2	17	1	38	5	0
Caravelli, Mike, Ogden*	1	2	.333	3.93	5	2	0	0	1	0	18.1	27	83	11	8	1	0	3	1	3	0	13	0	1
Cardona, Isbell, Ogden*	0	2	.000	7.04	3	3	0	0	0	0	15.1	26	73	13	12	1	0	0	0	7	0	9	0	0
Castillo, Vic, Medicine Hat	0	0	.000	0.00	2	0	0	0	1	0	2.0	5	14	5	0	0	0	0	0	0	0	2	0	1
Chapa, Javier, Great Falls	2	2	.500	5.69	13	9	0	0	1	0	49.0	54	217	36	31	4	0	3	2	17	0	37	5	0
Charbonneau, Marc, G. Falls*	4	1	.800	3.61	14	7	0	0	2	0	42.1	37	198	28	17	3	1	3	2	27	2	30	2	1
Clark, Chris, Idaho Falls	0	0	.000	4.50	1	1	0	0	0	0	6.0	3	24	3	3	1	0	0	0	4	0	9	1	0

Pitcher, Team	W	L	Pct.	ERA	G	GS	CG	ShO	GF	Sv.	IP	H	TBF	R	ER	HR	SH	SF	HB	BB	IBB	SO	WP	Bk.
Clement, Matt, Idaho Falls	6	3	.667	4.33	14	14	0	0	0	0	81.0	61	349	53	39	3	6	3	13	42	0	65	19	2
Collins, Edward, Helena	5	3	.625	5.86	14	13	0	0	0	0	55.1	50	274	44	36	2	0	2	7	63	0	33	6	1
Cooke, Alan, Ogden	0	5	.000	5.13	16	5	0	0	2	0	40.1	52	194	26	23	5	0	1	1	32	1	23	4	1
Corral, Ruben, Medicine Hat	4	8	.333	4.81	14	14	2	0	0	0	86.0	92	382	65	46	7	5	7	2	34	0	50	4	1
Davis, John, Great Falls	2	2	.500	2.81	11	1	0	0	3	0	32.0	24	137	20	10	6	0	0	3	19	2	26	5	1
Dawsey, Jason, Helena*	3	0	1.000	2.74	9	8	0	0	0	0	42.2	40	183	15	13	1	0	3	2	23	0	47	5	1
Dillon, Chad, Butte	0	5	.000	10.23	15	7	0	0	0	0	41.1	60	228	58	47	2	0	5	7	39	0	26	11	0
Done, Johnny, Medicine Hat	5	5	.500	4.59	22	1	0	0	13	1	33.1	35	156	25	17	1	4	1	2	15	3	29	6	2
Erdos, Todd, Idaho Falls	5	3	.625	3.48	32	0	0	0	20	1	41.1	34	185	19	16	1	3	2	5	30	2	48	8	0
Escobar, Kelvin, Med. Hat	3	3	.500	5.71	14	14	1	1	0	0	69.1	66	307	47	44	6	2	5	6	33	0	75	4	4
Estrada, Horacio, Helena*	1	2	.333	5.40	13	0	0	0	1	0	30.0	27	144	21	18	3	5	0	3	24	0	30	2	0
Falls, Curtis, Lethbridge	2	2	.500	3.71	24	4	1	0	5	1	53.1	56	238	27	22	3	2	3	3	19	1	49	3	2
Feliciano, Pedro, Great Falls*	0	0	.000	13.50	6	0	0	0	3	0	6.2	12	43	12	10	0	0	0	0	7	1	9	4	2
Fernandes, Jamie, Butte	4	4	.500	6.02	12	12	0	0	0	0	64.1	75	305	52	43	7	3	3	8	32	0	44	9	0
Fernandez, Omar, Great Falls	3	1	.750	4.84	19	2	0	0	6	0	35.1	39	166	28	19	4	0	3	1	21	2	27	8	0
Flores, Ignacio, Great Falls	6	4	.600	4.72	16	12	0	0	1	0	68.2	66	301	42	36	3	0	1	4	38	0	76	4	2
Fox, Ryan, Ogden	0	0	.000	7.71	2	0	0	0	1	0	2.1	7	16	6	2	1	0	0	1	0	0	2	1	0
Friedman, Matt, Lethbridge	0	8	.000	6.60	20	6	0	0	10	4	43.2	55	210	40	32	2	2	5	1	26	4	36	1	5
Gamez, Rene, Ogden	4	2	.667	6.29	10	10	0	0	0	0	54.1	53	247	41	38	1	1	5	5	30	1	42	7	3
Garcia, Eddy, Billings	3	2	.600	2.63	15	5	0	0	3	1	48.0	38	193	20	14	0	0	0	0	12	1	45	2	2
Gaskill, Derek, Helena	5	2	.714	3.70	31	0	0	0	10	3	56.0	50	243	30	23	3	0	1	4	23	0	59	10	0
Gomez, Miguel, Med. Hat	2	5	.286	5.10	14	14	1	0	0	0	72.1	79	326	55	41	10	2	1	6	32	0	46	5	2
Gooda, David, Helena*	4	4	.500	4.17	10	10	0	0	0	0	58.1	54	267	32	27	3	4	2	7	33	1	33	1	5
Graves, Jon, Idaho Falls	0	0	.000	13.50	4	0	0	0	0	0	4.0	5	26	7	6	0	0	1	1	12	0	0	2	0
Grote, Jason, Butte	2	5	.286	7.04	22	7	0	0	13	4	47.1	67	223	46	37	0	1	3	1	23	3	35	8	1
Guerrero, Sergio, Helena	0	0	.000	13.50	1	0	0	0	1	0	2.0	3	10	3	3	1	0	1	0	0	0	1	0	0
Gullard, Jack, Lethbridge*	0	2	.000	6.60	26	2	0	0	11	1	30.0	38	141	27	22	4	2	3	0	13	1	34	3	0
Guzman, Domingo, Id. Falls	2	1	.667	6.66	27	0	0	0	23	11	25.2	25	127	22	19	2	3	1	1	25	1	33	6	3
Harper, Terry, Ogd.-Let.	1	4	.200	8.33	23	1	0	0	8	0	31.1	35	163	36	29	6	4	0	7	25	0	39	4	1
Henderson, James, Id. Falls	3	0	1.000	2.25	4	4	0	0	0	0	20.0	19	81	6	5	0	0	1	3	9	0	16	4	1
Hibbard, Billy, Medicine Hat	1	1	.500	3.57	4	3	0	0	0	0	17.2	14	70	8	7	1	0	1	0	4	0	15	0	0
Hindy, Mark, Ogden*	2	3	.400	4.73	24	6	0	0	5	1	70.1	89	327	52	37	5	1	3	0	24	0	44	4	2
Hokanson, Don, Lethbridge	0	0	.000	7.98	8	0	0	0	1	0	14.2	32	81	21	13	0	0	1	0	7	0	7	1	0
Holding, Brook, Butte	4	3	.571	5.14	27	0	0	0	10	3	42.0	36	191	26	24	1	2	2	0	33	1	49	6	1
Hommel, Brian, Helena*	2	0	1.000	0.45	15	0	0	0	8	2	20.0	7	86	3	1	0	2	0	4	14	0	32	2	1
Irvine, Michael, Idaho Falls	2	1	.667	5.85	28	0	0	0	9	2	52.1	59	238	40	34	6	1	2	3	28	1	52	6	0
James, Jhon, Medicine Hat	0	0	.000	18.00	2	0	0	0	1	0	1.0	2	8	2	2	1	0	0	0	3	0	1	1	0
Jamie, Jorge, Ogden*	0	0	.000	4.32	10	0	0	0	6	1	16.2	22	74	8	8	1	1	0	1	4	0	12	1	0
Jenkins, Scott, Lethbridge	1	3	.250	6.51	15	6	0	0	4	0	47.0	56	239	49	34	8	0	2	7	40	0	43	9	1
Johnson, Mike, Med. Hat	4	1	.800	3.86	19	0	0	0	7	3	49.0	46	217	26	21	2	2	2	0	25	1	32	6	0
Johnson, Scott, Butte	0	2	.000	6.58	20	0	0	0	4	0	39.2	59	191	31	29	2	0	2	0	11	1	31	2	4
Jones, Matthew, Butte	0	1	.000	7.97	21	0	0	0	9	0	35.0	54	181	40	31	4	0	3	2	17	1	30	2	2
Judice, Bryan, Lethbridge	1	1	.500	3.00	7	0	0	0	7	3	6.0	5	27	4	2	0	1	1	0	3	0	8	0	0
Justiniano, Rene, Butte	0	8	.000	7.50	12	12	0	0	0	0	60.0	86	285	58	50	7	0	5	1	26	1	40	3	7
Kazama, Yuhito, Ogden	0	1	.000	14.04	6	1	0	0	1	0	8.1	16	48	17	13	4	0	0	2	8	0	4	2	0
King, Raymond, Billings*	3	0	1.000	1.67	28	0	0	0	15	5	43.0	31	169	11	8	1	2	0	0	15	3	43	1	1
Kirkman, Casey, Lethbridge	5	6	.455	4.55	15	15	1	0	0	0	95.0	94	404	56	48	4	2	4	3	39	0	91	3	1
Kline, Jason, Ogden*	3	4	.429	5.43	25	6	0	0	10	2	58.0	80	273	45	35	7	2	4	3	25	1	37	2	1
Kolb, Brandon, Idaho Falls	2	3	.400	7.04	9	8	0	0	0	0	38.1	42	181	33	30	1	2	2	2	29	0	21	5	0
Lapka, Rick, Billings	8	4	.667	3.76	14	14	0	0	0	0	79.0	66	334	36	33	2	2	2	6	43	3	46	7	2
LaRue, Shaun, Lethbridge	2	2	.500	2.97	26	0	0	0	8	0	36.1	30	163	13	12	1	1	2	2	24	2	42	3	0
Lawrence, Rich, Billings	0	1	.000	3.24	13	2	0	0	2	1	25.0	25	112	18	9	2	0	1	1	11	0	27	1	0
Lee, Calvin, Ogden	1	2	.333	7.52	5	5	0	0	0	0	20.1	21	102	23	17	1	0	0	2	21	0	15	3	0
Lenhardt, Bruce, Helena	0	1	.000	1.93	9	0	0	0	6	0	9.1	7	46	6	2	1	0	0	1	11	1	10	1	0
MacRae, Scott, Billings	0	1	.000	5.67	18	0	0	0	4	1	27.0	32	135	24	17	0	0	5	3	20	4	9	2	1
Mann, James, Medicine Hat	5	4	.556	4.29	14	14	1	1	0	0	77.2	78	347	47	37	5	3	2	7	37	0	66	6	0
Marine, Justin, Billings	1	0	1.000	1.75	18	0	0	0	7	2	25.2	20	114	14	5	0	1	1	4	11	0	20	2	0
Martin, Jeremy, Ogden*	1	1	.500	7.64	9	2	0	0	2	0	17.2	23	79	16	15	2	1	1	4	11	0	11	3	0
McMillan, Leonard, Butte	0	1	.000	9.88	10	0	0	0	1	0	13.2	18	78	17	15	2	1	0	1	18	1	15	2	1
Medero, Gadiel, Butte	0	0	.000	15.30	8	1	0	0	5	0	10.0	22	59	19	17	0	0	0	1	7	0	4	1	1
Mejia, Carlos, Butte*	2	1	.667	3.76	10	7	0	0	2	0	38.1	37	164	16	16	4	1	5	2	17	1	28	2	1
Merila, Mark, Idaho Falls	0	0	.000	45.00	1	0	0	0	1	0	1.0	5	9	5	5	0	0	0	1	1	0	0	0	0
Messick, J.T., But.-Let.	0	0	.000	9.00	1	0	0	0	1	0	1.0	2	5	1	1	1	0	0	0	0	0	2	0	0
Miller, Shawn, Helena	2	0	1.000	4.82	16	0	0	0	4	0	28.0	37	136	18	15	1	0	1	0	16	0	33	2	1
Mitchell, John, Medicine Hat	2	2	.500	2.50	25	0	0	0	23	11	36.0	20	150	15	10	1	3	1	1	17	1	50	5	1
Mullins, Greg, Helena*	4	0	1.000	2.74	4	4	0	0	0	0	23.0	22	98	7	7	0	0	0	2	6	0	14	0	2
Nakashima, Toni, Great Falls*	2	4	.333	5.60	20	3	0	0	4	2	35.1	39	171	25	22	1	1	0	2	20	0	32	2	0
Nate, Scott, Helena*	0	2	.000	9.00	3	0	0	0	2	1	2.0	4	10	3	2	1	1	0	0	0	0	2	0	0
Neal, Billy, G.F.-Let.	3	3	.500	3.72	16	9	1	0	3	0	65.1	74	290	42	27	1	1	2	4	24	1	55	6	3
Newman, Eric, Idaho Falls	8	4	.667	4.41	15	14	0	0	0	0	81.2	91	365	49	40	3	5	4	7	35	0	65	3	1
Novak, Troy, Ogden	5	1	.833	3.88	15	15	2	1	0	0	97.1	101	416	50	42	5	1	3	3	41	0	71	5	0
Ochsenfeld, Christopher, G.F.*	1	4	.200	6.86	14	7	0	0	2	1	42.0	50	209	45	32	1	0	4	1	33	0	32	5	0
O'Hearn, Paul, Ogden	1	4	.200	8.91	11	7	0	0	1	0	32.1	41	176	45	32	0	0	1	14	26	0	27	3	3
Padilla, Roy, Butte*	2	7	.222	5.91	15	14	0	0	0	0	70.0	80	340	60	46	1	2	4	7	54	0	49	11	0
Pasqualicchio, Michael, Helena*	3	0	1.000	3.16	8	7	0	0	0	0	31.1	30	142	14	11	2	0	1	1	20	0	21	1	3
Pavlovich, Tony, Helena	0	0	.000	0.93	9	0	0	0	9	4	9.2	4	37	1	1	1	0	0	1	3	0	14	1	0
Perez, Jayson, Idaho Falls	0	0	.000	0.00	1	0	0	0	0	0	1.0	1	4	0	0	0	0	0	0	0	0	2	0	0
Porzio, Mike, Ogden*	4	3	.571	6.38	8	8	2	0	0	0	48.0	66	220	39	34	4	0	3	2	15	0	26	6	0
Preston, George, Helena	1	0	1.000	8.10	3	2	0	0	1	0	6.2	11	36	9	6	3	0	0	2	2	0	9	0	0
Reed, Jason, Great Falls*	2	5	.286	4.09	15	12	0	0	1	1	72.2	79	323	42	33	2	1	2	5	28	1	45	0	1
Remington, Jake, Idaho Falls	5	5	.500	5.15	15	15	1	1	0	0	87.1	106	379	62	50	3	2	3	5	29	0	54	5	1
Richardson, Darrell, Let.	5	4	.556	5.00	15	15	1	0	0	0	84.2	106	393	63	47	6	1	1	5	38	0	85	10	1
Richardson, Jesse, Helena*	3	1	.750	4.62	25	0	0	0	6	2	39.0	44	182	23	20	6	2	0	2	27	0	34	1	0

Pitcher, Team	W	L	Pct.	ERA	G	GS	CG	ShO	GF	Sv.	IP	H	TBF	R	ER	HR	SH	SF	HB	BB	IBB	SO	WP	Bk.
Riedling, John, Billings	2	2	.500	7.04	13	7	0	0	2	1	38.1	51	192	38	30	4	0	3	1	21	2	28	8	0
Rivera, Oscar, Great Falls	2	1	.667	4.13	18	1	0	0	13	1	28.1	28	134	19	13	3	2	4	0	17	1	30	3	0
Robins, Doug, Lethbridge	2	2	.500	5.13	15	4	0	0	2	0	40.1	43	175	29	23	7	0	1	0	16	0	28	6	2
Rodriguez, Luis, Butte*	0	1	.000	9.49	7	0	0	0	2	0	12.1	12	61	14	13	1	0	1	1	12	0	10	2	0
Rodriguez, Sammy, Butte	0	0	.000	9.00	1	0	0	0	0	0	2.0	2	11	2	2	0	0	0	0	3	0	5	0	0
Rodriguez, Victor, Med. Hat	4	1	.800	3.88	17	2	0	0	0	0	58.0	42	255	31	25	5	3	2	9	40	0	45	11	0
Rosario, Nelson, Med. Hat*	0	1	.000	7.82	10	0	0	0	7	0	12.2	21	64	13	11	1	0	1	1	6	0	5	1	0
Sak, James, Idaho Falls	3	1	.750	1.65	13	0	0	0	3	1	32.2	15	123	9	6	1	1	0	0	12	1	55	1	1
Sangeado, Juan, Great Falls	1	3	.250	4.30	16	3	0	0	4	1	46.0	47	207	28	22	4	4	1	1	25	3	46	4	0
Schultea, Matt, Ogden	4	2	.667	4.67	34	0	0	0	10	1	54.0	59	244	37	28	1	3	3	4	18	4	43	3	1
Sheldon, Shane, Helena	0	0	.000	13.50	17	0	0	0	7	0	15.1	18	91	28	23	3	0	0	3	25	0	15	8	2
Smith, Ramon, Med. Hat*	1	4	.200	3.63	19	0	0	0	9	2	22.1	15	104	16	9	2	0	0	0	24	0	26	6	0
Smith, Travis, Helena	4	2	.667	2.41	20	7	0	0	11	5	56.0	41	224	16	15	4	0	7	19	0	63	4	2	
Spear, Russell, Idaho Falls	3	2	.600	6.21	14	13	0	0	0	0	66.2	83	324	65	46	7	0	5	4	36	0	53	8	0
Sweezey, Gary, Great Falls	2	1	.667	3.21	17	0	0	0	11	2	28.0	34	125	22	10	4	1	3	2	6	0	18	5	1
Taczy, Craig, Great Falls*	0	4	.000	3.52	18	2	0	0	7	0	30.2	25	145	20	12	1	0	1	2	28	0	24	6	1
Torres, Jackson, Great Falls	3	3	.500	4.59	14	8	0	0	2	1	51.0	66	242	37	26	1	2	1	9	11	3	32	8	1
Torres, Luis, Idaho Falls	0	1	.000	27.00	1	0	0	0	0	0	1.0	3	7	3	3	0	0	0	0	2	0	2	0	0
Upchurch, Wayne, Lethbridge	2	6	.250	5.60	9	9	1	1	0	0	53.0	68	247	44	33	6	0	3	4	19	0	39	2	0
Veniard, Jay, Medicine Hat	4	1	.800	2.71	11	10	0	0	0	0	63.0	67	280	34	19	2	2	3	3	21	0	43	6	2
Waites, Steve, Butte	2	5	.286	4.78	28	0	0	0	8	0	43.1	60	209	33	23	3	2	2	22	4	26	3	1	
Weiss, Marc, Billings	1	2	.333	7.62	18	1	0	0	6	1	26.0	36	127	26	22	0	0	1	15	2	14	1	1	
Whitson, Eric, Ogden	2	1	.667	5.82	22	0	0	0	17	4	29.1	35	142	33	28	8	1	1	2	16	2	31	5	1
Wright, Scott, Billings	2	0	1.000	3.62	17	0	0	0	4	0	27.1	28	123	15	11	1	1	0	2	7	0	29	0	2

COMBINATION SHUTOUTS: **Billings (4)**—Callahan-King, Callahan-King-Wright-Weiss-Marine-Bryant, Callahan-Weiss, Lapka-MacRae. **Butte (0)**—None. **Great Falls (0)**—None. **Helena (3)**—Dawsey-Gaskill-Richardson-Smith, Gooda-Gaskill-Hommel, Smith-Gaskill-Pavlovich. **Idaho Falls (2)**—Clement-Bales, Henderson-Campbell-Guzman. **Lethbridge (1)**—Robins-Falls-Gullard-Friedman. **Medicine Hat (1)**—Hibbard-Smith. **Ogden (0)**—None.

NO-HIT GAMES: Remington, Idaho Falls, defeated Helena, 6-0 (first game), June 23; Escobar, Medicine Hat, defeated Ogden, 2-0 (first game), July 20.

PITCHERS WITH TWO OR MORE TEAMS

Pitcher, Team	W	L	Pct.	ERA	G	GS	CG	ShO	GF	Sv.	IP	H	TBF	R	ER	HR	SH	SF	HB	BB	IBB	SO	WP	Bk.
Harper, Terry, Ogden	1	2	.333	11.81	8	1	0	0	4	0	10.2	14	61	21	14	4	0	3	11	0	11	1	0	
Harper, Terry, Lethbridge	0	2	.000	6.53	15	0	0	0	4	0	20.2	21	102	15	15	2	4	0	4	14	0	28	3	1
Neal, Billy, Great Falls	0	1	.000	5.84	6	1	0	0	3	0	12.1	19	61	12	8	0	1	0	2	4	1	8	0	2
Neal, Billy, Lethbridge	3	2	.600	3.23	10	8	1	0	0	0	53.0	55	229	30	19	1	0	2	2	20	0	47	6	1

1995 FIELDING

TEAM

Team	Pct.	G	PO	A	E	TC	DP	PB	Team	Pct.	G	PO	A	E	TC	DP	PB
Ogden	.959	70	1853	837	114	2804	72	24	Lethbridge	.950	72	1896	786	142	2824	49	26
Billings	.959	69	1839	780	112	2731	75	21	Butte	.948	70	1792	775	142	2709	60	15
Helena	.958	71	1848	798	117	2763	78	20	Medicine Hat	.939	72	1874	732	170	2776	60	19
Idaho Falls	.957	71	1904	861	123	2888	91	18	Great Falls	.938	69	1783	744	168	2695	55	19

INDIVIDUAL

FIRST BASEMEN

NOTE: All caps denotes fielding-percentage leader based on 36 games for catchers, 48 for all other non-pitchers and 72 innings for pitchers. *Throws lefthanded.

Player, Team	Pct.	G	PO	A	E	TC	DP
Allen, Dustin, Idaho Falls	1.000	3	39	1	0	40	3
Barkett, Andy, Butte*	.991	45	407	39	4	450	35
Bethea, Larry, Great Falls	1.000	8	19	2	0	21	1
Bramlett, Jeff, Great Falls	.992	27	112	13	1	126	16
Cook, John, Lethbridge	.993	46	379	32	3	414	22
Curl, John, Medicine Hat	.984	63	499	45	9	553	42
Dillingham, Daniel, Lethbridge	1.000	1	9	0	0	9	1
Hunt, Kenya, Helena	.939	9	30	1	2	33	4
Johnson, Anthony, Lethbridge	.987	28	213	20	3	236	13
JONES, Shane, Ogden	.989	70	656	46	8	710	68
Judge, Mike, Helena	.985	16	125	8	2	135	15
Kernan, Phil, Butte	.979	11	86	8	2	96	8
Kinkade, Mike, Helena	.995	21	174	14	1	189	26
Martinez, Rafael, Great Falls*	.984	58	449	39	8	496	30
Messick, J.T., But.-Let.	.962	4	24	1	1	26	1
O'Hearn, Paul, Ogden	1.000	1	5	0	0	5	0
Parent, Gerald, Helena	1.000	13	109	4	0	113	12
Parsons, Jason, Billings	.976	9	74	7	2	83	12
Sanchez, Marcos, Idaho Falls	1.000	3	25	3	0	28	6
Shanks, Cliff, Butte	.971	15	118	15	4	137	11
Smith, Rick, Helena	.992	27	218	25	2	245	19
Sorg, Jay, Billings	.987	62	567	30	8	605	54
Stewart, Paxton, Medicine Hat	.936	8	44	0	3	47	3
Timmons, Shayne, Med. Hat	.929	5	25	1	2	28	3
Valdespino, Jose, Med. Hat	1.000	2	16	0	0	16	2
Vallero, Rich, Ogden	1.000	1	2	0	0	2	0
Watkins, Sean, Idaho Falls*	.981	65	561	45	12	618	67

TRIPLE PLAY: Kinkade.

FIRST BASEMEN WITH TWO OR MORE TEAMS

Player, Team	Pct.	G	PO	A	E	TC	DP
Messick, J.T., Butte	.000	1	0	0	0	0	0
Messick, J.T., Lethbridge	.962	3	24	1	1	26	1

SECOND BASEMEN

Player, Team	Pct.	G	PO	A	E	TC	DP
Arevalos, Ryan, Helena	.921	12	21	37	5	63	9
Arrollado, Courtney, Butte	.933	58	133	185	23	341	41
Bramlett, Jeff, Great Falls	1.000	1	1	1	0	2	0
Bucci, Carmen, Idaho Falls	1.000	4	2	8	0	10	2
Burks, Donny, Lethbridge	.970	11	14	18	1	33	2
Carpentier, Mike, Great Falls	1.000	1	0	1	0	1	0
Coca, Mark, Ogden	.900	2	3	6	1	10	1
Demetral, Scott, Ogden	.973	38	84	95	5	184	33
Flores, Eric, Great Falls	1.000	4	1	4	0	5	0
Gama, Ricardo, Idaho Falls	.959	69	160	212	16	388	68
Gialella, Brian, Butte	.893	17	24	43	8	75	8
Goodhart, Steven, Billings	.957	65	128	187	14	329	47
Guerrero, Sergio, Helena	.977	7	17	26	1	44	9
HUTCHISON, Tom, Lethbridge	.972	53	106	137	7	250	23
Lewis, Dwayne, Lethbridge	.955	9	14	28	2	44	6
Lopez, Mickey, Helena	.968	26	56	66	4	126	20
Martinez, Erik, Ogden	.893	29	52	90	17	159	19
Martinez, Matt, Ogden	.750	2	4	2	2	8	1
Mateo, Jose, Great Falls	.833	4	3	2	1	6	1
Merila, Mark, Idaho Falls	1.000	2	5	9	0	14	4
Meyer, Bobby, Great Falls	.784	15	10	19	8	37	2
Ozuna, Rafael, Great Falls	.942	62	110	148	16	274	28
Peeples, Michael, Med. Hat	.873	45	88	90	26	204	14
Phair, Kelly, Ogden	.941	5	7	9	1	17	3
Ritter, Ryan, Helena	.940	27	53	57	7	117	15

Player, Team	Pct.	G	PO	A	E	TC	DP
Schock, Jared, Ogden	1.000	2	5	3	0	8	1
Snelling, Allen, Medicine Hat	.914	30	52	65	11	128	10
Walker, Rodney, Lethbridge	.857	8	14	16	5	35	4
Wilson, Brian, Billings	.976	8	17	23	1	41	2

THIRD BASEMEN

Player, Team	Pct.	G	PO	A	E	TC	DP
Arrollado, Courtney, Butte	.929	4	6	7	1	14	1
Barlock, Todd, Great Falls	.862	56	35	121	25	181	5
Bledsoe, Jim, Ogden	.850	5	4	13	3	20	0
Bucci, Carmen, Idaho Falls	.900	12	4	5	1	10	0
Burks, Donny, Lethbridge	.750	1	3	0	1	4	1
Demetral, Scott, Ogden	.979	13	15	32	1	48	7
DeSensi, Craig, Butte	.894	26	25	34	7	66	3
Guerrero, Sergio, Helena	.907	23	13	55	7	75	7
Hills, Richard, Idaho Falls	.951	32	16	62	4	82	3
Hutchison, Tom, Lethbridge	.818	8	6	12	4	22	3
Illig, Brett, Great Falls	.684	11	2	11	6	19	0
Judge, Mike, Helena	.750	1	2	1	1	4	0
Kinkade, Mike, Helena	.909	25	10	50	6	66	6
Kominek, Tobias, Helena	.909	6	4	16	2	22	2
Langdon, Trajan, Idaho Falls	.783	9	5	13	5	23	2
Lopez, Louis, Ogden	.930	44	33	114	11	158	11
Lopiccolo, Jamie, Ogden	.837	11	9	27	7	43	3
Manfredi, Joel, Great Falls	.900	19	8	28	4	40	3
McCarty, Matt, Lethbridge	.881	27	15	44	8	67	3
Merila, Mark, Idaho Falls	.867	36	23	75	15	113	7
Messick, J.T., But.-Let.	.921	31	12	46	5	63	4
Moreno, Victor, Lethbridge	.849	24	12	33	8	53	1
Parent, Gerald, Helena	.845	20	11	38	9	58	5
Peeples, Michael, Med. Hat	.667	1	2	0	1	3	0
PRESTON, Doyle, Billings	.929	64	48	136	14	198	18
Shanks, Cliff, Butte	.927	21	8	30	3	41	2
Shatley, Andy, Medicine Hat	.851	70	53	130	32	215	13
Timmons, Shayne, Med. Hat	.667	4	1	3	2	6	0
Walker, Rodney, Lethbridge	.931	10	6	21	2	29	3
Ward, Jason, Lethbridge	.897	11	10	16	3	29	0
Wilson, Brian, Billings	.885	11	4	19	3	26	3

THIRD BASEMEN WITH TWO OR MORE TEAMS

Player, Team	Pct.	G	PO	A	E	TC	DP
Messick, J.T., Butte	.933	29	12	44	4	60	4
Messick, J.T., Lethbridge	.667	2	0	2	1	3	0

SHORTSTOPS

Player, Team	Pct.	G	PO	A	E	TC	DP
Arevalos, Ryan, Helena	.922	35	44	98	12	154	22
Bucci, Carmen, Idaho Falls	.963	31	45	85	5	135	22
Burks, Donny, Lethbridge	.906	49	66	127	20	213	17
Carpentier, Mike, Great Falls	.917	6	9	13	2	24	2
Demetral, Scott, Ogden	1.000	7	8	23	0	31	4
DeSensi, Craig, Butte	1.000	1	1	2	0	3	1
Flores, Eric, Great Falls	.843	36	37	65	19	121	14
Gialella, Brian, Butte	.906	13	19	29	5	53	6
Guerrero, Sergio, Helena	.978	10	21	24	1	46	7
Hills, Richard, Idaho Falls	.947	30	58	103	9	170	28
Hokanson, Don, Lethbridge	1.000	1	0	3	0	3	0
Hutchison, Tom, Lethbridge	1.000	1	0	1	0	1	0
Illig, Brett, Great Falls	.833	10	9	6	3	18	2
Lewis, Dwayne, Lethbridge	.923	6	9	15	2	26	2
Lopez, Mickey, Helena	.899	31	54	88	16	158	20
Martinez, Erik, Ogden	.667	1	2	0	1	3	0
Martinez, Matt, Ogden	1.000	1	6	1	0	7	0
Mateo, Jose, Great Falls	.923	36	48	96	12	156	18
McCarty, Matt, G.F.-Let.	.838	14	6	25	6	37	3
Messick, J.T., Butte	.889	2	1	7	1	9	1
Meyer, Bobby, Great Falls	1.000	1	1	0	0	1	0
Montgomery, Andre, Billings	.878	33	41	81	17	139	15
Perez, Nelson, Butte	.893	61	84	176	31	291	36
PHAIR, Kelly, Ogden	.948	57	90	181	15	286	34
Ritter, Ryan, Helena	1.000	1	2	1	0	3	0
Rosario, Eliezer, Idaho Falls	.921	20	34	71	9	114	18
Srebroski, Andrew, Ogden	.895	10	18	33	6	57	5
Walker, Rodney, Lethbridge	.880	22	24	42	9	75	4
Wilson, Brian, Billings	.920	52	62	157	19	238	35
Woodward, Chris, Medicine Hat	.911	72	106	202	30	338	34

TRIPLE PLAY: Arevalos.

SHORTSTOPS WITH TWO OR MORE TEAMS

Player, Team	Pct.	G	PO	A	E	TC	DP
McCarty, Matt, Great Falls	.857	12	3	21	4	28	2
McCarty, Matt, Lethbridge	.778	2	3	4	2	9	1

OUTFIELDERS

Player, Team	Pct.	G	PO	A	E	TC	DP
Abernathy, George, Idaho Falls	.959	61	86	7	4	97	1
Allen, Dustin, Idaho Falls	1.000	12	12	1	0	13	0
Amerson, Gordon, Idaho Falls*	.951	45	70	7	4	81	0
Aviles, Ronnel, Lethbridge	.946	37	32	3	2	37	0
Baker, Jason, Great Falls*	.986	52	62	6	1	69	0
Barlock, Todd, Great Falls	1.000	1	1	0	0	1	0
Benner, Brian, Butte	.976	59	78	2	2	82	0
Bledsoe, Jim, Ogden	1.000	2	1	1	0	2	0
Bogle, Bryan, Butte	.000	2	0	0	1	1	0
Bramlett, Jeff, Great Falls	1.000	2	1	1	0	2	0
Bray, Notorris, Butte	.959	60	111	7	5	123	0
Brown, Eric, Great Falls	.978	36	45	0	1	46	0
Claybrook, Stephen, Billings	.975	63	110	6	3	119	1
Coca, Mark, Ogden	.953	69	109	12	6	127	0
Cornish, Tim, Ogden	.926	12	23	2	2	27	0
Cropper, Roger, Lethbridge	.961	64	94	5	4	103	1
Dillingham, Daniel, Lethbridge	.880	25	22	0	3	25	0
ELLIOTT, David, Helena	1.000	48	46	2	0	48	0
Farner, Matt, Medicine Hat*	.976	42	77	3	2	82	0
Garcia, Miguel, Great Falls	.942	55	109	5	7	121	2
Gonzalez, Manuel, Great Falls	.949	48	90	3	5	98	1
Goodman, Herbert, Billings	.900	32	26	1	3	30	0
Gordon, Herman, Med. Hat	.965	45	107	3	4	114	2
Gronowski, Craig, Ogden*	.917	10	10	1	1	12	0
Hall, Darran, Billings*	1.000	12	16	1	0	17	0
Hampton, Robbie, Med. Hat	.964	53	95	11	4	110	3
Hinds, Collin, Lethbridge	.937	69	124	10	9	143	1
Hunt, Kenya, Idaho Falls	1.000	8	3	1	0	4	0
Iapoce, Anthony, Helena*	.966	39	55	2	2	59	0
Jenkins, Geoff, Helena*	1.000	6	15	1	0	16	1
Johnson, Anthony, Lethbridge	.927	34	49	2	4	55	0
Johnson, Brian, Helena	.971	30	34	0	1	35	0
Johnson, Ledowick, Helena	.923	30	47	1	4	52	0
King, Brian, Ogden*	.929	8	13	0	1	14	0
Kominek, Tobias, Helena	1.000	6	4	1	0	5	0
Levias, Andres, Butte	.967	56	115	4	4	123	0
Lindsey, Rodney, Idaho Falls	.949	35	69	6	4	79	1
Lopiccolo, Jamie, Ogden	.983	58	112	7	2	121	0
Martinez, Erik, Ogden	1.000	1	0	0	0	1	0
Martinez, Obed, Idaho Falls	.893	51	48	2	6	56	0
McCormick, Andrew, Med. Hat	.961	67	112	11	5	128	2
Mealing, Al, Helena	.962	48	72	3	3	78	0
Moore, James, Idaho Falls	1.000	14	8	1	0	9	0
Morales, Rich, Ogden	1.000	1	1	0	0	1	0
Moreno, Victor, Lethbridge	.870	20	19	1	3	23	0
Morrison, Gregory, Great Falls*	.877	44	61	3	9	73	0
Parent, Gerald, Helena	.960	17	22	2	1	25	0
Peeples, Michael, Medicine Hat	1.000	8	22	0	0	22	0
Prokopec, Luke, Great Falls	1.000	34	30	4	0	34	0
Ritter, Ryan, Helena	1.000	17	13	3	0	16	0
Rojas, Christian, Billings	.980	68	140	8	3	151	2
Sanchez, Ismael, Ogden	.936	19	41	3	3	47	0
Sanchez, Marcos, Idaho Falls	1.000	2	1	0	0	1	0
Scheffer, Lawrence, Ogden	.938	41	42	3	3	48	0
Scott, Thomas, Billings	.990	66	94	6	1	101	0
Shapiro, Tony, Butte	.958	18	21	2	1	24	0
Smith, Ramon, Medicine Hat*	1.000	1	1	0	0	1	0
Stewart, Paxton, Med. Hat	.895	12	16	1	2	19	1
Stuckenschneider, Eric, G.F.	1.000	3	2	0	0	2	0
Zumwalt, Rusty, Butte*	.950	36	35	3	2	40	0

CATCHERS

Player, Team	Pct.	G	PO	A	E	TC	DP	PB
Andreopoulos, Alex, Helena	1.000	3	11	3	0	14	0	0
Burress, Andrew, Billings	.973	23	98	11	3	112	1	6
Cancel, Robinson, Helena	.978	45	349	53	9	411	5	7
Cook, John, Lethbridge	1.000	2	12	3	0	15	0	1
Davis, Ben, Idaho Falls	.985	48	362	44	6	412	0	1
Davis, Josh, Idaho Falls	.938	4	41	4	3	48	3	10
Ebbert, Chad, Idaho Falls	.889	1	7	1	1	9	0	0
Fehrenbach, Todd, Billings	.897	8	31	4	4	39	0	5
KEIGHLEY, Chris, Ogden	.987	44	260	33	4	297	1	9
Kinkade, Mike, Helena	.976	18	107	15	3	125	1	7
Knight, Brook, Helena	1.000	14	54	5	0	59	0	4
Larue, Michael, Billings	.980	54	346	46	8	400	7	10
Manfredi, Anthony, Id. Falls	1.000	12	26	1	0	27	0	3
Marnell, Anthony, Id. Falls	1.000	3	18	4	0	22	0	1
Mauch, Dennis, Great Falls	.947	28	163	15	10	188	1	6
Messick, J.T., Butte	.952	8	33	7	2	42	0	0
O'Neal, Troy, Let.-Hel.	.970	42	294	59	11	364	2	13
Paul, Kortney, Lethbridge	.967	38	305	44	12	361	5	14

Player, Team	Pct.	G	PO	A	E	TC	DP	PB
Pena, Angel, Great Falls	.980	45	297	42	7	346	3	9
Prokopec, Luke, Great Falls	1.000	2	10	1	0	11	0	1
Rodriguez, Sammy, Butte	.927	14	69	7	6	82	0	3
Sanchez, Marcos, Id. Falls	.968	19	132	19	5	156	1	6
Shanks, Cliff, Butte	1.000	2	1	0	0	1	0	0
Timmons, Shayne, Med. Hat.	.986	13	64	9	1	74	0	1
Underwood, Devin, Butte	.969	54	344	35	12	391	1	12
Valdespino, Jose, Med. Hat	.980	31	220	27	5	252	3	4
Vallero, Rich, Ogden	.966	36	200	26	8	234	0	15
Wilson, Craig, Medicine Hat	.982	35	237	29	5	271	3	14

TRIPLE PLAY: Cancel.

CATCHERS WITH TWO OR MORE TEAMS

Player, Team	Pct.	G	PO	A	E	TC	DP	PB
O'Neal, Troy, Lethbridge	.967	38	263	55	11	329	2	11
O'Neal, Troy, Helena	1.000	4	31	4	0	35	0	2

PITCHERS

Player, Team	Pct.	G	PO	A	E	TC	DP
Abreu, Juan, Butte*	.667	8	5	3	4	12	1
Alexander, Donald, Ogden	.889	19	0	8	1	9	0
Atchley, Justin, Billings*	.846	13	1	10	2	13	1
Bailey, Ben, Billings	.867	13	4	9	2	15	1
Bales, Daniel, Idaho Falls	1.000	10	1	2	0	3	1
Barnes, Larry, Helena	.667	3	0	2	1	3	0
Baron, Jim, Idaho Falls*	1.000	27	0	4	0	4	0
Battaglia, Chuck, Lethbridge	.800	4	1	3	1	5	1
Benny, Peter, Helena	.846	11	5	6	2	13	1
Berninger, Darren, Helena	.857	21	3	3	1	7	0
Bonilla, Welnis, Butte	.909	27	6	4	1	11	0
Bourbakis, Michael, Great Falls	1.000	11	1	1	0	2	0
Bowles, Matt, Helena	1.000	6	0	4	0	4	1
Brabec, William, Medicine Hat	1.000	19	0	3	0	3	0
Bryant, Adam, Billings	1.000	29	0	4	0	4	0
Burge, Jason, Lethbridge*	1.000	23	0	4	0	4	0
Callahan, Damon, Billings	.857	14	6	6	2	14	0
Camp, Jared, Helena	1.000	8	4	4	0	8	0
Campbell, Tim, Idaho Falls	.875	18	3	4	1	8	0
Caravelli, Mike, Ogden*	1.000	5	0	1	0	1	0
Cardona, Isbell, Butte	1.000	3	2	1	0	3	0
Chapa, Javier, Great Falls	.909	13	5	5	1	11	0
Charbonneau, Marc, Great Falls*	.786	14	2	9	3	14	0
Clement, Matt, Idaho Falls	.960	14	10	14	1	25	0
Collins, Edward, Helena	.889	14	2	6	1	9	0
Cooke, Alan, Ogden	1.000	16	2	5	0	7	1
Corral, Ruben, Medicine Hat	.895	14	3	14	2	19	1
Davis, John, Great Falls	1.000	11	1	1	0	2	0
Dawsey, Jason, Helena*	1.000	9	1	9	0	10	1
Dillon, Chad, Butte	.600	15	4	2	4	10	0
Done, Johnny, Medicine Hat	1.000	22	4	6	0	10	0
Erdos, Todd, Idaho Falls	1.000	32	1	2	0	3	0
Escobar, Kelvin, Medicine Hat	.909	14	7	3	1	11	0
Estrada, Horacio, Helena*	.900	13	2	7	1	10	1
Falls, Curtis, Lethbridge	.818	24	2	7	2	11	0
Fernandes, Jamie, Butte	.944	12	9	8	1	18	0
Fernandez, Omar, Great Falls	.857	19	2	4	1	7	0
Flores, Ignacio, Great Falls	.875	16	3	11	2	16	0
Friedman, Matt, Lethbridge	.917	20	4	7	1	12	0
Gamez, Rene, Ogden	1.000	10	7	6	0	13	0
Garcia, Eddy, Billings	.875	15	4	3	1	8	1
Gaskill, Derek, Helena	.818	31	3	6	2	11	0
Gomez, Miguel, Medicine Hat	.909	14	6	14	2	22	2
Gooda, David, Helena*	.938	10	6	9	1	16	0
Graves, Jon, Idaho Falls	1.000	4	2	1	0	3	0
Grote, Jason, Butte	.909	22	5	5	1	11	1
Gullard, Jack, Lethbridge*	1.000	26	1	4	0	5	0
Guzman, Domingo, Idaho Falls	.667	27	0	2	1	3	0
Harper, Terry, Ogd.-Let.	1.000	23	2	4	0	6	0
Henderson, James, Idaho Falls	.833	4	2	3	1	6	1
Hibbard, Billy, Medicine Hat	1.000	4	0	5	0	5	0
Hindy, Mark, Ogden*	.857	24	6	6	2	14	0
Hokanson, Don, Lethbridge	1.000	8	1	4	0	5	0
Holding, Brook, Butte	1.000	27	7	6	0	13	1
Hommel, Brian, Helena*	1.000	15	0	4	0	4	0

Player, Team	Pct.	G	PO	A	E	TC	DP
Irvine, Michael, Idaho Falls	1.000	28	3	3	0	6	1
Jamie, Jorge, Ogden*	1.000	10	0	4	0	4	0
Jenkins, Scott, Lethbridge	.778	15	1	6	2	9	0
Johnson, Mike, Medicine Hat	.875	19	1	13	2	16	0
Johnson, Scott, Butte	1.000	20	2	5	0	7	0
Jones, Matthew, Butte	1.000	21	1	2	0	3	0
Judice, Bryan, Lethbridge	1.000	7	0	1	0	1	0
Justiniano, Rene, Butte	.900	12	6	12	2	20	0
Kazama, Yuhito, Ogden	1.000	6	0	1	0	1	0
King, Raymond, Billings*	.909	28	7	3	1	11	0
Kirkman, Casey, Lethbridge	.913	15	13	8	2	23	0
Kline, Jason, Ogden*	.917	25	3	8	1	12	1
Kolb, Brandon, Idaho Falls	.750	9	0	3	1	4	0
Lapka, Rick, Billings	1.000	14	7	8	0	15	0
LaRue, Shaun, Lethbridge	1.000	26	3	10	0	13	0
Lawrence, Rich, Billings	1.000	13	0	3	0	3	1
Lee, Calvin, Ogden	.800	5	0	4	1	5	0
Lenhardt, Bruce, Helena	1.000	9	0	1	0	1	0
MacRae, Scott, Billings	1.000	18	1	3	0	4	0
Mann, James, Medicine Hat	.737	14	6	8	5	19	0
Marine, Justin, Billings	.500	18	1	0	1	2	0
Martin, Jeremy, Ogden*	1.000	9	0	1	0	1	0
McMillan, Leonard, Butte	1.000	10	0	1	0	1	0
Medero, Gadiel, Butte	1.000	8	2	2	0	4	0
Mejia, Carlos, Butte*	1.000	10	4	4	0	8	0
Miller, Shawn, Helena	1.000	16	2	0	0	2	1
Mitchell, John, Medicine Hat	.833	25	1	4	1	6	0
Mullins, Greg, Helena*	.889	4	3	5	1	9	1
Nakashima, Toni, Great Falls*	.667	20	1	1	1	3	0
Nate, Scott, Helena*	1.000	3	0	1	0	1	0
Neal, Billy, G.F.-Let.	.905	16	8	11	2	21	1
Newman, Eric, Idaho Falls	.900	15	6	12	2	20	1
NOVAK, Troy, Ogden	1.000	15	8	9	0	17	0
Ochsenfeld, Christopher, G. Falls*	.714	14	2	3	2	7	0
O'Hearn, Paul, Ogden	.889	11	3	5	1	9	0
Padilla, Roy, Butte*	.972	15	7	28	1	36	0
Pasqualicchio, Michael, Helena*	.800	8	5	3	2	10	0
Pavlovich, Tony, Helena	1.000	9	1	0	0	1	0
Porzio, Mike, Ogden*	1.000	8	0	6	0	6	0
Preston, George, Helena	.000	3	0	0	1	1	0
Reed, Jason, Great Falls*	.941	15	0	16	1	17	0
Remington, Jake, Idaho Falls	.955	15	8	13	1	22	0
Richardson, Darrell, Lethbridge	.933	15	7	7	1	15	0
Richardson, Jesse, Helena*	.833	25	0	5	1	6	0
Riedling, John, Billings	1.000	13	1	3	0	4	0
Rivera, Oscar, Great Falls	1.000	18	1	7	0	8	0
Robins, Doug, Lethbridge	1.000	15	4	6	0	10	1
Rodriguez, Luis, Butte*	1.000	7	0	1	0	1	0
Rodriguez, Victor, Med. Hat	.850	17	4	13	3	20	1
Rosario, Nelson, Med. Hat*	1.000	10	0	1	0	1	0
Sak, James, Idaho Falls	.857	13	1	5	1	7	0
Sangeado, Juan, Great Falls	.700	16	5	2	3	10	1
Schultea, Matt, Ogden	1.000	34	4	6	0	10	0
Sheldon, Shane, Helena	1.000	17	3	0	0	3	1
Smith, Ramon, Medicine Hat*	.778	19	1	6	2	9	1
Smith, Travis, Helena	.941	20	7	9	1	17	0
Spear, Russell, Idaho Falls	.667	14	3	3	3	9	0
Sweezey, Gary, Great Falls	1.000	17	2	5	0	7	1
Taczy, Craig, Great Falls*	1.000	18	3	1	0	4	0
Torres, Jackson, Great Falls	.545	14	0	6	5	11	3
Upchurch, Wayne, Lethbridge	.938	9	4	11	1	16	0
Veniard, Jay, Medicine Hat*	.667	11	4	12	8	24	0
Waites, Steve, Butte	1.000	28	1	5	0	6	1
Weiss, Marc, Billings	1.000	18	4	4	0	8	1
Whitson, Eric, Ogden	1.000	22	3	3	0	6	1
Wright, Scott, Billings	1.000	17	1	1	0	2	0

TRIPLE PLAY: Collins.

PITCHERS WITH TWO OR MORE TEAMS

Player, Team	Pct.	G	PO	A	E	TC	DP
Harper, Terry, Ogden	1.000	8	1	1	0	2	0
Harper, Terry, Lethbridge	1.000	15	1	3	0	4	0
Neal, Billy, Great Falls	1.000	6	1	1	0	2	0
Neal, Billy, Lethbridge	.895	10	7	10	2	19	1

The following players did not have any fielding statistics at the positions indicated or appeared only as a designated hitter, pinch-hitter or pinch-runner: Barkett, 3b; Besser, p; Bucci, p; Castillo, p; Clark, p; Elliott, ss; Feliciano, p; Fox, p; M. Garcia, ss; Gavello, dh; Guerrero, p; Illig, 2b; James, p; Keighley, of; B. King, 3b; Lewis, of; E. Martinez, 3b; McCarty, 2b; Merila, p; Messick, p; Meyer, of; Montgomery, of; O'Hearn, of; Ozuna, ss; J. Perez, p; D. Preston, ss; S. Rodriguez, p; Schock, 3b; Shapiro, c; Ri. Smith, ss, of; Snelling, 3b, ss; L. Torres, p; Walker, of; Whitson, of.

SUMMER CLASS A Pioneer League

Year	Team	Pct.
1939—	Twin Falls*	.581
1940—	Salt Lake City	.608
	Ogden (4th)*	.492
1941—	Boise	.623
	Ogden (2nd)*	.598
1942—	Pocatello†	.690
	Boise	.683
1943-44-45—	Did not operate.	
1946—	Twin Falls‡	.585
	Salt Lake City†	.585
1947—	Salt Lake City	.618
	Twin Falls†	.600
1948—	Pocatello	.611
	Twin Falls (2nd)*	.595
1949—	Twin Falls	.624
	Pocatello (3rd)*	.595
1950—	Pocatello	.635
	Billings (3rd)*	.571
1951—	Salt Lake City	.618
	Great Falls (3rd)*	.559
1952—	Pocatello	.595
	Idaho Falls (2nd)*	.573
1953—	Ogden	.679
	Salt Lake City (4th)*	.527
1954—	Salt Lake City	.595
	Great Falls (4th)*	.530
1955—	Boise	.588
	Magic Valley (4th)*	.489
1956—	Boise	.561
1957—	Salt Lake City	.650
	Billings†	.582

Year	Team	Pct.
1958—	Great Falls	.582
	Boise†	.615
1959—	Boise	.633
	Billings (2nd)*	.523
1960—	Boise†	.686
	Idaho Falls	.650
1961—	Boise	.638
	Great Falls*	.571
1962—	Boise§	.565
	Billings†	.706
1963—	Idaho Falls	.702
	Magic Valley†	.643
1964—	Treasure Valley	.615
1965—	Treasure Valley	.530
1966—	Ogden	.591
1967—	Ogden	.621
1968—	Ogden	.609
1969—	Ogden	.620
1970—	Idaho Falls	.629
1971—	Great Falls	.643
1972—	Billings	.694
1973—	Billings	.629
1974—	Idaho Falls	.569
1975—	Great Falls	.577
1976—	Great Falls	.577
1977—	Lethbridge	.629
1978—	Billings∞	.735
1979—	Helena	.623
	Lethbridge▲	.559
1980—	Lethbridge▲	.743
	Billings	.629

Year	Team	Pct.
1981—	Calgary	.657
	Butte▲	.557
1982—	Medicine Hat▲	.629
	Idaho Falls	.600
1983—	Billings▲	.614
	Calgary	.600
1984—	Billings	.691
	Helena▲	.647
1985—	Great Falls	.771
	Salt Lake City▲	.657
1986—	Salt Lake City◆	.643
	Great Falls	.571
1987—	Salt Lake City◆	.700
	Helena	.657
1988—	Great Falls◆	.754
	Butte	.629
1989—	Great Falls◆	.791
	Butte	.621
1990—	Great Falls◆	.706
	Salt Lake	.618
1991—	Salt Lake City◆	.700
	Great Falls	.657
1992—	Salt Lake	.697
	Billings◆	.697
1993—	Billings◆	.653
	Helena	.589
1994—	Billings◆	.694
	Helena	.611
1995—	Billings	.710
	Helena■	.690

*Won four-club playoff. †Won split-season playoff. ‡Ended first half in tie with Salt Lake City and won one-game playoff. §Ended first half in tie with Billings and Great Falls and won playoff. ∞Billings (first place) defeated Idaho Falls (second place) in first place-second place playoff. ▲League divided into Northern and Southern divisions; won two-club playoff. ◆Won two-club playoff. ■League divided into Northern and Southern divisions; won four-club playoff.

SUMMER CLASS A *Pioneer League*

MINOR LEAGUE INDEX

TEAMS AND CITIES